THE Catholic Youth Bible
INTERNATIONAL EDITION

For the text of the New Revised Standard Version (NRSV): Catholic Edition
Imprimatur: † Most Rev. Daniel E. Pilarczyk
President, National Conference of Catholic Bishops
Washington, D.C., 12 September 1991
Imprimatur: Canadian Conference of Catholic Bishops
Ottawa, 15 October 1991

Article writers: Eduardo Arnouil; Lisa-Marie Calderone-Stewart; Carmen María Cervantes; Catherine Cory; Gary Dreier; Karen Emmerich; Carole Goodwin; Ron Kenney; Edward P. Kunzman; Judi Lanciotti; Joseph A. Morris, CM; Daniel Ponsetto; Rosa Sanchez; Larry Schatz, FSC; Vikki Shepp; Valerie Shields; Brian Singer-Towns; Tony Tamberino; Michael Theisen; and Victor Valenzuela

The acknowledgments continue on page 1507.

Printed in China

Printing: 9 8 7 6 5 4

Year: 2012 11 10 09 08 07 06

ISBN-10: 0-88489-822-9
ISBN-13: 978-0-88489-822-1   5084204

Produced with the assistance of The Livingstone Corporation (www.LivingstoneCorp.com). Project staff includes: Chris Hudson, Ashley Taylor, Kathleen Ristow, Thomas Ristow, Kirk Luttrell, Rosalie Krusemark, and Joel Bartlett.

Library of Congress Cataloging-in-Publication Data

Bible. English. New Revised Standard. 2004.

The Catholic youth Bible : international edition : New Revised Standard Version, Catholic edition.

   p. cm.

ISBN 0-88489-822-9 (hardcover)

I. Title.

BS191.5A12004 W56 2004

220.5'20434—dc22

2004009239

THE
Catholic
Youth
Bible

INTERNATIONAL EDITION

New Revised Standard Version:
Catholic Edition

Saint Mary's Press®

Contents

The New Testament

Welcome!

THIS UNIQUE BIBLE IS FOR YOU.

The Catholic Youth Bible (CYB) is filled with things that will make it easier for you to understand the Bible's message. The authors, editors, designers, and artists involved in creating its special features were focused on you—a young person seeking answers to life's important questions. The *CYB* can be a true companion, helping you find the answers you seek and perhaps raising new questions along the way. It will help you see yourself in God's image and likeness, *A VITAL PART OF GOD'S SAVING WORK IN THE WORLD.*

WHAT MAKES THIS YOUTH BIBLE *CATHOLIC*? For starters, its introductions and articles reflect Catholic interpretation of the Bible and make connections to Catholic beliefs and traditions. In addition, this Bible contains all seventy-three books and letters that form a complete Catholic Bible, seven more than most other Bibles (see "The Case of the Missing Books," near Tob 1.16). Does this mean that other Christians cannot use *The Catholic Youth Bible*? Not at all. When it comes to the Scriptures, Christians from all cultures and denominations have more in common than we have differences.

AS YOU USE THIS BIBLE, keep in mind two important points. The first is that the Bible is for everyone. Wherever you are in your relationship with God, *the Bible can speak to you.* The articles in *The Catholic Youth Bible* invite you to consider what the church teaches about God's message in the Bible whether you are a committed Christian or a searcher with lots of questions.

The second point is that all the special features in *The Catholic Youth Bible* are designed to encourage you *to read the Bible itself.* It is the Bible's stories, poems, prophecies, and letters that carry this central message: *God desires a loving relationship with us.* The special features of this Bible can help you understand God's message. *BUT IT IS GOD'S WORD IN THE BIBLE THAT CAN CHANGE YOUR LIFE.*

Love one another

SPECIAL FEATURES

The Catholic Youth Bible is loaded with special features to help make it easier for you to read and understand the Bible. Here is a list of some of those features and where to find them.

HOW TO READ AND STUDY THE BIBLE

The chapter that follows this general introduction gives advice for interpreting the Bible and a process for studying the Bible alone or with a group.

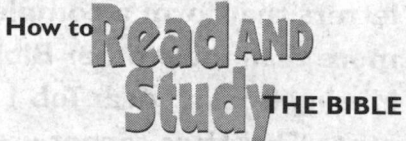

SUGGESTED READING PLANS

This chapter offers some great reading plans to get you started in studying the Bible.

SECTION INTRODUCTIONS

Each major section of the Bible (the Pentateuch, the historical books, the wisdom books, the prophetic books, the Gospels and the Acts of the Apostles, and the Letters and Revelation) begins with background on the books in that section.

BOOK INTRODUCTIONS

Introductions at the beginning of most books (sometimes two or three books share a single introduction) give insight into each book's central message and an overview of its contents.

LIVE IT!

The "Live It!" articles apply the Bible's messages to situations you may be facing now or will face in the future.

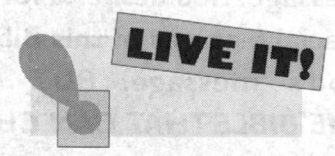

PRAY IT!

The "Pray It!" articles can help you use the Bible for personal prayer. They show the biblical basis for the prayer and sacramental life of the Catholic church.

DID YOU KNOW?

The "Did You Know?" articles provide background from biblical scholars to help you understand the culture and traditions of biblical times, or the church's interpretation of certain passages.

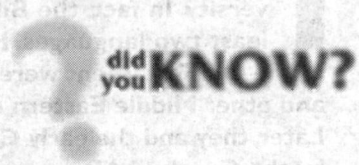

INTRODUCING . . .

The "Introducing . . ." articles give a quick introduction to the lives of important biblical people.

CATHOLIC CONNECTIONS

The "Catholic Connections" articles show the biblical basis for many Catholic Christian beliefs and practices.

WHERE DO I FIND IT?

Several indexes are located at the back of the Bible, before the maps. The first index contains several lists that can help you locate Bible passages on events, people, and teachings of Jesus. The second index helps you find Bible passages related to each sacrament. The third index helps you find Bible passages related to specific life and faith issues. The fourth index leads you to articles on specific topics throughout *The Catholic Youth Bible*. The first three indexes generally use Bible citations to guide you, and the fourth index uses page numbers.

STUDY AIDS

A concordance, color maps, and a timeline are found at the back of the Bible. The timeline and maps will help you locate where and when different biblical events occurred.

The Bible Is MULTICULTURAL

THE BIBLE developed in the midst of great cultural diversity. In fact, the Bible was originally written in at least two languages, Hebrew and Greek. The people of the Old Testament were influenced by Arabic, Egyptian, and other Middle Eastern cultures that surrounded them. Later, they and the early Christian church were influenced by the Greek and Roman cultures. In the Bible, God is revealed as the God of *all* nations and *all* cultures.

Christians believe that the Bible's core message of God's love for human beings speaks to people of any culture. That is one reason the Bible has been translated into more languages than any other book in the world. Christians also believe that God is at work in the lives of people of every culture, whether or not they have been formally introduced to the Christian message. Listening to other cultures' experience of God can deepen Christian people's appreciation of God's message present in the Bible.

We live in a multicultural world. *The Catholic Youth Bible* responds to this reality in two main ways. First, all the articles attempt to speak in a way that people of all cultures can appreciate and understand. Second, some articles have been specially written to represent cultural perspectives from around the world.

All the articles share cultural experiences and traditions, religious symbols, prayers, and poetry, and they connect all these elements to the Bible. "Cultural Connections," an entry in the subject index at the back of the Bible, lists the locations of all these articles.

The cultural perspectives represented in *The Catholic Youth Bible* are a small sampling of the many unique cultures in the world. Because of space restrictions, articles on many cultures could not be included. Despite these limitations, the multicultural articles can deepen your appreciation of the Bible's message and of the rich ways different cultures live that message.

NAVIGATING *The Catholic Youth Bible*

THE CATHOLIC YOUTH BIBLE has several aids to help you locate references to Bible books and the Bible's special features. The contents on pages iv–v will be your main guide in locating the different books and features. However, the last page in the color section (facing the back cover) lists all the Bible books alphabetically and gives their abbreviations and beginning page numbers. You will find this a useful and easy-to-locate guide. Also, the section "Where Do I Find It?" offers several types of indexes to help you locate specific passages and articles.

Throughout *The Catholic Youth Bible,* there are many references to specific Bible passages. These references are given in shorthand form, such as Jn 3.16–17. The initial letters are the abbreviation for (or, in a few cases, the full name of) the Bible book. The number before the period stands for the chapter, and the number(s) after the period stands for the verse(s). So Jn 3.16–17 refers to the Gospel According to John, chapter 3, verses 16 to 17.

NAME OF BOOK   VERSE(S)

Jn 3.16–17

CHAPTER

Most of the articles end with a citation identifying the Bible passage the article is based on. It is important to read the passage before reading the article.

QUESTIONS AND ANSWERS About the Bible

THE BIBLE—which is also called the sacred Scriptures—tells the story of the loving relationship between God and humankind. It brings people to a deeper relationship with God, teaches important truths about Christian faith, and challenges how we live our life and relate with other people. However, studying the Bible raises questions for many people. This section gives some answers to key questions from Catholic Christian teaching. Because these are brief answers to important questions, you may want to talk more about them with someone in your family, church, or school.

What does it mean to say that God inspired the Bible? Did God speak directly to the Bible's authors?

Christians make a fantastic claim about the Bible: God is the author of the sacred Scriptures. They believe the Bible is God's word, containing the truths that God wishes to reveal to humankind for our salvation. Through the Holy Spirit, God inspired the human authors of the Bible's books to reveal these truths in their writings. These two concepts—God's **inspiration** of the biblical authors and God's **revelation** in their writings of the truths about God and God's will for us—are two important Christian beliefs about the Bible.

To say that biblical authors were inspired by God does not mean that they took dictation directly from God. They were true authors using creative literary forms to communicate the people's experience of God. In fact, many of the books had more than one author. Some books went through several decades of development in which the stories were told and retold, written down, combined, and edited. The church believes the Holy Spirit was guiding the many people involved throughout this whole process.

How do I know that what is in the Bible is true? Aren't there mistakes in the Bible?

Christians believe that the Bible is true and without errors when it teaches the things God wishes to reveal for the sake of our salvation. This is called the inerrancy of the Bible.

Some Christians also believe that the Bible is without error in every respect, including all references to scientific and historical facts. But Catholic Christians, along with others, are cautious about making this claim. The Catholic church teaches that in order to interpret the Bible correctly, we must understand what the human authors intended to communicate at the time of their writing. To know what God wants to reveal through their words, we must take into account "the conditions of their time and culture, the literary genres in use at that time, and the modes of feeling, speaking, and narrating then current" (*Catechism of the Catholic Church*, no. 110).

In other words, from our modern viewpoint, some statements in the Bible may seem like mistakes. But these "mistakes" may be due to the difference between a biblical author's cultural perspective and our cultural perspective. Or they may be due to our misunderstanding of a biblical author's use of literary devices such as metaphors, fiction, and poetry. Or perhaps they are due to a biblical author's different understanding of science or history. In its introductions and articles, *The Catholic Youth Bible* will help you understand the biblical authors' intentions and the church's teaching about what God is revealing through them.

Why do Catholics believe that the Bible alone isn't enough to teach all the truths about the Christian faith?

All Christians believe that God's complete revelation—all that people need to know about God and about their relation to God—is expressed in Jesus Christ. They believe that Jesus is the living Word of God, "the image of the invisible God" (Col 1.15). All Christians believe that the Bible is a primary way of communicating God's revelation, which has its ultimate source in Christ.

But Catholic Christians believe that God's revelation is also communicated through **sacred Tradition**. Sacred Tradition, which is sometimes simply called Tradition, is all that the first Apostles learned from Jesus and the Holy Spirit. Under the guidance of the Holy Spirit, it is preserved, taught, and reinterpreted for each new generation by the Apostles' successors—the pope and bishops. Scripture and Tradition are closely related and support each other, having their common source in Jesus Christ. Some of the articles in *The Catholic Youth Bible* expand on the Bible's message with teaching from sacred Tradition.

Why does the Bible have two testaments?

The Bible reveals God's plan for humanity. It is divided into two parts. The Old Testament records the relationship between God and the descendants of Abraham, particularly the descendants of Abraham's grandson Jacob. At different times in their history, these descendants are called the Hebrews, the Israelites, and the Jews. The Old Testament contains their religious history, laws, and sacred stories. Because the Old Testament contains the sacred Scriptures of the Jewish people, many Christians also call the Old Testament the Hebrew Scriptures.

The New Testament presents Jesus as the full revelation of God. Jesus was a Jew, and he affirmed the core beliefs of the Jewish faith. He knew and cherished the Hebrew Scriptures. But he also revealed new insights into God's desired relationship with human beings. After his Resurrection, as his followers lived out the implications of his teachings, they eventually formed a new religious faith that came to be called Christianity. The books and letters in the New Testament record their central teachings and beliefs about Jesus.

The church teaches that there is a profound unity to the Old and New Testaments in relation to God's revelation. "The Old Testament prepares for the New and the New Testament fulfills the Old; the two shed light on each other; both are true Word of God" (*Catechism*, no. 140). This is why both the Old and New Testaments are used in Catholic liturgy and catechesis.

The Bible was written a long time ago. What does it have to do with my life today?

Christians believe the Bible's core message of God's desire to be in a loving relationship with human beings is greater than the difficulties caused by the passing of time and by cultural differences between the biblical era and our time. They believe that the more people read, reflect on, and study the Bible, the more they can discover what God is saying to people today. The Bible's message does not wear out or become obsolete. However, the Bible was originally written by and for people who lived in different historical circumstances. In order to make the Bible relevant to our time, people need to interpret it in its proper context (see the next chapter, "How to Read and Study the Bible," for help with this). This process of making the Bible's message current for our time is called **actualization**.

Each person, community, and culture brings its life experiences to interact with God's revelation in the Bible. God's word sheds light on our hopes and struggles and in so doing becomes a source of new life for us. Knowing that God forgives our sins, liberates us from the things that oppress and enslave us, and rejoices in our successes gives us the inner peace we all seek. The Bible tells us that we are entrusted with Jesus' mission to share God's peace, justice, and love—a mission that gives true meaning to our life.

Of course, the best way to discover what the Bible has to do with your life is to read and study it yourself. The same Holy Spirit who inspired the original authors will also be your companion as you spend time with the Bible—comforting, exciting, challenging, and encouraging you along your way.

How to Read AND Study THE BIBLE

MAKING SENSE OF THE BIBLE

> "The Word became flesh and lived among us" (Jn 1.14).

God's Word came to earth as a person, Jesus Christ. Jesus was fully human so that people could experience God's love firsthand. He was also fully God so that through him death is overcome and new life is breathed into sinful humanity.

The Bible is called God's word because it is closely linked to Jesus. Like Jesus, it can be said to be both human and divine. It is divine because it reveals to us God and God's plan. But it is also the work of human authors and reflects their knowledge, culture, and biases. It is through their words that the Bible reveals God's nature, God's saving work in the world (often called salvation history), and God's purpose for humanity—including our lives. It follows that an important part of understanding the Bible is understanding the human authors' intentions.

However, understanding the authors' intentions isn't enough either. We must also look at the message of any individual book or passage within the bigger picture of the entire Bible's message and the church's interpretation of it. Here are some suggestions for considering these different contexts when you read the Bible.

Consider the Book's Central Themes

The Bible's authors usually had a central theme or themes in mind when writing their particular book or letter. So when you are confused about the meaning of a particular verse or passage, it often helps to go back and read the whole chapter or even check out the introduction to the book. For example, you may wonder what Jesus is trying to teach us in the story of the prodigal son, Lk 15.11–32. You might try reading from the beginning of chapter 15. You'll find that Jesus told the story in response to people who criticized him for welcoming sinners. This helps us understand that the prodigal son story teaches that we are supposed to welcome sinners too.

Consider the Historical Situation and the Audience

Certain Bible passages do not make sense unless we understand the historical situation the author was trying to address. The introductions to each of the books in *The Catholic Youth Bible* help you with this. For example, in Am 5.21,23 God tells the people: "I hate, I despise your festivals. . . . / Take away from me the noise of your songs." Doesn't God like worship? In the introduction to Amos, we learn that God sent Amos to speak against the rich people who exploited the poor and then attended elaborate religious festivals to worship God. The hypocrisy was what God hated.

Consider the Teaching of the Whole Bible

An old saying calls us to "use the Bible to interpret the Bible." Some people focus on a single verse from the Bible and ignore other passages on the same subject. For example, some churches will not allow women in any position of leadership. They base this on 1 Cor 14.34, which says, "Women should be silent in the churches." But in doing this, they disregard other passages, such as those in which Paul pays respect to women who were ministers and leaders in the church.

Consider the Church's Interpretation

Most Christian churches have traditions and teachings for interpreting the Bible and applying its message. For Roman Catholics, bishops ultimately have the responsibility for properly interpreting God's revelation in the Bible. Many other people (Scripture scholars, priests, parish ministers, and teachers, for example) help us understand the bishops' interpretation of the Scriptures and how to apply it to our lives. *The Catholic Youth Bible* points out the Catholic church's established teaching for important passages, especially in the "Catholic Connections" articles. When in doubt, ask a priest, minister, parish leader, teacher, or parent for help in looking for the correct interpretation of a confusing passage.

HEAD AND HEART

Sometimes when you pick up the Bible, you want to study and learn. Maybe you want to learn some Bible history or understand more about Baptism. Maybe you want to know why the Gospel of John is so different from the other Gospels. These are things of the head, the intellect.

Sometimes when you pick up the Bible, you are hungry to grow closer to God. You want to experience God's presence in your life or receive guidance about a problem. These are things of the heart, the soul.

Ask God to touch both your head and heart when you read the Bible. It's important to be open to both because we were created to be whole people. *The Catholic Youth Bible* can help. Some of the articles, particularly the introductions to the books, the "Did You Know?" articles, and the "Catholic Connections" articles, give background to help your understanding for head reading. The "Live It!" and "Pray It!" articles are more for your heart reading.

THE PRIMA PROCESS

Prima is the Latin word for "first." In the PRIMA process, each letter of the word stands for a step in reading and studying the Bible individually or with a group. Using the PRIMA process helps you remember to keep God first in your life!

Pray. Begin with a prayer that your time with the Bible will draw you closer to God.

Read attentively, trusting that God will give you what you need to learn or grow.

Imagine what was going on when the passage was first written. What is its cultural and historical context? Try to put yourself into the story. What was the author trying to get across?

Meditate on what you have read. How does this fit in the context of the rest of the Bible's teaching? with the church's teaching? What do you think God is teaching you?

Apply what you have read to your life. God may be calling you to address a particular issue or relationship. Or you may find words of comfort and support you need at this particular time. Carry God's word into the rest of your day, the rest of your life!

PERSONAL AND GROUP STUDY

Personal Reading and Study

Faith is personal. Reading the Bible by yourself can help you grow in both your head and heart relationships with God. Choose a time that fits for you and make a commitment to read *The Catholic Youth Bible* regularly, at least once a week if not every day. The PRIMA process and the Bible reading plans in the next chapter will give you a structure for your personal reading.

Group Reading and Study

Your faith is personal, but it is not private. The Bible itself teaches that God calls us to be part of a Christian community. Reading and studying the Bible with a group can feed you and teach you in an exciting way. Consider starting a group Bible study by inviting some friends or family members to meet with you. Or check at your parish to see what Bible studies might already be going on.

Again, the PRIMA process and the Bible reading plans in this book can provide a structure for reading the Bible with a group. Check with your parish or school for other resources you can use with a group.

MAKING A PLAN

Note: All the reading plans described in this section are found on page xviii, "Suggested Reading Plans."

The Catholic church has an excellent plan for reading and studying the Bible, called the lectionary. The lectionary includes a cycle of Scripture passages read at Sunday Eucharist in the liturgy of the word. It is inspiring to know that other Catholics all over the world are hearing and reflecting on the same Scriptures at the same time. Studying the Sunday lectionary readings can make a big difference in your appreciation of the Eucharist. You can use reading plan 1, "Reading the Bible with the Church," to help you do this for part of the year. It lists the Sunday lectionary readings for the entire year.

Reading whole books of the Bible is important to fully understanding the Bible in context. But it rarely works to say, "I'm going to read the whole Bible cover to cover." Most people quit when they hit the detailed laws in the Book of Exodus. So as a start, you can use reading plan 2, "A Walk Through the Bible," which gives a four-week overview of the important events in the Bible. After that you might read one of the four Gospels—Mark is good because it is short and filled with action. Then try the Acts of the Apostles. Follow this by one of the letters from the New Testament—1 Corinthians is a good one to start with. Eventually, move on to Genesis and Exodus from the Old Testament to see how their themes are connected to the New Testament books you have read.

You could also make a plan to study themes in the Bible. To get started, pick from reading plans 3 to 8, which cover topics such as sin and salvation, suffering, God's call, and women in the Bible. Or use the article subject index in the back of *The Catholic Youth Bible* to create your own reading plan on a topic that interests you.

THE CHURCH YEAR

The feast days and holy days celebrated by Catholics and other Christians follow a yearly pattern. This pattern is called the liturgical year; it is different from the calendar year. Here is a description of the major seasons in the liturgical year. It might help you if you also take a look at the circular diagram of the liturgical year, found on page xvii.

Advent begins the liturgical year four Sundays before Christmas. It is a time of preparation for the coming of Christ. The Advent season can be found on the liturgical year wheel in November and December. It is represented by the small graphic of an Advent wreath.

The Christmas season lasts twelve days, beginning with Christmas Day and concluding with the feast of the Baptism of the Lord. This season is found at the top part of the liturgical year wheel. The cross reminds us that the wood of the manger becomes the wood of the cross.

Lent begins with Ash Wednesday and lasts forty days. It is a solemn time of fasting, prayer, and almsgiving in preparation for Easter. The small picture of the palms and cross in the liturgical year wheel symbolizes all of Lent as a journey toward Palm Sunday, when the same crowd that waves palms and yells "Hosanna!" ends up waving angry fists and shouting "Crucify him!"

The Easter Triduum is the celebration of Holy Thursday, Good Friday, and the Easter Vigil on Holy Saturday. At this one, continuous, three-day liturgy, Christians remember the Lord's Supper, Christ's Passion and death, and his Resurrection. These feasts are at the heart of the liturgical year. They are represented by the picture of the Easter candle, which makes its appearance in the darkness of the Easter Vigil. The vestments and altar cloths seen are red on Good Friday and white on the other two days.

The Easter Season lasts fifty days, beginning with Easter Sunday and ending with the feast of Pentecost. The symbol of the lamb represents Jesus, the innocent sacrificial lamb of God. The symbol of the Holy Spirit reminds us that the Holy Spirit came to the disciples, in the rush of wind and tongues of fire. The altar cloths and vestments are white throughout the Easter season, and then red on Pentecost. Red is the color of the Holy Spirit (as in Confirmation Mass) and of the celebration of feast days associated with martyrs, people killed for their faith (such as the feast of Saints Peter and Paul).

The season of Ordinary Time is made up of the days between Christmas and Lent, and the days between Easter and Advent. The bread and wine show us that the main focus of Ordinary Time is the ministry of Jesus, represented by the grapes and bread of communion. There are some special feast days during Ordinary Time that are not celebrated with green vestments and altar cloths, such as Trinity Sunday and the Feast of the Body and Blood of Christ, the first two Sundays after Pentecost, and the Feast of Christ the King, the last Sunday before Advent. You'll see white on all three of those days. The particular dates and days these feasts fall upon vary from year to year.

Christmas is always December 25, so counting backwards four Sundays shows the four Sundays of Advent. Sometimes Advent includes Thanksgiving weekend, and sometimes it doesn't, depending on which day of the week Christmas is.

Easter is always the first Sunday after the first full moon in the spring. Counting backwards six Sundays and then one Wednesday shows when Ash Wednesday and Lent begin. Sometimes Easter is in March, and sometimes it is in April.

On page xviii, you will find a Bible reading plan that corresponds to the readings of the Bible heard on Sundays throughout these seasons. That is an excellent way to get to know the Bible and the liturgical year at the same time.

Liturgical (Church) Year Calendar

Suggested Reading Plans

READING PLAN 1: Reading the Bible with the Church

This reading plan lists the Sunday readings for the liturgical year. The Scripture passages listed in the following table reflect those found in the official Catholic Lectionary for Mass, which uses New American Bible translation.

ADVENT AND CHRISTMAS

Cycle A (2004, 2007, 2010)	Cycle B (2005, 2008, 2011)	Cycle C (2006, 2009, 2012)
The First Sunday of Advent		
Isa 2.1–5	Isa 63.16–17; 64.1–8	Jer 33.14–16
Rom 13.11–14	1 Cor 1.3–9	1 Thess 3.12—4.2
Mt 24.37–44	Mk 13.33–37	Lk 21.25–28,34–36
The Second Sunday of Advent		
Isa 11.1–10	Isa 40.1–5,9–11	Bar 5.1–9
Rom 15.4–9	2 Pet 3.8–14	Phil 1.4–6,8–11
Mt 3.1–12	Mk 1.1–8	Lk 3.1–6
The Third Sunday of Advent		
Isa 35.1–6,10	Isa 61.1–2,10–11	Zeph 3.14–18
Jas 5.7–10	1 Thess 5.16–24	Phil 4.4–7
Mt 11.2–11	Jn 1.6–8,19–28	Lk 3.10–18
The Fourth Sunday of Advent		
Isa 7.10–14	2 Sam 7.1–5,8–11,16	Mic 5.2–4
Rom 1.1–7	Rom 16.25–27	Heb 10.5–10
Mt 1.18–24	Lk 1.26–38	Lk 1.39–45
Midnight Mass *(25 December, every year, readings are the same for all cycles)*		
Isa 9.2–7	Isa 9.2–7	Isa 9.2–7
Titus 2.11–14	Titus 2.11–14	Titus 2.11–14
Lk 2.1–14	Lk 2.1–14	Lk 2.1–14
Feast of the Holy Family		
Sir 3.2–6,12–14	Sir 3.2–6,12–14	Sir 3.2–6,12–14
Col 3.12–21	Col 3.12–21	Col 3.12–21
Mt 2.13–15,19–23	Lk 2.22–40	Lk 2.41–52
Solemnity of Mary, Mother of God *(1 January, every year, readings are the same for all cycles)*		
Num 6.22–27	Num 6.22–27	Num 6.22–27
Gal 4.4–7	Gal 4.4–7	Gal 4.4–7
Lk 2.16–21	Lk 2.16–21	Lk 2.16–21
Epiphany *(readings are the same for all cycles)*		
Isa 60.1–6	Isa 60.1–6	Isa 60.1–6
Eph 3.2–3,5–6	Eph 3.2–3,5–6	Eph 3.2–3,5–6
Mt 2.1–12	Mt 2.1–12	Mt 2.1–12
Baptism of the Lord		
Isa 42.1–4,6–7	Isa 42.1–4,6–7	Isa 42.1–4,6–7
Acts 10.34–38	Acts 10.34–38	Acts 10.34–38
Mt 3.13–17	Mk 1.7–11	Lk 3.15–16,21–22

LENT AND EASTER

Cycle A (2005, 2008, 2011)	Cycle B (2006, 2009, 2012)	Cycle C (2007, 2010, 2013)
Ash Wednesday *(readings are the same for all cycles)*		
Joel 2.12–18	Joel 2.12–18	Joel 2.12–18
2 Cor 5.20—6.2	2 Cor 5.20—6.2	2 Cor 5.20—6.2
Mt 6.1–6,16–18	Mt 6.1–6,16–18	Mt 6.1–6,16–18
The First Sunday of Lent		
Gen 2.7–9; 3.1–7	Gen 9.8–15	Deut 26.4–10
Rom 5.12–19	1 Pet 3.18–22	Rom 10.8–13
Mt 4.1–11	Mk 1.12–15	Lk 4.1–13

Cycle A (2005, 2008, 2011)	Cycle B (2006, 2009, 2012)	Cycle C (2007, 2010, 2013)
The Second Sunday of Lent		
Gen 12.1–4	Gen 22.1–2,9,10–13,15–18	Gen 15.5–12,17–18
2 Tim 1.8–10	Rom 8.31–34	Phil 3.17—4.1
Mt 17.1–9	Mk 9.2–10	Lk 9.28–36
The Third Sunday of Lent		
Ex 17.3–7	Ex 20.1–17	Ex 3.1–8,13–15
Rom 5.1–2,5–8	1 Cor 1.22–25	1 Cor 10.1–6,10–12
Jn 4.5–42	Jn 2.13–25	Lk 13.1–9
The Fourth Sunday of Lent		
1 Sam 16.1,6–7,10–13	2 Chr 36.14–17,19–23	Josh 5.9,10–12
Eph 5.8–14	Eph 2.4–10	2 Cor 5.17–21
Jn 9.1–41	Jn 3.14–21	Lk 15.1–3,11–32
The Fifth Sunday of Lent		
Ezek 37.12–14	Jer 31.31–34	Isa 43.16–21
Rom 8.8–11	Heb 5.7–9	Phil 3.8–14
Jn 11.1–45	Jn 12.20–33	Jn 8.1–11
Passion Sunday (Palm Sunday)		
Isa 50.4–7	Isa 50.4–7	Isa 50.4–7
Phil 2.6–11	Phil 2.6–11	Phil 2.6–11
Mt 26.14—27.66	Mk 14.1—15.47	Lk 22.14—23.56
Holy Thursday (*readings are the same for all cycles*)		
Ex 12.1–8,11–14	Ex 12.1–8,11–14	Ex 12.1–8,11–14
1 Cor 11.23–26	1 Cor 11.23–26	1 Cor 11.23–26
Jn 13.1–15	Jn 13.1–15	Jn 13.1–15
Good Friday (*readings are the same for all cycles*)		
Isa 52.13—53.12	Isa 52.13—53.12	Isa 52.13—53.12
Heb 4.14–16; 5.7–9	Heb 4.14–16; 5.7–9	Heb 4.14–16; 5.7–9
Jn 18.1—19.42	Jn 18.1—19.42	Jn 18.1—19.42
Easter Sunday (*readings are the same for all cycles*)		
Acts 10.34,37–43	Acts 10.34,37–43	Acts 10.34,37–43
Col 3.1–4 or 1 Cor 5.6–8	Col 3.1–4 or 1 Cor 5.6–8	Col 3.1–4 or 1 Cor 5.6–8
Jn 20.1–9	Jn 20.1–9	Jn 20.1–9
Second Sunday of Easter		
Acts 2.42–47	Acts 4.32–35	Acts 5.12–16
1 Pet 1.3–9	1 Jn 5.1–6	Rev 1.9–19
Jn 20.19–31	Jn 20.19–31	Jn 20.19–31
Third Sunday of Easter		
Acts 2.14,22–28	Acts 3.13–19	Acts 5.27–32,40–41
1 Pet 1.17–21	1 Jn 2.1–5	Rev 5.11–14
Lk 24.13–35	Lk 24.35–48	Jn 21.1–19
Fourth Sunday of Easter		
Acts 2.14,36–41	Acts 4.8–12	Acts 13.14,43–52
1 Pet 2.20–25	1 Jn 3.1–2	Rev 7.9,14–17
Jn 10.1–10	Jn 10.11–18	Jn 10.27–30
Fifth Sunday of Easter		
Acts 6.1–7	Acts 9.26–31	Acts 14.21–27
1 Pet 2.4–9	1 Jn 3.18–24	Rev 21.1–5
Jn 14.1–12	Jn 15.1–8	Jn 13.31–35
Sixth Sunday of Easter		
Acts 8.5–8,14–17	Acts 10.25–26,34–35,44–48	Acts 15.1–2,22–29
1 Pet 3.15–18	1 Jn 4.7–10	Rev 21.10–14,22–23
Jn 14.15–21	Jn 15.9–17	Jn 14.23–29
Seventh Sunday of Easter		
Acts 1.12–14	Acts 1.15–17,20–26	Acts 7.55–60
1 Pet 4.13–16	1 Jn 4.11–16	Rev 22.12–14,16–17,20
Jn 17.1–11	Jn 17.11–19	Jn 17.20–26
Pentecost Sunday (*readings are the same for all cycles*)		
Acts 2.1–11	Acts 2.1–11	Acts 2.1–11
1 Cor 12.3–7,12–13	1 Cor 12.3–7,12–13	1 Cor 12.3–7,12–13
Jn 20.19–23	Jn 20.19–23	Jn 20.19–23

ORDINARY TIME

	Cycle A (2005, 2008, 2011)	Cycle B (2006, 2009, 2012)	Cycle C (2007, 2010, 2013)

The First Sunday in Ordinary Time
(see the Feast of the Baptism of the Lord under "Advent and Christmas")

The Second Sunday in Ordinary Time

	Isa 49.3,5–6	1 Sam 3.3b–10,19	Isa 62.1–5
	1 Cor 1.1–3	1 Cor 6.13c–15a,17–20	1 Cor 12.4–11
	Jn 1.29–34	Jn 1.35–42	Jn 2.1–11

The Third Sunday in Ordinary Time

	Isa 8.23—9.3	Jon 3.1–5,10	Neh 8.2–4a,5–6,8–10
	1 Cor 1.10–13,17	1 Cor 7.29–31	1 Cor 12.12–30
	Mt 4.12–23	Mk 1.14–20	Lk 1.1–4; 4.14–21

The Fourth Sunday in Ordinary Time

	Zeph 2.3; 3.12–13	Deut 18.15–20	Jer 1.4–5,17–19
	1 Cor 1.26–31	1 Cor 7.32–35	1 Cor 12.31—13.13
	Mt 5.1–12a	Mk1.21–28	Lk 4.21–30

The Fifth Sunday in Ordinary Time

	Isa 58.7–10	Job 7.1–4,6–7	Isa 6.1–2a,3–8
	1 Cor 2.1–5	1 Cor 9,16–19,22–23	1 Cor 15.1–11
	Mt 5.13–16	Mk 1.29–39	Lk 5.1–11

The Sixth Sunday in Ordinary Time

	Sir 15.15–20	Lv 13.1–2,45–46	Jer 17.5–8
	1 Cor 2.6–10	1 Cor 10.31—11.1	1 Cor 15.12,16–20
	Mt 5.17–37	Mk 1.40–45	Lk 6.17,20–26

The Seventh Sunday in Ordinary Time

	Lev 19,1–2,17–18	Isa 43.18–19,21–22,24b–25	1 Sam 26.2,7–9,12–13,22–23
	1 Cor 3.16–23	2 Cor 1.18–22	1 Cor 15.45–49
	Mt 5.38–48	Mk 2.1–12	Lk 6.27–38

The Eighth Sunday in Ordinary Time

	Isa 49.14–15	Hos 2.16b,17b,21–22	Sir 27.4–7
	1 Cor 4.1–5	2 Cor 3.1b–6	1 Cor 15.54–58
	Mt 6.24–34	Mk 2.18–22	Lk 6.39–45

The Ninth Sunday in Ordinary Time

	Deut 11.18,26–28,32	Deut 5.12–15	1 Kings 8.41–43
	Rom 3.21–25a,28	2 Cor 4.6–11	Gal 1.1–2,6–10
	Mt 7.21–27	Mk 2.23—3.6	Lk 7.1–10

The Tenth Sunday in Ordinary Time

	Hos 6.3–6	Gen 3.9–15	1 Kings 17.17–24
	Rom 4.18–25	2 Cor 4.13—5.1	Gal 1.11–19
	Mt 9.9–13	Mk 3.20–35	Lk 7.11–17

The Eleventh Sunday in Ordinary Time

	Ex 19.2–6a	Ezek 17.22–24	2 Sam 12.7–10,13
	Rom 5.6–11	2 Cor 5.6–10	Gal 2.16,19–21
	Mt 9.36—10.8	Mk 4.26–34	Lk 7.36—8.3

The Twelfth Sunday in Ordinary Time

	Jer 20.10–13	Job 38.1,8–11	Zech 12.10–11; 13.1
	Rom 5.12–15	2 Cor 5.14–17	Gal 3.26–29
	Mt 10.26–33	Mk 4.35–41	Lk 9.18–24

The Thirteenth Sunday in Ordinary Time

	2 Kings 4.8–11,14–16a	Wis 1.13–15; 2.23–24	1 Kings 19.16b,19–21
	Rom 6.3–4,8–11	2 Cor 8.7,9,13–15	Gal 5.1,13–18
	Mt 10.37–42	Mk 5.21–43	Lk 9.51–62

The Fourteenth Sunday in Ordinary Time

	Zech 9.9–10	Ezek 2.2–5	Isa 66.10–14c
	Rom 8.9,11–13	2 Cor 12.7–10	Gal 6.14–18
	Mt 11.25–30	Mk 6.1–6	Lk 10.1–12,17–20

The Fifteenth Sunday in Ordinary Time

	Isa 55.10–11	Am 7.12–15	Deut 30.10–14
	Rom 8.18–23	Eph 1.3–14	Col 1.15–20
	Mt 13.1–23	Mk 6.7–13	Lk 10.25–37

The Sixteenth Sunday in Ordinary Time

	Wis 12.13,16–19	Jer 23.1–6	Gen 18.1–10a
	Rom 8.26–27	Eph 2.13–18	Col 1.24–28
	Mt 13.24–43	Mk 6.30–34	Lk 10.38–42

The Seventeenth Sunday in Ordinary Time

	1 Kings 3.5,7–12	2 Kings 4.42–44	Gen 18.20–32
	Rom 8.28–30	Eph 4.1–6	Col 2.12–14
	Mt 13.44–52	Jn 6.1–15	Lk 11.1–13

ORDINARY TIME (*continued*)

Cycle A (2005, 2008, 2011)	Cycle B (2006, 2009, 2012)	Cycle C (2007, 2010, 2013)
The Eighteenth Sunday in Ordinary Time		
Isa 55.1–3	Ex 16.2–4,12–15	Eccl 1.2; 2.21–23
Rom 8.35,37–39	Eph 4.17,20–24	Col 3.1–5,9–11
Mt 14.13–21	Jn 6.24–35	Lk 12.13–21
The Nineteenth Sunday in Ordinary Time		
1 Kings 19.9a,11–13a	1 Kings 19.4–8	Wis 18.6–9
Rom 9.1–5	Eph 4.30—5.2	Heb 11.1–2,8–19
Mt 14.22–33	Jn 6.41–51	Lk 12.32–48
The Twentieth Sunday in Ordinary Time		
Isa 56.1,6–7	Prov 9,1–6	Jer 38.4–6,8–10
Rom 11.13–15,29–32	Eph 5.15–20	Heb 12.1–4
Mt 15.21–28	Jn 6.51–58	Lk 12.49–53
The Twenty-First Sunday in Ordinary Time		
Isa 22.19–23	Josh 24.1–2a,15–17,18b	Isa 66.18–21
Rom 11.33–36	Eph 5.21–32	Heb 12.5–7,11–13
Mt 16.13–20	Jn 6.60–69	Lk 13.22–30
The Twenty-Second Sunday in Ordinary Time		
Jer 20.7–9	Deut 4.1–2,6–8	Sir 3.17–18,20,28–29
Rom 12.1–2	Jas 1.17–18,21b–22,27	Heb 12.18–19,22–24a
Mt 16.21–27	Mk 7.1–8,14–15,21–23	Lk 14.1,7–14
The Twenty-Third Sunday in Ordinary Time		
Ezek 33.7–9	Isa 35.4–7a	Wis 9.13–18b
Rom 13.8–10	Jas 2.1–5	Philem 9–10,12–17
Mt 18.15–20	Mk7.31–37	Lk 14.25–33
The Twenty-Fourth Sunday in Ordinary Time		
Isa 55.6–9	Isa 50.5–9a	Ex 32.7–11,13–14
Rom 14.7–9	Jas 2.14–18	1 Tim 1.12–17
Mt 18.21–35	Mk 8.27–35	Lk 15.1–32
The Twenty-Fifth Sunday in Ordinary Time		
Acts 2.14,22–28	Wis 2.12,17–20	Am 8.4–7
Phil 1.20c–24,27a	Jas 3.16—4.3	1 Tim 2.1–8
Mt 20.1–16a	Mk 9.30–37	Lk 16.1–13
The Twenty-Sixth Sunday in Ordinary Time		
Ezek 18.25–28	Num 11.25–29	Am 6.1a,4–7
Phil 2.1–11	Jas 5.1–6	1 Tim 6.11–16
Mt 21.28–32	Mk 9.38–43,45,47–48	Lk 16.19–31
The Twenty-Seventh Sunday in Ordinary Time		
Isa 5.1–7	Gen 2.18–24	Hab 1.2–3; 2.2–4
Phil 4.6–9	Heb 2.9–11	2 Tim 1.6–8,13–14
Mt 21.33–43	Mk 10.2–16	Lk 17.5–10
The Twenty-Eighth Sunday in Ordinary Time		
Isa 25.6–10a	Wis 7.7–11	2 Kings 5.14–17
Phil 4.12–14,19–20	Heb 4.12–13	2 Tim 2.8–13
Mt 22.1–14	Mk 10.17–30	Lk 17.11–19
The Twenty-Ninth Sunday in Ordinary Time		
Isa 45.1,4–6	Isa 52.10–11	Ex 17.8–13
1 Thess 1.1–5b	Heb 4.14–16	2 Tim 3.14—4.2
Mt 22.15–21	Mk 10.35–45	Lk 18.1–8
The Thirtieth Sunday in Ordinary Time		
Ex 22.20–26	Jer 31.7–9	Sir 35.12–14,16–18
1 Thess 1.5c–10	Heb 5.1–6	2 Tim 4.6–8,16–18
Mt 22.34–40	Mk 10.46–52	Lk 18.9–14
The Thirty-First Sunday in Ordinary Time		
Mal 1.14b—2.2b,8–10	Deut 6.2–6	Wis 11.22—12.2
1 Thess 2.7b–9,13	Heb 7.23–28	2 Thess 1.11—2.2
Mt 23.1–12	Mk 12.28b–34	Lk 19.1–10
The Thirty-Second Sunday in Ordinary Time		
Wis 6.12–16	1 Kings 17.10–16	2 Macc 7.1–2,9–14
1 Thess 5.1–6	Heb 9.24–28	2 Thess 2.16—3.5
Mt 25.14–30	Mk 12.38–44	Lk 20.27–38
The Thirty-Third Sunday in Ordinary Time		
Prov 31.10–13,19–20,30–31	Dan 12.1–3	Mal 3.19–20
Rom 8.35,37–39	Heb 10.11–14,18	2 Thess 3.7–12
Mt 14.13–21	Mk 13.24–32	Lk 21.5–19
The Thirty-Fourth Sunday in Ordinary Time (*The Solemnity of Our Lord Jesus Christ the King*)		
Ezek 34.11–12,15–17	Dan 7.13–14	2 Sam 5.1–3
1 Cor 15.20–26,28	Rev 1.5–8	Col 1.12–20
Mt 25.31–46	Jn 18.33b–37	Lk 23.35–43

READING PLAN 2:
A Walk Through the Bible

In four weeks, you can visit some of the highlights of the Bible in chronological order.

Day	Bible Reading	Story
❑ 1	Gen, chs 1–2	Creation
❑ 2	Gen, ch 3	the first sin
❑ 3	Gen 6.9—9.17	the Flood
❑ 4	Gen 17.1—18.15	God's covenant with Abraham
❑ 5	Gen, chs 37, 42–45	Joseph and his brothers
❑ 6	Ex, chs 2–4	the call of Moses
❑ 7	Ex, chs 12–14	God's victory over Pharaoh
❑ 8	Ex, chs 19–20	the Covenant at Sinai and the Ten Commandments
❑ 9	Judg, chs 13–16	Sampson
❑ 10	1 Sam, ch 17	David and Goliath
❑ 11	2 Sam, chs 6–7	God's promise to David
❑ 12	2 Chr, chs 1–3	King Solomon
❑ 13	2 Chr, chs 34–36	from King Josiah to the fall of Jerusalem
❑ 14	Ps 51, 139	David's repentance and God's presence
❑ 15	Wis, chs 7–9	God's wisdom
❑ 16	Mic, chs 1–3	the sins of Judah and Israel
❑ 17	Isa, chs 11–12	promises of hope
❑ 18	Mal, chs 3–4	the day of the Lord
❑ 19	Lk, ch 2	the birth and childhood of Jesus
❑ 20	Mt, chs 5–7	Jesus' Sermon on the Mount
❑ 21	Lk, chs 15–16	Jesus' parables
❑ 22	Mk, ch 15	the death of Jesus
❑ 23	Jn, ch 20	the Resurrection of Jesus
❑ 24	Acts 9.1–22	the conversion of Saul (Paul)
❑ 25	1 Cor, chs 12–14	Christian community
❑ 26	Gal, chs 1–3	faith and the Law
❑ 27	Jas	Christian living
❑ 28	Rev, chs 21–22	the new heaven and the new earth

READING PLAN 5:
The Justice of God

God, it seems, has a preference for the poor. Spend a week reading about God's justice in the Old Testament, and a week in the New Testament.

Day	Bible Reading	Theme
❑ 1	Gen 1.1—2.3	God's Creation is good.
❑ 2	Gen, ch 45	God sides with the youngest.
❑ 3	Ex 3.7–10	God sides with the oppressed.
❑ 4	Lev, ch 25	the Jubilee year
❑ 5	Deut 24.10–21	God is with the least.
❑ 6	Ps 82	justice to the needy
❑ 7	Am 5.21–24; 8.4–8	Let justice roll down.
❑ 8	Mt 5.43–48	Love your enemies.
❑ 9	Mt 19.13–15	Jesus welcomes little children.
❑ 10	Mt 25.31–46	Jesus identifies with the least.
❑ 11	Lk 1.46–56; 6.20–26	God reverses the world's order.
❑ 12	Lk 16.19–31	a rich man and poor Lazarus
❑ 13	Lk 22.24–27	Who is the greatest?
❑ 14	Jas 2.1–13	showing favorites?

READING PLAN 6:
Sin and Salvation

The truth is, none of us is perfect—we are all sinners. But God has a plan to save us. Take a two-week journey as you walk from sin to salvation.

Day	Bible Reading	Theme
❑ 1	Gen, ch 3	the first sin
❑ 2	Gen, ch 6	evil everywhere
❑ 3	Gen 12.1–9	God starts a relationship.
❑ 4	Ex 6.1–8	God rescues God's people.
❑ 5	Lev, ch 4	a sacrifice for sin
❑ 6	Jn 3.1–21	for God so loved the world
❑ 7	Mk 8.31–38	a new sacrifice
❑ 8	Rom 7.14–25	the predicament
❑ 9	Rom 6.1–8, 20–23	the promise
❑ 10	Gal 3.23–29	children of God
❑ 11	Joel 2.12–13; 1 Jn 1.8—2.2	return, repent, and confess
❑ 12	Ps 53	confession prayer
❑ 13	Heb 10.8–15	the only sacrifice
❑ 14	Mt 26.26–28	the Eucharist

READING PLAN 3:
Images of God

God has revealed the divine self to us in many wonderful ways. Enjoy two weeks of "seeing" the different pictures of our God.

Day	Bible Reading	Picture of God
❑ 1	Gen 1.26—3.24	Creator
❑ 2	Ex 3.13–15; 6.2–3	"I AM"
❑ 3	Lev 11.44–45; Mt 25.31–46	holy one and judge
❑ 4	Deut, ch 20	warrior and defender
❑ 5	Ps 12.5	advocate of the poor
❑ 6	Ps 23	great shepherd
❑ 7	Job 42.1–6; Jer 18.1–11	mysterious awesome one
❑ 8	Wis 6.12–20	feminine, wise
❑ 9	Isa 49.14–15	faithful mother
❑ 10	Jon 1.1–2; 3.5–10	universal God of all
❑ 11	Lk 11.1–4	father
❑ 12	Lk, ch 15	domestic God
❑ 13	Jn 1.1–18; Col 1.15–20	Jesus, the Word made flesh
❑ 14	1 Cor, ch 13; 1 Jn 4.7–8	love

READING PLAN 4:
Called by God

Throughout the Bible, God calls people to serve. You too are called to be a disciple. Take two weeks and pray about your call.

Day	Bible Reading	The One Called
❑ 1	Gen 12.1–9	Abram (Abraham)
❑ 2	Ex 3.1—4.17	Moses
❑ 3	Ruth	Ruth
❑ 4	1 Sam, ch 3	Samuel
❑ 5	1 Sam, ch 16	David
❑ 6	Isa 43.1–7	Isaiah
❑ 7	Jer 1.4–10	Jeremiah
❑ 8	Mt 4.18–22	the first disciples
❑ 9	Mk 8.31–38	any disciple
❑ 10	Lk 9.1–6	any disciple
❑ 11	Lk 18.18–30	a rich ruler
❑ 12	Acts 9.1–19	Saul (Paul)
❑ 13	Eph 5.1–20	any disciple
❑ 14	1 Pet 2.9–17	you!

READING PLAN 7:
Why Do We Suffer?

Why God allows suffering has been a question for many of the Bible's authors. During this two-week study, look for the growing awareness that God is with us in our suffering.

Day	Bible Reading	Theme or Article Title
❑ 1	introduction to Tob	God rescues the suffering?
❑ 2	Tob, ch 3	suffering and suicide
❑ 3	Job 1.13–21	suffering and faith
❑ 4	the article near Job 24.1	"A Long Debate"
❑ 5	the article near Job 38.1—42.6	"Why?"
❑ 6	Ps 6	praying for deliverance
❑ 7	the article near Lam 5.22	"Growing Through Loss"
❑ 8	Isa 52.13—53.12	the suffering servant
❑ 9	Jn 12.24–26	the paschal mystery
❑ 10	the article near Mk 15.16–20	"Facing the Hard Times"
❑ 11	the article near Mt 27.27–44	"Suffering Prayer"
❑ 12	2 Cor 1.3–11	God's presence
❑ 13	2 Cor 11.16–30	Paul's suffering
❑ 14	1 Pet 3.13—4.19	suffering as a Christian

READING PLAN 8:
Women in the Bible

In the ancient world, many people considered women to be inferior to men. But throughout the Bible, God shows otherwise. Here is a two-week look at women who have served God and the church.

Day	Bible Reading	Woman or Women
❑ 1	Gen 2.18—3.20	Eve
❑ 2	Gen 17.15–16; 21.1–7	Sarai (Sarah)
❑ 3	Ex 15.19–21	Miriam
❑ 4	Judg, chs 4–5	Deborah
❑ 5	Ruth	Ruth
❑ 6	1 Sam 1.1—2.11	Hannah
❑ 7	Esth, ch 8	Esther
❑ 8	Lk 1.5–25,57–66	Elizabeth
❑ 9	Lk 1.26—2.20	Mary, the mother of our Lord
❑ 10	Lk 2.36–38	Anna
❑ 11	Jn 20.1–18	Mary Magdalene
❑ 12	Jn 11.1–44; 12.1–8	Mary and Martha
❑ 13	Acts 16.11–15; ch 18	Lydia and Priscilla
❑ 14	Rom 16.1–7	Phoebe and Junia

Preface to the NRSV: Catholic Edition

This Catholic edition of the New Revised Standard Version of the Bible has been authorized by the National Conference of Catholic Bishops in the U.S.A. and by the National Council of the Churches of Christ in the U.S.A. It has received the ecclesiastical approval of the Catholic Bishops of both the United States and Canada. The undersigned, who prepared this edition, is a member of the Revised Standard Version Bible Translation Committee as well as an active member and past president of the Catholic Biblical Association of America.

Roman Catholics are already familiar with the accuracy and elegance of the New Revised Standard Version, first published in 1990. It has previously appeared in two major types of edition: an edition of the Old and New Testaments alone, the Bible of most Protestants; and an edition of the Old and New Testaments with the Apocryphal/Deuterocanonical Books placed between the two Testaments. The text of the latter edition received the Imprimatur (official approbation) of the United States and Canadian Catholic Bishops. The New Revised Standard Version is truly an ecumenical translation, for it was produced by Roman Catholic, Eastern Orthodox, Protestant, and Jewish scholars. Because of this Catholic presence no change in the translation was requested for this edition. The only exceptions are the Book of Esther, which exists in two different forms that are explained below, and the Book of Daniel, which includes the deuterocanonical portions that are listed below.

Regarding the number of the books of the Old Testament canon and their arrangement, however, Protestants and Jews on the one hand, and Roman Catholics and Orthodox Christians on the other, hold different beliefs. From the time of the Reformation in the sixteenth century, Protestants have adopted the Jewish canon of the Old Testament, which was established by the rabbis at the end of the first century of the Common Era. This canon includes only those books that were written in Hebrew and Aramaic. In addition to these books, however, Roman Catholics, following the ancient tradition of the Christian church, also hold the Deuterocanonical Books of the Old Testament to be sacred and inspired, and therefore canonical. Protestants and Jews call these books Apocrypha, a word that means "hidden or concealed," an inappropriate title for works that were part of the Greek Old Testament (the Septuagint) from pre-Christian times. The Roman Catholic canon, which was fixed by the time of the Council of Hippo in 393 and reaffirmed by the two Councils of Carthage in 397 and 419, was formally defined by the Council of Trent in 1546. This canon contains seven Deuterocanonical Books: Tobit, Judith, the Wisdom of Solomon, Sirach (the Wisdom of Ben Sira, also known as Ecclesiasticus), Baruch including the Letter of Jeremiah as chapter 6, and 1 and 2 Maccabees; and extra portions of two other books: the Additions to Esther; and the Prayer of Azariah and the Song of the Three Jews inserted between verses 23 and 24 of Daniel 3, Susanna as Daniel 13, and Bel and the Dragon as Daniel 14. Over and above these books and extra portions, the Bible of Greek and Slavonic Orthodox Christians includes 1 Esdras, the Prayer of Manasseh, Psalm 151, and 3 Maccabees. The Slavonic Bible also contains 2 Esdras, and an appendix to the Greek Bible includes 4 Maccabees.

Several of the Deuterocanonical Books were written originally in Hebrew or Aramaic, the rest in Greek. More than two-thirds of the Book of Sirach is now extant in Hebrew, and four fragments of the Book of Tobit in Hebrew and Aramaic were recovered from Qumran Cave IV. It seems certain that Judith and the additions to Daniel were also written originally in Hebrew. Hebrew is the original language of the prose parts of Baruch; the poetic parts were composed in Greek. The Wisdom of Solomon was written completely in Greek. The original language of 1 Maccabees was Hebrew while 2 Maccabees was composed in Greek.

The Book of Esther has two different forms: the short Hebrew original; and the longer Greek version that contains one hundred and seven additional verses comprising six distinct portions, A through F. It is the translation of the entire Greek version that appears in the Deuterocanonical section of the New Revised Standard Version. In this Catholic edition, however, the translation of the Greek portions has been inserted at the appropriate places of the translation of the Hebrew form of the book. Some of the Greek portions apparently had a Hebrew origin; the others were written in Greek.

What is distinctive about this Catholic edition—as well as every other edition published by Roman Catholics—is that the Deuterocanonical Books and portions are placed in their proper order among the other books of the Old Testament. Thus, Tobit, Judith, the long form of Esther, and 1 and 2 Maccabees are found among the so-called historical books directly after Nehemiah. The Wisdom of Solomon and the Book of Sirach follow after the Song of Solomon among the wisdom books. Because Baruch, the well-known secretary of Jeremiah, is said to be the author of the work that bears his name, the book is placed after Jeremiah and Lamentations. This order of books comes from the Latin Vulgate translated by St. Jerome in the late fourth and early fifth centuries. It is essentially the same order as that found in the fourth-century Codex Vaticanus, one of the oldest extant manuscripts of the Septuagint.

Roman Catholics will welcome this edition of the New Revised Standard Version of the Bible for personal reading and study as well as liturgical usage. Based on the latest manuscript discoveries and critical editions, it offers the fruits of the best biblical scholarship in the idiom of today while being sensitive to the contemporary concern for inclusive language when referring to human beings.

ALEXANDER A. DI LELLA, O.F.M.
Andrews-Kelly-Ryan Distinguished Professor of Biblical Studies
The Catholic University of America

September 30, 1992
Feast of St. Jerome

To the Reader

This preface is addressed to you by the Committee of translators, who wish to explain, as briefly as possible, the origin and character of our work. The publication of our revision is yet another step in the long, continual process of making the Bible available in the form of the English language that is most widely current in our day. To summarize in a single sentence: the New Revised Standard Version of the Bible is an authorized revision of the Revised Standard Version, published in 1952, which was a revision of the American Standard Version, published in 1901, which, in turn, embodied earlier revisions of the King James Version, published in 1611.

In the course of time, the King James Version came to be regarded as "the Authorized Version." With good reason it has been termed "the noblest monument of English prose," and it has entered, as no other book has, into the making of the personal character and the public institutions of the English-speaking peoples. We owe to it an incalculable debt.

Yet the King James Version has serious defects. By the middle of the nineteenth century, the development of biblical studies and the discovery of many biblical manuscripts more ancient than those on which the King James Version was based made it apparent that these defects were so many as to call for revision. The task was begun, by authority of the Church of England, in 1870. The (British) Revised Version of the Bible was published in 1881–1885; and the American Standard Version, its variant embodying the preferences of the American scholars associated with the work, was published, as was mentioned above, in 1901. In 1928 the copyright of the latter was acquired by the International Council of Religious Education and thus passed into the ownership of the churches of the United States and Canada that were associated in this Council through their boards of education and publication.

The Council appointed a committee of scholars to have charge of the text of the American Standard Version and to undertake inquiry concerning the need for further revision. After studying the questions whether or not revision should be undertaken, and if so, what its nature and extent should be, in 1937 the Council authorized a revision. The scholars who served as members of the Committee worked in two sections, one dealing with the Old Testament and one with the New Testament. In 1946 the Revised Standard Version of the New Testament was published. The publication of the Revised Standard Version of the Bible, containing the Old and New Testaments, took place on September 30, 1952. A translation of the Apocryphal/Deuterocanonical Books of the Old Testament followed in 1957. In 1977 this collection was issued in an expanded edition, containing three additional texts received by Eastern Orthodox communions (3 and 4 Maccabees and Psalm 151). Thereafter the Revised Standard Version gained the distinction of being officially authorized for use by all major Christian churches: Protestant, Anglican, Roman Catholic, and Eastern Orthodox.

The Revised Standard Version Bible Committee is a continuing body, comprising about thirty members, both men and women. Ecumenical in representation, it includes scholars affiliated with various Protestant denominations, as well as several Roman Catholic members, an Eastern Orthodox member, and a Jewish member who serves in the Old Testament section. For a period of time the Committee included several members from Canada and from England.

Because no translation of the Bible is perfect or is acceptable to all groups of readers, and because discoveries of older manuscripts and further investigation of linguistic features of the text continue to become available, renderings of the Bible have proliferated. During the years following the publication of the Revised Standard Version, twenty-six other English translations and revisions of the Bible were produced by committees and by individual scholars—not to mention twenty-five other translations and revisions of the New Testament alone. One of the latter was the second edition of the RSV New Testament, issued in 1971, twenty-five years after its initial publication.

Following the publication of the RSV Old Testament in 1952, significant advances were made in the discovery and interpretation of documents in Semitic languages related to Hebrew. In addition to the information that had become available in the late 1940s from the Dead Sea texts of Isaiah and Habakkuk, subsequent acquisitions from the same area brought to light many other early copies of all the books of the Hebrew Scriptures (except Esther), though most of these copies are fragmentary. During the same period early Greek manuscript copies of books of the New Testament also became available.

In order to take these discoveries into account, along with recent studies of documents in Semitic languages related to Hebrew, in 1974 the Policies Committee of the Revised Standard Version, which is a standing committee of the National Council of the Churches of Christ in the U.S.A., authorized the preparation of a revision of the entire RSV Bible.

For the Old Testament the Committee has made use of the *Biblia Hebraica Stuttgartensia* (1977; ed. sec. emendata, 1983). This is an edition of the Hebrew and Aramaic text as current early in the Christian era and fixed by Jewish scholars (the "Masoretes") of the sixth to the ninth centuries. The vowel signs, which were added by the Masoretes, are accepted in the main, but where a more probable and convincing reading can be obtained by assuming different vowels this has been done. No notes are given in such cases, because the vowel points are less ancient and reliable than the consonants. When an alternative reading given by the Masoretes is translated in a footnote, this is identified by the words "Another reading is."

Departures from the consonantal text of the best manuscripts have been made only where it seems clear that errors in copying had been made before the text was standardized. Most of the corrections adopted are based on the ancient versions (translations into Greek, Aramaic, Syriac, and Latin), which were made prior to the time of the work of the Masoretes and which therefore may reflect earlier forms of the Hebrew text. In such instances a footnote specifies the version or versions from which the correction has been derived and also gives a translation of the Masoretic Text. Where it was deemed appropriate to do so, information is supplied in footnotes from subsidiary Jewish traditions concerning other textual readings (the *Tiqqune Sopherim*, "emendations of the scribes"). These are identified in the footnotes as "Ancient Heb tradition."

Occasionally it is evident that the text has suffered in transmission and that none of the versions provides a satisfactory restoration. Here we can only follow the best judgment of competent scholars as to the most probable reconstruction of the original text. Such reconstructions are indicated in footnotes by the abbreviation Cn ("Correction"), and a translation of the Masoretic Text is added.

For the Apocryphal/Deuterocanonical Books of the Old Testament the Committee has made use of a number of texts. For most of these books the basic Greek text from which the present translation was made is the edition of the Septuagint prepared by Alfred Rahlfs and published by the Württemberg Bible Society (Stuttgart, 1935). For several of the books the more recently published individual volumes of the Göttingen Septuagint project were utilized. For the Book of Tobit it was decided to follow the form of the Greek text found in codex Sinaiticus (supported as it is by evidence from Qumran); where this text is defective, it was supplemented and corrected by other Greek manuscripts. For the three Additions to Daniel (namely, Susanna, the Prayer of Azariah and the Song of the Three Jews, and Bel and the Dragon) the Committee continued to use the Greek version attributed to Theodotion (the so-called "Theodotion-Daniel"). In translating Ecclesiasticus (Sirach), while constant reference was made to the Hebrew fragments of a large portion of this book (those discovered at Qumran and Masada as well as those recovered from the Cairo Geniza), the Committee generally followed the Greek text (including verse numbers) published by Joseph Ziegler in the Göttingen Septuagint (1965). But in many places the Committee has translated the Hebrew text when this provides a reading that is clearly superior to the Greek; the Syriac and Latin versions were also consulted throughout and occasionally adopted. Finally, in the Book of Esther we have placed the deuterocanonical portions, translated from Robert Hanhart's Göttingen edition of the Greek (1983), in their original context within the translation of the Hebrew text.

For the New Testament the Committee has based its work on the most recent edition of *The Greek New Testament*, prepared by an interconfessional and international committee and published by the United Bible Societies (1966, 3rd ed. corrected, 1983; information concerning changes to be introduced into the critical apparatus of the forthcoming 4th edition was available to the Committee). As in that edition, double brackets are used to enclose a few passages that are generally regarded to be later additions to the text, but which we have retained because of their evident antiquity and their importance in the textual tradition. Only in very rare instances have we replaced the text or the punctuation of the Bible Societies' edition by an alternative that seemed to us to be superior. Here and there in the footnotes the phrase, "Other ancient authorities read," identifies alternative readings preserved by Greek manuscripts and early versions. In both Testaments, alternative renderings of the text are indicated by the word "Or."

As for the style of English adopted for the present revision, among the mandates given to the Committee in 1980 by the Division of Education and Ministry of the National Council of the Churches of Christ (which now holds the copyright of the RSV Bible) was the directive to continue in the tradition of the King James Bible, but to introduce such changes as are warranted on the basis of accuracy, clarity, euphony, and current English usage. Within the constraints set by the original texts and by the mandates of the Division, the Committee has followed the maxim, "As literal as possible, as free as necessary." As a consequence, the New Revised Standard Version (NRSV) remains essentially a literal translation. Paraphrastic renderings have been adopted only sparingly, and then chiefly to compensate for a deficiency in the English language—the lack of a common gender third person singular pronoun.

During the almost half a century since the publication of the RSV, many in the churches have become sensitive to the danger of linguistic sexism arising from the inherent bias of the English language towards the masculine gender, a bias that in the case of the Bible has often restricted or obscured the meaning of the original text. The mandates from the Division specified that, in references to men and women, masculine-oriented language should be eliminated as far as this can be done without altering passages that reflect the historical situation of ancient patriarchal culture. As can be appreciated, more than once the Committee found that the several mandates stood in tension and even in conflict. The various concerns had to be balanced case by case in order to provide a faithful and acceptable rendering without using contrived English. Only very occasionally has the pronoun "he" or "him" been retained in passages where the reference may have been to a woman as well as to a man; for example, in several legal texts in

Leviticus and Deuteronomy. In such instances of formal, legal language, the options of either putting the passage in the plural or of introducing additional nouns to avoid masculine pronouns in English seemed to the Committee to obscure the historic structure and literary character of the original. In the vast majority of cases, however, inclusiveness has been attained by simple rephrasing or by introducing plural forms when this does not distort the meaning of the passage. Of course, in narrative and in parable no attempt was made to generalize the sex of individual persons.

Another aspect of style will be detected by readers who compare the more stately English rendering of the Old Testament with the less formal rendering adopted for the New Testament. For example, the traditional distinction between *shall* and *will* in English has been retained in the Old Testament as appropriate in rendering a document that embodies what may be termed the classic form of Hebrew, while in the New Testament the abandonment of such distinctions in the usage of the future tense in English reflects the more colloquial nature of the koine Greek used by most New Testament authors except when they are quoting the Old Testament.

Careful readers will notice that here and there in the Old Testament the word LORD (or in certain cases GOD) is printed in capital letters. This represents the traditional manner in English versions of rendering the Divine Name, the "Tetragrammaton" (see the notes on Exodus 3.14, 15), following the precedent of the ancient Greek and Latin translators and the long established practice in the reading of the Hebrew Scriptures in the synagogue. While it is almost if not quite certain that the Name was originally pronounced "Yahweh," this pronunciation was not indicated when the Masoretes added vowel sounds to the consonantal Hebrew text. To the four consonants YHWH of the Name, which had come to be regarded as too sacred to be pronounced, they attached vowel signs indicating that in its place should be read the Hebrew word *Adonai* meaning "Lord" (or *Elohim* meaning "God"). Ancient Greek translators employed the word *Kyrios* ("Lord") for the Name. The Vulgate likewise used the Latin word *Dominus* ("Lord"). The form "Jehovah" is of late medieval origin; it is a combination of the consonants of the Divine Name and the vowels attached to it by the Masoretes but belonging to an entirely different word. Although the American Standard Version (1901) had used "Jehovah" to render the Tetragrammaton (the sound of Y being represented by J and the sound of W by V, as in Latin), for two reasons the Committees that produced the RSV and the NRSV returned to the more familiar usage of the King James Version. (1) The word "Jehovah" does not accurately represent any form of the Name ever used in Hebrew. (2) The use of any proper name for the one and only God, as though there were other gods from whom the true God had to be distinguished, began to be discontinued in Judaism before the Christian era and is inappropriate for the universal faith of the Christian Church.

It will be seen that in the Psalms and in other prayers addressed to God the archaic second person singular pronouns (*thee, thou, thine*) and verb forms (*art, hast, hadst*) are no longer used. Although some readers may regret this change, it should be pointed out that in the original languages neither the Old Testament nor the New makes any linguistic distinction between addressing a human being and addressing the Deity. Furthermore, in the tradition of the King James Version one will not expect to find the use of capital letters for pronouns that refer to the Deity—such capitalization is an unnecessary innovation that has only recently been introduced into a few English translations of the Bible. Finally, we have left to the discretion of the licensed publishers such matters as section headings, cross-references, and clues to the pronunciation of proper names.

This new version seeks to preserve all that is best in the English Bible as it has been known and used through the years. It is intended for use in public reading and congregational worship, as well as in private study, instruction, and meditation. We have resisted the temptation to introduce terms and phrases that merely reflect current moods, and have tried to put the message of the Scriptures in simple, enduring words and expressions that are worthy to stand in the great tradition of the King James Bible and its predecessors.

In traditional Judaism and Christianity, the Bible has been more than a historical document to be preserved or a classic of literature to be cherished and admired; it is recognized as the unique record of God's dealings with people over the ages. The Old Testament sets forth the call of a special people to enter into covenant relation with the God of justice and steadfast love and to bring God's law to the nations. The New Testament records the life and work of Jesus Christ, the one in whom "the Word became flesh," as well as describes the rise and spread of the early Christian Church. The Bible carries its full message, not to those who regard it simply as a noble literary heritage of the past or who wish to use it to enhance political purposes and advance otherwise desirable goals, but to all persons and communities who read it so that they may discern and understand what God is saying to them. That message must not be disguised in phrases that are no longer clear, or hidden under words that have changed or lost their meaning; it must be presented in language that is direct and plain and meaningful to people today. It is the hope and prayer of the translators that this version of the Bible may continue to hold a large place in congregational life and to speak to all readers, young and old alike, helping them to understand and believe and respond to its message.

For the Committee,
BRUCE M. METZGER

Guide to the Pronunciation of Proper Names

This edition of the New Revised Standard Version includes a simplified self-pronunciation system for proper names. The system is designed to provide assistance to the reader without filling the text with a complicated variety of symbols, many of which provide unneeded pronunciation clues.

Well-known proper names such as Moses, Nazareth, and Timothy are printed without pronunciation marks of any kind. Such names are a familiar part of our cultural heritage, and they are instantly recognizable to most readers .

More difficult proper names (as well as certain transliterated non-English words) are shown in the text with simplified pronunciation markings. (Two notes of caution: The anglicized pronunciation of a name differs at times from that of the ancient language. Also, there are differences of opinion among speakers of English concerning the most desirable pronunciation of certain names.)

Three kinds of marks are used:

- ´ The acute accent mark: shows which syllable of a name is to be stressed. A compound name—with parts separated by a hyphen—has an accent mark in each part having more than one syllable.

- · The centered dot: shows where an unaccented syllable ends and another syllable begins.

- ‾ The macron: printed over a vowel that has a "long" sound. The macron is shown over the following vowels when they are sounded as indicated:

  a as in gate
  e as in key
  i as in ice
  o as in hope
  u as in use or rule
  y as in type

The macron also indicates the pronunciation of certain diphthongs, or vowel combinations:

  over the *a* in *ai* as in pail
  over the *i* in *ai* as in aisle

A vowel that does not have a "long" sound is printed with no pronunciation mark. In most cases the sound of such a vowel can be determined closely enough by observing how the name is spelled, divided into syllables, and accented.

Abbreviations Used in the Notes

In the notes to the books of the Old Testament the following abbreviations are used:

Ant.	Josephus, *Antiquities of the Jews*
Aram	Aramaic
Ch, chs	Chapter, chapters
Cn	Correction; made where the text has suffered in transmission and the versions provide no satisfactory restoration but where the Standard Bible Committee agrees with the judgment of competent scholars as to the most probable reconstruction of the original text
Gk	Septuagint, Greek version of the Old Testament
Heb	Hebrew of the consonantal Masoretic Text of the Old Testament
Josephus	Flavius Josephus (Jewish historian, about A.D. 37 to about 95)
Macc.	The book(s) of the Maccabees
Ms(s)	Manuscript(s)
MT	The Hebrew of the pointed Masoretic Text of the Old Testament
OL	Old Latin
Q Ms(s)	Manuscript(s) found at Qumran by the Dead Sea
Sam	Samaritan Hebrew text of the Old Testament
Syr	Syriac Version of the Old Testament
Syr H	Syriac Version of Origen's Hexapla
Tg	Targum
Vg	Vulgate, Latin Version of the Old Testament

THE *Old Testament*

Pentateuch

Did you ever get to a movie late? Did you end up bothering your friends who got there on time by asking: "What's happening? Why did he do that? What did she mean by that?" Like the first crucial minutes of a movie, the five books of the Pentateuch set the stage for much of what happens in the rest of the Bible. If you are not familiar with their wonderful stories, you might find yourself asking: "What's happening? Why is he doing that? Why did she say that?" when reading later books.

In-depth

THE NAME PENTATEUCH LITERALLY MEANS A "five-part writing." Thus, the Pentateuch is the first five books of the Old Testament: Genesis, Exodus, Leviticus, Numbers, and Deuteronomy. These books are special to Jewish and Christian believers because they tell of the origins of God's people and their unique relationship with God—sometimes called salvation history. They are the blueprint needed for properly understanding the rest of the Bible. The Pentateuch introduces the idea of a single God who is responsible for all creation. It also tells that this God is active in the world and in the lives of its people, and that the Israelites have been called into a special relationship with this God.

One of the central elements of the special relationship between God and the Israelites described in the Pentateuch is the Sinai Covenant. A covenant is a solemn promise between two parties, where both parties agree to fulfill certain obligations. The Sinai Covenant is the most famous one between God and Israel, with Moses as the mediator, which you will read about in Exodus. In Genesis, you will read about the covenants God makes with Noah, Abraham, and Jacob, which lead to the Sinai Covenant.

Reading the Pentateuch is like appreciating a fine tapestry. When you view a tapestry from the front, all the threads combine to make a beautiful, coherent image. In the same way, an overall look at the covenants, stories, and laws in the Pentateuch combines them to form a picture of the love relationship between God and the people of Israel. A close look at the back of a tapestry shows a more chaotic mix of colors and yarn. So too a closer look at the writings in the Pentateuch reveals not one story but many.

Biblical scholars speak of four primary sources for the stories and traditions in the Pentateuch. The sources reflect four different schools of thought about Israel's relationship with God. For convenience, each source is referred to as an individual author.

- The Yahwist used Yahweh as God's name. This writer focused on the southern kingdom of Judah, used lots of stories, emphasized God's closeness to humanity, and portrayed God acting as a human person.
- The Elohist referred to God as Elohim or Lord. The Elohist wrote about the northern kingdom of Israel and was concerned about idolatry and morality. The writings of the Elohist present God speaking through symbols such as a burning bush.
- The Deuteronomist emphasized the Law as the foundation of the kingdom of Judah. The Deuteronomist emerged toward the end of the monarchy (the time of the Israelite kings), when the Covenant Law seemed to have been forgotten.
- Finally, the Priestly writer emphasized religious rituals and the role of the priesthood. This writer portrayed God as more distant and used a more formal style. This source was written after the Babylonian Exile.

Knowing that these four sources contributed to the final form of the Pentateuch can help us understand that the Pentateuch books are not simply records of events as they occurred but rather faith accounts about the Israelites' growing relationship with God, inspired by God and told from different perspectives.

In the Pentateuch, God reveals how much God loves the human race collectively and how much God loves us personally. God wishes to be in a relationship with us today just as much as God did back then. The Pentateuch reminds us that we are all children of God.

Other Background

- Some of the most familiar stories and people of the Old Testament are found in Genesis and Exodus. Genesis includes the stories of Creation, Adam and Eve, Noah and the Flood, Abraham and Sarah, and Joseph and his brothers. Exodus contains the stories of Moses and the burning bush, Pharaoh and the ten plagues, the parting of the Red Sea, and the Ten Commandments.

- The Jews also refer to the five books of the Pentateuch as the Torah, meaning "teaching" or "instruction."

- An ancient tradition named Moses as the author of the Pentateuch. This was no doubt due to Moses' importance in the Pentateuch itself. But evidence suggests that most of the Pentateuch was written hundreds of years after Moses' death.

- The two types of writing in the Pentateuch are stories and laws. Genesis is all stories; Leviticus and Deuteronomy are mostly laws, and Exodus and Numbers are about half stories and half laws.

Displays of awesome cosmic power, tender love stories, tearful family reunions, and tales of deceit, rape, murder, and worldwide destruction. Does this sound like the script for next summer's blockbuster movie? No, it's the Book of Genesis! It is the story of how a world created for love and harmony goes astray because of human sin. Through it all, God is at work, forming a people to restore what was lost.

At a Glance

- **1.1—11.32.** the creation of the world and human beings by God
- **12.1—50.26.** stories of the ancestors (matriarchs and patriarchs) of Israel

In-depth

Genesis gathers together inspired stories and traditions that reveal God's nature and purpose, and the beginning of the Israelites' special relationship with God. Genesis has two main sections. The first section, chapters 1–11, contains some of the Bible's most memorable stories about Creation and the effect of sin. Chapters 1–2 tell two stories of Creation that portray the beauty and wonder of the natural world and emphasize the goodness and harmony that God intended in Creation. Creation culminates in human beings, made in God's own image. Those first human beings, Adam and Eve, live in a wonderful garden in harmony with God, Creation, and each other. But in chapter 3, sin enters the world, and as a result, Adam and Eve will experience separation, suffering, and ultimately death.

Quick Facts

Period Covered

The stories in the first eleven chapters are primeval history. Chapters 12–15 cover the period of the ancestors, or patriarchs and matriarchs (from 2000 to 1500 B.C.).

Author

An unknown author gathered oral traditions and stories from tribal peoples sometime from 1225 to 1000 B.C. (see Introduction to the Pentateuch)

Themes

the goodness of Creation, human responsibility, the effects of sin, covenant, God's bringing good out of evil

And sin spreads, first to the family (Cain and Abel in chapter 4), then to all society (Noah and the Flood in chapters 6–9). Even after the Flood and God's covenant with Noah, the story of the tower of Babel demonstrates that sin pits nation against nation. As you read these chapters, remember that they were written not as historical accounts or scientific explanations but as symbolic stories that shared faith experiences and taught important religious truths.

The second section of Genesis, chapters 12–50, tells the story of the origins of the Israelite people. It begins with Abraham and Sarah (originally called Abram and Sarai) and continues with Ishmael and Isaac and with Isaac and Rebekah's children, Esau and Jacob. Genesis ends with Joseph, one of Jacob's twelve sons, cleverly saving Egypt and Israel from famine. This section introduces the covenant God makes with Abraham and reminds the reader that God's plans will overcome human sin and weakness.

Genesis

Six Days of Creation and the Sabbath
(Gen 2.4b–9; Job 38.4–11; Jn 1.1–5)

1 In the beginning when God created[a] the heavens and the earth, 2 the earth was a formless void and darkness covered the face of the deep, while a wind from God[b] swept over the face of the waters. 3 Then God said, "Let there be light"; and there was light. 4 And God saw that the light was good; and God separated the light from the darkness. 5 God called the light Day, and the darkness he called Night. And there was evening and there was morning, the first day.

6 And God said, "Let there be a dome in the midst of the waters, and let it separate the waters from the waters." 7 So God made the dome and separated the waters that were under the dome from the waters that were above the dome. And it was so. 8 God called the dome Sky. And there was evening and there was morning, the second day.

9 And God said, "Let the waters under the sky be gathered together into one place, and let the dry land appear." And it was so. 10 God called the dry land Earth, and the waters that were gathered together he called Seas. And God saw that it was good. 11 Then God said, "Let the earth put forth vegetation: plants yielding seed, and fruit trees of every kind on earth that bear fruit with the seed in it." And it was so. 12 The earth brought forth vegetation: plants yielding seed of every kind, and trees of every kind bearing fruit with the seed in it. And God saw that it was good. 13 And there was evening and there was morning, the third day.

14 And God said, "Let there be lights in the dome of the sky to separate the day from the night; and let them be for signs and for seasons and for days and years, 15 and let them be lights in the dome of the sky to give light upon the earth." And it was so. 16 God made the two great lights—the greater light to rule the day and the lesser light to rule the night—and the stars. 17 God set them in the dome of the sky to give light upon the earth, 18 to rule over the day and over the night, and to separate the light from the darkness. And God saw that it was good. 19 And there was evening and there was morning, the fourth day.

20 And God said, "Let the waters bring forth swarms of living creatures, and let birds fly above the earth across the dome of the sky." 21 So God created the great sea monsters and every living creature that moves, of every kind, with which the waters swarm, and every winged bird of every kind. And God saw that it was good. 22 God blessed them, saying, "Be fruitful and multiply and fill the waters in the seas, and let birds multiply on the earth." 23 And there was evening and there was morning, the fifth day.

24 And God said, "Let the earth bring forth living creatures of every kind: cattle and creeping things and wild animals of the earth of every kind." And it was so. 25 God made the wild animals of the earth of every kind, and the cattle of every kind,

---

a Or *when God began to create* or *In the beginning God created*   *b* Or *while the spirit of God* or *while a mighty wind* and everything that creeps upon the ground of every kind. And God saw that it was good.

26 Then God said, "Let us make humankind*c* in our image, according to our likeness; and let them have dominion over the fish of the sea, and over the birds of the air, and over the cattle, and over all the wild animals of the earth,*d* and over every creeping thing that creeps upon the earth."

27 So God created humankind*c* in his image,
in the image of God he created them;*e*
male and female he created them.

28 God blessed them, and God said to them, "Be fruitful and multiply, and fill the earth and subdue it; and have dominion over the fish of the sea and over the birds of the air and over every living thing that moves upon the earth." 29 God said, "See, I have given you every plant yielding seed that is

did you KNOW?

Literary Genres

Some Christians believe that God actually created the world in seven twenty-four-hour days. Such a belief comes from a literal reading of the first chapter of Genesis, as though it were a scientific textbook. However, Genesis was written not as a science article but as symbolic stories, sometimes called mythic stories, that convey great moral and spiritual truths. We should not try to come to any scientific conclusions about the creation of the world from reading these stories.

Mythic stories are one literary type, or genre. You just have to look in a newspaper to see examples of different literary genres: news stories, advice columns, editorials, and comics. Each genre has different rules for interpreting its meaning. The Bible also contains many types of literary genres, including hero stories, poetry, laws, legends, fictional satire, debates, and letters. To properly understand the Bible, pay attention to the literary genre—otherwise, you might believe the Bible is saying something God doesn't intend.

▶ Gen 1.1—2.4

IN THE BEGINNING

"In the beginning when God created the heavens and the earth . . ." (Gen 1.1). This simple verse is one of the foundational beliefs of Christianity. We are not a random collection of atoms. The world is not a lucky combination of cosmic circumstances. The universe did not just accidentally happen.

The beginning of wisdom is acknowledging that a higher power is at work in our life, that the universe has purpose, and that everything was created by God. The ancient writers and editors of Genesis expressed these ideas in the Creation stories. The church affirms these beliefs. They are expressed in a prayer called the Apostles' Creed, which begins, "I believe in God the father almighty, creator of heaven and earth."

Genesis expresses another foundational belief: God created everything good! Read the story in chapter 1, and see how this belief is constantly repeated: And humankind is "very good," created in God's own image. This is God's message to you in the first chapter of the Bible: You carry God's image within you. You are very good! Don't let anyone ever convince you otherwise.

▶ Gen 1.1—2.4

upon the face of all the earth, and every tree with seed in its fruit; you shall have them for food. 30 And to every beast of the earth, and to every bird of the air, and to everything that creeps on the earth, everything that has the breath of life, I have given every green plant for food." And it was so. 31 God saw everything that he had made, and indeed, it was very good. And there was evening and there was morning, the sixth day.

2 Thus the heavens and the earth were finished, and all their multitude. 2 And on the seventh day God finished the work that he had done, and he rested on the seventh day from all the work that he had done. 3 So God blessed the seventh day and hallowed it, because on it God rested from all the work that he had done in creation.

4 These are the generations of the heavens and the earth when they were created.

---

c Heb *adam*   *d* Syr: Heb *and over all the earth*
e Heb *him*

PRAY IT!
The Sabbath

Even God needed to take a rest. The writer of Genesis makes this point to remind readers to set aside a day for rest and prayer, which Jewish people call the Sabbath. Honoring the Sabbath is an act of trust in God. It means we believe that the world will not fall apart if we stop our activity. The world is in God's hands. We can hear this truth echoed in Jesus' words:

Consider the lilies, how they grow: they neither toil nor spin; yet I tell you, even Solomon in all his glory was not clothed like one of these. But if God so clothes the grass of the field, which is alive today and tomorrow is thrown into the oven, how much more will he clothe you. (Lk 12.27–28)

Traditionally, Christians rest and pray on Sunday because it is the day on which Jesus was resurrected. In many cultures today, it seems that many people are losing this practice. What could we gain if we recommitted ourselves to a day of rest, celebration, and prayer? What can you do personally to more fully honor the concept of Sabbath rest?

▸ Gen 2.1–3

Another Account of the Creation
(Gen 1.26–30)

In the day that the LORD*f* God made the earth and the heavens, 5 when no plant of the field was yet in the earth and no herb of the field had yet sprung up—for the LORD God had not caused it to rain upon the earth, and there was no one to till the ground; 6 but a stream would rise from the earth, and water the whole face of the ground— 7 then the LORD God formed man from the dust of the ground,*g* and breathed into his nostrils the breath of life; and the man became a living being. 8 And the LORD God planted a garden in Eden, in the east; and there he put the man whom he had formed. 9 Out of the ground the LORD God made to grow every tree that is pleasant to the sight and good for food, the tree of life also in the midst of the garden, and the tree of the knowledge of good and evil.

10 A river flows out of Eden to water the garden, and from there it divides and becomes four branches. 11 The name of the first is Pi'shon; it is the one that flows around the whole land of Hav'i·lah, where there is gold; 12 and the gold of that land is good; bdellium and onyx stone are there. 13 The name of the second river is Gi'hon; it is the one that flows around the whole land of Cush. 14 The name of the third river is Tigris, which flows east of Assyria. And the fourth river is the Euphrates.

15 The LORD God took the man and put him in the garden of Eden to till it and keep it. 16 And the LORD God commanded the man, "You may freely eat of every tree of the garden; 17 but of the tree of the knowledge of good and evil you shall not eat, for in the day that you eat of it you shall die."

18 Then the LORD God said, "It is not good that the man should be alone; I will make him a helper

---

f Heb *YHWH*, as in other places where "LORD" is spelled with capital letters (see also Exod 3.14–15 with notes).
g Or *formed a man* (Heb *adam*) *of dust from the ground* (Heb *adamah*)

PRAY IT!
In God's Image

God does not make mistakes; people do. Some people might be tempted to deny their racial heritage, even to change their physical appearance in order to fit into the latest fad or the dominant cultural image of beauty. We must remember that physical features are not accidents. God planned for them—we are all made in God's image.

If we are to authentically love ourselves, we must love our whole selves. This includes a love for dark skin or light skin, straight hair or tight curly hair, wide nose or pug nose, and all the variations in between. Whatever our appearance, we are all blessed of God.

Dear God, I praise you for who I am on the inside and on the outside. Amen.

▸ Gen 1.26–27

GOD IS OUR CREATOR!

According to Genesis, chapters 1–2, God created the universe and is the source of order in all creation. Creation is good, and its goodness is reflected in the harmony, peace, and love between the Creator and his creatures, and among the creatures themselves. In Spanish-speaking theological traditions, this ideal relationship—symbolized by the way God and Adam and Eve relate in the Garden of Eden—is considered the foundation in which salvation history is rooted.

■ How are your relationships with God, your friends, your family, and nature characterized by harmony, peace, and love?

■ Reflect on how you can improve some of your strained relationships, and ask God's help to do it.

Human beings are created in God's image and likeness and share God's attributes: freedom, love, knowledge, and the ability to create. With these gifts comes the responsibility of caring for all creation.

■ Give thanks and praise to God for creation, especially for your own life and the lives of the people around you.

■ Think of how you, your family, and your community can take better care of all creation. Pray that you fully develop your capacity to love, to know the truth, and to use your freedom wisely.

God established a covenant with us at the moment of our creation, and we keep this covenant by freely placing ourselves in God's hands and being responsive to God's invitation to live in communion with God and people.

■ How do you use your freedom to respond to God's invitation?

■ Think about the aspects of your life for which you most need God's wisdom to live in harmony and love. Put yourself in God's hands, and let God help and direct you.

▶ Genesis, chapters 1–2

as his partner." 19 So out of the ground the LORD God formed every animal of the field and every bird of the air, and brought them to the man to see what he would call them; and whatever the man called every living creature, that was its name. 20 The man gave names to all cattle, and to the birds of the air, and to every animal of the field; but for the man[h] there was not found a helper as his partner. 21 So the LORD God caused a deep sleep to fall upon the man, and he slept; then he took one of his ribs and closed up its place with flesh. 22 And the rib that the LORD God had taken from the man he made into a woman and brought her to the man. 23 Then the man said,

"This at last is bone of my bones
    and flesh of my flesh;
this one shall be called Woman,[i]
    for out of Man[j] this one was taken."

24 Therefore a man leaves his father and his mother and clings to his wife, and they become one flesh. 25 And the man and his wife were both naked, and were not ashamed.

The First Sin and Its Punishment
(Rom 5.12–21)

3 Now the serpent was more crafty than any other wild animal that the LORD God had made. He said to the woman, "Did God say, 'You shall not eat from any tree in the garden'?" 2 The woman said to the serpent, "We may eat of the fruit of the trees in the garden; 3 but God said, 'You shall not eat of the fruit of the tree that is in the middle of the garden, nor shall you touch it, or you shall die.' " 4 But the serpent said to the woman, "You will not die; 5 for God knows that when you eat of it your eyes will be opened, and you will be like God,[k] knowing good and evil." 6 So when the woman saw that the tree was good for food, and

h Or for Adam   i Heb ishshah   j Heb ish   k Or gods

that it was a delight to the eyes, and that the tree was to be desired to make one wise, she took of its fruit and ate; and she also gave some to her husband, who was with her, and he ate. 7 Then the eyes of both were opened, and they knew that they were naked; and they sewed fig leaves together and made loincloths for themselves.

8 They heard the sound of the LORD God walking in the garden at the time of the evening breeze, and the man and his wife hid themselves from the presence of the LORD God among the trees of the garden. 9 But the LORD God called to the man, and said to him, "Where are you?" 10 He said, "I heard the sound of you in the garden, and I was afraid, because I was naked; and I hid myself." 11 He said, "Who told you that you were naked? Have you eaten from the tree of which I commanded you not to eat?" 12 The man said, "The woman whom you gave to be with me, she gave me fruit from the tree, and I ate." 13 Then the LORD God said to the woman, "What is this that you have done?" The woman said, "The serpent tricked me, and I ate."
14 The LORD God said to the serpent,

"Because you have done this,
    cursed are you among all animals
    and among all wild creatures;
upon your belly you shall go,
    and dust you shall eat
    all the days of your life.
15 I will put enmity between you and the
    woman,
    and between your offspring and hers;
he will strike your head,
    and you will strike his heel."
16 To the woman he said,

"I will greatly increase your pangs in
    childbearing;
    in pain you shall bring forth children,
yet your desire shall be for your
    husband,
    and he shall rule over you."
17 And to the man[l] he said,

"Because you have listened to the voice of
    your wife,
    and have eaten of the tree
about which I commanded you,
'You shall not eat of it,'
cursed is the ground because of you;
    in toil you shall eat of it all the days of
    your life;
18 thorns and thistles it shall bring forth
    for you;
    and you shall eat the plants of the
    field.
19 By the sweat of your face
    you shall eat bread

until you return to the ground,
    for out of it you were taken;
you are dust,
    and to dust you shall return."
20 The man named his wife Eve,[m] because she was the mother of all living. 21 And the LORD God made garments of skins for the man[n] and for his wife, and clothed them.

Catholic Connections

ORIGINAL SIN BREAKS OUR RELATIONSHIP WITH GOD

The story of Adam and Eve is about the human weakness for sinning and disobeying God. The serpent tells Adam and Eve they can be like God, and know good and evil. After disobeying God, they recognize that they are naked and feel shame. Their relationship of trust with God is broken. This story teaches that soon after men and women were created, sin entered human history and led to pain and suffering.

This reality—that every human person, beginning with our first ancestors, chooses to disobey God—the Catholic church calls original sin. Original sin is another way of saying that every person makes choices that separate him or her from God. We are born into this condition, which has been passed on from the beginning of the human race.

▶ Gen 3.1–24

22 Then the LORD God said, "See, the man has become like one of us, knowing good and evil; and now, he might reach out his hand and take also from the tree of life, and eat, and live forever"— 23 therefore the LORD God sent him forth from the garden of Eden, to till the ground from which he

---

l Or to Adam   m In Heb Eve resembles the word for living
n Or for Adam

Brothers and Sisters

"Am I my brother's keeper?" (Gen 4.9). With that famous question, Cain pretends that he does not know where his brother is. God does not answer Cain's question directly, but each of us knows the response. We are—each of us and all of us—responsible for one another: family, friends, and strangers. We are brothers and sisters because God has created us that way. We cannot avoid our obligation to watch out for one another.

Are there people in your life who need you to be a brother or sister to them? If so, commit yourself right now to reach out to them.

▶ Gen 4.9

was taken. 24 He drove out the man; and at the east of the garden of Eden he placed the cherubim, and a sword flaming and turning to guard the way to the tree of life.

Cain Murders Abel
(Lk 11.51; Heb 11.4; 12.24)

4 Now the man knew his wife Eve, and she conceived and bore Cain, saying, "I have produced*o* a man with the help of the LORD." 2 Next she bore his brother Abel. Now Abel was a keeper of sheep, and Cain a tiller of the ground. 3 In the course of time Cain brought to the LORD an offering of the fruit of the ground, 4 and Abel for his part brought of the firstlings of his flock, their fat portions. And the LORD had regard for Abel and his offering, 5 but for Cain and his offering he had no regard. So Cain was very angry, and his countenance fell. 6 The LORD said to Cain, "Why are you angry, and why has your countenance fallen? 7 If you do well, will you not be accepted? And if you do not do well, sin is lurking at the door; its desire is for you, but you must master it."

8 Cain said to his brother Abel, "Let us go out to the field."*p* And when they were in the field, Cain rose up against his brother Abel, and killed him. 9 Then the LORD said to Cain, "Where is your brother Abel?" He said, "I do not know; am I my brother's keeper?" 10 And the LORD said, "What have you done? Listen; your brother's blood is crying out to me from the ground! 11 And now you are cursed from the ground, which has opened its mouth to receive your brother's blood from your hand. 12 When you till the ground, it will no longer yield to you its strength; you will be a fugitive and a wanderer on the earth." 13 Cain said to the LORD, "My punishment is greater than I can bear! 14 Today you have driven me away from the soil, and I shall be hidden from your face; I shall be a fugitive and a wanderer on the earth, and anyone who meets me

may kill me." 15 Then the LORD said to him, "Not so!*q* Whoever kills Cain will suffer a sevenfold vengeance." And the LORD put a mark on Cain, so that no one who came upon him would kill him. 16 Then Cain went away from the presence of the LORD, and settled in the land of Nod,*r* east of Eden.

Beginnings of Civilization

17 Cain knew his wife, and she conceived and bore É'noch; and he built a city, and named it

---

o The verb in Heb resembles the word for *Cain*
p Sam Gk Syr Compare Vg: MT lacks *Let us go out to the field*   *q* Gk Syr Vg: Heb *Therefore*   *r* That is *Wandering*

THE CYCLE OF VIOLENCE

Cain was a murderer. Some might say he deserved the death penalty. But in Gen 4.15, God marks Cain so that he is protected from being killed. God seeks to stop the cycle of violence. Why kill someone to show that it is wrong to kill someone?

Think of a television show or movie with violent sequences that you have seen recently. What attitude did it portray toward violence? Often, violence in revenge is shown as justified, even satisfying. How does violence on television or in the movies affect your own attitude toward it? How might you respond to God's call to stop the cycle of violence?

▶ Gen 4.15

Ē'noch after his son Ē'noch. 18 To Ē'noch was born I'rad; and I'rad was the father of Me•hū'ja•el, and Me•hū'ja•el the father of Me•thū'sha•el, and Me•thū'sha•el the father of Lā'mech. 19 Lā'mech took two wives; the name of the one was Ā'dah, and the name of the other Zil'lah. 20 Ā'dah bore Jā'bal; he was the ancestor of those who live in tents and have livestock. 21 His brother's name was Jū'bal; he was the ancestor of all those who play the lyre and pipe. 22 Zil'lah bore Tū'bal-cāin, who made all kinds of bronze and iron tools. The sister of Tū'bal-cāin was Nā'a•mah.

23 Lā'mech said to his wives:

"Ā'dah and Zil'lah, hear my voice;
   you wives of Lā'mech, listen to what
      I say:
I have killed a man for wounding me,
   a young man for striking me.
24 If Cain is avenged sevenfold,
   truly Lā'mech seventy-sevenfold."

25 Adam knew his wife again, and she bore a son and named him Seth, for she said, "God has appointed[s] for me another child instead of Abel, because Cain killed him." 26 To Seth also a son was born, and he named him Ē'nosh. At that time people began to invoke the name of the LORD.

Adam's Descendants to Noah and His Sons
(1 Chr 1.1–4; Lk 3.36–38)

5 This is the list of the descendants of Adam. When God created humankind,[t] he made them[u] in the likeness of God. 2 Male and female he created them, and he blessed them and named them "Humankind"[t] when they were created.

3 When Adam had lived one hundred thirty years, he became the father of a son in his likeness, according to his image, and named him Seth. 4 The days of Adam after he became the father of Seth were eight hundred years; and he had other sons and daughters. 5 Thus all the days that Adam lived were nine hundred thirty years; and he died.

6 When Seth had lived one hundred five years, he became the father of Ē'nosh. 7 Seth lived after the birth of Ē'nosh eight hundred seven years, and had other sons and daughters. 8 Thus all the days of Seth were nine hundred twelve years; and he died.

9 When Ē'nosh had lived ninety years, he became the father of Kē'nan. 10 Ē'nosh lived after the birth of Kē'nan eight hundred fifteen years, and had other sons and daughters. 11 Thus all the days of Ē'nosh were nine hundred five years; and he died.

12 When Kē'nan had lived seventy years, he became the father of Ma•hal'a•lel. 13 Kē'nan lived after the birth of Ma•hal'a•lel eight hundred and forty years, and had other sons and daughters.

14 Thus all the days of Kē'nan were nine hundred and ten years; and he died.

15 When Ma•hal'a•lel had lived sixty-five years, he became the father of Jar'ed. 16 Ma•hal'a•lel lived after the birth of Jar'ed eight hundred thirty years, and had other sons and daughters. 17 Thus all the days of Ma•hal'a•lel were eight hundred ninety-five years; and he died.

18 When Jar'ed had lived one hundred sixty-two years he became the father of Ē'noch. 19 Jar'ed lived after the birth of Ē'noch eight hundred years, and had other sons and daughters. 20 Thus all the days of Jar'ed were nine hundred sixty-two years; and he died.

21 When Ē'noch had lived sixty-five years, he became the father of Me•thū'se•lah. 22 Ē'noch walked with God after the birth of Me•thū'se•lah three hundred years, and had other sons and daughters. 23 Thus all the days of Ē'noch were three hundred sixty-five years. 24 Ē'noch walked with God; then he was no more, because God took him.

25 When Me•thū'se•lah had lived one hundred eighty-seven years, he became the father of Lā'-mech. 26 Me•thū'se•lah lived after the birth of Lā'-mech seven hundred eighty-two years, and had other sons and daughters. 27 Thus all the days of Me•thū'se•lah were nine hundred sixty-nine years; and he died.

28 When Lā'mech had lived one hundred eighty-two years, he became the father of a son; 29 he named him Noah, saying, "Out of the ground that the LORD has cursed this one shall bring us relief from our work and from the toil of our hands." 30 Lā'mech lived after the birth of Noah five hundred ninety-five years, and had other sons and daughters. 31 Thus all the days of Lā'mech were seven hundred seventy-seven years; and he died.

32 After Noah was five hundred years old, Noah became the father of Shem, Ham, and Jā'pheth.

The Wickedness of Humankind

6 When people began to multiply on the face of the ground, and daughters were born to them, 2 the sons of God saw that they were fair; and they took wives for themselves of all that they chose. 3 Then the LORD said, "My spirit shall not abide[v] in mortals forever, for they are flesh; their days shall be one hundred twenty years." 4 The Neph'i•lim were on the earth in those days—and also afterward—when the sons of God went in to the daughters of humans, who bore children to

---

s The verb in Heb resembles the word for *Seth*
t Heb *adam*   u Heb *him*   v Meaning of Heb uncertain

them. These were the heroes that were of old, warriors of renown.

5 The LORD saw that the wickedness of humankind was great in the earth, and that every inclination of the thoughts of their hearts was only evil continually. 6 And the LORD was sorry that he had made humankind on the earth, and it grieved him to his heart. 7 So the LORD said, "I will blot out from the earth the human beings I have created—people

stroy from under heaven all flesh in which is the breath of life; everything that is on the earth shall die. 18 But I will establish my covenant with you; and you shall come into the ark, you, your sons, your wife, and your sons' wives with you. 19 And of every living thing, of all flesh, you shall bring two of every kind into the ark, to keep them alive with you; they shall be male and female. 20 Of the birds according to their kinds, and of the animals ac-

Sin Has Social Consequences

At the beginning of the Noah story, sin has continued to spread so that it has become an accepted part of society. The Great Flood, which wipes out a whole civilization, symbolizes the consequences of widespread sin. Later in Genesis, the story of the tower of Babel (11.1–9) symbolizes another consequence of the institutionalized sin of disobedience and pride.

When sin becomes part of our social systems and our institutions, the church calls it social sin. Social sin is a result of personal sin, but it is bigger than any one person's choice. Examples of social sin are the unequal distribution of the world's wealth, the exploitation of workers by corporations, and discrimination based on race or gender. The good news is that God's saving power is greater than social sin! What are the effects of social sin in your community? in your country? in the world? How are Christians in your church or community organizing to stand against social sin?

▶ Gen 6.1—9.17

together with animals and creeping things and birds of the air, for I am sorry that I have made them." 8 But Noah found favor in the sight of the LORD.

Noah Pleases God
(Heb 11.7; 1 Pet 3.20)

9 These are the descendants of Noah. Noah was a righteous man, blameless in his generation; Noah walked with God. 10 And Noah had three sons, Shem, Ham, and Jā'pheth.

11 Now the earth was corrupt in God's sight, and the earth was filled with violence. 12 And God saw that the earth was corrupt; for all flesh had corrupted its ways upon the earth. 13 And God said to Noah, "I have determined to make an end of all flesh, for the earth is filled with violence because of them; now I am going to destroy them along with the earth. 14 Make yourself an ark of cypressʷ wood; make rooms in the ark, and cover it inside and out with pitch. 15 This is how you are to make it: the length of the ark three hundred cubits, its width fifty cubits, and its height thirty cubits. 16 Make a roofˣ for the ark, and finish it to a cubit above; and put the door of the ark in its side; make it with lower, second, and third decks. 17 For my part, I am going to bring a flood of waters on the earth, to de-

cording to their kinds, of every creeping thing of the ground according to its kind, two of every kind shall come in to you, to keep them alive. 21 Also take with you every kind of food that is eaten, and store it up; and it shall serve as food for you and for them." 22 Noah did this; he did all that God commanded him.

The Great Flood
(Lk 17.26–27)

7 Then the LORD said to Noah, "Go into the ark, you and all your household, for I have seen that you alone are righteous before me in this generation. 2 Take with you seven pairs of all clean animals, the male and its mate; and a pair of the animals that are not clean, the male and its mate; 3 and seven pairs of the birds of the air also, male and female, to keep their kind alive on the face of all the earth. 4 For in seven days I will send rain on the earth for forty days and forty nights; and every living thing that I have made I will blot out from the face of the ground." 5 And Noah did all that the LORD had commanded him.

ʷ Meaning of Heb uncertain   ˣ Or *window*

did you KNOW?

The Flood

The sin of Adam and Eve in the garden starts a disastrous trend in which each generation adds to sin in the world. This sin leads to the corruption of the world and the destruction of human beings. The Great Flood illustrates the ancient belief that God washed the world clean of this sinfulness and gave another chance to those who were faithful to God.

Other ancient cultures had stories about great floods. But in those stories, vindictive gods caused the floods for petty reasons. These gods had no real love for humanity. The Bible's Flood story is unique because it insists that God acted out of justice and in response to great evil.

God takes great care to save Noah and his family because they are faithful to God. After the Flood, God makes a covenant with Noah, promising never to destroy the earth by flood again—another unique element not found in the stories of other cultures.

▶ Gen 6.1—9.17

6 Noah was six hundred years old when the flood of waters came on the earth. 7 And Noah with his sons and his wife and his sons' wives went into the ark to escape the waters of the flood. 8 Of clean animals, and of animals that are not clean, and of birds, and of everything that creeps on the ground, 9 two and two, male and female, went into the ark with Noah, as God had commanded Noah. 10 And after seven days the waters of the flood came on the earth.

11 In the six hundredth year of Noah's life, in the second month, on the seventeenth day of the month, on that day all the fountains of the great deep burst forth, and the windows of the heavens were opened. 12 The rain fell on the earth forty days and forty nights. 13 On the very same day Noah with his sons, Shem and Ham and Jā'pheth, and Noah's wife and the three wives of his sons entered the ark, 14they and every wild animal of every kind, and all domestic animals of every kind, and every creeping thing that creeps on the earth, and every bird of every kind—every bird, every winged

creature. 15 They went into the ark with Noah, two and two of all flesh in which there was the breath of life. 16 And those that entered, male and female of all flesh, went in as God had commanded him; and the LORD shut him in.

17 The flood continued forty days on the earth; and the waters increased, and bore up the ark, and it rose high above the earth. 18 The waters swelled and increased greatly on the earth; and the ark floated on the face of the waters. 19 The waters swelled so mightily on the earth that all the high mountains under the whole heaven were covered; 20 the waters swelled above the mountains, covering them fifteen cubits deep. 21 And all flesh died that moved on the earth, birds, domestic animals, wild animals, all swarming creatures that swarm on the earth, and all human beings; 22 everything on dry land in whose nostrils was the breath of life died. 23 He blotted out every living thing that was on the face of the ground, human beings and animals and creeping things and birds of the air; they were blotted out from the earth. Only Noah was left, and those that were with him in the ark. 24 And the waters swelled on the earth for one hundred fifty days.

The Flood Subsides

8 But God remembered Noah and all the wild animals and all the domestic animals that were with him in the ark. And God made a wind blow over the earth, and the waters subsided; 2 the fountains of the deep and the windows of the heavens were closed, the rain from the heavens was restrained, 3 and the waters gradually receded from the earth. At the end of one hundred fifty days the waters had abated; 4 and in the seventh month, on the seventeenth day of the month, the ark came to rest on the mountains of Ar'a•rat. 5 The waters continued to abate until the tenth month; in the tenth month, on the first day of the month, the tops of the mountains appeared.

6 At the end of forty days Noah opened the window of the ark that he had made 7 and sent out the raven; and it went to and fro until the waters were dried up from the earth. 8 Then he sent out the dove from him, to see if the waters had subsided from the face of the ground; 9 but the dove found no place to set its foot, and it returned to him to the ark, for the waters were still on the face of the whole earth. So he put out his hand and took it and brought it into the ark with him. 10 He waited another seven days, and again he sent out the dove from the ark; 11 and the dove came back to him in the evening, and there in its beak was a freshly plucked olive leaf; so Noah knew that the waters had subsided from the earth. 12 Then he

GEN

8.11

waited another seven days, and sent out the dove; and it did not return to him any more.

13 In the six hundred first year, in the first month, on the first day of the month, the waters were dried up from the earth; and Noah removed the covering of the ark, and looked, and saw that the face of the ground was drying. 14 In the second month, on the twenty-seventh day of the month, the earth was dry. 15 Then God said to Noah, 16 "Go out of the ark, you and your wife, and your sons and your sons' wives with you. 17 Bring out with you every living thing that is with you of all flesh—birds and animals and every creeping thing that creeps on the earth—so that they may abound on the earth, and be fruitful and multiply on the earth." 18 So Noah went out with his sons and his wife and his sons' wives. 19 And every animal, every creeping thing, and every bird, everything that moves on the earth, went out of the ark by families.

God's Promise to Noah

20 Then Noah built an altar to the LORD, and took of every clean animal and of every clean bird, and offered burnt offerings on the altar. 21 And when the LORD smelled the pleasing odor, the LORD said in his heart, "I will never again curse the ground because of humankind, for the inclination of the human heart is evil from youth; nor will I ever again destroy every living creature as I have done.
22 As long as the earth endures,
     seedtime and harvest, cold and
          heat,
     summer and winter, day and night,
          shall not cease."

The Covenant with Noah

9 God blessed Noah and his sons, and said to them, "Be fruitful and multiply, and fill the earth. 2 The fear and dread of you shall rest on every animal of the earth, and on every bird of the air, on everything that creeps on the ground, and on all the fish of the sea; into your hand they are delivered. 3 Every moving thing that lives shall be food for you; and just as I gave you the green plants, I give you everything. 4 Only, you shall not eat flesh with its life, that is, its blood. 5 For your own lifeblood I will surely require a reckoning: from every animal I will require it and from human beings, each one for the blood of another, I will require a reckoning for human life.
6   Whoever sheds the blood of a human,
        by a human shall that person's blood be
              shed;
     for in his own image
        God made humankind.
7 And you, be fruitful and multiply, abound on the earth and multiply in it."

8 Then God said to Noah and to his sons with him, 9 "As for me, I am establishing my covenant with you and your descendants after you, 10 and with every living creature that is with you, the birds, the domestic animals, and every animal of the earth with you, as many as came out of the ark.ʸ 11 I establish my covenant with you, that never again shall all flesh be cut off by the waters of a

---

ʸ Gk: Heb adds *every animal of the earth*

did you KNOW?
Water in the Bible

For the ancient Hebrews, although water often represented a source of life, it also represented forces of destruction over which God triumphs. In the story of Creation, God is portrayed as mastering the waters that represent chaos (Gen 1.1–2)—God constructs the upper and lower firmaments to hold back the waters. At the time of the Great Flood, God releases the waters, and they destroy life on the earth. At the time of the Exodus, God will once again display the divine mastery of the waters, as will Jesus Christ later on.

flood, and never again shall there be a flood to destroy the earth." 12 God said, "This is the sign of the covenant that I make between me and you and every living creature that is with you, for all future generations: 13 I have set my bow in the clouds, and it shall be a sign of the covenant between me

PRAY IT
The Rainbow

What do you see when you see a rainbow? Do you see a multicolored arc caused by the refraction of sunlight through droplets of water? Or do you see a wonder of nature that causes you to stop and stare in awe? Something as remarkable as a rainbow can never be reduced to a scientific explanation. It's no wonder that the writer of Genesis used it as a symbol of God's covenant promise. When God and Israel see the rainbow in the clouds, they will recall their covenant together.

God of imagination and color, only you could come up with the idea of a rainbow! Rainstorm and sunshine, harmony and diversity, mercy and hope, promise and joy, wonder and awe. Are these inside me, the wondrous creation you delight in? Guide me to the rainbows in my life!

▸ **Gen 9.8–17**

and the earth. 14 When I bring clouds over the earth and the bow is seen in the clouds, 15 I will remember my covenant that is between me and you and every living creature of all flesh; and the waters shall never again become a flood to destroy all flesh. 16 When the bow is in the clouds, I will see it and remember the everlasting covenant between God and every living creature of all flesh that is on the earth." 17 God said to Noah, "This is the sign of the covenant that I have established between me and all flesh that is on the earth."

Noah and His Sons

18 The sons of Noah who went out of the ark were Shem, Ham, and Jā′pheth. Ham was the father of Cā′naan. 19 These three were the sons of Noah; and from these the whole earth was peopled.

20 Noah, a man of the soil, was the first to plant a vineyard. 21 He drank some of the wine and became drunk, and he lay uncovered in his tent. 22 And Ham, the father of Cā′naan, saw the nakedness of his father, and told his two brothers outside. 23 Then Shem and Jā′pheth took a garment, laid it on both their shoulders, and walked backward and covered the nakedness of their father; their faces were turned away, and they did not see their father's nakedness. 24 When Noah awoke from his wine and knew what his youngest son had done to him, 25 he said,

"Cursed be Cā′naan;
　　lowest of slaves shall he be to his
　　　brothers."
26 He also said,
"Blessed by the LORD my God be
　　Shem;
　and let Cā′naan be his slave.
27 May God make space for*z* Jā′pheth,
　　and let him live in the tents of Shem;
　　and let Cā′naan be his slave."
28 After the flood Noah lived three hundred fifty years. 29 All the days of Noah were nine hundred fifty years; and he died.

Nations Descended from Noah
(1 Chr 1.5–27)

10 These are the descendants of Noah's sons, Shem, Ham, and Jā′pheth; children were born to them after the flood.

2 The descendants of Jā′pheth: Gō′mer, Mā′gog, Mā′daī, Jā′van, Tū′bal, Mē′shech, and Tī′ras. 3 The descendants of Gō′mer: Ash′ke•naz, Rī′phath, and Tō•gar′mah. 4 The descendants of Jā′van: E•lī′shah, Tar′shish, Kit′tim, and Rod′a•nim.*a* 5 From these the coastland peoples spread. These are the descendants of Jā′pheth*b* in their lands, with their own language, by their families, in their nations.

6 The descendants of Ham: Cush, Egypt, Put, and Cā′naan. 7 The descendants of Cush: Sē′ba, Hav′i•lah, Sab′tah, Rā′a•mah, and Sab′te•ca. The descendants of Rā′a•mah: Shē′ba and Dē′dan. 8 Cush became the father of Nim′rod; he was the first on earth to become a mighty warrior. 9 He was a mighty hunter before the LORD; therefore it is said, "Like Nim′rod a mighty hunter before the LORD." 10 The beginning of his kingdom was Bā′bel, Ē′rech, and Ac′cad, all of them in the land of Shī′nar. 11 From that land he went into Assyria, and built Nin′e•veh, Re•hō′both-ir, Cā′lah, and 12 Rē′sen between Nin′e•veh and Cā′lah; that is the great city. 13 Egypt became the father of Lū′dim, An′a•mim,

---

z Heb *yapht*, a play on *Japheth*　*a* Heb Mss Sam Gk See 1 Chr 1.7: MT *Dodanim*　*b* Compare verses 20, 31. Heb lacks *These are the descendants of Japheth*

A Barrier or a Bridge?

Language can be either a barrier or a bridge. Through our speech, we connect with other people. And we often hear it expressed that love, music, and a smile are universal languages. Yet, languages also separate, symbolizing differences between cultures and nations that can erupt in wars and other atrocities.

The story of the tower of Babel is an ancient explanation of why the separation between people, symbolized by different languages, occurs. The people ignore God's command to "fill the earth" (Gen 1.28). Instead, they gather in one place to try to build a tower reaching to heaven, a sin of pride and arrogance. God confuses their language to foil their plan. It is not language but pride that separates us.

In the Acts of the Apostles, chapter 2, language serves as a bridge. The Holy Spirit enables the people from many different lands to hear the Apostles speaking in their own languages. The Spirit serves to unify us, no matter what earthly language we speak. The Good News is universal and unites us!

▶ Gen 11.1–9

Le·hă′bim, Naph′tū·him, ¹⁴ Path·rŭ′sim, Cas·lŭ′him, and Caph′to·rim, from which the Phi·lis′tines come.*c*

15 Că′naan became the father of Sī′don his firstborn, and Heth, ¹⁶ and the Jeb′ū·sites, the Am′o·rītes, the Gir′ga·shītes, ¹⁷ the Hī′vītes, the Ar′kītes, the Sī′nītes, ¹⁸ the Ar′vad·ites, the Zem′a·rītes, and the Hă′math·ites. Afterward the families of the Că′naan·ites spread abroad. ¹⁹ And the territory of the Că′naan·ites extended from Sī′don, in the direction of Gĕ′rar, as far as Gā′za, and in the direction of Sod′om, Go·mor′rah, Ad′mah, and Ze·boi′im, as far as Lā′sha. ²⁰ These are the descendants of Ham, by their families, their languages, their lands, and their nations.

21 To Shem also, the father of all the children of Ē′ber, the elder brother of Jă′pheth, children were born. ²² The descendants of Shem: Ē′lam, As′shur, Ar·pach′shad, Lud, and Ar′am. ²³ The descendants of Ar′am: Uz, Hul, Gĕ′ther, and Mash. ²⁴ Ar·pach′shad became the father of Shĕ′lah; and Shĕ′lah became the father of Ē′ber. ²⁵ To Ē′ber were born two sons: the name of the one was Pĕ′leg,*d* for in his days the earth was divided, and his brother's name was Jok′tan. ²⁶ Jok′tan became the father of Al·mō′dad, Shĕ′leph, Hă·zar·mă′veth, Jĕ′rah, ²⁷ Ha·dor′am, Ū′zal, Dik′lah, ²⁸ Ō′bal, A·bim′a·el, Shĕ′ba, ²⁹ Ō′phir, Hav′i·lah, and Jō′bab; all these were the descendants of Jok′tan. ³⁰ The territory in which they lived extended from Mĕ′sha in the direction of Sĕ′phar, the hill country of the east. ³¹ These are the descendants of Shem, by their families, their languages, their lands, and their nations.

32 These are the families of Noah's sons, according to their genealogies, in their nations; and from these the nations spread abroad on the earth after the flood.

The Tower of Babel

11 Now the whole earth had one language and the same words. ² And as they migrated from the east,*e* they came upon a plain in the land of Shī′nar and settled there. ³ And they said to one another, "Come, let us make bricks, and burn them thoroughly." And they had brick for stone, and bitumen for mortar. ⁴ Then they said, "Come, let us build ourselves a city, and a tower with its top in the heavens, and let us make a name for ourselves; otherwise we shall be scattered abroad upon the face of the whole earth." ⁵ The LORD came down to see the city and the tower, which mortals had built. ⁶ And the LORD said, "Look, they are one people, and they have all one language; and this is only the beginning of what they will do; nothing that they propose to do will now be impossible for them. ⁷ Come, let us go down, and confuse their language there, so that they will not understand one another's speech." ⁸ So the LORD scattered them abroad from there over the face of all the earth, and they left off building the city. ⁹ Therefore it was called Bā′bel, because there the LORD confused*f* the language of all the earth; and from there the LORD scattered them abroad over the face of all the earth.

---

c Cn: Heb *Casluhim, from which the Philistines come, and Caphtorim*   *d* That is *Division*   *e* Or *migrated eastward*
f Heb *balal,* meaning *to confuse*

Descendants of Shem
(1 Chr 1.17–27; Lk 3.34–36)

10 These are the descendants of Shem. When Shem was one hundred years old, he became the father of Ar•pach'shad two years after the flood; 11 and Shem lived after the birth of Ar•pach'shad five hundred years, and had other sons and daughters.

12 When Ar•pach'shad had lived thirty-five years, he became the father of Shē'lah; 13 and Ar•pach'shad lived after the birth of Shē'lah four hundred three years, and had other sons and daughters.

14 When Shē'lah had lived thirty years, he became the father of Ē'ber; 15 and Shē'lah lived after the birth of Ē'ber four hundred three years, and had other sons and daughters.

16 When Ē'ber had lived thirty-four years, he became the father of Pē'leg; 17 and Ē'ber lived after the birth of Pē'leg four hundred thirty years, and had other sons and daughters.

18 When Pē'leg had lived thirty years, he became the father of Rē'ū; 19 and Pē'leg lived after the birth of Rē'ū two hundred nine years, and had other sons and daughters.

20 When Rē'ū had lived thirty-two years, he became the father of Sē'rug; 21 and Rē'ū lived after the birth of Sē'rug two hundred seven years, and had other sons and daughters.

22 When Sē'rug had lived thirty years, he became the father of Nā'hor; 23 and Sē'rug lived after the birth of Nā'hor two hundred years, and had other sons and daughters.

24 When Nā'hor had lived twenty-nine years, he became the father of Tē'rah; 25 and Nā'hor lived after the birth of Tē'rah one hundred nineteen years, and had other sons and daughters.

26 When Tē'rah had lived seventy years, he became the father of Abram, Nā'hor, and Har'an.

Descendants of Terah

27 Now these are the descendants of Tē'rah. Tē'rah was the father of Abram, Nā'hor, and Har'an; and Har'an was the father of Lot. 28 Har'an died before his father Tē'rah in the land of his birth, in Ūr of the Chal•dē'ans. 29 Abram and Nā'hor took wives; the name of Abram's wife was Sar'aī, and the name of Nā'hor's wife was Mil'cah. She was the daughter of Har'an the father of Mil'cah and Is'cah. 30 Now Sar'aī was barren; she had no child.

31 Tē'rah took his son Abram and his grandson Lot son of Har'an, and his daughter-in-law Sar'aī, his son Abram's wife, and they went out together from Ūr of the Chal•dē'ans to go into the land of Cā'naan; but when they came to Har'an, they set-

tled there. 32 The days of Tē'rah were two hundred five years; and Tē'rah died in Har'an.

The Call of Abram
(Acts 7.2–5)

12 Now the LORD said to Abram, "Go from your country and your kindred and your father's house to the land that I will show you. 2 I will make of you a great nation, and I will bless you, and make your name great, so that you will be a blessing. 3 I will bless those who bless you, and the one who curses you I will curse; and in you all the families of the earth shall be blessed."*g*

4 So Abram went, as the LORD had told him; and Lot went with him. Abram was seventy-five years old when he departed from Har'an. 5 Abram took his wife Sar'aī and his brother's son Lot, and all the possessions that they had gathered, and the persons whom they had acquired in Har'an; and they set forth to go to the land of Cā'naan. When they had come to the land of Cā'naan, 6 Abram passed through the land to the place at Shē'chem, to the oak*h* of Mō'reh. At that time the Cā'-naan•ītes were in the land. 7 Then the LORD appeared to Abram, and said, "To your offspring*i* I will give this land." So he built there an altar to the LORD, who had appeared to him. 8 From there he moved on to the hill country on the east of Beth'el, and pitched his tent, with Beth'el on the west and Ai on the east; and there he built an altar to the LORD and invoked the name of the LORD. 9 And Abram journeyed on by stages toward the Neg'eb.

Abram and Sarai in Egypt

10 Now there was a famine in the land. So Abram went down to Egypt to reside there as an alien, for the famine was severe in the land. 11 When he was about to enter Egypt, he said to his wife Sar'aī, "I know well that you are a woman beautiful in appearance; 12 and when the Egyptians see you, they will say, 'This is his wife'; then they will kill me, but they will let you live. 13 Say you are my sister, so that it may go well with me because of you, and that my life may be spared on your account." 14 When Abram entered Egypt the Egyptians saw that the woman was very beautiful. 15 When the officials of Pharaoh saw her, they praised her to Pharaoh. And the woman was taken into Pharaoh's house. 16 And for her sake he dealt well with Abram; and he had sheep, oxen, male donkeys, male and female slaves, female donkeys, and camels.

---

g Or by you all the families of the earth shall bless themselves   h Or terebinth   i Heb seed

17 But the LORD afflicted Pharaoh and his house with great plagues because of Sar'ai, Abram's wife. 18 So Pharaoh called Abram, and said, "What is this you have done to me? Why did you not tell me that she was your wife? 19 Why did you say, 'She is my sister,' so that I took her for my wife? Now then, here is your wife, take her, and be gone." 20 And Pharaoh gave his men orders concerning him; and they set him on the way, with his wife and all that he had.

Cā'naan•ites and the Per'iz•zītes lived in the land. 8 Then Abram said to Lot, "Let there be no strife between you and me, and between your herders and my herders; for we are kindred. 9 Is not the whole land before you? Separate yourself from me. If you take the left hand, then I will go to the right; or if you take the right hand, then I will go to the left." 10 Lot looked about him, and saw that the plain of the Jordan was well watered everywhere like the garden of the LORD, like the land of Egypt,

Introducing

▶ ABRAHAM AND SARAH

Abraham, whose name was originally Abram, is an important figure for three major world religions: Judaism, Christianity, and Islam. Abraham is regarded as the great example of faith in God. He first appears in Gen 11.26. For many years, Abram lives in Haran in northern Mesopotamia (see map 1, "The World of the Patriarchs") with his wife, Sarai. God calls Abram and Sarai to leave their home, seals a covenant with them, and changes their names to Abraham and Sarah. God's covenant promises that they will be the parents "of a multitude of nations" (17.5) and their descendants will be as numerous as the "stars of heaven" (22.17).

Later, God requests that Abraham sacrifice his son Isaac. God stops him from going through with it, but Abraham's willingness to cooperate with God and his complete trust in God become the foundation for Israel's faith. Not surprisingly, in the Old Testament, when a prophet or teacher needed an example of someone with unwavering trust in God, Abraham was often cited.

In the New Testament, Abraham is revered as the first patriarch to enter into a covenant with God (see Mt 1.1; Lk 16.19–31) and the great pioneer of Israel's faith (Acts 7.2–50; Rom 4.1–25; Heb 7.1–10).

Gen 12.1—25.11

Abram and Lot Separate

13 So Abram went up from Egypt, he and his wife, and all that he had, and Lot with him, into the Neg'eb.

2 Now Abram was very rich in livestock, in silver, and in gold. 3 He journeyed on by stages from the Neg'eb as far as Beth'el, to the place where his tent had been at the beginning, between Beth'el and Ai, 4 to the place where he had made an altar at the first; and there Abram called on the name of the LORD. 5 Now Lot, who went with Abram, also had flocks and herds and tents, 6 so that the land could not support both of them living together; for their possessions were so great that they could not live together, 7 and there was strife between the herders of Abram's livestock and the herders of Lot's livestock. At that time the

in the direction of Zō'ar; this was before the LORD had destroyed Sod'om and Go•mor'rah. 11 So Lot chose for himself all the plain of the Jordan, and Lot journeyed eastward; thus they separated from each other. 12 Abram settled in the land of Cā'naan, while Lot settled among the cities of the Plain and moved his tent as far as Sod'om. 13 Now the people of Sod'om were wicked, great sinners against the LORD.

14 The LORD said to Abram, after Lot had separated from him, "Raise your eyes now, and look from the place where you are, northward and southward and eastward and westward; 15 for all the land that you see I will give to you and to your offspring*j* forever. 16 I will make your offspring like

---

j Heb *seed*

GEN

the dust of the earth; so that if one can count the dust of the earth, your offspring also can be counted. 17 Rise up, walk through the length and the breadth of the land, for I will give it to you." 18 So Abram moved his tent, and came and settled by the oaks*k* of Mam're, which are at Hē'bron; and there he built an altar to the LORD.

Lot's Captivity and Rescue

14 In the days of King Am'ra·phel of Shī'nar, King Ar'i·och of El·lā'sar, King Ched·or·la·ō'mer of Ē'lam, and King Tī'dal of Goi'im, 2 these kings made war with King Bē'ra of Sod'om, King Bir'sha of Go·mor'rah, King Shī'nab of Ad'mah, King Shem·ē'ber of Ze·boi'im, and the king of Bē'la (that is, Zō'ar). 3 All these joined forces in the Valley of Sid'dim (that is, the Dead Sea).*l* 4 Twelve years they had served Ched·or·la·ō'mer, but in the thirteenth year they rebelled. 5 In the fourteenth year Ched·or·la·ō'mer and the kings who were with him came and subdued the Reph'a·im in Ash'te·roth-kar·nā'im, the Zū'zim in Ham, the Ē'mim in Shā'veh-kir·i·a·thā'im, 6 and the Hor'ītes in the hill country of Sē'ir as far as El-par'an on the edge of the wilderness; 7 then they turned back and came to En-mish'pat (that is, Kā'desh), and subdued all the country of the A·mal'e·kītes, and also the Am'o·rītes who lived in Haz'a·zon-tā'mar. 8 Then the king of Sod'om, the king of Go·mor'rah, the king of Ad'mah, the king of Ze·boi'im, and the king of Bē'la (that is, Zō'ar) went out, and they joined battle in the Valley of Sid'dim 9 with King Ched·or·la·ō'mer of Ē'lam, King Tī'dal of Goi'im, King Am'ra·phel of Shī'nar, and King Ar'i·och of El·lā'sar, four kings against five. 10 Now the Valley of Sid'dim was full of bitumen pits; and as the kings of Sod'om and Go·mor'rah fled, some fell into them, and the rest fled to the hill country. 11 So the enemy took all the goods of Sod'om and Go·mor'rah, and all their provisions, and went their way; 12 they also took Lot, the son of Abram's brother, who lived in Sod'om, and his goods, and departed.

13 Then one who had escaped came and told Abram the Hebrew, who was living by the oaks*k* of Mam're the Am'o·rīte, brother of Esh'col and of Ā'ner; these were allies of Abram. 14 When Abram heard that his nephew had been taken captive, he led forth his trained men, born in his house, three hundred eighteen of them, and went in pursuit as far as Dan. 15 He divided his forces against them by night, he and his servants, and routed them and pursued them to Hō'bah, north of Damascus. 16 Then he brought back all the goods, and also brought back his nephew Lot with his goods, and the women and the people.

Abram Blessed by Melchizedek
(Heb 7.1–2)

17 After his return from the defeat of Ched-or·la·ō'mer and the kings who were with him, the king of Sod'om went out to meet him at the Valley of Shā'veh (that is, the King's Valley). 18 And King Mel·chiz'e·dek of Salem brought out bread and wine; he was priest of God Most High.*m* 19 He blessed him and said,

"Blessed be Abram by God Most High,*m*
    maker of heaven and earth;
20   and blessed be God Most High,*m*
    who has delivered your enemies into your
        hand!"

BREAD AND WINE

Melchizedek, a king and priest, uses bread and wine in a ritual to bless Abram. Bread and wine served as an ancient symbol of nourishment and celebration. The sacrament of the Eucharist has its roots in rituals such as this one. See Heb 7.1–10 for a New Testament interpretation of Melchizedek's importance.

▶ Gen 14.17–20

And Abram gave him one-tenth of everything. 21 Then the king of Sod'om said to Abram, "Give me the persons, but take the goods for yourself." 22 But Abram said to the king of Sod'om, "I have sworn to the LORD, God Most High,*m* maker of heaven and earth, 23 that I would not take a thread or a sandal-thong or anything that is yours, so that you might not say, 'I have made Abram rich.' 24 I will take nothing but what the young men have eaten, and the share of the men who went with me—Ā'ner, Esh'col, and Mam're. Let them take their share."

---

k Or *terebinths*   *l* Heb *Salt Sea*   *m* Heb *El Elyon*

God's Covenant with Abram
(Heb 11.8–10)

15 After these things the word of the LORD came to Abram in a vision, "Do not be afraid, Abram, I am your shield; your reward shall be very great." 2 But Abram said, "O Lord GOD, what will you give me, for I continue childless, and the heir of my house is El•i•ē′zer of Damascus?"[n] 3 And Abram said, "You have given me no offspring, and so a slave born in my house is to be my heir." 4 But the

did **you KNOW?**

Fire

Fire appears frequently throughout the Old Testament, symbolizing two aspects of God: presence and holiness. Fire symbolizes a special presence of God in the sealing of the covenant with Abraham (Gen 15.17), in the burning bush (Ex 3.2), and in the pillar of fire leading Israel through the desert (Ex 13.21). Fire also symbolizes God's holiness appearing to purge and purify those who deviate from God's ways, as in Sodom and Gomorrah (Gen 19.24) and the seventh plague against Egypt (Ex 9.23).

▸ **Gen 15.17**

word of the LORD came to him, "This man shall not be your heir; no one but your very own issue shall be your heir." 5 He brought him outside and said, "Look toward heaven and count the stars, if you are able to count them." Then he said to him, "So shall your descendants be." 6 And he believed the LORD; and the LORD[o] reckoned it to him as righteousness.

7 Then he said to him, "I am the LORD who brought you from Ûr of the Chal•dē′ans, to give you this land to possess." 8 But he said, "O Lord GOD, how am I to know that I shall possess it?" 9 He said to him, "Bring me a heifer three years old, a female goat three years old, a ram three years old, a turtledove, and a young pigeon." 10 He brought him all these and cut them in two, laying each half over against the other; but he did not cut the birds in two. 11 And when birds of prey came down on the carcasses, Abram drove them away. 12 As the sun was going down, a deep sleep fell

upon Abram, and a deep and terrifying darkness descended upon him. 13 Then the LORD[n] said to Abram, "Know this for certain, that your offspring shall be aliens in a land that is not theirs, and shall be slaves there, and they shall be oppressed for four hundred years; 14 but I will bring judgment on the nation that they serve, and afterward they shall come out with great possessions. 15 As for yourself, you shall go to your ancestors in peace; you shall be buried in a good old age. 16 And they shall come back here in the fourth generation; for the iniquity of the Am′o•rites is not yet complete."

17 When the sun had gone down and it was dark, a smoking fire pot and a flaming torch passed between these pieces. 18 On that day the LORD made a covenant with Abram, saying, "To your descendants I give this land, from the river of Egypt to the great river, the river Euphrates, 19 the land of the Ken′ites, the Ken′iz•zites, the Kad′mon•ites, 20 the Hit′tites, the Per′iz•zites, the Reph′a•im, 21 the Am′o•rites, the Cā′naan•ites, the Gir′-ga•shites, and the Jeb′ū•sites."

The Birth of Ishmael

16 Now Sar′ai, Abram's wife, bore him no children. She had an Egyptian slave-girl whose name was Hā′gar, 2 and Sar′ai said to Abram, "You see that the LORD has prevented me from bearing children; go in to my slave-girl; it may be that I shall obtain children by her." And Abram listened to the voice of Sar′ai. 3 So, after Abram had lived ten years in the land of Cā′naan, Sar′ai, Abram's wife, took Hā′gar the Egyptian, her slave-girl, and gave her to her husband Abram as a wife. 4 He went in to Hā′gar, and she conceived; and when she saw that she had conceived, she looked with contempt on her mistress. 5 Then Sar′ai said to Abram, "May the wrong done to me be on you! I gave my slave-girl to your embrace, and when she saw that she had conceived, she looked on me with contempt. May the LORD judge between you and me!" 6 But Abram said to Sar′ai, "Your slave-girl is in your power; do to her as you please." Then Sar′ai dealt harshly with her, and she ran away from her.

7 The angel of the LORD found her by a spring of water in the wilderness, the spring on the way to Shur. 8 And he said, "Hā′gar, slave-girl of Sar′ai, where have you come from and where are you going?" She said, "I am running away from my mistress Sar′ai." 9 The angel of the LORD said to her, "Return to your mistress, and submit to her." 10 The angel of the LORD also said to her, "I will so greatly multiply your offspring that they cannot be

---

[n] Meaning of Heb uncertain · [o] Heb *he*

counted for multitude." ¹¹ And the angel of the LORD said to her,

"Now you have conceived and shall bear a son; you shall call him Ish′ma·el,ᵖ for the LORD has given heed to your affliction.
¹² He shall be a wild ass of a man, with his hand against everyone, and everyone's hand against him; and he shall live at odds with all his kin."

¹³ So she named the LORD who spoke to her, "You are El-roi";�q for she said, "Have I really seen God and remained alive after seeing him?"ʳ ¹⁴ Therefore the well was called Bē′er-la′haī-roi;ˢ it lies between Kā′desh and Bē′red.

¹⁵ Hā′gar bore Abram a son; and Abram named his son, whom Hā′gar bore, Ish′ma·el. ¹⁶ Abram was eighty-six years old when Hā′gar bore himᵗ Ish′ma·el.

The Sign of the Covenant
(Ex 12.43—13.2)

17 When Abram was ninety-nine years old, the LORD appeared to Abram, and said to him, "I am God Almighty;ᵘ walk before me, and be blameless. ² And I will make my covenant between me and you, and will make you exceedingly numerous." ³ Then Abram fell on his face; and God said to him, ⁴ "As for me, this is my covenant with you: You shall be the ancestor of a multitude of na-

tions. ⁵ No longer shall your name be Abram,ᵛ but your name shall be Abraham;ʷ for I have made you the ancestor of a multitude of nations. ⁶ I will make you exceedingly fruitful; and I will make nations of you, and kings shall come from you. ⁷ I will establish my covenant between me and you, and your offspring after you throughout their generations, for an everlasting covenant, to be God to you and to your offspringˣ after you. ⁸ And I will give to you, and to your offspring after you, the land where you are now an alien, all the land of Cā′naan, for a perpetual holding; and I will be their God."

⁹ God said to Abraham, "As for you, you shall keep my covenant, you and your offspring after you throughout their generations. ¹⁰ This is my covenant, which you shall keep, between me and you and your offspring after you: Every male among you shall be circumcised. ¹¹ You shall circumcise the flesh of your foreskins, and it shall be a sign of the covenant between me and you. ¹² Throughout your generations every male among you shall be circumcised when he is eight days old, including the slave born in your house and the one bought with your money from any foreigner who is not of your offspring. ¹³ Both the slave born in

ᵖ That is *God hears* q Perhaps *God of seeing* or *God who sees* ʳ Meaning of Heb uncertain ˢ That is *the Well of the Living One who sees me* ᵗ Heb *Abram* ᵘ Traditional rendering of Heb *El Shaddai* ᵛ That is *exalted ancestor* ʷ Here taken to mean *ancestor of a multitude* ˣ Heb *seed*

Love and Jealousy

LIVE IT!

A love triangle in the Bible! The relationship between Abram, Sarai, and Hagar is shocking by Christian moral standards but would not have been unusual in their time. A patriarch like Abram would often have children by several wives, slaves, and concubines (something like mistresses who lived with the household). It's not surprising that such relationships would have fostered jealousy and tension. The conflict between Hagar and Sarai must have been fierce for Hagar to leave the security of Abram's household.

So, why does God's angel seek out Hagar and ask her to return to a place where she is likely to be mistreated? To answer this, we have to remember that the writer of Genesis was concerned more with explaining the rise of nations than with teaching a moral lesson. Hagar must return to bear her son, Ishmael, so that the Ishmaelites (descendants of Ishmael) have a clear connection to Abraham as their ancestor.

Today, we encourage victims of abuse and harassment to speak out and take action. When we encounter people who have been abused or harassed, we need to help them seek justice and set things right. Remember the larger message in Genesis—that every person is created in God's image and is to be treated with the utmost dignity and respect. Carrying out this message is our responsibility as brothers and sisters to one another.

▶ Gen 16.1–16

Covenant

Covenant is a powerful word in the Bible, with deep religious significance because it expresses the intimate relationship between God and God's people. At its most basic level, a covenant is a promise by both parties involved to do certain things. In the covenant God makes with Noah, God promises never to destroy the earth again, and Noah's family promises to fill the earth and subdue it (Gen 9.1–17). In the covenant with Abraham, God promises that Abram's descendants will be numerous and become a great nation. In return, Abram and all the male members of his household and their male descendants must practice circumcision to mark that they belong to God (17.1–27). In the Covenant made at Mount Sinai with Moses (Ex 19.1–9) and the Hebrew people, God promises to give them the Promised Land. In return, they promise to follow the laws God gives to them.

As told by the author of Genesis, these covenants are always initiated by God, who wants to lead the people to a better way of life. But the people must respond to God's offer as a sign of their faith in God. The New Testament tells of a new and lasting Covenant for all people and for all time (2 Cor 3.3; Gal 4.21–31).

And so we, each of us, are part of these ancient promises. Like the many faithful people who have gone before us, we too are the descendants of Abraham and Sarah, believers in the one God and members of God's family. We too are heirs to a special, intimate relationship with the Holy One of Israel.

▸ **Gen 17.1–27**

your house and the one bought with your money must be circumcised. So shall my covenant be in your flesh an everlasting covenant. 14 Any uncircumcised male who is not circumcised in the flesh of his foreskin shall be cut off from his people; he has broken my covenant."

15 God said to Abraham, "As for Sar'ai your wife, you shall not call her Sar'ai, but Sarah shall be her name. 16 I will bless her, and moreover I will give you a son by her. I will bless her, and she shall give rise to nations; kings of peoples shall come from her." 17 Then Abraham fell on his face and laughed, and said to himself, "Can a child be born to a man who is a hundred years old? Can Sarah, who is ninety years old, bear a child?" 18 And Abraham said to God, "O that Ish'ma•el might live in your sight!" 19 God said, "No, but your wife Sarah shall bear you a son, and you shall name him Isaac.*y* I will establish my covenant with him as an everlasting covenant for his offspring after him. 20 As for Ish'ma•el, I have heard you; I will bless him and make him fruitful and exceedingly numerous; he shall be the father of twelve princes, and I will make him a great nation. 21 But my covenant I will establish with Isaac, whom Sarah shall bear to you at this season next year." 22 And when he had finished talking with him, God went up from Abraham.

23 Then Abraham took his son Ish'ma•el and all the slaves born in his house or bought with his money, every male among the men of Abraham's house, and he circumcised the flesh of their foreskins that very day, as God had said to him. 24 Abraham was ninety-nine years old when he was circumcised in the flesh of his foreskin. 25 And his son Ish'ma•el was thirteen years old when he was circumcised in the flesh of his foreskin. 26 That very day Abraham and his son Ish'ma•el were circumcised; 27 and all the men of his house, slaves born in the house and those bought with money from a foreigner, were circumcised with him.

A Son Promised to Abraham and Sarah
(Heb 13.2)

18 The LORD appeared to Abraham*z* by the oaks*a* of Mam're, as he sat at the entrance of his tent in the heat of the day. 2 He looked up and saw three men standing near him. When he saw them, he ran from the tent entrance to meet them, and bowed down to the ground. 3 He said, "My lord, if I find favor with you, do not pass by your servant. 4 Let a little water be brought, and wash your feet, and rest yourselves under the tree. 5 Let me bring a little bread, that you may refresh yourselves, and after that you may pass on—

---

y That is *he laughs*   *z* Heb *him*   *a* Or *terebinths*

did you KNOW?

Circumcision

Circumcision, the removal of the foreskin of the penis, was practiced by many
peoples in the ancient world. In Israel,
circumcision was performed shortly after
birth. It symbolized that this person belonged to the people of God, and was
required by the Covenant that God made
first with Abraham, then with Moses
and all Israel. Today, most Jews continue
circumcision as a religious practice, and
other people may be circumcised for
personal reasons.

In the early church, circumcision
became the center of a controversy about
whether Gentiles who wanted to become
Christians had to first become Jews (Acts
of the Apostles, chapter 15; Phil 3.2–9).

▶ **Gen 17.9–14**

it before them; and he stood by them under the
tree while they ate.

9 They said to him, "Where is your wife
Sarah?" And he said, "There, in the tent." 10 Then
one said, "I will surely return to you in due season,
and your wife Sarah shall have a son." And Sarah
was listening at the tent entrance behind him.
11 Now Abraham and Sarah were old, advanced in
age; it had ceased to be with Sarah after the manner of women. 12 So Sarah laughed to herself, saying, "After I have grown old, and my husband is
old, shall I have pleasure?" 13 The LORD said to
Abraham, "Why did Sarah laugh, and say, 'Shall I
indeed bear a child, now that I am old?' 14 Is anything too wonderful for the LORD? At the set time
I will return to you, in due season, and Sarah shall
have a son." 15 But Sarah denied, saying, "I did not
laugh"; for she was afraid. He said, "Oh yes, you
did laugh."

Judgment Pronounced on Sodom

16 Then the men set out from there, and they
looked toward Sod'om; and Abraham went with
them to set them on their way. 17 The LORD said,
"Shall I hide from Abraham what I am about to do,
18 seeing that Abraham shall become a great and
mighty nation, and all the nations of the earth
shall be blessed in him?*c* 19 No, for I have chosen*d*
him, that he may charge his children and his
household after him to keep the way of the LORD
by doing righteousness and justice; so that the
LORD may bring about for Abraham what he has
promised him." 20 Then the LORD said, "How great

---

b Heb *seahs*   *c* Or *and all the nations of the earth shall bless
themselves by him*   *d* Heb *known*

since you have come to your servant." So they said,
"Do as you have said." 6 And Abraham hastened
into the tent to Sarah, and said, "Make ready quickly three measures*b* of choice flour, knead it, and
make cakes." 7 Abraham ran to the herd, and took
a calf, tender and good, and gave it to the servant,
who hastened to prepare it. 8 Then he took curds
and milk and the calf that he had prepared, and set

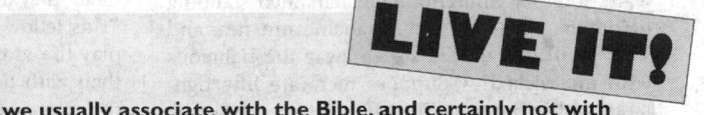

What's So Funny?   LIVE IT!

Laughter is not a word we usually associate with the Bible, and certainly not with
the Old Testament. Most of the stories are serious, filled with accounts of sacrifice, battles, and the Covenant. But here is Sarah, an old woman, long past childbearing age. She overhears one of Abraham's mysterious guests tell him that in
a year, he and Sarah will have a son (Gen 18.10). How can she help but laugh? She and
Abraham do produce, of course, a son called Isaac, whose Hebrew name, *Yishaq*, means
"laughed." Sarah's cynical chuckles must have turned to joyful laughs at the birth of her
beloved son. Laughter is a wonderful response to the gift of life and is a natural and often
spontaneous response to God's presence within us and around us.

"Is anything too wonderful for the LORD?" (verse 14). We are all tempted to laugh at
the notion that miracles can happen to us. As we grow in faith and open ourselves to
God's goodness, our laughter will change from cynical laughter to joyful laughter.

▶ **Gen 18.9–15**

PRAY IT?
Get Close to God

Our prayers reveal what we believe about God and what we value. Abraham's bargaining for the inhabitants of Sodom and Gomorrah shows his faith, his care for others, and his closeness with God. Although he is humble, he deals with God as a friend whom he is not afraid to be honest with.

We too must be honest with God in our prayer. Too many Christians simply do not trust God enough to be completely themselves with God. They are afraid to share their doubts, anger, grief, and frustrations. But God is big enough to handle it all. Find a way in your prayer to share your innermost thoughts and feelings with God. For some people, journaling helps; others yell and shout aloud at the Lord. Remember that God's healing touch cannot enter our life until we are willing to share our deepest feelings.

▶ **Gen 18.22–33**

is the outcry against Sod'om and Go•mor'rah and how very grave their sin! 21 I must go down and see whether they have done altogether according to the outcry that has come to me; and if not, I will know."

22 So the men turned from there, and went toward Sod'om, while Abraham remained standing before the LORD.*e* 23 Then Abraham came near and said, "Will you indeed sweep away the righteous with the wicked? 24 Suppose there are fifty righteous within the city; will you then sweep away the place and not forgive it for the fifty righteous who are in it? 25 Far be it from you to do such a thing, to slay the righteous with the wicked, so that the righteous fare as the wicked! Far be that from you! Shall not the Judge of all the earth do what is just?" 26 And the LORD said, "If I find at Sod'om fifty righteous in the city, I will forgive the whole place for their sake." 27 Abraham answered, "Let me take it upon myself to speak to the Lord, I who am but dust and ashes. 28 Suppose five of the fifty righteous are lacking? Will you destroy the whole city for lack of five?" And he said, "I will not destroy it if I find forty-five there." 29 Again he spoke to him, "Suppose forty are found there." He answered, "For

the sake of forty I will not do it." 30 Then he said, "Oh do not let the Lord be angry if I speak. Suppose thirty are found there." He answered, "I will not do it, if I find thirty there." 31 He said, "Let me take it upon myself to speak to the Lord. Suppose twenty are found there." He answered, "For the sake of twenty I will not destroy it." 32 Then he said, "Oh do not let the Lord be angry if I speak just once more. Suppose ten are found there." He answered, "For the sake of ten I will not destroy it." 33 And the LORD went his way, when he had finished speaking to Abraham; and Abraham returned to his place.

The Depravity of Sodom

19 The two angels came to Sod'om in the evening, and Lot was sitting in the gateway of Sod'om. When Lot saw them, he rose to meet them, and bowed down with his face to the ground. 2 He said, "Please, my lords, turn aside to your servant's house and spend the night, and wash your feet; then you can rise early and go on your way." They said, "No; we will spend the night in the square." 3vBut he urged them strongly; so they turned aside to him and entered his house; and he made them a feast, and baked unleavened bread, and they ate. 4 But before they lay down, the men of the city, the men of Sod'om, both young and old, all the people to the last man, surrounded the house; 5 and they called to Lot, "Where are the men who came to you tonight? Bring them out to us, so that we may know them." 6 Lot went out of the door to the men, shut the door after him, 7 and said, "I beg you, my brothers, do not act so wickedly. 8 Look, I have two daughters who have not known a man; let me bring them out to you, and do to them as you please; only do nothing to these men, for they have come under the shelter of my roof." 9 But they replied, "Stand back!" And they said, "This fellow came here as an alien, and he would play the judge! Now we will deal worse with you than with them." Then they pressed hard against the man Lot, and came near the door to break it down. 10 But the men inside reached out their hands and brought Lot into the house with them, and shut the door. 11 And they struck with blindness the men who were at the door of the house, both small and great, so that they were unable to find the door.

Sodom and Gomorrah Destroyed
(Mt 11.23–24; Lk 17.28–32)

12 Then the men said to Lot, "Have you anyone else here? Sons-in-law, sons, daughters, or anyone

---

e Another ancient tradition reads *while the LORD remained standing before Abraham*

Be Kind to Strangers

If our first gesture to outsiders were one of respect, kindness, and gracious hospitality, what might our world be like? The story of Sodom and Gomorrah shows us the results of disrespect, inhospitality, and the attempted abuse of strangers. Like Abraham, Lot is a wonderful host. But the people of Sodom want Lot's visitors for their own sexual pleasure (to "know" someone is often biblical language for sexual intercourse). For the author of Genesis, this horrendous crime calls for the most severe punishment.

As children of God, it is our responsibility to extend our kindness to stranger and friend alike. So how are visitors or new students treated in your school? How are visitors treated in your home?

▶ Gen 19.1–11

---

you have in the city—bring them out of the place. 13 For we are about to destroy this place, because the outcry against its people has become great before the LORD, and the LORD has sent us to destroy it." 14 So Lot went out and said to his sons-in-law, who were to marry his daughters, "Up, get out of this place; for the LORD is about to destroy the city." But he seemed to his sons-in-law to be jesting.

15 When morning dawned, the angels urged Lot, saying, "Get up, take your wife and your two daughters who are here, or else you will be consumed in the punishment of the city." 16 But he lingered; so the men seized him and his wife and his two daughters by the hand, the LORD being merciful to him, and they brought him out and left him outside the city. 17 When they had brought them outside, they*f* said, "Flee for your life; do not look back or stop anywhere in the Plain; flee to the hills, or else you will be consumed." 18 And Lot said to them, "Oh, no, my lords; 19 your servant has found favor with you, and you have shown me great kindness in saving my life; but I cannot flee to the hills, for fear the disaster will overtake me and I die. 20 Look, that city is near enough to flee to, and it is a little one. Let me escape there—is it not a little one?—and my life will be saved!" 21He said to him, "Very well, I grant you this favor too, and will not overthrow the city of which you have spoken. 22 Hurry, escape there; for I can do nothing until you arrive there." Therefore the city was called Zō'ar.*g* 23 The sun had risen on the earth when Lot came to Zō'ar.

24 Then the LORD rained on Sod'om and Gomor'rah sulfur and fire from the LORD out of heaven; 25 and he overthrew those cities, and all the Plain, and all the inhabitants of the cities, and what grew on the ground. 26 But Lot's wife, behind him, looked back, and she became a pillar of salt.

27 Abraham went early in the morning to the place where he had stood before the LORD; 28 and he looked down toward Sod'om and Go•mor'rah and toward all the land of the Plain and saw the smoke of the land going up like the smoke of a furnace.

29 So it was that, when God destroyed the cities of the Plain, God remembered Abraham, and sent Lot out of the midst of the overthrow, when he overthrew the cities in which Lot had settled.

The Shameful Origin of Moab and Ammon

30 Now Lot went up out of Zō'ar and settled in the hills with his two daughters, for he was afraid to stay in Zō'ar; so he lived in a cave with his two daughters. 31 And the firstborn said to the younger, "Our father is old, and there is not a man on earth to come in to us after the manner of all the world. 32 Come, let us make our father drink wine, and we will lie with him, so that we may preserve offspring through our father." 33 So they made their father drink wine that night; and the firstborn went in, and lay with her father; he did not know when she lay down or when she rose. 34 On the next day, the firstborn said to the younger, "Look, I lay last night with my father; let us make him drink wine tonight also; then you go in and lie with him, so that we may preserve offspring through our father." 35 So they made their father drink wine that night also; and the younger rose, and lay with him; and he did not know when she lay down or when she rose. 36 Thus both the daughters of Lot became pregnant by their father. 37 The firstborn bore a son, and named him Mō'ab; he is the ancestor of the Mō'ab•ites to this day. 38 The younger also bore a son and named him Ben-am'mī; he is the ancestor of the Am'mon•ites to this day.

---

f Gk Syr Vg: Heb *he*   *g* That is *Little*

GEN

Abraham and Sarah at Gerar

20 From there Abraham journeyed toward the region of the Neg'eb, and settled between Kā'desh and Shur. While residing in Gĕ'rar as an alien, 2 Abraham said of his wife Sarah, "She is my sister." And King A•bim'e•lech of Gĕ'rar sent and took Sarah. 3 But God came to A•bim'e•lech in a dream by night, and said to him, "You are about to die because of the woman whom you have taken; for she is a married woman." 4 Now A•bim'e•lech had not approached her; so he said, "Lord, will you destroy an innocent people? 5 Did he not himself say to me, 'She is my sister'? And she herself said, 'He is my brother.' I did this in the integrity of my heart and the innocence of my hands." 6 Then God said to him in the dream, "Yes, I know that you did this in the integrity of your heart; furthermore it was I who kept you from sinning against me. Therefore I did not let you touch her. 7 Now then, return the man's wife; for he is a prophet, and he will pray for you and you shall live. But if you do not restore her, know that you shall surely die, you and all that are yours."

8 So A•bim'e•lech rose early in the morning, and called all his servants and told them all these things; and the men were very much afraid. 9 Then A•bim'e•lech called Abraham, and said to him, "What have you done to us? How have I sinned against you, that you have brought such great guilt on me and my kingdom? You have done things to me that ought not to be done." 10 And A•bim'e•lech said to Abraham, "What were you thinking of, that you did this thing?" 11 Abraham said, "I did it because I thought, There is no fear of God at all in this place, and they will kill me because of my wife. 12 Besides, she is indeed my sister, the daughter of my father but not the daughter of my mother; and she became my wife. 13 And when God caused me to wander from my father's house, I said to her, 'This is the kindness you must do me: at every place to which we come, say of me, He is my brother.' " 14 Then A•bim'-e•lech took sheep and oxen, and male and female slaves, and gave them to Abraham, and restored his wife Sarah to him. 15 A•bim'e•lech said, "My land is before you; settle where it pleases you." 16 To Sarah he said, "Look, I have given your brother a thousand pieces of silver; it is your exoneration before all who are with you; you are completely vindicated." 17 Then Abraham prayed to God; and God healed A•bim'e•lech, and also healed his wife and female slaves so that they bore children. 18 For the LORD had closed fast all the wombs of the house of A•bim'e•lech because of Sarah, Abraham's wife.

The Birth of Isaac
(Heb 11.11)

21 The LORD dealt with Sarah as he had said, and the LORD did for Sarah as he had promised. 2 Sarah conceived and bore Abraham a son in his old age, at the time of which God had spoken to him. 3 Abraham gave the name Isaac to his son whom Sarah bore him. 4 And Abraham circumcised his son Isaac when he was eight days old, as God had commanded him. 5 Abraham was a hundred years old when his son Isaac was born to him. 6 Now Sarah said, "God has brought laughter for me; everyone who hears will laugh with me." 7 And she said, "Who would ever have said to Abraham that Sarah would nurse children? Yet I have borne him a son in his old age."

Hagar and Ishmael Sent Away
(Gal 4.21–30)

8 The child grew, and was weaned; and Abraham made a great feast on the day that Isaac was weaned. 9 But Sarah saw the son of Hā'gar the Egyptian, whom she had borne to Abraham, playing with her son Isaac.*h* 10 So she said to Abraham, "Cast out this slave woman with her son; for the son of this slave woman shall not inherit along with my son Isaac." 11 The matter was very distressing to Abraham on account of his son. 12 But God said to Abraham, "Do not be distressed because of the boy and because of your slave woman; whatever Sarah says to you, do as she tells you, for it is through Isaac that offspring shall be named for you. 13 As for the son of the slave woman, I will make a nation of him also, because he is your offspring." 14 So Abraham rose early in the morning, and took bread and a skin of water, and gave it to Hā'gar, putting it on her shoulder, along with the child, and sent her away. And she departed, and wandered about in the wilderness of Bĕ'er-shĕ'ba.

15 When the water in the skin was gone, she cast the child under one of the bushes. 16 Then she went and sat down opposite him a good way off, about the distance of a bowshot; for she said, "Do not let me look on the death of the child." And as she sat opposite him, she lifted up her voice and wept. 17 And God heard the voice of the boy; and the angel of God called to Hā'gar from heaven, and said to her, "What troubles you, Hā'gar? Do not be afraid; for God has heard the voice of the boy where he is. 18 Come, lift up the boy and hold him fast with your hand, for I will make a great nation of him." 19 Then God opened her eyes and she saw a well of water. She went, and filled the skin with water, and gave the boy a drink.

---

h Gk Vg: Heb lacks *with her son Isaac*

20 God was with the boy, and he grew up; he lived in the wilderness, and became an expert with the bow. 21 He lived in the wilderness of Par'an; and his mother got a wife for him from the land of Egypt.

PRAY IT
Hagar's Rescue

Genesis 21.8–21 is part 2 of the Hagar and Ishmael story begun in 16.1–16. Once again, Hagar is the victim of Sarah's jealousy. But this time God does not send her back. Seemingly facing certain death, Hagar receives from God the ability to see the opportunity for life in front of her. This time the writer of Genesis makes the point that God rescues the abused and abandoned. Hagar and Ishmael survive, and from their descendants, a great people emerges.

Hagar's story reminds us that God wants to rescue us from oppression, injustice, and abuse. Often, we want to ask God to magically take these things away. But because God has given human beings free will, we cannot always be spared from the abuse and injustice of others. In your prayer, you can always ask God to rescue you, to give you the vision to see the healthy choices you can make to improve your situation. Do that right now if you are in an unjust or abusive situation.

▶ Gen 21.8–21

Abraham and Abimelech Make a Covenant

22 At that time A·bim'e·lech, with Phi'col the commander of his army, said to Abraham, "God is with you in all that you do; 23 now therefore swear to me here by God that you will not deal falsely with me or with my offspring or with my posterity, but as I have dealt loyally with you, you will deal with me and with the land where you have resided as an alien." 24 And Abraham said, "I swear it."

25 When Abraham complained to A·bim'e·lech about a well of water that A·bim'e·lech's servants had seized, 26 A·bim'e·lech said, "I do not know who has done this; you did not tell me, and I have not heard of it until today." 27 So Abraham took sheep and oxen and gave them to A·bim'e·lech, and the two men made a covenant. 28 Abraham set apart seven ewe lambs of the flock. 29 And A·bim'e·lech said to Abraham, "What is the meaning of these seven ewe lambs that you have set apart?" 30 He said, "These seven ewe lambs you shall accept from my hand, in order that you may be a witness for me that I dug this well." 31 Therefore that place was called Bě'er-shě'ba;ⁱ because there both of them swore an oath. 32 When they had made a covenant at Bě'er-shě'ba, A·bim'e·lech, with Phi'col the commander of his army, left and returned to the land of the Phi·lis'tines. 33 Abraham𝗃 planted a tamarisk tree in Bě'er-shě'ba, and called there on the name of the Lᴏʀᴅ, the Everlasting God.ᵏ 34 And Abraham resided as an alien many days in the land of the Phi·lis'tines.

The Command to Sacrifice Isaac
(Heb 11.17–19)

22 After these things God tested Abraham. He said to him, "Abraham!" And he said, "Here I am." 2 He said, "Take your son, your only son Isaac, whom you love, and go to the land of Mō·rī'ah, and offer him there as a burnt offering on one of the mountains that I shall show you." 3 So Abraham rose early in the morning, saddled his donkey, and took two of his young men with him, and his son Isaac; he cut the wood for the burnt offering, and set out and went to the place in the distance that God had shown him. 4 On the third day Abraham looked up and saw the place far away. 5 Then Abraham said to his young men, "Stay here with the donkey; the boy and I will go over there; we will worship, and then we will come back to you." 6 Abraham took the wood of the burnt offering and laid it on his son Isaac, and he himself carried the fire and the knife. So the two of them walked on together. 7 Isaac said to his father Abraham, "Father!" And he said, "Here I am, my son." He said, "The fire and the wood are here, but where is the lamb for a burnt offering?" 8 Abraham said, "God himself will provide the lamb for a burnt offering, my son." So the two of them walked on together.

9 When they came to the place that God had shown him, Abraham built an altar there and laid the wood in order. He bound his son Isaac, and laid him on the altar, on top of the wood. 10 Then Abraham reached out his hand and took the knife to killˡ his son. 11 But the angel of the Lᴏʀᴅ called to him from heaven, and said, "Abraham,

---

ⁱ That is *Well of seven* or *Well of the oath*   𝗃 Heb *He*
ᵏ Or *the* Lᴏʀᴅ, *El Olam*   ˡ Or *to slaughter*

Abraham!" And he said, "Here I am." 12 He said, "Do not lay your hand on the boy or do anything to him; for now I know that you fear God, since you have not withheld your son, your only son, from me." 13 And Abraham looked up and saw a ram, caught in a thicket by its horns. Abraham went and took the ram and offered it up as a burnt offering instead of his son. 14 So Abraham called that place "The LORD will provide";*m* as it is said to this day, "On the mount of the LORD it shall be provided."*n*

15 The angel of the LORD called to Abraham a second time from heaven, 16 and said, "By myself I have sworn, says the LORD: Because you have done this, and have not withheld your son, your only son, 17 I will indeed bless you, and I will make your offspring as numerous as the stars of heaven and as the sand that is on the seashore. And your offspring shall possess the gate of their enemies, 18 and by your offspring shall all the nations of the earth gain blessing for themselves, because you have obeyed my voice." 19 So Abraham returned to his young men, and they arose and went together to Bē′er-shē′ba; and Abraham lived at Bē′er-shē′ba.

The Children of Nahor

20 Now after these things it was told Abraham, "Mil′cah also has borne children, to your brother Nā′hor: 21 Uz the firstborn, Buz his brother, Ke•mū′el the father of Ar′am, 22 Chē′sed, Hā′zō, Pil′dash, Jid′laph, and Be•thū′el." 23 Be•thū′el became the father of Rebekah. These eight Mil′cah bore to Nā′hor, Abraham's brother. 24 Moreover,

Chap. 22

Ultimate Trust in God!

To us it seems horrible that God would ask Abraham to sacrifice his son Isaac. But this story is meant to be a sign of Abraham's complete trust in God. Ultimately, God prevented the sacrifice because God wanted not Isaac's death but Abraham's faith. Because of his willingness to respond to God's demand, Abraham is recognized as the father of our faith. Our trust in God should be as total as Abraham's trust was.

We probably won't ever be faced with the test of Abraham, but the story shows us the power of faith. Because of Abraham's faith in God's promise, Isaac lived and became the father of Jacob, whose twelve sons became the twelve tribes of Israel. In your prayer, reflect or journal on the following questions:

- Because of your beliefs, have you ever had to give up someone or something that was precious to you?
- How has your life been enriched as a result of your trust in God in a difficult situation?

▸ Gen 22.1–19

his concubine, whose name was Re•ū′mah, bore Tē′bah, Gā′ham, Tā′hash, and Mā′a•cah.

Sarah's Death and Burial

23 Sarah lived one hundred twenty-seven years; this was the length of Sarah's life. 2 And Sarah died at Kir′i•ath-ar′ba (that is, Hē′bron) in the land of Cā′naan; and Abraham went in to mourn for Sarah and to weep for her. 3 Abraham rose up from beside his dead, and said to the Hit′tites, 4 "I am a stranger and an alien residing among you; give me property among you for a burying place, so that I may bury my dead out of my sight." 5 The Hit′tites answered Abraham, 6 "Hear us, my lord; you are a mighty prince among us. Bury your dead in the choicest of our burial places; none of us will withhold from you any burial ground for burying your dead." 7 Abra-

m Or *will see;* Heb traditionally transliterated *Jehovah Jireh* *n* Or *he shall be seen* ham rose and bowed to the Hit'tites, the people of the land. ⁸ He said to them, "If you are willing that I should bury my dead out of my sight, hear me, and entreat for me Ē'phron son of Zō'har, ⁹ so that he may give me the cave of Mach•pē'lah, which he owns; it is at the end of his field. For the full price let him give it to me in your presence as a possession for a burying place." ¹⁰ Now Ē'phron was sitting among the Hit'tites; and Ē'phron the Hit'tite answered Abraham in the hearing of the Hit'tites, of all who went in at the gate of his city, ¹¹ "No, my lord, hear me; I give you the field, and I give you the cave that is in it; in the presence of my people I give it to you; bury your dead." ¹² Then Abraham bowed down before the people of the land. ¹³ He said to Ē'phron in the hearing of the people of the land, "If you only will listen to me! I will give the price of the field; accept it from me, so that I may bury my dead there." ¹⁴ Ē'phron answered Abraham, ¹⁵ "My lord, listen to me; a piece of land worth four hundred shekels of silver—what is that between you and me? Bury your dead." ¹⁶ Abraham agreed with Ē'phron; and Abraham weighed out for Ē'phron the silver that he had named in the hearing of the Hit'tites, four hundred shekels of silver, according to the weights current among the merchants.

17 So the field of Ē'phron in Mach•pē'lah, which was to the east of Mam're, the field with the cave that was in it and all the trees that were in the field, throughout its whole area, passed ¹⁸ to Abraham as a possession in the presence of the Hit'tites, in the presence of all who went in at the gate of his city. ¹⁹ After this, Abraham buried Sarah his wife in the cave of the field of Mach•pē'lah facing Mam're (that is, Hē'bron) in the land of Cā'naan. ²⁰ The field and the cave that is in it passed from the Hit'tites into Abraham's possession as a burying place.

The Marriage of Isaac and Rebekah

24 Now Abraham was old, well advanced in years; and the LORD had blessed Abraham in all things. ² Abraham said to his servant, the oldest of his house, who had charge of all that he had, "Put your hand under my thigh ³ and I will make you swear by the LORD, the God of heaven and earth, that you will not get a wife for my son from the daughters of the Cā'naan•ites, among whom I live, ⁴ but will go to my country and to my kindred and get a wife for my son Isaac." ⁵ The servant said to him, "Perhaps the woman may not be willing to follow me to this land; must I then take your son back to the land from which you came?" ⁶ Abraham said to him, "See to it that you do not take my son back there. ⁷ The LORD, the God of heaven, who took me from my father's

house and from the land of my birth, and who spoke to me and swore to me, 'To your offspring I will give this land,' he will send his angel before you, and you shall take a wife for my son from there. ⁸ But if the woman is not willing to follow you, then you will be free from this oath of mine; only you must not take my son back there." ⁹ So the servant put his hand under the thigh of Abraham his master and swore to him concerning this matter.

10 Then the servant took ten of his master's camels and departed, taking all kinds of choice gifts from his master; and he set out and went to Ar'am-nā•ha•rā'im, to the city of Nā'hor. ¹¹ He made the camels kneel down outside the city by the well of water; it was toward evening, the time when women go out to draw water. ¹² And he said, "O LORD, God of my master Abraham, please grant me success today and show steadfast love to my master Abraham. ¹³ I am standing here by the spring of water, and the daughters of the townspeople are coming out to draw water. ¹⁴ Let the girl to whom I shall say, 'Please offer your jar that I may drink,' and who shall say, 'Drink, and I will water your camels'—let her be the one whom you have appointed for your servant Isaac. By this I shall know that you have shown steadfast love to my master."

15 Before he had finished speaking, there was Rebekah, who was born to Be•thū'el son of Mil'-cah, the wife of Nā'hor, Abraham's brother, coming out with her water jar on her shoulder. ¹⁶ The girl was very fair to look upon, a virgin, whom no man had known. She went down to the spring, filled her jar, and came up. ¹⁷ Then the servant ran to meet her and said, "Please let me sip a little water from your jar." ¹⁸ "Drink, my lord," she said, and quickly lowered her jar upon her hand and gave him a drink. ¹⁹ When she had finished giving him a drink, she said, "I will draw for your camels also, until they have finished drinking." ²⁰ So she quickly emptied her jar into the trough and ran again to the well to draw, and she drew for all his camels. ²¹ The man gazed at her in silence to learn whether or not the LORD had made his journey successful.

22 When the camels had finished drinking, the man took a gold nose-ring weighing a half shekel, and two bracelets for her arms weighing ten gold shekels, ²³ and said, "Tell me whose daughter you are. Is there room in your father's house for us to spend the night?" ²⁴ She said to him, "I am the daughter of Be•thū'el son of Mil'cah, whom she bore to Nā'hor." ²⁵ She added, "We have plenty of straw and fodder and a place to spend the night." ²⁶ The man bowed his head and worshiped the LORD ²⁷ and said, "Blessed be the LORD, the God of

GEN

my master Abraham, who has not forsaken his steadfast love and his faithfulness toward my master. As for me, the LORD has led me on the way to the house of my master's kin."

28 Then the girl ran and told her mother's household about these things. 29 Rebekah had a brother whose name was Lā'ban; and Lā'ban ran out to the man, to the spring. 30 As soon as he had seen the nose-ring, and the bracelets on his sister's arms, and when he heard the words of his sister Rebekah, "Thus the man spoke to me," he went to the man; and there he was, standing by the camels at the spring. 31 He said, "Come in, O blessed of the LORD. Why do you stand outside when I have prepared the house and a place for the camels?" 32 So the man came into the house; and Lā'ban unloaded the camels, and gave him straw and fodder for the camels, and water to wash his feet and the feet of the men who were with him. 33 Then food was set before him to eat; but he said, "I will not eat until I have told my errand." He said, "Speak on."

34 So he said, "I am Abraham's servant. 35 The LORD has greatly blessed my master, and he has become wealthy; he has given him flocks and herds, silver and gold, male and female slaves, camels and donkeys. 36 And Sarah my master's wife bore a son to my master when she was old; and he has given him all that he has. 37 My master made me swear, saying, 'You shall not take a wife for my son from the daughters of the Cā'naan•ites, in whose land I live; 38 but you shall go to my father's house, to my kindred, and get a wife for my son.' 39 I said to my master, 'Perhaps the woman will not follow me.' 40 But he said to me, 'The LORD, before whom I walk, will send his angel with you and make your way successful. You shall get a wife for my son from my kindred, from my father's house. 41 Then you will be free from my oath, when you come to my kindred; even if they will not give her to you, you will be free from my oath.'

42 "I came today to the spring, and said, 'O LORD, the God of my master Abraham, if now you will only make successful the way I am going! 43 I am standing here by the spring of water; let the young woman who comes out to draw, to whom I shall say, "Please give me a little water from your jar to drink," 44 and who will say to me, "Drink, and I will draw for your camels also"—let her be the woman whom the LORD has appointed for my master's son.'

45 "Before I had finished speaking in my heart, there was Rebekah coming out with her water jar on her shoulder, and she went down to the spring, and drew. I said to her, 'Please let me drink.' 46 She quickly let down her jar from her shoulder, and said, 'Drink, and I will also water your camels.' So

I drank, and she also watered the camels. 47 Then I asked her, 'Whose daughter are you?' She said, 'The daughter of Be•thū'el, Nā'hor's son, whom Mil'cah bore to him.' So I put the ring on her nose, and the bracelets on her arms. 48 Then I bowed my head and worshiped the LORD, and blessed the LORD, the God of my master Abraham, who had led me by the right way to obtain the daughter of my master's kinsman for his son. 49 Now then, if you will deal loyally and truly with my master, tell me; and if not, tell me, so that I may turn either to the right hand or to the left."

50 Then Lā'ban and Be•thū'el answered, "The thing comes from the LORD; we cannot speak to you anything bad or good. 51 Look, Rebekah is before you, take her and go, and let her be the wife of your master's son, as the LORD has spoken."

52 When Abraham's servant heard their words, he bowed himself to the ground before the LORD. 53 And the servant brought out jewelry of silver and of gold, and garments, and gave them to Rebekah; he also gave to her brother and to her mother costly ornaments. 54 Then he and the men who were with him ate and drank, and they spent the night there. When they rose in the morning, he said, "Send me back to my master." 55 Her brother and her mother said, "Let the girl remain with us a while, at least ten days; after that she may go." 56 But he said to them, "Do not delay me, since the LORD has made my journey successful; let me go that I may go to my master." 57 They said, "We will call the girl, and ask her." 58 And they called Rebekah, and said to her, "Will you go with this man?" She said, "I will." 59 So they sent away their sister Rebekah and her nurse along with Abraham's servant and his men. 60 And they blessed Rebekah and said to her,

"May you, our sister, become
    thousands of myriads;
may your offspring gain possession
    of the gates of their foes."

61 Then Rebekah and her maids rose up, mounted the camels, and followed the man; thus the servant took Rebekah, and went his way.

62 Now Isaac had come from° Bē'er-la'hai-roi, and was settled in the Neg'eb. 63 Isaac went out in the evening to walkᴾ in the field; and looking up, he saw camels coming. 64 And Rebekah looked up, and when she saw Isaac, she slipped quickly from the camel, 65 and said to the servant, "Who is the man over there, walking in the field to meet us?" The servant said, "It is my master." So she took her veil and covered herself. 66 And the servant told Isaac all the things that he had done. 67 Then Isaac

---

o Syr Tg: Heb *from coming to*   *p* Meaning of Heb word is uncertain brought her into his mother Sarah's tent. He took Rebekah, and she became his wife; and he loved her. So Isaac was comforted after his mother's death.

Abraham Marries Keturah
(1 Chr 1.32–33)

25 Abraham took another wife, whose name was Ke•tū′rah. [2] She bore him Zim′ran, Jok′shan, Mē′dan, Mid′i•an, Ish′bak, and Shū′ah. [3] Jok′shan was the father of Shē′ba and Dē′dan. The sons of Dē′dan were As•shū′rim, Le-tū′shim, and Le•um′mim. [4] The sons of Mid′i•an were Ē′phah, Ē′pher, Hā′noch, A•bī′da, and El•dā′-ah. All these were the children of Ke•tū′rah. [5] Abraham gave all he had to Isaac. [6] But to the sons of his concubines Abraham gave gifts, while he was still living, and he sent them away from his son Isaac, eastward to the east country.

The Death of Abraham

[7] This is the length of Abraham's life, one hundred seventy-five years. [8] Abraham breathed his last and died in a good old age, an old man and full of years, and was gathered to his people. [9] His sons Isaac and Ish′ma•el buried him in the cave of Mach•pē′lah, in the field of Ē′phron son of Zō′har the Hit′tīte, east of Mam′re, [10] the field that Abraham purchased from the Hit′tītes. There Abraham was buried, with his wife Sarah. [11] After the death of Abraham God blessed his son Isaac. And Isaac settled at Bē′er-la′haī-roi.

Ishmael's Descendants
(1 Chr 1.29–31)

[12] These are the descendants of Ish′ma•el, Abraham's son, whom Hā′gar the Egyptian, Sarah's slave-girl, bore to Abraham. [13] These are the names of the sons of Ish′ma•el, named in the order of their birth: Ne•bā′i•oth, the firstborn of Ish′ma•el; and Kē′dar, Ad′bē•el, Mib′sam, [14] Mish′ma, Dū′-mah, Mas′sa, [15] Hā′dad, Tē′ma, Jē′tur, Nā′phish, and Ked′e•mah. [16] These are the sons of Ish′ma•el and these are their names, by their villages and by their encampments, twelve princes according to their tribes. [17] (This is the length of the life of Ish′-ma•el, one hundred thirty-seven years; he breathed his last and died, and was gathered to his people.) [18] They settled from Hav′i•lah to Shur, which is opposite Egypt in the direction of Assyria; he settled down[q] alongside of[r] all his people.

The Birth and Youth of Esau and Jacob
(Rom 9.10–12)

[19] These are the descendants of Isaac, Abraham's son: Abraham was the father of Isaac, [20] and Isaac was forty years old when he married Rebekah,

did you KNOW?
Abraham's Descendants

God promised Hagar that her son Ishmael would be made "a great nation" (Gen 21.18). The Old Testament lists twelve princely tribes that descended from Abraham's older son (Gen 25.13–16), tribes traditionally associated with the people of ancient Edom. A much later Islamic tradition identifies Muhammad and his descendants—the Muslims—as "children of Ishmael."

Abraham's younger son, Isaac, was the father of Jacob. The Jewish people trace their lineage to Jacob and his twelve sons. Because Jesus was a Jew, Christians ultimately trace their ancestry through Jacob to Abraham as well.

Thus, three major world religions— Judaism, Christianity, and Islam—all see Abraham as their "father in faith."

▶ Gen 25.12–18

daughter of Be•thū′el the Ar•a•mē′an of Pad′dan-ar′am, sister of Lā′ban the Ar•a•mē′an. [21] Isaac prayed to the LORD for his wife, because she was barren; and the LORD granted his prayer, and his wife Rebekah conceived. [22] The children struggled together within her; and she said, "If it is to be this way, why do I live?"[s] So she went to inquire of the LORD. [23] And the LORD said to her,

"Two nations are in your womb,
and two peoples born of you shall be
divided;
the one shall be stronger than the other,
the elder shall serve the younger."

[24] When her time to give birth was at hand, there were twins in her womb. [25] The first came out red, all his body like a hairy mantle; so they named him Esau. [26] Afterward his brother came out, with his hand gripping Esau's heel; so he was named Jacob.[t] Isaac was sixty years old when she bore them.

[27] When the boys grew up, Esau was a skillful hunter, a man of the field, while Jacob was a quiet man, living in tents. [28] Isaac loved Esau, because he was fond of game; but Rebekah loved Jacob.

---

q Heb *he fell* *r* Or *down in opposition to* *s* Syr: Meaning of Heb uncertain *t* That is *He takes by the heel* or *He supplants*

GEN

Esau Sells His Birthright
(Heb 12.16)

29 Once when Jacob was cooking a stew, Esau came in from the field, and he was famished. 30 Esau said to Jacob, "Let me eat some of that red stuff, for I am famished!" (Therefore he was called Ê'dom.ᵘ) 31 Jacob said, "First sell me your birthright." 32 Esau said, "I am about to die; of what use is a birthright to me?" 33 Jacob said, "Swear to me first."ᵛ So he swore to him, and sold his birthright to Jacob. 34 Then Jacob gave Esau bread and lentil stew, and he ate and drank, and rose and went his way. Thus Esau despised his birthright.

PRAY IT?

Sibling Rivalry

It is common for siblings to have conflict in their relationship, but with Jacob and Esau, the conflict becomes extreme. Follow their story in Genesis, chapters 27–28, 33.

For another story of extreme sibling rivalry, see 37.12–36. Joseph's brothers (all sons of Jacob) are so jealous of him that they plot to kill him. But instead, he gets sold as a slave—and that turns out to be a great career move for him.

The story of the prodigal son in Lk 15.11–32 is yet another example of sibling rivalry.

Do you have any brothers or sisters? If so, how do you treat them? Do you ever pray for them? Do you ever tell them that you care about them—even if they make you angry at times?

If you don't have any brothers or sisters, how about cousins, neighbors, or friends? All relationships get better with prayer and care.

▸ Gen 25.19–34

Isaac and Abimelech

26 Now there was a famine in the land, besides the former famine that had occurred in the days of Abraham. And Isaac went to Gê'rar, to King A·bim'e·lech of the Phi·lis'tines. 2 The LORD appeared to Isaacʷ and said, "Do not go down to Egypt; settle in the land that I shall show you. 3 Reside in this land as an alien, and I will be with you, and will bless you; for to you and to your descendants I will give all these lands, and I will fulfill the oath that I swore to your father Abraham. 4 I will make your offspring as numerous as the stars of heaven, and will give to your offspring all these lands; and all the nations of the earth shall gain blessing for themselves through your offspring, 5 because Abraham obeyed my voice and kept my charge, my commandments, my statutes, and my laws."

6 So Isaac settled in Gê'rar. 7 When the men of the place asked him about his wife, he said, "She is my sister"; for he was afraid to say, "My wife," thinking, "or else the men of the place might kill me for the sake of Rebekah, because she is attractive in appearance." 8 When Isaac had been there a long time, King A·bim'e·lech of the Phi·lis'tines looked out of a window and saw him fondling his wife Rebekah. 9 So A·bim'e·lech called for Isaac, and said, "So she is your wife! Why then did you say, 'She is my sister'?" Isaac said to him, "Because I thought I might die because of her." 10 A·bim'e·lech said, "What is this you have done to us? One of the people might easily have lain with your wife, and you would have brought guilt upon us." 11 So A·bim'e·lech warned all the people, saying, "Whoever touches this man or his wife shall be put to death."

12 Isaac sowed seed in that land, and in the same year reaped a hundredfold. The LORD blessed him, 13 and the man became rich; he prospered more and more until he became very wealthy. 14 He had possessions of flocks and herds, and a great household, so that the Phi·lis'tines envied him. 15 (Now the Phi·lis'tines had stopped up and filled with earth all the wells that his father's servants had dug in the days of his father Abraham.) 16And A·bim'e·lech said to Isaac, "Go away from us; you have become too powerful for us."

17 So Isaac departed from there and camped in the valley of Gê'rar and settled there. 18 Isaac dug again the wells of water that had been dug in the days of his father Abraham; for the Phi·lis'tines had stopped them up after the death of Abraham; and he gave them the names that his father had given them. 19 But when Isaac's servants dug in the valley and found there a well of spring water, 20 the herders of Gê'rar quarreled with Isaac's herders, saying, "The water is ours." So he called the well Ê'sek,ˣ because they contended with him. 21 Then they dug another well, and they quarreled over that one also; so he called it Sit'nah.ʸ 22 He moved from

---

ᵘ That is *Red*   ᵛ Heb *today*   ʷ Heb *him*   ˣ That is *Contention*
ʸ That is *Enmity*

there and dug another well, and they did not quarrel over it; so he called it Re•hō'both,[z] saying, "Now the LORD has made room for us, and we shall be fruitful in the land."

23 From there he went up to Bē'er-shē'ba. 24 And that very night the LORD appeared to him and said, "I am the God of your father Abraham; do not be afraid, for I am with you and will bless you and make your offspring numerous for my servant Abraham's sake." 25 So he built an altar there, called on the name of the LORD, and pitched his tent there. And there Isaac's servants dug a well.

26 Then A•bim'e•lech went to him from Gē'rar, with A•huz'zath his adviser and Phi'col the commander of his army. 27 Isaac said to them, "Why have you come to me, seeing that you hate me and have sent me away from you?" 28 They said, "We see plainly that the LORD has been with you; so we say, let there be an oath between you and us, and let us make a covenant with you 29 so that you will do us no harm, just as we have not touched you and have done to you nothing but good and have sent you away in peace. You are now the blessed of the LORD." 30 So he made them a feast, and they ate and drank. 31 In the morning they rose early and exchanged oaths; and Isaac set them on their way, and they departed from him in peace. 32 That same day Isaac's servants came and told him about the well that they had dug, and said to him, "We have found water!" 33 He called it Shī'bah;[a] therefore the name of the city is Bē'er-shē'ba[b] to this day.

Esau's Hittite Wives

34 When Esau was forty years old, he married Judith daughter of Be•ē'rī the Hit'tīte, and Bas'emath daughter of Ē'lon the Hit'tīte; 35 and they made life bitter for Isaac and Rebekah.

Isaac Blesses Jacob

27 When Isaac was old and his eyes were dim so that he could not see, he called his elder son Esau and said to him, "My son"; and he answered, "Here I am." 2 He said, "See, I am old; I do not know the day of my death. 3 Now then, take your weapons, your quiver and your bow, and go out to the field, and hunt game for me. 4 Then prepare for me savory food, such as I like, and bring it to me to eat, so that I may bless you before I die."

5 Now Rebekah was listening when Isaac spoke to his son Esau. So when Esau went to the field to hunt for game and bring it, 6 Rebekah said to her son Jacob, "I heard your father say to your brother Esau, 7 'Bring me game, and prepare for me savory food to eat, that I may bless you before the LORD before I die.' 8 Now therefore, my son, obey my word as I command you. 9 Go to the flock, and get me two choice kids, so that I may prepare from them savory food for your father, such as he likes; 10 and you shall take it to your father to eat, so that he may bless you before he dies." 11 But Jacob said to his mother Rebekah, "Look, my brother Esau is

---

[z] That is *Broad places* or *Room*   [a] A word resembling the word for *oath*   [b] That is *Well of the oath* or *Well of seven*

Introducing ►JACOB

According to the Bible, Abraham was the father of Isaac, and Isaac was the father of Jacob, and Jacob was the father of twelve sons who became the leaders of the twelve tribes of Israel. Jacob, like his ancestors, participated in the covenant with God that promised a great land and many descendants. He is portrayed as a very human character with a wide range of emotions and actions, both good and bad. Jacob is a repentant brother, a kind father, and a successful herder, but he is also a trickster who steals his brother Esau's birthright and his father's blessing (Gen 25.29–34; 27.1–29). It is no wonder that Jacob's name means "supplanter" or "heel grabber."

In a dream, God renews the covenant promises to Jacob (28.10–17), and in another dream (35.9–15), God changes Jacob's name to Israel (Gen 32.22–32). Jacob's descendants become known as the Israelites. His story reveals that God's blessing continues to work even through flawed human beings.

Gen 25.19—50.14

GEN

a hairy man, and I am a man of smooth skin. [12] Perhaps my father will feel me, and I shall seem to be mocking him, and bring a curse on myself and not a blessing." [13] His mother said to him, "Let your curse be on me, my son; only obey my word, and go, get them for me." [14] So he went and got them and brought them to his mother; and his mother prepared savory food, such as his father loved. [15] Then Rebekah took the best garments of her elder son Esau, which were with her in the house, and put them on her younger son Jacob; [16] and she put the skins of the kids on his hands and on the smooth part of his neck. [17] Then she

did you KNOW?

God's Surprising Choice

In most ancient cultures, including Israel's, the oldest son of the family was expected to inherit his father's property (the birthright) and authority (the blessing). In the story of Esau and Jacob, Jacob tricks Esau (the oldest son) out of his birthright (Gen 25.29–34) and deceives his blind father into giving him the blessing (27.1–29).

It is surprising that Genesis makes no comment on the morality of Jacob's actions. However, the story is not about morality but about God's justice: God is not bound by human expectations. Again and again in the Old Testament, God defies human rules by choosing the "little ones" for big responsibilities: Jacob, Joseph, Ruth, David, and Esther, for example. Even the Israelites themselves were an unlikely choice on God's part. Why didn't God choose a nation of great wealth and power instead of a group that was enslaved?

The story of Jacob and Esau reminds us that God does not bow to human rules, expectations, or plans. God's ways are often surprising! (For more on God's surprising choices, see reading plan 5, "The Justice of God.")

▸ Gen 27.1–40

handed the savory food, and the bread that she had prepared, to her son Jacob.

18 So he went in to his father, and said, "My father"; and he said, "Here I am; who are you, my son?" [19] Jacob said to his father, "I am Esau your firstborn. I have done as you told me; now sit up and eat of my game, so that you may bless me." [20] But Isaac said to his son, "How is it that you have found it so quickly, my son?" He answered, "Because the LORD your God granted me success." [21] Then Isaac said to Jacob, "Come near, that I may feel you, my son, to know whether you are really my son Esau or not." [22] So Jacob went up to his father Isaac, who felt him and said, "The voice is Jacob's voice, but the hands are the hands of Esau." [23] He did not recognize him, because his hands were hairy like his brother Esau's hands; so he blessed him. [24] He said, "Are you really my son Esau?" He answered, "I am." [25] Then he said, "Bring it to me, that I may eat of my son's game and bless you." So he brought it to him, and he ate; and he brought him wine, and he drank. [26] Then his father Isaac said to him, "Come near and kiss me, my son." [27] So he came near and kissed him; and he smelled the smell of his garments, and blessed him, and said,

"Ah, the smell of my son
　　is like the smell of a field that the LORD
　　　　has blessed.
28 May God give you of the dew of heaven,
　　and of the fatness of the earth,
　　and plenty of grain and wine.
29 Let peoples serve you,
　　and nations bow down to you.
Be lord over your brothers,
　　and may your mother's sons bow down
　　　　to you.
Cursed be everyone who curses you,
　　and blessed be everyone who blesses you!"

Esau's Lost Blessing
(Heb 12.17)

30 As soon as Isaac had finished blessing Jacob, when Jacob had scarcely gone out from the presence of his father Isaac, his brother Esau came in from his hunting. [31] He also prepared savory food, and brought it to his father. And he said to his father, "Let my father sit up and eat of his son's game, so that you may bless me." [32] His father Isaac said to him, "Who are you?" He answered, "I am your firstborn son, Esau." [33] Then Isaac trembled violently, and said, "Who was it then that hunted game and brought it to me, and I ate it all[c] before you came, and I have blessed him?—yes, and blessed he shall be!" [34] When Esau heard his father's words,

---

c Cn: Heb of all

he cried out with an exceedingly great and bitter cry, and said to his father, "Bless me, me also, father!" 35 But he said, "Your brother came deceitfully, and he has taken away your blessing." 36 Esau said, "Is he not rightly named Jacob?d For he has supplanted me these two times. He took away my birthright; and look, now he has taken away my blessing." Then he said, "Have you not reserved a blessing for me?" 37 Isaac answered Esau, "I have already made him your lord, and I have given him all his brothers as servants, and with grain and wine I have sustained him. What then can I do for you, my son?" 38 Esau said to his father, "Have you only one blessing, father? Bless me, me also, father!" And Esau lifted up his voice and wept.

39 Then his father Isaac answered him:

"See, away frome the fatness of the earth shall
   your home be,
  and away fromf the dew of heaven on
   high.
40 By your sword you shall live,
  and you shall serve your brother;
but when you break loose,g
  you shall break his yoke from your neck."

Jacob Escapes Esau's Fury

41 Now Esau hated Jacob because of the blessing with which his father had blessed him, and Esau said to himself, "The days of mourning for my father are approaching; then I will kill my brother Jacob." 42 But the words of her elder son Esau were told to Rebekah; so she sent and called her younger son Jacob and said to him, "Your brother Esau is consoling himself by planning to kill you. 43 Now therefore, my son, obey my voice; flee at once to my brother Lā'ban in Har'an, 44 and stay with him a while, until your brother's fury turns away— 45 until your brother's anger against you turns away, and he forgets what you have done to him; then I will send, and bring you back from there. Why should I lose both of you in one day?"

46 Then Rebekah said to Isaac, "I am weary of my life because of the Hit'tīte women. If Jacob marries one of the Hit'tīte women such as these, one of the women of the land, what good will my life be to me?"

28

Then Isaac called Jacob and blessed him, and charged him, "You shall not marry one of the Cā'naan•īte women. 2 Go at once to Pad'dan-ar'am to the house of Be•thū'el, your mother's father; and take as wife from there one of the daughters of Lā'ban, your mother's brother. 3 May God Almightyh bless you and make you fruitful and numerous, that you may become a company of peoples. 4 May he give to you the blessing of Abraham, to you and to your offspring with you, so that you may take possession of the land where you now live

as an alien—land that God gave to Abraham." 5 Thus Isaac sent Jacob away; and he went to Pad'dan-ar'am, to Lā'ban son of Be•thū'el the Ar•a•mē'an, the brother of Rebekah, Jacob's and Esau's mother.

Esau Marries Ishmael's Daughter

6 Now Esau saw that Isaac had blessed Jacob and sent him away to Pad'dan-ar'am to take a wife from there, and that as he blessed him he charged him, "You shall not marry one of the Cā'naan•īte women," 7 and that Jacob had obeyed his father and his mother and gone to Pad'dan-ar'am. 8 So when Esau saw that the Cā'naan•īte women did not please his father Isaac, 9 Esau went to Ish'ma•el and took Mā'ha•lath daughter of Abraham's son Ish'ma•el, and sister of Ne•bā'i•oth, to be his wife in addition to the wives he had.

Jacob's Dream at Bethel

10 Jacob left Be'er-she'ba and went toward Har'an. 11 He came to a certain place and stayed there for the night, because the sun had set. Taking one of the stones of the place, he put it under his head and lay down in that place. 12 And he dreamed that there was a ladderi set up on the earth, the top of it reaching to heaven; and the angels of God were ascending and descending on it. 13 And the LORD stood beside himj and said, "I am the LORD, the God of Abraham your father and the God of Isaac; the land on which you lie I will give to you and to your offspring; 14 and your offspring shall be like the dust of the earth, and you shall spread abroad to the west and to the east and to the north and to the south; and all the families of the earth shall be blessedk in you and in your offspring. 15 Know that I am with you and will keep you wherever you go, and will bring you back to this land; for I will not leave you until I have done what I have promised you." 16 Then Jacob woke from his sleep and said, "Surely the LORD is in this place—and I did not know it!" 17 And he was afraid, and said, "How awesome is this place! This is none other than the house of God, and this is the gate of heaven."

18 So Jacob rose early in the morning, and he took the stone that he had put under his head and set it up for a pillar and poured oil on the top of it. 19 He called that place Beth'el;l but the name of the city was Luz at the first. 20 Then Jacob made a vow, saying, "If God will be with me, and will keep me

---

d That is He supplants or He takes by the heel   e Or See, of
f Or and of   g Meaning of Heb uncertain   h Traditional
rendering of Heb El Shaddai   i Or stairway or ramp
j Or stood above it   k Or shall bless themselves   l That is House
of God

in this way that I go, and will give me bread to eat and clothing to wear, 21 so that I come again to my father's house in peace, then the LORD shall be my God, 22 and this stone, which I have set up for a pillar, shall be God's house; and of all that you give me I will surely give one-tenth to you."

Jacob Meets Rachel

29 Then Jacob went on his journey, and came to the land of the people of the east. 2 As he looked, he saw a well in the field and three flocks of sheep lying there beside it; for out of

PRAY IT!
Friendship with God

Just as Jacob is leaving his home and everything he knows, God establishes a personal relationship with him through a dream. In this relationship, God and Jacob interact personally, are accountable to each other, and trust each other. Jacob will need this relationship to help him through the tough times ahead. See Gen 32.22–32 for further developments in Jacob's relationship with God.

God, I want to know your presence. Use my dreams and my waking thoughts; use my family, friends, and neighbors; use your holy word. Use them all to reach me. For I know your presence will sustain me on my most difficult journeys, as it did Jacob.

▶ **Gen 28.10–22**

that well the flocks were watered. The stone on the well's mouth was large, 3 and when all the flocks were gathered there, the shepherds would roll the stone from the mouth of the well, and water the sheep, and put the stone back in its place on the mouth of the well.

4 Jacob said to them, "My brothers, where do you come from?" They said, "We are from Har'an." 5 He said to them, "Do you know Lā'ban son of Nā'hor?" They said, "We do." 6 He said to them, "Is it well with him?" "Yes," they replied, "and here is his daughter Rachel, coming with the sheep." 7 He said, "Look, it is still broad daylight; it is not time for the animals to be gathered together. Water the sheep, and go, pasture them." 8 But they said, "We cannot until all the flocks are gathered together,

and the stone is rolled from the mouth of the well; then we water the sheep."

9 While he was still speaking with them, Rachel came with her father's sheep; for she kept them. 10 Now when Jacob saw Rachel, the daughter of his mother's brother Lā'ban, and the sheep of his mother's brother Lā'ban, Jacob went up and rolled the stone from the well's mouth, and watered the flock of his mother's brother Lā'ban. 11 Then Jacob kissed Rachel, and wept aloud. 12 And Jacob told Rachel that he was her father's kinsman, and that he was Rebekah's son; and she ran and told her father.

13 When Lā'ban heard the news about his sister's son Jacob, he ran to meet him; he embraced him and kissed him, and brought him to his house. Jacob[m] told Lā'ban all these things, 14 and Lā'ban said to him, "Surely you are my bone and my flesh!" And he stayed with him a month.

Jacob Marries Laban's Daughters

15 Then Lā'ban said to Jacob, "Because you are my kinsman, should you therefore serve me for nothing? Tell me, what shall your wages be?" 16 Now Lā'ban had two daughters; the name of the elder was Leah, and the name of the younger was Rachel. 17 Leah's eyes were lovely,[n] and Rachel was graceful and beautiful. 18 Jacob loved Rachel; so he said, "I will serve you seven years for your younger daughter Rachel." 19 Lā'ban said, "It is better that I give her to you than that I should give her to any other man; stay with me." 20 So Jacob served seven years for Rachel, and they seemed to him but a few days because of the love he had for her.

21 Then Jacob said to Lā'ban, "Give me my wife that I may go in to her, for my time is completed." 22 So Lā'ban gathered together all the people of the place, and made a feast. 23 But in the evening he took his daughter Leah and brought her to Jacob; and he went in to her. 24 (Lā'ban gave his maid Zil'pah to his daughter Leah to be her maid.) 25 When morning came, it was Leah! And Jacob said to Lā'ban, "What is this you have done to me? Did I not serve with you for Rachel? Why then have you deceived me?" 26 Lā'ban said, "This is not done in our country—giving the younger before the first-born. 27 Complete the week of this one, and we will give you the other also in return for serving me another seven years." 28 Jacob did so, and completed her week; then Lā'ban gave him his daughter Rachel as a wife. 29 (Lā'ban gave his maid Bil'hah to his daughter Rachel to be her maid.) 30 So Jacob went in to Rachel also, and he loved Rachel more than Leah. He served Lā'ban[o] for another seven years.

---

m Heb *He*   n Meaning of Heb uncertain   o Heb *him*

When Lies Boomerang

Predictably, Jacob becomes upset when he finds out that he has been deceived by Laban (Gen 29.25). Yet, the very reason Jacob is working for his uncle Laban is that he has fled from his brother Esau, whom he deceived several years ago (27.1–40). Jacob's lies and deceit have boomeranged, so now he is the victim.

Somehow, our lies, gossip, and manipulation of others often come back to haunt us. So it was with Jacob. So it will be with us if we follow his example.

▶ **Gen 29.15–30**

31 When the LORD saw that Leah was unloved, he opened her womb; but Rachel was barren. 32 Leah conceived and bore a son, and she named him Reuben;*p* for she said, "Because the LORD has looked on my affliction; surely now my husband will love me." 33 She conceived again and bore a son, and said, "Because the LORD has heard*q* that I am hated, he has given me this son also"; and she named him Sim′e·on. 34 Again she conceived and bore a son, and said, "Now this time my husband will be joined*r* to me, because I have borne him three sons"; therefore he was named Levi. 35 She conceived again and bore a son, and said, "This time I will praise*s* the LORD"; therefore she named him Judah; then she ceased bearing.

30 When Rachel saw that she bore Jacob no children, she envied her sister; and she said to Jacob, "Give me children, or I shall die!" 2 Jacob became very angry with Rachel and said, "Am I in the place of God, who has withheld from you the fruit of the womb?" 3 Then she said, "Here is my maid Bil′hah; go in to her, that she may bear upon my knees and that I too may have children through her." 4 So she gave him her maid Bil′hah as a wife; and Jacob went in to her. 5 And Bil′hah conceived and bore Jacob a son. 6 Then Rachel said, "God has judged me, and has also heard my voice and given me a son"; therefore she named him Dan.*t* 7 Rachel's maid Bil′hah conceived again and bore Jacob a second son. 8 Then Rachel said, "With mighty wrestlings I have wrestled*u* with my sister, and have prevailed"; so she named him Naph′ta·li. 9 When Leah saw that she had ceased bearing children, she took her maid Zil′pah and gave her to Jacob as a wife. 10 Then Leah's maid Zil′pah bore Jacob a son. 11 And Leah said, "Good fortune!" so she named him Gad.*v* 12 Leah's maid Zil′pah bore Jacob a second son. 13 And Leah said, "Happy am I! For the women will call me happy"; so she named him Ash′er.*w*

14 In the days of wheat harvest Reuben went and found mandrakes in the field, and brought them to his mother Leah. Then Rachel said to Leah, "Please give me some of your son's mandrakes." 15 But she said to her, "Is it a small matter that you have taken away my husband? Would you take away my son's mandrakes also?" Rachel said, "Then he may lie with you tonight for your son's mandrakes." 16 When Jacob came from the field in the evening, Leah went out to meet him, and said, "You must come in to me; for I have hired you with my son's mandrakes." So he lay with her that night. 17 And God heeded Leah, and she conceived and bore Jacob a fifth son. 18 Leah said, "God has given me my hire*x* because I gave my maid to my husband"; so she named him Is′sa·char. 19 And Leah conceived again, and she bore Jacob a sixth son. 20 Then Leah said, "God has endowed me with a good dowry; now my husband will honor*y* me, because I have borne him six sons"; so she named him Zeb′u·lun. 21 Afterwards she bore a daughter, and named her Di′nah.

22 Then God remembered Rachel, and God heeded her and opened her womb. 23 She conceived and bore a son, and said, "God has taken away my reproach"; 24 and she named him Joseph,*z* saying, "May the Lord add to me another son!"

Jacob Prospers at Laban's Expense

25 When Rachel had borne Joseph, Jacob said to Lā′ban, "Send me away, that I may go to my own home and country. 26 Give me my wives and my children for whom I have served you, and let me go; for you know very well the service I have given you." 27 But Lā′ban said to him, "If you will allow me to

p That is *See, a son* *q* Heb *shama* *r* Heb *lawah* *s* Heb *hodah* *t* That is *He judged* *u* Heb *niphtal* *v* That is *Fortune* *w* That is *Happy* *x* Heb *sakar* *y* Heb *zabal* *z* That is *He adds* say so, I have learned by divination that the LORD has blessed me because of you; 28 name your wages, and I will give it." 29 Jacob said to him, "You yourself know how I have served you, and how your cattle have fared with me. 30 For you had little before I came, and it has increased abundantly; and the LORD has blessed you wherever I turned. But now when shall I provide for my own household also?" 31 He said, "What shall I give you?" Jacob said, "You shall not give me anything; if you will do this for me, I will again feed your flock and keep it: 32 let me pass through all your flock today, removing from it every speckled and spotted sheep and every black lamb, and the spotted and speckled among the goats; and such shall be my wages. 33 So my honesty will answer for me later, when you come to look into my wages with you. Every one that is not speckled and spotted among the goats and black among the lambs, if found with me, shall be counted stolen." 34 Lā'ban said, "Good! Let it be as you have said." 35 But that day Lā'ban removed the male goats that were striped and spotted, and all the female goats that were speckled and spotted, every one that had white on it, and every lamb that was black, and put them in charge of his sons; 36 and he set a distance of three days' journey between himself and Jacob, while Jacob was pasturing the rest of Lā'ban's flock.

37 Then Jacob took fresh rods of poplar and almond and plane, and peeled white streaks in them, exposing the white of the rods. 38 He set the rods that he had peeled in front of the flocks in the troughs, that is, the watering places, where the flocks came to drink. And since they bred when they came to drink, 39 the flocks bred in front of the rods, and so the flocks produced young that were striped, speckled, and spotted. 40 Jacob separated the lambs, and set the faces of the flocks toward the striped and the completely black animals in the flock of Lā'ban; and he put his own droves apart, and did not put them with Lā'ban's flock. 41 Whenever the stronger of the flock were breeding, Jacob laid the rods in the troughs before the eyes of the flock, that they might breed among the rods, 42 but for the feebler of the flock he did not lay them there; so the feebler were Lā'ban's, and the stronger Jacob's. 43 Thus the man grew exceedingly rich, and had large flocks, and male and female slaves, and camels and donkeys.

Jacob Flees with Family and Flocks

31 Now Jacob heard that the sons of Lā'ban were saying, "Jacob has taken all that was our father's; he has gained all this wealth from what belonged to our father." 2 And Jacob saw that Lā'ban did not regard him as favorably as he did before. 3 Then the LORD said to Jacob, "Return to the land of your ancestors and to your kin-

dred, and I will be with you." 4 So Jacob sent and called Rachel and Leah into the field where his flock was, 5 and said to them, "I see that your father does not regard me as favorably as he did before. But the God of my father has been with me. 6 You know that I have served your father with all my strength; 7 yet your father has cheated me and changed my wages ten times, but God did not permit him to harm me. 8 If he said, 'The speckled shall be your wages,' then all the flock bore speckled; and if he said, 'The striped shall be your wages,' then all the flock bore striped. 9 Thus God has taken away the livestock of your father, and given them to me.

10 "During the mating of the flock I once had a dream in which I looked up and saw that the male goats that leaped upon the flock were striped, speckled, and mottled. 11 Then the angel of God said to me in the dream, 'Jacob,' and I said, 'Here I am!' 12 And he said, 'Look up and see that all the goats that leap on the flock are striped, speckled, and mottled; for I have seen all that Lā'ban is doing to you. 13 I am the God of Beth'el,[a] where you anointed a pillar and made a vow to me. Now leave this land at once and return to the land of your birth.' " 14 Then Rachel and Leah answered him, "Is there any portion or inheritance left to us in our father's house? 15 Are we not regarded by him as foreigners? For he has sold us, and he has been using up the money given for us. 16 All the property that God has taken away from our father belongs to us and to our children; now then, do whatever God has said to you."

17 So Jacob arose, and set his children and his wives on camels; 18 and he drove away all his livestock, all the property that he had gained, the livestock in his possession that he had acquired in Pad'dan-ar'am, to go to his father Isaac in the land of Cā'naan.

19 Now Lā'ban had gone to shear his sheep, and Rachel stole her father's household gods. 20 And Jacob deceived Lā'ban the Ar•a•mē'an, in that he did not tell him that he intended to flee. 21 So he fled with all that he had; starting out he crossed the Euphrates,[b] and set his face toward the hill country of Gil'e•ad.

Laban Overtakes Jacob

22 On the third day Lā'ban was told that Jacob had fled. 23 So he took his kinsfolk with him and pursued him for seven days until he caught up with him in the hill country of Gil'e•ad. 24 But God came to Lā'ban the Ar•a•mē'an in a dream by night, and said to him, "Take heed that you say not a word to Jacob, either good or bad."

---

a Cn: Meaning of Heb uncertain   b Heb *the river*

25 Lā'ban overtook Jacob. Now Jacob had pitched his tent in the hill country, and Lā'ban with his kinsfolk camped in the hill country of Gil'e•ad. 26 Lā'ban said to Jacob, "What have you done? You have deceived me, and carried away my daughters like captives of the sword. 27 Why did you flee secretly and deceive me and not tell me? I would have sent you away with mirth and songs, with tambourine and lyre. 28 And why did you not permit me to kiss my sons and my daughters farewell? What you have done is foolish. 29 It is in my power to do you harm; but the God of your father spoke to me last night, saying, 'Take heed that you speak to Jacob neither good nor bad.' 30 Even though you had to go because you longed greatly for your father's house, why did you steal my gods?" 31 Jacob answered Lā'ban, "Because I was afraid, for I thought that you would take your daughters from me by force. 32 But anyone with whom you find your gods shall not live. In the presence of our kinsfolk, point out what I have that is yours, and take it." Now Jacob did not know that Rachel had stolen the gods.*c*

33 So Lā'ban went into Jacob's tent, and into Leah's tent, and into the tent of the two maids, but he did not find them. And he went out of Leah's tent, and entered Rachel's. 34 Now Rachel had taken the household gods and put them in the camel's saddle, and sat on them. Lā'ban felt all about in the tent, but did not find them. 35 And she said to her father, "Let not my lord be angry that I cannot rise before you, for the way of women is upon me." So he searched, but did not find the household gods.

36 Then Jacob became angry, and upbraided Lā'ban. Jacob said to Lā'ban, "What is my offense? What is my sin, that you have hotly pursued me? 37 Although you have felt about through all my goods, what have you found of all your household goods? Set it here before my kinsfolk and your kinsfolk, so that they may decide between us two. 38 These twenty years I have been with you; your ewes and your female goats have not miscarried, and I have not eaten the rams of your flocks. 39 That which was torn by wild beasts I did not bring to you; I bore the loss of it myself; of my hand you required it, whether stolen by day or stolen by night. 40 It was like this with me: by day the heat consumed me, and the cold by night, and my sleep fled from my eyes. 41 These twenty years I have been in your house; I served you fourteen years for your two daughters, and six years for your flock, and you have changed my wages ten times. 42 If the God of my father, the God of Abraham and the Fear*d* of Isaac, had not been on my side, surely now you would have sent me away empty-handed. God saw my affliction and the labor of my hands, and rebuked you last night."

Laban and Jacob Make a Covenant

43 Then Lā'ban answered and said to Jacob, "The daughters are my daughters, the children are my children, the flocks are my flocks, and all that you see is mine. But what can I do today about these daughters of mine, or about their children whom they have borne? 44 Come now, let us make a covenant, you and I; and let it be a witness between you and me." 45 So Jacob took a stone, and set it up as a pillar. 46 And Jacob said to his kinsfolk, "Gather stones," and they took stones, and made a heap; and they ate there by the heap. 47 Lā'ban called it Jĕ'gar-sā•ha•dŭ'tha:*e* but Jacob called it Gal'e•ed.*f* 48 Lā'ban said, "This heap is a witness between you and me today." Therefore he called it Gal'e•ed, 49 and the pillar*g* Miz'pah,*h* for he said, "The LORD watch between you and me, when we are absent one from the other. 50 If you ill-treat my daughters, or if you take wives in addition to my daughters, though no one else is with us, remember that God is witness between you and me."

51 Then Lā'ban said to Jacob, "See this heap and see the pillar, which I have set between you and me. 52 This heap is a witness, and the pillar is a witness, that I will not pass beyond this heap to you, and you will not pass beyond this heap and this pillar to me, for harm. 53 May the God of Abraham and the God of Nā'hor"—the God of their father—"judge between us." So Jacob swore by the Fear*d* of his father Isaac, 54 and Jacob offered a sacrifice on the height and called his kinsfolk to eat bread; and they ate bread and tarried all night in the hill country.

55*i* Early in the morning Lā'ban rose up, and kissed his grandchildren and his daughters and blessed them; then he departed and returned home.

32 Jacob went on his way and the angels of God met him; 2 and when Jacob saw them he said, "This is God's camp!" So he called that place Mā•ha•nā'im.*j*

Jacob Sends Presents to Appease Esau

3 Jacob sent messengers before him to his brother Esau in the land of Sē'ir, the country of Ē'dom, 4 instructing them, "Thus you shall say to my lord Esau: Thus says your servant Jacob, 'I have lived with Lā'ban as an alien, and stayed until now;

---

c Heb *them*　*d* Meaning of Heb uncertain　*e* In Aramaic *The heap of witness*　*f* In Hebrew *The heap of witness*
g Compare Sam: MT lacks *the pillar*　*h* That is *Watchpost*
i Ch 32.1 in Heb　*j* Here taken to mean *Two camps*

GEN

5 and I have oxen, donkeys, flocks, male and female slaves; and I have sent to tell my lord, in order that I may find favor in your sight.' "

6 The messengers returned to Jacob, saying, "We came to your brother Esau, and he is coming to meet you, and four hundred men are with him." 7 Then Jacob was greatly afraid and distressed; and he divided the people that were with him, and the flocks and herds and camels, into two companies, 8 thinking, "If Esau comes to the one company and destroys it, then the company that is left will escape."

9 And Jacob said, "O God of my father Abraham and God of my father Isaac, O LORD who said to me, 'Return to your country and to your kindred, and I will do you good,' 10 I am not worthy of the least of all the steadfast love and all the faithfulness that you have shown to your servant, for with only my staff I crossed this Jordan; and now I have become two companies. 11 Deliver me, please, from the hand of my brother, from the hand of Esau, for I am afraid of him; he may come and kill us all, the mothers with the children. 12 Yet you have said, 'I will surely do you good, and make your offspring as the sand of the sea, which cannot be counted because of their number.' "

13 So he spent that night there, and from what he had with him he took a present for his brother Esau, 14 two hundred female goats and twenty male goats, two hundred ewes and twenty rams, 15 thirty milch camels and their colts, forty cows and ten bulls, twenty female donkeys and ten male donkeys. 16 These he delivered into the hand of his servants, every drove by itself, and said to his servants, "Pass on ahead of me, and put a space between drove and drove." 17 He instructed the foremost, "When Esau my brother meets you, and asks you, 'To whom do you belong? Where are you going? And whose are these ahead of you?' 18 then you shall say, 'They belong to your servant Jacob; they are a present sent to my lord Esau; and moreover he is behind us.' " 19 He likewise instructed the second and the third and all who followed the droves, "You shall say the same thing to Esau when you meet him, 20 and you shall say, 'Moreover your servant Jacob is behind us.' " For he thought, "I may appease him with the present that goes ahead of me, and afterwards I shall see his face; perhaps he will accept me." 21 So the present passed on ahead of him; and he himself spent that night in the camp.

Jacob Wrestles at Peniel

22 The same night he got up and took his two wives, his two maids, and his eleven children, and crossed the ford of the Jab'bok. 23 He took them and sent them across the stream, and likewise everything that he had. 24 Jacob was left alone; and

PRAY IT!
Wrestling with God

Even after twenty years, Jacob is anxious about meeting Esau again. This time, Jacob uses his craftiness not to deceive Esau but to gain Esau's good graces. Then while on the way home, he has an amazing religious experience. Many Scripture scholars believe that the strange wrestling encounter is a symbol that Jacob has become a changed person. He finally realizes that in all his troubles, God was his true opponent.

Perhaps at times you have wrestled with yourself or with God. It is not so much that God is your opponent or that you are in a contest. It is the wrestling itself that matters. When you face challenges, especially the big ones, you wrestle between the person you are now and the person God is calling you to be.

In your prayer, reflect or journal on the following questions:

- When does it seem like God is trying to wrestle with you? What does it feel like?
- Is God challenging you about something in your life right now?
- What blessings might you gain in accepting God's challenge and changing your life?

▶ Gen 32.22–32

a man wrestled with him until daybreak. 25 When the man saw that he did not prevail against Jacob, he struck him on the hip socket; and Jacob's hip was put out of joint as he wrestled with him. 26 Then he said, "Let me go, for the day is breaking." But Jacob said, "I will not let you go, unless you bless me." 27 So he said to him, "What is your name?" And he said, "Jacob." 28 Then the man[k] said, "You shall no longer be called Jacob, but Israel,[l] for you have striven with God and with humans,[m] and have prevailed." 29 Then Jacob asked him, "Please tell me your name." But he said, "Why is it that you ask my name?" And there he blessed him. 30 So Jacob called the place Pe•ni'el,[n] saying,

---

k Heb he l That is The one who strives with God or God strives m Or with divine and human beings n That is The face of God

GEN

"For I have seen God face to face, and yet my life is preserved." 31 The sun rose upon him as he passed Pe•nü'el, limping because of his hip. 32 Therefore to this day the Israelites do not eat the thigh muscle that is on the hip socket, because he struck Jacob on the hip socket at the thigh muscle.

Jacob and Esau Meet

33 Now Jacob looked up and saw Esau coming, and four hundred men with him. So he divided the children among Leah and Rachel and the two maids. 2 He put the maids with their children in front, then Leah with her children, and Rachel and Joseph last of all. 3 He himself went on ahead of them, bowing himself to the ground seven times, until he came near his brother.

4 But Esau ran to meet him, and embraced him, and fell on his neck and kissed him, and they wept. 5 When Esau looked up and saw the women and children, he said, "Who are these with you?" Jacob said, "The children whom God has graciously given your servant." 6 Then the maids drew near, they and their children, and bowed down; 7 Leah likewise and her children drew near and bowed down; and finally Joseph and Rachel drew near, and they bowed down. 8 Esau said, "What do you mean by all this company that I met?" Jacob answered, "To find favor with my lord." 9 But Esau said, "I have enough, my brother; keep what you have for yourself." 10 Jacob said, "No, please; if I find favor with you, then accept my present from my hand; for truly to see your face is like seeing the face of God—since you have received me with such favor. 11 Please accept my gift that is brought to you, because God has dealt graciously with me, and because I have everything I want." So he urged him, and he took it.

12 Then Esau said, "Let us journey on our way, and I will go alongside you." 13 But Jacob said to him, "My lord knows that the children are frail and that the flocks and herds, which are nursing, are a care to me; and if they are overdriven for one day, all the flocks will die. 14 Let my lord pass on ahead of his servant, and I will lead on slowly, according to the pace of the cattle that are before me and according to the pace of the children, until I come to my lord in Sē'ir."

15 So Esau said, "Let me leave with you some of the people who are with me." But he said, "Why should my lord be so kind to me?" 16 So Esau returned that day on his way to Sē'ir. 17 But Jacob journeyed to Suc'coth,o and built himself a house, and made booths for his cattle; therefore the place is called Suc'coth.

Jacob Reaches Shechem

18 Jacob came safely to the city of Shē'chem, which is in the land of Cā'naan, on his way from Pad'dan-ar'am; and he camped before the city. 19 And from the sons of Hā'mor, Shē'chem's father, he bought for one hundred pieces of moneyp the plot of land on which he had pitched his tent. 20 There he erected an altar and called it El-Ē•lō'he-Is'rā•el.q

---

o That is *Booths*   p Heb *one hundred qesitah*   q That is *God, the God of Israel*

Letting Go of the Past

Jacob is understandably apprehensive as he approaches his long-estranged twin brother. How will Esau react? But Esau, who was wronged by Jacob, runs to meet him and gives him a hug. All is forgiven, and the two are reconciled at last. This story is like the parable of the prodigal son in Lk 15.11–32.

All of us have wronged others, especially the people we care about most. All of us have also experienced forgiveness. Nothing is quite like the freedom that comes with genuine forgiveness and reconciliation. A burden is lifted. A heavy heart is made lighter. A vengeful attitude is transformed into a feeling of inner peace and harmony. This is the work of God's grace. Forgiveness and reconciliation are powerful signs of the presence of God. We can almost feel the enormous sense of relief experienced by Jacob as he realizes that his brother holds no grudge.

Does a relationship in your life need forgiveness and reconciliation? If so, what can you do to bring about healing in this relationship?

▶ Gen 33.1–17

GEN

The Rape of Dinah

34 Now Dī'nah the daughter of Leah, whom she had borne to Jacob, went out to visit the women of the region. 2 When Shē'chem son of Hā'mor the Hī'vite, prince of the region, saw her, he seized her and lay with her by force. 3 And his soul was drawn to Dī'nah daughter of Jacob; he loved the girl, and spoke tenderly to her. 4 So Shē'chem spoke to his father Hā'mor, saying, "Get me this girl to be my wife."

5 Now Jacob heard that Shē'chem[r] had defiled his daughter Dī'nah; but his sons were with his cattle in the field, so Jacob held his peace until they came. 6 And Hā'mor the father of Shē'chem went out to Jacob to speak with him, 7 just as the sons of Jacob came in from the field. When they heard of it, the men were indignant and very angry, because he had committed an outrage in Israel by lying with Jacob's daughter, for such a thing ought not to be done.

8 But Hā'mor spoke with them, saying, "The heart of my son Shē'chem longs for your daughter; please give her to him in marriage. 9 Make marriages with us; give your daughters to us, and take our daughters for yourselves. 10 You shall live with us; and the land shall be open to you; live and trade in it, and get property in it." 11 Shē'chem also said to her father and to her brothers, "Let me find favor with you, and whatever you say to me I will give. 12 Put the marriage present and gift as high as you like, and I will give whatever you ask me; only give me the girl to be my wife."

13 The sons of Jacob answered Shē'chem and his father Hā'mor deceitfully, because he had defiled their sister Dī'nah. 14 They said to them, "We cannot do this thing, to give our sister to one who is uncircumcised, for that would be a disgrace to us. 15 Only on this condition will we consent to you: that you will become as we are and every male among you be circumcised. 16 Then we will give our daughters to you, and we will take your daughters for ourselves, and we will live among you and become one people. 17 But if you will not listen to us and be circumcised, then we will take our daughter and be gone."

18 Their words pleased Hā'mor and Hā'mor's son Shē'chem. 19 And the young man did not delay to do the thing, because he was delighted with Jacob's daughter. Now he was the most honored of all his family. 20 So Hā'mor and his son Shē'chem came to the gate of their city and spoke to the men of their city, saying, 21 "These people are friendly with us; let them live in the land and trade in it, for the land is large enough for them; let us take their daughters in marriage, and let us give them our daughters. 22 Only on this condition will they agree to live among us, to become one people: that every male among us be circumcised as they are circumcised. 23 Will not their livestock, their property, and all their animals be ours? Only let us agree with them, and they will live among us." 24 And all who went out of the city gate heeded Hā'mor and his son Shē'chem; and every male was circumcised, all who went out of the gate of his city.

---

r Heb *he*

The men were INDIGNANT and very ANGRY, because he had committed an OUTRAGE in Israel by lying with Jacob's daughter, for such a thing ought not to be done.

34.7

Dinah's Brothers Avenge Their Sister

25 On the third day, when they were still in pain, two of the sons of Jacob, Sim'ē•on and Levi, Dī'nah's brothers, took their swords and came against the city unawares, and killed all the males. 2 They killed Hā'mor and his son Shē'chem with the sword, and took Di'nah out of Shē'chem's house, and went away. 27 And the other sons of Jacob came upon the slain, and plundered the city, because their sister had been defiled. 28 They took their flocks and their herds, their donkeys, and whatever was in the city and in the field. 29 All their wealth, all their little ones and their wives, all that was in the houses, they captured and made their prey. 30 Then Jacob said to Sim'ē•on and Levi, "You have brought trouble on me by making me odious to the inhabitants of the land, the Cā'naan•ītes and the Per'iz•zītes; my numbers are few, and if they gather themselves against me and attack me, I shall be destroyed, both I and my household." 31 But they said, "Should our sister be treated like a whore?"

Jacob Returns to Bethel

35 God said to Jacob, "Arise, go up to Beth'el, and settle there. Make an altar there to the God who appeared to you when you fled from your brother Esau." 2 So Jacob said to his household and to all who were with him, "Put away the foreign gods that are among you, and purify yourselves, and change your clothes; 3 then come, let us go up to Beth'el, that I may make an altar there to the God who answered me in the day of my distress and has been with me wherever I have gone." 4 So they gave to Jacob all the foreign gods that they had, and the rings that were in their ears; and Jacob hid them under the oak that was near Shē'chem.

5 As they journeyed, a terror from God fell upon the cities all around them, so that no one pursued them. 6 Jacob came to Luz (that is, Beth'el), which is in the land of Cā'naan, he and all the people who were with him, 7 and there he built an altar and called the place El-beth'el,ˢ because it was there that God had revealed himself to him when he fled from his brother. 8 And Deb'or•ah, Rebekah's nurse, died, and she was buried under an oak below Beth'el. So it was called Al'lon-bac'uth.ᵗ

9 God appeared to Jacob again when he came from Pad'dan-ar'am, and he blessed him. 10 God said to him, "Your name is Jacob; no longer shall you be called Jacob, but Israel shall be your name." So he was called Israel. 11 God said to him, "I am God Almighty:ᵘ be fruitful and multiply; a nation and a company of nations shall come from you, and kings shall spring from you. 12 The land that I gave to Abraham and Isaac I will give to you, and I will give the land to your offspring after you."

13 Then God went up from him at the place where he had spoken with him. 14 Jacob set up a pillar in the place where he had spoken with him, a pillar of stone; and he poured out a drink offering on it, and poured oil on it. 15 So Jacob called the place where God had spoken with him Beth'el.

The Birth of Benjamin and the Death of Rachel

16 Then they journeyed from Beth'el; and when they were still some distance from Eph'rath, Rachel was in childbirth, and she had hard labor. 17 When she was in her hard labor, the midwife said to her, "Do not be afraid; for now you will have another son." 18 As her soul was departing (for she died), she named him Ben-ō'ni;ᵛ but his father called him Benjamin.ʷ 19 So Rachel died, and she was buried on the way to Eph'rath (that is, Bethlehem), 20 and Jacob set up a pillar at her grave; it is the pillar of Rachel's tomb, which is there to this day. 21 Israel journeyed on, and pitched his tent beyond the tower of Ē'der.

22 While Israel lived in that land, Reuben went and lay with Bil'hah his father's concubine; and Israel heard of it.

Now the sons of Jacob were twelve. 23 The sons of Leah: Reuben (Jacob's firstborn), Sim'ē•on, Levi, Judah, Is'sa•char, and Zeb'ū•lun. 24 The sons of Rachel: Joseph and Benjamin. 25 The sons of Bil'hah, Rachel's maid: Dan and Naph'ta•lī. 26 The sons of Zil'pah, Leah's maid: Gad and Ash'er. These were the sons of Jacob who were born to him in Pad'dan-ar'am.

The Death of Isaac

27 Jacob came to his father Isaac at Mam're, or Kir'i•ath-ar'ba (that is, Hē'bron), where Abraham and Isaac had resided as aliens. 28 Now the days of Isaac were one hundred eighty years. 29 And Isaac breathed his last; he died and was gathered to his people, old and full of days; and his sons Esau and Jacob buried him.

Esau's Descendants
(1 Chr 1.35–42)

36 These are the descendants of Esau (that is, Ē'dom). 2 Esau took his wives from the Cā'naan•ītes: Ā'dah daughter of Ē'lon the Hit'tīte, Ō•hol•i•bā'mah daughter of An'ah sonˣ of Zib'ē•on the Hī'vīte, 3 and Bas'e•math, Ish'ma•el's daughter, sister of Ne•bā'i•oth. 4 Ā'dah bore E•li'phaz to Esau; Bas'e•math bore Reū'el; 5 and Ō•hol•i•bā'mah bore Jē'ush, Jā'lam, and Kō'rah.

ˢ That is *God of Bethel*   ᵗ That is *Oak of weeping*
ᵘ Traditional rendering of Heb *El Shaddai*
ᵛ That is *Son of my sorrow*   ʷ That is *Son of the right hand* or *Son of the South*   ˣ Sam Gk Syr: Heb *daughter*

GEN

These are the sons of Esau who were born to him in the land of Cā′naan.

6 Then Esau took his wives, his sons, his daughters, and all the members of his household, his cattle, all his livestock, and all the property he had acquired in the land of Cā′naan; and he moved to a land some distance from his brother Jacob. 7 For their possessions were too great for them to live together; the land where they were staying could not support them because of their livestock. 8 So Esau settled in the hill country of Sē′ir; Esau is Ē′dom.

9 These are the descendants of Esau, ancestor of the Ē′dom·ites, in the hill country of Sē′ir. 10 These are the names of Esau's sons: E·lī′phaz son of Ā′dah the wife of Esau; Reū′el, the son of Esau's wife Bas′e·math. 11 The sons of E·lī′phaz were Tē′man, Ō′mar, Zē′phō, Gā′tam, and Kē′naz. 12 (Tim′na was a concubine of E·lī′phaz, Esau's son; she bore Am′a·lek to E·lī′phaz.) These were the sons of Ā′dah, Esau's wife. 13 These were the sons of Reū′el: Nā′hath, Zē′rah, Sham′mah, and Miz′zah. These were the sons of Esau's wife, Bas′e·math. 14 These were the sons of Esau's wife Ō·hol·i·bā′mah, daughter of An′ah son[y] of Zib′ē·on: she bore to Esau Jē′ush, Jā′lam, and Kō′rah.

Clans and Kings of Edom

15 These are the clans[z] of the sons of Esau. The sons of E·lī′phaz the firstborn of Esau: the clans[z] Tē′man, Ō′mar, Zē′phō, Kē′naz, 16 Kō′rah, Gā′tam, and Am′a·lek; these are the clans[z] of E·lī′phaz in the land of Ē′dom; they are the sons of Ā′dah. 17 These are the sons of Esau's son Reū′el: the clans[z] Nā′hath, Zē′rah, Sham′mah, and Miz′zah; these are the clans[z] of Reū′el in the land of Ē′dom; they are the sons of Esau's wife Bas′e·math. 18 These are the sons of Esau's wife Ō·hol·i·bā′-mah: the clans[z] Jē′ush, Jā′lam, and Kō′rah; these are the clans[z] born of Esau's wife Ō·hol·i·bā′mah, the daughter of An′ah. 19 These are the sons of Esau (that is, Ē′dom), and these are their clans.[z]

20 These are the sons of Sē′ir the Hor′īte, the inhabitants of the land: Lō′tan, Shō′bal, Zib′ē·on, An′ah, 21 Dī′shon, Ē′zer, and Dī′shan; these are the clans[z] of the Hor′ītes, the sons of Sē′ir in the land of Ē′dom. 22 The sons of Lō′tan were Hō′rī and Hē′-man; and Lō′tan's sister was Tim′na. 23 These are the sons of Shō′bal: Al′van, Man′a·hath, Ē′bal, Shē′phō, and Ō′nam. 24 These are the sons of Zib′ē·on: Ā′i·ah and An′ah; he is the An′ah who found the springs[a] in the wilderness, as he pastured the donkeys of his father Zib′ē·on. 25 These are the children of An′ah: Dī′shon and Ō·hol·i·bā′mah daughter of An′ah. 26 These are the sons of Dī′shon: Hem′dan, Esh′ban, Ith′ran, and Chē′ran. 27 These are the sons of Ē′zer: Bil′han, Zā′a·van, and Ā′kan. 28 These are the sons of Dī′shan: Uz and Ar′an. 29 These are the

clans[z] of the Hor′ītes: the clans[z] Lō′tan, Shō′bal, Zib′ē·on, An′ah, 30 Dī′shon, Ē′zer, and Dī′shan; these are the clans[z] of the Hor′ītes, clan by clan[b] in the land of Sē′ir.

31 These are the kings who reigned in the land of Ē′dom, before any king reigned over the Israelites. 32 Bē′la son of Bē′or reigned in Ē′dom, the name of his city being Din′ha·bah. 33 Bē′la died, and Jō′bab son of Zē′rah of Boz′rah succeeded him as king. 34 Jō′bab died, and Hū′sham of the land of the Tē′man·ītes succeeded him as king. 35 Hū′sham died, and Hā′dad son of Bē′dad, who defeated Mid′i·an in the country of Mō′ab, succeeded him as king, the name of his city being Ā′vith. 36 Hā′dad died, and Sam′lah of Mas·rē′kah succeeded him as king. 37 Sam′lah died, and Shā′ūl of Re·hō′both on the Euphrates succeeded him as king. 38 Shā′ūl died, and Bā′al-hā′nan son of Ach′bor succeeded him as king. 39 Bā′al-hā′nan son of Ach′bor died, and Hā′dar succeeded him as king, the name of his city being Pā′ū; his wife's name was Me·het′a·bel, the daughter of Mā′tred, daughter of Me-za·hab′.

40 These are the names of the clans[z] of Esau, according to their families and their localities by their names: the clans[z] Tim′na, Al′vah, Jē′theth, 41 Ō·hol·i·bā′mah, Ē′lah, Pī′non, 42 Kē′naz, Tē′man, Mib′zar, 43 Mag′di·el, and I′ram; these are the clans[z] of Ē′dom (that is, Esau, the father of Ē′dom), according to their settlements in the land that they held.

Joseph Dreams of Greatness

37 Jacob settled in the land where his father had lived as an alien, the land of Cā′naan. 2 This is the story of the family of Jacob.

Joseph, being seventeen years old, was shepherding the flock with his brothers; he was a helper to the sons of Bil′hah and Zil′pah, his father's wives; and Joseph brought a bad report of them to their father. 3 Now Israel loved Joseph more than any other of his children, because he was the son of his old age; and he had made him a long robe with sleeves.[c] 4 But when his brothers saw that their father loved him more than all his brothers, they hated him, and could not speak peaceably to him.

5 Once Joseph had a dream, and when he told it to his brothers, they hated him even more. 6 He said to them, "Listen to this dream that I dreamed. 7 There we were, binding sheaves in the field. Suddenly my sheaf rose and stood upright; then your sheaves gathered around it, and bowed down to my sheaf." 8 His brothers said to him, "Are you

y Gk Syr: Heb *daughter*   z Or *chiefs*   a Meaning of Heb uncertain   b Or *chief by chief*   c Traditional rendering (compare Gk): *a coat of many colors*; meaning of Heb uncertain indeed to reign over us? Are you indeed to have dominion over us?" So they hated him even more because of his dreams and his words.

9 He had another dream, and told it to his brothers, saying, "Look, I have had another dream: the sun, the moon, and eleven stars were bowing down to me." 10 But when he told it to his father and to his brothers, his father rebuked him, and said to him, "What kind of dream is this that you have had? Shall we indeed come, I and your mother and your brothers, and bow to the ground before you?" 11 So his brothers were jealous of him, but his father kept the matter in mind.

Joseph Is Sold by His Brothers

12 Now his brothers went to pasture their father's flock near Shĕ′chem. 13 And Israel said to Joseph, "Are not your brothers pasturing the flock at Shĕ′chem? Come, I will send you to them." He answered, "Here I am." 14 So he said to him, "Go now, see if it is well with your brothers and with the flock; and bring word back to me." So he sent him from the valley of Hĕ′bron.

He came to Shĕ′chem, 15 and a man found him wandering in the fields; the man asked him, "What are you seeking?" 16 "I am seeking my brothers," he said; "tell me, please, where they are pasturing the flock." 17 The man said, "They have gone away, for I heard them say, 'Let us go to Dō′than.' " So Joseph went after his brothers, and found them at Dō′than. 18 They saw him

from a distance, and before he came near to them, they conspired to kill him. 19 They said to one another, "Here comes this dreamer. 20 Come now, let us kill him and throw him into one of the pits; then we shall say that a wild animal has devoured him, and we shall see what will become of his dreams." 21 But when Reuben heard it, he delivered him out of their hands, saying, "Let us not take his life." 22 Reuben said to them, "Shed no blood; throw him into this pit here in the wilderness, but lay no hand on him"—that he might rescue him out of their hand and restore him to his father. 23 So when Joseph came to his brothers, they stripped him of his robe, the long robe with sleeves[d] that he wore; 24 and they took him and threw him into a pit. The pit was empty; there was no water in it.

25 Then they sat down to eat; and looking up they saw a caravan of Ish′ma·el·ites coming from Gil′e·ad, with their camels carrying gum, balm, and resin, on their way to carry it down to Egypt. 26 Then Judah said to his brothers, "What profit is it if we kill our brother and conceal his blood? 27 Come, let us sell him to the Ish′ma·el·ites, and not lay our hands on him, for he is our brother, our own flesh." And his brothers agreed. 28 When some Mid′i·an·ite traders passed by, they drew Joseph up, lifting him out of the pit, and sold him

---

[d] See note on 37.3

▶ JOSEPH

Chapters 37–50 of Genesis contain one of the world's greatest stories of family, jealousy, betrayal, and forgiveness.

A son of Jacob and Rachel, Joseph carries to Egypt the divine promises of land and descendants, and eventually becomes the link with the story of Moses and the Exodus. As Jacob's favorite son, Joseph experiences the jealousy of his brothers, who sell him to Egyptian merchants. In Egypt, Joseph rises to power, becoming second-in-command to the Pharaoh. Later, when Joseph's brothers come to Egypt looking for food, he forgives them and becomes reconciled with them.

Joseph's story encourages us to forgive others, even when we have been unjustly treated by them. Whenever we have been greatly wronged, remembering Joseph will offer us hope and courage.

Gen 37.1—50.26

GEN

to the Ish'ma•el•ites for twenty pieces of silver. And they took Joseph to Egypt.

29 When Reuben returned to the pit and saw that Joseph was not in the pit, he tore his clothes. 30 He returned to his brothers, and said, "The boy is gone; and I, where can I turn?" 31 Then they took Joseph's robe, slaughtered a goat, and dipped the robe in the blood. 32 They had the long robe with sleeves*e* taken to their father, and they said, "This we have found; see now whether it is your son's robe or not." 33 He recognized it, and said, "It is my son's robe! A wild animal has devoured him; Joseph is without doubt torn to pieces." 34 Then Jacob tore his garments, and put sackcloth on his loins, and mourned for his son many days. 35 All his sons and all his daughters sought to comfort him; but he refused to be comforted, and said, "No, I shall go down to Shĕ'ōl to my son, mourning." Thus his father bewailed him. 36 Meanwhile the Mid'i•an•ites had sold him in Egypt to Pot'i•phar, one of Pharaoh's officials, the captain of the guard.

Judah and Tamar

38 It happened at that time that Judah went down from his brothers and settled near a certain A•dul'lam•ite whose name was Hī'rah. 2 There Judah saw the daughter of a certain Cā'naan•ite whose name was Shū'a; he married her and went in to her. 3 She conceived and bore a son; and he named him Er. 4 Again she conceived and bore a son whom she named Ō'nan. 5 Yet again she bore a son, and she named him Shĕ'lah. She*f* was in Chĕ'zib when she bore him. 6 Judah took a wife for Er his firstborn; her name was Tā'mar. 7 But Er, Judah's firstborn, was wicked in the sight of the LORD, and the LORD put him to death. 8 Then Judah said to Ō'nan, "Go in to your brother's wife and perform the duty of a brother-in-law to her; raise up offspring for your brother." 9 But since Ō'nan knew that the offspring would not be his, he spilled his semen on the ground whenever he went in to his brother's wife, so that he would not give offspring to his brother. 10 What he did was displeasing in the sight of the LORD, and he put him to death also. 11 Then Judah said to his daughter-in-law Tā'mar, "Remain a widow in your father's house until my son Shĕ'lah grows up"—for he feared that he too would die, like his brothers. So Tā'mar went to live in her father's house.

12 In course of time the wife of Judah, Shū'a's daughter, died; when Judah's time of mourning was over,*g* he went up to Tim'nah to his sheepshearers, he and his friend Hī'rah the A•dul'lam•ite. 13 When Tā'mar was told, "Your father-in-law is going up to Tim'nah to shear his sheep," 14 she put off her widow's garments, put on a veil, wrapped

herself up, and sat down at the entrance to E•nā'im, which is on the road to Tim'nah. She saw that Shĕ'lah was grown up, yet she had not been given to him in marriage. 15 When Judah saw her, he thought her to be a prostitute, for she had covered her face. 16 He went over to her at the roadside, and said, "Come, let me come in to you," for he did not know that she was his daughter-in-law. She said, "What will you give me, that you may come in to me?" 17 He answered, "I will send you a kid from the flock." And she said, "Only if you give me a pledge, until you send it." 18 He said, "What pledge shall I give you?" She replied, "Your signet and your cord, and the staff that is in your hand." So he gave them to her, and went in to her, and she conceived by him. 19 Then she got up and went away, and taking off her veil she put on the garments of her widowhood.

20 When Judah sent the kid by his friend the A•dul'lam•ite, to recover the pledge from the

---

e See note on 37.3   *f* Gk: Heb *He*   *g* Heb *when Judah was comforted* woman, he could not find her. 21 He asked the townspeople, "Where is the temple prostitute who was at E•na'im by the wayside?" But they said, "No prostitute has been here." 22 So he returned to Judah, and said, "I have not found her; moreover the townspeople said, 'No prostitute has been here.' " 23 Judah replied, "Let her keep the things as her own, otherwise we will be laughed at; you see, I sent this kid, and you could not find her."

24 About three months later Judah was told, "Your daughter-in-law Tā'mar has played the whore; moreover she is pregnant as a result of whoredom." And Judah said, "Bring her out, and let her be burned." 25 As she was being brought out, she sent word to her father-in-law, "It was the owner of these who made me pregnant." And she said, "Take note, please, whose these are, the signet and the cord and the staff." 26 Then Judah acknowledged them and said, "She is more in the right than I, since I did not give her to my son Shē'lah." And he did not lie with her again.

27 When the time of her delivery came, there were twins in her womb. 28 While she was in labor, one put out a hand; and the midwife took and bound on his hand a crimson thread, saying, "This one came out first." 29 But just then he drew back his hand, and out came his brother; and she said, "What a breach you have made for yourself!" Therefore he was named Per'ez.h 30 Afterward his brother came out with the crimson thread on his hand; and he was named Zē'rah.i

Joseph and Potiphar's Wife

39 Now Joseph was taken down to Egypt, and Pot'i•phar, an officer of Pharaoh, the captain of the guard, an Egyptian, bought him from the Ish'ma•el•ites who had brought him down there. 2 The LORD was with Joseph, and he became a successful man; he was in the house of his Egyptian master. 3 His master saw that the LORD was with him, and that the LORD caused all that he did to prosper in his hands. 4 So Joseph found favor in his sight and attended him; he made him overseer of his house and put him in charge of all that he had. 5 From the time that he made him overseer in his house and over all that he had, the LORD blessed the Egyptian's house for Joseph's sake; the blessing of the LORD was on all that he had, in house and field. 6 So he left all that he had in Joseph's charge; and, with him there, he had no concern for anything but the food that he ate.

Now Joseph was handsome and good-looking. 7 And after a time his master's wife cast her eyes on Joseph and said, "Lie with me." 8 But he refused and said to his master's wife, "Look, with me here, my master has no concern about anything in the house, and he has put everything that he has in my hand. 9 He is not greater in this house than I am, nor has he kept back anything from me except yourself, because you are his wife. How then could I do this great wickedness, and sin against God?" 10 And although she spoke to Joseph day after day, he would not consent to lie beside her or to be with her. 11 One day, however, when he went into the house to do his work, and while no one else was in the house, 12 she caught hold of his garment, saying, "Lie with me!" But he left his garment in her hand, and fled and ran outside. 13 When she saw that he had left his garment in her hand and had fled outside, 14 she called out to the members of her household and said to them, "See, my husbandj has brought among us a Hebrew to insult us! He came in to me to lie with me, and I cried out with a loud voice; 15 and when he heard me raise my voice and cry out, he left his garment beside me, and fled outside." 16 Then she kept his garment by her until his master came home, 17 and she told him the same story, saying, "The Hebrew servant, whom you have brought among us, came in to me to insult me; 18 but as soon as I raised my voice and cried out, he left his garment beside me, and fled outside."

19 When his master heard the words that his wife spoke to him, saying, "This is the way your servant treated me," he became enraged. 20 And Joseph's master took him and put him into the prison, the place where the king's prisoners were confined; he remained there in prison. 21 But the LORD was with Joseph and showed him steadfast love; he gave him favor in the sight of the chief jailer. 22 The chief jailer committed to Joseph's care all the prisoners who were in the prison, and whatever was done there, he was the one who did it. 23 The chief jailer paid no heed to anything that was in Joseph's care, because the LORD was with him; and whatever he did, the LORD made it prosper.

The Dreams of Two Prisoners

40 Some time after this, the cupbearer of the king of Egypt and his baker offended their lord the king of Egypt. 2 Pharaoh was angry with his two officers, the chief cupbearer and the chief baker, 3 and he put them in custody in the house of the captain of the guard, in the prison where Joseph was confined. 4 The captain of the guard charged Joseph with them, and he waited on them; and they continued for some time in custody. 5 One night they both dreamed—the cupbearer and the baker of the king of Egypt, who were confined in the prison—each his own dream, and

---

h That is A breach   i That is Brightness; perhaps alluding to the crimson thread   j Heb he

GEN

each dream with its own meaning. 6 When Joseph came to them in the morning, he saw that they were troubled. 7 So he asked Pharaoh's officers, who were with him in custody in his master's house, "Why are your faces downcast today?" 8 They said to him, "We have had dreams, and there is no one to interpret them." And Joseph said to them, "Do not interpretations belong to God? Please tell them to me."

9 So the chief cupbearer told his dream to Joseph, and said to him, "In my dream there was a vine before me, 10 and on the vine there were three branches. As soon as it budded, its blossoms came out and the clusters ripened into grapes. 11 Pharaoh's cup was in my hand; and I took the grapes and pressed them into Pharaoh's cup, and placed the cup in Pharaoh's hand." 12 Then Joseph said to him, "This is its interpretation: the three branches are three days; 13 within three days Pharaoh will lift up your head and restore you to your office; and you shall place Pharaoh's cup in his hand, just as you used to do when you were his cupbearer. 14 But remember me when it is well with you; please do me the kindness to make mention of me to Pharaoh, and so get me out of this place. 15 For in fact I was stolen out of the land of the Hebrews; and here also I have done nothing that they should have put me into the dungeon."

16 When the chief baker saw that the interpretation was favorable, he said to Joseph, "I also had a dream: there were three cake baskets on my head, 17 and in the uppermost basket there were all sorts of baked food for Pharaoh, but the birds were eating it out of the basket on my head." 18 And Joseph answered, "This is its interpretation: the three baskets are three days; 19 within three days Pharaoh will lift up your head—from you!—and hang you on a pole; and the birds will eat the flesh from you."

20 On the third day, which was Pharaoh's birthday, he made a feast for all his servants, and lifted up the head of the chief cupbearer and the head of the chief baker among his servants. 21 He restored the chief cupbearer to his cupbearing, and he placed the cup in Pharaoh's hand; 22 but the chief baker he hanged, just as Joseph had interpreted to them. 23 Yet the chief cupbearer did not remember Joseph, but forgot him.

Joseph Interprets Pharaoh's Dream

41 After two whole years, Pharaoh dreamed that he was standing by the Nile, 2 and there came up out of the Nile seven sleek and fat cows, and they grazed in the reed grass. 3 Then seven other cows, ugly and thin, came up out of the Nile after them, and stood by the other cows on the bank of the Nile. 4 The ugly and thin cows ate up the seven sleek and fat cows. And Pharaoh awoke. 5 Then he fell asleep and dreamed a second time; seven ears of grain, plump and good, were growing on one stalk. 6 Then seven ears, thin and blighted by the east wind, sprouted after them. 7 The thin ears swallowed up the seven plump and full ears. Pharaoh awoke, and it was a dream. 8 In the morning his spirit was troubled; so he sent and called for all the magicians of Egypt and all its wise men. Pharaoh told them his dreams, but there was no one who could interpret them to Pharaoh.

9 Then the chief cupbearer said to Pharaoh, "I remember my faults today. 10 Once Pharaoh was angry with his servants, and put me and the chief baker in custody in the house of the captain of the guard. 11 We dreamed on the same night, he and I, each having a dream with its own meaning. 12 A young Hebrew was there with us, a servant of the captain of the guard. When we told him, he interpreted our dreams to us, giving an interpretation to each according to his dream. 13 As he interpreted to us, so it turned out; I was restored to my office, and the baker was hanged."

14 Then Pharaoh sent for Joseph, and he was hurriedly brought out of the dungeon. When he had shaved himself and changed his clothes, he came in before Pharaoh. 15 And Pharaoh said to Joseph, "I have had a dream, and there is no one who can interpret it. I have heard it said of you that when you hear a dream you can interpret it." 16 Joseph answered Pharaoh, "It is not I; God will give Pharaoh a favorable answer." 17 Then Pharaoh said to Joseph, "In my dream I was standing on the banks of the Nile; 18 and seven cows, fat and sleek, came up out of the Nile and fed in the reed grass. 19 Then seven other cows came up after them, poor, very ugly, and thin. Never had I seen such ugly ones in all the land of Egypt. 20 The thin and ugly cows ate up the first seven fat cows, 21 but when they had eaten them no one would have known that they had done so, for they were still as ugly as before. Then I awoke. 22 I fell asleep a second time [k] and I saw in my dream seven ears of grain, full and good, growing on one stalk, 23 and seven ears, withered, thin, and blighted by the east wind, sprouting after them; 24 and the thin ears swallowed up the seven good ears. But when I told it to the magicians, there was no one who could explain it to me."

25 Then Joseph said to Pharaoh, "Pharaoh's dreams are one and the same; God has revealed to Pharaoh what he is about to do. 26 The seven good cows are seven years, and the seven good ears are seven years; the dreams are one. 27 The seven lean and ugly cows that came up after them are seven years, as are the seven empty ears blighted by the

---

k Gk Syr Vg: Heb lacks *I fell asleep a second time*

east wind. They are seven years of famine. [28] It is as I told Pharaoh; God has shown to Pharaoh what he is about to do. [29] There will come seven years of great plenty throughout all the land of Egypt. [30] After them there will arise seven years of famine, and all the plenty will be forgotten in the land of Egypt; the famine will consume the land. [31] The plenty will no longer be known in the land because of the famine that will follow, for it will be very grievous. [32] And the doubling of Pharaoh's dream means that the thing is fixed by God, and God will shortly bring it about. [33] Now therefore let Pharaoh select a man who is discerning and wise, and set him over the land of Egypt. [34] Let Pharaoh proceed to appoint overseers over the land, and take one-fifth of the produce of the land of Egypt during the seven plenteous years. [35] Let them gather all the food of these good years that are coming, and lay up grain under the authority of Pharaoh for food in the cities, and let them keep it. [36] That food shall be a reserve for the land against the seven years of famine that are to befall the land of Egypt, so that the land may not perish through the famine."

Joseph's Rise to Power

[37] The proposal pleased Pharaoh and all his servants. [38] Pharaoh said to his servants, "Can we find anyone else like this—one in whom is the spirit of God?" [39] So Pharaoh said to Joseph, "Since God has shown you all this, there is no one so discerning and wise as you. [40] You shall be over my house, and all my people shall order themselves as you command; only with regard to the throne will I be greater than you." [41] And Pharaoh said to Joseph, "See, I have set you over all the land of Egypt." [42] Removing his signet ring from his hand, Pharaoh put it on Joseph's hand; he arrayed him in garments of fine linen, and put a gold chain around his neck. [43] He had him ride in the chariot of his second-in-command; and they cried out in front of him, "Bow the knee!"[l] Thus he set him over all the land of Egypt. [44] Moreover Pharaoh said to Joseph, "I am Pharaoh, and without your consent no one shall lift up hand or foot in all the land of Egypt." [45] Pharaoh gave Joseph the name Zaph'e•nath-pa•ne'ah; and he gave him As'e•nath daughter of Po•ti'phe•ra, priest of On, as his wife. Thus Joseph gained authority over the land of Egypt.

[46] Joseph was thirty years old when he entered the service of Pharaoh king of Egypt. And Joseph went out from the presence of Pharaoh, and went through all the land of Egypt. [47] During the seven plenteous years the earth produced abundantly. [48] He gathered up all the food of the seven years when there was plenty[m] in the land of Egypt, and stored up food in the cities; he stored up in every city the food from the fields around it. [49] So Joseph stored up grain in such abundance—like the sand of the sea—that he stopped measuring it; it was beyond measure.

[50] Before the years of famine came, Joseph had two sons, whom As'e•nath daughter of Po•ti'-phe•ra, priest of On, bore to him. [51] Joseph named the firstborn Ma•nas'seh,[n] "For," he said, "God has made me forget all my hardship and all my father's house." [52] The second he named E'phra•im,[o] "For God has made me fruitful in the land of my misfortunes."

[53] The seven years of plenty that prevailed in the land of Egypt came to an end; [54] and the seven

did you KNOW?

Dreams

In the ancient world, belief in the reality and significance of dreams was widespread. The ancients believed that dreams and visions revealed messages, prophecies, and healing from their gods. Israel shared this view of the importance of dreams. Joseph is described as an interpreter of dreams, and this skill earns him Pharaoh's respect (Gen 41.37–45), as well as his brothers' jealousy (37.5–11).

In the Old Testament, the prophets are often referred to as seers because the word of God so often comes to them through dreams and visions. The focus, however, is always on the word of God and its meaning, not on the dream itself. In fact, God usually gives a character in the story the interpretation of the dream, which aims to lead the people to more faithful observance of the covenant. If the dream does not do this, it is to be considered a false dream. (See other references to dreams in Gen 28.10–22; Deut 13.2–6; Sir 34.1–4; Jer 27.9–10; 29.8–9; Joel 2.28; Zech 1.8; Mt 1.20; 2.13.)

▶ Gen 37.1–11; 40.1—41.36

---

l *Abrek,* apparently an Egyptian word similar in sound to the Hebrew word meaning *to kneel*   *m* Sam Gk: MT *the seven years that were*   *n* That is *Making to forget*   *o* From a Hebrew word meaning *to be fruitful*

GEN

years of famine began to come, just as Joseph had said. There was famine in every country, but throughout the land of Egypt there was bread. ⁵⁵ When all the land of Egypt was famished, the people cried to Pharaoh for bread. Pharaoh said to all the Egyptians, "Go to Joseph; what he says to you, do." ⁵⁶ And since the famine had spread over all the land, Joseph opened all the storehouses,ᵖ and sold to the Egyptians, for the famine was severe in the land of Egypt. ⁵⁷ Moreover, all the world came to Joseph in Egypt to buy grain, because the famine became severe throughout the world.

Joseph's Brothers Go to Egypt

42 When Jacob learned that there was grain in Egypt, he said to his sons, "Why do you keep looking at one another? ² I have heard," he said, "that there is grain in Egypt; go down and buy grain for us there, that we may live and not die." ³ So ten of Joseph's brothers went down to buy grain in Egypt. ⁴ But Jacob did not send Joseph's brother Benjamin with his brothers, for he feared that harm might come to him. ⁵ Thus the sons of Israel were among the other people who came to buy grain, for the famine had reached the land of Cā'naan.

6 Now Joseph was governor over the land; it was he who sold to all the people of the land. And Joseph's brothers came and bowed themselves before him with their faces to the ground. ⁷ When Joseph saw his brothers, he recognized them, but he treated them like strangers and spoke harshly to them. "Where do you come from?" he said. They said, "From the land of Cā'naan, to buy food." ⁸ Although Joseph had recognized his brothers, they did not recognize him. ⁹ Joseph also remembered the dreams that he had dreamed about them. He said to them, "You are spies; you have come to see the nakedness of the land!" ¹⁰ They said to him, "No, my lord; your servants have come to buy food. ¹¹ We are all sons of one man; we are honest men; your servants have never been spies." ¹² But he said to them, "No, you have come to see the nakedness of the land!" ¹³ They said, "We, your servants, are twelve brothers, the sons of a certain man in the land of Cā'naan; the youngest, however, is now with our father, and one is no more." ¹⁴ But Joseph said to them, "It is just as I have said to you; you are spies! ¹⁵ Here is how you shall be tested: as Pharaoh lives, you shall not leave this place unless your youngest brother comes here! ¹⁶ Let one of you go and bring your brother, while the rest of you remain in prison, in order that your words may be tested, whether there is truth in you; or else, as Pharaoh lives, surely you are spies." ¹⁷ And he put them all together in prison for three days.

18 On the third day Joseph said to them, "Do this and you will live, for I fear God: ¹⁹ if you are honest men, let one of your brothers stay here where you are imprisoned. The rest of you shall go and carry grain for the famine of your households, ²⁰ and bring your youngest brother to me. Thus your words will be verified, and you shall not die." And they agreed to do so. ²¹ They said to one another, "Alas, we are paying the penalty for what we did to our brother; we saw his anguish when he pleaded with us, but we would not listen. That is why this anguish has come upon us." ²² Then Reuben answered them, "Did I not tell you not to wrong the boy? But you would not listen. So now there comes a reckoning for his blood." ²³ They did not know that Joseph understood them, since he spoke with them through an interpreter. ²⁴ He turned away from them and wept; then he returned and spoke to them. And he picked out Sim'ē•on and had him bound before their eyes. ²⁵ Joseph then gave orders to fill their bags with grain, to return every man's money to his sack, and to give them provisions for their journey. This was done for them.

Joseph's Brothers Return to Canaan

26 They loaded their donkeys with their grain, and departed. ²⁷ When one of them opened his sack to give his donkey fodder at the lodging place, he saw his money at the top of the sack. ²⁸ He said to his brothers, "My money has been put back; here it is in my sack!" At this they lost heart and turned trembling to one another, saying, "What is this that God has done to us?"

29 When they came to their father Jacob in the land of Cā'naan, they told him all that had happened to them, saying, ³⁰ "The man, the lord of the land, spoke harshly to us, and charged us with spying on the land. ³¹ But we said to him, 'We are honest men, we are not spies. ³² We are twelve brothers, sons of our father; one is no more, and the youngest is now with our father in the land of Cā'naan.' ³³ Then the man, the lord of the land, said to us, 'By this I shall know that you are honest men: leave one of your brothers with me, take grain for the famine of your households, and go your way. ³⁴ Bring your youngest brother to me, and I shall know that you are not spies but honest men. Then I will release your brother to you, and you may trade in the land.' "

35 As they were emptying their sacks, there in each one's sack was his bag of money. When they and their father saw their bundles of money, they were dismayed. ³⁶ And their father Jacob said to

---

ᵖ Gk Vg Compare Syr: Heb *opened all that was in*
(or, *among*) *them*

them, "I am the one you have bereaved of children: Joseph is no more, and Sim'ē•on is no more, and now you would take Benjamin. All this has happened to me!" 37 Then Reuben said to his father, "You may kill my two sons if I do not bring him back to you. Put him in my hands, and I will bring him back to you." 38 But he said, "My son shall not go down with you, for his brother is dead, and he alone is left. If harm should come to him on the journey that you are to make, you would bring down my gray hairs with sorrow to Shē'ōl."

The Brothers Come Again, Bringing Benjamin

43 Now the famine was severe in the land. 2 And when they had eaten up the grain that they had brought from Egypt, their father said to them, "Go again, buy us a little more food." 3 But Judah said to him, "The man solemnly warned us, saying, 'You shall not see my face unless your brother is with you.' 4 If you will send our brother with us, we will go down and buy you food; 5 but if you will not send him, we will not go down, for the man said to us, 'You shall not see my face, unless your brother is with you.' " 6 Israel said, "Why did you treat me so badly as to tell the man that you had another brother?" 7 They replied, "The man questioned us carefully about ourselves and our kindred, saying, 'Is your father still alive? Have you another brother?' What we told him was in answer to these questions. Could we in any way know that he would say, 'Bring your brother down'?" 8 Then Judah said to his father Israel, "Send the boy with me, and let us be on our way, so that we may live and not die—you and we and also our little ones. 9 I myself will be surety for him; you can hold me accountable for him. If I do not bring him back to you and set him before you, then let me bear the blame forever. 10 If we had not delayed, we would now have returned twice."

11 Then their father Israel said to them, "If it must be so, then do this: take some of the choice fruits of the land in your bags, and carry them down as a present to the man—a little balm and a little honey, gum, resin, pistachio nuts, and almonds. 12 Take double the money with you. Carry back with you the money that was returned in the top of your sacks; perhaps it was an oversight. 13 Take your brother also, and be on your way again to the man; 14 may God Almighty*q* grant you mercy before the man, so that he may send back your other brother and Benjamin. As for me, if I am bereaved of my children, I am bereaved." 15 So the men took the present, and they took double the money with them, as well as Benjamin. Then they went on their way down to Egypt, and stood before Joseph.

16 When Joseph saw Benjamin with them, he said to the steward of his house, "Bring the men into the house, and slaughter an animal and make ready, for the men are to dine with me at noon." 17 The man did as Joseph said, and brought the men to Joseph's house. 18 Now the men were afraid because they were brought to Joseph's house, and they said, "It is because of the money, replaced in our sacks the first time, that we have been brought in, so that he may have an opportunity to fall upon us, to make slaves of us and take our donkeys." 19 So they went up to the steward of Joseph's house and spoke with him at the entrance to the house. 20 They said, "Oh, my lord, we came down the first time to buy food; 21 and when we came to the lodging place we opened our sacks, and there was each one's money in the top of his sack, our money in full weight. So we have brought it back with us. 22 Moreover we have brought down with us additional money to buy food. We do not know who put our money in our sacks." 23 He replied, "Rest assured, do not be afraid; your God and the God of your father must have put treasure in your sacks for you; I received your money." Then he brought Sim'ē•on out to them. 24 When the steward*r* had brought the men into Joseph's house, and given them water, and they had washed their feet, and when he had given their donkeys fodder, 25 they made the present ready for Joseph's coming at noon, for they had heard that they would dine there.

26 When Joseph came home, they brought him the present that they had carried into the house, and bowed to the ground before him. 27 He inquired about their welfare, and said, "Is your father well, the old man of whom you spoke? Is he still alive?" 28 They said, "Your servant our father is well; he is still alive." And they bowed their heads and did obeisance. 29 Then he looked up and saw his brother Benjamin, his mother's son, and said, "Is this your youngest brother, of whom you spoke to me? God be gracious to you, my son!" 30 With that, Joseph hurried out, because he was overcome with affection for his brother, and he was about to weep. So he went into a private room and wept there. 31 Then he washed his face and came out; and controlling himself he said, "Serve the meal." 32 They served him by himself, and them by themselves, and the Egyptians who ate with him by themselves, because the Egyptians could not eat with the Hebrews, for that is an abomination to the Egyptians. 33 When they were seated before him, the firstborn according to his birthright and the youngest according to his youth, the men looked at one another in amazement. 34 Portions were taken to them from Joseph's table, but

---

q Traditional rendering of Heb *El Shaddai*　　*r* Heb *the man*

Benjamin's portion was five times as much as any of theirs. So they drank and were merry with him.

Joseph Detains Benjamin

44 Then he commanded the steward of his house, "Fill the men's sacks with food, as much as they can carry, and put each man's money in the top of his sack. 2 Put my cup, the silver cup, in the top of the sack of the youngest, with his money for the grain." And he did as Joseph told him. 3 As soon as the morning was light, the men were sent away with their donkeys. 4 When they had gone only a short distance from the city, Joseph said to his steward, "Go, follow after the men; and when you overtake them, say to them, 'Why have you returned evil for good? Why have you stolen my silver cup?ᵍ 5 Is it not from this that my lord drinks? Does he not indeed use it for divination? You have done wrong in doing this.' "

6 When he overtook them, he repeated these words to them. 7 They said to him, "Why does my lord speak such words as these? Far be it from your servants that they should do such a thing! 8 Look, the money that we found at the top of our sacks, we brought back to you from the land of Cā'naan; why then would we steal silver or gold from your lord's house? 9 Should it be found with any one of your servants, let him die; moreover the rest of us will become my lord's slaves." 10 He said, "Even so; in accordance with your words, let it be: he with whom it is found shall become my slave, but the rest of you shall go free." 11 Then each one quickly lowered his sack to the ground, and each opened his sack. 12 He searched, beginning with the eldest and ending with the youngest; and the cup was found in Benjamin's sack. 13 At this they tore their clothes. Then each one loaded his donkey, and they returned to the city.

14 Judah and his brothers came to Joseph's house while he was still there; and they fell to the ground before him. 15 Joseph said to them, "What deed is this that you have done? Do you not know that one such as I can practice divination?" 16 And Judah said, "What can we say to my lord? What can we speak? How can we clear ourselves? God has found out the guilt of your servants; here we are then, my lord's slaves, both we and also the one in whose possession the cup has been found." 17 But he said, "Far be it from me that I should do so! Only the one in whose possession the cup was found shall be my slave; but as for you, go up in peace to your father."

Judah Pleads for Benjamin's Release

18 Then Judah stepped up to him and said, "O my lord, let your servant please speak a word in my lord's ears, and do not be angry with your ser-

vant; for you are like Pharaoh himself. 19 My lord asked his servants, saying, 'Have you a father or a brother?' 20 And we said to my lord, 'We have a father, an old man, and a young brother, the child of his old age. His brother is dead; he alone is left of his mother's children, and his father loves him.' 21 Then you said to your servants, 'Bring him down to me, so that I may set my eyes on him.' 22 We said to my lord, 'The boy cannot leave his father, for if he should leave his father, his father would die.' 23 Then you said to your servants, 'Unless your youngest brother comes down with you, you shall see my face no more.' 24 When we went back to your servant my father we told him the words of my lord. 25 And when our father said, 'Go again, buy us a little food,' 26 we said, 'We cannot go down. Only if our youngest brother goes with us, will we go down; for we cannot see the man's face unless our youngest brother is with us.' 27 Then your servant my father said to us, 'You know that my wife bore me two sons; 28 one left me, and I said, Surely he has been torn to pieces; and I have never seen him since. 29 If you take this one also from me, and harm comes to him, you will bring down my gray hairs in sorrow to Shē'ōl.' 30 Now therefore, when I come to your servant my father and the boy is not with us, then, as his life is bound up in the boy's life, 31 when he sees that the boy is not with us, he will die; and your servants will bring down the gray hairs of your servant our father with sorrow to Shē'ōl. 32 For your servant became surety for the boy to my father, saying, 'If I do not bring him back to you, then I will bear the blame in the sight of my father all my life.' 33 Now therefore, please let your servant remain as a slave to my lord in place of the boy; and let the boy go back with his brothers. 34 For how can I go back to my father if the boy is not with me? I fear to see the suffering that would come upon my father."

Joseph Reveals Himself to His Brothers

45 Then Joseph could no longer control himself before all those who stood by him, and he cried out, "Send everyone away from me." So no one stayed with him when Joseph made himself known to his brothers. 2 And he wept so loudly that the Egyptians heard it, and the household of Pharaoh heard it. 3 Joseph said to his brothers, "I am Joseph. Is my father still alive?" But his brothers could not answer him, so dismayed were they at his presence.

4 Then Joseph said to his brothers, "Come closer to me." And they came closer. He said, "I am

---

ᵍ Gk Compare Vg: Heb lacks *Why have you stolen my silver cup?*

your brother, Joseph, whom you sold into Egypt. 5 And now do not be distressed, or angry with yourselves, because you sold me here; for God sent me before you to preserve life. 6 For the famine has been in the land these two years; and there are five more years in which there will be neither plowing nor harvest. 7 God sent me before you to preserve for you a remnant on earth, and to keep alive for you many survivors. 8 So it was not you who sent me here, but God; he has made me a father to Pharaoh, and lord of all his house and ruler over all the land of Egypt. 9 Hurry and go up to my father and say to him, 'Thus says your son Joseph, God has made me lord of all Egypt; come down to me, do not delay. 10 You shall settle in the land of Gō'shen, and you shall be near me, you and your children and your children's children, as well as your flocks, your herds, and all that you have. 11 I will provide for you there—since there are five more years of famine to come—so that you and your household, and all that you have, will not come to poverty.' 12 And now your eyes and the eyes of my brother Benjamin see that it is my own mouth that speaks to you. 13 You must tell my father how greatly I am honored in Egypt, and all that you have seen. Hurry and bring my father down here." 14 Then he fell upon his brother Benjamin's neck and wept, while Benjamin wept upon his neck. 15 And he kissed all his brothers and wept upon them; and after that his brothers talked with him.

16 When the report was heard in Pharaoh's house, "Joseph's brothers have come," Pharaoh and his servants were pleased. 17 Pharaoh said to Joseph, "Say to your brothers, 'Do this: load your animals and go back to the land of Cā'naan. 18 Take your father and your households and come to me, so that I may give you the best of the land of Egypt, and you may enjoy the fat of the land.' 19 You are further charged to say, 'Do this: take wagons from the land of Egypt for your little ones and for your wives, and bring your father, and come. 20 Give no thought to your possessions, for the best of all the land of Egypt is yours.' "

21 The sons of Israel did so. Joseph gave them wagons according to the instruction of Pharaoh, and he gave them provisions for the journey. 22 To each one of them he gave a set of garments; but to Benjamin he gave three hundred pieces of silver and five sets of garments. 23 To his father he sent the following: ten donkeys loaded with the good things of Egypt, and ten female donkeys loaded with grain, bread, and provision for his father on the journey. 24 Then he sent his brothers on their way, and as they were leaving he said to them, "Do not quarrel*t* along the way."

25 So they went up out of Egypt and came to their father Jacob in the land of Cā'naan. 26 And they told him, "Joseph is still alive! He is even ruler over all the land of Egypt." He was stunned; he could not believe them. 27 But when they told him all the words of Joseph that he had said to them, and when he saw the wagons that Joseph had sent to carry him, the spirit of their father Jacob revived. 28 Israel said, "Enough! My son Joseph is still alive. I must go and see him before I die."

---

t Or *be agitated*

God's Master Plan

LIVE IT!

After Joseph's tearful reconciliation with his brothers, he tells them that their past treatment of him enabled him to save them from the famine. Because he ended up in Egypt and rose to power, he can now invite them to stay as guests of the Pharaoh.

Joseph realizes that good has come out of an evil act. He sees the events of his family's life as part of God's plan to preserve life and to make sure that the Covenant continues. Joseph's insight does not justify what his brothers did, but it does help us realize that good can come out of a tragic event. It is often hard for us to understand why something bad is happening, but as time passes, we often gain perspective and insight. These are the rewards of trust and faith. Joseph remained faithful, despite many difficulties. Let us strive to do the same, assured that not even human sinfulness can thwart God's saving plans.

When have you experienced good things coming out of a bad situation? Has it ever seemed like God has upset part of your life, only to result in something better than you expected?

▶ **Gen 45.5–8**

Jacob Brings His Whole Family to Egypt
(Ex 6.14–25)

46 When Israel set out on his journey with all that he had and came to Bĕ'er-shĕ'ba, he offered sacrifices to the God of his father Isaac. 2 God spoke to Israel in visions of the night, and said, "Jacob, Jacob." And he said, "Here I am." 3 Then he said, "I am God,u the God of your father; do not be afraid to go down to Egypt, for I will make of you a great nation there. 4 I myself will go down with you to Egypt, and I will also bring you up again; and Joseph's own hand shall close your eyes."

5 Then Jacob set out from Bĕ'er-shĕ'ba; and the sons of Israel carried their father Jacob, their little ones, and their wives, in the wagons that Pharaoh had sent to carry him. 6 They also took their livestock and the goods that they had acquired in the land of Cā'naan, and they came into Egypt, Jacob and all his offspring with him, 7 his sons, and his sons' sons with him, his daughters, and his sons' daughters; all his offspring he brought with him into Egypt.

8 Now these are the names of the Israelites, Jacob and his offspring, who came to Egypt. Reuben, Jacob's firstborn, 9 and the children of Reuben: Hā'noch, Pal'lū, Hez'ron, and Car'mī. 10 The children of Sim'ē·on: Je·mū'el, Jā'min, Ō'had, Jā'chin, Zō'har, and Shā'ūl,v the son of a Cā'naan·ite woman. 11 The children of Levi: Ger'shon, Kō'hath, and Me·rar'ī. 12 The children of Judah: Er, Ō'nan, Shē'lah, Per'ez, and Zē'rah (but Er and Ō'nan died in the land of Cā'naan); and the children of Per'ez were Hez'ron and Hā'mul. 13 The children of Is'sa·char: Tō'la, Pū'vah, Jash'ub,w and Shim'ron. 14 The children of Zeb'ū·lun: Sē'red, Ē'lon, and Jah'lē·el 15 (these are the sons of Leah, whom she bore to Jacob in Pad'dan-ar'am, together with his daughter Dī'nah; in all his sons and his daughters numbered thirty-three). 16 The children of Gad: Ziph'i·on, Hag'gī, Shū'nī, Ez'bon, Ē'rī, A·rō'dī, and A·rē'lī. 17 The children of Ash'er: Im'nah, Ish'vah, Ish'vī, Bē·rī'ah, and their sister Sē'rah. The children of Bē·rī'ah: Hē'ber and Mal'chi·el 18 (these are the children of Zil'pah, whom Lā'ban gave to his daughter Leah; and these she bore to Jacob—sixteen persons). 19 The children of Jacob's wife Rachel: Joseph and Benjamin. 20 To Joseph in the land of Egypt were born Ma·nas'seh and Ē'phra·im, whom As'e·nath daughter of Pō·ti'phe·ra, priest of On, bore to him. 21 The children of Benjamin: Bē'la, Bē'cher, Ash'bel, Gē'ra, Nā'a·man, Ē'hī, Rosh, Mup'pim, Hup'pim, and Ard 22 (these are the children of Rachel, who were born to Jacob—fourteen persons in all). 23 The children of Dan: Hā'shum.x 24 The children of Naph'ta·lī: Jah'zē·el, Gū'nī, Jē'-

zer, and Shil'lem 25 (these are the children of Bil'hah, whom Lā'ban gave to his daughter Rachel, and these she bore to Jacob—seven persons in all). 26 All the persons belonging to Jacob who came into Egypt, who were his own offspring, not including the wives of his sons, were sixty-six persons in all. 27 The children of Joseph, who were born to him in Egypt, were two; all the persons of the house of Jacob who came into Egypt were seventy.

Jacob Settles in Goshen

28 Israely sent Judah ahead to Joseph to lead the way before him into Gō'shen. When they came to the land of Gō'shen, 29 Joseph made ready his chariot and went up to meet his father Israel in Gō'shen. He presented himself to him, fell on his neck, and wept on his neck a good while. 30 Israel said to Joseph, "I can die now, having seen for myself that you are still alive." 31 Joseph said to his brothers and to his father's household, "I will go up and tell Pharaoh, and will say to him, 'My brothers and my father's household, who were in the land of Cā'naan, have come to me. 32 The men are shepherds, for they have been keepers of livestock; and they have brought their flocks, and their herds, and all that they have.' 33 When Pharaoh calls you, and says, 'What is your occupation?' 34 you shall say, 'Your servants have been keepers of livestock from our youth even until now, both we and our ancestors'—in order that you may settle in the land of Gō'shen, because all shepherds are abhorrent to the Egyptians."

47 So Joseph went and told Pharaoh, "My father and my brothers, with their flocks and herds and all that they possess, have come from the land of Cā'naan; they are now in the land of Gō'shen." 2 From among his brothers he took five men and presented them to Pharaoh. 3 Pharaoh said to his brothers, "What is your occupation?" And they said to Pharaoh, "Your servants are shepherds, as our ancestors were." 4 They said to Pharaoh, "We have come to reside as aliens in the land; for there is no pasture for your servants' flocks because the famine is severe in the land of Cā'naan. Now, we ask you, let your servants settle in the land of Gō'shen." 5 Then Pharaoh said to Joseph, "Your father and your brothers have come to you. 6 The land of Egypt is before you; settle your father and your brothers in the best part of the land; let them live in the land of Gō'shen; and if you know that there are capable men among them, put them in charge of my livestock."

7 Then Joseph brought in his father Jacob, and

---

u Heb *the God*   v Or *Saul*   w Compare Sam Gk Num 26.24; 1 Chr 7.1: MT *Iob*   x Gk: Heb *Hushim*   y Heb *He* presented him before Pharaoh, and Jacob blessed Pharaoh. 8 Pharaoh said to Jacob, "How many are the years of your life?" 9 Jacob said to Pharaoh, "The years of my earthly sojourn are one hundred thirty; few and hard have been the years of my life. They do not compare with the years of the life of my ancestors during their long sojourn." 10 Then Jacob blessed Pharaoh, and went out from the presence of Pharaoh. 11 Joseph settled his father and his brothers, and granted them a holding in the land of Egypt, in the best part of the land, in the land of Ram'e•sēs, as Pharaoh had instructed. 12 And Joseph provided his father, his brothers, and all his father's household with food, according to the number of their dependents.

The Famine in Egypt

13 Now there was no food in all the land, for the famine was very severe. The land of Egypt and the land of Cā'naan languished because of the famine. 14 Joseph collected all the money to be found in the land of Egypt and in the land of Cā'-naan, in exchange for the grain that they bought; and Joseph brought the money into Pharaoh's house. 15 When the money from the land of Egypt and from the land of Cā'naan was spent, all the Egyptians came to Joseph, and said, "Give us food! Why should we die before your eyes? For our money is gone." 16 And Joseph answered, "Give me your livestock, and I will give you food in exchange for your livestock, if your money is gone." 17 So they brought their livestock to Joseph; and Joseph gave them food in exchange for the horses, the flocks, the herds, and the donkeys. That year he supplied them with food in exchange for all their livestock. 18 When that year was ended, they came to him the following year, and said to him, "We can not hide from my lord that our money is all spent; and the herds of cattle are my lord's. There is nothing left in the sight of my lord but our bodies and our lands. 19 Shall we die before your eyes, both we and our land? Buy us and our land in exchange for food. We with our land will become slaves to Pharaoh; just give us seed, so that we may live and not die, and that the land may not become desolate."

20 So Joseph bought all the land of Egypt for Pharaoh. All the Egyptians sold their fields, because the famine was severe upon them; and the land became Pharaoh's. 21 As for the people, he made slaves of them z from one end of Egypt to the other. 22 Only the land of the priests he did not buy; for the priests had a fixed allowance from Pharaoh, and lived on the allowance that Pharaoh gave them; therefore they did not sell their land. 23 Then Joseph said to the people, "Now that I

have this day bought you and your land for Pharaoh, here is seed for you; sow the land. 24 And at the harvests you shall give one-fifth to Pharaoh, and four-fifths shall be your own, as seed for the field and as food for yourselves and your households, and as food for your little ones." 25 They said, "You have saved our lives; may it please my lord, we will be slaves to Pharaoh." 26 So Joseph made it a statute concerning the land of Egypt, and it stands to this day, that Pharaoh should have the fifth. The land of the priests alone did not become Pharaoh's.

The Last Days of Jacob

27 Thus Israel settled in the land of Egypt, in the region of Gō'shen; and they gained possessions in it, and were fruitful and multiplied exceedingly. 28 Jacob lived in the land of Egypt seventeen years; so the days of Jacob, the years of his life, were one hundred forty-seven years.

29 When the time of Israel's death drew near, he called his son Joseph and said to him, "If I have found favor with you, put your hand under my thigh and promise to deal loyally and truly with me. Do not bury me in Egypt. 30When I lie down with my ancestors, carry me out of Egypt and bury me in their burial place." He answered, "I will do as you have said." 31 And he said, "Swear to me"; and he swore to him. Then Israel bowed himself on the head of his bed.

Jacob Blesses Joseph's Sons
(Heb 11.21)

48 After this Joseph was told, "Your father is ill." So he took with him his two sons, Ma•nas'seh and Ē'phra•im. 2 When Jacob was told, "Your son Joseph has come to you," he a summoned his strength and sat up in bed. 3 And Jacob said to Joseph, "God Almighty b appeared to me at Luz in the land of Cā'naan, and he blessed me, 4 and said to me, 'I am going to make you fruitful and increase your numbers; I will make of you a company of peoples, and will give this land to your offspring after you for a perpetual holding.' 5 Therefore your two sons, who were born to you in the land of Egypt before I came to you in Egypt, are now mine; Ē'phra•im and Ma•nas'seh shall be mine, just as Reuben and Sim'ē•on are. 6 As for the offspring born to you after them, they shall be yours. They shall be recorded under the names of their brothers with regard to their inheritance. 7 For when I came from Pad'dan, Rachel, alas, died in the land of Cā'naan on the way, while there was

---

z Sam Gk Compare Vg: MT *He removed them to the cities*   a Heb *Israel*   b Traditional rendering of Heb *El Shaddai*

G
E
N

still some distance to go to Eph'rath; and I buried her there on the way to Eph'rath" (that is, Bethlehem).

8 When Israel saw Joseph's sons, he said, "Who are these?" 9 Joseph said to his father, "They are my sons, whom God has given me here." And he said, "Bring them to me, please, that I may bless them." 10 Now the eyes of Israel were dim with age, and he could not see well. So Joseph brought them near him; and he kissed them and embraced them. 11 Israel said to Joseph, "I did not expect to see your face; and here God has let me see your children also." 12 Then Joseph removed them from his father's knees,c and he bowed himself with his face to the earth. 13 Joseph took them both, E'phra·im in his right hand toward Israel's left, and Ma·nas'seh in his left hand toward Israel's right, and brought them near him. 14 But Israel stretched out his right hand and laid it on the head of E'phra·im, who was the younger, and his left hand on the head of Ma·nas'seh, crossing his hands, for Ma·nas'seh was the firstborn. 15 He blessed Joseph, and said,

"The God before whom my ancestors
      Abraham and Isaac walked,
the God who has been my shepherd all my life
      to this day,
16 the angel who has redeemed me from all
      harm, bless the boys;
and in them let my name be perpetuated, and
      the name of my ancestors Abraham
      and Isaac;
and let them grow into a multitude on the
      earth."

17 When Joseph saw that his father laid his right hand on the head of E'phra·im, it displeased him; so he took his father's hand, to remove it from E'phra·im's head to Ma·nas'seh's head. 18 Joseph said to his father, "Not so, my father! Since this one is the firstborn, put your right hand on his head." 19 But his father refused, and said, "I know, my son, I know; he also shall become a people, and he also shall be great. Nevertheless his younger brother shall be greater than he, and his offspring shall become a multitude of nations." 20 So he blessed them that day, saying,

"By youd Israel will invoke blessings,
      saying,
'God make youd like E'phra·im and like
      Ma·nas'seh.' "

So he put E'phra·im ahead of Ma·nas'seh. 21 Then Israel said to Joseph, "I am about to die, but God will be with you and will bring you again to the land of your ancestors. 22 I now give to you one portione more than to your brothers, the portione that I took from the hand of the Am'o·rites with my sword and with my bow."

Jacob's Last Words to His Sons

49 Then Jacob called his sons, and said: "Gather around, that I may tell you what will happen to you in days to come.

2 Assemble and hear, O sons of Jacob;
      listen to Israel your father.

3 Reuben, you are my firstborn,
      my might and the first fruits of my vigor,
      excelling in rank and excelling in power.
4 Unstable as water, you shall no longer excel
      because you went up onto your father's
            bed;
      then you defiled it—youf went up onto my
            couch!

5 Sim'e·on and Levi are brothers;
      weapons of violence are their swords.
6 May I never come into their council;
      may I not be joined to their company—
for in their anger they killed men,
      and at their whim they hamstrung oxen.
7 Cursed be their anger, for it is fierce,
      and their wrath, for it is cruel!
I will divide them in Jacob,
      and scatter them in Israel.

8 Judah, your brothers shall praise you;
      your hand shall be on the neck of your
            enemies;
      your father's sons shall bow down before
            you.
9 Judah is a lion's whelp;
      from the prey, my son, you have gone up.
He crouches down, he stretches out like a
            lion,
      like a lioness—who dares rouse him up?
10 The scepter shall not depart from Judah,
      nor the ruler's staff from between his feet,
until tribute comes to him;g
      and the obedience of the peoples is his.
11 Binding his foal to the vine
      and his donkey's colt to the choice vine,
he washes his garments in wine
      and his robe in the blood of grapes;
12 his eyes are darker than wine,
      and his teeth whiter than milk.

13 Zeb'u·lun shall settle at the shore of the sea;
      he shall be a haven for ships,
      and his border shall be at Si'don.

---

c Heb *from his knees*   d *you* here is singular in Heb
e Or *mountain slope* (Heb *shekem*, a play on the name of the
town and district of Shechem)   f Gk Syr Tg: Heb *he*   g Or
until Shiloh comes or *until he comes to Shiloh* or (with Syr)
until he comes to whom it belongs

14 Is'sa•char is a strong donkey,
    lying down between the sheepfolds;
15 he saw that a resting place was good,
    and that the land was pleasant;
so he bowed his shoulder to the
        burden,
    and became a slave at forced labor.

16 Dan shall judge his people
    as one of the tribes of Israel.
17 Dan shall be a snake by the roadside,
    a viper along the path,
that bites the horse's heels
    so that its rider falls backward.

18 I wait for your salvation, O LORD.

19 Gad shall be raided by raiders,
    but he shall raid at their heels.

20 Ash'er's[h] food shall be rich,
    and he shall provide royal delicacies.

21 Naph'ta•li is a doe let loose
    that bears lovely fawns.[i]

22 Joseph is a fruitful bough,
    a fruitful bough by a spring;
    his branches run over the wall.[j]
23 The archers fiercely attacked him;
    they shot at him and pressed him hard.
24 Yet his bow remained taut,
    and his arms[k] were made agile
by the hands of the Mighty One of Jacob,
    by the name of the Shepherd, the Rock of
        Israel,
25 by the God of your father, who will help you,
    by the Almighty[l] who will bless you
    with blessings of heaven above,
blessings of the deep that lies beneath,
    blessings of the breasts and of the womb.
26 The blessings of your father
    are stronger than the blessings of the
        eternal mountains,
    the bounties[m] of the everlasting hills;
    may they be on the head of Joseph,

---

h Gk Vg Syr: Heb *From Asher*   i Or *that gives beautiful
words*   j Meaning of Heb uncertain   k Heb *the arms of
his hands*   l Traditional rendering of Heb *Shaddai*   m Cn
Compare Gk: Heb *of my progenitors to the boundaries*

ASSEMBLE AND HEAR!

Genesis 49.1–2 is the first reading at Mass on the ninth day before Christmas. This is an important
day for Filipino Catholics because it marks the beginning of Simbang Gabi, or Dawn Worship.

On the nine days before Christmas, people gather to celebrate Mass in the dark of the
predawn—usually between four and five o'clock in the morning. Mass ends with chocolate and
buns and socializing. In fact, this is such a popular custom that even people who don't come to
Mass all year will make it for the nine Masses of Simbang Gabi! It is a special celebration of
thankfulness for the gift of their Catholic faith.

This Philippine tradition is an example of a Catholic custom called a novena. A novena is a
public or private prayer repeated nine times. It can be a prayer said every day for nine days, one
day a week for nine weeks, one day a month for nine months, or in any other pattern of nine.
Why not make up your own personal novena? Just think of a prayer in a form you find meaningful (journaling, singing, reading the Scriptures, or even praying silently), and repeat it once a day
for nine days or once a week for nine weeks. Happy praying!

▶ Gen 49.1–2

GEN

on the brow of him who was set apart from
his brothers.

27 Benjamin is a ravenous wolf,
    in the morning devouring the prey,
    and at evening dividing the spoil."

28 All these are the twelve tribes of Israel, and
this is what their father said to them when he
blessed them, blessing each one of them with a
suitable blessing.

Jacob's Death and Burial

29 Then he charged them, saying to them, "I
am about to be gathered to my people. Bury me
with my ancestors—in the cave in the field of
E´phron the Hit´tīte, 30 in the cave in the field at
Mach•pē´lah, near Mam´re, in the land of Cā´naan,
in the field that Abraham bought from E´phron the
Hit´tīte as a burial site. 31 There Abraham and his
wife Sarah were buried; there Isaac and his wife
Rebekah were buried; and there I buried Leah—
32 the field and the cave that is in it were purchased
from the Hit´tītes." 33 When Jacob ended his
charge to his sons, he drew up his feet into the
bed, breathed his last, and was gathered to his
people.

50 Then Joseph threw himself on his father's face and wept over him and
kissed him. 2 Joseph commanded the physicians in
his service to embalm his father. So the physicians
embalmed Israel; 3 they spent forty days in doing
this, for that is the time required for embalming.
And the Egyptians wept for him seventy days.

4 When the days of weeping for him were past,
Joseph addressed the household of Pharaoh, "If
now I have found favor with you, please speak to
Pharaoh as follows: 5 My father made me swear an
oath; he said, 'I am about to die. In the tomb that
I hewed out for myself in the land of Cā´naan,
there you shall bury me.' Now therefore let me go
up, so that I may bury my father; then I will return." 6 Pharaoh answered, "Go up, and bury your
father, as he made you swear to do."

7 So Joseph went up to bury his father. With him
went up all the servants of Pharaoh, the elders of his
household, and all the elders of the land of Egypt,
8 as well as all the household of Joseph, his brothers, and his father's household. Only their children,
their flocks, and their herds were left in the land of
Gō´shen. 9 Both chariots and charioteers went up
with him. It was a very great company. 10 When they
came to the threshing floor of Ā´tad, which is beyond the Jordan, they held there a very great and sorrowful lamentation; and he observed a time of
mourning for his father seven days. 11 When the
Cā´naan•īte inhabitants of the land saw the mourn-

ing on the threshing floor of Ă'tad, they said, "This is a grievous mourning on the part of the Egyptians." Therefore the place was named Ā'bel-miz'ra•im;[n] it is beyond the Jordan. 12 Thus his sons did for him as he had instructed them. 13 They carried him to the land of Cā'naan and buried him in the cave of the field at Mach•pē'lah, the field near Mam're, which Abraham bought as a burial site from Ē'phron the Hit'tīte. 14 After he had buried his father, Joseph returned to Egypt with his brothers and all who had gone up with him to bury his father.

Joseph Forgives His Brothers

15 Realizing that their father was dead, Joseph's brothers said, "What if Joseph still bears a grudge against us and pays us back in full for all the wrong that we did to him?" 16 So they approached[o] Joseph, saying, "Your father gave this instruction before he died, 17 'Say to Joseph: I beg you, forgive the crime of your brothers and the wrong they did in harming you.' Now therefore please forgive the crime of the servants of the God of your father." Joseph wept when they spoke to him. 18 Then his brothers also wept,[p] fell down before him, and said, "We are here as your slaves." 19 But Joseph said to them, "Do not be afraid! Am I in the place of God?

20 Even though you intended to do harm to me, God intended it for good, in order to preserve a numerous people, as he is doing today. 21 So have no fear; I myself will provide for you and your little ones." In this way he reassured them, speaking kindly to them.

Joseph's Last Days and Death
(Heb 11.22)

22 So Joseph remained in Egypt, he and his father's household; and Joseph lived one hundred ten years. 23 Joseph saw Ē'phra•im's children of the third generation; the children of Mā'chir son of Ma•nas'seh were also born on Joseph's knees.

24 Then Joseph said to his brothers, "I am about to die; but God will surely come to you, and bring you up out of this land to the land that he swore to Abraham, to Isaac, and to Jacob." 25 So Joseph made the Israelites swear, saying, "When God comes to you, you shall carry up my bones from here." 26 And Joseph died, being one hundred ten years old; he was embalmed and placed in a coffin in Egypt.

---

[n] That is *mourning* (or *meadow*) *of Egypt*   [o] Gk Syr: Heb *they commanded*   [p] Cn: Heb *also came*

The Book of Exodus

C lick! Chains snap shut around your ankles. Crack! The tip of a whip whistles past your head. Bang! A door shuts, leaving you in darkness. These are the sounds of slavery, and they come as a surprise at the beginning of the Book of Exodus. What happened after the happy ending in Genesis? Like an action-packed drama, Exodus tells a story of deceit and broken promises, and of how God's miraculous interventions delivered the Israelites from their slavery in Egypt.

At a Glance

- **Chapters 1–10.** Pharaoh's oppression, the call of Moses, the plagues
- **11.1—15.21.** the Passover, deliverance at the Red Sea
- **15.22—18.27.** the journey through the wilderness
- **19.1—35.3.** the Covenant at Mount Sinai, difficulty living the Covenant
- **35.4—40.38.** construction of the tabernacle

In-depth

The Book of Exodus is the story of Israel's liberation. Exodus literally means "departure," and this book's central story is of how God liberates the people from slavery in Egypt (an event called the Exodus). Its central character is Moses, who is chosen by God to become God's voice and the instrument of God's power. Exodus was written hundreds of years after these events, using oral traditions that described the origin of many of the Israelites' beliefs and religious rituals.

Exodus is divided into four main sections. The first two sections, chapters 1–18, begin with the Israelites enslaved in Egypt and prohibited from worshiping their God. Israel cries out to God, and God answers by sending Moses. When Pharaoh refuses to let the Israelites go, God sends ten devastating plagues, and Pharaoh finally gives in. Later, Pharaoh changes his mind and chases the Israelites, only to have his army destroyed after the Israelites' escape through the Red Sea. This section ends with the people wandering through the wilderness, sustained by food and water miraculously provided by God.

Sections three and four of Exodus, chapters 19–40, occur at Mount Sinai. There God enters into a covenant with all the people. God's part of the Sinai Covenant is to guarantee continued protection. Israel's part is to be faithful to God alone, a faithfulness marked by special laws (chapters 20–23) and special worship (chapters 24–31) that unite them as a people. Exodus ends with Israel still encamped at Mount Sinai, struggling to become a people of the Covenant.

The stories and laws in Exodus are at the heart of both Jewish and Christian belief in a God who saves, a God of freedom. You cannot fully appreciate the meaning of Jesus' life, death, and Resurrection without knowing these stories.

Quick Facts

Period Covered
sometime from 1500 to 1250 B.C.

Author
unknown author gathering oral traditions and stories from various tribal peoples

Themes
God liberates people from slavery and oppression. God sustains the Israelites in the wilderness. God forms a covenant marked by laws and rituals.

Exodus

14.21

1 These are the names of the sons of Israel who came to Egypt with Jacob, each with his household: ² Reuben, Sim'ē·on, Levi, and Judah, ³ Is'sa·char, Zeb'ū·lun, and Benjamin, ⁴ Dan and Naph'ta·lī, Gad and Ash'er. ⁵ The total number of people born to Jacob was seventy. Joseph was already in Egypt. ⁶ Then Joseph died, and all his brothers, and that whole generation. ⁷ But the Israelites were fruitful and prolific; they multiplied and grew exceedingly strong, so that the land was filled with them.

The Israelites Are Oppressed

8 Now a new king arose over Egypt, who did not know Joseph. ⁹ He said to his people, "Look, the Israelite people are more numerous and more powerful than we. ¹⁰ Come, let us deal shrewdly with them, or they will increase and, in the event of war, join our enemies and fight against us and escape from the land." ¹¹ Therefore they set taskmasters over them to oppress them with forced labor. They built supply cities, Pī'thom and Ram'e·sēs, for Pharaoh. ¹² But the more they were oppressed, the more they multiplied and spread, so that the Egyptians came to dread the Israelites. ¹³ The Egyptians became ruthless in imposing tasks on the Israelites, ¹⁴ and made their lives bitter with hard service in mortar and brick and in every kind of field labor. They were ruthless in all the tasks that they imposed on them.

15 The king of Egypt said to the Hebrew midwives, one of whom was named Shiph'rah and the other Pū'ah, ¹⁶ "When you act as midwives to the Hebrew women, and see them on the birthstool, if it is a boy, kill him; but if it is a girl, she shall live." ¹⁷ But the midwives feared God; they did not do as the king of Egypt commanded them, but they let the boys live. ¹⁸ So the king of Egypt summoned the midwives and said to them, "Why have you done this, and allowed the boys to live?" ¹⁹ The midwives said to Pharaoh, "Because the Hebrew women are not like the Egyptian women; for they are vigorous and give birth before the midwife comes to them." ²⁰ So God dealt well with the midwives; and the people multiplied and became very strong. ²¹ And because the midwives feared God, he gave them families. ²² Then Pharaoh commanded all his people, "Every boy that is born to the Hebrews*a* you shall throw into the Nile, but you shall let every girl live."

Birth and Youth of Moses
(Heb 11.23)

2 Now a man from the house of Levi went and married a Lē'vīte woman. ² The woman conceived and bore a son; and when she saw that he was a fine baby, she hid him three months. ³ When she could hide him no longer she got a papyrus basket for him, and plastered it with bitumen and pitch; she put the child in it and placed it among the reeds on the bank of the river. ⁴ His sister stood at a distance, to see what would happen to him.

---

a Sam Gk Tg: Heb lacks *to the Hebrews*

Saving Lives

In the story of the birth of Moses, Pharaoh ordered the Egyptian midwives to kill all the male Israelite babies at birth. The midwives recognized such killing as an atrocity and refused to obey Pharaoh. Their actions might be considered civil disobedience against unjust laws.

Some people claim that the right to have an abortion is a just law. Aren't they right? Consider this incident: At a youth group gathering, abortion was discussed, and a video was shown on how abortions are performed. One young man shared that although he did not believe in abortion, he used to believe exceptions could be made, such as in the case of rape or incest. After watching the video, he said that he no longer believed that such exceptions could be morally justified. A young woman said that the video had convinced her that abortion is in the same moral category as serial murder. These young people, like the midwives in Exodus, recognized that all human life is sacred.

▶ Ex 1.15–22

5 The daughter of Pharaoh came down to bathe at the river, while her attendants walked beside the river. She saw the basket among the reeds and sent her maid to bring it. 6 When she opened it, she saw the child. He was crying, and she took pity on him. "This must be one of the Hebrews' children," she said. 7 Then his sister said to Pharaoh's daughter, "Shall I go and get you a nurse from the Hebrew women to nurse the child for you?" 8 Pharaoh's daughter said to her, "Yes." So the girl went and called the child's mother. 9 Pharaoh's daughter said to her, "Take this child and nurse it for me, and I will give you your wages." So the woman took the child and nursed it. 10 When the child grew up, she brought him to Pharaoh's daughter, and she took him as her son. She named him Moses,[b] "because," she said, "I drew him out[c] of the water."

Moses Flees to Midian
(Heb 11.24–25)

11 One day, after Moses had grown up, he went out to his people and saw their forced labor. He saw

---

b Heb *Mosheh*   c Heb *mashah*

Introducing ▶ MOSES

Moses is, without doubt, the most important character in the Pentateuch, if not the entire Old Testament. Struggling to find language to describe his greatness, Deut 34.10 says, "Never since has there arisen a prophet in Israel like Moses, whom the LORD knew face to face." Born to a couple from the tribe of Levi and raised as an Egyptian by the Pharaoh's daughter, Moses was perfectly suited to negotiate Israel's freedom from slavery in Egypt. In event after event, the author of Exodus shows us Moses' wonder-working power, his prophetic skill, and his intimacy with God.

Despite all of Moses' great accomplishments, he never loses his humanness. He lacks confidence in his ability to speak (Ex 4.10); he is angry and frustrated with his people (17.4), and he bargains with God out of love for his people (32.11–14). Moses, noble but also knowing sadness, is elegantly portrayed in the passage where he dies within sight of the Promised Land (Deuteronomy, chapter 34). These qualities paint a picture of someone whose perseverance and trust allowed God to work through him.

A prophet is literally God's voice, and Moses was indeed God's voice, which shaped Israel to be a people of the Covenant. All other leaders and figures in the Old Testament are compared with Moses. In the New Testament, even Jesus is compared with Moses.

Cultural Connections

HOLY GROUND

E
X

In many Asian cultures, before people enter a home, they remove their shoes. People do this before entering a mosque too. Removing one's shoes is a common sign of respect. Moses is commanded to remove his sandals in Ex 3.5. Why? Because he is standing on holy ground. Why is the ground holy? Because God is present.

Moses is awestruck and humbled by his experience of God's presence. In today's multimedia culture, we are rarely awed by anything. Even the burning bush would be just another special effect. How can we regain our sense of awe at God's majesty? Some people experience it in nature, looking at a star-filled sky or the waves rolling in on the ocean. Others experience it in getting to know other people deeply. Still others find it in the amazing patterns that science reveals. The one common element to experiencing awe seems to be the ability to slow down, look closely, and appreciate what we discover.

So slow down, find your own holy ground, take your shoes off, and let God fill you with awe!

▶ Ex 3.1–6

---

an Egyptian beating a Hebrew, one of his kinsfolk. 12 He looked this way and that, and seeing no one he killed the Egyptian and hid him in the sand. 13 When he went out the next day, he saw two Hebrews fighting; and he said to the one who was in the wrong, "Why do you strike your fellow Hebrew?" 14 He answered, "Who made you a ruler and judge over us? Do you mean to kill me as you killed the Egyptian?" Then Moses was afraid and thought, "Surely the thing is known." 15 When Pharaoh heard of it, he sought to kill Moses.

But Moses fled from Pharaoh. He settled in the land of Mid′i·an, and sat down by a well. 16 The priest of Mid′i·an had seven daughters. They came to draw water, and filled the troughs to water their father's flock. 17 But some shepherds came and drove them away. Moses got up and came to their defense and watered their flock. 18 When they returned to their father Reü′el, he said, "How is it that you have come back so soon today?" 19 They said, "An Egyptian helped us against the shepherds; he even drew water for us and watered the flock." 20 He said to his daughters, "Where is he? Why did you leave the man? Invite him to break bread." 21 Moses agreed to stay with the man, and he gave Moses his daughter Zip•pō′rah in marriage. 22 She bore a son, and he named him Ger′shom; for he said, "I have been an alien[d] residing in a foreign land."

23 After a long time the king of Egypt died. The Israelites groaned under their slavery, and cried out. Out of the slavery their cry for help rose up to God. 24 God heard their groaning, and God remembered his covenant with Abraham, Isaac, and Jacob. 25 God looked upon the Israelites, and God took notice of them.

Moses at the Burning Bush
(Ex 6.2—7.7; 11.1–4; 12.35–36)

3 Moses was keeping the flock of his father-in-law Jeth′rō, the priest of Mid′i·an; he led his flock beyond the wilderness, and came to Hō′reb, the mountain of God. 2 There the angel of the LORD appeared to him in a flame of fire out of a bush; he looked, and the bush was blazing, yet it was not consumed. 3 Then Moses said, "I must turn aside and look at this great sight, and see why the bush is not burned up." 4 When the LORD saw that he had turned aside to see, God called to him out of the bush, "Moses, Moses!" And he said, "Here I am." 5 Then he said, "Come no closer! Remove the sandals from your feet, for the place on which you are standing is holy ground." 6 He said further, "I am the God of your father, the God of Abraham, the God of Isaac, and the God of Jacob." And Moses hid his face, for he was afraid to look at God.

7 Then the LORD said, "I have observed the

---

d Heb ger

EX

THE NAME OF GOD

Many Native American peoples, such as the Lakota and the Sioux, have several names for God. Wakan-Tanka and Tun-ka-shi-la are still commonly used today. These words for God are often translated as Great Spirit.

This is a good translation because Wakan is a word that brings together the concepts of mystery, sacredness, holiness, awe, and inspiration. Tanka describes something that is great.

Tun-ka-shi-la is often used the same way as Wakan-Tanka, but its meaning is slightly different. Tun-ka-shi-la is often translated as Grandfather or Great Grandfather, but it means the "one who is the oldest, so old that nothing or no one is older." Tun-ka-shi-la is a name that reflects the Great Spirit as the source of all things, the one who has existed from the beginning.

▶ Ex 3.13–15

---

misery of my people who are in Egypt; I have heard their cry on account of their taskmasters. Indeed, I know their sufferings, 8 and I have come down to deliver them from the Egyptians, and to bring them up out of that land to a good and broad land, a land flowing with milk and honey, to the country of the Cā′naan•ites, the Hit′tītes, the Am′o•rītes, the Per′iz•zītes, the Hī′vītes, and the Jeb′ū•sītes. 9 The cry of the Israelites has now come to me; I have also seen how the Egyptians oppress them. 10 So come, I will send you to Pharaoh to bring my people, the Israelites, out of Egypt." 11 But Moses said to God, "Who am I that I should go to Pharaoh, and bring the Israelites out of Egypt?" 12 He said, "I will be with you; and this shall be the sign for you that it is I who sent you: when you have brought the people out of Egypt, you shall worship God on this mountain."

The Divine Name Revealed

13 But Moses said to God, "If I come to the Israelites and say to them, 'The God of your ancestors has sent me to you,' and they ask me, 'What is his name?' what shall I say to them?" 14 God said to Moses, "I AM WHO I AM."*e* He said further, "Thus you shall say to the Israelites, 'I AM has sent me to you.' " 15 God also said to Moses, "Thus you shall say to the Israelites, 'The LORD,*f* the God of your ancestors, the God of Abraham, the God of Isaac, and the God of Jacob, has sent me to you':

---

e Or I AM WHAT I AM or I WILL BE WHAT I WILL BE   *f* The word "LORD" when spelled with capital letters stands for the divine name, YHWH, which is here connected with the verb hayah, "to be"

---

did you KNOW?
God's Mysterious Name

"I am who am"—one possible translation of Yahweh from Ex 3.14—seems more like a definition than a name. Some scholars have suggested Yahweh might be better translated "he causes to be what exists." In any case, the four Hebrew letters YHWH (or Yahweh in English) are difficult to translate. Over the centuries, the Jewish people stopped pronouncing the four letters out of reverence for God and replaced them with the word Adonai, meaning "my Lord." Most English translations of the Bible respect this long-standing tradition, translating the original YHWH as LORD. This mysterious name of God reminds us that no name or symbol can fully express who God is.

▶ Ex 3.13–15

This is my name forever,
and this my title for all generations.

16 Go and assemble the elders of Israel, and say to them, 'The LORD, the God of your ancestors, the God of Abraham, of Isaac, and of Jacob, has appeared to me, saying: I have given heed to you and to what has been done to you in Egypt. 17 I declare that I will bring you up out of the misery of Egypt, to the land of the Cā′naan•ites, the Hit′tītes, the Am′o•rītes, the Per′iz•zītes, the Hi′vītes, and the Jeb′ū•sītes, a land flowing with milk and honey.' 18 They will listen to your voice; and you and the elders of Israel shall go to the king of Egypt and say to him, 'The LORD, the God of the Hebrews, has met with us; let us now go a three days' journey into the wilderness, so that we may sacrifice to the LORD our God.' 19 I know, however, that the king of Egypt will not let you go unless compelled by a mighty hand.ᵍ 20 So I will stretch out my hand and strike Egypt with all my wonders that I will perform in it; after that he will let you go. 21 I will bring this people into such favor with the Egyptians that, when you go, you will not go empty-handed; 22 each woman shall ask her neighbor and any woman living in the neighbor's house for jewelry of silver and of gold, and clothing, and you shall put them on your sons

and on your daughters; and so you shall plunder the Egyptians."

Moses' Miraculous Power

4 Then Moses answered, "But suppose they do not believe me or listen to me, but say, 'The LORD did not appear to you.'" 2 The LORD said to him, "What is that in your hand?" He said, "A staff." 3 And he said, "Throw it on the ground." So he threw the staff on the ground, and it became a snake; and Moses drew back from it. 4 Then the LORD said to Moses, "Reach out your hand, and seize it by the tail"—so he reached out his hand and grasped it, and it became a staff in his hand— 5 "so that they may believe that the LORD, the God of their ancestors, the God of Abraham, the God of Isaac, and the God of Jacob, has appeared to you."

6 Again, the LORD said to him, "Put your hand inside your cloak." He put his hand into his cloak; and when he took it out, his hand was leprous,ʰ as white as snow. 7 Then God said, "Put your hand back into your cloak"—so he put his hand back into his cloak, and when he took it out, it was

---

ᵍ Gk Vg: Heb *no, not by a mighty hand*   ʰ A term for several skin diseases; precise meaning uncertain

GOD SENDS PROPHETS TO LIBERATE HIS PEOPLE!

God responded to the cry of his people, choosing Moses as a prophet and commissioning him to lead the Israelites to freedom. Despite Moses' first doubts, with God's assistance, Moses became an effective and powerful leader. God would not let Moses' excuses stand in the way of God's mission of liberation.

Christians share in Jesus Christ's prophetic work as well. We too need to speak out against injustice and help the victims of oppression. Like the prophets before us, we can only succeed with God's help.

In our time, great spiritual leaders have risen up to lead people to freedom: Mohandas Gandhi, Martin Luther King Jr., Dorothy Day, Archbishop Oscar Romero, and Cesar Chavez are just a few. As in the case of Moses, God inspired these leaders to see their people experiencing injustice and to seek to liberate them from oppressive powers. You can be sure that these people also had their doubts and relied on God for their strength and hope.

■ Are you aware of any group that is being oppressed today? How might God be calling you to help?
■ Ask God for wisdom, strength, and help in your mission.

▶ Ex 4.1–17

restored like the rest of his body— ⁸ "If they will not believe you or heed the first sign, they may believe the second sign. ⁹ If they will not believe even these two signs or heed you, you shall take some water from the Nile and pour it on the dry ground; and the water that you shall take from the Nile will become blood on the dry ground."

10 But Moses said to the LORD, "O my Lord, I have never been eloquent, neither in the past nor even now that you have spoken to your servant; but I am slow of speech and slow of tongue." ¹¹ Then the LORD said to him, "Who gives speech to mortals? Who makes them mute or deaf, seeing or blind? Is it not I, the LORD? ¹² Now go, and I will be with your mouth and teach you what you are to speak." ¹³ But he said, "O my Lord, please send someone else." ¹⁴ Then the anger of the LORD was kindled against Moses and he said, "What of your brother Aaron the Lē'vīte? I know that he can speak fluently; even now he is coming out to meet you, and when he sees you his heart will be glad. ¹⁵ You shall speak to him and put the words in his mouth; and I will be with your mouth and with his mouth, and will teach you what you shall do. ¹⁶ He indeed shall speak for you to the people; he shall serve as a mouth for you, and you shall serve as God for him. ¹⁷ Take in your hand this staff, with which you shall perform the signs."

Moses Returns to Egypt

18 Moses went back to his father-in-law Jeth'rō and said to him, "Please let me go back to my kindred in Egypt and see whether they are still living." And Jeth'rō said to Moses, "Go in peace." ¹⁹ The LORD said to Moses in Mid'i•an, "Go back to Egypt; for all those who were seeking your life are dead." ²⁰ So Moses took his wife and his sons, put them on a donkey, and went back to the land of Egypt; and Moses carried the staff of God in his hand.

21 And the LORD said to Moses, "When you go back to Egypt, see that you perform before Pharaoh all the wonders that I have put in your power; but I will harden his heart, so that he will not let the people go. ²² Then you shall say to Pharaoh, 'Thus says the LORD: Israel is my firstborn son. ²³ I said to you, "Let my son go that he may worship me." But you refused to let him go; now I will kill your firstborn son.' "

24 On the way, at a place where they spent the night, the LORD met him and tried to kill him. ²⁵ But Zip•pō'rah took a flint and cut off her son's foreskin, and touched Moses'ⁱ feet with it, and said, "Truly you are a bridegroom of blood to me!" ²⁶ So he let him alone. It was then she said, "A bridegroom of blood by circumcision."

27 The LORD said to Aaron, "Go into the wilderness to meet Moses." So he went; and he met him at the mountain of God and kissed him. ²⁸ Moses told Aaron all the words of the LORD with which he had sent him, and all the signs with which he had charged him. ²⁹ Then Moses and Aaron went and assembled all the elders of the Israelites. ³⁰ Aaron spoke all the words that the LORD had spoken to Moses, and performed the signs in the sight of the people. ³¹ The people believed; and when they heard that the LORD had given heed to the Israelites and that he had seen their misery, they bowed down and worshiped.

Bricks without Straw

5 Afterward Moses and Aaron went to Pharaoh and said, "Thus says the LORD, the God of Israel, 'Let my people go, so that they may celebrate a festival to me in the wilderness.' " ² But Pharaoh said, "Who is the LORD, that I should heed him and let Israel go? I do not know the LORD, and I will not let Israel go." ³ Then they said, "The God of the Hebrews has revealed himself to us; let us go a three days' journey into the wilderness to sacrifice to the LORD our God, or he will fall upon us with pestilence or sword." ⁴ But the king of Egypt said to them, "Moses and Aaron, why are you taking the people away from their work? Get to your labors!" ⁵ Pharaoh continued, "Now they are more numerous than the people of the landʲ and yet you want them to stop working!" ⁶ That same day Pharaoh commanded the taskmasters of the people, as well as their supervisors, ⁷ "You shall no longer give the people straw to make bricks, as before; let them go and gather straw for themselves. ⁸ But you shall require of them the same quantity of bricks as they have made previously; do not diminish it, for they are lazy; that is why they cry, 'Let us go and offer sacrifice to our God.' ⁹ Let heavier work be laid on them; then they will labor at it and pay no attention to deceptive words."

10 So the taskmasters and the supervisors of the people went out and said to the people, "Thus says Pharaoh, 'I will not give you straw. ¹¹ Go and get straw yourselves, wherever you can find it; but your work will not be lessened in the least.' " ¹² So the people scattered throughout the land of Egypt, to gather stubble for straw. ¹³ The taskmasters were urgent, saying, "Complete your work, the same daily assignment as when you were given straw." ¹⁴ And the supervisors of the Israelites, whom Pharaoh's taskmasters had set over them, were beaten, and were asked, "Why did you not finish the required quantity of bricks yesterday and today, as you did before?"

15 Then the Israelite supervisors came to Pharaoh and cried, "Why do you treat your servants like

---

ⁱ Heb *his*   ʲ Sam: Heb *The people of the land are now many* this? 16 No straw is given to your servants, yet they say to us, 'Make bricks!' Look how your servants are beaten! You are unjust to your own people."[k] 17 He said, "You are lazy, lazy; that is why you say, 'Let us go and sacrifice to the LORD.' 18 Go now, and work; for no straw shall be given you, but you shall still deliver the same number of bricks." 19 The Israelite supervisors saw that they were in trouble when they were told, "You shall not lessen your daily number of bricks." 20 As they left Pharaoh, they came upon Moses and Aaron who were waiting to meet them. 21 They said to them, "The LORD look upon you and judge! You have brought us into bad odor with Pharaoh and his officials, and have put a sword in their hand to kill us."

22 Then Moses turned again to the LORD and said, "O LORD, why have you mistreated this people? Why did you ever send me? 23 Since I first came to Pharaoh to speak in your name, he has mistreated this people, and you have done nothing at all to deliver your people."

Israel's Deliverance Assured
(Ex 3.1—4.17)

6 Then the LORD said to Moses, "Now you shall see what I will do to Pharaoh: Indeed, by a mighty hand he will let them go; by a mighty hand he will drive them out of his land."

2 God also spoke to Moses and said to him: "I am the LORD. 3 I appeared to Abraham, Isaac, and Jacob as God Almighty,[l] but by my name 'The LORD'[m] I did not make myself known to them. 4 I also established my covenant with them, to give them the land of Cā'naan, the land in which they resided as aliens. 5 I have also heard the groaning of the Israelites whom the Egyptians are holding as slaves, and I have remembered my covenant. 6 Say therefore to the Israelites, 'I am the LORD, and I will free you from the burdens of the Egyptians and deliver you from slavery to them. I will redeem you with an outstretched arm and with mighty acts of judgment. 7 I will take you as my people, and I will be your God. You shall know that I am the LORD your God, who has freed you from the burdens of the Egyptians. 8 I will bring you into the land that I swore to give to Abraham, Isaac, and Jacob; I will give it to you for a possession. I am the LORD.' " 9 Moses told this to the Israelites; but they would not listen to Moses, because of their broken spirit and their cruel slavery.

10 Then the LORD spoke to Moses, 11 "Go and tell Pharaoh king of Egypt to let the Israelites go out of his land." 12 But Moses spoke to the LORD, "The Israelites have not listened to me; how then shall Pharaoh listen to me, poor speaker that I am?"[n] 13 Thus the LORD spoke to Moses and Aaron, and gave them orders regarding the Israelites and Phar-

PRAY IT?
Why Me?

Read Ex 5.22–23. Can you imagine how Moses must have felt? He did what God told him to do, and things only got worse for the Israelites. But Moses was still able to talk to God, even if only to say, "Why did you send me?"

Thomas Merton, a famous Trappist monk and spiritual writer, knew that Christians sometimes feel like Moses did:

> The Christian
> must have the courage
> to follow Christ.
> The Christian
> who is risen in Christ
> must dare
> to be like Christ:
> he must dare
> to follow conscience
> even in unpopular causes.
> He must, if necessary,
> be able to disagree with the majority
> and make decisions
> that he knows
> to be according to the Gospel
> and teaching of Christ,
> even when others
> do not understand
> why he is acting this way.
> (He Is Risen, p. 22)

The next time you are feeling a little like Moses and wondering, Why me? try this prayer:

Faithful God, help me to trust in you during times of disappointment and disillusion. I want to believe you are working in ways I cannot see. Please help my disbelief, for I know that you will honor my best efforts and make things come out right in the end. Amen.

▶ Ex 5.22–23

aoh king of Egypt, charging them to free the Israelites from the land of Egypt.

---

k Gk Compare Syr Vg: Heb *beaten, and the sin of your people*
l Traditional rendering of Heb *El Shaddai* m Heb *YHWH*; see note at 3.15 n Heb *me? I am uncircumcised of lips*

EX

PRAY IT!
You Promised, God

The Israelite people had been slaves for so long, they were discouraged and did not believe Moses' liberating message in Ex 6.1–9. Moses probably sounded crazy to them. The writer of Exodus reminds us of God's faithfulness to God's promises and that God's plans cannot be stopped by human weakness. We too may find it hard to believe in God's power in our life when we feel burdened and oppressed, especially over a long time.

In your prayer, reflect or journal on the following questions and suggestion:

- When do you find it hard to believe in God's promises?
- What people do you know who find it hard to accept God's power in their life?
- What barriers are keeping them from accepting God?
- Make up your own prayer expressing your desire to count on God's promises.

▶ Ex 6.1–9

The Genealogy of Moses and Aaron
(Gen 46.8–27)

14 The following are the heads of their ancestral houses: the sons of Reuben, the firstborn of Israel: Hă′noch, Pal′lū, Hez′ron, and Car′mī; these are the families of Reuben. 15 The sons of Sim′ē•on: Je•mū′el, Jā′min, Ō′had, Jā′chin, Zō′har, and Shā′ūl,ᵒ the son of a Cā′naan•ite woman; these are the families of Sim′ē•on. 16 The following are the names of the sons of Levi according to their genealogies: Ger′shon,ᵖ Kō′hath, and Me•rar′ī, and the length of Levi's life was one hundred thirty-seven years. 17 The sons of Ger′shon:ᵖ Lib′nī and Shim′ē•ī, by their families. 18 The sons of Kō′hath: Am′ram, Iz′har, Hĕ′bron, and Uz′zi•el, and the length of Kō′hath's life was one hundred thirty three years. 19 The sons of Me•rar′ī: Mah′lī and Mū′shī. These are the families of the Lē′vītes according to their genealogies. 20 Am′ram married Joch′e•bed his father's sister and she bore him Aaron and Moses, and the length of Am′ram's life was one hundred thirty-seven years. 21 The sons of Iz′har: Kō′rah, Nĕ′pheg, and Zich′rī. 22 The sons of Uz′zi•el: Mish′a•el, El′za•phan, and Sith′rī. 23 Aaron married

E•lish′e•ba, daughter of Am•min′a•dab and sister of Nah′shon, and she bore him Nā′dab, A•bī′hū, El•ē•ā′zar, and Ith′a•mar. 24 The sons of Kō′rah: As′sir, El•kā′nah, and A•bī′a•saph; these are the families of the Kō′ra•hītes. 25 Aaron's son El•ē•ā′zar married one of the daughters of Pū′ti•el, and she bore him Phin′e•has. These are the heads of the ancestral houses of the Lē′vītes by their families.

26 It was this same Aaron and Moses to whom the LORD said, "Bring the Israelites out of the land of Egypt, company by company." 27 It was they who spoke to Pharaoh king of Egypt to bring the Israelites out of Egypt, the same Moses and Aaron.

Moses and Aaron Obey God's Commands

28 On the day when the LORD spoke to Moses in the land of Egypt, 29 he said to him, "I am the LORD; tell Pharaoh king of Egypt all that I am speaking to you." 30 But Moses said in the LORD's presence, "Since I am a poor speaker,�q why would Pharaoh listen to me?"

7 The LORD said to Moses, "See, I have made you like God to Pharaoh, and your brother Aaron shall be your prophet. 2 You shall speak all that I command you, and your brother Aaron shall tell Pharaoh to let the Israelites go out of his land. 3 But I will harden Pharaoh's heart, and I will multiply my signs and wonders in the land of Egypt. 4 When Pharaoh does not listen to you, I will lay my hand upon Egypt and bring my people the Israelites, company by company, out of the land of Egypt by great acts of judgment. 5 The Egyptians shall know that I am the LORD, when I stretch out my hand against Egypt and bring the Israelites out from among them." 6 Moses and Aaron did so; they did just as the LORD commanded them. 7 Moses was eighty years old and Aaron eighty-three when they spoke to Pharaoh.

Aaron's Miraculous Rod
(Ex 4.1–5)

8 The LORD said to Moses and Aaron, 9 "When Pharaoh says to you, 'Perform a wonder,' then you shall say to Aaron, 'Take your staff and throw it down before Pharaoh, and it will become a snake.'" 10 So Moses and Aaron went to Pharaoh and did as the LORD had commanded; Aaron threw down his staff before Pharaoh and his officials, and it became a snake. 11 Then Pharaoh summoned the wise men and the sorcerers; and they also, the magicians of Egypt, did the same by their secret arts. 12 Each one threw down his staff, and they became snakes; but Aaron's staff swallowed up theirs. 13 Still Pharaoh's heart was hardened, and he would not listen to them, as the LORD had said.

ᵒ Or Saul　ᵖ Also spelled Gershom; see 2.22　q Heb am uncircumcised of lips; see 6.12

did you KNOW?

Plagues and the Crossing of the Red Sea

The writer of Exodus combines several versions of what happened in describing the ten plagues and the crossing of the Red Sea. Like in a fine tapestry, the different strands are carefully woven together to produce a suspenseful story. When Pharaoh refuses to let the Israelites go, God sends ten plagues to convince Pharaoh to cooperate. The first nine plagues are exaggerations of naturally occurring events. For example, Exodus says that the first plague is the water of the Nile turning to blood. At times, silt and microbes pollute and redden the Nile, making the water undrinkable. The Israelite people see God at work in the timing of these natural events.

Finally, God must resort to drastic measures. For the tenth plague, God sends the angel of death to kill the first-born children of the Egyptians. Moses has the Israelites mark their doorposts with the blood of a lamb so that the angel of death "passes over" their homes. Pharaoh is now eager to get rid of the Israelites and releases them from service. They gladly begin their journey to God's Promised Land.

After the Israelites leave, Pharaoh regrets his decision and sends his army after them. As the Egyptians close in, the Israelites seem to be trapped at the marshlands by the Red Sea (see map 2, "The Exodus from Egypt"). Although the prose version of this situation in Exodus, chapter 14, and the poetic version in chapter 15 differ in many details, both stress that the Israelites are able to pass through a section of wetlands that was made nearly dry by a strong east wind. The chariot wheels of the Egyptians get stuck in the mud, and as the water returns, they drown. Again, it is the timing of God's help that enables the miraculous escape. God hears God's people and sets them free!

▶ Ex 7.1—14.31

The First Plague: Water Turned to Blood

14 Then the LORD said to Moses, "Pharaoh's heart is hardened; he refuses to let the people go. 15 Go to Pharaoh in the morning, as he is going out to the water; stand by at the river bank to meet him, and take in your hand the staff that was turned into a snake. 16 Say to him, 'The LORD, the God of the Hebrews, sent me to you to say, "Let my people go, so that they may worship me in the wilderness." But until now you have not listened. 17 Thus says the LORD, "By this you shall know that I am the LORD." See, with the staff that is in my hand I will strike the water that is in the Nile, and it shall be turned to blood. 18 The fish in the river shall die, the river itself shall stink, and the Egyptians shall be unable to drink water from the Nile.' " 19 The LORD said to Moses, "Say to Aaron, 'Take your staff and stretch out your hand over the waters of Egypt—over its rivers, its canals, and its ponds, and all its pools of water—so that they may become blood; and there shall be blood throughout the whole land of Egypt, even in vessels of wood and in vessels of stone.' "

20 Moses and Aaron did just as the LORD commanded. In the sight of Pharaoh and of his officials he lifted up the staff and struck the water in the river, and all the water in the river was turned into blood, 21 and the fish in the river died. The river stank so that the Egyptians could not drink its water, and there was blood throughout the whole land of Egypt. 22 But the magicians of Egypt did the same by their secret arts; so Pharaoh's heart remained hardened, and he would not listen to them, as the LORD had said. 23 Pharaoh turned and went into his house, and he did not take even this to heart. 24 And all the Egyptians had to dig along the Nile for water to drink, for they could not drink the water of the river.

25 Seven days passed after the LORD had struck the Nile.

The Second Plague: Frogs

8 ʳThen the LORD said to Moses, "Go to Pharaoh and say to him, 'Thus says the LORD: Let my people go, so that they may worship me. 2 If you refuse to let them go, I will plague your whole country with frogs. 3 The river shall swarm with frogs; they shall come up into your palace, into your bedchamber and your bed, and into the houses of your officials and of your people,ˢ and into your ovens and your kneading bowls. 4 The frogs shall come up on you and on your people and on all your officials.' " 5ᵗ And the LORD said to Moses, "Say to Aaron, 'Stretch out your hand with your staff over the rivers, the canals, and the pools,

---

ʳ Ch 7.26 in Heb   ˢ Gk: Heb upon your people   ᵗ Ch 8.1 in Heb

and make frogs come up on the land of Egypt.' "
6 So Aaron stretched out his hand over the waters
of Egypt; and the frogs came up and covered the
land of Egypt. 7 But the magicians did the same by
their secret arts, and brought frogs up on the land
of Egypt.

8 Then Pharaoh called Moses and Aaron, and
said, "Pray to the LORD to take away the frogs from
me and my people, and I will let the people go to
sacrifice to the LORD." 9 Moses said to Pharaoh,
"Kindly tell me when I am to pray for you and for
your officials and for your people, that the frogs
may be removed from you and your houses and be
left only in the Nile." 10 And he said, "Tomorrow."
Moses said, "As you say! So that you may know that
there is no one like the LORD our God, 11 the frogs
shall leave you and your houses and your officials
and your people; they shall be left only in the Nile."
12 Then Moses and Aaron went out from Pharaoh;
and Moses cried out to the LORD concerning the
frogs that he had brought upon Pharaoh.u 13 And
the LORD did as Moses requested: the frogs died in
the houses, the courtyards, and the fields. 14 And
they gathered them together in heaps, and the land
stank. 15 But when Pharaoh saw that there was a
respite, he hardened his heart, and would not listen
to them, just as the LORD had said.

The Third Plague: Gnats

16 Then the LORD said to Moses, "Say to Aaron,
'Stretch out your staff and strike the dust of the
earth, so that it may become gnats throughout the
whole land of Egypt.' " 17 And they did so; Aaron
stretched out his hand with his staff and struck the
dust of the earth, and gnats came on humans and
animals alike; all the dust of the earth turned into
gnats throughout the whole land of Egypt. 18 The
magicians tried to produce gnats by their secret arts,
but they could not. There were gnats on both humans and animals. 19 And the magicians said to
Pharaoh, "This is the finger of God!" But Pharaoh's
heart was hardened, and he would not listen to
them, just as the LORD had said.

The Fourth Plague: Flies

20 Then the LORD said to Moses, "Rise early in
the morning and present yourself before Pharaoh,
as he goes out to the water, and say to him, 'Thus
says the LORD: Let my people go, so that they may
worship me. 21 For if you will not let my people go,
I will send swarms of flies on you, your officials,
and your people, and into your houses; and the
houses of the Egyptians shall be filled with swarms
of flies; so also the land where they live. 22 But on
that day I will set apart the land of Gō'shen, where
my people live, so that no swarms of flies shall be
there, that you may know that I the LORD am in this

land. 23 Thus I will make a distinctionv between my
people and your people. This sign shall appear tomorrow.' " 24 The LORD did so, and great swarms of
flies came into the house of Pharaoh and into his
officials' houses; in all of Egypt the land was ruined
because of the flies.

25 Then Pharaoh summoned Moses and Aaron,
and said, "Go, sacrifice to your God within the
land." 26 But Moses said, "It would not be right to
do so; for the sacrifices that we offer to the LORD our
God are offensive to the Egyptians. If we offer in the
sight of the Egyptians sacrifices that are offensive to
them, will they not stone us? 27 We must go a three
days' journey into the wilderness and sacrifice to the
LORD our God as he commands us." 28 So Pharaoh
said, "I will let you go to sacrifice to the LORD your
God in the wilderness, provided you do not go very
far away. Pray for me." 29 Then Moses said, "As
soon as I leave you, I will pray to the LORD that the
swarms of flies may depart tomorrow from Pharaoh, from his officials, and from his people; only
do not let Pharaoh again deal falsely by not letting
the people go to sacrifice to the LORD."

30 So Moses went out from Pharaoh and
prayed to the LORD. 31 And the LORD did as Moses
asked: he removed the swarms of flies from Pharaoh, from his officials, and from his people; not
one remained. 32 But Pharaoh hardened his heart
this time also, and would not let the people go.

The Fifth Plague: Livestock Diseased

9 Then the LORD said to Moses, "Go to Pharaoh, and say to him, 'Thus says the LORD, the
God of the Hebrews: Let my people go, so that they
may worship me. 2 For if you refuse to let them go
and still hold them, 3 the hand of the LORD will
strike with a deadly pestilence your livestock in the
field: the horses, the donkeys, the camels, the herds,
and the flocks. 4 But the LORD will make a distinction between the livestock of Israel and the livestock of Egypt, so that nothing shall die of all that
belongs to the Israelites.' " 5 The LORD set a time,
saying, "Tomorrow the LORD will do this thing in
the land." 6 And on the next day the LORD did so;
all the livestock of the Egyptians died, but of the
livestock of the Israelites not one died. 7 Pharaoh
inquired and found that not one of the livestock of
the Israelites was dead. But the heart of Pharaoh
was hardened, and he would not let the people go.

The Sixth Plague: Boils
(Deut 28.27)

8 Then the LORD said to Moses and Aaron,
"Take handfuls of soot from the kiln, and let Moses

---

u Or frogs, as he had agreed with Pharaoh   v Gk Vg: Heb will
set redemption

throw it in the air in the sight of Pharaoh. 9 It shall become fine dust all over the land of Egypt, and shall cause festering boils on humans and animals throughout the whole land of Egypt." 10 So they took soot from the kiln, and stood before Pharaoh, and Moses threw it in the air, and it caused festering boils on humans and animals. 11 The magicians could not stand before Moses because of the boils, for the boils afflicted the magicians as well as all the Egyptians. 12 But the LORD hardened the heart of Pharaoh, and he would not listen to them, just as the LORD had spoken to Moses.

The Seventh Plague: Thunder and Hail

13 Then the LORD said to Moses, "Rise up early in the morning and present yourself before Pharaoh, and say to him, 'Thus says the LORD, the God of the Hebrews: Let my people go, so that they may worship me. 14 For this time I will send all my plagues upon you yourself, and upon your officials, and upon your people, so that you may know that there is no one like me in all the earth. 15 For by now I could have stretched out my hand and struck you and your people with pestilence, and you would have been cut off from the earth. 16 But this is why I have let you live: to show you my power, and to make my name resound through all the earth. 17 You are still exalting yourself against my people, and will not let them go. 18 Tomorrow at this time I will cause the heaviest hail to fall that has ever fallen in Egypt from the day it was founded until now. 19 Send, therefore, and have your livestock and everything that you have in the open field brought to a secure place; every human or animal that is in the open field and is not brought under shelter will die when the hail comes down upon them.' " 20 Those officials of Pharaoh who feared the word of the LORD hurried their slaves and livestock off to a secure place. 21 Those who did not regard the word of the LORD left their slaves and livestock in the open field.

22 The LORD said to Moses, "Stretch out your hand toward heaven so that hail may fall on the whole land of Egypt, on humans and animals and all the plants of the field in the land of Egypt." 23 Then Moses stretched out his staff toward heaven, and the LORD sent thunder and hail, and fire came down on the earth. And the LORD rained hail on the land of Egypt; 24 there was hail with fire flashing continually in the midst of it, such heavy hail as had never fallen in all the land of Egypt since it became a nation. 25 The hail struck down everything that was in the open field throughout all the land of Egypt, both human and animal; the hail also struck down all the plants of the field, and shattered every tree in the field. 26 Only in the land of Gō'shen, where the Israelites were, there was no hail.

27 Then Pharaoh summoned Moses and Aaron, and said to them, "This time I have sinned; the LORD is in the right, and I and my people are in the wrong. 28 Pray to the LORD! Enough of God's thunder and hail! I will let you go; you need stay no longer." 29 Moses said to him, "As soon as I have gone out of the city, I will stretch out my hands to the LORD; the thunder will cease, and there will be no more hail, so that you may know that the earth is the LORD's. 30 But as for you and your officials, I know that you do not yet fear the LORD God." 31 (Now the flax and the barley were ruined, for the barley was in the ear and the flax was in bud. 32 But the wheat and the spelt were not ruined, for they are late in coming up.) 33 So Moses left Pharaoh, went out of the city, and stretched out his hands to the LORD; then the thunder and the hail ceased, and the rain no longer poured down on the earth. 34 But when Pharaoh saw that the rain and the hail and the thunder had ceased, he sinned once more and hardened his heart, he and his officials. 35 So the heart of Pharaoh was hardened, and he would not let the Israelites go, just as the LORD had spoken through Moses.

The Eighth Plague: Locusts
(Joel 1.2–4)

10 Then the LORD said to Moses, "Go to Pharaoh; for I have hardened his heart and the heart of his officials, in order that I may show these signs of mine among them, 2 and that you may tell your children and grandchildren how I have made fools of the Egyptians and what signs I have done among them—so that you may know that I am the LORD."

3 So Moses and Aaron went to Pharaoh, and said to him, "Thus says the LORD, the God of the Hebrews, 'How long will you refuse to humble yourself before me? Let my people go, so that they may worship me. 4 For if you refuse to let my people go, tomorrow I will bring locusts into your country. 5 They shall cover the surface of the land, so that no one will be able to see the land. They shall devour the last remnant left you after the hail, and they shall devour every tree of yours that grows in the field. 6 They shall fill your houses, and the houses of all your officials and of all the Egyptians—something that neither your parents nor your grandparents have seen, from the day they came on earth to this day.' " Then he turned and went out from Pharaoh.

7 Pharaoh's officials said to him, "How long shall this fellow be a snare to us? Let the people go, so that they may worship the LORD their God; do you not yet understand that Egypt is ruined?" 8 So Moses and Aaron were brought back to Pharaoh, and he said to them, "Go, worship the LORD your

God! But which ones are to go?" 9 Moses said, "We will go with our young and our old; we will go with our sons and daughters and with our flocks and herds, because we have the LORD's festival to celebrate." 10 He said to them, "The LORD indeed will be with you, if ever I let your little ones go with you! Plainly, you have some evil purpose in mind. 11 No, never! Your men may go and worship the LORD, for that is what you are asking." And they were driven out from Pharaoh's presence.

12 Then the LORD said to Moses, "Stretch out your hand over the land of Egypt, so that the locusts may come upon it and eat every plant in the land, all that the hail has left." 13 So Moses stretched out his staff over the land of Egypt, and the LORD brought an east wind upon the land all that day and all that night; when morning came, the east wind had brought the locusts. 14 The locusts came upon all the land of Egypt and settled on the whole country of Egypt, such a dense swarm of locusts as had never been before, nor ever shall be again. 15 They covered the surface of the whole land, so that the land was black; and they ate all the plants in the land and all the fruit of the trees that the hail had left; nothing green was left, no tree, no plant in the field, in all the land of Egypt. 16 Pharaoh hurriedly summoned Moses and Aaron and said, "I have sinned against the LORD your God, and against you. 17 Do forgive my sin just this once, and pray to the LORD your God that at the least he remove this deadly thing from me." 18 So he went out from Pharaoh and prayed to the LORD. 19 The LORD changed the wind into a very strong west wind, which lifted the locusts and drove them into the Red Sea;*w* not a single locust was left in all the country of Egypt. 20 But the LORD hardened Pharaoh's heart, and he would not let the Israelites go.

The Ninth Plague: Darkness

21 Then the LORD said to Moses, "Stretch out your hand toward heaven so that there may be darkness over the land of Egypt, a darkness that can be felt." 22 So Moses stretched out his hand toward heaven, and there was dense darkness in all the land of Egypt for three days. 23 People could not see one another, and for three days they could not move from where they were; but all the Israelites had light where they lived. 24 Then Pharaoh summoned Moses, and said, "Go, worship the LORD. Only your flocks and your herds shall remain behind. Even your children may go with you." 25 But Moses said, "You must also let us have sacrifices and burnt offerings to sacrifice to the LORD our God. 26 Our livestock also must go with us; not a hoof shall be left behind, for we must choose some of them for the worship of the LORD our God, and we will not know what to use to worship the LORD

until we arrive there." 27 But the LORD hardened Pharaoh's heart, and he was unwilling to let them go. 28 Then Pharaoh said to him, "Get away from me! Take care that you do not see my face again, for on the day you see my face you shall die." 29 Moses said, "Just as you say! I will never see your face again."

Warning of the Final Plague
(Ex 3.21–22; 12.35–36)

11 The LORD said to Moses, "I will bring one more plague upon Pharaoh and upon Egypt; afterwards he will let you go from here; indeed, when he lets you go, he will drive you away. 2 Tell the people that every man is to ask his neighbor and every woman is to ask her neighbor for objects of silver and gold." 3 The LORD gave the people favor in the sight of the Egyptians. Moreover, Moses himself was a man of great importance in the land of Egypt, in the sight of Pharaoh's officials and in the sight of the people.

4 Moses said, "Thus says the LORD: About midnight I will go out through Egypt. 5 Every firstborn in the land of Egypt shall die, from the firstborn of Pharaoh who sits on his throne to the firstborn of the female slave who is behind the handmill, and all the firstborn of the livestock. 6 Then there will be a loud cry throughout the whole land of Egypt, such as has never been or will ever be again. 7 But not a dog shall growl at any of the Israelites—not at people, not at animals—so that you may know that the LORD makes a distinction between Egypt and Israel. 8 Then all these officials of yours shall come down to me, and bow low to me, saying, 'Leave us, you and all the people who follow you.' After that I will leave." And in hot anger he left Pharaoh.

9 The LORD said to Moses, "Pharaoh will not listen to you, in order that my wonders may be multiplied in the land of Egypt." 10 Moses and Aaron performed all these wonders before Pharaoh; but the LORD hardened Pharaoh's heart, and he did not let the people of Israel go out of his land.

The First Passover Instituted
(Num 9.1–14; Deut 16.1–8; Ezek 45.21–25)

12 The LORD said to Moses and Aaron in the land of Egypt: 2 This month shall mark for you the beginning of months; it shall be the first month of the year for you. 3 Tell the whole congregation of Israel that on the tenth of this month they are to take a lamb for each family, a lamb for each household. 4 If a household is too small for a whole lamb, it shall join its closest neighbor in obtaining one; the lamb shall be divided in proportion to the number of people who eat of it. 5 Your

---

w Or Sea of Reeds

lamb shall be without blemish, a year-old male; you may take it from the sheep or from the goats. 6 You shall keep it until the fourteenth day of this month; then the whole assembled congregation of Israel shall slaughter it at twilight. 7 They shall take some of the blood and put it on the two doorposts and the lintel of the houses in which they eat it. 8 They shall eat the lamb that same night; they shall eat it roasted over the fire with unleavened bread and bitter herbs. 9 Do not eat any of it raw or boiled in water, but roasted over the fire, with its head, legs, and inner organs. 10 You shall let none of it remain until the morning; anything that remains until the morning you shall burn. 11 This is how you shall eat it: your loins girded, your sandals on your feet, and your staff in your hand; and you shall eat it hurriedly. It is the passover of the LORD. 12 For I will pass through the land of Egypt that night, and I will strike down every firstborn in the land of Egypt, both human beings and animals; on all the gods of Egypt I will execute judgments: I am the LORD. 13 The blood shall be a sign for you on the houses where you live: when I see the blood, I will pass over you, and no plague shall destroy you when I strike the land of Egypt.

14 This day shall be a day of remembrance for you. You shall celebrate it as a festival to the LORD; throughout your generations you shall observe it as a perpetual ordinance. 15 Seven days you shall eat unleavened bread; on the first day you shall remove leaven from your houses, for whoever eats leavened bread from the first day until the seventh day shall be cut off from Israel. 16 On the first day you shall hold a solemn assembly, and on the seventh day a solemn assembly; no work shall be done on those days; only what everyone must eat, that alone may be prepared by you. 17 You shall observe the festival of unleavened bread, for on this very day I brought your companies out of the land of Egypt: you shall observe this day throughout your generations as a perpetual ordinance. 18 In the first month, from the evening of the fourteenth day until the evening of the twenty-first day, you shall eat unleavened bread. 19 For seven days no leaven shall be found in your houses; for whoever eats what is leavened shall be cut off from the congregation of Israel, whether an alien or a native of the land. 20 You shall eat nothing leavened; in all your settlements you shall eat unleavened bread.

21 Then Moses called all the elders of Israel and said to them, "Go, select lambs for your families, and slaughter the passover lamb. 22 Take a bunch of hyssop, dip it in the blood that is in the basin, and touch the lintel and the two doorposts with the blood in the basin. None of you shall go outside the door of your house until morning. 23 For the LORD will pass through to strike down the Egyp-

did you KNOW?

The Passover

"Why is this night so different from all other nights?" This question, asked by the youngest member of the family, is part of the Jewish celebration of the Passover. Jewish people continue to celebrate the Passover today in fulfillment of Moses' command, "You shall observe this rite as a perpetual ordinance for you and your children" (Ex 12.24).

The Passover is celebrated around a meal including lamb and unleavened bread. The lamb recalls the Passover lamb whose blood was placed on the doorpost to protect the firstborn from the angel of death. The unleavened bread recalls the haste in which the people prepared to depart. Retelling the ancient story, generations of Jews have remembered that "night of nights" when the angel of death passed over the Israelites' houses and struck down the firstborn of the Egyptians. On that night, the people of God were finally released from slavery. Thus, Passover is a celebration of God's gift of freedom—a religious Independence Day, so to speak.

It was during the Passover celebration that Jesus had his farewell dinner (see Jn 13.1), placing himself as the paschal sacrifice. Christians see Jesus as the new Passover; through his death and Resurrection, we are finally liberated from all bondage, including sin and death.

▸ Ex 12.14–28

tians; when he sees the blood on the lintel and on the two doorposts, the LORD will pass over that door and will not allow the destroyer to enter your houses to strike you down. 24 You shall observe this rite as a perpetual ordinance for you and your children. 25 When you come to the land that the LORD will give you, as he has promised, you shall keep this observance. 26 And when your children ask you, 'What do you mean by this observance?' 27 you shall say, 'It is the passover sacrifice to the LORD, for he passed over the houses of the Israelites in Egypt, when he struck down the Egyptians but spared our houses.' " And the people bowed down and worshiped.

28 The Israelites went and did just as the LORD had commanded Moses and Aaron.

The Tenth Plague: Death of the Firstborn
(Ex 11.1–10)

29 At midnight the LORD struck down all the firstborn in the land of Egypt, from the firstborn of Pharaoh who sat on his throne to the firstborn of the prisoner who was in the dungeon, and all the firstborn of the livestock. 30 Pharaoh arose in the night, he and all his officials and all the Egyptians; and there was a loud cry in Egypt, for there was not a house without someone dead. 31 Then he summoned Moses and Aaron in the night, and said, "Rise up, go away from my people, both you and the Israelites! Go, worship the LORD, as you said. 32 Take your flocks and your herds, as you said, and be gone. And bring a blessing on me too!"

The Exodus: From Rameses to Succoth

33 The Egyptians urged the people to hasten their departure from the land, for they said, "We shall all be dead." 34 So the people took their dough before it was leavened, with their kneading bowls wrapped up in their cloaks on their shoulders. 35 The Israelites had done as Moses told them; they had asked the Egyptians for jewelry of silver and gold, and for clothing, 36 and the LORD had given the people favor in the sight of the Egyptians, so that they let them have what they asked. And so they plundered the Egyptians.

37 The Israelites journeyed from Ram′e•ses to Suc′coth, about six hundred thousand men on foot, besides children. 38 A mixed crowd also went up with them, and livestock in great numbers, both flocks and herds. 39 They baked unleavened cakes of the dough that they had brought out of Egypt; it was not leavened, because they were driven out of Egypt and could not wait, nor had they prepared any provisions for themselves.

40 The time that the Israelites had lived in Egypt was four hundred thirty years. 41 At the end of four hundred thirty years, on that very day, all the companies of the LORD went out from the land of Egypt. 42 That was for the LORD a night of vigil, to bring them out of the land of Egypt. That same night is a vigil to be kept for the LORD by all the Israelites throughout their generations.

Directions for the Passover
(Gen 17.9–14; Ex 12.1–13)

43 The LORD said to Moses and Aaron: This is the ordinance for the passover: no foreigner shall eat of it, 44 but any slave who has been purchased may eat of it after he has been circumcised; 45 no

bound or hired servant may eat of it. 46 It shall be eaten in one house; you shall not take any of the animal outside the house, and you shall not break any of its bones. 47 The whole congregation of Israel shall celebrate it. 48 If an alien who resides with you wants to celebrate the passover to the LORD, all his males shall be circumcised; then he may draw near to celebrate it; he shall be regarded as a native of the land. But no uncircumcised person shall eat of it; 49 there shall be one law for the native and for the alien who resides among you.

50 All the Israelites did just as the LORD had commanded Moses and Aaron. 51 That very day the LORD brought the Israelites out of the land of Egypt, company by company.

13 The LORD said to Moses: 2 Consecrate to me all the firstborn; whatever is the first to open the womb among the Israelites, of human beings and animals, is mine.

The Festival of Unleavened Bread
(Ex 12.14–20)

3 Moses said to the people, "Remember this day on which you came out of Egypt, out of the house of slavery, because the LORD brought you out from there by strength of hand; no leavened bread shall be eaten. 4 Today, in the month of Ā′bib, you are going out. 5 When the LORD brings you into the land of the Cā′naan•ites, the Hit′tites, the Am′o•rites, the Hi′vites, and the Jeb′ū•sites, which he swore to your ancestors to give you, a land flowing with milk and honey, you shall keep this observance in this month. 6 Seven days you shall eat unleavened bread, and on the seventh day there shall be a festival to the LORD. 7 Unleavened bread shall be eaten for seven days; no leavened bread shall be seen in your possession, and no leaven shall be seen among you in all your territory. 8 You shall tell your child on that day, 'It is because of what the LORD did for me when I came out of Egypt.' 9 It shall serve for you as a sign on your hand and as a reminder on your forehead, so that the teaching of the LORD may be on your lips; for with a strong hand the LORD brought you out of Egypt. 10 You shall keep this ordinance at its proper time from year to year.

The Consecration of the Firstborn

11 "When the LORD has brought you into the land of the Cā′naan•ites, as he swore to you and your ancestors, and has given it to you, 12 you shall set apart to the LORD all that first opens the womb. All the firstborn of your livestock that are males shall be the LORD's. 13 But every firstborn donkey you shall redeem with a sheep; if you do not redeem it, you must break its neck. Every firstborn male among your children you shall redeem. 14 When in the future your child asks you, 'What does this

mean?' you shall answer, 'By strength of hand the LORD brought us out of Egypt, from the house of slavery. 15 When Pharaoh stubbornly refused to let us go, the LORD killed all the firstborn in the land of Egypt, from human firstborn to the firstborn of animals. Therefore I sacrifice to the LORD every male that first opens the womb, but every firstborn of my sons I redeem.' 16 It shall serve as a sign on your hand and as an emblemˣ on your forehead that by strength of hand the LORD brought us out of Egypt."

The Pillars of Cloud and Fire
(Ex 40.34–38; Num 9.15–23; 1 Kings 8.10–11)

17 When Pharaoh let the people go, God did not lead them by way of the land of the Phi•lis'tines, although that was nearer; for God thought, "If the people face war, they may change their minds and return to Egypt." 18 So God led the people by the roundabout way of the wilderness toward the Red Sea.ʸ The Israelites went up out of the

land of Egypt prepared for battle. 19 And Moses took with him the bones of Joseph who had required a solemn oath of the Israelites, saying, "God will surely take notice of you, and then you must carry my bones with you from here." 20 They set out from Suc'coth, and camped at E'tham, on the edge of the wilderness. 21 The LORD went in front of them in a pillar of cloud by day, to lead them along the way, and in a pillar of fire by night, to give them light, so that they might travel by day and by night. 22 Neither the pillar of cloud by day nor the pillar of fire by night left its place in front of the people.

Crossing the Red Sea

14 Then the LORD said to Moses: 2 Tell the Israelites to turn back and camp in front of Pī-ha•hī'roth, between Mig'dōl and the sea, in

---

ˣ Or *as a frontlet;* meaning of Heb uncertain   ʸ Or *Sea of Reeds*

EX

LOOK TO THE HILLS

This is a story told about two Israelites who, while crossing the Red Sea, kept looking down at their feet. One said: "Look at my feet. They're covered with mud. This is some fine mess that Moses led us into." They crossed the sea without ever looking up. They never saw the sea parted on either side. As they wiped the mud from their feet and garments, they completely missed the sea's closing and the Egyptians' being swallowed up at God's command!

Although it seems like it would have been impossible to miss something so fantastic as the parting of the Red Sea, it is sometimes easy to focus so much on the negative that the positive is missed. Some people—especially those facing oppression, rejection, injustice, and hardship—keep looking down and miss seeing God's power and their own talents and gifts. Looking down can almost become second nature, poisoning a person's whole attitude. People can waste a lot of time looking down at life's struggles and never looking up.

Brothers and sisters, the resurrected Christ has won victory for all, for people of every race and culture—so look up! Keep your eyes on the prize of the high calling of God in Christ Jesus. Remember the hopeful words in Psalm 121.1–2:

I lift up my eyes to the hills—
    from where will my help come?
My help comes from the LORD,
    who made heaven and earth.

What do you do when self-doubt and negativity tempt you to keep looking down? How can you encourage others when it seems that the injustices and struggles of life have beaten them down?

▸ Ex 14.1–31

Cultural Connections

GOD LIBERATES US FROM OPPRESSION!

Many centuries before Christ, the Israelites migrated to Egypt from Canaan, seeking food because of an extreme drought in their land. The Egyptians, taking advantage of the Israelites' need for food and shelter, set taskmasters to rule over them and made their lives bitter with hard service.

- Have you, your family, or your people ever experienced oppression through forced labor?
- Are you aware of situations in which people are being oppressed or exploited because of their immigrant status, their educational level, or their need for food and shelter?
- Pray for God's liberating power, and ask God to give you the strength to fight unjust situations and oppression.

The Israelite people groaned under their slavery and asked God for help. God responded to their plight and sent Moses to lead them into freedom. But they needed to overcome their fear of the unknown future and to step out in trust. Their liberation was accomplished when they responded to God's initiative to free themselves from a life of bondage. To be free, we must first be willing to admit that we are enslaved to something.

- What types of oppression or pressures have taken away your freedom to live according to God's will?
- How can your community help young people to recognize when they are enslaved by social and peer pressures?
- Pray with Psalm 54 to ask for God's help in your struggle. Or pray with Psalm 146 to praise and thank God for liberation that you have experienced.

▶ Ex 14.1–31

front of Bāʹal-zēʹphon; you shall camp opposite it, by the sea. 3 Pharaoh will say of the Israelites, "They are wandering aimlessly in the land; the wilderness has closed in on them." 4 I will harden Pharaoh's heart, and he will pursue them, so that I will gain glory for myself over Pharaoh and all his army; and the Egyptians shall know that I am the LORD. And they did so.

5 When the king of Egypt was told that the people had fled, the minds of Pharaoh and his officials were changed toward the people, and they said, "What have we done, letting Israel leave our service?" 6 So he had his chariot made ready, and took his army with him; 7 he took six hundred picked chariots and all the other chariots of Egypt with officers over all of them. 8 The LORD hardened the heart of Pharaoh king of Egypt and he pursued the Israelites, who were going out boldly. 9 The Egyptians pursued them, all Pharaoh's horses and chariots, his chariot drivers and his army; they overtook them camped by the sea, by Pī-ha•hī′roth, in front of Bāʹal-zēʹphon.

10 As Pharaoh drew near, the Israelites looked back, and there were the Egyptians advancing on them. In great fear the Israelites cried out to the LORD. 11 They said to Moses, "Was it because there were no graves in Egypt that you have taken us away to die in the wilderness? What have you done to us, bringing us out of Egypt? 12 Is this not the very thing we told you in Egypt, 'Let us alone and let us serve the Egyptians'? For it would have been better for us to serve the Egyptians than to die in the wilderness." 13 But Moses said to the people, "Do not be afraid, stand firm, and see the deliverance that the LORD will accomplish for you today; for the Egyptians whom you see today you shall never see again. 14 The LORD will fight for you, and you have only to keep still."

15 Then the LORD said to Moses, "Why do you cry out to me? Tell the Israelites to go forward. 16 But you lift up your staff, and stretch out your hand over the sea and divide it, that the Israelites may go into the sea on dry ground. 17 Then I will harden the hearts of the Egyptians so that they will

go in after them; and so I will gain glory for myself over Pharaoh and all his army, his chariots, and his chariot drivers. 18 And the Egyptians shall know that I am the LORD, when I have gained glory for myself over Pharaoh, his chariots, and his chariot drivers."

19 The angel of God who was going before the Israelite army moved and went behind them; and the pillar of cloud moved from in front of them and took its place behind them. 20 It came between the army of Egypt and the army of Israel. And so the cloud was there with the darkness, and it lit up the night; one did not come near the other all night. 21 Then Moses stretched out his hand over the sea. The LORD drove the sea back by a strong east wind all night, and turned the sea into dry land; and the waters were divided. 22 The Israelites went into the sea on dry ground, the waters forming a wall for them on their right and on their left. 23 The Egyptians pursued, and went into the sea after them, all of Pharaoh's horses, chariots, and chariot drivers. 24 At the morning watch the LORD in the pillar of fire and cloud looked down upon the Egyptian army, and threw the Egyptian army into panic. 25 He clogged[z] their chariot wheels so that they turned with difficulty. The Egyptians said, "Let us flee from the Israelites, for the LORD is fighting for them against Egypt."

The Pursuers Drowned

26 Then the LORD said to Moses, "Stretch out your hand over the sea, so that the water may come back upon the Egyptians, upon their chariots and chariot drivers." 27 So Moses stretched out his hand over the sea, and at dawn the sea returned to its normal depth. As the Egyptians fled before it, the LORD tossed the Egyptians into the sea. 28 The waters returned and covered the chariots and the chariot drivers, the entire army of Pharaoh that had followed them into the sea; not one of them remained. 29 But the Israelites walked on dry ground through the sea, the waters forming a wall for them on their right and on their left.

30 Thus the LORD saved Israel that day from the Egyptians; and Israel saw the Egyptians dead on the seashore. 31 Israel saw the great work that the LORD did against the Egyptians. So the people feared the LORD and believed in the LORD and in his servant Moses.

The Song of Moses
(Ex 14.13–14; Ps 78.12–14)

15
Then Moses and the Israelites sang this song to the LORD:

"I will sing to the LORD, for he has triumphed gloriously;

horse and rider he has thrown into the sea.
2 The LORD is my strength and my might,[a]
  and he has become my salvation;
  this is my God, and I will praise him,
  my father's God, and I will exalt him.
3 The LORD is a warrior;
  the LORD is his name.

4 "Pharaoh's chariots and his army he cast into
    the sea;
  his picked officers were sunk in the Red Sea.[b]

PRAY IT!
Miriam Leads the People in Praise

The Song at the Sea in Ex 15.1–21 is probably the oldest writing in the Bible. It is an example of how the Israelite people put stories of God's mighty deeds into song so that they could be remembered and passed on from generation to generation.

Verses 20–21 tell us that the prophetess Miriam led the prayer—singing and dancing. Miriam was Moses and Aaron's sister. The three of them formed a leadership team. Many biblical scholars believe that she may be the author of the song. This is one of the few biblical stories that clearly show a woman serving as a prayer leader.

▶ Ex 15.1–21

5 The floods covered them;
    they went down into the depths like a stone.
6 Your right hand, O LORD, glorious in power—
    your right hand, O LORD, shattered the
      enemy.
7 In the greatness of your majesty you overthrew
      your adversaries;
    you sent out your fury, it consumed them
      like stubble.
8 At the blast of your nostrils the waters piled up,
    the floods stood up in a heap;
    the deeps congealed in the heart of the sea.
9 The enemy said, 'I will pursue, I will overtake,
    I will divide the spoil, my desire shall have
      its fill of them.

---

z Sam Gk Syr: MT *removed*   a Or *song*   b Or *Sea of Reeds*

EX

I will draw my sword, my hand shall
 destroy them.'
10 You blew with your wind, the sea covered
 them;
 they sank like lead in the mighty waters.

11 "Who is like you, O LORD, among the gods?
 Who is like you, majestic in holiness,
 awesome in splendor, doing wonders?
12 You stretched out your right hand,
 the earth swallowed them.

13 "In your steadfast love you led the people
 whom you redeemed;
 you guided them by your strength to your
 holy abode.
14 The peoples heard, they trembled;
 pangs seized the inhabitants of Phi·lis'ti·a.
15 Then the chiefs of Ē'dom were dismayed;
 trembling seized the leaders of Mō'ab;
 all the inhabitants of Cā'naan melted
 away.
16 Terror and dread fell upon them;
 by the might of your arm, they became still
 as a stone
 until your people, O LORD, passed by,
 until the people whom you acquired
 passed by.
17 You brought them in and planted them on the
 mountain of your own possession,
 the place, O LORD, that you made your
 abode,
 the sanctuary, O LORD, that your hands
 have established.
18 The LORD will reign forever and ever."

19 When the horses of Pharaoh with his chariots and his chariot drivers went into the sea, the
LORD brought back the waters of the sea upon
them; but the Israelites walked through the sea on
dry ground.

The Song of Miriam
(Num 26.59)

20 Then the prophet Miriam, Aaron's sister,
took a tambourine in her hand; and all the women
went out after her with tambourines and with dancing. 21 And Miriam sang to them:
 "Sing to the LORD, for he has triumphed
 gloriously;
 horse and rider he has thrown into the sea."

Bitter Water Made Sweet

22 Then Moses ordered Israel to set out from
the Red Sea,c and they went into the wilderness of
Shur. They went three days in the wilderness and
found no water. 23 When they came to Mar'ah, they
could not drink the water of Mar'ah because it was

bitter. That is why it was called Mar'ah.d 24 And the
people complained against Moses, saying, "What
shall we drink?" 25 He cried out to the LORD; and
the LORD showed him a piece of wood;e he threw it
into the water, and the water became sweet.

There the LORDf made for them a statute and an
ordinance and there he put them to the test. 26 He
said, "If you will listen carefully to the voice of the
LORD your God, and do what is right in his sight,
and give heed to his commandments and keep all
his statutes, I will not bring upon you any of the
diseases that I brought upon the Egyptians; for I am
the LORD who heals you."

27 Then they came to Ē'lim, where there were
twelve springs of water and seventy palm trees; and
they camped there by the water.

Bread from Heaven

16 The whole congregation of the Israelites
set out from Ē'lim; and Israel came to the
wilderness of Sin, which is between Ē'lim and Sinai,
on the fifteenth day of the second month after they
had departed from the land of Egypt. 2 The whole
congregation of the Israelites complained against
Moses and Aaron in the wilderness. 3 The Israelites
said to them, "If only we had died by the hand of
the LORD in the land of Egypt, when we sat by the
fleshpots and ate our fill of bread; for you have
brought us out into this wilderness to kill this
whole assembly with hunger."

4 Then the LORD said to Moses, "I am going to
rain bread from heaven for you, and each day the
people shall go out and gather enough for that day.
In that way I will test them, whether they will follow my instruction or not. 5 On the sixth day, when
they prepare what they bring in, it will be twice as
much as they gather on other days." 6 So Moses and
Aaron said to all the Israelites, "In the evening you
shall know that it was the LORD who brought
you out of the land of Egypt, 7 and in the morning
you shall see the glory of the LORD, because he has
heard your complaining against the LORD. For what
are we, that you complain against us?" 8 And Moses
said, "When the LORD gives you meat to eat in the
evening and your fill of bread in the morning, because the LORD has heard the complaining that you
utter against him—what are we? Your complaining
is not against us but against the LORD."

9 Then Moses said to Aaron, "Say to the whole
congregation of the Israelites, 'Draw near to the
LORD, for he has heard your complaining.' " 10 And
as Aaron spoke to the whole congregation of the Israelites, they looked toward the wilderness, and
the glory of the LORD appeared in the cloud. 11 The
LORD spoke to Moses and said, 12 "I have heard the

---

c Or Sea of Reeds d That is Bitterness e Or a tree f Heb he

LIVE IT!

Those Whiny Israelites

It's so easy to complain, isn't it? As soon as things aren't quite the way we would like, we start fussing and whining and grumbling. We have all done it. We are no different from the Israelites who, despite having just been miraculously delivered from slavery, start complaining after a few days in the wilderness. "Why," they ask, "would God lead us through the Red Sea only to let us die of hunger?"

Perspective. Faith. That's what it takes. Once we have been through a crisis or spent time in a place where people are truly poor and hungry, we gain a perspective on our own culture, on our own tendency to want everything just the way we like it and as soon as possible. The next time we hear ourselves complaining about something, let's pause and try to see a bigger picture, perhaps the one that God sees. Then we can ask ourselves, Is this really worth complaining about?

▶ Ex 16.1–3

E
X

complaining of the Israelites; say to them, 'At twilight you shall eat meat, and in the morning you shall have your fill of bread; then you shall know that I am the LORD your God.' "

13 In the evening quails came up and covered the camp; and in the morning there was a layer of dew around the camp. 14 When the layer of dew lifted, there on the surface of the wilderness was a fine flaky substance, as fine as frost on the ground. 15 When the Israelites saw it, they said to one another, "What is it?"^{g} For they did not know what it was. Moses said to them, "It is the bread that the LORD has given you to eat. 16 This is what the LORD has commanded: 'Gather as much of it as each of you needs, an omer to a person according to the number of persons, all providing for those in their own tents.' " 17 The Israelites did so, some gathering more, some less. 18 But when they measured it with an omer, those who gathered much had nothing over, and those who gathered little had no shortage; they gathered as much as each of them needed. 19 And Moses said to them, "Let no one leave any of it over until morning." 20 But they did not listen to Moses; some left part of it until morning, and it bred worms and became foul. And Moses was angry with them. 21 Morning by morning they gathered it, as much as each needed; but when the sun grew hot, it melted.

22 On the sixth day they gathered twice as much food, two omers apiece. When all the leaders of the congregation came and told Moses, 23 he said to them, "This is what the LORD has commanded: 'Tomorrow is a day of solemn rest, a holy sabbath to the LORD; bake what you want to bake and boil what you want to boil, and all that is left over put aside to be kept until morning.' " 24 So they put it aside until morning, as Moses commanded them; and it did not become foul, and there were no

worms in it. 25 Moses said, "Eat it today, for today is a sabbath to the LORD; today you will not find it in the field. 26 Six days you shall gather it; but on the seventh day, which is a sabbath, there will be none."

27 On the seventh day some of the people went out to gather, and they found none. 28 The LORD said to Moses, "How long will you refuse to keep my commandments and instructions? 29 See! The LORD has given you the sabbath, therefore on the sixth day he gives you food for two days; each of you stay where you are; do not leave your place on the seventh day." 30 So the people rested on the seventh day.

31 The house of Israel called it manna; it was like coriander seed, white, and the taste of it was like wafers made with honey. 32 Moses said, "This is what the LORD has commanded: 'Let an omer of it be kept throughout your generations, in order that they may see the food with which I fed you in the wilderness, when I brought you out of the land of Egypt.' " 33 And Moses said to Aaron, "Take a jar, and put an omer of manna in it, and place it before the LORD, to be kept throughout your generations." 34 As the LORD commanded Moses, so Aaron placed it before the covenant,^{h} for safekeeping. 35 The Israelites ate manna forty years, until they came to a habitable land; they ate manna, until they came to the border of the land of Cā'naan. 36 An omer is a tenth of an ephah.

Water from the Rock
(Num 20.1–13)

17 From the wilderness of Sin the whole congregation of the Israelites journeyed by stages, as the LORD commanded. They camped at

---

^{g} Or "It is manna" (Heb *man hu*, see verse 31) ^{h} Or *treaty* or *testimony*; Heb *eduth*

EX

MANNA AND RICE

Rice is the symbol of our life
We eat rice daily
There are different kinds of rice
But we are one
as the rice-eating community
Rice is the symbol of celebration
We express our joy of harvest with it
There are many sufferings in Asia
but we anticipate the time of cosmic celebration.

(From Maren C. Tirabassi and Kathy Wonson Eddy, editors,
Gifts of Many Cultures, p. 186)

This poem from Japan by Masao and Fumiko Takenaka expresses their appreciation for rice, the most basic food of the Japanese. It unites them as a people and reminds them to be joyful. In a similar way, Exodus tells how the gift of manna united the Israelites and gave them a reason for celebration despite their many trials. What foods unite you and your friends? family? culture? What connections do you see between manna, rice, and the Eucharist?

▶ Ex 16.1–36

Reph'i•dim, but there was no water for the people to drink. 2 The people quarreled with Moses, and said, "Give us water to drink." Moses said to them, "Why do you quarrel with me? Why do you test the LORD?" 3 But the people thirsted there for water; and the people complained against Moses and said, "Why did you bring us out of Egypt, to kill us and our children and livestock with thirst?" 4 So Moses cried out to the LORD, "What shall I do with this people? They are almost ready to stone me." 5 The LORD said to Moses, "Go on ahead of the people, and take some of the elders of Israel with you; take in your hand the staff with which you struck the Nile, and go. 6 I will be standing there in front of you on the rock at Hō'reb. Strike the rock, and water will come out of it, so that the people may drink." Moses did so, in the sight of the elders of Israel. 7 He called the place Mas'sah[i] and Mer'i•bah,[j] because the Israelites quarreled and tested the LORD, saying, "Is the LORD among us or not?"

Amalek Attacks Israel and Is Defeated
(Gen 14.7; Num 13.29; 14.25)

8 Then Am'a•lek came and fought with Israel at Reph'i•dim. 9 Moses said to Joshua, "Choose some men for us and go out, fight with Am'a•lek. Tomorrow I will stand on the top of the hill with the staff of God in my hand." 10 So Joshua did as Moses told him, and fought with Am'a•lek, while Moses, Aaron, and Hur went up to the top of the hill. 11 Whenever Moses held up his hand, Israel prevailed; and whenever he lowered his hand, Am'a•lek prevailed. 12 But Moses' hands grew weary; so they took a stone and put it under him, and he sat on it. Aaron and Hur held up his hands, one on one side, and the other on the other side; so his hands were steady until the sun set. 13 And Joshua defeated Am'a•lek and his people with the sword.

14 Then the LORD said to Moses, "Write this as a reminder in a book and recite it in the hearing of Joshua: I will utterly blot out the remembrance of Am'a•lek from under heaven." 15 And Moses built an altar and called it, The LORD is my banner. 16 He said, "A hand upon the banner of the LORD![k] The LORD will have war with Am'a•lek from generation to generation."

---

i That is *Test*   *j* That is *Quarrel*   *k* Cn: Meaning of Heb uncertain

Prayer in Support of Others

During the battle against Amalek, Moses' outstretched arms could be understood as a prayer of support for the Israelites. It was an effective prayer, too, because as long as he was able to maintain it, the Israelites were winning. When he could not maintain the prayer by himself, Aaron and Hur helped.

Prayer makes a difference. Research has shown that prayer helps people's emotional and physical health and healing, though it cannot explain why. Spiritual energy is a proven, powerful force.

Prayer doesn't even need words. To hold someone in prayer, just think of the person, and quietly take his or her pain or joy into your heart.

▸ Ex 17.8–16

Jethro's Advice
(Deut 1.9–18)

18 Jeth'rō, the priest of Mid'i·an, Moses' father-in-law, heard of all that God had done for Moses and for his people Israel, how the LORD had brought Israel out of Egypt. 2 After Moses had sent away his wife Zip·pō'rah, his father-in-law

Jeth'rō took her back, 3 along with her two sons. The name of the one was Ger'shom (for he said, "I have been an alien[l] in a foreign land"), 4 and the name of the other, El·i·ē'zer[m] (for he said, "The God of my father was my help, and delivered me from the sword of Pharaoh"). 5 Jeth'rō, Moses' father-in-law, came into the wilderness where Moses was encamped at the mountain of God, bringing Moses' sons and wife to him. 6 He sent word to Moses, "I, your father-in-law Jeth'rō, am coming to you, with your wife and her two sons." 7 Moses went out to meet his father-in-law; he bowed down and kissed him; each asked after the other's welfare, and they went into the tent. 8 Then Moses told his father-in-law all that the LORD had done to Pharaoh and to the Egyptians for Israel's sake, all the hardship that had beset them on the way, and how the LORD had delivered them. 9 Jeth'rō rejoiced for all the good that the LORD had done to Israel, in delivering them from the Egyptians.

10 Jeth'rō said, "Blessed be the LORD, who has delivered you from the Egyptians and from Pharaoh. 11 Now I know that the LORD is greater than all gods, because he delivered the people from the Egyptians,[n] when they dealt arrogantly with them." 12 And Jeth'rō, Moses' father-in-law, brought a burnt offering and sacrifices to God; and Aaron came with all the elders of Israel to eat bread with Moses' father-in-law in the presence of God.

13 The next day Moses sat as judge for the people, while the people stood around him from morning until evening. 14 When Moses' father-in-law saw all that he was doing for the people, he

---

[l] Heb *ger*   [m] Heb *Eli,* my God; *ezer,* help   [n] The clause *because . . . Egyptians* has been transposed from verse 10

EX

LIVE IT!

Sharing Responsibility

Was Moses a workaholic (see Ex 18.18)? Maybe he just found himself suddenly overwhelmed by too many responsibilities. Fortunately for Moses, he had a wise father-in-law who could see an alternative that Moses could not see—or maybe did not want to see.

What person in this story do you feel most like?

■ Moses, surrounded by people clamoring for your attention
■ Jethro, concerned about Moses but able to offer some advice
■ one of the people, hoping that Moses has a few minutes to listen to your problem
■ one of the trustworthy judges, chosen by Moses to make sure that the Israelites experience justice in all their day-to-day business

When leaders share responsibility, they are saying to other people, "I trust you, we're in this together, and you are needed." When you are in a leadership position, remember Jethro's advice to Moses, and don't be a lone ranger; ask others to help!

▸ Ex 18.13–26

EX

said, "What is this that you are doing for the people? Why do you sit alone, while all the people stand around you from morning until evening?" 15 Moses said to his father-in-law, "Because the people come to me to inquire of God. 16 When they have a dispute, they come to me and I decide between one person and another, and I make known to them the statutes and instructions of God." 17 Moses' father-in-law said to him, "What you are doing is not good. 18 You will surely wear yourself out, both you and these people with you. For the task is too heavy for you; you cannot do it alone. 19 Now listen to me. I will give you counsel, and God be with you! You should represent the people before God, and you should bring their cases before God; 20 teach them the statutes and instructions and make known to them the way they are to go and the things they are to do. 21 You should also look for able men among all the people, men who fear God, are trustworthy, and hate dishonest gain; set such men over them as officers over thousands, hundreds, fifties, and tens. 22 Let them sit as judges for the people at all times; let them bring every important case to you, but decide every minor case themselves. So it will be easier for you, and they will bear the burden with you. 23 If you do this, and God so commands you, then you will be able to endure, and all these people will go to their home in peace."

24 So Moses listened to his father-in-law and did all that he had said. 25 Moses chose able men from all Israel and appointed them as heads over the people, as officers over thousands, hundreds, fifties, and tens. 26 And they judged the people at all times; hard cases they brought to Moses, but any minor case they decided themselves. 27 Then Moses let his father-in-law depart, and he went off to his own country.

The Israelites Reach Mount Sinai

19 On the third new moon after the Israelites had gone out of the land of Egypt, on that very day, they came into the wilderness of Sinai. 2 They had journeyed from Reph'i·dim, entered the wilderness of Sinai, and camped in the wilderness; Israel camped there in front of the mountain. 3 Then Moses went up to God; the LORD called to him from the mountain, saying, "Thus you shall say to the house of Jacob, and tell the Israelites: 4 You have seen what I did to the Egyptians, and how I bore you on eagles' wings and brought you to myself. 5 Now therefore, if you obey my voice and keep my covenant, you shall be my treasured possession out of all the peoples. Indeed, the whole earth is mine, 6 but you shall be for me a priestly kingdom and a holy nation. These are the words that you shall speak to the Israelites."

7 So Moses came, summoned the elders of the people, and set before them all these words that the LORD had commanded him. 8 The people all answered as one: "Everything that the LORD has spoken we will do." Moses reported the words of the people to the LORD. 9 Then the LORD said to Moses, "I am going to come to you in a dense cloud, in order that the people may hear when I speak with you and so trust you ever after."

The People Consecrated

When Moses had told the words of the people to the LORD, 10 the LORD said to Moses: "Go to the people and consecrate them today and tomorrow. Have them wash their clothes 11 and prepare for the third day, because on the third day the LORD will come down upon Mount Sinai in the sight of all the people. 12 You shall set limits for the people all around, saying, 'Be careful not to go up the mountain or to touch the edge of it. Any who touch the mountain shall be put to death. 13 No hand shall touch them, but they shall be stoned or shot with arrows;[o] whether animal or human being, they shall not live.' When the trumpet sounds a long blast, they may go up on the mountain." 14 So Moses went down from the mountain to the people. He consecrated the people, and they washed their clothes. 15 And he said to the people, "Prepare for the third day; do not go near a woman."

16 On the morning of the third day there was thunder and lightning, as well as a thick cloud on the mountain, and a blast of a trumpet so loud that all the people who were in the camp trembled. 17 Moses brought the people out of the camp to meet God. They took their stand at the foot of the mountain. 18 Now Mount Sinai was wrapped in smoke, because the LORD had descended upon it in fire; the smoke went up like the smoke of a kiln, while the whole mountain shook violently. 19 As the blast of the trumpet grew louder and louder, Moses would speak and God would answer him in thunder. 20 When the LORD descended upon Mount Sinai, to the top of the mountain, the LORD summoned Moses to the top of the mountain, and Moses went up. 21 Then the LORD said to Moses, "Go down and warn the people not to break through to the LORD to look; otherwise many of them will perish. 22 Even the priests who approach the LORD must consecrate themselves or the LORD will break out against them." 23 Moses said to the LORD, "The people are not permitted to come up to Mount Sinai; for you yourself warned us, saying, 'Set limits around the mountain and keep it holy.' " 24 The LORD said to him, "Go down, and come up

---

o Heb lacks *with arrows*

bringing Aaron with you; but do not let either the priests or the people break through to come up to the LORD; otherwise he will break out against them." 25 So Moses went down to the people and told them.

The Ten Commandments
(Deut 5.1–22)

20 Then God spoke all these words:
2 I am the LORD your God, who brought you out of the land of Egypt, out of the house of slavery; 3 you shall have no other gods before*p* me.

4 You shall not make for yourself an idol, whether in the form of anything that is in heaven above, or that is on the earth beneath, or that is in the water under the earth. 5 You shall not bow down to them or worship them; for I the LORD your God am a jealous God, punishing children for the iniquity of parents, to the third and the fourth generation of those who reject me, 6 but showing steadfast love to the thousandth generation*q* of those who love me and keep my commandments.

7 You shall not make wrongful use of the name of the LORD your God, for the LORD will not acquit anyone who misuses his name.

8 Remember the sabbath day, and keep it holy. 9 Six days you shall labor and do all your work. 10 But the seventh day is a sabbath to the LORD your God; you shall not do any work—you, your son or your daughter, your male or female slave, your livestock, or the alien resident in your towns. 11 For in six days the LORD made heaven and earth, the sea, and all that is in them, but rested the seventh day; therefore the LORD blessed the sabbath day and consecrated it.

12 Honor your father and your mother, so that your days may be long in the land that the LORD your God is giving you.

13 You shall not murder.*r*

14 You shall not commit adultery.

15 You shall not steal.

16 You shall not bear false witness against your neighbor.

17 You shall not covet your neighbor's house; you shall not covet your neighbor's wife, or male or female slave, or ox, or donkey, or anything that belongs to your neighbor.

18 When all the people witnessed the thunder and lightning, the sound of the trumpet, and the mountain smoking, they were afraid*s* and trembled and stood at a distance, 19 and said to Moses, "You speak to us, and we will listen; but do not let God speak to us, or we will die." 20 Moses said to the people, "Do not be afraid; for God has come only to test you and to put the fear of him upon you so that you do not sin." 21 Then the people stood at a distance, while Moses drew near to the thick darkness where God was.

The Law concerning the Altar

22 The LORD said to Moses: Thus you shall say to the Israelites: "You have seen for yourselves that I spoke with you from heaven. 23 You shall not make gods of silver alongside me, nor shall you make for yourselves gods of gold. 24 You need make for me only an altar of earth and sacrifice on it your burnt offerings and your offerings of well-being,

---

p Or *besides*   *q* Or *to thousands*   *r* Or *kill*   *s* Sam Gk Syr Vg: MT *they saw*

did you KNOW?
The Ten Commandments

The Covenant God made with the Israelites is often called the Sinai Covenant. The Ten Commandments are a handy summary of the Sinai Covenant—literally handy because they can be counted off on one's fingers. Because the Commandments are short (so short that they are sometimes called the Ten Words) and most of them begin with a similar phrase ("You shall not"), they are easily committed to memory. The ancient Israelites believed that everyone had to know and observe these basic rules if God's people were to live together in peace and security. Today, three major world religions—Jewish, Christian, and Islamic—continue to revere the Ten Commandments as basic building blocks of human community.

For the ancient Israelites, the Ten Commandments covered specific behaviors that made them different from the neighboring cultures. Over the centuries, Christians have applied the moral principles of the Ten Commandments to many other moral questions. In fact, the *Catechism of the Catholic Church* presents the Ten Commandments as the structure for teaching about many moral issues. For Jesus' teaching on the Commandments, see Mt 5.1—7.29; 22.34—40; Mk 12.28—34.

▶ Ex 20.1–17

EX

The TEN Commandments

1 I am the LORD your God . . . you shall have no other gods before me. **2** You shall not make wrongful use of the name of the LORD your God. **3** Remember the sabbath day, and keep it holy. **4** Honor your father and your mother. **5** You shall not murder. **6** You shall not commit adultery. **7** You shall not steal. **8** You shall not bear false witness against your neighbor. **9 & 10** You shall not covet your neighbor's house; you shall not covet your neighbor's wife . . . or anything that belongs to your neighbor.

20.2–17

your sheep and your oxen; in every place where I cause my name to be remembered I will come to you and bless you. 25 But if you make for me an altar of stone, do not build it of hewn stones; for if you use a chisel upon it you profane it. 26 You shall not go up by steps to my altar, so that your nakedness may not be exposed on it."

The Law concerning Slaves
(Deut 15.12–18)

21 These are the ordinances that you shall set before them:

2 When you buy a male Hebrew slave, he shall serve six years, but in the seventh he shall go out a free person, without debt. 3 If he comes in single, he shall go out single; if he comes in married, then his wife shall go out with him. 4 If his master gives him a wife and she bears him sons or daughters, the wife and her children shall be her master's and he shall go out alone. 5 But if the slave declares, "I love my master, my wife, and my children; I will not go out a free person," 6 then his master shall bring him before God.ᵗ He shall be brought to the door or the doorpost; and his master shall pierce his ear with an awl; and he shall serve him for life.

7 When a man sells his daughter as a slave, she shall not go out as the male slaves do. 8 If she does not please her master, who designated her for himself, then he shall let her be redeemed; he shall have no right to sell her to a foreign people, since he has

---

ᵗ Or *to the judges*

dealt unfairly with her. 9 If he designates her for his son, he shall deal with her as with a daughter. 10 If he takes another wife to himself, he shall not diminish the food, clothing, or marital rights of the first wife.u 11 And if he does not do these three things for her, she shall go out without debt, without payment of money.

The Law concerning Violence

12 Whoever strikes a person mortally shall be put to death. 13 If it was not premeditated, but came about by an act of God, then I will appoint for you a place to which the killer may flee. 14 But if someone willfully attacks and kills another by treachery, you shall take the killer from my altar for execution.

15 Whoever strikes father or mother shall be put to death.

16 Whoever kidnaps a person, whether that person has been sold or is still held in possession, shall be put to death.

17 Whoever curses father or mother shall be put to death.

18 When individuals quarrel and one strikes the other with a stone or fist so that the injured party, though not dead, is confined to bed, 19 but recovers and walks around outside with the help of a staff, then the assailant shall be free of liability, except to pay for the loss of time, and to arrange for full recovery.

20 When a slaveowner strikes a male or female slave with a rod and the slave dies immediately, the owner shall be punished. 21 But if the slave survives a day or two, there is no punishment; for the slave is the owner's property.

22 When people who are fighting injure a pregnant woman so that there is a miscarriage, and yet no further harm follows, the one responsible shall be fined what the woman's husband demands, paying as much as the judges determine. 23 If any harm follows, then you shall give life for life, 24 eye for eye, tooth for tooth, hand for hand, foot for foot, 25 burn for burn, wound for wound, stripe for stripe.

26 When a slaveowner strikes the eye of a male or female slave, destroying it, the owner shall let the slave go, a free person, to compensate for the eye. 27 If the owner knocks out a tooth of a male or female slave, the slave shall be let go, a free person, to compensate for the tooth.

Laws concerning Property

28 When an ox gores a man or a woman to death, the ox shall be stoned, and its flesh shall not be eaten; but the owner of the ox shall not be liable. 29 If the ox has been accustomed to gore in the past, and its owner has been warned but has not restrained it, and it kills a man or a woman, the ox shall be stoned, and its owner also shall be put to death. 30 If a ransom is imposed on the owner, then the owner shall pay whatever is imposed for the redemption of the victim's life. 31 If it gores a boy or a girl, the owner shall be dealt with according to this same rule. 32 If the ox gores a male or female slave, the owner shall pay to the slaveowner thirty shekels of silver, and the ox shall be stoned.

33 If someone leaves a pit open, or digs a pit and does not cover it, and an ox or a donkey falls into it, 34 the owner of the pit shall make restitution, giving money to its owner, but keeping the dead animal.

35 If someone's ox hurts the ox of another, so that it dies, then they shall sell the live ox and divide the price of it; and the dead animal they shall also divide. 36 But if it was known that the ox was

---

u Heb *of her*

Living the Ten Commandments

LIVE IT!

God gave the Israelites the Ten Commandments, which united them and required from them certain attitudes and behaviors toward God and their fellow Israelites. Obedience to the Commandments became the sign of faithfulness to the Covenant with God. Later, the prophets again and again held the Israelites accountable for this Covenant, calling them to repent and reconcile with God when they disobeyed God's Law.

The Ten Commandments continue to be the moral foundation for Jews and Christians today. How do you use them in making your moral decisions? How familiar are you with church teaching that applies the Ten Commandments today? Ask God for the understanding and the strength to keep God's Commandments, especially those that are the most difficult for you.

▶ Ex 20.1–17

accustomed to gore in the past, and its owner has not restrained it, the owner shall restore ox for ox, but keep the dead animal.

Laws of Restitution

22 *v* When someone steals an ox or a sheep, and slaughters it or sells it, the thief shall pay five oxen for an ox, and four sheep for a sheep.*w* The thief shall make restitution, but if unable to do so, shall be sold for the theft. 4 When the animal, whether ox or donkey or sheep, is found alive in the thief's possession, the thief shall pay double.

2*x* If a thief is found breaking in, and is beaten to death, no bloodguilt is incurred; 3 but if it happens after sunrise, bloodguilt is incurred.

of which one party says, "This is mine," the case of both parties shall come before God;*y* the one whom God condemns*z* shall pay double to the other.

10 When someone delivers to another a donkey, ox, sheep, or any other animal for safekeeping, and it dies or is injured or is carried off, without anyone seeing it, 11 an oath before the LORD shall decide between the two of them that the one has not laid hands on the property of the other; the owner shall accept the oath, and no restitution shall be made. 12 But if it was stolen, restitution shall be made to its owner. 13 If it was mangled by beasts, let it be brought as evidence; restitution shall not be made for the mangled remains.

Would You Do It?

"You shall not wrong or oppress a resident alien. . . . You shall not abuse any widow or orphan" (Ex 22.21–22). This section of the Sinai laws reminds the Israelites to take care of the poor and vulnerable in their midst. It reminds the Israelites not to become abusive like the Egyptians.

How can we care for poor people? Consider this story: Mike and Dave were spending some time in a large city. During a walk, they went by the train station, a place where many runaways and homeless people found refuge. They came across a young man hunched over with his back to the wall. His clothes were wet, and he was shivering. He was holding a cup, panhandling. Dave took out some change and threw it into the cup. Mike just stood and stared. Dave motioned to Mike to keep on moving, but Mike didn't move. Then Mike did something that amazed Dave. He sat down and took off his shoes, an almost brand-new pair of insulated leather hiking boots he had received for Christmas. He motioned to the young homeless man to do the same. He took his boots and socks and put them on the young man. Mike put on the young man's old canvas sneakers, stood up, and walked away. Dave followed in silence.

▶ **Ex 22.21–27**

5 When someone causes a field or vineyard to be grazed over, or lets livestock loose to graze in someone else's field, restitution shall be made from the best in the owner's field or vineyard.

6 When fire breaks out and catches in thorns so that the stacked grain or the standing grain or the field is consumed, the one who started the fire shall make full restitution.

7 When someone delivers to a neighbor money or goods for safekeeping, and they are stolen from the neighbor's house, then the thief, if caught, shall pay double. 8 If the thief is not caught, the owner of the house shall be brought before God,*y* to determine whether or not the owner had laid hands on the neighbor's goods.

9 In any case of disputed ownership involving ox, donkey, sheep, clothing, or any other loss,

14 When someone borrows an animal from another and it is injured or dies, the owner not being present, full restitution shall be made. 15 If the owner was present, there shall be no restitution; if it was hired, only the hiring fee is due.

Social and Religious Laws

16 When a man seduces a virgin who is not engaged to be married, and lies with her, he shall give the bride-price for her and make her his wife. 17 But if her father refuses to give her to him, he shall pay an amount equal to the bride-price for virgins.

18 You shall not permit a female sorcerer to live.

---

v Ch 21.37 in Heb   *w* Verses 2, 3, and 4 rearranged thus: 3b, 4, 2, 3a   *x* Ch 22.1 in Heb   *y* Or *before the judges*
z Or *the judges condemn*

19 Whoever lies with an animal shall be put to death.

20 Whoever sacrifices to any god, other than the LORD alone, shall be devoted to destruction.

21 You shall not wrong or oppress a resident alien, for you were aliens in the land of Egypt. 22 You shall not abuse any widow or orphan. 23 If you do abuse them, when they cry out to me, I will surely heed their cry; 24 my wrath will burn, and I will kill you with the sword, and your wives shall become widows and your children orphans.

25 If you lend money to my people, to the poor among you, you shall not deal with them as a creditor; you shall not exact interest from them. 26 If you take your neighbor's cloak in pawn, you shall restore it before the sun goes down; 27 for it may be your neighbor's only clothing to use as cover; in what else shall that person sleep? And if your neighbor cries out to me, I will listen, for I am compassionate.

28 You shall not revile God, or curse a leader of your people.

29 You shall not delay to make offerings from the fullness of your harvest and from the outflow of your presses.[a]

The firstborn of your sons you shall give to me. 30 You shall do the same with your oxen and with your sheep: seven days it shall remain with its mother; on the eighth day you shall give it to me.

31 You shall be people consecrated to me; therefore you shall not eat any meat that is mangled by beasts in the field; you shall throw it to the dogs.

Justice for All

23 You shall not spread a false report. You shall not join hands with the wicked to act as a malicious witness. 2 You shall not follow a majority in wrongdoing; when you bear witness in a lawsuit, you shall not side with the majority so as to pervert justice; 3 nor shall you be partial to the poor in a lawsuit.

4 When you come upon your enemy's ox or donkey going astray, you shall bring it back.

5 When you see the donkey of one who hates you lying under its burden and you would hold back from setting it free, you must help to set it free.[a]

6 You shall not pervert the justice due to your poor in their lawsuits. 7 Keep far from a false charge, and do not kill the innocent and those in the right, for I will not acquit the guilty. 8 You shall take no bribe, for a bribe blinds the officials, and subverts the cause of those who are in the right.

9 You shall not oppress a resident alien; you know the heart of an alien, for you were aliens in the land of Egypt.

Sabbatical Year and Sabbath

10 For six years you shall sow your land and gather in its yield; 11 but the seventh year you shall let it rest and lie fallow, so that the poor of your people may eat; and what they leave the wild animals may eat. You shall do the same with your vineyard, and with your olive orchard.

12 Six days you shall do your work, but on the seventh day you shall rest, so that your ox and your donkey may have relief, and your homeborn slave and the resident alien may be refreshed. 13 Be attentive to all that I have said to you. Do not invoke the names of other gods; do not let them be heard on your lips.

The Annual Festivals
(Ex 34.18–26; Deut 16.1–17)

14 Three times in the year you shall hold a festival for me. 15 You shall observe the festival of unleavened bread; as I commanded you, you shall eat unleavened bread for seven days at the appointed time in the month of Ā'bib, for in it you came out of Egypt.

No one shall appear before me empty-handed.

16 You shall observe the festival of harvest, of the first fruits of your labor, of what you sow in the field. You shall observe the festival of ingathering at the end of the year, when you gather in from the field the fruit of your labor. 17 Three times in the year all your males shall appear before the Lord GOD.

18 You shall not offer the blood of my sacrifice with anything leavened, or let the fat of my festival remain until the morning.

19 The choicest of the first fruits of your ground you shall bring into the house of the LORD your God.

You shall not boil a kid in its mother's milk.

The Conquest of Canaan Promised

20 I am going to send an angel in front of you, to guard you on the way and to bring you to the place that I have prepared. 21 Be attentive to him and listen to his voice; do not rebel against him, for he will not pardon your transgression; for my name is in him.

22 But if you listen attentively to his voice and do all that I say, then I will be an enemy to your enemies and a foe to your foes.

23 When my angel goes in front of you, and brings you to the Am'o•rites, the Hit'tites, the Per'iz•zites, the Cā'naan•ites, the Hi'vites, and the Jeb'ū•sites, and I blot them out, 24 you shall not bow down to their gods, or worship them, or follow their practices, but you shall utterly demolish

EX

---

a Meaning of Heb uncertain

them and break their pillars in pieces. 25 You shall worship the LORD your God, and I*b* will bless your bread and your water; and I will take sickness away from among you. 26 No one shall miscarry or be barren in your land; I will fulfill the number of your days. 27 I will send my terror in front of you, and will throw into confusion all the people against whom you shall come, and I will make all your enemies turn their backs to you. 28 And I will send the pestilence*c* in front of you, which shall drive out the Hi′vites, the Cā′naan•ites, and the Hit′tites from before you. 29 I will not drive them out from before you in one year, or the land would become desolate and the wild animals would multiply against you. 30 Little by little I will drive them out from before you, until you have increased and possess the land. 31 I will set your borders from the Red Sea*d* to the sea of the Phi•lis′tines, and from the wilderness to the Euphrates; for I will hand over to you the inhabitants of the land, and you shall drive them out before you. 32 You shall make no covenant with them and their gods. 33 They shall not live in your land, or they will make you sin against me; for if you worship their gods, it will surely be a snare to you.

The Blood of the Covenant

24 Then he said to Moses, "Come up to the LORD, you and Aaron, Nā′dab, and A•bi′hū, and seventy of the elders of Israel, and worship at a distance. 2 Moses alone shall come near the LORD; but the others shall not come near, and the people shall not come up with him."

3 Moses came and told the people all the words of the LORD and all the ordinances; and all the people answered with one voice, and said, "All the words that the LORD has spoken we will do." 4 And Moses wrote down all the words of the LORD. He rose early in the morning, and built an altar at the foot of the mountain, and set up twelve pillars, corresponding to the twelve tribes of Israel. 5 He sent young men of the people of Israel, who offered burnt offerings and sacrificed oxen as offerings of well-being to the LORD. 6 Moses took half of the blood and put it in basins, and half of the blood he dashed against the altar. 7 Then he took the book of the covenant, and read it in the hearing of the people; and they said, "All that the LORD has spoken we will do, and we will be obedient." 8 Moses took the blood and dashed it on the people, and said, "See the blood of the covenant that the LORD has made with you in accordance with all these words."

On the Mountain with God

9 Then Moses and Aaron, Nā′dab, and A•bi′hū, and seventy of the elders of Israel went up, 10 and they saw the God of Israel. Under his feet there was something like a pavement of sapphire stone, like the very heaven for clearness. 11 God*e* did not lay his hand on the chief men of the people of Israel; also they beheld God, and they ate and drank.

12 The LORD said to Moses, "Come up to me on the mountain, and wait there; and I will give you the tablets of stone, with the law and the commandment, which I have written for their instruction." 13 So Moses set out with his assistant Joshua, and Moses went up into the mountain of God.

b Gk Vg: Heb *he*   *c* Or *hornets:* Meaning of Heb uncertain *d* Or *Sea of Reeds*   *e* Heb *He*

did you KNOW?

Sacrifice and the Eucharist

Sacrifice is defined as an offering made to God that becomes holy by being set apart, blessed, and burned or consumed. Just as food and gifts were brought to a king as a form of tribute and worship, so too in Israel animals were brought to God and sacrificed, their blood splattered on the altar, and their meat cooked and eaten as a form of worship that brought communion with God. The blood symbolized God's gift of life, and when the blessed sacrifice was eaten, communion occurred between God and people. In Exodus, chapter 24, when Israel is about to ratify the Covenant with God, Moses smears the blood of the animal on the altar to assert the Israelites' union with God through the observance of the Covenant.

In the New Testament, the language Jesus uses at his Last Supper seems to reflect this sacrificial understanding. Jesus shares bread and wine as his body and blood and speaks about a New Covenant that will be ratified by the giving of his body and the shedding of his blood. Even today, Catholics celebrating the Eucharist in Jesus' memory encounter the real presence of Jesus in the sacred food of bread and wine, recalling the New Covenant of love he established through giving his body and shedding his blood.

▶ Ex 24.1–8

14 To the elders he had said, "Wait here for us, until we come to you again; for Aaron and Hur are with you; whoever has a dispute may go to them."

15 Then Moses went up on the mountain, and the cloud covered the mountain. 16 The glory of the LORD settled on Mount Sinai, and the cloud covered it for six days; on the seventh day he called to Moses out of the cloud. 17 Now the appearance of the glory of the LORD was like a devouring fire on the top of the mountain in the sight of the people of Israel. 18 Moses entered the cloud, and went up on the mountain. Moses was on the mountain for forty days and forty nights.

25.10–22

Offerings for the Tabernacle
(Ex 35.4–9)

25 The LORD said to Moses: 2 Tell the Israelites to take for me an offering; from all whose hearts prompt them to give you shall receive the offering for me. 3 This is the offering that you shall receive from them: gold, silver, and bronze, 4 blue, purple, and crimson yarns and fine linen, goats' hair, 5 tanned rams' skins, fine leather,*f* acacia wood, 6 oil for the lamps, spices for the anointing oil and for the fragrant incense, 7 onyx stones and gems to be set in the ephod and for the breastpiece. 8 And have them make me a sanctuary, so that I may dwell among them. 9 In accordance with all that I show you concerning the pattern of the tabernacle and of all its furniture, so you shall make it.

The Ark of the Covenant
(Ex 37.1–9)

10 They shall make an ark of acacia wood; it shall be two and a half cubits long, a cubit and a half wide, and a cubit and a half high. 11 You shall overlay it with pure gold, inside and outside you shall overlay it, and you shall make a molding of gold upon it all around. 12 You shall cast four rings of gold for it and put them on its four feet, two rings on the one side of it, and two rings on the other side. 13 You shall make poles of acacia wood, and overlay them with gold. 14 And you shall put the poles into the rings on the sides of the ark, by which to carry the ark. 15 The poles shall remain in the rings of the ark; they shall not be taken from it. 16 You shall put into the ark the covenant*g* that I shall give you.

17 Then you shall make a mercy seat*h* of pure gold; two cubits and a half shall be its length, and a cubit and a half its width. 18 You shall make two cherubim of gold; you shall make them of hammered work, at the two ends of the mercy seat.*i* 19 Make one cherub at the one end, and one cherub at the other; of one piece with the mercy seat*i* you shall make the cherubim at its two ends. 20 The cherubim shall spread out their wings above, overshadowing the mercy seat*i* with their wings. They shall face one to another; the faces of the cherubim shall be turned toward the mercy seat.*i* 21 You shall put the mercy seat*i* on the top of the ark; and in the ark you shall put the covenant*g* that I shall give you. 22 There I will meet with you, and from above the mercy seat,*i* from between the two cherubim that are on the ark of the covenant,*g* I will deliver to you all my commands for the Israelites.

The Table for the Bread of the Presence
(Ex 37.10–16)

23 You shall make a table of acacia wood, two cubits long, one cubit wide, and a cubit and a half high. 24 You shall overlay it with pure gold, and make a molding of gold around it. 25 You shall make around it a rim a handbreadth wide, and a molding of gold around the rim. 26 You shall make for it four rings of gold, and fasten the rings to the four corners at its four legs. 27 The rings that hold the poles used for carrying the table shall be close to the rim. 28 You shall make the poles of acacia wood, and overlay them with gold, and the table shall be carried with these. 29 You shall make its plates and dishes for incense, and its flagons and bowls with which to pour drink offerings; you shall make them of pure gold. 30 And you shall set the bread of the Presence on the table before me always.

The Lampstand
(Ex 37.17–24)

31 You shall make a lampstand of pure gold. The base and the shaft of the lampstand shall be

---

f Meaning of Heb uncertain   *g* Or *treaty,* or *testimony*; Heb *eduth*   *h* Or *a cover*   *i* Or *the cover* made of hammered work; its cups, its calyxes, and its petals shall be of one piece with it; 32 and there shall be six branches going out of its sides, three branches of the lampstand out of one side of it and three branches of the lampstand out of the other side of it; 33 three cups shaped like almond blossoms, each with calyx and petals, on one branch, and three cups shaped like almond blossoms, each with calyx and petals, on the other branch—so for the six branches going out of the lampstand. 34 On the lampstand itself there shall be four cups shaped like almond blossoms, each with its calyxes and petals. 35 There shall be a calyx of one piece with it under the first pair of branches, a calyx of one piece with it under the next pair of branches, and a calyx of one piece with it under the last pair of branches—so for the six branches that go out of the lampstand. 36 Their calyxes and their branches shall be of one piece with it, the whole of it one hammered piece of pure gold. 37 You shall make the seven lamps for it; and the lamps shall be set up so as to give light on the space in front of it. 38 Its snuffers and trays shall be of pure gold. 39 It, and all these utensils, shall be made from a talent of pure gold. 40 And see that you make them according to the pattern for them, which is being shown you on the mountain.

The Tabernacle
(Ex 36.8–38)

26 Moreover you shall make the tabernacle with ten curtains of fine twisted linen, and blue, purple, and crimson yarns; you shall make them with cherubim skillfully worked into them. 2 The length of each curtain shall be twenty-eight cubits, and the width of each curtain four cubits; all the curtains shall be of the same size. 3 Five curtains shall be joined to one another; and the other five curtains shall be joined to one another. 4 You shall make loops of blue on the edge of the outermost curtain in the first set; and likewise you shall make loops on the edge of the outermost curtain in the second set. 5 You shall make fifty loops on the one curtain, and you shall make fifty loops on the edge of the curtain that is in the second set; the loops shall be opposite one another. 6 You shall make fifty clasps of gold, and join the curtains to one another with the clasps, so that the tabernacle may be one whole.

7 You shall also make curtains of goats' hair for a tent over the tabernacle; you shall make eleven curtains. 8 The length of each curtain shall be thirty cubits, and the width of each curtain four cubits; the eleven curtains shall be of the same size. 9 You shall join five curtains by themselves, and six curtains by themselves, and the sixth curtain you shall double over at the front of the tent. 10 You shall

make fifty loops on the edge of the curtain that is outermost in one set, and fifty loops on the edge of the curtain that is outermost in the second set.

11 You shall make fifty clasps of bronze, and put the clasps into the loops, and join the tent together, so that it may be one whole. 12 The part that remains of the curtains of the tent, the half curtain that remains, shall hang over the back of the tabernacle. 13 The cubit on the one side, and the cubit on the other side, of what remains in the length of the curtains of the tent, shall hang over the sides of the tabernacle, on this side and that side, to cover it. 14 You shall make for the tent a covering of tanned rams' skins and an outer covering of fine leather.*j*

The Framework
15 You shall make upright frames of acacia wood for the tabernacle. 16 Ten cubits shall be the length of a frame, and a cubit and a half the width of each frame. 17 There shall be two pegs in each frame to fit the frames together; you shall make these for all the frames of the tabernacle. 18 You shall make the frames for the tabernacle: twenty frames for the south side; 19 and you shall make forty bases of silver under the twenty frames, two bases under the first frame for its two pegs, and two bases under the next frame for its two pegs; 20 and for the second side of the tabernacle, on the north side twenty frames, 21 and their forty bases of silver, two bases under the first frame, and two bases under the next frame; 22 and for the rear of the tabernacle westward you shall make six frames. 23 You shall make two frames for corners of the tabernacle in the rear; 24 they shall be separate beneath, but joined at the top, at the first ring; it shall be the same with both of them; they shall form the two corners. 25 And so there shall be eight frames, with their bases of silver, sixteen bases; two bases under the first frame, and two bases under the next frame.

26 You shall make bars of acacia wood, five for the frames of the one side of the tabernacle, 27 and five bars for the frames of the other side of the tabernacle, and five bars for the frames of the side of the tabernacle at the rear westward. 28 The middle bar, halfway up the frames, shall pass through from end to end. 29 You shall overlay the frames with gold, and shall make their rings of gold to hold the bars; and you shall overlay the bars with gold. 30 Then you shall erect the tabernacle according to the plan for it that you were shown on the mountain.

The Curtain
31 You shall make a curtain of blue, purple, and crimson yarns, and of fine twisted linen; it shall

---

j Meaning of Heb uncertain

be made with cherubim skillfully worked into it. 32 You shall hang it on four pillars of acacia overlaid with gold, which have hooks of gold and rest on four bases of silver. 33 You shall hang the curtain under the clasps, and bring the ark of the covenant*k* in there, within the curtain; and the curtain shall separate for you the holy place from the most holy. 34 You shall put the mercy seat*l* on the ark of the covenant*k* in the most holy place. 35 You shall set the table outside the curtain, and the lampstand on the south side of the tabernacle opposite the table; and you shall put the table on the north side.

36 You shall make a screen for the entrance of the tent, of blue, purple, and crimson yarns, and of fine twisted linen, embroidered with needlework. 37 You shall make for the screen five pillars of acacia, and overlay them with gold; their hooks shall be of gold, and you shall cast five bases of bronze for them.

The Altar of Burnt Offering
(Ex 38.1–7)

27 You shall make the altar of acacia wood, five cubits long and five cubits wide; the altar shall be square, and it shall be three cubits high. 2 You shall make horns for it on its four corners; its horns shall be of one piece with it, and you shall overlay it with bronze. 3 You shall make pots for it to receive its ashes, and shovels and basins and forks and firepans; you shall make all its utensils of bronze. 4 You shall also make for it a grating, a network of bronze; and on the net you shall make four bronze rings at its four corners. 5 You shall set it under the ledge of the altar so that the net shall extend halfway down the altar. 6 You shall make poles for the altar, poles of acacia wood, and overlay them with bronze; 7 the poles shall be put through the rings, so that the poles shall be on the two sides of the altar when it is carried. 8 You shall make it hollow, with boards. They shall be made just as you were shown on the mountain.

The Court and Its Hangings
(Ex 38.9–20)

9 You shall make the court of the tabernacle. On the south side the court shall have hangings of fine twisted linen one hundred cubits long for that side; 10 its twenty pillars and their twenty bases shall be of bronze, but the hooks of the pillars and their bands shall be of silver. 11 Likewise for its length on the north side there shall be hangings one hundred cubits long, their pillars twenty and their bases twenty, of bronze, but the hooks of the pillars and their bands shall be of silver. 12 For the width of the court on the west side there shall be fifty cubits of hangings, with ten pillars and ten bases. 13 The width of the court on the front to the east shall be fifty cubits. 14 There shall be fifteen cubits of hangings on the one side, with three pillars and three bases. 15 There shall be fifteen cubits of hangings on the other side, with three pillars and three bases. 16 For the gate of the court there shall be a screen twenty cubits long, of blue, purple, and crimson yarns, and of fine twisted linen, embroidered with needlework; it shall have four pillars and with them four bases. 17 All the pillars around the court shall be banded with silver; their hooks shall be of silver, and their bases of bronze. 18 The length of the court shall be one hundred cubits, the width fifty, and the height five cubits, with hangings of fine twisted linen and bases of bronze. 19 All the utensils of the tabernacle for every use, and all its pegs and all the pegs of the court, shall be of bronze.

The Oil for the Lamp
(Lev 24.1–4)

20 You shall further command the Israelites to bring you pure oil of beaten olives for the light, so that a lamp may be set up to burn regularly. 21 In the tent of meeting, outside the curtain that is before the covenant,*k* Aaron and his sons shall tend it from evening to morning before the LORD. It shall be a perpetual ordinance to be observed throughout their generations by the Israelites.

Vestments for the Priesthood
(Ex 39.1–7)

28 Then bring near to you your brother Aaron, and his sons with him, from among the Israelites, to serve me as priests—Aaron and Aaron's sons, Nă′dab and A•bī′hū, El•ē•ā′zar and Ith′a•mar. 2 You shall make sacred vestments for the glorious adornment of your brother Aaron. 3 And you shall speak to all who have ability, whom I have endowed with skill, that they make Aaron's vestments to consecrate him for my priesthood. 4 These are the vestments that they shall make: a breastpiece, an ephod, a robe, a checkered tunic, a turban, and a sash. When they make these sacred vestments for your brother Aaron and his sons to serve me as priests, 5 they shall use gold, blue, purple, and crimson yarns, and fine linen.

The Ephod

6 They shall make the ephod of gold, of blue, purple, and crimson yarns, and of fine twisted linen, skillfully worked. 7 It shall have two shoulder-pieces attached to its two edges, so that it may be joined together. 8 The decorated band on it shall be of the same workmanship and materials, of gold, of blue, purple, and crimson yarns, and of fine twisted linen. 9 You shall take two onyx stones, and

EX

---

k Or *treaty,* or *testimony;* Heb *eduth*   *l* Or *the cover* engrave on them the names of the sons of Israel, [10] six of their names on the one stone, and the names of the remaining six on the other stone, in the order of their birth. [11] As a gem-cutter engraves signets, so you shall engrave the two stones with the names of the sons of Israel; you shall mount them in settings of gold filigree. [12] You shall set the two stones on the shoulder-pieces of the ephod, as stones of remembrance for the sons of Israel; and Aaron shall bear their names before the LORD on his two shoulders for remembrance. [13] You shall make settings of gold filigree, [14] and two chains of pure gold, twisted like cords; and you shall attach the corded chains to the settings.

The Breastplate
(Ex 39.8–21)

15 You shall make a breastpiece of judgment, in skilled work; you shall make it in the style of the ephod; of gold, of blue and purple and crimson yarns, and of fine twisted linen you shall make it. [16] It shall be square and doubled, a span in length and a span in width. [17] You shall set in it four rows of stones. A row of carnelian,[m] chrysolite, and emerald shall be the first row; [18] and the second row a turquoise, a sapphire,[n] and a moonstone; [19] and the third row a jacinth, an agate, and an amethyst; [20] and the fourth row a beryl, an onyx, and a jasper; they shall be set in gold filigree. [21] There shall be twelve stones with names corresponding to the names of the sons of Israel; they shall be like signets, each engraved with its name, for the twelve tribes. [22] You shall make for the breastpiece chains of pure gold, twisted like cords; [23] and you shall make for the breastpiece two rings of gold, and put the two rings on the two edges of the breastpiece. [24] You shall put the two cords of gold in the two rings at the edges of the breastpiece; [25] the two ends of the two cords you shall attach to the two settings, and so attach it in front to the shoulder-pieces of the ephod. [26] You shall make two rings of gold, and put them at the two ends of the breastpiece, on its inside edge next to the ephod. [27] You shall make two rings of gold, and attach them in front to the lower part of the two shoulder-pieces of the ephod, at its joining above the decorated band of the ephod. [28] The breastpiece shall be bound by its rings to the rings of the ephod with a blue cord, so that it may lie on the decorated band of the ephod, and so that the breastpiece shall not come loose from the ephod. [29] So Aaron shall bear the names of the sons of Israel in the breastpiece of judgment on his heart when he goes into the holy place, for a continual remembrance before the LORD. [30] In the breastpiece of judgment you shall put the U'rim and the Thum'mim, and they shall be on Aaron's heart when he goes in before the LORD; thus Aaron shall

bear the judgment of the Israelites on his heart before the LORD continually.

Other Priestly Vestments
(Ex 39.22–31)

31 You shall make the robe of the ephod all of blue. [32] It shall have an opening for the head in the middle of it, with a woven binding around the opening, like the opening in a coat of mail,[o] so that it may not be torn. [33] On its lower hem you shall make pomegranates of blue, purple, and crimson yarns, all around the lower hem, with bells of gold between them all around— [34] a golden bell and a pomegranate alternating all around the lower hem of the robe. [35] Aaron shall wear it when he ministers, and its sound shall be heard when he goes into the holy place before the LORD, and when he comes out, so that he may not die.

36 You shall make a rosette of pure gold, and engrave on it, like the engraving of a signet, "Holy to the LORD." [37] You shall fasten it on the turban with a blue cord; it shall be on the front of the turban. [38] It shall be on Aaron's forehead, and Aaron shall take on himself any guilt incurred in the holy offering that the Israelites consecrate as their sacred donations; it shall always be on his forehead, in order that they may find favor before the LORD.

39 You shall make the checkered tunic of fine linen, and you shall make a turban of fine linen, and you shall make a sash embroidered with needlework.

40 For Aaron's sons you shall make tunics and sashes and headdresses; you shall make them for their glorious adornment. [41] You shall put them on your brother Aaron, and on his sons with him, and shall anoint them and ordain them and consecrate them, so that they may serve me as priests. [42] You shall make for them linen undergarments to cover their naked flesh; they shall reach from the hips to the thighs; [43] Aaron and his sons shall wear them when they go into the tent of meeting, or when they come near the altar to minister in the holy place; or they will bring guilt on themselves and die. This shall be a perpetual ordinance for him and for his descendants after him.

The Ordination of the Priests
(Lev 8.1–36)

29 Now this is what you shall do to them to consecrate them, so that they may serve me as priests. Take one young bull and two rams without blemish, [2] and unleavened bread, unleavened cakes mixed with oil, and unleavened wafers spread with oil. You shall make them of choice

---

m The identity of several of these stones is uncertain   n Or lapis lazuli   o Meaning of Heb uncertain wheat flour. 3 You shall put them in one basket and bring them in the basket, and bring the bull and the two rams. 4 You shall bring Aaron and his sons to the entrance of the tent of meeting, and wash them with water. 5 Then you shall take the vestments, and put on Aaron the tunic and the robe of the ephod, and the ephod, and the breastpiece, and gird him with the decorated band of the ephod; 6 and you shall set the turban on his head, and put the holy diadem on the turban. 7 You shall take the anointing oil, and pour it on his head and anoint him. 8 Then you shall bring his sons, and put tunics on them, 9 and you shall gird them with sashes*p* and tie headdresses on them; and the priesthood shall be theirs by a perpetual ordinance. You shall then ordain Aaron and his sons.

10 You shall bring the bull in front of the tent of meeting. Aaron and his sons shall lay their hands on the head of the bull, 11 and you shall slaughter the bull before the LORD, at the entrance of the tent of meeting, 12 and shall take some of the blood of the bull and put it on the horns of the altar with your finger, and all the rest of the blood you shall pour out at the base of the altar. 13 You shall take all the fat that covers the entrails, and the appendage of the liver, and the two kidneys with the fat that is on them, and turn them into smoke on the altar. 14 But the flesh of the bull, and its skin, and its dung, you shall burn with fire outside the camp; it is a sin offering.

15 Then you shall take one of the rams, and Aaron and his sons shall lay their hands on the head of the ram, 16 and you shall slaughter the ram, and shall take its blood and dash it against all sides of the altar. 17 Then you shall cut the ram into its parts, and wash its entrails and its legs, and put them with its parts and its head, 18 and turn the whole ram into smoke on the altar; it is a burnt offering to the LORD; it is a pleasing odor, an offering by fire to the LORD.

19 You shall take the other ram; and Aaron and his sons shall lay their hands on the head of the ram, 20 and you shall slaughter the ram, and take some of its blood and put it on the lobe of Aaron's right ear and on the lobes of the right ears of his sons, and on the thumbs of their right hands, and on the big toes of their right feet, and dash the rest of the blood against all sides of the altar. 21 Then you shall take some of the blood that is on the altar, and some of the anointing oil, and sprinkle it on Aaron and his vestments and on his sons and his sons' vestments with him; then he and his vestments shall be holy, as well as his sons and his sons' vestments.

22 You shall also take the fat of the ram, the fat tail, the fat that covers the entrails, the appendage of the liver, the two kidneys with the fat that is on them, and the right thigh (for it is a ram of ordination), 23 and one loaf of bread, one cake of bread made with oil, and one wafer, out of the basket of unleavened bread that is before the LORD; 24 and you shall place all these on the palms of Aaron and on the palms of his sons, and raise them as an elevation offering before the LORD. 25 Then you shall take them from their hands, and turn them into smoke on the altar on top of the burnt offering of pleasing odor before the LORD; it is an offering by fire to the LORD.

26 You shall take the breast of the ram of Aaron's ordination and raise it as an elevation offering before the LORD; and it shall be your portion. 27 You shall consecrate the breast that was raised as an elevation offering and the thigh that was raised as an elevation offering from the ram of ordination, from that which belonged to Aaron and his sons. 28 These things shall be a perpetual ordinance for Aaron and his sons from the Israelites, for this is an offering; and it shall be an offering by the Israelites from their sacrifice of offerings of well-being, their offering to the LORD.

29 The sacred vestments of Aaron shall be passed on to his sons after him; they shall be anointed in them and ordained in them. 30 The son who is priest in his place shall wear them seven days, when he comes into the tent of meeting to minister in the holy place.

31 You shall take the ram of ordination, and boil its flesh in a holy place; 32 and Aaron and his sons shall eat the flesh of the ram and the bread that is in the basket, at the entrance of the tent of meeting. 33 They themselves shall eat the food by which atonement is made, to ordain and consecrate them, but no one else shall eat of them, because they are holy. 34 If any of the flesh for the ordination, or of the bread, remains until the morning, then you shall burn the remainder with fire; it shall not be eaten, because it is holy.

35 Thus you shall do to Aaron and to his sons, just as I have commanded you; through seven days you shall ordain them. 36 Also every day you shall offer a bull as a sin offering for atonement. Also you shall offer a sin offering for the altar, when you make atonement for it, and shall anoint it, to consecrate it. 37 Seven days you shall make atonement for the altar, and consecrate it, and the altar shall be most holy; whatever touches the altar shall become holy.

The Daily Offerings
(Num 28.1–8)

38 Now this is what you shall offer on the altar: two lambs a year old regularly each day. 39 One

---

p Gk: Heb *sashes, Aaron and his sons*

lamb you shall offer in the morning, and the other lamb you shall offer in the evening; 40 and with the first lamb one-tenth of a measure of choice flour mixed with one-fourth of a hin of beaten oil, and one-fourth of a hin of wine for a drink offering. 41 And the other lamb you shall offer in the evening, and shall offer with it a grain offering and its drink offering, as in the morning, for a pleasing odor, an offering by fire to the LORD. 42 It shall be a regular burnt offering throughout your generations at the entrance of the tent of meeting before the LORD, where I will meet with you, to speak to you there. 43 I will meet with the Israelites there, and it shall be sanctified by my glory; 44 I will consecrate the tent of meeting and the altar; Aaron also and his sons I will consecrate, to serve me as priests. 45 I will dwell among the Israelites, and I will be their God. 46 And they shall know that I am the LORD their God, who brought them out of the land of Egypt that I might dwell among them; I am the LORD their God.

The Altar of Incense
(Ex 37.25–28)

30 You shall make an altar on which to offer incense; you shall make it of acacia wood. 2 It shall be one cubit long, and one cubit wide; it shall be square, and shall be two cubits high; its horns shall be of one piece with it. 3 You shall overlay it with pure gold, its top, and its sides all around and its horns; and you shall make for it a molding of gold all around. 4 And you shall make two golden rings for it; under its molding on two opposite sides of it you shall make them, and they shall hold the poles with which to carry it. 5 You shall make the poles of acacia wood, and overlay them with gold. 6 You shall place it in front of the curtain that is above the ark of the covenant,q in front of the mercy seatr that is over the covenant,q where I will meet with you. 7 Aaron shall offer fragrant incense on it; every morning when he dresses the lamps he shall offer it, 8 and when Aaron sets up the lamps in the evening, he shall offer it, a regular incense offering before the LORD throughout your generations. 9 You shall not offer unholy incense on it, or a burnt offering, or a grain offering; and you shall not pour a drink offering on it. 10 Once a year Aaron shall perform the rite of atonement on its horns. Throughout your generations he shall perform the atonement for it once a year with the blood of the atoning sin offering. It is most holy to the LORD.

The Half Shekel for the Sanctuary

11 The LORD spoke to Moses: 12 When you take a census of the Israelites to register them, at registration all of them shall give a ransom for their lives to the LORD, so that no plague may come upon them for being registered. 13 This is what each one who is registered shall give: half a shekel according to the shekel of the sanctuary (the shekel is twenty gerahs), half a shekel as an offering to the LORD. 14 Each one who is registered, from twenty years old and upward, shall give the LORD's offering. 15 The rich shall not give more, and the poor shall not give less, than the half shekel, when you bring this offering to the LORD to make atonement for your lives. 16 You shall take the atonement money from the Israelites and shall designate it for the service of the tent of meeting; before the LORD it will be a reminder to the Israelites of the ransom given for your lives.

The Bronze Basin

17 The LORD spoke to Moses: 18 You shall make a bronze basin with a bronze stand for washing. You shall put it between the tent of meeting and the altar, and you shall put water in it; 19 with the waters Aaron and his sons shall wash their hands and their feet. 20 When they go into the tent of meeting, or when they come near the altar to minister, to make an offering by fire to the LORD, they shall wash with water, so that they may not die. 21 They shall wash their hands and their feet, so that they may not die: it shall be a perpetual ordinance for them, for him and for his descendants throughout their generations.

The Anointing Oil and Incense
(Ex 37.29)

22 The LORD spoke to Moses: 23 Take the finest spices: of liquid myrrh five hundred shekels, and of sweet-smelling cinnamon half as much, that is, two hundred fifty, and two hundred fifty of aromatic cane, 24 and five hundred of cassia—measured by the sanctuary shekel—and a hin of olive oil; 25 and you shall make of these a sacred anointing oil blended as by the perfumer; it shall be a holy anointing oil. 26 With it you shall anoint the tent of meeting and the ark of the covenant,q 27 and the table and all its utensils, and the lampstand and its utensils, and the altar of incense, 28 and the altar of burnt offering with all its utensils, and the basin with its stand; 29 you shall consecrate them, so that they may be most holy; whatever touches them will become holy. 30 You shall anoint Aaron and his sons, and consecrate them, in order that they may serve me as priests. 31 You shall say to the Israelites, "This shall be my holy anointing oil throughout your generations. 32 It shall not be used in any ordinary anointing of the body, and you shall make

---

q Or *treaty*, or *testimony*; Heb *eduth*   r Or *the cover*
s Heb *it*

no other like it in composition; it is holy, and it shall be holy to you. 33 Whoever compounds any like it or whoever puts any of it on an unqualified person shall be cut off from the people."

34 The LORD said to Moses: Take sweet spices, stacte, and onycha, and galbanum, sweet spices with pure frankincense (an equal part of each), 35 and make an incense blended as by the perfumer, seasoned with salt, pure and holy; 36 and you shall beat some of it into powder, and put part of it before the covenant[t] in the tent of meeting where I shall meet with you; it shall be for you most holy. 37 When you make incense according to this composition, you shall not make it for yourselves; it shall be regarded by you as holy to the LORD. 38 Whoever makes any like it to use as perfume shall be cut off from the people.

Bezalel and Oholiab
(Ex 35.30—36.1)

31 The LORD spoke to Moses: 2 See, I have called by name Bez′a•lel son of U′rī son of Hur, of the tribe of Judah: 3 and I have filled him with divine spirit,[u] with ability, intelligence, and knowledge in every kind of craft, 4 to devise artistic designs, to work in gold, silver, and bronze, 5 in cutting stones for setting, and in carving wood, in every kind of craft. 6 Moreover, I have appointed with him Ŏ•hŏ′li•ab son of A•his′a•mach, of the tribe of Dan; and I have given skill to all the skillful, so that they may make all that I have commanded you: 7 the tent of meeting, and the ark of the covenant,[t] and the mercy seat[v] that is on it, and all the furnishings of the tent, 8 the table and its utensils, and the pure lampstand with all its utensils, and the altar of incense, 9 and the altar of burnt offering with all its utensils, and the basin with its stand, 10 and the finely worked vestments, the holy vestments for the priest Aaron and the vestments of his sons, for their service as priests, 11 and the anointing oil and the fragrant incense for the holy place. They shall do just as I have commanded you.

The Sabbath Law

12 The LORD said to Moses: 13 You yourself are to speak to the Israelites: "You shall keep my sabbaths, for this is a sign between me and you throughout your generations, given in order that you may know that I, the LORD, sanctify you. 14 You shall keep the sabbath, because it is holy for you; everyone who profanes it shall be put to death; whoever does any work on it shall be cut off from among the people. 15 Six days shall work be done, but the seventh day is a sabbath of solemn rest, holy to the LORD; whoever does any work on the sabbath day shall be put to death. 16 Therefore the

Israelites shall keep the sabbath, observing the sabbath throughout their generations, as a perpetual covenant. 17 It is a sign forever between me and the people of Israel that in six days the LORD made heaven and earth, and on the seventh day he rested, and was refreshed."

The Two Tablets of the Covenant

18 When God[w] finished speaking with Moses on Mount Sinai, he gave him the two tablets of the covenant,[t] tablets of stone, written with the finger of God.

The Golden Calf
(Deut 9.6–29)

32 When the people saw that Moses delayed to come down from the mountain, the people gathered around Aaron, and said to him, "Come, make gods for us, who shall go before us; as for this Moses, the man who brought us up out of the land of Egypt, we do not know what has become of him." 2 Aaron said to them, "Take off the gold rings that are on the ears of your wives, your sons, and your daughters, and bring them to me." 3 So all the people took off the gold rings from their ears, and brought them to Aaron. 4 He took the gold from them, formed it in a mold,[x] and cast an image of a calf; and they said, "These are your gods, O Israel, who brought you up out of the land of Egypt!" 5 When Aaron saw this, he built an altar before it; and Aaron made proclamation and said, "Tomorrow shall be a festival to the LORD." 6 They rose early the next day, and offered burnt offerings and brought sacrifices of well-being; and the people sat down to eat and drink, and rose up to revel.

7 The LORD said to Moses, "Go down at once! Your people, whom you brought up out of the land of Egypt, have acted perversely; 8 they have been quick to turn aside from the way that I commanded them; they have cast for themselves an image of a calf, and have worshiped it and sacrificed to it, and said, 'These are your gods, O Israel, who brought you up out of the land of Egypt!' " 9 The LORD said to Moses, "I have seen this people, how stiff-necked they are. 10 Now let me alone, so that my wrath may burn hot against them and I may consume them; and of you I will make a great nation."

11 But Moses implored the LORD his God, and said, "O LORD, why does your wrath burn hot against your people, whom you brought out of the land of Egypt with great power and with a mighty

---

t Or *treaty*, or *testimony*; Heb *eduth*   u Or *with the spirit of God*   v Or *the cover*   w Heb *he*   x Or *fashioned it with a graving tool*; Meaning of Heb uncertain

E
X

Caught Up in the Moment

Now that I think about it, it was a stupid thing to do. But it is so hard to be objective when you are caught up in the excitement of the moment. We had been waiting a long time for Moses—too long, it seems. We got bored and restless. You know how it is. Someone came up with the idea of the golden calf. It sounded like fun, something to pass the time and remind us of the old gods. And I have to admit, that calf did look pretty good!

I do feel sorry for Aaron. Moses saw what we had done and hurled the stone tablets to the ground in a fit of rage. Aaron tried to explain how it was, but Moses would hear none of it. He was upset. He had a right to be. There is no valid excuse for what we did. Aaron tried to pretend that the calf sort of formed itself, but it was a feeble excuse. We all knew it. And when we learned what was on the stone tablets, we knew we had done wrong. Moses had those tablets from the hands of God. This was to have been a solemn moment, followed by a great celebration. But instead, we had to face the wrath of Moses and pick up the shattered pieces of stone.

It is so easy to lose sight of what we are all about. It is so easy to do something stupid when we are bored and tired of waiting. And then we wonder how we could have let ourselves get so far off track. It is too easy, isn't it? We are all too human at times.

No, I don't blame Moses for losing his temper. He had every right. We let him down. We let ourselves down. But most of all, we let God down.

▶ Ex 32.1–35

---

hand? 12 Why should the Egyptians say, 'It was with evil intent that he brought them out to kill them in the mountains, and to consume them from the face of the earth'? Turn from your fierce wrath; change your mind and do not bring disaster on your people. 13 Remember Abraham, Isaac, and Israel, your servants, how you swore to them by your own self, saying to them, 'I will multiply your descendants like the stars of heaven, and all this land that I have promised I will give to your descendants, and they shall inherit it forever.' " 14 And the LORD changed his mind about the disaster that he planned to bring on his people.

15 Then Moses turned and went down from the mountain, carrying the two tablets of the covenant^y in his hands, tablets that were written on both sides, written on the front and on the back. 16 The tablets were the work of God, and the writing was the writing of God, engraved upon the tablets. 17 When Joshua heard the noise of the people as they shouted, he said to Moses, "There is a noise of war in the camp." 18 But he said,

"It is not the sound made by victors,
or the sound made by losers;
it is the sound of revelers that I hear."

19 As soon as he came near the camp and saw the calf and the dancing, Moses' anger burned hot, and he threw the tablets from his hands and broke them at the foot of the mountain. 20 He took the calf that they had made, burned it with fire, ground it to powder, scattered it on the water, and made the Israelites drink it.

21 Moses said to Aaron, "What did this people do to you that you have brought so great a sin upon them?" 22 And Aaron said, "Do not let the anger of my lord burn hot; you know the people, that they are bent on evil. 23 They said to me, 'Make us gods, who shall go before us; as for this Moses, the man who brought us up out of the land of Egypt, we do not know what has become of him.' 24 So I said to them, 'Whoever has gold, take it off'; so they gave it to me, and I threw it into the fire, and out came this calf!"

25 When Moses saw that the people were running wild (for Aaron had let them run wild, to the derision of their enemies), 26 then Moses stood in the gate of the camp, and said, "Who is on the LORD's side? Come to me!" And all the sons of Levi gathered around him. 27 He said to them, "Thus says the LORD, the God of Israel, 'Put your sword on your side, each of you! Go back and forth from gate to gate throughout the camp, and each of you kill your brother, your friend, and your neighbor.' " 28 The sons of Levi did as Moses commanded, and about three thousand of the people fell on that day. 29 Moses said, "Today you have ordained yourselves^z for the service of the LORD, each one at the

---

y Or *treaty,* or *testimony;* Heb *eduth*   z Gk Vg Compare Tg: Heb *Today ordain yourselves* cost of a son or a brother, and so have brought a blessing on yourselves this day."

30 On the next day Moses said to the people, "You have sinned a great sin. But now I will go up to the LORD; perhaps I can make atonement for your sin." 31 So Moses returned to the LORD and said, "Alas, this people has sinned a great sin; they have made for themselves gods of gold. 32 But now, if you will only forgive their sin—but if not, blot me out of the book that you have written." 33 But the LORD said to Moses, "Whoever has sinned against me I will blot out of my book. 34 But now go, lead the people to the place about which I have spoken to you; see, my angel shall go in front of you. Nevertheless, when the day comes for punishment, I will punish them for their sin."

35 Then the LORD sent a plague on the people, because they made the calf—the one that Aaron made.

The Command to Leave Sinai

33 The LORD said to Moses, "Go, leave this place, you and the people whom you have brought up out of the land of Egypt, and go to the land of which I swore to Abraham, Isaac, and Jacob, saying, 'To your descendants I will give it.' 2 I will send an angel before you, and I will drive out the Cā′naan•ites, the Am′o•rites, the Hit′tites, the Per′iz•zītes, the Hī′vītes, and the Jeb′ū•sītes. 3 Go up to a land flowing with milk and honey; but I will not go up among you, or I would consume you on the way, for you are a stiff-necked people."

4 When the people heard these harsh words, they mourned, and no one put on ornaments. 5 For the LORD had said to Moses, "Say to the Israelites, 'You are a stiff-necked people; if for a single moment I should go up among you, I would consume you. So now take off your ornaments, and I will decide what to do to you.' " 6 Therefore the Israelites stripped themselves of their ornaments, from Mount Hō′reb onward.

The Tent outside the Camp

7 Now Moses used to take the tent and pitch it outside the camp, far off from the camp; he called it the tent of meeting. And everyone who sought the LORD would go out to the tent of meeting, which was outside the camp. 8 Whenever Moses went out to the tent, all the people would rise and stand, each of them, at the entrance of their tents and watch Moses until he had gone into the tent. 9 When Moses entered the tent, the pillar of cloud would descend and stand at the entrance of the tent, and the LORD would speak with Moses. 10 When all the people saw the pillar of cloud standing at the entrance of the tent, all the people would rise and bow down, all of them, at the entrance of their tent. 11 Thus the LORD used to speak to Moses face to face, as one speaks to a friend. Then he would return to the camp; but his young assistant, Joshua son of Nun, would not leave the tent.

Moses' Intercession

12 Moses said to the LORD, "See, you have said to me, 'Bring up this people'; but you have not let me know whom you will send with me. Yet you have said, 'I know you by name, and you have also found favor in my sight.' 13 Now if I have found favor in your sight, show me your ways, so that I may know you and find favor in your sight. Consider too that this nation is your people." 14 He said, "My presence will go with you, and I will give you rest." 15 And he said to him, "If your presence will not go, do not carry us up from here. 16 For how shall it be known that I have found favor in your sight, I and your people, unless you go with us? In this way, we shall be distinct, I and your people, from every people on the face of the earth."

PRAY IT
God Passing By

How close can we get to God without actually seeing God's face? If anyone would know, it is Moses. His rather amazing encounter with God is recorded in Ex 33.17–23.

We too can experience, as many saints and mystics have, a deep intimacy with God. It is significant that God and Moses most often met in nature. If you are lucky, you have a favorite outdoor spot. Perhaps it is a place where you can simply sit and ponder as you gaze at the scenery before you. Perhaps during a sunset on a lovely summer evening or while gazing at the sea or a flowing stream, you somehow connect with God. You may not actually see or feel the hand of God, but somehow you know that God is with you and you are catching a glimpse of God's glory. You feel yourself held in the palm of God's gracious hand. And sometimes, like Moses (see 34.29), you are transformed by the power of God's presence.

Where do you most fully experience the presence of God?

▶ Ex 33.17–23

17 The Lord said to Moses, "I will do the very thing that you have asked; for you have found favor in my sight, and I know you by name." 18 Moses said, "Show me your glory, I pray." 19 And he said, "I will make all my goodness pass before you, and will proclaim before you the name, 'The Lord';a and I will be gracious to whom I will be gracious, and will show mercy on whom I will show mercy. 20 But," he said, "you cannot see my face; for no one shall see me and live." 21 And the Lord continued, "See, there is a place by me where you shall stand on the rock; 22 and while my glory passes by I will put you in a cleft of the rock, and I will cover you with my hand until I have passed by; 23 then I will take away my hand, and you shall see my back; but my face shall not be seen."

Moses Makes New Tablets
(Deut 10.1–5)

34 The Lord said to Moses, "Cut two tablets of stone like the former ones, and I will write on the tablets the words that were on the former tablets, which you broke. 2 Be ready in the morning, and come up in the morning to Mount Sinai and present yourself there to me, on the top of the mountain. 3 No one shall come up with you, and do not let anyone be seen throughout all the mountain; and do not let flocks or herds graze in front of that mountain." 4 So Moses cut two tablets of stone like the former ones; and he rose early in the morning and went up on Mount Sinai, as the Lord had commanded him, and took in his hand the two tablets of stone. 5 The Lord descended in the cloud and stood with him there, and proclaimed the name, "The Lord."a 6 The Lord passed before him, and proclaimed,

"The Lord, the Lord,
a God merciful and gracious,
slow to anger,
and abounding in steadfast love and
    faithfulness,
7 keeping steadfast love for the thousandth
    generation,b
forgiving iniquity and transgression
    and sin,
yet by no means clearing the guilty,
but visiting the iniquity of the parents
upon the children
and the children's children,
to the third and the fourth generation."

8 And Moses quickly bowed his head toward the earth, and worshiped. 9 He said, "If now I have found favor in your sight, O Lord, I pray, let the Lord go with us. Although this is a stiff-necked people, pardon our iniquity and our sin, and take us for your inheritance."

The Covenant Renewed
(Ex 23.14–19; Deut 7.1–6; 16.1–17)

10 He said: I hereby make a covenant. Before all your people I will perform marvels, such as have not been performed in all the earth or in any nation; and all the people among whom you live shall see the work of the Lord; for it is an awesome thing that I will do with you.

11 Observe what I command you today. See, I will drive out before you the Am'o•rites, the Ca'-naan•ites, the Hit'tites, the Per'iz•zites, the Hi'vites, and the Jeb'u•sites. 12 Take care not to make a covenant with the inhabitants of the land to which you are going, or it will become a snare among you. 13 You shall tear down their altars, break their pillars, and cut down their sacred polesc 14 (for you shall worship no other god, because the Lord, whose name is Jealous, is a jealous God). 15 You shall not make a covenant with the inhabitants of the land, for when they prostitute themselves to their gods and sacrifice to their gods, someone among them will invite you, and you will eat of the sacrifice. 16 And you will take wives from among their daughters for your sons, and their daughters who prostitute themselves to their gods will make your sons also prostitute themselves to their gods.

17 You shall not make cast idols.

18 You shall keep the festival of unleavened bread. Seven days you shall eat unleavened bread, as I commanded you, at the time appointed in the month of A'bib; for in the month of A'bib you came out from Egypt.

19 All that first opens the womb is mine, all your maled livestock, the firstborn of cow and sheep. 20 The firstborn of a donkey you shall redeem with a lamb, or if you will not redeem it you shall break its neck. All the firstborn of your sons you shall redeem.

No one shall appear before me empty-handed.

21 Six days you shall work, but on the seventh day you shall rest; even in plowing time and in harvest time you shall rest. 22 You shall observe the festival of weeks, the first fruits of wheat harvest, and the festival of ingathering at the turn of the year. 23 Three times in the year all your males shall appear before the Lord God, the God of Israel. 24 For I will cast out nations before you, and enlarge your borders; no one shall covet your land when you go up to appear before the Lord your God three times in the year.

25 You shall not offer the blood of my sacrifice with leaven, and the sacrifice of the festival of the passover shall not be left until the morning.

---

a Heb YHWH; see note at 3.15   b Or for thousands   c Heb Asherim   d Gk Theodotion Vg Tg: Meaning of Heb uncertain

26 The best of the first fruits of your ground you shall bring to the house of the LORD your God.

You shall not boil a kid in its mother's milk.

27 The LORD said to Moses: Write these words; in accordance with these words I have made a covenant with you and with Israel. 28 He was there with the LORD forty days and forty nights; he neither ate bread nor drank water. And he wrote on the tablets the words of the covenant, the ten commandments.e

The Shining Face of Moses

29 Moses came down from Mount Sinai. As he came down from the mountain with the two tablets of the covenantf in his hand, Moses did not know that the skin of his face shone because he had been talking with God. 30 When Aaron and all the Israelites saw Moses, the skin of his face was shining, and they were afraid to come near him. 31 But Moses called to them; and Aaron and all the leaders of the congregation returned to him, and Moses spoke with them. 32 Afterward all the Israelites came near, and he gave them in commandment all that the LORD had spoken with him on Mount Sinai. 33 When Moses had finished speaking with them, he put a veil on his face; 34 but whenever Moses went in before the LORD to speak with him, he would take the veil off, until he came out; and when he came out, and told the Israelites what he had been commanded, 35 the Israelites would see the face of Moses, that the skin of his face was shining; and Moses would put the veil on his face again, until he went in to speak with him.

Sabbath Regulations

35 Moses assembled all the congregation of the Israelites and said to them: These are the things that the LORD has commanded you to do:

2 Six days shall work be done, but on the seventh day you shall have a holy sabbath of solemn rest to the LORD; whoever does any work on it shall be put to death. 3 You shall kindle no fire in all your dwellings on the sabbath day.

Preparations for Making the Tabernacle
(Ex 25.1–9; 39.32–43)

4 Moses said to all the congregation of the Israelites: This is the thing that the LORD has commanded: 5 Take from among you an offering to the LORD; let whoever is of a generous heart bring the LORD's offering: gold, silver, and bronze; 6 blue, purple, and crimson yarns, and fine linen; goats' hair, 7 tanned rams' skins, and fine leather;g acacia

did you KNOW?

Major Jewish Feasts

The joyful anticipation that we feel before a major holiday seems to be shared by people of all cultures and religious traditions. Certainly, the Israelites had that feeling before the three festivals described in Ex 34.18–26 (and in 23.14–17). They looked forward to them the way we might look forward to Christmas or Easter. These three feasts were called pilgrimage feasts because they required males to travel to the Temple in Jerusalem.

The *feast of Unleavened Bread*, which began on the day after Passover and lasted a week, marked the beginning of the barley harvest. This feast probably originated in a pre-Passover agricultural holiday. Originally, unleavened bread—bread made without yeast—was eaten during this week to symbolize a fresh start. Later, the feast was connected to the Passover celebration, and the custom of eating unleavened bread came to be seen as a reminder of the haste with which the people had left Egypt—before having time to leaven their bread.

The *feast of Weeks*, or Pentecost, began seven weeks after the barley harvest, to celebrate the start of the wheat harvest. Later, the feast of Weeks took on added significance. Because the Israelites had arrived at Mount Sinai in the third month after their departure from Egypt (19.1), this weeklong feast came to be seen as a celebration of God's Covenant with Israel.

The third weeklong festival, the *feast of Booths*, was celebrated as the produce of the land was gathered. Much like our own Thanksgiving Day, it was a time set aside to thank God for the bounty of the earth. It is the most popular of the pilgrimage feasts. In Exodus, it is called the feast at the fruit harvest, and in other places, simply the festival (1 Kings 8.2).

▶ Ex 34.18–26

---

e Heb *words*   f Or *treaty*, or *testimony*; Heb *eduth*
g Meaning of Heb uncertain

wood, 8 oil for the light, spices for the anointing oil and for the fragrant incense, 9 and onyx stones and gems to be set in the ephod and the breast-piece.

10 All who are skillful among you shall come and make all that the LORD has commanded: the tabernacle, 11 its tent and its covering, its clasps and its frames, its bars, its pillars, and its bases; 12 the ark with its poles, the mercy seat,*h* and the curtain for the screen; 13 the table with its poles and all its utensils, and the bread of the Presence; 14 the lamp-stand also for the light, with its utensils and its lamps, and the oil for the light; 15 and the altar of incense, with its poles, and the anointing oil and the fragrant incense, and the screen for the en-trance, the entrance of the tabernacle; 16 the altar of burnt offering, with its grating of bronze, its poles, and all its utensils, the basin with its stand; 17 the hangings of the court, its pillars and its bases, and the screen for the gate of the court; 18 the pegs of the tabernacle and the pegs of the court, and their cords; 19 the finely worked vestments for minister-ing in the holy place, the holy vestments for the priest Aaron, and the vestments of his sons, for their service as priests.

Offerings for the Tabernacle

20 Then all the congregation of the Israelites withdrew from the presence of Moses. 21 And they came, everyone whose heart was stirred, and everyone whose spirit was willing, and brought the LORD's offering to be used for the tent of meeting, and for all its service, and for the sacred vestments. 22 So they came, both men and women; all who were of a willing heart brought brooches and earrings and signet rings and pen-dants, all sorts of gold objects, everyone bringing an offering of gold to the LORD. 23 And everyone who possessed blue or purple or crimson yarn or fine linen or goats' hair or tanned rams' skins or fine leather,*i* brought them. 24 Everyone who could make an offering of silver or bronze brought it as the LORD's offering; and everyone who possessed acacia wood of any use in the work, brought it. 25 All the skillful women spun with their hands, and brought what they had spun in blue and purple and crimson yarns and fine linen; 26 all the women whose hearts moved them to use their skill spun the goats' hair. 27 And the leaders brought onyx stones and gems to be set in the ephod and the breastpiece, 28 and spices and oil for the light, and for the anointing oil, and for the fragrant incense. 29 All the Israelite men and women whose hearts made them willing to bring anything for the work that the LORD had commanded by Moses to be done, brought it as a freewill offering to the LORD.

Bezalel and Oholiab
(Ex 31.1–11)

30 Then Moses said to the Israelites: See, the LORD has called by name Bez'a•lel son of U'rī son of Hur, of the tribe of Judah; 31 he has filled him with divine spirit,*j* with skill, intelligence, and knowl-edge in every kind of craft, 32 to devise artistic de-signs, to work in gold, silver, and bronze, 33 in cutting stones for setting, and in carving wood, in every kind of craft. 34 And he has inspired him to teach, both him and Ō•hō'li•ab son of A•his'-a•mach, of the tribe of Dan. 35 He has filled them with skill to do every kind of work done by an artisan or by a designer or by an embroiderer in blue, purple, and crimson yarns, and in fine linen, or by a weaver—by any sort of artisan or skilled de-signer.

36 Bez'a•lel and Ō•hō'li•ab and every skill-ful one to whom the LORD has given skill and understanding to know how to do any work in the construction of the sanctuary shall work in ac-cordance with all that the LORD has commanded.

2 Moses then called Bez'a•lel and Ō•hō'li•ab and every skillful one to whom the LORD had given skill, everyone whose heart was stirred to come to do the work; 3 and they received from Moses all the freewill offerings that the Israelites had brought for doing the work on the sanctuary. They still kept bringing him freewill offerings every morning, 4 so that all the artisans who were doing every sort of task on the sanctuary came, each from the task be-ing performed, 5 and said to Moses, "The people are bringing much more than enough for doing the work that the LORD has commanded us to do." 6 So Moses gave command, and word was proclaimed throughout the camp: "No man or woman is to make anything else as an offering for the sanctu-ary." So the people were restrained from bringing; 7 for what they had already brought was more than enough to do all the work.

Construction of the Tabernacle
(Ex 26.1–37)

8 All those with skill among the workers made the tabernacle with ten curtains; they were made of fine twisted linen, and blue, purple, and crimson yarns, with cherubim skillfully worked into them. 9 The length of each curtain was twenty-eight cu-bits, and the width of each curtain four cubits; all the curtains were of the same size.

10 He joined five curtains to one another, and the other five curtains he joined to one another. 11 He made loops of blue on the edge of the outer-most curtain of the first set; likewise he made them

---

h Or *the cover*   *i* Meaning of Heb uncertain   *j* Or *the spirit of God* on the edge of the outermost curtain of the second set; 12 he made fifty loops on the one curtain, and he made fifty loops on the edge of the curtain that was in the second set; the loops were opposite one another. 13 And he made fifty clasps of gold, and joined the curtains one to the other with clasps; so the tabernacle was one whole.

14 He also made curtains of goats' hair for a tent over the tabernacle; he made eleven curtains. 15 The length of each curtain was thirty cubits, and the width of each curtain four cubits; the eleven curtains were of the same size. 16 He joined five curtains by themselves, and six curtains by themselves. 17 He made fifty loops on the edge of the outermost curtain of the one set, and fifty loops on the edge of the other connecting curtain. 18 He made fifty clasps of bronze to join the tent together so that it might be one whole. 19 And he made for the tent a covering of tanned rams' skins and an outer covering of fine leather.k

20 Then he made the upright frames for the tabernacle of acacia wood. 21 Ten cubits was the length of a frame, and a cubit and a half the width of each frame. 22 Each frame had two pegs for fitting together; he did this for all the frames of the tabernacle. 23 The frames for the tabernacle he made in this way: twenty frames for the south side; 24 and he made forty bases of silver under the twenty frames, two bases under the first frame for its two pegs, and two bases under the next frame for its two pegs. 25 For the second side of the tabernacle, on the north side, he made twenty frames 26 and their forty bases of silver, two bases under the first frame and two bases under the next frame. 27 For the rear of the tabernacle westward he made six frames. 28 He made two frames for corners of the tabernacle in the rear. 29 They were separate beneath, but joined at the top, at the first ring; he made two of them in this way, for the two corners. 30 There were eight frames with their bases of silver: sixteen bases, under every frame two bases.

31 He made bars of acacia wood, five for the frames of the one side of the tabernacle, 32 and five bars for the frames of the other side of the tabernacle, and five bars for the frames of the tabernacle at the rear westward. 33 He made the middle bar to pass through from end to end halfway up the frames. 34 And he overlaid the frames with gold, and made rings of gold for them to hold the bars, and overlaid the bars with gold.

35 He made the curtain of blue, purple, and crimson yarns, and fine twisted linen, with cherubim skillfully worked into it. 36 For it he made four pillars of acacia, and overlaid them with gold; their hooks were of gold, and he cast for them four bases of silver. 37 He also made a screen for the entrance to the tent, of blue, purple, and crimson yarns, and fine twisted linen, embroidered with needlework; 38 and its five pillars with their hooks. He overlaid their capitals and their bases with gold, but their five bases were of bronze.

Making the Ark of the Covenant
(Ex 25.10–22)

37 Bez′a•lel made the ark of acacia wood; it was two and a half cubits long, a cubit and a half wide, and a cubit and a half high. 2 He overlaid it with pure gold inside and outside, and made a molding of gold around it. 3 He cast for it four rings of gold for its four feet, two rings on its one side and two rings on its other side. 4 He made poles of acacia wood, and overlaid them with gold, 5 and put the poles into the rings on the sides of the ark, to carry the ark. 6 He made a mercy seatl of pure gold; two cubits and a half was its length, and a cubit and a half its width. 7 He made two cherubim of hammered gold; at the two ends of the mercy seatm he made them, 8 one cherub at the one end, and one cherub at the other end; of one piece with the mercy seatm he made the cherubim at its two ends. 9 The cherubim spread out their wings above, overshadowing the mercy seatm with their wings. They faced one another; the faces of the cherubim were turned toward the mercy seat.m

Making the Table for the Bread of the Presence
(Ex 25.23–30)

10 He also made the table of acacia wood, two cubits long, one cubit wide, and a cubit and a half high. 11 He overlaid it with pure gold, and made a molding of gold around it. 12 He made around it a rim a handbreadth wide, and made a molding of gold around the rim. 13 He cast for it four rings of gold, and fastened the rings to the four corners at its four legs. 14 The rings that held the poles used for carrying the table were close to the rim. 15 He made the poles of acacia wood to carry the table, and overlaid them with gold. 16 And he made the vessels of pure gold that were to be on the table, its plates and dishes for incense, and its bowls and flagons with which to pour drink offerings.

Making the Lampstand
(Ex 25.31–40)

17 He also made the lampstand of pure gold. The base and the shaft of the lampstand were made of hammered work; its cups, its calyxes, and its petals were of one piece with it. 18 There were six branches going out of its sides, three branches of the lampstand out of one side of it and three branches of the lampstand out of the other side of

---

k Meaning of Heb uncertain　l Or a cover　m Or the cover

did you KNOW?

The Ark of the Covenant

The ark of the Covenant, which Bezalel made in fulfillment of God's command, was a portable box in which the Israelites kept the tablets of the Law (see Deut 10.1–5; 1 Kings 8.9) and possibly other sacred items. The large box was made of gold-plated wood, with four rings attached to its lower corners; through these rings, gold-plated poles were inserted for carrying the ark in procession. On top of the ark sat two golden angels facing each other, their wings touching over their heads.

The ark of the Covenant was a symbol of God's saving presence among the Israelites. It accompanied them during their forty years in the desert (Num 10.33–36) and was solemnly carried through the Jordan River when they entered the Promised Land (Josh 3.1–17). Later, the Israelite soldiers took the ark into battle, invoking God's strength against their enemies (1 Sam 4.1–11). After the ark was lost in battle to the Philistines, David retrieved it and brought it to Jerusalem (2 Sam 6.1–23), where his son Solomon eventually enthroned it in the Temple, in the holy of holies (1 Kings 8.1–11). The ark remained there until the destruction of Jerusalem in 587 B.C., when it was lost to history.

▸ Ex 37.1–9

snuffers and its trays of pure gold. 24 He made it and all its utensils of a talent of pure gold.

Making the Altar of Incense
(Ex 30.1–5)

25 He made the altar of incense of acacia wood, one cubit long, and one cubit wide; it was square, and was two cubits high; its horns were of one piece with it. 26 He overlaid it with pure gold, its top, and its sides all around, and its horns; and he made for it a molding of gold all around, 27 and made two golden rings for it under its molding, on two opposite sides of it, to hold the poles with which to carry it. 28 And he made the poles of acacia wood, and overlaid them with gold.

Making the Anointing Oil and the Incense
(Ex 30.22–38)

29 He made the holy anointing oil also, and the pure fragrant incense, blended as by the perfumer.

Making the Altar of Burnt Offering
(Ex 27.1–8)

38 He made the altar of burnt offering also of acacia wood; it was five cubits long, and five cubits wide; it was square, and three cubits high. 2 He made horns for it on its four corners; its horns were of one piece with it, and he overlaid it with bronze. 3 He made all the utensils of the altar, the pots, the shovels, the basins, the forks, and the firepans: all its utensils he made of bronze. 4 He made for the altar a grating, a network of bronze, under its ledge, extending halfway down. 5 He cast four rings on the four corners of the bronze grating to hold the poles; 6 he made the poles of acacia wood, and overlaid them with bronze. 7 And he put the poles through the rings on the sides of the altar, to carry it with them; he made it hollow, with boards.

8 He made the basin of bronze with its stand of bronze, from the mirrors of the women who served at the entrance to the tent of meeting.

Making the Court of the Tabernacle
(Ex 27.9–19)

9 He made the court; for the south side the hangings of the court were of fine twisted linen, one hundred cubits long; 10 its twenty pillars and their twenty bases were of bronze, but the hooks of the pillars and their bands were of silver. 11 For the north side there were hangings one hundred cubits long; its twenty pillars and their twenty bases were of bronze, but the hooks of the pillars and their bands were of silver. 12 For the west side there were hangings fifty cubits long, with ten pillars and ten bases; the hooks of the pillars and their bands were of silver. 13 And for the front to the east, fifty cubits.

it; 19 three cups shaped like almond blossoms, each with calyx and petals, on one branch, and three cups shaped like almond blossoms, each with calyx and petals, on the other branch—so for the six branches going out of the lampstand. 20 On the lampstand itself there were four cups shaped like almond blossoms, each with its calyxes and petals. 21 There was a calyx of one piece with it under the first pair of branches, a calyx of one piece with it under the next pair of branches, and a calyx of one piece with it under the last pair of branches. 22 Their calyxes and their branches were of one piece with it, the whole of it one hammered piece of pure gold. 23 He made its seven lamps and its

14 The hangings for one side of the gate were fifteen cubits, with three pillars and three bases. 15 And so for the other side; on each side of the gate of the court were hangings of fifteen cubits, with three pillars and three bases. 16 All the hangings around the court were of fine twisted linen. 17 The bases for the pillars were of bronze, but the hooks of the pillars and their bands were of silver; the overlaying of their capitals was also of silver, and all the pillars of the court were banded with silver. 18 The screen for the entrance to the court was embroidered with needlework in blue, purple, and crimson yarns and fine twisted linen. It was twenty cubits long and, along the width of it, five cubits high, corresponding to the hangings of the court. 19 There were four pillars; their four bases were of bronze, their hooks of silver, and the overlaying of their capitals and their bands of silver. 20 All the pegs for the tabernacle and for the court all around were of bronze.

Materials of the Tabernacle

21 These are the records of the tabernacle, the tabernacle of the covenant,[n] which were drawn up at the commandment of Moses, the work of the Lē'vītes being under the direction of Ith'a•mar son of the priest Aaron. 22 Bez'a•lel son of Ū'rī son of Hur, of the tribe of Judah, made all that the LORD commanded Moses; 23 and with him was Ō•hō'-li•ab son of A•his'a•mach, of the tribe of Dan, engraver, designer, and embroiderer in blue, purple, and crimson yarns, and in fine linen.

24 All the gold that was used for the work, in all the construction of the sanctuary, the gold from the offering, was twenty-nine talents and seven hundred thirty shekels, measured by the sanctuary shekel. 25 The silver from those of the congregation who were counted was one hundred talents and one thousand seven hundred seventy-five shekels, measured by the sanctuary shekel; 26 a beka a head (that is, half a shekel, measured by the sanctuary shekel), for everyone who was counted in the census, from twenty years old and upward, for six hundred three thousand, five hundred fifty men. 27 The hundred talents of silver were for casting the bases of the sanctuary, and the bases of the curtain; one hundred bases for the hundred talents, a talent for a base. 28 Of the thousand seven hundred seventy-five shekels he made hooks for the pillars, and overlaid their capitals and made bands for them. 29 The bronze that was contributed was seventy talents, and two thousand four hundred shekels; 30 with it he made the bases for the entrance of the tent of meeting, the bronze altar and the bronze grating for it and all the utensils of the altar, 31 the bases all around the court, and the bases of the gate of the court, all the pegs of the tabernacle, and all the pegs around the court.

Making the Vestments for the Priesthood
(Ex 28.1–43)

39 Of the blue, purple, and crimson yarns they made finely worked vestments, for ministering in the holy place; they made the sacred vestments for Aaron; as the LORD had commanded Moses.

2 He made the ephod of gold, of blue, purple, and crimson yarns, and of fine twisted linen. 3 Gold leaf was hammered out and cut into threads to work into the blue, purple, and crimson yarns and into the fine twisted linen, in skilled design. 4 They made for the ephod shoulder-pieces, joined to it at its two edges. 5 The decorated band on it was of the same materials and workmanship, of gold, of blue, purple, and crimson yarns, and of fine twisted linen; as the LORD had commanded Moses.

6 The onyx stones were prepared, enclosed in settings of gold filigree and engraved like the engravings of a signet, according to the names of the sons of Israel. 7 He set them on the shoulder-pieces of the ephod, to be stones of remembrance for the sons of Israel; as the LORD had commanded Moses.

8 He made the breastpiece, in skilled work, like the work of the ephod, of gold, of blue, purple, and crimson yarns, and of fine twisted linen. 9 It was square; the breastpiece was made double, a span in length and a span in width when doubled. 10 They set in it four rows of stones. A row of carnelian,[o] chrysolite, and emerald was the first row; 11 and the second row, a turquoise, a sapphire,[p] and a moonstone; 12 and the third row, a jacinth, an agate, and an amethyst; 13 and the fourth row, a beryl, an onyx, and a jasper; they were enclosed in settings of gold filigree. 14 There were twelve stones with names corresponding to the names of the sons of Israel; they were like signets, each engraved with its name, for the twelve tribes. 15 They made on the breastpiece chains of pure gold, twisted like cords; 16 and they made two settings of gold filigree and two gold rings, and put the two rings on the two edges of the breastpiece; 17 and they put the two cords of gold in the two rings at the edges of the breastpiece. 18 Two ends of the two cords they had attached to the two settings of filigree; in this way they attached it in front to the shoulder-pieces of the ephod. 19 Then they made two rings of gold, and put them at the two ends of the breastpiece, on its inside edge next to the ephod. 20 They made two rings of gold, and attached them in front to the lower part of the two shoulder-pieces of the ephod, at its joining above the decorated band of the ephod. 21 They bound the breastpiece by its rings to the rings of the ephod with a blue cord, so

---

n Or *treaty*, or *testimony*; Heb *eduth*   o The identification of several of these stones is uncertain   p Or *lapis lazuli* that it should lie on the decorated band of the ephod, and that the breastpiece should not come loose from the ephod; as the LORD had commanded Moses.

22 He also made the robe of the ephod woven all of blue yarn; 23 and the opening of the robe in the middle of it was like the opening in a coat of mail,*q* with a binding around the opening, so that it might not be torn. 24 On the lower hem of the robe they made pomegranates of blue, purple, and crimson yarns, and of fine twisted linen. 25 They also made bells of pure gold, and put the bells between the pomegranates on the lower hem of the robe all around, between the pomegranates; 26 a bell and a pomegranate, a bell and a pomegranate all around on the lower hem of the robe for ministering; as the LORD had commanded Moses.

27 They also made the tunics, woven of fine linen, for Aaron and his sons, 28 and the turban of fine linen, and the headdresses of fine linen, and the linen undergarments of fine twisted linen, 29 and the sash of fine twisted linen, and of blue, purple, and crimson yarns, embroidered with needlework; as the LORD had commanded Moses.

30 They made the rosette of the holy diadem of pure gold, and wrote on it an inscription, like the engraving of a signet, "Holy to the LORD." 31 They tied to it a blue cord, to fasten it on the turban above; as the LORD had commanded Moses.

The Work Completed
(Ex 35.10–19)

32 In this way all the work of the tabernacle of the tent of meeting was finished; the Israelites had done everything just as the LORD had commanded Moses. 33 Then they brought the tabernacle to Moses, the tent and all its utensils, its hooks, its frames, its bars, its pillars, and its bases; 34 the covering of tanned rams' skins and the covering of fine leather,*q* and the curtain for the screen; 35 the ark of the covenant*r* with its poles and the mercy seat;*s* 36 the table with all its utensils, and the bread of the Presence; 37 the pure lampstand with its lamps set on it and all its utensils, and the oil for the light; 38 the golden altar, the anointing oil and the fragrant incense, and the screen for the entrance of the tent; 39 the bronze altar, and its grating of bronze, its poles, and all its utensils; the basin with its stand; 40 the hangings of the court, its pillars, and its bases, and the screen for the gate of the court, its cords, and its pegs; and all the utensils for the service of the tabernacle, for the tent of meeting; 41 the finely worked vestments for ministering in the holy place, the sacred vestments for the priest Aaron, and the vestments of his sons to serve as priests. 42 The Israelites had done all of the work just as the LORD

had commanded Moses. 43 When Moses saw that they had done all the work just as the LORD had commanded, he blessed them.

The Tabernacle Erected and Its Equipment Installed

40 The LORD spoke to Moses: 2 On the first day of the first month you shall set up the tabernacle of the tent of meeting. 3 You shall put in it the ark of the covenant,*s* and you shall screen the ark with the curtain. 4 You shall bring in the table, and arrange its setting; and you shall bring in the lampstand, and set up its lamps. 5 You shall put the golden altar for incense before the ark of the covenant,*s* and set up the screen for the entrance of the tabernacle. 6 You shall set the altar of burnt offering before the entrance of the tabernacle of the tent of meeting, 7 and place the basin between the tent of meeting and the altar, and put water in it. 8 You shall set up the court all around, and hang up the screen for the gate of the court. 9 Then you shall take the anointing oil, and anoint the tabernacle and all that is in it, and consecrate it and all its furniture, so that it shall become holy. 10 You shall also anoint the altar of burnt offering and all its utensils, and consecrate the altar, so that the altar shall be most holy. 11 You shall also anoint the basin with its stand, and consecrate it. 12 Then you shall bring Aaron and his sons to the entrance of the tent of meeting, and shall wash them with water, 13 and put on Aaron the sacred vestments, and you shall anoint him and consecrate him, so that he may serve me as priest. 14 You shall bring his sons also and put tunics on them, 15 and anoint them, as you anointed their father, that they may serve me as priests: and their anointing shall admit them to a perpetual priesthood throughout all generations to come.

16 Moses did everything just as the LORD had commanded him. 17 In the first month in the second year, on the first day of the month, the tabernacle was set up. 18 Moses set up the tabernacle; he laid its bases, and set up its frames, and put in its poles, and raised up its pillars; 19 and he spread the tent over the tabernacle, and put the covering of the tent over it; as the LORD had commanded Moses. 20 He took the covenant*r* and put it into the ark, and put the poles on the ark, and set the mercy seat*s* above the ark; 21 and he brought the ark into the tabernacle, and set up the curtain for screening, and screened the ark of the covenant;*r* as the LORD had commanded Moses. 22 He put the table in the tent of meeting, on the north side of the tabernacle, outside the curtain, 23 and set the bread in order on it

---

q Meaning of Heb uncertain   *r* Or *treaty,* or *testimony;* Heb *eduth*   *s* Or *the cover*

Cultural Connections

UMBRELLAS, ARKS, AND TENTS

Umbrellas offer protection from the sun or rain. In Asian cultures, servants would hold umbrellas over emperors and kings. Catholics in Indonesia have adapted this custom for their worship. Often an umbrella is set up over the tabernacle. Umbrellas are held over a priest when he carries the Blessed Sacrament or over the statue of Jesus' Sacred Heart when it is carried in a procession. The umbrella has become a sign of reverence for something that symbolizes God's presence.

The ark of the Covenant was built to act like an umbrella, to protect and reverence the tablets of the Law (the Commandments). When the ark was not being carried, it rested in the tabernacle in the holy of holies, which was a special tent at the center of the Israelites' camp. The ark and the tent served the same practical purpose as an umbrella and had the same deeper meaning of reverencing God's presence.

The next time you use an umbrella, remember how umbrellas are used to show respect for that which is holy: the body of Christ, the Ten Commandments, and one of God's greatest creations, you!

▸ Ex 40.1–15

before the LORD; as the LORD had commanded Moses. ²⁴ He put the lampstand in the tent of meeting, opposite the table on the south side of the tabernacle, ²⁵ and set up the lamps before the LORD; as the LORD had commanded Moses. ²⁶ He put the golden altar in the tent of meeting before the curtain, ²⁷ and offered fragrant incense on it; as the LORD had commanded Moses. ²⁸ He also put in place the screen for the entrance of the tabernacle. ²⁹ He set the altar of burnt offering at the entrance of the tabernacle of the tent of meeting, and offered on it the burnt offering and the grain offering as the LORD had commanded Moses. ³⁰ He set the basin between the tent of meeting and the altar, and put water in it for washing, ³¹ with which Moses and Aaron and his sons washed their hands and their feet. ³² When they went into the tent of meeting, and when they approached the altar, they washed; as the LORD had commanded Moses. ³³ He set up the court around the tabernacle and the altar, and put up the screen at the gate of the court. So Moses finished the work.

The Cloud and the Glory
(Ex 13.21–22; Num 9.15–23)

34 Then the cloud covered the tent of meeting, and the glory of the LORD filled the tabernacle. ³⁵ Moses was not able to enter the tent of meeting because the cloud settled upon it, and the glory of the LORD filled the tabernacle. ³⁶ Whenever the cloud was taken up from the tabernacle, the Israelites would set out on each stage of their journey; ³⁷ but if the cloud was not taken up, then they did not set out until the day that it was taken up. ³⁸ For the cloud of the LORD was on the tabernacle by day, and fire was in the cloud*t* by night, before the eyes of all the house of Israel at each stage of their journey.

t Heb *it*

The Book of Leviticus

When approaching a stop sign, come to a complete stop before proceeding." "You are not allowed to pass when a yellow line is on your side of the road." Sometime soon you will be given a book to learn these rules of driving—unless you have already had the pleasure! These laws may be a pain to memorize, but without them driving would be chaos. The Book of Leviticus has a similar function. It is primarily a list of laws, rules, and instructions to ensure holiness and order in worship and the people's way of life.

At a Glance

- **Chapters 1–7.** laws regulating various sacrifices
- **Chapters 8–10.** the ordination ceremony of Aaron and his sons
- **Chapters 11–16.** purity laws and the celebration of Yom Kippur
- **Chapters 17–26.** holiness laws
- **Chapters 27–34.** the re-dedication of holy things

In-depth

Leviticus, the third book of the Pentateuch, or Torah, is named after the tribe of Levi, whose male members were designated priests in Israel. It was their responsibility to conduct appropriate worship of God. For that reason, the book has often been referred to as the Torah (Law) of the Priests.

Most Scripture scholars believe that the laws and regulations in Leviticus developed over hundreds of years after the people entered the Promised Land. The book was composed at a time when the priests were struggling to unify Israel as it lay in ruins from its Babylonian conquerers. They wished to gather the various traditions and regulations that governed Israel's way of life. The author of Leviticus, referred to as the Priestly writer, writes as if these gathered traditions and regulations were given by God to Moses at Mount Sinai as part of the original Law. The author wishes to show that these laws are an extension of the Sinai Covenant.

If the goal of Israel's existence is to "be holy, for I [the LORD] am holy" (Lev 11.45), then the Book of Leviticus records how holiness becomes part of every aspect of Israel's existence. Chapters 17–26 are described as the Holiness Code. The words on love of neighbor in 19.18 are quoted several times in the New Testament. The purpose of Leviticus is to call Israel to follow the Law, and thus become a holy people and make its land a suitable place for God to dwell.

The customs and rites in Jesus' time are observances of the laws in Leviticus. Many of those customs and rites were left behind as Christianity emerged as a distinct religion.

Quick Facts

Period Covered
after the Exodus, during the Israelites' encampment at Mount Sinai

Author
the Priestly writer writing after the Babylonian Exile

Theme
to teach the way of holiness through observance of the Law and religious ritual

Leviticus

Chap. 1

The Burnt Offering

1 The LORD summoned Moses and spoke to him from the tent of meeting, saying: 2 Speak to the people of Israel and say to them: When any of you bring an offering of livestock to the LORD, you shall bring your offering from the herd or from the flock.

3 If the offering is a burnt offering from the herd, you shall offer a male without blemish; you shall bring it to the entrance of the tent of meeting, for acceptance in your behalf before the LORD. 4 You shall lay your hand on the head of the burnt offering, and it shall be acceptable in your behalf as atonement for you. 5 The bull shall be slaughtered before the LORD; and Aaron's sons the priests shall offer the blood, dashing the blood against all sides of the altar that is at the entrance of the tent of meeting. 6 The burnt offering shall be flayed and cut up into its parts. 7 The sons of the priest Aaron shall put fire on the altar and arrange wood on the fire. 8 Aaron's sons the priests shall arrange the parts, with the head and the suet, on the wood that is on the fire on the altar; 9 but its entrails and its legs shall be washed with water. Then the priest shall turn the whole into smoke on the altar as a burnt offering, an offering by fire of pleasing odor to the LORD.

10 If your gift for a burnt offering is from the flock, from the sheep or goats, your offering shall be a male without blemish. 11 It shall be slaugh-tered on the north side of the altar before the LORD, and Aaron's sons the priests shall dash its blood against all sides of the altar. 12 It shall be cut up into its parts, with its head and its suet, and the priest shall arrange them on the wood that is on the fire on the altar; 13 but the entrails and the legs shall be washed with water. Then the priest shall offer the whole and turn it into smoke on the altar; it is a burnt offering, an offering by fire of pleasing odor to the LORD.

14 If your offering to the LORD is a burnt offer-ing of birds, you shall choose your offering from turtledoves or pigeons. 15 The priest shall bring it to the altar and wring off its head, and turn it into smoke on the altar; and its blood shall be drained out against the side of the altar. 16 He shall remove its crop with its contents[a] and throw it at the east side of the altar, in the place for ashes. 17 He shall tear it open by its wings without severing it. Then the priest shall turn it into smoke on the altar, on the wood that is on the fire; it is a burnt offering, an offering by fire of pleasing odor to the LORD.

Grain Offerings

2 When anyone presents a grain offering to the LORD, the offering shall be of choice flour; the worshiper shall pour oil on it, and put frankincense on it, 2 and bring it to Aaron's sons the priests. Af-ter taking from it a handful of the choice flour and

---

a Meaning of Heb uncertain

oil, with all its frankincense, the priest shall turn this token portion into smoke on the altar, an offering by fire of pleasing odor to the LORD. ³ And what is left of the grain offering shall be for Aaron and his sons, a most holy part of the offerings by fire to the LORD.

did you KNOW?

The Covenant Laws

Even though Christians are not bound by the Jewish religion—see the Letters to the Hebrews and to the Romans—the laws in Leviticus help us understand the meaning of life for the Israelites. These laws developed out of their experience of striving to be faithful to God and were interpreted and taught by the priests of the tribe of Levi.

The purity laws may seem the strangest to us today. They defined who or what was pure—that is, free from contamination—and therefore acceptable to God. They included laws on sickness, especially leprosy, because physical disease was understood as a symptom of sin or spiritual contamination. Purity laws also covered food, animals, bodily discharges, and corpses.

Other laws described proper relationships between people. These laws reflected more the intentions of the heart. Later, the prophets and Jesus would emphasize that impurity comes from the heart, not from something outside the person (Mk 7.1–23). Other laws regulated priestly ministry, and still others regulated social institutions. Nothing was left to chance. The laws of the Covenant made it clear that God was present in every aspect of the people's lives.

4 When you present a grain offering baked in the oven, it shall be of choice flour: unleavened cakes mixed with oil, or unleavened wafers spread with oil. ⁵ If your offering is grain prepared on a griddle, it shall be of choice flour mixed with oil, unleavened; ⁶ break it in pieces, and pour oil on it; it is a grain offering. ⁷ If your offering is grain prepared in a pan, it shall be made of choice flour in

oil. ⁸ You shall bring to the LORD the grain offering that is prepared in any of these ways; and when it is presented to the priest, he shall take it to the altar. ⁹ The priest shall remove from the grain offering its token portion and turn this into smoke on the altar, an offering by fire of pleasing odor to the LORD. ¹⁰ And what is left of the grain offering shall be for Aaron and his sons; it is a most holy part of the offerings by fire to the LORD.

11 No grain offering that you bring to the LORD shall be made with leaven, for you must not turn any leaven or honey into smoke as an offering by fire to the LORD. ¹² You may bring them to the LORD as an offering of choice products, but they shall not be offered on the altar for a pleasing odor. ¹³ You shall not omit from your grain offerings the salt of the covenant with your God; with all your offerings you shall offer salt.

14 If you bring a grain offering of first fruits to the LORD, you shall bring as the grain offering of your first fruits coarse new grain from fresh ears, parched with fire. ¹⁵ You shall add oil to it and lay frankincense on it; it is a grain offering. ¹⁶ And the priest shall turn a token portion of it into smoke— some of the coarse grain and oil with all its frankincense; it is an offering by fire to the LORD.

Offerings of Well-Being

3 If the offering is a sacrifice of well-being, if you offer an animal of the herd, whether male or female, you shall offer one without blemish before the LORD. ² You shall lay your hand on the head of the offering and slaughter it at the entrance of the tent of meeting; and Aaron's sons the priests shall dash the blood against all sides of the altar. ³ You shall offer from the sacrifice of well-being, as an offering by fire to the LORD, the fat that covers the entrails and all the fat that is around the entrails; ⁴ the two kidneys with the fat that is on them at the loins, and the appendage of the liver, which he shall remove with the kidneys. ⁵ Then Aaron's sons shall turn these into smoke on the altar, with the burnt offering that is on the wood on the fire, as an offering by fire of pleasing odor to the LORD.

6 If your offering for a sacrifice of well-being to the LORD is from the flock, male or female, you shall offer one without blemish. ⁷ If you present a sheep as your offering, you shall bring it before the LORD ⁸ and lay your hand on the head of the offering. It shall be slaughtered before the tent of meeting; and Aaron's sons shall dash its blood against all sides of the altar. ⁹ You shall present its fat from the sacrifice of well-being, as an offering by fire to the LORD: the whole broad tail, which shall be removed close to the backbone, the fat that covers the entrails, and all the fat that is around the entrails; ¹⁰ the two kidneys with the fat that is on them at

the loins, and the appendage of the liver, which you shall remove with the kidneys. 11 Then the priest shall turn these into smoke on the altar as a food offering by fire to the LORD.

12 If your offering is a goat, you shall bring it before the LORD 13 and lay your hand on its head; it shall be slaughtered before the tent of meeting; and the sons of Aaron shall dash its blood against all sides of the altar. 14 You shall present as your offering from it, as an offering by fire to the LORD, the fat that covers the entrails, and all the fat that is around the entrails; 15 the two kidneys with the fat that is on them at the loins, and the appendage of the liver, which you shall remove with the kidneys. 16 Then the priest shall turn these into smoke on the altar as a food offering by fire for a pleasing odor.

All fat is the LORD's. 17 It shall be a perpetual statute throughout your generations, in all your settlements: you must not eat any fat or any blood.

Sin Offerings

4 The LORD spoke to Moses, saying, 2 Speak to the people of Israel, saying: When anyone sins unintentionally in any of the LORD's commandments about things not to be done, and does any one of them:

3 If it is the anointed priest who sins, thus bringing guilt on the people, he shall offer for the sin that he has committed a bull of the herd without blemish as a sin offering to the LORD. 4 He shall bring the bull to the entrance of the tent of meeting before the LORD and lay his hand on the head of the bull; the bull shall be slaughtered before the LORD. 5 The anointed priest shall take some of the blood of the bull and bring it into the tent of meeting. 6 The priest shall dip his finger in the blood and sprinkle some of the blood seven times before the LORD in front of the curtain of the sanctuary. 7 The priest shall put some of the blood on the horns of the altar of fragrant incense that is in the tent of meeting before the LORD; and the rest of the blood of the bull he shall pour out at the base of the altar of burnt offering, which is at the entrance of the tent of meeting. 8 He shall remove all the fat from the bull of sin offering: the fat that covers the entrails and all the fat that is around the entrails; 9 the two kidneys with the fat that is on them at the loins; and the appendage of the liver, which he shall remove with the kidneys, 10 just as these are removed from the ox of the sacrifice of well-being. The priest shall turn them into smoke upon the altar of burnt offering. 11 But the skin of the bull and all its flesh, as well as its head, its legs, its entrails, and its dung— 12 all the rest of the bull—he shall carry out to a clean place outside the camp, to the

ash heap, and shall burn it on a wood fire; at the ash heap it shall be burned.

13 If the whole congregation of Israel errs unintentionally and the matter escapes the notice of the assembly, and they do any one of the things that by the LORD's commandments ought not to be done and incur guilt; 14 when the sin that they have committed becomes known, the assembly shall offer a bull of the herd for a sin offering and bring it before the tent of meeting. 15 The elders of the congregation shall lay their hands on the head of the bull before the LORD, and the bull shall be slaughtered before the LORD. 16 The anointed priest shall bring some of the blood of the bull into the tent of meeting, 17 and the priest shall dip his finger in the blood and sprinkle it seven times before the LORD, in front of the curtain. 18 He shall put some of the blood on the horns of the altar that is before the LORD in the tent of meeting; and the rest of the blood he shall pour out at the base of the altar of burnt offering that is at the entrance of the tent of meeting. 19 He shall remove all its fat and turn it into smoke on the altar. 20 He shall do with the bull just as is

PRAY IT?
Sin Offering

The sin offering laws probably seem strange to you. Because of Jesus' sacrifice, Christians have never had to make sin offerings. But they do serve an important role in understanding what Jesus' death and Resurrection mean for our own sin and salvation.

The Israelites understood that sin affects not only the sinner but also those whose life the sinner touches. They understood sin as incurring a debt that must be repaid. The sinner made a guilt offering to atone for the sin.

Isaiah said that God made the life of the suffering servant a guilt offering for those who were too far into debt to repay (Isa 53.10). At the Last Supper, Jesus told the Apostles, "This is my blood . . . which is poured out for many for the forgiveness of sins" (Mt 26.28). Jesus became our sin offering to take on the debt of our sin. In prayerful thanks for this great gift, read Eph 1.3–14.

▶ Lev 4.1—5.26

done with the bull of sin offering; he shall do the same with this. The priest shall make atonement for them, and they shall be forgiven. 21 He shall carry the bull outside the camp, and burn it as he burned the first bull; it is the sin offering for the assembly.

22 When a ruler sins, doing unintentionally any one of all the things that by commandments of the LORD his God ought not to be done and incurs guilt, 23 once the sin that he has committed is made known to him, he shall bring as his offering a male goat without blemish. 24 He shall lay his hand on the head of the goat; it shall be slaughtered at the spot where the burnt offering is slaughtered before the LORD; it is a sin offering. 25 The priest shall take some of the blood of the sin offering with his finger and put it on the horns of the altar of burnt offering, and pour out the rest of its blood at the base of the altar of burnt offering. 26 All its fat he shall turn into smoke on the altar, like the fat of the sacrifice of well-being. Thus the priest shall make atonement on his behalf for his sin, and he shall be forgiven.

27 If anyone of the ordinary people among you sins unintentionally in doing any one of the things that by the LORD's commandments ought not to be done and incurs guilt, 28 when the sin that you have committed is made known to you, you shall bring a female goat without blemish as your offering, for the sin that you have committed. 29 You shall lay your hand on the head of the sin offering; and the sin offering shall be slaughtered at the place of the burnt offering. 30 The priest shall take some of its blood with his finger and put it on the horns of the altar of burnt offering, and he shall pour out the rest of its blood at the base of the altar. 31 He shall remove all its fat, as the fat is removed from the offering of well-being; and the priest shall turn it into smoke on the altar for a pleasing odor to the LORD. Thus the priest shall make atonement on your behalf, and you shall be forgiven.

32 If the offering you bring as a sin offering is a sheep, you shall bring a female without blemish. 33 You shall lay your hand on the head of the sin offering; and it shall be slaughtered as a sin offering at the spot where the burnt offering is slaughtered. 34 The priest shall take some of the blood of the sin offering with his finger and put it on the horns of the altar of burnt offering, and pour out the rest of its blood at the base of the altar. 35 You shall remove all its fat, as the fat of the sheep is removed from the sacrifice of well-being, and the priest shall turn it into smoke on the altar, with the offerings by fire to the LORD. Thus the priest shall make atonement on your behalf for the sin that you have committed, and you shall be forgiven.

5 When any of you sin in that you have heard a public adjuration to testify and—though able to testify as one who has seen or learned of the mat-

ter—do not speak up, you are subject to punishment. 2 Or when any of you touch any unclean thing—whether the carcass of an unclean beast or the carcass of unclean livestock or the carcass of an unclean swarming thing—and are unaware of it, you have become unclean, and are guilty. 3 Or when you touch human uncleanness—any uncleanness by which one can become unclean—and are unaware of it, when you come to know it, you shall be guilty. 4 Or when any of you utter aloud a rash oath for a bad or a good purpose, whatever people utter in an oath, and are unaware of it, when you come to know it, you shall in any of these be guilty. 5 When you realize your guilt in any of these, you shall confess the sin that you have committed. 6 And you shall bring to the LORD, as your penalty for the sin that you have committed, a female from the flock, a sheep or a goat, as a sin offering; and the priest shall make atonement on your behalf for your sin.

7 But if you cannot afford a sheep, you shall bring to the LORD, as your penalty for the sin that you have committed, two turtledoves or two pigeons, one for a sin offering and the other for a burnt offering. 8 You shall bring them to the priest, who shall offer first the one for the sin offering, wringing its head at the nape without severing it. 9 He shall sprinkle some of the blood of the sin offering on the side of the altar, while the rest of the blood shall be drained out at the base of the altar; it is a sin offering. 10 And the second he shall offer for a burnt offering according to the regulation. Thus the priest shall make atonement on your behalf for the sin that you have committed, and you shall be forgiven.

11 But if you cannot afford two turtledoves or two pigeons, you shall bring as your offering for the sin that you have committed one-tenth of an ephah of choice flour for a sin offering; you shall not put oil on it or lay frankincense on it, for it is a sin offering. 12 You shall bring it to the priest, and the priest shall scoop up a handful of it as its memorial portion, and turn this into smoke on the altar, with the offerings by fire to the LORD; it is a sin offering. 13 Thus the priest shall make atonement on your behalf for whichever of these sins you have committed, and you shall be forgiven. Like the grain offering, the rest shall be for the priest.

Offerings with Restitution

14 The LORD spoke to Moses, saying: 15 When any of you commit a trespass and sin unintentionally in any of the holy things of the LORD, you shall bring, as your guilt offering to the LORD, a ram without blemish from the flock, convertible into silver by the sanctuary shekel; it is a guilt offering.

16 And you shall make restitution for the holy thing in which you were remiss, and shall add one-fifth to it and give it to the priest. The priest shall make atonement on your behalf with the ram of the guilt offering, and you shall be forgiven.

17 If any of you sin without knowing it, doing any of the things that by the LORD's commandments ought not to be done, you have incurred guilt, and are subject to punishment. 18 You shall bring to the priest a ram without blemish from the flock, or the equivalent, as a guilt offering; and the priest shall make atonement on your behalf for the error that you committed unintentionally, and you shall be forgiven. 19 It is a guilt offering; you have incurred guilt before the LORD.

6 *b* The LORD spoke to Moses, saying: 2 When any of you sin and commit a trespass against the LORD by deceiving a neighbor in a matter of a deposit or a pledge, or by robbery, or if you have defrauded a neighbor, 3 or have found something lost and lied about it—if you swear falsely regarding any of the various things that one may do and sin thereby— 4 when you have sinned and realize your guilt, and would restore what you took by robbery or by fraud or the deposit that was committed to you, or the lost thing that you found, 5 or anything else about which you have sworn falsely, you shall repay the principal amount and shall add one-fifth to it. You shall pay it to its owner when you realize your guilt. 6 And you shall bring to the priest, as your guilt offering to the LORD, a ram without blemish from the flock, or its equivalent, for a guilt offering. 7 The priest shall make atonement on your behalf before the LORD, and you shall be forgiven for any of the things that one may do and incur guilt thereby.

Instructions concerning Sacrifices

8*c* The LORD spoke to Moses, saying: 9 Command Aaron and his sons, saying: This is the ritual of the burnt offering. The burnt offering itself shall remain on the hearth upon the altar all night until the morning, while the fire on the altar shall be kept burning. 10 The priest shall put on his linen vestments after putting on his linen undergarments next to his body; and he shall take up the ashes to which the fire has reduced the burnt offering on the altar, and place them beside the altar. 11 Then he shall take off his vestments and put on other garments, and carry the ashes out to a clean place outside the camp. 12 The fire on the altar shall be kept burning; it shall not go out. Every morning the priest shall add wood to it, lay out the burnt offering on it, and turn into smoke the fat pieces of the offerings of well-being. 13 A perpetual fire shall be kept burning on the altar; it shall not go out.

14 This is the ritual of the grain offering: The sons of Aaron shall offer it before the LORD, in front of the altar. 15 They shall take from it a handful of the choice flour and oil of the grain offering, with all the frankincense that is on the offering, and they shall turn its memorial portion into smoke on the altar as a pleasing odor to the LORD. 16 Aaron and his sons shall eat what is left of it; it shall be eaten as unleavened cakes in a holy place; in the court of the tent of meeting they shall eat it. 17 It shall not be baked with leaven. I have given it as their portion of my offerings by fire; it is most holy, like the sin offering and the guilt offering. 18 Every male among the descendants of Aaron shall eat of it, as their perpetual due throughout your generations, from the LORD's offerings by fire; anything that touches them shall become holy.

19 The LORD spoke to Moses, saying: 20 This is the offering that Aaron and his sons shall offer to the LORD on the day when he is anointed: one-tenth of an ephah of choice flour as a regular offering, half of it in the morning and half in the evening. 21 It shall be made with oil on a griddle; you shall bring it well soaked, as a grain offering of baked*d* pieces, and you shall present it as a pleasing odor to the LORD. 22 And so the priest, anointed from among Aaron's descendants as a successor, shall prepare it; it is the LORD's—a perpetual due— to be turned entirely into smoke. 23 Every grain offering of a priest shall be wholly burned; it shall not be eaten.

24 The LORD spoke to Moses, saying: 25 Speak to Aaron and his sons, saying: This is the ritual of the sin offering. The sin offering shall be slaughtered before the LORD at the spot where the burnt offering is slaughtered; it is most holy. 26 The priest who offers it as a sin offering shall eat of it; it shall be eaten in a holy place, in the court of the tent of meeting. 27 Whatever touches its flesh shall become holy; and when any of its blood is spattered on a garment, you shall wash the bespattered part in a holy place. 28 An earthen vessel in which it was boiled shall be broken; but if it is boiled in a bronze vessel, that shall be scoured and rinsed in water. 29 Every male among the priests shall eat of it; it is most holy. 30 But no sin offering shall be eaten from which any blood is brought into the tent of meeting for atonement in the holy place; it shall be burned with fire.

7 This is the ritual of the guilt offering. It is most holy; 2 at the spot where the burnt offering is slaughtered, they shall slaughter the guilt offering, and its blood shall be dashed against all sides of the altar. 3 All its fat shall be offered: the broad tail, the fat that covers the entrails, 4 the two

---

b Ch 5.20 in Heb *c* Ch 6.1 in Heb *d* Meaning of Heb uncertain kidneys with the fat that is on them at the loins, and the appendage of the liver, which shall be removed with the kidneys. 5 The priest shall turn them into smoke on the altar as an offering by fire to the LORD; it is a guilt offering. 6 Every male among the priests shall eat of it; it shall be eaten in a holy place; it is most holy.

7 The guilt offering is like the sin offering, there is the same ritual for them; the priest who makes atonement with it shall have it. 8 So, too, the priest who offers anyone's burnt offering shall keep the skin of the burnt offering that he has offered. 9 And every grain offering baked in the oven, and all that is prepared in a pan or on a griddle, shall belong to the priest who offers it. 10 But every other grain offering, mixed with oil or dry, shall belong to all the sons of Aaron equally.

Further Instructions

11 This is the ritual of the sacrifice of the offering of well-being that one may offer to the LORD. 12 If you offer it for thanksgiving, you shall offer with the thank offering unleavened cakes mixed with oil, unleavened wafers spread with oil, and cakes of choice flour well soaked in oil. 13 With your thanksgiving sacrifice of well-being you shall bring your offering with cakes of leavened bread. 14 From this you shall offer one cake from each offering, as a gift to the LORD; it shall belong to the priest who dashes the blood of the offering of well-being. 15 And the flesh of your thanksgiving sacrifice of well-being shall be eaten on the day it is offered; you shall not leave any of it until morning. 16 But if the sacrifice you offer is a votive offering or a freewill offering, it shall be eaten on the day that you offer your sacrifice, and what is left of it shall be eaten the next day; 17 but what is left of the flesh of the sacrifice shall be burned up on the third day. 18 If any of the flesh of your sacrifice of well-being is eaten on the third day, it shall not be acceptable, nor shall it be credited to the one who offers it; it shall be an abomination, and the one who eats of it shall incur guilt.

19 Flesh that touches any unclean thing shall not be eaten; it shall be burned up. As for other flesh, all who are clean may eat such flesh. 20 But those who eat flesh from the LORD's sacrifice of well-being while in a state of uncleanness shall be cut off from their kin. 21 When any one of you touches any unclean thing—human uncleanness or an unclean animal or any unclean creature—and then eats flesh from the LORD's sacrifice of well-being, you shall be cut off from your kin.

22 The LORD spoke to Moses, saying: 23 Speak to the people of Israel, saying: You shall eat no fat of ox or sheep or goat. 24 The fat of an animal that died or was torn by wild animals may be put to any other use, but you must not eat it. 25 If any one of you eats the fat from an animal of which an offering by fire may be made to the LORD, you who eat it shall be cut off from your kin. 26 You must not eat any blood whatever, either of bird or of animal, in any of your settlements. 27 Any one of you who eats any blood shall be cut off from your kin.

28 The LORD spoke to Moses, saying: 29 Speak to the people of Israel, saying: Any one of you who would offer to the LORD your sacrifice of well-being must yourself bring to the LORD your offering from your sacrifice of well-being. 30 Your own hands shall bring the LORD's offering by fire; you shall bring the fat with the breast, so that the breast may be raised as an elevation offering before the LORD. 31 The priest shall turn the fat into smoke on the altar, but the breast shall belong to Aaron and his sons. 32 And the right thigh from your sacrifices of well-being you shall give to the priest as an offering; 33 the one among the sons of Aaron who offers the blood and fat of the offering of well-being shall have the right thigh for a portion. 34 For I have taken the breast of the elevation offering, and the thigh that is offered, from the people of Israel, from their sacrifices of well-being, and have given them to Aaron the priest and to his sons, as a perpetual due from the people of Israel. 35 This is the portion allotted to Aaron and to his sons from the offerings made by fire to the LORD, once they have been brought forward to serve the LORD as priests; 36 these the LORD commanded to be given them, when he anointed them, as a perpetual due from the people of Israel throughout their generations.

37 This is the ritual of the burnt offering, the grain offering, the sin offering, the guilt offering, the offering of ordination, and the sacrifice of well-being, 38 which the LORD commanded Moses on Mount Sinai, when he commanded the people of Israel to bring their offerings to the LORD, in the wilderness of Sinai.

The Rites of Ordination
(Ex 29.1–37)

8 The LORD spoke to Moses, saying: 2 Take Aaron and his sons with him, the vestments, the anointing oil, the bull of sin offering, the two rams, and the basket of unleavened bread; 3 and assemble the whole congregation at the entrance of the tent of meeting. 4 And Moses did as the LORD commanded him. When the congregation was assembled at the entrance of the tent of meeting, 5 Moses said to the congregation, "This is what the LORD has commanded to be done."

6 Then Moses brought Aaron and his sons forward, and washed them with water. 7 He put the tunic on him, fastened the sash around him, clothed him with the robe, and put the ephod on him. He

then put the decorated band of the ephod around him, tying the ephod to him with it. 8 He placed the breastpiece on him, and in the breastpiece he put the U'rim and the Thum'mim. 9 And he set the turban on his head, and on the turban, in front, he set the golden ornament, the holy crown, as the LORD commanded Moses.

10 Then Moses took the anointing oil and anointed the tabernacle and all that was in it, and consecrated them. 11 He sprinkled some of it on the altar seven times, and anointed the altar and all its utensils, and the basin and its base, to consecrate them. 12 He poured some of the anointing oil on Aaron's head and anointed him, to consecrate him. 13 And Moses brought forward Aaron's sons, and clothed them with tunics, and fastened sashes around them, and tied headdresses on them, as the LORD commanded Moses.

14 He led forward the bull of sin offering; and Aaron and his sons laid their hands upon the head of the bull of sin offering, 15 and it was slaughtered. Moses took the blood and with his finger put some on each of the horns of the altar, purifying the altar; then he poured out the blood at the base of the altar. Thus he consecrated it, to make atonement for it. 16 Moses took all the fat that was around the entrails, and the appendage of the liver, and the two kidneys with their fat, and turned them into smoke on the altar. 17 But the bull itself, its skin and flesh and its dung, he burned with fire outside the camp, as the LORD commanded Moses.

18 Then he brought forward the ram of burnt offering. Aaron and his sons laid their hands on the head of the ram, 19 and it was slaughtered. Moses dashed the blood against all sides of the altar. 20 The ram was cut into its parts, and Moses turned into smoke the head and the parts and the suet. 21 And after the entrails and the legs were washed with water, Moses turned into smoke the whole ram on the altar; it was a burnt offering for a pleasing odor, an offering by fire to the LORD, as the LORD commanded Moses.

22 Then he brought forward the second ram, the ram of ordination. Aaron and his sons laid their hands on the head of the ram, 23 and it was slaughtered. Moses took some of its blood and put it on the lobe of Aaron's right ear and on the thumb of his right hand and on the big toe of his right foot. 24 After Aaron's sons were brought forward, Moses put some of the blood on the lobes of their right ears and on the thumbs of their right hands and on the big toes of their right feet; and Moses dashed the rest of the blood against all sides of the altar. 25 He took the fat—the broad tail, all the fat that was around the entrails, the appendage of the liver, and the two kidneys with their fat—and the right thigh. 26 From the basket of unleavened bread that

was before the LORD, he took one cake of unleavened bread, one cake of bread with oil, and one wafer, and placed them on the fat and on the right thigh. 27 He placed all these on the palms of Aaron and on the palms of his sons, and raised them as an elevation offering before the LORD. 28 Then Moses took them from their hands and turned them into smoke on the altar with the burnt offering. This was an ordination offering for a pleasing odor, an offering by fire to the LORD. 29 Moses took the breast and raised it as an elevation offering before the LORD; it was Moses' portion of the ram of ordination, as the LORD commanded Moses.

30 Then Moses took some of the anointing oil and some of the blood that was on the altar and sprinkled them on Aaron and his vestments, and also on his sons and their vestments. Thus he consecrated Aaron and his vestments, and also his sons and their vestments.

31 And Moses said to Aaron and his sons, "Boil the flesh at the entrance of the tent of meeting, and eat it there with the bread that is in the basket of ordination offerings, as I was commanded, 'Aaron and his sons shall eat it'; 32 and what remains of the flesh and the bread you shall burn with fire. 33 You shall not go outside the entrance of the tent of meeting for seven days, until the day when your period of ordination is completed. For it will take seven days to ordain you; 34 as has been done today, the LORD has commanded to be done to make atonement for you. 35 You shall remain at the entrance of the tent of meeting day and night for seven days, keeping the LORD's charge so that you do not die; for so I am commanded." 36 Aaron and his sons did all the things that the LORD commanded through Moses.

Aaron's Priesthood Inaugurated

9 On the eighth day Moses summoned Aaron and his sons and the elders of Israel. 2 He said to Aaron, "Take a bull calf for a sin offering and a ram for a burnt offering, without blemish, and offer them before the LORD. 3 And say to the people of Israel, 'Take a male goat for a sin offering; a calf and a lamb, yearlings without blemish, for a burnt offering; 4 and an ox and a ram for an offering of well-being to sacrifice before the LORD; and a grain offering mixed with oil. For today the LORD will appear to you.' " 5 They brought what Moses commanded to the front of the tent of meeting; and the whole congregation drew near and stood before the LORD. 6 And Moses said, "This is the thing that the LORD commanded you to do, so that the glory of the LORD may appear to you." 7 Then Moses said to Aaron, "Draw near to the altar and sacrifice your sin offering and your burnt offering, and make atonement for yourself and for the people; and sacrifice

LEV

the offering of the people, and make atonement for them; as the LORD has commanded."

8 Aaron drew near to the altar, and slaughtered the calf of the sin offering, which was for himself. 9 The sons of Aaron presented the blood to him, and he dipped his finger in the blood and put it on the horns of the altar; and the rest of the blood he poured out at the base of the altar. 10 But the fat, the kidneys, and the appendage of the liver from the sin offering he turned into smoke on the altar, as the LORD commanded Moses; 11 and the flesh and the skin he burned with fire outside the camp.

12 Then he slaughtered the burnt offering. Aaron's sons brought him the blood, and he dashed it against all sides of the altar. 13 And they brought him the burnt offering piece by piece, and the head, which he turned into smoke on the altar. 14 He washed the entrails and the legs and, with the burnt offering, turned them into smoke on the altar.

15 Next he presented the people's offering. He took the goat of the sin offering that was for the people, and slaughtered it, and presented it as a sin offering like the first one. 16 He presented the burnt offering, and sacrificed it according to regulation. 17 He presented the grain offering, and, taking a handful of it, he turned it into smoke on the altar, in addition to the burnt offering of the morning.

18 He slaughtered the ox and the ram as a sacrifice of well-being for the people. Aaron's sons brought him the blood, which he dashed against all sides of the altar, 19 and the fat of the ox and of the ram—the broad tail, the fat that covers the entrails, the two kidneys and the fat on them,e and the appendage of the liver. 20 They first laid the fat on the breasts, and the fat was turned into smoke on the altar; 21 and the breasts and the right thigh Aaron raised as an elevation offering before the LORD, as Moses had commanded.

22 Aaron lifted his hands toward the people and blessed them; and he came down after sacrificing the sin offering, the burnt offering, and the offering of well-being. 23 Moses and Aaron entered the tent of meeting, and then came out and blessed the people; and the glory of the LORD appeared to all the people. 24 Fire came out from the LORD and consumed the burnt offering and the fat on the altar; and when all the people saw it, they shouted and fell on their faces.

Nadab and Abihu

10 Now Aaron's sons, Nā'dab and A•bī'hū, each took his censer, put fire in it, and laid incense on it; and they offered unholy fire before the LORD, such as he had not commanded them. 2 And fire came out from the presence of the LORD and consumed them, and they died before

the LORD. 3 Then Moses said to Aaron, "This is what the LORD meant when he said,

'Through those who are near me
    I will show myself holy,
and before all the people
    I will be glorified.' "

And Aaron was silent.

4 Moses summoned Mish'a•el and El'za•phan, sons of Uz'zi•el the uncle of Aaron, and said to them, "Come forward, and carry your kinsmen away from the front of the sanctuary to a place outside the camp." 5 They came forward and carried them by their tunics out of the camp, as Moses had ordered. 6 And Moses said to Aaron and to his sons El•ē•ā'zar and Ith'a•mar, "Do not dishevel your hair, and do not tear your vestments, or you will die and wrath will strike all the congregation; but your kindred, the whole house of Israel, may mourn the burning that the LORD has sent. 7 You shall not go outside the entrance of the tent of meeting, or you will die; for the anointing oil of the LORD is on you." And they did as Moses had ordered.

8 And the LORD spoke to Aaron: 9 Drink no wine or strong drink, neither you nor your sons, when you enter the tent of meeting, that you may not die; it is a statute forever throughout your generations. 10 You are to distinguish between the holy and the common, and between the unclean and the clean; 11 and you are to teach the people of Israel all the statutes that the LORD has spoken to them through Moses.

12 Moses spoke to Aaron and to his remaining sons, El•ē•ā'zar and Ith'a•mar: Take the grain offering that is left from the LORD's offerings by fire, and eat it unleavened beside the altar, for it is most holy; 13 you shall eat it in a holy place, because it is your due and your sons' due, from the offerings by fire to the LORD; for so I am commanded. 14 But the breast that is elevated and the thigh that is raised, you and your sons and daughters as well may eat in any clean place; for they have been assigned to you and your children from the sacrifices of the offerings of well-being of the people of Israel. 15 The thigh that is raised and the breast that is elevated they shall bring, together with the offerings by fire of the fat, to raise for an elevation offering before the LORD; they are to be your due and that of your children forever, as the LORD has commanded.

16 Then Moses made inquiry about the goat of the sin offering, and—it had already been burned! He was angry with El•ē•ā'zar and Ith'a•mar, Aaron's remaining sons, and said, 17 "Why did you not eat the sin offering in the sacred area? For it is most holy, and God f has given it to you that you may re-

---

e Gk: Heb the broad tail, and that which covers, and the kidneys
f Heb he

move the guilt of the congregation, to make atonement on their behalf before the LORD. 18 Its blood
was not brought into the inner part of the sanctuary. You should certainly have eaten it in the sanctuary, as I commanded." 19 And Aaron spoke to
Moses, "See, today they offered their sin offering
and their burnt offering before the LORD; and yet
such things as these have befallen me! If I had eaten
the sin offering today, would it have been agreeable
to the LORD?" 20 And when Moses heard that, he
agreed.

Clean and Unclean Foods
(Deut 14.3–21)

11 The LORD spoke to Moses and Aaron,
saying to them: 2 Speak to the people of
Israel, saying:

From among all the land animals, these are the
creatures that you may eat. 3 Any animal that has
divided hoofs and is cleft-footed and chews the
cud—such you may eat. 4 But among those that
chew the cud or have divided hoofs, you shall not
eat the following: the camel, for even though it
chews the cud, it does not have divided hoofs; it is
unclean for you. 5 The rock badger, for even though
it chews the cud, it does not have divided hoofs; it
is unclean for you. 6 The hare, for even though it
chews the cud, it does not have divided hoofs; it is
unclean for you. 7 The pig, for even though it has
divided hoofs and is cleft-footed, it does not chew
the cud; it is unclean for you. 8 Of their flesh you
shall not eat, and their carcasses you shall not
touch; they are unclean for you.

9 These you may eat, of all that are in the waters. Everything in the waters that has fins and
scales, whether in the seas or in the streams—such
you may eat. 10 But anything in the seas or the
streams that does not have fins and scales, of the
swarming creatures in the waters and among all
the other living creatures that are in the waters—
they are detestable to you 11 and detestable they
shall remain. Of their flesh you shall not eat, and
their carcasses you shall regard as detestable.
12 Everything in the waters that does not have fins
and scales is detestable to you.

13 These you shall regard as detestable among
the birds. They shall not be eaten; they are an
abomination: the eagle, the vulture, the osprey,
14 the buzzard, the kite of any kind; 15 every raven
of any kind; 16 the ostrich, the nighthawk, the sea
gull, the hawk of any kind; 17 the little owl, the cormorant, the great owl, 18 the water hen, the desert
owl,g the carrion vulture, 19 the stork, the heron of
any kind, the hoopoe, and the bat.h

20 All winged insects that walk upon all fours
are detestable to you. 21 But among the winged insects that walk on all fours you may eat those that

did you KNOW?
The Israelite Diet

The diet of the ancient Israelites consisted
mainly of breads, cereals, fruits, vegetables, and dairy products. Meat was served
only on special occasions because it was
expensive. A typical family meal was
made up of barley or wheat bread, grapes,
figs, olive oil, beans, cucumbers, onions,
and cheese. On festive occasions, beef or
lamb might grace the table.

The laws in Leviticus, chapter 11,
contain many restrictions regarding the
eating of animals. The reasons for these
restrictions are not clear, although many
scholars believe that one purpose was to
keep the Israelites from consuming animals used in pagan worship (for example,
the pig offered in Babylonian services).
Hygiene was likely another consideration.

The basic "meat laws" were as follows:

- Of the larger animals, those that
  chewed their cud and had split hooves
  could be eaten. Therefore, lamb was
  acceptable, but pork was not.
- Sea creatures only with both fins and
  scales could be eaten. Thus, catfish and
  eels were to be avoided.
- Eagles, vultures, buzzards, and many
  other birds were excluded from the
  table.
- Rodents, reptiles, and insects (except
  locusts and grasshoppers) were spurned
  altogether.

The blood from all animals had to be
drained completely before cooking because blood was seen as the life force and
therefore as belonging to God alone. In
addition, it was unlawful to touch or eat
any animal found dead; contact with any
dead body made one impure.

▶ Lev 11.1–47

have jointed legs above their feet, with which to
leap on the ground. 22 Of them you may eat: the locust according to its kind, the bald locust according
to its kind, the cricket according to its kind, and the

---

g Or *pelican*   h Identification of several of the birds in
verses 13-19 is uncertain

LEV

grasshopper according to its kind. 23 But all other winged insects that have four feet are detestable to you.

Unclean Animals

24 By these you shall become unclean; whoever touches the carcass of any of them shall be unclean until the evening, 25 and whoever carries any part of the carcass of any of them shall wash his clothes and be unclean until the evening. 26 Every animal that has divided hoofs but is not cleft-footed or does not chew the cud is unclean for you; everyone who touches one of them shall be unclean. 27 All that walk on their paws, among the animals that walk on all fours, are unclean for you; whoever touches the carcass of any of them shall be

unclean until the evening, 28 and the one who carries the carcass shall wash his clothes and be unclean until the evening; they are unclean for you.

29 These are unclean for you among the creatures that swarm upon the earth: the weasel, the mouse, the great lizard according to its kind, 30 the gecko, the land crocodile, the lizard, the sand lizard, and the chameleon. 31 These are unclean for you among all that swarm; whoever touches one of them when they are dead shall be unclean until the evening. 32 And anything upon which any of them falls when they are dead shall be unclean, whether an article of wood or cloth or skin or sacking, any article that is used for any purpose; it shall be dipped into water, and it shall be unclean until the evening, and then it shall be clean. 33 And if any of

A MOTHER'S PRAYER AT CHILDBIRTH

Sun, moon, stars,
you that move in the heavens,
hear this mother!
A new life has come among you.
Make its path smooth that it may reach
the brow of the first hill.

Winds, clouds, rain, mist,
all that move in the air,
hear this mother!
A new life has come among you.
Make its path smooth that it may reach
the brow of the second hill.

Hills, valleys, rivers, lakes, trees, grasses,
all of the earth,
hear this mother!
A new life has come among you.
Make its path smooth that it may reach
the brow of the third hill.

Birds that fly in the air,
animals that dwell in the forest,
insects that creep in the grasses and burrow
in the ground,
hear this mother!
A new life has come among you.
Make its path smooth that it may reach
the brow of the fourth hill.

All the heavens, air and earth,
hear this mother!
A new life has come among you.
Make its path smooth—then shall it travel
beyond the four hills!

(From Suzanne Slesin and
Emily Gwathmey, compilers, *Amen*, n.p.)

Like the Israelites, with their purification ritual described in Leviticus, chapter 12, most cultures have rituals and prayers associated with childbirth. In this mother's prayer of the North American Omaha tribe, the four hills refer to the four parts of human life—childhood, youth, adulthood, and old age. What a wonderful reminder that life is a journey and that all creation is invited to celebrate new life!

▶ Lev 12.1–8

them falls into any earthen vessel, all that is in it shall be unclean, and you shall break the vessel. 34 Any food that could be eaten shall be unclean if water from any such vessel comes upon it; and any liquid that could be drunk shall be unclean if it was in any such vessel. 35 Everything on which any part of the carcass falls shall be unclean; whether an oven or stove, it shall be broken in pieces; they are unclean, and shall remain unclean for you. 36 But a spring or a cistern holding water shall be clean, while whatever touches the carcass in it shall be unclean. 37 If any part of their carcass falls upon any seed set aside for sowing, it is clean; 38 but if water is put on the seed and any part of their carcass falls on it, it is unclean for you.

39 If an animal of which you may eat dies, anyone who touches its carcass shall be unclean until the evening. 40 Those who eat of its carcass shall wash their clothes and be unclean until the evening; and those who carry the carcass shall wash their clothes and be unclean until the evening. 41 All creatures that swarm upon the earth are detestable; they shall not be eaten. 42 Whatever moves on its belly, and whatever moves on all fours, or whatever has many feet, all the creatures that swarm upon the earth, you shall not eat; for they are detestable. 43 You shall not make yourselves detestable with any creature that swarms; you shall not defile yourselves with them, and so become unclean. 44 For I am the LORD your God; sanctify yourselves therefore, and be holy, for I am holy. You shall not defile yourselves with any swarming creature that moves on the earth. 45 For I am the LORD who brought you up from the land of Egypt, to be your God; you shall be holy, for I am holy. 46 This is the law pertaining to land animal and bird and every living creature that moves through the waters and every creature that swarms upon the earth, 47 to make a distinction between the unclean and the clean, and between the living creature that may be eaten and the living creature that may not be eaten.

Purification of Women after Childbirth
(Cp Lk 2.22–24)

12 The LORD spoke to Moses, saying: 2 Speak to the people of Israel, saying:

If a woman conceives and bears a male child, she shall be ceremonially unclean seven days; as at the time of her menstruation, she shall be unclean. 3 On the eighth day the flesh of his foreskin shall be circumcised. 4 Her time of blood purification shall be thirty-three days; she shall not touch any holy thing, or come into the sanctuary, until the days of her purification are completed. 5 If she bears a female child, she shall be unclean two weeks, as in

her menstruation; her time of blood purification shall be sixty-six days.

6 When the days of her purification are completed, whether for a son or for a daughter, she shall bring to the priest at the entrance of the tent of meeting a lamb in its first year for a burnt offering, and a pigeon or a turtledove for a sin offering. 7 He shall offer it before the LORD, and make atonement on her behalf; then she shall be clean from her flow of blood. This is the law for her who bears a child, male or female. 8 If she cannot afford a sheep, she shall take two turtledoves or two pigeons, one for a burnt offering and the other for a sin offering; and the priest shall make atonement on her behalf, and she shall be clean.

Leprosy, Varieties and Symptoms

13 The LORD spoke to Moses and Aaron, saying: 2 When a person has on the skin of his body a swelling or an eruption or a spot, and it turns into a leprous[i] disease on the skin of his body, he shall be brought to Aaron the priest or to one of his sons the priests. 3 The priest shall examine the disease on the skin of his body, and if the hair in the diseased area has turned white and the disease appears to be deeper than the skin of his body, it is a leprous[i] disease; after the priest has examined him he shall pronounce him ceremonially unclean. 4 But if the spot is white in the skin of his body, and appears no deeper than the skin, and the hair in it has not turned white, the priest shall confine the diseased person for seven days. 5 The priest shall examine him on the seventh day, and if he sees that the disease is checked and the disease has not spread in the skin, then the priest shall confine him seven days more. 6 The priest shall examine him again on the seventh day, and if the disease has abated and the disease has not spread in the skin, the priest shall pronounce him clean; it is only an eruption; and he shall wash his clothes, and be clean. 7 But if the eruption spreads in the skin after he has shown himself to the priest for his cleansing, he shall appear again before the priest. 8 The priest shall make an examination, and if the eruption has spread in the skin, the priest shall pronounce him unclean; it is a leprous[i] disease.

9 When a person contracts a leprous[i] disease, he shall be brought to the priest. 10 The priest shall make an examination, and if there is a white swelling in the skin that has turned the hair white, and there is quick raw flesh in the swelling, 11 it is a chronic leprous[i] disease in the skin of his body. The priest shall pronounce him unclean; he shall not

---

[i] A term for several skin diseases; precise meaning uncertain

confine him, for he is unclean. 12 But if the disease breaks out in the skin, so that it covers all the skin of the diseased person from head to foot, so far as the priest can see, 13 then the priest shall make an examination, and if the disease has covered all his body, he shall pronounce him clean of the disease; since it has all turned white, he is clean. 14 But if raw flesh ever appears on him, he shall be unclean; 15 the priest shall examine the raw flesh and pronounce him unclean. Raw flesh is unclean, for it is a leprous*j* disease. 16 But if the raw flesh again turns white, he shall come to the priest; 17 the priest shall examine him, and if the disease has turned white, the priest shall pronounce the diseased person clean. He is clean.

18 When there is on the skin of one's body a boil that has healed, 19 and in the place of the boil there appears a white swelling or a reddish-white spot, it shall be shown to the priest. 20 The priest shall make an examination, and if it appears deeper than the skin and its hair has turned white, the priest shall pronounce him unclean; this is a leprous*j* disease, broken out in the boil. 21 But if the priest examines it and the hair on it is not white, nor is it deeper than the skin but has abated, the priest shall confine him seven days. 22 If it spreads in the skin, the priest shall pronounce him unclean; it is diseased. 23 But if the spot remains in one place and does not spread, it is the scar of the boil; the priest shall pronounce him clean.

24 Or, when the body has a burn on the skin and the raw flesh of the burn becomes a spot, reddish-white or white, 25 the priest shall examine it. If the hair in the spot has turned white and it appears deeper than the skin, it is a leprous*j* disease; it has broken out in the burn, and the priest shall pronounce him unclean. This is a leprous*j* disease. 26 But if the priest examines it and the hair in the spot is not white, and it is no deeper than the skin but has abated, the priest shall confine him seven days. 27 The priest shall examine him the seventh day; if it is spreading in the skin, the priest shall pronounce him unclean. This is a leprous*j* disease. 28 But if the spot remains in one place and does not spread in the skin but has abated, it is a swelling from the burn, and the priest shall pronounce him clean; for it is the scar of the burn.

29 When a man or woman has a disease on the head or in the beard, 30 the priest shall examine the disease. If it appears deeper than the skin and the hair in it is yellow and thin, the priest shall pronounce him unclean; it is an itch, a leprous*j* disease of the head or the beard. 31 If the priest examines the itching disease, and it appears no deeper than the skin and there is no black hair in it, the priest shall confine the person with the itching disease for seven days. 32 On the seventh day the priest shall examine the itch; if the itch has not spread, and there is no yellow hair in it, and the itch appears to be no deeper than the skin, 33 he shall shave, but the itch he shall not shave. The priest shall confine the person with the itch for seven days more. 34 On the seventh day the priest shall examine the itch; if the itch has not spread in the skin and it appears to be no deeper than the skin, the priest shall pronounce him clean. He shall wash his clothes and be clean. 35 But if the itch spreads in the skin after he was pronounced clean, 36 the priest shall examine him. If the itch has spread in the skin, the priest need not seek for the yellow hair; he is unclean. 37 But if in his eyes the itch is checked, and black hair has grown in it, the itch is healed, he is clean; and the priest shall pronounce him clean.

38 When a man or a woman has spots on the skin of the body, white spots, 39 the priest shall make an examination, and if the spots on the skin of the body are of a dull white, it is a rash that has broken out on the skin; he is clean.

40 If anyone loses the hair from his head, he is bald but he is clean. 41 If he loses the hair from his forehead and temples, he has baldness of the forehead but he is clean. 42 But if there is on the bald head or the bald forehead a reddish-white diseased spot, it is a leprous*j* disease breaking out on his bald head or his bald forehead. 43 The priest shall examine him; if the diseased swelling is reddish-white on his bald head or on his bald forehead, which resembles a leprous*j* disease in the skin of the body, 44 he is leprous,*j* he is unclean. The priest shall pronounce him unclean; the disease is on his head.

45 The person who has the leprous*j* disease shall wear torn clothes and let the hair of his head be disheveled; and he shall cover his upper lip and cry out, "Unclean, unclean." 46 He shall remain unclean as long as he has the disease; he is unclean. He shall live alone; his dwelling shall be outside the camp.

47 Concerning clothing: when a leprous*j* disease appears in it, in woolen or linen cloth, 48 in warp or woof of linen or wool, or in a skin or in anything made of skin, 49 if the disease shows greenish or reddish in the garment, whether in warp or woof or in skin or in anything made of skin, it is a leprous*j* disease and shall be shown to the priest. 50 The priest shall examine the disease, and put the diseased article aside for seven days. 51 He shall examine the disease on the seventh day. If the disease has spread in the cloth, in warp or woof, or in the skin, whatever be the use of the skin, this is a spreading leprous*j* disease; it is unclean.

---

j A term for several skin diseases; precise meaning uncertain

52 He shall burn the clothing, whether diseased in warp or woof, woolen or linen, or anything of skin, for it is a spreading leprous[k] disease; it shall be burned in fire.

53 If the priest makes an examination, and the disease has not spread in the clothing, in warp or woof or in anything of skin, 54 the priest shall command them to wash the article in which the disease appears, and he shall put it aside seven days more. 55 The priest shall examine the diseased article after it has been washed. If the diseased spot has not changed color, though the disease has not spread, it is unclean; you shall burn it in fire, whether the leprous[k] spot is on the inside or on the outside.

56 If the priest makes an examination, and the disease has abated after it is washed, he shall tear the spot out of the cloth, in warp or woof, or out of skin. 57 If it appears again in the garment, in warp or woof, or in anything of skin, it is spreading; you shall burn with fire that in which the disease appears. 58 But the cloth, warp or woof, or anything of skin from which the disease disappears when you have washed it, shall then be washed a second time, and it shall be clean.

59 This is the ritual for a leprous[k] disease in a cloth of wool or linen, either in warp or woof, or in anything of skin, to decide whether it is clean or unclean.

Purification of Lepers and Leprous Houses
(Cp Mt 8.1–4; Lk 5.12–14)

14 The LORD spoke to Moses, saying: 2 This shall be the ritual for the leprous[k] person at the time of his cleansing:

He shall be brought to the priest; 3 the priest shall go out of the camp, and the priest shall make an examination. If the disease is healed in the leprous[k] person, 4 the priest shall command that two living clean birds and cedarwood and crimson yarn and hyssop be brought for the one who is to be cleansed. 5 The priest shall command that one of the birds be slaughtered over fresh water in an earthen vessel. 6 He shall take the living bird with the cedarwood and the crimson yarn and the hyssop, and dip them and the living bird in the blood of the bird that was slaughtered over the fresh water. 7 He shall sprinkle it seven times upon the one who is to be cleansed of the leprous[k] disease; then he shall pronounce him clean, and he shall let the living bird go into the open field. 8 The one who is to be cleansed shall wash his clothes, and shave off all his hair, and bathe himself in water, and he shall be clean. After that he shall come into the camp, but shall live outside his tent seven days. 9 On the seventh day he shall shave all his hair: of head, beard, eyebrows; he shall shave all his hair. Then he

shall wash his clothes, and bathe his body in water, and he shall be clean.

10 On the eighth day he shall take two male lambs without blemish, and one ewe lamb in its first year without blemish, and a grain offering of three-tenths of an ephah of choice flour mixed with oil, and one log[l] of oil. 11 The priest who cleanses shall set the person to be cleansed, along with these things, before the LORD, at the entrance of the tent of meeting. 12 The priest shall take one of the lambs, and offer it as a guilt offering, along with the log[l] of oil, and raise them as an elevation offering before the LORD. 13 He shall slaughter the lamb in the place where the sin offering and the burnt offering are slaughtered in the holy place; for the guilt offering, like the sin offering, belongs to the priest: it is most holy. 14 The priest shall take some of the blood of the guilt offering and put it on the lobe of the right ear of the one to be cleansed, and on the thumb of the right hand, and on the big toe of the right foot. 15 The priest shall take some of the log[l] of oil and pour it into the palm of his own left hand, 16 and dip his right finger in the oil that is in his left hand and sprinkle some oil with his finger seven times before the LORD. 17 Some of the oil that remains in his hand the priest shall put on the lobe of the right ear of the one to be cleansed, and on the thumb of the right hand, and on the big toe of the right foot, on top of the blood of the guilt offering. 18 The rest of the oil that is in the priest's hand he shall put on the head of the one to be cleansed. Then the priest shall make atonement on his behalf before the LORD: 19 the priest shall offer the sin offering, to make atonement for the one to be cleansed from his uncleanness. Afterward he shall slaughter the burnt offering; 20 and the priest shall offer the burnt offering and the grain offering on the altar. Thus the priest shall make atonement on his behalf and he shall be clean.

21 But if he is poor and cannot afford so much, he shall take one male lamb for a guilt offering to be elevated, to make atonement on his behalf, and one-tenth of an ephah of choice flour mixed with oil for a grain offering and a log[l] of oil; 22 also two turtledoves or two pigeons, such as he can afford, one for a sin offering and the other for a burnt offering. 23 On the eighth day he shall bring them for his cleansing to the priest, to the entrance of the tent of meeting, before the LORD; 24 and the priest shall take the lamb of the guilt offering and the log[l] of oil, and the priest shall raise them as an elevation offering before the LORD. 25 The priest shall slaughter the lamb of the guilt offering and shall take some of the blood of the guilt offering, and put it

---

k A term for several skin diseases; precise meaning uncertain   l A liquid measure on the lobe of the right ear of the one to be cleansed, and on the thumb of the right hand, and on the big toe of the right foot. 26 The priest shall pour some of the oil into the palm of his own left hand, 27 and shall sprinkle with his right finger some of the oil that is in his left hand seven times before the LORD. 28 The priest shall put some of the oil that is in his hand on the lobe of the right ear of the one to be cleansed, and on the thumb of the right hand, and the big toe of the right foot, where the blood of the guilt offering was placed. 29 The rest of the oil that is in the priest's hand he shall put on the head of the one to be cleansed, to make atonement on his behalf before the LORD. 30 And he shall offer, of the turtledoves or pigeons such as he can afford, 31 one[m] for a sin offering and the other for a burnt offering, along with a grain offering; and the priest shall make atonement before the LORD on behalf of the one being cleansed. 32 This is the ritual for the one who has a leprous[n] disease, who cannot afford the offerings for his cleansing.

33 The LORD spoke to Moses and Aaron, saying:

34 When you come into the land of Ca'naan, which I give you for a possession, and I put a leprous[n] disease in a house in the land of your possession, 35 the owner of the house shall come and tell the priest, saying, "There seems to me to be some sort of disease in my house." 36 The priest shall command that they empty the house before the priest goes to examine the disease, or all that is in the house will become unclean; and afterward the priest shall go in to inspect the house. 37 He shall examine the disease; if the disease is in the walls of the house with greenish or reddish spots, and if it appears to be deeper than the surface, 38 the priest shall go outside to the door of the house and shut up the house seven days. 39 The priest shall come again on the seventh day and make an inspection; if the disease has spread in the walls of the house, 40 the priest shall command that the stones in which the disease appears be taken out and thrown into an unclean place outside the city. 41 He shall have the inside of the house scraped thoroughly, and the plaster that is scraped off shall be dumped in an unclean place outside the city. 42 They shall take other stones and put them in the place of those stones, and take other plaster and plaster the house.

43 If the disease breaks out again in the house, after he has taken out the stones and scraped the house and plastered it, 44 the priest shall go and make inspection; if the disease has spread in the house, it is a spreading leprous[n] disease in the house; it is unclean. 45 He shall have the house torn down, its stones and timber and all the plaster of the house, and taken outside the city to an unclean place. 46 All who enter the house while it is shut up shall be unclean until the evening; 47 and all who sleep in the house shall wash their clothes; and all who eat in the house shall wash their clothes.

48 If the priest comes and makes an inspection, and the disease has not spread in the house after the house was plastered, the priest shall pronounce the house clean; the disease is healed. 49 For the cleansing of the house he shall take two birds, with cedarwood and crimson yarn and hyssop, 50 and shall slaughter one of the birds over fresh water in an earthen vessel, 51 and shall take the cedarwood and the hyssop and the crimson yarn, along with the living bird, and dip them in the blood of the slaughtered bird and the fresh water, and sprinkle the house seven times. 52 Thus he shall cleanse the house with the blood of the bird, and with the fresh water, and with the living bird, and with the cedarwood and hyssop and crimson yarn; 53 and he shall let the living bird go out of the city into the open field; so he shall make atonement for the house, and it shall be clean.

54 This is the ritual for any leprous[n] disease: for an itch, 55 for leprous[n] diseases in clothing and houses, 56 and for a swelling or an eruption or a spot, 57 to determine when it is unclean and when it is clean. This is the ritual for leprous[n] diseases.

Concerning Bodily Discharges

15 The LORD spoke to Moses and Aaron, saying: 2 Speak to the people of Israel and say to them:

When any man has a discharge from his member,[o] his discharge makes him ceremonially unclean. 3 The uncleanness of his discharge is this: whether his member[o] flows with his discharge, or his member[o] is stopped from discharging, it is uncleanness for him. 4 Every bed on which the one with the discharge lies shall be unclean; and everything on which he sits shall be unclean. 5 Anyone who touches his bed shall wash his clothes, and bathe in water, and be unclean until the evening. 6 All who sit on anything on which the one with the discharge has sat shall wash their clothes, and bathe in water, and be unclean until the evening. 7 All who touch the body of the one with the discharge shall wash their clothes, and bathe in water, and be unclean until the evening. 8 If the one with the discharge spits on persons who are clean, then they shall wash their clothes, and bathe in water, and be unclean until the evening. 9 Any saddle on which the one with the discharge rides shall be unclean. 10 All who touch anything that was under him shall be unclean until the evening, and all who carry such a thing shall wash their clothes, and bathe in

---

[m] Gk Syr: Heb *afford*, 31*such as he can afford, one*   [n] A term for several skin diseases; precise meaning uncertain   [o] Heb *flesh*

did you KNOW?

Monthly Periods

Not every woman suffers pain and swelling as part of her menstrual cycle, but many do. Imagine the life of women in Old Testament days. No sanitary supplies, just strips of cloth. Not much privacy. Not much sympathy from men. No understanding of human biology. Just the monthly flow of blood and the trouble and discomfort of dealing with it.

And on top of the discomfort, women were seen as unclean during their menstrual period. How unfair! How uncaring! How did this unclean concept in Lev 15.19–33 develop, anyway? It probably had to do with blood's being a powerful sign of life. To the ancient Israelites, the loss of blood may have symbolized illness and death.

Thankfully, we do not apply all the Mosaic laws to our life today. We have grown in our understanding of human biology and of human dignity. Let's never stop growing.

▸ Lev 15.19–33

water, and be unclean until the evening. 11 All those whom the one with the discharge touches without his having rinsed his hands in water shall wash their clothes, and bathe in water, and be unclean until the evening. 12 Any earthen vessel that the one with the discharge touches shall be broken; and every vessel of wood shall be rinsed in water.

13 When the one with a discharge is cleansed of his discharge, he shall count seven days for his cleansing; he shall wash his clothes and bathe his body in fresh water, and he shall be clean. 14 On the eighth day he shall take two turtledoves or two pigeons and come before the LORD to the entrance of the tent of meeting and give them to the priest. 15 The priest shall offer them, one for a sin offering and the other for a burnt offering; and the priest shall make atonement on his behalf before the LORD for his discharge.

16 If a man has an emission of semen, he shall bathe his whole body in water, and be unclean until the evening. 17 Everything made of cloth or of skin on which the semen falls shall be washed with water, and be unclean until the evening. 18 If a man

lies with a woman and has an emission of semen, both of them shall bathe in water, and be unclean until the evening.

19 When a woman has a discharge of blood that is her regular discharge from her body, she shall be in her impurity for seven days, and whoever touches her shall be unclean until the evening. 20 Everything upon which she lies during her impurity shall be unclean; everything also upon which she sits shall be unclean. 21 Whoever touches her bed shall wash his clothes, and bathe in water, and be unclean until the evening. 22 Whoever touches anything upon which she sits shall wash his clothes, and bathe in water, and be unclean until the evening; 23 whether it is the bed or anything upon which she sits, when he touches it he shall be unclean until the evening. 24 If any man lies with her, and her impurity falls on him, he shall be unclean seven days; and every bed on which he lies shall be unclean.

25 If a woman has a discharge of blood for many days, not at the time of her impurity, or if she has a discharge beyond the time of her impurity, all the days of the discharge she shall continue in uncleanness; as in the days of her impurity, she shall be unclean. 26 Every bed on which she lies during all the days of her discharge shall be treated as the bed of her impurity; and everything on which she sits shall be unclean, as in the uncleanness of her impurity. 27 Whoever touches these things shall be unclean, and shall wash his clothes, and bathe in water, and be unclean until the evening. 28 If she is cleansed of her discharge, she shall count seven days, and after that she shall be clean. 29 On the eighth day she shall take two turtledoves or two pigeons and bring them to the priest at the entrance of the tent of meeting. 30 The priest shall offer one for a sin offering and the other for a burnt offering; and the priest shall make atonement on her behalf before the LORD for her unclean discharge.

31 Thus you shall keep the people of Israel separate from their uncleanness, so that they do not die in their uncleanness by defiling my tabernacle that is in their midst.

32 This is the ritual for those who have a discharge: for him who has an emission of semen, becoming unclean thereby, 33 for her who is in the infirmity of her period, for anyone, male or female, who has a discharge, and for the man who lies with a woman who is unclean.

The Day of Atonement

16 The LORD spoke to Moses after the death of the two sons of Aaron, when they drew near before the LORD and died. 2 The LORD said to Moses:

Tell your brother Aaron not to come just at any

LEV

time into the sanctuary inside the curtain before the mercy seat*p* that is upon the ark, or he will die; for I appear in the cloud upon the mercy seat.*p* 3 Thus shall Aaron come into the holy place: with a young bull for a sin offering and a ram for a burnt offering. 4 He shall put on the holy linen tunic, and shall have the linen undergarments next to his body, fasten the linen sash, and wear the linen turban; these are the holy vestments. He shall bathe his body in water, and then put them on. 5 He shall take from the congregation of the people of Israel two male goats for a sin offering, and one ram for a burnt offering.

6 Aaron shall offer the bull as a sin offering for himself, and shall make atonement for himself and for his house. 7 He shall take the two goats and set them before the LORD at the entrance of the tent of meeting; 8 and Aaron shall cast lots on the two goats, one lot for the LORD and the other lot for Az'a•zel.*q* 9 Aaron shall present the goat on which the lot fell for the LORD, and offer it as a sin offering; 10 but the goat on which the lot fell for Az'a•zel*q* shall be presented alive before the LORD to make atonement over it, that it may be sent away into the wilderness to Az'a•zel.*q*

11 Aaron shall present the bull as a sin offering for himself, and shall make atonement for himself and for his house; he shall slaughter the bull as a sin offering for himself. 12 He shall take a censer full of coals of fire from the altar before the LORD, and two handfuls of crushed sweet incense, and he shall bring it inside the curtain 13 and put the incense on the fire before the LORD, that the cloud of the incense may cover the mercy seat*p* that is upon the covenant,*r* or he will die. 14 He shall take some of the blood of the bull, and sprinkle it with his finger on the front of the mercy seat,*p* and before the mercy seat*p* he shall sprinkle the blood with his finger seven times.

15 He shall slaughter the goat of the sin offering that is for the people and bring its blood inside the curtain, and do with its blood as he did with the blood of the bull, sprinkling it upon the mercy seat*p* and before the mercy seat.*p* 16 Thus he shall make atonement for the sanctuary, because of the uncleannesses of the people of Israel, and because of their transgressions, all their sins; and so he shall do for the tent of meeting, which remains with them in the midst of their uncleannesses. 17 No one shall be in the tent of meeting from the time he enters to make atonement in the sanctuary until he comes out and has made atonement for himself and for his house and for all the assembly of Israel. 18 Then he shall go out to the altar that is before the LORD and make atonement on its behalf, and shall take some of the blood of the bull and of the blood of the goat, and put it on each of the horns of the altar. 19 He shall sprinkle some of the blood on it with his finger seven times, and cleanse it and hallow it from the uncleannesses of the people of Israel.

20 When he has finished atoning for the holy place and the tent of meeting and the altar, he shall

---

p Or *the cover*   *q* Traditionally rendered *a scapegoat*   *r* Or *treaty,* or *testament;* Heb *eduth*

The Scapegoat

LIVE IT!

What an interesting tradition! In the Israelite ritual described in Lev 16.20–21, the leader symbolically transfers all the people's sins onto a goat and drives it away. It is a liberating act that allows a fresh start.

But today, the idea of a scapegoat conveys oppression rather than freedom. A person becomes the scapegoat when other people blame him or her for their problems. Here is an example:

Suppose you are on a sports team that expects this week's game to be easy, so no one works hard at practice. On game day, the score is tied near the end of the game. Your team is already thinking about going home when the other team scores a goal and wins the game. Everyone gets mad at the goalie for not preventing the goal. The goalie is the scapegoat, but all should share in the fault for the loss because they did not practice well or play their best.

- **Have you ever been the scapegoat for someone else's problems? If so, how did that feel? What did you do?**
- **Have you ever scapegoated someone else when you were partly to blame for some situation? What happened? How will you prevent scapegoating in the future?**

▸ **Lev 16.20–21**

present the live goat. 21 Then Aaron shall lay both his hands on the head of the live goat, and confess over it all the iniquities of the people of Israel, and all their transgressions, all their sins, putting them on the head of the goat, and sending it away into the wilderness by means of someone designated for the task.ˢ 22 The goat shall bear on itself all their iniquities to a barren region; and the goat shall be set free in the wilderness.

23 Then Aaron shall enter the tent of meeting, and shall take off the linen vestments that he put on when he went into the holy place, and shall leave them there. 24 He shall bathe his body in water in a holy place, and put on his vestments; then he shall come out and offer his burnt offering and the burnt offering of the people, making atonement for himself and for the people. 25 The fat of the sin offering he shall turn into smoke on the altar. 26 The one who sets the goat free for Az'a•zelᵗ shall wash his clothes and bathe his body in water, and afterward may come into the camp. 27 The bull of the sin offering and the goat of the sin offering, whose blood was brought in to make atonement in the holy place, shall be taken outside the camp; their skin and their flesh and their dung shall be consumed in fire. 28 The one who burns them shall wash his clothes and bathe his body in water, and afterward may come into the camp.

29 This shall be a statute to you forever: In the seventh month, on the tenth day of the month, you shall deny yourselves,ᵘ and shall do no work, neither the citizen nor the alien who resides among you. 30 For on this day atonement shall be made for you, to cleanse you; from all your sins you shall be clean before the LORD. 31 It is a sabbath of complete rest to you, and you shall deny yourselves;ᵘ it is a statute forever. 32 The priest who is anointed and consecrated as priest in his father's place shall make atonement, wearing the linen vestments, the holy vestments. 33 He shall make atonement for the sanctuary, and he shall make atonement for the tent of meeting and for the altar, and he shall make atonement for the priests and for all the people of the assembly. 34 This shall be an everlasting statute for you, to make atonement for the people of Israel once in the year for all their sins. And Moses did as the LORD had commanded him.

The Slaughtering of Animals

17 The LORD spoke to Moses: 2 Speak to Aaron and his sons and to all the people of Israel and say to them: This is what the LORD has commanded. 3 If anyone of the house of Israel slaughters an ox or a lamb or a goat in the camp, or slaughters it outside the camp, 4 and does not bring it to the entrance of the tent of meeting, to present it as an offering to the LORD before the tabernacle of the LORD, he shall be held guilty of bloodshed; he has shed blood, and he shall be cut off from the people. 5 This is in order that the people of Israel may bring their sacrifices that they offer in the open field, that they may bring them to the LORD, to the priest at the entrance of the tent of meeting, and offer them as sacrifices of well-being to the LORD. 6 The priest shall dash the blood against the altar of the LORD at the entrance of the tent of meeting, and turn the fat into smoke as a pleasing odor to the LORD, 7 so that they may no longer offer their sacrifices for goat-demons, to whom they prostitute themselves. This shall be a statute forever to them throughout their generations.

8 And say to them further: Anyone of the house of Israel or of the aliens who reside among them who offers a burnt offering or sacrifice, 9 and does not bring it to the entrance of the tent of meeting, to sacrifice it to the LORD, shall be cut off from the people.

Eating Blood Prohibited

10 If anyone of the house of Israel or of the aliens who reside among them eats any blood, I will set my face against that person who eats blood, and will cut that person off from the people. 11 For the life of the flesh is in the blood; and I have given it to you for making atonement for your lives on the altar; for, as life, it is the blood that makes atonement. 12 Therefore I have said to the people of Israel: No person among you shall eat blood, nor shall any alien who resides among you eat blood. 13 And anyone of the people of Israel, or of the aliens who reside among them, who hunts down an animal or bird that may be eaten shall pour out its blood and cover it with earth.

14 For the life of every creature—its blood is its life; therefore I have said to the people of Israel: You shall not eat the blood of any creature, for the life of every creature is its blood; whoever eats it shall be cut off. 15 All persons, citizens or aliens, who eat what dies of itself or what has been torn by wild animals, shall wash their clothes, and bathe themselves in water, and be unclean until the evening; then they shall be clean. 16 But if they do not wash themselves or bathe their body, they shall bear their guilt.

Sexual Relations

18 The LORD spoke to Moses, saying: 2 Speak to the people of Israel and say to them: I am the LORD your God. 3 You shall not do as they do in the land of Egypt, where you lived, and you shall not do as they do in the land of

LEV

ˢ Meaning of Heb uncertain   ᵗ Traditionally rendered *a scapegoat*   ᵘ Or *shall fast*

Cā'naan, to which I am bringing you. You shall not follow their statutes. 4 My ordinances you shall observe and my statutes you shall keep, following them: I am the LORD your God. 5 You shall keep my statutes and my ordinances; by doing so one shall live: I am the LORD.

6 None of you shall approach anyone near of kin to uncover nakedness: I am the LORD. 7 You shall not uncover the nakedness of your father, which is the nakedness of your mother; she is your mother, you shall not uncover her nakedness. 8 You shall not uncover the nakedness of your father's wife; it is the nakedness of your father. 9 You shall not uncover the nakedness of your sister, your father's daughter or your mother's daughter, whether born at home or born abroad. 10 You shall not uncover the nakedness of your son's daughter or of your daughter's daughter, for their nakedness is your own nakedness. 11 You shall not uncover the nakedness of your father's wife's daughter, begotten by your father, since she is your sister. 12 You shall not uncover the nakedness of your father's sister; she is your father's flesh. 13 You shall not uncover the nakedness of your mother's sister, for she is your mother's flesh. 14 You shall not uncover the nakedness of your father's brother, that is, you shall not approach his wife; she is your aunt. 15 You shall not uncover the nakedness of your daughter-in-law: she is your son's wife; you shall not uncover her nakedness. 16 You shall not uncover the nakedness of your brother's wife; it is your brother's nakedness. 17 You shall not uncover the nakedness of a woman and her daughter, and you shall not take^v her son's daughter or her daughter's daughter to uncover her nakedness; they are your^w flesh; it is depravity. 18 And you shall not take^v a woman as a rival to her sister, uncovering her nakedness while her sister is still alive.

19 You shall not approach a woman to uncover her nakedness while she is in her menstrual uncleanness. 20 You shall not have sexual relations with your kinsman's wife, and defile yourself with her. 21 You shall not give any of your offspring to sacrifice them^x to Mō'lech, and so profane the name of your God: I am the LORD. 22 You shall not lie with a male as with a woman; it is an abomination. 23 You shall not have sexual relations with any animal and defile yourself with it, nor shall any woman give herself to an animal to have sexual relations with it: it is perversion.

24 Do not defile yourselves in any of these ways, for by all these practices the nations I am casting out before you have defiled themselves. 25 Thus the land became defiled; and I punished it for its iniquity, and the land vomited out its inhabitants. 26 But you shall keep my statutes and my ordinances and commit none of these abominations, either the citizen or the alien who resides among you 27 (for the inhabitants of the land, who were before you, committed all of these abominations, and the land became defiled); 28 otherwise the land will vomit you out for defiling it, as it vomited out

---

^{v} Or marry ^{w} Gk: Heb lacks your ^{x} Heb to pass them over

LIVE IT!

A Very Special Gift

The laws about sexual relations in Leviticus, chapter 18, are another example of how holiness extended to all aspects of life for the Israelites. The people had experienced the sexual promiscuity of other cultures (see Genesis, chapter 19). To become a great nation, the children of God, they had to abandon unhealthy and unholy sexual practices and follow God's way.

Young people today also receive many confusing cultural messages about when it is okay to have sex. In movies, television, and music, sex happens all the time between unmarried people, with no consequences. But the church, parents, and teachers are saying to wait until marriage. What is a person to believe?

Think about this: Suppose you are receiving a special gift for Christmas. The gift has been wrapped up and then hidden until Christmas Day. How would it feel if you discovered the present and opened it before Christmas? You probably would initially feel some excitement and pleasure in opening the gift. But the special meaning of opening it on the right day would be lost—for both you and the one presenting it to you.

Sex is a wonderful gift from God, meant for that day when you say, "I do," to someone you are committed to for life. You can only appreciate the full beauty of the gift when it is shared in marriage. God wants us to wait so that it will be as special as it is meant to be.

▶ Lev 18.1–30

the nation that was before you. 29 For whoever commits any of these abominations shall be cut off from their people. 30 So keep my charge not to commit any of these abominations that were done before you, and not to defile yourselves by them: I am the LORD your God.

Ritual and Moral Holiness

19 The LORD spoke to Moses, saying: 2 Speak to all the congregation of the people of Israel and say to them: You shall be holy, for I the LORD your God am holy. 3 You shall each revere your mother and father, and you shall keep my sabbaths: I am the LORD your God. 4 Do not turn to idols or make cast images for yourselves: I am the LORD your God.

5 When you offer a sacrifice of well-being to the LORD, offer it in such a way that it is acceptable in your behalf. 6 It shall be eaten on the same day you offer it, or on the next day; and anything left over until the third day shall be consumed in fire. 7 If it is eaten at all on the third day, it is an abomination; it will not be acceptable. 8 All who eat it shall be subject to punishment, because they have profaned what is holy to the LORD; and any such person shall be cut off from the people.

9 When you reap the harvest of your land, you shall not reap to the very edges of your field, or gather the gleanings of your harvest. 10 You shall not strip your vineyard bare, or gather the fallen grapes of your vineyard; you shall leave them for the poor and the alien: I am the LORD your God.

11 You shall not steal; you shall not deal falsely; and you shall not lie to one another. 12 And you shall not swear falsely by my name, profaning the name of your God: I am the LORD.

13 You shall not defraud your neighbor; you shall not steal; and you shall not keep for yourself the wages of a laborer until morning. 14 You shall not revile the deaf or put a stumbling block before the blind; you shall fear your God: I am the LORD.

15 You shall not render an unjust judgment; you shall not be partial to the poor or defer to the great: with justice you shall judge your neighbor. 16 You shall not go around as a slanderer[y] among your people, and you shall not profit by the blood[z] of your neighbor: I am the LORD.

17 You shall not hate in your heart anyone of your kin; you shall reprove your neighbor, or you will incur guilt yourself. 18 You shall not take vengeance or bear a grudge against any of your people, but you shall love your neighbor as yourself: I am the LORD.

19 You shall keep my statutes. You shall not let your animals breed with a different kind; you shall not sow your field with two kinds of seed; nor shall you put on a garment made of two different materials.

20 If a man has sexual relations with a woman who is a slave, designated for another man but not ransomed or given her freedom, an inquiry shall be held. They shall not be put to death, since she has not been freed; 21 but he shall bring a guilt offering for himself to the LORD, at the entrance of the tent of meeting, a ram as guilt offering. 22 And the priest shall make atonement for him with the ram of guilt offering before the LORD for his sin that he committed; and the sin he committed shall be forgiven him.

23 When you come into the land and plant all kinds of trees for food, then you shall regard their fruit as forbidden;[a] three years it shall be forbidden[b] to you, it must not be eaten. 24 In the fourth year all their fruit shall be set apart for rejoicing in the LORD. 25 But in the fifth year you may eat of their fruit, that their yield may be increased for you: I am the LORD your God.

26 You shall not eat anything with its blood. You shall not practice augury or witchcraft. 27 You shall not round off the hair on your temples or mar the edges of your beard. 28 You shall not make any gashes in your flesh for the dead or tattoo any marks upon you: I am the LORD.

29 Do not profane your daughter by making her a prostitute, that the land not become prostituted and full of depravity. 30 You shall keep my sabbaths and reverence my sanctuary: I am the LORD.

31 Do not turn to mediums or wizards; do not seek them out, to be defiled by them: I am the LORD your God.

32 You shall rise before the aged, and defer to the old; and you shall fear your God: I am the LORD.

33 When an alien resides with you in your land, you shall not oppress the alien. 34 The alien who resides with you shall be to you as the citizen among you; you shall love the alien as yourself, for you were aliens in the land of Egypt: I am the LORD your God.

35 You shall not cheat in measuring length, weight, or quantity. 36 You shall have honest balances, honest weights, an honest ephah, and an honest hin: I am the LORD your God, who brought you out of the land of Egypt. 37 You shall keep all my statutes and all my ordinances, and observe them: I am the LORD.

Penalties for Violations of Holiness

20 The LORD spoke to Moses, saying: 2 Say further to the people of Israel:

Any of the people of Israel, or of the aliens who reside in Israel, who give any of their offspring to

---

y Meaning of Heb uncertain z Heb *stand against the blood*
a Heb *as their uncircumcision* b Heb *uncircumcision*

Mō'lech shall be put to death; the people of the land shall stone them to death. ³ I myself will set my face against them, and will cut them off from the people, because they have given of their offspring to Mō'lech, defiling my sanctuary and profaning my holy name. ⁴ And if the people of the land should ever close their eyes to them, when they give of their offspring to Mō'lech, and do not put them to death, ⁵ I myself will set my face against them and against their family, and will cut them off from among their people, them and all who follow them in prostituting themselves to Mō'lech.

6 If any turn to mediums and wizards, prostituting themselves to them, I will set my face against them, and will cut them off from the people. ⁷ Consecrate yourselves therefore, and be holy; for I am the LORD your God. ⁸ Keep my statutes, and observe them; I am the LORD; I sanctify you. ⁹ All who curse father or mother shall be put to death; having cursed father or mother, their blood is upon them.

10 If a man commits adultery with the wife of[c] his neighbor, both the adulterer and the adulteress shall be put to death. ¹¹ The man who lies with his father's wife has uncovered his father's nakedness; both of them shall be put to death; their blood is upon them. ¹² If a man lies with his daughter-in-law, both of them shall be put to death; they have committed perversion, their blood is upon them. ¹³ If a man lies with a male as with a woman, both of them have committed an abomination; they shall be put to death; their blood is upon them. ¹⁴ If a man takes a wife and her mother also, it is depravity; they shall be burned to death, both he and they, that there may be no depravity among you. ¹⁵ If a man has sexual relations with an animal, he shall be put to death; and you shall kill the animal. ¹⁶ If a woman approaches any animal and has sexual relations with it, you shall kill the woman and the animal; they shall be put to death, their blood is upon them.

17 If a man takes his sister, a daughter of his father or a daughter of his mother, and sees her nakedness, and she sees his nakedness, it is a disgrace, and they shall be cut off in the sight of their people; he has uncovered his sister's nakedness, he shall be subject to punishment. ¹⁸ If a man lies with a woman having her sickness and uncovers her nakedness, he has laid bare her flow and she has laid bare her flow of blood; both of them shall be cut off from their people. ¹⁹ You shall not uncover the nakedness of your mother's sister or of your father's sister, for that is to lay bare one's own flesh; they shall be subject to punishment. ²⁰ If a man lies with his uncle's wife, he has uncovered his uncle's nakedness; they shall be subject to punishment; they shall die childless. ²¹ If a

You Shall Be Holy

As the Israelites' image of God developed, so did their sense of how they needed to live as God's people. As God's chosen people, they felt called to behave according to God's plan for them by keeping themselves pure as individuals and as a community. The laws in the Book of Leviticus are examples of how they lived out the call to be holy. For them, holiness was not just for the Sabbath or the Temple but for every day and everything.

Think about the choices you make in the following areas. How do your choices help you to be holy as God is holy?

- what you eat
- what you watch
- what you wear
- what you buy
- what you listen to
- how you relate to other people

▸ Leviticus, chapters 19–20

man takes his brother's wife, it is impurity; he has uncovered his brother's nakedness; they shall be childless.

22 You shall keep all my statutes and all my ordinances, and observe them, so that the land to which I bring you to settle in may not vomit you out. ²³ You shall not follow the practices of the nation that I am driving out before you. Because they did all these things, I abhorred them. ²⁴ But I have said to you: You shall inherit their land, and I will give it to you to possess, a land flowing with milk and honey. I am the LORD your God; I have separated you from the peoples. ²⁵ You shall therefore make a distinction between the clean animal and the unclean, and between the unclean bird and the clean; you shall not bring abomination on yourselves by animal or by bird or by anything with which the ground teems, which I have set apart for you to hold unclean. ²⁶ You shall be holy to me; for I the LORD am holy, and I have separated you from the other peoples to be mine.

27 A man or a woman who is a medium or a wizard shall be put to death; they shall be stoned to death, their blood is upon them.

---

[c] Heb repeats *if a man commits adultery with the wife of*

The Holiness of Priests
(Cp Ezek 44.15–31)

21 The LORD said to Moses: Speak to the priests, the sons of Aaron, and say to them:

No one shall defile himself for a dead person among his relatives, 2 except for his nearest kin: his mother, his father, his son, his daughter, his brother; 3 likewise, for a virgin sister, close to him because she has had no husband, he may defile himself for her. 4 But he shall not defile himself as a husband among his people and so profane himself. 5 They shall not make bald spots upon their heads, or shave off the edges of their beards, or make any gashes in their flesh. 6 They shall be holy to their God, and not profane the name of their God; for they offer the LORD's offerings by fire, the food of their God; therefore they shall be holy. 7 They shall not marry a prostitute or a woman who has been defiled; neither shall they marry a woman divorced from her husband. For they are holy to their God, 8 and you shall treat them as holy, since they offer the food of your God; they shall be holy to you, for I the LORD, I who sanctify you, am holy. 9 When the daughter of a priest profanes herself through prostitution, she profanes her father; she shall be burned to death.

10 The priest who is exalted above his fellows, on whose head the anointing oil has been poured and who has been consecrated to wear the vestments, shall not dishevel his hair, nor tear his vestments. 11 He shall not go where there is a dead body; he shall not defile himself even for his father or mother. 12 He shall not go outside the sanctuary and thus profane the sanctuary of his God; for the consecration of the anointing oil of his God is upon him: I am the LORD. 13 He shall marry only a woman who is a virgin. 14 A widow, or a divorced woman, or a woman who has been defiled, a prostitute, these he shall not marry. He shall marry a virgin of his own kin, 15 that he may not profane his offspring among his kin; for I am the LORD; I sanctify him.

16 The LORD spoke to Moses, saying: 17 Speak to Aaron and say: No one of your offspring throughout their generations who has a blemish may approach to offer the food of his God. 18 For no one who has a blemish shall draw near, one who is blind or lame, or one who has a mutilated face or a limb too long, 19 or one who has a broken foot or a broken hand, 20 or a hunchback, or a dwarf, or a man with a blemish in his eyes or an itching disease or scabs or crushed testicles. 21 No descendant of Aaron the priest who has a blemish shall come near to offer the LORD's offerings by fire; since he has a blemish, he shall not come near to offer the food of his God. 22 He may eat the food of his God, of the most holy as well as of the holy. 23 But he shall not come near the curtain or approach the altar, because he has a blemish, that he may not profane my sanctuaries; for I am the LORD; I sanctify them. 24 Thus Moses spoke to Aaron and to his sons and to all the people of Israel.

The Use of Holy Offerings

22 The LORD spoke to Moses, saying: 2 Direct Aaron and his sons to deal carefully with the sacred donations of the people of Israel, which they dedicate to me, so that they may not profane my holy name; I am the LORD. 3 Say to them: If anyone among all your offspring throughout your generations comes near the sacred donations, which the people of Israel dedicate to the LORD, while he is in a state of uncleanness, that person shall be cut off from my presence: I am the LORD. 4 No one of Aaron's offspring who has a leprous*d* disease or suffers a discharge may eat of the sacred donations until he is clean. Whoever touches anything made unclean by a corpse or a man who has had an emission of semen, 5 and whoever touches any swarming thing by which he may be made unclean or any human being by whom he may be made unclean—whatever his uncleanness may be— 6 the person who touches any such shall be unclean until evening and shall not eat of the sacred donations unless he has washed his body in water. 7 When the sun sets he shall be clean; and afterward he may eat of the sacred donations, for they are his food. 8 That which died or was torn by wild animals he shall not eat, becoming unclean by it: I am the LORD. 9 They shall keep my charge, so that they may not incur guilt and die in the sanctuary *e* for having profaned it: I am the LORD; I sanctify them.

10 No lay person shall eat of the sacred donations. No bound or hired servant of the priest shall eat of the sacred donations; 11 but if a priest acquires anyone by purchase, the person may eat of them; and those that are born in his house may eat of his food. 12 If a priest's daughter marries a layman, she shall not eat of the offering of the sacred donations; 13 but if a priest's daughter is widowed or divorced, without offspring, and returns to her father's house, as in her youth, she may eat of her father's food. No lay person shall eat of it. 14 If a man eats of the sacred donation unintentionally, he shall add one-fifth of its value to it, and give the sacred donation to the priest. 15 No one shall profane the sacred donations of the people of Israel, which they offer to the LORD, 16 causing them to

---

d A term for several skin diseases; precise meaning uncertain   *e* Vg: Heb *incur guilt for it and die in it* bear guilt requiring a guilt offering, by eating their sacred donations: for I am the LORD; I sanctify them.

Acceptable Offerings

17 The LORD spoke to Moses, saying: 18 Speak to Aaron and his sons and all the people of Israel and say to them: When anyone of the house of Israel or of the aliens residing in Israel presents an offering, whether in payment of a vow or as a freewill offering that is offered to the LORD as a burnt offering, 19 to be acceptable in your behalf it shall be a male without blemish, of the cattle or the sheep or the goats. 20 You shall not offer anything that has a blemish, for it will not be acceptable in your behalf.

21 When anyone offers a sacrifice of well-being to the LORD, in fulfillment of a vow or as a freewill offering, from the herd or from the flock, to be acceptable it must be perfect; there shall be no blemish in it. 22 Anything blind, or injured, or maimed, or having a discharge or an itch or scabs—these you shall not offer to the LORD or put any of them on the altar as offerings by fire to the LORD. 23 An ox or a lamb that has a limb too long or too short you may present for a freewill offering; but it will not be accepted for a vow. 24 Any animal that has its testicles bruised or crushed or torn or cut, you shall not offer to the LORD; such you shall not do within your land, 25 nor shall you accept any such animals from a foreigner to offer as food to your God; since they are mutilated, with a blemish in them, they shall not be accepted in your behalf.

26 The LORD spoke to Moses, saying: 27 When an ox or a sheep or a goat is born, it shall remain seven days with its mother, and from the eighth day on it shall be acceptable as the LORD's offering by fire. 28 But you shall not slaughter, from the herd or the flock, an animal with its young on the same day. 29 When you sacrifice a thanksgiving offering to the LORD, you shall sacrifice it so that it may be acceptable in your behalf. 30 It shall be eaten on the same day; you shall not leave any of it until morning: I am the LORD.

31 Thus you shall keep my commandments and observe them: I am the LORD. 32 You shall not profane my holy name, that I may be sanctified among the people of Israel: I am the LORD; I sanctify you, 33 I who brought you out of the land of Egypt to be your God: I am the LORD.

Appointed Festivals

23 The LORD spoke to Moses, saying: 2 Speak to the people of Israel and say to them: These are the appointed festivals of the LORD that you shall proclaim as holy convocations, my appointed festivals.

The Sabbath, Passover, and Unleavened Bread
(Num 28.16–25)

3 Six days shall work be done; but the seventh day is a sabbath of complete rest, a holy convocation; you shall do no work: it is a sabbath to the LORD throughout your settlements.

4 These are the appointed festivals of the LORD, the holy convocations, which you shall celebrate at the time appointed for them. 5 In the first month, on the fourteenth day of the month, at twilight, *f* there shall be a passover offering to the LORD, 6 and on the fifteenth day of the same month is the festival of unleavened bread to the LORD; seven days you shall eat unleavened bread. 7 On the first day you shall have a holy convocation; you shall not work at your occupations. 8 For seven days you shall present the LORD's offerings by fire; on the seventh day there shall be a holy convocation: you shall not work at your occupations.

The Offering of First Fruits

9 The LORD spoke to Moses: 10 Speak to the people of Israel and say to them: When you enter the land that I am giving you and you reap its harvest, you shall bring the sheaf of the first fruits of your harvest to the priest. 11 He shall raise the sheaf before the LORD, that you may find acceptance; on the day after the sabbath the priest shall raise it. 12 On the day when you raise the sheaf, you shall offer a lamb a year old, without blemish, as a burnt offering to the LORD. 13 And the grain offering with it shall be two-tenths of an ephah of choice flour mixed with oil, an offering by fire of pleasing odor to the LORD; and the drink offering with it shall be of wine, one-fourth of a hin. 14 You shall eat no bread or parched grain or fresh ears until that very day, until you have brought the offering of your God: it is a statute forever throughout your generations in all your settlements.

The Festival of Weeks
(Ex 34.22; Num 28.26–31; Deut 16.9–10)

15 And from the day after the sabbath, from the day on which you bring the sheaf of the elevation offering, you shall count off seven weeks; they shall be complete. 16 You shall count until the day after the seventh sabbath, fifty days; then you shall present an offering of new grain to the LORD. 17 You shall bring from your settlements two loaves of bread as an elevation offering, each made of two-tenths of an ephah; they shall be of choice flour, baked with leaven, as first fruits to the LORD. 18 You shall present with the bread seven lambs a year old without blemish, one young bull, and two rams; they shall be a burnt offering to the LORD, along

---

f Heb *between the two evenings*

KOREAN FESTIVAL CUSTOMS

In preparation for the Lunar New Year (in January or February) and for the Moon Festival (a feast of thanksgiving in August), Korean families follow some traditional customs. These customs are similar to those of the Israelite festivals described in Leviticus, chapter 23.

In Korea, the day before each feast is used for purification. People take ceremonial baths symbolizing the total cleansing of their body, their spirit, and their attitudes. The baths wash away meanness, carelessness, and other faults. The people also wear new clothes and often get a haircut.

Before sunrise on the day of the feast, the people bow before a table holding name cards of their ancestors. They use incense, pour out wine, and pray to their ancestors, asking for their intercession and help. Family members pray silently for all their individual and family needs. During the day, families visit the homes of their extended family. During these visits, the prayer ritual is often repeated.

After a day of visiting, families return home for a feast of the best food and drink possible. The sharing of food is the most significant part of the meal. Neighbors exchange portions of food with one another and bring food to poor families. Families set food on a small table near the door as an offering of thanks to the Creator and sprinkle rice on the ground around their house in gratitude for the crops.

▶ Lev 23.4–44

with their grain offering and their drink offerings, an offering by fire of pleasing odor to the LORD. [19] You shall also offer one male goat for a sin offering, and two male lambs a year old as a sacrifice of well-being. [20] The priest shall raise them with the bread of the first fruits as an elevation offering before the LORD, together with the two lambs; they shall be holy to the LORD for the priest. [21] On that same day you shall make proclamation; you shall hold a holy convocation; you shall not work at your occupations. This is a statute forever in all your settlements throughout your generations.

[22] When you reap the harvest of your land, you shall not reap to the very edges of your field, or gather the gleanings of your harvest; you shall leave them for the poor and for the alien: I am the LORD your God.

The Festival of Trumpets
(Num 29.1–6)

[23] The LORD spoke to Moses, saying: [24] Speak to the people of Israel, saying: In the seventh month, on the first day of the month, you shall observe a day of complete rest, a holy convocation commemorated with trumpet blasts. [25] You shall

not work at your occupations; and you shall present the LORD's offering by fire.

The Day of Atonement
(Num 29.7–11)

[26] The LORD spoke to Moses, saying: [27] Now, the tenth day of this seventh month is the day of atonement; it shall be a holy convocation for you: you shall deny yourselves[g] and present the LORD's offering by fire; [28] and you shall do no work during that entire day; for it is a day of atonement, to make atonement on your behalf before the LORD your God. [29] For anyone who does not practice self-denial[h] during that entire day shall be cut off from the people. [30] And anyone who does any work during that entire day, such a one I will destroy from the midst of the people. [31] You shall do no work: it is a statute forever throughout your generations in all your settlements. [32] It shall be to you a sabbath of complete rest, and you shall deny yourselves;[g] on the ninth day of the month at evening, from evening to evening you shall keep your sabbath.

---

g Or *shall fast*   h Or *does not fast*

The Festival of Booths
(Num 29.12–40; Deut 16.13–17)

33 The LORD spoke to Moses, saying: 34 Speak to the people of Israel, saying: On the fifteenth day of this seventh month, and lasting seven days, there shall be the festival of booths[i] to the LORD. 35 The first day shall be a holy convocation; you shall not work at your occupations. 36 Seven days you shall present the LORD's offerings by fire; on the eighth day you shall observe a holy convocation and present the LORD's offerings by fire; it is a solemn assembly; you shall not work at your occupations.

37 These are the appointed festivals of the LORD, which you shall celebrate as times of holy convocation, for presenting to the LORD offerings by fire—burnt offerings and grain offerings, sacrifices and drink offerings, each on its proper day— 38 apart from the sabbaths of the LORD, and apart from your gifts, and apart from all your votive offerings, and apart from all your freewill offerings, which you give to the LORD.

39 Now, the fifteenth day of the seventh month, when you have gathered in the produce of the land, you shall keep the festival of the LORD, lasting seven days; a complete rest on the first day, and a complete rest on the eighth day. 40 On the first day you shall take the fruit of majestic[j] trees, branches of palm trees, boughs of leafy trees, and willows of the brook; and you shall rejoice before the LORD your God for seven days. 41 You shall keep it as a festival to the LORD seven days in the year; you shall keep it in the seventh month as a statute forever throughout your generations. 42 You shall live in booths for seven days; all that are citizens in Israel shall live in booths, 43 so that your generations may know that I made the people of Israel live in booths when I brought them out of the land of Egypt: I am the LORD your God.

44 Thus Moses declared to the people of Israel the appointed festivals of the LORD.

The Lamp
(Ex 27.20–21)

24 The LORD spoke to Moses, saying: 2 Command the people of Israel to bring you pure oil of beaten olives for the lamp, that a light may be kept burning regularly. 3 Aaron shall set it up in the tent of meeting, outside the curtain of the covenant,[k] to burn from evening to morning before the LORD regularly; it shall be a statute forever throughout your generations. 4 He shall set up the lamps on the lampstand of pure gold[l] before the LORD regularly.

The Bread for the Tabernacle

5 You shall take choice flour, and bake twelve loaves of it; two-tenths of an ephah shall be in each loaf. 6 You shall place them in two rows, six in a row, on the table of pure gold.[m] 7 You shall put pure frankincense with each row, to be a token offering for the bread, as an offering by fire to the LORD. 8 Every sabbath day Aaron shall set them in order before the LORD regularly as a commitment of the people of Israel, as a covenant forever. 9 They shall be for Aaron and his descendants, who shall eat them in a holy place, for they are most holy portions for him from the offerings by fire to the LORD, a perpetual due.

Blasphemy and Its Punishment

10 A man whose mother was an Israelite and whose father was an Egyptian came out among the people of Israel; and the Israelite woman's son and a certain Israelite began fighting in the camp. 11 The Israelite woman's son blasphemed the Name in a curse. And they brought him to Moses—now his mother's name was She•lō′mith, daughter of Dib′rī, of the tribe of Dan— 12 and they put him in custody, until the decision of the LORD should be made clear to them.

13 The LORD said to Moses, saying: 14 Take the blasphemer outside the camp; and let all who were within hearing lay their hands on his head, and let the whole congregation stone him. 15 And speak to the people of Israel, saying: Anyone who curses God shall bear the sin. 16 One who blasphemes the name of the LORD shall be put to death; the whole congregation shall stone the blasphemer. Aliens as well as citizens, when they blaspheme the Name, shall be put to death. 17 Anyone who kills a human being shall be put to death. 18 Anyone who kills an animal shall make restitution for it, life for life. 19 Anyone who maims another shall suffer the same injury in return: 20 fracture for fracture, eye for eye, tooth for tooth; the injury inflicted is the injury to be suffered. 21 One who kills an animal shall make restitution for it; but one who kills a human being shall be put to death. 22 You shall have one law for the alien and for the citizen: for I am the LORD your God. 23 Moses spoke thus to the people of Israel; and they took the blasphemer outside the camp, and stoned him to death. The people of Israel did as the LORD had commanded Moses.

The Sabbatical Year
(Deut 15.1–11)

25 The LORD spoke to Moses on Mount Sinai, saying: 2 Speak to the people of Israel and say to them: When you enter the land that I am giving you, the land shall observe a sabbath for

---

i Or tabernacles: Heb succoth   j Meaning of Heb uncertain
k Or treaty, or testament; Heb eduth   l Heb pure lampstand
m Heb pure table

did you KNOW?

7 x 7 + 1 = Jubilee!

In the Bible, seven is a special number. Just as the seventh day of the week was set aside as a day of rest in ancient Israel, so the seventh year was set aside as a year of rest for the land. Fields were to remain uncultivated during the seventh year; whatever fruits or grains grew on their own were to be left for the poor. The "sabbatical year" was a reminder to the people that the land actually belonged to God, not to them.

Seven may be a special number, but seven times seven plus one is very special. The fiftieth year—the year after seven times seven years—was declared the Jubilee year, and God's Law demanded some very special things to happen. The people were to take a year of vacation from their normal routine. This meant no planting for a farmer, no lending for a banker, and no big sales for a merchant. Why this break? Because God wanted the Jubilee year to be a time when everyone started over with a clean slate. During the Jubilee, all land was to be returned to its original owners, and all Israelite slaves were to be set free. Debts were to be forgiven and justly settled. The year of Jubilee was like the reset button on a computer, stopping everything and returning it to its original setting. It was a check against the unjust distribution of property and wealth.

The Catholic church has continued the custom of celebrating the fiftieth year, especially when it marks the end of a century. Faithful to its Jewish roots, the church sees the Jubilee year as a special time for renewal. In preparation for a Jubilee year, it asks individuals and communities to commit themselves to following Jesus more faithfully.

▸ Leviticus, chapter 25

for the LORD: you shall not sow your field or prune your vineyard. 5 You shall not reap the aftergrowth of your harvest or gather the grapes of your unpruned vine: it shall be a year of complete rest for the land. 6 You may eat what the land yields during its sabbath—you, your male and female slaves, your hired and your bound laborers who live with you; 7 for your livestock also, and for the wild animals in your land all its yield shall be for food.

The Year of Jubilee

8 You shall count off seven weeks[n] of years, seven times seven years, so that the period of seven weeks of years gives forty-nine years. 9 Then you shall have the trumpet sounded loud; on the tenth day of the seventh month—on the day of atonement—you shall have the trumpet sounded throughout all your land. 10 And you shall hallow the fiftieth year and you shall proclaim liberty throughout the land to all its inhabitants. It shall be a jubilee for you: you shall return, every one of you, to your property and every one of you to your family. 11 That fiftieth year shall be a jubilee for you: you shall not sow, or reap the aftergrowth, or harvest the unpruned vines. 12 For it is a jubilee; it shall be holy to you: you shall eat only what the field itself produces.

13 In this year of jubilee you shall return, every one of you, to your property. 14 When you make a sale to your neighbor or buy from your neighbor, you shall not cheat one another. 15 When you buy from your neighbor, you shall pay only for the number of years since the jubilee; the seller shall charge you only for the remaining crop years. 16 If the years are more, you shall increase the price, and if the years are fewer, you shall diminish the price; for it is a certain number of harvests that are being sold to you. 17 You shall not cheat one another, but you shall fear your God; for I am the LORD your God.

18 You shall observe my statutes and faithfully keep my ordinances, so that you may live on the land securely. 19 The land will yield its fruit, and you will eat your fill and live on it securely. 20 Should you ask, "What shall we eat in the seventh year, if we may not sow or gather in our crop?" 21 I will order my blessing for you in the sixth year, so that it will yield a crop for three years. 22 When you sow in the eighth year, you will be eating from the old crop; until the ninth year, when its produce comes in, you shall eat the old. 23 The land shall not be sold in perpetuity, for the land is mine; with me you are but aliens and tenants. 24 Throughout the land that you hold, you shall provide for the redemption of the land.

the LORD. 3 Six years you shall sow your field, and six years you shall prune your vineyard, and gather in their yield; 4 but in the seventh year there shall be a sabbath of complete rest for the land, a sabbath

---

n Or *sabbaths*

LEV

25 If anyone of your kin falls into difficulty and sells a piece of property, then the next of kin shall come and redeem what the relative has sold. 26 If the person has no one to redeem it, but then prospers and finds sufficient means to do so, 27 the years since its sale shall be computed and the difference shall be refunded to the person to whom it was sold, and the property shall be returned. 28 But if there are not sufficient means to recover it, what was sold shall remain with the purchaser until the year of jubilee; in the jubilee it shall be released, and the property shall be returned.

29 If anyone sells a dwelling house in a walled city, it may be redeemed until a year has elapsed since its sale; the right of redemption shall be one year. 30 If it is not redeemed before a full year has elapsed, a house that is in a walled city shall pass in perpetuity to the purchaser, throughout the generations; it shall not be released in the jubilee. 31 But houses in villages that have no walls around them shall be classed as open country; they may be redeemed, and they shall be released in the jubilee. 32 As for the cities of the Lĕ′vītes, the Lĕ′vītes shall forever have the right of redemption of the houses in the cities belonging to them. 33 Such property as may be redeemed from the Lĕ′vītes—houses sold in a city belonging to them—shall be released in the jubilee; because the houses in the cities of the Lĕ′vītes are their possession among the people of Israel. 34 But the open land around their cities may not be sold; for that is their possession for all time.

35 If any of your kin fall into difficulty and become dependent on you,[o] you shall support them; they shall live with you as though resident aliens. 36 Do not take interest in advance or otherwise make a profit from them, but fear your God; let them live with you. 37 You shall not lend them your money at interest taken in advance, or provide them food at a profit. 38 I am the LORD your God, who brought you out of the land of Egypt, to give you the land of Cā′naan, to be your God.

39 If any who are dependent on you become so impoverished that they sell themselves to you, you shall not make them serve as slaves. 40 They shall remain with you as hired or bound laborers. They shall serve with you until the year of the jubilee. 41 Then they and their children with them shall be free from your authority; they shall go back to their own family and return to their ancestral property. 42 For they are my servants, whom I brought out of the land of Egypt; they shall not be sold as slaves are sold. 43 You shall not rule over them with harshness, but shall fear your God. 44 As for the male and female slaves whom you may have, it is from the nations around you that you may acquire male and female slaves. 45 You may also acquire them from among the aliens residing with you, and from their families that are with you, who have been born in your land; and they may be your property. 46 You may keep them as a possession for your children after you, for them to inherit as property. These you may treat as slaves, but as for your fellow Israelites, no one shall rule over the other with harshness.

47 If resident aliens among you prosper, and if any of your kin fall into difficulty with one of them and sell themselves to an alien, or to a branch of the alien's family, 48 after they have sold themselves they shall have the right of redemption; one of their brothers may redeem them, 49 or their uncle or their uncle's son may redeem them, or anyone of their family who is of their own flesh may redeem them; or if they prosper they may redeem themselves. 50 They shall compute with the purchaser the total from the year when they sold themselves to the alien until the jubilee year; the price of the sale shall be applied to the number of years: the time they were with the owner shall be rated as the time of a hired laborer. 51 If many years remain, they shall pay for their redemption in proportion to the purchase price; 52 and if few years remain until the jubilee year, they shall compute thus: according to the years involved they shall make payment for their redemption. 53 As a laborer hired by the year they shall be under the alien's authority, who shall not, however, rule with harshness over them in your sight. 54 And if they have not been redeemed in any of these ways, they and their children with them shall go free in the jubilee year. 55 For to me the people of Israel are servants; they are my servants whom I brought out from the land of Egypt: I am the LORD your God.

Rewards for Obedience
(Deut 7.12–24; 28.1–14)

26 You shall make for yourselves no idols and erect no carved images or pillars, and you shall not place figured stones in your land, to worship at them; for I am the LORD your God. 2 You shall keep my sabbaths and reverence my sanctuary: I am the LORD.

3 If you follow my statutes and keep my commandments and observe them faithfully, 4 I will give you your rains in their season, and the land shall yield its produce, and the trees of the field shall yield their fruit. 5 Your threshing shall overtake the vintage, and the vintage shall overtake the sowing; you shall eat your bread to the full, and live securely in your land. 6 And I will grant peace in the land, and you shall lie down, and no one shall make you afraid; I will remove dangerous animals from the land, and no sword shall go through your

---

o Meaning of Heb uncertain

land. [7] You shall give chase to your enemies, and they shall fall before you by the sword. [8] Five of you shall give chase to a hundred, and a hundred of you shall give chase to ten thousand; your enemies shall fall before you by the sword. [9] I will look with favor upon you and make you fruitful and multiply you; and I will maintain my covenant with you. [10] You shall eat old grain long stored, and you shall have to clear out the old to make way for the new. [11] I will place my dwelling in your midst, and I shall not abhor you. [12] And I will walk among you, and will be your God, and you shall be my people. [13] I am the LORD your God who brought you out of the land of Egypt, to be their slaves no more; I have broken the bars of your yoke and made you walk erect.

Penalties for Disobedience
(Deut 28.15–68)

14 But if you will not obey me, and do not observe all these commandments, [15] if you spurn my statutes, and abhor my ordinances, so that you will not observe all my commandments, and you break my covenant, [16] I in turn will do this to you: I will bring terror on you; consumption and fever that waste the eyes and cause life to pine away. You shall sow your seed in vain, for your enemies shall eat it. [17] I will set my face against you, and you shall be struck down by your enemies; your foes shall rule over you, and you shall flee though no one pursues you. [18] And if in spite of this you will not obey me, I will continue to punish you sevenfold for your sins. [19] I will break your proud glory, and I will make your sky like iron and your earth like copper. [20] Your strength shall be spent to no purpose: your land shall not yield its produce, and the trees of the land shall not yield their fruit.

21 If you continue hostile to me, and will not obey me, I will continue to plague you sevenfold for your sins. [22] I will let loose wild animals against you, and they shall bereave you of your children and destroy your livestock; they shall make you few in number, and your roads shall be deserted.

23 If in spite of these punishments you have not turned back to me, but continue hostile to me, [24] then I too will continue hostile to you: I myself will strike you sevenfold for your sins. [25] I will bring the sword against you, executing vengeance for the covenant; and if you withdraw within your cities, I will send pestilence among you, and you shall be delivered into enemy hands. [26] When I break your staff of bread, ten women shall bake your bread in a single oven, and they shall dole out your bread by weight; and though you eat, you shall not be satisfied.

27 But if, despite this, you disobey me, and continue hostile to me, [28] I will continue hostile to you in fury; I in turn will punish you myself seven-fold for your sins. [29] You shall eat the flesh of your sons, and you shall eat the flesh of your daughters. [30] I will destroy your high places and cut down your incense altars; I will heap your carcasses on the carcasses of your idols. I will abhor you. [31] I will lay your cities waste, will make your sanctuaries desolate, and I will not smell your pleasing odors. [32] I will devastate the land, so that your enemies who come to settle in it shall be appalled at it. [33] And you I will scatter among the nations, and I will unsheathe the sword against you; your land shall be a desolation, and your cities a waste.

34 Then the land shall enjoy[q] its sabbath years as long as it lies desolate, while you are in the land of your enemies; then the land shall rest, and enjoy[p] its sabbath years. [35] As long as it lies desolate, it shall have the rest it did not have on your sabbaths when you were living on it. [36] And as for those of you who survive, I will send faintness into their hearts in the lands of their enemies; the sound of a driven leaf shall put them to flight, and they shall flee as one flees from the sword, and they shall fall though no one pursues. [37] They shall stumble over one another, as if to escape a sword, though no one pursues; and you shall have no power to stand against your enemies. [38] You shall perish among the nations, and the land of your enemies shall devour you. [39] And those of you who survive shall languish in the land of your enemies because of their iniquities; also they shall languish because of the iniquities of their ancestors.

40 But if they confess their iniquity and the iniquity of their ancestors, in that they committed treachery against me and, moreover, that they continued hostile to me— [41] so that I, in turn, continued hostile to them and brought them into the land of their enemies; if then their uncircumcised heart is humbled and they make amends for their iniquity, [42] then will I remember my covenant with Jacob; I will remember also my covenant with Isaac and also my covenant with Abraham, and I will remember the land. [43] For the land shall be deserted by them, and enjoy[p] its sabbath years by lying desolate without them, while they shall make amends for their iniquity, because they dared to spurn my ordinances, and they abhorred my statutes. [44] Yet for all that, when they are in the land of their enemies, I will not spurn them, or abhor them so as to destroy them utterly and break my covenant with them; for I am the LORD their God; [45] but I will remember in their favor the covenant with their ancestors whom I brought out of the land of Egypt in the sight of the nations, to be their God: I am the LORD.

46 These are the statutes and ordinances and

L
E
V

---

p Or *make up for*

laws that the LORD established between himself and the people of Israel on Mount Sinai through Moses.

Votive Offerings

27 The LORD spoke to Moses, saying: 2 Speak to the people of Israel and say to them: When a person makes an explicit vow to the LORD concerning the equivalent for a human being, 3 the equivalent for a male shall be: from twenty to sixty years of age the equivalent shall be fifty shekels of silver by the sanctuary shekel. 4 If the person is a female, the equivalent is thirty shekels. 5 If the age is from five to twenty years of age, the equivalent is twenty shekels for a male and ten shekels for a female. 6 If the age is from one month to five years, the equivalent for a male is five shekels of silver, and for a female the equivalent is three shekels of silver. 7 And if the person is sixty years old or over, then the equivalent for a male is fifteen shekels, and for a female ten shekels. 8 If any cannot afford the equivalent, they shall be brought before the priest and the priest shall assess them; the priest shall assess them according to what each one making a vow can afford.

9 If it concerns an animal that may be brought as an offering to the LORD, any such that may be given to the LORD shall be holy. 10 Another shall not be exchanged or substituted for it, either good for bad or bad for good; and if one animal is substituted for another, both that one and its substitute shall be holy. 11 If it concerns any unclean animal that may not be brought as an offering to the LORD, the animal shall be presented before the priest. 12 The priest shall assess it: whether good or bad, according to the assessment of the priest, so it shall be. 13 But if it is to be redeemed, one-fifth must be added to the assessment.

14 If a person consecrates a house to the LORD, the priest shall assess it: whether good or bad, as the priest assesses it, so it shall stand. 15 And if the one who consecrates the house wishes to redeem it, one-fifth shall be added to its assessed value, and it shall revert to the original owner.

16 If a person consecrates to the LORD any inherited landholding, its assessment shall be in accordance with its seed requirements: fifty shekels of silver to a homer of barley seed. 17 If the person consecrates the field as of the year of jubilee, that assessment shall stand; 18 but if the field is consecrated after the jubilee, the priest shall compute the price for it according to the years that remain until the year of jubilee, and the assessment shall be reduced. 19 And if the one who consecrates the field wishes to redeem it, then one-fifth shall be added to its assessed value, and it shall revert to the original owner; 20 but if the field is not redeemed, or if it has been sold to someone else, it shall no longer be redeemable. 21 But when the field is released in the jubilee, it shall be holy to the LORD as a devoted field; it becomes the priest's holding. 22 If someone consecrates to the LORD a field that has been purchased, which is not a part of the inherited landholding, 23 the priest shall compute for it the proportionate assessment up to the year of jubilee, and the assessment shall be paid as of that day, a sacred donation to the LORD. 24 In the year of jubilee the field shall return to the one from whom it was bought, whose holding the land is. 25 All assessments shall be by the sanctuary shekel: twenty gerahs shall make a shekel.

26 A firstling of animals, however, which as a firstling belongs to the LORD, cannot be consecrated by anyone; whether ox or sheep, it is the LORD's. 27 If it is an unclean animal, it shall be ransomed at its assessment, with one-fifth added; if it is not redeemed, it shall be sold at its assessment.

28 Nothing that a person owns that has been devoted to destruction for the LORD, be it human or animal, or inherited landholding, may be sold or redeemed; every devoted thing is most holy to the LORD. 29 No human beings who have been devoted to destruction can be ransomed; they shall be put to death.

30 All tithes from the land, whether the seed from the ground or the fruit from the tree, are the LORD's; they are holy to the LORD. 31 If persons wish to redeem any of their tithes, they must add one-fifth to them. 32 All tithes of herd and flock, every tenth one that passes under the shepherd's staff, shall be holy to the LORD. 33 Let no one inquire whether it is good or bad, or make substitution for it; if one makes substitution for it, then both it and the substitute shall be holy and cannot be redeemed.

34 These are the commandments that the LORD gave to Moses for the people of Israel on Mount Sinai.

Sound the trumpet, beat the drum, we are going to war! The call to arms brings out the best and the worst in people—courage and cowardice, love and hate, hope and fear. The Book of Numbers records the varied experiences of the Israelites as they prepare for the armed conquest of the Promised Land. But most important, it tells of God's insistence that they maintain their purity and holiness to be worthy recipients of God's promises.

At a Glance

- **1.1—10.10.** preparation at Mount Sinai for conquest of the Promised Land

- **10.11—25.18.** the desert journey and the death of the older generation

- **Chapters 26–36.** the birth of a new generation ready to enter the Promised Land

In-depth

Although the Book of Numbers is named for the two censuses mentioned in it (chapters 1 and 26), the book's original Hebrew name, meaning "in the desert," describes it better. Numbers picks up the story of the Israelites where Exodus leaves off. The first section begins with a census at Mount Sinai to determine who is eligible for military service. As the people prepare to enter the Promised Land, their leaders review the laws and regulations with them.

In the second section, the Israelites begin their journey to the Promised Land. Unfortunately, they have not learned to put their faith in God, and their journey is marked by grumbling, rebellion, and even idolatry. When the first army refuses to enter the Promised Land because of reports that it is inhabited by fierce giants (Num 13.32–33), God decrees that none of the older generation who left Egypt shall enter the Promised Land. So, the Israelites begin their desert wandering, which lasts thirty-eight years (see map 2, "The Exodus from Egypt").

The third section of Numbers paints a more hopeful picture. The people of the new generation are faithful and obedient as they prepare to enter the Land. They experience victory against the Midianites (chapter 31) and conquer the land east of the Jordan (chapter 32). The God who liberated their ancestors from Egypt, sustained and led them through the wilderness with Moses, is the same God who now makes ready to fulfill the promise of the Land to Israel.

Numbers was written by priestly scribes hundreds of years after these events, after the people had lost the Promised Land to the Babylonians. They fully appreciated the gift of the Land only after they had lost it. For the Israelites in the Babylonian Exile, Numbers portrayed the hopeful, grateful, and faithful hearts required of those whom God blesses.

Quick Facts

Period Covered
the thirty-eight years of wandering in the desert after the Exodus

Authors
priestly scribes writing during the Babylonian Exile (587–538 B.C.)

Theme
Faithfulness and gratefulness to God are necessary for Israel to obtain the Promised Land.

The Book of *Numbers*

Numbers

Chap. 31

The First Census of Israel
(Cp 2 Sam 24.1–9; 1 Chr 21.1–6)

1 The LORD spoke to Moses in the wilderness of Sinai, in the tent of meeting, on the first day of the second month, in the second year after they had come out of the land of Egypt, saying: 2 Take a census of the whole congregation of Israelites, in their clans, by ancestral houses, according to the number of names, every male individually; 3 from twenty years old and upward, everyone in Israel able to go to war. You and Aaron shall enroll them, company by company. 4 A man from each tribe shall be with you, each man the head of his ancestral house. 5 These are the names of the men who shall assist you:

From Reuben, E•li′zur son of Shed′e̅•ur.
6 From Sim′e̅•on, She•lu̅′mi•el son of
        Zū•ri•shad′daī.
7 From Judah, Nah′shon son of Am•min′a•dab.
8 From Is′sa•char, Ne•than′el son of Zū′ar.
9 From Zeb′ū•lun, E•li′ab son of He̅′lon.
10 From the sons of Joseph:
    from E̅′phra•im, E•lish′a•ma son of
        Am•mī′hud;
    from Ma•nas′seh, Ga•mā′li•el son of
        Pe•dah′zur.
11 From Benjamin, A•bī′dan son of Gid•e̅•o̅′ni.
12 From Dan, Ă•hī•e̅′zer son of Am•mi•shad′daī.
13 From Ash′er, Pā′gi•el son of Och′ran.

14 From Gad, E•li′a•saph son of Deū′el.
15 From Naph′ta•lī, A•hī′ra son of E̅′nan.
16 These were the ones chosen from the congregation, the leaders of their ancestral tribes, the heads of the divisions of Israel.

17 Moses and Aaron took these men who had been designated by name, 18 and on the first day of the second month they assembled the whole congregation together. They registered themselves in their clans, by their ancestral houses, according to the number of names from twenty years old and upward, individually, 19 as the LORD commanded Moses. So he enrolled them in the wilderness of Sinai.

20 The descendants of Reuben, Israel's firstborn, their lineage, in their clans, by their ancestral houses, according to the number of names, individually, every male from twenty years old and upward, everyone able to go to war: 21 those enrolled of the tribe of Reuben were forty-six thousand five hundred.

22 The descendants of Sim′e̅•on, their lineage, in their clans, by their ancestral houses, those of them that were numbered, according to the number of names, individually, every male from twenty years old and upward, everyone able to go to war: 23 those enrolled of the tribe of Sim′e̅•on were fifty-nine thousand three hundred.

24 The descendants of Gad, their lineage, in their clans, by their ancestral houses, according to

the number of the names, from twenty years old and upward, everyone able to go to war: 25 those enrolled of the tribe of Gad were forty-five thousand six hundred fifty.

26 The descendants of Judah, their lineage, in their clans, by their ancestral houses, according to the number of names, from twenty years old and upward, everyone able to go to war: 27 those enrolled of the tribe of Judah were seventy-four thousand six hundred.

28 The descendants of Is'sa•char, their lineage, in their clans, by their ancestral houses, according to the number of names, from twenty years old and upward, everyone able to go to war: 29 those enrolled of the tribe of Is'sa•char were fifty-four thousand four hundred.

30 The descendants of Zeb'ū•lun, their lineage, in their clans, by their ancestral houses, according to the number of names, from twenty years old and upward, everyone able to go to war: 31 those enrolled of the tribe of Zeb'ū•lun were fifty-seven thousand four hundred.

32 The descendants of Joseph, namely, the descendants of Ē'phra•im, their lineage, in their clans, by their ancestral houses, according to the number of names, from twenty years old and upward, everyone able to go to war: 33 those enrolled of the tribe of Ē'phra•im were forty thousand five hundred.

34 The descendants of Ma•nas'seh, their lineage, in their clans, by their ancestral houses, according to the number of names, from twenty years old and upward, everyone able to go to war: 35 those enrolled of the tribe of Ma•nas'seh were thirty-two thousand two hundred.

36 The descendants of Benjamin, their lineage, in their clans, by their ancestral houses, according to the number of names, from twenty years old and upward, everyone able to go to war: 37 those enrolled of the tribe of Benjamin were thirty-five thousand four hundred.

38 The descendants of Dan, their lineage, in their clans, by their ancestral houses, according to the number of names, from twenty years old and upward, everyone able to go to war: 39 those enrolled of the tribe of Dan were sixty-two thousand seven hundred.

40 The descendants of Ash'er, their lineage, in their clans, by their ancestral houses, according to the number of names, from twenty years old and upward, everyone able to go to war: 41 those enrolled of the tribe of Ash'er were forty-one thousand five hundred.

42 The descendants of Naph'ta•lī, their lineage, in their clans, by their ancestral houses, according to the number of names, from twenty years old and upward, everyone able to go to war: 43 those enrolled of the tribe of Naph'ta•lī were fifty-three thousand four hundred.

44 These are those who were enrolled, whom Moses and Aaron enrolled with the help of the leaders of Israel, twelve men, each representing his ancestral house. 45 So the whole number of the Israelites, by their ancestral houses, from twenty years old and upward, everyone able to go to war in Israel— 46 their whole number was six hundred three thousand five hundred fifty. 47 The Lē'vītes, however, were not numbered by their ancestral tribe along with them.

48 The LORD had said to Moses: 49 Only the tribe of Levi you shall not enroll, and you shall not take a census of them with the other Israelites. 50 Rather you shall appoint the Lē'vītes over the tabernacle of the covenant,*a* and over all its equipment, and over all that belongs to it; they are to carry the tabernacle and all its equipment, and they shall tend it, and shall camp around the tabernacle. 51 When the tabernacle is to set out, the Lē'vītes shall take it down; and when the tabernacle is to be pitched, the Lē'vītes shall set it up. And any outsider who comes near shall be put to death. 52 The other Israelites shall camp in their respective regimental camps, by companies; 53 but the Lē'vītes shall camp around the tabernacle of the covenant,*a* that there may be no wrath on the congregation of the Israelites; and the Lē'vītes shall perform the guard duty of the tabernacle of the covenant.*a* 54 The Israelites did so; they did just as the LORD commanded Moses.

The Order of Encampment and Marching

2 The LORD spoke to Moses and Aaron, saying: 2 The Israelites shall camp each in their respective regiments, under ensigns by their ancestral houses; they shall camp facing the tent of meeting on every side. 3 Those to camp on the east side toward the sunrise shall be of the regimental encampment of Judah by companies. The leader of the people of Judah shall be Nah'shon son of Am•min'a•dab, 4 with a company as enrolled of seventy-four thousand six hundred. 5 Those to camp next to him shall be the tribe of Is'sa•char. The leader of the Is'sa•char•ītes shall be Ne•than'el son of Zū'ar, 6 with a company as enrolled of fifty-four thousand four hundred. 7 Then the tribe of Zeb'ū•lun: The leader of the Zeb'ū•lun•ītes shall be E•lī'ab son of Hē'lon, 8 with a company as enrolled of fifty-seven thousand four hundred. 9 The total enrollment of the camp of Judah, by companies, is one hundred eighty-six thousand four hundred. They shall set out first on the march.

---

a Or *treaty,* or *testimony;* Heb *eduth*

?did you KNOW?

Holy War

The Book of Numbers begins with a census of "everyone in Israel able to go to war" (1.3). The people of Israel are preparing to take over the land God had promised to them, the Chosen People. This is no ordinary war but a Holy war, a war that they believe is divinely inspired, even a war God commands. In 31.2, God says to Moses, "Avenge the Israelites on the Midianites." The Israelites go on to kill every Midianite except for the young girls who are virgins.

How are we to understand this? Does God really order the killing of innocent people? To answer this, let's first remember that the writers of the Bible were influenced by their own cultural background and understanding of God. Three main things were probably on the mind of the writer of Numbers. First, the early Israelites viewed God as a warrior god fighting for them. Second, they believed the Canaanites were a wicked and idolatrous people who deserved punishment. And finally, they believed the Midianites deserved special punishment because they had led the Israelites into idolatry and sin at Shittim (see 25.1–5).

Holy wars are dangerous. Throughout history, people have committed atrocities in the name of God. Christians must interpret the Old Testament in the light of Jesus' teachings in the New Testament. Jesus clearly taught about a God of mercy and love, not a God of war and vengeance. This is one area where the New Testament teaching replaces an earlier Old Testament understanding. Holy wars have no place in the lives of Christians.

the Sim'ē•on•ites shall be She•lū'mi•el son of Zū•ri•shad'daī, 13 with a company as enrolled of fifty-nine thousand three hundred. 14 Then the tribe of Gad: The leader of the Gad'ites shall be E•li'a•saph son of Reū'el, 15 with a company as enrolled of forty-five thousand six hundred fifty. 16 The total enrollment of the camp of Reuben, by companies, is one hundred fifty-one thousand four hundred fifty. They shall set out second.

17 The tent of meeting, with the camp of the Lē'vītes, shall set out in the center of the camps; they shall set out just as they camp, each in position, by their regiments.

18 On the west side shall be the regimental encampment of Ē'phra•im by companies. The leader of the people of Ē'phra•im shall be E•lish'a•ma son of Am•mi'hud, 19 with a company as enrolled of forty thousand five hundred. 20 Next to him shall be the tribe of Ma•nas'seh. The leader of the people of Ma•nas'seh shall be Ga•mā'li•el son of Pe•dah'zur, 21 with a company as enrolled of thirty-two thousand two hundred. 22 Then the tribe of Benjamin: The leader of the Ben'ja•min•ites shall be A•bi'dan son of Gid•ē•ō'ni, 23 with a company as enrolled of thirty-five thousand four hundred. 24 The total enrollment of the camp of Ē'phra•im, by companies, is one hundred eight thousand one hundred. They shall set out third on the march.

25 On the north side shall be the regimental encampment of Dan by companies. The leader of the Dan'ites shall be Ā•hi•ē'zer son of Am•mi•shad'-daī, 26 with a company as enrolled of sixty-two thousand seven hundred. 27 Those to camp next to him shall be the tribe of Ash'er. The leader of the Ash'er•ites shall be Pā'gi•el son of Ōch'ran, 28 with a company as enrolled of forty-one thousand five hundred. 29 Then the tribe of Naph'ta•li: The leader of the Naph'ta•lites shall be A•hi'ra son of Ē'nan, 30 with a company as enrolled of fifty-three thousand four hundred. 31 The total enrollment of the camp of Dan is one hundred fifty-seven thousand six hundred. They shall set out last, by companies.[b]

32 This was the enrollment of the Israelites by their ancestral houses; the total enrollment in the camps by their companies was six hundred three thousand five hundred fifty. 33 Just as the LORD had commanded Moses, the Lē'vītes were not enrolled among the other Israelites.

34 The Israelites did just as the LORD had commanded Moses: They camped by regiments, and they set out the same way, everyone by clans, according to ancestral houses.

10 On the south side shall be the regimental encampment of Reuben by companies. The leader of the Reū'ben•ites shall be E•li'zur son of Shed'-ē•ur, 11 with a company as enrolled of forty-six thousand five hundred. 12 And those to camp next to him shall be the tribe of Sim'ē•on. The leader of

---

b Compare verses 9, 16, 24: Heb by their regiments

The Sons of Aaron
(Lev 10.1–7)

3 This is the lineage of Aaron and Moses at the time when the LORD spoke with Moses on Mount Sinai. 2 These are the names of the sons of Aaron: Nā′dab the firstborn, and A·bī′hū, El·ē·ā′zar, and Ith′a·mar; 3 these are the names of the sons of Aaron, the anointed priests, whom he ordained to minister as priests. 4 Nā′dab and A·bī′hū died before the LORD when they offered unholy fire before the LORD in the wilderness of Sinai, and they had no children. El·ē·ā′zar and Ith′a·mar served as priests in the lifetime of their father Aaron.

The Duties of the Levites

5 Then the LORD spoke to Moses, saying: 6 Bring the tribe of Levi near, and set them before Aaron the priest, so that they may assist him. 7 They shall perform duties for him and for the whole congregation in front of the tent of meeting, doing service at the tabernacle; 8 they shall be in charge of all the furnishings of the tent of meeting, and attend to the duties for the Israelites as they do service at the tabernacle. 9 You shall give the Lē′vītes to Aaron and his descendants; they are unreservedly given to him from among the Israelites. 10 But you shall make a register of Aaron and his descendants; it is they who shall attend to the priesthood, and any outsider who comes near shall be put to death.

11 Then the LORD spoke to Moses, saying: 12 I hereby accept the Lē′vītes from among the Israelites as substitutes for all the firstborn that open the womb among the Israelites. The Lē′vītes shall be mine, 13 for all the firstborn are mine; when I killed all the firstborn in the land of Egypt, I consecrated for my own all the firstborn in Israel, both human and animal; they shall be mine. I am the LORD.

A Census of the Levites
(Cp Num 1.47–54)

14 Then the LORD spoke to Moses in the wilderness of Sinai, saying: 15 Enroll the Lē′vītes by ancestral houses and by clans. You shall enroll every male from a month old and upward. 16 So Moses enrolled them according to the word of the LORD, as he was commanded. 17 The following were the sons of Levi, by their names: Ger′shon, Kō′hath, and Me·rar′ī. 18 These are the names of the sons of Ger′shon by their clans: Lib′nī and Shim′ē·ī. 19 The sons of Kō′hath by their clans: Am′ram, Iz′har, Hē′bron, and Uz′zi·el. 20 The sons of Me·rar′ī by their clans: Mah′lī and Mū′shī. These are the clans of the Lē′vītes, by their ancestral houses.

21 To Ger′shon belonged the clan of the Lib′nītes and the clan of the Shim′ē·ītes; these were the clans of the Ger′shon·ītes. 22 Their enrollment, counting all the males from a month old and upward, was seven thousand five hundred. 23 The clans of the Ger′shon·ītes were to camp behind the tabernacle on the west, 24 with E·lī′a·saph son of Lā′el as head of the ancestral house of Ger′shon·ītes. 25 The responsibility of the sons of Ger′shon in the tent of meeting was to be the tabernacle, the tent with its covering, the screen for the entrance of the tent of meeting, 26 the hangings of the court, the screen for the entrance of the court that is around the tabernacle and the altar, and its cords—all the service pertaining to these.

27 To Kō′hath belonged the clan of the Am′ram·ites, the clan of the Iz′har·ītes, the clan of the Hē′bron·ītes, and the clan of the Uz′zi·el·ītes; these are the clans of the Kō′hath·ītes. 28 Counting all the males, from a month old and upward, there were eight thousand six hundred, attending to the duties of the sanctuary. 29 The clans of the Kō′hath·ītes were to camp on the south side of the tabernacle, 30 with E·li·zā′phan son of Uz′zi·el as head of the ancestral house of the clans of the Kō′hath·ītes. 31 Their responsibility was to be the ark, the table, the lampstand, the altars, the vessels of the sanctuary with which the priests minister, and the screen—all the service pertaining to these. 32 El·ē·ā′zar son of Aaron the priest was to be chief over the leaders of the Lē′vītes, and to have oversight of those who had charge of the sanctuary.

33 To Me·rar′ī belonged the clan of the Mah′lītes and the clan of the Mū′shītes: these are the clans of Me·rar′ī. 34 Their enrollment, counting all the males from a month old and upward, was six thousand two hundred. 35 The head of the ancestral house of the clans of Me·rar′ī was Zū′ri·el son of Ab·i·hā′il; they were to camp on the north side of the tabernacle. 36 The responsibility assigned to the sons of Me·rar′ī was to be the frames of the tabernacle, the bars, the pillars, the bases, and all their accessories—all the service pertaining to these; 37 also the pillars of the court all around, with their bases and pegs and cords.

38 Those who were to camp in front of the tabernacle on the east—in front of the tent of meeting toward the east—were Moses and Aaron and Aaron's sons, having charge of the rites within the sanctuary, whatever had to be done for the Israelites; and any outsider who came near was to be put to death. 39 The total enrollment of the Lē′vītes whom Moses and Aaron enrolled at the commandment of the LORD, by their clans, all the males from a month old and upward, was twenty-two thousand.

NUM

The Redemption of the Firstborn

40 Then the LORD said to Moses: Enroll all the firstborn males of the Israelites, from a month old and upward, and count their names. 41 But you shall accept the Lē′vītes for me—I am the LORD—as substitutes for all the firstborn among the Israelites, and the livestock of the Lē′vītes as substitutes for all the firstborn among the livestock of the Israelites. 42 So Moses enrolled all the firstborn among the Israelites, as the LORD commanded him. 43 The total enrollment, all the firstborn males from a month old and upward, counting the number of names, was twenty-two thousand two hundred seventy-three.

44 Then the LORD spoke to Moses, saying: 45 Accept the Lē′vītes as substitutes for all the firstborn among the Israelites, and the livestock of the Lē′vītes as substitutes for their livestock; and the Lē′vītes shall be mine. I am the LORD. 46 As the price of redemption of the two hundred seventy-three of the firstborn of the Israelites, over and above the number of the Lē′vītes, 47 you shall accept five shekels apiece, reckoning by the shekel of the sanctuary, a shekel of twenty gerahs. 48 Give to Aaron and his sons the money by which the excess number of them is redeemed. 49 So Moses took the redemption money from those who were over and above those redeemed by the Lē′vītes; 50 from the firstborn of the Israelites he took the money, one thousand three hundred sixty-five shekels, reckoned by the shekel of the sanctuary; 51 and Moses gave the redemption money to Aaron and his sons, according to the word of the LORD, as the LORD had commanded Moses.

The Kohathites

4 The LORD spoke to Moses and Aaron, saying: 2 Take a census of the Kō′hath•ītes separate from the other Lē′vītes, by their clans and their ancestral houses, 3 from thirty years old up to fifty years old, all who qualify to do work relating to the tent of meeting. 4 The service of the Kō′hath•ītes relating to the tent of meeting concerns the most holy things.

5 When the camp is to set out, Aaron and his sons shall go in and take down the screening curtain, and cover the ark of the covenant[c] with it; 6 then they shall put on it a covering of fine leather,[d] and spread over that a cloth all of blue, and shall put its poles in place. 7 Over the table of the bread of the Presence they shall spread a blue cloth, and put on it the plates, the dishes for incense, the bowls, and the flagons for the drink offering; the regular bread also shall be on it; 8 then they shall spread over them a crimson cloth, and cover it with a covering of fine leather,[d] and shall put its poles in place. 9 They shall take a blue cloth, and cover the lampstand for the light, with its lamps, its snuffers, its trays, and all the vessels for oil with which it is supplied; 10 and they shall put it with all its utensils in a covering of fine leather,[d] and put it on the carrying frame. 11 Over the golden altar they shall spread a blue cloth, and cover it with a covering of fine leather,[d] and shall put its poles in place; 12 and they shall take all the utensils of the service that are used in the sanctuary, and put them in a blue cloth, and cover them with a covering of fine leather,[d] and put them on the carrying frame. 13 They shall take away the ashes from the altar, and spread a purple cloth over it; 14 and they shall put on it all the utensils of the altar, which are used for the service there, the firepans, the forks, the shovels, and the basins, all the utensils of the altar; and they shall spread on it a covering of fine leather,[d] and shall put its poles in place. 15 When Aaron and his sons have finished covering the sanctuary and all the furnishings of the sanctuary, as the camp sets out, after that the Kō′hath•ītes shall come to carry these, but they must not touch the holy things, or they will die. These are the things of the tent of meeting that the Kō′hath•ītes are to carry.

16 El•ē•ā′zar son of Aaron the priest shall have charge of the oil for the light, the fragrant incense, the regular grain offering, and the anointing oil, the oversight of all the tabernacle and all that is in it, in the sanctuary and in its utensils.

17 Then the LORD spoke to Moses and Aaron, saying: 18 You must not let the tribe of the clans of the Kō′hath•ītes be destroyed from among the Lē′vītes. 19 This is how you must deal with them in order that they may live and not die when they come near to the most holy things: Aaron and his sons shall go in and assign each to a particular task or burden. 20 But the Kō′hath•ītes[e] must not go in to look on the holy things even for a moment; otherwise they will die.

The Gershonites and Merarites

21 Then the LORD spoke to Moses, saying: 22 Take a census of the Ger′shon•ītes also, by their ancestral houses and by their clans; 23 from thirty years old up to fifty years old you shall enroll them, all who qualify to do work in the tent of meeting. 24 This is the service of the clans of the Ger′shon•ītes, in serving and bearing burdens: 25 They shall carry the curtains of the tabernacle, and the tent of meeting with its covering, and the outer covering of fine leather[d] that is on top of it, and the screen for the entrance of the tent of meeting, 26 and the hangings of the court, and the screen for the entrance of the gate of the court that is around

---

[c] Or *treaty*, or *testimony*; Heb *eduth*   [d] Meaning of Heb uncertain   [e] Heb *they*

the tabernacle and the altar, and their cords, and all the equipment for their service; and they shall do all that needs to be done with regard to them. 27 All the service of the Ger'shon•ites shall be at the command of Aaron and his sons, in all that they are to carry, and in all that they have to do; and you shall assign to their charge all that they are to carry. 28 This is the service of the clans of the Ger'shon•ites relating to the tent of meeting, and their responsibilities are to be under the oversight of Ith'a•mar son of Aaron the priest.

29 As for the Me•rar'ites, you shall enroll them by their clans and their ancestral houses; 30 from thirty years old up to fifty years old you shall enroll them, everyone who qualifies to do the work of the tent of meeting. 31 This is what they are charged to carry, as the whole of their service in the tent of meeting: the frames of the tabernacle, with its bars, pillars, and bases, 32 and the pillars of the court all around with their bases, pegs, and cords, with all their equipment and all their related service; and you shall assign by name the objects that they are required to carry. 33 This is the service of the clans of the Me•rar'ites, the whole of their service relating to the tent of meeting, under the hand of Ith'a•mar son of Aaron the priest.

Census of the Levites

34 So Moses and Aaron and the leaders of the congregation enrolled the Kō'hath•ites, by their clans and their ancestral houses, 35 from thirty years old up to fifty years old, everyone who qualified for work relating to the tent of meeting; 36 and their enrollment by clans was two thousand seven hundred fifty. 37 This was the enrollment of the clans of the Kō'hath•ites, all who served at the tent of meeting, whom Moses and Aaron enrolled according to the commandment of the LORD by Moses.

38 The enrollment of the Ger'shon•ites, by their clans and their ancestral houses, 39 from thirty years old up to fifty years old, everyone who qualified for work relating to the tent of meeting— 40 their enrollment by their clans and their ancestral houses was two thousand six hundred thirty. 41 This was the enrollment of the clans of the Ger'shon•ites, all who served at the tent of meeting, whom Moses and Aaron enrolled according to the commandment of the LORD.

42 The enrollment of the clans of the Me•rar'ites, by their clans and their ancestral houses, 43 from thirty years old up to fifty years old, everyone who qualified for work relating to the tent of meeting— 44 their enrollment by their clans was three thousand two hundred. 45 This is the enrollment of the clans of the Me•rar'ites, whom Moses and Aaron enrolled according to the commandment of the LORD by Moses.

46 All those who were enrolled of the Lē'vites, whom Moses and Aaron and the leaders of Israel enrolled, by their clans and their ancestral houses, 47 from thirty years old up to fifty years old, everyone who qualified to do the work of service and the work of bearing burdens relating to the tent of meeting, 48 their enrollment was eight thousand five hundred eighty. 49 According to the commandment of the LORD through Moses they were appointed to their several tasks of serving or carrying; thus they were enrolled by him, as the LORD commanded Moses.

Unclean Persons
(Cp Lev 15.1–33)

5 The LORD spoke to Moses, saying: 2 Command the Israelites to put out of the camp everyone who is leprous,*f* or has a discharge, and everyone who is unclean through contact with a corpse; 3 you shall put out both male and female, putting them outside the camp; they must not defile their camp, where I dwell among them. 4 The Israelites did so, putting them outside the camp; as the LORD had spoken to Moses, so the Israelites did.

Confession and Restitution
(Lev 6.1–7)

5 The LORD spoke to Moses, saying: 6 Speak to the Israelites: When a man or a woman wrongs another, breaking faith with the LORD, that person incurs guilt 7 and shall confess the sin that has been committed. The person shall make full restitution for the wrong, adding one-fifth to it, and giving it to the one who was wronged. 8 If the injured party has no next of kin to whom restitution may be made for the wrong, the restitution for wrong shall go to the LORD for the priest, in addition to the ram of atonement with which atonement is made for the guilty party. 9 Among all the sacred donations of the Israelites, every gift that they bring to the priest shall be his. 10 The sacred donations of all are their own; whatever anyone gives to the priest shall be his.

Concerning an Unfaithful Wife

11 The LORD spoke to Moses, saying: 12 Speak to the Israelites and say to them: If any man's wife goes astray and is unfaithful to him, 13 if a man has had intercourse with her but it is hidden from her husband, so that she is undetected though she has defiled herself, and there is no witness against her since she was not caught in the act; 14 if a spirit of

f A term for several skin diseases; precise meaning uncertain

N
U
M

jealousy comes on him, and he is jealous of his wife who has defiled herself; or if a spirit of jealousy comes on him, and he is jealous of his wife, though she has not defiled herself; 15 then the man shall bring his wife to the priest. And he shall bring the offering required for her, one-tenth of an ephah of barley flour. He shall pour no oil on it and put no frankincense on it, for it is a grain offering of jealousy, a grain offering of remembrance, bringing iniquity to remembrance.

16 Then the priest shall bring her near, and set her before the LORD; 17 the priest shall take holy water in an earthen vessel, and take some of the dust that is on the floor of the tabernacle and put it into the water. 18 The priest shall set the woman before the LORD, dishevel the woman's hair, and place in her hands the grain offering of remembrance, which is the grain offering of jealousy. In his own hand the priest shall have the water of bitterness that brings the curse. 19 Then the priest shall make her take an oath, saying, "If no man has lain with you, if you have not turned aside to uncleanness while under your husband's authority, be immune to this water of bitterness that brings the curse. 20 But if you have gone astray while under your husband's authority, if you have defiled yourself and some man other than your husband has had intercourse with you," 21—let the priest make the woman take the oath of the curse and say to the woman—"the LORD make you an execration and an oath among your people, when the LORD makes your uterus drop, your womb discharge; 22 now may this water that brings the curse enter your bowels and make your womb discharge, your uterus drop!" And the woman shall say, "Amen. Amen."

23 Then the priest shall put these curses in writing, and wash them off into the water of bitterness. 24 He shall make the woman drink the water of bitterness that brings the curse, and the water that brings the curse shall enter her and cause bitter pain. 25 The priest shall take the grain offering of jealousy out of the woman's hand, and shall elevate the grain offering before the LORD and bring it to the altar; 26 and the priest shall take a handful of the grain offering, as its memorial portion, and turn it into smoke on the altar, and afterward shall make the woman drink the water. 27 When he has made her drink the water, then, if she has defiled herself and has been unfaithful to her husband, the water that brings the curse shall enter into her and cause bitter pain, and her womb shall discharge, her uterus drop, and the woman shall become an execration among her people. 28 But if the woman has not defiled herself and is clean, then she shall be immune and be able to conceive children.

29 This is the law in cases of jealousy, when a wife, while under her husband's authority, goes astray and defiles herself, 30 or when a spirit of jealousy comes on a man and he is jealous of his wife; then he shall set the woman before the LORD, and the priest shall apply this entire law to her. 31 The man shall be free from iniquity, but the woman shall bear her iniquity.

The Nazirites

6 The LORD spoke to Moses, saying: 2 Speak to the Israelites and say to them: When either men or women make a special vow, the vow of a nazirite,g to separate themselves to the LORD, 3 they shall separate themselves from wine and strong drink; they shall drink no wine vinegar or other vinegar, and shall not drink any grape juice or eat grapes, fresh or dried. 4 All their days as naziritesh they shall eat nothing that is produced by the grapevine, not even the seeds or the skins.

5 All the days of their nazirite vow no razor shall come upon the head; until the time is completed for which they separate themselves to the LORD, they shall be holy; they shall let the locks of the head grow long.

6 All the days that they separate themselves to the LORD they shall not go near a corpse. 7 Even if their father or mother, brother or sister, should die, they may not defile themselves; because their consecration to God is upon the head. 8 All their days as naziritesh they are holy to the LORD.

9 If someone dies very suddenly nearby, defiling the consecrated head, then they shall shave the head on the day of their cleansing; on the seventh day they shall shave it. 10 On the eighth day they shall bring two turtledoves or two young pigeons to the priest at the entrance of the tent of meeting, 11 and the priest shall offer one as a sin offering and the other as a burnt offering, and make atonement for them, because they incurred guilt by reason of the corpse. They shall sanctify the head that same day, 12 and separate themselves to the LORD for their days as nazirites,h and bring a male lamb a year old as a guilt offering. The former time shall be void, because the consecrated head was defiled.

13 This is the law for the naziritesh when the time of their consecration has been completed: they shall be brought to the entrance of the tent of meeting, 14 and they shall offer their gift to the LORD, one male lamb a year old without blemish as a burnt offering, one ewe lamb a year old without blemish as a sin offering, one ram without blemish as an offering of well-being, 15 and a bas-

---

g That is *one* separated or *one consecrated*   h That is *those separated* or *those consecrated*

God Bless You

A very old blessing in Num 6.22–27
(some of which is repeated in Ps 4.6
and 67.1) was not originally a Christian
blessing, but its three parts remind us of
Christian blessings calling on the Trinity.

This blessing is a good one for special
occasions. You could write it on a card for
a birthday, a wedding anniversary, or any
other special event. Or you could use it
to make a poster or an engraving for a
first Communion, a wedding, or a Confirmation.

If this blessing sounds familiar, maybe
it's because on the feast of Mary, mother
of God, we hear it as the first reading.

▸ **Num 6.22–27**

The Priestly Benediction

22 The LORD spoke to Moses, saying: 23 Speak
to Aaron and his sons, saying, Thus you shall bless
the Israelites: You shall say to them,
24 The LORD bless you and keep you;
25 the LORD make his face to shine upon you, and
 be gracious to you;
26 the LORD lift up his countenance upon you,
 and give you peace.
27 So they shall put my name on the Israelites,
and I will bless them.

Offerings of the Leaders

7 On the day when Moses had finished setting
up the tabernacle, and had anointed and consecrated it with all its furnishings, and had anointed and consecrated the altar with all its utensils,
2 the leaders of Israel, heads of their ancestral
houses, the leaders of the tribes, who were over
those who were enrolled, made offerings. 3 They
brought their offerings before the LORD, six covered
wagons and twelve oxen, a wagon for every two of
the leaders, and for each one an ox; they presented
them before the tabernacle. 4 Then the LORD said to
Moses: 5 Accept these from them, that they may be
used in doing the service of the tent of meeting, and
give them to the Lě′vītes, to each according to his
service. 6 So Moses took the wagons and the oxen,
and gave them to the Lě′vītes. 7 Two wagons and
four oxen he gave to the Ger′shon•ites, according to
their service; 8 and four wagons and eight oxen he
gave to the Me•rar′ites, according to their service,
under the direction of Ith′a•mar son of Aaron the
priest. 9 But to the Kō′hath•ites he gave none, because they were charged with the care of the holy
things that had to be carried on the shoulders.

10 The leaders also presented offerings for the
dedication of the altar at the time when it was
anointed; the leaders presented their offering before the altar. 11 The LORD said to Moses: They shall
present their offerings, one leader each day, for the
dedication of the altar.

12 The one who presented his offering the first
day was Nah′shon son of Am•min′a•dab, of the
tribe of Judah; 13 his offering was one silver plate
weighing one hundred thirty shekels, one silver
basin weighing seventy shekels, according to the
shekel of the sanctuary, both of them full of choice
flour mixed with oil for a grain offering; 14 one
golden dish weighing ten shekels, full of incense;
15 one young bull, one ram, one male lamb a year
old, for a burnt offering; 16 one male goat for a sin
offering; 17 and for the sacrifice of well-being, two
oxen, five rams, five male goats, and five male

N
U
M

ket of unleavened bread, cakes of choice flour
mixed with oil and unleavened wafers spread with
oil, with their grain offering and their drink offerings. 16 The priest shall present them before the
LORD and offer their sin offering and burnt offering, 17 and shall offer the ram as a sacrifice of well-
being to the LORD, with the basket of unleavened
bread; the priest also shall make the accompanying grain offering and drink offering. 18 Then the
nazirites[i] shall shave the consecrated head at the
entrance of the tent of meeting, and shall take
the hair from the consecrated head and put it on
the fire under the sacrifice of well-being. 19 The
priest shall take the shoulder of the ram, when it
is boiled, and one unleavened cake out of the basket, and one unleavened wafer, and shall put them
in the palms of the nazirites,[i] after they have
shaved the consecrated head. 20 Then the priest
shall elevate them as an elevation offering before
the LORD; they are a holy portion for the priest, together with the breast that is elevated and the
thigh that is offered. After that the nazirites[i] may
drink wine.

21 This is the law for the nazirites[i] who take a
vow. Their offering to the LORD must be in accordance with the nazirite[j] vow, apart from what else
they can afford. In accordance with whatever vow
they take, so they shall do, following the law for
their consecration.

_____
[i] That is *those separated* or *those consecrated*   [j] That is *one*
separated or *one consecrated*

lambs a year old. This was the offering of Nah'shon son of Am·min'a·dab.

18 On the second day Ne·than'el son of Zū'ar, the leader of Is'sa·char, presented an offering; 19 he presented for his offering one silver plate weighing one hundred thirty shekels, one silver basin weighing seventy shekels, according to the shekel of the sanctuary, both of them full of choice flour mixed with oil for a grain offering; 20 one golden dish weighing ten shekels, full of incense; 21 one young bull, one ram, one male lamb a year old, as a burnt offering; 22 one male goat as a sin offering; 23 and for the sacrifice of well-being, two oxen, five rams, five male goats, and five male lambs a year old. This was the offering of Ne·than'el son of Zū'ar.

24 On the third day E·lī'ab son of Hē'lon, the leader of the Zeb'ū·lun·ītes: 25 his offering was one silver plate weighing one hundred thirty shekels, one silver basin weighing seventy shekels, according to the shekel of the sanctuary, both of them full of choice flour mixed with oil for a grain offering; 26 one golden dish weighing ten shekels, full of incense; 27 one young bull, one ram, one male lamb a year old, for a burnt offering; 28 one male goat for a sin offering; 29 and for the sacrifice of well-being, two oxen, five rams, five male goats, and five male lambs a year old. This was the offering of E·lī'ab son of Hē'lon.

30 On the fourth day E·lī'zur son of Shed'ē·ur, the leader of the Reū'ben·ītes: 31 his offering was one silver plate weighing one hundred thirty shekels, one silver basin weighing seventy shekels, according to the shekel of the sanctuary, both of them full of choice flour mixed with oil for a grain offering; 32 one golden dish weighing ten shekels, full of incense; 33 one young bull, one ram, one male lamb a year old, for a burnt offering; 34 one male goat for a sin offering; 35 and for the sacrifice of well-being, two oxen, five rams, five male goats, and five male lambs a year old. This was the offering of E·lī'zur son of Shed'ē·ur.

36 On the fifth day She·lū'mi·el son of Zū·ri·shad'daī, the leader of the Sim'ē·on·ītes: 37 his offering was one silver plate weighing one hundred thirty shekels, one silver basin weighing seventy shekels, according to the shekel of the sanctuary, both of them full of choice flour mixed with oil for a grain offering; 38 one golden dish weighing ten shekels, full of incense; 39 one young bull, one ram, one male lamb a year old, for a burnt offering; 40 one male goat for a sin offering; 41 and for the sacrifice of well-being, two oxen, five rams, five male goats, and five male lambs a year old. This was the offering of She·lū'mi·el son of Zū·ri·shad'daī.

42 On the sixth day E·lī'a·saph son of Deū'el, the leader of the Gad'ītes: 43 his offering was one

silver plate weighing one hundred thirty shekels, one silver basin weighing seventy shekels, according to the shekel of the sanctuary, both of them full of choice flour mixed with oil for a grain offering; 44 one golden dish weighing ten shekels, full of incense; 45 one young bull, one ram, one male lamb a year old, for a burnt offering; 46 one male goat for a sin offering; 47 and for the sacrifice of well-being, two oxen, five rams, five male goats, and five male lambs a year old. This was the offering of E·lī'a·saph son of Deū'el.

48 On the seventh day E·lish'a·ma son of Am·mī'hud, the leader of the Ē'phra·im·ītes: 49 his offering was one silver plate weighing one hundred thirty shekels, one silver basin weighing seventy shekels, according to the shekel of the sanctuary, both of them full of choice flour mixed with oil for a grain offering; 50 one golden dish weighing ten shekels, full of incense; 51 one young bull, one ram, one male lamb a year old, for a burnt offering; 52 one male goat for a sin offering; 53 and for the sacrifice of well-being, two oxen, five rams, five male goats, and five male lambs a year old. This was the offering of E·lish'a·ma son of Am·mī'hud.

54 On the eighth day Ga·mā'li·el son of Pe·dah'zur, the leader of the Ma·nas'sītes: 55 his offering was one silver plate weighing one hundred thirty shekels, one silver basin weighing seventy shekels, according to the shekel of the sanctuary, both of them full of choice flour mixed with oil for a grain offering; 56 one golden dish weighing ten shekels, full of incense; 57 one young bull, one ram, one male lamb a year old, for a burnt offering; 58 one male goat for a sin offering; 59 and for the sacrifice of well-being, two oxen, five rams, five male goats, and five male lambs a year old. This was the offering of Ga·mā'li·el son of Pe·dah'zur.

60 On the ninth day A·bī'dan son of Gid·ē·ō'ni, the leader of the Ben'ja·min·ītes: 61 his offering was one silver plate weighing one hundred thirty shekels, one silver basin weighing seventy shekels, according to the shekel of the sanctuary, both of them full of choice flour mixed with oil for a grain offering; 62 one golden dish weighing ten shekels, full of incense; 63 one young bull, one ram, one male lamb a year old, for a burnt offering; 64 one male goat for a sin offering; 65 and for the sacrifice of well-being, two oxen, five rams, five male goats, and five male lambs a year old. This was the offering of A·bī'dan son of Gid·ē·ō'ni.

66 On the tenth day Ā·hī·ē'zer son of Am·mi·shad'daī, the leader of the Dan'ītes: 67 his offering was one silver plate weighing one hundred thirty shekels, one silver basin weighing seventy shekels, according to the shekel of the sanctuary, both of them full of choice flour mixed with oil for a grain

offering; 68 one golden dish weighing ten shekels, full of incense; 69 one young bull, one ram, one male lamb a year old, for a burnt offering; 70 one male goat for a sin offering; 71 and for the sacrifice of well-being, two oxen, five rams, five male goats, and five male lambs a year old. This was the offering of Ă•hī•ĕ′zer son of Am•mi•shad′daī.

72 On the eleventh day Pā′gi•el son of Ōch′ran, the leader of the Ash′er•ites: 73 his offering was one silver plate weighing one hundred thirty shekels, one silver basin weighing seventy shekels, according to the shekel of the sanctuary, both of them full of choice flour mixed with oil for a grain offering; 74 one golden dish weighing ten shekels, full of incense; 75 one young bull, one ram, one male lamb a year old, for a burnt offering; 76 one male goat for a sin offering; 77 and for the sacrifice of well-being, two oxen, five rams, five male goats, and five male lambs a year old. This was the offering of Pā′gi•el son of Ōch′ran.

78 On the twelfth day A•hī′ra son of Ē′nan, the leader of the Naph′ta•lītes: 79 his offering was one silver plate weighing one hundred thirty shekels, one silver basin weighing seventy shekels, according to the shekel of the sanctuary, both of them full of choice flour mixed with oil for a grain offering; 80 one golden dish weighing ten shekels, full of incense; 81 one young bull, one ram, one male lamb a year old, for a burnt offering; 82 one male goat for a sin offering; 83 and for the sacrifice of well-being, two oxen, five rams, five male goats, and five male lambs a year old. This was the offering of A•hī′ra son of Ē′nan.

84 This was the dedication offering for the altar, at the time when it was anointed, from the leaders of Israel: twelve silver plates, twelve silver basins, twelve golden dishes, 85 each silver plate weighing one hundred thirty shekels and each basin seventy, all the silver of the vessels two thousand four hundred shekels according to the shekel of the sanctuary, 86 the twelve golden dishes, full of incense, weighing ten shekels apiece according to the shekel of the sanctuary, all the gold of the dishes being one hundred twenty shekels; 87 all the livestock for the burnt offering twelve bulls, twelve rams, twelve male lambs a year old, with their grain offering; and twelve male goats for a sin offering; 88 and all the livestock for the sacrifice of well-being twenty-four bulls, the rams sixty, the male goats sixty, the male lambs a year old sixty. This was the dedication offering for the altar, after it was anointed.

89 When Moses went into the tent of meeting to speak with the LORD,[k] he would hear the voice speaking to him from above the mercy seat[l] that was on the ark of the covenant[m] from between the two cherubim; thus it spoke to him.

The Seven Lamps
(Ex 25.31–40)

8 The LORD spoke to Moses, saying: 2 Speak to Aaron and say to him: When you set up the lamps, the seven lamps shall give light in front of the lampstand. 3 Aaron did so; he set up its lamps to give light in front of the lampstand, as the LORD had commanded Moses. 4 Now this was how the lampstand was made, out of hammered work of gold. From its base to its flowers, it was hammered work; according to the pattern that the LORD had shown Moses, so he made the lampstand.

Consecration and Service of the Levites

5 The LORD spoke to Moses, saying: 6 Take the Lē′vītes from among the Israelites and cleanse them. 7 Thus you shall do to them, to cleanse them: sprinkle the water of purification on them, have them shave their whole body with a razor and wash their clothes, and so cleanse themselves. 8 Then let them take a young bull and its grain offering of choice flour mixed with oil, and you shall take another young bull for a sin offering. 9 You shall bring the Lē′vītes before the tent of meeting, and assemble the whole congregation of the Israelites. 10 When you bring the Lē′vītes before the LORD, the Israelites shall lay their hands on the Lē′vītes, 11 and Aaron shall present the Lē′vītes before the LORD as an elevation offering from the Israelites, that they may do the service of the LORD. 12 The Lē′vītes shall lay their hands on the heads of the bulls, and he shall offer the one for a sin offering and the other for a burnt offering to the LORD, to make atonement for the Lē′vītes. 13 Then you shall have the Lē′vītes stand before Aaron and his sons, and you shall present them as an elevation offering to the LORD.

14 Thus you shall separate the Lē′vītes from among the other Israelites, and the Lē′vītes shall be mine. 15 Thereafter the Lē′vītes may go in to do service at the tent of meeting, once you have cleansed them and presented them as an elevation offering. 16 For they are unreservedly given to me from among the Israelites; I have taken them for myself, in place of all that open the womb, the firstborn of all the Israelites. 17 For all the firstborn among the Israelites are mine, both human and animal. On the day that I struck down all the firstborn in the land of Egypt I consecrated them for myself, 18 but I have taken the Lē′vītes in place of all the firstborn among the Israelites. 19 Moreover, I have given the Lē′vītes as a gift to Aaron and his sons from among the Israelites, to do the service for the Israelites at the tent of meeting, and to make atonement for the Israelites, in order that there may be

---

k Heb *him*   l Or *the cover*   m Or *treaty*, or *testimony*; Heb *eduth* no plague among the Israelites for coming too close to the sanctuary.

20 Moses and Aaron and the whole congregation of the Israelites did with the Lē′vītes accordingly; the Israelites did with the Lē′vītes just as the LORD had commanded Moses concerning them. 21 The Lē′vītes purified themselves from sin and washed their clothes; then Aaron presented them as an elevation offering before the LORD, and Aaron made atonement for them to cleanse them. 22 Thereafter the Lē′vītes went in to do their service in the tent of meeting in attendance on Aaron and his sons. As the LORD had commanded Moses concerning the Lē′vītes, so they did with them.

23 The LORD spoke to Moses, saying: 24 This applies to the Lē′vītes: from twenty-five years old and upward they shall begin to do duty in the service of the tent of meeting; 25 and from the age of fifty years they shall retire from the duty of the service and serve no more. 26 They may assist their brothers in the tent of meeting in carrying out their duties, but they shall perform no service. Thus you shall do with the Lē′vītes in assigning their duties.

The Passover at Sinai
(Ex 12.1–20)

9 The LORD spoke to Moses in the wilderness of Sinai, in the first month of the second year after they had come out of the land of Egypt, saying: 2 Let the Israelites keep the passover at its appointed time. 3 On the fourteenth day of this month, at twilight,[n] you shall keep it at its appointed time; according to all its statutes and all its regulations you shall keep it. 4 So Moses told the Israelites that they should keep the passover. 5 They kept the passover in the first month, on the fourteenth day of the month, at twilight,[n] in the wilderness of Sinai. Just as the LORD had commanded Moses, so the Israelites did. 6 Now there were certain people who were unclean through touching a corpse, so that they could not keep the passover on that day. They came before Moses and Aaron on that day, 7 and said to him, "Although we are unclean through touching a corpse, why must we be kept from presenting the LORD's offering at its appointed time among the Israelites?" 8 Moses spoke to them, "Wait, so that I may hear what the LORD will command concerning you."

9 The LORD spoke to Moses, saying: 10 Speak to the Israelites, saying: Anyone of you or your descendants who is unclean through touching a corpse, or is away on a journey, shall still keep the passover to the LORD. 11 In the second month on the fourteenth day, at twilight,[n] they shall keep it; they shall eat it with unleavened bread and bitter herbs. 12 They shall leave none of it until morning, nor break a bone of it; according to all the statute

for the passover they shall keep it. 13 But anyone who is clean and is not on a journey, and yet refrains from keeping the passover, shall be cut off from the people for not presenting the LORD's offering at its appointed time; such a one shall bear the consequences for the sin. 14 Any alien residing among you who wishes to keep the passover to the LORD shall do so according to the statute of the passover and according to its regulation; you shall have one statute for both the resident alien and the native.

The Cloud and the Fire
(Ex 13.21–22; 40.34–38)

15 On the day the tabernacle was set up, the cloud covered the tabernacle, the tent of the covenant;[o] and from evening until morning it was over the tabernacle, having the appearance of fire. 16 It was always so: the cloud covered it by day[p] and the appearance of fire by night. 17 Whenever the cloud lifted from over the tent, then the Israelites would set out; and in the place where the cloud settled down, there the Israelites would camp. 18 At the command of the LORD the Israelites would set out, and at the command of the LORD they would camp. As long as the cloud rested over the tabernacle, they would remain in camp. 19 Even when the cloud continued over the tabernacle many days, the Israelites would keep the charge of the LORD, and would not set out. 20 Sometimes the cloud would remain a few days over the tabernacle, and according to the command of the LORD they would remain in camp; then according to the command of the LORD they would set out. 21 Sometimes the cloud would remain from evening until morning; and when the cloud lifted in the morning, they would set out, or if it continued for a day and a night, when the cloud lifted they would set out. 22 Whether it was two days, or a month, or a longer time, that the cloud continued over the tabernacle, resting upon it, the Israelites would remain in camp and would not set out; but when it lifted they would set out. 23 At the command of the LORD they would camp, and at the command of the LORD they would set out. They kept the charge of the LORD, at the command of the LORD by Moses.

The Silver Trumpets

10 The LORD spoke to Moses, saying: 2 Make two silver trumpets; you shall make them of hammered work; and you shall use them for summoning the congregation, and for breaking camp. 3 When both are blown, the whole

---

n Heb *between the two evenings* o Or *treaty*, or *testimony*; Heb *eduth* p Gk Syr Vg: Heb lacks *by day* congregation shall assemble before you at the entrance of the tent of meeting. 4 But if only one is blown, then the leaders, the heads of the tribes of Israel, shall assemble before you. 5 When you blow an alarm, the camps on the east side shall set out; 6 when you blow a second alarm, the camps on the south side shall set out. An alarm is to be blown whenever they are to set out. 7 But when the assembly is to be gathered, you shall blow, but you shall not sound an alarm. 8 The sons of Aaron, the priests, shall blow the trumpets; this shall be a perpetual institution for you throughout your generations. 9 When you go to war in your land against the adversary who oppresses you, you shall sound an alarm with the trumpets, so that you may be remembered before the LORD your God and be saved from your enemies. 10 Also on your days of rejoicing, at your appointed festivals, and at the beginnings of your months, you shall blow the trumpets over your burnt offerings and over your sacrifices of well-being; they shall serve as a reminder on your behalf before the LORD your God: I am the LORD your God.

Departure from Sinai

11 In the second year, in the second month, on the twentieth day of the month, the cloud lifted from over the tabernacle of the covenant.*q* 12 Then the Israelites set out by stages from the wilderness of Sinai, and the cloud settled down in the wilderness of Par′an. 13 They set out for the first time at the command of the LORD by Moses. 14 The standard of the camp of Judah set out first, company by company, and over the whole company was Nah′shon son of Am·min′a·dab. 15 Over the company of the tribe of Is′sa·char was Ne·than′el son of Zū′ar; 16 and over the company of the tribe of Zeb′-ū·lun was E·li′ab son of Hē′lon.

17 Then the tabernacle was taken down, and the Ger′shon·ites and the Me·rar′ites, who carried the tabernacle, set out. 18 Next the standard of the camp of Reuben set out, company by company; and over the whole company was E·li′zur son of Shed′ē·ur. 19 Over the company of the tribe of Sim′ē·on was She·lū′mi·el son of Zū·ri·shad′daī, 20 and over the company of the tribe of Gad was E·li′a·saph son of Deū′el.

21 Then the Kō′hath·ites, who carried the holy things, set out; and the tabernacle was set up before their arrival. 22 Next the standard of the E′phra-im·ite camp set out, company by company, and over the whole company was E·lish′a·ma son of Am·mi′hud. 23 Over the company of the tribe of Ma·nas′seh was Ga·mā′li·el son of Pe·dah′zur, 24 and over the company of the tribe of Benjamin was A·bi′dan son of Gid·e·ō′ni. 25 Then the standard of the camp of Dan, act-

ing as the rear guard of all the camps, set out, company by company, and over the whole company was A·hi·ē′zer son of Am·mi·shad′daī. 26 Over the company of the tribe of Ash′er was Pā′gi·el son of Ōch′ran, 27 and over the company of the tribe of Naph′ta·li was A·hi′ra son of Ē′nan. 28 This was the order of march of the Israelites, company by company, when they set out.

29 Moses said to Hō′bab son of Reū′el the Mid′i·an·ite, Moses′ father-in-law, "We are setting out for the place of which the LORD said, 'I will give it to you'; come with us, and we will treat you well; for the LORD has promised good to Israel." 30 But he said to him, "I will not go, but I will go back to my own land and to my kindred." 31 He said, "Do not leave us, for you know where we should camp in the wilderness, and you will serve as eyes for us. 32 Moreover, if you go with us, whatever good the LORD does for us, the same we will do for you."

33 So they set out from the mount of the LORD three days′ journey with the ark of the covenant of the LORD going before them three days′ journey, to seek out a resting place for them, 34 the cloud of the LORD being over them by day when they set out from the camp.

35 Whenever the ark set out, Moses would say,
"Arise, O LORD, let your enemies be
scattered,
and your foes flee before you."
36 And whenever it came to rest, he would say,
"Return, O LORD of the ten thousand
thousands of Israel."*r*

Complaining in the Desert

11 Now when the people complained in the hearing of the LORD about their misfortunes, the LORD heard it and his anger was kindled. Then the fire of the LORD burned against them, and consumed some outlying parts of the camp. 2 But the people cried out to Moses; and Moses prayed to the LORD, and the fire abated. 3 So that place was called Tab′e·rah,*s* because the fire of the LORD burned against them.

4 The rabble among them had a strong craving; and the Israelites also wept again, and said, "If only we had meat to eat! 5 We remember the fish we used to eat in Egypt for nothing, the cucumbers, the melons, the leeks, the onions, and the garlic; 6 but now our strength is dried up, and there is nothing at all but this manna to look at."

7 Now the manna was like coriander seed, and its color was like the color of gum resin. 8 The people went around and gathered it, ground it in mills or beat it in mortars, then boiled it in pots and

N
U
M

---

q Or *treaty,* or *testimony;* Heb *eduth*   *r* Meaning of Heb uncertain   *s* That is *Burning* made cakes of it; and the taste of it was like the taste of cakes baked with oil. 9 When the dew fell on the camp in the night, the manna would fall with it.

10 Moses heard the people weeping throughout their families, all at the entrances of their tents. Then the LORD became very angry, and Moses was displeased. 11 So Moses said to the LORD, "Why have you treated your servant so badly? Why have I not found favor in your sight, that you lay the burden of all this people on me? 12 Did I conceive all this people? Did I give birth to them, that you should say to me, 'Carry them in your bosom, as a nurse carries a sucking child, to the land that you promised on oath to their ancestors'? 13 Where am I to get meat to give to all this people? For they come weeping to me and say, 'Give us meat to eat!' 14 I am not able to carry all this people alone, for they are too heavy for me. 15 If this is the way you are going to treat me, put me to death at once—if I have found favor in your sight—and do not let me see my misery."

The Seventy Elders

16 So the LORD said to Moses, "Gather for me seventy of the elders of Israel, whom you know to be the elders of the people and officers over them; bring them to the tent of meeting, and have them take their place there with you. 17 I will come down and talk with you there; and I will take some of the spirit that is on you and put it on them; and they shall bear the burden of the people along with you so that you will not bear it all by yourself. 18 And say to the people: Consecrate yourselves for tomorrow, and you shall eat meat; for you have wailed in the hearing of the LORD, saying, 'If only we had meat to eat! Surely it was better for us in Egypt.' Therefore the LORD will give you meat, and you shall eat. 19 You shall eat not only one day, or two days, or five days, or ten days, or twenty days, 20 but for a whole month—until it comes out of your nostrils and becomes loathsome to you—because you have rejected the LORD who is among you, and have wailed before him, saying, 'Why did we ever leave Egypt?' " 21 But Moses said, "The people I am with number six hundred thousand on foot; and you say, 'I will give them meat, that they may eat for a whole month'! 22 Are there enough flocks and herds to slaughter for them? Are there enough fish in the sea to catch for them?" 23 The LORD said to Moses, "Is the LORD's power limited?t Now you shall see whether my word will come true for you or not."

24 So Moses went out and told the people the words of the LORD; and he gathered seventy elders of the people, and placed them all around the tent. 25 Then the LORD came down in the cloud and spoke to him, and took some of the spirit that was on him and put it on the seventy elders; and when the spirit rested upon them, they prophesied. But they did not do so again.

26 Two men remained in the camp, one named El'dad, and the other named Mē'dad, and the spirit rested on them; they were among those registered, but they had not gone out to the tent, and so they prophesied in the camp. 27 And a young man ran and told Moses, "El'dad and Mē'dad are prophesying in the camp." 28 And Joshua son of Nun, the assistant of Moses, one of his chosen men,u said, "My lord Moses, stop them!" 29 But Moses said to him, "Are you jealous for my sake? Would that all the LORD's people were prophets, and that the LORD would put his spirit on them!" 30 And Moses and the elders of Israel returned to the camp.

The Quails

31 Then a wind went out from the LORD, and it brought quails from the sea and let them fall beside the camp, about a day's journey on this side and a day's journey on the other side, all around the camp, about two cubits deep on the ground. 32 So the people worked all that day and night and all the next day, gathering the quails; the least anyone gathered was ten homers; and they spread them out for themselves all around the camp. 33 But while the meat was still between their teeth, before it was consumed, the anger of the LORD was kindled against the people, and the LORD struck the people with a very great plague. 34 So that place was called Kib'roth-hat·tā'a·vah,v because there they buried the people who had the craving. 35 From Kib'roth-hat·tā'a·vah the people journeyed to Ha·zē'roth.

Aaron and Miriam Jealous of Moses

12 While they were at Ha·zē'roth, Miriam and Aaron spoke against Moses because of the Cū'shīte woman whom he had married (for he had indeed married a Cū'shīte woman); 2 and they said, "Has the LORD spoken only through Moses? Has he not spoken through us also?" And the LORD heard it. 3 Now the man Moses was very humble,w more so than anyone else on the face of the earth. 4 Suddenly the LORD said to Moses, Aaron, and Miriam, "Come out, you three, to the tent of meeting." So the three of them came out. 5 Then the LORD came down in a pillar of cloud, and stood at the entrance of the tent, and called Aaron and Miriam; and they both came forward. 6 And he said, "Hear my words:

---

t Heb LORD's hand too short? u Or of Moses from his youth v That is Graves of craving w Or devout

When there are prophets among you,
   I the LORD make myself known to them in
      visions;
   I speak to them in dreams.
7 Not so with my servant Moses;
   he is entrusted with all my house.
8 With him I speak face to face—clearly, not in
     riddles;
   and he beholds the form of the LORD.
Why then were you not afraid to speak against my servant Moses?" 9 And the anger of the LORD was kindled against them, and he departed.

10 When the cloud went away from over the tent, Miriam had become leprous,*x* as white as snow. And Aaron turned towards Miriam and saw that she was leprous. 11 Then Aaron said to Moses, "Oh, my lord, do not punish us*y* for a sin that we have so foolishly committed. 12 Do not let her be like one stillborn, whose flesh is half consumed when it comes out of its mother's womb." 13 And Moses cried to the LORD, "O God, please heal her." 14 But the LORD said to Moses, "If her father had but spit in her face, would she not bear her shame for seven days? Let her be shut out of the camp for seven days, and after that she may be brought in again." 15 So Miriam was shut out of the camp for seven days; and the people did not set out on the march until Miriam had been brought in again. 16 After that the people set out from Ha·zē′roth, and camped in the wilderness of Par′an.

Spies Sent into Canaan
(Deut 1.19–33)

13 The LORD said to Moses, 2 "Send men to spy out the land of Cā′naan, which I am giving to the Israelites; from each of their ancestral tribes you shall send a man, every one a leader among them." 3 So Moses sent them from the wilderness of Par′an, according to the command of the LORD, all of them leading men among the Israelites. 4 These were their names: From the tribe of Reuben, Sham′mū·a son of Zac′cur; 5 from the tribe of Sim′ē·on, Shā′phat son of Hō′rī; 6 from the tribe of Judah, Caleb son of Je·phūn′neh; 7 from the tribe of Is′sa·char, I′gal son of Joseph; 8 from the tribe of E′phra·im, Hō·shē′a son of Nun; 9 from the tribe of Benjamin, Pal′tī son of Rā′phū; 10 from the tribe of Zeb′ū·lun, Gad′di·el son of Sō′dī; 11 from the tribe of Joseph (that is, from the tribe of Ma·nas′seh), Gad′dī son of Sū′sī; 12 from the tribe of Dan, Am′mi·el son of Ge·mal′lī; 13 from the tribe of Ash′er, Seth′ur son of Michael; 14 from the tribe of Naph′ta·lī, Nah′bī son of Voph′sī; 15 from the tribe of Gad, Ge·ū′el son of Mā′chī. 16 These were the names of the men whom Moses sent to spy out the land. And Moses changed the name of Hō·shē′a son of Nun to Joshua.

17 Moses sent them to spy out the land of

x A term for several skin diseases; precise meaning uncertain   *y* Heb *do not lay sin upon us*

N U M

The Jealousy of Miriam and Aaron

Miriam. I don't know, Aaron. Sometimes Moses really gets to me. He seems to forget that we're all in this together.
Aaron. Yes, we are God's chosen people. All of us, not just Moses. And, of course, he married outside the fold. A Cushite, of all people.
Miriam. It really is a scandal. He is the self-appointed leader of our people, and yet he is not even married to an Israelite woman. That just doesn't sit well with our people.
Aaron. And he can be so aloof. I know he has a special connection with God, and I know it isn't easy being a leader. But he always seems to set himself apart, acting like he's better than the rest of us.
Miriam. What bothers me most is that Moses assumes that God speaks only through him.
Aaron. Yes, it's as if the rest of us have no role to play. What if I receive a revelation from God? Will Moses respond the same way we are expected to whenever he speaks? I doubt it!
Miriam. So do I. He pretends to be humble and to speak for God. I'm tired of it. We need to have a voice also.

Jealousy is like a dangerous cancer, growing until it affects your whole outlook on life (see what happens to Miriam in Num 12.10). What happens inside of you when you feel jealous? How does jealousy affect your attitudes toward other people?

▸ **Numbers, chapter 12**

Cā′naan, and said to them, "Go up there into the Neg′eb, and go up into the hill country, 18 and see what the land is like, and whether the people who live in it are strong or weak, whether they are few or many, 19 and whether the land they live in is good or bad, and whether the towns that they live in are unwalled or fortified, 20 and whether the land is rich or poor, and whether there are trees in it or not. Be bold, and bring some of the fruit of the land." Now it was the season of the first ripe grapes.

21 So they went up and spied out the land from the wilderness of Zin to Rě′hob, near Lě′bō-hă′math. 22 They went up into the Neg′eb, and came to Hě′bron; and A•hī′man, Shě′shai, and Tal′mai, the An′a•kītes, were there. (Hě′bron was built seven years before Zō′an in Egypt.) 23 And they came to the Wadi Esh′col, and cut down from there a branch with a single cluster of grapes, and they carried it on a pole between two of them. They also brought some pomegranates and figs. 24 That place was called the Wadi Esh′col,ᶻ because of the cluster that the Israelites cut down from there.

The Report of the Spies

25 At the end of forty days they returned from spying out the land. 26 And they came to Moses and Aaron and to all the congregation of the Israelites in the wilderness of Par′an, at Kā′desh; they brought back word to them and to all the congregation, and showed them the fruit of the land. 27 And they told him, "We came to the land to which you sent us; it flows with milk and honey, and this is its fruit. 28 Yet the people who live in the land are strong, and the towns are fortified and very large; and besides, we saw the descendants of Ā′nak there. 29 The A•mal′e•kītes live in the land of the Neg′eb; the Hit′tītes, the Jeb′ū•sītes, and the Am′o•rītes live in the hill country; and the Cā′naan•ītes live by the sea, and along the Jordan."

30 But Caleb quieted the people before Moses, and said, "Let us go up at once and occupy it, for we are well able to overcome it." 31 Then the men who had gone up with him said, "We are not able to go up against this people, for they are stronger than we." 32 So they brought to the Israelites an unfavorable report of the land that they had spied out, saying, "The land that we have gone through as spies is a land that devours its inhabitants; and all the people that we saw in it are of great size. 33 There we saw the Neph′i•lim (the An′a•kītes come from the Neph′i•lim); and to ourselves we seemed like grasshoppers, and so we seemed to them."

The People Rebel

14 Then all the congregation raised a loud cry, and the people wept that night. 2 And all the Israelites complained against Moses

and Aaron; the whole congregation said to them, "Would that we had died in the land of Egypt! Or would that we had died in this wilderness! 3 Why is the LORD bringing us into this land to fall by the sword? Our wives and our little ones will become booty; would it not be better for us to go back to Egypt?" 4 So they said to one another, "Let us choose a captain, and go back to Egypt."

5 Then Moses and Aaron fell on their faces before all the assembly of the congregation of the Israelites. 6 And Joshua son of Nun and Caleb son of Je•phūn′neh, who were among those who had spied out the land, tore their clothes 7 and said to all the congregation of the Israelites, "The land that we went through as spies is an exceedingly good land. 8 If the LORD is pleased with us, he will bring us into this land and give it to us, a land that flows with milk and honey. 9 Only, do not rebel against the LORD; and do not fear the people of the land, for they are no more than bread for us; their protection is removed from them, and the LORD is with us; do not fear them." 10 But the whole congregation threatened to stone them.

Then the glory of the LORD appeared at the tent of meeting to all the Israelites. 11 And the LORD said to Moses, "How long will this people despise me? And how long will they refuse to believe in me, in spite of all the signs that I have done among them? 12 I will strike them with pestilence and disinherit them, and I will make of you a nation greater and mightier than they."

Moses Intercedes for the People

13 But Moses said to the LORD, "Then the Egyptians will hear of it, for in your might you brought up this people from among them, 14 and they will tell the inhabitants of this land. They have heard that you, O LORD, are in the midst of this people; for you, O LORD, are seen face to face, and your cloud stands over them and you go in front of them, in a pillar of cloud by day and in a pillar of fire by night. 15 Now if you kill this people all at one time, then the nations who have heard about you will say, 16 'It is because the LORD was not able to bring this people into the land he swore to give them that he has slaughtered them in the wilderness.' 17 And now, therefore, let the power of the LORD be great in the way that you promised when you spoke, saying,
18 'The LORD is slow to anger,
and abounding in steadfast love,
forgiving iniquity and transgression,
but by no means clearing the guilty,
visiting the iniquity of the parents
upon the children
to the third and the fourth generation.'

ᶻ That is *Cluster*

19 Forgive the iniquity of this people according to the greatness of your steadfast love, just as you have pardoned this people, from Egypt even until now."

20 Then the LORD said, "I do forgive, just as you have asked; 21 nevertheless—as I live, and as all the earth shall be filled with the glory of the LORD— 22 none of the people who have seen my glory and the signs that I did in Egypt and in the wilderness, and yet have tested me these ten times and have not obeyed my voice, 23 shall see the land that I swore to give to their ancestors; none of those who despised me shall see it. 24 But my servant Caleb, because he has a different spirit and has followed me wholeheartedly, I will bring into the land into which he went, and his descendants shall possess it. 25 Now, since the A·mal′e·kites and the Cā′naan·ites live in the valleys, turn tomorrow and set out for the wilderness by the way to the Red Sea."*a*

An Attempted Invasion is Repulsed
(Deut 1.41–45)

26 And the LORD spoke to Moses and to Aaron, saying: 27 How long shall this wicked congregation complain against me? I have heard the complaints of the Israelites, which they complain against me. 28 Say to them, "As I live," says the LORD, "I will do to you the very things I heard you say: 29 your dead bodies shall fall in this very wilderness; and of all your number, included in the census, from twenty years old and upward, who have complained against me, 30 not one of you shall come into the land in which I swore to settle you, except Caleb son of Je·phun′neh and Joshua son of Nun. 31 But your little ones, who you said would become booty, I will bring in, and they shall know the land that you have despised. 32 But as for you, your dead bodies shall fall in this wilderness. 33 And your children shall be shepherds in the wilderness for forty years, and shall suffer for your faithlessness, until the last of your dead bodies lies in the wilderness. 34 According to the number of the days in which you spied out the land, forty days, for every day a year, you shall bear your iniquity, forty years, and you shall know my displeasure." 35 I the LORD have spoken; surely I will do thus to all this wicked congregation gathered together against me: in this wilderness they shall come to a full end, and there they shall die.

36 And the men whom Moses sent to spy out the land, who returned and made all the congregation complain against him by bringing a bad report about the land— 37 the men who brought an unfavorable report about the land died by a plague before the LORD. 38 But Joshua son of Nun and Caleb son of Je·phun′neh alone remained alive, of those men who went to spy out the land.

39 When Moses told these words to all the Israelites, the people mourned greatly. 40 They rose early in the morning and went up to the heights of the hill country, saying, "Here we are. We will go up to the place that the LORD has promised, for we have sinned." 41 But Moses said, "Why do you continue to transgress the command of the LORD? That will not succeed. 42 Do not go up, for the LORD is not with you; do not let yourselves be struck down before your enemies. 43 For the A·mal′e·kites and the Cā′naan·ites will confront you there, and you shall fall by the sword; because you have turned back from following the LORD, the LORD will not be with you." 44 But they presumed to go up to the heights of the hill country, even though the ark of the covenant of the LORD, and Moses, had not left the camp. 45 Then the A·mal′e·kites and the Cā′naan·ites who lived in that hill country came down and defeated them, pursuing them as far as Hor′mah.

Various Offerings

15 The LORD spoke to Moses, saying: 2 Speak to the Israelites and say to them: When you come into the land you are to inhabit, which I am giving you, 3 and you make an offering by fire to the LORD from the herd or from the flock—whether a burnt offering or a sacrifice, to fulfill a vow or as a freewill offering or at your appointed festivals—to make a pleasing odor for the LORD, 4 then whoever presents such an offering to the LORD shall present also a grain offering, one-tenth of an ephah of choice flour, mixed with one-fourth of a hin of oil. 5 Moreover, you shall offer one-fourth of a hin of wine as a drink offering with the burnt offering or the sacrifice, for each lamb. 6 For a ram, you shall offer a grain offering, two-tenths of an ephah of choice flour mixed with one-third of a hin of oil; 7 and as a drink offering you shall offer one-third of a hin of wine, a pleasing odor to the LORD. 8 When you offer a bull as a burnt offering or a sacrifice, to fulfill a vow or as an offering of well-being to the LORD, 9 then you shall present with the bull a grain offering, three-tenths of an ephah of choice flour, mixed with half a hin of oil, 10 and you shall present as a drink offering half a hin of wine, as an offering by fire, a pleasing odor to the LORD.

11 Thus it shall be done for each ox or ram, or for each of the male lambs or the kids. 12 According to the number that you offer, so you shall do with each and every one. 13 Every native Israelite shall do these things in this way, in presenting an

---

a Or Sea of Reeds

offering by fire, a pleasing odor to the LORD. 14 An alien who lives with you, or who takes up permanent residence among you, and wishes to offer an offering by fire, a pleasing odor to the LORD, shall do as you do. 15 As for the assembly, there shall be for both you and the resident alien a single statute, a perpetual statute throughout your generations; you and the alien shall be alike before the LORD. 16 You and the alien who resides with you shall have the same law and the same ordinance.

17 The LORD spoke to Moses, saying: 18 Speak to the Israelites and say to them: After you come into the land to which I am bringing you, 19 whenever you eat of the bread of the land, you shall present a donation to the LORD. 20 From your first batch of dough you shall present a loaf as a donation; you shall present it just as you present a donation from the threshing floor. 21 Throughout your generations you shall give to the LORD a donation from the first of your batch of dough.

22 But if you unintentionally fail to observe all these commandments that the LORD has spoken to Moses— 23 everything that the LORD has commanded you by Moses, from the day the LORD gave commandment and thereafter, throughout your generations— 24 then if it was done unintentionally without the knowledge of the congregation, the whole congregation shall offer one young bull for a burnt offering, a pleasing odor to the LORD, together with its grain offering and its drink offering, according to the ordinance, and one male goat for a sin offering. 25 The priest shall make atonement for all the congregation of the Israelites, and they shall be forgiven; it was unintentional, and they have brought their offering, an offering by fire to the LORD, and their sin offering before the LORD, for their error. 26 All the congregation of the Israelites shall be forgiven, as well as the aliens residing among them, because the whole people was involved in the error.

27 An individual who sins unintentionally shall present a female goat a year old for a sin offering. 28 And the priest shall make atonement before the LORD for the one who commits an error, when it is unintentional, to make atonement for the person, who then shall be forgiven. 29 For both the native among the Israelites and the alien residing among them—you shall have the same law for anyone who acts in error. 30 But whoever acts high-handedly, whether a native or an alien, affronts the LORD, and shall be cut off from among the people. 31 Because of having despised the word of the LORD and broken his commandment, such a person shall be utterly cut off and bear the guilt.

Penalty for Violating the Sabbath
(Ex 31.12–17)

32 When the Israelites were in the wilderness, they found a man gathering sticks on the sabbath day. 33 Those who found him gathering sticks brought him to Moses, Aaron, and to the whole congregation. 34 They put him in custody, because it was not clear what should be done to him. 35 Then the LORD said to Moses, "The man shall be put to death; all the congregation shall stone him outside the camp." 36 The whole congregation brought him outside the camp and stoned him to death, just as the LORD had commanded Moses.

Fringes on Garments

37 The LORD said to Moses: 38 Speak to the Israelites, and tell them to make fringes on the corners of their garments throughout their generations and to put a blue cord on the fringe at each corner. 39 You have the fringe so that, when you see it, you will remember all the commandments of the LORD and do them, and not follow the lust of your own heart and your own eyes. 40 So you shall remember and do all my commandments, and you shall be holy to your God. 41 I am the LORD your God, who brought you out of the land of Egypt, to be your God: I am the LORD your God.

Revolt of Korah, Dathan, and Abiram

16 Now Kō′rah son of Iz′har son of Kō′hath son of Levi, along with Dā′than and A•bī′ram sons of E•lī′ab, and On son of Pē′leth—descendants of Reuben—took 2 two hundred fifty Israelite men, leaders of the congregation, chosen from the assembly, well-known men,[b] and they confronted Moses. 3 They assembled against Moses and against Aaron, and said to them, "You have gone too far! All the congregation are holy, every one of them, and the LORD is among them. So why then do you exalt yourselves above the assembly of the LORD?" 4 When Moses heard it, he fell on his face. 5 Then he said to Kō′rah and all his company, "In the morning the LORD will make known who is his, and who is holy, and who will be allowed to approach him; the one whom he will choose he will allow to approach him. 6 Do this: take censers, Kō′rah and all your[c] company, 7 and tomorrow put fire in them, and lay incense on them before the LORD; and the man whom the LORD chooses shall be the holy one. You Lē′vītes have gone too far!" 8 Then Moses said to Kō′rah, "Hear now, you Lē′vītes! 9 Is it too little for you that the God of Israel has separated you from the congregation of Israel, to allow you to approach him in order to

---

b Cn: Heb and they confronted Moses, and two hundred fifty men . . . well-known men   c Heb his

N
U
M

perform the duties of the LORD's tabernacle, and to stand before the congregation and serve them? 10 He has allowed you to approach him, and all your brother Lĕ′vītes with you; yet you seek the priesthood as well! 11 Therefore you and all your company have gathered together against the LORD. What is Aaron that you rail against him?"

12 Moses sent for Dā′than and A•bī′ram sons of E•lī′ab; but they said, "We will not come! 13 Is it too little that you have brought us up out of a land flowing with milk and honey to kill us in the wilderness, that you must also lord it over us? 14 It is clear you have not brought us into a land flowing with milk and honey, or given us an inheritance of fields and vineyards. Would you put out the eyes of these men? We will not come!"

15 Moses was very angry and said to the LORD, "Pay no attention to their offering. I have not taken one donkey from them, and I have not harmed any one of them." 16 And Moses said to Kō′rah, "As for you and all your company, be present tomorrow before the LORD, you and they and Aaron; 17 and let each one of you take his censer, and put incense on it, and each one of you present his censer before the LORD, two hundred fifty censers; you also, and Aaron, each his censer." 18 So each man took his censer, and they put fire in the censers and laid incense on them, and they stood at the entrance of the tent of meeting with Moses and Aaron. 19 Then Kō′rah assembled the whole congregation against them at the entrance of the tent of meeting. And the glory of the LORD appeared to the whole congregation.

20 Then the LORD spoke to Moses and to Aaron, saying: 21 Separate yourselves from this congregation, so that I may consume them in a moment. 22 They fell on their faces, and said, "O God, the God of the spirits of all flesh, shall one person sin and you become angry with the whole congregation?"

23 And the LORD spoke to Moses, saying: 24 Say to the congregation: Get away from the dwellings of Kō′rah, Dā′than, and A•bī′ram. 25 So Moses got up and went to Dā′than and A•bī′ram; the elders of Israel followed him. 26 He said to the congregation, "Turn away from the tents of these wicked men, and touch nothing of theirs, or you will be swept away for all their sins." 27 So they got away from the dwellings of Kō′rah, Dā′than, and A•bī′ram; and Dā′than and A•bī′ram came out and stood at the entrance of their tents, together with their wives, their children, and their little ones. 28 And Moses said, "This is how you shall know that the LORD has sent me to do all these works; it has not been of my own accord: 29 If these people die a natural death, or if a natural fate comes on them, then the LORD has not sent me. 30 But if the LORD creates something new, and the ground opens its mouth and swallows them up, with all that belongs to them, and they go down alive into Shĕ′ōl, then you shall know that these men have despised the LORD."

31 As soon as he finished speaking all these words, the ground under them was split apart. 32 The earth opened its mouth and swallowed them up, along with their households—everyone who belonged to Kō′rah and all their goods. 33 So they with all that belonged to them went down alive into Shĕ′ōl; the earth closed over them, and they perished from the midst of the assembly. 34 All Israel around them fled at their outcry, for they said, "The earth will swallow us too!" 35 And fire came out from the LORD and consumed the two hundred fifty men offering the incense.

36d Then the LORD spoke to Moses, saying: 37 Tell El•ē•ā′zar son of Aaron the priest to take the censers out of the blaze; then scatter the fire far and wide. 38 For the censers of these sinners have become holy at the cost of their lives. Make them into hammered plates as a covering for the altar, for they presented them before the LORD and they became holy. Thus they shall be a sign to the Israelites. 39 So El•′ē•ā′zar the priest took the bronze censers that had been presented by those who were burned; and they were hammered out as a covering for the altar— 40 a reminder to the Israelites that no outsider, who is not of the descendants of Aaron, shall approach to offer incense before the LORD, so as not to become like Kō′rah and his company—just as the LORD had said to him through Moses.

41 On the next day, however, the whole congregation of the Israelites rebelled against Moses and against Aaron, saying, "You have killed the people of the LORD." 42 And when the congregation had assembled against them, Moses and Aaron turned toward the tent of meeting; the cloud had covered it and the glory of the LORD appeared. 43 Then Moses and Aaron came to the front of the tent of meeting, 44 and the LORD spoke to Moses, saying, 45 "Get away from this congregation, so that I may consume them in a moment." And they fell on their faces. 46 Moses said to Aaron, "Take your censer, put fire on it from the altar and lay incense on it, and carry it quickly to the congregation and make atonement for them. For wrath has gone out from the LORD; the plague has begun." 47 So Aaron took it as Moses had ordered, and ran into the middle of the assembly, where the plague had already begun among the people. He put on the incense, and made atonement for the people. 48 He stood between the dead and the living; and the plague was stopped. 49 Those who died by the plague were

NUM

---

d Ch 17.1 in Heb

fourteen thousand seven hundred, besides those who died in the affair of Kō'rah. 50 When the plague was stopped, Aaron returned to Moses at the entrance of the tent of meeting.

The Budding of Aaron's Rod

17 *e* The LORD spoke to Moses, saying: 2 Speak to the Israelites, and get twelve staffs from them, one for each ancestral house, from all the leaders of their ancestral houses. Write each man's name on his staff, 3 and write Aaron's name on the staff of Levi. For there shall be one staff for the head of each ancestral house. 4 Place them in the tent of meeting before the covenant,*f* where I meet with you. 5 And the staff of the man whom I choose shall sprout; thus I will put a stop to the complaints of the Israelites that they continually make against you. 6 Moses spoke to the Israelites; and all their leaders gave him staffs, one for each leader, according to their ancestral houses, twelve staffs; and the staff of Aaron was among theirs. 7 So Moses placed the staffs before the LORD in the tent of the covenant.*f*

8 When Moses went into the tent of the covenant*f* on the next day, the staff of Aaron for the house of Levi had sprouted. It put forth buds, produced blossoms, and bore ripe almonds. 9 Then Moses brought out all the staffs from before the LORD to all the Israelites; and they looked, and each man took his staff. 10 And the LORD said to Moses, "Put back the staff of Aaron before the covenant,*f* to be kept as a warning to rebels, so that you may make an end of their complaints against me, or else they will die." 11 Moses did so; just as the LORD commanded him, so he did.

12 The Israelites said to Moses, "We are perishing; we are lost, all of us are lost! 13 Everyone who approaches the tabernacle of the LORD will die. Are we all to perish?"

Responsibility of Priests and Levites

18 The LORD said to Aaron: You and your sons and your ancestral house with you shall bear responsibility for offenses connected with the sanctuary, while you and your sons alone shall bear responsibility for offenses connected with the priesthood. 2 So bring with you also your brothers of the tribe of Levi, your ancestral tribe, in order that they may be joined to you, and serve you while you and your sons with you are in front of the tent of the covenant. *f* 3 They shall perform duties for you and for the whole tent. But they must not approach either the utensils of the sanctuary or the altar, otherwise both they and you will die. 4 They are attached to you in order to perform the duties of the tent of meeting, for all the service of the tent; no outsider shall approach you. 5 You yourselves shall

perform the duties of the sanctuary and the duties of the altar, so that wrath may never again come upon the Israelites. 6 It is I who now take your brother Lē'vites from among the Israelites; they are now yours as a gift, dedicated to the LORD, to perform the service of the tent of meeting. 7 But you and your sons with you shall diligently perform your priestly duties in all that concerns the altar and the area behind the curtain. I give your priesthood as a gift;*g* any outsider who approaches shall be put to death.

The Priests' Portion

8 The LORD spoke to Aaron: I have given you charge of the offerings made to me, all the holy gifts of the Israelites; I have given them to you and your sons as a priestly portion due you in perpetuity. 9 This shall be yours from the most holy things, reserved from the fire: every offering of theirs that they render to me as a most holy thing, whether grain offering, sin offering, or guilt offering, shall belong to you and your sons. 10 As a most holy thing you shall eat it; every male may eat it; it shall be holy to you. 11 This also is yours: I have given to you, together with your sons and daughters, as a perpetual due, whatever is set aside from the gifts of all the elevation offerings of the Israelites; everyone who is clean in your house may eat them. 12 All the best of the oil and all the best of the wine and of the grain, the choice produce that they give to the LORD, I have given to you. 13 The first fruits of all that is in their land, which they bring to the LORD, shall be yours; everyone who is clean in your house may eat of it. 14 Every devoted thing in Israel shall be yours. 15 The first issue of the womb of all creatures, human and animal, which is offered to the LORD, shall be yours; but the firstborn of human beings you shall redeem, and the firstborn of unclean animals you shall redeem. 16 Their redemption price, reckoned from one month of age, you shall fix at five shekels of silver, according to the shekel of the sanctuary (that is, twenty gerahs). 17 But the firstborn of a cow, or the firstborn of a sheep, or the firstborn of a goat, you shall not redeem; they are holy. You shall dash their blood on the altar, and shall turn their fat into smoke as an offering by fire for a pleasing odor to the LORD; 18 but their flesh shall be yours, just as the breast that is elevated and as the right thigh are yours. 19 All the holy offerings that the Israelites present to the LORD I have given to you, together with your sons and daughters, as a perpetual due; it is a covenant of salt forever before the LORD for you and your descendants as well. 20 Then the LORD

---

e Ch 17.16 in Heb   *f* Or *treaty,* or *testimony;* Heb *eduth*
g Heb *as a service of gift*

said to Aaron: You shall have no allotment in their land, nor shall you have any share among them; I am your share and your possession among the Israelites.

21 To the Lē′vītes I have given every tithe in Israel for a possession in return for the service that they perform, the service in the tent of meeting. 22 From now on the Israelites shall no longer approach the tent of meeting, or else they will incur guilt and die. 23 But the Lē′vītes shall perform the service of the tent of meeting, and they shall bear responsibility for their own offenses; it shall be a perpetual statute throughout your generations. But among the Israelites they shall have no allotment, 24 because I have given to the Lē′vītes as their portion the tithe of the Israelites, which they set apart as an offering to the LORD. Therefore I have said of them that they shall have no allotment among the Israelites.

25 Then the LORD spoke to Moses, saying: 26 You shall speak to the Lē′vītes, saying: When you receive from the Israelites the tithe that I have given you from them for your portion, you shall set apart an offering from it to the LORD, a tithe of the tithe. 27 It shall be reckoned to you as your gift, the same as the grain of the threshing floor and the fullness of the wine press. 28 Thus you also shall set apart an offering to the LORD from all the tithes that you receive from the Israelites; and from them you shall give the LORD's offering to the priest Aaron. 29 Out of all the gifts to you, you shall set apart every offering due to the LORD; the best of all of them is the part to be consecrated. 30 Say also to them: When you have set apart the best of it, then the rest shall be reckoned to the Lē′vītes as produce of the threshing floor, and as produce of the wine press. 31 You may eat it in any place, you and your households; for it is your payment for your service in the tent of meeting. 32 You shall incur no guilt by reason of it, when you have offered the best of it. But you shall not profane the holy gifts of the Israelites, on pain of death.

Ceremony of the Red Heifer

19 The LORD spoke to Moses and Aaron, saying: 2 This is a statute of the law that the LORD has commanded: Tell the Israelites to bring you a red heifer without defect, in which there is no blemish and on which no yoke has been laid. 3 You shall give it to the priest El·ē·a′zar, and it shall be taken outside the camp and slaughtered in his presence. 4 The priest El·ē·a′zar shall take some of its blood with his finger and sprinkle it seven times towards the front of the tent of meeting. 5 Then the heifer shall be burned in his sight; its skin, its flesh, and its blood, with its dung, shall be

burned. 6 The priest shall take cedarwood, hyssop, and crimson material, and throw them into the fire in which the heifer is burning. 7 Then the priest shall wash his clothes and bathe his body in water, and afterwards he may come into the camp; but the priest shall remain unclean until evening. 8 The one who burns the heifer[h] shall wash his clothes in water and bathe his body in water; he shall remain unclean until evening. 9 Then someone who is clean shall gather up the ashes of the heifer, and deposit them outside the camp in a clean place; and they shall be kept for the congregation of the Israelites for the water for cleansing. It is a purification offering. 10 The one who gathers the ashes of the heifer shall wash his clothes and be unclean until evening.

This shall be a perpetual statute for the Israelites and for the alien residing among them. 11 Those who touch the dead body of any human being shall be unclean seven days. 12 They shall purify themselves with the water on the third day and on the seventh day, and so be clean; but if they do not purify themselves on the third day and on the seventh day, they will not become clean. 13 All who touch a corpse, the body of a human being who has died, and do not purify themselves, defile the tabernacle of the LORD; such persons shall be cut off from Israel. Since water for cleansing was not dashed on them, they remain unclean; their uncleanness is still on them.

14 This is the law when someone dies in a tent: everyone who comes into the tent, and everyone who is in the tent, shall be unclean seven days. 15 And every open vessel with no cover fastened on it is unclean. 16 Whoever in the open field touches one who has been killed by a sword, or who has died naturally,[i] or a human bone, or a grave, shall be unclean seven days. 17 For the unclean they shall take some ashes of the burnt purification offering, and running water shall be added in a vessel; 18 then a clean person shall take hyssop, dip it in the water, and sprinkle it on the tent, on all the furnishings, on the persons who were there, and on whoever touched the bone, the slain, the corpse, or the grave. 19 The clean person shall sprinkle the unclean ones on the third day and on the seventh day, thus purifying them on the seventh day. Then they shall wash their clothes and bathe themselves in water, and at evening they shall be clean. 20 Any who are unclean but do not purify themselves, those persons shall be cut off from the assembly, for they have defiled the sanctuary of the LORD. Since the water for cleansing has not been dashed on them, they are unclean.

21 It shall be a perpetual statute for them. The one who sprinkles the water for cleansing shall

NUM

---

h Heb it   i Heb lacks *naturally*

wash his clothes, and whoever touches the water for cleansing shall be unclean until evening. 22 Whatever the unclean person touches shall be unclean, and anyone who touches it shall be unclean until evening.

The Waters of Meribah
(Ex 17.1–7)

20 The Israelites, the whole congregation, came into the wilderness of Zin in the first month, and the people stayed in Kā′desh. Miriam died there, and was buried there.

2 Now there was no water for the congregation; so they gathered together against Moses and against Aaron. 3 The people quarreled with Moses and said, "Would that we had died when our kindred died before the LORD! 4 Why have you brought the assembly of the LORD into this wilderness for us and our livestock to die here? 5 Why have you brought us up out of Egypt, to bring us to this wretched place? It is no place for grain, or figs, or vines, or pomegranates; and there is no water to drink." 6 Then Moses and Aaron went away from the assembly to the entrance of the tent of meeting; they fell on their faces, and the glory of the LORD appeared to them. 7 The LORD spoke to Moses, saying: 8 Take the staff, and assemble the congregation, you and your brother Aaron, and command the rock before their eyes to yield its water. Thus you shall bring water out of the rock for them; thus you shall provide drink for the congregation and their livestock.

9 So Moses took the staff from before the LORD, as he had commanded him. 10 Moses and Aaron gathered the assembly together before the rock, and he said to them, "Listen, you rebels, shall we bring water for you out of this rock?" 11 Then Moses lifted up his hand and struck the rock twice with his staff; water came out abundantly, and the congregation and their livestock drank. 12 But the LORD said to Moses and Aaron, "Because you did not trust in me, to show my holiness before the eyes of the Israelites, therefore you shall not bring this assembly into the land that I have given them." 13 These are the waters of Mer′i•bah, j where the people of Israel quarreled with the LORD, and by which he showed his holiness.

Passage through Edom Refused

14 Moses sent messengers from Kā′desh to the king of Ē′dom, "Thus says your brother Israel: You know all the adversity that has befallen us: 15 how our ancestors went down to Egypt, and we lived in Egypt a long time; and the Egyptians oppressed us and our ancestors; 16 and when we cried to the LORD, he heard our voice, and sent an angel and brought us out of Egypt; and here we are in Kā′desh,

a town on the edge of your territory. 17 Now let us pass through your land. We will not pass through field or vineyard, or drink water from any well; we will go along the King's Highway, not turning aside to the right hand or to the left until we have passed through your territory."

18 But Ē′dom said to him, "You shall not pass through, or we will come out with the sword against you." 19 The Israelites said to him, "We will stay on the highway; and if we drink of your water, we and our livestock, then we will pay for it. It is only a small matter; just let us pass through on foot." 20 But he said, "You shall not pass through." And Ē′dom came out against them with a large force, heavily armed. 21 Thus Ē′dom refused to give Israel passage through their territory; so Israel turned away from them.

The Death of Aaron

22 They set out from Kā′desh, and the Israelites, the whole congregation, came to Mount Hor. 23 Then the LORD said to Moses and Aaron at Mount Hor, on the border of the land of Ē′dom, 24 "Let Aaron be gathered to his people. For he shall not enter the land that I have given to the Israelites, because you rebelled against my command at the waters of Mer′i•bah. 25 Take Aaron and his son El•ē•ā′zar, and bring them up Mount Hor; 26 strip Aaron of his vestments, and put them on his son El•ē•ā′zar. But Aaron shall be gathered to his people,k and shall die there." 27 Moses did as the LORD had commanded; they went up Mount Hor in the sight of the whole congregation. 28 Moses stripped Aaron of his vestments, and put them on his son El•ē•ā′zar; and Aaron died there on the top of the mountain. Moses and El•ē•ā′zar came down from the mountain. 29 When all the congregation saw that Aaron had died, all the house of Israel mourned for Aaron thirty days.

The Bronze Serpent

21 When the Cā′naan•īte, the king of Ar′ad, who lived in the Neg′eb, heard that Israel was coming by the way of Ath′a•rim, he fought against Israel and took some of them captive. 2 Then Israel made a vow to the LORD and said, "If you will indeed give this people into our hands, then we will utterly destroy their towns." 3 The LORD listened to the voice of Israel, and handed over the Cā′naan•ites; and they utterly destroyed them and their towns; so the place was called Hor′mah.l

4 From Mount Hor they set out by the way to the Red Sea,m to go around the land of Ē′dom; but the people became impatient on the way. 5 The

j That is Quarrel   k Heb lacks to his people   l Heb Destruction   m Or Sea of Reeds people spoke against God and against Moses, "Why have you brought us up out of Egypt to die in the wilderness? For there is no food and no water, and we detest this miserable food." [6] Then the LORD sent poisonous[n] serpents among the people, and they bit the people, so that many Israelites died. [7] The people came to Moses and said, "We have sinned by speaking against the LORD and against you; pray to the LORD to take away the serpents from us." So Moses prayed for the people. [8] And the LORD said to Moses, "Make a poisonous[o] serpent, and set it on a pole; and everyone who is bitten shall look at it and live." [9] So Moses made a serpent of bronze, and put it upon a pole; and whenever a serpent bit someone, that person would look at the serpent of bronze and live.

The Journey to Moab

10 The Israelites set out, and camped in Ō'both. [11] They set out from Ō'both, and camped at Ī'ye-ab'a•rim, in the wilderness bordering Mō'ab toward the sunrise. [12] From there they set out, and camped in the Wadi Zē'red. [13] From there they set out, and camped on the other side of the Ar'non, in[p] the wilderness that extends from the boundary of the Am'o•rītes; for the Ar'non is the boundary of Mō'ab, between Mō'ab and the Am'o•rītes. [14] Wherefore it is said in the Book of the Wars of the LORD,

> "Wa'heb in Sū'phah and the wadis.
> The Ar'non [15] and the slopes of the wadis
>   that extend to the seat of Ar,
> and lie along the border of Mō'ab."[q]

16 From there they continued to Bē'er;[r] that is the well of which the LORD said to Moses, "Gather the people together, and I will give them water." [17] Then Israel sang this song:

> "Spring up, O well!—Sing to it!—
> [18] the well that the leaders sank,
>   that the nobles of the people dug,
>   with the scepter, with the staff."

From the wilderness to Mat'ta•nah, [19] from Mat'ta•nah to Na•hal'i•el, from Na•hal'i•el to Bā'moth, [20] and from Bā'moth to the valley lying in the region of Mō'ab by the top of Pis'gah that overlooks the wasteland.[s]

King Sihon Defeated
(Deut 2.26–37)

21 Then Israel sent messengers to King Sī'hon of the Am'o•rītes, saying, [22] "Let me pass through your land; we will not turn aside into field or vineyard; we will not drink the water of any well; we will go by the King's Highway until we have passed through your territory." [23] But Sī'hon would not allow Israel to pass through his territory. Sī'hon gathered all his people together, and went out against

Chap. 21

Israel to the wilderness; he came to Jā'haz, and fought against Israel. [24] Israel put him to the sword, and took possession of his land from the Ar'non to the Jab'bok, as far as to the Am'mon•ītes; for boundary of the Am'mon•ītes was strong. [25] Israel took all these towns, and Israel settled in all the towns of the Am'o•rītes, in Hesh'bon, and in all its villages. [26] For Hesh'bon was the city of King Sī'hon of the Am'o•rītes, who had fought against the former king of Mō'ab and captured all his land as far as the Ar'non. [27] Therefore the ballad singers say,

> "Come to Hesh'bon, let it be built;
>   let the city of Sī'hon be established.
> [28] For fire came out from Hesh'bon,
>   flame from the city of Sī'hon.
> It devoured Ar of Mō'ab,
>   and swallowed up[t] the heights of the
>   Ar'non.
> [29] Woe to you, O Mō'ab!
>   You are undone, O people of Chē'mosh!
> He has made his sons fugitives,
>   and his daughters captives,
>   to an Am'o•rīte king, Sī'hon.
> [30] So their posterity perished
>   from Hesh'bon[u] to Dī'bon,
> and we laid waste until fire spread to
>   Med'e•ba."[v]

31 Thus Israel settled in the land of the Am'o•rītes. [32] Moses sent to spy out Jā'zer; and they captured its villages, and dispossessed the Am'o•rītes who were there.

---

[n] Or *fiery*; Heb *seraphim*   [o] Or *fiery*; Heb *seraph*   [p] Gk: Heb *which is in*   [q] Meaning of Heb uncertain   [r] That is *Well*   [s] Or *Jeshimon*   [t] Gk: Heb *and the lords of*   [u] Gk: Heb *we have shot at them; Heshbon has perished*   [v] Compare Sam Gk: Meaning of MT uncertain

King Og Defeated
(Deut 3.1–22)

33 Then they turned and went up the road to Bā'shan; and King Og of Bā'shan came out against them, he and all his people, to battle at Ed're·ī. 34 But the LORD said to Moses, "Do not be afraid of him; for I have given him into your hand, with all his people, and all his land. You shall do to him as you did to King Sī'hon of the Am'o·rītes, who ruled in Hesh'bon." 35 So they killed him, his sons, and all his people, until there was no survivor left; and they took possession of his land.

Balak Summons Balaam to Curse Israel

22 The Israelites set out, and camped in the plains of Mō'ab across the Jordan from Jericho. 2 Now Bā'lak son of Zip'por saw all that Israel had done to the Am'o·rītes. 3 Mō'ab was in great dread of the people, because they were so numerous; Mō'ab was overcome with fear of the people of Israel. 4 And Mō'ab said to the elders of Mid'i·an, "This horde will now lick up all that is around us, as an ox licks up the grass of the field." Now Bā'lak son of Zip'por was king of Mō'ab at that time. 5 He sent messengers to Bā'laam son of Bē'or at Pē'thor, which is on the Euphrates, in the land of Ā'maw,ʷ to summon him, saying, "A people has come out of Egypt; they have spread over the face of the earth, and they have settled next to me. 6 Come now, curse this people for me, since they are stronger than I; perhaps I shall be able to defeat them and drive them from the land; for I know that whomever you bless is blessed, and whomever you curse is cursed."

7 So the elders of Mō'ab and the elders of Mid'i·an departed with the fees for divination in their hand; and they came to Bā'laam, and gave him Bā'lak's message. 8 He said to them, "Stay here tonight, and I will bring back word to you, just as the LORD speaks to me"; so the officials of Mō'ab stayed with Bā'laam. 9 God came to Bā'laam and said, "Who are these men with you?" 10 Bā'laam said to God, "King Bā'lak son of Zip'por of Mō'ab, has sent me this message: 11 'A people has come out of Egypt and has spread over the face of the earth; now come, curse them for me; perhaps I shall be able to fight against them and drive them out.'" 12 God said to Bā'laam, "You shall not go with them; you shall not curse the people, for they are blessed." 13 So Bā'laam rose in the morning, and said to the officials of Bā'lak, "Go to your own land, for the LORD has refused to let me go with you." 14 So the officials of Mō'ab rose and went to Bā'lak, and said, "Bā'laam refuses to come with us."

15 Once again Bā'lak sent officials, more numerous and more distinguished than these. 16 They came to Bā'laam and said to him, "Thus says Bā'lak son of Zip'por: 'Do not let anything hinder you from coming to me; 17 for I will surely do you great honor, and whatever you say to me I will do; come, curse this people for me.'" 18 But Bā'laam replied to the servants of Bā'lak, "Although Bā'lak were to give me his house full of silver and gold, I could not go beyond the command of the LORD my God, to do less or more. 19 You remain here, as the others did, so that I may learn what more the LORD may say to me." 20 That night God came to Bā'laam and said to him, "If the men have come to summon you, get up and go with them; but do only what I tell you to do." 21 So Bā'laam got up in the morning, saddled his donkey, and went with the officials of Mō'ab.

Balaam, the Donkey, and the Angel

22 God's anger was kindled because he was going, and the angel of the LORD took his stand in the road as his adversary. Now he was riding on the donkey, and his two servants were with him. 23 The donkey saw the angel of the LORD standing in the road, with a drawn sword in his hand; so the donkey turned off the road, and went into the field; and Bā'laam struck the donkey, to turn it back onto the road. 24 Then the angel of the LORD stood in a narrow path between the vineyards, with a wall on either side. 25 When the donkey saw the angel of the LORD, it scraped against the wall, and scraped Bā'laam's foot against the wall; so he struck it again. 26 Then the angel of the LORD went ahead, and stood in a narrow place, where there was no way to turn either to the right or to the left. 27 When the donkey saw the angel of the LORD, it lay down under Bā'laam; and Bā'laam's anger was kindled, and he struck the donkey with his staff. 28 Then the LORD opened the mouth of the donkey, and it said to Bā'laam, "What have I done to you, that you have struck me these three times?" 29 Bā'laam said to the donkey, "Because you have made a fool of me! I wish I had a sword in my hand! I would kill you right now!" 30 But the donkey said to Bā'laam, "Am I not your donkey, which you have ridden all your life to this day? Have I been in the habit of treating you this way?" And he said, "No."

31 Then the LORD opened the eyes of Bā'laam, and he saw the angel of the LORD standing in the road, with his drawn sword in his hand; and he bowed down, falling on his face. 32 The angel of the LORD said to him, "Why have you struck your donkey these three times? I have come out as an adversary, because your way is perverseˣ before me. 33 The donkey saw me, and turned away from me these three times. If it had not turned away from me, surely just now I would have killed you and let

---

w Or *land of his kinsfolk*   *x* Meaning of Heb uncertain

PRAY IT!

The Talking Donkey

Balaam is an interesting biblical character. He is not an Israelite and seems
to be a sort of prophet for hire. Balak,
the king of Moab, hires him to prophesy
against Israel. But Balaam, hearing a
message from God through his donkey,
instead of cursing the Israelites, blesses
them four times. Even though the Israelites were unfaithful, God continues
to be with them, to bless them.

Balaam is a sign of the universal character of God's call, and the donkey is a
symbol of the poor and oppressed. The
complaining and whining donkey represents those who usually are not heard but
are given a voice through the prophets.

This story gives us two insights into
prayer. First, if God can use a donkey to
talk to Balaam, God can use anything
to talk to us. God speaks to us in many
ways—through our experiences, the
Scriptures, poetry and music, our relationship with nature, and more. Are we
paying attention? Second, God wants us
to hear the often unheard voice of the
poor and oppressed. Do you hear God's
voice expressed through them?

▸ **Num 22.22–35**

it live." 34 Then Bā'laam said to the angel of the
LORD, "I have sinned, for I did not know that you
were standing in the road to oppose me. Now therefore, if it is displeasing to you, I will return home."
35 The angel of the LORD said to Bā'laam, "Go with
the men; but speak only what I tell you to speak." So
Bā'laam went on with the officials of Bā'lak.

36 When Bā'lak heard that Bā'laam had come,
he went out to meet him at Ir-mō'ab, on the boundary formed by the Ar'non, at the farthest point of
the boundary. 37 Bā'lak said to Bā'laam, "Did I not
send to summon you? Why did you not come to
me? Am I not able to honor you?" 38 Bā'laam said
to Bā'lak, "I have come to you now, but do I have
power to say just anything? The word God puts in
my mouth, that is what I must say." 39 Then
Bā'laam went with Bā'lak, and they came to
Kir'i·ath-hū'zoth. 40 Bā'lak sacrificed oxen and
sheep, and sent them to Bā'laam and to the officials
who were with him.

Balaam's First Oracle

41 On the next day Bā'lak took Bā'laam and
brought him up to Bā'moth-bā'al; and from there he

23 could see part of the people of Israel.*y* 1 Then
Bā'laam said to Bā'lak, "Build me seven
altars here, and prepare seven bulls and seven rams
for me." 2 Bā'lak did as Bā'laam had said; and
Bā'lak and Bā'laam offered a bull and a ram on each
altar. 3 Then Bā'laam said to Bā'lak, "Stay here beside your burnt offerings while I go aside. Perhaps
the LORD will come to meet me. Whatever he shows
me I will tell you." And he went to a bare height.

4 Then God met Bā'laam; and Bā'laam said to
him, "I have arranged the seven altars, and have offered a bull and a ram on each altar." 5 The LORD
put a word in Bā'laam's mouth, and said, "Return
to Bā'lak, and this is what you must say." 6 So he returned to Bā'lak,*z* who was standing beside his
burnt offerings with all the officials of Mō'ab.
7 Then Bā'laam*a* uttered his oracle, saying:

"Bā'lak has brought me from Ar'am,
    the king of Mō'ab from the eastern
        mountains:
'Come, curse Jacob for me;
    Come, denounce Israel!'
8 How can I curse whom God has not cursed?
    How can I denounce those whom the LORD
        has not denounced?
9 For from the top of the crags I see him,
    from the hills I behold him.
Here is a people living alone,
    and not reckoning itself among the nations!
10 Who can count the dust of Jacob,
    or number the dust-cloud*b* of Israel?
Let me die the death of the upright,
    and let my end be like his!"

11 Then Bā'lak said to Bā'laam, "What have you
done to me? I brought you to curse my enemies,
but now you have done nothing but bless them."
12 He answered, "Must I not take care to say what
the LORD puts into my mouth?"

Balaam's Second Oracle

13 So Bā'lak said to him, "Come with me to
another place from which you may see them; you
shall see only part of them, and shall not see them
all; then curse them for me from there." 14 So he
took him to the field of Zō'phim, to the top of Pis'-
gah. He built seven altars, and offered a bull and a
ram on each altar. 15 Bā'laam said to Bā'lak, "Stand
here beside your burnt offerings, while I meet the
LORD over there." 16 The LORD met Bā'laam, put a
word into his mouth, and said, "Return to Bā'lak,
and this is what you shall say." 17 When he came to

NUM

---

y Heb lacks *of Israel*   *z* Heb *him*   *a* Heb *he*   *b* Or *fourth
part*

him, he was standing beside his burnt offerings with the officials of Mō′ab. Bă′lak said to him, "What has the LORD said?" 18 Then Bă′laam uttered his oracle, saying:

"Rise, Bă′lak, and hear;
listen to me, O son of Zip′por:
19 God is not a human being, that he should lie,
or a mortal, that he should change his mind.
Has he promised, and will he not do it?
Has he spoken, and will he not fulfill it?
20 See, I received a command to bless;
he has blessed, and I cannot revoke it.
21 He has not beheld misfortune in Jacob,
nor has he seen trouble in Israel.
The LORD their God is with them,
acclaimed as a king among them.
22 God, who brings them out of Egypt,
is like the horns of a wild ox for them.
23 Surely there is no enchantment against Jacob,
no divination against Israel;
now it shall be said of Jacob and Israel,
'See what God has done!'
24 Look, a people rising up like a lioness,
and rousing itself like a lion!
It does not lie down until it has eaten the prey
and drunk the blood of the slain."

25 Then Bă′lak said to Bă′laam, "Do not curse them at all, and do not bless them at all." 26 But Bă′laam answered Bă′lak, "Did I not tell you, 'Whatever the LORD says, that is what I must do'?"

27 So Bă′lak said to Bă′laam, "Come now, I will take you to another place; perhaps it will please God that you may curse them for me from there." 28 So Bă′lak took Bă′laam to the top of Pē′or, which overlooks the wasteland.c 29 Bă′laam said to Bă′lak, "Build me seven altars here, and prepare seven bulls and seven rams for me." 30 So Bă′lak did as Bă′laam had said, and offered a bull and a ram on each altar.

Balaam's Third Oracle

24 Now Bă′laam saw that it pleased the LORD to bless Israel, so he did not go, as at other times, to look for omens, but set his face toward the wilderness. 2 Bă′laam looked up and saw Israel camping tribe by tribe. Then the spirit of God came upon him, 3 and he uttered his oracle, saying:

"The oracle of Bă′laam son of Bē′or,
the oracle of the man whose eye is clear,d
4 the oracle of one who hears the words of God,
who sees the vision of the Almighty,e
who falls down, but with eyes uncovered:
5 how fair are your tents, O Jacob,
your encampments, O Israel!
6 Like palm groves that stretch far away,
like gardens beside a river,

like aloes that the LORD has planted,
like cedar trees beside the waters.
7 Water shall flow from his buckets,
and his seed shall have abundant water,
his king shall be higher than Ă′gag,
and his kingdom shall be exalted.
8 God who brings him out of Egypt,
is like the horns of a wild ox for him;
he shall devour the nations that are his foes
and break their bones.
He shall strike with his arrows.f
9 He crouched, he lay down like a lion,
and like a lioness; who will rouse him up?
Blessed is everyone who blesses you,
and cursed is everyone who curses you."

10 Then Bă′lak's anger was kindled against Bă′laam, and he struck his hands together. Bă′lak said to Bă′laam, "I summoned you to curse my enemies, but instead you have blessed them these three times. 11 Now be off with you! Go home! I said, 'I will reward you richly,' but the LORD has denied you any reward." 12 And Bă′laam said to Bă′lak, "Did I not tell your messengers whom you sent to me, 13 'If Bă′lak should give me his house full of silver and gold, I would not be able to go beyond the word of the LORD, to do either good or bad of my own will; what the LORD says, that is what I will say'? 14 So now, I am going to my people; let me advise you what this people will do to your people in days to come."

Balaam's Fourth Oracle

15 So he uttered his oracle, saying:
"The oracle of Bă′laam son of Bē′or,
the oracle of the man whose eye is clear,d
16 the oracle of one who hears the words of God,
and knows the knowledge of the Most High,g
who sees the vision of the Almighty,e
who falls down, but with his eyes uncovered:
17 I see him, but not now;
I behold him, but not near—
a star shall come out of Jacob,
and a scepter shall rise out of Israel;
it shall crush the borderlandsh of Mō′ab,
and the territoryi of all the Sheth′ites.
18 Ē′dom will become a possession,
Sē′ir a possession of its enemies,j
while Israel does valiantly.
19 One out of Jacob shall rule,
and destroy the survivors of Ir."

---

c Or *overlooks Jeshimon* d Or *closed* or *open* e Traditional rendering of Heb *Shaddai* f Meaning of Heb uncertain g Or *of Elyon* h Or *forehead* i Some Mss read *skull* j Heb *Seir, its enemies, a possession*

20 Then he looked on Am′a•lek, and uttered his oracle, saying:

"First among the nations was Am′a•lek,
    but its end is to perish forever."

21 Then he looked on the Ken′īte, and uttered his oracle, saying:

"Enduring is your dwelling place,
    and your nest is set in the rock;
22   yet Kāin is destined for burning.
    How long shall As′shur take you away
        captive?"

23 Again he uttered his oracle, saying:

"Alas, who shall live when God does this?
24   But ships shall come from Kit′tim
and shall afflict As′shur and Ē′ber;
    and he also shall perish forever."

25 Then Bā′laam got up and went back to his place, and Bā′lak also went his way.

Worship of Baal of Peor

25 While Israel was staying at Shit′tim, the people began to have sexual relations with the women of Mō′ab. 2 These invited the people to the sacrifices of their gods, and the people ate and bowed down to their gods. 3 Thus Israel yoked itself to the Bā′al of Pē′or, and the LORD′s anger was kindled against Israel. 4 The LORD said to Moses, "Take all the chiefs of the people, and impale them in the sun before the LORD, in order that the fierce anger of the LORD may turn away from Israel." 5 And Moses said to the judges of Israel, "Each of you shall kill any of your people who have yoked themselves to the Bā′al of Pē′or."

6 Just then one of the Israelites came and brought a Mid′i•an•īte woman into his family, in the sight of Moses and in the sight of the whole congregation of the Israelites, while they were weeping at the entrance of the tent of meeting. 7 When Phin′e•has son of El•ē•ā′zar, son of Aaron the priest, saw it, he got up and left the congregation. Taking a spear in his hand, 8 he went after the Israelite man into the tent, and pierced the two of them, the Israelite and the woman, through the belly. So the plague was stopped among the people of Israel. 9 Nevertheless those that died by the plague were twenty-four thousand.

10 The LORD spoke to Moses, saying: 11 "Phin′-e•has son of El•ē•ā′zar, son of Aaron the priest, has turned back my wrath from the Israelites by manifesting such zeal among them on my behalf that in my jealousy I did not consume the Israelites. 12 Therefore say, 'I hereby grant him my covenant of peace. 13 It shall be for him and for his descendants after him a covenant of perpetual priesthood, because he was zealous for his God, and made atonement for the Israelites.' "

14 The name of the slain Israelite man, who was killed with the Mid′i•an•īte woman, was Zim′rī son of Sa′lū, head of an ancestral house belonging to the Sim′ē•on•ites. 15 The name of the Mid′-i•an•īte woman who was killed was Cōz′bī daughter of Zur, who was the head of a clan, an ancestral house in Mid′i•an.

16 The LORD said to Moses, 17 "Harass the Mid′-i•an•ītes, and defeat them; 18 for they have harassed you by the trickery with which they deceived you in the affair of Pē′or, and in the affair of Cōz′bī, the daughter of a leader of Mid′i•an, their sister; she was killed on the day of the plague that resulted from Pē′or."

A Census of the New Generation

26 After the plague the LORD said to Moses and to El•ē•ā′zar son of Aaron the priest, 2 "Take a census of the whole congregation of the Israelites, from twenty years old and upward, by their ancestral houses, everyone in Israel able to go to war." 3 Moses and El•ē•ā′zar the priest spoke with them in the plains of Mō′ab by the Jordan opposite Jericho, saying, 4 "Take a census of the people,[k] from twenty years old and upward," as the LORD commanded Moses.

The Israelites, who came out of the land of Egypt, were:

5 Reuben, the firstborn of Israel. The descendants of Reuben: of Hā′noch, the clan of the Hā′noch•ites; of Pal′lū, the clan of the Pal′lū•ites; 6 of Hez′ron, the clan of the Hez′ron•ites; of Car′mī, the clan of the Car′mītes. 7 These are the clans of the Reū′ben•ites; the number of those enrolled was forty-three thousand seven hundred thirty. 8 And the descendants of Pal′lū: E•lī′ab. 9 The descendants of E•lī′ab: Nem′ū•el, Dā′than, and A•bī′ram. These are the same Dā′than and A•bī′ram, chosen from the congregation, who rebelled against Moses and Aaron in the company of Kō′rah, when they rebelled against the LORD, 10 and the earth opened its mouth and swallowed them up along with Kō′rah, when that company died, when the fire devoured two hundred fifty men; and they became a warning. 11 Notwithstanding, the sons of Kō′rah did not die.

12 The descendants of Sim′ē•on by their clans: of Nem′ū•el, the clan of the Nem′ū•el•ites; of Jā′min, the clan of the Jā′min•ites; of Jā′chin, the clan of the Jā′chin•ites; 13 of Zē′rah, the clan of the Zē′ra•hites; of Shā′ūl, the clan of the Shā′u•lites.[l] 14 These are the clans of the Sim′ē•on•ites, twenty-two thousand two hundred.

15 The children of Gad by their clans: of Zē′phon, the clan of the Zē′phon•ites; of Hag′gī, the clan of the Hag′gītes; of Shū′nī, the clan of the

N
U
M

---

k Heb lacks *take a census of the people*: Compare verse 2
l Or *Saul . . . Saulites*

Shū′nītes; 16 of Oz′nī, the clan of the Oz′nītes; of Ē′rī, the clan of the Ē′rītes; 17 of Ar′od, the clan of the Ar′o•dītes; of A•rē′lī, the clan of the A•rē′lītes. 18 These are the clans of the Gad′ītes: the number of those enrolled was forty thousand five hundred.

19 The sons of Judah: Er and Ō′nan; Er and Ō′nan died in the land of Cā′naan. 20 The descendants of Judah by their clans were: of Shē′lah, the clan of the Shē′la•nītes; of Per′ez, the clan of the Per′e•zītes; of Zē′rah, the clan of the Zē′ra•hītes. 21 The descendants of Per′ez were: of Hez′ron, the clan of the Hez′ron•ītes; of Hā′mul, the clan of the Hā′mul•ītes. 22 These are the clans of Judah: the number of those enrolled was seventy-six thousand five hundred.

23 The descendants of Is′sa•char by their clans: of Tō′la, the clan of the Tō′la•ītes; of Pū′vah, the clan of the Pū′nītes; 24 of Jash′ub, the clan of the Jash′ub•ītes; of Shim′ron, the clan of the Shim′ron′ītes. 25 These are the clans of Is′sa•char: sixty-four thousand three hundred enrolled.

26 The descendants of Zeb′ū•lun by their clans: of Sē′red, the clan of the Sē′red•ītes; of Ē′lon, the clan of the Ē′lon•ītes; of Jah′lē•el, the clan of the Jah′lē•el•ītes. 27 These are the clans of the Zeb′ū•lun•ītes; the number of those enrolled was sixty thousand five hundred.

28 The sons of Joseph by their clans: Ma•nas′seh and Ē′phra•im. 29 The descendants of Ma•nas′seh: of Mā′chir, the clan of the Mā′chir•ītes; and Mā′chir was the father of Gil′e•ad; of Gil′e•ad, the clan of the Gil′e•ad•ītes. 30 These are the descendants of Gil′e•ad: of Ī•ē′zer, the clan of the Ī•ē′zer•ītes; of Hē′lek, the clan of the Hē′lek•ītes; 31 and of As′ri•el, the clan of the As′ri•el•ītes; and of Shē′chem, the clan of the Shē′chem•ītes; 32 and of She•mī′da, the clan of the She•mī′da•ītes; and of Hē′pher, the clan of the Hē′pher•ītes. 33 Now Ze•loph′e•had son of Hē′pher had no sons, but daughters: and the names of the daughters of Ze•loph′e•had were Mah′lah, Noah, Hog′lah, Mil′cah, and Tir′zah. 34 These are the clans of Ma•nas′seh; the number of those enrolled was fifty-two thousand seven hundred.

35 These are the descendants of Ē′phra•im according to their clans: of Shū•thē′lah, the clan of the Shū•the•lā′hītes; of Bē′cher, the clan of the Bē′cher•ītes; of Tā′han, the clan of the Tā′ha•nītes. 36 And these are the descendants of Shū•thē′lah: of Ē′ran, the clan of the Ē′ran•ītes. 37 These are the clans of the Ē′phra•im•ītes: the number of those enrolled was thirty-two thousand five hundred. These are the descendants of Joseph by their clans.

38 The descendants of Benjamin by their clans: of Bē′la, the clan of the Bē′la•ītes; of Ash′bel, the clan of the Ash′bel•ītes; of A•hī′ram, the clan of the A•hī′ram•ītes; 39 of She•phū′pham, the clan of the Shū′pham•ītes; of Hū′pham, the clan of the Hū′pham•ītes. 40 And the sons of Bē′la were Ard and Nā′a•man: of Ard, the clan of the Ard′ītes; of Nā′a•man, the clan of the Nā′a•mītes. 41 These are the descendants of Benjamin by their clans; the number of those enrolled was forty-five thousand six hundred.

42 These are the descendants of Dan by their clans: of Shū′ham, the clan of the Shū′ham•ītes. These are the clans of Dan by their clans. 43 All the clans of the Shū′ham•ītes: sixty-four thousand four hundred enrolled.

44 The descendants of Ash′er by their families: of Im′nah, the clan of the Im′nītes; of Ish′vī, the clan of the Ish′vītes; of Bē•rī′ah, the clan of the Bē•rī′ītes. 45 Of the descendants of Bē•rī′ah: of Hē′ber, the clan of the Hē′ber•ītes; of Mal′chi•el, the clan of the Mal′chi•el•ītes. 46 And the name of the daughter of Ash′er was Sē′rah. 47 These are the clans of the Ash′er•ītes: the number of those enrolled was fifty-three thousand four hundred.

48 The descendants of Naph′ta•lī by their clans: of Jah′zē•el, the clan of the Jah′zē•el•ītes; of Gū′nī, the clan of the Gū′nītes; 49 of Jē′zer, the clan of the Jē′zer•ītes; of Shil′lem, the clan of the Shil′lem•ītes. 50 These are the Naph′ta•lītes*m* by their clans: the number of those enrolled was forty-five thousand four hundred.

51 This was the number of the Israelites enrolled: six hundred and one thousand seven hundred thirty.

52 The LORD spoke to Moses, saying: 53 To these the land shall be apportioned for inheritance according to the number of names. 54 To a large tribe you shall give a large inheritance, and to a small tribe you shall give a small inheritance; every tribe shall be given its inheritance according to its enrollment. 55 But the land shall be apportioned by lot; according to the names of their ancestral tribes they shall inherit. 56 Their inheritance shall be apportioned according to lot between the larger and the smaller.

57 This is the enrollment of the Lē′vites by their clans: of Ger′shon, the clan of the Ger′shon•ītes; of Kō′hath, the clan of the Kō′hath•ītes; of Me•rar′ī, the clan of the Me•rar′ītes. 58 These are the clans of Levi: the clan of the Lib′nītes, the clan of the Hē′bron•ītes, the clan of the Mah′lītes, the clan of the Mū′shītes, the clan of the Kō′ra•hītes. Now Kō′hath was the father of Am′ram. 59 The name of Am′ram's wife was Joch′e•bed daughter of Levi, who was born to Levi in Egypt; and she bore to Am′ram: Aaron, Moses, and their sister Miriam. 60 To Aaron were born Nā′dab, A•bī′hū, El•ē•ā′zar, and Ith′a•mar. 61 But Nā′dab and A•bī′hū died when they offered

_m_ Heb clans of Naphtali

unholy fire before the LORD. 62 The number of those enrolled was twenty-three thousand, every male one month old and upward; for they were not enrolled among the Israelites because there was no allotment given to them among the Israelites.

63 These were those enrolled by Moses and El'·ē·ā'zar the priest, who enrolled the Israelites in the plains of Mō'ab by the Jordan opposite Jericho. 64 Among these there was not one of those enrolled by Moses and Aaron the priest, who had enrolled the Israelites in the wilderness of Sinai. 65 For the LORD had said of them, "They shall die in the wilderness." Not one of them was left, except Caleb son of Je·phūn'neh and Joshua son of Nun.

The Daughters of Zelophehad

27 Then the daughters of Ze·loph'e·had came forward. Ze·loph'e·had was son of Hē'pher son of Gil'e·ad son of Mā'chir son of Ma·nas'seh son of Joseph, a member of the Ma·nas'sīte clans. The names of his daughters were: Mah'lah, Noah, Hog'lah, Mil'cah, and Tir'zah. 2 They stood before Moses, El·ē·ā'zar the priest, the leaders, and all the congregation, at the entrance of the tent of meeting, and they said, 3 "Our father died in the wilderness; he was not among the company of those who gathered themselves together against the LORD in the company of Kō'rah, but died for his own sin; and he had no sons. 4 Why should the name of our father be taken away from his clan because he had no son? Give to us a possession among our father's brothers."

5 Moses brought their case before the LORD. 6 And the LORD spoke to Moses, saying: 7 The daughters of Ze·loph'e·had are right in what they are saying; you shall indeed let them possess an inheritance among their father's brothers and pass the inheritance of their father on to them. 8 You shall also say to the Israelites, "If a man dies, and has no son, then you shall pass his inheritance on to his daughter. 9 If he has no daughter, then you shall give his inheritance to his brothers. 10 If he has no brothers, then you shall give his inheritance to his father's brothers. 11 And if his father has no brothers, then you shall give his inheritance to the nearest kinsman of his clan, and he shall possess it. It shall be for the Israelites a statute and ordinance, as the LORD commanded Moses."

Joshua Appointed Moses' Successor
(Deut 31.1–8)

12 The LORD said to Moses, "Go up this mountain of the Ab'a·rim range, and see the land that I have given to the Israelites. 13 When you have seen it, you also shall be gathered to your people, as your brother Aaron was, 14 because you rebelled against my word in the wilderness of Zin when the congre-

gation quarreled with me.[n] You did not show my holiness before their eyes at the waters." (These are the waters of Mer'i·bath-kā'desh in the wilderness of Zin.) 15 Moses spoke to the LORD, saying, 16 "Let the LORD, the God of the spirits of all flesh, appoint someone over the congregation 17 who shall go out before them and come in before them, who shall lead them out and bring them in, so that the congregation of the LORD may not be like sheep without a shepherd." 18 So the LORD said to Moses, "Take Joshua son of Nun, a man in whom is the spirit, and lay your hand upon him; 19 have him stand before El·ē·ā'zar the priest and all the congregation, and commission him in their sight. 20 You shall give him some of your authority, so that all the congregation of the Israelites may obey. 21 But he shall stand before El·ē·ā'zar the priest, who shall inquire for him by the decision of the Ū'rim before the LORD; at his word they shall go out and at his word they shall come in, both he and all the Israelites with him, the whole congregation." 22 So Moses did as the LORD commanded him. He took Joshua and had him stand before El·ē·ā'zar the priest and the whole congregation; 23 he laid his hands on him and commissioned him—as the LORD had directed through Moses.

Daily Offerings
(Ex 29.38–46)

28 The LORD spoke to Moses, saying: 2 Command the Israelites, and say to them: My offering, the food for my offerings by fire, my pleasing odor, you shall take care to offer to me at its appointed time. 3 And you shall say to them, This is the offering by fire that you shall offer to the LORD: two male lambs a year old without blemish, daily, as a regular offering. 4 One lamb you shall offer in the morning, and the other lamb you shall offer at twilight;[o] 5 also one-tenth of an ephah of choice flour for a grain offering, mixed with one-fourth of a hin of beaten oil. 6 It is a regular burnt offering, ordained at Mount Sinai for a pleasing odor, an offering by fire to the LORD. 7 Its drink offering shall be one-fourth of a hin for each lamb; in the sanctuary you shall pour out a drink offering of strong drink to the LORD. 8 The other lamb you shall offer at twilight[o] with a grain offering and a drink offering like the one in the morning; you shall offer it as an offering by fire, a pleasing odor to the LORD.

Sabbath Offerings

9 On the sabbath day: two male lambs a year old without blemish, and two-tenths of an ephah of choice flour for a grain offering, mixed with oil,

---

[n] Heb lacks *with me*   [o] Heb *between the two evenings*

and its drink offering— 10 this is the burnt offering for every sabbath, in addition to the regular burnt offering and its drink offering.

Monthly Offerings

11 At the beginnings of your months you shall offer a burnt offering to the LORD: two young bulls, one ram, seven male lambs a year old without blemish; 12 also three-tenths of an ephah of choice flour for a grain offering, mixed with oil, for each bull; and two-tenths of choice flour for a grain offering, mixed with oil, for the one ram; 13 and one-tenth of choice flour mixed with oil as a grain offering for every lamb—a burnt offering of pleasing odor, an offering by fire to the LORD. 14 Their drink offerings shall be half a hin of wine for a bull, one-third of a hin for a ram, and one-fourth of a hin for a lamb. This is the burnt offering of every month throughout the months of the year. 15 And there shall be one male goat for a sin offering to the LORD; it shall be offered in addition to the regular burnt offering and its drink offering.

Offerings at Passover
(Lev 23.5–14)

16 On the fourteenth day of the first month there shall be a passover offering to the LORD. 17 And on the fifteenth day of this month is a festival; seven days shall unleavened bread be eaten. 18 On the first day there shall be a holy convocation. You shall not work at your occupations. 19 You shall offer an offering by fire, a burnt offering to the LORD: two young bulls, one ram, and seven male lambs a year old; see that they are without blemish. 20 Their grain offering shall be of choice flour mixed with oil: three-tenths of an ephah shall you offer for a bull, and two-tenths for a ram; 21 one-tenth shall you offer for each of the seven lambs; 22 also one male goat for a sin offering, to make atonement for you. 23 You shall offer these in addition to the burnt offering of the morning, which belongs to the regular burnt offering. 24 In the same way you shall offer daily, for seven days, the food of an offering by fire, a pleasing odor to the LORD; it shall be offered in addition to the regular burnt offering and its drink offering. 25 And on the seventh day you shall have a holy convocation; you shall not work at your occupations.

Offerings at the Festival of Weeks
(Lev 23.15–22)

26 On the day of the first fruits, when you offer a grain offering of new grain to the LORD at your festival of weeks, you shall have a holy convocation; you shall not work at your occupations. 27 You shall offer a burnt offering, a pleasing odor to the LORD: two young bulls, one ram, seven male lambs

a year old. 28 Their grain offering shall be of choice flour mixed with oil, three-tenths of an ephah for each bull, two-tenths for one ram, 29 one-tenth for each of the seven lambs; 30 with one male goat, to make atonement for you. 31 In addition to the regular burnt offering with its grain offering, you shall offer them and their drink offering. They shall be without blemish.

Offerings at the Festival of Trumpets
(Lev 23.23–25)

29 On the first day of the seventh month you shall have a holy convocation; you shall not work at your occupations. It is a day for you to blow the trumpets, 2 and you shall offer a burnt offering, a pleasing odor to the LORD: one young bull, one ram, seven male lambs a year old without blemish. 3 Their grain offering shall be of choice flour mixed with oil, three-tenths of one ephah for the bull, two-tenths for the ram, 4 and one-tenth for each of the seven lambs; 5 with one male goat for a sin offering, to make atonement for you. 6 These are in addition to the burnt offering of the new moon and its grain offering, and the regular burnt offering and its grain offering, and their drink offerings, according to the ordinance for them, a pleasing odor, an offering by fire to the LORD.

Offerings on the Day of Atonement
(Lev 23.26–32)

7 On the tenth day of this seventh month you shall have a holy convocation, and deny yourselves;p you shall do no work. 8 You shall offer a burnt offering to the LORD, a pleasing odor: one young bull, one ram, seven male lambs a year old. They shall be without blemish. 9 Their grain offering shall be of choice flour mixed with oil, three-tenths of an ephah for the bull, two-tenths for the one ram, 10 one-tenth for each of the seven lambs; 11 with one male goat for a sin offering, in addition to the sin offering of atonement, and the regular burnt offering and its grain offering, and their drink offerings.

Offerings at the Festival of Booths
(Lev 23.33–44)

12 On the fifteenth day of the seventh month you shall have a holy convocation; you shall not work at your occupations. You shall celebrate a festival to the LORD seven days. 13 You shall offer a burnt offering, an offering by fire, a pleasing odor to the LORD: thirteen young bulls, two rams, fourteen male lambs a year old. They shall be without

---

p Or and fast

did you KNOW?

Other Jewish Feasts

In chapter 29 of Numbers, we find the instructions for two more Jewish festivals. (For other Jewish festivals, see Ex 34.18–26.) The *feast of Trumpets* is a fall celebration prescribed for "the first day of the seventh month" (Num 29.1). This day of rest, marked by trumpet blasts and sacrifices, came to be called Rosh Hashanah (head of the year), the beginning of the Jewish New Year.

On the tenth day of the seventh month, the Israelites celebrated the Day of Atonement (Yom Kippur). On this solemn day of penance and fasting, the high priest laid the sins of the people on a so-called scapegoat (see Lev 16.20–21), then ran the beast into the wilderness, thus symbolically purifying the nation.

▸ **Num 29.1–11**

one male goat for a sin offering, in addition to the regular burnt offering, its grain offering and its drink offering.

26 On the fifth day: nine bulls, two rams, fourteen male lambs a year old without blemish, 27 with the grain offering and the drink offerings for the bulls, for the rams, and for the lambs, as prescribed in accordance with their number; 28 also one male goat for a sin offering, in addition to the regular burnt offering and its grain offering and its drink offering.

29 On the sixth day: eight bulls, two rams, fourteen male lambs a year old without blemish, 30 with the grain offering and the drink offerings for the bulls, for the rams, and for the lambs, as prescribed in accordance with their number; 31 also one male goat for a sin offering, in addition to the regular burnt offering, its grain offering, and its drink offerings.

32 On the seventh day: seven bulls, two rams, fourteen male lambs a year old without blemish, 33 with the grain offering and the drink offerings for the bulls, for the rams, and for the lambs, as prescribed in accordance with their number; 34 also one male goat for a sin offering, besides the regular burnt offering, its grain offering, and its drink offering.

35 On the eighth day you shall have a solemn assembly; you shall not work at your occupations. 36 You shall offer a burnt offering, an offering by fire, a pleasing odor to the LORD: one bull, one ram, seven male lambs a year old without blemish, 37 and the grain offering and the drink offerings for the bull, for the ram, and for the lambs, as prescribed in accordance with their number; 38 also one male goat for a sin offering, in addition to the regular burnt offering and its grain offering and its drink offering.

39 These you shall offer to the LORD at your appointed festivals, in addition to your votive offerings and your freewill offerings, as your burnt offerings, your grain offerings, your drink offerings, and your offerings of well-being.

40*q* So Moses told the Israelites everything just as the LORD had commanded Moses.

blemish. 14 Their grain offering shall be of choice flour mixed with oil, three-tenths of an ephah for each of the thirteen bulls, two-tenths for each of the two rams, 15 and one-tenth for each of the fourteen lambs; 16 also one male goat for a sin offering, in addition to the regular burnt offering, its grain offering and its drink offering.

17 On the second day: twelve young bulls, two rams, fourteen male lambs a year old without blemish, 18 with the grain offering and the drink offerings for the bulls, for the rams, and for the lambs, as prescribed in accordance with their number; 19 also one male goat for a sin offering, in addition to the regular burnt offering and its grain offering, and their drink offerings.

20 On the third day: eleven bulls, two rams, fourteen male lambs a year old without blemish, 21 with the grain offering and the drink offerings for the bulls, for the rams, and for the lambs, as prescribed in accordance with their number; 22 also one male goat for a sin offering, in addition to the regular burnt offering and its grain offering and its drink offering.

23 On the fourth day: ten bulls, two rams, fourteen male lambs a year old without blemish, 24 with the grain offering and the drink offerings for the bulls, for the rams, and for the lambs, as prescribed in accordance with their number; 25 also

Vows Made by Women

30

Then Moses said to the heads of the tribes of the Israelites: This is what the LORD has commanded. 2 When a man makes a vow to the LORD, or swears an oath to bind himself by a pledge, he shall not break his word; he shall do according to all that proceeds out of his mouth.

3 When a woman makes a vow to the LORD, or binds herself by a pledge, while within her father's

q Ch 30.1 in Heb

did you KNOW?

Making a Vow

Vow.

Such a simple word, really. Three letters. One syllable. But its simplicity masks its meaning. If a word's length were directly related to its significance, *vow* would have to become a long word indeed. It is a heavy word, one that we use sparingly. We tend to associate it with marriage or the life commitment of priests and religious sisters and brothers. Vows can be public or private, solemn or simple.

From a faith perspective, a person making a vow is making a deep, binding promise before God. A vow cannot really be captured on paper. A vow must be lived out. It must be internalized. It is the foundation for a life choice. We know, deep in our heart, that God is part of our vows.

The Israelites also took vows seriously. Numbers, chapter 30, is devoted to laws about vows. The laws were sexist by our standards. For example, a father or a husband could veto a woman's vows. Such laws were deemed acceptable in the Israelites' patriarchal society, but they are not in ours.

▸ **Num 30.2–5**

house, in her youth, 4 and her father hears of her vow or her pledge by which she has bound herself, and says nothing to her; then all her vows shall stand, and any pledge by which she has bound herself shall stand. 5 But if her father expresses disapproval to her at the time that he hears of it, no vow of hers, and no pledge by which she has bound herself, shall stand; and the LORD will forgive her, because her father had expressed to her his disapproval.

6 If she marries, while obligated by her vows or any thoughtless utterance of her lips by which she has bound herself, 7 and her husband hears of it and says nothing to her at the time that he hears, then her vows shall stand, and her pledges by which she has bound herself shall stand. 8 But if, at the time that her husband hears of it, he expresses disapproval to her, then he shall nullify

the vow by which she was obligated, or the thoughtless utterance of her lips, by which she bound herself; and the LORD will forgive her. 9 (But every vow of a widow or of a divorced woman, by which she has bound herself, shall be binding upon her.) 10 And if she made a vow in her husband's house, or bound herself by a pledge with an oath, 11 and her husband heard it and said nothing to her, and did not express disapproval to her, then all her vows shall stand, and any pledge by which she bound herself shall stand. 12 But if her husband nullifies them at the time that he hears them, then whatever proceeds out of her lips concerning her vows, or concerning her pledge of herself, shall not stand. Her husband has nullified them, and the LORD will forgive her. 13 Any vow or any binding oath to deny herself,*r* her husband may allow to stand, or her husband may nullify. 14 But if her husband says nothing to her from day to day,*s* then he validates all her vows, or all her pledges, by which she is obligated; he has validated them, because he said nothing to her at the time that he heard of them. 15 But if he nullifies them some time after he has heard of them, then he shall bear her guilt.

16 These are the statutes that the LORD commanded Moses concerning a husband and his wife, and a father and his daughter while she is still young and in her father's house.

War against Midian

31 The LORD spoke to Moses, saying, 2 "Avenge the Israelites on the Mid·i·an·ites; afterward you shall be gathered to your people." 3 So Moses said to the people, "Arm some of your number for the war, so that they may go against Mid'i·an, to execute the LORD's vengeance on Mid'i·an. 4 You shall send a thousand from each of the tribes of Israel to the war." 5 So out of the thousands of Israel, a thousand from each tribe were conscripted, twelve thousand armed for battle. 6 Moses sent them to the war, a thousand from each tribe, along with Phin'e·has son of El·e·a'zar the priest,*t* with the vessels of the sanctuary and the trumpets for sounding the alarm in his hand. 7 They did battle against Mid'i·an, as the LORD had commanded Moses, and killed every male. 8 They killed the kings of Mid'i·an: E'vi, Re'kem, Zur, Hur, and Re'ba, the five kings of Mid'i·an, in addition to others who were slain by them; and they also killed Ba'laam son of Be'or with the sword. 9 The Israelites took the women of Mid'i·an and their little ones captive; and they took all their cattle, their flocks, and

---

r Or *to fast* *s* Or *from that day to the next* *t* Gk: Heb adds *to the war* all their goods as booty. 10 All their towns where they had settled, and all their encampments, they burned, 11 but they took all the spoil and all the booty, both people and animals. 12 Then they brought the captives and the booty and the spoil to Moses, to El•ē•ā′zar the priest, and to the congregation of the Israelites, at the camp on the plains of Mō′ab by the Jordan at Jericho.

Return from the War

13 Moses, El•ē•ā′zar the priest, and all the leaders of the congregation went to meet them outside the camp. 14 Moses became angry with the officers of the army, the commanders of thousands and the commanders of hundreds, who had come from service in the war. 15 Moses said to them, "Have you allowed all the women to live? 16 These women here, on Bā′laam's advice, made the Israelites act treacherously against the LORD in the affair of Pē′or, so that the plague came among the congregation of the LORD. 17 Now therefore, kill every male among the little ones, and kill every woman who has known a man by sleeping with him. 18 But all the young girls who have not known a man by sleeping with him, keep alive for yourselves. 19 Camp outside the camp seven days; whoever of you has killed any person or touched a corpse, purify yourselves and your captives on the third and on the seventh day. 20 You shall purify every garment, every article of skin, everything made of goats' hair, and every article of wood."

21 El•ē•ā′zar the priest said to the troops who had gone to battle: "This is the statute of the law that the LORD has commanded Moses: 22 gold, silver, bronze, iron, tin, and lead— 23 everything that can withstand fire, shall be passed through fire, and it shall be clean. Nevertheless it shall also be purified with the water for purification; and whatever cannot withstand fire, shall be passed through the water. 24 You must wash your clothes on the seventh day, and you shall be clean; afterward you may come into the camp."

Disposition of Captives and Booty

25 The LORD spoke to Moses, saying, 26 "You and El•ē•ā′zar the priest and the heads of the ancestral houses of the congregation make an inventory of the booty captured, both human and animal. 27 Divide the booty into two parts, between the warriors who went out to battle and all the congregation. 28 From the share of the warriors who went out to battle, set aside as tribute for the LORD, one item out of every five hundred, whether persons, oxen, donkeys, sheep, or goats. 29 Take it from their half and give it to El•ē•ā′zar the priest as an offering to the LORD. 30 But from the Israelites' half you shall take one out of every fifty, whether persons, oxen, donkeys, sheep, or goats—all the animals—and give them to the Lē′vites who have charge of the tabernacle of the LORD."

31 Then Moses and El•ē•ā′zar the priest did as the LORD had commanded Moses:

32 The booty remaining from the spoil that the troops had taken totaled six hundred seventy-five thousand sheep, 33 seventy-two thousand oxen, 34 sixty-one thousand donkeys, 35 and thirty-two thousand persons in all, women who had not known a man by sleeping with him.

36 The half-share, the portion of those who had gone out to war, was in number three hundred thirty-seven thousand five hundred sheep and goats, 37 and the LORD's tribute of sheep and goats was six hundred seventy-five. 38 The oxen were thirty-six thousand, of which the LORD's tribute was seventy-two. 39 The donkeys were thirty thousand five hundred, of which the LORD's tribute was sixty-one. 40 The persons were sixteen thousand, of which the LORD's tribute was thirty-two persons. 41 Moses gave the tribute, the offering for the LORD, to El•ē•ā′zar the priest, as the LORD had commanded Moses.

42 As for the Israelites' half, which Moses separated from that of the troops, 43 the congregation's half was three hundred thirty-seven thousand five hundred sheep and goats, 44 thirty-six thousand oxen, 45 thirty thousand five hundred donkeys, 46 and sixteen thousand persons. 47 From the Israelites' half Moses took one of every fifty, both of persons and of animals, and gave them to the Lē′vites who had charge of the tabernacle of the LORD; as the LORD had commanded Moses.

48 Then the officers who were over the thousands of the army, the commanders of thousands and the commanders of hundreds, approached Moses, 49 and said to Moses, "Your servants have counted the warriors who are under our command, and not one of us is missing. 50 And we have brought the LORD's offering, what each of us found, articles of gold, armlets and bracelets, signet rings, earrings, and pendants, to make atonement for ourselves before the LORD." 51 Moses and El•ē•ā′zar the priest received the gold from them, all in the form of crafted articles. 52 And all the gold of the offering that they offered to the LORD, from the commanders of thousands and the commanders of hundreds, was sixteen thousand seven hundred fifty shekels. 53 (The troops had all taken plunder for themselves.) 54 So Moses and El•ē•ā′zar the priest received the gold from the commanders of thousands and of hundreds, and brought it into the tent of meeting as a memorial for the Israelites before the LORD.

Conquest and Division of Transjordan
(Deut 3.12–22)

32 Now the Reŭ′ben•ītes and the Gad′ītes owned a very great number of cattle. When they saw that the land of Jā′zer and the land of Gil′e•ad was a good place for cattle, 2 the Gad′ītes and the Reŭ′ben•ītes came and spoke to Moses, to El•ē•ā′zar the priest, and to the leaders of the congregation, saying, 3 "At′a•roth, Dī′bon, Jā′zer, Nim′rah, Hesh′bon, Ĕ•le•ā′leh, Sĕ′bam, Nĕ′bō, and Bĕ′on— 4 the land that the LORD subdued before the congregation of Israel—is a land for cattle; and your servants have cattle." 5 They continued, "If we have found favor in your sight, let this land be given to your servants for a possession; do not make us cross the Jordan."

6 But Moses said to the Gad′ītes and to the Reŭ′ben•ītes, "Shall your brothers go to war while you sit here? 7 Why will you discourage the hearts of the Israelites from going over into the land that the LORD has given them? 8 Your fathers did this, when I sent them from Kā′desh-bar′nē•a to see the land. 9 When they went up to the Wadi Esh′col and saw the land, they discouraged the hearts of the Israelites from going into the land that the LORD had given them. 10 The LORD′s anger was kindled on that day and he swore, saying, 11 'Surely none of the people who came up out of Egypt, from twenty years old and upward, shall see the land that I swore to give to Abraham, to Isaac, and to Jacob, because they have not unreservedly followed me— 12 none except Caleb son of Je•phŭn′neh the Ken′iz•zīte and Joshua son of Nun, for they have unreservedly followed the LORD.' 13 And the LORD′s anger was kindled against Israel, and he made them wander in the wilderness for forty years, until all the generation that had done evil in the sight of the LORD had disappeared. 14 And now you, a brood of sinners, have risen in place of your fathers, to increase the LORD′s fierce anger against Israel! 15 If you turn away from following him, he will again abandon them in the wilderness; and you will destroy all this people."

16 Then they came up to him and said, "We will build sheepfolds here for our flocks, and towns for our little ones, 17 but we will take up arms as a vanguard[u] before the Israelites, until we have brought them to their place. Meanwhile our little ones will stay in the fortified towns because of the inhabitants of the land. 18 We will not return to our homes until all the Israelites have obtained their inheritance. 19 We will not inherit with them on the other side of the Jordan and beyond, because our inheritance has come to us on this side of the Jordan to the east."

20 So Moses said to them, "If you do this—if you take up arms to go before the LORD for the war, 21 and all those of you who bear arms cross the Jordan before the LORD, until he has driven out his enemies from before him 22 and the land is subdued before the LORD—then after that you may return and be free of obligation to the LORD and to Israel, and this land shall be your possession before the LORD. 23 But if you do not do this, you have sinned against the LORD; and be sure your sin will find you out. 24 Build towns for your little ones, and folds for your flocks; but do what you have promised."

25 Then the Gad′ītes and the Reŭ′ben•ītes said to Moses, "Your servants will do as my lord commands. 26 Our little ones, our wives, our flocks, and all our livestock shall remain there in the towns of Gil′e•ad; 27 but your servants will cross over, everyone armed for war, to do battle for the LORD, just as my lord orders."

28 So Moses gave command concerning them to El•ē•ā′zar the priest, to Joshua son of Nun, and to the heads of the ancestral houses of the Israelite tribes. 29 And Moses said to them, "If the Gad′ītes and the Reŭ′ben•ītes, everyone armed for battle before the LORD, will cross over the Jordan with you and the land shall be subdued before you, then you shall give them the land of Gil′e•ad for a possession; 30 but if they will not cross over with you armed, they shall have possessions among you in the land of Cā′naan." 31 The Gad′ītes and the Reŭ′ben•ītes answered, "As the LORD has spoken to your servants, so we will do. 32 We will cross over armed before the LORD into the land of Cā′naan, but the possession of our inheritance shall remain with us on this side of[v] the Jordan."

33 Moses gave to them—to the Gad′ītes and to the Reŭ′ben•ītes and to the half-tribe of Ma•nas′seh son of Joseph—the kingdom of King Sī′hon of the Am′o•rītes and the kingdom of King Og of Bā′shan, the land and its towns, with the territories of the surrounding towns. 34 And the Gad′ītes rebuilt Dī′bon, At′a•roth, A•rō′er, 35 At′roth-shō′phan, Jā′zer, Jog′be•hah, 36 Beth-nim′rah, and Beth-har′an, fortified cities, and folds for sheep. 37 And the Reŭ′ben•ītes rebuilt Hesh′bon, Ĕ•le•ā′leh, Kir•i•a•thā′im, 38 Nĕ′bō, and Bā′al-mē′on (some names being changed), and Sib′mah; and they gave names to the towns that they rebuilt. 39 The descendants of Mā′chir son of Ma•nas′seh went to Gil′e•ad, captured it, and dispossessed the Am′o•rītes who were there; 40 so Moses gave Gil′e•ad to Mā′chir son of Ma•nas′seh, and he settled there. 41 Jā′ir son of Ma•nas′seh went and captured their villages, and renamed them Hav′voth-jā′ir.[w] 42 And Nō′bah went and captured Kĕ′nath and its villages, and renamed it Nō′bah after himself.

---

u Cn: Heb *hurrying*   v Heb *beyond*   w That is *the villages of Jair*

The Stages of Israel's Journey from Egypt

33 These are the stages by which the Israelites went out of the land of Egypt in military formation under the leadership of Moses and Aaron. 2 Moses wrote down their starting points, stage by stage, by command of the LORD; and these are their stages according to their starting places. 3 They set out from Ram'e•sēs in the first month, on the fifteenth day of the first month; on the day after the passover the Israelites went out boldly in the sight of all the Egyptians, 4 while the Egyptians were burying all their first-born, whom the LORD had struck down among them. The LORD executed judgments even against their gods.

5 So the Israelites set out from Ram'e•sēs, and camped at Suc'coth. 6 They set out from Suc'coth, and camped at Ē'tham, which is on the edge of the wilderness. 7 They set out from Ē'tham, and turned back to Pī-ha•hī'roth, which faces Bā'al-zē'phon; and they camped before Mig'dōl. 8 They set out from Pī-ha•hī'roth, passed through the sea into the wilderness, went a three days' journey in the wilderness of Ē'tham, and camped at Mar'ah. 9 They set out from Mar'ah and came to Ē'lim; at Ē'lim there were twelve springs of water and seventy palm trees, and they camped there. 10 They set out from Ē'lim and camped by the Red Sea.*x* 11 They set out from the Red Sea*x* and camped in the wilderness of Sin. 12 They set out from the wilderness of Sin and camped at Doph'kah. 13 They set out from Doph'kah and camped at Ā'lush. 14 They set out from Ā'lush and camped at Reph'i•dim, where there was no water for the people to drink. 15 They set out from Reph'i•dim and camped in the wilderness of Sinai. 16 They set out from the wilderness of Sinai and camped at Kib'roth-hat•tā'a•vah. 17 They set out from Kib'roth-hat•tā'a•vah and camped at Ha•zē'roth. 18 They set out from Ha•zē'roth and camped at Rith'mah. 19 They set out from Rith'mah and camped at Rim'mon-per'ez. 20 They set out from Rim'mon-per'ez and camped at Lib'nah. 21 They set out from Lib'nah and camped at Ris'sah. 22 They set out from Ris'sah and camped at Kē•he•lā'thah. 23 They set out from Kē•he•lā'thah and camped at Mount Shē'pher. 24 They set out from Mount Shē'pher and camped at Ha•rā'dah. 25 They set out from Ha•rā'dah and camped at Mak•hē'loth. 26 They set out from Mak•hē'loth and camped at Tā'hath. 27 They set out from Tā'hath and camped at Tē'rah. 28 They set out from Tē'rah and camped at Mith'kah. 29 They set out from Mith'kah and camped at Hash•mō'nah. 30 They set out from Hash•mō'nah and camped at Mō•sē'roth. 31 They set out from Mō•sē'roth and camped at Ben'ē-jā'a•kan. 32 They set out from Ben'ē-jā'a•kan and camped at Hor-hag•gid'gad. 33 They set out from Hor-hag•gid'gad and camped at Jot'ba•thah. 34 They set out from Jot'ba•thah and camped at A•brō'nah. 35 They set out from A•brō'nah and camped at Ē'zi•on-gē'ber. 36 They set out from Ē'zi•on-gē'ber and camped in the wilderness of Zin (that is, Kā'desh). 37 They set out from Kā'desh and camped at Mount Hor, on the edge of the land of Ē'dom.

38 Aaron the priest went up Mount Hor at the command of the LORD and died there in the fortieth year after the Israelites had come out of the land of Egypt, on the first day of the fifth month. 39 Aaron was one hundred twenty-three years old when he died on Mount Hor.

40 The Cā'naan•ite, the king of Ar'ad, who lived in the Neg'eb in the land of Cā'naan, heard of the coming of the Israelites.

41 They set out from Mount Hor and camped at Zal•mō'nah. 42 They set out from Zal•mō'nah and camped at Pū'non. 43 They set out from Pū'non and camped at Ō'both. 44 They set out from Ō'both and camped at I'ye-ab'a•rim, in the territory of Mō'ab. 45 They set out from I'yim and camped at Dī'bon-gad. 46 They set out from Dī'bon-gad and camped at Al'mon-dib•la•thā'im. 47 They set out from Al'mon-dib•la•thā'im and camped in the mountains of Ab'a•rim, before Nē'bō. 48 They set out from the mountains of Ab'a•rim and camped in the plains of Mō'ab by the Jordan at Jericho; 49 they camped by the Jordan from Beth-jesh'i•moth as far as A'bel-shit'tim in the plains of Mō'ab.

Directions for the Conquest of Canaan

50 In the plains of Mō'ab by the Jordan at Jericho, the LORD spoke to Moses, saying: 51 Speak to the Israelites, and say to them: When you cross over the Jordan into the land of Cā'naan, 52 you shall drive out all the inhabitants of the land from before you, destroy all their figured stones, destroy all their cast images, and demolish all their high places. 53 You shall take possession of the land and settle in it, for I have given you the land to possess. 54 You shall apportion the land by lot according to your clans; to a large one you shall give a large inheritance, and to a small one you shall give a small inheritance; the inheritance shall belong to the person on whom the lot falls; according to your ancestral tribes you shall inherit. 55 But if you do not drive out the inhabitants of the land from before you, then those whom you let remain shall be as barbs in your eyes and thorns in your sides; they shall trouble you in the land where you are settling. 56 And I will do to you as I thought to do to them.

x Or *Sea of Reeds*

The Boundaries of the Land

34 The LORD spoke to Moses, saying: 2 Command the Israelites, and say to them: When you enter the land of Cā′naan (this is the land that shall fall to you for an inheritance, the land of Cā′naan, defined by its boundaries), 3 your south sector shall extend from the wilderness of Zin along the side of Ē′dom. Your southern boundary shall begin from the end of the Dead Sea*y* on the east; 4 your boundary shall turn south of the ascent of Ak•rab′bim, and cross to Zin, and its outer limit shall be south of Kā′desh-bar′nē•a; then it shall go on to Hā′zar-ad′dar, and cross to Az′mon; 5 the boundary shall turn from Az′mon to the Wadi of Egypt, and its termination shall be at the Sea.

6 For the western boundary, you shall have the Great Sea and its*z* coast; this shall be your western boundary.

7 This shall be your northern boundary: from the Great Sea you shall mark out your line to Mount Hor; 8 from Mount Hor you shall mark it out to Lē′bō-hā′math, and the outer limit of the boundary shall be at Zē′dad; 9 then the boundary shall extend to Ziph′ron, and its end shall be at Hā′zar-ē′nan; this shall be your northern boundary.

10 You shall mark out your eastern boundary from Hā′zar-ē′nan to Shē′pham; 11 and the boundary shall continue down from Shē′pham to Rib′lah on the east side of Ā′in; and the boundary shall go down, and reach the eastern slope of the sea of Chin′ne•reth; 12 and the boundary shall go down to the Jordan, and its end shall be at the Dead Sea.*y* This shall be your land with its boundaries all around.

13 Moses commanded the Israelites, saying: This is the land that you shall inherit by lot, which the LORD has commanded to give to the nine tribes and to the half-tribe; 14 for the tribe of the Reū′-ben•ites by their ancestral houses and the tribe of the Gad′ites by their ancestral houses have taken their inheritance, and also the half-tribe of Ma-nas′seh; 15 the two tribes and the half-tribe have taken their inheritance beyond the Jordan at Jericho eastward, toward the sunrise.

Tribal Leaders

16 The LORD spoke to Moses, saying: 17 These are the names of the men who shall apportion the land to you for inheritance: the priest El•ē•ā′zar and Joshua son of Nun. 18 You shall take one leader of every tribe to apportion the land for inheritance. 19 These are the names of the men: Of the tribe of Judah, Caleb son of Je•phūn′neh. 20 Of the tribe of the Sim′ē•on•ites, She•mū′el son of Am•mī′hud. 21 Of the tribe of Benjamin, Ē•li′dad son of Chis′-lon. 22 Of the tribe of the Dan′ites a leader, Buk′ki son of Jog′li. 23 Of the Jō′seph•ites: of the tribe of the Ma•nas′sites a leader, Han′ni•el son of Ē′phod,

24 and of the tribe of the Ē′phra•im•ites a leader, Kemū′el son of Shiph′tan. 25 Of the tribe of the Zeb′ū•lun•ites a leader, Ē′li-zā′phan son of Par′-nach. 26 Of the tribe of the Is′sa•char•ites a leader, Pal′ti•el son of Az′zan. 27 And of the tribe of the Ash′er•ites a leader, A•hi′hud son of She•lō′mi. 28 Of the tribe of the Naph′ta•lites a leader, Pe•dah′el son of Ammi′hud. 29 These were the ones whom the LORD commanded to apportion the inheritance for the Israelites in the land of Cā′naan.

Cities for the Levites

35 In the plains of Mō′ab by the Jordan at Jericho, the LORD spoke to Moses, saying: 2 Command the Israelites to give, from the inheritance that they possess, towns for the Lē′vites to live in; you shall also give to the Lē′vites pasture lands surrounding the towns. 3 The towns shall be theirs to live in, and their pasture lands shall be for their cattle, for their livestock, and for all their animals. 4 The pasture lands of the towns, which you shall give to the Lē′vites, shall reach from the wall of the town outward a thousand cubits all around. 5 You shall measure, outside the town, for the east side two thousand cubits, for the south side two thousand cubits, for the west side two thousand cubits, and for the north side two thousand cubits, with the town in the middle; this shall belong to them as pasture land for their towns.

6 The towns that you give to the Lē′vites shall include the six cities of refuge, where you shall permit a slayer to flee, and in addition to them you shall give forty-two towns. 7 The towns that you give to the Lē′vites shall total forty-eight, with their pasture lands. 8 And as for the towns that you shall give from the possession of the Israelites, from the larger tribes you shall take many, and from the smaller tribes you shall take few; each, in proportion to the inheritance that it obtains, shall give of its towns to the Lē′vites.

Cities of Refuge
(Deut 19.1–13; Josh 20.1–9)

9 The LORD spoke to Moses, saying: 10 Speak to the Israelites, and say to them: When you cross the Jordan into the land of Cā′naan, 11 then you shall select cities to be cities of refuge for you, so that a slayer who kills a person without intent may flee there. 12 The cities shall be for you a refuge from the avenger, so that the slayer may not die until there is a trial before the congregation.

13 The cities that you designate shall be six cities of refuge for you: 14 you shall designate three cities beyond the Jordan, and three cities in the land of Cā′naan, to be cities of refuge. 15 These six cities

---

y Heb *Salt Sea*   *z* Syr: Heb lacks *its*

shall serve as refuge for the Israelites, for the resident or transient alien among them, so that anyone who kills a person without intent may flee there.

Concerning Murder and Blood Revenge

16 But anyone who strikes another with an iron object, and death ensues, is a murderer; the murderer shall be put to death. 17 Or anyone who strikes another with a stone in hand that could cause death, and death ensues, is a murderer; the murderer shall be put to death. 18 Or anyone who strikes another with a weapon of wood in hand that could cause death, and death ensues, is a murderer; the murderer shall be put to death. 19 The avenger of blood is the one who shall put the murderer to death; when they meet, the avenger of blood shall execute the sentence. 20 Likewise, if someone pushes another from hatred, or hurls something at another, lying in wait, and death ensues, 21 or in enmity strikes another with the hand, and death ensues, then the one who struck the blow shall be put to death; that person is a murderer; the avenger of blood shall put the murderer to death, when they meet.

22 But if someone pushes another suddenly without enmity, or hurls any object without lying in wait, 23 or, while handling any stone that could cause death, unintentionally*a* drops it on another and death ensues, though they were not enemies, and no harm was intended, 24 then the congregation shall judge between the slayer and the avenger of blood, in accordance with these ordinances; 25 and the congregation shall rescue the slayer from the avenger of blood. Then the congregation shall send the slayer back to the original city of refuge. The slayer shall live in it until the death of the high priest who was anointed with the holy oil. 26 But if the slayer shall at any time go outside the bounds of the original city of refuge, 27 and is found by the avenger of blood outside the bounds of the city of refuge, and is killed by the avenger, no bloodguilt shall be incurred. 28 For the slayer must remain in the city of refuge until the death of the high priest; but after the death of the high priest the slayer may return home.

29 These things shall be a statute and ordinance for you throughout your generations wherever you live.

30 If anyone kills another, the murderer shall be put to death on the evidence of witnesses; but no one shall be put to death on the testimony of a single witness. 31 Moreover you shall accept no ransom for the life of a murderer who is subject to the death penalty; a murderer must be put to death. 32 Nor shall you accept ransom for one who has fled to a city of refuge, enabling the fugitive to return to live in the land before the death of the high priest. 33 You shall not pollute the land in which you live; for blood pollutes the land, and no expiation can be made for the land, for the blood that is shed in it, except by the blood of the one who shed it. 34 You shall not defile the land in which you live, in which I also dwell; for I the LORD dwell among the Israelites.

Marriage of Female Heirs

36 The heads of the ancestral houses of the clans of the descendants of Gil'e•ad son of Mā'chir son of Ma•nas'seh, of the Jō'seph•īte clans, came forward and spoke in the presence of Moses and the leaders, the heads of the ancestral houses of the Israelites; 2 they said, "The LORD commanded my lord to give the land for inheritance by lot to the Israelites; and my lord was commanded by the LORD to give the inheritance of our brother Ze•loph'e•had to his daughters. 3 But if they are married into another Israelite tribe, then their inheritance will be taken from the inheritance of our ancestors and added to the inheritance of the tribe into which they marry; so it will be taken away from the allotted portion of our inheritance. 4 And when the jubilee of the Israelites comes, then their inheritance will be added to the inheritance of the tribe into which they have married; and their inheritance will be taken from the inheritance of our ancestral tribe."

5 Then Moses commanded the Israelites according to the word of the LORD, saying, "The descendants of the tribe of Joseph are right in what they are saying. 6 This is what the LORD commands concerning the daughters of Ze•loph'e•had, 'Let them marry whom they think best; only it must be into a clan of their father's tribe that they are married, 7 so that no inheritance of the Israelites shall be transferred from one tribe to another; for all Israelites shall retain the inheritance of their ancestral tribes. 8 Every daughter who possesses an inheritance in any tribe of the Israelites shall marry one from the clan of her father's tribe, so that all Israelites may continue to possess their ancestral inheritance. 9 No inheritance shall be transferred from one tribe to another; for each of the tribes of the Israelites shall retain its own inheritance.' "

10 The daughters of Ze•loph'e•had did as the LORD had commanded Moses. 11 Mah'lah, Tir'zah, Hog'lah, Mil'cah, and Noah, the daughters of Ze•loph'e•had, married sons of their father's brothers. 12 They were married into the clans of the descendants of Ma•nas'seh son of Joseph, and their inheritance remained in the tribe of their father's clan.

13 These are the commandments and the ordinances that the LORD commanded through Moses to the Israelites in the plains of Mō'ab by the Jordan at Jericho.

a Heb without seeing

The Book of Deuteronomy

I magine this touching scene: You are standing at the bedside of your aging grandparent with all your cousins and family members. Your grandfather or grandmother begins to speak, sharing stories about the lessons he or she has learned from life. You listen to the familiar stories as if for the first time, and you are awed by the wisdom and love they contain. This is the scene Deuteronomy sets up—Moses is like the wise, aging grandparent, sharing his instructions and encouragement before dying.

At a Glance

- **1.1—4.43.** Moses reviews Israel's history.
- **4.44—11.32.** Moses proclaims obedience to the Torah.
- **Chapters 12–26.** Moses adapts the Covenant for settlement in the Land.
- **Chapters 27–34.** Moses gives a farewell address and dies.

In-depth

The word Deuteronomy means "second law" in Greek. The first Law given on Mount Sinai was proposed by God to guide Israel in its wilderness journey. Written at a time when Israel was settled in the Promised Land and in need of religious reformation, Deuteronomy is a "second Law," adapted to the new situation of a people that needs to be reminded of its Covenant with God.

Deuteronomy has four sections:

- In the first section (1.1—4.43), Moses addresses Israel by reviewing its history since Mount Horeb (Deuteronomy's term for Mount Sinai). Moses calls Israel to faithfulness and loyalty.
- In the second section (4.44—11.32), Moses reviews the Ten Commandments and the essence of the Law. He reminds the Israelites of the rewards for obeying and the consequences of disobeying the Law.
- In the third section (chapters 12–26), the most important section of Deuteronomy, Moses spells out a law to shape and govern the Israelites' new life as they settle in the Land.
- Finally, in the fourth section (chapters 27–34), Moses gives his last will and testament, offers a final blessing, and dies. His death is portrayed as the "sealing" of the second Law.

More than anything else, Deuteronomy stresses Israel as one people, with one God, one sanctuary, and now one Land. These elements not only make Israel a unique people but also bind it together in unity and solidarity. The Land of Promise now becomes a symbol of God's blessing and favor, the fulfillment of God's promises in the Covenant.

Quick Facts

Period Covered
just before the Israelites enter the Promised Land

Authors
scribes from the eighth century B.C. adapting the earlier Covenant Law to Israel's changing situation

Theme
the importance of the Covenant, the total commitment required by God's law

Deuteronomy

1.1

Events at Horeb Recalled

1 These are the words that Moses spoke to all Israel beyond the Jordan—in the wilderness, on the plain opposite Sūph, between Par'an and Tō'phel, Lā'ban, Ha•zē'roth, and Di-za•hab'. 2 (By the way of Mount Sē'ir it takes eleven days to reach Kā'desh-bar'nē•a from Hō'reb.) 3 In the fortieth year, on the first day of the eleventh month, Moses spoke to the Israelites just as the LORD had commanded him to speak to them. 4 This was after he had defeated King Sī'hon of the Am'o•rites, who reigned in Hesh'bon, and King Og of Bā'shan, who reigned in Ash'ta•roth and*a* in Ed'rē•ī. 5 Beyond the Jordan in the land of Mō'ab, Moses undertook to expound this law as follows:

6 The LORD our God spoke to us at Hō'reb, saying, "You have stayed long enough at this mountain. 7 Resume your journey, and go into the hill country of the Am'o•rites as well as into the neighboring regions—the Ar'a•bah, the hill country, the She•phē'lah, the Neg'eb, and the seacoast—the land of the Cā'naan•ītes and the Lebanon, as far as the great river, the river Euphrates. 8 See, I have set the land before you; go in and take possession of the land that I*b* swore to your ancestors, to Abraham, to Isaac, and to Jacob, to give to them and to their descendants after them."

Appointment of Tribal Leaders
(Ex 18.13–27)

9 At that time I said to you, "I am unable by myself to bear you. 10 The LORD your God has multiplied you, so that today you are as numerous as the stars of heaven. 11 May the LORD, the God of your ancestors, increase you a thousand times more and bless you, as he has promised you! 12 But how can I bear the heavy burden of your disputes all by myself? 13 Choose for each of your tribes individuals who are wise, discerning, and reputable to be your leaders." 14 You answered me, "The plan you have proposed is a good one." 15 So I took the leaders of your tribes, wise and reputable individuals, and installed them as leaders over you, commanders of thousands, commanders of hundreds, commanders of fifties, commanders of tens, and officials, throughout your tribes. 16 I charged your judges at that time: "Give the members of your community a fair hearing, and judge rightly between one person and another, whether citizen or resident alien. 17 You must not be partial in judging: hear out the small and the great alike; you shall not be intimidated

---

a Gk Syr Vg Compare Josh 12.4: Heb lacks *and*   *b* Sam Gk: MT *the* LORD by anyone, for the judgment is God's. Any case that is too hard for you, bring to me, and I will hear it." 18 So I charged you at that time with all the things that you should do.

Israel's Refusal to Enter the Land
(Num 13.1–33)

19 Then, just as the LORD our God had ordered us, we set out from Hŏ′reb and went through all that great and terrible wilderness that you saw, on the way to the hill country of the Am′o•rītes, until we reached Kā′desh-bar′nē•a. 20 I said to you, "You have reached the hill country of the Am′o•rītes, which the LORD our God is giving us. 21 See, the LORD your God has given the land to you; go up, take possession, as the LORD, the God of your ancestors, has promised you; do not fear or be dismayed."

22 All of you came to me and said, "Let us send men ahead of us to explore the land for us and bring back a report to us regarding the route by which we should go up and the cities we will come to." 23 The plan seemed good to me, and I selected twelve of you, one from each tribe. 24 They set out and went up into the hill country, and when they reached the Valley of Esh′col they spied it out 25 and gathered some of the land's produce, which they brought down to us. They brought back a report to us, and said, "It is a good land that the LORD our God is giving us."

26 But you were unwilling to go up. You rebelled against the command of the LORD your God; 27 you grumbled in your tents and said, "It is because the LORD hates us that he has brought us out of the land of Egypt, to hand us over to the Am′o•rītes to destroy us. 28 Where are we headed? Our kindred have made our hearts melt by reporting, 'The people are stronger and taller than we; the cities are large and fortified up to heaven! We actually saw there the offspring of the An′a•kim!' " 29 I said to you, "Have no dread or fear of them. 30 The LORD your God, who goes before you, is the one who will fight for you, just as he did for you in Egypt before your very eyes, 31 and in the wilderness, where you saw how the LORD your God carried you, just as one carries a child, all the way that you traveled until you reached this place. 32 But in spite of this, you have no trust in the LORD your God, 33 who goes before you on the way to seek out a place for you to camp, in fire by night, and in the cloud by day, to show you the route you should take."

The Penalty for Israel's Rebellion
(Num 14.20–45)

34 When the LORD heard your words, he was wrathful and swore: 35 "Not one of these—not one

of this evil generation—shall see the good land that I swore to give to your ancestors, 36 except Caleb son of Je•phŭn′neh. He shall see it, and to him and to his descendants I will give the land on which he set foot, because of his complete fidelity to the LORD." 37 Even with me the LORD was angry on your account, saying, "You also shall not enter there. 38 Joshua son of Nun, your assistant, shall enter there; encourage him, for he is the one who will secure Israel's possession of it. 39 And as for your little ones, who you thought would become booty, your children, who today do not yet know right from wrong, they shall enter there; to them I will give it, and they shall take possession of it. 40 But as for you, journey back into the wilderness, in the direction of the Red Sea."c

41 You answered me, "We have sinned against the LORD! We are ready to go up and fight, just as the LORD our God commanded us." So all of you strapped on your battle gear, and thought it easy to go up into the hill country. 42 The LORD said to me, "Say to them, 'Do not go up and do not fight, for I am not in the midst of you; otherwise you will be defeated by your enemies.' " 43 Although I told you, you would not listen. You rebelled against the command of the LORD and presumptuously went up into the hill country. 44 The Am′o•rītes who lived in that hill country then came out against you and chased you as bees do. They beat you down in Sē′ir as far as Hor′mah. 45 When you returned and wept before the LORD, the LORD would neither heed your voice nor pay you any attention.

The Desert Years

46 After you had stayed at Kā′desh as many days as you did, 1 we journeyed back into the wilderness, in the direction of the Red Sea,c as the LORD had told me and skirted Mount Sē′ir for many days. 2 Then the LORD said to me: 3 "You have been skirting this hill country long enough. Head north, 4 and charge the people as follows: You are about to pass through the territory of your kindred, the descendants of Esau, who live in Sē′ir. They will be afraid of you, so, be very careful 5 not to engage in battle with them, for I will not give you even so much as a foot's length of their land, since I have given Mount Sē′ir to Esau as a possession. 6 You shall purchase food from them for money, so that you may eat; and you shall also buy water from them for money, so that you may drink. 7 Surely the LORD your God has blessed you in all your undertakings; he knows your going through this great wilderness. These forty years the LORD your God has been with you; you have

---

c Or *Sea of Reeds*

DEUT

lacked nothing." 8 So we passed by our kin, the descendants of Esau who live in Sē'ir, leaving behind the route of the Ar'a•bah, and leaving behind Ē'lath and Ē'zi•on-gē'ber.

When we had headed out along the route of the wilderness of Mō'ab, 9 the LORD said to me: "Do not harass Mō'ab or engage them in battle, for I will not give you any of its land as a possession, since I have given Ar as a possession to the descendants of Lot." 10 (The Ē'mim—a large and numerous people, as tall as the An'a•kim—had formerly inhabited it. 11 Like the An'a•kim, they are usually reckoned as Reph'a•im, though the Mō'ab•ītes call them Ē'mim. 12 Moreover, the Hō'rim had formerly inhabited Sē'ir, but the descendants of Esau dispossessed them, destroying them and settling in their place, as Israel has done in the land that the LORD gave them as a possession.) 13 "Now then, proceed to cross over the Wadi Zē'red."

So we crossed over the Wadi Zē'red. 14 And the length of time we had traveled from Kā'desh-bar'nē•a until we crossed the Wadi Zē'red was thirty-eight years, until the entire generation of warriors had perished from the camp, as the LORD had sworn concerning them. 15 Indeed, the LORD's own hand was against them, to root them out from the camp, until all had perished.

16 Just as soon as all the warriors had died off from among the people, 17 the LORD spoke to me, saying, 18 "Today you are going to cross the boundary of Mō'ab at Ar. 19 When you approach the frontier of the Am'mon•ītes, do not harass them or engage them in battle, for I will not give the land of the Am'mon•ītes to you as a possession, because I have given it to the descendants of Lot." 20 (It also is usually reckoned as a land of Reph'a•im. Reph'a•im formerly inhabited it, though the Am'mon•ītes call them Zam•zum'-mim, 21 a strong and numerous people, as tall as the An'a•kim. But the LORD destroyed them from before the Am'mon•ītes so that they could dispossess them and settle in their place. 22 He did the same for the descendants of Esau, who live in Sē'ir, by destroying the Hō'rim before them so that they could dispossess them and settle in their place even to this day. 23 As for the Av'vim, who had lived in settlements in the vicinity of Gā'za, the Caph'to•rim, who came from Caph'tor, destroyed them and settled in their place.) 24 "Proceed on your journey and cross the Wadi Ar'non. See, I have handed over to you King Sī'hon the Am'o•rīte of Hesh'bon, and his land. Begin to take possession by engaging him in battle. 25 This day I will begin to put the dread and fear of you upon the peoples everywhere under heaven; when they hear report of you, they will tremble and be in anguish because of you."

Defeat of King Sihon
(Num 21.21–32)

26 So I sent messengers from the wilderness of Ked'e•moth to King Sī'hon of Hesh'bon with the following terms of peace: 27 "If you let me pass through your land, I will travel only along the road; I will turn aside neither to the right nor to the left. 28 You shall sell me food for money, so that I may eat, and supply me water for money, so that I may drink. Only allow me to pass through on foot— 29 just as the descendants of Esau who live in Sē'ir have done for me and likewise the Mō'ab•ītes who live in Ar—until I cross the Jordan into the land that the LORD our God is giving us." 30 But King Sī'hon of Hesh'bon was not willing to let us pass through, for the LORD your God had hardened his spirit and made his heart defiant in order to hand him over to you, as he has now done.

31 The LORD said to me, "See, I have begun to give Sī'hon and his land over to you. Begin now to take possession of his land." 32 So when Sī'hon came out against us, he and all his people for battle at Jā'haz, 33 the LORD our God gave him over to us; and we struck him down, along with his offspring and all his people. 34 At that time we captured all his towns, and in each town we utterly destroyed men, women, and children. We left not a single survivor. 35 Only the livestock we kept as spoil for ourselves, as well as the plunder of the towns that we had captured. 36 From A•rō'er on the edge of the Wadi Ar'non (including the town that is in the wadi itself) as far as Gil'e•ad, there was no citadel too high for us. The LORD our God gave everything to us. 37 You did not encroach, however, on the land of the Am'mon•ītes, avoiding the whole upper region of the Wadi Jab'bok as well as the towns of the hill country, just asd the LORD our God had charged.

Defeat of King Og
(Num 21.33–35)

3 When we headed up the road to Bā'shan, King Og of Bā'shan came out against us, he and all his people, for battle at Ed'rē•ī. 2 The LORD said to me, "Do not fear him, for I have handed him over to you, along with his people and his land. Do to him as you did to King Sī'hon of the Am'o•rītes, who reigned in Hesh'bon." 3 So the LORD our God also handed over to us King Og of Bā'shan and all his people. We struck him down until not a single survivor was left. 4 At that time we captured all his towns; there was no citadel that we did not take from them—sixty towns, the whole region of Ar'-gob, the kingdom of Og in Bā'shan. 5 All these were fortress towns with high walls, double gates, and

---

d Gk Tg: Heb *and all*

bars, besides a great many villages. 6 And we utterly destroyed them, as we had done to King Sī′hon of Hesh′bon, in each city utterly destroying men, women, and children. 7 But all the livestock and the plunder of the towns we kept as spoil for ourselves.

8 So at that time we took from the two kings of the Am′o•rītes the land beyond the Jordan, from the Wadi Ar′non to Mount Hermon 9 (the Sī•dō′ni•ans call Hermon Sir′i•on, while the Am′o•rītes call it Sē′nir), 10 all the towns of the tableland, the whole of Gil′e•ad, and all of Bā′shan, as far as Sal′e•cah and Ed′rē•ī, towns of Og′s kingdom in Bā′shan. 11 (Now only King Og of Bā′shan was left of the remnant of the Reph′a•im. In fact his bed, an iron bed, can still be seen in Rab′bah of the Am′mon•ītes. By the common cubit it is nine cubits long and four cubits wide.) 12 As for the land that we took possession of at that time, I gave to the Reū′ben•ītes and Gad′ītes the territory north of A•rō′er,*e* that is on the edge of the Wadi Ar′non, as well as half the hill country of Gil′e•ad with its towns, 13 and I gave to the half-tribe of Ma•nas′seh the rest of Gil′e•ad and all of Bā′shan, Og′s kingdom. (The whole region of Ar′gob: all that portion of Bā′shan used to be called a land of Reph′a•im; 14 Jā′ir the Ma•nas′sīte acquired the whole region of Ar′gob as far as the border of the Gesh′u•rītes and the Mā′a•ca•thītes, and he named them—that is, Bā′shan—after himself, Hav′voth-jā′ir,*f* as it is to this day.) 15 To Mā′chir I gave Gil′e•ad. 16 And to the Reū′ben•ītes and the Gad′ītes I gave the territory from Gil′e•ad as far as the Wadi Ar′non, with the middle of the wadi as a boundary, and up to the Jab′bok, the wadi being boundary of the Am′mon•ītes; 17 the Ar′a•bah also, with the Jordan and its banks, from Chin′ne•reth down to the sea of the Ar′a•bah, the Dead Sea,*g* with the lower slopes of Pis′gah on the east.

18 At that time, I charged you as follows: "Although the LORD your God has given you this land to occupy, all your troops shall cross over armed as the vanguard of your Israelite kin. 19 Only your wives, your children, and your livestock—I know that you have much livestock—shall stay behind in the towns that I have given to you. 20 When the LORD gives rest to your kindred, as to you, and they too have occupied the land that the LORD your God is giving them beyond the Jordan, then each of you may return to the property that I have given to you." 21 And I charged Joshua as well at that time, saying: "Your own eyes have seen everything that the LORD your God has done to these two kings; so the LORD will do to all the kingdoms into which you are about to cross. 22 Do not fear them, for it is the LORD your God who fights for you."

Moses Views Canaan from Pisgah

23 At that time, too, I entreated the LORD, saying: 24 "O Lord GOD, you have only begun to show your servant your greatness and your might; what god in heaven or on earth can perform deeds and mighty acts like yours! 25 Let me cross over to see the good land beyond the Jordan, that good hill country and the Lebanon." 26 But the LORD was angry with me on your account and would not heed me. The LORD said to me, "Enough from you! Never speak to me of this matter again! 27 Go up to the top of Pis′gah and look around you to the west, to the north, to the south, and to the east. Look well, for you shall not cross over this Jordan. 28 But charge Joshua, and encourage and strengthen him, because it is he who shall cross over at the head of this people and who shall secure their possession of the land that you will see." 29 So we remained in the valley opposite Beth-pē′or.

Moses Commands Obedience

4 So now, Israel, give heed to the statutes and ordinances that I am teaching you to observe, so that you may live to enter and occupy the land that the LORD, the God of your ancestors, is giving you. 2 You must neither add anything to what I command you nor take away anything from it, but keep the commandments of the LORD your God with which I am charging you. 3 You have seen for yourselves what the LORD did with regard to the Bā′al of Pē′or—how the LORD your God destroyed from among you everyone who followed the Bā′al of Pē′or, 4 while those of you who held fast to the LORD your God are all alive today.

5 See, just as the LORD my God has charged me, I now teach you statutes and ordinances for you to observe in the land that you are about to enter and occupy. 6 You must observe them diligently, for this will show your wisdom and discernment to the peoples, who, when they hear all these statutes, will say, "Surely this great nation is a wise and discerning people!" 7 For what other great nation has a god so near to it as the LORD our God is whenever we call to him? 8 And what other great nation has statutes and ordinances as just as this entire law that I am setting before you today?

9 But take care and watch yourselves closely, so as neither to forget the things that your eyes have seen nor to let them slip from your mind all the days of your life; make them known to your children and your children's children— 10 how you once stood before the LORD your God at Hō′reb, when the LORD said to me, "Assemble the people for me, and I will let them hear my words, so that

e Heb *territory from Aroer*   *f* That is *Settlement of Jair*
g Heb *Salt Sea*

they may learn to fear me as long as they live on the earth, and may teach their children so"; 11 you approached and stood at the foot of the mountain while the mountain was blazing up to the very heavens, shrouded in dark clouds. 12 Then the LORD spoke to you out of the fire. You heard the sound of words but saw no form; there was only a voice. 13 He declared to you his covenant, which he charged you to observe, that is, the ten commandments;[h] and he wrote them on two stone tablets. 14 And the LORD charged me at that time to teach you statutes and ordinances for you to observe in the land that you are about to cross into and occupy.

15 Since you saw no form when the LORD spoke to you at Hō'reb out of the fire, take care and watch yourselves closely, 16 so that you do not act corruptly by making an idol for yourselves, in the form of any figure—the likeness of male or female, 17 the likeness of any animal that is on the earth, the likeness of any winged bird that flies in the air, 18 the likeness of anything that creeps on the ground, the likeness of any fish that is in the water under the earth. 19 And when you look up to the heavens and see the sun, the moon, and the stars, all the host of heaven, do not be led astray and bow down to them and serve them, things that the LORD your God has allotted to all the peoples everywhere under heaven. 20 But the LORD has taken you and brought you out of the iron-smelter, out of Egypt, to become a people of his very own possession, as you are now.

21 The LORD was angry with me because of you, and he vowed that I should not cross the Jordan and that I should not enter the good land that the LORD your God is giving for your possession. 22 For I am going to die in this land without crossing over the Jordan, but you are going to cross over to take possession of that good land. 23 So be careful not to forget the covenant that the LORD your God made with you, and not to make for yourselves an idol in the form of anything that the LORD your God has forbidden you. 24 For the LORD your God is a devouring fire, a jealous God.

25 When you have had children and children's children, and become complacent in the land, if you act corruptly by making an idol in the form of anything, thus doing what is evil in the sight of the LORD your God, and provoking him to anger, 26 I call heaven and earth to witness against you today that you will soon utterly perish from the land that you are crossing the Jordan to occupy; you will not live long on it, but will be utterly destroyed. 27 The LORD will scatter you among the peoples; only a few of you will be left among the nations where the LORD will lead you. 28 There you will serve other gods made by human hands, objects of wood and stone that neither see, nor hear, nor eat, nor smell.

29 From there you will seek the LORD your God, and you will find him if you search after him with all your heart and soul. 30 In your distress, when all these things have happened to you in time to come, you will return to the LORD your God and heed him. 31 Because the LORD your God is a merciful God, he will neither abandon you nor destroy you; he will not forget the covenant with your ancestors that he swore to them.

32 For ask now about former ages, long before your own, ever since the day that God created human beings on the earth; ask from one end of heaven to the other: has anything so great as this ever happened or has its like ever been heard of? 33 Has any people ever heard the voice of a god speaking out of a fire, as you have heard, and lived? 34 Or has any god ever attempted to go and take a nation for himself from the midst of another nation, by trials, by signs and wonders, by war, by a mighty hand and an outstretched arm, and by terrifying displays of power, as the LORD your God did for you in Egypt before your very eyes? 35 To you it was shown so that you would acknowledge that the LORD is God; there is no other besides him. 36 From heaven he made you hear his voice to discipline you. On earth he showed you his great fire, while you heard his words coming out of the fire. 37 And because he loved your ancestors, he chose their descendants after them. He brought you out of Egypt with his own presence, by his great power, 38 driving out before you nations greater and mightier than yourselves, to bring you in, giving you their land for a possession, as it is still today. 39 So acknowledge today and take to heart that the LORD is God in heaven above and on the earth beneath; there is no other. 40 Keep his statutes and his commandments, which I am commanding you today for your own well-being and that of your descendants after you, so that you may long remain in the land that the LORD your God is giving you for all time.

Cities of Refuge East of the Jordan

41 Then Moses set apart on the east side of the Jordan three cities 42 to which a homicide could flee, someone who unintentionally kills another person, the two not having been at enmity before; the homicide could flee to one of these cities and live: 43 Bē'zer in the wilderness on the tableland belonging to the Reū'ben•ites, Rā'moth in Gil'e•ad belonging to the Gad'ītes, and Gō'lan in Bā'shan belonging to the Ma•nas'sītes.

Transition to the Second Address

44 This is the law that Moses set before the Israelites. 45 These are the decrees and the statutes

---

h Heb *the ten words*

and ordinances that Moses spoke to the Israelites when they had come out of Egypt, 46 beyond the Jordan in the valley opposite Beth-pē'or, in the land of King Sī'hon of the Am'o•rītes, who reigned at Hesh'bon, whom Moses and the Israelites defeated when they came out of Egypt. 47 They occupied his land and the land of King Og of Bā'shan, the two kings of the Am'o•rītes on the eastern side of the Jordan: 48 from A•rō'er, which is on the edge of the Wadi Ar'non, as far as Mount Sir'i•on[i] (that is, Hermon), 49 together with all the Ar'a•bah on the east side of the Jordan as far as the Sea of the Ar'a•bah, under the slopes of Pis'gah.

The Ten Commandments
(Ex 20.1–17)

5 Moses convened all Israel, and said to them: Hear, O Israel, the statutes and ordinances that I am addressing to you today; you shall learn them and observe them diligently. 2 The LORD our God made a covenant with us at Hō'reb. 3 Not with our ancestors did the LORD make this covenant, but with us, who are all of us here alive today. 4 The LORD spoke with you face to face at the mountain, out of the fire. 5 (At that time I was standing between the LORD and you to declare to you the words[j] of the LORD; for you were afraid because of the fire and did not go up the mountain.) And he said:

6 I am the LORD your God, who brought you out of the land of Egypt, out of the house of slavery; 7 you shall have no other gods before[k] me.

8 You shall not make for yourself an idol, whether in the form of anything that is in heaven above, or that is on the earth beneath, or that is in the water under the earth. 9 You shall not bow down to them or worship them; for I the LORD your God am a jealous God, punishing children for the iniquity of parents, to the third and fourth generation of those who reject me, 10 but showing steadfast love to the thousandth generation[l] of those who love me and keep my commandments.

11 You shall not make wrongful use of the name of the LORD your God, for the LORD will not acquit anyone who misuses his name.

12 Observe the sabbath day and keep it holy, as the LORD your God commanded you. 13 Six days you shall labor and do all your work. 14 But the seventh day is a sabbath to the LORD your God; you shall not do any work—you, or your son or your daughter, or your male or female slave, or your ox or your donkey, or any of your livestock, or the resident alien in your towns, so that your male and female slave may rest as well as you. 15 Remember that you were a slave in the land of Egypt, and the LORD your God brought you out from there with a mighty hand and an outstretched arm; therefore the LORD your God commanded you to keep the sabbath day.

16 Honor your father and your mother, as the LORD your God commanded you, so that your days may be long and that it may go well with you in the land that the LORD your God is giving you.

17 You shall not murder.[m]

18 Neither shall you commit adultery.

19 Neither shall you steal.

20 Neither shall you bear false witness against your neighbor.

21 Neither shall you covet your neighbor's wife. Neither shall you desire your neighbor's house, or field, or male or female slave, or ox, or donkey, or anything that belongs to your neighbor.

Moses the Mediator of God's Will
(Ex 20.18–21)

22 These words the LORD spoke with a loud voice to your whole assembly at the mountain, out of the fire, the cloud, and the thick darkness, and he added no more. He wrote them on two stone tablets, and gave them to me. 23 When you heard the voice out of the darkness, while the mountain was burning with fire, you approached me, all the heads of your tribes and your elders; 24 and you said, "Look, the LORD our God has shown us his glory and greatness, and we have heard his voice out of the fire. Today we have seen that God may speak to someone and the person may still live. 25 So now why should we die? For this great fire will consume us; if we hear the voice of the LORD our God any longer, we shall die. 26 For who is there of all flesh that has heard the voice of the living God speaking out of fire, as we have, and remained alive? 27 Go near, you yourself, and hear all that the LORD our God will say. Then tell us everything that the LORD our God tells you, and we will listen and do it."

28 The LORD heard your words when you spoke to me, and the LORD said to me: "I have heard the words of this people, which they have spoken to you; they are right in all that they have spoken. 29 If only they had such a mind as this, to fear me and to keep all my commandments always, so that it might go well with them and with their children forever! 30 Go say to them, 'Return to your tents.' 31 But you, stand here by me, and I will tell you all the commandments, the statutes and the ordinances, that you shall teach them, so that they may do them in the land that I am giving them to possess." 32 You must therefore be careful to do as the LORD your God has commanded you; you shall not turn to the right or to the left. 33 You must follow

---

i Syr: Heb *Sion*   j Q Mss Sam Gk Syr Vg Tg: MT *word*
k Or *besides*   l Or *to thousands*   m Or *kill*

THE LAKOTA CODE

See how similar these guidelines from a Native American tribal code are to the Ten Commandments (Deut 5.1–21), not to mention our own civil laws, school policies, and even family rules. What can we learn from them?

- Love one another.
- Pity orphan children. Be kind to them because they are poor; feed them and clothe them.
- Do not kill one another.
- Do not steal anything from anyone, especially from your own people.
- Do not tell lies to anyone, or lie about anyone.
- Respect your brothers and sisters. Do not marry in your own family.
- The ability to make good speech is a great gift from their maker, owner of all things, to the people. This is why you should not talk badly about anyone. Bad talk can hurt one's family or everyday life.
- Never quarrel among one another. Be good to others and always be friendly to whomever you meet, wherever you meet them.
- Do not brag about yourself, or try to hurt another's feelings. The generous person is the one who is respected.

(Ron Zeilinger, *Sacred Ground*, pp. 74–75)

▶ **Deut 5.1–21**

exactly the path that the LORD your God has commanded you, so that you may live, and that it may go well with you, and that you may live long in the land that you are to possess.

The Great Commandment

6 Now this is the commandment—the statutes and the ordinances—that the LORD your God charged me to teach you to observe in the land that you are about to cross into and occupy, 2 so that you and your children and your children's children may fear the LORD your God all the days of your life, and keep all his decrees and his commandments that I am commanding you, so that your days may be long. 3 Hear therefore, O Israel, and observe them diligently, so that it may go well with you, and so that you may multiply greatly in a land flowing with milk and honey, as the LORD, the God of your ancestors, has promised you.

4 Hear, O Israel: The LORD is our God, the LORD alone.*n* 5 You shall love the LORD your God with all your heart, and with all your soul, and with all your might. 6 Keep these words that I am commanding you today in your heart. 7 Recite them to your children and talk about them when you are at home and when you are away, when you lie down and when you rise. 8 Bind them as a sign on your hand, fix them as an emblem*o* on your forehead, 9 and write them on the doorposts of your house and on your gates.

Caution against Disobedience

10 When the LORD your God has brought you into the land that he swore to your ancestors, to Abraham, to Isaac, and to Jacob, to give you—a land with fine, large cities that you did not build, 11 houses filled with all sorts of goods that you did not fill, hewn cisterns that you did not hew, vineyards and olive groves that you did not plant—and when you have eaten your fill, 12 take care that you do not forget the LORD, who brought you out of the land of Egypt, out of the house of slavery. 13 The LORD your God you shall fear; him you shall serve, and by his name alone you shall swear. 14 Do not follow other gods, any of the gods of the peoples who are all around you, 15 because the LORD your

---

n Or *The* LORD *our God is one* LORD, or *The* LORD *our God, the* LORD *is one,* or *The* LORD *is our God, the* LORD *is one*
o Or *as a frontlet*

PRAY IT!

The Shema: Putting God First

Deuteronomy 6.4 is the most famous declaration of faith in the Old Testament: "Hear, O Israel: The LORD is our God, the LORD alone." This short verse, part of a prayer called the Shema, is uttered daily by faithful Jews. It has been so important that the commands of verses 8–9 often have been interpreted literally. The Pharisees of Jesus' day, for example, wore miniature copies of the prayer on their bodies and attached other copies to their doorposts. Orthodox Jews today continue this tradition. Keeping the law of God is a privilege—something to be "worn" with pride!

The Shema reminds Jewish people to put God first and to love God with all their heart, soul, and might. Think about people who seem to carry God in their heart all the time. Are they lost and frustrated? Do they seem angry and hate filled? Chances are they seem more relaxed and sure of themselves than most people do. Having God in your sights at all times will help in more ways than you could ever imagine!

▸ **Deut 6.4–9**

God, who is present with you, is a jealous God. The anger of the LORD your God would be kindled against you and he would destroy you from the face of the earth.

16 Do not put the LORD your God to the test, as you tested him at Mas'sah. 17 You must diligently keep the commandments of the LORD your God, and his decrees, and his statutes that he has commanded you. 18 Do what is right and good in the sight of the LORD, so that it may go well with you, and so that you may go in and occupy the good land that the LORD swore to your ancestors to give you, 19 thrusting out all your enemies from before you, as the LORD has promised.

20 When your children ask you in time to come, "What is the meaning of the decrees and the statutes and the ordinances that the LORD our God has commanded you?" 21 then you shall say to your children, "We were Pharaoh's slaves in Egypt, but the LORD brought us out of Egypt with a mighty hand. 22 The LORD displayed before our eyes great and awesome signs and wonders against Egypt, against Pharaoh and all his household. 23 He brought us out from there in order to bring us in, to give us the land that he promised on oath to our ancestors. 24 Then the LORD commanded us to observe all these statutes, to fear the LORD our God, for our lasting good, so as to keep us alive, as is now the case. 25 If we diligently observe this entire commandment before the LORD our God, as he has commanded us, we will be in the right."

A Chosen People
(Ex 34.10–16)

7 When the LORD your God brings you into the land that you are about to enter and occupy, and he clears away many nations before you—the Hit′tites, the Gir′ga·shites, the Am′o·rites, the Cā′naan·ites, the Per′iz·zites, the Hī′vites, and the Jeb′ū·sites, seven nations mightier and more numerous than you— 2 and when the LORD your God gives them over to you and you defeat them, then you must utterly destroy them. Make no covenant with them and show them no mercy. 3 Do not intermarry with them, giving your daughters to their sons or taking their daughters for your sons, 4 for that would turn away your children from following me, to serve other gods. Then the anger of the LORD would be kindled against you, and he would destroy you quickly. 5 But this is how you must deal with them: break down their altars, smash their pillars, hew down their sacred poles,*p* and burn their idols with fire. 6 For you are a people holy to the LORD your God; the LORD your God has chosen you out of all the peoples on earth to be his people, his treasured possession.

7 It was not because you were more numerous than any other people that the LORD set his heart on you and chose you—for you were the fewest of all peoples. 8 It was because the LORD loved you and kept the oath that he swore to your ancestors, that the LORD has brought you out with a mighty hand, and redeemed you from the house of slavery, from the hand of Pharaoh king of Egypt. 9 Know therefore that the LORD your God is God, the faithful God who maintains covenant loyalty with those who love him and keep his commandments, to a thousand generations, 10 and who repays in their own person those who reject him. He does not delay but repays in their own person those who reject him. 11 Therefore, observe diligently the commandment—the statutes and the ordinances—that I am commanding you today.

p Heb *Asherim*

Blessings for Obedience
(Lev 26.1–13; Deut 28.1–14)

12 If you heed these ordinances, by diligently observing them, the LORD your God will maintain with you the covenant loyalty that he swore to your ancestors; 13 he will love you, bless you, and multiply you; he will bless the fruit of your womb and the fruit of your ground, your grain and your wine and your oil, the increase of your cattle and the issue of your flock, in the land that he swore to your ancestors to give you. 14 You shall be the most blessed of peoples, with neither sterility nor barrenness among you or your livestock. 15 The LORD will turn away from you every illness; all the dread diseases of Egypt that you experienced, he will not inflict on you, but he will lay them on all who hate you. 16 You shall devour all the peoples that the LORD your God is giving over to you, showing them no pity; you shall not serve their gods, for that would be a snare to you.

17 If you say to yourself, "These nations are more numerous than I; how can I dispossess them?" 18 do not be afraid of them. Just remember what the LORD your God did to Pharaoh and to all Egypt, 19 the great trials that your eyes saw, the signs and wonders, the mighty hand and the outstretched arm by which the LORD your God brought you out. The LORD your God will do the same to all the peoples of whom you are afraid. 20 Moreover, the LORD your God will send the pestilence *q* against them, until even the survivors and the fugitives are destroyed. 21 Have no dread of them, for the LORD your God, who is present with you, is a great and awesome God. 22 The LORD your God will clear away these nations before you little by little; you will not be able to make a quick end of them, otherwise the wild animals would become too numerous for you. 23 But the LORD your God will give them over to you, and throw them into great panic, until they are destroyed. 24 He will hand their kings over to you and you shall blot out their name from under heaven; no one will be able to stand against you, until you have destroyed them. 25 The images of their gods you shall burn with fire. Do not covet the silver or the gold that is on them and take it for yourself, because you could be ensnared by it; for it

q Or hornets: Meaning of Heb uncertain

DON'T LOSE YOUR LANGUAGE!

"Qui perd sa langue, perd sa foi." This French Canadian proverb means, "Lose your language, lose your faith."

As Canada was being settled, the French were afraid that the English culture would dominate the land and culture. Most of the French were Catholic, and most of the English were Protestant. The French believed their faith was so tied to their language that the loss of their language would mean a loss to their faith and how they expressed it culturally.

This same fear is present in the Bible. Peter was afraid to eat with the Gentiles—those who were not Jews (see Gal 2.12). The Samaritan woman at the well knew that Jesus, a Jew, should have nothing to do with her because Samaritans were considered "half-Jews" due to intermarriage (Jn 4.9).

Chapter 7 of Deuteronomy portrays this fear in a frightening way. Israelites were told not just to avoid pagans but to destroy them. Intermarriage would mean losing Jewish language, culture, and faith—and sooner or later would lead to worshiping false gods. (See also Ex 23.23–26.)

Yet Jesus treated the Samaritan woman with dignity. Paul challenged Peter to eat with the uncircumcised and to let them become Christians without first becoming Jews. We need not be afraid of those who are different from us. We can treat others with dignity and even build friendship without the fear of losing our language or our faith.

▶ Deut 7.1–5

DEUT

is abhorrent to the LORD your God. 26 Do not bring an abhorrent thing into your house, or you will be set apart for destruction like it. You must utterly detest and abhor it, for it is set apart for destruction.

A Warning Not to Forget God in Prosperity

8 This entire commandment that I command you today you must diligently observe, so that you may live and increase, and go in and occupy the land that the LORD promised on oath to your ancestors. 2 Remember the long way that the LORD your God has led you these forty years in the wilderness, in order to humble you, testing you to know what was in your heart, whether or not you would keep his commandments. 3 He humbled you by letting you hunger, then by feeding you with manna, with which neither you nor your ancestors were acquainted, in order to make you understand that one

does not live by bread alone, but by every word that comes from the mouth of the LORD.ʳ 4 The clothes on your back did not wear out and your feet did not swell these forty years. 5 Know then in your heart that as a parent disciplines a child so the LORD your God disciplines you. 6 Therefore keep the commandments of the LORD your God, by walking in his ways and by fearing him. 7 For the LORD your God is bringing you into a good land, a land with flowing streams, with springs and underground waters welling up in valleys and hills, 8 a land of wheat and barley, of vines and fig trees and pomegranates, a land of olive trees and honey, 9 a land where you may eat bread without scarcity, where you will lack nothing, a land whose stones are iron and from whose hills you may mine copper. 10 You shall eat

---

ʳ Or *by anything that the LORD decrees*

THE PRINCIPLE OF *UJIMA*

Decades before the Civil War in the United States of America, the Underground Railroad helped thousands of African slaves find their way to freedom. The Underground Railroad was not a real railroad but a loose network of antislavery northerners—mostly African Americans—who helped escaped slaves reach safety in the free states or Canada. People called conductors guided groups of fugitive slaves through isolated areas at night so that they wouldn't be spotted. Others opened their homes and farms to give them safe places to stay during the day. It was dangerous work because professional slave catchers and local officials were always looking for escaped slaves to return for financial rewards.

The Underground Railroad is just one example of what can be accomplished through the Kwanzaa principle of ujima (see "Kwanzaa as a Way of Life," Deut 10.12–22), which is collective work and responsibility. African American ancestors in the United States worked together bravely for the common good. Many members of the Underground Railroad were former slaves themselves and took responsibility for freeing others as they had been freed. Today, we need young people with the same sense of responsibility and the willingness to work together to free others from poverty, violence, and addiction.

Martin Luther King Jr. did this. In his last speech, he said to you and me: "I've been to the Mountain top, and I've seen the Promised Land. I may not get there with you, but I want you to know that we as a people will get to the Promised Land." He knew that he would not live to see his people freed from prejudice and discrimination. But he spent his whole life working with others toward that goal.

The author of Deuteronomy wrote long after Moses' time. Many of the Chosen People had indeed become wealthy, so he used Moses' authority to remind them of how they had gotten to where they were. Their ancestors—escaped, impoverished slaves—trusted in God and worked together over a long time to bring prosperity to the nation. This is the mentality we too must cultivate to bring success to ourselves and our people.

▶ Deut 8.11–18

your fill and bless the LORD your God for the good land that he has given you.

11 Take care that you do not forget the LORD your God, by failing to keep his commandments, his ordinances, and his statutes, which I am commanding you today. 12 When you have eaten your fill and have built fine houses and live in them, 13 and when your herds and flocks have multiplied, and your silver and gold is multiplied, and all that you have is multiplied, 14 then do not exalt yourself, forgetting the LORD your God, who brought you out of the land of Egypt, out of the house of slavery, 15 who led you through the great and terrible wilderness, an arid wasteland with poisonous[s] snakes and scorpions. He made water flow for you from flint rock, 16 and fed you in the wilderness with manna that your ancestors did not know, to humble you and to test you, and in the end to do you good. 17 Do not say to yourself, "My power and the might of my own hand have gotten me this wealth." 18 But remember the LORD your God, for it is he who gives you power to get wealth, so that he may confirm his covenant that he swore to your ancestors, as he is doing today. 19 If you do forget the LORD your God and follow other gods to serve and worship them, I solemnly warn you today that you shall surely perish. 20 Like the nations that the LORD is destroying before you, so shall you perish, because you would not obey the voice of the LORD your God.

The Consequences of Rebelling against God
(Ex 32.1–35)

9 Hear, O Israel! You are about to cross the Jordan today, to go in and dispossess nations larger and mightier than you, great cities, fortified to the heavens, 2 a strong and tall people, the offspring of the An'a•kim, whom you know. You have heard it said of them, "Who can stand up to the An'a•kim?" 3 Know then today that the LORD your God is the one who crosses over before you as a devouring fire; he will defeat them and subdue them before you, so that you may dispossess and destroy them quickly, as the LORD has promised you.

4 When the LORD your God thrusts them out before you, do not say to yourself, "It is because of my righteousness that the LORD has brought me in to occupy this land"; it is rather because of the wickedness of these nations that the LORD is dispossessing them before you. 5 It is not because of your righteousness or the uprightness of your heart that you are going in to occupy their land; but because of the wickedness of these nations the LORD your God is dispossessing them before you, in order to fulfill the promise that the LORD made on oath to your ancestors, to Abraham, to Isaac, and to Jacob.

6 Know, then, that the LORD your God is not giving you this good land to occupy because of your righteousness; for you are a stubborn people. 7 Remember and do not forget how you provoked the LORD your God to wrath in the wilderness; you have been rebellious against the LORD from the day you came out of the land of Egypt until you came to this place.

8 Even at Hō'reb you provoked the LORD to wrath, and the LORD was so angry with you that he was ready to destroy you. 9 When I went up the mountain to receive the stone tablets, the tablets of the covenant that the LORD made with you, I remained on the mountain forty days and forty nights; I neither ate bread nor drank water. 10 And the LORD gave me the two stone tablets written with the finger of God; on them were all the words that the LORD had spoken to you at the mountain out of the fire on the day of the assembly. 11 At the end of forty days and forty nights the LORD gave me the two stone tablets, the tablets of the covenant. 12 Then the LORD said to me, "Get up, go down quickly from here, for your people whom you have brought from Egypt have acted corruptly. They have been quick to turn from the way that I commanded them; they have cast an image for themselves." 13 Furthermore the LORD said to me, "I have seen that this people is indeed a stubborn people. 14 Let me alone that I may destroy them and blot out their name from under heaven; and I will make of you a nation mightier and more numerous than they."

15 So I turned and went down from the mountain, while the mountain was ablaze; the two tablets of the covenant were in my two hands. 16 Then I saw that you had indeed sinned against the LORD your God, by casting for yourselves an image of a calf; you had been quick to turn from the way that the LORD had commanded you. 17 So I took hold of the two tablets and flung them from my two hands, smashing them before your eyes. 18 Then I lay prostrate before the LORD as before, forty days and forty nights; I neither ate bread nor drank water, because of all the sin you had committed, provoking the LORD by doing what was evil in his sight. 19 For I was afraid that the anger that the LORD bore against you was so fierce that he would destroy you. But the LORD listened to me that time also. 20 The LORD was so angry with Aaron that he was ready to destroy him, but I interceded also on behalf of Aaron at that same time. 21 Then I took the sinful thing you had made, the calf, and burned it with fire and crushed it, grinding it thoroughly, until it was reduced to dust; and I threw the dust of it into the stream that runs down the mountain.

DEUT

---

s Or *fiery*; Heb *seraph*

22 At Tab'e•rah also, and at Mas'sah, and at Kib'roth-hat•tā'a•vah, you provoked the LORD to wrath. 23 And when the LORD sent you from Kā'desh-bar'nē•a, saying, "Go up and occupy the land that I have given you," you rebelled against the command of the LORD your God, neither trusting him nor obeying him. 24 You have been rebellious against the LORD as long as he has[t] known you.

25 Throughout the forty days and forty nights that I lay prostrate before the LORD when the LORD intended to destroy you, 26 I prayed to the LORD and said, "Lord GOD, do not destroy the people who are your very own possession, whom you redeemed in your greatness, whom you brought out of Egypt with a mighty hand. 27 Remember your servants, Abraham, Isaac, and Jacob; pay no attention to the stubbornness of this people, their wickedness and their sin, 28 otherwise the land from which you have brought us might say, 'Because the LORD was not able to bring them into the land that he promised them, and because he hated them, he has brought them out to let them die in the wilderness.' 29 For they are the people of your very own possession, whom you brought out by your great power and by your outstretched arm."

The Second Pair of Tablets
(Ex 34.1–9)

10 At that time the LORD said to me, "Carve out two tablets of stone like the former ones, and come up to me on the mountain, and make an ark of wood. 2 I will write on the tablets the words that were on the former tablets, which you smashed, and you shall put them in the ark." 3 So I made an ark of acacia wood, cut two tablets of stone like the former ones, and went up the mountain with the two tablets in my hand. 4 Then he wrote on the tablets the same words as before, the ten commandments[u] that the LORD had spoken to you on the mountain out of the fire on the day of the assembly; and the LORD gave them to me. 5 So I turned and came down from the mountain, and put the tablets in the ark that I had made; and there they are, as the LORD commanded me.

6 (The Israelites journeyed from Be•er'oth-be'nē-jā'a•kan[v] to Mō•sē'rah. There Aaron died, and there he was buried; his son El•ē•ā'zar succeeded him as priest. 7 From there they journeyed to Gud'gō•dah, and from Gud'gō•dah to Jot'ba•thah, a land with flowing streams. 8 At that time the LORD set apart the tribe of Levi to carry the ark of the covenant of the LORD, to stand before the LORD to minister to him, and to bless in his name, to this day. 9 Therefore Levi has no allotment or inheritance with his kindred; the LORD is his inheritance, as the LORD your God promised him.)

10 I stayed on the mountain forty days and forty nights, as I had done the first time. And once again the LORD listened to me. The LORD was unwilling to destroy you. 11 The LORD said to me, "Get up, go on your journey at the head of the people, that they may go in and occupy the land that I swore to their ancestors to give them."

The Essence of the Law

12 So now, O Israel, what does the LORD your God require of you? Only to fear the LORD your God, to walk in all his ways, to love him, to serve the LORD your God with all your heart and with all your soul, 13 and to keep the commandments of the LORD your God[w] and his decrees that I am commanding you today, for your own well-being. 14 Although heaven and the heaven of heavens belong to the LORD your God, the earth with all that is in it, 15 yet the LORD set his heart in love on your ancestors alone and chose you, their descendants after them, out of all the peoples, as it is today. 16 Circumcise, then, the foreskin of your heart, and do not be stubborn any longer. 17 For the LORD your God is God of gods and Lord of lords, the great God, mighty and awesome, who is not partial and takes no bribe, 18 who executes justice for the orphan and the widow, and who loves the strangers, providing them food and clothing. 19 You shall also love the stranger, for you were strangers in the land of Egypt. 20 You shall fear the LORD your God; him alone you shall worship; to him you shall hold fast, and by his name you shall swear. 21 He is your praise; he is your God, who has done for you these great and awesome things that your own eyes have seen. 22 Your ancestors went down to Egypt seventy persons; and now the LORD your God has made you as numerous as the stars in heaven.

Rewards for Obedience

11 You shall love the LORD your God, therefore, and keep his charge, his decrees, his ordinances, and his commandments always. 2 Remember today that it was not your children (who have not known or seen the discipline of the LORD your God), but it is you who must acknowledge his greatness, his mighty hand and his outstretched arm, 3 his signs and his deeds that he did in Egypt to Pharaoh, the king of Egypt, and to all his land; 4 what he did to the Egyptian army, to their horses and chariots, how he made the water of the Red Sea[x] flow over them as they pursued you, so that the LORD has destroyed them to this day; 5 what he did to you in the wilderness, until you came to this

---

t Sam Gk: MT *I have*   *u* Heb *the ten words*   *v* Or *the wells of the Bene-jaakan*   *w* Q Ms Gk Syr: MT lacks *your God*   *x* Or *Sea of Reeds*

KWANZAA AS A WAY OF LIFE

The heart of the Law is love, our love for God and God's love for us. We express that love through the values we live out. Conflicts occur when the way we rank our values comes into conflict with the way others rank their values.

For example: You may place a value on completing all your schoolwork, studying, and excelling in school. Another person sitting near you in class may not place the same high value on school. The two of you may come into conflict because this person disrupts the class and makes it difficult for you to understand what the teacher is explaining.

This is why a universal value system is important. It is why the Book of Deuteronomy has laws on everything from worship to sanitation. These laws gave the Israelites a common value system.

Kwanzaa is the name of a value system accepted by many African peoples. It was developed by Maulana Karenga after studying many different cultures throughout Africa. In 1965, he codified the unifying aspects of each of these cultures into the seven principles of Kwanzaa (also known as the Nguzo Saba). The seven principles are written in Swahili (an African trade and business language) and speak to the holistic development of the individual, family, community, nation, and race. Kwanzaa is celebrated from 26 December to 1 January. It is good that more and more African Americans are celebrating it each year, but these principles must be fully put into practice year-round as a way of life.

Kwanzaa is not a religion or a religious holiday, but it can strengthen the faith that you already practice. Look up the Bible passages listed with the following Kwanzaa principles to learn more about each one:

1. *umoja* (unity): Psalm 133; 1 Cor 12.12–26
2. *kujichagulia* (self-determination): Jdt 8.9–36
3. *ujima* (collective work and responsibility): Deut 8.11–18
4. *ujamaa* (cooperative economics): Mt 16.25
5. *nia* (purpose): Rom 8.28
6. *kuumba* (creativity): Mt 25.14–30
7. *imani* (faith): Gal 6.9

▶ Deut 10.12–22

place; 6 and what he did to Dā′than and A•bī′ram, sons of E•li′ab son of Reuben, how in the midst of all Israel the earth opened its mouth and swallowed them up, along with their households, their tents, and every living being in their company; 7 for it is your own eyes that have seen every great deed that the LORD did.

8 Keep, then, this entire commandment that I am commanding you today, so that you may have strength to go in and occupy the land that you are crossing over to occupy, 9 and so that you may live long in the land that the LORD swore to your ancestors to give them and to their descendants, a land flowing with milk and honey. 10 For the land that you are about to enter to occupy is not like the land of Egypt, from which you have come, where you sow your seed and irrigate by foot like a vegetable garden. 11 But the land that you are crossing over to occupy is a land of hills and valleys, watered by rain from the sky, 12 a land that the LORD your God looks after. The eyes of the LORD your God are always on it, from the beginning of the year to the end of the year.

13 If you will only heed his every commandment[y] that I am commanding you today—loving the LORD your God, and serving him with all your

DEUT

---
y Compare Gk: Heb *my commandments*

heart and with all your soul— 14 then he[z] will give the rain for your land in its season, the early rain and the later rain, and you will gather in your grain, your wine, and your oil; 15 and he[z] will give grass in your fields for your livestock, and you will eat your fill. 16 Take care, or you will be seduced into turning away, serving other gods and worshiping them, 17 for then the anger of the LORD will be kindled against you and he will shut up the heavens, so that there will be no rain and the land will yield no fruit; then you will perish quickly off the good land that the LORD is giving you.

18 You shall put these words of mine in your heart and soul, and you shall bind them as a sign on your hand, and fix them as an emblem[a] on your forehead. 19 Teach them to your children, talking about them when you are at home and when you are away, when you lie down and when you rise. 20 Write them on the doorposts of your house and on your gates, 21 so that your days and the days of your children may be multiplied in the land that the LORD swore to your ancestors to give them, as long as the heavens are above the earth.

22 If you will diligently observe this entire commandment that I am commanding you, loving the LORD your God, walking in all his ways, and holding fast to him, 23 then the LORD will drive out all these nations before you, and you will dispossess nations larger and mightier than yourselves. 24 Every place on which you set foot shall be yours; your territory shall extend from the wilderness to the Lebanon and from the River, the river Euphrates, to the Western Sea. 25 No one will be able to stand against you; the LORD your God will put the fear and dread of you on all the land on which you set foot, as he promised you.

26 See, I am setting before you today a blessing and a curse: 27 the blessing, if you obey the commandments of the LORD your God that I am commanding you today; 28 and the curse, if you do not obey the commandments of the LORD your God, but turn from the way that I am commanding you today, to follow other gods that you have not known.

29 When the LORD your God has brought you into the land that you are entering to occupy, you shall set the blessing on Mount Ger'i•zim and the curse on Mount E'bal. 30 As you know, they are beyond the Jordan, some distance to the west, in the land of the Ca'naan•ites who live in the Ar'a•bah, opposite Gil'gal, beside the oak[b] of Mo'reh. 31 When you cross the Jordan to go in to occupy the land that the LORD your God is giving you, and when you occupy and live in it, 32 you must diligently observe all the statutes and ordinances that I am setting before you today.

Pagan Shrines to Be Destroyed

12 These are the statutes and ordinances that you must diligently observe in the land that the LORD, the God of your ancestors, has given you to occupy all the days that you live on the earth.

2 You must demolish completely all the places where the nations whom you are about to dispossess served their gods, on the mountain heights, on the hills, and under every leafy tree. 3 Break down their altars, smash their pillars, burn their sacred poles[c] with fire, and hew down the idols of their gods, and thus blot out their name from their places. 4 You shall not worship the LORD your God in such ways. 5 But you shall seek the place that the LORD your God will choose out of all your tribes as his habitation to put his name there. You shall go there, 6 bringing there your burnt offerings and your sacrifices, your tithes and your donations, your votive gifts, your freewill offerings, and the firstlings of your herds and flocks. 7 And you shall eat there in the presence of the LORD your God, you and your households together, rejoicing in all the undertakings in which the LORD your God has blessed you.

8 You shall not act as we are acting here today, all of us according to our own desires, 9 for you have not yet come into the rest and the possession that the LORD your God is giving you. 10 When you cross over the Jordan and live in the land that the LORD your God is allotting to you, and when he gives you rest from your enemies all around so that you live in safety, 11 then you shall bring everything that I command you to the place that the LORD your God will choose as a dwelling for his name: your burnt offerings and your sacrifices, your tithes and your donations, and all your choice votive gifts that you vow to the LORD. 12 And you shall rejoice before the LORD your God, you together with your sons and your daughters, your male and female slaves, and the Le'vites who reside in your towns (since they have no allotment or inheritance with you).

A Prescribed Place of Worship

13 Take care that you do not offer your burnt offerings at any place you happen to see. 14 But only at the place that the LORD will choose in one of your tribes—there you shall offer your burnt offerings and there you shall do everything I command you.

15 Yet whenever you desire you may slaughter and eat meat within any of your towns, according to the blessing that the LORD your God has given you; the unclean and the clean may eat of it, as they

---

z Sam Gk Vg: MT *I*   a Or *as a frontlet*   b Gk Syr: Compare Gen 12.6; Heb *oaks* or *terebinths*   c Heb *Asherim* would of gazelle or deer. [16] The blood, however, you must not eat; you shall pour it out on the ground like water. [17] Nor may you eat within your towns the tithe of your grain, your wine, and your oil, the firstlings of your herds and your flocks, any of your votive gifts that you vow, your freewill offerings, or your donations; [18] these you shall eat in the presence of the LORD your God at the place that the LORD your God will choose, you together with your son and your daughter, your male and female slaves, and the Lē´vītes resident in your towns, rejoicing in the presence of the LORD your God in all your undertakings. [19] Take care that you do not neglect the Lē´vite as long as you live in your land.

[20] When the LORD your God enlarges your territory, as he has promised you, and you say, "I am going to eat some meat," because you wish to eat meat, you may eat meat whenever you have the desire. [21] If the place where the LORD your God will choose to put his name is too far from you, and you slaughter as I have commanded you any of your herd or flock that the LORD has given you, then you may eat within your towns whenever you desire. [22] Indeed, just as gazelle or deer is eaten, so you may eat it; the unclean and the clean alike may eat it. [23] Only be sure that you do not eat the blood; for the blood is the life, and you shall not eat the life with the meat. [24] Do not eat it; you shall pour it out on the ground like water. [25] Do not eat it, so that all may go well with you and your children after you, because you do what is right in the sight of the LORD. [26] But the sacred donations that are due from you, and your votive gifts, you shall bring to the place that the LORD will choose. [27] You shall present your burnt offerings, both the meat and the blood, on the altar of the LORD your God; the blood of your other sacrifices shall be poured out beside[d] the altar of the LORD your God, but the meat you may eat.

[28] Be careful to obey all these words that I command you today,[e] so that it may go well with you and with your children after you forever, because you will be doing what is good and right in the sight of the LORD your God.

Warning against Idolatry

[29] When the LORD your God has cut off before you the nations whom you are about to enter to dispossess them, when you have dispossessed them and live in their land, [30] take care that you are not snared into imitating them, after they have been destroyed before you: do not inquire concerning their gods, saying, "How did these nations worship their gods? I also want to do the same." [31] You must not do the same for the LORD your God, because every abhorrent thing that the LORD hates they have done for their gods. They would even burn their sons and their daughters in the fire to their gods. [32] [f]You must diligently observe everything that I command you; do not add to it or take anything from it.

13 [g]If prophets or those who divine by dreams appear among you and promise you omens or portents, [2] and the omens or the portents declared by them take place, and they say, "Let us follow other gods" (whom you have not known) "and let us serve them," [3] you must not heed the words of those prophets or those who divine by dreams; for the LORD your God is testing you, to know whether you indeed love the LORD your God with all your heart and soul. [4] The LORD your God you shall follow, him alone you shall fear, his commandments you shall keep, his voice you shall obey, him you shall serve, and to him you shall hold fast. [5] But those prophets or those who divine by dreams shall be put to death for having spoken treason against the LORD your God—who brought you out of the land of Egypt and redeemed you from the house of slavery—to turn you from the way in which the LORD your God commanded you to walk. So you shall purge the evil from your midst.

[6] If anyone secretly entices you—even if it is your brother, your father's son or[h] your mother's son, or your own son or daughter, or the wife you embrace, or your most intimate friend—saying, "Let us go worship other gods," whom neither you nor your ancestors have known, [7] any of the gods of the peoples that are around you, whether near you or far away from you, from one end of the earth to the other, [8] you must not yield to or heed any such persons. Show them no pity or compassion and do not shield them. [9] But you shall surely kill them; your own hand shall be first against them to execute them, and afterwards the hand of all the people. [10] Stone them to death for trying to turn you away from the LORD your God, who brought you out of the land of Egypt, out of the house of slavery. [11] Then all Israel shall hear and be afraid, and never again do any such wickedness.

[12] If you hear it said about one of the towns that the LORD your God is giving you to live in, [13] that scoundrels from among you have gone out and led the inhabitants of the town astray, saying, "Let us go and worship other gods," whom you have not known, [14] then you shall inquire and make a thorough investigation. If the charge is established that such an abhorrent thing has been done among you, [15] you shall put the inhabitants of that town to the sword, utterly destroying it and everything in it—even putting its livestock to the

---

[d] Or *on*   [e] Gk Sam Syr: MT lacks *today*   [f] Ch 13.1 in Heb   [g] Ch 13.2 in Heb   [h] Sam Gk Compare Tg: MT lacks *your father's son or*

sword. 16 All of its spoil you shall gather into its public square; then burn the town and all its spoil with fire, as a whole burnt offering to the LORD your God. It shall remain a perpetual ruin, never to be rebuilt. 17 Do not let anything devoted to destruction stick to your hand, so that the LORD may turn from his fierce anger and show you compassion, and in his compassion multiply you, as he swore to your ancestors, 18 if you obey the voice of the LORD your God by keeping all his commandments that I am commanding you today, doing what is right in the sight of the LORD your God.

Pagan Practices Forbidden

14 You are children of the LORD your God. You must not lacerate yourselves or shave your forelocks for the dead. 2 For you are a people holy to the LORD your God; it is you the LORD has chosen out of all the peoples on earth to be his people, his treasured possession.

14.3–21

Clean and Unclean Foods
(Lev 11.1–47)

3 You shall not eat any abhorrent thing. 4 These are the animals you may eat: the ox, the sheep, the goat, 5 the deer, the gazelle, the roebuck, the wild goat, the ibex, the antelope, and the mountain-sheep. 6 Any animal that divides the hoof and has the hoof cleft in two, and chews the cud, among the animals, you may eat. 7 Yet of those that chew the cud or have the hoof cleft you shall not eat these: the camel, the hare, and the rock badger, because they chew the cud but do not divide the hoof; they are unclean for you. 8 And the pig, because it divides the hoof but does not chew the cud, is un-

clean for you. You shall not eat their meat, and you shall not touch their carcasses.

9 Of all that live in water you may eat these: whatever has fins and scales you may eat. 10 And whatever does not have fins and scales you shall not eat; it is unclean for you.

11 You may eat any clean birds. 12 But these are the ones that you shall not eat: the eagle, the vulture, the osprey, 13 the buzzard, the kite of any kind; 14 every raven of any kind; 15 the ostrich, the nighthawk, the sea gull, the hawk of any kind; 16 the little owl and the great owl, the water hen 17 and the desert owl,*i* the carrion vulture and the cormorant, 18 the stork, the heron of any kind; the hoopoe and the bat.*j* 19 And all winged insects are unclean for you; they shall not be eaten. 20 You may eat any clean winged creature.

21 You shall not eat anything that dies of itself; you may give it to aliens residing in your towns for them to eat, or you may sell it to a foreigner. For you are a people holy to the LORD your God.

You shall not boil a kid in its mother's milk.

Regulations concerning Tithes

22 Set apart a tithe of all the yield of your seed that is brought in yearly from the field. 23 In the presence of the LORD your God, in the place that he will choose as a dwelling for his name, you shall eat the tithe of your grain, your wine, and your oil, as well as the firstlings of your herd and flock, so that you may learn to fear the LORD your God always. 24 But if, when the LORD your God has blessed you, the distance is so great that you are unable to transport it, because the place where the LORD your God will choose to set his name is too far away from you, 25 then you may turn it into money. With the money secure in hand, go to the place that the LORD your God will choose; 26 spend the money for whatever you wish—oxen, sheep, wine, strong drink, or whatever you desire. And you shall eat there in the presence of the LORD your God, you and your household rejoicing together. 27 As for the Lē'vītes resident in your towns, do not neglect them, because they have no allotment or inheritance with you.

28 Every third year you shall bring out the full tithe of your produce for that year, and store it within your towns; 29 the Lē'vītes, because they have no allotment or inheritance with you, as well as the resident aliens, the orphans, and the widows in your towns, may come and eat their fill so that the LORD your God may bless you in all the work that you undertake.

---

i Or *pelican* *j* Identification of several of the birds in verses 12-18 is uncertain

Laws concerning the Sabbatical Year
(Ex 21.1–11; Lev 25.1–7)

15 Every seventh year you shall grant a re- mission of debts. 2 And this is the man- ner of the remission: every creditor shall remit the claim that is held against a neighbor, not exacting it of a neighbor who is a member of the community, because the LORD's remission has been proclaimed. 3 Of a foreigner you may exact it, but you must re- mit your claim on whatever any member of your community owes you. 4 There will, however, be no one in need among you, because the LORD is sure to bless you in the land that the LORD your God is giv- ing you as a possession to occupy, 5 if only you will obey the LORD your God by diligently observing this entire commandment that I command you to- day. 6 When the LORD your God has blessed you, as he promised you, you will lend to many nations, but you will not borrow; you will rule over many nations, but they will not rule over you.

7 If there is among you anyone in need, a member of your community in any of your towns within the land that the LORD your God is giving you, do not be hard-hearted or tight-fisted toward your needy neighbor. 8 You should rather open your hand, willingly lending enough to meet the need, whatever it may be. 9 Be careful that you do not entertain a mean thought, thinking, "The sev- enth year, the year of remission, is near," and therefore view your needy neighbor with hostility and give nothing; your neighbor might cry to the LORD against you, and you would incur guilt. 10 Give liberally and be ungrudging when you do so, for on this account the LORD your God will bless you in all your work and in all that you un- dertake. 11 Since there will never cease to be some in need on the earth, I therefore command you, "Open your hand to the poor and needy neighbor in your land."

12 If a member of your community, whether a Hebrew man or a Hebrew woman, is sold[k] to you and works for you six years, in the seventh year you shall set that person free. 13 And when you send a male slave[l] out from you a free person, you shall not send him out empty-handed. 14 Provide liberally out of your flock, your threshing floor, and your wine press, thus giving to him some of the bounty with which the LORD your God has blessed you. 15 Remember that you were a slave in the land of Egypt, and the LORD your God re- deemed you; for this reason I lay this command upon you today. 16 But if he says to you, "I will not go out from you," because he loves you and your household, since he is well off with you,[l] 17 then you shall take an awl and thrust it through his ear- lobe into the door, and he shall be your slave[m] forever.

You shall do the same with regard to your female slave.[n]

18 Do not consider it a hardship when you send them out from you free persons, because for six years they have given you services worth the wages of hired laborers; and the LORD your God will bless you in all that you do.

The Firstborn of Livestock

19 Every firstling male born of your herd and flock you shall consecrate to the LORD your God; you shall not do work with your firstling ox nor shear the firstling of your flock. 20 You shall eat it, you together with your household, in the presence of the LORD your God year by year at the place that the LORD will choose. 21 But if it has any defect— any serious defect, such as lameness or blindness— you shall not sacrifice it to the LORD your God; 22 within your towns you may eat it, the unclean and the clean alike, as you would a gazelle or deer. 23 Its blood, however, you must not eat; you shall pour it out on the ground like water.

The Passover Reviewed
(Ex 12.1–20; 23.14–19; 34.18–26)

16 Observe the month[o] of Ā'bib by keep- ing the passover to the LORD your God, for in the month of Ā'bib the LORD your God brought you out of Egypt by night. 2 You shall of- fer the passover sacrifice to the LORD your God, from the flock and the herd, at the place that the LORD will choose as a dwelling for his name. 3 You must not eat with it anything leavened. For seven days you shall eat unleavened bread with it—the bread of affliction—because you came out of the land of Egypt in great haste, so that all the days of your life you may remember the day of your de- parture from the land of Egypt. 4 No leaven shall be seen with you in all your territory for seven days; and none of the meat of what you slaughter on the evening of the first day shall remain until morning. 5 You are not permitted to offer the passover sacrifice within any of your towns that the LORD your God is giving you. 6 But at the place that the LORD your God will choose as a dwelling for his name, only there shall you offer the passover sacrifice, in the evening at sunset, the time of day when you departed from Egypt. 7 You shall cook it and eat it at the place that the LORD your God will choose; the next morning you may go back to your tents. 8 For six days you shall continue to eat un- leavened bread, and on the seventh day there shall be a solemn assembly for the LORD your God, when you shall do no work.

DEUT

---

k Or *sells himself or herself* l Heb *him* m Or *bondman*
n Or *bondwoman* o Or *new moon*

The Festival of Weeks Reviewed
(Ex 34.22; Lev 23.15–21; Num 28.26–31)

9 You shall count seven weeks; begin to count the seven weeks from the time the sickle is first put to the standing grain. 10 Then you shall keep the festival of weeks to the LORD your God, contributing a freewill offering in proportion to the blessing that you have received from the LORD your God. 11 Rejoice before the LORD your God—you and your sons and your daughters, your male and female slaves, the Lē′vītes resident in your towns, as well as the strangers, the orphans, and the widows who are among you—at the place that the LORD your God will choose as a dwelling for his name. 12 Remember that you were a slave in Egypt, and diligently observe these statutes.

The Festival of Booths Reviewed
(Lev 23.33–43; Num 29.12–40)

13 You shall keep the festival of booths*p* for seven days, when you have gathered in the produce from your threshing floor and your wine press. 14 Rejoice during your festival, you and your sons and your daughters, your male and female slaves, as well as the Lē′vītes, the strangers, the orphans, and the widows resident in your towns. 15 Seven days you shall keep the festival to the LORD your God at the place that the LORD will choose; for the LORD your God will bless you in all your produce and in all your undertakings, and you shall surely celebrate.

16 Three times a year all your males shall appear before the LORD your God at the place that he will choose: at the festival of unleavened bread, at the festival of weeks, and at the festival of booths.*p* They shall not appear before the LORD empty-handed; 17 all shall give as they are able, according to the blessing of the LORD your God that he has given you.

Municipal Judges and Officers

18 You shall appoint judges and officials throughout your tribes, in all your towns that the LORD your God is giving you, and they shall render just decisions for the people. 19 You must not distort justice; you must not show partiality; and you must not accept bribes, for a bribe blinds the eyes of the wise and subverts the cause of those who are in the right. 20 Justice, and only justice, you shall pursue, so that you may live and occupy the land that the LORD your God is giving you.

Forbidden Forms of Worship

21 You shall not plant any tree as a sacred pole*q* beside the altar that you make for the LORD your God; 22 nor shall you set up a stone pillar—things that the LORD your God hates.

17 You must not sacrifice to the LORD your God an ox or a sheep that has a defect, anything seriously wrong; for that is abhorrent to the LORD your God.

2 If there is found among you, in one of your towns that the LORD your God is giving you, a man or woman who does what is evil in the sight of the LORD your God, and transgresses his covenant 3 by going to serve other gods and worshiping them—whether the sun or the moon or any of the host of heaven, which I have forbidden— 4 and if it is reported to you or you hear of it, and you make a thorough inquiry, and the charge is proved true that such an abhorrent thing has occurred in Israel, 5 then you shall bring out to your gates that man or that woman who has committed this crime and you shall stone the man or woman to death. 6 On the evidence of two or three witnesses the death sentence shall be executed; a person must not be put to death on the evidence of only one witness. 7 The hands of the witnesses shall be the first raised against the person to execute the death penalty, and afterward the hands of all the people. So you shall purge the evil from your midst.

Legal Decisions by Priests and Judges

8 If a judicial decision is too difficult for you to make between one kind of bloodshed and another, one kind of legal right and another, or one kind of assault and another—any such matters of dispute in your towns—then you shall immediately go up to the place that the LORD your God will choose, 9 where you shall consult with the levitical priests and the judge who is in office in those days; they shall announce to you the decision in the case. 10 Carry out exactly the decision that they announce to you from the place that the LORD will choose, diligently observing everything they instruct you. 11 You must carry out fully the law that they interpret for you or the ruling that they announce to you; do not turn aside from the decision that they announce to you, either to the right or to the left. 12 As for anyone who presumes to disobey the priest appointed to minister there to the LORD your God, or the judge, that person shall die. So you shall purge the evil from Israel. 13 All the people will hear and be afraid, and will not act presumptuously again.

Limitations of Royal Authority

14 When you have come into the land that the LORD your God is giving you, and have taken possession of it and settled in it, and you say, "I will set a king over me, like all the nations that are around me," 15 you may indeed set over you a king whom

---

p Or *tabernacles*; Heb *succoth*   *q* Heb *Asherah*

did you KNOW?

The Torah

The Hebrew word Torah means "instruction" or "teaching," and only over time has come to mean "the Law." Torah refers most fundamentally to the Law that was recorded as given by God to Moses on Mount Sinai. As the people of Israel lived the Torah, it became equated with their very life and existence. It was the key for their organization as a people and gave consistency to their struggle to live their Covenant with God.

Jewish people refer to the first five books of the Bible (the Pentateuch) as the Torah because those books contain the Law and instructions on how to live it. The other books of the Old Testament are also strongly connected to the Torah. The historical books record how the people and their kings kept the Torah or disobeyed it. When they obeyed, they were blessed with happiness, health, and prosperity. When they disobeyed, they were punished with barrenness, destruction, and death. The prophets in the prophetic books call the people to faithfulness to the Law. They condemn idolatry and injustice and call the people to live the spirit of the Torah.

What law are Christians called to live by? For a hint, see the Letter of Paul to the Galatians and the Letter of James.

▶ Deut 17.8–11

---

the LORD your God will choose. One of your own community you may set as king over you; you are not permitted to put a foreigner over you, who is not of your own community. 16 Even so, he must not acquire many horses for himself, or return the people to Egypt in order to acquire more horses, since the LORD has said to you, "You must never return that way again." 17 And he must not acquire many wives for himself, or else his heart will turn away; also silver and gold he must not acquire in great quantity for himself. 18 When he has taken the throne of his kingdom, he shall have a copy of this law written for him in the presence of the levitical priests. 19 It shall remain with him and he shall

read in it all the days of his life, so that he may learn to fear the LORD his God, diligently observing all the words of this law and these statutes, 20 neither exalting himself above other members of the community nor turning aside from the commandment, either to the right or to the left, so that he and his descendants may reign long over his kingdom in Israel.

Privileges of Priests and Levites

18 The levitical priests, the whole tribe of Levi, shall have no allotment or inheritance within Israel. They may eat the sacrifices that are the LORD's portion[r] 2 but they shall have no inheritance among the other members of the community; the LORD is their inheritance, as he promised them.

3 This shall be the priests' due from the people, from those offering a sacrifice, whether an ox or a sheep: they shall give to the priest the shoulder, the two jowls, and the stomach. 4 The first fruits of your grain, your wine, and your oil, as well as the first of the fleece of your sheep, you shall give him. 5 For the LORD your God has chosen Levi[s] out of all your tribes, to stand and minister in the name of the LORD, him and his sons for all time.

6 If a Lĕʹvite leaves any of your towns, from wherever he has been residing in Israel, and comes to the place that the LORD will choose (and he may come whenever he wishes), 7 then he may minister in the name of the LORD his God, like all his fellow-Lĕʹvites who stand to minister there before the LORD. 8 They shall have equal portions to eat, even though they have income from the sale of family possessions.[r]

Child-Sacrifice, Divination, and Magic Prohibited

9 When you come into the land that the LORD your God is giving you, you must not learn to imitate the abhorrent practices of those nations. 10 No one shall be found among you who makes a son or daughter pass through fire, or who practices divination, or is a soothsayer, or an augur, or a sorcerer, 11 or one who casts spells, or who consults ghosts or spirits, or who seeks oracles from the dead. 12 For whoever does these things is abhorrent to the LORD; it is because of such abhorrent practices that the LORD your God is driving them out before you. 13 You must remain completely loyal to the LORD your God. 14 Although these nations that you are about to dispossess do give heed to soothsayers and diviners, as for you, the LORD your God does not permit you to do so.

---

r Meaning of Heb uncertain   s Heb *him*

DEUT

A New Prophet Like Moses

15 The LORD your God will raise up for you a prophet[t] like me from among your own people; you shall heed such a prophet.[u] 16 This is what you requested of the LORD your God at Hō′reb on the day of the assembly when you said: "If I hear the voice of the LORD my God any more, or ever again see this great fire, I will die." 17 Then the LORD replied to me: "They are right in what they have said. 18 I will raise up for them a prophet[t] like you from among their own people; I will put my words in the mouth of the prophet,[v] who shall speak to them everything that I command. 19 Anyone who does not heed the words that the prophet[w] shall speak in my name, I myself will hold accountable. 20 But any prophet who speaks in the name of other gods, or who presumes to speak in my name a word that I have not commanded the prophet to speak—that prophet shall die." 21 You may say to yourself, "How can we recognize a word that the LORD has not spoken?" 22 If a prophet speaks in the name of the LORD but the thing does not take place or prove true, it is a word that the LORD has not spoken. The prophet has spoken it presumptuously; do not be frightened by it.

Laws concerning the Cities of Refuge
(Num 35.9–28; Josh 20.1–9)

19 When the LORD your God has cut off the nations whose land the LORD your God is giving you, and you have dispossessed them and settled in their towns and in their houses, 2 you shall set apart three cities in the land that the LORD your God is giving you to possess. 3 You shall calculate the distances[x] and divide into three regions the land that the LORD your God gives you as a possession, so that any homicide can flee to one of them.

4 Now this is the case of a homicide who might flee there and live, that is, someone who has killed another person unintentionally when the two had not been at enmity before: 5 Suppose someone goes into the forest with another to cut wood, and when one of them swings the ax to cut down a tree, the head slips from the handle and strikes the other person who then dies; the killer may flee to one of these cities and live. 6 But if the distance is too great, the avenger of blood in hot anger might pursue and overtake and put the killer to death, although a death sentence was not deserved, since the two had not been at enmity before. 7 Therefore I command you: You shall set apart three cities.

8 If the LORD your God enlarges your territory, as he swore to your ancestors—and he will give you all the land that he promised your ancestors to give you, 9 provided you diligently observe this entire commandment that I command you today, by loving the LORD your God and walking always in his ways—then you shall add three more cities to these three, 10 so that the blood of an innocent person may not be shed in the land that the LORD your God is giving you as an inheritance, thereby bringing bloodguilt upon you.

11 But if someone at enmity with another lies in wait and attacks and takes the life of that person, and flees into one of these cities, 12 then the elders of the killer's city shall send to have the culprit taken from there and handed over to the avenger of blood to be put to death. 13 Show no pity; you shall purge the guilt of innocent blood from Israel, so that it may go well with you.

Property Boundaries

14 You must not move your neighbor's boundary marker, set up by former generations, on the property that will be allotted to you in the land that the LORD your God is giving you to possess.

Law concerning Witnesses

15 A single witness shall not suffice to convict a person of any crime or wrongdoing in connection with any offense that may be committed. Only on the evidence of two or three witnesses shall a charge be sustained. 16 If a malicious witness comes forward to accuse someone of wrongdoing, 17 then both parties to the dispute shall appear before the LORD, before the priests and the judges who are in office in those days, 18 and the judges shall make a thorough inquiry. If the witness is a false witness, having testified falsely against another, 19 then you shall do to the false witness just as the false witness had meant to do to the other. So you shall purge the evil from your midst. 20 The rest shall hear and be afraid, and a crime such as this shall never again be committed among you. 21 Show no pity: life for life, eye for eye, tooth for tooth, hand for hand, foot for foot.

Rules of Warfare

20 When you go out to war against your enemies, and see horses and chariots, an army larger than your own, you shall not be afraid of them; for the LORD your God is with you, who brought you up from the land of Egypt. 2 Before you engage in battle, the priest shall come forward and speak to the troops, 3 and shall say to them: "Hear, O Israel! Today you are drawing near to do battle against your enemies. Do not lose heart, or be afraid, or panic, or be in dread of them; 4 for it is the LORD your God who goes with you, to fight for you against your enemies, to give you victory."

---

t Or prophets   u Or such prophets   v Or mouths of the prophets   w Heb he   x Or prepare roads to them

5 Then the officials shall address the troops, saying, "Has anyone built a new house but not dedicated it? He should go back to his house, or he might die in the battle and another dedicate it. 6 Has anyone planted a vineyard but not yet enjoyed its fruit? He should go back to his house, or he might die in the battle and another be first to enjoy its fruit. 7 Has anyone become engaged to a woman but not yet married her? He should go back to his house, or he might die in the battle and another marry her." 8 The officials shall continue to address the troops, saying, "Is anyone afraid or disheartened? He should go back to his house, or he might cause the heart of his comrades to melt like his own." 9 When the officials have finished addressing the troops, then the commanders shall take charge of them.

10 When you draw near to a town to fight against it, offer it terms of peace. 11 If it accepts your terms of peace and surrenders to you, then all the people in it shall serve you at forced labor. 12 If it does not submit to you peacefully, but makes war against you, then you shall besiege it; 13 and when the LORD your God gives it into your hand, you shall put all its males to the sword. 14 You may, however, take as your booty the women, the children, livestock, and everything else in the town, all its spoil. You may enjoy the spoil of your enemies, which the LORD your God has given you. 15 Thus you shall treat all the towns that are very far from you, which are not towns of the nations here. 16 But as for the towns of these peoples that the LORD your God is giving you as an inheritance, you must not let anything that breathes remain alive. 17 You shall annihilate them—the Hit'tītes and the Am'o•rītes, the Cā'naan•ītes and the Per'iz•zītes, the Hī'vītes and the Jeb'ū•sītes—just as the LORD your God has commanded, 18 so that they may not teach you to do all the abhorrent things that they do for their gods, and you thus sin against the LORD your God.

19 If you besiege a town for a long time, making war against it in order to take it, you must not destroy its trees by wielding an ax against them. Although you may take food from them, you must not cut them down. Are trees in the field human beings that they should come under siege from you? 20 You may destroy only the trees that you know do not produce food; you may cut them down for use in building siegeworks against the town that makes war with you, until it falls.

Law concerning Murder by Persons Unknown

21 If, in the land that the LORD your God is giving you to possess, a body is found lying in open country, and it is not known who struck the person down, 2 then your elders and your judges shall come out to measure the distances to the towns that are near the body. 3 The elders of the town nearest the body shall take a heifer that has never been worked, one that has not pulled in the yoke; 4 the elders of that town shall bring the heifer down to a wadi with running water, which is neither plowed nor sown, and shall break the heifer's neck there in the wadi. 5 Then the priests, the sons of Levi, shall come forward, for the LORD your God has chosen them to minister to him and to pronounce blessings in the name of the LORD, and by their decision all cases of dispute and assault shall be settled. 6 All the elders of that town nearest the body shall wash their hands over the heifer whose neck was broken in the wadi, 7 and they shall declare: "Our hands did not shed this blood, nor were we witnesses to it. 8 Absolve, O LORD, your people Israel, whom you redeemed; do not let the guilt of innocent blood remain in the midst of your people Israel." Then they will be absolved of bloodguilt.

DEUT

Facing Life's Battles

LIVE IT!

What are the wars in your life? Where do you experience conflict and lack of peace? We all hope that we will not face war in armed conflict. But in a sense, war is around us in the conflicts of everyday life.

We have fights with family and friends. We battle the pressures of society and our peers. We are at odds with the future. Deuteronomy 20.1 tells us that we are not to fear times of war because our God is with us and will be our strength.

When we face conflict, our faith will be tested, but we must hold strong and true to what God tells us. If we let our heart be filled with God, the wars that we face will become opportunities for God's love to triumph.

What conflicts do you encounter these days? Do you sense that God is with you in these conflicts? If so, how? Pray for peace-filled ways to resolve conflict.

▶ **Deut 20.1**

9 So you shall purge the guilt of innocent blood from your midst, because you must do what is right in the sight of the LORD.

Female Captives

10 When you go out to war against your enemies, and the LORD your God hands them over to you and you take them captive, 11 suppose you see among the captives a beautiful woman whom you desire and want to marry, 12 and so you bring her home to your house: she shall shave her head, pare her nails, 13 discard her captive's garb, and shall remain in your house a full month, mourning for her father and mother; after that you may go in to her and be her husband, and she shall be your wife. 14 But if you are not satisfied with her, you shall let her go free and not sell her for money. You must not treat her as a slave, since you have dishonored her.

The Right of the Firstborn

15 If a man has two wives, one of them loved and the other disliked, and if both the loved and the disliked have borne him sons, the firstborn being the son of the one who is disliked, 16 then on the day when he wills his possessions to his sons, he is not permitted to treat the son of the loved as the firstborn in preference to the son of the disliked, who is the firstborn. 17 He must acknowledge as firstborn the son of the one who is disliked, giving him a double portion*y* of all that he has; since he is the first issue of his virility, the right of the firstborn is his.

Rebellious Children

18 If someone has a stubborn and rebellious son who will not obey his father and mother, who does not heed them when they discipline him, 19 then his father and his mother shall take hold of him and bring him out to the elders of his town at the gate of that place. 20 They shall say to the elders of his town, "This son of ours is stubborn and rebellious. He will not obey us. He is a glutton and a drunkard." 21 Then all the men of the town shall stone him to death. So you shall purge the evil from your midst; and all Israel will hear, and be afraid.

Miscellaneous Laws

22 When someone is convicted of a crime punishable by death and is executed, and you hang him on a tree, 23 his corpse must not remain all night upon the tree; you shall bury him that same day, for anyone hung on a tree is under God's curse. You must not defile the land that the LORD your God is giving you for possession.

22 You shall not watch your neighbor's ox or sheep straying away and ignore them; you shall take them back to their owner. 2 If the owner does not reside near you or you do not know who the owner is, you shall bring it to your own house, and it shall remain with you until the owner claims it; then you shall return it. 3 You shall do the same with a neighbor's donkey; you shall do the same with a neighbor's garment; and you shall do the same with anything else that your neighbor loses and you find. You may not withhold your help.

4 You shall not see your neighbor's donkey or ox fallen on the road and ignore it; you shall help to lift it up.

5 A woman shall not wear a man's apparel, nor shall a man put on a woman's garment; for whoever does such things is abhorrent to the LORD your God.

6 If you come on a bird's nest, in any tree or on the ground, with fledglings or eggs, with the mother sitting on the fledglings or on the eggs, you shall not take the mother with the young. 7 Let the mother go, taking only the young for yourself, in order that it may go well with you and you may live long.

8 When you build a new house, you shall make a parapet for your roof; otherwise you might have bloodguilt on your house, if anyone should fall from it.

9 You shall not sow your vineyard with a second kind of seed, or the whole yield will have to be forfeited, both the crop that you have sown and the yield of the vineyard itself.

10 You shall not plow with an ox and a donkey yoked together.

11 You shall not wear clothes made of wool and linen woven together.

12 You shall make tassels on the four corners of the cloak with which you cover yourself.

Laws concerning Sexual Relations

13 Suppose a man marries a woman, but after going in to her, he dislikes her 14 and makes up charges against her, slandering her by saying, "I married this woman; but when I lay with her, I did not find evidence of her virginity." 15 The father of the young woman and her mother shall then submit the evidence of the young woman's virginity to the elders of the city at the gate. 16 The father of the young woman shall say to the elders: "I gave my daughter in marriage to this man but he dislikes her; 17 now he has made up charges against her, saying, 'I did not find evidence of your daughter's virginity.' But here is the evidence of my daughter's virginity." Then they shall spread out the cloth before the elders of the town. 18 The elders of that town shall take the man and punish him; 19 they shall fine him one hundred shekels of silver (which they shall give to the young woman's father) be-

y Heb two-thirds

D
E
U
T

cause he has slandered a virgin of Israel. She shall remain his wife; he shall not be permitted to divorce her as long as he lives.

20 If, however, this charge is true, that evidence of the young woman's virginity was not found, [21] then they shall bring the young woman out to the entrance of her father's house and the men of her town shall stone her to death, because she committed a disgraceful act in Israel by prostituting herself in her father's house. So you shall purge the evil from your midst.

22 If a man is caught lying with the wife of another man, both of them shall die, the man who lay with the woman as well as the woman. So you shall purge the evil from Israel.

23 If there is a young woman, a virgin already engaged to be married, and a man meets her in the town and lies with her, [24] you shall bring both of them to the gate of that town and stone them to death, the young woman because she did not cry for help in the town and the man because he violated his neighbor's wife. So you shall purge the evil from your midst.

25 But if the man meets the engaged woman in the open country, and the man seizes her and lies with her, then only the man who lay with her shall die. [26] You shall do nothing to the young woman; the young woman has not committed an offense punishable by death, because this case is like that of someone who attacks and murders a neighbor. [27] Since he found her in the open country, the engaged woman may have cried for help, but there was no one to rescue her.

28 If a man meets a virgin who is not engaged, and seizes her and lies with her, and they are caught in the act, [29] the man who lay with her shall give fifty shekels of silver to the young woman's father, and she shall become his wife. Because he violated her he shall not be permitted to divorce her as long as he lives.

30[z] A man shall not marry his father's wife, thereby violating his father's rights.[a]

Those Excluded from the Assembly

23 No one whose testicles are crushed or whose penis is cut off shall be admitted to the assembly of the LORD.

2 Those born of an illicit union shall not be admitted to the assembly of the LORD. Even to the tenth generation, none of their descendants shall be admitted to the assembly of the LORD.

3 No Am′mon·ite or Mō′ab·ite shall be admitted to the assembly of the LORD. Even to the tenth generation, none of their descendants shall be admitted to the assembly of the LORD, 4 because they did not meet you with food and water on your journey out of Egypt, and because they hired against

you Bā′laam son of Bē′or, from Pē′thor of Mes·o·po·tā′mi·a, to curse you. 5 (Yet the LORD your God refused to heed Bā′laam; the LORD your God turned the curse into a blessing for you, because the LORD your God loved you.) 6 You shall never promote their welfare or their prosperity as long as you live.

7 You shall not abhor any of the Ē′dom·ites, for they are your kin. You shall not abhor any of the Egyptians, because you were an alien residing in their land. 8 The children of the third generation that are born to them may be admitted to the assembly of the LORD.

Sanitary, Ritual, and Humanitarian Precepts

9 When you are encamped against your enemies you shall guard against any impropriety.

10 If one of you becomes unclean because of a nocturnal emission, then he shall go outside the camp; he must not come within the camp. 11 When evening comes, he shall wash himself with water, and when the sun has set, he may come back into the camp.

12 You shall have a designated area outside the camp to which you shall go. 13 With your utensils you shall have a trowel; when you relieve yourself outside, you shall dig a hole with it and then cover up your excrement. 14 Because the LORD your God travels along with your camp, to save you and to hand over your enemies to you, therefore your camp must be holy, so that he may not see anything indecent among you and turn away from you.

15 Slaves who have escaped to you from their owners shall not be given back to them. 16 They shall reside with you, in your midst, in any place they choose in any one of your towns, wherever they please; you shall not oppress them.

17 None of the daughters of Israel shall be a temple prostitute; none of the sons of Israel shall be a temple prostitute. 18 You shall not bring the fee of a prostitute or the wages of a male prostitute[b] into the house of the LORD your God in payment for any vow, for both of these are abhorrent to the LORD your God.

19 You shall not charge interest on loans to another Israelite, interest on money, interest on provisions, interest on anything that is lent. 20 On loans to a foreigner you may charge interest, but on loans to another Israelite you may not charge interest, so that the LORD your God may bless you in all your undertakings in the land that you are about to enter and possess.

21 If you make a vow to the LORD your God, do not postpone fulfilling it; for the LORD your God will surely require it of you, and you would incur

DEUT

---

z Ch 23.1 in Heb   a Heb *uncovering his father's skirt*   b Heb *a dog* guilt. 22 But if you refrain from vowing, you will not incur guilt. 23 Whatever your lips utter you must diligently perform, just as you have freely vowed to the LORD your God with your own mouth.

24 If you go into your neighbor's vineyard, you may eat your fill of grapes, as many as you wish, but you shall not put any in a container.

25 If you go into your neighbor's standing grain, you may pluck the ears with your hand, but you shall not put a sickle to your neighbor's standing grain.

Laws concerning Marriage and Divorce

24 Suppose a man enters into marriage with a woman, but she does not please him because he finds something objectionable about her, and so he writes her a certificate of divorce, puts it in her hand, and sends her out of his house; she then leaves his house 2 and goes off to become another man's wife. 3 Then suppose the second man dislikes her, writes her a bill of divorce, puts it in her hand, and sends her out of his house (or the second man who married her dies); 4 her first husband, who sent her away, is not permitted to take her again to be his wife after she has been defiled; for that would be abhorrent to the LORD, and you shall not bring guilt on the land that the LORD your God is giving you as a possession.

Miscellaneous Laws

5 When a man is newly married, he shall not go out with the army or be charged with any related duty. He shall be free at home one year, to be happy with the wife whom he has married.

6 No one shall take a mill or an upper millstone in pledge, for that would be taking a life in pledge.

7 If someone is caught kidnaping another Israelite, enslaving or selling the Israelite, then that kidnaper shall die. So you shall purge the evil from your midst.

8 Guard against an outbreak of a leprous[c] skin disease by being very careful; you shall carefully observe whatever the levitical priests instruct you, just as I have commanded them. 9 Remember what the LORD your God did to Miriam on your journey out of Egypt.

10 When you make your neighbor a loan of any kind, you shall not go into the house to take the pledge. 11 You shall wait outside, while the person to whom you are making the loan brings the pledge out to you. 12 If the person is poor, you shall not sleep in the garment given you as[d] the pledge. 13 You shall give the pledge back by sunset, so that your neighbor may sleep in the cloak and bless you; and it will be to your credit before the LORD your God.

14 You shall not withhold the wages of poor

did you KNOW?

The Poor, the Strangers, the Widows, and the Orphans

One remarkable aspect of Israel's Covenant was the command to care for the poor, the "aliens" or strangers, the widows, and the orphans. These four groups were the outsiders in ancient Israel because they fell outside Israel's socioeconomic system. The poor often had no means to sustain themselves. Strangers, or aliens, were not part of Israel's tribal organization. Widows depended on the charity of others. Orphans were destitute because they had no family to help them survive.

God provides a reason why Israel must care for the poor and oppressed. Just as the Israelites were enslaved in Egypt—when they were poor, oppressed, orphans in a foreign land—and God responded to their cry for help, so they must care for the poor, oppressed, forgotten, and marginalized in their midst. Can this be any less true for us today?

▶ Deut 24.10–21

and needy laborers, whether other Israelites or aliens who reside in your land in one of your towns. 15 You shall pay them their wages daily before sunset, because they are poor and their livelihood depends on them; otherwise they might cry to the LORD against you, and you would incur guilt.

16 Parents shall not be put to death for their children, nor shall children be put to death for their parents; only for their own crimes may persons be put to death.

17 You shall not deprive a resident alien or an orphan of justice; you shall not take a widow's garment in pledge. 18 Remember that you were a slave in Egypt and the LORD your God redeemed you from there; therefore I command you to do this.

19 When you reap your harvest in your field and forget a sheaf in the field, you shall not go back to get it; it shall be left for the alien, the orphan,

---

c A term for several skin diseases; precise meaning uncertain   d Heb lacks *the garment given you as*

DEUT

and the widow, so that the LORD you[r]
bless you in all your undertakings. 20
beat your olive trees, do not strip what is
shall be for the alien, the orphan, and the wid[ow.]

21 When you gather the grapes of your vineyard, do not glean what is left; it shall be for the
alien, the orphan, and the widow. 22 Remember
that you were a slave in the land of Egypt; therefore
I am commanding you to do this.

25 Suppose two persons have a dispute and
enter into litigation, and the judges decide between them, declaring one to be in the right
and the other to be in the wrong. 2 If the one in the
wrong deserves to be flogged, the judge shall make
that person lie down and be beaten in his presence
with the number of lashes proportionate to the offense. 3 Forty lashes may be given but not more; if
more lashes than these are given, your neighbor
will be degraded in your sight.

4 You shall not muzzle an ox while it is treading
out the grain.

Levirate Marriage

5 When brothers reside together, and one of
them dies and has no son, the wife of the deceased
shall not be married outside the family to a
stranger. Her husband's brother shall go in to her,
taking her in marriage, and performing the duty of
a husband's brother to her, 6 and the firstborn
whom she bears shall succeed to the name of the
deceased brother, so that his name may not be blotted out of Israel. 7 But if the man has no desire to
marry his brother's widow, then his brother's widow shall go up to the elders at the gate and say, "My
husband's brother refuses to perpetuate his brother's name in Israel; he will not perform the duty of
a husband's brother to me." 8 Then the elders of his
town shall summon him and speak to him. If he
persists, saying, "I have no desire to marry her,"
9 then his brother's wife shall go up to him in the
presence of the elders, pull his sandal off his foot,
spit in his face, and declare, "This is what is done
to the man who does not build up his brother's
house." 10 Throughout Israel his family shall be
known as "the house of him whose sandal was
pulled off."

Various Commands

11 If men get into a fight with one another, and
the wife of one intervenes to rescue her husband
from the grip of his opponent by reaching out and
seizing his genitals, 12 you shall cut off her hand;
show no pity.

13 You shall not have in your bag two kinds of
weights, large and small. 14 You shall not have in
your house two kinds of measures, large and small.
15 You shall have only a full and honest weight; you

only a full and honest measure, so that
may be long in the land that the LORD
y[is] giving you. 16 For all who do such
[is] act dishonestly, are abhorrent to the

struck d[own?] what Am'a·lek did to you on
fear God. [in] Egypt, 18 how he attacked you
given you rest, were faint and weary, and
in the land that th[e] LORD your God has
an inheritance to pos[sess,] enemies on every hand,
membrance of Am'a·lek God is giving you as
forget. all blot out the re-
heaven; do not

First Fruits and Tith[es]

26 When you have come into the [l]and that
the LORD your God is giving yo[u] as an
inheritance to possess, and you possess it, and settle in it, 2 you shall take some of the first of all the
fruit of the ground, which you harvest from the
land that the LORD your God is giving you, and you
shall put it in a basket and go to the place that the
LORD your God will choose as a dwelling for his
name. 3 You shall go to the priest who is in office at
that time, and say to him, "Today I declare to the
LORD your God that I have come into the land that
the LORD swore to our ancestors to give us." 4 When
the priest takes the basket from your hand and sets
it down before the altar of the LORD your God,
5 you shall make this response before the LORD
your God: "A wandering Ar·a·mē'an was my ancestor; he went down into Egypt and lived there as an
alien, few in number, and there he became a great
nation, mighty and populous. 6 When the Egyptians treated us harshly and afflicted us, by imposing hard labor on us, 7 we cried to the LORD, the
God of our ancestors; the LORD heard our voice and
saw our affliction, our toil, and our oppression.
8 The LORD brought us out of Egypt with a mighty
hand and an outstretched arm, with a terrifying display of power, and with signs and wonders; 9 and
he brought us into this place and gave us this land,
a land flowing with milk and honey. 10 So now I
bring the first of the fruit of the ground that you,
O LORD, have given me." You shall set it down before the LORD your God and bow down before the
LORD your God. 11 Then you, together with the
Lē'vītes and the aliens who reside among you, shall
celebrate with all the bounty that the LORD your
God has given to you and to your house.

12 When you have finished paying all the tithe
of your produce in the third year (which is the year
of the tithe), giving it to the Lē'vītes, the aliens, the
orphans, and the widows, so that they may eat their
fill within your towns, 13 then you shall say before

the LORD your God: "I have r~~e~~and-
portion from the house, and ~~n~~either
Lē'vītes, the resident aliens, ~~c~~ommand-
widows, in accordance with mourning;
ment that you comman~~d~~ was unclean;
transgressed nor forgott~~en~~ the dead. I have
ments: 14 I have not ea~~t~~ing just as you com-
I have not removed ~~fr~~om your holy habita-
and I have not offer~~ed~~ ss your people Israel and
obeyed the LORD ~~bless~~ as your people Israel and
manded me. 15 ~~g~~ive given us, as you swore
tion, from hea~~ven~~ land flowing with milk and
the ground th~~at~~land flowing with milk and
to our ance~~stors,~~
honey."

~~C~~oncluding Exhortation

~~16 Th~~is very day the LORD your God is com-
mand~~ing~~ you to observe these statutes· and ordi-
nan~~c~~es; so observe them diligently with all your
heart and with all your soul. 17 Today you have obtained the LORD's agreement: to be your God; and
for you to walk in his ways, to keep his statutes, his
commandments, and his ordinances, and to obey
him. 18 Today the LORD has obtained your agreement: to be his treasured people, as he promised
you, and to keep his commandments; 19 for him to
set you high above all nations that he has made, in
praise and in fame and in honor; and for you to be
a people holy to the LORD your God, as he promised.

The Inscribed Stones and Altar on Mount Ebal

27 Then Moses and the elders of Israel
charged all the people as follows: Keep
the entire commandment that I am commanding
you today. 2 On the day that you cross over the Jordan into the land that the LORD your God is giving
you, you shall set up large stones and cover them
with plaster. 3 You shall write on them all the words
of this law when you have crossed over, to enter the
land that the LORD your God is giving you, a land
flowing with milk and honey, as the LORD, the God
of your ancestors, promised you. 4 So when you
have crossed over the Jordan, you shall set up these
stones, about which I am commanding you today,
on Mount Ē'bal, and you shall cover them with
plaster. 5 And you shall build an altar there to the
LORD your God, an altar of stones on which you
have not used an iron tool. 6 You must build the altar of the LORD your God of unhewn*e* stones. Then
offer up burnt offerings on it to the LORD your God,
7 make sacrifices of well-being, and eat them there,
rejoicing before the LORD your God. 8 You shall
write on the stones all the words of this law very
clearly.

9 Then Moses and the levitical priests spoke to
all Israel, saying: Keep silence and hear, O Israel!
This very day you have become the people of the
LORD your God. 10 Therefore obey the LORD your
God, observing his commandments and his
statutes that I am commanding you today.

Twelve Curses

11 The same day Moses charged the people as
follows: 12 When you have crossed over the Jordan,
these shall stand on Mount Ger'i·zim for the blessing of the people: Sim'ē·on, Levi, Judah, Is'sa·char,
Joseph, and Benjamin. 13 And these shall stand on
Mount Ē'bal for the curse: Reuben, Gad, Ash'er,
Zeb'ū·lun, Dan, and Naph'ta·lī. 14 Then the Lē'vītes
shall declare in a loud voice to all the Israelites:

15 "Cursed be anyone who makes an idol or
casts an image, anything abhorrent to the LORD, the
work of an artisan, and sets it up in secret." All the
people shall respond, saying, "Amen!"

16 "Cursed be anyone who dishonors father or
mother." All the people shall say, "Amen!"

17 "Cursed be anyone who moves a neighbor's
boundary marker." All the people shall say,
"Amen!"

18 "Cursed be anyone who misleads a blind
person on the road." All the people shall say,
"Amen!"

19 "Cursed be anyone who deprives the alien,
the orphan, and the widow of justice." All the people shall say, "Amen!"

20 "Cursed be anyone who lies with his father's
wife, because he has violated his father's rights."*f* All
the people shall say, "Amen!"

21 "Cursed be anyone who lies with any animal." All the people shall say, "Amen!"

22 "Cursed be anyone who lies with his sister,
whether the daughter of his father or the daughter
of his mother." All the people shall say, "Amen!"

23 "Cursed be anyone who lies with his mother-
in-law." All the people shall say, "Amen!"

24 "Cursed be anyone who strikes down a
neighbor in secret." All the people shall say,
"Amen!"

25 "Cursed be anyone who takes a bribe to shed
innocent blood." All the people shall say, "Amen!"

26 "Cursed be anyone who does not uphold
the words of this law by observing them." All the
people shall say, "Amen!"

Blessings for Obedience
(Lev 26.1–13; Deut 7.12–24)

28 If you will only obey the LORD your
God, by diligently observing all his
commandments that I am commanding you today,
the LORD your God will set you high above all the

---

e Heb *whole*   *f* Heb *uncovered his father's skirt*

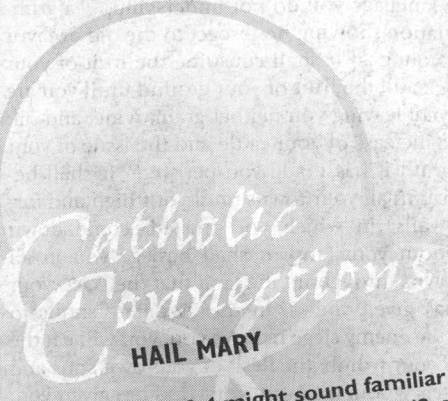

Catholic Connections

HAIL MARY

Deuteronomy 28.4 might sound familiar to you. These words, also found in Lk 1.42, are part of a prayer called the Hail Mary. In this passage, Moses reminds the Israelites that they shall be blessed because of their obedience, and Mary is the ultimate example of the blessings that come from obedience to God's will.

▶ Deut 28.1–6

nations of the earth; 2 all these blessings shall come upon you and overtake you, if you obey the LORD your God:

3 Blessed shall you be in the city, and blessed shall you be in the field.

4 Blessed shall be the fruit of your womb, the fruit of your ground, and the fruit of your livestock, both the increase of your cattle and the issue of your flock.

5 Blessed shall be your basket and your kneading bowl.

6 Blessed shall you be when you come in, and blessed shall you be when you go out.

7 The LORD will cause your enemies who rise against you to be defeated before you; they shall come out against you one way, and flee before you seven ways. 8 The LORD will command the blessing upon you in your barns, and in all that you undertake; he will bless you in the land that the LORD your God is giving you. 9 The LORD will establish you as his holy people, as he has sworn to you, if you keep the commandments of the LORD your God and walk in his ways. 10 All the peoples of the earth shall see that you are called by the name of the LORD, and they shall be afraid of you. 11 The LORD will make you abound in prosperity, in the fruit of your womb, in the fruit of your livestock, and in the fruit of your ground in the land that the LORD swore to your ancestors to give you. 12 The LORD will open for you his rich storehouse, the

... the rain of your land in its season ... your undertakings. You will lend to ... but you will not borrow. 13 The ... the head, and not the tail; you ... top, and not at the bottom—if ... the commandments of the LORD your ... commanding you today, by diligently ... and if you do not turn aside from any ... that I am commanding ing other gods to ... or to the left, follow-

Warnings against Disobedience
(Ex 9.8–12; Lev 26.14–46)

15 But if you will not obey the LORD your God by diligently observing all his commandments and decrees, which I am commanding you today, then all these curses shall come upon you and overtake you:

16 Cursed shall you be in the city, and cursed shall you be in the field.

17 Cursed shall be your basket and your kneading bowl.

18 Cursed shall be the fruit of your womb, the fruit of your ground, the increase of your cattle and the issue of your flock.

19 Cursed shall you be when you come in, and cursed shall you be when you go out.

20 The LORD will send upon you disaster, panic, and frustration in everything you attempt to do, until you are destroyed and perish quickly, on account of the evil of your deeds, because you have forsaken me. 21 The LORD will make the pestilence cling to you until it has consumed you off the land that you are entering to possess. 22 The LORD will afflict you with consumption, fever, inflammation, with fiery heat and drought, and with blight and mildew; they shall pursue you until you perish. 23 The sky over your head shall be bronze, and the earth under you iron. 24 The LORD will change the rain of your land into powder, and only dust shall come down upon you from the sky until you are destroyed.

25 The LORD will cause you to be defeated before your enemies; you shall go out against them one way and flee before them seven ways. You shall become an object of horror to all the kingdoms of the earth. 26 Your corpses shall be food for every bird of the air and animal of the earth, and there shall be no one to frighten them away. 27 The LORD will afflict you with the boils of Egypt, with ulcers, scurvy, and itch, of which you cannot be healed. 28 The LORD will afflict you with madness, blindness, and confusion of mind; 29 you shall grope about at noon as blind people grope in darkness, but you shall be unable to find your way; and you shall be continually abused and robbed, without

anyone to help. 30 You sha_You shall
woman, but another man 31 Your ox
shall build a house, but but you shall
plant a vineyard, but no olen in front of
shall be butchered befcyou. Your sheep
not eat of it. Your don without anyone to
you, and shall not b ghters shall be given
shall be given to yo ou look on; you will
help you. 32 Your s or them all day but be
to another peopl strain your eyes g. 33 A people whom you
powerless to do up the fruit of your ground
do not know sors; you shall be continually
and of all you, 34 and driven mad by the sight
abused and call see. 35 The LORD will strike you
that your ey nd or the legs with grievous boils of
on the kne not be haled, from the sole of your
which you own of your head. 36 The LORD will
foot to the ng whom you set over you, to
bring yo nation that neither you nor your ancestors have
known, where you shall serve other gods, of wood
and stone. 37 You shall become an object of horror,
a proverb, and a byword among all the peoples
where the LORD will lead you.

38 You shall carry much seed into the field but
shall gather little in, for the locust shall consume it.
39 You shall plant vineyards and dress them, but
you shall neither drink the wine nor gather the
grapes, for the worm shall eat them. 40 You shall
have olive trees throughout all your territory, but
you shall not anoint yourself with the oil, for your
olives shall drop off. 41 You shall have sons and
daughters, but they shall not remain yours, for they
shall go into captivity. 42 All your trees and the fruit
of your ground the cicada shall take over. 43 Aliens
residing among you shall ascend above you higher
and higher, while you shall descend lower and lower. 44 They shall lend to you but you shall not lend
to them; they shall be the head an you shall be
the tail.

45 All these curses shall come upon you, pursuing and overtaking you until you are destroyed, because you did not obey the LORD your God, by
observing the commandments and the decrees that
he commanded you. 46 They shall be among you
and your descendants as a sign and a portent forever.

47 Because you did not serve the LORD your
God joyfully and with gladness of heart for the
abundance of everything, 48 therefore you shall
serve your enemies whom the LORD will send
against you, in hunger and thirst, in nakedness and
lack of everything. He will put an iron yoke on your
neck until he has destroyed you. 49 The LORD will
bring a nation from far away, from the end of the
earth, to swoop down on you like an eagle, a nation

whose language you do not understand, 50 a grim-
faced nation showing no respect to the old or favor
to the young. 51 It shall consume the fruit of your
livestock and the fruit of your ground until you are
destroyed, leaving you neither grain, wine, and oil,
nor the increase of your cattle and the issue of your
flock, until it has made you perish. 52 It shall besiege you in all your towns until your high and fortified walls, in which you trusted, come down
throughout your land; it shall besiege you in all
your towns throughout the land that the LORD your
God has given you. 53 In the desperate straits to
which the enemy siege reduces you, you will eat the
fruit of your womb, the flesh of your own sons and
daughters whom the LORD your God has given you.
54 Even the most refined and gentle of men among
you will begrudge food to his own brother, to the
wife whom he embraces, and to the last of his remaining children, 55 giving to none of them any of
the flesh of his children whom he is eating, because
nothing else remains to him, in the desperate straits
to which the enemy siege will reduce you in all your
towns. 56 She who is the most refined and gentle
among you, so gentle and refined that she does not
venture to set the sole of her foot on the ground,
will begrudge food to the husband whom she embraces, to her own son, and to her own daughter,
57 begrudging even the afterbirth that comes out
from between her thighs, and the children that she
bears, because she is eating them in secret for lack
of anything else, in the desperate straits to which
the enemy siege will reduce you in your towns.

58 If you do not diligently observe all the words
of this law that are written in this book, fearing this
glorious and awesome name, the LORD your God,
59 then the LORD will overwhelm both you and
your offspring with severe and lasting afflictions
and grievous and lasting maladies. 60 He will bring
back upon you all the diseases of Egypt, of which
you were in dread, and they shall cling to you.
61 Every other malady and affliction, even though
not recorded in the book of this law, the LORD will
inflict on you until you are destroyed. 62 Although
once you were as numerous as the stars in heaven,
you shall be left few in number, because you did
not obey the LORD your God. 63 And just as the
LORD took delight in making you prosperous and
numerous, so the LORD will take delight in bringing
you to ruin and destruction; you shall be plucked
off the land that you are entering to possess. 64 The
LORD will scatter you among all peoples, from one
end of the earth to the other; and there you shall
serve other gods, of wood and stone, which neither
you nor your ancestors have known. 65 Among
those nations you shall find no ease, no resting
place for the sole of your foot. There the LORD will
give you a trembling heart, failing eyes, and a lan-

DEUT

guishing spirit. 66 Your life shall hang in doubt before you; night and day you shall be in dread, with no assurance of your life. 67 In the morning you shall say, "If only it were evening!" and at evening you shall say, "If only it were morning!"—because of the dread that your heart shall feel and the sights that your eyes shall see. 68 The LORD will bring you back in ships to Egypt, by a route that I promised you would never see again; and there you shall offer yourselves for sale to your enemies as male and female slaves, but there will be no buyer.

29 8 These are the words of the covenant that the LORD commanded Moses to make with the Israelites in the land of Mō'ab, in addition to the covenant that he had made with them at Hō'reb.

The Covenant Renewed in Moab

2h Moses summoned all Israel and said to them: You have seen all that the LORD did before your eyes in the land of Egypt, to Pharaoh and to all his servants and to all his land, 3 the great trials that your eyes saw, the signs, and those great wonders. 4 But to this day the LORD has not given you a mind to understand, or eyes to see, or ears to hear. 5 I have led you forty years in the wilderness. The clothes on your back have not worn out, and the sandals on your feet have not worn out; 6 you have not eaten bread, and you have not drunk wine or strong drink—so that you may know that I am the LORD your God. 7 When you came to this place, King Sī'hon of Hesh'bon and King Og of Bā'shan came out against us for battle, but we defeated them. 8 We took their land and gave it as an inheritance to the Reū'ben•ites, the Gad'ites, and the half-tribe of Ma•nas'seh. 9 Therefore diligently observe the words of this covenant, in order that you may succeedi in everything that you do.

10 You stand assembled today, all of you, before the LORD your God—the leaders of your tribes,j your elders, and your officials, all the men of Israel, 11 your children, your women, and the aliens who are in your camp, both those who cut your wood and those who draw your water— 12 to enter into the covenant of the LORD your God, sworn by an oath, which the LORD your God is making with you today; 13 in order that he may establish you today as his people, and that he may be your God, as he promised you and as he swore to your ancestors, to Abraham, to Isaac, and to Jacob. 14 I am making this covenant, sworn by an oath, not only with you who stand here with us today before the LORD our God, 15 but also with those who are not here with us today. 16 You know how we lived in the land of Egypt, and how we came through the midst of the nations through which you passed. 17 You have seen their detestable things, the filthy idols of wood and stone, of silver and gold, that were among them. 18 It may be that there is among you a man or woman, or a family or tribe, whose heart is already turning away from the LORD our God to serve the gods of those nations. It may be that there is among you a root sprouting poisonous and bitter growth. 19 All who hear the words of this oath and bless themselves, thinking in their hearts, "We are safe even though we go our own stubborn ways" (thus bringing disaster on moist and dry alike)k— 20 the LORD will be unwilling to pardon them, for the LORD's anger and passion will smoke against them. All the curses written in this book will descend on them, and the LORD will blot out their names from under heaven. 21 The LORD will single them out from all the tribes of Israel for calamity, in accordance with all the curses of the covenant written in this book of the law. 22 The next generation, your children who rise up after you, as well as the foreigner who comes from a distant country, will see the devastation of that land and the afflictions with which the LORD has afflicted it— 23 all its soil burned out by sulfur and salt, nothing planted, nothing sprouting, unable to support any vegetation, like the destruction of Sod'om and Go•mor'rah, Ad'mah and Ze•boi'im, which the LORD destroyed in his fierce anger— 24 they and indeed all the nations will wonder, "Why has the LORD done thus to this land? What caused this great display of anger?" 25 They will conclude, "It is because they abandoned the covenant of the LORD, the God of their ancestors, which he made with them when he brought them out of the land of Egypt. 26 They turned and served other gods, worshiping them, gods whom they had not known and whom he had not allotted to them; 27 so the anger of the LORD was kindled against that land, bringing on it every curse written in this book. 28 The LORD uprooted them from their land in anger, fury, and great wrath, and cast them into another land, as is now the case." 29 The secret things belong to the LORD our God, but the revealed things belong to us and to our children forever, to observe all the words of this law.

God's Fidelity Assured

30 When all these things have happened to you, the blessings and the curses that I have set before you, if you call them to mind among all the nations where the LORD your God has driven you, 2 and return to the LORD your God, and you and your children obey him with all your heart and with all your soul, just as I am

D
E
U
T

---

8 Ch 28.69 in Heb h Ch 29.1 in Heb i Or *deal wisely*
j Gk Syr: Heb *your leaders, your tribes* k Meaning of Heb uncertain

commanding you today, ³ then the LORD your God will restore your fortunes and have compassion on you, gathering you again from all the peoples among whom the LORD your God has scattered you. ⁴ Even if you are exiled to the ends of the world,ˡ from there the LORD your God will gather you, and from there he will bring you back. ⁵ The LORD your God will bring you into the land that your ancestors possessed, and you will possess it; he will make you more prosperous and numerous than your ancestors.

6 Moreover, the LORD your God will circumcise your heart and the heart of your descendants, so that you will love the LORD your God with all your heart and with all your soul, in order that you may live. ⁷ The LORD your God will put all these curses on your enemies and on the adversaries who took advantage of you. ⁸ Then you shall again obey the LORD, observing all his commandments that I am commanding you today, ⁹ and the LORD your God will make you abundantly prosperous in all your undertakings, in the fruit of your body, in the fruit of your livestock, and in the fruit of your soil. For the LORD will again take delight in prospering you, just as he delighted in prospering your ancestors, ¹⁰ when you obey the LORD your God by observing his commandments and decrees that are written in this book of the law, because you turn to the LORD your God with all your heart and with all your soul.

Exhortation to Choose Life

11 Surely, this commandment that I am commanding you today is not too hard for you, nor is it too far away. ¹² It is not in heaven, that you should say, "Who will go up to heaven for us, and get it for us so that we may hear it and observe it?" ¹³ Neither is it beyond the sea, that you should say, "Who will cross to the other side of the sea for us,

and get it for us so that we may hear it and observe it?" ¹⁴ No, the word is very near to you; it is in your mouth and in your heart for you to observe.

15 See, I have set before you today life and prosperity, death and adversity. ¹⁶ If you obey the commandments of the LORD your God^m that I am commanding you today, by loving the LORD your God, walking in his ways, and observing his commandments, decrees, and ordinances, then you shall live and become numerous, and the LORD your God will bless you in the land that you are entering to possess. ¹⁷ But if your heart turns away and you do not hear, but are led astray to bow down to other gods and serve them, ¹⁸ I declare to you today that you shall perish; you shall not live long in the land that you are crossing the Jordan to enter and possess. ¹⁹ I call heaven and earth to witness against you today that I have set before you life and death, blessings and curses. Choose life so that you and your descendants may live, ²⁰ loving the LORD your God, obeying him, and holding fast to him; for that means life to you and length of days, so that you may live in the land that the LORD swore to give to your ancestors, to Abraham, to Isaac, and to Jacob.

Joshua Becomes Moses' Successor
(Num 27.12–23)

31 When Moses had finished speaking all^n these words to all Israel, ² he said to them: "I am now one hundred twenty years old. I am no longer able to get about, and the LORD has told me, 'You shall not cross over this Jordan.' ³ The LORD your God himself will cross over before you. He will destroy these nations before you, and you

---

ˡ Heb *of heaven*   *m* Gk: Heb lacks *If you obey the commandments of the LORD your God*   *n* Q Ms Gk: MT *Moses went and spoke*

"Choose life."

LIVE IT!

This statement is a powerful summons to all of us who are believers. We live in a culture that is constantly filled and refilled with images of violence and death, especially in the media and entertainment. Many people seem to choose options that lead to death rather than life. Temptations to do so are everywhere.

God calls us to choose life—every time. What options before us lead to life rather than death? What choices give life to others?

Life is what we are called to—a full life, lived out in God's presence, a life lived in service to others. Think about the choices you make each day. Your decision to greet someone or smile at someone can make a big difference. That difference can be life giving. Choose life. It is always the right choice!

▶ **Deut 30.19**

Moses and Joshua Receive God's Charge

14 The LORD said to Moses, "Your time to die is near; call Joshua and present yourselves in the tent of meeting, so that I may commission him." So Moses and Joshua went and presented themselves in the tent of meeting, 15 and the LORD appeared at the tent in a pillar of cloud; the pillar of cloud stood at the entrance to the tent.

16 The LORD said to Moses, "Soon you will lie down with your ancestors. Then this people will begin to prostitute themselves to the foreign gods in their midst, the gods of the land into which they are going; they will forsake me, breaking my covenant that I have made with them. 17 My anger will be kindled against them in that day. I will forsake them and hide my face from them; they will become easy prey, and many terrible troubles will come upon them. In that day they will say, 'Have not these troubles come upon us because our God is not in our midst?' 18 On that day I will surely hide my face on account of all the evil they have done by turning to other gods. 19 Now therefore write this song, and teach it to the Israelites; put it in their mouths, in order that this song may be a witness for me against the Israelites. 20 For when I have brought them into the land flowing with milk and honey, which I promised on oath to their ancestors, and they have eaten their fill and grown fat, they will turn to other gods and serve them, despising me and breaking my covenant. 21 And when many terrible troubles come upon them, this song will confront them as a witness, because it will not be lost from the mouths of their descendants. For I know what they are inclined to do even now, before I have brought them into the land that I promised them on oath." 22 That very day Moses wrote this song and taught it to the Israelites.

23 Then the LORD commissioned Joshua son of Nun and said, "Be strong and bold, for you shall bring the Israelites into the land that I promised them; I will be with you."

24 When Moses had finished writing down in a book the words of this law to the very end, 25 Moses commanded the Lē′vites who carried the ark of the covenant of the LORD, saying, 26 "Take this book of the law and put it beside the ark of the covenant of the LORD your God; let it remain there as a witness against you. 27 For I know well how rebellious and stubborn you are. If you already have been so rebellious toward the LORD while I am still alive among you, how much more after my death! 28 Assemble to me all the elders of your tribes and your officials, so that I may recite these words·in their hearing and call heaven and earth to witness against them. 29 For I know that after my death you

shall dispossess them. Joshua also will cross over before you, as the LORD promised. 4 The LORD will do to them as he did to Si′hon and Og, the kings of the Am′o·rītes, and to their land, when he destroyed them. 5 The LORD will give them over to you and you shall deal with them in full accord with the command that I have given to you. 6 Be strong and bold; have no fear or dread of them, because it is the LORD your God who goes with you; he will not fail you or forsake you."

7 Then Moses summoned Joshua and said to him in the sight of all Israel: "Be strong and bold, for you are the one who will go with this people into the land that the LORD has sworn to their ancestors to give them; and you will put them in possession of it. 8 It is the LORD who goes before you. He will be with you; he will not fail you or forsake you. Do not fear or be dismayed."

The Law to Be Read Every Seventh Year

9 Then Moses wrote down this law, and gave it to the priests, the sons of Levi, who carried the ark of the covenant of the LORD, and to all the elders of Israel. 10 Moses commanded them: "Every seventh year, in the scheduled year of remission, during the festival of booths,ᵒ 11 when all Israel comes to appear before the LORD your God at the place that he will choose, you shall read this law before all Israel in their hearing. 12 Assemble the people—men, women, and children, as well as the aliens residing in your towns—so that they may hear and learn to fear the LORD your God and to observe diligently all the words of this law, 13 and so that their children, who have not known it, may hear and learn to fear the LORD your God, as long as you live in the land that you are crossing over the Jordan to possess."

DEUT

Cultural Connections

LIVE THE HISTORY OF SALVATION!

As Moses did, contemporary cultures express their faith in the Lord of history:

Lord, you who are the Lord of all,
we, the Hispanic people of the United States,
conscious of being a people with its own identity,
born of common roots,
cultural traditions, language, and faith,
and in diversity united,
direct this prayer to you.

Lord and master of history,
we, a people, as we experience the same hungers and hurts,
make a preferential option for the poor,
and we stand in solidarity with this suffering humanity.

From your creative womb, we have been born;
we are your family, your believing people.
In this moment of grace, we feel ourselves called
to a "prophetic mission";
working together and participating in community,
we speak in your name to church and society.

Raised up as a people, intent on being authors
of our own history,
we walk with hope and in a progressive process.
Together we contribute to the coming of
the Kingdom of God here and now,
struggling to establish the new society, with an economy, relationships, and values based on the
*   love and the justice of your Son, Jesus Christ.*

We ask this in company with Mary,
the mother of all believers.
Amen.

(Secretariat for Hispanic Affairs of the USA National Conference
of Catholic Bishops, *Prophetic Voices*, p. 23)

will surely act corruptly, turning aside from the way that I have commanded you. In time to come trouble will befall you, because you will do what is evil in the sight of the LORD, provoking him to anger through the work of your hands."

The Song of Moses

30 Then Moses recited the words of this song, to the very end, in the hearing of the whole assembly of Israel:

32 Give ear, O heavens, and I will speak;
     let the earth hear the words of my
         mouth.
2 May my teaching drop like the rain,

my speech condense like the dew;
  like gentle rain on grass,
    like showers on new growth.
3 For I will proclaim the name of the LORD;
     ascribe greatness to our God!

4 The Rock, his work is perfect,
     and all his ways are just.
   A faithful God, without deceit,
     just and upright is he;
5 yet his degenerate children have dealt falsely
         with him,*p*

---

p Meaning of Heb uncertain

DEUT

a perverse and crooked generation.
6 Do you thus repay the LORD,
     O foolish and senseless people?
Is not he your father, who created you,
     who made you and established you?
7 Remember the days of old,
     consider the years long past;
ask your father, and he will inform you;
     your elders, and they will tell you.
8 When the Most High*q* apportioned the nations,
     when he divided humankind,
he fixed the boundaries of the peoples
     according to the number of the gods;*r*
9 the LORD's own portion was his people,
     Jacob his allotted share.

10 He sustained*s* him in a desert land,
     in a howling wilderness waste;
he shielded him, cared for him,
     guarded him as the apple of his eye.
11 As an eagle stirs up its nest,
     and hovers over its young;
as it spreads its wings, takes them up,
     and bears them aloft on its pinions,
12 the LORD alone guided him;
     no foreign god was with him.
13 He set him atop the heights of the land,
     and fed him with*t* produce of the field;
he nursed him with honey from the crags,
     with oil from flinty rock;
14 curds from the herd, and milk from the flock,
     with fat of lambs and rams;
Bā'shan bulls and goats,
     together with the choicest wheat—
     you drank fine wine from the blood of
         grapes.
15 Jacob ate his fill;*u*
     Jesh'ū·run grew fat, and kicked.
     You grew fat, bloated, and gorged!
He abandoned God who made him,
     and scoffed at the Rock of his salvation.
16 They made him jealous with strange gods,
     with abhorrent things they provoked him.
17 They sacrificed to demons, not God,
     to deities they had never known,
to new ones recently arrived,
     whom your ancestors had not feared.
18 You were unmindful of the Rock that bore
         you;*v*
     you forgot the God who gave you birth.

19 The LORD saw it, and was jealous;*w*
     he spurned*x* his sons and daughters.
20 He said: I will hide my face from them,
     I will see what their end will be;
for they are a perverse generation,
     children in whom there is no faithfulness.

21 They made me jealous with what is no god,
     provoked me with their idols.
So I will make them jealous with what is no
         people,
     provoke them with a foolish nation.
22 For a fire is kindled by my anger,
     and burns to the depths of Shĕ'ōl;
it devours the earth and its increase,
     and sets on fire the foundations of the
         mountains.
23 I will heap disasters upon them,
     spend my arrows against them:
24 wasting hunger,
     burning consumption,
     bitter pestilence.
The teeth of beasts I will send against them,
     with venom of things crawling in the dust.
25 In the street the sword shall bereave,
     and in the chambers terror,
for young man and woman alike,
     nursing child and old gray head.
26 I thought to scatter them*y*
     and blot out the memory of them from
         humankind;
27 but I feared provocation by the enemy,
     for their adversaries might misunderstand
and say, "Our hand is triumphant;
     it was not the LORD who did all this."

28 They are a nation void of sense;
     there is no understanding in them.
29 If they were wise, they would understand this;
     they would discern what the end would be.
30 How could one have routed a thousand,
     and two put a myriad to flight,
unless their Rock had sold them,
     the LORD had given them up?
31 Indeed their rock is not like our Rock;
     our enemies are fools.*y*
32 Their vine comes from the vinestock of
         Sod'om,
     from the vineyards of Go·mor'rah;
their grapes are grapes of poison,
     their clusters are bitter;
33 their wine is the poison of serpents,
     the cruel venom of asps.

34 Is not this laid up in store with me,
     sealed up in my treasuries?
35 Vengeance is mine, and recompense,
     for the time when their foot shall slip;

D
E
U
T

---

q Traditional rendering of Heb *Elyon*   *r* Q Ms Compare Gk
Tg: MT *the Israelites*   *s* Sam Gk Compare Tg: MT *found*
t Sam Gk Syr Tg: MT *he ate*   *u* Q Mss Sam Gk: MT lacks
Jacob ate his fill   *v* Or *that begot you*   *w* Q Mss Gk: MT lacks
was jealous   *x* Cn: Heb *he spurned because of provocation*
y Gk: Meaning of Heb uncertain

because the day of their calamity is at hand,
their doom comes swiftly.

36 Indeed the LORD will vindicate his people,
have compassion on his servants,
when he sees that their power is gone,
neither bond nor free remaining.
37 Then he will say: Where are their gods,
the rock in which they took refuge,
38 who ate the fat of their sacrifices,
and drank the wine of their libations?
Let them rise up and help you,
let them be your protection!

39 See now that I, even I, am he;
there is no god besides me.
I kill and I make alive;
I wound and I heal;
and no one can deliver from my hand.
40 For I lift up my hand to heaven,
and swear: As I live forever,
41 when I whet my flashing sword,
and my hand takes hold on judgment;
I will take vengeance on my adversaries,
and will repay those who hate me.
42 I will make my arrows drunk with blood,
and my sword shall devour flesh—
with the blood of the slain and the captives,
from the long-haired enemy.

43 Praise, O heavens,*z* his people,
worship him, all you gods!*a*
For he will avenge the blood of his children,*b*
and take vengeance on his adversaries;
he will repay those who hate him,*a*
and cleanse the land for his people.*c*

44 Moses came and recited all the words of this song in the hearing of the people, he and Joshua*d* son of Nun. 45 When Moses had finished reciting all these words to all Israel, 46 he said to them: "Take to heart all the words that I am giving in witness against you today; give them as a command to your children, so that they may diligently observe all the words of this law. 47 This is no trifling matter for you, but rather your very life; through it you may live long in the land that you are crossing over the Jordan to possess."

Moses' Death Foretold

48 On that very day the LORD addressed Moses as follows: 49 "Ascend this mountain of the Ab'-a•rim, Mount Nē'bō, which is in the land of Mō'ab, across from Jericho, and view the land of Cā'naan, which I am giving to the Israelites for a possession; 50 you shall die there on the mountain that you ascend and shall be gathered to your kin, as your brother Aaron died on Mount Hor and was gath-

ered to his kin; 51 because both of you broke faith with me among the Israelites at the waters of Mer'i•bath-kā'desh in the wilderness of Zin, by failing to maintain my holiness among the Israelites. 52 Although you may view the land from a distance, you shall not enter it—the land that I am giving to the Israelites."

Moses' Final Blessing on Israel

33 This is the blessing with which Moses, the man of God, blessed the Israelites before his death. 2 He said:
The LORD came from Sinai,
and dawned from Sē'ir upon us;*e*
he shone forth from Mount Par'an.
With him were myriads of holy ones;*f*
at his right, a host of his own.*g*
3 Indeed, O favorite among*h* peoples,
all his holy ones were in your charge;
they marched at your heels,
accepted direction from you.
4 Moses charged us with the law,
as a possession for the assembly of Jacob.
5 There arose a king in Jesh'ū•run,
when the leaders of the people
assembled—
the united tribes of Israel.

6 May Reuben live, and not die out,
even though his numbers are few.

7 And this he said of Judah:
O LORD, give heed to Judah,
and bring him to his people;
strengthen his hands for him,*i*
and be a help against his adversaries.

8 And of Levi he said:
Give to Levi*j* your Thum'mim,
and your Ū'rim to your loyal one,
whom you tested at Mas'sah,
with whom you contended at the waters
of Mer'i•bah;
9 who said of his father and mother,
"I regard them not";
he ignored his kin,
and did not acknowledge his children.
For they observed your word,
and kept your covenant.

---

z Q Ms Gk: MT *nations*   *a* Q Ms Gk: MT lacks this line
b Q Ms Gk: MT *his servants*   *c* Q Ms Sam Gk Vg: MT *his land his people*   *d* Sam Gk Syr Vg: MT *Hoshea*   *e* Gk Syr Vg Compare Tg: Heb *upon them*   *f* Cn Compare Gk Sam Syr Vg: MT *He came from Ribeboth-kodesh*,   *g* Cn Compare Gk: meaning of Heb uncertain   *h* Or *O lover of the*   *i* Cn: Heb *with his hands he contended*   *j* Q Ms Gk: MT lacks *Give to Levi*

10 They teach Jacob your ordinances,
   and Israel your law;
they place incense before you,
   and whole burnt offerings on your altar.
11 Bless, O LORD, his substance,
   and accept the work of his hands;
crush the loins of his adversaries,
   of those that hate him, so that they do not
      rise again.

12 Of Benjamin he said:
The beloved of the LORD rests in safety—
the High God*k* surrounds him all day long—
   the beloved*l* rests between his shoulders.

13 And of Joseph he said:
Blessed by the LORD be his land,
   with the choice gifts of heaven above,
   and of the deep that lies beneath;
14 with the choice fruits of the sun,
   and the rich yield of the months;
15 with the finest produce of the ancient
      mountains,
   and the abundance of the everlasting
      hills;
16 with the choice gifts of the earth and its
      fullness,
   and the favor of the one who dwells on
      Sinai.*m*
Let these come on the head of Joseph,
   on the brow of the prince among his
      brothers.
17 A firstborn*n* bull—majesty is his!
   His horns are the horns of a wild ox;
with them he gores the peoples,
   driving them to*o* the ends of the earth;
such are the myriads of E'phra·im,
   such are the thousands of Ma·nas'seh.

18 And of Zeb'u·lun he said:
Rejoice, Zeb'u·lun, in your going out;
   and Is'sa·char, in your tents.
19 They call peoples to the mountain;
   there they offer the right sacrifices;
for they suck the affluence of the seas
   and the hidden treasures of the sand.

20 And of Gad he said:
Blessed be the enlargement of Gad!
   Gad lives like a lion;
   he tears at arm and scalp.
21 He chose the best for himself,
   for there a commander's allotment was
      reserved;
he came at the head of the people,
   he executed the justice of the LORD,
   and his ordinances for Israel.

22 And of Dan he said:
Dan is a lion's whelp
   that leaps forth from Ba'shan.

23 And of Naph'ta·li he said:
O Naph'ta·li, sated with favor,
   full of the blessing of the LORD,
   possess the west and the south.

24 And of Ash'er he said:
Most blessed of sons be Ash'er;
   may he be the favorite of his brothers,
   and may he dip his foot in oil.
25 Your bars are iron and bronze;
   and as your days, so is your strength.

26 There is none like God, O Jesh'u·run,
   who rides through the heavens to your
      help,
   majestic through the skies.
27 He subdues the ancient gods,*p*
   shatters*q* the forces of old;*r*
he drove out the enemy before you,
   and said, "Destroy!"
28 So Israel lives in safety,
   untroubled is Jacob's abode*s*
in a land of grain and wine,
   where the heavens drop down dew.
29 Happy are you, O Israel! Who is like you,
   a people saved by the LORD,
the shield of your help,
   and the sword of your triumph!
Your enemies shall come fawning to you,
   and you shall tread on their backs.

Moses Dies and Is Buried in the Land of Moab

34 Then Moses went up from the plains of Mo'ab to Mount Ne'bo, to the top of Pis'gah, which is opposite Jericho, and the LORD showed him the whole land: Gil'e·ad as far as Dan, 2 all Naph'ta·li, the land of E'phra·im and Ma-nas'seh, all the land of Judah as far as the Western Sea, 3 the Neg'eb, and the Plain—that is, the valley of Jericho, the city of palm trees—as far as Zo'ar. 4 The LORD said to him, "This is the land of which I swore to Abraham, to Isaac, and to Jacob, saying, 'I will give it to your descendants'; I have let you see it with your eyes, but you shall not cross over there." 5 Then Moses, the servant of the LORD, died there in the land of Mo'ab, at the LORD's command. 6 He was buried in a valley in the land of Mo'ab, opposite Beth-pe'or, but no one knows his burial

---

k Heb *above him*   *l* Heb *he*   *m* Cn: Heb *in the bush*
n Q Ms Gk Syr Vg: MT *His firstborn*   *o* Cn: Heb *the peoples, together*   *p* Or *The eternal God is a dwelling place*   *q* Cn: Heb *from underneath*   *r* Or *the everlasting arms*   *s* Or *fountain*

DEUT

MOSES' DEATH

Why did Moses die on the brink of entering the Promised Land? This question has disturbed many generations of believers. The one who received God's call to lead the Israelites out of slavery, who amazed Pharaoh with wonders and called down plagues on Egypt, who opened the Red Sea and received the tablets of the Law on Mount Sinai—this great leader did not get to enjoy the success of his work (Num 20.12)! Deuteronomy 34.1–6 simply tells us that Moses died on Mount Nebo and that his burial place was forgotten.

But consider this: By the time Deuteronomy was written, Moses had become a legendary figure. Many of the details of his life had been forgotten. Perhaps it is fitting that Moses' story ends as it began: shrouded in mystery, tragedy, and hope. What hope? The hope for another prophet like Moses (18.15) that remained alive and strong in the Israelites' hearts.

▶ **Deuteronomy, chapter 34**

place to this day. 7 Moses was one hundred twenty years old when he died; his sight was unimpaired and his vigor had not abated. 8 The Israelites wept for Moses in the plains of Mō′ab thirty days; then the period of mourning for Moses was ended.

9 Joshua son of Nun was full of the spirit of wisdom, because Moses had laid his hands on him; and the Israelites obeyed him, doing as the LORD had commanded Moses.

10 Never since has there arisen a prophet in Israel like Moses, whom the LORD knew face to face. 11 He was unequaled for all the signs and wonders that the LORD sent him to perform in the land of Egypt, against Pharaoh and all his servants and his entire land, 12 and for all the mighty deeds and all the terrifying displays of power that Moses performed in the sight of all Israel.

Introduction to the

Historical
Books

Have you ever noticed that many older people enjoy telling stories about the past? Sometimes, it seems that their past experiences are more real to them than present-day events. Those of us who are younger may get tired of hearing about the "good old days." Still, a lot is to be gained from listening carefully to the memories of our elders. The sixteen historical books of the Old Testament, like the voices of respected elders, tell the stories of God at work in ancient Israel. In reading these stories, we can see more clearly how God works in today's world.

In-depth

THE HISTORICAL BOOKS RECOUNT THE PERIOD of Israelite history from 1250 to 100 B.C. In those books, we read about the following events:

- the Israelites' settlement in the Promised Land and their struggle to protect themselves from their enemies (the Books of Joshua and Judges)
- the rise of a united kingdom under David (1 and 2 Samuel, 1 Kings)
- the division of the kingdom into northern and southern kingdoms, and the various kings and prophets of each, until the fall of Jerusalem in 587 B.C. (1 and 2 Kings, 1 and 2 Chronicles)
- the return from Exile and the rebuilding of the nation (Ezra and Nehemiah)
- the Jewish resistance to Greek domination in the second century before Christ (1 and 2 Maccabees)

In addition, the books contain three "novels" about the human challenge to trust God in difficult times (Tobit, Judith, and Esther).

The historical books of the Old Testament are not like the history books that we read in school. Those who write history books today generally try to report the facts with little interpretation. "Let the events speak for themselves," they say. However, those who wrote the historical books of the Old Testament had a different purpose: "Let us tell you what the events *mean in the light of our faith in God."* Thus, the history contained in these books is often called sacred history because it reveals God's message and God's purpose in history.

Scripture scholars find evidence of two general groups shaping the final form of the historical books. The first group is called the Deuteronomic school of writers because it was responsible for the highly influential Book of Deuteronomy. This group also wrote Joshua, Judges, 1 and 2 Samuel, and 1 and 2 Kings. The Deuteronomists were convinced that God rewarded the good and punished the wicked in this world. Thus, you will find in these books a repeated pattern of (1) God's offer of love, (2) the people's faithlessness and sin, (3) God's just punishment, (4) the people's repentance and cry for help, (5) God's forgiveness and mercy, and (6) the people's repeated sin.

The second group (or person), sometimes called the Chronicler, is responsible for 1 and 2 Chronicles, and probably Ezra and Nehemiah. The Chronicler still emphasized that God rewards the faithful and punishes the unfaithful, but the measurement for what is faithful had changed. Instead of emphasizing faithfulness to the Sinai Covenant, the Chronicler emphasized faithfulness to proper worship, particularly worship at the Temple in Jerusalem. The Chronicler wrote after the destruction of the northern and southern kingdoms, to nurture the faith of a small community trying to rebuild itself.

Some of the religious truths you will learn from reading these books are as follows:

- God is not removed from the affairs of this world but cares deeply about what is happening in human history.
- People are happier when they follow the law of God than when they turn away from the Law.
- All human beings, from the beginning of history, are joined in a common struggle to find sense and meaning in the ups and downs of life.

As you read these books, remember that the authors' understanding of God is not the same as Jesus' understanding. Although not denying the truths about God taught by these books, Christians have a larger context for understanding God's unconditional love and unlimited mercy: Jesus' teaching in the New Testament.

Other Background

- **The Book of Ruth was not originally one of the historical books. It was written later than the books it is now sandwiched between.**

- **The Books of 1 and 2 Chronicles review the same historical period as 1 and 2 Samuel and 1 and 2 Kings.**

- **Tobit, Judith, and Esther are fictional works that use history only as a backdrop. Their purpose is to encourage fidelity to God's law in hard times.**

- **Tobit, Judith, 1 and 2 Maccabees, and parts of Esther are not found in every translation of the Old Testament and are not contained in many Protestant Bibles. See "The Case of the Missing Books," near Tobit 1.16.**

When you were young, did you ask to hear your favorite story over and over again? Do you remember feeling secure because you knew how the story would turn out? Often, familiar stories appeal to us because of their simple justice: evil is punished, and good is rewarded. The author of the Book of Joshua applies this simple justice to the conquest of the Promised Land: those who follow God are rewarded, and those who do not are destroyed.

In-depth

The Book of Joshua is named after the Israelite hero who succeeds Moses and leads the people in their takeover of the Promised Land. At the beginning of the book, Joshua promises the Israelites that they will conquer the land of Canaan and make it their own if they are faithful to the Covenant of Moses. They respond with enthusiasm, "Just as we obeyed Moses in all things, so we will obey you" (1.17). The author describes how by remaining true to the Commandments of God, the various Israelite tribes, under Joshua's leadership, take over the land and settle in it with their families and livestock (see map 2, "The Exodus from Egypt").

Today, biblical scholars doubt that the conquest of the Promised Land by the twelve tribes of Israel was as complete and easy as it is written in Joshua. Archaeologists have found evidence that Canaanites continued to live in the area after the "conquest." The historical memories preserved in the book were reshaped by the author to emphasize an important lesson of faith: God would preserve the Israelites on their land as long as they obeyed the Commandments.

The belief in the triumph of good and the punishment of evil is at the heart of the Book of Joshua. Like Judges, 1 and 2 Samuel, and 1 and 2 Kings, the Book of Joshua is inspired by the Book of Deuteronomy, which insists that God rewards the just and punishes the wicked in this world (see Deut 30.15–20). The Book of Joshua challenges us to remember that God is our surest hope in all the ups and downs of history.

At a Glance

- **Chapters 1–12.** the conquest of the land of Canaan

- **Chapters 13–22.** the division of the land among the twelve tribes

- **Chapters 23–24.** Joshua's last words and death

Quick Facts

Period Covered
after the desert wandering, from about 1250 to 1200 B.C.

Author
unknown, from the Deuteronomic tradition, writing in the seventh or sixth century B.C.

Themes
Israel's conquest of the Promised Land, the triumph of good and the punishment of evil

Of Note
The name Jesus is the Greek form of Joshua, which means "God saves."

Joshua

3.14

God's Commission to Joshua

After the death of Moses the servant of the LORD, the LORD spoke to Joshua son of Nun, Moses' assistant, saying, 2 "My servant Moses is dead. Now proceed to cross the Jordan, you and all this people, into the land that I am giving to them, to the Israelites. 3 Every place that the sole of your foot will tread upon I have given to you, as I promised to Moses. 4 From the wilderness and the Lebanon as far as the great river, the river Euphrates, all the land of the Hit′tites, to the Great Sea in the west shall be your territory. 5 No one shall be able to stand against you all the days of your life. As I was with Moses, so I will be with you; I will not fail you or forsake you. 6 Be strong and courageous; for you shall put this people in possession of the land that I swore to their ancestors to give them. 7 Only be strong and very courageous, being careful to act in accordance with all the law that my servant Moses commanded you; do not turn from it to the right hand or to the left, so that you may be successful wherever you go. 8 This book of the law shall not depart out of your mouth; you shall meditate on it day and night, so that you may be careful to act in accordance with all that is written in it. For then you shall make your way prosperous, and then you shall be successful. 9 I hereby command you: Be strong and courageous; do not be frightened or dismayed, for the LORD your God is with you wherever you go."

Preparations for the Invasion

10 Then Joshua commanded the officers of the people, 11 "Pass through the camp, and command the people: 'Prepare your provisions; for in three days you are to cross over the Jordan, to go in to take possession of the land that the LORD your God gives you to possess.'"

12 To the Reū′ben·ites, the Gad′ites, and the half-tribe of Ma·nas′seh Joshua said, 13 "Remember the word that Moses the servant of the LORD commanded you, saying, 'The LORD your God is providing you a place of rest, and will give you this land.' 14 Your wives, your little ones, and your livestock shall remain in the land that Moses gave you beyond the Jordan. But all the warriors among you shall cross over armed before your kindred and shall help them, 15 until the LORD gives rest to your kindred as well as to you, and they too take possession of the land that the LORD your God is giving them. Then you shall return to your own land and take possession of it, the land that Moses the servant of the LORD gave you beyond the Jordan to the east."

16 They answered Joshua: "All that you have commanded us we will do, and wherever you send us we will go. 17 Just as we obeyed Moses in all things, so we will obey you. Only may the LORD your God be with you, as he was with Moses! 18 Whoever rebels against your orders and disobeys your words, whatever you command, shall be put to death. Only be strong and courageous."

Be Not Afraid

"Be strong and courageous; do not be frightened or dismayed, for the LORD your God is with you wherever you go" (Josh 1.9).

Living proof:

Saint Joan of Arc was a humble, uneducated peasant maiden from fifteenth-century France. Inspired by saintly voices, she overcame numerous obstacles to lead the French troops into battle against British invaders.

Saint Thomas More, a distinguished scholar and lawyer, refused to approve King Henry VIII's divorce and remarriage and establishment of the Church of England.

Dorothy Day, twentieth-century American cofounder of the Catholic Worker Movement, challenged all Christians to serve poor and homeless people and dedicated her life to nonviolence.

Archbishop Oscar Romero of El Salvador was shot while saying Mass in 1980 because he dared to speak against the military groups that were terrorizing and killing the poor people of his diocese.

These four people, along with many others, have taken to heart God's words to Joshua. If you are not familiar with their stories, take time to learn more about these Catholic heroes.

▸ Josh 1.5–9

Spies Sent to Jericho
(Heb 11.31)

2 Then Joshua son of Nun sent two men secretly from Shit'tim as spies, saying, "Go, view the land, especially Jericho." So they went, and entered the house of a prostitute whose name was Rā'hab, and spent the night there. 2 The king of Jericho was told, "Some Israelites have come here tonight to search out the land." 3 Then the king of Jericho sent orders to Rā'hab, "Bring out the men who have come to you, who entered your house, for they have come only to search out the whole land." 4 But the woman took the two men and hid them. Then she said, "True, the men came to me, but I did not know where they came from. 5 And when it was time to close the gate at dark, the men went out. Where the men went I do not know. Pursue them quickly, for you can overtake them." 6 She had, however, brought them up to the roof and hidden them with the stalks of flax that she had laid out on the roof. 7 So the men pursued them on the way to the Jordan as far as the fords. As soon as the pursuers had gone out, the gate was shut.

8 Before they went to sleep, she came up to them on the roof 9 and said to the men: "I know that the LORD has given you the land, and that dread of you has fallen on us, and that all the inhabitants of the land melt in fear before you. 10 For we have heard how the LORD dried up the water of the Red Sea[a] before you when you came out of Egypt, and what you did to the two kings of the

Am'o•rītes that were beyond the Jordan, to Sī'hon and Og, whom you utterly destroyed. 11 As soon as we heard it, our hearts melted, and there was no courage left in any of us because of you. The LORD your God is indeed God in heaven above and on earth below. 12 Now then, since I have dealt kindly with you, swear to me by the LORD that you in turn will deal kindly with my family. Give me a sign of good faith 13 that you will spare my father and mother, my brothers and sisters, and all who belong to them, and deliver our lives from death." 14 The men said to her, "Our life for yours! If you do not tell this business of ours, then we will deal kindly and faithfully with you when the LORD gives us the land."

15 Then she let them down by a rope through the window, for her house was on the outer side of the city wall and she resided within the wall itself. 16 She said to them, "Go toward the hill country, so that the pursuers may not come upon you. Hide yourselves there three days, until the pursuers have returned; then afterward you may go your way." 17 The men said to her, "We will be released from this oath that you have made us swear to you 18 if we invade the land and you do not tie this crimson cord in the window through which you let us down, and you do not gather into your house your father and mother, your brothers, and all your family. 19 If any of you go out of the doors of your

---

a Or Sea of Reeds

house into the street, they shall be responsible for their own death, and we shall be innocent; but if a hand is laid upon any who are with you in the house, we shall bear the responsibility for their death. 20 But if you tell this business of ours, then we shall be released from this oath that you made us swear to you." 21 She said, "According to your words, so be it." She sent them away and they departed. Then she tied the crimson cord in the window.

22 They departed and went into the hill country and stayed there three days, until the pursuers returned. The pursuers had searched all along the way and found nothing. 23 Then the two men came down again from the hill country. They crossed over, came to Joshua son of Nun, and told him all that had happened to them. 24 They said to Joshua, "Truly the LORD has given all the land into our hands; moreover all the inhabitants of the land melt in fear before us."

PRAY IT?

A Prayer Against Prejudice

Creator of diverse people, the Israelites united themselves with Rahab, someone outside their group, and trusted her. Lead me to be open to befriending those who are different from me so that I may learn to trust them as well.

Forgive my friends and me for every time we have looked at someone different and considered that person to be of lesser quality. Forgive us for each time we have talked about certain people as if we were superior. Forgive our cliques that look down on others and won't associate with them. Help us forgive those who have looked down on us. Amen.

▸ **Joshua, chapter 2**

Israel Crosses the Jordan

3 Early in the morning Joshua rose and set out from Shit'tim with all the Israelites, and they came to the Jordan. They camped there before crossing over. 2 At the end of three days the officers went through the camp 3 and commanded the people, "When you see the ark of the covenant of the LORD your God being carried by the levitical priests,

then you shall set out from your place. Follow it, 4 so that you may know the way you should go, for you have not passed this way before. Yet there shall be a space between you and it, a distance of about two thousand cubits; do not come any nearer to it." 5 Then Joshua said to the people, "Sanctify yourselves; for tomorrow the LORD will do wonders among you." 6 To the priests Joshua said, "Take up the ark of the covenant, and pass on in front of the people." So they took up the ark of the covenant and went in front of the people.

7 The LORD said to Joshua, "This day I will begin to exalt you in the sight of all Israel, so that they may know that I will be with you as I was with Moses. 8 You are the one who shall command the priests who bear the ark of the covenant, 'When you come to the edge of the waters of the Jordan, you shall stand still in the Jordan.' " 9 Joshua then said to the Israelites, "Draw near and hear the words of the LORD your God." 10 Joshua said, "By this you shall know that among you is the living God who without fail will drive out from before you the Cā'-naan•ītes, Hit'tītes, Hī'vītes, Per'iz•zītes, Gir'ga-shītes, Am'o•rītes, and Jeb'ū•sītes: 11 the ark of the covenant of the Lord of all the earth is going to pass before you into the Jordan. 12 So now select twelve men from the tribes of Israel, one from each tribe. 13 When the soles of the feet of the priests who bear the ark of the LORD, the Lord of all the earth, rest in the waters of the Jordan, the waters of the Jordan flowing from above shall be cut off; they shall stand in a single heap."

14 When the people set out from their tents to cross over the Jordan, the priests bearing the ark of the covenant were in front of the people. 15 Now the Jordan overflows all its banks throughout the time of harvest. So when those who bore the ark had come to the Jordan, and the feet of the priests bearing the ark were dipped in the edge of the water, 16 the waters flowing from above stood still, rising up in a single heap far off at Adam, the city that is beside Zar'e•than, while those flowing toward the sea of the Ar'a•bah, the Dead Sea,*b* were wholly cut off. Then the people crossed over opposite Jericho. 17 While all Israel were crossing over on dry ground, the priests who bore the ark of the covenant of the LORD stood on dry ground in the middle of the Jordan, until the entire nation finished crossing over the Jordan.

Twelve Stones Set Up at Gilgal

4 When the entire nation had finished crossing over the Jordan, the LORD said to Joshua: 2 "Select twelve men from the people, one from each tribe, 3 and command them, 'Take twelve

---

b Heb *Salt Sea*

JOSH

stones from here out of the middle of the Jordan, from the place where the priests' feet stood, carry them over with you, and lay them down in the place where you camp tonight.' " 4 Then Joshua summoned the twelve men from the Israelites, whom he had appointed, one from each tribe. 5 Joshua said to them, "Pass on before the ark of the LORD your God into the middle of the Jordan, and each of you take up a stone on his shoulder, one for each of the tribes of the Israelites, 6 so that this may be a sign among you. When your children ask in time to come, 'What do those stones mean to you?' 7 then you shall tell them that the waters of the Jordan were cut off in front of the ark of the covenant of the LORD. When it crossed over the Jordan, the waters of the Jordan were cut off. So these stones shall be to the Israelites a memorial forever."

8 The Israelites did as Joshua commanded. They took up twelve stones out of the middle of the Jordan, according to the number of the tribes of the Israelites, as the LORD told Joshua, carried them over with them to the place where they camped, and laid them down there. 9 (Joshua set up twelve stones in the middle of the Jordan, in the place where the feet of the priests bearing the ark of the covenant had stood; and they are there to this day.)

10 The priests who bore the ark remained standing in the middle of the Jordan, until everything was finished that the LORD commanded Joshua to tell the people, according to all that Moses had commanded Joshua. The people crossed over in haste. 11 As soon as all the people had finished crossing over, the ark of the LORD, and the priests, crossed over in front of the people. 12 The Reü′ben·ites, the Gad′ites, and the half-tribe of Ma·nas′seh crossed over armed before the Israelites, as Moses had ordered them. 13 About forty thousand armed for war crossed over before the LORD to the plains of Jericho for battle.

14 On that day the LORD exalted Joshua in the sight of all Israel; and they stood in awe of him, as they had stood in awe of Moses, all the days of his life.

15 The LORD said to Joshua, 16 "Command the priests who bear the ark of the covenant,c to come up out of the Jordan." 17 Joshua therefore commanded the priests, "Come up out of the Jordan." 18 When the priests bearing the ark of the covenant of the LORD came up from the middle of the Jordan, and the soles of the priests' feet touched dry ground, the waters of the Jordan returned to their place and overflowed all its banks, as before.

19 The people came up out of the Jordan on the tenth day of the first month, and they camped in Gil′gal on the east border of Jericho. 20 Those twelve stones, which they had taken out of the Jordan, Joshua set up in Gil′gal, 21 saying to the Israelites,

"When your children ask their parents in time to come, 'What do these stones mean?' 22 then you shall let your children know, 'Israel crossed over the Jordan here on dry ground.' 23 For the LORD your God dried up the waters of the Jordan for you until you crossed over, as the LORD your God did to the Red Sea,d which he dried up for us until we crossed over, 24 so that all the peoples of the earth may know that the hand of the LORD is mighty, and so that you may fear the LORD your God forever."

The New Generation Circumcised

5 When all the kings of the Am′o·rites beyond the Jordan to the west, and all the kings of the Ca′naan·ites by the sea, heard that the LORD had dried up the waters of the Jordan for the Israelites until they had crossed over, their hearts melted, and there was no longer any spirit in them, because of the Israelites.

2 At that time the LORD said to Joshua, "Make flint knives and circumcise the Israelites a second time." 3 So Joshua made flint knives, and circumcised the Israelites at Gib′e·ath-ha·ar′a·loth.e 4 This is the reason why Joshua circumcised them: all the males of the people who came out of Egypt, all the warriors, had died during the journey through the wilderness after they had come out of Egypt. 5 Although all the people who came out had been circumcised, yet all the people born on the journey through the wilderness after they had come out of Egypt had not been circumcised. 6 For the Israelites traveled forty years in the wilderness, until all the nation, the warriors who came out of Egypt, perished, not having listened to the voice of the LORD. To them the LORD swore that he would not let them see the land that he had sworn to their ancestors to give us, a land flowing with milk and honey. 7 So it was their children, whom he raised up in their place, that Joshua circumcised; for they were uncircumcised, because they had not been circumcised on the way.

8 When the circumcising of all the nation was done, they remained in their places in the camp until they were healed. 9 The LORD said to Joshua, "Today I have rolled away from you the disgrace of Egypt." And so that place is called Gil′galf to this day.

The Passover at Gilgal

10 While the Israelites were camped in Gil′gal they kept the passover in the evening on the fourteenth day of the month in the plains of Jericho. 11 On the day after the passover, on that very day,

---

c Or treaty, or testimony; Heb eduth   d Or Sea of Reeds
e That is the Hill of the Foreskins   f Related to Heb galal
to roll

they ate the produce of the land, unleavened cakes and parched grain. 12 The manna ceased on the day they ate the produce of the land, and the Israelites no longer had manna; they ate the crops of the land of Cā'naan that year.

Joshua's Vision

13 Once when Joshua was by Jericho, he looked up and saw a man standing before him with a drawn sword in his hand. Joshua went to him and said to him, "Are you one of us, or one of our adversaries?" 14 He replied, "Neither; but as commander of the army of the LORD I have now come." And Joshua fell on his face to the earth and worshiped, and he said to him, "What do you command your servant, my lord?" 15 The commander of the army of the LORD said to Joshua, "Remove the sandals from your feet, for the place where you stand is holy." And Joshua did so.

Jericho Taken and Destroyed

6 Now Jericho was shut up inside and out because of the Israelites; no one came out and no one went in. 2 The LORD said to Joshua, "See, I have handed Jericho over to you, along with its king and soldiers. 3 You shall march around the city, all the warriors circling the city once. Thus you shall do for six days, 4 with seven priests bearing seven trumpets of rams' horns before the ark. On the seventh day you shall march around the city seven times, the priests blowing the trumpets. 5 When they make a long blast with the ram's horn, as soon as you hear the sound of the trumpet, then all the people shall shout with a great shout; and the wall of the city will fall down flat, and all the people shall charge straight ahead." 6 So Joshua son of Nun summoned the priests and said to them, "Take up the ark of the covenant, and have seven priests carry seven trumpets of rams' horns in front of the ark of the LORD." 7 To the people he said, "Go forward and march around the city; have the armed men pass on before the ark of the LORD."

8 As Joshua had commanded the people, the seven priests carrying the seven trumpets of rams' horns before the LORD went forward, blowing the trumpets, with the ark of the covenant of the LORD following them. 9 And the armed men went before the priests who blew the trumpets; the rear guard came after the ark, while the trumpets blew continually. 10 To the people Joshua gave this command: "You shall not shout or let your voice be heard, nor shall you utter a word, until the day I tell you to shout. Then you shall shout." 11 So the ark of the LORD went around the city, circling it once; and they came into the camp, and spent the night in the camp.

12 Then Joshua rose early in the morning, and the priests took up the ark of the LORD. 13 The seven priests carrying the seven trumpets of rams' horns before the ark of the LORD passed on, blowing the trumpets continually. The armed men went before them, and the rear guard came after the ark of the LORD, while the trumpets blew continually. 14 On the second day they marched around the city once and then returned to the camp. They did this for six days.

15 On the seventh day they rose early, at dawn, and marched around the city in the same manner seven times. It was only on that day that they marched around the city seven times. 16 And at the seventh time, when the priests had blown the trumpets, Joshua said to the people, "Shout! For the LORD has given you the city. 17 The city and all that is in it shall be devoted to the LORD for destruction. Only Rā'hab the prostitute and all who are with her in her house shall live because she hid the messengers we sent. 18 As for you, keep away from the things devoted to destruction, so as not to covet*g* and take any of the devoted things and make the camp of Israel an object for destruction, bringing trouble upon it. 19 But all silver and gold, and vessels of bronze and iron, are sacred to the LORD; they shall go into the treasury of the LORD." 20 So the people shouted, and the trumpets were blown. As soon as the people heard the sound of the trumpets, they raised a great shout, and the wall fell down flat; so the people charged straight ahead into the city and captured it. 21 Then they devoted to destruction by the edge of the sword all in the city, both men and women, young and old, oxen, sheep, and donkeys.

22 Joshua said to the two men who had spied out the land, "Go into the prostitute's house, and bring the woman out of it and all who belong to her, as you swore to her." 23 So the young men who had been spies went in and brought Rā'hab out, along with her father, her mother, her brothers, and all who belonged to her—they brought all her kindred out—and set them outside the camp of Israel. 24 They burned down the city, and everything in it; only the silver and gold, and the vessels of bronze and iron, they put into the treasury of the house of the LORD. 25 But Rā'hab the prostitute, with her family and all who belonged to her, Joshua spared. Her family*h* has lived in Israel ever since. For she hid the messengers whom Joshua sent to spy out Jericho.

26 Joshua then pronounced this oath, saying,
"Cursed before the LORD be anyone who tries
   to build this city—this Jericho!
At the cost of his firstborn he shall lay its
   foundation,

---

g Gk: Heb *devote to destruction* Compare 7.21   *h* Heb *She*

and at the cost of his youngest he shall set
up its gates!"

27 So the LORD was with Joshua; and his fame
was in all the land.

The Sin of Achan and Its Punishment

7 But the Israelites broke faith in regard to the
devoted things: Ā'chan son of Car'mī son of
Zab'dī son of Zē'rah, of the tribe of Judah, took
some of the devoted things; and the anger of the
LORD burned against the Israelites.

2 Joshua sent men from Jericho to Aī, which is
near Beth-ā'ven, east of Beth'el, and said to them,
"Go up and spy out the land." And the men went
up and spied out Aī. 3 Then they returned to Joshua
and said to him, "Not all the people need go up;
about two or three thousand men should go up and
attack Aī. Since they are so few, do not make the
whole people toil up there." 4 So about three thousand of the people went up there; and they fled before the men of Aī. 5 The men of Aī killed about
thirty-six of them, chasing them from outside the
gate as far as Sheb'a•rim and killing them on the
slope. The hearts of the people melted and turned
to water.

6 Then Joshua tore his clothes, and fell to the
ground on his face before the ark of the LORD until
the evening, he and the elders of Israel; and they
put dust on their heads. 7 Joshua said, "Ah, Lord
GOD! Why have you brought this people across the
Jordan at all, to hand us over to the Am'o•rites so as
to destroy us? Would that we had been content to
settle beyond the Jordan! 8 O Lord, what can I say,
now that Israel has turned their backs to their enemies! 9 The Cā'naan•ites and all the inhabitants of
the land will hear of it, and surround us, and cut off
our name from the earth. Then what will you do for
your great name?"

10 The LORD said to Joshua, "Stand up! Why
have you fallen upon your face? 11 Israel has sinned;
they have transgressed my covenant that I imposed
on them. They have taken some of the devoted
things; they have stolen, they have acted deceitfully, and they have put them among their own belongings. 12 Therefore the Israelites are unable to
stand before their enemies; they turn their backs to
their enemies, because they have become a thing
devoted for destruction themselves. I will be with
you no more, unless you destroy the devoted things
from among you. 13 Proceed to sanctify the people,
and say, 'Sanctify yourselves for tomorrow; for thus
says the LORD, the God of Israel, "There are devoted
things among you, O Israel; you will be unable to
stand before your enemies until you take away the
devoted things from among you." 14 In the morning therefore you shall come forward tribe by tribe.
The tribe that the LORD takes shall come near by

clans, the clan that the LORD takes shall come near
by households, and the household that the LORD
takes shall come near one by one. 15 And the one
who is taken as having the devoted things shall be
burned with fire, together with all that he has, for
having transgressed the covenant of the LORD, and
for having done an outrageous thing in Israel.' "

16 So Joshua rose early in the morning, and
brought Israel near tribe by tribe, and the tribe of
Judah was taken. 17 He brought near the clans of Judah, and the clan of the Zē'ra•hites was taken; and
he brought near the clan of the Zē'ra•hites, family
by family,[i] and Zab'dī was taken. 18 And he brought
near his household one by one, and Ā'chan son of
Car'mī son of Zab'dī son of Zē'rah, of the tribe of
Judah, was taken. 19 Then Joshua said to Ā'chan,
"My son, give glory to the LORD God of Israel and
make confession to him. Tell me now what you
have done; do not hide it from me." 20 And Ā'chan
answered Joshua, "It is true; I am the one who
sinned against the LORD God of Israel. This is what
I did: 21 when I saw among the spoil a beautiful
mantle from Shi'nar, and two hundred shekels of
silver, and a bar of gold weighing fifty shekels, then
I coveted them and took them. They now lie hidden
in the ground inside my tent, with the silver underneath."

22 So Joshua sent messengers, and they ran to
the tent; and there it was, hidden in his tent with
the silver underneath. 23 They took them out of the
tent and brought them to Joshua and all the Israelites; and they spread them out before the LORD.
24 Then Joshua and all Israel with him took Ā'chan
son of Zē'rah, with the silver, the mantle, and the
bar of gold, with his sons and daughters, with his
oxen, donkeys, and sheep, and his tent and all that
he had; and they brought them up to the Valley of
Ā'chor. 25 Joshua said, "Why did you bring trouble
on us? The LORD is bringing trouble on you today."
And all Israel stoned him to death; they burned
them with fire, cast stones on them, 26 and raised
over him a great heap of stones that remains to this
day. Then the LORD turned from his burning anger.
Therefore that place to this day is called the Valley
of Ā'chor.[j]

Ai Captured by a Stratagem and Destroyed

8 Then the LORD said to Joshua, "Do not fear or
be dismayed; take all the fighting men with
you, and go up now to Aī. See, I have handed over
to you the king of Aī with his people, his city, and
his land. 2 You shall do to Aī and its king as you did
to Jericho and its king; only its spoil and its livestock you may take as booty for yourselves. Set an
ambush against the city, behind it."

---

[i] Mss Syr: MT *man by man*   [j] That is *Trouble*

3 So Joshua and all the fighting men set out to go up against Ai. Joshua chose thirty thousand warriors and sent them out by night 4 with the command, "You shall lie in ambush against the city, behind it; do not go very far from the city, but all of you stay alert. 5 I and all the people who are with me will approach the city. When they come out against us, as before, we shall flee from them. 6 They will come out after us until we have drawn them away from the city; for they will say, 'They are fleeing from us, as before.' While we flee from them, 7 you shall rise up from the ambush and seize the city; for the LORD your God will give it into your hand. 8 And when you have taken the city, you shall set the city on fire, doing as the LORD has ordered; see, I have commanded you." 9 So Joshua sent them out; and they went to the place of ambush, and lay between Beth'el and Ai, to the west of Ai; but Joshua spent that night in the camp.[k]

10 In the morning Joshua rose early and mustered the people, and went up, with the elders of Israel, before the people to Ai. 11 All the fighting men who were with him went up, and drew near before the city, and camped on the north side of Ai, with a ravine between them and Ai. 12 Taking about five thousand men, he set them in ambush between Beth'el and Ai, to the west of the city. 13 So they stationed the forces, the main encampment that was north of the city and its rear guard west of the city. But Joshua spent that night in the valley. 14 When the king of Ai saw this, he and all his people, the inhabitants of the city, hurried out early in the morning to the meeting place facing the Ar'a·bah to meet Israel in battle; but he did not know that there was an ambush against him behind the city. 15 And Joshua and all Israel made a pretense of being beaten before them, and fled in the direction of the wilderness. 16 So all the people who were in the city were called together to pursue them, and as they pursued Joshua they were drawn away from the city. 17 There was not a man left in Ai or Beth'el who did not go out after Israel; they left the city open, and pursued Israel.

18 Then the LORD said to Joshua, "Stretch out the sword that is in your hand toward Ai; for I will give it into your hand." And Joshua stretched out the sword that was in his hand toward the city. 19 As soon as he stretched out his hand, the troops in ambush rose quickly out of their place and rushed forward. They entered the city, took it, and at once set the city on fire. 20 So when the men of Ai looked back, the smoke of the city was rising to the sky. They had no power to flee this way or that, for the people who fled to the wilderness turned back against the pursuers. 21 When Joshua and all Israel saw that the ambush had taken the city and that the smoke of the city was rising, then they turned back and struck down the men of Ai. 22 And the others came out from the city against them; so they were surrounded by Israelites, some on one side, and some on the other; and Israel struck them down until no one was left who survived or escaped. 23 But the king of Ai was taken alive and brought to Joshua.

24 When Israel had finished slaughtering all the inhabitants of Ai in the open wilderness where they pursued them, and when all of them to the very last had fallen by the edge of the sword, all Israel returned to Ai, and attacked it with the edge of the

---

k Heb *among the people*

Catholic Connections

THE IMPORTANCE OF ALTARS

As soon as the Israelites were able, they built an altar in the Promised Land and renewed their Covenant with God. The altar was a visible sign of the constant need for rededication and renewal.

The altar is an important symbol for Catholics. Catholics gather around the altar to remember and celebrate Jesus' sacrificial death, his Resurrection, and our new Covenant with God. We gather around the altar to share a meal. We remember the story of our faith, and we are joined together as a community of faith.

The next time you are in church, look at the altar and think about all the other altars in Catholic churches around the world. Think about all the other people who are celebrating the Mass even as you sit there. Think about all the people, beginning with Jesus and the Apostles, who have celebrated their Christian faith around an altar. You are united with them just as surely as the Israelite people were united with one another at Mount Ebal.

▶ Josh 8.30–35

JOSH

sword. 25 The total of those who fell that day, both men and women, was twelve thousand—all the people of Aī. 26 For Joshua did not draw back his hand, with which he stretched out the sword, until he had utterly destroyed all the inhabitants of Aī. 27 Only the livestock and the spoil of that city Israel took as their booty, according to the word of the LORD that he had issued to Joshua. 28 So Joshua burned Aī, and made it forever a heap of ruins, as it is to this day. 29 And he hanged the king of Aī on a tree until evening; and at sunset Joshua commanded, and they took his body down from the tree, threw it down at the entrance of the gate of the city, and raised over it a great heap of stones, which stands there to this day.

Joshua Renews the Covenant
(Cp Deut 27.4–5)

30 Then Joshua built on Mount Ē′bal an altar to the LORD, the God of Israel, 31 just as Moses the servant of the LORD had commanded the Israelites, as it is written in the book of the law of Moses, "an altar of unhewn[l] stones, on which no iron tool has been used"; and they offered on it burnt offerings to the LORD, and sacrificed offerings of well-being. 32 And there, in the presence of the Israelites, Joshua[m] wrote on the stones a copy of the law of Moses, which he had written. 33 All Israel, alien as well as citizen, with their elders and officers and their judges, stood on opposite sides of the ark in front of the levitical priests who carried the ark of the covenant of the LORD, half of them in front of Mount Ger′i•zim and half of them in front of Mount Ē′bal, as Moses the servant of the LORD had commanded at the first, that they should bless the people of Israel. 34 And afterward he read all the words of the law, blessings and curses, according to all that is written in the book of the law. 35 There was not a word of all that Moses commanded that Joshua did not read before all the assembly of Israel, and the women, and the little ones, and the aliens who resided among them.

The Gibeonites Save Themselves by Trickery

9 Now when all the kings who were beyond the Jordan in the hill country and in the lowland all along the coast of the Great Sea toward Lebanon—the Hit′tites, the Am′o•rites, the Cā′naan•ites, the Per′iz•zites, the Hi′vites, and the Jeb′u•sites—heard of this, 2 they gathered together with one accord to fight Joshua and Israel.

3 But when the inhabitants of Gib′ē•on heard what Joshua had done to Jericho and to Aī, 4 they on their part acted with cunning: they went and prepared provisions,[n] and took worn-out sacks for their donkeys, and wineskins, worn-out and torn and mended, 5 with worn-out, patched sandals on their feet, and worn-out clothes; and all their provisions were dry and moldy. 6 They went to Joshua in the camp at Gil′gal, and said to him and to the Israelites, "We have come from a far country; so now make a treaty with us." 7 But the Israelites said to the Hi′vites, "Perhaps you live among us; then how can we make a treaty with you?" 8 They said to Joshua, "We are your servants." And Joshua said to them, "Who are you? And where do you come from?" 9 They said to him, "Your servants have come from a very far country, because of the name of the LORD your God; for we have heard a report of him, of all that he did in Egypt, 10 and of all that he did to the two kings of the Am′o•rites who were beyond the Jordan, King Sī′hon of Hesh′bon, and King Og of Bā′shan who lived in Ash′ta•roth. 11 So our elders and all the inhabitants of our country said to us, 'Take provisions in your hand for the journey; go to meet them, and say to them, "We are your servants; come now, make a treaty with us." ' 12 Here is our bread; it was still warm when we took it from our houses as our food for the journey, on the day we set out to come to you, but now, see, it is dry and moldy; 13 these wineskins were new when we filled them, and see, they are burst; and these garments and sandals of ours are worn out from the very long journey." 14 So the leaders[o] partook of their provisions, and did not ask direction from the LORD. 15 And Joshua made peace with them, guaranteeing their lives by a treaty; and the leaders of the congregation swore an oath to them.

16 But when three days had passed after they had made a treaty with them, they heard that they were their neighbors and were living among them. 17 So the Israelites set out and reached their cities on the third day. Now their cities were Gib′ē•on, Chē•phī′rah, Be•er′oth, and Kir′i•ath-jē′a•rim. 18 But the Israelites did not attack them, because the leaders of the congregation had sworn to them by the LORD, the God of Israel. Then all the congregation murmured against the leaders. 19 But all the leaders said to all the congregation, "We have sworn to them by the LORD, the God of Israel, and now we must not touch them. 20 This is what we will do to them: We will let them live, so that wrath may not come upon us, because of the oath that we swore to them." 21 The leaders said to them, "Let them live." So they became hewers of wood and drawers of water for all the congregation, as the leaders had decided concerning them.

22 Joshua summoned them, and said to them, "Why did you deceive us, saying, 'We are very far from you,' while in fact you are living among us?

---

l Heb whole   m Heb he   n Cn: Meaning of Heb uncertain
o Gk: Heb men

23 Now therefore you are cursed, and some of you shall always be slaves, hewers of wood and drawers of water for the house of my God." 24 They answered Joshua, "Because it was told to your servants for a certainty that the LORD your God had commanded his servant Moses to give you all the land, and to destroy all the inhabitants of the land before you; so we were in great fear for our lives because of you, and did this thing. 25 And now we are in your hand: do as it seems good and right in your sight to do to us." 26 This is what he did for them: he saved them from the Israelites; and they did not kill them. 27 But on that day Joshua made them hewers of wood and drawers of water for the congregation and for the altar of the LORD, to continue to this day, in the place that he should choose.

The Sun Stands Still

10 When King A·dō'ni-zē'dek of Jerusalem heard how Joshua had taken Aī, and had utterly destroyed it, doing to Aī and its king as he had done to Jericho and its king, and how the inhabitants of Gib'ē·on had made peace with Israel and were among them, 2 he *p* became greatly frightened, because Gib'ē·on was a large city, like one of the royal cities, and was larger than Aī, and all its men were warriors. 3 So King A·dō'ni-zē'dek of Jerusalem sent a message to King Hō'ham of Hē'bron, to King Pī'ram of Jar'muth, to King Ja·phī'a of Lā'chish, and to King Dē'bir of Eg'lon, saying, 4 "Come up and help me, and let us attack Gib'ē·on; for it has made peace with Joshua and with the Israelites." 5 Then the five kings of the Am'o·rītes—the king of Jerusalem, the king of Hē'bron, the king of Jar'muth, the king of Lā'chish, and the king of Eg'lon—gathered their forces, and went up with all their armies and camped against Gib'ē·on, and made war against it.

6 And the Gib'ē·on·ītes sent to Joshua at the camp in Gil'gal, saying, "Do not abandon your servants; come up to us quickly, and save us, and help us; for all the kings of the Am'o·rītes who live in the hill country are gathered against us." 7 So Joshua went up from Gil'gal, he and all the fighting force with him, all the mighty warriors. 8 The LORD said to Joshua, "Do not fear them, for I have handed them over to you; not one of them shall stand before you." 9 So Joshua came upon them suddenly, having marched up all night from Gil'gal. 10 And the LORD threw them into a panic before Israel, who inflicted a great slaughter on them at Gib'ē·on, chased them by the way of the ascent of Beth-hō'ron, and struck them down as far as A·zē'kah and Mak·kē'dah. 11 As they fled before Israel, while they were going down the slope of Beth-hō'ron, the LORD threw down huge stones from heaven on them as far as A·zē'kah, and they died; there were more who died because of the hailstones than the Israelites killed with the sword.

12 On the day when the LORD gave the Am'-o·rītes over to the Israelites, Joshua spoke to the LORD; and he said in the sight of Israel,

"Sun, stand still at Gib'ē·on,
        and Moon, in the valley of Aī'ja·lon."
13 And the sun stood still, and the moon stopped,
        until the nation took vengeance on their
                enemies.

Is this not written in the Book of Jash'ar? The sun stopped in midheaven, and did not hurry to set for about a whole day. 14 There has been no day like it before or since, when the LORD heeded a human voice; for the LORD fought for Israel.

15 Then Joshua returned, and all Israel with him, to the camp at Gil'gal.

Five Kings Defeated

16 Meanwhile, these five kings fled and hid themselves in the cave at Mak·kē'dah. 17 And it was told Joshua, "The five kings have been found, hidden in the cave at Mak·kē'dah." 18 Joshua said, "Roll large stones against the mouth of the cave, and set men by it to guard them; 19 but do not stay there yourselves; pursue your enemies, and attack them from the rear. Do not let them enter their towns, for the LORD your God has given them into your hand." 20 When Joshua and the Israelites had finished inflicting a very great slaughter on them, until they were wiped out, and when the survivors had entered into the fortified towns, 21 all the people returned safe to Joshua in the camp at Mak·kē'dah; no one dared to speak *q* against any of the Israelites.

22 Then Joshua said, "Open the mouth of the cave, and bring those five kings out to me from the cave." 23 They did so, and brought the five kings out to him from the cave, the king of Jerusalem, the king of Hē'bron, the king of Jar'muth, the king of Lā'chish, and the king of Eg'lon. 24 When they brought the kings out to Joshua, Joshua summoned all the Israelites, and said to the chiefs of the warriors who had gone with him, "Come near, put your feet on the necks of these kings." Then they came near and put their feet on their necks. 25 And Joshua said to them, "Do not be afraid or dismayed; be strong and courageous; for thus the LORD will do to all the enemies against whom you fight." 26 Afterward Joshua struck them down and put them to death, and he hung them on five trees. And they hung on the trees until evening. 27 At sunset Joshua commanded, and they took them down from the trees and threw them into the cave where they had hidden themselves; they set large stones against the mouth of the cave, which remain to this very day.

---

p Heb *they*   *q* Heb *moved his tongue*

JOSH

28 Joshua took Mak•kē'dah on that day, and struck it and its king with the edge of the sword; he utterly destroyed every person in it; he left no one remaining. And he did to the king of Mak•kē'dah as he had done to the king of Jericho.

29 Then Joshua passed on from Mak•kē'dah, and all Israel with him, to Lib'nah, and fought against Lib'nah. 30 The LORD gave it also and its king into the hand of Israel; and he struck it with the edge of the sword, and every person in it; he left no one remaining in it; and he did to its king as he had done to the king of Jericho.

31 Next Joshua passed on from Lib'nah, and all Israel with him, to Lā'chish, and laid siege to it, and assaulted it. 32 The LORD gave Lā'chish into the hand of Israel, and he took it on the second day, and struck it with the edge of the sword, and every person in it, as he had done to Lib'nah.

33 Then King Hō'ram of Gē'zer came up to help Lā'chish; and Joshua struck him and his people, leaving him no survivors.

34 From Lā'chish Joshua passed on with all Israel to Eg'lon; and they laid siege to it, and assaulted it; 35 and they took it that day, and struck it with the edge of the sword; and every person in it he utterly destroyed that day, as he had done to Lā'chish.

36 Then Joshua went up with all Israel from Eg'lon to Hē'bron; they assaulted it, 37 and took it, and struck it with the edge of the sword, and its king and its towns, and every person in it; he left no one remaining, just as he had done to Eg'lon, and utterly destroyed it with every person in it.

38 Then Joshua, with all Israel, turned back to Dē'bir and assaulted it, 39 and he took it with its king and all its towns; they struck them with the edge of the sword, and utterly destroyed every person in it; he left no one remaining; just as he had done to Hē'bron, and, as he had done to Lib'nah and its king, so he did to Dē'bir and its king.

40 So Joshua defeated the whole land, the hill country and the Neg'eb and the lowland and the slopes, and all their kings; he left no one remaining, but utterly destroyed all that breathed, as the LORD God of Israel commanded. 41 And Joshua defeated them from Kā'desh-bar'nē•a to Gā'za, and all the country of Gō'shen, as far as Gib'e•on. 42 Joshua took all these kings and their land at one time, because the LORD God of Israel fought for Israel. 43 Then Joshua returned, and all Israel with him, to the camp at Gil'gal.

The United Kings
of Northern Canaan Defeated

11 When King Jā'bin of Hā'zor heard of this, he sent to King Jō'bab of Mā'don, to the king of Shim'ron, to the king of Ach'shaph, 2 and to the kings who were in the northern hill country, and in the Ar'a•bah south of Chin'ne•roth, and in the lowland, and in Nā'photh-dor on the west, 3 to the Cā'naan•ites in the east and the west, the Am'o•rītes, the Hit'tītes, the Per'iz•zītes, and the Jeb'ū•sītes inthe hill country, and the Hī'vītes under Hermon in the land of Miz'pah. 4 They came out, with all their troops, a great army, in number like the sand on the seashore, with very many horses and chariots. 5 All these kings joined their forces, and came and camped together at the waters of Mē'rom, to fight with Israel.

6 And the LORD said to Joshua, "Do not be afraid of them, for tomorrow at this time I will hand over all of them, slain, to Israel; you shall hamstring their horses, and burn their chariots with fire." 7 So Joshua came suddenly upon them with all his fighting force, by the waters of Mē'rom, and fell upon them. 8 And the LORD handed them over to Israel, who attacked them and chased them as far as Great Sī'don and Mis'rē•photh-mā'im, and eastward as far as the valley of Miz'peh. They struck them down, until they had left no one remaining. 9 And Joshua did to them as the LORD commanded him; he hamstrung their horses, and burned their chariots with fire.

10 Joshua turned back at that time, and took Hā'zor, and struck its king down with the sword. Before that time Hā'zor was the head of all those kingdoms. 11 And they put to the sword all who were in it, utterly destroying them; there was no one left who breathed, and he burned Hā'zor with fire. 12 And all the towns of those kings, and all their kings, Joshua took, and struck them with the edge of the sword, utterly destroying them, as Moses the servant of the LORD had commanded. 13 But Israel burned none of the towns that stood on mounds except Hā'zor, which Joshua did burn. 14 All the spoil of these towns, and the livestock, the Israelites took for their booty; but all the people they struck down with the edge of the sword, until they had destroyed them, and they did not leave any who breathed. 15 As the LORD had commanded his servant Moses, so Moses commanded Joshua, and so Joshua did; he left nothing undone of all that the LORD had commanded Moses.

Summary of Joshua's Conquests

16 So Joshua took all that land: the hill country and all the Neg'eb and all the land of Gō'shen and the lowland and the Ar'a•bah and the hill country of Israel and its lowland, 17 from Mount Hā'lak, which rises toward Sē'ir, as far as Bā'al-gad in the valley of Lebanon below Mount Hermon. He took all their kings, struck them down, and put them to death. 18 Joshua made war a long time with all those kings. 19 There was not a town that made peace with the Israelites, except the Hī'vītes, the in-

habitants of Gib′e•on; all were taken in battle. 20 For it was the LORD's doing to harden their hearts so that they would come against Israel in battle, in order that they might be utterly destroyed, and might receive no mercy, but be exterminated, just as the LORD had commanded Moses.

21 At that time Joshua came and wiped out the An′a•kim from the hill country, from Hē′bron, from Dē′bir, from Ā′nab, and from all the hill country of Judah, and from all the hill country of Israel; Joshua utterly destroyed them with their towns. 22 None of the An′a•kim was left in the land of the Israelites; some remained only in Gā′za, in Gath, and in Ash′dod. 23 So Joshua took the whole land, according to all that the LORD had spoken to Moses; and Joshua gave it for an inheritance to Israel according to their tribal allotments. And the land had rest from war.

The Kings Conquered by Moses
(Cp Num 21.21–35)

12 Now these are the kings of the land, whom the Israelites defeated, whose land they occupied beyond the Jordan toward the east, from the Wadi Ar′non to Mount Hermon, with all the Ar′a•bah eastward: 2 King Sī′hon of the Am′o•rītes who lived at Hesh′bon, and ruled from A•rō′er, which is on the edge of the Wadi Ar′non, and from the middle of the valley as far as the river Jab′bok, the boundary of the Am′mon•ites, that is, half of Gil′e•ad, 3 and the Ar′a•bah to the Sea of Chin′ne•roth eastward, and in the direction of Beth-jesh′i•moth, to the sea of the Ar′a•bah, the Dead Sea,ʳ southward to the foot of the slopes of Pis′gah; 4 and King Ogˢ of Bā′shan, one of the last of the Reph′a•im, who lived at Ash′ta•roth and at Ed′rē•ī 5 and ruled over Mount Hermon and Sal′e•cah and all Bā′shan to the boundary of the Gesh′ū•rītes and the Mā′a•ca•thītes, and over half of Gil′e•ad to the boundary of King Sī′hon of Hesh′bon. 6 Moses, the servant of the LORD, and the Israelites defeated them; and Moses the servant of the LORD gave their land for a possession to the Reū′ben•ites and the Gad′ītes and the half-tribe of Ma•nas′seh.

The Kings Conquered by Joshua

7 The following are the kings of the land whom Joshua and the Israelites defeated on the west side of the Jordan, from Bā′al-gad in the valley of Lebanon to Mount Hā′lak, that rises toward Sē′ir (and Joshua gave their land to the tribes of Israel as a possession according to their allotments, 8 in the hill country, in the lowland, in the Ar′a•bah, in the slopes, in the wilderness, and in the Neg′eb, the land of the Hit′tītes, Am′o•rītes, Cā′naan•ites, Per′iz•zītes, Hī′vītes, and Jeb′ū•sītes):

did you KNOW?
The Conquest of Canaan

A strong parallel connects the beginning of the story of Joshua—the crossing of the Jordan River, God's direction and protection of the Israelites (symbolized by the ark), and the renewal of the Covenant at Mount Ebal—and the events of the Exodus from Egypt. The parallel reinforces how the conquest of Canaan was part of God's continued liberation of the Chosen People and a key moment in the history of Israel.

As the Israelites moved in on the Promised Land, the Canaanites were one of several groups of people that the Israelites had to deal with. Joshua 12.8 also mentions Hittites, Amorites, Perizzites, Hivites, and Jebusites. But the Canaanites seemed to be the dominant inhabitants. They were primarily an agricultural society and believed that their gods, called baals, controlled the rains, the seasons, and the fertility of the soil. For the Israelites, God was revealed as the only God over all creation and history.

The conquest of the Canaanites through violence might make you wonder what the Israelites believed about God. Basically, they believed that the Canaanite baals were an offense against God. Because the Canaanites would not change, the Israelites felt justified in killing them and taking their land. (See "Holy War," Num 2.1.) Later, Christians would not be able to justify such actions because of Jesus' teaching that everyone is loved by God and that we must love even our enemies. But at the time Joshua was written, God and God's plan for humanity had not yet been fully revealed.

▶ Joshua, chapter 12

9 the king of Jericho	one
the king of Aī, which is next to Beth′el	one
10 the king of Jerusalem	one
the king of Hē′bron	one

ʳ Heb *Salt Sea*   ˢ Gk: Heb *the boundary of King Og*

¹¹ the king of Jar′muth   one
the king of Lā′chish   one
¹² the king of Eg′lon   one
the king of Ge′zer   one
¹³ the king of De′bir   one
the king of Ge′der   one
¹⁴ the king of Hor′mah   one
the king of Ar′ad   one
¹⁵ the king of Lib′nah   one
the king of A·dul′lam   one
¹⁶ the king of Mak·ke′dah   one
the king of Beth′el   one
¹⁷ the king of Tap′pu·ah   one
the king of He′pher   one
¹⁸ the king of Ā′phek   one
the king of La·shar′on   one
¹⁹ the king of Mā′don   one
the king of Hā′zor   one
²⁰ the king of Shim′ron-me′ron   one
the king of Ach′shaph   one
²¹ the king of Tā′a·nach   one
the king of Me·gid′do   one
²² the king of Ke′desh   one
the king of Jok′ne·am in Car′mel   one
²³ the king of Dor in Nā′phath-dor   one
the king of Goi′im in Galilee,^t   one
²⁴ the king of Tir′zah   one
thirty-one kings in all.

The Parts of Canaan Still Unconquered

13 Now Joshua was old and advanced in years; and the LORD said to him, "You are old and advanced in years, and very much of the land still remains to be possessed. ² This is the land that still remains: all the regions of the Phi·lis′tines, and all those of the Gesh′u·rites ³ (from the Shī′hor, which is east of Egypt, northward to the boundary of Ek′ron, it is reckoned as Cā′naan·ite; there are five rulers of the Phi·lis′tines, those of Gā′za, Ash′dod, Ash′ke·lon, Gath, and Ek′ron), and those of the Av′vim ⁴ in the south; all the land of the Cā′naan·ites, and Mear′ah that belongs to the Si·dō′ni·ans, to Ā′phek, to the boundary of the Am′o·rites, ⁵ and the land of the Ge′bal·ites, and all Lebanon, toward the east, from Bā′al-gad below Mount Hermon to Le′bō-hā′math, ⁶ all the inhabitants of the hill country from Lebanon to Mis′re·photh-mā′im, even all the Si·dō′ni·ans. I will myself drive them out from before the Israelites; only allot the land to Israel for an inheritance, as I have commanded you. ⁷ Now therefore divide this land for an inheritance to the nine tribes and the half-tribe of Ma·nas′seh."

The Territory East of the Jordan

⁸ With the other half-tribe of Ma·nas′seh^u the Reu′ben·ites and the Gad′ites received their inheritance, which Moses gave them, beyond the Jordan eastward, as Moses the servant of the LORD gave them: ⁹ from A·rō′er, which is on the edge of the Wadi Ar′non, and the town that is in the middle of the valley, and all the tableland from^v Med′e·ba as far as Dī′bon; ¹⁰ and all the cities of King Sī′hon of the Am′o·rites, who reigned in Hesh′bon, as far as the boundary of the Am′mon·ites; ¹¹ and Gil′e·ad, and the region of the Gesh′u·rites and Mā′a·ca·thītes, and all Mount Hermon, and all Bā′shan to Sal′e·cah; ¹² all the kingdom of Og in Bā′shan, who reigned in Ash′ta·roth and in Ed′re·ī (he alone was left of the survivors of the Reph′a·im); these Moses had defeated and driven out. ¹³ Yet the Israelites did not drive out the Gesh′u·rites or the Mā′a·ca·thītes; but Ge′shur and Mā′a·cath live within Israel to this day.

¹⁴ To the tribe of Levi alone Moses gave no inheritance; the offerings by fire to the LORD God of Israel are their inheritance, as he said to them.

The Territory of Reuben

¹⁵ Moses gave an inheritance to the tribe of the Reu′ben·ites according to their clans. ¹⁶ Their territory was from A·rō′er, which is on the edge of the Wadi Ar′non, and the town that is in the middle of the valley, and all the tableland by Med′e·ba; ¹⁷ with Hesh′bon, and all its towns that are in the tableland; Dī′bon, and Bā′moth-bā′al, and Beth-bā′al-me′on, ¹⁸ and Jā′haz, and Ked′e·moth, and Meph′a·ath, ¹⁹ and Kir·i·a·thā′im, and Sib′mah, and Ze′reth-shā′har on the hill of the valley, ²⁰ and Beth-pe′or, and the slopes of Pis′gah, and Beth-jesh′i·moth, ²¹ that is, all the towns of the tableland, and all the kingdom of King Sī′hon of the Am′o·rites, who reigned in Hesh′bon, whom Moses defeated with the leaders of Mid′i·an, E′vi and Re′kem and Zur and Hur and Re′ba, as princes of Sī′hon, who lived in the land. ²² Along with the rest of those they put to death, the Israelites also put to the sword Bā′laam son of Be′or, who practiced divination. ²³ And the border of the Reu′ben·ites was the Jordan and its banks. This was the inheritance of the Reu′ben·ites according to their families, with their towns and villages.

The Territory of Gad

²⁴ Moses gave an inheritance also to the tribe of the Gad′ites, according to their families. ²⁵ Their territory was Jā′zer, and all the towns of Gil′e·ad, and half the land of the Am′mon·ites, to A·rō′er, which is east of Rab′bah, ²⁶ and from Hesh′bon to Rā′math-miz′peh and Bet′ō·nim, and from Mā·ha·nā′im to the territory of De′bir,^w ²⁷ and in the valley Beth-hā′ram, Beth-nim′rah, Suc′coth, and Zā′phon,

---

^t Gk: Heb *Gilgal*   ^u Cn: Heb *With it*   ^v Compare Gk: Heb lacks *from*   ^w Gk Syr Vg: Heb *Lidebir*

the rest of the kingdom of King Sī′hon of Hesh′bon, the Jordan and its banks, as far as the lower end of the Sea of Chin′ne•reth, eastward beyond the Jordan. 28 This is the inheritance of the Gad′ītes according to their clans, with their towns and villages.

The Territory of the Half-Tribe of Manasseh (East)

29 Moses gave an inheritance to the half-tribe of Ma•nas′seh; it was allotted to the half-tribe of the Ma•nas′sītes according to their families. 30 Their territory extended from Mā•ha•nā′im, through all Bā′shan, the whole kingdom of King Og of Bā′shan, and all the settlements of Jā′ir, which are in Bā′shan, sixty towns, 31 and half of Gil′e•ad, and Ash′ta•roth, and Ed′rē•ī, the towns of the kingdom of Og in Bā′shan; these were allotted to the people of Mā′chir son of Ma•nas′seh according to their clans—for half the Mā′chir•ītes.

32 These are the inheritances that Moses distributed in the plains of Mō′ab, beyond the Jordan east of Jericho. 33 But to the tribe of Levi Moses gave no inheritance; the LORD God of Israel is their inheritance, as he said to them.

The Distribution of Territory West of the Jordan

14 These are the inheritances that the Israelites received in the land of Cā′naan, which the priest El•ē•ā′zar, and Joshua son of Nun, and the heads of the families of the tribes of the Israelites distributed to them. 2 Their inheritance was by lot, as the LORD had commanded Moses for the nine and one-half tribes. 3 For Moses had given an inheritance to the two and one-half tribes beyond the Jordan; but to the Lē′vītes he gave no inheritance among them. 4 For the people of Joseph were two tribes, Ma•nas′seh and Ē′phra•im; and no portion was given to the Lē′vītes in the land, but only towns to live in, with their pasture lands for their flocks and herds. 5 The Israelites did as the LORD commanded Moses; they allotted the land.

Hebron Allotted to Caleb

6 Then the people of Judah came to Joshua at Gil′gal; and Caleb son of Je•phūn′neh the Ken′iz-zīte said to him, "You know what the LORD said to Moses the man of God in Kā′desh-bar′nē•a concerning you and me. 7 I was forty years old when Moses the servant of the LORD sent me from Kā′desh-bar′nē•a to spy out the land; and I brought him an honest report. 8 But my companions who went up with me made the heart of the people melt; yet I wholeheartedly followed the LORD my God. 9 And Moses swore on that day, saying, 'Surely the land on which your foot has trodden shall be an inheritance for you and your children forever, be-

cause you have wholeheartedly followed the LORD my God.' 10 And now, as you see, the LORD has kept me alive, as he said, these forty-five years since the time that the LORD spoke this word to Moses, while Israel was journeying through the wilderness; and here I am today, eighty-five years old. 11 I am still as strong today as I was on the day that Moses sent me; my strength now is as my strength was then, for war, and for going and coming. 12 So now give me this hill country of which the LORD spoke on that day; for you heard on that day how the An′a•kim were there, with great fortified cities; it may be that the LORD will be with me, and I shall drive them out, as the LORD said."

13 Then Joshua blessed him, and gave Hē′bron to Caleb son of Je•phūn′neh for an inheritance. 14 So Hē′bron became the inheritance of Caleb son of Je•phūn′neh the Ken′iz•zīte to this day, because he wholeheartedly followed the LORD, the God of Israel. 15 Now the name of Hē′bron formerly was Kir′i•ath-ar′ba;ˣ this Ar′ba wasʸ the greatest man among the An′a•kim. And the land had rest from war.

The Territory of Judah

15 The lot for the tribe of the people of Judah according to their families reached southward to the boundary of Ē′dom, to the wilderness of Zin at the farthest south. 2 And their south boundary ran from the end of the Dead Sea,ᶻ from the bay that faces southward; 3 it goes out southward of the ascent of Ak•rab′bim, passes along to Zin, and goes up south of Kā′desh-bar′nē•a, along by Hez′ron, up to Ad′dar, makes a turn to Kar′ka, 4 passes along to Az′mon, goes out by the Wadi of Egypt, and comes to its end at the sea. This shall be your south boundary. 5 And the east boundary is the Dead Sea,ᶻ to the mouth of the Jordan. And the boundary on the north side runs from the bay of the sea at the mouth of the Jordan; 6 and the boundary goes up to Beth-hog′lah, and passes along north of Beth-ar′a•bah; and the boundary goes up to the Stone of Bō′han, Reuben's son; 7 and the boundary goes up to Dē′bir from the Valley of Ā′chor, and so northward, turning toward Gil′gal, which is opposite the ascent of A•dum′mim, which is on the south side of the valley; and the boundary passes along to the waters of En-shē′mesh, and ends at En-rō′gel; 8 then the boundary goes up by the valley of the son of Hin′nom at the southern slope of the Jeb′ū•sites (that is, Jerusalem); and the boundary goes up to the top of the mountain that lies over against the valley of Hin′nom, on the west, at the northern end of the valley of Reph′a•im; 9 then the boundary extends from the top of the mountain to

---

ˣ That is *the city of Arba*   ʸ Heb lacks *this Arba was*   ᶻ Heb *Salt Sea* the spring of the Waters of Neph•tō'ah, and from there to the towns of Mount Ē'phron; then the boundary bends around to Bā'a•lah (that is, Kir'i•ath-jē'a•rim); 10 and the boundary circles west of Bā'a•lah to Mount Sē'ir, passes along to the northern slope of Mount Jē'a•rim (that is, Ches'-a•lon), and goes down to Beth-shē'mesh, and passes along by Tim'nah; 11 the boundary goes out to the slope of the hill north of Ek'ron, then the boundary bends around to Shik'ke•ron, and passes along to Mount Bā'a•lah, and goes out to Jab'nē•el; then the boundary comes to an end at the sea. 12 And the west boundary was the Mediterranean with its coast. This is the boundary surrounding the people of Judah according to their families.

Caleb Occupies His Portion
(Judg 1.11–15)

13 According to the commandment of the LORD to Joshua, he gave to Caleb son of Je•phūn'neh a portion among the people of Judah, Kir'i•ath-ar'ba,[a] that is, Hē'bron (Ar'ba was the father of Ā'nak). 14 And Caleb drove out from there the three sons of Ā'nak: Shē'shaī, A•hī'man, and Tal'maī, the descendants of Ā'nak. 15 From there he went up against the inhabitants of Dē'bir; now the name of Dē'bir formerly was Kir'i•ath-sē'pher. 16 And Caleb said, "Whoever attacks Kir'i•ath-sē'pher and takes it, to him I will give my daughter Ach'sah as wife." 17 Oth'ni•el son of Kē'naz, the brother of Caleb, took it; and he gave him his daughter Ach'sah as wife. 18 When she came to him, she urged him to ask her father for a field. As she dismounted from her donkey, Caleb said to her, "What do you wish?" 19 She said to him, "Give me a present; since you have set me in the land of the Neg'eb, give me springs of water as well." So Caleb gave her the upper springs and the lower springs.

The Towns of Judah

20 This is the inheritance of the tribe of the people of Judah according to their families. 21 The towns belonging to the tribe of the people of Judah in the extreme south, toward the boundary of Ē'dom, were Kab'zē•el, Ē'der, Jā'gur, 22 Kī'nah, Di•mō'nah, A•dā'dah, 23 Kē'desh, Hā'zor, Ith'nan, 24 Ziph, Tē'lem, Be•ā'loth, 25 Hā'zor-ha•dat'tah, Ker'i•oth-hez'ron (that is, Hā'zor), 26 Ā'mam, Shē'-ma, Mō'la•dah, 27 Hā'zar-gad'dah, Hesh'mon, Beth-pel'et, 28 Hā'zar-shū'al, Bē'er-shē'ba, Biz•i•o•thī'ah, 29 Bā'a•lah, Ī'im, Ē'zem, 30 El•tō'lad, Chē'sil, Hor'-mah, 31 Zik'lag, Mad•man'nah, San•san'nah, 32 Le•bā'oth, Shil'him, Ā'in, and Rim'mon: in all, twenty-nine towns, with their villages.

33 And in the lowland, Esh'tā•ol, Zō'rah, Ash'-nah, 34 Za•nō'ah, En-gan'nim, Tap'pū•ah, Ē'nam, 35 Jar'muth, A•dul'lam, Sō'cōh, A•zē'kah, 36 Shā•a-

rā'im, Ad•i•thā'im, Ge•dē'rah, Ged•e•rō•thā'im: fourteen towns with their villages.

37 Zē'nan, Ha•dash'ah, Mig'dal-gad, 38 Dil'an, Miz'peh, Jok'thē-el, 39 Lā'chish, Boz'kath, Eg'lon, 40 Cab'bon, Lah'mam, Chit'lish, 41 Ge•dē'roth, Beth-dā'gon, Nā'a•mah, and Mak•kē'dah: sixteen towns with their villages.

42 Lib'nah, Ē'ther, Ā'shan, 43 Iph'tah, Ash'nah, Nē'zib, 44 Kē•ī'lah, Ach'zib, and Ma•rē'shah: nine towns with their villages.

45 Ek'ron, with its dependencies and its villages; 46 from Ek'ron to the sea, all that were near Ash'dod, with their villages.

47 Ash'dod, its towns and its villages; Gā'za, its towns and its villages; to the Wadi of Egypt, and the Great Sea with its coast.

48 And in the hill country, Shā'mir, Jat'tir, Sō'cōh, 49 Dan'nah, Kir'i•ath-san'nah (that is, Dē'bir), 50 Ā'nab, Esh'te•mōh, Ā'nim, 51 Gō'shen, Hō'lon, and Gī'lōh: eleven towns with their villages.

52 A'rab, Dū'mah, Ē'shan, 53 Jā'nim, Beth-tap'pū•ah, A•phē'kah, 54 Hum'tah, Kir'i•ath-ar'ba (that is, Hē'bron), and Zī'or: nine towns with their villages.

55 Mā'on, Car'mel, Ziph, Jut'tah, 56 Jez'rē•el, Jok'dē•am, Za•nō'ah, 57 Kāin, Gib'ē•ah, and Tim'-nah: ten towns with their villages.

58 Hal'hul, Beth-zur, Gē'dor, 59 Mā'a•rath, Beth-ā'noth, and El'tē•kon: six towns with their villages.

60 Kir'i•ath-bā'al (that is, Kir'i•ath-jē'a•rim) and Rab'bah: two towns with their villages.

61 In the wilderness, Beth-ar'a•bah, Mid'din, Se•cā'cah, 62 Nib'shan, the City of Salt, and En-ge'di: six towns with their villages.

63 But the people of Judah could not drive out the Jeb'ū•sītes, the inhabitants of Jerusalem; so the Jeb'ū•sītes live with the people of Judah in Jerusalem to this day.

The Territory of Ephraim

16 The allotment of the Jō'seph•ītes went from the Jordan by Jericho, east of the waters of Jericho, into the wilderness, going up from Jericho into the hill country to Beth'el; 2 then going from Beth'el to Luz, it passes along to At'a•roth, the territory of the Ar'chites; 3 then it goes down westward to the territory of the Japh'let•ītes, as far as the territory of Lower Beth-hō'ron, then to Gē'zer, and it ends at the sea.

4 The Jō'seph•ītes—Ma•nas'seh and Ē'phra•im—received their inheritance.

5 The territory of the Ē'phra•im•ītes by their families was as follows: the boundary of their inheritance on the east was At'a•roth-ad'dar as far as

---

a That is the city of Arba

Upper Beth-hō′ron, 6 and the boundary goes from there to the sea; on the north is Mich•mē′thath; then on the east the boundary makes a turn toward Tā′a•nath-shī′lōh, and passes along beyond it on the east to Ja•nō′ah, 7 then it goes down from Ja•nō′ah to At′a•roth and to Nā′a•rah, and touches Jericho, ending at the Jordan. 8 From Tap′pū•ah the boundary goes westward to the Wadi Kā′nah, and ends at the sea. Such is the inheritance of the tribe of the Ē′phra•im•ītes by their families, 9 together with the towns that were set apart for the Ē′phra•im•ītes within the inheritance of the Ma•nas′sītes, all those towns with their villages. 10 They did not, however, drive out the Cā′naan•ītes who lived in Gē′zer: so the Cā′naan•ītes have lived within Ē′phra•im to this day but have been made to do forced labor.

The Other Half-Tribe of Manasseh (West)

17 Then allotment was made to the tribe of Ma•nas′seh, for he was the firstborn of Joseph. To Mā′chir the firstborn of Ma•nas′seh, the father of Gil′e•ad, were allotted Gil′e•ad and Bā′shan, because he was a warrior. 2 And allotments were made to the rest of the tribe of Ma•nas′seh, by their families, Ā•bi•ē′zer, Hē′lek, As′ri•el, Shē′chem, Hē′pher, and She•mī′da; these were the male descendants of Ma•nas′seh son of Joseph, by their families.

3 Now Ze•loph′e•had son of Hē′pher son of Gil′e•ad son of Mā′chir son of Ma•nas′seh had no sons, but only daughters; and these are the names of his daughters: Mah′lah, Noah, Hog′lah, Mil′cah, and Tir′zah. 4 They came before the priest El•ē•ā′zar and Joshua son of Nun and the leaders, and said, "The LORD commanded Moses to give us an inheritance along with our male kin." So according to the commandment of the LORD he gave them an inheritance among the kinsmen of their father. 5 Thus there fell to Ma•nas′seh ten portions, besides the land of Gil′e•ad and Bā′shan, which is on the other side of the Jordan, 6 because the daughters of Ma•nas′seh received an inheritance along with his sons. The land of Gil′e•ad was allotted to the rest of the Ma•nas′sītes.

7 The territory of Ma•nas′seh reached from Ash′er to Mich•mē′thath, which is east of Shē′chem; then the boundary goes along southward to the inhabitants of En-tap′pū•ah. 8 The land of Tap′pū•ah belonged to Ma•nas′seh, but the town of Tap′pū•ah on the boundary of Ma•nas′seh belonged to the Ē′phra•im•ītes. 9 Then the boundary went down to the Wadi Kā′nah. The towns here, to the south of the wadi, among the towns of Ma•nas′seh, belong to Ē′phra•im. Then the boundary of Ma•nas′seh goes along the north side of the wadi and ends at the sea. 10 The land to the south is Ē′phra•im′s and that to the north is Ma•nas′seh′s, with the sea forming its boundary; on the north Ash′er is reached, and on

the east Is′sa•char. 11 Within Is′sa•char and Ash′er, Ma•nas′seh had Beth-shē′an and its villages, Ib′lē•am and its villages, the inhabitants of Dor and its villages, the inhabitants of En-dor and its villages, the inhabitants of Tā′a•nach and its villages, and the inhabitants of Me•gid′dō and its villages (the third is Nā′phath).*b* 12 Yet the Ma•nas′sītes could not take possession of those towns; but the Cā′naan•ītes continued to live in that land. 13 But when the Israelites grew strong, they put the Cā′naan•ītes to forced labor, but did not utterly drive them out.

The Tribe of Joseph Protests

14 The tribe of Joseph spoke to Joshua, saying, "Why have you given me but one lot and one portion as an inheritance, since we are a numerous people, whom all along the LORD has blessed?" 15 And Joshua said to them, "If you are a numerous people, go up to the forest, and clear ground there for yourselves in the land of the Per′iz•zītes and the Reph′a•im, since the hill country of Ē′phra•im is too narrow for you." 16 The tribe of Joseph said, "The hill country is not enough for us; yet all the Cā′naan•ītes who live in the plain have chariots of iron, both those in Beth-shē′an and its villages and those in the Valley of Jez′rē•el." 17 Then Joshua said to the house of Joseph, to Ē′phra•im and Ma•nas′seh, "You are indeed a numerous people, and have great power; you shall not have one lot only, 18 but the hill country shall be yours, for though it is a forest, you shall clear it and possess it to its farthest borders; for you shall drive out the Cā′naan•ītes, though they have chariots of iron, and though they are strong."

The Territories of the Remaining Tribes

18 Then the whole congregation of the Israelites assembled at Shī′lōh, and set up the tent of meeting there. The land lay subdued before them.

2 There remained among the Israelites seven tribes whose inheritance had not yet been apportioned. 3 So Joshua said to the Israelites, "How long will you be slack about going in and taking possession of the land that the LORD, the God of your ancestors, has given you? 4 Provide three men from each tribe, and I will send them out that they may begin to go throughout the land, writing a description of it with a view to their inheritances. Then come back to me. 5 They shall divide it into seven portions, Judah continuing in its territory on the south, and the house of Joseph in their territory on the north. 6 You shall describe the land in seven divisions and bring the description here to me; and I will cast lots for you here before the LORD our God.

---

b Meaning of Heb uncertain

7 The Lē′vītes have no portion among you, for the priesthood of the LORD is their heritage; and Gad and Reuben and the half-tribe of Ma•nas′seh have received their inheritance beyond the Jordan eastward, which Moses the servant of the LORD gave them."

8 So the men started on their way; and Joshua charged those who went to write the description of the land, saying, "Go throughout the land and write a description of it, and come back to me; and I will cast lots for you here before the LORD in Shī′lōh." 9 So the men went and traversed the land and set down in a book a description of it by towns in seven divisions; then they came back to Joshua in the camp at Shī′lōh, 10 and Joshua cast lots for them in Shī′lōh before the LORD; and there Joshua apportioned the land to the Israelites, to each a portion.

The Territory of Benjamin

11 The lot of the tribe of Benjamin according to its families came up, and the territory allotted to it fell between the tribe of Judah and the tribe of Joseph. 12 On the north side their boundary began at the Jordan; then the boundary goes up to the slope of Jericho on the north, then up through the hill country westward; and it ends at the wilderness of Beth-ā′ven. 13 From there the boundary passes along southward in the direction of Luz, to the slope of Luz (that is, Beth′el), then the boundary goes down to At′a•roth-ad′dar, on the mountain that lies south of Lower Beth-hō′ron. 14 Then the boundary goes in another direction, turning on the western side southward from the mountain that lies to the south, opposite Beth-hō′ron, and it ends at Kir′i•ath-bā′al (that is, Kir′i•ath-jē′a•rim), a town belonging to the tribe of Judah. This forms the western side. 15 The southern side begins at the outskirts of Kir′i•ath-jē′a•rim; and the boundary goes from there to Ē′phron,c to the spring of the Waters of Neph•tō′ah; 16 then the boundary goes down to the border of the mountain that overlooks the valley of the son of Hin′nom, which is at the north end of the valley of Reph′a•im; and it then goes down the valley of Hin′nom, south of the slope of the Jeb′u•sītes, and downward to En-rō′gel; 17 then it bends in a northerly direction going on to En-shē′mesh, and from there goes to Ge•li′loth, which is opposite the ascent of A•dum′mim; then it goes down to the Stone of Bō′han, Reuben′s son; 18 and passing on to the north of the slope of Beth-ar′a•bahd it goes down to the Ar′a•bah; 19 then the boundary passes on to the north of the slope of Beth-hog′lah; and the boundary ends at the northern bay of the Dead Sea,e at the south end of the Jordan: this is the southern border. 20 The Jordan forms its boundary on the eastern side. This is the inheritance of the tribe of Benjamin, according to its families, boundary by boundary all around.

21 Now the towns of the tribe of Benjamin according to their families were Jericho, Beth-hog′lah, Ē′mek-kē′ziz, 22 Beth-ar′a•bah, Zem•a•rā′im, Beth′el, 23 Av′vim, Par′ah, Oph′rah, 24 Chē′pharam′mo•nī, Oph′nī, and Gē′ba—twelve towns with their villages: 25 Gib′ē•on, Rā′mah, Be•er′oth, 26 Miz′peh, Chē•phī′rah, Mō′zah, 27 Rē′kem, Ir′pē•el, Tar′a•lah, 28 Zē′la, Ha•ē′leph, Jē′busf (that is, Jerusalem), Gib′ē•ah g and Kir′i•ath-jē′a•rim h—fourteen towns with their villages. This is the inheritance of the tribe of Benjamin according to its families.

The Territory of Simeon

19 The second lot came out for Sim′ē•on, for the tribe of Sim′ē•on, according to its families; its inheritance lay within the inheritance of the tribe of Judah. 2 It had for its inheritance Bē′er-shē′ba, Shē′ba, Mō′la•dah, 3 Hā′zar-shū′al, Bā′lah, Ē′zem, 4 El-tō′lad, Bē′thul, Hor′mah, 5 Zik′lag, Beth-mar′ca•both, Hā′zar-sū′sah, 6 Beth-le•bā′oth, and Sha•rū′hen—thirteen towns with their villages; 7 Ā′in, Rim′mon, Ē′ther, and Ā′shan—four towns with their villages; 8 together with all the villages all around these towns as far as Bā′a•lath-bē′er, Rā′mah of the Neg′eb. This was the inheritance of the tribe of Sim′ē•on according to its families. 9 The inheritance of the tribe of Sim′ē•on formed part of the territory of Judah; because the portion of the tribe of Judah was too large for them, the tribe of Sim′ē•on obtained an inheritance within their inheritance.

The Territory of Zebulun

10 The third lot came up for the tribe of Zeb′u•lun, according to its families. The boundary of its inheritance reached as far as Sā′rid; 11 then its boundary goes up westward, and on to Mar′a•lah, and touches Dab′be•sheth, then the wadi that is east of Jok′nē•am; 12 from Sā′rid it goes in the other direction eastward toward the sunrise to the boundary of Chis′loth-tā′bor; from there it goes to Dab′e•rath, then up to Ja•phī′a; 13 from there it passes along on the east toward the sunrise to Gath-hē′pher, to Eth-kā′zin, and going on to Rim′mon it bends toward Nē′ah; 14 then on the north the boundary makes a turn to Han•na′thon, and it ends at the valley of Iph′tah-el; 15 and Kat′tath, Na•hal′al, Shim′ron, I′da•lah, and Bethlehem—twelve towns with their villages. 16 This is the inheritance of the tribe of Zeb′u•lun, according to its families—these towns with their villages.

---

c Cn See 15.9. Heb *westward*   d Gk: Heb *to the slope over against the Arabah*   e Heb *Salt Sea*   f Gk Syr Vg: Heb *the Jebusite*   g Heb *Gibeath*   h Gk: Heb *Kiriath*

The Territory of Issachar

17 The fourth lot came out for Is'sa·char, for the tribe of Is'sa·char, according to its families. 18 Its territory included Jez're'·el, Che·sul'loth, Shū'nem, 19 Haph·a·rā'im, Shī'on, A·nā'ha·rath, 20 Rab'bith, Kish'i·on, Ē'bez, 21 Rē'meth, En-gan'nim, En-had'-dah, Beth-paz'zez; 22 the boundary also touches Tā'-bor, Sha·ha·zū'mah, and Beth-shē'mesh, and its boundary ends at the Jordan—sixteen towns with their villages. 23 This is the inheritance of the tribe of Is'sa·char, according to its families—the towns with their villages.

The Territory of Asher

24 The fifth lot came out for the tribe of Ash'er according to its families. 25 Its boundary included Hel'kath, Hā'lī, Bē'ten, Ach'shaph, 26 Al·lam'-me·lech, Ā'mad, and Mi'shal; on the west it touch-es Car'mel and Shī·hor-lib'nath, 27 then it turns eastward, goes to Beth-dā'gon, and touches Zeb'-ū·lun and the valley of Iph'tah-el northward to Beth-ē'mek and Nē·ī'el; then it continues in the north to Cā'bul, 28 Ē'bron, Rē'hob, Ham'mon, Kā'-nah, as far as Great Sī'don; 29 then the boundary turns to Rā'mah, reaching to the fortified city of Tȳre; then the boundary turns to Hō'sah, and it ends at the sea; Ma·hā'lab,*i* Ach'zib, 30 Um'mah, Ā'phek, and Rē'hob—twenty-two towns with their villages. 31 This is the inheritance of the tribe of Ash'er according to its families—these towns with their villages.

The Territory of Naphtali

32 The sixth lot came out for the tribe of Naph'-ta·lī, for the tribe of Naph'ta·lī, according to its families. 33 And its boundary ran from Hē'leph, from the oak in Zā·a·nan'nim, and Ad'a·mī-nek'eb, and Jab'nē·el, as far as Lak'kum; and it ended at the Jordan; 34 then the boundary turns westward to Az'noth-tā'bor, and goes from there to Huk'kok, touching Zeb'ū·lun at the south, and Ash'er on the west, and Judah on the east at the Jordan. 35 The fortified towns are Zid'dim, Zer, Ham'math, Rak'kath, Chin'ne·reth, 36 Ad'a·mah, Rā'mah, Hā'-zor, 37 Kē'desh, Ed'rē·ī, En-hā'zor, 38 Ī'ron, Mig'dal-el, Hō'rem, Beth-ā'nath, and Beth-shē'mesh—nineteen towns with their villages. 39 This is the in-heritance of the tribe of Naph'ta·lī according to its families—the towns with their villages.

The Territory of Dan

40 The seventh lot came out for the tribe of Dan, according to its families. 41 The territory of its inheritance included Zō'rah, Esh'tā·ol, Ir-shē'mesh, 42 Shā·a·lab'bin, Aī'ja·lon, Ith'lah, 43 Ē'lon, Tim'-nah, Ek'ron, 44 El'tē·keh, Gib'be·thon, Bā'a·lath, 45 Jē'hud, Ben'ē-bē'rak, Gath-rim'mon, 46 Me-

jar'kon, and Rak'kon at the border opposite Jop'pa. 47 When the territory of the Dan'ites was lost to them, the Dan'ites went up and fought against Lē'-shem, and after capturing it and putting it to the sword, they took possession of it and settled in it, calling Lē'shem, Dan, after their ancestor Dan. 48 This is the inheritance of the tribe of Dan, accord-ing to their families—these towns with their villages.

Joshua's Inheritance

49 When they had finished distributing the sev-eral territories of the land as inheritances, the Is-raelites gave an inheritance among them to Joshua son of Nun. 50 By command of the LORD they gave him the town that he asked for, Tim'nath-sē'rah in the hill country of Ē'phra·im; he rebuilt the town, and settled in it.

51 These are the inheritances that the priest El·ē·ā'zar and Joshua son of Nun and the heads of the families of the tribes of the Israelites distributed by lot at Shī'lōh before the LORD, at the entrance of the tent of meeting. So they finished dividing the land.

The Cities of Refuge
(Num 35.9–28; Deut 19.1–13)

20 Then the LORD spoke to Joshua, saying, 2 "Say to the Israelites, 'Appoint the cities of refuge, of which I spoke to you through Moses, 3 so that anyone who kills a person without intent or by mistake may flee there; they shall be for you a refuge from the avenger of blood. 4 The slay-er shall flee to one of these cities and shall stand at the entrance of the gate of the city, and explain the case to the elders of that city; then the fugitive shall be taken into the city, and given a place, and shall remain with them. 5 And if the avenger of blood is in pursuit, they shall not give up the slayer, because the neighbor was killed by mistake, there having been no enmity between them before. 6 The slayer shall remain in that city until there is a trial before the congregation, until the death of the one who is high priest at the time: then the slayer may return home, to the town in which the deed was done.' "

7 So they set apart Kē'desh in Galilee in the hill country of Naph'ta·lī, and Shē'chem in the hill country of Ē'phra·im, and Kir'i·ath-ar'ba (that is, Hē'bron) in the hill country of Judah. 8 And be-yond the Jordan east of Jericho, they appointed Bē'zer in the wilderness on the tableland, from the tribe of Reuben, and Rā'moth in Gil'e·ad, from the tribe of Gad, and Gō'lan in Bā'shan, from the tribe of Ma·nas'seh. 9 These were the cities designated for all the Israelites, and for the aliens residing among them, that anyone who killed a person without

---

i Cn Compare Gk: Heb *Mehebel*

intent could flee there, so as not to die by the hand of the avenger of blood, until there was a trial before the congregation.

Cities Allotted to the Levites
(1 Chr 6.54–81)

21 Then the heads of the families of the Lĕ'vītes came to the priest El•ĕ•ā'zar and to Joshua son of Nun and to the heads of the families of the tribes of the Israelites; 2 they said to them at Shī'lōh in the land of Cā'naan, "The LORD commanded through Moses that we be given towns to live in, along with their pasture lands for our livestock." 3 So by command of the LORD the Israelites gave to the Lĕ'vītes the following towns and pasture lands out of their inheritance.

4 The lot came out for the families of the Kō'hath•ītes. So those Lĕ'vītes who were descendants of Aaron the priest received by lot thirteen towns from the tribes of Judah, Sim'ē•on, and Benjamin.

5 The rest of the Kō'hath•ītes received by lot ten towns from the families of the tribe of Ē'phra•im, from the tribe of Dan, and the half-tribe of Manas'seh.

6 The Ger'shon•ītes received by lot thirteen towns from the families of the tribe of Is'sa•char, from the tribe of Ash'er, from the tribe of Naph'ta•lī, and from the half-tribe of Ma•nas'seh in Bā'shan.

7 The Me•rar'ītes according to their families received twelve towns from the tribe of Reuben, the tribe of Gad, and the tribe of Zeb'ū•lun.

8 These towns and their pasture lands the Israelites gave by lot to the Lĕ'vītes, as the LORD had commanded through Moses.

9 Out of the tribe of Judah and the tribe of Sim'ē•on they gave the following towns mentioned by name, 10 which went to the descendants of Aaron, one of the families of the Kō'hath•ītes who belonged to the Lĕ'vītes, since the lot fell to them first. 11 They gave them Kir'i•ath-ar'ba (Ar'ba being the father of Ā'nak), that is Hē'bron, in the hill country of Judah, along with the pasture lands around it. 12 But the fields of the town and its villages had been given to Caleb son of Je•phūn'neh as his holding.

13 To the descendants of Aaron the priest they gave Hē'bron, the city of refuge for the slayer, with its pasture lands, Lib'nah with its pasture lands, 14 Jat'tir with its pasture lands, Esh•te•mō'a with its pasture lands, 15 Hō'lon with its pasture lands, Dē'bir with its pasture lands, 16 Ā'in with its pasture lands, Jut'tah with its pasture lands, and Beth-shē'mesh with its pasture lands—nine towns out of these two tribes. 17 Out of the tribe of Benjamin: Gib'ē•on with its pasture lands, Gē'ba with its pas-

ture lands, 18 An'a•thoth with its pasture lands, and Al'mon with its pasture lands—four towns. 19 The towns of the descendants of Aaron—the priests—were thirteen in all, with their pasture lands.

20 As to the rest of the Kō'hath•ītes belonging to the Kō'hath•īte families of the Lĕ'vītes, the towns allotted to them were out of the tribe of Ē'phra•im. 21 To them were given Shē'chem, the city of refuge for the slayer, with its pasture lands in the hill country of Ē'phra•im, Gē'zer with its pasture lands, 22 Kib'zā•im with its pasture lands, and Beth-hō'ron with its pasture lands—four towns. 23 Out of the tribe of Dan: El'tē•ke with its pasture lands, Gib'be•thon with its pasture lands, 24 Aī'ja•lon with its pasture lands, Gath-rim'mon with its pasture lands—four towns. 25 Out of the half-tribe of Ma•nas'seh: Tā'a•nach with its pasture lands, and Gath-rim'mon with its pasture lands—two towns. 26 The towns of the families of the rest of the Kō'hath•ītes were ten in all, with their pasture lands.

27 To the Ger'shon•ītes, one of the families of the Lĕ'vītes, were given out of the half-tribe of Ma•nas'seh, Gō'lan in Bā'shan with its pasture lands, the city of refuge for the slayer, and Be•esh•tē'rah with its pasture lands—two towns. 28 Out of the tribe of Is'sa•char: Kish'i•on with its pasture lands, Dab'e•rath with its pasture lands, 29 Jar'muth with its pasture lands, En-gan'nim with its pasture lands—four towns. 30 Out of the tribe of Ash'er: Mī'shal with its pasture lands, Ab'don with its pasture lands, 31 Hel'kath with its pasture lands, and Rē'hob with its pasture lands—four towns. 32 Out of the tribe of Naph'ta•lī: Kē'desh in Galilee with its pasture lands, the city of refuge for the slayer, Ham'moth-dor with its pasture lands, and Kar'tan with its pasture lands—three towns. 33 The towns of the several families of the Ger'shon•ītes were in all thirteen, with their pasture lands.

34 To the rest of the Lĕ'vītes—the Me•rar'īte families—were given out of the tribe of Zeb'ū•lun: Jok'nē•am with its pasture lands, Kar'tah with its pasture lands, 35 Dim'nah with its pasture lands, Na•hal'al with its pasture lands—four towns. 36 Out of the tribe of Reuben: Bē'zer with its pasture lands, Jah'zah with its pasture lands, 37 Ked'e•moth with its pasture lands, and Meph'a•ath with its pasture lands—four towns. 38 Out of the tribe of Gad: Rā'moth in Gil'e•ad with its pasture lands, the city of refuge for the slayer, Mā•ha•nā'im with its pasture lands, 39 Hesh'bon with its pasture lands, Jā'zer with its pasture lands—four towns in all. 40 As for the towns of the several Me•rar'īte families, that is, the remainder of the families of the Lĕ'vītes, those allotted to them were twelve in all.

41 The towns of the Lĕ'vītes within the holdings of the Israelites were in all forty-eight towns with

their pasture lands. 42 Each of these towns had its pasture lands around it; so it was with all these towns.

43 Thus the LORD gave to Israel all the land that he swore to their ancestors that he would give them; and having taken possession of it, they settled there. 44 And the LORD gave them rest on every side just as he had sworn to their ancestors; not one of all their enemies had withstood them, for the LORD had given all their enemies into their hands. 45 Not one of all the good promises that the LORD had made to the house of Israel had failed; all came to pass.

The Eastern Tribes Return to Their Territory

22 Then Joshua summoned the Reū'ben·ites, the Gad'ites, and the half-tribe of Ma·nas'seh, 2 and said to them, "You have observed all that Moses the servant of the LORD commanded you, and have obeyed me in all that I have commanded you; 3 you have not forsaken your kindred these many days, down to this day, but have been careful to keep the charge of the LORD your God. 4 And now the LORD your God has given rest to your kindred, as he promised them; therefore turn and go to your tents in the land where your possession lies, which Moses the servant of the LORD gave you on the other side of the Jordan. 5 Take good care to observe the commandment and instruction that Moses the servant of the LORD commanded you, to love the LORD your God, to walk in all his ways, to keep his commandments, and to hold fast to him, and to serve him with all your heart and with all your soul." 6 So Joshua blessed them and sent them away, and they went to their tents.

7 Now to the one half of the tribe of Ma·nas'seh Moses had given a possession in Bā'shan; but to the other half Joshua had given a possession beside their fellow Israelites in the land west of the Jordan. And when Joshua sent them away to their tents and blessed them, 8 he said to them, "Go back to your tents with much wealth, and with very much livestock, with silver, gold, bronze, and iron, and with a great quantity of clothing; divide the spoil of your enemies with your kindred." 9 So the Reū'ben·ites and the Gad'ites and the half-tribe of Ma·nas'seh returned home, parting from the Israelites at Shī'lōh, which is in the land of Cā'naan, to go to the land of Gil'e·ad, their own land of which they had taken possession by command of the LORD through Moses.

A Memorial Altar East of the Jordan

10 When they came to the regionʲ near the Jordan that lies in the land of Cā'naan, the Reū'ben·ites and the Gad'ites and the half-tribe of Ma·nas'seh built there an altar by the Jordan, an altar of great size. 11 The Israelites heard that the Reū'ben·ites and the Gad'ites and the half-tribe of Ma·nas'seh had built an altar at the frontier of the land of Cā'naan, in the region ᵏ near the Jordan, on the side that belongs to the Israelites. 12 And when the people of Israel heard of it, the whole assembly of the Israelites gathered at Shī'lōh, to make war against them.

13 Then the Israelites sent the priest Phin'e·has son of El·ē·ā'zar to the Reū'ben·ites and the Gad'ites and the half-tribe of Ma·nas'seh, in the land of Gil'e·ad, 14 and with him ten chiefs, one from each of the tribal families of Israel, every one of them the head of a family among the clans of Israel. 15 They came to the Reū'ben·ites, the Gad'ites, and the half-tribe of Ma·nas'seh, in the land of Gil'e·ad, and they said to them, 16 "Thus says the

ʲ Or to Geliloth   ᵏ Or at Geliloth

PRAY IT!
A Prayer for Understanding

When the Israelite tribes located east of the Jordan build a large altar to worship God, the Israelite tribes who settled west of the Jordan become concerned. They think that by building more altars, the tribes to the east are compromising their belief in one God. Some are ready to go to war over this issue. But maintaining unity among the tribes is also important. So, the western tribes wisely send Phinehas and others to insist on the importance of one place of worship. Listening to the eastern tribes, Phinehas understands their good intentions, and war is avoided.

Think about times when you have jumped to conclusions about other people's actions. Then say the following prayer:

God of love and wisdom, a misunderstanding almost led to war among the Israelites. Help me to avoid jumping to conclusions about the actions of others. Help me to listen and understand their intentions, as Phinehas did. And let me be gracious in recognizing when I am wrong. Amen.

▸ Josh 22.13–20

whole congregation of the LORD, 'What is this treachery that you have committed against the God of Israel in turning away today from following the LORD, by building yourselves an altar today in rebellion against the LORD? ¹⁷ Have we not had enough of the sin at Pĕ'or from which even yet we have not cleansed ourselves, and for which a plague came upon the congregation of the LORD, ¹⁸ that you must turn away today from following the LORD! If you rebel against the LORD today, he will be angry with the whole congregation of Israel tomorrow. ¹⁹ But now, if your land is unclean, cross over into the LORD's land where the LORD's tabernacle now stands, and take for yourselves a possession among us; only do not rebel against the LORD, or rebel against us*ˡ* by building yourselves an altar other than the altar of the LORD our God. ²⁰ Did not Ā'chan son of Zĕ'rah break faith in the matter of the devoted things, and wrath fell upon all the congregation of Israel? And he did not perish alone for his iniquity!' "

21 Then the Reū'ben•ītes, the Gad'ītes, and the half-tribe of Ma•nas'seh said in answer to the heads of the families of Israel, ²² "The LORD, God of gods! The LORD, God of gods! He knows; and let Israel itself know! If it was in rebellion or in breach of faith toward the LORD, do not spare us today ²³ for building an altar to turn away from following the LORD; or if we did so to offer burnt offerings or grain offerings or offerings of well-being on it, may the LORD himself take vengeance. ²⁴ No! We did it from fear that in time to come your children might say to our children, 'What have you to do with the LORD, the God of Israel? ²⁵ For the LORD has made the Jordan a boundary between us and you, you Reū'ben•ītes and Gad'ītes; you have no portion in the LORD.' So your children might make our children cease to worship the LORD. ²⁶ Therefore we said, 'Let us now build an altar, not for burnt offering, nor for sacrifice, ²⁷ but to be a witness between us and you, and between the generations after us, that we do perform the service of the LORD in his presence with our burnt offerings and sacrifices and offerings of well-being; so that your children may never say to our children in time to come, "You have no portion in the LORD." ' ²⁸ And we thought, If this should be said to us or to our descendants in time to come, we could say, 'Look at this copy of the altar of the LORD, which our ancestors made, not for burnt offerings, nor for sacrifice, but to be a witness between us and you.' ²⁹ Far be it from us that we should rebel against the LORD, and turn away this day from following the LORD by building an altar for burnt offering, grain offering, or sacrifice, other than the altar of the LORD our God that stands before his tabernacle!"

30 When the priest Phin'e•has and the chiefs of the congregation, the heads of the families of Israel who were with him, heard the words that the Reū'ben•ītes and the Gad'ītes and the Ma•nas'sītes spoke, they were satisfied. ³¹ The priest Phin'e•has son of El•ē•ā'zar said to the Reū'ben•ītes and the Gad'ītes and the Ma•nas'sītes, "Today we know that the LORD is among us, because you have not committed this treachery against the LORD; now you have saved the Israelites from the hand of the LORD."

32 Then the priest Phin'e•has son of El•ē•ā'zar and the chiefs returned from the Reū'ben•ītes and the Gad'ītes in the land of Gil'e•ad to the land of Cā'naan, to the Israelites, and brought back word to them. ³³ The report pleased the Israelites; and the Israelites blessed God and spoke no more of making war against them, to destroy the land where the Reū'ben•ītes and the Gad'ītes were settled. ³⁴ The Reū'ben•ītes and the Gad'ītes called the altar Witness;*ᵐ* "For," said they, "it is a witness between us that the LORD is God."

Joshua Exhorts the People

23 A long time afterward, when the LORD had given rest to Israel from all their enemies all around, and Joshua was old and well advanced in years, ² Joshua summoned all Israel, their elders and heads, their judges and officers, and said to them, "I am now old and well advanced in years; ³ and you have seen all that the LORD your God has done to all these nations for your sake, for it is the LORD your God who has fought for you. ⁴ I have allotted to you as an inheritance for your tribes those nations that remain, along with all the nations that I have already cut off, from the Jordan to the Great Sea in the west. ⁵ The LORD your God will push them back before you, and drive them out of your sight; and you shall possess their land, as the LORD your God promised you. ⁶ Therefore be very steadfast to observe and do all that is written in the book of the law of Moses, turning aside from it neither to the right nor to the left, ⁷ so that you may not be mixed with these nations left here among you, or make mention of the names of their gods, or swear by them, or serve them, or bow yourselves down to them, ⁸ but hold fast to the LORD your God, as you have done to this day. ⁹ For the LORD has driven out before you great and strong nations; and as for you, no one has been able to withstand you to this day. ¹⁰ One of you puts to flight a thousand, since it is the LORD your God who fights for you, as he promised you. ¹¹ Be very careful, therefore, to love the LORD your God. ¹² For if you turn back, and join the survivors of these nations left here among you,

---

ˡ Or *make rebels of us*   *ᵐ* Cn Compare Syr: Heb lacks *Witness* and intermarry with them, so that you marry their women and they yours, [13] know assuredly that the LORD your God will not continue to drive out these nations before you; but they shall be a snare and a trap for you, a scourge on your sides, and thorns in your eyes, until you perish from this good land that the LORD your God has given you.

[14] "And now I am about to go the way of all the earth, and you know in your hearts and souls, all of you, that not one thing has failed of all the good things that the LORD your God promised concerning you; all have come to pass for you, not one of them has failed. [15] But just as all the good things that the LORD your God promised concerning you have been fulfilled for you, so the LORD will bring upon you all the bad things, until he has destroyed you from this good land that the LORD your God has given you. [16] If you transgress the covenant of the LORD your God, which he enjoined on you, and go and serve other gods and bow down to them, then the anger of the LORD will be kindled against you, and you shall perish quickly from the good land that he has given to you."

The Tribes Renew the Covenant
(Cp Ex 24.9–18)

24 Then Joshua gathered all the tribes of Israel to Shĕ'chem, and summoned the elders, the heads, the judges, and the officers of Is-

rael; and they presented themselves before God. [2] And Joshua said to all the people, "Thus says the LORD, the God of Israel: Long ago your ancestors— Tĕ'rah and his sons Abraham and Nā'hor—lived beyond the Euphrates and served other gods. [3] Then I took your father Abraham from beyond the River and led him through all the land of Cā'naan and made his offspring many. I gave him Isaac; [4] and to Isaac I gave Jacob and Esau. I gave Esau the hill country of Sĕ'ir to possess, but Jacob and his children went down to Egypt. [5] Then I sent Moses and Aaron, and I plagued Egypt with what I did in its midst; and afterwards I brought you out. [6] When I brought your ancestors out of Egypt, you came to the sea; and the Egyptians pursued your ancestors with chariots and horsemen to the Red Sea.[n] [7] When they cried out to the LORD, he put darkness between you and the Egyptians, and made the sea come upon them and cover them; and your eyes saw what I did to Egypt. Afterwards you lived in the wilderness a long time. [8] Then I brought you to the land of the Am'o•rītes, who lived on the other side of the Jordan; they fought with you, and I handed them over to you, and you took possession of their land, and I destroyed them before you. [9] Then King Bā'lak son of Zip'por of Mō'ab, set out to fight against Israel. He sent and invited Bā'laam son of

---

[n] Or *Sea of Reeds*

Living the Covenant Today

Some people think that the Israelites were completely homogenous and without differences, but nothing could be further from the truth. Joshua 24.1 tells how Joshua summoned the leaders of the twelve tribes to present themselves before God. In this gathering, they embraced their common faith in God and renewed the Covenant of Sinai, setting aside their differences and political struggles.

People don't have to be identical, or even similar, to be united. They just have to be tolerant of one another's differences and see a reason to celebrate the richness of their diversity.

Imagine if all Christian churches could come together, as the tribes did in Joshua's time, and embrace a common identity before God. Imagine if all the clubs, cliques, and gangs in our schools and neighborhoods could come together that way. What strength we would have to help one another face life's challenges!

What can you do to foster this type of unity in your local schools, churches, and neighborhoods?

Who are some adults and young people you know who might help you work toward this goal?

▸ Josh 24.1–28

Bĕ'or to curse you, 10 but I would not listen to Bā'laam; therefore he blessed you; so I rescued you out of his hand. 11 When you went over the Jordan and came to Jericho, the citizens of Jericho fought against you, and also the Am'o•rītes, the Per'iz•zītes, the Cā'naan•ītes, the Hit'tītes, the Gir'-ga•shītes, the Hī'vītes, and the Jeb'ū•sītes; and I handed them over to you. 12 I sent the hornetᵒ ahead of you, which drove out before you the two kings of the Am'o•rītes; it was not by your sword or by your bow. 13 I gave you a land on which you had not labored, and towns that you had not built, and you live in them; you eat the fruit of vineyards and oliveyards that you did not plant.

14 "Now therefore revere the LORD, and serve him in sincerity and in faithfulness; put away the gods that your ancestors served beyond the River and in Egypt, and serve the LORD. 15 Now if you are unwilling to serve the LORD, choose this day whom you will serve, whether the gods your ancestors served in the region beyond the River or the gods of the Am'o•rītes in whose land you are living; but as for me and my household, we will serve the LORD."

16 Then the people answered, "Far be it from us that we should forsake the LORD to serve other gods; 17 for it is the LORD our God who brought us and our ancestors up from the land of Egypt, out of the house of slavery, and who did those great signs in our sight. He protected us along all the way that we went, and among all the peoples through whom we passed; 18 and the LORD drove out before us all the peoples, the Am'o•rītes who lived in the land. Therefore we also will serve the LORD, for he is our God."

19 But Joshua said to the people, "You cannot serve the LORD, for he is a holy God. He is a jealous God; he will not forgive your transgressions or your sins. 20 If you forsake the LORD and serve foreign gods, then he will turn and do you harm, and consume you, after having done you good." 21 And the people said to Joshua, "No, we will serve the LORD!" 22 Then Joshua said to the people, "You are witnesses against yourselves that you have chosen the LORD, to serve him." And they said, "We are witnesses." 23 He said, "Then put away the foreign gods that are among you, and incline your hearts to the LORD, the God of Israel." 24 The people said to Joshua, "The LORD our God we will serve, and him we will obey." 25 So Joshua made a covenant with the people that day, and made statutes and ordinances for them at Shĕ'chem. 26 Joshua wrote these

Revere the LORD, and serve him in sincerity and in faithfulness

24.14

words in the book of the law of God; and he took a large stone, and set it up there under the oak in the sanctuary of the LORD. 27 Joshua said to all the people, "See, this stone shall be a witness against us; for it has heard all the words of the LORD that he spoke to us; therefore it shall be a witness against you, if you deal falsely with your God." 28 So Joshua sent the people away to their inheritances.

Death of Joshua and Eleazar

29 After these things Joshua son of Nun, the servant of the LORD, died, being one hundred ten years old. 30 They buried him in his own inheritance at Tim'nath-sē'rah, which is in the hill country of Ē'phra•im, north of Mount Gā'ash.

31 Israel served the LORD all the days of Joshua, and all the days of the elders who outlived Joshua and had known all the work that the LORD did for Israel.

32 The bones of Joseph, which the Israelites had brought up from Egypt, were buried at Shĕ'chem, in the portion of ground that Jacob had bought from the children of Hā'mor, the father of Shĕ'chem, for one hundred pieces of money;ᵖ it became an inheritance of the descendants of Joseph.

33 El•ē•ā'zar son of Aaron died; and they buried him at Gib'ē•ah, the town of his son Phin'e•has, which had been given him in the hill country of Ē'phra•im.

ᵒ Meaning of Heb uncertain   ᵖ Heb *one hundred qesitah*

The teenage years often feel like an in-between time, when young people pass from being children to becoming adults who must take responsibility for their own life. This time of transition holds many challenges. In some ways, the Book of Judges is about Israel's "teenage years." It tells about the difficulties faced by God's people in an in-between time: the two hundred years between the conquest of Canaan under Joshua and the establish-ment of the kingdom of Israel under Saul.

At a Glance

- **1.1—3.6.** historical introduction
- **3.7—16.31.** the stories of individual judges
- **Chapters 17–21.** two appendices

In-depth

In the Book of Judges, the twelve tribes of Israel face two especially difficult challenges: how to live peacefully with one another and how to withstand the attacks of foreign armies. God answers the Israelites' prayers for help by raising up extraordinary men and women to lead the tribes. These famous leaders— Gideon, Deborah, Samson, and nine others—are called judges, but they aren't judges in courtrooms wearing black robes. They are local elders and military heroes who are chosen by God's spirit to lead the Israelites in times of crisis.

The pattern that we observed in the Book of Joshua also appears in the Book of Judges: when the people obey God's laws, they thrive; when they are disobedient, they suffer and need to be rescued by a leader raised up by God's spirit. The stories in Judges probably began as regional tales about local heroes. As they were collected and edited by the author of Judges, they became national stories influenced by the message of Deuteronomy: faithfulness to God is the only road to personal and tribal security.

Judges reminds us that the challenges of life, especially in the in-between times, are best handled through prayer and reliance on God. God can be trusted to lead us through all difficulties, both great and small.

Quick Facts

Period Covered
from 1220 to 1000 B.C.

Author
The book was put into final form by an unknown person from the Deuteronomic school, sometime during the Israelite monarchy.

Themes
God raises up mighty heroes to protect the people. God works even through flawed heroes.

The Book of Judges

235

Judges

Chap. 5

Israel's Failure to Complete the Conquest of Canaan
(Josh 15.13–19)

1 After the death of Joshua, the Israelites inquired of the LORD, "Who shall go up first for us against the Cā′naan·ites, to fight against them?" ² The LORD said, "Judah shall go up. I hereby give the land into his hand." ³ Judah said to his brother Sim′ē·on, "Come up with me into the territory allotted to me, that we may fight against the Cā′naan·ites; then I too will go with you into the territory allotted to you." So Sim′ē·on went with him. ⁴ Then Judah went up and the LORD gave the Cā′naan·ites and the Per′iz·zītes into their hand; and they defeated ten thousand of them at Bē′zek. ⁵ They came upon A·dō′ni-bē′zek at Bē′zek, and fought against him, and defeated the Cā′naan·ites and the Per′iz·zītes. ⁶ A·dō′ni-bē′zek fled; but they pursued him, and caught him, and cut off his thumbs and big toes. ⁷ A·dō′ni-bē′zek said, "Seventy kings with their thumbs and big toes cut off used to pick up scraps under my table; as I have done, so God has paid me back." They brought him to Jerusalem, and he died there.

8 Then the people of Judah fought against Jerusalem and took it. They put it to the sword and set the city on fire. ⁹ Afterward the people of Judah went down to fight against the Cā′naan·ites who lived in the hill country, in the Neg′eb, and in the lowland. ¹⁰ Judah went against the Cā′naan·ites who lived in Hē′bron (the name of Hē′bron was formerly Kir′i·ath-ar′ba); and they defeated Shē′shaī and A·hī′man and Tal′maī.

11 From there they went against the inhabitants of Dē′bir (the name of Dē′bir was formerly Kir′i·ath-sē′pher). ¹² Then Caleb said, "Whoever attacks Kir′i·ath-sē′pher and takes it, I will give him my daughter Ach′sah as wife." ¹³ And Oth′ni·el son of Kē′naz, Caleb's younger brother, took it; and he gave him his daughter Ach′sah as wife. ¹⁴ When she came to him, she urged him to ask her father for a field. As she dismounted from her donkey, Caleb said to her, "What do you wish?" ¹⁵ She said to him, "Give me a present; since you have set me in the land of the Neg′eb, give me also Gul′loth-māy′im."[a] So Caleb gave her Upper Gul′loth and Lower Gul′loth.

16 The descendants of Hō′bab[b] the Ken′īte, Moses' father-in-law, went up with the people of Judah from the city of palms into the wilderness of Judah, which lies in the Neg′eb near Ar′ad. Then they went and settled with the A·mal′e·kītes.[c] ¹⁷ Judah went with his brother Sim′ē·on, and they defeated

---

a That is *Basins of Water*   *b* Gk: Heb lacks *Hobab*
c See 1 Sam 15.6: Heb *people*

PRAY IT!
Water in the Desert

Caleb's daughter, Achsah, asks for Gulloth-mayim (Judg 1.15) as her wedding present. Gulloth-mayim means "basins of water," and presumably, she was asking for a place with springs of fresh water. Achsah's new home will be in the desert, and she knows that her family will need water. She's not afraid to ask for what she needs.

In your prayer, reflect or journal on the following questions:

■ What parts of your life are like a barren desert, that is, dry and lifeless?

■ What could act as a spring for these parts of your life, bringing new life to them? Be bold in asking God to bring that new life.

▸ Judg 1.14–15

---

the Cā'naan•ites who inhabited Zē'phath, and devoted it to destruction. So the city was called Hor'mah. 18 Judah took Gā'za with its territory, Ash'ke•lon with its territory, and Ek'ron with its territory. 19 The LORD was with Judah, and he took possession of the hill country, but could not drive out the inhabitants of the plain, because they had chariots of iron. 20 Hē'bron was given to Caleb, as Moses had said; and he drove out from it the three sons of Ā'nak. 21 But the Ben'ja•min•ites did not drive out the Jeb'ū•sītes who lived in Jerusalem; so the Jeb'ū•sītes have lived in Jerusalem among the Ben'ja•min•ites to this day.

22 The house of Joseph also went up against Beth'el; and the LORD was with them. 23 The house of Joseph sent out spies to Beth'el (the name of the city was formerly Luz). 24 When the spies saw a man coming out of the city, they said to him, "Show us the way into the city, and we will deal kindly with you." 25 So he showed them the way into the city; and they put the city to the sword, but they let the man and all his family go. 26 So the man went to the land of the Hit'tītes and built a city, and named it Luz; that is its name to this day.

27 Ma•nas'seh did not drive out the inhabitants of Beth-shē'an and its villages, or Tā'a•nach and its villages, or the inhabitants of Dor and its villages, or the inhabitants of Ib'lē•am and its villages, or the inhabitants of Me•gid'dō and its villages; but the Cā'naan•ites continued to live in that land. 28 When

Israel grew strong, they put the Cā'naan•ites to forced labor, but did not in fact drive them out. 29 And Ē'phra•im did not drive out the Cā-naan•ites who lived in Gē'zer; but the Cā'naan•ites lived among them in Gē'zer. 30 Zeb'ū•lun did not drive out the inhabitants of Kit'ron, or the inhabitants of Na•hal'ol; but the Cā'naan•ites lived among them, and became subject to forced labor. 31 Ash'er did not drive out the inhabitants of Ac'cō, or the inhabitants of Sī'don, or of Ah'lab, or of Ach'zib, or of Hel'bah, or of Ā'phik, or of Rē'hob; 32 but the Ash'er•ites lived among the Cā'naan•ites, the inhabitants of the land; for they did not drive them out.

33 Naph'ta•lī did not drive out the inhabitants of Beth-shē'mesh, or the inhabitants of Beth-ā'nath, but lived among the Cā'naan•ites, the inhabitants of the land; nevertheless the inhabitants of Beth-shē'mesh and of Beth-ā'nath became subject to forced labor for them.

34 The Am'o•rites pressed the Dan'ites back into the hill country; they did not allow them to come down to the plain. 35 The Am'o•rites continued to live in Har-hēr'es, in Aī'ja•lon, and in Shā-al'bim, but the hand of the house of Joseph rested heavily on them, and they became subject to forced labor. 36 The border of the Am'o•rites ran from the ascent of Ak•rab'bim, from Sē'la and upward.

Israel's Disobedience

2 Now the angel of the LORD went up from Gil'gal to Bō'chim, and said, "I brought you up from Egypt, and brought you into the land that I had promised to your ancestors. I said, 'I will never break my covenant with you. 2 For your part, do not make a covenant with the inhabitants of this land; tear down their altars.' But you have not obeyed my command. See what you have done! 3 So now I say, I will not drive them out before you; but they shall become adversaries[d] to you, and their gods shall be a snare to you." 4 When the angel of the LORD spoke these words to all the Israelites, the people lifted up their voices and wept. 5 So they named that place Bō'chim,[e] and there they sacrificed to the LORD.

Death of Joshua
(Josh 24.29–31)

6 When Joshua dismissed the people, the Israelites all went to their own inheritances to take possession of the land. 7 The people worshiped the LORD all the days of Joshua, and all the days of the elders who outlived Joshua, who had seen all

---

d OL Vg Compare Gk: Heb *sides*   e That is *Weepers*

the great work that the LORD had done for Israel. [8] Joshua son of Nun, the servant of the LORD, died at the age of one hundred ten years. [9] So they buried him within the bounds of his inheritance in Tim′nath-hĕ′rēs, in the hill country of Ĕ′phra•im, north of Mount Gā′ash. [10] Moreover, that whole generation was gathered to their ancestors, and another generation grew up after them, who did not know the LORD or the work that he had done for Israel.

Israel's Unfaithfulness

[11] Then the Israelites did what was evil in the sight of the LORD and worshiped the Bā′als; [12] and they abandoned the LORD, the God of their ancestors, who had brought them out of the land of Egypt; they followed other gods, from among the gods of the peoples who were all around them, and bowed down to them; and they provoked the LORD to anger. [13] They abandoned the LORD, and worshiped Bā′al and the As•tar′tēs. [14] So the anger of the LORD was kindled against Israel, and he gave them over to plunderers who plundered them, and he sold them into the power of their enemies all around, so that they could no longer withstand their enemies. [15] Whenever they marched out, the hand of the LORD was against them to bring misfortune, as the LORD had warned them and sworn to them; and they were in great distress.

[16] Then the LORD raised up judges, who delivered them out of the power of those who plundered them. [17] Yet they did not listen even to their judges; for they lusted after other gods and bowed down to them. They soon turned aside from the way in which their ancestors had walked, who had obeyed the commandments of the LORD; they did not follow their example. [18] Whenever the LORD raised up judges for them, the LORD was with the judge, and he delivered them from the hand of their enemies all the days of the judge; for the LORD would be moved to pity by their groaning because of those who persecuted and oppressed them. [19] But whenever the judge died, they would relapse and behave worse than their ancestors, following other gods, worshiping them and bowing down to them. They would not drop any of their practices or their stubborn ways. [20] So the anger of the LORD was kindled against Israel; and he said, "Because this people have transgressed my covenant that I commanded their ancestors, and have not obeyed my voice, [21] I will no longer drive out before them any of the nations that Joshua left when he died." [22] In order to test Israel, whether or not they would take care to walk in the way of the LORD as their ancestors did, [23] the LORD had left those nations, not driving them out at once, and had not handed them over to Joshua.

Nations Remaining in the Land

3 Now these are the nations that the LORD left to test all those in Israel who had no experience of any war in Cā′naan [2] (it was only that successive generations of Israelites might know war, to teach those who had no experience of it before): [3] the five lords of the Phi•lis′tines, and all the Cā′-naan•ītes, and the Sī•dō′ni•ans, and the Hī′vītes who lived on Mount Lebanon, from Mount Bā′al-her′mon as far as Lĕ′bō-hā′math. [4] They were for the testing of Israel, to know whether Israel would obey the commandments of the LORD, which he commanded their ancestors by Moses. [5] So the Israelites lived among the Cā′naan•ites, the Hit′tites,

Obeying Authority

Have you ever decided to disobey your parents, your teachers, or maybe a boss at work? What were the consequences? Disobedience to legitimate authority tends to bring about bad consequences. Just read Judg 2.11–15. The people turned from God, and their separation from God led to defeat at the hands of their enemies.

God places parents, teachers, and other authority figures in our life to protect and support us. Their love and caring are an extension of God's love and caring. From their vantage point, they often see a bigger picture than we do. When we disobey their reasonable requests, we build walls between them and us, preventing God's love from reaching us. On the other hand, obedience leads to more trust, responsibility, and freedom. Of course, as Jesus himself showed us, no one is obligated to obey requests or directions that are abusive, demeaning, or immoral.

So, the next time you are having a problem with a person in authority, ask yourself, "Might obedience in this situation somehow bring me closer to God?"

▶ Judg 2.10–15

the Am′o•rītes, the Per′iz•zītes, the Hī′vītes, and the Jeb′ū•sītes; 6 and they took their daughters as wives for themselves, and their own daughters they gave to their sons; and they worshiped their gods.

Othniel

7 The Israelites did what was evil in the sight of the LORD, forgetting the LORD their God, and worshiping the Bā′als and the A•shē′rahs. 8 Therefore the anger of the LORD was kindled against Israel, and he sold them into the hand of King Cū′shan-rish•a•thā′im of Ar′am-nā•ha•rā′im; and the Israelites served Cū′shan-rish•a•thā′im eight years. 9 But when the Israelites cried out to the LORD, the LORD raised up a deliverer for the Israelites, who delivered them, Oth′ni•el son of Kē′naz, Caleb′s younger brother. 10 The spirit of the LORD came upon him, and he judged Israel; he went out to war, and the LORD gave King Cū′shan-rish•a•thā′im of Ar′am into his hand; and his hand prevailed over Cū′shan-rish•a•thā′im. 11 So the land had rest forty years. Then Oth′ni•el son of Kē′naz died.

Ehud

12 The Israelites again did what was evil in the sight of the LORD; and the LORD strengthened King Eg′lon of Mō′ab against Israel, because they had done what was evil in the sight of the LORD. 13 In alliance with the Am′mon•ites and the A•mal′e•kītes, he went and defeated Israel; and they took possession of the city of palms. 14 So the Israelites served King Eg′lon of Mō′ab eighteen years.

15 But when the Israelites cried out to the LORD, the LORD raised up for them a deliverer, Ē′hud son of Gē′ra, the Ben′ja•min•īte, a left-handed man. The Israelites sent tribute by him to King Eg′lon of Mō′ab. 16 Ē′hud made for himself a sword with two edges, a cubit in length; and he fastened it on his right thigh under his clothes. 17 Then he presented the tribute to King Eg′lon of Mō′ab. Now Eg′lon was a very fat man. 18 When Ē′hud had finished presenting the tribute, he sent the people who carried the tribute on their way. 19 But he himself turned back at the sculptured stones near Gil′gal, and said, "I have a secret message for you, O king." So the king said,f "Silence!" and all his attendants went out from his presence. 20 Ē′hud came to him, while he was sitting alone in his cool roof chamber, and said, "I have a message from God for you." So he rose from his seat. 21 Then Ē′hud reached with his left hand, took the sword from his right thigh, and thrust it into Eg′lon′sg belly; 22 the hilt also went in after the blade, and the fat closed over the blade, for he did not draw the sword out of his belly; and the dirt came out.h 23 Then Ē′hud went out into the vestibule,i and closed the doors of the roof chamber on him, and locked them.

24 After he had gone, the servants came. When they saw that the doors of the roof chamber were locked, they thought, "He must be relieving himselfj in the cool chamber." 25 So they waited until they were embarrassed. When he still did not open the doors of the roof chamber, they took the key and opened them. There was their lord lying dead on the floor.

26 Ē′hud escaped while they delayed, and passed beyond the sculptured stones, and escaped to Sē•ī′rah. 27 When he arrived, he sounded the trumpet in the hill country of Ē′phra•im; and the Israelites went down with him from the hill country, having him at their head. 28 He said to them, "Follow after me; for the LORD has given your enemies the Mō′ab•ītes into your hand." So they went down after him, and seized the fords of the Jordan against the Mō′ab•ītes, and allowed no one to cross over. 29 At that time they killed about ten thousand of the Mō′ab•ītes, all strong, able-bodied men; no one escaped. 30 So Mō′ab was subdued that day under the hand of Israel. And the land had rest eighty years.

Shamgar

31 After him came Sham′gar son of Ā′nath, who killed six hundred of the Phi•lis′tines with an ox-goad. He too delivered Israel.

Deborah and Barak

4 The Israelites again did what was evil in the sight of the LORD, after Ē′hud died. 2 So the LORD sold them into the hand of King Jā′bin of Cā′-naan, who reigned in Hā′zor; the commander of his army was Sis′e•ra, who lived in Ha•rō′sheth-ha-goi′im. 3 Then the Israelites cried out to the LORD for help; for he had nine hundred chariots of iron, and had oppressed the Israelites cruelly twenty years.

4 At that time Deb′or•ah, a prophetess, wife of Lap′pi•doth, was judging Israel. 5 She used to sit under the palm of Deb′or•ah between Rā′mah and Beth′el in the hill country of Ē′phra•im; and the Israelites came up to her for judgment. 6 She sent and summoned Bar′ak son of A•bin′ō•am from Kē′desh in Naph′ta•lī, and said to him, "The LORD, the God of Israel, commands you, 'Go, take position at Mount Tā′bor, bringing ten thousand from the tribe of Naph′ta•lī and the tribe of Zeb′ū•lun. 7 I will draw out Sis′e•ra, the general of Jā′bin's army, to meet you by the Wadi Kī′shon with his chariots and his troops; and I will give him into your hand.' " 8 Bar′ak said to her, "If you will go with me, I will

---

f Heb *he said*   g Heb *his*   h With Tg Vg: Meaning of Heb uncertain   i Meaning of Heb uncertain   j Heb *covering his feet* go; but if you will not go with me, I will not go." 9 And she said, "I will surely go with you; nevertheless, the road on which you are going will not lead to your glory, for the LORD will sell Sis′e·ra into the hand of a woman." Then Deb′or·ah got up and went with Bar′ak to Kē′desh. 10 Bar′ak summoned Zeb′ū·lun and Naph′ta·lī to Kē′desh; and ten thousand warriors went up behind him; and Deb′or·ah went up with him.

11 Now Hē′ber the Ken′īte had separated from the other Ken′ītes,*k* that is, the descendants of Hō′bab the father-in-law of Moses, and had encamped as far away as Ē′lon-be·zā-a·nan′nim, which is near Kē′desh.

12 When Sis′e·ra was told that Bar′ak son of A·bin′ō·am had gone up to Mount Tā′bor, 13 Sis′e·ra called out all his chariots, nine hundred chariots of iron, and all the troops who were with

him, from Ha·rō′sheth-ha-goi′im to the Wadi Kī′shon. 14 Then Deb′or·ah said to Bar′ak, "Up! For this is the day on which the LORD has given Sis′e·ra into your hand. The LORD is indeed going out before you." So Bar′ak went down from Mount Tā′bor with ten thousand warriors following him. 15 And the LORD threw Sis′e·ra and all his chariots and all his army into a panic*l* before Bar′ak; Sis′e·ra got down from his chariot and fled away on foot, 16 while Bar′ak pursued the chariots and the army to Ha·rō′sheth-ha-goi′im. All the army of Sis′e·ra fell by the sword; no one was left.

17 Now Sis′e·ra had fled away on foot to the tent of Jā′el wife of Hē′ber the Ken′īte; for there was peace between King Jā′bin of Hā′zor and the clan of Hē′ber the Ken′īte. 18 Jā′el came out to meet Sis′e·ra, and said to him, "Turn aside, my lord, turn aside to me; have no fear." So he turned aside to her into the tent, and she covered him with a rug. 19 Then he said to her, "Please give me a little water to drink; for I am thirsty." So she opened a skin of milk and gave him a drink and covered him. 20 He said to her, "Stand at the entrance of the tent, and if anybody comes and asks you, 'Is anyone here?' say, 'No.' " 21 But Jā′el wife of Hē′ber took a tent peg, and took a hammer in her hand, and went softly to him and drove the peg into his temple, until it went down into the ground—he was lying fast asleep from weariness—and he died. 22 Then, as Bar′ak came in pursuit of Sis′e·ra, Jā′el went out to meet him, and said to him, "Come, and I will show you the man whom you are seeking." So he went into her tent; and there was Sis′e·ra lying dead, with the tent peg in his temple.

23 So on that day God subdued King Jā′bin of Cā′naan before the Israelites. 24 Then the hand of the Israelites bore harder and harder on King Jā′bin of Cā′naan, until they destroyed King Jā′bin of Cā′naan.

PRAY IT?

Wartime Women

In Judges, chapter 4, Deborah, a judge and prophet, rallies Barak and the Israelites to war, and Jael, another woman (who is not an Israelite), delivers the final blow to the enemy's commander, Sisera. In chapter 5, Deborah leads the victory celebration with an elaborate prayer-song that is probably one of the oldest texts in the Bible (see also Exodus, chapter 15).

In the Bible, women are often innocent victims of war. Usually, they do not do the fighting but are raped, killed, or widowed. Is Jael's violence the answer to this abuse? Is Jael a hero? Or is she still a victim of war, forced to make a violent choice in order to survive in a violent world? The writer of the Book of Judges gives no judgment on her actions.

When we are no longer victims but have become people who abuse others, has the situation really improved? Or are we just doing to others what we would never want done to ourselves? In light of Jesus' teachings, these are important questions to ask. Let us pray:

God of love, please deliver us from being both victims of violence and agents of violence. Amen.

▸ **Judges, chapter 4**

The Song of Deborah

5 Then Deb′or·ah and Bar′ak son of A·bin′ō·am sang on that day, saying:
2 "When locks are long in Israel,
    when the people offer themselves
        willingly—
    bless*m* the LORD!

3 "Hear, O kings; give ear, O princes;
    to the LORD I will sing,
    I will make melody to the LORD, the God
        of Israel.

---

k Heb *from the Kain* *l* Heb adds *to the sword;* compare verse 16 *m* Or *You who offer yourselves willingly among the people, bless*

The Battle Within

Although the story of Deborah is inspiring, partly because so few women leaders are portrayed in the Bible, it is also a story of war and violence. The Book of Judges records one battle after another. It is wearying to read of so much fighting and of rejoicing over someone's having a tent peg pounded into his head.

We need to keep our perspective here and understand that the way the Israelites viewed life at that time was simple: If they were victorious, God was with them. If they were defeated, God had been offended and had turned away from them.

What can we learn from this story? It teaches that God never turns away from us. The real victories to celebrate are the personal battles that we win each day as we strive to become more faithful to God. Jesus calls us to make peace rather than war. Our greatest enemy is often within, as we strive to be the person God wants us to be, whether our name is Deborah or Joshua, Jennifer or Carlos.

What battle is going on inside you today? What choice in this battle leads to greater faithfulness to God?

▸ **Judges, chapter 4**

---

4 "LORD, when you went out from Sĕ'ir,
    when you marched from the region of
        E'dom,
the earth trembled,
    and the heavens poured,
    the clouds indeed poured water.
5 The mountains quaked before the LORD, the
        One of Sinai,
    before the LORD, the God of Israel.

6 "In the days of Sham'gar son of Ā'nath,
    in the days of Jā'el, caravans ceased
    and travelers kept to the byways.
7 The peasantry prospered in Israel,
    they grew fat on plunder,
because you arose, Deb'or•ah,
    arose as a mother in Israel.
8 When new gods were chosen,
    then war was in the gates.
Was shield or spear to be seen
    among forty thousand in Israel?
9 My heart goes out to the commanders of Israel
    who offered themselves willingly among
        the people.
    Bless the LORD.

10 "Tell of it, you who ride on white donkeys,
    you who sit on rich carpets[n]
    and you who walk by the way.
11 To the sound of musicians[n] at the watering
        places,
    there they repeat the triumphs of the LORD,
    the triumphs of his peasantry in Israel.

"Then down to the gates marched the people
    of the LORD.

12 "Awake, awake, Deb'or•ah!
    Awake, awake, utter a song!
Arise, Bar'ak, lead away your captives,
    O son of A•bin'ō•am.
13 Then down marched the remnant of the noble;
    the people of the LORD marched down for
        him[o] against the mighty.
14 From E'phra•im they set out[p] into the valley,[q]
    following you, Benjamin, with your kin;
from Mā'chir marched down the commanders,
    and from Zeb'ū•lun those who bear the
        marshal's staff;
15 the chiefs of Is'sa•char came with
        Deb'or•ah,
    and Is'sa•char faithful to Bar'ak;
    into the valley they rushed out at his heels.
Among the clans of Reuben
    there were great searchings of heart.
16 Why did you tarry among the sheepfolds,
    to hear the piping for the flocks?
Among the clans of Reuben
    there were great searchings of heart.
17 Gil'e•ad stayed beyond the Jordan;
    and Dan, why did he abide with the ships?
Ash'er sat still at the coast of the sea,
    settling down by his landings.
18 Zeb'ū•lun is a people that scorned death;
    Naph'ta•lī too, on the heights of the field.

19 "The kings came, they fought;
    then fought the kings of Cā'naan,
at Tā'a•nach, by the waters of Me•gid'dō;
    they got no spoils of silver.

---

n Meaning of Heb uncertain o Gk: Heb me p Cn: Heb
From Ephraim their root q Gk: Heb in Amalek

J
U
D
G

20 The stars fought from heaven,
   from their courses they fought against
      Sis'e•ra.
21 The torrent Kī'shon swept them away,
   the onrushing torrent, the torrent Kī'shon.
   March on, my soul, with might!

22 "Then loud beat the horses' hoofs
   with the galloping, galloping of his steeds.

23 "Curse Mē'roz, says the angel of the LORD,
   curse bitterly its inhabitants,
   because they did not come to the help of the
      LORD,
   to the help of the LORD against the mighty.

24 "Most blessed of women be Jā'el,
   the wife of Hē'ber the Ken'īte,
   of tent-dwelling women most blessed.
25 He asked water and she gave him milk,
   she brought him curds in a lordly bowl.
26 She put her hand to the tent peg
   and her right hand to the workmen's
      mallet;
   she struck Sis'e•ra a blow,
   she crushed his head,
   she shattered and pierced his temple.
27 He sank, he fell,
   he lay still at her feet;
   at her feet he sank, he fell;
   where he sank, there he fell dead.

28 "Out of the window she peered,
   the mother of Sis'e•ra gazedʳ through the
      lattice:
   'Why is his chariot so long in coming?
   Why tarry the hoofbeats of his chariots?'
29 Her wisest ladies make answer,
   indeed, she answers the question herself:
30 'Are they not finding and dividing the spoil?—
   A girl or two for every man;
   spoil of dyed stuffs for Sis'e•ra,
   spoil of dyed stuffs embroidered,
   two pieces of dyed work embroidered for
      my neck as spoil?'

31 "So perish all your enemies, O LORD!
   But may your friends be like the sun as it
      rises in its might."

And the land had rest forty years.

The Midianite Oppression

6 The Israelites did what was evil in the sight of the LORD, and the LORD gave them into the hand of Mid'i•an seven years. 2 The hand of Mid'i•an prevailed over Israel; and because of Mid'i•an the Israelites provided for themselves hiding places in the mountains, caves and strongholds. 3 For whenever the Israelites put in seed, the Mid'i•an•ites and the A•mal'e•kītes and the people of the east would come up against them. 4 They would encamp against them and destroy the produce of the land, as far as the neighborhood of Gā'za, and leave no sustenance in Israel, and no sheep or ox or donkey. 5 For they and their livestock would come up, and they would even bring their tents, as thick as locusts; neither they nor their camels could be counted; so they wasted the land as they came in. 6 Thus Israel was greatly impoverished because of Mid'i•an; and the Israelites cried out to the LORD for help.

7 When the Israelites cried to the LORD on account of the Mid'i•an•ites, 8 the LORD sent a prophet to the Israelites; and he said to them, "Thus says the LORD, the God of Israel: I led you up from Egypt, and brought you out of the house of slavery; 9 and I delivered you from the hand of the Egyptians, and from the hand of all who oppressed you, and drove them out before you, and gave you their land; 10 and I said to you, 'I am the LORD your God; you shall not pay reverence to the gods of the Am'o•rītes, in whose land you live.' But you have not given heed to my voice."

The Call of Gideon

11 Now the angel of the LORD came and sat under the oak at Oph'rah, which belonged to Jō'ash the Ā•bi•ez'rīte, as his son Gideon was beating out wheat in the wine press, to hide it from the Mid'i•an•ites. 12 The angel of the LORD appeared to him and said to him, "The LORD is with you, you mighty warrior." 13 Gideon answered him, "But sir, if the LORD is with us, why then has all this happened to us? And where are all his wonderful deeds that our ancestors recounted to us, saying, 'Did not the LORD bring us up from Egypt?' But now the LORD has cast us off, and given us into the hand of Mid'i•an." 14 Then the LORD turned to him and said, "Go in this might of yours and deliver Israel from the hand of Mid'i•an; I hereby commission you." 15 He responded, "But sir, how can I deliver Israel? My clan is the weakest in Ma•nas'seh, and I am the least in my family." 16 The LORD said to him, "But I will be with you, and you shall strike down the Mid'i•an•ites, every one of them." 17 Then he said to him, "If now I have found favor with you, then show me a sign that it is you who speak with me. 18 Do not depart from here until I come to you, and bring out my present, and set it before you." And he said, "I will stay until you return."

19 So Gideon went into his house and prepared

ʳ Gk Compare Tg: Heb *exclaimed*

a kid, and unleavened cakes from an ephah of flour; the meat he put in a basket, and the broth he put in a pot, and brought them to him under the oak and presented them. 20 The angel of God said to him, "Take the meat and the unleavened cakes, and put them on this rock, and pour out the broth." And he did so. 21 Then the angel of the LORD reached out the tip of the staff that was in his hand, and touched the meat and the unleavened cakes; and fire sprang up from the rock and consumed the meat and the unleavened cakes; and the angel of the LORD vanished from his sight. 22 Then Gideon perceived that it was the angel of the LORD; and Gideon said, "Help me, Lord GOD! For I have seen the angel of the LORD face to face." 23 But the LORD said to him, "Peace be to you; do not fear, you shall not die." 24 Then Gideon built an altar there to the LORD, and called it, The LORD is peace. To this day it still stands at Oph'rah, which belongs to the Ā•bi•ez'rītes.

25 That night the LORD said to him, "Take your father's bull, the second bull seven years old, and pull down the altar of Bā'al that belongs to your father, and cut down the sacred poles that is beside it; 26 and build an altar to the LORD your God on the top of the stronghold here, in proper order; then take the second bull, and offer it as a burnt offering with the wood of the sacred poles that you shall cut down." 27 So Gideon took ten of his servants, and did as the LORD had told him; but because he was too afraid of his family and the townspeople to do it by day, he did it by night.

Gideon Destroys the Altar of Baal

28 When the townspeople rose early in the morning, the altar of Bā'al was broken down, and the sacred poles beside it was cut down, and the second bull was offered on the altar that had been built. 29 So they said to one another, "Who has done this?" After searching and inquiring, they were told, "Gideon son of Jō'ash did it." 30 Then the townspeople said to Jō'ash, "Bring out your son, so that he may die, for he has pulled down the altar of Bā'al and cut down the sacred poles beside it." 31 But Jō'ash said to all who were arrayed against him, "Will you contend for Bā'al? Or will you defend his cause? Whoever contends for him shall be put to death by morning. If he is a god, let him contend for himself, because his altar has been pulled down." 32 Therefore on that day Gideont was called Jer•ub•bā'al, that is to say, "Let Bā'al contend against him," because he pulled down his altar.

33 Then all the Mid'i•an•ītes and the A•mal'e•kītes and the people of the east came together, and crossing the Jordan they encamped in the Valley of Jez'rē•el. 34 But the spirit of the LORD took possession of Gideon; and he sounded the trumpet,

and the Ā•bi•ez'rītes were called out to follow him. 35 He sent messengers throughout all Ma•nas'seh, and they too were called out to follow him. He also sent messengers to Ash'er, Zeb'ū•lun, and Naph'-ta•lī, and they went up to meet them.

The Sign of the Fleece

36 Then Gideon said to God, "In order to see whether you will deliver Israel by my hand, as you have said, 37 I am going to lay a fleece of wool on the threshing floor; if there is dew on the fleece alone, and it is dry on all the ground, then I shall know that you will deliver Israel by my hand, as you have said." 38 And it was so. When he rose early next morning and squeezed the fleece, he wrung enough dew from the fleece to fill a bowl with water. 39 Then Gideon said to God, "Do not let your anger burn against me, let me speak one more time; let me, please, make trial with the fleece just once more; let it be dry only on the fleece, and on all the ground let there be dew." 40 And God did so that night. It was dry on the fleece only, and on all the ground there was dew.

---

s Heb *Asherah*   t Heb *he*

PRAY IT!
Trusting God

The true test of love is loving without testing.

Gideon keeps testing God; he cannot bring himself to believe God's promises. Judges, chapters 6–8, gives a full picture of this hero who never quite understands what loving God is all about. Even after his victory and his words of devotion to God, he makes a gold idol (Judg 8.22–28).

Most people are tempted to test God in some way: "God, I'll know you are there for me if I get this job." Fortunately, God is big enough to accept our testing. Just do not expect God to answer every request—at least not exactly the way you would like God to answer it.

How do you test God? Is your prayer more trusting than Gideon's prayer? The next time you feel anxious or afraid, use one of these Scripture passages for your prayer: Psalm 25; Psalm 27; John, chapter 14; 1 Jn 4.7–21. Challenge yourself to trust God without testing.

▶ Judg 6.36–40

Gideon Surprises and Routs the Midianites

7 Then Jer·ub·bā′al (that is, Gideon) and all the troops that were with him rose early and encamped beside the spring of Har′od; and the camp of Mid′i·an was north of them, below[u] the hill of Mō′reh, in the valley.

2 The LORD said to Gideon, "The troops with you are too many for me to give the Mid′i·an·ites into their hand. Israel would only take the credit away from me, saying, 'My own hand has delivered me.' 3 Now therefore proclaim this in the hearing of the troops, 'Whoever is fearful and trembling, let him return home.' " Thus Gideon sifted them out;[v] twenty-two thousand returned, and ten thousand remained.

4 Then the LORD said to Gideon, "The troops are still too many; take them down to the water and I will sift them out for you there. When I say, 'This one shall go with you,' he shall go with you; and when I say, 'This one shall not go with you,' he shall not go." 5 So he brought the troops down to the water; and the LORD said to Gideon, "All those who lap the water with their tongues, as a dog laps, you shall put to one side; all those who kneel down to drink, putting their hands to their mouths,[w] you shall put to the other side." 6 The number of those that lapped was three hundred; but all the rest of the troops knelt down to drink water. 7 Then the LORD said to Gideon, "With the three hundred that lapped I will deliver you, and give the Mid′i·an·ites into your hand. Let all the others go to their homes." 8 So he took the jars of the troops from their hands,[x] and their trumpets; and he sent all the rest of Israel back to their own tents, but retained the three hundred. The camp of Mid′i·an was below him in the valley.

9 That same night the LORD said to him, "Get up, attack the camp; for I have given it into your hand. 10 But if you fear to attack, go down to the camp with your servant Pū′rah; 11 and you shall hear what they say, and afterward your hands shall be strengthened to attack the camp." Then he went down with his servant Pū′rah to the outposts of the armed men that were in the camp. 12 The Mid′i·an·ites and the A·mal′e·kites and all the people of the east lay along the valley as thick as locusts; and their camels were without number, countless as the sand on the seashore. 13 When Gideon arrived, there was a man telling a dream to his comrade; and he said, "I had a dream, and in it a cake of barley bread tumbled into the camp of Mid′i·an, and came to the tent, and struck it so that it fell; it turned upside down, and the tent collapsed." 14 And his comrade answered, "This is no other than the sword of Gideon son of Jō′ash, a man of Israel; into his hand God has given Mid′i·an and all the army."

15 When Gideon heard the telling of the dream and its interpretation, he worshiped; and he returned to the camp of Israel, and said, "Get up; for the LORD has given the army of Mid′i·an into your hand." 16 After he divided the three hundred men into three companies, and put trumpets into the hands of all of them, and empty jars, with torches inside the jars, 17 he said to them, "Look at me, and do the same; when I come to the outskirts of the camp, do as I do. 18 When I blow the trumpet, I and all who are with me, then you also blow the trumpets around the whole camp, and shout, 'For the LORD and for Gideon!' "

19 So Gideon and the hundred who were with him came to the outskirts of the camp at the beginning of the middle watch, when they had just set the watch; and they blew the trumpets and smashed the jars that were in their hands. 20 So the three companies blew the trumpets and broke the jars, holding in their left hands the torches, and in their right hands the trumpets to blow; and they cried, "A sword for the LORD and for Gideon!" 21 Every man stood in his place all around the camp, and all the men in camp ran; they cried out and fled. 22 When they blew the three hundred trumpets, the LORD set every man's sword against his fellow and against all the army; and the army fled as far as Beth-shit′tah toward Zer′e·rah,[y] as far as the border of Ā′bel-me·hō′lah, by Tab′bath. 23 And the men of Israel were called out from Naph′ta·li and from Ash′er and from all Ma·nas′seh, and they pursued after the Mid′i·an·ites.

24 Then Gideon sent messengers throughout all the hill country of E′phra·im, saying, "Come down against the Mid′i·an·ites and seize the waters against them, as far as Beth-bar′ah, and also the Jordan." So all the men of E′phra·im were called out, and they seized the waters as far as Beth-bar′ah, and also the Jordan. 25 They captured the two captains of Mid′i·an, Or′eb and Zē′eb; they killed Or′eb at the rock of Or′eb, and Zē′eb they killed at the wine press of Zē′eb, as they pursued the Mid′i·an·ites. They brought the heads of Or′eb and Zē′eb to Gideon beyond the Jordan.

Gideon's Triumph and Vengeance

8 Then the E′phra·im·ites said to him, "What have you done to us, not to call us when you went to fight against the Mid′i·an·ites?" And they upbraided him violently. 2 So he said to them, "What have I done now in comparison with you? Is not the gleaning of the grapes of E′phra·im better

---

u Heb *from*   v Cn: Heb *home, and depart from Mount Gilead'* "
w Heb places the words *putting their hands to their mouths*
after the word *lapped* in verse 6   x Cn: Heb *So the people
took provisions in their hands*   y Another reading is *Zeredah*

than the vintage of Ă·bi·ĕ′zer? [3] God has given into your hands the captains of Mid′i·an, Or′eb and Zĕ′eb; what have I been able to do in comparison with you?" When he said this, their anger against him subsided.

[4] Then Gideon came to the Jordan and crossed over, he and the three hundred who were with him, exhausted and famished.[z] [5] So he said to the people of Suc′coth, "Please give some loaves of bread to my followers, for they are exhausted, and I am pursuing Zĕ′bah and Zal·mun′na, the kings of Mid′i·an." [6] But the officials of Suc′coth said, "Do you already have in your possession the hands of Zĕ′bah and Zal·mun′na, that we should give bread to your army?" [7] Gideon replied, "Well then, when the LORD has given Zĕ′bah and Zal·mun′na into my hand, I will trample your flesh on the thorns of the wilderness and on briers." [8] From there he went up to Pe·nū′el, and made the same request of them; and the people of Pe·nū′el answered him as the people of Suc′coth had answered. [9] So he said to the people of Pe·nū′el, "When I come back victorious, I will break down this tower."

[10] Now Zĕ′bah and Zal·mun′na were in Kar′kor with their army, about fifteen thousand men, all who were left of all the army of the people of the east; for one hundred twenty thousand men bearing arms had fallen. [11] So Gideon went up by the caravan route east of Nō′bah and Jog′be·hah, and attacked the army; for the army was off its guard. [12] Zĕ′bah and Zal·mun′na fled; and he pursued them and took the two kings of Mid′i·an, Zĕ′bah and Zal·mun′na, and threw all the army into a panic.

[13] When Gideon son of Jō′ash returned from the battle by the ascent of Heres, [14] he caught a young man, one of the people of Suc′coth, and questioned him; and he listed for him the officials and elders of Suc′coth, seventy-seven people. [15] Then he came to the people of Suc′coth, and said, "Here are Zĕ′bah and Zal·mun′na, about whom you taunted me, saying, 'Do you already have in your possession the hands of Zĕ′bah and Zal·mun′na, that we should give bread to your troops who are exhausted?' " [16] So he took the elders of the city and he took thorns of the wilderness and briers and with them he trampled[a] the people of Suc′coth. [17] He also broke down the tower of Pe·nū′el, and killed the men of the city.

[18] Then he said to Zĕ′bah and Zal·mun′na, "What about the men whom you killed at Tā′bor?" They answered, "As you are, so were they, every one of them; they resembled the sons of a king." [19] And he replied, "They were my brothers, the sons of my mother; as the LORD lives, if you had saved them alive, I would not kill you." [20] So he said to Jĕ′ther his firstborn, "Go kill them!" But the boy did not draw his sword, for he was afraid, because he was still a boy. [21] Then Zĕ′bah and Zal·mun′na said, "You come and kill us; for as the man is, so is his strength." So Gideon proceeded to kill Zĕ′bah and Zal·mun′na; and he took the crescents that were on the necks of their camels.

Gideon's Idolatry

[22] Then the Israelites said to Gideon, "Rule over us, you and your son and your grandson also; for you have delivered us out of the hand of Mid′i·an." [23] Gideon said to them, "I will not rule over you, and my son will not rule over you; the LORD will rule over you." [24] Then Gideon said to them, "Let me make a request of you; each of you give me an earring he has taken as booty." (For the enemy[b] had golden earrings, because they were Ish′ma·el·ītes.) [25] "We will willingly give them," they answered. So they spread a garment, and each threw into it an earring he had taken as booty. [26] The weight of the golden earrings that he requested was one thousand seven hundred shekels of gold (apart from the crescents and the pendants and the purple garments worn by the kings of Mid′i·an, and the collars that were on the necks of their camels). [27] Gideon made an ephod of it and put it in his town, in Oph′rah; and all Israel prostituted themselves to it there, and it became a snare to Gideon and to his family. [28] So Mid′i·an was subdued before the Israelites, and they lifted up their heads no more. So the land had rest forty years in the days of Gideon.

Death of Gideon

[29] Jer·ub·bā′al son of Jō′ash went to live in his own house. [30] Now Gideon had seventy sons, his own offspring, for he had many wives. [31] His concubine who was in Shĕ′chem also bore him a son, and he named him A·bim′e·lech. [32] Then Gideon son of Jō′ash died at a good old age, and was buried in the tomb of his father Jō′ash at Oph′rah of the Ă·bi·ez′rītes.

[33] As soon as Gideon died, the Israelites relapsed and prostituted themselves with the Bā′als, making Bā′al-bēr′ith their god. [34] The Israelites did not remember the LORD their God, who had rescued them from the hand of all their enemies on every side; [35] and they did not exhibit loyalty to the house of Jer·ub·bā′al (that is, Gideon) in return for all the good that he had done to Israel.

Abimelech Attempts to Establish a Monarchy

9 Now A·bim′e·lech son of Jer·ub·bā′al went to Shĕ′chem to his mother's kinsfolk and said to them and to the whole clan of his mother's family,

---

z Gk: Heb *pursuing*   a With verse 7, Compare Gk: Heb *he taught*   b Heb *they*

2 "Say in the hearing of all the lords of Shĕ′chem, 'Which is better for you, that all seventy of the sons of Jer·ub·bā′al rule over you, or that one rule over you?' Remember also that I am your bone and your flesh." 3 So his mother's kinsfolk spoke all these words on his behalf in the hearing of all the lords of Shĕ′chem; and their hearts inclined to follow A·bim′e·lech, for they said, "He is our brother." 4 They gave him seventy pieces of silver out of the temple of Bā′al-bĕ′rith with which A·bim′e·lech hired worthless and reckless fellows, who followed him. 5 He went to his father's house at Oph′rah, and killed his brothers the sons of Jer·ub·bā′al, seventy men, on one stone; but Jō′tham, the youngest son of Jer·ub·bā′al, survived, for he hid himself. 6 Then all the lords of Shĕ′chem and all Beth-mil′lō came together, and they went and made A·bim′-e·lech king, by the oak of the pillar[c] at Shĕ′chem.

The Parable of the Trees

7 When it was told to Jō′tham, he went and stood on the top of Mount Ger′i·zim, and cried aloud and said to them, "Listen to me, you lords of Shĕ′chem, so that God may listen to you.

8 The trees once went out
  to anoint a king over themselves.
So they said to the olive tree,
  'Reign over us.'
9 The olive tree answered them,
  'Shall I stop producing my rich oil
    by which gods and mortals are
    honored,
    and go to sway over the trees?'
10 Then the trees said to the fig tree,
  'You come and reign over us.'
11 But the fig tree answered them,
  'Shall I stop producing my sweetness
    and my delicious fruit,
    and go to sway over the trees?'
12 Then the trees said to the vine,
  'You come and reign over us.'
13 But the vine said to them,
  'Shall I stop producing my wine
    that cheers gods and mortals,
    and go to sway over the trees?'
14 So all the trees said to the bramble,
  'You come and reign over us.'
15 And the bramble said to the trees,
  'If in good faith you are anointing me king
    over you,
    then come and take refuge in my shade;
    but if not, let fire come out of the bramble
    and devour the cedars of Lebanon.'
16 "Now therefore, if you acted in good faith and honor when you made A·bim′e·lech king, and if you have dealt well with Jer·ub·bā′al and his house, and have done to him as his actions de-

served— 17 for my father fought for you, and risked his life, and rescued you from the hand of Mid′i·an; 18 but you have risen up against my father's house this day, and have killed his sons, seventy men on one stone, and have made A·bim′e·lech, the son of his slave woman, king over the lords of Shĕ′chem, because he is your kinsman— 19 if, I say, you have acted in good faith and honor with Je·rub·bā′al and with his house this day, then rejoice in A·bim′-e·lech, and let him also rejoice in you; 20 but if not, let fire come out from A·bim′e·lech, and devour the lords of Shĕ′chem, and Beth-mil′lō; and let fire come out from the lords of Shĕ′chem, and from Beth-mil′lō, and devour A·bim′e·lech." 21 Then Jō′tham ran away and fled, going to Bĕ′er, where he remained for fear of his brother A·bim′e·lech.

The Downfall of Abimelech

22 A·bim′e·lech ruled over Israel three years. 23 But God sent an evil spirit between A·bim′e·lech and the lords of Shĕ′chem; and the lords of Shĕ′chem dealt treacherously with A·bim′e·lech. 24 This happened so that the violence done to the seventy sons of Jer·ub·bā′al might be avenged[d] and their blood be laid on their brother A·bim′e·lech, who killed them, and on the lords of Shĕ′chem, who strengthened his hands to kill his brothers. 25 So, out of hostility to him, the lords of Shĕ′chem set ambushes on the mountain tops. They robbed all who passed by them along that way; and it was reported to A·bim′e·lech.

26 When Gā′al son of Ĕ′bed moved into Shĕ′chem with his kinsfolk, the lords of Shĕ′chem put confidence in him. 27 They went out into the field and gathered the grapes from their vineyards, trod them, and celebrated. Then they went into the temple of their god, ate and drank, and ridiculed A·bim′e·lech. 28 Gā′al son of Ĕ′bed said, "Who is A·bim′e·lech, and who are we of Shĕ′chem, that we should serve him? Did not the son of Jer·ub·bā′al and Zĕ′bul his officer serve the men of Hā′mor father of Shĕ′chem? Why then should we serve him? 29 If only this people were under my command! Then I would remove A·bim′e·lech; I would say[e] to him, 'Increase your army, and come out.' "

30 When Zĕ′bul the ruler of the city heard the words of Gā′al son of Ĕ′bed, his anger was kindled. 31 He sent messengers to A·bim′e·lech at A·rū′mah,[f] saying, "Look, Gā′al son of Ĕ′bed and his kinsfolk have come to Shĕ′chem, and they are stirring up[g] the city against you. 32 Now therefore, go by night, you and the troops that are with you, and lie in wait in the fields. 33 Then early in the morning, as soon

---

c Cn: Meaning of Heb uncertain *d* Heb *might come* *e* Gk: Heb *and he said* *f* Cn See 9.41. Heb *Tormah* *g* Cn: Heb *are besieging* as the sun rises, get up and rush on the city; and when he and the troops that are with him come out against you, you may deal with them as best you can."

34 So A•bim′e•lech and all the troops with him got up by night and lay in wait against Shě′chem in four companies. 35 When Gā′al son of Ě′bed went out and stood in the entrance of the gate of the city, A•bim′e•lech and the troops with him rose from the ambush. 36 And when Gā′al saw them, he said to Zě′bul, "Look, people are coming down from the mountain tops!" And Zě′bul said to him, "The shadows on the mountains look like people to you." 37 Gā′al spoke again and said, "Look, people are coming down from Tab•būr′-e′rez, and one company is coming from the direction of Ě′lon-me•on′e•nim."ʰ 38 Then Zě′bul said to him, "Where is your boastⁱ now, you who said, 'Who is A•bim′e•lech, that we should serve him?' Are not these the troops you made light of? Go out now and fight with them." 39 So Gā′al went out at the head of the lords of Shě′chem, and fought with A•bim′e•lech. 40 A•bim′e•lech chased him, and he fled before him. Many fell wounded, up to the entrance of the gate. 41 So A•bim′e•lech resided at A•rū′mah; and Zě′bul drove out Gā′al and his kinsfolk, so that they could not live on at Shě′chem.

42 On the following day the people went out into the fields. When A•bim′e•lech was told, 43 he took his troops and divided them into three companies, and lay in wait in the fields. When he looked and saw the people coming out of the city, he rose against them and killed them. 44 A•bim′-e•lech and the company that wasʲ with him rushed forward and stood at the entrance of the gate of the city, while the two companies rushed on all who were in the fields and killed them. 45 A•bim′e•lech fought against the city all that day; he took the city, and killed the people that were in it; and he razed the city and sowed it with salt.

46 When all the lords of the Tower of Shě′chem heard of it, they entered the stronghold of the temple of El-bě′rith. 47 A•bim′e•lech was told that all the lords of the Tower of Shě′chem were gathered together. 48 So A•bim′e•lech went up to Mount Zal′-mon, he and all the troops that were with him. A•bim′e•lech took an ax in his hand, cut down a bundle of brushwood, and took it up and laid it on his shoulder. Then he said to the troops with him, "What you have seen me do, do quickly, as I have done." 49 So every one of the troops cut down a bundle and following A•bim′e•lech put it against the stronghold, and they set the stronghold on fire over them, so that all the people of the Tower of Shě′chem also died, about a thousand men and women.

50 Then A•bim′e•lech went to Thě′bez, and en-

camped against Thě′bez, and took it. 51 But there was a strong tower within the city, and all the men and women and all the lords of the city fled to it and shut themselves in; and they went to the roof of the tower. 52 A•bim′e•lech came to the tower, and fought against it, and came near to the entrance of the tower to burn it with fire. 53 But a certain woman threw an upper millstone on A•bim′e•lech's head, and crushed his skull. 54 Immediately he called to the young man who carried his armor and said to him, "Draw your sword and kill me, so people will not say about me, 'A woman killed him.' " So the young man thrust him through, and he died. 55 When the Israelites saw that A•bim′e•lech was dead, they all went home. 56 Thus God repaid A•bim′e•lech for the crime he committed against his father in killing his seventy brothers; 57 and God also made all the wickedness of the people of Shě′chem fall back on their heads, and on them came the curse of Jō′tham son of Jer•ub•bā′al.

Tola and Jair

10 After A•bim′e•lech, Tō′la son of Pū′ah son of Dō′dō, a man of Is′sa•char, who lived at Shā′mir in the hill country of Ě′phra•im, rose to deliver Israel. 2 He judged Israel twenty-three years. Then he died, and was buried at Shā′mir.

3 After him came Jā′ir the Gil′e•ad•īte, who judged Israel twenty-two years. 4 He had thirty sons who rode on thirty donkeys; and they had thirty towns, which are in the land of Gil′e•ad, and are called Hav′voth-jā′ir to this day. 5 Jā′ir died, and was buried in Kā′mon.

Oppression by the Ammonites

6 The Israelites again did what was evil in the sight of the LORD, worshiping the Bā′als and the As•tar′tēs, the gods of Ar′am, the gods of Sī′don, the gods of Mō′ab, the gods of the Am′mon•ītes, and the gods of the Phi•lis′tines. Thus they abandoned the LORD, and did not worship him. 7 So the anger of the LORD was kindled against Israel, and he sold them into the hand of the Phi•lis′tines and into the hand of the Am′mon•ītes, 8 and they crushed and oppressed the Israelites that year. For eighteen years they oppressed all the Israelites that were beyond the Jordan in the land of the Am′o•rītes, which is in Gil′e•ad. 9 The Am′mon•ītes also crossed the Jordan to fight against Judah and against Benjamin and against the house of Ě′phra•im; so that Israel was greatly distressed.

10 So the Israelites cried to the LORD, saying, "We have sinned against you, because we have

---

ʰ That is *Diviners' Oak*   ⁱ Heb *mouth*   ʲ Vg and some Gk Mss: Heb *companies that were*

J
U
D
G

abandoned our God and have worshiped the Bā'als." [11] And the LORD said to the Israelites, "Did I not deliver you[k] from the Egyptians and from the Am'o·rites, from the Am'mon·ites and from the Phi·lis'tines? [12] The Sī·dō'ni·ans also, and the A·mal'e·kītes, and the Mā'on·ītes, oppressed you; and you cried to me, and I delivered you out of their hand. [13] Yet you have abandoned me and worshiped other gods; therefore I will deliver you no more. [14] Go and cry to the gods whom you have chosen; let them deliver you in the time of your distress." [15] And the Israelites said to the LORD, "We have sinned; do to us whatever seems good to you; but deliver us this day!" [16] So they put away the foreign gods from among them and worshiped the LORD; and he could no longer bear to see Israel suffer.

[17] Then the Am'mon·ites were called to arms, and they encamped in Gil'e·ad; and the Israelites came together, and they encamped at Miz'pah.

PRAY IT!
The Effects of Sin

Once again, the Israelites lapse into sin and worship other gods (Judg 10.6). Once again, they cry out to God to save them (verse 10). Did they think their sins would have no effect on their lives?

Listen to these words from Pope John Paul II:

There is no sin, not even the most intimate and secret one, the most strictly individual one, that exclusively concerns the person committing it. With greater or lesser violence, with greater or lesser harm, every sin has repercussions on the . . . whole human family.

Have you done anything today that brought harm to you or others? Have you used your gifts and talents as God intended them to be used? Have you neglected an opportunity to share God's love with another person?

LORD, you know all things. Look on me with love, and hear my prayer. Forgive my sins, and give me strength to turn away from the lure of sin. Help me to be more generous in serving you and my neighbor. Help me to be a true follower of your Son, Jesus. Amen.

▶ Judg 10.10–16

[18] The commanders of the people of Gil'e·ad said to one another, "Who will begin the fight against the Am'mon·ites? He shall be head over all the inhabitants of Gil'e·ad."

Jephthah

11 Now Jeph'thah the Gil'e·ad·īte, the son of a prostitute, was a mighty warrior. Gil'e·ad was the father of Jeph'thah. [2] Gil'e·ad's wife also bore him sons; and when his wife's sons grew up, they drove Jeph'thah away, saying to him, "You shall not inherit anything in our father's house; for you are the son of another woman." [3] Then Jeph'thah fled from his brothers and lived in the land of Tob. Outlaws collected around Jeph'thah and went raiding with him.

[4] After a time the Am'mon·ites made war against Israel. [5] And when the Am'mon·ites made war against Israel, the elders of Gil'e·ad went to bring Jeph'thah from the land of Tob. [6] They said to Jeph'thah, "Come and be our commander, so that we may fight with the Am'mon·ites." [7] But Jeph'thah said to the elders of Gil'e·ad, "Are you not the very ones who rejected me and drove me out of my father's house? So why do you come to me now when you are in trouble?" [8] The elders of Gil'e·ad said to Jeph'thah, "Nevertheless, we have now turned back to you, so that you may go with us and fight with the Am'mon·ites, and become head over us, over all the inhabitants of Gil'e·ad." [9] Jeph'thah said to the elders of Gil'e·ad, "If you bring me home again to fight with the Am'mon·ites, and the LORD gives them over to me, I will be your head." [10] And the elders of Gil'e·ad said to Jeph'thah, "The LORD will be witness between us; we will surely do as you say." [11] So Jeph'thah went with the elders of Gil'e·ad, and the people made him head and commander over them; and Jeph'thah spoke all his words before the LORD at Miz'pah.

[12] Then Jeph'thah sent messengers to the king of the Am'mon·ites and said, "What is there between you and me, that you have come to me to fight against my land?" [13] The king of the Am'mon·ites answered the messengers of Jeph'thah, "Because Israel, on coming from Egypt, took away my land from the Ar'non to the Jab'bok and to the Jordan; now therefore restore it peaceably." [14] Once again Jeph'thah sent messengers to the king of the Am'mon·ites [15] and said to him: "Thus says Jeph'thah: Israel did not take away the land of Mō'ab or the land of the Am'mon·ites, [16] but when they came up from Egypt, Israel went through the wilderness to the Red Sea[l] and came to Kā'desh. [17] Israel then sent messengers to the king of Ē'dom,

---

k Heb lacks *Did I not deliver you*   *l* Or *Sea of Reeds* saying, 'Let us pass through your land'; but the king of Ē′dom would not listen. They also sent to the king of Mō′ab, but he would not consent. So Israel remained at Kā′desh. 18 Then they journeyed through the wilderness, went around the land of Ē′dom and the land of Mō′ab, arrived on the east side of the land of Mō′ab, and camped on the other side of the Ar′non. They did not enter the territory of Mō′ab, for the Ar′non was the boundary of Mō′ab. 19 Israel then sent messengers to King Sī′hon of the Am′o•rītes, king of Hesh′bon; and Israel said to him, 'Let us pass through your land to our country.' 20 But Sī′hon did not trust Israel to pass through his territory; so Sī′hon gathered all his people together, and encamped at Jā′haz, and fought with Israel. 21 Then the LORD, the God of Israel, gave Sī′hon and all his people into the hand of Israel, and they defeated them; so Israel occupied all the land of the Am′o•rītes, who inhabited that country. 22 They occupied all the territory of the Am′o•rītes from the Ar′non to the Jab′bok and from the wilderness to the Jordan. 23 So now the LORD, the God of Israel, has conquered the Am′o•rītes for the benefit of his people Israel. Do you intend to take their place? 24 Should you not possess what your god Chē′mosh gives you to possess? And should we not be the ones to possess everything that the LORD our God has conquered for our benefit? 25 Now are you any better than King Bā′lak son of Zip′por of Mō′ab? Did he ever enter into conflict with Israel, or did he ever go to war with them? 26 While Israel lived in Hesh′bon and its villages, and in A•rō′er and its villages, and in all the towns that are along the Ar′non, three hundred years, why did you not recover them within that time? 27 It is not I who have sinned against you, but you are the one who does me wrong by making war on me. Let the LORD, who is judge, decide today for the Israelites or for the Am′mon•ītes." 28 But the king of the Am′mon•ītes did not heed the message that Jeph′thah sent him.

Jephthah's Vow

29 Then the spirit of the LORD came upon Jeph′thah, and he passed through Gil′e•ad and Ma•nas′seh. He passed on to Miz′pah of Gil′e•ad, and from Miz′pah of Gil′e•ad he passed on to the Am′mon•ītes. 30 And Jeph′thah made a vow to the LORD, and said, "If you will give the Am′mon•ītes into my hand, 31 then whoever comes out of the doors of my house to meet me, when I return victorious from the Am′mon•ītes, shall be the LORD's, to be offered up by me as a burnt offering." 32 So Jeph′thah crossed over to the Am′mon•ītes to fight against them; and the LORD gave them into his hand. 33 He inflicted a massive defeat on them from A•rō′er to the neighborhood of Min′nith, twenty towns, and as far as Ā′bel-ker′a•mim. So the Am′mon•ītes were subdued before the people of Israel.

Jephthah's Daughter

34 Then Jeph′thah came to his home at Miz′-pah; and there was his daughter coming out to meet him with timbrels and with dancing. She was his only child; he had no son or daughter except her. 35 When he saw her, he tore his clothes, and said, "Alas, my daughter! You have brought me very low; you have become the cause of great trouble to me. For I have opened my mouth to the LORD, and I cannot take back my vow." 36 She said to him, "My father, if you have opened your mouth to the LORD, do to me according to what has gone out of your mouth, now that the LORD has given you vengeance against your enemies, the Am′mon•ītes." 37 And she said to her father, "Let this thing be done for me: Grant me two months, so that I may go and wander*m* on the mountains, and bewail my virginity, my companions and I." 38 "Go," he said and sent her away for two months. So she departed, she and her companions, and bewailed her virginity on the mountains. 39 At the end of two months, she returned to her father, who did with her according to the vow he had made. She had never slept with a man. So there arose an Israelite custom that 40 for four days every year the daughters of Israel would go out to lament the daughter of Jeph′thah the Gil′e•ad•ite.

Intertribal Dissension

12 The men of Ē′phra•im were called to arms, and they crossed to Zā′phon and said to Jeph′thah, "Why did you cross over to fight against the Am′mon•ītes, and did not call us to go with you? We will burn your house down over you!" 2 Jeph′thah said to them, "My people and I were engaged in conflict with the Am′mon•ītes who oppressed us*n* severely. But when I called you, you did not deliver me from their hand. 3 When I saw that you would not deliver me, I took my life in my hand, and crossed over against the Am′mon•ītes, and the LORD gave them into my hand. Why then have you come up to me this day, to fight against me?" 4 Then Jeph′thah gathered all the men of Gil′e•ad and fought with Ē′phra•im; and the men of Gil′e•ad defeated Ē′phra•im, because they said, "You are fugitives from Ē′phra•im, you Gil′e•ad•ites—in the heart of Ē′phra•im and Ma•nas′-seh."*o* 5 Then the Gil′e•ad•ites took the fords of the Jordan against the Ē′phra•im•ītes. Whenever one of the fugitives of Ē′phra•im said, "Let me go over,"

---

m Cn: Heb *go down*　*n* Gk OL, Syr H: Heb lacks *who oppressed us*　*o* Meaning of Heb uncertain: Gk omits *because . . . Manasseh*

the men of Gil'e•ad would say to him, "Are you an
E'phra•im•īte?" When he said, "No," 6 they said to
him, "Then say Shib'bo•leth," and he said,
"Sib'bo•leth," for he could not pronounce it right.
Then they seized him and killed him at the fords of
the Jordan. Forty-two thousand of the E'phra•im•ites
fell at that time.

7 Jeph'thah judged Israel six years. Then
Jeph'thah the Gil'e•ad•īte died, and was buried in
his town in Gil'e•ad. *p*

Ibzan, Elon, and Abdon

8 After him Ib'zan of Bethlehem judged Israel.
9 He had thirty sons. He gave his thirty daughters in
marriage outside his clan and brought in thirty
young women from outside for his sons. He judged
Israel seven years. 10 Then Ib'zan died, and was
buried at Bethlehem.

11 After him E'lon the Zeb'ū•lun•ite judged Israel; and he judged Israel ten years. 12 Then E'lon
the Zeb'ū•lun•ite died, and was buried at Aī'ja•lon
in the land of Zeb'ū•lun.

13 After him Ab'don son of Hil'lel the
Pir'a•thon•īte judged Israel. 14 He had forty sons
and thirty grandsons, who rode on seventy donkeys; he judged Israel eight years. 15 Then Ab'don
son of Hil'lel the Pir'a•thon•īte died, and was
buried at Pir'a•thon in the land of E'phra•im, in the
hill country of the A•mal'e•kītes.

The Birth of Samson
(Cp Num 6.1–21)

13 The Israelites again did what was evil in
the sight of the LORD, and the LORD gave
them into the hand of the Phi•lis'tines forty years.

2 There was a certain man of Zō'rah, of the tribe
of the Dan'ites, whose name was Ma•nō'ah. His
wife was barren, having borne no children. 3 And
the angel of the LORD appeared to the woman and
said to her, "Although you are barren, having borne
no children, you shall conceive and bear a son.
4 Now be careful not to drink wine or strong drink,
or to eat anything unclean, 5 for you shall conceive
and bear a son. No razor is to come on his head, for
the boy shall be a nazirite*q* to God from birth. It is
he who shall begin to deliver Israel from the hand
of the Phi•lis'tines." 6 Then the woman came and
told her husband, "A man of God came to me, and
his appearance was like that of an angel*r* of God,
most awe-inspiring; I did not ask him where he
came from, and he did not tell me his name; 7 but
he said to me, 'You shall conceive and bear a son.
So then drink no wine or strong drink, and eat
nothing unclean, for the boy shall be a nazirite*q* to
God from birth to the day of his death.' "

8 Then Ma•nō'ah entreated the LORD, and said,
"O LORD, I pray, let the man of God whom you sent
come to us again and teach us what we are to do
concerning the boy who will be born." 9 God listened to Ma•nō'ah, and the angel of God came
again to the woman as she sat in the field; but her
husband Ma•nō'ah was not with her. 10 So the
woman ran quickly and told her husband, "The
man who came to me the other day has appeared to
me." 11 Ma•nō'ah got up and followed his wife, and
came to the man and said to him, "Are you the man
who spoke to this woman?" And he said, "I am."

p Gk: Heb *in the towns of Gilead*   *q* That is *one separated* or
one consecrated   *r* Or *the angel*

Introducing ▶ SAMSON

**The story of Samson in Judges, chapters 13–16, is one of the most well-known in the Bible.
Most of us know Samson for his great feats of strength, such as killing a lion bare-handed
and slaying a thousand men with the jawbone of a donkey. But did you also know that
Samson's birth was announced by an angel and that the Book of Judges says "the spirit of
the LORD rushed on him" more often for Samson than for any other judge? Samson was
a Nazirite as well as a judge. Nazirites took vows to abstain from alcohol, avoid contact
with dead bodies, and refrain from cutting their hair.**

    **Like many of the other judges, Samson was a flawed hero. He broke all his Nazirite
vows, was controlled by lust, and used his great strength for personal revenge. Despite
these flaws, God chose to use Samson. Samson paid for his sins, but ultimately, his tragic
death brought victory over the Philistines. Once again, God's purposes were accomplished,
even through a flawed and sinful human being.**

12 Then Ma·nō′ah said, "Now when your words come true, what is to be the boy's rule of life; what is he to do?" 13 The angel of the LORD said to Ma·nō′ah, "Let the woman give heed to all that I said to her. 14 She may not eat of anything that comes from the vine. She is not to drink wine or strong drink, or eat any unclean thing. She is to observe everything that I commanded her."

15 Ma·nō′ah said to the angel of the LORD, "Allow us to detain you, and prepare a kid for you." 16 The angel of the LORD said to Ma·nō′ah, "If you detain me, I will not eat your food; but if you want to prepare a burnt offering, then offer it to the LORD." (For Ma·nō′ah did not know that he was the angel of the LORD.) 17 Then Ma·nō′ah said to the angel of the LORD, "What is your name, so that we may honor you when your words come true?" 18 But the angel of the LORD said to him, "Why do you ask my name? It is too wonderful."

19 So Ma·nō′ah took the kid with the grain offering, and offered it on the rock to the LORD, to him who works[s] wonders.[t] 20 When the flame went up toward heaven from the altar, the angel of the LORD ascended in the flame of the altar while Ma·nō′ah and his wife looked on; and they fell on their faces to the ground. 21 The angel of the LORD did not appear again to Ma·nō′ah and his wife. Then Ma·nō′ah realized that it was the angel of the LORD. 22 And Ma·nō′ah said to his wife, "We shall surely die, for we have seen God." 23 But his wife said to him, "If the LORD had meant to kill us, he would not have accepted a burnt offering and a grain offering at our hands, or shown us all these things, or now announced to us such things as these."

24 The woman bore a son, and named him Samson. The boy grew, and the LORD blessed him. 25 The spirit of the LORD began to stir him in Mā′ha·neh-dan, between Zō′rah and Esh′tā·ol.

Samson's Marriage

14 Once Samson went down to Tim′nah, and at Tim′nah he saw a Phi·lis′tine woman. 2 Then he came up, and told his father and mother, "I saw a Phi·lis′tine woman at Tim′nah; now get her for me as my wife." 3 But his father and mother said to him, "Is there not a woman among your kin, or among all our[u] people, that you must go to take a wife from the uncircumcised Phi·lis′tines?" But Samson said to his father, "Get her for me, because she pleases me." 4 His father and mother did not know that this was from the LORD; for he was seeking a pretext to act against the Phi·lis′tines. At that time the Phi·lis′tines had dominion over Israel.

5 Then Samson went down with his father and mother to Tim′nah. When he came to the vineyards of Tim′nah, suddenly a young lion roared at him.

6 The spirit of the LORD rushed on him, and he tore the lion apart barehanded as one might tear apart a kid. But he did not tell his father or his mother what he had done. 7 Then he went down and talked with the woman, and she pleased Samson. 8 After a while he returned to marry her, and he turned aside to see the carcass of the lion, and there was a swarm of bees in the body of the lion, and honey. 9 He scraped it out into his hands, and went on, eating as he went. When he came to his father and mother, he gave some to them, and they ate it. But he did not tell them that he had taken the honey from the carcass of the lion.

10 His father went down to the woman, and Samson made a feast there as the young men were accustomed to do. 11 When the people saw him, they brought thirty companions to be with him. 12 Samson said to them, "Let me now put a riddle to you. If you can explain it to me within the seven days of the feast, and find it out, then I will give you thirty linen garments and thirty festal garments. 13 But if you cannot explain it to me, then you shall give me thirty linen garments and thirty festal garments." So they said to him, "Ask your riddle; let us hear it." 14 He said to them,

"Out of the eater came something to eat.
Out of the strong came something sweet."

But for three days they could not explain the riddle.

15 On the fourth[v] day they said to Samson's wife, "Coax your husband to explain the riddle to us, or we will burn you and your father's house with fire. Have you invited us here to impoverish us?" 16 So Samson's wife wept before him, saying, "You hate me; you do not really love me. You have asked a riddle of my people, but you have not explained it to me." He said to her, "Look, I have not told my father or my mother. Why should I tell you?" 17 She wept before him the seven days that their feast lasted; and because she nagged him, on the seventh day he told her. Then she explained the riddle to her people. 18 The men of the town said to him on the seventh day before the sun went down,

"What is sweeter than honey?
What is stronger than a lion?"

And he said to them,

"If you had not plowed with my heifer,
you would not have found out my riddle."

19 Then the spirit of the LORD rushed on him, and he went down to Ash′ke·lon. He killed thirty men of the town, took their spoil, and gave the festal garments to those who had explained the riddle. In hot anger he went back to his father's house. 20 And Samson's wife was given to his companion, who had been his best man.

---

[s] Gk Vg: Heb *and working*   [t] Heb *wonders, while Manoah and his wife looked on*   [u] Cn: Heb *my*   [v] Gk Syr: Heb *seventh*

J
U
D
G

Samson Defeats the Philistines

15 After a while, at the time of the wheat harvest, Samson went to visit his wife, bringing along a kid. He said, "I want to go into my wife's room." But her father would not allow him to go in. 2 Her father said, "I was sure that you had rejected her; so I gave her to your companion. Is not her younger sister prettier than she? Why not take her instead?" 3 Samson said to them, "This time, when I do mischief to the Phi·lis'tines, I will be without blame." 4 So Samson went and caught three hundred foxes, and took some torches; and he turned the foxes[w] tail to tail, and put a torch between each pair of tails. 5 When he had set fire to the torches, he let the foxes go into the standing grain of the Phi·lis'tines, and burned up the shocks and the standing grain, as well as the vineyards and[x] olive groves. 6 Then the Phi·lis'tines asked, "Who has done this?" And they said, "Samson, the son-in-law of the Tim'nite, because he has taken Samson's wife and given her to his companion." So the Phi·lis'tines came up, and burned her and her father. 7 Samson said to them, "If this is what you do, I swear I will not stop until I have taken revenge on you." 8 He struck them down hip and thigh with great slaughter; and he went down and stayed in the cleft of the rock of E'tam.

9 Then the Phi·lis'tines came up and encamped in Judah, and made a raid on Le'hi. 10 The men of Judah said, "Why have you come up against us?" They said, "We have come up to bind Samson, to do to him as he did to us." 11 Then three thousand men of Judah went down to the cleft of the rock of E'tam, and they said to Samson, "Do you not know that the Phi·lis'tines are rulers over us? What then have you done to us?" He replied, "As they did to me, so I have done to them." 12 They said to him, "We have come down to bind you, so that we may give you into the hands of the Phi·lis'tines." Samson answered them, "Swear to me that you yourselves will not attack me." 13 They said to him, "No, we will only bind you and give you into their hands; we will not kill you." So they bound him with two new ropes, and brought him up from the rock.

14 When he came to Le'hi, the Phi·lis'tines came shouting to meet him; and the spirit of the LORD rushed on him, and the ropes that were on his arms became like flax that has caught fire, and his bonds melted off his hands. 15 Then he found a fresh jawbone of a donkey, reached down and took it, and with it he killed a thousand men. 16 And Samson said,

"With the jawbone of a donkey,
  heaps upon heaps,
with the jawbone of a donkey
  I have slain a thousand men."

17 When he had finished speaking, he threw away the jawbone; and that place was called Ra'math-le'hi. y 18 By then he was very thirsty, and he called on the LORD, saying, "You have granted this great victory by the hand of your servant. Am I now to die of thirst, and fall into the hands of the uncircumcised?" 19 So God split open the hollow place that is at Le'hi, and water came from it. When he drank, his spirit returned, and he revived. Therefore it was named En-hak·kor'e,[z] which is at Le'hi to this day. 20 And he judged Israel in the days of the Phi·lis'-tines twenty years.

Samson and Delilah

16 Once Samson went to Ga'za, where he saw a prostitute and went in to her. 2 The Ga'zites were told,[a] "Samson has come here." So they circled around and lay in wait for him all night at the city gate. They kept quiet all night, thinking, "Let us wait until the light of the morning; then we will kill him." 3 But Samson lay only until midnight. Then at midnight he rose up, took hold of the doors of the city gate and the two posts, pulled them up, bar and all, put them on his shoulders, and carried them to the top of the hill that is in front of He'bron.

4 After this he fell in love with a woman in the valley of So'rek, whose name was De·li'lah. 5 The lords of the Phi·lis'tines came to her and said to her, "Coax him, and find out what makes his strength so great, and how we may overpower him, so that we may bind him in order to subdue him; and we will each give you eleven hundred pieces of silver." 6 So De·li'lah said to Samson, "Please tell me what makes your strength so great, and how you could be bound, so that one could subdue you." 7 Samson said to her, "If they bind me with seven fresh bowstrings that are not dried out, then I shall become weak, and be like anyone else." 8 Then the lords of the Phi·lis'tines brought her seven fresh bowstrings that had not dried out, and she bound him with them. 9 While men were lying in wait in an inner chamber, she said to him, "The Phi·lis'tines are upon you, Samson!" But he snapped the bowstrings, as a strand of fiber snaps when it touches the fire. So the secret of his strength was not known.

10 Then De·li'lah said to Samson, "You have mocked me and told me lies; please tell me how you could be bound." 11 He said to her, "If they bind me with new ropes that have not been used, then I shall become weak, and be like anyone else." 12 So De·li'lah took new ropes and bound him with them, and said to him, "The Phi·lis'tines are upon

---

w Heb *them*   x Gk Tg Vg: Heb lacks *and*   y That is *The Hill of the Jawbone*   z That is *The Spring of the One who Called*
a Gk: Heb lacks *were told*

Manipulation

You'd think that Samson would catch on, wouldn't you? Delilah tries to coax from Samson the secret of his strength. By the third attempt, it seems rather obvious that she wants to betray him to the Philistines. Nonetheless, Samson finally is pestered into revealing his secret, and Delilah uses the information to betray him.

Have you ever had a confidence betrayed? Have you ever trusted someone with a secret only to discover later that your secret is out? It makes it that much harder to trust again, to be open and to share yourself with another. When the person who betrays your confidence is someone you love, the betrayal is even more painful.

We need to do some soul-searching here. Ask yourself: Am I the kind of person who can be trusted with someone's secret? Have I ever betrayed a confidence?

It is easier than we like to think to be like Delilah—abusing the trust built up in a relationship and manipulating another person, even someone we care deeply about. We need to resolve to be people of integrity, who would never betray a confidence for personal gain.

▸ Judg 16.4–22

J
U
D
G

you, Samson!" (The men lying in wait were in an inner chamber.) But he snapped the ropes off his arms like a thread.

13 Then Dē·lī'lah said to Samson, "Until now you have mocked me and told me lies; tell me how you could be bound." He said to her, "If you weave the seven locks of my head with the web and make it tight with the pin, then I shall become weak, and be like anyone else." 14 So while he slept, Dē·lī'lah took the seven locks of his head and wove them into the web,[b] and made them tight with the pin. Then she said to him, "The Phi·lis'tines are upon you, Samson!" But he awoke from his sleep, and pulled away the pin, the loom, and the web.

15 Then she said to him, "How can you say, 'I love you,' when your heart is not with me? You have mocked me three times now and have not told me what makes your strength so great." 16 Finally, after she had nagged him with her words day after day, and pestered him, he was tired to death. 17 So he told her his whole secret, and said to her, "A razor has never come upon my head; for I have been a nazirite[c] to God from my mother's womb. If my head were shaved, then my strength would leave me; I would become weak, and be like anyone else."

18 When Dē·lī'lah realized that he had told her his whole secret, she sent and called the lords of the Phi·lis'tines, saying, "This time come up, for he has told his whole secret to me." Then the lords of the Phi·lis'tines came up to her, and brought the money in their hands. 19 She let him fall asleep on her lap; and she called a man, and had him shave off the seven locks of his head. He began to weaken,[d] and his strength left him. 20 Then she said, "The Phi·lis'tines are upon you, Samson!" When he

awoke from his sleep, he thought, "I will go out as at other times, and shake myself free." But he did not know that the LORD had left him. 21 So the Phi·lis'tines seized him and gouged out his eyes. They brought him down to Gā'za and bound him with bronze shackles; and he ground at the mill in the prison. 22 But the hair of his head began to grow again after it had been shaved.

Samson's Death

23 Now the lords of the Phi·lis'tines gathered to offer a great sacrifice to their god Dā'gon, and to rejoice; for they said, "Our god has given Samson our enemy into our hand." 24 When the people saw him, they praised their god; for they said, "Our god has given our enemy into our hand, the ravager of our country, who has killed many of us." 25 And when their hearts were merry, they said, "Call Samson, and let him entertain us." So they called Samson out of the prison, and he performed for them. They made him stand between the pillars; 26 and Samson said to the attendant who held him by the hand, "Let me feel the pillars on which the house rests, so that I may lean against them." 27 Now the house was full of men and women; all the lords of the Phi·lis'tines were there, and on the roof there were about three thousand men and women, who looked on while Samson performed.

28 Then Samson called to the LORD and said, "Lord GOD, remember me and strengthen me only this once, O God, so that with this one act of revenge I may pay back the Phi·lis'tines for my two

---

b Compare Gk: in verses 13-14, Heb lacks *and make it tight . . . into the web*   c That is *one separated* or *one consecrated*   d Gk: Heb *She began to torment him*

JUDG

16.28–31

eyes."*e* 29 And Samson grasped the two middle pillars on which the house rested, and he leaned his weight against them, his right hand on the one and his left hand on the other. 30 Then Samson said, "Let me die with the Phi·lis'tines." He strained with all his might; and the house fell on the lords and all the people who were in it. So those he killed at his death were more than those he had killed during his life. 31 Then his brothers and all his family came down and took him and brought him up and buried him between Zō'rah and Esh'tā·ol in the tomb of his father Ma·nō'ah. He had judged Israel twenty years.

Micah and the Levite

17 There was a man in the hill country of Ē'phra·im whose name was Mī'cah. 2 He said to his mother, "The eleven hundred pieces of silver that were taken from you, about which you uttered a curse, and even spoke it in my hearing,— that silver is in my possession; I took it; but now I will return it to you."*f* And his mother said, "May my son be blessed by the LORD!" 3 Then he returned the eleven hundred pieces of silver to his mother; and his mother said, "I consecrate the silver to the LORD from my hand for my son, to make an idol of cast metal." 4 So when he returned the money to his mother, his mother took two hundred pieces of silver, and gave it to the silversmith, who made it into an idol of cast metal; and it was in the house of Mī'cah. 5 This man Mī'cah had a shrine, and he made an ephod and teraphim, and installed one of his sons, who became his priest. 6 In those days there was no king in Israel; all the people did what was right in their own eyes.

7 Now there was a young man of Bethlehem in

Judah, of the clan of Judah. He was a Lē'vīte residing there. 8 This man left the town of Bethlehem in Judah, to live wherever he could find a place. He came to the house of Mī'cah in the hill country of Ē'phra·im to carry on his work.*g* 9 Mī'cah said to him, "From where do you come?" He replied, "I am a Lē'vīte of Bethlehem in Judah, and I am going to live wherever I can find a place." 10 Then Mī'cah said to him, "Stay with me, and be to me a father and a priest, and I will give you ten pieces of silver a year, a set of clothes, and your living."*h* 11 The Lē'vīte agreed to stay with the man; and the young man became to him like one of his sons. 12 So Mī'cah installed the Lē'vīte, and the young man became his priest, and was in the house of Mī'cah. 13 Then Mī'cah said, "Now I know that the LORD will prosper me, because the Lē'vīte has become my priest."

The Migration of Dan

18 In those days there was no king in Israel. And in those days the tribe of the Dan'ītes was seeking for itself a territory to live in; for until then no territory among the tribes of Israel had been allotted to them. 2 So the Dan'ītes sent five valiant men from the whole number of their clan, from Zō'rah and from Esh'tā·ol, to spy out the land and to explore it; and they said to them, "Go, explore the land." When they came to the hill country of Ē'phra·im, to the house of Mī'cah, they stayed there. 3 While they were at Mī'cah's house, they recognized the voice of the young Lē'vīte; so they went over and asked him, "Who brought you here? What are you doing in this place? What is your business here?" 4 He said to them, "Mī'cah did such and such for me, and he hired me, and I have become his priest." 5 Then they said to him, "Inquire of God that we may know whether the mission we are undertaking will succeed." 6 The priest replied, "Go in peace. The mission you are on is under the eye of the LORD."

7 The five men went on, and when they came to Lā'ish, they observed the people who were there living securely, after the manner of the Sī·dō'ni·ans, quiet and unsuspecting, lacking*i* nothing on earth, and possessing wealth.*j* Furthermore, they were far from the Sī·dō'ni·ans and had no dealings with Ar'am.*k* 8 When they came to their kinsfolk at Zō'rah and Esh'tā·ol, they said to them, "What do you report?" 9 They said, "Come, let us go up against them; for we have seen the land, and it is

e Or *so that I may be avenged upon the Philistines for one of my two eyes* *f* The words *but now I will return it to you* are transposed from the end of verse 3 in Heb *g* Or *Ephraim, continuing his journey* *h* Heb *living, and the Levite went* *i* Cn Compare 18.10: Meaning of Heb uncertain *j* Meaning of Heb uncertain *k* Symmachus: Heb *with anyone* very good. Will you do nothing? Do not be slow to go, but enter in and possess the land. 10 When you go, you will come to an unsuspecting people. The land is broad—God has indeed given it into your hands—a place where there is no lack of anything on earth."

11 Six hundred men of the Dan'ite clan, armed with weapons of war, set out from Zō'rah and Esh'-tā•ol, 12 and went up and encamped at Kir'i•ath-jē'a•rim in Judah. On this account that place is called Mā'ha•neh-dan*l* to this day; it is west of Kir'i•ath-jē'a•rim. 13 From there they passed on to the hill country of Ē'phra•im, and came to the house of Mī'cah.

14 Then the five men who had gone to spy out the land (that is, Lā'ish) said to their comrades, "Do you know that in these buildings there are an ephod, teraphim, and an idol of cast metal? Now therefore consider what you will do." 15 So they turned in that direction and came to the house of the young Lē'vite, at the home of Mī'cah, and greeted him. 16 While the six hundred men of the Dan'-ites, armed with their weapons of war, stood by the entrance of the gate, 17 the five men who had gone to spy out the land proceeded to enter and take the idol of cast metal, the ephod, and the teraphim.*m* The priest was standing by the entrance of the gate with the six hundred men armed with weapons of war. 18 When the men went into Mī'cah's house and took the idol of cast metal, the ephod, and the teraphim, the priest said to them, "What are you doing?" 19 They said to him, "Keep quiet! Put your hand over your mouth, and come with us, and be to us a father and a priest. Is it better for you to be priest to the house of one person, or to be priest to a tribe and clan in Israel?" 20 Then the priest accepted the offer. He took the ephod, the teraphim, and the idol, and went along with the people.

21 So they resumed their journey, putting the little ones, the livestock, and the goods in front of them. 22 When they were some distance from the home of Mī'cah, the men who were in the houses near Mī'cah's house were called out, and they overtook the Dan'ites. 23 They shouted to the Dan'ites, who turned around and said to Mī'cah, "What is the matter that you come with such a company?" 24 He replied, "You take my gods that I made, and the priest, and go away, and what have I left? How then can you ask me, 'What is the matter?' " 25 And the Dan'ites said to him, "You had better not let your voice be heard among us or else hot-tempered fellows will attack you, and you will lose your life and the lives of your household." 26 Then the Dan'ites went their way. When Mī'cah saw that they were too strong for him, he turned and went back to his home.

The Danites Settle in Laish

27 The Dan'ites, having taken what Mī'cah had made, and the priest who belonged to him, came to Lā'ish, to a people quiet and unsuspecting, put them to the sword, and burned down the city. 28 There was no deliverer, because it was far from Sī'don and they had no dealings with Ar'am.*n* It was in the valley that belongs to Beth-rē'hob. They rebuilt the city, and lived in it. 29 They named the city Dan, after their ancestor Dan, who was born to Israel; but the name of the city was formerly Lā'ish. 30 Then the Dan'ites set up the idol for themselves. Jonathan son of Ger'shom, son of Moses,*o* and his sons were priests to the tribe of the Dan'ites until the time the land went into captivity. 31 So they maintained as their own Mī'cah's idol that he had made, as long as the house of God was at Shī'lōh.

The Levite's Concubine

19 In those days, when there was no king in Israel, a certain Lē'vite, residing in the remote parts of the hill country of Ē'phra•im, took to himself a concubine from Bethlehem in Judah. 2 But his concubine became angry with*p* him, and she went away from him to her father's house at Bethlehem in Judah, and was there some four months. 3 Then her husband set out after her, to speak tenderly to her and bring her back. He had with him his servant and a couple of donkeys. When he reached*q* her father's house, the girl's father saw him and came with joy to meet him. 4 His father-in-law, the girl's father, made him stay, and he remained with him three days; so they ate and drank, and he*r* stayed there. 5 On the fourth day they got up early in the morning, and he prepared to go; but the girl's father said to his son-in-law, "Fortify yourself with a bit of food, and after that you may go." 6 So the two men sat and ate and drank together; and the girl's father said to the man, "Why not spend the night and enjoy yourself?" 7 When the man got up to go, his father-in-law kept urging him until he spent the night there again. 8 On the fifth day he got up early in the morning to leave; and the girl's father said, "Fortify yourself." So they lingered*s* until the day declined, and the two of them ate and drank.*t* 9 When the man with his concubine and his servant got up to leave, his father-in-law, the girl's father, said to him, "Look, the day has worn on until it is almost evening. Spend the night. See, the day has drawn to a close.

---

l That is *Camp of Dan*   *m* Compare 17.4, 5; 18.14: Heb *teraphim and the cast metal*   *n* Cn Compare verse 7: Heb *with anyone*   *o* Another reading is *son of Manasseh*   *p* Gk OL: Heb *prostituted herself against*   *q* Gk: Heb *she brought him to*   *r* Compare verse 7 and Gk: Heb *they*   *s* Cn: Heb *Linger*   *t* Gk: Heb lacks *and drank*

Spend the night here and enjoy yourself. Tomorrow you can get up early in the morning for your journey, and go home."

10 But the man would not spend the night; he got up and departed, and arrived opposite Jē'bus (that is, Jerusalem). He had with him a couple of saddled donkeys, and his concubine was with him. 11 When they were near Jē'bus, the day was far spent, and the servant said to his master, "Come now, let us turn aside to this city of the Jeb'ū·sītes, and spend the night in it." 12 But his master said to him, "We will not turn aside into a city of foreigners, who do not belong to the people of Israel; but we will continue on to Gib'ē·ah." 13 Then he said to his servant, "Come, let us try to reach one of these places, and spend the night at Gib'ē·ah or at Rā'mah." 14 So they passed on and went their way; and the sun went down on them near Gib'ē·ah, which belongs to Benjamin. 15 They turned aside there, to go in and spend the night at Gib'ē·ah. He went in and sat down in the open square of the city, but no one took them in to spend the night.

16 Then at evening there was an old man coming from his work in the field. The man was from the hill country of Ē'phra·im, and he was residing in Gib'ē·ah. (The people of the place were Ben'-ja·min·ītes.) 17 When the old man looked up and saw the wayfarer in the open square of the city, he said, "Where are you going and where do you come from?" 18 He answered him, "We are passing from Bethlehem in Judah to the remote parts of the hill country of Ē'phra·im, from which I come. I went to Bethlehem in Judah; and I am going to my home.ᵘ Nobody has offered to take me in. 19 We your servants have straw and fodder for our donkeys, with bread and wine for me and the woman and the young man along with us. We need nothing more." 20 The old man said, "Peace be to you. I will care for all your wants; only do not spend the night in the square." 21 So he brought him into his house, and fed the donkeys; they washed their feet, and ate and drank.

Gibeah's Crime

22 While they were enjoying themselves, the men of the city, a perverse lot, surrounded the house, and started pounding on the door. They said to the old man, the master of the house, "Bring out the man who came into your house, so that we may have intercourse with him." 23 And the man, the master of the house, went out to them and said to them, "No, my brothers, do not act so wickedly. Since this man is my guest, do not do this vile thing. 24 Here are my virgin daughter and his concubine; let me bring them out now. Ravish them and do whatever you want to them; but against this man do not do such a vile thing." 25 But the men

would not listen to him. So the man seized his concubine, and put her out to them. They wantonly raped her, and abused her all through the night until the morning. And as the dawn began to break, they let her go. 26 As morning appeared, the woman came and fell down at the door of the man's house where her master was, until it was light.

27 In the morning her master got up, opened the doors of the house, and when he went out to go on his way, there was his concubine lying at the door of the house, with her hands on the threshold. 28 "Get up," he said to her, "we are going." But there was no answer. Then he put her on the donkey; and the man set out for his home. 29 When he had entered his house, he took a knife, and grasping his concubine he cut her into twelve pieces, limb by limb, and sent her throughout all the territory of Israel. 30 Then he commanded the men whom he sent, saying, "Thus shall you say to all the Israelites, 'Has such a thing ever happenedᵛ since the day that the Israelites came up from the land of Egypt until this day? Consider it, take counsel, and speak out.' "

The Other Tribes Attack Benjamin

20 Then all the Israelites came out, from Dan to Bē'er-shē'ba, including the land of Gil'e·ad, and the congregation assembled in one body before the LORD at Miz'pah. 2 The chiefs of all the people, of all the tribes of Israel, presented themselves in the assembly of the people of God, four hundred thousand foot-soldiers bearing arms. 3 (Now the Ben'ja·min·ītes heard that the people of Israel had gone up to Miz'pah.) And the Israelites said, "Tell us, how did this criminal act come about?" 4 The Lē'vīte, the husband of the woman who was murdered, answered, "I came to Gib'ē·ah that belongs to Benjamin, I and my concubine, to spend the night. 5 The lords of Gib'ē·ah rose up against me, and surrounded the house at night. They intended to kill me, and they raped my concubine until she died. 6 Then I took my concubine and cut her into pieces, and sent her throughout the whole extent of Israel's territory; for they have committed a vile outrage in Israel. 7 So now, you Israelites, all of you, give your advice and counsel here."

8 All the people got up as one, saying, "We will not any of us go to our tents, nor will any of us return to our houses. 9 But now this is what we will do to Gib'ē·ah: we will go upʷ against it by lot. 10 We will take ten men of a hundred throughout all the tribes of Israel, and a hundred of a thousand, and a thousand of ten thousand, to bring provi-

---

ᵘ Gk Compare 19.29. Heb *to the house of the LORD*
ᵛ Compare Gk: Heb 30*And all who saw it said, "Such a thing has not happened or been seen* ʷ Gk: Heb lacks *we will go up*

sions for the troops, who are going to repay^x
Gib′ē·ah of Benjamin for all the disgrace that they
have done in Israel." 11 So all the men of Israel
gathered against the city, united as one.

12 The tribes of Israel sent men through all the
tribe of Benjamin, saying, "What crime is this that
has been committed among you? 13 Now then,
hand over those scoundrels in Gib′ē·ah, so that we
may put them to death, and purge the evil from Israel." But the Ben′ja·min·ītes would not listen to
their kinsfolk, the Israelites. 14 The Ben′ja·min·ītes
came together out of the towns to Gib′ē·ah, to go
out to battle against the Israelites. 15 On that day
the Ben′ja·min·ītes mustered twenty-six thousand
armed men from their towns, besides the inhabitants of Gib′ē·ah. 16 Of all this force, there were sev-
en hundred picked men who were left-handed;
every one could sling a stone at a hair, and not
miss. 17 And the Israelites, apart from Benjamin,
mustered four hundred thousand armed men, all of
them warriors.

18 The Israelites proceeded to go up to Beth′el,
where they inquired of God, "Which of us shall go
up first to battle against the Ben′ja·min·ītes?" And
the LORD answered, "Judah shall go up first."

19 Then the Israelites got up in the morning,
and encamped against Gib′ē·ah. 20 The Israelites
went out to battle against Benjamin; and the Israelites drew up the battle line against them at
Gib′ē·ah. 21 The Ben′ja·min·ītes came out of
Gib′ē·ah, and struck down on that day twenty-two
thousand of the Israelites. 23^yThe Israelites went up
and wept before the LORD until the evening; and
they inquired of the LORD, "Shall we again draw
near to battle against our kinsfolk the Ben′ja-
min·ītes?" And the LORD said, "Go up against
them." 22 The Israelites took courage, and again
formed the battle line in the same place where they
had formed it on the first day.

24 So the Israelites advanced against the Ben′-
ja·min·ītes the second day. 25 Benjamin moved out
against them from Gib′ē·ah the second day, and
struck down eighteen thousand of the Israelites, all
of them armed men. 26 Then all the Israelites, the
whole army, went back to Beth′el and wept, sitting
there before the LORD; they fasted that day until
evening. Then they offered burnt offerings and sacrifices of well-being before the LORD. 27 And the Israelites inquired of the LORD (for the ark of the
covenant of God was there in those days, 28 and
Phin′e·has son of El·e·ā′zar, son of Aaron, ministered before it in those days), saying, "Shall we go
out once more to battle against our kinsfolk the
Ben′ja·min·ītes, or shall we desist?" The LORD answered, "Go up, for tomorrow I will give them into
your hand."

29 So Israel stationed men in ambush around

Gib′ē·ah. 30 Then the Israelites went up against the
Ben′ja·min·ītes on the third day, and set themselves
in array against Gib′ē·ah, as before. 31 When the
Ben′ja·min·ītes went out against the army, they
were drawn away from the city. As before they began to inflict casualties on the troops, along the
main roads, one of which goes up to Beth′el and the
other to Gib′ē·ah, as well as in the open country,
killing about thirty men of Israel. 32 The Ben′-
ja·min·ītes thought, "They are being routed before
us, as previously." But the Israelites said, "Let us retreat and draw them away from the city toward the
roads." 33 The main body of the Israelites drew back
its battle line to Bā′al-tā′mar, while those Israelites
who were in ambush rushed out of their place west^z
of Gē′ba. 34 There came against Gib′ē·ah ten thousand picked men out of all Israel, and the battle was
fierce. But the Ben′ja·min·ītes did not realize that
disaster was close upon them.

35 The LORD defeated Benjamin before Israel;
and the Israelites destroyed twenty-five thousand
one hundred men of Benjamin that day, all of them
armed.

36 Then the Ben′ja·min·ītes saw that they were
defeated.^a The Israelites gave ground to Benjamin,
because they trusted to the troops in ambush that
they had stationed against Gib′ē·ah. 37 The troops
in ambush rushed quickly upon Gib′ē·ah. Then
they put the whole city to the sword. 38 Now the
agreement between the main body of Israel and the
men in ambush was that when they sent up a cloud
of smoke out of the city 39 the main body of Israel
should turn in battle. But Benjamin had begun to
inflict casualties on the Israelites, killing about thirty of them; so they thought, "Surely they are defeated before us, as in the first battle." 40 But when the
cloud, a column of smoke, began to rise out of the
city, the Ben′ja·min·ītes looked behind them—and
there was the whole city going up in smoke toward
the sky! 41 Then the main body of Israel turned, and
the Ben′ja·min·ītes were dismayed, for they saw
that disaster was close upon them. 42 Therefore they
turned away from the Israelites in the direction of
the wilderness; but the battle overtook them, and
those who came out of the city^b were slaughtering
them in between.^c 43 Cutting down^d the Ben′-
ja·min·ītes, they pursued them from Nō′hah^e and
trod them down as far as a place east of Gib′ē·ah.
44 Eighteen thousand Ben′ja·min·ītes fell, all of
them courageous fighters. 45 When they turned and
fled toward the wilderness to the rock of Rim′mon,

---

x Compare Gk: Meaning of Heb uncertain   y Verses 22 and
23 are transposed   z Gk Vg: Heb *in the plain*   a This
sentence is continued by verse 45.   b Compare Vg and
some Gk Mss: Heb *cities*   c Compare Syr: Meaning of Heb
uncertain   d Gk: Heb *Surrounding*   e Gk: Heb *pursued them
at their resting place*

five thousand of them were cut down on the main roads, and they were pursued as far as Gi′dom, and two thousand of them were slain. 46 So all who fell that day of Benjamin were twenty-five thousand arms-bearing men, all of them courageous fighters. 47 But six hundred turned and fled toward the wilderness to the rock of Rim′mon, and remained at the rock of Rim′mon for four months. 48 Meanwhile, the Israelites turned back against the Ben′ja•min•ites, and put them to the sword—the city, the people, the animals, and all that remained. Also the remaining towns they set on fire.

The Benjaminites Saved from Extinction

21 Now the Israelites had sworn at Miz′pah, "No one of us shall give his daughter in marriage to Benjamin." 2 And the people came to Beth′el, and sat there until evening before God, and they lifted up their voices and wept bitterly. 3 They said, "O LORD, the God of Israel, why has it come to pass that today there should be one tribe lacking in Israel?" 4 On the next day, the people got up early, and built an altar there, and offered burnt offerings and sacrifices of well-being. 5 Then the Israelites said, "Which of all the tribes of Israel did not come up in the assembly to the LORD?" For a solemn oath had been taken concerning whoever did not come up to the LORD to Miz′pah, saying, "That one shall be put to death." 6 But the Israelites had compassion for Benjamin their kin, and said, "One tribe is cut off from Israel this day. 7 What shall we do for wives for those who are left, since we have sworn by the LORD that we will not give them any of our daughters as wives?"

8 Then they said, "Is there anyone from the tribes of Israel who did not come up to the LORD to Miz′pah?" It turned out that no one from Ja′besh-gil′ē•ad had come to the camp, to the assembly. 9 For when the roll was called among the people, not one of the inhabitants of Ja′besh-gil′ē•ad was there. 10 So the congregation sent twelve thousand soldiers there and commanded them, "Go, put the inhabitants of Ja′besh-gil′ē•ad to the sword, including the women and the little ones. 11 This is what you shall do; every male and every woman that has lain with a male you shall devote to destruction." 12 And they found among the inhabitants of Ja′besh-gil′ē•ad four hundred young virgins who had never slept with a man and brought them to the camp at Shi′lōh, which is in the land of Cā′naan.

13 Then the whole congregation sent word to the Ben′ja•min•ites who were at the rock of Rim′mon, and proclaimed peace to them. 14 Benjamin returned at that time; and they gave them the women whom they had saved alive of the women of Ja′besh-gil′ē•ad; but they did not suffice for them.

15 The people had compassion on Benjamin because the LORD had made a breach in the tribes of Israel. 16 So the elders of the congregation said, "What shall we do for wives for those who are left, since there are no women left in Benjamin?" 17 And they said, "There must be heirs for the survivors of Benjamin, in order that a tribe may not be blotted out from Israel. 18 Yet we cannot give any of our daughters to them as wives." For the Israelites had sworn, "Cursed be anyone who gives a wife to Benjamin." 19 So they said, "Look, the yearly festival of the LORD is taking place at Shi′lōh, which is north of Beth′el, on the east of the highway that goes up from Beth′el to Shē′chem, and south of Le•bō′nah." 20 And they instructed the Ben′ja•min•ites, saying, "Go and lie in wait in the vineyards, 21 and watch; when the young women of Shi′lōh come out to dance in the dances, then come out of the vineyards and each of you carry off a wife for himself from the young women of Shi′lōh, and go to the land of Benjamin. 22 Then if their fathers or their brothers come to complain to us, we will say to them, 'Be generous and allow us to have them; because we did not capture in battle a wife for each man. But neither did you incur guilt by giving your daughters to them.' " 23 The Ben′ja•min•ites did so; they took wives for each of them from the dancers whom they abducted. Then they went and returned to their territory, and rebuilt the towns, and lived in them. 24 So the Israelites departed from there at that time by tribes and families, and they went out from there to their own territories.

25 In those days there was no king in Israel; all the people did what was right in their own eyes.

Tracing one's family tree has become a popular pastime. People comb through courthouse files, study old tombstones in search of names and dates, and write to churches in foreign countries looking for baptismal and marriage records. In learning about our ancestors, we gain a better sense of our place in history and who we should be in light of that history. Ruth is a beautiful story of love and loyalty about one of Israel's ancestors. The story helps God's people understand who they are and how they should live.

At a Glance

- **Chapter 1.** Ruth goes with her mother-in-law to Bethlehem.

- **Chapters 2–3.** Ruth encounters Boaz.

- **Chapter 4.** the marriage of Ruth and Boaz, Ruth's descendants

In-depth

The Book of Ruth offers a surprising revelation about the family tree of King David: Ruth, King David's great-grandmother, was a foreigner, born and reared in the land of Moab. The Book of Ruth was written long after the death of her famous great-grandson, but it seems to preserve an accurate memory: King David was of mixed ancestry. Many Israelites were probably shocked that God worked through a member of an enemy tribe to advance the divine plan.

The Book of Ruth is sandwiched between Judges and 1 Samuel because its events take place during the time of the judges. It teaches some extremely important lessons:

- Ruth was faithful to Naomi, her mother-in-law, even though she was of a different race and different faith. Ruth challenged the ancient Israelites, who tended to view foreigners with suspicion and to see nothing good in their enemies.
- If God's plan included a Moabite woman among David's ancestors, then God's love and favor must extend beyond the boundaries of Israel. After the Exile, when Jewish marriages to foreigners were outlawed, the little Book of Ruth presented a huge challenge!
- God works through the faithfulness of ordinary people living ordinary lives. No kings, wars, or dramatic miracles appear in the Book of Ruth.

The Book of Ruth is action packed and full of dialog; it is a dramatic story like the Books of Judith and Tobit. Some of the traditions of ancient Israel may seem strange to us today, but we can still gain a deeper understanding of ourselves and our faith by reading the story of King David's great-grandmother.

Quick Facts

Period Covered
sometime from 1200 to 1000 B.C.

Author
unknown, probably writing sometime during the monarchy (1000–800 B.C.)

Themes
God's plan includes non-Israelites. God works through ordinary people.

The Book of *Ruth*

Ruth

Elimelech's Family Goes to Moab

1 In the days when the judges ruled, there was a famine in the land, and a certain man of Bethlehem in Judah went to live in the country of Mō'ab, he and his wife and two sons. 2 The name of the man was Ē•lim'e•lech and the name of his wife Nā'o•mī, and the names of his two sons were Mah'lon and Chil'i•on; they were Eph'ra•thītes from Bethlehem in Judah. They went into the country of Mō'ab and remained there. 3 But Ē•lim'e•lech, the husband of Nā'o•mī, died, and she was left with her two sons. 4 These took Mō'ab•īte wives; the name of the one was Or'pah and the name of the other Ruth. When they had lived there about ten years, 5 both Mah'lon and Chil'i•on also died, so that the woman was left without her two sons and her husband.

Naomi and Her Moabite Daughters-in-Law

6 Then she started to return with her daughters-in-law from the country of Mō'ab, for she had heard in the country of Mō'ab that the LORD had considered his people and given them food. 7 So she set out from the place where she had been living, she and her two daughters-in-law, and they went on their way to go back to the land of Judah. 8 But Nā'o•mī said to her two daughters-in-law, "Go back each of you to your mother's house. May the LORD deal kindly with you, as you have dealt with the dead and with me. 9 The LORD grant that you may find security, each of you in the house of your husband." Then she kissed them, and they wept aloud. 10 They said to her, "No, we will return with you to your people." 11 But Nā'o•mī said, "Turn back, my daughters, why will you go with me? Do I still have sons in my womb that they may become your husbands? 12 Turn back, my daughters, go your way, for I am too old to have a husband. Even if I thought there was hope for me, even if I should have a husband tonight and bear sons, 13 would you then wait until they were grown? Would you then refrain from marrying? No, my daughters, it has been far more bitter for me than for you, because the hand of the LORD has turned against me." 14 Then they wept aloud again. Or'pah kissed her mother-in-law, but Ruth clung to her.

15 So she said, "See, your sister-in-law has gone back to her people and to her gods; return after your sister-in-law." 16 But Ruth said,

"Do not press me to leave you
    or to turn back from following you!
Where you go, I will go;
    where you lodge, I will lodge;
your people shall be my people,
    and your God my God.
17 Where you die, I will die—
    there will I be buried.
May the LORD do thus and so to me,
    and more as well,
if even death parts me from you!"

18 When Nā'o•mī saw that she was determined to go with her, she said no more to her.

Stand by Me

Loyalty is one of those old-fashioned words, isn't it? How often do we hear it mentioned these days? And what exactly does it mean to be loyal? The story of Naomi and Ruth gives us an inspiring example of loyalty. After Ruth's husband dies and her mother-in-law decides to return home to Bethlehem, Naomi tells her two widowed daughters-in-law that they should return to their homes and marry again. But Ruth decides to stay with Naomi, which means leaving her own land of Moab and settling in Judea, a foreign land. Ruth's words to Naomi are a powerful statement of what it means to be loyal: "Where you go, I will go; where you lodge, I will lodge; your people shall be my people, and your God my God" (Ruth 1.16). In other words, "No matter what, I will stand by you."

We are also called to be loyal—especially to our families and friends. In other words, we are to stand by the people we are close to, especially when they are experiencing hard times. Even when it's tough to do so, we are to remain faithful. Loyalty creates trust and deepens relationships.

None of us wants to be disloyal. Think about Peter's reaction at Jesus' Passion when he realized he had denied knowing Jesus three times!

Reflect on the times in your life when you have experienced loyalty. How have your friends or family members proven their loyalty to you? How and when have you proven your loyalty to another? God is always loyal to us; are we loyal to God?

▸ **Ruth 1.1–18**

RUTH

19 So the two of them went on until they came to Bethlehem. When they came to Bethlehem, the whole town was stirred because of them; and the women said, "Is this Nā′o•mī?" 20 She said to them,
"Call me no longer Nā′o•mī,*a*
    call me Mar′a,*b*
    for the Almighty*c* has dealt bitterly with me.
21 I went away full,
    but the LORD has brought me back empty;
why call me Nā′o•mī
    when the LORD has dealt harshly with*d* me,
    and the Almighty*c* has brought calamity
        upon me?"
22 So Nā′o•mī returned together with Ruth the Mō′ab•īte, her daughter-in-law, who came back with her from the country of Mō′ab. They came to Bethlehem at the beginning of the barley harvest.

Ruth Meets Boaz

2 Now Nā′o•mī had a kinsman on her husband's side, a prominent rich man, of the family of Ē′lim′ē•lech, whose name was Bō′az. 2 And Ruth the Mō′ab•īte said to Nā′o•mī, "Let me go to the field and glean among the ears of grain, behind someone in whose sight I may find favor." She said to her, "Go, my daughter." 3 So she went. She came and gleaned in the field behind the reapers. As it happened, she came to the part of the field belonging to Bō′az, who was of the family of Ē′lim′ē•lech. 4 Just then Bō′az came from Bethle-

hem. He said to the reapers, "The LORD be with you." They answered, "The LORD bless you." 5 Then Bō′az said to his servant who was in charge of the reapers, "To whom does this young woman belong?" 6 The servant who was in charge of the reapers answered, "She is the Mō′ab•īte who came back with Nā′o•mī from the country of Mō′ab. 7 She said, 'Please, let me glean and gather among the sheaves behind the reapers.' So she came, and she has been on her feet from early this morning until now, without resting even for a moment."*e*

8 Then Bō′az said to Ruth, "Now listen, my daughter, do not go to glean in another field or leave this one, but keep close to my young women. 9 Keep your eyes on the field that is being reaped, and follow behind them. I have ordered the young men not to bother you. If you get thirsty, go to the vessels and drink from what the young men have drawn." 10 Then she fell prostrate, with her face to the ground, and said to him, "Why have I found favor in your sight, that you should take notice of me, when I am a foreigner?" 11 But Bō′az answered her, "All that you have done for your mother-in-law since the death of your husband has been fully told me, and how you left your father and mother and your native land and came to a people that you did

---

a That is *Pleasant*   *b* That is *Bitter*   *c* Traditional rendering of Heb *Shaddai*   *d* Or *has testified against*   *e* Compare Gk Vg: Meaning of Heb uncertain

R
U
T
H

not know before. 12 May the LORD reward you for your deeds, and may you have a full reward from the LORD, the God of Israel, under whose wings you have come for refuge!" 13 Then she said, "May I continue to find favor in your sight, my lord, for you have comforted me and spoken kindly to your servant, even though I am not one of your servants."

14 At mealtime Bō'az said to her, "Come here, and eat some of this bread, and dip your morsel in the sour wine." So she sat beside the reapers, and he heaped up for her some parched grain. She ate until she was satisfied, and she had some left over. 15 When she got up to glean, Bō'az instructed his young men, "Let her glean even among the standing sheaves, and do not reproach her. 16 You must also pull out some handfuls for her from the bundles, and leave them for her to glean, and do not rebuke her."

17 So she gleaned in the field until evening. Then she beat out what she had gleaned, and it was about an ephah of barley. 18 She picked it up and came into the town, and her mother-in-law saw how much she had gleaned. Then she took out and gave her what was left over after she herself had been satisfied. 19 Her mother-in-law said to her, "Where did you glean today? And where have you worked? Blessed be the man who took notice of you." So she told her mother-in-law with whom she had worked, and said, "The name of the man with whom I worked today is Bō'az." 20 Then

Nā'o•mī said to her daughter-in-law, "Blessed be he by the LORD, whose kindness has not forsaken the living or the dead!" Nā'o•mī also said to her, "The man is a relative of ours, one of our nearest kin."*f* 21 Then Ruth the Mō'ab•īte said, "He even said to me, 'Stay close by my servants, until they have finished all my harvest.' " 22 Nā'o•mī said to Ruth, her daughter-in-law, "It is better, my daughter, that you go out with his young women, otherwise you might be bothered in another field." 23 So she stayed close to the young women of Bō'az, gleaning until the end of the barley and wheat harvests; and she lived with her mother-in-law.

Ruth and Boaz at the Threshing Floor

3 Nā'o•mī her mother-in-law said to her, "My daughter, I need to seek some security for you, so that it may be well with you. 2 Now here is our kinsman Bō'az, with whose young women you have been working. See, he is winnowing barley tonight at the threshing floor. 3 Now wash and anoint yourself, and put on your best clothes and go down to the threshing floor; but do not make yourself known to the man until he has finished eating and drinking. 4 When he lies down, observe the place where he lies; then, go and uncover his feet and lie down; and he will tell you what to do." 5 She said to her, "All that you tell me I will do."

6 So she went down to the threshing floor and

---

f Or *one with the right to redeem*

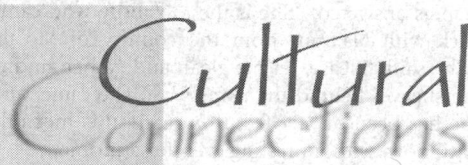

SERVICE TO THE POOR AND THE COMMUNITY!

The story of Ruth was a challenge to the Israelites' tendency to distrust foreigners. It is also an example of how service to the poor was an integral part of Israel's society. For in the story, Boaz, a wealthy and respected person, both provides for the poor and looks beyond the differences of race and faith to marry Ruth. Boaz's goal is to do God's will. His marriage to Ruth ensures that Naomi's land is redeemed and that she will have descendants to claim the land. Ruth's faithfulness and Boaz's integrity serve to gradually restore Naomi's hope in God's care.

In the New Testament, it becomes even clearer that God makes no distinctions between people of different races and cultures. And Jesus teaches that caring for the poor is one of the requirements for being God's people.

- How do you treat people of different races, and how much is service to poor people a part of your life?
- Pray that you can follow Ruth and Boaz's example and be an instrument of faith, hope, and justice for people in need.

did just as her mother-in-law had instructed her. 7 When Bō′az had eaten and drunk, and he was in a contented mood, he went to lie down at the end of the heap of grain. Then she came stealthily and uncovered his feet, and lay down. 8 At midnight the man was startled, and turned over, and there, lying at his feet, was a woman! 9 He said, "Who are you?" And she answered, "I am Ruth, your servant; spread your cloak over your servant, for you are next-of-kin."ᵍ 10 He said, "May you be blessed by the LORD, my daughter; this last instance of your loyalty is better than the first; you have not gone after young men, whether poor or rich. 11 And now, my daughter, do not be afraid, I will do for you all that you ask, for all the assembly of my people know that you are a worthy woman. 12 But now, though it is true that I am a near kinsman, there is another kinsman more closely related than I. 13 Remain this night, and in the morning, if he will act as next-of-kinᵍ for you, good; let him do it. If he is not willing to act as next-of-kinᵍ for you, then, as the LORD lives, I will act as next-of-kinᵍ for you. Lie down until the morning." 14 So she lay at his feet until morning, but got up before one person could recognize another; for he said, "It must not be known that the woman came to the threshing floor." 15 Then he said, "Bring the cloak you are wearing and hold it out." So she held it, and he measured out six measures of barley, and put it on her back; then he went into the city. 16 She came to her mother-in-law, who said, "How did things go with you,ʰ my daughter?" Then she told her all that the man had done for her, 17 saying, "He gave me these six measures of barley, for he said, 'Do not go back to your mother-in-law empty-handed.' " 18 She replied, "Wait, my daughter, until you learn how the matter turns out, for the man will not rest, but will settle the matter today."

The Marriage of Boaz and Ruth

4 No sooner had Bō′az gone up to the gate and sat down there than the next-of-kin,ᵍ of whom Bō′az had spoken, came passing by. So Bō′az said, "Come over, friend; sit down here." And he went over and sat down. 2 Then Bō′az took ten men of the elders of the city, and said, "Sit down here"; so they sat down. 3 He then said to the next-of-kin,ᵍ "Nā′o•mī, who has come back from the country of Mō′ab, is selling the parcel of land that belonged to our kinsman Ē•lim′e•lech. 4 So I thought I would tell you of it, and say: Buy it in the presence of those sitting here, and in the presence of the elders of my people. If you will redeem it, redeem it; but if you will not, tell me, so that I may know; for there is no one prior to you to redeem it, and I come after you." So he said, "I will redeem it." 5 Then Bō′az said, "The day you acquire the field from the hand of Nā′o•mī, you are also acquiring Ruthⁱ the Mō′ab•īte, the widow of the dead man, to maintain the dead man's name on his inheritance." 6 At this, the next-of-kinᵍ said, "I cannot redeem it for myself without damaging my own inheritance. Take my right of redemption yourself, for I cannot redeem it."

7 Now this was the custom in former times in Israel concerning redeeming and exchanging: to confirm a transaction, the one took off a sandal and gave it to the other; this was the manner of attesting in Israel. 8 So when the next-of-kinᵍ said to Bō′az, "Acquire it for yourself," he took off his sandal. 9 Then Bō′az said to the elders and all the people, "Today you are witnesses that I have acquired from the hand of Nā′o•mī all that belonged to Ē•lim′-e•lech and all that belonged to Chil′i•on and Mah′lon. 10 I have also acquired Ruth the Mō′-ab•īte, the wife of Mah′lon, to be my wife, to maintain the dead man's name on his inheritance, in order that the name of the dead may not be cut off from his kindred and from the gate of his native place; today you are witnesses." 11 Then all the people who were at the gate, along with the elders, said, "We are witnesses. May the LORD make the woman who is coming into your house like Rachel and

ᵍ Or one with the right to redeem   ʰ Or "Who are you,
ⁱ OL Vg: Heb from the hand of Naomi and from Ruth

PRAY IT!
Wherever You Go

Ruth is under no obligation to leave her homeland and go to Israel with her mother-in-law, very likely facing a life of poverty. But her loyalty is rewarded, and she finds new life among God's people.

After reading Ruth's story, reflect on these questions:

- What do you find inspiring in Ruth's story?
- To whom are you faithful?
- What would have to be present in a relationship for you to have the kind of loyalty Ruth showed to Naomi?
- Can you make Ruth's words to Naomi your prayer to God?

Where you lead, I will follow; where you direct me, I will live; your people shall be my family, and your God shall always be my God. (Adapted from Ruth 1.16)

RUTH

Leah, who together built up the house of Israel. May you produce children in Eph'ra•thah and bestow a name in Bethlehem; 12 and, through the children that the LORD will give you by this young woman, may your house be like the house of Per'ez, whom Tā'mar bore to Judah."

The Genealogy of David
(Matt 1.2–6)

13 So Bō'az took Ruth and she became his wife. When they came together, the LORD made her conceive, and she bore a son. 14 Then the women said to Nā'o•mī, "Blessed be the LORD, who has not left you this day without next-of-kin;*j* and may his name be renowned in Israel! 15 He shall be to you a restorer of life and a nourisher of your old age; for your daughter-in-law who loves you, who is more to you than seven sons, has borne him." 16 Then Nā'o•mī took the child and laid him in her bosom, and became his nurse. 17 The women of the neighborhood gave him a name, saying, "A son has been born to Nā'o•mī." They named him Ō'bed; he became the father of Jesse, the father of David.

18 Now these are the descendants of Per'ez: Per'ez became the father of Hez'ron, 19 Hez'ron of Ram, Ram of Am•min'a•dab, 20 Am•min'a•dab of Nah'shon, Nah'shon of Sal'mon, 21 Sal'mon of Bō'az, Bō'az of Ō'bed, 22 Ō'bed of Jesse, and Jesse of David.

---

j Or one with the right to redeem

The First Book of Samuel reflects a tension in Israel as the days of the judges come to an end and the first kings make their appearance. This period of Israelite history is filled with mighty struggles and colorful personalities, including a king who gradually loses his sanity and the shining hero who replaces him.

At a Glance

- **Chapters 1–7.** stories of Eli and Samuel
- **Chapters 8–15.** the beginning of Saul's kingship
- **Chapters 16–31.** stories of King Saul and the young David

In-depth

This book is named after Samuel, the last of the judges and a reluctant king-maker. Samuel, a prophet anointed to speak God's word to the nation, represents one way of governing. God works through the prophet's words to remind the people of Israel to be faithful to the terms of the Covenant. A second way of governing is represented by Saul, the first king anointed by Samuel to rule over the whole nation. God works through the king's laws and regulations to ensure that the people of Israel are faithful to the terms of the Covenant. In 1 Samuel, the former way of governing the Israelite nation gradually gives way to the latter, with an obvious gain and an obvious loss for the people.

When kings begin to rule Israel in place of judges and prophets, the people gain a more structured way of life and develop a greater national identity. These changes also make them stronger in facing threats from other nations. But at the same time, the people lose a great deal of personal freedom and independence. They are taxed and even forced into labor to support the king's government and building plans. Echoes of this debate on governing styles can be found throughout 1 Samuel (see "Doublets," near 9.1).

Israel's kings were understood as being chosen by God and as being responsible for God's interests. First Samuel clearly emphasizes that the success of kings depends on their obedience to God's law. First Samuel reminds us that final authority in human affairs rests in no human being, but in God alone. Human systems are never perfect, but must constantly be reviewed and renewed.

Quick Facts

Period Covered
approximately 1080 to 1040 B.C.

Author
unknown, from the Deuteronomic tradition, probably using ancient court records and hero stories

Theme
tension between the need for a king and the people's reliance on God

Of Note
First and Second Samuel, originally one book, were made into two books when they were translated from Hebrew into Greek.

The First Book of Samuel

1 Samuel

Samuel's Birth and Dedication

1 There was a certain man of Rā·ma·thā'im, a Zuph'īte[a] from the hill country of Ē'phra·im, whose name was El·kā'nah son of Je·rō'ham son of E·lī'hū son of Tō'hū son of Zuph, an Ē'phra·im·īte. [2] He had two wives; the name of the one was Hannah, and the name of the other Pe·nin'nah. Pe·nin'nah had children, but Hannah had no children.

[3] Now this man used to go up year by year from his town to worship and to sacrifice to the LORD of hosts at Shī'lōh, where the two sons of Ē'lī, Hoph'nī and Phin'e·has, were priests of the LORD. [4] On the day when El·kā'nah sacrificed, he would give portions to his wife Pe·nin'nah and to all her sons and daughters; [5] but to Hannah he gave a double portion,[b] because he loved her, though the LORD had closed her womb. [6] Her rival used to provoke her severely, to irritate her, because the LORD had closed her womb. [7] So it went on year by year; as often as she went up to the house of the LORD, she used to provoke her. Therefore Hannah wept and would not eat. [8] Her husband El·kā'nah said to her, "Hannah, why do you weep? Why do you not eat? Why is your heart sad? Am I not more to you than ten sons?"

[9] After they had eaten and drunk at Shī'lōh, Hannah rose and presented herself before the LORD.[c] Now Ē'lī the priest was sitting on the seat beside the doorpost of the temple of the LORD. [10] She was deeply distressed and prayed to the LORD, and wept bitterly. [11] She made this vow: "O LORD of hosts, if only you will look on the misery of your servant, and remember me, and not forget your servant, but will give to your servant a male child, then I will set him before you as a nazirite[d] until the day of his death. He shall drink neither wine nor intoxicants,[e] and no razor shall touch his head."

[12] As she continued praying before the LORD, Ē'lī observed her mouth. [13] Hannah was praying silently; only her lips moved, but her voice was not heard; therefore Ē'lī thought she was drunk. [14] So Ē'lī said to her, "How long will you make a drunken spectacle of yourself? Put away your wine." [15] But Hannah answered, "No, my lord, I am a woman deeply troubled; I have drunk neither wine nor strong drink, but I have been pouring out my soul before the LORD. [16] Do not regard your servant as a worthless woman, for I have been speaking out of my great anxiety and vexation all this time." [17] Then Ē'lī answered, "Go in peace; the God of Israel grant the petition you have made to him." [18] And she said, "Let your servant find favor in your sight." Then the woman went to her quarters,[f] ate

---

a Compare Gk and 1 Chr 6.35-36: Heb *Ramathaim-zophim*
b Syr: Meaning of Heb uncertain *c* Gk: Heb lacks *and presented herself before the LORD* *d* That is *one separated* or *one consecrated* *e* Cn Compare Gk Q Ms 1.22: MT *then I will give him to the LORD all the days of his life* *f* Gk: Heb *went her way*

PRAY IT!

Prayers of Strong and Holy Women

Compare Hannah's prayer in I Sam 2.1–10 to Mary's prayer in Lk 1.46–55. Notice the joy, the confident faith in God's way, and the understanding that God will raise up those who are hungry, poor, and in need. Notice also how God will deal with the proud, the powerful, and the rich, especially in Mary's prayer. These holy women identify in their lives and in their prayers the bigger picture of what God is all about.

What strong and holy women in your life keep you in their prayers?

▸ I Sam 2.1–10

and drank with her husband,*g* and her countenance was sad no longer.*h*

19 They rose early in the morning and worshiped before the LORD; then they went back to their house at Rā′mah. El•kā′nah knew his wife Hannah, and the LORD remembered her. 20 In due time Hannah conceived and bore a son. She named him Samuel, for she said, "I have asked him of the LORD."

21 The man El•kā′nah and all his household went up to offer to the LORD the yearly sacrifice, and to pay his vow. 22 But Hannah did not go up, for she said to her husband, "As soon as the child is weaned, I will bring him, that he may appear in the presence of the LORD, and remain there forever; I will offer him as a nazirite*i* for all time."*j* 23 Her husband El•kā′nah said to her, "Do what seems best to you, wait until you have weaned him; only— may the LORD establish his word."*k* So the woman remained and nursed her son, until she weaned him. 24 When she had weaned him, she took him up with her, along with a three-year-old bull,*l* an ephah of flour, and a skin of wine. She brought him to the house of the LORD at Shī′lōh; and the child was young. 25 Then they slaughtered the bull, and they brought the child to Ē′lī. 26 And she said, "Oh, my lord! As you live, my lord, I am the woman who was standing here in your presence, praying to the LORD. 27 For this child I prayed; and the LORD has granted me the petition that I made to him. 28 Therefore I have lent him to the LORD; as long as he lives, he is given to the LORD."

She left him there for*m* the LORD.

Hannah's Prayer
(Cp Lk 1.46–55)

2 Hannah prayed and said,
"My heart exults in the LORD;
    my strength is exalted in my God.*n*
My mouth derides my enemies,
    because I rejoice in my*o* victory.

2 "There is no Holy One like the LORD,
    no one besides you;
    there is no Rock like our God.
3 Talk no more so very proudly,
    let not arrogance come from your mouth;
for the LORD is a God of knowledge,
    and by him actions are weighed.
4 The bows of the mighty are broken,
    but the feeble gird on strength.
5 Those who were full have hired themselves out
        for bread,
    but those who were hungry are fat with spoil.
The barren has borne seven,
    but she who has many children is forlorn.
6 The LORD kills and brings to life;
    he brings down to Shē′ōl and raises up.
7 The LORD makes poor and makes rich;
    he brings low, he also exalts.
8 He raises up the poor from the dust;
    he lifts the needy from the ash heap,
to make them sit with princes
    and inherit a seat of honor.*p*
For the pillars of the earth are the LORD's,
    and on them he has set the world.

9 "He will guard the feet of his faithful ones,
    but the wicked shall be cut off in darkness;
    for not by might does one prevail.
10 The LORD! His adversaries shall be shattered;
    the Most High*q* will thunder in heaven.
The LORD will judge the ends of the earth;
    he will give strength to his king,
    and exalt the power of his anointed."

Eli's Wicked Sons

11 Then El•kā′nah went home to Rā′mah, while the boy remained to minister to the LORD, in the presence of the priest Ē′lī.

12 Now the sons of Ē′lī were scoundrels; they

g Gk: Heb lacks *and drank with her husband*   *h* Gk: Meaning of Heb uncertain   *i* That is *one separated* or *one consecrated*   *j* Cn Compare Q Ms: MT lacks *I will offer him as a nazirite for all time*   *k* MT: Q Ms Gk Compare Syr *that which goes out of your mouth*   *l* Q Ms Gk Syr: MT *three bulls*   *m* Gk (Compare Q Ms) and Gk at 2.11: MT *And he (that is, Elkanah) worshiped there before*   *n* Gk: Heb *the* LORD   *o* Q Ms: MT *your*   *p* Gk (Compare Q Ms) adds *He grants the vow of the one who vows, and blesses the years of the just*   *q* Cn Heb *against him he* had no regard for the LORD [13] or for the duties of the priests to the people. When anyone offered sacrifice, the priest's servant would come, while the meat was boiling, with a three-pronged fork in his hand, [14] and he would thrust it into the pan, or kettle, or caldron, or pot; all that the fork brought up the priest would take for himself.[r] This is what they did at Shiʹlōh to all the Israelites who came there. [15] Moreover, before the fat was burned, the priest's servant would come and say to the one who was sacrificing, "Give meat for the priest to roast; for he will not accept boiled meat from you, but only raw." [16] And if the man said to him, "Let them burn the fat first, and then take whatever you wish," he would say, "No, you must give it now; if not, I will take it by force." [17] Thus the sin of the young men was very great in the sight of the LORD; for they treated the offerings of the LORD with contempt.

The Child Samuel at Shiloh

18 Samuel was ministering before the LORD, a boy wearing a linen ephod. [19] His mother used to make for him a little robe and take it to him each year, when she went up with her husband to offer the yearly sacrifice. [20] Then Ēʹli would bless Elʹkāʹnah and his wife, and say, "May the LORD repay[s] you with children by this woman for the gift that she made to[t] the LORD"; and then they would return to their home.

21 And[u] the LORD took note of Hannah; she conceived and bore three sons and two daughters. And the boy Samuel grew up in the presence of the LORD.

Prophecy against Eli's Household

22 Now Ēʹli was very old. He heard all that his sons were doing to all Israel, and how they lay with the women who served at the entrance to the tent of meeting. [23] He said to them, "Why do you do such things? For I hear of your evil dealings from all these people. [24] No, my sons; it is not a good report that I hear the people of the LORD spreading abroad. [25] If one person sins against another, someone can intercede for the sinner with the LORD;[v] but if someone sins against the LORD, who can make intercession?" But they would not listen to the voice of their father; for it was the will of the LORD to kill them.

26 Now the boy Samuel continued to grow both in stature and in favor with the LORD and with the people.

27 A man of God came to Ēʹli and said to him, "Thus the LORD has said, 'I revealed[w] myself to the family of your ancestor in Egypt when they were slaves[x] to the house of Pharaoh. [28] I chose him out of all the tribes of Israel to be my priest, to go up to my altar, to offer incense, to wear an ephod before me; and I gave to the family of your ancestor all my offerings by fire from the people of Israel. [29] Why then look with greedy eye[y] at my sacrifices and my offerings that I commanded, and honor your sons more than me by fattening yourselves on the choicest parts of every offering of my people Israel?' [30] Therefore the LORD the God of Israel declares: 'I promised that your family and the family of your ancestor should go in and out before me forever'; but now the LORD declares: 'Far be it from me; for those who honor me I will honor, and those who despise me shall be treated with contempt. [31] See, a time is coming when I will cut off your strength and the strength of your ancestor's family, so that no one in your family will live to old age. [32] Then in distress you will look with greedy eye[z] on all the prosperity that shall be bestowed upon Israel; and no one in your family shall ever live to old age. [33] The only one of you whom I shall not cut off from my altar shall be spared to weep out his[a] eyes and grieve his[b] heart; all the members of your household shall die by the sword.[c] [34] The fate of your two sons, Hophʹni and Phinʹeʹhas, shall be the sign to you—both of them shall die on the same day. [35] I will raise up for myself a faithful priest, who shall do according to what is in my heart and in my mind. I will build him a sure house, and he shall go in and out before my anointed one forever. [36] Everyone who is left in your family shall come to implore him for a piece of silver or a loaf of bread, and shall say, Please put me in one of the priest's places, that I may eat a morsel of bread.' "

Samuel's Calling and Prophetic Activity

3 Now the boy Samuel was ministering to the LORD under Ēʹli. The word of the LORD was rare in those days; visions were not widespread.

2 At that time Ēʹli, whose eyesight had begun to grow dim so that he could not see, was lying down in his room; [3] the lamp of God had not yet gone out, and Samuel was lying down in the temple of the LORD, where the ark of God was. [4] Then the LORD called, "Samuel! Samuel!"[d] and he said, "Here I am!" [5] and ran to Ēʹli, and said, "Here I am, for you called me." But he said, "I did not call; lie down again." So he went and lay down. [6] The LORD called again, "Samuel!" Samuel got up and went to Ēʹli, and said, "Here I am, for you called me." But he said, "I did not call, my son; lie down again."

---

[r] Gk Syr Vg: Heb *with it*   [s] Q Ms Gk: MT *give*   [t] Q Ms Gk: MT *for the petition that she asked of*   [u] Q Ms Gk: MT *When*   [v] Gk Compare Q Ms: MT *another, God will mediate for him*   [w] Gk Tg Syr: Heb *Did I reveal*   [x] Q Ms Gk: MT lacks *slaves*   [y] Q Ms Gk: MT *then kick*   [z] Q Ms Gk: MT *will kick*   [a] Q Ms Gk: MT *your*   [b] Q Ms Gk: Heb *your*   [c] Q Ms See Gk: MT *die like mortals*   [d] Q Ms Gk See 3.10: MT *the LORD called Samuel*

PRAY IT!

Eli Teaches Samuel How to Pray

Eli taught Samuel to listen to God's voice with a simple sentence: "Speak, LORD, for your servant is listening" (1 Sam 3.9). Let's look at that sentence as a prayer:

"*Speak, LORD . . .*" This is an invitation. It shows openness and readiness. It shows your recognition of God: "You are the Almighty, and I am ready to hear what you have to say."

"*. . . for your servant . . .*" This shows humility. It is a recognition of yourself: "I am your servant. It is my desire to do what you want. My life's purpose is to serve you."

"*. . . is listening.*" This demonstrates your response: "I am not going to ignore you. I am not going to daydream or just pretend to pay attention. I will take in your message, and it will become part of me."

▸ 1 Sam 3.1–19

---

7 Now Samuel did not yet know the LORD, and the word of the LORD had not yet been revealed to him. 8 The LORD called Samuel again, a third time. And he got up and went to Ēʹlī, and said, "Here I am, for you called me." Then Ēʹlī perceived that the LORD was calling the boy. 9 Therefore Ēʹlī said to Samuel, "Go, lie down; and if he calls you, you shall say, 'Speak, LORD, for your servant is listening.' " So Samuel went and lay down in his place.

10 Now the LORD came and stood there, calling as before, "Samuel! Samuel!" And Samuel said, "Speak, for your servant is listening." 11 Then the LORD said to Samuel, "See, I am about to do something in Israel that will make both ears of anyone who hears of it tingle. 12 On that day I will fulfill against Ēʹlī all that I have spoken concerning his house, from beginning to end. 13 For I have told him that I am about to punish his house forever, for the iniquity that he knew, because his sons were blaspheming God,*e* and he did not restrain them. 14 Therefore I swear to the house of Ēʹlī that the iniquity of Ēʹlī's house shall not be expiated by sacrifice or offering forever."

15 Samuel lay there until morning; then he opened the doors of the house of the LORD. Samuel was afraid to tell the vision to Ēʹlī. 16 But Ēʹlī called Samuel and said, "Samuel, my son." He said, "Here I am." 17 Ēʹlī said, "What was it that he told you? Do not hide it from me. May God do so to you and more also, if you hide anything from me of all that he told you." 18 So Samuel told him everything and hid nothing from him. Then he said, "It is the LORD; let him do what seems good to him."

19 As Samuel grew up, the LORD was with him and let none of his words fall to the ground. 20 And all Israel from Dan to Bēʹer-shēʹba knew that Samuel was a trustworthy prophet of the LORD. 21 The LORD continued to appear at Shīʹlōh, for the LORD revealed himself to Samuel at Shīʹlōh by the word

4 of the LORD. 1 And the word of Samuel came to all Israel.

The Ark of God Captured

In those days the Phiʹlisʹtines mustered for war against Israel,*f* and Israel went out to battle against them;*g* they encamped at Ebʹeʹnēʹzer, and the Phiʹlisʹtines encamped at Āʹphek. 2 The Phiʹlisʹtines drew up in line against Israel, and when the battle was joined,*h* Israel was defeated by the Phiʹlisʹtines, who killed about four thousand men on the field of battle. 3 When the troops came to the camp, the elders of Israel said, "Why has the LORD put us to rout today before the Phiʹlisʹtines? Let us bring the ark of the covenant of the LORD here from Shīʹlōh, so that he may come among us and save us from the power of our enemies." 4 So the people sent to Shīʹlōh, and brought from there the ark of the covenant of the LORD of hosts, who is enthroned on the cherubim. The two sons of Ēʹlī, Hophʹnī and Phinʹeʹhas, were there with the ark of the covenant of God.

5 When the ark of the covenant of the LORD came into the camp, all Israel gave a mighty shout, so that the earth resounded. 6 When the Phiʹlisʹtines heard the noise of the shouting, they said, "What does this great shouting in the camp of the Hebrews mean?" When they learned that the ark of the LORD had come to the camp, 7 the Phiʹlisʹtines were afraid; for they said, "Gods have*i* come into the camp." They also said, "Woe to us! For nothing like this has happened before. 8 Woe to us! Who can deliver us from the power of these mighty gods? These are the gods who struck the Egyptians with every sort of plague in the wilderness. 9 Take courage, and be men, O Phiʹlisʹtines, in

---

e Another reading is *for themselves*   *f* Gk: Heb lacks *In those days the Philistines mustered for war against Israel*   *g* Gk: Heb *against the Philistines*   *h* Meaning of Heb uncertain   *i* Or *A god has* order not to become slaves to the Hebrews as they have been to you; be men and fight."

10 So the Phi·lis'tines fought; Israel was defeated, and they fled, everyone to his home. There was a very great slaughter, for there fell of Israel thirty thousand foot soldiers. 11 The ark of God was captured; and the two sons of É'lī, Hoph'nī and Phin'e·has, died.

Death of Eli

12 A man of Benjamin ran from the battle line, and came to Shī'lōh the same day, with his clothes torn and with earth upon his head. 13 When he arrived, É'lī was sitting upon his seat by the road watching, for his heart trembled for the ark of God. When the man came into the city and told the news, all the city cried out. 14 When É'lī heard the sound of the outcry, he said, "What is this uproar?" Then the man came quickly and told É'lī. 15 Now É'lī was ninety-eight years old and his eyes were set, so that he could not see. 16 The man said to É'lī, "I have just come from the battle; I fled from the battle today." He said, "How did it go, my son?" 17 The messenger replied, "Israel has fled before the Phi·lis'tines, and there has also been a great slaughter among the troops; your two sons also, Hoph'nī and Phin'e·has, are dead, and the ark of God has been captured." 18 When he mentioned the ark of God, É'lī[j] fell over backward from his seat by the side of the gate; and his neck was broken and he died, for he was an old man, and heavy. He had judged Israel forty years.

19 Now his daughter-in-law, the wife of Phin'e·has, was pregnant, about to give birth. When she heard the news that the ark of God was captured, and that her father-in-law and her husband were dead, she bowed and gave birth; for her labor pains overwhelmed her. 20 As she was about to die, the women attending her said to her, "Do not be afraid, for you have borne a son." But she did not answer or give heed. 21 She named the child Ich'a-bod, meaning, "The glory has departed from Israel," because the ark of God had been captured and because of her father-in-law and her husband. 22 She said, "The glory has departed from Israel, for the ark of God has been captured."

The Philistines and the Ark

5 When the Phi·lis'tines captured the ark of God, they brought it from Eb·e·nē'zer to Ash'-dod; 2 then the Phi·lis'tines took the ark of God and brought it into the house of Dā'gon and placed it beside Dā'gon. 3 When the people of Ash'dod rose early the next day, there was Dā'gon, fallen on his face to the ground before the ark of the LORD. So they took Dā'gon and put him back in his place. 4 But when they rose early on the next morning,

Dā'gon had fallen on his face to the ground before the ark of the LORD, and the head of Dā'gon and both his hands were lying cut off upon the threshold; only the trunk of[k] Dā'gon was left to him. 5 This is why the priests of Dā'gon and all who enter the house of Dā'gon do not step on the threshold of Dā'gon in Ash'dod to this day.

6 The hand of the LORD was heavy upon the people of Ash'dod, and he terrified and struck them with tumors, both in Ash'dod and in its territory. 7 And when the inhabitants of Ash'dod saw how things were, they said, "The ark of the God of Israel must not remain with us; for his hand is heavy on us and on our god Dā'gon." 8 So they sent and gathered together all the lords of the Phi·lis'tines, and said, "What shall we do with the ark of the God of Israel?" The inhabitants of Gath replied, "Let the ark of God be moved on to us."[l] So they moved the ark of the God of Israel to Gath.[m] 9 But after they had brought it to Gath,[n] the hand of the LORD was against the city, causing a very great panic; he struck the inhabitants of the city, both young and old, so that tumors broke out on them. 10 So they sent the ark of the God of Israel[o] to Ek'ron. But when the ark of God came to Ek'ron, the people of Ek'ron cried out, "Why[p] have they brought around to us[q] the ark of the God of Israel to kill us[q] and our[r] people?" 11 They sent therefore and gathered together all the lords of the Phi·lis'tines, and said, "Send away the ark of the God of Israel, and let it return to its own place, that it may not kill us and our people." For there was a deathly panic[s] throughout the whole city. The hand of God was very heavy there; 12 those who did not die were stricken with tumors, and the cry of the city went up to heaven.

The Ark Returned to Israel

6 The ark of the LORD was in the country of the Phi·lis'tines seven months. 2 Then the Phi·lis'-tines called for the priests and the diviners and said, "What shall we do with the ark of the LORD? Tell us what we should send with it to its place." 3 They said, "If you send away the ark of the God of Israel, do not send it empty, but by all means return him a guilt offering. Then you will be healed and will be ransomed;[t] will not his hand then turn from you?" 4 And they said, "What is the guilt offering that we shall return to him?" They answered, "Five gold tumors and five gold mice, according to the number of the lords of the Phi·lis'tines; for the same plague was upon all of you and upon your lords. 5 So you

---

j Heb he k Heb lacks *the trunk of* l Gk Compare Q Ms:
MT *They answered, "Let the ark of the God of Israel be brought
around to Gath."* m Gk: Heb lacks *to Gath* n Q Ms: MT
lacks *to Gath* o Q Ms Gk: MT lacks *of Israel* p Q Ms Gk:
MT lacks *Why* q Heb *me* r Heb *my* s Q Ms reads *a panic
from the LORD* t Q Ms Gk: MT *and it will be known to you*

must make images of your tumors and images of your mice that ravage the land, and give glory to the God of Israel; perhaps he will lighten his hand on you and your gods and your land. 6 Why should you harden your hearts as the Egyptians and Pharaoh hardened their hearts? After he had made fools of them, did they not let the people go, and they departed? 7 Now then, get ready a new cart and two milch cows that have never borne a yoke, and yoke the cows to the cart, but take their calves home, away from them. 8 Take the ark of the LORD and place it on the cart, and put in a box at its side the figures of gold, which you are returning to him as a guilt offering. Then send it off, and let it go its way. 9 And watch; if it goes up on the way to its own land, to Beth-she′mesh, then it is he who has done us this great harm; but if not, then we shall know that it is not his hand that struck us; it happened to us by chance."

10 The men did so; they took two milch cows and yoked them to the cart, and shut up their calves at home. 11 They put the ark of the LORD on the cart, and the box with the gold mice and the images of their tumors. 12 The cows went straight in the direction of Beth-she′mesh along one highway, lowing as they went; they turned neither to the right nor to the left, and the lords of the Phi·lis′tines went after them as far as the border of Beth-she′mesh.

13 Now the people of Beth-she′mesh were reaping their wheat harvest in the valley. When they looked up and saw the ark, they went with rejoicing to meet it.ᵘ 14 The cart came into the field of Joshua of Beth-she′mesh, and stopped there. A large stone was there; so they split up the wood of the cart and offered the cows as a burnt offering to the LORD. 15 The Le′vites took down the ark of the LORD and the box that was beside it, in which were the gold objects, and set them upon the large stone. Then the people of Beth-she′mesh offered burnt offerings and presented sacrifices on that day to the LORD. 16 When the five lords of the Phi·lis′tines saw it, they returned that day to Ek′ron.

17 These are the gold tumors, which the Phi·lis′tines returned as a guilt offering to the LORD: one for Ash′dod, one for Ga′za, one for Ash′ke·lon, one for Gath, one for Ek′ron; 18 also the gold mice, according to the number of all the cities of the Phi·lis′tines belonging to the five lords, both fortified cities and unwalled villages. The great stone, beside which they set down the ark of the LORD, is a witness to this day in the field of Joshua of Beth-she′mesh.

The Ark at Kiriath-jearim

19 The descendants of Jec·o·ni′ah did not rejoice with the people of Beth-she′mesh when they greetedᵛ the ark of the LORD; and he killed seventy

men of them.ʷ The people mourned because the LORD had made a great slaughter among the people. 20 Then the people of Beth-she′mesh said, "Who is able to stand before the LORD, this holy God? To whom shall he go so that we may be rid of him?" 21 So they sent messengers to the inhabitants of Kir′i·ath-je′a·rim, saying, "The Phi·lis′tines have returned the ark of the LORD. Come down and take it up to you." 1 And the people of Kir′i·ath-je′a·rim came and took up the ark of the LORD, and brought it to the house of A·bin′a·dab on the hill. They consecrated his son, El·e·a′zar, to have charge of the ark of the LORD.

2 From the day that the ark was lodged at Kir′i·ath-je′a·rim, a long time passed, some twenty years, and all the house of Israel lamentedˣ after the LORD.

Samuel as Judge

3 Then Samuel said to all the house of Israel, "If you are returning to the LORD with all your heart, then put away the foreign gods and the As·tar′tes from among you. Direct your heart to the LORD, and serve him only, and he will deliver you out of the hand of the Phi·lis′tines." 4 So Israel put away the Ba′als and the As·tar′tes, and they served the LORD only.

5 Then Samuel said, "Gather all Israel at Miz′-pah, and I will pray to the LORD for you." 6 So they gathered at Miz′pah, and drew water and poured it out before the LORD. They fasted that day, and said, "We have sinned against the LORD." And Samuel judged the people of Israel at Miz′pah.

7 When the Phi·lis′tines heard that the people of Israel had gathered at Miz′pah, the lords of the Phi·lis′tines went up against Israel. And when the people of Israel heard of it they were afraid of the Phi·lis′tines. 8 The people of Israel said to Samuel, "Do not cease to cry out to the LORD our God for us, and pray that he may save us from the hand of the Phi·lis′tines." 9 So Samuel took a sucking lamb and offered it as a whole burnt offering to the LORD; Samuel cried out to the LORD for Israel, and the LORD answered him. 10 As Samuel was offering up the burnt offering, the Phi·lis′tines drew near to attack Israel; but the LORD thundered with a mighty voice that day against the Phi·lis′tines and threw them into confusion; and they were routed before Israel. 11 And the men of Israel went out of Miz′pah and pursued the Phi·lis′tines, and struck them down as far as beyond Beth-car.

12 Then Samuel took a stone and set it up

ᵘ Gk: Heb *rejoiced to see it*   ᵛ Gk: Heb *And he killed some of the people of Beth-shemesh, because they looked into*   ʷ Heb *killed seventy men, fifty thousand men*   ˣ Meaning of Heb uncertain between Miz'pah and Je•shā'nah,[y] and named it Eb•e•nē'zer;[z] for he said, "Thus far the LORD has helped us." 13 So the Phi•lis'tines were subdued and did not again enter the territory of Israel; the hand of the LORD was against the Phi•lis'tines all the days of Samuel. 14 The towns that the Phi•lis'tines had taken from Israel were restored to Israel, from Ek'ron to Gath; and Israel recovered their territory from the hand of the Phi•lis'tines. There was peace also between Israel and the Am'o•rītes.

15 Samuel judged Israel all the days of his life. 16 He went on a circuit year by year to Beth'el, Gil'-gal, and Miz'pah; and he judged Israel in all these places. 17 Then he would come back to Rā'mah, for his home was there; he administered justice there to Israel, and built there an altar to the LORD.

Israel Demands a King

8 When Samuel became old, he made his sons judges over Israel. 2 The name of his firstborn son was Jō'el, and the name of his second, A•bī'jah; they were judges in Bē'er-shē'ba. 3 Yet his sons did not follow in his ways, but turned aside after gain; they took bribes and perverted justice.

4 Then all the elders of Israel gathered together and came to Samuel at Rā'mah, 5 and said to him, "You are old and your sons do not follow in your ways; appoint for us, then, a king to govern us, like other nations." 6 But the thing displeased Samuel when they said, "Give us a king to govern us." Samuel prayed to the LORD, 7 and the LORD said to Samuel, "Listen to the voice of the people in all that they say to you; for they have not rejected you, but they have rejected me from being king over them. 8 Just as they have done to me,[a] from the day I brought them up out of Egypt to this day, forsaking me and serving other gods, so also they are doing to you. 9 Now then, listen to their voice; only—you shall solemnly warn them, and show them the ways of the king who shall reign over them."

10 So Samuel reported all the words of the LORD to the people who were asking him for a king. 11 He said, "These will be the ways of the king who will reign over you: he will take your sons and appoint them to his chariots and to be his horsemen, and to run before his chariots; 12 and he will appoint for himself commanders of thousands and command-ers of fifties, and some to plow his ground and to reap his harvest, and to make his implements of war and the equipment of his chariots. 13 He will take your daughters to be perfumers and cooks and bak-ers. 14 He will take the best of your fields and vine-yards and olive orchards and give them to his courtiers. 15 He will take one-tenth of your grain and of your vineyards and give it to his officers and his courtiers. 16 He will take your male and female slaves, and the best of your cattle[b] and donkeys, and

did you KNOW?

Doublets

Often, more than one version of a story is recorded in the Bible. Genesis has two stories of the Creation (1.1—2.4; 2.4–25). The First Book of Samuel has two differ-ent attitudes toward the request to have a king in Israel. Compare the anti-king passages of 8.10–22 and 10.17–19 with the pro-king passages of 9.15–16 and chapter 11. Most likely, the difference of opinion comes from different parts of Israel. The Bible often combines two versions of a story, called doublets, to allow considera-tion of both sides of an issue.

put them to his work. 17 He will take one-tenth of your flocks, and you shall be his slaves. 18 And in that day you will cry out because of your king, whom you have chosen for yourselves; but the LORD will not answer you in that day."

Israel's Request for a King Granted

19 But the people refused to listen to the voice of Samuel; they said, "No! but we are determined to have a king over us, 20 so that we also may be like other nations, and that our king may govern us and go out before us and fight our battles." 21 When Samuel had heard all the words of the people, he repeated them in the ears of the LORD. 22 The LORD said to Samuel, "Listen to their voice and set a king over them." Samuel then said to the people of Is-rael, "Each of you return home."

Saul Chosen to Be King

9 There was a man of Benjamin whose name was Kish son of A•bī'el son of Zē'ror son of Be•cō'rath son of A•phī'ah, a Ben'ja•min•īte, a man of wealth. 2 He had a son whose name was Saul, a handsome young man. There was not a man among the people of Israel more handsome than he; he stood head and shoulders above everyone else.

3 Now the donkeys of Kish, Saul's father, had strayed. So Kish said to his son Saul, "Take one of the boys with you; go and look for the donkeys." 4 He passed through the hill country of E'phra•im and passed through the land of Shal'i•shah, but

---

[y] Gk Syr: Heb *Shen*   [z] That is *Stone of Help*   [a] Gk: Heb lacks *to me*   [b] Gk: Heb *young men*

they did not find them. And they passed through the land of Shā′a•lim, but they were not there. Then he passed through the land of Benjamin, but they did not find them.

5 When they came to the land of Zuph, Saul said to the boy who was with him, "Let us turn back, or my father will stop worrying about the donkeys and worry about us." 6 But he said to him, "There is a man of God in this town; he is a man held in honor. Whatever he says always comes true. Let us go there now; perhaps he will tell us about the journey on which we have set out." 7 Then Saul replied to the boy, "But if we go, what can we bring the man? For the bread in our sacks is gone, and there is no present to bring to the man of God. What have we?" 8 The boy answered Saul again, "Here, I have with me a quarter shekel of silver; I will give it to the man of God, to tell us our way." 9 (Formerly in Israel, anyone who went to inquire of God would say, "Come, let us go to the seer"; for the one who is now called a prophet was formerly called a seer.) 10 Saul said to the boy, "Good; come, let us go." So they went to the town where the man of God was.

11 As they went up the hill to the town, they met some girls coming out to draw water, and said to them, "Is the seer here?" 12 They answered, "Yes, there he is just ahead of you. Hurry; he has come just now to the town, because the people have a sacrifice today at the shrine. 13 As soon as you enter the town, you will find him, before he goes up to the shrine to eat. For the people will not eat until he comes, since he must bless the sacrifice; afterward those eat who are invited. Now go up, for you will meet him immediately." 14 So they went up to the town. As they were entering the town, they saw Samuel coming out toward them on his way up to the shrine.

15 Now the day before Saul came, the LORD had revealed to Samuel: 16 "Tomorrow about this time I will send to you a man from the land of Benjamin, and you shall anoint him to be ruler over my people Israel. He shall save my people from the hand of the Phi•lis′tines; for I have seen the suffering of[c] my people, because their outcry has come to me." 17 When Samuel saw Saul, the LORD told him, "Here is the man of whom I spoke to you. He it is who shall rule over my people." 18 Then Saul approached Samuel inside the gate, and said, "Tell me, please, where is the house of the seer?" 19 Samuel answered Saul, "I am the seer; go up before me to the shrine, for today you shall eat with me, and in the morning I will let you go and will tell you all that is on your mind. 20 As for your donkeys that were lost three days ago, give no further thought to them, for they have been found. And on whom is all Israel's desire fixed, if not on you and

on all your ancestral house?" 21 Saul answered, "I am only a Ben′ja•min•ite, from the least of the tribes of Israel, and my family is the humblest of all the families of the tribe of Benjamin. Why then have you spoken to me in this way?"

22 Then Samuel took Saul and his servant-boy and brought them into the hall, and gave them a place at the head of those who had been invited, of whom there were about thirty. 23 And Samuel said to the cook, "Bring the portion I gave you, the one I asked you to put aside." 24 The cook took up the thigh and what went with it[d] and set them before Saul. Samuel said, "See, what was kept is set before you. Eat; for it is set[e] before you at the appointed time, so that you might eat with the guests."[f]

So Saul ate with Samuel that day. 25 When they came down from the shrine into the town, a bed was spread for Saul[g] on the roof, and he lay down to sleep.[h] 26 Then at the break of dawn[i] Samuel called to Saul upon the roof, "Get up, so that I may send you on your way." Saul got up, and both he and Samuel went out into the street.

Samuel Anoints Saul

27 As they were going down to the outskirts of the town, Samuel said to Saul, "Tell the boy to go on before us, and when he has passed on, stop here yourself for a while, that I may make known to you

10 the word of God." 1 Samuel took a vial of oil and poured it on his head, and kissed him; he said, "The LORD has anointed you ruler over his people Israel. You shall reign over the people of the LORD and you will save them from the hand of their enemies all around. Now this shall be the sign to you that the LORD has anointed you ruler[j] over his heritage: 2 When you depart from me today you will meet two men by Rachel's tomb in the territory of Benjamin at Zel′zah; they will say to you, 'The donkeys that you went to seek are found, and now your father has stopped worrying about them and is worrying about you, saying: What shall I do about my son?' 3 Then you shall go on from there further and come to the oak of Tā′bor; three men going up to God at Beth′el will meet you there, one carrying three kids, another carrying three loaves of bread, and another carrying a skin of wine. 4 They will greet you and give you two loaves of bread, which you shall accept from them. 5 After that you shall come to Gib′ē•ath-e•lō′him,[k] at the place where the Phi•lis′tine garrison is; there, as you

---

c Gk: Heb lacks the suffering of   d Meaning of Heb uncertain   e Q Ms Gk: MT it was kept   f Cn: Heb it was kept for you, saying, I have invited the people   g Gk: Heb and he spoke with Saul   h Gk: Heb lacks and he lay down to sleep   i Gk: Heb and they arose early and at break of dawn   j Gk: Heb lacks over his people Israel. You shall . . . anointed you ruler   k Or the Hill of God

1
S
A
M

come to the town, you will meet a band of prophets coming down from the shrine with harp, tambourine, flute, and lyre playing in front of them; they will be in a prophetic frenzy. 6 Then the spirit of the LORD will possess you, and you will be in a prophetic frenzy along with them and be turned into a different person. 7 Now when these signs meet you, do whatever you see fit to do, for God is with you. 8 And you shall go down to Gil'gal ahead of me; then I will come down to you to present burnt offerings and offer sacrifices of well-being. Seven days you shall wait, until I come to you and show you what you shall do."

Saul Prophesies

9 As he turned away to leave Samuel, God gave him another heart; and all these signs were fulfilled that day. 10 When they were going from there*l* to Gib'ē·ah,*m* a band of prophets met him; and the spirit of God possessed him, and he fell into a prophetic frenzy along with them. 11 When all who knew him before saw how he prophesied with the prophets, the people said to one another, "What has come over the son of Kish? Is Saul also among the prophets?" 12 A man of the place answered, "And who is their father?" Therefore it became a proverb, "Is Saul also among the prophets?" 13 When his prophetic frenzy had ended, he went home.*n*

14 Saul's uncle said to him and to the boy, "Where did you go?" And he replied, "To seek the donkeys; and when we saw they were not to be found, we went to Samuel." 15 Saul's uncle said, "Tell me what Samuel said to you." 16 Saul said to his uncle, "He told us that the donkeys had been found." But about the matter of the kingship, of which Samuel had spoken, he did not tell him anything.

Saul Proclaimed King

17 Samuel summoned the people to the LORD at Miz'pah 18 and said to them,*o* "Thus says the LORD, the God of Israel, 'I brought up Israel out of Egypt, and I rescued you from the hand of the Egyptians and from the hand of all the kingdoms that were oppressing you.' 19 But today you have rejected your God, who saves you from all your calamities and your distresses; and you have said, 'No! but set a king over us.' Now therefore present yourselves before the LORD by your tribes and by your clans."

20 Then Samuel brought all the tribes of Israel near, and the tribe of Benjamin was taken by lot. 21 He brought the tribe of Benjamin near by its families, and the family of the Mā'trites was taken by lot. Finally he brought the family of the Mā'trites near man by man,*p* and Saul the son of Kish was taken by lot. But when they sought him, he could not be found. 22 So they inquired again of the LORD, "Did the man come here?"*q* and the LORD said, "See, he has hidden himself among the baggage." 23 Then they ran and brought him from there. When he took his stand among the people, he was head and shoulders taller than any of them. 24 Samuel said to all the people, "Do you see the one whom the LORD has chosen? There is no one like him among all the people." And all the people shouted, "Long live the king!"

25 Samuel told the people the rights and duties of the kingship; and he wrote them in a book and laid it up before the LORD. Then Samuel sent all the people back to their homes. 26 Saul also went to his home at Gib'ē·ah, and with him went warriors whose hearts God had touched. 27 But some worthless fellows said, "How can this man save us?" They despised him and brought him no present. But he held his peace.

Now Nā'hash, king of the Am'mon·ites, had been grievously oppressing the Gad'ites and the Reū'ben·ites. He would gouge out the right eye of each of them and would not grant Israel a deliverer. No one was left of the Israelites across the Jordan whose right eye Nā'hash, king of the Am'mon·ites, had not gouged out. But there were seven thousand men who had escaped from the Am'mon·ites and had entered Jā'besh-gil'ē·ad.*r*

Saul Defeats the Ammonites

11 About a month later,*s* Nā'hash the Am'-mon·ite went up and besieged Jā'besh-gil'ē·ad; and all the men of Jā'besh said to Nā'hash, "Make a treaty with us, and we will serve you." 2 But Nā'hash the Am'mon·ite said to them, "On this condition I will make a treaty with you, namely that I gouge out everyone's right eye, and thus put disgrace upon all Israel." 3 The elders of Jā'besh said to him, "Give us seven days' respite that we may send messengers through all the territory of Israel. Then, if there is no one to save us, we will give ourselves up to you." 4 When the messengers came to Gib'ē·ah of Saul, they reported the matter in the hearing of the people; and all the people wept aloud.

5 Now Saul was coming from the field behind the oxen; and Saul said, "What is the matter with the people, that they are weeping?" So they told him the message from the inhabitants of Jā'besh. 6 And the spirit of God came upon Saul in power when he heard these words, and his anger was

---

l Gk: Heb *they came there* *m* Or *the hill* *n* Cn: Heb *he came to the shrine* *o* Heb *to the people of Israel* *p* Gk: Heb lacks *Finally . . . man by man* *q* Gk: Heb *Is there yet a man to come here?* *r* Q Ms Compare Josephus, *Antiquities* VI.v.1 (68-71): MT lacks *Now Nahash . . . entered Jabesh-gilead.* *s* Q Ms Gk: MT lacks *About a month later* greatly kindled. 7 He took a yoke of oxen, and cut them in pieces and sent them throughout all the territory of Israel by messengers, saying, "Whoever does not come out after Saul and Samuel, so shall it be done to his oxen!" Then the dread of the LORD fell upon the people, and they came out as one. 8 When he mustered them at Bē′zek, those from Israel were three hundred thousand, and those from Judah seventy[t] thousand. 9 They said to the messengers who had come, "Thus shall you say to the inhabitants of Jā′besh-gil′e·ad: 'Tomorrow, by the time the sun is hot, you shall have deliverance.' " When the messengers came and told the inhabitants of Jā′besh, they rejoiced. 10 So the inhabitants of Jā′besh said, "Tomorrow we will give ourselves up to you, and you may do to us whatever seems good to you." 11 The next day Saul put the people in three companies. At the morning watch they came into the camp and cut down the Am′mon·ites until the heat of the day; and those who survived were scattered, so that no two of them were left together.

12 The people said to Samuel, "Who is it that said, 'Shall Saul reign over us?' Give them to us so that we may put them to death." 13 But Saul said, "No one shall be put to death this day, for today the LORD has brought deliverance to Israel."

14 Samuel said to the people, "Come, let us go to Gil′gal and there renew the kingship." 15 So all the people went to Gil′gal, and there they made Saul king before the LORD in Gil′gal. There they sacrificed offerings of well-being before the LORD, and there Saul and all the Israelites rejoiced greatly.

Samuel's Farewell Address

12 Samuel said to all Israel, "I have listened to you in all that you have said to me, and have set a king over you. 2 See, it is the king who leads you now; I am old and gray, but my sons are with you. I have led you from my youth until this day. 3 Here I am; testify against me before the LORD and before his anointed. Whose ox have I taken? Or whose donkey have I taken? Or whom have I defrauded? Whom have I oppressed? Or from whose hand have I taken a bribe to blind my eyes with it? Testify against me[u] and I will restore it to you." 4 They said, "You have not defrauded us or oppressed us or taken anything from the hand of anyone." 5 He said to them, "The LORD is witness against you, and his anointed is witness this day, that you have not found anything in my hand." And they said, "He is witness."

6 Samuel said to the people, "The LORD is witness, who[v] appointed Moses and Aaron and brought your ancestors up out of the land of Egypt. 7 Now therefore take your stand, so that I may enter into judgment with you before the LORD, and I will declare to you[w] all the saving deeds of the LORD

that he performed for you and for your ancestors. 8 When Jacob went into Egypt and the Egyptians oppressed them,[x] then your ancestors cried to the LORD and the LORD sent Moses and Aaron, who brought forth your ancestors out of Egypt, and settled them in this place. 9 But they forgot the LORD their God; and he sold them into the hand of Sis′e·ra, commander of the army of King Jā′bin of[y] Hā′zor, and into the hand of the Phi·lis′tines, and into the hand of the king of Mō′ab; and they fought against them. 10 Then they cried to the LORD, and said, 'We have sinned, because we have forsaken the LORD, and have served the Bā′als and the As·tar′tēs; but now rescue us out of the hand of our enemies, and we will serve you.' 11 And the LORD sent Jer·ub·bā′al and Bar′ak,[z] and Jeph′thah, and Samson,[a] and rescued you out of the hand of your enemies on every side; and you lived in safety. 12 But when you saw that King Nā′hash of the Am′mon·ites came against you, you said to me, 'No, but a king shall reign over us,' though the LORD your God was your king. 13 See, here is the king whom you have chosen, for whom you have asked; see, the LORD has set a king over you. 14 If you will fear the LORD and serve him and heed his voice and not rebel against the commandment of the LORD, and if both you and the king who reigns over you will follow the LORD your God, it will be well; 15 but if you will not heed the voice of the LORD, but rebel against the commandment of the LORD, then the hand of the LORD will be against you and your king.[b] 16 Now therefore take your stand and see this great thing that the LORD will do before your eyes. 17 Is it not the wheat harvest today? I will call upon the LORD, that he may send thunder and rain; and you shall know and see that the wickedness that you have done in the sight of the LORD is great in demanding a king for yourselves." 18 So Samuel called upon the LORD, and the LORD sent thunder and rain that day; and all the people greatly feared the LORD and Samuel.

19 All the people said to Samuel, "Pray to the LORD your God for your servants, so that we may not die; for we have added to all our sins the evil of demanding a king for ourselves." 20 And Samuel said to the people, "Do not be afraid; you have done all this evil, yet do not turn aside from following the LORD, but serve the LORD with all your heart; 21 and do not turn aside after useless things that cannot profit or save, for they are useless. 22 For the LORD will not cast away his people, for

---

t Q Ms Gk: MT *thirty*   u Gk: Heb lacks *Testify against me*
v Gk: Heb lacks *is witness, who*   w Gk: Heb lacks *and I will
declare to you*   x Gk: Heb lacks *and the Egyptians oppressed
them*   y Gk: Heb lacks *King Jabin of*   z Gk Syr: Heb *Bedan*
a Gk: Heb *Samuel*   b Gk: Heb *and your ancestors*

his great name's sake, because it has pleased the LORD to make you a people for himself. 23 Moreover as for me, far be it from me that I should sin against the LORD by ceasing to pray for you; and I will instruct you in the good and the right way. 24 Only fear the LORD, and serve him faithfully with all your heart; for consider what great things he has done for you. 25 But if you still do wickedly, you shall be swept away, both you and your king."

Saul's Unlawful Sacrifice

13 Saul was . . .c years old when he began to reign; and he reigned . . . and twod years over Israel.

2 Saul chose three thousand out of Israel; two thousand were with Saul in Mich'mash and the hill country of Beth'el, and a thousand were with Jonathan in Gib'ě·ah of Benjamin; the rest of the people he sent home to their tents. 3 Jonathan defeated the garrison of the Phi·lis'tines that was at Gě'ba; and the Phi·lis'tines heard of it. And Saul blew the trumpet throughout all the land, saying, "Let the Hebrews hear!" 4 When all Israel heard that Saul had defeated the garrison of the Phi·lis'tines, and also that Israel had become odious to the Phi·lis'tines, the people were called out to join Saul at Gil'gal.

5 The Phi·lis'tines mustered to fight with Israel, thirty thousand chariots, and six thousand horsemen, and troops like the sand on the seashore in multitude; they came up and encamped at Mich'-mash, to the east of Beth-a'ven. 6 When the Israelites saw that they were in distress (for the troops were hard pressed), the people hid themselves in caves and in holes and in rocks and in tombs and in cisterns. 7 Some Hebrews crossed the Jordan to the land of Gad and Gil'e·ad. Saul was still at Gil'-gal, and all the people followed him trembling.

8 He waited seven days, the time appointed by Samuel; but Samuel did not come to Gil'gal, and the people began to slip away from Saul.e 9 So Saul said, "Bring the burnt offering here to me, and the offerings of well-being." And he offered the burnt offering. 10 As soon as he had finished offering the burnt offering, Samuel arrived; and Saul went out to meet him and salute him. 11 Samuel said, "What have you done?" Saul replied, "When I saw that the people were slipping away from me, and that you did not come within the days appointed, and that the Phi·lis'tines were mustering at Mich'mash, 12 I said, 'Now the Phi·lis'tines will come down upon me at Gil'gal, and I have not entreated the favor of the LORD'; so I forced myself, and offered the burnt offering." 13 Samuel said to Saul, "You have done foolishly; you have not kept the commandment of the LORD your God, which he commanded you. The LORD would have established your kingdom

over Israel forever, 14 but now your kingdom will not continue; the LORD has sought out a man after his own heart; and the LORD has appointed him to be ruler over his people, because you have not kept what the LORD commanded you." 15 And Samuel left and went on his way from Gil'gal.f The rest of the people followed Saul to join the army; they went up from Gil'gal toward Gib'ě·ah of Benjamin.g

Preparations for Battle

Saul counted the people who were present with him, about six hundred men. 16 Saul, his son Jonathan, and the people who were present with them stayed in Gě'ba of Benjamin; but the Phi·lis'tines encamped at Mich'mash. 17 And raiders came out of the camp of the Phi·lis'tines in three companies; one company turned toward Oph'rah, to the land of Shū'al, 18 another company turned toward Beth-hō'ron, and another company turned toward the mountainh that looks down upon the valley of Ze·bō'im toward the wilderness.

19 Now there was no smith to be found throughout all the land of Israel; for the Phi·lis'-tines said, "The Hebrews must not make swords or spears for themselves"; 20 so all the Israelites went down to the Phi·lis'tines to sharpen their plow-shares, mattocks, axes, or sickles;i 21 The charge was two-thirds of a shekelj for the plowshares and for the mattocks, and one-third of a shekel for sharpening the axes and for setting the goads.k 22 So on the day of the battle neither sword nor spear was to be found in the possession of any of the people with Saul and Jonathan; but Saul and his son Jonathan had them.

Jonathan Surprises and Routs the Philistines

14 23 Now a garrison of the Phi·lis'tines had gone out to the pass of Mich'mash. 1 One day Jonathan son of Saul said to the young man who carried his armor, "Come, let us go over to the Phi·lis'tine garrison on the other side." But he did not tell his father. 2 Saul was staying in the outskirts of Gib'ě·ah under the pomegranate tree that is at Mig'ron; the troops that were with him were about six hundred men, 3 along with A·hī'jah son of A·hī'tub, Ich'a·bod's brother, son of Phin'e·has son of Ē'lī, the priest of the LORD in Shī'lōh, carrying an ephod. Now the people did not know that Jonathan had gone. 4 In the pass,l by which Jonathan tried to go over to the Phi·lis'tine

---

c The number is lacking in the Heb text (the verse is lacking in the Septuagint).   d Two is not the entire number; something has dropped out.   e Heb him   f Gk: Heb went up from Gilgal to Gibeah of Benjamin   g Gk: Heb lacks The rest . . . of Benjamin   h Cn Compare Gk: Heb toward the border   i Gk: Heb plowshare   j Heb was a pim   k Cn: Meaning of Heb uncertain   l Heb Between the passes garrison, there was a rocky crag on one side and a rocky crag on the other; the name of the one was Bō′zez, and the name of the other Sĕ′neh. 5 One crag rose on the north in front of Mich′mash, and the other on the south in front of Gĕ′ba.

6 Jonathan said to the young man who carried his armor, "Come, let us go over to the garrison of these uncircumcised; it may be that the LORD will act for us; for nothing can hinder the LORD from saving by many or by few." 7 His armor-bearer said to him, "Do all that your mind inclines to.*m* I am with you; as your mind is, so is mine."*n* 8 Then Jonathan said, "Now we will cross over to those men and will show ourselves to them. 9 If they say to us, 'Wait until we come to you,' then we will stand still in our place, and we will not go up to them. 10 But if they say, 'Come up to us,' then we will go up; for the LORD has given them into our hand. That will be the sign for us." 11 So both of them showed themselves to the garrison of the Phi·lis′tines; and the Phi·lis′tines said, "Look, Hebrews are coming out of the holes where they have hidden themselves." 12 The men of the garrison hailed Jonathan and his armor-bearer, saying, "Come up to us, and we will show you something." Jonathan said to his armor-bearer, "Come up after me; for the LORD has given them into the hand of Israel." 13 Then Jonathan climbed up on his hands and feet, with his armor-bearer following after him. The Phi·lis′tines*o* fell before Jonathan, and his armor-bearer, coming after him, killed them. 14 In that first slaughter Jonathan and his armor-bearer killed about twenty men within an area about half a furrow long in an acre*p* of land. 15 There was a panic in the camp, in the field, and among all the people; the garrison and even the raiders trembled; the earth quaked; and it became a very great panic.

16 Saul's lookouts in Gib′ē·ah of Benjamin were watching as the multitude was surging back and forth.*q* 17 Then Saul said to the troops that were with him, "Call the roll and see who has gone from us." When they had called the roll, Jonathan and his armor-bearer were not there. 18 Saul said to A·hi′jah, "Bring the ark*r* of God here." For at that time the ark*r* of God went with the Israelites. 19 While Saul was talking to the priest, the tumult in the camp of the Phi·lis′tines increased more and more; and Saul said to the priest, "Withdraw your hand." 20 Then Saul and all the people who were with him rallied and went into the battle; and every sword was against the other, so that there was very great confusion. 21 Now the Hebrews who previously had been with the Phi·lis′tines and had gone up with them into the camp turned and joined the Israelites who were with Saul and Jonathan. 22 Likewise, when all the Israelites who had gone into hiding in the hill country of Ē′phra·im heard

that the Phi·lis′tines were fleeing, they too followed closely after them in the battle. 23 So the LORD gave Israel the victory that day.

The battle passed beyond Beth-a′ven, and the troops with Saul numbered altogether about ten thousand men. The battle spread out over the hill country of Ē′phra·im.

Saul's Rash Oath

24 Now Saul committed a very rash act on that day.*s* He had laid an oath on the troops, saying, "Cursed be anyone who eats food before it is evening and I have been avenged on my enemies." So none of the troops tasted food. 25 All the troops*t* came upon a honeycomb; and there was honey on the ground. 26 When the troops came upon the honeycomb, the honey was dripping out; but they did not put their hands to their mouths, for they feared the oath. 27 But Jonathan had not heard his father charge the troops with the oath; so he extended the staff that was in his hand, and dipped the tip of it in the honeycomb, and put his hand to his mouth; and his eyes brightened. 28 Then one of the soldiers said, "Your father strictly charged the troops with an oath, saying, 'Cursed be anyone who eats food this day.' And so the troops are faint." 29 Then Jonathan said, "My father has troubled the land; see how my eyes have brightened because I tasted a little of this honey. 30 How much better if today the troops had eaten freely of the spoil taken from their enemies; for now the slaughter among the Phi·lis′tines has not been great."

31 After they had struck down the Phi·lis′tines that day from Mich′mash to Aï′ja·lon, the troops were very faint; 32 so the troops flew upon the spoil, and took sheep and oxen and calves, and slaughtered them on the ground; and the troops ate them with the blood. 33 Then it was reported to Saul, "Look, the troops are sinning against the LORD by eating with the blood." And he said, "You have dealt treacherously; roll a large stone before me here."*u* 34 Saul said, "Disperse yourselves among the troops, and say to them, 'Let all bring their oxen or their sheep, and slaughter them here, and eat; and do not sin against the LORD by eating with the blood.' " So all of the troops brought their oxen with them that night, and slaughtered them there. 35 And Saul built an altar to the LORD; it was the first altar that he built to the LORD.

Jonathan in Danger of Death

36 Then Saul said, "Let us go down after the Phi·lis′tines by night and despoil them until the

---

m Gk: Heb *Do all that is in your mind. Turn*　*n* Gk: Heb lacks *so is mine*　*o* Heb *They*　*p* Heb *yoke*　*q* Gk: Heb *they went and there*　*r* Gk *the ephod*　*s* Gk: Heb *The Israelites were distressed that day*　*t* Heb *land*　*u* Gk: Heb *me this day* morning light; let us not leave one of them." They said, "Do whatever seems good to you." But the priest said, "Let us draw near to God here." ³⁷ So Saul inquired of God, "Shall I go down after the Phi·lis′tines? Will you give them into the hand of Israel?" But he did not answer him that day. ³⁸ Saul said, "Come here, all you leaders of the people; and let us find out how this sin has arisen today. ³⁹ For as the LORD lives who saves Israel, even if it is in my son Jonathan, he shall surely die!" But there was no one among all the people who answered him. ⁴⁰ He said to all Israel, "You shall be on one side, and I and my son Jonathan will be on the other side." The people said to Saul, "Do what seems good to you." ⁴¹ Then Saul said, "O LORD God of Israel, why have you not answered your servant today? If this guilt is in me or in my son Jonathan, O LORD God of Israel, give Ūʹrim; but if this guilt is in your people Israel,ᵛ give Thumʹmim." And Jonathan and Saul were indicated by the lot, but the people were cleared. ⁴² Then Saul said, "Cast the lot between me and my son Jonathan." And Jonathan was taken.

⁴³ Then Saul said to Jonathan, "Tell me what you have done." Jonathan told him, "I tasted a little honey with the tip of the staff that was in my hand; here I am, I will die." ⁴⁴ Saul said, "God do so to me and more also; you shall surely die, Jonathan!" ⁴⁵ Then the people said to Saul, "Shall Jonathan die, who has accomplished this great victory in Israel? Far from it! As the LORD lives, not one hair of his head shall fall to the ground; for he has worked with God today." So the people ransomed Jonathan, and he did not die. ⁴⁶ Then Saul withdrew from pursuing the Phi·lis′tines; and the Phi·lis′tines went to their own place.

Saul's Continuing Wars

⁴⁷ When Saul had taken the kingship over Israel, he fought against all his enemies on every side—against Mōʹab, against the Am′mon·ites, against Ēʹdom, against the kings of Zōʹbah, and against the Phi·lis′tines; wherever he turned he routed them. ⁴⁸ He did valiantly, and struck down the A·malʹe·kītes, and rescued Israel out of the hands of those who plundered them.

⁴⁹ Now the sons of Saul were Jonathan, Ishʹvī, and Mal·chi·shūʹa; and the names of his two daughters were these: the name of the firstborn was Mēʹrab, and the name of the younger, Miʹchal. ⁵⁰ The name of Saul's wife was A·hin′ō·am daughter of A·him′a·az. And the name of the commander of his army was Abner son of Ner, Saul's uncle; ⁵¹ Kish was the father of Saul, and Ner the father of Abner was the son of A·biʹel.

⁵² There was hard fighting against the Phi·lis′tines all the days of Saul; and when Saul saw any strong or valiant warrior, he took him into his service.

Saul Defeats the Amalekites but Spares Their King

15 Samuel said to Saul, "The LORD sent me to anoint you king over his people Israel; now therefore listen to the words of the LORD. ² Thus says the LORD of hosts, 'I will punish the A·malʹe·kītes for what they did in opposing the Israelites when they came up out of Egypt. ³ Now go and attack Am′a·lek, and utterly destroy all that they have; do not spare them, but kill both man and woman, child and infant, ox and sheep, camel and donkey.' "

⁴ So Saul summoned the people, and numbered them in Te·lāʹim, two hundred thousand foot soldiers, and ten thousand soldiers of Judah. ⁵ Saul came to the city of the A·malʹe·kītes and lay in wait in the valley. ⁶ Saul said to the Ken′ītes, "Go! Leave! Withdraw from among the A·malʹe·kītes, or I will

---

ᵛ Vg Compare Gk: Heb ⁴¹*Saul said to the LORD, the God of Israel*

Power and Corruption

Power corrupts. We have often heard that phrase. And in 1 Sam 15.22–23, we have a vivid example. King Saul once again has decided to take matters in his own hands and goes against the word of the LORD. He seems to assume that his role as king exempts him from obedience to God. But Samuel reminds Saul that he has assumed way too much. No king, no president, no prime minster is above the law. Especially when that Law comes from God.

Have you ever been in a position of leadership and been tempted to abuse your privileges?

▸ **1 Sam 15.22–23**

destroy you with them; for you showed kindness to all the people of Israel when they came up out of Egypt." So the Ken′ites withdrew from the A•mal′-e•kītes. 7 Saul defeated the A•mal′e•kītes, from Hav′i•lah as far as Shur, which is east of Egypt. 8 He took King Ā′gag of the A•mal′e•kītes alive, but utterly destroyed all the people with the edge of the sword. 9 Saul and the people spared Ā′gag, and the best of the sheep and of the cattle and of the fatlings, and the lambs, and all that was valuable, and would not utterly destroy them; all that was despised and worthless they utterly destroyed.

Saul Rejected as King

10 The word of the LORD came to Samuel: 11 "I regret that I made Saul king, for he has turned back from following me, and has not carried out my commands." Samuel was angry; and he cried out to the LORD all night. 12 Samuel rose early in the morning to meet Saul, and Samuel was told, "Saul went to Car′mel, where he set up a monument for himself, and on returning he passed on down to Gil′gal." 13 When Samuel came to Saul, Saul said to him, "May you be blessed by the LORD; I have carried out the command of the LORD." 14 But Samuel said, "What then is this bleating of sheep in my ears, and the lowing of cattle that I hear?" 15 Saul said, "They have brought them from the A•mal′e•kītes; for the people spared the best of the sheep and the cattle, to sacrifice to the LORD your God; but the rest we have utterly destroyed." 16 Then Samuel said to Saul, "Stop! I will tell you what the LORD said to me last night." He replied, "Speak."

17 Samuel said, "Though you are little in your own eyes, are you not the head of the tribes of Israel? The LORD anointed you king over Israel. 18 And the LORD sent you on a mission, and said, 'Go, utterly destroy the sinners, the A•mal′e•kītes, and fight against them until they are consumed.' 19 Why then did you not obey the voice of the LORD? Why did you swoop down on the spoil, and do what was evil in the sight of the LORD?" 20 Saul said to Samuel, "I have obeyed the voice of the LORD, I have gone on the mission on which the LORD sent me, I have brought Ā′gag the king of Am′a•lek, and I have utterly destroyed the A•mal′e•kītes. 21 But from the spoil the people took sheep and cattle, the best of the things devoted to destruction, to sacrifice to the LORD your God in Gil′gal." 22 And Samuel said,

"Has the LORD as great delight in burnt
    offerings and sacrifices,
      as in obedience to the voice of the LORD?
Surely, to obey is better than sacrifice,
    and to heed than the fat of rams.
23 For rebellion is no less a sin than divination,

and stubbornness is like iniquity and
    idolatry.
Because you have rejected the word of the
    LORD,
    he has also rejected you from being king."

24 Saul said to Samuel, "I have sinned; for I have transgressed the commandment of the LORD and your words, because I feared the people and obeyed their voice. 25 Now therefore, I pray, pardon my sin, and return with me, so that I may worship the LORD." 26 Samuel said to Saul, "I will not return with you; for you have rejected the word of the LORD, and the LORD has rejected you from being king over Israel." 27 As Samuel turned to go away, Saul caught hold of the hem of his robe, and it tore. 28 And Samuel said to him, "The LORD has torn the kingdom of Israel from you this very day, and has given it to a neighbor of yours, who is better than you. 29 Moreover the Glory of Israel will not recant[w] or change his mind; for he is not a mortal, that he should change his mind." 30 Then Saul[x] said, "I have sinned; yet honor me now before the elders of my people and before Israel, and return with me, so that I may worship the LORD your God." 31 So Samuel turned back after Saul; and Saul worshiped the LORD.

32 Then Samuel said, "Bring Ā′gag king of the A•mal′e•kītes here to me." And Ā′gag came to him haltingly.[y] Ā′gag said, "Surely this is the bitterness of death."[z] 33 But Samuel said,

"As your sword has made women childless,
    so your mother shall be childless among
      women."
And Samuel hewed Ā′gag in pieces before the LORD in Gil′gal.

34 Then Samuel went to Rā′mah; and Saul went up to his house in Gib′ē•ah of Saul. 35 Samuel did not see Saul again until the day of his death, but Samuel grieved over Saul. And the LORD was sorry that he had made Saul king over Israel.

David Anointed as King

16 The LORD said to Samuel, "How long will you grieve over Saul? I have rejected him from being king over Israel. Fill your horn with oil and set out; I will send you to Jesse the Beth′le•hem•ite, for I have provided for myself a king among his sons." 2 Samuel said, "How can I go? If Saul hears of it, he will kill me." And the LORD said, "Take a heifer with you, and say, 'I have come to sacrifice to the LORD.' 3 Invite Jesse to the sacrifice, and I will show you what you shall do; and you shall anoint for me the one whom I name

1
S
A
M

---

w Q Ms Gk: MT *deceive*   x Heb *he*   y Cn Compare Gk: Meaning of Heb uncertain   z Q Ms Gk: MT *Surely the bitterness of death is past* to you." 4 Samuel did what the LORD commanded, and came to Bethlehem. The elders of the city came to meet him trembling, and said, "Do you come peaceably?" 5 He said, "Peaceably; I have come to sacrifice to the LORD; sanctify yourselves and come with me to the sacrifice." And he sanctified Jesse and his sons and invited them to the sacrifice.

6 When they came, he looked on E·li′ab and thought, "Surely the LORD's anointed is now before the LORD."*a* 7 But the LORD said to Samuel, "Do not look on his appearance or on the height of his stature, because I have rejected him; for the LORD does not see as mortals see; they look on the outward appearance, but the LORD looks on the heart."

But the LORD said to Samuel, "Do not look on his appearance or on the height of his stature, because I have rejected him; for the LORD does not see as mortals see; they look on the outward appearance, but the LORD looks on the heart. 16.7

8 Then Jesse called A·bin′a·dab, and made him pass before Samuel. He said, "Neither has the LORD chosen this one." 9 Then Jesse made Sham′mah pass by. And he said, "Neither has the LORD chosen this one." 10 Jesse made seven of his sons pass before Samuel, and Samuel said to Jesse, "The LORD has not chosen any of these." 11 Samuel said to Jesse, "Are all your sons here?" And he said, "There remains yet the youngest, but he is keeping the sheep." And Samuel said to Jesse, "Send and bring him; for we will not sit down until he comes here." 12 He sent and brought him in. Now he was ruddy, and had beautiful eyes, and was handsome. The LORD said, "Rise and anoint him; for this is the one." 13 Then Samuel took the horn of oil, and anointed him in the presence of his brothers; and the spirit of the LORD came mightily upon David from that day forward. Samuel then set out and went to Rā′mah.

David Plays the Lyre for Saul

14 Now the spirit of the LORD departed from Saul, and an evil spirit from the LORD tormented him. 15 And Saul's servants said to him, "See now, an evil spirit from God is tormenting you. 16 Let our lord now command the servants who attend you to look for someone who is skillful in playing the lyre; and when the evil spirit from God is upon you, he will play it, and you will feel better." 17 So Saul said to his servants, "Provide for me someone who can play well, and bring him to me." 18 One of the young men answered, "I have seen a son of Jesse the Beth′le·hem·īte who is skillful in playing, a man of valor, a warrior, prudent in speech, and a man of good presence; and the LORD is with him." 19 So Saul sent messengers to Jesse, and said, "Send me your son David who is with the sheep." 20 Jesse took a donkey loaded with bread, a skin of wine, and a kid, and sent them by his son David to Saul. 21 And David came to Saul, and entered his service. Saul loved him greatly, and he became his armor-bearer. 22 Saul sent to Jesse, saying, "Let David remain in my service, for he has found favor in my sight." 23 And whenever the evil spirit from God came upon Saul, David took the lyre and played it with his hand, and Saul would be relieved and feel better, and the evil spirit would depart from him.

David and Goliath

17 Now the Phi·lis′tines gathered their armies for battle; they were gathered at Sō′cōh, which belongs to Judah, and encamped between Sō′cōh and A·zē′kah, in Ē′phes-dam′mim. 2 Saul and the Israelites gathered and encamped in the valley of Ē′lah, and formed ranks against the Phi·lis′tines. 3 The Phi·lis′tines stood on the mountain on the one side, and Israel stood on the mountain on the other side, with a valley between them. 4 And there came out from the camp of the Phi·lis′tines a champion named Goliath, of Gath, whose height was six*b* cubits and a span. 5 He had a helmet of bronze on his head, and he was armed with a coat of mail; the weight of the coat was five thousand shekels of bronze. 6 He had greaves of bronze on his legs and a javelin of bronze slung between his shoulders. 7 The shaft of his spear was like a weaver's beam, and his spear's head weighed six hundred shekels of iron; and his shield-bearer went before him. 8 He stood and shouted to the ranks of Israel, "Why have you come out to draw up for battle? Am I not a Phi·lis′tine, and are you not servants of Saul? Choose a man for yourselves, and let him come down to me. 9 If he is able to fight with me and kill me, then we will be your servants; but if I prevail against him and kill him, then you

---

a Heb *him*   *b* MT: Q Ms Gk *four*

16.13

of Jesse had followed Saul to the battle; the names of his three sons who went to the battle were E·li'ab the firstborn, and next to him A·bin'adab, and the third Sham'mah. 14 David was the youngest; the three eldest followed Saul, 15 but David went back and forth from Saul to feed his father's sheep at Bethlehem. 16 For forty days the Phi·lis'tine came forward and took his stand, morning and evening.

17 Jesse said to his son David, "Take for your brothers an ephah of this parched grain and these ten loaves, and carry them quickly to the camp to your brothers; 18 also take these ten cheeses to the commander of their thousand. See how your brothers fare, and bring some token from them."

19 Now Saul, and they, and all the men of Israel, were in the valley of E'lah, fighting with the Phi·lis'tines. 20 David rose early in the morning, left the sheep with a keeper, took the provisions, and went as Jesse had commanded him. He came to the encampment as the army was going forth to the battle line, shouting the war cry. 21 Israel and the Phi·lis'tines drew up for battle, army against army. 22 David left the things in charge of the keeper of the baggage, ran to the ranks, and went and greeted his brothers. 23 As he talked with them, the champion, the Phi·lis'tine of Gath, Goliath by name, came up

shall be our servants and serve us." 10 And the Phi·lis'tine said, "Today I defy the ranks of Israel! Give me a man, that we may fight together." 11 When Saul and all Israel heard these words of the Phi·lis'tine, they were dismayed and greatly afraid.

12 Now David was the son of an Eph'ra·thite of Bethlehem in Judah, named Jesse, who had eight sons. In the days of Saul the man was already old and advanced in years.*c* 13 The three eldest sons

---

c Gk Syr: Heb *among men*

1
S
A
M

Introducing ▶DAVID

Who cannot love David? This shepherd-turned-king is one of the great tragic heroes of the Old Testament. David, whose name means "beloved," was the successor to Saul and the second king (1000–961 B.C.) of the new nation formed out of the twelve tribes of Israel. The youngest son of Jesse of the tribe of Judah, David was a member of Saul's court as a young man. Later, when Saul disappointed God, Samuel the prophet anointed David as Saul's successor. After Saul was killed, David established the neutral city of Jerusalem as his capital (see map 3, "The Kingdom Years"). He moved the ark of the LORD there, making this city the new religious center of Israel. Jerusalem is also known as the City of David.

David was a successful warrior, a capable king, and a gifted poet, having himself written some of the Psalms. He was also capable of great sin. His affair with Bathsheba seemed to lead to a string of violence and betrayal affecting his whole family. One of his sons, Absalom, even inspired a revolt against David. But through it all, David was passionately in love with God. God recognized this and promised David that someone from his house would sit upon the throne in Israel.

When Israel was destroyed and its kings taken prisoners, the people developed a hope that another anointed one, a messiah from the house of David, would rise up and lead Israel in God's ways once again. It is this hope for the Davidic messiah that is fulfilled by Jesus in the New Testament.

out of the ranks of the Phi·lis'tines, and spoke the same words as before. And David heard him.

24 All the Israelites, when they saw the man, fled from him and were very much afraid. 25 The Israelites said, "Have you seen this man who has come up? Surely he has come up to defy Israel. The king will greatly enrich the man who kills him, and will give him his daughter and make his family free in Israel." 26 David said to the men who stood by him, "What shall be done for the man who kills this Phi·lis'tine, and takes away the reproach from Israel? For who is this uncircumcised Phi·lis'tine that he should defy the armies of the living God?" 27 The people answered him in the same way, "So shall it be done for the man who kills him."

28 His eldest brother E·li'ab heard him talking to the men; and E·li'ab's anger was kindled against David. He said, "Why have you come down? With whom have you left those few sheep in the wilderness? I know your presumption and the evil of your heart; for you have come down just to see the battle." 29 David said, "What have I done now? It was only a question." 30 He turned away from him toward another and spoke in the same way; and the people answered him again as before.

31 When the words that David spoke were heard, they repeated them before Saul; and he sent for him. 32 David said to Saul, "Let no one's heart fail because of him; your servant will go and fight with this Phi·lis'tine." 33 Saul said to David, "You are not able to go against this Phi·lis'tine to fight with him; for you are just a boy, and he has been a warrior from his youth." 34 But David said to Saul, "Your servant used to keep sheep for his father; and whenever a lion or a bear came, and took a lamb from the flock, 35 I went after it and struck it down, rescuing the lamb from its mouth; and if it turned against me, I would catch it by the jaw, strike it down, and kill it. 36 Your servant has killed both lions and bears; and this uncircumcised Phi·lis'tine shall be like one of them, since he has defied the armies of the living God." 37 David said, "The LORD, who saved me from the paw of the lion and from the paw of the bear, will save me from the hand of this Phi·lis'tine." So Saul said to David, "Go, and may the LORD be with you!"

38 Saul clothed David with his armor; he put a bronze helmet on his head and clothed him with a coat of mail. 39 David strapped Saul's sword over the armor, and he tried in vain to walk, for he was not used to them. Then David said to Saul, "I cannot walk with these; for I am not used to them." So David removed them. 40 Then he took his staff in his hand, and chose five smooth stones from the wadi, and put them in his shepherd's bag, in the pouch; his sling was in his hand, and he drew near to the Phi·lis'tine.

41 The Phi·lis'tine came on and drew near to David, with his shield-bearer in front of him. 42 When the Phi·lis'tine looked and saw David, he disdained him, for he was only a youth, ruddy and handsome in appearance. 43 The Phi·lis'tine said to David, "Am I a dog, that you come to me with sticks?" And the Phi·lis'tine cursed David by his gods. 44 The Phi·lis'tine said to David, "Come to me, and I will give your flesh to the birds of the air and to the wild animals of the field." 45 But David said to the Phi·lis'tine, "You come to me with sword and spear and javelin; but I come to you in the name of the LORD of hosts, the God of the armies of Israel, whom you have defied. 46 This very day the LORD will deliver you into my hand, and I will strike you down and cut off your head; and I will give the dead bodies of the Phi·lis'tine army

Taking On Goliath

David makes it look so easy. A slingshot, a stone, a skillful aim, and it is all over. Goliath is dead, and the Israelites win the day. It is a story that gives hope to anyone who has ever been bullied or harassed.

A David lives in each of us, and plenty of Goliaths are out there ready to defeat us. The Goliaths we encounter can include peer pressure, an addiction, an abusive situation, or simply self-doubt. We may feel overpowered by these Goliaths, sure that they are too big for us to handle. But they are not! Those of us who believe in God, as David did, know that we are not alone. As followers of Jesus, we rely not on violence but on love and the support of the Christian community to defeat the Goliaths in our life. We can make David's story our own.

Identify a Goliath in your life right now, and journal about it. What stepping-stone can you take in defeating it?

▶ 1 Samuel, chapter 17

this very day to the birds of the air and to the wild animals of the earth, so that all the earth may know that there is a God in Israel, 47 and that all this assembly may know that the LORD does not save by sword and spear; for the battle is the LORD's and he will give you into our hand."

48 When the Phi•lis'tine drew nearer to meet David, David ran quickly toward the battle line to meet the Phi•lis'tine. 49 David put his hand in his bag, took out a stone, slung it, and struck the Phi•lis'tine on his forehead; the stone sank into his forehead, and he fell face down on the ground.

50 So David prevailed over the Phi•lis'tine with a sling and a stone, striking down the Phi•lis'tine and killing him; there was no sword in David's hand. 51 Then David ran and stood over the Phi•lis'-tine; he grasped his sword, drew it out of its sheath, and killed him; then he cut off his head with it. When the Phi•lis'tines saw that their champion was dead, they fled. 52 The troops of Israel and Judah rose up with a shout and pursued the Phi•lis'tines as far as Gath[d] and the gates of Ek'ron, so that the wounded Phi•lis'tines fell on the way from Shā•a•rā'im as far as Gath and Ek'ron. 53 The Israelites came back from chasing the Phi•lis'tines, and they plundered their camp. 54 David took the head of the Phi•lis'tine and brought it to Jerusalem; but he put his armor in his tent.

55 When Saul saw David go out against the Phi•lis'tine, he said to Abner, the commander of the army, "Abner, whose son is this young man?" Abner said, "As your soul lives, O king, I do not know." 56 The king said, "Inquire whose son the stripling is." 57 On David's return from killing the Phi•lis'tine, Abner took him and brought him before Saul, with the head of the Phi•lis'tine in his hand. 58 Saul said to him, "Whose son are you, young man?" And David answered, "I am the son of your servant Jesse the Beth'le•hem•īte."

Jonathan's Covenant with David

18 When David[e] had finished speaking to Saul, the soul of Jonathan was bound to the soul of David, and Jonathan loved him as his own soul. 2 Saul took him that day and would not let him return to his father's house. 3 Then Jonathan made a covenant with David, because he loved him as his own soul. 4 Jonathan stripped himself of the robe that he was wearing, and gave it to David, and his armor, and even his sword and his bow and his belt. 5 David went out and was successful wherever Saul sent him; as a result, Saul set him over the army. And all the people, even the servants of Saul, approved.

6 As they were coming home, when David returned from killing the Phi•lis'tine, the women came out of all the towns of Israel, singing and dancing, to meet King Saul, with tambourines, with songs of joy, and with musical instruments.[f] 7 And the women sang to one another as they made merry,

"Saul has killed his thousands,
and David his ten thousands."

8 Saul was very angry, for this saying displeased him. He said, "They have ascribed to David ten thousands, and to me they have ascribed thousands; what more can he have but the kingdom?" 9 So Saul eyed David from that day on.

Saul Tries to Kill David

10 The next day an evil spirit from God rushed upon Saul, and he raved within his house, while David was playing the lyre, as he did day by day. Saul had his spear in his hand; 11 and Saul threw the spear, for he thought, "I will pin David to the wall." But David eluded him twice.

12 Saul was afraid of David, because the LORD was with him but had departed from Saul. 13 So Saul removed him from his presence, and made him a commander of a thousand; and David marched out and came in, leading the army. 14 David had success in all his undertakings; for the LORD was with him. 15 When Saul saw that he had great success, he stood in awe of him. 16 But all Israel and Judah loved David; for it was he who marched out and came in leading them.

David Marries Michal

17 Then Saul said to David, "Here is my elder daughter Mē'rab; I will give her to you as a wife; only be valiant for me and fight the LORD's battles." For Saul thought, "I will not raise a hand against him; let the Phi•lis'tines deal with him." 18 David said to Saul, "Who am I and who are my kinsfolk, my father's family in Israel, that I should be son-in-law to the king?" 19 But at the time when Saul's daughter Mē'rab should have been given to David, she was given to Ā'dri•el the Me•hō'la•thīte as a wife.

20 Now Saul's daughter Mī'chal loved David. Saul was told, and the thing pleased him. 21 Saul thought, "Let me give her to him that she may be a snare for him and that the hand of the Phi•lis'tines may be against him." Therefore Saul said to David a second time,[g] "You shall now be my son-in-law." 22 Saul commanded his servants, "Speak to David in private and say, 'See, the king is delighted with you, and all his servants love you; now then, become the king's son-in-law.' " 23 So Saul's servants reported these words to David in private. And David said, "Does it seem to you a little thing to

---

[d] Gk Syr: Heb Gai　[e] Heb he　[f] Or triangles, or three-stringed instruments　[g] Heb by two

become the king's son-in-law, seeing that I am a poor man and of no repute?" 24 The servants of Saul told him, "This is what David said." 25 Then Saul said, "Thus shall you say to David, 'The king desires no marriage present except a hundred foreskins of the Phi·lis'tines, that he may be avenged on the king's enemies.' " Now Saul planned to make David fall by the hand of the Phi·lis'tines. 26 When his servants told David these words, David was well pleased to be the king's son-in-law. Before the time had expired, 27 David rose and went, along with his men, and killed one hundred*h* of the Phi·lis'tines; and David brought their foreskins, which were given in full number to the king, that he might become the king's son-in-law. Saul gave him his daughter Mi'chal as a wife. 28 But when Saul realized that the LORD was with David, and that Saul's daughter Mi'chal loved him, 29 Saul was still more afraid of David. So Saul was David's enemy from that time forward.

30 Then the commanders of the Phi·lis'tines came out to battle; and as often as they came out, David had more success than all the servants of Saul, so that his fame became very great.

Jonathan Intercedes for David

19 Saul spoke with his son Jonathan and with all his servants about killing David. But Saul's son Jonathan took great delight in David. 2 Jonathan told David, "My father Saul is trying to kill you; therefore be on guard tomorrow morning; stay in a secret place and hide yourself. 3 I will go out and stand beside my father in the field where you are, and I will speak to my father about you; if I learn anything I will tell you." 4 Jonathan spoke well of David to his father Saul, saying to him, "The king should not sin against his servant David, because he has not sinned against you, and because his deeds have been of good service to you; 5 for he took his life in his hand when he attacked the Phi·lis'tine, and the LORD brought about a great victory for all Israel. You saw it, and rejoiced; why then will you sin against an innocent person by killing David without cause?" 6 Saul heeded the voice of Jonathan; Saul swore, "As the LORD lives, he shall not be put to death." 7 So Jonathan called David and related all these things to him. Jonathan then brought David to Saul, and he was in his presence as before.

Michal Helps David Escape from Saul

8 Again there was war, and David went out to fight the Phi·lis'tines. He launched a heavy attack on them, so that they fled before him. 9 Then an evil spirit from the LORD came upon Saul, as he sat in his house with his spear in his hand, while David was playing music. 10 Saul sought to pin David to the wall with the spear; but he eluded Saul, so that he struck the spear into the wall. David fled and escaped that night.

11 Saul sent messengers to David's house to keep watch over him, planning to kill him in the morning. David's wife Mi'chal told him, "If you do not save your life tonight, tomorrow you will be killed." 12 So Mi'chal let David down through the window; he fled away and escaped. 13 Mi'chal took an idol*i* and laid it on the bed; she put a net*j* of goats' hair on its head, and covered it with the clothes. 14 When Saul sent messengers to take David, she said, "He is sick." 15 Then Saul sent the messengers to see David for themselves. He said, "Bring him up to me in the bed, that I may kill him." 16 When the messengers came in, the idol*k* was in the bed, with the covering*j* of goats' hair on its head. 17 Saul said to Mi'chal, "Why have you deceived me like this, and let my enemy go, so that he has escaped?" Mi'chal answered Saul, "He said to me, 'Let me go; why should I kill you?' "

David Joins Samuel in Ramah

18 Now David fled and escaped; he came to Samuel at Ra'mah, and told him all that Saul had done to him. He and Samuel went and settled at Nai'oth. 19 Saul was told, "David is at Nai'oth in Ra'mah." 20 Then Saul sent messengers to take David. When they saw the company of the prophets in a frenzy, with Samuel standing in charge of*j* them, the spirit of God came upon the messengers of Saul, and they also fell into a prophetic frenzy. 21 When Saul was told, he sent other messengers, and they also fell into a frenzy. Saul sent messengers again the third time, and they also fell into a frenzy. 22 Then he himself went to Ra'mah. He came to the great well that is in Se'cu;*l* he asked, "Where are Samuel and David?" And someone said, "They are at Nai'oth in Ra'mah." 23 He went there, toward Nai'oth in Ra'mah; and the spirit of God came upon him. As he was going, he fell into a prophetic frenzy, until he came to Nai'oth in Ra'mah. 24 He too stripped off his clothes, and he too fell into a frenzy before Samuel. He lay naked all that day and all that night. Therefore it is said, "Is Saul also among the prophets?"

The Friendship of David and Jonathan

20 David fled from Nai'oth in Ra'mah. He came before Jonathan and said, "What have I done? What is my guilt? And what is my sin against your father that he is trying to take my life?" 2 He said to him, "Far from it! You shall not die. My

---

h Gk Compare 2 Sam 3.14: Heb *two hundred*   *i* Heb *took the teraphim*   *j* Meaning of Heb uncertain   *k* Heb *the teraphim*   *l* Gk reads *to the well of the threshing floor on the bare height*

Friends Forever

David and Jonathan have one of the most touching stories of friendship in the Bible. In 1 Sam 18.1–4, Jonathan makes a special covenant with David. In chapter 20, their deep love leads them to risk their lives for each other. Saul, the king and Jonathan's father, is acting like a madman. He is insanely jealous of David and wants him dead.

Yet, Jonathan and David bring God into their relationship. This gives them the wisdom to see what is right and do it. When they have to part (see 20.41–42), they weep and kiss and remind each other of their vows.

Not many teenagers deal with situations as drastic as this, but tension with parents over your choice of friends can be common. Parents may not understand why you like a person whom they dislike. It can leave you with a sense of being stuck in the middle.

Your response should be like David and Jonathan's, keeping God part of all your relationships. Each friendship then becomes a living prayer, and God will guide you through conflicts and help you make good decisions.

▶ 1 Samuel, chapter 20

father does nothing either great or small without disclosing it to me; and why should my father hide this from me? Never!" 3 But David also swore, "Your father knows well that you like me; and he thinks, 'Do not let Jonathan know this, or he will be grieved.' But truly, as the LORD lives and as you yourself live, there is but a step between me and death." 4 Then Jonathan said to David, "Whatever you say, I will do for you." 5 David said to Jonathan, "Tomorrow is the new moon, and I should not fail to sit with the king at the meal; but let me go, so that I may hide in the field until the third evening. 6 If your father misses me at all, then say, 'David earnestly asked leave of me to run to Bethlehem his city; for there is a yearly sacrifice there for all the family.' 7 If he says, 'Good!' it will be well with your servant; but if he is angry, then know that evil has been determined by him. 8 Therefore deal kindly with your servant, for you have brought your servant into a sacred covenant[m] with you. But if there is guilt in me, kill me yourself; why should you bring me to your father?" 9 Jonathan said, "Far be

it from you! If I knew that it was decided by my father that evil should come upon you, would I not tell you?" 10 Then David said to Jonathan, "Who will tell me if your father answers you harshly?" 11 Jonathan replied to David, "Come, let us go out into the field." So they both went out into the field.

12 Jonathan said to David, "By the LORD, the God of Israel! When I have sounded out my father, about this time tomorrow, or on the third day, if he is well disposed toward David, shall I not then send and disclose it to you? 13 But if my father intends to do you harm, the LORD do so to Jonathan, and more also, if I do not disclose it to you, and send you away, so that you may go in safety. May the LORD be with you, as he has been with my father. 14 If I am still alive, show me the faithful love of the LORD; but if I die,[n] 15 never cut off your faithful love from my house, even if the LORD were to cut off every one of the enemies of David from the face of the earth." 16 Thus Jonathan made a covenant with the house of David, saying, "May the LORD seek out the enemies of David." 17 Jonathan made David swear again by his love for him; for he loved him as he loved his own life.

18 Jonathan said to him, "Tomorrow is the new moon; you will be missed, because your place will be empty. 19 On the day after tomorrow, you shall go a long way down; go to the place where you hid yourself earlier, and remain beside the stone there.[n] 20 I will shoot three arrows to the side of it, as though I shot at a mark. 21 Then I will send the boy, saying, 'Go, find the arrows.' If I say to the boy, 'Look, the arrows are on this side of you, collect them,' then you are to come, for, as the LORD lives, it is safe for you and there is no danger. 22 But if I say to the young man, 'Look, the arrows are beyond you,' then go; for the LORD has sent you away. 23 As for the matter about which you and I have spoken, the LORD is witness[o] between you and me forever."

24 So David hid himself in the field. When the new moon came, the king sat at the feast to eat. 25 The king sat upon his seat, as at other times, upon the seat by the wall. Jonathan stood, while Abner sat by Saul's side; but David's place was empty.

26 Saul did not say anything that day; for he thought, "Something has befallen him; he is not clean, surely he is not clean." 27 But on the second day, the day after the new moon, David's place was empty. And Saul said to his son Jonathan, "Why has the son of Jesse not come to the feast, either yesterday or today?" 28 Jonathan answered Saul, "David earnestly asked leave of me to go to Bethlehem;

---

m Heb *a covenant of the LORD*   n Meaning of Heb uncertain   o Gk: Heb lacks *witness*

29 he said, 'Let me go; for our family is holding a sacrifice in the city, and my brother has command-ed me to be there. So now, if I have found favor in your sight, let me get away, and see my brothers.' For this reason he has not come to the king's table."

30 Then Saul's anger was kindled against Jonathan. He said to him, "You son of a perverse, rebellious woman! Do I not know that you have chosen the son of Jesse to your own shame, and to the shame of your mother's nakedness? 31 For as long as the son of Jesse lives upon the earth, neither you nor your kingdom shall be established. Now send and bring him to me, for he shall surely die." 32 Then Jonathan answered his father Saul, "Why should he be put to death? What has he done?" 33 But Saul threw his spear at him to strike him; so Jonathan knew that it was the decision of his father to put David to death. 34 Jonathan rose from the table in fierce anger and ate no food on the second day of the month, for he was grieved for David, and because his father had disgraced him.

35 In the morning Jonathan went out into the field to the appointment with David, and with him was a little boy. 36 He said to the boy, "Run and find the arrows that I shoot." As the boy ran, he shot an arrow beyond him. 37 When the boy came to the place where Jonathan's arrow had fallen, Jonathan called after the boy and said, "Is the arrow not be-yond you?" 38 Jonathan called after the boy, "Hurry, be quick, do not linger." So Jonathan's boy gathered up the arrows and came to his master. 39 But the boy knew nothing; only Jonathan and David knew the arrangement. 40 Jonathan gave his weapons to the boy and said to him, "Go and carry them to the city." 41 As soon as the boy had gone, David rose from beside the stone heap *p* and prostrated himself with his face to the ground. He bowed three times, and they kissed each other, and wept with each oth-er; David wept the more.*q* 42 Then Jonathan said to David, "Go in peace, since both of us have sworn in the name of the LORD, saying, 'The LORD shall be be-tween me and you, and between my descendants and your descendants, forever.' " He got up and left; and Jonathan went into the city.*r*

David and the Holy Bread

21 *s*David came to Nob to the priest A•him′-e•lech. A•him′e•lech came trembling to meet David, and said to him, "Why are you alone, and no one with you?" 2 David said to the priest A•him′e•lech, "The king has charged me with a mat-ter, and said to me, 'No one must know anything of the matter about which I send you, and with which I have charged you.' I have made an appointment*t* with the young men for such and such a place. 3 Now then, what have you at hand? Give me five loaves of bread, or whatever is here." 4 The priest

answered David, "I have no ordinary bread at hand, only holy bread—provided that the young men have kept themselves from women." 5 David an-swered the priest, "Indeed women have been kept from us as always when I go on an expedition; the vessels of the young men are holy even when it is a common journey; how much more today will their vessels be holy?" 6 So the priest gave him the holy bread; for there was no bread there except the bread of the Presence, which is removed from before the LORD, to be replaced by hot bread on the day it is taken away.

7 Now a certain man of the servants of Saul was there that day, detained before the LORD; his name was Dō′eg the Ē′dom•ite, the chief of Saul's shep-herds.

8 David said to A•him′e•lech, "Is there no spear or sword here with you? I did not bring my sword or my weapons with me, because the king's busi-ness required haste." 9 The priest said, "The sword of Goliath the Phi•lis′tine, whom you killed in the valley of Ē′lah, is here wrapped in a cloth behind the ephod; if you will take that, take it, for there is none here except that one." David said, "There is none like it; give it to me."

David Flees to Gath

10 David rose and fled that day from Saul; he went to King Ā′chish of Gath. 11 The servants of Ā′chish said to him, "Is this not David the king of the land? Did they not sing to one another of him in dances,

'Saul has killed his thousands,
  and David his ten thousands'?"

12 David took these words to heart and was very much afraid of King Ā′chish of Gath. 13 So he changed his behavior before them; he pretended to be mad when in their presence.*u* He scratched marks on the doors of the gate, and let his spittle run down his beard. 14 Ā′chish said to his servants, "Look, you see the man is mad; why then have you brought him to me? 15 Do I lack madmen, that you have brought this fellow to play the madman in my presence? Shall this fellow come into my house?"

David and His Followers at Adullam

22 David left there and escaped to the cave of A•dul′lam; when his brothers and all his father's house heard of it, they went down there to him. 2 Everyone who was in distress, and every-one who was in debt, and everyone who was dis-contented gathered to him; and he became captain over them. Those who were with him numbered about four hundred.

3 David went from there to Miz'peh of Mō'ab. He said to the king of Mō'ab, "Please let my father and mother come^v to you, until I know what God will do for me." 4 He left them with the king of Mō'ab, and they stayed with him all the time that David was in the stronghold. 5 Then the prophet Gad said to David, "Do not remain in the stronghold; leave, and go into the land of Judah." So David left, and went into the forest of Hē'reth.

Saul Slaughters the Priests at Nob

6 Saul heard that David and those who were with him had been located. Saul was sitting at Gib'ē·ah, under the tamarisk tree on the height, with his spear in his hand, and all his servants were standing around him. 7 Saul said to his servants who stood around him, "Hear now, you Ben'-ja·min·ites; will the son of Jesse give every one of you fields and vineyards, will he make you all commanders of thousands and commanders of hundreds? 8 Is that why all of you have conspired against me? No one discloses to me when my son makes a league with the son of Jesse, none of you is sorry for me or discloses to me that my son has stirred up my servant against me, to lie in wait, as he is doing today." 9 Dō'eg the Ē'dom·ite, who was in charge of Saul's servants, answered, "I saw the son of Jesse coming to Nob, to A·him'e·lech son of A·hī'tub; 10 he inquired of the LORD for him, gave him provisions, and gave him the sword of Goliath the Phi·lis'tine."

11 The king sent for the priest A·him'e·lech son of A·hī'tub and for all his father's house, the priests who were at Nob; and all of them came to the king. 12 Saul said, "Listen now, son of A·hī'tub." He answered, "Here I am, my lord." 13 Saul said to him, "Why have you conspired against me, you and the son of Jesse, by giving him bread and a sword, and by inquiring of God for him, so that he has risen against me, to lie in wait, as he is doing today?"

14 Then A·him'e·lech answered the king, "Who among all your servants is so faithful as David? He is the king's son-in-law, and is quick^w to do your bidding, and is honored in your house. 15 Is today the first time that I have inquired of God for him? By no means! Do not let the king impute anything to his servant or to any member of my father's house; for your servant has known nothing of all this, much or little." 16 The king said, "You shall surely die, A·him'e·lech, you and all your father's house." 17 The king said to the guard who stood around him, "Turn and kill the priests of the LORD, because their hand also is with David; they knew that he fled, and did not disclose it to me." But the servants of the king would not raise their hand to

attack the priests of the LORD. 18 Then the king said to Dō'eg, "You, Dō'eg, turn and attack the priests." Dō'eg the Ē'dom·ite turned and attacked the priests; on that day he killed eighty-five who wore the linen ephod. 19 Nob, the city of the priests, he put to the sword; men and women, children and infants, oxen, donkeys, and sheep, he put to the sword.

20 But one of the sons of A·him'e·lech son of A·hī'tub, named A·bī'a·thar, escaped and fled after David. 21 A·bī'a·thar told David that Saul had killed the priests of the LORD. 22 David said to A·bī'a·thar, "I knew on that day, when Dō'eg the Ē'dom·ite was there, that he would surely tell Saul. I am responsible^x for the lives of all your father's house. 23 Stay with me, and do not be afraid; for the one who seeks my life seeks your life; you will be safe with me."

David Saves the City of Keilah

23 Now they told David, "The Phi·lis'tines are fighting against Kē·i'lah, and are robbing the threshing floors." 2 David inquired of the LORD, "Shall I go and attack these Phi·lis'tines?" The LORD said to David, "Go and attack the Phi·lis'tines and save Kē·i'lah." 3 But David's men said to him, "Look, we are afraid here in Judah; how much more then if we go to Kē·i'lah against the armies of the Phi·lis'tines?" 4 Then David inquired of the LORD again. The LORD answered him, "Yes, go down to Kē·i'lah; for I will give the Phi·lis'tines into your hand." 5 So David and his men went to Kē·i'lah, fought with the Phi·lis'tines, brought away their livestock, and dealt them a heavy defeat. Thus David rescued the inhabitants of Kē·i'lah.

6 When A·bī'a·thar son of A·him'e·lech fled to David at Kē·i'lah, he came down with an ephod in his hand. 7 Now it was told Saul that David had come to Kē·i'lah. And Saul said, "God has given^y him into my hand; for he has shut himself in by entering a town that has gates and bars." 8 Saul summoned all the people to war, to go down to Kē·i'lah, to besiege David and his men. 9 When David learned that Saul was plotting evil against him, he said to the priest A·bī'a·thar, "Bring the ephod here." 10 David said, "O LORD, the God of Israel, your servant has heard that Saul seeks to come to Kē·i'lah, to destroy the city on my account. 11 And now, will^z Saul come down as your servant has heard? O LORD, the God of Israel, I beseech you, tell your servant." The LORD said, "He will come down." 12 Then David said, "Will the men of

---

^{v} Syr Vg: Heb *come out* ^{w} Heb *and turns aside* ^{x} Gk Vg: Meaning of Heb uncertain ^{y} Gk Tg: Heb *made a stranger of* ^{z} Q Ms Compare Gk: MT *Will the men of Keilah surrender me into his hand? Will*

Kē·ī'lah surrender me and my men into the hand of Saul?" The LORD said, "They will surrender you." 13 Then David and his men, who were about six hundred, set out and left Kē·ī'lah; they wandered wherever they could go. When Saul was told that David had escaped from Kē·ī'lah, he gave up the expedition. 14 David remained in the strongholds in the wilderness, in the hill country of the Wilderness of Ziph. Saul sought him every day, but the LORD *a* did not give him into his hand.

David Eludes Saul in the Wilderness

15 David was in the Wilderness of Ziph at Hō'resh when he learned that*b* Saul had come out to seek his life. 16 Saul's son Jonathan set out and came to David at Hō'resh; there he strengthened his hand through the LORD.*c* 17 He said to him, "Do not be afraid; for the hand of my father Saul shall not find you; you shall be king over Israel, and I shall be second to you; my father Saul also knows that this is so." 18 Then the two of them made a covenant before the LORD; David remained at Hō'resh, and Jonathan went home.

19 Then some Ziph'ites went up to Saul at Gib'ē·ah and said, "David is hiding among us in the strongholds of Hō'resh, on the hill of Ha·chī'lah, which is south of Jē·shī'mon. 20 Now, O king, whenever you wish to come down, do so; and our part will be to surrender him into the king's hand." 21 Saul said, "May you be blessed by the LORD for showing me compassion! 22 Go and make sure once more; find out exactly where he is, and who has seen him there; for I am told that he is very cunning. 23 Look around and learn all the hiding places where he lurks, and come back to me with sure information. Then I will go with you; and if he is in the land, I will search him out among all the thousands of Judah." 24 So they set out and went to Ziph ahead of Saul.

David and his men were in the wilderness of Mā'on, in the Ar'a·bah to the south of Jē·shī'mon. 25 Saul and his men went to search for him. When David was told, he went down to the rock and stayed in the wilderness of Mā'on. When Saul heard that, he pursued David into the wilderness of Mā'on. 26 Saul went on one side of the mountain, and David and his men on the other side of the mountain. David was hurrying to get away from Saul, while Saul and his men were closing in on David and his men to capture them. 27 Then a messenger came to Saul, saying, "Hurry and come; for the Phi·lis'tines have made a raid on the land." 28 So Saul stopped pursuing David, and went against the Phi·lis'tines; therefore that place was called the Rock of Escape.*d* 29 *e*David then went up from there, and lived in the strongholds of En-ge'di.

David Spares Saul's Life

24 When Saul returned from following the Phi·lis'tines, he was told, "David is in the wilderness of En-ge'di." 2 Then Saul took three thousand chosen men out of all Israel, and went to look for David and his men in the direction of the Rocks of the Wild Goats. 3 He came to the sheepfolds beside the road, where there was a cave; and Saul went in to relieve himself.*f* Now David and his men were sitting in the innermost parts of the cave. 4 The men of David said to him, "Here is the day of which the LORD said to you, 'I will give your enemy into your hand, and you shall do to him as it seems good to you.' " Then David went and stealthily cut

---

a Q Ms Gk: MT *God*   *b* Or *saw that*   *c* Compare Q Ms Gk: MT *God*   *d* Or *Rock of Division*; meaning of Heb uncertain   *e* Ch 24.1 in Heb   *f* Heb *to cover his feet*

did you KNOW?

The LORD's Anointed

Throughout human history, oil has been used as medicine, perfume, and a symbol of blessing. The Israelite kings and prophets were anointed with oil to symbolize the powerful spirit of God present to them as they fulfilled their important role. Often it was olive oil mixed with a small amount of perfume. Oil plays a symbolic role throughout the Bible and has historically played an important role in the life of the church. In many Old Testament texts, oil was reserved for priests, kings, and people of high importance. Today we use oil in most of the sacraments of the church because we are the "priestly people."

The Hebrew word *mashiah*, translated in 1 Sam 24.6 as "anointed [one]," is the root of the English word *messiah*. Often applied to kings in the Old Testament, this title was attached in the second century B.C. to the one "like David" who was expected to come (see Dan 9.25). *Mashiah* translated in Greek is *christos*, which became the title given to Jesus by his followers: Jesus, the Christ; Jesus, the anointed one; Jesus, the Messiah.

off a corner of Saul's cloak. [5] Afterward David was stricken to the heart because he had cut off a corner of Saul's cloak. [6] He said to his men, "The LORD forbid that I should do this thing to my lord, the LORD's anointed, to raise my hand against him; for he is the LORD's anointed." [7] So David scolded his men severely and did not permit them to attack Saul. Then Saul got up and left the cave, and went on his way.

[8] Afterwards David also rose up and went out of the cave and called after Saul, "My lord the king!" When Saul looked behind him, David bowed with his face to the ground, and did obeisance. [9] David said to Saul, "Why do you listen to the words of those who say, 'David seeks to do you harm'? [10] This very day your eyes have seen how the LORD gave you into my hand in the cave; and some urged me to kill you, but I spared[g] you. I said, 'I will not raise my hand against my lord; for he is the LORD's anointed.' [11] See, my father, see the corner of your cloak in my hand; for by the fact that I cut off the corner of your cloak, and did not kill you, you may know for certain that there is no wrong or treason in my hands. I have not sinned against you, though you are hunting me to take my life. [12] May the LORD judge between me and you! May the LORD avenge me on you; but my hand shall not be against you. [13] As the ancient proverb says, 'Out of the wicked comes forth wickedness'; but my hand shall not be against you. [14] Against whom has the king of Israel come out? Whom do you pursue? A dead dog? A single flea? [15] May the LORD therefore be judge, and give sentence between me and you. May he see to it, and plead my cause, and vindicate me against you."

[16] When David had finished speaking these words to Saul, Saul said, "Is this your voice, my son David?" Saul lifted up his voice and wept. [17] He said to David, "You are more righteous than I; for you have repaid me good, whereas I have repaid you evil. [18] Today you have explained how you have dealt well with me, in that you did not kill me when the LORD put me into your hands. [19] For who has ever found an enemy, and sent the enemy safely away? So may the LORD reward you with good for what you have done to me this day. [20] Now I know that you shall surely be king, and that the kingdom of Israel shall be established in your hand. [21] Swear to me therefore by the LORD that you will not cut off my descendants after me, and that you will not wipe out my name from my father's house." [22] So David swore this to Saul. Then Saul went home; but David and his men went up to the stronghold.

Death of Samuel

25 Now Samuel died; and all Israel assembled and mourned for him. They buried him at his home in Rā'mah.

Then David got up and went down to the wilderness of Par'an.

David and the Wife of Nabal

[2] There was a man in Mā'on, whose property was in Car'mel. The man was very rich; he had three thousand sheep and a thousand goats. He was shearing his sheep in Car'mel. [3] Now the name of the man was Nā'bal, and the name of his wife Ab'i·gāil. The woman was clever and beautiful, but the man was surly and mean; he was a Cā'leb·ite. [4] David heard in the wilderness that Nā'bal was shearing his sheep. [5] So David sent ten young men; and David said to the young men, "Go up to Car'mel, and go to Nā'bal, and greet him in my name. [6] Thus you shall salute him: 'Peace be to you, and peace be to your house, and peace be to all that you have. [7] I hear that you have shearers; now your shepherds have been with us, and we did them no harm, and they missed nothing, all the time they were in Car'mel. [8] Ask your young men, and they will tell you. Therefore let my young men find favor in your sight; for we have come on a feast day. Please give whatever you have at hand to your servants and to your son David.' "

[9] When David's young men came, they said all this to Nā'bal in the name of David; and then they waited. [10] But Nā'bal answered David's servants, "Who is David? Who is the son of Jesse? There are many servants today who are breaking away from their masters. [11] Shall I take my bread and my water and the meat that I have butchered for my shearers, and give it to men who come from I do not know where?" [12] So David's young men turned away, and came back and told him all this. [13] David said to his men, "Every man strap on his sword!" And every one of them strapped on his sword; David also strapped on his sword; and about four hundred men went up after David, while two hundred remained with the baggage.

[14] But one of the young men told Ab'i·gāil, Nā'bal's wife, "David sent messengers out of the wilderness to salute our master; and he shouted insults at them. [15] Yet the men were very good to us, and we suffered no harm, and we never missed anything when we were in the fields, as long as we were with them; [16] they were a wall to us both by night and by day, all the while we were with them keeping the sheep. [17] Now therefore know this and consider what you should do; for evil has been decided against our master and against all his house; he is so ill-natured that no one can speak to him."

[18] Then Ab'i·gāil hurried and took two hundred loaves, two skins of wine, five sheep ready dressed, five measures of parched grain, one hundred

---

g Gk Syr Tg Vg: Heb *it* (my eye) *spared*

clusters of raisins, and two hundred cakes of figs. She loaded them on donkeys 19 and said to her young men, "Go on ahead of me; I am coming after you." But she did not tell her husband Nā′bal. 20 As she rode on the donkey and came down under cover of the mountain, David and his men came down toward her; and she met them. 21 Now David had said, "Surely it was in vain that I protected all that this fellow has in the wilderness, so that nothing was missed of all that belonged to him; but he has returned me evil for good. 22 God do so to David[h] and more also, if by morning I leave so much as one male of all who belong to him."

23 When Ab′i•gāil saw David, she hurried and alighted from the donkey, and fell before David on her face, bowing to the ground. 24 She fell at his feet and said, "Upon me alone, my lord, be the guilt; please let your servant speak in your ears, and hear the words of your servant. 25 My lord, do not take seriously this ill-natured fellow, Nā′bal; for as his name is, so is he; Nā′bal[i] is his name, and folly is with him; but I, your servant, did not see the young men of my lord, whom you sent.

26 "Now then, my lord, as the LORD lives, and as you yourself live, since the LORD has restrained you from bloodguilt and from taking vengeance with your own hand, now let your enemies and those who seek to do evil to my lord be like Nā′bal. 27 And now let this present that your servant has brought to my lord be given to the young men who follow my lord. 28 Please forgive the trespass of your servant; for the LORD will certainly make my lord a sure house, because my lord is fighting the battles of the LORD; and evil shall not be found in you so long as you live. 29 If anyone should rise up to pursue you and to seek your life, the life of my lord shall be bound in the bundle of the living under the care of the LORD your God; but the lives of your enemies he shall sling out as from the hollow of a sling. 30 When the LORD has done to my lord according to all the good that he has spoken concerning you, and has appointed you prince over Israel, 31 my lord shall have no cause of grief, or pangs of conscience, for having shed blood without cause or for having saved himself. And when the LORD has dealt well with my lord, then remember your servant."

32 David said to Ab′i•gāil, "Blessed be the LORD, the God of Israel, who sent you to meet me today! 33 Blessed be your good sense, and blessed be you, who have kept me today from bloodguilt and from avenging myself by my own hand! 34 For as surely as the LORD the God of Israel lives, who has restrained me from hurting you, unless you had hurried and come to meet me, truly by morning there would not have been left to Nā′bal so much as one male." 35 Then David received from her

hand what she had brought him; he said to her, "Go up to your house in peace; see, I have heeded your voice, and I have granted your petition."

36 Ab′i•gāil came to Nā′bal; he was holding a feast in his house, like the feast of a king. Nā′bal's heart was merry within him, for he was very drunk; so she told him nothing at all until the morning light. 37 In the morning, when the wine had gone out of Nā′bal, his wife told him these things, and his heart died within him; he became like a stone. 38 About ten days later the LORD struck Nā′bal, and he died.

39 When David heard that Nā′bal was dead, he said, "Blessed be the LORD who has judged the case of Nā′bal's insult to me, and has kept back his servant from evil; the LORD has returned the evildoing of Nā′bal upon his own head." Then David sent and wooed Ab′i•gāil, to make her his wife. 40 When David's servants came to Ab′i•gāil at Car′mel, they said to her, "David has sent us to you to take you to him as his wife." 41 She rose and bowed down, with her face to the ground, and said, "Your servant is a slave to wash the feet of the servants of my lord." 42 Ab′i•gāil got up hurriedly and rode away on a donkey; her five maids attended her. She went after the messengers of David and became his wife.

43 David also married A•hin′ō•am of Jez′rē•el; both of them became his wives. 44 Saul had given his daughter Mī′chal, David's wife, to Pal′tī son of Lā′ish, who was from Gal′lim.

David Spares Saul's Life a Second Time

26 Then the Ziph′ītes came to Saul at Gib′ē•ah, saying, "David is in hiding on the hill of Ha•chī′lah, which is opposite Jē•shī′-mon."[j] 2 So Saul rose and went down to the Wilderness of Ziph, with three thousand chosen men of Israel, to seek David in the Wilderness of Ziph. 3 Saul encamped on the hill of Ha•chī′lah, which is opposite Jē•shī′mon[j] beside the road. But David remained in the wilderness. When he learned that Saul had come after him into the wilderness, 4 David sent out spies, and learned that Saul had indeed arrived. 5 Then David set out and came to the place where Saul had encamped; and David saw the place where Saul lay, with Abner son of Ner, the commander of his army. Saul was lying within the encampment, while the army was encamped around him.

6 Then David said to A•him′e•lech the Hit′tīte, and to Jō′ab's brother A•bi′shaī son of Ze•rū′i•ah, "Who will go down with me into the camp to Saul?" A•bi′shaī said, "I will go down with you." 7 So David and A•bi′shaī went to the army by night;

---

h Gk Compare Syr: Heb *the enemies of David*   i That is *Fool*
j Or *opposite the wasteland*

there Saul lay sleeping within the encampment, with his spear stuck in the ground at his head; and Abner and the army lay around him. 8 A·bi′shaī said to David, "God has given your enemy into your hand today; now therefore let me pin him to the ground with one stroke of the spear; I will not strike him twice." 9 But David said to A·bi′shaī, "Do not destroy him; for who can raise his hand against the LORD's anointed, and be guiltless?" 10 David said, "As the LORD lives, the LORD will strike him down; or his day will come to die; or he will go down into battle and perish. 11 The LORD forbid that I should raise my hand against the LORD's anointed; but now take the spear that is at his head, and the water jar, and let us go." 12 So David took the spear that was at Saul's head and the water jar, and they went away. No one saw it, or knew it, nor did anyone awake; for they were all asleep, because a deep sleep from the LORD had fallen upon them.

13 Then David went over to the other side, and stood on top of a hill far away, with a great distance between them. 14 David called to the army and to Abner son of Ner, saying, "Abner! Will you not answer?" Then Abner replied, "Who are you that calls to the king?" 15 David said to Abner, "Are you not a man? Who is like you in Israel? Why then have you not kept watch over your lord the king? For one of the people came in to destroy your lord the king. 16 This thing that you have done is not good. As the LORD lives, you deserve to die, because you have not kept watch over your lord, the LORD's anointed. See now, where is the king's spear, or the water jar that was at his head?"

17 Saul recognized David's voice, and said, "Is this your voice, my son David?" David said, "It is my voice, my lord, O king." 18 And he added, "Why does my lord pursue his servant? For what have I done? What guilt is on my hands? 19 Now therefore let my lord the king hear the words of his servant. If it is the LORD who has stirred you up against me, may he accept an offering; but if it is mortals, may they be cursed before the LORD, for they have driven me out today from my share in the heritage of the LORD, saying, 'Go, serve other gods.' 20 Now therefore, do not let my blood fall to the ground, away from the presence of the LORD; for the king of Israel has come out to seek a single flea, like one who hunts a partridge in the mountains."

21 Then Saul said, "I have done wrong; come back, my son David, for I will never harm you again, because my life was precious in your sight today; I have been a fool, and have made a great mistake." 22 David replied, "Here is the spear, O king! Let one of the young men come over and get it. 23 The LORD rewards everyone for his righteousness and his faithfulness; for the LORD gave you into my hand today, but I would not raise my hand against the LORD's anointed. 24 As your life was precious today in my sight, so may my life be precious in the sight of the LORD, and may he rescue me from all tribulation." 25 Then Saul said to David, "Blessed be you, my son David! You will do many things and will succeed in them." So David went his way, and Saul returned to his place.

David Serves King Achish of Gath

27 David said in his heart, "I shall now perish one day by the hand of Saul; there is nothing better for me than to escape to the land of the Phi·lis′tines; then Saul will despair of seeking me any longer within the borders of Israel, and I shall escape out of his hand." 2 So David set out and went over, he and the six hundred men who were with him, to King Ā′chish son of Mā′och of Gath. 3 David stayed with Ā′chish at Gath, he and his troops, every man with his household, and David with his two wives, A·hin′ō·am of Jez′rē·el, and Ab′i·gāil of Car′mel, Nā′bal's widow. 4 When Saul was told that David had fled to Gath, he no longer sought for him.

5 Then David said to Ā′chish, "If I have found favor in your sight, let a place be given me in one of the country towns, so that I may live there; for why should your servant live in the royal city with you?" 6 So that day Ā′chish gave him Zik′lag; therefore Zik′lag has belonged to the kings of Judah to this day. 7 The length of time that David lived in the country of the Phi·lis′tines was one year and four months.

8 Now David and his men went up and made raids on the Gesh′ū·rītes, the Gir′zītes, and the A·mal′e·kītes; for these were the landed settlements from Tē′lam[k] on the way to Shur and on to the land of Egypt. 9 David struck the land, leaving neither man nor woman alive, but took away the sheep, the oxen, the donkeys, the camels, and the clothing, and came back to Ā′chish. 10 When Ā′chish asked, "Against whom[l] have you made a raid today?" David would say, "Against the Neg′eb of Judah," or "Against the Neg′eb of the Je·rah′mē·el·ītes," or, "Against the Neg′eb of the Ken′ītes." 11 David left neither man nor woman alive to be brought back to Gath, thinking, "They might tell about us, and say, 'David has done so and so.' " Such was his practice all the time he lived in the country of the Phi·lis′tines. 12 Ā′chish trusted David, thinking, "He has made himself utterly abhorrent to his people Israel; therefore he shall always be my servant."

28 In those days the Phi·lis′tines gathered their forces for war, to fight against Israel. Ā′chish said to David, "You know, of course,

---

k Compare Gk 15.4: Heb *from of old* l Q Ms Gk Vg: MT lacks *whom* that you and your men are to go out with me in the army." 2 David said to Ā'chish, "Very well, then you shall know what your servant can do." Ā'chish said to David, "Very well, I will make you my bodyguard for life."

Saul Consults a Medium
(Cp Deut 18.9–14)

3 Now Samuel had died, and all Israel had mourned for him and buried him in Rā'mah, his own city. Saul had expelled the mediums and the wizards from the land. 4 The Phi•lis'tines assembled, and came and encamped at Shū'nem. Saul gathered all Israel, and they encamped at Gil•bō'a. 5 When Saul saw the army of the Phi•lis'tines, he was afraid, and his heart trembled greatly. 6 When Saul inquired of the LORD, the LORD did not answer him, not by dreams, or by Ū'rim, or by prophets. 7 Then Saul said to his servants, "Seek out for me a woman who is a medium, so that I may go to her and inquire of her." His servants said to him, "There is a medium at En'dor."

8 So Saul disguised himself and put on other clothes and went there, he and two men with him. They came to the woman by night. And he said, "Consult a spirit for me, and bring up for me the one whom I name to you." 9 The woman said to him, "Surely you know what Saul has done, how he has cut off the mediums and the wizards from the land. Why then are you laying a snare for my life to bring about my death?" 10 But Saul swore to her by the LORD, "As the LORD lives, no punishment shall come upon you for this thing." 11 Then the woman said, "Whom shall I bring up for you?" He answered, "Bring up Samuel for me." 12 When the woman saw Samuel, she cried out with a loud voice; and the woman said to Saul, "Why have you deceived me? You are Saul!" 13 The king said to her, "Have no fear; what do you see?" The woman said to Saul, "I see a divine being^m coming up out of the ground." 14 He said to her, "What is his appearance?" She said, "An old man is coming up; he is wrapped in a robe." So Saul knew that it was Samuel, and he bowed with his face to the ground, and did obeisance.

15 Then Samuel said to Saul, "Why have you disturbed me by bringing me up?" Saul answered, "I am in great distress, for the Phi•lis'tines are warring against me, and God has turned away from me and answers me no more, either by prophets or by dreams; so I have summoned you to tell me what I should do." 16 Samuel said, "Why then do you ask me, since the LORD has turned from you and become your enemy? 17 The LORD has done to you just as he spoke by me; for the LORD has torn the kingdom out of your hand, and given it to your neighbor, David. 18 Because you did not obey the voice of the LORD, and did not carry out his fierce wrath against Am'a•lek, therefore the LORD has done this thing to you today. 19 Moreover the LORD will give Israel along with you into the hands of the Phi•lis'tines; and tomorrow you and your sons shall be with me; the LORD will also give the army of Israel into the hands of the Phi•lis'tines."

20 Immediately Saul fell full length on the ground, filled with fear because of the words of Samuel; and there was no strength in him, for he had eaten nothing all day and all night. 21 The woman came to Saul, and when she saw that he was terrified, she said to him, "Your servant has listened to you; I have taken my life in my hand, and have listened to what you have said to me. 22 Now therefore, you also listen to your servant; let me set a morsel of bread before you. Eat, that you may have strength when you go on your way." 23 He refused, and said, "I will not eat." But his servants, together with the woman, urged him; and he listened to their words. So he got up from the ground and sat on the bed. 24 Now the woman had a fatted calf in the house. She quickly slaughtered it, and she took flour, kneaded it, and baked unleavened cakes. 25 She put them before Saul and his servants, and they ate. Then they rose and went away that night.

The Philistines Reject David

29 Now the Phi•lis'tines gathered all their forces at Ā'phek, while the Israelites were encamped by the fountain that is in Jez'rē•el. 2 As the lords of the Phi•lis'tines were passing on by hundreds and by thousands, and David and his men were passing on in the rear with Ā'chish, 3 the commanders of the Phi•lis'tines said, "What are these Hebrews doing here?" Ā'chish said to the commanders of the Phi•lis'tines, "Is this not David, the servant of King Saul of Israel, who has been with me now for days and years? Since he deserted to me I have found no fault in him to this day." 4 But the commanders of the Phi•lis'tines were angry with him; and the commanders of the Phi•lis'tines said to him, "Send the man back, so that he may return to the place that you have assigned to him; he shall not go down with us to battle, or else he may become an adversary to us in the battle. For how could this fellow reconcile himself to his lord? Would it not be with the heads of the men here? 5 Is this not David, of whom they sing to one another in dances,

'Saul has killed his thousands,
and David his ten thousands'?"

6 Then Ā'chish called David and said to him, "As the LORD lives, you have been honest, and to me it seems right that you should march out and in

---

^m Or a god; or gods

with me in the campaign; for I have found nothing wrong in you from the day of your coming to me until today. Nevertheless the lords do not approve of you. 7 So go back now; and go peaceably; do nothing to displease the lords of the Phi·lis'tines." 8 David said to Ā'chish, "But what have I done? What have you found in your servant from the day I entered your service until now, that I should not go and fight against the enemies of my lord the king?" 9 Ā'chish replied to David, "I know that you are as blameless in my sight as an angel of God; nevertheless, the commanders of the Phi·lis'tines have said, 'He shall not go up with us to the battle.' 10 Now then rise early in the morning, you and the servants of your lord who came with you, and go to the place that I appointed for you. As for the evil report, do not take it to heart, for you have done well before me.[n] Start early in the morning, and leave as soon as you have light." 11 So David set out with his men early in the morning, to return to the land of the Phi·lis'tines. But the Phi·lis'tines went up to Jez're·el.

David Avenges the Destruction of Ziklag

30 Now when David and his men came to Zik'lag on the third day, the A·mal'e·kites had made a raid on the Neg'eb and on Zik'lag. They had attacked Zik'lag, burned it down, 2 and taken captive the women and all[o] who were in it, both small and great; they killed none of them, but carried them off, and went their way. 3 When David and his men came to the city, they found it burned down, and their wives and sons and daughters taken captive. 4 Then David and the people who were with him raised their voices and wept, until they had no more strength to weep. 5 David's two wives also had been taken captive, A·hin'ō·am of Jez're·el, and Ab'i·gāil the widow of Nā'bal of Car'mel. 6 David was in great danger; for the people spoke of stoning him, because all the people were bitter in spirit for their sons and daughters. But David strengthened himself in the LORD his God.

7 David said to the priest A·bi'a·thar son of A·him'e·lech, "Bring me the ephod." So A·bi'a·thar brought the ephod to David. 8 David inquired of the LORD, "Shall I pursue this band? Shall I overtake them?" He answered him, "Pursue; for you shall surely overtake and shall surely rescue." 9 So David set out, he and the six hundred men who were with him. They came to the Wadi Bē'sor, where those stayed who were left behind. 10 But David went on with the pursuit, he and four hundred men; two hundred stayed behind, too exhausted to cross the Wadi Bē'sor.

11 In the open country they found an Egyptian, and brought him to David. They gave him bread and he ate; they gave him water to drink; 12 they also gave him a piece of fig cake and two clusters of raisins. When he had eaten, his spirit revived; for he had not eaten bread or drunk water for three days and three nights. 13 Then David said to him, "To whom do you belong? Where are you from?" He said, "I am a young man of Egypt, servant to an A·mal'e·kite. My master left me behind because I fell sick three days ago. 14 We had made a raid on the Neg'eb of the Cher'e·thites and on that which belongs to Judah and on the Neg'eb of Caleb; and we burned Zik'lag down." 15 David said to him, "Will you take me down to this raiding party?" He said, "Swear to me by God that you will not kill me, or hand me over to my master, and I will take you down to them."

16 When he had taken him down, they were spread out all over the ground, eating and drinking and dancing, because of the great amount of spoil they had taken from the land of the Phi·lis'tines and from the land of Judah. 17 David attacked them from twilight until the evening of the next day. Not one of them escaped, except four hundred young men, who mounted camels and fled. 18 David recovered all that the A·mal'e·kites had taken; and David rescued his two wives. 19 Nothing was missing, whether small or great, sons or daughters, spoil or anything that had been taken; David brought back everything. 20 David also captured all the flocks and herds, which were driven ahead of the other cattle; people said, "This is David's spoil."

21 Then David came to the two hundred men who had been too exhausted to follow David, and who had been left at the Wadi Bē'sor. They went out to meet David and to meet the people who were with him. When David drew near to the people he saluted them. 22 Then all the corrupt and worthless fellows among the men who had gone with David said, "Because they did not go with us, we will not give them any of the spoil that we have recovered, except that each man may take his wife and children, and leave." 23 But David said, "You shall not do so, my brothers, with what the LORD has given us; he has preserved us and handed over to us the raiding party that attacked us. 24 Who would listen to you in this matter? For the share of the one who goes down into the battle shall be the same as the share of the one who stays by the baggage; they shall share alike." 25 From that day forward he made it a statute and an ordinance for Israel; it continues to the present day.

26 When David came to Zik'lag, he sent part of the spoil to his friends, the elders of Judah, saying, "Here is a present for you from the spoil of the enemies of the LORD"; 27 it was for those in Beth'el, in

---

[n] Gk: Heb lacks *and go to the place . . . done well before me*
[o] Gk: Heb lacks *and all*

Suicide Is Not an Answer

In I Sam 31.4, Saul commits suicide out of fear of what his enemies would do to him. His death leaves a gap for the Israelites, and David, Saul's enemy, deeply mourns his death in 2 Samuel, chapter 1.

A popular newspaper advice columnist printed a letter from someone who was writing to share a thought on suicide. He had decided that his life was not worth living anymore and planned to kill himself. The moment before he was about to do it, he thought about who would find him, and then he stopped. He realized that he couldn't put someone through the pain and suffering of finding him dead from suicide. Because he thought of another, he no longer looked at his life as hopeless.

No life is worthless! No pain is invincible! No matter how overwhelming your struggles and challenges seem, there are people who can help you, and people who could not bear to lose you. Seek God for help, seek others for help—suicide is never a solution!

For more on suicide, see "Judas's Suicide," Mt 27.3–10.

▶ I Sam 31.1–6

Rā'moth of the Neg'eb, in Jat'tir, 28 in A•rŏ'er, in Siph'moth, in Esh•te•mŏ'a, 29 in Rā'cal, in the towns of the Je•rah'mē•el•ītes, in the towns of the Ken'ītes, 30 in Hor'mah, in Bor-ash'an, in Ā'thach, 31 in Hĕ'bron, all the places where David and his men had roamed.

The Death of Saul and His Sons
(1 Chr 10.1–14)

31 Now the Phi•lis'tines fought against Is-rael; and the men of Israel fled before the Phi•lis'tines, and many fell *p* on Mount Gil•bō'a. 2 The Phi•lis'tines overtook Saul and his sons; and the Phi•lis'tines killed Jonathan and A•bin'a•dab and Mal•chī•shū'a, the sons of Saul. 3 The battle pressed hard upon Saul; the archers found him, and he was badly wounded by them. 4 Then Saul said to his armor-bearer, "Draw your sword and thrust me through with it, so that these uncircumcised may not come and thrust me through, and make sport of me." But his armor-bearer was unwilling; for he was terrified. So Saul took his own sword and fell upon it. 5 When his armor-bearer saw that Saul was dead, he also fell upon his sword and died with him. 6 So Saul and his three sons and his armor-bearer and all

his men died together on the same day. 7 When the men of Israel who were on the other side of the valley and those beyond the Jordan saw that the men of Israel had fled and that Saul and his sons were dead, they forsook their towns and fled; and the Phi•lis'tines came and occupied them.

8 The next day, when the Phi•lis'tines came to strip the dead, they found Saul and his three sons fallen on Mount Gil•bō'a. 9 They cut off his head, stripped off his armor, and sent messengers throughout the land of the Phi•lis'tines to carry the good news to the houses of their idols and to the people. 10 They put his armor in the temple of As-tar'tē;*q* and they fastened his body to the wall of Beth-shan. 11 But when the inhabitants of Jā'besh-gil'ē•ad heard what the Phi•lis'tines had done to Saul, 12 all the valiant men set out, traveled all night long, and took the body of Saul and the bodies of his sons from the wall of Beth-shan. They came to Jā'besh and burned them there. 13 Then they took their bones and buried them under the tamarisk tree in Jā'besh, and fasted seven days.

---

p Heb *and they fell slain*   *q* Heb plural

1
S
A
M

Politician Guilty of Taking Foreign Bribes!" "Minister Accused of Sexual Misconduct!" "Athlete Arrested on Drug Charges!" Sometimes it seems as if the news is filled with one scandal after another. "What's happening in the world today?" we may ask in despair. "Are there no honest, decent people left?" After reading 2 Samuel, you will realize that scandals among the rich and powerful are nothing new. But somehow, God's will is accomplished despite human sin.

At a Glance

- **Chapter 1.** David mourns Saul's death.
- **Chapters 2–20.** the reign of David
- **Chapters 21–24.** miscellaneous texts, including David's last words

In-depth

The main character in 2 Samuel is King David, whom we already met in 1 Samuel. The youngest of Jesse's sons, David is secretly anointed to succeed King Saul; he kills Goliath, plays music in Saul's court, and is befriended by the king's son Jonathan. At the beginning of 2 Samuel, when David takes the throne and quickly extends Israel's boundaries in every direction, everything looks hopeful for the nation.

As 2 Samuel continues, however, we discover that this hero is far from perfect: he sleeps with Bathsheba, the wife of one of his soldiers, and then tries to deceive the man when Bathsheba reports that she is pregnant. Later, he has the soldier killed and takes Bathsheba as his own. Soon, several tragedies befall his family, and further bad decisions hurt his reign, leaving us with a mixed picture of the second king of Israel. Was David a great saint or a great sinner?

It was through David that God established a new Covenant with the people of Israel (7.1–17). This fact is underlined in a memorable way when David, after completing his own magnificent palace, declares that he will build a house for God. But God does not want a temple; God wishes to maintain a covenantal relationship with the people of Israel through all history: "Your throne shall be established forever" (verse 16).

Although a talented military leader and a powerful ruler, King David shared our broken human nature. The author of 2 Samuel reminds us that even the great and the mighty stand in need of God's help and mercy; even they must keep God's Covenant. Because of David's reliance on God, he became a symbol of the ideal king and of the future messiah. David's greatness—and our own—comes from a willing reliance on God.

Quick Facts

Period Covered
from 1000 to 961 B.C.

Author
same as for 1 Samuel

Theme
David's rise to power and his fall into sin

Of Note
Samuel does not appear in this book, although it carries his name.

2 Samuel

David Mourns for Saul and Jonathan

1 After the death of Saul, when David had returned from defeating the A·mal'e·kites, David remained two days in Zik'lag. 2 On the third day, a man came from Saul's camp, with his clothes torn and dirt on his head. When he came to David, he fell to the ground and did obeisance. 3 David said to him, "Where have you come from?" He said to him, "I have escaped from the camp of Israel." 4 David said to him, "How did things go? Tell me!" He answered, "The army fled from the battle, but also many of the army fell and died; and Saul and his son Jonathan also died." 5 Then David asked the young man who was reporting to him, "How do you know that Saul and his son Jonathan died?" 6 The young man reporting to him said, "I happened to be on Mount Gil·bo'a; and there was Saul leaning on his spear, while the chariots and the horsemen drew close to him. 7 When he looked behind him, he saw me, and called to me. I answered, 'Here sir.' 8 And he said to me, 'Who are you?' I answered him, 'I am an A·mal'e·kite.' 9 He said to me, 'Come, stand over me and kill me; for convulsions have seized me, and yet my life still lingers.' 10 So I stood over him, and killed him, for I knew that he could not live after he had fallen. I took the crown that was

on his head and the armlet that was on his arm, and I have brought them here to my lord."

11 Then David took hold of his clothes and tore them; and all the men who were with him did the same. 12 They mourned and wept, and fasted until evening for Saul and for his son Jonathan, and for the army of the LORD and for the house of Israel, because they had fallen by the sword. 13 David said to the young man who had reported to him, "Where do you come from?" He answered, "I am the son of a resident alien, an A·mal'e·kite." 14 David said to him, "Were you not afraid to lift your hand to destroy the LORD's anointed?" 15 Then David called one of the young men and said, "Come here and strike him down." So he struck him down and he died. 16 David said to him, "Your blood be on your head; for your own mouth has testified against you, saying, 'I have killed the LORD's anointed.' "

17 David intoned this lamentation over Saul and his son Jonathan. 18 (He ordered that The Song of the Bow*a* be taught to the people of Judah; it is written in the Book of Jash'ar.) He said:
19 Your glory, O Israel, lies slain upon your
high places!
How the mighty have fallen!

---

a Heb *that The Bow*

20 Tell it not in Gath,
   proclaim it not in the streets of
      Ash·ke·lon;
   or the daughters of the Phi·lis'tines will
      rejoice,
   the daughters of the uncircumcised will
      exult.

21 You mountains of Gil·bō'a,
   let there be no dew or rain upon you,
   nor bounteous fields!*b*
   For there the shield of the mighty was
      defiled,
   the shield of Saul, anointed with oil no
      more.

22 From the blood of the slain,
   from the fat of the mighty,
   the bow of Jonathan did not turn back,
   nor the sword of Saul return empty.

23 Saul and Jonathan, beloved and lovely!
   In life and in death they were not
      divided;
   they were swifter than eagles,
   they were stronger than lions.

24 O daughters of Israel, weep over Saul,
   who clothed you with crimson, in luxury,
   who put ornaments of gold on your
      apparel.

25 How the mighty have fallen
   in the midst of the battle!

Jonathan lies slain upon your high places.
26   I am distressed for you, my brother Jonathan;
   greatly beloved were you to me;
      your love to me was wonderful,
      passing the love of women.

27 How the mighty have fallen,
   and the weapons of war perished!

David Anointed King of Judah

2 After this David inquired of the LORD, "Shall I go up into any of the cities of Judah?" The LORD said to him, "Go up." David said, "To which shall I go up?" He said, "To Hē'bron." 2 So David went up there, along with his two wives, A·hin'-ō·am of Jez're·el, and Ab'i·gāil the widow of Nā'bal of Car'mel. 3 David brought up the men who were with him, every one with his household; and they settled in the towns of Hē'bron. 4 Then the people of Judah came, and there they anointed David king over the house of Judah.

When they told David, "It was the people of Jā'besh-gil'ē·ad who buried Saul," 5 David sent messengers to the people of Jā'besh-gil'ē·ad, and said to them, "May you be blessed by the LORD, because you showed this loyalty to Saul your lord, and buried him! 6 Now may the LORD show steadfast love and faithfulness to you! And I too will reward you because you have done this thing. 7 Therefore let your hands be strong, and be valiant; for Saul your lord is dead, and the house of Judah has anointed me king over them."

---

b Meaning of Heb uncertain

2
S
A
M

David the Musician

LIVE IT!

Most of us know that music can be a powerful force. Most of us listen to music every day. It helps us get through hard times. It is also an essential part of most celebrations. What would a wedding be like without music? What would a party be like without music? No doubt each of us has a favorite song or musician we turn to often, especially when we need a lift. And no doubt God works through music to touch our hearts.

David also knew the power of music. His song of mourning for Saul and Jonathan is an emotional tribute to both men, but especially to his close friend, Jonathan. If you are a musician, you know that God also works through you to touch the hearts of others and speak to them. Let David be your inspiration. He played the lyre (harp), sang, and wrote beautiful songs, which we call psalms. He prayed through music. There is a saying that goes, "Those who sing pray twice." David seemed to live that out in his life.

What are the songs and music that help you to pray and to recall God's presence? If you are a musician, when have you felt God's presence while making music?

▶ 2 Sam 1.17–27

Ishbaal King of Israel

8 But Abner son of Ner, commander of Saul's army, had taken Ish'bā·al^c son of Saul, and brought him over to Mā·ha·nā'im. 9 He made him king over Gil'e·ad, the Ash'ur·ites, Jez're'el, E'phra·im, Benjamin, and over all Israel. 10 Ish'bā·al,^c Saul's son, was forty years old when he began to reign over Israel, and he reigned two years. But the house of Judah followed David. 11 The time that David was king in Hē'bron over the house of Judah was seven years and six months.

The Battle of Gibeon

12 Abner son of Ner, and the servants of Ish'bā·al^c son of Saul, went out from Mā·ha·nā'im to Gib'e·on. 13 Jō'ab son of Ze·rū'i·ah, and the servants of David, went out and met them at the pool of Gib'e·on. One group sat on one side of the pool, while the other sat on the other side of the pool. 14 Abner said to Jō'ab, "Let the young men come forward and have a contest before us." Jō'ab said, "Let them come forward." 15 So they came forward and were counted as they passed by, twelve for Benjamin and Ish'bā·al^c son of Saul, and twelve of the servants of David. 16 Each grasped his opponent by the head, and thrust his sword in his opponent's side; so they fell down together. Therefore that place was called Hel'kath-haz·zū'rim,^d which is at Gib'e·on. 17 The battle was very fierce that day; and Abner and the men of Israel were beaten by the servants of David.

18 The three sons of Ze·rū'i·ah were there, Jō'ab, A·bi'shaī, and As'a·hel. Now As'a·hel was as swift of foot as a wild gazelle. 19 As'a·hel pursued Abner, turning neither to the right nor to the left as he followed him. 20 Then Abner looked back and said, "Is it you, As'a·hel?" He answered, "Yes, it is." 21 Abner said to him, "Turn to your right or to your left, and seize one of the young men, and take his spoil." But As'a·hel would not turn away from following him. 22 Abner said again to As'a·hel, "Turn away from following me; why should I strike you to the ground? How then could I show my face to your brother Jō'ab?" 23 But he refused to turn away. So Abner struck him in the stomach with the butt of his spear, so that the spear came out at his back. He fell there, and died where he lay. And all those who came to the place where As'a·hel had fallen and died, stood still.

24 But Jō'ab and A·bi'shaī pursued Abner. As the sun was going down they came to the hill of Am'mah, which lies before Gi'ah on the way to the wilderness of Gib'e·on. 25 The Ben'ja·min·ites rallied around Abner and formed a single band; they took their stand on the top of a hill. 26 Then Abner called to Jō'ab, "Is the sword to keep devouring forever? Do you not know that the end will be bitter?

How long will it be before you order your people to turn from the pursuit of their kinsmen?" 27 Jō'ab said, "As God lives, if you had not spoken, the people would have continued to pursue their kinsmen, not stopping until morning." 28 Jō'ab sounded the trumpet and all the people stopped; they no longer pursued Israel or engaged in battle any further.

29 Abner and his men traveled all that night through the Ar'a·bah; they crossed the Jordan, and, marching the whole forenoon,^e they came to Mā·ha·nā'im. 30 Jō'ab returned from the pursuit of Abner; and when he had gathered all the people together, there were missing of David's servants nineteen men besides As'a·hel. 31 But the servants of David had killed of Benjamin three hundred sixty of Abner's men. 32 They took up As'a·hel and buried him in the tomb of his father, which was at Bethlehem. Jō'ab and his men marched all night, and the day broke upon them at Hē'bron.

Abner Defects to David

3 There was a long war between the house of Saul and the house of David; David grew stronger and stronger, while the house of Saul became weaker and weaker.

2 Sons were born to David at Hē'bron: his firstborn was Am'non, of A·hin'ō·am of Jez're'el; 3 his second, Chil'ē·ab, of Ab'i·gāil the widow of Nā'bal of Car'mel; the third, Ab'sa·lom son of Mā'a·cah, daughter of King Tal'maī of Gē'shur; 4 the fourth, Ad·o·nī'jah son of Hag'gith; the fifth, Sheph·a·tī'ah son of A·bī'tal; 5 and the sixth, Ith're·am, of David's wife Eg'lah. These were born to David in Hē'bron.

6 While there was war between the house of Saul and the house of David, Abner was making himself strong in the house of Saul. 7 Now Saul had a concubine whose name was Riz'pah daughter of Ā'i·ah. And Ish'bā·al^f said to Abner, "Why have you gone in to my father's concubine?" 8 The words of Ish'bā·al^c made Abner very angry; he said, "Am I a dog's head for Judah? Today I keep showing loyalty to the house of your father Saul, to his brothers, and to his friends, and have not given you into the hand of David; and yet you charge me now with a crime concerning this woman. 9 So may God do to Abner and so may he add to it! For just what the LORD has sworn to David, that will I accomplish for him, 10 to transfer the kingdom from the house of Saul, and set up the throne of David over Israel and over Judah, from Dan to Bē'er-shē'ba." 11 And Ish'bā·al^f could not answer Abner another word, because he feared him.

---

^c Gk Compare 1 Chr 8.33; 9.39: Heb *Ish-bosheth*, "man of shame"   ^d That is *Field of Sword-edges*   ^e Meaning of Heb uncertain   ^f Heb *And he*

12 Abner sent messengers to David at Hĕ′bron,*g* saying, "To whom does the land belong? Make your covenant with me, and I will give you my support to bring all Israel over to you." 13 He said, "Good; I will make a covenant with you. But one thing I require of you: you shall never appear in my presence unless you bring Saul's daughter Mĭ′chal when you come to see me." 14 Then David sent messengers to Saul's son Ish′bā•al,*h* saying, "Give me my wife Mĭ′chal, to whom I became engaged at the price of one hundred foreskins of the Phi•lis′tines." 15 Ish′bā•al*h* sent and took her from her husband Pal′ti•el the son of Lā′ish. 16 But her husband went with her, weeping as he walked behind her all the way to Ba•hŭ′rim. Then Abner said to him, "Go back home!" So he went back.

17 Abner sent word to the elders of Israel, saying, "For some time past you have been seeking David as king over you. 18 Now then bring it about; for the LORD has promised David: Through my servant David I will save my people Israel from the hand of the Phi•lis′tines, and from all their enemies." 19 Abner also spoke directly to the Ben′ja•min•ites; then Abner went to tell David at Hĕ′bron all that Israel and the whole house of Benjamin were ready to do.

20 When Abner came with twenty men to David at Hĕ′bron, David made a feast for Abner and the men who were with him. 21 Abner said to David, "Let me go and rally all Israel to my lord the king, in order that they may make a covenant with you, and that you may reign over all that your heart desires." So David dismissed Abner, and he went away in peace.

Abner Is Killed by Joab

22 Just then the servants of David arrived with Jŏ′ab from a raid, bringing much spoil with them. But Abner was not with David at Hĕ′bron, for David*i* had dismissed him, and he had gone away in peace. 23 When Jŏ′ab and all the army that was with him came, it was told Jŏ′ab, "Abner son of Ner came to the king, and he has dismissed him, and he has gone away in peace." 24 Then Jŏ′ab went to the king and said, "What have you done? Abner came to you; why did you dismiss him, so that he got away? 25 You know that Abner son of Ner came to deceive you, and to learn your comings and goings and to learn all that you are doing."

26 When Jŏ′ab came out from David's presence, he sent messengers after Abner, and they brought him back from the cistern of Sĭ′rah; but David did not know about it. 27 When Abner returned to Hĕ′bron, Jŏ′ab took him aside in the gateway to speak with him privately, and there he stabbed him in the stomach. So he died for shedding*j* the blood of As′a•hel, Jŏ′ab's*k* brother. 28 Afterward, when David heard of it, he said, "I and my kingdom are forever guiltless before the LORD for the blood of Abner son of Ner. 29 May the guilt*l* fall on the head of Jŏ′ab, and on all his father's house; and may the house of Jŏ′ab never be without one who has a discharge, or who is leprous,*m* or who holds a spindle, or who falls by the sword, or who lacks food!" 30 So Jŏ′ab and his brother A•bi′shai murdered Abner because he had killed their brother As′a•hel in the battle at Gib′e•on.

31 Then David said to Jŏ′ab and to all the people who were with him, "Tear your clothes, and put on sackcloth, and mourn over Abner." And King David followed the bier. 32 They buried Abner at Hĕ′bron. The king lifted up his voice and wept at the grave of Abner, and all the people wept. 33 The king lamented for Abner, saying,

"Should Abner die as a fool dies?
34 Your hands were not bound,
      your feet were not fettered;
as one falls before the wicked
      you have fallen."

And all the people wept over him again. 35 Then all the people came to persuade David to eat something while it was still day; but David swore, saying, "So may God do to me, and more, if I taste bread or anything else before the sun goes down!" 36 All the people took notice of it, and it pleased them; just as everything the king did pleased all the people. 37 So all the people and all Israel understood that day that the king had no part in the killing of Abner son of Ner. 38 And the king said to his servants, "Do you not know that a prince and a great man has fallen this day in Israel? 39 Today I am powerless, even though anointed king; these men, the sons of Ze•rŭ′i•ah, are too violent for me. The LORD pay back the one who does wickedly in accordance with his wickedness!"

Ishbaal Assassinated

4 When Saul's son Ish′bā•al*n* heard that Abner had died at Hĕ′bron, his courage failed, and all Israel was dismayed. 2 Saul's son had two captains of raiding bands; the name of the one was Bā′a•nah, and the name of the other Rĕ′chab. They were sons of Rim′mon a Ben′ja•min•ite from Be•er′oth—for Be•er′oth is considered to belong to Benjamin. 3 (Now the people of Be•er′oth had fled to Git′ta•im and are there as resident aliens to this day).

4 Saul's son Jonathan had a son who was crippled in his feet. He was five years old when the news about Saul and Jonathan came from Jez′re•el.

g Gk: Heb *where he was*   *h* Heb *Ish-bosheth*   *i* Heb *he*
j Heb lacks *shedding*   *k* Heb *his*   *l* Heb *May it*   *m* A term for several skin diseases; precise meaning uncertain   *n* Heb lacks *Ishbaal*

His nurse picked him up and fled; and, in her haste to flee, it happened that he fell and became lame. His name was Me·phib'o·sheth.⁰

5 Now the sons of Rim'mon the Be·er'oth·ite, Re'chab and Ba'a·nah, set out, and about the heat of the day they came to the house of Ish'ba·al,ᵖ while he was taking his noonday rest. 6 They came inside the house as though to take wheat, and they struck him in the stomach; then Re'chab and his brother Ba'a·nah escaped.�q 7 Now they had come into the house while he was lying on his couch in his bed-chamber; they attacked him, killed him, and be-headed him. Then they took his head and traveled by way of the Ar'a·bah all night long. 8 They brought the head of Ish'ba·alʳ to David at He'bron and said to the king, "Here is the head of Ish'ba·al,ᵖ son of Saul, your enemy, who sought your life; the LORD has avenged my lord the king this day on Saul and on his offspring."

9 David answered Re'chab and his brother Ba'a·nah, the sons of Rim'mon the Be·er'oth·ite, "As the LORD lives, who has redeemed my life out of every adversity, 10 when the one who told me, 'See, Saul is dead,' thought he was bringing good news, I seized him and killed him at Zik'lag—this was the reward I gave him for his news. 11 How much more then, when wicked men have killed a righteous man on his bed in his own house! And now shall I not require his blood at your hand, and destroy you from the earth?" 12 So David commanded the young men, and they killed them; they cut off their hands and feet, and hung their bodies beside the pool at He'bron. But the head of Ish'ba·alᵖ they took and buried in the tomb of Abner at He'bron.

David Anointed King of All Israel
(1 Chr 11.1–3)

5 Then all the tribes of Israel came to David at He'bron, and said, "Look, we are your bone and flesh. 2 For some time, while Saul was king over us, it was you who led out Israel and brought it in. The LORD said to you: It is you who shall be shep-herd of my people Israel, you who shall be ruler over Israel." 3 So all the elders of Israel came to the king at He'bron; and King David made a covenant with them at He'bron before the LORD, and they anointed David king over Israel. 4 David was thirty years old when he began to reign, and he reigned forty years. 5 At He'bron he reigned over Judah sev-en years and six months; and at Jerusalem he reigned over all Israel and Judah thirty-three years.

Jerusalem Made Capital of
the United Kingdom
(1 Chr 11.4–9; 14.1–7)

6 The king and his men marched to Jerusalem against the Jeb'u·sites, the inhabitants of the land, who said to David, "You will not come in here, even the blind and the lame will turn you back"—think-ing, "David cannot come in here." 7 Nevertheless David took the stronghold of Zion, which is now the city of David. 8 David had said on that day, "Whoever would strike down the Jeb'u·sites, let him get up the water shaft to attack the lame and the blind, those whom David hates."ʳ Therefore it is said, "The blind and the lame shall not come into the house." 9 David occupied the stronghold, and named it the city of David. David built the city all around from the Mil'lō inward. 10 And David be-came greater and greater, for the LORD, the God of hosts, was with him.

11 King Hiram of Tỹre sent messengers to David, along with cedar trees, and carpenters and masons who built David a house. 12 David then perceived that the LORD had established him king over Israel, and that he had exalted his kingdom for the sake of his people Israel.

13 In Jerusalem, after he came from He'bron, David took more concubines and wives; and more sons and daughters were born to David. 14 These are the names of those who were born to him in Jerusalem: Sham'mu·a, Sho'bab, Nathan, Solomon, ¹⁵Ib'har, E·lish'u·a, Ne'pheg, Ja·phi'a, ¹⁶E·lish'a·ma, E·li'a·da, and E·liph'e·let.

Philistine Attack Repulsed
(1 Chr 14.8–17)

17 When the Phi·lis'tines heard that David had been anointed king over Israel, all the Phi·lis'tines went up in search of David; but David heard about it and went down to the stronghold. 18 Now the Phi·lis'tines had come and spread out in the valley of Reph'a·im. 19 David inquired of the LORD, "Shall I go up against the Phi·lis'tines? Will you give them into my hand?" The LORD said to David, "Go up; for I will certainly give the Phi·lis'tines into your hand." 20 So David came to Ba'al-pe·ra'zim, and David defeated them there. He said, "The LORD has burst forth againstˢ my enemies before me, like a bursting flood." Therefore that place is called Ba'al-pe·ra'zim.ᵗ 21 The Phi·lis'tines abandoned their idols there, and David and his men carried them away.

22 Once again the Phi·lis'tines came up, and were spread out in the valley of Reph'a·im. 23 When David inquired of the LORD, he said, "You shall not go up; go around to their rear, and come upon them opposite the balsam trees. 24 When you hear the sound of marching in the tops of the balsam

---

⁰ In 1 Chr 8.34 and 9.40, *Merib-baal*   ᵖ Heb *Ish-bosheth*
�q Meaning of Heb of verse 6 uncertain   ʳ Another reading is *those who hate David*   ˢ Heb *paraz*   ᵗ That is *Lord of Bursting Forth*

trees, then be on the alert; for then the LORD has gone out before you to strike down the army of the Phi·lis'tines." 25 David did just as the LORD had commanded him; and he struck down the Phi·lis'tines from Gē'ba all the way to Gē'zer.

David Brings the Ark to Jerusalem
(1 Chr 13.1–14; 15.25—16.3)

6 David again gathered all the chosen men of Israel, thirty thousand. 2 David and all the people with him set out and went from Bā'a·lējū'dah, to bring up from there the ark of God, which is called by the name of the LORD of hosts who is enthroned on the cherubim. 3 They carried the ark of God on a new cart, and brought it out of the house of A·bin'a·dab, which was on the hill. Uz'zah and A·hi'ō,*u* the sons of A·bin'a·dab, were driving the new cart 4 with the ark of God;*v* and A·hi'ō*u* went in front of the ark. 5 David and all the house of Israel were dancing before the LORD with all their might, with songs*w* and lyres and harps and tambourines and castanets and cymbals.

6 When they came to the threshing floor of Na'con, Uz'zah reached out his hand to the ark of God and took hold of it, for the oxen shook it. 7 The anger of the LORD was kindled against Uz'zah; and God struck him there because he reached out his hand to the ark;*x* and he died there beside the ark of God. 8 David was angry because the LORD had burst forth with an outburst upon Uz'zah; so that place is called Per'ez-uz'zah,*y* to this day. 9 David was afraid of the LORD that day; he said, "How can the ark of the LORD come into my care?" 10 So David was unwilling to take the ark of the LORD into his care in the city of David; instead David took it to the house of Ō'bed-ē'dom the Git'tite. 11 The ark of the LORD

remained in the house of Ō'bed-ē'dom the Git'tite three months; and the LORD blessed Ō'bed-ē'dom and all his household.

12 It was told King David, "The LORD has blessed the household of Ō'bed-ē'dom and all that belongs to him, because of the ark of God." So David went and brought up the ark of God from the house of Ō'bed-ē'dom to the city of David with rejoicing; 13 and when those who bore the ark of the LORD had gone six paces, he sacrificed an ox and a fatling. 14 David danced before the LORD with all his might; David was girded with a linen ephod. 15 So David and all the house of Israel brought up the ark of the LORD with shouting, and with the sound of the trumpet.

16 As the ark of the LORD came into the city of David, Mī'chal daughter of Saul looked out of the window, and saw King David leaping and dancing before the LORD; and she despised him in her heart.

17 They brought in the ark of the LORD, and set it in its place, inside the tent that David had pitched for it; and David offered burnt offerings and offerings of well-being before the LORD. 18 When David had finished offering the burnt offerings and the offerings of well-being, he blessed the people in the name of the LORD of hosts, 19 and distributed food among all the people, the whole multitude of Israel, both men and women, to each a cake of bread, a portion of meat,*z* and a cake of raisins. Then all the people went back to their homes.

---

u Or *and his brother*   *v* Compare Gk: Heb *and brought it out of the house of Abinadab, which was on the hill with the ark of God*   *w* Q Ms Gk 1 Chr 13.8: Heb *fir trees*   *x* 1 Chr 13.10 Compare Q Ms: Meaning of Heb uncertain   *y* That is *Bursting Out Against Uzzah*   *z* Vg: Meaning of Heb uncertain

---

LIVE IT!

The Dance of Life

It's a party! How else could we describe the festivities surrounding the triumphant bringing of the ark of the LORD into Jerusalem? And King David is leading the way, dancing before the LORD "with all his might" (2 Sam 6.14). What a scene that must have been! What a wonderfully uninhibited way for David to express his great joy at escorting the ark into the city he has made his own.

So often we attend religious rituals as mere observers, much like Michal, David's wife, being critical and uninvolved. David shows us the true way to celebrate—with singing and dancing and eating. We need to celebrate together the presence of the LORD in our life! Here, David is our role model. Let us sing the song in our heart and dance to the music God has planted within us.

How can we do a better job of celebrating the LORD in our life? Are we observers or participants in the dance of life?

▶ 2 Sam 6.11–19

20 David returned to bless his household. But Mi'chal the daughter of Saul came out to meet David, and said, "How the king of Israel honored himself today, uncovering himself today before the eyes of his servants' maids, as any vulgar fellow might shamelessly uncover himself!" 21 David said to Mi'chal, "It was before the LORD, who chose me in place of your father and all his household, to appoint me as prince over Israel, the people of the LORD, that I have danced before the LORD. 22 I will make myself yet more contemptible than this, and I will be abased in my own eyes; but by the maids of whom you have spoken, by them I shall be held in honor." 23 And Mi'chal the daughter of Saul had no child to the day of her death.

God's Covenant with David
(1 Chr 17.1–15)

7 Now when the king was settled in his house, and the LORD had given him rest from all his enemies around him, 2 the king said to the prophet Nathan, "See now, I am living in a house of cedar, but the ark of God stays in a tent." 3 Nathan said to the king, "Go, do all that you have in mind; for the LORD is with you."

4 But that same night the word of the LORD came to Nathan: 5 Go and tell my servant David: Thus says the LORD: Are you the one to build me a house to live in? 6 I have not lived in a house since the day I brought up the people of Israel from Egypt to this day, but I have been moving about in a tent and a tabernacle. 7 Wherever I have moved about among all the people of Israel, did I ever speak a word with any of the tribal leaders[a] of Israel, whom I commanded to shepherd my people Israel, saying, "Why have you not built me a house of cedar?" 8 Now therefore thus you shall say to my servant David: Thus says the LORD of hosts: I took you from the pasture, from following the sheep to be prince over my people Israel; 9 and I have been with you wherever you went, and have cut off all your enemies from before you; and I will make for you a great name, like the name of the great ones of the earth. 10 And I will appoint a place for my people Israel and will plant them, so that they may live in their own place, and be disturbed no more; and evildoers shall afflict them no more, as formerly, 11 from the time that I appointed judges over my people Israel; and I will give you rest from all your enemies. Moreover the LORD declares to you that the LORD will make you a house. 12 When your days are fulfilled and you lie down with your ancestors, I will raise up your offspring after you, who shall come forth from your body, and I will establish his kingdom. 13 He shall build a house for my name, and I will establish the throne of his kingdom forever. 14 I will be a father to him, and he shall be a

PRAY IT!
David Praises God

Then King David went in and sat before the LORD, and said, "Who am I, O Lord GOD, and what is my house, that you have brought me thus far?" (2 Sam 7.18). When was the last time you brought yourself before God, like King David, simply to offer praise for all God has done for you?

It is easy for us to feel too busy to take time for God. Then we complain and get frustrated because God does not seem to be around, giving our life direction. Taking quiet moments to place ourselves in humility before our God and to praise God for the good we experience is important.

Find a quiet place, take just fifteen minutes. No radio, no television, no book. Think of all the positive and happy things in your life, and in your own words, say, "Thank you, God, for caring for me and the people I love!"

▶ 2 Sam 7.18–29

son to me. When he commits iniquity, I will punish him with a rod such as mortals use, with blows inflicted by human beings. 15 But I will not take[b] my steadfast love from him, as I took it from Saul, whom I put away from before you. 16 Your house and your kingdom shall be made sure forever before me;[c] your throne shall be established forever. 17 In accordance with all these words and with all this vision, Nathan spoke to David.

David's Prayer
(1 Chr 17.16–27)

18 Then King David went in and sat before the LORD, and said, "Who am I, O Lord GOD, and what is my house, that you have brought me thus far? 19 And yet this was a small thing in your eyes, O Lord GOD; you have spoken also of your servant's house for a great while to come. May this be instruction for the people,[d] O Lord GOD! 20 And what more can David say to you? For you know your servant, O Lord GOD! 21 Because of your promise, and

a Or any of the tribes   b Gk Syr Vg 1 Chr 17.13: Heb *shall not depart*   c Gk Heb Mss: MT *before you*; Compare 2 Sam 7.26, 29   d Meaning of Heb uncertain according to your own heart, you have wrought all this greatness, so that your servant may know it. 22 Therefore you are great, O LORD God; for there is no one like you, and there is no God besides you, according to all that we have heard with our ears. 23 Who is like your people, like Israel? Is there another*e* nation on earth whose God went to redeem it as a people, and to make a name for himself, doing great and awesome things for them,*f* by driving out*g* before his people nations and their gods?*h* 24 And you established your people Israel for yourself to be your people forever; and you, O LORD, became their God. 25 And now, O LORD God, as for the word that you have spoken concerning your servant and concerning his house, confirm it forever; do as you have promised. 26 Thus your name will be magnified forever in the saying, 'The LORD of hosts is God over Israel'; and the house of your servant David will be established before you. 27 For you, O LORD of hosts, the God of Israel, have made this revelation to your servant, saying, 'I will build you a house'; therefore your servant has found courage to pray this prayer to you. 28 And now, O Lord GOD, you are God, and your words are true, and you have promised this good thing to your servant; 29 now therefore may it please you to bless the house of your servant, so that it may continue forever before you; for you, O Lord GOD, have spoken, and with your blessing shall the house of your servant be blessed forever."

David's Wars
(1 Chr 18.1–13)

8 Some time afterward, David attacked the Phi·lis'tines and subdued them; David took Meth'eg-am'mah out of the hand of the Phi·lis'tines. 2 He also defeated the Mō'ab·ites and, making them lie down on the ground, measured them off with a cord; he measured two lengths of cord for those who were to be put to death, and one length*i* for those who were to be spared. And the Mō'ab·ites became servants to David and brought tribute. 3 David also struck down King Had·a·dē'zer son of Rē'hob of Zō'bah, as he went to restore his monument*j* at the river Euphrates. 4 David took from him one thousand seven hundred horsemen, and twenty thousand foot soldiers. David hamstrung all the chariot horses, but left enough for a hundred chariots. 5 When the Ar·a·mē'ans of Damascus came to help King Had·a·dē'zer of Zō'bah, David killed twenty-two thousand men of the Ar·amē'ans. 6 Then David put garrisons among the Ara·mē'ans of Damascus; and the Ar·a·mē'ans became servants to David and brought tribute. The LORD gave victory to David wherever he went. 7 David took the gold shields that were carried by the servants of

Had·a·dē'zer, and brought them to Jerusalem. 8 From Bē'tah and from Be·rō'thaī, towns of Had·a·dē'zer, King David took a great amount of bronze.

9 When King Tō'i of Hā'math heard that David had defeated the whole army of Had·a·dē'zer, 10 Tō'i sent his son Jō'ram to King David, to greet him and to congratulate him because he had fought against Had·a·dē'zer and defeated him. Now Had·a·dē'zer had often been at war with Tō'i. Jō'ram brought with him articles of silver, gold, and bronze; 11 these also King David dedicated to the LORD, together with the silver and gold that he dedicated from all the nations he subdued, 12 from Ē'dom, Mō'ab, the Am'mon·ites, the Phi·lis'tines, Am'a·lek, and from the spoil of King Had·a·dē'zer son of Rē'hob of Zō'bah.

13 David won a name for himself. When he returned, he killed eighteen thousand Ē'dom·ites*k* in the Valley of Salt. 14 He put garrisons in Ē'dom; throughout all Ē'dom he put garrisons, and all the Ē'dom·ites became David's servants. And the LORD gave victory to David wherever he went.

David's Officers
(1 Chr 18.14–17)

15 So David reigned over all Israel; and David administered justice and equity to all his people. 16 Jō'ab son of Ze·rū'i·ah was over the army; Je·hosh'a·phat son of A·hī'lud was recorder; 17 Zā'dok son of A·hī'tub and A·him'e·lech son of A·bī'a·thar were priests; Se·rāi'ah was secretary; 18 Be·nā'i·ah son of Je·hoi'a·da was over*l* the Cher'e·thītes and the Pel'eth·ītes; and David's sons were priests.

David's Kindness to Mephibosheth

9 David asked, "Is there still anyone left of the house of Saul to whom I may show kindness for Jonathan's sake?" 2 Now there was a servant of the house of Saul whose name was Zī'ba, and he was summoned to David. The king said to him, "Are you Zī'ba?" And he said, "At your service!" 3 The king said, "Is there anyone remaining of the house of Saul to whom I may show the kindness of God?" Zī'ba said to the king, "There remains a son of Jonathan; he is crippled in his feet." 4 The king said to him, "Where is he?" Zī'ba said to the king, "He is in the house of Mā'chir son of Am'mi·el, at Lō-dē'bar." 5 Then King David sent and brought him from the house of Mā'chir son of Am'mi·el, at

e Gk: Heb *one*   *f* Heb *you*   *g* Gk 1 Chr 17.21: Heb *for your land*   *h* Cn: Heb *before your people, whom you redeemed for yourself from Egypt, nations and its gods*   *i* Heb *one full length*   *j* Compare 1 Sam 15.12 and 2 Sam 18.18   *k* Gk: Heb *returned from striking down eighteen thousand Arameans*   *l* Syr Tg Vg 20.23; 1 Chr 18.17: Heb lacks *was over*

Lō-dē'bar. 6 Me•phib'o•sheth^m son of Jonathan son of Saul came to David, and fell on his face and did obeisance. David said, "Me•phib'o•sheth!"^m He answered, "I am your servant." 7 David said to him, "Do not be afraid, for I will show you kindness for the sake of your father Jonathan; I will restore to you all the land of your grandfather Saul, and you yourself shall eat at my table always." 8 He did obeisance and said, "What is your servant, that you should look upon a dead dog such as I?"

9 Then the king summoned Saul's servant Zī'ba, and said to him, "All that belonged to Saul and to all his house I have given to your master's grandson. 10 You and your sons and your servants shall till the land for him, and shall bring in the produce, so that your master's grandson may have food to eat; but your master's grandson Me•phib'o•sheth^m shall always eat at my table." Now Zī'ba had fifteen sons and twenty servants. 11 Then Zī'ba said to the king, "According to all that my lord the king commands his servant, so your servant will do." Me•phib'-o•sheth^m ate at David's^n table, like one of the king's sons. 12 Me•phib'o•sheth^m had a young son whose name was Mī'ca. And all who lived in Zī'ba's house became Me•phib'o•sheth's^o servants. 13 Me•phib'-o•sheth^m lived in Jerusalem, for he always ate at the king's table. Now he was lame in both his feet.

The Ammonites and Arameans Are Defeated
(1 Chr 19.1–19)

10 Some time afterward, the king of the Am'mon•ites died, and his son Hā'nun succeeded him. 2 David said, "I will deal loyally with Hā'nun son of Nā'hash, just as his father dealt loyally with me." So David sent envoys to console him concerning his father. When David's envoys came into the land of the Am'mon•ites, 3 the princes of the Am'mon•ites said to their lord Hā'-nun, "Do you really think that David is honoring your father just because he has sent messengers with condolences to you? Has not David sent his envoys to you to search the city, to spy it out, and to overthrow it?" 4 So Hā'nun seized David's envoys, shaved off half the beard of each, cut off their garments in the middle at their hips, and sent them away. 5 When David was told, he sent to meet them, for the men were greatly ashamed. The king said, "Remain at Jericho until your beards have grown, and then return."

6 When the Am'mon•ites saw that they had become odious to David, the Am'mon•ites sent and hired the Ar•a•mē'ans of Beth-rē'hob and the Ar•a•mē'ans of Zō'bah, twenty thousand foot soldiers, as well as the king of Mā'a•cah, one thousand men, and the men of Tob, twelve thousand men. 7 When David heard of it, he sent Jō'ab and all the army with the warriors. 8 The Am'mon•ites came out and drew up in battle array at the entrance of the gate; but the Ar•a•mē'ans of Zō'bah and of Rē'hob, and the men of Tob and Mā'a•cah, were by themselves in the open country.

9 When Jō'ab saw that the battle was set against him both in front and in the rear, he chose some of the picked men of Israel, and arrayed them against the Ar•a•mē'ans; 10 the rest of his men he put in the charge of his brother A•bi'shaī, and he arrayed them against the Am'mon•ites. 11 He said, "If the Ar•a•mē'ans are too strong for me, then you shall help me; but if the Am'mon•ites are too strong for you, then I will come and help you. 12 Be strong, and let us be courageous for the sake of our people, and for the cities of our God; and may the LORD do what seems good to him." 13 So Jō'ab and the people who were with him moved forward into battle against the Ar•a•mē'ans; and they fled before him. 14 When the Am'mon•ites saw that the Ar•a•mē'ans fled, they likewise fled before A•bi'shaī, and entered the city. Then Jō'ab returned from fighting against the Am'mon•ites, and came to Jerusalem.

15 But when the Ar•a•mē'ans saw that they had been defeated by Israel, they gathered themselves together. 16 Had•a•dē'zer sent and brought out the Ar•a•mē'ans who were beyond the Euphrates; and they came to Hē'lam, with Shō'bach the commander of the army of Had•a•dē'zer at their head. 17 When it was told David, he gathered all Israel together, and crossed the Jordan, and came to Hē'lam. The Ar•a•mē'ans arrayed themselves against David and fought with him. 18 The Ar•a•mē'ans fled before Israel; and David killed of the Ar•a•mē'ans seven hundred chariot teams, and forty thousand horsemen,^p and wounded Shō'bach the commander of their army, so that he died there. 19 When all the kings who were servants of Had•a•dē'zer saw that they had been defeated by Israel, they made peace with Israel, and became subject to them. So the Ar•a•mē'ans were afraid to help the Am'-mon•ites any more.

David Commits Adultery with Bathsheba

11 In the spring of the year, the time when kings go out to battle, David sent Jō'ab with his officers and all Israel with him; they ravaged the Am'mon•ites, and besieged Rab'bah. But David remained at Jerusalem.

2 It happened, late one afternoon, when David rose from his couch and was walking about on the roof of the king's house, that he saw from the roof a woman bathing; the woman was very beautiful.

m Or *Merib-baal*: See 4.4 note   n Gk: Heb *my*   o Or *Merib-baal's*: See 4.4 note   p 1 Chr 19.18 and some Gk Mss read *foot soldiers*

LIVE IT!

Lust and Its Consequences

What the king wants, the king gets.

That seems to be the message of 2 Sam 11.1–5. We are spared many of the details about the encounter between David and Bathsheba, but we do know this: Bathsheba is married to Uriah, so David has coveted another man's wife and committed adultery. When Bathsheba becomes pregnant, David attempts to deceive Uriah into thinking the baby is Uriah's, by bringing him home to have sex with Bathsheba. But Uriah refuses to do so because he and his comrades are in the midst of a war. Finally, David arranges for Uriah to be murdered in battle.

In one brief episode, David has broken four commandments. He has given in to lust, and it has led him into a situation that will affect his family, his kingship, and the whole nation of Israel.

It is so easy to give in to temptation, especially lust, because it can be so alluring, and because we generally fail to think beyond the moment. A dangerous thing.

However, God can still use us, despite our sinfulness, as God used David.

▶ 2 Sam 11.1–5

---

3 David sent someone to inquire about the woman. It was reported, "This is Bath·she′ba daughter of E·li′am, the wife of U·ri′ah the Hit′tite." 4 So David sent messengers to get her, and she came to him, and he lay with her. (Now she was purifying herself after her period.) Then she returned to her house. 5 The woman conceived; and she sent and told David, "I am pregnant."

6 So David sent word to Jō′ab, "Send me U·ri′ah the Hit′tite." And Jō′ab sent U·ri′ah to David. 7 When U·ri′ah came to him, David asked how Jō′ab and the people fared, and how the war was going. 8 Then David said to U·ri′ah, "Go down to your house, and wash your feet." U·ri′ah went out of the king's house, and there followed him a present from the king. 9 But U·ri′ah slept at the entrance of the king's house with all the servants of his lord, and did not go down to his house. 10 When they told David, "U·ri′ah did not go down to his house," David said to U·ri′ah, "You have just come from a journey. Why did you not go down to your house?" 11 U·ri′ah said to David, "The ark and Israel and Judah remain in booths;q and my lord Jō′ab and the servants of my lord are camping in the open field; shall I then go to my house, to eat and to drink, and to lie with my wife? As you live, and as your soul lives, I will not do such a thing." 12 Then David said to U·ri′ah, "Remain here today also, and tomorrow I will send you back." So U·ri′ah remained in Jerusalem that day. On the next day, 13 David invited him to eat and drink in his presence and made him drunk; and in the evening he went out to lie on his couch with the servants of his lord, but he did not go down to his house.

David Has Uriah Killed

14 In the morning David wrote a letter to Jō′ab, and sent it by the hand of U·ri′ah. 15 In the letter he wrote, "Set U·ri′ah in the forefront of the hardest fighting, and then draw back from him, so that he may be struck down and die." 16 As Jō′ab was besieging the city, he assigned U·ri′ah to the place where he knew there were valiant warriors. 17 The men of the city came out and fought with Jō′ab; and some of the servants of David among the people fell. U·ri′ah the Hit′tite was killed as well. 18 Then Jō′ab sent and told David all the news about the fighting; 19 and he instructed the messenger, "When you have finished telling the king all the news about the fighting, 20 then, if the king's anger rises, and if he says to you, 'Why did you go so near the city to fight? Did you not know that they would shoot from the wall? 21 Who killed A·bim′e·lech son of Jer·ub·bā′al?r Did not a woman throw an upper millstone on him from the wall, so that he died at Thē′bez? Why did you go so near the wall?' then you shall say, 'Your servant U·ri′ah the Hit′tite is dead too.'"

22 So the messenger went, and came and told David all that Jō′ab had sent him to tell. 23 The messenger said to David, "The men gained an advantage over us, and came out against us in the field; but we drove them back to the entrance of the gate. 24 Then the archers shot at your servants from the wall; some of the king's servants are dead; and your servant U·ri′ah the Hit′tite is dead also." 25 David said to the messenger, "Thus you shall say

---

q Or at Succoth   r Gk Syr Judg 7.1: Heb Jerubbesheth

2
S
A
M

to Jō'ab, 'Do not let this matter trouble you, for the sword devours now one and now another; press your attack on the city, and overthrow it.' And encourage him."

26 When the wife of Ū·rī'ah heard that her husband was dead, she made lamentation for him. 27 When the mourning was over, David sent and brought her to his house, and she became his wife, and bore him a son.

Nathan Condemns David

But the thing that David had done displeased the LORD, 1 and the LORD sent Nathan to David. He came to him, and said to him, "There were two men in a certain city, the one rich and the other poor. 2 The rich man had very many flocks and herds; 3 but the poor man had nothing but one little ewe lamb, which he had bought. He brought it up, and it grew up with him and with his children; it used to eat of his meager fare, and drink from his cup, and lie in his bosom, and it was like a daughter to him. 4 Now there came a traveler to the rich man, and he was loath to take one of his own flock or herd to prepare for the wayfarer who had come to him, but he took the poor man's lamb, and prepared that for the guest who had come to him." 5 Then David's anger was greatly kindled against the man. He said to Nathan, "As the LORD lives, the man who has done this deserves to die; 6 he shall restore the lamb fourfold, because he did this thing, and because he had no pity."

7 Nathan said to David, "You are the man! Thus says the LORD, the God of Israel: I anointed you king over Israel, and I rescued you from the hand of Saul; 8 I gave you your master's house, and your master's wives into your bosom, and gave you the house of Israel and of Judah; and if that had been too little, I would have added as much more. 9 Why have you despised the word of the LORD, to do what is evil in his sight? You have struck down Ū·rī'ah the Hit'tite with the sword, and have taken his wife to be your wife, and have killed him with the sword of the Am'mon·ites. 10 Now therefore the sword shall never depart from your house, for you have despised me, and have taken the wife of Ū·rī'ah the Hit'tite to be your wife. 11 Thus says the LORD: I will raise up trouble against you from within your own house; and I will take your wives before your eyes, and give them to your neighbor, and he shall lie with your wives in the sight of this very sun. 12 For you did it secretly; but I will do this thing before all Israel, and before the sun." 13 David said to Nathan, "I have sinned against the LORD." Nathan said to David, "Now the LORD has put away your sin; you shall not die. 14 Nevertheless, because by this deed you have utterly scorned the LORD,s the child that is born to you shall die." 15 Then Nathan went to his house.

Bathsheba's Child Dies

The LORD struck the child that Ū·rī'ah's wife bore to David, and it became very ill. 16 David therefore pleaded with God for the child; David fasted, and went in and lay all night on the ground. 17 The elders of his house stood beside him, urging him to rise from the ground; but he would not, nor did he eat food with them. 18 On the seventh day the child

---

s Ancient scribal tradition: Compare 1 Sam 25.22 note: Heb *scorned the enemies of the LORD*

The Power of a Good Story   LIVE IT!

A story can be a powerful thing. Jesus knew the power of stories, so he often responded to questions by telling a story.

The prophet Nathan also knew the power of stories. His challenge was to force David to come to grips with what he had done with Bathsheba and Uriah. In 2 Samuel, Nathan cleverly creates a story in which David is to assume his familiar role as judge. David hears the case and is furious at the actions of the rich man in it, declaring that he should die for what he has done. Then, with four words, Nathan turns David's world upside down:

"You are the man!" (12.7).

What can David say? He just condemned himself, and he knows it. Nathan has cleverly forced him into a moment of truth. You may want to read Psalm 51, which poetically records David's confession.

Yes, a story can be a powerful thing. Just ask Nathan. Or David. Or Jesus.

▶ 2 Sam 12.1–12

died. And the servants of David were afraid to tell him that the child was dead; for they said, "While the child was still alive, we spoke to him, and he did not listen to us; how then can we tell him the child is dead? He may do himself some harm." 19 But when David saw that his servants were whispering together, he perceived that the child was dead; and David said to his servants, "Is the child dead?" They said, "He is dead."

20 Then David rose from the ground, washed, anointed himself, and changed his clothes. He went into the house of the LORD, and worshiped; he then went to his own house; and when he asked, they set food before him and he ate. 21 Then his servants said to him, "What is this thing that you have done? You fasted and wept for the child while it was alive; but when the child died, you rose and ate food." 22 He said, "While the child was still alive, I fasted and wept; for I said, 'Who knows? The LORD may be gracious to me, and the child may live.' 23 But now he is dead; why should I fast? Can I bring him back again? I shall go to him, but he will not return to me."

Solomon Is Born

24 Then David consoled his wife Bath·she′ba, and went to her, and lay with her; and she bore a son, and he named him Solomon. The LORD loved him, 25 and sent a message by the prophet Nathan; so he named him Jed·i·di′ah,t because of the LORD.

The Ammonites Crushed
(1 Chr 20.1–3)

26 Now Jo′ab fought against Rab′bah of the Am′mon·ites, and took the royal city. 27 Jo′ab sent messengers to David, and said, "I have fought against Rab′bah; moreover, I have taken the water city. 28 Now, then, gather the rest of the people together, and encamp against the city, and take it; or I myself will take the city, and it will be called by my name." 29 So David gathered all the people together and went to Rab′bah, and fought against it and took it. 30 He took the crown of Mil′comu from his head; the weight of it was a talent of gold, and in it was a precious stone; and it was placed on David's head. He also brought forth the spoil of the city, a very great amount. 31 He brought out the people who were in it, and set them to work with saws and iron picks and iron axes, or sent them to the brickworks. Thus he did to all the cities of the Am′mon·ites. Then David and all the people returned to Jerusalem.

Amnon and Tamar

13 Some time passed. David's son Ab′sa·lom had a beautiful sister whose name was Ta′mar; and David's son Am′non fell in

love with her. 2 Am′non was so tormented that he made himself ill because of his sister Ta′mar, for she was a virgin and it seemed impossible to Am′non to do anything to her. 3 But Am′non had a friend whose name was Jon′a·dab, the son of David's brother Shim′ē·ah; and Jon′a·dab was a very crafty man. 4 He said to him, "O son of the king, why are you so haggard morning after morning? Will you not tell me?" Am′non said to him, "I love Ta′mar, my brother Ab′sa·lom's sister." 5 Jon′a·dab said to him, "Lie down on your bed, and pretend to be ill; and when your father comes to see you, say to him, 'Let my sister Ta′mar come and give me something to eat, and prepare the food in my sight, so that I may see it and eat it from her hand.' " 6 So Am′non lay down, and pretended to be ill; and when the king came to see him, Am′non said to the king, "Please let my sister Ta′mar come and make a couple of cakes in my sight, so that I may eat from her hand."

7 Then David sent home to Ta′mar, saying, "Go to your brother Am′non's house, and prepare food for him." 8 So Ta′mar went to her brother Am′non's house, where he was lying down. She took dough, kneaded it, made cakes in his sight, and baked the cakes. 9 Then she took the pan and set themv out before him, but he refused to eat. Am′non said, "Send out everyone from me." So everyone went out from him. 10 Then Am′non said to Ta′mar, "Bring the food into the chamber, so that I may eat from your hand." So Ta′mar took the cakes she had made, and brought them into the chamber to Am′non her brother. 11 But when she brought them near him to eat, he took hold of her, and said to her, "Come, lie with me, my sister." 12 She answered him, "No, my brother, do not force me; for such a thing is not done in Israel; do not do anything so vile! 13 As for me, where could I carry my shame? And as for you, you would be as one of the scoundrels in Israel. Now therefore, I beg you, speak to the king; for he will not withhold me from you." 14 But he would not listen to her; and being stronger than she, he forced her and lay with her.

15 Then Am′non was seized with a very great loathing for her; indeed, his loathing was even greater than the lust he had felt for her. Am′non said to her, "Get out!" 16 But she said to him, "No, my brother;w for this wrong in sending me away is greater than the other that you did to me." But he would not listen to her. 17 He called the young man who served him and said, "Put this woman out of my presence, and bolt the door after her." 18 (Now she was wearing a long robe with sleeves; for this is

---

t That is Beloved of the LORD   u Gk See 1 Kings 11.5, 33: Heb their kings   v Heb and poured   w Cn Compare Gk Vg: Meaning of Heb uncertain

Family Violence

How should we react to the story of the rape of Tamar by her half-brother, Amnon, and the subsequent murder of Amnon by Absalom to avenge his sister's disgrace? This brutal story of lust, cruelty, and revenge has all the makings of a TV movie or a best-selling paperback. So, what is it doing in the Bible?

We have to remind ourselves that these are all David's children. We also have to remind ourselves that after Nathan confronts David about his affair with Bathsheba and his arrangement of Uriah's death, he tells David that "the sword shall never depart from your house" (2 Sam 12.10).

This prophecy finds fulfillment with the deaths of David's sons Amnon (see 2 Sam 13.28-29) and Absalom (see 2 Sam 18.14). Just as David allowed his lust for Bathsheba to get the best of him, Amnon follows in his father's footsteps, but by deceiving and forcing himself upon his sister, he has magnified the offense. And then in disgust, he wants nothing to do with Tamar. Tamar's brother Absalom bides his time, and when the opportunity presents itself, he has Amnon killed in front of the rest of his brothers to avenge his sister. Absalom himself dies shortly thereafter when he gets tangled up in a tree and an enemy takes advantage of his misfortune.

This is a tragic story and, unfortunately, all too human. The men and women of the Scriptures had to deal with the same horrors and family violence that we do, three thousand years later. The words of Ecclesiastes seem sadly true in this case:

"What has been is what will be,
    and what has been done is what will be done;
    there is nothing new under the sun."

(1.9)

At least in this story, the old axiom "Those who live by the sword die by the sword" has come true.

▶ 2 Sam 13

how the virgin daughters of the king were clothed in earlier times.ˣ) So his servant put her out, and bolted the door after her. 19 But Tā'mar put ashes on her head, and tore the long robe that she was wearing; she put her hand on her head, and went away, crying aloud as she went.

20 Her brother Ab'sa•lom said to her, "Has Am'non your brother been with you? Be quiet for now, my sister; he is your brother; do not take this to heart." So Tā'mar remained, a desolate woman, in her brother Ab'sa•lom's house. 21 When King David heard of all these things, he became very angry, but he would not punish his son Am'non, because he loved him, for he was his firstborn.ʸ 22 But Ab'sa•lom spoke to Am'non neither good nor bad; for Ab'sa•lom hated Am'non, because he had raped his sister Tā'mar.

Absalom Avenges the Violation of His Sister

23 After two full years Ab'sa•lom had sheepshearers at Bā'al-hā'zor, which is near É'phra•im, and Ab'sa•lom invited all the king's sons. 24 Ab'sa•lom came to the king, and said, "Your servant has sheepshearers; will the king and his servants please go with your servant?" 25 But the king said to Ab'sa•lom, "No, my son, let us not all go, or else we will be burdensome to you." He pressed him, but he would not go but gave him his blessing. 26 Then Ab'sa•lom said, "If not, please let my brother Am'non go with us." The king said to him, "Why should he go with you?" 27 But Ab'sa•lom pressed him until he let Am'non and all the king's sons go with him. Ab'sa•lom made a feast like a king's feast.ᶻ 28 Then Ab'sa•lom commanded his servants, "Watch when Am'non's heart is merry with wine, and when I say to you, 'Strike Am'non,' then kill him. Do not be afraid; have I not myself commanded you? Be courageous and valiant." 29 So the servants of Ab'sa•lom did to Am'non as Ab'sa•lom had commanded. Then all the king's sons rose, and each mounted his mule and fled.

30 While they were on the way, the report came to David that Ab'sa•lom had killed all the king's sons, and not one of them was left. 31 The king rose,

---

ˣ Cn: Heb *were clothed in robes* ʸ Q Ms Gk: MT lacks *but he would not punish . . . firstborn* ᶻ Gk Compare Q Ms: MT lacks *Absalom made a feast like a king's feast* tore his garments, and lay on the ground; and all his servants who were standing by tore their garments. 32 But Jon′a·dab, the son of David's brother Shim′ē·ah, said, "Let not my lord suppose that they have killed all the young men the king's sons; Am′non alone is dead. This has been determined by Ab′sa·lom from the day Am′non*a* raped his sister Tā′mar. 33 Now therefore, do not let my lord the king take it to heart, as if all the king's sons were dead; for Am′non alone is dead."

34 But Ab′sa·lom fled. When the young man who kept watch looked up, he saw many people coming from the Hor·ō·nā′im road*b* by the side of the mountain. 35 Jon′a·dab said to the king, "See, the king's sons have come; as your servant said, so it has come about." 36 As soon as he had finished speaking, the king's sons arrived, and raised their voices and wept; and the king and all his servants also wept very bitterly.

37 But Ab′sa·lom fled, and went to Tal′maī son of Am·mī′hud, king of Gē′shur. David mourned for his son day after day. 38 Ab′sa·lom, having fled to Gē′shur, stayed there three years. 39 And the heart of*c* the king went out, yearning for Ab′sa·lom; for he was now consoled over the death of Am′non.

Absalom Returns to Jerusalem

14 Now Jō′ab son of Ze·rū′i·ah perceived that the king's mind was on Ab′sa·lom. 2 Jō′ab sent to Te·kō′a and brought from there a wise woman. He said to her, "Pretend to be a mourner; put on mourning garments, do not anoint yourself with oil, but behave like a woman who has been mourning many days for the dead. 3 Go to the king and speak to him as follows." And Jō′ab put the words into her mouth.

4 When the woman of Te·kō′a came to the king, she fell on her face to the ground and did obeisance, and said, "Help, O king!" 5 The king asked her, "What is your trouble?" She answered, "Alas, I am a widow; my husband is dead. 6 Your servant had two sons, and they fought with one another in the field; there was no one to part them, and one struck the other and killed him. 7 Now the whole family has risen against your servant. They say, 'Give up the man who struck his brother, so that we may kill him for the life of his brother whom he murdered, even if we destroy the heir as well.' Thus they would quench my one remaining ember, and leave to my husband neither name nor remnant on the face of the earth."

8 Then the king said to the woman, "Go to your house, and I will give orders concerning you." 9 The woman of Te·kō′a said to the king, "On me be the guilt, my lord the king, and on my father's house; let the king and his throne be guiltless." 10 The king said, "If anyone says anything to you, bring him to me, and he shall never touch you again." 11 Then she said, "Please, may the king keep the LORD your God in mind, so that the avenger of blood may kill no more, and my son not be destroyed." He said, "As the LORD lives, not one hair of your son shall fall to the ground."

12 Then the woman said, "Please let your servant speak a word to my lord the king." He said, "Speak." 13 The woman said, "Why then have you planned such a thing against the people of God? For in giving this decision the king convicts himself, inasmuch as the king does not bring his banished one home again. 14 We must all die; we are like water spilled on the ground, which cannot be gathered up. But God will not take away a life; he will devise plans so as not to keep an outcast banished forever from his presence.*d* 15 Now I have come to say this to my lord the king because the people have made me afraid; your servant thought, 'I will speak to the king; it may be that the king will perform the request of his servant. 16 For the king will hear, and deliver his servant from the hand of the man who would cut both me and my son off from the heritage of God.' 17 Your servant thought, 'The word of my lord the king will set me at rest'; for my lord the king is like the angel of God, discerning good and evil. The LORD your God be with you!"

18 Then the king answered the woman, "Do not withhold from me anything I ask you." The woman said, "Let my lord the king speak." 19 The king said, "Is the hand of Jō′ab with you in all this?" The woman answered and said, "As surely as you live, my lord the king, one cannot turn right or left from anything that my lord the king has said. For it was your servant Jō′ab who commanded me; it was he who put all these words into the mouth of your servant. 20 In order to change the course of affairs your servant Jō′ab did this. But my lord has wisdom like the wisdom of the angel of God to know all things that are on the earth."

21 Then the king said to Jō′ab, "Very well, I grant this; go, bring back the young man Ab′sa·lom." 22 Jō′ab prostrated himself with his face to the ground and did obeisance, and blessed the king; and Jō′ab said, "Today your servant knows that I have found favor in your sight, my lord the king, in that the king has granted the request of his servant." 23 So Jō′ab set off, went to Gē′shur, and brought Ab′sa·lom to Jerusalem. 24 The king said, "Let him go to his own house; he is not to come into my presence." So Ab′sa·lom went to his own house, and did not come into the king's presence.

2
S
A
M

---

a Heb *he*   *b* Cn Compare Gk: Heb *the road behind him*
c Q Ms Gk: MT *And David*   *d* Meaning of Heb uncertain

David Forgives Absalom

25 Now in all Israel there was no one to be praised so much for his beauty as Ab'sa•lom; from the sole of his foot to the crown of his head there was no blemish in him. 26 When he cut the hair of his head (for at the end of every year he used to cut it; when it was heavy on him, he cut it), he weighed the hair of his head, two hundred shekels by the king's weight. 27 There were born to Ab'sa•lom three sons, and one daughter whose name was Tā'mar; she was a beautiful woman.

28 So Ab'sa•lom lived two full years in Jerusalem, without coming into the king's presence. 29 Then Ab'sa•lom sent for Jō'ab to send him to the king; but Jō'ab would not come to him. He sent a second time, but Jō'ab would not come. 30 Then he said to his servants, "Look, Jō'ab's field is next to mine, and he has barley there; go and set it on fire." So Ab'sa•lom's servants set the field on fire. 31 Then Jō'ab rose and went to Ab'sa•lom at his house, and said to him, "Why have your servants set my field on fire?" 32 Ab'sa•lom answered Jō'ab, "Look, I sent word to you: Come here, that I may send you to the king with the question, 'Why have I come from Gē'shur? It would be better for me to be there still.' Now let me go into the king's presence; if there is guilt in me, let him kill me!" 33 Then Jō'ab went to the king and told him; and he summoned Ab'sa•lom. So he came to the king and prostrated himself with his face to the ground before the king; and the king kissed Ab'sa•lom.

Absalom Usurps the Throne

15 After this Ab'sa•lom got himself a chariot and horses, and fifty men to run ahead of him. 2 Ab'sa•lom used to rise early and stand beside the road into the gate; and when anyone brought a suit before the king for judgment, Ab'sa•lom would call out and say, "From what city are you?" When the person said, "Your servant is of such and such a tribe in Israel," 3 Ab'sa•lom would say, "See, your claims are good and right; but there is no one deputed by the king to hear you." 4 Ab'sa•lom said moreover, "If only I were judge in the land! Then all who had a suit or cause might come to me, and I would give them justice." 5 Whenever people came near to do obeisance to him, he would put out his hand and take hold of them, and kiss them. 6 Thus Ab'sa•lom did to every Israelite who came to the king for judgment; so Ab'sa•lom stole the hearts of the people of Israel.

7 At the end of four*e* years Ab'sa•lom said to the king, "Please let me go to Hē'bron and pay the vow that I have made to the LORD. 8 For your servant made a vow while I lived at Gē'shur in Ar'am: If the LORD will indeed bring me back to Jerusalem, then I will worship the LORD in Hē'bron."*f* 9 The king

said to him, "Go in peace." So he got up, and went to Hē'bron. 10 But Ab'sa•lom sent secret messengers throughout all the tribes of Israel, saying, "As soon as you hear the sound of the trumpet, then shout: Ab'sa•lom has become king at Hē'bron!" 11 Two hundred men from Jerusalem went with Ab'sa•lom; they were invited guests, and they went in their innocence, knowing nothing of the matter. 12 While Ab'sa•lom was offering the sacrifices, he sent for*g* A•hith'o•phel the Gi'lo•nīte, David's counselor, from his city Gī'lōh. The conspiracy grew in strength, and the people with Ab'sa•lom kept increasing.

David Flees from Jerusalem

13 A messenger came to David, saying, "The hearts of the Israelites have gone after Ab'sa•lom." 14 Then David said to all his officials who were with him at Jerusalem, "Get up! Let us flee, or there will be no escape for us from Ab'sa•lom. Hurry, or he will soon overtake us, and bring disaster down upon us, and attack the city with the edge of the sword." 15 The king's officials said to the king, "Your servants are ready to do whatever our lord the king decides." 16 So the king left, followed by all his household, except ten concubines whom he left behind to look after the house. 17 The king left, followed by all the people; and they stopped at the last house. 18 All his officials passed by him; and all the Cher'e•thītes, and all the Pel'eth•ites, and all the six hundred Git'tītes who had followed him from Gath, passed on before the king.

19 Then the king said to It'taī the Git'tīte, "Why are you also coming with us? Go back, and stay with the king; for you are a foreigner, and also an exile from your home. 20 You came only yesterday, and shall I today make you wander about with us, while I go wherever I can? Go back, and take your kinsfolk with you; and may the LORD show*h* steadfast love and faithfulness to you." 21 But It'taī answered the king, "As the LORD lives, and as my lord the king lives, wherever my lord the king may be, whether for death or for life, there also your servant will be." 22 David said to It'taī, "Go then, march on." So It'taī the Git'tīte marched on, with all his men and all the little ones who were with him. 23 The whole country wept aloud as all the people passed by; the king crossed the Wadi Kid'ron, and all the people moved on toward the wilderness.

24 A•bi'a•thar came up, and Zā'dok also, with all the Lē'vītes, carrying the ark of the covenant of God. They set down the ark of God, until the people had all passed out of the city. 25 Then the king said to Zā'dok, "Carry the ark of God back into the

---

e Gk Syr: Heb *forty*   *f* Gk Mss: Heb lacks *in Hebron*
g Or *he sent*   *h* Gk Compare 2.6: Heb lacks *may the* LORD *show*

city. If I find favor in the eyes of the LORD, he will bring me back and let me see both it and the place where it stays. 26 But if he says, 'I take no pleasure in you,' here I am, let him do to me what seems good to him." 27 The king also said to the priest Zā'dok, "Look,[i] go back to the city in peace, you and A•bī'a•thar,[j] with your two sons, A•him'a•az your son, and Jonathan son of A•bī'a•thar. 28 See, I will wait at the fords of the wilderness until word comes from you to inform me." 29 So Zā'dok and A•bī'a•thar carried the ark of God back to Jerusalem, and they remained there.

30 But David went up the ascent of the Mount of Olives, weeping as he went, with his head covered and walking barefoot; and all the people who were with him covered their heads and went up, weeping as they went. 31 David was told that A•hith'o•phel was among the conspirators with Ab'sa•lom. And David said, "O LORD, I pray you, turn the counsel of A•hith'o•phel into foolishness."

Hushai Becomes David's Spy

32 When David came to the summit, where God was worshiped, Hū'shaī the Ar'chīte came to meet him with his coat torn and earth on his head. 33 David said to him, "If you go on with me, you will be a burden to me. 34 But if you return to the city and say to Ab'sa•lom, 'I will be your servant, O king; as I have been your father's servant in time past, so now I will be your servant,' then you will defeat for me the counsel of A•hith'o•phel. 35 The priests Zā'dok and A•bī'a•thar will be with you there. So whatever you hear from the king's house, tell it to the priests Zā'dok and A•bī'a•thar. 36 Their two sons are with them there, Zā'dok's son A•him'a•az and A•bī'a•thar's son Jonathan; and by them you shall report to me everything you hear." 37 So Hū'shaī, David's friend, came into the city, just as Ab'sa•lom was entering Jerusalem.

David's Adversaries

16 When David had passed a little beyond the summit, Zī'ba the servant of Me•phib'o•sheth[k] met him, with a couple of donkeys saddled, carrying two hundred loaves of bread, one hundred bunches of raisins, one hundred of summer fruits, and one skin of wine. 2 The king said to Zī'ba, "Why have you brought these?" Zī'ba answered, "The donkeys are for the king's household to ride, the bread and summer fruit for the young men to eat, and the wine is for those to drink who faint in the wilderness." 3 The king said, "And where is your master's son?" Zī'ba said to the king, "He remains in Jerusalem; for he said, 'Today the house of Israel will give me back my grandfather's kingdom.' " 4 Then the king said to Zī'ba, "All that belonged to Me•phib'o•sheth[m] is now yours." Zī'ba

said, "I do obeisance; let me find favor in your sight, my lord the king."

Shimei Curses David

5 When King David came to Ba•hū'rim, a man of the family of the house of Saul came out whose name was Shim'ē•ī son of Gē'ra; he came out cursing. 6 He threw stones at David and at all the servants of King David; now all the people and all the warriors were on his right and on his left. 7 Shim'ē•ī shouted while he cursed, "Out! Out! Murderer! Scoundrel! 8 The LORD has avenged on all of you the blood of the house of Saul, in whose place you have reigned; and the LORD has given the kingdom into the hand of your son Ab'sa•lom. See, disaster has overtaken you; for you are a man of blood."

9 Then A•bi'shaī son of Ze•rū'i•ah said to the king, "Why should this dead dog curse my lord the king? Let me go over and take off his head." 10 But the king said, "What have I to do with you, you sons of Ze•rū'i•ah? If he is cursing because the LORD has said to him, 'Curse David,' who then shall say, 'Why have you done so?' " 11 David said to A•bi'shaī and to all his servants, "My own son seeks my life; how much more now may this Ben'ja•min•īte! Let him alone, and let him curse; for the LORD has bidden him. 12 It may be that the LORD will look on my distress,[l] and the LORD will repay me with good for this cursing of me today." 13 So David and his men went on the road, while Shim'ē•ī went along on the hillside opposite him and cursed as he went, throwing stones and flinging dust at him. 14 The king and all the people who were with him arrived weary at the Jordan;[m] and there he refreshed himself.

The Counsel of Ahithophel

15 Now Ab'sa•lom and all the Israelites[n] came to Jerusalem; A•hith'o•phel was with him. 16 When Hū'shaī the Ar'chīte, David's friend, came to Ab'sa•lom, Hū'shaī said to Ab'sa•lom, "Long live the king! Long live the king!" 17 Ab'sa•lom said to Hū'shaī, "Is this your loyalty to your friend? Why did you not go with your friend?" 18 Hū'shaī said to Ab'sa•lom, "No; but the one whom the LORD and this people and all the Israelites have chosen, his I will be, and with him I will remain. 19 Moreover, whom should I serve? Should it not be his son? Just as I have served your father, so I will serve you."

20 Then Ab'sa•lom said to A•hith'o•phel, "Give us your counsel; what shall we do?" 21 A•hith'-o•phel said to Ab'sa•lom, "Go in to your father's concubines, the ones he has left to look after the

---

i Gk: Heb *Are you a seer* or *Do you see?*   j Cn: Heb lacks *and Abiathar*   k Or *Merib-baal*: See 4.4 note   l Gk Vg: Heb *iniquity*   m Gk: Heb lacks *at the Jordan*   n Gk: Heb *all the people, the men of Israel* house; and all Israel will hear that you have made yourself odious to your father, and the hands of all who are with you will be strengthened." 22 So they pitched a tent for Ab'sa•lom upon the roof; and Ab'sa•lom went in to his father's concubines in the sight of all Israel. 23 Now in those days the counsel that A•hith'o•phel gave was as if one consulted the oracle⁰ of God; so all the counsel of A•hith'o•phel was esteemed, both by David and by Ab'sa•lom.

17 Moreover A•hith'o•phel said to Ab'-sa•lom, "Let me choose twelve thousand men, and I will set out and pursue David tonight. 2 I will come upon him while he is weary and discouraged, and throw him into a panic; and all the people who are with him will flee. I will strike down only the king, 3 and I will bring all the people back to you as a bride comes home to her husband. You seek the life of only one man,ᵖ and all the people will be at peace." 4 The advice pleased Ab'sa•lom and all the elders of Israel.

The Counsel of Hushai

5 Then Ab'sa•lom said, "Call Hū'shaī the Ar'chīte also, and let us hear too what he has to say." 6 When Hū'shaī came to Ab'sa•lom, Ab'sa•lom said to him, "This is what A•hith'o•phel has said; shall we do as he advises? If not, you tell us." 7 Then Hū'shaī said to Ab'sa•lom, "This time the counsel that A•hith'o•phel has given is not good." 8 Hū'shaī continued, "You know that your father and his men are warriors, and that they are enraged, like a bear robbed of her cubs in the field. Besides, your father is expert in war; he will not spend the night with the troops. 9 Even now he has hidden himself in one of the pits, or in some other place. And when some of our troopsᑫ fall at the first attack, whoever hears it will say, 'There has been a slaughter among the troops who follow Ab'sa•lom.' 10 Then even the valiant warrior, whose heart is like the heart of a lion, will utterly melt with fear; for all Israel knows that your father is a warrior, and that those who are with him are valiant warriors. 11 But my counsel is that all Israel be gathered to you, from Dan to Bē'er-shē'ba, like the sand by the sea for multitude, and that you go to battle in person. 12 So we shall come upon him in whatever place he may be found, and we shall light on him as the dew falls on the ground; and he will not survive, nor will any of those with him. 13 If he withdraws into a city, then all Israel will bring ropes to that city, and we shall drag it into the valley, until not even a pebble is to be found there." 14 Ab'sa•lom and all the men of Israel said, "The counsel of Hū'shaī the Ar'chīte is better than the counsel of A•hith'o•phel." For the LORD had ordained to defeat the good counsel of A•hith'o•phel, so that the LORD might bring ruin on Ab'sa•lom.

Hushai Warns David to Escape

15 Then Hū'shaī said to the priests Zā'dok and A•bī'a•thar, "Thus and so did A•hith'o•phel counsel Ab'sa•lom and the elders of Israel; and thus and so I have counseled. 16 Therefore send quickly and tell David, 'Do not lodge tonight at the fords of the wilderness, but by all means cross over; otherwise the king and all the people who are with him will be swallowed up.' " 17 Jonathan and A•him'a•az were waiting at En-rō'gel; a servant-girl used to go and tell them, and they would go and tell King David; for they could not risk being seen entering the city. 18 But a boy saw them, and told Ab'sa•lom; so both of them went away quickly, and came to the house of a man at Ba•hū'rim, who had a well in his courtyard; and they went down into it. 19 The man's wife took a covering, stretched it over the well's mouth, and spread out grain on it; and nothing was known of it. 20 When Ab'sa•lom's servants came to the woman at the house, they said, "Where are A•him'a•az and Jonathan?" The woman said to them, "They have crossed over the brookʳ of water." And when they had searched and could not find them, they returned to Jerusalem.

21 After they had gone, the men came up out of the well, and went and told King David. They said to David, "Go and cross the water quickly; for thus and so has A•hith'o•phel counseled against you." 22 So David and all the people who were with him set out and crossed the Jordan; by daybreak not one was left who had not crossed the Jordan.

23 When A•hith'o•phel saw that his counsel was not followed, he saddled his donkey and went off home to his own city. He set his house in order, and hanged himself; he died and was buried in the tomb of his father.

24 Then David came to Mā•ha•nā'im, while Ab'sa•lom crossed the Jordan with all the men of Israel. 25 Now Ab'sa•lom had set A•mā'sa over the army in the place of Jō'ab. A•mā'sa was the son of a man named Ith'ra the Ish'ma•el•īte,ˢ who had married Ab'i•gāl daughter of Nā'hash, sister of Ze•rū'-i•ah, Jō'ab's mother. 26 The Israelites and Ab'sa•lom encamped in the land of Gil'e•ad.

27 When David came to Mā•ha•nā'im, Shō'bī son of Nā'hash from Rab'bah of the Am'mon•ītes, and Mā'chir son of Am'mi•el from Lō-dē'bar, and Bar•zil'laī the Gil'e•ad•īte from Rō'ge•lim, 28 brought beds, basins, and earthen vessels, wheat, barley, meal, parched grain, beans and lentils,ᵗ 29 honey and curds, sheep, and cheese from the herd, for David and the people with him to eat; for they said,

---

⁰ Heb word   ᵖ Gk: Heb *like the return of the whole (is) the man whom you seek*   ᑫ Gk Mss: Heb *some of them*
ʳ Meaning of Heb uncertain   ˢ 1 Chr 2.17: Heb *Israelite*
ᵗ Heb *and lentils and parched grain*

"The troops are hungry and weary and thirsty in the wilderness."

The Defeat and Death of Absalom

18 Then David mustered the men who were with him, and set over them commanders of thousands and commanders of hundreds. 2 And David divided the army into three groups:ᵘ one third under the command of Jō′ab, one third under the command of A•bi′shaī son of Ze•rū′i•ah, Jō′ab's brother, and one third under the command of It′taī the Git′tīte. The king said to the men, "I myself will also go out with you." 3 But the men said, "You shall not go out. For if we flee, they will not care about us. If half of us die, they will not care about us. But you are worth ten thousand of us;ᵛ therefore it is better that you send us help from the city." 4 The king said to them, "Whatever seems best to you I will do." So the king stood at the side of the gate, while all the army marched out by hundreds and by thousands. 5 The king ordered Jō′ab and A•bi′shaī and It′taī, saying, "Deal gently for my sake with the young man Ab′sa•lom." And all the people heard when the king gave orders to all the commanders concerning Ab′sa•lom.

6 So the army went out into the field against Israel; and the battle was fought in the forest of E′phra•im. 7 The men of Israel were defeated there by the servants of David, and the slaughter there was great on that day, twenty thousand men. 8 The battle spread over the face of all the country; and the forest claimed more victims that day than the sword.

9 Ab′sa•lom happened to meet the servants of David. Ab′sa•lom was riding on his mule, and the mule went under the thick branches of a great oak. His head caught fast in the oak, and he was left hangingʷ between heaven and earth, while the mule that was under him went on. 10 A man saw it, and told Jō′ab, "I saw Ab′sa•lom hanging in an oak." 11 Jō′ab said to the man who told him, "What, you saw him! Why then did you not strike him there to the ground? I would have been glad to give you ten pieces of silver and a belt." 12 But the man said to Jō′ab, "Even if I felt in my hand the weight of a thousand pieces of silver, I would not raise my hand against the king's son; for in our hearing the king commanded you and A•bi′shaī and It′taī, saying: For my sake protect the young man Ab′sa•lom! 13 On the other hand, if I had dealt treacherously against his lifeˣ (and there is nothing hidden from the king), then you yourself would have stood aloof." 14 Jō′ab said, "I will not waste time like this with you." He took three spears in his hand, and thrust them into the heart of Ab′sa•lom, while he was still alive in the oak. 15 And ten young men, Jō′ab's armor-bearers, surrounded Ab′sa•lom and struck him, and killed him.

16 Then Jō′ab sounded the trumpet, and the troops came back from pursuing Israel, for Jō′ab restrained the troops. 17 They took Ab′sa•lom, threw him into a great pit in the forest, and raised over him a very great heap of stones. Meanwhile all the Israelites fled to their homes. 18 Now Ab′salom in his lifetime had taken and set up for himself a pillar that is in the King's Valley, for he said, "I have no son to keep my name in remembrance"; he called the pillar by his own name. It is called Ab′sa•lom's Monument to this day.

David Hears of Absalom's Death

19 Then A•him′a•az son of Zā′dok said, "Let me run, and carry tidings to the king that the LORD has delivered him from the power of his enemies." 20 Jō′ab said to him, "You are not to carry tidings today; you may carry tidings another day, but today you shall not do so, because the king's son is dead." 21 Then Jō′ab said to a Cū′shīte, "Go, tell the king what you have seen." The Cū′shīte bowed before Jō′ab, and ran. 22 Then A•him′a•az son of Zā′dok said again to Jō′ab, "Come what may, let me also run after the Cū′shīte." And Jō′ab said, "Why will you run, my son, seeing that you have no rewardʸ for the tidings?" 23 "Come what may," he said, "I will run." So he said to him, "Run." Then A•him′a•az ran by the way of the Plain, and outran the Cū′shīte.

24 Now David was sitting between the two gates. The sentinel went up to the roof of the gate by the wall, and when he looked up, he saw a man running alone. 25 The sentinel shouted and told the king. The king said, "If he is alone, there are tidings in his mouth." He kept coming, and drew near. 26 Then the sentinel saw another man running; and the sentinel called to the gatekeeper and said, "See, another man running alone!" The king said, "He also is bringing tidings." 27 The sentinel said, "I think the running of the first one is like the running of A•him′a•az son of Zā′dok." The king said, "He is a good man, and comes with good tidings."

28 Then A•him′a•az cried out to the king, "All is well!" He prostrated himself before the king with his face to the ground, and said, "Blessed be the LORD your God, who has delivered up the men who raised their hand against my lord the king." 29 The king said, "Is it well with the young man Ab′sa•lom?" A•him′a•az answered, "When Jō′ab sent your servant,ᶻ I saw a great tumult, but I do not know what it was." 30 The king said, "Turn aside, and stand here." So he turned aside, and stood still.

ᵘ Gk: Heb *sent forth the army*   ᵛ Gk Vg Symmachus: Heb *for now there are ten thousand such as we*   ʷ Gk Syr Tg: Heb *was put*   ˣ Another reading is *at the risk of my life*   ʸ Meaning of Heb uncertain   ᶻ Heb *the king's servant, your servant*

31 Then the Cū'shīte came; and the Cū'shīte said, "Good tidings for my lord the king! For the LORD has vindicated you this day, delivering you from the power of all who rose up against you." 32 The king said to the Cū'shīte, "Is it well with the young man Ab'sa•lom?" The Cū'shīte answered, "May the enemies of my lord the king, and all who rise up to do you harm, be like that young man."

David Mourns for Absalom

33[a] The king was deeply moved, and went up to the chamber over the gate, and wept; and as he went, he said, "O my son Ab'sa•lom, my son, my son Ab'sa•lom! Would I had died instead of you, O Ab'sa•lom, my son, my son!"

19 It was told Jō'ab, "The king is weeping and mourning for Ab'sa•lom." 2 So the victory that day was turned into mourning for all the troops; for the troops heard that day, "The king is grieving for his son." 3 The troops stole into the city that day as soldiers steal in who are ashamed when they flee in battle. 4 The king covered his face, and the king cried with a loud voice, "O my son Ab'sa•lom, O Ab'sa•lom, my son, my son!" 5 Then Jō'ab came into the house to the king, and said, "Today you have covered with shame the faces of all your officers who have saved your life today, and the lives of your sons and your daughters, and the lives of your wives and your concubines, 6 for love of those who hate you and for hatred of those who love you. You have made it clear today that commanders and officers are nothing to you; for I perceive that if Ab'sa•lom were alive and all of us were dead today, then you would be pleased. 7 So go out at once and speak kindly to your servants; for I swear by the LORD, if you do not go, not a man will stay with you this night; and this will be worse for you than any disaster that has come upon you from your youth until now." 8 Then the king got up and took his seat in the gate. The troops were all told, "See, the king is sitting in the gate"; and all the troops came before the king.

David Recalled to Jerusalem

Meanwhile, all the Israelites had fled to their homes. 9 All the people were disputing throughout all the tribes of Israel, saying, "The king delivered us from the hand of our enemies, and saved us from the hand of the Phi•lis'tines; and now he has fled out of the land because of Ab'sa•lom. 10 But Ab'salom, whom we anointed over us, is dead in battle. Now therefore why do you say nothing about bringing the king back?"

11 King David sent this message to the priests Zā'dok and A•bī'a•thar, "Say to the elders of Judah, 'Why should you be the last to bring the king back to his house? The talk of all Israel has come to the king.[b] 12 You are my kin, you are my bone and my flesh; why then should you be the last to bring back the king?' 13 And say to A•mā'sa, 'Are you not my bone and my flesh? So may God do to me, and more, if you are not the commander of my army from now on, in place of Jō'ab.'" 14 A•mā'sa[c] swayed the hearts of all the people of Judah as one, and they sent word to the king, "Return, both you and all your servants." 15 So the king came back to the Jordan; and Judah came to Gil'gal to meet the king and to bring him over the Jordan.

16 Shim'ē•ī son of Gē'ra, the Ben'ja•min•īte, from Ba•hū'rim, hurried to come down with the people of Judah to meet King David; 17 with him were a thousand people from Benjamin. And Zī'ba, the servant of the house of Saul, with his fifteen sons and his twenty servants, rushed down to the Jordan ahead of the king, 18 while the crossing was taking place,[d] to bring over the king's household, and to do his pleasure.

David's Mercy to Shimei

Shim'ē•ī son of Gē'ra fell down before the king, as he was about to cross the Jordan, 19 and said to the king, "May my lord not hold me guilty or remember how your servant did wrong on the day my lord the king left Jerusalem; may the king not bear it in mind. 20 For your servant knows that I have sinned; therefore, see, I have come this day, the first of all the house of Joseph to come down to meet my lord the king." 21 A•bi'shaī son of Ze•rū'i•ah answered, "Shall not Shim'ē•ī be put to death for this, because he cursed the LORD's anointed?" 22 But David said, "What have I to do with you, you sons of Ze•rū'i•ah,

---

a Ch 19.1 in Heb   b Gk: Heb to the king, to his house
c Heb He   d Cn: Heb the ford crossed

that you should today become an adversary to me? Shall anyone be put to death in Israel this day? For do I not know that I am this day king over Israel?" 23 The king said to Shim′e•ī, "You shall not die." And the king gave him his oath.

David and Mephibosheth Meet

24 Me•phib′o•sheth*e* grandson of Saul came down to meet the king; he had not taken care of his feet, or trimmed his beard, or washed his clothes, from the day the king left until the day he came back in safety. 25 When he came from Jerusalem to meet the king, the king said to him, "Why did you not go with me, Me•phib′o•sheth?"*e* 26 He answered, "My lord, O king, my servant deceived me; for your servant said to him, 'Saddle a donkey for me,*f* so that I may ride on it and go with the king.' For your servant is lame. 27 He has slandered your servant to my lord the king. But my lord the king is like the angel of God; do therefore what seems good to you. 28 For all my father's house were doomed to death before my lord the king; but you set your servant among those who eat at your table. What further right have I, then, to appeal to the king?" 29 The king said to him, "Why speak any more of your affairs? I have decided: you and Zī′ba shall divide the land." 30 Me•phib′o•sheth*e* said to the king, "Let him take it all, since my lord the king has arrived home safely."

David's Kindness to Barzillai

31 Now Bar•zil′laī the Gil′e•ad•ite had come down from Rō′ge•lim; he went on with the king to the Jordan, to escort him over the Jordan. 32 Bar•zil′laī was a very aged man, eighty years old.

He had provided the king with food while he stayed at Mā•ha•nā′im, for he was a very wealthy man. 33 The king said to Bar•zil′laī, "Come over with me, and I will provide for you in Jerusalem at my side." 34 But Bar•zil′laī said to the king, "How many years have I still to live, that I should go up with the king to Jerusalem? 35 Today I am eighty years old; can I discern what is pleasant and what is not? Can your servant taste what he eats or what he drinks? Can I still listen to the voice of singing men and singing women? Why then should your servant be an added burden to my lord the king? 36 Your servant will go a little way over the Jordan with the king. Why should the king recompense me with such a reward? 37 Please let your servant return, so that I may die in my own town, near the graves of my father and my mother. But here is your servant Chim′ham; let him go over with my lord the king; and do for him whatever seems good to you." 38 The king answered, "Chim′ham shall go over with me, and I will do for him whatever seems good to you; and all that you desire of me I will do for you." 39 Then all the people crossed over the Jordan, and the king crossed over; the king kissed Bar•zil′laī and blessed him, and he returned to his own home. 40 The king went on to Gil′gal, and Chim′ham went on with him; all the people of Judah, and also half the people of Israel, brought the king on his way.

41 Then all the people of Israel came to the king, and said to him, "Why have our kindred the people of Judah stolen you away, and brought the king and his household over the Jordan, and all David's men

---

e Or *Merib-baal*: See 4.4 note   *f* Gk Syr Vg: Heb *said, 'I will saddle a donkey for myself*

Surviving Grief

There is no greater loss for parents than the death of a child. In 2 Sam 18.33, King David is devastated by the death of his son Absalom, despite Absalom's betrayal. There is no easy answer or explanation when someone we love dies. How could God allow this? It is too hard to understand. What helps is to allow ourselves to mourn like David and to place ourselves into God's healing hands.

Life continues. Joab challenges David not to forget the people who have served him faithfully and count on his leadership (verses 6–8). In our grief, we must not forget the family and friends who grieve with us. We need them, and they need us to heal the pain of loss.

▶ 2 Sam 19.1–9

with him?" 42 All the people of Judah answered the people of Israel, "Because the king is near of kin to us. Why then are you angry over this matter? Have we eaten at all at the king's expense? Or has he given us any gift?" 43 But the people of Israel answered the people of Judah, "We have ten shares in the king, and in David also we have more than you. Why then did you despise us? Were we not the first to speak of bringing back our king?" But the words of the people of Judah were fiercer than the words of the people of Israel.

The Rebellion of Sheba

20 Now a scoundrel named She'ba son of Bich'rī, a Ben'ja·min·ite, happened to be there. He sounded the trumpet and cried out,

"We have no portion in David,
no share in the son of Jesse!
Everyone to your tents, O Israel!"

2 So all the people of Israel withdrew from David and followed She'ba son of Bich'rī; but the people of Judah followed their king steadfastly from the Jordan to Jerusalem.

3 David came to his house at Jerusalem; and the king took the ten concubines whom he had left to look after the house, and put them in a house under guard, and provided for them, but did not go in to them. So they were shut up until the day of their death, living as if in widowhood.

4 Then the king said to A·mā'sa, "Call the men of Judah together to me within three days, and be here yourself." 5 So A·mā'sa went to summon Judah; but he delayed beyond the set time that had been appointed him. 6 David said to A·bi'shaī, "Now She'ba son of Bich'rī will do us more harm than Ab'sa·lom; take your lord's servants and pursue him, or he will find fortified cities for himself, and escape from us." 7 Jō'ab's men went out after him, along with the Cher'e·thites, the Pel'eth·ītes, and all the warriors; they went out from Jerusalem to pursue She'ba son of Bich'rī. 8 When they were at the large stone that is in Gib'e·on, A·mā'sa came to meet them. Now Jō'ab was wearing a soldier's garment and over it was a belt with a sword in its sheath fastened at his waist; as he went forward it fell out. 9 Jō'ab said to A·mā'sa, "Is it well with you, my brother?" And Jō'ab took A·mā'sa by the beard with his right hand to kiss him. 10 But A·mā'sa did not notice the sword in Jō'ab's hand; Jō'ab struck him in the belly so that his entrails poured out on the ground, and he died. He did not strike a second blow.

Then Jō'ab and his brother A·bi'shaī pursued She'ba son of Bich'rī. 11 And one of Jō'ab's men took his stand by A·mā'sa, and said, "Whoever favors Jō'ab, and whoever is for David, let him follow Jō'ab." 12 A·mā'sa lay wallowing in his blood on the highway, and the man saw that all the people were stopping. Since he saw that all who came by him were stopping, he carried A·mā'sa from the highway into a field, and threw a garment over him. 13 Once he was removed from the highway, all the people went on after Jō'ab to pursue She'ba son of Bich'rī.

14 She'ba*g* passed through all the tribes of Israel to Abel of Beth-mā'a·cah;*h* and all the Bich'rītes*i* assembled, and followed him inside. 15 Jō'ab's forces*j* came and besieged him in Abel of Beth-mā'a·cah; they threw up a siege ramp against the city, and it stood against the rampart. Jō'ab's forces were battering the wall to break it down. 16 Then a wise woman called from the city, "Listen! Listen! Tell Jō'ab, 'Come here, I want to speak to you.' " 17 He came near her; and the woman said, "Are you Jō'ab?" He answered, "I am." Then she said to him, "Listen to the words of your servant." He answered, "I am listening." 18 Then she said, "They used to say in the old days, 'Let them inquire at Abel'; and so they would settle a matter. 19 I am one of those who are peaceable and faithful in Israel; you seek to destroy a city that is a mother in Israel; why will you swallow up the heritage of the LORD?" 20 Jō'ab answered, "Far be it from me, far be it, that I should swallow up or destroy! 21 That is not the case! But a man of the hill country of E'phra·im, called She'ba son of Bich'rī, has lifted up his hand against King David; give him up alone, and I will withdraw from the city." The woman said to Jō'ab, "His head shall be thrown over the wall to you." 22 Then the woman went to all the people with her wise plan. And they cut off the head of She'ba son of Bich'rī, and threw it out to Jō'ab. So he blew the trumpet, and they dispersed from the city, and all went to their homes, while Jō'ab returned to Jerusalem to the king.

23 Now Jō'ab was in command of all the army of Israel;*k* Be·nā'i·ah son of Je·hoi'a·da was in command of the Cher'e·thites and the Pel'eth·ītes; 24 A·dor'am was in charge of the forced labor; Je·hosh'a·phat son of A·hī'lud was the recorder; 25 She'va was secretary; Zā'dok and A·bī'a·thar were priests; 26 and Ira the Jā'i·rīte was also David's priest.

David Avenges the Gibeonites

21 Now there was a famine in the days of David for three years, year after year; and David inquired of the LORD. The LORD said, "There is bloodguilt on Saul and on his house, because he put the Gib'e·on·ītes to death." 2 So the king called the Gib'e·on·ītes and spoke to them. (Now the

---

g Heb *He*   *h* Compare 20.15: Heb *and Beth-maacah*
i Compare Gk Vg: Heb *Berites*   *j* Heb *They*   *k* Cn: Heb *Joab to all the army, Israel*

Gib′ē•on•ītes were not of the people of Israel, but of the remnant of the Am′o•rītes; although the people of Israel had sworn to spare them, Saul had tried to wipe them out in his zeal for the people of Israel and Judah.) [3] David said to the Gib′ē•on•ītes, "What shall I do for you? How shall I make expiation, that you may bless the heritage of the LORD?" [4] The Gib′ē•on•ītes said to him, "It is not a matter of silver or gold between us and Saul or his house; neither is it for us to put anyone to death in Israel." He said, "What do you say that I should do for you?" [5] They said to the king, "The man who consumed us and planned to destroy us, so that we should have no place in all the territory of Israel— [6] let seven of his sons be handed over to us, and we will impale them before the LORD at Gib′ē•on on the mountain of the LORD."[l] The king said, "I will hand them over."

[7] But the king spared Me•phib′o•sheth,[m] the son of Saul's son Jonathan, because of the oath of the LORD that was between them, between David and Jonathan son of Saul. [8] The king took the two sons of Riz′pah daughter of Ā′i•ah, whom she bore to Saul, Ar•mō′ni and Me•phib′o•sheth;[m] and the five sons of Mē′rab[n] daughter of Saul, whom she bore to Ā′dri•el son of Bar•zil′laī the Me•hō′la•thīte; [9] he gave them into the hands of the Gib′ē•on•ītes, and they impaled them on the mountain before the LORD. The seven of them perished together. They were put to death in the first days of harvest, at the beginning of barley harvest.

[10] Then Riz′pah the daughter of Ā′i•ah took sackcloth, and spread it on a rock for herself, from the beginning of harvest until rain fell on them from the heavens; she did not allow the birds of the air to come on the bodies[o] by day, or the wild animals by night. [11] When David was told what Riz′pah daughter of Ā′i•ah, the concubine of Saul, had done, [12] David went and took the bones of Saul and the bones of his son Jonathan from the people of Jā′besh-gil′ē•ad, who had stolen them from the public square of Beth-shan, where the Phi•lis′tines had hung them up, on the day the Phi•lis′tines killed Saul on Gil•bō′a. [13] He brought up from there the bones of Saul and the bones of his son Jonathan; and they gathered the bones of those who had been impaled. [14] They buried the bones of Saul and of his son Jonathan in the land of Benjamin in Zē′la, in the tomb of his father Kish; they did all that the king commanded. After that, God heeded supplications for the land.

Exploits of David's Men
(1 Chr 20.4–8)

[15] The Phi•lis′tines went to war again with Israel, and David went down together with his servants. They fought against the Phi•lis′tines, and David grew weary. [16] Ish′bi-bē′nob, one of the de-scendants of the giants, whose spear weighed three hundred shekels of bronze, and who was fitted out with new weapons,[p] said he would kill David. [17] But A•bi′shaī son of Ze•rū′i•ah came to his aid, and attacked the Phi•lis′tine and killed him. Then David's men swore to him, "You shall not go out with us to battle any longer, so that you do not quench the lamp of Israel."

[18] After this a battle took place with the Phi•lis′tines, at Gob; then Sib′be•caī the Hū′sha•thīte killed Saph, who was one of the descendants of the giants. [19] Then there was another battle with the Phi•lis′tines at Gob; and El•hā′nan son of Jā′a•rē-or′e•gim, the Beth′le•hem•ite, killed Goliath the Git′tīte, the shaft of whose spear was like a weaver's beam. [20] There was again war at Gath, where there was a man of great size, who had six fingers on each hand, and six toes on each foot, twenty-four in number; he too was descended from the giants. [21] When he taunted Israel, Jonathan son of David's brother Shim′ē•ī, killed him. [22] These four were de-scended from the giants in Gath; they fell by the hands of David and his servants.

David's Song of Thanksgiving
(Ps 18.1–50)

22 David spoke to the LORD the words of this song on the day when the LORD delivered him from the hand of all his enemies, and from the hand of Saul. [2] He said:

> The LORD is my rock, my fortress, and my
>   deliverer,
> [3]   my God, my rock, in whom I take refuge,
> my shield and the horn of my salvation,
>   my stronghold and my refuge,
>   my savior; you save me from violence.
> [4] I call upon the LORD, who is worthy to be
>   praised,
> and I am saved from my enemies.
>
> [5] For the waves of death encompassed me,
>   the torrents of perdition assailed me;
> [6] the cords of Shē′ōl entangled me,
>   the snares of death confronted me.
>
> [7] In my distress I called upon the LORD;
>   to my God I called.
> From his temple he heard my voice,
>   and my cry came to his ears.
>
> [8] Then the earth reeled and rocked;
>   the foundations of the heavens trembled

---

[l] Cn Compare Gk and 21.9: Heb *at Gibeah of Saul, the chosen of the LORD*   [m] Or *Merib-baal:* See 4.4 note   [n] Two Heb Mss Syr Compare Gk: MT *Michal*   [o] Heb *them*   [p] Heb *was belted anew*

The Lord Is My Rock

Build on the rock! What exactly does that mean? Have you ever watched a house being built? One of the first things that a contractor does is level the ground and put in a foundation. Upon the foundation, the structure begins to grow. A solid foundation will enable that house to stand for many years.

The same goes for our life, both personally and communally. What is your foundation—the rock—that your life is built on? In 2 Sam 22.2, King David says to the LORD, "[You are] my rock, my fortress, and my deliverer." David built his life on the rock and foundation of the LORD. As a result, he found refuge in times of fear. It was this rock that saved David and the people of Israel from the hands of their enemies. Because of David's reliance on God, his kingdom is seen by later generations of Jews as the ideal kingdom for Israel.

You too can find this same refuge, this same saving grace. Starting today, build your life with the Lord as your foundation (see Mt 7.24–27). The next time you face a battle, be it drugs or envy or anger or lust, *stand on the rock!*

▶ **2 Sam 22.1–4**

and quaked, because he was angry.
9 Smoke went up from his nostrils,
   and devouring fire from his mouth;
   glowing coals flamed forth from him.
10 He bowed the heavens, and came down;
   thick darkness was under his feet.
11 He rode on a cherub, and flew;
   he was seen upon the wings of the wind.
12 He made darkness around him a canopy,
   thick clouds, a gathering of water.
13 Out of the brightness before him
   coals of fire flamed forth.
14 The LORD thundered from heaven;
   the Most High uttered his voice.
15 He sent out arrows, and scattered them
   —lightning, and routed them.
16 Then the channels of the sea were seen,
   the foundations of the world were laid bare
at the rebuke of the LORD,
   at the blast of the breath of his nostrils.

17 He reached from on high, he took me,
   he drew me out of mighty waters.
18 He delivered me from my strong enemy,
   from those who hated me;
   for they were too mighty for me.
19 They came upon me in the day of my calamity,
   but the LORD was my stay.
20 He brought me out into a broad place;
   he delivered me, because he delighted in
   me.

21 The LORD rewarded me according to my
   righteousness;
   according to the cleanness of my hands he
   recompensed me.

22 For I have kept the ways of the LORD,
   and have not wickedly departed from my
      God.
23 For all his ordinances were before me,
   and from his statutes I did not turn aside.
24 I was blameless before him,
   and I kept myself from guilt.
25 Therefore the LORD has recompensed me
      according to my righteousness,
   according to my cleanness in his sight.

26 With the loyal you show yourself loyal;
   with the blameless you show yourself
      blameless;
27 with the pure you show yourself pure,
   and with the crooked you show yourself
      perverse.
28 You deliver a humble people,
   but your eyes are upon the haughty to bring
      them down.
29 Indeed, you are my lamp, O LORD,
   the LORD lightens my darkness.
30 By you I can crush a troop,
   and by my God I can leap over a wall.
31 This God—his way is perfect;
   the promise of the LORD proves true;
   he is a shield for all who take refuge
      in him.

32 For who is God, but the LORD?
   And who is a rock, except our God?
33 The God who has girded me with strength[q]
   has opened wide my path.[r]

---

[q] Q Ms Gk Syr Vg Compare Ps 18.32: MT *God is my strong refuge*   [r] Meaning of Heb uncertain

34 He made my[s] feet like the feet of deer,
  and set me secure on the heights.
35 He trains my hands for war,
  so that my arms can bend a bow of bronze.
36 You have given me the shield of your salvation,
  and your help[t] has made me great.
37 You have made me stride freely,
  and my feet do not slip;
38 I pursued my enemies and destroyed them,
  and did not turn back until they were
    consumed.
39 I consumed them; I struck them down, so that
    they did not rise;
  they fell under my feet.
40 For you girded me with strength for the battle;
  you made my assailants sink under me.
41 You made my enemies turn their backs to me,
  those who hated me, and I destroyed them.
42 They looked, but there was no one to save
    them;
  they cried to the LORD, but he did not
    answer them.
43 I beat them fine like the dust of the earth,
  I crushed them and stamped them down
    like the mire of the streets.

44 You delivered me from strife with the peoples;[u]
  you kept me as the head of the nations;
  people whom I had not known served me.
45 Foreigners came cringing to me;
  as soon as they heard of me, they obeyed me.
46 Foreigners lost heart,
  and came trembling out of their
    strongholds.

47 The LORD lives! Blessed be my rock,
  and exalted be my God, the rock of my
    salvation,
48 the God who gave me vengeance
  and brought down peoples under me,
49 who brought me out from my enemies;
  you exalted me above my adversaries,
  you delivered me from the violent.

50 For this I will extol you, O LORD, among the
    nations,
  and sing praises to your name.
51 He is a tower of salvation for his king,
  and shows steadfast love to his anointed,
  to David and his descendants forever.

The Last Words of David

23 Now these are the last words of David:
  The oracle of David, son of Jesse,
  the oracle of the man whom God exalted,[v]
the anointed of the God of Jacob,
  the favorite of the Strong One of Israel:

2 The spirit of the LORD speaks through me,
  his word is upon my tongue.

3 The God of Israel has spoken,
  the Rock of Israel has said to me:
One who rules over people justly,
  ruling in the fear of God,
4 is like the light of morning,
  like the sun rising on a cloudless morning,
  gleaming from the rain on the grassy land.

5 Is not my house like this with God?
  For he has made with me an everlasting
    covenant,
  ordered in all things and secure.
Will he not cause to prosper
  all my help and my desire?
6 But the godless are [w] all like thorns that are
    thrown away;
  for they cannot be picked up with the hand;
7 to touch them one uses an iron bar
  or the shaft of a spear.
And they are entirely consumed in fire on
    the spot.[x]

David's Mighty Men
(1 Chr 11.10–47)

8 These are the names of the warriors whom David had: Jo'sheb-bas·she'beth a Tah·che'mo·nīte;[y] he was chief of the Three;[y] he wielded his spear[z] against eight hundred whom he killed at one time.

9 Next to him among the three warriors was El·e·a'zar son of Do'do son of A·ho'hī. He was with David when they defied the Phi·lis'tines who were gathered there for battle. The Israelites withdrew, 10 but he stood his ground. He struck down the Phi·lis'tines until his arm grew weary, though his hand clung to the sword. The LORD brought about a great victory that day. Then the people came back to him—but only to strip the dead.

11 Next to him was Sham'mah son of A'gee, the Har'a·rīte. The Phi·lis'tines gathered together at Le'hī, where there was a plot of ground full of lentils; and the army fled from the Phi·lis'tines. 12 But he took his stand in the middle of the plot, defended it, and killed the Phi·lis'tines; and the LORD brought about a great victory.

13 Towards the beginning of harvest three of the thirty[c] chiefs went down to join David at the cave of A·dul'lam, while a band of Phi·lis'tines was encamped in the valley of Reph'a·im. 14 David was

---

s Another reading is *his*   t Q Ms: MT *your answering*
u Gk: Heb *from strife with my people*   v Q Ms: MT *who was
raised on high*   w Heb *But worthlessness*   x Heb *in sitting*
y Gk Vg Compare 1 Chr 11.11: Meaning of Heb
uncertain   z 1 Chr 11.11: Meaning of Heb uncertain
a Heb adds *head*

then in the stronghold; and the garrison of the Phi•lis′tines was then at Bethlehem. 15 David said longingly, "O that someone would give me water to drink from the well of Bethlehem that is by the gate!" 16 Then the three warriors broke through the camp of the Phi•lis′tines, drew water from the well of Bethlehem that was by the gate, and brought it to David. But he would not drink of it; he poured it out to the LORD, 17 for he said, "The LORD forbid that I should do this. Can I drink the blood of the men who went at the risk of their lives?" Therefore he would not drink it. The three warriors did these things.

18 Now A•bi′shai son of Ze•ru′i•ah, the brother of Jō′ab, was chief of the Thirty.b With his spear he fought against three hundred men and killed them, and won a name beside the Three. 19 He was the most renowned of the Thirty,c and became their commander; but he did not attain to the Three.

20 Be•na′i•ah son of Je•hoi′a•da was a valiant warriord from Kab′zē•el, a doer of great deeds; he struck down two sons of Ar′i•ele of Mō′ab. He also went down and killed a lion in a pit on a day when snow had fallen. 21 And he killed an Egyptian, a handsome man. The Egyptian had a spear in his hand; but Be•na′i•ah went against him with a staff, snatched the spear out of the Egyptian's hand, and killed him with his own spear. 22 Such were the things Be•na′i•ah son of Je•hoi′a•da did, and won a name beside the three warriors. 23 He was renowned among the Thirty, but he did not attain to the Three. And David put him in charge of his bodyguard.

24 Among the Thirty were As′a•hel brother of Jō′ab; El•hā′nan son of Dō′dō of Bethlehem; 25 Sham′mah of Har′od; E•li′ka of Har′od; 26 Hē′lez the Pal′tīte; Ira son of Ik′kesh of Te•kō′a; 27 Ā′bi•ē′zer of An′a•thoth; Me•bun′nai the Hū′sha•thīte; 28 Zal′mon the A•hō′hīte; Mā′ha•rai of Ne•toph′ah; 29 Hē′leb son of Bā′a•nah of Ne•toph′ah; It′tai son of Rī′bai of Gib′ē•ah of the Ben′ja•min•ītes; 30 Be•na′i•ah of Pir′a•thon; Hid′dai of the torrents of Gā′ash; 31 Ā′bi-al′bon the Ar′ba•thīte; Az′ma•veth of Ba•hū′rim; 32 Ē•li′ah•ba of Shā•al′bon; the sons of Jā′shen: Jonathan 33 son off Sham′mah the Har′a•rīte; A•hī′am son of Shar′ar the Har′a•rīte; 34 E•liph′e•let son of A•has′bai of Mā′a•cah; E•li′am son of A•hith′o•phel the Gi′lo•nīte; 35 Hez′rog of Car′mel; Pā′a•rai the Ar′bīte; 36 I′gal son of Nathan of Zō′bah; Bā′nī the Gad′īte; 37 Zē′lek the Am′mon•īte; Nā′ha•rai of Be•er′oth, the armor-bearer of Jō′ab son of Ze•ru′i•ah; 38 Ira the Ith′rīte; Gā′reb the Ith′rīte; 39 Ū•rī′ah the Hit′tīte—thirty-seven in all.

David's Census of Israel and Judah
(1 Chr 21.1–6)

24 Again the anger of the LORD was kindled against Israel; and he incited David against them, saying, "Go, count the people of Israel and Judah." 2 So the king said to Jō′ab and the commanders of the army,h who were with him, "Go through all the tribes of Israel, from Dan to Bē′er-shē′ba, and take a census of the people, so that I may know how many there are." 3 But Jō′ab said to the king, "May the LORD your God increase the number of the people a hundredfold, while the eyes of my lord the king can still see it! But why does my lord the king want to do this?" 4 But the king's word prevailed against Jō′ab and the commanders of the army. So Jō′ab and the commanders of the army went out from the presence of the king to take a census of the people of Israel. 5 They crossed the Jordan, and began fromi A•rō′er and from the city that is in the middle of the valley, toward Gad and on to Jā′zer. 6 Then they came to Gil′e•ad, and to Kā′desh in the land of the Hit′tītes;j and they came to Dan, and from Dank they went around to Sī′don, 7 and came to the fortress of Tȳre and to all the cities of the Hī′vītes and Cā′naan•ites; and they went out to the Neg′eb of Judah at Bē′er-shē′ba. 8 So when they had gone through all the land, they came back to Jerusalem at the end of nine months and twenty days. 9 Jō′ab reported to the king the number of those who had been recorded: in Israel there were eight hundred thousand soldiers able to draw the sword, and those of Judah were five hundred thousand.

Judgment on David's Sin
(1 Chr 21.7–17)

10 But afterward, David was stricken to the heart because he had numbered the people. David said to the LORD, "I have sinned greatly in what I have done. But now, O LORD, I pray you, take away the guilt of your servant; for I have done very foolishly." 11 When David rose in the morning, the word of the LORD came to the prophet Gad, David's seer, saying, 12 "Go and say to David: Thus says the LORD: Three things I offerl you; choose one of them, and I will do it to you." 13 So Gad came to David and told him; he asked him, "Shall threem years of famine come to you on your land? Or will you flee three months before your foes while they pursue you? Or shall there be three days' pestilence in your land? Now consider, and decide what answer I shall return to the one who sent me." 14 Then David said to Gad, "I am in great distress; let us fall

---

b Two Heb Mss Syr: MT *Three*   c Syr Compare 1 Chr 11.25: Heb *Was he the most renowned of the Three?*   d Another reading is *the son of Ish-hai*   e Gk: Heb lacks *sons of*   f Gk: Heb lacks *son of*   g Another reading is *Hezrai*   h 1 Chr 21.2 Gk: Heb *to Joab the commander of the army*   i Gk Mss: Heb *encamped in Aroer south of*   j Gk: Heb *to the land of Tahtim-hodshi*   k Cn Compare Gk: Heb *they came to Dan-jaan and*   l Or *hold over*   m 1 Chr 21.12 Gk: Heb *seven* into the hand of the LORD, for his mercy is great; but let me not fall into human hands."

15 So the LORD sent a pestilence on Israel from that morning until the appointed time; and seventy thousand of the people died, from Dan to Bě'er-shě'ba. 16 But when the angel stretched out his hand toward Jerusalem to destroy it, the LORD relented concerning the evil, and said to the angel who was bringing destruction among the people, "It is enough; now stay your hand." The angel of the LORD was then by the threshing floor of A·rau'nah the Jeb'ū·sīte. 17 When David saw the angel who was destroying the people, he said to the LORD, "I alone have sinned, and I alone have done wickedly; but these sheep, what have they done? Let your hand, I pray, be against me and against my father's house."

David's Altar on the Threshing Floor
(1 Chr 21.18–27)

18 That day Gad came to David and said to him, "Go up and erect an altar to the LORD on the threshing floor of A·rau'nah the Jeb'ū·sīte." 19 Following Gad's instructions, David went up, as the LORD had commanded. 20 When A·rau'nah looked down, he saw the king and his servants coming toward him; and A·rau'nah went out and prostrated himself before the king with his face to the ground. 21 A·rau'nah said, "Why has my lord the king come to his servant?" David said, "To buy the threshing floor from you in order to build an altar to the LORD, so that the plague may be averted from the people." 22 Then A·rau'nah said to David, "Let my lord the king take and offer up what seems good to him; here are the oxen for the burnt offering, and the threshing sledges and the yokes of the oxen for the wood. 23 All this, O king, A·rau'nah gives to the king." And A·rau'nah said to the king, "May the LORD your God respond favorably to you."

24 But the king said to A·rau'nah, "No, but I will buy them from you for a price; I will not offer burnt offerings to the LORD my God that cost me nothing." So David bought the threshing floor and the oxen for fifty shekels of silver. 25 David built there an altar to the LORD, and offered burnt offerings and offerings of well-being. So the LORD answered his supplication for the land, and the plague was averted from Israel.

Kings

The ancient Egyptians had an advanced civilization, yet today the remains of their handiwork lie buried under centuries of sand. The great Roman Empire spanned the Western world at the time of Jesus, yet today, only scattered ruins testify to its existence. The same is true of the glorious but short-lived Israelite kingdom. The Books of 1 and 2 Kings trace its tragic collapse from the glories of Solomon's Temple to the Babylonian Exile.

At a Glance

- **1 Kings, chapters 1–11.** the reign of King Solomon

- **1 Kings, chapter 12, to 2 Kings, chapter 17.** the various kings of Israel and Judah

- **2 Kings, chapters 18–30.** the kingdom of Judah until its fall in 587 B.C.

In-depth

If the kingships of Saul and David could be described as the spring and summer of the Israelite kingdom, the Books of 1 and 2 Kings describe its fall and winter. The beginning of 1 Kings covers the glorious late summer under King Solomon. Solomon accumulated great riches, constructed a beautiful Temple, and built Jerusalem into a city rivaling any other center of power. But the summer was quickly over at Solomon's death, when the kingdom was split in two (see map 3, "The Kingdom Years"). The northern kingdom, called Israel, and the southern kingdom, called Judah, were ruled by a succession of kings, most of whom proved to be weak and sinful leaders. Their incompetence had disastrous consequences: the two kingdoms fell to foreign powers. Israel fell to the Assyrians in 722 B.C., and Judah to the Babylonians in 587 B.C.

The sorrow that we hear in 1 and 2 Kings is accompanied by a clear explanation: the people have fallen because of their wickedness and the wickedness of their leaders. Not surprisingly, the author of 1 and 2 Kings fashioned the history of God's people into a kind of morality tale, emphasizing the importance of faithfulness to the Covenant and the Law.

Of special interest in these books is the appearance of the classical prophet. Unlike the prophets of other lands, who were mere tools in the ruler's hand, the great prophets of Israel and Judah, like Elijah and Elisha, often directly opposed royal decisions and actions. Their job was not to pamper the ruler's pride, but to speak God's word clearly and boldly.

As we read about the terrible crises that the kingdoms of Judah and Israel faced, we can reflect on one of the basic truths of human history: Apart from God there is no hope. Only one thing remains as history passes: God's promise.

Quick Facts

Period Covered
from 961 to 587 B.C.

Author
unknown, from the Deuteronomic tradition, writing after the fall of Jerusalem

Theme
the history of Israel's and Judah's kings from Solomon until the fall of Jerusalem

Of Note
The two books of Kings were originally one book.

322

1 Kings

10.23

The Struggle for the Succession

1 King David was old and advanced in years; and although they covered him with clothes, he could not get warm. ² So his servants said to him, "Let a young virgin be sought for my lord the king, and let her wait on the king, and be his attendant; let her lie in your bosom, so that my lord the king may be warm." ³ So they searched for a beautiful girl throughout all the territory of Israel, and found Ab'i·shag the Shū'nam·mīte, and brought her to the king. ⁴ The girl was very beautiful. She became the king's attendant and served him, but the king did not know her sexually.

5 Now Ad·o·nī'jah son of Hag'gith exalted himself, saying, "I will be king"; he prepared for himself chariots and horsemen, and fifty men to run before him. ⁶ His father had never at any time displeased him by asking, "Why have you done thus and so?" He was also a very handsome man, and he was born next after Ab'sa·lom. ⁷ He conferred with Jō'ab son of Ze·rū'i·ah and with the priest A·bī'athar, and they supported Ad·o·nī'jah. ⁸ But the priest Zā'dok, and Be·nā'i·ah son of Je·hoi'a·da, and the prophet Nathan, and Shim'e·ī, and Rē'ī, and David's own warriors did not side with Ad·o·nī'jah.

9 Ad·o·nī'jah sacrificed sheep, oxen, and fatted cattle by the stone Zō'he·leth, which is beside En·rō'gel, and he invited all his brothers, the king's sons, and all the royal officials of Judah, ¹⁰ but he did not invite the prophet Nathan or Be·nā'i·ah or the warriors or his brother Solomon.

11 Then Nathan said to Bath·shē'ba, Solomon's mother, "Have you not heard that Ad·o·nī'jah son of Hag'gith has become king and our lord David does not know it? ¹² Now therefore come, let me give you advice, so that you may save your own life and the life of your son Solomon. ¹³ Go in at once to King David, and say to him, 'Did you not, my lord the king, swear to your servant, saying: Your son Solomon shall succeed me as king, and he shall sit on my throne? Why then is Ad·o·nī'jah king?' ¹⁴ Then while you are still there speaking with the king, I will come in after you and confirm your words."

15 So Bath·shē'ba went to the king in his room. The king was very old; Ab'i·shag the Shū'nam·mīte was attending the king. ¹⁶ Bath·shē'ba bowed and did obeisance to the king, and the king said, "What do you wish?" ¹⁷ She said to him, "My lord, you swore to your servant by the LORD your God, saying: Your son Solomon shall succeed me as king, and he shall sit on my throne. ¹⁸ But now suddenly Ad·o·nī'jah has become king, though you, my lord the king, do not know it. ¹⁹ He has sacrificed oxen, fatted cattle, and sheep in abundance, and has invited all the children of the king, the priest A·bī'a·thar, and Jō'ab the commander of the army; but your servant Solomon he has not invited. ²⁰ But you, my lord the king—the eyes of all Israel are on you to tell them who shall sit on the throne of my lord the king after him. ²¹ Otherwise it will come to pass, when my lord the king sleeps with his

Introducing... ▶SOLOMON

Solomon was one of the sons of David and Bathsheba. He ruled for forty years after King David died, and he was the third and last king to rule over the united kingdom of Israel.

There is an old saying that often our personal strengths are our greatest weaknesses. This is true of Solomon. He was a tremendous organizer, an able ruler, a clever politician, and a great builder—it was during his reign that the first Temple was built in Jerusalem. To fulfill these great accomplishments, however, Solomon taxed his people heavily, married foreign women to seal political alliances with other nations, and used forced labor to complete his building projects. These things offended God and made Solomon unpopular with the people of Israel.

When Solomon died, ten of the original twelve tribes from the northern part of Israel left the kingdom owing to these harsh practices and set up their own kingdom. Israel never again existed as a united kingdom ruled by an Israelite king. The author of Kings attributes this more to Solomon's acceptance of other gods near the end of his life than to his political mistakes.

---

ancestors, that my son Solomon and I will be counted offenders."

22 While she was still speaking with the king, the prophet Nathan came in. 23 The king was told, "Here is the prophet Nathan." When he came in before the king, he did obeisance to the king, with his face to the ground. 24 Nathan said, "My lord the king, have you said, 'Ad•o•ni′jah shall succeed me as king, and he shall sit on my throne'? 25 For today he has gone down and has sacrificed oxen, fatted cattle, and sheep in abundance, and has invited all the king's children, Jō′ab the commander*a* of the army, and the priest A•bī′a•thar, who are now eating and drinking before him, and saying, 'Long live King Ad•o•ni′jah!' 26 But he did not invite me, your servant, and the priest Zā′dok, and Be•nā′i•ah son of Je•hoi′a•da, and your servant Solomon. 27 Has this thing been brought about by my lord the king and you have not let your servants know who should sit on the throne of my lord the king after him?"

The Accession of Solomon
(1 Chr 29.22b–25)

28 King David answered, "Summon Bath•shē′ba to me." So she came into the king's presence, and stood before the king. 29 The king swore, saying, "As the LORD lives, who has saved my life from every adversity, 30 as I swore to you by the LORD, the God of Israel, 'Your son Solomon shall succeed me as king, and he shall sit on my throne in my place,' so will I do this day." 31 Then Bath•shē′ba bowed with her face to the ground, and did obeisance to the king, and said, "May my lord King David live forever!"

32 King David said, "Summon to me the priest Zā′dok, the prophet Nathan, and Be•nā′i•ah son of Je•hoi′a•da." When they came before the king, 33 the king said to them, "Take with you the servants of your lord, and have my son Solomon ride on my own mule, and bring him down to Gī′hon. 34 There let the priest Zā′dok and the prophet Nathan anoint him king over Israel; then blow the trumpet, and say, 'Long live King Solomon!' 35 You shall go up following him. Let him enter and sit on my throne; he shall be king in my place; for I have appointed him to be ruler over Israel and over Judah." 36 Be•nā′i•ah son of Je•hoi′a•da answered the king, "Amen! May the LORD, the God of my lord the king, so ordain. 37 As the LORD has been with my lord the king, so may he be with Solomon, and make his throne greater than the throne of my lord King David."

38 So the priest Zā′dok, the prophet Nathan, and Be•nā′i•ah son of Je•hoi′a•da, and the Cher′e•thites and the Pel′eth•ites, went down and had Solomon ride on King David's mule, and led him to Gī′hon. 39 There the priest Zā′dok took the horn of oil from the tent and anointed Solomon. Then they blew the trumpet, and all the people said, "Long live King Solomon!" 40 And all the people went up following him, playing on pipes and rejoicing with great joy, so that the earth quaked at their noise.

41 Ad•o•ni′jah and all the guests who were with him heard it as they finished feasting. When Jō′ab heard the sound of the trumpet, he said, "Why is the city in an uproar?" 42 While he was still speak-

---

a Gk: Heb *the commanders*

ing, Jonathan son of the priest A·bī′a·thar arrived. Ad·o·nī′jah said, "Come in, for you are a worthy man and surely you bring good news." 43 Jonathan answered Ad·o·nī′jah, "No, for our lord King David has made Solomon king; 44 the king has sent with him the priest Zā′dok, the prophet Nathan, and Be·nā′i·ah son of Je·hoi′a·da, and the Cher′e·thītes and the Pel′eth·ītes; and they had him ride on the king's mule; 45 the priest Zā′dok and the prophet Nathan have anointed him king at Gi′hon; and they have gone up from there rejoicing, so that the city is in an uproar. This is the noise that you heard. 46 Solomon now sits on the royal throne. 47 Moreover the king's servants came to congratulate our lord King David, saying, 'May God make the name of Solomon more famous than yours, and make his throne greater than your throne.' The king bowed in worship on the bed 48 and went on to pray thus, 'Blessed be the LORD, the God of Israel, who today has granted one of my offspring*b* to sit on my throne and permitted me to witness it.' "

49 Then all the guests of Ad·o·nī′jah got up trembling and went their own ways. 50 Ad·o·nī′jah, fearing Solomon, got up and went to grasp the horns of the altar. 51 Solomon was informed, "Ad·o·nī′jah is afraid of King Solomon; see, he has laid hold of the horns of the altar, saying, 'Let King Solomon swear to me first that he will not kill his servant with the sword.' " 52 So Solomon responded, "If he proves to be a worthy man, not one of his hairs shall fall to the ground; but if wickedness is found in him, he shall die." 53 Then King Solomon sent to have him brought down from the altar. He came to do obeisance to King Solomon; and Solomon said to him, "Go home."

David's Instruction to Solomon

2 When David's time to die drew near, he charged his son Solomon, saying: 2 "I am about to go the way of all the earth. Be strong, be courageous, 3 and keep the charge of the LORD your God, walking in his ways and keeping his statutes, his commandments, his ordinances, and his testimonies, as it is written in the law of Moses, so that you may prosper in all that you do and wherever you turn. 4 Then the LORD will establish his word that he spoke concerning me: 'If your heirs take heed to their way, to walk before me in faithfulness with all their heart and with all their soul, there shall not fail you a successor on the throne of Israel.'

5 "Moreover you know also what Jō′ab son of Ze·rū′i·ah did to me, how he dealt with the two commanders of the armies of Israel, Abner son of Ner, and A·mā′sa son of Jē′ther, whom he murdered, retaliating in time of peace for blood that had been shed in war, and putting the blood of war on the belt around his waist, and on the sandals on his feet. 6 Act therefore according to your wisdom, but do not let his gray head go down to Shē′ōl in peace. 7 Deal loyally, however, with the sons of Bar·zil′lai the Gil′e·ad·īte, and let them be among those who eat at your table; for with such loyalty they met me when I fled from your brother Ab′sa·lom. 8 There is also with you Shim′ē·i son of Gē′ra, the Ben′ja·min·īte from Ba·hū′rim, who cursed me with a terrible curse on the day when I went to Mā·ha·nā′im; but when he came down to meet me at the Jordan, I swore to him by the LORD, 'I will not put you to death with the sword.' 9 Therefore do not hold him guiltless, for you are a wise man; you will know what you ought to do to him, and you must bring his gray head down with blood to Shē′ōl."

Death of David
(1 Chr 3.4; 29.26–28)

10 Then David slept with his ancestors, and was buried in the city of David. 11 The time that David reigned over Israel was forty years; he reigned seven years in Hē′bron, and thirty-three years in Jerusalem. 12 So Solomon sat on the throne of his father David; and his kingdom was firmly established.

Solomon Consolidates His Reign

13 Then Ad·o·nī′jah son of Hag′gith came to Bath·shē′ba, Solomon's mother. She asked, "Do you come peaceably?" He said, "Peaceably." 14 Then he said, "May I have a word with you?" She said, "Go on." 15 He said, "You know that the kingdom was mine, and that all Israel expected me to reign; however, the kingdom has turned about and become my brother's, for it was his from the LORD. 16 And now I have one request to make of you; do not refuse me." She said to him, "Go on." 17 He said, "Please ask King Solomon—he will not refuse you—to give me Ab′i·shag the Shū′nam·mīte as my wife." 18 Bath·shē′ba said, "Very well; I will speak to the king on your behalf."

19 So Bath·shē′ba went to King Solomon, to speak to him on behalf of Ad·o·nī′jah. The king rose to meet her, and bowed down to her; then he sat on his throne, and had a throne brought for the king's mother, and she sat on his right. 20 Then she said, "I have one small request to make of you; do not refuse me." And the king said to her, "Make your request, my mother; for I will not refuse you." 21 She said, "Let Ab′i·shag the Shū′nam·mīte be given to your brother Ad·o·nī′jah as his wife." 22 King Solomon answered his mother, "And why do you ask Ab′i·shag the Shū′nam·mīte for Ado·nī′jah? Ask for him the kingdom as well! For he is my elder brother; ask not only for him but also for the priest

---

b Gk: Heb *one*

A•bī′a•thar and for Jō′ab son of Ze•rū′i•ah!" 23 Then King Solomon swore by the LORD, "So may God do to me, and more also, for Ad•o•nī′jah has devised this scheme at the risk of his life! 24 Now therefore as the LORD lives, who has established me and placed me on the throne of my father David, and who has made me a house as he promised, today Ad•o•nī′jah shall be put to death." 25 So King Solomon sent Be•nā′i•ah son of Je•hoi′a•da; he struck him down, and he died.

26 The king said to the priest A•bī′a•thar, "Go to An′a•thoth, to your estate; for you deserve death. But I will not at this time put you to death, because you carried the ark of the Lord GOD before my father David, and because you shared in all the hardships my father endured." 27 So Solomon banished A•bī′a•thar from being priest to the LORD, thus fulfilling the word of the LORD that he had spoken concerning the house of Ē′li in Shī′lōh.

28 When the news came to Jō′ab—for Jō′ab had supported Ad•o•nī′jah though he had not supported Ab′sa•lom—Jō′ab fled to the tent of the LORD and grasped the horns of the altar. 29 When it was told King Solomon, "Jō′ab has fled to the tent of the LORD and now is beside the altar," Solomon sent Be•nā′i•ah son of Je•hoi′a•da, saying, "Go, strike him down." 30 So Be•nā′i•ah came to the tent of the LORD and said to him, "The king commands, 'Come out.' " But he said, "No, I will die here." Then Be•nā′i•ah brought the king word again, saying, "Thus said Jō′ab, and thus he answered me." 31 The king replied to him, "Do as he has said, strike him down and bury him; and thus take away from me and from my father's house the guilt for the blood that Jō′ab shed without cause. 32 The LORD will bring back his bloody deeds on his own head, because, without the knowledge of my father David, he attacked and killed with the sword two men more righteous and better than himself, Abner son of Ner, commander of the army of Israel, and A•mā′sa son of Jē′ther, commander of the army of Judah. 33 So shall their blood come back on the head of Jō′ab and on the head of his descendants forever; but to David, and to his descendants, and to his house, and to his throne, there shall be peace from the LORD forevermore." 34 Then Be•nā′-i•ah son of Je•hoi′a•da went up and struck him down and killed him; and he was buried at his own house near the wilderness. 35 The king put Be•nā′i•ah son of Je•hoi′a•da over the army in his place, and the king put the priest Zā′dok in the place of A•bī′a•thar.

36 Then the king sent and summoned Shim′ē•ī, and said to him, "Build yourself a house in Jerusalem, and live there, and do not go out from there to any place whatever. 37 For on the day you go out, and cross the Wadi Kid′ron, know for certain that you shall die; your blood shall be on your own head." 38 And Shim′ē•ī said to the king, "The sentence is fair; as my lord the king has said, so will your servant do." So Shim′ē•ī lived in Jerusalem many days.

39 But it happened at the end of three years that two of Shim′ē•ī's slaves ran away to King Ā′chish son of Mā′a•cah of Gath. When it was told Shim′ē•ī, "Your slaves are in Gath," 40 Shim′ē•ī arose and saddled a donkey, and went to Ā′chish in Gath, to search for his slaves; Shim′ē•ī went and brought his slaves from Gath. 41 When Solomon was told that Shim′ē•ī had gone from Jerusalem to Gath and returned, 42 the king sent and summoned Shim′ē•ī, and said to him, "Did I not make you swear by the LORD, and solemnly adjure you, saying, 'Know for certain that on the day you go out and go to any place whatever, you shall die'? And you said to me, 'The sentence is fair; I accept.' 43 Why then have you not kept your oath to the LORD and the commandment with which I charged you?" 44 The king also said to Shim′ē•ī, "You know in your own heart all the evil that you did to my father David; so the LORD will bring back your evil on your own head. 45 But King Solomon shall be blessed, and the throne of David shall be established before the LORD forever." 46 Then the king commanded Be•nā′i•ah son of Je•hoi′a•da; and he went out and struck him down, and he died.

So the kingdom was established in the hand of Solomon.

Solomon's Prayer for Wisdom
(2 Chr 1.2–13)

3 Solomon made a marriage alliance with Pharaoh king of Egypt; he took Pharaoh's daughter and brought her into the city of David, until he had finished building his own house and the house of the LORD and the wall around Jerusalem. 2 The people were sacrificing at the high places, however, because no house had yet been built for the name of the LORD.

3 Solomon loved the LORD, walking in the statutes of his father David; only, he sacrificed and offered incense at the high places. 4 The king went to Gib′ē•on to sacrifice there, for that was the principal high place; Solomon used to offer a thousand burnt offerings on that altar. 5 At Gib′ē•on the LORD appeared to Solomon in a dream by night; and God said, "Ask what I should give you." 6 And Solomon said, "You have shown great and steadfast love to your servant my father David, because he walked before you in faithfulness, in righteousness, and in uprightness of heart toward you; and you have kept for him this great and steadfast love, and have given him a son to sit on his throne today. 7 And now, O LORD my God, you have made your servant king

GOD, GIVE ME WISDOM!

At the beginning of his reign, Solomon asked God for wisdom to govern his people. Under the advice of the prophet Nathan, Solomon became a great king. His failure came later because he betrayed God by accepting other gods and exploiting his people with work and taxes to build his magnificent royal city of Jerusalem.

Whenever you are in a leadership position, remember that you must use the power or authority you have in service to God and God's people; never use it to exploit others or for your own selfishness.
- Ask God for the wisdom necessary to discern how to respond to the needs of people you lead.
- Examine your leadership style frequently to see if you remain faithful to God's call to be a servant of those in need.

▶ 1 Kings 3.4–15

in place of my father David, although I am only a little child; I do not know how to go out or come in. 8 And your servant is in the midst of the people whom you have chosen, a great people, so numerous they cannot be numbered or counted. 9 Give your servant therefore an understanding mind to govern your people, able to discern between good and evil; for who can govern this your great people?"

10 It pleased the Lord that Solomon had asked this. 11 God said to him, "Because you have asked this, and have not asked for yourself long life or riches, or for the life of your enemies, but have asked for yourself understanding to discern what is right, 12 I now do according to your word. Indeed I give you a wise and discerning mind; no one like you has been before you and no one like you shall arise after you. 13 I give you also what you have not asked, both riches and honor all your life; no other king shall compare with you. 14 If you will walk in my ways, keeping my statutes and my commandments, as your father David walked, then I will lengthen your life."

15 Then Solomon awoke; it had been a dream. He came to Jerusalem where he stood before the ark of the covenant of the LORD. He offered up burnt offerings and offerings of well-being, and provided a feast for all his servants.

Solomon's Wisdom in Judgment

16 Later, two women who were prostitutes came to the king and stood before him. 17 The one woman said, "Please, my lord, this woman and I live in the same house; and I gave birth while she was in the house. 18 Then on the third day after I gave birth, this woman also gave birth. We were together; there was no one else with us in the house, only the two of us were in the house. 19 Then this woman's son died in the night, because she lay on him. 20 She got up in the middle of the night and took my son from beside me while your servant slept. She laid him at her breast, and laid her dead son at my breast. 21 When I rose in the morning to nurse my son, I saw that he was dead; but when I looked at him closely in the morning, clearly it was not the son I had borne." 22 But the other woman said, "No, the living son is mine, and the dead son is yours." The first said, "No, the dead son is yours, and the living son is mine." So they argued before the king.

23 Then the king said, "The one says, 'This is my son that is alive, and your son is dead'; while the other says, 'Not so! Your son is dead, and my son is the living one.' " 24 So the king said, "Bring me a sword," and they brought a sword before the king. 25 The king said, "Divide the living boy in two; then give half to the one, and half to the other." 26 But the woman whose son was alive said to the king—because compassion for her son burned within her—"Please, my lord, give her the living boy; certainly do not kill him!" The other said, "It shall be neither mine nor yours; divide it." 27 Then the king responded: "Give the first woman the living boy; do not kill him. She is his mother." 28 All

PRAY IT!
A Wise Heart

A famous prayer, often called the Peace Prayer, by Saint Francis of Assisi (A.D. 1181–1226), contains the line "LORD, grant that I may not so much seek to be . . . understood, as to understand."

It is almost as if Saint Francis is echoing the prayer of King Solomon, who lived two thousand years before him. The request is the same. Both men ask God to give them the gift of a wise heart—the ability to see things as God sees them.

What a difference wisdom can make in our life. What a wonderful thing to pray for. What a blessing to increase the amount of wisdom in our world. What inspiring examples we have in the prayers of Solomon a millennium before Jesus, and of Francis a millennium after.

Let us ask God daily for a wise heart.

▶ 1 Kings 3.9

Israel heard of the judgment that the king had rendered; and they stood in awe of the king, because they perceived that the wisdom of God was in him, to execute justice.

Solomon's Administrative Officers

4 King Solomon was king over all Israel, 2 and these were his high officials: Az·a·rī′ah son of Zā′dok was the priest; 3 El·i·hōr′eph and A·hī′jah sons of Shī′sha were secretaries; Je·hosh′a·phat son of A·hī′lud was recorder; 4 Be·nā′i·ah son of Je·hoi′a·da was in command of the army; Zā′dok and A·bī′a·thar were priests; 5 Az·a·rī′ah son of Nathan was over the officials; Zā′bud son of Nathan was priest and king's friend; 6 A·hī′shar was in charge of the palace; and Ad·o·nī′ram son of Ab′da was in charge of the forced labor.

7 Solomon had twelve officials over all Israel, who provided food for the king and his household; each one had to make provision for one month in the year. 8 These were their names: Ben-hur, in the hill country of Ē′phra·im; 9 Ben-dē′ker, in Mā′kaz, Shā·al′bim, Beth-shē′mesh, and Ē′lon-beth-hā′nan; 10 Ben-hē′sed, in A·rūb′both (to him belonged Sō′cōh and all the land of Hē′pher); 11 Ben-a·bin′a·dab, in all Nā′phath-dor (he had Tā′phath, Solomon's daughter, as his wife); 12 Bā′a·na son of A·hī′lud, in Tā′a·nach, Me·gid′dō, and all Beth-

shē′an, which is beside Zar′e·than below Jez′rē·el, and from Beth-shē′an to Ā′bel-me·hō′lah, as far as the other side of Jok′mē·am; 13 Ben-gē′ber, in Rā′moth-gil′ē·ad (he had the villages of Jā′ir son of Ma-nas′seh, which are in Gil′e·ad, and he had the region of Ar′gob, which is in Bā′shan, sixty great cities with walls and bronze bars); 14 A·hin′a·dab son of Id′dō, in Mā·ha·nā′im; 15 A·him′a·az, in Naph′ta·lī (he had taken Bas′e·math, Solomon's daughter, as his wife); 16 Bā′a·na son of Hū′shai, in Ash′er and Be·ā′loth; 17 Je·hosh′a·phat son of Pa·rū′ah, in Is′sa·char; 18 Shim′ē·ī son of Ē′la, in Benjamin; 19 Gē′ber son of Ū′rī, in the land of Gil′e·ad, the country of King Sī′hon of the Am′o·rītes and of King Og of Bā′shan. And there was one official in the land of Judah.

Magnificence of Solomon's Rule

20 Judah and Israel were as numerous as the sand by the sea; they ate and drank and were happy. 21 ᶜSolomon was sovereign over all the kingdoms from the Euphrates to the land of the Phi·lis′tines, even to the border of Egypt; they brought tribute and served Solomon all the days of his life.

22 Solomon's provision for one day was thirty cors of choice flour, and sixty cors of meal, 23 ten fat oxen, and twenty pasture-fed cattle, one hundred sheep, besides deer, gazelles, roebucks, and fatted fowl. 24 For he had dominion over all the region west of the Euphrates from Tiph′sah to Gā′za, over all the kings west of the Euphrates; and he had peace on all sides. 25 During Solomon's lifetime Judah and Israel lived in safety, from Dan even to Bē′er-shē′ba, all of them under their vines and fig trees. 26 Solomon also had forty thousand stalls of horses for his chariots, and twelve thousand horsemen. 27 Those officials supplied provisions for King Solomon and for all who came to King Solomon's table, each one in his month; they let nothing be lacking. 28 They also brought to the required place barley and straw for the horses and swift steeds, each according to his charge.

Fame of Solomon's Wisdom

29 God gave Solomon very great wisdom, discernment, and breadth of understanding as vast as the sand on the seashore, 30 so that Solomon's wisdom surpassed the wisdom of all the people of the east, and all the wisdom of Egypt. 31 He was wiser than anyone else, wiser than Ē′than the Ez′ra·hīte, and Hē′man, Cal′col, and Dar′da, children of Mā′hol; his fame spread throughout all the surrounding nations. 32 He composed three thousand proverbs, and his songs numbered a thousand and

---

ᶜ Ch 5.1 in Heb

five. 33 He would speak of trees, from the cedar that is in the Lebanon to the hyssop that grows in the wall; he would speak of animals, and birds, and reptiles, and fish. 34 People came from all the nations to hear the wisdom of Solomon; they came from all the kings of the earth who had heard of his wisdom.

Preparations and Materials for the Temple
(2 Chr 2.1–18)

5 *d* Now King Hiram of Tyre sent his servants to Solomon, when he heard that they had anointed him king in place of his father; for Hiram had always been a friend to David. 2 Solomon sent word to Hiram, saying, 3 "You know that my father David could not build a house for the name of the LORD his God because of the warfare with which his enemies surrounded him, until the LORD put them under the soles of his feet.*e* 4 But now the LORD my God has given me rest on every side; there is neither adversary nor misfortune. 5 So I intend to build a house for the name of the LORD my God, as the LORD said to my father David, 'Your son, whom I will set on your throne in your place, shall build the house for my name.' 6 Therefore command that cedars from the Lebanon be cut for me. My servants will join your servants, and I will give you whatever wages you set for your servants; for you know that there is no one among us who knows how to cut timber like the Si·dō′ni·ans."

7 When Hiram heard the words of Solomon, he rejoiced greatly, and said, "Blessed be the LORD to-day, who has given to David a wise son to be over this great people." 8 Hiram sent word to Solomon, "I have heard the message that you have sent to me;

I will fulfill all your needs in the matter of cedar and cypress timber. 9 My servants shall bring it down to the sea from the Lebanon; I will make it into rafts to go by sea to the place you indicate. I will have them broken up there for you to take away. And you shall meet my needs by providing food for my household." 10 So Hiram supplied Solomon's every need for timber of cedar and cypress. 11 Solomon in turn gave Hiram twenty thousand cors of wheat as food for his household, and twenty cors of fine oil. Solomon gave this to Hiram year by year. 12 So the LORD gave Solomon wisdom, as he promised him. There was peace between Hiram and Solomon; and the two of them made a treaty.

13 King Solomon conscripted forced labor out of all Israel; the levy numbered thirty thousand men. 14 He sent them to the Lebanon, ten thousand a month in shifts; they would be a month in the Lebanon and two months at home; Ad·o·nī′ram was in charge of the forced labor. 15 Solomon also had seventy thousand laborers and eighty thousand stonecutters in the hill country, 16 besides Solomon's three thousand three hundred supervisors who were over the work, having charge of the people who did the work. 17 At the king's command, they quarried out great, costly stones in order to lay the foundation of the house with dressed stones. 18 So Solomon's builders and Hiram's builders and the Gē′bal·ites did the stonecutting and prepared the timber and the stone to build the house.

---

d Ch 5.15 in Heb   *e* Gk Tg Vg: Heb *my feet* or *his feet*

HOW EXCELLENT

The First Book of Kings says, "Solomon's wisdom surpassed the wisdom of all the people of the east, and all the wisdom of Egypt" (4.30).

The people of Egypt and of the East are dark-skinned people. Ancient southern Egypt included the country of modern Ethiopia. The people in these countries must have been well known for their wisdom in order for the biblical author to use them in a comparison with Solomon.

▶ I Kings 5.10

Solomon Builds the Temple
(2 Chr 3.1–14)

6 In the four hundred eightieth year after the Israelites came out of the land of Egypt, in the fourth year of Solomon's reign over Israel, in the month of Ziv, which is the second month, he began to build the house of the LORD. 2 The house that King Solomon built for the LORD was sixty cubits long, twenty cubits wide, and thirty cubits high. 3 The vestibule in front of the nave of the house was twenty cubits wide, across the width of the house. Its depth was ten cubits in front of the house. 4 For the house he made windows with recessed frames.*f* 5 He also built a structure against the wall of the house, running around the walls of the house, both the nave and the inner sanctuary; and he made side chambers all around. 6 The lowest story*g* was five cubits wide, the middle one was six cubits wide, and the third was seven cubits wide; for around the outside of the house he made offsets on the wall in order that the supporting beams should not be inserted into the walls of the house.

7 The house was built with stone finished at the quarry, so that neither hammer nor ax nor any tool of iron was heard in the temple while it was being built.

8 The entrance for the middle story was on the south side of the house: one went up by winding stairs to the middle story, and from the middle story to the third. 9 So he built the house, and finished it; he roofed the house with beams and planks of cedar. 10 He built the structure against the whole house, each story*h* five cubits high, and it was joined to the house with timbers of cedar.

11 Now the word of the LORD came to Solomon, 12 "Concerning this house that you are building, if you will walk in my statutes, obey my ordinances, and keep all my commandments by walking in them, then I will establish my promise with you, which I made to your father David. 13 I will dwell among the children of Israel, and will not forsake my people Israel."

14 So Solomon built the house, and finished it. 15 He lined the walls of the house on the inside with boards of cedar; from the floor of the house to the rafters of the ceiling, he covered them on the inside with wood; and he covered the floor of the house with boards of cypress. 16 He built twenty cubits of the rear of the house with boards of cedar from the floor to the rafters, and he built this within as an inner sanctuary, as the most holy place. 17 The house, that is, the nave in front of the inner sanctuary, was forty cubits long. 18 The cedar within the house had carvings of gourds and open flowers; all was cedar, no stone was seen. 19 The inner sanctuary he prepared in the innermost part of the house, to set there the ark of the covenant of the LORD. 20 The interior of the inner sanctuary was twenty cubits long, twenty cubits wide, and twenty cubits high; he overlaid it with pure gold. He also overlaid the altar with cedar.*i* 21 Solomon overlaid the inside of the house with pure gold, then he drew chains of gold across, in front of the inner sanctuary, and overlaid it with gold. 22 Next he overlaid the whole house with gold, in order that the whole house might be perfect; even the whole altar that belonged to the inner sanctuary he overlaid with gold.

---

f Gk: Meaning of Heb uncertain   *g* Gk: Heb *structure*   *h* Heb lacks *each story*   *i* Meaning of Heb uncertain

The Temple of Solomon

1 Kings, chap. 6

Holy of Holies

Storeroom

Storeroom

Holy Place
(Nave)

Porch

Pillar   Pillar

Steps

Sea of Bronze   Altar

The Furnishings of the Temple
(2 Chr 4.1–10, 19–22; 5.1)

23 In the inner sanctuary he made two cherubim of olivewood, each ten cubits high. 24 Five cubits was the length of one wing of the cherub, and five cubits the length of the other wing of the cherub; it was ten cubits from the tip of one wing to the tip of the other. 25 The other cherub also measured ten cubits; both cherubim had the same measure and the same form. 26 The height of one cherub was ten cubits, and so was that of the other cherub. 27 He put the cherubim in the innermost part of the house; the wings of the cherubim were spread out so that a wing of one was touching the one wall, and a wing of the other cherub was touching the other wall; their other wings toward the center of the house were touching wing to wing. 28 He also overlaid the cherubim with gold.

29 He carved the walls of the house all around about with carved engravings of cherubim, palm trees, and open flowers, in the inner and outer rooms. 30 The floor of the house he overlaid with gold, in the inner and outer rooms.

31 For the entrance to the inner sanctuary he made doors of olivewood; the lintel and the doorposts were five-sided.*j* 32 He covered the two doors of olivewood with carvings of cherubim, palm trees, and open flowers; he overlaid them with gold, and spread gold on the cherubim and on the palm trees.

33 So also he made for the entrance to the nave doorposts of olivewood, four-sided each, 34 and two doors of cypress wood; the two leaves of the one door were folding, and the two leaves of the other door were folding. 35 He carved cherubim, palm trees, and open flowers, overlaying them with gold evenly applied upon the carved work. 36 He built the inner court with three courses of dressed stone to one course of cedar beams.

37 In the fourth year the foundation of the house of the LORD was laid, in the month of Ziv. 38 In the eleventh year, in the month of Bul, which is the eighth month, the house was finished in all its parts, and according to all its specifications. He was seven years in building it.

Solomon's Palace and Other Buildings

7 Solomon was building his own house thirteen years, and he finished his entire house. 2 He built the House of the Forest of the Lebanon one hundred cubits long, fifty cubits wide, and thirty cubits high, built on four rows of cedar pillars, with cedar beams on the pillars. 3 It was roofed with cedar on the forty-five rafters, fifteen in each row, which were on the pillars. 4 There were window frames in the three rows, facing each other in the three rows. 5 All the doorways and doorposts had four-sided frames, opposite, facing each other in the three rows.

6 He made the Hall of Pillars fifty cubits long and thirty cubits wide. There was a porch in front with pillars, and a canopy in front of them.

7 He made the Hall of the Throne where he was to pronounce judgment, the Hall of Justice, covered with cedar from floor to floor.

8 His own house where he would reside, in the other court back of the hall, was of the same construction. Solomon also made a house like this hall for Pharaoh's daughter, whom he had taken in marriage.

9 All these were made of costly stones, cut according to measure, sawed with saws, back and front, from the foundation to the coping, and from outside to the great court. 10 The foundation was of costly stones, huge stones, stones of eight and ten cubits. 11 There were costly stones above, cut to measure, and cedarwood. 12 The great court had three courses of dressed stone to one layer of cedar beams all around; so had the inner court of the house of the LORD, and the vestibule of the house.

Products of Hiram the Bronzeworker
(2 Chr 3.15–17; 4.11–18)

13 Now King Solomon invited and received Hiram from Tyre. 14 He was the son of a widow of the tribe of Naph'ta•li, whose father, a man of Tyre, had been an artisan in bronze; he was full of skill, intelligence, and knowledge in working bronze. He came to King Solomon, and did all his work.

15 He cast two pillars of bronze. Eighteen cubits was the height of the one, and a cord of twelve cubits would encircle it; the second pillar was the same.*k* 16 He also made two capitals of molten bronze, to set on the tops of the pillars; the height of the one capital was five cubits, and the height of the other capital was five cubits. 17 There were nets of checker work with wreaths of chain work for the capitals on the tops of the pillars; seven*l* for the one capital, and seven*l* for the other capital. 18 He made the columns with two rows around each latticework to cover the capitals that were above the pomegranates; he did the same with the other capital. 19 Now the capitals that were on the tops of the pillars in the vestibule were of lily-work, four cubits high. 20 The capitals were on the two pillars and also above the rounded projection that was beside the latticework; there were two hundred pomegranates in rows all around; and so with the other capital. 21 He set up the pillars at the vestibule of the temple; he set up the pillar on the south and called it

j Meaning of Heb uncertain   *k* Cn: Heb *and a cord of twelve cubits encircled the second pillar;* Compare Jer 52.21
l Heb: Gk *a net*

Jă'chin; and he set up the pillar on the north and called it Bō'az. 22 On the tops of the pillars was lily-work. Thus the work of the pillars was finished.

23 Then he made the molten sea; it was round, ten cubits from brim to brim, and five cubits high. A line of thirty cubits would encircle it completely. 24 Under its brim were panels all around it, each of ten cubits, surrounding the sea; there were two rows of panels, cast when it was cast. 25 It stood on twelve oxen, three facing north, three facing west, three facing south, and three facing east; the sea was set on them. The hindquarters of each were toward the inside. 26 Its thickness was a handbreadth; its brim was made like the brim of a cup, like the flower of a lily; it held two thousand baths.*m*

27 He also made the ten stands of bronze; each stand was four cubits long, four cubits wide, and three cubits high. 28 This was the construction of the stands: they had borders; the borders were within the frames; 29 on the borders that were set in the frames were lions, oxen, and cherubim. On the frames, both above and below the lions and oxen, there were wreaths of beveled work. 30 Each stand had four bronze wheels and axles of bronze; at the four corners were supports for a basin. The supports were cast with wreaths at the side of each. 31 Its opening was within the crown whose height was one cubit; its opening was round, as a pedestal is made; it was a cubit and a half wide. At its opening there were carvings; its borders were four-sided, not round. 32 The four wheels were underneath the borders; the axles of the wheels were in the stands; and the height of a wheel was a cubit and a half. 33 The wheels were made like a chariot wheel; their axles, their rims, their spokes, and their hubs were all cast. 34 There were four supports at the four corners of each stand; the supports were of one piece with the stands. 35 On the top of the stand there was a round band half a cubit high; on the top of the stand, its stays and its borders were of one piece with it. 36 On the surfaces of its stays and on its borders he carved cherubim, lions, and palm trees, where each had space, with wreaths all around. 37 In this way he made the ten stands; all of them were cast alike, with the same size and the same form.

38 He made ten basins of bronze; each basin held forty baths,*l* each basin measured four cubits; there was a basin for each of the ten stands. 39 He set five of the stands on the south side of the house, and five on the north side of the house; he set the sea on the southeast corner of the house.

40 Hiram also made the pots, the shovels, and the basins. So Hiram finished all the work that he did for King Solomon on the house of the LORD: 41 the two pillars, the two bowls of the capitals that were on the tops of the pillars, the two latticeworks to cover the two bowls of the capitals that were on the tops of the pillars; 42 the four hundred pomegranates for the two latticeworks, two rows of pomegranates for each latticework, to cover the two bowls of the capitals that were on the pillars; 43 the ten stands, the ten basins on the stands; 44 the one sea, and the twelve oxen underneath the sea.

45 The pots, the shovels, and the basins, all these vessels that Hiram made for King Solomon for the house of the LORD were of burnished bronze. 46 In the plain of the Jordan the king cast them, in the clay ground between Suc'coth and Zar'e•than. 47 Solomon left all the vessels unweighed, because there were so many of them; the weight of the bronze was not determined.

48 So Solomon made all the vessels that were in the house of the LORD: the golden altar, the golden table for the bread of the Presence, 49 the lampstands of pure gold, five on the south side and five on the north, in front of the inner sanctuary; the flowers, the lamps, and the tongs, of gold; 50 the cups, snuffers, basins, dishes for incense, and firepans, of pure gold; the sockets for the doors of the innermost part of the house, the most holy place, and for the doors of the nave of the temple, of gold.

51 Thus all the work that King Solomon did on the house of the LORD was finished. Solomon brought in the things that his father David had dedicated, the silver, the gold, and the vessels, and stored them in the treasuries of the house of the LORD.

Dedication of the Temple
(2 Chr 5.2—6.2)

8 Then Solomon assembled the elders of Israel and all the heads of the tribes, the leaders of the ancestral houses of the Israelites, before King Solomon in Jerusalem, to bring up the ark of the covenant of the LORD out of the city of David, which is Zion. 2 All the people of Israel assembled to King Solomon at the festival in the month Eth'a•nim, which is the seventh month. 3 And all the elders of Israel came, and the priests carried the ark. 4 So they brought up the ark of the LORD, the tent of meeting, and all the holy vessels that were in the tent; the priests and the Lē'vītes brought them up. 5 King Solomon and all the congregation of Israel, who had assembled before him, were with him before the ark, sacrificing so many sheep and oxen that they could not be counted or numbered. 6 Then the priests brought the ark of the covenant of the LORD to its place, in the inner sanctuary of the house, in the most holy place, underneath the wings of the cherubim. 7 For the cherubim spread out their wings over the place of the ark, so that the

---

m A Heb measure of volume

cherubim made a covering above the ark and its poles. 8 The poles were so long that the ends of the poles were seen from the holy place in front of the inner sanctuary; but they could not be seen from outside; they are there to this day. 9 There was nothing in the ark except the two tablets of stone that Moses had placed there at Hō′reb, where the LORD made a covenant with the Israelites, when they came out of the land of Egypt. 10 And when the priests came out of the holy place, a cloud filled the house of the LORD, 11 so that the priests could not stand to minister because of the cloud; for the glory of the LORD filled the house of the LORD.

12 Then Solomon said,

"The LORD has said that he would dwell in
    thick darkness.
13 I have built you an exalted house,
    a place for you to dwell in forever."

Solomon's Speech
(2 Chr 6.3–11)

14 Then the king turned around and blessed all the assembly of Israel, while all the assembly of Israel stood. 15 He said, "Blessed be the LORD, the God of Israel, who with his hand has fulfilled what he promised with his mouth to my father David, saying, 16 'Since the day that I brought my people Israel out of Egypt, I have not chosen a city from any of the tribes of Israel in which to build a house, that my name might be there; but I chose David to be over my people Israel.' 17 My father David had it in mind to build a house for the name of the LORD, the God of Israel. 18 But the LORD said to my father David, 'You did well to consider building a house for my name; 19 nevertheless you shall not build the house, but your son who shall be born to you shall build the house for my name.' 20 Now the LORD has upheld the promise that he made; for I have risen in the place of my father David; I sit on the throne of Israel, as the LORD promised, and have built the house for the name of the LORD, the God of Israel. 21 There I have provided a place for the ark, in which is the covenant of the LORD that he made with our ancestors when he brought them out of the land of Egypt."

Solomon's Prayer of Dedication
(2 Chr 6.12–39)

22 Then Solomon stood before the altar of the LORD in the presence of all the assembly of Israel, and spread out his hands to heaven. 23 He said, "O LORD, God of Israel, there is no God like you in heaven above or on earth beneath, keeping covenant and steadfast love for your servants who walk before you with all their heart, 24 the covenant that you kept for your servant my father David as you declared to him; you promised with your mouth and have this day fulfilled with your hand. 25 Therefore, O LORD, God of Israel, keep for your servant my father David that which you promised him, saying, 'There shall never fail you a successor before me to sit on the throne of Israel, if only your children look to their way, to walk before me as you have walked before me.' 26 Therefore, O God of Israel, let your word be confirmed, which you promised to your servant my father David.

27 "But will God indeed dwell on the earth? Even heaven and the highest heaven cannot contain you, much less this house that I have built! 28 Regard your servant's prayer and his plea, O LORD my God, heeding the cry and the prayer that your servant prays to you today; 29 that your eyes may be open night and day toward this house, the place of which you said, 'My name shall be there,' that you may heed the prayer that your servant prays toward this place. 30 Hear the plea of your servant and of your people Israel when they pray toward this place; O hear in heaven your dwelling place; heed and forgive.

31 "If someone sins against a neighbor and is given an oath to swear, and comes and swears before your altar in this house, 32 then hear in heaven, and act, and judge your servants, condemning the guilty by bringing their conduct on their own head,

PRAY IT?
Holy Places

Solomon knows that the Temple will not hold God. Holy places are not cages to keep God contained. People need holy places more than God does. We gather together in public holy places to experience God's presence as a community. But we can also meet God one-on-one in private holy places, special to us alone.

Try creating a holy space in your bedroom. Clear out a corner, and put in it a small table and a chair or rug to sit on. On the table, put your Bible and an object or two to help you focus on God. You might use a candle, a special picture or statue, or something from a retreat or a special place. Try to spend a little time each day in your holy space with God.

▶ I Kings 8.27–30

and vindicating the righteous by rewarding them according to their righteousness.

33 "When your people Israel, having sinned against you, are defeated before an enemy but turn again to you, confess your name, pray and plead with you in this house, 34 then hear in heaven, forgive the sin of your people Israel, and bring them again to the land that you gave to their ancestors.

35 "When heaven is shut up and there is no rain because they have sinned against you, and then they pray toward this place, confess your name, and turn from their sin, because you punish[n] them, 36 then hear in heaven, and forgive the sin of your servants, your people Israel, when you teach them the good way in which they should walk; and grant rain on your land, which you have given to your people as an inheritance.

37 "If there is famine in the land, if there is plague, blight, mildew, locust, or caterpillar; if their enemy besieges them in any[o] of their cities; whatever plague, whatever sickness there is; 38 whatever prayer, whatever plea there is from any individual or from all your people Israel, all knowing the afflictions of their own hearts so that they stretch out their hands toward this house; 39 then hear in heaven your dwelling place, forgive, act, and render to all whose hearts you know—according to all their ways, for only you know what is in every human heart— 40 so that they may fear you all the days that they live in the land that you gave to our ancestors.

41 "Likewise when a foreigner, who is not of your people Israel, comes from a distant land because of your name 42—for they shall hear of your great name, your mighty hand, and your outstretched arm—when a foreigner comes and prays toward this house, 43 then hear in heaven your dwelling place, and do according to all that the foreigner calls to you, so that all the peoples of the earth may know your name and fear you, as do your people Israel, and so that they may know that your name has been invoked on this house that I have built.

44 "If your people go out to battle against their enemy, by whatever way you shall send them, and they pray to the LORD toward the city that you have chosen and the house that I have built for your name, 45 then hear in heaven their prayer and their plea, and maintain their cause.

46 "If they sin against you—for there is no one who does not sin—and you are angry with them and give them to an enemy, so that they are carried away captive to the land of the enemy, far off or near; 47 yet if they come to their senses in the land to which they have been taken captive, and repent, and plead with you in the land of their captors, saying, 'We have sinned, and have done wrong; we have acted wickedly'; 48 if they repent with all their heart and soul in the land of their enemies, who took them captive, and pray to you toward their land, which you gave to their ancestors, the city that you have chosen, and the house that I have built for your name; 49 then hear in heaven your dwelling place their prayer and their plea, maintain their cause 50 and forgive your people who have sinned against you, and all their transgressions that they have committed against you; and grant them compassion in the sight of their captors, so that they may have compassion on them 51 (for they are your people and heritage, which you brought out of Egypt, from the midst of the iron-smelter). 52 Let your eyes be open to the plea of your servant, and to the plea of your people Israel, listening to them whenever they call to you. 53 For you have separated them from among all the peoples of the earth, to be your heritage, just as you promised through Moses, your servant, when you brought our ancestors out of Egypt, O Lord GOD."

Solomon Blesses the Assembly
(2 Chr 6.40–42)

54 Now when Solomon finished offering all this prayer and this plea to the LORD, he arose from facing the altar of the LORD, where he had knelt with hands outstretched toward heaven; 55 he stood and blessed all the assembly of Israel with a loud voice:

56 "Blessed be the LORD, who has given rest to his people Israel according to all that he promised; not one word has failed of all his good promise, which he spoke through his servant Moses. 57 The LORD our God be with us, as he was with our ancestors; may he not leave us or abandon us, 58 but incline our hearts to him, to walk in all his ways, and to keep his commandments, his statutes, and his ordinances, which he commanded our ancestors. 59 Let these words of mine, with which I pleaded before the LORD, be near to the LORD our God day and night, and may he maintain the cause of his servant and the cause of his people Israel, as each day requires; 60 so that all the peoples of the earth may know that the LORD is God; there is no other. 61 Therefore devote yourselves completely to the LORD our God, walking in his statutes and keeping his commandments, as at this day."

Solomon Offers Sacrifices
(2 Chr 7.4–11)

62 Then the king, and all Israel with him, offered sacrifice before the LORD. 63 Solomon offered as sacrifices of well-being to the LORD twenty-two thousand oxen and one hundred twenty thousand sheep. So the king and all the people of Israel dedicated the house of the LORD. 64 The same day the king consecrated the middle of the court that was in

---

[n] Or *when you answer*   [o] Gk Syr: Heb *in the land*

front of the house of the LORD; for there he offered the burnt offerings and the grain offerings and the fat pieces of the sacrifices of well-being, because the bronze altar that was before the LORD was too small to receive the burnt offerings and the grain offerings and the fat pieces of the sacrifices of well-being.

65 So Solomon held the festival at that time, and all Israel with him—a great assembly, people from Lē′bō-hā′math to the Wadi of Egypt—before the LORD our God, seven days.ᵖ 66 On the eighth day he sent the people away; and they blessed the king, and went to their tents, joyful and in good spirits because of all the goodness that the LORD had shown to his servant David and to his people Israel.

God Appears Again to Solomon
(2 Chr 7.11–22)

9 When Solomon had finished building the house of the LORD and the king's house and all that Solomon desired to build, 2 the LORD appeared to Solomon a second time, as he had appeared to him at Gib′ē-on. 3 The LORD said to him, "I have heard your prayer and your plea, which you made before me; I have consecrated this house that you have built, and put my name there forever; my eyes and my heart will be there for all time. 4 As for you, if you will walk before me, as David your father walked, with integrity of heart and uprightness,

doing according to all that I have commanded you, and keeping my statutes and my ordinances, 5 then I will establish your royal throne over Israel forever, as I promised your father David, saying, 'There shall not fail you a successor on the throne of Israel.'

6 "If you turn aside from following me, you or your children, and do not keep my commandments and my statutes that I have set before you, but go and serve other gods and worship them, 7 then I will cut Israel off from the land that I have given them; and the house that I have consecrated for my name I will cast out of my sight; and Israel will become a proverb and a taunt among all peoples. 8 This house will become a heap of ruins;�q everyone passing by it will be astonished, and will hiss; and they will say, 'Why has the LORD done such a thing to this land and to this house?' 9 Then they will say, 'Because they have forsaken the LORD their God, who brought their ancestors out of the land of Egypt, and embraced other gods, worshiping them and serving them; therefore the LORD has brought this disaster upon them.' "

10 At the end of twenty years, in which Solomon had built the two houses, the house of the LORD and the king's house, 11 King Hiram of Tȳre having supplied Solomon with cedar and cypress timber and gold, as much as he desired, King Solomon gave to Hiram twenty cities in the land of Galilee. 12 But when Hiram came from Tȳre to see the cities that Solomon had given him, they did not please him. 13 Therefore he said, "What kind of cities are these that you have given me, my brother?" So they are called the land of Cā′bulʳ to this day. 14 But Hiram had sent to the king one hundred twenty talents of gold.

Other Acts of Solomon
(2 Chr 8.3–16)

15 This is the account of the forced labor that King Solomon conscripted to build the house of the LORD and his own house, the Mil′lō and the wall of Jerusalem, Hā′zor, Me•gid′dō, Gē′zer 16 (Pharaoh king of Egypt had gone up and captured Gē′zer and burned it down, had killed the Cā′naan•ites who lived in the city, and had given it as dowry to his daughter, Solomon's wife; 17 so Solomon rebuilt Gē′zer), Lower Beth-hō′ron, 18 Bā′a•lath, Tā′mar in the wilderness, within the land, 19 as well as all of Solomon's storage cities, the cities for his chariots, the cities for his cavalry, and whatever Solomon desired to build, in Jerusalem, in Lebanon, and in all the land of his dominion. 20 All the people who were left of the Am′o•rītes, the Hit′tītes, the

Catholic Connections

BLESSING THE COMMUNITY

The community is a phrase used to describe people gathered to pray together. Think of how the community is blessed at the end of Mass. With raised hands, the priest speaks with words similar to Solomon's in 1 Kings 8.56–61. The people are sent forth to know God's love and to do what God wants.

Let us praise God, who loves us, and let us go in peace to love and serve God and one another.

▶ 1 Kings 8.56–61

ᵖ Compare Gk: Heb *seven days and seven days, fourteen days*   q Syr Old Latin: Heb *will become high*   r Perhaps meaning *a land good for nothing*

Per'iz•zītes, the Hī'vītes, and the Jeb'ū•sītes, who were not of the people of Israel— 21 their descendants who were still left in the land, whom the Israelites were unable to destroy completely—these Solomon conscripted for slave labor, and so they are to this day. 22 But of the Israelites Solomon made no slaves; they were the soldiers, they were his officials, his commanders, his captains, and the commanders of his chariotry and cavalry.

23 These were the chief officers who were over Solomon's work: five hundred fifty, who had charge of the people who carried on the work.

24 But Pharaoh's daughter went up from the city of David to her own house that Solomon had built for her; then he built the Mil'lō.

25 Three times a year Solomon used to offer up burnt offerings and sacrifices of well-being on the altar that he built for the LORD, offering incense[s] before the LORD. So he completed the house.

Solomon's Commercial Activity
(2 Chr 8.17–18)

26 King Solomon built a fleet of ships at Ē'zi•on-gē'ber, which is near Ē'loth on the shore of the Red Sea,[t] in the land of Ē'dom. 27 Hiram sent his servants with the fleet, sailors who were familiar with the sea, together with the servants of Solomon. 28 They went to Ō'phir, and imported from there four hundred twenty talents of gold, which they delivered to King Solomon.

Visit of the Queen of Sheba
(2 Chr 9.1–28)

10 When the queen of Shē'ba heard of the fame of Solomon (fame due to[u] the name of the LORD), she came to test him with hard questions. 2 She came to Jerusalem with a very great retinue, with camels bearing spices, and very much gold, and precious stones; and when she came to Solomon, she told him all that was on her mind. 3 Solomon answered all her questions; there was nothing hidden from the king that he could not explain to her. 4 When the queen of Shē'ba had observed all the wisdom of Solomon, the house that he had built, 5 the food of his table, the seating of his officials, and the attendance of his servants, their clothing, his valets, and his burnt offerings that he offered at the house of the LORD, there was no more spirit in her.

6 So she said to the king, "The report was true that I heard in my own land of your accomplishments and of your wisdom, 7 but I did not believe the reports until I came and my own eyes had seen it. Not even half had been told me; your wisdom and prosperity far surpass the report that I had heard. 8 Happy are your wives![v] Happy are these your servants, who continually attend you and hear

your wisdom! 9 Blessed be the LORD your God, who has delighted in you and set you on the throne of Israel! Because the LORD loved Israel forever, he has made you king to execute justice and righteousness." 10 Then she gave the king one hundred twenty talents of gold, a great quantity of spices, and precious stones; never again did spices come in such quantity as that which the queen of Shē'ba gave to King Solomon.

11 Moreover, the fleet of Hiram, which carried gold from Ō'phir, brought from Ō'phir a great quantity of almug wood and precious stones. 12 From the almug wood the king made supports for the house of the LORD, and for the king's house, lyres also and harps for the singers; no such almug wood has come or been seen to this day.

13 Meanwhile King Solomon gave to the queen of Shē'ba every desire that she expressed, as well as what he gave her out of Solomon's royal bounty. Then she returned to her own land, with her servants.

14 The weight of gold that came to Solomon in one year was six hundred sixty-six talents of gold, 15 besides that which came from the traders and from the business of the merchants, and from all the kings of Arabia and the governors of the land. 16 King Solomon made two hundred large shields of beaten gold; six hundred shekels of gold went into each large shield; 17 He made three hundred shields of beaten gold; three minas of gold went into each shield; and the king put them in the House of the Forest of Lebanon. 18 The king also made a great ivory throne, and overlaid it with the finest gold. 19 The throne had six steps. The top of the throne was rounded in the back, and on each side of the seat were arm rests and two lions standing beside the arm rests, 20 while twelve lions were standing, one on each end of a step on the six steps. Nothing like it was ever made in any kingdom. 21 All King Solomon's drinking vessels were of gold, and all the vessels of the House of the Forest of Lebanon were of pure gold; none were of silver—it was not considered as anything in the days of Solomon. 22 For the king had a fleet of ships of Tar'shish at sea with the fleet of Hiram. Once every three years the fleet of ships of Tar'shish used to come bringing gold, silver, ivory, apes, and peacocks.[w]

23 Thus King Solomon excelled all the kings of the earth in riches and in wisdom. 24 The whole earth sought the presence of Solomon to hear his wisdom, which God had put into his mind. 25 Every one of them brought a present, objects of

---

[s] Gk: Heb *offering incense with it that was*   [t] Or *Sea of Reeds*   [u] Meaning of Heb uncertain   [v] Gk Syr: Heb *men*   [w] Or *baboons*

silver and gold, garments, weaponry, spices, horses, and mules, so much year by year.

26 Solomon gathered together chariots and horses; he had fourteen hundred chariots and twelve thousand horses, which he stationed in the chariot cities and with the king in Jerusalem. 27 The king made silver as common in Jerusalem as stones, and he made cedars as numerous as the sycamores of the She·phē′lah. 28 Solomon's import of horses was from Egypt and Kū′e, and the king's traders received them from Kū′e at a price. 29 A chariot could be imported from Egypt for six hundred shekels of silver, and a horse for one hundred fifty; so through the king's traders they were exported to all the kings of the Hit′tītes and the kings of Ar′am.

Solomon's Errors

11 King Solomon loved many foreign women along with the daughter of Pharaoh: Mō′ab·īte, Am′mon·īte, Ē′dom·īte, Sī·dō′ni·an, and Hit′tīte women, 2 from the nations concerning which the LORD had said to the Israelites, "You shall not enter into marriage with them, neither shall they with you; for they will surely incline your

PRAY IT?
Solomon's Sin

Sometimes, when we think we are strongest, we are actually weakest. Solomon replaces his poverty of spirit with pride (see 1 Kings 3.4–14). He seems to believe that he is strong enough to go against God's command not to take foreign wives and that he can withstand the influence of their foreign gods. But Solomon falls into the sin of idolatry (worshiping other gods), breaking the Covenant.

Have you ever considered doing something that you knew was wrong? Did you tell yourself, "It won't hurt to do it just this once"? Maybe that is what Solomon said when he took his first foreign wife.

In your prayer time, reflect or journal on the following questions:

- What takes your attention away from God?
- Have you ever used the excuse, "I'm strong enough to handle this," to lead you into doing something wrong?
- Pray Ps 86.11 to end your prayer.

▶ 1 Kings 11.1–8

heart to follow their gods"; Solomon clung to these in love. 3 Among his wives were seven hundred princesses and three hundred concubines; and his wives turned away his heart. 4 For when Solomon was old, his wives turned away his heart after other gods; and his heart was not true to the LORD his God, as was the heart of his father David. 5 For Solomon followed As·tar′tē the goddess of the Sī·dō′ni·ans, and Mil′com the abomination of the Am′mon·ītes. 6 So Solomon did what was evil in the sight of the LORD, and did not completely follow the LORD, as his father David had done. 7 Then Solomon built a high place for Chē′mosh the abomination of Mō′ab, and for Mō′lech the abomination of the Am′mon·ītes, on the mountain east of Jerusalem. 8 He did the same for all his foreign wives, who offered incense and sacrificed to their gods.

9 Then the LORD was angry with Solomon, because his heart had turned away from the LORD, the God of Israel, who had appeared to him twice, 10 and had commanded him concerning this matter, that he should not follow other gods; but he did not observe what the LORD commanded. 11 Therefore the LORD said to Solomon, "Since this has been your mind and you have not kept my covenant and my statutes that I have commanded you, I will surely tear the kingdom from you and give it to your servant. 12 Yet for the sake of your father David I will not do it in your lifetime; I will tear it out of the hand of your son. 13 I will not, however, tear away the entire kingdom; I will give one tribe to your son, for the sake of my servant David and for the sake of Jerusalem, which I have chosen."

Adversaries of Solomon

14 Then the LORD raised up an adversary against Solomon, Hā′dad the Ē′dom·īte; he was of the royal house in Ē′dom. 15 For when David was in Ē′dom, and Jō′ab the commander of the army went up to bury the dead, he killed every male in Ē′dom 16 (for Jō′ab and all Israel remained there six months, until he had eliminated every male in Ē′dom); 17 but Hā′dad fled to Egypt with some Ē′dom·ītes who were servants of his father. He was a young boy at that time. 18 They set out from Mid′i·an and came to Par′an; they took people with them from Par′an and came to Egypt, to Pharaoh king of Egypt, who gave him a house, assigned him an allowance of food, and gave him land. 19 Hā′dad found great favor in the sight of Pharaoh, so that he gave him his sister-in-law for a wife, the sister of Queen Tah′pe·nēs. 20 The sister of Tah′pe·nēs gave birth by him to his son Ge·nū′bath, whom Tah′pe·nēs weaned in Pharaoh's house; Ge·nū′bath was in Pharaoh's house among the children of Pharaoh. 21 When Hā′dad heard in Egypt that

David slept with his ancestors and that Jō′ab the commander of the army was dead, Hā′dad said to Pharaoh, "Let me depart, that I may go to my own country." 22 But Pharaoh said to him, "What do you lack with me that you now seek to go to your own country?" And he said, "No, do let me go."

23 God raised up another adversary against Solomon,ˣ Rē′zon son of E•lī′a•da, who had fled from his master, King Had•a•dē′zer of Zō′bah. 24 He gathered followers around him and became leader of a marauding band, after the slaughter by David; they went to Damascus, settled there, and made him king in Damascus. 25 He was an adversary of Israel all the days of Solomon, making trouble as Hā′dad did; he despised Israel and reigned over Ar′am.

Jeroboam's Rebellion

26 Jer•o•bō′am son of Nē′bat, an Ē′phra•im•ite of Zer′e•dah, a servant of Solomon, whose mother's name was Ze•rū′ah, a widow, rebelled against the king. 27 The following was the reason he rebelled against the king. Solomon built the Mil′lō, and closed up the gap in the wallʸ of the city of his father David. 28 The man Jer•o•bō′am was very able, and when Solomon saw that the young man was industrious he gave him charge over all the forced labor of the house of Joseph. 29 About that time, when Jer•o•bō′am was leaving Jerusalem, the prophet A•hī′jah the Shī′lo•nīte found him on the road. A•hī′jah had clothed himself with a new garment. The two of them were alone in the open country 30 when A•hī′jah laid hold of the new garment he was wearing and tore it into twelve pieces. 31 He then said to Jer•o•bō′am: Take for yourself ten pieces; for thus says the LORD, the God of Israel, "See, I am about to tear the kingdom from the hand of Solomon, and will give you ten tribes. 32 One tribe will remain his, for the sake of my servant David and for the sake of Jerusalem, the city that I have chosen out of all the tribes of Israel. 33 This is because he hasᶻ forsaken me, worshiped As•tar′tē the goddess of the Sī•dō′ni•ans, Chē′mosh the god of Mō′ab, and Mil′com the god of the Am′mon•ites, and hasᶻ not walked in my ways, doing what is right in my sight and keeping my statutes and my ordinances, as his father David did. 34 Nevertheless I will not take the whole kingdom away from him but will make him ruler all the days of his life, for the sake of my servant David whom I chose and who did keep my commandments and my statutes; 35 but I will take the kingdom away from his son and give it to you—that is, the ten tribes. 36 Yet to his son I will give one tribe, so that my servant David may always have a lamp before me in Jerusalem, the city where I have chosen to put my name. 37 I will take you, and you shall reign over all that your soul desires; you shall be king over Israel.

38 If you will listen to all that I command you, walk in my ways, and do what is right in my sight by keeping my statutes and my commandments, as David my servant did, I will be with you, and will build you an enduring house, as I built for David, and I will give Israel to you. 39 For this reason I will punish the descendants of David, but not forever." 40 Solomon sought therefore to kill Jer•o•bō′am; but Jer•o•bō′am promptly fled to Egypt, to King Shī′shak of Egypt, and remained in Egypt until the death of Solomon.

Death of Solomon
(2 Chr 9.29–31)

41 Now the rest of the acts of Solomon, all that he did as well as his wisdom, are they not written in the Book of the Acts of Solomon? 42 The time that Solomon reigned in Jerusalem over all Israel was forty years. 43 Solomon slept with his ancestors and was buried in the city of his father David; and his son Rē•ho•bō′am succeeded him.

The Northern Tribes Secede
(2 Chr 10.1–19)

12 Rē•ho•bō′am went to Shē′chem, for all Israel had come to Shē′chem to make him king. 2 When Jer•o•bō′am son of Nē′bat heard of it (for he was still in Egypt, where he had fled from King Solomon), then Jer•o•bō′am returned fromᵃ Egypt. 3 And they sent and called him; and Jer•o•bō′am and all the assembly of Israel came and said to Rē•ho•bō′am, 4 "Your father made our yoke heavy. Now therefore lighten the hard service of your father and his heavy yoke that he placed on us, and we will serve you." 5 He said to them, "Go away for three days, then come again to me." So the people went away.

6 Then King Rē•ho•bō′am took counsel with the older men who had attended his father Solomon while he was still alive, saying, "How do you advise me to answer this people?" 7 They answered him, "If you will be a servant to this people today and serve them, and speak good words to them when you answer them, then they will be your servants forever." 8 But he disregarded the advice that the older men gave him, and consulted with the young men who had grown up with him and now attended him. 9 He said to them, "What do you advise that we answer this people who have said to me, 'Lighten the yoke that your father put on us'?" 10 The young men who had grown up with him said to him, "Thus you should say to this people who spoke to you, 'Your father made our yoke heavy, but you must lighten it for us'; thus you

---

ˣ Heb *him*   ʸ Heb lacks *in the wall*   ᶻ Gk Syr Vg: Heb *they have*   ᵃ Gk Vg Compare 2 Chr 10.2: Heb *lived in*

did you KNOW?

The Kingdom of Israel Splits

When the people of Israel first came to settle in Canaan, they organized into twelve tribes, ruled by chieftains, that supported and protected one another. As Israel grew in size, it was necessary to have one central ruler who would unite the tribes into one nation. Saul was the first king of this united Israel. David followed Saul and expanded the kingdom's territory. David's son Solomon continued ruling over the expanded kingdom and engaged in expensive building projects.

At Solomon's death, many Israelites wanted a less demanding king. They had suffered under the burden of heavy taxes and forced labor. When Solomon's son Rehoboam refused to make any changes (1 Kings 12.11), ten of the northern tribes pulled away and placed their own king, Jeroboam, on the throne. The northern kingdom was called Israel. The southern kingdom, composed of two tribes, was called Judah (see map 3, "The Kingdom Years"). The kingdom was now split in two, and it was never again reunited.

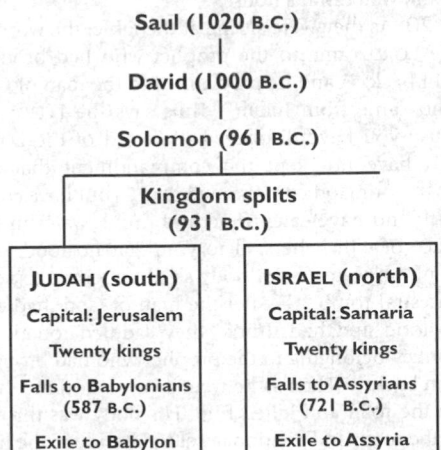

Saul (1020 B.C.)
|
David (1000 B.C.)
|
Solomon (961 B.C.)

Kingdom splits
(931 B.C.)

JUDAH (south)	ISRAEL (north)
Capital: Jerusalem	Capital: Samaria
Twenty kings	Twenty kings
Falls to Babylonians (587 B.C.)	Falls to Assyrians (721 B.C.)
Exile to Babylon	Exile to Assyria

▸ 1 Kings 12.1–19

should say to them, 'My little finger is thicker than my father's loins. 11 Now, whereas my father laid on you a heavy yoke, I will add to your yoke. My father disciplined you with whips, but I will discipline you with scorpions.' "

12 So Jer·o·bō'am and all the people came to Rē·ho·bō'am the third day, as the king had said, "Come to me again the third day." 13 The king answered the people harshly. He disregarded the advice that the older men had given him 14 and spoke to them according to the advice of the young men, "My father made your yoke heavy, but I will add to your yoke; my father disciplined you with whips, but I will discipline you with scorpions." 15 So the king did not listen to the people, because it was a turn of affairs brought about by the LORD that he might fulfill his word, which the LORD had spoken by A·hī'jah the Shī'lo·nīte to Jer·o·bō'am son of Nĕ'bat.

16 When all Israel saw that the king would not listen to them, the people answered the king,

"What share do we have in David?
　　We have no inheritance in the son of Jesse.
To your tents, O Israel!
　　Look now to your own house, O David."

So Israel went away to their tents. 17 But Rē·ho·bō'am reigned over the Israelites who were living in the towns of Judah. 18 When King Rē·ho·bō'am sent A·dor'am, who was taskmaster over the forced labor, all Israel stoned him to death. King Rē·ho·bō'am then hurriedly mounted his chariot to flee to Jerusalem. 19 So Israel has been in rebellion against the house of David to this day.

First Dynasty: Jeroboam Reigns over Israel
(2 Chr 11.1–4)

20 When all Israel heard that Jer·o·bō'am had returned, they sent and called him to the assembly and made him king over all Israel. There was no one who followed the house of David, except the tribe of Judah alone.

21 When Rē·ho·bō'am came to Jerusalem, he assembled all the house of Judah and the tribe of Benjamin, one hundred eighty thousand chosen troops to fight against the house of Israel, to restore the kingdom to Rē·ho·bō'am son of Solomon. 22 But the word of God came to She·mai'ah the man of God: 23 Say to King Rē·ho·bō'am of Judah, son of Solomon, and to all the house of Judah and Benjamin, and to the rest of the people, 24 "Thus says the LORD, You shall not go up or fight against your kindred the people of Israel. Let everyone go home, for this thing is from me." So they heeded the word of the LORD and went home again, according to the word of the LORD.

Jeroboam's Golden Calves

25 Then Jer·o·bō'am built Shě'chem in the hill country of Ē'phra·im, and resided there; he went out from there and built Pe·nū'el. 26 Then Jer·o·bō'am said to himself, "Now the kingdom may well revert to the house of David. 27 If this people continues to go up to offer sacrifices in the house of the LORD at Jerusalem, the heart of this people will turn again to their master, King Rē·ho·bō'am of Judah; they will kill me and return to King Rē·ho·bō'am of Judah." 28 So the king took counsel, and made two calves of gold. He said to the people,*b* "You have gone up to Jerusalem long enough. Here are your gods, O Israel, who brought you up out of the land of Egypt." 29 He set one in Beth'el, and the other he put in Dan. 30 And this thing became a sin, for the people went to worship before the one at Beth'el and before the other as far as Dan.*c* 31 He also made houses*d* on high places, and appointed priests from among all the people, who were not Lē'vītes. 32 Jer·o·bō'am appointed a festival on the fifteenth day of the eighth month like the festival that was in Judah, and he offered sacrifices on the altar; so he did in Beth'el, sacrificing to the calves that he had made. And he placed in Beth'el the priests of the high places that he had made. 33 He went up to the altar that he had made in Beth'el on the fifteenth day in the eighth month, in the month that he alone had devised; he appointed a festival for the people of Israel, and he went up to the altar to offer incense.

A Man of God from Judah

13 While Jer·o·bō'am was standing by the altar to offer incense, a man of God came out of Judah by the word of the LORD to Beth'el 2 and proclaimed against the altar by the word of the LORD, and said, "O altar, altar, thus says the LORD: 'A son shall be born to the house of David, Jō·sī'ah by name; and he shall sacrifice on you the priests of the high places who offer incense on you, and human bones shall be burned on you.' " 3 He gave a sign the same day, saying, "This is the sign that the LORD has spoken: 'The altar shall be torn down, and the ashes that are on it shall be poured out.' " 4 When the king heard what the man of God cried out against the altar at Beth'el, Jer·o·bō'am stretched out his hand from the altar, saying, "Seize him!" But the hand that he stretched out against him withered so that he could not draw it back to himself. 5 The altar also was torn down, and the ashes poured out from the altar, according to the sign that the man of God had given by the word of the LORD. 6 The king said to the man of God, "Entreat now the favor of the LORD your God, and pray for me, so that my hand may be restored to me." So the man of God entreated the LORD; and the king's hand was restored to him, and became as it was before. 7 Then the king said to the

man of God, "Come home with me and dine, and I will give you a gift." 8 But the man of God said to the king, "If you give me half your kingdom, I will not go in with you; nor will I eat food or drink water in this place. 9 For thus I was commanded by the word of the LORD: You shall not eat food, or drink water, or return by the way that you came." 10 So he went another way, and did not return by the way that he had come to Beth'el.

11 Now there lived an old prophet in Beth'el. One of his sons came and told him all that the man of God had done that day in Beth'el; the words also that he had spoken to the king, they told to their father. 12 Their father said to them, "Which way did he go?" And his sons showed him the way that the man of God who came from Judah had gone. 13 Then he said to his sons, "Saddle a donkey for me." So they saddled a donkey for him, and he mounted it. 14 He went after the man of God, and found him sitting under an oak tree. He said to him, "Are you the man of God who came from Judah?" He answered, "I am." 15 Then he said to him, "Come home with me and eat some food." 16 But he said, "I cannot return with you, or go in with you; nor will I eat food or drink water with you in this place; 17 for it was said to me by the word of the LORD: You shall not eat food or drink water there, or return by the way that you came." 18 Then the other*e* said to him, "I also am a prophet as you are, and an angel spoke to me by the word of the LORD: Bring him back with you into your house so that he may eat food and drink water." But he was deceiving him. 19 Then the man of God*e* went back with him, and ate food and drank water in his house.

20 As they were sitting at the table, the word of the LORD came to the prophet who had brought him back; 21 and he proclaimed to the man of God who came from Judah, "Thus says the LORD: Because you have disobeyed the word of the LORD, and have not kept the commandment that the LORD your God commanded you, 22 but have come back and have eaten food and drunk water in the place of which he said to you, 'Eat no food, and drink no water,' your body shall not come to your ancestral tomb." 23 After the man of God*e* had eaten food and had drunk, they saddled for him a donkey belonging to the prophet who had brought him back. 24 Then as he went away, a lion met him on the road and killed him. His body was thrown in the road, and the donkey stood beside it; the lion also stood beside the body. 25 People passed by and saw the body thrown in the road, with the lion standing by the body. And they came and told it in the town where the old prophet lived.

---

b Gk: Heb *to them*   *c* Compare Gk: Heb *went to the one as far as Dan*   *d* Gk Vg Compare 13.32: Heb *a house*   *e* Heb *he*

26 When the prophet who had brought him back from the way heard of it, he said, "It is the man of God who disobeyed the word of the LORD; therefore the LORD has given him to the lion, which has torn him and killed him according to the word that the LORD spoke to him." 27 Then he said to his sons, "Saddle a donkey for me." So they saddled one, 28 and he went and found the body thrown in the road, with the donkey and the lion standing beside the body. The lion had not eaten the body or attacked the donkey. 29 The prophet took up the body of the man of God, laid it on the donkey, and brought it back to the city,*f* to mourn and to bury him. 30 He laid the body in his own grave; and they mourned over him, saying, "Alas, my brother!" 31 After he had buried him, he said to his sons, "When I die, bury me in the grave in which the man of God is buried; lay my bones beside his bones. 32 For the saying that he proclaimed by the word of the LORD against the altar in Beth'el, and against all the houses of the high places that are in the cities of Sa·mār′i·a, shall surely come to pass."

33 Even after this event Jer·o·bō′am did not turn from his evil way, but made priests for the high places again from among all the people; any who wanted to be priests he consecrated for the high places. 34 This matter became sin to the house of Jer·o·bō′am, so as to cut it off and to destroy it from the face of the earth.

Judgment on the House of Jeroboam

14 At that time A·bī′jah son of Jer·o·bō′am fell sick. 2 Jer·o·bō′am said to his wife, "Go, disguise yourself, so that it will not be known that you are the wife of Jer·o·bō′am, and go to Shī′lōh; for the prophet A·hī′jah is there, who said of me that I should be king over this people. 3 Take with you ten loaves, some cakes, and a jar of honey, and go to him; he will tell you what shall happen to the child."

4 Jer·o·bō′am's wife did so; she set out and went to Shī′lōh, and came to the house of A·hī′jah. Now A·hī′jah could not see, for his eyes were dim because of his age. 5 But the LORD said to A·hī′jah, "The wife of Jer·o·bō′am is coming to inquire of you concerning her son; for he is sick. Thus and thus you shall say to her."

When she came, she pretended to be another woman. 6 But when A·hī′jah heard the sound of her feet, as she came in at the door, he said, "Come in, wife of Jer·o·bō′am; why do you pretend to be another? For I am charged with heavy tidings for you. 7 Go, tell Jer·o·bō′am, 'Thus says the LORD, the God of Israel: Because I exalted you from among the people, made you leader over my people Israel, 8 and tore the kingdom away from the house of David to give it to you; yet you have not been like

my servant David, who kept my commandments and followed me with all his heart, doing only that which was right in my sight, 9 but you have done evil above all those who were before you and have gone and made for yourself other gods, and cast images, provoking me to anger, and have thrust me behind your back; 10 therefore, I will bring evil upon the house of Jer·o·bō′am. I will cut off from Jer·o·bō′am every male, both bond and free in Israel, and will consume the house of Jer·o·bō′am, just as one burns up dung until it is all gone. 11 Anyone belonging to Jer·o·bō′am who dies in the city, the dogs shall eat; and anyone who dies in the open country, the birds of the air shall eat; for the LORD has spoken.' 12 Therefore set out, go to your house. When your feet enter the city, the child shall die. 13 All Israel shall mourn for him and bury him; for he alone of Jer·o·bō′am's family shall come to the grave, because in him there is found something pleasing to the LORD, the God of Israel, in the house of Jer·o·bō′am. 14 Moreover the LORD will raise up for himself a king over Israel, who shall cut off the house of Jer·o·bō′am today, even right now!*g*

15 "The LORD will strike Israel, as a reed is shaken in the water; he will root up Israel out of this good land that he gave to their ancestors, and scatter them beyond the Euphrates, because they have made their sacred poles,*h* provoking the LORD to anger. 16 He will give Israel up because of the sins of Jer·o·bō′am, which he sinned and which he caused Israel to commit."

17 Then Jer·o·bō′am's wife got up and went away, and she came to Tir′zah. As she came to the threshold of the house, the child died. 18 All Israel buried him and mourned for him, according to the word of the LORD, which he spoke by his servant the prophet A·hī′jah.

Death of Jeroboam

19 Now the rest of the acts of Jer·o·bō′am, how he warred and how he reigned, are written in the Book of the Annals of the Kings of Israel. 20 The time that Jer·o·bō′am reigned was twenty-two years; then he slept with his ancestors, and his son Nā′dab succeeded him.

Rehoboam Reigns over Judah
(2 Chr 11.5—12.16)

21 Now Rē·ho·bō′am son of Solomon reigned in Judah. Rē·ho·bō′am was forty-one years old when he began to reign, and he reigned seventeen years in Jerusalem, the city that the LORD had chosen out of all the tribes of Israel, to put his name there. His mother's name was Nā′a·mah the

---

f Gk: Heb *he came to the town of the old prophet*   *g* Meaning of Heb uncertain   *h* Heb *Asherim*

Am'mon•īte. 22 Judah did what was evil in the sight of the LORD; they provoked him to jealousy with their sins that they committed, more than all that their ancestors had done. 23 For they also built for themselves high places, pillars, and sacred poles[i] on every high hill and under every green tree; 24 there were also male temple prostitutes in the land. They committed all the abominations of the nations that the LORD drove out before the people of Israel.

25 In the fifth year of King Rē•ho•bō'am, King Shī'shak of Egypt came up against Jerusalem; 26 he took away the treasures of the house of the LORD and the treasures of the king's house; he took everything. He also took away all the shields of gold that Solomon had made; 27 so King Rē•ho•bō'am made shields of bronze instead, and committed them to the hands of the officers of the guard, who kept the door of the king's house. 28 As often as the king went into the house of the LORD, the guard carried them and brought them back to the guardroom.

29 Now the rest of the acts of Rē•ho•bō'am, and all that he did, are they not written in the Book of the Annals of the Kings of Judah? 30 There was war between Rē•ho•bō'am and Jer•o•bō'am continually. 31 Rē•ho•bō'am slept with his ancestors and was buried with his ancestors in the city of David. His mother's name was Nā'a•mah the Am'mon•īte. His son A•bī'jam succeeded him.

Abijam Reigns over Judah: Idolatry and War
(2 Chr 13.1—14.1)

15 Now in the eighteenth year of King Jer•o•bō'am son of Nē'bat, A•bī'jam began to reign over Judah. 2 He reigned for three years in Jerusalem. His mother's name was Mā'a•cah daughter of A•bish'a•lom. 3 He committed all the sins that his father did before him; his heart was not true to the LORD his God, like the heart of his father David. 4 Nevertheless for David's sake the LORD his God gave him a lamp in Jerusalem, setting up his son after him, and establishing Jerusalem; 5 because David did what was right in the sight of the LORD, and did not turn aside from anything that he commanded him all the days of his life, except in the matter of Ū•rī'ah the Hit'tīte. 6 The war begun between Rē•ho•bō'am and Jer•o•bō'am continued all the days of his life. 7 The rest of the acts of A•bī'jam, and all that he did, are they not written in the Book of the Annals of the Kings of Judah? There was war between A•bī'jam and Jer•o•bō'am. 8 A•bī'jam slept with his ancestors, and they buried him in the city of David. Then his son Asa succeeded him.

Asa Reigns over Judah
(2 Chr 14.1—15.19)

9 In the twentieth year of King Jer•o•bō'am of Israel, Asa began to reign over Judah; 10 he reigned forty-one years in Jerusalem. His mother's name was Mā'a•cah daughter of A•bish'a•lom. 11 Asa did what was right in the sight of the LORD, as his father David had done. 12 He put away the male temple prostitutes out of the land, and removed all the idols that his ancestors had made. 13 He also removed his mother Mā'a•cah from being queen mother, because she had made an abominable image for A•shē'rah; Asa cut down her image and burned it at the Wadi Kid'ron. 14 But the high places were not taken away. Nevertheless the heart of Asa was true to the LORD all his days. 15 He brought into the house of the LORD the votive gifts of his father and his own votive gifts—silver, gold, and utensils.

Alliance with Aram against Israel
(2 Chr 16.1—17.1)

16 There was war between Asa and King Bā'a•sha of Israel all their days. 17 King Bā'a•sha of Israel went up against Judah, and built Rā'mah, to prevent anyone from going out or coming in to King Asa of Judah. 18 Then Asa took all the silver and the gold that were left in the treasures of the house of the LORD and the treasures of the king's house, and gave them into the hands of his servants. King Asa sent them to King Ben-hā'dad son of Tab•rim'mon son of Hē'zi•on of Ar'am, who resided in Damascus, saying, 19 "Let there be an alliance between me and you, like that between my father and your father: I am sending you a present of silver and gold; go, break your alliance with King Bā'a•sha of Israel, so that he may withdraw from me." 20 Ben-hā'dad listened to King Asa, and sent the commanders of his armies against the cities of Israel. He conquered Ī'jon, Dan, Ā'bel-beth-mā'a•cah, and all Chin'ne•roth, with all the land of Naph'ta•lī. 21 When Bā'a•sha heard of it, he stopped building Rā'mah and lived in Tir'zah. 22 Then King Asa made a proclamation to all Judah, none was exempt: they carried away the stones of Rā'mah and its timber, with which Bā'a•sha had been building; with them King Asa built Gē'ba of Benjamin and Miz'pah. 23 Now the rest of all the acts of Asa, all his power, all that he did, and the cities that he built, are they not written in the Book of the Annals of the Kings of Judah? But in his old age he was diseased in his feet. 24 Then Asa slept with his ancestors, and was buried with his ancestors in the city of his father David; his son Je•hosh'a•phat succeeded him.

Nadab Reigns over Israel

25 Nā'dab son of Jer•o•bō'am began to reign over Israel in the second year of King Asa of Judah; he reigned over Israel two years. 26 He did what was evil in the sight of the LORD, walking in the way of

---

i Heb *Asherim*

his ancestor and in the sin that he caused Israel to commit.

27 Bāʹaʹsha son of Aʹhīʹjah, of the house of Isʹsaʹchar, conspired against him; and Bāʹaʹsha struck him down at Gibʹbeʹthon, which belonged to the Phiʹlisʹtines; for Nāʹdab and all Israel were laying siege to Gibʹbeʹthon. 28 So Bāʹaʹsha killed Nāʹdabʲ in the third year of King Asa of Judah, and succeeded him. 29 As soon as he was king, he killed all the house of Jerʹoʹbōʹam; he left to the house of Jerʹoʹbōʹam not one that breathed, until he had destroyed it, according to the word of the LORD that he spoke by his servant Aʹhīʹjah the Shīʹloʹnīte— 30 because of the sins of Jerʹoʹbōʹam that he committed and that he caused Israel to commit, and because of the anger to which he provoked the LORD, the God of Israel.

31 Now the rest of the acts of Nāʹdab, and all that he did, are they not written in the Book of the Annals of the Kings of Israel? 32 There was war between Asa and King Bāʹaʹsha of Israel all their days.

Second Dynasty: Baasha Reigns over Israel

33 In the third year of King Asa of Judah, Bāʹaʹsha son of Aʹhīʹjah began to reign over all Israel at Tirʹzah; he reigned twenty-four years. 34 He did what was evil in the sight of the LORD, walking in the way of Jerʹoʹbōʹam and in the sin that he caused Israel to commit.

16 The word of the LORD came to Jěʹhū son of Haʹnāʹnī against Bāʹaʹsha, saying, 2 "Since I exalted you out of the dust and made you leader over my people Israel, and you have walked in the way of Jerʹoʹbōʹam, and have caused my people Israel to sin, provoking me to anger with their sins, 3 therefore, I will consume Bāʹaʹsha and his house, and I will make your house like the house of Jerʹoʹbōʹam son of Něʹbat. 4 Anyone belonging to Bāʹaʹsha who dies in the city the dogs shall eat; and anyone of his who dies in the field the birds of the air shall eat."

5 Now the rest of the acts of Bāʹaʹsha, what he did, and his power, are they not written in the Book of the Annals of the Kings of Israel? 6 Bāʹaʹsha slept with his ancestors, and was buried at Tirʹzah; and his son Ēʹlah succeeded him. 7 Moreover the word of the LORD came by the prophet Jěʹhū son of Haʹnāʹnī against Bāʹaʹsha and his house, both because of all the evil that he did in the sight of the LORD, provoking him to anger with the work of his hands, in being like the house of Jerʹoʹbōʹam, and also because he destroyed it.

Elah Reigns over Israel

8 In the twenty-sixth year of King Asa of Judah, Ēʹlah son of Bāʹaʹsha began to reign over Israel in Tirʹzah; he reigned two years. 9 But his servant Zimʹrī, commander of half his chariots, conspired against him. When he was at Tirʹzah, drinking himself drunk in the house of Arʹza, who was in charge of the palace at Tirʹzah, 10 Zimʹrī came in and struck him down and killed him, in the twenty-seventh year of King Asa of Judah, and succeeded him.

11 When he began to reign, as soon as he had seated himself on his throne, he killed all the house of Bāʹaʹsha; he did not leave him a single male of his kindred or his friends. 12 Thus Zimʹrī destroyed all the house of Bāʹaʹsha, according to the word of the LORD, which he spoke against Bāʹaʹsha by the prophet Jěʹhū— 13 because of all the sins of Bāʹaʹsha and the sins of his son Ēʹlah that they committed, and that they caused Israel to commit, provoking the LORD God of Israel to anger with their idols. 14 Now the rest of the acts of Ēʹlah, and all that he did, are they not written in the Book of the Annals of the Kings of Israel?

Third Dynasty: Zimri Reigns over Israel

15 In the twenty-seventh year of King Asa of Judah, Zimʹrī reigned seven days in Tirʹzah. Now the troops were encamped against Gibʹbeʹthon, which belonged to the Phiʹlisʹtines, 16 and the troops who were encamped heard it said, "Zimʹrī has conspired, and he has killed the king"; therefore all Israel made Omʹrī, the commander of the army, king over Israel that day in the camp. 17 So Omʹrī went up from Gibʹbeʹthon, and all Israel with him, and they besieged Tirʹzah. 18 When Zimʹrī saw that the city was taken, he went into the citadel of the king's house; he burned down the king's house over himself with fire, and died— 19 because of the sins that he committed, doing evil in the sight of the LORD, walking in the way of Jerʹoʹbōʹam, and for the sin that he committed, causing Israel to sin. 20 Now the rest of the acts of Zimʹrī, and the conspiracy that he made, are they not written in the Book of the Annals of the Kings of Israel?

Fourth Dynasty: Omri Reigns over Israel

21 Then the people of Israel were divided into two parts; half of the people followed Tibʹnī son of Gīʹnath, to make him king, and half followed Omʹrī. 22 But the people who followed Omʹrī overcame the people who followed Tibʹnī son of Gīʹnath; so Tibʹnī died, and Omʹrī became king. 23 In the thirty-first year of King Asa of Judah, Omʹrī began to reign over Israel; he reigned for twelve years, six of them in Tirʹzah.

Samaria the New Capital

24 He bought the hill of Saʹmārʹiʹa from Shěʹmer for two talents of silver; he fortified the hill,

---

ʲ Heb *Him*

and called the city that he built, Sa·mār′i·a, after the name of Shē′mer, the owner of the hill.

25 Om′rī did what was evil in the sight of the LORD; he did more evil than all who were before him. 26 For he walked in all the way of Jer·o·bō′am son of Nē′bat, and in the sins that he caused Israel to commit, provoking the LORD, the God of Israel, to anger by their idols. 27 Now the rest of the acts of Om′rī that he did, and the power that he showed, are they not written in the Book of the Annals of the Kings of Israel? 28 Om′rī slept with his ancestors, and was buried in Sa·mār′i·a; his son Ā′hab succeeded him.

Ahab Reigns over Israel

29 In the thirty-eighth year of King Asa of Judah, Ā′hab son of Om′rī began to reign over Israel; Ā′hab son of Om′rī reigned over Israel in Sa·mār′i·a twenty-two years. 30 Ā′hab son of Om′rī did evil in the sight of the LORD more than all who were before him.

Ahab Marries Jezebel and Worships Baal

31 And as if it had been a light thing for him to walk in the sins of Jer·o·bō′am son of Nē′bat, he took as his wife Jez′e·bel daughter of King Eth·ba′al of the Sī·dō′ni·ans, and went and served Bā′al, and worshiped him. 32 He erected an altar for Bā′al in the house of Bā′al, which he built in Sa·mār′i·a. 33 Ā′hab also made a sacred pole.*k* Ā′hab did more to provoke the anger of the LORD, the God of Israel, than had all the kings of Israel who were before him. 34 In his days Hī′el of Beth′el built Jericho; he laid its foundation at the cost of A·bī′ram his firstborn, and set up its gates at the cost of his youngest son Sē′gub, according to the word of the LORD, which he spoke by Joshua son of Nun.

Elijah Predicts a Drought

17 Now E·lī′jah the Tish′bīte, of Tish′bē*l* in Gil′e·ad, said to Ā′hab, "As the LORD the God of Israel lives, before whom I stand, there shall be neither dew nor rain these years, except by my word." 2 The word of the LORD came to him, saying, 3 "Go from here and turn eastward, and hide yourself by the Wadi Chē′rith, which is east of the Jordan. 4 You shall drink from the wadi, and I have commanded the ravens to feed you there." 5 So he went and did according to the word of the LORD; he went and lived by the Wadi Chē′rith, which is east of the

---

k Heb *Asherah*   *l* Gk: Heb *of the settlers*

Introducing ▶ELIJAH AND ELISHA

You didn't want to mess with Elijah and Elisha. They were take-no-prisoners kinds of prophets. According to 1 Kings, Elijah has 450 prophets of Baal killed after publicly humiliating them (18.40). And when a bunch of boys call Elisha "baldhead," they are attacked by bears (2 Kings 2.23–24).

Elijah, whose name means "Yahweh is my God," shows up in the second half of 1 Kings reminding the Israelites that God is their God alone and that keeping God's Covenant means not worshiping the Canaanite baals (gods). In a dramatic story, he shows the idol-worshiping King Ahab and Queen Jezebel that God is superior to their false gods (1 Kings 18.21–40).

Elijah was recorded as being carried to heaven in a fiery chariot (2 Kings 2.11) as a sign of his greatness, and he was expected to reappear before the "day of the LORD" arrived (Mal 4.5). By New Testament times, Elijah had come to represent the prophets as Moses had come to represent the Law. Referring to Moses and Elijah was a way of summarizing everything that God had revealed before Christ.

Elisha was Elijah's disciple and successor. He plays an important role in the first half of 2 Kings. Elisha's name means "God is salvation." He was a man of wisdom and a miracle worker.

These "tough guys" also had tender hearts. Both miraculously multiplied food for widows (1 Kings 17.16; 2 Kings 4.5), and both brought a dead child back to life (1 Kings 17.22; 2 Kings 4.34). Elijah and Elisha are revered both for their uncompromising faith and for their compassion for the "little ones."

Jordan. 6 The ravens brought him bread and meat in the morning, and bread and meat in the evening; and he drank from the wadi. 7 But after a while the wadi dried up, because there was no rain in the land.

The Widow of Zarephath

8 Then the word of the LORD came to him, saying, 9 "Go now to Zar'e•phath, which belongs to Sī'-don, and live there; for I have commanded a widow there to feed you." 10 So he set out and went to Zar'e•phath. When he came to the gate of the town, a widow was there gathering sticks; he called to her and said, "Bring me a little water in a vessel, so that I may drink." 11 As she was going to bring it, he called to her and said, "Bring me a morsel of bread in your hand." 12 But she said, "As the LORD your God lives, I have nothing baked, only a handful of meal in a jar, and a little oil in a jug; I am now gathering a couple of sticks, so that I may go home and prepare it for myself and my son, that we may eat it, and die." 13 E•lī'jah said to her, "Do not be afraid; go and do as you have said; but first make me a little cake of it and bring it to me, and afterwards make something for yourself and your son. 14 For thus says the LORD the God of Israel: The jar of meal will not be emptied and the jug of oil will not fail until the day that the LORD sends rain on the earth." 15 She went and did as E•lī'jah said, so that she as well as he and her household ate for many days. 16 The jar of meal was not emptied, neither did the jug of oil fail, according to the word of the LORD that he spoke by E•lī'jah.

Elijah Revives the Widow's Son

17 After this the son of the woman, the mistress of the house, became ill; his illness was so severe that there was no breath left in him. 18 She then said to E•lī'jah, "What have you against me, O man of God? You have come to me to bring my sin to remembrance, and to cause the death of my son!" 19 But he said to her, "Give me your son." He took him from her bosom, carried him up into the upper chamber where he was lodging, and laid him on his own bed. 20 He cried out to the LORD, "O LORD my God, have you brought calamity even upon the widow with whom I am staying, by killing her son?" 21 Then he stretched himself upon the child three times, and cried out to the LORD, "O LORD my God, let this child's life come into him again." 22 The LORD listened to the voice of E•lī'jah; the life of the child came into him again, and he revived. 23 E•lī'jah took the child, brought him down from the upper chamber into the house, and gave him to his mother; then E•lī'jah said, "See, your son is alive." 24 So the woman said to E•lī'jah, "Now I know that you are a man of God, and that the word of the LORD in your mouth is truth."

Elijah's Message to Ahab

18 After many days the word of the LORD came to E•lī'jah, in the third year of the drought,*m* saying, "Go, present yourself to Ā'hab; I will send rain on the earth." 2 So E•lī'jah went to present himself to Ā'hab. The famine was severe in Sa•mār'i•a. 3 Ā'hab summoned Ō•ba•dī'ah, who was in charge of the palace. (Now Ō•ba•dī'ah revered the LORD greatly; 4 when Jez'e•bel was killing off the prophets of the LORD, Ō•ba•dī'ah took a hundred prophets, hid them fifty to a cave, and provided them with bread and water.) 5 Then Ā'hab said to Ō•ba•dī'ah, "Go through the land to all the springs of water and to all the wadis; perhaps we may find grass to keep the horses and mules alive, and not lose some of the animals." 6 So they divided the land between them to pass through it; Ā'hab went in one direction by himself, and Ō•ba•dī'ah went in another direction by himself.

7 As Ō•ba•dī'ah was on the way, E•lī'jah met him; Ō•ba•dī'ah recognized him, fell on his face, and said, "Is it you, my lord E•lī'jah?" 8 He answered him, "It is I. Go, tell your lord that E•lī'jah is here." 9 And he said, "How have I sinned, that you would hand your servant over to Ā'hab, to kill me? 10 As the LORD your God lives, there is no nation or kingdom to which my lord has not sent to seek you; and when they would say, 'He is not here,' he would require an oath of the kingdom or nation, that they had not found you. 11 But now you say, 'Go, tell your lord that E•lī'jah is here.' 12 As soon as I have gone from you, the spirit of the LORD will carry you I know not where; so, when I come and tell Ā'hab and he cannot find you, he will kill me, although I your servant have revered the LORD from my youth. 13 Has it not been told my lord what I did when Jez'e•bel killed the prophets of the LORD, how I hid a hundred of the LORD's prophets fifty to a cave, and provided them with bread and water? 14 Yet now you say, 'Go, tell your lord that E•lī'jah is here'; he will surely kill me." 15 E•lī'jah said, "As the LORD of hosts lives, before whom I stand, I will surely show myself to him today." 16 So Ō•ba•dī'ah went to meet Ā'hab, and told him; and Ā'hab went to meet E•lī'jah.

17 When Ā'hab saw E•lī'jah, Ā'hab said to him, "Is it you, you troubler of Israel?" 18 He answered, "I have not troubled Israel; but you have, and your father's house, because you have forsaken the commandments of the LORD and followed the Bā'als. 19 Now therefore have all Israel assemble for me at Mount Car'mel, with the four hundred fifty prophets of Bā'al and the four hundred prophets of A•shē'rah, who eat at Jez'e•bel's table."

1
K
I
N
G
S

---

m Heb lacks *of the drought*

Elijah's Triumph over the Priests of Baal

20 So Ā'hab sent to all the Israelites, and assembled the prophets at Mount Car'mel. 21 E•lī'jah then came near to all the people, and said, "How long will you go limping with two different opinions? If the LORD is God, follow him; but if Bā'al, then follow him." The people did not answer him a word. 22 Then E•lī'jah said to the people, "I, even I only, am left a prophet of the LORD; but Bā'al's prophets number four hundred fifty. 23 Let two bulls be given to us; let them choose one bull for themselves, cut it in pieces, and lay it on the wood, but put no fire to it; I will prepare the other bull and lay it on the wood, but put no fire to it. 24 Then you call on the name of your god and I will call on the name of the LORD; the god who answers by fire is indeed God." All the people answered, "Well spoken!" 25 Then E•lī'jah said to the prophets of Bā'al, "Choose for yourselves one bull and prepare it first, for you are many; then call on the name of your god, but put no fire to it." 26 So they took the bull that was given them, prepared it, and called on the name of Bā'al from morning until noon, crying, "O Bā'al, answer us!" But there was no voice, and no answer. They limped about the altar that they had made. 27 At noon E•lī'jah mocked them, saying, "Cry aloud! Surely he is a god; either he is meditating, or he has wandered away, or he is on a journey, or perhaps he is asleep and must be awakened." 28 Then they cried aloud and, as was their custom, they cut themselves with swords and lances until the blood gushed out over them. 29 As midday passed, they raved on until the time of the offering of the oblation, but there was no voice, no answer, and no response.

30 Then E•lī'jah said to all the people, "Come closer to me"; and all the people came closer to him. First he repaired the altar of the LORD that had been thrown down; 31 E•lī'jah took twelve stones, according to the number of the tribes of the sons of Jacob, to whom the word of the LORD came, saying, "Israel shall be your name"; 32 with the stones he built an altar in the name of the LORD. Then he made a trench around the altar, large enough to contain two measures of seed. 33 Next he put the wood in order, cut the bull in pieces, and laid it on the wood. He said, "Fill four jars with water and pour it on the burnt offering and on the wood." 34 Then he said, "Do it a second time"; and they did it a second time. Again he said, "Do it a third time"; and they did it a third time, 35 so that the water ran all around the altar, and filled the trench also with water.

36 At the time of the offering of the oblation, the prophet E•lī'jah came near and said, "O LORD, God of Abraham, Isaac, and Israel, let it be known this day that you are God in Israel, that I am your servant, and that I have done all these things at your bidding. 37 Answer me, O LORD, answer me, so that this people may know that you, O LORD, are God, and that you have turned their hearts back." 38 Then the fire of the LORD fell and consumed the burnt offering, the wood, the stones, and the dust, and even licked up the water that was in the trench. 39 When all the people saw it, they fell on their faces and said, "The LORD indeed is God; the LORD indeed is God." 40 E•lī'jah said to them, "Seize the prophets of Bā'al; do not let one of them escape." Then they seized them; and E•lī'jah brought them down to the Wadi Kī'shon, and killed them there.

The Drought Ends

41 E•lī'jah said to Ā'hab, "Go up, eat and drink; for there is a sound of rushing rain." 42 So Ā'hab went up to eat and to drink. E•lī'jah went up to the top of Car'mel; there he bowed himself down upon the earth and put his face between his knees. 43 He said to his servant, "Go up now, look toward the sea." He went up and looked, and said, "There is nothing." Then he said, "Go again seven times." 44 At the seventh time he said, "Look, a little cloud no bigger than a person's hand is rising out of the sea." Then he said, "Go say to Ā'hab, 'Harness your chariot and go down before the rain stops you.' " 45 In a little while the heavens grew black with clouds and wind; there was a heavy rain. Ā'hab rode off and went to Jez're•el. 46 But the hand of the LORD was on E•lī'jah; he girded up his loins and ran in front of Ā'hab to the entrance of Jez'rē•el.

Elijah Flees from Jezebel

19 Ā'hab told Jez'e•bel all that E•lī'jah had done, and how he had killed all the prophets with the sword. 2 Then Jez'e•bel sent a messenger to E•lī'jah, saying, "So may the gods do to me, and more also, if I do not make your life like the life of one of them by this time tomorrow." 3 Then he was afraid; he got up and fled for his life, and came to Bē'er-shē'ba, which belongs to Judah; he left his servant there.

4 But he himself went a day's journey into the wilderness, and came and sat down under a solitary broom tree. He asked that he might die: "It is enough; now, O LORD, take away my life, for I am no better than my ancestors." 5 Then he lay down under the broom tree and fell asleep. Suddenly an angel touched him and said to him, "Get up and eat." 6 He looked, and there at his head was a cake baked on hot stones, and a jar of water. He ate and drank, and lay down again. 7 The angel of the LORD came a second time, touched him, and said, "Get up and eat, otherwise the journey will be too much for you." 8 He got up, and ate and drank; then he went in the strength of that food forty days and

PRAY IT!
Looking for God

Elijah was told to meet God on the mountain. God's presence could have been in fire, an earthquake, a great wind, but God was in none of these. God was in the tiny whispering sound.

All of us have a need for God. We might not know it, but it is there: a God-shaped hole in our soul that no one and nothing else can fill. Without God we will always feel empty.

Sometimes, we look for things to fill that empty space. And we still feel empty.

The irony is that through all this, God is there, in the quiet depths of our heart. We need to be like Elijah—tuning out things that are not God and tuning in to God's presence. Taking quiet time to think and pray is a great start.

▸ 1 Kings 19.9–13

---

forty nights to Hō'reb the mount of God. 9 At that place he came to a cave, and spent the night there.

Then the word of the LORD came to him, saying, "What are you doing here, E·lī'jah?" 10 He answered, "I have been very zealous for the LORD, the God of hosts; for the Israelites have forsaken your covenant, thrown down your altars, and killed your prophets with the sword. I alone am left, and they are seeking my life, to take it away."

Elijah Meets God at Horeb

11 He said, "Go out and stand on the mountain before the LORD, for the LORD is about to pass by." Now there was a great wind, so strong that it was splitting mountains and breaking rocks in pieces before the LORD, but the LORD was not in the wind; and after the wind an earthquake, but the LORD was not in the earthquake; 12 and after the earthquake a fire, but the LORD was not in the fire; and after the fire a sound of sheer silence. 13 When E·lī'jah heard it, he wrapped his face in his mantle and went out and stood at the entrance of the cave. Then there came a voice to him that said, "What are you doing here, E·lī'jah?" 14 He answered, "I have been very zealous for the LORD, the God of hosts; for the Is-

---

raelites have forsaken your covenant, thrown down your altars, and killed your prophets with the sword. I alone am left, and they are seeking my life, to take it away." 15 Then the LORD said to him, "Go, return on your way to the wilderness of Damascus; when you arrive, you shall anoint Haz'a·el as king over Ar'am. 16 Also you shall anoint Jē'hū son of Nim'shī as king over Israel; and you shall anoint E·lī'sha son of Shā'phat of Ā'bel-me·hō'lah as prophet in your place. 17 Whoever escapes from the sword of Haz'a·el, Jē'hū shall kill; and whoever escapes from the sword of Jē'hū, E·lī'sha shall kill. 18 Yet I will leave seven thousand in Israel, all the knees that have not bowed to Bā'al, and every mouth that has not kissed him."

Elisha Becomes Elijah's Disciple

19 So he set out from there, and found E·lī'sha son of Shā'phat, who was plowing. There were twelve yoke of oxen ahead of him, and he was with the twelfth. E·lī'jah passed by him and threw his mantle over him. 20 He left the oxen, ran after E·lī'jah, and said, "Let me kiss my father and my mother, and then I will follow you." Then E·lī'jah[n] said to him, "Go back again; for what have I done to you?" 21 He returned from following him, took the yoke of oxen, and slaughtered them; using the equipment from the oxen, he boiled their flesh, and gave it to the people, and they ate. Then he set out and followed E·lī'jah, and became his servant.

Ahab's Wars with the Arameans

20 King Ben-hā'dad of Ar'am gathered all his army together; thirty-two kings were with him, along with horses and chariots. He marched against Sa·mār'i·a, laid siege to it, and attacked it. 2 Then he sent messengers into the city to King Ā'hab of Israel, and said to him: "Thus says Ben-hā'dad: 3 Your silver and gold are mine; your fairest wives and children also are mine." 4 The king of Israel answered, "As you say, my lord, O king, I am yours, and all that I have." 5 The messengers came again and said: "Thus says Ben-hā'dad: I sent to you, saying, 'Deliver to me your silver and gold, your wives and children'; 6 nevertheless I will send my servants to you tomorrow about this time, and they shall search your house and the houses of your servants, and lay hands on whatever pleases them,[o] and take it away."

7 Then the king of Israel called all the elders of the land, and said, "Look now! See how this man is seeking trouble; for he sent to me for my wives, my children, my silver, and my gold; and I did not refuse him." 8 Then all the elders and all the people said to him, "Do not listen or consent." 9 So he said

---

n Heb *he*　o Gk Syr Vg: Heb *you*

to the messengers of Ben-hā′dad, "Tell my lord the king: All that you first demanded of your servant I will do; but this thing I cannot do." The messengers left and brought him word again. 10 Ben-hā′dad sent to him and said, "The gods do so to me, and more also, if the dust of Sa·mār′i·a will provide a handful for each of the people who follow me." 11 The king of Israel answered, "Tell him: One who puts on armor should not brag like one who takes it off." 12 When Ben-hā′dad heard this message— now he had been drinking with the kings in the booths—he said to his men, "Take your positions!" And they took their positions against the city.

Prophetic Opposition to Ahab

13 Then a certain prophet came up to King Ā′hab of Israel and said, "Thus says the LORD, Have you seen all this great multitude? Look, I will give it into your hand today; and you shall know that I am the LORD." 14 Ā′hab said, "By whom?" He said, "Thus says the LORD, By the young men who serve the district governors." Then he said, "Who shall begin the battle?" He answered, "You." 15 Then he mustered the young men who served the district governors, two hundred thirty-two; after them he mustered all the people of Israel, seven thousand.

16 They went out at noon, while Ben-hā′dad was drinking himself drunk in the booths, he and the thirty-two kings allied with him. 17 The young men who served the district governors went out first. Ben-hā′dad had sent out scouts,*p* and they reported to him, "Men have come out from Sa·mār′i·a." 18 He said, "If they have come out for peace, take them alive; if they have come out for war, take them alive."

19 But these had already come out of the city: the young men who served the district governors, and the army that followed them. 20 Each killed his man; the Ar·a·mē′ans fled and Israel pursued them, but King Ben-hā′dad of Ar′am escaped on a horse with the cavalry. 21 The king of Israel went out, attacked the horses and chariots, and defeated the Ar·a·mē′ans with a great slaughter.

22 Then the prophet approached the king of Israel and said to him, "Come, strengthen yourself, and consider well what you have to do; for in the spring the king of Ar′am will come up against you."

The Arameans Are Defeated

23 The servants of the king of Ar′am said to him, "Their gods are gods of the hills, and so they were stronger than we; but let us fight against them in the plain, and surely we shall be stronger than they. 24 Also do this: remove the kings, each from his post, and put commanders in place of them; 25 and muster an army like the army that you have

lost, horse for horse, and chariot for chariot; then we will fight against them in the plain, and surely we shall be stronger than they." He heeded their voice, and did so.

26 In the spring Ben-hā′dad mustered the Ar·a·mē′ans and went up to Ā′phek to fight against Israel. 27 After the Israelites had been mustered and provisioned, they went out to engage them; the people of Israel encamped opposite them like two little flocks of goats, while the Ar·a·mē′ans filled the country. 28 A man of God approached and said to the king of Israel, "Thus says the LORD: Because the Ar·a·mē′ans have said, 'The LORD is a god of the hills but he is not a god of the valleys,' therefore I will give all this great multitude into your hand, and you shall know that I am the LORD." 29 They encamped opposite one another seven days. Then on the seventh day the battle began; the Israelites killed one hundred thousand Ar·a·mē′an foot soldiers in one day. 30 The rest fled into the city of Ā′phek; and the wall fell on twenty-seven thousand men that were left.

Ben-hā′dad also fled, and entered the city to hide. 31 His servants said to him, "Look, we have heard that the kings of the house of Israel are merciful kings; let us put sackcloth around our waists and ropes on our heads, and go out to the king of Israel; perhaps he will spare your life." 32 So they tied sackcloth around their waists, put ropes on their heads, went to the king of Israel, and said, "Your servant Ben-hā′dad says, 'Please let me live.' " And he said, "Is he still alive? He is my brother." 33 Now the men were watching for an omen; they quickly took it up from him and said, "Yes, Ben-hā′dad is your brother." Then he said, "Go and bring him." So Ben-hā′dad came out to him; and he had him come up into the chariot. 34 Ben-hā′dad*q* said to him, "I will restore the towns that my father took from your father; and you may establish bazaars for yourself in Damascus, as my father did in Sa·mār′i·a." The king of Israel responded,*r* "I will let you go on those terms." So he made a treaty with him and let him go.

A Prophet Condemns Ahab

35 At the command of the LORD a certain member of a company of prophets*s* said to another, "Strike me!" But the man refused to strike him. 36 Then he said to him, "Because you have not obeyed the voice of the LORD, as soon as you have left me, a lion will kill you." And when he had left him, a lion met him and killed him. 37 Then he found another man and said, "Strike me!" So the man hit him, striking and wounding him. 38 Then

---

p Heb lacks *scouts* *q* Heb *He* *r* Heb lacks *The king of Israel responded* *s* Heb *of the sons of the prophets* the prophet departed, and waited for the king along the road, disguising himself with a bandage over his eyes. 39 As the king passed by, he cried to the king and said, "Your servant went out into the thick of the battle; then a soldier turned and brought a man to me, and said, 'Guard this man; if he is missing, your life shall be given for his life, or else you shall pay a talent of silver.' 40 While your servant was busy here and there, he was gone." The king of Israel said to him, "So shall your judgment be; you yourself have decided it." 41 Then he quickly took the bandage away from his eyes. The king of Israel recognized him as one of the prophets. 42 Then he said to him, "Thus says the LORD, 'Because you have let the man go whom I had devoted to destruction, therefore your life shall be for his life, and your people for his people.' " 43 The king of Israel set out toward home, resentful and sullen, and came to Sa·mār′i·a.

Naboth's Vineyard

21 Later the following events took place: Nā′both the Jez′rē·el·īte had a vineyard in Jez′rē·el, beside the palace of King Ā′hab of Sa·mār′i·a. 2 And Ā′hab said to Nā′both, "Give me your vineyard, so that I may have it for a vegetable garden, because it is near my house; I will give you a better vineyard for it; or, if it seems good to you, I will give you its value in money." 3 But Nā′both said to Ā′hab, "The LORD forbid that I should give you my ancestral inheritance." 4 Ā′hab went home resentful and sullen because of what Nā′both the Jez′rē·el·īte had said to him; for he had said, "I will not give you my ancestral inheritance." He lay down on his bed, turned away his face, and would not eat.

5 His wife Jez′e·bel came to him and said, "Why are you so depressed that you will not eat?" 6 He said to her, "Because I spoke to Nā′both the Jez′rē·el·īte and said to him, 'Give me your vineyard for money; or else, if you prefer, I will give you another vineyard for it'; but he answered, 'I will not give you my vineyard.' " 7 His wife Jez′e·bel said to him, "Do you now govern Israel? Get up, eat some food, and be cheerful; I will give you the vineyard of Nā′both the Jez′rē·el·īte."

8 So she wrote letters in Ā′hab's name and sealed them with his seal; she sent the letters to the elders and the nobles who lived with Nā′both in his city. 9 She wrote in the letters, "Proclaim a fast, and seat Nā′both at the head of the assembly; 10 seat two scoundrels opposite him, and have them bring a charge against him, saying, 'You have cursed God and the king.' Then take him out, and stone him to death." 11 The men of his city, the elders and the nobles who lived in his city, did as Jez′e·bel had sent word to them. Just as it was written in the letters that she had sent to them, 12 they proclaimed a

fast and seated Nā′both at the head of the assembly. 13 The two scoundrels came in and sat opposite him; and the scoundrels brought a charge against Nā′both, in the presence of the people, saying, "Nā′both cursed God and the king." So they took him outside the city, and stoned him to death. 14 Then they sent to Jez′e·bel, saying, "Nā′both has been stoned; he is dead."

15 As soon as Jez′e·bel heard that Nā′both had been stoned and was dead, Jez′e·bel said to Ā′hab, "Go, take possession of the vineyard of Nā′both the Jez′rē·el·īte, which he refused to give you for money; for Nā′both is not alive, but dead." 16 As soon as Ā′hab heard that Nā′both was dead, Ā′hab set out to go down to the vineyard of Nā′both the Jez′rē·el·īte, to take possession of it.

Elijah Pronounces God's Sentence

17 Then the word of the LORD came to E·lī′jah the Tish′bīte, saying: 18 Go down to meet King Ā′hab of Israel, who rules[t] in Sa·mār′i·a; he is now in the vineyard of Nā′both, where he has gone to take possession. 19 You shall say to him, "Thus says the LORD: Have you killed, and also taken possession?" You shall say to him, "Thus says the LORD: In the place where dogs licked up the blood of Nā′both, dogs will also lick up your blood."

20 Ā′hab said to E·lī′jah, "Have you found me, O my enemy?" He answered, "I have found you. Because you have sold yourself to do what is evil in the sight of the LORD, 21 I will bring disaster on you; I will consume you, and will cut off from Ā′hab every male, bond or free, in Israel; 22 and I will make your house like the house of Jer·o·bō′am son of Nē′bat, and like the house of Bā′a·sha son of A·hī′jah, because you have provoked me to anger and have caused Israel to sin. 23 Also concerning Jez′e·bel the LORD said, 'The dogs shall eat Jez′e·bel within the bounds of Jez′rē·el.' 24 Anyone belonging to Ā′hab who dies in the city the dogs shall eat; and anyone of his who dies in the open country the birds of the air shall eat."

25 (Indeed, there was no one like Ā′hab, who sold himself to do what was evil in the sight of the LORD, urged on by his wife Jez′e·bel. 26 He acted most abominably in going after idols, as the Am′o·rītes had done, whom the LORD drove out before the Israelites.)

27 When Ā′hab heard those words, he tore his clothes and put sackcloth over his bare flesh; he fasted, lay in the sackcloth, and went about dejectedly. 28 Then the word of the LORD came to E·lī′jah the Tish′bīte: 29 "Have you seen how Ā′hab has humbled himself before me? Because he has humbled himself before me, I will not bring the disaster

---

t Heb *who is*

1 K I N G S

in his days; but in his son's days I will bring the disaster on his house."

Joint Campaign with Judah against Aram
(2 Chr 18.1–11)

22 For three years Ar'am and Israel continued without war. 2 But in the third year King Je·hosh'a·phat of Judah came down to the king of Israel. 3 The king of Israel said to his servants, "Do you know that Rā'moth-gil'ē·ad belongs to us, yet we are doing nothing to take it out of the hand of the king of Ar'am?" 4 He said to Je·hosh'a·phat, "Will you go with me to battle at Rā'moth-gil'ē·ad?" Je·hosh'a·phat replied to the king of Israel, "I am as you are; my people are your people, my horses are your horses."

5 But Je·hosh'a·phat also said to the king of Israel, "Inquire first for the word of the LORD." 6 Then the king of Israel gathered the prophets together, about four hundred of them, and said to them, "Shall I go to battle against Rā'moth-gil'ē·ad, or shall I refrain?" They said, "Go up; for the LORD will give it into the hand of the king." 7 But Je·hosh'a·phat said, "Is there no other prophet of the LORD here of whom we may inquire?" 8 The king of Israel said to Je·hosh'a·phat, "There is still one other by whom we may inquire of the LORD, Mī·cāi'ah son of Im'lah; but I hate him, for he never prophesies anything favorable about me, but only disaster." Je·hosh'a·phat said, "Let the king not say such a thing." 9 Then the king of Israel summoned an officer and said, "Bring quickly Mī·cāi'ah son of Im'lah." 10 Now the king of Israel and King Je·hosh'a·phat of Judah were sitting on their thrones, arrayed in their robes, at the threshing floor at the entrance of the gate of Sa·mār'i·a; and all the prophets were prophesying before them. 11 Zed·e·kī'ah son of Che·nā'a·nah made for himself horns of iron, and he said, "Thus says the LORD: With these you shall gore the Ar·a·mē'ans until they are destroyed." 12 All the prophets were prophesying the same and saying, "Go up to Rā'moth-gil'ē·ad and triumph; the LORD will give it into the hand of the king."

Micaiah Predicts Failure
(2 Chr 18.12–27)

13 The messenger who had gone to summon Mī·cāi'ah said to him, "Look, the words of the prophets with one accord are favorable to the king; let your word be like the word of one of them, and speak favorably." 14 But Mī·cāi'ah said, "As the LORD lives, whatever the LORD says to me, that I will speak."

15 When he had come to the king, the king said to him, "Mī·cāi'ah, shall we go to Rā'moth-gil'ē·ad to battle, or shall we refrain?" He answered him, "Go up and triumph; the LORD will give it into the hand of the king." 16 But the king said to him, "How many times must I make you swear to tell me nothing but the truth in the name of the LORD?" 17 Then Mī·cāi'ahᵘ said, "I saw all Israel scattered on the mountains, like sheep that have no shepherd; and the LORD said, 'These have no master; let each one go home in peace.' " 18 The king of Israel said to Je·hosh'a·phat, "Did I not tell you that he would not prophesy anything favorable about me, but only disaster?"

19 Then Mī·cāi'ahᵘ said, "Therefore hear the word of the LORD: I saw the LORD sitting on his throne, with all the host of heaven standing beside him to the right and to the left of him. 20 And the LORD said, 'Who will entice Ā'hab, so that he may go up and fall at Rā'moth-gil'ē·ad?' Then one said one thing, and another said another, 21 until a spirit came forward and stood before the LORD, saying, 'I will entice him.' 22 'How?' the LORD asked him. He replied, 'I will go out and be a lying spirit in the mouth of all his prophets.' Then the LORDᵘ said, 'You are to entice him, and you shall succeed; go out and do it.' 23 So you see, the LORD has put a lying spirit in the mouth of all these your prophets; the LORD has decreed disaster for you."

24 Then Zed·e·kī'ah son of Che·nā'a·nah came up to Mī·cāi'ah, slapped him on the cheek, and said, "Which way did the spirit of the LORD pass from me to speak to you?" 25 Mī·cāi'ah replied, "You will find out on that day when you go in to hide in an inner chamber." 26 The king of Israel then ordered, "Take Mī·cāi'ah, and return him to Ā'mon the governor of the city and to Jō'ash the king's son, 27 and say, 'Thus says the king: Put this fellow in prison, and feed him on reduced rations of bread and water until I come in peace.' " 28 Mī·cāi'ah said, "If you return in peace, the LORD has not spoken by me." And he said, "Hear, you peoples, all of you!"

Defeat and Death of Ahab
(2 Chr 18.28–34)

29 So the king of Israel and King Je·hosh'a·phat of Judah went up to Rā'moth-gil'ē·ad. 30 The king of Israel said to Je·hosh'a·phat, "I will disguise myself and go into battle, but you wear your robes." So the king of Israel disguised himself and went into battle. 31 Now the king of Ar'am had commanded the thirty-two captains of his chariots, "Fight with no one small or great, but only with the king of Israel." 32 When the captains of the chariots saw Je·hosh'a·phat, they said, "It is surely the king of Israel." So they turned to fight against him; and Je·hosh'a·phat cried out. 33 When the captains of

ᵘ Heb *he*

the chariots saw that it was not the king of Israel, they turned back from pursuing him. 34 But a certain man drew his bow and unknowingly struck the king of Israel between the scale armor and the breastplate; so he said to the driver of his chariot, "Turn around, and carry me out of the battle, for I am wounded." 35 The battle grew hot that day, and the king was propped up in his chariot facing the Ar•a•mē′ans, until at evening he died; the blood from the wound had flowed into the bottom of the chariot. 36 Then about sunset a shout went through the army, "Every man to his city, and every man to his country!"

37 So the king died, and was brought to Sa•mār′i•a; they buried the king in Sa•mār′i•a. 38 They washed the chariot by the pool of Sa•mār′-i•a; the dogs licked up his blood, and the prostitutes washed themselves in it,ᵛ according to the word of the LORD that he had spoken. 39 Now the rest of the acts of Ā′hab, and all that he did, and the ivory house that he built, and all the cities that he built, are they not written in the Book of the Annals of the Kings of Israel? 40 So Ā′hab slept with his ancestors; and his son A•ha•zī′ah succeeded him.

Jehoshaphat Reigns over Judah
(2 Chr 20.31—21.1)

41 Je•hosh′a•phat son of Asa began to reign over Judah in the fourth year of King Ā′hab of Israel. 42 Je•hosh′a•phat was thirty-five years old when he began to reign, and he reigned twenty-five years in Jerusalem. His mother's name was A•zū′bah daughter of Shil′hī. 43 He walked in all the way of his father Asa; he did not turn aside from it, doing what was right in the sight of the LORD; yet the high places were not taken away, and the people still sacrificed and offered incense on the high places. 44 Je•hosh′a•phat also made peace with the king of Israel.

45 Now the rest of the acts of Je•hosh′a•phat, and his power that he showed, and how he waged war, are they not written in the Book of the Annals of the Kings of Judah? 46 The remnant of the male temple prostitutes who were still in the land in the days of his father Asa, he exterminated.

47 There was no king in É′dom; a deputy was king. 48 Je•hosh′a•phat made ships of the Tar′shish type to go to Ō′phir for gold; but they did not go, for the ships were wrecked at É′zi•on-gē′ber. 49 Then A•ha•zī′ah son of Ā′hab said to Je•hosh′aphat, "Let my servants go with your servants in the ships," but Je•hosh′a•phat was not willing. 50 Je•hosh′a•phat slept with his ancestors and was buried with his ancestors in the city of his father David; his son Je•hō′ram succeeded him.

Ahaziah Reigns over Israel

51 A•ha•zī′ah son of Ā′hab began to reign over Israel in Sa•mār′i•a in the seventeenth year of King Je•hosh′a•phat of Judah; he reigned two years over Israel. 52 He did what was evil in the sight of the LORD, and walked in the way of his father and mother, and in the way of Jer•o•bō′am son of Nĕ′-bat, who caused Israel to sin. 53 He served Bā′al and worshiped him; he provoked the LORD, the God of Israel, to anger, just as his father had done.

ᵛ Heb lacks *in it*

2 Kings

Chap. 25

Elijah Denounces Ahaziah

1 After the death of Ā'hab, Mō'ab rebelled against Israel.

2 A•ha•zī'ah had fallen through the lattice in his upper chamber in Sa•mār'i•a, and lay injured; so he sent messengers, telling them, "Go, inquire of Bā'al-zē'bub, the god of Ek'ron, whether I shall recover from this injury." 3 But the angel of the LORD said to E•lī'jah the Tish'bīte, "Get up, go to meet the messengers of the king of Sa•mār'i•a, and say to them, 'Is it because there is no God in Israel that you are going to inquire of Bā'al-zē'bub, the god of Ek'ron?' 4 Now therefore thus says the LORD, 'You shall not leave the bed to which you have gone, but you shall surely die.' " So E•lī'jah went.

5 The messengers returned to the king, who said to them, "Why have you returned?" 6 They answered him, "There came a man to meet us, who said to us, 'Go back to the king who sent you, and say to him: Thus says the LORD: Is it because there is no God in Israel that you are sending to inquire of Bā'al-zē'bub, the god of Ek'ron? Therefore you shall not leave the bed to which you have gone, but shall surely die.' " 7 He said to them, "What sort of man was he who came to meet you and told you these things?" 8 They answered him, "A hairy man, with a leather belt around his waist." He said, "It is E•lī'jah the Tish'bīte."

9 Then the king sent to him a captain of fifty with his fifty men. He went up to E•lī'jah, who was sitting on the top of a hill, and said to him, "O man of God, the king says, 'Come down.' " 10 But E•lī'jah answered the captain of fifty, "If I am a man of God, let fire come down from heaven and consume you and your fifty." Then fire came down from heaven, and consumed him and his fifty.

11 Again the king sent to him another captain of fifty with his fifty. He went up[a] and said to him, "O man of God, this is the king's order: Come down quickly!" 12 But E•lī'jah answered them, "If I am a man of God, let fire come down from heaven and consume you and your fifty." Then the fire of God came down from heaven and consumed him and his fifty.

13 Again the king sent the captain of a third fifty with his fifty. So the third captain of fifty went up, and came and fell on his knees before E•lī'jah, and entreated him, "O man of God, please let my life, and the life of these fifty servants of yours, be precious in your sight. 14 Look, fire came down from heaven and consumed the two former captains of fifty men with their fifties; but now let my life be precious in your sight." 15 Then the angel of the LORD said to E•lī'jah, "Go down with him; do not be afraid of him." So he set out and went down with him to the king, 16 and said to him, "Thus says the LORD: Because you have sent messengers to inquire of Bā'al-zē'bub, the god of Ek'ron,—is it be-

a Gk Compare verses 9, 13: Heb *He answered*

352

cause there is no God in Israel to inquire of his word?—therefore you shall not leave the bed to which you have gone, but you shall surely die."

Death of Ahaziah

17 So he died according to the word of the LORD that E•li′jah had spoken. His brother,[b] Je•hō′ram succeeded him as king in the second year of King Je•hō′ram son of Je•hosh′a•phat of Judah, because A•ha•zi′ah had no son. 18 Now the rest of the acts of A•ha•zi′ah that he did, are they not written in the Book of the Annals of the Kings of Israel?

Elijah Ascends to Heaven

2 Now when the LORD was about to take E•li′-jah up to heaven by a whirlwind, E•li′jah and E•li′sha were on their way from Gil′gal. 2 E•li′jah said to E•li′sha, "Stay here; for the LORD has sent me as far as Beth′el." But E•li′sha said, "As the LORD lives, and as you yourself live, I will not leave you." So they went down to Beth′el. 3 The company of prophets[c] who were in Beth′el came out to E•li′sha, and said to him, "Do you know that today the LORD will take your master away from you?" And he said, "Yes, I know; keep silent."

4 E•li′jah said to him, "E•li′sha, stay here; for the LORD has sent me to Jericho." But he said, "As the LORD lives, and as you yourself live, I will not leave you." So they came to Jericho. 5 The company of prophets[c] who were at Jericho drew near to E•li′-sha, and said to him, "Do you know that today the LORD will take your master away from you?" And he answered, "Yes, I know; be silent."

6 Then E•li′jah said to him, "Stay here; for the LORD has sent me to the Jordan." But he said, "As the LORD lives, and as you yourself live, I will not leave you." So the two of them went on. 7 Fifty men of the company of prophets[c] also went, and stood at some distance from them, as they both were standing by the Jordan. 8 Then E•li′jah took his mantle and rolled it up, and struck the water; the water was parted to the one side and to the other, until the two of them crossed on dry ground.

9 When they had crossed, E•li′jah said to E•li′sha, "Tell me what I may do for you, before I am taken from you." E•li′sha said, "Please let me inherit a double share of your spirit." 10 He responded, "You have asked a hard thing; yet, if you see me as I am being taken from you, it will be granted you; if not, it will not." 11 As they continued walking and talking, a chariot of fire and horses of fire separated the two of them, and E•li′jah ascended in a

---

b Gk Syr: Heb lacks *His brother*   c Heb *sons of the prophets*

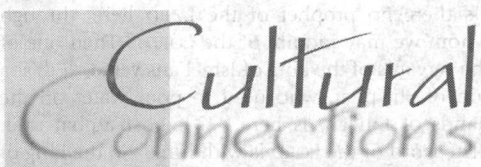

ELIJAH, PROPHET OF GOD IN SOLIDARITY WITH THE PEOPLE!

Elijah was a passionate prophet who read the history of the monarchy (Israel's kings) from the perspective of God. He saw division in the people of Israel. On the one hand were the kings, the noblemen, and the leaders of the army; on the other hand were the peasants, the widows, and the persecuted prophets. The Covenant had been broken. Elijah denounced the unfaithfulness of Queen Jezebel and Kings Ahab and Ahaziah. They had introduced idolatry in the form of the false god Baal, who favored the powerful and allowed injustices.

Elijah's faithfulness to the Covenant and his solidarity with the poor led him to speak against kings and queens, to fight false prophets, and to intervene in national affairs. The powerful rulers wanted to kill him and silence his voice. After his dramatic departure (2 Kings 2.11), the people never forgot him; they always expected his return.

- If you saw today's world through the prism that Elijah used to view the world of his time, what would you see? Whom would you support with your words and actions? Whom would you challenge?
- Through your Baptism, you are called to be a prophet. As a prophet, how can you promote justice in society?

2
K
I
N
G
S

whirlwind into heaven. 12 E•li′sha kept watching and crying out, "Father, father! The chariots of Israel and its horsemen!" But when he could no longer see him, he grasped his own clothes and tore them in two pieces.

Elisha Succeeds Elijah

13 He picked up the mantle of E•li′jah that had fallen from him, and went back and stood on the bank of the Jordan. 14 He took the mantle of E•li′jah that had fallen from him, and struck the water, saying, "Where is the LORD, the God of E•li′jah?" When he had struck the water, the water was parted to the one side and to the other, and E•li′sha went over.

15 When the company of prophets*d* who were at Jericho saw him at a distance, they declared, "The spirit of E•li′jah rests on E•li′sha." They came to meet him and bowed to the ground before him. 16 They said to him, "See now, we have fifty strong men among your servants; please let them go and seek your master; it may be that the spirit of the LORD has caught him up and thrown him down on some mountain or into some valley." He responded, "No, do not send them." 17 But when they urged him until he was ashamed, he said, "Send them." So they sent fifty men who searched for three days but did not find him. 18 When they came back to him (he had remained at Jericho), he said to them, "Did I not say to you, Do not go?"

Elisha Performs Miracles

19 Now the people of the city said to E•li′sha, "The location of this city is good, as my lord sees; but the water is bad, and the land is unfruitful." 20 He said, "Bring me a new bowl, and put salt in it." So they brought it to him. 21 Then he went to the spring of water and threw the salt into it, and said, "Thus says the LORD, I have made this water wholesome; from now on neither death nor miscarriage shall come from it." 22 So the water has been wholesome to this day, according to the word that E•li′sha spoke.

23 He went up from there to Beth′el; and while he was going up on the way, some small boys came out of the city and jeered at him, saying, "Go away, baldhead! Go away, baldhead!" 24 When he turned around and saw them, he cursed them in the name of the LORD. Then two she-bears came out of the woods and mauled forty-two of the boys. 25 From there he went on to Mount Car′mel, and then returned to Sa•mār′i•a.

Jehoram Reigns over Israel

3 In the eighteenth year of King Je•hosh′a•phat of Judah, Je•hō′ram son of Ā′hab became king over Israel in Sa•mār′i•a; he reigned twelve years.

2 He did what was evil in the sight of the LORD, though not like his father and mother, for he removed the pillar of Bā′al that his father had made. 3 Nevertheless he clung to the sin of Jer•o•bō′am son of Nē′bat, which he caused Israel to commit; he did not depart from it.

War with Moab

4 Now King Mē′sha of Mō′ab was a sheep breeder, who used to deliver to the king of Israel one hundred thousand lambs, and the wool of one hundred thousand rams. 5 But when Ā′hab died, the king of Mō′ab rebelled against the king of Israel. 6 So King Je•hō′ram marched out of Sa•mār′i•a at that time and mustered all Israel. 7 As he went he sent word to King Je•hosh′a•phat of Judah, "The king of Mō′ab has rebelled against me; will you go with me to battle against Mō′ab?" He answered, "I will; I am with you, my people are your people, my horses are your horses." 8 Then he asked, "By which way shall we march?" Je•hō′ram answered, "By the way of the wilderness of Ē′dom."

9 So the king of Israel, the king of Judah, and the king of Ē′dom set out; and when they had made a roundabout march of seven days, there was no water for the army or for the animals that were with them. 10 Then the king of Israel said, "Alas! The LORD has summoned us, three kings, only to be handed over to Mō′ab." 11 But Je•hosh′a•phat said, "Is there no prophet of the LORD here, through whom we may inquire of the LORD?" Then one of the servants of the king of Israel answered, "E•li′sha son of Shā′phat, who used to pour water on the hands of E•li′jah, is here." 12 Je•hosh′a•phat said, "The word of the LORD is with him." So the king of Israel and Je•hosh′a•phat and the king of Ē′dom went down to him.

13 E•li′sha said to the king of Israel, "What have I to do with you? Go to your father's prophets or to your mother's." But the king of Israel said to him, "No; it is the LORD who has summoned us, three kings, only to be handed over to Mō′ab." 14 E•li′sha said, "As the LORD of hosts lives, whom I serve, were it not that I have regard for King Je•hosh′a•phat of Judah, I would give you neither a look nor a glance. 15 But get me a musician." And then, while the musician was playing, the power of the LORD came on him. 16 And he said, "Thus says the LORD, 'I will make this wadi full of pools.' 17 For thus says the LORD, 'You shall see neither wind nor rain, but the wadi shall be filled with water, so that you shall drink, you, your cattle, and your animals.' 18 This is only a trifle in the sight of the LORD, for he will also hand Mō′ab over to you. 19 You shall conquer every fortified city and every choice city; every good tree

---

d Heb *sons of the prophets*

you shall fell, all springs of water you shall stop up, and every good piece of land you shall ruin with stones." 20 The next day, about the time of the morning offering, suddenly water began to flow from the direction of Ē′dom, until the country was filled with water.

21 When all the Mō′ab•ites heard that the kings had come up to fight against them, all who were able to put on armor, from the youngest to the oldest, were called out and were drawn up at the frontier. 22 When they rose early in the morning, and the sun shone upon the water, the Mō′ab•ites saw the water opposite them as red as blood. 23 They said, "This is blood; the kings must have fought together, and killed one another. Now then, Mō′ab, to the spoil!" 24 But when they came to the camp of Israel, the Israelites rose up and attacked the Mō′ab•ites, who fled before them; as they entered Mō′ab they continued the attack.*e* 25 The cities they overturned, and on every good piece of land everyone threw a stone, until it was covered; every spring of water they stopped up, and every good tree they felled. Only at Kir-har′eseth did the stone walls remain, until the slingers surrounded and attacked it. 26 When the king of Mō′ab saw that the battle was going against him, he took with him seven hundred swordsmen to break through, opposite the king of Ē′dom; but they could not. 27 Then he took his firstborn son who was to succeed him, and offered him as a burnt offering on the wall. And great wrath came upon Israel, so they withdrew from him and returned to their own land.

Elisha and the Widow's Oil
(Cp 1 Kings 17.14–16)

4 Now the wife of a member of the company of prophets*f* cried to E•lī′sha, "Your servant my husband is dead; and you know that your servant feared the LORD, but a creditor has come to take my two children as slaves." 2 E•lī′sha said to her, "What shall I do for you? Tell me, what do you have in the house?" She answered, "Your servant has nothing in the house, except a jar of oil." 3 He said, "Go outside, borrow vessels from all your neighbors, empty vessels and not just a few. 4 Then go in, and shut the door behind you and your children, and start pouring into all these vessels; when each is full, set it aside." 5 So she left him and shut the door behind her and her children; they kept bringing vessels to her, and she kept pouring. 6 When the vessels were full, she said to her son, "Bring me another vessel." But he said to her, "There are no more." Then the oil stopped flowing. 7 She came and told the man of God, and he said, "Go sell the oil and pay your debts, and you and your children can live on the rest."

Elisha Raises the Shunammite's Son
(Cp 1 Kings 17.17–24)

8 One day E•lī′sha was passing through Shū′nem, where a wealthy woman lived, who urged him to have a meal. So whenever he passed that way, he would stop there for a meal. 9 She said to her husband, "Look, I am sure that this man who regularly passes our way is a holy man of God. 10 Let us make a small roof chamber with walls, and put there for him a bed, a table, a chair, and a lamp, so that he can stay there whenever he comes to us."

11 One day when he came there, he went up to the chamber and lay down there. 12 He said to his servant Ge•hā′zī, "Call the Shū′nam•mite woman." When he had called her, she stood before him. 13 He said to him, "Say to her, Since you have taken all this trouble for us, what may be done for you? Would you have a word spoken on your behalf to the king or to the commander of the army?" She answered, "I live among my own people." 14 He said, "What then may be done for her?" Ge•hā′zī answered, "Well, she has no son, and her husband is old." 15 He said, "Call her." When he had called her, she stood at the door. 16 He said, "At this season, in due time, you shall embrace a son." She replied, "No, my lord, O man of God; do not deceive your servant."

17 The woman conceived and bore a son at that season, in due time, as E•lī′sha had declared to her.

18 When the child was older, he went out one day to his father among the reapers. 19 He complained to his father, "Oh, my head, my head!" The father said to his servant, "Carry him to his mother." 20 He carried him and brought him to his

---

e Compare Gk Syr: Meaning of Heb uncertain　*f* Heb *the sons of the prophets*

4.1–7

mother; the child sat on her lap until noon, and he died. 21 She went up and laid him on the bed of the man of God, closed the door on him, and left. 22 Then she called to her husband, and said, "Send me one of the servants and one of the donkeys, so that I may quickly go to the man of God and come back again." 23 He said, "Why go to him today? It is neither new moon nor sabbath." She said, "It will be all right." 24 Then she saddled the donkey and said to her servant, "Urge the animal on; do not hold back for me unless I tell you." 25 So she set out, and came to the man of God at Mount Car′mel.

When the man of God saw her coming, he said to Ge•hā′zī his servant, "Look, there is the Shū′-nam•mīte woman; 26 run at once to meet her, and say to her, Are you all right? Is your husband all right? Is the child all right?" She answered, "It is all right." 27 When she came to the man of God at the mountain, she caught hold of his feet. Ge•hā′zī approached to push her away. But the man of God said, "Let her alone, for she is in bitter distress; the LORD has hidden it from me and has not told me." 28 Then she said, "Did I ask my lord for a son? Did I not say, Do not mislead me?" 29 He said to Ge′-hā′zī, "Gird up your loins, and take my staff in your hand, and go. If you meet anyone, give no greeting, and if anyone greets you, do not answer; and lay my staff on the face of the child." 30 Then the mother of the child said, "As the LORD lives, and as you yourself live, I will not leave without you." So he rose up and followed her. 31 Ge•hā′zī went on ahead and laid the staff on the face of the child, but there was no sound or sign of life. He came back to meet him and told him, "The child has not awakened."

32 When E•lī′sha came into the house, he saw the child lying dead on his bed. 33 So he went in and closed the door on the two of them, and prayed to the LORD. 34 Then he got up on the bed*g* and lay upon the child, putting his mouth upon his mouth, his eyes upon his eyes, and his hands upon his hands; and while he lay bent over him, the flesh of the child became warm. 35 He got down, walked once to and fro in the room, then got up again and bent over him; the child sneezed seven times, and the child opened his eyes. 36 E•lī′sha*h* summoned Ge•hā′zī and said, "Call the Shū′nam•mīte woman." So he called her. When she came to him, he said, "Take your son." 37 She came and fell at his feet, bowing to the ground; then she took her son and left.

Elisha Purifies the Pot of Stew

38 When E•lī′sha returned to Gil′gal, there was a famine in the land. As the company of prophets was*i* sitting before him, he said to his servant, "Put the large pot on, and make some stew for the company of prophets."*j* 39 One of them went out into the field to gather herbs; he found a wild vine and

gathered from it a lapful of wild gourds, and came and cut them up into the pot of stew, not knowing what they were. 40 They served some for the men to eat. But while they were eating the stew, they cried out, "O man of God, there is death in the pot!" They could not eat it. 41 He said, "Then bring some flour." He threw it into the pot, and said, "Serve the people and let them eat." And there was nothing harmful in the pot.

Elisha Feeds One Hundred Men
(Cp Mt 14.13–21; 15.32–39)

42 A man came from Bā′al-shal′i•shah, bringing food from the first fruits to the man of God: twenty loaves of barley and fresh ears of grain in his sack. E•lī′sha said, "Give it to the people and let them eat." 43 But his servant said, "How can I set this before a hundred people?" So he repeated, "Give it to the people and let them eat, for thus says the LORD, 'They shall eat and have some left.'" 44 He set it before them, they ate, and had some left, according to the word of the LORD.

The Healing of Naaman

5 Nā′a•man, commander of the army of the king of Ar′am, was a great man and in high favor with his master, because by him the LORD had

---

g Heb lacks *on the bed* *h* Heb *he* *i* Heb *sons of the prophets were* *j* Heb *sons of the prophets* given victory to Ar'am. The man, though a mighty warrior, suffered from leprosy.[k] 2 Now the Ar·a·mē'ans on one of their raids had taken a young girl captive from the land of Israel, and she served Nā'a·man's wife. 3 She said to her mistress, "If only my lord were with the prophet who is in Sa·mār'i·a! He would cure him of his leprosy."[k] 4 So Nā'a·man[l] went in and told his lord just what the girl from the land of Israel had said. 5 And the king of Ar'am said, "Go then, and I will send along a letter to the king of Israel."

He went, taking with him ten talents of silver, six thousand shekels of gold, and ten sets of garments. 6 He brought the letter to the king of Israel, which read, "When this letter reaches you, know that I have sent to you my servant Nā'a·man, that you may cure him of his leprosy."[k] 7 When the king of Israel read the letter, he tore his clothes and said, "Am I God, to give death or life, that this man sends word to me to cure a man of his leprosy?[k] Just look and see how he is trying to pick a quarrel with me."

8 But when E·li'sha the man of God heard that the king of Israel had torn his clothes, he sent a message to the king, "Why have you torn your clothes? Let him come to me, that he may learn that there is a prophet in Israel." 9 So Nā'a·man came with his horses and chariots, and halted at the entrance of E·li'sha's house. 10 E·li'sha sent a messenger to him, saying, "Go, wash in the Jordan seven times, and your flesh shall be restored and you shall be clean." 11 But Nā'a·man became angry and went away, saying, "I thought that for me he would surely come out, and stand and call on the name of the LORD his God, and would wave his hand over the spot, and cure the leprosy![k] 12 Are not A·bā'na[m] and Phar'par, the rivers of Damascus, better than all the waters of Israel? Could I not wash in them, and be clean?" He turned and went away in a rage. 13 But his servants approached and said to him, "Father, if

the prophet had commanded you to do something difficult, would you not have done it? How much more, when all he said to you was, 'Wash, and be clean'?" 14 So he went down and immersed himself seven times in the Jordan, according to the word of the man of God; his flesh was restored like the flesh of a young boy, and he was clean.

15 Then he returned to the man of God, he and all his company; he came and stood before him and said, "Now I know that there is no God in all the earth except in Israel; please accept a present from your servant." 16 But he said, "As the LORD lives, whom I serve, I will accept nothing!" He urged him to accept, but he refused. 17 Then Nā'a·man said, "If not, please let two mule-loads of earth be given to your servant; for your servant will no longer offer burnt offering or sacrifice to any god except the LORD. 18 But may the LORD pardon your servant on one count: when my master goes into the house of Rim'mon to worship there, leaning on my arm, and I bow down in the house of Rim'mon, when I do bow down in the house of Rim'mon, may the LORD pardon your servant on this one count." 19 He said to him, "Go in peace."

Gehazi's Greed

But when Nā'a·man had gone from him a short distance, 20 Ge·hā'zī, the servant of E·li'sha the man of God, thought, "My master has let that Ar·a·mē'an Nā'a·man off too lightly by not accepting from him what he offered. As the LORD lives, I will run after him and get something out of him." 21 So Ge·hā'zī went after Nā'a·man. When Nā'a·man saw someone running after him, he jumped down from the chariot to meet him and said, "Is everything all right?" 22 He replied, "Yes, but my master has sent

---

[k] A term for several skin diseases; precise meaning uncertain   [l] Heb he   [m] Another reading is Amana

---

Feed Your Soul

LIVE IT!

Elisha's miracle in 2 Kings 4.44 fed the body, but it is just as important to feed the appetite of the soul, such as the need for hope, for affirmation, and for being loved. It's easy to satisfy your physical appetite, but when it comes to feeding your soul, where do you go?

God gives us plenty of opportunities to feed our soul. We just need to take advantage of them. Go to church. Participate in your youth program. Start a Bible study. Go on a retreat or to a youth conference. Talk to friends about your faith and theirs. Take a walk and pray. You'll find that feeding your faith can be fun.

▶ 2 Kings 4.42–44

me to say, 'Two members of a company of prophets[n] have just come to me from the hill country of Ē'phra·im; please give them a talent of silver and two changes of clothing.' " [23] Nā'a·man said, "Please accept two talents." He urged him, and tied up two talents of silver in two bags, with two changes of clothing, and gave them to two of his servants, who carried them in front of Ge·hā'zī.[o] [24] When he came to the citadel, he took the bags[p] from them, and stored them inside; he dismissed the men, and they left.

[25] He went in and stood before his master; and E·lī'sha said to him, "Where have you been, Ge·hā'zī?" He answered, "Your servant has not gone anywhere at all." [26] But he said to him, "Did I not go with you in spirit when someone left his chariot to meet you? Is this a time to accept money and to accept clothing, olive orchards and vineyards, sheep and oxen, and male and female slaves? [27] Therefore the leprosy[q] of Nā'a·man shall cling to you, and to your descendants forever." So he left his presence leprous,[q] as white as snow.

The Miracle of the Ax Head

6 Now the company of prophets[n] said to E·lī'sha, "As you see, the place where we live under your charge is too small for us. [2] Let us go to the Jordan, and let us collect logs there, one for each of us, and build a place there for us to live." He answered, "Do so." [3] Then one of them said, "Please come with your servants." And he answered, "I will." [4] So he went with them. When they came to the Jordan, they cut down trees. [5] But as one was felling a log, his ax head fell into the water; he cried out, "Alas, master! It was borrowed." [6] Then the man of God said, "Where did it fall?" When he showed him the place, he cut off a stick, and threw it in there, and made the iron float. [7] He said, "Pick it up." So he reached out his hand and took it.

The Aramean Attack Is Thwarted

[8] Once when the king of Ar'am was at war with Israel, he took counsel with his officers. He said, "At such and such a place shall be my camp." [9] But the man of God sent word to the king of Israel, "Take care not to pass this place, because the Ar·a·mē'ans are going down there." [10] The king of Israel sent word to the place of which the man of God spoke. More than once or twice he warned such a place[r] so that it was on the alert.

[11] The mind of the king of Ar'am was greatly perturbed because of this; he called his officers and said to them, "Now tell me who among us sides with the king of Israel?" [12] Then one of his officers said, "No one, my lord king. It is E·lī'sha, the prophet in Israel, who tells the king of Israel the words that you speak in your bedchamber." [13] He

said, "Go and find where he is; I will send and seize him." He was told, "He is in Dō'than." [14] So he sent horses and chariots there and a great army; they came by night, and surrounded the city.

[15] When an attendant of the man of God rose early in the morning and went out, an army with horses and chariots was all around the city. His servant said, "Alas, master! What shall we do?" [16] He replied, "Do not be afraid, for there are more with us than there are with them." [17] Then E·lī'sha prayed: "O LORD, please open his eyes that he may see." So the LORD opened the eyes of the servant, and he saw; the mountain was full of horses and chariots of fire all around E·lī'sha. [18] When the Ar·a·mē'ans[s] came down against him, E·lī'sha prayed to the LORD, and said, "Strike this people, please, with blindness." So he struck them with blindness as E·lī'sha had asked. [19] E·lī'sha said to them, "This is not the way, and this is not the city; follow me, and I will bring you to the man whom you seek." And he led them to Sa·mār'i·a.

[20] As soon as they entered Sa·mār'i·a, E·lī'sha said, "O LORD, open the eyes of these men so that they may see." The LORD opened their eyes, and they saw that they were inside Sa·mār'i·a. [21] When the king of Israel saw them he said to E·lī'sha, "Father, shall I kill them? Shall I kill them?" [22] He answered, "No! Did you capture with your sword and your bow those whom you want to kill? Set food and water before them so that they may eat and drink; and let them go to their master." [23] So he prepared for them a great feast; after they ate and drank, he sent them on their way, and they went to their master. And the Ar·a·mē'ans no longer came raiding into the land of Israel.

Ben-hadad's Siege of Samaria

[24] Some time later King Ben-hā'dad of Ar'am mustered his entire army; he marched against Sa·mār'i·a and laid siege to it. [25] As the siege continued, famine in Sa·mār'i·a became so great that a donkey's head was sold for eighty shekels of silver, and one-fourth of a kab of dove's dung for five shekels of silver. [26] Now as the king of Israel was walking on the city wall, a woman cried out to him, "Help, my lord king!" [27] He said, "No! Let the LORD help you. How can I help you? From the threshing floor or from the wine press?" [28] But then the king asked her, "What is your complaint?" She answered, "This woman said to me, 'Give up your son; we will eat him today, and we will eat my son tomorrow.' [29] So we cooked my son and ate him. The next day I said to her, 'Give up your son and we will eat him.'

---

[n] Heb *sons of the prophets*   [o] Heb *him*   [p] Heb lacks *the bags*
[q] A term for several skin diseases; precise meaning uncertain   [r] Heb *warned it*   [s] Heb *they*

But she has hidden her son." 30 When the king heard the words of the woman he tore his clothes—now since he was walking on the city wall, the people could see that he had sackcloth on his body underneath— 31 and he said, "So may God do to me, and more, if the head of E•li′sha son of Shā′-phat stays on his shoulders today." 32 So he dispatched a man from his presence.

Now E•li′sha was sitting in his house, and the elders were sitting with him. Before the messenger arrived, E•li′sha said to the elders, "Are you aware that this murderer has sent someone to take off my head? When the messenger comes, see that you shut the door and hold it closed against him. Is not the sound of his master′s feet behind him?" 33 While he was still speaking with them, the king[t] came down to him and said, "This trouble is from the LORD! Why should I hope in the LORD any longer?" 1 But E•li′sha said, "Hear the word of the LORD: thus says the LORD, Tomorrow about this time a measure of choice meal shall be sold for a shekel, and two measures of barley for a shekel, at the gate of Sa•mār′i•a." 2 Then the captain on whose hand the king leaned said to the man of God, "Even if the LORD were to make windows in the sky, could such a thing happen?" But he said, "You shall see it with your own eyes, but you shall not eat from it."

The Arameans Flee

3 Now there were four leprous[u] men outside the city gate, who said to one another, "Why should we sit here until we die? 4 If we say, 'Let us enter the city,' the famine is in the city, and we shall die there; but if we sit here, we shall also die. Therefore, let us desert to the Ar•a•mē′an camp; if they spare our lives, we shall live; and if they kill us, we shall but die." 5 So they arose at twilight to go to the Ar•a•mē′an camp; but when they came to the edge of the Ar•a•mē′an camp, there was no one there at all. 6 For the Lord had caused the Ar•a•mē′an army to hear the sound of chariots, and of horses, the sound of a great army, so that they said to one another, "The king of Israel has hired the kings of the Hit′tītes and the kings of Egypt to fight against us." 7 So they fled away in the twilight and abandoned their tents, their horses, and their donkeys leaving the camp just as it was, and fled for their lives. 8 When these leprous[u] men had come to the edge of the camp, they went into a tent, ate and drank, carried off silver, gold, and clothing, and went and hid them. Then they came back, entered another tent, carried off things from it, and went and hid them. 9 Then they said to one another, "What we are doing is wrong. This is a day of good news; if we are silent and wait until the morning light, we will be found guilty; therefore let us go and tell the king′s

household." 10 So they came and called to the gatekeepers of the city, and told them, "We went to the Ar•a•mē′an camp, but there was no one to be seen or heard there, nothing but the horses tied, the donkeys tied, and the tents as they were." 11 Then the gatekeepers called out and proclaimed it to the king′s household. 12 The king got up in the night, and said to his servants, "I will tell you what the Ar•a•mē′ans have prepared against us. They know that we are starving; so they have left the camp to hide themselves in the open country, thinking, 'When they come out of the city, we shall take them alive and get into the city.' " 13 One of his servants said, "Let some men take five of the remaining horses, since those left here will suffer the fate of the whole multitude of Israel that have perished already;[v] let us send and find out." 14 So they took two mounted men, and the king sent them after the Ar•a•mē′an army, saying, "Go and find out." 15 So they went after them as far as the Jordan; the whole way was littered with garments and equipment that the Ar•a•mē′ans had thrown away in their haste. So the messengers returned, and told the king.

16 Then the people went out, and plundered the camp of the Ar•a•mē′ans. So a measure of choice meal was sold for a shekel, and two measures of barley for a shekel, according to the word of the LORD. 17 Now the king had appointed the captain on whose hand he leaned to have charge of the gate; the people trampled him to death in the gate, just as the man of God had said when the king came down to him. 18 For when the man of God had said to the king, "Two measures of barley shall be sold for a shekel, and a measure of choice meal for a shekel, about this time tomorrow in the gate of Sa•mār′i•a," 19 the captain had answered the man of God, "Even if the LORD were to make windows in the sky, could such a thing happen?" And he had answered, "You shall see it with your own eyes, but you shall not eat from it." 20 It did indeed happen to him; the people trampled him to death in the gate.

The Shunammite Woman′s Land Restored

Now E•li′sha had said to the woman whose son he had restored to life, "Get up and go with your household, and settle wherever you can; for the LORD has called for a famine, and it will come on the land for seven years." 2 So the woman got up and did according to the word of the man of God; she went with her household and settled in the land of the Phi•lis′tines seven years. 3 At the end of the seven years, when the woman returned from the land of the Phi•lis′tines, she set out to appeal to

t See 7.2: Heb messenger   u A term for several skin diseases; precise meaning uncertain   v Compare Gk Syr Vg: Meaning of Heb uncertain

2
K
I
N
G
S

the king for her house and her land. 4 Now the king was talking with Ge•hā′zī the servant of the man of God, saying, "Tell me all the great things that E•lī′sha has done." 5 While he was telling the king how E•lī′sha had restored a dead person to life, the woman whose son he had restored to life appealed to the king for her house and her land. Ge•hā′zī said, "My lord king, here is the woman, and here is her son whom E•lī′sha restored to life." 6 When the king questioned the woman, she told him. So the king appointed an official for her, saying, "Restore all that was hers, together with all the revenue of the fields from the day that she left the land until now."

Death of Ben-hadad

7 E•lī′sha went to Damascus while King Ben-hā′dad of Ar′am was ill. When it was told him, "The man of God has come here," 8 the king said to Haz′a•el, "Take a present with you and go to meet the man of God. Inquire of the LORD through him, whether I shall recover from this illness." 9 So Haz′a•el went to meet him, taking a present with him, all kinds of goods of Damascus, forty camel loads. When he entered and stood before him, he said, "Your son King Ben-hā′dad of Ar′am has sent me to you, saying, 'Shall I recover from this illness?' " 10 E•lī′sha said to him, "Go, say to him, 'You shall certainly recover'; but the LORD has shown me that he shall certainly die." 11 He fixed his gaze and stared at him, until he was ashamed. Then the man of God wept. 12 Haz′a•el asked, "Why does my lord weep?" He answered, "Because I know the evil that you will do to the people of Israel; you will set their fortresses on fire, you will kill their young men with the sword, dash in pieces their little ones, and rip up their pregnant women." 13 Haz′a•el said, "What is your servant, who is a mere dog, that he should do this great thing?" E•lī′sha answered, "The LORD has shown me that you are to be king over Ar′am." 14 Then he left E•lī′sha, and went to his master Ben-hā′dad,ʷ who said to him, "What did E•lī′sha say to you?" And he answered, "He told me that you would certainly recover." 15 But the next day he took the bed-cover and dipped it in water and spread it over the king's face, until he died. And Haz′a•el succeeded him.

Jehoram Reigns over Judah
(2 Chr 21.1–20)

16 In the fifth year of King Jō′ram son of Ā′hab of Israel,ˣ Je•hō′ram son of King Je•hosh′a•phat of Judah began to reign. 17 He was thirty-two years old when he became king, and he reigned eight years in Jerusalem. 18 He walked in the way of the kings of Israel, as the house of Ā′hab had done, for the daughter of Ā′hab was his wife. He did what was

Grading Kings

As you read the remaining chapters of Second Kings, notice that the author gives a kind of report card for each of the rulers of Israel and Judah. Jehoram, for example, receives an F: "He did what was evil in the sight of the LORD" (8.18). Josiah receives an A: "He did what was right in the sight of the LORD" (22.2). The author, who wrote after the fall of both kingdoms, provides a theological reason for Israel's and Judah's failure. Because most of the rulers continually violated God's law, they were largely responsible for the fall of the kingdoms.

evil in the sight of the LORD. 19 Yet the LORD would not destroy Judah, for the sake of his servant David, since he had promised to give a lamp to him and to his descendants forever.

20 In his days Ē′dom revolted against the rule of Judah, and set up a king of their own. 21 Then Jō′ram crossed over to Zā′ir with all his chariots. He set out by night and attacked the Ē′dom•ites and their chariot commanders who had surrounded him;ʸ but his army fled home. 22 So Ē′dom has been in revolt against the rule of Judah to this day. Lib′nah also revolted at the same time. 23 Now the rest of the acts of Jō′ram, and all that he did, are they not written in the Book of the Annals of the Kings of Judah? 24 So Jō′ram slept with his ancestors, and was buried with them in the city of David; his son A•ha•zī′ah succeeded him.

Ahaziah Reigns over Judah
(2 Chr 22.1–6)

25 In the twelfth year of King Jō′ram son of Ā′hab of Israel, A•ha•zī′ah son of King Je•hō′ram of Judah began to reign. 26 A•ha•zī′ah was twenty-two years old when he began to reign; he reigned one year in Jerusalem. His mother's name was Ath-a•lī′ah, a granddaughter of King Om′rī of Israel. 27 He also walked in the way of the house of Ā′hab, doing what was evil in the sight of the LORD, as the house of Ā′hab had done, for he was son-in-law to the house of Ā′hab.

ʷ Heb lacks *Ben-hadad* ˣ Gk Syr: Heb adds *Jehoshaphat being king of Judah,* ʸ Meaning of Heb uncertain

28 He went with Jō'ram son of Ā'hab to wage war against King Haz'a•el of Ar'am at Rā'moth-gil'ē•ad, where the Ar•a•mē'ans wounded Jō'ram. 29 King Jō'ram returned to be healed in Jez'rē•el of the wounds that the Ar•a•mē'ans had inflicted on him at Rā'mah, when he fought against King Haz'a•el of Ar'am. King A•ha•zī'ah son of Je•hō'ram of Judah went down to see Jō'ram son of Ā'hab in Jez'rē•el, because he was wounded.

Anointing of Jehu

9 Then the prophet E•lī'sha called a member of the company of prophets*z* and said to him, "Gird up your loins; take this flask of oil in your hand, and go to Rā'moth-gil'ē•ad. 2 When you arrive, look there for Jē'hū son of Je•hosh'a•phat, son of Nim'shī; go in and get him to leave his companions, and take him into an inner chamber. 3 Then take the flask of oil, pour it on his head, and say, 'Thus says the LORD: I anoint you king over Israel.' Then open the door and flee; do not linger."

4 So the young man, the young prophet, went to Rā'moth-gil'ē•ad. 5 He arrived while the commanders of the army were in council, and he announced, "I have a message for you, commander." "For which one of us?" asked Jē'hū. "For you, commander." 6 So Jē'hū*a* got up and went inside; the young man poured the oil on his head, saying to him, "Thus says the LORD the God of Israel: I anoint you king over the people of the LORD, over Israel. 7 You shall strike down the house of your master Ā'hab, so that I may avenge on Jez'e•bel the blood of my servants the prophets, and the blood of all the servants of the LORD. 8 For the whole house of Ā'hab shall perish; I will cut off from Ā'hab every male, bond or free, in Israel. 9 I will make the house of Ā'hab like the house of Jer•o•bō'am son of Nē'bat, and like the house of Bā'a•sha son of A•hī'jah. 10 The dogs shall eat Jez'e•bel in the territory of Jez'rē•el, and no one shall bury her." Then he opened the door and fled.

11 When Jē'hū came back to his master's officers, they said to him, "Is everything all right? Why did that madman come to you?" He answered them, "You know the sort and how they babble." 12 They said, "Liar! Come on, tell us!" So he said, "This is just what he said to me: 'Thus says the LORD, I anoint you king over Israel.' " 13 Then hurriedly they all took their cloaks and spread them for him on the bare*b* steps; and they blew the trumpet, and proclaimed, "Jē'hū is king."

Joram of Israel Killed

14 Thus Jē'hū son of Je•hosh'a•phat son of Nim'shī conspired against Jō'ram. Jō'ram with all Israel had been on guard at Rā'moth-gil'ē•ad against King Haz'a•el of Ar'am; 15 but King Jō'ram had returned to be healed in Jez'rē•el of the wounds that the Ar•a•mē'ans had inflicted on him, when he fought against King Haz'a•el of Ar'am. So Jē'hū said, "If this is your wish, then let no one slip out of the city to go and tell the news in Jez'rē•el." 16 Then Jē'hū mounted his chariot and went to Jez'rē•el, where Jō'ram was lying ill. King A•ha•zī'ah of Judah had come down to visit Jō'ram.

17 In Jez'rē•el, the sentinel standing on the tower spied the company of Jē'hū arriving, and said, "I see a company." Jō'ram said, "Take a horseman; send him to meet them, and let him say, 'Is it peace?' " 18 So the horseman went to meet him; he said, "Thus says the king, 'Is it peace?' " Jē'hū responded, "What have you to do with peace? Fall in behind me." The sentinel reported, saying, "The messenger reached them, but he is not coming back." 19 Then he sent out a second horseman, who came to them and said, "Thus says the king, 'Is it peace?' " Jē'hū answered, "What have you to do with peace? Fall in behind me." 20 Again the sentinel reported, "He reached them, but he is not coming back. It looks like the driving of Jē'hū son of Nim'shī; for he drives like a maniac."

21 Jō'ram said, "Get ready." And they got his chariot ready. Then King Jō'ram of Israel and King A•ha•zī'ah of Judah set out, each in his chariot, and went to meet Jē'hū; they met him at the property of Nā'both the Jez'rē•el•īte. 22 When Jō'ram saw Jē'hū, he said, "Is it peace, Jē'hū?" He answered, "What peace can there be, so long as the many whoredoms and sorceries of your mother Jez'e•bel continue?" 23 Then Jō'ram reined about and fled, saying to A•ha•zī'ah, "Treason, A•ha•zī'ah!" 24 Jē'hū drew his bow with all his strength, and shot Jō'ram between the shoulders, so that the arrow pierced his heart; and he sank in his chariot. 25 Jē'hū said to his aide Bid'kar, "Lift him out, and throw him on the plot of ground belonging to Nā'both the Jez'rē•el•īte; for remember, when you and I rode side by side behind his father Ā'hab how the LORD uttered this oracle against him: 26 'For the blood of Nā'both and for the blood of his children that I saw yesterday, says the LORD, I swear I will repay you on this very plot of ground.' Now therefore lift him out and throw him on the plot of ground, in accordance with the word of the LORD."

Ahaziah of Judah Killed
(2 Chr 22.7–9)

27 When King A•ha•zī'ah of Judah saw this, he fled in the direction of Beth-hag'gan. Jē'hū pursued him, saying, "Shoot him also!" And they shot him*c*

---

z Heb *sons of the prophets*   *a* Heb *he*   *b* Meaning of Heb uncertain   *c* Syr Vg Compare Gk: Heb lacks *and they shot him* in the chariot at the ascent to Gur, which is by Ib′le·am. Then he fled to Me·gid′dō, and died there. 28 His officers carried him in a chariot to Jerusalem, and buried him in his tomb with his ancestors in the city of David.

29 In the eleventh year of Jō′ram son of Ā′hab, A·ha·zī′ah began to reign over Judah.

Jezebel's Violent Death

30 When Jē′hū came to Jez′re·el, Jez′e·bel heard of it; she painted her eyes, and adorned her head, and looked out of the window. 31 As Jē′hū entered the gate, she said, "Is it peace, Zim′rī, murderer of your master?" 32 He looked up to the window and said, "Who is on my side? Who?" Two or three eunuchs looked out at him. 33 He said, "Throw her down." So they threw her down; some of her blood spattered on the wall and on the horses, which trampled on her. 34 Then he went in and ate and drank; he said, "See to that cursed woman and bury her; for she is a king's daughter." 35 But when they went to bury her, they found no more of her than the skull and the feet and the palms of her hands. 36 When they came back and told him, he said, "This is the word of the LORD, which he spoke by his servant E·lī′jah the Tish′bīte, 'In the territory of Jez′re·el the dogs shall eat the flesh of Jez′e·bel; 37 the corpse of Jez′e·bel shall be like dung on the field in the territory of Jez′re·el, so that no one can say, This is Jez′e·bel.' "

Massacre of Ahab's Descendants

10 Now Ā′hab had seventy sons in Sa·mār′i·a. So Jē′hū wrote letters and sent them to Sa·mār′i·a, to the rulers of Jez′re·el,d to the elders, and to the guardians of the sons ofe Ā′hab, saying, 2 "Since your master's sons are with you and you have at your disposal chariots and horses, a fortified city, and weapons, 3 select the son of your master who is the best qualified, set him on his father's throne, and fight for your master's house." 4 But they were utterly terrified and said, "Look, two kings could not withstand him; how then can we stand?" 5 So the steward of the palace, and the governor of the city, along with the elders and the guardians, sent word to Jē′hū: "We are your servants; we will do anything you say. We will not make anyone king; do whatever you think right." 6 Then he wrote them a second letter, saying, "If you are on my side, and if you are ready to obey me, take the heads of your master's sons and come to me at Jez′re·el tomorrow at this time." Now the king's sons, seventy persons, were with the leaders of the city, who were charged with their upbringing. 7 When the letter reached them, they took the king's sons and killed them, seventy persons; they put their heads in baskets and sent them to him at Jez′re·el. 8 When the messenger came and told him, "They have brought the heads of the king's sons," he said, "Lay them in two heaps at the entrance of the gate until the morning." 9 Then in the morning when he went out, he stood and said to all the people, "You are innocent. It was I who conspired against my master and killed him; but who struck down all these? 10 Know then that there shall fall to the earth nothing of the word of the LORD, which the LORD spoke concerning the house of Ā′hab; for the LORD has done what he said through his servant E·lī′jah." 11 So Jē′hū killed all who were left of the house of Ā′hab in Jez′re·el, all his leaders, close friends, and priests, until he left him no survivor.

12 Then he set out and went to Sa·mār′i·a. On the way, when he was at Beth-ek′ed of the Shepherds, 13 Jē′hū met relatives of King A·ha·zī′ah of Judah and said, "Who are you?" They answered, "We are kin of A·ha·zī′ah; we have come down to visit the royal princes and the sons of the queen mother." 14 He said, "Take them alive." They took them alive, and slaughtered them at the pit of Beth-ek′ed, forty-two in all; he spared none of them.

15 When he left there, he met Je·hon′a·dab son of Rē′chab coming to meet him; he greeted him, and said to him, "Is your heart as true to mine as mine is to yours?"f Je·hon′a·dab answered, "It is." Jē′hū said,g "If it is, give me your hand." So he gave him his hand. Jē′hū took him up with him into the chariot. 16 He said, "Come with me, and see my zeal for the LORD." So he h had him ride in his chariot. 17 When he came to Sa·mār′i·a, he killed all who were left to Ā′hab in Sa·mār′i·a, until he had wiped them out, according to the word of the LORD that he spoke to E·lī′jah.

Slaughter of Worshipers of Baal

18 Then Jē′hū assembled all the people and said to them, "Ā′hab offered Bā′al small service; but Jē′hū will offer much more. 19 Now therefore summon to me all the prophets of Bā′al, all his worshipers, and all his priests; let none be missing, for I have a great sacrifice to offer to Bā′al; whoever is missing shall not live." But Jē′hū was acting with cunning in order to destroy the worshipers of Bā′al. 20 Jē′hū decreed, "Sanctify a solemn assembly for Bā′al." So they proclaimed it. 21 Jē′hū sent word throughout all Israel; all the worshipers of Bā′al came, so that there was no one left who did not come. They entered the temple of Bā′al, until the temple of Bā′al was filled from wall to wall. 22 He said to the keeper of the wardrobe, "Bring out the vestments for all the wor-

---

d Or of the city; Vg Compare Gk   e Gk: Heb lacks of the sons of   f Gk: Heb Is it right with your heart, as my heart is with your heart?   g Gk: Heb lacks Jehu said   h Gk Syr Tg: Heb they shipers of Bā′al." So he brought out the vestments for them. 23 Then Jē′hū entered the temple of Bā′al with Je·hon′a·dab son of Rē′chab; he said to the worshipers of Bā′al, "Search and see that there is no worshiper of the LORD here among you, but only worshipers of Bā′al." 24 Then they proceeded to offer sacrifices and burnt offerings.

Now Jē′hū had stationed eighty men outside, saying, "Whoever allows any of those to escape whom I deliver into your hands shall forfeit his life." 25 As soon as he had finished presenting the burnt offering, Jē′hū said to the guards and to the officers, "Come in and kill them; let no one escape." So they put them to the sword. The guards and the officers threw them out, and then went into the citadel of the temple of Bā′al. 26 They brought out the pillar*i* that was in the temple of Bā′al, and burned it. 27 Then they demolished the pillar of Bā′al, and destroyed the temple of Bā′al, and made it a latrine to this day.

28 Thus Jē′hū wiped out Bā′al from Israel. 29 But Jē′hū did not turn aside from the sins of Jer·o·bō′am son of Nē′bat, which he caused Israel to commit—the golden calves that were in Beth′el and in Dan. 30 The LORD said to Jē′hū, "Because you have done well in carrying out what I consider right, and in accordance with all that was in my heart have dealt with the house of Ā′hab, your sons of the fourth generation shall sit on the throne of Israel." 31 But Jē′hū was not careful to follow the law of the LORD the God of Israel with all his heart; he did not turn from the sins of Jer·o·bō′am, which he caused Israel to commit.

Death of Jehu

32 In those days the LORD began to trim off parts of Israel. Haz′a·el defeated them throughout the territory of Israel: 33 from the Jordan eastward, all the land of Gil′e·ad, the Gad′ītes, the Reū′ben·ites, and the Ma·nas′sītes, from A·rō′er, which is by the Wadi Ar′non, that is, Gil′e·ad and Bā′shan. 34 Now the rest of the acts of Jē′hū, all that he did, and all his power, are they not written in the Book of the Annals of the Kings of Israel? 35 So Jē′hū slept with his ancestors, and they buried him in Sa·mār′i·a. His son Je·hō′a·haz succeeded him. 36 The time that Jē′hū reigned over Israel in Sa·mār′i·a was twenty-eight years.

Athaliah Reigns over Judah
(2 Chr 22.10–12)

11 Now when Ath·a·lī′ah, A·ha·zī′ah's mother, saw that her son was dead, she set about to destroy all the royal family. 2 But Je·hosh′e·ba, King Jō′ram's daughter, A·ha·zī′ah's sister, took Jō′ash son of A·ha·zī′ah, and stole him away from among the king's children who were

about to be killed; she put*j* him and his nurse in a bedroom. Thus she*k* hid him from Ath·a·lī′ah, so that he was not killed; 3 he remained with her six years, hidden in the house of the LORD, while Ath·a·lī′ah reigned over the land.

Jehoiada Anoints the Child Joash
(2 Chr 23.1–11)

4 But in the seventh year Je·hoi′a·da summoned the captains of the Cār′ītes and of the guards and had them come to him in the house of the LORD. He made a covenant with them and put them under oath in the house of the LORD; then he showed them the king's son. 5 He commanded them, "This is what you are to do: one-third of you, those who go off duty on the sabbath and guard the king's house 6 (another third being at the gate Sur and a third at the gate behind the guards), shall guard the palace; 7 and your two divisions that come on duty in force on the sabbath and guard the house of the LORD*l* 8 shall surround the king, each with weapons in hand; and whoever approaches the ranks is to be killed. Be with the king in his comings and goings."

9 The captains did according to all that the priest Je·hoi′a·da commanded; each brought his men who were to go off duty on the sabbath, with those who were to come on duty on the sabbath, and came to the priest Je·hoi′a·da. 10 The priest delivered to the captains the spears and shields that had been King David's, which were in the house of the LORD; 11 the guards stood, every man with his weapons in his hand, from the south side of the house to the north side of the house, around the altar and the house, to guard the king on every side. 12 Then he brought out the king's son, put the crown on him, and gave him the covenant;*m* they proclaimed him king, and anointed him; they clapped their hands and shouted, "Long live the king!"

Death of Athaliah
(2 Chr 23.12—24.1)

13 When Ath·a·lī′ah heard the noise of the guard and of the people, she went into the house of the LORD to the people; 14 when she looked, there was the king standing by the pillar, according to custom, with the captains and the trumpeters beside the king, and all the people of the land rejoicing and blowing trumpets. Ath·a·lī′ah tore her clothes and cried, "Treason! Treason!" 15 Then the priest Je·hoi′a·da commanded the captains who were set over the army, "Bring her out between the

---

i Gk Vg Syr Tg: Heb *pillars*   *j* With 2 Chr 22.11: Heb lacks *she put*   *k* Gk Syr Vg Compare 2 Chr 22.11: Heb *they*   *l* Heb *the LORD to the king*   *m* Or *treaty* or *testimony*; Heb *eduth* ranks, and kill with the sword anyone who follows her." For the priest said, "Let her not be killed in the house of the LORD." 16 So they laid hands on her; she went through the horses' entrance to the king's house, and there she was put to death.

17 Je·hoi′a·da made a covenant between the LORD and the king and people, that they should be the LORD's people; also between the king and the people. 18 Then all the people of the land went to the house of Bā′al, and tore it down; his altars and his images they broke in pieces, and they killed Mat′tan, the priest of Bā′al, before the altars. The priest posted guards over the house of the LORD. 19 He took the captains, the Cār′ītes, the guards, and all the people of the land; then they brought the king down from the house of the LORD, marching through the gate of the guards to the king's house. He took his seat on the throne of the kings. 20 So all the people of the land rejoiced; and the city was quiet after Ath·a·lī′ah had been killed with the sword at the king's house.

21[n] Je·hō′ash[o] was seven years old when he began to reign.

The Temple Repaired
(2 Chr 24.1–14)

12 In the seventh year of Jē′hū, Je·hō′ash began to reign; he reigned forty years in Jerusalem. His mother's name was Zib′i·ah of Bē′er·shē′ba. 2 Je·hō′ash did what was right in the sight of the LORD all his days, because the priest Je·hoi′a·da instructed him. 3 Nevertheless the high places were not taken away; the people continued to sacrifice and make offerings on the high places.

4 Je·hō′ash said to the priests, "All the money offered as sacred donations that is brought into the house of the LORD, the money for which each person is assessed—the money from the assessment of persons—and the money from the voluntary offerings brought into the house of the LORD, 5 let the priests receive from each of the donors; and let them repair the house wherever any need of repairs is discovered." 6 But by the twenty-third year of King Je·hō′ash the priests had made no repairs on the house. 7 Therefore King Je·hō′ash summoned the priest Je·hoi′a·da with the other priests and said to them, "Why are you not repairing the house? Now therefore do not accept any more money from your donors but hand it over for the repair of the house." 8 So the priests agreed that they would neither accept more money from the people nor repair the house.

9 Then the priest Je·hoi′a·da took a chest, made a hole in its lid, and set it beside the altar on the right side as one entered the house of the LORD; the priests who guarded the threshold put in it all the money that was brought into the house of the

LORD. 10 Whenever they saw that there was a great deal of money in the chest, the king's secretary and the high priest went up, counted the money that was found in the house of the LORD, and tied it up in bags. 11 They would give the money that was weighed out into the hands of the workers who had the oversight of the house of the LORD; then they paid it out to the carpenters and the builders who worked on the house of the LORD, 12 to the masons and the stonecutters, as well as to buy timber and quarried stone for making repairs on the house of the LORD, as well as for any outlay for repairs of the house. 13 But for the house of the LORD no basins of silver, snuffers, bowls, trumpets, or any vessels of gold, or of silver, were made from the money that was brought into the house of the LORD, 14 for that was given to the workers who were repairing the house of the LORD with it. 15 They did not ask an accounting from those into whose hand they delivered the money to pay out to the workers, for they dealt honestly. 16 The money from the guilt offerings and the money from the sin offerings was not brought into the house of the LORD; it belonged to the priests.

Hazael Threatens Jerusalem

17 At that time King Haz′a·el of Ar′am went up, fought against Gath, and took it. But when Haz′a·el set his face to go up against Jerusalem, 18 King Je·hō′ash of Judah took all the votive gifts that Je·hosh′a·phat, Je·hō′ram, and A·ha·zī′ah, his ancestors, the kings of Judah, had dedicated, as well as his own votive gifts, all the gold that was found in the treasuries of the house of the LORD and of the king's house, and sent these to King Haz′a·el of Ar′am. Then Haz′a·el withdrew from Jerusalem.

Death of Joash
(2 Chr 24.23–27)

19 Now the rest of the acts of Jō′ash, and all that he did, are they not written in the Book of the Annals of the Kings of Judah? 20 His servants arose, devised a conspiracy, and killed Jō′ash in the house of Mil′lo, on the way that goes down to Sil′la. 21 It was Jō′za·car son of Shim′ē·ath and Je·hō′za·bad son of Shō′mer, his servants, who struck him down, so that he died. He was buried with his ancestors in the city of David; then his son Am·a·zī′ah succeeded him.

Jehoahaz Reigns over Israel

13 In the twenty-third year of King Jō′ash son of A·ha·zī′ah of Judah, Je·hō′a·haz son of Jē′hū began to reign over Israel in Sa·mār′i·a; he reigned seventeen years. 2 He did what was evil

---

[n] Ch 12.1 in Heb   [o] Another spelling is *Joash*; see verse 19

in the sight of the LORD, and followed the sins of Jer·o·bō′am son of Nē′bat, which he caused Israel to sin; he did not depart from them. [3] The anger of the LORD was kindled against Israel, so that he gave them repeatedly into the hand of King Haz′a·el of Ar′am, then into the hand of Ben-hā′dad son of Haz′a·el. [4] But Je·hō′a·haz entreated the LORD, and the LORD heeded him; for he saw the oppression of Israel, how the king of Ar′am oppressed them. [5] Therefore the LORD gave Israel a savior, so that they escaped from the hand of the Ar·a·mē′ans; and the people of Israel lived in their homes as former-ly. [6] Nevertheless they did not depart from the sins of the house of Jer·o·bō′am, which he caused Israel to sin, but walked[p] in them; the sacred pole[q] also remained in Sa·mār′i·a. [7] So Je·hō′a·haz was left with an army of not more than fifty horsemen, ten chariots and ten thousand footmen; for the king of Ar′am had destroyed them and made them like the dust at threshing. [8] Now the rest of the acts of Je·hō′a·haz and all that he did, including his might, are they not written in the Book of the Annals of the Kings of Israel? [9] So Je·hō′a·haz slept with his an-cestors, and they buried him in Sa·mār′i·a; then his son Jō′ash succeeded him.

Jehoash Reigns over Israel

10 In the thirty-seventh year of King Jō′ash of Judah, Je·hō′ash son of Je·hō′a·haz began to reign over Israel in Sa·mār′i·a; he reigned sixteen years. [11] He also did what was evil in the sight of the LORD; he did not depart from all the sins of Jer·o·bō′am son of Nē′bat, which he caused Israel to sin, but he walked in them. [12] Now the rest of the acts of Jō′ash, and all that he did, as well as the might with which he fought against King Am·a-zī′ah of Judah, are they not written in the Book of the Annals of the Kings of Israel? [13] So Jō′ash slept with his ancestors, and Jer·o·bō′am sat upon his throne; Jō′ash was buried in Sa·mār′i·a with the kings of Israel.

Death of Elisha

14 Now when E·lī′sha had fallen sick with the illness of which he was to die, King Jō′ash of Israel went down to him, and wept before him, crying, "My father, my father! The chariots of Israel and its horsemen!" [15] E·lī′sha said to him, "Take a bow and arrows"; so he took a bow and arrows. [16] Then he said to the king of Israel, "Draw the bow"; and he drew it. E·lī′sha laid his hands on the king's hands. [17] Then he said, "Open the window east-ward"; and he opened it. E·lī′sha said, "Shoot"; and he shot. Then he said, "The LORD's arrow of victory, the arrow of victory over Ar′am! For you shall fight the Ar·a·mē′ans in Ā′phek until you have made an end of them." [18] He continued, "Take the arrows";

and he took them. He said to the king of Israel, "Strike the ground with them"; he struck three times, and stopped. [19] Then the man of God was angry with him, and said, "You should have struck five or six times; then you would have struck down Ar′am until you had made an end of it, but now you will strike down Ar′am only three times."

20 So E·lī′sha died, and they buried him. Now bands of Mō′ab·ītes used to invade the land in the spring of the year. [21] As a man was being buried, a marauding band was seen and the man was thrown into the grave of E·lī′sha; as soon as the man touched the bones of E·lī′sha, he came to life and stood on his feet.

Israel Recaptures Cities from Aram

22 Now King Haz′a·el of Ar′am oppressed Israel all the days of Je·hō′a·haz. [23] But the LORD was gra-cious to them and had compassion on them; he turned toward them, because of his covenant with Abraham, Isaac, and Jacob, and would not destroy them; nor has he banished them from his presence until now.

24 When King Haz′a·el of Ar′am died, his son Ben-hā′dad succeeded him. [25] Then Je·hō′ash son of Je·hō′a·haz took again from Ben-hā′dad son of Haz′a·el the towns that he had taken from his father Je·hō′a·haz in war. Three times Jō′ash defeated him and recovered the towns of Israel.

Amaziah Reigns over Judah
(2 Chr 25.1—26.2)

14 In the second year of King Jō′ash son of Jō′a·haz of Israel, King Am·a·zī′ah son of Jō′ash of Judah, began to reign. [2] He was twenty-five years old when he began to reign, and he reigned twenty-nine years in Jerusalem. His moth-er's name was Jē·hō·ad′din of Jerusalem. [3] He did what was right in the sight of the LORD, yet not like his ancestor David; in all things he did as his father Jō′ash had done. [4] But the high places were not re-moved; the people still sacrificed and made offer-ings on the high places. [5] As soon as the royal power was firmly in his hand he killed his servants who had murdered his father the king. [6] But he did not put to death the children of the murderers; ac-cording to what is written in the book of the law of Moses, where the LORD commanded, "The parents shall not be put to death for the children, or the children be put to death for the parents; but all shall be put to death for their own sins."

7 He killed ten thousand Ē′dom·ītes in the Val-ley of Salt and took Sē′la by storm; he called it Jok′thē-el, which is its name to this day.

8 Then Am·a·zī′ah sent messengers to King

---

[p] Gk Syr Tg Vg: Heb *he walked*   [q] Heb *Asherah*

Je•hō′ash son of Je•hō′a•haz, son of Jē′hū, of Israel, saying, "Come, let us look one another in the face." 9 King Je•hō′ash of Israel sent word to King Am•a•zī′ah of Judah, "A thornbush on Lebanon sent to a cedar on Lebanon, saying, 'Give your daughter to my son for a wife'; but a wild animal of Lebanon passed by and trampled down the thornbush. 10 You have indeed defeated Ē′dom, and your heart has lifted you up. Be content with your glory, and stay at home; for why should you provoke trouble so that you fall, you and Judah with you?"

11 But Am•a•zī′ah would not listen. So King Je•hō′ash of Israel went up; he and King Am•a•zī′ah of Judah faced one another in battle at Beth-shē′mesh, which belongs to Judah. 12 Judah was defeated by Israel; everyone fled home. 13 King Je•hō′ash of Israel captured King Am•a•zī′ah of Judah son of Je•hō′ash, son of A•ha•zī′ah, at Beth-shē′mesh; he came to Jerusalem, and broke down the wall of Jerusalem from the Ē′phra•im Gate to the Corner Gate, a distance of four hundred cubits. 14 He seized all the gold and silver, and all the vessels that were found in the house of the LORD and in the treasuries of the king's house, as well as hostages; then he returned to Sa•mār′i•a.

15 Now the rest of the acts that Je•hō′ash did, his might, and how he fought with King Am•a•zī′ah of Judah, are they not written in the Book of the Annals of the Kings of Israel? 16 Je•hō′ash slept with his ancestors, and was buried in Sa•mār′i•a with the kings of Israel; then his son Jer•o•bō′am succeeded him.

17 King Am•a•zī′ah son of Jō′ash of Judah lived fifteen years after the death of King Je•hō′ash son of Je•hō′a•haz of Israel. 18 Now the rest of the deeds of Am•a•zī′ah, are they not written in the Book of the Annals of the Kings of Judah? 19 They made a conspiracy against him in Jerusalem, and he fled to Lā′chish. But they sent after him to Lā′chish, and killed him there. 20 They brought him on horses; he was buried in Jerusalem with his ancestors in the city of David. 21 All the people of Judah took Az•a•rī′ah, who was sixteen years old, and made him king to succeed his father Am•a•zī′ah. 22 He rebuilt Ē′lath and restored it to Judah, after King Am•a•zī′ah[r] slept with his ancestors.

Jeroboam II Reigns over Israel

23 In the fifteenth year of King Am•a•zī′ah son of Jō′ash of Judah, King Jer•o•bō′am son of Jō′ash of Israel began to reign in Sa•mār′i•a; he reigned forty-one years. 24 He did what was evil in the sight of the LORD; he did not depart from all the sins of Jer•o•bō′am son of Nē′bat, which he caused Israel to sin. 25 He restored the border of Israel from Lē′bo-hā′math as far as the Sea of the Ar′a•bah, according to the word of the LORD, the God of Israel, which he

spoke by his servant Jonah son of A•mit′taī, the prophet, who was from Gath-hē′pher. 26 For the LORD saw that the distress of Israel was very bitter; there was no one left, bond or free, and no one to help Israel. 27 But the LORD had not said that he would blot out the name of Israel from under heaven, so he saved them by the hand of Jer•o•bō′am son of Jō′ash.

28 Now the rest of the acts of Jer•o•bō′am, and all that he did, and his might, how he fought, and how he recovered for Israel Damascus and Hā′math, which had belonged to Judah, are they not written in the Book of the Annals of the Kings of Israel? 29 Jer•o•bō′am slept with his ancestors, the kings of Israel; his son Zech•a•rī′ah succeeded him.

Azariah Reigns over Judah
(2 Chr 26.3–23)

15 In the twenty-seventh year of King Jer•o•bō′am of Israel King Az•a•rī′ah son of Am•a•zī′ah of Judah began to reign. 2 He was sixteen years old when he began to reign, and he reigned fifty-two years in Jerusalem. His mother's name was Jec•o•lī′ah of Jerusalem. 3 He did what was right in the sight of the LORD, just as his father Am•a•zī′ah had done. 4 Nevertheless the high places were not taken away; the people still sacrificed and made offerings on the high places. 5 The LORD struck the king, so that he was leprous[s] to the day of his death, and lived in a separate house. Jō′tham the king's son was in charge of the palace, governing the people of the land. 6 Now the rest of the acts of Az•a•rī′ah, and all that he did, are they not written in the Book of the Annals of the Kings of Judah? 7 Az•a•rī′ah slept with his ancestors; they buried him with his ancestors in the city of David; his son Jō′tham succeeded him.

Zechariah Reigns over Israel

8 In the thirty-eighth year of King Az•a•rī′ah of Judah, Zech•a•rī′ah son of Jer•o•bō′am reigned over Israel in Sa•mār′i•a six months. 9 He did what was evil in the sight of the LORD, as his ancestors had done. He did not depart from the sins of Jer•o•bō′am son of Nē′bat, which he caused Israel to sin. 10 Shal′lum son of Jā′besh conspired against him, and struck him down in public and killed him, and reigned in place of him. 11 Now the rest of the deeds of Zech•a•rī′ah are written in the Book of the Annals of the Kings of Israel. 12 This was the promise of the LORD that he gave to Jē′hū, "Your sons shall sit on the throne of Israel to the fourth generation." And so it happened.

---

r Heb *the king*   s A term for several skin diseases; precise meaning uncertain

Shallum Reigns over Israel

13 Shal'lum son of Jā'besh began to reign in the thirty-ninth year of King Uz•zī'ah of Judah; he reigned one month in Sa•mār'i•a. 14 Then Men'a-hem son of Gā'dī came up from Tir'zah and came to Sa•mār'i•a; he struck down Shal'lum son of Jā'besh in Sa•mār'i•a and killed him; he reigned in place of him. 15 Now the rest of the deeds of Shal'lum, including the conspiracy that he made, are written in the Book of the Annals of the Kings of Israel. 16 At that time Men'a•hem sacked Tiph'-sah, all who were in it and its territory from Tir'zah on; because they did not open it to him, he sacked it. He ripped open all the pregnant women in it.

Menahem Reigns over Israel

17 In the thirty-ninth year of King Az•a•rī'ah of Judah, Men'a•hem son of Gā'dī began to reign over Israel; he reigned ten years in Sa•mār'i•a. 18 He did what was evil in the sight of the LORD; he did not depart all his days from any of the sins of Jer•o•bō'am son of Nē'bat, which he caused Israel to sin. 19 King Pūl of Assyria came against the land; Men'a•hem gave Pūl a thousand talents of silver, so that he might help him confirm his hold on the royal power. 20 Men'a•hem exacted the money from Israel, that is, from all the wealthy, fifty shekels of silver from each one, to give to the king of Assyria. So the king of Assyria turned back, and did not stay there in the land. 21 Now the rest of the deeds of Men'a•hem, and all that he did, are they not written in the Book of the Annals of the Kings of Israel? 22 Men'a•hem slept with his ancestors, and his son Pek•a•hī'ah succeeded him.

Pekahiah Reigns over Israel

23 In the fiftieth year of King Az•a•rī'ah of Ju-dah, Pek•a•hī'ah son of Men'a•hem began to reign over Israel in Sa•mār'i•a; he reigned two years. 24 He did what was evil in the sight of the LORD; he did not turn away from the sins of Jer•o•bō'am son of Nē'bat, which he caused Israel to sin. 25 Pē'kah son of Rem•a•lī'ah, his captain, conspired against him with fifty of the Gil'e•ad•ites, and attacked him in Sa•mār'i•a, in the citadel of the palace along with Ar'gob and A•ri'eh; he killed him, and reigned in place of him. 26 Now the rest of the deeds of Pek•a•hī'ah, and all that he did, are written in the Book of the Annals of the Kings of Israel.

Pekah Reigns over Israel

27 In the fifty-second year of King Az•a•rī'ah of Judah, Pē'kah son of Rem•a•lī'ah began to reign over Israel in Sa•mār'i•a; he reigned twenty years. 28 He did what was evil in the sight of the LORD; he did not depart from the sins of Jer•o•bō'am son of Nē'bat, which he caused Israel to sin.

29 In the days of King Pē'kah of Israel, King Tig'lath-pi•lē'ser of Assyria came and captured I'jon, Ā'bel-beth-mā'a•cah, Ja•nō'ah, Kē'desh, Hā'zor, Gil'e•ad, and Galilee, all the land of Naph'ta•lī; and he carried the people captive to Assyria. 30 Then Hō•shē'a son of Ē'lah made a conspiracy against Pē'kah son of Rem•a•lī'ah, attacked him, and killed him; he reigned in place of him, in the twentieth year of Jō'tham son of Uz•zī'ah. 31 Now the rest of the acts of Pē'kah, and all that he did, are written in the Book of the Annals of the Kings of Israel.

Jotham Reigns over Judah
(2 Chr 27.1–9)

32 In the second year of King Pē'kah son of Rem•a•lī'ah of Israel, King Jō'tham son of Uz•zī'ah of Judah began to reign. 33 He was twenty-five years old when he began to reign and reigned sixteen years in Jerusalem. His mother's name was Je•rū'sha daughter of Zā'dok. 34 He did what was right in the sight of the LORD, just as his father Uz•zī'ah had done. 35 Nevertheless the high places were not re-moved; the people still sacrificed and made offer-ings on the high places. He built the upper gate of the house of the LORD. 36 Now the rest of the acts of Jō'tham, and all that he did, are they not written in the Book of the Annals of the Kings of Judah? 37 In those days the LORD began to send King Rē'zin of Ar'am and Pē'kah son of Rem•a•lī'ah against Judah. 38 Jō'tham slept with his ancestors, and was buried with his ancestors in the city of David, his ancestor; his son Ā'haz succeeded him.

Ahaz Reigns over Judah
(2 Chr 28.1–27)

16 In the seventeenth year of Pē'kah son of Rem•a•lī'ah, King Ā'haz son of Jō'tham of Judah began to reign. 2 Ā'haz was twenty years old when he began to reign; he reigned sixteen years in Jerusalem. He did not do what was right in the sight of the LORD his God, as his ancestor David had done, 3 but he walked in the way of the kings of Israel. He even made his son pass through fire, according to the abominable practices of the na-tions whom the LORD drove out before the people of Israel. 4 He sacrificed and made offerings on the high places, on the hills, and under every green tree.

5 Then King Rē'zin of Ar'am and King Pē'kah son of Rem•a•lī'ah of Israel came up to wage war on Jerusalem; they besieged Ā'haz but could not con-quer him. 6 At that time the king of Ē'dom[t] recov-ered Ē'lath for Ē'dom,[u] and drove the Judeans from Ē'lath; and the Ē'dom•ites came to Ē'lath, where they live to this day. 7 Ā'haz sent messengers to King Tig'lath-pi•lē'ser of Assyria, saying, "I am your

---

t Cn: Heb *King Rezin of Aram*   u Cn: Heb *Aram*

servant and your son. Come up, and rescue me from the hand of the king of Ar′am and from the hand of the king of Israel, who are attacking me." [8] Ā′haz also took the silver and gold found in the house of the LORD and in the treasures of the king's house, and sent a present to the king of Assyria. [9] The king of Assyria listened to him; the king of Assyria marched up against Damascus, and took it, carrying its people captive to Kir; then he killed Rē′zin.

[10] When King Ā′haz went to Damascus to meet King Tig′lath-pī·lē′ser of Assyria, he saw the altar that was at Damascus. King Ā′haz sent to the priest Ū·rī′ah a model of the altar, and its pattern, exact in all its details. [11] The priest Ū·rī′ah built the altar; in accordance with all that King Ā′haz had sent from Damascus, just so did the priest Ū·rī′ah build it, before King Ā′haz arrived from Damascus. [12] When the king came from Damascus, the king viewed the altar. Then the king drew near to the altar, went up on it, [13] and offered his burnt offering and his grain offering, poured his drink offering, and dashed the blood of his offerings of well-being against the altar. [14] The bronze altar that was before the LORD he removed from the front of the house, from the place between his altar and the house of the LORD, and put it on the north side of his altar. [15] King Ā′haz commanded the priest Ū·rī′ah, saying, "Upon the great altar offer the morning burnt offering, and the evening grain offering, and the king's burnt offering, and his grain offering, with the burnt offering of all the people of the land, their grain offering, and their drink offering; then dash against it all the blood of the burnt offering, and all the blood of the sacrifice; but the bronze altar shall be for me to inquire by." [16] The priest Ū·rī′ah did everything that King Ā′haz commanded.

[17] Then King Ā′haz cut off the frames of the stands, and removed the laver from them; he removed the sea from the bronze oxen that were under it, and put it on a pediment of stone. [18] The covered portal for use on the sabbath that had been built inside the palace, and the outer entrance for the king he removed from[v] the house of the LORD. He did this because of the king of Assyria. [19] Now the rest of the acts of Ā′haz that he did, are they not written in the Book of the Annals of the Kings of Judah? [20] Ā′haz slept with his ancestors, and was buried with his ancestors in the city of David; his son Hez·e·kī′ah succeeded him.

Hoshea Reigns over Israel

17 In the twelfth year of King Ā′haz of Judah, Hō·shē′a son of Ē′lah began to reign in Sa·mār′i·a over Israel; he reigned nine years. [2] He did what was evil in the sight of the LORD, yet not like the kings of Israel who were be-

fore him. [3] King Shal·man·ē′ser of Assyria came up against him; Hō·shē′a became his vassal, and paid him tribute. [4] But the king of Assyria found treachery in Hō·shē′a; for he had sent messengers to King So of Egypt, and offered no tribute to the king of Assyria, as he had done year by year; therefore the king of Assyria confined him and imprisoned him.

Israel Carried Captive to Assyria

[5] Then the king of Assyria invaded all the land and came to Sa·mār′i·a; for three years he besieged it. [6] In the ninth year of Hō·shē′a the king of Assyria captured Sa·mār′i·a; he carried the Israelites away to Assyria. He placed them in Hā′lah, on the Hā′bor, the river of Gō′zan, and in the cities of the Mēdes.

[7] This occurred because the people of Israel had sinned against the LORD their God, who had brought them up out of the land of Egypt from under the hand of Pharaoh king of Egypt. They had worshiped other gods [8] and walked in the customs of the nations whom the LORD drove out before the people of Israel, and in the customs that the kings of Israel had introduced.[w] [9] The people of Israel secretly did things that were not right against the LORD their God. They built for themselves high places at all their towns, from watchtower to fortified city; [10] they set up for themselves pillars and sa-

---

[v] Cn: Heb lacks *from*   [w] Meaning of Heb uncertain

did you KNOW?

The First Captivity

The Second Book of Kings describes two captivities and exiles. The first one is the Assyrian conquest of the northern kingdom, Israel, which occurred in 721 B.C. (see map 4, "The Assyrian Empire"). According to the author of 2 Kings, Israel fell first because its kings and people were even less faithful to God than the kings and people of Judah, the southern kingdom. Notice that the Assyrian conquest is described in the briefest detail (17.5–6), but the reasons for it are described in great detail (verses 7–18).

▶ 2 Kings 17.5–18

cred poles*x* on every high hill and under every green tree; 11 there they made offerings on all the high places, as the nations did whom the LORD carried away before them. They did wicked things, provoking the LORD to anger; 12 they served idols, of which the LORD had said to them, "You shall not do this." 13 Yet the LORD warned Israel and Judah by every prophet and every seer, saying, "Turn from your evil ways and keep my commandments and my statutes, in accordance with all the law that I commanded your ancestors and that I sent to you by my servants the prophets." 14 They would not listen but were stubborn, as their ancestors had been, who did not believe in the LORD their God. 15 They despised his statutes, and his covenant that he made with their ancestors, and the warnings that he gave them. They went after false idols and became false; they followed the nations that were around them, concerning whom the LORD had commanded them that they should not do as they did. 16 They rejected all the commandments of the LORD their God and made for themselves cast images of two calves; they made a sacred pole,*y* worshiped all the host of heaven, and served Bā'al. 17 They made their sons and their daughters pass through fire; they used divination and augury; and they sold themselves to do evil in the sight of the LORD, provoking him to anger. 18 Therefore the LORD was very angry with Israel and removed them out of his sight; none was left but the tribe of Judah alone.

19 Judah also did not keep the commandments of the LORD their God but walked in the customs that Israel had introduced. 20 The LORD rejected all the descendants of Israel; he punished them and gave them into the hand of plunderers, until he had banished them from his presence.

21 When he had torn Israel from the house of David, they made Jer•o•bō'am son of Nē'bat king. Jer•o•bō'am drove Israel from following the LORD and made them commit great sin. 22 The people of Israel continued in all the sins that Jer•o•bō'am committed; they did not depart from them 23 until the LORD removed Israel out of his sight, as he had foretold through all his servants the prophets. So Israel was exiled from their own land to Assyria until this day.

Assyria Resettles Samaria

24 The king of Assyria brought people from Babylon, Cū'thah, Av'va, Hā'math, and Seph•ar•vā'im, and placed them in the cities of Sa•mār'i•a in place of the people of Israel; they took possession of Sa•mār'i•a, and settled in its cities. 25 When they first settled there, they did not worship the LORD; therefore the LORD sent lions among them, which killed some of them. 26 So the king of Assyria was told, "The nations that you have carried away and placed in the cities of Sa•mār'i•a do not know the law of the god of the land; therefore he has sent lions among them; they are killing them, because they do not know the law of the god of the land." 27 Then the king of Assyria commanded, "Send there one of the priests whom you carried away from there; let him*z* go and live there, and teach them the law of the god of the land." 28 So one of the priests whom they had carried away from Sa•mār'i•a came and lived in Beth'el; he taught them how they should worship the LORD.

29 But every nation still made gods of its own and put them in the shrines of the high places that the people of Sa•mār'i•a had made, every nation in the cities in which they lived; 30 the people of Babylon made Suc'coth-bē'noth, the people of Cuth made Ner'gal, the people of Hā'math made A•shī'ma; 31 the Av'vītes made Nib'haz and Tar'tak; the Se•phar'vītes burned their children in the fire to A•dram'me•lech and A•nam'me•lech, the gods of Seph•ar•vā'im. 32 They also worshiped the LORD and appointed from among themselves all sorts of people as priests of the high places, who sacrificed for them in the shrines of the high places. 33 So they worshiped the LORD but also served their own gods, after the manner of the nations from among whom they had been carried away. 34 To this day they continue to practice their former customs.

They do not worship the LORD and they do not follow the statutes or the ordinances or the law or the commandment that the LORD commanded the children of Jacob, whom he named Israel. 35 The LORD had made a covenant with them and commanded them, "You shall not worship other gods or bow yourselves to them or serve them or sacrifice to them, 36 but you shall worship the LORD, who brought you out of the land of Egypt with great power and with an outstretched arm; you shall bow yourselves to him, and to him you shall sacrifice. 37 The statutes and the ordinances and the law and the commandment that he wrote for you, you shall always be careful to observe. You shall not worship other gods; 38 you shall not forget the covenant that I have made with you. You shall not worship other gods, 39 but you shall worship the LORD your God; he will deliver you out of the hand of all your enemies." 40 They would not listen, however, but they continued to practice their former custom.

41 So these nations worshiped the LORD, but also served their carved images; to this day their children and their children's children continue to do as their ancestors did.

---

x Heb *Asherim*　*y* Heb *Asherah*　*z* Syr Vg: Heb *them*

Hezekiah's Reign over Judah
(2 Chr 29.1–2; 31.1)

18 In the third year of King Hō·shě'a son of Ē'lah of Israel, Hez·e·kī'ah son of King Ā'haz of Judah began to reign. 2 He was twenty-five years old when he began to reign; he reigned twenty-nine years in Jerusalem. His mother's name was Ā'bī daughter of Zech·a·rī'ah. 3 He did what was right in the sight of the LORD just as his ancestor David had done. 4 He removed the high places, broke down the pillars, and cut down the sacred pole.[a] He broke in pieces the bronze serpent that Moses had made, for until those days the people of Israel had made offerings to it; it was called Ne·hush'tan. 5 He trusted in the LORD the God of Israel; so that there was no one like him among all the kings of Judah after him, or among those who were before him. 6 For he held fast to the LORD; he did not depart from following him but kept the commandments that the LORD commanded Moses. 7 The LORD was with him; wherever he went, he prospered. He rebelled against the king of Assyria and would not serve him. 8 He attacked the Phi·lis'tines as far as Gā'za and its territory, from watchtower to fortified city.

9 In the fourth year of King Hez·e·kī'ah, which was the seventh year of King Hō·shě'a son of Ē'lah of Israel, King Shal·man·ě'ser of Assyria came up against Sa·mār'i·a, besieged it, 10 and at the end of three years, took it. In the sixth year of Hez·e·kī'ah, which was the ninth year of King Hō·shě'a of Israel, Sa·mār'i·a was taken. 11 The king of Assyria carried the Israelites away to Assyria, settled them in Hā'lah, on the Hā'bor, the river of Gō'zan, and in the cities of the Mēdes, 12 because they did not obey the voice of the LORD their God but transgressed his covenant—all that Moses the servant of the LORD had commanded; they neither listened nor obeyed.

Sennacherib Invades Judah
(Isa 36.1–22; 2 Chr 32.1–19)

13 In the fourteenth year of King Hez·e·kī'ah, King Sen·nach'e·rib of Assyria came up against all the fortified cities of Judah and captured them. 14 King Hez·e·kī'ah of Judah sent to the king of Assyria at Lā'chish, saying, "I have done wrong; withdraw from me; whatever you impose on me I will bear." The king of Assyria demanded of King Hez·e·kī'ah of Judah three hundred talents of silver and thirty talents of gold. 15 Hez·e·kī'ah gave him all the silver that was found in the house of the LORD and in the treasuries of the king's house. 16 At that time Hez·e·kī'ah stripped the gold from the doors of the temple of the LORD, and from the doorposts that King Hez·e·kī'ah of Judah had overlaid and gave it to the king of Assyria. 17 The king of Assyria sent the Tar'tan, the Rab·sar'is, and the Rab'sha·keh with a great army from Lā'chish to King Hez·e·kī'ah at Jerusalem. They went up and came to Jerusalem. When they arrived, they came and stood by the conduit of the upper pool, which is on the highway to the Fuller's Field. 18 When they called for the king, there came out to them E·lī'a·kim son of Hil·kī'ah, who was in charge of the palace, and Sheb'nah the secretary, and Jō'ah son of Ā'saph, the recorder.

19 The Rab'sha·keh said to them, "Say to Hez·e·kī'ah: Thus says the great king, the king of Assyria: On what do you base this confidence of yours? 20 Do you think that mere words are strategy and power for war? On whom do you now rely, that you have rebelled against me? 21 See, you are relying now on Egypt, that broken reed of a staff, which will pierce the hand of anyone who leans on it. Such is Pharaoh king of Egypt to all who rely on him. 22 But if you say to me, 'We rely on the LORD our God,' is it not he whose high places and altars Hez·e·kī'ah has removed, saying to Judah and to Jerusalem, 'You shall worship before this altar in Jerusalem'? 23 Come now, make a wager with my master the king of Assyria: I will give you two thousand horses, if you are able on your part to set riders on them. 24 How then can you repulse a single captain among the least of my master's servants, when you rely on Egypt for chariots and for horsemen? 25 Moreover, is it without the LORD that I have come up against this place to destroy it? The LORD said to me, Go up against this land, and destroy it."

26 Then E·lī'a·kim son of Hil·kī'ah, and Sheb'nah, and Jō'ah said to the Rab'sha·keh, "Please speak to your servants in the Ar·a·mā'ic language, for we understand it; do not speak to us in the language of Judah within the hearing of the people who are on the wall." 27 But the Rab'sha·keh said to them, "Has my master sent me to speak these words to your master and to you, and not to the people sitting on the wall, who are doomed with you to eat their own dung and to drink their own urine?"

28 Then the Rab'sha·keh stood and called out in a loud voice in the language of Judah, "Hear the word of the great king, the king of Assyria! 29 Thus says the king: 'Do not let Hez·e·kī'ah deceive you, for he will not be able to deliver you out of my hand. 30 Do not let Hez·e·kī'ah make you rely on the LORD by saying, The LORD will surely deliver us, and this city will not be given into the hand of the king of Assyria.' 31 Do not listen to Hez·e·kī'ah; for thus says the king of Assyria: 'Make your peace with me and come out to me; then every one of you will eat from your own vine and your own fig tree, and drink water from your own cistern, 32 until I come and take you away to a land like your own land, a

_____

a Heb Asherah

land of grain and wine, a land of bread and vineyards, a land of olive oil and honey, that you may
live and not die. Do not listen to Hez•e•kī′ah when
he misleads you by saying, The LORD will deliver us.
33 Has any of the gods of the nations ever delivered
its land out of the hand of the king of Assyria?
34 Where are the gods of Hā′math and Ar′pad?
Where are the gods of Seph•ar•vā′im, Hē′na, and
Iv′vah? Have they delivered Sa•mār′i•a out of my
hand? 35 Who among all the gods of the countries
have delivered their countries out of my hand, that
the LORD should deliver Jerusalem out of my hand?' "

36 But the people were silent and answered
him not a word, for the king's command was, "Do
not answer him." 37 Then E•lī′a•kim son of Hil•kī′-
ah, who was in charge of the palace, and Sheb′na
the secretary, and Jō′ah son of Ā′saph, the recorder,
came to Hez•e•kī′ah with their clothes torn and told
him the words of the Rab′sha•keh.

Hezekiah Consults Isaiah
(Isa 37.1–7)

19 When King Hez•e•kī′ah heard it, he tore
his clothes, covered himself with sackcloth, and went into the house of the LORD. 2 And
he sent E•lī′a•kim, who was in charge of the palace,
and Sheb′na the secretary, and the senior priests,
covered with sackcloth, to the prophet Ī•sāi′ah son
of Ā′moz. 3 They said to him, "Thus says Hez•e•
kī′ah, This day is a day of distress, of rebuke, and of
disgrace; children have come to the birth, and there
is no strength to bring them forth. 4 It may be that
the LORD your God heard all the words of the
Rab′sha•keh, whom his master the king of Assyria
has sent to mock the living God, and will rebuke
the words that the LORD your God has heard; therefore lift up your prayer for the remnant that is left."
5 When the servants of King Hez•e•kī′ah came to
Ī•sāi′ah, 6 Ī•sāi′ah said to them, "Say to your master,
'Thus says the LORD: Do not be afraid because of the
words that you have heard, with which the servants
of the king of Assyria have reviled me. 7 I myself
will put a spirit in him, so that he shall hear a rumor and return to his own land; I will cause him to
fall by the sword in his own land.' "

Sennacherib's Threat
(Isa 37.8–13)

8 The Rab′sha•keh returned, and found the king
of Assyria fighting against Lib′nah; for he had heard
that the king had left Lā′chish. 9 When the king[b]
heard concerning King Tir•hā′kah of Ethiopia,[c]
"See, he has set out to fight against you," he sent
messengers again to Hez•e•kī′ah, saying, 10 "Thus
shall you speak to King Hez•e•kī′ah of Judah: Do
not let your God on whom you rely deceive you by
promising that Jerusalem will not be given into the

hand of the king of Assyria. 11 See, you have heard
what the kings of Assyria have done to all lands, destroying them utterly. Shall you be delivered?
12 Have the gods of the nations delivered them, the
nations that my predecessors destroyed, Gō′zan,
Har′an, Rē′zeph, and the people of Eden who were
in Te•las′sar? 13 Where is the king of Hā′math, the
king of Ar′pad, the king of the city of Seph•ar•vā′im,
the king of Hē′na, or the king of Iv′vah?"

Hezekiah's Prayer
(Isa 37.14–35)

14 Hez•e•kī′ah received the letter from the hand
of the messengers and read it; then Hez•e•kī′ah
went up to the house of the LORD and spread it before the LORD. 15 And Hez•e•kī′ah prayed before the
LORD, and said: "O LORD the God of Israel, who are
enthroned above the cherubim, you are God, you
alone, of all the kingdoms of the earth; you have
made heaven and earth. 16 Incline your ear, O
LORD, and hear; open your eyes, O LORD, and see;
hear the words of Sen•nach′e•rib, which he has sent
to mock the living God. 17 Truly, O LORD, the kings
of Assyria have laid waste the nations and their
lands, 18 and have hurled their gods into the fire,
though they were no gods but the work of human
hands—wood and stone—and so they were destroyed. 19 So now, O LORD our God, save us, I pray
you, from his hand, so that all the kingdoms of the
earth may know that you, O LORD, are God alone."

20 Then Ī•sāi′ah son of Ā′moz sent to Hez•e•
kī′ah, saying, "Thus says the LORD, the God of Israel: I have heard your prayer to me about King
Sen•nach′e•rib of Assyria. 21 This is the word that
the LORD has spoken concerning him:

She despises you, she scorns you—
    virgin daughter Zion;
she tosses her head—behind your back,
    daughter Jerusalem.

22 "Whom have you mocked and reviled?
    Against whom have you raised your
      voice
    and haughtily lifted your eyes?
    Against the Holy One of Israel!
23 By your messengers you have mocked the Lord,
    and you have said, 'With my many chariots
  I have gone up the heights of the mountains,
    to the far recesses of Lebanon;
  I felled its tallest cedars,
    its choicest cypresses;
  I entered its farthest retreat,
    its densest forest.
24 I dug wells
    and drank foreign waters,

---

b Heb *he* c Or *Nubia*; Heb *Cush*

I dried up with the sole of my foot
    all the streams of Egypt.'

25 "Have you not heard
        that I determined it long ago?
    I planned from days of old
        what now I bring to pass,
    that you should make fortified cities
        . crash into heaps of ruins,
26 while their inhabitants, shorn of strength,
        are dismayed and confounded;
    they have become like plants of the field
        and like tender grass,
    like grass on the housetops,
        blighted before it is grown.

27 "But I know your rising*d* and your sitting,
        your going out and coming in,
        and your raging against me.
28 Because you have raged against me
        and your arrogance has come to
            my ears,
    I will put my hook in your nose
        and my bit in your mouth;
    I will turn you back on the way
        by which you came.

29 "And this shall be the sign for you: This year you shall eat what grows of itself, and in the second year what springs from that; then in the third year sow, reap, plant vineyards, and eat their fruit. 30 The surviving remnant of the house of Judah shall again take root downward, and bear fruit upward; 31 for from Jerusalem a remnant shall go out, and from Mount Zion a band of survivors. The zeal of the LORD of hosts will do this.

32 "Therefore thus says the LORD concerning the king of Assyria: He shall not come into this city, shoot an arrow there, come before it with a shield, or cast up a siege ramp against it. 33 By the way that he came, by the same he shall return; he shall not come into this city, says the LORD. 34 For I will defend this city to save it, for my own sake and for the sake of my servant David."

Sennacherib's Defeat and Death
(Isa 37.36–38; 2 Chr 32.20–23)

35 That very night the angel of the LORD set out and struck down one hundred eighty-five thousand in the camp of the Assyrians; when morning dawned, they were all dead bodies. 36 Then King Sen·nach'e·rib of Assyria left, went home, and lived at Nin'e·veh. 37 As he was worshiping in the house of his god Nis'roch, his sons A·dram'me·lech and Sha·rē'zer killed him with the sword, and they escaped into the land of Ar'a·rat. His son Ē'sar-had'don succeeded him.

Hezekiah's Illness
(2 Chr 32.24–26; Isa 38.1–8)

20 In those days Hez·e·ki'ah became sick and was at the point of death. The prophet I·sāi'ah son of Ā'moz came to him, and said to him, "Thus says the LORD: Set your house in order, for you shall die; you shall not recover." 2 Then Hez·e·ki'ah turned his face to the wall and prayed to the LORD: 3 "Remember now, O LORD, I implore you, how I have walked before you in faithfulness with a whole heart, and have done what is good in your sight." Hez·e·ki'ah wept bitterly. 4 Before I·sāi'ah had gone out of the middle court, the word of the LORD came to him: 5 "Turn back, and say to Hez·e·ki'ah prince of my people, Thus says the LORD, the God of your ancestor David: I have heard your prayer, I have seen your tears; indeed, I will heal you; on the third day you shall go up to the house of the LORD. 6 I will add fifteen years to your life. I will deliver you and this city out of the hand of the king of Assyria; I will defend this city for my own sake and for my servant David's sake." 7 Then I·sāi'ah said, "Bring a lump of figs. Let them take it and apply it to the boil, so that he may recover."

8 Hez·e·ki'ah said to I·sāi'ah, "What shall be the sign that the LORD will heal me, and that I shall go up to the house of the LORD on the third day?" 9 I·sāi'ah said, "This is the sign to you from the LORD, that the LORD will do the thing that he has promised: the shadow has now advanced ten intervals; shall it retreat ten intervals?" 10 Hez·e·ki'ah answered, "It is normal for the shadow to lengthen ten intervals; rather let the shadow retreat ten intervals." 11 The prophet I·sāi'ah cried to the LORD; and he brought the shadow back the ten intervals, by which the sun*e* had declined on the dial of Ā'haz.

Envoys from Babylon
(Isa 39.1–8)

12 At that time King Mer'o·dach-bal'a·dan son of Bal'a·dan of Babylon sent envoys with letters and a present to Hez·e·ki'ah, for he had heard that Hez·e·ki'ah had been sick. 13 Hez·e·ki'ah welcomed them;*f* he showed them all his treasure house, the silver, the gold, the spices, the precious oil, his armory, all that was found in his storehouses; there was nothing in his house or in all his realm that Hez·e·ki'ah did not show them. 14 Then the prophet I·sāi'ah came to King Hez·e·ki'ah, and said to him, "What did these men say? From where did they come to you?" Hez·e·ki'ah answered, "They

---

d Gk Compare Isa 37.27 Q Ms: MT lacks *rising*   *e* Syr See Isa 38.8 and Tg: Heb *it*   *f* Gk Vg Syr: Heb *When Hezekiah heard about them*

have come from a far country, from Babylon."
15 He said, "What have they seen in your house?"
Hez•e•kī'ah answered, "They have seen all that is in
my house; there is nothing in my storehouses that I
did not show them."

16 Then Ī•sāi'ah said to Hez•e•kī'ah, "Hear the
word of the LORD: 17 Days are coming when all that
is in your house, and that which your ancestors
have stored up until this day, shall be carried to
Babylon; nothing shall be left, says the LORD.
18 Some of your own sons who are born to you
shall be taken away; they shall be eunuchs in the
palace of the king of Babylon." 19 Then Hez•e•kī'ah
said to Ī•sāi'ah, "The word of the LORD that you
have spoken is good." For he thought, "Why not, if
there will be peace and security in my days?"

Death of Hezekiah
(2 Chr 32.32–33)

20 The rest of the deeds of Hez•e•kī'ah, all his
power, how he made the pool and the conduit and
brought water into the city, are they not written in
the Book of the Annals of the Kings of Judah?
21 Hez•e•kī'ah slept with his ancestors; and his son
Ma•nas'seh succeeded him.

Manasseh Reigns over Judah
(2 Chr 33.1–20)

21 Ma•nas'seh was twelve years old when
he began to reign; he reigned fifty-five
years in Jerusalem. His mother's name was Heph'-
zi•bah. 2 He did what was evil in the sight of the
LORD, following the abominable practices of the
nations that the LORD drove out before the people
of Israel. 3 For he rebuilt the high places that his father Hez•e•kī'ah had destroyed; he erected altars for
Bā'al, made a sacred pole,⁸ as King Ā'hab of Israel
had done, worshiped all the host of heaven, and
served them. 4 He built altars in the house of the
LORD, of which the LORD had said, "In Jerusalem I
will put my name." 5 He built altars for all the host
of heaven in the two courts of the house of the
LORD. 6 He made his son pass through fire; he practiced soothsaying and augury, and dealt with mediums and with wizards. He did much evil in the
sight of the LORD, provoking him to anger. 7 The
carved image of A•shē'rah that he had made he set
in the house of which the LORD said to David and
to his son Solomon, "In this house, and in
Jerusalem, which I have chosen out of all the tribes
of Israel, I will put my name forever; 8 I will not
cause the feet of Israel to wander any more out of
the land that I gave to their ancestors, if only they
will be careful to do according to all that I have
commanded them, and according to all the law that
my servant Moses commanded them." 9 But they
did not listen; Ma•nas'seh misled them to do more

evil than the nations had done that the LORD destroyed before the people of Israel.

10 The LORD said by his servants the prophets,
11 "Because King Ma•nas'seh of Judah has committed these abominations, has done things more
wicked than all that the Am'o•rītes did, who were
before him, and has caused Judah also to sin with
his idols; 12 therefore thus says the LORD, the God
of Israel, I am bringing upon Jerusalem and Judah
such evil that the ears of everyone who hears of it
will tingle. 13 I will stretch over Jerusalem the
measuring line for Sa•mār'i•a, and the plummet
for the house of Ā'hab; I will wipe Jerusalem as
one wipes a dish, wiping it and turning it upside
down. 14 I will cast off the remnant of my heritage,
and give them into the hand of their enemies; they
shall become a prey and a spoil to all their enemies, 15 because they have done what is evil in my
sight and have provoked me to anger, since the
day their ancestors came out of Egypt, even to this
day."

16 Moreover Ma•nas'seh shed very much innocent blood, until he had filled Jerusalem from one
end to another, besides the sin that he caused Judah
to sin so that they did what was evil in the sight of
the LORD.

17 Now the rest of the acts of Ma•nas'seh, all
that he did, and the sin that he committed, are they
not written in the Book of the Annals of the Kings
of Judah? 18 Ma•nas'seh slept with his ancestors,
and was buried in the garden of his house, in the
garden of Uz'za. His son Ā'mon succeeded him.

Amon Reigns over Judah
(2 Chr 33.21–25)

19 Ā'mon was twenty-two years old when he began to reign; he reigned two years in Jerusalem. His
mother's name was Me•shul'le•meth daughter of
Hā'ruz of Jot'bah. 20 He did what was evil in the
sight of the LORD, as his father Ma•nas'seh had
done. 21 He walked in all the way in which his father walked, served the idols that his father served,
and worshiped them; 22 he abandoned the LORD,
the God of his ancestors, and did not walk in the
way of the LORD. 23 The servants of Ā'mon conspired against him, and killed the king in his house.
24 But the people of the land killed all those who
had conspired against King Ā'mon, and the people
of the land made his son Jō•sī'ah king in place of
him. 25 Now the rest of the acts of Ā'mon that he
did, are they not written in the Book of the Annals
of the Kings of Judah? 26 He was buried in his tomb
in the garden of Uz'za; then his son Jō•sī'ah succeeded him.

8 Heb *Asherah*

Josiah Reigns over Judah
(2 Chr 34.1–2)

22 Jō·sī'ah was eight years old when he began to reign; he reigned thirty-one years in Jerusalem. His mother's name was Je·dī'dah daughter of A·dāi'ah of Boz'kath. 2 He did what was right in the sight of the LORD, and walked in all the way of his father David; he did not turn aside to the right or to the left.

Hilkiah Finds the Book of the Law
(2 Chr 34.8–28)

3 In the eighteenth year of King Jō·sī'ah, the king sent Shā'phan son of Az·a·lī'ah, son of Me-shul'lam, the secretary, to the house of the LORD, saying, 4 "Go up to the high priest Hil·kī'ah, and have him count the entire sum of the money that has been brought into the house of the LORD, which the keepers of the threshold have collected from the people; 5 let it be given into the hand of the workers who have the oversight of the house of the LORD; let them give it to the workers who are at the house of the LORD, repairing the house, 6 that is, to the carpenters, to the builders, to the masons; and let them use it to buy timber and quarried stone to repair the house. 7 But no accounting shall be asked from them for the money that is delivered into their hand, for they deal honestly."

8 The high priest Hil·kī'ah said to Shā'phan the secretary, "I have found the book of the law in the house of the LORD." When Hil·kī'ah gave the book to Shā'phan, he read it. 9 Then Shā'phan the secretary came to the king, and reported to the king, "Your servants have emptied out the money that was found in the house, and have delivered it into the hand of the workers who have oversight of the house of the LORD." 10 Shā'phan the secretary informed the king, "The priest Hil·kī'ah has given me a book." Shā'phan then read it aloud to the king.

11 When the king heard the words of the book of the law, he tore his clothes. 12 Then the king commanded the priest Hil·kī'ah, A·hī'kam son of Shā'phan, Ach'bor son of Mī·cāi'ah, Shā'phan the secretary, and the king's servant A·sāi'ah, saying, 13 "Go, inquire of the LORD for me, for the people, and for all Judah, concerning the words of this book that has been found; for great is the wrath of the LORD that is kindled against us, because our ancestors did not obey the words of this book, to do according to all that is written concerning us."

14 So the priest Hil·kī'ah, A·hī'kam, Ach'bor, Shā'phan, and A·sāi'ah went to the prophetess Hul'dah the wife of Shal'lum son of Tik'vah, son of Har'has, keeper of the wardrobe; she resided in Jerusalem in the Second Quarter, where they consulted her. 15 She declared to them, "Thus says the LORD, the God of Israel: Tell the man who sent you

PRAY IT!

Josiah Brings Back the Ways of God

What happened to the Covenant? What happened to the Israelites' true traditions and prayer rituals? After worshiping false gods for so long, it seems as if people just forgot about the Covenant! Then in 2 Kings 22.8, Hilkiah discovers an old book, King Josiah reads it, and a religious reform is started. Josiah's reform is an effort to know and obey God's law and to restore worship to the one, true God. The holy days and holy ways of God are back—at least for a while (see also 2 Chronicles, chapters 34–35).

Reading can be powerful. Christians have a tremendous tradition of spiritual writings that inspire and renew faith. Spiritual autobiographies like *The Confessions of Saint Augustine*; *The Story of a Soul*, by Saint Thérèse of Lisieux; and *The Seven Storey Mountain*, by Thomas Merton, are classics. You might try starting with entertaining fictional books with a strong spiritual message, like the seven volumes of *The Chronicles of Narnia*, by C. S. Lewis, or the *Joshua* books, by Joseph F. Girzone. For other suggestions of spiritual writings you might enjoy, ask a parent, youth minister, teacher, or pastor.

▶ 2 Kings, chapters 22–23

to me, 16 Thus says the LORD, I will indeed bring disaster on this place and on its inhabitants—all the words of the book that the king of Judah has read. 17 Because they have abandoned me and have made offerings to other gods, so that they have provoked me to anger with all the work of their hands, therefore my wrath will be kindled against this place, and it will not be quenched. 18 But as to the king of Judah, who sent you to inquire of the LORD, thus shall you say to him, Thus says the LORD, the God of Israel: Regarding the words that you have heard, 19 because your heart was penitent, and you humbled yourself before the LORD, when you heard how I spoke against this place, and against its inhabitants, that they should become a desolation and a curse, and because you have torn your clothes and wept before me, I also have heard you, says the LORD. 20 Therefore, I will gather you to your ancestors, and you shall be gathered to your grave in peace; your eyes shall not see all the disaster that I will bring on this place." They took the message back to the king.

Josiah's Reformation
(2 Chr 34.29–33)

23 Then the king directed that all the elders of Judah and Jerusalem should be gathered to him. 2 The king went up to the house of the LORD, and with him went all the people of Judah, all the inhabitants of Jerusalem, the priests, the prophets, and all the people, both small and great; he read in their hearing all the words of the book of the covenant that had been found in the house of the LORD. 3 The king stood by the pillar and made a covenant before the LORD, to follow the LORD, keeping his commandments, his decrees, and his statutes, with all his heart and all his soul, to perform the words of this covenant that were written in this book. All the people joined in the covenant.

4 The king commanded the high priest Hilki'ah, the priests of the second order, and the guardians of the threshold, to bring out of the temple of the LORD all the vessels made for Ba'al, for A•she'rah, and for all the host of heaven; he burned them outside Jerusalem in the fields of the Kid'ron, and carried their ashes to Beth'el. 5 He deposed the idolatrous priests whom the kings of Judah had ordained to make offerings in the high places at the cities of Judah and around Jerusalem; those also who made offerings to Ba'al, to the sun, the moon, the constellations, and all the host of the heavens. 6 He brought out the image of[h] A•she'rah from the house of the LORD, outside Jerusalem, to the Wadi Kid'ron, burned it at the Wadi Kid'ron, beat it to dust and threw the dust of it upon the graves of the common people. 7 He broke down the houses of the male temple prostitutes that were in the house of the LORD, where the women did weaving for A•she'rah. 8 He brought all the priests out of the towns of Judah, and defiled the high places where the priests had made offerings, from Ge'ba to Be'er-she'ba; he broke down the high places of the gates that were at the entrance of the gate of Joshua the governor of the city, which were on the left at the gate of the city. 9 The priests of the high places, however, did not come up to the altar of the LORD in Jerusalem, but ate unleavened bread among their kindred. 10 He defiled To'pheth, which is in the valley of Ben-hin'nom, so that no one would make a son or a daughter pass through fire as an offering to Mo'lech. 11 He removed the horses that the kings of Judah had dedicated to the sun, at the entrance to the house of the LORD, by the chamber of the eunuch Na'than-me'lech, which were in the precincts;[i] then he burned the chariots of the sun with fire.

12 The altars on the roof of the upper chamber of A'haz, which the kings of Judah had made, and the altars that Ma•nas'seh had made in the two courts of the house of the LORD, he pulled down from there and broke in pieces, and threw the rubble into the Wadi Kid'ron. 13 The king defiled the high places that were east of Jerusalem, to the south of the Mount of Destruction, which King Solomon of Israel had built for As•tar'te the abomination of the Si•do'ni•ans, for Che'mosh the abomination of Mo'ab, and for Mil'com the abomination of the Am'mon•ites. 14 He broke the pillars in pieces, cut down the sacred poles,[j] and covered the sites with human bones.

15 Moreover, the altar at Beth'el, the high place erected by Jer•o•bo'am son of Ne'bat, who caused Israel to sin—he pulled down that altar along with the high place. He burned the high place, crushing it to dust; he also burned the sacred pole.[k] 16 As Jo•si'ah turned, he saw the tombs there on the mount; and he sent and took the bones out of the tombs, and burned them on the altar, and defiled it, according to the word of the LORD that the man of God proclaimed,[l] when Jer•o•bo'am stood by the altar at the festival; he turned and looked up at the tomb of the man of God who had predicted these things. 17 Then he said, "What is that monument that I see?" The people of the city told him, "It is the tomb of the man of God who came from Judah and predicted these things that you have done against the altar at Beth'el." 18 He said, "Let him rest; let no one move his bones." So they let his bones alone, with the bones of the prophet who came out of Sa•mar'i•a. 19 Moreover, Jo•si'ah removed all the shrines of the high places that were in the towns of Sa•mar'i•a, which kings of Israel had made, provoking the LORD to anger; he did to them just as he had done at Beth'el. 20 He slaughtered on the altars all the priests of the high places who were there, and burned human bones on them. Then he returned to Jerusalem.

The Passover Celebrated
(2 Chr 35.1–19)

21 The king commanded all the people, "Keep the passover to the LORD your God as prescribed in this book of the covenant." 22 No such passover had been kept since the days of the judges who judged Israel, even during all the days of the kings of Israel and of the kings of Judah; 23 but in the eighteenth year of King Jo•si'ah this passover was kept to the LORD in Jerusalem.

24 Moreover Jo•si'ah put away the mediums,

---

h Heb lacks *image of*   *i* Meaning of Heb uncertain   *j* Heb *Asherim*   *k* Heb *Asherah*   *l* Gk: Heb *proclaimed, who had predicted these things*

wizards, teraphim,ᵐ idols, and all the abominations that were seen in the land of Judah and in
Jerusalem, so that he established the words of the
law that were written in the book that the priest
Hil·kī′ah had found in the house of the LORD. 25 Before him there was no king like him, who turned to
the LORD with all his heart, with all his soul, and
with all his might, according to all the law of
Moses; nor did any like him arise after him.

26 Still the LORD did not turn from the fierceness of his great wrath, by which his anger was kindled against Judah, because of all the provocations
with which Ma·nas′seh had provoked him. 27 The
LORD said, "I will remove Judah also out of my
sight, as I have removed Israel; and I will reject this
city that I have chosen, Jerusalem, and the house of
which I said, My name shall be there."

Josiah Dies in Battle
(2 Chr 35.20—36.1)

28 Now the rest of the acts of Jō·sī′ah, and all
that he did, are they not written in the Book of the
Annals of the Kings of Judah? 29 In his days Pharaoh
Nē′cō king of Egypt went up to the king of Assyria to
the river Euphrates. King Jō·sī′ah went to meet him;
but when Pharaoh Nē′cō met him at Me·gid′dō, he
killed him. 30 His servants carried him dead in a
chariot from Me·gid′dō, brought him to Jerusalem,
and buried him in his own tomb. The people of the
land took Je·hō′a·haz son of Jō·sī′ah, anointed him,
and made him king in place of his father.

Reign and Captivity of Jehoahaz
(2 Chr 36.1–4)

31 Je·hō′a·haz was twenty-three years old when
he began to reign; he reigned three months in
Jerusalem. His mother's name was Ha·mū′tal
daughter of Jer·e·mī′ah of Lib′nah. 32 He did what
was evil in the sight of the LORD, just as his ancestors had done. 33 Pharaoh Nē′cō confined him at
Rib′lah in the land of Hā′math, so that he might not
reign in Jerusalem, and imposed tribute on the land
of one hundred talents of silver and a talent of gold.
34 Pharaoh Nē′cō made E·lī′a·kim son of Jō·sī′ah
king in place of his father Jō·sī′ah, and changed his
name to Je·hoi′a·kim. But he took Je·hō′a·haz away;
he came to Egypt, and died there. 35 Je·hoi′a·kim
gave the silver and the gold to Pharaoh, but he
taxed the land in order to meet Pharaoh's demand
for money. He exacted the silver and the gold from
the people of the land, from all according to their
assessment, to give it to Pharaoh Nē′cō.

Jehoiakim Reigns over Judah
(2 Chr 36.5–8)

36 Je·hoi′a·kim was twenty-five years old when
he began to reign; he reigned eleven years in Jeru-

salem. His mother's name was Ze·bī′dah daughter
of Pe·dāi′ah of Rū′mah. 37 He did what was evil in
the sight of the LORD, just as all his ancestors had
done.

Judah Overrun by Enemies

24 In his days King Ne·bū·chad·nez′zar of
Babylon came up; Je·hoi′a·kim became
his servant for three years; then he turned and rebelled against him. 2 The LORD sent against him
bands of the Chal·dē′ans, bands of the Ar·a·mē′ans,
bands of the Mō′ab·ītes, and bands of the Am′-
mon·ītes; he sent them against Judah to destroy it,
according to the word of the LORD that he spoke by
his servants the prophets. 3 Surely this came upon
Judah at the command of the LORD, to remove
them out of his sight, for the sins of Ma·nas′seh, for
all that he had committed, 4 and also for the innocent blood that he had shed; for he filled Jerusalem
with innocent blood, and the LORD was not willing
to pardon. 5 Now the rest of the deeds of Je·hoi′-
a·kim, and all that he did, are they not written in
the Book of the Annals of the Kings of Judah? 6 So
Je·hoi′a·kim slept with his ancestors; then his son
Je·hoi′a·chin succeeded him. 7 The king of Egypt
did not come again out of his land, for the king of
Babylon had taken over all that belonged to the
king of Egypt from the Wadi of Egypt to the River
Euphrates.

Reign and Captivity of Jehoiachin
(2 Chr 36.9–10)

8 Je·hoi′a·chin was eighteen years old when he
began to reign; he reigned three months in Jerusalem. His mother's name was Ne·hush′ta daughter
of El·nā′than of Jerusalem. 9 He did what was evil
in the sight of the LORD, just as his father had done.

10 At that time the servants of King Ne·bū·
chad·nez′zar of Babylon came up to Jerusalem, and
the city was besieged. 11 King Ne·bū·chad·nez′zar of
Babylon came to the city, while his servants were
besieging it; 12 King Je·hoi′a·chin of Judah gave
himself up to the king of Babylon, himself, his
mother, his servants, his officers, and his palace officials. The king of Babylon took him prisoner in
the eighth year of his reign.

Capture of Jerusalem

13 He carried off all the treasures of the house
of the LORD, and the treasures of the king's house;
he cut in pieces all the vessels of gold in the temple
of the LORD, which King Solomon of Israel had
made, all this as the LORD had foretold. 14 He carried away all Jerusalem, all the officials, all the warriors, ten thousand captives, all the artisans and the

---

m Or *household gods*

smiths; no one remained, except the poorest people of the land. 15 He carried away Je·hoi′a·chin to Babylon; the king's mother, the king's wives, his officials, and the elite of the land, he took into captivity from Jerusalem to Babylon. 16 The king of Babylon brought captive to Babylon all the men of valor, seven thousand, the artisans and the smiths, one thousand, all of them strong and fit for war. 17 The king of Babylon made Mat·ta·ni′ah, Je·hoi′a·chin's uncle, king in his place, and changed his name to Zed·e·ki′ah.

Zedekiah Reigns over Judah
(2 Chr 36.11–14; Jer 52.1–3a)

18 Zed·e·ki′ah was twenty-one years old when he began to reign; he reigned eleven years in Jerusalem. His mother's name was Ha·mu′tal daughter of Jer·e·mi′ah of Lib′nah. 19 He did what was evil in the sight of the LORD, just as Je·hoi′a·kim had done. 20 Indeed, Jerusalem and Judah so angered the LORD that he expelled them from his presence.

The Fall and Captivity of Judah
(2 Chr 36.15–21; Jer 52.3b–30)

Zed·e·ki′ah rebelled against the king of Babylon.

25 1 And in the ninth year of his reign, in the tenth month, on the tenth day of the month, King Ne·bu·chad·nez′zar of Babylon came with all his army against Jerusalem, and laid siege to it; they built siegeworks against it all around. 2 So the city was besieged until the eleventh year of King Zed·e·ki′ah. 3 On the ninth day of the fourth month the famine became so severe in the city that there was no food for the people of the land. 4 Then a breach was made in the city wall;n the king with all the soldiers fled° by night by the way of the gate between the two walls, by the king's garden, though the Chal·de′ans were all around the city. They went in the direction of the Ar′a·bah. 5 But the army of the Chal·de′ans pursued the king, and overtook him in the plains of Jericho; all his army was scattered, deserting him. 6 Then they captured the king and brought him up to the king of Babylon at Rib′lah, who passed sentence on him. 7 They slaughtered the sons of Zed·e·ki′ah before his eyes, then put out the eyes of Zed·e·ki′ah; they bound him in fetters and took him to Babylon.

8 In the fifth month, on the seventh day of the month—which was the nineteenth year of King Ne·bu·chad·nez′zar, king of Babylon—Ne·bu·za·rad′an, the captain of the bodyguard, a servant of the king of Babylon, came to Jerusalem. 9 He burned the house of the LORD, the king's house, and all the houses of Jerusalem; every great house he burned down. 10 All the army of the Chal·de′ans who were with the captain of the guard broke down

the walls around Jerusalem. 11 Ne·bu·za·rad′an the captain of the guard carried into exile the rest of the people who were left in the city and the deserters who had defected to the king of Babylon—all the rest of the population. 12 But the captain of the guard left some of the poorest people of the land to be vinedressers and tillers of the soil.

13 The bronze pillars that were in the house of the LORD, as well as the stands and the bronze sea that were in the house of the LORD, the Chal·de′ans broke in pieces, and carried the bronze to Babylon. 14 They took away the pots, the shovels, the snuffers, the dishes for incense, and all the bronze vessels used in the temple service, 15 as well as the firepans and the basins. What was made of gold the captain of the guard took away for the gold, and what was made of silver, for the silver. 16 As for the two pillars, the one sea, and the stands, which Solomon had made for the house of the LORD, the bronze of all these vessels was beyond weighing. 17 The height of the one pillar was eighteen cubits, and on it was a bronze capital; the height of the capital was three cubits; latticework and pomegranates, all of bronze, were on the capital all around.

---

n Heb lacks *wall*   ° Gk Compare Jer 39.4; 52.7: Heb lacks *the king* and lacks *fled*

---

did you KNOW?
The Fall of Jerusalem

The second conquest and exile described in 2 Kings (see "The First Captivity," 17.5–18, for the first) involves the southern kingdom, Judah. Judah was conquered by the Babylonians in 587 B.C., which is why that event is often referred to as the Babylonian Exile (see map 5, "The Babylonian Empire"). The author of Kings implies that the kingdom of Judah lasted longer than the kingdom of Israel because it had faithful reformer kings like Hezekiah and Josiah. The fall of Judah was particularly devastating because both Jerusalem, David's city, and the Temple, the central place of worship, were destroyed. The whole Book of Lamentations is an expression of the sorrow and grief the people experienced as a result.

▶ **2 Kings 25.1–21**

2 K I N G S

The second pillar had the same, with the lattice-work.

18 The captain of the guard took the chief priest Se•rāi′ah, the second priest Zeph•a•nī′ah, and the three guardians of the threshold; 19 from the city he took an officer who had been in command of the soldiers, and five men of the king's council who were found in the city; the secretary who was the commander of the army who mustered the people of the land; and sixty men of the people of the land who were found in the city. 20 Ne•bū•za•rad′an the captain of the guard took them, and brought them to the king of Babylon at Rib′lah. 21 The king of Babylon struck them down and put them to death at Rib′lah in the land of Hā′math. So Judah went into exile out of its land.

Gedaliah Made Governor of Judah
(Jer 40.5—41.18)

22 He appointed Ged•a•lī′ah son of A•hī′kam son of Shā′phan as governor over the people who remained in the land of Judah, whom King Ne•bū•chad•nez′zar of Babylon had left. 23 Now when all the captains of the forces and their men heard that the king of Babylon had appointed Ged•a•lī′ah as governor, they came with their men to Ged•a•lī′ah at Miz′pah, namely, Ish′ma•el son of Neth•a•nī′ah, Jō•hā′nan son of Ka•rē′ah, Se•rāi′ah son of Tan′hu•meth the Ne•toph′a•thīte, and Jā•az-a•nī′ah son of the Mā′a•ca•thīte. 24 Ged•a•lī′ah swore to them and their men, saying, "Do not be afraid because of the Chal•dē′an officials; live in the land, serve the king of Babylon, and it shall be well with you." 25 But in the seventh month, Ish′ma•el son of Neth•a•nī′ah son of E•lish′a•ma, of the royal family, came with ten men; they struck down Ged•a•lī′ah so that he died, along with the Judeans and Chal•dē′ans who were with him at Miz′pah. 26 Then all the people, high and low,[p] and the captains of the forces set out and went to Egypt; for they were afraid of the Chal•dē′ans.

Jehoiachin Released from Prison
(Jer 52.31–34)

27 In the thirty-seventh year of the exile of King Je•hoi′a•chin of Judah, in the twelfth month, on the twenty-seventh day of the month, King Ē′vil-me•rō′dach of Babylon, in the year that he began to reign, released King Je•hoi′a•chin of Judah from prison; 28 he spoke kindly to him, and gave him a seat above the other seats of the kings who were with him in Babylon. 29 So Je•hoi′a•chin put aside his prison clothes. Every day of his life he dined regularly in the king's presence. 30 For his allowance, a regular allowance was given him by the king, a portion every day, as long as he lived.

---

p Or *young and old*

Have you ever had a friendly disagreement with someone over the interpretation of something? Did you each emphasize different aspects to support your interpretation? The First and Second Books of Chronicles are another interpretation of the history of the people of Israel. These books downplay the Covenant and emphasize the importance of institutional ritual and worship of God.

In-depth

The Chronicler is the name given to the unknown author (or authors) of 1 and 2 Chronicles. The Chronicler, writing after the Israelites returned from the Exile in Babylon, has a unique perspective, so unique that he almost never mentions the Sinai Covenant or Moses (central themes throughout other parts of the Old Testament). Because the Israelites cannot have their own king, the Chronicler emphasizes a new type of reign, one governed by priests instead of kings.

The Chronicler uses two types of material—genealogies and lively sermons—to summarize Israel's history from the Creation to around 525 B.C. But he primarily focuses on Kings David and Solomon. They are praised extensively because of their role in centralizing worship in Jerusalem and building the Temple. Many of the negative stories about David from 2 Samuel—such as his affair with Bathsheba—are not even mentioned. The Chronicler wants nothing to tarnish the people's memory of an ideal kingdom that might one day be restored.

Second Chronicles also focuses on the southern kingdom of Judah and ignores the northern kingdom of Israel after Solomon's death. This may well be due to a bias of the priestly class in Jerusalem against the religious practice of the northern tribes. This bias lasted into Jesus' time.

The goal of 1 and 2 Chronicles was to give the Israelites hope for the future after returning from the Exile. The Chronicler reminded them that if they maintained their religious practices and worship of God, they would continue to be God's people.

At a Glance

- **1 Chronicles, chapters 1–9.** genealogies of Israel
- **1 Chronicles, chapters 10–29.** David's kingship
- **2 Chronicles, chapters 1–9.** Solomon's kingship
- **2 Chronicles, chapters 10–36.** the kings of Judah after Solomon's death

Quick Facts

Period Covered
Creation to the end of the Babylonian captivity

Author
a Levite cantor and scribe writing after the return to Jerusalem around 400 B.C.

Theme
Israel can secure its future by continuing its worship in the pattern established by David.

1 Chronicles

Chap. 15

From Adam to Abraham
(Gen 5.1–32; 10.1–32; 11.10–26; Lk 3.34–38)

1 Adam, Seth, Ē′nosh; ² Kē′nan, Ma•hal′a•lel, Jar′ed; ³ Ē′noch, Me•thū′se•lah, Lā′mech; ⁴ Noah, Shem, Ham, and Jā′pheth.

5 The descendants of Jā′pheth: Gō′mer, Mā′gog, Mā′daī, Jā′van, Tū′bal, Mē′shech, and Tī′ras. ⁶ The descendants of Gō′mer: Ash′ke•naz, Dī′phath,*a* and Tō•gar′mah. ⁷ The descendants of Jā′van: E•li′shah, Tar′shish, Kit′tim, and Rod′a•nim.*b*

8 The descendants of Ham: Cush, Egypt, Put, and Cā′naan. ⁹ The descendants of Cush: Sē′ba, Hav′i•lah, Sab′ta, Rā′a•ma, and Sab′te•ca. The descendants of Rā′a•mah: Shē′ba and Dē′dan. ¹⁰ Cush became the father of Nim′rod; he was the first to be a mighty one on the earth.

11 Egypt became the father of Lū′dim, An′a•mim, Le•hā′bim, Naph′tū•him, ¹² Path•rū′sim, Cas•lū′him, and Caph′to•rim, from whom the Phi•lis′tines come.*c*

13 Cā′naan became the father of Sī′don his firstborn, and Heth, ¹⁴ and the Jeb′ū•sītes, the Am′o•rītes, the Gir′ga•shītes, ¹⁵ the Hī′vītes, the Ar′kītes, the Sī′nītes, ¹⁶ the Ar′vad•ītes, the Zem′a•rītes, and the Hā′math•ītes.

17 The descendants of Shem: Ē′lam, As′shur, Ar•pach′shad, Lud, Ar′am, Uz, Hul, Gē′ther, and Mē′shech.*d* ¹⁸ Ar•pach′shad became the father of Shē′lah; and Shē′lah became the father of Ē′ber. ¹⁹ To Ē′ber were born two sons: the name of the one

was Pē′leg (for in his days the earth was divided), and the name of his brother Jok′tan. ²⁰ Jok′tan became the father of Al•mō′dad, Shē′leph, Hā•zar•mā′veth, Jē′rah, ²¹ Ha•dor′am, Ū′zal, Dik′lah, ²² Ē′bal, A•bim′a•el, Shē′ba, ²³ Ō′phir, Hav′i•lah, and Jō′bab; all these were the descendants of Jok′tan.

24 Shem, Ar•pach′shad, Shē′lah; ²⁵ Ē′ber, Pē′leg, Rē′ū; ²⁶ Sē′rug, Nā′hor, Tē′rah; ²⁷ Abram, that is, Abraham.

From Abraham to Jacob
(Gen 25.1–4, 12–16; 36.1–30)

28 The sons of Abraham: Isaac and Ish′ma•el. ²⁹ These are their genealogies: the firstborn of Ish′ma•el, Ne•bā′i•oth; and Kē′dar, Ad′bē•el, Mib′sam, ³⁰ Mish′ma, Dū′mah, Mas′sa, Hā′dad, Tē′ma, ³¹ Jē′tur, Nā′phish, and Ked′e•mah. These are the sons of Ish′ma•el. ³² The sons of Ke•tū′rah, Abraham's concubine: she bore Zim′ran, Jok′shan, Mē′dan, Mid′i•an, Ish′bak, and Shū′ah. The sons of Jok′shan: Shē′ba and Dē′dan. ³³ The sons of Mid′i•an: Ē′phah, Ē′pher, Hā′noch, A•bī′da, and El•dā′ah. All these were the descendants of Ke•tū′rah.

34 Abraham became the father of Isaac. The sons of Isaac: Esau and Israel. ³⁵ The sons of Esau: E•lī′phaz, Reū′el, Jē′ush, Jā′lam, and Kō′rah. ³⁶ The

---

a Gen 10.3 *Ripath*; See Gk Vg   *b* Gen 10.4 *Dodanim*; See Syr Vg   *c* Heb *Casluhim, from which the Philistines come, Caphtorim*; See Am 9.7, Jer 47.4   *d* *Mash* in Gen 10.23

sons of E•lī′phaz: Tē′man, Ō′mar, Zē′phī, Gā′tam, Kē′naz, Tim′na, and Am′a•lek. 37 The sons of Reū′el: Nā′hath, Zē′rah, Sham′mah, and Miz′zah.

38 The sons of Sē′ir: Lō′tan, Shō′bal, Zib′ē•on, An′ah, Dī′shon, Ē′zer, and Dī′shan. 39 The sons of Lō′tan: Hō′rī and Hō′mam; and Lō′tan′s sister was Tim′na. 40 The sons of Shō′bal: Al′i•an, Man′a•hath, Ē′bal, Shē′phī, and Ō′nam. The sons of Zib′ē•on: Ā′i•ah and An′ah. 41 The sons of An′ah: Dī′shon. The sons of Dī′shon: Ham′ran, Esh′ban, Ith′ran, and Chē′ran. 42 The sons of Ē′zer: Bil′han, Zā′a•van, and Jā′a•kan.*e* The sons of Dī′shan: *f* Uz and Ar′an.

43 These are the kings who reigned in the land of Ē′dom before any king reigned over the Israelites: Bē′la son of Bē′or, whose city was called Din′ha•bah. 44 When Bē′la died, Jō′bab son of Zē′rah of Boz′rah succeeded him. 45 When Jō′bab died, Hū′sham of the land of the Tē′man•ites succeeded him. 46 When Hū′sham died, Hā′dad son of Bē′dad, who defeated Mid′i•an in the country of Mō′ab, succeeded him; and the name of his city was Ā′vith. 47 When Hā′dad died, Sam′lah of Mas•rē′kah succeeded him. 48 When Sam′lah died, Shā′ul*g* of Re•hō′both on the Euphrates succeeded him. 49 When Shā′ul*g* died, Bā′al-hā′nan son of Ach′bor succeeded him. 50 When Bā′al-hā′nan died, Hā′dad succeeded him; the name of his city was Pā′ī, and his wife′s name Me•het′a•bel daughter of Mā′tred, daughter of Me-za•hab′. 51 And Hā′dad died.

The clans*h* of Ē′dom were: clans*h* Tim′na, Al′i•ah,*i* Jē′theth, 52 Ō•hol•i•bā′mah, Ē′lah, Pī′non, 53 Kē′naz, Tē′man, Mib′zar, 54 Mag′di•el, and Ī′ram; these are the clans*h* of Ē′dom.

The Sons of Israel and the Descendants of Judah
(Gen 29.31–30.24; 35.16–18; 46.8–25; Ruth 4.18–22; Mt 1.2–6; Lk 33.1–33)

2 These are the sons of Israel: Reuben, Sim′ē•on, Levi, Judah, Is′sa•char, Zeb′ū•lun, 2 Dan, Joseph, Benjamin, Naph′ta•lī, Gad, and Ash′er. 3 The sons of Judah: Er, Ō′nan, and Shē′lah; these three the Cā′naan•ite woman Bath-shū′a bore to him. Now Er, Judah′s firstborn, was wicked in the sight of the LORD, and he put him to death. 4 His daughter-in-law Tā′mar also bore him Per′ez and Zē′rah. Judah had five sons in all.

5 The sons of Per′ez: Hez′ron and Hā′mul. 6 The sons of Zē′rah: Zim′rī, Ē′than, Hē′man, Cal′col, and Dar′a,*j* five in all. 7 The sons of Car′mī: Ā′char, the troubler of Israel, who transgressed in the matter of the devoted thing; 8 and Ē′than′s son was Az•a•rī′ah.

9 The sons of Hez′ron, who were born to him: Je•rah′mē•el, Ram, and Che•lū′bai. 10 Ram became the father of Am•min′a•dab, and Am•min′a•dab became the father of Nah′shon, prince of the sons of Judah. 11 Nah′shon became the father of Sal′ma,

Sal′ma of Bō′az, 12 Bō′az of Ō′bed, Ō′bed of Jesse. 13 Jesse became the father of E•lī′ab his firstborn, A•bin′a•dab the second, Shim′ē•a the third, 14 Ne•than′el the fourth, Rad′dai the fifth, 15 Ō′zem the sixth, David the seventh; 16 and their sisters were Ze•rū′i•ah and Ab′i•gāil. The sons of Ze•rū′i•ah: A•bi′shai, Jō′ab, and As′a•hel, three. 17 Ab′i•gāil bore A•mā′sa, and the father of A•mā′sa was Jē′ther the Ish′ma•el•īte.

18 Caleb son of Hez′ron had children by his wife A•zū′bah, and by Jer′i•oth; these were her sons: Jē′sher, Shō′bab, and Ar′don. 19 When A•zū′bah died, Caleb married Eph′rath, who bore him Hur. 20 Hur became the father of Ū′rī, and Ū′rī became the father of Bez′a•lel.

21 Afterward Hez′ron went in to the daughter of Mā′chir father of Gil′e•ad, whom he married when he was sixty years old; and she bore him Sē′gub; 22 and Sē′gub became the father of Jā′ir, who had twenty-three towns in the land of Gil′e•ad. 23 But Gē′shur and Ar′am took from them Hav′voth-jā′ir, Kē′nath and its villages, sixty towns. All these were descendants of Mā′chir, father of Gil′e•ad. 24 After the death of Hez′ron, in Cā′leb-eph′ra•thah, A•bī′jah wife of Hez′ron bore him Ash′hur, father of Te•kō′a.

25 The sons of Je•rah′mē•el, the firstborn of Hez′ron: Ram his firstborn, Bū′nah, Ō′ren, Ō′zem, and A•hī′jah. 26 Je•rah′mē•el also had another wife, whose name was At′a•rah; she was the mother of Ō′nam. 27 The sons of Ram, the firstborn of Je•rah′mē•el: Mā′az, Jā′min, and Ē′ker. 28 The sons of Ō′nam: Sham′maī and Jā′da. The sons of Sham′maī: Nā′dab and A•bī′shur. 29 The name of A•bī′shur′s wife was Ab•i•hā′il, and she bore him Ah′ban and Mō′lid. 30 The sons of Nā′dab: Sē′led and Ap′pa•im; and Sē′led died childless. 31 The son*k* of Ap′pa•im: Ish′ī. The son*k* of Ish′ī: Shē′shan. The son*k* of Shē′shan: Ah′laī. 32 The sons of Jā′da, Sham′maī′s brother: Jē′ther and Jonathan; and Jē′ther died childless. 33 The sons of Jonathan: Pē′leth and Zā′za. These were the descendants of Je•rah′mē•el. 34 Now Shē′shan had no sons, only daughters; but Shē′shan had an Egyptian slave, whose name was Jar′ha. 35 So Shē′shan gave his daughter in marriage to his slave Jar′ha; and she bore him At′taī. 36 At′taī became the father of Nathan, and Nathan of Zā′bad. 37 Zā′bad became the father of Eph′lal, and Eph′lal of Ō′bed. 38 Ō′bed became the father of Jē′hū, and Jē′hū of Az•a•rī′ah. 39 Az•a•rī′ah became the father of Hē′lez, and Hē′lez of El•e•ā′sah. 40 El•e•ā′sah became the father of Sis′maī, and Sis′maī of Shal′lum.

---

e Or *and Akan; See* Gen 36.27   *f* See 1.38: Heb *Dishon*
g Or *Saul*   *h* Or *chiefs*   *i* Or *Alvah; See* Gen 36.40   *j* Or *Darda;* Compare Syr Tg some Gk Mss; See 1 Kings 4.31
k Heb *sons*

41 Shal'lum became the father of Jek•a•mī'ah, and Jek•a•mī'ah of E•lish'a•ma.

42 The sons of Caleb brother of Je•rah'mē•el: Mē'sha[l] his firstborn, who was father of Ziph. The sons of Ma•rē'shah father of Hē'bron. 43 The sons of Hē'bron: Kō'rah, Tap'pū•ah, Rē'kem, and Shē'ma. 44 Shē'ma became father of Rā'ham, father of Jor'kē•am; and Rē'kem became the father of Sham'mai. 45 The son of Sham'mai: Mā'on; and Mā'on was the father of Beth-zur. 46 Ē'phah also, Caleb's concubine, bore Har'an, Mō'za, and Gā'zez; and Har'an became the father of Gā'zez. 47 The sons of Jah'dai: Rē'gem, Jō'tham, Gē'shan, Pē'let, Ē'phah, and Shā'aph. 48 Mā'a•cah, Caleb's concubine, bore Shē'ber and Tir'ha•nah. 49 She also bore Shā'aph father of Mad•man'nah, Shē'va father of Mach•bē'nah and father of Gib'ē•a; and the daughter of Caleb was Ach'sah. 50 These were the descendants of Caleb.

The sons[m] of Hur the firstborn of Eph'ra•thah: Shō'bal father of Kir'i•ath-jē'a•rim, 51 Sal'ma father of Bethlehem, and Har'eph father of Beth-gā'der. 52 Shō'bal father of Kir'i•ath-jē'a•rim had other sons: Ha•rō'eh, half of the Me•nū'hoth. 53 And the families of Kir'i•ath-jē'a•rim: the Ith'rītes, the Pū'thītes, the Shū'ma•thītes, and the Mish'ra•ītes; from these came the Zō'ra•thītes and the Esh'ta•o•lītes. 54 The sons of Sal'ma: Bethlehem, the Ne•toph'a•thītes, At'roth-beth-jō'ab, and half of the Man•a•hā'thītes, the Zō'rites. 55 The families also of the scribes that lived at Jā'bez: the Tī'ra•thītes, the Shim'ē•a•thītes, and the Sū'ca•thītes. These are the Ken'ītes who came from Ham'math, father of the house of Rē'chab.

Descendants of David and Solomon
(Mt 1.6–12)

3 These are the sons of David who were born to him in Hē'bron: the firstborn Am'non, by A•hin'ō•am the Jez'rē•el•īte; the second Daniel, by Ab'i•gail the Car'mel•īte; 2 the third Ab'sa•lom, son of Mā'a•cah, daughter of King Tal'mai of Gē'shur; the fourth Ad•o•nī'jah, son of Hag'gith; 3 the fifth Sheph•a•tī'ah, by A•bi'tal; the sixth Ith'rē•am, by his wife Eg'lah; 4 six were born to him in Hē'bron, where he reigned for seven years and six months. And he reigned thirty-three years in Jerusalem. 5 These were born to him in Jerusalem: Shim'ē•a, Shō'bab, Nathan, and Solomon, four by Bath-shū'a, daughter of Am'mi•el; 6 then Ib'har, E•lish'a•ma, E•liph'e•let, 7 Nō'gah, Nē'pheg, Ja•phi'a, 8 E•lish'a•ma, E•lī'a•da, and E•liph'e•let, nine. 9 All these were David's sons, besides the sons of the concubines; and Tā'mar was their sister.

10 The descendants of Solomon: Rē•ho•bō'am, A•bī'jah his son, Asa his son, Je•hosh'a•phat his son, 11 Jō'ram his son, A•ha•zī'ah his son, Jō'ash his son,

12 Am•a•zī'ah his son, Az•a•rī'ah his son, Jō'tham his son, 13 Ā'haz his son, Hez•e•kī'ah his son, Ma•nas'seh his son, 14 Ā'mon his son, Jō•sī'ah his son. 15 The sons of Jō•sī'ah: Jō•hā'nan the firstborn, the second Je•hoi'a•kim, the third Zed•e•kī'ah, the fourth Shal'lum. 16 The descendants of Je•hoi'a•kim: Jec•o•nī'ah his son, Zed•e•kī'ah his son; 17 and the sons of Jec•o•nī'ah, the captive: She•al'ti•el his son, 18 Mal•chī'ram, Pe•dāi'ah, Shen•az'zar, Jek•a•mī'ah, Hosh'a•ma, and Ned•a•bī'ah; 19 The sons of Pe•dāi'ah: Ze•rub'ba•bel and Shim'ē•ī; and the sons of Ze•rub'ba•bel: Me•shul'lam and Han•a•nī'ah, and She•lō'mith was their sister; 20 and Ha•shū'bah, Ō'hel, Ber•e•chī'ah, Has•a•dī'ah, and Jū'shab-hē'sed, five. 21 The sons of Han•a•nī'ah: Pel•a•tī'ah and Je•shā'i•ah, his son[n] Reph•āi'ah, his son[n] Ar'nan, his son[n] Ō•ba•dī'ah, his son[n] Shec•a•nī'ah. 22 The son[o] of Shec•a•nī'ah: She•māi'ah. And the sons of She•māi'ah: Hat'tush, Ī'gal, Ba•rī'ah, Nē•a•rī'ah, and Shā'phat, six. 23 The sons of

---

[l] Gk reads *Mareshah*　[m] Gk Vg: Heb *son*　[n] Gk Compare Syr Vg: Heb *sons of*　[o] Heb *sons*

did you KNOW?

Genealogies

Look at all these names! Our present-day interest in family trees obviously has ancient roots. The first nine chapters of 1 Chronicles consist entirely of family trees—or genealogies—tracing the history of Israel from Adam to Saul. In a culture where not only money and identity but also the offices of priest and king passed from one generation to another, it was essential to be able to trace one's bloodline.

The many genealogies of the Old Testament answer important questions: How were the various tribes related to one another? Who were a particular tribe's ancestors? What right did a certain group or person have to the office of priest or king? The Chronicler lists the genealogies of David and Levi in considerable detail. The kingship and the priesthood were clearly of special interest to him.

▶ **1 Chronicles, chapters 1–9**

Nē·a·rī'ah: El·i·ō·ē'naī, Hiz·kī'ah, and Az·rī'kam, three. 24 The sons of El·i·ō·ē'naī: Hod·a·vī'ah, E·lī'a·shib, Pe·lāi'ah, Ak'kub, Jō·hā'nan, De·laī'ah, and A·nā'nī, seven.

Descendants of Judah

4 The sons of Judah: Per'ez, Hez'ron, Car'mī, Hur, and Shō'bal. 2 Rē·āi'ah son of Shō'bal became the father of Jā'hath, and Jā'hath became the father of A·hū'māi and Lā'had. These were the families of the Zō'ra·thītes. 3 These were the sons[p] of Ē'tam: Jez'rē·el, Ish'ma, and Id'bash; and the name of their sister was Haz·ze·lel·pō'nī, 4 and Pe·nū'el was the father of Gē'dor, and Ē'zer the father of Hū'shah. These were the sons of Hur, the firstborn of Eph'ra·thah, the father of Bethlehem. 5 Ash'hur father of Te·kō'a had two wives, Hē'lah and Nā'a·rah; 6 Nā'a·rah bore him A·huz'zam, Hē'pher, Tē'me·nī, and Hā·a·hash'ta·rī.[q] These were the sons of Nā'a·rah. 7 The sons of Hē'lah: Zē'reth, Iz'har,[r] and Eth'nan. 8 Koz became the father of Ā'nub, Zō·bē'bah, and the families of A·har'hel son of Har'um. 9 Jā'bez was honored more than his brothers; and his mother named him Jā'bez, saying, "Because I bore him in pain." 10 Jā'bez called on the God of Israel, saying, "Oh that you would bless me and enlarge my border, and that your hand might be with me, and that you would keep me from hurt and harm!" And God granted what he asked. 11 Chē'lub the brother of Shū'hah became the father of Mē'hir, who was the father of Esh'ton. 12 Esh'ton became the father of Beth-rā'pha, Pa·sē'ah, and Te·hin'nah the father of Ir-nā'hash. These are the men of Rē'cah. 13 The sons of Kē'naz: Oth'ni·el and Se·rāi'ah; and the sons of Oth'ni·el: Hā'thath and Me·ō'no·thaī.[s] 14 Me·ō'no·thaī became the father of Oph'rah; and Se·rāi'ah became the father of Jō'ab father of Gē-har'a·shim,[t] so-called because they were artisans. 15 The sons of Caleb son of Je·phūn'neh: I'rū, Ē'lah, and Nā'am; and the son[u] of Ē'lah: Kē'naz. 16 The sons of Je·hal'le·lel: Ziph, Zī'phah, Tir'i·a, and As'a·rel. 17 The sons of Ez'rah: Jē'ther, Mē'red, Ē'pher, and Jā'lon. These are the sons of Bith'i·ah, daughter of Pharaoh, whom Mē'red married;[v] and she conceived and bore[w] Miriam, Sham'maī, and Ish'bah father of Esh·te·mō'a. 18 And his Judean wife bore Jē'red father of Gē'dor, Hē'ber father of Sō'cō, and Je·kū'thi·el father of Za·nō'ah. 19 The sons of the wife of Hō·dī'ah, the sister of Nā'ham, were the fathers of Kē·ī'lah the Gar'mīte and Esh·te·mō'a the Mā'a·ca·thīte. 20 The sons of Shī'mon: Am'non, Rin'nah, Ben-hā'nan, and Ti'lon. The sons of Ish'ī: Zō'heth and Ben-zō'heth. 21 The sons of Shē'lah son of Judah: Er father of Lē'cah, Lā'a·dah father of Ma·rē'shah, and the families of the guild of linen workers at Beth-ash·bē'a; 22 and Jō'kim, and the men of Cō·zē'ba, and Jō'ash, and Sar'aph, who married into Mō'ab but returned to Lē'hem[x] (now the records[y] are ancient). 23 These were the potters and inhabitants of Ne·tā'im and Ge·dē'rah; they lived there with the king in his service.

Descendants of Simeon
(Gen 46.10)

24 The sons of Sim'ē·on: Nem'ū·el, Jā'min, Jā'rib, Zē'rah, Shā'ūl;[z] 25 Shal'lum was his son, Mib'sam his son, Mish'ma his son. 26 The sons of Mish'ma: Ham'mū·el his son, Zac'cur his son, Shim'ē·ī his son. 27 Shim'ē·ī had sixteen sons and six daughters; but his brothers did not have many children, nor did all their family multiply like the Judeans. 28 They lived in Bē'er-shē'ba, Mō'la·dah, Hā'zar-shū'al, 29 Bil'hah, Ē'zem, Tō'lad, 30 Be·thū'el, Hor'mah, Zik'lag, 31 Beth-mar'ca·both, Hā'zar-sū'sim, Beth-bi'rī, and Shā·a·rā'im. These were their towns until David became king. 32 And their villages were Ē'tam, Ā'in, Rim'mon, Tō'chen, and Ā'shan, five towns, 33 along with all their villages that were around these towns as far as Bā'al. These were their settlements. And they kept a genealogical record.

34 Me·shō'bab, Jam'lech, Jō'shah son of Am·a·zī'ah, 35 Jō'el, Jē'hū son of Josh·i·bī'ah son of Se·rāi'ah son of As'i·el, 36 El·i·ō·ē'naī, Jā·a·kō'bah, Jesh·ō·hāi'ah, A·sāi'ah, Ad'i·el, Je·sim'i·el, Be·nā'i·ah, 37 Zī'za son of Shī'phī son of Al'lon son of Je·daī'ah son of Shim'rī son of She·māi'ah— 38 these mentioned by name were leaders in their families, and their clans increased greatly. 39 They journeyed to the entrance of Gē'dor, to the east side of the valley, to seek pasture for their flocks, 40 where they found rich, good pasture, and the land was very broad, quiet, and peaceful; for the former inhabitants there belonged to Ham. 41 These, registered by name, came in the days of King Hez·e·kī'ah of Judah, and attacked their tents and the Me·ū'nim who were found there, and exterminated them to this day, and settled in their place, because there was pasture there for their flocks. 42 And some of them, five hundred men of the Sim'ē·on·ītes, went to Mount Sē'ir, having as their leaders Pel·a·tī'ah, Nē·a·rī'ah, Reph·āi'ah, and Uz'zi·el, sons of Ish'ī; 43 they destroyed the remnant of the A·mal'e·kītes that had escaped, and they have lived there to this day.

---

p Gk Compare Vg: Heb the father   q Or Ahashtari
r Another reading is Zohar   s Gk Vg: Heb lacks and Meonothai   t That is Valley of artisans   u Heb sons   v The clause: These are . . . married is transposed from verse 18
w Heb lacks and bore   x Vg Compare Gk: Heb and Jashubi-lahem   y Or matters   z Or Saul

Descendants of Reuben
(Gen 46.8–9)

5 The sons of Reuben the firstborn of Israel. (He was the firstborn, but because he defiled his father's bed his birthright was given to the sons of Joseph son of Israel, so that he is not enrolled in the genealogy according to the birthright; 2 though Judah became prominent among his brothers and a ruler came from him, yet the birthright belonged to Joseph.) 3 The sons of Reuben, the firstborn of Israel: Hā′noch, Pal′lū, Hez′ron, and Car′mī. 4 The sons of Jō′el: She•māi′ah his son, Gog his son, Shim′ē•ī his son, 5 Mī′cah his son, Rē•āi′ah his son, Bā′al his son, 6 Be•er′ah his son, whom King Til′gath-pil•nē′ser of Assyria carried away into exile; he was a chieftain of the Reū′ben•ites. 7 And his kindred by their families, when the genealogy of their generations was reckoned: the chief, Je•ī′el, and Zech•a•rī′ah, 8 and Bē′la son of Ā′zaz, son of Shē′ma, son of Jō′el, who lived in A•rō′er, as far as Nē′bō and Bā′al-me′on. 9 He also lived to the east as far as the beginning of the desert this side of the Euphrates, because their cattle had multiplied in the land of Gil′e•ad. 10 And in the days of Saul they made war on the Hag′rītes, who fell by their hand; and they lived in their tents throughout all the region east of Gil′e•ad.

Descendants of Gad

11 The sons of Gad lived beside them in the land of Bā′shan as far as Sal′e•cah: 12 Jō′el the chief, Shā′pham the second, Jā′naī, and Shā′phat in Bā′shan. 13 And their kindred according to their clans: Michael, Me•shul′lam, Shē′ba, Jō′raī, Jā′can, Zī′a, and Ē′ber, seven. 14 These were the sons of Ab•i•hā′il son of Hū′rī, son of Ja•rō′ah, son of Gil′e•ad, son of Michael, son of Je•shish′aī, son of Jah′dō, son of Buz; 15 Ā′hī son of Ab′di•el, son of Gū′nī, was chief in their clan; 16 and they lived in Gil′e•ad, in Bā′shan and in its towns, and in all the pasture lands of Sharon to their limits. 17 All of these were enrolled by genealogies in the days of King Jō′tham of Judah, and in the days of King Jer•o•bō′am of Israel.

18 The Reū′ben•ites, the Gad′ītes, and the half-tribe of Ma•nas′seh had valiant warriors, who carried shield and sword, and drew the bow, expert in war, forty-four thousand seven hundred sixty, ready for service. 19 They made war on the Hag′rītes, Jē′tur, Nā′phish, and Nō′dab; 20 and when they received help against them, the Hag′rītes and all who were with them were given into their hands, for they cried to God in the battle, and he granted their entreaty because they trusted in him. 21 They captured their livestock: fifty thousand of their camels, two hundred fifty thousand sheep, two thousand donkeys, and one hundred thousand captives.

22 Many fell slain, because the war was of God. And they lived in their territory until the exile.

The Half-Tribe of Manasseh

23 The members of the half-tribe of Ma•nas′seh lived in the land; they were very numerous from Bā′shan to Bā′al-her′mon, Sē′nir, and Mount Hermon. 24 These were the heads of their clans: Ē′pher,[a] Ish′ī, E•lī′el, Az′rī•el, Jer•e•mī′ah, Hod•a•vī′ah, and Jah′di•el, mighty warriors, famous men, heads of their clans. 25 But they transgressed against the God of their ancestors, and prostituted themselves to the gods of the peoples of the land, whom God had destroyed before them. 26 So the God of Israel stirred up the spirit of King Pūl of Assyria, the spirit of King Til′gath-pil•nē′ser of Assyria, and he carried them away, namely, the Reū′ben•ites, the Gad′ītes, and the half-tribe of Ma•nas′seh, and brought them to Hā′lah, Hā′bor, Hār′a, and the river Gō′zan, to this day.

Descendants of Levi
(Gen 46.11)

6 [b]The sons of Levi: Ger′shom,[c] Kō′hath, and Me•rar′ī. 2 The sons of Kō′hath: Am′ram, Iz′har, Hē′bron, and Uz′zi•el. 3 The children of Am′ram: Aaron, Moses, and Miriam. The sons of Aaron: Nā′dab, A•bī′hū, El•ē•ā′zar, and Ith′a•mar. 4 El•ē•ā′zar became the father of Phin′e•has, Phin′e•has of Ab•i•shū′a, 5 Ab•i•shū′a of Buk′kī, Buk′kī of Uz′zī, 6 Uz′zī of Zer•a•hī′ah, Zer•a•hī′ah of Me•rā′i•oth, 7 Me•rā′i•oth of Am•a•rī′ah, Am•a•rī′ah of A•hī′tub, 8 A•hī′tub of Zā′dok, Zā′dok of A•him′a•az, 9 A•him′a•az of Az•a•rī′ah, Az•a•rī′ah of Jō•hā′nan, 10 and Jō•hā′nan of Az•a•rī′ah (it was he who served as priest in the house that Solomon built in Jerusalem). 11 Az•a•rī′ah became the father of Am•a•rī′ah, Am•a•rī′ah of A•hī′tub, 12 A•hī′tub of Zā′dok, Zā′dok of Shal′lum, 13 Shal′lum of Hil•kī′ah, Hil•kī′ah of Az•a•rī′ah, 14 Az•a•rī′ah of Se•rāi′ah, Se•rāi′ah of Je•hoz′a•dak; 15 and Je•hoz′a•dak went into exile when the LORD sent Judah and Jerusalem into exile by the hand of Ne•bū•chad•nez′zar.

16[d] The sons of Levi: Ger′shom, Kō′hath, and Me•rar′ī. 17 These are the names of the sons of Ger′shom: Lib′nī and Shim′ē•ī. 18 The sons of Kō′hath: Am′ram, Iz′har, Hē′bron, and Uz′zi•el. 19 The sons of Me•rar′ī: Mah′lī and Mū′shī. These are the clans of the Lē′vītes according to their ancestry. 20 Of Ger′shom: Lib′nī his son, Jā′hath his son, Zim′mah his son, 21 Jō′ah his son, Id′dō his son, Zē′rah his son, Jē•ath′e•raī his son. 22 The sons of Kō′hath: Am•min′a•dab his son, Kō′rah his son, As′sir his son, 23 El•kā′nah his son, E•bī′a•saph his

---

a Gk Vg: Heb *and Epher*   b Ch 5.27 in Heb   c Heb *Gershon,* variant of *Gershom;* See 6.16   d Ch 6.1 in Heb son, As'sir his son, 24 Tā'thath his son, Ū•rī'el his son, Uz•zī'ah his son, and Shā'ūl his son. 25 The sons of El•kā'nah: A•mā'saī and A•hī'moth, 26 El•kā'nah his son, Zō'phaī his son, Nā'hath his son, 27 E•lī'ab his son, Je•rō'ham his son, El•kā'nah his son. 28 The sons of Samuel: Jō'el[e] his firstborn, the second A•bī'-jah.[f] 29 The sons of Me•rar'ī: Mah'lī, Lib'nī his son, Shim'ē•ī his son, Uz'zah his son, 30 Shim'ē•a his son, Hag•gī'ah his son, and A•sāi'ah his son.

Musicians Appointed by David

31 These are the men whom David put in charge of the service of song in the house of the LORD, after the ark came to rest there. 32 They ministered with song before the tabernacle of the tent of meeting, until Solomon had built the house of the LORD in Jerusalem; and they performed their service in due order. 33 These are the men who served; and their sons were: Of the Kō'hath•ītes: Hē'man, the singer, son of Jō'el, son of Samuel, 34 son of El•kā'nah, son of Je•rō'ham, son of E•lī'el, son of Tō'ah, 35 son of Zuph, son of El•kā'nah, son of Mā'hath, son of A•mā'saī, 36 son of El•kā'nah, son of Jō'el, son of Az•a•rī'ah, son of Zeph•a•nī'ah, 37 son of Tā'hath, son of As'sir, son of E•bī'a•saph, son of Kō'rah, 38 son of Iz'har, son of Kō'hath, son of Levi, son of Israel; 39 and his brother Ā'saph, who stood on his right, namely, Ā'saph son of Be•re•chī'ah, son of Shim'ē•a, 40 son of Michael, son of Bā•a•sē'i•ah, son of Mal•chī'jah, 41 son of Eth'nī, son of Zē'rah, son of A•dāi'ah, 42 son of Ē'than, son of Zim'mah, son of Shim'ē•ī, 43 son of Jā'hath, son of Ger'shom, son of Levi. 44 On the left were their kindred the sons of Me•rar'ī: Ē'than son of Kish'ī, son of Ab'dī, son of Mal'luch, 45 son of Hash•a•bī'ah, son of Am•a•zī'ah, son of Hil•kī'ah, 46 son of Am'zī, son of Bā'nī, son of Shē'mer, 47 son of Mah'lī, son of Mū'shī, son of Me•rar'ī, son of Levi; 48 and their kindred the Lē'vītes were appointed for all the service of the tabernacle of the house of God.

49 But Aaron and his sons made offerings on the altar of burnt offering and on the altar of incense, doing all the work of the most holy place, to make atonement for Israel, according to all that Moses the servant of God had commanded. 50 These are the sons of Aaron: El•ē•ā'zar his son, Phin'e•has his son, Ab•i•shū'a his son, 51 Buk'kī his son, Uz'zī his son, Zer•a•hī'ah his son, 52 Me•rā'-i•oth his son, Am•a•rī'ah his son, A•hī'tub his son, 53 Zā'dok his son, A•him'a•az his son.

Settlements of the Levites
(Josh 21.1–42)

54 These are their dwelling places according to their settlements within their borders: to the sons of Aaron of the families of Kō'hath•ītes—for the lot

fell to them first— 55 to them they gave Hē'bron in the land of Judah and its surrounding pasture lands, 56 but the fields of the city and its villages they gave to Caleb son of Je•phūn'neh. 57 To the sons of Aaron they gave the cities of refuge: Hē'bron, Lib'nah with its pasture lands, Jat'tir, Esh•te•mō'a with its pasture lands, 58 Hī'len[g] with its pasture lands, Dē'bir with its pasture lands, 59 Ā'shan with its pasture lands, and Beth-shē'mesh with its pasture lands. 60 From the tribe of Benjamin, Gē'ba with its pasture lands, Al'e•meth with its pasture lands, and An'a•thoth with its pasture lands. All their towns throughout their families were thirteen.

61 To the rest of the Kō'hath•ītes were given by lot out of the family of the tribe, out of the half-tribe, the half of Ma•nas'seh, ten towns. 62 To the Ger'shom•ītes according to their families were allotted thirteen towns out of the tribes of Is'sa•char, Ash'er, Naph'ta•lī, and Ma•nas'seh in Bā'shan. 63 To the Me•rar'ītes according to their families were allotted twelve towns out of the tribes of Reuben, Gad, and Zeb'ū•lun. 64 So the people of Israel gave the Lē'vītes the towns with their pasture lands. 65 They also gave them by lot out of the tribes of Judah, Sim'ē•on, and Benjamin these towns that are mentioned by name.

66 And some of the families of the sons of Kō'hath had towns of their territory out of the tribe of E'phra•im. 67 They were given the cities of refuge: Shē'chem with its pasture lands in the hill country of E'phra•im, Gē'zer with its pasture lands, 68 Jok'mē•am with its pasture lands, Beth-hō'ron with its pasture lands, 69 Aī'ja•lon with its pasture lands, Gath-rim'mon with its pasture lands; 70 and out of the half-tribe of Ma•nas'seh, Ā'ner with its pasture lands, and Bil'ē•am with its pasture lands, for the rest of the families of the Kō'hath•ītes.

71 To the Ger'shom•ītes: out of the half-tribe of Ma•nas'seh: Gō'lan in Bā'shan with its pasture lands and Ash'ta•roth with its pasture lands; 72 and out of the tribe of Is'sa•char: Kē'desh with its pasture lands, Dab'e•rath[h] with its pasture lands, 73 Rā'-moth with its pasture lands, and Ā'nem with its pasture lands; 74 out of the tribe of Ash'er: Mā'shal with its pasture lands, Ab'don with its pasture lands, 75 Hū'kok with its pasture lands, and Rē'hob with its pasture lands; 76 and out of the tribe of Naph'-ta•lī: Kē'desh in Galilee with its pasture lands, Ham'mon with its pasture lands, and Kir•i•a•thā'im with its pasture lands. 77 To the rest of the Me•rar'-ītes out of the tribe of Zeb'ū•lun: Rim'mo•nō with

---

e Gk Syr Compare verse 33 and 1 Sam 8.2: Heb lacks *Joel*
f Heb reads *Vashni, and Abijah* for *the second Abijah,* taking *the second* as a proper name   g Other readings *Hilez, Holon;* See Josh 21.15   h Or *Dobrath*

its pasture lands, Tā′bor with its pasture lands, 78 and across the Jordan from Jericho, on the east side of the Jordan, out of the tribe of Reuben: Bē′zer in the steppe with its pasture lands, Jah′zah with its pasture lands, 79 Ked′e•moth with its pasture lands, and Meph′a•ath with its pasture lands; 80 and out of the tribe of Gad: Rā′moth in Gil′e•ad with its pasture lands, Mā•ha•nā′im with its pasture lands, 81 Hesh′bon with its pasture lands, and Jā′zer with its pasture lands.

Descendants of Issachar
(Gen 46.13)

7 The sons[i] of Is′sa•char: Tō′la, Pū′ah, Jash′ub, and Shim′ron, four. 2 The sons of Tō′la: Uz′zī, Reph•āi′ah, Jē′ri•el, Jah′mai, Ib′sam, and She•mū′el, heads of their ancestral houses, namely of Tō′la, mighty warriors of their generations, their number in the days of David being twenty-two thousand six hundred. 3 The son[j] of Uz′zī: Iz•ra•hī′ah. And the sons of Iz•ra•hī′ah: Michael, Ō•ba•dī′ah, Jō′el, and Is•shī′ah, five, all of them chiefs; 4 and along with them, by their generations, according to their ancestral houses, were units of the fighting force, thirty-six thousand, for they had many wives and sons. 5 Their kindred belonging to all the families of Is′sa•char were in all eighty-seven thousand mighty warriors, enrolled by genealogy.

Descendants of Benjamin
(Gen 46.21)

6 The sons of Benjamin: Bē′la, Bē′cher, and Je•dī′a•el, three. 7 The sons of Bē′la: Ez′bon, Uz′zī, Uz′zi•el, Jer′i•moth, and Ī′rī, five, heads of ancestral houses, mighty warriors; and their enrollment by genealogies was twenty-two thousand thirty-four. 8 The sons of Bē′cher: Ze•mī′rah, Jō′ash, El•i•ē′zer, El•i•ō•ē′nai, Om′rī, Jer′e•moth, A•bī′jah, An′a•thoth, and Al′e•meth. All these were the sons of Bē′cher; 9 and their enrollment by genealogies, according to their generations, as heads of their ancestral houses, mighty warriors, was twenty thousand two hundred. 10 The sons of Je•dī′a•el: Bil′han. And the sons of Bil′han: Jē′ush, Benjamin, Ē′hud, Che•nā′a•nah, Zē′than, Tar′shish, and A•hish′a•har. 11 All these were the sons of Je•dī′a•el according to the heads of their ancestral houses, mighty warriors, seventeen thousand two hundred, ready for service in war. 12 And Shup′pim and Hup′pim were the sons of Ir, Hū′shim the son[j] of A′her.

Descendants of Naphtali
(Gen 46.24)

13 The descendants of Naph′ta•lī: Jah′zi•el, Gū′nī, Jē′zer, and Shal′lum, the descendants of Bil′hah.

Descendants of Manasseh

14 The sons of Ma•nas′seh: As′ri•el, whom his Ar•a•mē′an concubine bore; she bore Mā′chir the father of Gil′e•ad. 15 And Mā′chir took a wife for Hup′pim and for Shup′pim. The name of his sister was Mā′a•cah. And the name of the second was Ze•loph′e•had; and Ze•loph′e•had had daughters. 16 Mā′a•cah the wife of Mā′chir bore a son, and she named him Pē′resh; the name of his brother was Shē′resh; and his sons were Ū′lam and Rē′kem. 17 The son[j] of Ū′lam: Bē′dan. These were the sons of Gil′e•ad son of Mā′chir, son of Ma•nas′seh. 18 And his sister Ham•mō′le•cheth bore Ish′hod, Ā•bi•ē′zer, and Mah′lah. 19 The sons of She•mī′da were A•hī′an, Shē′chem, Lik′hī, and A•nī′am.

Descendants of Ephraim

20 The sons of Ē′phra•im: Shū•thē′lah, and Bē′red his son, Tā′hath his son, El•ē•ā′dah his son, Tā′hath his son, 21 Zā′bad his son, Shū•thē′lah his son, and Ē′zer and Ē′lē•ad. Now the people of Gath, who were born in the land, killed them, because they came down to raid their cattle. 22 And their father Ē′phra•im mourned many days, and his brothers came to comfort him. 23 Ē′phra•im[k] went in to his wife, and she conceived and bore a son; and he named him Bē•rī′ah, because disaster[l] had befallen his house. 24 His daughter was Shē′e•rah, who built both Lower and Upper Beth-hō′ron, and Uz′zen-shē′e•rah. 25 Rē′phah was his son, Rē′sheph his son, Tē′lah his son, Tā′han his son, 26 Lā′dan his son, Am•mī′hud his son, E•lish′a•ma his son, 27 Nun[m] his son, Joshua his son. 28 Their possessions and settlements were Beth′el and its towns, and eastward Nā′a•ran, and westward Gē′zer and its towns, Shē′chem and its towns, as far as Āy′yah and its towns; 29 also along the borders of the Ma•nas′sites, Beth-shē′an and its towns, Tā′a•nach and its towns, Me•gid′dō and its towns, Dor and its towns. In these lived the sons of Joseph son of Israel.

Descendants of Asher
(Gen 46.17)

30 The sons of Ash′er: Im′nah, Ish′vah, Ish′vī, Bē•rī′ah, and their sister Sē′rah. 31 The sons of Bē•rī′ah: Hē′ber and Mal′chi•el, who was the father of Bir′za•ith. 32 Hē′ber became the father of Japh′let, Shō′mer, Hō′tham, and their sister Shū′a. 33 The sons of Japh′let: Pā′sach, Bim′hal, and Ash′vath. These are the sons of Japh′let. 34 The sons of Shē′mer: A′hī, Rōh′gah, Hub′bah, and Ar′am. 35 The sons of Hē′lem[n] his brother: Zō′phah, Im′na, Shē′lesh, and Ā′mal. 36 The sons of Zō′phah: Sū′ah

---

i Syr Compare Vg: Heb *And to the sons*   j Heb *sons*   k Heb *He*   l Heb *beraah*   m Here spelled *Non*; see Ex 33.11   n Or *Hotham*; see 7.32

Har·ne·pher, Shū′al, Bē′rī, Im′rah, [37] Bē′zer, Hod, Sham′ma, Shil′shah, Ith′ran, and Be·ē′ra. [38] The sons of Jē′ther: Je·phūn′neh, Pis′pa, and Ar′a. [39] The sons of Ul′la: Ā′rah, Han′ni·el, and Rī·zī′a. [40] All of these were men of Ash′er, heads of ancestral houses, select mighty warriors, chief of the princes. Their number enrolled by genealogies, for service in war, was twenty-six thousand men.

Descendants of Benjamin
(Gen 46.21)

8 Benjamin became the father of Bē′la his firstborn, Ash′bel the second, A′har·ah the third, [2] Nō′hah the fourth, and Rā′pha the fifth. [3] And Bē′la had sons: Ad′dar, Gē′ra, A·bī′hud,[o] [4] A·bi·shū′a, Nā′a·man, A·hō′ah, [5] Gē′ra, She·phū′phan, and Hū′ram. [6] These are the sons of Ē′hud (they were heads of ancestral houses of the inhabitants of Gē′ba, and they were carried into exile to Man′a·hath): [7] Nā′a·man,[p] A·hī′jah, and Gē′ra, that is, Heg′lam,[q] who became the father of Uz′za and A·hī′hud. [8] And Shā·ha·rā′im had sons in the country of Mō′ab after he had sent away his wives Hū′shim and Bā′a·ra. [9] He had sons by his wife Hō′desh: Jō′bab, Zib′i·a, Mē′sha, Mal′cam, [10] Jē′uz, Sa·chī′a, and Mir′mah. These were his sons, heads of ancestral houses. [11] He also had sons by Hū′shim: A·bī′tub and El·pā′al. [12] The sons of El·pā′al: Ē′ber, Mī′sham, and Shē′med, who built Ō′nō and Lod with its towns, [13] and Bē·rī′ah and Shē′ma (they were heads of ancestral houses of the inhabitants of Aī′ja·lon, who put to flight the inhabitants of Gath); [14] and A·hī′ō, Shā′shak, and Jer′e·moth. [15] Zeb·a·dī′ah, Ar′ad, Ē′der, [16] Michael, Ish′pah, and Jō′ha were sons of Bē·rī′ah. [17] Zeb·a·dī′ah, Me·shul′lam, Hiz′kī, Hē′ber, [18] Ish′me·raī, Iz·lī′ah, and Jō′bab were the sons of El·pā′al. [19] Jā′kim, Zich′rī, Zab′dī, [20] E·li·ē′naī, Zil′le·thaī, E·lī′el, [21] A·dāi′ah, Be·rā′i·ah, and Shim′rath were the sons of Shim′ē·ī. [22] Ish′pan, Ē′ber, E·lī′el, [23] Ab′don, Zich′rī, Hā′nan, [24] Han·a·nī′ah, Ē′lam, An·tho·thī′jah, [25] Iph·dē′i·ah, and Pe·nū′el were the sons of Shā′shak. [26] Sham′she·raī, Shē·ha·rī′ah, Ath·a·lī′ah, [27] Jā·ar·e·shī′ah, E·lī′jah, and Zich′rī were the sons of Je·rō′ham. [28] These were the heads of ancestral houses, according to their generations, chiefs. These lived in Jerusalem.

[29] Je·i′el[r] the father of Gib′ē·on lived in Gib′ē·on, and the name of his wife was Mā′a·cah. [30] His firstborn son: Ab′don, then Zur, Kish, Bā′al,[s] Nā′dab, [31] Gē′dor, A·hī′ō, Zē′cher, [32] and Mik′loth, who became the father of Shim′ē·ah. Now these also lived opposite their kindred in Jerusalem, with their kindred. [33] Ner became the father of Kish, Kish of Saul,[t] Saul[t] of Jonathan, Mal·chi·shū′a, A·bin′a·dab, and Esh-bā′al; [34] and the son of Jonathan was Mer′ib-bā′al; and Mer′ib-bā′al became the father of Mī′cah. [35] The sons of Mī′cah: Pī′thon, Mē′lech, Ta·rē′a, and Ā′haz. [36] Ā′haz became the father of Je·hō′ad·dah; and Je·hō′ad·dah became the father of Al′e·meth, Az′ma·veth, and Zim′rī; Zim′rī became the father of Mō′za. [37] Mō′za became the father of Bin′ē·a; Rā′phah was his son, El·e·ā′sah his son, Ā′zel his son. [38] Ā′zel had six sons, and these are their names: Az·rī′kam, Bō′che·rū, Ish′ma·el, Shē·a·rī′ah, Ō·ba·dī′ah, and Hā′nan; all these were the sons of Ā′zel. [39] The sons of his brother Ē′shek: Ū′lam his firstborn, Jē′ush the second, and E·liph′e·let the third. [40] The sons of Ū′lam were mighty warriors, archers, having many children and grandchildren, one hundred fifty. All these were Ben′ja·min·ites.

9 So all Israel was enrolled by genealogies; and these are written in the Book of the Kings of Israel. And Judah was taken into exile in Babylon because of their unfaithfulness. [2] Now the first to live again in their possessions in their towns were Israelites, priests, Lē′vītes, and temple servants.

Inhabitants of Jerusalem after the Exile

[3] And some of the people of Judah, Benjamin, Ē′phra·im, and Ma·nas′seh lived in Jerusalem: [4] Ū′thaī son of Am·mī′hud, son of Om′rī, son of Im′rī, son of Bā′nī, from the sons of Per′ez son of Judah. [5] And of the Shī′lo·nītes: A·sāi′ah the firstborn, and his sons. [6] Of the sons of Zē′rah: Je·ū′el and their kin, six hundred ninety. [7] Of the Ben′ja·min·ites: Sal′lū son of Me·shul′lam, son of Hod·a·vī′ah, son of Has·se·nū′ah, [8] Ib·nē′i·ah son of Je·rō′ham, Ē′lah son of Uz′zī, son of Mich′rī, and Me·shul′lam son of Sheph·a·tī′ah, son of Reū′el, son of Ib·nī′jah; [9] and their kindred according to their generations, nine hundred fifty-six. All these were heads of families according to their ancestral houses.

Priestly Families

[10] Of the priests: Je·daī′ah, Je·hoi′a·rib, Jā′chin, [11] and Az·a·rī′ah son of Hil·kī′ah, son of Me·shul′lam, son of Zā′dok, son of Me·rā′i·oth, son of A·hī′tub, the chief officer of the house of God; [12] and A·dāi′ah son of Je·rō′ham, son of Pash′hur, son of Mal·chī′jah, and Mā′a·saī son of Ad′i·el, son of Jah′ze·rah, son of Me·shul′lam, son of Me·shil′le·mith, son of Im′mer; [13] besides their kindred, heads of their ancestral houses, one thousand seven hundred sixty, qualified for the work of the service of the house of God.

---

o Or *father of Ehud;* see 8.6   *p* Heb *and Naaman*   *q* Or *he carried them into exile*   *r* Compare 9.35: Heb lacks *Jeiel*   *s* Gk Ms adds *Ner;* Compare 8.33 and 9.36   *t* Or *Shaul*

1
C
H
R

Levitical Families

14 Of the Lē′vītes: She•māi′ah son of Has′shub, son of Az•rī′kam, son of Hash•a•bi′ah, of the sons of Me•rar′ī; 15 and Bak•bak′kar, Hē′resh, Gā′lal, and Matta •nī′ah son of Mī′ca, son of Zich′rī, son of Ā′saph; 16 and Ō •ba •dī′ah son of She •māi′ah, son of Gā′lal, son of Je •dū′thun, and Ber •e •chī′ah son of Asa, son of El •kā′nah, who lived in the villages of the Netoph′a •thītes.

17 The gatekeepers were: Shal′lum, Ak′kub, Tal′mon, A•hī′man; and their kindred Shal′lum was the chief, 18 stationed previously in the king′s gate on the east side. These were the gatekeepers of the camp of the Lē′vītes. 19 Shal′lum son of Kō′re, son of E•bī′a•saph, son of Kō′rah, and his kindred of his ancestral house, the Kō′ra•hītes, were in charge of the work of the service, guardians of the thresholds of the tent, as their ancestors had been in charge of the camp of the LORD, guardians of the entrance. 20 And Phin′e•has son of El•e•ā′zar was chief over them in former times; the LORD was with him. 21 Zech•a•rī′ah son of Me•shel•e•mī′ah was gatekeeper at the entrance of the tent of meeting. 22 All these, who were chosen as gatekeepers at the thresholds, were two hundred twelve. They were enrolled by genealogies in their villages. David and the seer Samuel established them in their office of trust. 23 So they and their descendants were in charge of the gates of the house of the LORD, that is, the house of the tent, as guards. 24 The gatekeepers were on the four sides, east, west, north, and south; 25 and their kindred who were in their villages were obliged to come in every seven days, in turn, to be with them; 26 for the four chief gatekeepers, who were Lē′vītes, were in charge of the chambers and the treasures of the house of God. 27 And they would spend the night near the house of God; for on them lay the duty of watching, and they had charge of opening it every morning.

28 Some of them had charge of the utensils of service, for they were required to count them when they were brought in and taken out. 29 Others of them were appointed over the furniture, and over all the holy utensils, also over the choice flour, the wine, the oil, the incense, and the spices. 30 Others, of the sons of the priests, prepared the mixing of the spices, 31 and Mat•ti•thī′ah, one of the Lē′vītes, the firstborn of Shal′lum the Kō′ra•hīte, was in charge of making the flat cakes. 32 Also some of their kindred of the Kō′hath•ītes had charge of the rows of bread, to prepare them for each sabbath.

33 Now these are the singers, the heads of ancestral houses of the Lē′vītes, living in the chambers of the temple free from other service, for they were on duty day and night. 34 These were heads of ancestral houses of the Lē′vītes, according to their generations; these leaders lived in Jerusalem.

The Family of King Saul

35 In Gib′ē•on lived the father of Gib′ē•on, Je•ī′el, and the name of his wife was Mā′a•cah. 36 His firstborn son was Ab′don, then Zur, Kish, Bā′al, Ner, Nā′dab, 37 Gē′dor, A•hī′ō, Zech•a•rī′ah, and Mik′loth; 38 and Mik′loth became the father of Shim′ē•am; and these also lived opposite their kindred in Jerusalem, with their kindred. 39 Ner became the father of Kish, Kish of Saul, Saul of Jonathan, Mal•chī•shū′a, A•bin′a•dab, and Eshbā′al; 40 and the son of Jonathan was Mer′ib-bā′al; and Mer′ib-bā′al became the father of Mī′cah. 41 The sons of Mī′cah: Pī′thon, Mē′lech, Tah′rē•a, and Ā′haz;ᵘ 42 and Ā′haz became the father of Jar′ah, and Jar′ah of Al′e•meth, Az′ma•veth, and Zim′rī; and Zim′rī became the father of Mō′za. 43 Mō′za became the father of Bin′ē•a; and Reph•āi′ah was his son, El•e•ā′sah his son, Ā′zel his son. 44 Ā′zel had six sons, and these are their names: Az•rī′kam, Bō′che•rū, Ish′ma•el, Shē•a•rī′ah, Ō•ba′dī•ah, and Hā′nan; these were the sons of Ā′zel.

Death of Saul and His Sons
(1 Sam 31.1–13)

10 Now the Phi•lis′tines fought against Israel; and the men of Israel fled before the Phi•lis′tines, and fell slain on Mount Gil•bō′a. 2 The Phi•lis′tines overtook Saul and his sons; and the Phi•lis′tines killed Jonathan and A•bin′a•dab and Mal•chi•shū′a, sons of Saul. 3 The battle pressed hard on Saul; and the archers found him, and he was wounded by the archers. 4 Then Saul said to his armor-bearer, "Draw your sword, and thrust me through with it, so that these uncircumcised may not come and make sport of me." But his armor-bearer was unwilling, for he was terrified. So Saul took his own sword and fell on it. 5 When his armor-bearer saw that Saul was dead, he also fell on his sword and died. 6 Thus Saul died; he and his three sons and all his house died together. 7 When all the men of Israel who were in the valley saw that the armyᵛ had fled and that Saul and his sons were dead, they abandoned their towns and fled; and the Phi•lis′tines came and occupied them.

8 The next day when the Phi•lis′tines came to strip the dead, they found Saul and his sons fallen on Mount Gil•bō′a. 9 They stripped him and took his head and his armor, and sent messengers throughout the land of the Phi•lis′tines to carry the good news to their idols and to the people. 10 They put his armor in the temple of their gods, and fastened his head in the temple of Dā′gon. 11 But when all Jā′besh-gil′ē•ad heard everything that the Phi•lis′tines had done to Saul, 12 all the valiant war

---

ᵘ Compare 8.35: Heb lacks *and Ahaz*   ᵛ Heb *they*

riors got up and took away the body of Saul and the bodies of his sons, and brought them to Jā′besh. Then they buried their bones under the oak in Jā′besh, and fasted seven days.

13 So Saul died for his unfaithfulness; he was unfaithful to the LORD in that he did not keep the command of the LORD; moreover, he had consulted a medium, seeking guidance, 14 and did not seek guidance from the LORD. Therefore the LORD*w* put him to death and turned the kingdom over to David son of Jesse.

David Anointed King of All Israel
(2 Sam 5.1–3)

11 Then all Israel gathered together to David at Hē′bron and said, "See, we are your bone and flesh. 2 For some time now, even while Saul was king, it was you who commanded the army of Israel. The LORD your God said to you: It is you who shall be shepherd of my people Israel, you who shall be ruler over my people Israel." 3 So all the elders of Israel came to the king at Hē′bron, and David made a covenant with them at Hē′bron before the LORD. And they anointed David king over Israel, according to the word of the LORD by Samuel.

Jerusalem Captured
(2 Sam 5.6–10)

4 David and all Israel marched to Jerusalem, that is Jē′bus, where the Jeb′ū•sītes were, the inhabitants of the land. 5 The inhabitants of Jē′bus said to David, "You will not come in here." Nevertheless David took the stronghold of Zion, now the city of David. 6 David had said, "Whoever attacks the Jeb′ū•sītes first shall be chief and commander." And Jō′ab son of Ze•rū′i•ah went up first, so he became chief. 7 David resided in the stronghold; therefore it was called the city of David. 8 He built the city all around, from the Mil′lō in complete circuit; and Jō′ab repaired the rest of the city. 9 And David became greater and greater, for the LORD of hosts was with him.

David's Mighty Men and Their Exploits
(2 Sam 23.8–39)

10 Now these are the chiefs of David's warriors, who gave him strong support in his kingdom, together with all Israel, to make him king, according to the word of the LORD concerning Israel. 11 This is an account of David's mighty warriors: Ja•shō′-bē•am, son of Hach′mo•nī,*x* was chief of the Three;*y* he wielded his spear against three hundred whom he killed at one time.

12 And next to him among the three warriors was El•ē•ā′zar son of Dō′dō, the A•hō′hīte. 13 He was with David at Pas-dam′mim when the Phi•lis′-

tines were gathered there for battle. There was a plot of ground full of barley. Now the people had fled from the Phi•lis′tines, 14 but he and David took their stand in the middle of the plot, defended it, and killed the Phi•lis′tines; and the LORD saved them by a great victory.

15 Three of the thirty chiefs went down to the rock to David at the cave of A•dul′lam, while the army of Phi•lis′tines was encamped in the valley of Reph′a•im. 16 David was then in the stronghold; and the garrison of the Phi•lis′tines was then at Bethlehem. 17 David said longingly, "O that someone would give me water to drink from the well of Bethlehem that is by the gate!" 18 Then the Three broke through the camp of the Phi•lis′tines, and drew water from the well of Bethlehem that was by the gate, and they brought it to David. But David would not drink of it; he poured it out to the LORD, 19 and said, "My God forbid that I should do this. Can I drink the blood of these men? For at the risk of their lives they brought it." Therefore he would not drink it. The three warriors did these things.

20 Now A•bi′shaī,*z* the brother of Jō′ab, was chief of the Thirty.*a* With his spear he fought against three hundred and killed them, and won a name beside the Three. 21 He was the most renowned*b* of the Thirty,*a* and became their commander; but he did not attain to the Three.

22 Be•nā′i•ah son of Je•hoi′a•da was a valiant man*c* of Kab′zē•el, a doer of great deeds; he struck down two sons of*d* Ar′i•el of Mō′ab. He also went down and killed a lion in a pit on a day when snow had fallen. 23 And he killed an Egyptian, a man of great stature, five cubits tall. The Egyptian had in his hand a spear like a weaver's beam; but Be•nā′i•ah went against him with a staff, snatched the spear out of the Egyptian's hand, and killed him with his own spear. 24 Such were the things Be•nā′i•ah son of Je•hoi′a•da did, and he won a name beside the three warriors. 25 He was renowned among the Thirty, but he did not attain to the Three. And David put him in charge of his bodyguard.

26 The warriors of the armies were As′a•hel brother of Jō′ab, El•hā′nan son of Dō′dō of Bethlehem, 27 Sham′moth of Har′od,*e* Hē′lez the Pel′-o•nīte, 28 Ira son of Ik′kesh of Te•kō′a, Ā•bi•ē′zer of An′a•thoth, 29 Sib′be•caī the Hū′sha•thīte, I′lai the A•hō′hīte, 30 Mā′ha•raī of Ne•toph′ah, Hē′led son of Bā′a•nah of Ne•toph′ah, 31 Ith′aī son of Rī′baī of Gib′ē•ah of the Ben′ja•min•ītes, Be•nā′i•ah of Pir′-a•thon, 32 Hū′raī of the wadis of Gā′ash, A•bī′el the

---

w Heb he   x Or a Hachmonite   y Compare 2 Sam 23.8: Heb Thirty or captains   z Gk Vg Tg Compare 2 Sam 23.18: Heb Abshai   a Syr: Heb Three   b Compare 2 Sam 23.19: Heb more renowned among the two   c Syr: Heb the son of a valiant man   d See 2 Sam 23.20: Heb lacks sons of   e Compare 2 Sam 23.25: Heb the Harorite

Ar·ba·thīte, 33 Az′ma·veth of Ba·hā′rum, Ê·lī′ah·ba of Shā·al′bon, 34 Hā′shem*f* the Gī′zō·nīte, Jonathan son of Shā′gee the Har′a·rīte, 35 A·hī′am son of Sā′char the Har′a·rīte, E·lī′phal son of Ūr, 36 Hē′pher the Me·chē′ra·thīte, A·hī′jah the Pel′o·nīte, 37 Hez′rō of Car′mel, Nā′a·raī son of Ez′baī, 38 Jō′el the brother of Nathan, Mib′har son of Hag′rī, 39 Zē′lek the Am′mon·īte, Nā′ha·raī of Be·er′oth, the armor-bearer of Jō′ab son of Ze·rū′i·ah, 40 Ira the Ith′rīte, Gā′reb the Ith′rīte, 41 Ū·rī′ah the Hit′tīte, Zā′bad son of Ah′laī, 42 Ad′i·na son of Shī′za the Reū′ben·īte, a leader of the Reū′ben·ītes, and thirty with him, 43 Hā′nan son of Mā′a·cah, and Josh′a·phat the Mith′nīte, 44 Uz·zī′a the Ash′te·ra·thīte, Shā′ma and Je·ī′el sons of Hō′tham the A·rō′er·īte, 45 Je·dī′a·el son of Shim′rī, and his brother Jō′ha the Tī′zīte, 46 E·lī′el the Mā′ha·vīte, and Jer′i·baī and Josh·a·vī′ah sons of El′nā·am, and Ith′mah the Mō′ab·īte, 47 E·lī′el, and Ō′bed, and Jā·a·sī′el the Me·zō′ba·īte.

David's Followers in the Wilderness
(1 Sam 22.1–2)

12 The following are those who came to David at Zik′lag, while he could not move about freely because of Saul son of Kish; they were among the mighty warriors who helped him in war. 2 They were archers, and could shoot arrows and sling stones with either the right hand or the left; they were Ben′ja·min·ītes, Saul's kindred. 3 The chief was Ā·hī·ē′zer, then Jō′ash, both sons of She·mā′ah of Gib′ē·ah; also Jē′zi·el and Pē′let sons of Az′ma·veth; Ber′a·cah, Jē′hū of An′a·thoth, 4 Ish-mā′i·ah of Gib′ē·on, a warrior among the Thirty and a leader over the Thirty; Jer·e·mī′ah,*g* Ja·hā′zi·el, Jō·hā′nan, Joz′a·bad of Ge·dē′rah, 5 E·lū′zaī,*h* Jer′i·moth, Be·a·lī′ah, Shem·a·rī′ah, Sheph·a·tī′ah the Ha·rū′phīte; 6 El·kā′nah, Is·shī′ah, Az′a·rel, Jō·ē′zer, and Ja·shō′bē·am, the Kō′ra·hītes; 7 and Jō·ē′lah and Zeb·a·dī′ah, sons of Je·rō′ham of Gē′dor.

8 From the Gad′ītes there went over to David at the stronghold in the wilderness mighty and experienced warriors, expert with shield and spear, whose faces were like the faces of lions, and who were swift as gazelles on the mountains: 9 Ē′zer the chief, Ō·ba·dī′ah second, E·lī′ab third, 10 Mishman′nah fourth, Jer·e·mī′ah fifth, 11 At′taī sixth, E·lī′el seventh, 12 Jō·hā′nan eighth, El·zā′bad ninth, 13 Jer·e·mī′ah tenth, Mach′ban·naī eleventh. 14 These Gad′ītes were officers of the army, the least equal to a hundred and the greatest to a thousand. 15 These are the men who crossed the Jordan in the first month, when it was overflowing all its banks, and put to flight all those in the valleys, to the east and to the west.

16 Some Ben′ja·min·ītes and Jū′dah·ītes came to the stronghold to David. 17 David went out to

meet them and said to them, "If you have come to me in friendship, to help me, then my heart will be knit to you; but if you have come to betray me to my adversaries, though my hands have done no wrong, then may the God of our ancestors see and give judgment." 18 Then the spirit came upon A·mā′saī, chief of the Thirty, and he said,

"We are yours, O David;
    and with you, O son of Jesse!
Peace, peace to you,
    and peace to the one who helps you!
For your God is the one who helps you."

Then David received them, and made them officers of his troops.

19 Some of the Ma·nas′sites deserted to David when he came with the Phi·lis′tines for the battle against Saul. (Yet he did not help them, for the rulers of the Phi·lis′tines took counsel and sent him away, saying, "He will desert to his master Saul at the cost of our heads.") 20 As he went to Zik′lag these Ma·nas′sites deserted to him: Ad′nah, Joz′a·bad, Je·dī′a·el, Michael, Joz′a·bad, E·lī′hū, and Zil′le·thaī, chiefs of the thousands in Ma·nas′seh. 21 They helped David against the band of raiders,*i* for they were all warriors and commanders in the army. 22 Indeed from day to day people kept coming to David to help him, until there was a great army, like an army of God.

David's Army at Hebron

23 These are the numbers of the divisions of the armed troops who came to David in Hē′bron to turn the kingdom of Saul over to him, according to the word of the LORD. 24 The people of Judah bearing shield and spear numbered six thousand eight hundred armed troops. 25 Of the Sim′e·on·ītes, mighty warriors, seven thousand one hundred. 26 Of the Lē′vītes four thousand six hundred. 27 Je-hoi′a·da, leader of the house of Aaron, and with him three thousand seven hundred. 28 Zā′dok, a young warrior, and twenty-two commanders from his own ancestral house. 29 Of the Ben′ja·min·ītes, the kindred of Saul, three thousand, of whom the majority had continued to keep their allegiance to the house of Saul. 30 Of the Ē′phra·im·ītes, twenty thousand eight hundred, mighty warriors, notables in their ancestral houses. 31 Of the half-tribe of Ma·nas′seh, eighteen thousand, who were expressly named to come and make David king. 32 Of Is·sa·char, those who had understanding of the times, to know what Israel ought to do, two hundred chiefs, and all their kindred under their com-

---

f Compare Gk and 2 Sam 23.32: Heb *the sons of Hashem*
g Heb verse 5   *h* Heb verse 6   *i* Or *as officers of his troops*

mand. 33 Of Zeb′ū•lun, fifty thousand seasoned troops, equipped for battle with all the weapons of war, to help David[j] with singleness of purpose. 34 Of Naph′ta•lī, a thousand commanders, with whom there were thirty-seven thousand armed with shield and spear. 35 Of the Dan′ītes, twenty-eight thousand six hundred equipped for battle. 36 Of Ash′er, forty thousand seasoned troops ready for battle. 37 Of the Reū′ben•ites and Gad′ītes and the half-tribe of Ma•nas′seh from beyond the Jordan, one hundred twenty thousand armed with all the weapons of war.

38 All these, warriors arrayed in battle order, came to Hē′bron with full intent to make David king over all Israel; likewise all the rest of Israel were of a single mind to make David king. 39 They were there with David for three days, eating and drinking, for their kindred had provided for them. 40 And also their neighbors, from as far away as Is′sa•char and Zeb′ū•lun and Naph′ta•lī, came bringing food on donkeys, camels, mules, and oxen—abundant provisions of meal, cakes of figs, clusters of raisins, wine, oil, oxen, and sheep, for there was joy in Israel.

The Ark Brought from Kiriath-jearim
(2 Sam 6.1–11)

13 David consulted with the commanders of the thousands and of the hundreds, with every leader. 2 David said to the whole assembly of Israel, "If it seems good to you, and if it is the will of the LORD our God, let us send abroad to our kindred who remain in all the land of Israel, including the priests and Lē′vītes in the cities that have pasture lands, that they may come together to us. 3 Then let us bring again the ark of our God to us; for we did not turn to it in the days of Saul." 4 The whole assembly agreed to do so, for the thing pleased all the people.

5 So David assembled all Israel from the Shī′hor of Egypt to Lē′bō-hā′math, to bring the ark of God from Kir′i•ath-jē′a•rim. 6 And David and all Israel went up to Bā′a•lah, that is, to Kir′i•ath-jē′a•rim, which belongs to Judah, to bring up from there the ark of God, the LORD, who is enthroned on the cherubim, which is called by his[k] name. 7 They carried the ark of God on a new cart, from the house of A•bin′a•dab, and Uz′zah and A•hī′ō[l] were driving the cart. 8 David and all Israel were dancing before God with all their might, with song and lyres and harps and tambourines and cymbals and trumpets.

9 When they came to the threshing floor of Chi′don, Uz′zah put out his hand to hold the ark, for the oxen shook it. 10 The anger of the LORD was kindled against Uz′zah; he struck him down because he put out his hand to the ark; and he died there before God. 11 David was angry because the LORD had burst out against Uz′zah; so that place is called Per′ez-uz′zah[m] to this day. 12 David was afraid of God that day; he said, "How can I bring the ark of God into my care?" 13 So David did not take the ark into his care into the city of David; he took it instead to the house of Ō′bed-ē′dom the Git′tīte. 14 The ark of God remained with the household of Ō′bed-ē′dom in his house three months, and the LORD blessed the household of Ō′bed-ē′dom and all that he had.

David Established at Jerusalem
(2 Sam 5.11–16)

14 King Hiram of Tȳre sent messengers to David, along with cedar logs, and masons and carpenters to build a house for him. 2 David then perceived that the LORD had established him as king over Israel, and that his kingdom was highly exalted for the sake of his people Israel.

3 David took more wives in Jerusalem, and David became the father of more sons and daughters. 4 These are the names of the children whom he had in Jerusalem: Sham′mū•a, Shō′bab, and Nathan; Solomon, 5 Ib′har, E•lish′ū•a, and El′pe•let; 6 Nō′gah, Nē′pheg, and Ja•phi′a; 7 E•lish′a•ma, Bē•e•lī′a•da, and E•liph′e•let.

Defeat of the Philistines
(2 Sam 5.17–25)

8 When the Phi•lis′tines heard that David had been anointed king over all Israel, all the Phi•lis′tines went up in search of David; and David heard of it and went out against them. 9 Now the Phi•lis′tines had come and made a raid in the valley of Reph′a•im. 10 David inquired of God, "Shall I go up against the Phi•lis′tines? Will you give them into my hand?" The LORD said to him, "Go up, and I will give them into your hand." 11 So he went up to Bā′al-pe•rā′zim, and David defeated them there. David said, "God has burst out[n] against my enemies by my hand, like a bursting flood." Therefore that place is called Bā′al-pe•rā′zim.[o] 12 They abandoned their gods there, and at David's command they were burned.

13 Once again the Phi•lis′tines made a raid in the valley. 14 When David again inquired of God, God said to him, "You shall not go up after them; go around and come on them opposite the balsam trees. 15 When you hear the sound of marching in the tops of the balsam trees, then go out to battle; for God has gone out before you to strike down the army of the Phi•lis′tines." 16 David did as God had commanded him, and they struck down the

---

j Gk: Heb lacks *David*   k Heb lacks *his*   l Or *and his brother*   m That is *Bursting Out Against Uzzah*   n Heb *paraz*   o That is *Lord of Bursting Out*

Phi•lis′tine army from Gib′ē•on to Gē′zer. 17 The fame of David went out into all lands, and the LORD brought the fear of him on all nations.

The Ark Brought to Jerusalem
(2 Sam 6.12–16)

15 David*p* built houses for himself in the city of David, and he prepared a place for the ark of God and pitched a tent for it. 2 Then David commanded that no one but the Lē′vītes were to carry the ark of God, for the LORD had chosen them to carry the ark of the LORD and to minister to him forever. 3 David assembled all Israel in Jerusalem to bring up the ark of the LORD to its place, which he had prepared for it. 4 Then David gathered together the descendants of Aaron and the Lē′vītes: 5 of the sons of Kō′hath, Ū•rī′el the chief, with one hundred twenty of his kindred; 6 of the sons of Me•rar′ī, A•sāi′ah the chief, with two hundred twenty of his kindred; 7 of the sons of Ger′shom, Jō′el the chief, with one hundred thirty of his kindred; 8 of the sons of E•li•zā′phan, She•māi′ah the chief, with two hundred of his kindred; 9 of the sons of Hē′bron, E•lī′el the chief, with eighty of his kindred; 10 of the sons of Uz′zi•el, Am•min′a•dab the chief, with one hundred twelve of his kindred.

11 David summoned the priests Zā′dok and A•bī′a•thar, and the Lē′vītes Ū•rī′el, A•sāi′ah, Jō′el, She•māi′ah, E•lī′el, and Am•min′a•dab. 12 He said to them, "You are the heads of families of the Lē′vītes; sanctify yourselves, you and your kindred, so that you may bring up the ark of the LORD, the God of Israel, to the place that I have prepared for it. 13 Because you did not carry it the first time,*q* the LORD our God burst out against us, because we did not give it proper care." 14 So the priests and the Lē′vītes sanctified themselves to bring up the ark of the LORD, the God of Israel. 15 And the Lē′vītes carried the ark of God on their shoulders with the poles, as Moses had commanded according to the word of the LORD.

16 David also commanded the chiefs of the Lē′vītes to appoint their kindred as the singers to play on musical instruments, on harps and lyres and cymbals, to raise loud sounds of joy. 17 So the Lē′vītes appointed Hē′man son of Jō′el; and of his kindred Ā′saph son of Ber•e•chī′ah; and of the sons of Me•rar′ī, their kindred, Ē′than son of Kū•shā′i•ah; 18 and with them their kindred of the second order, Zech•a•rī′ah, Ja•ā′zi•el, She•mir′a•moth, Je•hī′el, Un′nī, E•lī′ab, Be•nā′i•ah, Mā•a•sēi′ah, Mat•ti•thī′ah, E•liph′e•le•hū, and Mik•nē′i•ah, and the gatekeepers Ō′bed-ē′dom and Je•ī′el. 19 The singers Hē′man, Ā′saph, and Ē′than were to sound bronze cymbals; 20 Zech•a•rī′ah, Ā′zi•el, She•mir′a•moth, Je•hī′el, Un′nī, E•lī′ab, Mā•a•sēi′ah, and Be•nā′i•ah were to play harps according to Al′a•moth; 21 but Mat•ti•thī′ah, E•liph′e•le•hū, Mik•nē′i•ah, Ō′bed-ē′dom, Je•ī′el, and Az•a•zī′ah were to lead with lyres according to the Shem′i•nith. 22 Chen•a•nī′ah, leader of the Lē′vītes in music, was to direct the music, for he understood it. 23 Ber•e•chī′ah and El•kā′nah were to be gatekeepers for the ark. 24 Sheb•a•nī′ah, Josh′a•phat, Ne•than′el, A•mā′sai, Zech•a•rī′ah, Be•nā′i•ah, and El•i•e′zer, the priests, were to blow the trumpets before the ark of God. Ō′bed-ē′dom and Je•hī′ah also were to be gatekeepers for the ark.

25 So David and the elders of Israel, and the commanders of the thousands, went to bring up the ark of the covenant of the LORD from the house of Ō′bed-ē′dom with rejoicing. 26 And because God helped the Lē′vītes who were carrying the ark of the covenant of the LORD, they sacrificed seven bulls and seven rams. 27 David was clothed with a robe of fine linen, as also were all the Lē′vītes who were carrying the ark, and the singers, and Chen•a•nī′ah the leader of the music of the singers; and David wore a linen ephod. 28 So all Israel brought up the ark of the covenant of the LORD with shouting, to the sound of the horn, trumpets, and cymbals, and made loud music on harps and lyres.

29 As the ark of the covenant of the LORD came to the city of David, Mī′chal daughter of Saul looked out of the window, and saw King David leaping and dancing; and she despised him in her heart.

The Ark Placed in the Tent
(2 Sam 6.17–19)

16 They brought in the ark of God, and set it inside the tent that David had pitched for it; and they offered burnt offerings and offerings of well-being before God. 2 When David had finished offering the burnt offerings and the offerings of well-being, he blessed the people in the name of the LORD; 3 and he distributed to every person in Israel—man and woman alike—to each a loaf of bread, a portion of meat,*r* and a cake of raisins.

4 He appointed certain of the Lē′vītes as ministers before the ark of the LORD, to invoke, to thank, and to praise the LORD, the God of Israel. 5 Ā′saph was the chief, and second to him Zech•a•rī′ah, Je•ī′el, She•mir′a•moth, Je•hī′el, Mat•ti•thī′ah, E•lī′ab, Be•nā′i•ah, Ō′bed-ē′dom, and Je•ī′el, with harps and lyres; Ā′saph was to sound the cymbals, 6 and the priests Be•nā′i•ah and Ja•hā′zi•el were to blow trumpets regularly, before the ark of the covenant of God.

---

p Heb *He*   *q* Meaning of Heb uncertain   *r* Compare Gk Syr Vg: Meaning of Heb uncertain

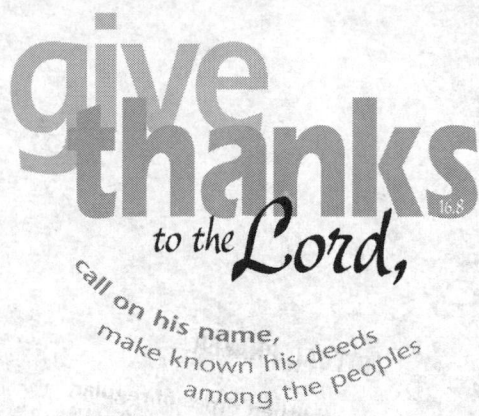

give thanks to the Lord,

call on his name,
make known his deeds
among the peoples

16.8

David's Psalm of Thanksgiving
(Ps 96.1–13; 105.1–15; 106.1, 47–48)

7 Then on that day David first appointed the singing of praises to the LORD by Ā'saph and his kindred.

8 O give thanks to the LORD, call on his name,
   make known his deeds among the peoples.
9 Sing to him, sing praises to him,
   tell of all his wonderful works.
10 Glory in his holy name;
    let the hearts of those who seek the LORD
       rejoice.
11 Seek the LORD and his strength,
    seek his presence continually.
12 Remember the wonderful works he has done,
    his miracles, and the judgments he uttered,
13 O offspring of his servant Israel,ˢ
    children of Jacob, his chosen ones.

14 He is the LORD our God;
    his judgments are in all the earth.
15 Remember his covenant forever,
    the word that he commanded, for a
       thousand generations,
16 the covenant that he made with Abraham,
    his sworn promise to Isaac,
17 which he confirmed to Jacob as a statute,
    to Israel as an everlasting covenant,
18 saying, "To you I will give the land of Cā'naan
    as your portion for an inheritance."

19 When they were few in number,
    of little account, and strangers in the land,ᵗ
20 wandering from nation to nation,
    from one kingdom to another people,
21 he allowed no one to oppress them;
    he rebuked kings on their account,
22 saying, "Do not touch my anointed ones;
    do my prophets no harm."

23 Sing to the LORD, all the earth.
    Tell of his salvation from day to day.
24 Declare his glory among the nations,
    his marvelous works among all the
       peoples.
25 For great is the LORD, and greatly to be
       praised;
    he is to be revered above all gods.
26 For all the gods of the peoples are idols,
    but the LORD made the heavens.
27 Honor and majesty are before him;
    strength and joy are in his place.

28 Ascribe to the LORD, O families of the peoples,
    ascribe to the LORD glory and strength.
29 Ascribe to the LORD the glory due his name;
    bring an offering, and come before him.
   Worship the LORD in holy splendor;
30   tremble before him, all the earth.
   The world is firmly established; it shall
       never be moved.
31 Let the heavens be glad, and let the earth
       rejoice,
    and let them say among the nations,
       "The LORD is king!"
32 Let the sea roar, and all that fills it;
    let the field exult, and everything in it.
33 Then shall the trees of the forest sing for joy
    before the LORD, for he comes to judge the
       earth.
34 O give thanks to the LORD, for he is good;
    for his steadfast love endures forever.

35 Say also:
   "Save us, O God of our salvation,
       and gather and rescue us from among the
          nations,
    that we may give thanks to your holy name,
       and glory in your praise.
36 Blessed be the LORD, the God of Israel,
    from everlasting to everlasting."
Then all the people said "Amen!" and praised the LORD.

Regular Worship Maintained

37 David left Ā'saph and his kinsfolk there before the ark of the covenant of the LORD to minister regularly before the ark as each day required, 38 and also Ō'bed-ē'dom and hisᵘ sixty-eight kinsfolk; while Ō'bed-ē'dom son of Je·dū'thun and Hō'sah were to be gatekeepers. 39 And he left the priest Zā'dok and his kindred the priests before the tabernacle of the LORD in the high place that was at Gib'ē·on, 40 to offer burnt offerings to the LORD on the altar of

---

ˢ Another reading is *Abraham* (compare Ps 105.6)   ᵗ Heb
in it   ᵘ Gk Syr Vg: Heb *their*

burnt offering regularly, morning and evening, according to all that is written in the law of the LORD that he commanded Israel. ⁴¹ With them were Hĕ′-man and Je•dū′thun, and the rest of those chosen and expressly named to render thanks to the LORD, for his steadfast love endures forever. ⁴² Hĕ′man and Je•dū′thun had with them trumpets and cymbals for the music, and instruments for sacred song. The sons of Je•dū′thun were appointed to the gate.

43 Then all the people departed to their homes, and David went home to bless his household.

God's Covenant with David
(2 Sam 7.1–17)

17 Now when David settled in his house, David said to the prophet Nathan, "I am living in a house of cedar, but the ark of the covenant of the LORD is under a tent." ² Nathan said to David, "Do all that you have in mind, for God is with you."

3 But that same night the word of the LORD came to Nathan, saying: ⁴ Go and tell my servant David: Thus says the LORD: You shall not build me a house to live in. ⁵ For I have not lived in a house since the day I brought out Israel to this very day, but I have lived in a tent and a tabernacle.ᵛ ⁶ Wherever I have moved about among all Israel, did I ever speak a word with any of the judges of Israel, whom I commanded to shepherd my people, saying, Why have you not built me a house of cedar? ⁷ Now therefore thus you shall say to my servant David: Thus says the LORD of hosts: I took you from the pasture, from following the sheep, to be ruler over my people Israel; ⁸ and I have been with you wherever you went, and have cut off all your enemies before you; and I will make for you a name, like the name of the great ones of the earth. ⁹ I will appoint a place for my people Israel, and will plant them, so that they may live in their own place, and be disturbed no more; and evildoers shall wear them down no more, as they did formerly, ¹⁰ from the time that I appointed judges over my people Israel; and I will subdue all your enemies.

Moreover I declare to you that the LORD will build you a house. ¹¹ When your days are fulfilled to go to be with your ancestors, I will raise up your offspring after you, one of your own sons, and I will establish his kingdom. ¹² He shall build a house for me, and I will establish his throne forever. ¹³ I will be a father to him, and he shall be a son to me. I will not take my steadfast love from him, as I took it from him who was before you, ¹⁴ but I will confirm him in my house and in my kingdom forever, and his throne shall be established forever. ¹⁵ In accordance with all these words and all this vision, Nathan spoke to David.

Catholic Connections

RITUAL PRAYER

King David established times of regular, ritual prayer at the ark. Regular, ritual prayer is a practice of many of the world's great religions and, in the eyes of the Chronicler, is a key ingredient of true religious practice. Catholics also have ancient traditions of regular, ritual prayer. (Regular, in this instance, does not mean "ordinary," but rather "at certain, established times.") We start the day with prayer, we end the day with prayer, we have special blessings for special occasions, and we gather to celebrate the Eucharist each week. Regular, ritual prayer helps to remind us of God's presence and of our identity as God's people.

How do you pray? Do you pray regularly? Do you have any personal rituals as part of your prayer life?

▶ I Chr 16.37–43

David's Prayer
(2 Sam 7.18–29)

16 Then King David went in and sat before the LORD, and said, "Who am I, O LORD God, and what is my house, that you have brought me thus far? ¹⁷ And even this was a small thing in your sight, O God; you have also spoken of your servant's house for a great while to come. You regard me as someone of high rank,ʷ O LORD God! ¹⁸ And what more can David say to you for honoring your servant? You know your servant. ¹⁹ For your servant's sake, O LORD, and according to your own heart, you have done all these great deeds, making known all these great things. ²⁰ There is no one like you, O LORD, and there is no God besides you, according to all that we have heard with our ears. ²¹ Who is like your people Israel, one nation on the earth whom

---

ᵛ Gk 2 Sam 7.6: Heb *but I have been from tent to tent and from tabernacle* ʷ Meaning of Heb uncertain

God went to redeem to be his people, making for yourself a name for great and terrible things, in driving out nations before your people whom you redeemed from Egypt? 22 And you made your people Israel to be your people forever; and you, O LORD, became their God.

23 "And now, O LORD, as for the word that you have spoken concerning your servant and concerning his house, let it be established forever, and do as you have promised. 24 Thus your name will be established and magnified forever in the saying, 'The LORD of hosts, the God of Israel, is Israel's God'; and the house of your servant David will be established in your presence. 25 For you, my God, have revealed to your servant that you will build a house for him; therefore your servant has found it possible to pray before you. 26 And now, O LORD, you are God, and you have promised this good thing to your servant; 27 therefore may it please you to bless the house of your servant, that it may continue forever before you. For you, O LORD, have blessed and are blessed^x forever."

David's Kingdom Established and Extended
(2 Sam 8.1–14)

18 Some time afterward, David attacked the Phi·lis'tines and subdued them; he took Gath and its villages from the Phi·lis'tines.

2 He defeated Mō'ab, and the Mō'ab·ites became subject to David and brought tribute.

3 David also struck down King Had·a·dē'zer of Zō'bah, toward Hā'math,^y as he went to set up a monument at the river Euphrates. 4 David took from him one thousand chariots, seven thousand cavalry, and twenty thousand foot soldiers. David hamstrung all the chariot horses, but left one hundred of them. 5 When the Ar·a·mē'ans of Damascus came to help King Had·a·dē'zer of Zō'bah, David killed twenty-two thousand Ar·a·mē'ans. 6 Then David put garrisons^z in Ar'am of Damascus; and the Ar·a·mē'ans became subject to David, and brought tribute. The LORD gave victory to David wherever he went. 7 David took the gold shields that were carried by the servants of Had·a·dē'zer, and brought them to Jerusalem. 8 From Tib'hath and from Cūn, cities of Had·a·dē'zer, David took a vast quantity of bronze; with it Solomon made the bronze sea and the pillars and the vessels of bronze.

9 When King Tō'ū of Hā'math heard that David had defeated the whole army of King Had·a·dē'zer of Zō'bah, 10 he sent his son Ha·dor'am to King David, to greet him and to congratulate him, because he had fought against Had·a·dē'zer and defeated him. Now Had·a·dē'zer had often been at war with Tō'ū. He sent all sorts of articles of gold, of silver, and of bronze; 11 these also King David dedicated to the LORD, together with the silver and gold that he had carried off from all the nations, from Ē'dom, Mō'ab, the Am'mon·ites, the Phi·lis'tines, and Am'a·lek.

12 A·bi'shai son of Ze·rū'i·ah killed eighteen thousand Ē'dom·ites in the Valley of Salt. 13 He put garrisons in Ē'dom; and all the Ē'dom·ites became subject to David. And the LORD gave victory to David wherever he went.

---

x Or *and it is blessed*   *y* Meaning of Heb uncertain   *z* Gk Vg 2 Sam 8.6 Compare Syr: Heb lacks *garrisons*

Where Do We Place God?

LIVE IT!

How the world loves boxes and containers and compartments! Remember the old saying, "A place for everything and everything in its place?" There is something comforting in knowing that everything is where it should be.

Don't we often try to put God away in a special place? Isn't it more convenient to think of God as residing "up there" in the tabernacle or sanctuary? Perhaps that is why in 1 Chr 17.4–6, God seems less than enthusiastic about David's desire to build a temple. The danger is clear: identify God with a building, however grand and beautiful, and in people's minds, God *stays* there.

When we enter a chapel or a church, we become reverent, sensing that we are in the presence of God. And, indeed, we are. But we need to remember that we do not leave God behind when we step out of that structure. Simply put, God cannot and will not be confined, despite our best efforts.

Our God walks with us. God's place is everywhere.

How can you practice living in the constant presence of God?

▸ 1 Chr 17.1–15

David's Administration
(2 Sam 8.15–18)

14 So David reigned over all Israel; and he administered justice and equity to all his people. 15 Jo'ab son of Ze·ru'i·ah was over the army; Je·hosh'a·phat son of A·hi'lud was recorder; 16 Za'dok son of A·hi'tub and A·him'e·lech son of A·bi'a·thar were priests; Shav'sha was secretary; 17 Be·na'i·ah son of Je·hoi'a·da was over the Cher'e·thites and the Pel'eth·ites; and David's sons were the chief officials in the service of the king.

Defeat of the Ammonites and Arameans
(2 Sam 10.1–19)

19 Some time afterward, King Na'hash of the Am'mon·ites died, and his son succeeded him. 2 David said, "I will deal loyally with Ha'nun son of Na'hash, for his father dealt loyally with me." So David sent messengers to console him concerning his father. When David's servants came to Ha'nun in the land of the Am'mon·ites, to console him, 3 the officials of the Am'mon·ites said to Ha'nun, "Do you think, because David has sent consolers to you, that he is honoring your father? Have not his servants come to you to search and to overthrow and to spy out the land?" 4 So Ha'nun seized David's servants, shaved them, cut off their garments in the middle at their hips, and sent them away; 5 and they departed. When David was told about the men, he sent messengers to them, for they felt greatly humiliated. The king said, "Remain at Jericho until your beards have grown, and then return."

6 When the Am'mon·ites saw that they had made themselves odious to David, Ha'nun and the Am'mon·ites sent a thousand talents of silver to hire chariots and cavalry from Mes·o·po·ta'mi·a, from Ar'am-ma'a·cah and from Zo'bah. 7 They hired thirty-two thousand chariots and the king of Ma'a·cah with his army, who came and camped before Med'e·ba. And the Am'mon·ites were mustered from their cities and came to battle. 8 When David heard of it, he sent Jo'ab and all the army of the warriors. 9 The Am'mon·ites came out and drew up in battle array at the entrance of the city, and the kings who had come were by themselves in the open country.

10 When Jo'ab saw that the line of battle was set against him both in front and in the rear, he chose some of the picked men of Israel and arrayed them against the Ar·a·me'ans; 11 the rest of his troops he put in the charge of his brother A·bi'shai, and they were arrayed against the Am'mon·ites. 12 He said, "If the Ar·a·me'ans are too strong for me, then you shall help me; but if the Am'mon·ites are too strong for you, then I will help you. 13 Be strong, and let us be courageous for our people and for the cities of

our God; and may the LORD do what seems good to him." 14 So Jo'ab and the troops who were with him advanced toward the Ar·a·me'ans for battle; and they fled before him. 15 When the Am'mon·ites saw that the Ar·a·me'ans fled, they likewise fled before A·bi'shai, Jo'ab's brother, and entered the city. Then Jo'ab came to Jerusalem.

16 But when the Ar·a·me'ans saw that they had been defeated by Israel, they sent messengers and brought out the Ar·a·me'ans who were beyond the Euphrates, with Sho'phach the commander of the army of Had·a·de'zer at their head. 17 When David was informed, he gathered all Israel together, crossed the Jordan, came to them, and drew up his forces against them. When David set the battle in array against the Ar·a·me'ans, they fought with him. 18 The Ar·a·me'ans fled before Israel; and David killed seven thousand Ar·a·me'an charioteers and forty thousand foot soldiers, and also killed Sho'phach the commander of their army. 19 When the servants of Had·a·de'zer saw that they had been defeated by Israel, they made peace with David, and became subject to him. So the Ar·a·me'ans were not willing to help the Am'mon·ites any more.

Siege and Capture of Rabbah
(2 Sam 11.1; 12.26–31)

20 In the spring of the year, the time when kings go out to battle, Jo'ab led out the army, ravaged the country of the Am'mon·ites, and came and besieged Rab'bah. But David remained at Jerusalem. Jo'ab attacked Rab'bah, and overthrew it. 2 David took the crown of Mil'com*a* from his head; he found that it weighed a talent of gold, and in it was a precious stone; and it was placed on David's head. He also brought out the booty of the city, a very great amount. 3 He brought out the people who were in it, and set them to work*b* with saws and iron picks and axes.*c* Thus David did to all the cities of the Am'mon·ites. Then David and all the people returned to Jerusalem.

Exploits against the Philistines
(2 Sam 21.15–22)

4 After this, war broke out with the Phi·lis'tines at Ge'zer; then Sib'be·cai the Hu'sha·thite killed Sip'pai, who was one of the descendants of the giants; and the Phi·lis'tines were subdued. 5 Again there was war with the Phi·lis'tines; and El·ha'nan son of Ja'ir killed Lah'mi the brother of Goliath the Git'tite, the shaft of whose spear was like a weaver's beam. 6 Again there was war at Gath, where there was a man of great size, who had six fingers on each

---

a Gk Vg See 1 Kings 11.5, 33: MT *of their king*   *b* Compare 2 Sam 12.31: Heb *and he sawed*   *c* Compare 2 Sam 12.31: Heb *saws* hand, and six toes on each foot, twenty-four in number; he also was descended from the giants. 7 When he taunted Israel, Jonathan son of Shim'ē•a, David's brother, killed him. 8 These were descended from the giants in Gath; they fell by the hand of David and his servants.

The Census and Plague
(2 Sam 24.1–17)

21 Satan stood up against Israel, and incited David to count the people of Israel. 2 So David said to Jō'ab and the commanders of the army, "Go, number Israel, from Bē'er-shē'ba to Dan, and bring me a report, so that I may know their number." 3 But Jō'ab said, "May the LORD increase the number of his people a hundredfold! Are they not, my lord the king, all of them my lord's servants? Why then should my lord require this? Why should he bring guilt on Israel?" 4 But the king's word prevailed against Jō'ab. So Jō'ab departed and went throughout all Israel, and came back to Jerusalem. 5 Jō'ab gave the total count of the people to David. In all Israel there were one million one hundred thousand men who drew the sword, and in Judah four hundred seventy thousand who drew the sword. 6 But he did not include Levi and Benjamin in the numbering, for the king's command was abhorrent to Jō'ab.

7 But God was displeased with this thing, and he struck Israel. 8 David said to God, "I have sinned greatly in that I have done this thing. But now, I pray you, take away the guilt of your servant; for I have done very foolishly." 9 The LORD spoke to Gad, David's seer, saying, 10 "Go and say to David, 'Thus says the LORD: Three things I offer you; choose one of them, so that I may do it to you.'" 11 So Gad came to David and said to him, "Thus says the LORD, 'Take your choice: 12 either three years of famine; or three months of devastation by your foes, while the sword of your enemies overtakes you; or three days of the sword of the LORD, pestilence on the land, and the angel of the LORD destroying throughout all the territory of Israel.' Now decide what answer I shall return to the one who sent me." 13 Then David said to Gad, "I am in great distress; let me fall into the hand of the LORD, for his mercy is very great; but let me not fall into human hands."

14 So the LORD sent a pestilence on Israel; and seventy thousand persons fell in Israel. 15 And God sent an angel to Jerusalem to destroy it; but when he was about to destroy it, the LORD took note and relented concerning the calamity; he said to the destroying angel, "Enough! Stay your hand." The angel of the LORD was then standing by the threshing floor of Or'nan the Jeb'ū•site. 16 David looked up and saw the angel of the LORD standing between

PRAY IT!
True Repentance

Think of a time when you said, "I'm sorry," just because you felt you had to. Now think of a time when you were truly sorry for causing harm to another by doing something God had commanded you not to do. There is a big difference between going through the motions of repentance and being truly repentant before another and before God. For example, David sinned by ordering a census to count his people (1 Chr 21.2). He accepted a consequence that he hoped would be the easiest (verse 13). But when he saw the harm he had caused, he became truly repentant and asked God's mercy upon the Israelites (verse 17).

Repentance requires true sorrow and asking God to change our heart. It leads to an active response to make amends with God and with the church. Such repentance is called reconciliation, and Catholics celebrate it in the sacrament of Reconciliation.

▸ 1 Chr 21.1–17

earth and heaven, and in his hand a drawn sword stretched out over Jerusalem. Then David and the elders, clothed in sackcloth, fell on their faces. 17 And David said to God, "Was it not I who gave the command to count the people? It is I who have sinned and done very wickedly. But these sheep, what have they done? Let your hand, I pray, O LORD my God, be against me and against my father's house; but do not let your people be plagued!"

David's Altar and Sacrifice
(2 Sam 24.18–25)

18 Then the angel of the LORD commanded Gad to tell David that he should go up and erect an altar to the LORD on the threshing floor of Or'nan the Jeb'ū•site. 19 So David went up following Gad's instructions, which he had spoken in the name of the LORD. 20 Or'nan turned and saw the angel; and while his four sons who were with him hid themselves, Or'nan continued to thresh wheat. 21 As David came to Or'nan, Or'nan looked and saw David; he went out from the threshing floor, and did obeisance to David with his face to the ground. 22 David said to Or'nan, "Give me the site of the

threshing floor that I may build on it an altar to the LORD—give it to me at its full price—so that the plague may be averted from the people." 23 Then Or'nan said to David, "Take it; and let my lord the king do what seems good to him; see, I present the oxen for burnt offerings, and the threshing sledges for the wood, and the wheat for a grain offering. I give it all." 24 But King David said to Or'nan, "No; I will buy them for the full price. I will not take for the LORD what is yours, nor offer burnt offerings that cost me nothing." 25 So David paid Or'nan six hundred shekels of gold by weight for the site. 26 David built there an altar to the LORD and presented burnt offerings and offerings of well-being. He called upon the LORD, and he answered him with fire from heaven on the altar of burnt offering. 27 Then the LORD commanded the angel, and he put his sword back into its sheath.

The Place Chosen for the Temple

28 At that time, when David saw that the LORD had answered him at the threshing floor of Or'nan the Jeb'ū·sīte, he made his sacrifices there. 29 For the tabernacle of the LORD, which Moses had made in the wilderness, and the altar of burnt offering were at that time in the high place at Gib'ē·on; 30 but David could not go before it to inquire of God, for he was afraid of the sword of the angel of the LORD.

22 1 Then David said, "Here shall be the house of the LORD God and here the altar of burnt offering for Israel."

David Prepares to Build the Temple

2 David gave orders to gather together the aliens who were residing in the land of Israel, and he set stonecutters to prepare dressed stones for building the house of God. 3 David also provided great stores of iron for nails for the doors of the gates and for clamps, as well as bronze in quantities beyond weighing, 4 and cedar logs without number—for the Sī·dō'ni·ans and Tȳ'ri·ans brought great quantities of cedar to David. 5 For David said, "My son Solomon is young and inexperienced, and the house that is to be built for the LORD must be exceedingly magnificent, famous and glorified throughout all lands; I will therefore make preparation for it." So David provided materials in great quantity before his death.

David's Charge to Solomon and the Leaders

6 Then he called for his son Solomon and charged him to build a house for the LORD, the God of Israel. 7 David said to Solomon, "My son, I had planned to build a house to the name of the LORD my God. 8 But the word of the LORD came to me, saying, 'You have shed much blood and have waged great wars; you shall not build a house to my name, because you have shed so much blood in my sight on the earth. 9 See, a son shall be born to you; he shall be a man of peace. I will give him peace from all his enemies on every side; for his name shall be Solomon,[d] and I will give peace[e] and quiet to Israel in his days. 10 He shall build a house for my name. He shall be a son to me, and I will be a father to him, and I will establish his royal throne in Israel forever.' 11 Now, my son, the LORD be with you, so that you may succeed in building the house of the LORD your God, as he has spoken concerning you. 12 Only, may the LORD grant you discretion and understanding, so that when he gives you charge over Israel you may keep the law of the LORD your God. 13 Then you will prosper if you are careful to observe the statutes and the ordinances that the LORD commanded Moses for Israel. Be strong and of good courage. Do not be afraid or dismayed. 14 With great pains I have provided for the house of the LORD one hundred thousand talents of gold, one million talents of silver, and bronze and iron beyond weighing, for there is so much of it; timber and stone too I have provided. To these you must add more. 15 You have an abundance of workers: stonecutters, masons, carpenters, and all kinds of artisans without number, skilled in working 16 gold, silver, bronze, and iron. Now begin the work, and the LORD be with you."

17 David also commanded all the leaders of Israel to help his son Solomon, saying, 18 "Is not the LORD your God with you? Has he not given you peace on every side? For he has delivered the inhabitants of the land into my hand; and the land is subdued before the LORD and his people. 19 Now set your mind and heart to seek the LORD your God. Go and build the sanctuary of the LORD God so that the ark of the covenant of the LORD and the holy vessels of God may be brought into a house built for the name of the LORD."

Families of the Levites and Their Functions

23 When David was old and full of days, he made his son Solomon king over Israel. 2 David assembled all the leaders of Israel and the priests and the Lē'vītes. 3 The Lē'vītes, thirty years old and upward, were counted, and the total was thirty-eight thousand. 4 "Twenty-four thousand of these," David said, "shall have charge of the work in the house of the LORD, six thousand shall be officers and judges, 5 four thousand gatekeepers, and four thousand shall offer praises to the LORD with the instruments that I have made for praise." 6 And David organized them in divisions corresponding to the sons of Levi: Ger'shon,[f] Kō'hath, and Me·rar'i.

---

d Heb *Shelomoh*   e Heb *shalom*   f Or *Gershom*; See 1 Chr 6.1, note, and 23.15

7 The sons of Ger'shon*g* were La'dan and Shim'ē·ī. 8 The sons of La'dan: Je·hī'el the chief, Zē'tham, and Jō'el, three. 9 The sons of Shim'ē·ī: She·lō'moth, Ha'zi·el, and Har'an, three. These were the heads of families of La'dan. 10 And the sons of Shim'ē·ī: Ja'hath, Zī'na, Jē'ush, and Bē·rī'ah. These four were the sons of Shim'ē·ī. 11 Ja'hath was the chief, and Zī'zah the second; but Jē'ush and Be·rī'ah did not have many sons, so they were enrolled as a single family.

12 The sons of Kō'hath: Am'ram, Iz'har, Hē'bron, and Uz'zi·el, four. 13 The sons of Am'ram: Aaron and Moses. Aaron was set apart to consecrate the most holy things, so that he and his sons forever should make offerings before the LORD, and minister to him and pronounce blessings in his name forever; 14 but as for Moses the man of God, his sons were to be reckoned among the tribe of Levi. 15 The sons of Moses: Ger'shom and El·i·ē'zer. 16 The sons of Ger'shom: She·bū'el the chief. 17 The sons of El·i·ē'zer: Rē·ha·bī'ah the chief; El·i·ē'zer had no other sons, but the sons of Rē·ha·bī'ah were very numerous. 18 The sons of Iz'har: She·lō'mith the chief. 19 The sons of Hē'bron: Je·rī'ah the chief, Am·a·rī'ah the second, Ja·hā'zi·el the third, and Jek·a·mē'am the fourth. 20 The sons of Uz'zi·el: Mī'cah the chief and Is·shī'ah the second.

21 The sons of Me·rar'ī: Mah'lī and Mū'shī. The sons of Mah'lī: El·ē·ā'zar and Kish. 22 El·ē·ā'zar died having no sons, but only daughters; their kindred, the sons of Kish, married them. 23 The sons of Mū'shī: Mah'lī, Ē'der, and Jer'e·moth, three.

24 These were the sons of Levi by their ancestral houses, the heads of families as they were enrolled according to the number of the names of the individuals from twenty years old and upward who were to do the work for the service of the house of the LORD. 25 For David said, "The LORD, the God of Israel, has given rest to his people; and he resides in Jerusalem forever. 26 And so the Lē'vītes no longer need to carry the tabernacle or any of the things for its service"— 27 for according to the last words of David these were the number of the Lē'vītes from twenty years old and upward— 28 "but their duty shall be to assist the descendants of Aaron for the service of the house of the LORD, having the care of the courts and the chambers, the cleansing of all that is holy, and any work for the service of the house of God; 29 to assist also with the rows of bread, the choice flour for the grain offering, the wafers of unleavened bread, the baked offering, the offering mixed with oil, and all measures of quantity or size. 30 And they shall stand every morning, thanking and praising the LORD, and likewise at evening, 31 and whenever burnt offerings are offered to the LORD on sabbaths, new moons, and appointed festivals, according to the number required of them,

regularly before the LORD. 32 Thus they shall keep charge of the tent of meeting and the sanctuary, and shall attend the descendants of Aaron, their kindred, for the service of the house of the LORD."

Divisions of the Priests

24 The divisions of the descendants of Aaron were these. The sons of Aaron: Na'dab, A·bī'hū, El·ē·ā'zar, and Ith'a·mar. 2 But Na'dab and A·bī'hū died before their father, and had no sons; so El·ē·ā'zar and Ith'a·mar became the priests. 3 Along with Zā'dok of the sons of El·ē·ā'zar, and A·him'e·lech of the sons of Ith'a·mar, David organized them according to the appointed duties in their service. 4 Since more chief men were found among the sons of El·ē·ā'zar than among the sons of Ith'a·mar, they organized them under sixteen heads of ancestral houses of the sons of El·ē·ā'zar, and eight of the sons of Ith'a·mar. 5 They organized them by lot, all alike, for there were officers of the sanctuary and officers of God among both the sons of El·ē·ā'zar and the sons of Ith'a·mar. 6 The scribe She·māi'ah son of Ne·than'el, a Lē'vīte, recorded them in the presence of the king, and the officers, and Zā'dok the priest, and A·him'e·lech son of A·bī'a·thar, and the heads of ancestral houses of the priests and of the Lē'vītes; one ancestral house being chosen for El·ē·ā'zar and one chosen for Ith'a·mar.

7 The first lot fell to Je·hoi'a·rib, the second to Je·dai'ah, 8 the third to Ha'rim, the fourth to Se·ō'rim, 9 the fifth to Mal·chī'jah, the sixth to Mij'a·min, 10 the seventh to Hak'koz, the eighth to A·bī'jah, 11 the ninth to Jesh'ū·a, the tenth to Shec·a·nī'ah, 12 the eleventh to E·lī'a·shib, the twelfth to Ja'kim, 13 the thirteenth to Hup'pah, the fourteenth to Je·sheb'e·ab, 14 the fifteenth to Bil'gah, the sixteenth to Im'mer, 15 the seventeenth to Hē'zir, the eighteenth to Hap'piz·zez, 16 the nineteenth to Peth·a·hī'ah, the twentieth to Je·hez'kel, 17 the twenty-first to Ja'chin, the twenty-second to Gā'mūl, 18 the twenty-third to De·lai'ah, the twenty-fourth to Mā·a·zī'ah. 19 These had as their appointed duty in their service to enter the house of the LORD according to the procedure established for them by their ancestor Aaron, as the LORD God of Israel had commanded him.

Other Levites

20 And of the rest of the sons of Levi: of the sons of Am'ram, Shū'ba·el; of the sons of Shū'ba·el, Jeh·dē'i·ah. 21 Of Rē·ha·bī'ah: of the sons of Rē·ha·bī'ah, Is·shī'ah the chief. 22 Of the Iz'har·ītes, She·lō'moth; of the sons of She·lō'moth, Ja'hath. 23 The sons of Hē'bron:*h* Je·rī'ah the chief,*i*

---

g Vg Compare Gk Syr: Heb *to the Gershonite*   *h* See 23.19: Heb lacks *Hebron*   *i* See 23.19: Heb lacks *the chief*

Am·a·rī'ah the second, Ja·hā'zi·el the third, Jek·a·mē'am the fourth. 24 The sons of Uz'zi·el, Mī'cah; of the sons of Mī'cah, Shā'mir. 25 The brother of Mī'cah, Is·shī'ah; of the sons of Is·shī'ah, Zech·a·rī'ah. 26 The sons of Me·rar'ī: Mah'li and Mū'shī. The sons of Jā·a·zī'ah: Bĕ'no.*j* 27 The sons of Me·rar'ī: of Jā·a·zī'ah, Bĕ'no,*j* Shō'ham, Zac'cur, and Ib'rī. 28 Of Mah'lī: El·ē·ā'zar, who had no sons. 29 Of Kish, the sons of Kish: Je·rah'mē·el. 30 The sons of Mū'shī: Mah'li, Ē'der, and Jer'i·moth. These were the sons of the Lē'vītes according to their ancestral houses. 31 These also cast lots corresponding to their kindred, the descendants of Aaron, in the presence of King David, Zā'dok, A·him'e·lech, and the heads of ancestral houses of the priests and of the Lē'vītes, the chief as well as the youngest brother.

The Temple Musicians

25 David and the officers of the army also set apart for the service the sons of Ā'saph, and of Hē'man, and of Je·dū'thun, who should prophesy with lyres, harps, and cymbals. The list of those who did the work and of their duties was: 2 Of the sons of Ā'saph: Zac'cur, Joseph, Neth·a·nī'ah, and As·a·rē'lah, sons of Ā'saph, under the direction of Ā'saph, who prophesied under the direction of the king. 3 Of Je·dū'thun, the sons of Je·dū'thun: Ged·a·lī'ah, Zĕ'rī, Je·shā'i·ah, Shim'ē·ī,*k* Hash·a·bī'ah, and Mat·ti·thī'ah, six, under the direction of their father Jed·ū'thun, who prophesied with the lyre in thanksgiving and praise to the LORD. 4 Of Hē'man, the sons of Hē'man: Buk·kī'ah, Mat·ta·nī'ah, Uz'zi·el, She·bū'el, and Jer'i·moth, Han·a·nī'ah, Ha·nā'nī, E·lī'a·thah, Gid·dal'tī, and Rō·mam'ti-ē'zer, Josh·be·kash'ah, Mal·lō'thī, Hō'thir, Ma·hā'zi·oth. 5 All these were the sons of Hē'man the king's seer, according to the promise of God to exalt him; for God had given Hē'man fourteen sons and three daughters. 6 They were all under the direction of their father for the music in the house of the LORD with cymbals, harps, and lyres for the service of the house of God. Ā'saph, Je·dū'thun, and Hē'man were under the order of the king. 7 They and their kindred, who were trained in singing to the LORD, all of whom were skillful, numbered two hundred eighty-eight. 8 And they cast lots for their duties, small and great, teacher and pupil alike.

9 The first lot fell for Ā'saph to Joseph; the second to Ged·a·lī'ah, to him and his brothers and his sons, twelve; 10 the third to Zac'cur, his sons and his brothers, twelve; 11 the fourth to Iz'rī, his sons and his brothers, twelve; 12 the fifth to Neth·a·nī'ah, his sons and his brothers, twelve; 13 the sixth to Buk·kī'ah, his sons and his brothers, twelve; 14 the seventh to Jes·a·rē'lah,*l* his sons and his brothers, twelve; 15 the eighth to Je·shā'i·ah, his sons and his brothers,

twelve; 16 the ninth to Mat·ta·nī'ah, his sons and his brothers, twelve; 17 the tenth to Shim'ē·ī, his sons and his brothers, twelve; 18 the eleventh to Az'a·rel, his sons and his brothers, twelve; 19 the twelfth to Hash·a·bī'ah, his sons and his brothers, twelve; 20 to the thirteenth, Shū'ba·el, his sons and his brothers, twelve; 21 to the fourteenth, Mat·ti·thī'ah, his sons and his brothers, twelve; 22 to the fifteenth, to Jer'e·moth, his sons and his brothers, twelve; 23 to the sixteenth, to Han·a·nī'ah, his sons and his brothers, twelve; 24 to the seventeenth, to Josh·be·kash'ah, his sons and his brothers, twelve; 25 to the eighteenth, to Ha·nā'nī, his sons and his brothers, twelve; 26 to the nineteenth, to Mal·lō'thī, his sons and his brothers, twelve; 27 to the twentieth, to E·lī'a·thah, his sons and his brothers, twelve; 28 to the twenty-first, to Hō'thir, his sons and his brothers, twelve; 29 to the twenty-second, to Gid·dal'tī, his sons and his brothers, twelve; 30 to the twenty-third, to Ma·hā'zi·oth, his sons and his brothers, twelve; 31 to the twenty-fourth, to Rō·mam'ti-ē'zer, his sons and his brothers, twelve.

The Gatekeepers

26 As for the divisions of the gatekeepers: of the Kō'ra·hītes, Me·shel·e·mī'ah son of Kō're, of the sons of Ā'saph. 2 Me·shel·e·mī'ah had sons: Zech·a·rī'ah the firstborn, Je·dī'a·el the second, Zeb·a·dī'ah the third, Jath'ni·el the fourth, 3 Ē'lam the fifth, Jē·hō·hā'nan the sixth, El·i·ē·hō·ē'naī the seventh. 4 Ō'bed-ē'dom had sons: She·māi'ah the firstborn, Je·hō'za·bad the second, Jō'ah the third, Sā'char the fourth, Ne·than'el the fifth, 5 Am'mi·el the sixth, Is'sa·char the seventh, Pe·ul'le·thaī the eighth; for God blessed him. 6 Also to his son She·māi'ah sons were born who exercised authority in their ancestral houses, for they were men of great ability. 7 The sons of She·māi'ah: Oth'nī, Reph'a·el, Ō'bed, and El·zā'bad, whose brothers were able men, E·lī'hū and Sem·a·chī'ah. 8 All these, sons of Ō'bed-ē'dom with their sons and brothers, were able men qualified for the service; sixty-two of Ō'bed-ē'dom. 9 Me·shel·e·mī'ah had sons and brothers, able men, eighteen. 10 Hō'sah, of the sons of Me·rar'ī, had sons: Shim'rī the chief (for though he was not the firstborn, his father made him chief), 11 Hil·kī'ah the second, Teb·a·lī'ah the third, Zech·a·rī'ah the fourth: all the sons and brothers of Hō'sah totaled thirteen.

12 These divisions of the gatekeepers, corresponding to their leaders, had duties, just as their kindred did, ministering in the house of the LORD; 13 and they cast lots by ancestral houses, small and great alike, for their gates. 14 The lot for the east fell

j Or *his son*: Meaning of Heb uncertain   *k* One Ms: Gk: MT lacks *Shimei*   *l* Or *Asarelah*; see 25.2

to Shel·e·mi′ah. They cast lots also for his son Zech·a·ri′ah, a prudent counselor, and his lot came out for the north. 15 Ō′bed-ē′dom's came out for the south, and to his sons was allotted the storehouse. 16 For Shup′pim and Hō′sah it came out for the west, at the gate of Shal′le·cheth on the ascending road. Guard corresponded to guard. 17 On the east there were six Lē′vītes each day,[m] on the north four each day, on the south four each day, as well as two and two at the storehouse; 18 and for the colonnade[n] on the west there were four at the road and two at the colonnade.[n] 19 These were the divisions of the gatekeepers among the Kō′ra·hītes and the sons of Me·rar′ī.

The Treasurers, Officers, and Judges

20 And of the Lē′vītes, A·hi′jah had charge of the treasuries of the house of God and the treasuries of the dedicated gifts. 21 The sons of Lā′dan, the sons of the Ger′shon·ītes belonging to Lā′dan, the heads of families belonging to Lā′dan the Ger′shon·īte: Je·hi′e·lī.[o]

22 The sons of Je·hi′e·lī, Zē′tham and his brother Jō′el, were in charge of the treasuries of the house of the LORD. 23 Of the Am′ram·ītes, the Iz′har·ītes, the Hē′bron·ītes, and the Uz′zi·el·ītes: 24 She·bū′el son of Ger′shom, son of Moses, was chief officer in charge of the treasuries. 25 His brothers: from El·i·e′zer were his son Rē·ha·bi′ah, his son Je·shā′i·ah, his son Jō′ram, his son Zich′rī, and his son She·lō′moth. 26 This She·lō′moth and his brothers were in charge of all the treasuries of the dedicated gifts that King David, and the heads of families, and the officers of the thousands and the hundreds, and the commanders of the army, had dedicated. 27 From booty won in battles they dedicated gifts for the maintenance of the house of the LORD. 28 Also all that Samuel the seer, and Saul son of Kish, and Abner son of Ner, and Jō′ab son of Ze·ru′i·ah had dedicated—all dedicated gifts were in the care of She·lō′moth[p] and his brothers.

29 Of the Iz′har·ītes, Chen·a·ni′ah and his sons were appointed to outside duties for Israel, as officers and judges. 30 Of the Hē′bron·ītes, Hash·a·bī′ah and his brothers, one thousand seven hundred men of ability, had the oversight of Israel west of the Jordan for all the work of the LORD and for the service of the king. 31 Of the Hē′bron·ītes, Je·rī′jah was chief of the Hē′bron·ītes. (In the fortieth year of David's reign search was made, of whatever genealogy or family, and men of great ability among them were found at Jā′zer in Gil′e·ad.) 32 King David appointed him and his brothers, two thousand seven hundred men of ability, heads of families, to have the oversight of the Reū′ben·ītes, the Gad′ītes, and the half-tribe of the Ma·nas′sītes for everything pertaining to God and for the affairs of the king.

The Military Divisions

27 This is the list of the people of Israel, the heads of families, the commanders of the thousands and the hundreds, and their officers who served the king in all matters concerning the divisions that came and went, month after month throughout the year, each division numbering twenty-four thousand: 2 Ja·shō′bē·am son of Zab′di·el was in charge of the first division in the first month; in his division were twenty-four thousand. 3 He was a descendant of Per′ez, and was chief of all the commanders of the army for the first month. 4 Dō′dai the A·hō′hīte was in charge of the division of the second month; Mik′loth was the chief officer of his division. In his division were twenty-four thousand. 5 The third commander, for the third month, was Be·nā′i·ah son of the priest Je·hoi′a·da, as chief; in his division were twenty-four thousand. 6 This is the Be·nā′i·ah who was a mighty man of the Thirty and in command of the Thirty; his son Am·miz′a·bad was in charge of his division.[q] 7 As′a·hel brother of Jō′ab was fourth, for the fourth month, and his son Zeb·a·di′ah after him; in his division were twenty-four thousand. 8 The fifth commander, for the fifth month, was Sham′huth, the Iz′ra·hīte; in his division were twenty-four thousand. 9 Sixth, for the sixth month, was Ira son of Ik′kesh the Te·kō′īte; in his division were twenty-four thousand. 10 Seventh, for the seventh month, was Hē′lez the Pel′o·nīte, of the Ē′phra·im·ītes; in his division were twenty-four thousand. 11 Eighth, for the eighth month, was Sib′be·caī the Hū′sha·thīte, of the Zē′ra·hītes; in his division were twenty-four thousand. 12 Ninth, for the ninth month, was Ā·bi·ē′zer of An′a·thoth, a Ben′ja·min·īte; in his division were twenty-four thousand. 13 Tenth, for the tenth month, was Mā′ha·raī of Ne·toph′ah, of the Zē′ra·hītes; in his division were twenty-four thousand. 14 Eleventh, for the eleventh month, was Be·nā′i·ah of Pir′a·thon, of the Ē′phra·im·ītes; in his division were twenty-four thousand. 15 Twelfth, for the twelfth month, was Hel′daī the Ne·toph′a·thīte, of Oth′ni·el; in his division were twenty-four thousand.

Leaders of Tribes

16 Over the tribes of Israel, for the Reū′ben·ītes, El·i·e′zer son of Zich′rī was chief officer; for the Sim′ē·on·ītes, Sheph·a·tī′ah son of Mā′a·cah; 17 for Levi, Hash·a·bī′ah son of Ke·mū′el; for Aaron, Zā′dok; 18 for Judah, E·li′hū, one of David's brothers; for Is′sa·char, Om′rī son of Michael; 19 for

---

m Gk: Heb lacks *each day*   n Heb *parbar*: meaning uncertain   o The Hebrew text of verse 21 is confused   p Gk Compare 26.28: Heb *Shelomith*   q Gk Vg: Heb *Ammizabad was his division*

Zeb'ū·lun, Ish•mā'i•ah son of Ō·ba·dī'ah; for Naph'-ta·lī, Jer'i•moth son of Az'ri•el; 20 for the Ē'phra·im•ites, Hō·shē'a son of Az•a·zī'ah; for the half-tribe of Ma•nas'seh, Jō'el son of Pe·dāi'ah; 21 for the half-tribe of Ma•nas'seh in Gil'e·ad, Id'dō son of Zech•a·rī'ah; for Benjamin, Jā•a·sī'el son of Abner; 22 for Dan, Az'a·rel son of Je·rō'ham. These were the leaders of the tribes of Israel. 23 David did not count those below twenty years of age, for the LORD had promised to make Israel as numerous as the stars of heaven. 24 Jō'ab son of Ze·rū'i·ah began to count them, but did not finish; yet wrath came upon Israel for this, and the number was not entered into the account of the Annals of King David.

Other Civic Officials

25 Over the king's treasuries was Az'ma•veth son of Ad'i•el. Over the treasuries in the country, in the cities, in the villages and in the towers, was Jonathan son of Uz•zī'ah. 26 Over those who did the work of the field, tilling the soil, was Ez'rī son of Chē'lub. 27 Over the vineyards was Shim'ē•ī the Rā'ma•thīte. Over the produce of the vineyards for the wine cellars was Zab'dī the Shiph'mīte. 28 Over the olive and sycamore trees in the She•phē'lah was Bā'al-hā'nan the Ge•dē'rīte. Over the stores of oil was Jō'ash. 29 Over the herds that pastured in Sharon was Shit'rāī the Shār'on•īte. Over the herds in the valleys was Shā'phat son of Ad'lā•ī. 30 Over the camels was Ō'bil the Ish'ma•el•īte. Over the donkeys was Jeh•dē'i·ah the Me•ron'o•thīte. Over the flocks was Jā'ziz the Hag'rīte. 31 All these were stewards of King David's property.

32 Jonathan, David's uncle, was a counselor, being a man of understanding and a scribe; Je•hī'el son of Hach'mo•nī attended the king's sons. 33 A•hith'o•phel was the king's counselor, and Hū'shaī the Ar'chīte was the king's friend. 34 After A•hith'o•phel came Je•hoi'a·da son of Be•nā'i·ah, and A•bī'a·thar. Jō'ab was commander of the king's army.

Solomon Instructed to Build the Temple

28 David assembled at Jerusalem all the officials of Israel, the officials of the tribes, the officers of the divisions that served the king, the commanders of the thousands, the commanders of the hundreds, the stewards of all the property and cattle of the king and his sons, together with the palace officials, the mighty warriors, and all the warriors. 2 Then King David rose to his feet and said: "Hear me, my brothers and my people. I had planned to build a house of rest for the ark of the covenant of the LORD, for the footstool of our God; and I made preparations for building. 3 But God said to me, 'You shall not build a house for my name, for you are a warrior and have shed blood.'

4 Yet the LORD God of Israel chose me from all my ancestral house to be king over Israel forever; for he chose Judah as leader, and in the house of Judah my father's house, and among my father's sons he took delight in making me king over all Israel. 5 And of all my sons, for the LORD has given me many, he has chosen my son Solomon to sit upon the throne of the kingdom of the LORD over Israel. 6 He said to me, 'It is your son Solomon who shall build my house and my courts, for I have chosen him to be a son to me, and I will be a father to him. 7 I will establish his kingdom forever if he continues resolute in keeping my commandments and my ordinances, as he is today.' 8 Now therefore in the sight of all Israel, the assembly of the LORD, and in the hearing of our God, observe and search out all the commandments of the LORD your God; that you may possess this good land, and leave it for an inheritance to your children after you forever.

9 "And you, my son Solomon, know the God of your father, and serve him with single mind and willing heart; for the LORD searches every mind, and understands every plan and thought. If you seek him, he will be found by you; but if you forsake him, he will abandon you forever. 10 Take heed now, for the LORD has chosen you to build a house as the sanctuary; be strong, and act."

11 Then David gave his son Solomon the plan of the vestibule of the temple, and of its houses, its treasuries, its upper rooms, and its inner chambers, and of the room for the mercy seat;r 12 and the plan of all that he had in mind: for the courts of the house of the LORD, all the surrounding chambers, the treasuries of the house of God, and the treasuries for dedicated gifts; 13 for the divisions of the priests and of the Lē'vītes, and all the work of the service in the house of the LORD; for all the vessels for the service in the house of the LORD, 14 the weight of gold for all golden vessels for each service, the weight of silver vessels for each service, 15 the weight of the golden lampstands and their lamps, the weight of gold for each lampstand and its lamps, the weight of silver for a lampstand and its lamps, according to the use of each in the service, 16 the weight of gold for each table for the rows of bread, the silver for the silver tables, 17 and pure gold for the forks, the basins, and the cups; for the golden bowls and the weight of each; for the silver bowls and the weight of each; 18 for the altar of incense made of refined gold, and its weight; also his plan for the golden chariot of the cherubim that spread their wings and covered the ark of the covenant of the LORD.

19 "All this, in writing at the LORD's direction, he made clear to me—the plan of all the works."

---

r Or the cover

20 David said further to his son Solomon, "Be strong and of good courage, and act. Do not be afraid or dismayed; for the LORD God, my God, is with you. He will not fail you or forsake you, until all the work for the service of the house of the LORD is finished. 21 Here are the divisions of the priests and the Lē'vītes for all the service of the house of God; and with you in all the work will be every volunteer who has skill for any kind of service; also the officers and all the people will be wholly at your command."

Offerings for Building the Temple

29 King David said to the whole assembly, "My son Solomon, whom alone God has chosen, is young and inexperienced, and the work is great; for the temple[s] will not be for mortals but for the LORD God. 2 So I have provided for the house of my God, so far as I was able, the gold for the things of gold, the silver for the things of silver, and the bronze for the things of bronze, the iron for the things of iron, and wood for the things of wood, besides great quantities of onyx and stones for setting, antimony, colored stones, all sorts of precious stones, and marble in abundance. 3 Moreover, in addition to all that I have provided for the holy house, I have a treasure of my own of gold and silver, and because of my devotion to the house of my God I give it to the house of my God: 4 three thousand talents of gold, of the gold of Ō'phir, and seven thousand talents of refined silver, for overlaying the walls of the house, 5 and for all the work to be done by artisans, gold for the things of gold and silver for the things of silver. Who then will offer willingly, consecrating themselves today to the LORD?"

6 Then the leaders of ancestral houses made their freewill offerings, as did also the leaders of the tribes, the commanders of the thousands and of the hundreds, and the officers over the king's work. 7 They gave for the service of the house of God five thousand talents and ten thousand darics of gold, ten thousand talents of silver, eighteen thousand talents of bronze, and one hundred thousand talents of iron. 8 Whoever had precious stones gave them to the treasury of the house of the LORD, into the care of Je•hi'el the Ger'shon•ite. 9 Then the people rejoiced because these had given willingly, for with single mind they had offered freely to the LORD; King David also rejoiced greatly.

David's Praise to God

10 Then David blessed the LORD in the presence of all the assembly; David said: "Blessed are you, O LORD, the God of our ancestor Israel, forever and ever. 11 Yours, O LORD, are the greatness, the power, the glory, the victory, and the majesty; for all that is in the heavens and on the earth is yours; yours is the kingdom, O LORD, and you are exalted as head above all. 12 Riches and honor come from you, and you rule over all. In your hand are power and might; and it is in your hand to make great and to give strength to all. 13 And now, our God,

---

[s] Heb *fortress*

GOD'S NAME

As David neared the end of his life and reign, he blessed God's name in the midst of the people. The Israelites, who believed in one God, were surrounded by other cultures who believed in many different gods, both good and evil. The name of the Israelites' one God was sacred and precious to them, and they often associated God's name with power, glory, majesty, and victory over all creation.

In Hmong, the name of God is Huab Tais Ntuj, which can be translated as Highest One or Emperor Spirit or Overriding Spirit. The Hmong culture developed as a subculture within the Central Highlands of China. The Hmong believed in different spirits, both good and evil, angelic and demonic. So, in naming God Highest Emperor, overriding all other spirits, they clearly also developed a belief in one God with power over all creation.

▶ **I Chr 29.10–22**

we give thanks to you and praise your glorious name.

14 "But who am I, and what is my people, that we should be able to make this freewill offering? For all things come from you, and of your own have we given you. 15 For we are aliens and transients before you, as were all our ancestors; our days on the earth are like a shadow, and there is no hope. 16 O LORD our God, all this abundance that we have provided for building you a house for your holy name comes from your hand and is all your own. 17 I know, my God, that you search the heart, and take pleasure in uprightness; in the uprightness of my heart I have freely offered all these things, and now I have seen your people, who are present here, offering freely and joyously to you. 18 O LORD, the God of Abraham, Isaac, and Israel, our ancestors, keep forever such purposes and thoughts in the hearts of your people, and direct their hearts toward you. 19 Grant to my son Solomon that with single mind he may keep your commandments, your decrees, and your statutes, performing all of them, and that he may build the temple[t] for which I have made provision."

20 Then David said to the whole assembly, "Bless the LORD your God." And all the assembly blessed the LORD, the God of their ancestors, and bowed their heads and prostrated themselves before the LORD and the king. 21 On the next day they offered sacrifices and burnt offerings to the LORD, a thousand bulls, a thousand rams, and a thousand lambs, with their libations, and sacrifices in abundance for all Israel; 22 and they ate and drank before the LORD on that day with great joy.

Solomon Anointed King
(1 Kings 1.38–40; 2.12)

They made David's son Solomon king a second time; they anointed him as the LORD's prince, and Zā′dok as priest. 23 Then Solomon sat on the throne of the LORD, succeeding his father David as king; he prospered, and all Israel obeyed him. 24 All the leaders and the mighty warriors, and also all the sons of King David, pledged their allegiance to King Solomon. 25 The LORD highly exalted Solomon in the sight of all Israel, and bestowed upon him such royal majesty as had not been on any king before him in Israel.

Summary of David's Reign

26 Thus David son of Jesse reigned over all Israel. 27 The period that he reigned over Israel was forty years; he reigned seven years in Hē′bron, and thirty-three years in Jerusalem. 28 He died in a good old age, full of days, riches, and honor; and his son Solomon succeeded him. 29 Now the acts of King David, from first to last, are written in the records of the seer Samuel, and in the records of the prophet Nathan, and in the records of the seer Gad, 30 with accounts of all his rule and his might and of the events that befell him and Israel and all the kingdoms of the earth.

---

t Heb *fortress*

2 Chronicles

For background on this book, see the introduction to 1 and 2 Chronicles.

Chap. 3

Solomon Requests Wisdom
(1 Kings 3.1–15)

1 Solomon son of David established himself in his kingdom; the LORD his God was with him and made him exceedingly great.

2 Solomon summoned all Israel, the commanders of the thousands and of the hundreds, the judges, and all the leaders of all Israel, the heads of families. 3 Then Solomon, and the whole assembly with him, went to the high place that was at Gib'ē•on; for God's tent of meeting, which Moses the servant of the LORD had made in the wilderness, was there. 4 (But David had brought the ark of God up from Kir'i•ath-jē'a•rim to the place that David had prepared for it; for he had pitched a tent for it in Jerusalem.) 5 Moreover the bronze altar that Bez'a•lel son of Ū'rī, son of Hur, had made, was there in front of the tabernacle of the LORD. And Solomon and the assembly inquired at it. 6 Solomon went up there to the bronze altar before the LORD, which was at the tent of meeting, and offered a thousand burnt offerings on it.

7 That night God appeared to Solomon, and said to him, "Ask what I should give you." 8 Solomon said to God, "You have shown great and steadfast love to my father David, and have made me succeed him as king. 9 O LORD God, let your promise to my father David now be fulfilled, for you have made me king over a people as numerous as the dust of the earth. 10 Give me now wisdom and knowledge to go out and come in before this people, for who can rule this great people of yours?" 11 God answered Solomon, "Because this was in your heart, and you have not asked for possessions, wealth, honor, or the life of those who hate you, and have not even asked for long life, but have asked for wisdom and knowledge for yourself that you may rule my people over whom I have made you king, 12 wisdom and knowledge are granted to you. I will also give you riches, possessions, and honor, such as none of the kings had who were before you, and none after you shall have the like." 13 So Solomon came from[a] the high place at Gib'ē•on, from the tent of meeting, to Jerusalem. And he reigned over Israel.

Solomon's Military and Commercial Activity
(1 Kings 10.26–29; 2 Chr 9.25–28)

14 Solomon gathered together chariots and horses; he had fourteen hundred chariots and twelve thousand horses, which he stationed in the chariot cities and with the king in Jerusalem. 15 The king made silver and gold as common in Jerusalem as stone, and he made cedar as plentiful as the sycamore of the She•phē'lah. 16 Solomon's horses were imported from Egypt and Kū'e; the king's traders received them from Kū'e at the prevailing price. 17 They imported from Egypt, and then

---

a Gk Vg: Heb *to*

did you **KNOW?**

Wisdom and the Torah

What a deal for Solomon! God tells him to ask for anything and Solomon will have it (2 Chr 1.7). Solomon prays to be wise (verse 10), which pleases God because it indicates Solomon's desire to rule God's people according to God's will. But what is wisdom? For the Chronicler, wisdom is ultimately living one's life in conformity with God's instruction, or the Torah (see Deut 17.8–11). Wisdom is evident in the person who worships God correctly and lives a moral life in keeping with the Law, and in the king who governs justly. To learn more about the Israelites' view of wisdom, take a look at the wisdom books in the next section of the Old Testament. For a New Testament perspective, see Lk 2.41–52; 1 Cor 1.18–31.

▸ 2 Chr 1.7–12

exported, a chariot for six hundred shekels of silver, and a horse for one hundred fifty; so through them these were exported to all the kings of the Hit′tītes and the kings of Ar′am.

Preparations for Building the Temple

2 [b] Solomon decided to build a temple for the name of the LORD, and a royal palace for himself. 2 [c] Solomon conscripted seventy thousand laborers and eighty thousand stonecutters in the hill country, with three thousand six hundred to oversee them.

Alliance with Huram of Tyre
(1 Kings 5.1–18)

3 Solomon sent word to King Hū′ram of Tyre: "Once you dealt with my father David and sent him cedar to build himself a house to live in. 4 I am now about to build a house for the name of the LORD my God and dedicate it to him for offering fragrant incense before him, and for the regular offering of the rows of bread, and for burnt offerings morning and evening, on the sabbaths and the new moons and the appointed festivals of the LORD our God, as ordained forever for Israel. 5 The house that I am about to build will be great, for our God is greater than other gods. 6 But who is able to build him a

house, since heaven, even highest heaven, cannot contain him? Who am I to build a house for him, except as a place to make offerings before him? 7 So now send me an artisan skilled to work in gold, silver, bronze, and iron, and in purple, crimson, and blue fabrics, trained also in engraving, to join the skilled workers who are with me in Judah and Jerusalem, whom my father David provided. 8 Send me also cedar, cypress, and algum timber from Lebanon, for I know that your servants are skilled in cutting Lebanon timber. My servants will work with your servants 9 to prepare timber for me in abundance, for the house I am about to build will be great and wonderful. 10 I will provide for your servants, those who cut the timber, twenty thousand cors of crushed wheat, twenty thousand cors of barley, twenty thousand baths [d] of wine, and twenty thousand baths of oil."

11 Then King Hū′ram of Tyre answered in a letter that he sent to Solomon, "Because the LORD loves his people he has made you king over them." 12 Hū′ram also said, "Blessed be the LORD God of Israel, who made heaven and earth, who has given King David a wise son, endowed with discretion and understanding, who will build a temple for the LORD, and a royal palace for himself. 13 "I have dispatched Hū′ram-ā′bī, a skilled artisan, endowed with understanding, 14 the son of one of the Dan′īte women, his father a Ty′rian. He is trained to work in gold, silver, bronze, iron, stone, and wood, and in purple, blue, and crimson fabrics and fine linen, and to do all sorts of engraving and execute any design that may be assigned him, with your artisans, the artisans of my lord, your father David. 15 Now, as for the wheat, barley, oil, and wine, of which my lord has spoken, let him send them to his servants. 16 We will cut whatever timber you need from Lebanon, and bring it to you as rafts by sea to Jop′pa; you will take it up to Jerusalem."

17 Then Solomon took a census of all the aliens who were residing in the land of Israel, after the census that his father David had taken; and there were found to be one hundred fifty-three thousand six hundred. 18 Seventy thousand of them he assigned as laborers, eighty thousand as stonecutters in the hill country, and three thousand six hundred as overseers to make the people work.

Solomon Builds the Temple
(1 Kings 6.1–22)

3 Solomon began to build the house of the LORD in Jerusalem on Mount Mō•rī′ah, where the LORD had appeared to his father David, at the

---

[b] Ch 1.18 in Heb   [c] Ch 2.1 in Heb   [d] A Hebrew measure of volume

place that David had designated, on the threshing floor of Or′nan the Jeb′u·site. 2 He began to build on the second day of the second month of the fourth year of his reign. 3 These are Solomon's measurements[e] for building the house of God: the length, in cubits of the old standard, was sixty cubits, and the width twenty cubits. 4 The vestibule in front of the nave of the house was twenty cubits long, across the width of the house;[f] and its height was one hundred twenty cubits. He overlaid it on the inside with pure gold. 5 The nave he lined with cypress, covered it with fine gold, and made palms and chains on it. 6 He adorned the house with settings of precious stones. The gold was gold from Par·va′im. 7 So he lined the house with gold—its beams, its thresholds, its walls, and its doors; and he carved cherubim on the walls.

8 He made the most holy place; its length, corresponding to the width of the house, was twenty cubits, and its width was twenty cubits; he overlaid it with six hundred talents of fine gold. 9 The weight of the nails was fifty shekels of gold. He overlaid the upper chambers with gold.

10 In the most holy place he made two carved cherubim and overlaid[g] them with gold. 11 The wings of the cherubim together extended twenty cubits: one wing of the one, five cubits long, touched the wall of the house, and its other wing, five cubits long, touched the wing of the other cherub; 12 and of this cherub, one wing, five cubits long, touched the wall of the house, and the other wing, also five cubits long, was joined to the wing of the first cherub. 13 The wings of these cherubim extended twenty cubits; the cherubim[h] stood on their feet, facing the nave. 14 And Solomon[i] made the curtain of blue and purple and crimson fabrics and fine linen, and worked cherubim into it.

15 In front of the house he made two pillars thirty-five cubits high, with a capital of five cubits on the top of each. 16 He made encircling[j] chains and put them on the tops of the pillars; and he made one hundred pomegranates, and put them on the chains. 17 He set up the pillars in front of the temple, one on the right, the other on the left; the one on the right he called Ja′chin, and the one on the left, Bo′az.

Furnishings of the Temple
(1 Kings 6.23–38; 7.13–51)

4 He made an altar of bronze, twenty cubits long, twenty cubits wide, and ten cubits high. 2 Then he made the molten sea; it was round, ten cubits from rim to rim, and five cubits high. A line of thirty cubits would encircle it completely. 3 Under it were panels all around, each of ten cubits, surrounding the sea; there were two rows of panels, cast when it was cast. 4 It stood on twelve oxen,

three facing north, three facing west, three facing south, and three facing east; the sea was set on them. The hindquarters of each were toward the inside. 5 Its thickness was a handbreadth; its rim was made like the rim of a cup, like the flower of a lily; it held three thousand baths.[k] 6 He also made ten basins in which to wash, and set five on the right side, and five on the left. In these they were to rinse what was used for the burnt offering. The sea was for the priests to wash in.

7 He made ten golden lampstands as prescribed, and set them in the temple, five on the south side and five on the north. 8 He also made ten tables and placed them in the temple, five on the right side and five on the left. And he made one hundred basins of gold. 9 He made the court of the priests, and the great court, and doors for the court; he overlaid their doors with bronze. 10 He set the sea at the southeast corner of the house.

11 And Hu′ram made the pots, the shovels, and the basins. Thus Hu′ram finished the work that he did for King Solomon on the house of God: 12 the two pillars, the bowls, and the two capitals on the top of the pillars; and the two latticeworks to cover the two bowls of the capitals that were on the top of the pillars; 13 the four hundred pomegranates for the two latticeworks, two rows of pomegranates for each latticework, to cover the two bowls of the capitals that were on the pillars. 14 He made the stands, the basins on the stands, 15 the one sea, and the twelve oxen underneath it. 16 The pots, the shovels, the forks, and all the equipment for these Hu′ram-a′bi made of burnished bronze for King Solomon for the house of the LORD. 17 In the plain of the Jordan the king cast them, in the clay ground between Suc′coth and Zer′e·dah. 18 Solomon made all these things in great quantities, so that the weight of the bronze was not determined.

19 So Solomon made all the things that were in the house of God: the golden altar, the tables for the bread of the Presence, 20 the lampstands and their lamps of pure gold to burn before the inner sanctuary, as prescribed; 21 the flowers, the lamps, and the tongs, of purest gold; 22 the snuffers, basins, ladles, and firepans, of pure gold. As for the entrance to the temple: the inner doors to the most holy place and the doors of the nave of the temple were of gold.

5 Thus all the work that Solomon did for the house of the LORD was finished. Solomon brought in the things that his father David had dedicated, and stored the silver, the gold, and all the vessels in the treasuries of the house of God.

---

e Syr: Heb *foundations*   f Compare 1 Kings 6.3: Meaning of Heb uncertain   g Heb *they overlaid*   h Heb *they*   i Heb *he*   j Cn: Heb *in the inner sanctuary*   k A Hebrew measure of volume

The Ark Brought into the Temple
(1 Kings 8.1–11)

2 Then Solomon assembled the elders of Israel and all the heads of the tribes, the leaders of the ancestral houses of the people of Israel, in Jerusalem, to bring up the ark of the covenant of the LORD out of the city of David, which is Zion. 3 And all the Israelites assembled before the king at the festival that is in the seventh month. 4 And all the elders of Israel came, and the Lĕ′vītes carried the ark. 5 So they brought up the ark, the tent of meeting, and all the holy vessels that were in the tent; the priests and the Lĕ′vītes brought them up. 6 King Solomon and all the congregation of Israel, who had assembled before him, were before the ark, sacrificing so many sheep and oxen that they could not be numbered or counted. 7 Then the priests brought the ark of the covenant of the LORD to its place, in the inner sanctuary of the house, in the most holy place, underneath the wings of the cherubim. 8 For the cherubim spread out their wings over the place of the ark, so that the cherubim made a covering above the ark and its poles. 9 The poles were so long that the ends of the poles were seen from the holy place in front of the inner sanctuary; but they could not be seen from outside; they are there to this day. 10 There was nothing in the ark except the two tablets that Moses put there at Hō′reb, where the LORD made a covenant[l] with the people of Israel after they came out of Egypt.

11 Now when the priests came out of the holy place (for all the priests who were present had sanctified themselves, without regard to their divisions), 12 all the levitical singers, Ā′saph, Hĕ′man, and Je•dū′thun, their sons and kindred, arrayed in fine linen, with cymbals, harps, and lyres, stood east of the altar with one hundred twenty priests who were trumpeters. 13 It was the duty of the trumpeters and singers to make themselves heard in unison in praise and thanksgiving to the LORD, and when the song was raised, with trumpets and cymbals and other musical instruments, in praise to the LORD,

"For he is good,
  for his steadfast love endures forever,"
the house, the house of the LORD, was filled with a cloud, 14 so that the priests could not stand to minister because of the cloud; for the glory of the LORD filled the house of God.

Dedication of the Temple
(1 Kings 8.12–21)

6 Then Solomon said, "The LORD has said that he would reside in thick darkness. 2 I have built you an exalted house, a place for you to reside in forever."

3 Then the king turned around and blessed all the assembly of Israel, while all the assembly of Israel stood. 4 And he said, "Blessed be the LORD, the God of Israel, who with his hand has fulfilled what he promised with his mouth to my father David, saying, 5 'Since the day that I brought my people out of the land of Egypt, I have not chosen a city from any of the tribes of Israel in which to build a house, so that my name might be there, and I chose no one as ruler over my people Israel; 6 but I have chosen Jerusalem in order that my name may be there, and I have chosen David to be over my people Israel.' 7 My father David had it in mind to build a house for the name of the LORD, the God of Israel. 8 But the LORD said to my father David, 'You did well to consider building a house for my name; 9 nevertheless you shall not build the house, but your son who shall be born to you shall build the house for my name.' 10 Now the LORD has fulfilled his promise that he made; for I have succeeded my father David, and sit on the throne of Israel, as the LORD promised, and have built the house for the name of the LORD, the God of Israel. 11 There I have set the ark, in which is the covenant of the LORD that he made with the people of Israel."

Solomon's Prayer of Dedication
(1 Kings 8.22–53)

12 Then Solomon[m] stood before the altar of the LORD in the presence of the whole assembly of Israel, and spread out his hands. 13 Solomon had made a bronze platform five cubits long, five cubits wide, and three cubits high, and had set it in the court; and he stood on it. Then he knelt on his knees in the presence of the whole assembly of Israel, and spread out his hands toward heaven. 14 He said, "O LORD, God of Israel, there is no God like you, in heaven or on earth, keeping covenant in steadfast love with your servants who walk before you with all their heart— 15 you who have kept for your servant, my father David, what you promised to him. Indeed, you promised with your mouth and this day have fulfilled with your hand. 16 Therefore, O LORD, God of Israel, keep for your servant, my father David, that which you promised him, saying, 'There shall never fail you a successor before me to sit on the throne of Israel, if only your children keep to their way, to walk in my law as you have walked before me.' 17 Therefore, O LORD, God of Israel, let your word be confirmed, which you promised to your servant David.

18 "But will God indeed reside with mortals on earth? Even heaven and the highest heaven cannot contain you, how much less this house that I have built! 19 Regard your servant's prayer and his plea, O LORD my God, heeding the cry and the prayer that your servant prays to you. 20 May your eyes be

---

l Heb lacks *a covenant*   *m* Heb *he*

open day and night toward this house, the place where you promised to set your name, and may you heed the prayer that your servant prays toward this place. 21 And hear the plea of your servant and of your people Israel, when they pray toward this place; may you hear from heaven your dwelling place; hear and forgive.

22 "If someone sins against another and is required to take an oath and comes and swears before your altar in this house, 23 may you hear from heaven, and act, and judge your servants, repaying the guilty by bringing their conduct on their own head, and vindicating those who are in the right by rewarding them in accordance with their righteousness.

24 "When your people Israel, having sinned against you, are defeated before an enemy but turn again to you, confess your name, pray and plead with you in this house, 25 may you hear from heaven, and forgive the sin of your people Israel, and bring them again to the land that you gave to them and to their ancestors.

26 "When heaven is shut up and there is no rain because they have sinned against you, and then they pray toward this place, confess your name, and turn from their sin, because you punish them, 27 may you hear in heaven, forgive the sin of your servants, your people Israel, when you teach them the good way in which they should walk; and send down rain upon your land, which you have given to your people as an inheritance.

28 "If there is famine in the land, if there is plague, blight, mildew, locust, or caterpillar; if their enemies besiege them in any of the settlements of the lands; whatever suffering, whatever sickness there is; 29 whatever prayer, whatever plea from any individual or from all your people Israel, all knowing their own suffering and their own sorrows so that they stretch out their hands toward this house; 30 may you hear from heaven, your dwelling place, forgive, and render to all whose heart you know, according to all their ways, for only you know the human heart. 31 Thus may they fear you and walk in your ways all the days that they live in the land that you gave to our ancestors.

32 "Likewise when foreigners, who are not of your people Israel, come from a distant land because of your great name, and your mighty hand, and your outstretched arm, when they come and pray toward this house, 33 may you hear from heaven your dwelling place, and do whatever the foreigners ask of you, in order that all the peoples of the earth may know your name and fear you, as do your people Israel, and that they may know that your name has been invoked on this house that I have built.

34 "If your people go out to battle against their enemies, by whatever way you shall send them, and they pray to you toward this city that you have chosen and the house that I have built for your name, 35 then hear from heaven their prayer and their plea, and maintain their cause.

36 "If they sin against you—for there is no one who does not sin—and you are angry with them and give them to an enemy, so that they are carried away captive to a land far or near; 37 then if they come to their senses in the land to which they have been taken captive, and repent, and plead with you in the land of their captivity, saying, 'We have sinned, and have done wrong; we have acted wickedly'; 38 if they repent with all their heart and soul in the land of their captivity, to which they were taken captive, and pray toward their land, which you gave to their ancestors, the city that you have chosen, and the house that I have built for your name, 39 then hear from heaven your dwelling place their prayer and their pleas, maintain their cause and forgive your people who have sinned against you. 40 Now, O my God, let your eyes be open and your ears attentive to prayer from this place.

41 "Now rise up, O LORD God, and go to your
        resting place,
    you and the ark of your might.
Let your priests, O LORD God, be clothed with
        salvation,
    and let your faithful rejoice in your
        goodness.
42 O LORD God, do not reject your anointed one.
    Remember your steadfast love for your
        servant David."

Solomon Dedicates the Temple
(1 Kings 8.62–66)

7 When Solomon had ended his prayer, fire came down from heaven and consumed the burnt offering and the sacrifices; and the glory of the LORD filled the temple. 2 The priests could not enter the house of the LORD, because the glory of the LORD filled the LORD's house. 3 When all the people of Israel saw the fire come down and the glory of the LORD on the temple, they bowed down on the pavement with their faces to the ground, and worshiped and gave thanks to the LORD, saying,
    "For he is good,
        for his steadfast love endures forever."
4 Then the king and all the people offered sacrifice before the LORD. 5 King Solomon offered as a sacrifice twenty-two thousand oxen and one hundred twenty thousand sheep. So the king and all the people dedicated the house of God. 6 The priests stood at their posts; the Lēvites also, with the instruments for music to the LORD that King David had made for giving thanks to the LORD—for

his steadfast love endures forever—whenever David offered praises by their ministry. Opposite them the priests sounded trumpets; and all Israel stood.

7 Solomon consecrated the middle of the court that was in front of the house of the LORD; for there he offered the burnt offerings and the fat of the offerings of well-being because the bronze altar Solomon had made could not hold the burnt offering and the grain offering and the fat parts.

8 At that time Solomon held the festival for seven days, and all Israel with him, a very great congregation, from Lĕʹbō-haʹmath to the Wadi of Egypt. 9 On the eighth day they held a solemn assembly; for they had observed the dedication of the altar seven days and the festival seven days. 10 On the twenty-third day of the seventh month he sent the people away to their homes, joyful and in good spirits because of the goodness that the LORD had shown to David and to Solomon and to his people Israel.

11 Thus Solomon finished the house of the LORD and the king's house; all that Solomon had planned to do in the house of the LORD and in his own house he successfully accomplished.

God's Second Appearance to Solomon
(1 Kings 9.1–9)

12 Then the LORD appeared to Solomon in the night and said to him: "I have heard your prayer, and have chosen this place for myself as a house of sacrifice. 13 When I shut up the heavens so that there is no rain, or command the locust to devour the land, or send pestilence among my people, 14 if my people who are called by my name humble themselves, pray, seek my face, and turn from their wicked ways, then I will hear from heaven, and will forgive their sin and heal their land. 15 Now my eyes will be open and my ears attentive to the prayer that is made in this place. 16 For now I have chosen and consecrated this house so that my name may be there forever; my eyes and my heart will be there for all time. 17 As for you, if you walk before me, as your father David walked, doing according to all that I have commanded you and keeping my statutes and my ordinances, 18 then I will establish your royal throne, as I made covenant with your father David saying, 'You shall never lack a successor to rule over Israel.'

19 "But if you[n] turn aside and forsake my statutes and my commandments that I have set before you, and go and serve other gods and worship them, 20 then I will pluck you[o] up from the land that I have given you;[o] and this house, which I have consecrated for my name, I will cast out of my sight, and will make it a proverb and a byword among all peoples. 21 And regarding this house, now exalted, everyone passing by will be astonished, and say,

'Why has the LORD done such a thing to this land and to this house?' 22 Then they will say, 'Because they abandoned the LORD the God of their ancestors who brought them out of the land of Egypt, and they adopted other gods, and worshiped them and served them; therefore he has brought all this calamity upon them.' "

Various Activities of Solomon
(1 Kings 9.10–28)

8 At the end of twenty years, during which Solomon had built the house of the LORD and his own house, 2 Solomon rebuilt the cities that Hūʹram had given to him, and settled the people of Israel in them.

3 Solomon went to Hāʹmath-zōʹbah, and captured it. 4 He built Tadʹmor in the wilderness and all the storage towns that he built in Hāʹmath. 5 He also built Upper Beth-hōʹron and Lower Beth-hōʹron, fortified cities, with walls, gates, and bars, 6 and Bāʹa•lath, as well as all Solomon's storage towns, and all the towns for his chariots, the towns for his cavalry, and whatever Solomon desired to build, in Jerusalem, in Lebanon, and in all the land of his dominion. 7 All the people who were left of the Hitʹtītes, the Amʹo•rītes, the Perʹiz•zītes, the Hīʹvītes, and the Jebʹū•sītes, who were not of Israel, 8 from their descendants who were still left in the land, whom the people of Israel had not destroyed—these Solomon conscripted for forced labor, as is still the case today. 9 But of the people of Israel Solomon made no slaves for his work; they were soldiers, and his officers, the commanders of his chariotry and cavalry. 10 These were the chief officers of King Solomon, two hundred fifty of them, who exercised authority over the people.

11 Solomon brought Pharaoh's daughter from the city of David to the house that he had built for her, for he said, "My wife shall not live in the house of King David of Israel, for the places to which the ark of the LORD has come are holy."

12 Then Solomon offered up burnt offerings to the LORD on the altar of the LORD that he had built in front of the vestibule, 13 as the duty of each day required, offering according to the commandment of Moses for the sabbaths, the new moons, and the three annual festivals—the festival of unleavened bread, the festival of weeks, and the festival of booths. 14 According to the ordinance of his father David, he appointed the divisions of the priests for their service, and the Lĕʹvītes for their offices of praise and ministry alongside the priests as the duty of each day required, and the gatekeepers in their divisions for the several gates; for so David the man of God had commanded. 15 They did not turn away

---

n The word *you* in this verse is plural   o Heb *them*

from what the king had commanded the priests and Lĕ′vītes regarding anything at all, or regarding the treasuries.

16 Thus all the work of Solomon was accomplished from[p] the day the foundation of the house of the LORD was laid until the house of the LORD was finished completely.

17 Then Solomon went to Ē′zi•on-gē′ber and Ē′loth on the shore of the sea, in the land of Ē′dom. [18] Hū′ram sent him, in the care of his servants, ships and servants familiar with the sea. They went to Ō′phir, together with the servants of Solomon, and imported from there four hundred fifty talents of gold and brought it to King Solomon.

Chap. 9

Visit of the Queen of Sheba
(1 Kings 10.1–13)

9 When the queen of Shĕ′ba heard of the fame of Solomon, she came to Jerusalem to test him with hard questions, having a very great retinue and camels bearing spices and very much gold and precious stones. When she came to Solomon, she discussed with him all that was on her mind. [2] Solomon answered all her questions; there was nothing hidden from Solomon that he could not explain to her. [3] When the queen of Shĕ′ba had observed the wisdom of Solomon, the house that he had built, [4] the food of his table, the seating of his officials, and the attendance of his servants, and their clothing, his valets, and their clothing, and his burnt offerings[q] that he offered at the house of the LORD, there was no more spirit left in her.

5 So she said to the king, "The report was true that I heard in my own land of your accomplish-

ments and of your wisdom, [6] but I did not believe the[r] reports until I came and my own eyes saw it. Not even half of the greatness of your wisdom had been told to me; you far surpass the report that I had heard. [7] Happy are your people! Happy are these your servants, who continually attend you and hear your wisdom! [8] Blessed be the LORD your God, who has delighted in you and set you on his throne as king for the LORD your God. Because your God loved Israel and would establish them forever, he has made you king over them, that you may execute justice and righteousness." [9] Then she gave the king one hundred twenty talents of gold, a very great quantity of spices, and precious stones: there were no spices such as those that the queen of Shĕ′ba gave to King Solomon.

10 Moreover the servants of Hū′ram and the servants of Solomon who brought gold from Ō′phir brought algum wood and precious stones. [11] From the algum wood, the king made steps[s] for the house of the LORD and for the king's house, lyres also and harps for the singers; there never was seen the like of them before in the land of Judah.

12 Meanwhile King Solomon granted the queen of Shĕ′ba every desire that she expressed, well beyond what she had brought to the king. Then she returned to her own land, with her servants.

Solomon's Great Wealth
(1 Kings 10.14–29; 2 Chr 1.14–17)

13 The weight of gold that came to Solomon in one year was six hundred sixty-six talents of gold, [14] besides that which the traders and merchants brought; and all the kings of Arabia and the governors of the land brought gold and silver to Solomon. [15] King Solomon made two hundred large shields of beaten gold; six hundred shekels of beaten gold went into each large shield. [16] He made three hundred shields of beaten gold; three hundred shekels of gold went into each shield; and the king put them in the House of the Forest of Lebanon. [17] The king also made a great ivory throne, and overlaid it with pure gold. [18] The throne had six steps and a footstool of gold, which were attached to the throne, and on each side of the seat were arm rests and two lions standing beside the arm rests, [19] while twelve lions were standing, one on each end of a step on the six steps. The like of it was never made in any kingdom. [20] All King Solomon's drinking vessels were of gold, and all the vessels of the House of the Forest of Lebanon were of pure gold; silver was not considered as anything in the days of Solomon. [21] For the king's ships went to Tar′shish with the servants of Hū′ram; once every

---

p Gk Syr Vg: Heb *to*   *q* Gk Syr Vg 1 Kings 10.5: Heb *ascent*
r Heb *their*   *s* Gk Vg: Meaning of Heb uncertain

Money Talks

You can't take it with you.

How often have we heard this statement? We know it's true. Yet we are so easily impressed with wealth and riches. King Solomon, whose wealth is described in 2 Chr 9.13–28, would be right at home in our world, which seems so taken with the rich and the famous.

The Chronicler seems to suggest that Solomon's wealth is a sign of his being blessed by God (see 1.12). And some Jews and Christians still see wealth as a sign of God's blessing. But we need to remember Jesus' words, "Where your treasure is, there your heart will be also" (Mt 6.21), and "Blessed are you who are poor, / for yours is the kingdom of God" (Lk 6.20). Jesus saw that the accumulation of wealth in his time was frequently the result of injustice (see "The Greed Trap," Lk 12.13–21). Simply put, Jesus probably would not have approved of Solomon's wealth. How do you view wealth? What is your attitude toward poor people?

▸ 2 Chr 9.13–28

three years the ships of Tar'shish used to come bringing gold, silver, ivory, apes, and peacocks.[t]

22 Thus King Solomon excelled all the kings of the earth in riches and in wisdom. 23 All the kings of the earth sought the presence of Solomon to hear his wisdom, which God had put into his mind. 24 Every one of them brought a present, objects of silver and gold, garments, weaponry, spices, horses, and mules, so much year by year. 25 Solomon had four thousand stalls for horses and chariots, and twelve thousand horses, which he stationed in the chariot cities and with the king in Jerusalem. 26 He ruled over all the kings from the Euphrates to the land of the Phi·lis'tines, and to the border of Egypt. 27 The king made silver as common in Jerusalem as stone, and cedar as plentiful as the sycamore of the She·phe'lah. 28 Horses were imported for Solomon from Egypt and from all lands.

Death of Solomon
(1 Kings 11.41–43)

29 Now the rest of the acts of Solomon, from first to last, are they not written in the history of the prophet Nathan, and in the prophecy of A·hi'jah the Shi'lo·nite, and in the visions of the seer Id'do concerning Jer·o·bo'am son of Ne'bat? 30 Solomon reigned in Jerusalem over all Israel forty years. 31 Solomon slept with his ancestors and was buried in the city of his father David; and his son Re·ho·bo'am succeeded him.

The Revolt against Rehoboam
(1 Kings 12.1–19)

10 Re·ho·bo'am went to She'chem, for all Israel had come to She'chem to make him king. 2 When Jer·o·bo'am son of Ne'bat heard of it (for he was in Egypt, where he had fled from

King Solomon), then Jer·o·bo'am returned from Egypt. 3 They sent and called him; and Jer·o·bo'am and all Israel came and said to Re·ho·bo'am, 4 "Your father made our yoke heavy. Now therefore lighten the hard service of your father and his heavy yoke that he placed on us, and we will serve you." 5 He said to them, "Come to me again in three days." So the people went away.

6 Then King Re·ho·bo'am took counsel with the older men who had attended his father Solomon while he was still alive, saying, "How do you advise me to answer this people?" 7 They answered him, "If you will be kind to this people and please them, and speak good words to them, then they will be your servants forever." 8 But he rejected the advice that the older men gave him, and consulted the young men who had grown up with him and now attended him. 9 He said to them, "What do you advise that we answer this people who have said to me, 'Lighten the yoke that your father put on us'?" 10 The young men who had grown up with him said to him, "Thus should you speak to the people who said to you, 'Your father made our yoke heavy, but you must lighten it for us'; tell them, 'My little finger is thicker than my father's loins. 11 Now, whereas my father laid on you a heavy yoke, I will add to your yoke. My father disciplined you with whips, but I will discipline you with scorpions.' "

12 So Jer·o·bo'am and all the people came to Re·ho·bo'am the third day, as the king had said, "Come to me again the third day." 13 The king answered them harshly. King Re·ho·bo'am rejected the advice of the older men; 14 he spoke to them in accordance with the advice of the young men, "My father made your yoke heavy, but I will add to it;

[t] Or baboons

my father disciplined you with whips, but I will discipline you with scorpions." 15 So the king did not listen to the people, because it was a turn of affairs brought about by God so that the LORD might fulfill his word, which he had spoken by A·hi′jah the Shi′lo·nite to Jer·o·bo′am son of Ne′bat.

16 When all Israel saw that the king would not listen to them, the people answered the king,

"What share do we have in David?
We have no inheritance in the son of Jesse.
Each of you to your tents, O Israel!
Look now to your own house, O David."

So all Israel departed to their tents. 17 But Rē·ho·bo′am reigned over the people of Israel who were living in the cities of Judah. 18 When King Rē·ho·bo′am sent Ha·dor′am, who was taskmaster over the forced labor, the people of Israel stoned him to death. King Rē·ho·bo′am hurriedly mounted his chariot to flee to Jerusalem. 19 So Israel has been in rebellion against the house of David to this day.

Judah and Benjamin Fortified
(1 Kings 12.20–24)

11 When Rē·ho·bo′am came to Jerusalem, he assembled one hundred eighty thousand chosen troops of the house of Judah and Benjamin to fight against Israel, to restore the kingdom to Rē·ho·bo′am. 2 But the word of the LORD came to She·mai′ah the man of God: 3 Say to King Rē·ho·bo′am of Judah, son of Solomon, and to all Israel in Judah and Benjamin, 4 "Thus says the LORD: You shall not go up or fight against your kindred. Let everyone return home, for this thing is from me." So they heeded the word of the LORD and turned back from the expedition against Jer·o·bo′am.

5 Rē·ho·bo′am resided in Jerusalem, and he built cities for defense in Judah. 6 He built up Bethlehem, Ē′tam, Te·ko′a, 7 Beth-zur, Sō′cō, A·dul′lam, 8 Gath, Ma·rē′shah, Ziph, 9 Ad·o·rā′im, Lā′chish, A·zē′kah, 10 Zō′rah, Aī′ja·lon, and Hē′bron, fortified cities that are in Judah and in Benjamin. 11 He made the fortresses strong, and put commanders in them, and stores of food, oil, and wine. 12 He also put large shields and spears in all the cities, and made them very strong. So he held Judah and Benjamin.

Priests and Levites Support Rehoboam
(1 Kings 14.21–24)

13 The priests and the Lē′vites who were in all Israel presented themselves to him from all their territories. 14 The Lē′vites had left their common lands and their holdings and had come to Judah and Jerusalem, because Jer·o·bo′am and his sons had prevented them from serving as priests of the LORD, 15 and had appointed his own priests for the high places, and for the goat-demons, and for the calves that he had made. 16 Those who had set

their hearts to seek the LORD God of Israel came after them from all the tribes of Israel to Jerusalem to sacrifice to the LORD, the God of their ancestors. 17 They strengthened the kingdom of Judah, and for three years they made Rē·ho·bo′am son of Solomon secure, for they walked for three years in the way of David and Solomon.

Rehoboam's Marriages

18 Rē·ho·bo′am took as his wife Mā′ha·lath daughter of Jer′i·moth son of David, and of Ab·i·hā′il daughter of E·li′ab son of Jesse. 19 She bore him sons: Jē′ush, Shem·a·ri′ah, and Zā′ham. 20 After her he took Mā′a·cah daughter of Ab′-sa·lom, who bore him A·bi′jah, At′tai, Zī′za, and She·lō′mith. 21 Rē·ho·bo′am loved Mā′a·cah daughter of Ab′sa·lom more than all his other wives and concubines (he took eighteen wives and sixty concubines, and became the father of twenty-eight sons and sixty daughters). 22 Rē·ho·bo′am appointed A·bi′jah son of Mā′a·cah as chief prince among his brothers, for he intended to make him king. 23 He dealt wisely, and distributed some of his sons through all the districts of Judah and Benjamin, in all the fortified cities; he gave them abundant provisions, and found many wives for them.

Egypt Attacks Judah
(1 Kings 14.25–28)

12 When the rule of Rē·ho·bo′am was established and he grew strong, he abandoned the law of the LORD, he and all Israel with him. 2 In the fifth year of King Rē·ho·bo′am, because they had been unfaithful to the LORD, King Shi′shak of Egypt came up against Jerusalem 3 with twelve hundred chariots and sixty thousand cavalry. A countless army came with him from Egypt—Libyans, Suk′ki·im, and Ethiopians.ᵘ 4 He took the fortified cities of Judah and came as far as Jerusalem. 5 Then the prophet She·mai′ah came to Rē·ho·bo′am and to the officers of Judah, who had gathered at Jerusalem because of Shi′shak, and said to them, "Thus says the LORD: You abandoned me, so I have abandoned you to the hand of Shi′shak." 6 Then the officers of Israel and the king humbled themselves and said, "The LORD is in the right." 7 When the LORD saw that they humbled themselves, the word of the LORD came to She·mai′ah, saying: "They have humbled themselves; I will not destroy them, but I will grant them some deliverance, and my wrath shall not be poured out on Jerusalem by the hand of Shi′shak. 8 Nevertheless they shall be his servants, so that they may know the difference between serving me and serving the kingdoms of other lands."

ᵘ Or *Nubians;* Heb *Cushites*

9 So King Shī'shak of Egypt came up against Jerusalem; he took away the treasures of the house of the LORD and the treasures of the king's house; he took everything. He also took away the shields of gold that Solomon had made; 10 but King Re·ho·bō'am made in place of them shields of bronze, and committed them to the hands of the officers of the guard, who kept the door of the king's house. 11 Whenever the king went into the house of the LORD, the guard would come along bearing them, and would then bring them back to the guardroom. 12 Because he humbled himself the wrath of the LORD turned from him, so as not to destroy them completely; moreover, conditions were good in Judah.

mother's name was Mī·cāi'ah daughter of Ū·rī'el of Gib'ē·ah.

Now there was war between A·bī'jah and Jer·o·bō'am. 3 A·bī'jah engaged in battle, having an army of valiant warriors, four hundred thousand picked men; and Jer·o·bō'am drew up his line of battle against him with eight hundred thousand picked mighty warriors. 4 Then A·bī'jah stood on the slope of Mount Zem·a·rā'im that is in the hill country of Ē'phra·im, and said, "Listen to me, Jer·o·bō'am and all Israel! 5 Do you not know that the LORD God of Israel gave the kingship over Israel forever to David and his sons by a covenant of salt? 6 Yet Jer·o·bō'am son of Nē'bat, a servant of Solo-

Selling Out

King Rehoboam, son of Solomon, sold out and abandoned the law of the LORD after he thought his rule was secure (2 Chr 12.1). The Chronicler tells us that the LORD abandoned Rehoboam to the Egyptians because of this. Fortunately, Rehoboam and his officers repented, and the LORD showed mercy on them.

It is tempting to compromise our values in order to succeed and become popular, even though doing this ends up hurting the people around us. Maybe you have experienced some success like Rehoboam and figure you can have even more if you just bend the rules a bit. Maybe you feel life has given you a rotten deal and the only way to get ahead is to forget your principles. But before you sell out, think again. Ultimately, abandoning your good and holy principles won't get you ahead; it will only lead to your downfall.

▶ 2 Chr 12.1–12

Death of Rehoboam
(1 Kings 14.21–22, 29–31)

13 So King Rē·ho·bō'am established himself in Jerusalem and reigned. Rē·ho·bō'am was forty-one years old when he began to reign; he reigned seventeen years in Jerusalem, the city that the LORD had chosen out of all the tribes of Israel to put his name there. His mother's name was Nā'a·mah the Am'mon·īte. 14 He did evil, for he did not set his heart to seek the LORD.

15 Now the acts of Rē·ho·bō'am, from first to last, are they not written in the records of the prophet She·māi'ah and of the seer Id'dō, recorded by genealogy? There were continual wars between Rē·ho·bō'am and Jer·o·bō'am. 16 Rē·ho·bō'am slept with his ancestors and was buried in the city of David; and his son A·bī'jah succeeded him.

Abijah Reigns over Judah
(1 Kings 15.1–8)

13 In the eighteenth year of King Jer·o·bō'am, A·bī'jah began to reign over Judah. 2 He reigned for three years in Jerusalem. His

mon son of David, rose up and rebelled against his lord; 7 and certain worthless scoundrels gathered around him and defied Rē·ho·bō'am son of Solomon, when Rē·ho·bō'am was young and irresolute and could not withstand them.

8 "And now you think that you can withstand the kingdom of the LORD in the hand of the sons of David, because you are a great multitude and have with you the golden calves that Jer·o·bō'am made as gods for you. 9 Have you not driven out the priests of the LORD, the descendants of Aaron, and the Lē'vītes, and made priests for yourselves like the peoples of other lands? Whoever comes to be consecrated with a young bull or seven rams becomes a priest of what are no gods. 10 But as for us, the LORD is our God, and we have not abandoned him. We have priests ministering to the LORD who are descendants of Aaron, and Lē'vītes for their service. 11 They offer to the LORD every morning and every evening burnt offerings and fragrant incense, set out the rows of bread on the table of pure gold, and care for the golden lampstand so that its lamps may burn every evening; for we keep the charge of the

LORD our God, but you have abandoned him. 12 See, God is with us at our head, and his priests have their battle trumpets to sound the call to battle against you. O Israelites, do not fight against the LORD, the God of your ancestors; for you cannot succeed."

13 Jer·o·bo'am had sent an ambush around to come on them from behind; thus his troops[v] were in front of Judah, and the ambush was behind them. 14 When Judah turned, the battle was in front of them and behind them. They cried out to the LORD, and the priests blew the trumpets. 15 Then the people of Judah raised the battle shout. And when the people of Judah shouted, God defeated Jer·o·bo'am and all Israel before A·bi'jah and Judah. 16 The Israelites fled before Judah, and God gave them into their hands. 17 A·bi'jah and his army defeated them with great slaughter; five hundred thousand picked men of Israel fell slain. 18 Thus the Israelites were subdued at that time, and the people of Judah prevailed, because they relied on the LORD, the God of their ancestors. 19 A·bi'jah pursued Jer·o·bo'am, and took cities from him: Beth'el with its villages and Je·sha'nah with its villages and E'phron[w] with its villages. 20 Jer·o·bo'am did not recover his power in the days of A·bi'jah; the LORD struck him down, and he died. 21 But A·bi'jah grew strong. He took fourteen wives, and became the father of twenty-two sons and sixteen daughters. 22 The rest of the acts of A·bi'jah, his behavior and his deeds, are written in the story of the prophet Id'do.

Asa Reigns
(1 Kings 15.9–15)

14 [x] So A·bi'jah slept with his ancestors, and they buried him in the city of David. His son Asa succeeded him. In his days the land had rest for ten years. 2[y] Asa did what was good and right in the sight of the LORD his God. 3 He took away the foreign altars and the high places, broke down the pillars, hewed down the sacred poles,[z] 4 and commanded Judah to seek the LORD, the God of their ancestors, and to keep the law and the commandment. 5 He also removed from all the cities of Judah the high places and the incense altars. And the kingdom had rest under him. 6 He built fortified cities in Judah while the land had rest. He had no war in those years, for the LORD gave him peace. 7 He said to Judah, "Let us build these cities, and surround them with walls and towers, gates and bars; the land is still ours because we have sought the LORD our God; we have sought him, and he has given us peace on every side." So they built and prospered. 8 Asa had an army of three hundred thousand from Judah, armed with large shields and spears, and two hundred eighty thousand troops from Benjamin who carried shields and drew bows; all these were mighty warriors.

Ethiopian Invasion Repulsed

9 Ze'rah the Ethiopian[a] came out against them with an army of a million men and three hundred chariots, and came as far as Ma·re'shah. 10 Asa went out to meet him, and they drew up their lines of battle in the valley of Zeph'a·thah at Ma·re'shah. 11 Asa cried to the LORD his God, "O LORD, there is no difference for you between helping the mighty and the weak. Help us, O LORD our God, for we rely on you, and in your name we have come against this multitude. O LORD, you are our God; let no mortal prevail against you." 12 So the LORD defeated the Ethiopians[b] before Asa and before Judah, and the Ethiopians[b] fled. 13 Asa and the army with him pursued them as far as Ge'rar, and the Ethiopians[b] fell until no one remained alive; for they were broken before the LORD and his army. The people of Judah[c] carried away a great quantity of booty. 14 They defeated all the cities around Ge'rar, for the fear of the LORD was on them. They plundered all the cities; for there was much plunder in them. 15 They also attacked the tents of those who had livestock,[d] and carried away sheep and goats in abundance, and camels. Then they returned to Jerusalem.

15 The spirit of God came upon Az·a·ri'ah son of O'ded. 2 He went out to meet Asa and said to him, "Hear me, Asa, and all Judah and Benjamin: The LORD is with you, while you are with him. If you seek him, he will be found by you, but if you abandon him, he will abandon you. 3 For a long time Israel was without the true God, and without a teaching priest, and without law; 4 but when in their distress they turned to the LORD, the God of Israel, and sought him, he was found by them. 5 In those times it was not safe for anyone to go or come, for great disturbances afflicted all the inhabitants of the lands. 6 They were broken in pieces, nation against nation and city against city, for God troubled them with every sort of distress. 7 But you, take courage! Do not let your hands be weak, for your work shall be rewarded."

8 When Asa heard these words, the prophecy of Az·a·ri'ah son of O'ded,[e] he took courage, and put away the abominable idols from all the land of Judah and Benjamin and from the towns that he had taken in the hill country of E'phra·im. He repaired the altar of the LORD that was in front of the vestibule of the house of the LORD.[f] 9 He gathered

---

v Heb *they*   w Another reading is *Ephrain*   x Ch 13.23 in Heb   y Ch 14.1 in Heb   z Heb *Asherim*   a Or *Nubian*; Heb *Cushite*   b Or *Nubians*; Heb *Cushites*   c Heb *They*   d Meaning of Heb uncertain   e Compare Syr Vg: Heb *the prophecy, the prophet Obed*   f Heb *the vestibule of the LORD*

Keep On Turning

Conversion.

A very important word for Christians. Its Latin root means "to turn around." We turn from sin and toward God, as individuals and as a people. In 2 Chr 15.8–15, we read about King Asa and his people hearing the words of the prophet Azariah and then turning away from idols and turning back to God.

Conversion is not a one-time event. It is a process all of us go through again and again as our faith and understanding grow. We are reminded of that especially during the season of Lent. On Ash Wednesday, as individuals and as a community, we hear the words, "Turn away from sin and be faithful to the gospel" (*Sacramentary*, p. 77). The Israelites went through the same thing. Again and again, they were called to turn back to God.

If we are committed to following Jesus, conversion is a lifelong process of deepening our faith. Where are you most in need of conversion? Where is our nation most in need of conversion?

▸ 2 Chr 15.8–15

all Judah and Benjamin, and those from Ēʹphra·im, Ma·nasʹseh, and Simʹē·on who were residing as aliens with them, for great numbers had deserted to him from Israel when they saw that the LORD his God was with him. 10 They were gathered at Jerusalem in the third month of the fifteenth year of the reign of Asa. 11 They sacrificed to the LORD on that day, from the booty that they had brought, seven hundred oxen and seven thousand sheep. 12 They entered into a covenant to seek the LORD, the God of their ancestors, with all their heart and with all their soul. 13 Whoever would not seek the LORD, the God of Israel, should be put to death, whether young or old, man or woman. 14 They took an oath to the LORD with a loud voice, and with shouting, and with trumpets, and with horns. 15 All Judah rejoiced over the oath; for they had sworn with all their heart, and had sought him with their whole desire, and he was found by them, and the LORD gave them rest all around.

16 King Asa even removed his mother Māʹa·cah from being queen mother because she had made an abominable image for A·shēʹrah. Asa cut down her image, crushed it, and burned it at the Wadi Kidʹron. 17 But the high places were not taken out of Israel. Nevertheless the heart of Asa was true all his days. 18 He brought into the house of God the votive gifts of his father and his own votive gifts— silver, gold, and utensils. 19 And there was no more war until the thirty-fifth year of the reign of Asa.

Alliance with Aram Condemned
(1 Kings 15.16–22)

16 In the thirty-sixth year of the reign of Asa, King Bāʹa·sha of Israel went up against Judah, and built Rāʹmah, to prevent anyone from going out or coming into the territory ofᵍ King Asa of Judah. 2 Then Asa took silver and gold from the treasures of the house of the LORD and the king's house, and sent them to King Ben-hāʹdad of Arʹam, who resided in Damascus, saying, 3 "Let there be an alliance between me and you, like that between my father and your father; I am sending to you silver and gold; go, break your alliance with King Bāʹa·sha of Israel, so that he may withdraw from me." 4 Ben-hāʹdad listened to King Asa, and sent the commanders of his armies against the cities of Israel. They conquered Iʹjon, Dan, Āʹbel-māʹim, and all the store-cities of Naphʹta·lī. 5 When Bāʹa·sha heard of it, he stopped building Rāʹmah, and let his work cease. 6 Then King Asa brought all Judah, and they carried away the stones of Rāʹmah and its timber, with which Bāʹa·sha had been building, and with them he built up Gēʹba and Mizʹpah.

7 At that time the seer Ha·nāʹnī came to King Asa of Judah, and said to him, "Because you relied on the king of Arʹam, and did not rely on the LORD your God, the army of the king of Arʹam has escaped you. 8 Were not the Ethiopiansʰ and the Libyans a huge army with exceedingly many chariots and cavalry? Yet because you relied on the LORD, he gave them into your hand. 9 For the eyes of the LORD range throughout the entire earth, to strengthen those whose heart is true to him. You have done foolishly in this; for from now on you will have wars." 10 Then Asa was angry with the seer, and put him in the stocks, in prison, for he was in a rage with him because of this. And Asa inflicted cruelties on some of the people at the same time.

ᵍ Heb lacks *the territory of* ʰ Or *Nubians*; Heb *Cushites*

Asa's Disease and Death
(1 Kings 15.23–24)

11 The acts of Asa, from first to last, are written in the Book of the Kings of Judah and Israel. 12 In the thirty-ninth year of his reign Asa was diseased in his feet, and his disease became severe; yet even in his disease he did not seek the LORD, but sought help from physicians. 13 Then Asa slept with his ancestors, dying in the forty-first year of his reign. 14 They buried him in the tomb that he had hewn out for himself in the city of David. They laid him on a bier that had been filled with various kinds of spices prepared by the perfumer's art; and they made a very great fire in his honor.

Jehoshaphat's Reign

17 His son Je·hosh′a·phat succeeded him, and strengthened himself against Israel. 2 He placed forces in all the fortified cities of Judah, and set garrisons in the land of Judah, and in the cities of E′phra·im that his father Asa had taken. 3 The LORD was with Je·hosh′a·phat, because he walked in the earlier ways of his father;[i] he did not seek the Ba′als, 4 but sought the God of his father and walked in his commandments, and not according to the ways of Israel. 5 Therefore the LORD established the kingdom in his hand. All Judah brought tribute to Je·hosh′a·phat, and he had great riches and honor. 6 His heart was courageous in the ways of the LORD; and furthermore he removed the high places and the sacred poles[j] from Judah.

7 In the third year of his reign he sent his officials, Ben-ha′il, O·ba·di′ah, Zech·a·ri′ah, Ne·than′el, and Mi·cai′ah, to teach in the cities of Judah. 8 With them were the Le′vites, She·mai′ah, Neth·a·ni′ah, Zeb·a·di′ah, As′a·hel, She·mir′a·moth, Je·hon′a·than, Ad·o·ni′jah, To·bi′jah, and Tob-ad·o·ni′jah; and with these Le′vites, the priests E·lish′a·ma and Je·ho′ram. 9 They taught in Judah, having the book of the law of the LORD with them; they went around through all the cities of Judah and taught among the people.

10 The fear of the LORD fell on all the kingdoms of the lands around Judah, and they did not make war against Je·hosh′a·phat. 11 Some of the Phi·lis′tines brought Je·hosh′a·phat presents, and silver for tribute; and the Arabs also brought him seven thousand seven hundred rams and seven thousand seven hundred male goats. 12 Je·hosh′a·phat grew steadily greater. He built fortresses and storage cities in Judah. 13 He carried out great works in the cities of Judah. He had soldiers, mighty warriors, in Jerusalem. 14 This was the muster of them by ancestral houses: Of Judah, the commanders of the thousands: Ad′nah the commander, with three hundred thousand mighty warriors, 15 and next to him Je·ho·ha′nan the commander, with two hundred

eighty thousand, 16 and next to him Am·a·si′ah son of Zich′ri, a volunteer for the service of the LORD, with two hundred thousand mighty warriors. 17 Of Benjamin: E·li′a·da, a mighty warrior, with two hundred thousand armed with bow and shield, 18 and next to him Je·ho′za·bad with one hundred eighty thousand armed for war. 19 These were in the service of the king, besides those whom the king had placed in the fortified cities throughout all Judah.

Micaiah Predicts Failure
(1 Kings 22.1–28)

18 Now Je·hosh′a·phat had great riches and honor; and he made a marriage alliance with A′hab. 2 After some years he went down to A′hab in Sa·mar′i·a. A′hab slaughtered an abundance of sheep and oxen for him and for the people who were with him, and induced him to go up against Ra′moth-gil′e·ad. 3 King A′hab of Israel said to King Je·hosh′a·phat of Judah, "Will you go with me to Ra′moth-gil′e·ad?" He answered him, "I am with you, my people are your people. We will be with you in the war."

4 But Je·hosh′a·phat also said to the king of Israel, "Inquire first for the word of the LORD." 5 Then the king of Israel gathered the prophets together, four hundred of them, and said to them, "Shall we go to battle against Ra′moth-gil′e·ad, or shall I refrain?" They said, "Go up; for God will give it into the hand of the king." 6 But Je·hosh′a·phat said, "Is there no other prophet of the LORD here of whom we may inquire?" 7 The king of Israel said to Je·hosh′a·phat, "There is still one other by whom we may inquire of the LORD, Mi·cai′ah son of Im′lah; but I hate him, for he never prophesies anything favorable about me, but only disaster." Je·hosh′a·phat said, "Let the king not say such a thing." 8 Then the king of Israel summoned an officer and said, "Bring quickly Mi·cai′ah son of Im′lah." 9 Now the king of Israel and King Je·hosh′a·phat of Judah were sitting on their thrones, arrayed in their robes; and they were sitting at the threshing floor at the entrance of the gate of Sa·mar′i·a; and all the prophets were prophesying before them. 10 Zed·e·ki′ah son of Che·na′a·nah made for himself horns of iron, and he said, "Thus says the LORD: With these you shall gore the Ar·a·me′ans until they are destroyed." 11 All the prophets were prophesying the same and saying, "Go up to Ra′moth-gil′e·ad and triumph; the LORD will give it into the hand of the king."

12 The messenger who had gone to summon Mi·cai′ah said to him, "Look, the words of the prophets with one accord are favorable to the king;

---

i Another reading is *his father David*   j Heb *Asherim*

let your word be like the word of one of them, and speak favorably." 13 But Mĭ·cāi'ah said, "As the LORD lives, whatever my God says, that I will speak."

14 When he had come to the king, the king said to him, "Mĭ·cāi'ah, shall we go to Rā'moth-gil'ē·ad to battle, or shall I refrain?" He answered, "Go up and triumph; they will be given into your hand." 15 But the king said to him, "How many times must I make you swear to tell me nothing but the truth in the name of the LORD?" 16 Then Mĭ·cāi'ah[k] said, "I saw all Israel scattered on the mountains, like sheep without a shepherd; and the LORD said, 'These have no master; let each one go home in peace.' " 17 The king of Israel said to Je·hosh'a·phat, "Did I not tell you that he would not prophesy anything favorable about me, but only disaster?"

18 Then Mĭ·cāi'ah[k] said, "Therefore hear the word of the LORD: I saw the LORD sitting on his throne, with all the host of heaven standing to the right and to the left of him. 19 And the LORD said, 'Who will entice King Ā'hab of Israel, so that he may go up and fall at Rā'moth-gil'ē·ad?' Then one said one thing, and another said another, 20 until a spirit came forward and stood before the LORD, saying, 'I will entice him.' The LORD asked him, 'How?' 21 He replied, 'I will go out and be a lying spirit in the mouth of all his prophets.' Then the LORD[k] said, 'You are to entice him, and you shall succeed; go out and do it.' 22 So you see, the LORD has put a lying spirit in the mouth of these your prophets; the LORD has decreed disaster for you."

23 Then Zed·e·kī'ah son of Che·nā'a·nah came up to Mĭ·cāi'ah, slapped him on the cheek, and said, "Which way did the spirit of the LORD pass from me to speak to you?" 24 Mĭ·cāi'ah replied, "You will find out on that day when you go in to hide in an inner chamber." 25 The king of Israel then ordered, "Take Mĭ·cāi'ah, and return him to Ā'mon the governor of the city and to Jō'ash the king's son; 26 and say, 'Thus says the king: Put this fellow in prison, and feed him on reduced rations of bread and water until I return in peace.' " 27 Mĭ·cāi'ah said, "If you return in peace, the LORD has not spoken by me." And he said, "Hear, you peoples, all of you!"

Defeat and Death of Ahab
(1 Kings 22.29–40)

28 So the king of Israel and King Je·hosh'a·phat of Judah went up to Rā'moth-gil'ē·ad. 29 The king of Israel said to Je·hosh'a·phat, "I will disguise myself and go into battle, but you wear your robes." So the king of Israel disguised himself, and they went into battle. 30 Now the king of Ar'am had commanded the captains of his chariots, "Fight with no one small or great, but only with the king of Israel." 31 When the captains of the chariots saw Je-

hosh'a·phat, they said, "It is the king of Israel." So they turned to fight against him; and Je·hosh'a·phat cried out, and the LORD helped him. God drew them away from him, 32 for when the captains of the chariots saw that it was not the king of Israel, they turned back from pursuing him. 33 But a certain man drew his bow and unknowingly struck the king of Israel between the scale armor and the breastplate; so he said to the driver of his chariot, "Turn around, and carry me out of the battle, for I am wounded." 34 The battle grew hot that day, and the king of Israel propped himself up in his chariot facing the Ar·a·mē'ans until evening; then at sunset he died.

19

King Je·hosh'a·phat of Judah returned in safety to his house in Jerusalem. 2 Jē'hū son of Ha·nā'nī the seer went out to meet him and said to King Je·hosh'a·phat, "Should you help the wicked and love those who hate the LORD? Because of this, wrath has gone out against you from the LORD. 3 Nevertheless, some good is found in you, for you destroyed the sacred poles[l] out of the land, and have set your heart to seek God."

The Reforms of Jehoshaphat

4 Je·hosh'a·phat resided at Jerusalem; then he went out again among the people, from Bē'er-shē'ba to the hill country of Ē'phra·im, and brought them back to the LORD, the God of their ancestors. 5 He appointed judges in the land in all the fortified cities of Judah, city by city, 6 and said to the judges, "Consider what you are doing, for you judge not on behalf of human beings but on the LORD's behalf; he is with you in giving judgment. 7 Now, let the fear of the LORD be upon you; take care what you do, for there is no perversion of justice with the LORD our God, or partiality, or taking of bribes."

8 Moreover in Jerusalem Je·hosh'a·phat appointed certain Lē'vites and priests and heads of families of Israel, to give judgment for the LORD and to decide disputed cases. They had their seat at Jerusalem. 9 He charged them: "This is how you shall act: in the fear of the LORD, in faithfulness, and with your whole heart; 10 whenever a case comes to you from your kindred who live in their cities, concerning bloodshed, law or commandment, statutes or ordinances, then you shall instruct them, so that they may not incur guilt before the LORD and wrath may not come on you and your kindred. Do so, and you will not incur guilt. 11 See, Am·a·rī'ah the chief priest is over you in all matters of the LORD; and Zeb·a·dī'ah son of Ish'ma·el, the governor of the house of Judah, in all the king's matters; and the Lē'vites will serve you as officers. Deal courageously, and may the LORD be with the good!"

---

k Heb *he*   *l* Heb *Asheroth*

Invasion from the East

20 After this the Mō·ab·ītes and Am'mon-ītes, and with them some of the Me·ū'-nītes,[m] came against Je·hosh'a·phat for battle. [2] Messengers[n] came and told Je·hosh'a·phat, "A great multitude is coming against you from E'dom,[o] from beyond the sea; already they are at Haz'a·zon-tā'mar" (that is, En-ge'di). [3] Je·hosh'a·phat was afraid; he set himself to seek the LORD, and proclaimed a fast throughout all Judah. [4] Judah assembled to seek help from the LORD; from all the towns of Judah they came to seek the LORD.

Jehoshaphat's Prayer and Victory

[5] Je·hosh'a·phat stood in the assembly of Judah and Jerusalem, in the house of the LORD, before the new court, [6] and said, "O LORD, God of our ancestors, are you not God in heaven? Do you not rule over all the kingdoms of the nations? In your hand are power and might, so that no one is able to withstand you. [7] Did you not, O our God, drive out the inhabitants of this land before your people Israel, and give it forever to the descendants of your friend Abraham? [8] They have lived in it, and in it have built you a sanctuary for your name, saying, [9] 'If disaster comes upon us, the sword, judgment,[p] or pestilence, or famine, we will stand before this house, and before you, for your name is in this house, and cry to you in our distress, and you will hear and save.' [10] See now, the people of Am'mon, Mō'ab, and Mount Sē'ir, whom you would not let Israel invade when they came from the land of Egypt, and whom they avoided and did not destroy— [11] they reward us by coming to drive us out of your possession that you have given us to inherit. [12] O our God, will you not execute judgment upon them? For we are powerless against this great multitude that is coming against us. We do not know what to do, but our eyes are on you."

[13] Meanwhile all Judah stood before the LORD, with their little ones, their wives, and their children. [14] Then the spirit of the LORD came upon Ja·hā'zi·el son of Zech·a·rī'ah, son of Be·nā'i·ah, son of Je·ī'el, son of Mat·ta·nī'ah, a Lē'vīte of the sons of Ā'saph, in the middle of the assembly. [15] He said, "Listen, all Judah and inhabitants of Jerusalem, and King Je·hosh'a·phat: Thus says the LORD to you: 'Do not fear or be dismayed at this great multitude; for the battle is not yours but God's. [16] Tomorrow go down against them; they will come up by the ascent of Ziz; you will find them at the end of the valley, before the wilderness of Je·rū'el. [17] This battle is not for you to fight; take your position, stand still, and see the victory of the LORD on your behalf, O Judah and Jerusalem.' Do not fear or be dismayed; tomorrow go out against them, and the LORD will be with you."

[18] Then Je·hosh'a·phat bowed down with his face to the ground, and all Judah and the inhabitants of Jerusalem fell down before the LORD, worshiping the LORD. [19] And the Lē'vītes, of the Kō'hath·ītes and the Kō'ra·hītes, stood up to praise the LORD, the God of Israel, with a very loud voice.

[20] They rose early in the morning and went out into the wilderness of Te·kō'a; and as they went out, Je·hosh'a·phat stood and said, "Listen to me, O Judah and inhabitants of Jerusalem! Believe in the LORD your God and you will be established; believe his prophets." [21] When he had taken counsel with the people, he appointed those who were to sing to the LORD and praise him in holy splendor, as they went before the army, saying,

"Give thanks to the LORD,
    for his steadfast love endures forever."

[22] As they began to sing and praise, the LORD set an ambush against the Am'mon·ītes, Mō'ab, and Mount Sē'ir, who had come against Judah, so that they were routed. [23] For the Am'mon·ītes and Mō'ab attacked the inhabitants of Mount Sē'ir, destroying them utterly; and when they had made an end of the inhabitants of Sē'ir, they all helped to destroy one another.

[24] When Judah came to the watchtower of the wilderness, they looked toward the multitude; they were corpses lying on the ground; no one had escaped. [25] When Je·hosh'a·phat and his people came to take the booty from them, they found livestock[q] in great numbers, goods, clothing, and precious things, which they took for themselves until they could carry no more. They spent three days taking the booty, because of its abundance. [26] On the fourth day they assembled in the Valley of Ber'a·cah, for there they blessed the LORD; therefore that place has been called the Valley of Ber'a·cah[r] to this day. [27] Then all the people of Judah and Jerusalem, with Je·hosh'a·phat at their head, returned to Jerusalem with joy, for the LORD had enabled them to rejoice over their enemies. [28] They came to Jerusalem, with harps and lyres and trumpets, to the house of the LORD. [29] The fear of God came on all the kingdoms of the countries when they heard that the LORD had fought against the enemies of Israel. [30] And the realm of Je·hosh'a·phat was quiet, for his God gave him rest all around.

The End of Jehoshaphat's Reign
(1 Kings 22.41–50)

[31] So Je·hosh'a·phat reigned over Judah. He was thirty-five years old when he began to reign; he reigned twenty-five years in Jerusalem. His mother's

---

m Compare 26.7: Heb *Ammonites*   *n* Heb *They*   *o* One Ms: MT *Aram*   *p* Or *the sword of judgment*   *q* Gk: Heb *among them*   *r* That is *Blessing* name was A•zū′bah daughter of Shil′hī. 32 He walked in the way of his father Asa and did not turn aside from it, doing what was right in the sight of the LORD. 33 Yet the high places were not removed; the people had not yet set their hearts upon the God of their ancestors.

34 Now the rest of the acts of Je•hosh′a•phat, from first to last, are written in the Annals of Jē′hū son of Ha•nā′nī, which are recorded in the Book of the Kings of Israel.

35 After this King Je•hosh′a•phat of Judah joined with King A•ha•zī′ah of Israel, who did wickedly. 36 He joined him in building ships to go to Tar′shish; they built the ships in Ē′zi•on-gē′ber. 37 Then El•i•ē′zer son of Dō•dav′a•hū of Ma•rē′shah prophesied against Je•hosh′a•phat, saying, "Because you have joined with A•ha•zī′ah, the LORD will destroy what you have made." And the ships were wrecked and were not able to go to Tar′shish.

Jehoram's Reign
(1 Kings 22.50; 2 Kings 8.16–19)

21 Je•hosh′a•phat slept with his ancestors and was buried with his ancestors in the city of David; his son Je•hō′ram succeeded him. 2 He had brothers, the sons of Je•hosh′a•phat: Az•a•rī′ah, Je•hī′el, Zech•a•rī′ah, Az•a•rī′ah, Michael, and Sheph•a•tī′ah; all these were the sons of King Je•hosh′a•phat of Judah.ˢ 3 Their father gave them many gifts, of silver, gold, and valuable possessions, together with fortified cities in Judah; but he gave the kingdom to Je•hō′ram, because he was the first-born. 4 When Je•hō′ram had ascended the throne of his father and was established, he put all his brothers to the sword, and also some of the officials of Israel. 5 Je•hō′ram was thirty-two years old when he began to reign; he reigned eight years in Jerusalem. 6 He walked in the way of the kings of Israel, as the house of Ā′hab had done; for the daughter of Ā′hab was his wife. He did what was evil in the sight of the LORD. 7 Yet the LORD would not destroy the house of David because of the covenant that he had made with David, and since he had promised to give a lamp to him and to his descendants forever.

Revolt of Edom
(2 Kings 8.20–22)

8 In his days Ē′dom revolted against the rule of Judah and set up a king of their own. 9 Then Je•hō′ram crossed over with his commanders and all his chariots. He set out by night and attacked the Ē′dom•ites, who had surrounded him and his chariot commanders. 10 So Ē′dom has been in revolt against the rule of Judah to this day. At that time Lib′nah also revolted against his rule, because he had forsaken the LORD, the God of his ancestors.

Elijah's Letter

11 Moreover he made high places in the hill country of Judah, and led the inhabitants of Jerusalem into unfaithfulness, and made Judah go astray. 12 A letter came to him from the prophet E•lī′jah, saying: "Thus says the LORD, the God of your father David: Because you have not walked in the ways of your father Je•hosh′a•phat or in the ways of King Asa of Judah, 13 but have walked in the way of the kings of Israel, and have led Judah and the inhabitants of Jerusalem into unfaithfulness, as the house of Ā′hab led Israel into unfaithfulness, and because you also have killed your brothers, members of your father's house, who were better than yourself, 14 see, the LORD will bring a great plague on your people, your children, your wives, and all your possessions, 15 and you yourself will have a severe sickness with a disease of your bowels, until your bowels come out, day after day, because of the disease."

did you KNOW?

The Role of the Prophet

The letter from Elijah to King Jehoram discussed in 2 Chr 21.12–15 underscores the principal role of the Hebrew prophet: to be God's voice, the one who speaks for God. Although many early figures are called prophets, including Moses and Deborah, the classical prophet—*nabi'* in Hebrew—appeared later in Israelite history. The primary function of the prophet was not to foretell the future but to announce God's judgment, to confront those who violated God's law, and to console those who suffered. In short, the prophets were the conscience of the Israelite nation.

▸ **2 Chr 21.12–15**

16 The LORD aroused against Je•hō′ram the anger of the Phi•lis′tines and of the Arabs who are near the Ethiopians.ᵗ 17 They came up against Judah, invaded it, and carried away all the possessions they found that belonged to the king's house, along with his sons and his wives, so that no son was left to him except Je•hō′a•haz, his youngest son.

ˢ Gk Syr: Heb *Israel*   ᵗ Or *Nubians;* Heb *Cushites*

Disease and Death of Jehoram
(2 Kings 8.23–24)

18 After all this the LORD struck him in his bowels with an incurable disease. 19 In course of time, at the end of two years, his bowels came out because of the disease, and he died in great agony. His people made no fire in his honor, like the fires made for his ancestors. 20 He was thirty-two years old when he began to reign; he reigned eight years in Jerusalem. He departed with no one's regret. They buried him in the city of David, but not in the tombs of the kings.

Ahaziah's Reign
(2 Kings 8.25–29; 9.14–16, 27–29)

22 The inhabitants of Jerusalem made his youngest son A•ha•zī′ah king as his successor; for the troops who came with the Arabs to the camp had killed all the older sons. So A•ha•zī′ah son of Je•hō′ram reigned as king of Judah. 2 A•ha•zī′ah was forty-two years old when he began to reign; he reigned one year in Jerusalem. His mother's name was Ath•a•lī′ah, a granddaughter of Om′rī. 3 He also walked in the ways of the house of Ā′hab, for his mother was his counselor in doing wickedly. 4 He did what was evil in the sight of the LORD, as the house of Ā′hab had done; for after the death of his father they were his counselors, to his ruin. 5 He even followed their advice, and went with Je•hō′ram son of King Ā′hab of Israel to make war against King Haz′a•el of Ar′am at Rā′moth-gil′e̅•ad. The Ar•a•me̅′ans wounded Jō′ram, 6 and he returned to be healed in Jez′re̅•el of the wounds that he had received at Rā′mah, when he fought King Haz′a•el of Ar′am. And A•ha•zī′ah son of King Je•hō′ram of Judah went down to see Jō′ram son of Ā′hab in Jez′re̅•el, because he was sick.

7 But it was ordained by God that the downfall of A•ha•zī′ah should come about through his going to visit Jō′ram. For when he came there he went out with Je•hō′ram to meet Jē′hū son of Nim′shī, whom the LORD had anointed to destroy the house of Ā′hab. 8 When Jē′hū was executing judgment on the house of Ā′hab, he met the officials of Judah and the sons of A•ha•zī′ah's brothers, who attended A•ha•zī′ah, and he killed them. 9 He searched for A•ha•zī′ah, who was captured while hiding in Sa•mār′i•a and was brought to Jē′hū, and put to death. They buried him, for they said, "He is the grandson of Je•hosh′a•phat, who sought the LORD with all his heart." And the house of A•ha•zī′ah had no one able to rule the kingdom.

Athaliah Seizes the Throne
(2 Kings 11.1–8)

10 Now when Ath•a•lī′ah, A•ha•zī′ah's mother, saw that her son was dead, she set about to destroy all the royal family of the house of Judah. 11 But Jē•hō•shab′e•ath, the king's daughter, took Jō′ash son of A•ha•zī′ah, and stole him away from among the king's children who were about to be killed; she put him and his nurse in a bedroom. Thus Jē•hō•shab′e•ath, daughter of King Je•hō′ram and wife of the priest Je•hoi′a•da—because she was a sister of A•ha•zī′ah—hid him from Ath•a•lī′ah, so that she did not kill him; 12 he remained with them six years, hidden in the house of God, while Ath•a•lī′ah reigned over the land.

23 But in the seventh year Je•hoi′a•da took courage, and entered into a compact with the commanders of the hundreds, Az•a•rī′ah son of Je•rō′ham, Ish′ma•el son of Jē•hō•hā′nan, Az•a•rī′ah son of Ō′bed, Mā•a•sēi′ah son of A•dāi′ah, and El•i•shā′phat son of Zich′rī. 2 They went around through Judah and gathered the Lē′vītes from all the towns of Judah, and the heads of families of Israel, and they came to Jerusalem. 3 Then the whole assembly made a covenant with the king in the house of God. Je•hoi′a•daᵘ said to them, "Here is the king's son! Let him reign, as the LORD promised concerning the sons of David. 4 This is what you are to do: one-third of you, priests and Lē′vītes, who come on duty on the sabbath, shall be gatekeepers, 5 one-third shall be at the king's house, and one-third at the Gate of the Foundation; and all the people shall be in the courts of the house of the LORD. 6 Do not let anyone enter the house of the LORD except the priests and ministering Lē′vītes; they may enter, for they are holy, but all the otherᵛ people shall observe the instructions of the LORD. 7 The Lē′vītes shall surround the king, each with his weapons in his hand; and whoever enters the house shall be killed. Stay with the king in his comings and goings."

Joash Crowned King
(2 Kings 11.9–12)

8 The Lē′vītes and all Judah did according to all that the priest Je•hoi′a•da commanded; each brought his men, who were to come on duty on the sabbath, with those who were to go off duty on the sabbath; for the priest Je•hoi′a•da did not dismiss the divisions. 9 The priest Je•hoi′a•da delivered to the captains the spears and the large and small shields that had been King David's, which were in the house of God; 10 and he set all the people as a guard for the king, everyone with weapon in hand, from the south side of the house to the north side of the house, around the altar and the house. 11 Then he brought out the king's son, put the crown on him, and gave him the covenant;ʷ they proclaimed him king, and Je•hoi′a•da and his sons

---

ᵘ Heb *He*   ᵛ Heb lacks *other*   ʷ Or *treaty,* or *testimony;* Heb *eduth* anointed him; and they shouted, "Long live the king!"

Athaliah Murdered
(2 Kings 11.13–20)

12 When Ath·a·liʹah heard the noise of the people running and praising the king, she went into the house of the LORD to the people; 13 and when she looked, there was the king standing by his pillar at the entrance, and the captains and the trumpeters beside the king, and all the people of the land rejoicing and blowing trumpets, and the singers with their musical instruments leading in the celebration. Ath·a·liʹah tore her clothes, and cried, "Treason! Treason!" 14 Then the priest Je·hoiʹa·da brought out the captains who were set over the army, saying to them, "Bring her out between the ranks; anyone who follows her is to be put to the sword." For the priest said, "Do not put her to death in the house of the LORD." 15 So they laid hands on her; she went into the entrance of the Horse Gate of the king's house, and there they put her to death.

16 Je·hoiʹa·da made a covenant between himself and all the people and the king that they should be the LORD's people. 17 Then all the people went to the house of Baʹal, and tore it down; his altars and his images they broke in pieces, and they killed Matʹtan, the priest of Baʹal, in front of the altars. 18 Je·hoiʹa·da assigned the care of the house of the LORD to the levitical priests whom David had organized to be in charge of the house of the LORD, to offer burnt offerings to the LORD, as it is written in the law of Moses, with rejoicing and with singing, according to the order of David. 19 He stationed the gatekeepers at the gates of the house of the LORD so that no one should enter who was in any way unclean. 20 And he took the captains, the nobles, the governors of the people, and all the people of the land, and they brought the king down from the house of the LORD, marching through the upper gate to the king's house. They set the king on the royal throne. 21 So all the people of the land rejoiced, and the city was quiet after Ath·a·liʹah had been killed with the sword.

Joash Repairs the Temple
(2 Kings 11.21—12.16)

24 Joʹash was seven years old when he began to reign; he reigned forty years in Jerusalem; his mother's name was Zibʹi·ah of Beʹer·sheʹba. 2 Joʹash did what was right in the sight of the LORD all the days of the priest Je·hoiʹa·da. 3 Je·hoiʹa·da got two wives for him, and he became the father of sons and daughters.

4 Some time afterward Joʹash decided to restore the house of the LORD. 5 He assembled the priests and the Leʹvites and said to them, "Go out to the cities of Judah and gather money from all Israel to repair the house of your God, year by year; and see that you act quickly." But the Leʹvites did not act quickly. 6 So the king summoned Je·hoiʹa·da the chief, and said to him, "Why have you not required the Leʹvites to bring in from Judah and Jerusalem the tax levied by Moses, the servant of the LORD, on*x* the congregation of Israel for the tent of the covenant?"*y* 7 For the children of Ath·a·liʹah, that wicked woman, had broken into the house of God, and had even used all the dedicated things of the house of the LORD for the Baʹals.

8 So the king gave command, and they made a chest, and set it outside the gate of the house of the LORD. 9 A proclamation was made throughout Judah and Jerusalem to bring in for the LORD the tax that Moses the servant of God laid on Israel in the wilderness. 10 All the leaders and all the people rejoiced and brought their tax and dropped it into the chest until it was full. 11 Whenever the chest was brought to the king's officers by the Leʹvites, when they saw that there was a large amount of money in it, the king's secretary and the officer of the chief priest would come and empty the chest and take it and return it to its place. So they did day after day, and collected money in abundance. 12 The king and Je·hoiʹa·da gave it to those who had charge of the work of the house of the LORD, and they hired masons and carpenters to restore the house of the LORD, and also workers in iron and bronze to repair the house of the LORD. 13 So those who were engaged in the work labored, and the repairing went forward at their hands, and they restored the house of God to its proper condition and strengthened it. 14 When they had finished, they brought the rest of the money to the king and Je·hoiʹa·da, and with it were made utensils for the house of the LORD, utensils for the service and for the burnt offerings, and ladles, and vessels of gold and silver. They offered burnt offerings in the house of the LORD regularly all the days of Je·hoiʹa·da.

Apostasy of Joash

15 But Je·hoiʹa·da grew old and full of days, and died; he was one hundred thirty years old at his death. 16 And they buried him in the city of David among the kings, because he had done good in Israel, and for God and his house.

17 Now after the death of Je·hoiʹa·da the officials of Judah came and did obeisance to the king; then the king listened to them. 18 They abandoned the house of the LORD, the God of their ancestors, and served the sacred poles*z* and the idols. And wrath came upon Judah and Jerusalem for this guilt

---

x Compare Vg: Heb *and*   *y* Or *treaty,* or *testimony;*
Heb *eduth*   *z* Heb *Asherim*

of theirs. 19 Yet he sent prophets among them to bring them back to the LORD; they testified against them, but they would not listen.

20 Then the spirit of God took possession of[a] Zech•a•rī′ah son of the priest Je•hoi′a•da; he stood above the people and said to them, "Thus says God: Why do you transgress the commandments of the LORD, so that you cannot prosper? Because you have forsaken the LORD, he has also forsaken you." 21 But they conspired against him, and by command of the king they stoned him to death in the court of the house of the LORD. 22 King Jō′ash did not remember the kindness that Je•hoi′a•da, Zech•a•rī′ah's father, had shown him, but killed his son. As he was dying, he said, "May the LORD see and avenge!"

Death of Joash
(2 Kings 12.19–21)

23 At the end of the year the army of Ar′am came up against Jō′ash. They came to Judah and Jerusalem, and destroyed all the officials of the people from among them, and sent all the booty they took to the king of Damascus. 24 Although the army of Ar′am had come with few men, the LORD delivered into their hand a very great army, because they had abandoned the LORD, the God of their ancestors. Thus they executed judgment on Jō′ash.

25 When they had withdrawn, leaving him severely wounded, his servants conspired against him because of the blood of the son[b] of the priest Je•hoi′a•da, and they killed him on his bed. So he died; and they buried him in the city of David, but they did not bury him in the tombs of the kings. 26 Those who conspired against him were Zā′bad son of Shim′ē•ath the Am′mon•ite, and Je•hō′za•bad son of Shim′rith the Mō′ab•ite. 27 Accounts of his sons, and of the many oracles against him, and of the rebuilding[c] of the house of God are written in the Commentary on the Book of the Kings. And his son Am•a•zī′ah succeeded him.

Reign of Amaziah
(2 Kings 14.1–6)

25 Am•a•zī′ah was twenty-five years old when he began to reign, and he reigned twenty-nine years in Jerusalem. His mother's name was Jē•hō•ad′dan of Jerusalem. 2 He did what was right in the sight of the LORD, yet not with a true heart. 3 As soon as the royal power was firmly in his hand he killed his servants who had murdered his father the king. 4 But he did not put their children to death, according to what is written in the law, in the book of Moses, where the LORD commanded, "The parents shall not be put to death for the children, or the children be put to death for the parents; but all shall be put to death for their own sins."

Slaughter of the Edomites
(2 Kings 14.7)

5 Am•a•zī′ah assembled the people of Judah, and set them by ancestral houses under commanders of the thousands and of the hundreds for all Judah and Benjamin. He mustered those twenty years old and upward, and found that they were three hundred thousand picked troops fit for war, able to handle spear and shield. 6 He also hired one hundred thousand mighty warriors from Israel for one hundred talents of silver. 7 But a man of God came to him and said, "O king, do not let the army of Israel go with you, for the LORD is not with Israel—all these Ē′phra•im•ites. 8 Rather, go by yourself and act; be strong in battle, or God will fling you down before the enemy; for God has power to help or to overthrow." 9 Am•a•zī′ah said to the man of God, "But what shall we do about the hundred talents that I have given to the army of Israel?" The man of God answered, "The LORD is able to give you much more than this." 10 Then Ama•zī′ah discharged the army that had come to him from Ē′phra•im, letting them go home again. But they became very angry with Judah, and returned home in fierce anger.

11 Am•a•zī′ah took courage, and led out his people; he went to the Valley of Salt, and struck down ten thousand men of Sē′ir. 12 The people of Judah captured another ten thousand alive, took them to the top of Sē′la, and threw them down from the top of Sē′la, so that all of them were dashed to pieces. 13 But the men of the army whom Am•a•zī′ah sent back, not letting them go with him to battle, fell on the cities of Judah from Sa•mār′i•a to Beth-hō′ron; they killed three thousand people in them, and took much booty.

14 Now after Am•a•zī′ah came from the slaughter of the Ē′dom•ites, he brought the gods of the people of Sē′ir, set them up as his gods, and worshiped them, making offerings to them. 15 The LORD was angry with Am•a•zī′ah and sent to him a prophet, who said to him, "Why have you resorted to a people's gods who could not deliver their own people from your hand?" 16 But as he was speaking the king[d] said to him, "Have we made you a royal counselor? Stop! Why should you be put to death?" So the prophet stopped, but said, "I know that God has determined to destroy you, because you have done this and have not listened to my advice."

Israel Defeats Judah
(2 Kings 14.8–14)

17 Then King Am•a•zī′ah of Judah took counsel and sent to King Jō′ash son of Je•hō′a•haz son of Jē′hū of Israel, saying, "Come, let us look one

---

a Heb *clothed itself with*   b Gk Vg: Heb *sons*   c Heb *founding*   d Heb *he* another in the face." 18 King Jō'ash of Israel sent word to King Am·a·zī'ah of Judah, "A thornbush on Lebanon sent to a cedar on Lebanon, saying, 'Give your daughter to my son for a wife'; but a wild animal of Lebanon passed by and trampled down the thornbush. 19 You say, 'See, I have defeated Ē'dom,' and your heart has lifted you up in boastfulness. Now stay at home; why should you provoke trouble so that you fall, you and Judah with you?"

20 But Am·a·zī'ah would not listen—it was God's doing, in order to hand them over, because they had sought the gods of Ē'dom. 21 So King Jō'ash of Israel went up; he and King Am·a·zī'ah of Judah faced one another in battle at Beth-shē'mesh, which belongs to Judah. 22 Judah was defeated by Israel; everyone fled home. 23 King Jō'ash of Israel captured King Am·a·zī'ah of Judah, son of Jō'ash, son of A·ha·zī'ah, at Beth-shē'mesh; he brought him to Jerusalem, and broke down the wall of Jerusalem from the Ē'phra·im Gate to the Corner Gate, a distance of four hundred cubits. 24 He seized all the gold and silver, and all the vessels that were found in the house of God, and O'bed-ē'dom with them; he seized also the treasuries of the king's house, also hostages; then he returned to Sa·mār'i·a.

Death of Amaziah
(2 Kings 14.17–20)

25 King Am·a·zī'ah son of Jō'ash of Judah, lived fifteen years after the death of King Jō'ash son of Je·hō'a·haz of Israel. 26 Now the rest of the deeds of Am·a·zī'ah, from first to last, are they not written in the Book of the Kings of Judah and Israel? 27 From the time that Am·a·zī'ah turned away from the LORD they made a conspiracy against him in Jerusalem, and he fled to Lā'chish. But they sent after him to Lā'chish, and killed him there. 28 They brought him back on horses; he was buried with his ancestors in the city of David.

Reign of Uzziah
(2 Kings 14.21–22; 15.1–3)

26 Then all the people of Judah took Uz·zī'ah, who was sixteen years old, and made him king to succeed his father Am·a·zī'ah. 2 He rebuilt Ē'loth and restored it to Judah, after the king slept with his ancestors. 3 Uz·zī'ah was sixteen years old when he began to reign, and he reigned fifty-two years in Jerusalem. His mother's name was Jec·o·lī'ah of Jerusalem. 4 He did what was right in the sight of the LORD, just as his father Am·a·zī'ah had done. 5 He set himself to seek God in the days of Zech·a·rī'ah, who instructed him in the fear of God; and as long as he sought the LORD, God made him prosper.

6 He went out and made war against the Phi·lis'tines, and broke down the wall of Gath and the wall of Jab'neh and the wall of Ash'dod; he built cities in the territory of Ash'dod and elsewhere among the Phi·lis'tines. 7 God helped him against the Phi·lis'tines, against the Arabs who lived in Gur-bā'al, and against the Me·ū'nītes. 8 The Am'mon·ītes paid tribute to Uz·zī'ah, and his fame spread even to the border of Egypt, for he became very strong. 9 Moreover Uz·zī'ah built towers in Jerusalem at the Corner Gate, at the Valley Gate, and at the Angle, and fortified them. 10 He built towers in the wilderness and hewed out many cisterns, for he had large herds, both in the She·phē'lah and in the plain, and he had farmers and vinedressers in the hills and in the fertile lands, for he loved the soil. 11 Moreover Uz·zī'ah had an army of soldiers, fit for war, in divisions according to the numbers in the muster made by the secretary Je·i'el and the officer Mā·a·sēi'ah, under the direction of Han·a·nī'ah, one of the king's commanders. 12 The whole number of the heads of ancestral houses of mighty warriors was two thousand six hundred. 13 Under their command was an army of three hundred seven thousand five hundred, who could make war with mighty power, to help the king against the enemy. 14 Uz·zī'ah provided for all the army the shields, spears, helmets, coats of mail, bows, and stones for slinging. 15 In Jerusalem he set up machines, invented by skilled workers, on the towers and the corners for shooting arrows and large stones. And his fame spread far, for he was marvelously helped until he became strong.

Pride and Apostasy
(2 Kings 15.4–7)

16 But when he had become strong he grew proud, to his destruction. For he was false to the LORD his God, and entered the temple of the LORD to make offering on the altar of incense. 17 But the priest Az·a·rī'ah went in after him, with eighty priests of the LORD who were men of valor; 18 they withstood King Uz·zī'ah, and said to him, "It is not for you, Uz·zī'ah, to make offering to the LORD, but for the priests the descendants of Aaron, who are consecrated to make offering. Go out of the sanctuary; for you have done wrong, and it will bring you no honor from the LORD God." 19 Then Uz·zī'ah was angry. Now he had a censer in his hand to make offering, and when he became angry with the priests a leprous[e] disease broke out on his forehead, in the presence of the priests in the house of the LORD, by the altar of incense. 20 When the chief priest Az·a·rī'ah, and all the priests, looked at him, he was leprous[e] in his forehead. They hurried him

---

[e] A term for several skin diseases; precise meaning uncertain

out, and he himself hurried to get out, because the LORD had struck him. 21 King Uz‧zi′ah was leprous*f* to the day of his death, and being leprous*f* lived in a separate house, for he was excluded from the house of the LORD. His son Jō′tham was in charge of the palace of the king, governing the people of the land.

22 Now the rest of the acts of Uz‧zi′ah, from first to last, the prophet Ĭ‧sai′ah son of Ā′moz wrote. 23 Uz‧zi′ah slept with his ancestors; they buried him near his ancestors in the burial field that belonged to the kings, for they said, "He is leprous."*f* His son Jō′tham succeeded him.

Reign of Jotham
(2 Kings 15.32–38)

27 Jō′tham was twenty-five years old when he began to reign; he reigned sixteen years in Jerusalem. His mother's name was Je‧ru′shah daughter of Zā′dok. 2 He did what was right in the sight of the LORD just as his father Uz‧zi′ah had done—only he did not invade the temple of the LORD. But the people still followed corrupt practices. 3 He built the upper gate of the house of the LORD, and did extensive building on the wall of O′phel. 4 Moreover he built cities in the hill country of Judah, and forts and towers on the wooded hills. 5 He fought with the king of the Am′‑mon‧ītes and prevailed against them. The Am′‑mon‧ītes gave him that year one hundred talents of silver, ten thousand cors of wheat and ten thousand of barley. The Am′mon‧ītes paid him the same amount in the second and the third years. 6 So Jō′tham became strong because he ordered his ways before the LORD his God. 7 Now the rest of the acts of Jō′tham, and all his wars and his ways, are written in the Book of the Kings of Israel and Judah. 8 He was twenty-five years old when he began to reign; he reigned sixteen years in Jerusalem. 9 Jō′tham slept with his ancestors, and they buried him in the city of David; and his son Ā′haz succeeded him.

Reign of Ahaz
(2 Kings 16.1–4)

28 Ā′haz was twenty years old when he began to reign; he reigned sixteen years in Jerusalem. He did not do what was right in the sight of the LORD, as his ancestor David had done, 2 but he walked in the ways of the kings of Israel. He even made cast images for the Bā′als; 3 and he made offerings in the valley of the son of Hin′nom, and made his sons pass through fire, according to the abominable practices of the nations whom the LORD drove out before the people of Israel. 4 He sacrificed and made offerings on the high places, on the hills, and under every green tree.

Aram and Israel Defeat Judah
(2 Kings 16.5–6; Isa 7.1)

5 Therefore the LORD his God gave him into the hand of the king of Ar′am, who defeated him and took captive a great number of his people and brought them to Damascus. He was also given into the hand of the king of Israel, who defeated him with great slaughter. 6 Pē′kah son of Rem‧a‧li′ah killed one hundred twenty thousand in Judah in one day, all of them valiant warriors, because they had abandoned the LORD, the God of their ancestors. 7 And Zich′rī, a mighty warrior of Ē′phra‧im, killed the king's son Mā‧a‧sēi′ah, Az‧rī′kam the commander of the palace, and El‧kā′nah the next in authority to the king.

Intervention of Oded

8 The people of Israel took captive two hundred thousand of their kin, women, sons, and daughters; they also took much booty from them and brought the booty to Sa‧mār′i‧a. 9 But a prophet of the LORD was there, whose name was Ō′ded; he went out to meet the army that came to Sa‧mār′i‧a, and said to them, "Because the LORD, the God of your ancestors, was angry with Judah, he gave them into your hand, but you have killed them in a rage that has reached up to heaven. 10 Now you intend to subjugate the people of Judah and Jerusalem, male and female, as your slaves. But what have you except sins against the LORD your God? 11 Now hear me, and send back the captives whom you have taken from your kindred, for the fierce wrath of the LORD is upon you." 12 Moreover, certain chiefs of the Ē′phra‧im‧ites, Az‧a‧ri′ah son of Jō‧hā′nan, Ber‧e‧chi′ah son of Me‧shil′le‧moth, Jē‧hiz‧ki′ah son of Shal′lum, and A‧mā′sa son of Had′lai, stood up against those who were coming from the war, 13 and said to them, "You shall not bring the captives in here, for you propose to bring on us guilt against the LORD in addition to our present sins and guilt. For our guilt is already great, and there is fierce wrath against Israel." 14 So the warriors left the captives and the booty before the officials and all the assembly. 15 Then those who were mentioned by name got up and took the captives, and with the booty they clothed all that were naked among them; they clothed them, gave them sandals, provided them with food and drink, and anointed them; and carrying all the feeble among them on donkeys, they brought them to their kindred at Jericho, the city of palm trees. Then they returned to Sa‧mār′i‧a.

---

f A term for several skin diseases; precise meaning uncertain

2 CHR

Assyria Refuses to Help Judah
(2 Kings 16.7–9)

16 At that time King Ā′haz sent to the kings[g] of Assyria for help. 17 For the Ē′dom•ītes had again invaded and defeated Judah, and carried away captives. 18 And the Phi•lis′tines had made raids on the cities in the She•phē′lah and the Neg′eb of Judah, and had taken Beth-shē′mesh, Aī′ja•lon, Ge•dē′roth, Sō′cō with its villages, Tim′nah with its villages, and Gim′zō with its villages; and they settled there. 19 For the LORD brought Judah low because of King Ā′haz of Israel, for he had behaved without restraint in Judah and had been faithless to the LORD. 20 So King Til′gath-pil•nē′ser of Assyria came against him, and oppressed him instead of strengthening him. 21 For Ā′haz plundered the house of the LORD and the houses of the king and of the officials, and gave tribute to the king of Assyria; but it did not help him.

Apostasy and Death of Ahaz
(2 Kings 16.12–20)

22 In the time of his distress he became yet more faithless to the LORD—this same King Ā′haz. 23 For he sacrificed to the gods of Damascus, which had defeated him, and said, "Because the gods of the kings of Ar′am helped them, I will sacrifice to them so that they may help me." But they were the ruin of him, and of all Israel. 24 Ā′haz gathered together the utensils of the house of God, and cut in pieces the utensils of the house of God. He shut up the doors of the house of the LORD and made himself altars in every corner of Jerusalem. 25 In every city of Judah he made high places to make offerings to other gods, provoking to anger the LORD, the God of his ancestors. 26 Now the rest of his acts and all his ways, from first to last, are written in the Book of the Kings of Judah and Israel. 27 Ā′haz slept with his ancestors, and they buried him in the city, in Jerusalem; but they did not bring him into the tombs of the kings of Israel. His son Hez•e•kī′ah succeeded him.

Reign of Hezekiah
(2 Kings 18.1–3)

29 Hez•e•kī′ah began to reign when he was twenty-five years old; he reigned twenty-nine years in Jerusalem. His mother's name was A•bī′jah daughter of Zech•a•rī′ah. 2 He did what was right in the sight of the LORD, just as his ancestor David had done.

The Temple Cleansed

3 In the first year of his reign, in the first month, he opened the doors of the house of the LORD and repaired them. 4 He brought in the priests and the Lē′vītes and assembled them in the square on the east. 5 He said to them, "Listen to me, Lē′vītes! Sanctify yourselves, and sanctify the house of the LORD, the God of your ancestors, and carry out the filth from the holy place. 6 For our ancestors have been unfaithful and have done what was evil in the sight of the LORD our God; they have forsaken him, and have turned away their faces from the dwelling of the LORD, and turned their backs. 7 They also shut the doors of the vestibule and put out the lamps, and have not offered incense or made burnt offerings in the holy place to the God of Israel. 8 Therefore the wrath of the LORD came upon Judah and Jerusalem, and he has made them an object of horror, of astonishment, and of hissing, as you see with your own eyes. 9 Our fathers have fallen by the sword and our sons and our daughters and our wives are in captivity for this. 10 Now it is in my heart to make a covenant with the LORD, the God of Israel, so that his fierce anger may turn away from us. 11 My sons, do not now be negligent, for the LORD has chosen you to stand in his presence to minister to him, and to be his ministers and make offerings to him."

---

g Gk Syr Vg Compare 2 Kings 16.7: Heb *kings*

PRAY IT!
Renewing Your Prayer Life

Hezekiah was one of Judah's reformer kings. Before he became king, the people had neglected the Temple in Jerusalem for a long time. At the beginning of Hezekiah's reign, the Temple needed some intense effort to get it back in order.

Sometimes our prayer life suffers from neglect too. We get busy and do not take enough time to pray, or we forget to pray altogether. When we decide to commit ourselves to regular prayer, it may take some intense effort to get rid of our bad habits.

Imagine your prayer life as being like the Temple. How does it look? Is it in need of a little dusting? full of cobwebs? ready for major renovation? What steps can you take to make sure you do not neglect your prayer life?

▶ 2 Chr 29.1–11

12 Then the Lē'vītes arose, Mā'hath son of A•mā'saī, and Jō'el son of Az•a•rī'ah, of the sons of the Kō'hath•ītes; and of the sons of Me•rar'ī, Kish son of Ab'dī, and Az•a•rī'ah son of Je•hal'le•lel; and of the Ger'shon•ītes, Jō'ah son of Zim'mah, and Eden son of Jō'ah; 13 and of the sons of E•li•zā'-phan, Shim'rī and Je•ū'el; and of the sons of Ā'saph, Zech•a•rī'ah and Mat•ta•nī'ah; 14 and of the sons of Hē'man, Jē•hū'el and Shim'ē•ī; and of the sons of Je•dū'thun, She•māi'ah and Uz'zi•el. 15 They gathered their brothers, sanctified themselves, and went in as the king had commanded, by the words of the LORD, to cleanse the house of the LORD. 16 The priests went into the inner part of the house of the LORD to cleanse it, and they brought out all the unclean things that they found in the temple of the LORD into the court of the house of the LORD; and the Lē'vītes took them and carried them out to the Wadi Kid'ron. 17 They began to sanctify on the first day of the first month, and on the eighth day of the month they came to the vestibule of the LORD; then for eight days they sanctified the house of the LORD, and on the sixteenth day of the first month they finished. 18 Then they went inside to King Hez•e•kī'ah and said, "We have cleansed all the house of the LORD, the altar of burnt offering and all its utensils, and the table for the rows of bread and all its utensils. 19 All the utensils that King Ā'haz repudiated during his reign when he was faithless, we have made ready and sanctified; see, they are in front of the altar of the LORD."

Temple Worship Restored

20 Then King Hez•e•kī'ah rose early, assembled the officials of the city, and went up to the house of the LORD. 21 They brought seven bulls, seven rams, seven lambs, and seven male goats for a sin offering for the kingdom and for the sanctuary and for Judah. He commanded the priests the descendants of Aaron to offer them on the altar of the LORD. 22 So they slaughtered the bulls, and the priests received the blood and dashed it against the altar; they slaughtered the rams and their blood was dashed against the altar; they also slaughtered the lambs and their blood was dashed against the altar. 23 Then the male goats for the sin offering were brought to the king and the assembly; they laid their hands on them, 24 and the priests slaughtered them and made a sin offering with their blood at the altar, to make atonement for all Israel. For the king commanded that the burnt offering and the sin offering should be made for all Israel.

25 He stationed the Lē'vītes in the house of the LORD with cymbals, harps, and lyres, according to the commandment of David and of Gad the king's seer and of the prophet Nathan, for the commandment was from the LORD through his prophets.

26 The Lē'vītes stood with the instruments of David, and the priests with the trumpets. 27 Then Hez•e•kī'ah commanded that the burnt offering be offered on the altar. When the burnt offering began, the song to the LORD began also, and the trumpets, accompanied by the instruments of King David of Israel. 28 The whole assembly worshiped, the singers sang, and the trumpeters sounded; all this continued until the burnt offering was finished. 29 When the offering was finished, the king and all who were present with him bowed down and worshiped. 30 King Hez•e•kī'ah and the officials commanded the Lē'vītes to sing praises to the LORD with the words of David and of the seer Ā'saph. They sang praises with gladness, and they bowed down and worshiped.

31 Then Hez•e•kī'ah said, "You have now consecrated yourselves to the LORD; come near, bring sacrifices and thank offerings to the house of the LORD." The assembly brought sacrifices and thank offerings; and all who were of a willing heart brought burnt offerings. 32 The number of the burnt offerings that the assembly brought was seventy bulls, one hundred rams, and two hundred lambs; all these were for a burnt offering to the LORD. 33 The consecrated offerings were six hundred bulls and three thousand sheep. 34 But the priests were too few and could not skin all the burnt offerings, so, until other priests had sanctified themselves, their kindred, the Lē'vītes, helped them until the work was finished—for the Lē'vītes were more conscientious[h] than the priests in sanctifying themselves. 35 Besides the great number of burnt offerings there was the fat of the offerings of well-being, and there were the drink offerings for the burnt offerings. Thus the service of the house of the LORD was restored. 36 And Hez•e•kī'ah and all the people rejoiced because of what God had done for the people; for the thing had come about suddenly.

The Great Passover

30 Hez•e•kī'ah sent word to all Israel and Judah, and wrote letters also to Ē'phra-im and Ma•nas'seh, that they should come to the house of the LORD at Jerusalem, to keep the passover to the LORD the God of Israel. 2 For the king and his officials and all the assembly in Jerusalem had taken counsel to keep the passover in the second month 3 (for they could not keep it at its proper time because the priests had not sanctified themselves in sufficient number, nor had the people assembled in Jerusalem). 4 The plan seemed right to the king and all the assembly. 5 So they decreed to make a proclamation throughout all Israel, from Bē'er-shē'ba to Dan, that the people should

---

h Heb *upright in heart*

come and keep the passover to the LORD the God of Israel, at Jerusalem; for they had not kept it in great numbers as prescribed. 6 So couriers went throughout all Israel and Judah with letters from the king and his officials, as the king had commanded, saying, "O people of Israel, return to the LORD, the God of Abraham, Isaac, and Israel, so that he may turn again to the remnant of you who have escaped from the hand of the kings of Assyria. 7 Do not be like your ancestors and your kindred, who were faithless to the LORD God of their ancestors, so that he made them a desolation, as you see. 8 Do not now be stiff-necked as your ancestors were, but yield yourselves to the LORD and come to his sanctuary, which he has sanctified forever, and serve the LORD your God, so that his fierce anger may turn away from you. 9 For as you return to the LORD, your kindred and your children will find compassion with their captors, and return to this land. For the LORD your God is gracious and merciful, and will not turn away his face from you, if you return to him."

10 So the couriers went from city to city through the country of Ē'phra·im and Ma·nas'seh, and as far as Zeb'ū·lun; but they laughed them to scorn, and mocked them. 11 Only a few from Ash'er, Ma·nas'seh, and Zeb'ū·lun humbled themselves and came to Jerusalem. 12 The hand of God was also on Judah to give them one heart to do what the king and the officials commanded by the word of the LORD.

13 Many people came together in Jerusalem to keep the festival of unleavened bread in the second month, a very large assembly. 14 They set to work and removed the altars that were in Jerusalem, and all the altars for offering incense they took away and threw into the Wadi Kid'ron. 15 They slaughtered the passover lamb on the fourteenth day of the second month. The priests and the Lē'vītes were ashamed, and they sanctified themselves and brought burnt offerings into the house of the LORD. 16 They took their accustomed posts according to the law of Moses the man of God; the priests dashed the blood that they received[i] from the hands of the Lē'vītes. 17 For there were many in the assembly who had not sanctified themselves; therefore the Lē'vītes had to slaughter the passover lamb for everyone who was not clean, to make it holy to the LORD. 18 For a multitude of the people, many of them from Ē'phra·im, Ma·nas'seh, Is'sa·char, and Zeb'ū·lun, had not cleansed themselves, yet they ate the passover otherwise than as prescribed. But Hez·e·ki'ah prayed for them, saying, "The good LORD pardon all 19 who set their hearts to seek God, the LORD the God of their ancestors, even though not in accordance with the sanctuary's rules of cleanness." 20 The LORD heard Hez·e·ki'ah, and

healed the people. 21 The people of Israel who were present at Jerusalem kept the festival of unleavened bread seven days with great gladness; and the Lē'vītes and the priests praised the LORD day by day, accompanied by loud instruments for the LORD. 22 Hez·e·ki'ah spoke encouragingly to all the Lē'vītes who showed good skill in the service of the LORD. So the people ate the food of the festival for seven days, sacrificing offerings of well-being and giving thanks to the LORD the God of their ancestors.

23 Then the whole assembly agreed together to keep the festival for another seven days; so they kept it for another seven days with gladness. 24 For King Hez·e·ki'ah of Judah gave the assembly a thousand bulls and seven thousand sheep for offerings, and the officials gave the assembly a thousand bulls and ten thousand sheep. The priests sanctified themselves in great numbers. 25 The whole assembly of Judah, the priests and the Lē'vītes, and the whole assembly that came out of Israel, and the resident aliens who came out of the land of Israel, and the resident aliens who lived in Judah, rejoiced. 26 There was great joy in Jerusalem, for since the time of Solomon son of King David of Israel there had been nothing like this in Jerusalem. 27 Then the priests and the Lē'vītes stood up and blessed the people, and their voice was heard; their prayer came to his holy dwelling in heaven.

Pagan Shrines Destroyed
(2 Kings 18.4)

31 Now when all this was finished, all Israel who were present went out to the cities of Judah and broke down the pillars, hewed down the sacred poles,[j] and pulled down the high places and the altars throughout all Judah and Benjamin, and in Ē'phra·im and Ma·nas'seh, until they had destroyed them all. Then all the people of Israel returned to their cities, all to their individual properties.

2 Hez·e·ki'ah appointed the divisions of the priests and of the Lē'vītes, division by division, everyone according to his service, the priests and the Lē'vītes, for burnt offerings and offerings of well-being, to minister in the gates of the camp of the LORD and to give thanks and praise. 3 The contribution of the king from his own possessions was for the burnt offerings: the burnt offerings of morning and evening, and the burnt offerings for the sabbaths, the new moons, and the appointed festivals, as it is written in the law of the LORD. 4 He commanded the people who lived in Jerusalem to give the portion due to the priests and the Lē'vītes, so that they might devote themselves to the law of the LORD. 5 As soon as the word spread, the people

---

i Heb lacks *that they received*   j Heb *Asherim*

Giving the Best of the Best

LIVE IT!

In 2 Chr 31.5, we read about how the people "gave in abundance the first fruits of grain, wine, oil, honey, and of all the produce of the field." They gave the best of the best, in gratitude for the gifts from God. That is what being generous is all about. True generosity springs from the heart and motivates us to give the best of what we have, not just what we do not want or need anymore.

The word *tithe* appears in this verse. For the Israelites, to tithe meant to give 10 percent of one's earnings as a tax for the upkeep of the Temple. Some Christians continue the spirit of tithing by giving 10 percent of all they earn to the church and other charities. They are offering God their best, the firstfruits of their labor (see Lk 21.1–4 and Acts 4.32–37).

We all need to search our heart and continue this tradition of offering our best back to God—not because it makes us look good and gives us "extra points" with God, but because it comes from our gratitude for the gifts we have received.

▶ 2 Chr 31.2–10

of Israel gave in abundance the first fruits of grain, wine, oil, honey, and of all the produce of the field; and they brought in abundantly the tithe of everything. 6 The people of Israel and Judah who lived in the cities of Judah also brought in the tithe of cattle and sheep, and the tithe of the dedicated things that had been consecrated to the LORD their God, and laid them in heaps. 7 In the third month they began to pile up the heaps, and finished them in the seventh month. 8 When Hez·e·ki'ah and the officials came and saw the heaps, they blessed the LORD and his people Israel. 9 Hez·e·ki'ah questioned the priests and the Lē'vītes about the heaps. 10 The chief priest Az·a·rī'ah, who was of the house of Zā'dok, answered him, "Since they began to bring the contributions into the house of the LORD, we have had enough to eat and have plenty to spare; for the LORD has blessed his people, so that we have this great supply left over."

Reorganization of Priests and Levites

11 Then Hez·e·ki'ah commanded them to prepare store-chambers in the house of the LORD; and they prepared them. 12 Faithfully they brought in the contributions, the tithes and the dedicated things. The chief officer in charge of them was Con·a·ni'ah the Lē'vīte, with his brother Shim'ē·ī as second; 13 while Je·hi'el, Az·a·zi'ah, Nā'hath, As'a·hel, Jer'i·moth, Joz'a·bad, E·li'el, Is·ma·chi'ah, Mā'hath, and Be·nā'i·ah were overseers assisting Con·a·ni'ah and his brother Shim'ē·ī, by the appointment of King Hez·e·ki'ah and of Az·a·rī'ah the chief officer of the house of God. 14 Kō're son of Im'nah the Lē'vīte, keeper of the east gate, was in charge of the freewill offerings to God, to apportion the contribution reserved for the LORD and the most holy offerings. 15 Eden, Mi·ni'a·min, Jesh'ū·a,

She·māi'ah, Am·a·rī'ah, and Shec·a·ni'ah were faithfully assisting him in the cities of the priests, to distribute the portions to their kindred, old and young alike, by divisions, 16 except those enrolled by genealogy, males from three years old and upwards, all who entered the house of the LORD as the duty of each day required, for their service according to their offices, by their divisions. 17 The enrollment of the priests was according to their ancestral houses; that of the Lē'vītes from twenty years old and upwards was according to their offices, by their divisions. 18 The priests were enrolled with all their little children, their wives, their sons, and their daughters, the whole multitude; for they were faithful in keeping themselves holy. 19 And for the descendants of Aaron, the priests, who were in the fields of common land belonging to their towns, town by town, the people designated by name were to distribute portions to every male among the priests and to everyone among the Lē'vītes who was enrolled.

20 Hez·e·ki'ah did this throughout all Judah; he did what was good and right and faithful before the LORD his God. 21 And every work that he undertook in the service of the house of God, and in accordance with the law and the commandments, to seek his God, he did with all his heart; and he prospered.

Sennacherib's Invasion
(2 Kings 18.13—19.34; Isa 36.2–22)

32 After these things and these acts of faithfulness, King Sen·nach'e·rib of Assyria came and invaded Judah and encamped against the fortified cities, thinking to win them for himself. 2 When Hez·e·ki'ah saw that Sen·nach'e·rib had come and intended to fight against Jerusalem, 3 he planned with his officers and his warriors to stop the flow of the springs that were outside the city; and they helped him. 4 A great many people were gathered, and they stopped all the springs and the wadi that flowed through the land, saying, "Why should the Assyrian kings come and find water in abundance?" 5 Hez·e·kī′ah*k* set to work resolutely and built up the entire wall that was broken down, and raised towers on it,*l* and outside it he built another wall; he also strengthened the Mil′lō in the city of David, and made weapons and shields in abundance. 6 He appointed combat commanders over the people, and gathered them together to him in the square at the gate of the city and spoke encouragingly to them, saying, 7 "Be strong and of good courage. Do not be afraid or dismayed before the king of Assyria and all the horde that is with him; for there is one greater with us than with him. 8 With him is an arm of flesh; but with us is the LORD our God, to help us and to fight our battles." The people were encouraged by the words of King Hez·e·kī′ah of Judah.

9 After this, while King Sen·nach′e·rib of Assyria was at Lā′chish with all his forces, he sent his servants to Jerusalem to King Hez·e·kī′ah of Judah and to all the people of Judah that were in Jerusalem, saying, 10 "Thus says King Sen·nach′e·rib of Assyria: On what are you relying, that you undergo the siege of Jerusalem? 11 Is not Hez·e·kī′ah misleading you, handing you over to die by famine and by thirst, when he tells you, 'The LORD our God will save us from the hand of the king of Assyria'? 12 Was it not this same Hez·e·kī′ah who took away his high places and his altars and commanded Judah and Jerusalem, saying, 'Before one altar you shall worship, and upon it you shall make your offerings'? 13 Do you not know what I and my ancestors have done to all the peoples of other lands? Were the gods of the nations of those lands at all able to save their lands out of my hand? 14 Who among all the gods of those nations that my ancestors utterly destroyed was able to save his people from my hand, that your God should be able to save you from my hand? 15 Now therefore do not let Hez·e·kī′ah deceive you or mislead you in this fashion, and do not believe him, for no god of any nation or kingdom has been able to save his people from my hand or from the hand of my ancestors. How much less will your God save you out of my hand!"

16 His servants said still more against the Lord GOD and against his servant Hez·e·kī′ah. 17 He also wrote letters to throw contempt on the LORD the God of Israel and to speak against him, saying, "Just as the gods of the nations in other lands did not rescue their people from my hands, so the God of Hez·e·kī′ah will not rescue his people from my hand." 18 They shouted it with a loud voice in the language of Judah to the people of Jerusalem who were on the wall, to frighten and terrify them, in order that they might take the city. 19 They spoke of the God of Jerusalem as if he were like the gods of the peoples of the earth, which are the work of human hands.

Sennacherib's Defeat and Death
(2 Kings 19.35–37)

20 Then King Hez·e·kī′ah and the prophet Ī·sāi′ah son of Ā′moz prayed because of this and cried to heaven. 21 And the LORD sent an angel who cut off all the mighty warriors and commanders and officers in the camp of the king of Assyria. So he returned in disgrace to his own land. When he came into the house of his god, some of his own sons struck him down there with the sword. 22 So the LORD saved Hez·e·kī′ah and the inhabitants of Jerusalem from the hand of King Sen·nach′e·rib of Assyria and from the hand of all his enemies; he gave them rest*m* on every side. 23 Many brought gifts to the LORD in Jerusalem and precious things to King Hez·e·kī′ah of Judah, so that he was exalted in the sight of all nations from that time onward.

Hezekiah's Sickness
(2 Kings 20.1–11; Isa 38.1–8)

24 In those days Hez·e·kī′ah became sick and was at the point of death. He prayed to the LORD, and he answered him and gave him a sign. 25 But Hez·e·kī′ah did not respond according to the benefit done to him, for his heart was proud. Therefore wrath came upon him and upon Judah and Jerusalem. 26 Then Hez·e·kī′ah humbled himself for the pride of his heart, both he and the inhabitants of Jerusalem, so that the wrath of the LORD did not come upon them in the days of Hez·e·kī′ah.

Hezekiah's Prosperity and Achievements
(2 Kings 20.12–21; Isa 39.1–8)

27 Hez·e·kī′ah had very great riches and honor; and he made for himself treasuries for silver, for gold, for precious stones, for spices, for shields, and for all kinds of costly objects; 28 storehouses also for the yield of grain, wine, and oil; and stalls for all kinds of cattle, and sheepfolds.*n* 29 He likewise provided cities for himself, and flocks and herds in abundance; for God had given him very great possessions. 30 This same Hez·e·kī′ah closed the upper outlet of the waters of Gī′hon and directed them down to the west side of the city of David. Hez·e·kī′ah prospered in all his works. 31 So also in the matter of the envoys of the officials of Babylon,

---

k Heb *He*　*l* Vg: Heb *and raised on the towers*　*m* Gk Vg: Heb *guided them*　*n* Gk Vg: Heb *flocks for folds*

Perseverance in Leadership

King Hezekiah persevered and prospered. He had many riches and provided for the people in his kingdom. One great accomplishment was a tunnel he had dug under the City of David (2 Chr 32.30). The tunnel allowed the springs of Gihon to flow into the city so that the people had easier access to the water.

That tunnel, more than seventeen hundred feet long, was carved through the stone. Today, it would not take much to complete such a task, but in Hezekiah's time, it was done little by little with simple tools.

A great leader needs perseverance. People can get discouraged and lose heart when faced with difficult tasks. A good leader provides the encouragement and vision to get the job done. Who is an encouraging leader in your life? How do you encourage other people you work or go to school or live with?

▶ 2 Chr 32.27–33

---

who had been sent to him to inquire about the sign that had been done in the land, God left him to himself, in order to test him and to know all that was in his heart.

32 Now the rest of the acts of Hez·e·kī'ah, and his good deeds, are written in the vision of the prophet Ī·sāi'ah son of Ā'moz in the Book of the Kings of Judah and Israel. 33 Hez·e·kī'ah slept with his ancestors, and they buried him on the ascent to the tombs of the descendants of David; and all Judah and the inhabitants of Jerusalem did him honor at his death. His son Ma·nas'seh succeeded him.

Reign of Manasseh
(2 Kings 21.1–9)

33 Ma·nas'seh was twelve years old when he began to reign; he reigned fifty-five years in Jerusalem. 2 He did what was evil in the sight of the LORD, according to the abominable practices of the nations whom the LORD drove out before the people of Israel. 3 For he rebuilt the high places that his father Hez·e·kī'ah had pulled down, and erected altars to the Bā'als, made sacred poles,ᵒ worshiped all the host of heaven, and served them. 4 He built altars in the house of the LORD, of which the LORD had said, "In Jerusalem shall my name be forever." 5 He built altars for all the host of heaven in the two courts of the house of the LORD. 6 He made his son pass through fire in the valley of the son of Hin'nom, practiced soothsaying and augury and sorcery, and dealt with mediums and with wizards. He did much evil in the sight of the LORD, provoking him to anger. 7 The carved image of the idol that he had made he set in the house of God, of which God said to David and to his son Solomon, "In this house, and in Jerusalem, which I have chosen out of all the tribes of Israel, I will put my name forever; 8 I will never again remove the feet of Israel

from the land that I appointed for your ancestors, if only they will be careful to do all that I have commanded them, all the law, the statutes, and the ordinances given through Moses." 9 Ma·nas'seh misled Judah and the inhabitants of Jerusalem, so that they did more evil than the nations whom the LORD had destroyed before the people of Israel.

Manasseh Restored after Repentance

10 The LORD spoke to Ma·nas'seh and to his people, but they gave no heed. 11 Therefore the LORD brought against them the commanders of the army of the king of Assyria, who took Ma·nas'seh captive in manacles, bound him with fetters, and brought him to Babylon. 12 While he was in distress he entreated the favor of the LORD his God and humbled himself greatly before the God of his ancestors. 13 He prayed to him, and God received his entreaty, heard his plea, and restored him again to Jerusalem and to his kingdom. Then Ma·nas'seh knew that the LORD indeed was God.

14 Afterward he built an outer wall for the city of David west of Gī'hon, in the valley, reaching the entrance at the Fish Gate; he carried it around O'phel, and raised it to a very great height. He also put commanders of the army in all the fortified cities in Judah. 15 He took away the foreign gods and the idol from the house of the LORD, and all the altars that he had built on the mountain of the house of the LORD and in Jerusalem, and he threw them out of the city. 16 He also restored the altar of the LORD and offered on it sacrifices of well-being and of thanksgiving; and he commanded Judah to serve the LORD the God of Israel. 17 The people, however, still sacrificed at the high places, but only to the LORD their God.

ᵒ Heb *Asheroth*

Death of Manasseh
(2 Kings 21.17–18)

18 Now the rest of the acts of Ma·nas′seh, his prayer to his God, and the words of the seers who spoke to him in the name of the LORD God of Israel, these are in the Annals of the Kings of Israel. 19 His prayer, and how God received his entreaty, all his sin and his faithlessness, the sites on which he built high places and set up the sacred poles*p* and the images, before he humbled himself, these are written in the records of the seers.*q* 20 So Ma·nas′seh slept with his ancestors, and they buried him in his house. His son Ā′mon succeeded him.

Amon's Reign and Death
(2 Kings 21.19–26)

21 Ā′mon was twenty-two years old when he began to reign; he reigned two years in Jerusalem. 22 He did what was evil in the sight of the LORD, as his father Ma·nas′seh had done. Ā′mon sacrificed to all the images that his father Ma·nas′seh had made, and served them. 23 He did not humble himself before the LORD, as his father Ma·nas′seh had humbled himself, but this Ā′mon incurred more and more guilt. 24 His servants conspired against him and killed him in his house. 25 But the people of the land killed all those who had conspired against King Ā′mon; and the people of the land made his son Jō·sī′ah king to succeed him.

Reign of Josiah
(2 Kings 22.1–2)

34 Jō·sī′ah was eight years old when he began to reign; he reigned thirty-one years in Jerusalem. 2 He did what was right in the sight of the LORD, and walked in the ways of his ancestor David; he did not turn aside to the right or to the left. 3 For in the eighth year of his reign, while he was still a boy, he began to seek the God of his ancestor David, and in the twelfth year he began to purge Judah and Jerusalem of the high places, the sacred poles,*p* and the carved and the cast images. 4 In his presence they pulled down the altars of the Bā′als; he demolished the incense altars that stood above them. He broke down the sacred poles*p* and the carved and the cast images; he made dust of them and scattered it over the graves of those who had sacrificed to them. 5 He also burned the bones of the priests on their altars, and purged Judah and Jerusalem. 6 In the towns of Ma·nas′seh, Ē′phra·im, and Sim′ē·on, and as far as Naph′ta·lī, in their ruins*r* all around, 7 he broke down the altars, beat the sacred poles*p* and the images into powder, and demolished all the incense altars throughout all the land of Israel. Then he returned to Jerusalem.

Discovery of the Book of the Law
(2 Kings 22.3–20)

8 In the eighteenth year of his reign, when he had purged the land and the house, he sent Shā′phan son of Az·a·lī′ah, Mā·a·sēi′ah the governor of the city, and Jō′ah son of Jō′a·haz, the recorder, to repair the house of the LORD his God. 9 They came to the high priest Hil·kī′ah and delivered the money that had been brought into the house of God, which the Lē′vītes, the keepers of the threshold, had collected from Ma·nas′seh and Ē′phra·im and from all the remnant of Israel and from all Judah and Benjamin and from the inhabitants of Jerusalem. 10 They delivered it to the workers who had the oversight of the house of the LORD, and the workers who were working in the house of the LORD gave it for repairing and restoring the house. 11 They gave it to the carpenters and the builders to buy quarried stone, and timber for binders, and beams for the buildings that the kings of Judah had let go to ruin. 12 The people did the work faithfully. Over them were appointed the Lē′vītes Jā′hath and Ō·ba·dī′ah, of the sons of Me·rar′ī, along with Zech·a·rī′ah and Me·shul′lam, of the sons of the Kō′hath·ītes, to have oversight. Other Lē′vītes, all skillful with instruments of music, 13 were over the burden bearers and directed all who did work in every kind of service; and some of the Lē′vītes were scribes, and officials, and gatekeepers.

14 While they were bringing out the money that had been brought into the house of the LORD, the priest Hil·kī′ah found the book of the law of the LORD given through Moses. 15 Hil·kī′ah said to the secretary Shā′phan, "I have found the book of the law in the house of the LORD"; and Hil·kī′ah gave the book to Shā′phan. 16 Shā′phan brought the book to the king, and further reported to the king, "All that was committed to your servants they are doing. 17 They have emptied out the money that was found in the house of the LORD and have delivered it into the hand of the overseers and the workers." 18 The secretary Shā′phan informed the king, "The priest Hil·kī′ah has given me a book." Shā′phan then read it aloud to the king.

19 When the king heard the words of the law he tore his clothes. 20 Then the king commanded Hil·kī′ah, A·hī′kam son of Shā′phan, Ab′don son of Mī′cah, the secretary Shā′phan, and the king's servant A·sāi′ah: 21 "Go, inquire of the LORD for me and for those who are left in Israel and in Judah, concerning the words of the book that has been found; for the wrath of the LORD that is poured out on us is great, because our ancestors did not keep

---

p Heb *Asherim*   *q* One Ms Gk: MT *of Hozai*   *r* Meaning of Heb uncertain the word of the LORD, to act in accordance with all that is written in this book."

The Prophet Huldah Consulted

22 So Hil·ki′ah and those whom the king had sent went to the prophet Hul′dah, the wife of Shal′lum son of Tok′hath son of Has′rah, keeper of the wardrobe (who lived in Jerusalem in the Second Quarter) and spoke to her to that effect. 23 She declared to them, "Thus says the LORD, the God of Israel: Tell the man who sent you to me, 24 Thus says the LORD: I will indeed bring disaster upon this place and upon its inhabitants, all the curses that are written in the book that was read before the king of Judah. 25 Because they have forsaken me and have made offerings tc other gods, so that they have provoked me to anger with all the works of their hands, my wrath will be poured out on this place and will not be quenched. 26 But as to the king of Judah, who sent you to inquire of the LORD, thus shall you say to him: Thus says the LORD, the God of Israel: Regarding the words that you have heard, 27 because your heart was penitent and you humbled yourself before God when you heard his words against this place and its inhabitants, and you have humbled yourself before me, and have torn your clothes and wept before me, I also have heard you, says the LORD. 28 I will gather you to your ancestors and you shall be gathered to your grave in peace; your eyes shall not see all the disaster that I will bring on this place and its inhabitants." They took the message back to the king.

The Covenant Renewed
(2 Kings 23.1–20)

29 Then the king sent word and gathered together all the elders of Judah and Jerusalem. 30 The king went up to the house of the LORD, with all the people of Judah, the inhabitants of Jerusalem, the priests and the Le′vites, all the people both great and small; he read in their hearing all the words of the book of the covenant that had been found in the house of the LORD. 31 The king stood in his place and made a covenant before the LORD, to follow the LORD, keeping his commandments, his decrees, and his statutes, with all his heart and all his soul, to perform the words of the covenant that were written in this book. 32 Then he made all who were present in Jerusalem and in Benjamin pledge themselves to it. And the inhabitants of Jerusalem acted according to the covenant of God, the God of their ancestors. 33 Jo·si′ah took away all the abominations from all the territory that belonged to the people of Israel, and made all who were in Israel worship the LORD their God. All his days they did not turn away from following the LORD the God of their ancestors.

Celebration of the Passover
(2 Kings 23.21–23)

35 Jo·si′ah kept a passover to the LORD in Jerusalem; they slaughtered the passover lamb on the fourteenth day of the first month. 2 He appointed the priests to their offices and encouraged them in the service of the house of the LORD. 3 He said to the Le′vites who taught all Israel and who were holy to the LORD, "Put the holy ark in the house that Solomon son of David, king of Israel, built; you need no longer carry it on your shoulders. Now serve the LORD your God and his people Israel. 4 Make preparations by your ancestral houses by your divisions, following the written directions of King David of Israel and the written directions of his son Solomon. 5 Take position in the holy place according to the groupings of the ancestral houses of your kindred the people, and let there be Le′vites for each division of an ancestral house.ˢ 6 Slaughter the passover lamb, sanctify yourselves, and on behalf of your kindred make preparations, acting according to the word of the LORD by Moses."

7 Then Jo·si′ah contributed to the people, as passover offerings for all that were present, lambs and kids from the flock to the number of thirty thousand, and three thousand bulls; these were from the king's possessions. 8 His officials contributed willingly to the people, to the priests, and to the Le′vites. Hil·ki′ah, Zech·a·ri′ah, and Je·hi′el, the chief officers of the house of God, gave to the priests for the passover offerings two thousand six hundred lambs and kids and three hundred bulls. 9 Con·a·ni′ah also, and his brothers She·mai′ah and Ne·than′el, and Hash·a·bi′ah and Je·i′el and Joz′a·bad, the chiefs of the Le′vites, gave to the Le′vites for the passover offerings five thousand lambs and kids and five hundred bulls.

10 When the service had been prepared for, the priests stood in their place, and the Le′vites in their divisions according to the king's command. 11 They slaughtered the passover lamb, and the priests dashed the blood that they receivedᵗ from them, while the Le′vites did the skinning. 12 They set aside the burnt offerings so that they might distribute them according to the groupings of the ancestral houses of the people, to offer to the LORD, as it is written in the book of Moses. And they did the same with the bulls. 13 They roasted the passover lamb with fire according to the ordinance; and they boiled the holy offerings in pots, in caldrons, and in pans, and carried them quickly to all the people. 14 Afterward they made preparations for themselves and for the priests, because the priests the descendants of Aaron were occupied in offering the burnt offerings and the fat parts until night; so the Le′vites made preparations

---

ˢ Meaning of Heb uncertain   ᵗ Heb lacks *that they received* for themselves and for the priests, the descendants of Aaron. 15 The singers, the descendants of Ā'saph, were in their place according to the command of David, and Ā'saph, and Hē'man, and the king's seer Je·dū'thun. The gatekeepers were at each gate; they did not need to interrupt their service, for their kindred the Lē'vītes made preparations for them.

16 So all the service of the LORD was prepared that day, to keep the passover and to offer burnt offerings on the altar of the LORD, according to the command of King Jō·sī'ah. 17 The people of Israel who were present kept the passover at that time, and the festival of unleavened bread seven days. 18 No passover like it had been kept in Israel since the days of the prophet Samuel; none of the kings of Israel had kept such a passover as was kept by Jō·sī'ah, by the priests and the Lē'vītes, by all Judah and Israel who were present, and by the inhabitants of Jerusalem. 19 In the eighteenth year of the reign of Jō·sī'ah this passover was kept.

Defeat by Pharaoh Neco and Death of Josiah
(2 Kings 23.28–30)

20 After all this, when Jō·sī'ah had set the temple in order, King Nē'cō of Egypt went up to fight at Car'chem·ish on the Euphrates, and Jō·sī'ah went out against him. 21 But Nē'cōᵘ sent envoys to him, saying, "What have I to do with you, king of Judah? I am not coming against you today, but against the house with which I am at war; and God has commanded me to hurry. Cease opposing God, who is with me, so that he will not destroy you." 22 But Jō·sī'ah would not turn away from him, but disguised himself in order to fight with him. He did not listen to the words of Nē'cō from the mouth of God, but joined battle in the plain of Me·gid'dō. 23 The archers shot King Jō·sī'ah; and the king said to his servants, "Take me away, for I am badly wounded." 24 So his servants took him out of the chariot and carried him in his second chariotᵛ and brought him to Jerusalem. There he died, and was buried in the tombs of his ancestors. All Judah and Jerusalem mourned for Jō·sī'ah. 25 Jer·e·mī'ah also uttered a lament for Jō·sī'ah, and all the singing men and singing women have spoken of Jō·sī'ah in their laments to this day. They made these a custom in Israel; they are recorded in the Laments. 26 Now the rest of the acts of Jō·sī'ah and his faithful deeds in accordance with what is written in the law of the LORD, 27 and his acts, first and last, are written in the Book of the Kings of Israel and Judah.

Reign of Jehoahaz
(2 Kings 23.31–33)

36 The people of the land took Je·hō'a·haz son of Jō·sī'ah and made him king to succeed his father in Jerusalem. 2 Je·hō'a·haz was twenty-three years old when he began to reign; he reigned three months in Jerusalem. 3 Then the king of Egypt deposed him in Jerusalem and laid on the land a tribute of one hundred talents of silver and one talent of gold. 4 The king of Egypt made his brother E·lī'a·kim king over Judah and Jerusalem, and changed his name to Je·hoi'a·kim; but Nē'cō took his brother Je·hō'a·haz and carried him to Egypt.

Reign and Captivity of Jehoiakim
(2 Kings 23.34—24.7)

5 Je·hoi'a·kim was twenty-five years old when he began to reign; he reigned eleven years in Jerusalem. He did what was evil in the sight of the LORD his God. 6 Against him King Ne·bū·chad·nez'zar of Babylon came up, and bound him with fetters to take him to Babylon. 7 Ne·bū·chad·nez'zar also carried some of the vessels of the house of the LORD to Babylon and put them in his palace in Babylon. 8 Now the rest of the acts of Je·hoi'a·kim, and the abominations that he did, and what was found against him, are written in the Book of the Kings of Israel and Judah; and his son Je·hoi'a·chin succeeded him.

Reign and Captivity of Jehoiachin
(2 Kings 24.8–17)

9 Je·hoi'a·chin was eight years old when he began to reign; he reigned three months and ten days in Jerusalem. He did what was evil in the sight of the LORD. 10 In the spring of the year King Ne·bū·chad·nez'zar sent and brought him to Babylon, along with the precious vessels of the house of the LORD, and made his brother Zed·e·kī'ah king over Judah and Jerusalem.

Reign of Zedekiah
(2 Kings 24.18–20; Jer 52.1–3a)

11 Zed·e·kī'ah was twenty-one years old when he began to reign; he reigned eleven years in Jerusalem. 12 He did what was evil in the sight of the LORD his God. He did not humble himself before the prophet Jer·e·mī'ah who spoke from the mouth of the LORD. 13 He also rebelled against King Ne·bū·chad·nez'zar, who had made him swear by God; he stiffened his neck and hardened his heart against turning to the LORD, the God of Israel. 14 All the leading priests and the people also were exceedingly unfaithful, following all the abominations of the nations; and they polluted the house of the LORD that he had consecrated in Jerusalem.

The Fall of Jerusalem
(2 Kings 25.1–21; Jer 52.3b–30)

15 The LORD, the God of their ancestors, sent persistently to them by his messengers, because he

---

ᵘ Heb *he* ᵛ Or *the chariot of his deputy*

LIVE IT!

Stiff Necks

It happened so quickly. I was waiting at a stoplight when the car behind me slammed into my car and my neck snapped back. Whiplash! It hurt, but it didn't seem very serious. I was much more upset at the damage that had been done to my car. But by the next morning, I was in agony. I could barely move my head, and my neck was stiff and sore. By the end of the day, my neck was in a brace, and I was taking pain medication.

Now I understand a little better why the Bible so often uses the metaphor of stiff-necked people (2 Chr 36.13). To be unable or unwilling to turn their heads deprives people of the ability to look toward God. They just keep looking straight ahead as if it were not possible to look in any other direction. You miss out on a lot if you don't or can't look from side to side, believe me!

How often have you refused to turn toward God or to gain a new perspective on life?

▸ 2 Chr 36.11–14

---

had compassion on his people and on his dwelling place; 16 but they kept mocking the messengers of God, despising his words, and scoffing at his prophets, until the wrath of the LORD against his people became so great that there was no remedy.

17 Therefore he brought up against them the king of the Chal·dē′ans, who killed their youths with the sword in the house of their sanctuary, and had no compassion on young man or young woman, the aged or the feeble; he gave them all into his hand. 18 All the vessels of the house of God, large and small, and the treasures of the house of the LORD, and the treasures of the king and of his officials, all these he brought to Babylon. 19 They burned the house of God, broke down the wall of Jerusalem, burned all its palaces with fire, and destroyed all its precious vessels. 20 He took into exile in Babylon those who had escaped from the sword, and they became servants to him and to his sons

until the establishment of the kingdom of Persia, 21 to fulfill the word of the LORD by the mouth of Jer·e·mī′ah, until the land had made up for its sabbaths. All the days that it lay desolate it kept sabbath, to fulfill seventy years.

Cyrus Proclaims Liberty for the Exiles
(Ezra 1.1–4)

22 In the first year of King Cyrus of Persia, in fulfillment of the word of the LORD spoken by Jer·e·mī′ah, the LORD stirred up the spirit of King Cyrus of Persia so that he sent a herald throughout all his kingdom and also declared in a written edict: 23 "Thus says King Cyrus of Persia: The LORD, the God of heaven, has given me all the kingdoms of the earth, and he has charged me to build him a house at Jerusalem, which is in Judah. Whoever is among you of all his people, may the LORD his God be with him! Let him go up."

The Books of Ezra and Nehemiah

I magine the worst holiday ever. The car breaks down twice, you are sick almost the whole time, and the weather is awful. You can't wait to get home—but when you walk in the front door, the house is trashed. Now, imagine how the Israelites felt. They didn't just have a bad holiday; they spent fifty years as captives in a foreign land. When they finally returned home, they faced the overwhelming task of rebuilding Jerusalem and starting their new life. Fortunately, they had Ezra and Nehemiah to help lead and encourage them.

At a Glance

- **Ezra, chapters 1–6.** Israel's return to Judah
- **Ezra, chapters 7–10.** Ezra's coming and works
- **Neh 1.1–7.72.** Nehemiah's appointment as governor
- **Neh 7.73–9.38.** Ezra's proclaiming of the Torah
- **Nehemiah, chapters 10–13.** the various reforms of Nehemiah

In-depth

In 587 B.C., the land of Judah and the city of Jerusalem were conquered by the Babylonians, and many Israelites were exiled to Babylon. The Books of Ezra and Nehemiah pick up the story with the return of some Israelites from Babylon to Judah in 538 B.C. The two books were originally a single work, perhaps written in their final form by the same person (or persons) who wrote 1 and 2 Chronicles.

Ezra, a descendant of Israelite priests, was born in Babylonian captivity and became a priest. Because priests couldn't exercise their religious functions during the Exile, they dedicated themselves to studying the Scriptures. Eventually, Ezra was sent to Judah by the Persian emperor Artaxerxes to restore Israel's faithfulness to God. Ezra appointed scribes and judges to establish civil and moral order in the new community returned from Exile.

Nehemiah was a Jewish cupbearer for Emperor Artaxerxes (a cupbearer tastes the contents of whatever the emperor drinks to assure it is not poisoned). When Nehemiah heard reports of Jerusalem's poverty and ruin, he persuaded the emperor to appoint him governor of Judah to help rebuild the city. Nehemiah turned out to be a gifted governor. Under Nehemiah's direction, Jerusalem's walls were rebuilt, and economic and social reforms helped restore order and hope to the community.

Ezra and Nehemiah's leadership was extremely important to Israel as the people returned and began the difficult task of rebuilding Jerusalem. The need to save the faith and customs of the Israelites led to a strict observance of the Law and the beginnings of modern Judaism.

Quick Facts

Period Covered
from the Exiles' return to Jerusalem through Nehemiah's tenure as governor of Judah, from 538 to about 400 B.C.

Author
a scribe (the Chronicler) drawing on Ezra's and Nehemiah's memoirs and other sources

Themes
the return of the Israelites from captivity, the rebuilding of Jerusalem and the Temple

Ezra

6.3

End of the Babylonian Captivity
(2 Chr 36.22–23)

1 In the first year of King Cyrus of Persia, in order that the word of the Lord by the mouth of Jer·e·miʹah might be accomplished, the Lord stirred up the spirit of King Cyrus of Persia so that he sent a herald throughout all his kingdom, and also in a written edict declared:

2 "Thus says King Cyrus of Persia: The Lord, the God of heaven, has given me all the kingdoms of the earth, and he has charged me to build him a house at Jerusalem in Judah. 3 Any of those among you who are of his people—may their God be with them!—are now permitted to go up to Jerusalem in Judah, and rebuild the house of the Lord, the God of Israel—he is the God who is in Jerusalem; 4 and let all survivors, in whatever place they reside, be assisted by the people of their place with silver and gold, with goods and with animals, besides freewill offerings for the house of God in Jerusalem."

5 The heads of the families of Judah and Benjamin, and the priests and the Lēʹvītes—everyone whose spirit God had stirred—got ready to go up and rebuild the house of the Lord in Jerusalem. 6 All their neighbors aided them with silver vessels, with gold, with goods, with animals, and with valuable gifts, besides all that was freely offered. 7 King Cyrus himself brought out the vessels of the house of the Lord that Ne·bū·chad·nezʹzar had carried away from Jerusalem and placed in the house of his gods. 8 King Cyrus of Persia had them released into the charge of Mithʹre·dath the treasurer, who count-

ed them out to Shesh·bazʹzar the prince of Judah. 9 And this was the inventory: gold basins, thirty; silver basins, one thousand; knives,ᵃ twenty-nine; 10 gold bowls, thirty; other silver bowls, four hundred ten; other vessels, one thousand; 11 the total of the gold and silver vessels was five thousand four hundred. All these Shesh·bazʹzar brought up, when the exiles were brought up from Babylonia to Jerusalem.

List of the Returned Exiles
(Neh 7.6–73)

2 Now these were the people of the province who came from those captive exiles whom King Ne·bū·chad·nezʹzar of Babylon had carried captive to Babylonia; they returned to Jerusalem and Judah, all to their own towns. 2 They came with Ze·rubʹba·bel, Jeshʹū·a, Nē·he·mīʹah, Se·rāiʹah, Rē·el·āiʹah, Morʹde·caī, Bilʹshan, Misʹpar, Bigʹvaī, Rēʹhum, and Bāʹa·nah.

The number of the Israelite people: 3 the descendants of Pāʹrosh, two thousand one hundred seventy-two. 4 Of Sheph·a·tīʹah, three hundred seventy-two. 5 Of Āʹrah, seven hundred seventy-five. 6 Of Pāʹhath-mōʹab, namely the descendants of Jeshʹū·a and Jōʹab, two thousand eight hundred twelve. 7 Of Ēʹlam, one thousand two hundred fifty-four. 8 Of Zatʹtū, nine hundred forty-five. 9 Of Zacʹcaī, seven hundred sixty. 10 Of Bāʹnī, six hundred forty-two. 11 Of Bēʹbaī, six hundred twenty-three. 12 Of Azʹgad,

---

ᵃ Vg: Meaning of Heb uncertain

Thus says King Cyrus of Persia:

The **LORD,**
the **God** of heaven,
has given me
all the **kingdoms** of the earth,
and he has charged me to build **him** a house
1.2   at **Jerusalem** in Judah.

one thousand two hundred twenty-two. ¹³ Of Ad·o·nī'kam, six hundred sixty-six. ¹⁴ Of Big'vaī, two thousand fifty-six. ¹⁵ Of Ā'din, four hundred fifty-four. ¹⁶ Of Ā'ter, namely of Hez·e·kī'ah, ninety-eight. ¹⁷ Of Bē'zaī, three hundred twenty-three. ¹⁸ Of Jō'rah, one hundred twelve. ¹⁹ Of Hā'shum, two hundred twenty-three. ²⁰ Of Gib'bar, ninety-five. ²¹ Of Bethlehem, one hundred twenty-three. ²² The people of Ne·toph'ah, fifty-six. ²³ Of An'a·thoth, one hundred twenty-eight. ²⁴ The descendants of Az'ma·veth, forty-two. ²⁵ Of Kir·i·ath-ar'im, Chē·phī'rah, and Be·er'oth, seven hundred forty-three. ²⁶ Of Rā'mah and Gē'ba, six hundred twenty-one. ²⁷ The people of Mich'mas, one hundred twenty-two. ²⁸ Of Beth'el and Aī, two hundred twenty-three. ²⁹ The descendants of Nē'bō, fifty-two. ³⁰ Of Mag'bish, one hundred fifty-six. ³¹ Of the other Ē'lam, one thousand two hundred fifty-four. ³² Of Hā'rim, three hundred twenty. ³³ Of Lod, Hā'did, and Ō'nō, seven hundred twenty-five. ³⁴ Of Jericho, three hundred forty-five. ³⁵ Of Se·nā'ah, three thousand six hundred thirty.

³⁶ The priests: the descendants of Je·daī'ah, of the house of Jesh'ū·a, nine hundred seventy-three. ³⁷ Of Im'mer, one thousand fifty-two. ³⁸ Of Pash'hur, one thousand two hundred forty-seven. ³⁹ Of Hā'rim, one thousand seventeen.

⁴⁰ The Lē'vītes: the descendants of Jesh'ū·a and Kad'mi·el, of the descendants of Hod·a·vī'ah, seventy-four. ⁴¹ The singers: the descendants of Ā'saph, one hundred twenty-eight. ⁴² The descendants of the gatekeepers: of Shal'lum, of Ā'ter, of

Tal'mon, of Ak'kub, of Ha·tī'ta, and of Shō'baī, in all one hundred thirty-nine.

⁴³ The temple servants: the descendants of Zī'ha, Ha·sū'pha, Tab·bā'oth, ⁴⁴ Kē'ros, Sī'a·ha, Pā'don, ⁴⁵ Le·bā'nah, Hag'a·bah, Ak'kub, ⁴⁶ Hā'gab, Sham'laī, Hā'nan, ⁴⁷ Gid'del, Gā'har, Rē·āi'ah, ⁴⁸ Rē'zin, Ne·kō'da, Gaz'zam, ⁴⁹ Uz'za, Pa·sē'ah, Bē'saī, ⁵⁰ As'nah, Me·ū'nim, Ne·phi'sim, ⁵¹ Bak'buk, Ha·kū'pha, Har'hur, ⁵² Baz'luth, Me·hī'da, Har'sha,⁵³ Bar'kos, Sis'e·ra, Tē'mah, ⁵⁴ Ne·zī'ah, and Ha·tī'pha.

⁵⁵ The descendants of Solomon's servants: Sō'taī, Has·sō'phe·reth, Pe·rū'da, ⁵⁶ Jā'a·lah, Dar'kon, Gid'del, ⁵⁷ Sheph·a·tī'ah, Hat'til, Pō'che·reth-haz·ze·bā'im, and Ā'mī.

⁵⁸ All the temple servants and the descendants of Solomon's servants were three hundred ninety-two.

⁵⁹ The following were those who came up from Tel-mē'lah, Tel-har'sha, Chē'rub, Ad'dan, and Im'mer, though they could not prove their families or their descent, whether they belonged to Israel: ⁶⁰ the descendants of De·laī'ah, Tō·bī'ah, and Ne·kō'da, six hundred fifty-two. ⁶¹ Also, of the descendants of the priests: the descendants of Ha·baī'ah, Hak'koz, and Bar·zil'laī (who had married one of the daughters of Bar·zil'laī the Gil'e·ad·ite, and was called by their name). ⁶² These looked for their entries in the genealogical records, but they were not found there, and so they were excluded from the priesthood as unclean; ⁶³ the governor told them that they were not to partake of the most holy food, until there should be a priest to consult Ū'rim and Thum'mim.

64 The whole assembly together was forty-two thousand three hundred sixty, 65 besides their male and female servants, of whom there were seven thousand three hundred thirty-seven; and they had two hundred male and female singers. 66 They had seven hundred thirty-six horses, two hundred forty-five mules, 67 four hundred thirty-five camels, and six thousand seven hundred twenty donkeys.

68 As soon as they came to the house of the LORD in Jerusalem, some of the heads of families made freewill offerings for the house of God, to erect it on its site. 69 According to their resources they gave to the building fund sixty-one thousand darics of gold, five thousand minas of silver, and one hundred priestly robes.

70 The priests, the Lē′vītes, and some of the people lived in Jerusalem and its vicinity;*b* and the singers, the gatekeepers, and the temple servants lived in their towns, and all Israel in their towns.

Worship Restored at Jerusalem

3 When the seventh month came, and the Israelites were in the towns, the people gathered together in Jerusalem. 2 Then Jesh′ū•a son of Jō′za•dak, with his fellow priests, and Ze•rub′ba•bel son of She•al′ti•el with his kin set out to build the altar of the God of Israel, to offer burnt offerings on it, as prescribed in the law of Moses the man of God. 3 They set up the altar on its foundation, because they were in dread of the neighboring peoples, and they offered burnt offerings upon it to the LORD, morning and evening. 4 And they kept the festival of booths,*c* as prescribed, and offered the daily burnt offerings by number according to the ordinance, as required for each day, 5 and after that the regular burnt offerings, the offerings at the new moon and at all the sacred festivals of the LORD, and the offerings of everyone who made a freewill offering to the LORD. 6 From the first day of the seventh month they began to offer burnt offerings to the LORD. But the foundation of the temple of the LORD was not yet laid. 7 So they gave money to the masons and the carpenters, and food, drink, and oil to the Sī•dō′ni•ans and the Tȳ′ri•ans to bring cedar trees from Lebanon to the sea, to Jop′pa, according to the grant that they had from King Cyrus of Persia.

Foundation Laid for the Temple

8 In the second year after their arrival at the house of God at Jerusalem, in the second month, Ze•rub′ba•bel son of She•al′ti•el and Jesh′ū•a son of Jō′za•dak made a beginning, together with the rest of their people, the priests and the Lē′vītes and all who had come to Jerusalem from the captivity. They appointed the Lē′vītes, from twenty years old and upward, to have the oversight of the work on

the house of the LORD. 9 And Jesh′ū•a with his sons and his kin, and Kad′mi•el and his sons, Bin′nū•i and Hod•a•vī′ah*d* along with the sons of Hen′a•dad, the Lē′vītes, their sons and kin, together took charge of the workers in the house of God.

10 When the builders laid the foundation of the temple of the LORD, the priests in their vestments were stationed to praise the LORD with trumpets, and the Lē′vītes, the sons of Ā′saph, with cymbals, according to the directions of King David of Israel; 11 and they sang responsively, praising and giving thanks to the LORD,

"For he is good,
  for his steadfast love endures forever toward
      Israel."

And all the people responded with a great shout when they praised the LORD, because the foundation of the house of the LORD was laid. 12 But many of the priests and Lē′vītes and heads of families, old people who had seen the first house on its foundations, wept with a loud voice when they saw this house, though many shouted aloud for joy, 13 so that the people could not distinguish

---

b 1 Esdras 5.46: Heb lacks *lived in Jerusalem and its vicinity*
c Or *tabernacles;* Heb *succoth*   *d* Compare 2.40; Neh 7.43;
1 Esdras 5.58: Heb *sons of Judah*

PRAY IT!
Holy Tears

Ezra 3.12 tells us that many of the older Israelites who remembered the first Temple wept at the grand celebration that marked its rebirth. Were they shedding tears of joy that the Temple was being built again? Or were they shedding tears of sorrow over what they had lost and never regained? Most likely, they were doing both.

Weeping can be a holy and healing part of life. Unfortunately, some people believe that strong men and women never cry. But tears are appropriate on many occasions: the loss of a dear friend or family member, a reconciliation with someone after a long separation, and the moment we recognize we have sinned and hurt someone deeply, to name a few. We should bring our tears to God in prayer. They will turn into holy tears as God's healing love enters our life.

▶ Ezra 3.10–13

EZRA

the sound of the joyful shout from the sound of the people's weeping, for the people shouted so loudly that the sound was heard far away.

Resistance to Rebuilding the Temple

4 When the adversaries of Judah and Benjamin heard that the returned exiles were building a temple to the LORD, the God of Israel, 2 they approached Ze·rub'ba·bel and the heads of families and said to them, "Let us build with you, for we worship your God as you do, and we have been sacrificing to him ever since the days of King Ē'sar-had'don of Assyria who brought us here." 3 But Ze·rub'ba·bel, Jesh'ū·a, and the rest of the heads of families in Israel said to them, "You shall have no part with us in building a house to our God; but we alone will build to the LORD, the God of Israel, as King Cyrus of Persia has commanded us."

4 Then the people of the land discouraged the people of Judah, and made them afraid to build, 5 and they bribed officials to frustrate their plan throughout the reign of King Cyrus of Persia and until the reign of King Da·rī'us of Persia.

Rebuilding of Jerusalem Opposed

6 In the reign of A·has·ū·ē'rus, in his accession year, they wrote an accusation against the inhabitants of Judah and Jerusalem.

7 And in the days of Ar·ta·xerx'ēs, Bish'lam and Mith're·dath and Tā'bē·el and the rest of their associates wrote to King Ar·ta·xerx'ēs of Persia; the letter was written in Ar·a·mā'ic and translated.[e] 8 Rē'hum the royal deputy and Shim'shaī the scribe wrote a letter against Jerusalem to King Ar·ta·xerx'ēs as follows 9 (then Rē'hum the royal deputy, Shim'shaī the scribe, and the rest of their associates, the judges, the envoys, the officials, the Persians, the people of Ē'rech, the Babylonians, the people of Su'sa, that is, the Ē'lam·ites, 10 and the rest of the nations whom the great and noble Os·nap'par deported and settled in the cities of Sa·mār'i·a and in the rest of the province Beyond the River wrote—and now 11 this is a copy of the letter that they sent):

"To King Ar·ta·xerx'ēs: Your servants, the people of the province Beyond the River, send greeting. And now 12 may it be known to the king that the Jews who came up from you to us have gone to Jerusalem. They are rebuilding that rebellious and wicked city; they are finishing the walls and repairing the foundations. 13 Now may it be known to the king that, if this city is rebuilt and the walls finished, they will not pay tribute, custom, or toll, and the royal revenue will be reduced. 14 Now because we share the salt of the palace and it is not fitting for us to witness the king's dishonor, therefore we send and inform the king, 15 so that a search may be made in the annals of your ancestors. You will

discover in the annals that this is a rebellious city, hurtful to kings and provinces, and that sedition was stirred up in it from long ago. On that account this city was laid waste. 16 We make known to the king that, if this city is rebuilt and its walls finished, you will then have no possession in the province Beyond the River."

17 The king sent an answer: "To Rē'hum the royal deputy and Shim'shaī the scribe and the rest of their associates who live in Sa·mār'i·a and in the rest of the province Beyond the River, greeting. And now 18 the letter that you sent to us has been read in translation before me. 19 So I made a decree, and someone searched and discovered that this city has risen against kings from long ago, and that rebellion and sedition have been made in it. 20 Jerusalem has had mighty kings who ruled over the whole province Beyond the River, to whom tribute, custom, and toll were paid. 21 Therefore issue an order that these people be made to cease, and that this city not be rebuilt, until I make a decree. 22 Moreover, take care not to be slack in this matter; why should damage grow to the hurt of the king?"

23 Then when the copy of King Ar·ta·xerx'ēs' letter was read before Rē'hum and the scribe Shim'shaī and their associates, they hurried to the Jews in Jerusalem and by force and power made them cease. 24 At that time the work on the house of God in

---

e Heb adds *in Aramaic*, indicating that 4.8—6.18 is in Aramaic. Another interpretation is *The letter was written in the Aramaic script and set forth in the Aramaic language*

Jerusalem stopped and was discontinued until the second year of the reign of King Da·rī'us of Persia.

Restoration of the Temple Resumed
(Hag 1.1; Zech 1.1)

5 Now the prophets, Hag'gai*f* and Zech·a·rī'ah son of Id'dō, prophesied to the Jews who were in Judah and Jerusalem, in the name of the God of Israel who was over them. 2 Then Ze·rub'-ba·bel son of She·al'ti·el and Jesh'ū·a son of Jō'za·dak set out to rebuild the house of God in Jerusalem; and with them were the prophets of God, helping them.

3 At the same time Tat'te·naī the governor of the province Beyond the River and Shĕ'thar-boz'e·naī and their associates came to them and spoke to them thus, "Who gave you a decree to build this house and to finish this structure?" 4 They*g* also asked them this, "What are the names of the men who are building this building?" 5 But the eye of their God was upon the elders of the Jews, and they did not stop them until a report reached Da·rī'us and then answer was returned by letter in reply to it.

6 The copy of the letter that Tat'te·naī the governor of the province Beyond the River and Shĕ'thar-boz'e·naī and his associates the envoys who were in the province Beyond the River sent to King Da·rī'us; 7 they sent him a report, in which was written as follows: "To Da·rī'us the king, all peace! 8 May it be known to the king that we went to the province of Judah, to the house of the great God. It is being built of hewn stone, and timber is laid in the walls; this work is being done diligently and prospers in their hands. 9 Then we spoke to those elders and asked them, 'Who gave you a decree to build this house and to finish this structure?' 10 We also asked them their names, for your information, so that we might write down the names of the men at their head. 11 This was their reply to us: 'We are the servants of the God of heaven and earth, and we are rebuilding the house that was built many years ago, which a great king of Israel built and finished. 12 But because our ancestors had angered the God of heaven, he gave them into the hand of King Ne·bū·chad·nez'zar of Babylon, the Chal·dē'an, who destroyed this house and carried away the

---

f Aram adds *the prophet*   *g* Gk Syr: Aram *We*

THE REBIRTH OF A NATION

Among the first things oppressive governments often do, historically speaking, is destroy or shut down religious establishments and make religious gatherings illegal. This is what happened to the Israelites taken into exile. But when oppressive governments can no longer hold the people down, when oppressive methods lose their grip, among the first things the people do is bring back religious establishments and religious gatherings. This is what the Israelites did upon return to their land.

The reopening of the Catholic Cathedral in Moscow, Russia, in December 1999, marked the symbolic end of Roman Catholic religious persecution in Russia. For over eighty years, radical socialist, Marxist, and communist political leaders persecuted almost all religious communities in Russia, especially Roman Catholics. Faith and religion were seen as not just unimportant but as unnecessary and unwanted, to say the least.

Russia now struggles to rise above those years of oppression, and not just the religious oppression but the social and economic oppression as well. Many see the reopening of the Catholic Cathedral as an important step toward rebuilding the wounded country and leading it out of its past woes.

Have you ever felt uncomfortable speaking about your beliefs in a group of people? What kinds of statements did people make that caused you to feel uncomfortable sharing your beliefs? How can you help to eliminate intolerance of this kind?

▶ Ezra, chapter 5

E
Z
R
A

people to Babylonia. 13 However, King Cyrus of Babylon, in the first year of his reign, made a decree that this house of God should be rebuilt. 14 Moreover, the gold and silver vessels of the house of God, which Ne•bu•chad•nez'zar had taken out of the temple in Jerusalem and had brought into the temple of Babylon, these King Cyrus took out of the temple of Babylon, and they were delivered to a man named Shesh•baz'zar, whom he had made governor. 15 He said to him, "Take these vessels; go and put them in the temple in Jerusalem, and let the house of God be rebuilt on its site." 16 Then this Shesh•baz'zar came and laid the foundations of the house of God in Jerusalem; and from that time until now it has been under construction, and it is not yet finished.' 17 And now, if it seems good to the king, have a search made in the royal archives there in Babylon, to see whether a decree was issued by King Cyrus for the rebuilding of this house of God in Jerusalem. Let the king send us his pleasure in this matter."

The Decree of Darius

6 Then King Da•ri'us made a decree, and they searched the archives where the documents were stored in Babylon. 2 But it was in Ec•bat'a•na, the capital in the province of Med'i•a, that a scroll was found on which this was written: "A record. 3 In the first year of his reign, King Cyrus issued a decree: Concerning the house of God at Jerusalem, let the house be rebuilt, the place where sacrifices are offered and burnt offerings are brought;*h* its height shall be sixty cubits and its width sixty cubits, 4 with three courses of hewn stones and one course of timber; let the cost be paid from the royal treasury. 5 Moreover, let the gold and silver vessels of the house of God, which Ne•bu•chad•nez'zar took out of the temple in Jerusalem and brought to Babylon, be restored and brought back to the temple in Jerusalem, each to its place; you shall put them in the house of God."

6 "Now you, Tat'te•nai, governor of the province Beyond the River, She'thar-boz'e•nai, and you, their associates, the envoys in the province Beyond the River, keep away; 7 let the work on this house of God alone; let the governor of the Jews and the elders of the Jews rebuild this house of God on its site. 8 Moreover I make a decree regarding what you shall do for these elders of the Jews for the rebuilding of this house of God: the cost is to be paid to these people, in full and without delay, from the royal revenue, the tribute of the province Beyond the River. 9 Whatever is needed—young bulls, rams, or sheep for burnt offerings to the God of heaven, wheat, salt, wine, or oil, as the priests in Jerusalem require—let that be given to them day by day without fail, 10 so that they may offer pleas-

ing sacrifices to the God of heaven, and pray for the life of the king and his children. 11 Furthermore I decree that if anyone alters this edict, a beam shall be pulled out of the house of the perpetrator, who then shall be impaled on it. The house shall be made a dunghill. 12 May the God who has established his name there overthrow any king or people that shall put forth a hand to alter this, or to destroy this house of God in Jerusalem. I, Da•ri'us, make a decree; let it be done with all diligence."

Completion and Dedication of the Temple

13 Then, according to the word sent by King Da•ri'us, Tat'te•nai, the governor of the province Beyond the River, She'thar-boz'e•nai, and their associates did with all diligence what King Da•ri'us had ordered. 14 So the elders of the Jews built and prospered, through the prophesying of the prophet Hag'gai and Zech•a•ri'ah son of Id'do. They finished their building by command of the God of Israel and by decree of Cyrus, Da•ri'us, and King Ar•ta•xerx'es of Persia; 15 and this house was finished on the third day of the month of A'dar, in the sixth year of the reign of King Da•ri'us.

16 The people of Israel, the priests and the Le'vites, and the rest of the returned exiles, celebrated the dedication of this house of God with joy. 17 They offered at the dedication of this house of God one hundred bulls, two hundred rams, four hundred lambs, and as a sin offering for all Israel, twelve male goats, according to the number of the tribes of Israel. 18 Then they set the priests in their divisions and the Le'vites in their courses for the service of God at Jerusalem, as it is written in the book of Moses.

The Passover Celebrated
(Cp Deut 16.1–8)

19 On the fourteenth day of the first month the returned exiles kept the passover. 20 For both the priests and the Le'vites had purified themselves; all of them were clean. So they killed the passover lamb for all the returned exiles, for their fellow priests, and for themselves. 21 It was eaten by the people of Israel who had returned from exile, and also by all who had joined them and separated themselves from the pollutions of the nations of the land to worship the LORD, the God of Israel. 22 With joy they celebrated the festival of unleavened bread seven days; for the LORD had made them joyful, and had turned the heart of the king of Assyria to them, so that he aided them in the work on the house of God, the God of Israel.

---

h Meaning of Aram uncertain

The Coming and Work of Ezra

7 After this, in the reign of King Ar·ta·xerx′ēs of Persia, Ezra son of Se·rāi′ah, son of Az·a·rī′ah, son of Hil·kī′ah, ² son of Shal′lum, son of Zā′dok, son of A·hī′tub, ³ son of Am·a·rī′ah, son of Az·a·rī′ah, son of Me·rā′i·oth, ⁴ son of Zer·a·hī′ah, son of Uz′zī, son of Buk′kī, ⁵ son of Ab·i·shū′a, son of Phin′e·has, son of El·e·ā′zar, son of the chief priest Aaron— ⁶ this Ezra went up from Babylonia. He was a scribe skilled in the law of Moses that the LORD the God of Israel had given; and the king granted him all that he asked, for the hand of the LORD his God was upon him.

7 Some of the people of Israel, and some of the priests and Lē′vītes, the singers and gatekeepers, and the temple servants also went up to Jerusalem, in the seventh year of King Ar·ta·xerx′ēs. ⁸ They came to Jerusalem in the fifth month, which was in the seventh year of the king. ⁹ On the first day of the first month the journey up from Babylon was begun, and on the first day of the fifth month he came to Jerusalem, for the gracious hand of his God was upon him. ¹⁰ For Ezra had set his heart to study the law of the LORD, and to do it, and to teach the statutes and ordinances in Israel.

The Letter of Artaxerxes to Ezra

11 This is a copy of the letter that King Ar·ta·xerx′ēs gave to the priest Ezra, the scribe, a scholar of the text of the commandments of the LORD and his statutes for Israel: ¹² "Ar·ta·xerx′ēs, king of kings, to the priest Ezra, the scribe of the law of the God of heaven: Peace.ⁱ And now ¹³ I decree that any of the people of Israel or their priests or Lē′vītes in my kingdom who freely offers to go to Jerusalem may go with you. ¹⁴ For you are sent by the king and his seven counselors to make inquiries about Judah and Jerusalem according to the law of your God, which is in your hand, ¹⁵ and also to convey the silver and gold that the king and his counselors have freely offered to the God of Israel, whose dwelling is in Jerusalem, ¹⁶ with all the silver and gold that you shall find in the whole province of Babylonia, and with the freewill offerings of the people and the priests, given willingly for the house of their God in Jerusalem. ¹⁷ With this money, then, you shall with all diligence buy bulls, rams, and lambs, and their grain offerings and their drink offerings, and you shall offer them on the altar of the house of your God in Jerusalem. ¹⁸ Whatever seems good to you and your colleagues to do with the rest of the silver and gold, you may do, according to the will of your God. ¹⁹ The vessels that have been given you for the service of the house of your God, you shall deliver before the God of Jerusalem. ²⁰ And whatever else is required for the house of your God, which you are responsible for providing, you may provide out of the king's treasury.

21 "I, King Ar·ta·xerx′ēs, decree to all the treasurers in the province Beyond the River: Whatever the priest Ezra, the scribe of the law of the God of heaven, requires of you, let it be done with all diligence, ²² up to one hundred talents of silver, one hundred cors of wheat, one hundred bathsʲ of wine, one hundred bathsʲ of oil, and unlimited salt. ²³ Whatever is commanded by the God of heaven, let it be done with zeal for the house of the God of heaven, or wrath will come upon the realm of the king and his heirs. ²⁴ We also notify you that it shall not be lawful to impose tribute, custom, or toll on any of the priests, the Lē′vītes, the singers, the door-keepers, the temple servants, or other servants of this house of God.

25 "And you, Ezra, according to the God-given wisdom you possess, appoint magistrates and judges who may judge all the people in the province Beyond the River who know the laws of your God; and you shall teach those who do not know them. ²⁶ All who will not obey the law of your God and the law of the king, let judgment be strictly executed on them, whether for death or for banishment or for confiscation of their goods or for imprisonment."

27 Blessed be the LORD, the God of our ancestors, who put such a thing as this into the heart of the king to glorify the house of the LORD in Jerusalem, ²⁸ and who extended to me steadfast love before the king and his counselors, and before all the king's mighty officers. I took courage, for the hand of the LORD my God was upon me, and I gathered leaders from Israel to go up with me.

Heads of Families Who Returned with Ezra

8 These are their family heads, and this is the genealogy of those who went up with me from Babylonia, in the reign of King Ar·ta·xerx′ēs: ² Of the descendants of Phin′e·has, Ger′shom. Of Ith′a·mar, Daniel. Of David, Hat′tush, ³ of the descendants of Shec·a·nī′ah. Of Pā′rosh, Zech·a·rī′ah, with whom were registered one hundred fifty males. ⁴ Of the descendants of Pā′hath-mō′ab, El·i·ē·hō·ē′nai son of Zer·a·hī′ah, and with him two hundred males. ⁵ Of the descendants of Zat′tū,ᵏ Shec·a·nī′ah son of Ja·hā′zi·el, and with him three hundred males. ⁶ Of the descendants of Ā′din, Ē′bed son of Jonathan, and with him fifty males. ⁷ Of the descendants of Ē′lam, Je·shā′i·ah son of Ath·a·lī′ah, and with him seventy males. ⁸ Of the descendants of Sheph·a·tī′ah, Zeb·a·dī′ah son of Michael, and with him eighty males. ⁹ Of the descendants of Jō′ab, Ō·ba·dī′ah son of Je·hī′el, and with him two hundred eighteen males. ¹⁰ Of the

---

ⁱ Syr Vg 1 Esdras 8.9: Aram *Perfect*   ʲ A Heb measure of volume   ᵏ Gk 1 Esdras 8.32: Heb lacks *of Zattu* descendants of Bā'nī,[l] She•lō'mith son of Jos•i•phī'-ah, and with him one hundred sixty males. 11 Of the descendants of Bē'baī, Zech•a•rī'ah son of Bē'baī, and with him twenty-eight males. 12 Of the descendants of Az'gad, Jō•hā'nan son of Hak'ka•tan, and with him one hundred ten males. 13 Of the descendants of Ad•o•nī'kam, those who came later, their names being E•liph'e•let, Je•ū'el, and She•māi'ah, and with them sixty males. 14 Of the descendants of Big'vaī, Ū'thaī and Zac'cur, and with them seventy males.

Servants for the Temple

15 I gathered them by the river that runs to A•hā'va, and there we camped three days. As I reviewed the people and the priests, I found there none of the descendants of Levi. 16 Then I sent for El•i•ē'zer, Ar'i•el, She•māi'ah, El•nā'than, Jā'rib, El•nā'than, Nathan, Zech•a•rī'ah, and Me•shul'lam, who were leaders, and for Joi'a•rib and El•nā'than, who were wise, 17 and sent them to Id'dō, the leader at the place called Cas•i•phī'a, telling them what to say to Id'dō and his colleagues the temple servants at Cas•i•phī'a, namely, to send us ministers for the house of our God. 18 Since the gracious hand of our God was upon us, they brought us a man of discretion, of the descendants of Mah'lī son of Levi son of Israel, namely Sher•e•bī'ah, with his sons and kin, eighteen; 19 also Hash•a•bī'ah and with him Je•shā'i•ah of the descendants of Me•rar'ī, with his kin and their sons, twenty; 20 besides two hundred twenty of the temple servants, whom David and his officials had set apart to attend the Lē'vītes. These were all mentioned by name.

Fasting and Prayer for Protection

21 Then I proclaimed a fast there, at the river A•hā'va, that we might deny ourselves[m] before our God, to seek from him a safe journey for ourselves, our children, and all our possessions. 22 For I was ashamed to ask the king for a band of soldiers and cavalry to protect us against the enemy on our way, since we had told the king that the hand of our God is gracious to all who seek him, but his power and his wrath are against all who forsake him. 23 So we fasted and petitioned our God for this, and he listened to our entreaty.

Gifts for the Temple

24 Then I set apart twelve of the leading priests: Sher•e•bī'ah, Hash•a•bī'ah, and ten of their kin with them. 25 And I weighed out to them the silver and the gold and the vessels, the offering for the house of our God that the king, his counselors, his lords, and all Israel there present had offered; 26 I weighed out into their hand six hundred fifty talents of silver, and one hundred silver vessels worth . . . talents,[n] and one hundred talents of gold, 27 twenty gold bowls worth a thousand darics, and two vessels of fine polished bronze as precious as gold. 28 And I said to them, "You are holy to the LORD, and the vessels are holy; and the silver and the gold are a freewill offering to the LORD, the God of your ancestors. 29 Guard them and keep them until you weigh them before the chief priests and the Lē'vītes and the heads of families in Israel at Jerusalem, within the chambers of the house of the LORD." 30 So the priests and the Lē'vītes took over the silver, the gold, and the vessels as they were weighed out, to bring them to Jerusalem, to the house of our God.

The Return to Jerusalem

31 Then we left the river A•hā'va on the twelfth day of the first month, to go to Jerusalem; the hand of our God was upon us, and he delivered us from the hand of the enemy and from ambushes along the way. 32 We came to Jerusalem and remained there three days. 33 On the fourth day, within the house of our God, the silver, the gold, and the vessels were weighed into the hands of the priest Mer'e•moth son of Ū•rī'ah, and with him was El•ē•ā'zar son of Phin'e•has, and with them were the Lē'vītes, Joz'a•bad son of Jesh'ū•a and Nō•a•dī'ah son of Bin'nū•ī. 34 The total was counted and weighed, and the weight of everything was recorded.

35 At that time those who had come from captivity, the returned exiles, offered burnt offerings to the God of Israel, twelve bulls for all Israel, ninety-six rams, seventy-seven lambs, and as a sin offering twelve male goats; all this was a burnt offering to the LORD. 36 They also delivered the king's commissions to the king's satraps and to the governors of the province Beyond the River; and they supported the people and the house of God.

Denunciation of Mixed Marriages

9 After these things had been done, the officials approached me and said, "The people of Israel, the priests, and the Lē'vītes have not separated themselves from the peoples of the lands with their abominations, from the Cā'naan•ītes, the Hit'tītes, the Per'iz•zītes, the Jeb'ū•sītes, the Am'mon•ītes, the Mō'ab•ītes, the Egyptians, and the Am'o•rītes. 2 For they have taken some of their daughters as wives for themselves and for their sons. Thus the holy seed has mixed itself with the peoples of the lands, and in this faithlessness the officials and leaders have led the way." 3 When I heard this, I tore my garment and my mantle, and pulled hair from my head and beard, and sat appalled. 4 Then all who trembled at the words of the God of Israel, because

---

[l] Gk 1 Esdras 8.36: Heb lacks Bani   [m] Or might fast   [n] The number of talents is lacking

of the faithlessness of the returned exiles, gathered around me while I sat appalled until the evening sacrifice.

Ezra's Prayer

5 At the evening sacrifice I got up from my fasting, with my garments and my mantle torn, and fell on my knees, spread out my hands to the LORD my God, 6 and said,

"O my God, I am too ashamed and embarrassed to lift my face to you, my God, for our iniquities have risen higher than our heads, and our guilt has mounted up to the heavens. 7 From the days of our ancestors to this day we have been deep in guilt, and for our iniquities we, our kings, and our priests have been handed over to the kings of the lands, to the sword, to captivity, to plundering, and to utter shame, as is now the case. 8 But now for a brief moment favor has been shown by the LORD our God, who has left us a remnant, and given us a stake in his holy place, in order that he[o] may brighten our eyes and grant us a little sustenance in our slavery. 9 For we are slaves; yet our God has not forsaken us in our slavery, but has extended to us his steadfast love before the kings of Persia, to give us new life to set up the house of our God, to repair its ruins, and to give us a wall in Judea and Jerusalem.

10 "And now, our God, what shall we say after this? For we have forsaken your commandments, 11 which you commanded by your servants the prophets, saying, 'The land that you are entering to possess is a land unclean with the pollutions of the peoples of the lands, with their abominations. They have filled it from end to end with their uncleanness. 12 Therefore do not give your daughters to their sons, neither take their daughters for your sons, and never seek their peace or prosperity, so that you may be strong and eat the good of the land and leave it for an inheritance to your children forever.' 13 After all that has come upon us for our evil deeds and for our great guilt, seeing that you, our God, have punished us less than our iniquities deserved and have given us such a remnant as this, 14 shall we break your commandments again and intermarry with the peoples who practice these abominations? Would you not be angry with us until you destroy us without remnant or survivor? 15 O LORD, God of Israel, you are just, but we have escaped as a remnant, as is now the case. Here we are before you in our guilt, though no one can face you because of this."

The People's Response

10 While Ezra prayed and made confession, weeping and throwing himself down before the house of God, a very great assembly of men, women, and children gathered to him out of Israel; the people also wept bitterly. 2 Shec·a·ni'ah son of Je·hi'el, of the descendants of E'lam, addressed Ezra, saying, "We have broken faith with our God and have married foreign women from the peoples of the land, but even now there is hope for Israel in spite of this. 3 So now let us make a covenant with our God to send away all these wives and their children, according to the counsel of my lord and of those who tremble at the commandment of our God; and let it be done according to the law. 4 Take action, for it is your duty, and we are with you; be strong, and do it." 5 Then Ezra stood up and made the leading priests, the Le'vites, and all Israel swear that they would do as had been said. So they swore.

---

[o] Heb *our God*

Who Belongs, and Who Does Not?   LIVE IT!

In Ezra, chapters 9–10, Ezra tells the people to reject their foreign wives and children. Nehemiah does the same in Neh 13.23–27. This probably strikes us as harsh, but we can try to understand the Israelites' situation. Only a remnant of the Israelites was left to re-establish Israel's identity. History had taught the Israelites that intermarriage led to a watering down of their faith and of the people's loyalty to their religious practices. The only way to survive as a people was to separate themselves from outsiders.

This separation led to an even greater animosity between the Jews from Judah and their cousins in faith, the Samaritans. We see some of this prejudice in the Gospels (see Jn 4.1–42 and "Discrimination in Jesus' Time," Lk 10.25–37). Christians have had similar separations throughout our history. Today, the church teaches us to be faithful to our beliefs but also to be open to others who believe differently and discover together what we have in common.

▸ **Ezra, chapters 9–10**

Foreign Wives and Their Children Rejected

6 Then Ezra withdrew from before the house of God, and went to the chamber of Jē•hō•hā'nan son of E•lī'a•shib, where he spent the night.*p* He did not eat bread or drink water, for he was mourning over the faithlessness of the exiles. 7 They made a proclamation throughout Judah and Jerusalem to all the returned exiles that they should assemble at Jerusalem, 8 and that if any did not come within three days, by order of the officials and the elders all their property should be forfeited, and they themselves banned from the congregation of the exiles.

9 Then all the people of Judah and Benjamin assembled at Jerusalem within the three days; it was the ninth month, on the twentieth day of the month. All the people sat in the open square before the house of God, trembling because of this matter and because of the heavy rain. 10 Then Ezra the priest stood up and said to them, "You have trespassed and married foreign women, and so increased the guilt of Israel. 11 Now make confession to the LORD the God of your ancestors, and do his will; separate yourselves from the peoples of the land and from the foreign wives." 12 Then all the assembly answered with a loud voice, "It is so; we must do as you have said. 13 But the people are many, and it is a time of heavy rain; we cannot stand in the open. Nor is this a task for one day or for two, for many of us have transgressed in this matter. 14 Let our officials represent the whole assembly, and let all in our towns who have taken foreign wives come at appointed times, and with them the elders and judges of every town, until the fierce wrath of our God on this account is averted from us." 15 Only Jonathan son of As'a•hel and Jahzēi'ah son of Tik'vah opposed this, and Me•shul'lam and Shab'be•thai the Lē'vites supported them.

16 Then the returned exiles did so. Ezra the priest selected men,*q* heads of families, according to their families, each of them designated by name. On the first day of the tenth month they sat down to examine the matter. 17 By the first day of the first month they had come to the end of all the men who had married foreign women.

18 There were found of the descendants of the priests who had married foreign women, of the descendants of Jesh'ū•a son of Jō'za•dak and his brothers: Mā•a•sēi'ah, El•i•ē'zer, Jā'rib, and Ged•a•li'ah. 19 They pledged themselves to send away their wives, and their guilt offering was a ram of the flock for their guilt. 20 Of the descendants of Im'mer: Ha•nā'nī and Zeb•a•dī'ah. 21 Of the descendants of Hā'rim: Mā•a•sēi'ah, E•lī'jah, She•māi'ah, Je•hī'el, and Uz•zī'ah. 22 Of the descendants of Pash'hur: El•i•ō•ē'nai, Mā•a•sēi'ah, Ish'ma•el, Ne•than'el, Joz'a•bad, and El•ā'sah.

23 Of the Lē'vites: Joz'a•bad, Shim'ē•ī, Ke•lāi'ah (that is, Ke•lī'ta), Peth•a•hī'ah, Judah, and El•i•ē'zer. 24 Of the singers: E•lī'a•shib. Of the gatekeepers: Shal'lum, Tē'lem, and Ū'rī.

25 And of Israel: of the descendants of Pā'rosh: Ra•mī'ah, Iz•zī'ah, Mal•chī'jah, Mij'a•min, El•ē•ā'zar, Hash•a•bī'ah,*r* and Be•nā'i•ah. 26 Of the descendants of Ē'lam: Mat•ta•nī'ah, Zech•a•rī'ah, Je•hī'el, Ab'dī, Jer'e•moth, and E•lī'jah. 27 Of the descendants of Zat'tū: El•i•ō•ē'nai, E•lī'a•shib, Mat•ta•nī'ah, Jer'e•moth, Zā'bad, and A•zī'za. 28 Of the descendants of Bē'bai: Jē•hō•hā'nan, Han•a•nī'ah, Zab'bai, and Ath'lai. 29 Of the descendants of Bā'nī: Me•shul'lam, Mal'luch, A•dāi'ah, Jash'ub, Shē'al, and Jer'e•moth. 30 Of the descendants of Pā'hath-mō'ab: Ad'na, Chē'lal, Be•nā'i•ah, Mā•a•sēi'ah, Mat•ta•nī'ah, Bez'a•lel, Bin'nū•ī, and Ma•nas'seh. 31 Of the descendants of Hā'rim: El•i•ē'zer, Is•shī'jah, Mal•chī'jah, She•māi'ah, Shim'ē•on, 32 Benjamin, Mal'luch, and Shem•a•rī'ah. 33 Of the descendants of Hā'shum: Mat•tē'nai, Mat•tat'tah, Zā'bad, E•liph'e•let, Jer'e•mai, Ma•nas'seh, and Shim'ē•ī. 34 Of the descendants of Bā'nī: Mā•a•dā'ī, Am'ram, Ū'el, 35 Be•nā'i•ah, Bē•dēi'ah, Chel'ū•hi, 36 Va•nī'ah, Mer'e•moth, E•lī'a•shib, 37 Mat•ta•nī'ah, Mat•tē'nai, and Jā•a'sū. 38 Of the descendants of Bin'nū•ī:*s* Shim'ē•ī, 39 Shel•e•mī'ah, Nathan, A•dāi'ah, 40 Machnad'e•bai, Shā'shai, Shā'rai, 41 Az'a•rel, Shel•e•mī'ah, Shem•a•rī'ah, 42 Shal'lum, Am•a•rī'ah, and Joseph. 43 Of the descendants of Nē'bō: Je•ī'el, Mat•ti•thī'ah, Zā'bad, Ze•bī'na, Jad'dai, Jō'el, and Be•nā'i•ah. 44 All these had married foreign women, and they sent them away with their children.*t*

---

p 1 Esdras 9.2: Heb *where he went*   *q* 1 Esdras 9.16: Syr: Heb *And there were selected Ezra,*   *r* 1 Esdras 9.26 Gk: Heb *Malchijah*   *s* Gk: Heb *Bani, Binnui*   *t* 1 Esdras 9.36; meaning of Heb uncertain

Nehemiah

For background on this book, see the introduction to Ezra and Nehemiah.

Nehemiah Prays for His People

1 The words of Nĕ•he•mī'ah son of Hac•a•lī'ah. In the month of Chis'lev, in the twentieth year, while I was in Su'sa the capital, 2 one of my brothers, Ha•nā'ni, came with certain men from Judah; and I asked them about the Jews that survived, those who had escaped the captivity, and about Jerusalem. 3 They replied, "The survivors there in the province who escaped captivity are in great trouble and shame; the wall of Jerusalem is broken down, and its gates have been destroyed by fire."

4 When I heard these words I sat down and wept, and mourned for days, fasting and praying before the God of heaven. 5 I said, "O LORD God of heaven, the great and awesome God who keeps covenant and steadfast love with those who love him and keep his commandments; 6 let your ear be attentive and your eyes open to hear the prayer of your servant that I now pray before you day and night for your servants, the people of Israel, confessing the sins of the people of Israel, which we have sinned against you. Both I and my family have sinned. 7 We have offended you deeply, failing to keep the commandments, the statutes, and the ordinances that you commanded your servant Moses. 8 Remember the word that you commanded your servant Moses, 'If you are unfaithful, I will scatter you among the peoples; 9 but if you return to me and keep my commandments and do them, though your outcasts are under the farthest skies, I will gather them from there and bring them to the place at which I have chosen to establish my name.' 10 They are your servants and your people, whom you redeemed by your great power and your strong hand. 11 O Lord, let your ear be attentive to the prayer of your servant, and to the prayer of your servants who delight in revering your name. Give success to your servant today, and grant him mercy in the sight of this man!"

At the time, I was cupbearer to the king.

Nehemiah Sent to Judah

2 In the month of Nī'san, in the twentieth year of King Ar•ta•xerx'ēs, when wine was served him, I carried the wine and gave it to the king. Now, I had never been sad in his presence before. 2 So the king said to me, "Why is your face sad, since you are not sick? This can only be sadness of the heart." Then I was very much afraid. 3 I said to the king, "May the king live forever! Why should my face not be sad, when the city, the place of my ancestors' graves, lies waste, and its gates have been destroyed by fire?" 4 Then the king said to me, "What do you request?" So I prayed to the God of heaven. 5 Then I said to the king, "If it pleases the king, and if your servant has found favor with you, I ask that you send me to Judah, to the city of my ancestors' graves, so that I may rebuild it." 6 The king said to me (the queen also was sitting beside him), "How long will you be gone, and when will you return?"

447

PRAY IT!

Nehemiah Prepares for Action

Do you ever hear the news and think, Why bother trying to make the world a better place? Christians are called to social action—action for justice, action to make the world a better place. But social sin can scare Christians away from social action. Social sin—such as poverty, racism, violence, materialism, and indifference—seems too big for any individual to do much about. In the overwhelming face of social sin, it is easy to say, "I give up."

But then we have Nehemiah's example. When Nehemiah heard of the results of Israel's collective sin, he could have said, "I give up." Instead, he turned to God in fasting and prayer. Fasting and prayer help us focus on what is important. Fasting and prayer help us remember that God calls us only to be faithful in taking action. Let God worry about the results.

In your prayer, reflect or journal on the following questions:

- What social issue are you concerned about?
- What can you fast from to help yourself gain a new perspective on that issue? (You can fast from many things: food, television, a particular activity, a particular place.)
- What group can you get involved with to address this concern?
- What do you need to bring to God in prayer?

▶ Nehemiah, chapter 1

So it pleased the king to send me, and I set him a date. 7 Then I said to the king, "If it pleases the king, let letters be given me to the governors of the province Beyond the River, that they may grant me passage until I arrive in Judah; 8 and a letter to Ā′saph, the keeper of the king's forest, directing him to give me timber to make beams for the gates of the temple fortress, and for the wall of the city, and for the house that I shall occupy." And the king granted me what I asked, for the gracious hand of my God was upon me.

9 Then I came to the governors of the province Beyond the River, and gave them the king's letters. Now the king had sent officers of the army and cavalry with me. 10 When San•bal′lat the Hor′o•nite and Tō•bi′ah the Am′mon•ite official heard this, it displeased them greatly that someone had come to seek the welfare of the people of Israel.

Nehemiah's Inspection of the Walls

11 So I came to Jerusalem and was there for three days. 12 Then I got up during the night, I and a few men with me; I told no one what my God had put into my heart to do for Jerusalem. The only animal I took was the animal I rode. 13 I went out by night by the Valley Gate past the Dragon's Spring and to the Dung Gate, and I inspected the walls of Jerusalem that had been broken down and its gates that had been destroyed by fire. 14 Then I went on to the Fountain Gate and to the King's Pool; but there was no place for the animal I was riding to continue. 15 So I went up by way of the valley by night and inspected the wall. Then I turned back and entered by the Valley Gate, and so returned. 16 The officials did not know where I had gone or what I was doing; I had not yet told the Jews, the priests, the nobles, the officials, and the rest that were to do the work.

Decision to Restore the Walls

17 Then I said to them, "You see the trouble we are in, how Jerusalem lies in ruins with its gates burned. Come, let us rebuild the wall of Jerusalem, so that we may no longer suffer disgrace." 18 I told them that the hand of my God had been gracious upon me, and also the words that the king had spoken to me. Then they said, "Let us start building!" So they committed themselves to the common good. 19 But when San•bal′lat the Hor′o•nite and Tō•bi′ah the Am′mon•ite official, and Gē′shem the A′rab heard of it, they mocked and ridiculed us, saying, "What is this that you are doing? Are you rebelling against the king?" 20 Then I replied to them, "The God of heaven is the one who will give us success, and we his servants are going to start building; but you have no share or claim or historic right in Jerusalem."

Organization of the Work

3 Then the high priest E•li′a•shib set to work with his fellow priests and rebuilt the Sheep Gate. They consecrated it and set up its doors; they consecrated it as far as the Tower of the Hundred and as far as the Tower of Ha•nan′el. 2 And the men of Jericho built next to him. And next to them*a* Zac′cur son of Im′ri built.

---

a Heb *him*

did you KNOW?

Rebuilding Hiroshima

You may have heard the term *Ground Zero* used in reference to the sites of many recent disasters that have occurred in our world, especially in reference to the site of the twin towers at the former World Trade Center in the United States. The term was originally used in reference to the site in Hiroshima, Japan, where the first atomic bomb was dropped on a civilian population, on August 6, 1945.

Luckily, our world has not seen the destructive power that a nuclear weapon would cause if dropped on a populated area. Sadly, we do know what the A-bomb, as it is often called, can do. It flattened a major city with an incredible heat and wind that melted and destroyed objects and people within 1.5 miles of its epicenter.

Although the effects of the A-bomb were catastrophic, the blast did not wipe out the human spirit. Since that day, citizens of Hiroshima have been recovering and rebuilding, first by burying the dead, then by rebuilding homes, stores, churches, and temples. Today, Hiroshima is a thriving city of one million people. The destruction and rebuilding of Hiroshima are probably best summarized in this haiku, written by Yasuhiko Shigemoto, who was a teenager when the bomb hit:

How freely
butterflies are flying about
in the A-bomb Dome!
("My Haiku of Hiroshima")

▶ Neh 2.17–18

3 The sons of Has•se•nā'ah built the Fish Gate; they laid its beams and set up its doors, its bolts, and its bars. 4 Next to them Mer'e•moth son of Ū•rī'ah son of Hak'koz made repairs. Next to them Me•shul'lam son of Ber•e•chī'ah son of Me•shez'-a•bel made repairs. Next to them Zā'dok son of Bā'a•na made repairs. 5 Next to them the Te•kō'ites made repairs; but their nobles would not put their shoulders to the work of their Lord.*b*

6 Joi'a•da son of Pa•sē'ah and Me•shul'lam son of Bes•o•dēi'ah repaired the Old Gate; they laid its beams and set up its doors, its bolts, and its bars. 7 Next to them repairs were made by Me•la•tī'ah the Gib'ē•on•īte and Jā'don the Me•ron'o•thīte—the men of Gib'ē•on and of Miz'pah—who were under the jurisdiction of*c* the governor of the province Beyond the River. 8 Next to them Uz'zi•el son of Har•haī'ah, one of the goldsmiths, made repairs. Next to him Han•a•nī'ah, one of the perfumers, made repairs; and they restored Jerusalem as far as the Broad Wall. 9 Next to them Reph•āi'ah son of Hur, ruler of half the district of*d* Jerusalem, made repairs. 10 Next to them Je•daī'ah son of Har•ū'-maph made repairs opposite his house; and next to him Hat'tush son of Hash•ab•neī'ah made repairs. 11 Mal•chī'jah son of Hā'rim and Has'shub son of Pā'hath-mō'ab repaired another section and the Tower of the Ovens. 12 Next to him Shal'lum son of Hal•lō'hesh, ruler of half the district of*d* Jerusalem, made repairs, he and his daughters.

13 Hā'nun and the inhabitants of Za•nō'ah repaired the Valley Gate; they rebuilt it and set up its doors, its bolts, and its bars, and repaired a thousand cubits of the wall, as far as the Dung Gate.

14 Mal•chī'jah son of Rē'chab, ruler of the district of*e* Beth-hac•chē'rem, repaired the Dung Gate; he rebuilt it and set up its doors, its bolts, and its bars.

15 And Shal'lum son of Col-hō'zeh, ruler of the district of*e* Miz'pah, repaired the Fountain Gate; he rebuilt it and covered it and set up its doors, its bolts, and its bars; and he built the wall of the Pool of Shē'lah of the king's garden, as far as the stairs that go down from the City of David. 16 After him Nē•he•mī'ah son of Az'buk, ruler of half the district of*d* Beth-zur, repaired from a point opposite the graves of David, as far as the artificial pool and the house of the warriors. 17 After him the Lē'vites made repairs: Rē'hum son of Bā'nī; next to him Hash•a•bī'ah, ruler of half the district of*d* Kē•ī'lah, made repairs for his district. 18 After him their kin made repairs: Bin'nū•ī,*f* son of Hen'a•dad, ruler of half the district of*d* Kē•ī'lah; 19 next to him Ē'zer son of Jesh'ū•a, ruler*g* of Miz'pah, repaired another section opposite the ascent to the armory at the Angle. 20 After him Bar'uch son of Zab'baī repaired another section from the Angle to the door of the house of the high priest E•lī'a•shib. 21 After him Mer'e•moth son of Ū•rī'ah son of Hak'koz repaired another section from the door of the house of E•lī'a•shib to the end of the house of E•lī'a•shib. 22 After him the priests, the men of the surrounding area, made repairs.

N
E
H

---

b Or *lords*   *c* Meaning of Heb uncertain   *d* Or *supervisor of half the portion assigned to*   *e* Or *supervisor of the portion assigned to*   *f* Gk Syr Compare verse 24, 10.9: Heb *Bavvai*   *g* Or *supervisor*

Nehemiah's Strength

Many young people have traumatic experiences, such as the divorce of their parents, domestic and community violence, the death of a parent or sibling, prejudice, and poverty. Some young people come through these experiences as victims, unable to take any control of their life. Others take the attitude If you can't beat them, join them, and become cynical, violent, or antisocial. But some rise above their hurt to live a happy and healthy life. What can account for the difference in people's reactions?

Perhaps Nehemiah provides a clue. He was confronted by cynical people (Neh 4.2–3) and violent people (4.7–9). But he trusted in something bigger than himself. "The God of heaven is the one who will give us success" (2.20), he proclaimed to those with negative attitudes.

Prayer and faith in God gave Nehemiah strength to take action in difficult times. They can work for us too. Don't let life's traumas make you powerless. Don't let them make you cynical and part of the problem. Pray and have faith, and you too will have the strength to meet your problems with action.

▸ **Nehemiah, chapter 4**

23 After them Benjamin and Has'shub made repairs opposite their house. After them Az·a·rī'ah son of Mā·a·sēī'ah son of An·a·nī'ah made repairs beside his own house. 24 After him Bin'nū·ī son of Hen'a·dad repaired another section, from the house of Az·a·rī'ah to the Angle and to the corner. 25 Pā'lal son of Ū'zaī repaired opposite the Angle and the tower projecting from the upper house of the king at the court of the guard. After him Pe·dāi'ah son of Pā'rosh 26 and the temple servants living^h on Ō'phel made repairs up to a point opposite the Water Gate on the east and the projecting tower. 27 After him the Te·kō'ītes repaired another section opposite the great projecting tower as far as the wall of Ō'phel.

28 Above the Horse Gate the priests made repairs, each one opposite his own house. 29 After them Zā'dok son of Im'mer made repairs opposite his own house. After him She·māi'ah son of Shec·a·nī'ah, the keeper of the East Gate, made repairs. 30 After him Han·a·nī'ah son of Shel·e·mī'ah and Hā'nun sixth son of Zā'laph repaired another section. After him Me·shul'lam son of Ber·e·chī'ah made repairs opposite his living quarters. 31 After him Mal·chī'jah, one of the goldsmiths, made repairs as far as the house of the temple servants and of the merchants, opposite the Muster Gate,^{i} and to the upper room of the corner. 32 And between the upper room of the corner and the Sheep Gate the goldsmiths and the merchants made repairs.

Hostile Plots Thwarted

4 ^{j} Now when San·bal'lat heard that we were building the wall, he was angry and greatly enraged, and he mocked the Jews. 2 He said in the presence of his associates and of the army of Sa·mār'i·a, "What are these feeble Jews doing? Will they restore things? Will they sacrifice? Will they finish it in a day? Will they revive the stones out of the heaps of rubbish—and burned ones at that?" 3 Tō·bī'ah the Am'mon·ite was beside him, and he said, "That stone wall they are building—any fox going up on it would break it down!" 4 Hear, O our God, for we are despised; turn their taunt back on their own heads, and give them over as plunder in a land of captivity. 5 Do not cover their guilt, and do not let their sin be blotted out from your sight; for they have hurled insults in the face of the builders.

6 So we rebuilt the wall, and all the wall was joined together to half its height; for the people had a mind to work.

7^k But when San·bal'lat and Tō·bī'ah and the Arabs and the Am'mon·ites and the Ash'dod·ites heard that the repairing of the walls of Jerusalem was going forward and the gaps were beginning to be closed, they were very angry, 8 and all plotted together to come and fight against Jerusalem and to cause confusion in it. 9 So we prayed to our God, and set a guard as a protection against them day and night.

10 But Judah said, "The strength of the burden bearers is failing, and there is too much rubbish so that we are unable to work on the wall." 11 And our enemies said, "They will not know or see anything before we come upon them and kill them and stop the work." 12 When the Jews who lived near them came, they said to us ten times, "From all the places

---

^{h} Cn: Heb *were living* ^{i} Or *Hammiphkad Gate* ^{j} Ch 3.33 in Heb ^{k} Ch 4.1 in Heb

where they live[l] they will come up against us."[m]
13 So in the lowest parts of the space behind the wall, in open places, I stationed the people according to their families,[n] with their swords, their spears, and their bows. 14 After I looked these things over, I stood up and said to the nobles and the officials and the rest of the people, "Do not be afraid of them. Remember the LORD, who is great and awesome, and fight for your kin, your sons, your daughters, your wives, and your homes."

15 When our enemies heard that their plot was known to us, and that God had frustrated it, we all returned to the wall, each to his work. 16 From that day on, half of my servants worked on construction, and half held the spears, shields, bows, and body-armor; and the leaders posted themselves behind the whole house of Judah, 17 who were building the wall. The burden bearers carried their loads in such a way that each labored on the work with one hand and with the other held a weapon. 18 And each of the builders had his sword strapped at his side while he built. The man who sounded the trumpet was beside me. 19 And I said to the nobles, the officials, and the rest of the people, "The work is great and widely spread out, and we are separated far from one another on the wall. 20 Rally to us wherever you hear the sound of the trumpet. Our God will fight for us."

21 So we labored at the work, and half of them held the spears from break of dawn until the stars came out. 22 I also said to the people at that time, "Let every man and his servant pass the night inside Jerusalem, so that they may be a guard for us by night and may labor by day." 23 So neither I nor my brothers nor my servants nor the men of the guard who followed me ever took off our clothes; each kept his weapon in his right hand.[o]

Nehemiah Deals with Oppression

5 Now there was a great outcry of the people and of their wives against their Jewish kin. 2 For there were those who said, "With our sons and our daughters, we are many; we must get grain, so that we may eat and stay alive." 3 There were also those who said, "We are having to pledge our fields, our vineyards, and our houses in order to get grain during the famine." 4 And there were those who said, "We are having to borrow money on our fields and vineyards to pay the king's tax. 5 Now our flesh is the same as that of our kindred; our children are the same as their children; and yet we are forcing our sons and daughters to be slaves, and some of our daughters have been ravished; we are powerless, and our fields and vineyards now belong to others."

NEH

---

[l] Cn: Heb *you return* [m] Compare Gk Syr: Meaning of Heb uncertain [n] Meaning of Heb uncertain [o] Cn: Heb *each his weapon the water*

Hunger Pains

LIVE IT!

"I'm hungry."

"Yeah, I'm starved. Let's go get something to eat."

How many times have we uttered those words or heard them said? It's so easy. If we're hungry, we eat. If we're thirsty, we grab something to drink. If we're not feeling well, we get something to make us feel better. We forget sometimes that our way of doing things is the exception in the world, not the rule. Right now, people in this country and in the rest of the world are starving and have no idea where their next meal is coming from.

When Nehemiah's people were hungry, he saw the problem right away. The problem was not a lack of food. It was that some people were using their wealth and influence to control who got the food (Neh 5.7–8). Nehemiah took the radical step of demanding that the powerful and wealthy stop taking advantage of those less well off. He demanded that the wealthy restore the money and property that they had taken from others through unjust charging of interest (verses 10–11).

Experts tell us that much the same is true today. People are starving not because food is scarce but because political and economic conditions prevent them from getting the food. If only we could be like Nehemiah and demand that the powerful and wealthy reform. Well, you know what? We can! We can educate ourselves and speak out through letters and phone calls to elected officials. And while we are calling for society to change, let's volunteer at a neighborhood pantry or soup kitchen to help feed the poor people in our own backyard.

▸ Nehemiah, chapter 5

6 I was very angry when I heard their outcry and these complaints. 7 After thinking it over, I brought charges against the nobles and the officials; I said to them, "You are all taking interest from your own people." And I called a great assembly to deal with them, 8 and said to them, "As far as we were able, we have bought back our Jewish kindred who had been sold to other nations; but now you are selling your own kin, who must then be bought back by us!" They were silent, and could not find a word to say. 9 So I said, "The thing that you are doing is not good. Should you not walk in the fear of our God, to prevent the taunts of the nations our enemies? 10 Moreover I and my brothers and my servants are lending them money and grain. Let us stop this taking of interest. 11 Restore to them, this very day, their fields, their vineyards, their olive orchards, and their houses, and the interest on money, grain, wine, and oil that you have been exacting from them." 12 Then they said, "We will restore everything and demand nothing more from them. We will do as you say." And I called the priests, and made them take an oath to do as they had promised. 13 I also shook out the fold of my garment and said, "So may God shake out everyone from house and from property who does not perform this promise. Thus may they be shaken out and emptied." And all the assembly said, "Amen," and praised the LORD. And the people did as they had promised.

The Generosity of Nehemiah

14 Moreover from the time that I was appointed to be their governor in the land of Judah, from the twentieth year to the thirty-second year of King Ar•ta•xerx′ēs, twelve years, neither I nor my brothers ate the food allowance of the governor. 15 The former governors who were before me laid heavy burdens on the people, and took food and wine from them, besides forty shekels of silver. Even their servants lorded it over the people. But I did not do so, because of the fear of God. 16 Indeed, I devoted myself to the work on this wall, and acquired no land; and all my servants were gathered there for the work. 17 Moreover there were at my table one hundred fifty people, Jews and officials, besides those who came to us from the nations around us. 18 Now that which was prepared for one day was one ox and six choice sheep; also fowls were prepared for me, and every ten days skins of wine in abundance; yet with all this I did not demand the food allowance of the governor, because of the heavy burden of labor on the people. 19 Remember for my good, O my God, all that I have done for this people.

Intrigues of Enemies Foiled

6 Now when it was reported to San•bal′lat and Tō•bī′ah and to Gē′shem the A′rab and to the rest of our enemies that I had built the wall and that

there was no gap left in it (though up to that time I had not set up the doors in the gates), 2 San•bal′lat and Gē′shem sent to me, saying, "Come and let us meet together in one of the villages in the plain of Ō′nō." But they intended to do me harm. 3 So I sent messengers to them, saying, "I am doing a great work and I cannot come down. Why should the work stop while I leave it to come down to you?" 4 They sent to me four times in this way, and I answered them in the same manner. 5 In the same way San•bal′lat for the fifth time sent his servant to me with an open letter in his hand. 6 In it was written, "It is reported among the nations—and Gē′shem*p* also says it—that you and the Jews intend to rebel; that is why you are building the wall; and according to this report you wish to become their king. 7 You have also set up prophets to proclaim in Jerusalem concerning you, 'There is a king in Judah!' And now it will be reported to the king according to these words. So come, therefore, and let us confer together." 8 Then I sent to him, saying, "No such things as you say have been done; you are inventing them out of your own mind" 9—for they all wanted to frighten us, thinking, "Their hands will drop from the work, and it will not be done." But now, O God, strengthen my hands.

10 One day when I went into the house of She•mā′iah son of De•laī′ah son of Me•het′a•bel, who was confined to his house, he said, "Let us meet together in the house of God, within the temple, and let us close the doors of the temple, for they are coming to kill you; indeed, tonight they are coming to kill you." 11 But I said, "Should a man like me run away? Would a man like me go into the temple to save his life? I will not go in!" 12 Then I perceived and saw that God had not sent him at all, but he had pronounced the prophecy against me because Tō•bī′ah and San•bal′lat had hired him. 13 He was hired for this purpose, to intimidate me and make me sin by acting in this way, and so they could give me a bad name, in order to taunt me. 14 Remember Tō•bī′ah and San•bal′lat, O my God, according to these things that they did, and also the prophetess Nō•a•dī′ah and the rest of the prophets who wanted to make me afraid.

The Wall Completed

15 So the wall was finished on the twenty-fifth day of the month Ē′lul, in fifty-two days. 16 And when all our enemies heard of it, all the nations around us were afraid*q* and fell greatly in their own esteem; for they perceived that this work had been accomplished with the help of our God. 17 Moreover in those days the nobles of Judah sent many

---

p Heb *Gashmu*   *q* Another reading is *saw*

letters to Tō•bī′ah, and Tō•bī′ah's letters came to them. [18] For many in Judah were bound by oath to him, because he was the son-in-law of Shec•a•nī′ah son of Ā′rah: and his son Jē•hō•hā′nan had married the daughter of Me•shul′lam son of Ber•e•chī′ah. [19] Also they spoke of his good deeds in my presence, and reported my words to him. And Tō•bī′ah sent letters to intimidate me.

7 Now when the wall had been built and I had set up the doors, and the gatekeepers, the singers, and the Lē′vītes had been appointed, [2] I gave my brother Ha•nā′nī charge over Jerusalem, along with Han•a•nī′ah the commander of the citadel—for he was a faithful man and feared God more than many. [3] And I said to them, "The gates of Jerusalem are not to be opened until the sun is hot; while the gatekeepers[r] are still standing guard, let them shut and bar the doors. Appoint guards from among the inhabitants of Jerusalem, some at their watch posts, and others before their own houses." [4] The city was wide and large, but the people within it were few and no houses had been built.

Lists of the Returned Exiles
(Ezra 2.1–70)

5 Then my God put it into my mind to assemble the nobles and the officials and the people to be enrolled by genealogy. And I found the book of the genealogy of those who were the first to come back, and I found the following written in it:

6 These are the people of the province who came up out of the captivity of those exiles whom King Ne•bū•chad•nez′zar of Babylon had carried into exile; they returned to Jerusalem and Judah, each to his town. [7] They came with Ze•rub′ba•bel, Jesh′ū•a, Nē•he•mī′ah, Az•a•rī′ah, Rā•a•mī′ah, Nā•ham′a•nī, Mor′de•caī, Bil′shan, Mis′pe•reth, Big′vaī, Nē′hum, Bā′a•nah.

The number of the Israelite people: [8] the descendants of Pā′rosh, two thousand one hundred seventy-two. [9] Of Sheph•a•tī′ah, three hundred seventy-two. [10] Of Ā′rah, six hundred fifty-two. [11] Of Pā′hath-mō′ab, namely the descendants of Jesh′ū•a and Jō′ab, two thousand eight hundred eighteen. [12] Of Ē′lam, one thousand two hundred fifty-four. [13] Of Zat′tū, eight hundred forty-five. [14] Of Zac′caī, seven hundred sixty. [15] Of Bin′nū•ī, six hundred forty-eight. [16] Of Bē′baī, six hundred twenty-eight. [17] Of Az′gad, two thousand three hundred twenty-two. [18] Of Ad•o•nī′kam, six hundred sixty-seven. [19] Of Big′vaī, two thousand sixty-seven. [20] Of Ā′din, six hundred fifty-five. [21] Of Ā′ter, namely of Hez•e•kī′ah, ninety-eight. [22] Of Hā′shum, three hundred twenty-eight. [23] Of Bē′zaī, three hundred twenty-four. [24] Of Hā′riph, one hundred twelve. [25] Of Gib′ē•on, ninety-five. [26] The people of Bethlehem and Ne•toph′ah, one hundred

eighty-eight. [27] Of An′a•thoth, one hundred twenty-eight. [28] Of Beth-az′ma•veth, forty-two. [29] Of Kir′i•ath-jē′a•rim, Chē•phī′rah, and Be•er′oth, seven hundred forty-three. [30] Of Rā′mah and Gē′ba, six hundred twenty-one. [31] Of Mich′mas, one hundred twenty-two. [32] Of Beth′el and Aī, one hundred twenty-three. [33] Of the other Nē′bō, fifty-two. [34] The descendants of the other Ē′lam, one thousand two hundred fifty-four. [35] Of Hā′rim, three hundred twenty. [36] Of Jericho, three hundred forty-five. [37] Of Lod, Hā′did, and Ō′nō, seven hundred twenty-one. [38] Of Se•nā′ah, three thousand nine hundred thirty.

39 The priests: the descendants of Je•daī′ah, namely the house of Jesh′ū•a, nine hundred seventy-three. [40] Of Im′mer, one thousand fifty-two. [41] Of Pash′hur, one thousand two hundred forty-seven. [42] Of Hā′rim, one thousand seventeen.

43 The Lē′vītes: the descendants of Jesh′ū•a, namely of Kad′mi•el of the descendants of Hō′de•vah, seventy-four. [44] The singers: the descendants of Ā′saph, one hundred forty-eight. [45] The gatekeepers: the descendants of Shal′lum, of Ā′ter, of Tal′mon, of Ak′kub, of Ha•tī′ta, of Shō′baī, one hundred thirty-eight.

46 The temple servants: the descendants of Zī′ha, of Ha•sū′pha, of Tab•bā′oth, [47] of Kē′ros, of Sī′a, of Pā′don, [48] of Le•bā′na, of Hag′a•ba, of Shal′maī, [49] of Hā′nan, of Gid′del, of Gā′har, [50] of Rē•āi′ah, of Rē′zin, of Ne•kō′da, [51] of Gaz′zam, of Uz′za, of Pa•sē′ah, [52] of Bē′saī, of Me•ū′nim, of Ne•phūsh′e•sim, [53] of Bak′buk, of Ha•kū′pha, of Har′hur, [54] of Baz′lith, of Me•hī′da, of Har′sha, [55] of Bar′kos, of Sis′e•ra, of Tē′mah, [56] of Ne•zī′ah, of Ha•tī′pha.

57 The descendants of Solomon's servants: of Sō′taī, of Sō′phe•reth, of Pe•rī′da, [58] of Jā′a•la, of Dar′kon, of Gid′del, [59] of Sheph•a•tī′ah, of Hat′til, of Pō′che•reth-haz•ze•bā′im, of Ā′mon.

60 All the temple servants and the descendants of Solomon's servants were three hundred ninety-two.

61 The following were those who came up from Tel-mē′lah, Tel-har′sha, Chē′rub, Ad′don, and Im′mer, but they could not prove their ancestral houses or their descent, whether they belonged to Israel: [62] the descendants of De•laī′ah, of Tō•bī′ah, of Ne•kō′da, six hundred forty-two. [63] Also, of the priests: the descendants of Hō•baī′ah, of Hak′koz, of Bar•zil′laī (who had married one of the daughters of Bar•zil′laī the Gil′e•ad•īte and was called by their name). [64] These sought their registration among those enrolled in the genealogies, but it was not found there, so they were excluded from the priesthood as unclean; [65] the governor told them that they were not to partake of the most holy food, until a priest with Ū′rim and Thum′mim should come.

---

r Heb *while they*

66 The whole assembly together was forty-two thousand three hundred sixty, 67 besides their male and female slaves, of whom there were seven thousand three hundred thirty-seven; and they had two hundred forty-five singers, male and female. 68 They had seven hundred thirty-six horses, two hundred forty-five mules,ˢ 69 four hundred thirty-five camels, and six thousand seven hundred twenty donkeys.

70 Now some of the heads of ancestral houses contributed to the work. The governor gave to the treasury one thousand darics of gold, fifty basins, and five hundred thirty priestly robes. 71 And some of the heads of ancestral houses gave into the building fund twenty thousand darics of gold and two thousand two hundred minas of silver. 72 And what the rest of the people gave was twenty thousand darics of gold, two thousand minas of silver, and sixty-seven priestly robes.

73 So the priests, the Lĕ´vītes, the gatekeepers, the singers, some of the people, the temple servants, and all Israel settled in their towns.

Ezra Summons the People to Obey the Law

When the seventh month came—the people of Israel being settled in their towns— 1 all the people gathered together into the square before the Water Gate. They told the scribe Ezra to bring the book of the law of Moses, which the LORD had given to Israel. 2 Accordingly, the priest Ezra brought the law before the assembly, both men and women and all who could hear with understanding. This was on the first day of the seventh month. 3 He read from it facing the square before the Water Gate from early morning until midday, in the presence of the men and the women and those who could understand; and the ears of all the people were attentive to the book of the law. 4 The scribe Ezra stood on a wooden platform that had been made for the purpose; and beside him stood Mat-ti·thī´ah, Shĕ´ma, A·naī´ah, Ū·rī´ah, Hil·kī´ah, and Mā·a·sēi´ah on his right hand; and Pe·dāi´ah, Mish´a·el, Mal·chī´jah, Hā´shum, Hash-bad´da·nah, Zech·a·rī´ah, and Me·shul´lam on his left hand. 5 And Ezra opened the book in the sight of all the people, for he was standing above all the people; and when he opened it, all the people stood up. 6 Then Ezra blessed the LORD, the great God, and all the people answered, "Amen, Amen," lifting up their hands. Then they bowed their heads and worshiped the LORD with their faces to the ground. 7 Also Jesh´ū·a, Bā´nī, Sher·e·bī´ah, Jā´min, Ak´kub, Shab´be·thai, Hō·dī´ah, Mā·a·sēi´ah, Ke·lī´ta, Az·a·rī´ah, Joz´a·bad, Hā´nan, Pe·lāi´ah, the Lĕ´vītes,ᵗ helped the people to understand the law, while the people remained in their places. 8 So they read from the book, from the law of God, with interpretation.

They gave the sense, so that the people understood the reading.

9 And Nĕ·he·mī´ah, who was the governor, and Ezra the priest and scribe, and the Lĕ´vītes who taught the people said to all the people, "This day is holy to the LORD your God; do not mourn or weep." For all the people wept when they heard the words of the law. 10 Then he said to them, "Go your way, eat the fat and drink sweet wine and send portions of them to those for whom nothing is prepared, for this day is holy to our LORD; and do not be grieved, for the joy of the LORD is your strength." 11 So the Lĕ´vītes stilled all the people, saying, "Be quiet, for this day is holy; do not be grieved." 12 And all the people went their way to eat and drink and to send portions and to make great rejoicing, because they had understood the words that were declared to them.

The Festival of Booths Celebrated
(Cp Lev 23.33–43)

13 On the second day the heads of ancestral houses of all the people, with the priests and the Lĕ´vītes, came together to the scribe Ezra in order to study the words of the law. 14 And they found it written in the law, which the LORD had commanded by Moses, that the people of Israel should live in boothsᵘ during the festival of the seventh month, 15 and that they should publish and proclaim in all their towns and in Jerusalem as follows, "Go out to the hills and bring branches of olive, wild olive, myrtle, palm, and other leafy trees to make booths,ᵘ as it is written." 16 So the people went out and brought them, and made boothsᵘ for themselves, each on the roofs of their houses, and in their courts and in the courts of the house of God, and in the square at the Water Gate and in the square at the Gate of Ē´phra·im. 17 And all the assembly of those who had returned from the captivity made boothsᵘ and lived in them; for from the days of Jesh´ū·a son of Nun to that day the people of Israel had not done so. And there was very great rejoicing. 18 And day by day, from the first day to the last day, he read from the book of the law of God. They kept the festival seven days; and on the eighth day there was a solemn assembly, according to the ordinance.

National Confession

9 Now on the twenty-fourth day of this month the people of Israel were assembled with fasting and in sackcloth, and with earth on their heads.ᵛ 2 Then those of Israelite descent separated

---

ˢ Ezra 2.66 and the margins of some Hebrew Mss: MT lacks *They had . . . forty-five mules*   ᵗ 1 Esdras 9.48 Vg: Heb *and the Levites*   ᵘ Or *tabernacles*; Heb *succoth*   ᵛ Heb *on them* and **bless the LORD your God** from everlasting to everlasting *9.5* UP STAND

themselves from all foreigners, and stood and confessed their sins and the iniquities of their ancestors. 3 They stood up in their place and read from the book of the law of the LORD their God for a fourth part of the day, and for another fourth they made confession and worshiped the LORD their God. 4 Then Jesh′ū·a, Bā′nī, Kad′mi·el, Sheb·a·nī′-ah, Bun′nī, Sher·e·bī′ah, Bā′nī, and Che·nā′nī stood on the stairs of the Lē′vītes and cried out with a loud voice to the LORD their God. 5 Then the Lē′-vītes, Jesh′ū·a, Kad′mi·el, Bā′nī, Hash·ab·neī′ah, Sher·e·bī′ah, Hō·dī′ah, Sheb·a·nī′ah, and Peth·a·hī′-ah, said, "Stand up and bless the LORD your God from everlasting to everlasting. Blessed be your glorious name, which is exalted above all blessing and praise."

6 And Ezra said:*w* "You are the LORD, you alone; you have made heaven, the heaven of heavens, with all their host, the earth and all that is on it, the seas and all that is in them. To all of them you give life, and the host of heaven worships you. 7 You are the LORD, the God who chose Abram and brought him out of Ūr of the Chal·dē′ans and gave him the name Abraham; 8 and you found his heart faithful before you, and made with him a covenant to give to his descendants the land of the Cā′naan·īte, the Hit′tīte, the Am′o·rīte, the Per′iz·zīte, the Jeb′ū·sīte, and the Gir′ga·shīte; and you have fulfilled your promise, for you are righteous.

9 "And you saw the distress of our ancestors in Egypt and heard their cry at the Red Sea.*x* 10 You performed signs and wonders against Pharaoh and all his servants and all the people of his land, for you knew that they acted insolently against our ancestors. You made a name for yourself, which remains to this day. 11 And you divided the sea before them, so that they passed through the sea on dry land, but you threw their pursuers into the depths, like a stone into mighty waters. 12 Moreover, you

led them by day with a pillar of cloud, and by night with a pillar of fire, to give them light on the way in which they should go. 13 You came down also upon Mount Sinai, and spoke with them from heaven, and gave them right ordinances and true laws, good statutes and commandments, 14 and you made known your holy sabbath to them and gave them commandments and statutes and a law through your servant Moses. 15 For their hunger you gave them bread from heaven, and for their thirst you brought water for them out of the rock, and you told them to go in to possess the land that you swore to give them.

16 "But they and our ancestors acted presumptuously and stiffened their necks and did not obey your commandments; 17 they refused to obey, and were not mindful of the wonders that you performed among them; but they stiffened their necks and determined to return to their slavery in Egypt. But you are a God ready to forgive, gracious and merciful, slow to anger and abounding in steadfast love, and you did not forsake them. 18 Even when they had cast an image of a calf for themselves and said, 'This is your God who brought you up out of Egypt,' and had committed great blasphemies, 19 you in your great mercies did not forsake them in the wilderness; the pillar of cloud that led them in the way did not leave them by day, nor the pillar of fire by night that gave them light on the way by which they should go. 20 You gave your good spirit to instruct them, and did not withhold your manna from their mouths, and gave them water for their thirst. 21 Forty years you sustained them in the wilderness so that they lacked nothing; their clothes did not wear out and their feet did not swell. 22 And you gave them kingdoms and peoples, and allotted to them every corner,*y* so they took possession of the land of King Sī′hon of Hesh′bon and the land of King Og of Bā′shan. 23 You multiplied their descendants like the stars of heaven, and brought them into the land that you had told their ancestors to enter and possess. 24 So the descendants went in and possessed the land, and you subdued before them the inhabitants of the land, the Cā′-naan·ītes, and gave them into their hands, with their kings and the peoples of the land, to do with them as they pleased. 25 And they captured fortress cities and a rich land, and took possession of houses filled with all sorts of goods, hewn cisterns, vineyards, olive orchards, and fruit trees in abundance; so they ate, and were filled and became fat, and delighted themselves in your great goodness.

26 "Nevertheless they were disobedient and rebelled against you and cast your law behind their

---

w Gk: Heb lacks *And Ezra said*   *x* Or *Sea of Reeds*   *y* Meaning of Heb uncertain backs and killed your prophets, who had warned them in order to turn them back to you, and they committed great blasphemies. 27 Therefore you gave them into the hands of their enemies, who made them suffer. Then in the time of their suffering they cried out to you and you heard them from heaven, and according to your great mercies you gave them saviors who saved them from the hands of their enemies. 28 But after they had rest, they again did evil before you, and you abandoned them to the hands of their enemies, so that they had dominion over them; yet when they turned and cried to you, you heard from heaven, and many times you rescued them according to your mercies. 29 And you warned them in order to turn them back to your law. Yet they acted presumptuously and did not obey your commandments, but sinned against your ordinances, by the observance of which a person shall live. They turned a stubborn shoulder and stiffened their neck and would not obey. 30 Many years you were patient with them, and warned them by your spirit through your prophets; yet they would not listen. Therefore you handed them over to the peoples of the lands. 31 Nevertheless, in your great mercies you did not make an end of them or forsake them, for you are a gracious and merciful God.

32 "Now therefore, our God—the great and mighty and awesome God, keeping covenant and steadfast love—do not treat lightly all the hardship that has come upon us, upon our kings, our officials, our priests, our prophets, our ancestors, and all your people, since the time of the kings of Assyria until today. 33 You have been just in all that has come upon us, for you have dealt faithfully and we have acted wickedly; 34 our kings, our officials, our priests, and our ancestors have not kept your law or heeded the commandments and the warnings that you gave them. 35 Even in their own kingdom, and in the great goodness you bestowed on them, and in the large and rich land that you set before them, they did not serve you and did not turn from their wicked works. 36 Here we are, slaves to this day—slaves in the land that you gave to our ancestors to enjoy its fruit and its good gifts. 37 Its rich yield goes to the kings whom you have set over us because of our sins; they have power also over our bodies and over our livestock at their pleasure, and we are in great distress."

Those Who Signed the Covenant

38z Because of all this we make a firm agreement in writing, and on that sealed document are inscribed the names of our officials, our Lēˈvites, and our priests.

10a Upon the sealed document are the names of Nēˈheˈmiˈah the governor, son of Hacˈaˈliˈah, and Zedˈeˈkiˈah; 2 Seˈraiˈah, Azˈaˈriˈ-

ah, Jerˈeˈmiˈah, 3 Pashˈhur, Amˈaˈriˈah, Malˈchiˈjah, 4 Hatˈtush, Shebˈaˈniˈah, Malˈluch, 5 Hāˈrim, Merˈeˈmoth, Ōˈbaˈdiˈah, 6 Daniel, Ginˈneˈthon, Barˈuch, 7 Meˈshulˈlam, Aˈbiˈjah, Mijˈaˈmin, 8 Māˈaˈziˈah, Bilˈgai, Sheˈmaiˈah; these are the priests. 9 And the Lēˈvites: Jeshˈuˈa son of Azˈaˈniˈah, Binˈnuˈi of the sons of Henˈaˈdad, Kadˈmiˈel; 10 and their associates, Shebˈaˈniˈah, Hōˈdiˈah, Keˈliˈta, Peˈlāiˈah, Hāˈnan, 11 Miˈca, Rēˈhob, Hash-aˈbiˈah, 12 Zacˈcur, Sherˈeˈbiˈah, Shebˈaˈniˈah, 13 Hōˈdiˈah, Bāˈni, Beˈniˈnū. 14 The leaders of the people: Pāˈrosh, Pāˈhath-mōˈab, Ēˈlam, Zatˈtū, Bāˈni, 15 Bunˈni, Azˈgad, Bēˈbai, 16 Adˈoˈniˈjah, Bigˈvai, Āˈdin, 17 Āˈter, Hezˈeˈkiˈah, Azˈzur, 18 Hōˈdiˈah, Hāˈshum, Bēˈzai, 19 Hāˈriph, Anˈaˈthoth, Nēˈbai, 20 Magˈpiˈash, Meshulˈlam, Hēˈzir, 21 Meˈshezˈaˈbel, Zāˈdok, Jadˈdūˈa, 22 Pelˈaˈtiˈah, Hāˈnan, Aˈnaiˈah, 23 Hōˈshēˈa, Hanˈaˈniˈah, Hasˈshub, 24 Halˈlōˈhesh, Pilˈha, Shōˈbek, 25 Rēˈhum, Haˈshabˈnah, Māˈaˈsēiˈah, 26 Aˈhiˈah, Hāˈnan, Āˈnan, 27 Malˈluch, Hāˈrim, and Bāˈaˈnah.

Summary of the Covenant

28 The rest of the people, the priests, the Lēˈvites, the gatekeepers, the singers, the temple servants, and all who have separated themselves from the peoples of the lands to adhere to the law of God, their wives, their sons, their daughters, all who have knowledge and understanding, 29 join with their kin, their nobles, and enter into a curse and an oath to walk in God's law, which was given by Moses the servant of God, and to observe and do all the commandments of the LORD our Lord and his ordinances and his statutes. 30 We will not give our daughters to the peoples of the land or take their daughters for our sons; 31 and if the peoples of the land bring in merchandise or any grain on the sabbath day to sell, we will not buy it from them on the sabbath or on a holy day; and we will forego the crops of the seventh year and the exaction of every debt.

32 We also lay on ourselves the obligation to charge ourselves yearly one-third of a shekel for the service of the house of our God: 33 for the rows of bread, the regular grain offering, the regular burnt offering, the sabbaths, the new moons, the appointed festivals, the sacred donations, and the sin offerings to make atonement for Israel, and for all the work of the house of our God. 34 We have also cast lots among the priests, the Lēˈvites, and the people, for the wood offering, to bring it into the house of our God, by ancestral houses, at appointed times, year by year, to burn on the altar of the LORD our God, as it is written in the law. 35 We obligate ourselves to bring the first fruits of our soil and the first fruits of all fruit of every tree, year by

---

z Ch 10.1 in Heb   a Ch 10.2 in Heb

year, to the house of the LORD; 36 also to bring to the house of our God, to the priests who minister in the house of our God, the firstborn of our sons and of our livestock, as it is written in the law, and the firstlings of our herds and of our flocks; 37 and to bring the first of our dough, and our contributions, the fruit of every tree, the wine and the oil, to the priests, to the chambers of the house of our God; and to bring to the Lĕ′vītes the tithes from our soil, for it is the Lĕ′vītes who collect the tithes in all our rural towns. 38 And the priest, the descendant of Aaron, shall be with the Lĕ′vītes when the Lĕ′vītes receive the tithes; and the Lĕ′vītes shall bring up a tithe of the tithes to the house of our God, to the chambers of the storehouse. 39 For the people of Israel and the sons of Levi shall bring the contribution of grain, wine, and oil to the storerooms where the vessels of the sanctuary are, and where the priests that minister, and the gatekeepers and the singers are. We will not neglect the house of our God.

Population of the City Increased

11 Now the leaders of the people lived in Jerusalem; and the rest of the people cast lots to bring one out of ten to live in the holy city Jerusalem, while nine-tenths remained in the other towns. 2 And the people blessed all those who willingly offered to live in Jerusalem.

3 These are the leaders of the province who lived in Jerusalem; but in the towns of Judah all lived on their property in their towns: Israel, the priests, the Lĕ′vītes, the temple servants, and the descendants of Solomon's servants. 4 And in Jerusalem lived some of the Jŭ′dah•ītes and of the Ben′ja•min•ītes. Of the Jŭ′dah•ītes: A•thaī′ah son of Uz•zī′ah son of Zech•a•rī′ah son of Am•a•rī′ah son of Sheph•a•tī′ah son of Ma•hal′a•lel, of the descendants of Per′ez; 5 and Mā•a•sēi′ah son of Bar′uch son of Col-hō′zeh son of Ha•zaī′ah son of A•dāi′ah son of Joi′a•rib son of Zech•a•rī′ah son of the Shī′lo•nīte. 6 All the descendants of Per′ez who lived in Jerusalem were four hundred sixty-eight valiant warriors.

7 And these are the Ben′ja•min•ītes: Sal′lū son of Me•shul′lam son of Jō′ed son of Pe•dāi′ah son of Kō′laī′ah son of Mā•a•sēi′ah son of Ith′i•el son of Je•shā′i•ah. 8 And his brothers[b] Gab•bā′ī, Sal′laī: nine hundred twenty-eight. 9 Jō′el son of Zich′rī was their overseer; and Judah son of Has•se•nū′ah was second in charge of the city.

10 Of the priests: Je•daī′ah son of Joi′a•rib, Jā′chin, 11 Se•rāi′ah son of Hil•kī′ah son of Me•shul′lam son of Zā′dok son of Me•rā′i•oth son of A•hī′tub, officer of the house of God, 12 and their associates who did the work of the house, eight hundred twenty-two; and A•dāi′ah son of Je•rō′ham son of Pel•a•lī′ah son of Am′zī son of Zech•a•rī′ah son of Pash′hur son of Mal•chī′jah, 13 and his associates, heads of ancestral houses, two hundred forty-two; and A•mash′sai son of Az′a•rel son of Ah′zaī son of Me•shil′le•moth son of Im′mer, 14 and their associates, valiant warriors, one hundred twenty-eight; their overseer was Zab′di•el son of Hag•ge•dō′lim.

15 And of the Lĕ′vītes: She•māi′ah son of Has′shub son of Az•rī′kam son of Hash•a•bī′ah son of Bun′nī; 16 and Shab′be•thaī and Joz′a•bad, of the leaders of the Lĕ′vītes, who were over the outside work of the house of God; 17 and Mat•ta•nī′ah son of Mī′ca son of Zab′dī son of Ā′saph, who was the leader to begin the thanksgiving in prayer, and Bak•bū•kī′ah, the second among his associates; and Ab′da son of Sham′mū•a son of Gā′lal son of Je•dū′thun. 18 All the Lĕ′vītes in the holy city were two hundred eighty-four.

19 The gatekeepers, Ak′kub, Tal′mon and their associates, who kept watch at the gates, were one hundred seventy-two. 20 And the rest of Israel, and of the priests and the Lĕ′vītes, were in all the towns of Judah, all of them in their inheritance. 21 But the temple servants lived on Ō′phel; and Zī′ha and Gish′pa were over the temple servants.

22 The overseer of the Lĕ′vītes in Jerusalem was Uz′zī son of Bā′nī son of Hash•a•bī′ah son of Mat•ta•nī′ah son of Mī′ca, of the descendants of Ā′saph, the singers, in charge of the work of the house of God. 23 For there was a command from the king concerning them, and a settled provision for the singers, as was required every day. 24 And Peth•a•hī′ah son of Me•shez′a•bel, of the descendants of Zĕ′rah son of Judah, was at the king's hand in all matters concerning the people.

Villages outside Jerusalem

25 And as for the villages, with their fields, some of the people of Judah lived in Kir′i•ath-ar′ba and its villages, and in Dī′bon and its villages, and in Je•kab′zĕ•el and its villages, 26 and in Jesh′ū•a and in Mō′la•dah and Beth-pel′et, 27 in Hā′zar-shū′al, in Bĕ′er-shĕ′ba and its villages, 28 in Zik′lag, in Mē•cō′nah and its villages, 29 in En-rim′mon, in Zō′rah, in Jar′muth, 30 Za•nō′ah, A•dul′lam, and their villages, Lā′chish and its fields, and A•zĕ′kah and its villages. So they camped from Bĕ′er-shĕ′ba to the valley of Hin′nom. 31 The people of Benjamin also lived from Gĕ′ba onward, at Mich′mash, Āi′ja, Beth′el and its villages, 32 An′a•thoth, Nob, An•a•nī′ah, 33 Hā′zor, Rā′mah, Git′ta•im, 34 Hā′did, Ze•bō′im, Ne•bal′lat, 35 Lod, and Ō′nō, the valley of artisans. 36 And certain divisions of the Lĕ′vītes in Judah were joined to Benjamin.

---

b Gk Mss: Heb *And after him*

A List of Priests and Levites
(Cp Ezra 2.36–40)

12 These are the priests and the Lē'vītes who came up with Ze·rub'ba·bel son of She·al'ti·el, and Jesh'ū·a: Se·rāi'ah, Jer·e·mī'ah, Ezra, 2 Am·a·rī'ah, Mal'luch, Hat'tush, 3 Shec·a·nī'ah, Rē'hum, Mer'e·moth, 4 Id'dō, Gin'ne·thoi, A·bī'jah, 5 Mij'a·min, Mā·a·dī'ah, Bil'gah, 6 She·māi'ah, Joi'a·rib, Je·daī'ah, 7 Sal'lū, Ā'mok, Hil·kī'ah, Je·daī'ah. These were the leaders of the priests and of their associates in the days of Jesh'ū·a.

8 And the Lē'vītes: Jesh'ū·a, Bin'nū·ī, Kad'mi·el, Sher·e·bī'ah, Judah, and Mat·ta·nī'ah, who with his associates was in charge of the songs of thanksgiving. 9 And Bak·bū·kī'ah and Un'nō their associates stood opposite them in the service. 10 Jesh'ū·a was the father of Joi'a·kim, Joi'a·kim the father of E·lī'a·shib, E·lī'a·shib the father of Joi'a·da, 11 Joi'a·da the father of Jonathan, and Jonathan the father of Jad'dū·a.

12 In the days of Joi'a·kim the priests, heads of ancestral houses, were: of Se·rāi'ah, Me·raī'ah; of Jer·e·mī'ah, Han·a·nī'ah; 13 of Ezra, Me·shul'lam; of Am·a·rī'ah, Jē·hō·ha'nan; 14 of Mal'lu·chī, Jona·than; of Sheb·a·nī'ah, Joseph; 15 of Hā'rim, Ad'na; of Me·rā'i·oth, Hel'kaī; 16 of Id'dō, Zech·a·rī'ah; of Gin'ne·thon, Me·shul'lam; 17 of A·bī'jah, Zich'rī; of Mi·nī'a·min, of Mō·a·dī'ah, Pil'taī; 18 of Bil'gah, Sham'mū·a; of She·māi'ah, Je·hon'a·than; 19 of Joi'a·rib, Mat·tē'naī; of Je·daī'ah, Uz'zī; 20 of Sal'laī, Kal'laī; of Ā'mok, Ē'ber; 21 of Hil·kī'ah, Hash·a·bī'ah; of Je·daī'ah, Ne·than'el.

22 As for the Lē'vītes, in the days of E·lī'a·shib, Joi'a·da, Jō·hā'nan, and Jad'dū·a, there were recorded the heads of ancestral houses; also the priests until the reign of Da·rī'us the Persian. 23 The Lē'vītes, heads of ancestral houses, were recorded in the Book of the Annals until the days of Jō·hā'nan son of E·lī'a·shib. 24 And the leaders of the Lē'vītes: Hash·a·bī'ah, Sher·e·bī'ah, and Jesh'ū·a son of Kad'mi·el, with their associates over against them, to praise and to give thanks, according to the commandment of David the man of God, section opposite to section. 25 Mat·ta·nī'ah, Bak·bū·kī'ah, Ō·ba·dī'ah, Me·shul'lam, Tal'mon, and Ak'kub were gatekeepers standing guard at the storehouses of the gates. 26 These were in the days of Joi'a·kim son of Jesh'ū·a son of Jō'za·dak, and in the days of the governor Nē·he·mī'ah and of the priest Ezra, the scribe.

Dedication of the City Wall

27 Now at the dedication of the wall of Jerusalem they sought out the Lē'vītes in all their places, to bring them to Jerusalem to celebrate the dedication with rejoicing, with thanksgivings and with singing, with cymbals, harps, and lyres. 28 The companies of the singers gathered together from the circuit around Jerusalem and from the villages of the Ne·toph'a·thītes; 29 also from Beth-gil'gal and from the region of Gē'ba and Az'ma·veth; for the singers had built for themselves villages around Jerusalem. 30 And the priests and the Lē'vītes purified themselves; and they purified the people and the gates and the wall.

31 Then I brought the leaders of Judah up onto the wall, and appointed two great companies that gave thanks and went in procession. One went to the right on the wall to the Dung Gate; 32 and after them went Hō·shai'ah and half the officials of Judah, 33 and Az·a·rī'ah, Ezra, Me·shul'lam, 34 Judah, Benjamin, She·māi'ah, and Jer·e·mī'ah, 35 and some of the young priests with trumpets: Zech·a·rī'ah son of Jonathan son of She·māi'ah son of Mat·ta·nī'ah son of Mī·cāi'ah son of Zac'cur son of Ā'saph; 36 and his kindred, She·māi'ah, Az'a·rel, Mil'a·laī, Gil'a·laī, Mā'aī, Ne·than'el, Judah, and Ha·nā'nī, with the musical instruments of David the man of God; and the scribe Ezra went in front of them. 37 At the Fountain Gate, in front of them, they went straight up by the stairs of the city of David, at the ascent of the wall, above the house of David, to the Water Gate on the east.

38 The other company of those who gave thanks went to the left,*c* and I followed them with half of the people on the wall, above the Tower of the Ovens, to the Broad Wall, 39 and above the Gate of E'phra·im, and by the Old Gate, and by the Fish Gate and the Tower of Ha·nan'el and the Tower of the Hundred, to the Sheep Gate; and they came to a halt at the Gate of the Guard. 40 So both companies of those who gave thanks stood in the house of God, and I and half of the officials with me; 41 and the priests E·lī'a·kim, Mā·a·sēi'ah, Mi·nī'a·min, Mī·cāi'ah, El·i·ō·ē'naī, Zech·a·rī'ah, and Han·a·nī'ah, with trumpets; 42 and Mā·a·sēi'ah, She·māi'ah, El·ē·ā'zar, Uz'zī, Jē·hō·hā'nan, Mal·chī'jah, Ē'lam, and Ē'zer. And the singers sang with Jez·ra·hī'ah as their leader. 43 They offered great sacrifices that day and rejoiced, for God had made them rejoice with great joy; the women and children also rejoiced. The joy of Jerusalem was heard far away.

Temple Responsibilities

44 On that day men were appointed over the chambers for the stores, the contributions, the first fruits, and the tithes, to gather into them the portions required by the law for the priests and for the Lē'vītes from the fields belonging to the towns; for Judah rejoiced over the priests and the Lē'vītes who ministered. 45 They performed the service of their God and the service of purification, as did the

---

c Cn: Heb *opposite*

singers and the gatekeepers, according to the command of David and his son Solomon. 46 For in the days of David and Ā'saph long ago there was a leader of the singers, and there were songs of praise and thanksgiving to God. 47 In the days of Ze·rub'ba·bel and in the days of Nĕ·he·mī'ah all Israel gave the daily portions for the singers and the gatekeepers. They set apart that which was for the Lĕ'vītes; and the Lĕ'vītes set apart that which was for the descendants of Aaron.

Foreigners Separated from Israel
(Num 22.1—24.25)

13 On that day they read from the book of Moses in the hearing of the people; and in it was found written that no Am'mon·ite or Mō'ab·ite should ever enter the assembly of God, 2 because they did not meet the Israelites with bread and water, but hired Bā'laam against them to curse them—yet our God turned the curse into a blessing. 3 When the people heard the law, they separated from Israel all those of foreign descent.

The Reforms of Nehemiah

4 Now before this, the priest E·lī'a·shib, who was appointed over the chambers of the house of our God, and who was related to Tō·bī'ah, 5 prepared for Tō·bī'ah a large room where they had previously put the grain offering, the frankincense, the vessels, and the tithes of grain, wine, and oil, which were given by commandment to the Lĕ'vītes, singers, and gatekeepers, and the contributions for the priests. 6 While this was taking place I was not in Jerusalem, for in the thirty-second year of King Ar·ta·xerx'ēs of Babylon I went to the king. After some time I asked leave of the king 7 and returned to Jerusalem. I then discovered the wrong that E·lī'a·shib had done on behalf of Tō·bī'ah, preparing a room for him in the courts of the house of God. 8 And I was very angry, and I threw all the household furniture of Tō·bī'ah out of the room. 9 Then I gave orders and they cleansed the chambers, and I brought back the vessels of the house of God, with the grain offering and the frankincense.

10 I also found out that the portions of the Lĕ'vītes had not been given to them; so that the Lĕ'vītes and the singers, who had conducted the service, had gone back to their fields. 11 So I remonstrated with the officials and said, "Why is the house of God forsaken?" And I gathered them together and set them in their stations. 12 Then all Judah brought the tithe of the grain, wine, and oil into the storehouses. 13 And I appointed as treasurers over the storehouses the priest Shel·e·mī'ah, the scribe Zā'dok, and Pe·dāi'ah of the Lĕ'vītes, and as their assistant Hā'nan son of Zac'cur son of

Mat·ta·nī'ah, for they were considered faithful; and their duty was to distribute to their associates. 14 Remember me, O my God, concerning this, and do not wipe out my good deeds that I have done for the house of my God and for his service.

Sabbath Reforms Begun

15 In those days I saw in Judah people treading wine presses on the sabbath, and bringing in heaps of grain and loading them on donkeys; and also wine, grapes, figs, and all kinds of burdens, which they brought into Jerusalem on the sabbath day; and I warned them at that time against selling food. 16 Tȳ'ri·ans also, who lived in the city, brought in fish and all kinds of merchandise and sold them on the sabbath to the people of Judah, and in Jerusalem. 17 Then I remonstrated with the nobles of Judah and said to them, "What is this evil thing that you are doing, profaning the sabbath day? 18 Did not your ancestors act in this way, and did not our God bring all this disaster on us and on this city? Yet you bring more wrath on Israel by profaning the sabbath."

19 When it began to be dark at the gates of Jerusalem before the sabbath, I commanded that the doors should be shut and gave orders that they should not be opened until after the sabbath. And I set some of my servants over the gates, to prevent any burden from being brought in on the sabbath day. 20 Then the merchants and sellers of all kinds of merchandise spent the night outside Jerusalem once or twice. 21 But I warned them and said to them, "Why do you spend the night in front of the wall? If you do so again, I will lay hands on you." From that time on they did not come on the sabbath. 22 And I commanded the Lĕ'vītes that they should purify themselves and come and guard the gates, to keep the sabbath day holy. Remember this also in my favor, O my God, and spare me according to the greatness of your steadfast love.

Mixed Marriages Condemned
(Cp Ezra 9.1–4)

23 In those days also I saw Jews who had married women of Ash'dod, Am'mon, and Mō'ab; 24 and half of their children spoke the language of Ash'dod, and they could not speak the language of Judah, but spoke the language of various peoples. 25 And I contended with them and cursed them and beat some of them and pulled out their hair; and I made them take an oath in the name of God, saying, "You shall not give your daughters to their sons, or take their daughters for your sons or for yourselves. 26 Did not King Solomon of Israel sin on account of such women? Among the many nations there was no king like him, and he was

N
E
H

NEH

beloved by his God, and God made him king over all Israel; nevertheless, foreign women made even him to sin. 27 Shall we then listen to you and do all this great evil and act treacherously against our God by marrying foreign women?"

28 And one of the sons of Je•hoi′a•da, son of the high priest E•li′a•shib, was the son-in-law of San•bal′lat the Hor′o•nīte; I chased him away from me. 29 Remember them, O my God, because they have defiled the priesthood, the covenant of the priests and the Lē′vītes.

30 Thus I cleansed them from everything foreign, and I established the duties of the priests and Lē′vītes, each in his work; 31 and I provided for the wood offering, at appointed times, and for the first fruits. Remember me, O my God, for good.

Good people suffering, love that must overcome a frightening obstacle, an undercover angel—the Book of Tobit has it all. Part fairy tale, part love story, this book will bring a smile to your face and perhaps a tear to your eye. Enjoy!

In-depth

For the author of the Book of Tobit, understanding God's will was not difficult. The conviction that God rewards good people, especially those who have experienced great suffering, is evident on every page. In the story, the faithful Tobit, who is blinded after doing a good deed, and the virtuous Sarah, who is ridiculed because she has had seven husbands die on their wedding night, pray for death because of their suffering and humiliation. In answer to their prayers, God sends the angel Raphael to lead Tobit's son Tobias on a journey to Sarah's town. The story ends happily—but you will have to read it yourself to find out exactly how.

The Book of Tobit is a novel, that is, a fiction book. The author was writing at a time when the Jews were governed by oppressive Greek rulers, and the people needed the reassurance of this happy tale. They had not forgotten the fall of Jerusalem or the Exile in Babylon, and Israel's suffering weighed heavily on them. What was the advantage of following God's law if all they had to look forward to was more suffering? (Belief in an afterlife had not yet developed among the Jewish people.) The book assured the faithful that God would eventually reward them: it was just a matter of time.

Although the book's miraculous answers may seem too simple to modern-day readers, its insistence on God's presence in human life and God's concern for those who suffer remains as important as ever. All people—even Christians who believe in life after death—need encouragement to face the challenges of this world with faith and hope.

At a Glance

- **Chapters 1–3.** the sufferings of Tobit and Sarah
- **Chapters 4–10.** the journey of Tobias and his marriage to Sarah
- **Chapters 11–12.** Tobias's homecoming and Tobit's cure
- **Chapters 13–14.** Tobit's prayer of thanksgiving, and death

Quick Facts

Setting
although fictional, the book reflects the historical situation of the Israelites deported from Israel to Ninevah in 721 B.C.

Author
unknown, writing sometime in the second century B.C.

Theme
In time, God will aid the faithful who suffer.

Of Note
Raphael is one of only three angels named in the Bible; the others are Michael and Gabriel.

The Book of Tobit

Tobit

1 This book tells the story of Tō′bit son of Tō′bi•el son of Ha•nan′i•el son of A•dū′el son of Gab′a•el son of Raph′a•el son of Rag′ū•el of the descendants[a] of As′i•el, of the tribe of Naph′ta•lī, [2] who in the days of King Shal•man•ē′ser[b] of the Assyrians was taken into captivity from This′bē, which is to the south of Kē′desh Naph′ta•lī in Upper Galilee, above Ash′er toward the west, and north of Phō′gor.

Tobit's Youth and Virtuous Life
(Cp Deut 12.11–14; 16.16; 1 Kings 12.28–29)

[3] I, Tō′bit, walked in the ways of truth and righteousness all the days of my life. I performed many acts of charity for my kindred and my people who had gone with me in exile to Nin′e•veh in the land of the Assyrians. [4] When I was in my own country, in the land of Israel, while I was still a young man, the whole tribe of my ancestor Naph′-ta•lī deserted the house of David and Jerusalem. This city had been chosen from among all the tribes of Israel, where all the tribes of Israel should offer sacrifice and where the temple, the dwelling of God, had been consecrated and established for all generations forever. [5] All my kindred and our ancestral house of Naph′ta•lī sacrificed to the calf[c] that King Jer•o-bō′am of Israel had erected in Dan and on all the mountains of Galilee. [6] But I alone went often to Jerusalem for the festivals, as it is prescribed for all

Israel by an everlasting decree. I would hurry off to Jerusalem with the first fruits of the crops and the firstlings of the flock, the tithes of the cattle, and the first shearings of the sheep. [7] I would give these to the priests, the sons of Aaron, at the altar; likewise the tenth of the grain, wine, olive oil, pomegranates, figs, and the rest of the fruits to the sons of Levi who ministered at Jerusalem. Also for six years I would save up a second tenth in money and go and distribute it in Jerusalem. [8] A third tenth[d] I would give to the orphans and widows and to the converts who had attached themselves to Israel. I would bring it and give it to them in the third year, and we would eat it according to the ordinance decreed concerning it in the law of Moses and according to the instructions of Deb′or•ah, the mother of my father Tō′bi•el,[e] for my father had died and left me an orphan. [9] When I became a man I married a woman,[f] a member of our own family, and by her I became the father of a son whom I named Tō•bī′as.

Taken Captive to Nineveh

[10] After I was carried away captive to Assyria and came as a captive to Nin′e•veh, everyone of my kin-

---

[a] Other ancient authorities lack *of Raphael son of Raguel of the descendants* [b] Gk *Enemessaros* [c] Other ancient authorities read *heifer* [d] *A third tenth* added from other ancient authorities [e] Lat: Gk *Hananiel* [f] Other ancient authorities add *Anna*

dred and my people ate the food of the Gentiles, 11 but I kept myself from eating the food of the Gentiles. 12 Because I was mindful of God with all my heart, 13 the Most High gave me favor and good standing with Shal•man•ē′ser,[g] and I used to buy everything he needed. 14 Until his death I used to go into Mēd′i•a, and buy for him there. While in the country of Mēd′i•a I left bags of silver worth ten talents in trust with Gab′a•el, the brother of Gā′brī. 15 But when Shal•man•ē′ser[g] died, and his son Sennach′e•rib reigned in his place, the highways into Mēd′i•a became unsafe and I could no longer go there.

Courage in Burying the Dead
(Cp Num 19.11–13)

16 In the days of Shal•man•ē′ser[g] I performed many acts of charity to my kindred, those of my tribe. 17 I would give my food to the hungry and my clothing to the naked; and if I saw the dead body of any of my people thrown out behind the wall of Nin′e•veh, I would bury it. 18 I also buried any whom King Sen•nach′e•rib put to death when he came fleeing from Judea in those days of judgment that the king of heaven executed upon him because of his blasphemies. For in his anger he put to death many Israelites; but I would secretly remove the bodies and bury them. So when Sen•nach′e•rib looked for them he could not find them. 19 Then one of the Nin′e•vites went and informed the king about me, that I was burying them; so I hid myself. But when I realized that the king knew about me and that I was being searched for to be put to death, I was afraid and ran away. 20 Then all my property was confiscated; nothing was left to me that was not taken into the royal treasury except my wife Anna and my son Tō•bī′as.

21 But not forty[h] days passed before two of Sen•nach′e•rib′s[i] sons killed him, and they fled to the mountains of Ar′a•rat, and his son Ē′sar-had′don[j] reigned after him. He appointed A•hī′kar, the son of my brother Han′a•el[k] over all the accounts of his kingdom, and he had authority over the entire administration. 22 A•hī′kar interceded for me, and I returned to Nin′e•veh. Now A•hī′kar was chief cupbearer, keeper of the signet, and in charge of administration of the accounts under King Sennach′e•rib of Assyria; so Ē′sar-had′don[j] reappointed him. He was my nephew and so a close relative.

2 Then during the reign of Ē′sar-had′don[j] I returned home, and my wife Anna and my son Tō•bī′as were restored to me. At our festival of Pentecost, which is the sacred festival of weeks, a good dinner was prepared for me and I reclined to eat. 2 When the table was set for me and an abundance of food placed before me, I said to my son Tō•bī′as, "Go, my child, and bring whatever poor person you may find of our people among the exiles in

did you KNOW?

The Case of the Missing Books

The Book of Tobit is treated differently in some versions of the Bible. Some put it in a section of books separated from the rest of the Old Testament. Some do not include it at all. We can find an explanation to this puzzle if we look back in time.

Sometime in the second or third century B.C., Jewish scholars translated the Scriptures from Hebrew and Aramaic into Greek. Many Jews living throughout the Mediterranean world spoke Greek, which had become a common language in that area at the time. For Greek-speaking Jews, this translation, called the Septuagint, was the Bible that they used. Because most of the early Christians spoke Greek, including Jews such as Paul, the Septuagint was adopted by the church as its Bible (Old Testament).

After the destruction of the Jerusalem Temple by the Romans in A.D. 70, leading rabbis strove to reorganize Jewish worship, which could no longer center on the Temple in Jerusalem. They reviewed the existing editions of the Bible and developed an official list of thirty-nine holy books. They rejected certain books contained in the Greek Sepuagint for which there was no existing original Hebrew or Aramaic text, such as Tobit, Judith, 1 and 2 Maccabees, Wisdom, Sirach, Baruch, and additions to the Books of Esther and Daniel.

Many centuries later, the Christian reformer Martin Luther used the Jewish canon of the Old Testament in his translation of the Bible. He placed the additional books in a separate section, entitling them the Apocrypha (from the Greek for "hidden"). The Catholic church and the Orthodox churches continue to use the fuller Greek canon, preferring the term *deuterocanonical* (from the Greek for "second canon") for the disputed books.

TOB

---

[g] Gk Enemessaros [h] Other ancient authorities read either *forty-five* or *fifty* [i] Gk *his* [j] Gk *Sacherdonos* [k] Other authorities read *Hananael*

Nin'e•veh, who is wholeheartedly mindful of God,[l] and he shall eat together with me. I will wait for you, until you come back." ³ So Tō•bī'as went to look for some poor person of our people. When he had returned he said, "Father!" And I replied, "Here I am, my child." Then he went on to say, "Look, father, one of our own people has been murdered and thrown into the market place, and now he lies there strangled." ⁴ Then I sprang up, left the dinner before even tasting it, and removed the body[m] from the square[n] and laid it[m] in one of the rooms until sunset when I might bury it.[m] ⁵ When I returned, I washed myself and ate my food in sorrow. ⁶ Then I remembered the prophecy of Ā'mos, how he said against Beth'el,[o]

"Your festivals shall be turned into
    mourning,
and all your songs into lamentation."
And I wept.

Tobit Becomes Blind

⁷ When the sun had set, I went and dug a grave and buried him. ⁸ And my neighbors laughed and said, "Is he still not afraid? He has already been hunted down to be put to death for doing this, and he ran away; yet here he is again burying the dead!" ⁹ That same night I washed myself and went into my courtyard and slept by the wall of the courtyard; and my face was uncovered because of the heat. ¹⁰ I did not know that there were sparrows on the wall; their fresh droppings fell into my eyes and produced white films. I went to physicians to be healed, but the more they treated me with ointments the more my vision was obscured by the white films, until I became completely blind. For four years I remained unable to see. All my kindred were sorry for me, and A•hī'kar took care of me for two years before he went to El•y•mā'is.

Tobit's Wife Earns Their Livelihood

¹¹ At that time, also, my wife Anna earned money at women's work. ¹² She used to send what she made to the owners and they would pay wages to her. One day, the seventh of Dys'trus, when she cut off a piece she had woven and sent it to the owners, they paid her full wages and also gave her a young goat for a meal. ¹³ When she returned to me, the goat began to bleat. So I called her and said, "Where did you get this goat? It is surely not stolen, is it? Return it to the owners; for we have no right to eat anything stolen." ¹⁴ But she said to me, "It was given to me as a gift in addition to my wages." But I did not believe her, and told her to return it to the owners. I became flushed with anger against her over this. Then she replied to me, "Where are your acts of charity? Where are your righteous deeds? These things are known about you!"[p]

Tobit's Prayer

3 Then with much grief and anguish of heart I wept, and with groaning began to pray:
² "You are righteous, O Lord,
    and all your deeds are just;
all your ways are mercy and truth;
    you judge the world.[q]
³ And now, O Lord, remember me
    and look favorably upon me.
Do not punish me for my sins
    and for my unwitting offenses
    and those that my ancestors committed
        before you.
They sinned against you,
⁴   and disobeyed your commandments.
So you gave us over to plunder, exile, and
        death,
    to become the talk, the byword, and an
        object of reproach
    among all the nations among whom you
        have dispersed us.
⁵ And now your many judgments are true
    in exacting penalty from me for my sins.
For we have not kept your commandments
    and have not walked in accordance with
        truth before you.
⁶ So now deal with me as you will;
    command my spirit to be taken from me,
    so that I may be released from the face of
        the earth and become dust.
For it is better for me to die than to live,
    because I have had to listen to undeserved
        insults,
    and great is the sorrow within me.
Command, O Lord, that I be released from this
        distress;
    release me to go to the eternal home,
    and do not, O Lord, turn your face away
        from me.
For it is better for me to die
    than to see so much distress in my life
    and to listen to insults."

Sarah Falsely Accused

7 On the same day, at Ec•bat'a•na in Mēd'i•a, it also happened that Sarah, the daughter of Rag'ū•el, was reproached by one of her father's maids. ⁸ For she had been married to seven husbands, and the wicked demon As•mō•dē'us had killed each of them before they had been with her as is customary for wives. So the maid said to her, "You are the one

---

[l] Lat: Gk *wholeheartedly mindful*   [m] Gk *him*   [n] Other ancient authorities lack *from the square*   [o] Other ancient authorities read *against Bethlehem*   [p] Or *to you*; Gk *with you*   [q] Other ancient authorities read *you render true and righteous judgment forever*

PRAY IT?

Praying for Death?

Tobit and Sarah are at the end of their rope. They have experienced such suffering and disgrace that life no longer has any meaning for them. They know suicide is wrong, so they each pray that God will send death to end their suffering and humiliation (Tob 3.6,10).

It is not uncommon for people who are very sick or in great pain or very old to pray for death, like Tobit. Unfortunately, young people who have experienced great loss or trauma often wish for death too, like Sarah. No one can completely explain the mystery of why we—both young and old—suffer. But through our loving actions and prayers, we can support one another in our suffering.

What people do you know who are suffering to the point of despair? Take a few moments every day to remember those people in prayer, and call or write to let them know you are thinking of them.

▶ Tobit, chapter 3

who kills[r] your husbands! See, you have already been married to seven husbands and have not borne the name of[s] a single one of them. 9 Why do you beat us? Because your husbands are dead? Go with them! May we never see a son or daughter of yours!"

Sarah's Prayer for Death

10 On that day she was grieved in spirit and wept. When she had gone up to her father's upper room, she intended to hang herself. But she thought it over and said, "Never shall they reproach my father, saying to him, 'You had only one beloved daughter but she hanged herself because of her distress.' And I shall bring my father in his old age down in sorrow to Hades. It is better for me not to hang myself, but to pray the Lord that I may die and not listen to these reproaches anymore." 11 At that same time, with hands outstretched toward the window, she prayed and said,

"Blessed are you, merciful God!
    Blessed is your name forever;
    let all your works praise you forever.
12 And now, Lord,[t] I turn my face to you,

and raise my eyes toward you.
13 Command that I be released from the earth
    and not listen to such reproaches any more.
14 You know, O Master, that I am innocent
    of any defilement with a man,
15 and that I have not disgraced my name
    or the name of my father in the land of my
        exile.
I am my father's only child;
    he has no other child to be his heir;
and he has no close relative or other kindred
    for whom I should keep myself as wife.
Already seven husbands of mine have died.
    Why should I still live?
But if it is not pleasing to you, O Lord, to take
        my life,
    hear me in my disgrace."

An Answer to Prayer
(Num 36.6–9)

16 At that very moment, the prayers of both of them were heard in the glorious presence of God. 17 So Raph'a•el was sent to heal both of them: Tō'bit, by removing the white films from his eyes, so that he might see God's light with his eyes; and Sarah, daughter of Rag'u•el, by giving her in marriage to Tō•bī'as son of Tō'bit, and by setting her free from the wicked demon As•mō•dě'us. For Tō•bī'as was entitled to have her before all others who had desired to marry her. At the same time that Tō'bit returned from the courtyard into his house, Sarah daughter of Rag'u•el came down from her upper room.

Tobit Gives Instructions to His Son
(Deut 15.7–8; Mt 6.2–4)

4 That same day Tō'bit remembered the money that he had left in trust with Gab'a•el at Rā'gēs in Mēd'i•a, 2 and he said to himself, "Now I have asked for death. Why do I not call my son Tō•bī'as and explain to him about the money before I die?" 3 Then he called his son Tō•bī'as, and when he came to him he said, "My son, when I die,[u] give me a proper burial. Honor your mother and do not abandon her all the days of her life. Do whatever pleases her, and do not grieve her in anything. 4 Remember her, my son, because she faced many dangers for you while you were in her womb. And when she dies, bury her beside me in the same grave.

5 "Revere the Lord all your days, my son, and refuse to sin or to transgress his commandments. Live uprightly all the days of your life, and do not

---

r Other ancient authorities read *strangles*   s Other ancient authorities read *have had no benefit from*   t Other ancient authorities lack *Lord*   u Lat walk in the ways of wrongdoing; 6 for those who act in accordance with truth will prosper in all their activities. To all those who practice righteousness^v 7 give alms from your possessions, and do not let your eye begrudge the gift when you make it. Do not turn your face away from anyone who is poor, and the face of God will not be turned away from you. 8 If you have many possessions, make your gift from them in proportion; if few, do not be afraid to give according to the little you have. 9 So you will be laying up a good treasure for yourself against the day of necessity. 10 For almsgiving delivers from death and keeps you from going into the Darkness. 11 Indeed, almsgiving, for all who practice it, is an excellent offering in the presence of the Most High.

12 "Beware, my son, of every kind of fornication. First of all, marry a woman from among the descendants of your ancestors; do not marry a foreign woman, who is not of your father's tribe; for we are the descendants of the prophets. Remember, my son, that Noah, Abraham, Isaac, and Jacob, our ancestors of old, all took wives from among their kindred. They were blessed in their children, and their posterity will inherit the land. 13 So now, my son, love your kindred, and in your heart do not disdain your kindred, the sons and daughters of your people, by refusing to take a wife for yourself from among them. For in pride there is ruin and great confusion. And in idleness there is loss and dire poverty, because idleness is the mother of famine.

14 "Do not keep over until the next day the wages of those who work for you, but pay them at once. If you serve God you will receive payment. Watch yourself, my son, in everything you do, and discipline yourself in all your conduct. 15 And what you hate, do not do to anyone. Do not drink wine to excess or let drunkenness go with you on your way. 16 Give some of your food to the hungry, and some of your clothing to the naked. Give all your surplus as alms, and do not let your eye begrudge your giving of alms. 17 Place your bread on the grave of the righteous, but give none to sinners. 18 Seek advice from every wise person and do not despise any useful counsel. 19 At all times bless the Lord God, and ask him that your ways may be made straight and that all your paths and plans may prosper. For none of the nations has understanding, but the Lord himself will give them good counsel; but if he chooses otherwise, he casts down to deepest Hades. So now, my child, remember these commandments, and do not let them be erased from your heart.

Money Left in Trust with Gabael

20 "And now, my son, let me explain to you that I left ten talents of silver in trust with Gab′a•el son of Ga′bri•as, at Ra′gēs in Mēd′i•a. 21 Do not be afraid, my son, because we have become poor. You have great wealth if you fear God and flee from

---

v The text of codex Sinaiticus goes directly from verse 6 to verse 19, reading *To those who practice righteousness* 19*the Lord will give good counsel.* In order to fill the lacuna verses 7 to 18 are derived from other ancient authorities

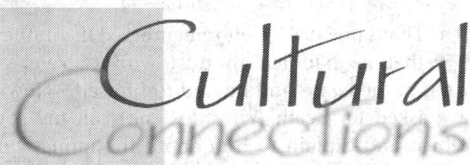

GIVE FOOD TO THE HUNGRY

In China, whenever you see a friend, it is customary to ask whether he or she has eaten a meal yet. If your friend responds, "No, I haven't eaten yet," it may mean that his or her last meal was yesterday or even the day before that. Then, you invite your friend to your home and share whatever food you have. This custom goes back to the great famine of China (1958–59), when people were dying of starvation and even eating tree bark.

Tobit gives his son good advice when he instructs him to share his food with the hungry and his clothing with the poor (Tob 4.16). Read Mt 25.31–46 to hear how seriously Jesus wants us to follow this advice.

▶ Tob 4.16

every sin and do what is good in the sight of the Lord your God."

The Angel Raphael
(Heb 13.2)

5 Then Tō·bī'as answered his father Tō'bit, "I will do everything that you have commanded me, father; 2 but how can I obtain the money[w] from him, since he does not know me and I do not know him? What evidence[x] am I to give him so that he will recognize and trust me, and give me the money? Also, I do not know the roads to Mēd'i·a, or how to get there." 3 Then Tō'bit answered his son Tō·bī'as, "He gave me his bond and I gave him my bond. I[y] divided his in two; we each took one part, and I put one with the money. And now twenty years have passed since I left this money in trust. So now, my son, find yourself a trustworthy man to go with you, and we will pay him wages until you return. But get back the money from Gab'a·el."[z]

4 So Tō·bī'as went out to look for a man to go with him to Mēd'i·a, someone who was acquainted with the way. He went out and found the angel Raph'a·el standing in front of him; but he did not perceive that he was an angel of God. 5 Tō·bī'as[a] said to him, "Where do you come from, young man?" "From your kindred, the Israelites," he replied, "and I have come here to work." Then Tōbi'as[b] said to him, "Do you know the way to go to Mēd'i·a?" 6 "Yes," he replied, "I have been there many times; I am acquainted with it and know all the roads. I have often traveled to Mēd'i·a, and would stay with our kinsman Gab'a·el who lives in Rā'gēs of Mēd'i·a. It is a journey of two days from Ec·bat'a·na to Rā'gēs; for it lies in a mountainous area, while Ec·bat'a·na is in the middle of the plain." 7 Then Tō·bī'as said to him, "Wait for me, young man, until I go in and tell my father; for I do need you to travel with me, and I will pay you your wages." 8 He replied, "All right, I will wait; but do not take too long."

9 So Tō·bī'as[b] went in to tell his father Tō'bit and said to him, "I have just found a man who is one of our own Israelite kindred!" He replied, "Call the man in, my son, so that I may learn about his family and to what tribe he belongs, and whether he is trustworthy enough to go with you."

10 Then Tō·bī'as went out and called him, and said, "Young man, my father is calling for you." So he went in to him, and Tō'bit greeted him first. He replied, "Joyous greetings to you!" But Tō'bit retorted, "What joy is left for me any more? I am a man without eyesight; I cannot see the light of heaven, but I lie in darkness like the dead who no longer see the light. Although still alive, I am among the dead. I hear people but I cannot see them." But the young man[b] said, "Take courage; the time is near for God

to heal you; take courage." Then Tō'bit said to him, "My son Tō·bī'as wishes to go to Mēd'i·a. Can you accompany him and guide him? I will pay your wages, brother." He answered, "I can go with him and I know all the roads, for I have often gone to Mēd'i·a and have crossed all its plains, and I am familiar with its mountains and all of its roads."

11 Then Tō'bit[b] said to him, "Brother, of what family are you and from what tribe? Tell me, brother." 12 He replied, "Why do you need to know my tribe?" But Tō'bit[b] said, "I want to be sure, brother, whose son you are and what your name is." 13 He replied, "I am Az·a·rī'ah, the son of the great Han·a·nī'ah, one of your relatives." 14 Then Tō'bit said to him, "Welcome! God save you, brother. Do not feel bitter toward me, brother, because I wanted to be sure about your ancestry. It turns out that you are a kinsman, and of good and noble lineage. For I knew Han·a·nī'ah and Nathan,[c] the two sons of Shem·e·lī'ah,[d] and they used to go with me to Jerusalem and worshiped with me there, and were not led astray. Your kindred are good people; you come of good stock. Hearty welcome!"

15 Then he added, "I will pay you a drachma a day as wages, as well as expenses for yourself and my son. So go with my son, 16 and[e] I will add something to your wages." Raph'a·el[a] answered, "I will go with him; so do not fear. We shall leave in good health and return to you in good health, because the way is safe." 17 So Tō'bit[b] said to him, "Blessings be upon you, brother."

Then he called his son and said to him, "Son, prepare supplies for the journey and set out with your brother. May God in heaven bring you safely there and return you in good health to me; and may his angel, my son, accompany you both for your safety."

Before he went out to start his journey, he kissed his father and mother. Tō'bit then said to him, "Have a safe journey."

18 But his mother[f] began to weep, and said to Tō'bit, "Why is it that you have sent my child away? Is he not the staff of our hand as he goes in and out before us? 19 Do not heap money upon money, but let it be a ransom for our child. 20 For the life that is given to us by the Lord is enough for us." 21 Tō'bit[a] said to her, "Do not worry; our child will leave in good health and return to us in good health. Your eyes will see him on the day when he returns to you in good health. Say no more! Do not fear for them, my sister. 22 For a good angel will accompany him;

---

[w] Gk it   [x] Gk sign   [y] Other authorities read He [z] Gk from him   [a] Gk He   [b] Gk he   [c] Other ancient authorities read Jathan or Nathaniah   [d] Other ancient authorities read Shemaiah   [e] Other ancient authorities add when you return safely   [f] Other ancient authorities add Anna

his journey will be successful, and he will come back in good health." [1] So she stopped weeping.

6

Journey to Rages

The young man went out and the angel went with him; [2] and the dog came out with him and went along with them. So they both journeyed along, and when the first night overtook them they camped by the Tigris river. [3] Then the young man went down to wash his feet in the Tigris river. Suddenly a large fish leaped up from the water and tried to swallow the young man's foot, and he cried out. [4] But the angel said to the young man, "Catch hold of the fish and hang on to it!" So the young man grasped the fish and drew it up on the land. [5] Then the angel said to him, "Cut open the fish and take out its gall, heart, and liver. Keep them with you, but throw away the intestines. For its gall, heart, and liver are useful as medicine." [6] So after cutting open the fish the young man gathered together the gall, heart, and liver; then he roasted and ate some of the fish, and kept some to be salted.

The two continued on their way together until they were near Med'i·a[g] [7] Then the young man questioned the angel and said to him, "Brother Az·a·ri'ah, what medicinal value is there in the fish's heart and liver, and in the gall?" [8] He replied, "As for the fish's heart and liver, you must burn them to make a smoke in the presence of a man or woman afflicted by a demon or evil spirit, and every affliction will flee away and never remain with that person any longer. [9] And as for the gall, anoint a person's eyes where white films have appeared on them; blow upon them, upon the white films, and the eyes[h] will be healed."

Raphael's Instructions

(Num 36.6–9)

[10] When he entered Med'i·a and already was approaching Ec·bat·a·na,[i] [11] Raph'a·el said to the young man, "Brother To·bi'as." "Here I am," he answered. Then Raph'a·el[j] said to him, "We must stay this night in the home of Rag'ü·el. He is your relative, and he has a daughter named Sarah. [12] He has no male heir and no daughter except Sarah only, and you, as next of kin to her, have before all other men a hereditary claim on her. Also it is right for you to inherit her father's possessions. Moreover, the girl is sensible, brave, and very beautiful, and her father is a good man." [13] He continued, "You have every right to take her in marriage. So listen to me, brother; tonight I will speak to her father about the girl, so that we may take her to be your bride. When we return from Ra'ges we will celebrate her marriage. For I know that Rag'ü·el can by no means keep her from you or promise her to another man without incurring the penalty of death according to

the decree of the book of Moses. Indeed he knows that you, rather than any other man, are entitled to marry his daughter. So now listen to me, brother, and tonight we shall speak concerning the girl and arrange her engagement to you. And when we return from Ra'ges we will take her and bring her back with us to your house."

[14] Then To·bi'as said in answer to Raph'a·el, "Brother Az·a·ri'ah, I have heard that she already has been married to seven husbands and that they died in the bridal chamber. On the night when they went in to her, they would die. I have heard people saying that it was a demon that killed them. [15] It does not harm her, but it kills anyone who desires to approach her. So now, since I am the only son my father has, I am afraid that I may die and bring my father's and mother's life down to their grave, grieving for me—and they have no other son to bury them."

[16] But Raph'a·el[j] said to him, "Do you not remember your father's orders when he commanded you to take a wife from your father's house? Now listen to me, brother, and say no more about this demon. Take her. I know that this very night she will be given to you in marriage. [17] When you enter the bridal chamber, take some of the fish's liver and heart, and put them on the embers of the incense. An odor will be given off; [18] the demon will smell it and flee, and will never be seen near her any more. Now when you are about to go to bed with her, both of you must first stand up and pray, imploring the Lord of heaven that mercy and safety may be granted to you. Do not be afraid, for she was set apart for you before the world was made. You will save her, and she will go with you. I presume that you will have children by her, and they will be as brothers to you. Now say no more!" When To·bi'as heard the words of Raph'a·el and learned that she was his kinswoman,[k] related through his father's lineage, he loved her very much, and his heart was drawn to her.

Arrival at Home of Raguel

7

Now when they[l] entered Ec·bat·a·na, To·bi'as[j] said to him, "Brother Az·a·ri'ah, take me straight to our brother Rag'ü·el." So he took him to Rag'ü·el's house, where they found him sitting beside the courtyard door. They greeted him first, and he replied, "Joyous greetings, brothers; welcome and good health!" Then he brought them into his house. [2] He said to his wife Edna, "How much the young man resembles my kinsman To'bit!" [3] Then Edna questioned them, saying, "Where are you

---

g Other ancient authorities read *Ecbatana*   h Gk *they*
i Other ancient authorities read *Rages*   j Gk *he*
k Gk *sister*   l Other ancient authorities read *he*

from, brothers?" They answered, "We belong to the descendants of Naph'ta•lī who are exiles in Nin'e•veh." [4] She said to them, "Do you know our kinsman Tō'bit?" And they replied, "Yes, we know him." Then she asked them, "Is he[m] in good health?" [5] They replied, "He is alive and in good health." And Tō•bī'as added, "He is my father!" [6] At that Rag'ū•el jumped up and kissed him and wept. [7] He also spoke to him as follows, "Blessings on you, my child, son of a good and noble father![n] O most miserable of calamities that such an upright and beneficent man has become blind!" He then embraced his kinsman Tō•bī'as and wept. [8] His wife Edna also wept for him, and their daughter Sarah likewise wept. [9] Then Rag'ū•el[o] slaughtered a ram from the flock and received them very warmly.

Marriage of Tobias and Sarah

When they had bathed and washed themselves and had reclined to dine, Tō•bī'as said to Raph'a•el, "Brother Az•a•rī'ah, ask Rag'ū•el to give me my kinswoman[p] Sarah." [10] But Rag'ū•el overheard it and said to the lad, "Eat and drink, and be merry tonight. For no one except you, brother, has the right to marry my daughter Sarah. Likewise I am not at liberty to give her to any other man than yourself, because you are my nearest relative. But let me explain to you the true situation more fully, my child. [11] I have given her to seven men of our kinsmen, and all died on the night when they went in to her. But now, my child, eat and drink, and the Lord will act on behalf of you both." But Tō•bī'as said, "I will neither eat nor drink anything until you settle the things that pertain to me." So Rag'ū•el said, "I will do so. She is given to you in accordance with the decree in the book of Moses, and it has been decreed from heaven that she be given to you. Take your kinswoman;[p] from now on you are her brother and she is your sister. She is given to you from today and forever. May the Lord of heaven, my child, guide and prosper you both this night and grant you mercy and peace." [12] Then Rag'ū•el summoned his daughter Sarah. When she came to him he took her by the hand and gave her to Tō•bī'as,[q] saying, "Take her to be your wife in accordance with the law and decree written in the book of Moses. Take her and bring her safely to your father. And may the God of heaven prosper your journey with his peace." [13] Then he called her mother and told her to bring writing material; and he wrote out a copy of a marriage contract, to the effect that he gave her to him as wife according to the decree of the law of Moses. [14] Then they began to eat and drink.

[15] Rag'ū•el called his wife Edna and said to her, "Sister, get the other room ready, and take her there." [16] So she went and made the bed in the room as he had told her, and brought Sarah[r] there. She wept for her daughter.[r] Then, wiping away the tears,[s] she said to her, "Take courage, my daughter; the Lord of heaven grant you joy[t] in place of your sorrow. Take courage, my daughter." Then she went out.

Tobias Routs the Demon
(Cp Mt 12.43–45)

8 When they had finished eating and drinking they wanted to retire; so they took the young man and brought him into the bedroom. [2] Then Tō•bī'as remembered the words of Raph'a•el, and he took the fish's liver and heart out of the bag where he had them and put them on the embers of the incense. [3] The odor of the fish so repelled the demon that he fled to the remotest parts[u] of Egypt. But Raph'a•el followed him, and at once bound him there hand and foot.

[4] When the parents[v] had gone out and shut the door of the room, Tō•bī'as got out of bed and said to Sarah,[r] "Sister, get up, and let us pray and implore our Lord that he grant us mercy and safety." [5] So she got up, and they began to pray and implore that they might be kept safe. Tō•bī'as[w] began by saying,

"Blessed are you, O God of our ancestors,
    and blessed is your name in all generations
        forever.
Let the heavens and the whole creation bless
        you forever.
[6] You made Adam, and for him you made his
        wife Eve
    as a helper and support.
From the two of them the human race has
        sprung.
You said, 'It is not good that the man should
        be alone;
    let us make a helper for him like himself.'
[7] I now am taking this kinswoman of mine,
    not because of lust,
    but with sincerity.
Grant that she and I may find mercy
    and that we may grow old together."

[8] And they both said, "Amen, Amen." [9] Then they went to sleep for the night.

But Rag'ū•el arose and called his servants to him, and they went and dug a grave, [10] for he said, "It is possible that he will die and we will become an object of ridicule and derision." [11] When they had

---

[m] Other ancient authorities add *alive and*   [n] Other ancient authorities add *When he heard that Tobit had lost his sight, he was stricken with grief and wept. Then he said,*   [o] Gk *he*   [p] Gk *sister*   [q] Gk *him*   [r] Gk *her*   [s] Other ancient authorities read *the tears of her daughter*   [t] Other ancient authorities read *favor*   [u] Or *fled through the air to the parts*   [v] Gk *they*   [w] Gk *He*

Angels Among Us

Many older Catholics were taught as children that they were to leave a bit of space on their chair for their guardian angel. We smile at that story, partly because it was a creative way to make angels real in the lives of children, and partly because it points to a truth about God's presence in our life.

In the fictional story of Tobit, we meet the angel Raphael. In other parts of the Bible, angels serve primarily as God's messengers. But Raphael is much more than a messenger. He disguises himself as a kindly but unknown relative who guides Tobias to the secrets he needs to know to relieve both Tobit's and Sarah's suffering.

The truth is that many angels are around us. Most of us have heard stories about kind strangers who appear seemingly out of nowhere to help and then disappear. Our seat may not have a lot of room for an angel, but our world certainly does. They remind us that God is with us, protecting us and guiding us.

Have you or someone you know been touched by an angel? In return, why don't you look for opportunities to be someone else's "angel"?

finished digging the grave, Rag′ū•el went into his house and called his wife, 12 saying, "Send one of the maids and have her go in to see if he is alive. But if he is dead, let us bury him without anyone knowing it." 13 So they sent the maid, lit a lamp, and opened the door; and she went in and found them sound asleep together. 14 Then the maid came out and informed them that he was alive and that nothing was wrong. 15 So they blessed the God of heaven, and Rag′ū•el[x] said,

"Blessed are you, O God, with every pure
    blessing;
let all your chosen ones bless you.[y]
Let them bless you forever.

16 Blessed are you because you have made me
    glad.
It has not turned out as I expected,
but you have dealt with us according to
    your great mercy.

17 Blessed are you because you had compassion
    on two only children.
Be merciful to them, O Master, and keep them
    safe;
bring their lives to fulfillment
in happiness and mercy."

18 Then he ordered his servants to fill in the grave before daybreak.

Wedding Feast

19 After this he asked his wife to bake many loaves of bread; and he went out to the herd and brought two steers and four rams and ordered them to be slaughtered. So they began to make preparations. 20 Then he called for Tō•bī′as and swore on oath to him in these words:[z] "You shall not leave here for fourteen days, but shall stay here eating and drinking with me; and you shall cheer up my daughter, who has been depressed. 21 Take at once half of what I own and return in safety to your father; the other half will be yours when my wife and I die. Take courage, my child. I am your father and Edna is your mother, and we belong to you as well as to your wife[a] now and forever. Take courage, my child."

The Money Recovered

9 Then Tō•bī′as called Raph′a•el and said to him, 2 "Brother Az•a•rī′ah, take four servants and two camels with you and travel to Rā′gēs. Go to the home of Gab′a•el, give him the bond, get the money, and then bring him with you to the wedding celebration. 4 For you know that my father must be counting the days, and if I delay even one day I will upset him very much. 3 You are witness to the oath Rag′ū•el has sworn, and I cannot violate his oath."[b] 5 So Raph′a•el with the four servants and two camels went to Rā′gēs in Mēd′i•a and stayed with Gab′a•el. Raph′a•el[c] gave him the bond and informed him that Tō′bit's son Tō•bī′as had married and was inviting him to the wedding celebration. So Gab′a•el[d] got up and counted out to him the money bags, with their seals intact; then they loaded them on the camels.[e] 6 In the morning they both got up early and went to the wedding celebration. When they came into Rag′ū•el's house they found Tō•bī′as reclining at table. He sprang up and greeted Gab′a•el,[f] who wept and blessed him with the words, "Good and noble son of a father good

---

x Gk *they*   y Other ancient authorities lack this line
z Other ancient authorities read *Tobias and said to him*
a Gk *sister*   b In other ancient authorities verse 3 precedes verse 4   c Gk *He*   d Gk *he*   e Other ancient authorities lack *on the camels*   f Gk *him*

and noble, upright and generous! May the Lord grant the blessing of heaven to you and your wife, and to your wife's father and mother. Blessed be God, for I see in Tō·bī′as the very image of my cousin Tō′bit."

Anxiety of the Parents

10 Now, day by day, Tō′bit kept counting how many days Tō·bī′as[s] would need for going and for returning. And when the days had passed and his son did not appear, 2 he said, "Is it possible that he has been detained? Or that Gab′a·el has died, and there is no one to give him the money?" 3 And he began to worry. 4 His wife Anna said, "My child has perished and is no longer among the living." And she began to weep and mourn for her son, saying, 5 "Woe to me, my child, the light of my eyes, that I let you make the journey." 6 But Tō′bit kept saying to her, "Be quiet and stop worrying, my dear;[h] he is all right. Probably something unexpected has happened there. The man who went with him is trustworthy and is one of our own kin. Do not grieve for him, my dear;[h] he will soon be here." 7 She answered him, "Be quiet yourself! Stop trying to deceive me! My child has perished." She would rush out every day and watch the road her son had taken, and would heed no one.[i] When the sun had set she would go in and mourn and weep all night long, getting no sleep at all.

Tobias and Sarah Start for Home

Now when the fourteen days of the wedding celebration had ended that Rag′ū·el had sworn to observe for his daughter, Tō·bī′as came to him and said, "Send me back, for I know that my father and mother do not believe that they will see me again. So I beg of you, father, to let me go so that I may return to my own father. I have already explained to you how I left him." 8 But Rag′ū·el said to Tō·bī′as, "Stay, my child, stay with me; I will send messengers to your father Tō′bit and they will inform him about you." 9 But he said, "No! I beg you to send me back to my father." 10 So Rag′ū·el promptly gave Tō·bī′as his wife Sarah, as well as half of all his property: male and female slaves, oxen and sheep, donkeys and camels, clothing, money, and household goods. 11 Then he saw them safely off; he embraced Tō·bī′as[j] and said, "Farewell, my child; have a safe journey. The Lord of heaven prosper you and your wife Sarah, and may I see children of yours before I die." 12 Then he kissed his daughter Sarah and said to her, "My daughter, honor your father-in-law and your mother-in-law,[k] since from now on they are as much your parents as those who gave you birth. Go in peace, daughter, and may I hear a good report about you as long as I live." Then he bade

them farewell and let them go. Then Edna said to Tō·bī′as, "My child and dear brother, the Lord of heaven bring you back safely, and may I live long enough to see children of you and of my daughter Sarah before I die. In the sight of the Lord I entrust my daughter to you; do nothing to grieve her all the days of your life. Go in peace, my child. From now on I am your mother and Sarah is your beloved wife.[h] May we all prosper together all the days of our lives." Then she kissed them both and saw them safely off. 13 Tō·bī′as parted from Rag′ū·el with happiness and joy, praising the Lord of heaven and earth, King over all, because he had made his journey a success. Finally, he blessed Rag′ū·el and his wife Edna, and said, "I have been commanded by the Lord to honor you all the days of my life."[l]

Homeward Journey

11 When they came near to Ka·ser′in, which is opposite Nin′e·veh, Raph′a·el said, 2 "You are aware of how we left your father. 3 Let us run ahead of your wife and prepare the house while they are still on the way." 4 As they went on together Raph′a·el[s] said to him, "Have the gall ready." And the dog[m] went along behind them.

5 Meanwhile Anna sat looking intently down the road by which her son would come. 6 When she caught sight of him coming, she said to his father, "Look, your son is coming, and the man who went with him!"

Tobit's Sight Restored
(Cp Acts 9.18)

7 Raph′a·el said to Tō·bī′as, before he had approached his father, "I know that his eyes will be opened. 8 Smear the gall of the fish on his eyes; the medicine will make the white films shrink and peel off from his eyes, and your father will regain his sight and see the light." 9 Then Anna ran up to her son and threw her arms around him, saying, "Now that I have seen you, my child, I am ready to die." And she wept. 10 Then Tō′bit got up and came stumbling out through the courtyard door. Tō·bī′as went up to him, 11 with the gall of the fish in his hand, and holding him firmly, he blew into his eyes, saying, "Take courage, father." With this he applied the medicine on his eyes, 12 and it made them smart.[l] 13 Next, with both his hands he peeled off the white films from the corners of his eyes. Then Tō′bit[s] saw his son and[n] threw his arms around him, 14 and he

---

s Gk *he*   h Gk *sister*   i Other ancient authorities read *and she would eat nothing*   j Gk *him*   k Other ancient authorities lack parts of *Then . . . mother-in-law*   l Lat: Meaning of Gk uncertain   m Codex Sinaiticus reads *And the Lord*   n Other ancient authorities lack *saw his son and* wept and said to him, "I see you, my son, the light of my eyes!" Then he said,

"Blessed be God,
and blessed be his great name,
and blessed be all his holy angels.
May his holy name be blessed[o]
throughout all the ages.
15 Though he afflicted me,
he has had mercy upon me.[p]
Now I see my son Tŏ·bī'as!"

So Tŏ'bit went in rejoicing and praising God at the top of his voice. Tŏ·bī'as reported to his father that his journey had been successful, that he had brought the money, that he had married Rag'ū·el's daughter Sarah, and that she was, indeed, on her way there, very near to the gate of Nin'e·veh.

16 Then Tŏ'bit, rejoicing and praising God, went out to meet his daughter-in-law at the gate of Nin'e·veh. When the people of Nin'e·veh saw him coming, walking along in full vigor and with no one leading him, they were amazed. 17 Before them all, Tŏ'bit acknowledged that God had been merciful to him and had restored his sight. When Tŏ'bit met Sarah the wife of his son Tŏ·bī'as, he blessed her saying, "Come in, my daughter, and welcome. Blessed be your God who has brought you to us, my daughter. Blessed be your father and your mother, blessed be my son Tŏ·bī'as, and blessed be you, my daughter. Come in now to your home, and welcome, with blessing and joy. Come in, my daughter." So on that day there was rejoicing among all the Jews who were in Nin'e·veh. 18 A·hī'kar and his nephew Nā'dab were also present to share Tŏ'bit's joy. With merriment they celebrated Tŏ·bī'as's wedding feast for seven days, and many gifts were given to him.[q]

Raphael's Wages

12 When the wedding celebration was ended, Tŏ'bit called his son Tŏ·bī'as and said to him, "My child, see to paying the wages of the man who went with you, and give him a bonus as well." 2 He replied, "Father, how much shall I pay him? It would do no harm to give him half of the possessions brought back with me. 3 For he has led me back to you safely, he cured my wife, he brought the money back with me, and he healed you. How much extra shall I give him as a bonus?" 4 Tŏ'bit said, "He deserves, my child, to receive half of all that he brought back." 5 So Tŏ·bī'as[r] called him and said, "Take for your wages half of all that you brought back, and farewell."

Raphael's Exhortation
(Sir 29.8–13; Mt 6.1–18)

6 Then Raph'a·el[r] called the two of them privately and said to them, "Bless God and acknowl-

edge him in the presence of all the living for the good things he has done for you. Bless and sing praise to his name. With fitting honor declare to all people the deeds[s] of God. Do not be slow to acknowledge him. 7 It is good to conceal the secret of a king, but to acknowledge and reveal the works of God, and with fitting honor to acknowledge him. Do good and evil will not overtake you. 8 Prayer with fasting[t] is good, but better than both is almsgiving with righteousness. A little with righteousness is better than wealth with wrongdoing.[u] It is better to give alms than to lay up gold. 9 For almsgiving saves from death and purges away every sin. Those who give alms will enjoy a full life, 10 but those who commit sin and do wrong are their own worst enemies.

Raphael Discloses His Identity

11 "I will now declare the whole truth to you and will conceal nothing from you. Already I have declared it to you when I said, 'It is good to conceal the secret of a king, but to reveal with due honor the works of God.' 12 So now when you and Sarah prayed, it was I who brought and read[v] the record of your prayer before the glory of the Lord, and likewise whenever you would bury the dead. 13 And that time when you did not hesitate to get up and leave your dinner to go and bury the dead, 14 I was sent to you to test you. And at the same time God sent me to heal you and Sarah your daughter-in-law. 15 I am Raph'a·el, one of the seven angels who stand ready and enter before the glory of the Lord."

16 The two of them were shaken; they fell face down, for they were afraid. 17 But he said to them, "Do not be afraid; peace be with you. Bless God forevermore. 18 As for me, when I was with you, I was not acting on my own will, but by the will of God. Bless him each and every day; sing his praises. 19 Although you were watching me, I really did not eat or drink anything—but what you saw was a vision. 20 So now get up from the ground,[w] and acknowledge God. See, I am ascending to him who sent me. Write down all these things that have happened to you." And he ascended. 21 Then they stood up, and could see him no more. 22 They kept blessing God and singing his praises, and they acknowledged God for these marvelous deeds of his, when an angel of God had appeared to them.

---

o Codex Sinaiticus reads *May his great name be upon us and blessed be all the angels*   p Lat: Gk lacks this line   q Gk *he*
ancient authorities lack parts of this sentence   r Gk *he*
s Gk *words*; other ancient authorities read *words of the deeds*   t Codex Sinaiticus *with sincerity*   u Lat   v Lat: Gk lacks *and read*   w Other ancient authorities read *now bless the Lord on earth*

Tobit's Thanksgiving to God
(Rev 21.9—22.5)

13 Then Tō′bit*x* said:
"Blessed be God who lives forever,
  because his kingdom*y* lasts throughout all
    ages.
2 For he afflicts, and he shows mercy;
  he leads down to Hades in the lowest
    regions of the earth,
  and he brings up from the great abyss,*z*
  and there is nothing that can escape his
    hand.
3 Acknowledge him before the nations,
    O children of Israel;
  for he has scattered you among them.
4   He has shown you his greatness even there.
  Exalt him in the presence of every living being,
    because he is our Lord and he is our God;
    he is our Father and he is God forever.
5 He will afflict*a* you for your iniquities,
    but he will again show mercy on all of you.
  He will gather you from all the nations
    among whom you have been scattered.
6 If you turn to him with all your heart and with
      all your soul,
    to do what is true before him,
  then he will turn to you
    and will no longer hide his face from you.

So now see what he has done for you;
    acknowledge him at the top of your voice.
Bless the Lord of righteousness,
    and exalt the King of the ages.*b*
In the land of my exile I acknowledge him,
    and show his power and majesty to a
      nation of sinners:
'Turn back, you sinners, and do what is right
      before him;
    perhaps he may look with favor upon you
      and show you mercy.'
7 As for me, I exalt my God,
    and my soul rejoices in the King of heaven.
8 Let all people speak of his majesty,
    and acknowledge him in Jerusalem.
9 O Jerusalem, the holy city,
    he afflicted*c* you for the deeds of your
      hands,*d*
    but will again have mercy on the children
      of the righteous.
10 Acknowledge the Lord, for he is good,*e*

---

x Gk *he*   *y* Other ancient authorities read *forever, and his
kingdom*   *z* Gk *from destruction*   *a* Other ancient authorities
read *He afflicted*   *b* The lacuna in codex Sinaiticus, verses
6b to 10a, is filled in from other ancient authorities
c Other ancient authorities read *will afflict*   *d* Other ancient
authorities read *your children*   *e* Other ancient authorities
read *Lord worthily*

T
O
B

HOPE FOR THE FAITHFUL!

When the Jews lived under the influence of Greek culture, there was a great need for hope. The story of Tobit and Tobias, whose names mean "goodness" and "God is good," was written to give hope to those who continue to be faithful to God, even in difficult times.

Tobit is the model of the good Israelite at all times and places. God's saving actions for him and his family symbolize God's actions toward Israel. In this spirit, before his death, Tobit sings a beautiful hymn in thanksgiving for God's goodness and with hope in the triumph of Jerusalem over its oppressors.

■ Recognize the goodness of God in your life and the way in which you fail God.
■ Take a moment to pray in Tobit's style. Praise God for the blessings in your life; ask forgiveness for the times you have failed God; give thanks for the times God has answered your prayers in a wiser way than what you had asked for. Pray not only for yourself but for all people, with hope for the triumph of God's love and peace over the egoism, hatred, and violence so common today.

▶ **Tobit, chapter 13**

and bless the King of the ages,
   so that his tent*f* may be rebuilt in you in joy.
May he cheer all those within you who are
     captives,
   and love all those within you who are
     distressed,
   to all generations forever.
11 A bright light will shine to all the ends of the
     earth;
   many nations will come to you from far
     away,
the inhabitants of the remotest parts of the
     earth to your holy name,
   bearing gifts in their hands for the King of
     heaven.
Generation after generation will give joyful
     praise in you;
   the name of the chosen city will endure
     forever.
12 Cursed are all who speak a harsh word against
     you;
   cursed are all who conquer you
   and pull down your walls,
all who overthrow your towers
   and set your homes on fire.
   But blessed forever will be all who revere
     you.*g*
13 Go, then, and rejoice over the children of the
     righteous,
   for they will be gathered together
   and will praise the Lord of the ages.
14 Happy are those who love you,
   and happy are those who rejoice in your
     prosperity.
   Happy also are all people who grieve with you
     because of your afflictions;
   for they will rejoice with you
     and witness all your glory forever.
15 My soul blesses*h* the Lord, the great King!
16   For Jerusalem will be built*i* as his house for
     all ages.
How happy I will be if a remnant of my
     descendants should survive
   to see your glory and acknowledge the King
     of heaven.
The gates of Jerusalem will be built with
     sapphire and emerald,
   and all your walls with precious stones.
The towers of Jerusalem will be built with gold,
   and their battlements with pure gold.
The streets of Jerusalem will be paved
     with ruby and with stones of Ō′phir.
17 The gates of Jerusalem will sing hymns of joy,
     and all her houses will cry, 'Hallelujah!
Blessed be the God of Israel!'
   and the blessed will bless the holy name
     forever and ever."

Tobit's Final Counsel
(Nah 1.2—3.19; Zech 8.20—23)

14 So ended Tō′bit's words of praise.
2 Tō′bit*j* died in peace when he was one
hundred twelve years old, and was buried with
great honor in Nin′e•veh. He was sixty-two*k* years
old when he lost his eyesight, and after regaining it
he lived in prosperity, giving alms and continually
blessing God and acknowledging God's majesty.

3 When he was about to die, he called his son
Tō•bī′as and the seven sons of Tō•bī′as*l* and gave
this command: "My son, take your children 4 and
hurry off to Mēd′i•a, for I believe the word of God
that Nā′hum spoke about Nin′e•veh, that all these
things will take place and overtake Assyria and
Nin′e•veh. Indeed, everything that was spoken by
the prophets of Israel, whom God sent, will occur.
None of all their words will fail, but all will come
true at their appointed times. So it will be safer in
Mēd′i•a than in Assyria and Babylon. For I know
and believe that whatever God has said will be fulfilled and will come true; not a single word of the
prophecies will fail. All of our kindred, inhabitants
of the land of Israel, will be scattered and taken as
captives from the good land; and the whole land of
Israel will be desolate, even Sa•mār′i•a and Jerusalem will be desolate. And the temple of God in it
will be burned to the ground, and it will be desolate
for a while.*m*

5 "But God will again have mercy on them, and
God will bring them back into the land of Israel;
and they will rebuild the temple of God, but not
like the first one until the period when the times of
fulfillment shall come. After this they all will return
from their exile and will rebuild Jerusalem in splendor; and in it the temple of God will be rebuilt, just
as the prophets of Israel have said concerning it.
6 Then the nations in the whole world will all be
converted and worship God in truth. They will all
abandon their idols, which deceitfully have led
them into their error; 7 and in righteousness they
will praise the eternal God. All the Israelites who
are saved in those days and are truly mindful of
God will be gathered together; they will go to
Jerusalem and live in safety forever in the land of
Abraham, and it will be given over to them. Those
who sincerely love God will rejoice, but those who
commit sin and injustice will vanish from all the
earth. 8,9 So now, my children, I command you,
serve God faithfully and do what is pleasing in his
sight. Your children are also to be commanded to

---

f Or *tabernacle*   *g* Other ancient authorities read *who build
you up*   *h* Or *O my soul, bless*   *i* Other ancient authorities
add *for a city*   *j* Gk *He*   *k* Other ancient authorities read
fifty-eight   *l* Lat: Gk lacks *and the seven sons of Tobias*   *m* Lat:
Other ancient authorities read *of God will be in distress and
will be burned for a while*

do what is right and to give alms, and to be mindful of God and to bless his name at all times with sincerity and with all their strength. So now, my son, leave Nin′e•veh; do not remain here. 10 On whatever day you bury your mother beside me, do not stay overnight within the confines of the city. For I see that there is much wickedness within it, and that much deceit is practiced within it, while the people are without shame. See, my son, what Nā′dab did to A•hī′kar who had reared him. Was he not, while still alive, brought down into the earth? For God repaid him to his face for this shameful treatment. A•hī′kar came out into the light, but Nā′dab went into the eternal darkness, because he tried to kill A•hī′kar. Because he gave alms, A•hī′kar[n] escaped the fatal trap that Nā′dab had set for him, but Nā′dab fell into it himself, and was destroyed. 11 So now, my children, see what almsgiving accomplishes, and what injustice does—it brings death! But now my breath fails me."

Death of Tobit and Anna

Then they laid him on his bed, and he died; and he received an honorable funeral. 12 When Tōbī′as′s mother died, he buried her beside his father. Then he and his wife and children[o] returned to Mēd′i•a and settled in Ec•bat′a•na with Rag′ū•el his father-in-law. 13 He treated his parents-in-law[p] with great respect in their old age, and buried them in Ec•bat′a•na of Mēd′i•a. He inherited both the property of Rag′ū•el and that of his father Tō′bit. 14 He died highly respected at the age of one hundred seventeen[q] years. 15 Before he died he heard[r] of the destruction of Nin′e•veh, and he saw its prisoners being led into Mēd′i•a, those whom King Cȳ•ax′a•rēs[s] of Mēd′i•a had taken captive. Tō•bī′as[t] praised God for all he had done to the people of Nin′e•veh and Assyria; before he died he rejoiced over Nin′e•veh, and he blessed the Lord God forever and ever. Amen.[u]

---

n Gk *he*; other ancient authorities read *Manasses*   o Codex Sinaiticus lacks *and children*   p Gk *them*   q Other authorities read other numbers   r Codex Sinaiticus reads *saw and heard*   s Cn: Codex Sinaiticus *Ahikar*; other ancient authorities read *Nebuchadnezzar and Ahasuerus*   t Gk *He*   u Other ancient authorities lack *Amen*

Do you like to cheer for the underdog? If so, you are like most people. Whether in a law court, on a football field, or in politics, we get a thrill from seeing the high and mighty toppled by a courageous and determined underdog. This theme is evident in some of the most popular stories of the Old Testament: a group of Hebrew slaves escapes from Pharaoh's army; the teenage David topples the giant Goliath; the prophet Daniel escapes injury in the lions' den. Judith's story is another in which the little people —against all odds—somehow come out on top.

At a Glance

- **Chapters 1–7.** the Jews in danger
- **Chapters 8–16.** Judith to the rescue

In-depth

As the Book of Judith opens, the mighty Assyrian army is on the march against Jerusalem. To block the advance, the citizens of the small town of Bethulia are asked by the high priest to resist the army's movement. With little hope of success but a great deal of courage, the Bethulians accept the challenge. When they are at the point of surrender, a childless widow named Judith steps forward. Putting all her trust in "the God of the lowly, helper of the oppressed, upholder of the weak, protector of the forsaken, savior of those without hope" (Jdt 9.11), she bravely delivers her nation from certain defeat.

The story of Judith must have presented a challenge to the male-dominated world of the Israelites. As a childless widow, Judith would have had little social standing. Yet she succeeds where the king, the priests, and the leaders of the city fail. It is interesting that the name Judith is probably not even a proper name. It simply means "Jewish woman." In a sense, Judith stands for all the Jewish women of the past who have served God through their faith, courage, and decisive action.

Because of its many historical errors, the Book of Judith is clearly a fictional work. With remarkable storytelling flair, the author underlines one of the major elements of Hebrew faith: "O Lord, you are great and glorious, / wonderful in strength, invincible" (16.13). This was the kind of faith that the underdog people of God needed as they faced the growing might of the Roman Empire.

Quick Facts

Setting
a fictional book without a clear historical setting

Author
unknown, writing at the end of the second or the beginning of the first century B.C.

Themes
a woman of faith and courage, God's saving power

The Book of Judith

Judith

Chap. 10

Arphaxad Fortifies Ecbatana
(Cp Ezra 6.2)

1 It was the twelfth year of the reign of Ne·bū·chad·nez′zar, who ruled over the Assyrians in the great city of Nin′e·veh. In those days Ar·phā′xad ruled over the Mēdes in Ec·bat′a·na. ² He built walls around Ec·bat′a·na with hewn stones three cubits thick and six cubits long; he made the walls seventy cubits high and fifty cubits wide. ³ At its gates he raised towers one hundred cubits high and sixty cubits wide at the foundations. ⁴ He made its gates seventy cubits high and forty cubits wide to allow his armies to march out in force and his infantry to form their ranks. ⁵ Then King Ne·bū·chad-nez′zar made war against King Ar·phā′xad in the great plain that is on the borders of Rā′gau. ⁶ There rallied to him all the people of the hill country and all those who lived along the Euphrates, the Tigris, and the Hȳ·das′pēs, and, on the plain, Ar′i·och, king of the El·y·mē′ans. Thus, many nations joined the forces of the Chal·dē′ans.[a]

Nebuchadnezzar Issues Ultimatum

7 Then Ne·bū·chad·nez′zar, king of the Assyrians, sent messengers to all who lived in Persia and to all who lived in the west, those who lived in Ci·li′ci·a and Damascus, Lebanon and An·ti·leb′a·non, and all who lived along the seacoast, ⁸ and those among the nations of Car′mel and Gil′e·ad, and Upper Galilee and the great plain of Es·dra·ē′lon, ⁹ and all who were in Sa·mār′i·a and its towns, and beyond the Jordan as far as Jerusalem and Beth′a·ny and Chel′ous and Kā′desh and the river of Egypt, and Tah′pan·hēs and Rā·am′sēs and the whole land of Gō′shen, ¹⁰ even beyond Tā′nis and Memphis, and all who lived in Egypt as far as the borders of Ethiopia. ¹¹ But all who lived in the whole region disregarded the summons of Ne·bū·chad·nez′zar, king of the Assyrians, and refused to join him in the war; for they were not afraid of him, but regarded him as only one man.[b] So they sent back his messengers empty-handed and in disgrace.

12 Then Ne·bū·chad·nez′zar became very angry with this whole region, and swore by his throne and kingdom that he would take revenge on the whole territory of Ci·li′ci·a and Damascus and Syria, that he would kill with his sword also all the inhabitants of the land of Mō′ab, and the people of Am′mon, and all Judea, and every one in Egypt, as far as the coasts of the two seas.

Arphaxad Is Defeated

13 In the seventeenth year he led his forces against King Ar·phā′xad and defeated him in battle, overthrowing the whole army of Ar·phā′xad and all

---

[a] Syr: Gk *Cheleoudites*   [b] Or *a man*

his cavalry and all his chariots. 14 Thus he took possession of his towns and came to Ec•bat'a•na, captured its towers, plundered its markets, and turned its glory into disgrace. 15 He captured Ar•phã'xad in the mountains of Rã'gau and struck him down with his spears, thus destroying him once and for all. 16 Then he returned to Nin'e•veh, he and all his combined forces, a vast body of troops; and there he and his forces rested and feasted for one hundred twenty days.

The Expedition against the West

2 In the eighteenth year, on the twenty-second day of the first month, there was talk in the palace of Ne•bū•chad•nez'zar, king of the Assyrians, about carrying out his revenge on the whole region, just as he had said. 2 He summoned all his ministers and all his nobles and set before them his secret plan and recounted fully, with his own lips, all the wickedness of the region.c 3 They decided that every one who had not obeyed his command should be destroyed.

4 When he had completed his plan, Ne•bū-chad•nez'zar, king of the Assyrians, called Hol•o-fer'nēs, the chief general of his army, second only to himself, and said to him, 5 "Thus says the Great King, the lord of the whole earth: Leave my presence and take with you men confident in their strength, one hundred twenty thousand foot soldiers and twelve thousand cavalry. 6 March out against all the land to the west, because they disobeyed my orders. 7 Tell them to prepare earth and water, for I am coming against them in my anger, and will cover the whole face of the earth with the feet of my troops, to whom I will hand them over to be plundered. 8 Their wounded shall fill their ravines and gullies, and the swelling river shall be filled with their dead. 9 I will lead them away captive to the ends of the whole earth. 10 You shall go and seize all their territory for me in advance. They must yield themselves to you, and you shall hold them for me until the day of their punishment. 11 But to those who resist show no mercy, but hand them over to slaughter and plunder throughout your whole region. 12 For as I live, and by the power of my kingdom, what I have spoken I will accomplish by my own hand. 13 And you—take care not to transgress any of your lord's commands, but carry them out exactly as I have ordered you; do it without delay."

Campaign of Holofernes

14 So Hol•o•fer'nēs left the presence of his lord, and summoned all the commanders, generals, and officers of the Assyrian army. 15 He mustered the picked troops by divisions as his lord had ordered him to do, one hundred twenty thousand of them,

together with twelve thousand archers on horseback, 16 and he organized them as a great army is marshaled for a campaign. 17 He took along a vast number of camels and donkeys and mules for transport, and innumerable sheep and oxen and goats for food; 18 also ample rations for everyone, and a huge amount of gold and silver from the royal palace.

19 Then he set out with his whole army, to go ahead of King Ne•bū•chad•nez'zar and to cover the whole face of the earth to the west with their chariots and cavalry and picked foot soldiers. 20 Along with them went a mixed crowd like a swarm of locusts, like the dustd of the earth—a multitude that could not be counted.

21 They marched for three days from Nin'e•veh to the plain of Bec'ti•leth, and camped opposite Bec'ti•leth near the mountain that is to the north of Upper Ci•li'ci•a. 22 From there Hol•o•fer'nēse took his whole army, the infantry, cavalry, and chariots, and went up into the hill country. 23 He ravaged Put and Lud, and plundered all the Ras'si•sites and the Ish'ma•el•ītes on the border of the desert, south of the country of the Chel'le•ans. 24 Then he followedf the Euphrates and passed through Mes•o-po•tã'mi•a and destroyed all the fortified towns along the brook Ab'ron, as far as the sea. 25 He also seized the territory of Ci•li'ci•a, and killed everyone who resisted him. Then he came to the southern borders of Jã'pheth, facing Arabia. 26 He surrounded all the Mid'i•an•ītes, and burned their tents and plundered their sheepfolds. 27 Then he went down into the plain of Damascus during the wheat harvest, and burned all their fields and destroyed their flocks and herds and sacked their towns and ravaged their lands and put all their young men to the sword.

28 So fear and dread of him fell upon all the people who lived along the seacoast, at Sĩ'don and Tÿre, and those who lived in Sur and Ō•cĩ'na and all who lived in Jam'ni•a. Those who lived in A•zõ'tus and As'ca•lon feared him greatly.

Entreaties for Peace
(Cp Dan 3.1–7)

3 They therefore sent messengers to him to sue for peace in these words: 2 "We, the servants of Ne•bū•chad•nez'zar, the Great King, lie prostrate before you. Do with us whatever you will. 3 See, our buildings and all our land and all our wheat fields and our flocks and herds and all our encampmentsg lie before you; do with them as you please. 4 Our towns and their inhabitants are also your slaves; come and deal with them as you see fit."

---

c Meaning of Gk uncertain   d Gk sand   e Gk he
f Or crossed   g Gk all the sheepfolds of our tents

5 The men came to Hol•o•fer′nēs and told him all this. 6 Then he went down to the seacoast with his army and stationed garrisons in the fortified towns and took picked men from them as auxiliaries. 7 These people and all in the countryside welcomed him with garlands and dances and tambourines. 8 Yet he demolished all their shrines*h* and cut down their sacred groves; for he had been commissioned to destroy all the gods of the land, so that all nations should worship Ne•bū•chad•nez′zar alone, and that all their dialects and tribes should call upon him as a god.

9 Then he came toward Es•dra•ē′lon, near Dō′than, facing the great ridge of Judea; 10 he camped between Gē′ba and Scyth•op′o•lis, and remained for a whole month in order to collect all the supplies for his army.

Judea on the Alert

4 When the Israelites living in Judea heard of everything that Hol•o•fer′nēs, the general of Ne•bū•chad•nez′zar, the king of the Assyrians, had done to the nations, and how he had plundered and destroyed all their temples, 2 they were therefore greatly terrified at his approach; they were alarmed both for Jerusalem and for the temple of the Lord their God. 3 For they had only recently returned from exile, and all the people of Judea had just now gathered together, and the sacred vessels and the altar and the temple had been consecrated after their profanation. 4 So they sent word to every district of Sa•mār′i•a, and to Kō′na, Beth-hō′ron, Bel′māin, and Jericho, and to Chō′ba and Aē•sor′a, and the valley of Salem. 5 They immediately seized all the high hilltops and fortified the villages on them and stored up food in preparation for war—since their fields had recently been harvested.

6 The high priest, Jō′a•kim, who was in Jerusalem at the time, wrote to the people of Beth•ū′li•a and Bet•o•mes•thā′im, which faces Es•dra•ē′lon opposite the plain near Dō′than, 7 ordering them to seize the mountain passes, since by them Judea could be invaded; and it would be easy to stop any who tried to enter, for the approach was narrow, wide enough for only two at a time to pass.

Prayer and Penance

8 So the Israelites did as they had been ordered by the high priest Jō′a•kim and the senate of the whole people of Israel, in session at Jerusalem. 9 And every man of Israel cried out to God with great fervor, and they humbled themselves with much fasting. 10 They and their wives and their children and their cattle and every resident alien and hired laborer and purchased slave—they all put sackcloth around their waists. 11 And all the Israelite men, women, and children living at Jerusalem prostrated themselves before the temple and put ashes on their heads and spread out their sackcloth before the Lord. 12 They even draped the altar with sackcloth and cried out in unison, praying fervently to the God of Israel not to allow their infants to be carried off and their wives to be taken as booty, and the towns they had inherited to be destroyed, and the sanctuary to be profaned and desecrated to the malicious joy of the Gentiles.

13 The Lord heard their prayers and had regard for their distress; for the people fasted many days throughout Judea and in Jerusalem before the sanctuary of the Lord Almighty. 14 The high priest Jō′a•kim and all the priests who stood before the Lord and ministered to the Lord, with sackcloth around their loins, offered the daily burnt offerings, the votive offerings, and freewill offerings of the people. 15 With ashes on their turbans, they cried out to the Lord with all their might to look with favor on the whole house of Israel.

Council against the Israelites

5 It was reported to Hol•o•fer′nēs, the general of the Assyrian army, that the people of Israel had prepared for war and had closed the mountain passes and fortified all the high hilltops and set up barricades in the plains. 2 In great anger he called together all the princes of Mō′ab and the commanders of Am′mon and all the governors of the coastland, 3 and said to them, "Tell me, you Cā′naan•ītes, what people is this that lives in the hill country? What towns do they inhabit? How large is their army, and in what does their power and strength consist? Who rules over them as king and leads their army? 4 And why have they alone, of all who live in the west, refused to come out and meet me?"

Achior's Report
(Gen 11.27—12.5; Ex 7.1—12.46; 14.21–22)

5 Then Ā′chi•or, the leader of all the Am′mon•ītes, said to him, "May my lord please listen to a report from the mouth of your servant, and I will tell you the truth about this people that lives in the mountain district near you. No falsehood shall come from your servant's mouth. 6 These people are descended from the Chal•dē′ans. 7 At one time they lived in Mes•o•po•tā′mi•a, because they did not wish to follow the gods of their ancestors who were in Chal•dē′a. 8 Since they had abandoned the ways of their ancestors, and worshiped the God of heaven, the God they had come to know, their ancestors*i* drove them out from the presence of their gods. So they fled to Mes•o•po•tā′mi•a, and lived there for a long time. 9 Then their God commanded them to

h Syr: Gk *borders*   *i* Gk *they*

leave the place where they were living and go to the land of Cā′naan. There they settled, and grew very prosperous in gold and silver and very much livestock. 10 When a famine spread over the land of Cā′naan they went down to Egypt and lived there as long as they had food. There they became so great a multitude that their race could not be counted. 11 So the king of Egypt became hostile to them; he exploited them and forced them to make bricks. 12 They cried out to their God, and he afflicted the whole land of Egypt with incurable plagues. So the Egyptians drove them out of their sight. 13 Then God dried up the Red Sea before them, 14 and he led them by the way of Sinai and Kā′desh-bar′nē·a. They drove out all the people of the desert, 15 and took up residence in the land of the Am′o·rītes, and by their might destroyed all the inhabitants of Hesh′bon; and crossing over the Jordan they took possession of all the hill country. 16 They drove out before them the Cā′naan·ītes, the Per′iz·zītes, the Jeb′ū·sītes, the Shē·chem·ītes, and all the Ger′ge-sītes, and lived there a long time.

17 "As long as they did not sin against their God they prospered, for the God who hates iniquity is with them. 18 But when they departed from the way he had prescribed for them, they were utterly defeated in many battles and were led away captive to a foreign land. The temple of their God was razed to the ground, and their towns were occupied by their enemies. 19 But now they have returned to their God, and have come back from the places where they were scattered, and have occupied Jerusalem, where their sanctuary is, and have settled in the hill country, because it was uninhabited.

20 "So now, my master and lord, if there is any oversight in this people and they sin against their God and we find out their offense, then we can go up and defeat them. 21 But if they are not a guilty nation, then let my lord pass them by; for their Lord and God will defend them, and we shall become the laughingstock of the whole world."

22 When Ā′chi·or had finished saying these things, all the people standing around the tent began to complain; Hol·o·fer′nēs' officers and all the inhabitants of the seacoast and Mō′ab insisted that he should be cut to pieces. 23 They said, "We are not afraid of the Israelites; they are a people with no strength or power for making war. 24 Therefore let us go ahead, Lord Hol·o·fer′nēs, and your vast army will swallow them up."

Achior Handed over to the Israelites

6 When the disturbance made by the people outside the council had died down, Hol·o·fer′nēs, the commander of the Assyrian army, said to Ā′chi·or[j] in the presence of all the foreign contingents:

2 "Who are you, Ā′chi·or and you mercenaries of E′phra·im, to prophesy among us as you have done today and tell us not to make war against the people of Israel because their God will defend them? What god is there except Ne·bū·chad·nez′zar? He will send his forces and destroy them from the face of the earth. Their God will not save them; 3 we the king's[k] servants will destroy them as one man. They cannot resist the might of our cavalry. 4 We will overwhelm them;[l] their mountains will be drunk with their blood, and their fields will be full of their dead. Not even their footprints will survive our attack; they will utterly perish. So says King Ne·bū·chad·nez′zar, lord of the whole earth. For he has spoken; none of his words shall be in vain.

5 "As for you, Ā′chi·or, you Am′mon·īte mercenary, you have said these words in a moment of perversity; you shall not see my face again from this day until I take revenge on this race that came out of Egypt. 6 Then at my return the sword of my army and the spear[m] of my servants shall pierce your sides, and you shall fall among their wounded. 7 Now my slaves are going to take you back into the hill country and put you in one of the towns beside the passes. 8 You will not die until you perish along with them. 9 If you really hope in your heart that they will not be taken, then do not look downcast! I have spoken, and none of my words shall fail to come true."

10 Then Hol·o·fer′nēs ordered his slaves, who waited on him in his tent, to seize Ā′chi·or and take him away to Beth·ū′li·a and hand him over to the Israelites. 11 So the slaves took him and led him out of the camp into the plain, and from the plain they went up into the hill country and came to the springs below Beth·ū′li·a. 12 When the men of the town saw them,[n] they seized their weapons and ran out of the town to the top of the hill, and all the slingers kept them from coming up by throwing stones at them. 13 So having taken shelter below the hill, they bound Ā′chi·or and left him lying at the foot of the hill, and returned to their master.

14 Then the Israelites came down from their town and found him; they untied him and brought him into Beth·ū′li·a and placed him before the magistrates of their town, 15 who in those days were Uz·zī′ah son of Mī′cah, of the tribe of Sim′ē·on, and Chab′ris son of Gō·thon′i·el, and Char′mis son of Mel′chi·el. 16 They called together all the elders of the town, and all their young men and women ran to the assembly. They set Ā′chi·or in the midst of all

---

j Other ancient authorities add *and to all the Moabites*
k Gk *his* l Other ancient authorities add *with it* m Lat Syr: Gk *people* n Other ancient authorities add *on the top of the hill*

their people, and Uz·zī'ah questioned him about what had happened. 17 He answered and told them what had taken place at the council of Hol·o·fer'nēs, and all that he had said in the presence of the Assyrian leaders, and all that Hol·o·fer'nēs had boasted he would do against the house of Israel. 18 Then the people fell down and worshiped God, and cried out:

19 "O Lord God of heaven, see their arrogance, and have pity on our people in their humiliation, and look kindly today on the faces of those who are consecrated to you."

20 Then they reassured Ā'chi·or, and praised him highly. 21 Uz·zī'ah took him from the assembly to his own house and gave a banquet for the elders; and all that night they called on the God of Israel for help.

The Campaign against Bethulia

7 The next day Hol·o·fer'nēs ordered his whole army, and all the allies who had joined him, to break camp and move against Beth·ū'li·a, and to seize the passes up into the hill country and make war on the Israelites. 2 So all their warriors marched off that day; their fighting forces numbered one hundred seventy thousand infantry and twelve thousand cavalry, not counting the baggage and the foot soldiers handling it, a very great multitude. 3 They encamped in the valley near Beth·ū'li·a, beside the spring, and they spread out in breadth over Dō'than as far as Bal·bā'im and in length from Beth·ū'li·a to Cȳ'a·mon, which faces Es·dra·ē'lon.

4 When the Israelites saw their vast numbers, they were greatly terrified and said to one another, "They will now strip clean the whole land; neither the high mountains nor the valleys nor the hills will bear their weight." 5 Yet they all seized their weapons, and when they had kindled fires on their towers, they remained on guard all that night.

6 On the second day Hol·o·fer'nēs led out all his cavalry in full view of the Israelites in Beth·ū'li·a. 7 He reconnoitered the approaches to their town, and visited the springs that supplied their water; he seized them and set guards of soldiers over them, and then returned to his army.

8 Then all the chieftains of the Ē'dom·ites and all the leaders of the Mō'ab·ites and the commanders of the coastland came to him and said, 9 "Listen to what we have to say, my lord, and your army will suffer no losses. 10 This people, the Israelites, do not rely on their spears but on the height of the mountains where they live, for it is not easy to reach the tops of their mountains. 11 Therefore, my lord, do not fight against them in regular formation, and not a man of your army will fall. 12 Remain in your camp, and keep all the men in your forces with you; let your servants take possession of the spring of water that flows from the foot of the mountain, 13 for this is where all the people of Beth·ū'li·a get their water. So thirst will destroy them, and they will surrender their town. Meanwhile, we and our people will go up to the tops of the nearby mountains and camp there to keep watch to see that no one gets out of the town. 14 They and their wives and children will waste away with famine, and before the sword reaches them they will be strewn about in the streets where they live. 15 Thus you will pay them back with evil, because they rebelled and did not receive you peaceably."

16 These words pleased Hol·o·fer'nēs and all his attendants, and he gave orders to do as they had said. 17 So the army of the Am'mon·ites moved forward, together with five thousand Assyrians, and they encamped in the valley and seized the water supply and the springs of the Israelites. 18 And the Ē'dom·ites and Am'mon·ites went up and encamped in the hill country opposite Dō'than; and they sent some of their men toward the south and the east, toward Eg're·beh, which is near Chū'sī beside the Wadi Moch'mur. The rest of the Assyrian army encamped in the plain, and covered the whole face of the land. Their tents and supply trains spread out in great number, and they formed a vast multitude.

The Distress of the Israelites

19 The Israelites then cried out to the Lord their God, for their courage failed, because all their enemies had surrounded them, and there was no way of escape from them. 20 The whole Assyrian army, their infantry, chariots, and cavalry, surrounded them for thirty-four days, until all the water containers of every inhabitant of Beth·ū'li·a were empty; 21 their cisterns were going dry, and on no day did they have enough water to drink, for their drinking water was rationed. 22 Their children were listless, and the women and young men fainted from thirst and were collapsing in the streets of the town and in the gateways; they no longer had any strength.

23 Then all the people, the young men, the women, and the children, gathered around Uz·zī'ah and the rulers of the town and cried out with a loud voice, and said before all the elders, 24 "Let God judge between you and us! You have done us a great injury in not making peace with the Assyrians. 25 For now we have no one to help us; God has sold us into their hands, to be strewn before them in thirst and exhaustion. 26 Now summon them and surrender the whole town as booty to the army of Hol·o·fer'nēs and to all his forces. 27 For it would be better for us to be captured by them.ᵒ We shall indeed become slaves, but our lives will be spared,

---

ᵒ Other ancient authorities add *than to die of thirst*

and we shall not witness our little ones dying before our eyes, and our wives and children drawing
their last breath. 28 We call to witness against you
heaven and earth and our God, the Lord of our ancestors, who punishes us for our sins and the sins of
our ancestors; do today the things that we have described!"

29 Then great and general lamentation arose
throughout the assembly, and they cried out to the
Lord God with a loud voice. 30 But Uz·zi'ah said to
them, "Courage, my brothers and sisters!ᵖ Let us
hold out for five days more; by that time the Lord
our God will turn his mercy to us again, for he will
not forsake us utterly. 31 But if these days pass by,
and no help comes for us, I will do as you say."

32 Then he dismissed the people to their various posts, and they went up on the walls and towers of their town. The women and children he sent
home. In the town they were in great misery.

The Character of Judith

8 Now in those days Judith heard about these
things: she was the daughter of Me·rar'ī son
of Ox son of Joseph son of O'zi·el son of El·kī'ah

son of An·a·nī'as son of Gideon son of Raph'a·in
son of A·hī'tub son of E·lī'jah son of Hil·kī'ah son
of E·lī'ab son of Na·than'a·el son of Sa·lā'mi·el son
of Sar·a·sad'aī son of Israel. 2 Her husband Ma·nas'-
seh, who belonged to her tribe and family, had died
during the barley harvest. 3 For as he stood overseeing those who were binding sheaves in the field, he
was overcome by the burning heat, and took to his
bed and died in his town Beth·ū'li·a. So they buried
him with his ancestors in the field between Dō'than
and Bal'a·mon. 4 Judith remained as a widow for
three years and four months 5 at home where she
set up a tent for herself on the roof of her house.
She put sackcloth around her waist and dressed in
widow's clothing. 6 She fasted all the days of her
widowhood, except the day before the sabbath and
the sabbath itself, the day before the new moon
and the day of the new moon, and the festivals and
days of rejoicing of the house of Israel. 7 She was
beautiful in appearance, and was very lovely to behold. Her husband Ma·nas'seh had left her gold
and silver, men and women slaves, livestock, and

ᵖ Gk Courage, brothers

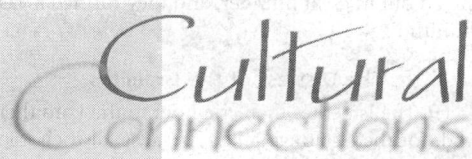

THE PRINCIPLE OF *KUJICHAGULIA*

**"That man over there says that women need to be helped into carriages, and lifted over
ditches, and to have the best place everywhere. Nobody ever helps me into carriages, or over
mud puddles, or gives me any best place! And ain't I a woman?" (Sojourner Truth, 1851)**

When people who are abused cower quietly in corners, injustice lives on. Bent heads, muffled
voices, and terrified spirits invite wrongs to continue.

Judith was a biblical heroine who refused to let her role be determined by others. As a
woman and a widow, she had little social standing in ancient Israel. Yet, she did not let this keep
her from speaking out and challenging the community leaders to action.

Sojourner Truth was a modern hero who refused to keep quiet despite being mistreated and
devalued. Her womanhood was slighted, and her personhood was trampled, yet she traveled
America to tell all who would listen about the evils of slavery.

The African Kwanzaa principle of *kujichagulia* (see "Kwanzaa as a Way of Life," Deut
10.12–22), or self-determination, sometimes requires us to stand up and speak out. Silence can
be compliance. Thank God for the gift of boldness of speech! It gives us the power to speak the
truth even in the most oppressive situations.

*Dear God, give me the boldness of Judith and Sojourner Truth to address the wrongs of this world.
Amen.*

▶ Jdt 8.9–36

JDT

fields; and she maintained this estate. 8 No one spoke ill of her, for she feared God with great devotion.

Judith and the Elders
(Gen 22.1–18; 29.1—31.55; Deut 6.16;
Rom 11.33–34)

9 When Judith heard the harsh words spoken by the people against the ruler, because they were faint for lack of water, and when she heard all that Uz·zi′ah said to them, and how he promised them under oath to surrender the town to the Assyrians after five days, 10 she sent her maid, who was in charge of all she possessed, to summon Uz·zi′ah and*q* Chab′ris and Char′mis, the elders of her town. 11 They came to her, and she said to them:

"Listen to me, rulers of the people of Beth·u̅′li·a! What you have said to the people today is not right; you have even sworn and pronounced this oath between God and you, promising to surrender the town to our enemies unless the Lord turns and helps us within so many days. 12 Who are you to put God to the test today, and to set yourselves up in the place of*r* God in human affairs? 13 You are putting the Lord Almighty to the test, but you will never learn anything! 14 You cannot plumb the depths of the human heart or understand the workings of the human mind; how do you expect to search out God, who made all these things, and find out his mind or comprehend his thought? No, my brothers, do not anger the Lord our God. 15 For if he does not choose to help us within these five days, he has power to protect us within any time he pleases, or even to destroy us in the presence of our enemies. 16 Do not try to bind the purposes of the Lord our God; for God is not like a human being, to be threatened, or like a mere mortal, to be won over by pleading. 17 Therefore, while we wait for his deliverance, let us call upon him to help us, and he will hear our voice, if it pleases him.

18 "For never in our generation, nor in these present days, has there been any tribe or family or people or town of ours that worships gods made with hands, as was done in days gone by. 19 That was why our ancestors were handed over to the sword and to pillage, and so they suffered a great catastrophe before our enemies. 20 But we know no other god but him, and so we hope that he will not disdain us or any of our nation. 21 For if we are captured, all Judea will be captured and our sanctuary will be plundered; and he will make us pay for its desecration with our blood. 22 The slaughter of our kindred and the captivity of the land and the desolation of our inheritance—all this he will bring on our heads among the Gentiles, wherever we serve as slaves; and we shall be an offense and a disgrace in the eyes of those who acquire us. 23 For our slavery

will not bring us into favor, but the Lord our God will turn it to dishonor.

24 "Therefore, my brothers, let us set an example for our kindred, for their lives depend upon us, and the sanctuary—both the temple and the altar—rests upon us. 25 In spite of everything let us give thanks to the Lord our God, who is putting us to the test as he did our ancestors. 26 Remember what he did with Abraham, and how he tested Isaac, and what happened to Jacob in Syrian Mes·o·po·ta̅′mi·a, while he was tending the sheep of La̅′ban, his mother's brother. 27 For he has not tried us with fire, as he did them, to search their hearts, nor has he taken vengeance on us; but the Lord scourges those who are close to him in order to admonish them."

28 Then Uz·zi′ah said to her, "All that you have said was spoken out of a true heart, and there is no one who can deny your words. 29 Today is not the first time your wisdom has been shown, but from the beginning of your life all the people have recognized your understanding, for your heart's disposition is right. 30 But the people were so thirsty that they compelled us to do for them what we have promised, and made us take an oath that we cannot break. 31 Now since you are a God-fearing woman, pray for us, so that the Lord may send us rain to fill our cisterns. Then we will no longer feel faint from thirst."

32 Then Judith said to them, "Listen to me. I am about to do something that will go down through all generations of our descendants. 33 Stand at the town gate tonight so that I may go out with my maid; and within the days after which you have promised to surrender the town to our enemies, the Lord will deliver Israel by my hand. 34 Only, do not try to find out what I am doing; for I will not tell you until I have finished what I am about to do."

35 Uz·zi′ah and the rulers said to her, "Go in peace, and may the Lord God go before you, to take vengeance on our enemies." 36 So they returned from the tent and went to their posts.

The Prayer of Judith
(Gen 34.1–31)

9 Then Judith prostrated herself, put ashes on her head, and uncovered the sackcloth she was wearing. At the very time when the evening incense was being offered in the house of God in Jerusalem, Judith cried out to the Lord with a loud voice, and said,

2 "O Lord God of my ancestor Sim′e·on, to whom you gave a sword to take revenge on those strangers who had torn off a virgin's clothing*s* to defile her, and exposed her thighs to put her to shame,

---
q Other ancient authorities lack *Uzziah and* (see verses 28 and 35) *r* Or *above* *s* Cn: Gk *loosed her womb*

and polluted her womb to disgrace her; for you said, 'It shall not be done'—yet they did it; 3 so you gave up their rulers to be killed, and their bed, which was ashamed of the deceit they had practiced, was stained with blood, and you struck down slaves along with princes, and princes on their thrones. 4 You gave up their wives for booty and their daughters to captivity, and all their booty to be divided among your beloved children who burned with zeal for you and abhorred the pollution of their blood and called on you for help. O God, my God, hear me also, a widow.

5 "For you have done these things and those that went before and those that followed. You have designed the things that are now, and those that are to come. What you had in mind has happened; 6 the things you decided on presented themselves and said, 'Here we are!' For all your ways are prepared in advance, and your judgment is with foreknowledge.

7 "Here now are the Assyrians, a greatly increased force, priding themselves in their horses and riders, boasting in the strength of their foot soldiers, and trusting in shield and spear, in bow and sling. They do not know that you are the Lord who crushes wars; the Lord is your name. 8 Break their strength by your might, and bring down their power in your anger; for they intend to defile your sanctuary, and to pollute the tabernacle where your glorious name resides, and to break off the horns[t] of your altar with the sword. 9 Look at their pride, and send your wrath upon their heads. Give to me, a widow, the strong hand to do what I plan. 10 By the deceit of my lips strike down the slave with the prince and the prince with his servant; crush their arrogance by the hand of a woman.

11 "For your strength does not depend on numbers, nor your might on the powerful. But you are the God of the lowly, helper of the oppressed, upholder of the weak, protector of the forsaken, savior of those without hope. 12 Please, please, God of my father, God of the heritage of Israel, Lord of heaven and earth, Creator of the waters, King of all your creation, hear my prayer! 13 Make my deceitful words bring wound and bruise on those who have planned cruel things against your covenant, and against your sacred house, and against Mount Zion, and against the house your children possess. 14 Let your whole nation and every tribe know and understand that you are God, the God of all power and might, and that there is no other who protects the people of Israel but you alone!"

Judith Prepares to Go to Holofernes

10 When Judith[u] had stopped crying out to the God of Israel, and had ended all these words, 2 she rose from where she lay pros-

Catholic Connections

THE BODY PRAYER

To pray, Judith prostrated herself, which means she lay face down on the ground. This position demonstrates humility and surrender. Judith also wore ashes and sackcloth, additional symbols of repentance and sorrow.

You will see this prayer posture on Good Friday, when the priests lie down on the floor at the beginning of the service. It is a sign of reverence and humility as we remember in a special way Jesus' sacrifice on the cross. You will see priest and deacon candidates prostrate themselves during the ordination ceremony as a sign of humility and their dependence on God's strength to carry out their ministry—a sign not just for themselves but for the whole Christian community.

▶ Jdt 9.1

trate. She called her maid and went down into the house where she lived on sabbaths and on her festal days. 3 She removed the sackcloth she had been wearing, took off her widow's garments, bathed her body with water, and anointed herself with precious ointment. She combed her hair, put on a tiara, and dressed herself in the festive attire that she used to wear while her husband Ma•nas'seh was living. 4 She put sandals on her feet, and put on her anklets, bracelets, rings, earrings, and all her other jewelry. Thus she made herself very beautiful, to entice the eyes of all the men who might see her. 5 She gave her maid a skin of wine and a flask of oil, and filled a bag with roasted grain, dried fig cakes, and fine bread;[v] then she wrapped up all her dishes and gave them to her to carry.

6 Then they went out to the town gate of Beth•u'li•a and found Uz•zi'ah standing there with the elders of the town, Chab'ris and Char'mis.

---

t Syr: Gk *horn*   u Gk *she*   v Other ancient authorities add *and cheese*

7 When they saw her transformed in appearance and dressed differently, they were very greatly astounded at her beauty and said to her, 8 "May the God of our ancestors grant you favor and fulfill your plans, so that the people of Israel may glory and Jerusalem may be exalted." She bowed down to God.

9 Then she said to them, "Order the gate of the town to be opened for me so that I may go out and accomplish the things you have just said to me." So they ordered the young men to open the gate for her, as she requested. 10 When they had done this, Judith went out, accompanied by her maid. The men of the town watched her until she had gone down the mountain and passed through the valley, where they lost sight of her.

Judith Is Captured

11 As the women[w] were going straight on through the valley, an Assyrian patrol met her 12 and took her into custody. They asked her, "To what people do you belong, and where are you coming from, and where are you going?" She replied, "I am a daughter of the Hebrews, but I am fleeing from them, for they are about to be handed over to you to be devoured. 13 I am on my way to see Hol·o·fer′nēs the commander of your army, to give him a true report; I will show him a way by which he can go and capture all the hill country without losing one of his men, captured or slain."

14 When the men heard her words, and observed her face—she was in their eyes marvelously beautiful—they said to her, 15 "You have saved your life by hurrying down to see our lord. Go at once to his tent; some of us will escort you and hand you over to him. 16 When you stand before him, have no fear in your heart, but tell him what you have just said, and he will treat you well."

17 They chose from their number a hundred men to accompany her and her maid, and they brought them to the tent of Hol·o·fer′nēs. 18 There was great excitement in the whole camp, for her arrival was reported from tent to tent. They came and gathered around her as she stood outside the tent of Hol·o·fer′nēs, waiting until they told him about her. 19 They marveled at her beauty and admired the Israelites, judging them by her. They said to one another, "Who can despise these people, who have women like this among them? It is not wise to leave one of their men alive, for if we let them go they will be able to beguile the whole world!"

Judith Is Brought before Holofernes

20 Then the guards of Hol·o·fer′nēs and all his servants came out and led her into the tent. 21 Hol·o·fer′nēs was resting on his bed under a canopy that was woven with purple and gold, emeralds and other precious stones. 22 When they told him of her, he came to the front of the tent, with silver lamps carried before him. 23 When Judith came into the presence of Hol·o·fer′nēs[x] and his servants, they all marveled at the beauty of her face. She prostrated herself and did obeisance to him, but his slaves raised her up.

11 Then Hol·o·fer′nēs said to her, "Take courage, woman, and do not be afraid in your heart, for I have never hurt anyone who chose to serve Ne·bū·chad·nez′zar, king of all the earth. 2 Even now, if your people who live in the hill country had not slighted me, I would never have lifted my spear against them. They have brought this on themselves. 3 But now tell me why you have fled from them and have come over to us. In any event, you have come to safety. Take courage! You will live tonight and ever after. 4 No one will hurt you. Rather, all will treat you well, as they do the servants of my lord King Ne·bū·chad·nez′zar."

Judith Explains Her Presence

5 Judith answered him, "Accept the words of your slave, and let your servant speak in your presence. I will say nothing false to my lord this night. 6 If you follow out the words of your servant, God will accomplish something through you, and my lord will not fail to achieve his purposes. 7 By the life of Ne·bū·chad·nez′zar, king of the whole earth, and by the power of him who has sent you to direct every living being! Not only do human beings serve him because of you, but also the animals of the field and the cattle and the birds of the air will live, because of your power, under Ne·bū·chad·nez′zar and all his house. 8 For we have heard of your wisdom and skill, and it is reported throughout the whole world that you alone are the best in the whole kingdom, the most informed and the most astounding in military strategy.

9 "Now as for Ā′chi·or′s speech in your council, we have heard his words, for the people of Beth·ū′li·a spared him and he told them all he had said to you. 10 Therefore, lord and master, do not disregard what he said, but keep it in your mind, for it is true. Indeed our nation cannot be punished, nor can the sword prevail against them, unless they sin against their God.

11 "But now, in order that my lord may not be defeated and his purpose frustrated, death will fall upon them, for a sin has overtaken them by which they are about to provoke their God to anger when they do what is wrong. 12 Since their food supply is exhausted and their water has almost given out, they have planned to kill their livestock and have determined to use all that God by his laws has

---

w Gk *they*   x Gk *him*

J D T

forbidden them to eat. 13 They have decided to consume the first fruits of the grain and the tithes of the wine and oil, which they had consecrated and set aside for the priests who minister in the presence of our God in Jerusalem—things it is not lawful for any of the people even to touch with their hands. 14 Since even the people in Jerusalem have been doing this, they have sent messengers there in order to bring back permission from the council of the elders. 15 When the response reaches them and they act upon it, on that very day they will be handed over to you to be destroyed.

16 "So when I, your slave, learned all this, I fled from them. God has sent me to accomplish with you things that will astonish the whole world wherever people shall hear about them. 17 Your servant is indeed God-fearing and serves the God of heaven night and day. So, my lord, I will remain with you; but every night your servant will go out into the valley and pray to God. He will tell me when they have committed their sins. 18 Then I will come and tell you, so that you may go out with your whole army, and not one of them will be able to withstand you. 19 Then I will lead you through Judea, until you come to Jerusalem; there I will set your throne.ʸ You will drive them like sheep that have no shepherd, and no dog will so much as growl at you. For this was told me to give me foreknowledge; it was announced to me, and I was sent to tell you."

20 Her words pleased Hol·o·fer′nēs and all his servants. They marveled at her wisdom and said, 21 "No other woman from one end of the earth to the other looks so beautiful or speaks so wisely!" 22 Then Hol·o·fer′nēs said to her, "God has done well to send you ahead of the people, to strengthen our hands and bring destruction on those who have despised my lord. 23 You are not only beautiful in appearance, but wise in speech. If you do as you have said, your God shall be my God, and you shall live in the palace of King Ne·bū·chad·nez′zar and be renowned throughout the whole world."

Judith as a Guest of Holofernes
(Cp Dan 1.3–8)

12 Then he commanded them to bring her in where his silver dinnerware was kept, and ordered them to set a table for her with some of his own delicacies, and with some of his own wine to drink. 2 But Judith said, "I cannot partake of them, or it will be an offense; but I will have enough with the things I brought with me." 3 Hol·o·fer′nēs said to her, "If your supply runs out, where can we get you more of the same? For none of your people are here with us." 4 Judith replied, "As surely as you live, my lord, your servant will not use up the supplies I have with me before the Lord carries out by my hand what he has determined."

5 Then the servants of Hol·o·fer′nēs brought her into the tent, and she slept until midnight. Toward the morning watch she got up 6 and sent this message to Hol·o·fer′nēs: "Let my lord now give orders to allow your servant to go out and pray." 7 So Hol·o·fer′nēs commanded his guards not to hinder her. She remained in the camp three days. She went out each night to the valley of Beth·ū′li·a, and bathed at the spring in the camp.ᶻ 8 After bathing, she prayed the Lord God of Israel to direct her way for the triumph of hisᵃ people. 9 Then she returned purified and stayed in the tent until she ate her food toward evening.

Judith Attends Holofernes' Banquet

10 On the fourth day Hol·o·fer′nēs held a banquet for his personal attendants only, and did not invite any of his officers. 11 He said to Ba·gō′as, the eunuch who had charge of his personal affairs, "Go and persuade the Hebrew woman who is in your care to join us and to eat and drink with us. 12 For it would be a disgrace if we let such a woman go without having intercourse with her. If we do not seduce her, she will laugh at us."

13 So Ba·gō′as left the presence of Hol·o·fer′nēs, and approached her and said, "Let this pretty girl not hesitate to come to my lord to be honored in his presence, and to enjoy drinking wine with us, and to become today like one of the Assyrian women who serve in the palace of Ne·bū·chad·nez′zar." 14 Judith replied, "Who am I to refuse my lord? Whatever pleases him I will do at once, and it will be a joy to me until the day of my death." 15 So

---

ʸ Or *chariot*   ᶻ Other ancient authorities lack *in the camp*
ᵃ Other ancient authorities read *her*

Dead Drunk!

Have you ever wondered why people get drunk? Why would anyone want to drink enough alcohol to pass out? Getting drunk has lots of negative consequences, and getting very drunk can even be fatal.

In the Book of Judith, chapter 13, Judith takes advantage of Holofernes' drunkenness to kill him. She gives the term *dead drunk* **a whole new meaning. If you do not believe that getting drunk can destroy your life, then think again. It doesn't take a widow with a sword to help drunkenness destroy your life.**

▸ Jdt 12.15—13.10

she proceeded to dress herself in all her woman's finery. Her maid went ahead and spread for her on the ground before Hol·o·fer′nēs the lambskins she had received from Ba·gō′as for her daily use in reclining.

16 Then Judith came in and lay down. Hol·ofer′nēs' heart was ravished with her and his passion was aroused, for he had been waiting for an opportunity to seduce her from the day he first saw her. 17 So Hol·o·fer′nēs said to her, "Have a drink and be merry with us!" 18 Judith said, "I will gladly drink, my lord, because today is the greatest day in my whole life." 19 Then she took what her maid had prepared and ate and drank before him. 20 Hol·o·fer′nēs was greatly pleased with her, and drank a great quantity of wine, much more than he had ever drunk in any one day since he was born.

Judith Beheads Holofernes

13 When evening came, his slaves quickly withdrew. Ba·gō′as closed the tent from outside and shut out the attendants from his master's presence. They went to bed, for they all were weary because the banquet had lasted so long. 2 But Judith was left alone in the tent, with Hol·o·fer′nēs stretched out on his bed, for he was dead drunk.

3 Now Judith had told her maid to stand outside the bedchamber and to wait for her to come out, as she did on the other days; for she said she would be going out for her prayers. She had said the same thing to Ba·gō′as. 4 So everyone went out, and no one, either small or great, was left in the bedchamber. Then Judith, standing beside his bed, said in her heart, "O Lord God of all might, look in this hour on the work of my hands for the exaltation of Jerusalem. 5 Now indeed is the time to help your heritage and to carry out my design to destroy the enemies who have risen up against us."

6 She went up to the bedpost near Hol·o·fer′nēs' head, and took down his sword that hung there. 7 She came close to his bed, took hold of the hair of his head, and said, "Give me strength today,

O Lord God of Israel!" 8 Then she struck his neck twice with all her might, and cut off his head. 9 Next she rolled his body off the bed and pulled down the canopy from the posts. Soon afterward she went out and gave Hol·o·fer′nēs' head to her maid, 10 who placed it in her food bag.

Judith Returns to Bethulia

Then the two of them went out together, as they were accustomed to do for prayer. They passed through the camp, circled around the valley, and went up the mountain to Beth·ū′li·a, and came to its gates. 11 From a distance Judith called out to the sentries at the gates, "Open, open the gate! God, our God, is with us, still showing his power in Israel and his strength against our enemies, as he has done today!"

12 When the people of her town heard her voice, they hurried down to the town gate and summoned the elders of the town. 13 They all ran together, both small and great, for it seemed unbelievable that she had returned. They opened the gate and welcomed them. Then they lit a fire to give light, and gathered around them. 14 Then she said to them with a loud voice, "Praise God, O praise him! Praise God, who has not withdrawn his mercy from the house of Israel, but has destroyed our enemies by my hand this very night!"

15 Then she pulled the head out of the bag and showed it to them, and said, "See here, the head of Hol·o·fer′nēs, the commander of the Assyrian army, and here is the canopy beneath which he lay in his drunken stupor. The Lord has struck him down by the hand of a woman. 16 As the Lord lives, who has protected me in the way I went, I swear that it was my face that seduced him to his destruction, and that he committed no sin with me, to defile and shame me."

17 All the people were greatly astonished. They bowed down and worshiped God, and said with one accord, "Blessed are you our God, who have this day humiliated the enemies of your people."

JDT

did you KNOW?

Is God a Fan of Violence?

Is it hard to believe that God strengthened Judith to cut off Holofernes' head (Jdt 13.7–8)? Or that God was angry at Saul for not destroying Agag and his possessions (1 Sam 15.18–19)? Or that Jephthah had to sacrifice his daughter because of a vow he had made (Jdg 11.29–40)? The violence portrayed in the Old Testament is often horrifying, especially when the Old Testament authors view it as part of God's will.

In the ancient world, tribes and nations viewed their gods as the leaders of their armies. The Hebrews were no exception. One of God's oldest titles is "LORD God of hosts" (Ps 89.9; Isa 6.3); the image is of an almighty warrior who fought on Israel's side (see Ex 15.3; 1 Sam 14.23). The enemies of Israel were seen as God's enemies, and their destruction as God's will. The military victories of Joshua, Saul, and David were understood as proof of heaven's blessing on the nation.

Later in history, as the Israelites experienced one agonizing defeat after another and the prophets challenged them to consider God's love for all nations, a new understanding of God's will began to develop in certain Jewish circles. Later prophets spoke of beating "swords into plowshares" (Isa 2.4), of making "a covenant of peace" (Ezek 37.26), of seeking "to do justice, and to love kindness, / and to walk humbly with your God" (Mic 6.8). From their own painful history, the Chosen People started to see that war and violence always meant unspeakable suffering for many, and they began to question whether holy war was part of God's will.

▸ Jdt 13.1–10

18 Then Uz·zi′ah said to her, "O daughter, you are blessed by the Most High God above all other women on earth; and blessed be the Lord God, who created the heavens and the earth, who has guided you to cut off the head of the leader of our enemies.

19 Your praise[b] will never depart from the hearts of those who remember the power of God. 20 May God grant this to be a perpetual honor to you, and may he reward you with blessings, because you risked your own life when our nation was brought low, and you averted our ruin, walking in the straight path before our God." And all the people said, "Amen. Amen."

Judith's Counsel

14 Then Judith said to them, "Listen to me, my friends. Take this head and hang it upon the parapet of your wall. 2 As soon as day breaks and the sun rises on the earth, each of you take up your weapons, and let every able-bodied man go out of the town; set a captain over them, as if you were going down to the plain against the Assyrian outpost; only do not go down. 3 Then they will seize their arms and go into the camp and rouse the officers of the Assyrian army. They will rush into the tent of Hol·o·fer′nes and will not find him. Then panic will come over them, and they will flee before you. 4 Then you and all who live within the borders of Israel will pursue them and cut them down in their tracks. 5 But before you do all this, bring Ā′chi·or the Am′mon·ite to me so that he may see and recognize the man who despised the house of Israel and sent him to us as if to his death."

6 So they summoned Ā′chi·or from the house of Uz·zī′ah. When he came and saw the head of Hol·o·fer′nes in the hand of one of the men in the assembly of the people, he fell down on his face in a faint. 7 When they raised him up he threw himself at Judith's feet, and did obeisance to her, and said, "Blessed are you in every tent of Judah! In every nation those who hear your name will be alarmed. 8 Now tell me what you have done during these days."

So Judith told him in the presence of the people all that she had done, from the day she left until the moment she began speaking to them. 9 When she had finished, the people raised a great shout and made a joyful noise in their town. 10 When Ā′chi·or saw all that the God of Israel had done, he believed firmly in God. So he was circumcised, and joined the house of Israel, remaining so to this day.

Holofernes' Death Is Discovered

11 As soon as it was dawn they hung the head of Hol·o·fer′nes on the wall. Then they all took their weapons, and they went out in companies to the mountain passes. 12 When the Assyrians saw them they sent word to their commanders, who then went to the generals and the captains and to all their other officers. 13 They came to Hol·o·fer-

---

b Other ancient authorities read *hope*

J D T

nĕs' tent and said to the steward in charge of all his personal affairs, "Wake up our lord, for the slaves have been so bold as to come down against us to give battle, to their utter destruction."

14 So Ba•gō'as went in and knocked at the entry of the tent, for he supposed that he was sleeping with Judith. 15 But when no one answered, he opened it and went into the bedchamber and found him sprawled on the floor dead, with his head missing. 16 He cried out with a loud voice and wept and groaned and shouted, and tore his clothes. 17 Then he went to the tent where Judith had stayed, and when he did not find her, he rushed out to the people and shouted, 18 "The slaves have tricked us! One Hebrew woman has brought disgrace on the house of King Ne•bū•chad-nez'zar. Look, Hol•o•fer'nēs is lying on the ground, and his head is missing!"

19 When the leaders of the Assyrian army heard this, they tore their tunics and were greatly dismayed, and their loud cries and shouts rose up throughout the camp.

The Assyrians Flee in Panic

15 When the men in the tents heard it, they were amazed at what had happened. 2 Overcome with fear and trembling, they did not wait for one another, but with one impulse all rushed out and fled by every path across the plain and through the hill country. 3 Those who had camped in the hills around Beth•ū'li•a also took to flight. Then the Israelites, everyone that was a soldier, rushed out upon them. 4 Uz•zi'ah sent men to Bet•o•mas•thā'im^c and Chō'ba and Kō'la, and to all the frontiers of Israel, to tell what had taken place and to urge all to rush out upon the enemy to destroy them. 5 When the Israelites heard it, with one accord they fell upon the enemy,^d and cut them down as far as Chō'ba. Those in Jerusalem and all the hill country also came, for they were told what had happened in the camp of the enemy. The men in Gil'e•ad and in Galilee outflanked them with great slaughter, even beyond Damascus and its borders. 6 The rest of the people of Beth•ū'li•a fell upon the Assyrian camp and plundered it, acquiring great riches. 7 And the Israelites, when they returned from the slaughter, took possession of what remained. Even the villages and towns in the hill country and in the plain got a great amount of booty, since there was a vast quantity of it.

The Israelites Celebrate Their Victory
(Cp 1 Sam 18.6)

8 Then the high priest Jō'a•kim and the elders of the Israelites who lived in Jerusalem came to witness the good things that the Lord had done for Israel, and to see Judith and to wish her well. 9 When they met her, they all blessed her with one accord and said to her, "You are the glory of Jerusalem, you are the great boast of Israel, you are the great pride of our nation! 10 You have done all this with your own hand; you have done great good to Israel, and God is well pleased with it. May the Almighty Lord bless you forever!" And all the people said, "Amen."

11 All the people plundered the camp for thirty days. They gave Judith the tent of Hol•o•fer'nēs and all his silver dinnerware, his beds, his bowls, and all his furniture. She took them and loaded her mules and hitched up her carts and piled the things on them.

12 All the women of Israel gathered to see her, and blessed her, and some of them performed a dance in her honor. She took ivy-wreathed wands in her hands and distributed them to the women who were with her; 13 and she and those who were with her crowned themselves with olive wreaths. She went before all the people in the dance, leading all the women, while all the men of Israel followed, bearing their arms and wearing garlands and singing hymns.

Judith Offers Her Hymn of Praise
(Cp Ex 15.20–21; Judg 5.1–31; Tob 13.1–17)

14 Judith began this thanksgiving before all Israel, and all the people loudly sang this song of **16** praise. 1 And Judith said,

Begin a song to my God with
    tambourines,
sing to my Lord with cymbals.
Raise to him a new psalm;^e
    exalt him, and call upon his name.
2 For the Lord is a God who crushes wars;
    he sets up his camp among his people;
    he delivered me from the hands of my
        pursuers.
3 The Assyrian came down from the mountains
       of the north;
    he came with myriads of his warriors;
    their numbers blocked up the wadis,
    and their cavalry covered the hills.
4 He boasted that he would burn up my
       territory,
    and kill my young men with the sword,
    and dash my infants to the ground,
    and seize my children as booty,
    and take my virgins as spoil.

5 But the Lord Almighty has foiled them
    by the hand of a woman.^f

---

^c Other ancient authorities add *and Bebai*   ^d Gk *them*
^e Other ancient authorities read *a psalm and praise*   ^f Other ancient authorities add *he has confounded them*

PRAY IT!

Judith Leads the Prayer-Song

In the Book of Judith, chapter 16, Judith sings praises to God and leads the people in a holy celebration after victory over the enemy.

Notice the similarity to Miriam's song (Exodus, chapter 15), Deborah's song (Judges, chapter 5), and even Tobit's song (Tobit, chapter 13).

Singing, dancing, and retelling special stories go hand in hand with praising God.

▶ Jdt 16.1–20

6 For their mighty one did not fall by the hands
    of the young men,
  nor did the sons of the Titans strike him
    down,
  nor did tall giants set upon him;
but Judith daughter of Me•rar′i
  with the beauty of her countenance undid
    him.

7 For she put away her widow's clothing
    to exalt the oppressed in Israel.
She anointed her face with perfume;
8 she fastened her hair with a tiara
    and put on a linen gown to beguile him.
9 Her sandal ravished his eyes,
  her beauty captivated his mind,
  and the sword severed his neck!
10 The Persians trembled at her boldness,
  the Mēdes were daunted at her daring.

11 Then my oppressed people shouted;
  my weak people cried out,[g] and the enemy[h]
    trembled;
  they lifted up their voices, and the enemy[h]
    were turned back.
12 Sons of slave-girls pierced them through
  and wounded them like the children of
    fugitives;
  they perished before the army of my Lord.

13 I will sing to my God a new song:
O Lord, you are great and glorious,
  wonderful in strength, invincible.
14 Let all your creatures serve you,

for you spoke, and they were made.
You sent forth your spirit,[i] and it formed
    them;[j]
  there is none that can resist your voice.
15 For the mountains shall be shaken to their
    foundations with the waters;
  before your glance the rocks shall melt like
    wax.
But to those who fear you
  you show mercy.
16 For every sacrifice as a fragrant offering is a
    small thing,
  and the fat of all whole burnt offerings to
    you is a very little thing;
but whoever fears the Lord is great forever.

17 Woe to the nations that rise up against my
    people!
  The Lord Almighty will take vengeance on
    them in the day of judgment;
  he will send fire and worms into their flesh;
  they shall weep in pain forever.

18 When they arrived at Jerusalem, they worshiped God. As soon as the people were purified, they offered their burnt offerings, their freewill offerings, and their gifts. 19 Judith also dedicated to God all the possessions of Hol•o•fer′nes, which the people had given her; and the canopy that she had taken for herself from his bedchamber she gave as a votive offering. 20 For three months the people continued feasting in Jerusalem before the sanctuary, and Judith remained with them.

The Renown and Death of Judith

21 After this they all returned home to their own inheritances. Judith went to Beth•ū′li•a, and remained on her estate. For the rest of her life she was honored throughout the whole country. 22 Many desired to marry her, but she gave herself to no man all the days of her life after her husband Ma•nas′seh died and was gathered to his people. 23 She became more and more famous, and grew old in her husband's house, reaching the age of one hundred five. She set her maid free. She died in Beth•ū′li•a, and they buried her in the cave of her husband Ma•nas′seh; 24 and the house of Israel mourned her for seven days. Before she died she distributed her property to all those who were next of kin to her husband Ma•nas′seh, and to her own nearest kindred. 25 No one ever again spread terror among the Israelites during the lifetime of Judith, or for a long time after her death.

---

g Other ancient authorities read feared   h Gk they   i Or breath   j Other ancient authorities read they were created

Most of us cannot understand what would possess a group of people to plot the complete destruction of another group of people. Yet, in our own time, ethnic groups have been targeted for extinction through wars, concentration camps, and death squads. The Book of Esther is the story of a genocidal plot against a Jewish population and how that plot was prevented by Mordecai and his courageous cousin Esther.

In-depth

In the five centuries before Jesus, many of the Jewish people who were uprooted from their homeland had to be on the lookout for their safety. Several of the late Old Testament books—Sirach, Tobit, and Daniel—reflect the challenges that these emigrant Jews had to face. The fictional story of Queen Esther belongs to this group. Like Joseph in Egypt, Esther rose to a position of power in a foreign government. When a plot was hatched to destroy the Jews, she used her influence with the king of Persia to save her people. Each year, Esther's victory is celebrated in the Jewish feast of Purim (Esth 9.18–32)—the feast of little people who have triumphed over larger forces.

Like Daniel, the Book of Esther has come down to us in two versions: the Hebrew and the Greek. The difference in style between these two versions is obvious:

- The shorter Hebrew text is clearly fictional and does not even mention God's name. The Greek text, a later reworking of the Hebrew, adds sections to bring out the religious dimension of the story and to make the book appear more historical.
- The Hebrew version emphasizes the human actors; the Greek version, the divine Actor. The two versions stress different aspects of the same truth: God is the savior of the Chosen People (Greek) but works through human beings to achieve that goal (Hebrew).

Despite the confusing numbering, the book reads as a unified story; it's full of action and has a happy ending. What is more, it challenges us to recognize in our hatred of others the seeds of unthinkable destruction.

Quick Facts

Setting
Persia after the Babylonian Exile

Authors
Hebrew version. unknown, probably writing in the late fourth century B.C.
Greek version. unknown, writing about two centuries later

Themes
God's love for the little ones, the origin of the feast of Purim

Of Note
Catholic Bibles include the Greek version of Esther, inserted as additions A to F.

The Book of Esther

Esther

Chap. 15

NOTE: The deuterocanonical portions of the Book of Esther are several additional passages found in the Greek translation of the Hebrew Book of Esther, a translation that differs also in other respects from the Hebrew text (the latter is translated in the NRSV Old Testament). The disordered chapter numbers come from the displacement of the additions to the end of the canonical Book of Esther by Jerome in his Latin translation and from the subsequent division of the Bible into chapters by Stephen Langton, who numbered the additions consecutively as though they formed a direct continuation of the Hebrew text. So that the additions may be read in their proper context, the whole of the Greek version is here translated, though certain familiar names are given according to their Hebrew rather than their Greek form; for example, Mordecai and Vashti instead of Mardocheus and Astin. The order followed is that of the Greek text, but the chapter and verse numbers conform to those of the King James or Authorized Version. The additions, conveniently indicated by the letters A—F, are located as follows: A, before 1.1; B, after 3.13; C and D, after 4.17; E, after 8.12; F, after 10.3.

ADDITION A

Mordecai's Dream

11 *a* 2 In the second year of the reign of A·has·u·e′rus the Great, on the first day of Nī′san, Mor′de·caī son of Jā′ir son of Shim′ē·ī*b* son of Kish, of the tribe of Benjamin, had a dream. 3 He was a Jew living in the city of Su′sa, a great man, serving in the court of the king. 4 He was one of the captives whom King Ne·bū·chad·nez′zar of Babylon had brought from Jerusalem with King Jec·o·nī′ah of Judah. And this was his dream: 5 Noises*c* and confusion, thunders and earthquake, tumult on the earth! 6 Then two great dragons came forward, both ready to fight, and they roared terri-

bly. 7 At their roaring every nation prepared for war, to fight against the righteous nation. 8 It was a day of darkness and gloom, of tribulation and distress, affliction and great tumult on the earth! 9 And the whole righteous nation was troubled; they feared the evils that threatened them,*d* and were ready to perish. 10 Then they cried out to God; and at their outcry, as though from a tiny spring, there came a great river, with abundant water; 11 light came, and the sun rose, and the lowly were exalted and devoured those held in honor.

12 Mor′de·caī saw in this dream what God had

a Chapters 11.2—12.6 correspond to chapter A 1-17 in some translations. *b* Gk *Semeios* *c* Or *Voices* *d* Gk *their own evils* determined to do, and after he awoke he had it on his mind, seeking all day to understand it in every detail.

A Plot against the King

12 Now Mor·de·caī took his rest in the courtyard with Big'than and Tē'resh, the two eunuchs of the king who kept watch in the courtyard. 2 He overheard their conversation and inquired into their purposes, and learned that they were preparing to lay hands on King A·has·ū·ē'rus; and he informed the king concerning them. 3 Then the king examined the two eunuchs, and after they had confessed it, they were led away to execution. 4 The king made a permanent record of these things, and Mor·de·caī wrote an account of them. 5 And the king ordered Mor·de·caī to serve in the court, and rewarded him for these things. 6 But Hā'man son of Ham·me·dā'tha the Ag'ag·īte, who was in great honor with the king, determined to injure Mor·de·caī and his people because of the two eunuchs of the king.

END OF ADDITION A

King Ahasuerus Deposes Queen Vashti

1 This happened in the days of A·has·ū·ē'rus, the same A·has·ū·ē'rus who ruled over one hundred twenty-seven provinces from India to Ethiopia.*e* 2 In those days when King A·has·ū·ē'rus sat on his royal throne in the citadel of Su'sa, 3 in the third year of his reign, he gave a banquet for all his officials and ministers. The army of Persia and Mēd'i·a and the nobles and governors of the provinces were present, 4 while he displayed the great wealth of his kingdom and the splendor and pomp of his majesty for many days, one hundred eighty days in all.

5 When these days were completed, the king gave for all the people present in the citadel of Su'sa, both great and small, a banquet lasting for seven days, in the court of the garden of the king's palace. 6 There were white cotton curtains and blue hangings tied with cords of fine linen and purple to silver rings*f* and marble pillars. There were couches of gold and silver on a mosaic pavement of porphyry, marble, mother-of-pearl, and colored stones. 7 Drinks were served in golden goblets, goblets of different kinds, and the royal wine was lavished according to the bounty of the king. 8 Drinking was by flagons, without restraint; for the king had given orders to all the officials of his palace to do as each one desired. 9 Furthermore, Queen Vash'tī gave a banquet for the women in the palace of King A·has·ū·ē'rus.

10 On the seventh day, when the king was merry with wine, he commanded Me·hū'man, Biz'tha, Har·bō'na, Big'tha and A·bag'tha, Zē'thar and Car'kas, the seven eunuchs who attended him, 11 to bring Queen Vash'tī before the king, wearing the royal crown, in order to show the peoples and the officials her beauty; for she was fair to behold. 12 But Queen Vash'tī refused to come at the king's command conveyed by the eunuchs. At this the king was enraged, and his anger burned within him.

13 Then the king consulted the sages who knew the laws*g* (for this was the king's procedure toward all who were versed in law and custom, 14 and those next to him were Car·shē'na, Shē'thar, Ad·mā'tha, Tar'shish, Mē'rēs, Mar·sē'na, and Mē·mū'can, the seven officials of Persia and Mēd'i·a, who had access to the king, and sat first in the kingdom): 15 "According to the law, what is to be done to Queen Vash'tī because she has not performed the command of King A·has·ū·ē'rus conveyed by the eunuchs?" 16 Then Mē·mū'can said in the presence of the king and the officials, "Not only has Queen Vash'tī done wrong to the king, but also to all the officials and all the peoples who are in all the provinces of King A·has·ū·ē'rus. 17 For this deed of the queen will be made known to all women, causing them to look with contempt on their husbands, since they will say, 'King A·has·ū·ē'rus commanded Queen Vash'tī to be brought before him, and she did not come.' 18 This very day the noble ladies of Persia and Mēd'i·a who have heard of the queen's behavior will rebel against*h* the king's officials, and there will be no end of contempt and wrath! 19 If it pleases the king, let a royal order go out from him, and let it be written among the laws of the Persians and the Mēdes so that it may not be altered, that Vash'tī is never again to come before King A·has·ū·ē'rus; and let the king give her royal position to another who is better than she. 20 So when the decree made by the king is proclaimed throughout all his kingdom, vast as it is, all women will give honor to their husbands, high and low alike."

21 This advice pleased the king and the officials, and the king did as Mē·mū'can proposed; 22 he sent letters to all the royal provinces, to every province in its own script and to every people in its own language, declaring that every man should be master in his own house.*i*

Esther Becomes Queen

2 After these things, when the anger of King A·has·ū·ē'rus had abated, he remembered Vash'tī and what she had done and what had been

---

e Or *Nubia;* Heb *Cush*   *f* Or *rods*   *g* Cn: Heb *times*   *h* Cn: Heb *will tell*   *i* Heb adds *and speak according to the language of his people*

E
S
T
H

decreed against her. 2 Then the king's servants who attended him said, "Let beautiful young virgins be sought out for the king. 3 And let the king appoint commissioners in all the provinces of his kingdom to gather all the beautiful young virgins to the harem in the citadel of Su'sa under custody of Heg'aī, the king's eunuch, who is in charge of the women; let their cosmetic treatments be given them. 4 And let the girl who pleases the king be queen instead of Vash'tī." This pleased the king, and he did so.

did you KNOW?

Diaspora Jews

The fictional story of Esther implies that Mordecai and Esther were members of the Diaspora. The Greek word *diaspora* means "scattered abroad." It refers to the Jews who lived outside of Palestine. When the Babylonians destroyed Jerusalem (587 B.C.), many of the Jews who were forced to leave the land of Israel decided to settle in various Greco-Roman cities and not return home. They maintained their Jewish identity by adapting the language and customs of their new home into their Jewish traditions. The Diaspora Jews were responsible for the translation of the Hebrew Bible into Greek, a translation called the Septuagint.

E
S
T
H

5 Now there was a Jew in the citadel of Su'sa whose name was Mor'de•caī son of Jā'ir son of Shim'ē•ī son of Kish, a Ben'ja•min•īte. 6 Kish*j* had been carried away from Jerusalem among the captives carried away with King Jec•o•nī'ah of Judah, whom King Ne•bū•chad•nez'zar of Babylon had carried away. 7 Mor'de•caī*k* had brought up Ha•das'-sah, that is Esther, his cousin, for she had neither father nor mother; the girl was fair and beautiful, and when her father and her mother died, Mor'de•caī adopted her as his own daughter. 8 So when the king's order and his edict were proclaimed, and when many young women were gathered in the citadel of Su'sa in custody of Heg'aī, Esther also was taken into the king's palace and put in custody of Heg'aī, who had charge of the women. 9 The girl pleased him and won his favor, and he quickly pro-

vided her with her cosmetic treatments and her portion of food, and with seven chosen maids from the king's palace, and advanced her and her maids to the best place in the harem. 10 Esther did not reveal her people or kindred, for Mor'de•caī had charged her not to tell. 11 Every day Mor'de•caī would walk around in front of the court of the harem, to learn how Esther was and how she fared.

12 The turn came for each girl to go in to King A•has•ū•ē'rus, after being twelve months under the regulations for the women, since this was the regular period of their cosmetic treatment, six months with oil of myrrh and six months with perfumes and cosmetics for women. 13 When the girl went in to the king she was given whatever she asked for to take with her from the harem to the king's palace. 14 In the evening she went in; then in the morning she came back to the second harem in custody of Sha•ash'gaz, the king's eunuch, who was in charge of the concubines; she did not go in to the king again, unless the king delighted in her and she was summoned by name.

15 When the turn came for Esther daughter of Ab•i•hā'il the uncle of Mor'de•caī, who had adopted her as his own daughter, to go in to the king, she asked for nothing except what Heg'aī the king's eunuch, who had charge of the women, advised. Now Esther was admired by all who saw her. 16 When Esther was taken to King A•has•ū•ē'rus in his royal palace in the tenth month, which is the month of Tē'beth, in the seventh year of his reign, 17 the king loved Esther more than all the other women; of all the virgins she won his favor and devotion, so that he set the royal crown on her head and made her queen instead of Vash'tī. 18 Then the king gave a great banquet to all his officials and ministers—"Esther's banquet." He also granted a holiday*l* to the provinces, and gave gifts with royal liberality.

Mordecai Discovers a Plot

19 When the virgins were being gathered together,*m* Mor'de•caī was sitting at the king's gate. 20 Now Esther had not revealed her kindred or her people, as Mor'de•caī had charged her; for Esther obeyed Mor'de•caī just as when she was brought up by him. 21 In those days, while Mor'de•caī was sitting at the king's gate, Big'than and Tē'resh, two of the king's eunuchs, who guarded the threshold, became angry and conspired to assassinate*n* King A•has•ū•ē'rus. 22 But the matter came to the knowledge of Mor'de•caī, and he told it to Queen Esther, and Esther told the king in the name of Mor'de•caī. 23 When the affair was investigated and found to be

---

j Heb *a Benjaminite* 6*who*   *k* Heb *He*   *l* Or *an amnesty*
m Heb adds *a second time*   *n* Heb *to lay hands on*

so, both the men were hanged on the gallows. It was recorded in the book of the annals in the presence of the king.

Haman Undertakes to Destroy the Jews

3 After these things King A•has•ū•ē'rus promoted Hā'man son of Ham•me•dā'tha the Ag'ag•īte, and advanced him and set his seat above all the officials who were with him. 2 And all the king's servants who were at the king's gate bowed down and did obeisance to Hā'man; for the king had so commanded concerning him. But Mor'de•caī did not bow down or do obeisance. 3 Then the king's servants who were at the king's gate said to Mor'de•caī, "Why do you disobey the king's command?" 4 When they spoke to him day after day and he would not listen to them, they told Hā'man, in order to see whether Mor'de•caī's words would avail; for he had told them that he was a Jew. 5 When Hā'man saw that Mor'de•caī did not bow down or do obeisance to him, Hā'man was infuriated. 6 But he thought it beneath him to lay hands on Mor'de•caī alone. So, having been told who Mor'de•caī's people were, Hā'man plotted to destroy all the Jews, the people of Mor'de•caī, throughout the whole kingdom of A•has•ū•ē'rus.

7 In the first month, which is the month of Nī'san, in the twelfth year of King A•has•ū•ē'rus, they cast Pūr—which means "the lot"—before Hā'man for the day and for the month, and the lot fell on the thirteenth day° of the twelfth month, which is the month of Ā'dar. 8 Then Hā'man said to King A•has•ū•ē'rus, "There is a certain people scattered and separated among the peoples in all the provinces of your kingdom; their laws are different from those of every other people, and they do not keep the king's laws, so that it is not appropriate for the king to tolerate them. 9 If it pleases the king, let a decree be issued for their destruction, and I will pay ten thousand talents of silver into the hands of those who have charge of the king's business, so that they may put it into the king's treasuries." 10 So the king took his signet ring from his hand and gave it to Hā'man son of Ham•me•dā'tha the Ag'ag•īte, the enemy of the Jews. 11 The king said to Hā'man, "The money is given to you, and the people as well, to do with them as it seems good to you."

12 Then the king's secretaries were summoned on the thirteenth day of the first month, and an edict, according to all that Hā'man commanded, was written to the king's satraps and to the governors over all the provinces and to the officials of all the peoples, to every province in its own script and every people in its own language; it was written in the name of King A•has•ū•ē'rus and sealed with the king's ring. 13 Letters were sent by couriers to all the king's provinces, giving orders to destroy, to kill, and to annihilate all Jews, young and old, women and children, in one day, the thirteenth day of the twelfth month, which is the month of Ā'dar, and to plunder their goods.

° Cn Compare Gk and verse 13 below: Heb *the twelfth month*

Body Count

LIVE IT!

Genocide. Such a frightening word. The complete destruction of a people. This is what King Ahasuerus plots in the Book of Esther: to destroy all the Jews in his kingdom. Fortunately, he does not succeed.

In our time, we know only too well that the past two centuries have been marked by many attempts to exterminate whole groups of people. The most systematic and ambitious of these attempts was that of Adolf Hitler and the Third Reich. Six million Jews were put to death in Nazi concentration camps, along with four million other "undesirables."

Such atrocities begin with a them-and-us attitude. The first step is to set apart a group of people and blame them for whatever is going wrong. The second is to give them a label, like "savages" or "communists," to make them seem less human and easier to destroy. The ghosts of too many victims of genocide remind us that the only accurate pronoun to describe our human family is *we*.

▶ Esth 3.1–7

ADDITION B

The King's Letter

13 *p* This is a copy of the letter: "The Great King, A•has•ū•ē'rus, writes the following to the governors of the hundred twenty-seven provinces from India to Ethiopia and to the officials under them:

2 "Having become ruler of many nations and master of the whole world (not elated with presumption of authority but always acting reasonably and with kindness), I have determined to settle the lives of my subjects in lasting tranquility and, in order to make my kingdom peaceable and open to travel throughout all its extent, to restore the peace desired by all people.

3 "When I asked my counselors how this might be accomplished, Hā'man—who excels among us in sound judgment, and is distinguished for his unchanging goodwill and steadfast fidelity, and has attained the second place in the kingdom— 4 pointed out to us that among all the nations in the world there is scattered a certain hostile people, who have laws contrary to those of every nation and continually disregard the ordinances of kings, so that the unifying of the kingdom that we honorably intend cannot be brought about. 5 We understand that this people, and it alone, stands constantly in opposition to every nation, perversely following a strange manner of life and laws, and is ill-disposed to our government, doing all the harm they can so that our kingdom may not attain stability.

6 "Therefore we have decreed that those indicated to you in the letters written by Hā'man, who is in charge of affairs and is our second father, shall all—wives and children included—be utterly destroyed by the swords of their enemies, without pity or restraint, on the fourteenth day of the twelfth month, Ā'dar, of this present year, 7 so that those who have long been hostile and remain so may in a single day go down in violence to Hades, and leave our government completely secure and untroubled hereafter."

END OF ADDITION B

3 14 A copy of the document was to be issued as a decree in every province by proclamation, calling on all the peoples to be ready for that day. 15 The couriers went quickly by order of the king, and the decree was issued in the citadel of Su'sa. The king and Hā'man sat down to drink; but the city of Su'sa was thrown into confusion.

Esther Agrees to Help the Jews

4 When Mor'de•caī learned all that had been done, Mor'de•caī tore his clothes and put on sackcloth and ashes, and went through the city, wailing with a loud and bitter cry; 2 he went up to the entrance of the king's gate, for no one might enter the king's gate clothed with sackcloth. 3 In every province, wherever the king's command and his decree came, there was great mourning among the Jews, with fasting and weeping and lamenting, and most of them lay in sackcloth and ashes.

4 When Esther's maids and her eunuchs came and told her, the queen was deeply distressed; she sent garments to clothe Mor'de•caī, so that he might take off his sackcloth; but he would not accept them. 5 Then Esther called for Hā'thach, one of the king's eunuchs, who had been appointed to attend her, and ordered him to go to Mor'de•caī to learn what was happening and why. 6 Hā'thach went out to Mor'de•caī in the open square of the city in front of the king's gate, 7 and Mor'de•caī told him all that had happened to him, and the exact sum of money that Hā'man had promised to pay into the king's treasuries for the destruction of the Jews. 8 Mor'de•caī also gave him a copy of the written decree issued in Su'sa for their destruction, that he might show it to Esther, explain it to her, and charge her to go to the king to make supplication to him and entreat him for her people.

9 Hā'thach went and told Esther what Mor'de•caī had said. 10 Then Esther spoke to Hā'thach and gave him a message for Mor'de•caī, saying, 11 "All the king's servants and the people of the king's provinces know that if any man or woman goes to the king inside the inner court without being called, there is but one law—all alike are to be put to death. Only if the king holds out the golden scepter to someone, may that person live. I myself have not been called to come in to the king for thirty days." 12 When they told Mor'de•caī what Esther had said, 13 Mor'de•caī told them to reply to Esther, "Do not think that in the king's palace you will escape any more than all the other Jews. 14 For if you keep silence at such a time as this, relief and deliverance will rise for the Jews from another quarter, but you and your father's family will perish. Who knows? Perhaps you have come to royal dignity for just such a time as this." 15 Then Esther said in reply to Mor'de•caī, 16 "Go, gather all the Jews to be found in Su'sa, and hold a fast on my behalf, and neither eat nor drink for three days, night or day. I and my maids will also fast as you do. After that I will go to the king, though it is against the law; and if I perish, I perish." 17 Mor'de•caī then

---

p Chapter 13.1-7 corresponds to chapter B 1-7 in some translations.

did you KNOW?

The Silent Women of the Bible

"Mordecai then went away and did everything as Esther had ordered him" (Esth 4.17). What a surprise: to hear of a man in the ancient world taking orders from a woman! Esther, like Judith, has an exceptional role in the Old Testament. Many other important women are not even named: Jephthah's daughter, Samson's mother, and Job's wife, for instance. Even the Hebrew women whose names have become famous—Sarah, Rebekah, Rachel, Miriam, Bathsheba—played second fiddle to their more famous husbands. They depended on indirect influence or trickery to get what they wanted.

In the biblical world, a woman was defined by her relationships with men. Before marriage, she belonged to her father's household and had no status outside of it. Once married, a woman left her father's family and joined the family of her husband. If her husband died, she remained in the new family, rearing children for her deceased spouse or, if childless, marrying a brother-in-law. Although many women undoubtedly lived happily under this system, many others just as surely suffered abuse or felt oppressed. The stories of Lot's daughters (Gen 19.8) and the woman of Gibeah (Judg 19.24–30) testify to this horrifying truth.

A system of scriptural interpretation that was developed during recent decades attempts to give voice to the many silent, forgotten, abused women of the Bible. More and more biblical scholars reread the familiar stories, searching for quiet messages that have long been overlooked. All of us—males and females alike—can benefit from this effort to listen to the voices of these women who have been silenced for so many centuries.

▸ Esth 4.15—C.1

went away and did everything as Esther had ordered him.

ADDITION C

Mordecai's Prayer

13 8 q Then Mor'de·cai[r] prayed to the Lord, calling to remembrance all the works of the Lord.

9 He said, "O Lord, Lord, you rule as King over all things, for the universe is in your power and there is no one who can oppose you when it is your will to save Israel, 10 for you have made heaven and earth and every wonderful thing under heaven. 11 You are Lord of all, and there is no one who can resist you, the Lord. 12 You know all things; you know, O Lord, that it was not in insolence or pride or for any love of glory that I did this, and refused to bow down to this proud Hā'man; 13 for I would have been willing to kiss the soles of his feet to save Israel! 14 But I did this so that I might not set human glory above the glory of God, and I will not bow down to anyone but you, who are my Lord; and I will not do these things in pride. 15 And now, O Lord God and King, God of Abraham, spare your people; for the eyes of our foes are upon us[s] to annihilate us, and they desire to destroy the inheritance that has been yours from the beginning. 16 Do not neglect your portion, which you redeemed for yourself out of the land of Egypt. 17 Hear my prayer, and have mercy upon your inheritance; turn our mourning into feasting that we may live and sing praise to your name, O Lord; do not destroy the lips[t] of those who praise you."

18 And all Israel cried out mightily, for their death was before their eyes.

Esther's Prayer

14 Then Queen Esther, seized with deadly anxiety, fled to the Lord. 2 She took off her splendid apparel and put on the garments of distress and mourning, and instead of costly perfumes she covered her head with ashes and dung, and she utterly humbled her body; every part that she loved to adorn she covered with her tangled hair. 3 She prayed to the Lord God of Israel, and said: "O my Lord, you only are our king; help me, who am alone and have no helper but you, 4 for my danger is in my hand. 5 Ever since I was born I have heard in the tribe of my family that you, O Lord, took Israel out of all the nations, and our ancestors from among all their forebears, for an everlasting

ESTH

---

q Chapters 13.8—15.16 correspond to chapters C 1-30 and D 1-16 in some translations.   r Gk *he*   s Gk *for they are eying us*   t Gk *mouth* inheritance, and that you did for them all that you promised. 6 And now we have sinned before you, and you have handed us over to our enemies 7 because we glorified their gods. You are righteous, O Lord! 8 And now they are not satisfied that we are in bitter slavery, but they have covenanted with their idols 9 to abolish what your mouth has ordained, and to destroy your inheritance, to stop the mouths of those who praise you and to quench your altar and the glory of your house, 10 to open the mouths of the nations for the praise of vain idols, and to magnify forever a mortal king.

11 "O Lord, do not surrender your scepter to what has no being; and do not let them laugh at our downfall; but turn their plan against them, and make an example of him who began this against us. 12 Remember, O Lord; make yourself known in this time of our affliction, and give me courage, O King of the gods and Master of all dominion! 13 Put eloquent speech in my mouth before the lion, and turn his heart to hate the man who is fighting against us, so that there may be an end of him and those who agree with him. 14 But save us by your hand, and help me, who am alone and have no helper but you, O Lord. 15 You have knowledge of all things, and you know that I hate the splendor of the wicked and abhor the bed of the uncircumcised and of any alien. 16 You know my necessity—that I abhor the sign of my proud position, which is upon my head on days when I appear in public. I abhor it like a filthy rag, and I do not wear it on the days when I am at leisure. 17 And your servant has not eaten at Hā′man's table, and I have not honored the king's feast or drunk the wine of libations. 18 Your servant has had no joy since the day that I was brought here until now, except in you, O Lord God of Abraham. 19 O God, whose might is over all, hear the voice of the despairing, and save us from the hands of evildoers. And save me from my fear!"

END OF ADDITION C

ADDITION D

Esther Is Received by the King
(Esth 5.1–2)

15 On the third day, when she ended her prayer, she took off the garments in which she had worshiped, and arrayed herself in splendid attire. 2 Then, majestically adorned, after invoking the aid of the all-seeing God and Savior, she took two maids with her; 3 on one she leaned gently for support, 4 while the other followed, carrying her train. 5 She was radiant with perfect beauty, and she looked happy, as if beloved, but her heart was frozen with fear. 6 When she had gone

through all the doors, she stood before the king. He was seated on his royal throne, clothed in the full array of his majesty, all covered with gold and precious stones. He was most terrifying.

7 Lifting his face, flushed with splendor, he looked at her in fierce anger. The queen faltered, and turned pale and faint, and collapsed on the head of the maid who went in front of her. 8 Then God changed the spirit of the king to gentleness, and in alarm he sprang from his throne and took her in his arms until she came to herself. He comforted her with soothing words, and said to her, 9 "What is it, Esther? I am your husband.*u* Take courage; 10 You shall not die, for our law applies only to our subjects.*v* Come near."

11 Then he raised the golden scepter and touched her neck with it; 12 he embraced her, and said, "Speak to me." 13 She said to him, "I saw you, my lord, like an angel of God, and my heart was shaken with fear at your glory. 14 For you are wonderful, my lord, and your countenance is full of grace." 15 And while she was speaking, she fainted and fell. 16 Then the king was agitated, and all his servants tried to comfort her.

END OF ADDITION D

Esther's Banquet

5*w* 3 The king said to her, "What is it, Queen Esther? What is your request? It shall be given you, even to the half of my kingdom." 4 Then Esther said, "If it pleases the king, let the king and Hā′man come today to a banquet that I have prepared for the king." 5 Then the king said, "Bring Hā′man quickly, so that we may do as Esther desires." So the king and Hā′man came to the banquet that Esther had prepared. 6 While they were drinking wine, the king said to Esther, "What is your petition? It shall be granted you. And what is your request? Even to the half of my kingdom, it shall be fulfilled." 7 Then Esther said, "This is my petition and request: 8 If I have won the king's favor, and if it pleases the king to grant my petition and fulfill my request, let the king and Hā′man come tomorrow to the banquet that I will prepare for them, and then I will do as the king has said."

Haman Plans to Have Mordecai Hanged

9 Hā′man went out that day happy and in good spirits. But when Hā′man saw Mor′de•caī in the king's gate, and observed that he neither rose nor trembled before him, he was infuriated with Mor′de•caī; 10 nevertheless Hā′man restrained him-

---

u Gk *brother*   *v* Meaning of Gk uncertain   *w* In Greek, Chapter D replaces verses 1 and 2 in Hebrew.

self and went home. Then he sent and called for his friends and his wife Zĕ′resh, [11] and Hā′man recounted to them the splendor of his riches, the number of his sons, all the promotions with which the king had honored him, and how he had advanced him above the officials and the ministers of the king. [12] Hā′man added, "Even Queen Esther let no one but myself come with the king to the banquet that she prepared. Tomorrow also I am invited by her, together with the king. [13] Yet all this does me no good so long as I see the Jew Mor′de•caī sitting at the king's gate." [14] Then his wife Zĕ′resh and all his friends said to him, "Let a gallows fifty cubits high be made, and in the morning tell the king to have Mor′de•caī hanged on it; then go with the king to the banquet in good spirits." This advice pleased Hā′man, and he had the gallows made.

The King Honors Mordecai

6 On that night the king could not sleep, and he gave orders to bring the book of records, the annals, and they were read to the king. [2] It was found written how Mor′de•caī had told about Big•thā′na and Tĕ′resh, two of the king's eunuchs, who guarded the threshold, and who had conspired to assassinate[x] King A•has•ū•ē′rus. [3] Then the king said, "What honor or distinction has been bestowed on Mor′de•caī for this?" The king's servants who attended him said, "Nothing has been done for him." [4] The king said, "Who is in the court?" Now Hā′man had just entered the outer court of the king's palace to speak to the king about having Mor′de•caī hanged on the gallows that he had prepared for him. [5] So the king's servants told him, "Hā′man is there, standing in the court." The king said, "Let him come in." [6] So Hā′man came in, and the king said to him, "What shall be done for the man whom the king wishes to honor?" Hā′man said to himself, "Whom would the king wish to honor more than me?" [7] So Hā′man said to the king, "For the man whom the king wishes to honor, [8] let royal robes be brought, which the king has worn, and a horse that the king has ridden, with a royal crown on its head. [9] Let the robes and the horse be handed over to one of the king's most noble officials; let him[y] robe the man whom the king wishes to honor, and let him[y] conduct the man on horseback through the open square of the city, proclaiming before him: 'Thus shall it be done for the man whom the king wishes to honor.' " [10] Then the king said to Hā′man, "Quickly, take the robes and the horse, as you have said, and do so to the Jew Mor′de•caī who sits at the king's gate. Leave out nothing that you have mentioned." [11] So Hā′man took the robes and the horse and robed Mor′de•caī and led him riding through the open square of the city, proclaiming, "Thus shall it be done for the man whom the king wishes to honor."

[12] Then Mor′de•caī returned to the king's gate, but Hā′man hurried to his house, mourning and with his head covered. [13] When Hā′man told his wife Zĕ′resh and all his friends everything that had happened to him, his advisers and his wife Zĕ′resh said to him, "If Mor′de•caī, before whom your downfall has begun, is of the Jewish people, you will not prevail against him, but will surely fall before him."

Haman's Downfall
and Mordecai's Advancement

[14] While they were still talking with him, the king's eunuchs arrived and hurried Hā′man off to the banquet that Esther had prepared. **7** [1] So the king and Hā′man went in to feast with Queen Esther. [2] On the second day, as they were drinking wine, the king again said to Esther, "What is your petition, Queen Esther? It shall be granted you. And what is your request? Even to the half of my kingdom, it shall be fulfilled." [3] Then Queen Esther answered, "If I have won your favor, O king, and if it pleases the king, let my life be given me— that is my petition—and the lives of my people— that is my request. [4] For we have been sold, I and my people, to be destroyed, to be killed, and to be annihilated. If we had been sold merely as slaves, men and women, I would have held my peace; but no enemy can compensate for this damage to the king."[z] [5] Then King A•has•ū•ē′rus said to Queen Esther, "Who is he, and where is he, who has presumed to do this?" [6] Esther said, "A foe and enemy, this wicked Hā′man!" Then Hā′man was terrified before the king and the queen. [7] The king rose from the feast in wrath and went into the palace garden, but Hā′man stayed to beg his life from Queen Esther, for he saw that the king had determined to destroy him. [8] When the king returned from the palace garden to the banquet hall, Hā′man had thrown himself on the couch where Esther was reclining; and the king said, "Will he even assault the queen in my presence, in my own house?" As the words left the mouth of the king, they covered Hā′man's face. [9] Then Har•bō′na, one of the eunuchs in attendance on the king, said, "Look, the very gallows that Hā′man has prepared for Mor′de•caī, whose word saved the king, stands at Hā′man's house, fifty cubits high." And the king said, "Hang him on that." [10] So they hanged Hā′man on the gallows that he had prepared for Mor′de•caī. Then the anger of the king abated. **8** [1] On that day King A•has•ū•ē′rus gave to Queen Esther the house of Hā′man, the enemy of the Jews; and Mor′de•caī came before the king, for Esther had told what he

---

x Heb *to lay hands on*   y Heb *them*   z Meaning of Heb uncertain

ESTH

was to her. 2 Then the king took off his signet ring, which he had taken from Hā′man, and gave it to Mor′de•caī. So Esther set Mor′de•caī over the house of Hā′man.

Esther Saves the Jews

3 Then Esther spoke again to the king; she fell at his feet, weeping and pleading with him to avert the evil design of Hā′man the Ag′ag•īte and the plot that he had devised against the Jews. 4 The king held out the golden scepter to Esther, 5 and Esther rose and stood before the king. She said, "If it pleases the king, and if I have won his favor, and if the thing seems right before the king, and I have his approval, let an order be written to revoke the letters devised by Hā′man son of Ham•me•dā′tha the Ag′-ag•īte, which he wrote giving orders to destroy the Jews who are in all the provinces of the king. 6 For how can I bear to see the calamity that is coming on my people? Or how can I bear to see the destruction of my kindred?" 7 Then King A•has•ū•ē′rus said to Queen Esther and to the Jew Mor′de•caī, "See, I have given Esther the house of Hā′man, and they have hanged him on the gallows, because he plotted to lay hands on the Jews. 8 You may write as you please with regard to the Jews, in the name of the king, and seal it with the king's ring; for an edict written in the name of the king and sealed with the king's ring cannot be revoked."

9 The king's secretaries were summoned at that time, in the third month, which is the month of Sī′-van, on the twenty-third day; and an edict was written, according to all that Mor′de•caī commanded, to the Jews and to the satraps and the governors and the officials of the provinces from India to Ethiopia,*a* one hundred twenty-seven provinces, to every province in its own script and to every people in its own language, and also to the Jews in their script and their language. 10 He wrote letters in the name of King A•has•ū•ē′rus, sealed them with the king's ring, and sent them by mounted couriers riding on fast steeds bred from the royal herd.*b* 11 By these letters the king allowed the Jews who were in every city to assemble and defend their lives, to destroy, to kill, and to annihilate any armed force of any people or province that might attack them, with their children and women, and to plunder their goods 12 on a single day throughout all the provinces of King A•has•ū•ē′rus, on the thirteenth day of the twelfth month, which is the month of Ā′dar.

Addition E

The Decree of Ahasuerus

16 *c* The following is a copy of this letter: "The Great King, A•has•ū•ē′rus, to the

governors of the provinces from India to Ethiopia, one hundred twenty-seven provinces, and to those who are loyal to our government, greetings.

2 "Many people, the more they are honored with the most generous kindness of their benefactors, the more proud do they become, 3 and not only seek to injure our subjects, but in their inability to stand prosperity, they even undertake to scheme against their own benefactors. 4 They not only take away thankfulness from others, but, carried away by the boasts of those who know nothing of goodness, they even assume that they will escape the evil-hating justice of God, who always sees everything. 5 And often many of those who are set in places of authority have been made in part responsible for the shedding of innocent blood, and have been involved in irremediable calamities, by the persuasion of friends who have been entrusted with the administration of public affairs, 6 when these persons by the false trickery of their evil natures beguile the sincere goodwill of their sovereigns.

7 "What has been wickedly accomplished through the pestilent behavior of those who exercise authority unworthily can be seen, not so much from the more ancient records that we hand on, as from investigation of matters close at hand.*d* 8 In the future we will take care to render our kingdom quiet and peaceable for all, 9 by changing our methods and always judging what comes before our eyes with more equitable consideration. 10 For Hā′man son of Ham•me•dā′tha, a Mac•e•dō′ni•an (really an alien to the Persian blood, and quite devoid of our kindliness), having become our guest, 11 enjoyed so fully the goodwill that we have for every nation that he was called our father and was continually bowed down to by all as the person second to the royal throne. 12 But, unable to restrain his arrogance, he undertook to deprive us of our kingdom and our life,*e* 13 and with intricate craft and deceit asked for the destruction of Mor′de•caī, our savior and perpetual benefactor, and of Esther, the blameless partner of our kingdom, together with their whole nation. 14 He thought that by these methods he would catch us undefended and would transfer the kingdom of the Persians to the Mac•e•dō′ni•ans.

15 "But we find that the Jews, who were consigned to annihilation by this thrice-accursed man, are not evildoers, but are governed by most righteous laws 16 and are children of the living God, most high, most mighty,*f* who has directed the kingdom both for us and for our ancestors in the most excellent order.

---

a Or *Nubia;* Heb *Cush*   *b* Meaning of Heb uncertain
c Chapter 16.1-24 corresponds to chapter E 1-24 in some translations.   *d* Gk *matters beside* (your) *feet*
e Gk *our spirit*   *f* Gk *greatest*

17 "You will therefore do well not to put in execution the letters sent by Hā′man son of Ham•me•dā′tha, 18 since he, the one who did these things, has been hanged at the gate of Su′sa with all his household—for God, who rules over all things, has speedily inflicted on him the punishment that he deserved.

19 "Therefore post a copy of this letter publicly in every place, and permit the Jews to live under their own laws. 20 And give them reinforcements, so that on the thirteenth day of the twelfth month, Ā′dar, on that very day, they may defend themselves against those who attack them at the time of oppression. 21 For God, who rules over all things, has made this day to be a joy for his chosen people instead of a day of destruction for them.

22 "Therefore you shall observe this with all good cheer as a notable day among your commemorative festivals, 23 so that both now and hereafter it may represent deliverance for you*g* and the loyal Persians, but that it may be a reminder of destruction for those who plot against us.

24 "Every city and country, without exception, that does not act accordingly shall be destroyed in wrath with spear and fire. It shall be made not only impassable for human beings, but also most hateful to wild animals and birds for all time."

END OF ADDITION E

---

8 13 A copy of the writ was to be issued as a decree in every province and published to all peoples, and the Jews were to be ready on that day to take revenge on their enemies. 14 So the couriers, mounted on their swift royal steeds, hurried out, urged by the king's command. The decree was issued in the citadel of Su′sa.

15 Then Mor′de•caī went out from the presence of the king, wearing royal robes of blue and white, with a great golden crown and a mantle of fine linen and purple, while the city of Su′sa shouted and rejoiced. 16 For the Jews there was light and gladness, joy and honor. 17 In every province and in every city, wherever the king's command and his edict came, there was gladness and joy among the Jews, a festival and a holiday. Furthermore, many of the peoples of the country professed to be Jews, because the fear of the Jews had fallen upon them.

Destruction of the Enemies of the Jews
(Cp 1 Macc 7.49)

9 Now in the twelfth month, which is the month of Ā′dar, on the thirteenth day, when the king's command and edict were about to be executed, on the very day when the enemies of the Jews hoped to gain power over them, but which

had been changed to a day when the Jews would gain power over their foes, 2 the Jews gathered in their cities throughout all the provinces of King A•has•ū•ē′rus to lay hands on those who had sought their ruin; and no one could withstand them, because the fear of them had fallen upon all peoples. 3 All the officials of the provinces, the satraps and the governors, and the royal officials were supporting the Jews, because the fear of Mor′de•caī had fallen upon them. 4 For Mor′de•caī was powerful in the king's house, and his fame spread throughout all the provinces as the man Mor′de•caī grew more and more powerful. 5 So the Jews struck down all their enemies with the sword, slaughtering, and destroying them, and did as they pleased to those who hated them. 6 In the citadel of Su′sa the Jews killed and destroyed five hundred people. 7 They killed Par•shan•dā′tha, Dal′phon, As•pā′tha, 8 Pō•rā′tha, A•dā′li•a, Ar•i•dā′tha, 9 Par•mash′ta, Ar′i•saī, Ar′i•daī, Vaī•zā′tha, 10 the ten sons of Hā′man son of Ham•me•dā′tha, the enemy of the Jews; but they did not touch the plunder.

11 That very day the number of those killed in the citadel of Su′sa was reported to the king. 12 The king said to Queen Esther, "In the citadel of Su′sa the Jews have killed five hundred people and also the ten sons of Hā′man. What have they done in the rest of the king's provinces? Now what is your petition? It shall be granted you. And what further is your request? It shall be fulfilled." 13 Esther said, "If it pleases the king, let the Jews who are in Su′sa be allowed tomorrow also to do according to this day's edict, and let the ten sons of Hā′man be hanged on the gallows." 14 So the king commanded this to be done; a decree was issued in Su′sa, and the ten sons of Hā′man were hanged. 15 The Jews who were in Su′sa gathered also on the fourteenth day of the month of Ā′dar and they killed three hundred persons in Su′sa; but they did not touch the plunder.

16 Now the other Jews who were in the king's provinces also gathered to defend their lives, and gained relief from their enemies, and killed seventy-five thousand of those who hated them; but they laid no hands on the plunder. 17 This was on the thirteenth day of the month of Ā′dar, and on the fourteenth day they rested and made that a day of feasting and gladness.

The Feast of Purim Inaugurated
(Esth 3.7)

18 But the Jews who were in Su′sa gathered on the thirteenth day and on the fourteenth, and rested on the fifteenth day, making that a day of feasting and gladness. 19 Therefore the Jews of the villages, who live in the open towns, hold the

---

g Other ancient authorities read *for us*

ESTH

fourteenth day of the month of Ā'dar as a day for gladness and feasting, a holiday on which they send gifts of food to one another.

20 Mor'de•caī recorded these things, and sent letters to all the Jews who were in all the provinces of King A•has•ū•ē'rus, both near and far, 21 enjoining them that they should keep the fourteenth day of the month Ā'dar and also the fifteenth day of the same month, year by year, 22 as the days on which the Jews gained relief from their enemies, and as the month that had been turned for them from sorrow into gladness and from mourning into a holiday; that they should make them days of feasting and gladness, days for sending gifts of food to one another and presents to the poor. 23 So the Jews adopted as a custom what they had begun to do, as Mor'de•caī had written to them.

did you KNOW?

Purim

The feast of Purim ("lots" in Hebrew) commemorates the legendary victory of Queen Esther and Mordecai. A minor festival in the Jewish calendar, Purim is celebrated in late winter and is marked by the exchange of gifts and the sharing of meals.

▶ Esth 9.20–32

24 Hā'man son of Ham•me•dā'tha the Ag'ag•īte, the enemy of all the Jews, had plotted against the Jews to destroy them, and had cast Pūr—that is "the lot"—to crush and destroy them; 25 but when Esther came before the king, he gave orders in writing that the wicked plot that he had devised against the Jews should come upon his own head, and that he and his sons should be hanged on the gallows. 26 Therefore these days are called Pūr'im, from the word Pūr. Thus because of all that was written in this letter, and of what they had faced in this matter, and of what had happened to them, 27 the Jews established and accepted as a custom for themselves and their descendants and all who joined them, that without fail they would continue to observe these two days every year, as it was written and at the time appointed. 28 These days should be remembered and kept throughout every generation,

in every family, province, and city; and these days of Pūr'im should never fall into disuse among the Jews, nor should the commemoration of these days cease among their descendants.

29 Queen Esther daughter of Ab•i•hā'il, along with the Jew Mor'de•caī, gave full written authority, confirming this second letter about Pūr'im. 30 Letters were sent wishing peace and security to all the Jews, to the one hundred twenty-seven provinces of the kingdom of A•has•ū•ē'rus, 31 and giving orders that these days of Pūr'im should be observed at their appointed seasons, as the Jew Mor'de•caī and Queen Esther enjoined on the Jews, just as they had laid down for themselves and for their descendants regulations concerning their fasts and their lamentations. 32 The command of Queen Esther fixed these practices of Pūr'im, and it was recorded in writing.

10 King A•has•ū•ē'rus laid tribute on the land and on the islands of the sea. 2 All the acts of his power and might, and the full account of the high honor of Mor'de•caī, to which the king advanced him, are they not written in the annals of the kings of Mēd'i•a and Persia? 3 For Mor'de•caī the Jew was next in rank to King A•has•ū•ē'rus, and he was powerful among the Jews and popular with his many kindred, for he sought the good of his people and interceded for the welfare of all his descendants.

ADDITION F

Mordecai's Dream Fulfilled

4 h And Mor'de•caī said, "These things have come from God; 5 for I remember the dream that I had concerning these matters, and none of them has failed to be fulfilled. 6 There was the little spring that became a river, and there was light and sun and abundant water—the river is Esther, whom the king married and made queen. 7 The two dragons are Hā'man and myself. 8 The nations are those that gathered to destroy the name of the Jews. 9 And my nation, this is Israel, who cried out to God and was saved. The Lord has saved his people; the Lord has rescued us from all these evils; God has done great signs and wonders, wonders that have never happened among the nations. 10 For this purpose he made two lots, one for the people of God and one for all the nations, 11 and these two lots came to the hour and moment and day of decision before God and among all the nations. 12 And God remembered his people and vindicated his inheritance. 13 So they will observe these days in the

---

h Chapter 10.4–13 and 11.1 correspond to chapter F 1–11 in some translations.

month of Ā′dar, on the fourteenth and fifteenth[i] of that month, with an assembly and joy and gladness before God, from generation to generation forever among his people Israel."

Postscript

11 [1] In the fourth year of the reign of Ptol′e•my and Cleopatra, Dō•sith′e•us, who said that he was a priest and a Lē′vīte,[j] and his son Ptol′e•my brought to Egypt[k] the preceding Let-ter about Pūr′im, which they said was authentic and had been translated by Lȳ•sim′a•chus son of Ptol′e•my, one of the residents of Jerusalem.

END OF ADDITION F

_____

i Other ancient authorities lack *and fifteenth*　j Or *priest, and Levitas*　k Cn: Gk *brought in*

Have you ever listened as two fighting siblings tell their parents about a conflict? Usually, each child blames the other one and protests his or her complete innocence. Sometimes you have to wonder if they are even talking about the same fight. In a similar way, the author of 1 Maccabees, reporting on the Jewish resistance to the persecution of the Seleucid (Greek) rulers, tells one version of the story. The book defends the violent resistance of the family of Mattathias. Second Maccabees, on the other hand, has a broader perspective in telling of other forms of Jewish resistance.

At a Glance

- **Chapters 1–2.** the revolt of the Jews

- **3.1—9.22.** the leadership of Judas Maccabeus

- **9.23—16.24.** the leadership of Judas's brothers Jonathan and Simon

In-depth

The writer of 1 Maccabees has a clear purpose in mind: to defend the family of Mattathias, whose sons—the Maccabees—held positions of authority in the Jewish community. The most famous of them, Judas Maccabeus, led the Jews in a successful revolt (167–164 B.C.) against the Greek persecution—an incredible feat given the military might of the Greeks. After Judas's death, his brothers and nephews held positions of power, and Israel remained free from foreign domination for the next hundred years.

For traditional Jews, the power of the Maccabees posed a problem: because Mattathias's bloodline could be traced to neither King David nor Aaron the priest, by what right had his descendants assumed kingly and priestly authority? Against such criticism, the author of 1 Maccabees tries to prove that God's plan was accomplished through Mattathias's family.

The interpretation of Jewish history contained in 1 Maccabees invites us to believe in God's choice of Mattathias's sons as saviors of the nation. Even more important, it invites us to believe in the utter reliability of God: "And so observe, from generation to generation, that none of those who put their trust in [God] will lack strength" (2.61).

Quick Facts

Period Covered
from 175 to 134 B.C.

Author
unknown, writing around 100 B.C.

Theme
God brings Israel to freedom through the family of Mattathias.

Of Note
First Maccabees is not found in some Protestant Bibles (see "The Case of the Missing Books," Tob 1.16).

1 Maccabees

Alexander the Great

1 After Alexander son of Philip, the Mac•e•dō'ni•an, who came from the land of Kit'tim, had defeated[a] King Da•rī'us of the Persians and the Mēdes, he succeeded him as king. (He had previously become king of Greece.) 2 He fought many battles, conquered strongholds, and put to death the kings of the earth. 3 He advanced to the ends of the earth, and plundered many nations. When the earth became quiet before him, he was exalted, and his heart was lifted up. 4 He gathered a very strong army and ruled over countries, nations, and princes, and they became tributary to him.

5 After this he fell sick and perceived that he was dying. 6 So he summoned his most honored officers, who had been brought up with him from youth, and divided his kingdom among them while he was still alive. 7 And after Alexander had reigned twelve years, he died.

8 Then his officers began to rule, each in his own place. 9 They all put on crowns after his death, and so did their descendants after them for many years; and they caused many evils on the earth.

Antiochus Epiphanes and Renegade Jews
(2 Macc 4.7–17)

10 From them came forth a sinful root, An•tī'o•chus E•piph'a•nēs, son of King An•tī'o•chus; he had been a hostage in Rome. He began to reign in the one hundred thirty-seventh year of the kingdom of the Greeks.[b]

11 In those days certain renegades came out from Israel and misled many, saying, "Let us go and make a covenant with the Gentiles around us, for since we separated from them many disasters have come upon us." 12 This proposal pleased them, 13 and some of the people eagerly went to the king, who authorized them to observe the ordinances of the Gentiles. 14 So they built a gymnasium in Jerusalem, according to Gentile custom, 15 and removed the marks of circumcision, and abandoned the holy covenant. They joined with the Gentiles and sold themselves to do evil.

Antiochus in Egypt
(2 Macc 5.1, 11–26)

16 When An•tī'o•chus saw that his kingdom was established, he determined to become king of the land of Egypt, in order that he might reign over both kingdoms. 17 So he invaded Egypt with a strong force, with chariots and elephants and cavalry and with a large fleet. 18 He engaged King Ptol'e•my of Egypt in battle, and Ptol'e•my turned and fled before him, and many were wounded and fell. 19 They captured the fortified cities in the land of Egypt, and he plundered the land of Egypt.

Persecution of the Jews

20 After subduing Egypt, An•tī'o•chus returned in the one hundred forty-third year.[c] He went up

---

[a] Gk adds *and he defeated*   [b] 175 B.C.   [c] 169 B.C.

505

against Israel and came to Jerusalem with a strong force. 21 He arrogantly entered the sanctuary and took the golden altar, the lampstand for the light, and all its utensils. 22 He took also the table for the bread of the Presence, the cups for drink offerings, the bowls, the golden censers, the curtain, the crowns, and the gold decoration on the front of the temple; he stripped it all off. 23 He took the silver and the gold, and the costly vessels; he took also the hidden treasures that he found. 24 Taking them all, he went into his own land.

He shed much blood,
    and spoke with great arrogance.
25 Israel mourned deeply in every community,
26   rulers and elders groaned,
young women and young men became faint,
    the beauty of the women faded.
27 Every bridegroom took up the lament;
    she who sat in the bridal chamber was
      mourning.
28 Even the land trembled for its inhabitants,
    and all the house of Jacob was clothed with
      shame.

The Occupation of Jerusalem

29 Two years later the king sent to the cities of Judah a chief collector of tribute, and he came to Jerusalem with a large force. 30 Deceitfully he spoke peaceable words to them, and they believed him; but he suddenly fell upon the city, dealt it a severe blow, and destroyed many people of Israel. 31 He plundered the city, burned it with fire, and tore down its houses and its surrounding walls. 32 They took captive the women and children, and seized the livestock. 33 Then they fortified the city of David with a great strong wall and strong towers, and it became their citadel. 34 They stationed there a sinful people, men who were renegades. These strengthened their position; 35 they stored up arms and food, and collecting the spoils of Jerusalem they stored them there, and became a great menace,
36   for the citadel*d* became an ambush against the
      sanctuary,
    an evil adversary of Israel at all times.
37 On every side of the sanctuary they shed
      innocent blood;
    they even defiled the sanctuary.
38 Because of them the residents of Jerusalem
      fled;
    she became a dwelling of strangers;
she became strange to her offspring,
    and her children forsook her.
39 Her sanctuary became desolate like a
      desert;
    her feasts were turned into mourning,
her sabbaths into a reproach,
    her honor into contempt.

40   Her dishonor now grew as great as her glory;
    her exaltation was turned into mourning.

Installation of Gentile Cults
(Cp 2 Macc 6.1–17; Mt 24.15; Mk 13.14)

41 Then the king wrote to his whole kingdom that all should be one people, 42 and that all should give up their particular customs. 43 All the Gentiles accepted the command of the king. Many even from Israel gladly adopted his religion; they sacrificed to idols and profaned the sabbath. 44 And the king sent letters by messengers to Jerusalem and the towns of Judah; he directed them to follow customs strange to the land, 45 to forbid burnt offerings and sacrifices and drink offerings in the sanctuary, to profane sabbaths and festivals, 46 to defile the sanctuary and the priests, 47 to build altars and sacred precincts and shrines for idols, to sacrifice swine and other unclean animals, 48 and to leave their sons uncircumcised. They were to make themselves abominable by everything unclean and profane, 49 so that they would forget the law and change all the ordinances. 50 He added,*e* "And whoever does not obey the command of the king shall die."

51 In such words he wrote to his whole kingdom. He appointed inspectors over all the people and commanded the towns of Judah to offer sacrifice, town by town. 52 Many of the people, everyone who forsook the law, joined them, and they did evil in the land; 53 they drove Israel into hiding in every place of refuge they had.

54 Now on the fifteenth day of Chis'lev, in the one hundred forty-fifth year,*f* they erected a desolating sacrilege on the altar of burnt offering. They also built altars in the surrounding towns of Judah, 55 and offered incense at the doors of the houses and in the streets. 56 The books of the law that they found they tore to pieces and burned with fire. 57 Anyone found possessing the book of the covenant, or anyone who adhered to the law, was condemned to death by decree of the king. 58 They kept using violence against Israel, against those who were found month after month in the towns. 59 On the twenty-fifth day of the month they offered sacrifice on the altar that was on top of the altar of burnt offering. 60 According to the decree, they put to death the women who had their children circumcised, 61 and their families and those who circumcised them; and they hung the infants from their mothers' necks.

62 But many in Israel stood firm and were resolved in their hearts not to eat unclean food. 63 They chose to die rather than to be defiled by food or to profane the holy covenant; and they did die. 64 Very great wrath came upon Israel.

---

d Gk it   *e* Gk lacks *He added*   *f* 167 B.C.

Mattathias and His Sons

2 In those days Mat•ta•thi′as son of John son of Sim′ē•on, a priest of the family of Jō′a•rib, moved from Jerusalem and settled in Mō′dēin. ² He had five sons, John surnamed Gad′dī, ³ Simon called Thas′sī, ⁴ Judas called Mac•ca•bē′us, ⁵ El•ē•ā′-zar called Av′a•ran, and Jonathan called Ap′phus. ⁶ He saw the blasphemies being committed in Judah and Jerusalem, ⁷ and said,

"Alas! Why was I born to see this,
the ruin of my people, the ruin of the holy
city,
and to live there when it was given over to the
enemy,
the sanctuary given over to aliens?
8 Her temple has become like a person without
honor;ᵍ
9 her glorious vessels have been carried into
exile.
Her infants have been killed in her streets,
her youths by the sword of the foe.
10 What nation has not inherited her palacesʰ
and has not seized her spoils?
11 All her adornment has been taken away;
no longer free, she has become a slave.
12 And see, our holy place, our beauty,
and our glory have been laid waste;
the Gentiles have profaned them.
13 Why should we live any longer?"

14 Then Mat•ta•thi′as and his sons tore their clothes, put on sackcloth, and mourned greatly.

Pagan Worship Refused

15 The king's officers who were enforcing the apostasy came to the town of Mō′dēin to make them offer sacrifice. ¹⁶ Many from Israel came to them; and Mat•ta•thi′as and his sons were assembled. ¹⁷ Then the king's officers spoke to Mat•ta•thi′as as follows: "You are a leader, honored and great in this town, and supported by sons and brothers. ¹⁸ Now be the first to come and do what the king commands, as all the Gentiles and the people of Judah and those that are left in Jerusalem have done.

Then you and your sons will be numbered among the Friends of the king, and you and your sons will be honored with silver and gold and many gifts."

19 But Mat•ta•thi′as answered and said in a loud voice: "Even if all the nations that live under the rule of the king obey him, and have chosen to obey his commandments, everyone of them abandoning the religion of their ancestors, ²⁰ I and my sons and my brothers will continue to live by the covenant of our ancestors. ²¹ Far be it from us to desert the law and the ordinances. ²² We will not obey the king's words by turning aside from our religion to the right hand or to the left."

23 When he had finished speaking these words, a Jew came forward in the sight of all to offer sacrifice on the altar in Mō′dēin, according to the king's command. ²⁴ When Mat•ta•thi′as saw it, he burned with zeal and his heart was stirred. He gave vent to righteous anger; he ran and killed him on the altar. ²⁵ At the same time he killed the king's officer who was forcing them to sacrifice, and he tore down the altar. ²⁶ Thus he burned with zeal for the law, just as Phin′e•has did against Zim′rī son of Sa′lū.

27 Then Mat•ta•thi′as cried out in the town with a loud voice, saying: "Let every one who is zealous for the law and supports the covenant come out with me!" ²⁸ Then he and his sons fled to the hills and left all that they had in the town.

29 At that time many who were seeking righteousness and justice went down to the wilderness to live there, ³⁰ they, their sons, their wives, and their livestock, because troubles pressed heavily upon them. ³¹ And it was reported to the king's officers, and to the troops in Jerusalem the city of David, that those who had rejected the king's command had gone down to the hiding places in the wilderness. ³² Many pursued them, and overtook them; they encamped opposite them and prepared for battle against them on the sabbath day. ³³ They said to them, "Enough of this! Come out and do

---

ᵍ Meaning of Gk uncertain   ʰ Other ancient authorities read *has not had a part in her kingdom*

Religious Persecution

LIVE IT!

The Jews were facing a societal attack on their faith. But Mattathias and his sons chose to fight the official and cultural pressure to turn away from their faith.
Are there times when you feel persecuted because of your belief in God? In what subtle ways does contemporary society ridicule people with religious beliefs? If you were to be persecuted because of your religion, how would you respond?

▶ 1 Macc 2.19–22

what the king commands, and you will live." 34 But they said, "We will not come out, nor will we do what the king commands and so profane the sabbath day." 35 Then the enemy*i* quickly attacked them. 36 But they did not answer them or hurl a stone at them or block up their hiding places, 37 for they said, "Let us all die in our innocence; heaven and earth testify for us that you are killing us unjustly." 38 So they attacked them on the sabbath, and they died, with their wives and children and livestock, to the number of a thousand persons.

39 When Mat•ta•thi'as and his friends learned of it, they mourned for them deeply. 40 And all said to their neighbors: "If we all do as our kindred have done and refuse to fight with the Gentiles for our lives and for our ordinances, they will quickly destroy us from the earth." 41 So they made this decision that day: "Let us fight against anyone who comes to attack us on the sabbath day; let us not all die as our kindred died in their hiding places."

Counter-Attack

42 Then there united with them a company of Has•i•dē'ans, mighty warriors of Israel, all who offered themselves willingly for the law. 43 And all who became fugitives to escape their troubles joined them and reinforced them. 44 They organized an army, and struck down sinners in their anger and renegades in their wrath; the survivors fled to the Gentiles for safety. 45 And Mat•ta•thi'as and his friends went around and tore down the altars; 46 they forcibly circumcised all the uncircumcised boys that they found within the borders of Israel. 47 They hunted down the arrogant, and the work prospered in their hands. 48 They rescued the law out of the hands of the Gentiles and kings, and they never let the sinner gain the upper hand.

The Last Words of Mattathias
(Gen 22.1–18; 39.1—45.28; Num 13.1—14.10;
Josh 1.1–9)

49 Now the days drew near for Mat•ta•thi'as to die, and he said to his sons: "Arrogance and scorn have now become strong; it is a time of ruin and furious anger. 50 Now, my children, show zeal for the law, and give your lives for the covenant of our ancestors.

51 "Remember the deeds of the ancestors, which they did in their generations; and you will receive great honor and an everlasting name. 52 Was not Abraham found faithful when tested, and it was reckoned to him as righteousness? 53 Joseph in the time of his distress kept the commandment, and became lord of Egypt. 54 Phin'e•has our ancestor, because he was deeply zealous, received the covenant of everlasting priesthood. 55 Joshua, because he fulfilled the command, became a judge in

Israel. 56 Caleb, because he testified in the assembly, received an inheritance in the land. 57 David, because he was merciful, inherited the throne of the kingdom forever. 58 E•li'jah, because of great zeal for the law, was taken up into heaven. 59 Han•a•ni'ah, Az•a•ri'ah, and Mish'a•el believed and were saved from the flame. 60 Daniel, because of his innocence, was delivered from the mouth of the lions.

61 "And so observe, from generation to generation, that none of those who put their trust in him will lack strength. 62 Do not fear the words of sinners, for their splendor will turn into dung and worms. 63 Today they will be exalted, but tomorrow they will not be found, because they will have returned to the dust, and their plans will have perished. 64 My children, be courageous and grow strong in the law, for by it you will gain honor.

65 "Here is your brother Sim'e•on who, I know, is wise in counsel; always listen to him; he shall be your father. 66 Judas Mac•ca•bē'us has been a mighty warrior from his youth; he shall command the army for you and fight the battle against the peoples.*j* 67 You shall rally around you all who observe the law, and avenge the wrong done to your people. 68 Pay back the Gentiles in full, and obey the commands of the law."

69 Then he blessed them, and was gathered to his ancestors. 70 He died in the one hundred forty-sixth year*k* and was buried in the tomb of his ancestors at Mō'dein. And all Israel mourned for him with great lamentation.

The Early Victories of Judas
(2 Macc 8.1–7)

3 Then his son Judas, who was called Mac•ca•bē'us, took command in his place. 2 All his brothers and all who had joined his father helped him; they gladly fought for Israel.

3 He extended the glory of his people.
   Like a giant he put on his breastplate;
 he bound on his armor of war and waged
      battles,
   protecting the camp by his sword.
4 He was like a lion in his deeds,
   like a lion's cub roaring for prey.
5 He searched out and pursued those who broke
      the law;
   he burned those who troubled his people.
6 Lawbreakers shrank back for fear of him;
   all the evildoers were confounded;
   and deliverance prospered by his hand.
7 He embittered many kings,
   but he made Jacob glad by his deeds,
   and his memory is blessed forever.

---

i Gk *they*   *j* Or *of the people*   *k* 166 B.C.

8 He went through the cities of Judah;
　　he destroyed the ungodly out of the land;[l]
　　thus he turned away wrath from Israel.
9 He was renowned to the ends of the earth;
　　he gathered in those who were perishing.

10 Ap•ol•lō′ni•us now gathered together Gentiles and a large force from Sa•mār′i•a to fight against Israel. 11 When Judas learned of it, he went out to meet him, and he defeated and killed him. Many were wounded and fell, and the rest fled. 12 Then they seized their spoils; and Judas took the sword of Ap•ol•lō′ni•us, and used it in battle the rest of his life.

13 When Sēr′on, the commander of the Syrian army, heard that Judas had gathered a large company, including a body of faithful soldiers who stayed with him and went out to battle, 14 he said, "I will make a name for myself and win honor in the kingdom. I will make war on Judas and his companions, who scorn the king's command." 15 Once again a strong army of godless men went up with him to help him, to take vengeance on the Israelites.

16 When he approached the ascent of Beth-hō′ron, Judas went out to meet him with a small company. 17 But when they saw the army coming to meet them, they said to Judas, "How can we, few as we are, fight against so great and so strong a multitude? And we are faint, for we have eaten nothing today." 18 Judas replied, "It is easy for many to be hemmed in by few, for in the sight of Heaven there is no difference between saving by many or by few. 19 It is not on the size of the army that victory in battle depends, but strength comes from Heaven. 20 They come against us in great insolence and lawlessness to destroy us and our wives and our children, and to despoil us; 21 but we fight for our lives and our laws. 22 He himself will crush them before us; as for you, do not be afraid of them."

23 When he finished speaking, he rushed suddenly against Sēr′on and his army, and they were crushed before him. 24 They pursued them[m] down the descent of Beth-hō′ron to the plain; eight hundred of them fell, and the rest fled into the land of the Phi•lis′tines. 25 Then Judas and his brothers began to be feared, and terror fell on the Gentiles all around them. 26 His fame reached the king, and the Gentiles talked of the battles of Judas.

The Policy of Antiochus

27 When King An•ti′o•chus heard these reports, he was greatly angered; and he sent and gathered all the forces of his kingdom, a very strong army. 28 He opened his coffers and gave a year's pay to his forces, and ordered them to be ready for any need. 29 Then he saw that the money in the treasury was exhausted, and that the revenues from the country were small because of the dissension and disaster that he had caused in the land by abolishing the laws that had existed from the earliest days. 30 He feared that he might not have such funds as he had before for his expenses and for the gifts that he used to give more lavishly than preceding kings. 31 He was greatly perplexed in mind; then he determined to go to Persia and collect the revenues from those regions and raise a large fund.

32 He left Lys′i•as, a distinguished man of royal lineage, in charge of the king's affairs from the river Euphrates to the borders of Egypt. 33 Lys′i•as was also to take care of his son An•ti′o•chus until he returned. 34 And he turned over to Lys′i•as[n] half of his forces and the elephants, and gave him orders about all that he wanted done. As for the residents of Judea and Jerusalem, 35 Lys′i•as was to send a force against them to wipe out and destroy the strength of Israel and the remnant of Jerusalem; he was to banish the memory of them from the place, 36 settle aliens in all their territory, and distribute their land by lot. 37 Then the king took the remaining half of his forces and left An′ti•och his capital in the one hundred and forty-seventh year.[o] He crossed the Euphrates river and went through the upper provinces.

Preparations for Battle
(2 Macc 8.8–20)

38 Lys′i•as chose Ptol′e•my son of Dor•ym′e•nēs, and Nī•cā′nor and Gor′gi•as, able men among the Friends of the king, 39 and sent with them forty thousand infantry and seven thousand cavalry to go into the land of Judah and destroy it, as the king had commanded. 40 So they set out with their entire force, and when they arrived they encamped near Em•mā′us in the plain. 41 When the traders of the region heard what was said to them, they took silver and gold in immense amounts, and fetters,[p] and went to the camp to get the Israelites for slaves. And forces from Syria and the land of the Phi•lis′-tines joined with them.

42 Now Judas and his brothers saw that misfortunes had increased and that the forces were encamped in their territory. They also learned what the king had commanded to do to the people to cause their final destruction. 43 But they said to one another, "Let us restore the ruins of our people, and fight for our people and the sanctuary." 44 So the congregation assembled to be ready for battle, and to pray and ask for mercy and compassion.
45 Jerusalem was uninhabited like a wilderness;
　　not one of her children went in or out.
　The sanctuary was trampled down,

---

[l] Gk it　[m] Other ancient authorities read him　[n] Gk him
[o] 165 B.C.　[p] Syr: Gk Mss, Vg slaves

and aliens held the citadel;
    it was a lodging place for the Gentiles.
Joy was taken from Jacob;
    the flute and the harp ceased to play.

46 Then they gathered together and went to Miz'pah, opposite Jerusalem, because Israel formerly had a place of prayer in Miz'pah. 47 They fasted that day, put on sackcloth and sprinkled ashes on their heads, and tore their clothes. 48 And they opened the book of the law to inquire into those matters about which the Gentiles consulted the likenesses of their gods. 49 They also brought the vestments of the priesthood and the first fruits and the tithes, and they stirred up the nazirites*q* who had completed their days; 50 and they cried aloud to Heaven, saying,

"What shall we do with these?
    Where shall we take them?
51 Your sanctuary is trampled down and
        profaned,
    and your priests mourn in humiliation.
52 Here the Gentiles are assembled against us to
        destroy us;
    you know what they plot against us.
53 How will we be able to withstand them,
    if you do not help us?"

54 Then they sounded the trumpets and gave a loud shout. 55 After this Judas appointed leaders of the people, in charge of thousands and hundreds and fifties and tens. 56 Those who were building houses, or were about to be married, or were planting a vineyard, or were fainthearted, he told to go home again, according to the law. 57 Then the army marched out and encamped to the south of Em·ma'us.

58 And Judas said, "Arm yourselves and be courageous. Be ready early in the morning to fight with these Gentiles who have assembled against us to destroy us and our sanctuary. 59 It is better for us to die in battle than to see the misfortunes of our nation and of the sanctuary. 60 But as his will in heaven may be, so shall he do."

The Battle at Emmaus
(2 Macc 8.21–29, 34–36)

4 Now Gor'gi·as took five thousand infantry and one thousand picked cavalry, and this division moved out by night 2 to fall upon the camp of the Jews and attack them suddenly. Men from the citadel were his guides. 3 But Judas heard of it, and he and his warriors moved out to attack the king's force in Em·ma'us 4 while the division was still absent from the camp. 5 When Gor'gi·as entered the camp of Judas by night, he found no one there, so he looked for them in the hills, because he said, "These men are running away from us."

6 At daybreak Judas appeared in the plain with three thousand men, but they did not have armor and swords such as they desired. 7 And they saw the camp of the Gentiles, strong and fortified, with cavalry all around it; and these men were trained in war. 8 But Judas said to those who were with him, "Do not fear their numbers or be afraid when they charge. 9 Remember how our ancestors were saved at the Red Sea, when Pharaoh with his forces pursued them. 10 And now, let us cry to Heaven, to see whether he will favor us and remember his covenant with our ancestors and crush this army before us today. 11 Then all the Gentiles will know that there is one who redeems and saves Israel."

12 When the foreigners looked up and saw them coming against them, 13 they went out from their camp to battle. Then the men with Judas blew their trumpets 14 and engaged in battle. The Gentiles were crushed, and fled into the plain, 15 and all those in the rear fell by the sword. They pursued them to Ga·zā'ra, and to the plains of Id·ū·mē'a, and to A·zō'tus and Jam'ni·a; and three thousand of them fell. 16 Then Judas and his force turned back from pursuing them, 17 and he said to the people, "Do not be greedy for plunder, for there is a battle before us; 18 Gor'gi·as and his force are near us in the hills. But stand now against our enemies and fight them, and afterward seize the plunder boldly."

19 Just as Judas was finishing this speech, a detachment appeared, coming out of the hills. 20 They saw that their army*r* had been put to flight, and that the Jews*r* were burning the camp, for the smoke that was seen showed what had happened. 21 When they perceived this, they were greatly frightened, and when they also saw the army of Judas drawn up in the plain for battle, 22 they all fled into the land of the Phi·lis'tines. 23 Then Judas returned to plunder the camp, and they seized a great amount of gold and silver, and cloth dyed blue and sea purple, and great riches. 24 On their return they sang hymns and praises to Heaven— "For he is good, for his mercy endures forever." 25 Thus Israel had a great deliverance that day.

First Campaign of Lysias
(2 Macc 11.1–12)

26 Those of the foreigners who escaped went and reported to Lys'i·as all that had happened. 27 When he heard it, he was perplexed and discouraged, for things had not happened to Israel as he had intended, nor had they turned out as the king had ordered. 28 But the next year he mustered sixty thousand picked infantry and five thousand cavalry to subdue them. 29 They came into Id·ū·mē'a and encamped at Beth-zur, and Judas met them with ten thousand men.

---

q That is *those separated* or *those consecrated*   *r* Gk *they*

30 When he saw that their army was strong, he prayed, saying, "Blessed are you, O Savior of Israel, who crushed the attack of the mighty warrior by the hand of your servant David, and gave the camp of the Phi•lis'tines into the hands of Jonathan son of Saul, and of the man who carried his armor. 31 Hem in this army by the hand of your people Israel, and let them be ashamed of their troops and their cavalry. 32 Fill them with cowardice; melt the boldness of their strength; let them tremble in their destruction. 33 Strike them down with the sword of those who love you, and let all who know your name praise you with hymns."

34 Then both sides attacked, and there fell of the army of Lys'i•as five thousand men; they fell in action.s 35 When Lys'i•as saw the rout of his troops and observed the boldness that inspired those of Judas, and how ready they were either to live or to die nobly, he withdrew to An'ti•och and enlisted mercenaries in order to invade Judea again with an even larger army.

Cleansing and Dedication of the Temple
(2 Macc 10.1–9)

36 Then Judas and his brothers said, "See, our enemies are crushed; let us go up to cleanse the sanctuary and dedicate it." 37 So all the army assembled and went up to Mount Zion. 38 There they saw the sanctuary desolate, the altar profaned, and the gates burned. In the courts they saw bushes sprung up as in a thicket, or as on one of the mountains. They saw also the chambers of the priests in ruins. 39 Then they tore their clothes and mourned with great lamentation; they sprinkled themselves with ashes 40 and fell face down on the ground. And when the signal was given with the trumpets, they cried out to Heaven.

41 Then Judas detailed men to fight against those in the citadel until he had cleansed the sanctuary. 42 He chose blameless priests devoted to the law, 43 and they cleansed the sanctuary and removed the defiled stones to an unclean place. 44 They deliberated what to do about the altar of burnt offering, which had been profaned. 45 And they thought it best to tear it down, so that it would not be a lasting shame to them that the Gentiles had defiled it. So they tore down the altar, 46 and stored the stones in a convenient place on the temple hill until a prophet should come to tell what to do with them. 47 Then they took unhewnt stones, as the law directs, and built a new altar like the former one. 48 They also rebuilt the sanctuary and the interior of the temple, and consecrated the courts. 49 They made new holy vessels, and brought the lampstand, the altar of incense, and the table into the temple. 50 Then they offered incense on the altar and lit the lamps on the lampstand, and these gave light in the temple. 51 They placed the bread on the table and hung up the curtains. Thus they finished all the work they had undertaken.

52 Early in the morning on the twenty-fifth day of the ninth month, which is the month of Chis'lev, in the one hundred forty-eighth year,u 53 they rose and offered sacrifice, as the law directs, on the new altar of burnt offering that they had built. 54 At the very season and on the very day that the Gentiles had profaned it, it was dedicated with songs and harps and lutes and cymbals. 55 All the people fell on their faces and worshiped and blessed Heaven, who had prospered them. 56 So they celebrated the dedication of the altar for eight days, and joyfully offered burnt offerings; they offered a sacrifice of well-being and a thanksgiving offering. 57 They decorated the front of the temple with golden crowns and small shields; they restored the gates and the chambers for the priests, and fitted them with doors. 58 There was very great joy among the people, and the disgrace brought by the Gentiles was removed.

59 Then Judas and his brothers and all the assembly of Israel determined that every year at that season the days of dedication of the altar should be observed with joy and gladness for eight days, beginning with the twenty-fifth day of the month of Chis'lev.

60 At that time they fortified Mount Zion with high walls and strong towers all around, to keep the Gentiles from coming and trampling them down as

---

did you KNOW?

Hanukkah

Hanukkah, or the feast of Dedication, is a joyful eight-day celebration in the month of Chislev (December). On each night of the festival, a candle is lit in joyful remembrance of the Maccabees' rededication of the Temple in Jerusalem after it was robbed and desecrated by Antiochus IV Epiphanes (1 Macc 4.56). Even more deeply, the candlelight symbolizes the gratitude of the Jewish people for the survival, often against great odds, of their age-old faith.

▶ **1 Macc 4.52–59**

---

s Or *and some fell on the opposite side*   t Gk *whole*
u 164 B.C.

they had done before. [61] Judas[v] stationed a garrison there to guard it; he also fortified Beth-zur to guard it, so that the people might have a stronghold that faced Id•ū•mē′a.

Wars with Neighboring Peoples
(2 Macc 10.14–33)

5 When the Gentiles all around heard that the altar had been rebuilt and the sanctuary dedicated as it was before, they became very angry, [2] and they determined to destroy the descendants of Jacob who lived among them. So they began to kill and destroy among the people. [3] But Judas made war on the descendants of Esau in Id•ū•mē′a, at Ak•ra•bat′te•nē, because they kept lying in wait for Israel. He dealt them a heavy blow and humbled them and despoiled them. [4] He also remembered the wickedness of the sons of Baē′an, who were a trap and a snare to the people and ambushed them on the highways. [5] They were shut up by him in their[w] towers; and he encamped against them, vowed their complete destruction, and burned with fire their towers and all who were in them. [6] Then he crossed over to attack the Am′mon•ites, where he found a strong band and many people, with Timothy as their leader. [7] He engaged in many battles with them, and they were crushed before him; he struck them down. [8] He also took Jā′zer and its villages; then he returned to Judea.

Liberation of Galilean Jews
(2 Macc 12.10–25)

9 Now the Gentiles in Gil′e•ad gathered together against the Israelites who lived in their territory, and planned to destroy them. But they fled to the stronghold of Dath′e•ma, [10] and sent to Judas and his brothers a letter that said, "The Gentiles around us have gathered together to destroy us. [11] They are preparing to come and capture the stronghold to which we have fled, and Timothy is leading their forces. [12] Now then, come and rescue us from their hands, for many of us have fallen, [13] and all our kindred who were in the land of Tob have been killed; the enemy[x] have captured their wives and children and goods, and have destroyed about a thousand persons there."

14 While the letter was still being read, other messengers, with their garments torn, came from Galilee and made a similar report; [15] they said that the people of Ptol•e•mā′is and Tȳre and Sī′don, and all Galilee of the Gentiles,[y] had gathered together against them "to annihilate us." [16] When Judas and the people heard these messages, a great assembly was called to determine what they should do for their kindred who were in distress and were being attacked by enemies.[z] [17] Then Judas said to his brother Simon, "Choose your men and go and res-

cue your kindred in Galilee; Jonathan my brother and I will go to Gil′e•ad." [18] But he left Joseph, son of Zech•a•rī′ah, and Az•a•rī′ah, a leader of the people, with the rest of the forces, in Judea to guard it; [19] and he gave them this command, "Take charge of this people, but do not engage in battle with the Gentiles until we return." [20] Then three thousand men were assigned to Simon to go to Galilee, and eight thousand to Judas for Gil′e•ad.

21 So Simon went to Galilee and fought many battles against the Gentiles, and the Gentiles were crushed before him. [22] He pursued them to the gate of Ptol•e•mā′is; as many as three thousand of the Gentiles fell, and he despoiled them. [23] Then he took the Jews[a] of Galilee and Ar•bat′ta, with their wives and children, and all they possessed, and led them to Judea with great rejoicing.

Judas and Jonathan in Gilead

24 Judas Mac•ca•bē′us and his brother Jonathan crossed the Jordan and made three days' journey into the wilderness. [25] They encountered the Na•ba•tē′ans, who met them peaceably and told them all that had happened to their kindred in Gil′e•ad: [26] "Many of them have been shut up in Boz′rah and Bō′sor, in Al′e•ma and Chas′phō, Mā′ked and Car′na•im"—all these towns were strong and large— [27] "and some have been shut up in the other towns of Gil′e•ad; the enemy[x] are getting ready to attack the strongholds tomorrow and capture and destroy all these people in a single day."

28 Then Judas and his army quickly turned back by the wilderness road to Boz′rah; and he took the town, and killed every male by the edge of the sword; then he seized all its spoils and burned it with fire. [29] He left the place at night, and they went all the way to the stronghold of Dath′e•ma.[b] [30] At dawn they looked out and saw a large company, which could not be counted, carrying ladders and engines of war to capture the stronghold, and attacking the Jews within.[c] [31] So Judas saw that the battle had begun and that the cry of the town went up to Heaven, with trumpets and loud shouts, [32] and he said to the men of his forces, "Fight today for your kindred!" [33] Then he came up behind them in three companies, who sounded their trumpets and cried aloud in prayer. [34] And when the army of Timothy realized that it was Mac•ca•bē′us, they fled before him, and he dealt them a heavy blow. As many as eight thousand of them fell that day.

35 Next he turned aside to Mā′a•pha,[d] and

[v] Gk He   [w] Gk her   [x] Gk they   [y] Gk aliens   [z] Gk them
[a] Gk those   [b] Gk lacks of Dathema. See verse 9   [c] Gk and they were attacking them   [d] Other ancient authorities read Alema

fought against it and took it; and he killed every male in it, plundered it, and burned it with fire. 36 From there he marched on and took Chas′phō, Mā′ked, and Bō′sor, and the other towns of Gil′e•ad.

37 After these things Timothy gathered another army and encamped opposite Rā′phon, on the other side of the stream. 38 Judas sent men to spy out the camp, and they reported to him, "All the Gentiles around us have gathered to him; it is a very large force. 39 They also have hired Arabs to help them, and they are encamped across the stream, ready to come and fight against you." And Judas went to meet them.

40 Now as Judas and his army drew near to the stream of water, Timothy said to the officers of his forces, "If he crosses over to us first, we will not be able to resist him, for he will surely defeat us. 41 But if he shows fear and camps on the other side of the river, we will cross over to him and defeat him." 42 When Judas approached the stream of water, he stationed the officers[e] of the army at the stream and gave them this command, "Permit no one to encamp, but make them all enter the battle." 43 Then he crossed over against them first, and the whole army followed him. All the Gentiles were defeated before him, and they threw away their arms and fled into the sacred precincts at Car′na•im. 44 But he took the town and burned the sacred precincts with fire, together with all who were in them. Thus Car′na•im was conquered; they could stand before Judas no longer.

The Return to Jerusalem
(2 Macc 12.26–31)

45 Then Judas gathered together all the Israelites in Gil′e•ad, the small and the great, with their wives and children and goods, a very large company, to go to the land of Judah. 46 So they came to Ē′phron. This was a large and very strong town on the road, and they could not go around it to the right or to the left; they had to go through it. 47 But the people of the town shut them out and blocked up the gates with stones.

48 Judas sent them this friendly message, "Let us pass through your land to get to our land. No one will do you harm; we will simply pass by on foot." But they refused to open to him. 49 Then Judas ordered proclamation to be made to the army that all should encamp where they were. 50 So the men of the forces encamped, and he fought against the town all that day and all the night, and the town was delivered into his hands. 51 He destroyed every male by the edge of the sword, and razed and plundered the town. Then he passed through the town over the bodies of the dead.

52 Then they crossed the Jordan into the large plain before Beth-shan. 53 Judas kept rallying the laggards and encouraging the people all the way until he came to the land of Judah. 54 So they went up to Mount Zion with joy and gladness, and offered burnt offerings, because they had returned in safety; not one of them had fallen.

Joseph and Azariah Defeated

55 Now while Judas and Jonathan were in Gil′e•ad and their[f] brother Simon was in Galilee before Ptol•e•mā′is, 56 Joseph son of Zech•a•rī′ah, and Az•a•rī′ah, the commanders of the forces, heard of their brave deeds and of the heroic war they had fought. 57 So they said, "Let us also make a name for ourselves; let us go and make war on the Gentiles around us." 58 So they issued orders to the men of the forces that were with them and marched against Jam′ni•a. 59 Gor′gi•as and his men came out of the town to meet them in battle. 60 Then Joseph and Az•a•rī′ah were routed, and were pursued to the borders of Judea; as many as two thousand of the people of Israel fell that day. 61 Thus the people suffered a great rout because, thinking to do a brave deed, they did not listen to Judas and his brothers. 62 But they did not belong to the family of those men through whom deliverance was given to Israel.

63 The man Judas and his brothers were greatly honored in all Israel and among all the Gentiles, wherever their name was heard. 64 People gathered to them and praised them.

Success at Hebron and Philistia

65 Then Judas and his brothers went out and fought the descendants of Esau in the land to the south. He struck Hē′bron and its villages and tore down its strongholds and burned its towers on all sides. 66 Then he marched off to go into the land of the Phi•lis′tines, and passed through Mar′i•sa.[g] 67 On that day some priests, who wished to do a brave deed, fell in battle, for they went out to battle unwisely. 68 But Judas turned aside to A•zō′tus in the land of the Phi•lis′tines; he tore down their altars, and the carved images of their gods he burned with fire; he plundered the towns and returned to the land of Judah.

The Last Days of Antiochus Epiphanes
(2 Macc 1.11–17; 9.1–29; 10.9–13)

6 King An•ti′o•chus was going through the upper provinces when he heard that El•y•mā′is in Persia was a city famed for its wealth in silver and gold. 2 Its temple was very rich, containing golden shields, breastplates, and weapons left there by Alexander son of Philip, the Mac•e•dō′ni•an king who first reigned over the Greeks. 3 So he came and

---

e Or scribes   f Gk his   g Other ancient authorities read Samaria tried to take the city and plunder it, but he could not because his plan had become known to the citizens 4 and they withstood him in battle. So he fled and in great disappointment left there to return to Babylon.

5 Then someone came to him in Persia and reported that the armies that had gone into the land of Judah had been routed; 6 that Lys'i·as had gone first with a strong force, but had turned and fled before the Jews;h that the Jews i had grown strong from the arms, supplies, and abundant spoils that they had taken from the armies they had cut down; 7 that they had torn down the abomination that he had erected on the altar in Jerusalem; and that they had surrounded the sanctuary with high walls as before, and also Beth-zur, his town.

8 When the king heard this news, he was astounded and badly shaken. He took to his bed and became sick from disappointment, because things had not turned out for him as he had planned. 9 He lay there for many days, because deep disappointment continually gripped him, and he realized that he was dying. 10 So he called all his Friends and said to them, "Sleep has departed from my eyes and I am downhearted with worry. 11 I said to myself, 'To what distress I have come! And into what a great flood I now am plunged! For I was kind and beloved in my power.' 12 But now I remember the wrong I did in Jerusalem. I seized all its vessels of silver and gold, and I sent to destroy the inhabitants of Judah without good reason. 13 I know that it is because of this that these misfortunes have come upon me; here I am, perishing of bitter disappointment in a strange land."

14 Then he called for Philip, one of his Friends, and made him ruler over all his kingdom. 15 He gave him the crown and his robe and the signet, so that he might guide his son An·ti'o·chus and bring him up to be king. 16 Thus King An·ti'o·chus died there in the one hundred forty-ninth year.j 17 When Lys'i·as learned that the king was dead, he set up An·ti'o·chus the king'sk son to reign. Lys'i·asl had brought him up from boyhood; he named him Eū'pa·tor.

Renewed Attacks from Syria
(2 Macc 11.22–26; 13.1–26)

18 Meanwhile the garrison in the citadel kept hemming Israel in around the sanctuary. They were trying in every way to harm them and strengthen the Gentiles. 19 Judas therefore resolved to destroy them, and assembled all the people to besiege them. 20 They gathered together and besieged the citadelm in the one hundred fiftieth year;n and he built siege towers and other engines of war. 21 But some of the garrison escaped from the siege and some of the ungodly Israelites joined them.

22 They went to the king and said, "How long will you fail to do justice and to avenge our kindred? 23 We were happy to serve your father, to live by what he said, and to follow his commands. 24 For this reason the sons of our people besieged the citadel o and became hostile to us; moreover, they have put to death as many of us as they have caught, and they have seized our inheritances. 25 It is not against us alone that they have stretched out their hands; they have also attacked all the lands on their borders. 26 And see, today they have encamped against the citadel in Jerusalem to take it; they have fortified both the sanctuary and Beth-zur; 27 unless you quickly prevent them, they will do still greater things, and you will not be able to stop them."

28 The king was enraged when he heard this. He assembled all his Friends, the commanders of his forces and those in authority.p 29 Mercenary forces also came to him from other kingdoms and from islands of the seas. 30 The number of his forces was one hundred thousand foot soldiers, twenty thousand horsemen, and thirty-two elephants accustomed to war. 31 They came through Id·ū·mē'a and encamped against Beth-zur, and for many days they fought and built engines of war; but the Jews i sallied out and burned these with fire, and fought courageously.

The Battle at Beth-zechariah

32 Then Judas marched away from the citadel and encamped at Beth-zech·a·rī'ah, opposite the camp of the king. 33 Early in the morning the king set out and took his army by a forced march along the road to Beth-zech·a·rī'ah, and his troops made ready for battle and sounded their trumpets. 34 They offered the elephants the juice of grapes and mulberries, to arouse them for battle. 35 They distributed the animals among the phalanxes; with each elephant they stationed a thousand men armed with coats of mail, and with brass helmets on their heads; and five hundred picked horsemen were assigned to each beast. 36 These took their position beforehand wherever the animal was; wherever it went, they went with it, and they never left it. 37 On the elephantsh were wooden towers, strong and covered; they were fastened on each animal by special harness, and on each were fourq armed men who fought from there, and also its Indian driver. 38 The rest of the cavalry were stationed on either side, on the two flanks of the army, to harass the enemy while being themselves protected by the

---

h Gk them   i Gk they   j 163 B.C.   k Gk his   l Gk He   m Gk it   n 162 B.C.   o Meaning of Gk uncertain   p Gk those over the reins   q Cn: Some authorities read thirty; others thirty-two

did you KNOW?

A Just War

Have you ever believed in something so strongly that you could justify a war to protect it? The Maccabees did, and they led a violent resistance against terrible religious persecution.

The Catholic church teaches that "all citizens and all governments are obliged to work for the avoidance of war" (*Catechism*, no. 2308). But it also teaches that there can be occasions for legitimate defense by military force (no. 2309), or what is sometimes called a just war. The criteria for a just war are as follows:

- All other means to avoid war must be exhausted.
- The damage done by the aggressor must be grave and certain.
- There must be serious prospects of success.
- The use of arms must not produce evils that are greater than the evil to be eliminated.

No Catholic Christian can participate in good conscience in any war that does not meet all these criteria.

War is not the answer; peace is. But at times in history, some Christians have felt that the only response to a grave injustice was violent resistance. However, no Christian is obligated to fight in a war if doing so goes against his or her conscience—although he or she may be required to serve the community in some other way—and nonviolent resistance is always an option (see "Nonviolent Resistance," 2 Macc 7.42).

phalanxes. 39 When the sun shone on the shields of gold and brass, the hills were ablaze with them and gleamed like flaming torches.

40 Now a part of the king's army was spread out on the high hills, and some troops were on the plain, and they advanced steadily and in good order. 41 All who heard the noise made by their multitude, by the marching of the multitude and the clanking of their arms, trembled, for the army was very large and strong. 42 But Judas and his army advanced to the battle, and six hundred of the king's

army fell. 43 Now El•ē•ā′zar, called Av′a•ran, saw that one of the animals was equipped with royal armor. It was taller than all the others, and he supposed that the king was on it. 44 So he gave his life to save his people and to win for himself an everlasting name. 45 He courageously ran into the midst of the phalanx to reach it; he killed men right and left, and they parted before him on both sides. 46 He got under the elephant, stabbed it from beneath, and killed it; but it fell to the ground upon him and he died. 47 When the Jews[r] saw the royal might and the fierce attack of the forces, they turned away in flight.

The Siege of the Temple

48 The soldiers of the king's army went up to Jerusalem against them, and the king encamped in Judea and at Mount Zion. 49 He made peace with the people of Beth-zur, and they evacuated the town because they had no provisions there to withstand a siege, since it was a sabbatical year for the land. 50 So the king took Beth-zur and stationed a guard there to hold it. 51 Then he encamped before the sanctuary for many days. He set up siege towers, engines of war to throw fire and stones, machines to shoot arrows, and catapults. 52 The Jews[r] also made engines of war to match theirs, and fought for many days. 53 But they had no food in storage,[s] because it was the seventh year; those who had found safety in Judea from the Gentiles had consumed the last of the stores. 54 Only a few men were left in the sanctuary; the rest scattered to their own homes, for the famine proved too much for them.

Syria Offers Terms

55 Then Lys′i•as heard that Philip, whom King An•tī′o•chus while still living had appointed to bring up his son An•tī′o•chus to be king, 56 had returned from Persia and Mēd′i•a with the forces that had gone with the king, and that he was trying to seize control of the government. 57 So he quickly gave orders to withdraw, and said to the king, to the commanders of the forces, and to the troops, "Daily we grow weaker, our food supply is scant, the place against which we are fighting is strong, and the affairs of the kingdom press urgently on us. 58 Now then let us come to terms with these people, and make peace with them and with all their nation. 59 Let us agree to let them live by their laws as they did before; for it was on account of their laws that we abolished that they became angry and did all these things."

60 The speech pleased the king and the commanders, and he sent to the Jews[t] an offer of peace,

---

r Gk *they*   s Other ancient authorities read *in the sanctuary*
t Gk *them*

1 MACC

and they accepted it. 61 So the king and the commanders gave them their oath. On these conditions the Jews^u evacuated the stronghold. 62 But when the king entered Mount Zion and saw what a strong fortress the place was, he broke the oath he had sworn and gave orders to tear down the wall all around. 63 Then he set off in haste and returned to An'ti·och. He found Philip in control of the city, but he fought against him, and took the city by force.

Expedition of Bacchides and Alcimus
(2 Macc 14.1–14)

7 In the one hundred fifty-first year^v De·mē'-tri·us son of Se·leū'cus set out from Rome, sailed with a few men to a town by the sea, and there began to reign. 2 As he was entering the royal palace of his ancestors, the army seized An·tī'o·chus and Lys'i·as to bring them to him. 3 But when this act became known to him, he said, "Do not let me see their faces!" 4 So the army killed them, and De·mē'tri·us took his seat on the throne of his kingdom.

5 Then there came to him all the renegade and godless men of Israel; they were led by Al'ci·mus, who wanted to be high priest. 6 They brought to the king this accusation against the people: "Judas and his brothers have destroyed all your Friends, and have driven us out of our land. 7 Now then send a man whom you trust; let him go and see all the ruin that Judas^w has brought on us and on the land of the king, and let him punish them and all who help them."

8 So the king chose Bac'chi·dēs, one of the king's Friends, governor of the province Beyond the River; he was a great man in the kingdom and was faithful to the king. 9 He sent him, and with him he sent the ungodly Al'ci·mus, whom he made high priest; and he commanded him to take vengeance on the Israelites. 10 So they marched away and came with a large force into the land of Judah; and he sent messengers to Judas and his brothers with peaceable but treacherous words. 11 But they paid no attention to their words, for they saw that they had come with a large force.

12 Then a group of scribes appeared in a body before Al'ci·mus and Bac'chi·dēs to ask for just terms. 13 The Has·i·dē'ans were first among the Israelites to seek peace from them, 14 for they said, "A priest of the line of Aaron has come with the army, and he will not harm us." 15 Al'-ci·mus^x spoke peaceable words to them and swore this oath to them, "We will not seek to injure you or your friends." 16 So they trusted him; but he seized sixty of them and killed them in one day, in accordance with the word that was written,

17 "The flesh of your faithful ones and their blood
     they poured out all around Jerusalem,
     and there was no one to bury them."

18 Then the fear and dread of them fell on all the people, for they said, "There is no truth or justice in them, for they have violated the agreement and the oath that they swore."

19 Then Bac'chi·dēs withdrew from Jerusalem and encamped in Beth-zā'ith. And he sent and seized many of the men who had deserted to him,^y and some of the people, and killed them and threw them into a great pit. 20 He placed Al'ci·mus in charge of the country and left with him a force to help him; then Bac'chi·dēs went back to the king.

21 Al'ci·mus struggled to maintain his high priesthood, 22 and all who were troubling their people joined him. They gained control of the land of Judah and did great damage in Israel. 23 And Judas saw all the wrongs that Al'ci·mus and those with him had done among the Israelites; it was more than the Gentiles had done. 24 So Judas^w went out into all the surrounding parts of Judea, taking vengeance on those who had deserted and preventing those in the city^z from going out into the country. 25 When Al'ci·mus saw that Judas and those with him had grown strong, and realized that he could not withstand them, he returned to the king and brought malicious charges against them.

Nicanor in Judea
(2 Macc 14.15—15.19)

26 Then the king sent Nī·cā'nor, one of his honored princes, who hated and detested Israel, and he commanded him to destroy the people. 27 So Nī·cā'nor came to Jerusalem with a large force, and treacherously sent to Judas and his brothers this peaceable message, 28 "Let there be no fighting between you and me; I shall come with a few men to see you face to face in peace."

29 So he came to Judas, and they greeted one another peaceably; but the enemy were preparing to kidnap Judas. 30 It became known to Judas that Nī·cā'nor^w had come to him with treacherous intent, and he was afraid of him and would not meet him again. 31 When Nī·cā'nor learned that his plan had been disclosed, he went out to meet Judas in battle near Caph'ar-sal'a·ma. 32 About five hundred of the army of Nī·cā'nor fell, and the rest^u fled into the city of David.

Nicanor Threatens the Temple

33 After these events Nī·cā'nor went up to Mount Zion. Some of the priests from the sanctuary and some of the elders of the people came out to

---

^u Gk they ^v 161 B.C. ^w Gk he ^x Gk He ^y Or many of his men who had deserted ^z Gk and they were prevented greet him peaceably and to show him the burnt offering that was being offered for the king. 34 But he mocked them and derided them and defiled them and spoke arrogantly, 35 and in anger he swore this oath, "Unless Judas and his army are delivered into my hands this time, then if I return safely I will burn up this house." And he went out in great anger. 36 At this the priests went in and stood before the altar and the temple; they wept and said,

37 "You chose this house to be called by your
        name,
    and to be for your people a house of prayer
        and supplication.
38 Take vengeance on this man and on his army,
    and let them fall by the sword;
    remember their blasphemies,
    and let them live no longer."

The Death of Nicanor
(2 Macc 15.20–37)

39 Now Nĭ•că′nor went out from Jerusalem and encamped in Beth-hō′ron, and the Syrian army joined him. 40 Judas encamped in Ad′a•sa with three thousand men. Then Judas prayed and said, 41 "When the messengers from the king spoke blasphemy, your angel went out and struck down one hundred eighty-five thousand of the Assyrians.*a* 42 So also crush this army before us today; let the rest learn that Nĭ•că′nor*b* has spoken wickedly against the sanctuary, and judge him according to this wickedness."

43 So the armies met in battle on the thirteenth day of the month of Ă′dar. The army of Nĭ•că′nor was crushed, and he himself was the first to fall in the battle. 44 When his army saw that Nĭ•că′nor had fallen, they threw down their arms and fled. 45 The Jews*c* pursued them a day's journey, from Ad′a•sa as far as Ga•ză′ra, and as they followed they kept sounding the battle call on the trumpets. 46 People came out of all the surrounding villages of Judea, and they outflanked the enemy*d* and drove them back to their pursuers,*e* so that they all fell by the sword; not even one of them was left. 47 Then the Jews*c* seized the spoils and the plunder; they cut off Nĭ•că′nor's head and the right hand that he had so arrogantly stretched out, and brought them and displayed them just outside Jerusalem. 48 The people rejoiced greatly and celebrated that day as a day of great gladness. 49 They decreed that this day should be celebrated each year on the thirteenth day of Ă′dar. 50 So the land of Judah had rest for a few days.

A Eulogy of the Romans

8 Now Judas heard of the fame of the Romans, that they were very strong and were well-disposed toward all who made an alliance with them, that they pledged friendship to those who came to them, 2 and that they were very strong. He had been told of their wars and of the brave deeds that they were doing among the Gauls, how they had defeated them and forced them to pay tribute, 3 and what they had done in the land of Spain to get control of the silver and gold mines there, 4 and how they had gained control of the whole region by their planning and patience, even though the place was far distant from them. They also subdued the kings who came against them from the ends of the earth, until they crushed them and inflicted great disaster on them; the rest paid them tribute every year. 5 They had crushed in battle and conquered Philip, and King Per′sē•us of the Mac•e•dō′ni•ans,*f* and the others who rose up against them. 6 They also had defeated An•tĭ′o•chus the Great, king of Asia, who went to fight against them with one hundred twenty elephants and with cavalry and chariots and a very large army. He was crushed by them; 7 they took him alive and decreed that he and those who would reign after him should pay a heavy tribute and give hostages and surrender some of their best provinces, 8 the countries of India, Mēd′i•a, and Lyd′i•a. These they took from him and gave to King Eū′me•nēs. 9 The Greeks planned to come and destroy them, 10 but this became known to them, and they sent a general against the Greeks*d* and attacked them. Many of them were wounded and fell, and the Romans*c* took captive their wives and children; they plundered them, conquered the land, tore down their strongholds, and enslaved them to this day. 11 The remaining kingdoms and islands, as many as ever opposed them, they destroyed and enslaved; 12 but with their friends and those who rely on them they have kept friendship. They have subdued kings far and near, and as many as have heard of their fame have feared them. 13 Those whom they wish to help and to make kings, they make kings, and those whom they wish they depose; and they have been greatly exalted. 14 Yet for all this not one of them has put on a crown or worn purple as a mark of pride, 15 but they have built for themselves a senate chamber, and every day three hundred twenty senators constantly deliberate concerning the people, to govern them well. 16 They trust one man each year to rule over them and to control all their land; they all heed the one man, and there is no envy or jealousy among them.

An Alliance with Rome

17 So Judas chose Eū′pol′e•mus son of John son of Ac′cos, and Jason son of El•ē•ă′zar, and sent them to Rome to establish friendship and alliance, 18 and to free themselves from the yoke; for they

---

a Gk *of them*   *b* Gk *he*   *c* Gk *they*   *d* Gk *them*
e Gk *these*   *f* Or *Kittim*

saw that the kingdom of the Greeks was enslaving Israel completely. 19 They went to Rome, a very long journey; and they entered the senate chamber and spoke as follows: 20 "Judas, who is also called Mac•ca•bē'us, and his brothers and the people of the Jews have sent us to you to establish alliance and peace with you, so that we may be enrolled as your allies and friends." 21 The proposal pleased them, 22 and this is a copy of the letter that they wrote in reply, on bronze tablets, and sent to Jerusalem to remain with them there as a memorial of peace and alliance:

23 "May all go well with the Romans and with the nation of the Jews at sea and on land forever, and may sword and enemy be far from them. 24 If war comes first to Rome or to any of their allies in all their dominion, 25 the nation of the Jews shall act as their allies wholeheartedly, as the occasion may indicate to them. 26 To the enemy that makes war they shall not give or supply grain, arms, money, or ships, just as Rome has decided; and they shall keep their obligations without receiving any return. 27 In the same way, if war comes first to the nation of the Jews, the Romans shall willingly act as their allies, as the occasion may indicate to them. 28 And to their enemies there shall not be given grain, arms, money, or ships, just as Rome has decided; and they shall keep these obligations and do so without deceit. 29 Thus on these terms the Romans make a treaty with the Jewish people. 30 If after these terms are in effect both parties shall determine to add or delete anything, they shall do so at their discretion, and any addition or deletion that they may make shall be valid.

31 "Concerning the wrongs that King De•mē'-tri•us is doing to them, we have written to him as follows, 'Why have you made your yoke heavy on our friends and allies the Jews? 32 If now they appeal again for help against you, we will defend their rights and fight you on sea and on land.' "

Bacchides Returns to Judea

9 When De•mē'tri•us heard that Ni•cā'nor and his army had fallen in battle, he sent Bac'chi•dēs and Al'ci•mus into the land of Judah a second time, and with them the right wing of the army. 2 They went by the road that leads to Gil'gal and encamped against Mes'a•loth in Ar•bē'la, and they took it and killed many people. 3 In the first month of the one hundred fifty-second year g they encamped against Jerusalem; 4 then they marched off and went to Be•rē'a with twenty thousand foot soldiers and two thousand cavalry.

5 Now Judas was encamped in El'a•sa, and with him were three thousand picked men. 6 When they saw the huge number of the enemy forces, they were greatly frightened, and many slipped away

from the camp, until no more than eight hundred of them were left.

7 When Judas saw that his army had slipped away and the battle was imminent, he was crushed in spirit, for he had no time to assemble them. 8 He became faint, but he said to those who were left, "Let us get up and go against our enemies. We may have the strength to fight them." 9 But they tried to dissuade him, saying, "We do not have the strength. Let us rather save our own lives now, and let us come back with our kindred and fight them; we are too few." 10 But Judas said, "Far be it from us to do such a thing as to flee from them. If our time has come, let us die bravely for our kindred, and leave no cause to question our honor."

The Last Battle of Judas

11 Then the army of Bac'chi•dēs h marched out from the camp and took its stand for the encounter. The cavalry was divided into two companies, and the slingers and the archers went ahead of the army, as did all the chief warriors. 12 Bac'chi•dēs was on the right wing. Flanked by the two companies, the phalanx advanced to the sound of the trumpets; and the men with Judas also blew their trumpets. 13 The earth was shaken by the noise of the armies, and the battle raged from morning until evening.

14 Judas saw that Bac'chi•dēs and the strength of his army were on the right; then all the stouthearted men went with him, 15 and they crushed the right wing, and he pursued them as far as Mount A•zō'tus. 16 When those on the left wing saw that the right wing was crushed, they turned and followed close behind Judas and his men. 17 The battle became desperate, and many on both sides were wounded and fell. 18 Judas also fell, and the rest fled.

19 Then Jonathan and Simon took their brother Judas and buried him in the tomb of their ancestors at Mō'dein, 20 and wept for him. All Israel made great lamentation for him; they mourned many days and said,

21 "How is the mighty fallen,
    the savior of Israel!"

22 Now the rest of the acts of Judas, and his wars and the brave deeds that he did, and his greatness, have not been recorded, but they were very many.

Jonathan Succeeds Judas

23 After the death of Judas, the renegades emerged in all parts of Israel; all the wrongdoers reappeared. 24 In those days a very great famine occurred, and the country went over to their side. 25 Bac'chi•dēs chose the godless and put them in charge of the country. 26 They made inquiry and searched for the friends of Judas, and brought them

---

g 160 B.C.   h Gk lacks of Bacchides

What Makes a Hero?

History is full of heroes, those bigger-than-life men and women like Judas Maccabeus who have made a difference because of their courageous acts and their willingness to take risks that frighten other people. What makes someone a hero? Is each of us capable of heroism?

Someone we have grown up with, who now seems ordinary, could one day be a hero. None of us knows when we could be called on to do something heroic. We need an openness to God's call and a willingness to take a risk—to let go of our fears and to reach deep within ourselves for courage and strength. You may amaze yourself at what you can accomplish in extraordinary situations. The stuff of heroes, of great and brave persons such as Judas Maccabeus, is already within us. We need only to believe in ourselves and believe that God is with us.

You may not end up in a history book or be memorialized in a statue, but you can make a difference in the life of one or perhaps many people. What really counts is to be a hero in the eyes of God.

▶ 1 Macc 9.19–22

---

to Bac'chi•dēs, who took vengeance on them and made sport of them. 27 So there was great distress in Israel, such as had not been since the time that prophets ceased to appear among them.

28 Then all the friends of Judas assembled and said to Jonathan, 29 "Since the death of your brother Judas there has been no one like him to go against our enemies and Bac'chi•dēs, and to deal with those of our nation who hate us. 30 Now therefore we have chosen you today to take his place as our ruler and leader, to fight our battle." 31 So Jonathan accepted the leadership at that time in place of his brother Judas.

The Campaigns of Jonathan

32 When Bac'chi•dēs learned of this, he tried to kill him. 33 But Jonathan and his brother Simon and all who were with him heard of it, and they fled into the wilderness of Te•kō'a and camped by the water of the pool of As'phar. 34 Bac'chi•dēs found this out on the sabbath day, and he with all his army crossed the Jordan.

35 So Jonathan[i] sent his brother as leader of the multitude and begged the Na•ba•tē'ans, who were his friends, for permission to store with them the great amount of baggage that they had. 36 But the family of Jam'brī from Med'e•ba came out and seized John and all that he had, and left with it.

37 After these things it was reported to Jonathan and his brother Simon, "The family of Jam'brī are celebrating a great wedding, and are conducting the bride, a daughter of one of the great nobles of Cā'naan, from Nad'a•bath with a large escort." 38 Remembering how their brother John had been killed, they went up and hid under cover of the mountain.

39 They looked out and saw a tumultuous procession with a great amount of baggage; and the bridegroom came out with his friends and his brothers to meet them with tambourines and musicians and many weapons. 40 Then they rushed on them from the ambush and began killing them. Many were wounded and fell, and the rest fled to the mountain; and the Jews[j] took all their goods. 41 So the wedding was turned into mourning and the voice of their musicians into a funeral dirge. 42 After they had fully avenged the blood of their brother, they returned to the marshes of the Jordan.

43 When Bac'chi•dēs heard of this, he came with a large force on the sabbath day to the banks of the Jordan. 44 And Jonathan said to those with him, "Let us get up now and fight for our lives, for today things are not as they were before. 45 For look! the battle is in front of us and behind us; the water of the Jordan is on this side and on that, with marsh and thicket; there is no place to turn. 46 Cry out now to Heaven that you may be delivered from the hands of our enemies." 47 So the battle began, and Jonathan stretched out his hand to strike Bac'chi•dēs, but he eluded him and went to the rear. 48 Then Jonathan and the men with him leaped into the Jordan and swam across to the other side, and the enemy[j] did not cross the Jordan to attack them. 49 And about one thousand of Bac'chi•dēs' men fell that day.

Bacchides Builds Fortifications

50 Then Bac'chi•dēs[i] returned to Jerusalem and built strong cities in Judea: the fortress in Jericho,

---

i Gk he   j Gk they

1
M
A
C
C

and Em·mā'us, and Beth-hō'ron, and Beth'el, and Tim'nath, and[k] Phar'a·thon, and Tē'phon, with high walls and gates and bars. 51 And he placed garrisons in them to harass Israel. 52 He also fortified the town of Beth-zur, and Ga·zā'ra, and the citadel, and in them he put troops and stores of food. 53 And he took the sons of the leading men of the land as hostages and put them under guard in the citadel at Jerusalem.

54 In the one hundred and fifty-third year,[l] in the second month, Al'ci·mus gave orders to tear down the wall of the inner court of the sanctuary. He tore down the work of the prophets! 55 But he only began to tear it down, for at that time Al'ci·mus was stricken and his work was hindered; his mouth was stopped and he was paralyzed, so that he could no longer say a word or give commands concerning his house. 56 And Al'ci·mus died at that time in great agony. 57 When Bac'chi·dēs saw that Al'ci·mus was dead, he returned to the king, and the land of Judah had rest for two years.

The End of the War

58 Then all the lawless plotted and said, "See! Jonathan and his men are living in quiet and confidence. So now let us bring Bac'chi·dēs back, and he will capture them all in one night." 59 And they went and consulted with him. 60 He started to come with a large force, and secretly sent letters to all his allies in Judea, telling them to seize Jonathan and his men; but they were unable to do it, because their plan became known. 61 And Jonathan's men[m] seized about fifty of the men of the country who were leaders in this treachery, and killed them.

62 Then Jonathan with his men, and Simon, withdrew to Beth·bā'sī in the wilderness; he rebuilt the parts of it that had been demolished, and they fortified it. 63 When Bac'chi·dēs learned of this, he assembled all his forces, and sent orders to the men of Judea. 64 Then he came and encamped against Beth·bā'sī; he fought against it for many days and made machines of war. 65 But Jonathan left his brother Simon in the town, while he went out into the country; and he went out with only a few men. 66 He struck down Od·o·mē'ra and his kindred and the people of Phas'i·ron in their tents. 67 Then he[n] began to attack and went into battle with his forces; and Simon and his men sallied out from the town and set fire to the machines of war. 68 They fought with Bac'chi·dēs, and he was crushed by them. They pressed him very hard, for his plan and his expedition had been in vain. 69 So he was very angry at the renegades who had counseled him to come into the country, and he killed many of them. Then he decided to go back to his own land. 70 When Jonathan learned of this, he sent am-

bassadors to him to make peace with him and obtain release of the captives. 71 He agreed, and did as he said; and he swore to Jonathan[o] that he would not try to harm him as long as he lived. 72 He restored to him the captives whom he had taken previously from the land of Judah; then he turned and went back to his own land, and did not come again into their territory. 73 Thus the sword ceased from Israel. Jonathan settled in Mich'mash and began to judge the people; and he destroyed the godless out of Israel.

Revolt of Alexander Epiphanes

10 In the one hundred sixtieth year[p] Alexander E·piph'a·nēs, son of An·tī'o·chus, landed and occupied Ptol·e·mā'is. They welcomed him, and there he began to reign. 2 When King De·mē'tri·us heard of it, he assembled a very large army and marched out to meet him in battle. 3 De·mē'tri·us sent Jonathan a letter in peaceable words to honor him; 4 for he said to himself, "Let us act first to make peace with him[q] before he makes peace with Alexander against us, 5 for he will remember all the wrongs that we did to him and to his brothers and his nation." 6 So De·mē'tri·us[r] gave him authority to recruit troops, to equip them with arms, and to become his ally; and he commanded that the hostages in the citadel should be released to him.

7 Then Jonathan came to Jerusalem and read the letter in the hearing of all the people and of those in the citadel. 8 They were greatly alarmed when they heard that the king had given him authority to recruit troops. 9 But those in the citadel released the hostages to Jonathan, and he returned them to their parents.

10 And Jonathan took up residence in Jerusalem and began to rebuild and restore the city. 11 He directed those who were doing the work to build the walls and encircle Mount Zion with squared stones, for better fortification; and they did so. 12 Then the foreigners who were in the strongholds that Bac'chi·dēs had built fled; 13 all of them left their places and went back to their own lands. 14 Only in Beth-zur did some remain who had forsaken the law and the commandments, for it served as a place of refuge.

15 Now King Alexander heard of all the promises that De·mē'tri·us had sent to Jonathan, and he heard of the battles that Jonathan[r] and his brothers had fought, of the brave deeds that they had done, and of the troubles that they had endured. 16 So he

---

[k] Some authorities omit *and* [l] 159 B.C. [m] Gk *they*
[n] Other ancient authorities read *they* [o] Gk *him*
[p] 152 B.C. [q] Gk *them* [r] Gk *he*

said, "Shall we find another such man? Come now, we will make him our friend and ally." 17 And he wrote a letter and sent it to him, in the following words:

Jonathan Becomes High Priest

18 "King Alexander to his brother Jonathan, greetings. 19 We have heard about you, that you are a mighty warrior and worthy to be our friend. 20 And so we have appointed you today to be the high priest of your nation; you are to be called the king's Friend and you are to take our side and keep friendship with us." He also sent him a purple robe and a golden crown.

21 So Jonathan put on the sacred vestments in the seventh month of the one hundred sixtieth year,^{s} at the festival of booths,^{t} and he recruited troops and equipped them with arms in abundance. 22 When De·mē′tri·us heard of these things he was distressed and said, 23 "What is this that we have done? Alexander has gotten ahead of us in forming a friendship with the Jews to strengthen himself. 24 I also will write them words of encouragement and promise them honor and gifts, so that I may have their help." 25 So he sent a message to them in the following words:

A Letter from Demetrius to Jonathan

"King De·mē′tri·us to the nation of the Jews, greetings. 26 Since you have kept your agreement with us and have continued your friendship with us, and have not sided with our enemies, we have heard of it and rejoiced. 27 Now continue still to keep faith with us, and we will repay you with good for what you do for us. 28 We will grant you many immunities and give you gifts.

29 "I now free you and exempt all the Jews from payment of tribute and salt tax and crown levies, 30 and instead of collecting the third of the grain and the half of the fruit of the trees that I should receive, I release them from this day and henceforth. I will not collect them from the land of Judah or from the three districts added to it from Sa·mār′i·a and Galilee, from this day and for all time. 31 Jerusalem and its environs, its tithes and its revenues, shall be holy and free from tax. 32 I release also my control of the citadel in Jerusalem and give it to the high priest, so that he may station in it men of his own choice to guard it. 33 And everyone of the Jews taken as a captive from the land of Judah into any part of my kingdom, I set free without payment; and let all officials cancel also the taxes on their livestock.

34 "All the festivals and sabbaths and new moons and appointed days, and the three days before a festival and the three after a festival—let them all be days of immunity and release for all the Jews

who are in my kingdom. 35 No one shall have authority to exact anything from them or annoy any of them about any matter.

36 "Let Jews be enrolled in the king's forces to the number of thirty thousand men, and let the maintenance be given them that is due to all the forces of the king. 37 Let some of them be stationed in the great strongholds of the king, and let some of them be put in positions of trust in the kingdom. Let their officers and leaders be of their own number, and let them live by their own laws, just as the king has commanded in the land of Judah.

38 "As for the three districts that have been added to Judea from the country of Sa·mār′i·a, let them be annexed to Judea so that they may be considered to be under one ruler and obey no other authority than the high priest. 39 Ptol·e·mā′is and the land adjoining it I have given as a gift to the sanctuary in Jerusalem, to meet the necessary expenses of the sanctuary. 40 I also grant fifteen thousand shekels of silver yearly out of the king's revenues from appropriate places. 41 And all the additional funds that the government officials have not paid as they did in the first years,^{u} they shall give from now on for the service of the temple.^{v} 42 Moreover, the five thousand shekels of silver that my officials^w have received every year from the income of the services of the temple, this too is canceled, because it belongs to the priests who minister there. 43 And all who take refuge at the temple in Jerusalem, or in any of its precincts, because they owe money to the king or are in debt, let them be released and receive back all their property in my kingdom.

44 "Let the cost of rebuilding and restoring the structures of the sanctuary be paid from the revenues of the king. 45 And let the cost of rebuilding the walls of Jerusalem and fortifying it all around, and the cost of rebuilding the walls in Judea, also be paid from the revenues of the king."

Death of Demetrius

46 When Jonathan and the people heard these words, they did not believe or accept them, because they remembered the great wrongs that De·mē′-tri·us^x had done in Israel and how much he had oppressed them. 47 They favored Alexander, because he had been the first to speak peaceable words to them, and they remained his allies all his days.

48 Now King Alexander assembled large forces and encamped opposite De·mē′tri·us. 49 The two kings met in battle, and the army of De·mē′tri·us fled, and Alexander^y pursued him and defeated them. 50 He pressed the battle strongly until the sun set, and on that day De·mē′tri·us fell.

^{s} 152 B.C. ^{t} Or *tabernacles* ^{u} Meaning of Gk uncertain
^{v} Gk *house* ^{w} Gk *they* ^{x} Gk *he* ^{y} Other ancient
authorities read *Alexander fled, and Demetrius*

Treaty of Ptolemy and Alexander

51 Then Alexander sent ambassadors to Ptol'e•my king of Egypt with the following message: 52 "Since I have returned to my kingdom and have taken my seat on the throne of my ancestors, and established my rule—for I crushed De•mē'tri•us and gained control of our country; 53 I met him in battle, and he and his army were crushed by us, and we have taken our seat on the throne of his kingdom— 54 now therefore let us establish friendship with one another; give me now your daughter as my wife, and I will become your son-in-law, and will make gifts to you and to her in keeping with your position."

55 Ptol'e•my the king replied and said, "Happy was the day on which you returned to the land of your ancestors and took your seat on the throne of their kingdom. 56 And now I will do for you as you wrote, but meet me at Ptol•e•mā'is, so that we may see one another, and I will become your father-in-law, as you have said."

57 So Ptol'e•my set out from Egypt, he and his daughter Cleopatra, and came to Ptol•e•mā'is in the one hundred sixty-second year.[z] 58 King Alexander met him, and Ptol'e•my[a] gave him his daughter Cleopatra in marriage, and celebrated her wedding at Ptol•e•mā'is with great pomp, as kings do.

59 Then King Alexander wrote to Jonathan to come and meet him. 60 So he went with pomp to Ptol•e•mā'is and met the two kings; he gave them and their Friends silver and gold and many gifts, and found favor with them. 61 A group of malcontents from Israel, renegades, gathered together against him to accuse him; but the king paid no attention to them. 62 The king gave orders to take off Jonathan's garments and to clothe him in purple, and they did so. 63 The king also seated him at his side; and he said to his officers, "Go out with him into the middle of the city and proclaim that no one is to bring charges against him about any matter, and let no one annoy him for any reason." 64 When his accusers saw the honor that was paid him, in accord with the proclamation, and saw him clothed in purple, they all fled. 65 Thus the king honored him and enrolled him among his chief[b] Friends, and made him general and governor of the province. 66 And Jonathan returned to Jerusalem in peace and gladness.

Apollonius Is Defeated by Jonathan

67 In the one hundred sixty-fifth year[c] De•mē'tri•us son of De•mē'tri•us came from Crete to the land of his ancestors. 68 When King Alexander heard of it, he was greatly distressed and returned to An'ti•och. 69 And De•mē'tri•us appointed Ap•ol- lō'ni•us the governor of Coē•le•syr'i•a, and he assembled a large force and encamped against Jam'ni•a. Then he sent the following message to the high priest Jonathan:

70 "You are the only one to rise up against us, and I have fallen into ridicule and disgrace because of you. Why do you assume authority against us in the hill country? 71 If you now have confidence in your forces, come down to the plain to meet us, and let us match strength with each other there, for I have with me the power of the cities. 72 Ask and learn who I am and who the others are that are helping us. People will tell you that you cannot stand before us, for your ancestors were twice put to flight in their own land. 73 And now you will not be able to withstand my cavalry and such an army in the plain, where there is no stone or pebble, or place to flee."

74 When Jonathan heard the words of Ap•ol-lō'ni•us, his spirit was aroused. He chose ten thousand men and set out from Jerusalem, and his brother Simon met him to help him. 75 He encamped before Jop'pa, but the people of the city closed its gates, for Ap•ol•lō'ni•us had a garrison in Jop'pa. 76 So they fought against it, and the people of the city became afraid and opened the gates, and Jonathan gained possession of Jop'pa.

77 When Ap•ol•lō'ni•us heard of it, he mustered three thousand cavalry and a large army, and went to A•zō'tus as though he were going farther. At the same time he advanced into the plain, for he had a large troop of cavalry and put confidence in it. 78 Jonathan[a] pursued him to A•zō'tus, and the armies engaged in battle. 79 Now Ap•ol•lō'ni•us had secretly left a thousand cavalry behind them. 80 Jonathan learned that there was an ambush behind him, for they surrounded his army and shot arrows at his men from early morning until late afternoon. 81 But his men stood fast, as Jonathan had commanded, and the enemy's[d] horses grew tired.

82 Then Simon brought forward his force and engaged the phalanx in battle (for the cavalry was exhausted); they were overwhelmed by him and fled, 83 and the cavalry was dispersed in the plain. They fled to A•zō'tus and entered Beth-dā'gon, the temple of their idol, for safety. 84 But Jonathan burned A•zō'tus and the surrounding towns and plundered them; and the temple of Dā'gon, and those who had taken refuge in it, he burned with fire. 85 The number of those who fell by the sword, with those burned alive, came to eight thousand.

86 Then Jonathan left there and encamped against As'ka•lon, and the people of the city came out to meet him with great pomp.

87 He and those with him then returned to Jerusalem with a large amount of booty. 88 When King Alexander heard of these things, he honored

z 150 B.C.   a Gk he   b Gk first   c 147 B.C.   d Gk their

Jonathan still more; [89] and he sent to him a golden buckle, such as it is the custom to give to the King's Kinsmen. He also gave him Ek'ron and all its environs as his possession.

Ptolemy Invades Syria

11 Then the king of Egypt gathered great forces, like the sand by the seashore, and many ships; and he tried to get possession of Alexander's kingdom by trickery and add it to his own kingdom. [2] He set out for Syria with peaceable words, and the people of the towns opened their gates to him and went to meet him, for King Alexander had commanded them to meet him, since he was Alexander's[e] father-in-law. [3] But when Ptol'e•my entered the towns he stationed forces as a garrison in each town.

[4] When he[f] approached A•zō'tus, they showed him the burnt-out temple of Dā'gon, and A•zō'tus and its suburbs destroyed, and the corpses lying about, and the charred bodies of those whom Jonathan[g] had burned in the war, for they had piled them in heaps along his route. [5] They also told the king what Jonathan had done, to throw blame on him; but the king kept silent. [6] Jonathan met the king at Jop'pa with pomp, and they greeted one another and spent the night there. [7] And Jonathan went with the king as far as the river called E•leū'ther•us; then he returned to Jerusalem.

[8] So King Ptol'e•my gained control of the coastal cities as far as Se•leū'ci•a by the sea, and he kept devising wicked designs against Alexander. [9] He sent envoys to King De•mē'tri•us, saying, "Come, let us make a covenant with each other, and I will give you in marriage my daughter who was Alexander's wife, and you shall reign over your father's kingdom. [10] I now regret that I gave him my daughter, for he has tried to kill me." [11] He threw blame on Alexander[h] because he coveted his kingdom. [12] So he took his daughter away from him and gave her to De•mē'tri•us. He was estranged from Alexander, and their enmity became manifest.

[13] Then Ptol'e•my entered An'ti•och and put on the crown of Asia. Thus he put two crowns on his head, the crown of Egypt and that of Asia. [14] Now King Alexander was in Ci•li'ci•a at that time, because the people of that region were in revolt. [15] When Alexander heard of it, he came against him in battle. Ptol'e•my marched out and met him with a strong force, and put him to flight. [16] So Alexander fled into Arabia to find protection there, and King Ptol'e•my was triumphant. [17] Zab'di•el the A'rab cut off the head of Alexander and sent it to Ptol'e•my. [18] But King Ptol'e•my died three days later, and his troops in the strongholds were killed by the inhabitants of the strongholds. [19] So De•mē'tri•us became king in the one hundred sixty-seventh year.[i]

Jonathan's Diplomacy

[20] In those days Jonathan assembled the Judeans to attack the citadel in Jerusalem, and he built many engines of war to use against it. [21] But certain renegades who hated their nation went to the king and reported to him that Jonathan was besieging the citadel. [22] When he heard this he was angry, and as soon as he heard it he set out and came to Ptol•e•mā'is; and he wrote Jonathan not to continue the siege, but to meet him for a conference at Ptol•e•mā'is as quickly as possible.

[23] When Jonathan heard this, he gave orders to continue the siege. He chose some of the elders of Israel and some of the priests, and put himself in danger, [24] for he went to the king at Ptol•e•mā'is, taking silver and gold and clothing and numerous other gifts. And he won his favor. [25] Although certain renegades of his nation kept making complaints against him, [26] the king treated him as his predecessors had treated him; he exalted him in the presence of all his Friends. [27] He confirmed him in the high priesthood and in as many other honors as he had formerly had, and caused him to be reckoned among his chief[j] Friends. [28] Then Jonathan asked the king to free Judea and the three districts of Sa•mār'i•a[k] from tribute, and promised him three hundred talents. [29] The king consented, and wrote a letter to Jonathan about all these things; its contents were as follows:

[30] "King De•mē'tri•us to his brother Jonathan and to the nation of the Jews, greetings. [31] This copy of the letter that we wrote concerning you to our kinsman Las'the•nēs we have written to you also, so that you may know what it says. [32] 'King De•mē'tri•us to his father Las'the•nēs, greetings. [33] We have determined to do good to the nation of the Jews, who are our friends and fulfill their obligations to us, because of the goodwill they show toward us. [34] We have confirmed as their possession both the territory of Judea and the three districts of A•phāir'e•ma and Lyd'da and Rath'a•min; the latter, with all the region bordering them, were added to Judea from Sa•mār'i•a. To all those who offer sacrifice in Jerusalem we have granted release from[l] the royal taxes that the king formerly received from them each year, from the crops of the land and the fruit of the trees. [35] And the other payments henceforth due to us of the tithes, and the taxes due to us, and the salt pits and the crown taxes due to us— from all these we shall grant them release. [36] And not one of these grants shall be canceled from this time on forever. [37] Now therefore take care to make

---

e Gk his f Other ancient authorities read *they* g Gk *he*
h Gk *him* i 145 B.C. j Gk *first* k Cn: Gk *the three districts and Samaria* l Or *Samaria, for all those who offer sacrifice in Jerusalem, in place of*

a copy of this, and let it be given to Jonathan and put up in a conspicuous place on the holy mountain.' "

The Intrigue of Trypho

38 When King De·mē′tri·us saw that the land was quiet before him and that there was no opposition to him, he dismissed all his troops, all of them to their own homes, except the foreign troops that he had recruited from the islands of the nations. So all the troops who had served under his predecessors hated him. 39 A certain Trȳ′phō had formerly been one of Alexander's supporters; he saw that all the troops were grumbling against De·mē′tri·us. So he went to I·mal′kū·ē the A′rab, who was bringing up An·tī′o·chus, the young son of Alexander, 40 and insistently urged him to hand An·tī′o·chus[m] over to him, to become king in place of his father. He also reported to I·mal′kū·ē[m] what De·mē′tri·us had done and told of the hatred that the troops of De·mē′tri·us[n] had for him; and he stayed there many days.

41 Now Jonathan sent to King De·mē′tri·us the request that he remove the troops of the citadel from Jerusalem, and the troops in the strongholds; for they kept fighting against Israel. 42 And De·mē′tri·us sent this message back to Jonathan: "Not only will I do these things for you and your nation, but I will confer great honor on you and your nation, if I find an opportunity. 43 Now then you will do well to send me men who will help me, for all my troops have revolted." 44 So Jonathan sent three thousand stalwart men to him at An·tī′o·ch, and when they came to the king, the king rejoiced at their arrival.

45 Then the people of the city assembled within the city, to the number of a hundred and twenty thousand, and they wanted to kill the king. 46 But the king fled into the palace. Then the people of the city seized the main streets of the city and began to fight. 47 So the king called the Jews to his aid, and they all rallied around him and then spread out through the city; and they killed on that day about one hundred thousand. 48 They set fire to the city and seized a large amount of spoil on that day, and saved the king. 49 When the people of the city saw that the Jews had gained control of the city as they pleased, their courage failed and they cried out to the king with this entreaty: 50 "Grant us peace, and make the Jews stop fighting against us and our city." 51 And they threw down their arms and made peace. So the Jews gained glory in the sight of the king and of all the people in his kingdom, and they returned to Jerusalem with a large amount of spoil.

52 So King De·mē′tri·us sat on the throne of his kingdom, and the land was quiet before him. 53 But he broke his word about all that he had promised; he became estranged from Jonathan and did not repay the favors that Jonathan[o] had done him, but treated him very harshly.

Trypho Seizes Power

54 After this Trȳ′phō returned, and with him the young boy An·tī′o·chus who began to reign and put on the crown. 55 All the troops that De·mē′tri·us had discharged gathered around him; they fought against De·mē′tri·us,[m] and he fled and was routed. 56 Trȳ′phō captured the elephants[p] and gained control of An·tī′o·ch. 57 Then the young An·tī′o·chus wrote to Jonathan, saying, "I confirm you in the high priesthood and set you over the four districts and make you one of the king's Friends." 58 He also sent him gold plate and a table service, and granted him the right to drink from gold cups and dress in purple and wear a gold buckle. 59 He appointed Jonathan's[q] brother Simon governor from the Ladder of Tȳre to the borders of Egypt.

Campaigns of Jonathan and Simon

60 Then Jonathan set out and traveled beyond the river and among the towns, and all the army of Syria gathered to him as allies. When he came to As′ka·lon, the people of the city met him and paid him honor. 61 From there he went to Gā′za, but the people of Gā′za shut him out. So he besieged it and burned its suburbs with fire and plundered them. 62 Then the people of Gā′za pleaded with Jonathan, and he made peace with them, and took the sons of their rulers as hostages and sent them to Jerusalem. And he passed through the country as far as Damascus.

63 Then Jonathan heard that the officers of De·mē′tri·us had come to Kā′desh in Galilee with a large army, intending to remove him from office. 64 He went to meet them, but left his brother Simon in the country. 65 Simon encamped before Beth-zur and fought against it for many days and hemmed it in. 66 Then they asked him to grant them terms of peace, and he did so. He removed them from there, took possession of the town, and set a garrison over it.

67 Jonathan and his army encamped by the waters of Gen·nes′a·ret. Early in the morning they marched to the plain of Hā′zor, 68 and there in the plain the army of the foreigners met him; they had set an ambush against him in the mountains, but they themselves met him face to face. 69 Then the men in ambush emerged from their places and joined battle. 70 All the men with Jonathan fled; not one of them was left except Mat·ta·thī′as son of Ab′sa·lom and Judas son of Chal′phi, commanders

m Gk *him*   *n* Gk *his troops*   *o* Gk *he*   *p* Gk *animals*
q Gk *his*

of the forces of the army. 71 Jonathan tore his clothes, put dust on his head, and prayed. 72 Then he turned back to the battle against the enemy[r] and routed them, and they fled. 73 When his men who were fleeing saw this, they returned to him and joined him in the pursuit as far as Kā'desh, to their camp, and there they encamped. 74 As many as three thousand of the foreigners fell that day. And Jonathan returned to Jerusalem.

Alliances with Rome and Sparta

12 Now when Jonathan saw that the time was favorable for him, he chose men and sent them to Rome to confirm and renew the friendship with them. 2 He also sent letters to the same effect to the Spartans and to other places. 3 So they went to Rome and entered the senate chamber and said, "The high priest Jonathan and the Jewish nation have sent us to renew the former friendship and alliance with them." 4 And the Romans[s] gave them letters to the people in every place, asking them to provide for the envoys[r] safe conduct to the land of Judah.

5 This is a copy of the letter that Jonathan wrote to the Spartans: 6 "The high priest Jonathan, the senate of the nation, the priests, and the rest of the Jewish people to their brothers the Spartans, greetings. 7 Already in time past a letter was sent to the high priest Ō•nī'as from Ar'i•us,[t] who was king among you, stating that you are our brothers, as the appended copy shows. 8 Ō•nī'as welcomed the envoy with honor, and received the letter, which contained a clear declaration of alliance and friendship. 9 Therefore, though we have no need of these things, since we have as encouragement the holy books that are in our hands, 10 we have undertaken to send to renew our family ties and friendship with you, so that we may not become estranged from you, for considerable time has passed since you sent your letter to us. 11 We therefore remember you constantly on every occasion, both at our festivals and on other appropriate days, at the sacrifices that we offer and in our prayers, as it is right and proper to remember brothers. 12 And we rejoice in your glory. 13 But as for ourselves, many trials and many wars have encircled us; the kings around us have waged war against us. 14 We were unwilling to annoy you and our other allies and friends with these wars, 15 for we have the help that comes from Heaven for our aid, and so we were delivered from our enemies, and our enemies were humbled. 16 We therefore have chosen Nū•mē'ni•us son of An•ti'o•chus and An•tip'a•ter son of Jason, and have sent them to Rome to renew our former friendship and alliance with them. 17 We have commanded them to go also to you and greet you and deliver to you this letter from us concerning the renewal of our family ties. 18 And now please send us a reply to this."

19 This is a copy of the letter that they sent to Ō•nī'as: 20 "King Ar'i•us of the Spartans, to the high priest Ō•nī'as, greetings. 21 It has been found in writing concerning the Spartans and the Jews that they are brothers and are of the family of Abraham. 22 And now that we have learned this, please write us concerning your welfare; 23 we on our part write to you that your livestock and your property belong to us, and ours belong to you. We therefore command that our envoys[s] report to you accordingly."

Further Campaigns of Jonathan and Simon

24 Now Jonathan heard that the commanders of De•mē'tri•us had returned, with a larger force than before, to wage war against him. 25 So he marched away from Jerusalem and met them in the region of Hā'math, for he gave them no opportunity to invade his own country. 26 He sent spies to their camp, and they returned and reported to him that the enemy[s] were being drawn up in formation to attack the Jews[r] by night. 27 So when the sun had set, Jonathan commanded his troops to be alert and to keep their arms at hand so as to be ready all night for battle, and he stationed outposts around the camp. 28 When the enemy heard that Jonathan and his troops were prepared for battle, they were afraid and were terrified at heart; so they kindled fires in their camp and withdrew.[u] 29 But Jonathan and his troops did not know it until morning, for they saw the fires burning. 30 Then Jonathan pursued them, but he did not overtake them, for they had crossed the E•leū'ther•us river. 31 So Jonathan turned aside against the A'rabs who are called Zab•a•dē'ans, and he crushed them and plundered them. 32 Then he broke camp and went to Damascus, and marched through all that region.

33 Simon also went out and marched through the country as far as As'ka•lon and the neighboring strongholds. He turned aside to Jop'pa and took it by surprise, 34 for he had heard that they were ready to hand over the stronghold to those whom De•mē'tri•us had sent. And he stationed a garrison there to guard it.

35 When Jonathan returned he convened the elders of the people and planned with them to build strongholds in Judea, 36 to build the walls of Jerusalem still higher, and to erect a high barrier between the citadel and the city to separate it from the city, in order to isolate it so that its garrison[s] could neither buy nor sell. 37 So they gathered together to rebuild the city; part of the wall on the valley to the

---

r Gk *them*   s Gk *they*   t Vg Compare verse 20: Gk *Darius*
u Other ancient authorities omit *and withdrew*

12.50

east had fallen, and he repaired the section called Cha·phen′a·tha. 38 Simon also built Ad′i·da in the She·phē′lah; he fortified it and installed gates with bolts.

Trypho Captures Jonathan

39 Then Trỹ′phō attempted to become king in Asia and put on the crown, and to raise his hand against King An·ti′o·chus. 40 He feared that Jonathan might not permit him to do so, but might make war on him, so he kept seeking to seize and kill him, and he marched out and came to Beth-shan. 41 Jonathan went out to meet him with forty thousand picked warriors, and he came to Beth-shan. 42 When Trỹ′phō saw that he had come with a large army, he was afraid to raise his hand against him. 43 So he received him with honor and com-mended him to all his Friends, and he gave him gifts and commanded his Friends and his troops to obey him as they would himself. 44 Then he said to Jonathan, "Why have you put all these people to so much trouble when we are not at war? 45 Dismiss them now to their homes and choose for yourself a few men to stay with you, and come with me to Ptol·e·mā′is. I will hand it over to you as well as the other strongholds and the remaining troops and all the officials, and will turn around and go home. For that is why I am here."

46 Jonathan[v] trusted him and did as he said; he sent away the troops, and they returned to the land of Judah. 47 He kept with himself three thousand men, two thousand of whom he left in Galilee, while one thousand accompanied him. 48 But when Jonathan entered Ptol·e·mā′is, the people of Ptol·e·mā′is closed the gates and seized him, and they killed with the sword all who had entered with him.

49 Then Trỹ′phō sent troops and cavalry into Galilee and the Great Plain to destroy all Jona-than's soldiers. 50 But they realized that Jonathan had been seized and had perished along with his men, and they encouraged one another and kept marching in close formation, ready for battle. 51 When their pursuers saw that they would fight for their lives, they turned back. 52 So they all reached the land of Judah safely, and they mourned for Jonathan and his companions and were in great fear; and all Israel mourned deeply. 53 All the na-tions around them tried to destroy them, for they said, "They have no leader or helper. Now therefore let us make war on them and blot out the memory of them from humankind."

Simon Takes Command

13 Simon heard that Trỹ′phō had assem-bled a large army to invade the land of Judah and destroy it, 2 and he saw that the people were trembling with fear. So he went up to Je-rusalem, and gathering the people together 3 he en-couraged them, saying to them, "You yourselves know what great things my brothers and I and the house of my father have done for the laws and the sanctuary; you know also the wars and the difficul-ties that my brothers and I have seen. 4 By reason of this all my brothers have perished for the sake of Is-rael, and I alone am left. 5 And now, far be it from me to spare my life in any time of distress, for I am not better than my brothers. 6 But I will avenge my nation and the sanctuary and your wives and chil-dren, for all the nations have gathered together out of hatred to destroy us."

7 The spirit of the people was rekindled when they heard these words, 8 and they answered in a loud voice, "You are our leader in place of Judas and your brother Jonathan. 9 Fight our battles, and all that you say to us we will do." 10 So he assem-bled all the warriors and hurried to complete the walls of Jerusalem, and he fortified it on every side. 11 He sent Jonathan son of Ab′sa·lom to Jop′pa, and with him a considerable army; he drove out its oc-cupants and remained there.

Deceit and Treachery of Trypho

12 Then Trỹ′phō left Ptol·e·mā′is with a large army to invade the land of Judah, and Jonathan was with him under guard. 13 Simon encamped in Ad′i·da, facing the plain. 14 Trỹ′phō learned that Si-mon had risen up in place of his brother Jonathan, and that he was about to join battle with him, so he sent envoys to him and said, 15 "It is for the money that your brother Jonathan owed the royal treasury, in connection with the offices he held, that we are

---

v Gk *he*

detaining him. [16] Send now one hundred talents of silver and two of his sons as hostages, so that when released he will not revolt against us, and we will release him."

[17] Simon knew that they were speaking deceitfully to him, but he sent to get the money and the sons, so that he would not arouse great hostility among the people, who might say, [18] "It was because Simon[w] did not send him the money and the sons, that Jonathan[x] perished." [19] So he sent the sons and the hundred talents, but Try'pho[y] broke his word and did not release Jonathan.

[20] After this Try'pho came to invade the country and destroy it, and he circled around by the way to A·dor'a. But Simon and his army kept marching along opposite him to every place he went. [21] Now the men in the citadel kept sending envoys to Try'pho urging him to come to them by way of the wilderness and to send them food. [22] So Try'pho got all his cavalry ready to go, but that night a very heavy snow fell, and he did not go because of the snow. He marched off and went into the land of Gil'e·ad. [23] When he approached Bas'ka·ma, he killed Jonathan, and he was buried there. [24] Then Try'pho turned and went back to his own land.

Jonathan's Tomb

[25] Simon sent and took the bones of his brother Jonathan, and buried him in Mō'dein, the city of his ancestors. [26] All Israel bewailed him with great lamentation, and mourned for him many days. [27] And Simon built a monument over the tomb of his father and his brothers; he made it high so that it might be seen, with polished stone at the front and back. [28] He also erected seven pyramids, opposite one another, for his father and mother and four brothers. [29] For the pyramids[y] he devised an elaborate setting, erecting about them great columns, and on the columns he put suits of armor for a permanent memorial, and beside the suits of armor he carved ships, so that they could be seen by all who sail the sea. [30] This is the tomb that he built in Mō'dein; it remains to this day.

Judea Gains Independence

[31] Try'pho dealt treacherously with the young King An·ti'o·chus; he killed him [32] and became king in his place, putting on the crown of Asia; and he brought great calamity on the land. [33] But Simon built up the strongholds of Judea and walled them all around, with high towers and great walls and gates and bolts, and he stored food in the strongholds. [34] Simon also chose emissaries and sent them to King De·me'tri·us with a request to grant relief to the country, for all that Try'pho did was to plunder. [35] King De·me'tri·us sent him a favorable reply to this request, and wrote him a letter

as follows, [36] "King De·me'tri·us to Simon, the high priest and friend of kings, and to the elders and nation of the Jews, greetings. [37] We have received the gold crown and the palm branch that you[z] sent, and we are ready to make a general peace with you and to write to our officials to grant you release from tribute. [38] All the grants that we have made to you remain valid, and let the strongholds that you have built be your possession. [39] We pardon any errors and offenses committed to this day, and cancel the crown tax that you owe; and whatever other tax has been collected in Jerusalem shall be collected no longer. [40] And if any of you are qualified to be enrolled in our bodyguard,[a] let them be enrolled, and let there be peace between us."

[41] In the one hundred seventieth year[b] the yoke of the Gentiles was removed from Israel, [42] and the people began to write in their documents and contracts, "In the first year of Simon the great high priest and commander and leader of the Jews."

The Capture of Gazara by Simon

[43] In those days Simon[x] encamped against Ga·za'ra[c] and surrounded it with troops. He made a siege engine, brought it up to the city, and battered and captured one tower. [44] The men in the siege engine leaped out into the city, and a great tumult arose in the city. [45] The men in the city, with their wives and children, went up on the wall with their clothes torn, and they cried out with a loud voice, asking Simon to make peace with them; [46] they said, "Do not treat us according to our wicked acts but according to your mercy." [47] So Simon reached an agreement with them and stopped fighting against them. But he expelled them from the city and cleansed the houses in which the idols were located, and then entered it with hymns and praise. [48] He removed all uncleanness from it, and settled in it those who observed the law. He also strengthened its fortifications and built in it a house for himself.

Simon Regains the Citadel at Jerusalem

[49] Those who were in the citadel at Jerusalem were prevented from going in and out to buy and sell in the country. So they were very hungry, and many of them perished from famine. [50] Then they cried to Simon to make peace with them, and he did so. But he expelled them from there and cleansed the citadel from its pollutions. [51] On the twenty-third day of the second month, in the one hundred seventy-first year,[d] the Jews[e] entered it with praise and palm branches, and with harps and

---

w Gk I x Gk he y Gk For these z The word you in verses 37-40 is plural a Or court b 142 B.C. c Cn: Gk Gaza d 141 B.C. e Gk they cymbals and stringed instruments, and with hymns and songs, because a great enemy had been crushed and removed from Israel. 52 Simon*f* decreed that every year they should celebrate this day with rejoicing. He strengthened the fortifications of the temple hill alongside the citadel, and he and his men lived there. 53 Simon saw that his son John had reached manhood, and so he made him commander of all the forces; and he lived at Ga•zā′ra.

Capture of Demetrius

14 In the one hundred seventy-second year*g* King De•mē′tri•us assembled his forces and marched into Mēd′i•a to obtain help, so that he could make war against Trȳ′phō. 2 When King Ar′sa•cēs of Persia and Mēd′i•a heard that De•mē′tri•us had invaded his territory, he sent one of his generals to take him alive. 3 The general*f* went and defeated the army of De•mē′tri•us, and seized him and took him to Ar′sa•cēs, who put him under guard.

Eulogy of Simon

4 The land*h* had rest all the days of Simon.
      He sought the good of his nation;
his rule was pleasing to them,
      as was the honor shown him, all his days.
5 To crown all his honors he took Jop′pa for a
            harbor,
      and opened a way to the isles of the sea.
6 He extended the borders of his nation,
      and gained full control of the country.
7 He gathered a host of captives;
      he ruled over Ga•zā′ra and Beth-zur and the
            citadel,
and he removed its uncleanness from it;
      and there was none to oppose him.
8 They tilled their land in peace;
      the ground gave its increase,
      and the trees of the plains their fruit.
9 Old men sat in the streets;
      they all talked together of good things,
      and the youths put on splendid military
            attire.
10 He supplied the towns with food,
      and furnished them with the means of
            defense,
      until his renown spread to the ends of the
            earth.
11 He established peace in the land,
      and Israel rejoiced with great joy.
12 All the people sat under their own vines and fig
            trees,
      and there was none to make them
            afraid.
13 No one was left in the land to fight them,
      and the kings were crushed in those days.

14 He gave help to all the humble among his
            people;
      he sought out the law,
      and did away with all the renegades and
            outlaws.
15 He made the sanctuary glorious,
      and added to the vessels of the sanctuary.

Diplomacy with Rome and Sparta

16 It was heard in Rome, and as far away as Sparta, that Jonathan had died, and they were deeply grieved. 17 When they heard that his brother Simon had become high priest in his stead, and that he was ruling over the country and the towns in it, 18 they wrote to him on bronze tablets to renew with him the friendship and alliance that they had established with his brothers Judas and Jonathan. 19 And these were read before the assembly in Jerusalem.

20 This is a copy of the letter that the Spartans sent:

"The rulers and the city of the Spartans to the high priest Simon and to the elders and the priests and the rest of the Jewish people, our brothers, greetings. 21 The envoys who were sent to our people have told us about your glory and honor, and we rejoiced at their coming. 22 We have recorded what they said in our public decrees, as follows, 'Nū•mē′ni•us son of An•ti′o•chus and An•tip′a•ter son of Jason, envoys of the Jews, have come to us to renew their friendship with us. 23 It has pleased our people to receive these men with honor and to put a copy of their words in the public archives, so that the people of the Spartans may have a record of them. And they have sent a copy of this to the high priest Simon.' "

24 After this Simon sent Nū•mē′ni•us to Rome with a large gold shield weighing one thousand minas, to confirm the alliance with the Romans.*i*

Official Honors for Simon

25 When the people heard these things they said, "How shall we thank Simon and his sons? 26 For he and his brothers and the house of his father have stood firm; they have fought and repulsed Israel's enemies and established its freedom." 27 So they made a record on bronze tablets and put it on pillars on Mount Zion.

This is a copy of what they wrote: "On the eighteenth day of Ē′lul, in the one hundred seventy-second year,*g* which is the third year of the great high priest Simon, 28 in A•sar′a•mel,*j* in the great as-

---

f Gk *He*   *g* 140 B.C.   *h* Other ancient authorities add *of Judah*   *i* Gk *them*   *j* This word resembles the Hebrew words for *the court of the people of God* or *the prince of the people of God* sembly of the priests and the people and the rulers of the nation and the elders of the country, the following was proclaimed to us:

29 "Since wars often occurred in the country, Simon son of Mat·ta·thi′as, a priest of the sons[k] of Jo′a·rib, and his brothers, exposed themselves to danger and resisted the enemies of their nation, in order that their sanctuary and the law might be preserved; and they brought great glory to their nation. 30 Jonathan rallied the[l] nation, became their high priest, and was gathered to his people. 31 When their enemies decided to invade their country and lay hands on their sanctuary, 32 then Simon rose up and fought for his nation. He spent great sums of his own money; he armed the soldiers of his nation and paid them wages. 33 He fortified the towns of Judea, and Beth-zur on the borders of Judea, where formerly the arms of the enemy had been stored, and he placed there a garrison of Jews. 34 He also fortified Jop′pa, which is by the sea, and Ga·za′ra, which is on the borders of A·zo′tus, where the enemy formerly lived. He settled Jews there, and provided in those towns[m] whatever was necessary for their restoration.

35 "The people saw Simon's faithfulness[n] and the glory that he had resolved to win for his nation, and they made him their leader and high priest, because he had done all these things and because of the justice and loyalty that he had maintained toward his nation. He sought in every way to exalt his people. 36 In his days things prospered in his hands, so that the Gentiles were put out of the[l] country, as were also those in the city of David in Jerusalem, who had built themselves a citadel from which they used to sally forth and defile the environs of the sanctuary, doing great damage to its purity. 37 He settled Jews in it and fortified it for the safety of the country and of the city, and built the walls of Jerusalem higher.

38 "In view of these things King De·me′tri·us confirmed him in the high priesthood, 39 made him one of his Friends, and paid him high honors. 40 For he had heard that the Jews were addressed by the Romans as friends and allies and brothers, and that the Romans[o] had received the envoys of Simon with honor.

41 "The Jews and their priests have resolved that Simon should be their leader and high priest forever, until a trustworthy prophet should arise, 42 and that he should be governor over them and that he should take charge of the sanctuary and appoint officials over its tasks and over the country and the weapons and the strongholds, and that he should take charge of the sanctuary, 43 and that he should be obeyed by all, and that all contracts in the country should be written in his name, and that he should be clothed in purple and wear gold.

44 "None of the people or priests shall be permitted to nullify any of these decisions or to oppose what he says, or to convene an assembly in the country without his permission, or to be clothed in purple or put on a gold buckle. 45 Whoever acts contrary to these decisions or rejects any of them shall be liable to punishment."

46 All the people agreed to grant Simon the right to act in accordance with these decisions. 47 So Simon accepted and agreed to be high priest, to be commander and ethnarch of the Jews and priests, and to be protector of them all.[p] 48 And they gave orders to inscribe this decree on bronze tablets, to put them up in a conspicuous place in the precincts of the sanctuary, 49 and to deposit copies of them in the treasury, so that Simon and his sons might have them.

Letter of Antiochus VII

15 An·ti′o·chus, son of King De·me′tri·us, sent a letter from the islands of the sea to Simon, the priest and ethnarch of the Jews, and to all the nation; 2 its contents were as follows: "King An·ti′o·chus to Simon the high priest and ethnarch and to the nation of the Jews, greetings. 3 Whereas certain scoundrels have gained control of the kingdom of our ancestors, and I intend to lay claim to the kingdom so that I may restore it as it formerly was, and have recruited a host of mercenary troops and have equipped warships, 4 and intend to make a landing in the country so that I may proceed against those who have destroyed our country and those who have devastated many cities in my kingdom, 5 now therefore I confirm to you all the tax remissions that the kings before me have granted you, and a release from all the other payments from which they have released you. 6 I permit you to mint your own coinage as money for your country, 7 and I grant freedom to Jerusalem and the sanctuary. All the weapons that you have prepared and the strongholds that you have built and now hold shall remain yours. 8 Every debt you owe to the royal treasury and any such future debts shall be canceled for you from henceforth and for all time. 9 When we gain control of our kingdom, we will bestow great honor on you and your nation and the temple, so that your glory will become manifest in all the earth."

10 In the one hundred seventy-fourth year[q] An·ti′o·chus set out and invaded the land of his ancestors. All the troops rallied to him, so that there were only a few with Try′pho. 11 An·ti′o·chus pursued him, and Try′pho[r] came in his flight to Dor,

---

k Meaning of Gk uncertain   l Gk their   m Gk them
n Other ancient authorities read conduct   o Gk they   p Or to preside over them all   q 138 B.C.   r Gk he

which is by the sea; 12 for he knew that troubles had converged on him, and his troops had deserted him. 13 So An•ti′o•chus encamped against Dor, and with him were one hundred twenty thousand warriors and eight thousand cavalry. 14 He surrounded the town, and the ships joined battle from the sea; he pressed the town hard from land and sea, and permitted no one to leave or enter it.

Rome Supports the Jews

15 Then Nū•mē′ni•us and his companions arrived from Rome, with letters to the kings and countries, in which the following was written: 16 "Lucius, consul of the Romans, to King Ptol′-e•my, greetings. 17 The envoys of the Jews have come to us as our friends and allies to renew our ancient friendship and alliance. They had been sent by the high priest Simon and by the Jewish people 18 and have brought a gold shield weighing one thousand minas. 19 We therefore have decided to write to the kings and countries that they should not seek their harm or make war against them and their cities and their country, or make alliance with those who war against them. 20 And it has seemed good to us to accept the shield from them. 21 Therefore if any scoundrels have fled to you from their country, hand them over to the high priest Simon, so that he may punish them according to their law."

22 The consul*s* wrote the same thing to King De•mē′tri•us and to At′ta•lus and Ar•i•a•rā′thēs and Ar′sa•cēs, 23 and to all the countries, and to Samp′-sa•mēs,*t* and to the Spartans, and to Dē′los, and to Myn′dos, and to Si′cy•on, and to Cār′i•a, and to Sā′-mos, and to Pam•phyl′i•a, and to Ly′ci•a, and to Hal•i•car•nas′sus, and to Rhōdes, and to Pha•sē′lis, and to Cōs, and to Si′de, and to Ar′a•dus and Gor•tý′na and Cnī′dus and Cyprus and Cý•rē′nē. 24 They also sent a copy of these things to the high priest Simon.

Antiochus VII Threatens Simon

25 King An•ti′o•chus besieged Dor for the second time, continually throwing his forces against it and making engines of war; and he shut Trý′phō up and kept him from going out or in. 26 And Simon sent to An•ti′o•chus*u* two thousand picked troops, to fight for him, and silver and gold and a large amount of military equipment. 27 But he refused to receive them, and broke all the agreements he formerly had made with Simon, and became estranged from him. 28 He sent to him Ath•e•nō′bi•us, one of his Friends, to confer with him, saying, "You hold control of Jop′pa and Ga•za′ra and the citadel in Jerusalem; they are cities of my kingdom. 29 You have devastated their territory, you have done great damage in the land, and you have taken possession of many places in my kingdom. 30 Now then, hand over the cities that you have seized and the tribute money of the places that you have conquered outside the borders of Judea; 31 or else pay me five hundred talents of silver for the destruction that you have caused and five hundred talents more for the tribute money of the cities. Otherwise we will come and make war on you."

32 So Ath•e•nō′bi•us, the king's Friend, came to Jerusalem, and when he saw the splendor of Simon, and the sideboard with its gold and silver plate, and his great magnificence, he was amazed. Then he reported to him the king's message, 33 Simon said to him in reply: "We have neither taken foreign land nor seized foreign property, but only the inheritance of our ancestors, which at one time had been unjustly taken by our enemies. 34 Now that we have the opportunity, we are firmly holding the inheritance of our ancestors. 35 As for Jop′pa and Ga•za′ra, which you demand, they were causing great damage among the people and to our land; for them we will give you one hundred talents."

Ath•e•nō′bi•us*s* did not answer him a word, 36 but returned in wrath to the king and reported to him these words, and also the splendor of Simon and all that he had seen. And the king was very angry.

Victory over Cendebeus

37 Meanwhile Trý′phō embarked on a ship and escaped to Or•thō′si•a. 38 Then the king made Cen•de•bē′us commander-in-chief of the coastal country, and gave him troops of infantry and cavalry. 39 He commanded him to encamp against Judea, to build up Kēd′ron and fortify its gates, and to make war on the people; but the king pursued Trý′phō. 40 So Cen•de•bē′us came to Jam′ni•a and began to provoke the people and invade Judea and take the people captive and kill them. 41 He built up Kēd′ron and stationed horsemen and troops there, so that they might go out and make raids along the highways of Judea, as the king had ordered him.

16 John went up from Ga•za′ra and reported to his father Simon what Cen•de•bē′us had done. 2 And Simon called in his two eldest sons Judas and John, and said to them: "My brothers and I and my father's house have fought the wars of Israel from our youth until this day, and things have prospered in our hands so that we have delivered Israel many times. 3 But now I have grown old, and you by Heaven's*v* mercy are mature in years. Take my place and my brother's, and go out and fight for our nation, and may the help that comes from Heaven be with you."

---

s Gk *He*   *t* The name is uncertain   *u* Gk *him*   *v* Gk *his*

4 So John[w] chose out of the country twenty thousand warriors and cavalry, and they marched against Cen·de·bē'us and camped for the night in Mō'dein. 5 Early in the morning they started out and marched into the plain, where a large force of infantry and cavalry was coming to meet them; and a stream lay between them. 6 Then he and his army lined up against them. He saw that the soldiers were afraid to cross the stream, so he crossed over first; and when his troops saw him, they crossed over after him. 7 Then he divided the army and placed the cavalry in the center of the infantry, for the cavalry of the enemy were very numerous. 8 They sounded the trumpets, and Cen·de·bē'us and his army were put to flight; many of them fell wounded and the rest fled into the stronghold. 9 At that time Judas the brother of John was wounded, but John pursued them until Cen·de·bē'us[w] reached Kēd'ron, which he had built. 10 They also fled into the towers that were in the fields of A·zō'tus, and John[x] burned it with fire, and about two thousand of them fell. He then returned to Judea safely.

Murder of Simon and His Sons

11 Now Ptol'e·my son of A·bū'bus had been appointed governor over the plain of Jericho; he had a large store of silver and gold, 12 for he was son-in-law of the high priest. 13 His heart was lifted up; he determined to get control of the country, and made treacherous plans against Simon and his sons, to do away with them. 14 Now Simon was visiting the towns of the country and attending to their needs, and he went down to Jericho with his sons Mat·ta·thī'as and Judas, in the one hundred seventy-seventh year,[y] in the eleventh month, which is the month of She·bat'. 15 The son of A·bū'bus received them treacherously in the little stronghold called Dok, which he had built; he gave them a great banquet, and hid men there. 16 When Simon and his sons were drunk, Ptol'e·my and his men rose up, took their weapons, rushed in against Simon in the banquet hall and killed him and his two sons, as well as some of his servants. 17 So he committed an act of great treachery and returned evil for good.

John Succeeds Simon

18 Then Ptol'e·my wrote a report about these things and sent it to the king, asking him to send troops to aid him and to turn over to him the towns and the country. 19 He sent other troops to Ga·zā'ra to do away with John; he sent letters to the captains asking them to come to him so that he might give them silver and gold and gifts; 20 and he sent other troops to take possession of Jerusalem and the temple hill. 21 But someone ran ahead and reported to John at Ga·zā'ra that his father and brothers had perished, and that "he has sent men to kill you also." 22 When he heard this, he was greatly shocked; he seized the men who came to destroy him and killed them, for he had found out that they were seeking to destroy him.

23 The rest of the acts of John and his wars and the brave deeds that he did, and the building of the walls that he completed, and his achievements, 24 are written in the annals of his high priesthood, from the time that he became high priest after his father.

---

w Other ancient authorities read he   x Gk he   y 134 B.C.

When you are suffering, what is your first response? to escape? to look for relief? to cry out in pain? These are normal and healthy responses: no well-adjusted person chooses to suffer willingly. Sometimes, though, people inflict unspeakable suffering on one another, especially through violence such as rape and torture. What meaning could there be in such suffering? In response, 2 Maccabees insists that God will vindicate all those who suffer innocently at the hands of the unjust.

At a Glance

- **Chapters 1–2.** two letters to the Jews in Egypt, the author's preface

- **Chapters 3–7.** the persecution of the Jews

- **8.1—10.9.** the victory of Judas

- **10.10—15.39.** the renewal of persecution

In-depth

In 167 B.C., the Jewish people faced a new persecution under the Seleucid (Greek) king Antiochus IV Epiphanes. In an effort to unify the many different peoples under his rule, Antiochus imposed his own language, customs, and religion on all of them, including the Jews. Second Maccabees covers some of the same history as First Maccabees but with different purposes: to show the variety of ways the Jews resisted persecution and to give hope to persecuted Jews in the author's time.

The Book of Job had already struggled with the mystery of human suffering and concluded that only God could understand it. Not content with this answer, the author of 2 Maccabees presses forward with new insights:

- In the famous story of the martyrdom of a Jewish mother and her seven sons (7.1–42), 2 Maccabees talks about the resurrection of the dead.
- In chapter 12, the value of praying for the dead is commended.
- In chapter 15, the book speaks confidently of the prayers of the saints in heaven for those on earth.

Second Maccabees is less concerned with the facts of history than with the meaning of history. It insists that whenever God's faithful people suffer, they can be assured of receiving justice—if not in this life, then in the resurrection. The book shows how the Jewish faith continued to develop as it faced the sometimes painful events of history.

Quick Facts

Period Covered
from 180 to 161 B.C.
Author
someone around 100 B.C., summarizing a lost work by Jason of Cyrene
Themes
differing responses to persecution, the just and suffering
Of Note
Second Maccabees is not found in every translation of the Old Testament (see "The Case of the Missing Books," Tob 1.16).

2 Maccabees

A Letter to the Jews in Egypt

1 The Jews in Jerusalem and those in the land of Judea,
To their Jewish kindred in Egypt,
Greetings and true peace.

2 May God do good to you, and may he remember his covenant with Abraham and Isaac and Jacob, his faithful servants. 3 May he give you all a heart to worship him and to do his will with a strong heart and a willing spirit. 4 May he open your heart to his law and his commandments, and may he bring peace. 5 May he hear your prayers and be reconciled to you, and may he not forsake you in time of evil. 6 We are now praying for you here.

7 In the reign of De·mē′tri·us, in the one hundred sixty-ninth year,[a] we Jews wrote to you, in the critical distress that came upon us in those years after Jason and his company revolted from the holy land and the kingdom 8 and burned the gate and shed innocent blood. We prayed to the Lord and were heard, and we offered sacrifice and grain offering, and we lit the lamps and set out the loaves. 9 And now see that you keep the festival of booths in the month of Chis′lev, in the one hundred eighty-eighth year.[b]

A Letter to Aristobulus
(Cp 1 Macc 6.1–4)

10 The people of Jerusalem and of Judea and the senate and Judas,

To Ar·is·tob′ū·lus, who is of the family of the anointed priests, teacher of King Ptol′e·my, and to the Jews in Egypt,
Greetings and good health.

11 Having been saved by God out of grave dangers we thank him greatly for taking our side against the king,[c] 12 for he drove out those who fought against the holy city. 13 When the leader reached Persia with a force that seemed irresistible, they were cut to pieces in the temple of Na·nē′a by a deception employed by the priests of the goddess[d] Na·nē′a. 14 On the pretext of intending to marry her, An·tī′o·chus came to the place together with his Friends, to secure most of its treasures as a dowry. 15 When the priests of the temple of Na·nē′a had set out the treasures and An·tī′o·chus had come with a few men inside the wall of the sacred precinct, they closed the temple as soon as he entered it. 16 Opening a secret door in the ceiling, they threw stones and struck down the leader and his men; they dismembered them and cut off their heads and threw them to the people outside. 17 Blessed in every way be our God, who has brought judgment on those who have behaved impiously.

Fire Consumes Nehemiah's Sacrifice

18 Since on the twenty-fifth day of Chis′lev we shall celebrate the purification of the temple, we

---

a 143 B.C. *b* 124 B.C. *c* Cn: Gk *as those who array themselves against a king* *d* Gk lacks *the goddess* thought it necessary to notify you, in order that you also may celebrate the festival of booths and the festival of the fire given when Nē•he•mī′ah, who built the temple and the altar, offered sacrifices.

19 For when our ancestors were being led captive to Persia, the pious priests of that time took some of the fire of the altar and secretly hid it in the hollow of a dry cistern, where they took such precautions that the place was unknown to anyone. 20 But after many years had passed, when it pleased God, Nē•he•mī′ah, having been commissioned by the king of Persia, sent the descendants of the priests who had hidden the fire to get it. And when they reported to us that they had not found fire but only a thick liquid, he ordered them to dip it out and bring it. 21 When the materials for the sacrifices were presented, Nē•he•mī′ah ordered the priests to sprinkle the liquid on the wood and on the things laid upon it. 22 When this had been done and some time had passed, and when the sun, which had been clouded over, shone out, a great fire blazed up, so that all marveled. 23 And while the sacrifice was being consumed, the priests offered prayer— the priests and everyone. Jonathan led, and the rest responded, as did Nē•he•mī′ah. 24 The prayer was to this effect:

"O Lord, Lord God, Creator of all things, you are awe-inspiring and strong and just and merciful, you alone are king and are kind, 25 you alone are bountiful, you alone are just and almighty and eternal. You rescue Israel from every evil; you chose the ancestors and consecrated them. 26 Accept this sacrifice on behalf of all your people Israel and preserve your portion and make it holy. 27 Gather together our scattered people, set free those who are slaves among the Gentiles, look on those who are rejected and despised, and let the Gentiles know that you are our God. 28 Punish those who oppress and are insolent with pride. 29 Plant your people in your holy place, as Moses promised."

30 Then the priests sang the hymns. 31 After the materials of the sacrifice had been consumed, Nē•he•mī′ah ordered that the liquid that was left should be poured on large stones. 32 When this was done, a flame blazed up; but when the light from the altar shone back, it went out. 33 When this matter became known, and it was reported to the king of the Persians that, in the place where the exiled priests had hidden the fire, the liquid had appeared with which Nē•he•mī′ah and his associates had burned the materials of the sacrifice, 34 the king investigated the matter, and enclosed the place and made it sacred. 35 And with those persons whom the king favored he exchanged many excellent gifts. 36 Nē•he•mī′ah and his associates called this "nephthar," which means purification, but by most people it is called naphtha.[e]

Jeremiah Hides the Tent, Ark, and Altar

2 One finds in the records that the prophet Jer•e•mī′ah ordered those who were being deported to take some of the fire, as has been mentioned, 2 and that the prophet, after giving them the law, instructed those who were being deported not to forget the commandments of the Lord, or to be led astray in their thoughts on seeing the gold and silver statues and their adornment. 3 And with other similar words he exhorted them that the law should not depart from their hearts.

4 It was also in the same document that the prophet, having received an oracle, ordered that the tent and the ark should follow with him, and that he went out to the mountain where Moses had gone up and had seen the inheritance of God. 5 Jer•e•mī′ah came and found a cave-dwelling, and he brought there the tent and the ark and the altar of incense; then he sealed up the entrance. 6 Some of those who followed him came up intending to mark the way, but could not find it. 7 When Jer•e•mī′ah learned of it, he rebuked them and declared: "The place shall remain unknown until God gathers his people together again and shows his mercy. 8 Then the Lord will disclose these things, and the glory of the Lord will appear, as they were shown in the case of Moses, and as Solomon asked that the place should be specially consecrated."

9 It was also made clear that being possessed of wisdom Solomon[f] offered sacrifice for the dedication and completion of the temple. 10 Just as Moses prayed to the Lord, and fire came down from heaven and consumed the sacrifices, so also Solomon prayed, and the fire came down and consumed the whole burnt offerings. 11 And Moses said, "They were consumed because the sin offering had not been eaten." 12 Likewise Solomon also kept the eight days.

13 The same things are reported in the records and in the memoirs of Nē•he•mī′ah, and also that he founded a library and collected the books about the kings and prophets, and the writings of David, and letters of kings about votive offerings. 14 In the same way Judas also collected all the books that had been lost on account of the war that had come upon us, and they are in our possession. 15 So if you have need of them, send people to get them for you.

16 Since, therefore, we are about to celebrate the purification, we write to you. Will you therefore please keep the days? 17 It is God who has saved all his people, and has returned the inheritance to all, and the kingship and the priesthood and the consecration, 18 as he promised through the law. We

---

[e] Gk nephthai   [f] Gk he

have hope in God that he will soon have mercy on us and will gather us from everywhere under heaven into his holy place, for he has rescued us from great evils and has purified the place.

The Compiler's Preface

19 The story of Judas Mac·ca·bē'us and his brothers, and the purification of the great temple, and the dedication of the altar, 20 and further the wars against An·ti'o·chus E·piph'a·nēs and his son Eū'pa·tor, 21 and the appearances that came from heaven to those who fought bravely for Jū'da·ism, so that though few in number they seized the whole land and pursued the barbarian hordes, 22 and regained possession of the temple famous throughout the world, and liberated the city, and re-established the laws that were about to be abolished, while the Lord with great kindness became gracious to them—23 all this, which has been set forth by Jason of Cȳ·rē'nē in five volumes, we shall attempt to condense into a single book. 24 For considering the flood of statistics involved and the difficulty there is for those who wish to enter upon the narratives of history because of the mass of material, 25 we have aimed to please those who wish to read, to make it easy for those who are inclined to memorize, and to profit all readers. 26 For us who have undertaken the toil of abbreviating, it is no light matter but calls for sweat and loss of sleep, 27 just as it is not easy for one who prepares a banquet and seeks the benefit of others. Nevertheless, to secure the gratitude of many we will gladly endure the uncomfortable toil, 28 leaving the responsibility for exact details to the compiler, while devoting our effort to arriving at the outlines of the condensation. 29 For as the master builder of a new house must be concerned with the whole construction, while the one who undertakes its painting and decoration has to consider only what is suitable for its adornment, such in my judgment is the case with us. 30 It is the duty of the original historian to occupy the ground, to discuss matters from every side, and to take trouble with details, 31 but the one who recasts the narrative should be allowed to strive for brevity of expression and to forego exhaustive treatment. 32 At this point therefore let us begin our narrative, without adding any more to what has already been said; for it would be foolish to lengthen the preface while cutting short the history itself.

Arrival of Heliodorus in Jerusalem

3 While the holy city was inhabited in unbroken peace and the laws were strictly observed because of the piety of the high priest Ō·nī'as and his hatred of wickedness, 2 it came about that the kings themselves honored the place and glorified

the temple with the finest presents, 3 even to the extent that King Se·leū'cus of Asia defrayed from his own revenues all the expenses connected with the service of the sacrifices.

4 But a man named Simon, of the tribe of Benjamin, who had been made captain of the temple, had a disagreement with the high priest about the administration of the city market. 5 Since he could not prevail over Ō·nī'as, he went to Ap·ol·lō'ni·us of Tar'sus,g who at that time was governor of Coē·le·syr'i·a and Phoe·ni'ci·a, 6 and reported to him that the treasury in Jerusalem was full of untold sums of money, so that the amount of the funds could not be reckoned, and that they did not belong to the account of the sacrifices, but that it was possible for them to fall under the control of the king. 7 When Ap·ol·lō'ni·us met the king, he told him of the money about which he had been informed. The kingh chose Hē·li·o·dor'us, who was in charge of his affairs, and sent him with commands to effect the removal of the reported wealth. 8 Hē·li·o·dor'us at once set out on his journey, ostensibly to make a tour of inspection of the cities of Coē·le·syr'i·a and Phoe·ni'ci·a, but in fact to carry out the king's purpose.

9 When he had arrived at Jerusalem and had been kindly welcomed by the high priest ofi the city, he told about the disclosure that had been made and stated why he had come, and he inquired whether this really was the situation. 10 The high priest explained that there were some deposits belonging to widows and orphans, 11 and also some money of Hyr·cā'nus son of Tō·bī'as, a man of very prominent position, and that it totaled in all four hundred talents of silver and two hundred of gold. To such an extent the impious Simon had misrepresented the facts. 12 And he said that it was utterly impossible that wrong should be done to those people who had trusted in the holiness of the place and in the sanctity and inviolability of the temple that is honored throughout the whole world.

Heliodorus Plans to Rob the Temple

13 But Hē·li·o·dor'us, because of the orders he had from the king, said that this money must in any case be confiscated for the king's treasury. 14 So he set a day and went in to direct the inspection of these funds.

There was no little distress throughout the whole city. 15 The priests prostrated themselves before the altar in their priestly vestments and called toward heaven upon him who had given the law about deposits, that he should keep them safe for those who had deposited them. 16 To see the appearance of the

---

g Gk *Apollonius son of Tharseas*   h Gk *He*   i Other ancient authorities read *and* high priest was to be wounded at heart, for his face and the change in his color disclosed the anguish of his soul. [17] For terror and bodily trembling had come over the man, which plainly showed to those who looked at him the pain lodged in his heart. [18] People also hurried out of their houses in crowds to make a general supplication because the holy place was about to be brought into dishonor. [19] Women, girded with sackcloth under their breasts, thronged the streets. Some of the young women who were kept indoors ran together to the gates, and some to the walls, while others peered out of the windows. [20] And holding up their hands to heaven, they all made supplication. [21] There was something pitiable in the prostration of the whole populace and the anxiety of the high priest in his great anguish.

The Lord Protects His Temple

22 While they were calling upon the Almighty Lord that he would keep what had been entrusted safe and secure for those who had entrusted it, [23] Hē·li·o·dor′us went on with what had been decided. [24] But when he arrived at the treasury with his bodyguard, then and there the Sovereign of spirits and of all authority caused so great a manifestation that all who had been so bold as to accompany him were astounded by the power of God, and became faint with terror. [25] For there appeared to them a magnificently caparisoned horse, with a rider of frightening mien; it rushed furiously at Hē·li·o·dor′us and struck at him with its front hoofs. Its rider was seen to have armor and weapons of gold. [26] Two young men also appeared to him, remarkably strong, gloriously beautiful and splendidly dressed, who stood on either side of him and flogged him continuously, inflicting many blows on him. [27] When he suddenly fell to the ground and deep darkness came over him, his men took him up, put him on a stretcher, [28] and carried him away—this man who had just entered the aforesaid treasury with a great retinue and all his bodyguard but was now unable to help himself. They recognized clearly the sovereign power of God.

Onias Prays for Heliodorus

29 While he lay prostrate, speechless because of the divine intervention and deprived of any hope of recovery, [30] they praised the Lord who had acted marvelously for his own place. And the temple, which a little while before was full of fear and disturbance, was filled with joy and gladness, now that the Almighty Lord had appeared. [31] Some of Hē·li·o·dor′us's friends quickly begged Ō·nī′as to call upon the Most High to grant life to one who was lying quite at his last breath.

[32] So the high priest, fearing that the king might get the notion that some foul play had been perpetrated by the Jews with regard to Hē·li·o·dor′us, offered sacrifice for the man's recovery. [33] While the high priest was making an atonement, the same young men appeared again to Hē·li·o·dor′us dressed in the same clothing, and they stood and said, "Be very grateful to the high priest Ō·nī′as, since for his sake the Lord has granted you your life. [34] And see that you, who have been flogged by heaven, report to all people the majestic power of God." Having said this they vanished.

The Conversion of Heliodorus

35 Then Hē·li·o·dor′us offered sacrifice to the Lord and made very great vows to the Savior of his life, and having bidden Ō·nī′as farewell, he marched off with his forces to the king. [36] He bore testimony to all concerning the deeds of the supreme God, which he had seen with his own eyes. [37] When the king asked Hē·li·o·dor′us what sort of person would be suitable to send on another mission to Jerusalem, he replied, [38] "If you have any enemy or plotter against your government, send him there, for you will get him back thoroughly flogged, if he survives at all; for there is certainly some power of God about the place. [39] For he who has his dwelling in heaven watches over that place himself and brings it aid, and he strikes and destroys those who come to do it injury." [40] This was the outcome of the episode of Hē·li·o·dor′us and the protection of the treasury.

Simon Accuses Onias

4 The previously mentioned Simon, who had informed about the money against[i] his own country, slandered Ō·nī′as, saying that it was he who had incited Hē·li·o·dor′us and had been the real cause of the misfortune. [2] He dared to designate as a plotter against the government the man who was the benefactor of the city, the protector of his compatriots, and a zealot for the laws. [3] When his hatred progressed to such a degree that even murders were committed by one of Simon's approved agents, [4] Ō·nī′as recognized that the rivalry was serious and that Ap·ol·lō′ni·us son of Me·nes′-thē·us,[k] and governor of Coē·le·syr′i·a and Phoe·ni′-ci·a, was intensifying the malice of Simon. [5] So he appealed to the king, not accusing his compatriots but having in view the welfare, both public and private, of all the people. [6] For he saw that without the king's attention public affairs could not again reach a peaceful settlement, and that Simon would not stop his folly.

---

i Gk *and* *k* Vg Compare verse 21: Meaning of Gk uncertain

PRAY IT?

Arrogance

Arrogance seems to run in the family of Simon. First, Simon seeks to embarrass the high priest, Onias, because of a minor disagreement (2 Macc 3.1–14). When that fails, he falsely accuses Onias of a crime (4.1–6). Several years later, Simon's brother bribes his way into power (verses 23–29).

We have all encountered arrogant people who think that they can do no wrong, and when they do err, cover it up by attacking others. Many of us are intimidated by such people and resent that we felt talked down to or easily dismissed as unimportant. So, how should we respond to arrogant people? The most obvious solution is to ignore them. If that is not possible, then we need to react to them calmly and confidently. Finally, we should keep them in our prayers. Their arrogance can be masking an insecurity or a hurt that needs God's healing touch.

In your prayer, reflect or journal on the following questions:

- Who intimidates you by her or his arrogant behavior?
- How could you respond in a loving and just way?
- What do you need to bring to God in prayer?

▶ 2 Macc 3.1—4.29

Jason's Reforms

(Cp 1 Macc 1.10–19)

7 When Se·leū'cus died and An·tī'o·chus, who was called E·piph'a·nēs, succeeded to the kingdom, Jason the brother of Ō·nī'as obtained the high priesthood by corruption, 8 promising the king at an interview*[l]* three hundred sixty talents of silver, and from another source of revenue eighty talents. 9 In addition to this he promised to pay one hundred fifty more if permission were given to establish by his authority a gymnasium and a body of youth for it, and to enroll the people of Jerusalem as citizens of An'ti·och. 10 When the king assented and Jason*[m]* came to office, he at once shifted his compatriots over to the Greek way of life. 11 He set aside the existing royal concessions to the Jews, secured through John the father of

Eū·pol'e·mus, who went on the mission to establish friendship and alliance with the Romans; and he destroyed the lawful ways of living and introduced new customs contrary to the law. 12 He took delight in establishing a gymnasium right under the citadel, and he induced the noblest of the young men to wear the Greek hat. 13 There was such an extreme of Hellenization and increase in the adoption of foreign ways because of the surpassing wickedness of Jason, who was ungodly and no true*[n]* high priest, 14 that the priests were no longer intent upon their service at the altar. Despising the sanctuary and neglecting the sacrifices, they hurried to take part in the unlawful proceedings in the wrestling arena after the signal for the discus-throwing, 15 disdaining the honors prized by their ancestors and putting the highest value upon Greek forms of prestige. 16 For this reason heavy disaster overtook them, and those whose ways of living they admired and wished to imitate completely became their enemies and punished them. 17 It is no light thing to show irreverence to the divine laws—a fact that later events will make clear.

Jason Introduces Greek Customs

18 When the quadrennial games were being held at Tȳre and the king was present, 19 the vile Jason sent envoys, chosen as being An·ti·och'i·an citizens from Jerusalem, to carry three hundred silver drachmas for the sacrifice to Hercules. Those who carried the money, however, thought best not to use it for sacrifice, because that was inappropriate, but to expend it for another purpose. 20 So this money was intended by the sender for the sacrifice to Hercules, but by the decision of its carriers it was applied to the construction of triremes. 21 When Ap·ol·lō'ni·us son of Me·nes'thē·us was sent to Egypt for the coronation*[o]* of Phil·o·mē'tor as king, An·tī'o·chus learned that Phil·o·mē'tor*[m]* had become hostile to his government, and he took measures for his own security. Therefore upon arriving at Jop'pa he proceeded to Jerusalem. 22 He was welcomed magnificently by Jason and the city, and ushered in with a blaze of torches and with shouts. Then he marched his army into Phoe·ni'ci·a.

Menelaus Becomes High Priest

23 After a period of three years Jason sent Men·e·lā'us, the brother of the previously mentioned Simon, to carry the money to the king and to complete the records of essential business. 24 But he, when presented to the king, extolled him with an air of authority, and secured the high priesthood

l Or *by a petition*   *m* Gk *he*   *n* Gk lacks *true*   *o* Meaning of Gk uncertain for himself, outbidding Jason by three hundred talents of silver. 25 After receiving the king's orders he returned, possessing no qualification for the high priesthood, but having the hot temper of a cruel tyrant and the rage of a savage wild beast. 26 So Jason, who after supplanting his own brother was supplanted by another man, was driven as a fugitive into the land of Am'mon. 27 Although Men•e•lā'us continued to hold the office, he did not pay regularly any of the money promised to the king. 28 When Sos'tra•tus the captain of the citadel kept requesting payment—for the collection of the revenue was his responsibility—the two of them were summoned by the king on account of this issue. 29 Men•e•lā'us left his own brother Lȳ•sim'a•chus as deputy in the high priesthood, while Sos'tra•tus left Crā'tēs, the commander of the Cyp'ri•an troops.

The Murder of Onias

30 While such was the state of affairs, it happened that the people of Tar'sus and of Mal'lus revolted because their cities had been given as a present to An•tī'o•chis, the king's concubine. 31 So the king went hurriedly to settle the trouble, leaving An•dron'i•cus, a man of high rank, to act as his deputy. 32 But Men•e•lā'us, thinking he had obtained a suitable opportunity, stole some of the gold vessels of the temple and gave them to Andron'i•cus; other vessels, as it happened, he had sold to Tȳre and the neighboring cities. 33 When Ō•nī'as became fully aware of these acts, he publicly exposed them, having first withdrawn to a place of sanctuary at Daphne near An'ti•och. 34 Therefore Men•e•lā'us, taking An•dron'i•cus aside, urged him to kill Ō•nī'as. An•dron'i•cus*p* came to Ō•nī'as, and resorting to treachery, offered him sworn pledges and gave him his right hand; he persuaded him, though still suspicious, to come out from the place of sanctuary; then, with no regard for justice, he immediately put him out of the way.

Andronicus Is Punished

35 For this reason not only Jews, but many also of other nations, were grieved and displeased at the unjust murder of the man. 36 When the king returned from the region of Ci•li'ci•a, the Jews in the city*q* appealed to him with regard to the unreasonable murder of Ō•nī'as, and the Greeks shared their hatred of the crime. 37 Therefore An•tī'o•chus was grieved at heart and filled with pity, and wept because of the moderation and good conduct of the deceased. 38 Inflamed with anger, he immediately stripped off the purple robe from An•dron'i•cus, tore off his clothes, and led him around the whole city to that very place where he had committed the outrage against Ō•nī'as, and there he dispatched the bloodthirsty fellow. The Lord thus repaid him with the punishment he deserved.

Unpopularity of Lysimachus and Menelaus

39 When many acts of sacrilege had been committed in the city by Lȳ•sim'a•chus with the connivance of Men•e•lā'us, and when report of them had spread abroad, the populace gathered against Lȳ•sim'a•chus, because many of the gold vessels had already been stolen. 40 Since the crowds were becoming aroused and filled with anger, Lȳ•sim'a•chus armed about three thousand men and launched an unjust attack, under the leadership of a certain Au•rā'nus, a man advanced in years and no less advanced in folly. 41 But when the Jews*r* became aware that Lȳ•sim'a•chus was attacking them, some picked up stones, some blocks of wood, and others took handfuls of the ashes that were lying around, and threw them in wild confusion at Lȳ•sim'a•chus and his men. 42 As a result, they wounded many of them, and killed some, and put all the rest to flight; the temple robber himself they killed close by the treasury.

43 Charges were brought against Men•e•lā'us about this incident. 44 When the king came to Tȳre, three men sent by the senate presented the case before him. 45 But Men•e•lā'us, already as good as beaten, promised a substantial bribe to Ptol'e•my son of Dor•ym'e•nēs to win over the king. 46 Therefore Ptol'e•my, taking the king aside into a colonnade as if for refreshment, induced the king to change his mind. 47 Men•e•lā'us, the cause of all the trouble, he acquitted of the charges against him, while he sentenced to death those unfortunate men, who would have been freed uncondemned if they had pleaded even before Scyth'i•ans. 48 And so those who had spoken for the city and the villages*s* and the holy vessels quickly suffered the unjust penalty. 49 Therefore even the Tȳ'ri•ans, showing their hatred of the crime, provided magnificently for their funeral. 50 But Men•e•lā'us, because of the greed of those in power, remained in office, growing in wickedness, having become the chief plotter against his compatriots.

Jason Tries to Regain Control

5 About this time An•tī'o•chus made his second invasion of Egypt. 2 And it happened that, for almost forty days, there appeared over all the city golden-clad cavalry charging through the air, in companies fully armed with lances and drawn swords— 3 troops of cavalry drawn up, attacks and counterattacks made on this side and on that, brandishing of shields, massing of spears, hurling of

---

p Gk He   q Or in each city   r Gk they   s Other ancient authorities read the people missiles, the flash of golden trappings, and armor of all kinds. 4 Therefore everyone prayed that the apparition might prove to have been a good omen.

5 When a false rumor arose that An•ti'o•chus was dead, Jason took no fewer than a thousand men and suddenly made an assault on the city. When the troops on the wall had been forced back and at last the city was being taken, Men•e•lā'us took refuge in the citadel. 6 But Jason kept relentlessly slaughtering his compatriots, not realizing that success at the cost of one's kindred is the greatest misfortune, but imagining that he was setting up trophies of victory over enemies and not over compatriots. 7 He did not, however, gain control of the government; in the end he got only disgrace from his conspiracy, and fled again into the country of the Am'mon•ites. 8 Finally he met a miserable end. Accused[t] before Ar'e•tas the ruler of the A'rabs, fleeing from city to city, pursued by everyone, hated as a rebel against the laws, and abhorred as the executioner of his country and his compatriots, he was cast ashore in Egypt. 9 There he who had driven many from their own country into exile died in exile, having embarked to go to the Lac•e•dae•mō'-ni•ans in hope of finding protection because of their kinship. 10 He who had cast out many to lie unburied had no one to mourn for him; he had no funeral of any sort and no place in the tomb of his ancestors.

11 When news of what had happened reached the king, he took it to mean that Judea was in revolt. So, raging inwardly, he left Egypt and took the city by storm. 12 He commanded his soldiers to cut down relentlessly everyone they met and to kill those who went into their houses. 13 Then there was massacre of young and old, destruction of boys, women, and children, and slaughter of young girls and infants. 14 Within the total of three days eighty thousand were destroyed, forty thousand in hand-to-hand fighting, and as many were sold into slavery as were killed.

Pillage of the Temple
(1 Macc 1.20–40)

15 Not content with this, An•ti'o•chus[u] dared to enter the most holy temple in all the world, guided by Men•e•lā'us, who had become a traitor both to the laws and to his country. 16 He took the holy vessels with his polluted hands, and swept away with profane hands the votive offerings that other kings had made to enhance the glory and honor of the place. 17 An•ti'o•chus was elated in spirit, and did not perceive that the Lord was angered for a little while because of the sins of those who lived in the city, and that this was the reason he was disregarding the holy place. 18 But if it had not happened that they were involved in many sins, this man

would have been flogged and turned back from his rash act as soon as he came forward, just as Hē•li-o•dor'us had been, whom King Se•leū'cus sent to inspect the treasury. 19 But the Lord did not choose the nation for the sake of the holy place, but the place for the sake of the nation. 20 Therefore the place itself shared in the misfortunes that befell the nation and afterward participated in its benefits; and what was forsaken in the wrath of the Almighty was restored again in all its glory when the great Lord became reconciled.

21 So An•ti'o•chus carried off eighteen hundred talents from the temple, and hurried away to An'ti•och, thinking in his arrogance that he could sail on the land and walk on the sea, because his mind was elated. 22 He left governors to oppress the people: at Jerusalem, Philip, by birth a Phryg'i•an and in character more barbarous than the man who appointed him; 23 and at Ger'i•zim, An•dron'i•cus; and besides these Men•e•lā'us, who lorded it over his compatriots worse than the others did. In his malice toward the Jewish citizens,[v] 24 An•ti'o•chus[u] sent Ap•ol•lō'ni•us, the captain of the My'si•ans, with an army of twenty-two thousand, and commanded him to kill all the grown men and to sell the women and boys as slaves. 25 When this man arrived in Jerusalem, he pretended to be peaceably disposed and waited until the holy sabbath day; then, finding the Jews not at work, he ordered his troops to parade under arms. 26 He put to the sword all those who came out to see them, then rushed into the city with his armed warriors and killed great numbers of people.

27 But Judas Mac•ca•bē'us, with about nine others, got away to the wilderness, and kept himself and his companions alive in the mountains as wild animals do; they continued to live on what grew wild, so that they might not share in the defilement.

The Suppression of Judaism
(1 Macc 1.41–64)

6 Not long after this, the king sent an Athenian[w] senator[x] to compel the Jews to forsake the laws of their ancestors and no longer to live by the laws of God; 2 also to pollute the temple in Jerusalem and to call it the temple of Olympian Zeūs, and to call the one in Ger'i•zim the temple of Zeūs-the-Friend-of-Strangers, as did the people who lived in that place.

3 Harsh and utterly grievous was the onslaught of evil. 4 For the temple was filled with debauchery and reveling by the Gentiles, who dallied with prostitutes and had intercourse with women within the

---

t Cn: Gk *Imprisoned*   u Gk *he*   v Or *worse than the others did in his malice toward the Jewish citizens*   w Other ancient authorities read *Antiochian*   x Or *Geron an Athenian* sacred precincts, and besides brought in things for sacrifice that were unfit. 5 The altar was covered with abominable offerings that were forbidden by the laws. 6 People could neither keep the sabbath, nor observe the festivals of their ancestors, nor so much as confess themselves to be Jews.

7 On the monthly celebration of the king's birthday, the Jews[y] were taken, under bitter constraint, to partake of the sacrifices; and when a festival of Di•o•ny′sus was celebrated, they were compelled to wear wreaths of ivy and to walk in the procession in honor of Di•o•ny′sus. 8 At the suggestion of the people of Ptol•e•ma′is[z] a decree was issued to the neighboring Greek cities that they should adopt the same policy toward the Jews and make them partake of the sacrifices, 9 and should kill those who did not choose to change over to Greek customs. One could see, therefore, the misery that had come upon them. 10 For example, two women were brought in for having circumcised their children. They publicly paraded them around the city, with their babies hanging at their breasts, and then hurled them down headlong from the wall. 11 Others who had assembled in the caves nearby, in order to observe the seventh day secretly, were betrayed to Philip and were all burned together, because their piety kept them from defending themselves, in view of their regard for that most holy day.

Providential Significance of the Persecution

12 Now I urge those who read this book not to be depressed by such calamities, but to recognize that these punishments were designed not to destroy but to discipline our people. 13 In fact, it is a sign of great kindness not to let the impious alone for long, but to punish them immediately. 14 For in the case of the other nations the Lord waits patiently to punish them until they have reached the full measure of their sins; but he does not deal in this way with us, 15 in order that he may not take vengeance on us afterward when our sins have reached their height. 16 Therefore he never withdraws his mercy from us. Although he disciplines us with calamities, he does not forsake his own people. 17 Let what we have said serve as a reminder; we must go on briefly with the story.

The Martyrdom of Eleazar
(Lev 11.7–8; 4 Macc 5—7)

18 El•e•a′zar, one of the scribes in high position, a man now advanced in age and of noble presence, was being forced to open his mouth to eat swine's flesh. 19 But he, welcoming death with honor rather than life with pollution, went up to the rack of his own accord, spitting out the flesh, 20 as all ought to go who have the courage to refuse things that it is not right to taste, even for the natural love of life.

21 Those who were in charge of that unlawful sacrifice took the man aside because of their long acquaintance with him, and privately urged him to bring meat of his own providing, proper for him to use, and to pretend that he was eating the flesh of the sacrificial meal that had been commanded by the king, 22 so that by doing this he might be saved from death, and be treated kindly on account of his old friendship with them. 23 But making a high resolve, worthy of his years and the dignity of his old age and the gray hairs that he had reached with

---

y Gk they z Cn: Gk suggestion of the Ptolemies (or of Ptolemy)

HE NEVER DRAWS HIS MERCY FROM US
HE DOES NOT FORSAKE HIS OWN PEOPLE

distinction and his excellent life even from childhood, and moreover according to the holy God-given law, he declared himself quickly, telling them to send him to Hades.

24 "Such pretense is not worthy of our time of life," he said, "for many of the young might suppose that El·ē·a′zar in his ninetieth year had gone over to an alien religion, 25 and through my pretense, for the sake of living a brief moment longer, they would be led astray because of me, while I defile and disgrace my old age. 26 Even if for the present I would avoid the punishment of mortals, yet whether I live or die I will not escape the hands of the Almighty. 27 Therefore, by bravely giving up my life now, I will show myself worthy of my old age 28 and leave to the young a noble example of how to die a good death willingly and nobly for the revered and holy laws."

When he had said this, he went[a] at once to the rack. 29 Those who a little before had acted toward him with goodwill now changed to ill will, because

the words he had uttered were in their opinion sheer madness.[b] 30 When he was about to die under the blows, he groaned aloud and said: "It is clear to the Lord in his holy knowledge that, though I might have been saved from death, I am enduring terrible sufferings in my body under this beating, but in my soul I am glad to suffer these things because I fear him."

31 So in this way he died, leaving in his death an example of nobility and a memorial of courage, not only to the young but to the great body of his nation.

The Martyrdom of Seven Brothers

(4 Macc 8—18)

7 It happened also that seven brothers and their mother were arrested and were being compelled by the king, under torture with whips and

---

[a] Other ancient authorities read *was dragged*　[b] Meaning of Gk uncertain

I WILL SACRIFICE MYSELF

If I were a bird
and able to fly afar,
I would like to be a white dove
to guide the people to freedom.
If I were the cloud in the sky,
I would shelter and bring rains
to the rice field.
If I were a grain of sand

I would throw myself down
to make a path for the people.
I will sacrifice my life
for the suffering people.
I would sacrifice myself
no matter how many times
I would have to die.

("For the People," by Nid Thialand, in *Your Will Be Done*)

This song was written by a twenty-two-year-old Thai student. He was later shot and killed by police officers at a demonstration against the return of a corrupt leader. His love for Thailand echoes the love of the mother and her seven sons for God and their Jewish faith in chapter 7 of 2 Maccabees.

▶ 2 Maccabees, chapter 7

thongs, to partake of unlawful swine's flesh. 2 One of them, acting as their spokesman, said, "What do you intend to ask and learn from us? For we are ready to die rather than transgress the laws of our ancestors."

3 The king fell into a rage, and gave orders to have pans and caldrons heated. 4 These were heated immediately, and he commanded that the tongue of their spokesman be cut out and that they scalp him and cut off his hands and feet, while the rest of the brothers and the mother looked on. 5 When he was utterly helpless, the king*c* ordered them to take him to the fire, still breathing, and to fry him in a pan. The smoke from the pan spread widely, but the brothers*d* and their mother encouraged one another to die nobly, saying, 6 "The Lord God is watching over us and in truth has compassion on us, as Moses declared in his song that bore witness against the people to their faces, when he said, 'And he will have compassion on his servants.' "*e*

7 After the first brother had died in this way, they brought forward the second for their sport. They tore off the skin of his head with the hair, and asked him, "Will you eat rather than have your body punished limb by limb?" 8 He replied in the language of his ancestors and said to them, "No." Therefore he in turn underwent tortures as the first brother had done. 9 And when he was at his last breath, he said, "You accursed wretch, you dismiss us from this present life, but the King of the universe will raise us up to an everlasting renewal of life, because we have died for his laws."

10 After him, the third was the victim of their sport. When it was demanded, he quickly put out his tongue and courageously stretched forth his hands, 11 and said nobly, "I got these from Heaven, and because of his laws I disdain them, and from him I hope to get them back again." 12 As a result the king himself and those with him were astonished at the young man's spirit, for he regarded his sufferings as nothing.

13 After he too had died, they maltreated and tortured the fourth in the same way. 14 When he was near death, he said, "One cannot but choose to die at the hands of mortals and to cherish the hope God gives of being raised again by him. But for you there will be no resurrection to life!"

15 Next they brought forward the fifth and maltreated him. 16 But he looked at the king,*f* and said, "Because you have authority among mortals, though you also are mortal, you do what you please. But do not think that God has forsaken our people. 17 Keep on, and see how his mighty power will torture you and your descendants!"

18 After them they brought forward the sixth. And when he was about to die, he said, "Do not deceive yourself in vain. For we are suffering these things on our own account, because of our sins against our own God. Therefore*g* astounding things have happened. 19 But do not think that you will go unpunished for having tried to fight against God!"

20 The mother was especially admirable and worthy of honorable memory. Although she saw her seven sons perish within a single day, she bore it with good courage because of her hope in the Lord. 21 She encouraged each of them in the language of their ancestors. Filled with a noble spirit, she reinforced her woman's reasoning with a man's courage, and said to them, 22 "I do not know how you came into being in my womb. It was not I who gave you life and breath, nor I who set in order the elements within each of you. 23 Therefore the Creator of the world, who shaped the beginning of humankind and devised the origin of all things, will in his mercy give life and breath back to you again, since you now forget yourselves for the sake of his laws."

24 An•ti'o•chus felt that he was being treated with contempt, and he was suspicious of her reproachful tone. The youngest brother being still alive, An•ti'o•chus*c* not only appealed to him in words, but promised with oaths that he would make him rich and enviable if he would turn from the ways of his ancestors, and that he would take him for his Friend and entrust him with public affairs. 25 Since the young man would not listen to him at all, the king called the mother to him and urged her to advise the youth to save himself. 26 After much urging on his part, she undertook to persuade her son. 27 But, leaning close to him, she spoke in their native language as follows, deriding the cruel tyrant: "My son, have pity on me. I carried you nine months in my womb, and nursed you for three years, and have reared you and brought you up to this point in your life, and have taken care of you.*h* 28 I beg you, my child, to look at the heaven and the earth and see everything that is in them, and recognize that God did not make them out of things that existed.*i* And in the same way the human race came into being. 29 Do not fear this butcher, but prove worthy of your brothers. Accept death, so that in God's mercy I may get you back again along with your brothers."

30 While she was still speaking, the young man said, "What are you*j* waiting for? I will not obey the king's command, but I obey the command of the law that was given to our ancestors through Moses. 31 But you,*k* who have contrived all sorts of evil

---

c Gk *he*   *d* Gk *they*   *e* Gk *slaves*   *f* Gk *at him*   *g* Lat: Other ancient authorities lack *Therefore*   *h* Or *have borne the burden of your education*   *i* Or *God made them out of things that did not exist*   *j* The Gk here for *you* is plural   *k* The Gk here for *you* is singular against the Hebrews, will certainly not escape the hands of God. 32 For we are suffering because of our own sins. 33 And if our living Lord is angry for a little while, to rebuke and discipline us, he will again be reconciled with his own servants.[l] 34 But you, unholy wretch, you most defiled of all mortals, do not be elated in vain and puffed up by uncertain hopes, when you raise your hand against the children of heaven. 35 You have not yet escaped the judgment of the almighty, all-seeing God. 36 For our brothers after enduring a brief suffering have drunk[m] of ever-flowing life, under God's covenant; but you, by the judgment of God, will receive just punishment for your arrogance. 37 I, like my brothers, give up body and life for the laws of our ancestors, appealing to God to show mercy soon to our nation and by trials and plagues to make you confess that he alone is God, 38 and through me and my brothers to bring to an end the wrath of the Almighty that has justly fallen on our whole nation."

39 The king fell into a rage, and handled him worse than the others, being exasperated at his scorn. 40 So he died in his integrity, putting his whole trust in the Lord.

41 Last of all, the mother died, after her sons.

42 Let this be enough, then, about the eating of sacrifices and the extreme tortures.

The Revolt of Judas Maccabeus
(1 Macc 3.1–26)

8 Meanwhile Judas, who was also called Mac-ca·bē′us, and his companions secretly entered the villages and summoned their kindred and enlisted those who had continued in the Jewish faith, and so they gathered about six thousand. 2 They implored the Lord to look upon the people who were oppressed by all; and to have pity on the temple that had been profaned by the godless; 3 to have mercy on the city that was being destroyed and about to be leveled to the ground; to hearken to the blood that cried out to him; 4 to remember also the lawless destruction of the innocent babies and the blasphemies committed against his name; and to show his hatred of evil.

5 As soon as Mac·ca·bē′us got his army organized, the Gentiles could not withstand him, for the wrath of the Lord had turned to mercy. 6 Coming without warning, he would set fire to towns and villages. He captured strategic positions and put to flight not a few of the enemy. 7 He found the nights most advantageous for such attacks. And talk of his valor spread everywhere.

8 When Philip saw that the man was gaining ground little by little, and that he was pushing ahead with more frequent successes, he wrote to Ptol′e·my, the governor of Coē·le·syr′i·a and Phoe·ni′ci·a, to come to the aid of the king's gov-

did you KNOW?
Nonviolent Resistance

The article "A Just War," 1 Macc 6.32, discusses just war as a response to the Seleucid persecution of the Jews. Second Maccabees, chapters 6–7, hints at another response—nonviolent resistance. Despite being ordered to forsake their faith and to adopt Greek customs, Jews resisted. We read of women continuing to have their baby boys circumcised (6.10), of secret gatherings to celebrate the Sabbath (6.11), and of martyrs refusing to eat unlawful meat (6.19; 7.1). Although the stories focus on the violent responses and tortures inflicted by the Greeks, they indicate that at least part of the population neither gave up their religious practices nor took up arms in violent conflict.

Christians have continued to develop the concept of nonviolent resistance—sometimes called pacifism. Nonviolent resistance is rooted in Jesus' teachings to turn the other cheek (Mt 5.39) and "love your enemies" (5.44). Nonviolent resistance is not passive. It confronts evil and refuses to cooperate with it without resorting to violence. Those who practice nonviolent resistance accept the suffering that results because they know God can bring good out of the suffering of the just. The Catholic church teaches that nonviolent resistance gives witness to God's redeeming love and that no person who objects to committing violence should be forced into military service.

Christian nonviolence is a challenge for everyone. How do you practice it in your relationships with others? In what situations, if any, do you think it is necessary to respond with violence? In what situations would you refuse to participate in military service?

ernment. 9 Then Ptol′e·my[n] promptly appointed Ni·cā′nor son of Pa·trō′clus, one of the king's chief[o] Friends, and sent him, in command of no fewer than twenty thousand Gentiles of all nations, to

---

[l] Gk slaves   [m] Cn: Gk fallen   [n] Gk he   [o] Gk one of the first

wipe out the whole race of Judea. He associated with him Gor′gi•as, a general and a man of experience in military service. ¹⁰ Nĭ•cā′nor determined to make up for the king the tribute due to the Romans, two thousand talents, by selling the captured Jews into slavery. ¹¹ So he immediately sent to the towns on the seacoast, inviting them to buy Jewish slaves and promising to hand over ninety slaves for a talent, not expecting the judgment from the Almighty that was about to overtake him.

Preparation for Battle
(1 Macc 3.38–53)

12 Word came to Judas concerning Nĭ•cā′nor′s invasion; and when he told his companions of the arrival of the army, ¹³ those who were cowardly and distrustful of God′s justice ran off and got away. ¹⁴ Others sold all their remaining property, and at the same time implored the Lord to rescue those who had been sold by the ungodly Nĭ•cā′nor before he ever met them, ¹⁵ if not for their own sake, then for the sake of the covenants made with their ancestors, and because he had called them by his holy and glorious name. ¹⁶ But Mac•ca•bē′us gathered his forces together, to the number six thousand, and exhorted them not to be frightened by the enemy and not to fear the great multitude of Gentiles who were wickedly coming against them, but to fight nobly, ¹⁷ keeping before their eyes the lawless outrage that the Gentilesᵖ had committed against the holy place, and the torture of the derided city, and besides, the overthrow of their ancestral way of life. ¹⁸ "For they trust to arms and acts of daring," he said, "but we trust in the Almighty God, who is able with a single nod to strike down those who are coming against us, and even, if necessary, the whole world."

19 Moreover, he told them of the occasions when help came to their ancestors; how, in the time of Sen•nach′e•rib, when one hundred eighty-five thousand perished, ²⁰ and the time of the battle against the Galatians that took place in Babylonia, when eight thousand Jews�q fought along with four thousand Mac•e•dō′ni•ans; yet when the Mac•e•dō′ni•ans were hard pressed, the eight thousand, by the help that came to them from heaven, destroyed one hundred twenty thousand Galatiansʳ and took a great amount of booty.

Judas Defeats Nicanor
(1 Macc 3.54—4.25)

21 With these words he filled them with courage and made them ready to die for their laws and their country; then he divided his army into four parts. ²² He appointed his brothers also, Simon and Joseph and Jonathan, each to command a division, putting fifteen hundred men under each.

23 Besides, he appointed El•e•ā′zar to read aloudˢ from the holy book, and gave the watchword, "The help of God"; then, leading the first division himself, he joined battle with Nĭ•cā′nor.

24 With the Almighty as their ally, they killed more than nine thousand of the enemy, and wounded and disabled most of Nĭ•cā′nor′s army, and forced them all to flee. ²⁵ They captured the money of those who had come to buy them as slaves. After pursuing them for some distance, they were obliged to return because the hour was late. ²⁶ It was the day before the sabbath, and for that reason they did not continue their pursuit. ²⁷ When they had collected the arms of the enemy and stripped them of their spoils, they kept the sabbath, giving great praise and thanks to the Lord, who had preserved them for that day and allotted it to them as the beginning of mercy. ²⁸ After the sabbath they gave some of the spoils to those who had been tortured and to the widows and orphans, and distributed the rest among themselves and their children. ²⁹ When they had done this, they made common supplication and implored the merciful Lord to be wholly reconciled with his servants.ᵗ

Judas Defeats Timothy and Bacchides

30 In encounters with the forces of Timothy and Bac′chi•dēs they killed more than twenty thousand of them and got possession of some exceedingly high strongholds, and they divided a very large amount of plunder, giving to those who had been tortured and to the orphans and widows, and also to the aged, shares equal to their own. ³¹ They collected the arms of the enemy,ᵘ and carefully stored all of them in strategic places; the rest of the spoils they carried to Jerusalem. ³² They killed the commander of Timothy′s forces, a most wicked man, and one who had greatly troubled the Jews. ³³ While they were celebrating the victory in the city of their ancestors, they burned those who had set fire to the sacred gates, Cal•lis′the•nēs and some others, who had fled into one little house; so these received the proper reward for their impiety.ˢ

34 The thrice-accursed Nĭ•cā′nor, who had brought the thousand merchants to buy the Jews, ³⁵ having been humbled with the help of the Lord by opponents whom he regarded as of the least account, took off his splendid uniform and made his way alone like a runaway slave across the country until he reached An′ti•och, having succeeded chiefly in the destruction of his own army! ³⁶ So he who had undertaken to secure tribute for the Romans by the capture of the people of Jerusalem proclaimed that the Jews had a Defender, and that therefore the

---

ᵖ Gk *they*   �q Gk lacks *Jews*   ʳ Gk lacks *Galatians*
ˢ Meaning of Gk uncertain   ᵗ Gk *slaves*   ᵘ Gk *their arms*

Jews were invulnerable, because they followed the laws ordained by him.

The Last Campaign of Antiochus Epiphanes
(1 Macc 6.1–7; 2 Macc 1.11–17)

9 About that time, as it happened, An•tī'o•chus had retreated in disorder from the region of Persia. 2 He had entered the city called Per•sep'o•lis and attempted to rob the temples and control the city. Therefore the people rushed to the rescue with arms, and An•tī'o•chus and his army were defeated,*v* with the result that An•tī'o•chus was put to flight by the inhabitants and beat a shameful retreat. 3 While he was in Ec•bat'a•na, news came to him of what had happened to Nī•cā'nor and the forces of Timothy. 4 Transported with rage, he conceived the idea of turning upon the Jews the injury done by those who had put him to flight; so he ordered his charioteer to drive without stopping until he completed the journey. But the judgment of heaven rode with him! For in his arrogance he said, "When I get there I will make Jerusalem a cemetery of Jews."

5 But the all-seeing Lord, the God of Israel, struck him with an incurable and invisible blow. As soon as he stopped speaking he was seized with a pain in his bowels, for which there was no relief, and with sharp internal tortures— 6 and that very justly, for he had tortured the bowels of others with many and strange inflictions. 7 Yet he did not in any way stop his insolence, but was even more filled with arrogance, breathing fire in his rage against the Jews, and giving orders to drive even faster. And so it came about that he fell out of his chariot as it was rushing along, and the fall was so hard as to torture every limb of his body. 8 Thus he who only a little while before had thought in his superhuman arrogance that he could command the waves of the sea, and had imagined that he could weigh the high mountains in a balance, was brought down to earth and carried in a litter, making the power of God manifest to all. 9 And so the ungodly man's body swarmed with worms, and while he was still living in anguish and pain, his flesh rotted away, and because of the stench the whole army felt revulsion at his decay. 10 Because of his intolerable stench no one was able to carry the man who a little while before had thought that he could touch the stars of heaven. 11 Then it was that, broken in spirit, he began to lose much of his arrogance and to come to his senses under the scourge of God, for he was tortured with pain every moment. 12 And when he could not endure his own stench, he uttered these words, "It is right to be subject to God; mortals should not think that they are equal to God."*w*

Antiochus Makes a Promise to God
(1 Macc 6.8–17)

13 Then the abominable fellow made a vow to the Lord, who would no longer have mercy on him, stating 14 that the holy city, which he was hurrying to level to the ground and to make a cemetery, he was now declaring to be free; 15 and the Jews, whom he had not considered worth burying but had planned to throw out with their children for the wild animals and for the birds to eat, he would make, all of them, equal to citizens of Athens; 16 and the holy sanctuary, which he had formerly plundered, he would adorn with the finest offerings; and all the holy vessels he would give back, many times over; and the expenses incurred for the sacrifices he would provide from his own revenues; 17 and in addition to all this he also would become a Jew and would visit every inhabited place to proclaim the power of God. 18 But when his sufferings did not in any way abate, for the judgment of God had justly come upon him, he gave up all hope for himself and wrote to the Jews the following letter, in the form of a supplication. This was its content:

Antiochus's Letter and Death

19 "To his worthy Jewish citizens, An•tī'o•chus their king and general sends hearty greetings and good wishes for their health and prosperity. 20 If you and your children are well and your affairs are as you wish, I am glad. As my hope is in heaven, 21 I remember with affection your esteem and goodwill. On my way back from the region of Persia I suffered an annoying illness, and I have deemed it necessary to take thought for the general security of all. 22 I do not despair of my condition, for I have good hope of recovering from my illness, 23 but I observed that my father, on the occasions when he made expeditions into the upper country, appointed his successor, 24 so that, if anything unexpected happened or any unwelcome news came, the people throughout the realm would not be troubled, for they would know to whom the government was left. 25 Moreover, I understand how the princes along the borders and the neighbors of my kingdom keep watching for opportunities and waiting to see what will happen. So I have appointed my son An•tī'o•chus to be king, whom I have often entrusted and commended to most of you when I hurried off to the upper provinces; and I have written to him what is written here. 26 I therefore urge and beg you to remember the public and private services rendered to you and to maintain your present goodwill, each of you, toward me and my son. 27 For I am sure

---

v Gk *they were defeated*   *w* Or *not think thoughts proper only to God* that he will follow my policy and will treat you with moderation and kindness."

28 So the murderer and blasphemer, having endured the more intense suffering, such as he had inflicted on others, came to the end of his life by a most pitiable fate, among the mountains in a strange land. 29 And Philip, one of his courtiers, took his body home; then, fearing the son of An·ti′o·chus, he withdrew to Ptol′e·my Phil·o·mē′tor in Egypt.

Purification of the Temple
(1 Macc 4.36–61)

10 Now Mac·ca·bē′us and his followers, the Lord leading them on, recovered the temple and the city; 2 they tore down the altars that had been built in the public square by the foreigners, and also destroyed the sacred precincts. 3 They purified the sanctuary, and made another altar of sacrifice; then, striking fire out of flint, they offered sacrifices, after a lapse of two years, and they offered incense and lighted lamps and set out the bread of the Presence. 4 When they had done this, they fell prostrate and implored the Lord that they might never again fall into such misfortunes, but that, if they should ever sin, they might be disciplined by him with forbearance and not be handed over to blasphemous and barbarous nations. 5 It happened that on the same day on which the sanctuary had been profaned by the foreigners, the purification of the sanctuary took place, that is, on the twenty-fifth day of the same month, which was Chis′lev. 6 They celebrated it for eight days with rejoicing, in the manner of the festival of booths, remembering how not long before, during the festival of booths, they had been wandering in the mountains and caves like wild animals. 7 Therefore, carrying ivy-wreathed wands and beautiful branches and also fronds of palm, they offered hymns of thanksgiving to him who had given success to the purifying of his own holy place. 8 They decreed by public edict, ratified by vote, that the whole nation of the Jews should observe these days every year.

9 Such then was the end of An·ti′o·chus, who was called E·piph′a·nēs.

Accession of Antiochus Eupator
(1 Macc 6.17)

10 Now we will tell what took place under An·ti′o·chus Eū′pa·tor, who was the son of that ungodly man, and will give a brief summary of the principal calamities of the wars. 11 This man, when he succeeded to the kingdom, appointed one Lys′i·as to have charge of the government and to be chief governor of Coē·le·syr′i·a and Phoe·ni′ci·a. 12 Ptol′e·my, who was called Mā′cron, took the lead in showing justice to the Jews because of the wrong

10.6

that had been done to them, and attempted to maintain peaceful relations with them. 13 As a result he was accused before Eū′pa·tor by the king's Friends. He heard himself called a traitor at every turn, because he had abandoned Cyprus, which Phil·o·mē′tor had entrusted to him, and had gone over to An·ti′o·chus E·piph′a·nēs. Unable to command the respect due his office,[x] he took poison and ended his life.

Campaign in Idumea
(1 Macc 5.1–8)

14 When Gor′gi·as became governor of the region, he maintained a force of mercenaries, and at every turn kept attacking the Jews. 15 Besides this, the Id·ū·mē′ans, who had control of important strongholds, were harassing the Jews; they received those who were banished from Jerusalem, and endeavored to keep up the war. 16 But Mac·ca·bē′us and his forces, after making solemn supplication and imploring God to fight on their side, rushed to the strongholds of the Id·ū·mē′ans. 17 Attacking them vigorously, they gained possession of the places, and beat off all who fought upon the wall, and slaughtered those whom they encountered, killing no fewer than twenty thousand.

18 When at least nine thousand took refuge in two very strong towers well equipped to withstand a siege, 19 Mac·ca·bē′us left Simon and Joseph, and also Zac·chae′us and his troops, a force sufficient to besiege them; and he himself set off for places where he was more urgently needed. 20 But those with Simon, who were money-hungry, were bribed by some of those who were in the towers, and on receiving seventy thousand drachmas let some of

---

x Cn: Meaning of Gk uncertain

them slip away. 21 When word of what had happened came to Mac·ca·bē′us, he gathered the leaders of the people, and accused these men of having sold their kindred for money by setting their enemies free to fight against them. 22 Then he killed these men who had turned traitor, and immediately captured the two towers. 23 Having success at arms in everything he undertook, he destroyed more than twenty thousand in the two strongholds.

Judas Defeats Timothy

24 Now Timothy, who had been defeated by the Jews before, gathered a tremendous force of mercenaries and collected the cavalry from Asia in no small number. He came on, intending to take Judea by storm. 25 As he drew near, Mac·ca·bē′us and his men sprinkled dust on their heads and girded their loins with sackcloth, in supplication to God. 26 Falling upon the steps before the altar, they implored him to be gracious to them and to be an enemy to their enemies and an adversary to their adversaries, as the law declares. 27 And rising from their prayer they took up their arms and advanced a considerable distance from the city; and when they came near the enemy they halted. 28 Just as dawn was breaking, the two armies joined battle, the one having as pledge of success and victory not only their valor but also their reliance on the Lord, while the other made rage their leader in the fight.

29 When the battle became fierce, there appeared to the enemy from heaven five resplendent men on horses with golden bridles, and they were leading the Jews. 30 Two of them took Mac·ca·bē′us between them, and shielding him with their own armor and weapons, they kept him from being wounded. They showered arrows and thunderbolts on the enemy, so that, confused and blinded, they were thrown into disorder and cut to pieces. 31 Twenty thousand five hundred were slaughtered, besides six hundred cavalry.

32 Timothy himself fled to a stronghold called Ga·zā′ra, especially well garrisoned, where Chaēr′e·as was commander. 33 Then Mac·ca·bē′us and his men were glad, and they besieged the fort for four days. 34 The men within, relying on the strength of the place, kept blaspheming terribly and uttering wicked words. 35 But at dawn of the fifth day, twenty young men in the army of Mac·ca·bē′us, fired with anger because of the blasphemies, bravely stormed the wall and with savage fury cut down everyone they met. 36 Others who came up in the same way wheeled around against the defenders and set fire to the towers; they kindled fires and burned the blasphemers alive. Others broke open the gates and let in the rest of the force, and they occupied the city. 37 They killed Timothy, who was

hiding in a cistern, and his brother Chaēr′e·as, and Ap·ol·loph′a·nēs. 38 When they had accomplished these things, with hymns and thanksgivings they blessed the Lord who shows great kindness to Israel and gives them the victory.

Lysias Besieges Beth-zur
(1 Macc 4.26–35)

11 Very soon after this, Lys′i·as, the king's guardian and kinsman, who was in charge of the government, being vexed at what had happened, 2 gathered about eighty thousand infantry and all his cavalry and came against the Jews. He intended to make the city a home for Greeks, 3 and to levy tribute on the temple as he did on the sacred places of the other nations, and to put up the high priesthood for sale every year. 4 He took no account whatever of the power of God, but was elated with his ten thousands of infantry, and his thousands of cavalry, and his eighty elephants. 5 Invading Judea, he approached Beth-zur, which was a fortified place about five stadia*y* from Jerusalem, and pressed it hard.

6 When Mac·ca·bē′us and his men got word that Lys′i·as*z* was besieging the strongholds, they and all the people, with lamentations and tears, prayed the Lord to send a good angel to save Israel. 7 Mac·ca·bē′us himself was the first to take up arms, and he urged the others to risk their lives with him to aid their kindred. Then they eagerly rushed off together. 8 And there, while they were still near Jerusalem, a horseman appeared at their head, clothed in white and brandishing weapons of gold. 9 And together they all praised the merciful God, and were strengthened in heart, ready to assail not only humans but the wildest animals or walls of iron. 10 They advanced in battle order, having their heavenly ally, for the Lord had mercy on them. 11 They hurled themselves like lions against the enemy, and laid low eleven thousand of them and sixteen hundred cavalry, and forced all the rest to flee. 12 Most of them got away stripped and wounded, and Lys′i·as himself escaped by disgraceful flight.

Lysias Makes Peace with the Jews
(1 Macc 6.55–63)

13 As he was not without intelligence, he pondered over the defeat that had befallen him, and realized that the Hebrews were invincible because the mighty God fought on their side. So he sent to them 14 and persuaded them to settle everything on just terms, promising that he would persuade the king, constraining him to be their friend.*y* 15 Mac·ca·bē′us, having regard for the common good, agreed to all that Lys′i·as urged. For the king

---

y Meaning of Gk uncertain   *z* Gk *he*

granted every request in behalf of the Jews which Mac·ca·bē'us delivered to Lys'i·as in writing.

16 The letter written to the Jews by Lys'i·as was to this effect:

"Lys'i·as to the people of the Jews, greetings. 17 John and Ab'sa·lom, who were sent by you, have delivered your signed communication and have asked about the matters indicated in it. 18 I have informed the king of everything that needed to be brought before him, and he has agreed to what was possible. 19 If you will maintain your goodwill toward the government, I will endeavor in the future to help promote your welfare. 20 And concerning such matters and their details, I have ordered these men and my representatives to confer with you. 21 Farewell. The one hundred forty-eighth year,[a] Dī·os·co·rin'thi·us twenty-fourth."

22 The king's letter ran thus:

"King An·tī'o·chus to his brother Lys'i·as, greetings. 23 Now that our father has gone on to the gods, we desire that the subjects of the kingdom be undisturbed in caring for their own affairs. 24 We have heard that the Jews do not consent to our father's change to Greek customs, but prefer their own way of living and ask that their own customs be allowed them. 25 Accordingly, since we choose that this nation also should be free from disturbance, our decision is that their temple be restored to them and that they shall live according to the customs of their ancestors. 26 You will do well, therefore, to send word to them and give them pledges of friendship, so that they may know our policy and be of good cheer and go on happily in the conduct of their own affairs."

27 To the nation the king's letter was as follows:

"King An·tī'o·chus to the senate of the Jews and to the other Jews, greetings. 28 If you are well, it is as we desire. We also are in good health. 29 Men·e·lā'us has informed us that you wish to return home and look after your own affairs. 30 Therefore those who go home by the thirtieth of Xan'thi·cus will have our pledge of friendship and full permission 31 for the Jews to enjoy their own food and laws, just as formerly, and none of them shall be molested in any way for what may have been done in ignorance. 32 And I have also sent Men·e·lā'us to encourage you. 33 Farewell. The one hundred forty-eighth year,[a] Xan'thi·cus fifteenth."

34 The Romans also sent them a letter, which read thus:

"Quin'tus Mem'mi·us and Titus Mā'ni·us, envoys of the Romans, to the people of the Jews, greetings. 35 With regard to what Lys'i·as the kinsman of the king has granted you, we also give consent. 36 But as to the matters that he decided are to be referred to the king, as soon as you have considered them, send some one promptly so that we may make pro-posals appropriate for you. For we are on our way to An'ti·och. 37 Therefore make haste and send messengers so that we may have your judgment. 38 Farewell. The one hundred forty-eighth year,[a] Xan'thi·cus fifteenth."

Incidents at Joppa and Jamnia

12 When this agreement had been reached, Lys'i·as returned to the king, and the Jews went about their farming.

2 But some of the governors in various places, Timothy and Ap·ol·lō'ni·us son of Gen·naē'us, as well as Hī·e·ron'y·mus and Dem'o·phon, and in addition to these Nī·cā'nor the governor of Cyprus, would not let them live quietly and in peace. 3 And the people of Jop'pa did so ungodly a deed as this: they invited the Jews who lived among them to embark, with their wives and children, on boats that they had provided, as though there were no ill will to the Jews;[b] 4 and this was done by public vote of the city. When they accepted, because they wished to live peaceably and suspected nothing, the people of Jop'pa[c] took them out to sea and drowned them, at least two hundred. 5 When Judas heard of the cruelty visited on his compatriots, he gave orders to his men 6 and, calling upon God, the righteous judge, attacked the murderers of his kindred. He set fire to the harbor by night, burned the boats, and massacred those who had taken refuge there. 7 Then, because the city's gates were closed, he withdrew, intending to come again and root out the whole community of Jop'pa. 8 But learning that the people in Jam'ni·a meant in the same way to wipe out the Jews who were living among them, 9 he attacked the Jam'nites by night and set fire to the harbor and the fleet, so that the glow of the light was seen in Jerusalem, thirty miles[d] distant.

The Campaign in Gilead
(1 Macc 5.9–36)

10 When they had gone more than a mile[e] from there, on their march against Timothy, at least five thousand A'rabs with five hundred cavalry attacked them. 11 After a hard fight, Judas and his companions, with God's help, were victorious. The defeated nomads begged Judas to grant them pledges of friendship, promising to give him livestock and to help his people[f] in all other ways. 12 Judas, realizing that they might indeed be useful in many ways, agreed to make peace with them; and after receiving his pledges they went back to their tents.

13 He also attacked a certain town that was

---

[a] 164 B.C.   [b] Gk to them   [c] Gk they   [d] Gk two hundred forty stadia   [e] Gk nine stadia   [f] Gk them

strongly fortified with earthworks*g* and walls, and inhabited by all sorts of Gentiles. Its name was Cas'pin. 14 Those who were within, relying on the strength of the walls and on their supply of provisions, behaved most insolently toward Judas and his men, railing at them and even blaspheming and saying unholy things. 15 But Judas and his men, calling upon the great Sovereign of the world, who without battering rams or engines of war overthrew Jericho in the days of Joshua, rushed furiously upon the walls. 16 They took the town by the will of God, and slaughtered untold numbers, so that the adjoining lake, a quarter of a mile*h* wide, appeared to be running over with blood.

Judas Defeats Timothy's Army
(1 Macc 5.37–44)

17 When they had gone ninety-five miles*i* from there, they came to Chār'ax, to the Jews who are called Toū•bi•ā'nī. 18 They did not find Timothy in that region, for he had by then left there without accomplishing anything, though in one place he had left a very strong garrison. 19 Dō•sith'e•us and Sō•sip'a•ter, who were captains under Mac•ca•bē'us, marched out and destroyed those whom Timothy had left in the stronghold, more than ten thousand men. 20 But Mac•ca•bē'us arranged his army in divisions, set men*j* in command of the divisions, and hurried after Timothy, who had with him one hundred twenty thousand infantry and two thousand five hundred cavalry. 21 When Timothy learned of the approach of Judas, he sent off the women and the children and also the baggage to a place called Car'na•im; for that place was hard to besiege and difficult of access because of the narrowness of all the approaches. 22 But when Judas's first division appeared, terror and fear came over the enemy at the manifestation to them of him who sees all things. In their flight they rushed headlong in every direction, so that often they were injured by their own men and pierced by the points of their own swords. 23 Judas pressed the pursuit with the utmost vigor, putting the sinners to the sword, and destroyed as many as thirty thousand.

24 Timothy himself fell into the hands of Dō•sith'e•us and Sō•sip'a•ter and their men. With great guile he begged them to let him go in safety, because he held the parents of most of them, and the brothers of some, to whom no consideration would be shown. 25 And when with many words he had confirmed his solemn promise to restore them unharmed, they let him go, for the sake of saving their kindred.

Judas Wins Other Victories
(1 Macc 5.45–54)

26 Then Judas*k* marched against Car'na•im and the temple of A•tar'ga•tis, and slaughtered twenty-

five thousand people. 27 After the rout and destruction of these, he marched also against E'phron, a fortified town where Lys'i•as lived with multitudes of people of all nationalities.*g* Stalwart young men took their stand before the walls and made a vigorous defense; and great stores of war engines and missiles were there. 28 But the Jews*l* called upon the Sovereign who with power shatters the might of his enemies, and they got the town into their hands, and killed as many as twenty-five thousand of those who were in it.

29 Setting out from there, they hastened to Scyth•op'o•lis, which is seventy-five miles*m* from Jerusalem. 30 But when the Jews who lived there bore witness to the goodwill that the people of Scyth•op'o•lis had shown them and their kind treatment of them in times of misfortune, 31 they thanked them and exhorted them to be well disposed to their race in the future also. Then they went up to Jerusalem, as the festival of weeks was close at hand.

Judas Defeats Gorgias

32 After the festival called Pentecost, they hurried against Gor'gi•as, the governor of Id•u•mē'a, 33 who came out with three thousand infantry and four hundred cavalry. 34 When they joined battle, it happened that a few of the Jews fell. 35 But a certain Dō•sith'e•us, one of Ba•cē'nor's men, who was on horseback and was a strong man, caught hold of Gor'gi•as, and grasping his cloak was dragging him off by main strength, wishing to take the accursed man alive, when one of the Thrā'ci•an cavalry bore down on him and cut off his arm; so Gor'gi•as escaped and reached Mar'i•sa.

36 As Es'dris and his men had been fighting for a long time and were weary, Judas called upon the Lord to show himself their ally and leader in the battle. 37 In the language of their ancestors he raised the battle cry, with hymns; then he charged against Gor'gi•as's troops when they were not expecting it, and put them to flight.

Prayers for Those Killed in Battle

38 Then Judas assembled his army and went to the city of A•dul'lam. As the seventh day was coming on, they purified themselves according to the custom, and kept the sabbath there.

39 On the next day, as had now become necessary, Judas and his men went to take up the bodies of the fallen and to bring them back to lie with their kindred in the sepulchres of their ancestors. 40 Then under the tunic of each one of the dead they found

---

g Meaning of Gk uncertain *h* Gk *two stadia* *i* Gk *seven hundred fifty stadia* *j* Gk *them* *k* Gk *he* *l* Gk *they* *m* Gk *six hundred stadia* sacred tokens of the idols of Jam′ni•a, which the law forbids the Jews to wear. And it became clear to all that this was the reason these men had fallen. [41] So they all blessed the ways of the Lord, the righteous judge, who reveals the things that are hidden; [42] and they turned to supplication, praying that the sin that had been committed might be wholly blotted out. The noble Judas exhorted the people to keep themselves free from sin, for they had seen with their own eyes what had happened as the result of the sin of those who had fallen. [43] He also took up a collection, man by man, to the amount of two thousand drachmas of silver, and sent it to Jerusalem to provide for a sin offering. In doing this he acted very well and honorably, taking account of the resurrection. [44] For if he were not expecting that those who had fallen would rise again, it would have been superfluous and foolish to pray for the dead. [45] But if he was looking to the splendid reward that is laid up for those who fall asleep in godliness, it was a holy and pious thought. Therefore he made atonement for the dead, so that they might be delivered from their sin.

Menelaus Is Put to Death

13 In the one hundred forty-ninth year[n] word came to Judas and his men that An•ti′o•chus Eū′pa•tor was coming with a great army against Judea, [2] and with him Lys′i•as, his guardian, who had charge of the government. Each of them had a Greek force of one hundred ten thousand infantry, five thousand three hundred cavalry, twenty-two elephants, and three hundred chariots armed with scythes.

[3] Men•e•lā′us also joined them and with utter hypocrisy urged An•ti′o•chus on, not for the sake of his country's welfare, but because he thought that he would be established in office. [4] But the King of kings aroused the anger of An•ti′o•chus against the scoundrel; and when Lys′i•as informed him that this man was to blame for all the trouble, he ordered them to take him to Be•roē′a and to put him to death by the method that is customary in that place. [5] For there is a tower there, fifty cubits high, full of ashes, and it has a rim running around it that on all sides inclines precipitously into the ashes. [6] There they all push to destruction anyone guilty of sacrilege or notorious for other crimes. [7] By such a fate it came about that Men•e•lā′us the lawbreaker died, without even burial in the earth. [8] And this was eminently just; because he had committed many sins against the altar whose fire and ashes were holy, he met his death in ashes.

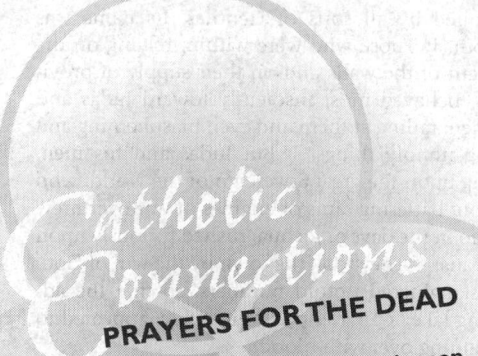

Catholic Connections

PRAYERS FOR THE DEAD

The story of Judas Maccabeus and his men praying for their fallen comrades provides an early witness to the practice of praying for the dead. Some Christian churches maintain that prayers for the dead have absolutely no effect. The Roman Catholic church, on the contrary, has always taught that prayers for the dead do have an effect and should be an important part of Christian practice.

This belief is related to the Catholic doctrine of Purgatory. The church teaches that when a person dies, there is a moment of judgment—particular judgment. While some people immediately enter heaven and others may be condemned to hell, some souls need a further cleansing of the effects of sin. They need to grow in holiness. This process is called Purgatory.

The members of the church, those already in heaven and those still on earth, pray and intercede for those who are in thi transitional state. The prayers of the faithfu call on God's mercy and grace to bring home to glory those who long for total union with God.

Did you know that the church prays fo the dead at every celebration of the Eu charist? Usually toward the end of the Eu charistic prayer, the priest offers a remembrance for the dead. One of the prayers reads, "Remember those who ha died in the peace of Christ and all the d whose faith is known to you alone" (Sac mentary, p. 560). Praying for the dead is one of the spiritual works of mercy. Try include prayers for the dead as part of daily spiritual practice.

▸ 2 Macc 12.38–45

A Battle Near the City of Modein
(1 Macc 6.43–46)

9 The king with barbarous arrogance was coming to show the Jews things far worse than those that had been done *o* in his father's time. 10 But when Judas heard of this, he ordered the people to call upon the Lord day and night, now if ever to help those who were on the point of being deprived of the law and their country and the holy temple, 11 and not to let the people who had just begun to revive fall into the hands of the blasphemous Gentiles. 12 When they had all joined in the same petition and had implored the merciful Lord with weeping and fasting and lying prostrate for three days without ceasing, Judas exhorted them and ordered them to stand ready.

13 After consulting privately with the elders, he determined to march out and decide the matter by the help of God before the king's army could enter Judea and get possession of the city. 14 So, committing the decision to the Creator of the world and exhorting his troops to fight bravely to the death for the laws, temple, city, country, and commonwealth, he pitched his camp near Mō′dēin. 15 He gave his troops the watchword, "God's victory," and with a picked force of the bravest young men, he attacked the king's pavilion at night and killed as many as two thousand men in the camp. He stabbed*p* the leading elephant and its rider. 16 In the end they filled the camp with terror and confusion and withdrew in triumph. 17 This happened, just as day was dawning, because the Lord's help protected him.

Antiochus Makes a Treaty with the Jews
(1 Macc 6.48–63)

18 The king, having had a taste of the daring of the Jews, tried strategy in attacking their positions. 19 He advanced against Beth-zur, a strong fortress of the Jews, was turned back, attacked again,*q* and was defeated. 20 Judas sent in to the garrison whatever was necessary. 21 But Rhod′o•cus, a man from the ranks of the Jews, gave secret information to the enemy; he was sought for, caught, and put in prison. 22 The king negotiated a second time with the people in Beth-zur, gave pledges, received theirs, withdrew, attacked Judas and his men, was defeated; 23 he got word that Philip, who had been left in charge of the government, had revolted in An′ti•och; he was dismayed, called in the Jews, yielded and swore to observe all their rights, settled with them and offered sacrifice, honored the sanctuary and showed generosity to the holy place. 24 He received Mac•ca•bē′us, left Heg•e•mō′ni•dēs as governor from Ptol•e•mā′is to Gē′rar, 25 and went to Ptol•e•mā′is. The people of Ptol•e•mā′is were indignant over the treaty; in fact they were so angry that

they wanted to annul its terms.*p* 26 Lys′i•as took the public platform, made the best possible defense, convinced them, appeased them, gained their goodwill, and set out for An′ti•och. This is how the king's attack and withdrawal turned out.

Alcimus Speaks against Judas
(1 Macc 7.1–25)

14 Three years later, word came to Judas and his men that De•mē′tri•us son of Se•leū′cus had sailed into the harbor of Trip′o•lis with a strong army and a fleet, 2 and had taken possession of the country, having made away with An•tī′o•chus and his guardian Lys′i•as.

3 Now a certain Al′ci•mus, who had formerly been high priest but had willfully defiled himself in the times of separation,*r* realized that there was no way for him to be safe or to have access again to the holy altar, 4 and went to King De•mē′tri•us in about the one hundred fifty-first year,*s* presenting to him a crown of gold and a palm, and besides these some of the customary olive branches from the temple. During that day he kept quiet. 5 But he found an opportunity that furthered his mad purpose when he was invited by De•mē′tri•us to a meeting of the council and was asked about the attitude and intentions of the Jews. He answered:

6 "Those of the Jews who are called Has•i•dē′ans, whose leader is Judas Mac•ca•bē′us, are keeping up war and stirring up sedition, and will not let the kingdom attain tranquility. 7 Therefore I have laid aside my ancestral glory—I mean the high priesthood—and have now come here, 8 first because I am genuinely concerned for the interests of the king, and second because I have regard also for my compatriots. For through the folly of those whom I have mentioned our whole nation is now in no small misfortune. 9 Since you are acquainted, O king, with the details of this matter, may it please you to take thought for our country and our hard-pressed nation with the gracious kindness that you show to all. 10 For as long as Judas lives, it is impossible for the government to find peace." 11 When he had said this, the rest of the king's Friends,*t* who were hostile to Judas, quickly inflamed De•mē′tri•us still more. 12 He immediately chose Nī•cā′nor, who had been in command of the elephants, appointed him governor of Judea, and sent him off 13 with orders to kill Judas and scatter his troops, and to install Al′ci•mus as high priest of the great*u* temple. 14 And the Gentiles throughout Judea, who had fled before*p* Judas, flocked to join

---

o Or *the worst of the things that had been done*   *p* Meaning of Gk uncertain   *q* Or *faltered*   *r* Other ancient authorities read *of mixing*   *s* 161 B.C.   *t* Gk *of the Friends*   *u* Gk *greatest*

Nĭ•cā'nor, thinking that the misfortunes and calamities of the Jews would mean prosperity for themselves.

Nicanor Makes Friends with Judas
(1 Macc 7.26–28)

15 When the Jews[v] heard of Nĭ•cā'nor's coming and the gathering of the Gentiles, they sprinkled dust on their heads and prayed to him who established his own people forever and always upholds his own heritage by manifesting himself. 16 At the command of the leader, they[w] set out from there immediately and engaged them in battle at a village called Des'sau.[x] 17 Simon, the brother of Judas, had encountered Nĭ•cā'nor, but had been temporarily[y] checked because of the sudden consternation created by the enemy.

18 Nevertheless Nĭ•cā'nor, hearing of the valor of Judas and his troops and their courage in battle for their country, shrank from deciding the issue by bloodshed. 19 Therefore he sent Pos•i•dō'ni•us, Thē•od'o•tus, and Mat•ta•thī'as to give and receive pledges of friendship. 20 When the terms had been fully considered, and the leader had informed the people, and it had appeared that they were of one mind, they agreed to the covenant. 21 The leaders[z] set a day on which to meet by themselves. A chariot came forward from each army; seats of honor were set in place; 22 Judas posted armed men in readiness at key places to prevent sudden treachery on the part of the enemy; so they duly held the consultation.

23 Nĭ•cā'nor stayed on in Jerusalem and did nothing out of the way, but dismissed the flocks of people that had gathered. 24 And he kept Judas always in his presence; he was warmly attached to the man. 25 He urged him to marry and have children; so Judas[w] married, settled down, and shared the common life.

Nicanor Turns against Judas
(1 Macc 7.29–30)

26 But when Al'ci•mus noticed their goodwill for one another, he took the covenant that had been made and went to De•mē'tri•us. He told him that Nĭ•cā'nor was disloyal to the government, since he had appointed that conspirator against the kingdom, Judas, to be his successor. 27 The king became excited and, provoked by the false accusations of that depraved man, wrote to Nĭ•cā'nor, stating that he was displeased with the covenant and commanding him to send Mac•ca•bē'us to An'ti•och as a prisoner without delay.

28 When this message came to Nĭ•cā'nor, he was troubled and grieved that he had to annul their agreement when the man had done no wrong. 29 Since it was not possible to oppose the king, he watched for an opportunity to accomplish this by a stratagem. 30 But Mac•ca•bēus, noticing that Nĭ•cā'nor was more austere in his dealings with him and was meeting him more rudely than had been his custom, concluded that this austerity did not spring from the best motives. So he gathered not a few of his men, and went into hiding from Nĭ•cā'nor. 31 When the latter became aware that he had been cleverly outwitted by the man, he went to the great[a] and holy temple while the priests were offering the customary sacrifices, and commanded them to hand the man over. 32 When they declared on oath that they did not know where the man was whom he wanted, 33 he stretched out his right hand toward the sanctuary, and swore this oath: "If you do not hand Judas over to me as a prisoner, I will level this shrine of God to the ground and tear down the altar, and build here a splendid temple to Dī•o•nỹ'sus."

34 Having said this, he went away. Then the priests stretched out their hands toward heaven and called upon the constant Defender of our nation, in these words: 35 "O Lord of all, though you have need of nothing, you were pleased that there should be a temple for your habitation among us; 36 so now, O holy One, Lord of all holiness, keep undefiled forever this house that has been so recently purified."

Razis Dies for His Country

37 A certain Rā'zis, one of the elders of Jerusalem, was denounced to Nĭ•cā'nor as a man who loved his compatriots and was very well thought of and for his goodwill was called father of the Jews. 38 In former times, when there was no mingling with the Gentiles, he had been accused of Jū'da•ism, and he had most zealously risked body and life for Jū'da•ism. 39 Nĭ•cā'nor, wishing to exhibit the enmity that he had for the Jews, sent more than five hundred soldiers to arrest him; 40 for he thought that by arresting[x] him he would do them an injury. 41 When the troops were about to capture the tower and were forcing the door of the courtyard, they ordered that fire be brought and the doors burned. Being surrounded, Rā'zis[w] fell upon his own sword, 42 preferring to die nobly rather than to fall into the hands of sinners and suffer outrages unworthy of his noble birth. 43 But in the heat of the struggle he did not hit exactly, and the crowd was now rushing in through the doors. He courageously ran up on the wall, and bravely threw himself down into the crowd. 44 But as they quickly drew back, a space opened and he fell in the middle of the empty space. 45 Still alive and aflame

---

v Gk *they*   *w* Gk *he*   *x* Meaning of Gk uncertain   *y* Other ancient authorities read *slowly*   *z* Gk *They*   *a* Gk *greatest* with anger, he rose, and though his blood gushed forth and his wounds were severe he ran through the crowd; and standing upon a steep rock, 46 with his blood now completely drained from him, he tore out his entrails, took them in both hands and hurled them at the crowd, calling upon the Lord of life and spirit to give them back to him again. This was the manner of his death.

Nicanor's Arrogance

15 When Nī•cā′nor heard that Judas and his troops were in the region of Sa•mār′i•a, he made plans to attack them with complete safety on the day of rest. 2 When the Jews who were compelled to follow him said, "Do not destroy so savagely and barbarously, but show respect for the day that he who sees all things has honored and hallowed above other days," 3 the thrice-accursed wretch asked if there were a sovereign in heaven who had commanded the keeping of the sabbath day. 4 When they declared, "It is the living Lord himself, the Sovereign in heaven, who ordered us to observe the seventh day," 5 he replied, "But I am a sovereign also, on earth, and I command you to take up arms and finish the king's business." Nevertheless, he did not succeed in carrying out his abominable design.

Judas Prepares the Jews for Battle

6 This Nī•cā′nor in his utter boastfulness and arrogance had determined to erect a public monument of victory over Judas and his forces. 7 But Mac•ca•bē′us did not cease to trust with all confidence that he would get help from the Lord. 8 He exhorted his troops not to fear the attack of the Gentiles, but to keep in mind the former times when help had come to them from heaven, and so to look for the victory that the Almighty would give them. 9 Encouraging them from the law and the prophets, and reminding them also of the struggles they had won, he made them the more eager. 10 When he had aroused their courage, he issued his orders, at the same time pointing out the perfidy of the Gentiles and their violation of oaths. 11 He armed each of them not so much with confidence in shields and spears as with the inspiration of brave words, and he cheered them all by relating a dream, a sort of vision,*b* which was worthy of belief.

12 What he saw was this: Ō•nī′as, who had been high priest, a noble and good man, of modest bearing and gentle manner, one who spoke fittingly and had been trained from childhood in all that belongs to excellence, was praying with outstretched hands for the whole body of the Jews. 13 Then in the same fashion another appeared, distinguished by his gray hair and dignity, and of marvelous majesty and authority. 14 And Ō•nī′as spoke,

saying, "This is a man who loves the family of Israel and prays much for the people and the holy city—Jer•e•mī′ah, the prophet of God." 15 Jer•e•mī′ah stretched out his right hand and gave to Judas a golden sword, and as he gave it he addressed him thus: 16 "Take this holy sword, a gift from God, with which you will strike down your adversaries."

17 Encouraged by the words of Judas, so noble and so effective in arousing valor and awaking courage in the souls of the young, they determined not to carry on a campaign*c* but to attack bravely, and to decide the matter by fighting hand to hand with all courage, because the city and the sanctuary and the temple were in danger. 18 Their concern for wives and children, and also for brothers and sisters*d* and relatives, lay upon them less heavily; their greatest and first fear was for the consecrated sanctuary. 19 And those who had to remain in the city were in no little distress, being anxious over the encounter in the open country.

The Defeat and Death of Nicanor
(1 Macc 7.39–50)

20 When all were now looking forward to the coming issue, and the enemy was already close at hand with their army drawn up for battle, the elephants*e* strategically stationed and the cavalry deployed on the flanks, 21 Mac•ca•bē′us, observing the masses that were in front of him and the varied supply of arms and the savagery of the elephants, stretched out his hands toward heaven and called upon the Lord who works wonders; for he knew that it is not by arms, but as the Lord*f* decides, that he gains the victory for those who deserve it. 22 He called upon him in these words: "O Lord, you sent your angel in the time of King Hez•e•kī′ah of Judea, and he killed fully one hundred eighty-five thousand in the camp of Sen•nach′e•rib. 23 So now, O Sovereign of the heavens, send a good angel to spread terror and trembling before us. 24 By the might of your arm may these blasphemers who come against your holy people be struck down." With these words he ended his prayer.

25 Nī•cā′nor and his troops advanced with trumpets and battle songs, 26 but Judas and his troops met the enemy in battle with invocations to God and prayers. 27 So, fighting with their hands and praying to God in their hearts, they laid low at least thirty-five thousand, and were greatly gladdened by God's manifestation.

28 When the action was over and they were returning with joy, they recognized Nī•cā′nor, lying dead, in full armor. 29 Then there was shouting and tumult, and they blessed the Sovereign Lord in the

---

b Meaning of Gk uncertain   *c* Or *to remain in camp*
d Gk *for brothers*   *e* Gk *animals*   *f* Gk *he*

language of their ancestors. ³⁰ Then the man who was ever in body and soul the defender of his people, the man who maintained his youthful goodwill toward his compatriots, ordered them to cut off Nĭ•cā′nor's head and arm and carry them to Jerusalem. ³¹ When he arrived there and had called his compatriots together and stationed the priests before the altar, he sent for those who were in the citadel. ³² He showed them the vile Nĭ•cā′nor's head and that profane man's arm, which had been boastfully stretched out against the holy house of the Almighty. ³³ He cut out the tongue of the ungodly Nĭ•cā′nor and said that he would feed it piecemeal to the birds and would hang up these rewards of his folly opposite the sanctuary. ³⁴ And they all, looking to heaven, blessed the Lord who had manifested himself, saying, "Blessed is he who has kept his own place undefiled!" ³⁵ Judas[g] hung Nĭ•cā′nor's head from the citadel, a clear and conspicuous sign to everyone of the help of the Lord. ³⁶ And they all decreed by public vote never to let this day go unobserved, but to celebrate the thirteenth day of the twelfth month—which is called Ā′dar in the Ar•a•mā′ic language—the day before Mor′de•cai's day.

_g Gk He_

Introducing ▶ JEWISH SECTS

In the last two centuries before Christ, a diversity of ways of being Jewish emerged. Different groups arose emphasizing different ways of remaining faithful to their Jewish heritage. These groups, or factions, within a religion are sometimes called sects. Primarily three sects emerged within Judaism.

Pharisees. The Pharisees were descendants of the Hasidim, Jews devoted to a strict observance of the Law who opposed King Antiochus IV Epiphanes' attempts to destroy the Jewish religion. Pharisee means "separated" and probably reflects the Pharisees' rigorous observance of the Law. They were often greatly respected. In the New Testament, Jesus argues with some Pharisees but is also a guest of others. Saint Paul was a Pharisee. Not surprisingly, some of the Pharisees' teachings were similar to those of the early Christians.

Sadducees. The Sadducees were a conservative Jewish sect that emerged in the first century B.C. and lasted only to around A.D 70. The Sadducees were wealthy and politically influential landowners, and some of them had important roles in the Temple. They emphasized the necessity of worshiping at the Temple in Jerusalem. Unlike the Pharisees, they did not believe in the resurrection of the body.

Essenes. The Essenes, like the Pharisees, seem to have descended from the Hasidim. They existed in the first century B.C. and disappeared after A.D. 70. The name Essene can mean "healer" or "pious." The Essenes did not believe in the necessity of Temple sacrifice and often lived together in isolated communities where they practiced a simple lifestyle. Some of them were connected with the desert monastery at Qumran and were responsible for writing the Dead Sea Scrolls. John the Baptist's preaching and some of Jesus' teaching in the Gospels closely reflected the writings and teachings of the Essenes.

37 This, then, is how matters turned out with Ni·ca′nor, and from that time the city has been in the possession of the Hebrews. So I will here end my story.

The Compiler's Epilogue

38 If it is well told and to the point, that is what I myself desired; if it is poorly done and mediocre, that was the best I could do. 39 For just as it is harmful to drink wine alone, or, again, to drink water alone, while wine mixed with water is sweet and delicious and enhances one's enjoyment, so also the style of the story delights the ears of those who read the work. And here will be the end.

Introduction to the

Wisdom

and *Poetry Books*

The LORD is my shepherd, I shall not want.
(Ps 23.1)

A soft answer turns away wrath,
but a harsh word stirs up anger.
(Prov 15.1)

For everything there is a season, and a time
for every matter under heaven.
(Eccl 3.1)

The books these words are taken from, the wisdom and poetry books of the Old Testament, are among the most quoted books of the Bible. The distilled wisdom they contain and the beauty of the language they use have universal appeal. Across cultures and across time, these books touch thoughtful minds and inquiring hearts.

In-depth

THIS SECTION OF THE BIBLE CONTAINS A VARIETY of books. The Book of Psalms consists of religious hymns, many written for use in Jewish worship. The Song of Solomon is a love poem. The Book of Job is a debate on why innocent people suffer. The Wisdom of Solomon, Proverbs, and Sirach give advice on moral and virtuous living. And Ecclesiastes is a sort of journal on the purpose of human life. The most obvious common element among these books is the use of poetic language to convey their message. Not that these are the only books of the Old Testament that use poetry. But they make such extensive application of it that a little background on the nature of Hebrew poetry is helpful for reading them.

The most important feature of Hebrew poetry is parallelism. Parallelism involves the repetition of words or ideas in successive lines of a verse. Sometimes, the second line contrasts with the first:

> For the LORD watches over the way of the
> righteous,
> but the way of the wicked will perish.
> (Ps 1.6)

Other times, the second line completes the thought of the first:

> The LORD looks down from heaven on humankind
> to see if there are any who are wise.
>
> (14.2)

Still other times, the second line seems to restate the first line more forcefully:

> For I know my transgressions,
> and my sin is ever before me.
>
> (51.3)

In its many forms, parallelism—not a rhythmic pattern or rhyming words—is the organizing principle of Hebrew poetry.

Hebrew poetry also uses symbolic language that is characteristic of poetry in any language. This includes metaphors ("The LORD is my rock" [18.2]) and similes ("As a deer longs for flowing streams, / so my soul longs for you, O God" [42.1]). To appreciate the beauty of Old Testament poetry and feel its impact, one must be willing to wrestle with symbolic ways of interpreting words and phrases.

Whereas the other books of the Old Testament emphasize ancient Israel's distinctive religious values, the wisdom and poetry books focus on its unique view of wisdom. Wisdom literature is something the ancient Israelites shared with neighboring cultures. The Egyptians, Sumerians, and Babylonians all had literature that offered practical, time-tested advice for people seeking trustworthy guidance. For the Israelites, however, true wisdom was more than mere common sense: it was a gift from God given to those who sought it. Some passages of the wisdom literature even describe wisdom as a divine person, a beautiful, eternal, holy, and feminine depiction of God (see Wis 7.22—8.8 and Sirach, chapter 1).

In general, the wisdom writings have these characteristics:
- few references to the Law or the Covenant
- a minimal interest in Israel's history
- a search for harmony and the meaning of life
- a willingness to explore the difficult mysteries of life, such as suffering and death
- a commitment to discovering the moral lessons of everyday experiences
- a fundamental belief that good and wise living is rewarded whereas evil and foolish ways lead to ruin

The poetry and wisdom books of the Old Testament had an enormous influence on the writers of the New Testament and continue to be popular. Their poetic structure, which often makes them difficult to comprehend, also gives them a richness and depth that centuries of reading and rereading have not exhausted. Each time you read from these books, you will discover new treasures to enrich your life.

Other Background

- **The Book of Psalms is quoted more often in the New Testament than is any other Old Testament book. Also, it is used extensively in the church's liturgy.**

- **Job and Ecclesiastes posed serious challenges to the traditional understanding of Israelite faith. For help in understanding why, see the introductions to these books.**

- **Solomon's reputation for wisdom was so great that he was indicated as the author of four books actually written by others: Proverbs and Ecclesiastes, and two books that carry his name, the Song of Solomon and the Wisdom of Solomon.**

- **The Wisdom of Solomon and Sirach are not found in all translations of the Old Testament (see "The Case of the Missing Books," Tob 1.16).**

You've seen the picture—a mother holding her poor, dead child, against the background of a country ravaged by drought. Or perhaps you have watched someone you love suffer from a devastating illness. And you found yourself wondering, Why, God? This is the basic question struggled with in the Book of Job. How can God allow innocent people to suffer?

In-depth

At the time Job was written, most Israelites believed that if they obeyed God's commandments, God would bless them and protect them. The Israelites also believed that if people were suffering or poor, God was punishing them for some sin they or their parents had committed, even if they did not know what that sin was. The Israelites' thinking was extremely logical—because God is all-powerful and completely just, God will not allow people or communities to suffer unless they have sinned in some way.

The Book of Job challenges that way of thinking. Job is a good man who has received great wealth and a wonderful family from God. In fact, Job's final defense in chapter 31 is one of the finest summaries of the Old Testament vision of a righteous person. The Book of Job begins with God allowing Job's wealth and children and health to be taken from him. Three friends come to mourn with Job. In a series of lengthy debates, they point out that his misfortunes must be the result of some sin or wrong he has committed. Job maintains his innocence, sometimes forcefully, and demands another explanation from God. Finally, God appears to Job and overwhelms him with questions about the nature of the universe. Job realizes that God is beyond human knowledge and that some mysteries—including suffering—can never be completely understood; they can only be accepted.

The Book of Job does not give the final answer about why bad things happen to good people. But it does make it clear that good people do suffer and their suffering is not a punishment sent by God. And Job is a reminder to the Israelites and to us that God's purposes are too far beyond human understanding for anyone to claim to know everything there is to know about God.

At a Glance

- **Chapters 1–2.** God and an adversary (Satan) agree to test Job.

- **Chapters 3–37.** Job and his friends debate the cause of his suffering.

- **38.1—42.6.** God responds to Job.

- **42.7–17.** The story has a happy ending.

Quick Facts

Author
unknown, writing between the seventh and fifth centuries B.C.

Theme
Why do good people suffer?

Of Note
Job is a story within a story: chapters 1–2 and 42.7–17 constitute a folktale; set within that tale, in 3.1—42.6, is a poetic debate about the cause of suffering.

The Book of Job

Job

1.20

Job and His Family

1 There was once a man in the land of Uz whose name was Jōb. That man was blameless and upright, one who feared God and turned away from evil. 2 There were born to him seven sons and three daughters. 3 He had seven thousand sheep, three thousand camels, five hundred yoke of oxen, five hundred donkeys, and very many servants; so that this man was the greatest of all the people of the east. 4 His sons used to go and hold feasts in one another's houses in turn; and they would send and invite their three sisters to eat and drink with them. 5 And when the feast days had run their course, Jōb would send and sanctify them, and he would rise early in the morning and offer burnt offerings according to the number of them all; for Jōb said, "It may be that my children have sinned, and cursed God in their hearts." This is what Jōb always did.

Attack on Job's Character

6 One day the heavenly beings[a] came to present themselves before the LORD, and Satan[b] also came among them. 7 The LORD said to Satan,[b] "Where have you come from?" Satan[b] answered the LORD, "From going to and fro on the earth, and from walking up and down on it." 8 The LORD said to Satan,[b] "Have you considered my servant Jōb? There is no one like him on the earth, a blameless and upright man who fears God and turns away from evil." 9 Then Satan[b] answered the LORD, "Does Jōb fear God for nothing? 10 Have you not put a fence

around him and his house and all that he has, on every side? You have blessed the work of his hands, and his possessions have increased in the land. 11 But stretch out your hand now, and touch all that he has, and he will curse you to your face." 12 The LORD said to Satan,[b] "Very well, all that he has is in your power; only do not stretch out your hand against him!" So Satan[b] went out from the presence of the LORD.

Job Loses Property and Children

13 One day when his sons and daughters were eating and drinking wine in the eldest brother's house, 14 a messenger came to Jōb and said, "The oxen were plowing and the donkeys were feeding beside them, 15 and the Sa•bē'ans fell on them and carried them off, and killed the servants with the edge of the sword; I alone have escaped to tell you." 16 While he was still speaking, another came and said, "The fire of God fell from heaven and burned up the sheep and the servants, and consumed them; I alone have escaped to tell you." 17 While he was still speaking, another came and said, "The Chal•dē'ans formed three columns, made a raid on the camels and carried them off, and killed the servants with the edge of the sword; I alone have escaped to tell you." 18 While he was still speaking, another came and said, "Your sons and daughters were eating and drinking wine in their eldest brother's house, 19 and suddenly a great wind came

---

a Heb *sons of God*   *b* Or *the Accuser*; Heb *ha-satan*

In Good Times and Bad

Have you ever felt so angry at the loss of something that you cursed and swore at God? Have you ever felt like just giving up on God because of your loss? In Job 1.13–19, a man named Job experiences an unimaginable loss. His children, his home, and his property are all destroyed at the same time. Job responds with great anger and great pain, but instead of cursing or blaming God, he blesses (praises) God (verse 21).

Job never loses his faith in God, even when he loses so much else. Through most of the rest of this book, he struggles to understand why this has happened to him. Job is an important model. When faced with great suffering, he does not lose his belief in the goodness of God, nor does he let his friends talk him into false confessions of sinfulness. Like Job, we must not fall into the trap of thinking that when bad things happen, God is punishing us.

▶ Job 1.13–21

---

across the desert, struck the four corners of the house, and it fell on the young people, and they are dead; I alone have escaped to tell you."

20 Then Jōb arose, tore his robe, shaved his head, and fell on the ground and worshiped. 21 He said, "Naked I came from my mother's womb, and naked shall I return there; the LORD gave, and the LORD has taken away; blessed be the name of the LORD."

22 In all this Jōb did not sin or charge God with wrongdoing.

Attack on Job's Health

2 One day the heavenly beings[c] came to present themselves before the LORD, and Satan[d] also came among them to present himself before the LORD. 2 The LORD said to Satan,[d] "Where have you come from?" Satan[e] answered the LORD, "From going to and fro on the earth, and from walking up and down on it." 3 The LORD said to Satan,[d] "Have

---

c Heb sons of God   d Or the Accuser; Heb ha-satan   e Or The Accuser; Heb ha-satan

---

Introducing ▶ SATAN

Does the word Satan conjure for you an image of a demon with horns and a tail, torturing people in the fires of hell? or perhaps an evil presence wandering the world looking for souls to corrupt? Does it surprise you that Job 1.6 and Zech 3.1 present Satan as actually working for God? In fact, the word Satan is more of a job description than a name; it means "adversary." In the Old Testament, Satan is depicted as a member of God's court whose responsibility it was to accuse or test humans before God. (Although, contrary to popular belief, the snake in the Garden of Eden is never identified as Satan in the Bible!)

It is only much later that Satan is seen as the enemy of God and the controller of the forces of evil. The notion of Satan as an evildoer seems to have been borrowed from a similar figure in Persian religion and developed in Israel as time passed. By the New Testament period, Satan is identified as a powerful agent of evil fighting against God (1 Thess 2.18), is instrumental in Jesus' death (Lk 22.3), tempts people to sin (1 Cor 7.5), and is called the devil (Rev 12.9). The good news is that in the death and Resurrection of Jesus, God overcomes the evil associated with Satan, both now and forever.

Job 1.6—2.10

you considered my servant Jōb? There is no one like him on the earth, a blameless and upright man who fears God and turns away from evil. He still persists in his integrity, although you incited me against him, to destroy him for no reason." 4 Then Satanᶠ answered the LORD, "Skin for skin! All that people have they will give to save their lives.ᵍ 5 But stretch out your hand now and touch his bone and his flesh, and he will curse you to your face." 6 The LORD said to Satan,ᶠ "Very well, he is in your power; only spare his life."

7 So Satanᶠ went out from the presence of the LORD, and inflicted loathsome sores on Jōb from the sole of his foot to the crown of his head. 8 Jōbʰ took a potsherd with which to scrape himself, and sat among the ashes.

9 Then his wife said to him, "Do you still persist in your integrity? Curseⁱ God, and die." 10 But he said to her, "You speak as any foolish woman would speak. Shall we receive the good at the hand of God, and not receive the bad?" In all this Jōb did not sin with his lips.

Job's Three Friends

11 Now when Jōb's three friends heard of all these troubles that had come upon him, each of them set out from his home—E•li′phaz the Tē′man•īte, Bil′dad the Shū′hīte, and Zō′phar the Nā′a•ma•thīte. They met together to go and console and comfort him. 12 When they saw him from a distance, they did not recognize him, and they raised their voices and wept aloud; they tore their robes and threw dust in the air upon their heads. 13 They sat with him on the ground seven days and seven nights, and no one spoke a word to him, for they saw that his suffering was very great.

Job Curses the Day He Was Born

3 After this Jōb opened his mouth and cursed the day of his birth. 2 Jōb said:
3 "Let the day perish in which I was born,
   and the night that said,
   'A man-child is conceived.'
4 Let that day be darkness!
   May God above not seek it,
   or light shine on it.
5 Let gloom and deep darkness claim it.
   Let clouds settle upon it;
   let the blackness of the day terrify it.
6 That night—let thick darkness seize it!
   let it not rejoice among the days of the year;
   let it not come into the number of the
       months.
7 Yes, let that night be barren;
   let no joyful cry be heardʲ in it.
8 Let those curse it who curse the Sea,ᵏ
   those who are skilled to rouse up
       Le•vī′a•than.
9 Let the stars of its dawn be dark;
   let it hope for light, but have none;
   may it not see the eyelids of the morning—
10 because it did not shut the doors of my
       mother's womb,
   and hide trouble from my eyes.

11 "Why did I not die at birth,
   come forth from the womb and expire?
12 Why were there knees to receive me,

ᶠ Or the Accuser; Heb ha-satan   ᵍ Or All that the man has he will give for his life   ʰ Heb He   ⁱ Heb Bless   ʲ Heb come   ᵏ Cn: Heb day

Being There

LIVE IT!

What is the best way to respond to the suffering of another?

In Job 2.11–13, Job was visited by three friends. They did not recognize him at first because of his great suffering; then they cried. And then something remarkable happened: "They sat down upon the ground with him seven days and seven nights, but none of them spoke a word to him; for they saw how great was his suffering."

We must give Job's friends credit for being there, for spending time with him, and for letting him know they cared, especially when they first arrived. That is all we have to do for a friend who is hurting—offer a hug and a simple "I'm sorry," and then just stay around. Though this sounds easy, it can be very hard; we can feel so helpless. We need to keep in mind that what matters most is that we are there. That is what will be remembered.

If you know people are suffering or grieving, don't avoid them. Go up to them, let them know how you feel, and just be there for them. That is all. And that is a lot.

▶ Job 2.11–13

J
O
B

or breasts for me to suck?

13 Now I would be lying down and quiet;
  I would be asleep; then I would be at rest

14 with kings and counselors of the earth
  who rebuild ruins for themselves,

15 or with princes who have gold,
  who fill their houses with silver.

16 Or why was I not buried like a stillborn child,
  like an infant that never sees the light?

17 There the wicked cease from troubling,
  and there the weary are at rest.

18 There the prisoners are at ease together;
  they do not hear the voice of the
    taskmaster.

19 The small and the great are there,
  and the slaves are free from their masters.

20 "Why is light given to one in misery,
  and life to the bitter in soul,

21 who long for death, but it does not come,
  and dig for it more than for hidden
    treasures;

22 who rejoice exceedingly,
  and are glad when they find the grave?

23 Why is light given to one who cannot see the way,
  whom God has fenced in?

24 For my sighing comes like^l my bread,
  and my groanings are poured out like water.

25 Truly the thing that I fear comes upon me,
  and what I dread befalls me.

26 I am not at ease, nor am I quiet;
  I have no rest; but trouble comes."

Eliphaz Speaks: Job Has Sinned

4 Then E·li′phaz the Tē′man·ite answered:
2 "If one ventures a word with you, will you
    be offended?
  But who can keep from speaking?

3 See, you have instructed many;
  you have strengthened the weak hands.

4 Your words have supported those who were
    stumbling,
  and you have made firm the feeble knees.

5 But now it has come to you, and you are
    impatient;
  it touches you, and you are dismayed.

6 Is not your fear of God your confidence,
  and the integrity of your ways your hope?

7 "Think now, who that was innocent ever
    perished?
  Or where were the upright cut off?

8 As I have seen, those who plow iniquity
  and sow trouble reap the same.

9 By the breath of God they perish,
  and by the blast of his anger they are
    consumed.

10 The roar of the lion, the voice of the fierce lion,
  and the teeth of the young lions are broken.

11 The strong lion perishes for lack of prey,
  and the whelps of the lioness are scattered.

12 "Now a word came stealing to me,
  my ear received the whisper of it.

13 Amid thoughts from visions of the night,
  when deep sleep falls on mortals,

14 dread came upon me, and trembling,
  which made all my bones shake.

15 A spirit glided past my face;
  the hair of my flesh bristled.

16 It stood still,
  but I could not discern its appearance.
  A form was before my eyes;
  there was silence, then I heard a voice:

17 'Can mortals be righteous before^m God?
  Can human beings be pure before^m their
    Maker?

18 Even in his servants he puts no trust,
  and his angels he charges with error;

19 how much more those who live in houses of
    clay,
  whose foundation is in the dust,
  who are crushed like a moth.

20 Between morning and evening they are
    destroyed;
  they perish forever without any regarding it.

21 Their tent-cord is plucked up within them,
  and they die devoid of wisdom.'

Job Is Corrected by God

5 "Call now; is there anyone who will answer
    you?
  To which of the holy ones will you turn?

2 Surely vexation kills the fool,
  and jealousy slays the simple.

3 I have seen fools taking root,
  but suddenly I cursed their dwelling.

4 Their children are far from safety,
  they are crushed in the gate,
  and there is no one to deliver them.

5 The hungry eat their harvest,
  and they take it even out of the thorns;^{n}
  and the thirsty^o pant after their wealth.

6 For misery does not come from the earth,
  nor does trouble sprout from the ground;

7 but human beings are born to trouble
  just as sparks^p fly upward.

8 "As for me, I would seek God,
  and to God I would commit my cause.

---

^{l} Heb *before* ^{m} Or *more than* ^{n} Meaning of Heb
uncertain ^{o} Aquila Symmachus Syr Vg: Heb *snare*
^{p} Or *birds*; Heb *sons of Resheph*

9 He does great things and unsearchable,
 marvelous things without number.
10 He gives rain on the earth
 and sends waters on the fields;
11 he sets on high those who are lowly,
 and those who mourn are lifted to safety.
12 He frustrates the devices of the crafty,
 so that their hands achieve no success.
13 He takes the wise in their own craftiness;
 and the schemes of the wily are brought to
  a quick end.
14 They meet with darkness in the daytime,
 and grope at noonday as in the night.
15 But he saves the needy from the sword of their
  mouth,
 from the hand of the mighty.
16 So the poor have hope,
 and injustice shuts its mouth.

17 "How happy is the one whom God
  reproves;
 therefore do not despise the discipline of
  the Almighty.*q*
18 For he wounds, but he binds up;
 he strikes, but his hands heal.
19 He will deliver you from six troubles;
 in seven no harm shall touch you.
20 In famine he will redeem you from death,
 and in war from the power of the sword.
21 You shall be hidden from the scourge of the
  tongue,
 and shall not fear destruction when it
  comes.
22 At destruction and famine you shall laugh,
 and shall not fear the wild animals of the
  earth.
23 For you shall be in league with the stones of
  the field,
 and the wild animals shall be at peace with
  you.
24 You shall know that your tent is safe,
 you shall inspect your fold and miss
  nothing.
25 You shall know that your descendants will be
  many,
 and your offspring like the grass of the
  earth.
26 You shall come to your grave in ripe old age,
 as a shock of grain comes up to the
  threshing floor in its season.
27 See, we have searched this out; it is true.
 Hear, and know it for yourself."

Job Replies: My Complaint Is Just

6 Then Job answered:
2 "O that my vexation were weighed,
 and all my calamity laid in the balances!

3 For then it would be heavier than the sand of
  the sea;
 therefore my words have been rash.
4 For the arrows of the Almighty*q* are in me;
 my spirit drinks their poison;
 the terrors of God are arrayed against me.
5 Does the wild ass bray over its grass,
 or the ox low over its fodder?
6 Can that which is tasteless be eaten without
  salt,
 or is there any flavor in the juice of
  mallows?*r*
7 My appetite refuses to touch them;
 they are like food that is loathsome to me.*r*

8 "O that I might have my request,
 and that God would grant my desire;
9 that it would please God to crush me,
 that he would let loose his hand and cut
  me off!
10 This would be my consolation;
 I would even exult*r* in unrelenting pain;
 for I have not denied the words of the Holy
  One.
11 What is my strength, that I should wait?
 And what is my end, that I should be
  patient?
12 Is my strength the strength of stones,
 or is my flesh bronze?
13 In truth I have no help in me,
 and any resource is driven from me.

14 "Those who withhold*s* kindness from a friend
 forsake the fear of the Almighty.*q*
15 My companions are treacherous like a
  torrent-bed,
 like freshets that pass away,
16 that run dark with ice,
 turbid with melting snow.
17 In time of heat they disappear;
 when it is hot, they vanish from their place.
18 The caravans turn aside from their course;
 they go up into the waste, and perish.
19 The caravans of Tē'ma look,
 the travelers of Shē'ba hope.
20 They are disappointed because they were
  confident;
 they come there and are confounded.
21 Such you have now become to me;*t*
 you see my calamity, and are afraid.
22 Have I said, 'Make me a gift'?
 Or, 'From your wealth offer a bribe for me'?

---

q Traditional rendering of Heb *Shaddai*   *r* Meaning of Heb
uncertain   *s* Syr Vg Compare Tg: Meaning of Heb uncertain
t Cn Compare Gk Syr: Meaning of Heb uncertain

JOB

23 Or, 'Save me from an opponent's hand'?
   Or, 'Ransom me from the hand of
      oppressors'?

24 "Teach me, and I will be silent;
   make me understand how I have gone
      wrong.
25 How forceful are honest words!
   But your reproof, what does it reprove?
26 Do you think that you can reprove words,
   as if the speech of the desperate were wind?
27 You would even cast lots over the orphan,
   and bargain over your friend.

28 "But now, be pleased to look at me;
   for I will not lie to your face.
29 Turn, I pray, let no wrong be done.
   Turn now, my vindication is at stake.
30 Is there any wrong on my tongue?
   Cannot my taste discern calamity?

Job: My Suffering Is without End

7 "Do not human beings have a hard service
      on earth,
   and are not their days like the days of a
      laborer?
2 Like a slave who longs for the shadow,
   and like laborers who look for their wages,
3 so I am allotted months of emptiness,
   and nights of misery are apportioned to me.
4 When I lie down I say, 'When shall I rise?'
   But the night is long,
   and I am full of tossing until dawn.
5 My flesh is clothed with worms and dirt;
   my skin hardens, then breaks out again.
6 My days are swifter than a weaver's shuttle,
   and come to their end without hope.ᵘ

7 "Remember that my life is a breath;
   my eye will never again see good.
8 The eye that beholds me will see me no more;
   while your eyes are upon me, I shall be gone.
9 As the cloud fades and vanishes,
   so those who go down to Shĕ'ōl do not
      come up;
10 they return no more to their houses,
   nor do their places know them any more.

11 "Therefore I will not restrain my mouth;
   I will speak in the anguish of my spirit;
   ·I will complain in the bitterness of my soul.
12 Am I the Sea, or the Dragon,
   that you set a guard over me?
13 When I say, 'My bed will comfort me,
   my couch will ease my complaint,'
14 then you scare me with dreams
   and terrify me with visions,

PRAY IT?
Suffering

Job's words in Job, chapter 7, are almost a prayer describing his suffering and asking, Why me? Job isn't worried about being polite; he says it like it is. What can you learn from Job about prayer during suffering?

First, you need to be honest with God and yourself. If you are hurt or in pain, don't play games with God. Tell God what you are feeling in your own words. Write it down in a journal if you want to. And be honest. Because if you aren't honest with God, you probably aren't being honest with yourself.

Second, let all your feelings out, just like Job did—including your anger. God is big enough to handle it. When you suppress your negative feelings, they may come out in unhealthy ways. So, let God help you deal with them.

Finally, let your prayer lead you to take some action. Job debated with his friends. That's probably how people did counseling back then! Your prayer to God for help might lead you to a counselor, a minister, or a support group. God works in many ways.

▸ Job 7.1–21

15 so that I would choose strangling
   and death rather than this body.
16 I loathe my life; I would not live forever.
   Let me alone, for my days are a breath.
17 What are human beings, that you make so
      much of them,
   that you set your mind on them,
18 visit them every morning,
   test them every moment?
19 Will you not look away from me for a
      while,
   let me alone until I swallow my spittle?
20 If I sin, what do I do to you, you watcher of
      humanity?
   Why have you made me your target?
   Why have I become a burden to you?
21 Why do you not pardon my transgression
   and take away my iniquity?

ᵘ Or *as the thread runs out*

For now I shall lie in the earth;
 you will seek me, but I shall not be."

Bildad Speaks: Job Should Repent

8 Then Bil'dad the Shū'hīte answered:
 2 "How long will you say these things,
  and the words of your mouth be a great
   wind?
3 Does God pervert justice?
 Or does the Almighty[v] pervert the right?
4 If your children sinned against him,
 he delivered them into the power of their
  transgression.
5 If you will seek God
 and make supplication to the Almighty,[v]
6 if you are pure and upright,
 surely then he will rouse himself for you
 and restore to you your rightful place.
7 Though your beginning was small,
 your latter days will be very great.

8 "For inquire now of bygone generations,
 and consider what their ancestors have
  found;
9 for we are but of yesterday, and we know
  nothing,
 for our days on earth are but a shadow.
10 Will they not teach you and tell you
 and utter words out of their understanding?
11 "Can papyrus grow where there is no marsh?
 Can reeds flourish where there is no water?
12 While yet in flower and not cut down,
 they wither before any other plant.
13 Such are the paths of all who forget God;
 the hope of the godless shall perish.
14 Their confidence is gossamer,
 a spider's house their trust.
15 If one leans against its house, it will not stand;
 if one lays hold of it, it will not endure.
16 The wicked thrive[w] before the sun,
 and their shoots spread over the garden.
17 Their roots twine around the stoneheap;
 they live among the rocks.[x]
18 If they are destroyed from their place,
 then it will deny them, saying, 'I have never
  seen you.'
19 See, these are their happy ways,[y]
 and out of the earth still others will spring.

20 "See, God will not reject a blameless person,
 nor take the hand of evildoers.
21 He will yet fill your mouth with laughter,
 and your lips with shouts of joy.
22 Those who hate you will be clothed with
  shame,
 and the tent of the wicked will be no
  more."

Job Replies: There Is No Mediator

9 Then Job answered:
 2 "Indeed I know that this is so;
 but how can a mortal be just before God?
3 If one wished to contend with him,
 one could not answer him once in a
  thousand.
4 He is wise in heart, and mighty in strength
 —who has resisted him, and succeeded?—
5 he who removes mountains, and they do not
  know it,
 when he overturns them in his anger;
6 who shakes the earth out of its place,
 and its pillars tremble;
7 who commands the sun, and it does not rise;
 who seals up the stars;
8 who alone stretched out the heavens
 and trampled the waves of the Sea;[z]
9 who made the Bear and Ō·rī'on,
 the Plēi'a·dēs and the chambers of the south;
10 who does great things beyond understanding,
 and marvelous things without number.
11 Look, he passes by me, and I do not see him;
 he moves on, but I do not perceive him.
12 He snatches away; who can stop him?
 Who will say to him, 'What are you doing?'

13 "God will not turn back his anger;
 the helpers of Rā'hab bowed beneath him.
14 How then can I answer him,
 choosing my words with him?
15 Though I am innocent, I cannot answer him;
 I must appeal for mercy to my accuser.[a]
16 If I summoned him and he answered me,
 I do not believe that he would listen to my
  voice.
17 For he crushes me with a tempest,
 and multiplies my wounds without
  cause;
18 he will not let me get my breath,
 but fills me with bitterness.
19 If it is a contest of strength, he is the strong
  one!
 If it is a matter of justice, who can summon
  him?[b]
20 Though I am innocent, my own mouth would
  condemn me;
 though I am blameless, he would prove me
  perverse.
21 I am blameless; I do not know myself;
 I loathe my life.
22 It is all one; therefore I say,

---

[v] Traditional rendering of Heb *Shaddai*   [w] Heb *He thrives*
[x] Gk Vg: Meaning of Heb uncertain   [y] Meaning of Heb
uncertain   [z] Or *trampled the back of the sea dragon*   [a] Or *for
my right*   [b] Compare Gk: Heb *me*

he destroys both the blameless and the
wicked.

23 When disaster brings sudden death,
he mocks at the calamity*c* of the innocent.

24 The earth is given into the hand of the wicked;
he covers the eyes of its judges—
if it is not he, who then is it?

25 "My days are swifter than a runner;
they flee away, they see no good.

26 They go by like skiffs of reed,
like an eagle swooping on the prey.

27 If I say, 'I will forget my complaint;
I will put off my sad countenance and be of
good cheer,'

28 I become afraid of all my suffering,
for I know you will not hold me innocent.

29 I shall be condemned;
why then do I labor in vain?

30 If I wash myself with soap
and cleanse my hands with lye,

31 yet you will plunge me into filth,
and my own clothes will abhor me.

32 For he is not a mortal, as I am, that I might
answer him,
that we should come to trial together.

33 There is no umpire*d* between us,
who might lay his hand on us both.

34 If he would take his rod away from me,
and not let dread of him terrify me,

35 then I would speak without fear of him,
for I know I am not what I am thought
to be.*e*

Job: I Loathe My Life

10 "I loathe my life;
I will give free utterance to my
complaint;
I will speak in the bitterness of my soul.

2 I will say to God, Do not condemn me;
let me know why you contend against me.

3 Does it seem good to you to oppress,
to despise the work of your hands
and favor the schemes of the wicked?

4 Do you have eyes of flesh?
Do you see as humans see?

5 Are your days like the days of mortals,
or your years like human years,

6 that you seek out my iniquity
and search for my sin,

7 although you know that I am not guilty,
and there is no one to deliver out of your
hand?

8 Your hands fashioned and made me;
and now you turn and destroy me.*f*

9 Remember that you fashioned me like clay;
and will you turn me to dust again?

10 Did you not pour me out like milk
and curdle me like cheese?

11 You clothed me with skin and flesh,
and knit me together with bones and
sinews.

12 You have granted me life and steadfast love,
and your care has preserved my spirit.

13 Yet these things you hid in your heart;
I know that this was your purpose.

14 If I sin, you watch me,
and do not acquit me of my iniquity.

15 If I am wicked, woe to me!
If I am righteous, I cannot lift up my head,
for I am filled with disgrace
and look upon my affliction.

16 Bold as a lion you hunt me;
you repeat your exploits against me.

17 You renew your witnesses against me,
and increase your vexation toward me;
you bring fresh troops against me.*g*

18 "Why did you bring me forth from the womb?
Would that I had died before any eye had
seen me,

19 and were as though I had not been,
carried from the womb to the grave.

20 Are not the days of my life few?*h*
Let me alone, that I may find a little
comfort*i*

21 before I go, never to return,
to the land of gloom and deep darkness,

22 the land of gloom*j* and chaos,
where light is like darkness."

Zophar Speaks: Job's Guilt Deserves Punishment

11 Then Zō'phar the Nā'a·ma·thīte answered:

2 "Should a multitude of words go unanswered,
and should one full of talk be vindicated?

3 Should your babble put others to silence,
and when you mock, shall no one shame
you?

4 For you say, 'My conduct*k* is pure,
and I am clean in God's*l* sight.'

5 But O that God would speak,
and open his lips to you,

6 and that he would tell you the secrets of
wisdom!

---

c Meaning of Heb uncertain   *d* Another reading is *Would
that there were an umpire*   *e* Cn: Heb *for I am not so in
myself*   *f* Cn Compare Gk Syr: Heb *made me together all
around, and you destroy me*   *g* Cn Compare Gk: Heb *toward
me; changes and a troop are with me*   *h* Cn Compare Gk Syr:
Heb *Are not my days few? Let him cease!*   *i* Heb *that I may
brighten up a little*   *j* Heb *gloom as darkness, deep darkness*
k Gk: Heb *teaching*   *l* Heb *your*

For wisdom is many-sided.[m]
Know then that God exacts of you less than
   your guilt deserves.

7 "Can you find out the deep things of God?
   Can you find out the limit of the
      Almighty?[n]
8 It is higher than heaven[o]—what can you do?
   Deeper than Shĕ'ōl—what can you know?
9 Its measure is longer than the earth,
   and broader than the sea.
10 If he passes through, and imprisons,
   and assembles for judgment, who can
      hinder him?
11 For he knows those who are worthless;
   when he sees iniquity, will he not consider
      it?
12 But a stupid person will get understanding,
   when a wild ass is born human.[m]

13 "If you direct your heart rightly,
   you will stretch out your hands toward him.
14 If iniquity is in your hand, put it far away,
   and do not let wickedness reside in your
      tents.
15 Surely then you will lift up your face without
      blemish;
   you will be secure, and will not fear.
16 You will forget your misery;
   you will remember it as waters that have
      passed away.
17 And your life will be brighter than the
      noonday;
   its darkness will be like the morning.
18 And you will have confidence, because there is
      hope;
   you will be protected[p] and take your rest in
      safety.
19 You will lie down, and no one will make you
      afraid;
   many will entreat your favor.
20 But the eyes of the wicked will fail;
   all way of escape will be lost to them,
   and their hope is to breathe their last."

Job Replies: I Am a Laughingstock

12 Then Job answered:
2   "No doubt you are the people,
   and wisdom will die with you.
3 But I have understanding as well as you;
   I am not inferior to you.
   Who does not know such things as these?
4 I am a laughingstock to my friends;
   I, who called upon God and he
      answered me,
   a just and blameless man, I am a
      laughingstock.

5 Those at ease have contempt for misfortune,[m]
   but it is ready for those whose feet are
      unstable.
6 The tents of robbers are at peace,
   and those who provoke God are secure,
   who bring their god in their hands.[q]

7 "But ask the animals, and they will teach you;
   the birds of the air, and they will tell you;
8 ask the plants of the earth,[r] and they will teach
      you;
   and the fish of the sea will declare to you.
9 Who among all these does not know
   that the hand of the LORD has done this?
10 In his hand is the life of every living thing
   and the breath of every human being.
11 Does not the ear test words
   as the palate tastes food?
12 Is wisdom with the aged,
   and understanding in length of days?

13 "With God[s] are wisdom and strength;
   he has counsel and understanding.
14 If he tears down, no one can rebuild;
   if he shuts someone in, no one can
      open up.
15 If he withholds the waters, they dry up;
   if he sends them out, they overwhelm the
      land.
16 With him are strength and wisdom;
   the deceived and the deceiver are his.
17 He leads counselors away stripped,
   and makes fools of judges.
18 He looses the sash of kings,
   and binds a waistcloth on their loins.
19 He leads priests away stripped,
   and overthrows the mighty.
20 He deprives of speech those who are trusted,
   and takes away the discernment of the
      elders.
21 He pours contempt on princes,
   and looses the belt of the strong.
22 He uncovers the deeps out of darkness,
   and brings deep darkness to light.
23 He makes nations great, then destroys them;
   he enlarges nations, then leads them away.
24 He strips understanding from the leaders[t] of
      the earth,
   and makes them wander in a pathless
      waste.
25 They grope in the dark without light;
   he makes them stagger like a drunkard.

---

m Meaning of Heb uncertain   n Traditional rendering of
Heb *Shaddai*   o Heb *The heights of heaven*   p Or *you will
look around*   q Or *whom God brought forth by his hand;*
Meaning of Heb uncertain   r Or *speak to the earth*
s Heb *him*   t Heb adds *of the people*

13

"Look, my eye has seen all this,
    my ear has heard and understood it.

2 What you know, I also know;
    I am not inferior to you.

3 But I would speak to the Almighty,[u]
    and I desire to argue my case with God.

4 As for you, you whitewash with lies;
    all of you are worthless physicians.

5 If you would only keep silent,
    that would be your wisdom!

6 Hear now my reasoning,
    and listen to the pleadings of my lips.

7 Will you speak falsely for God,
    and speak deceitfully for him?

8 Will you show partiality toward him,
    will you plead the case for God?

9 Will it be well with you when he searches you
    out?
    Or can you deceive him, as one person
    deceives another?

10 He will surely rebuke you
    if in secret you show partiality.

11 Will not his majesty terrify you,
    and the dread of him fall upon you?

12 Your maxims are proverbs of ashes,
    your defenses are defenses of clay.

13 "Let me have silence, and I will speak,
    and let come on me what may.

14 I will take my flesh in my teeth,
    and put my life in my hand.[v]

15 See, he will kill me; I have no hope;[w]
    but I will defend my ways to his face.

16 This will be my salvation,
    that the godless shall not come before him.

17 Listen carefully to my words,
    and let my declaration be in your ears.

18 I have indeed prepared my case;
    I know that I shall be vindicated.

19 Who is there that will contend with me?
    For then I would be silent and die.

Job's Despondent Prayer

20 Only grant two things to me,
    then I will not hide myself from your face:

21 withdraw your hand far from me,
    and do not let dread of you terrify me.

22 Then call, and I will answer;
    or let me speak, and you reply to me.

23 How many are my iniquities and my sins?
    Make me know my transgression and my
    sin.

24 Why do you hide your face,
    and count me as your enemy?

25 Will you frighten a windblown leaf
    and pursue dry chaff?

26 For you write bitter things against me,

and make me reap[x] the iniquities of my
    youth.

27 You put my feet in the stocks,
    and watch all my paths;
    you set a bound to the soles of my feet.

28 One wastes away like a rotten thing,
    like a garment that is moth-eaten.

14

"A mortal, born of woman, few of days
    and full of trouble,

2 comes up like a flower and withers,
    flees like a shadow and does not last.

3 Do you fix your eyes on such a one?
    Do you bring me into judgment with you?

4 Who can bring a clean thing out of an unclean?
    No one can.

5 Since their days are determined,
    and the number of their months is known
    to you,
    and you have appointed the bounds that
    they cannot pass,

6 look away from them, and desist,[y]
    that they may enjoy, like laborers, their
    days.

7 "For there is hope for a tree,
    if it is cut down, that it will sprout again,
    and that its shoots will not cease.

8 Though its root grows old in the earth,
    and its stump dies in the ground,

9 yet at the scent of water it will bud
    and put forth branches like a young plant.

10 But mortals die, and are laid low;
    humans expire, and where are they?

11 As waters fail from a lake,
    and a river wastes away and dries up,

12 so mortals lie down and do not rise again;
    until the heavens are no more, they will not
    awake
    or be roused out of their sleep.

13 O that you would hide me in She'ōl,
    that you would conceal me until your wrath
    is past,
    that you would appoint me a set time, and
    remember me!

14 If mortals die, will they live again?
    All the days of my service I would wait
    until my release should come.

15 You would call, and I would answer you;
    you would long for the work of your hands.

16 For then you would not[z] number my steps,
    you would not keep watch over my sin;

---

u Traditional rendering of Heb *Shaddai*   v Gk: Heb *Why
should I take . . . in my hand?*   w Or *Though he kill me, yet I
will trust in him*   x Heb *inherit*   y Cn: Heb *that they
may desist*   z Syr: Heb lacks *not*

17 my transgression would be sealed up in a bag,
     and you would cover over my iniquity.

18 "But the mountain falls and crumbles away,
     and the rock is removed from its place;
19 the waters wear away the stones;
     the torrents wash away the soil of the earth;
     so you destroy the hope of mortals.
20 You prevail forever against them, and they pass
          away;
     you change their countenance, and send
          them away.
21 Their children come to honor, and they do not
          know it;
     they are brought low, and it goes
          unnoticed.
22 They feel only the pain of their own bodies,
     and mourn only for themselves."

Eliphaz Speaks: Job Undermines Religion

15 Then E·li′phaz the Te′man·ite answered:
2 "Should the wise answer with windy
          knowledge,
     and fill themselves with the east wind?
3 Should they argue in unprofitable talk,
     or in words with which they can do no
          good?
4 But you are doing away with the fear of God,
     and hindering meditation before God.
5 For your iniquity teaches your mouth,
     and you choose the tongue of the crafty.
6 Your own mouth condemns you, and not I;
     your own lips testify against you.

7 "Are you the firstborn of the human race?
     Were you brought forth before the hills?
8 Have you listened in the council of God?
     And do you limit wisdom to yourself?
9 What do you know that we do not know?
     What do you understand that is not clear
          to us?
10 The gray-haired and the aged are on our side,
     those older than your father.
11 Are the consolations of God too small for you,
     or the word that deals gently with you?
12 Why does your heart carry you away,
     and why do your eyes flash,*a*
13 so that you turn your spirit against God,
     and let such words go out of your mouth?
14 What are mortals, that they can be clean?
     Or those born of woman, that they can be
          righteous?
15 God puts no trust even in his holy ones,
     and the heavens are not clean in his sight;
16 how much less one who is abominable and
          corrupt,
     one who drinks iniquity like water!

17 "I will show you; listen to me;
     what I have seen I will declare—
18 what sages have told,
     and their ancestors have not hidden,
19 to whom alone the land was given,
     and no stranger passed among them.
20 The wicked writhe in pain all their days,
     through all the years that are laid up for the
          ruthless.
21 Terrifying sounds are in their ears;
     in prosperity the destroyer will come upon
          them.
22 They despair of returning from darkness,
     and they are destined for the sword.
23 They wander abroad for bread, saying, 'Where
          is it?'
     They know that a day of darkness is ready at
          hand;
24 distress and anguish terrify them;
     they prevail against them, like a king
          prepared for battle.
25 Because they stretched out their hands against
          God,
     and bid defiance to the Almighty,*b*
26 running stubbornly against him
     with a thick-bossed shield;
27 because they have covered their faces with their
          fat,
     and gathered fat upon their loins,
28 they will live in desolate cities,
     in houses that no one should inhabit,
     houses destined to become heaps of
          ruins;
29 they will not be rich, and their wealth will not
          endure,
     nor will they strike root in the earth;*c*
30 they will not escape from darkness;
     the flame will dry up their shoots,
     and their blossom*d* will be swept away*e* by
          the wind.
31 Let them not trust in emptiness, deceiving
          themselves;
     for emptiness will be their recompense.
32 It will be paid in full before their time,
     and their branch will not be green.
33 They will shake off their unripe grape, like the
          vine,
     and cast off their blossoms, like the olive
          tree.
34 For the company of the godless is barren,
     and fire consumes the tents of bribery.
35 They conceive mischief and bring forth evil
     and their heart prepares deceit."

---

a Meaning of Heb uncertain   *b* Traditional rendering of
Heb *Shaddai*   *c* Vg: Meaning of Heb uncertain   *d* Gk: Heb
mouth   *e* Cn: Heb *will depart*

J
O
B

Job Reaffirms His Innocence

16 Then Job answered:
² "I have heard many such things;
miserable comforters are you all.
3 Have windy words no limit?
Or what provokes you that you keep on
talking?
4 I also could talk as you do,
if you were in my place;
I could join words together against you,
and shake my head at you.
5 I could encourage you with my mouth,
and the solace of my lips would assuage
your pain.

6 "If I speak, my pain is not assuaged,
and if I forbear, how much of it leaves me?
7 Surely now God has worn me out;
he has*f* made desolate all my company.
8 And he has*f* shriveled me up,
which is a witness against me;
my leanness has risen up against me,
and it testifies to my face.
9 He has torn me in his wrath, and hated me;
he has gnashed his teeth at me;
my adversary sharpens his eyes against me.
10 They have gaped at me with their mouths;
they have struck me insolently on the
cheek;
they mass themselves together against me.
11 God gives me up to the ungodly,
and casts me into the hands of the wicked.
12 I was at ease, and he broke me in two;
he seized me by the neck and dashed me to
pieces;
he set me up as his target;
13 his archers surround me.
He slashes open my kidneys, and shows no
mercy;
he pours out my gall on the ground.
14 He bursts upon me again and again;
he rushes at me like a warrior.
15 I have sewed sackcloth upon my skin,
and have laid my strength in the dust.
16 My face is red with weeping,
and deep darkness is on my eyelids,
17 though there is no violence in my hands,
and my prayer is pure.

18 "O earth, do not cover my blood;
let my outcry find no resting place.
19 Even now, in fact, my witness is in heaven,
and he that vouches for me is on high.
20 My friends scorn me;
my eye pours out tears to God,
21 that he would maintain the right of a mortal
with God,

as*g* one does for a neighbor.
22 For when a few years have come,
I shall go the way from which I shall not
return.

Job Prays for Relief

17 My spirit is broken, my days are extinct,
the grave is ready for me.
² Surely there are mockers around me,
and my eye dwells on their provocation.

3 "Lay down a pledge for me with yourself;
who is there that will give surety for me?
4 Since you have closed their minds to
understanding,
therefore you will not let them triumph.
5 Those who denounce friends for reward—
the eyes of their children will fail.

6 "He has made me a byword of the peoples,
and I am one before whom people spit.
7 My eye has grown dim from grief,
and all my members are like a shadow.
8 The upright are appalled at this,
and the innocent stir themselves up against
the godless.
9 Yet the righteous hold to their way,
and they that have clean hands grow
stronger and stronger.
10 But you, come back now, all of you,
and I shall not find a sensible person
among you.
11 My days are past, my plans are broken off,
the desires of my heart.
12 They make night into day;
'The light,' they say, 'is near to the
darkness.'*h*
13 If I look for Shē'ōl as my house,
if I spread my couch in darkness,
14 if I say to the Pit, 'You are my father,'
and to the worm, 'My mother,' or 'My
sister,'
15 where then is my hope?
Who will see my hope?
16 Will it go down to the bars of Shē'ōl?
Shall we descend together into the dust?"

Bildad Speaks: God Punishes the Wicked

18 Then Bil'dad the Shū'hite answered:
² "How long will you hunt for words?
Consider, and then we shall speak.
3 Why are we counted as cattle?
Why are we stupid in your sight?
4 You who tear yourself in your anger—

---

f Heb *you have*   *g* Syr Vg Tg: Heb *and*   *h* Meaning of Heb
uncertain

shall the earth be forsaken because of you,
or the rock be removed out of its place?

5 "Surely the light of the wicked is put out,
and the flame of their fire does not shine.
6 The light is dark in their tent,
and the lamp above them is put out.
7 Their strong steps are shortened,
and their own schemes throw them down.
8 For they are thrust into a net by their own feet,
and they walk into a pitfall.
9 A trap seizes them by the heel;
a snare lays hold of them.
10 A rope is hid for them in the ground,
a trap for them in the path.
11 Terrors frighten them on every side,
and chase them at their heels.
12 Their strength is consumed by hunger,[i]
and calamity is ready for their stumbling.
13 By disease their skin is consumed,[j]
the firstborn of Death consumes their
limbs.
14 They are torn from the tent in which they
trusted,
and are brought to the king of terrors.
15 In their tents nothing remains;
sulfur is scattered upon their habitations.
16 Their roots dry up beneath,
and their branches wither above.
17 Their memory perishes from the earth,
and they have no name in the street.
18 They are thrust from light into darkness,
and driven out of the world.
19 They have no offspring or descendant among
their people,
and no survivor where they used to live.
20 They of the west are appalled at their fate,
and horror seizes those of the east.
21 Surely such are the dwellings of the
ungodly,
such is the place of those who do not know
God."

Job Replies: I Know That My Redeemer Lives

19 Then Job answered:
2 "How long will you torment me,
and break me in pieces with words?
3 These ten times you have cast reproach
upon me;
are you not ashamed to wrong me?
4 And even if it is true that I have erred,
my error remains with me.
5 If indeed you magnify yourselves against me,
and make my humiliation an argument
against me,
6 know then that God has put me in the wrong,
and closed his net around me.

7 Even when I cry out, 'Violence!' I am not
answered;
I call aloud, but there is no justice.
8 He has walled up my way so that I cannot pass,
and he has set darkness upon my paths.
9 He has stripped my glory from me,
and taken the crown from my head.
10 He breaks me down on every side, and I am
gone,
he has uprooted my hope like a tree.
11 He has kindled his wrath against me,
and counts me as his adversary.
12 His troops come on together;
they have thrown up siegeworks[k]
against me,
and encamp around my tent.

13 "He has put my family far from me,
and my acquaintances are wholly estranged
from me.
14 My relatives and my close friends have
failed me;
15 the guests in my house have forgotten me;
my serving girls count me as a stranger;
I have become an alien in their eyes.
16 I call to my servant, but he gives me no answer;
I must myself plead with him.
17 My breath is repulsive to my wife;
I am loathsome to my own family.
18 Even young children despise me;
when I rise, they talk against me.
19 All my intimate friends abhor me,
and those whom I loved have turned
against me.
20 My bones cling to my skin and to my flesh,
and I have escaped by the skin of my teeth.
21 Have pity on me, have pity on me, O you my
friends,
for the hand of God has touched me!
22 Why do you, like God, pursue me,
never satisfied with my flesh?

23 "O that my words were written down!
O that they were inscribed in a book!
24 O that with an iron pen and with lead
they were engraved on a rock forever!
25 For I know that my Redeemer[l] lives,
and that at the last he[m] will stand upon the
earth;[n]
26 and after my skin has been thus destroyed,
then in[o] my flesh I shall see God,[p]
27 whom I shall see on my side,[q]

---

i Or *Disaster is hungry for them*   j Cn: Heb *It consumes the
limbs of his skin*   k Cn: Heb *their way*   l Or *Vindicator*
m Or *that he the Last*   n Heb *dust*   o Or *without*   p Meaning
of Heb of this verse uncertain   q Or *for myself*

JOB

and my eyes shall behold, and not another.
My heart faints within me!
28 If you say, 'How we will persecute him!'
and, 'The root of the matter is found in
him';
29 be afraid of the sword,
for wrath brings the punishment of the
sword,
so that you may know there is a judgment."

Zophar Speaks: Wickedness Receives Just Retribution

20 Then Zō'phar the Nā'a•ma•thīte answered:
2 "Pay attention! My thoughts urge me
to answer,
because of the agitation within me.
3 I hear censure that insults me,
and a spirit beyond my understanding
answers me.
4 Do you not know this from of old,
ever since mortals were placed on earth,
5 that the exulting of the wicked is short,
and the joy of the godless is but for a
moment?
6 Even though they mount up high as the
heavens,
and their head reaches to the clouds,
7 they will perish forever like their own dung;
those who have seen them will say, 'Where
are they?'
8 They will fly away like a dream, and not be
found;
they will be chased away like a vision of the
night.
9 The eye that saw them will see them no more,
nor will their place behold them any
longer.
10 Their children will seek the favor of the poor,
and their hands will give back their wealth.
11 Their bodies, once full of youth,
will lie down in the dust with them.

12 "Though wickedness is sweet in their mouth,
though they hide it under their tongues,
13 though they are loath to let it go,
and hold it in their mouths,
14 yet their food is turned in their stomachs;
it is the venom of asps within them.
15 They swallow down riches and vomit them up
again;
God casts them out of their bellies.
16 They will suck the poison of asps;
the tongue of a viper will kill them.
17 They will not look on the rivers,
the streams flowing with honey and curds.
18 They will give back the fruit of their toil,
and will not swallow it down;

from the profit of their trading
they will get no enjoyment.
19 For they have crushed and abandoned the
poor,
they have seized a house that they did not
build.

20 "They knew no quiet in their bellies;
in their greed they let nothing escape.
21 There was nothing left after they had eaten;
therefore their prosperity will not endure.
22 In full sufficiency they will be in distress;
all the force of misery will come upon
them.
23 To fill their belly to the full
God^r will send his fierce anger into them,
and rain it upon them as their food.^{s}
24 They will flee from an iron weapon;
a bronze arrow will strike them through.
25 It is drawn forth and comes out of their body,
and the glittering point comes out of their
gall;
terrors come upon them.
26 Utter darkness is laid up for their treasures;
a fire fanned by no one will devour them;
what is left in their tent will be consumed.
27 The heavens will reveal their iniquity,
and the earth will rise up against them.
28 The possessions of their house will be carried
away,
dragged off in the day of God's^t wrath.
29 This is the portion of the wicked from God,
the heritage decreed for them by God."

Job Replies: The Wicked Often Go Unpunished

21 Then Jōb answered:
2 "Listen carefully to my words,
and let this be your consolation.
3 Bear with me, and I will speak;
then after I have spoken, mock on.
4 As for me, is my complaint addressed to
mortals?
Why should I not be impatient?
5 Look at me, and be appalled,
and lay your hand upon your mouth.
6 When I think of it I am dismayed,
and shuddering seizes my flesh.
7 Why do the wicked live on,
reach old age, and grow mighty in power?
8 Their children are established in their presence,
and their offspring before their eyes.
9 Their houses are safe from fear,
and no rod of God is upon them.

---

r Heb *he* s Cn: Meaning of Heb uncertain t Heb *his*

10 Their bull breeds without fail;
   their cow calves and never miscarries.
11 They send out their little ones like a flock,
   and their children dance around.
12 They sing to the tambourine and the lyre,
   and rejoice to the sound of the pipe.
13 They spend their days in prosperity,
   and in peace they go down to Shĕ′ōl.
14 They say to God, 'Leave us alone!
   We do not desire to know your ways.
15 What is the Almighty,ᵘ that we should serve
      him?
   And what profit do we get if we pray to
      him?'
16 Is not their prosperity indeed their own
      achievement?ᵛ
   The plans of the wicked are repugnant
      to me.

17 "How often is the lamp of the wicked put out?
   How often does calamity come upon them?
   How often does Godʷ distribute pains in
      his anger?
18 How often are they like straw before the wind,
   and like chaff that the storm carries away?
19 You say, 'God stores up their iniquity for their
      children.'
   Let it be paid back to them, so that they
      may know it.
20 Let their own eyes see their destruction,
   and let them drink of the wrath of the
      Almighty.ᵘ
21 For what do they care for their household after
      them,
   when the number of their months is cut
      off?
22 Will any teach God knowledge,
   seeing that he judges those that are on
      high?
23 One dies in full prosperity,
   being wholly at ease and secure,
24 his loins full of milk
   and the marrow of his bones moist.
25 Another dies in bitterness of soul,
   never having tasted of good.
26 They lie down alike in the dust,
   and the worms cover them.

27 "Oh, I know your thoughts,
   and your schemes to wrong me.
28 For you say, 'Where is the house of the prince?
   Where is the tent in which the wicked
      lived?'
29 Have you not asked those who travel the roads,
   and do you not accept their testimony,
30 that the wicked are spared in the day of
      calamity,

and are rescued in the day of wrath?
31 Who declares their way to their face,
   and who repays them for what they have
      done?
32 When they are carried to the grave,
   a watch is kept over their tomb.
33 The clods of the valley are sweet to them;
   everyone will follow after,
   and those who went before are
      innumerable.
34 How then will you comfort me with empty
      nothings?
   There is nothing left of your answers but
      falsehood."

Eliphaz Speaks: Job's Wickedness Is Great

22 Then E·li′phaz the Tĕ′man·ite answered:
   2 "Can a mortal be of use to God?
   Can even the wisest be of service to him?
3 Is it any pleasure to the Almightyᵘ if you are
      righteous,
   or is it gain to him if you make your ways
      blameless?
4 Is it for your piety that he reproves you,
   and enters into judgment with you?
5 Is not your wickedness great?
   There is no end to your iniquities.
6 For you have exacted pledges from your family
      for no reason,
   and stripped the naked of their clothing.
7 You have given no water to the weary to drink,
   and you have withheld bread from the
      hungry.
8 The powerful possess the land,
   and the favored live in it.
9 You have sent widows away empty-handed,
   and the arms of the orphans you have
      crushed.ˣ
10 Therefore snares are around you,
   and sudden terror overwhelms you,
11 or darkness so that you cannot see;
   a flood of water covers you.

12 "Is not God high in the heavens?
   See the highest stars, how lofty they are!
13 Therefore you say, 'What does God know?
   Can he judge through the deep darkness?
14 Thick clouds enwrap him, so that he does not
      see,
   and he walks on the dome of heaven.'
15 Will you keep to the old way
   that the wicked have trod?
16 They were snatched away before their time;

ᵘ Traditional rendering of Heb *Shaddai*   ᵛ Heb *in their hand*   ʷ Heb *he*   ˣ Gk Syr Tg Vg: Heb *were crushed*

J
O
B

their foundation was washed away by a
flood.

17 They said to God, 'Leave us alone,'
and 'What can the Almighty*y* do to us?'*z*

18 Yet he filled their houses with good things—
but the plans of the wicked are repugnant
to me.

19 The righteous see it and are glad;
the innocent laugh them to scorn,

20 saying, 'Surely our adversaries are cut off,
and what they left, the fire has
consumed.'

21 "Agree with God,*a* and be at peace;
in this way good will come to you.

22 Receive instruction from his mouth,
and lay up his words in your heart.

23 If you return to the Almighty,*y* you will be
restored,
if you remove unrighteousness from your
tents,

24 if you treat gold like dust,
and gold of O'phir like the stones of the
torrent-bed,

25 and if the Almighty*y* is your gold
and your precious silver,

26 then you will delight yourself in the Almighty,*y*
and lift up your face to God.

27 You will pray to him, and he will hear you,
and you will pay your vows.

28 You will decide on a matter, and it will be
established for you,
and light will shine on your ways.

29 When others are humiliated, you say it is
pride;
for he saves the humble.

30 He will deliver even those who are guilty;
they will escape because of the cleanness of
your hands."*b*

Job Replies: My Complaint Is Bitter

23 Then Job answered:
2 "Today also my complaint is bitter;*c*
his*d* hand is heavy despite my groaning.

3 Oh, that I knew where I might find him,
that I might come even to his dwelling!

4 I would lay my case before him,
and fill my mouth with arguments.

5 I would learn what he would answer me,
and understand what he would say to me.

6 Would he contend with me in the greatness of
his power?
No; but he would give heed to me.

7 There an upright person could reason with
him,
and I should be acquitted forever by my
judge.

8 "If I go forward, he is not there;
or backward, I cannot perceive him;

9 on the left he hides, and I cannot behold him;
I turn*e* to the right, but I cannot see him.

10 But he knows the way that I take;
when he has tested me, I shall come out
like gold.

11 My foot has held fast to his steps;
I have kept his way and have not turned
aside.

12 I have not departed from the commandment of
his lips;
I have treasured in*f* my bosom the words of
his mouth.

13 But he stands alone and who can dissuade
him?
What he desires, that he does.

14 For he will complete what he appoints for me;
and many such things are in his mind.

15 Therefore I am terrified at his presence;
when I consider, I am in dread of him.

16 God has made my heart faint;
the Almighty*y* has terrified me;

17 If only I could vanish in darkness,
and thick darkness would cover my face!*g*

Job Complains of Violence on the Earth

24 "Why are times not kept by the Almighty,*y*
and why do those who know him
never see his days?

2 The wicked*h* remove landmarks;
they seize flocks and pasture them.

3 They drive away the donkey of the orphan;
they take the widow's ox for a pledge.

4 They thrust the needy off the road;
the poor of the earth all hide themselves.

5 Like wild asses in the desert
they go out to their toil,
scavenging in the wasteland
food for their young.

6 They reap in a field not their own
and they glean in the vineyard of the
wicked.

7 They lie all night naked, without clothing,
and have no covering in the cold.

8 They are wet with the rain of the mountains,
and cling to the rock for want of shelter.

9 "There are those who snatch the orphan child
from the breast,
and take as a pledge the infant of the poor.

---

y Traditional rendering of Heb *Shaddai* *z* Gk Syr: Heb
them *a* Heb *him* *b* Meaning of Heb uncertain *c* Syr Vg
Tg: Heb *rebellious* *d* Gk Syr: Heb *my* *e* Syr Vg: Heb *he
turns* *f* Gk Vg: Heb *from* *g* Or *But I am not destroyed by the
darkness; he has concealed the thick darkness from me* *h* Gk:
Heb *they*

did you KNOW?

A Long Debate

Why are Job's friends so insistent that sin and suffering are connected? Why do they go on, chapter after chapter, telling Job that his suffering is a punishment for his sins? The author of the Book of Job uses the debate of Job and his friends to contrast two positions. The position of Job's friends is that God rewards people who are good and punishes those who are wicked: if Job is suffering terribly, then Job must have sinned terribly. Job's repeated denial of sin reveals the second position, which is that sometimes innocent people suffer. This second position is harder to argue because it leaves a huge question: Why?

Because Job has too much integrity to repent for sins he never committed (Job 27.1–6), he keeps searching for another answer. Finally, Job makes an oath of innocence. Such an oath has God as its witness, and if it is false, it requires God to strike down the person who made it. But God appears to Job in an awesome show of power (chapters 38–41) and reminds Job that human intelligence is too limited to comprehend the deeper mysteries of creation. God alone knows why innocent people suffer; Job must trust God's plan.

Read chapters 20–24 to get a sense of the long debate in Job about human suffering. This debate reflects the long history of the Israelites wrestling with this complex question.

10 They go about naked, without clothing;
        though hungry, they carry the sheaves;
11 between their terraces^i they press out oil;
        they tread the wine presses, but suffer thirst.
12 From the city the dying groan,
        and the throat of the wounded cries for
            help;
        yet God pays no attention to their prayer.

13 "There are those who rebel against the light,
        who are not acquainted with its ways,
        and do not stay in its paths.

14 The murderer rises at dusk
        to kill the poor and needy,
        and in the night is like a thief.
15 The eye of the adulterer also waits for the
            twilight,
        saying, 'No eye will see me';
        and he disguises his face.
16 In the dark they dig through houses;
        by day they shut themselves up;
        they do not know the light.
17 For deep darkness is morning to all of them;
        for they are friends with the terrors of deep
            darkness.

18 "Swift are they on the face of the waters;
        their portion in the land is cursed;
        no treader turns toward their vineyards.
19 Drought and heat snatch away the snow
            waters;
        so does Shē'ōl those who have sinned.
20 The womb forgets them;
        the worm finds them sweet;
    they are no longer remembered;
        so wickedness is broken like a tree.

21 "They harm^j the childless woman,
        and do no good to the widow.
22 Yet God^k prolongs the life of the mighty by his
            power;
        they rise up when they despair of life.
23 He gives them security, and they are
            supported;
        his eyes are upon their ways.
24 They are exalted a little while, and then are
            gone;
        they wither and fade like the mallow;^l
        they are cut off like the heads of grain.
25 If it is not so, who will prove me a liar,
        and show that there is nothing in what I
            say?"

Bildad Speaks: How Can a Mortal Be Righteous Before God?

25 Then Bil'dad the Shū'hīte answered:
    2   "Dominion and fear are with God;^m
        he makes peace in his high heaven.
3 Is there any number to his armies?
        Upon whom does his light not arise?
4 How then can a mortal be righteous before
            God?
        How can one born of woman be pure?
5 If even the moon is not bright
        and the stars are not pure in his sight,

---

^i Meaning of Heb uncertain ^j Gk Tg: Heb *feed on* or
associate with ^k Heb *he* ^l Gk: Heb *like all others*
^m Heb *him*

6 how much less a mortal, who is a maggot,
   and a human being, who is a worm!"

Job Replies: God's Majesty Is Unsearchable

26 Then Jōb answered:
2 "How you have helped one who has
     no power!
  How you have assisted the arm that has no
     strength!
3 How you have counseled one who has no
     wisdom,
   and given much good advice!
4 With whose help have you uttered words,
   and whose spirit has come forth
     from you?
5 The shades below tremble,
   the waters and their inhabitants.
6 Shĕ'ōl is naked before God,
   and A·bad'don has no covering.
7 He stretches out Zā'phon[n] over the void,
   and hangs the earth upon nothing.
8 He binds up the waters in his thick clouds,
   and the cloud is not torn open by them.
9 He covers the face of the full moon,
   and spreads over it his cloud.
10 He has described a circle on the face of the
     waters,
   at the boundary between light and
     darkness.
11 The pillars of heaven tremble,
   and are astounded at his rebuke.
12 By his power he stilled the Sea;
   by his understanding he struck down
     Rā'hab.
13 By his wind the heavens were made fair;
   his hand pierced the fleeing serpent.
14 These are indeed but the outskirts of his ways;
   and how small a whisper do we hear of
     him!
   But the thunder of his power who can
     understand?"

Job Maintains His Integrity

27 Jōb again took up his discourse and said:
2 "As God lives, who has taken away
     my right,
  and the Almighty,[o] who has made my soul
     bitter,
3 as long as my breath is in me
   and the spirit of God is in my nostrils,
4 my lips will not speak falsehood,
   and my tongue will not utter deceit.
5 Far be it from me to say that you are right;
   until I die I will not put away my integrity
     from me.
6 I hold fast my righteousness, and will not let
   it go;

   my heart does not reproach me for any of
     my days.

7 "May my enemy be like the wicked,
   and may my opponent be like the
     unrighteous.
8 For what is the hope of the godless when God
     cuts them off,
   when God takes away their lives?
9 Will God hear their cry
   when trouble comes upon them?
10 Will they take delight in the Almighty?[o]
   Will they call upon God at all times?
11 I will teach you concerning the hand of God;
   that which is with the Almighty[o] I will not
     conceal.
12 All of you have seen it yourselves;
   why then have you become altogether vain?

13 "This is the portion of the wicked with God,
   and the heritage that oppressors receive
     from the Almighty:[o]
14 If their children are multiplied, it is for the
     sword;
   and their offspring have not enough to eat.
15 Those who survive them the pestilence buries,
   and their widows make no lamentation.
16 Though they heap up silver like dust,
   and pile up clothing like clay—
17 they may pile it up, but the just will wear it,
   and the innocent will divide the silver.
18 They build their houses like nests,
   like booths made by sentinels of the
     vineyard.
19 They go to bed with wealth, but will do so no
     more;
   they open their eyes, and it is gone.
20 Terrors overtake them like a flood;
   in the night a whirlwind carries them off.
21 The east wind lifts them up and they are gone;
   it sweeps them out of their place.
22 It[p] hurls at them without pity;
   they flee from its[q] power in headlong flight.
23 It[p] claps its[q] hands at them,
   and hisses at them from its[q] place.

Interlude: Where Wisdom Is Found

28 "Surely there is a mine for silver,
    and a place for gold to be refined.
2 Iron is taken out of the earth,
   and copper is smelted from ore.
3 Miners put[r] an end to darkness,
   and search out to the farthest bound
   the ore in gloom and deep darkness.

---

[n] Or *the North*   [o] Traditional rendering of Heb *Shaddai*
[p] Or *He* (that is God)   [q] Or *his*   [r] Heb *He puts*

4 They open shafts in a valley away from human
        habitation;
    they are forgotten by travelers,
    they sway suspended, remote from people.
5 As for the earth, out of it comes bread;
    but underneath it is turned up as by fire.
6 Its stones are the place of sapphires,ˢ
    and its dust contains gold.

7 "That path no bird of prey knows,
    and the falcon's eye has not seen it.
8 The proud wild animals have not trodden it;
    the lion has not passed over it.

9 "They put their hand to the flinty rock,
    and overturn mountains by the roots.
10 They cut out channels in the rocks,
    and their eyes see every precious thing.
11 The sources of the rivers they probe;ᵗ
    hidden things they bring to light.

12 "But where shall wisdom be found?
    And where is the place of understanding?
13 Mortals do not know the way to it,ᵘ
    and it is not found in the land of the living.
14 The deep says, 'It is not in me,'
    and the sea says, 'It is not with me.'
15 It cannot be gotten for gold,
    and silver cannot be weighed out as its
        price.
16 It cannot be valued in the gold of O'phir,
    in precious onyx or sapphire.ˢ
17 Gold and glass cannot equal it,
    nor can it be exchanged for jewels of fine
        gold.
18 No mention shall be made of coral or of
        crystal;
    the price of wisdom is above pearls.
19 The chrysolite of Ethiopiaᵛ cannot compare
        with it,
    nor can it be valued in pure gold.

20 "Where then does wisdom come from?
    And where is the place of understanding?
21 It is hidden from the eyes of all living,
    and concealed from the birds of the air.
22 A•bad'don and Death say,
    'We have heard a rumor of it with our ears.'

23 "God understands the way to it,
    and he knows its place.
24 For he looks to the ends of the earth,
    and sees everything under the heavens.
25 When he gave to the wind its weight,
    and apportioned out the waters by measure;
26 when he made a decree for the rain,
    and a way for the thunderbolt;

27 then he saw it and declared it;
    he established it, and searched it out.
28 And he said to humankind,
    'Truly, the fear of the Lord, that is wisdom;
    and to depart from evil is understanding.' "

Job Finishes His Defense

29 Jōb again took up his discourse and said:
    2 "O that I were as in the months of
        old,
    as in the days when God watched over me;
3 when his lamp shone over my head,
    and by his light I walked through darkness;
4 when I was in my prime,
    when the friendship of God was upon my
        tent;
5 when the Almightyʷ was still with me,
    when my children were around me;
6 when my steps were washed with milk,
    and the rock poured out for me streams of
        oil!
7 When I went out to the gate of the city,
    when I took my seat in the square,
8 the young men saw me and withdrew,
    and the aged rose up and stood;
9 the nobles refrained from talking,
    and laid their hands on their mouths;
10 the voices of princes were hushed,
    and their tongues stuck to the roof of their
        mouths.
11 When the ear heard, it commended me,
    and when the eye saw, it approved;
12 because I delivered the poor who cried,
    and the orphan who had no helper.
13 The blessing of the wretched came upon me,
    and I caused the widow's heart to sing for
        joy.
14 I put on righteousness, and it clothed me;
    my justice was like a robe and a turban.
15 I was eyes to the blind,
    and feet to the lame.
16 I was a father to the needy,
    and I championed the cause of the stranger.
17 I broke the fangs of the unrighteous,
    and made them drop their prey from their
        teeth.
18 Then I thought, 'I shall die in my nest,
    and I shall multiply my days like the
        phoenix;ˣ
19 my roots spread out to the waters,
    with the dew all night on my branches;
20 my glory was fresh with me,
    and my bow ever new in my hand.'

ˢ Or *lapis lazuli*   ᵗ Gk Vg: Heb *bind*   ᵘ Gk: Heb *its price*
ᵛ Or *Nubia*; Heb *Cush*   ʷ Traditional rendering of Heb
Shaddai   ˣ Or *like sand*

21 "They listened to me, and waited,
    and kept silence for my counsel.
22 After I spoke they did not speak again,
    and my word dropped upon them like
        dew.*y*
23 They waited for me as for the rain;
    they opened their mouths as for the spring
        rain.
24 I smiled on them when they had no
        confidence;
    and the light of my countenance they did
        not extinguish.*z*
25 I chose their way, and sat as chief,
    and I lived like a king among his troops,
    like one who comforts mourners.

30 "But now they make sport of me,
        those who are younger than I,
  whose fathers I would have disdained
    to set with the dogs of my flock.
2 What could I gain from the strength of their
        hands?
    All their vigor is gone.
3 Through want and hard hunger
    they gnaw the dry and desolate ground,
4 they pick mallow and the leaves of bushes,
    and to warm themselves the roots of
        broom.
5 They are driven out from society;
    people shout after them as after a thief.
6 In the gullies of wadis they must live,
    in holes in the ground, and in the rocks.
7 Among the bushes they bray;

    under the nettles they huddle together.
8 A senseless, disreputable brood,
    they have been whipped out of the land.

9 "And now they mock me in song;
    I am a byword to them.
10 They abhor me, they keep aloof from me;
    they do not hesitate to spit at the sight
        of me.
11 Because God has loosed my bowstring and
        humbled me,
    they have cast off restraint in my presence.
12 On my right hand the rabble rise up;
    they send me sprawling,
    and build roads for my ruin.
13 They break up my path,
    they promote my calamity;
    no one restrains*a* them.
14 As through a wide breach they come;
    amid the crash they roll on.
15 Terrors are turned upon me;
    my honor is pursued as by the wind,
    and my prosperity has passed away like a
        cloud.

16 "And now my soul is poured out within me;
    days of affliction have taken hold of me.
17 The night racks my bones,
    and the pain that gnaws me takes no rest.
18 With violence he seizes my garment;*b*

---

y Heb lacks *like dew*   *z* Meaning of Heb uncertain   *a* Cn:
Heb *helps*   *b* Gk: Heb *my garment is disfigured*

Hey, God! Did You Hear Me?

How do we know that God hears and answers our prayers? The Books of Job and
the Psalms describe many instances of both cries for help and God's responses to
those cries. In our day-to-day reality, however, we can't always tell when God is
answering our prayers. It isn't like we walk by trees that burn and speak to us, or
hear whispers in the wind that call our name, or see and hear angels who give us God's
answer. But God does hear and answer our prayers. One way to determine how God is
answering our prayers is through discernment.

    In the discernment process, an adult mentor or spiritual director can help you figure
out what God is trying to say to you. If you don't already have someone who can help you
in this way (like a priest, religion teacher, campus or youth minister, or parent), you can
ask at your parish or school for help in finding an adult mentor. This spiritual director will
be able to tell you more about the discernment process and whether it is the right process for you at this time in your life.

    With a spiritual director, you will learn how to hear God's answers to your prayers.

▶ Job 30.20

he grasps me by*c* the collar of my tunic.

19 He has cast me into the mire,
    and I have become like dust and ashes.
20 I cry to you and you do not answer me;
    I stand, and you merely look at me.
21 You have turned cruel to me;
    with the might of your hand you
        persecute me.
22 You lift me up on the wind, you make me ride
        on it,
    and you toss me about in the roar of the
        storm.
23 I know that you will bring me to death,
    and to the house appointed for all living.

24 "Surely one does not turn against the needy,*d*
    when in disaster they cry for help.*e*
25 Did I not weep for those whose day was hard?
    Was not my soul grieved for the poor?
26 But when I looked for good, evil came;
    and when I waited for light, darkness came.
27 My inward parts are in turmoil, and are never
        still;
    days of affliction come to meet me.
28 I go about in sunless gloom;
    I stand up in the assembly and cry for help.
29 I am a brother of jackals,
    and a companion of ostriches.
30 My skin turns black and falls from me,
    and my bones burn with heat.
31 My lyre is turned to mourning,
    and my pipe to the voice of those who
        weep.

31

"I have made a covenant with my eyes;
    how then could I look upon a virgin?
2 What would be my portion from God above,
    and my heritage from the Almighty*f* on
        high?
3 Does not calamity befall the unrighteous,
    and disaster the workers of iniquity?
4 Does he not see my ways,
    and number all my steps?

5 "If I have walked with falsehood,
    and my foot has hurried to deceit—
6 let me be weighed in a just balance,
    and let God know my integrity!—
7 if my step has turned aside from the way,
    and my heart has followed my eyes,
    and if any spot has clung to my hands;
8 then let me sow, and another eat;
    and let what grows for me be rooted out.

9 "If my heart has been enticed by a woman,
    and I have lain in wait at my neighbor's
        door;

10 then let my wife grind for another,
    and let other men kneel over her.
11 For that would be a heinous crime;
    that would be a criminal offense;
12 for that would be a fire consuming down to
        A·bad'don,
    and it would burn to the root all my
        harvest.

13 "If I have rejected the cause of my male or
        female slaves,
    when they brought a complaint against me;
14 what then shall I do when God rises up?
    When he makes inquiry, what shall I
        answer him?
15 Did not he who made me in the womb make
        them?
    And did not one fashion us in the womb?

16 "If I have withheld anything that the poor
        desired,
    or have caused the eyes of the widow to fail,
17 or have eaten my morsel alone,
    and the orphan has not eaten from it—
18 for from my youth I reared the orphan*g* like a
        father,
    and from my mother's womb I guided the
        widow*h*—
19 if I have seen anyone perish for lack of
        clothing,
    or a poor person without covering,
20 whose loins have not blessed me,
    and who was not warmed with the fleece of
        my sheep;
21 if I have raised my hand against the orphan,
    because I saw I had supporters at the gate;
22 then let my shoulder blade fall from my
        shoulder,
    and let my arm be broken from its socket.
23 For I was in terror of calamity from God,
    and I could not have faced his majesty.

24 "If I have made gold my trust,
    or called fine gold my confidence;
25 if I have rejoiced because my wealth was great,
    or because my hand had gotten much;
26 if I have looked at the sun*i* when it shone,
    or the moon moving in splendor,
27 and my heart has been secretly enticed,
    and my mouth has kissed my hand;
28 this also would be an iniquity to be punished
        by the judges,
    for I should have been false to God above.

---

c Heb *like*   *d* Heb *ruin*   *e* Cn: Meaning of Heb uncertain
f Traditional rendering of Heb *Shaddai*   *g* Heb *him*
h Heb *her*   *i* Heb *the light*

29 "If I have rejoiced at the ruin of those who
    hated me,
    or exulted when evil overtook them—
30 I have not let my mouth sin
    by asking for their lives with a curse—
31 if those of my tent ever said,
    'O that we might be sated with his flesh!'*j*—
32 the stranger has not lodged in the street;
    I have opened my doors to the traveler—
33 if I have concealed my transgressions as
        others do,*k*
    by hiding my iniquity in my bosom,
34 because I stood in great fear of the
        multitude,
    and the contempt of families terrified me,
    so that I kept silence, and did not go out of
        doors—
35 O that I had one to hear me!
    (Here is my signature! Let the Almighty*l*
    answer me!)
    O that I had the indictment written by my
        adversary!
36 Surely I would carry it on my shoulder;
    I would bind it on me like a crown;
37 I would give him an account of all my steps;
    like a prince I would approach him.

38 "If my land has cried out against me,
    and its furrows have wept together;
39 if I have eaten its yield without payment,
    and caused the death of its owners;
40 let thorns grow instead of wheat,
    and foul weeds instead of barley."

The words of Jōb are ended.

Elihu Rebukes Job's Friends

32 So these three men ceased to answer Jōb,
because he was righteous in his own
eyes. 2 Then E·lī'hū son of Bar'a·chel the Būz'īte, of
the family of Ram, became angry. He was angry at
Jōb because he justified himself rather than God;
3 he was angry also at Jōb's three friends because
they had found no answer, though they had declared Jōb to be in the wrong.*m* 4 Now E·lī'hū had
waited to speak to Jōb, because they were older
than he. 5 But when E·lī'hū saw that there was no
answer in the mouths of these three men, he became angry.

6 E·lī'hū son of Bar'a·chel the Būz'īte answered:
"I am young in years,
    and you are aged;
therefore I was timid and afraid
    to declare my opinion to you.
7 I said, 'Let days speak,
    and many years teach wisdom.'
8 But truly it is the spirit in a mortal,

But truly it is the spirit in a mortal, the breath of the Almighty, that makes for understanding. 32.8

    the breath of the Almighty,*l* that makes for
        understanding.
9 It is not the old*n* that are wise,
    nor the aged that understand what is right.
10 Therefore I say, 'Listen to me;
    let me also declare my opinion.'

11 "See, I waited for your words,
    I listened for your wise sayings,
    while you searched out what to say.
12 I gave you my attention,
    but there was in fact no one that confuted
        Jōb,
    no one among you that answered his
        words.
13 Yet do not say, 'We have found wisdom;
    God may vanquish him, not a human.'
14 He has not directed his words against me,
    and I will not answer him with your
        speeches.

15 "They are dismayed, they answer no more;
    they have not a word to say.
16 And am I to wait, because they do not speak,
    because they stand there, and answer no
        more?
17 I also will give my answer;
    I also will declare my opinion.
18 For I am full of words;
    the spirit within me constrains me.
19 My heart is indeed like wine that has no vent;
    like new wineskins, it is ready to burst.
20 I must speak, so that I may find relief;
    I must open my lips and answer.
21 I will not show partiality to any person

---

j Meaning of Heb uncertain   *k* Or *as Adam did*
l Traditional rendering of Heb *Shaddai*   *m* Another ancient
tradition reads *answer, and had put God in the wrong*   *n* Gk
Syr Vg: Heb *many*

or use flattery toward anyone.
22 For I do not know how to flatter—
   or my Maker would soon put an end to me!

Elihu Rebukes Job

33 "But now, hear my speech, O Job,
   and listen to all my words.
2 See, I open my mouth;
   the tongue in my mouth speaks.
3 My words declare the uprightness of my heart,
   and what my lips know they speak
      sincerely.
4 The spirit of God has made me,
   and the breath of the Almighty*o* gives me
      life.
5 Answer me, if you can;
   set your words in order before me; take
      your stand.
6 See, before God I am as you are;
   I too was formed from a piece of clay.
7 No fear of me need terrify you;
   my pressure will not be heavy on you.

8 "Surely, you have spoken in my hearing,
   and I have heard the sound of your words.
9 You say, 'I am clean, without transgression;
   I am pure, and there is no iniquity in me.
10 Look, he finds occasions against me,
   he counts me as his enemy;
11 he puts my feet in the stocks,
   and watches all my paths.'

12 "But in this you are not right. I will answer
      you:
   God is greater than any mortal.
13 Why do you contend against him,
   saying, 'He will answer none of my*p* words'?
14 For God speaks in one way,
   and in two, though people do not
      perceive it.
15 In a dream, in a vision of the night,
   when deep sleep falls on mortals,
   while they slumber on their beds,
16 then he opens their ears,
   and terrifies them with warnings,
17 that he may turn them aside from their
      deeds,
   and keep them from pride,
18 to spare their souls from the Pit,
   their lives from traversing the River.
19 They are also chastened with pain upon their
      beds,
   and with continual strife in their bones,
20 so that their lives loathe bread,
   and their appetites dainty food.
21 Their flesh is so wasted away that it cannot be
      seen;

and their bones, once invisible, now stick
   out.
22 Their souls draw near the Pit,
   and their lives to those who bring death.
23 Then, if there should be for one of them an
      angel,
   a mediator, one of a thousand,
   one who declares a person upright,
24 and he is gracious to that person, and says,
   'Deliver him from going down into the Pit;
   I have found a ransom;
25 let his flesh become fresh with youth;
   let him return to the days of his youthful
      vigor';
26 then he prays to God, and is accepted by him,
   he comes into his presence with joy,
and God*q* repays him for his righteousness.
27   That person sings to others and says,
'I sinned, and perverted what was right,
   and it was not paid back to me.
28 He has redeemed my soul from going down to
      the Pit,
   and my life shall see the light.'

29 "God indeed does all these things,
   twice, three times, with mortals,
30 to bring back their souls from the Pit,
   so that they may see the light of life.*r*
31 Pay heed, Job, listen to me;
   be silent, and I will speak.
32 If you have anything to say, answer me;
   speak, for I desire to justify you.
33 If not, listen to me;
   be silent, and I will teach you wisdom."

Elihu Proclaims God's Justice

34 Then E•li´hū continued and said:
2   "Hear my words, you wise men,
   and give ear to me, you who know;
3 for the ear tests words
   as the palate tastes food.
4 Let us choose what is right;
   let us determine among ourselves what is
      good.
5 For Job has said, 'I am innocent,
   and God has taken away my right;
6 in spite of being right I am counted a liar;
   my wound is incurable, though I am
      without transgression.'
7 Who is there like Job,
   who drinks up scoffing like water,
8 who goes in company with evildoers
   and walks with the wicked?

---

o Traditional rendering of Heb *Shaddai*   *p* Compare Gk:
Heb *his*   *q* Heb *he*   *r* Syr: Heb *to be lighted with the light
of life*

J
O
B

9 For he has said, 'It profits one nothing
    to take delight in God.'

10 "Therefore, hear me, you who have sense,
    far be it from God that he should do
        wickedness,
    and from the Almighty[s] that he should do
        wrong.
11 For according to their deeds he will repay
        them,
    and according to their ways he will make it
        befall them.
12 Of a truth, God will not do wickedly,
    and the Almighty[s] will not pervert justice.
13 Who gave him charge over the earth
    and who laid on him[t] the whole world?
14 If he should take back his spirit[u] to himself,
    and gather to himself his breath,
15 all flesh would perish together,
    and all mortals return to dust.

16 "If you have understanding, hear this;
    listen to what I say.
17 Shall one who hates justice govern?
    Will you condemn one who is righteous
        and mighty,
18 who says to a king, 'You scoundrel!'
    and to princes, 'You wicked men!';
19 who shows no partiality to nobles,
    nor regards the rich more than the poor,
    for they are all the work of his hands?
20 In a moment they die;
    at midnight the people are shaken and pass
        away,
    and the mighty are taken away by no
        human hand.

21 "For his eyes are upon the ways of mortals,
    and he sees all their steps.
22 There is no gloom or deep darkness
    where evildoers may hide themselves.
23 For he has not appointed a time[v] for anyone
    to go before God in judgment.
24 He shatters the mighty without investigation,
    and sets others in their place.
25 Thus, knowing their works,
    he overturns them in the night, and they
        are crushed.
26 He strikes them for their wickedness
    while others look on,
27 because they turned aside from following
        him,
    and had no regard for any of his ways,
28 so that they caused the cry of the poor to come
        to him,
    and he heard the cry of the afflicted—
29 When he is quiet, who can condemn?

When he hides his face, who can behold
    him,
    whether it be a nation or an individual?—
30 so that the godless should not reign,
    or those who ensnare the people.

31 "For has anyone said to God,
    'I have endured punishment; I will not
        offend any more;
32 teach me what I do not see;
    if I have done iniquity, I will do it no
        more'?
33 Will he then pay back to suit you,
    because you reject it?
For you must choose, and not I;
    therefore declare what you know.[w]
34 Those who have sense will say to me,
    and the wise who hear me will say,
35 'Jōb speaks without knowledge,
    his words are without insight.'
36 Would that Jōb were tried to the limit,
    because his answers are those of the wicked.
37 For he adds rebellion to his sin;
    he claps his hands among us,
    and multiplies his words against God."

Elihu Condemns Self-Righteousness

35 E·li'hū continued and said:
2 "Do you think this to be just?
You say, 'I am in the right before God.'
3 If you ask, 'What advantage have I?
    How am I better off than if I had sinned?'
4 I will answer you
    and your friends with you.
5 Look at the heavens and see;
    observe the clouds, which are higher than
        you.
6 If you have sinned, what do you accomplish
        against him?
    And if your transgressions are multiplied,
        what do you do to him?
7 If you are righteous, what do you give to him;
    or what does he receive from your hand?
8 Your wickedness affects others like you,
    and your righteousness, other human
        beings.

9 "Because of the multitude of oppressions
        people cry out;
    they call for help because of the arm of the
        mighty.
10 But no one says, 'Where is God my Maker,
    who gives strength in the night,

---

[s] Traditional rendering of Heb *Shaddai*   [t] Heb lacks *on him*   [u] Heb *his heart his spirit*   [v] Cn: Heb *yet*   [w] Meaning of Heb of verses 29-33 uncertain

11 who teaches us more than the animals of the
      earth,
      and makes us wiser than the birds of the
      air?'
12 There they cry out, but he does not answer,
      because of the pride of evildoers.
13 Surely God does not hear an empty cry,
      nor does the Almighty[x] regard it.
14 How much less when you say that you do not
      see him,
      that the case is before him, and you are
      waiting for him!
15 And now, because his anger does not punish,
      and he does not greatly heed transgression,[y]
16 Jōb opens his mouth in empty talk,
      he multiplies words without knowledge."

Elihu Exalts God's Goodness

36 E·lī'hū continued and said:
2 "Bear with me a little, and I will
      show you,
      for I have yet something to say on God's
      behalf.
3 I will bring my knowledge from far away,
      and ascribe righteousness to my Maker.
4 For truly my words are not false;
      one who is perfect in knowledge is with
      you.

5 "Surely God is mighty and does not despise
      any;
      he is mighty in strength of understanding.
6 He does not keep the wicked alive,
      but gives the afflicted their right.
7 He does not withdraw his eyes from the
      righteous,
      but with kings on the throne
      he sets them forever, and they are exalted.
8 And if they are bound in fetters
      and caught in the cords of affliction,
9 then he declares to them their work
      and their transgressions, that they are
      behaving arrogantly.
10 He opens their ears to instruction,
      and commands that they return from
      iniquity.
11 If they listen, and serve him,
      they complete their days in prosperity,
      and their years in pleasantness.
12 But if they do not listen, they shall perish by
      the sword,
      and die without knowledge.

13 "The godless in heart cherish anger;
      they do not cry for help when he binds
      them.
14 They die in their youth,

and their life ends in shame.[z]
15 He delivers the afflicted by their affliction,
      and opens their ear by adversity.
16 He also allured you out of distress
      into a broad place where there was no
      constraint,
      and what was set on your table was full of
      fatness.

17 "But you are obsessed with the case of the
      wicked;
      judgment and justice seize you.
18 Beware that wrath does not entice you into
      scoffing,
      and do not let the greatness of the ransom
      turn you aside.
19 Will your cry avail to keep you from
      distress,
      or will all the force of your strength?
20 Do not long for the night,
      when peoples are cut off in their place.
21 Beware! Do not turn to iniquity;
      because of that you have been tried by
      affliction.
22 See, God is exalted in his power;
      who is a teacher like him?
23 Who has prescribed for him his way,
      or who can say, 'You have done wrong'?

Elihu Proclaims God's Majesty

24 "Remember to extol his work,
      of which mortals have sung.
25 All people have looked on it;
      everyone watches it from far away.
26 Surely God is great, and we do not know
      him;
      the number of his years is unsearchable.
27 For he draws up the drops of water;
      he distills[a] his mist in rain,
28 which the skies pour down
      and drop upon mortals abundantly.
29 Can anyone understand the spreading of the
      clouds,
      the thunderings of his pavilion?
30 See, he scatters his lightning around him
      and covers the roots of the sea.
31 For by these he governs peoples;
      he gives food in abundance.
32 He covers his hands with the lightning,
      and commands it to strike the mark.
33 Its crashing[b] tells about him;
      he is jealous[b] with anger against iniquity.

---

x Traditional rendering of Heb *Shaddai*   y Theodotion
Symmachus Compare Vg: Meaning of Heb uncertain
z Heb *ends among the temple prostitutes*   a Cn: Heb *they
distill*   b Meaning of Heb uncertain

37

"At this also my heart trembles,
and leaps out of its place.

2 Listen, listen to the thunder of his voice
and the rumbling that comes from his
mouth.

3 Under the whole heaven he lets it loose,
and his lightning to the corners of the
earth.

4 After it his voice roars;
he thunders with his majestic voice
and he does not restrain the lightnings*c*
when his voice is heard.

5 God thunders wondrously with his voice;
he does great things that we cannot
comprehend.

6 For to the snow he says, 'Fall on the earth';
and the shower of rain, his heavy shower
of rain,

7 serves as a sign on everyone's hand,
so that all whom he has made may
know it.*d*

8 Then the animals go into their lairs
and remain in their dens.

9 From its chamber comes the whirlwind,
and cold from the scattering winds.

10 By the breath of God ice is given,
and the broad waters are frozen fast.

11 He loads the thick cloud with moisture;
the clouds scatter his lightning.

12 They turn round and round by his
guidance,
to accomplish all that he commands them
on the face of the habitable world.

13 Whether for correction, or for his land,
or for love, he causes it to happen.

14 "Hear this, O Jōb;
stop and consider the wondrous works of
God.

15 Do you know how God lays his command
upon them,
and causes the lightning of his cloud to
shine?

16 Do you know the balancings of the clouds,
the wondrous works of the one whose
knowledge is perfect,

17 you whose garments are hot
when the earth is still because of the south
wind?

18 Can you, like him, spread out the skies,
hard as a molten mirror?

19 Teach us what we shall say to him;
we cannot draw up our case because of
darkness.

20 Should he be told that I want to speak?
Did anyone ever wish to be swallowed up?

21 Now, no one can look on the light

when it is bright in the skies,
when the wind has passed and cleared them.

22 Out of the north comes golden splendor;
around God is awesome majesty.

23 The Almighty*e*—we cannot find him;
he is great in power and justice,
and abundant righteousness he will not
violate.

24 Therefore mortals fear him;
he does not regard any who are wise in
their own conceit."

The LORD Answers Job
(Cp Gen 1.1–10)

38

Then the LORD answered Jōb out of the
whirlwind:

2 "Who is this that darkens counsel by words
without knowledge?

3 Gird up your loins like a man,
I will question you, and you shall declare
to me.

4 "Where were you when I laid the foundation of
the earth?
Tell me, if you have understanding.

5 Who determined its measurements—surely you
know!
Or who stretched the line upon it?

6 On what were its bases sunk,
or who laid its cornerstone

7 when the morning stars sang together
and all the heavenly beings*f* shouted for
joy?

8 "Or who shut in the sea with doors
when it burst out from the womb?—

9 when I made the clouds its garment,
and thick darkness its swaddling band,

10 and prescribed bounds for it,
and set bars and doors,

11 and said, 'Thus far shall you come, and no
farther,
and here shall your proud waves be
stopped'?

12 "Have you commanded the morning since
your days began,
and caused the dawn to know its place,

13 so that it might take hold of the skirts of the
earth,
and the wicked be shaken out of it?

14 It is changed like clay under the seal,
and it is dyed*g* like a garment.

---

c Heb *them*   *d* Meaning of Heb of verse 7 uncertain
e Traditional rendering of Heb *Shaddai*   *f* Heb *sons
of God*   *g* Cn: Heb *and they stand forth*

did you KNOW?

Heaven and Earth

The questions God asks Job about the formation of the cosmos (Job 38.4–38) give us a clue about how the ancient Israelites thought the universe was put together. They believed that God had created it in three levels: the heavens, which were contained in a giant vault above the earth; the earth itself, which was a disk that rested on the waters of the abyss; and the abyss, which was the underworld. Over time, the heavens and the earth developed symbolic meanings. The heavens became known as the place where God dwells and the earth as the place that humans inhabit. Even later, the abyss became known as the place of the dead.

▶ Job 38.4–38

15 Light is withheld from the wicked,
      and their uplifted arm is broken.

16 "Have you entered into the springs of the sea,
      or walked in the recesses of the deep?
17 Have the gates of death been revealed to you,
      or have you seen the gates of deep
        darkness?
18 Have you comprehended the expanse of the
        earth?
      Declare, if you know all this.

19 "Where is the way to the dwelling of light,
      and where is the place of darkness,
20 that you may take it to its territory
      and that you may discern the paths to its
        home?
21 Surely you know, for you were born then,
      and the number of your days is great!

22 "Have you entered the storehouses of the
        snow,
      or have you seen the storehouses of the
        hail,
23 which I have reserved for the time of trouble,
      for the day of battle and war?
24 What is the way to the place where the light is
        distributed,

or where the east wind is scattered upon the
      earth?
25 "Who has cut a channel for the torrents of rain,
      and a way for the thunderbolt,
26 to bring rain on a land where no one lives,
      on the desert, which is empty of human
        life,
27 to satisfy the waste and desolate land,
      and to make the ground put forth grass?

28 "Has the rain a father,
      or who has begotten the drops of dew?
29 From whose womb did the ice come forth,
      and who has given birth to the hoarfrost of
        heaven?
30 The waters become hard like stone,
      and the face of the deep is frozen.

31 "Can you bind the chains of the Plēi'a•dēs,
      or loose the cords of Ō•rī'on?
32 Can you lead forth the Maz'za•roth in their
        season,
      or can you guide the Bear with its
        children?
33 Do you know the ordinances of the heavens?
      Can you establish their rule on the earth?

34 "Can you lift up your voice to the clouds,
      so that a flood of waters may cover you?
35 Can you send forth lightnings, so that they
        may go
      and say to you, 'Here we are'?
36 Who has put wisdom in the inward parts,[h]
      or given understanding to the mind?[h]
37 Who has the wisdom to number the clouds?
      Or who can tilt the waterskins of the
        heavens,
38 when the dust runs into a mass
      and the clods cling together?

39 "Can you hunt the prey for the lion,
      or satisfy the appetite of the young lions,
40 when they crouch in their dens,
      or lie in wait in their covert?
41 Who provides for the raven its prey,
      when its young ones cry to God,
      and wander about for lack of food?

39

"Do you know when the mountain
        goats give birth?
      Do you observe the calving of the deer?
2 Can you number the months that they fulfill,
      and do you know the time when they give
        birth,

---

h Meaning of Heb uncertain

3 when they crouch to give birth to their
  offspring,
  and are delivered of their young?
4 Their young ones become strong, they grow up
  in the open;
  they go forth, and do not return to them.

5 "Who has let the wild ass go free?
  Who has loosed the bonds of the swift ass,
6 to which I have given the steppe for its home,
  the salt land for its dwelling place?
7 It scorns the tumult of the city;
  it does not hear the shouts of the driver.
8 It ranges the mountains as its pasture,
  and it searches after every green thing.

9 "Is the wild ox willing to serve you?
  Will it spend the night at your crib?
10 Can you tie it in the furrow with ropes,
  or will it harrow the valleys after you?
11 Will you depend on it because its strength is
  great,
  and will you hand over your labor to it?
12 Do you have faith in it that it will return,
  and bring your grain to your threshing
  floor?*i*

13 "The ostrich's wings flap wildly,
  though its pinions lack plumage.*j*
14 For it leaves its eggs to the earth,
  and lets them be warmed on the ground,
15 forgetting that a foot may crush them,
  and that a wild animal may trample them.
16 It deals cruelly with its young, as if they were
  not its own;
  though its labor should be in vain, yet it
  has no fear;
17 because God has made it forget wisdom,
  and given it no share in understanding.
18 When it spreads its plumes aloft,*k*
  it laughs at the horse and its rider.

19 "Do you give the horse its might?
  Do you clothe its neck with mane?
20 Do you make it leap like the locust?
  Its majestic snorting is terrible.
21 It paws*j* violently, exults mightily;
  it goes out to meet the weapons.
22 It laughs at fear, and is not dismayed;
  it does not turn back from the sword.
23 Upon it rattle the quiver,
  the flashing spear, and the javelin.
24 With fierceness and rage it swallows the
  ground;
  it cannot stand still at the sound of the
  trumpet.
25 When the trumpet sounds, it says 'Aha!'

From a distance it smells the battle,
  the thunder of the captains, and the
  shouting.
26 "Is it by your wisdom that the hawk soars,
  and spreads its wings toward the south?
27 Is it at your command that the eagle
  mounts up
  and makes its nest on high?
28 It lives on the rock and makes its home
  in the fastness of the rocky crag.
29 From there it spies the prey;
  its eyes see it from far away.
30 Its young ones suck up blood;
  and where the slain are, there it is."

40 And the LORD said to Jōb:
2 "Shall a faultfinder contend with
  the Almighty?*l*
Anyone who argues with God must
  respond."

Job's Response to God

3 Then Jōb answered the LORD:
4 "See, I am of small account; what shall I
  answer you?
  I lay my hand on my mouth.
5 I have spoken once, and I will not answer;
  twice, but will proceed no further."

God's Challenge to Job

6 Then the LORD answered Jōb out of the whirlwind:
7 "Gird up your loins like a man;
  I will question you, and you declare to me.
8 Will you even put me in the wrong?
  Will you condemn me that you may be
  justified?
9 Have you an arm like God,
  and can you thunder with a voice
  like his?

10 "Deck yourself with majesty and dignity;
  clothe yourself with glory and splendor.
11 Pour out the overflowings of your anger,
  and look on all who are proud, and abase
  them.
12 Look on all who are proud, and bring them
  low;
  tread down the wicked where they stand.
13 Hide them all in the dust together;
  bind their faces in the world below.*m*
14 Then I will also acknowledge to you

---

i Heb *your grain and your threshing floor*   *j* Meaning of Heb
uncertain   *k* Gk Syr Vg: Heb *they dig*   *l* Traditional
rendering of Heb *Shaddai*   *m* Heb *the hidden place*

PRAY IT!
Too Big to Understand

All the questions God asks Job about creation and good and evil in Job, chapters 38–41, are intended to make one simple point: "You can never understand me. I am too big. You are too small."

The author of Job seems to be saying to readers, "If you think you've got God all figured out—like Job's friends thought they had or like even Job wanted to have—you're wrong." The author is reminding readers that God is a mystery —powerful and awesome beyond our imagination and control.

In your prayer, reflect or journal on the following questions:
- Do you expect God to provide you with happiness? peace? friends?
- What happens if God doesn't meet your expectations in the way you want them to be met? Can you let go of your expectations and trust in God's love? Why or why not?

▶ Job, chapters 38–41

that your own right hand can give you
    victory.

15 "Look at Bē'he·moth,
    which I made just as I made you;
    it eats grass like an ox.
16 Its strength is in its loins,
    and its power in the muscles of its belly.
17 It makes its tail stiff like a cedar;
    the sinews of its thighs are knit together.
18 Its bones are tubes of bronze,
    its limbs like bars of iron.

19 "It is the first of the great acts of God—
    only its Maker can approach it with the
        sword.
20 For the mountains yield food for it
    where all the wild animals play.
21 Under the lotus plants it lies,
    in the covert of the reeds and in the marsh.
22 The lotus trees cover it for shade;
    the willows of the wadi surround it.
23 Even if the river is turbulent, it is not
    frightened;

it is confident though Jordan rushes against
    its mouth.
24 Can one take it with hooks[n]
    or pierce its nose with a snare?

41 [o] "Can you draw out Le·vī'a·than[p] with
      a fishhook,
    or press down its tongue with a cord?
2 Can you put a rope in its nose,
    or pierce its jaw with a hook?
3 Will it make many supplications to you?
    Will it speak soft words to you?
4 Will it make a covenant with you
    to be taken as your servant forever?
5 Will you play with it as with a bird,
    or will you put it on leash for your girls?
6 Will traders bargain over it?
    Will they divide it up among the
      merchants?
7 Can you fill its skin with harpoons,
    or its head with fishing spears?
8 Lay hands on it;
    think of the battle; you will not do it again!
9[q] Any hope of capturing it[r] will be disappointed;
    were not even the gods[s] overwhelmed at the
      sight of it?
10 No one is so fierce as to dare to stir it up.
    Who can stand before it?[t]
11 Who can confront it[t] and be safe?[u]
    —under the whole heaven, who?[v]

12 "I will not keep silence concerning its limbs,
    or its mighty strength, or its splendid frame.
13 Who can strip off its outer garment?
    Who can penetrate its double coat of mail?[w]
14 Who can open the doors of its face?
    There is terror all around its teeth.
15 Its back[x] is made of shields in rows,
    shut up closely as with a seal.
16 One is so near to another
    that no air can come between them.
17 They are joined one to another;
    they clasp each other and cannot be
      separated.
18 Its sneezes flash forth light,
    and its eyes are like the eyelids of the dawn.
19 From its mouth go flaming torches;
    sparks of fire leap out.
20 Out of its nostrils comes smoke,
    as from a boiling pot and burning rushes.
21 Its breath kindles coals,

---

[n] Cn: Heb *in his eyes*   [o] Ch 40.25 in Heb   [p] Or *the crocodile*   [q] Ch 41.1 in Heb   [r] Heb *of it*   [s] Cn Compare Symmachus Syr: Heb *one is*   [t] Heb *me*   [u] Gk: Heb *that I shall repay*   [v] Heb *to me*   [w] Gk: Heb *bridle*   [x] Cn Compare Gk Vg: Heb *pride*

J
O
B

and a flame comes out of its mouth.

22 In its neck abides strength,
and terror dances before it.

23 The folds of its flesh cling together;
it is firmly cast and immovable.

24 Its heart is as hard as stone,
as hard as the lower millstone.

25 When it raises itself up the gods are afraid;
at the crashing they are beside themselves.

26 Though the sword reaches it, it does not avail,
nor does the spear, the dart, or the javelin.

27 It counts iron as straw,
and bronze as rotten wood.

28 The arrow cannot make it flee;
slingstones, for it, are turned to chaff.

29 Clubs are counted as chaff;
it laughs at the rattle of javelins.

30 Its underparts are like sharp potsherds;
it spreads itself like a threshing sledge on
the mire.

31 It makes the deep boil like a pot;
it makes the sea like a pot of ointment.

32 It leaves a shining wake behind it;
one would think the deep to be white-haired.

33 On earth it has no equal,
a creature without fear.

34 It surveys everything that is lofty;
it is king over all that are proud."

Job Is Humbled and Satisfied

42 Then Jōb answered the LORD:
2 "I know that you can do all things,
and that no purpose of yours can be
thwarted.

3 'Who is this that hides counsel without
knowledge?'
Therefore I have uttered what I did not
understand,
things too wonderful for me, which I did
not know.

4 'Hear, and I will speak;
I will question you, and you declare to me.'

5 I had heard of you by the hearing of the ear,
but now my eye sees you;

6 therefore I despise myself,
and repent in dust and ashes."

Job's Friends Are Humiliated

7 After the LORD had spoken these words to Jōb, the LORD said to E·lī'phaz the Tē'man·īte: "My wrath is kindled against you and against your two friends; for you have not spoken of me what is right, as my servant Jōb has. 8 Now therefore take seven bulls and seven rams, and go to my servant Jōb, and offer up for yourselves a burnt offering; and my servant Jōb shall pray for you, for I will accept his prayer not to deal with you according to your folly; for you have not spoken of me what is right, as my servant Jōb has done." 9 So E·lī'phaz the Tē'man·īte and Bil'dad the Shū'hīte and Zō'phar the Nā'a·ma·thīte went and did what the LORD had told them; and the LORD accepted Jōb's prayer.

Job's Fortunes Are Restored Twofold

10 And the LORD restored the fortunes of Jōb when he had prayed for his friends; and the LORD gave Jōb twice as much as he had before. 11 Then there came to him all his brothers and sisters and

Why?

LIVE IT!

So, that's it? God just shows up, overwhelms Job with a bunch of questions he can't answer, and then gives Job back double everything he lost? God doesn't even answer Job's question about why he had to suffer!

And what about *our* questions? Why do innocent children die? Why is someone we love taken from us? Why do people die from hunger in a world that has so much? Why did that plane crash? Why did our friend die?

Why was Job satisfied with God's response? Perhaps Job's mind and his heart struggled with God's answer, and his heart won. Maybe his heart told him to trust in God's love even when his mind couldn't understand the mystery of his suffering.

With Job, the Israelite people began to see the suffering of innocent people as mystery and not as punishment. In the New Testament, this suffering would continue to be seen as mystery but also as something more. The death of Jesus—the ultimate innocent suffering person—and his Resurrection led to the understanding that God ultimately brings good out of the suffering of faithful people (see Jn 12.24–25 and the introduction to 1 Peter).

▶ Job 38.1—42.6

all who had known him before, and they ate bread with him in his house; they showed him sympathy and comforted him for all the evil that the LORD had brought upon him; and each of them gave him a piece of money^y and a gold ring. 12 The LORD blessed the latter days of Jōb more than his beginning; and he had fourteen thousand sheep, six thousand camels, a thousand yoke of oxen, and a thousand donkeys. 13 He also had seven sons and three daughters. 14 He named the first Je•mī′mah, the second Ke•zī′ah, and the third Ker′en-hap′puch. 15 In all the land there were no women so beautiful as Jōb's daughters; and their father gave them an inheritance along with their brothers. 16 After this Jōb lived one hundred and forty years, and saw his children, and his children's children, four generations. 17 And Jōb died, old and full of days.

---

y Heb *a qesitah*

We each have our own favorite music that somehow resonates with our being, and maybe even expresses our attitude and philosophy toward life. So much so that we often refer to it as *our* music, even though it was written by someone else. In the same way, we can say that the Psalms are Israel's music. They are the hymns or songs that Israel used in its Temple worship. They give voice to the souls of the Israelites and tell about the ups and downs of the Israelites' relationship with God.

At a Glance

Psalms is divided into five books without any particular organizing theme:

- **Psalms 1–41.** Book I
- **Psalms 42–72.** Book II
- **Psalms 73–89.** Book III
- **Psalms 90–106.** Book IV
- **Psalms 107–150.** Book V

In-depth

The Hebrew version of Psalms is titled Tehillim, or Praises, because its hymns praise God. The Greek translation calls them Psalmoi, or Psalms, which means "religious songs performed to music." The 150 Psalms can be grouped into one or more of five general categories:

- The *hymns of praise and thanksgiving* sing of God's majesty, power, and wisdom (for example, Psalms 8, 24, 47, 93, 95–99, 113–118, 136, and 150).
- The *hymns of lament or petition* include both individual and communal cries to God for help in some need (for example, Psalms 38, 51, 55, 58, 59, 74, 78, 105, and 106).
- The *hymns of wisdom* sing of Israel's insights into how to live according to God's law and what brings true happiness (for example, Psalms 1, 34, 37, 49, 73, 112, and 128).
- The *liturgical or worship psalms* are used for entrance hymns at liturgies or during worship services at the Temple (for example, Psalms 15, 24, and 134).
- The *historical psalms* sing of the great wonders God has worked throughout the history of Israel (for example, Psalms 78, 105, 106, 135, and 136).

Quick Facts

Authors
many, sometimes called psalmists

Themes
a variety

Of Note
The psalms are used by Catholic Christians regularly at Mass and in the church's official prayer, the Liturgy of the Hours.

Because of King David's reputation for writing and performing music, he is named as the author of many of the Psalms. Actually, though, many of them were written long after his death. It is more accurate to understand the Psalms as a collection of songs that reflect different times and experiences throughout Israel's existence. Just as your favorite music might tell others what you value as a person, the Psalms tell us about Israel and its wondrous relationship with God.

The Book of Psalms

Psalms

BOOK I
(Psalms 1–41)

Psalm 1

The Two Ways

1 Happy are those
  who do not follow the advice of the
      wicked,
  or take the path that sinners tread,
    or sit in the seat of scoffers;
2 but their delight is in the law of
      the LORD,
  and on his law they meditate day and
      night.
3 They are like trees
    planted by streams of water,
  which yield their fruit in its season,
    and their leaves do not wither.
  In all that they do, they prosper.

4 The wicked are not so,
    but are like chaff that the wind drives
      away.
5 Therefore the wicked will not stand in the
      judgment,
    nor sinners in the congregation of the
      righteous;
6 for the LORD watches over the way of the
      righteous,
    but the way of the wicked will perish.

Psalm 2

God's Promise to His Anointed

(Acts 4.23–31)

1 Why do the nations conspire,
    and the peoples plot in vain?
2 The kings of the earth set themselves,
    and the rulers take counsel together,
    against the LORD and his anointed, saying,
3 "Let us burst their bonds asunder,
    and cast their cords from us."

4 He who sits in the heavens laughs;
    the LORD has them in derision.
5 Then he will speak to them in his wrath,
    and terrify them in his fury, saying,
6 "I have set my king on Zion, my holy hill."

7 I will tell of the decree of the LORD:
  He said to me, "You are my son;
    today I have begotten you.
8 Ask of me, and I will make the nations your
      heritage,
    and the ends of the earth your possession.
9 You shall break them with a rod of iron,
    and dash them in pieces like a potter's
      vessel."

10 Now therefore, O kings, be wise;
    be warned, O rulers of the earth.

P
S
A
L
M
S

?did you KNOW?
Understanding the Psalms

"Praise God!" "Why am I suffering?" "Save us from oppression and injustice." "God, give me rest." These phrases illustrate types of prayer: praise, lament, and petition. The Book of Psalms includes these and many other kinds of prayer, made by individuals, small groups, or the whole Jewish nation. Yet, throughout the Psalms, there is one constant: human experience is viewed through the eyes of faith. For example, Psalm 3 reflects the human experience of being attacked by others (verses 1–2). The writer of this psalm, rather than losing all hope, calls God to the rescue (verse 7). In a similar way, all the Psalms teach us that every human experience can also be a faith experience.

11 Serve the LORD with fear,
     with trembling 12 kiss his feet,*a*
or he will be angry, and you will perish in the way;
     for his wrath is quickly kindled.

Happy are all who take refuge in him.

Psalm 3

Trust in God under Adversity

A Psalm of David, when he fled from his son Ab′sa•lom.

1 O LORD, how many are my foes!
     Many are rising against me;
2 many are saying to me,
     "There is no help for you*b* in God."   *Sĕ′lah*

3 But you, O LORD, are a shield around me,
     my glory, and the one who lifts up my head.
4 I cry aloud to the LORD,
     and he answers me from his holy hill.   *Sĕ′lah*

5 I lie down and sleep;
     I wake again, for the LORD sustains me.
6 I am not afraid of ten thousands of people
     who have set themselves against me all around.

7 Rise up, O LORD!
     Deliver me, O my God!
For you strike all my enemies on the cheek;
     you break the teeth of the wicked.

8 Deliverance belongs to the LORD;
     may your blessing be on your people!
                                                    Sĕ′lah

Psalm 4

Confident Plea for Deliverance from Enemies

To the leader: with stringed instruments.
A Psalm of David.

1 Answer me when I call, O God of my right!
     You gave me room when I was in distress.
     Be gracious to me, and hear my prayer.

2 How long, you people, shall my honor suffer shame?
     How long will you love vain words, and seek after lies?   *Sĕ′lah*
3 But know that the LORD has set apart the faithful for himself;
     the LORD hears when I call to him.

4 When you are disturbed,*c* do not sin;
     ponder it on your beds, and be silent.
                                                    Sĕ′lah
5 Offer right sacrifices,
     and put your trust in the LORD.

6 There are many who say, "O that we might see some good!
     Let the light of your face shine on us, O LORD!"
7 You have put gladness in my heart
     more than when their grain and wine abound.

8 I will both lie down and sleep in peace;
     for you alone, O LORD, make me lie down in safety.

Psalm 5

Trust in God for Deliverance from Enemies

To the leader: for the flutes. A Psalm of David.

1 Give ear to my words, O LORD;
     give heed to my sighing.
2 Listen to the sound of my cry,
     my King and my God, for to you I pray.

---

a Cn: Meaning of Heb of verses 11b and 12a is uncertain
b Syr: Heb *him*   *c* Or *are angry*

3 O LORD, in the morning you hear my voice;
in the morning I plead my case to you, and
watch.

4 For you are not a God who delights in
wickedness;
evil will not sojourn with you.
5 The boastful will not stand before your eyes;
you hate all evildoers.
6 You destroy those who speak lies;
the LORD abhors the bloodthirsty and
deceitful.

7 But I, through the abundance of your steadfast
love,
will enter your house,
I will bow down toward your holy temple
in awe of you.
8 Lead me, O LORD, in your righteousness
because of my enemies;
make your way straight before me.

9 For there is no truth in their mouths;
their hearts are destruction;
their throats are open graves;
they flatter with their tongues.
10 Make them bear their guilt, O God;
let them fall by their own counsels;
because of their many transgressions cast them
out,
for they have rebelled against you.

11 But let all who take refuge in you rejoice;
let them ever sing for joy.
Spread your protection over them,
so that those who love your name may
exult in you.
12 For you bless the righteous, O LORD;
you cover them with favor as with a shield.

Psalm 6

Prayer for Recovery

To the leader: with stringed instruments; according to
The Shem'i•nith. A Psalm of David.

1 O LORD, do not rebuke me in your
anger,
or discipline me in your wrath.
2 Be gracious to me, O LORD, for I am
languishing;
O LORD, heal me, for my bones are shaking
with terror.
3 My soul also is struck with terror,
while you, O LORD—how long?

4 Turn, O LORD, save my life;
deliver me for the sake of your steadfast
love.
5 For in death there is no remembrance
of you;
in Shē'ōl who can give you praise?

6 I am weary with my moaning;
every night I flood my bed with
tears;
I drench my couch with my weeping.
7 My eyes waste away because of grief;
they grow weak because of all
my foes.

8 Depart from me, all you workers of evil,
for the LORD has heard the sound of my
weeping.
9 The LORD has heard my supplication;
the LORD accepts my prayer.
10 All my enemies shall be ashamed and struck
with terror;
they shall turn back, and in a moment be
put to shame.

Our Cross to Bear

In Psalm 6, the psalmist is praying for deliverance from physical and mental suffering. Christians often refer to the suffering or sacrifice that comes as part of life as
their cross to bear, because they see it as connected to Jesus' own suffering on the
cross. Indeed, we all have crosses to bear. Some crosses are heavier than others,
and like the psalmist, we ask God to deliver us from them. But unlike the psalmist, Christians also pray that God will transform their suffering and use it in some way for the good
of others.

What are some of the crosses that you have had to bear? How were you saved from
your suffering? How has someone else's suffering or sacrifice helped or inspired you?

▶ Psalm 6

Psalm 7

Plea for Help against Persecutors

A Shig•gāi'on of David, which he sang to the LORD
concerning Cush, a Ben'ja•min•ite.

1 O LORD my God, in you I take refuge;
  save me from all my pursuers, and deliver
    me,
2 or like a lion they will tear me apart;
  they will drag me away, with no one to
    rescue.

3 O LORD my God, if I have done this,
  if there is wrong in my hands,
4 if I have repaid my ally with harm
  or plundered my foe without cause,
5 then let the enemy pursue and overtake me,
  trample my life to the ground,
  and lay my soul in the dust.   *Se'lah*

6 Rise up, O LORD, in your anger;
  lift yourself up against the fury of my
    enemies;
  awake, O my God;*d* you have appointed a
    judgment.
7 Let the assembly of the peoples be gathered
    around you,
  and over it take your seat*e* on high.
8 The LORD judges the peoples;
  judge me, O LORD, according to my
    righteousness
  and according to the integrity that is in me.

9 O let the evil of the wicked come to an end,
  but establish the righteous,
you who test the minds and hearts,
  O righteous God.
10 God is my shield,
  who saves the upright in heart.
11 God is a righteous judge,
  and a God who has indignation
    every day.

12 If one does not repent, God*f* will whet his
    sword;
  he has bent and strung his bow;
13 he has prepared his deadly weapons,
  making his arrows fiery shafts.
14 See how they conceive evil,
  and are pregnant with mischief,
  and bring forth lies.
15 They make a pit, digging it out,
  and fall into the hole that they have made.
16 Their mischief returns upon their own
    heads,
  and on their own heads their violence
    descends.

17 I will give to the LORD the thanks due to his
    righteousness,
  and sing praise to the name of the LORD,
    the Most High.

Psalm 8

Divine Majesty and Human Dignity

To the leader: according to The Git'tith.
A Psalm of David.

1 O LORD, our Sovereign,
  how majestic is your name in all the earth!

You have set your glory above the heavens.
2   Out of the mouths of babes and infants
  you have founded a bulwark because of your
    foes,
  to silence the enemy and the avenger.

3 When I look at your heavens, the work of your
    fingers,
  the moon and the stars that you have
    established;
4 what are human beings that you are mindful of
    them,
  mortals*g* that you care for them?

5 Yet you have made them a little lower than
    God,*h*
  and crowned them with glory and honor.
6 You have given them dominion over the works
    of your hands;
  you have put all things under their feet,
7 all sheep and oxen,
  and also the beasts of the field,
8 the birds of the air, and the fish of the sea,
  whatever passes along the paths of the
    seas.

9 O LORD, our Sovereign,
  how majestic is your name in all the
    earth!

Psalm 9

God's Power and Justice

To the leader: according to Muth-lab'ben.
A Psalm of David.

1 I will give thanks to the LORD with my whole
    heart;
  I will tell of all your wonderful deeds.

---

d Or *awake for me*   *e* Cn: Heb *return*   *f* Heb *he*   *g* Heb *ben
adam*, lit. *son of man*   *h* Or *than the divine beings* or *angels*:
Heb *elohim*

2 I will be glad and exult in you;
 I will sing praise to your name, O Most
  High.

3 When my enemies turned back,
 they stumbled and perished before you.
4 For you have maintained my just cause;
 you have sat on the throne giving righteous
  judgment.

5 You have rebuked the nations, you have
  destroyed the wicked;
 you have blotted out their name forever
  and ever.
6 The enemies have vanished in everlasting ruins;
 their cities you have rooted out;
 the very memory of them has perished.

7 But the LORD sits enthroned forever,
 he has established his throne for judgment.
8 He judges the world with righteousness;
 he judges the peoples with equity.

9 The LORD is a stronghold for the oppressed,
 a stronghold in times of trouble.
10 And those who know your name put their trust
  in you,
 for you, O LORD, have not forsaken those
  who seek you.

11 Sing praises to the LORD, who dwells in Zion.
 Declare his deeds among the peoples.
12 For he who avenges blood is mindful of them;
 he does not forget the cry of the afflicted.

13 Be gracious to me, O LORD.
 See what I suffer from those who hate me;
 you are the one who lifts me up from the
  gates of death,
14 so that I may recount all your praises,

and, in the gates of daughter Zion,
 rejoice in your deliverance.

15 The nations have sunk in the pit that they
  made;
 in the net that they hid has their own foot
  been caught.
16 The LORD has made himself known, he has
  executed judgment;
 the wicked are snared in the work of their
  own hands. *Hig·gāiʹon. Sěʹlah*

17 The wicked shall depart to Shěʹōl,
 all the nations that forget God.

18 For the needy shall not always be forgotten,
 nor the hope of the poor perish forever.

19 Rise up, O LORD! Do not let mortals
  prevail;
 let the nations be judged before you.
20 Put them in fear, O LORD;
 let the nations know that they are only
  human. *Sěʹlah*

Psalm 10

Prayer for Deliverance from Enemies

1 Why, O LORD, do you stand far off?
 Why do you hide yourself in times of
  trouble?
2 In arrogance the wicked persecute the poor—
 let them be caught in the schemes they have
  devised.

3 For the wicked boast of the desires of their
  heart,
 those greedy for gain curse and renounce
  the LORD.

Write Your Own Psalm

As you may know, there are many types of psalms (see the introduction to the Book of Psalms). You may also know that more than one person wrote the Psalms. Even today there are psalmists, people who write songs or poems similar in tone and style to the Psalms in the Bible. Would you like to write your own psalm? Try it in your journal:

- Choose the type of psalm you want to write.
- Use poetic language and symbolism.
- Illustrate your psalm.
- Set it to music (like the original ones).
- Or, choose an existing Psalm and rewrite it to reflect a current issue.

P
S
A
L
M
S

4 In the pride of their countenance the wicked
        say, "God will not seek it out";
    all their thoughts are, "There is no God."

5 Their ways prosper at all times;
        your judgments are on high, out of their
            sight;
    as for their foes, they scoff at them.
6 They think in their heart, "We shall not be
            moved;
        throughout all generations we shall not
            meet adversity."

7 Their mouths are filled with cursing and deceit
            and oppression;
        under their tongues are mischief and
            iniquity.
8 They sit in ambush in the villages;
        in hiding places they murder the innocent.

    Their eyes stealthily watch for the helpless;
9   they lurk in secret like a lion in its covert;
    they lurk that they may seize the poor;
        they seize the poor and drag them off in
            their net.

10 They stoop, they crouch,
        and the helpless fall by their might.
11 They think in their heart, "God has forgotten,
        he has hidden his face, he will never
            see it."

12 Rise up, O LORD; O God, lift up your hand;
        do not forget the oppressed.
13 Why do the wicked renounce God,
        and say in their hearts, "You will not call us
            to account"?

14 But you do see! Indeed you note trouble and
            grief,
        that you may take it into your hands;
    the helpless commit themselves to you;
        you have been the helper of the orphan.

15 Break the arm of the wicked and evildoers;
        seek out their wickedness until you find
            none.
16 The LORD is king forever and ever;
        the nations shall perish from his land.

17 O LORD, you will hear the desire of the meek;
        you will strengthen their heart, you will
            incline your ear
18 to do justice for the orphan and the
            oppressed,
        so that those from earth may strike terror
            no more.[i]

Psalm 11

Song of Trust in God

To the leader. Of David.

1 In the LORD I take refuge; how can you say
        to me,
    "Flee like a bird to the mountains;[j]
2 for look, the wicked bend the bow,
        they have fitted their arrow to the string,
        to shoot in the dark at the upright in heart.
3 If the foundations are destroyed,
        what can the righteous do?"

4 The LORD is in his holy temple;
        the LORD's throne is in heaven.
    His eyes behold, his gaze examines
        humankind.
5 The LORD tests the righteous and the wicked,
        and his soul hates the lover of violence.
6 On the wicked he will rain coals of fire and
            sulfur;
        a scorching wind shall be the portion of
            their cup.
7 For the LORD is righteous;
    he loves righteous deeds;
        the upright shall behold his face.

Psalm 12

Plea for Help in Evil Times

To the leader: according to The Shem'i•nith.
A Psalm of David.

1 Help, O LORD, for there is no longer anyone
        who is godly;
        the faithful have disappeared from
            humankind.
2 They utter lies to each other;
        with flattering lips and a double heart they
            speak.

3 May the LORD cut off all flattering lips,
        the tongue that makes great boasts,
4 those who say, "With our tongues we will
            prevail;
        our lips are our own—who is our master?"

5 "Because the poor are despoiled, because the
            needy groan,
        I will now rise up," says the LORD;
    "I will place them in the safety for which
            they long."
6 The promises of the LORD are promises that are
        pure,

---

i Meaning of Heb uncertain   j Gk Syr Jerome Tg: Heb *flee
to your mountain, O bird*

silver refined in a furnace on the ground,
purified seven times.

7 You, O LORD, will protect us;
you will guard us from this generation
forever.
8 On every side the wicked prowl,
as vileness is exalted among humankind.

Psalm 13

Prayer for Deliverance from Enemies
To the leader. A Psalm of David.

1 How long, O LORD? Will you forget me
forever?
How long will you hide your face from me?
2 How long must I bear pain[k] in my soul,
and have sorrow in my heart all day long?
How long shall my enemy be exalted over me?

3 Consider and answer me, O LORD my God!
Give light to my eyes, or I will sleep the
sleep of death,
4 and my enemy will say, "I have prevailed";
my foes will rejoice because I am shaken.

5 But I trusted in your steadfast love;
my heart shall rejoice in your salvation.
6 I will sing to the LORD,
because he has dealt bountifully with me.

Psalm 14

Denunciation of Godlessness
(Ps 53.1–6)
To the leader. Of David.

1 Fools say in their hearts, "There is no God."
They are corrupt, they do abominable
deeds;
there is no one who does good.

2 The LORD looks down from heaven on
humankind
to see if there are any who are wise,
who seek after God.

3 They have all gone astray, they are all alike
perverse;
there is no one who does good,
no, not one.

4 Have they no knowledge, all the
evildoers
who eat up my people as they eat
bread,
and do not call upon the LORD?

5 There they shall be in great terror,
for God is with the company of the
righteous.

k Syr: Heb *hold counsels*

Believing

Angel. My LORD, the earth is filled with those who say, "There is no God!"
God. So, my messenger, what do we do with these people?
Angel. My LORD, they are fools.
God. Perhaps, but they are free. I force no one to believe in me.
Angel. Yet, the wise always seem to find you.
God. That is because they seek me. Those who seek—
Angel. Yes, I know, LORD, they shall find. But how do we get through to those others, the godless ones?
God. You must trust. My signs and wonders surround them. There is the witness of those who believe. And there are a few angels.
Angel. But they keep explaining all that away.
God. So they do. They are free, after all. Their destiny is in their hands, in the choices they make.
Angel. Including the most basic choice of all.
God. Yes. Especially that. True love is not forced. It gives and awaits a response. We must trust in love.
Angel. And hope?
God. Yes, always hope.

▸ Psalm 14

LIVING IN YOUR TENT, ON YOUR HOLY HILL

Native Americans can appreciate the imagery of Psalm 15. Both tents and hills have a sacred meaning for them. The Lakota have the phrase *mit-a-ku-ye O-ya-sin*, which means "all my relatives." This phrase is often used at the end of a prayer, much like *amen*. It expresses the deep belief that all human beings are our brothers and sisters, and we all belong in the Holy Tent of the Great Spirit. All creatures—the two legged and the four legged, those that crawl and those that fly—are our relatives. In fact, we are related to all of creation—the sea, the rocks, the caves, the sky, the trees, the holy hills. Native Americans understand human beings as connected to all creation, and they believe that any harm we do to creation we do to ourselves.

▸ Psalm 15

6 You would confound the plans of the poor,
    but the LORD is their refuge.

7 O that deliverance for Israel would come from
        Zion!
    When the LORD restores the fortunes of his
        people,
    Jacob will rejoice; Israel will be glad.

Psalm 15

Who Shall Abide in God's Sanctuary?

A Psalm of David.

1 O LORD, who may abide in your tent?
    Who may dwell on your holy hill?

2 Those who walk blamelessly, and do what is
        right,
    and speak the truth from their heart;
3 who do not slander with their tongue,
        and do no evil to their friends,
        nor take up a reproach against their
            neighbors;
4 in whose eyes the wicked are despised,
        but who honor those who fear the LORD;
    who stand by their oath even to their hurt;
5 who do not lend money at interest,
        and do not take a bribe against the
            innocent.

Those who do these things shall never be
    moved.

Psalm 16

Song of Trust and Security in God

A Mik'tam of David.

1 Protect me, O God, for in you I take
        refuge.
2 I say to the LORD, "You are my Lord;
    I have no good apart from you."[l]

3 As for the holy ones in the land, they are the
        noble,
    in whom is all my delight.

4 Those who choose another god multiply their
        sorrows;[m]
    their drink offerings of blood I will not
        pour out
    or take their names upon my lips.

5 The LORD is my chosen portion and my cup;
        you hold my lot.
6 The boundary lines have fallen for me in
        pleasant places;

    I have a goodly heritage.
7 I bless the LORD who gives me counsel;
    in the night also my heart instructs me.
8 I keep the LORD always before me;
        because he is at my right hand, I shall not
            be moved.

---

l Jerome Tg: Meaning of Heb uncertain   *m* Cn: Meaning of Heb uncertain

9 Therefore my heart is glad, and my soul
　　rejoices;
　　my body also rests secure.
10 For you do not give me up to Shĕ'ōl,
　　or let your faithful one see the Pit.

11 You show me the path of life.
　　In your presence there is fullness of joy;
　　in your right hand are pleasures
　　　forevermore.

Psalm 17

Prayer for Deliverance from Persecutors

A Prayer of David.

1 Hear a just cause, O LORD; attend to my cry;
　　give ear to my prayer from lips free of
　　　deceit.
2 From you let my vindication come;
　　let your eyes see the right.

3 If you try my heart, if you visit me by night,
　　if you test me, you will find no wickedness
　　　in me;
　　my mouth does not transgress.
4 As for what others do, by the word of your
　　　lips
　　I have avoided the ways of the violent.
5 My steps have held fast to your paths;
　　my feet have not slipped.

6 I call upon you, for you will answer me,
　　O God;
　　incline your ear to me, hear my words.
7 Wondrously show your steadfast love,
　　O savior of those who seek refuge
　　from their adversaries at your right
　　　hand.

8 Guard me as the apple of the eye;
　　hide me in the shadow of your wings,
9 from the wicked who despoil me,
　　my deadly enemies who surround me.
10 They close their hearts to pity;
　　with their mouths they speak arrogantly.
11 They track me down;[n] now they surround me;
　　they set their eyes to cast me to the
　　　ground.
12 They are like a lion eager to tear,
　　like a young lion lurking in ambush.

13 Rise up, O LORD, confront them, overthrow
　　　them!
　　By your sword deliver my life from the
　　　wicked,
14 from mortals—by your hand, O LORD—

from mortals whose portion in life is in this
　　world.
May their bellies be filled with what you have
　　stored up for them;
may their children have more than
　　enough;
may they leave something over to their little
　　ones.

15 As for me, I shall behold your face in
　　righteousness;
　　when I awake I shall be satisfied, beholding
　　your likeness.

Psalm 18

Royal Thanksgiving for Victory

(2 Sam 22.1–51)

*To the leader. A Psalm of David the servant of the LORD,
who addressed the words of this song to the LORD on the
day when the LORD delivered him from the hand of all
his enemies, and from the hand of Saul. He said:*

1 I love you, O LORD, my strength.
2 The LORD is my rock, my fortress, and my
　　deliverer,
　　my God, my rock in whom I take refuge,
　　my shield, and the horn of my salvation,
　　my stronghold.
3 I call upon the LORD, who is worthy to be
　　praised,
　　so I shall be saved from my enemies.

4 The cords of death encompassed me;
　　the torrents of perdition assailed me;
5 the cords of Shĕ'ōl entangled me;
　　the snares of death confronted me.

6 In my distress I called upon the LORD;
　　to my God I cried for help.
From his temple he heard my voice,
　　and my cry to him reached his ears.

7 Then the earth reeled and rocked;
　　the foundations also of the mountains
　　　trembled
　　and quaked, because he was angry.
8 Smoke went up from his nostrils,
　　and devouring fire from his mouth;
　　glowing coals flamed forth from him.
9 He bowed the heavens, and came down;
　　thick darkness was under his feet.
10 He rode on a cherub, and flew;
　　he came swiftly upon the wings of the
　　　wind.

---

n One Ms Compare Syr: MT *Our steps*

P
S
A
L
M
S

11 He made darkness his covering around him,
   his canopy thick clouds dark with water.
12 Out of the brightness before him
      there broke through his clouds
      hailstones and coals of fire.
13 The LORD also thundered in the heavens,
      and the Most High uttered his voice.*o*
14 And he sent out his arrows, and scattered them;
      he flashed forth lightnings, and routed
         them.
15 Then the channels of the sea were seen,
      and the foundations of the world were laid
         bare
   at your rebuke, O LORD,
      at the blast of the breath of your nostrils.

16 He reached down from on high, he took me;
   he drew me out of mighty waters.
17 He delivered me from my strong enemy,
      and from those who hated me;
   for they were too mighty for me.
18 They confronted me in the day of my calamity;
   but the LORD was my support.
19 He brought me out into a broad place;
   he delivered me, because he delighted
      in me.

20 The LORD rewarded me according to my
      righteousness;
   according to the cleanness of my hands he
      recompensed me.
21 For I have kept the ways of the LORD,
   and have not wickedly departed from my
      God.
22 For all his ordinances were before me,
   and his statutes I did not put away
      from me.
23 I was blameless before him,
   and I kept myself from guilt.
24 Therefore the LORD has recompensed me
      according to my righteousness,
   according to the cleanness of my hands in
      his sight.

25 With the loyal you show yourself loyal;
   with the blameless you show yourself
      blameless;
26 with the pure you show yourself pure;
   and with the crooked you show yourself
      perverse.
27 For you deliver a humble people,
   but the haughty eyes you bring down.
28 It is you who light my lamp;
   the LORD, my God, lights up my darkness.
29 By you I can crush a troop,
   and by my God I can leap over a wall.
30 This God—his way is perfect;

   the promise of the LORD proves true;
   he is a shield for all who take refuge in him.

31 For who is God except the LORD?
   And who is a rock besides our God?—
32 the God who girded me with strength,
   and made my way safe.
33 He made my feet like the feet of a deer,
   and set me secure on the heights.
34 He trains my hands for war,
   so that my arms can bend a bow of bronze.
35 You have given me the shield of your salvation,
   and your right hand has supported me;
   your help*p* has made me great.
36 You gave me a wide place for my steps
      under me,
   and my feet did not slip.
37 I pursued my enemies and overtook them;
      and did not turn back until they were
         consumed.
38 I struck them down, so that they were not able
      to rise;
   they fell under my feet.
39 For you girded me with strength for the battle;
   you made my assailants sink under me.
40 You made my enemies turn their backs to me,
   and those who hated me I destroyed.
41 They cried for help, but there was no one to
      save them;
   they cried to the LORD, but he did not
      answer them.
42 I beat them fine, like dust before the wind;
   I cast them out like the mire of the streets.

43 You delivered me from strife with the peoples;*q*
   you made me head of the nations;
   people whom I had not known served me.
44 As soon as they heard of me they obeyed me;
   foreigners came cringing to me.
45 Foreigners lost heart,
   and came trembling out of their strongholds.

46 The LORD lives! Blessed be my rock,
   and exalted be the God of my salvation,
47 the God who gave me vengeance
   and subdued peoples under me;
48 who delivered me from my enemies;
   indeed, you exalted me above my
      adversaries;
   you delivered me from the violent.

49 For this I will extol you, O LORD, among the
      nations,
   and sing praises to your name.

---

o Gk See 2 Sam 22.14: Heb adds *hailstones and coals of fire*
p Or *gentleness*   *q* Gk Tg: Heb *people*

50 Great triumphs he gives to his king,
       and shows steadfast love to his anointed,
       to David and his descendants forever.

Psalm 19

God's Glory in Creation and the Law
To the leader. A Psalm of David.

1 The heavens are telling the glory of God;
       and the firmament[r] proclaims his
          handiwork.
2 Day to day pours forth speech,
       and night to night declares knowledge.
3 There is no speech, nor are there words;
       their voice is not heard;
4 yet their voice[s] goes out through all the earth,
       and their words to the end of the world.

   In the heavens[t] he has set a tent for the sun,
5 which comes out like a bridegroom from his
          wedding canopy,
       and like a strong man runs its course with
          joy.

"The Heavens Are Telling the Glory of God"

Does that opening line of Psalm 19 sound familiar? Perhaps you've seen it on a poster or sung it at Mass. The sky constantly tells us how glorious and magnificent God is!

Have you ever watched the awesome show of a thunder and lightning storm? been delighted by a rainbow? marveled at the power behind a tornado or a hurricane? been tickled by a gentle spring breeze? caught snowflakes on your tongue? had leaves dance around you in a brisk autumn wind? lost yourself looking up into a star-filled night? felt breathless watching a magnificent sunset?

As amazing as the sky is, it only hints at how amazing God is! And in the second half of Psalm 19, the psalmist reminds us that God's law is equally wonderful. Read Psalm 19 as your own prayer of praise to God for the many ways God communicates to us.

▶ Psalm 19

6 Its rising is from the end of the heavens,
       and its circuit to the end of them;
       and nothing is hid from its heat.

7 The law of the LORD is perfect,
       reviving the soul;
   the decrees of the LORD are sure,
       making wise the simple;
8 the precepts of the LORD are right,
       rejoicing the heart;
   the commandment of the LORD is clear,
       enlightening the eyes;
9 the fear of the LORD is pure,
       enduring forever;
    the ordinances of the LORD are true
       and righteous altogether.
10 More to be desired are they than gold,
       even much fine gold;
   sweeter also than honey,
       and drippings of the honeycomb.

11 Moreover by them is your servant warned;
       in keeping them there is great reward.
12 But who can detect their errors?
       Clear me from hidden faults.
13 Keep back your servant also from the insolent;[u]
       do not let them have dominion over me.
   Then I shall be blameless,
       and innocent of great transgression.

14 Let the words of my mouth and the meditation
          of my heart
       be acceptable to you,
       O LORD, my rock and my redeemer.

Psalm 20

Prayer for Victory
To the leader. A Psalm of David.

1 The LORD answer you in the day of trouble!
       The name of the God of Jacob protect you!
2 May he send you help from the sanctuary,
       and give you support from Zion.
3 May he remember all your offerings,
       and regard with favor your burnt sacrifices.
                                              Sĕ′lah

4 May he grant you your heart's desire,
       and fulfill all your plans.
5 May we shout for joy over your victory,
       and in the name of our God set up our
          banners.
   May the LORD fulfill all your petitions.

---

r Or *dome*   s Gk Jerome Compare Syr: Heb *line*
t Heb *In them*   u Or *from proud thoughts*

6 Now I know that the LORD will help his
anointed;
he will answer him from his holy heaven
with mighty victories by his right hand.
7 Some take pride in chariots, and some in
horses,
but our pride is in the name of the LORD
our God.
8 They will collapse and fall,
but we shall rise and stand upright.

9 Give victory to the king, O LORD;
answer us when we call.*v*

Psalm 21

Thanksgiving for Victory

To the leader. A Psalm of David.

1 In your strength the king rejoices, O LORD,
and in your help how greatly he exults!
2 You have given him his heart's desire,
and have not withheld the request of his
lips.   *Selah*
3 For you meet him with rich blessings;
you set a crown of fine gold on his head.
4 He asked you for life; you gave it to him—
length of days forever and ever.
5 His glory is great through your help;
splendor and majesty you bestow
on him.
6 You bestow on him blessings forever;
you make him glad with the joy of your
presence.
7 For the king trusts in the LORD,
and through the steadfast love of the Most
High he shall not be moved.

8 Your hand will find out all your enemies;
your right hand will find out those who
hate you.
9 You will make them like a fiery furnace
when you appear.
The LORD will swallow them up in his wrath,
and fire will consume them.
10 You will destroy their offspring from the
earth,
and their children from among
humankind.
11 If they plan evil against you,
if they devise mischief, they will not
succeed.
12 For you will put them to flight;
you will aim at their faces with your bows.

13 Be exalted, O LORD, in your strength!
We will sing and praise your power.

Psalm 22

Plea for Deliverance from Suffering
and Hostility

*To the leader: according to The Deer of the Dawn.
A Psalm of David.*

1 My God, my God, why have you forsaken me?
Why are you so far from helping me, from
the words of my groaning?
2 O my God, I cry by day, but you do not
answer;
and by night, but find no rest.

3 Yet you are holy,
enthroned on the praises of Israel.
4 In you our ancestors trusted;
they trusted, and you delivered them.
5 To you they cried, and were saved;
in you they trusted, and were not put to
shame.

6 But I am a worm, and not human;
scorned by others, and despised by the
people.
7 All who see me mock at me;
they make mouths at me, they shake their
heads;
8 "Commit your cause to the LORD; let him
deliver—
let him rescue the one in whom he
delights!"

9 Yet it was you who took me from the
womb;
you kept me safe on my mother's breast.
10 On you I was cast from my birth,
and since my mother bore me you have
been my God.
11 Do not be far from me,
for trouble is near
and there is no one to help.

12 Many bulls encircle me,
strong bulls of Ba'shan surround me;
13 they open wide their mouths at me,
like a ravening and roaring lion.

14 I am poured out like water,
and all my bones are out of joint;
my heart is like wax;
it is melted within my breast;
15 my mouth*w* is dried up like a potsherd,
and my tongue sticks to my jaws;
you lay me in the dust of death.

---

v Gk: Heb *give victory, O LORD; let the King answer us when
we call*   *w* Cn: Heb *strength*

16 For dogs are all around me;
        a company of evildoers encircles me.
    My hands and feet have shriveled;*

17 I can count all my bones.
    They stare and gloat over me;

18 they divide my clothes among
            themselves,
        and for my clothing they cast lots.

19 But you, O LORD, do not be far away!
        O my help, come quickly to my aid!

20 Deliver my soul from the sword,
        my life *y* from the power of the dog!

21   Save me from the mouth of the lion!

    From the horns of the wild oxen you have
            rescued *z* me.

22 I will tell of your name to my brothers and
            sisters; *a*
        in the midst of the congregation I will
            praise you:

23 You who fear the LORD, praise him!
        All you offspring of Jacob, glorify him;
        stand in awe of him, all you offspring of
            Israel!

24 For he did not despise or abhor
        the affliction of the afflicted;
    he did not hide his face from me, *b*
        but heard when I *c* cried to him.

25 From you comes my praise in the great
            congregation;
        my vows I will pay before those who fear
            him.

26 The poor *d* shall eat and be satisfied;
        those who seek him shall praise the
            LORD.
        May your hearts live forever!

27 All the ends of the earth shall remember
        and turn to the LORD;
    and all the families of the nations
        shall worship before him. *e*

28 For dominion belongs to the LORD,
        and he rules over the nations.

29 To him, *f* indeed, shall all who sleep in *g* the
            earth bow down;
        before him shall bow all who go down to
            the dust,
        and I shall live for him. *h*

30 Posterity will serve him;
        future generations will be told about the
            Lord,

31 and *i* proclaim his deliverance to a people yet
            unborn,
        saying that he has done it.

Catholic Connections

HOPE IN DESPAIR

The Gospel writers make many references to Psalm 22 in telling the story of Jesus' suffering and death. During the long Gospel readings on Palm Sunday and Good Friday, you will hear them. Try reading Mt 27.45–50 and then reading Psalm 22. What sound like words of despair in Matthew are actually words of promise for those familiar with the psalm. This is because Psalm 22 is a hymn of hope, which ends by praising God for hearing and rescuing those who cry out. So, even in the horrible suffering of Jesus' death, there was already the promise of God's saving action.

▸ **Psalm 22**

Psalm 23

The Divine Shepherd

A Psalm of David.

1 The LORD is my shepherd, I shall not want.

2   He makes me lie down in green pastures;
    he leads me beside still waters; *j*

3   he restores my soul. *k*
    He leads me in right paths *l*
        for his name's sake.

4   Even though I walk through the darkest
            valley, *m*
        I fear no evil;
    for you are with me;
        your rod and your staff—
        they comfort me.

---

x Meaning of Heb uncertain   *y* Heb *my only one*   *z* Heb *answered*   *a* Or *kindred*   *b* Heb *him*   *c* Heb *he*   *d* Or *afflicted*   *e* Gk Syr Jerome: Heb *you*   *f* Cn: Heb *They have eaten and*   *g* Cn: Heb *all the fat ones*   *h* Compare Gk Syr Vg: Heb *and he who cannot keep himself alive*   *i* Compare Gk: Heb *it will be told about the Lord to the generation,* *31they will come and*   *j* Heb *waters of rest*   *k* Or *life*   *l* Or *paths of righteousness*   *m* Or *the valley of the shadow of death*

P
S
A
L
M
S

THE GOOD SHEPHERD LOOKS AFTER US!

The famous Psalm 23 offers two images of God: the Good Shepherd and a generous host. Both images speak of God's nearness and gentle care for us. In the New Testament, Jesus appears as the Good Shepherd who gives his life for the life of his sheep (Jn 10.1–29). He also appears several times as a host, particularly in the stories about the multiplication of the loaves and the Last Supper.

Similar images repeat time and again in Hispanic homes. The following traditional sayings are just some examples of the caring and generous attitudes among Latin American families: "My home is your home" (Mi casa es su casa); "God help you! What can I do for you?" (¡Dios te ampare! ¿Cómo puedo ayudarte?); "Where two eat, three eat; where six eat, seven eat" (Donde comen dos comen tres; donde comen seis comen siete); "Welcome! We just add water to the beans" (¡Bienvenidos! Le echamos más agua a los frijoles); and "Stay with us! From wall to wall, all is mattress" (¡Quédense con nosotros! De pared a pared todo es colchón!).

As a Christian, you should pray Psalm 23 feeling the nearness of Jesus, the Good Shepherd, and asking his help to be a good shepherd for people in need:
- Pray the psalm slowly, letting God fill you with peace and security.
- Pray the psalm again, this time thinking of friends who might be feeling like sheep without a shepherd. How can you lead them to Jesus? How can you care more for them?

▶ Psalm 23

5 You prepare a table before me
    in the presence of my enemies;
you anoint my head with oil;
    my cup overflows.
6 Surely[n] goodness and mercy[o] shall follow me
    all the days of my life,
and I shall dwell in the house of the LORD
    my whole life long.[p]

Psalm 24

Entrance into the Temple

Of David. A Psalm.

1 The earth is the LORD's and all that is in it,
    the world, and those who live in it;
2 for he has founded it on the seas,
    and established it on the rivers.

3 Who shall ascend the hill of the LORD?
    And who shall stand in his holy place?
4 Those who have clean hands and pure hearts,
    who do not lift up their souls to what is false,

    and do not swear deceitfully.
5 They will receive blessing from the LORD,
    and vindication from the God of their salvation.
6 Such is the company of those who seek him,
    who seek the face of the God of Jacob.[q]

Sĕ'lah

7 Lift up your heads, O gates!
    and be lifted up, O ancient doors!
    that the King of glory may come in.
8 Who is the King of glory?
    The LORD, strong and mighty,
    the LORD, mighty in battle.
9 Lift up your heads, O gates!
    and be lifted up, O ancient doors!
    that the King of glory may come in.
10 Who is this King of glory?
    The LORD of hosts,
    he is the King of glory.

Sĕ'lah

---

n Or *Only* o Or *kindness* p Heb *for length of days*
q Gk Syr: Heb *your face, O Jacob*

Psalm 25

Prayer for Guidance and for Deliverance
Of David.

1 To you, O LORD, I lift up my soul.
2 O my God, in you I trust;
    do not let me be put to shame;
    do not let my enemies exult over me.
3 Do not let those who wait for you be put to
        shame;
    let them be ashamed who are wantonly
        treacherous.

did you KNOW?

Temple Worship

When Israel was ruled by kings (1000–587 B.C.), worship in the Temple at Jerusalem was an important part of the people's religious life. Many of the psalms, like Psalm 24, refer to going up to the Temple (the "holy place" in verse 3). Although the first Temple was destroyed in 587 B.C., it was later rebuilt. Temple worship started again and continued into Jesus' time. This is what the priests did during some of the Temple ceremonies:

Daily Temple worship
■ every morning, presented a burnt offering (a year-old male lamb), grain, drink, and an incense offering
■ every evening, presented a second burnt offering and a cereal offering

Sabbath (weekly) Temple worship
■ gave two additional burnt offerings
■ replaced the twelve loaves of bread, called the bread of Presence (1 Kings 7.48; Mt 12.4 & Heb 9.2), recalling the manna with which God fed Israel in the desert
■ made an incense offering

Monthly and festival Temple worship
■ blew the trumpet
■ presented additional burnt offerings and a sin offering (a male goat)
■ on the Day of Atonement, laid their hands on a living goat while confessing the people's sins and then sent the goat away into the wilderness

4 Make me to know your ways, O LORD;
    teach me your paths.
5 Lead me in your truth, and teach me,
    for you are the God of my salvation;
    for you I wait all day long.

6 Be mindful of your mercy, O LORD, and of
        your steadfast love,
    for they have been from of old.
7 Do not remember the sins of my youth or my
        transgressions;
    according to your steadfast love
        remember me,
    for your goodness' sake, O LORD!

8 Good and upright is the LORD;
    therefore he instructs sinners in the way.
9 He leads the humble in what is right,
    and teaches the humble his way.
10 All the paths of the LORD are steadfast love and
        faithfulness,
    for those who keep his covenant and his
        decrees.

11 For your name's sake, O LORD,
    pardon my guilt, for it is great.
12 Who are they that fear the LORD?
    He will teach them the way that they
        should choose.

13 They will abide in prosperity,
    and their children shall possess the land.
14 The friendship of the LORD is for those who
        fear him,
    and he makes his covenant known to them.
15 My eyes are ever toward the LORD,
    for he will pluck my feet out of the net.

16 Turn to me and be gracious to me,
    for I am lonely and afflicted.
17 Relieve the troubles of my heart,
    and bring me[r] out of my distress.
18 Consider my affliction and my trouble,
    and forgive all my sins.

19 Consider how many are my foes,
    and with what violent hatred they hate me.
20 O guard my life, and deliver me;
    do not let me be put to shame, for I take
        refuge in you.
21 May integrity and uprightness preserve me,
    for I wait for you.

22 Redeem Israel, O God,
    out of all its troubles.

---

r Or *The troubles of my heart are enlarged; bring me*

Psalm 26

Plea for Justice and Declaration
of Righteousness

Of David.

1 Vindicate me, O LORD,
    for I have walked in my integrity,
    and I have trusted in the LORD without
        wavering.
2 Prove me, O LORD, and try me;
    test my heart and mind.
3 For your steadfast love is before my eyes,
    and I walk in faithfulness to you.[s]

4 I do not sit with the worthless,
    nor do I consort with hypocrites;
5 I hate the company of evildoers,
    and will not sit with the wicked.

6 I wash my hands in innocence,
    and go around your altar, O LORD,
7 singing aloud a song of thanksgiving,
    and telling all your wondrous deeds.

8 O LORD, I love the house in which you
        dwell,
    and the place where your glory abides.
9 Do not sweep me away with sinners,
    nor my life with the bloodthirsty,
10 those in whose hands are evil devices,
    and whose right hands are full of bribes.

11 But as for me, I walk in my integrity;
    redeem me, and be gracious to me.
12 My foot stands on level ground;
    in the great congregation I will bless the
        LORD.

Psalm 27

Triumphant Song of Confidence

Of David.

1 The LORD is my light and my salvation;
    whom shall I fear?
The LORD is the stronghold[t] of my life;
    of whom shall I be afraid?

2 When evildoers assail me
        to devour my flesh—
my adversaries and foes—
        they shall stumble and fall.

3 Though an army encamp against me,
    my heart shall not fear;
though war rise up against me,
    yet I will be confident.

PRAY IT
Integrity and Values

People with integrity know what they value and have a commitment to being consistent in what they believe and what they do. It is impossible for us to have integrity if we follow one set of values in one situation and another set of values in a different situation. The integrity of the writer of Psalm 26 comes from following God in everything (Ps 26.1). The psalmist even wants to be tested by God (verse 2) to be sure of complete faithfulness! To have the kind of integrity that the psalmist writes about, we have to let God be the only ruler of our life. Being able to do that takes a lifetime of growth and conversion.

What values are you committed to consistently? Can you think of times when your actions did not reflect your values or beliefs? Pray that God will give you strength to do what is right, even when it is most difficult.

▸ **Psalm 26**

4 One thing I asked of the LORD,
    that will I seek after:
to live in the house of the LORD
    all the days of my life,
to behold the beauty of the LORD,
    and to inquire in his temple.

5 For he will hide me in his shelter
    in the day of trouble;
he will conceal me under the cover of his tent;
    he will set me high on a rock.

6 Now my head is lifted up
    above my enemies all around me,
and I will offer in his tent
    sacrifices with shouts of joy;
I will sing and make melody to the LORD.

7 Hear, O LORD, when I cry aloud,
    be gracious to me and answer me!
8 "Come," my heart says, "seek his face!"
    Your face, LORD, do I seek.
9   Do not hide your face from me.

---

s Or *in your faithfulness*   t Or *refuge*

Do not turn your servant away in anger,
    you who have been my help.
Do not cast me off, do not forsake me,
    O God of my salvation!
10 If my father and mother forsake me,
    the LORD will take me up.

11 Teach me your way, O LORD,
    and lead me on a level path
    because of my enemies.
12 Do not give me up to the will of my
        adversaries,
    for false witnesses have risen against me,
    and they are breathing out violence.

13 I believe that I shall see the goodness of the
        LORD
    in the land of the living.
14 Wait for the LORD;
    be strong, and let your heart take courage;
    wait for the LORD!

Psalm 28

Prayer for Help and Thanksgiving for It

Of David.

1 To you, O LORD, I call;
    my rock, do not refuse to hear me,
for if you are silent to me,
    I shall be like those who go down
        to the Pit.
2 Hear the voice of my supplication,
    as I cry to you for help,
as I lift up my hands
    toward your most holy sanctuary.^u

3 Do not drag me away with the wicked,
    with those who are workers of evil,
who speak peace with their neighbors,
    while mischief is in their hearts.
4 Repay them according to their work,
    and according to the evil of their deeds;
repay them according to the work of their
        hands;
    render them their due reward.
5 Because they do not regard the works of the
        LORD,
    or the work of his hands,
he will break them down and build them up
        no more.

6 Blessed be the LORD,
    for he has heard the sound of my
        pleadings.
7 The LORD is my strength and my shield;
    in him my heart trusts;

so I am helped, and my heart exults,
    and with my song I give thanks to him.

8 The LORD is the strength of his people;
    he is the saving refuge of his anointed.
9 O save your people, and bless your heritage;
    be their shepherd, and carry them forever.

Psalm 29

The Voice of God in a Great Storm

A Psalm of David.

1 Ascribe to the LORD, O heavenly beings,^v
    ascribe to the LORD glory and strength.
2 Ascribe to the LORD the glory of his name;
    worship the LORD in holy splendor.

3 The voice of the LORD is over the waters;
    the God of glory thunders,
    the LORD, over mighty waters.
4 The voice of the LORD is powerful;
    the voice of the LORD is full of majesty.

5 The voice of the LORD breaks the cedars;
    the LORD breaks the cedars of Lebanon.
6 He makes Lebanon skip like a calf,
    and Sir'i•on like a young wild ox.

---

u Heb *your innermost sanctuary*   v Heb *sons of gods*

The Eye of the Storm

Thunderstorms can be frightening. They often come up quickly and without warning. The winds and lightning that accompany them can be destructive. Children and animals (okay, lots of adults too) are often afraid at the sheer force of it all.

It would be difficult to read Psalm 29 aloud and not be expressive. Phrases such as "the God of glory thunders" (verse 3), and "the voice of the LORD breaks the cedars" (verse 5) and "flashes forth flames of fire" (verse 7) evoke a divine splendor that we do not often hear about. The psalmist speaks with admiration about the power and majesty of God.

When have you experienced the awesome power of God?

▶ Psalm 29

7 The voice of the LORD flashes forth flames of
fire.
8 The voice of the LORD shakes the wilderness;
the LORD shakes the wilderness of Kā′desh.

9 The voice of the LORD causes the oaks to
whirl,[w]
and strips the forest bare;
and in his temple all say, "Glory!"

10 The LORD sits enthroned over the flood;
the LORD sits enthroned as king forever.
11 May the LORD give strength to his people!
May the LORD bless his people with
peace!

Psalm 30

Thanksgiving for Recovery from Grave Illness

A Psalm. A Song at the dedication of the temple.
Of David.

1 I will extol you, O LORD, for you have drawn
me up,
and did not let my foes rejoice over me.
2 O LORD my God, I cried to you for help,
and you have healed me.
3 O LORD, you brought up my soul from
Shē′ōl,
restored me to life from among those gone
down to the Pit.[x]

4 Sing praises to the LORD, O you his faithful
ones,
and give thanks to his holy name.
5 For his anger is but for a moment;
his favor is for a lifetime.
Weeping may linger for the night,
but joy comes with the morning.

6 As for me, I said in my prosperity,
"I shall never be moved."
7 By your favor, O LORD,
you had established me as a strong
mountain;
you hid your face;
I was dismayed.

8 To you, O LORD, I cried,
and to the LORD I made supplication:
9 "What profit is there in my death,
if I go down to the Pit?
Will the dust praise you?
Will it tell of your faithfulness?
10 Hear, O LORD, and be gracious to me!
O LORD, be my helper!"

11 You have turned my mourning into dancing;
you have taken off my sackcloth
and clothed me with joy,
12 so that my soul[y] may praise you and not be
silent.
O LORD my God, I will give thanks to you
forever.

Psalm 31

Prayer and Praise for Deliverance from Enemies

To the leader. A Psalm of David.

1 In you, O LORD, I seek refuge;
do not let me ever be put to shame;
in your righteousness deliver me.
2 Incline your ear to me;
rescue me speedily.
Be a rock of refuge for me,
a strong fortress to save me.

3 You are indeed my rock and my fortress;
for your name's sake lead me and guide me,
4 take me out of the net that is hidden for me,
for you are my refuge.
5 Into your hand I commit my spirit;
you have redeemed me, O LORD, faithful
God.

6 You hate[z] those who pay regard to worthless
idols,
but I trust in the LORD.
7 I will exult and rejoice in your steadfast love,
because you have seen my affliction;
you have taken heed of my adversities,
8 and have not delivered me into the hand of the
enemy;
you have set my feet in a broad place.

9 Be gracious to me, O LORD, for I am in distress;
my eye wastes away from grief,
my soul and body also.
10 For my life is spent with sorrow,
and my years with sighing;
my strength fails because of my misery,[a]
and my bones waste away.

11 I am the scorn of all my adversaries,
a horror[b] to my neighbors,
an object of dread to my acquaintances;
those who see me in the street flee
from me.

---

w Or *causes the deer to calve*   *x* Or *that I should not go down to*
the Pit   *y* Heb *that glory*   *z* One Heb Ms Gk Syr Jerome: MT
I hate   *a* Gk Syr: Heb *my iniquity*   *b* Cn: Heb *exceedingly*

Cultural Connections

COURAGE

Psalm 31 ends "Be strong, and let your heart take courage, / all you who wait in the LORD" (verse 24). Courage is an important value for many Native American peoples. For the Lakota tribe, it is one of four primary values. The Lakota word for courage is *woo-hit-i-ka.*

Leaders particularly have to be brave. It takes courage to make unpopular decisions and to go against peer pressure. It takes courage to do the right thing when the wrong thing might be easier or more enjoyable. It takes courage to protect others and to care for their needs. Because these kinds of actions take courage, practicing them will earn you honor.

What is the most courageous thing you have done for the sake of someone else?

To explore the other primary Lakota virtues, see the Cultural Connections article for Psalm 73.

▶ Psalm 31

12 I have passed out of mind like one who is dead;
    I have become like a broken vessel.
13 For I hear the whispering of many—
    terror all around!—
  as they scheme together against me,
    as they plot to take my life.

14 But I trust in you, O LORD;
    I say, "You are my God."
15 My times are in your hand;
    deliver me from the hand of my enemies
      and persecutors.
16 Let your face shine upon your servant;
    save me in your steadfast love.
17 Do not let me be put to shame, O LORD,
    for I call on you;
  let the wicked be put to shame;
    let them go dumbfounded to Shĕ′ōl.
18 Let the lying lips be stilled
    that speak insolently against the righteous
    with pride and contempt.

19 O how abundant is your goodness
    that you have laid up for those who fear you,
  and accomplished for those who take refuge in
      you,
    in the sight of everyone!
20 In the shelter of your presence you hide them
    from human plots;
  you hold them safe under your shelter
    from contentious tongues.

21 Blessed be the LORD,
    for he has wondrously shown his steadfast
      love to me
    when I was beset as a city under siege.
22 I had said in my alarm,
    "I am driven far*c* from your sight."
  But you heard my supplications
    when I cried out to you for help.

23 Love the LORD, all you his saints.
    The LORD preserves the faithful,
    but abundantly repays the one who acts
      haughtily.
24 Be strong, and let your heart take
      courage,
    all you who wait for the LORD.

Psalm 32

The Joy of Forgiveness
Of David. A Mas′kil.

1 Happy are those whose transgression is
      forgiven,
    whose sin is covered.
2 Happy are those to whom the LORD imputes
      no iniquity,
    and in whose spirit there is no deceit.

---

c Another reading is *cut off*

3 While I kept silence, my body wasted away
　　through my groaning all day long.
4 For day and night your hand was heavy
　　　　upon me;
　　my strength was dried up[d] as by the heat
　　　　of summer.　　　　　　　*Sĕ'lah*

5 Then I acknowledged my sin to you,
　　and I did not hide my iniquity;
　I said, "I will confess my transgressions to the
　　LORD,"
　　and you forgave the guilt of my sin.　*Sĕ'lah*

6 Therefore let all who are faithful
　　offer prayer to you;
　at a time of distress,[e] the rush of mighty
　　　　waters
　　shall not reach them.
7 You are a hiding place for me;
　　you preserve me from trouble;
　　you surround me with glad cries of
　　　　deliverance.　　　　　　*Sĕ'lah*

8 I will instruct you and teach you the way you
　　　　should go;
　　I will counsel you with my eye upon you.
9 Do not be like a horse or a mule, without
　　　　understanding,
　　whose temper must be curbed with bit and
　　　　bridle,
　　else it will not stay near you.

10 Many are the torments of the wicked,
　　but steadfast love surrounds those who trust
　　　　in the LORD.
11 Be glad in the LORD and rejoice, O righteous,
　　and shout for joy, all you upright in
　　　　heart.

Psalm 33

The Greatness and Goodness of God

1 Rejoice in the LORD, O you righteous.
　　Praise befits the upright.
2 Praise the LORD with the lyre;
　　make melody to him with the harp of ten
　　　　strings.
3 Sing to him a new song;
　　play skillfully on the strings, with loud
　　　　shouts.

4 For the word of the LORD is upright,
　　and all his work is done in faithfulness.
5 He loves righteousness and justice;
　　the earth is full of the steadfast love of the
　　　　LORD.

6 By the word of the LORD the heavens were made,
　　and all their host by the breath of his
　　　　mouth.
7 He gathered the waters of the sea as in a bottle;
　　he put the deeps in storehouses.

8 Let all the earth fear the LORD;
　　let all the inhabitants of the world stand in
　　　　awe of him.
9 For he spoke, and it came to be;
　　he commanded, and it stood firm.

10 The LORD brings the counsel of the nations to
　　　　nothing;
　　he frustrates the plans of the peoples.
11 The counsel of the LORD stands forever,
　　the thoughts of his heart to all generations.
12 Happy is the nation whose God is the LORD,
　　the people whom he has chosen as his
　　　　heritage.

13 The LORD looks down from heaven;
　　he sees all humankind.
14 From where he sits enthroned he watches
　　all the inhabitants of the earth—
15 he who fashions the hearts of them all,
　　and observes all their deeds.
16 A king is not saved by his great army;
　　a warrior is not delivered by his great
　　　　strength.
17 The war horse is a vain hope for victory,
　　and by its great might it cannot save.

18 Truly the eye of the LORD is on those who fear
　　　　him,
　　on those who hope in his steadfast love,
19 to deliver their soul from death,
　　and to keep them alive in famine.

20 Our soul waits for the LORD;
　　he is our help and shield.
21 Our heart is glad in him,
　　because we trust in his holy name.
22 Let your steadfast love, O LORD, be upon us,
　　even as we hope in you.

Psalm 34

Praise for Deliverance from Trouble

*Of David, when he feigned madness before A•bim'e•lech,
　so that he drove him out, and he went away.*

1 I will bless the LORD at all times;
　　his praise shall continually be in my
　　　　mouth.

---

[d] Meaning of Heb uncertain　[e] Cn: Heb *at a time of
finding only*

2 My soul makes its boast in the LORD;
    let the humble hear and be glad.
3 O magnify the LORD with me,
    and let us exalt his name together.

4 I sought the LORD, and he answered me,
    and delivered me from all my fears.
5 Look to him, and be radiant;
    so your*f* faces shall never be ashamed.
6 This poor soul cried, and was heard by the
        LORD,
    and was saved from every trouble.
7 The angel of the LORD encamps
    around those who fear him, and delivers
        them.
8 O taste and see that the LORD is good;
    happy are those who take refuge in
        him.
9 O fear the LORD, you his holy ones,
    for those who fear him have no want.
10 The young lions suffer want and hunger,
    but those who seek the LORD lack no good
        thing.

11 Come, O children, listen to me;
    I will teach you the fear of the LORD.
12 Which of you desires life,
    and covets many days to enjoy good?
13 Keep your tongue from evil,
    and your lips from speaking deceit.
14 Depart from evil, and do good;
    seek peace, and pursue it.

15 The eyes of the LORD are on the
        righteous,
    and his ears are open to their cry.
16 The face of the LORD is against evildoers,
    to cut off the remembrance of them from
        the earth.
17 When the righteous cry for help, the LORD
        hears,
    and rescues them from all their
        troubles.
18 The LORD is near to the brokenhearted,
    and saves the crushed in spirit.

19 Many are the afflictions of the righteous,
    but the LORD rescues them from
        them all.
20 He keeps all their bones;
    not one of them will be broken.
21 Evil brings death to the wicked,
    and those who hate the righteous will be
        condemned.
22 The LORD redeems the life of his servants;
    none of those who take refuge in him will
        be condemned.

Psalm 35

Prayer for Deliverance from Enemies
Of David.

1 Contend, O LORD, with those who contend
        with me;
    fight against those who fight against me!
2 Take hold of shield and buckler,
    and rise up to help me!
3 Draw the spear and javelin
        against my pursuers;
    say to my soul,
        "I am your salvation."

4 Let them be put to shame and dishonor
        who seek after my life.
    Let them be turned back and confounded
        who devise evil against me.
5 Let them be like chaff before the wind,
    with the angel of the LORD driving them on.
6 Let their way be dark and slippery,
    with the angel of the LORD pursuing them.

7 For without cause they hid their net*g* for me;
    without cause they dug a pit*h* for my life.
8 Let ruin come on them unawares.
    And let the net that they hid ensnare them;
        let them fall in it—to their ruin.

9 Then my soul shall rejoice in the LORD,
    exulting in his deliverance.
10 All my bones shall say,
        "O LORD, who is like you?
    You deliver the weak
        from those too strong for them,
        the weak and needy from those who
            despoil them."

11 Malicious witnesses rise up;
    they ask me about things I do not know.
12 They repay me evil for good;
    my soul is forlorn.
13 But as for me, when they were sick,
    I wore sackcloth;
    I afflicted myself with fasting.
    I prayed with head bowed*i* on my bosom,
14   as though I grieved for a friend or a brother;
    I went about as one who laments for a mother,
        bowed down and in mourning.

15 But at my stumbling they gathered in glee,
        they gathered together against me;
    ruffians whom I did not know
        tore at me without ceasing;

---

f Gk Syr Jerome: Heb *their*   *g* Heb *a pit, their net*   *h* The
word *pit* is transposed from the preceding line   *i* Or *My
prayer turned back*

P
S
A
L
M
S

16 they impiously mocked more and more,*j*
    gnashing at me with their teeth.

17 How long, O LORD, will you look on?
    Rescue me from their ravages,
    my life from the lions!
18 Then I will thank you in the great
        congregation;
    in the mighty throng I will praise you.

19 Do not let my treacherous enemies rejoice
        over me,
    or those who hate me without cause wink
        the eye.
20 For they do not speak peace,
    but they conceive deceitful words
    against those who are quiet in the land.
21 They open wide their mouths against me;
    they say, "Aha, Aha,
    our eyes have seen it."

22 You have seen, O LORD; do not be silent!
    O Lord, do not be far from me!
23 Wake up! Bestir yourself for my defense,
    for my cause, my God and my Lord!
24 Vindicate me, O LORD, my God,
    according to your righteousness,
    and do not let them rejoice over me.
25 Do not let them say to themselves,
    "Aha, we have our heart's desire."
    Do not let them say, "We have swallowed
    you*k* up."

26 Let all those who rejoice at my calamity
    be put to shame and confusion;
    let those who exalt themselves against me
    be clothed with shame and dishonor.

27 Let those who desire my vindication
    shout for joy and be glad,
    and say evermore,
    "Great is the LORD,
    who delights in the welfare of his servant."
28 Then my tongue shall tell of your
        righteousness
    and of your praise all day long.

Psalm 36

Human Wickedness and
Divine Goodness

To the leader. Of David, the servant of the LORD.

1 Transgression speaks to the wicked
    deep in their hearts;
there is no fear of God
    before their eyes.

2 For they flatter themselves in their own eyes
    that their iniquity cannot be found out and
        hated.
3 The words of their mouths are mischief and
        deceit;
    they have ceased to act wisely and do
        good.
4 They plot mischief while on their beds;
    they are set on a way that is not good;
    they do not reject evil.

5 Your steadfast love, O LORD, extends to the
        heavens,
    your faithfulness to the clouds.
6 Your righteousness is like the mighty
        mountains,
    your judgments are like the great deep;
    you save humans and animals alike,
        O LORD.

7 How precious is your steadfast love, O God!
    All people may take refuge in the shadow of
        your wings.
8 They feast on the abundance of your house,
    and you give them drink from the river of
        your delights.
9 For with you is the fountain of life;
    in your light we see light.

10 O continue your steadfast love to those who
        know you,
    and your salvation to the upright of heart!
11 Do not let the foot of the arrogant tread
        on me,
    or the hand of the wicked drive me away.
12 There the evildoers lie prostrate;
    they are thrust down, unable to rise.

Psalm 37

Exhortation to Patience and Trust

Of David.

1 Do not fret because of the wicked;
    do not be envious of wrongdoers,
2 for they will soon fade like the grass,
    and wither like the green herb.

3 Trust in the LORD, and do good;
    so you will live in the land, and enjoy
        security.
4 Take delight in the LORD,
    and he will give you the desires of your
        heart.

---

j Cn Compare Gk: Heb *like the profanest of mockers of
a cake*   *k* Heb *him*

5 Commit your way to the LORD;
   trust in him, and he will act.
6 He will make your vindication shine like the
     light,
   and the justice of your cause like the
     noonday.

7 Be still before the LORD, and wait patiently for
     him;
   do not fret over those who prosper in their
     way,
   over those who carry out evil devices.

8 Refrain from anger, and forsake wrath.
   Do not fret—it leads only to evil.
9 For the wicked shall be cut off,
   but those who wait for the LORD shall
     inherit the land.

10 Yet a little while, and the wicked will be no
     more;
   though you look diligently for their place,
     they will not be there.
11 But the meek shall inherit the land,
   and delight themselves in abundant
     prosperity.

12 The wicked plot against the righteous,
   and gnash their teeth at them;
13 but the LORD laughs at the wicked,
   for he sees that their day is coming.

14 The wicked draw the sword and bend their
     bows
   to bring down the poor and needy,
   to kill those who walk uprightly;
15 their sword shall enter their own heart,
   and their bows shall be broken.

16 Better is a little that the righteous person has
   than the abundance of many wicked.
17 For the arms of the wicked shall be broken,
   but the LORD upholds the righteous.

18 The LORD knows the days of the blameless,
   and their heritage will abide forever;
19 they are not put to shame in evil times,
   in the days of famine they have abundance.

20 But the wicked perish,
   and the enemies of the LORD are like the
     glory of the pastures;
   they vanish—like smoke they vanish away.

21 The wicked borrow, and do not pay back,
   but the righteous are generous and keep
     giving;

22 for those blessed by the LORD shall inherit the
     land,
   but those cursed by him shall be cut off.

23 Our steps[l] are made firm by the LORD,
   when he delights in our[m] way;
24 though we stumble,[n] we[o] shall not fall
     headlong,
   for the LORD holds us[p] by the hand.

25 I have been young, and now am old,
   yet I have not seen the righteous forsaken
   or their children begging bread.
26 They are ever giving liberally and lending,
   and their children become a blessing.

27 Depart from evil, and do good;
   so you shall abide forever.
28 For the LORD loves justice;
   he will not forsake his faithful ones.

The righteous shall be kept safe forever,
   but the children of the wicked shall be cut
     off.
29 The righteous shall inherit the land,
   and live in it forever.

30 The mouths of the righteous utter wisdom,
   and their tongues speak justice.
31 The law of their God is in their hearts;
   their steps do not slip.

32 The wicked watch for the righteous,
   and seek to kill them.
33 The LORD will not abandon them to their
     power,
   or let them be condemned when they are
     brought to trial.

34 Wait for the LORD, and keep to his way,
   and he will exalt you to inherit the land;
   you will look on the destruction of the
     wicked.

35 I have seen the wicked oppressing,
   and towering like a cedar of Lebanon.[q]
36 Again I[r] passed by, and they were no more;
   though I sought them, they could not be
     found.

37 Mark the blameless, and behold the upright,
   for there is posterity for the peaceable.

---

l Heb *A man's steps*   *m* Heb *his*   *n* Heb *he stumbles*
o Heb *he*   *p* Heb *him*   *q* Gk: Meaning of Heb uncertain
r Gk Syr Jerome: Heb *he*

38 But transgressors shall be altogether destroyed;
       the posterity of the wicked shall be cut off.

39 The salvation of the righteous is from the
           LORD;
       he is their refuge in the time of trouble.
40 The LORD helps them and rescues them;
       he rescues them from the wicked, and saves
           them,
       because they take refuge in him.

Psalm 38

A Penitent Sufferer's Plea for Healing
A Psalm of David, for the memorial offering.

1 O LORD, do not rebuke me in your anger,
       or discipline me in your wrath.
2 For your arrows have sunk into me,
       and your hand has come down on me.

3 There is no soundness in my flesh
           because of your indignation;
   there is no health in my bones
           because of my sin.
4 For my iniquities have gone over my head;
       they weigh like a burden too heavy for me.

5 My wounds grow foul and fester
       because of my foolishness;
6 I am utterly bowed down and prostrate;
       all day long I go around mourning.
7 For my loins are filled with burning,
       and there is no soundness in my flesh.
8 I am utterly spent and crushed;
       I groan because of the tumult of my heart.

9 O Lord, all my longing is known to you;
       my sighing is not hidden from you.
10 My heart throbs, my strength fails me;
       as for the light of my eyes—it also has gone
           from me.
11 My friends and companions stand aloof from
           my affliction,
       and my neighbors stand far off.

12 Those who seek my life lay their snares;
       those who seek to hurt me speak of ruin,
       and meditate treachery all day long.

13 But I am like the deaf, I do not hear;
       like the mute, who cannot speak.
14 Truly, I am like one who does not hear,
       and in whose mouth is no retort.

15 But it is for you, O LORD, that I wait;
       it is you, O Lord my God, who will answer.

16 For I pray, "Only do not let them rejoice
           over me,
       those who boast against me when my foot
           slips."

17 For I am ready to fall,
       and my pain is ever with me.
18 I confess my iniquity;
       I am sorry for my sin.
19 Those who are my foes without cause[s] are
           mighty,
       and many are those who hate me
           wrongfully.
20 Those who render me evil for good
       are my adversaries because I follow after
           good.

21 Do not forsake me, O LORD;
       O my God, do not be far from me;
22 make haste to help me,
       O Lord, my salvation.

Psalm 39

Prayer for Wisdom and Forgiveness
To the leader: to Je•dū'thun. A Psalm of David.

1 I said, "I will guard my ways
       that I may not sin with my tongue;
   I will keep a muzzle on my mouth
       as long as the wicked are in my presence."
2 I was silent and still;
       I held my peace to no avail;
   my distress grew worse,
3   my heart became hot within me.
   While I mused, the fire burned;
       then I spoke with my tongue:

4 "LORD, let me know my end,
       and what is the measure of my days;
       let me know how fleeting my life is.
5 You have made my days a few handbreadths,
       and my lifetime is as nothing in your sight.
   Surely everyone stands as a mere breath.
                                                   Sě'lah
6   Surely everyone goes about like a shadow.
   Surely for nothing they are in turmoil;
       they heap up, and do not know who will
           gather.

7 "And now, O Lord, what do I wait for?
       My hope is in you.
8 Deliver me from all my transgressions.
       Do not make me the scorn of the fool.
9 I am silent; I do not open my mouth,

_____
s Q Ms: MT *my living foes*

for it is you who have done it.
10 Remove your stroke from me;
   I am worn down by the blows[t] of your
      hand.

11 "You chastise mortals
   in punishment for sin,
consuming like a moth what is dear to them;
   surely everyone is a mere breath.   *Se'lah*

12 "Hear my prayer, O LORD,
   and give ear to my cry;
   do not hold your peace at my tears.
For I am your passing guest,
   an alien, like all my forebears.
13 Turn your gaze away from me, that I may smile
      again,
   before I depart and am no more."

Psalm 40

Thanksgiving for Deliverance and
Prayer for Help

(Ps 70.1–5)

To the leader. Of David. A Psalm.

1 I waited patiently for the LORD;
   he inclined to me and heard my cry.
2 He drew me up from the desolate pit,[u]
   out of the miry bog,
and set my feet upon a rock,
   making my steps secure.
3 He put a new song in my mouth,
   a song of praise to our God.
Many will see and fear,
   and put their trust in the LORD.

4 Happy are those who make
   the LORD their trust,
who do not turn to the proud,
   to those who go astray after false gods.
5 You have multiplied, O LORD my God,
   your wondrous deeds and your thoughts
      toward us;
   none can compare with you.
Were I to proclaim and tell of them,
   they would be more than can be counted.

6 Sacrifice and offering you do not desire,
   but you have given me an open ear.[v]
Burnt offering and sin offering
   you have not required.
7 Then I said, "Here I am;
   in the scroll of the book it is written
      of me.[w]
8 I delight to do your will, O my God;
   your law is within my heart."

9 I have told the glad news of deliverance
   in the great congregation;
see, I have not restrained my lips,
   as you know, O LORD.
10 I have not hidden your saving help within my
      heart,
   I have spoken of your faithfulness and your
      salvation;
I have not concealed your steadfast love and
   your faithfulness
from the great congregation.

11 Do not, O LORD, withhold
   your mercy from me;
let your steadfast love and your faithfulness
   keep me safe forever.
12 For evils have encompassed me
   without number;
my iniquities have overtaken me,
   until I cannot see;
they are more than the hairs of my head,
   and my heart fails me.

13 Be pleased, O LORD, to deliver me;
   O LORD, make haste to help me.
14 Let all those be put to shame and confusion
   who seek to snatch away my life;
let those be turned back and brought to
      dishonor
   who desire my hurt.
15 Let those be appalled because of their shame
   who say to me, "Aha, Aha!"

16 But may all who seek you
   rejoice and be glad in you;
may those who love your salvation
   say continually, "Great is the LORD!"
17 As for me, I am poor and needy,
   but the Lord takes thought for me.
You are my help and my deliverer;
   do not delay, O my God.

Psalm 41

Assurance of God's Help and
a Plea for Healing

To the leader. A Psalm of David.

1 Happy are those who consider the poor;[x]
   the LORD delivers them in the day of
      trouble.
2 The LORD protects them and keeps them alive;
   they are called happy in the land.
   You do not give them up to the will of their
      enemies.

---

*t Heb hostility   u Cn: Heb pit of tumult   v Heb ears you have
dug for me   w Meaning of Heb uncertain   x Or weak*

3 The LORD sustains them on their sickbed;
 in their illness you heal all their
  infirmities.*y*

4 As for me, I said, "O LORD, be gracious to me;
 heal me, for I have sinned against you."
5 My enemies wonder in malice
 when I will die, and my name perish.
6 And when they come to see me, they utter
  empty words,
 while their hearts gather mischief;
 when they go out, they tell it abroad.
7 All who hate me whisper together about me;
 they imagine the worst for me.

8 They think that a deadly thing has fastened
  on me,
 that I will not rise again from where
  I lie.
9 Even my bosom friend in whom I trusted,
 who ate of my bread, has lifted the heel
  against me.
10 But you, O LORD, be gracious to me,
 and raise me up, that I may repay them.

11 By this I know that you are pleased with me;
 because my enemy has not triumphed
  over me.
12 But you have upheld me because of my
  integrity,
 and set me in your presence forever.
13 Blessed be the LORD, the God of Israel,
 from everlasting to everlasting.
  Amen and Amen.

BOOK II
(Psalms 42–72)
Psalm 42

Longing for God and His
Help in Distress

To the leader. A Mas'kil of the Kō'ra•hītes.

1 As a deer longs for flowing streams,
 so my soul longs for you, O God.
2 My soul thirsts for God,
 for the living God.
When shall I come and behold
 the face of God?
3 My tears have been my food
 day and night,
while people say to me continually,
 "Where is your God?"

4 These things I remember,
 as I pour out my soul:
how I went with the throng,*z*

and led them in procession to the house of
  God,
with glad shouts and songs of thanksgiving,
 a multitude keeping festival.
5 Why are you cast down, O my soul,
 and why are you disquieted within me?
Hope in God; for I shall again praise him,
 my help 6 and my God.

My soul is cast down within me;
 therefore I remember you
from the land of Jordan and of Hermon,
 from Mount Mī'zar.
7 Deep calls to deep
 at the thunder of your cataracts;
all your waves and your billows
 have gone over me.
8 By day the LORD commands his steadfast love,
 and at night his song is with me,
 a prayer to the God of my life.

9 I say to God, my rock,
 "Why have you forgotten me?
Why must I walk about mournfully
 because the enemy oppresses me?"
10 As with a deadly wound in my body,
 my adversaries taunt me,
while they say to me continually,
 "Where is your God?"

11 Why are you cast down, O my soul,
 and why are you disquieted within me?
Hope in God; for I shall again praise him,
 my help and my God.

---

y Heb *you change all his bed*   *z* Meaning of Heb uncertain

42.1*b*

and I will praise you with the harp,
    O God, my God.

5 Why are you cast down, O my soul,
    and why are you disquieted within me?
Hope in God; for I shall again praise him,
    my help and my God.

PRAY IT

Randy's First Day of School

Randy and his family have just moved to a new town. Randy is hopeful about this move because he didn't like his old neighborhood and school. There he was often made fun of for his size. So he figures this will be a new start for him, and just maybe the kids here will give him a chance.

The first day of school is exciting. Randy is nervous but can't wait to meet some new people. As the principal walks him down to his new homeroom, he has hopeful visions of how great it will be. When they walk into the classroom, all that changes. As the principal introduces him, someone yells from the back of the room, "Hey, hey, hey, it's Fat Albert!" Everyone laughs. Randy smiles, only to hide the pain and anger he feels inside.

Have you ever experienced painful moments like the one Randy went through? Psalm 42 is a good prayer to turn to during moments like these. Verse 5 says, "Hope in God; for I shall again, praise him, / my help and my God." If you follow this advice, the situation may not change, but your heart may find peace rather than anger.

▸ Psalm 42

Psalm 43

Prayer to God in Time of Trouble

1 Vindicate me, O God, and defend my cause
    against an ungodly people;
from those who are deceitful and unjust
    deliver me!
2 For you are the God in whom I take refuge;
    why have you cast me off?
Why must I walk about mournfully
    because of the oppression of the enemy?

3 O send out your light and your truth;
    let them lead me;
let them bring me to your holy hill
    and to your dwelling.
4 Then I will go to the altar of God,
    to God my exceeding joy;

Psalm 44

National Lament and Prayer for Help

To the leader. Of the Kō'ra•hites. A Mas'kil.

1 We have heard with our ears, O God,
    our ancestors have told us,
what deeds you performed in their days,
    in the days of old:
2 you with your own hand drove out the
        nations,
    but them you planted;
you afflicted the peoples,
    but them you set free;
3 for not by their own sword did they win the
        land,
    nor did their own arm give them victory;
but your right hand, and your arm,
    and the light of your countenance,
    for you delighted in them.

4 You are my King and my God;
    you command[a] victories for Jacob.
5 Through you we push down our foes;
    through your name we tread down our
        assailants.
6 For not in my bow do I trust,
    nor can my sword save me.
7 But you have saved us from our foes,
    and have put to confusion those who
        hate us.
8 In God we have boasted continually,
    and we will give thanks to your name
        forever.   *Sĕ'lah*

9 Yet you have rejected us and abased us,
    and have not gone out with our armies.
10 You made us turn back from the foe,
    and our enemies have gotten spoil.
11 You have made us like sheep for slaughter,
    and have scattered us among the nations.
12 You have sold your people for a trifle,
    demanding no high price for them.

13 You have made us the taunt of our neighbors,
    the derision and scorn of those around us.
14 You have made us a byword among the
        nations,

---

a Gk Syr: Heb *You are my King, O God; command*

a laughingstock[b] among the peoples.

15 All day long my disgrace is before me,
   and shame has covered my face
16 at the words of the taunters and revilers,
   at the sight of the enemy and the avenger.

17 All this has come upon us,
   yet we have not forgotten you,
   or been false to your covenant.
18 Our heart has not turned back,
   nor have our steps departed from your way,
19 yet you have broken us in the haunt of jackals,
   and covered us with deep darkness.

20 If we had forgotten the name of our God,
   or spread out our hands to a strange god,
21 would not God discover this?
   For he knows the secrets of the heart.
22 Because of you we are being killed all day long,
   and accounted as sheep for the slaughter.

23 Rouse yourself! Why do you sleep, O Lord?
   Awake, do not cast us off forever!
24 Why do you hide your face?
   Why do you forget our affliction and
   oppression?
25 For we sink down to the dust;
   our bodies cling to the ground.
26 Rise up, come to our help.
   Redeem us for the sake of your steadfast love.

Psalm 45

Ode for a Royal Wedding

To the leader: according to Lilies. Of the Kō'ra•hītes.
A Mas'kil. A love song.

1 My heart overflows with a goodly theme;
   I address my verses to the king;
   my tongue is like the pen of a ready scribe.

2 You are the most handsome of men;
   grace is poured upon your lips;
   therefore God has blessed you forever.
3 Gird your sword on your thigh, O mighty one,
   in your glory and majesty.

4 In your majesty ride on victoriously
   for the cause of truth and to defend[c] the
   right;
   let your right hand teach you dread deeds.
5 Your arrows are sharp
   in the heart of the king's enemies;
   the peoples fall under you.

6 Your throne, O God,[d] endures forever and ever.
   Your royal scepter is a scepter of equity;

7 you love righteousness and hate
   wickedness.
Therefore God, your God, has anointed you
   with the oil of gladness beyond your
   companions;
8 your robes are all fragrant with myrrh and
   aloes and cassia.
From ivory palaces stringed instruments make
   you glad;
9 daughters of kings are among your ladies of
   honor;
   at your right hand stands the queen in gold
   of Ō'phir.

10 Hear, O daughter, consider and incline your
   ear;
   forget your people and your father's house,
11 and the king will desire your beauty.
Since he is your lord, bow to him;
12 the people[e] of Tȳre will seek your favor
   with gifts,
   the richest of the people 13 with all kinds of
   wealth.

The princess is decked in her chamber with
   gold-woven robes;[f]
14 in many-colored robes she is led to the
   king;
   behind her the virgins, her companions,
   follow.
15 With joy and gladness they are led along
   as they enter the palace of the king.

16 In the place of ancestors you, O king,[g] shall
   have sons;
   you will make them princes in all the earth.
17 I will cause your name to be celebrated in all
   generations;
   therefore the peoples will praise you forever
   and ever.

Psalm 46

God's Defense of His City and People

To the leader. Of the Kō'ra•hītes.
According to Al'a•moth. A Song.

1 God is our refuge and strength,
   a very present[h] help in trouble.
2 Therefore we will not fear, though the earth
   should change,
   though the mountains shake in the heart of
   the sea;

---

b Heb *a shaking of the head*   c Cn: Heb *and the meekness of*
d Or *Your throne is a throne of God, it*   e Heb *daughter*   f Or
people. 13*All glorious is the princess within, gold embroidery is
her clothing*   g Heb lacks *O king*   h Or *well proved*

3 though its waters roar and foam,
    though the mountains tremble with its
        tumult.   *Sĕ'lah*

4 There is a river whose streams make glad the
        city of God,
    the holy habitation of the Most High.
5 God is in the midst of the city;*ᶦ* it shall not be
        moved;
    God will help it when the morning
        dawns.
6 The nations are in an uproar, the kingdoms
        totter;
    he utters his voice, the earth melts.
7 The LORD of hosts is with us;
    the God of Jacob is our refuge.*ʲ*   *Sĕ'lah*

8 Come, behold the works of the LORD;
    see what desolations he has brought on the
        earth.
9 He makes wars cease to the end of the earth;
    he breaks the bow, and shatters the
        spear;
    he burns the shields with fire.
10 "Be still, and know that I am God!
    I am exalted among the nations,
    I am exalted in the earth."
11 The LORD of hosts is with us;
    the God of Jacob is our refuge.*ʲ*   *Sĕ'lah*

Psalm 47

God's Rule over the Nations
To the leader. Of the Kŏ'ra•hites. A Psalm.

1 Clap your hands, all you peoples;
    shout to God with loud songs of joy.
2 For the LORD, the Most High, is awesome,
    a great king over all the earth.
3 He subdued peoples under us,
    and nations under our feet.
4 He chose our heritage for us,
    the pride of Jacob whom he loves.   *Sĕ'lah*

5 God has gone up with a shout,
    the LORD with the sound of a trumpet.
6 Sing praises to God, sing praises;
    sing praises to our King, sing praises.
7 For God is the king of all the earth;
    sing praises with a psalm.*ᵏ*

8 God is king over the nations;
    God sits on his holy throne.
9 The princes of the peoples gather
    as the people of the God of Abraham.
    For the shields of the earth belong to God;
        he is highly exalted.

Psalm 48

The Glory and Strength of Zion
A Song. A Psalm of the Kŏ'ra•hites.

1 Great is the LORD and greatly to be praised
        in the city of our God.
    His holy mountain, 2 beautiful in elevation,
        is the joy of all the earth,
    Mount Zion, in the far north,
        the city of the great King.
3 Within its citadels God
    has shown himself a sure defense.

4 Then the kings assembled,
    they came on together.
5 As soon as they saw it, they were astounded;
    they were in panic, they took to flight;
6 trembling took hold of them there,
    pains as of a woman in labor,
7 as when an east wind shatters
    the ships of Tar'shish.
8 As we have heard, so have we seen
    in the city of the LORD of hosts,
    in the city of our God,
        which God establishes forever.   *Sĕ'lah*

9 We ponder your steadfast love, O God,
    in the midst of your temple.
10 Your name, O God, like your praise,
    reaches to the ends of the earth.
    Your right hand is filled with victory.
11   Let Mount Zion be glad,
    let the towns*ˡ* of Judah rejoice
        because of your judgments.

12 Walk about Zion, go all around it,
        count its towers,
13 consider well its ramparts;
        go through its citadels,
    that you may tell the next generation
14   that this is God,
    our God forever and ever.
        He will be our guide forever.

Psalm 49

The Folly of Trust in Riches
To the leader. Of the Kŏ'ra•hites. A Psalm.

1 Hear this, all you peoples;
    give ear, all inhabitants of the world,
2 both low and high,
    rich and poor together.
3 My mouth shall speak wisdom;

ᶦ Heb *of it*   *ʲ* Or *fortress*   *ᵏ* Heb *Maskil*
ˡ Heb *daughters*

the meditation of my heart shall be
    understanding.
4 I will incline my ear to a proverb;
    I will solve my riddle to the music of the
        harp.

5 Why should I fear in times of trouble,
    when the iniquity of my persecutors
        surrounds me,
6 those who trust in their wealth
    and boast of the abundance of their
        riches?
7 Truly, no ransom avails for one's life,*m*
    there is no price one can give to God
        for it.
8 For the ransom of life is costly,
    and can never suffice,
9 that one should live on forever
    and never see the grave.*n*

10 When we look at the wise, they die;
    fool and dolt perish together
    and leave their wealth to others.
11 Their graves*o* are their homes forever,
    their dwelling places to all generations,
    though they named lands their own.
12 Mortals cannot abide in their pomp;
    they are like the animals that perish.

13 Such is the fate of the foolhardy,
    the end of those*p* who are pleased with
        their lot.   *Se͞'lah*
14 Like sheep they are appointed for She͞'ōl;
    Death shall be their shepherd;
  straight to the grave they descend,*q*
    and their form shall waste away;
    She͞'ōl shall be their home.*r*
15 But God will ransom my soul from the power
    of She͞'ōl,
    for he will receive me.   *Se͞'lah*

16 Do not be afraid when some become rich,
    when the wealth of their houses
        increases.
17 For when they die they will carry nothing
    away;
    their wealth will not go down after
        them.
18 Though in their lifetime they count themselves
    happy
    —for you are praised when you do well for
        yourself—
19 they*s* will go to the company of their
    ancestors,
    who will never again see the light.
20 Mortals cannot abide in their pomp;
    they are like the animals that perish.

Psalm 50
The Acceptable Sacrifice
A Psalm of Ā'saph.

1 The mighty one, God the LORD,
    speaks and summons the earth
    from the rising of the sun to its setting.
2 Out of Zion, the perfection of beauty,
    God shines forth.

3 Our God comes and does not keep silence,
    before him is a devouring fire,
    and a mighty tempest all around him.
4 He calls to the heavens above
    and to the earth, that he may judge his
        people:
5 "Gather to me my faithful ones,
    who made a covenant with me by
        sacrifice!"
6 The heavens declare his righteousness,
    for God himself is judge.   *Se͞'lah*

7 "Hear, O my people, and I will speak,
    O Israel, I will testify against you.
    I am God, your God.
8 Not for your sacrifices do I rebuke you;
    your burnt offerings are continually
        before me.
9 I will not accept a bull from your house,
    or goats from your folds.
10 For every wild animal of the forest is mine,
    the cattle on a thousand hills.
11 I know all the birds of the air,*t*
    and all that moves in the field is mine.

12 "If I were hungry, I would not tell you,
    for the world and all that is in it is mine.
13 Do I eat the flesh of bulls,
    or drink the blood of goats?
14 Offer to God a sacrifice of thanksgiving,*u*
    and pay your vows to the Most High.
15 Call on me in the day of trouble;
    I will deliver you, and you shall
        glorify me."

16 But to the wicked God says:
    "What right have you to recite my
        statutes,
    or take my covenant on your lips?
17 For you hate discipline,
    and you cast my words behind you.

---

m Another reading is *no one can ransom a brother*   *n* Heb
the pit   *o* Gk Syr Compare Tg: Heb *their inward* (thought)
p Tg: Heb *after them*   *q* Cn: Heb *the upright shall have
dominion over them in the morning*   *r* Meaning of Heb
uncertain   *s* Cn: Heb *you*   *t* Gk Syr Tg: Heb *mountains*
u Or *make thanksgiving your sacrifice to God*

18 You make friends with a thief when you see
  one,
  and you keep company with adulterers.

19 "You give your mouth free rein for evil,
  and your tongue frames deceit.
20 You sit and speak against your kin;
  you slander your own mother's child.
21 These things you have done and I have been
  silent;
  you thought that I was one just like
  yourself.
  But now I rebuke you, and lay the charge
  before you.

22 "Mark this, then, you who forget God,
  or I will tear you apart, and there will be no
  one to deliver.
23 Those who bring thanksgiving as their sacrifice
  honor me;
  to those who go the right way^v
  I will show the salvation of God."

Psalm 51

Prayer for Cleansing and Pardon

*To the leader. A Psalm of David, when the prophet
Nathan came to him, after he had gone
in to Bath•she′ba.*

1 Have mercy on me, O God,
  according to your steadfast love;
  according to your abundant mercy
  blot out my transgressions.

2 Wash me thoroughly from my iniquity,
  and cleanse me from my sin.

3 For I know my transgressions,
  and my sin is ever before me.
4 Against you, you alone, have I sinned,
  and done what is evil in your sight,
  so that you are justified in your sentence
  and blameless when you pass judgment.
5 Indeed, I was born guilty,
  a sinner when my mother conceived me.

6 You desire truth in the inward being;^{w}
  therefore teach me wisdom in my secret
  heart.
7 Purge me with hyssop, and I shall be clean;
  wash me, and I shall be whiter than snow.
8 Let me hear joy and gladness;
  let the bones that you have crushed rejoice.
9 Hide your face from my sins,
  and blot out all my iniquities.

10 Create in me a clean heart, O God,
  and put a new and right^x spirit within me.
11 Do not cast me away from your presence,
  and do not take your holy spirit from me.
12 Restore to me the joy of your salvation,
  and sustain in me a willing^y spirit.

13 Then I will teach transgressors your ways,
  and sinners will return to you.

---

^{v} Heb *who set a way* ^{w} Meaning of Heb uncertain
^{x} Or *steadfast* ^{y} Or *generous*

*Have mercy on me, O God
according to your steadfast love*

*Create in me a clean heart, O God
and put a new and right spirit within me*

14 Deliver me from bloodshed, O God,
 O God of my salvation,
 and my tongue will sing aloud of your
  deliverance.

15 O Lord, open my lips,
 and my mouth will declare your praise.
16 For you have no delight in sacrifice;
 if I were to give a burnt offering, you would
  not be pleased.
17 The sacrifice acceptable to God*z* is a broken
  spirit;
 a broken and contrite heart, O God, you
  will not despise.

18 Do good to Zion in your good pleasure;
 rebuild the walls of Jerusalem,
19 then you will delight in right sacrifices,
 in burnt offerings and whole burnt
  offerings;
 then bulls will be offered on your altar.

Psalm 52

Judgment on the Deceitful

*To the leader. A Mas'kil of David, when Dō'eg the
Ē'dom•ite came to Saul and said to him, "David has
come to the house of A•him'e•lech."*

1 Why do you boast, O mighty one,
 of mischief done against the godly?*a*
 All day long 2 you are plotting destruction.
 Your tongue is like a sharp razor,
 you worker of treachery.
3 You love evil more than good,
 and lying more than speaking the truth.
         Se'lah
4 You love all words that devour,
 O deceitful tongue.

5 But God will break you down forever;
 he will snatch and tear you from your tent;
 he will uproot you from the land of the
  living.   *Se'lah*
6 The righteous will see, and fear,
 and will laugh at the evildoer,*b* saying,
7 "See the one who would not take
  refuge in God,
 but trusted in abundant riches,
 and sought refuge in wealth!"*c*

8 But I am like a green olive tree
 in the house of God.
 I trust in the steadfast love of God
 forever and ever.
9 I will thank you forever,
 because of what you have done.

In the presence of the faithful
 I will proclaim*d* your name, for it is good.

Psalm 53

Denunciation of Godlessness

(Ps 14.1–7)

*To the leader: according to Mă'ha•lath.
A Mas'kil of David.*

1 Fools say in their hearts, "There is no God."
 They are corrupt, they commit abominable
  acts;
 there is no one who does good.

2 God looks down from heaven on humankind
 to see if there are any who are wise,
 who seek after God.

3 They have all fallen away, they are all alike
  perverse;
 there is no one who does good,
 no, not one.

4 Have they no knowledge, those evildoers,
 who eat up my people as they eat bread,
 and do not call upon God?

5 There they shall be in great terror,
 in terror such as has not been.
For God will scatter the bones of the
  ungodly;*e*
 they will be put to shame,*f* for God has
  rejected them.

6 O that deliverance for Israel would come from
  Zion!
 When God restores the fortunes of his
  people,
 Jacob will rejoice; Israel will be glad.

Psalm 54

Prayer for Vindication

*To the leader: with stringed instruments. A Mas'kil
of David, when the Ziph'ites went and told Saul,
"David is in hiding among us."*

1 Save me, O God, by your name,
 and vindicate me by your might.
2 Hear my prayer, O God;
 give ear to the words of my mouth.

---

z Or *My sacrifice, O God,* *a* Cn Compare Syr: Heb *the
kindness of God* *b* Heb *him* *c* Syr Tg: Heb *in his destruction*
d Cn: Heb *wait for* *e* Cn Compare Gk Syr: Heb *him who
encamps against you* *f* Gk: Heb *you have put (them) to
shame*

3 For the insolent have risen against me,
    the ruthless seek my life;
    they do not set God before them.   *Sĕ'lah*

4 But surely, God is my helper;
    the Lord is the upholder of*g* my life.
5 He will repay my enemies for their evil.
    In your faithfulness, put an end to them.

6 With a freewill offering I will sacrifice to you;
    I will give thanks to your name, O LORD,
        for it is good.
7 For he has delivered me from every trouble,
    and my eye has looked in triumph on my
        enemies.

Psalm 55

Complaint about a Friend's Treachery

To the leader: with stringed instruments.
A Mas'kil of David.

1 Give ear to my prayer, O God;
    do not hide yourself from my supplication.
2 Attend to me, and answer me;
    I am troubled in my complaint.
I am distraught 3 by the noise of the enemy,
    because of the clamor of the wicked.
For they bring*h* trouble upon me,

PRAY IT!
Betrayed!

Maybe you don't have enemies quite as
bad as the enemies described in Psalm
55, but you may be able to sympathize
with the psalmist when he writes this:
    My companion laid hands on a friend
        and violated a covenant with me
        (Verse 20)
    When you feel betrayed by others
like the psalmist does—maybe betrayed
by a friend who didn't keep a promise or
by a parent who seemed to treat you
unfairly or by anyone else for whatever
reason—call on God, and say a prayer
like the following:

I trust you, God; I want to believe you are
with me. Help me to know you are here
and that I am not alone. Amen.

▸ **Psalm 55**

and in anger they cherish enmity
    against me.

4 My heart is in anguish within me,
    the terrors of death have fallen upon me.
5 Fear and trembling come upon me,
    and horror overwhelms me.
6 And I say, "O that I had wings like a dove!
    I would fly away and be at rest;
7 truly, I would flee far away;
    I would lodge in the wilderness;   *Sĕ'lah*
8 I would hurry to find a shelter for myself
    from the raging wind and tempest."

9 Confuse, O Lord, confound their speech;
    for I see violence and strife in the city.
10 Day and night they go around it
    on its walls,
and iniquity and trouble are within it;
11   ruin is in its midst;
oppression and fraud
    do not depart from its marketplace.

12 It is not enemies who taunt me—
    I could bear that;
it is not adversaries who deal insolently
        with me—
    I could hide from them.
13 But it is you, my equal,
    my companion, my familiar friend,
14 with whom I kept pleasant company;
    we walked in the house of God with the
        throng.
15 Let death come upon them;
    let them go down alive to Shĕ'ōl;
    for evil is in their homes and in their hearts.

16 But I call upon God,
    and the LORD will save me.
17 Evening and morning and at noon
    I utter my complaint and moan,
    and he will hear my voice.
18 He will redeem me unharmed
    from the battle that I wage,
    for many are arrayed against me.
19 God, who is enthroned from of old,   *Sĕ'lah*
    will hear, and will humble them—
because they do not change,
    and do not fear God.

20 My companion laid hands on a friend
    and violated a covenant with me *i*
21 with speech smoother than butter,

---

g Gk Syr Jerome: Heb *is of those who uphold* or *is with those*
who uphold   *h* Cn Compare Gk: Heb *they cause to totter*
i Heb lacks *with me*

but with a heart set on war;
with words that were softer than oil,
but in fact were drawn swords.

22 Cast your burden^j on the LORD,
and he will sustain you;
he will never permit
the righteous to be moved.

23 But you, O God, will cast them down
into the lowest pit;
the bloodthirsty and treacherous
shall not live out half their days.
But I will trust in you.

Psalm 56

Trust in God under Persecution

*To the leader: according to The Dove
on Far-off Terebinths. Of David. A Mik'tam,
when the Phi•lis'tines seized him in Gath.*

1 Be gracious to me, O God, for people trample
on me;
all day long foes oppress me;
2 my enemies trample on me all day long,
for many fight against me.
O Most High, 3 when I am afraid,
I put my trust in you.
4 In God, whose word I praise,
in God I trust; I am not afraid;
what can flesh do to me?

5 All day long they seek to injure my cause;
all their thoughts are against me for evil.
6 They stir up strife, they lurk,
they watch my steps.
As they hoped to have my life,
7 so repay^k them for their crime;
in wrath cast down the peoples, O God!

8 You have kept count of my tossings;
put my tears in your bottle.
Are they not in your record?
9 Then my enemies will retreat
in the day when I call.
This I know, that^l God is for me.
10 In God, whose word I praise,
in the LORD, whose word I praise,
11 in God I trust; I am not afraid.
What can a mere mortal do to me?

12 My vows to you I must perform, O God;
I will render thank offerings to you.
13 For you have delivered my soul from death,
and my feet from falling,
so that I may walk before God
in the light of life.

Psalm 57

Praise and Assurance under Persecution

(Cp Ps 108.1–5)

*To the leader: Do Not Destroy. Of David. A Mik'tam,
when he fled from Saul, in the cave.*

1 Be merciful to me, O God, be merciful to me,
for in you my soul takes refuge;
in the shadow of your wings I will take refuge,
until the destroying storms pass by.
2 I cry to God Most High,
to God who fulfills his purpose for me.
3 He will send from heaven and save me,
he will put to shame those who trample
on me.   *Sě'lah*
God will send forth his steadfast love and his
faithfulness.

4 I lie down among lions
that greedily devour^m human prey;
their teeth are spears and arrows,
their tongues sharp swords.

5 Be exalted, O God, above the heavens.
Let your glory be over all the earth.

6 They set a net for my steps;
my soul was bowed down.
They dug a pit in my path,
but they have fallen into it themselves.
Sě'lah

7 My heart is steadfast, O God,
my heart is steadfast.
I will sing and make melody.
8   Awake, my soul!
Awake, O harp and lyre!
I will awake the dawn.
9 I will give thanks to you, O Lord, among the
peoples;
I will sing praises to you among the
nations.
10 For your steadfast love is as high as the
heavens;
your faithfulness extends to the clouds.

11 Be exalted, O God, above the heavens.
Let your glory be over all the earth.

Psalm 58

Prayer for Vengeance

To the leader: Do Not Destroy. Of David. A Mik'tam.

1 Do you indeed decree what is right, you gods?^{n}
Do you judge people fairly?

---

^{j} Or *Cast what he has given you* ^{k} Cn: Heb *rescue* ^{l} Or
because ^{m} Cn: Heb *are aflame for* ^{n} Or *mighty lords*

2 No, in your hearts you devise wrongs;
     your hands deal out violence on earth.

3 The wicked go astray from the womb;
     they err from their birth, speaking lies.
4 They have venom like the venom of a serpent,
     like the deaf adder that stops its ear,
5 so that it does not hear the voice of charmers
     or of the cunning enchanter.

6 O God, break the teeth in their mouths;
     tear out the fangs of the young lions,
          O LORD!
7 Let them vanish like water that runs away;
     like grass let them be trodden down[o] and
          wither.
8 Let them be like the snail that dissolves into
          slime;
     like the untimely birth that never sees the
          sun.
9 Sooner than your pots can feel the heat of
          thorns,
     whether green or ablaze, may he sweep
          them away!

10 The righteous will rejoice when they see
          vengeance done;
     they will bathe their feet in the blood of the
          wicked.
11 People will say, "Surely there is a reward for
          the righteous;
     surely there is a God who judges on earth."

Psalm 59

Prayer for Deliverance from Enemies

To the leader: Do Not Destroy. Of David.
A Mik'tam, when Saul ordered his house
to be watched in order to kill him.

1 Deliver me from my enemies, O my God;
     protect me from those who rise up
          against me.
2 Deliver me from those who work evil;
     from the bloodthirsty save me.

3 Even now they lie in wait for my life;
     the mighty stir up strife against me.
   For no transgression or sin of mine, O LORD,
4   for no fault of mine, they run and make
          ready.

   Rouse yourself, come to my help and see!
5   You, LORD God of hosts, are God of Israel.
   Awake to punish all the nations;
     spare none of those who treacherously plot
          evil.   *Sĕ'lah*

6 Each evening they come back,
     howling like dogs
     and prowling about the city.
7 There they are, bellowing with their mouths,
     with sharp words[p] on their lips—
     for "Who," they think,[q] "will hear us?"

8 But you laugh at them, O LORD;
     you hold all the nations in derision.
9 O my strength, I will watch for you;
     for you, O God, are my fortress.
10 My God in his steadfast love will meet me;
     my God will let me look in triumph on my
          enemies.

11 Do not kill them, or my people may forget;
     make them totter by your power, and bring
          them down,
          O Lord, our shield.
12 For the sin of their mouths, the words of their lips,
     let them be trapped in their pride.
   For the cursing and lies that they utter,
13   consume them in wrath;
     consume them until they are no more.
   Then it will be known to the ends of the earth
     that God rules over Jacob.   *Sĕ'lah*

14 Each evening they come back,
     howling like dogs
     and prowling about the city.
15 They roam about for food,
     and growl if they do not get their fill.

16 But I will sing of your might;
     I will sing aloud of your steadfast love in
          the morning.
   For you have been a fortress for me
     and a refuge in the day of my distress.
17 O my strength, I will sing praises to you,
     for you, O God, are my fortress,
     the God who shows me steadfast love.

Psalm 60

Prayer for National Victory after Defeat

(*Cp Ps 108.6–13*)

To the leader: according to the Lily of the Covenant.
A Mik'tam of David; for instruction; when he struggled
with Ar'am-nā•ha•rā'im and with Ar'am-zō'bah, and
when Jō'ab on his return killed twelve thousand
Ē'dom•ites in the Valley of Salt.

1 O God, you have rejected us, broken our
          defenses;
     you have been angry; now restore us!

---

o Cn: Meaning of Heb uncertain   *p* Heb *with swords*
q Heb lacks *they think*

P
S
A
L
M
S

The Agony of Defeat

The athletic team that has never lost does not exist. As a matter of fact, losing is what often inspires athletic teams to get stronger or faster or score more points. The psalmist who sang Psalm 60 knew how it felt to lose. Although this Psalm was written after defeat in battle, its spirit has echoed through the ages by athletic teams and all others who have competed and lost. The next time your team loses, read verses 1–5, and think about how the psalmist calls on God as a helper.

▶ **Psalm 60.1–5**

2 You have caused the land to quake; you have
    torn it open;
  repair the cracks in it, for it is tottering.
3 You have made your people suffer hard things;
    you have given us wine to drink that made
    us reel.

4 You have set up a banner for those who fear
    you,
    to rally to it out of bowshot.[r]   *Sĕ'lah*
5 Give victory with your right hand, and
    answer us,[s]
    so that those whom you love may be
    rescued.

6 God has promised in his sanctuary:[t]
    "With exultation I will divide up Shĕ'chem,
    and portion out the Vale of Suc'coth.
7 Gil'e•ad is mine, and Ma•nas'seh is mine;
    E'phra•im is my helmet;
    Judah is my scepter.
8 Mō'ab is my washbasin;
    on E'dom I hurl my shoe;
    over Phi•lis'ti•a I shout in triumph."

9 Who will bring me to the fortified city?
    Who will lead me to E'dom?
10 Have you not rejected us, O God?
    You do not go out, O God, with our armies.
11 O grant us help against the foe,
    for human help is worthless.
12 With God we shall do valiantly;
    it is he who will tread down our foes.

Psalm 61
Assurance of God's Protection
To the leader: with stringed instruments. Of David.

1 Hear my cry, O God;
    listen to my prayer.
2 From the end of the earth I call to you,
    when my heart is faint.

Lead me to the rock
    that is higher than I;
3 for you are my refuge,
    a strong tower against the enemy.

4 Let me abide in your tent forever,
    find refuge under the shelter of your wings.
                Sĕ'lah
5 For you, O God, have heard my vows;
    you have given me the heritage of those
    who fear your name.

6 Prolong the life of the king;
    may his years endure to all generations!
7 May he be enthroned forever before God;
    appoint steadfast love and faithfulness to
    watch over him!

8 So I will always sing praises to your
    name,
    as I pay my vows day after day.

Psalm 62
Song of Trust in God Alone
To the leader: according to Je•dū'thun.
A Psalm of David.

1 For God alone my soul waits in silence;
    from him comes my salvation.
2 He alone is my rock and my salvation,
    my fortress; I shall never be shaken.

3 How long will you assail a person,
    will you batter your victim, all of you,
    as you would a leaning wall, a tottering
    fence?
4 Their only plan is to bring down a person of
    prominence.
    They take pleasure in falsehood;

---

r Gk Syr Jerome: Heb *because of the truth*   s Another reading
is *me* t Or *by his holiness*

they bless with their mouths,
    but inwardly they curse.   *Sĕʾlah*

5 For God alone my soul waits in silence,
    for my hope is from him.
6 He alone is my rock and my salvation,
    my fortress; I shall not be shaken.
7 On God rests my deliverance and my
        honor;
    my mighty rock, my refuge is in God.

8 Trust in him at all times, O people;
    pour out your heart before him;
    God is a refuge for us.   *Sĕʾlah*

9 Those of low estate are but a breath,
    those of high estate are a delusion;
    in the balances they go up;
    they are together lighter than a breath.
10 Put no confidence in extortion,
    and set no vain hopes on robbery;
    if riches increase, do not set your heart on
        them.

11 Once God has spoken;
    twice have I heard this:
    that power belongs to God,
12   and steadfast love belongs to you,
        O Lord.
    For you repay to all
    according to their work.

PRAY IT!
Decide!

Whom are you going to trust? Where will you find your power? in the right people? in the right clothes? in money? in the right job?

    Or can you trust God to be your rock and your salvation (Ps 62.2)? Will you let God be your refuge (61.4; 62.7) in times of hardship? Why is it so hard sometimes to let your soul wait for God in silence (62.1)?

God, I am weak. Help me every day to put my trust in you.

    Help me to believe that you and I can do anything together.

▶ **Psalm 62**

Psalm 63
Comfort and Assurance in God's Presence
A Psalm of David, when he was in the Wilderness of Judah.

1 O God, you are my God, I seek you,
    my soul thirsts for you;
my flesh faints for you,
    as in a dry and weary land where there is no
        water.
2 So I have looked upon you in the sanctuary,
    beholding your power and glory.
3 Because your steadfast love is better than life,
    my lips will praise you.
4 So I will bless you as long as I live;
    I will lift up my hands and call on your
        name.

5 My soul is satisfied as with a rich feast,[u]
    and my mouth praises you with joyful
        lips
6 when I think of you on my bed,
    and meditate on you in the watches of the
        night;
7 for you have been my help,
    and in the shadow of your wings I sing for
        joy.
8 My soul clings to you;
    your right hand upholds me.

9 But those who seek to destroy my life
    shall go down into the depths of the earth;
10 they shall be given over to the power of the
        sword,
    they shall be prey for jackals.
11 But the king shall rejoice in God;
    all who swear by him shall exult,
    for the mouths of liars will be stopped.

Psalm 64
Prayer for Protection from Enemies
To the leader. A Psalm of David.

1 Hear my voice, O God, in my complaint;
    preserve my life from the dread enemy.
2 Hide me from the secret plots of the wicked,
    from the scheming of evildoers,
3 who whet their tongues like swords,
    who aim bitter words like arrows,
4 shooting from ambush at the blameless;
    they shoot suddenly and without fear.
5 They hold fast to their evil purpose;
    they talk of laying snares secretly,
thinking, "Who can see us?[v]

u Heb *with fat and fatness*   *v* Syr: Heb *them*

6   Who can search out our crimes?*w*
We have thought out a cunningly conceived
     plot."
For the human heart and mind are deep.

7 But God will shoot his arrow at them;
    they will be wounded suddenly.
8 Because of their tongue he will bring them to
    ruin;*x*
    all who see them will shake with horror.
9 Then everyone will fear;
    they will tell what God has brought about,
    and ponder what he has done.

10 Let the righteous rejoice in the LORD
    and take refuge in him.
Let all the upright in heart glory.

Psalm 65

Thanksgiving for Earth's Bounty

To the leader. A Psalm of David. A Song.

1 Praise is due to you,
    O God, in Zion;
and to you shall vows be performed,
2   O you who answer prayer!
To you all flesh shall come.
3 When deeds of iniquity overwhelm us,
    you forgive our transgressions.
4 Happy are those whom you choose and bring
    near
    to live in your courts.
We shall be satisfied with the goodness of your
    house,
    your holy temple.

5 By awesome deeds you answer us with
    deliverance,
    O God of our salvation;
you are the hope of all the ends of the earth
    and of the farthest seas.
6 By your*y* strength you established the
    mountains;
    you are girded with might.
7 You silence the roaring of the seas,
    the roaring of their waves,
    the tumult of the peoples.
8 Those who live at earth's farthest bounds are
    awed by your signs;
you make the gateways of the morning and the
    evening shout for joy.

9 You visit the earth and water it,
    you greatly enrich it;
the river of God is full of water;
    you provide the people with grain,

for so you have prepared it.
10 You water its furrows abundantly,
    settling its ridges,
softening it with showers,
    and blessing its growth.
11 You crown the year with your bounty;
    your wagon tracks overflow with richness.
12 The pastures of the wilderness overflow,
    the hills gird themselves with joy,
13 the meadows clothe themselves with flocks,
    the valleys deck themselves with grain,
    they shout and sing together for joy.

Psalm 66

Praise for God's Goodness to Israel

To the leader. A Song. A Psalm.

1 Make a joyful noise to God, all the earth;
2   sing the glory of his name;
    give to him glorious praise.
3 Say to God, "How awesome are your deeds!
    Because of your great power, your enemies
     cringe before you.
4 All the earth worships you;
    they sing praises to you,
    sing praises to your name."   *Sĕ'lah*

5 Come and see what God has done:
    he is awesome in his deeds among mortals.
6 He turned the sea into dry land;
    they passed through the river on foot.
There we rejoiced in him,
7   who rules by his might forever,
whose eyes keep watch on the nations—
    let the rebellious not exalt themselves.   *Sĕ'lah*

8 Bless our God, O peoples,
    let the sound of his praise be heard,
9 who has kept us among the living,
    and has not let our feet slip.
10 For you, O God, have tested us;
    you have tried us as silver is tried.
11 You brought us into the net;
    you laid burdens on our backs;
12 you let people ride over our heads;
    we went through fire and through water;
yet you have brought us out to a spacious
    place.*z*

13 I will come into your house with burnt
    offerings;

---

w Cn: Heb *They search out crimes*   *x* Cn: Heb *They will bring
him to ruin, their tongue being against them*   *y* Gk Jerome:
Heb *his*   *z* Cn Compare Gk Syr Jerome Tg: Heb *to a
saturation*

I will pay you my vows,
14 those that my lips uttered
   and my mouth promised when I was in
      trouble.
15 I will offer to you burnt offerings of fatlings,
   with the smoke of the sacrifice of rams;
   I will make an offering of bulls and goats.
                                        Se̅'lah

16 Come and hear, all you who fear God,
   and I will tell what he has done for me.
17 I cried aloud to him,
   and he was extolled with my tongue.
18 If I had cherished iniquity in my heart,
   the Lord would not have listened.
19 But truly God has listened;
   he has given heed to the words of my
      prayer.

20 Blessed be God,
   because he has not rejected my prayer
   or removed his steadfast love from me.

Psalm 67

The Nations Called to Praise God

To the leader: with stringed instruments.
A Psalm. A Song.

1 May God be gracious to us and bless us
   and make his face to shine upon us,
                                        Se̅'lah
2 that your way may be known upon earth,
   your saving power among all nations.
3 Let the peoples praise you, O God;
   let all the peoples praise you.

4 Let the nations be glad and sing for joy,
   for you judge the peoples with equity
   and guide the nations upon earth. *Se̅'lah*
5 Let the peoples praise you, O God;
   let all the peoples praise you.

6 The earth has yielded its increase;
   God, our God, has blessed us.
7 May God continue to bless us;
   let all the ends of the earth revere him.

Psalm 68

Praise and Thanksgiving

To the leader. Of David. A Psalm. A Song.

1 Let God rise up, let his enemies be scattered;
   let those who hate him flee before him.
2 As smoke is driven away, so drive them away;
   as wax melts before the fire,
   let the wicked perish before God.

3 But let the righteous be joyful;
   let them exult before God;
   let them be jubilant with joy.

4 Sing to God, sing praises to his name;
   lift up a song to him who rides upon the
      clouds[a]—
   his name is the LORD—
   be exultant before him.

5 Father of orphans and protector of widows
   is God in his holy habitation.
6 God gives the desolate a home to live in;
   he leads out the prisoners to prosperity,
   but the rebellious live in a parched
      land.

7 O God, when you went out before your
      people,
   when you marched through the wilderness,
                                        Se̅'lah
8 the earth quaked, the heavens poured down
      rain
   at the presence of God, the God of Sinai,
   at the presence of God, the God of Israel.
9 Rain in abundance, O God, you showered
      abroad;
   you restored your heritage when it
      languished;
10 your flock found a dwelling in it;
   in your goodness, O God, you provided for
      the needy.

11 The Lord gives the command;
   great is the company of those[b] who bore
      the tidings:
12 "The kings of the armies, they flee, they
      flee!"
   The women at home divide the spoil,
13 though they stay among the sheepfolds—
   the wings of a dove covered with silver,
   its pinions with green gold.
14 When the Almighty[c] scattered kings there,
   snow fell on Zal'mon.

15 O mighty mountain, mountain of Bā'shan;
   O many-peaked mountain, mountain of
      Bā'shan!
16 Why do you look with envy, O many-peaked
      mountain,
   at the mount that God desired for his
      abode,
   where the LORD will reside forever?

---

a Or *cast up a highway for him who rides through the deserts*
b Or *company of the women*   c Traditional rendering of
Heb *Shaddai*

P
S
A
L
M
S

BLACK PEOPLE PRAISE THE Lord

Psalm 68 commands us to sing praises to the LORD. We are told to praise the LORD because God is the "Father of orphans and protector of widows" (verse 5), "gives the desolate a home to live in" and "leads out the prisoners to prosperity" (verse 6), "daily bears us up" (verse 19), and "will shatter the heads of his enemies" (verse 21).

Near the end of all this praise, the psalmist says, "Let bronze be brought from Egypt; / let Ethiopia hasten to stretch out its hands to God" (verse 31). The psalmist's call to Egypt and Ethiopia is significant because the Egyptians and the Ethiopians were North African black people.

Nevertheless, the message of Psalm 68 is for all people, whether they are black, brown, red, yellow, or white. All people ought to submit to the LORD, all people ought to praise the LORD, and all people ought to render their whole self and their whole substance to the LORD. It matters not who we are or where we come from; the LORD is God and worthy of all praise!

▶ Psalm 68

17 With mighty chariotry, twice ten thousand,
  thousands upon thousands,
  the Lord came from Sinai into the holy
    place.*d*
18 You ascended the high mount,
  leading captives in your train
  and receiving gifts from people,
  even from those who rebel against the LORD
    God's abiding there.
19 Blessed be the Lord,
  who daily bears us up;
  God is our salvation.   *Sĕ'lah*
20 Our God is a God of salvation,
  and to GOD, the Lord, belongs escape from
    death.

21 But God will shatter the heads of his enemies,
  the hairy crown of those who walk in their
    guilty ways.
22 The Lord said,
  "I will bring them back from Bā'shan,
  I will bring them back from the depths of the
    sea,
23 so that you may bathe*e* your feet in blood,
  so that the tongues of your dogs may have
    their share from the foe."

24 Your solemn processions are seen,*f* O God,
  the processions of my God, my King, into
    the sanctuary—

25 the singers in front, the musicians last,
  between them girls playing tambourines:
26 "Bless God in the great congregation,
  the LORD, O you who are of Israel's
    fountain!"
27 There is Benjamin, the least of them, in the lead,
  the princes of Judah in a body,
  the princes of Zeb'ū•lun, the princes of
    Naph'ta•li.

28 Summon your might, O God;
  show your strength, O God, as you have
    done for us before.
29 Because of your temple at Jerusalem
  kings bear gifts to you.
30 Rebuke the wild animals that live among the
    reeds,
  the herd of bulls with the calves of the
    peoples.
  Trample*g* under foot those who lust after
    tribute;
  scatter the peoples who delight in war.*h*
31 Let bronze be brought from Egypt;
  let Ethiopia*i* hasten to stretch out its hands
    to God.

---

d Cn: Heb *The Lord among them Sinai in the holy* (place)
e Gk Syr Tg: Heb *shatter*   *f* Or *have been seen*   *g* Cn: Heb
Trampling   *h* Meaning of Heb of verse 30 is uncertain
i Or *Nubia*; Heb *Cush*

32 Sing to God, O kingdoms of the earth;
   sing praises to the Lord, *Sĕ'lah*
33 O rider in the heavens, the ancient heavens;
   listen, he sends out his voice, his mighty
   voice.
34 Ascribe power to God,
   whose majesty is over Israel;
   and whose power is in the skies.
35 Awesome is God in his *j* sanctuary,
   the God of Israel;
   he gives power and strength to his people.

Blessed be God!

Psalm 69

Prayer for Deliverance from Persecution

To the leader: according to Lilies. Of David.

1 Save me, O God,
   for the waters have come up to my neck.
2 I sink in deep mire,
   where there is no foothold;
 I have come into deep waters,
   and the flood sweeps over me.
3 I am weary with my crying;
   my throat is parched.
 My eyes grow dim
   with waiting for my God.

4 More in number than the hairs of my head
   are those who hate me without cause;
 many are those who would destroy me,
   my enemies who accuse me falsely.
 What I did not steal
   must I now restore?
5 O God, you know my folly;
   the wrongs I have done are not hidden
     from you.

6 Do not let those who hope in you be put to
     shame because of me,
   O Lord GOD of hosts;
 do not let those who seek you be dishonored
     because of me,
   O God of Israel.
7 It is for your sake that I have borne reproach,
   that shame has covered my face.
8 I have become a stranger to my kindred,
   an alien to my mother's children.

9 It is zeal for your house that has
     consumed me;
   the insults of those who insult you have
     fallen on me.
10 When I humbled my soul with fasting,*k*
   they insulted me for doing so.

11 When I made sackcloth my clothing,
   I became a byword to them.
12 I am the subject of gossip for those who sit in
     the gate,
   and the drunkards make songs about me.

13 But as for me, my prayer is to you, O LORD.
   At an acceptable time, O God,
   in the abundance of your steadfast love,
     answer me.
 With your faithful help 14 rescue me
   from sinking in the mire;
 let me be delivered from my enemies
   and from the deep waters.
15 Do not let the flood sweep over me,
   or the deep swallow me up,
   or the Pit close its mouth over me.

16 Answer me, O LORD, for your steadfast love is
     good;
   according to your abundant mercy, turn
     to me.
17 Do not hide your face from your servant,
   for I am in distress—make haste to
     answer me.
18 Draw near to me, redeem me,
   set me free because of my enemies.

19 You know the insults I receive,
   and my shame and dishonor;
   my foes are all known to you.
20 Insults have broken my heart,
   so that I am in despair.
 I looked for pity, but there was none;
   and for comforters, but I found none.
21 They gave me poison for food,
   and for my thirst they gave me vinegar to
     drink.

22 Let their table be a trap for them,
   a snare for their allies.
23 Let their eyes be darkened so that they cannot
     see,
   and make their loins tremble continually.
24 Pour out your indignation upon them,
   and let your burning anger overtake them.
25 May their camp be a desolation;
   let no one live in their tents.
26 For they persecute those whom you have struck
     down,
   and those whom you have wounded, they
     attack still more.*l*
27 Add guilt to their guilt;

---

j Gk: Heb *from your* *k* Gk Syr: Heb *I wept, with fasting my
soul,* or *I made my soul mourn with fasting* *l* Gk Syr: Heb
recount the pain of

P
S
A
L
M
S

may they have no acquittal from you.
28 Let them be blotted out of the book of the
    living;
    let them not be enrolled among the righteous.
29 But I am lowly and in pain;
    let your salvation, O God, protect me.

30 I will praise the name of God with a song;
    I will magnify him with thanksgiving.
31 This will please the LORD more than an ox
    or a bull with horns and hoofs.
32 Let the oppressed see it and be glad;
    you who seek God, let your hearts revive.
33 For the LORD hears the needy,
    and does not despise his own that are in
    bonds.

34 Let heaven and earth praise him,
    the seas and everything that moves in them.
35 For God will save Zion
    and rebuild the cities of Judah;
    and his servants shall live[m] there and possess it;
36 the children of his servants shall inherit it,
    and those who love his name shall live
    in it.

Psalm 70

Prayer for Deliverance from Enemies

(Ps 40.13–17)

To the leader. Of David, for the memorial offering.

1 Be pleased, O God, to deliver me.
    O LORD, make haste to help me!
2 Let those be put to shame and confusion
    who seek my life.
  Let those be turned back and brought to
    dishonor
    who desire to hurt me.
3 Let those who say, "Aha, Aha!"
    turn back because of their shame.

4 Let all who seek you
    rejoice and be glad in you.
  Let those who love your salvation
    say evermore, "God is great!"
5 But I am poor and needy;
    hasten to me, O God!
  You are my help and my deliverer;
    O LORD, do not delay!

Psalm 71

Prayer for Lifelong Protection and Help

1 In you, O LORD, I take refuge;
    let me never be put to shame.

2 In your righteousness deliver me and rescue me;
    incline your ear to me and save me.
3 Be to me a rock of refuge,
    a strong fortress,[n] to save me,
    for you are my rock and my fortress.

4 Rescue me, O my God, from the hand of the
    wicked,
    from the grasp of the unjust and cruel.
5 For you, O Lord, are my hope,
    my trust, O LORD, from my youth.
6 Upon you I have leaned from my birth;
    it was you who took me from my mother's
    womb.
  My praise is continually of you.

7 I have been like a portent to many,
    but you are my strong refuge.
8 My mouth is filled with your praise,
    and with your glory all day long.
9 Do not cast me off in the time of old age;
    do not forsake me when my strength is
    spent.
10 For my enemies speak concerning me,
    and those who watch for my life consult
    together.
11 They say, "Pursue and seize that person
    whom God has forsaken,
    for there is no one to deliver."

12 O God, do not be far from me;
    O my God, make haste to help me!
13 Let my accusers be put to shame and
    consumed;
    let those who seek to hurt me
    be covered with scorn and disgrace.
14 But I will hope continually,
    and will praise you yet more and more.
15 My mouth will tell of your righteous acts,
    of your deeds of salvation all day long,
    though their number is past my knowledge.
16 I will come praising the mighty deeds of the
    Lord GOD,
    I will praise your righteousness, yours alone.

17 O God, from my youth you have taught me,
    and I still proclaim your wondrous deeds.
18 So even to old age and gray hairs,
    O God, do not forsake me,
  until I proclaim your might
    to all the generations to come.[o]
  Your power 19 and your righteousness, O God,
    reach the high heavens.

---

m Syr: Heb *and they shall live*   n Gk Compare 31.3: Heb *to come continually you have commanded*   o Gk Compare Syr: Heb *to a generation, to all that come*

You who have done great things,
  O God, who is like you?
20 You who have made me see many troubles and
    calamities
  will revive me again;
from the depths of the earth
  you will bring me up again.
21 You will increase my honor,
  and comfort me once again.

22 I will also praise you with the harp
  for your faithfulness, O my God;
I will sing praises to you with the lyre,
  O Holy One of Israel.
23 My lips will shout for joy
  when I sing praises to you;
my soul also, which you have rescued.
24 All day long my tongue will talk of your
    righteous help,
for those who tried to do me harm
  have been put to shame, and disgraced.

Psalm 72

Prayer for Guidance and Support for the King
Of Solomon.

1 Give the king your justice, O God,
  and your righteousness to a king's son.

2 May he judge your people with righteousness,
  and your poor with justice.
3 May the mountains yield prosperity for the
    people,
  and the hills, in righteousness.
4 May he defend the cause of the poor of the
    people,
  give deliverance to the needy,
  and crush the oppressor.

5 May he live*p* while the sun endures,
  and as long as the moon, throughout all
    generations.
6 May he be like rain that falls on the mown
    grass,
  like showers that water the earth.
7 In his days may righteousness flourish
  and peace abound, until the moon is no
    more.

8 May he have dominion from sea to sea,
  and from the River to the ends of the earth.
9 May his foes*q* bow down before him,
  and his enemies lick the dust.
10 May the kings of Tar'shish and of the isles
  render him tribute,

---

p Gk: Heb *may they fear you*   *q* Cn: Heb *those who live in the wilderness*

OPEN UP YOUR TREASURE

Eccl 3.1 says, "For everything there is a season, and a time for every matter under heaven." And from Psalm 72, we see there is a timing for God's call to us.

Psalm 72.10 says the kings of Sheba and Seba shall come to pay tribute to the King of Israel. Sheba, or Seba, was an ancient kingdom, located near Ethiopia, that included black-skinned people.

In Matthew's story of Jesus' birth, God sends a message in the heavens to inform the dark-skinned wise men from the East when it is time to come and open up their treasures to the King.

God is sending a star to us now. God is talking loud to us, including blacks as a people. "Get yourself ready, and be prepared to bring your gifts to me," God says. God has opened the door for us to come, but we must be willing to fall down and worship God and open up our treasures. If we do that, we too will be wise people who acknowledge the One who is born King. Are you ready to acknowledge our real King?

▶ **Psalm 72.10–11**

P
S
A
L
M
S

may the kings of Shĕ'ba and Sĕ'ba
    bring gifts.
11 May all kings fall down before him,
    all nations give him service.

12 For he delivers the needy when they call,
    the poor and those who have no helper.
13 He has pity on the weak and the needy,
    and saves the lives of the needy.
14 From oppression and violence he redeems their
      life;
    and precious is their blood in his sight.

15 Long may he live!
    May gold of Shĕ'ba be given to him.
May prayer be made for him continually,
    and blessings invoked for him all day long.
16 May there be abundance of grain in the land;
    may it wave on the tops of the mountains;
    may its fruit be like Lebanon;
and may people blossom in the cities
    like the grass of the field.
17 May his name endure forever,
    his fame continue as long as the sun.
May all nations be blessed in him;*r*
    may they pronounce him happy.

18 Blessed be the LORD, the God of Israel,
    who alone does wondrous things.
19 Blessed be his glorious name forever;
    may his glory fill the whole earth.
        Amen and Amen.

20 The prayers of David son of Jesse are ended.

BOOK III
(Psalms 73–89)
Psalm 73

Plea for Relief from Oppressors

A Psalm of Ā'saph.

1 Truly God is good to the upright,*s*
    to those who are pure in heart.
2 But as for me, my feet had almost stumbled;
    my steps had nearly slipped.
3 For I was envious of the arrogant;
    I saw the prosperity of the wicked.

4 For they have no pain;
    their bodies are sound and sleek.
5 They are not in trouble as others are;
    they are not plagued like other people.
6 Therefore pride is their necklace;
    violence covers them like a garment.
7 Their eyes swell out with fatness;
    their hearts overflow with follies.
8 They scoff and speak with malice;

    loftily they threaten oppression.
9 They set their mouths against heaven,
    and their tongues range over the earth.

10 Therefore the people turn and praise them,*t*
    and find no fault in them.*u*
11 And they say, "How can God know?
    Is there knowledge in the Most High?"
12 Such are the wicked;
    always at ease, they increase in riches.
13 All in vain I have kept my heart clean
    and washed my hands in innocence.
14 For all day long I have been plagued,
    and am punished every morning.

15 If I had said, "I will talk on in this way,"
    I would have been untrue to the circle of
      your children.
16 But when I thought how to understand this,
    it seemed to me a wearisome task,
17 until I went into the sanctuary of God;
    then I perceived their end.
18 Truly you set them in slippery places;
    you make them fall to ruin.
19 How they are destroyed in a moment,
    swept away utterly by terrors!
20 They are*v* like a dream when one awakes;
    on awaking you despise their
      phantoms.

21 When my soul was embittered,
    when I was pricked in heart,
22 I was stupid and ignorant;
    I was like a brute beast toward you.
23 Nevertheless I am continually with you;
    you hold my right hand.
24 You guide me with your counsel,
    and afterward you will receive me with
      honor.*w*
25 Whom have I in heaven but you?
    And there is nothing on earth that I desire
     other than you.
26 My flesh and my heart may fail,
    but God is the strength*x* of my heart and my
      portion forever.

27 Indeed, those who are far from you will
     perish;
    you put an end to those who are false to
     you.
28 But for me it is good to be near God;
    I have made the Lord GOD my refuge,
    to tell of all your works.

---

*r Or bless themselves by him   s Or good to Israel   t Cn: Heb
his people return here   u Cn: Heb abundant waters are drained
by them   v Cn: Heb Lord   w Or to glory   x Heb rock*

Cultural Connections

WISDOM

Psalm 73 explores the common wisdom question of why the wicked prosper (verse 3). The psalmist finally sees clearly that the wicked eventually fall to ruin (verse 17). The gift of wisdom is also an important value for Native American peoples; in the Lakota tribe, it is one of four primary values. The Lakota word for wisdom is *wok-sa-pe*.

Wisdom is the ability to see clearly and not be taken in by illusions or outer appearances. The wise person knows that what is inside someone is more important than what is outside. The wise person also knows that we are nothing without the power of Wakan-Tanka, the Great Spirit. Because the sun helps us see things the way they really are, many Native Americans face the rising sun each day to pray to God for wisdom.

To explore the other primary Lakota virtues, see the Cultural Connections article for Psalm 31.

▸ **Psalm 73**

Psalm 74

Plea for Help in Time of National Humiliation

A Mas'kil of Ā'saph.

1 O God, why do you cast us off forever?
  Why does your anger smoke against the
    sheep of your pasture?
2 Remember your congregation, which you
    acquired long ago,
  which you redeemed to be the tribe of your
    heritage.
  Remember Mount Zion, where you came to
    dwell.

3 Direct your steps to the perpetual ruins;
  the enemy has destroyed everything in the
    sanctuary.

4 Your foes have roared within your holy
    place;
  they set up their emblems there.
5 At the upper entrance they hacked
  the wooden trellis with axes.*y*
6 And then, with hatchets and hammers,
  they smashed all its carved work.
7 They set your sanctuary on fire;
  they desecrated the dwelling place of your
    name,
  bringing it to the ground.
8 They said to themselves, "We will utterly
    subdue them";

they burned all the meeting places of God
  in the land.

9 We do not see our emblems;
  there is no longer any prophet,
  and there is no one among us who knows
    how long.
10 How long, O God, is the foe to scoff?
  Is the enemy to revile your name
    forever?
11 Why do you hold back your hand;
  why do you keep your hand in*z* your
    bosom?

12 Yet God my King is from of old,
  working salvation in the earth.
13 You divided the sea by your might;
  you broke the heads of the dragons in the
    waters.
14 You crushed the heads of Le•vi'a•than;
  you gave him as food*a* for the creatures of
    the wilderness.
15 You cut openings for springs and torrents;
  you dried up ever-flowing streams.
16 Yours is the day, yours also the night;
  you established the luminaries*b* and the
    sun.

---

y Cn Compare Gk Syr: Meaning of Heb uncertain
z Cn: Heb *do you consume your right hand from*   *a* Heb *food for the people*   *b* Or *moon*; Heb *light*

P
S
A
L
M
S

17 You have fixed all the bounds of the earth;
   you made summer and winter.

18 Remember this, O LORD, how the enemy scoffs,
   and an impious people reviles your name.
19 Do not deliver the soul of your dove to the
       wild animals;
   do not forget the life of your poor forever.

20 Have regard for your*c* covenant,
   for the dark places of the land are full of the
       haunts of violence.
21 Do not let the downtrodden be put to shame;
   let the poor and needy praise your name.
22 Rise up, O God, plead your cause;
   remember how the impious scoff at you all
       day long.
23 Do not forget the clamor of your foes,
   the uproar of your adversaries that goes up
       continually.

Psalm 75

Thanksgiving for God's
Wondrous Deeds

To the leader: Do Not Destroy.
A Psalm of Ā'saph. A Song.

1 We give thanks to you, O God;
   we give thanks; your name is near.
People tell of your wondrous deeds.

2 At the set time that I appoint
   I will judge with equity.
3 When the earth totters, with all its inhabitants,
   it is I who keep its pillars steady.   *Sĕ'lah*
4 I say to the boastful, "Do not boast,"
   and to the wicked, "Do not lift up your
       horn;
5 do not lift up your horn on high,
   or speak with insolent neck."

6 For not from the east or from the west
   and not from the wilderness comes lifting up;
7 but it is God who executes judgment,
   putting down one and lifting up another.
8 For in the hand of the LORD there is a cup
   with foaming wine, well mixed;
he will pour a draught from it,
   and all the wicked of the earth
   shall drain it down to the dregs.
9 But I will rejoice*d* forever;
   I will sing praises to the God of Jacob.

10 All the horns of the wicked I will cut off,
    but the horns of the righteous shall be
        exalted.

Psalm 76

Israel's God—Judge of All the Earth

To the leader: with stringed instruments.
A Psalm of Ā'saph. A Song.

1 In Judah God is known,
   his name is great in Israel.
2 His abode has been established in Ṣalem,
   his dwelling place in Zion.
3 There he broke the flashing arrows,
   the shield, the sword, and the weapons of
       war.   *Sĕ'lah*

4 Glorious are you, more majestic
   than the everlasting mountains.*e*
5 The stouthearted were stripped of their spoil;
   they sank into sleep;
none of the troops
   was able to lift a hand.
6 At your rebuke, O God of Jacob,
   both rider and horse lay stunned.

7 But you indeed are awesome!
   Who can stand before you
   when once your anger is roused?
8 From the heavens you uttered judgment;
   the earth feared and was still
9 when God rose up to establish judgment,
   to save all the oppressed of the earth.
       Sĕ'lah

10 Human wrath serves only to praise you,
    when you bind the last bit of your*f* wrath
        around you.
11 Make vows to the LORD your God, and perform
        them;
    let all who are around him bring gifts
        to the one who is awesome,
12 who cuts off the spirit of princes,
    who inspires fear in the kings of the earth.

Psalm 77

God's Mighty Deeds Recalled

To the leader: according to Je•dŭ'thun.
Of Ā'saph. A Psalm.

1 I cry aloud to God,
   aloud to God, that he may hear me.
2 In the day of my trouble I seek the Lord;
   in the night my hand is stretched out
       without wearying;
   my soul refuses to be comforted.
3 I think of God, and I moan;
   I meditate, and my spirit faints.   *Sĕ'lah*

---

c Gk Syr: Heb *the*   *d* Gk: Heb *declare*   *e* Gk: Heb *the*
mountains of prey   *f* Heb lacks *your*

4 You keep my eyelids from closing;
  I am so troubled that I cannot speak.
5 I consider the days of old,
  and remember the years of long ago.
6 I commune*g* with my heart in the night;
  I meditate and search my spirit:*h*
7 "Will the Lord spurn forever,
  and never again be favorable?
8 Has his steadfast love ceased forever?
  Are his promises at an end for all
    time?
9 Has God forgotten to be gracious?
  Has he in anger shut up his compassion?"
                                            Sĕ'lah
10 And I say, "It is my grief
   that the right hand of the Most High has
     changed."

11 I will call to mind the deeds of the LORD;
   I will remember your wonders of old.
12 I will meditate on all your work,
   and muse on your mighty deeds.
13 Your way, O God, is holy.
   What god is so great as our God?
14 You are the God who works wonders;
   you have displayed your might among the
     peoples.
15 With your strong arm you redeemed your
     people,
   the descendants of Jacob and Joseph. *Sĕ'lah*

16 When the waters saw you, O God,
   when the waters saw you, they were afraid;
   the very deep trembled.
17 The clouds poured out water;
   the skies thundered;
   your arrows flashed on every side.
18 The crash of your thunder was in the
     whirlwind;
   your lightnings lit up the world;
   the earth trembled and shook.
19 Your way was through the sea,
   your path, through the mighty waters;
   yet your footprints were unseen.
20 You led your people like a flock
   by the hand of Moses and Aaron.

Psalm 78

God's Goodness and Israel's Ingratitude

A Mas'kil of Ă'saph.

1 Give ear, O my people, to my teaching;
  incline your ears to the words of my mouth.
2 I will open my mouth in a parable;
  I will utter dark sayings from of old,
3 things that we have heard and known,
  that our ancestors have told us.
4 We will not hide them from their children;

g Gk Syr: Heb *My music*   *h* Syr Jerome: Heb *my spirit searches*

The Big Picture

Perspective is a valuable thing. It is easy for us to get caught up in the moment, overwhelmed by the urgency of school assignments, sports, and time with family and friends. As difficult as it is, we need to step back for a moment or two and try to grasp the big picture.

When we look back at our life and see where we have come from, the path often makes sense. The twists and turns that were so frustrating and confusing can now be recognized as temporary diversions on our journey. Everything we experienced—the good and the bad—contains lessons for us. The question is, How good a student are we?

The key to wisdom is reflection. Psalm 77 keeps saying this in different ways: "I meditate" (verses 3, 6, 12), "I consider" (verse 5), and "I will call to mind" (verse 11). How do you take the time to remember where you have been and to meditate on where you hope to go? Do you learn from the great teacher, life experience? Do you see the whole forest or only the trees right in front of you?

If you don't already spend some time at the end of each day reflecting on the events of that day, begin doing so. Perhaps keep a journal on how you felt or what you learned. Over time, you will see the big picture emerge and even have a greater sense of God's presence in your life.

▶ Psalm 77

we will tell to the coming generation
 the glorious deeds of the LORD, and his might,
 and the wonders that he has done.

5 He established a decree in Jacob,
 and appointed a law in Israel,
 which he commanded our ancestors
 to teach to their children;
6 that the next generation might know them,
 the children yet unborn,
 and rise up and tell them to their children,
7 so that they should set their hope in God,
 and not forget the works of God,
 but keep his commandments;
8 and that they should not be like their
 ancestors,
 a stubborn and rebellious generation,
 a generation whose heart was not steadfast,
 whose spirit was not faithful to God.

9 The Eʹphra·im·ites, armed with[i] the bow,
 turned back on the day of battle.
10 They did not keep God's covenant,
 but refused to walk according to his law.
11 They forgot what he had done,
 and the miracles that he had shown them.
12 In the sight of their ancestors he worked
 marvels
 in the land of Egypt, in the fields of Zōʹan.
13 He divided the sea and let them pass
 through it,
 and made the waters stand like a heap.
14 In the daytime he led them with a cloud,
 and all night long with a fiery light.
15 He split rocks open in the wilderness,
 and gave them drink abundantly as from
 the deep.
16 He made streams come out of the rock,
 and caused waters to flow down like rivers.

17 Yet they sinned still more against him,
 rebelling against the Most High in the
 desert.
18 They tested God in their heart
 by demanding the food they craved.
19 They spoke against God, saying,
 "Can God spread a table in the wilderness?
20 Even though he struck the rock so that water
 gushed out
 and torrents overflowed,
 can he also give bread,
 or provide meat for his people?"

21 Therefore, when the LORD heard, he was full of
 rage;
 a fire was kindled against Jacob,
 his anger mounted against Israel,

22 because they had no faith in God,
 and did not trust his saving power.
23 Yet he commanded the skies above,
 and opened the doors of heaven;
24 he rained down on them manna to eat,
 and gave them the grain of heaven.
25 Mortals ate of the bread of angels;
 he sent them food in abundance.
26 He caused the east wind to blow in the
 heavens,
 and by his power he led out the south
 wind;
27 he rained flesh upon them like dust,
 winged birds like the sand of the seas;
28 he let them fall within their camp,
 all around their dwellings.
29 And they ate and were well filled,
 for he gave them what they craved.
30 But before they had satisfied their craving,
 while the food was still in their mouths,
31 the anger of God rose against them
 and he killed the strongest of them,
 and laid low the flower of Israel.

32 In spite of all this they still sinned;
 they did not believe in his wonders.
33 So he made their days vanish like a breath,
 and their years in terror.
34 When he killed them, they sought for him;
 they repented and sought God earnestly.
35 They remembered that God was their rock,
 the Most High God their redeemer.
36 But they flattered him with their mouths;
 they lied to him with their tongues.
37 Their heart was not steadfast toward him;
 they were not true to his covenant.
38 Yet he, being compassionate,
 forgave their iniquity,
 and did not destroy them;
 often he restrained his anger,
 and did not stir up all his wrath.
39 He remembered that they were but flesh,
 a wind that passes and does not come
 again.
40 How often they rebelled against him in the
 wilderness
 and grieved him in the desert!
41 They tested God again and again,
 and provoked the Holy One of Israel.
42 They did not keep in mind his power,
 or the day when he redeemed them from
 the foe;
43 when he displayed his signs in Egypt,
 and his miracles in the fields of Zōʹan.
44 He turned their rivers to blood,

---

i Heb *armed with shooting*

so that they could not drink of their
  streams.
45 He sent among them swarms of flies, which
    devoured them,
  and frogs, which destroyed them.
46 He gave their crops to the caterpillar,
  and the fruit of their labor to the locust.
47 He destroyed their vines with hail,
  and their sycamores with frost.
48 He gave over their cattle to the hail,
  and their flocks to thunderbolts.
49 He let loose on them his fierce anger,
  wrath, indignation, and distress,
  a company of destroying angels.
50 He made a path for his anger;
  he did not spare them from death,
  but gave their lives over to the plague.
51 He struck all the firstborn in Egypt,
  the first issue of their strength in the tents
    of Ham.
52 Then he led out his people like sheep,
  and guided them in the wilderness like a
    flock.
53 He led them in safety, so that they were not
    afraid;
  but the sea overwhelmed their enemies.
54 And he brought them to his holy hill,
  to the mountain that his right hand had
    won.
55 He drove out nations before them;
  he apportioned them for a possession
  and settled the tribes of Israel in their tents.

56 Yet they tested the Most High God,
  and rebelled against him.
  They did not observe his decrees,
57 but turned away and were faithless like their
    ancestors;
  they twisted like a treacherous bow.
58 For they provoked him to anger with their high
    places;
  they moved him to jealousy with their
    idols.
59 When God heard, he was full of wrath,
  and he utterly rejected Israel.
60 He abandoned his dwelling at Shi′lōh,
  the tent where he dwelt among mortals,
61 and delivered his power to captivity,
  his glory to the hand of the foe.
62 He gave his people to the sword,
  and vented his wrath on his heritage.
63 Fire devoured their young men,
  and their girls had no marriage song.
64 Their priests fell by the sword,
  and their widows made no lamentation.
65 Then the Lord awoke as from sleep,
  like a warrior shouting because of wine.

66 He put his adversaries to rout;
  he put them to everlasting disgrace.

67 He rejected the tent of Joseph,
  he did not choose the tribe of Ē′phra•im;
68 but he chose the tribe of Judah,
  Mount Zion, which he loves.
69 He built his sanctuary like the high heavens,
  like the earth, which he has founded
    forever.
70 He chose his servant David,
  and took him from the sheepfolds;
71 from tending the nursing ewes he brought him
  to be the shepherd of his people Jacob,
  of Israel, his inheritance.
72 With upright heart he tended them,
  and guided them with skillful hand.

Psalm 79

Plea for Mercy for Jerusalem
A Psalm of Ā′saph.

1 O God, the nations have come into your
      inheritance;
    they have defiled your holy temple;
    they have laid Jerusalem in ruins.
2 They have given the bodies of your servants
      to the birds of the air for food,
    the flesh of your faithful to the wild
      animals of the earth.
3 They have poured out their blood like water
    all around Jerusalem,
    and there was no one to bury them.
4 We have become a taunt to our neighbors,
    mocked and derided by those around us.

5 How long, O LORD? Will you be angry forever?
    Will your jealous wrath burn like fire?
6 Pour out your anger on the nations
      that do not know you,
  and on the kingdoms
      that do not call on your name.
7 For they have devoured Jacob
    and laid waste his habitation.

8 Do not remember against us the iniquities of
      our ancestors;
    let your compassion come speedily to
      meet us,
    for we are brought very low.
9 Help us, O God of our salvation,
    for the glory of your name;
  deliver us, and forgive our sins,
    for your name's sake.
10 Why should the nations say,
    "Where is their God?"

Let the avenging of the outpoured blood of
    your servants
  be known among the nations before our
    eyes.

11 Let the groans of the prisoners come before
    you;
  according to your great power preserve
    those doomed to die.
12 Return sevenfold into the bosom of our
    neighbors
  the taunts with which they taunted you,
    O Lord!
13 Then we your people, the flock of your pasture,
  will give thanks to you forever;
  from generation to generation we will
    recount your praise.

Psalm 80

Prayer for Israel's Restoration

*To the leader: on Lilies, a Covenant.
Of Ā'saph. A Psalm.*

1 Give ear, O Shepherd of Israel,
    you who lead Joseph like a flock!
  You who are enthroned upon the cherubim,
    shine forth
2   before Ē'phra•im and Benjamin and
    Ma•nas'seh.
  Stir up your might,
    and come to save us!

3 Restore us, O God;
    let your face shine, that we may be saved.

4 O LORD God of hosts,
    how long will you be angry with your
    people's prayers?
5 You have fed them with the bread of tears,
    and given them tears to drink in full
    measure.
6 You make us the scorn*j* of our neighbors;
    our enemies laugh among themselves.

7 Restore us, O God of hosts;
    let your face shine, that we may be saved.

8 You brought a vine out of Egypt;
    you drove out the nations and planted it.
9 You cleared the ground for it;
    it took deep root and filled the land.
10 The mountains were covered with its shade,
    the mighty cedars with its branches;
11 it sent out its branches to the sea,
    and its shoots to the River.
12 Why then have you broken down its walls,

so that all who pass along the way pluck its
    fruit?
13 The boar from the forest ravages it,
    and all that move in the field feed on it.

14 Turn again, O God of hosts;
    look down from heaven, and see;
  have regard for this vine,
15   the stock that your right hand planted.*k*
16 They have burned it with fire, they have cut it
    down;*l*
  may they perish at the rebuke of your
    countenance.
17 But let your hand be upon the one at your
    right hand,
  the one whom you made strong for
    yourself.
18 Then we will never turn back from you;
    give us life, and we will call on your
    name.

19 Restore us, O LORD God of hosts;
    let your face shine, that we may be saved.

Psalm 81

God's Appeal to Stubborn Israel

To the leader: according to The Git'tith. Of Ā'saph.

1 Sing aloud to God our strength;
    shout for joy to the God of Jacob.
2 Raise a song, sound the tambourine,
    the sweet lyre with the harp.
3 Blow the trumpet at the new moon,
    at the full moon, on our festal day.
4 For it is a statute for Israel,
    an ordinance of the God of Jacob.
5 He made it a decree in Joseph,
    when he went out over*m* the land of
    Egypt.

I hear a voice I had not known:
6 "I relieved your*n* shoulder of the burden;
    your*n* hands were freed from the basket.
7 In distress you called, and I rescued you;
    I answered you in the secret place of
    thunder;
  I tested you at the waters of Mer'i•bah.
                                    Sē'lah

8 Hear, O my people, while I admonish you;
    O Israel, if you would but listen to me!
9 There shall be no strange god among you;
    you shall not bow down to a foreign god.
10 I am the LORD your God,

---

j Syr: Heb *strife*   *k* Heb adds from verse 17 *and upon the
one whom you made strong for yourself*   *l* Cn: Heb *it is
cut down*   *m* Or *against*   *n* Heb *his*

who brought you up out of the land of
Egypt.
Open your mouth wide and I will fill it.

11 "But my people did not listen to my voice;
Israel would not submit to me.
12 So I gave them over to their stubborn hearts,
to follow their own counsels.
13 O that my people would listen to me,
that Israel would walk in my ways!
14 Then I would quickly subdue their enemies,
and turn my hand against their foes.
15 Those who hate the LORD would cringe before
him,
and their doom would last forever.
16 I would feed you[o] with the finest of the wheat,
and with honey from the rock I would
satisfy you."

Psalm 82

A Plea for Justice

A Psalm of Ā'saph.

1 God has taken his place in the divine council;
in the midst of the gods he holds
judgment:
2 "How long will you judge unjustly
and show partiality to the wicked?   *Sĕ'lah*
3 Give justice to the weak and the orphan;
maintain the right of the lowly and the
destitute.
4 Rescue the weak and the needy;
deliver them from the hand of the wicked."

5 They have neither knowledge nor
understanding,
they walk around in darkness;
all the foundations of the earth are shaken.

6 I say, "You are gods,
children of the Most High, all of you;
7 nevertheless, you shall die like mortals,
and fall like any prince."[p]

8 Rise up, O God, judge the earth;
for all the nations belong to you!

Psalm 83

Prayer for Judgment on Israel's Foes

A Song. A Psalm of Ā'saph.

1 O God, do not keep silence;
do not hold your peace or be still, O God!
2 Even now your enemies are in tumult;
those who hate you have raised their heads.
3 They lay crafty plans against your people;
they consult together against those you
protect.
4 They say, "Come, let us wipe them out as a
nation;
let the name of Israel be remembered no
more."
5 They conspire with one accord;
against you they make a covenant—

---

o Cn Compare verse 16b: Heb *he would feed him*   *p* Or *fall
as one man, O princes*

AIDS—a Matter of Compassion

Jerry died of complications due to the AIDS virus. The paper carried an article
about his life. The writer said: "His worst fears were not realized. His church did
not reject him in the end. It surrounded him with love." What an awesome example of love and justice. Jerry's parish did not condemn him; it showed compassion
for his life.

We are tempted, in our society, to blame the weakest and the poorest for their situation and to excuse ourselves from any need to help. We say that people who are poor are
too lazy to work. That those who are hungry should get a job. That people dying of AIDS
deserve it because of their choices. These attitudes portray a cold justice without mercy.
They are not from the mind of God. For God, mercy and justice go hand in hand. Thank
goodness, the people of Jerry's parish understood that.

Psalm 82 is a plea for God's justice, a cry to "maintain the right of the lowly" (verse 3).
Take these words to heart, pray for those who judge without mercy, and remember the
reporter's words about Jerry: "His church . . . surrounded him with love."

 Psalm 82

6 the tents of Ē′dom and the Ish′ma•el•ites,
    Mō′ab and the Hag′rītes,
7 Gē′bal and Am′mon and Am′a•lek,
    Phi•lis′ti•a with the inhabitants of Tȳre;
8 Assyria also has joined them;
    they are the strong arm of the children of
      Lot.   *Sĕ′lah*

9 Do to them as you did to Mid′i•an,
    as to Sis′e•ra and Jā′bin at the Wadi Kī′shon,
10 who were destroyed at En-dor,
    who became dung for the ground.
11 Make their nobles like Or′eb and Zĕ′eb,
    all their princes like Zĕ′bah and Zal•mun′na,
12 who said, "Let us take the pastures of God
    for our own possession."

13 O my God, make them like whirling dust,*q*
    like chaff before the wind.
14 As fire consumes the forest,
    as the flame sets the mountains ablaze,
15 so pursue them with your tempest
    and terrify them with your hurricane.
16 Fill their faces with shame,
    so that they may seek your name, O LORD.
17 Let them be put to shame and dismayed
    forever;
    let them perish in disgrace.
18 Let them know that you alone,
    whose name is the LORD,
    are the Most High over all the earth.

Psalm 84

The Joy of Worship in the Temple

To the leader: according to The Git′tith.
Of the Kō′ra•hites. A Psalm.

1 How lovely is your dwelling place,
    O LORD of hosts!
2 My soul longs, indeed it faints
    for the courts of the LORD;
    my heart and my flesh sing for joy
    to the living God.

3 Even the sparrow finds a home,
    and the swallow a nest for herself,
    where she may lay her young,
    at your altars, O LORD of hosts,
    my King and my God.
4 Happy are those who live in your house,
    ever singing your praise.   *Sĕ′lah*

5 Happy are those whose strength is in you,
    in whose heart are the highways to Zion.*r*
6 As they go through the valley of Bā′ca
    they make it a place of springs;

the early rain also covers it with pools.
7 They go from strength to strength;
    the God of gods will be seen in Zion.

8 O LORD God of hosts, hear my prayer;
    give ear, O God of Jacob!   *Sĕ′lah*
9 Behold our shield, O God;
    look on the face of your anointed.

10 For a day in your courts is better
    than a thousand elsewhere.
I would rather be a doorkeeper in the house of
    my God
    than live in the tents of wickedness.
11 For the LORD God is a sun and shield;
    he bestows favor and honor.
No good thing does the LORD withhold
    from those who walk uprightly.
12 O LORD of hosts,
    happy is everyone who trusts in you.

Psalm 85

Prayer for the Restoration
of God's Favor

To the leader. Of the Kō′ra•hites. A Psalm.

1 LORD, you were favorable to your land;
    you restored the fortunes of Jacob.
2 You forgave the iniquity of your people;
    you pardoned all their sin.   *Sĕ′lah*
3 You withdrew all your wrath;
    you turned from your hot anger.

4 Restore us again, O God of our salvation,
    and put away your indignation toward us.
5 Will you be angry with us forever?
    Will you prolong your anger to all
    generations?
6 Will you not revive us again,
    so that your people may rejoice in you?
7 Show us your steadfast love, O LORD,
    and grant us your salvation.

8 Let me hear what God the LORD will speak,
    for he will speak peace to his people,
    to his faithful, to those who turn to him in
    their hearts.*s*
9 Surely his salvation is at hand for those who
    fear him,
    that his glory may dwell in our land.

10 Steadfast love and faithfulness will meet;
    righteousness and peace will kiss each
    other.

---

*q Or a tumbleweed   r Heb lacks to Zion   s Gk: Heb but let
them not turn back to folly*

11 Faithfulness will spring up from the ground,
       and righteousness will look down from the
           sky.
12 The LORD will give what is good,
       and our land will yield its increase.
13 Righteousness will go before him,
       and will make a path for his steps.

Psalm 86

Supplication for Help against Enemies

A Prayer of David.

1 Incline your ear, O LORD, and answer me,
       for I am poor and needy.
2 Preserve my life, for I am devoted to you;
       save your servant who trusts in you.
   You are my God; 3 be gracious to me, O Lord,
       for to you do I cry all day long.
4 Gladden the soul of your servant,
       for to you, O Lord, I lift up my soul.
5 For you, O Lord, are good and forgiving,
       abounding in steadfast love to all who call
           on you.
6 Give ear, O LORD, to my prayer;
       listen to my cry of supplication.
7 In the day of my trouble I call on you,
       for you will answer me.

8 There is none like you among the gods,
       O Lord,
   nor are there any works like yours.
9 All the nations you have made shall come
   and bow down before you, O Lord,
   and shall glorify your name.
10 For you are great and do wondrous things;
       you alone are God.
11 Teach me your way, O LORD,
       that I may walk in your truth;
       give me an undivided heart to revere your
           name.
12 I give thanks to you, O Lord my God, with my
           whole heart,
       and I will glorify your name forever.
13 For great is your steadfast love toward me;
       you have delivered my soul from the depths
           of Shĕ'ōl.

14 O God, the insolent rise up against me;
       a band of ruffians seeks my life,
       and they do not set you before them.
15 But you, O Lord, are a God merciful and
           gracious,
       slow to anger and abounding in steadfast
           love and faithfulness.
16 Turn to me and be gracious to me;
       give your strength to your servant;

save the child of your serving girl.
17 Show me a sign of your favor,
       so that those who hate me may see it and
           be put to shame,
       because you, LORD, have helped me and
           comforted me.

Psalm 87

The Joy of Living in Zion

Of the Kŏ'ra•hītes. A Psalm. A Song.

1 On the holy mount stands the city he founded;
2   the LORD loves the gates of Zion
       more than all the dwellings of Jacob.
3 Glorious things are spoken of you,
       O city of God.   *Sĕ'lah*

4 Among those who know me I mention Rā'hab
           and Babylon;
       Phi•lis'ti•a too, and Tȳre, with Ethiopiaᵗ—
       "This one was born there," they say.

5 And of Zion it shall be said,
       "This one and that one were born in it";
       for the Most High himself will establish it.
6 The LORD records, as he registers the peoples,
       "This one was born there."   *Sĕ'lah*

7 Singers and dancers alike say,
       "All my springs are in you."

Psalm 88

Prayer for Help in Despondency

A Song. A Psalm of the Kŏ'ra•hītes. To the leader:
according to Mā'ha•lath Le•an'noth. A Mas'kil
of Hĕ'man the Ez'ra•hite.

1 O LORD, God of my salvation,
       when, at night, I cry out in your presence,
2 let my prayer come before you;
       incline your ear to my cry.

3 For my soul is full of troubles,
       and my life draws near to Shĕ'ōl.
4 I am counted among those who go down to
           the Pit;
       I am like those who have no help,
5 like those forsaken among the dead,
       like the slain that lie in the grave,
   like those whom you remember no more,
       for they are cut off from your hand.
6 You have put me in the depths of the Pit,
       in the regions dark and deep.
7 Your wrath lies heavy upon me,

ᵗ Or *Nubia;* Heb *Cush*

and you overwhelm me with all your
  waves.   *Se̅'lah*

8 You have caused my companions to shun me;
    you have made me a thing of horror to
      them.
  I am shut in so that I cannot escape;
9   my eye grows dim through sorrow.
  Every day I call on you, O LORD;
    I spread out my hands to you.
10 Do you work wonders for the dead?
    Do the shades rise up to praise you? *Se̅'lah*
11 Is your steadfast love declared in the grave,
    or your faithfulness in A•bad'don?
12 Are your wonders known in the darkness,
    or your saving help in the land of
      forgetfulness?

13 But I, O LORD, cry out to you;
    in the morning my prayer comes before
      you.
14 O LORD, why do you cast me off?
    Why do you hide your face from me?
15 Wretched and close to death from my
      youth up,
    I suffer your terrors; I am desperate.*u*
16 Your wrath has swept over me;
    your dread assaults destroy me.
17 They surround me like a flood all day long;
    from all sides they close in on me.
18 You have caused friend and neighbor to
      shun me;
    my companions are in darkness.

Psalm 89

God's Covenant with David

A Mas'kil of E̅'than the Ez'ra•hite.

1 I will sing of your steadfast love, O LORD,*v*
      forever;
    with my mouth I will proclaim your
      faithfulness to all generations.
2 I declare that your steadfast love is established
      forever;
    your faithfulness is as firm as the heavens.

3 You said, "I have made a covenant with my
      chosen one,
    I have sworn to my servant David:
4 'I will establish your descendants forever,
    and build your throne for all generations.' "
                                    Se̅'lah

5 Let the heavens praise your wonders, O LORD,
    your faithfulness in the assembly of the
      holy ones.

6 For who in the skies can be compared to the
      LORD?
    Who among the heavenly beings is like the
      LORD,
7 a God feared in the council of the holy ones,
    great and awesome *w* above all that are
      around him?
8 O LORD God of hosts,
    who is as mighty as you, O LORD?
    Your faithfulness surrounds you.
9 You rule the raging of the sea;
    when its waves rise, you still them.
10 You crushed Ra̅'hab like a carcass;
    you scattered your enemies with your
      mighty arm.
11 The heavens are yours, the earth also is yours;
    the world and all that is in it—you have
      founded them.
12 The north and the south*x*—you created them;
    Ta̅'bor and Hermon joyously praise your
      name.
13 You have a mighty arm;
    strong is your hand, high your right hand.
14 Righteousness and justice are the foundation of
      your throne;
    steadfast love and faithfulness go before
      you.
15 Happy are the people who know the festal
      shout,
    who walk, O LORD, in the light of your
      countenance;
16 they exult in your name all day long,
    and extol*y* your righteousness.
17 For you are the glory of their strength;
    by your favor our horn is exalted.
18 For our shield belongs to the LORD,
    our king to the Holy One of Israel.

19 Then you spoke in a vision to your faithful
      one, and said:
    "I have set the crown*z* on one who is
      mighty,
    I have exalted one chosen from the people.
20 I have found my servant David;
    with my holy oil I have anointed him;
21 my hand shall always remain with him;
    my arm also shall strengthen him.
22 The enemy shall not outwit him,
    the wicked shall not humble him.
23 I will crush his foes before him
    and strike down those who hate him.
24 My faithfulness and steadfast love shall be with
      him;

---

u Meaning of Heb uncertain *v* Gk: Heb *the steadfast love of
the LORD* *w* Gk Syr: Heb *greatly awesome* *x* Or *Zaphon and
Yamin* *y* Cn: Heb *are exalted in* *z* Cn: Heb *help*

He shall cry to me,

"**You are
my Father,
my God,
and the Rock
of my salvation!**"

89.26

and in my name his horn shall be exalted.
25 I will set his hand on the sea
    and his right hand on the rivers.
26 He shall cry to me, 'You are my Father,
    my God, and the Rock of my salvation!'
27 I will make him the firstborn,
    the highest of the kings of the earth.
28 Forever I will keep my steadfast love for him,
    and my covenant with him will stand firm.
29 I will establish his line forever,
    and his throne as long as the heavens
    endure.
30 If his children forsake my law
    and do not walk according to my
    ordinances,
31 if they violate my statutes
    and do not keep my commandments,
32 then I will punish their transgression with the
    rod
    and their iniquity with scourges;
33 but I will not remove from him my steadfast
    love,
    or be false to my faithfulness.
34 I will not violate my covenant,
    or alter the word that went forth from my
    lips.
35 Once and for all I have sworn by my holiness;
    I will not lie to David.
36 His line shall continue forever,
    and his throne endure before me like the
    sun.
37 It shall be established forever like the moon,
    an enduring witness in the skies."   *Se'lah*

38 But now you have spurned and rejected him;
    you are full of wrath against your anointed.
39 You have renounced the covenant with your
    servant;
    you have defiled his crown in the dust.
40 You have broken through all his walls;
    you have laid his strongholds in ruins.
41 All who pass by plunder him;
    he has become the scorn of his
    neighbors.
42 You have exalted the right hand of his foes;
    you have made all his enemies rejoice.
43 Moreover, you have turned back the edge of his
    sword,
    and you have not supported him in battle.
44 You have removed the scepter from his
    hand,*a*
    and hurled his throne to the ground.
45 You have cut short the days of his youth;
    you have covered him with shame.   *Se'lah*

46 How long, O LORD? Will you hide yourself
    forever?
    How long will your wrath burn like fire?
47 Remember how short my time is— *b*
    for what vanity you have created all
    mortals!
48 Who can live and never see death?
    Who can escape the power of She'ōl? *Se'lah*

---

a Cn: Heb *removed his cleanness*   *b* Meaning of Heb
uncertain

49 Lord, where is your steadfast love of old,
   which by your faithfulness you swore to
      David?
50 Remember, O Lord, how your servant is
      taunted;
   how I bear in my bosom the insults of the
      peoples,c
51 with which your enemies taunt, O LORD,
   with which they taunted the footsteps of
      your anointed.

52 Blessed be the LORD forever.
      Amen and Amen.

BOOK IV
(Psalms 90–106)
Psalm 90

God's Eternity and Human Frailty

A Prayer of Moses, the man of God.

1 Lord, you have been our dwelling placed
   in all generations.
2 Before the mountains were brought forth,
   or ever you had formed the earth and the
      world,
   from everlasting to everlasting you are God.

3 You turn use back to dust,
   and say, "Turn back, you mortals."
4 For a thousand years in your sight
   are like yesterday when it is past,
   or like a watch in the night.

5 You sweep them away; they are like a dream,
   like grass that is renewed in the morning;
6 in the morning it flourishes and is renewed;
   in the evening it fades and withers.

7 For we are consumed by your anger;
   by your wrath we are overwhelmed.
8 You have set our iniquities before you,
   our secret sins in the light of your
      countenance.

9 For all our days pass away under your wrath;
   our years come to an endf like a sigh.
10 The days of our life are seventy years,
   or perhaps eighty, if we are strong;
   even then their spang is only toil and trouble;
   they are soon gone, and we fly away.

11 Who considers the power of your anger?
   Your wrath is as great as the fear that is due
      you.
12 So teach us to count our days
   that we may gain a wise heart.

13 Turn, O LORD! How long?
   Have compassion on your servants!
14 Satisfy us in the morning with your steadfast
      love,
   so that we may rejoice and be glad all our
      days.
15 Make us glad as many days as you have
      afflicted us,
   and as many years as we have seen evil.
16 Let your work be manifest to your servants,
   and your glorious power to their children.
17 Let the favor of the Lord our God be upon us,
   and prosper for us the work of our hands—
   O prosper the work of our hands!

Psalm 91

Assurance of God's Protection

1 You who live in the shelter of the Most High,
   who abide in the shadow of the Almighty,h
2 will say to the LORD, "My refuge and my
      fortress;
   my God, in whom I trust."
3 For he will deliver you from the snare of the
      fowler
   and from the deadly pestilence;
4 he will cover you with his pinions,
   and under his wings you will find refuge;
   his faithfulness is a shield and buckler.
5 You will not fear the terror of the night,
   or the arrow that flies by day,
6 or the pestilence that stalks in darkness,
   or the destruction that wastes at noonday.

7 A thousand may fall at your side,
   ten thousand at your right hand,
   but it will not come near you.
8 You will only look with your eyes
   and see the punishment of the wicked.

9 Because you have made the LORD your refuge,i
   the Most High your dwelling place,
10 no evil shall befall you,
   no scourge come near your tent.

11 For he will command his angels concerning
      you
   to guard you in all your ways.
12 On their hands they will bear you up,
   so that you will not dash your foot against
      a stone.

---

c Cn: Heb *bosom all of many peoples*   d Another reading is
our refuge   e Heb *humankind*   f Syr: Heb *we bring our years
to an end*   g Cn Compare Gk Syr Jerome Tg: Heb *pride*
h Traditional rendering of Heb *Shaddai*   i Cn: Heb *Because
you, LORD, are my refuge; you have made*

13 You will tread on the lion and the adder,
    the young lion and the serpent you will
        trample under foot.

14 Those who love me, I will deliver;
    I will protect those who know my name.
15 When they call to me, I will answer them;
    I will be with them in trouble,
    I will rescue them and honor them.
16 With long life I will satisfy them,
    and show them my salvation.

PRAY IT!
Have You Sung This Before?

Psalm 91 might sound familiar! It expresses confidence that God will protect us, no matter what.

**And He will raise you up on eagle's wings,
bear you on the breath of dawn,
make you to shine like the sun,
and hold you in the palm of His hand.
(Michael Joncas, "On Eagle's Wings")**

**Blest be the Lord; blest be the Lord,
the God of mercy, the God who saves.
I shall not fear the dark of night,
nor the arrow that flies by day.
(Dan Schutte, "Blest Be the Lord")**

▶ **Psalm 91**

Psalm 92
Thanksgiving for Vindication
A Psalm. A Song for the Sabbath Day.

1 It is good to give thanks to the LORD,
    to sing praises to your name,
        O Most High;
2 to declare your steadfast love in the morning,
    and your faithfulness by night,
3 to the music of the lute and the harp,
    to the melody of the lyre.
4 For you, O LORD, have made me glad by your
        work;
    at the works of your hands I sing for joy.

5 How great are your works, O LORD!
    Your thoughts are very deep!
6 The dullard cannot know,
    the stupid cannot understand this:
7 though the wicked sprout like grass
    and all evildoers flourish,
    they are doomed to destruction forever,
8   but you, O LORD, are on high forever.
9 For your enemies, O LORD,
    for your enemies shall perish;
    all evildoers shall be scattered.

10 But you have exalted my horn like that of the
        wild ox;
    you have poured over me[j] fresh oil.
11 My eyes have seen the downfall of my
        enemies;
    my ears have heard the doom of my evil
        assailants.

12 The righteous flourish like the palm tree,
    and grow like a cedar in Lebanon.
13 They are planted in the house of the LORD;
    they flourish in the courts of our God.
14 In old age they still produce fruit;
    they are always green and full of sap,
15 showing that the LORD is upright;
    he is my rock, and there is no
        unrighteousness in him.

Psalm 93
The Majesty of God's Rule

1 The LORD is king, he is robed in majesty;
    the LORD is robed, he is girded with
        strength.
    He has established the world; it shall never be
        moved;
2   your throne is established from of old;
    you are from everlasting.

3 The floods have lifted up, O LORD,
    the floods have lifted up their voice;
    the floods lift up their roaring.
4 More majestic than the thunders of mighty
        waters,
    more majestic than the waves[k] of
        the sea,
    majestic on high is the LORD!

5 Your decrees are very sure;
    holiness befits your house,
    O LORD, forevermore.

---

j Syr: Meaning of Heb uncertain   *k* Cn: Heb *majestic are the waves*

Psalm 94

God the Avenger of the Righteous

1 O LORD, you God of vengeance,
   you God of vengeance, shine forth!
2 Rise up, O judge of the earth;
   give to the proud what they deserve!
3 O LORD, how long shall the wicked,
   how long shall the wicked exult?

4 They pour out their arrogant words;
   all the evildoers boast.
5 They crush your people, O LORD,
   and afflict your heritage.
6 They kill the widow and the stranger,
   they murder the orphan,
7 and they say, "The LORD does not see;
   the God of Jacob does not perceive."

8 Understand, O dullest of the people;
   fools, when will you be wise?
9 He who planted the ear, does he not hear?
   He who formed the eye, does he not see?
10 He who disciplines the nations,
   he who teaches knowledge to humankind,
   does he not chastise?
11 The LORD knows our thoughts,[1]
   that they are but an empty breath.

12 Happy are those whom you discipline,
   O LORD,
   and whom you teach out of your law,
13 giving them respite from days of trouble,
   until a pit is dug for the wicked.
14 For the LORD will not forsake his people;
   he will not abandon his heritage;
15 for justice will return to the righteous,
   and all the upright in heart will follow it.

16 Who rises up for me against the wicked?
   Who stands up for me against evildoers?
17 If the LORD had not been my help,
   my soul would soon have lived in the land
   of silence.
18 When I thought, "My foot is slipping,"
   your steadfast love, O LORD, held me up.
19 When the cares of my heart are many,
   your consolations cheer my soul.
20 Can wicked rulers be allied with you,
   those who contrive mischief by statute?
21 They band together against the life of the
   righteous,
   and condemn the innocent to death.
22 But the LORD has become my stronghold,
   and my God the rock of my refuge.
23 He will repay them for their iniquity
   and wipe them out for their wickedness;
   the LORD our God will wipe them out.

O sing to the LORD a new song; sing to the LORD, all the earth. Sing to the LORD, bless his name; tell of his salvation from day to day.

Sing to the LORD

96.1–2

Psalm 95

A Call to Worship and Obedience

1 O come, let us sing to the LORD;
   let us make a joyful noise to the rock of our
   salvation!
2 Let us come into his presence with
   thanksgiving;
   let us make a joyful noise to him with
   songs of praise!
3 For the LORD is a great God,
   and a great King above all gods.
4 In his hand are the depths of the earth;
   the heights of the mountains are his also.
5 The sea is his, for he made it,
   and the dry land, which his hands have
   formed.

6 O come, let us worship and bow down,
   let us kneel before the LORD, our Maker!
7 For he is our God,
   and we are the people of his pasture,
   and the sheep of his hand.

O that today you would listen to his voice!
8   Do not harden your hearts, as at Mer'i·bah,
   as on the day at Mas'sah in the wilderness,
9 when your ancestors tested me,
   and put me to the proof, though they had
   seen my work.
10 For forty years I loathed that generation
   and said, "They are a people whose hearts
   go astray,
   and they do not regard my ways."
11 Therefore in my anger I swore,
   "They shall not enter my rest."

---

[1] Heb *the thoughts of humankind*

Psalm 96

Praise to God Who Comes in Judgment
(1 Chr 16.23–33)

1 O sing to the LORD a new song;
   sing to the LORD, all the earth.
2 Sing to the LORD, bless his name;
   tell of his salvation from day to day.
3 Declare his glory among the nations,
   his marvelous works among all the peoples.
4 For great is the LORD, and greatly to be praised;
   he is to be revered above all gods.
5 For all the gods of the peoples are idols,
   but the LORD made the heavens.
6 Honor and majesty are before him;
   strength and beauty are in his sanctuary.

7 Ascribe to the LORD, O families of the peoples,
   ascribe to the LORD glory and strength.
8 Ascribe to the LORD the glory due his name;
   bring an offering, and come into his courts.
9 Worship the LORD in holy splendor;
   tremble before him, all the earth.

10 Say among the nations, "The LORD is king!
    The world is firmly established; it shall
       never be moved.

He will judge the peoples with equity."
11 Let the heavens be glad, and let the earth
       rejoice;
   let the sea roar, and all that fills it;
12   let the field exult, and everything in it.
Then shall all the trees of the forest sing for joy
13   before the LORD; for he is coming,
   for he is coming to judge the earth.
He will judge the world with righteousness,
   and the peoples with his truth.

Psalm 97

The Glory of God's Reign

1 The LORD is king! Let the earth rejoice;
   let the many coastlands be glad!
2 Clouds and thick darkness are all around him;
   righteousness and justice are the foundation
       of his throne.
3 Fire goes before him,
   and consumes his adversaries on every
       side.
4 His lightnings light up the world;
   the earth sees and trembles.
5 The mountains melt like wax before the LORD,
   before the Lord of all the earth.

LEBANESE CATHOLICS

Catholics are a celebratory people. By holding feasts, we celebrate our great God and the wondrous ways in which God has shown love for us. We also hold feasts in remembrance of the saints who have gone before us. The saints are shining examples of individuals leading lives in unity with the will of God.

In some parts of the Middle East, like Lebanon, Catholic feast days are extravagant events. Each town has a patron saint, and on the eve of his or her feast day, nearly everyone in the community comes to the church. All night long the townspeople pray, eat, and dance in the church, and some even sleep there. Feast days in Lebanon are celebrations that include great processions, festive liturgies, and the participation of the whole community.

In other parts of the world where there are congregations of Middle Eastern Catholics, similar events take place. Some occur on a large scale with overnight festivities, and some occur on a smaller scale, but all have common characteristics: great processions, festive liturgies, good food, and the participation of the whole parish community.

Consider trying to get your youth group or campus ministry team to begin a similar tradition on the feast day of your parish or school.

▶ Psalm 96

6 The heavens proclaim his righteousness;
   and all the peoples behold his glory.
7 All worshipers of images are put to shame,
   those who make their boast in worthless idols;
   all gods bow down before him.
8 Zion hears and is glad,
   and the towns[m] of Judah rejoice,
   because of your judgments, O God.
9 For you, O LORD, are most high over all the earth;
   you are exalted far above all gods.

10 The LORD loves those who hate[n] evil;
   he guards the lives of his faithful;
   he rescues them from the hand of the wicked.
11 Light dawns[o] for the righteous,
   and joy for the upright in heart.
12 Rejoice in the LORD, O you righteous,
   and give thanks to his holy name!

Psalm 98

Praise the Judge of the World

A Psalm.

1 O sing to the LORD a new song,
   for he has done marvelous things.
   His right hand and his holy arm
   have gotten him victory.
2 The LORD has made known his victory;
   he has revealed his vindication in the sight of the nations.
3 He has remembered his steadfast love and faithfulness
   to the house of Israel.
   All the ends of the earth have seen
   the victory of our God.

4 Make a joyful noise to the LORD, all the earth;
   break forth into joyous song and sing praises.
5 Sing praises to the LORD with the lyre,
   with the lyre and the sound of melody.
6 With trumpets and the sound of the horn
   make a joyful noise before the King, the LORD.

7 Let the sea roar, and all that fills it;
   the world and those who live in it.
8 Let the floods clap their hands;
   let the hills sing together for joy
9 at the presence of the LORD, for he is coming to judge the earth.
   He will judge the world with righteousness,
   and the peoples with equity.

Psalm 99

Praise to God for His Holiness

1 The LORD is king; let the peoples tremble!
   He sits enthroned upon the cherubim; let the earth quake!
2 The LORD is great in Zion;
   he is exalted over all the peoples.
3 Let them praise your great and awesome name.
   Holy is he!
4 Mighty King,[p] lover of justice,
   you have established equity;
   you have executed justice
   and righteousness in Jacob.
5 Extol the LORD our God;
   worship at his footstool.
   Holy is he!

6 Moses and Aaron were among his priests,
   Samuel also was among those who called on his name.
   They cried to the LORD, and he answered them.
7 He spoke to them in the pillar of cloud;
   they kept his decrees,
   and the statutes that he gave them.

8 O LORD our God, you answered them;
   you were a forgiving God to them,
   but an avenger of their wrongdoings.
9 Extol the LORD our God,
   and worship at his holy mountain;
   for the LORD our God is holy.

Psalm 100

All Lands Summoned to Praise God

A Psalm of thanksgiving.

1 Make a joyful noise to the LORD, all the earth.
2   Worship the LORD with gladness;
   come into his presence with singing.

3 Know that the LORD is God.
   It is he that made us, and we are his;[q]
   we are his people, and the sheep of his pasture.

4 Enter his gates with thanksgiving,
   and his courts with praise.
   Give thanks to him, bless his name.

5 For the LORD is good;
   his steadfast love endures forever,
   and his faithfulness to all generations.

---

m Heb *daughters* n Cn: Heb *You who love the LORD hate*
o Gk Syr Jerome: Heb *is sown* p Cn: Heb *And a king's strength* q Another reading is *and not we ourselves*

Psalm 101

A Sovereign's Pledge of Integrity and Justice

Of David. A Psalm.

1 I will sing of loyalty and of justice;
  to you, O LORD, I will sing.

2 I will study the way that is blameless.
  When shall I attain it?

  I will walk with integrity of heart
    within my house;
3 I will not set before my eyes
    anything that is base.

  I hate the work of those who fall away;
    it shall not cling to me.
4 Perverseness of heart shall be far from me;
    I will know nothing of evil.

5 One who secretly slanders a neighbor
    I will destroy.
  A haughty look and an arrogant heart
    I will not tolerate.

6 I will look with favor on the faithful in the
    land,
    so that they may live with me;
  whoever walks in the way that is blameless
    shall minister to me.

7 No one who practices deceit
    shall remain in my house;
  no one who utters lies
    shall continue in my presence.

8 Morning by morning I will destroy
    all the wicked in the land,
  cutting off all evildoers
    from the city of the LORD.

Psalm 102

Prayer to the Eternal King for Help

*A prayer of one afflicted, when faint and pleading
before the LORD.*

1 Hear my prayer, O LORD;
    let my cry come to you.
2 Do not hide your face from me
    in the day of my distress.
  Incline your ear to me;
    answer me speedily in the day when I call.

3 For my days pass away like smoke,
    and my bones burn like a furnace.
4 My heart is stricken and withered like grass;
    I am too wasted to eat my bread.

5 Because of my loud groaning
    my bones cling to my skin.
6 I am like an owl of the wilderness,
    like a little owl of the waste places.
7 I lie awake;
    I am like a lonely bird on the housetop.
8 All day long my enemies taunt me;
    those who deride me use my name for a
      curse.
9 For I eat ashes like bread,
    and mingle tears with my drink,
10 because of your indignation and anger;
    for you have lifted me up and thrown me
      aside.
11 My days are like an evening shadow;
    I wither away like grass.

12 But you, O LORD, are enthroned forever;
    your name endures to all generations.
13 You will rise up and have compassion on Zion,
    for it is time to favor it;
    the appointed time has come.
14 For your servants hold its stones dear,
    and have pity on its dust.
15 The nations will fear the name of the LORD,
    and all the kings of the earth your glory.
16 For the LORD will build up Zion;
    he will appear in his glory.
17 He will regard the prayer of the destitute,
    and will not despise their prayer.

18 Let this be recorded for a generation to come,
    so that a people yet unborn may praise the
      LORD:
19 that he looked down from his holy height,
    from heaven the LORD looked at the earth,
20 to hear the groans of the prisoners,
    to set free those who were doomed
      to die;
21 so that the name of the LORD may be declared
      in Zion,
    and his praise in Jerusalem,
22 when peoples gather together,
    and kingdoms, to worship the LORD.

23 He has broken my strength in midcourse;
    he has shortened my days.
24 "O my God," I say, "do not take me away
    at the midpoint of my life,
  you whose years endure
    throughout all generations."

25 Long ago you laid the foundation of the earth,
    and the heavens are the work of your
      hands.
26 They will perish, but you endure;
    they will all wear out like a garment.

You change them like clothing, and they pass
　away;
27　but you are the same, and your years have
　　no end.
28　The children of your servants shall live secure;
　　their offspring shall be established in your
　　presence.

Psalm 103

Thanksgiving for God's Goodness

Of David.

1　Bless the LORD, O my soul,
　　and all that is within me,
　　bless his holy name.
2　Bless the LORD, O my soul,
　　and do not forget all his benefits—
3　who forgives all your iniquity,
　　who heals all your diseases,
4　who redeems your life from the Pit,
　　who crowns you with steadfast love and
　　　mercy,
5　who satisfies you with good as long as you live[r]
　　so that your youth is renewed like the
　　　eagle's.

6　The LORD works vindication
　　and justice for all who are oppressed.
7　He made known his ways to Moses,
　　his acts to the people of Israel.
8　The LORD is merciful and gracious,
　　slow to anger and abounding in steadfast
　　　love.

9　He will not always accuse,
　　nor will he keep his anger forever.
10　He does not deal with us according to our sins,
　　nor repay us according to our iniquities.
11　For as the heavens are high above the earth,
　　so great is his steadfast love toward those
　　　who fear him;
12　as far as the east is from the west,
　　so far he removes our transgressions
　　　from us.
13　As a father has compassion for his children,
　　so the LORD has compassion for those who
　　　fear him.
14　For he knows how we were made;
　　he remembers that we are dust.

15　As for mortals, their days are like grass;
　　they flourish like a flower of the field;
16　for the wind passes over it, and it is gone,
　　and its place knows it no more.
17　But the steadfast love of the LORD is from
　　　everlasting to everlasting
　　on those who fear him,
　　and his righteousness to children's children,
18　to those who keep his covenant
　　and remember to do his commandments.

19　The LORD has established his throne in the
　　　heavens,
　　and his kingdom rules over all.
20　Bless the LORD, O you his angels,
　　you mighty ones who do his bidding,

---

r Meaning of Heb uncertain

Letting Go of Anger

Psalm 103 is a beautiful prayer praising God's love and compassion. Verse 9 reminds us that God will not stay angry forever. What better lesson could we learn from our God? Anger is a natural human emotion—but in imitation of God, we should not hold on to it. When we let go of our anger, we build better relationships, because hidden anger puts other people on the defensive and destroys trust.

How do you let go of anger? Here are some suggestions:

■ Express your feelings in a letter or a journal.
■ Tell the person you are angry with how you feel and that you would like to reconcile.
■ Go for a fast walk or run, or use another form of exercise to "vent" your anger.
■ Relax with some quiet, reflective music.
■ Try to identify why you feel angry—often, anger is a symptom of another feeling such as hurt, disappointment, or even tiredness.
■ Express your anger in prayer to God, and ask for help in forgiveness.

God's way and God's goodness can be yours if you desire them. Make an effort; God does!

▶ Psalm 103

obedient to his spoken word.
21 Bless the LORD, all his hosts,
    his ministers that do his will.
22 Bless the LORD, all his works,
    in all places of his dominion.
Bless the LORD, O my soul.

Psalm 104

God the Creator and Provider

(Cp Gen 1.1–31)

1 Bless the LORD, O my soul.
    O LORD my God, you are very great.
You are clothed with honor and majesty,
2   wrapped in light as with a garment.
You stretch out the heavens like a tent,
3   you set the beams of your[s] chambers on the
        waters,
    you make the clouds your[s] chariot,
    you ride on the wings of the wind,
4 you make the winds your[s] messengers,
    fire and flame your[s] ministers.

5 You set the earth on its foundations,
    so that it shall never be shaken.
6 You cover it with the deep as with a garment;
    the waters stood above the mountains.
7 At your rebuke they flee;
    at the sound of your thunder they take to
        flight.
8 They rose up to the mountains, ran down to
        the valleys
    to the place that you appointed for them.
9 You set a boundary that they may not pass,
    so that they might not again cover the
        earth.

10 You make springs gush forth in the valleys;
    they flow between the hills,
11 giving drink to every wild animal;
    the wild asses quench their thirst.
12 By the streams[t] the birds of the air have their
        habitation;
    they sing among the branches.
13 From your lofty abode you water the
        mountains;
    the earth is satisfied with the fruit of your
        work.

14 You cause the grass to grow for the cattle,
    and plants for people to use,[u]
to bring forth food from the earth,
15   and wine to gladden the human heart,
    oil to make the face shine,
        and bread to strengthen the human heart.
16 The trees of the LORD are watered abundantly,

the cedars of Lebanon that he planted.
17 In them the birds build their nests;
    the stork has its home in the fir trees.
18 The high mountains are for the wild goats;
    the rocks are a refuge for the coneys.
19 You have made the moon to mark the
        seasons;
    the sun knows its time for setting.
20 You make darkness, and it is night,
    when all the animals of the forest come
        creeping out.
21 The young lions roar for their prey,
    seeking their food from God.
22 When the sun rises, they withdraw
    and lie down in their dens.
23 People go out to their work
    and to their labor until the evening.

24 O LORD, how manifold are your works!
    In wisdom you have made them all;
    the earth is full of your creatures.
25 Yonder is the sea, great and wide,
    creeping things innumerable are there,
    living things both small and great.
26 There go the ships,
    and Le•vi′a•than that you formed to sport
        in it.

27 These all look to you
    to give them their food in due season;
28 when you give to them, they gather it up;
    when you open your hand, they are filled
        with good things.
29 When you hide your face, they are dismayed;
    when you take away their breath, they die
    and return to their dust.
30 When you send forth your spirit,[v] they are
        created;
    and you renew the face of the ground.

31 May the glory of the LORD endure forever;
    may the LORD rejoice in his works—
32 who looks on the earth and it trembles,
    who touches the mountains and they
        smoke.
33 I will sing to the LORD as long as I live;
    I will sing praise to my God while I have
        being.
34 May my meditation be pleasing to him,
    for I rejoice in the LORD.
35 Let sinners be consumed from the earth,
    and let the wicked be no more.
Bless the LORD, O my soul.
Praise the LORD!

---

[s] Heb *his*   [t] Heb *By them*   [u] Or *to cultivate*
[v] Or *your breath*

Psalm 105

God's Faithfulness to Israel

(Ex 7.8—11.10; 1 Chr 16.8–22)

1 O give thanks to the LORD, call on his name,
   make known his deeds among the peoples.
2 Sing to him, sing praises to him;
   tell of all his wonderful works.
3 Glory in his holy name;
   let the hearts of those who seek the LORD
      rejoice.
4 Seek the LORD and his strength;
   seek his presence continually.
5 Remember the wonderful works he has done,
   his miracles, and the judgments he has
      uttered,
6 O offspring of his servant Abraham,*w*
   children of Jacob, his chosen ones.

7 He is the LORD our God;
   his judgments are in all the earth.
8 He is mindful of his covenant forever,
   of the word that he commanded, for a
      thousand generations,
9 the covenant that he made with Abraham,
   his sworn promise to Isaac,
10 which he confirmed to Jacob as a statute,
   to Israel as an everlasting covenant,
11 saying, "To you I will give the land of Ca'naan
   as your portion for an inheritance."

12 When they were few in number,
   of little account, and strangers in it,
13 wandering from nation to nation,
   from one kingdom to another people,
14 he allowed no one to oppress them;
   he rebuked kings on their account,
15 saying, "Do not touch my anointed ones;
   do my prophets no harm."

16 When he summoned famine against the land,
   and broke every staff of bread,
17 he had sent a man ahead of them,
   Joseph, who was sold as a slave.
18 His feet were hurt with fetters,
   his neck was put in a collar of iron;
19 until what he had said came to pass,
   the word of the LORD kept testing him.
20 The king sent and released him;
   the ruler of the peoples set him free.
21 He made him lord of his house,
   and ruler of all his possessions,
22 to instruct*x* his officials at his pleasure,
   and to teach his elders wisdom.

23 Then Israel came to Egypt;
   Jacob lived as an alien in the land of Ham.

24 And the LORD made his people very fruitful,
   and made them stronger than their foes,
25 whose hearts he then turned to hate his
      people,
   to deal craftily with his servants.

26 He sent his servant Moses,
   and Aaron whom he had chosen.
27 They performed his signs among them,
   and miracles in the land of Ham.
28 He sent darkness, and made the land dark;
   they rebelled*y* against his words.
29 He turned their waters into blood,
   and caused their fish to die.
30 Their land swarmed with frogs,
   even in the chambers of their kings.
31 He spoke, and there came swarms of flies,
   and gnats throughout their country.
32 He gave them hail for rain,
   and lightning that flashed through their
      land.
33 He struck their vines and fig trees,
   and shattered the trees of their country.
34 He spoke, and the locusts came,
   and young locusts without number;
35 they devoured all the vegetation in their land,
   and ate up the fruit of their ground.
36 He struck down all the firstborn in their land,
   the first issue of all their strength.

37 Then he brought Israel*z* out with silver and
      gold,
   and there was no one among their tribes
      who stumbled.
38 Egypt was glad when they departed,
   for dread of them had fallen upon it.
39 He spread a cloud for a covering,
   and fire to give light by night.
40 They asked, and he brought quails,
   and gave them food from heaven in
      abundance.
41 He opened the rock, and water gushed out;
   it flowed through the desert like a river.
42 For he remembered his holy promise,
   and Abraham, his servant.

43 So he brought his people out with joy,
   his chosen ones with singing.
44 He gave them the lands of the nations,
   and they took possession of the wealth of
      the peoples,
45 that they might keep his statutes
   and observe his laws.
   Praise the LORD!

---

w Another reading is *Israel* (compare 1 Chr 16.13)   *x* Gk
Syr Jerome: Heb *to bind*   *y* Cn Compare Gk Syr: Heb *they
did not rebel*   *z* Heb *them*

Psalm 106

A Confession of Israel's Sins

1 Praise the LORD!
   O give thanks to the LORD, for he is good;
   for his steadfast love endures forever.
2 Who can utter the mighty doings of the LORD,
   or declare all his praise?
3 Happy are those who observe justice,
   who do righteousness at all times.

4 Remember me, O LORD, when you show favor
            to your people;
   help me when you deliver them;
5 that I may see the prosperity of your chosen
            ones,
      that I may rejoice in the gladness of your
            nation,
      that I may glory in your heritage.

6 Both we and our ancestors have sinned;
   we have committed iniquity, have done
            wickedly.
7 Our ancestors, when they were in Egypt,
   did not consider your wonderful works;
   they did not remember the abundance of your
            steadfast love,
   but rebelled against the Most High*a* at the
            Red Sea.*b*
8 Yet he saved them for his name's sake,
   so that he might make known his mighty
            power.
9 He rebuked the Red Sea,*b* and it became dry;
   he led them through the deep as through a
            desert.
10 So he saved them from the hand of the foe,
   and delivered them from the hand of the
            enemy.
11 The waters covered their adversaries;
   not one of them was left.
12 Then they believed his words;
   they sang his praise.

13 But they soon forgot his works;
   they did not wait for his counsel.
14 But they had a wanton craving in the
            wilderness,
   and put God to the test in the desert;
15 he gave them what they asked,
   but sent a wasting disease among them.

16 They were jealous of Moses in the camp,
   and of Aaron, the holy one of the LORD.
17 The earth opened and swallowed up Dā′than,
   and covered the faction of A·bī′ram.
18 Fire also broke out in their company;
   the flame burned up the wicked.

19 They made a calf at Hō′reb
   and worshiped a cast image.
20 They exchanged the glory of God*c*
   for the image of an ox that eats grass.
21 They forgot God, their Savior,
   who had done great things in Egypt,
22 wondrous works in the land of Ham,
   and awesome deeds by the Red Sea.*b*
23 Therefore he said he would destroy them—
   had not Moses, his chosen one,
   stood in the breach before him,
      to turn away his wrath from destroying
            them.

24 Then they despised the pleasant land,
   having no faith in his promise.
25 They grumbled in their tents,
   and did not obey the voice of the LORD.
26 Therefore he raised his hand and swore to
            them
      that he would make them fall in the
            wilderness,
27 and would disperse *d* their descendants among
            the nations,
   scattering them over the lands.

28 Then they attached themselves to the Bā′al of
            Pĕ′or,
   and ate sacrifices offered to the dead;
29 they provoked the LORD to anger with their
            deeds,
   and a plague broke out among them.
30 Then Phin′e·has stood up and interceded,
   and the plague was stopped.
31 And that has been reckoned to him as
            righteousness
      from generation to generation forever.

32 They angered the LORD*e* at the waters of
            Mer′i·bah,
   and it went ill with Moses on their account;
33 for they made his spirit bitter,
   and he spoke words that were rash.

34 They did not destroy the peoples,
   as the LORD commanded them,
35 but they mingled with the nations
   and learned to do as they did.
36 They served their idols,
   which became a snare to them.
37 They sacrificed their sons
   and their daughters to the demons;
38 they poured out innocent blood,

---

a Cn Compare 78.17, 56: Heb *rebelled at the sea*   *b* Or *Sea
of Reeds*   *c* Compare Gk Mss: Heb *exchanged their glory*
d Syr Compare Ezek 20.23: Heb *cause to fall*   *e* Heb *him*

the blood of their sons and daughters,
whom they sacrificed to the idols of Cā'naan;
and the land was polluted with blood.
39 Thus they became unclean by their acts,
and prostituted themselves in their
doings.

40 Then the anger of the LORD was kindled against
his people,
and he abhorred his heritage;
41 he gave them into the hand of the nations,
so that those who hated them ruled over
them.
42 Their enemies oppressed them,
and they were brought into subjection
under their power.
43 Many times he delivered them,
but they were rebellious in their
purposes,
and were brought low through their
iniquity.
44 Nevertheless he regarded their distress
when he heard their cry.
45 For their sake he remembered his covenant,
and showed compassion according to the
abundance of his steadfast love.
46 He caused them to be pitied
by all who held them captive.

47 Save us, O LORD our God,
and gather us from among the nations,
that we may give thanks to your holy name
and glory in your praise.

48 Blessed be the LORD, the God of Israel,
from everlasting to everlasting.
And let all the people say, "Amen."
Praise the LORD!

BOOK V
(Psalms 107–150)
Psalm 107

Thanksgiving for Deliverance
from Many Troubles

1 O give thanks to the LORD, for he is good;
for his steadfast love endures forever.
2 Let the redeemed of the LORD say so,
those he redeemed from trouble,
3 and gathered in from the lands,
from the east and from the west,
from the north and from the south.ƒ

4 Some wandered in desert wastes,
finding no way to an inhabited town;
5 hungry and thirsty,

their soul fainted within them.
6 Then they cried to the LORD in their trouble,
and he delivered them from their distress;
7 he led them by a straight way,
until they reached an inhabited town.
8 Let them thank the LORD for his steadfast love,
for his wonderful works to humankind.
9 For he satisfies the thirsty,
and the hungry he fills with good things.

10 Some sat in darkness and in gloom,
prisoners in misery and in irons,
11 for they had rebelled against the words of God,
and spurned the counsel of the Most High.
12 Their hearts were bowed down with hard
labor;
they fell down, with no one to help.
13 Then they cried to the LORD in their trouble,
and he saved them from their distress;
14 he brought them out of darkness and gloom,
and broke their bonds asunder.
15 Let them thank the LORD for his steadfast love,
for his wonderful works to humankind.
16 For he shatters the doors of bronze,
and cuts in two the bars of iron.

17 Some were sickᵍ through their sinful ways,
and because of their iniquities endured
affliction;
18 they loathed any kind of food,
and they drew near to the gates of death.
19 Then they cried to the LORD in their trouble,
and he saved them from their distress;
20 he sent out his word and healed them,
and delivered them from destruction.
21 Let them thank the LORD for his steadfast love,
for his wonderful works to humankind.
22 And let them offer thanksgiving sacrifices,
and tell of his deeds with songs of joy.

23 Some went down to the sea in ships,
doing business on the mighty waters;
24 they saw the deeds of the LORD,
his wondrous works in the deep.
25 For he commanded and raised the stormy
wind,
which lifted up the waves of the sea.
26 They mounted up to heaven, they went down
to the depths;
their courage melted away in their calamity;
27 they reeled and staggered like drunkards,
and were at their wits' end.
28 Then they cried to the LORD in their trouble,
and he brought them out from their
distress;

ƒ Cn: Heb *sea*　ᵍ Cn: Heb *fools*

THANKFULNESS

It's good and natural for people to express thankfulness for their blessings. Psalm 107 is an extended thanksgiving for God's love and saving power. Indonesians have a custom for offering thanks on certain special occasions, such as after a new house is built, during the seventh month of pregnancy, and thirty-five days after the birth of a child.

During a thanksgiving for a new house, the family gathers in the house and offers prayers for the people who will live, eat, work, and die there. Similar prayers are said for a mother during pregnancy and for a child after birth—in thanksgiving for their health, well-being, and happiness. After the prayers, those who are gathered share a simple traditional meal of rice, vegetables, fish or chicken, and fruit.

▶ Psalm 107

29 he made the storm be still,
    and the waves of the sea were hushed.
30 Then they were glad because they had quiet,
    and he brought them to their desired
        haven.
31 Let them thank the LORD for his steadfast love,
    for his wonderful works to humankind.
32 Let them extol him in the congregation of the
        people,
    and praise him in the assembly of the
        elders.

33 He turns rivers into a desert,
    springs of water into thirsty ground,
34 a fruitful land into a salty waste,
    because of the wickedness of its inhabitants.
35 He turns a desert into pools of water,
    a parched land into springs of water.
36 And there he lets the hungry live,
    and they establish a town to live in;
37 they sow fields, and plant vineyards,
    and get a fruitful yield.
38 By his blessing they multiply greatly,
    and he does not let their cattle decrease.

39 When they are diminished and brought low
    through oppression, trouble, and sorrow,
40 he pours contempt on princes
    and makes them wander in trackless wastes;
41 but he raises up the needy out of distress,
    and makes their families like flocks.
42 The upright see it and are glad;
    and all wickedness stops its mouth.

43 Let those who are wise give heed to these
        things,
    and consider the steadfast love of the LORD.

Psalm 108

Praise and Prayer for Victory

(Ps 57.7–11; 60.5–12)

A Song. A Psalm of David.

1 My heart is steadfast, O God, my heart is
        steadfast;*h*
    I will sing and make melody.
    Awake, my soul!*i*
2 Awake, O harp and lyre!
    I will awake the dawn.
3 I will give thanks to you, O LORD, among the
        peoples,
    and I will sing praises to you among the
        nations.
4 For your steadfast love is higher than the
        heavens,
    and your faithfulness reaches to the clouds.

5 Be exalted, O God, above the heavens,
    and let your glory be over all the earth.
6 Give victory with your right hand, and
        answer me,
    so that those whom you love may be
        rescued.

---

h Heb Mss Gk Syr: MT lacks *my heart is steadfast*   *i* Compare
57.8: Heb *also my soul*

P
S
A
L
M
S

7 God has promised in his sanctuary:[j]
"With exultation I will divide up Shē'chem,
and portion out the Vale of Suc'coth.
8 Gil'e•ad is mine; Ma•nas'seh is mine;
Ē'phra•im is my helmet;
Judah is my scepter.
9 Mō'ab is my washbasin;
on Ē'dom I hurl my shoe;
over Phi•lis'ti•a I shout in triumph."

10 Who will bring me to the fortified city?
Who will lead me to Ē'dom?
11 Have you not rejected us, O God?
You do not go out, O God, with our
armies.
12 O grant us help against the foe,
for human help is worthless.
13 With God we shall do valiantly;
it is he who will tread down our foes.

Psalm 109

Prayer for Vindication and Vengeance

To the leader. Of David. A Psalm.

1 Do not be silent, O God of my praise.
2 For wicked and deceitful mouths are opened
against me,
speaking against me with lying tongues.
3 They beset me with words of hate,
and attack me without cause.
4 In return for my love they accuse me,
even while I make prayer for them.[k]
5 So they reward me evil for good,
and hatred for my love.

6 They say,[l] "Appoint a wicked man against
him;
let an accuser stand on his right.
7 When he is tried, let him be found guilty;
let his prayer be counted as sin.
8 May his days be few;
may another seize his position.
9 May his children be orphans,
and his wife a widow.
10 May his children wander about and beg;
may they be driven out of[m] the ruins they
inhabit.
11 May the creditor seize all that he has;
may strangers plunder the fruits of his toil.
12 May there be no one to do him a kindness,
nor anyone to pity his orphaned children.
13 May his posterity be cut off;
may his name be blotted out in the second
generation.
14 May the iniquity of his father[n] be remembered
before the LORD,

and do not let the sin of his mother be
blotted out.
15 Let them be before the LORD continually,
and may his[o] memory be cut off from the
earth.
16 For he did not remember to show kindness,
but pursued the poor and needy
and the brokenhearted to their death.
17 He loved to curse; let curses come on him.
He did not like blessing; may it be far from
him.
18 He clothed himself with cursing as his coat,
may it soak into his body like water,
like oil into his bones.
19 May it be like a garment that he wraps around
himself,
like a belt that he wears every day."

20 May that be the reward of my accusers from
the LORD,
of those who speak evil against my life.
21 But you, O LORD my Lord,
act on my behalf for your name's sake;
because your steadfast love is good,
deliver me.
22 For I am poor and needy,
and my heart is pierced within me.
23 I am gone like a shadow at evening;
I am shaken off like a locust.
24 My knees are weak through fasting;
my body has become gaunt.
25 I am an object of scorn to my accusers;
when they see me, they shake their heads.

26 Help me, O LORD my God!
Save me according to your steadfast
love.
27 Let them know that this is your hand;
you, O LORD, have done it.
28 Let them curse, but you will bless.
Let my assailants be put to shame;[p] may
your servant be glad.
29 May my accusers be clothed with dishonor;
may they be wrapped in their own shame
as in a mantle.
30 With my mouth I will give great thanks to the
LORD;
I will praise him in the midst of the
throng.
31 For he stands at the right hand of the needy,
to save them from those who would
condemn them to death.

---

j Or *by his holiness*   k Syr: Heb *I prayer*   l Heb lacks
They say   m Gk: Heb *and seek*   n Cn: Heb *fathers*
o Gk: Heb *their*   p Gk: Heb *They have risen up and have been
put to shame*

Psalm 110

Assurance of Victory for God's Priest-King

(Mt 22.44; Acts 2.34–35)

Of David. A Psalm.

1 The LORD says to my lord,
  "Sit at my right hand
until I make your enemies your footstool."

2 The LORD sends out from Zion
    your mighty scepter.
    Rule in the midst of your foes.
3 Your people will offer themselves willingly
    on the day you lead your forces
    on the holy mountains.*q*
From the womb of the morning,
    like dew, your youth*r* will come to you.
4 The LORD has sworn and will not change his
    mind,
  "You are a priest forever according to the
    order of Mel•chiz′e•dek."*s*

5 The Lord is at your right hand;
    he will shatter kings on the day of his
    wrath.
6 He will execute judgment among the nations,
    filling them with corpses;
he will shatter heads
    over the wide earth.
7 He will drink from the stream by the path;
    therefore he will lift up his head.

Psalm 111

Praise for God's Wonderful Works

1 Praise the LORD!
I will give thanks to the LORD with my whole
    heart,
  in the company of the upright, in the
    congregation.
2 Great are the works of the LORD,
    studied by all who delight in them.
3 Full of honor and majesty is his work,
    and his righteousness endures forever.
4 He has gained renown by his wonderful deeds;
    the LORD is gracious and merciful.
5 He provides food for those who fear him;
    he is ever mindful of his covenant.
6 He has shown his people the power of his
    works,
  in giving them the heritage of the nations.
7 The works of his hands are faithful and just;
    all his precepts are trustworthy.
8 They are established forever and ever,
    to be performed with faithfulness and
    uprightness.

9 He sent redemption to his people;
    he has commanded his covenant forever.
    Holy and awesome is his name.
10 The fear of the LORD is the beginning of
    wisdom;
  all those who practice it*t* have a good
    understanding.
    His praise endures forever.

Psalm 112

Blessings of the Righteous

1 Praise the LORD!
    Happy are those who fear the LORD,
    who greatly delight in his commandments.
2 Their descendants will be mighty in the land;
    the generation of the upright will be
    blessed.
3 Wealth and riches are in their houses,
    and their righteousness endures forever.
4 They rise in the darkness as a light for the
    upright;
    they are gracious, merciful, and righteous.
5 It is well with those who deal generously and
    lend,
    who conduct their affairs with justice.
6 For the righteous will never be moved;
    they will be remembered forever.
7 They are not afraid of evil tidings;
    their hearts are firm, secure in the LORD.
8 Their hearts are steady, they will not be afraid;
    in the end they will look in triumph on
    their foes.
9 They have distributed freely, they have given to
    the poor;
    their righteousness endures forever;
    their horn is exalted in honor.
10 The wicked see it and are angry;
    they gnash their teeth and melt away;
    the desire of the wicked comes to nothing.

Psalm 113

God the Helper of the Needy

1 Praise the LORD!
Praise, O servants of the LORD;
    praise the name of the LORD.

2 Blessed be the name of the LORD
    from this time on and forevermore.
3 From the rising of the sun to its setting
    the name of the LORD is to be praised.

---

q Another reading is *in holy splendor* *r* Cn: Heb *the dew of
your youth* *s* Or *forever, a rightful king by my edict* *t* Gk Syr:
Heb *them*

THE LORD IS HIGH ABOVE ALL NATIONS,

He raises the poor from the dust,
and lifts the needy from the ash heap,
to make them sit with princes,
with the princes of his people.

AND HIS GLORY ABOVE THE HEAVENS.

4 The LORD is high above all nations,
and his glory above the heavens.

5 Who is like the LORD our God,
who is seated on high,
6 who looks far down
on the heavens and the earth?
7 He raises the poor from the dust,
and lifts the needy from the ash heap,
8 to make them sit with princes,
with the princes of his people.
9 He gives the barren woman a home,
making her the joyous mother of
children.
Praise the LORD!

Psalm 114

God's Wonders at the Exodus
(Cp Ex 14.1–31)

1 When Israel went out from Egypt,
the house of Jacob from a people of strange
language,
2 Judah became God's^u sanctuary,
Israel his dominion.

3 The sea looked and fled;
Jordan turned back.
4 The mountains skipped like rams,
the hills like lambs.

5 Why is it, O sea, that you flee?
O Jordan, that you turn back?
6 O mountains, that you skip like rams?
O hills, like lambs?

7 Tremble, O earth, at the presence of the LORD,
at the presence of the God of Jacob,
8 who turns the rock into a pool of water,
the flint into a spring of water.

Psalm 115

The Impotence of Idols and
the Greatness of God

1 Not to us, O LORD, not to us, but to your name
give glory,
for the sake of your steadfast love and your
faithfulness.
2 Why should the nations say,
"Where is their God?"

3 Our God is in the heavens;
he does whatever he pleases.
4 Their idols are silver and gold,
the work of human hands.
5 They have mouths, but do not speak;
eyes, but do not see.
6 They have ears, but do not hear;

---

u Heb his

noses, but do not smell.
7 They have hands, but do not feel;
  feet, but do not walk;
  they make no sound in their throats.
8 Those who make them are like them;
  so are all who trust in them.

9 O Israel, trust in the LORD!
  He is their help and their shield.
10 O house of Aaron, trust in the LORD!
  He is their help and their shield.
11 You who fear the LORD, trust in the LORD!
  He is their help and their shield.

12 The LORD has been mindful of us; he will bless us;
  he will bless the house of Israel;
  he will bless the house of Aaron;
13 he will bless those who fear the LORD,
  both small and great.

14 May the LORD give you increase,
  both you and your children.
15 May you be blessed by the LORD,
  who made heaven and earth.

16 The heavens are the LORD's heavens,
  but the earth he has given to human beings.
17 The dead do not praise the LORD,
  nor do any that go down into silence.
18 But we will bless the LORD
  from this time on and forevermore.
  Praise the LORD!

Psalm 116
Thanksgiving for Recovery from Illness

1 I love the LORD, because he has heard
  my voice and my supplications.
2 Because he inclined his ear to me,
  therefore I will call on him as long as I live.
3 The snares of death encompassed me;

the pangs of Shĕ'ōl laid hold on me;
  I suffered distress and anguish.
4 Then I called on the name of the LORD:
  "O LORD, I pray, save my life!"

5 Gracious is the LORD, and righteous;
  our God is merciful.
6 The LORD protects the simple;
  when I was brought low, he saved me.
7 Return, O my soul, to your rest,
  for the LORD has dealt bountifully with you.

8 For you have delivered my soul from death,
  my eyes from tears,
  my feet from stumbling.
9 I walk before the LORD
  in the land of the living.
10 I kept my faith, even when I said,
  "I am greatly afflicted";
11 I said in my consternation,
  "Everyone is a liar."

12 What shall I return to the LORD
  for all his bounty to me?
13 I will lift up the cup of salvation
  and call on the name of the LORD,
14 I will pay my vows to the LORD
  in the presence of all his people.
15 Precious in the sight of the LORD
  is the death of his faithful ones.
16 O LORD, I am your servant;
  I am your servant, the child of your serving
    girl.
  You have loosed my bonds.
17 I will offer to you a thanksgiving sacrifice
  and call on the name of the LORD.
18 I will pay my vows to the LORD
  in the presence of all his people,
19 in the courts of the house of the LORD,
  in your midst, O Jerusalem.
  Praise the LORD!

P
S
A
L
M
S

What Lasts?

LIVE IT!

Will a car last forever? a house? the sun? Does anything other than God truly have
no end? No matter how much you look, you won't find such a thing. So, why do
we spend much of our time with what won't last, rather than what *will* last?
       Psalm 115 proclaims the greatness of God and the foolishness of idols. In the
end, the things that matter most won't be how many awards you were given, how much
money you made, or how many possessions you had, but rather how much you loved others,
how much you served, and how much you loved God!

▶ Psalm 115

P
S
A
L
M
S

Gratitude

LIVE IT!

Roy. Thank God, I'm feeling better.
Maria. Exactly!
Roy. Exactly what?
Maria. That's exactly what Psalm 116 is all about. Feeling better and thanking God for it.
Roy. Really? I thought the Psalms were about praising God and winning victories.
Maria. Some are. In a way, that's what Psalm 116 is about too. You can use it to praise God for your victory over illness.
Roy. I never really thought of it that way.
Maria. You prayed to get well, didn't you?
Roy. Yes, a lot.
Maria. Well, there you are. God heard your prayers. Now, how about some genuine gratitude?
Roy. You're right. Thank you, God! I'm feeling so much better!
Maria. Amen!

▶ Psalm 116

Psalm 117

Universal Call to Worship

1 Praise the LORD, all you nations!
     Extol him, all you peoples!
2 For great is his steadfast love toward us,
     and the faithfulness of the LORD endures
          forever.
   Praise the LORD!

Psalm 118

A Song of Victory

1 O give thanks to the LORD, for he is good;
     his steadfast love endures forever!

2 Let Israel say,
     "His steadfast love endures forever."
3 Let the house of Aaron say,
     "His steadfast love endures forever."
4 Let those who fear the LORD say,
     "His steadfast love endures forever."

5 Out of my distress I called on the
          LORD;
     the LORD answered me and set me in a
          broad place.
6 With the LORD on my side I do not fear.
     What can mortals do to me?
7 The LORD is on my side to help me;
     I shall look in triumph on those who
          hate me.
8 It is better to take refuge in the LORD
     than to put confidence in mortals.

9 It is better to take refuge in the LORD
     than to put confidence in princes.

10 All nations surrounded me;
     in the name of the LORD I cut them off!
11 They surrounded me, surrounded me on every
          side;
     in the name of the LORD I cut them off!
12 They surrounded me like bees;
     they blazed[v] like a fire of thorns;
     in the name of the LORD I cut them off!
13 I was pushed hard,[w] so that I was falling,
     but the LORD helped me.
14 The LORD is my strength and my might;
     he has become my salvation.

15 There are glad songs of victory in the tents of
          the righteous:
   "The right hand of the LORD does valiantly;
16   the right hand of the LORD is exalted;
       the right hand of the LORD does
            valiantly."
17 I shall not die, but I shall live,
     and recount the deeds of the LORD.
18 The LORD has punished me severely,
     but he did not give me over to death.

19 Open to me the gates of righteousness,
     that I may enter through them
     and give thanks to the LORD.

---

v Gk: Heb *were extinguished*   w Gk Syr Jerome: Heb *You pushed me hard*

20 This is the gate of the LORD;
    the righteous shall enter through it.

21 I thank you that you have answered me
    and have become my salvation.
22 The stone that the builders rejected
    has become the chief cornerstone.
23 This is the LORD's doing;
    it is marvelous in our eyes.
24 This is the day that the LORD has made;
    let us rejoice and be glad in it.ˣ
25 Save us, we beseech you, O LORD!
    O LORD, we beseech you, give us success!

26 Blessed is the one who comes in the name of
    the LORD.ʸ
    We bless you from the house of the LORD.
27 The LORD is God,
    and he has given us light.
    Bind the festal procession with branches,
    up to the horns of the altar.ᶻ

28 You are my God, and I will give thanks to you;
    you are my God, I will extol you.

29 O give thanks to the LORD, for he is good,
    for his steadfast love endures forever.

Psalm 119

The Glories of God's Law

1 Happy are those whose way is blameless,
    who walk in the law of the LORD.
2 Happy are those who keep his decrees,
    who seek him with their whole heart,
3 who also do no wrong,
    but walk in his ways.
4 You have commanded your precepts
    to be kept diligently.
5 O that my ways may be steadfast
    in keeping your statutes!
6 Then I shall not be put to shame,
    having my eyes fixed on all your
      commandments.
7 I will praise you with an upright heart,
    when I learn your righteous ordinances.
8 I will observe your statutes;
    do not utterly forsake me.

9 How can young people keep their way pure?
    By guarding it according to your word.
10 With my whole heart I seek you;
    do not let me stray from your
      commandments.
11 I treasure your word in my heart,
    so that I may not sin against you.

12 Blessed are you, O LORD;
    teach me your statutes.
13 With my lips I declare
    all the ordinances of your mouth.
14 I delight in the way of your decrees
    as much as in all riches.
15 I will meditate on your precepts,
    and fix my eyes on your ways.
16 I will delight in your statutes;
    I will not forget your word.

17 Deal bountifully with your servant,
    so that I may live and observe your word.
18 Open my eyes, so that I may behold
    wondrous things out of your law.
19 I live as an alien in the land;
    do not hide your commandments from me.
20 My soul is consumed with longing
    for your ordinances at all times.
21 You rebuke the insolent, accursed ones,

ˣ Or *in him* ʸ Or *Blessed in the name of the LORD is the one who comes* ᶻ Meaning of Heb uncertain

PRAY IT

The Longest Psalm

Psalm 119 is the longest psalm. Also, it has an interesting structure that you cannot appreciate in the English translation: it consists of twenty-two sections, and all the lines of a particular section begin with the same letter of the Hebrew alphabet. All the lines of the first section begin with *Aleph,* the Hebrew equivalent of the letter A. All the lines of the second section begin with *Beth,* the Hebrew equivalent of the letter B. And so on through the whole Hebrew alphabet!

This structure is called an acrostic. An acrostic is a poem in which the beginning letters of each line form a word or a phrase or a logical sequence. You may have written a poem like this in grade school using the word *mother* or *father.*

Write your own acrostic prayer, beginning the lines of the prayer with the letters of your name or of the name of someone or something you would like to pray for.

▶ **Psalm 119**

who wander from your commandments;
22 take away from me their scorn and contempt,
for I have kept your decrees.
23 Even though princes sit plotting against me,
your servant will meditate on your statutes.
24 Your decrees are my delight,
they are my counselors.

25 My soul clings to the dust;
revive me according to your word.
26 When I told of my ways, you answered me;
teach me your statutes.
27 Make me understand the way of your precepts,
and I will meditate on your wondrous
works.
28 My soul melts away for sorrow;
strengthen me according to your word.
29 Put false ways far from me;
and graciously teach me your law.
30 I have chosen the way of faithfulness;
I set your ordinances before me.
31 I cling to your decrees, O LORD;
let me not be put to shame.
32 I run the way of your commandments,
for you enlarge my understanding.

33 Teach me, O LORD, the way of your statutes,
and I will observe it to the end.
34 Give me understanding, that I may keep your
law
and observe it with my whole heart.
35 Lead me in the path of your commandments,
for I delight in it.
36 Turn my heart to your decrees,
and not to selfish gain.
37 Turn my eyes from looking at vanities;
give me life in your ways.
38 Confirm to your servant your promise,
which is for those who fear you.
39 Turn away the disgrace that I dread,
for your ordinances are good.
40 See, I have longed for your precepts;
in your righteousness give me life.

41 Let your steadfast love come to me, O LORD,
your salvation according to your promise.
42 Then I shall have an answer for those who
taunt me,
for I trust in your word.
43 Do not take the word of truth utterly out of my
mouth,
for my hope is in your ordinances.
44 I will keep your law continually,
forever and ever.
45 I shall walk at liberty,
for I have sought your precepts.
46 I will also speak of your decrees before kings,

and shall not be put to shame;
47 I find my delight in your commandments,
because I love them.
48 I revere your commandments, which I love,
and I will meditate on your statutes.

49 Remember your word to your servant,
in which you have made me hope.
50 This is my comfort in my distress,
that your promise gives me life.
51 The arrogant utterly deride me,
but I do not turn away from your law.
52 When I think of your ordinances from of old,
I take comfort, O LORD.
53 Hot indignation seizes me because of the
wicked,
those who forsake your law.
54 Your statutes have been my songs
wherever I make my home.
55 I remember your name in the night, O LORD,
and keep your law.
56 This blessing has fallen to me,
for I have kept your precepts.

57 The LORD is my portion;
I promise to keep your words.
58 I implore your favor with all my heart;
be gracious to me according to your
promise.
59 When I think of your ways,
I turn my feet to your decrees;
60 I hurry and do not delay
to keep your commandments.
61 Though the cords of the wicked ensnare me,
I do not forget your law.
62 At midnight I rise to praise you,
because of your righteous ordinances.
63 I am a companion of all who fear you,
of those who keep your precepts.
64 The earth, O LORD, is full of your steadfast
love;
teach me your statutes.

65 You have dealt well with your servant,
O LORD, according to your word.
66 Teach me good judgment and knowledge,
for I believe in your commandments.
67 Before I was humbled I went astray,
but now I keep your word.
68 You are good and do good;
teach me your statutes.
69 The arrogant smear me with lies,
but with my whole heart I keep your
precepts.
70 Their hearts are fat and gross,
but I delight in your law.
71 It is good for me that I was humbled,

so that I might learn your statutes.

72 The law of your mouth is better to me
than thousands of gold and silver pieces.

73 Your hands have made and fashioned me;
give me understanding that I may learn
your commandments.

74 Those who fear you shall see me and rejoice,
because I have hoped in your word.

75 I know, O LORD, that your judgments are right,
and that in faithfulness you have
humbled me.

76 Let your steadfast love become my comfort
according to your promise to your servant.

77 Let your mercy come to me, that I may live;
for your law is my delight.

78 Let the arrogant be put to shame,
because they have subverted me with guile;
as for me, I will meditate on your precepts.

79 Let those who fear you turn to me,
so that they may know your decrees.

80 May my heart be blameless in your statutes,
so that I may not be put to shame.

81 My soul languishes for your salvation;
I hope in your word.

82 My eyes fail with watching for your promise;
I ask, "When will you comfort me?"

83 For I have become like a wineskin in the
smoke,
yet I have not forgotten your statutes.

84 How long must your servant endure?
When will you judge those who
persecute me?

85 The arrogant have dug pitfalls for me;
they flout your law.

86 All your commandments are enduring;
I am persecuted without cause; help me!

87 They have almost made an end of me on earth;
but I have not forsaken your precepts.

88 In your steadfast love spare my life,
so that I may keep the decrees of your
mouth.

89 The LORD exists forever;
your word is firmly fixed in heaven.

90 Your faithfulness endures to all generations;
you have established the earth, and it
stands fast.

91 By your appointment they stand today,
for all things are your servants.

92 If your law had not been my delight,
I would have perished in my misery.

93 I will never forget your precepts,
for by them you have given me life.

94 I am yours; save me,
for I have sought your precepts.

95 The wicked lie in wait to destroy me,
but I consider your decrees.

96 I have seen a limit to all perfection,
but your commandment is exceedingly
broad.

97 Oh, how I love your law!
It is my meditation all day long.

98 Your commandment makes me wiser than my
enemies,
for it is always with me.

99 I have more understanding than all my
teachers,
for your decrees are my meditation.

100 I understand more than the aged,
for I keep your precepts.

101 I hold back my feet from every evil way,
in order to keep your word.

102 I do not turn away from your ordinances,
for you have taught me.

103 How sweet are your words to my taste,
sweeter than honey to my mouth!

104 Through your precepts I get understanding;
therefore I hate every false way.

105 Your word is a lamp to my feet
and a light to my path.

106 I have sworn an oath and confirmed it,
to observe your righteous ordinances.

107 I am severely afflicted;
give me life, O LORD, according to your
word.

108 Accept my offerings of praise, O LORD,
and teach me your ordinances.

109 I hold my life in my hand continually,
but I do not forget your law.

110 The wicked have laid a snare for me,
but I do not stray from your precepts.

111 Your decrees are my heritage forever;
they are the joy of my heart.

112 I incline my heart to perform your statutes
forever, to the end.

113 I hate the double-minded,
but I love your law.

114 You are my hiding place and my shield;
I hope in your word.

115 Go away from me, you evildoers,
that I may keep the commandments of my
God.

116 Uphold me according to your promise, that I
may live,
and let me not be put to shame in my
hope.

117 Hold me up, that I may be safe
and have regard for your statutes
continually.

PSALMS

118 You spurn all who go astray from your statutes;
    for their cunning is in vain.
119 All the wicked of the earth you count as dross;
    therefore I love your decrees.
120 My flesh trembles for fear of you,
    and I am afraid of your judgments.

121 I have done what is just and right;
    do not leave me to my oppressors.
122 Guarantee your servant's well-being;
    do not let the godless oppress me.
123 My eyes fail from watching for your salvation,
    and for the fulfillment of your righteous
        promise.
124 Deal with your servant according to your
        steadfast love,
    and teach me your statutes.
125 I am your servant; give me understanding,
    so that I may know your decrees.
126 It is time for the LORD to act,
    for your law has been broken.
127 Truly I love your commandments
    more than gold, more than fine gold.
128 Truly I direct my steps by all your precepts;*a*
    I hate every false way.

129 Your decrees are wonderful;
    therefore my soul keeps them.
130 The unfolding of your words gives light;
    it imparts understanding to the simple.
131 With open mouth I pant,
    because I long for your commandments.
132 Turn to me and be gracious to me,
    as is your custom toward those who love
        your name.
133 Keep my steps steady according to your promise,
    and never let iniquity have dominion over me.
134 Redeem me from human oppression,
    that I may keep your precepts.
135 Make your face shine upon your servant,
    and teach me your statutes.
136 My eyes shed streams of tears
    because your law is not kept.

137 You are righteous, O LORD,
    and your judgments are right.
138 You have appointed your decrees in
        righteousness
    and in all faithfulness.
139 My zeal consumes me
    because my foes forget your words.
140 Your promise is well tried,
    and your servant loves it.
141 I am small and despised,
    yet I do not forget your precepts.
142 Your righteousness is an everlasting
        righteousness,

and your law is the truth.
143 Trouble and anguish have come upon me,
    but your commandments are my delight.
144 Your decrees are righteous forever;
    give me understanding that I may live.

145 With my whole heart I cry; answer me, O LORD.
    I will keep your statutes.
146 I cry to you; save me,
    that I may observe your decrees.
147 I rise before dawn and cry for help;
    I put my hope in your words.
148 My eyes are awake before each watch of the
        night,
    that I may meditate on your promise.
149 In your steadfast love hear my voice;
    O LORD, in your justice preserve my life.
150 Those who persecute me with evil purpose
        draw near;
    they are far from your law.
151 Yet you are near, O LORD,
    and all your commandments are true.
152 Long ago I learned from your decrees
    that you have established them forever.

153 Look on my misery and rescue me,
    for I do not forget your law.
154 Plead my cause and redeem me;
    give me life according to your promise.
155 Salvation is far from the wicked,
    for they do not seek your statutes.
156 Great is your mercy, O LORD;
    give me life according to your justice.
157 Many are my persecutors and my adversaries,
    yet I do not swerve from your decrees.
158 I look at the faithless with disgust,
    because they do not keep your commands.
159 Consider how I love your precepts;
    preserve my life according to your steadfast
        love.
160 The sum of your word is truth;
    and every one of your righteous ordinances
        endures forever.

161 Princes persecute me without cause,
    but my heart stands in awe of your words.
162 I rejoice at your word
    like one who finds great spoil.
163 I hate and abhor falsehood,
    but I love your law.
164 Seven times a day I praise you
    for your righteous ordinances.
165 Great peace have those who love your law;
    nothing can make them stumble.
166 I hope for your salvation, O LORD,

---

a Gk Jerome: Meaning of Heb uncertain

and I fulfill your commandments.
167 My soul keeps your decrees;
    I love them exceedingly.
168 I keep your precepts and decrees,
    for all my ways are before you.

169 Let my cry come before you, O LORD;
    give me understanding according to your word.
170 Let my supplication come before you;
    deliver me according to your promise.
171 My lips will pour forth praise,
    because you teach me your statutes.
172 My tongue will sing of your promise,
    for all your commandments are right.
173 Let your hand be ready to help me,
    for I have chosen your precepts.
174 I long for your salvation, O LORD,
    and your law is my delight.
175 Let me live that I may praise you,
    and let your ordinances help me.
176 I have gone astray like a lost sheep; seek out
        your servant,
    for I do not forget your commandments.

Psalm 120

Prayer for Deliverance from Slanderers

A Song of Ascents.

1 In my distress I cry to the LORD,
    that he may answer me:
2 "Deliver me, O LORD,
    from lying lips,
    from a deceitful tongue."

3 What shall be given to you?
    And what more shall be done to you,
    you deceitful tongue?
4 A warrior's sharp arrows,
    with glowing coals of the broom tree!

5 Woe is me, that I am an alien in Mē'shech,
    that I must live among the tents of Kē'dar.
6 Too long have I had my dwelling
    among those who hate peace.
7 I am for peace;
    but when I speak,
    they are for war.

Psalm 121

Assurance of God's Protection

A Song of Ascents.

1 I lift up my eyes to the hills—
    from where will my help come?
2 My help comes from the LORD,
    who made heaven and earth.

3 He will not let your foot be moved;
    he who keeps you will not slumber.
4 He who keeps Israel
    will neither slumber nor sleep.

5 The LORD is your keeper;
    the LORD is your shade at your right hand.
6 The sun shall not strike you by day,
    nor the moon by night.

7 The LORD will keep you from all evil;
    he will keep your life.
8 The LORD will keep
    your going out and your coming in
    from this time on and forevermore.

Psalm 122

Song of Praise and Prayer for Jerusalem

A Song of Ascents. Of David.

1 I was glad when they said to me,
    "Let us go to the house of the LORD!"
2 Our feet are standing
    within your gates, O Jerusalem.

3 Jerusalem—built as a city
    that is bound firmly together.
4 To it the tribes go up,
    the tribes of the LORD,
as was decreed for Israel,
    to give thanks to the name of the LORD.
5 For there the thrones for judgment were
        set up,
    the thrones of the house of David.

6 Pray for the peace of Jerusalem:
    "May they prosper who love you.
7 Peace be within your walls,
    and security within your towers."
8 For the sake of my relatives and friends
    I will say, "Peace be within you."
9 For the sake of the house of the LORD our God,
    I will seek your good.

Psalm 123

Supplication for Mercy

A Song of Ascents.

1 To you I lift up my eyes,
    O you who are enthroned in the heavens!
2 As the eyes of servants
    look to the hand of their master,
as the eyes of a maid
    to the hand of her mistress,
so our eyes look to the LORD our God,
    until he has mercy upon us.

3 Have mercy upon us, O LORD, have mercy
upon us,
for we have had more than enough of
contempt.
4 Our soul has had more than its fill
of the scorn of those who are at ease,
of the contempt of the proud.

Psalm 124

Thanksgiving for Israel's Deliverance

A Song of Ascents. Of David.

1 If it had not been the LORD who was on our
side
—let Israel now say—
2 if it had not been the LORD who was on our
side,
when our enemies attacked us,
3 then they would have swallowed us up
alive,
when their anger was kindled
against us;
4 then the flood would have swept us
away,
the torrent would have gone over us;
5 then over us would have gone
the raging waters.

6 Blessed be the LORD,
who has not given us
as prey to their teeth.
7 We have escaped like a bird
from the snare of the fowlers;
the snare is broken,
and we have escaped.

8 Our help is in the name of the LORD,
who made heaven and earth.

Psalm 125

The Security of God's People

A Song of Ascents.

1 Those who trust in the LORD are like Mount
Zion,
which cannot be moved, but abides
forever.
2 As the mountains surround Jerusalem,
so the LORD surrounds his people,
from this time on and forevermore.
3 For the scepter of wickedness shall not rest
on the land allotted to the righteous,
so that the righteous might not stretch out
their hands to do wrong.
4 Do good, O LORD, to those who are good,
and to those who are upright in their
hearts.
5 But those who turn aside to their own crooked
ways
the LORD will lead away with evildoers.
Peace be upon Israel!

Psalm 126

A Harvest of Joy

A Song of Ascents.

1 When the LORD restored the fortunes of
Zion,[b]
we were like those who dream.
2 Then our mouth was filled with laughter,
and our tongue with shouts of joy;
then it was said among the nations,
"The LORD has done great things for them."
3 The LORD has done great things for us,
and we rejoiced.

---

b Or *brought back those who returned to Zion*

The LORD Was on Our Side

You often hear a team or group that has just played well or completed a great task
say, "God was with us." The writer of Psalm 124 expressed the same sentiment in
verses 1–2. What a gift it is to recognize God's help in our life. It is God who carries us when we are down, who rescues us when we are in trouble, and who gives
us the talent that we have.

Are you ever afraid, or do you ever feel lost? Read Psalm 124, and be assured that
others have felt the same way. Whether you are unsure about school, a job, a relationship,
or your future, just remember, "Our help is in the name of the LORD, / who made heaven
and earth" (verse 8).

▶ Psalm 124

4 Restore our fortunes, O LORD,
     like the watercourses in the Neg'eb.
5 May those who sow in tears
     reap with shouts of joy.
6 Those who go out weeping,
     bearing the seed for sowing,
shall come home with shouts of joy,
     carrying their sheaves.

Psalm 127

God's Blessings in the Home

A Song of Ascents. Of Solomon.

1 Unless the LORD builds the house,
     those who build it labor in vain.
Unless the LORD guards the city,
     the guard keeps watch in vain.
2 It is in vain that you rise up early
     and go late to rest,
eating the bread of anxious toil;
     for he gives sleep to his beloved.*c*

3 Sons are indeed a heritage from the LORD,
     the fruit of the womb a reward.
4 Like arrows in the hand of a warrior
     are the sons of one's youth.
5 Happy is the man who has
     his quiver full of them.
He shall not be put to shame
     when he speaks with his enemies in the gate.

Psalm 128

The Happy Home of the Faithful

A Song of Ascents.

1 Happy is everyone who fears the LORD,
     who walks in his ways.
2 You shall eat the fruit of the labor of your
     hands;
     you shall be happy, and it shall go well
     with you.

3 Your wife will be like a fruitful vine
     within your house;
your children will be like olive shoots
     around your table.
4 Thus shall the man be blessed
     who fears the LORD.

5 The LORD bless you from Zion.
     May you see the prosperity of
       Jerusalem
     all the days of your life.
6 May you see your children's children.
     Peace be upon Israel!

Psalm 129

Prayer for the Downfall of Israel's Enemies

A Song of Ascents.

1 "Often have they attacked me from my youth"
     —let Israel now say—
2 "often have they attacked me from my youth,
     yet they have not prevailed against me.
3 The plowers plowed on my back;
     they made their furrows long."
4 The LORD is righteous;
     he has cut the cords of the wicked.
5 May all who hate Zion
     be put to shame and turned backward.
6 Let them be like the grass on the housetops
     that withers before it grows up,
7 with which reapers do not fill their hands
     or binders of sheaves their arms,
8 while those who pass by do not say,
     "The blessing of the LORD be upon you!
     We bless you in the name of the LORD!"

Psalm 130

Waiting for Divine Redemption

A Song of Ascents.

1 Out of the depths I cry to you, O LORD.
2   Lord, hear my voice!
Let your ears be attentive
     to the voice of my supplications!

3 If you, O LORD, should mark iniquities,
     Lord, who could stand?
4 But there is forgiveness with you,
     so that you may be revered.

5 I wait for the LORD, my soul waits,
     and in his word I hope;
6 my soul waits for the Lord
     more than those who watch for the morning,
     more than those who watch for the morning.

7 O Israel, hope in the LORD!
     For with the LORD there is steadfast love,
     and with him is great power to redeem.
8 It is he who will redeem Israel
     from all its iniquities.

Psalm 131

Song of Quiet Trust

A Song of Ascents. Of David.

1 O LORD, my heart is not lifted up,
     my eyes are not raised too high;

---

c Or for he provides for his beloved during sleep

I do not occupy myself with things
    too great and too marvelous for me.
2 But I have calmed and quieted my soul,
    like a weaned child with its mother;
    my soul is like the weaned child that is
      with me.*d*

3 O Israel, hope in the LORD
    from this time on and forevermore.

PRAY IT!

Hold Me, Mother God

Psalm 131 is a humble prayer of child-like trust. It gives the wonderful image of God holding us like a child in a mother's lap. Like a mother, God hugs us close and keeps us safe and warm and protected. We don't need to solve problems or be concerned about our performance. We are loved just because we are us. God created us; God loves us and cradles us.

Do you remember sitting quietly in your mother's or grandmother's lap when you were a small child? If so, do you recall her telling you stories or singing you lullabies? If you do not have such memories, have you ever seen a mother calm her child with songs and stories? How is God's love like that? In prayer, imagine being held by God, as a child is held by a mother. You might be surprised at how safe and secure you feel!

▸ **Psalm 131**

Psalm 132

The Eternal Dwelling of God in Zion

A Song of Ascents.

1 O LORD, remember in David's favor
    all the hardships he endured;
2 how he swore to the LORD
    and vowed to the Mighty One of
      Jacob,
3 "I will not enter my house
    or get into my bed;
4 I will not give sleep to my eyes
    or slumber to my eyelids,
5 until I find a place for the LORD,
    a dwelling place for the Mighty One of
      Jacob."

6 We heard of it in Eph′ra•thah;
    we found it in the fields of Jā′ar.
7 "Let us go to his dwelling place;
    let us worship at his footstool."

8 Rise up, O LORD, and go to your resting place,
    you and the ark of your might.
9 Let your priests be clothed with righteousness,
    and let your faithful shout for joy.
10 For your servant David's sake
    do not turn away the face of your
      anointed one.

11 The LORD swore to David a sure oath
    from which he will not turn back:
"One of the sons of your body
    I will set on your throne.
12 If your sons keep my covenant
    and my decrees that I shall teach them,
their sons also, forevermore,
    shall sit on your throne."

13 For the LORD has chosen Zion;
    he has desired it for his habitation:
14 "This is my resting place forever;
    here I will reside, for I have desired it.
15 I will abundantly bless its provisions;
    I will satisfy its poor with bread.
16 Its priests I will clothe with salvation,
    and its faithful will shout for joy.
17 There I will cause a horn to sprout up for
      David;
    I have prepared a lamp for my
      anointed one.
18 His enemies I will clothe with disgrace,
    but on him, his crown will gleam."

Psalm 133

The Blessedness of Unity

A Song of Ascents.

1 How very good and pleasant it is
    when kindred live together in unity!
2 It is like the precious oil on the head,
    running down upon the beard,
on the beard of Aaron,
    running down over the collar of his
      robes.
3 It is like the dew of Hermon,
    which falls on the mountains of Zion.
For there the LORD ordained his blessing,
    life forevermore.

---

d Or *my soul within me is like a weaned child*

did you KNOW?

Jerusalem, Zion, City of David

Jerusalem, Zion, City of David—you have probably noticed that these three names keep popping up throughout the Psalms. They all refer to the heart of Israel, the city of Jerusalem. When David became king of the united tribes of Israel, he needed a neutral place between the northern and southern tribes. He conquered Jerusalem and elevated it as the political and religious center—thus, Jerusalem was also known as the City of David. Mount Zion, located within Jerusalem, was the site of the Temple—the sacred place where God dwelt. So, Zion became another way to refer to Jerusalem.

At that time, the Israelites felt that Jerusalem was invincible because it was God's dwelling place. But eventually, Jerusalem and the Temple were destroyed. Afterward, a hope arose that one day, a messiah from David's line would renew Jerusalem and true worship of God on Zion. The New Testament portrays Jesus as the fulfillment of this hope.

▸ Psalm 132

Psalm 134

Praise in the Night

A Song of Ascents.

1 Come, bless the LORD, all you servants of the
     LORD,
     who stand by night in the house of the
       LORD!
2 Lift up your hands to the holy place,
     and bless the LORD.

3 May the LORD, maker of heaven and
       earth,
     bless you from Zion.

Psalm 135

Praise for God's Goodness and Might

1 Praise the LORD!
     Praise the name of the LORD;
     give praise, O servants of the LORD,
2 you that stand in the house of the LORD,
     in the courts of the house of our God.
3 Praise the LORD, for the LORD is good;
     sing to his name, for he is gracious.
4 For the LORD has chosen Jacob for himself,
     Israel as his own possession.

5 For I know that the LORD is great;
     our Lord is above all gods.
6 Whatever the LORD pleases he does,
     in heaven and on earth,
     in the seas and all deeps.
7 He it is who makes the clouds rise at the end of
       the earth;
     he makes lightnings for the rain
     and brings out the wind from his
       storehouses.

8 He it was who struck down the firstborn of
       Egypt,
     both human beings and animals;
9 he sent signs and wonders
     into your midst, O Egypt,
     against Pharaoh and all his servants.
10 He struck down many nations
     and killed mighty kings—
11 Si'hon, king of the Am'o•rītes,
     and Og, king of Bā'shan,
     and all the kingdoms of Cā'naan—
12 and gave their land as a heritage,
     a heritage to his people Israel.

13 Your name, O LORD, endures forever,
     your renown, O LORD, throughout all
       ages.
14 For the LORD will vindicate his people,
     and have compassion on his servants.

15 The idols of the nations are silver and
       gold,
     the work of human hands.
16 They have mouths, but they do not speak;
     they have eyes, but they do not see;
17 they have ears, but they do not hear,
     and there is no breath in their mouths.
18 Those who make them
     and all who trust them
     shall become like them.

19 O house of Israel, bless the LORD!
     O house of Aaron, bless the LORD!
20 O house of Levi, bless the LORD!
     You that fear the LORD, bless the LORD!
21 Blessed be the LORD from Zion,
     he who resides in Jerusalem.
Praise the LORD!

2 O give thanks to the God of gods,
   for his steadfast love endures forever.
3 O give thanks to the Lord of lords,
   for his steadfast love endures forever;

4 who alone does great wonders,
   for his steadfast love endures forever;
5 who by understanding made the heavens,
   for his steadfast love endures forever;
6 who spread out the earth on the waters,
   for his steadfast love endures forever;
7 who made the great lights,
   for his steadfast love endures forever;
8 the sun to rule over the day,
   for his steadfast love endures forever;
9 the moon and stars to rule over the night,
   for his steadfast love endures forever;

10 who struck Egypt through their firstborn,
   for his steadfast love endures forever;
11 and brought Israel out from among them,
   for his steadfast love endures forever;
12 with a strong hand and an outstretched
      arm,
   for his steadfast love endures forever;
13 who divided the Red Sea[e] in two,
   for his steadfast love endures forever;
14 and made Israel pass through the midst
      of it,
   for his steadfast love endures forever;
15 but overthrew Pharaoh and his army in the
      Red Sea,[e]
   for his steadfast love endures forever;
16 who led his people through the
      wilderness,
   for his steadfast love endures forever;
17 who struck down great kings,
   for his steadfast love endures forever;
18 and killed famous kings,
   for his steadfast love endures forever;
19 Si'hon, king of the Am'o•rites,
   for his steadfast love endures forever;
20 and Og, king of Ba'shan,
   for his steadfast love endures forever;
21 and gave their land as a heritage,
   for his steadfast love endures forever;
22 a heritage to his servant Israel,
   for his steadfast love endures forever.

23 It is he who remembered us in our low estate,
   for his steadfast love endures forever;
24 and rescued us from our foes,
   for his steadfast love endures forever;
25 who gives food to all flesh,
   for his steadfast love endures forever.

---

e Or *Sea of Reeds*

Catholic Connections

CALLED TO RESPOND

Have you ever been to a sporting event where the cheering becomes a rousing anthem, expressing enthusiastic support for the team?

In a similar way, Psalm 136 must have been a prayer that managed to rouse the Israelites in their praise of God. Imagine a cantor starting slowly and softly with the first part of the first verse and then building in enthusiasm and volume through the succeeding verses as the community continuously responds, "for his steadfast love endures forever." That kind of prayer and response would have been a powerful way for the community to pray.

The Psalms are prayers that lend themselves well to such call-and-response techniques. We pray one of these ancient song-prayers at every Mass. After the first reading of the Mass, the community is called to respond to God's word by participating (ideally in song) in the responsorial psalm. God has spoken, and the community responds with gratitude, praise, and faith in sung prayer. The responsorial psalm invites us to open our hearts and to dialogue with God, who has spoken first.

This Sunday at Mass, pay close attention to the responsorial psalm. Be sure to sing the response (remember, you don't need a great voice to sing in church), and as you do, imagine that God is hanging on to your every word.

▶ Psalm 136

Psalm 136

God's Work in Creation and in History

1 O give thanks to the LORD, for he is good,
   for his steadfast love endures forever.

P
S
A
L
M
S

26 O give thanks to the God of heaven,
    for his steadfast love endures forever.

Psalm 137

Lament over the Destruction of Jerusalem

1 By the rivers of Babylon—
    there we sat down and there we wept
    when we remembered Zion.
2 On the willows*f* there
    we hung up our harps.
3 For there our captors
    asked us for songs,
and our tormentors asked for mirth, saying,
    "Sing us one of the songs of Zion!"

4 How could we sing the LORD's song
    in a foreign land?
5 If I forget you, O Jerusalem,
    let my right hand wither!
6 Let my tongue cling to the roof of my
      mouth,
    if I do not remember you,

if I do not set Jerusalem
    above my highest joy.

7 Remember, O LORD, against the É'dom•ites
    the day of Jerusalem's fall,
how they said, "Tear it down! Tear it down!
    Down to its foundations!"
8 O daughter Babylon, you devastator!*g*
    Happy shall they be who pay you back
    what you have done to us!
9 Happy shall they be who take your little ones
    and dash them against the rock!

Psalm 138

Thanksgiving and Praise
Of David.

1 I give you thanks, O LORD, with my whole
      heart;
    before the gods I sing your praise;

---

f Or *poplars*   *g* Or *you who are devastated*

CELTIC TRADITIONS

Many people of the British Isles, especially the Irish, have for hundreds of years celebrated their Celtic traditions. Over the years, their Celtic traditions have become fused with their expressions of their Catholic faith. One of the central Celtic Christian themes is the presence and protection of God. Like the psalmist who wrote Psalm 139, the author of "Saint Patrick's Breastplate" illustrates how the Celts call God into their life and world:

> Christ be with me, Christ within me
> Christ behind me, Christ before me,
> Christ beside me, Christ to win me,
> Christ to comfort and restore me,
> Christ beneath me, Christ above me,
> Christ in quiet, Christ in danger,
> Christ in the hearts of all that love me,
> Christ in mouth of friend or stranger.
> (in Ian Bradley, *The Celtic Way*, p. 33)

The next time you want to pray for the presence of God, try praying in the Celtic tradition so beautifully expressed in "Saint Patrick's Breastplate."

▶ Psalm 139

P
S
A
L
M
S

The Sacredness of Life

"For it was you who formed my inward parts; / you knit me together in my mother's womb" (Ps 139.13).

Psalm 139 speaks poetically of God's intimate care for each of us, long before we were even formed. It is perhaps the most powerful argument against abortion in the entire Bible. Who can deny that God gave us life long before we actually saw the light of day? How can we deny that every unborn child is fashioned by the hand of God?

It is easy to get caught up in arguments about individual rights and scientific terminology. But this is not about science or government or even when life begins. It is about poetry and love and the faith that God has knit together each of us in our mother's womb. God has great plans for each of us, whether we have been born, are in the womb, or have not yet even been thought of. God knows and loves us, and has through all eternity.

What else is there to say?

▶ **Psalm 139**

2 I bow down toward your holy temple
        and give thanks to your name for your
            steadfast love and your faithfulness;
        for you have exalted your name and your
            word
        above everything.*h*
3 On the day I called, you answered me,
        you increased my strength of soul.*i*

4 All the kings of the earth shall praise you,
            O LORD,
        for they have heard the words of your mouth.
5 They shall sing of the ways of the LORD,
        for great is the glory of the LORD.
6 For though the LORD is high, he regards the
            lowly;
        but the haughty he perceives from far
            away.

7 Though I walk in the midst of trouble,
        you preserve me against the wrath of my
            enemies;
    you stretch out your hand,
        and your right hand delivers me.
8 The LORD will fulfill his purpose for me;
        your steadfast love, O LORD, endures
            forever.
        Do not forsake the work of your hands.

Psalm 139

The Inescapable God

To the leader. Of David. A Psalm.

1 O LORD, you have searched me and known me.
2 You know when I sit down and when I rise up;
        you discern my thoughts from far away.

3 You search out my path and my lying down,
        and are acquainted with all my ways.
4 Even before a word is on my tongue,
        O LORD, you know it completely.
5 You hem me in, behind and before,
        and lay your hand upon me.
6 Such knowledge is too wonderful for me;
        it is so high that I cannot attain it.

7 Where can I go from your spirit?
        Or where can I flee from your presence?
8 If I ascend to heaven, you are there;
        if I make my bed in She'ōl, you are there.
9 If I take the wings of the morning
        and settle at the farthest limits of the sea,
10 even there your hand shall lead me,
        and your right hand shall hold me fast.
11 If I say, "Surely the darkness shall cover me,
        and the light around me become night,"
12 even the darkness is not dark to you;
        the night is as bright as the day,
        for darkness is as light to you.

13 For it was you who formed my inward parts;
        you knit me together in my mother's
            womb.
14 I praise you, for I am fearfully and wonderfully
            made.
        Wonderful are your works;
        that I know very well.
15   My frame was not hidden from you,
    when I was being made in secret,
        intricately woven in the depths of the earth.

h Cn: Heb *you have exalted your word above all your name*
i Syr Compare Gk Tg: Heb *you made me arrogant in my soul with strength*

16 Your eyes beheld my unformed substance.
In your book were written
    all the days that were formed for me,
    when none of them as yet existed.
17 How weighty to me are your thoughts,
    O God!
How vast is the sum of them!
18 I try to count them—they are more than the
        sand;
I come to the end*j*—I am still with you.

19 O that you would kill the wicked, O God,
    and that the bloodthirsty would depart
        from me—
20 those who speak of you maliciously,
    and lift themselves up against you for
        evil!*k*
21 Do I not hate those who hate you,
    O LORD?
And do I not loathe those who rise up
        against you?
22 I hate them with perfect hatred;

I count them my enemies.
23 Search me, O God, and know my heart;
    test me and know my thoughts.
24 See if there is any wicked*l* way in me,
    and lead me in the way everlasting.*m*

Psalm 140

Prayer for Deliverance from Enemies

To the leader. A Psalm of David.

1 Deliver me, O LORD, from evildoers;
    protect me from those who are violent,
2 who plan evil things in their minds
    and stir up wars continually.
3 They make their tongue sharp as a snake's,
    and under their lips is the venom of vipers.
                    Se'lah

---

j Or *I awake*   *k* Cn: Meaning of Heb uncertain
l Heb *hurtful*   *m* Or *the ancient way.* Compare Jer 6.16

GOD CARES FOR THOSE WHO SUFFER PERSECUTION!

Many of us like to think that persecution rarely occurs. Unfortunately, this is not true. All too frequently, people are persecuted because of their color, their ethnic origin, their political beliefs, or even their faith. Harassment can be as subtle as a rude comment or a patronizing attitude, or as aggressive as a beating or death. Young people know the feeling of persecution. They may experience it because of their origin, the way they look or talk, or what they believe.

    Psalm 140 is one of several psalms (see also Psalms 35, 86) and prayers seeking God's help in times of persecution. These typically have two parts. The first part asks for God's protection against persecutors, and the second part praises God's love, justice, and mercy. This illustrates the continual tension for all believers: feeling the need for God's action while at the same time being certain that God cares for them in the midst of their persecution.

    For Christians, Jesus is the perfect model of the persecuted person. He was persecuted without reason (Lk 23.4), and he felt God's absence (Mk 15.34), but he still put his entire faith and trust in God's will (Mt 26.39). Following Jesus' example, Christians throughout history have bravely endured persecution, and even death, for their faith.

- Have you or your family experienced some kind of persecution? If so, how and why? If you have ever participated in some kind of persecution of someone else, pray for forgiveness, and if possible make amends.
- Thank God for the blessings you have, and ask God for the strength to endure whatever persecutions come your way. Pray for those who are suffering persecution, regardless of the motive.

▶ **Psalm 140**

4 Guard me, O LORD, from the hands of the
wicked;
protect me from the violent
who have planned my downfall.
5 The arrogant have hidden a trap for me,
and with cords they have spread a net,n
along the road they have set snares for me.
Se̱'lah

6 I say to the LORD, "You are my God;
give ear, O LORD, to the voice of my
supplications."
7 O LORD, my Lord, my strong deliverer,
you have covered my head in the day of
battle.
8 Do not grant, O LORD, the desires of the
wicked;
do not further their evil plot.o
Se̱'lah

9 Those who surround me lift up their
heads;p
let the mischief of their lips overwhelm
them!
10 Let burning coals fall on them!
Let them be flung into pits, no more
to rise!
11 Do not let the slanderer be established in the
land;
let evil speedily hunt down the violent!

12 I know that the LORD maintains the cause of
the needy,
and executes justice for the poor.
13 Surely the righteous shall give thanks to your
name;
the upright shall live in your presence.

Psalm 141

Prayer for Preservation from Evil

A Psalm of David.

1 I call upon you, O LORD; come quickly
to me;
give ear to my voice when I call to you.
2 Let my prayer be counted as incense before
you,
and the lifting up of my hands as an
evening sacrifice.

3 Set a guard over my mouth, O LORD;
keep watch over the door of my lips.
4 Do not turn my heart to any evil,
to busy myself with wicked deeds
in company with those who work
iniquity;
do not let me eat of their delicacies.

5 Let the righteous strike me;
let the faithful correct me.
Never let the oil of the wicked anoint my
head,q
for my prayer is continuallyr against their
wicked deeds.
6 When they are given over to those who shall
condemn them,
then they shall learn that my words were
pleasant.
7 Like a rock that one breaks apart and shatters
on the land,
so shall their bones be strewn at the mouth
of She̱'ōl.s

8 But my eyes are turned toward you, O GOD,
my Lord;
in you I seek refuge; do not leave me
defenseless.
9 Keep me from the trap that they have laid
for me,
and from the snares of evildoers.
10 Let the wicked fall into their own nets,
while I alone escape.

Psalm 142

Prayer for Deliverance
from Persecutors

A Mas'kil of David. When he was in the cave.
A Prayer.

1 With my voice I cry to the LORD;
with my voice I make supplication to the
LORD.
2 I pour out my complaint before him;
I tell my trouble before him.
3 When my spirit is faint,
you know my way.

In the path where I walk
they have hidden a trap for me.
4 Look on my right hand and see—
there is no one who takes notice of me;
no refuge remains to me;
no one cares for me.

5 I cry to you, O LORD;
I say, "You are my refuge,
my portion in the land of the living."
6 Give heed to my cry,
for I am brought very low.

---

n Or *they have spread cords as a net* o Heb adds *they are*
exalted p Cn Compare Gk: Heb *those who surround me are*
uplifted in head; Heb divides verses 8 and 9 differently
q Gk: Meaning of Heb uncertain r Cn: Heb *for continually*
and my prayer s Meaning of Heb of verses 5-7 is uncertain

Save me from my persecutors,
for they are too strong for me.
7 Bring me out of prison,
so that I may give thanks to your name.
The righteous will surround me,
for you will deal bountifully with me.

Psalm 143

Prayer for Deliverance from Enemies
A Psalm of David.

1 Hear my prayer, O LORD;
give ear to my supplications in your
faithfulness;
answer me in your righteousness.
2 Do not enter into judgment with your
servant,
for no one living is righteous before you.

3 For the enemy has pursued me,
crushing my life to the ground,
making me sit in darkness like those long
dead.
4 Therefore my spirit faints within me;
my heart within me is appalled.

5 I remember the days of old,
I think about all your deeds,
I meditate on the works of your hands.
6 I stretch out my hands to you;
my soul thirsts for you like a parched land.
Sĕ'lah

7 Answer me quickly, O LORD;
my spirit fails.
Do not hide your face from me,
or I shall be like those who go down to the
Pit.
8 Let me hear of your steadfast love in the
morning,
for in you I put my trust.
Teach me the way I should go,
for to you I lift up my soul.

9 Save me, O LORD, from my enemies;
I have fled to you for refuge.[t]
10 Teach me to do your will,
for you are my God.
Let your good spirit lead me
on a level path.

11 For your name's sake, O LORD, preserve my
life.
In your righteousness bring me out of
trouble.
12 In your steadfast love cut off my enemies,

and destroy all my adversaries,
for I am your servant.

Psalm 144

Prayer for National Deliverance and Security
Of David.

1 Blessed be the LORD, my rock,
who trains my hands for war, and my
fingers for battle;
2 my rock[u] and my fortress,
my stronghold and my deliverer,
my shield, in whom I take refuge,
who subdues the peoples[v] under me.

3 O LORD, what are human beings that you
regard them,
or mortals that you think of them?
4 They are like a breath;
their days are like a passing shadow.

5 Bow your heavens, O LORD, and come
down;
touch the mountains so that they smoke.
6 Make the lightning flash and scatter them;
send out your arrows and rout them.
7 Stretch out your hand from on high;
set me free and rescue me from the mighty
waters,
from the hand of aliens,

---

t One Heb Ms Gk: MT *to you I have hidden*   u With 18.2
and 2 Sam 22.2: Heb *my steadfast love*   v Heb Mss Syr
Aquila Jerome: MT *my people*

PRAY IT
A Prayer for the Young

*We praise you, God, for all our nation's blessings!
We thank you for our young people, our sons and daughters who come forward to serve the people of God.
We ask you to make them strong, to call them into a trusting relationship with you, and to help them live a faithful life and to be leaders and examples for others.
Happy the people whose God is the LORD!*

▶ **Psalm 144**

8 whose mouths speak lies,
  and whose right hands are false.

9 I will sing a new song to you, O God;
  upon a ten-stringed harp I will play
      to you,
10 the one who gives victory to kings,
  who rescues his servant David.
11 Rescue me from the cruel sword,
  and deliver me from the hand of aliens,
whose mouths speak lies,
  and whose right hands are false.

12 May our sons in their youth
  be like plants full grown,
our daughters like corner pillars,
  cut for the building of a palace.
13 May our barns be filled,
  with produce of every kind;
may our sheep increase by thousands,
  by tens of thousands in our fields,
14 and may our cattle be heavy with
      young.
May there be no breach in the walls,*w* no
      exile,
  and no cry of distress in our streets.

15 Happy are the people to whom such blessings
      fall;
  happy are the people whose God is the
  LORD.

Psalm 145

The Greatness and the Goodness of God

Praise. Of David.

1 I will extol you, my God and King,
  and bless your name forever and ever.
2 Every day I will bless you,
  and praise your name forever and ever.
3 Great is the LORD, and greatly to be
      praised;
  his greatness is unsearchable.

4 One generation shall laud your works to
      another,
  and shall declare your mighty acts.
5 On the glorious splendor of your majesty,
  and on your wondrous works, I will
      meditate.
6 The might of your awesome deeds shall be
      proclaimed,
  and I will declare your greatness.
7 They shall celebrate the fame of your abundant
      goodness,
  and shall sing aloud of your righteousness.

8 The LORD is gracious and merciful,
  slow to anger and abounding in steadfast
  love.
9 The LORD is good to all,
  and his compassion is over all that he has
  made.

10 All your works shall give thanks to you,
      O LORD,
  and all your faithful shall bless you.
11 They shall speak of the glory of your
      kingdom,
  and tell of your power,
12 to make known to all people your*x* mighty
      deeds,
  and the glorious splendor of your*y*
  kingdom.
13 Your kingdom is an everlasting kingdom,
  and your dominion endures throughout all
      generations.

The LORD is faithful in all his words,
  and gracious in all his deeds.*z*
14 The LORD upholds all who are falling,
  and raises up all who are bowed down.
15 The eyes of all look to you,
  and you give them their food in due
  season.
16 You open your hand,
  satisfying the desire of every living thing.
17 The LORD is just in all his ways,
  and kind in all his doings.
18 The LORD is near to all who call on him,
  to all who call on him in truth.
19 He fulfills the desire of all who fear him;
  he also hears their cry, and saves them.
20 The LORD watches over all who love him,
  but all the wicked he will destroy.

21 My mouth will speak the praise of the LORD,
  and all flesh will bless his holy name
  forever and ever.

Psalm 146

Praise for God's Help

1 Praise the LORD!
Praise the LORD, O my soul!
2 I will praise the LORD as long as I live;
  I will sing praises to my God all my life
  long.

3 Do not put your trust in princes,
  in mortals, in whom there is no help.

w Heb lacks *in the walls*   x Gk Jerome Syr: Heb *his*
y Heb *his*   z These two lines supplied by Q Ms Gk Syr

4 When their breath departs, they return to the
      earth;
    on that very day their plans perish.

5 Happy are those whose help is the God of
      Jacob,
    whose hope is in the LORD their God,
6 who made heaven and earth,
    the sea, and all that is in them;
  who keeps faith forever;
7   who executes justice for the oppressed;
    who gives food to the hungry.

  The LORD sets the prisoners free;
8   the LORD opens the eyes of the blind.
  The LORD lifts up those who are bowed down;
    the LORD loves the righteous.
9 The LORD watches over the strangers;
    he upholds the orphan and the widow,
    but the way of the wicked he brings to
      ruin.

10 The LORD will reign forever,
    your God, O Zion, for all generations.
  Praise the LORD!

Psalm 147

Praise for God's Care for Jerusalem

1 Praise the LORD!
  How good it is to sing praises to our God;
    for he is gracious, and a song of praise is
      fitting.
2 The LORD builds up Jerusalem;
    he gathers the outcasts of Israel.
3 He heals the brokenhearted,
    and binds up their wounds.
4 He determines the number of the stars;
    he gives to all of them their names.
5 Great is our Lord, and abundant in power;

his understanding is beyond measure.
6 The LORD lifts up the downtrodden;
    he casts the wicked to the ground.

7 Sing to the LORD with thanksgiving;
    make melody to our God on the lyre.
8 He covers the heavens with clouds,
    prepares rain for the earth,
    makes grass grow on the hills.
9 He gives to the animals their food,
    and to the young ravens when they cry.
10 His delight is not in the strength of the
      horse,
    nor his pleasure in the speed of a runner;[a]
11 but the LORD takes pleasure in those who fear
      him,
    in those who hope in his steadfast love.

12 Praise the LORD, O Jerusalem!
    Praise your God, O Zion!
13 For he strengthens the bars of your gates;
    he blesses your children within you.
14 He grants peace[b] within your borders;
    he fills you with the finest of wheat.
15 He sends out his command to the earth;
    his word runs swiftly.
16 He gives snow like wool;
    he scatters frost like ashes.
17 He hurls down hail like crumbs—
    who can stand before his cold?
18 He sends out his word, and melts them;
    he makes his wind blow, and the waters
      flow.
19 He declares his word to Jacob,
    his statutes and ordinances to Israel.
20 He has not dealt thus with any other nation;
    they do not know his ordinances.
  Praise the LORD!

---

a Heb legs of a person   b Or prosperity

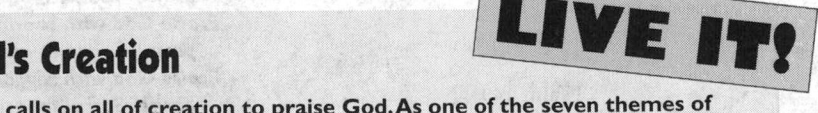

Care for God's Creation

LIVE IT!

Psalm 148 calls on all of creation to praise God. As one of the seven themes of
Catholic social teaching, caring for God's creation is one way we can respond to
God and the needs of others. Working to keep water clean for safe drinking and
for the protection of sea life, educating ourselves and others about the effects of
pollution on animal habitats and nesting sites, and protecting endangered species and all
of creation are some of the ways we can fulfill our call to care for God's creation. Psalm
148 asks us to complete a cycle—God creates; we are called to care for God's creation,
and all of creation continues in its praise of God.

▶ Psalm 148

Psalm 148
Praise for God's Universal Glory

1 Praise the LORD!
  Praise the LORD from the heavens;
    praise him in the heights!
2 Praise him, all his angels;
    praise him, all his host!

3 Praise him, sun and moon;
    praise him, all you shining stars!
4 Praise him, you highest heavens,
    and you waters above the heavens!

5 Let them praise the name of the LORD,
    for he commanded and they were
      created.
6 He established them forever and ever;
    he fixed their bounds, which cannot be
      passed.[c]

7 Praise the LORD from the earth,
    you sea monsters and all deeps,
8 fire and hail, snow and frost,
    stormy wind fulfilling his command!

9 Mountains and all hills,
    fruit trees and all cedars!
10 Wild animals and all cattle,
    creeping things and flying birds!

11 Kings of the earth and all peoples,
    princes and all rulers of the earth!
12 Young men and women alike,
    old and young together!

13 Let them praise the name of the LORD,
    for his name alone is exalted;
    his glory is above earth and heaven.
14 He has raised up a horn for his people,
    praise for all his faithful,
    for the people of Israel who are close to
      him.
  Praise the LORD!

Psalm 149
Praise for God's Goodness to Israel

1 Praise the LORD!
  Sing to the LORD a new song,
    his praise in the assembly of the faithful.
2 Let Israel be glad in its Maker;
    let the children of Zion rejoice in their
      King.
3 Let them praise his name with dancing,
    making melody to him with tambourine
      and lyre.

4 For the LORD takes pleasure in his people;
    he adorns the humble with victory.
5 Let the faithful exult in glory;
    let them sing for joy on their couches.
6 Let the high praises of God be in their
      throats
    and two-edged swords in their hands,
7 to execute vengeance on the nations
    and punishment on the peoples,
8 to bind their kings with fetters
    and their nobles with chains of iron,
9 to execute on them the judgment
      decreed.
  This is glory for all his faithful ones.
  Praise the LORD!

Psalm 150
Praise for God's Surpassing Greatness

1 Praise the LORD!
  Praise God in his sanctuary;
    praise him in his mighty firmament![d]

---

c Or he set a law that cannot pass away   d Or dome

PRAY IT!
Psalm 150, Part 2

Praise God with clarinet and saxophone;
  praise God with flute and oboe!
Praise God with French horn and tuba;
  praise God with marimba and
    xylophone!
Praise God with guitar and fiddle;
  praise God with banjo and ukulele!
Praise God with bagpipe and accordion;
  praise God with piano and calliope!
Praise God with steel drum and harmonica;
  praise God with bongo and maracas!
Praise God with soaring classical music;
  praise God with mellow blues and tango!
Praise God with reggae and rap;
  praise God with jazz and rock!
Praise God with square dancing and line
    dancing;
  praise God with polka and waltz!
Let everyone who has breath and hands
    and feet and voices—
  sopranos, altos, tenors, and basses—
  praise the LORD!

▶ Psalm 150

2 Praise him for his mighty deeds;
    praise him according to his surpassing
      greatness!

3 Praise him with trumpet sound;
    praise him with lute and harp!

4 Praise him with tambourine and dance;
    praise him with strings and pipe!

5 Praise him with clanging cymbals;
    praise him with loud clashing cymbals!

6 Let everything that breathes praise the LORD!
    Praise the LORD!

When we pick up the daily newspaper, many of us turn first to the advice columns. "My mom just doesn't understand me" we read. "Why won't she let me make my own decisions?" Or "All my friends take drugs. How do I resist the pressure?" The Book of Proverbs is the advice column of the Old Testament. It covers everything from raising children to choosing friends.

At a Glance

- **Chapters 1–9.** introduction and instructions for young people

- **10.1—31.9.** assorted collections of proverbs

- **31.10–31.** a reflection on being a good wife

In-depth

"Hear, my child" (Prov 1.8)—this, in a nutshell, is the teaching of Proverbs. The wise person listens to the "voices" of history: experience, intelligence, and common sense. The ancient Israelites had a long tradition of reflecting on the challenges of life. Over the centuries, a whole body of writings developed to record their reflections. These writings gave advice on common problems and questions that people faced, and directions for wise living.

Proverbs is the best-known example of this type of literature in the Old Testament. It contains two basic kinds of writings: longer instructions addressed to young people and short sayings addressed to all. With advice on matters ranging from laziness (6.6–11), cheating (11.1), pride (16.18), and the training of children (22.6), to laughter (14.13), eyewinks (16.30), visiting neighbors (25.17), and being a good wife (31.10–31), Proverbs is a treasure chest of advice from the ancient world. Although some of the sayings may seem outdated or funny to us today, the overall lesson is something that Jesus insists on in the Gospels: Faith is not just a matter of right believing; it is also a matter of right living.

The poetic structure of this book—a feature of most wisdom literature—reveals another basic insight of our ancestors in faith: How something is said is as important as what is said. In addition, parallelism makes the generally short sayings in this book easy to memorize. We would do well to consult Proverbs regularly for good advice, and to remember what we read. To all who care to hear, this book tells of the rewards of virtue and the dangers of vice.

Quick Facts

Author

King Solomon is introduced as the author, probably because of his legendary wisdom. However, the actual author is unknown, writing from the reign of King Solomon (970–931 B.C.) to sometime after the Babylonian Exile (587–538 B.C.).

Of Note

The book is made up of several collections of proverbs.

The Book of Proverbs

Proverbs

TRUST IN THE LORD WITH ALL YOUR HEART" 3.5a

1 The proverbs of Solomon son of David, king of Israel:

Prologue

2 For learning about wisdom and instruction,
  for understanding words of insight,
3 for gaining instruction in wise dealing,
  righteousness, justice, and equity;
4 to teach shrewdness to the simple,
  knowledge and prudence to the young—
5 let the wise also hear and gain in learning,
  and the discerning acquire skill,
6 to understand a proverb and a figure,
  the words of the wise and their riddles.

7 The fear of the LORD is the beginning of
    knowledge;
  fools despise wisdom and instruction.

Warnings against Evil Companions

8 Hear, my child, your father's instruction,
  and do not reject your mother's teaching;
9 for they are a fair garland for your head,
  and pendants for your neck.
10 My child, if sinners entice you,
  do not consent.
11 If they say, "Come with us, let us lie in wait for
    blood;
  let us wantonly ambush the innocent;
12 like Shĕ'ōl let us swallow them alive

and whole, like those who go down to the
    Pit.
13 We shall find all kinds of costly things;
  we shall fill our houses with booty.
14 Throw in your lot among us;
  we will all have one purse"—
15 my child, do not walk in their way,
  keep your foot from their paths;
16 for their feet run to evil,
  and they hurry to shed blood.
17 For in vain is the net baited
  while the bird is looking on;
18 yet they lie in wait—to kill themselves!
  and set an ambush—for their own lives!
19 Such is the end[a] of all who are greedy for gain;
  it takes away the life of its possessors.

The Call of Wisdom

20 Wisdom cries out in the street;
  in the squares she raises her voice.
21 At the busiest corner she cries out;
  at the entrance of the city gates she speaks:
22 "How long, O simple ones, will you love being
    simple?
  How long will scoffers delight in their scoffing
  and fools hate knowledge?
23 Give heed to my reproof;
  I will pour out my thoughts to you;

---

a Gk: Heb *are the ways*

Media Literacy

Our society today has a powerful, persuasive tool. It is called the media. We are influenced in many ways by what we read, watch, and hear in the many forms of modern media.

We might buy things because something we read says it's the best. We might look the other way when someone is being robbed because we see so much violence at the movies that it doesn't seem to bother us. We might dance to the beat of a song and not even realize that the words are suggesting an immoral behavior.

Certainly not all the messages in the media are bad. But to resist the influence of the media's negative messages, we must educate ourselves to watch for them. In Prov 1.10, we read "My child, if sinners entice you, / do not consent." Take time to really think about a message in the media before you choose to follow it. Verse 7 says it best: Only a fool despises wisdom!

▶ **Prov 1.10**

PROV

I will make my words known to you.
24 Because I have called and you refused,
    have stretched out my hand and no one
        heeded,
25 and because you have ignored all my counsel
    and would have none of my reproof,
26 I also will laugh at your calamity;
    I will mock when panic strikes you,
27 when panic strikes you like a storm,
    and your calamity comes like a whirlwind,
    when distress and anguish come upon you.
28 Then they will call upon me, but I will not
        answer;
    they will seek me diligently, but will not
        find me.
29 Because they hated knowledge
    and did not choose the fear of the LORD,
30 would have none of my counsel,
    and despised all my reproof,
31 therefore they shall eat the fruit of their way
    and be sated with their own devices.
32 For waywardness kills the simple,
    and the complacency of fools destroys
        them;
33 but those who listen to me will be secure
    and will live at ease, without dread of
        disaster."

The Value of Wisdom

2 My child, if you accept my words
    and treasure up my commandments
        within you,
2 making your ear attentive to wisdom
    and inclining your heart to understanding;
3 if you indeed cry out for insight,
    and raise your voice for understanding;
4 if you seek it like silver,

and search for it as for hidden treasures—
5 then you will understand the fear of the LORD
    and find the knowledge of God.
6 For the LORD gives wisdom;
    from his mouth come knowledge and
        understanding;
7 he stores up sound wisdom for the upright;
    he is a shield to those who walk
        blamelessly,
8 guarding the paths of justice
    and preserving the way of his faithful ones.
9 Then you will understand righteousness and
        justice
    and equity, every good path;
10 for wisdom will come into your heart,
    and knowledge will be pleasant to your
        soul;
11 prudence will watch over you;
    and understanding will guard you.
12 It will save you from the way of evil,
    from those who speak perversely,
13 who forsake the paths of uprightness
    to walk in the ways of darkness,
14 who rejoice in doing evil
    and delight in the perverseness of evil;
15 those whose paths are crooked,
    and who are devious in their ways.
16 You will be saved from the loose[b] woman,
    from the adulteress with her smooth
        words,
17 who forsakes the partner of her youth
    and forgets her sacred covenant;
18 for her way[c] leads down to death,
    and her paths to the shades;

---

b Heb *strange*   c Cn: Heb *house*

¹⁹ those who go to her never come back,
    nor do they regain the paths of life.

²⁰ Therefore walk in the way of the good,
    and keep to the paths of the just.
²¹ For the upright will abide in the land,
    and the innocent will remain in it;
²² but the wicked will be cut off from the land,
    and the treacherous will be rooted out of it.

Admonition to Trust and Honor God

3 My child, do not forget my teaching,
    but let your heart keep my
        commandments;
² for length of days and years of life
    and abundant welfare they will give you.

³ Do not let loyalty and faithfulness forsake you;
    bind them around your neck,
    write them on the tablet of your heart.
⁴ So you will find favor and good repute
    in the sight of God and of people.

⁵ Trust in the LORD with all your heart,
    and do not rely on your own insight.
⁶ In all your ways acknowledge him,
    and he will make straight your paths.
⁷ Do not be wise in your own eyes;
    fear the LORD, and turn away from evil.
⁸ It will be a healing for your flesh
    and a refreshment for your body.

⁹ Honor the LORD with your substance
    and with the first fruits of all your produce;
¹⁰ then your barns will be filled with plenty,
    and your vats will be bursting with wine.

¹¹ My child, do not despise the LORD's discipline
    or be weary of his reproof,
¹² for the LORD reproves the one he loves,
    as a father the son in whom he delights.

The True Wealth

¹³ Happy are those who find wisdom,
    and those who get understanding,
¹⁴ for her income is better than silver,
    and her revenue better than gold.
¹⁵ She is more precious than jewels,
    and nothing you desire can compare with
        her.
¹⁶ Long life is in her right hand;
    in her left hand are riches and honor.
¹⁷ Her ways are ways of pleasantness,
    and all her paths are peace.
¹⁸ She is a tree of life to those who lay hold
        of her;
    those who hold her fast are called happy.

PRAY IT?
Your Future

Read Prov 3.5–8 and think about your plans for the future. How does God play a part in them? Do they include discernment of (prayerful listening to) God's plans for you? Here are some clues for discerning where God is calling you:

- Pray about your future, and ask for God's direction.
- Look at your talents and interests. These are gifts from God to be used for the good of others as well as yourself.
- Imagine yourself doing whatever you are considering. What feelings surface? Peace and joy are usually signs of God's presence. Excessive anxiety, fear, and shame are usually signs of God's absence.
- Talk with a trusted adult about your options. If this person is wise, she or he will not give you a direct answer but will help you sort out where God is leading.

▶ **Prov 3.5–8**

God's Wisdom in Creation

¹⁹ The LORD by wisdom founded the earth;
    by understanding he established the
        heavens;
²⁰ by his knowledge the deeps broke open,
    and the clouds drop down the dew.

The True Security

²¹ My child, do not let these escape from your
        sight:
    keep sound wisdom and prudence,
²² and they will be life for your soul
    and adornment for your neck.
²³ Then you will walk on your way securely
    and your foot will not stumble.
²⁴ If you sit down,^d you will not be afraid;
    when you lie down, your sleep will be
        sweet.
²⁵ Do not be afraid of sudden panic,
    or of the storm that strikes the wicked;
²⁶ for the LORD will be your confidence
    and will keep your foot from being caught.

---

d Gk: Heb *lie down*

TRUE SECURITY

How do we know how to get going? Where do we get going to? Our faith gives us good advice and wise counsel (Prov 3.21). Prayer keeps us close to God (verse 26). And knowing we have made the right decision is true security.

When the going gets tough, first the tough get faithful, and prayerful, and thoughtful. Then they get going.

▶ Prov 3.21–26

27 Do not withhold good from those to whom it is due,[e]
    when it is in your power to do it.
28 Do not say to your neighbor, "Go, and come again,
    tomorrow I will give it"—when you have it with you.
29 Do not plan harm against your neighbor
    who lives trustingly beside you.
30 Do not quarrel with anyone without cause,
    when no harm has been done to you.
31 Do not envy the violent
    and do not choose any of their ways;
32 for the perverse are an abomination to the LORD,
    but the upright are in his confidence.
33 The LORD's curse is on the house of the wicked,
    but he blesses the abode of the righteous.
34 Toward the scorners he is scornful,
    but to the humble he shows favor.
35 The wise will inherit honor,
    but stubborn fools, disgrace.

Parental Advice

4 Listen, children, to a father's instruction,
    and be attentive, that you may gain[f] insight;
2 for I give you good precepts:
    do not forsake my teaching.
3 When I was a son with my father,
    tender, and my mother's favorite,
4 he taught me, and said to me,
    "Let your heart hold fast my words;
    keep my commandments, and live.
5 Get wisdom; get insight: do not forget, nor turn away

    from the words of my mouth.
6 Do not forsake her, and she will keep you;
    love her, and she will guard you.
7 The beginning of wisdom is this: Get wisdom,
    and whatever else you get, get insight.
8 Prize her highly, and she will exalt you;
    she will honor you if you embrace her.
9 She will place on your head a fair garland;
    she will bestow on you a beautiful crown."

Admonition to Keep to the Right Path

10 Hear, my child, and accept my words,
    that the years of your life may be many.
11 I have taught you the way of wisdom;
    I have led you in the paths of uprightness.
12 When you walk, your step will not be hampered;
    and if you run, you will not stumble.
13 Keep hold of instruction; do not let go;
    guard her, for she is your life.
14 Do not enter the path of the wicked,
    and do not walk in the way of evildoers.
15 Avoid it; do not go on it;
    turn away from it and pass on.
16 For they cannot sleep unless they have done wrong;
    they are robbed of sleep unless they have made someone stumble.
17 For they eat the bread of wickedness
    and drink the wine of violence.
18 But the path of the righteous is like the light of dawn,
    which shines brighter and brighter until full day.
19 The way of the wicked is like deep darkness;
    they do not know what they stumble over.
20 My child, be attentive to my words;
    incline your ear to my sayings.
21 Do not let them escape from your sight;
    keep them within your heart.
22 For they are life to those who find them,
    and healing to all their flesh.
23 Keep your heart with all vigilance,
    for from it flow the springs of life.
24 Put away from you crooked speech,
    and put devious talk far from you.
25 Let your eyes look directly forward,
    and your gaze be straight before you.
26 Keep straight the path of your feet,
    and all your ways will be sure.
27 Do not swerve to the right or to the left;
    turn your foot away from evil.

---

e Heb *from its owners*   f Heb *know*

PROV

Warning against Impurity and Infidelity

5 My child, be attentive to my wisdom;
    incline your ear to my understanding,

2 so that you may hold on to prudence,
    and your lips may guard knowledge.

3 For the lips of a loose*g* woman drip honey,
    and her speech is smoother than oil;

4 but in the end she is bitter as wormwood,
    sharp as a two-edged sword.

5 Her feet go down to death;
    her steps follow the path to Shĕ′ŏl.

6 She does not keep straight to the path of life;
    her ways wander, and she does not
      know it.

7 And now, my child,*h* listen to me,
    and do not depart from the words of my
      mouth.

8 Keep your way far from her,
    and do not go near the door of her house;

9 or you will give your honor to others,
    and your years to the merciless,

10 and strangers will take their fill of your wealth,
    and your labors will go to the house of an
      alien;

11 and at the end of your life you will groan,
    when your flesh and body are consumed,

12 and you say, "Oh, how I hated discipline,
    and my heart despised reproof!

13 I did not listen to the voice of my teachers
    or incline my ear to my instructors.

14 Now I am at the point of utter ruin
    in the public assembly."

15 Drink water from your own cistern,
    flowing water from your own well.

16 Should your springs be scattered abroad,
streams of water in the streets?

17 Let them be for yourself alone,
    and not for sharing with strangers.

18 Let your fountain be blessed,
    and rejoice in the wife of your youth,

19   a lovely deer, a graceful doe.
May her breasts satisfy you at all times;
    may you be intoxicated always by her love.

20 Why should you be intoxicated, my son, by
      another woman
    and embrace the bosom of an adulteress?

21 For human ways are under the eyes of the
      LORD,
    and he examines all their paths.

22 The iniquities of the wicked ensnare them,
    and they are caught in the toils of their sin.

23 They die for lack of discipline,
    and because of their great folly they are lost.

Practical Admonitions

6 My child, if you have given your pledge to
    your neighbor,
    if you have bound yourself to another,*i*

2 you are snared by the utterance of your lips,*j*
    caught by the words of your mouth.

3 So do this, my child, and save yourself,
    for you have come into your neighbor's
      power:
    go, hurry,*k* and plead with your neighbor.

4 Give your eyes no sleep
    and your eyelids no slumber;

5 save yourself like a gazelle from the hunter,*l*
    like a bird from the hand of the fowler.

---

g Heb *strange*   *h* Gk Vg: Heb *children*   *i* Or *a stranger*   *j* Cn
Compare Gk Syr: Heb *the words of your mouth*   *k* Or *humble
yourself*   *l* Cn: Heb *from the hand*

All the Days of My Life

LIVE IT!

The words "all the days of my life" have been repeated by countless couples on their wedding day, and for some of those couples, they are prophetic. The husband and wife will be together till death separates them, and then they will be reunited in heaven. Many couples make it through all the trials and difficulties and are around to celebrate their twenty-fifth and fiftieth anniversaries.

The writer of Prov 5.15–23 is warning men, in particular, against adultery, which remains, even today, a primary reason marriages break up. But the author's wish in verse 19 could easily be rephrased to address both husbands and wives: "May you always be invigorated by each other's love."

What a wonderful wedding toast!

▶ Prov 5.15–23

6 Go to the ant, you lazybones;
  consider its ways, and be wise.
7 Without having any chief
  or officer or ruler,
8 it prepares its food in summer,
  and gathers its sustenance in harvest.
9 How long will you lie there, O lazybones?
  When will you rise from your sleep?
10 A little sleep, a little slumber,
   a little folding of the hands to rest,
11 and poverty will come upon you like a robber,
   and want, like an armed warrior.

12 A scoundrel and a villain
   goes around with crooked speech,
13 winking the eyes, shuffling the feet,
   pointing the fingers,
14 with perverted mind devising evil,
   continually sowing discord;
15 on such a one calamity will descend suddenly;
   in a moment, damage beyond repair.

16 There are six things that the LORD hates,
   seven that are an abomination to him:
17 haughty eyes, a lying tongue,
   and hands that shed innocent blood,
18 a heart that devises wicked plans,
   feet that hurry to run to evil,

19 a lying witness who testifies falsely,
   and one who sows discord in a family.
20 My child, keep your father's commandment,
   and do not forsake your mother's teaching.
21 Bind them upon your heart always;
   tie them around your neck.
22 When you walk, they^m will lead you;
   when you lie down, they^m will watch over
      you;
   and when you awake, they^m will talk with
      you.

23 For the commandment is a lamp and the
      teaching a light,
   and the reproofs of discipline are the way of
      life,
24 to preserve you from the wife of another,^n
   from the smooth tongue of the adulteress.
25 Do not desire her beauty in your heart,
   and do not let her capture you with her
      eyelashes;
26 for a prostitute's fee is only a loaf of bread,^o
   but the wife of another stalks a man's very
      life.
27 Can fire be carried in the bosom
   without burning one's clothes?
28 Or can one walk on hot coals
   without scorching the feet?
29 So is he who sleeps with his neighbor's wife;
   no one who touches her will go
      unpunished.
30 Thieves are not despised who steal only
   to satisfy their appetite when they are hungry.
31 Yet if they are caught, they will pay sevenfold;
   they will forfeit all the goods of their house.
32 But he who commits adultery has no sense;
   he who does it destroys himself.
33 He will get wounds and dishonor,
   and his disgrace will not be wiped away.
34 For jealousy arouses a husband's fury,
   and he shows no restraint when he takes
      revenge.
35 He will accept no compensation,
   and refuses a bribe no matter how great.

The False Attractions of Adultery

7 My child, keep my words
  and store up my commandments
     with you;

---

m Heb *it*   n Gk: MT *the evil woman*   o Cn Compare Gk Syr
Vg Tg: Heb *for because of a harlot to a piece of bread*

Leaders with Character

Look at the list of the things the LORD hates in Prov 6.17–19. It looks like a popular description of a corrupt politician or businessperson! Now take the list and put it in the positive: humble eyes, a truthful tongue, hands that protect the innocent, a heart that plans good, feet that hurry to help, a truthful witness, and someone who brings harmony to families. That's the kind of leader everyone wants!

The author of Proverbs is constantly reminding us to be of good character. Especially when you are called to be a leader—and we all will be at some time in our life—keep the advice of Proverbs in mind. Be a leader of character by doing the things the LORD loves, not the things the LORD hates.

▸ Prov 6.16–19

2 keep my commandments and live,
    keep my teachings as the apple of your eye;
3 bind them on your fingers,
    write them on the tablet of your heart.
4 Say to wisdom, "You are my sister,"
    and call insight your intimate friend,
5 that they may keep you from the loose *p*
        woman,
    from the adulteress with her smooth words.

6 For at the window of my house
    I looked out through my lattice,
7 and I saw among the simple ones,
    I observed among the youths,
    a young man without sense,
8 passing along the street near her corner,
    taking the road to her house
9 in the twilight, in the evening,
    at the time of night and darkness.

10 Then a woman comes toward him,
    decked out like a prostitute, wily of heart.*q*
11 She is loud and wayward;
    her feet do not stay at home;
12 now in the street, now in the squares,
    and at every corner she lies in wait.
13 She seizes him and kisses him,
    and with impudent face she says to him:
14 "I had to offer sacrifices,
    and today I have paid my vows;
15 so now I have come out to meet you,
    to seek you eagerly, and I have found you!
16 I have decked my couch with coverings,
    colored spreads of Egyptian linen;
17 I have perfumed my bed with myrrh,
    aloes, and cinnamon.
18 Come, let us take our fill of love until morning;
    let us delight ourselves with love.
19 For my husband is not at home;
    he has gone on a long journey.
20 He took a bag of money with him;
    he will not come home until full moon."

21 With much seductive speech she persuades
        him;
    with her smooth talk she compels him.
22 Right away he follows her,
    and goes like an ox to the slaughter,
or bounds like a stag toward the trap*r*
23   until an arrow pierces its entrails.
He is like a bird rushing into a snare,
    not knowing that it will cost him his life.

24 And now, my children, listen to me,
    and be attentive to the words of my mouth.
25 Do not let your hearts turn aside to her ways;
    do not stray into her paths.

26 For many are those she has laid low,
    and numerous are her victims.
27 Her house is the way to Shĕ′ōl,
    going down to the chambers of death.

The Gifts of Wisdom

8 Does not wisdom call,
    and does not understanding raise
        her voice?
2 On the heights, beside the way,
    at the crossroads she takes her stand;
3 beside the gates in front of the town,
    at the entrance of the portals she cries out:
4 "To you, O people, I call,
    and my cry is to all that live.
5 O simple ones, learn prudence;
    acquire intelligence, you who lack it.
6 Hear, for I will speak noble things,
    and from my lips will come what is right;
7 for my mouth will utter truth;
    wickedness is an abomination to my lips.
8 All the words of my mouth are righteous;
    there is nothing twisted or crooked in them.
9 They are all straight to one who understands
    and right to those who find knowledge.
10 Take my instruction instead of silver,

---

p Heb *strange*   *q* Meaning of Heb uncertain   *r* Cn Compare
Gk: Meaning of Heb uncertain

PRAY IT!

The Gifts of Wisdom

To gain wisdom, you have to hunger for
it, really want it, and actively seek it
out. You will not find it by yourself: wisdom is found where other people are—
"beside the gates" where people meet
(Prov 8.3).

    Wisdom's gifts described in Proverbs,
chapter 8, include prudence, insight,
truth, knowledge, instruction or understanding, strength, and justice. Which of
these gifts do you have? Which would you
like to develop? Who could help you?
Write a prayer to the Holy Spirit, asking
for the strength and courage to seek out
these gifts.

▶ Prov 8.1–21

Introducing...

►LADY WISDOM

As you read the description of wisdom in Prov 8.1—9.6, you might get the impression that you are reading about a goddess. But that's not the case. The wisdom writers borrowed from neighboring cultures the idea of describing wisdom as a beautiful and eternal aspect of God. They exquisitely embodied the idea of wisdom in the figure of Lady Wisdom. Lady Wisdom comes from God. She was present at the Creation of the world, and she has a special understanding of the world and its workings. For the wisdom writers, Lady Wisdom was an aspect of God that wise people would want to pursue because she reveals the right ways to live and behave.

Prov 8.1—9.6

and knowledge rather than choice gold;
11 for wisdom is better than jewels,
  and all that you may desire cannot compare
    with her.
12 I, wisdom, live with prudence,[s]
  and I attain knowledge and discretion.
13 The fear of the LORD is hatred of evil.
  Pride and arrogance and the way of evil
    and perverted speech I hate.
14 I have good advice and sound wisdom;
  I have insight, I have strength.
15 By me kings reign,
  and rulers decree what is just;
16 by me rulers rule,
  and nobles, all who govern rightly.
17 I love those who love me,
  and those who seek me diligently find me.
18 Riches and honor are with me,
  enduring wealth and prosperity.
19 My fruit is better than gold, even fine gold,
  and my yield than choice silver.
20 I walk in the way of righteousness,
  along the paths of justice,
21 endowing with wealth those who love me,
  and filling their treasuries.

Wisdom's Part in Creation
(Cp Jn 1.1-3)

22 The LORD created me at the beginning[t] of his
    work,[u]
  the first of his acts of long ago.
23 Ages ago I was set up,
  at the first, before the beginning of the
    earth.
24 When there were no depths I was brought
    forth,
  when there were no springs abounding with
    water.

25 Before the mountains had been shaped,
  before the hills, I was brought forth—
26 when he had not yet made earth and fields,[s]
  or the world's first bits of soil.
27 When he established the heavens, I was
    there,
  when he drew a circle on the face of the
    deep,
28 when he made firm the skies above,
  when he established the fountains of the
    deep,
29 when he assigned to the sea its limit,
  so that the waters might not transgress his
    command,
  when he marked out the foundations of the
    earth,
30   then I was beside him, like a master
    worker;[v]
and I was daily his[w] delight,
  rejoicing before him always,
31 rejoicing in his inhabited world
  and delighting in the human race.

32 "And now, my children, listen to me:
  happy are those who keep my ways.
33 Hear instruction and be wise,
  and do not neglect it.
34 Happy is the one who listens to me,
  watching daily at my gates,
  waiting beside my doors.
35 For whoever finds me finds life
  and obtains favor from the LORD;
36 but those who miss me injure themselves;
  all who hate me love death."

---

[s] Meaning of Heb uncertain   [t] Or *me as the beginning*
[u] Heb *way*   [v] Another reading is *little child*   [w] Gk: Heb
lacks *his*

Wisdom's Feast

9 Wisdom has built her house,
 she has hewn her seven pillars.
2 She has slaughtered her animals, she has
 mixed her wine,
 she has also set her table.
3 She has sent out her servant-girls, she calls
 from the highest places in the town,
4 "You that are simple, turn in here!"
 To those without sense she says,
5 "Come, eat of my bread
 and drink of the wine I have mixed.
6 Lay aside immaturity,ˣ and live,
 and walk in the way of insight."

General Maxims

7 Whoever corrects a scoffer wins abuse;
 whoever rebukes the wicked gets hurt.
8 A scoffer who is rebuked will only hate you;
 the wise, when rebuked, will love you.
9 Give instructionʸ to the wise, and they will
 become wiser still;
 teach the righteous and they will gain in
 learning.
10 The fear of the LORD is the beginning of
 wisdom,
 and the knowledge of the Holy One is
 insight.

The fear of the **Lord**
is the beginning of

wisdom,

and the knowledge
of the **Holy One** is

insight

9.10

11 For by me your days will be multiplied,
 and years will be added to your life.
12 If you are wise, you are wise for yourself;
 if you scoff, you alone will bear it.

Folly's Invitation and Promise

13 The foolish woman is loud;
 she is ignorant and knows nothing.
14 She sits at the door of her house,
 on a seat at the high places of the town,
15 calling to those who pass by,
 who are going straight on their way,
16 "You who are simple, turn in here!"
 And to those without sense she says,
17 "Stolen water is sweet,
 and bread eaten in secret is pleasant."
18 But they do not know that the deadᶻ are there,
 that her guests are in the depths of Shĕ'ōl.

Wise Sayings of Solomon

10 The proverbs of Solomon.

A wise child makes a glad father,
 but a foolish child is a mother's grief.
2 Treasures gained by wickedness do not profit,
 but righteousness delivers from death.
3 The LORD does not let the righteous go hungry,
 but he thwarts the craving of the wicked.
4 A slack hand causes poverty,
 but the hand of the diligent makes rich.
5 A child who gathers in summer is prudent,
 but a child who sleeps in harvest brings
 shame.
6 Blessings are on the head of the righteous,
 but the mouth of the wicked conceals
 violence.
7 The memory of the righteous is a blessing,
 but the name of the wicked will rot.
8 The wise of heart will heed commandments,
 but a babbling fool will come to ruin.
9 Whoever walks in integrity walks securely,
 but whoever follows perverse ways will be
 found out.
10 Whoever winks the eye causes trouble,
 but the one who rebukes boldly makes
 peace.ᵃ
11 The mouth of the righteous is a fountain of
 life,
 but the mouth of the wicked conceals
 violence.
12 Hatred stirs up strife,
 but love covers all offenses.
13 On the lips of one who has understanding
 wisdom is found,
 but a rod is for the back of one who lacks
 sense.
14 The wise lay up knowledge,
 but the babbling of a fool brings ruin near.
15 The wealth of the rich is their fortress;
 the poverty of the poor is their ruin.
16 The wage of the righteous leads to life,
 the gain of the wicked to sin.

---

x Or *simpleness*   *y* Heb lacks *instruction*   *z* Heb *shades*
a Gk: Heb *but a babbling fool will come to ruin*

did you KNOW?

Live Justly

In Proverbs 10, we are given a list of the benefits of being a just person. In this chapter, a just person is one who is fair, right, moral, honest, and truthful. We read that a just person not only receives blessings, life, wisdom, and joy; he or she, by acting justly, also fulfills God's will.

Throughout the New Testament, Jesus tells his followers that his way is the just way. The parables of the Good Samaritan (see Lk 10.29-37) and the Unforgiving Servant (see Mt 18.21-35) are reminders of this. Living as a just person may not be easy, but it is what Christ asks of his followers.

▸ **Proverbs, chapter 10**

17 Whoever heeds instruction is on the path to
     life,
     but one who rejects a rebuke goes astray.
18 Lying lips conceal hatred,
     and whoever utters slander is a fool.
19 When words are many, transgression is not
     lacking,
     but the prudent are restrained in speech.
20 The tongue of the righteous is choice silver;
     the mind of the wicked is of little worth.
21 The lips of the righteous feed many,

     but fools die for lack of sense.
22 The blessing of the LORD makes rich,
     and he adds no sorrow with it.[b]
23 Doing wrong is like sport to a fool,
     but wise conduct is pleasure to a person of
     understanding.
24 What the wicked dread will come upon them,
     but the desire of the righteous will be
     granted.
25 When the tempest passes, the wicked are no
     more,
     but the righteous are established forever.
26 Like vinegar to the teeth, and smoke to the
     eyes,
     so are the lazy to their employers.
27 The fear of the LORD prolongs life,
     but the years of the wicked will be short.
28 The hope of the righteous ends in gladness,
     but the expectation of the wicked comes to
     nothing.
29 The way of the LORD is a stronghold for the
     upright,
     but destruction for evildoers.
30 The righteous will never be removed,
     but the wicked will not remain in the land.
31 The mouth of the righteous brings forth
     wisdom,
     but the perverse tongue will be cut off.
32 The lips of the righteous know what is
     acceptable,
     but the mouth of the wicked what is
     perverse.

11 A false balance is an abomination to
     the LORD,
     but an accurate weight is his delight.

---

b Or *and toil adds nothing to it*

Doing wrong is like sport to a fool,

but wise conduct is pleasure to a person of understanding.

10.23

2 When pride comes, then comes disgrace;
    but wisdom is with the humble.
3 The integrity of the upright guides them,
    but the crookedness of the treacherous
    destroys them.
4 Riches do not profit in the day of wrath,
    but righteousness delivers from death.
5 The righteousness of the blameless keeps their
    ways straight,
    but the wicked fall by their own
    wickedness.
6 The righteousness of the upright saves them,
    but the treacherous are taken captive by
    their schemes.
7 When the wicked die, their hope perishes,
    and the expectation of the godless comes to
    nothing.
8 The righteous are delivered from trouble,
    and the wicked get into it instead.
9 With their mouths the godless would destroy
    their neighbors,
    but by knowledge the righteous are
    delivered.
10 When it goes well with the righteous, the city
    rejoices;
    and when the wicked perish, there is
    jubilation.
11 By the blessing of the upright a city is exalted,
    but it is overthrown by the mouth of the
    wicked.
12 Whoever belittles another lacks sense,
    but an intelligent person remains silent.
13 A gossip goes about telling secrets,
    but one who is trustworthy in spirit keeps a
    confidence.
14 Where there is no guidance, a nation*c* falls,
    but in an abundance of counselors there is
    safety.
15 To guarantee loans for a stranger brings
    trouble,
    but there is safety in refusing to do so.
16 A gracious woman gets honor,
    but she who hates virtue is covered with
    shame.*d*
    The timid become destitute,*e*
    but the aggressive gain riches.
17 Those who are kind reward themselves,
    but the cruel do themselves harm.
18 The wicked earn no real gain,
    but those who sow righteousness get a true
    reward.
19 Whoever is steadfast in righteousness will live,
    but whoever pursues evil will die.
20 Crooked minds are an abomination to the
    LORD,
    but those of blameless ways are his delight.
21 Be assured, the wicked will not go unpunished,

but those who are righteous will escape.
22 Like a gold ring in a pig's snout
    is a beautiful woman without good sense.
23 The desire of the righteous ends only in good;
    the expectation of the wicked in wrath.
24 Some give freely, yet grow all the richer;
    others withhold what is due, and only
    suffer want.
25 A generous person will be enriched,
    and one who gives water will get water.
26 The people curse those who hold back grain,
    but a blessing is on the head of those who
    sell it.
27 Whoever diligently seeks good seeks favor,
    but evil comes to the one who searches
    for it.
28 Those who trust in their riches will wither,*f*
    but the righteous will flourish like green
    leaves.
29 Those who trouble their households will
    inherit wind,
    and the fool will be servant to the wise.
30 The fruit of the righteous is a tree of life,
    but violence*g* takes lives away.

c Or *an army*   *d* Compare Gk Syr: Heb lacks *but she . . .
shame*   *e* Gk: Heb lacks *The timid . . . destitute*   *f* Cn:
Heb *fall*   *g* Cn Compare Gk Syr: Heb *a wise man*

PRAY IT!
Gossip

Oh, God, forgive me!
    I gossiped about someone's family
today.
I don't even know if what I said was true.
But it made me feel important to tell it to
    my friends.
Help me keep my mouth shut!
When someone tells me a secret, seal it into
    my heart,
and keep it away from my lips!
Gossip can seem like fun, but it hurts
    people.
I can't stop thinking about how the target
    of my gossip would feel
if she or he knew what I said about the
    family.
Oh, God, teach me to be trustworthy!
Amen.

▶ **Prov 11.13**

31 If the righteous are repaid on earth,
how much more the wicked and the sinner!

12

Whoever loves discipline loves
knowledge,
but those who hate to be rebuked are
stupid.
2 The good obtain favor from the LORD,
but those who devise evil he condemns.
3 No one finds security by wickedness,
but the root of the righteous will never be
moved.
4 A good wife is the crown of her husband,
but she who brings shame is like rottenness
in his bones.
5 The thoughts of the righteous are just;
the advice of the wicked is treacherous.
6 The words of the wicked are a deadly ambush,
but the speech of the upright delivers them.
7 The wicked are overthrown and are no more,
but the house of the righteous will stand.
8 One is commended for good sense,
but a perverse mind is despised.
9 Better to be despised and have a servant,
than to be self-important and lack food.
10 The righteous know the needs of their animals,
but the mercy of the wicked is cruel.
11 Those who till their land will have plenty of
food,
but those who follow worthless pursuits
have no sense.
12 The wicked covet the proceeds of wickedness,[h]
but the root of the righteous bears fruit.
13 The evil are ensnared by the transgression of
their lips,
but the righteous escape from trouble.
14 From the fruit of the mouth one is filled with
good things,
and manual labor has its reward.
15 Fools think their own way is right,
but the wise listen to advice.
16 Fools show their anger at once,
but the prudent ignore an insult.
17 Whoever speaks the truth gives honest
evidence,
but a false witness speaks deceitfully.
18 Rash words are like sword thrusts,
but the tongue of the wise brings healing.
19 Truthful lips endure forever,
but a lying tongue lasts only a moment.
20 Deceit is in the mind of those who plan evil,
but those who counsel peace have joy.
21 No harm happens to the righteous,
but the wicked are filled with trouble.
22 Lying lips are an abomination to the LORD,
but those who act faithfully are his delight.
23 One who is clever conceals knowledge,
but the mind of a fool[i] broadcasts folly.

24 The hand of the diligent will rule,
while the lazy will be put to forced labor.
25 Anxiety weighs down the human heart,
but a good word cheers it up.
26 The righteous gives good advice to friends,[j]
but the way of the wicked leads astray.
27 The lazy do not roast[k] their game,
but the diligent obtain precious wealth.[k]
28 In the path of righteousness there is life,
in walking its path there is no death.

13

A wise child loves discipline,[l]
but a scoffer does not listen to
rebuke.
2 From the fruit of their words good persons eat
good things,
but the desire of the treacherous is for
wrongdoing.
3 Those who guard their mouths preserve their
lives;
those who open wide their lips come to
ruin.
4 The appetite of the lazy craves, and gets
nothing,
while the appetite of the diligent is richly
supplied.
5 The righteous hate falsehood,
but the wicked act shamefully and
disgracefully.
6 Righteousness guards one whose way is
upright,
but sin overthrows the wicked.
7 Some pretend to be rich, yet have nothing;
others pretend to be poor, yet have great
wealth.
8 Wealth is a ransom for a person's life,
but the poor get no threats.
9 The light of the righteous rejoices,
but the lamp of the wicked goes out.
10 By insolence the heedless make strife,
but wisdom is with those who take advice.
11 Wealth hastily gotten[m] will dwindle,
but those who gather little by little will
increase it.
12 Hope deferred makes the heart sick,
but a desire fulfilled is a tree of life.
13 Those who despise the word bring destruction
on themselves,
but those who respect the commandment
will be rewarded.
14 The teaching of the wise is a fountain of life,
so that one may avoid the snares of death.
15 Good sense wins favor,

---

h Or covet the catch of the wicked   i Heb the heart of fools
j Syr: Meaning of Heb uncertain   k Meaning of Heb
uncertain   l Cn: Heb A wise child the discipline of his
father   m Gk Vg: Heb from vanity

Break the Cycle of Hopelessness

When Lucy joined the gang, she thought she had finally found a place to belong and that her new "family" would do anything for her. The gang offered many things she didn't find at home or in school. She spent a great deal of time with her new friends. Before long, they were encouraging her to do things she didn't feel comfortable doing. When they were able to sell what she had stolen, the money was good, and the gang enjoyed freely spending it. Lucy is now in prison.

Proverbs 13.11 tells us that quick wealth doesn't last. Verse 20 says that the companion of fools will not do well in life. For many youth in detention centers or prisons, Lucy's story sounds familiar. That's wisdom they and many others—maybe we too—need to hear.

In the absence of caring adults, healthy role models, and detention center ministers, the cycle of hopelessness is free to continue and often results in stories like Lucy's. Find out how your parish or youth group can help youth and other young people in prison. Help them break the cycle of hopelessness.

▸ **Prov 13.11–20**

PROV

but the way of the faithless is their ruin.[n]

16 The clever do all things intelligently,
   but the fool displays folly.
17 A bad messenger brings trouble,
   but a faithful envoy, healing.
18 Poverty and disgrace are for the one who
   ignores instruction,
   but one who heeds reproof is honored.
19 A desire realized is sweet to the soul,
   but to turn away from evil is an
   abomination to fools.
20 Whoever walks with the wise becomes wise,
   but the companion of fools suffers harm.
21 Misfortune pursues sinners,
   but prosperity rewards the righteous.
22 The good leave an inheritance to their
   children's children,
   but the sinner's wealth is laid up for the
   righteous.
23 The field of the poor may yield much food,
   but it is swept away through injustice.
24 Those who spare the rod hate their
   children,
   but those who love them are diligent to
   discipline them.
25 The righteous have enough to satisfy their
   appetite,
   but the belly of the wicked is empty.

14 The wise woman[o] builds her house,
   but the foolish tears it down with her
   own hands.
2 Those who walk uprightly fear the LORD,
   but one who is devious in conduct despises
   him.
3 The talk of fools is a rod for their backs,[p]

but the lips of the wise preserve them.
4 Where there are no oxen, there is no grain;
   abundant crops come by the strength
   of the ox.
5 A faithful witness does not lie,
   but a false witness breathes out lies.
6 A scoffer seeks wisdom in vain,
   but knowledge is easy for one who
   understands.
7 Leave the presence of a fool,
   for there you do not find words of
   knowledge.
8 It is the wisdom of the clever to understand
   where they go,
   but the folly of fools misleads.
9 Fools mock at the guilt offering,[q]
   but the upright enjoy God's favor.
10 The heart knows its own bitterness,
   and no stranger shares its joy.
11 The house of the wicked is destroyed,
   but the tent of the upright flourishes.
12 There is a way that seems right to a person,
   but its end is the way to death.[r]
13 Even in laughter the heart is sad,
   and the end of joy is grief.
14 The perverse get what their ways deserve,
   and the good, what their deeds deserve.[s]
15 The simple believe everything,
   but the clever consider their steps.
16 The wise are cautious and turn away from evil,

---

n Cn Compare Gk Syr Vg Tg: Heb *is enduring*   o Heb
Wisdom of women   p Cn: Heb *a rod of pride*   q Meaning of
Heb uncertain   r Heb *ways of death*   s Cn: Heb *from
upon him*

but the fool throws off restraint and is
    careless.
17 One who is quick-tempered acts foolishly,
    and the schemer is hated.
18 The simple are adorned with^t folly,
    but the clever are crowned with knowledge.
19 The evil bow down before the good,
    the wicked at the gates of the righteous.
20 The poor are disliked even by their neighbors,
    but the rich have many friends.
21 Those who despise their neighbors are sinners,
    but happy are those who are kind to the
    poor.
22 Do they not err that plan evil?
    Those who plan good find loyalty and
    faithfulness.
23 In all toil there is profit,
    but mere talk leads only to poverty.
24 The crown of the wise is their wisdom,^u
    but folly is the garland^v of fools.
25 A truthful witness saves lives,
    but one who utters lies is a betrayer.
26 In the fear of the Lord one has strong
    confidence,
    and one's children will have a refuge.
27 The fear of the Lord is a fountain of life,
    so that one may avoid the snares of death.
28 The glory of a king is a multitude of people;
    without people a prince is ruined.
29 Whoever is slow to anger has great
    understanding,
    but one who has a hasty temper exalts folly.
30 A tranquil mind gives life to the flesh,
    but passion makes the bones rot.
31 Those who oppress the poor insult their Maker,
    but those who are kind to the needy honor
    him.
32 The wicked are overthrown by their evildoing,
    but the righteous find a refuge in their
    integrity.^w
33 Wisdom is at home in the mind of one who
    has understanding,
    but it is not^x known in the heart of fools.
34 Righteousness exalts a nation,
    but sin is a reproach to any people.
35 A servant who deals wisely has the king's favor,
    but his wrath falls on one who acts
    shamefully.

15

A soft answer turns away wrath,
    but a harsh word stirs up anger.
2 The tongue of the wise dispenses knowledge,^y
    but the mouths of fools pour out folly.
3 The eyes of the Lord are in every place,
    keeping watch on the evil and the good.
4 A gentle tongue is a tree of life,
    but perverseness in it breaks the spirit.
5 A fool despises a parent's instruction,

but the one who heeds admonition is
    prudent.
6 In the house of the righteous there is much
    treasure,
    but trouble befalls the income of the
    wicked.
7 The lips of the wise spread knowledge;
    not so the minds of fools.
8 The sacrifice of the wicked is an abomination
    to the Lord,
    but the prayer of the upright is his delight.
9 The way of the wicked is an abomination to
    the Lord,
    but he loves the one who pursues
    righteousness.
10 There is severe discipline for one who forsakes
    the way,
    but one who hates a rebuke will die.
11 Shĕ'ōl and A·bad'don lie open before the Lord,
    how much more human hearts!
12 Scoffers do not like to be rebuked;
    they will not go to the wise.
13 A glad heart makes a cheerful countenance,
    but by sorrow of heart the spirit is broken.
14 The mind of one who has understanding seeks
    knowledge,
    but the mouths of fools feed on folly.
15 All the days of the poor are hard,
    but a cheerful heart has a continual feast.
16 Better is a little with the fear of the Lord
    than great treasure and trouble with it.
17 Better is a dinner of vegetables where love is
    than a fatted ox and hatred with it.
18 Those who are hot-tempered stir up strife,
    but those who are slow to anger calm
    contention.
19 The way of the lazy is overgrown with thorns,
    but the path of the upright is a level
    highway.
20 A wise child makes a glad father,
    but the foolish despise their mothers.
21 Folly is a joy to one who has no sense,
    but a person of understanding walks
    straight ahead.
22 Without counsel, plans go wrong,
    but with many advisers they succeed.
23 To make an apt answer is a joy to anyone,
    and a word in season, how good it is!
24 For the wise the path of life leads upward,
    in order to avoid Shĕ'ōl below.
25 The Lord tears down the house of the proud,
    but maintains the widow's boundaries.
26 Evil plans are an abomination to the Lord,

---

^t Or *inherit* ^u Cn Compare Gk: Heb *riches* ^v Cn: Heb *is
the folly* ^w Gk Syr: Heb *in their death* ^x Gk Syr: Heb
lacks *not* ^y Cn: Heb *makes knowledge good*

but gracious words are pure.

27 Those who are greedy for unjust gain make
     trouble for their households,
   but those who hate bribes will live.
28 The mind of the righteous ponders how to
     answer,
   but the mouth of the wicked pours out evil.
29 The LORD is far from the wicked,
   but he hears the prayer of the righteous.
30 The light of the eyes rejoices the heart,
   and good news refreshes the body.
31 The ear that heeds wholesome admonition
   will lodge among the wise.
32 Those who ignore instruction despise
     themselves,
   but those who heed admonition gain
     understanding.
33 The fear of the LORD is instruction in wisdom,
   and humility goes before honor.

16 The plans of the mind belong to
         mortals,
   but the answer of the tongue is from the
     LORD.
2 All one's ways may be pure in one's own eyes,
   but the LORD weighs the spirit.
3 Commit your work to the LORD,
   and your plans will be established.

PRAY IT!

Offering Your Day
to God

Follow the advice of Prov 16.3, and start
each day with a prayer like this one:

*Dearest LORD, today I offer you all my
thoughts, deeds, and words. Let everything I
do reflect your love and goodness. Amen.*

▶ **Prov 16.3**

4 The LORD has made everything for its purpose,
   even the wicked for the day of trouble.
5 All those who are arrogant are an abomination
     to the LORD;
   be assured, they will not go unpunished.
6 By loyalty and faithfulness iniquity is atoned
     for,
   and by the fear of the LORD one avoids evil.
7 When the ways of people please the LORD,
   he causes even their enemies to be at peace
     with them.

8 Better is a little with righteousness
   than large income with injustice.
9 The human mind plans the way,
   but the LORD directs the steps.
10 Inspired decisions are on the lips of a king;
   his mouth does not sin in judgment.
11 Honest balances and scales are the LORD's;
   all the weights in the bag are his work.
12 It is an abomination to kings to do evil,
   for the throne is established by
     righteousness.
13 Righteous lips are the delight of a king,
   and he loves those who speak what is right.
14 A king's wrath is a messenger of death,
   and whoever is wise will appease it.
15 In the light of a king's face there is life,
   and his favor is like the clouds that bring
     the spring rain.
16 How much better to get wisdom than gold!
   To get understanding is to be chosen rather
     than silver.
17 The highway of the upright avoids evil;
   those who guard their way preserve their
     lives.
18 Pride goes before destruction,
   and a haughty spirit before a fall.
19 It is better to be of a lowly spirit among the
     poor
   than to divide the spoil with the proud.
20 Those who are attentive to a matter will
     prosper,
   and happy are those who trust in the LORD.
21 The wise of heart is called perceptive,
   and pleasant speech increases
     persuasiveness.
22 Wisdom is a fountain of life to one who has it,
   but folly is the punishment of fools.
23 The mind of the wise makes their speech
     judicious,
   and adds persuasiveness to their lips.
24 Pleasant words are like a honeycomb,
   sweetness to the soul and health to the
     body.
25 Sometimes there is a way that seems to be
     right,
   but in the end it is the way to death.
26 The appetite of workers works for them;
   their hunger urges them on.
27 Scoundrels concoct evil,
   and their speech is like a scorching fire.
28 A perverse person spreads strife,
   and a whisperer separates close friends.
29 The violent entice their neighbors,
   and lead them in a way that is not good.
30 One who winks the eyes plans[z] perverse things;

───────────────────────

z Gk Syr Vg Tg: Heb *to plan*

P
R
O
V

one who compresses the lips brings evil to
    pass.
31 Gray hair is a crown of glory;
    it is gained in a righteous life.
32 One who is slow to anger is better than the mighty,
    and one whose temper is controlled than
      one who captures a city.
33 The lot is cast into the lap,
    but the decision is the LORD's alone.

17 Better is a dry morsel with quiet
      than a house full of feasting with
        strife.
2 A slave who deals wisely will rule over a child
    who acts shamefully,
    and will share the inheritance as one of the
      family.
3 The crucible is for silver, and the furnace is for
    gold,
    but the LORD tests the heart.
4 An evildoer listens to wicked lips;
    and a liar gives heed to a mischievous
      tongue.
5 Those who mock the poor insult their Maker;
    those who are glad at calamity will not go
      unpunished.
6 Grandchildren are the crown of the aged,
    and the glory of children is their parents.
7 Fine speech is not becoming to a fool;
    still less is false speech to a ruler.*a*
8 A bribe is like a magic stone in the eyes of
      those who give it;
    wherever they turn they prosper.
9 One who forgives an affront fosters friendship,
    but one who dwells on disputes will
      alienate a friend.

10 A rebuke strikes deeper into a discerning
      person
    than a hundred blows into a fool.
11 Evil people seek only rebellion,
    but a cruel messenger will be sent against
      them.
12 Better to meet a she-bear robbed of its cubs
    than to confront a fool immersed in folly.
13 Evil will not depart from the house
    of one who returns evil for good.
14 The beginning of strife is like letting out water;
    so stop before the quarrel breaks out.
15 One who justifies the wicked and one who
      condemns the righteous
    are both alike an abomination to the LORD.
16 Why should fools have a price in hand
    to buy wisdom, when they have no mind to
      learn?
17 A friend loves at all times,
    and kinsfolk are born to share adversity.
18 It is senseless to give a pledge,
    to become surety for a neighbor.
19 One who loves transgression loves strife;
    one who builds a high threshold invites
      broken bones.
20 The crooked of mind do not prosper,
    and the perverse of tongue fall into
      calamity.
21 The one who begets a fool gets trouble;
    the parent of a fool has no joy.
22 A cheerful heart is a good medicine,
    but a downcast spirit dries up the bones.
23 The wicked accept a concealed bribe

---

a Or *a noble person*

Count to Ten

"The beginning of strife is like letting out water; so stop before the quarrel breaks out" (Prov 17.14).

Have you ever noticed how people quickly congregate whenever a fight breaks out, especially at school? Many of the spectators seem to be in entertainment mode and are generally on one side or the other. Others want the fight to stop but lack the courage or confidence to break it up. So, everyone ends up waiting until someone in authority comes along to intervene or until one of the contenders is hurt and the fight stops.

A fight can begin so quickly. A word. A taunting phrase. A sudden turn and a punch. And there is an instant fight. Some of us have a shorter fuse than others. Some of us have a temper that flares easily or an ego that won't allow us to walk away when provoked. To paraphrase the image used in Prov 17.14, once the water breaks through the dam, it is very hard to stop.

How do you react when you see a quarrel or a fight? How quickly do you get involved in fights or quarrels? If you have a quick temper, what can you do to control it?

▶ Prov 17.14

to pervert the ways of justice.
24 The discerning person looks to wisdom,
   but the eyes of a fool to the ends of the
      earth.
25 Foolish children are a grief to their father
   and bitterness to her who bore them.
26 To impose a fine on the innocent is not right,
   or to flog the noble for their integrity.
27 One who spares words is knowledgeable;
   one who is cool in spirit has understanding.
28 Even fools who keep silent are considered
      wise;
   when they close their lips, they are deemed
      intelligent.

18
The one who lives alone is
         self-indulgent,
   showing contempt for all who have sound
      judgment.[b]
2 A fool takes no pleasure in understanding,
   but only in expressing personal opinion.
3 When wickedness comes, contempt comes
      also;
   and with dishonor comes disgrace.
4 The words of the mouth are deep waters;
   the fountain of wisdom is a gushing stream.
5 It is not right to be partial to the guilty,
   or to subvert the innocent in judgment.
6 A fool's lips bring strife,
   and a fool's mouth invites a flogging.
7 The mouths of fools are their ruin,
   and their lips a snare to themselves.
8 The words of a whisperer are like delicious
      morsels;
   they go down into the inner parts of the
      body.
9 One who is slack in work
   is close kin to a vandal.
10 The name of the LORD is a strong tower;
   the righteous run into it and are safe.
11 The wealth of the rich is their strong city;
   in their imagination it is like a high wall.
12 Before destruction one's heart is haughty,
   but humility goes before honor.
13 If one gives answer before hearing,
   it is folly and shame.
14 The human spirit will endure sickness;
   but a broken spirit—who can bear?
15 An intelligent mind acquires knowledge,
   and the ear of the wise seeks knowledge.
16 A gift opens doors;
   it gives access to the great.
17 The one who first states a case seems right,
   until the other comes and cross-examines.
18 Casting the lot puts an end to disputes
   and decides between powerful contenders.
19 An ally offended is stronger than a city;[c]
   such quarreling is like the bars of a castle.

20 From the fruit of the mouth one's stomach is
      satisfied;
   the yield of the lips brings satisfaction.
21 Death and life are in the power of the tongue,
   and those who love it will eat its fruits.
22 He who finds a wife finds a good thing,
   and obtains favor from the LORD.
23 The poor use entreaties,
   but the rich answer roughly.
24 Some[d] friends play at friendship[e]
   but a true friend sticks closer than one's
      nearest kin.

19
Better the poor walking in integrity
      than one perverse of speech who is a
         fool.
2 Desire without knowledge is not good,
   and one who moves too hurriedly misses
      the way.
3 One's own folly leads to ruin,
   yet the heart rages against the LORD.
4 Wealth brings many friends,
   but the poor are left friendless.
5 A false witness will not go unpunished,
   and a liar will not escape.
6 Many seek the favor of the generous,
   and everyone is a friend to a giver of gifts.
7 If the poor are hated even by their kin,
   how much more are they shunned by their
      friends!
When they call after them, they are not there.[b]
8 To get wisdom is to love oneself;
   to keep understanding is to prosper.
9 A false witness will not go unpunished,
   and the liar will perish.
10 It is not fitting for a fool to live in luxury,
   much less for a slave to rule over princes.
11 Those with good sense are slow to anger,
   and it is their glory to overlook an offense.
12 A king's anger is like the growling of a lion,
   but his favor is like dew on the grass.
13 A stupid child is ruin to a father,
   and a wife's quarreling is a continual
      dripping of rain.
14 House and wealth are inherited from parents,
   but a prudent wife is from the LORD.
15 Laziness brings on deep sleep;
   an idle person will suffer hunger.
16 Those who keep the commandment will live;
   those who are heedless of their ways will
      die.
17 Whoever is kind to the poor lends to the LORD,
   and will be repaid in full.
18 Discipline your children while there is hope;

---

b Meaning of Heb uncertain   c Gk Syr Vg Tg: Meaning of
Heb uncertain   d Syr Tg: Heb *A man of*   e Cn Compare Syr
Vg Tg: Meaning of Heb uncertain

do not set your heart on their destruction.

19 A violent tempered person will pay the penalty;
   if you effect a rescue, you will only have to
      do it again.*f*

20 Listen to advice and accept instruction,
   that you may gain wisdom for the future.

21 The human mind may devise many plans,
   but it is the purpose of the LORD that will
      be established.

22 What is desirable in a person is loyalty,
   and it is better to be poor than a liar.

23 The fear of the LORD is life indeed;
   filled with it one rests secure
   and suffers no harm.

PRAY IT!

Fear of the LORD

The phrase "fear of the LORD" is used fourteen times in Proverbs (see, for example, 19.23). You might ask why the author of Proverbs keeps telling us to be afraid of God. But in the Bible, fear of the LORD has less to do with terror and fright than with awe, reverence, and respect. It's a reminder that God is far from ordinary. To fear the LORD is to take God very seriously.

Take some time to reflect or journal on the question What does it mean to fear the LORD? Describe a time when you were awed by something about God. Explain how you give God respect.

▶ **Prov 19.23**

24 The lazy person buries a hand in the dish,
   and will not even bring it back to the
      mouth.

25 Strike a scoffer, and the simple will learn
      prudence;
   reprove the intelligent, and they will gain
      knowledge.

26 Those who do violence to their father and
      chase away their mother
   are children who cause shame and bring
      reproach.

27 Cease straying, my child, from the words of
      knowledge,
   in order that you may hear instruction.

28 A worthless witness mocks at justice,
   and the mouth of the wicked devours
      iniquity.

29 Condemnation is ready for scoffers,

and flogging for the backs of fools.

20 Wine is a mocker, strong drink a
      brawler,
   and whoever is led astray by it is not wise.

2 The dread anger of a king is like the growling
      of a lion;
   anyone who provokes him to anger forfeits
      life itself.

3 It is honorable to refrain from strife,
   but every fool is quick to quarrel.

4 The lazy person does not plow in season;
   harvest comes, and there is nothing to be
      found.

5 The purposes in the human mind are like deep
      water,
   but the intelligent will draw them out.

6 Many proclaim themselves loyal,
   but who can find one worthy of trust?

7 The righteous walk in integrity—
   happy are the children who follow them!

8 A king who sits on the throne of judgment
   winnows all evil with his eyes.

9 Who can say, "I have made my heart clean;
   I am pure from my sin"?

10 Diverse weights and diverse measures
   are both alike an abomination to the LORD.

11 Even children make themselves known by their
      acts,
   by whether what they do is pure and right.

12 The hearing ear and the seeing eye—
   the LORD has made them both.

13 Do not love sleep, or else you will come to
      poverty;
   open your eyes, and you will have plenty of
      bread.

14 "Bad, bad," says the buyer,
   then goes away and boasts.

15 There is gold, and abundance of costly stones;
   but the lips informed by knowledge are a
      precious jewel.

16 Take the garment of one who has given surety
      for a stranger;
   seize the pledge given as surety for
      foreigners.

17 Bread gained by deceit is sweet,
   but afterward the mouth will be full of
      gravel.

18 Plans are established by taking advice;
   wage war by following wise guidance.

19 A gossip reveals secrets;
   therefore do not associate with a babbler.

20 If you curse father or mother,
   your lamp will go out in utter darkness.

21 An estate quickly acquired in the beginning
   will not be blessed in the end.

---

f Meaning of Heb uncertain

22 Do not say, "I will repay evil";
    wait for the LORD, and he will help you.
23 Differing weights are an abomination to the
    LORD,
    and false scales are not good.
24 All our steps are ordered by the LORD;
    how then can we understand our own
    ways?
25 It is a snare for one to say rashly, "It is holy,"
    and begin to reflect only after making a
    vow.
26 A wise king winnows the wicked,
    and drives the wheel over them.
27 The human spirit is the lamp of the LORD,
    searching every inmost part.
28 Loyalty and faithfulness preserve the king,
    and his throne is upheld by righteousness.g
29 The glory of youths is their strength,
    but the beauty of the aged is their gray hair.
30 Blows that wound cleanse away evil;
    beatings make clean the innermost parts.

21 The king's heart is a stream of water in
    the hand of the LORD;
    he turns it wherever he will.
2 All deeds are right in the sight of the doer,
    but the LORD weighs the heart.
3 To do righteousness and justice
    is more acceptable to the LORD than
    sacrifice.
4 Haughty eyes and a proud heart—
    the lamp of the wicked—are sin.
5 The plans of the diligent lead surely to
    abundance,
    but everyone who is hasty comes only to
    want.
6 The getting of treasures by a lying tongue
    is a fleeting vapor and a snareh of death.
7 The violence of the wicked will sweep them
    away,
    because they refuse to do what is just.
8 The way of the guilty is crooked,
    but the conduct of the pure is right.
9 It is better to live in a corner of the housetop
    than in a house shared with a contentious
    wife.
10 The souls of the wicked desire evil;
    their neighbors find no mercy in their eyes.
11 When a scoffer is punished, the simple become
    wiser;
    when the wise are instructed, they increase
    in knowledge.
12 The Righteous One observes the house of the
    wicked;
    he casts the wicked down to ruin.
13 If you close your ear to the cry of the poor,
    you will cry out and not be heard.
14 A gift in secret averts anger;

and a concealed bribe in the bosom, strong
    wrath.
15 When justice is done, it is a joy to the
    righteous,
    but dismay to evildoers.
16 Whoever wanders from the way of
    understanding
    will rest in the assembly of the dead.
17 Whoever loves pleasure will suffer want;
    whoever loves wine and oil will not be
    rich.
18 The wicked is a ransom for the righteous,
    and the faithless for the upright.
19 It is better to live in a desert land
    than with a contentious and fretful wife.
20 Precious treasure remainsi in the house of the
    wise,
    but the fool devours it.
21 Whoever pursues righteousness and kindness
    will find lifej and honor.
22 One wise person went up against a city of
    warriors
    and brought down the stronghold in which
    they trusted.
23 To watch over mouth and tongue
    is to keep out of trouble.
24 The proud, haughty person, named "Scoffer,"
    acts with arrogant pride.
25 The craving of the lazy person is fatal,
    for lazy hands refuse to labor.
26 All day long the wicked covet,k
    but the righteous give and do not hold
    back.
27 The sacrifice of the wicked is an abomination;
    how much more when brought with evil
    intent.
28 A false witness will perish,
    but a good listener will testify successfully.
29 The wicked put on a bold face,
    but the upright give thought tol their ways.
30 No wisdom, no understanding, no counsel,
    can avail against the LORD.
31 The horse is made ready for the day of battle,
    but the victory belongs to the LORD.

22 A good name is to be chosen rather
    than great riches,
    and favor is better than silver or gold.
2 The rich and the poor have this in common:
    the LORD is the maker of them all.
3 The clever see danger and hide;
    but the simple go on, and suffer for it.
4 The reward for humility and fear of the LORD
    is riches and honor and life.

---

g Gk: Heb loyalty   h Gk: Heb seekers   i Gk: Heb and oil
j Gk: Heb life and righteousness   k Gk: Heb all day long one
covets covetously   l Another reading is establish

5 Thorns and snares are in the way of the
      perverse;
   the cautious will keep far from them.
6 Train children in the right way,
   and when old, they will not stray.
7 The rich rule over the poor,
   and the borrower is the slave of the lender.
8 Whoever sows injustice will reap calamity,
   and the rod of anger will fail.
9 Those who are generous are blessed,
   for they share their bread with the poor.
10 Drive out a scoffer, and strife goes out;
   quarreling and abuse will cease.
11 Those who love a pure heart and are gracious
      in speech
   will have the king as a friend.
12 The eyes of the LORD keep watch over
      knowledge,
   but he overthrows the words of the
      faithless.
13 The lazy person says, "There is a lion outside!
   I shall be killed in the streets!"
14 The mouth of a loose*m* woman is a deep pit;
   he with whom the LORD is angry falls
      into it.
15 Folly is bound up in the heart of a boy,
   but the rod of discipline drives it far away.
16 Oppressing the poor in order to enrich
      oneself,
   and giving to the rich, will lead only to loss.

Sayings of the Wise

17   The words of the wise:

   Incline your ear and hear my words,*n*
      and apply your mind to my teaching;
18 for it will be pleasant if you keep them within
      you,
   if all of them are ready on your lips.
19 So that your trust may be in the LORD,
   I have made them known to you today—
      yes, to you.
20 Have I not written for you thirty sayings
   of admonition and knowledge,
21 to show you what is right and true,
   so that you may give a true answer to those
      who sent you?

22 Do not rob the poor because they are poor,
   or crush the afflicted at the gate;
23 for the LORD pleads their cause
   and despoils of life those who despoil
      them.
24 Make no friends with those given to anger,
   and do not associate with hotheads,
25 or you may learn their ways
   and entangle yourself in a snare.

26 Do not be one of those who give pledges,
   who become surety for debts.
27 If you have nothing with which to pay,
   why should your bed be taken from under
      you?
28 Do not remove the ancient landmark
   that your ancestors set up.
29 Do you see those who are skillful in their
      work?
   They will serve kings;
   they will not serve common people.

23 When you sit down to eat with a ruler,
      observe carefully what*o* is before
      you,
2 and put a knife to your throat
   if you have a big appetite.
3 Do not desire the ruler's*p* delicacies,
   for they are deceptive food.
4 Do not wear yourself out to get rich;
   be wise enough to desist.
5 When your eyes light upon it, it is gone;
   for suddenly it takes wings to itself,
   flying like an eagle toward heaven.
6 Do not eat the bread of the stingy;
   do not desire their delicacies;
7 for like a hair in the throat, so are they.*q*
   "Eat and drink!" they say to you;
   but they do not mean it.
8 You will vomit up the little you have eaten,
   and you will waste your pleasant words.
9 Do not speak in the hearing of a fool,
   who will only despise the wisdom of your
      words.
10 Do not remove an ancient landmark
   or encroach on the fields of orphans,
11 for their redeemer is strong;
   he will plead their cause against you.
12 Apply your mind to instruction
   and your ear to words of knowledge.
13 Do not withhold discipline from your children;
   if you beat them with a rod, they will not
      die.
14 If you beat them with the rod,
   you will save their lives from Shĕ′ōl.
15 My child, if your heart is wise,
   my heart too will be glad.
16 My soul will rejoice
   when your lips speak what is right.
17 Do not let your heart envy sinners,
   but always continue in the fear of the LORD.
18 Surely there is a future,
   and your hope will not be cut off.

---

m Heb *strange*   *n* Cn Compare Gk: Heb *Incline your ear, and
hear the words of the wise*   *o* Or *who*   *p* Heb *his*   *q* Meaning
of Heb uncertain

¹⁹ Hear, my child, and be wise,
  and direct your mind in the way.
²⁰ Do not be among winebibbers,
  or among gluttonous eaters of meat;
²¹ for the drunkard and the glutton will come to
      poverty,
  and drowsiness will clothe them with rags.

²² Listen to your father who begot you,
  and do not despise your mother when she
      is old.
²³ Buy truth, and do not sell it;
  buy wisdom, instruction, and
      understanding.
²⁴ The father of the righteous will greatly rejoice;
  he who begets a wise son will be glad in him.
²⁵ Let your father and mother be glad;
  let her who bore you rejoice.

²⁶ My child, give me your heart,
  and let your eyes observe^r my ways.
²⁷ For a prostitute is a deep pit;
  an adulteress^s is a narrow well.
²⁸ She lies in wait like a robber
  and increases the number of the faithless.

²⁹ Who has woe? Who has sorrow?
  Who has strife? Who has complaining?
  Who has wounds without cause?
  Who has redness of eyes?
³⁰ Those who linger late over wine,
  those who keep trying mixed wines.

³¹ Do not look at wine when it is red,
  when it sparkles in the cup
  and goes down smoothly.
³² At the last it bites like a serpent,
  and stings like an adder.
³³ Your eyes will see strange things,
  and your mind utter perverse things.
³⁴ You will be like one who lies down in the
      midst of the sea,
  like one who lies on the top of a mast.^t
³⁵ "They struck me," you will say,^u "but I was not
      hurt;
  they beat me, but I did not feel it.
When shall I awake?
  I will seek another drink."

24 Do not envy the wicked,
  nor desire to be with them;
² for their minds devise violence,
  and their lips talk of mischief.

³ By wisdom a house is built,
  and by understanding it is established;
⁴ by knowledge the rooms are filled
  with all precious and pleasant riches.
⁵ Wise warriors are mightier than strong ones,^v
  and those who have knowledge than those
      who have strength;
⁶ for by wise guidance you can wage your war,

---

^r Another reading is *delight in*   ^s Heb *an alien woman*
^t Meaning of Heb uncertain   ^u Gk Syr Vg Tg: Heb lacks *you
will say*   ^v Gk Compare Syr Tg: Heb *A wise man is strength*

WISDOM AND THE ELDERS

"By wisdom a house is built . . . / by knowledge the rooms are filled" (Prov 24.3–4). Becoming wise is like building and furnishing a house. It doesn't happen all at once; it takes time, experience, and work. Native American cultures understand this. Wisdom is an important value for them.

In many Native American cultures, the elders have the highest place of honor because of their wisdom. Native Americans understand that it takes an entire life to grow wise. The elders have lived through much, and their advice is always worth seeking. They are relied on to settle disagreements because they have learned to judge people by their heart and their integrity, not by their money or possessions. The others in the tribe know that through listening to the elders, they too, over time, will grow wise.

▶ **Prov 24.3–4**

and in abundance of counselors there is
victory.
7 Wisdom is too high for fools;
in the gate they do not open their mouths.

8 Whoever plans to do evil
will be called a mischief-maker.
9 The devising of folly is sin,
and the scoffer is an abomination to all.

10 If you faint in the day of adversity,
your strength being small;
11 if you hold back from rescuing those taken
away to death,
those who go staggering to the
slaughter;
12 if you say, "Look, we did not know this"—
does not he who weighs the heart
perceive it?
Does not he who keeps watch over your soul
know it?
And will he not repay all according to their
deeds?

13 My child, eat honey, for it is good,
and the drippings of the honeycomb are
sweet to your taste.
14 Know that wisdom is such to your soul;
if you find it, you will find a future,
and your hope will not be cut off.

15 Do not lie in wait like an outlaw against the
home of the righteous;
do no violence to the place where the
righteous live;
16 for though they fall seven times, they will rise
again;
but the wicked are overthrown by
calamity.

17 Do not rejoice when your enemies fall,
and do not let your heart be glad when
they stumble,
18 or else the LORD will see it and be
displeased,
and turn away his anger from them.

19 Do not fret because of evildoers.
Do not envy the wicked;
20 for the evil have no future;
the lamp of the wicked will go out.

21 My child, fear the LORD and the king,
and do not disobey either of them;w
22 for disaster comes from them suddenly,
and who knows the ruin that both can
bring?

Further Sayings of the Wise

23 These also are sayings of the wise:

Partiality in judging is not good.
24 Whoever says to the wicked, "You are innocent,"
will be cursed by peoples, abhorred by
nations;
25 but those who rebuke the wicked will have
delight,
and a good blessing will come upon them.
26 One who gives an honest answer
gives a kiss on the lips.

27 Prepare your work outside,
get everything ready for you in the field;
and after that build your house.

28 Do not be a witness against your neighbor
without cause,
and do not deceive with your lips.
29 Do not say, "I will do to others as they have
done to me;
I will pay them back for what they have done."

30 I passed by the field of one who was lazy,
by the vineyard of a stupid person;
31 and see, it was all overgrown with thorns;
the ground was covered with nettles,
and its stone wall was broken down.
32 Then I saw and considered it;
I looked and received instruction.
33 A little sleep, a little slumber,
a little folding of the hands to rest,
34 and poverty will come upon you like a robber,
and want, like an armed warrior.

Further Wise Sayings of Solomon

25 These are other proverbs of Solomon
that the officials of King Hez·e·ki′ah of
Judah copied.

2 It is the glory of God to conceal things,
but the glory of kings is to search things
out.
3 Like the heavens for height, like the earth for
depth,
so the mind of kings is unsearchable.
4 Take away the dross from the silver,
and the smith has material for a vessel;
5 take away the wicked from the presence of the
king,
and his throne will be established in
righteousness.
6 Do not put yourself forward in the king's
presence

---

w Gk: Heb do not associate with those who change

or stand in the place of the great;
7 for it is better to be told, "Come up here,"
    than to be put lower in the presence of a
      noble.

What your eyes have seen
8   do not hastily bring into court;
for[x] what will you do in the end,
    when your neighbor puts you to shame?
9 Argue your case with your neighbor directly,
    and do not disclose another's secret;
10 or else someone who hears you will bring
      shame upon you,
    and your ill repute will have no end.

11 A word fitly spoken
    is like apples of gold in a setting of silver.
12 Like a gold ring or an ornament of gold
    is a wise rebuke to a listening ear.
13 Like the cold of snow in the time of harvest
    are faithful messengers to those who send
      them;
    they refresh the spirit of their masters.
14 Like clouds and wind without rain
    is one who boasts of a gift never given.
15 With patience a ruler may be persuaded,
    and a soft tongue can break bones.
16 If you have found honey, eat only enough for
      you,
    or else, having too much, you will vomit it.
17 Let your foot be seldom in your neighbor's
      house,
    otherwise the neighbor will become weary
      of you and hate you.
18 Like a war club, a sword, or a sharp arrow
    is one who bears false witness against a
      neighbor.
19 Like a bad tooth or a lame foot
    is trust in a faithless person in time of trouble.
20 Like vinegar on a wound[y]
    is one who sings songs to a heavy heart.
Like a moth in clothing or a worm in wood,
    sorrow gnaws at the human heart.[z]
21 If your enemies are hungry, give them bread to
      eat;
    and if they are thirsty, give them water to
      drink;
22 for you will heap coals of fire on their heads,
    and the LORD will reward you.
23 The north wind produces rain,
    and a backbiting tongue, angry looks.
24 It is better to live in a corner of the housetop
    than in a house shared with a contentious
      wife.
25 Like cold water to a thirsty soul,
    so is good news from a far country.
26 Like a muddied spring or a polluted fountain

are the righteous who give way before the
    wicked.
27 It is not good to eat much honey,
    or to seek honor on top of honor.
28 Like a city breached, without walls,
    is one who lacks self-control.

26 Like snow in summer or rain in
      harvest,
    so honor is not fitting for a fool.
2 Like a sparrow in its flitting, like a swallow in
      its flying,
    an undeserved curse goes nowhere.
3 A whip for the horse, a bridle for the donkey,
    and a rod for the back of fools.
4 Do not answer fools according to their folly,
    or you will be a fool yourself.
5 Answer fools according to their folly,
    or they will be wise in their own eyes.
6 It is like cutting off one's foot and drinking
      down violence,
    to send a message by a fool.
7 The legs of a disabled person hang limp;
    so does a proverb in the mouth of a fool.
8 It is like binding a stone in a sling
    to give honor to a fool.
9 Like a thornbush brandished by the hand of a
      drunkard
    is a proverb in the mouth of a fool.
10 Like an archer who wounds everybody
    is one who hires a passing fool or
      drunkard.[a]
11 Like a dog that returns to its vomit
    is a fool who reverts to his folly.
12 Do you see persons wise in their own eyes?
    There is more hope for fools than for them.
13 The lazy person says, "There is a lion in the
      road!
    There is a lion in the streets!"
14 As a door turns on its hinges,
    so does a lazy person in bed.
15 The lazy person buries a hand in the dish,
    and is too tired to bring it back to the
      mouth.
16 The lazy person is wiser in self-esteem
    than seven who can answer discreetly.
17 Like somebody who takes a passing dog by the
      ears
    is one who meddles in the quarrel of
      another.
18 Like a maniac who shoots deadly firebrands
      and arrows,
19 so is one who deceives a neighbor
    and says, "I am only joking!"

---

x Cn: Heb *or else*   y Gk: Heb *Like one who takes off a garment
on a cold day, like vinegar on lye*   z Gk Syr Tg: Heb *lacks Like
a moth . . . human heart*   a Meaning of Heb uncertain

20 For lack of wood the fire goes out,
　　and where there is no whisperer, quarreling
　　　ceases.
21 As charcoal is to hot embers and wood to fire,
　　so is a quarrelsome person for kindling
　　　strife.
22 The words of a whisperer are like delicious
　　morsels;
　　they go down into the inner parts of the
　　　body.
23 Like the glaze[b] covering an earthen vessel
　　are smooth[c] lips with an evil heart.
24 An enemy dissembles in speaking
　　while harboring deceit within;
25 when an enemy speaks graciously, do not
　　believe it,
　　for there are seven abominations concealed
　　　within;
26 though hatred is covered with guile,
　　the enemy's wickedness will be exposed in
　　　the assembly.
27 Whoever digs a pit will fall into it,
　　and a stone will come back on the one who
　　　starts it rolling.
28 A lying tongue hates its victims,
　　and a flattering mouth works ruin.

27 Do not boast about tomorrow,
　　　for you do not know what a day may
　　　bring.
2 Let another praise you, and not your own
　　mouth—
　　a stranger, and not your own lips.
3 A stone is heavy, and sand is weighty,
　　but a fool's provocation is heavier than
　　　both.
4 Wrath is cruel, anger is overwhelming,
　　but who is able to stand before jealousy?
5 Better is open rebuke
　　than hidden love.
6 Well meant are the wounds a friend inflicts,
　　but profuse are the kisses of an enemy.

7 The sated appetite spurns honey,
　　but to a ravenous appetite even the bitter is
　　　sweet.
8 Like a bird that strays from its nest
　　is one who strays from home.
9 Perfume and incense make the heart glad,
　　but the soul is torn by trouble.[d]
10 Do not forsake your friend or the friend of
　　　your parent;
　　do not go to the house of your kindred in
　　　the day of your calamity.
　Better is a neighbor who is nearby
　　than kindred who are far away.
11 Be wise, my child, and make my heart glad,
　　so that I may answer whoever
　　　reproaches me.
12 The clever see danger and hide;
　　but the simple go on, and suffer for it.
13 Take the garment of one who has given surety
　　　for a stranger;
　　seize the pledge given as surety for
　　　foreigners.[e]
14 Whoever blesses a neighbor with a loud
　　　voice,
　　rising early in the morning,
　　will be counted as cursing.
15 A continual dripping on a rainy day
　　and a contentious wife are alike;
16 to restrain her is to restrain the wind
　　or to grasp oil in the right hand.[f]
17 Iron sharpens iron,
　　and one person sharpens the wits[g] of
　　　another.
18 Anyone who tends a fig tree will eat its fruit,
　　and anyone who takes care of a master will
　　　be honored.
19 Just as water reflects the face,
　　so one human heart reflects another.
20 She′ol and A·bad′don are never satisfied,
　　and human eyes are never satisfied.
21 The crucible is for silver, and the furnace is for
　　　gold,
　　so a person is tested[h] by being praised.
22 Crush a fool in a mortar with a pestle
　　along with crushed grain,
　　but the folly will not be driven out.

23 Know well the condition of your flocks,
　　and give attention to your herds;
24 for riches do not last forever,
　　nor a crown for all generations.
25 When the grass is gone, and new growth
　　　appears,

---

b Cn: Heb *silver of dross*　c Gk: Heb *burning*　d Gk: Heb *the
sweetness of a friend is better than one's own counsel*　e Vg and
20.16: Heb *for a foreign woman*　f Meaning of Heb
uncertain　g Heb *face*　h Heb lacks *is tested*

and the herbage of the mountains is
    gathered,

26 the lambs will provide your clothing,
    and the goats the price of a field;

27 there will be enough goats' milk for your food,
    for the food of your household
    and nourishment for your servant-girls.

28

The wicked flee when no one pursues,
    but the righteous are as bold as
    a lion.

2 When a land rebels
    it has many rulers;
but with an intelligent ruler
    there is lasting order.*i*

3 A ruler*j* who oppresses the poor
    is a beating rain that leaves no food.

4 Those who forsake the law praise the wicked,
    but those who keep the law struggle against
    them.

5 The evil do not understand justice,
    but those who seek the LORD understand it
    completely.

6 Better to be poor and walk in integrity
    than to be crooked in one's ways even
    though rich.

PRAY IT!
Integrity

A person with integrity does the right thing, even if it doesn't lead to fame or riches. A person with integrity won't lie, steal, or cheat; won't gossip, betray, or insult—not even when everyone else seems to be doing it. A person with integrity is trustworthy, dependable, and reliable. Such a person admits making mistakes and apologizes. Such a person forgives freely and doesn't hold grudges.

LORD, I'm far from perfect. But with every word I speak, every action I take, every choice I make, may I become more aware of how I am growing into a person of integrity.

▶ Prov 28.6

7 Those who keep the law are wise children,
    but companions of gluttons shame their
    parents.

8 One who augments wealth by exorbitant
    interest
gathers it for another who is kind to the
    poor.

9 When one will not listen to the law,
    even one's prayers are an abomination.

10 Those who mislead the upright into evil ways
    will fall into pits of their own making,
    but the blameless will have a goodly
    inheritance.

11 The rich is wise in self-esteem,
    but an intelligent poor person sees through
    the pose.

12 When the righteous triumph, there is great
    glory,
    but when the wicked prevail, people go into
    hiding.

13 No one who conceals transgressions will
    prosper,
    but one who confesses and forsakes them
    will obtain mercy.

14 Happy is the one who is never without fear,
    but one who is hard-hearted will fall into
    calamity.

15 Like a roaring lion or a charging bear
    is a wicked ruler over a poor people.

16 A ruler who lacks understanding is a cruel
    oppressor;
    but one who hates unjust gain will enjoy a
    long life.

17 If someone is burdened with the blood of
    another,
    let that killer be a fugitive until death;
    let no one offer assistance.

18 One who walks in integrity will be safe,
    but whoever follows crooked ways will fall
    into the Pit.*k*

19 Anyone who tills the land will have plenty of
    bread,
    but one who follows worthless pursuits will
    have plenty of poverty.

20 The faithful will abound with blessings,
    but one who is in a hurry to be rich will not
    go unpunished.

21 To show partiality is not good—
    yet for a piece of bread a person may do
    wrong.

22 The miser is in a hurry to get rich
    and does not know that loss is sure to
    come.

23 Whoever rebukes a person will afterward find
    more favor
    than one who flatters with the
    tongue.

24 Anyone who robs father or mother
    and says, "That is no crime,"
    is partner to a thug.

25 The greedy person stirs up strife,

---

i Meaning of Heb uncertain   *j* Cn: Heb *A poor person*
k Syr: Heb *fall all at once*

PROV

but whoever trusts in the LORD will be
enriched.
26 Those who trust in their own wits are fools;
but those who walk in wisdom come
through safely.
27 Whoever gives to the poor will lack nothing,
but one who turns a blind eye will get
many a curse.
28 When the wicked prevail, people go into
hiding;
but when they perish, the righteous
increase.

29

One who is often reproved, yet remains
stubborn,
will suddenly be broken beyond healing.
2 When the righteous are in authority, the people
rejoice;
but when the wicked rule, the people groan.
3 A child who loves wisdom makes a parent
glad,
but to keep company with prostitutes is to
squander one's substance.
4 By justice a king gives stability to the land,
but one who makes heavy exactions
ruins it.
5 Whoever flatters a neighbor
is spreading a net for the neighbor's feet.
6 In the transgression of the evil there is a snare,
but the righteous sing and rejoice.
7 The righteous know the rights of the poor;
the wicked have no such understanding.
8 Scoffers set a city aflame,
but the wise turn away wrath.
9 If the wise go to law with fools,
there is ranting and ridicule without
relief.
10 The bloodthirsty hate the blameless,
and they seek the life of the upright.
11 A fool gives full vent to anger,
but the wise quietly holds it back.
12 If a ruler listens to falsehood,
all his officials will be wicked.
13 The poor and the oppressor have this in
common:
the LORD gives light to the eyes of both.
14 If a king judges the poor with equity,
his throne will be established forever.
15 The rod and reproof give wisdom,
but a mother is disgraced by a neglected
child.
16 When the wicked are in authority,
transgression increases,
but the righteous will look upon their
downfall.
17 Discipline your children, and they will give you
rest;
they will give delight to your heart.

18 Where there is no prophecy, the people cast off
restraint,
but happy are those who keep the law.
19 By mere words servants are not disciplined,
for though they understand, they will not
give heed.
20 Do you see someone who is hasty in speech?
There is more hope for a fool than for
anyone like that.
21 A slave pampered from childhood
will come to a bad end.[l]
22 One given to anger stirs up strife,
and the hothead causes much transgression.
23 A person's pride will bring humiliation,
but one who is lowly in spirit will obtain
honor.
24 To be a partner of a thief is to hate one's own
life;
one hears the victim's curse, but discloses
nothing.[m]
25 The fear of others[n] lays a snare,
but one who trusts in the LORD is secure.
26 Many seek the favor of a ruler,
but it is from the LORD that one gets justice.
27 The unjust are an abomination to the
righteous,
but the upright are an abomination to the
wicked.

Sayings of Agur

30

The words of Ā′gur son of Jā′keh. An oracle.

Thus says the man: I am weary, O God,
I am weary, O God. How can I prevail?[o]
2 Surely I am too stupid to be human;
I do not have human understanding.
3 I have not learned wisdom,
nor have I knowledge of the holy ones.[p]
4 Who has ascended to heaven and come down?
Who has gathered the wind in the hollow
of the hand?
Who has wrapped up the waters in a garment?
Who has established all the ends of the
earth?
What is the person's name?
And what is the name of the person's
child?
Surely you know!

5 Every word of God proves true;
he is a shield to those who take refuge
in him.

---

[l] Vg: Meaning of Heb uncertain   [m] Meaning of Heb
uncertain   [n] Or *human fear*   [o] Or *I am spent.* Meaning of
Heb uncertain   [p] Or *Holy One*

Ravens and Vultures

LIVE IT!

> **The eye that mocks a father**
>   **and scorns to obey a mother**
> **will be pecked out by the ravens of the valley**
>   **and eaten by the vultures.**
>   **(Prov 30.17)**

If this passage reflected reality, most of us would already have been eaten by those vultures hovering overhead. For who among us has not at one time mocked our parents, if not to their face, then perhaps to our friends? And is there anyone who has not disobeyed a parent?

The vast majority of us are loved by our parents. In most cases, they are trying their hardest to do what is best for us, even though it doesn't always seem that way. If we can accept this, then it might be easier to forgive them their faults and overlook some of the things they do that irritate us.

Let's keep the vultures far away!

■ **What can you do to let your parents know that you love them?**
■ **What can you do today to show them more respect?**

▶ **Prov 30.17**

PROV

6 Do not add to his words,
    or else he will rebuke you, and you will be
        found a liar.

7 Two things I ask of you;
    do not deny them to me before I die:
8 Remove far from me falsehood and lying;
    give me neither poverty nor riches;
    feed me with the food that I need,
9 or I shall be full, and deny you,
    and say, "Who is the LORD?"
or I shall be poor, and steal,
    and profane the name of my God.

10 Do not slander a servant to a master,
    or the servant will curse you, and you will
        be held guilty.

11 There are those who curse their fathers
    and do not bless their mothers.
12 There are those who are pure in their own
        eyes
    yet are not cleansed of their filthiness.
13 There are those—how lofty are their eyes,
    how high their eyelids lift!—
14 there are those whose teeth are swords,
    whose teeth are knives,
to devour the poor from off the earth,
    the needy from among mortals.

15 The leech*q* has two daughters;
    "Give, give," they cry.
Three things are never satisfied;
    four never say, "Enough":
16 Shĕ'ōl, the barren womb,
    the earth ever thirsty for water,
    and the fire that never says, "Enough."*q*

17 The eye that mocks a father
    and scorns to obey a mother
will be pecked out by the ravens of the valley
    and eaten by the vultures.

18 Three things are too wonderful for me;
    four I do not understand:
19 the way of an eagle in the sky,
    the way of a snake on a rock,
the way of a ship on the high seas,
    and the way of a man with a girl.

20 This is the way of an adulteress:
    she eats, and wipes her mouth,
    and says, "I have done no wrong."

21 Under three things the earth trembles;
    under four it cannot bear up:
22 a slave when he becomes king,

---

q Meaning of Heb uncertain

and a fool when glutted with food;
23 an unloved woman when she gets a husband,
and a maid when she succeeds her mistress.

24 Four things on earth are small,
yet they are exceedingly wise:
25 the ants are a people without strength,
yet they provide their food in the summer;
26 the badgers are a people without power,
yet they make their homes in the rocks;
27 the locusts have no king,
yet all of them march in rank;
28 the lizard[r] can be grasped in the hand,
yet it is found in kings' palaces.

29 Three things are stately in their stride;
four are stately in their gait:
30 the lion, which is mightiest among wild
animals
and does not turn back before any;
31 the strutting rooster,[s] the he-goat,
and a king striding before[t] his people.

32 If you have been foolish, exalting yourself,
or if you have been devising evil,
put your hand on your mouth.
33 For as pressing milk produces curds,
and pressing the nose produces blood,
so pressing anger produces strife.

The Teaching of King Lemuel's Mother

31 The words of King Lem'u·el. An oracle
that his mother taught him:

2 No, my son! No, son of my womb!
No, son of my vows!
3 Do not give your strength to women,
your ways to those who destroy kings.
4 It is not for kings, O Lem'u·el,
it is not for kings to drink wine,
or for rulers to desire[u] strong drink;
5 or else they will drink and forget what has
been decreed,
and will pervert the rights of all the afflicted.
6 Give strong drink to one who is perishing,
and wine to those in bitter distress;
7 let them drink and forget their poverty,
and remember their misery no more.
8 Speak out for those who cannot speak,
for the rights of all the destitute.[v]
9 Speak out, judge righteously,
defend the rights of the poor and needy.

Ode to a Capable Wife

10 A capable wife who can find?
She is far more precious than jewels.
11 The heart of her husband trusts in her,

did you KNOW?

A Woman's Place

You've probably noticed that women had a much different role in biblical times than they do now. Then it was common, and expected, for women to be in the home—either their father's or their husband's—doing household chores.

Today, the Catholic church teaches that women and men share equality and that both deserve respect and mutual appreciation. It is not appropriate or just, therefore, to say that a woman's place is in the home. Women now choose where they spend their time!

Thousands of women today hold leadership positions at parish, diocesan, archdiocesan, and national levels. The church celebrates the inclusion of women in leadership positions and continues to strive for and support a more even distribution of men and women in these positions. If you are a young woman or young man interested in working for the church, ask for more information at your parish or school.

▸ **Prov 31.10–31**

and he will have no lack of gain.
12 She does him good, and not harm,
all the days of her life.
13 She seeks wool and flax,
and works with willing hands.
14 She is like the ships of the merchant,
she brings her food from far away.
15 She rises while it is still night
and provides food for her household
and tasks for her servant-girls.
16 She considers a field and buys it;
with the fruit of her hands she plants a
vineyard.
17 She girds herself with strength,
and makes her arms strong.
18 She perceives that her merchandise is
profitable.
Her lamp does not go out at night.

---

[r] Or *spider* [s] Gk Syr Tg Compare Vg: Meaning of Heb uncertain [t] Meaning of Heb uncertain [u] Cn: Heb *where* [v] Heb *all children of passing away*

19 She puts her hands to the distaff,
   and her hands hold the spindle.
20 She opens her hand to the poor,
   and reaches out her hands to the needy.
21 She is not afraid for her household when it
     snows,
   for all her household are clothed in
     crimson.
22 She makes herself coverings;
   her clothing is fine linen and purple.
23 Her husband is known in the city gates,
   taking his seat among the elders of the
     land.
24 She makes linen garments and sells them;
   she supplies the merchant with sashes.
25 Strength and dignity are her clothing,

   and she laughs at the time to come.
26 She opens her mouth with wisdom,
   and the teaching of kindness is on her
     tongue.
27 She looks well to the ways of her household,
   and does not eat the bread of idleness.
28 Her children rise up and call her happy;
   her husband too, and he praises her:
29 "Many women have done excellently,
   but you surpass them all."
30 Charm is deceitful, and beauty is vain,
   but a woman who fears the LORD is to be
     praised.
31 Give her a share in the fruit of her hands,
   and let her works praise her in the city
     gates.

The Book of Ecclesiastes

There is nothing new under the sun."
"Sorrow is better than laughter."
"No one can anticipate the time of disaster."
If you saw these comments on the Internet, what would you think? That you had just found the Web site of the National Association of Pessimists? Would you be surprised to learn that all these lines come from the Bible? The author of Ecclesiastes, who was called the Teacher (Eccl 1.1), wrote all of them. Yet, the book is hardly a defense of pessimism. The Teacher was pointing out to the Israelites the need for a new understanding of God and life.

At a Glance

- **1.1—6.9.** thoughts on life's difficulties, along with the Teacher's advice

- **6.10—12.8.** thoughts on the future

- **12.9–14.** the final editor's addition, affirming the traditional teaching

In-depth

After a long life of careful observation, the author of Ecclesiastes was disturbed by many things:

- that wise people perished just like fools (2.12–17)
- that those who worked hard for a living had to leave their possessions behind in death (5.13–17)
- that sometimes bad people lived longer than good people (7.15)
- that the most deserving did not always get what they had earned (9.11–12)

Observing these puzzling things, the Teacher asked the obvious question: "Why should we work so hard to be wise and good?" For centuries, believers had struggled to be honest, law-abiding people in the hope of being rewarded by God. And what had they gotten? Sickness, suffering, and death—like everyone else! "Something's wrong!" the Teacher insisted. "Something's terribly wrong!"

After raising the question, the author of Ecclesiastes did not provide an answer—nor is a convincing one to be found in the writings of others in the Old Testament. However, later generations of Jews, pondering the possibility of life after death—a concept that developed late in Jewish religion—began to see things in a different light. Does God possibly reward the faithful in a life beyond the grave? For Christians, the New Testament answers that question with a resounding yes.

The Book of Ecclesiastes stands as a reminder to believers that all things change, even our understanding of God. The Teacher was not a pessimist, but a realist with a mission—to stretch the traditional understanding of faith in order to embrace the difficult questions of life.

Quick Facts

Author
the Teacher, writing in the fourth or third century B.C.

Themes
Life is not always fair. There are no easy answers.

Of Note
Ecclesiastes is often attributed to King Solomon, although he did not write it.

Ecclesiastes

1.3

Reflections of a Royal Philosopher

1 The words of the Teacher,[a] the son of David, king in Jerusalem.

2 Vanity of vanities, says the Teacher,[a]
   vanity of vanities! All is vanity.

3 What do people gain from all the toil
   at which they toil under the sun?

4 A generation goes, and a generation
      comes,
   but the earth remains forever.

5 The sun rises and the sun goes down,
   and hurries to the place where it rises.

6 The wind blows to the south,
   and goes around to the north;
round and round goes the wind,
   and on its circuits the wind returns.

7 All streams run to the sea,
   but the sea is not full;
to the place where the streams flow,
   there they continue to flow.

8 All things[b] are wearisome;
   more than one can express;
the eye is not satisfied with seeing,
   or the ear filled with hearing.

9 What has been is what will be,
   and what has been done is what will be
      done;
   there is nothing new under the sun.

10 Is there a thing of which it is said,
   "See, this is new"?
It has already been,
   in the ages before us.

11 The people of long ago are not
      remembered,
   nor will there be any remembrance
of people yet to come
   by those who come after them.

The Futility of Seeking Wisdom

12 I, the Teacher,[a] when king over Israel in Jerusalem, 13 applied my mind to seek and to search out by wisdom all that is done under heaven; it is an unhappy business that God has given to human beings to be busy with. 14 I saw all the deeds that are done under the sun; and see, all is vanity and a chasing after wind.[c]

15 What is crooked cannot be made straight,
   and what is lacking cannot be counted.

16 I said to myself, "I have acquired great wisdom, surpassing all who were over Jerusalem before me; and my mind has had great experience of wisdom and knowledge." 17 And I applied my mind to know wisdom and to know madness and folly. I perceived that this also is but a chasing after wind.[c]

18 For in much wisdom is much vexation,
   and those who increase knowledge increase
      sorrow.

---

[a] Heb Qoheleth, traditionally rendered Preacher
[b] Or words [c] Or a feeding on wind. See Hos 12.1

New and Improved!

NEW! IMPROVED! These two words are basic to many ad campaigns. No matter how good a product is, sooner or later, it will be "new and improved." The reason is simple: the advertisers want us to think the product is even better.

The writer of Ecclesiastes would not be very impressed with the claims of advertisers today. The author sounds skeptical in 1.9: "There is nothing new under the sun." The Teacher is not going to be taken in by claims that something is new and improved. This person has seen it all before.

Advertising can get us thinking that our life isn't good enough, that we have to have more things and new things in order to be happy. In fact, we need to have a little bit of the attitude of the Teacher if we want to find contentment. Throughout the Book of Ecclesiastes, this writer invites us to enjoy what we have now.

Have you ever gotten something because of its advertising, only to be disappointed afterward? Are you enjoying the things you have right now?

▸ Eccl 1.1–11

The Futility of Self-Indulgence
(Cp 1 Kings 4.20–28)

2 I said to myself, "Come now, I will make a test of pleasure; enjoy yourself." But again, this also was vanity. 2 I said of laughter, "It is mad," and of pleasure, "What use is it?" 3 I searched with my mind how to cheer my body with wine—my mind still guiding me with wisdom—and how to lay hold on folly, until I might see what was good for mortals to do under heaven during the few days of their life. 4 I made great works; I built houses and planted vineyards for myself; 5 I made myself gardens and parks, and planted in them all kinds of fruit trees. 6 I made myself pools from which to water the forest of growing trees. 7 I bought male and female slaves, and had slaves who were born in my house; I also had great possessions of herds and flocks, more than any who had been before me in Jerusalem. 8 I also gathered for myself silver and gold and the treasure of kings and of the provinces; I got singers, both men and women, and delights of the flesh, and many concubines.[d]

9 So I became great and surpassed all who were before me in Jerusalem; also my wisdom remained with me. 10 Whatever my eyes desired I did not keep from them; I kept my heart from no pleasure, for my heart found pleasure in all my toil, and this was my reward for all my toil. 11 Then I considered all that my hands had done and the toil I had spent in doing it, and again, all was vanity and a chasing after wind,[e] and there was nothing to be gained under the sun.

Wisdom and Joy Given to One Who Pleases God

12 So I turned to consider wisdom and madness and folly; for what can the one do who comes after the king? Only what has already been done. 13 Then I saw that wisdom excels folly as light excels darkness.

14 The wise have eyes in their head,
   but fools walk in darkness.

Yet I perceived that the same fate befalls all of them. 15 Then I said to myself, "What happens to the fool will happen to me also; why then have I been so very wise?" And I said to myself that this also is vanity. 16 For there is no enduring remembrance of the wise or of fools, seeing that in the days to come all will have been long forgotten. How can the wise die just like fools? 17 So I hated life, because what is done under the sun was grievous to me; for all is vanity and a chasing after wind.[e]

18 I hated all my toil in which I had toiled under the sun, seeing that I must leave it to those who come after me 19—and who knows whether they will be wise or foolish? Yet they will be master of all for which I toiled and used my wisdom under the sun. This also is vanity. 20 So I turned and gave my heart up to despair concerning all the toil of my labors under the sun, 21 because sometimes one who has toiled with wisdom and knowledge and skill must leave all to be enjoyed by another who did not toil for it. This also is vanity and a great evil. 22 What do mortals get from all the toil and strain with which they toil under the sun? 23 For all their days are full of pain, and their work is a vexation; even at night their minds do not rest. This also is vanity.

24 There is nothing better for mortals than to

---

d Meaning of Heb uncertain   *e* Or *a feeding on wind*. See Hos 12.1

ECCL

eat and drink, and find enjoyment in their toil. This also, I saw, is from the hand of God; 25 for apart from him *f* who can eat or who can have enjoyment? 26 For to the one who pleases him God gives wisdom and knowledge and joy; but to the sinner he gives the work of gathering and heaping, only to give to one who pleases God. This also is vanity and a chasing after wind. *g*

Everything Has Its Time

3 For everything there is a season, and a time for every matter under heaven:
2 a time to be born, and a time to die;
a time to plant, and a time to pluck up what is planted;
3 a time to kill, and a time to heal;
a time to break down, and a time to build up;
4 a time to weep, and a time to laugh;
a time to mourn, and a time to dance;
5 a time to throw away stones, and a time to gather stones together;
a time to embrace, and a time to refrain from embracing;
6 a time to seek, and a time to lose;
a time to keep, and a time to throw away;
7 a time to tear, and a time to sew;
a time to keep silence, and a time to speak;
8 a time to love, and a time to hate;
a time for war, and a time for peace.

The God-Given Task

9 What gain have the workers from their toil? 10 I have seen the business that God has given to everyone to be busy with. 11 He has made everything suitable for its time; moreover he has put a sense of past and future into their minds, yet they cannot find out what God has done from the beginning to the end. 12 I know that there is nothing better for them than to be happy and enjoy themselves as long as they live; 13 moreover, it is God's gift that all should eat and drink and take pleasure in all their toil. 14 I know that whatever God does endures forever; nothing can be added to it, nor anything taken from it; God has done this, so that all should stand in awe before him. 15 That which is, already has been; that which is to be, already is; and God seeks out what has gone by. *h*

Judgment and the Future Belong to God

16 Moreover I saw under the sun that in the place of justice, wickedness was there, and in the place of righteousness, wickedness was there as well. 17 I said in my heart, God will judge the righteous and the wicked, for he has appointed a time for every matter, and for every work. 18 I said in my heart with regard to human beings that God is

f Gk Syr: Heb *apart from me*   *g* Or *a feeding on wind.* See Hos 12.1   *h* Heb *what is pursued*

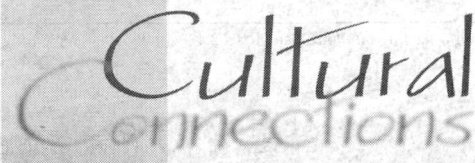

A TIME FOR CONNECTIONS

The Tao te Ching (pronounced "Dow deh JING") is the ancient Chinese Book of the Way. This piece of Chinese wisdom literature was written by Lao-tzu, who probably lived about 500 B.C., close to the time of the author of Ecclesiastes. See how similar the following passage from the Tao te Ching is to Eccl 3.1–8:

There is a time for being ahead,
a time for being behind;
a time for being in motion,
a time for being at rest;
a time for being vigorous,
a time for being exhausted;
a time for being safe,
a time for being in danger.
(Stephen Mitchell, translator, *Tao te Ching*, no. 29)

▶ Eccl 3.1–8

PRAY IT!

The Balance of Life

God of all seasons,
Help me to remember the sun when it
  is raining.
Help me to remember the rain when the sun
  is shining.
Teach me to respect the seniors when I am a
  sophomore.
Teach me to respect the sophomores when I
  am a senior.
When I win on the field, let me remember
  the times I lost.
When I lose on the field, let me remember
  the times I won.
Guide me to appreciate studying when I'm
  taking a hard test.
Guide me to appreciate hard tests when I'm
  studying.
During times with friends, remind me of
  times alone.
During times alone, remind me of times with
  friends.
Help me to live all moments and remember
  there is a balance to life.
Amen.

▸ Eccl 3.1–8

testing them to show that they are but animals.
19 For the fate of humans and the fate of animals is
the same; as one dies, so dies the other. They all
have the same breath, and humans have no advantage over the animals; for all is vanity. 20 All go to
one place; all are from the dust, and all turn to dust
again. 21 Who knows whether the human spirit
goes upward and the spirit of animals goes downward to the earth? 22 So I saw that there is nothing
better than that all should enjoy their work, for that
is their lot; who can bring them to see what will be
after them?

4 Again I saw all the oppressions that are practiced under the sun. Look, the tears of the
oppressed—with no one to comfort them! On the
side of their oppressors there was power—with no
one to comfort them. 2 And I thought the dead,
who have already died, more fortunate than the living, who are still alive; 3 but better than both is the
one who has not yet been, and has not seen the evil
deeds that are done under the sun.

4 Then I saw that all toil and all skill in work
come from one person's envy of another. This also
is vanity and a chasing after wind.[i]

5 Fools fold their hands
    and consume their own flesh.
6 Better is a handful with quiet
    than two handfuls with toil,
    and a chasing after wind.[i]
7 Again, I saw vanity under the sun: 8 the case of

---

[i] Or *a feeding on wind.* See Hos 12.1

LIVE IT!

Eat, Drink, and Be Merry

Shirley. Do you know what the Bible says about the purpose of life?
Brian. Well, it says a lot of things. What did you find?
Shirley. Eat, drink, and be merry!
Brian. What? Where did you find that?
Shirley. Ecclesiastes 3.13.
Brian. It really says that?
Shirley. It says, "It is God's gift that all should eat and drink and take pleasure in all their
    toil." So, eat, drink, and be merry!
Brian. But remember the first part of the passage: "It is God's gift." To look on the simple
    pleasures of life as gifts from God changes the focus a bit.
Shirley. You're right. It adds a deeper purpose to the enjoyment. All those pleasures are
    gifts from a God who wants us to be happy and enjoy ourselves as long as we live, as it
    says in verse 12.
Brian. Yes, and verse 1 says, "For everything there is a season, and a time for every matter
    under heaven."
Shirley. I guess this is a time to be grateful for the simple gifts!

▸ Eccl 3.9–15

ECCL

solitary individuals, without sons or brothers; yet there is no end to all their toil, and their eyes are never satisfied with riches. "For whom am I toiling," they ask, "and depriving myself of pleasure?" This also is vanity and an unhappy business.

The Value of a Friend

9 Two are better than one, because they have a good reward for their toil. 10 For if they fall, one will lift up the other; but woe to one who is alone and falls and does not have another to help. 11 Again, if two lie together, they keep warm; but how can one keep warm alone? 12 And though one might prevail against another, two will withstand one. A threefold cord is not quickly broken.

13 Better is a poor but wise youth than an old but foolish king, who will no longer take advice. 14 One can indeed come out of prison to reign, even though born poor in the kingdom. 15 I saw all the living who, moving about under the sun, follow that*j* youth who replaced the king;*k* 16 there was no end to all those people whom he led. Yet those who come later will not rejoice in him. Surely this also is vanity and a chasing after wind.*l*

Reverence, Humility, and Contentment

5 *m* Guard your steps when you go to the house of God; to draw near to listen is better than the sacrifice offered by fools; for they do not know how to keep from doing evil.*n* 2 *o*Never be rash with your mouth, nor let your heart be quick to utter a word before God, for God is in heaven, and you upon earth; therefore let your words be few.

3 For dreams come with many cares, and a fool's voice with many words.

4 When you make a vow to God, do not delay fulfilling it; for he has no pleasure in fools. Fulfill what you vow. 5 It is better that you should not vow than that you should vow and not fulfill it. 6 Do not let your mouth lead you into sin, and do not say before the messenger that it was a mistake; why should God be angry at your words, and destroy the work of your hands?

7 With many dreams come vanities and a multitude of words;*p* but fear God.

8 If you see in a province the oppression of the poor and the violation of justice and right, do not be amazed at the matter; for the high official is watched by a higher, and there are yet higher ones over them. 9 But all things considered, this is an advantage for a land: a king for a plowed field.*p*

10 The lover of money will not be satisfied with money; nor the lover of wealth, with gain. This also is vanity.

11 When goods increase, those who eat them increase; and what gain has their owner but to see them with his eyes?

12 Sweet is the sleep of laborers, whether they eat little or much; but the surfeit of the rich will not let them sleep.

13 There is a grievous ill that I have seen under the sun: riches were kept by their owners to their hurt, 14 and those riches were lost in a bad venture; though they are parents of children, they have nothing in their hands. 15 As they came from their mother's womb, so they shall go again, naked as they came; they shall take nothing for their toil, which they may carry away with their hands. 16 This also is a grievous ill: just as they came, so shall they go; and what gain do they have from toiling for the

---

j Heb *the second*   *k* Heb *him*   *l* Or *a feeding on wind*. See Hos 12.1   *m* Ch 4.17 in Heb   *n* Cn: Heb *they do not know how to do evil*   *o* Ch 5.1 in Heb   *p* Meaning of Heb uncertain

E
C
C
L

How Much Is Enough?

LIVE IT!

How much wealth does one need? According to the Teacher, in Eccl 5.10, those who love money will always want more. What is God trying to tell us here? Maybe that real happiness is not found in material wealth. The more we want, the less satisfied we are. Money can be an evil when it is all we want and think about.

For a week, try to do things with your family and friends that do not cost anything. Play board games, go for walks or hikes, even volunteer some time at a community organization. Consider taking the money you save and donating it to a worthy cause.

▶ Eccl 5.10

wind? 17 Besides, all their days they eat in darkness, in much vexation and sickness and resentment.

18 This is what I have seen to be good: it is fitting to eat and drink and find enjoyment in all the toil with which one toils under the sun the few days of the life God gives us; for this is our lot. 19 Likewise all to whom God gives wealth and possessions and whom he enables to enjoy them, and to accept their lot and find enjoyment in their toil—this is the gift of God. 20 For they will scarcely brood over the days of their lives, because God keeps them occupied with the joy of their hearts.

The Frustration of Desires

6 There is an evil that I have seen under the sun, and it lies heavy upon humankind: 2 those to whom God gives wealth, possessions, and honor, so that they lack nothing of all that they desire, yet God does not enable them to enjoy these things, but a stranger enjoys them. This is vanity; it is a grievous ill. 3 A man may beget a hundred children, and live many years; but however many are the days of his years, if he does not enjoy life's good things, or has no burial, I say that a stillborn child is better off than he. 4 For it comes into vanity and goes into darkness, and in darkness its name is covered; 5 moreover it has not seen the sun or known anything; yet it finds rest rather than he. 6 Even though he should live a thousand years twice over, yet enjoy no good—do not all go to one place?

7 All human toil is for the mouth, yet the appetite is not satisfied. 8 For what advantage have the wise over fools? And what do the poor have who know how to conduct themselves before the living? 9 Better is the sight of the eyes than the wandering of desire; this also is vanity and a chasing after wind.*q*

10 Whatever has come to be has already been named, and it is known what human beings are, and that they are not able to dispute with those who are stronger. 11 The more words, the more vanity, so how is one the better? 12 For who knows what is good for mortals while they live the few days of their vain life, which they pass like a shadow? For who can tell them what will be after them under the sun?

A Disillusioned View of Life

7 A good name is better than precious
  ointment,
    and the day of death, than the day of
  birth.
2 It is better to go to the house of mourning
    than to go to the house of feasting;
  for this is the end of everyone,
    and the living will lay it to heart.
3 Sorrow is better than laughter,

for by sadness of countenance the heart is
    made glad.
4 The heart of the wise is in the house of
    mourning;
  but the heart of fools is in the house of
    mirth.
5 It is better to hear the rebuke of the wise
    than to hear the song of fools.
6 For like the crackling of thorns under a pot,
    so is the laughter of fools;
  this also is vanity.
7 Surely oppression makes the wise foolish,
    and a bribe corrupts the heart.
8 Better is the end of a thing than its beginning;
    the patient in spirit are better than the
      proud in spirit.
9 Do not be quick to anger,
    for anger lodges in the bosom of fools.
10 Do not say, "Why were the former days better
      than these?"
  For it is not from wisdom that you ask this.
11 Wisdom is as good as an inheritance,
    an advantage to those who see the sun.
12 For the protection of wisdom is like the
      protection of money,
  and the advantage of knowledge is that
    wisdom gives life to the one who
      possesses it.
13 Consider the work of God;
  who can make straight what he has made
    crooked?

14 In the day of prosperity be joyful, and in the day of adversity consider; God has made the one as well as the other, so that mortals may not find out anything that will come after them.

The Riddles of Life

15 In my vain life I have seen everything; there are righteous people who perish in their righteousness, and there are wicked people who prolong their life in their evildoing. 16 Do not be too righteous, and do not act too wise; why should you destroy yourself? 17 Do not be too wicked, and do not be a fool; why should you die before your time? 18 It is good that you should take hold of the one, without letting go of the other; for the one who fears God shall succeed with both.

19 Wisdom gives strength to the wise more than ten rulers that are in a city.

20 Surely there is no one on earth so righteous as to do good without ever sinning.

21 Do not give heed to everything that people say, or you may hear your servant cursing you; 22 your heart knows that many times you have yourself cursed others.

---

q Or *a feeding on wind.* See Hos 12.1

23 All this I have tested by wisdom; I said, "I will be wise," but it was far from me. 24 That which is, is far off, and deep, very deep; who can find it out? 25 I turned my mind to know and to search out and to seek wisdom and the sum of things, and to know that wickedness is folly and that foolishness is madness. 26 I found more bitter than death the woman who is a trap, whose heart is snares and nets, whose hands are fetters; one who pleases God escapes her, but the sinner is taken by her. 27 See, this is what I found, says the Teacher,ʳ adding one thing to another to find the sum, 28 which my mind has sought repeatedly, but I have not found. One man among a thousand I found, but a woman among all these I have not found. 29 See, this alone I found, that God made human beings straightforward, but they have devised many schemes.

Obey the King and Enjoy Yourself

8 Who is like the wise man?
And who knows the interpretation of a thing?
Wisdom makes one's face shine,
and the hardness of one's countenance is changed.

2 Keepˢ the king's command because of your sacred oath. 3 Do not be terrified; go from his presence, do not delay when the matter is unpleasant, for he does whatever he pleases. 4 For the word of the king is powerful, and who can say to him, "What are you doing?" 5 Whoever obeys a command will meet no harm, and the wise mind will know the time and way. 6 For every matter has its time and way, although the troubles of mortals lie heavy upon them. 7 Indeed, they do not know what is to be, for who can tell them how it will be? 8 No one has power over the windᵗ to restrain the wind,ᵗ or power over the day of death; there is no discharge from the battle, nor does wickedness deliver those who practice it. 9 All this I observed, applying my mind to all that is done under the sun, while one person exercises authority over another to the other's hurt.

God's Ways Are Inscrutable

10 Then I saw the wicked buried; they used to go in and out of the holy place, and were praised in the city where they had done such things.ᵘ This also is vanity. 11 Because sentence against an evil deed is not executed speedily, the human heart is fully set to do evil. 12 Though sinners do evil a hundred times and prolong their lives, yet I know that it will be well with those who fear God, because they stand in fear before him, 13 but it will not be well with the wicked, neither will they prolong their days like a shadow, because they do not stand in fear before God.

14 There is a vanity that takes place on earth, that there are righteous people who are treated according to the conduct of the wicked, and there are wicked people who are treated according to the conduct of the righteous. I said that this also is vanity. 15 So I commend enjoyment, for there is nothing better for people under the sun than to eat, and drink, and enjoy themselves, for this will go with them in their toil through the days of life that God gives them under the sun.

16 When I applied my mind to know wisdom, and to see the business that is done on earth, how one's eyes see sleep neither day nor night, 17 then I saw all the work of God, that no one can find out what is happening under the sun. However much they may toil in seeking, they will not find it out; even though those who are wise claim to know, they cannot find it out.

Take Life as It Comes

9 All this I laid to heart, examining it all, how the righteous and the wise and their deeds are in the hand of God; whether it is love or hate one does not know. Everything that confronts them 2 is vanity,ᵛ since the same fate comes to all,

---

ʳ *Qoheleth*, traditionally rendered *Preacher*   ˢ Heb *I keep*   ᵗ Or *breath*   ᵘ Meaning of Heb uncertain   ᵛ Syr Compare Gk: Heb *Everything that confronts them* 2*is everything*

did you KNOW?

Imagine There Is No Heaven

Some people assume that the ancient Israelites believed in an afterlife as we do today. However, Ecclesiastes speaks of the end of earthly life without any hint of eternal life: "The dead know nothing; they have no more reward, and even the memory of them is lost" (9.5). The book reflects the author's belief that all life ends with death. It was not until the last two centuries before Jesus that the idea of life after death began to take root among the Jewish people.

▸ **Eccl 9.5**

ECCL

to the righteous and the wicked, to the good and the evil,[w] to the clean and the unclean, to those who sacrifice and those who do not sacrifice. As are the good, so are the sinners; those who swear are like those who shun an oath. 3 This is an evil in all that happens under the sun, that the same fate comes to everyone. Moreover, the hearts of all are full of evil; madness is in their hearts while they live, and after that they go to the dead. 4 But whoever is joined with all the living has hope, for a living dog is better than a dead lion. 5 The living know that they will die, but the dead know nothing; they have no more reward, and even the memory of them is lost. 6 Their love and their hate and their envy have already perished; never again will they have any share in all that happens under the sun.

7 Go, eat your bread with enjoyment, and drink your wine with a merry heart; for God has long ago approved what you do. 8 Let your garments always be white; do not let oil be lacking on your head. 9 Enjoy life with the wife whom you love, all the days of your vain life that are given you under the sun, because that is your portion in life and in your toil at which you toil under the sun. 10 Whatever your hand finds to do, do with your might; for there is no work or thought or knowledge or wisdom in Shĕ'ōl, to which you are going.

11 Again I saw that under the sun the race is not to the swift, nor the battle to the strong, nor bread to the wise, nor riches to the intelligent, nor favor to the skillful; but time and chance happen to them all. 12 For no one can anticipate the time of disaster. Like fish taken in a cruel net, and like birds caught in a snare, so mortals are snared at a time of calamity, when it suddenly falls upon them.

9.7

Wisdom Superior to Folly

13 I have also seen this example of wisdom under the sun, and it seemed great to me. 14 There was a little city with few people in it. A great king came against it and besieged it, building great siegeworks against it. 15 Now there was found in it a poor wise man, and he by his wisdom delivered the city. Yet no one remembered that poor man. 16 So I said, "Wisdom is better than might; yet the poor man's wisdom is despised, and his words are not heeded."

17 The quiet words of the wise are more to be heeded
    than the shouting of a ruler among fools.
18 Wisdom is better than weapons of war,
    but one bungler destroys much good.

Miscellaneous Observations

10 Dead flies make the perfumer's
    ointment give off a foul odor;
so a little folly outweighs wisdom and
    honor.
2 The heart of the wise inclines to the right,
    but the heart of a fool to the left.
3 Even when fools walk on the road, they lack
    sense,
    and show to everyone that they are fools.
4 If the anger of the ruler rises against you, do
    not leave your post,
    for calmness will undo great offenses.

5 There is an evil that I have seen under the sun, as great an error as if it proceeded from the ruler: 6 folly is set in many high places, and the rich sit in a low place. 7 I have seen slaves on horseback, and princes walking on foot like slaves.

8 Whoever digs a pit will fall into it;
    and whoever breaks through a wall will be
      bitten by a snake.
9 Whoever quarries stones will be hurt by them;
    and whoever splits logs will be endangered
      by them.
10 If the iron is blunt, and one does not whet the
    edge,
    then more strength must be exerted;
    but wisdom helps one to succeed.
11 If the snake bites before it is charmed,
    there is no advantage in a charmer.

12 Words spoken by the wise bring them favor,
    but the lips of fools consume them.
13 The words of their mouths begin in
    foolishness,
    and their talk ends in wicked madness;
14 yet fools talk on and on.
    No one knows what is to happen,
    and who can tell anyone what the future holds?

---

w Gk Syr Vg: Heb lacks *and the evil*

LIVE IT!

Carpe Diem—"Seize the Day"!

"Youth is wasted on the young."

Perhaps you have heard that statement uttered by not-so-young adults struggling with growing older. There is some truth in it: many young people do not reflect on life and do not pause to appreciate being young.

The Teacher says some beautiful and profound things about youthfulness. He advises young people to "follow the inclination of your heart" (Eccl 11.9) and to "banish anxiety from your mind" (verse 10). Someone like the Teacher might say today: "Follow your heart, and do not spend so much time worrying. It is a blessing to be young, to have so much energy and so many dreams. There are many pressures and stresses on young people today, but do not let them dominate your life. Enjoy this special time of growth and discovery."

It is good to be young. Seize the day!

▸ Eccl 11.7–10

---

15 The toil of fools wears them out,
    for they do not even know the way to town.

16 Alas for you, O land, when your king is a
        servant,x
    and your princes feast in the morning!
17 Happy are you, O land, when your king is a
        nobleman,
    and your princes feast at the proper time—
    for strength, and not for drunkenness!
18 Through sloth the roof sinks in,
    and through indolence the house leaks.
19 Feasts are made for laughter;
    wine gladdens life,
    and money meets every need.
20 Do not curse the king, even in your thoughts,
    or curse the rich, even in your bedroom;
    for a bird of the air may carry your voice,
    or some winged creature tell the matter.

The Value of Diligence

11

Send out your bread upon the waters,
    for after many days you will get
        it back.
2 Divide your means seven ways, or even eight,
    for you do not know what disaster may
        happen on earth.
3 When clouds are full,
    they empty rain on the earth;
whether a tree falls to the south or to the north,
    in the place where the tree falls, there it will
        lie.
4 Whoever observes the wind will not sow;
    and whoever regards the clouds will not
        reap.
5 Just as you do not know how the breath comes to the bones in the mother's womb, so you do not know the work of God, who makes everything.

6 In the morning sow your seed, and at evening do not let your hands be idle; for you do not know which will prosper, this or that, or whether both alike will be good.

Youth and Old Age

7 Light is sweet, and it is pleasant for the eyes to see the sun.

8 Even those who live many years should rejoice in them all; yet let them remember that the days of darkness will be many. All that comes is vanity.

9 Rejoice, young man, while you are young, and let your heart cheer you in the days of your youth. Follow the inclination of your heart and the desire of your eyes, but know that for all these things God will bring you into judgment.

10 Banish anxiety from your mind, and put away pain from your body; for youth and the dawn of life are vanity.

12

Remember your creator in the days of your youth, before the days of trouble come, and the years draw near when you will say, "I have no pleasure in them"; 2 before the sun and the light and the moon and the stars are darkened and the clouds return withy the rain; 3 in the day when the guards of the house tremble, and the strong men are bent, and the women who grind cease working because they are few, and those who look through the windows see dimly; 4 when the doors on the street are shut, and the sound of the grinding is low, and one rises up at the sound of a bird, and all the daughters of song are brought low; 5 when one is afraid of heights, and terrors are in the road; the almond tree blossoms, the grasshopper drags itself alongz and desire fails; because all must go to their eternal home, and the mourners

---

x Or a child   y Or after; Heb 'ahar   z Or is a burden

Remember the Elderly

Ecclesiastes 12.1–8 is a bittersweet poem about the difficulties of the aging process. To understand it, you need to be aware of the metaphors used, like these:
- Guards of the house = arms and hands
- Strong men = legs
- Women who grind = teeth
- Windows = eyes
- Doors = ears or lips
- Silver cord, golden bowl = life itself

Aging is a natural part of life, but it is a struggle for many people. No one enjoys its accompanying loss of mobility, loss of strength, and problems with seeing and hearing. The struggle is even greater if one is alone. If you have aging grandparents, family friends, or neighbors, keep in mind how much they need to be noticed by you. Stay in touch with them so that you can learn from their wisdom and they can be strengthened by your youth!

▶ Eccl 12.1–8

will go about the streets; 6 before the silver cord is snapped,[a] and the golden bowl is broken, and the pitcher is broken at the fountain, and the wheel broken at the cistern, 7 and the dust returns to the earth as it was, and the breath[b] returns to God who gave it. 8 Vanity of vanities, says the Teacher;[c] all is vanity.

Epilogue

9 Besides being wise, the Teacher[c] also taught the people knowledge, weighing and studying and arranging many proverbs. 10 The Teacher[c] sought to find pleasing words, and he wrote words of truth plainly.

11 The sayings of the wise are like goads, and like nails firmly fixed are the collected sayings that are given by one shepherd.[d] 12 Of anything beyond these, my child, beware. Of making many books there is no end, and much study is a weariness of the flesh.

13 The end of the matter; all has been heard. Fear God, and keep his commandments; for that is the whole duty of everyone. 14 For God will bring every deed into judgment, including[e] every secret thing, whether good or evil.

---

[a] Syr Vg Compare Gk: Heb *is removed*   [b] Or *the spirit*
[c] *Qoheleth*, traditionally rendered *Preacher*   [d] Meaning of Heb uncertain   [e] Or *into the judgment on*

ECCL

Sex sells. When we see an ad with a beautiful woman slipping out of a sports car or a bare-chested man grabbing an ice-cold soda, we sit up and take notice. Advertisers love to take advantage of our fascination with sex. Once they have our attention, they can sell us something we might not even be interested in! The Song of Solomon—a collection of ancient love poems—reminds us that this powerful force is ultimately a gift from God.

At a Glance

- **1.1–6.** introduction
- **1.7—2.7.** opening dialog between the lovers
- **2.8—8.4.** various reflections and other dialogs
- **8.5–14.** final thoughts

In-depth

From an advertiser's point of view, the Song of Solomon is a well-kept secret. How many people are aware of its explicit sexual images? Consider these verses:

- "Let him kiss me with the kisses of his mouth!" (1.2).
- "Your lips distill nectar, my bride; / honey and milk are under your tongue" (4.11).
- "O may your breasts be like clusters of the vine, / and the scent of your breath like apples" (7.8).

Some people find these images so surprising that they wonder why the Song of Solomon is found in the Bible at all.

Scholars believe that the naming of King Solomon in the Song's first verse is the main reason that this book was preserved and eventually included with the Jewish holy books. Although written long after Solomon's death, this book—like Proverbs and Ecclesiastes—was attributed to him to give it authority.

Through the centuries, some people have not been able to accept the Song of Solomon as simply love poetry and have hunted for a deeper meaning. Many people believe that the lover and the beloved in this book stand for Israel and God, or for Jesus and the church. Modern-day scholars, however, begin their interpretation of the Song of Solomon at the literal level, that is, as a collection of love poems. The book's inclusion among the other holy books, they insist, is an affirmation of the goodness of human sexuality: human love is holy because it is a gift from God. The passion and beauty of human sexual attraction is a reflection of the passion and beauty of God's love for us!

Quick Facts

Author
unknown, probably writing after the Jews' return from the Babylonian Exile in 538 B.C.

Theme
poetry that expresses the goodness and passion of human love

Of Note
In other translations, this book is called the Song of Songs or the Canticle of Canticles.

The Song of Solomon

Song of Solomon

1 The Song of Songs, which is Solomon's.

Love's Desires

2 Let him kiss me with the kisses of his mouth!
For your love is better than wine,
3   your anointing oils are fragrant,
your name is perfume poured out;
   therefore the maidens love you.
4 Draw me after you, let us make haste.
   The king has brought me into his
      chambers.
We will exult and rejoice in you;
   we will extol your love more than wine;
rightly do they love you.

Love's Boast

5 I am black and beautiful,
   O daughters of Jerusalem,
like the tents of Kē′dar,
   like the curtains of Solomon.
6 Do not gaze at me because I am dark,
   because the sun has gazed on me.
My mother's sons were angry with me;
   they made me keeper of the
      vineyards,
but my own vineyard I have not kept!
7 Tell me, you whom my soul loves,
   where you pasture your flock,
   where you make it lie down at noon;

for why should I be like one who is veiled
   beside the flocks of your companions?

8 If you do not know,
   O fairest among women,
follow the tracks of the flock,
   and pasture your kids
   beside the shepherds' tents.

Vision of the Beloved

9 I compare you, my love,
   to a mare among Pharaoh's chariots.
10 Your cheeks are comely with ornaments,
   your neck with strings of jewels.
11 We will make you ornaments of gold,
   studded with silver.

12 While the king was on his couch,
   my nard gave forth its fragrance.
13 My beloved is to me a bag of myrrh
   that lies between my breasts.
14 My beloved is to me a cluster of henna
      blossoms
   in the vineyards of En-ge′di.

15 Ah, you are beautiful, my love;
   ah, you are beautiful;
   your eyes are doves.
16 Ah, you are beautiful, my beloved,
   truly lovely.

BLACK AND BEAUTIFUL

I am black and beautiful,
  O daughters of Jerusalem,
like the tents of Kēʹdar,
  like the curtains of Solomon.
         (Song 1.5)

Who is speaking to us in this Scripture text? Who is so boldly and confidently proclaiming to us that she is black and beautiful? Some traditions say this is the bride of Solomon, the son of David and the third king of Israel.

Many of the people in the Old Testament world were black Africans or Afro-Asiatics (Asians of black African heritage). They had various shades of dark skin. In Song 1.5, the bride describes herself as black like the tents of Kēʹdar; in 5.10, she describes her lover as ruddy (reddish) in color.

Some Africans are ruddy; others are darker. Together, all Africans are a rainbow of blackness. Whatever shade they are, it is good. And if you are one of them, you are black and beautiful!

▶ Song 1.5

Our couch is green;
17   the beams of our house are cedar,
    our rafters[a] are pine.

2 I am a rose[b] of Sharon,
    a lily of the valleys.

2 As a lily among brambles,
  so is my love among maidens.

3 As an apple tree among the trees of the wood,
  so is my beloved among young men.
With great delight I sat in his shadow,
  and his fruit was sweet to my taste.

4 He brought me to the banqueting house,
  and his intention toward me was
    love.

5 Sustain me with raisins,
  refresh me with apples;
for I am faint with love.

6 O that his left hand were under my head,
  and that his right hand embraced me!

7 I adjure you, O daughters of Jerusalem,
  by the gazelles or the wild does:
do not stir up or awaken love
  until it is ready!

Springtime Rhapsody

8 The voice of my beloved!
  Look, he comes,
leaping upon the mountains,
  bounding over the hills.

9 My beloved is like a gazelle
  or a young stag.
Look, there he stands
  behind our wall,
gazing in at the windows,
  looking through the lattice.

10 My beloved speaks and says to me:
"Arise, my love, my fair one,
  and come away;

11 for now the winter is past,
  the rain is over and gone.

12 The flowers appear on the earth;
  the time of singing has come,
and the voice of the turtledove
  is heard in our land.

13 The fig tree puts forth its figs,
  and the vines are in blossom;
  they give forth fragrance.
Arise, my love, my fair one,

---

a Meaning of Heb uncertain b Heb *crocus*

S
O
N
G

you have ravished my heart with a glance of
    your eyes,
with one jewel of your necklace.

10 How sweet is your love, my sister, my bride!
    how much better is your love than
        wine,
    and the fragrance of your oils than any
        spice!
11 Your lips distill nectar, my bride;
    honey and milk are under your tongue;
    the scent of your garments is like the scent
        of Lebanon.
12 A garden locked is my sister, my bride,
    a garden locked, a fountain sealed.
13 Your channels is an orchard of pomegranates
    with all choicest fruits,
    henna with nard,
14 nard and saffron, calamus and cinnamon,
    with all trees of frankincense,
    myrrh and aloes,
    with all chief spices—
15 a garden fountain, a well of living water,
    and flowing streams from Lebanon.

16 Awake, O north wind,
    and come, O south wind!
    Blow upon my garden
    that its fragrance may be wafted abroad.
    Let my beloved come to his garden,
    and eats its choicest fruits.

5 I come to my garden, my sister, my bride;
    I gather my myrrh with my spice,
    I eat my honeycomb with my honey,
    I drink my wine with my milk.

Eat, friends, drink,
    and be drunk with love.

Another Dream

2 I slept, but my heart was awake.
    Listen! my beloved is knocking.
    "Open to me, my sister, my love,
    my dove, my perfect one;
    for my head is wet with dew,
    my locks with the drops of the night."
3 I had put off my garment;
    how could I put it on again?
    I had bathed my feet;
    how could I soil them?
4 My beloved thrust his hand into the opening,
    and my inmost being yearned for him.
5 I arose to open to my beloved,
    and my hands dripped with myrrh,
    my fingers with liquid myrrh,
    upon the handles of the bolt.
6 I opened to my beloved,
    but my beloved had turned and was gone.
    My soul failed me when he spoke.

---

s Meaning of Heb uncertain

Sexuality and Dialogue

LIVE IT!

A number of the love songs included in the Song of Solomon are addressed to the bridegroom and the beloved. It is as if a romantic dialogue has been recorded as lovers express the depth of feeling and desire they have for each other.

Dialogue is an essential aspect in any relationship. Open and honest communication provides the basis for maintaining and deepening the bonds of respect, friendship, and love.

Here is a time-honored test for any deep relationship: Is it possible for the two of you to speak honestly with each other about anything—especially problems and difficulties? Are you willing and able to discuss all dimensions of your love—including sexual feelings and desires?

Young couples often avoid such sensitive conversations. They fall victim to embarrassment and confusion and often leave important things unsaid. Such failure to communicate can result in hurt feelings, misunderstandings, and even behaviors that can lead to manipulation, selfishness, and sin.

Don't be afraid to discuss sexual issues. Always be ready to examine the nature of your relationships, especially when the power and passion of sexuality are present. True sexual love is rooted in dialogue, honest communication, and commitment. It finds its fullest expression in the context of marriage.

▶ Song of Solomon, chapters 2–7

PRAY IT!
The Song of Songs

If human love is a reflection of divine love, then could parts of this love poem called the Song of Songs be understood as prayers? Could you read parts of it as your words to God, and other parts as God's words to you? Look at these sections:

- **2.2–6.** a prayer describing your passion for God
- **5.6–8.** a prayer to God when God seems absent
- **8.6–7.** God's words of love to you

The words may seem strange in this context, but if we are passionate about pursuing a human relationship, why can't we be passionate about pursuing our relationship with God? Some of the greatest saints expressed their love of God as a passionate, romantic love. You can do the same in your prayer with God!

I sought him, but did not find him;
  I called him, but he gave no answer.
7 Making their rounds in the city
  the sentinels found me;
they beat me, they wounded me,
  they took away my mantle,
  those sentinels of the walls.
8 I adjure you, O daughters of Jerusalem,
  if you find my beloved,
tell him this:
  I am faint with love.

Praise for the Bridegroom

9 What is your beloved more than another
    beloved,
  O fairest among women?
What is your beloved more than another
    beloved,
  that you thus adjure us?

10 My beloved is all radiant and ruddy,
  distinguished among ten thousand.
11 His head is the finest gold;
  his locks are wavy,
  black as a raven.
12 His eyes are like doves
  beside springs of water,
bathed in milk,
  fitly set.*h*
13 His cheeks are like beds of spices,
  yielding fragrance.

His lips are lilies,
  distilling liquid myrrh.
14 His arms are rounded gold,
  set with jewels.
His body is ivory work,*h*
  encrusted with sapphires.*i*
15 His legs are alabaster columns,
  set upon bases of gold.
His appearance is like Lebanon,
  choice as the cedars.
16 His speech is most sweet,
  and he is altogether desirable.
This is my beloved and this is my friend,
  O daughters of Jerusalem.

6 Where has your beloved gone,
    O fairest among women?
Which way has your beloved turned,
  that we may seek him with you?

2 My beloved has gone down to his garden,
  to the beds of spices,
to pasture his flock in the gardens,
  and to gather lilies.
3 I am my beloved's and my beloved is mine;
  he pastures his flock among the lilies.

The Bride's Matchless Beauty

4 You are beautiful as Tir'zah, my love,
  comely as Jerusalem,
  terrible as an army with banners.
5 Turn away your eyes from me,
  for they overwhelm me!
Your hair is like a flock of goats,
  moving down the slopes of Gil'e•ad.
6 Your teeth are like a flock of ewes,
  that have come up from the washing;
all of them bear twins,
  and not one among them is bereaved.
7 Your cheeks are like halves of a pomegranate
  behind your veil.
8 There are sixty queens and eighty concubines,
  and maidens without number.
9 My dove, my perfect one, is the only one,
  the darling of her mother,
  flawless to her that bore her.
The maidens saw her and called her happy;
  the queens and concubines also, and they
    praised her.
10 "Who is this that looks forth like the dawn,
  fair as the moon, bright as the sun,
  terrible as an army with banners?"

11 I went down to the nut orchard,
  to look at the blossoms of the valley,

---

h Meaning of Heb uncertain   *i* Heb *lapis lazuli*

to see whether the vines had budded,
  whether the pomegranates were in bloom.
12 Before I was aware, my fancy set me
  in a chariot beside my prince.*j*

13*k* Return, return, O Shū'lam•mīte!
  Return, return, that we may look upon you.

Why should you look upon the Shū'lam•mīte,
  as upon a dance before two armies?*l*

Expressions of Praise

7 How graceful are your feet in sandals,
  O queenly maiden!
Your rounded thighs are like jewels,
  the work of a master hand.
2 Your navel is a rounded bowl
  that never lacks mixed wine.
Your belly is a heap of wheat,
  encircled with lilies.
3 Your two breasts are like two fawns,
  twins of a gazelle.
4 Your neck is like an ivory tower.
Your eyes are pools in Hesh'bon,
  by the gate of Bath-rab'bim.
Your nose is like a tower of Lebanon,
  overlooking Damascus.
5 Your head crowns you like Car'mel,
  and your flowing locks are like purple;
  a king is held captive in the tresses.*m*

6 How fair and pleasant you are,
  O loved one, delectable maiden!*n*
7 You are stately*o* as a palm tree,
  and your breasts are like its clusters.
8 I say I will climb the palm tree
  and lay hold of its branches.
O may your breasts be like clusters of the
  vine,
  and the scent of your breath like apples,
9 and your kisses*p* like the best wine
  that goes down*q* smoothly,
  gliding over lips and teeth.*r*

10 I am my beloved's,
  and his desire is for me.
11 Come, my beloved,
  let us go forth into the fields,
  and lodge in the villages;
12 let us go out early to the vineyards,
  and see whether the vines have budded,
whether the grape blossoms have opened
  and the pomegranates are in bloom.
There I will give you my love.
13 The mandrakes give forth fragrance,
  and over our doors are all choice fruits,
new as well as old,

did you KNOW?
Sex in the Old Testament

Through its surprisingly graphic sexual content (see, for example, 7.1–9), the Song of Solomon has surprised many generations of readers. It reminds us that one of the richest images of the Old Testament is a sexual one: God as the faithful lover of Israel. In Ex 20.5, we hear of God's jealous love of the Chosen People. By the time of the early prophets, the image of God as lover was fully developed: "On that day, says the LORD, you will call me 'My husband'" (Hos 2.16).

Because of ancient Israel's conviction that human love reflects divine love—and vice versa—there was a high regard for human sexuality. This regard was reflected in Israel's sexual morality. Free-for-all sex stood in clear contradiction of the holiness of God, whose faithful love was the model for all human love. The Ten Commandments prohibit not only having sex with someone else's spouse but also desiring someone else's spouse.

Despite these high standards, some Bible stories do not comment on the morality of behavior that would be unacceptable in Christian morality. They make no comment on the many patriarchs and kings who have more than one wife, and take for granted an inferior status of women in marriage. Because of problems like these, we must remember to read biblical passages in light of the *whole* Bible and the Christian tradition. In the Old Testament, we find the seeds of Christian sexual morality, not its full flower.

which I have laid up for you, O my
  beloved.
8 O that you were like a brother to me,
  who nursed at my mother's breast!
If I met you outside, I would kiss you,
  and no one would despise me.
2 I would lead you and bring you

---

j Cn: Meaning of Heb uncertain   *k* Ch 7.1 in Heb   *l* Or *dance of Mahanaim*   *m* Meaning of Heb uncertain   *n* Syr: Heb *in delights*   *o* Heb *This your stature is*   *p* Heb *palate*   *q* Heb *down for my lover*   *r* Gk Syr Vg: Heb *lips of sleepers*

into the house of my mother,
and into the chamber of the one who
    bore me.[s]
I would give you spiced wine to drink,
    the juice of my pomegranates.

3 O that his left hand were under my head,
    and that his right hand embraced me!
4 I adjure you, O daughters of Jerusalem,
    do not stir up or awaken love
    until it is ready!

Homecoming

5 Who is that coming up from the wilderness,
    leaning upon her beloved?

Under the apple tree I awakened you.
There your mother was in labor with you;
    there she who bore you was in labor.
6 Set me as a seal upon your heart,
    as a seal upon your arm;
for love is strong as death,
    passion fierce as the grave.
Its flashes are flashes of fire,
    a raging flame.
7 Many waters cannot quench love,
    neither can floods drown it.
If one offered for love
    all the wealth of one's house,
    it would be utterly scorned.

8 We have a little sister,
    and she has no breasts.

What shall we do for our sister,
    on the day when she is spoken for?
9 If she is a wall,
    we will build upon her a battlement of
        silver;
but if she is a door,
    we will enclose her with boards of cedar.
10 I was a wall,
    and my breasts were like towers;
then I was in his eyes
    as one who brings[t] peace.
11 Solomon had a vineyard at Bā′al-hā′mon;
    he entrusted the vineyard to keepers;
    each one was to bring for its fruit a
        thousand pieces of silver.
12 My vineyard, my very own, is for myself;
    you, O Solomon, may have the
        thousand,
    and the keepers of the fruit two hundred!

13 O you who dwell in the gardens,
    my companions are listening for your
        voice;
    let me hear it.

14 Make haste, my beloved,
    and be like a gazelle
or a young stag
    upon the mountains of spices!

---

s Gk Syr: Heb *my mother; she (or you) will teach me*
t Or *finds*

The Wisdom of Solomon

Do you know what life was like for your great-grandparents? How much of their history do you know? Time and distance have a way of fading the memories that keep our roots alive. The same was true for the ancient Jewish people after they had set-tled in different countries. The Wisdom of Solomon was written to remind them of their roots and the wisdom of their traditions.

At a Glance

In-depth

The Jewish people living in Alexandria, Egypt, in the first century B.C. had long forgotten the difficult transition their ancestors had experienced in moving from Judea. In fact, they had come to feel so much at home in Alexandria that certain leaders began to fear that the Jewish faith and way of life might be lost (see "Diaspora Jews," Esth 2.5). One of those leaders wrote the Wisdom of Solomon to encourage the "displaced" Jews to remain faithful to their heritage. Although incorporating new ideas into traditional arguments, the author insists that true wisdom is, in fact, very old. Its course can be traced "from the beginning of creation" (Wis 6.22).

The Wisdom of Solomon grapples with another problem—good versus evil—in a refreshing way. The author is convinced that there will be a final judgment, in which good people "will stand with great confidence," and evil people will shake "with dreadful fear" (5.1–2). What is more, the good will live forever (5.15), whereas the evil will disappear without a trace (4.18–19). Like Second Maccabees, the Wisdom of Solomon sees life after death as the answer to the troubling question, Why do innocent people suffer although God is good and just?

The Wisdom of Solomon claims King Solomon as its honorary author, even though it was written long after his death. In this quiet way, it reminds the Jewish faithful that they must never forget their roots in their ancient faith, even though they feel at home in their new land. The book shows how people of faith take the best of their history and tradition to find new answers in new situations.

Quick Facts

Author
unknown, writing around 50 B.C., making this the latest of all Old Testament books

Theme
the reward of the righteous, the praise of wisdom, the importance of trust in God

Of Note
The book is not found in every translation of the Old Testament (see "The Case of the Missing Books," Tob 1.16).

Wisdom

6.12

Exhortation to Uprightness

(Wis 6.1–11)

1 Love righteousness, you rulers of the earth,
  think of the Lord in goodness
and seek him with sincerity of heart;
2 because he is found by those who do not put
    him to the test,
  and manifests himself to those who do not
    distrust him.
3 For perverse thoughts separate people
    from God,
  and when his power is tested, it exposes the
    foolish;
4 because wisdom will not enter a deceitful
    soul,
  or dwell in a body enslaved to sin.
5 For a holy and disciplined spirit will flee from
    deceit,
  and will leave foolish thoughts behind,
  and will be ashamed at the approach of
    unrighteousness.

6 For wisdom is a kindly spirit,
  but will not free blasphemers from the guilt of
    their words;
  because God is witness of their inmost feelings,
  and a true observer of their hearts, and a hearer
    of their tongues.
7 Because the spirit of the Lord has filled the
    world,

and that which holds all things together knows
    what is said,
8 therefore those who utter unrighteous things
    will not escape notice,
  and justice, when it punishes, will not pass
    them by.
9 For inquiry will be made into the counsels of
    the ungodly,
  and a report of their words will come to the
    Lord,
  to convict them of their lawless deeds;
10 because a jealous ear hears all things,
  and the sound of grumbling does not go
    unheard.
11 Beware then of useless grumbling,
  and keep your tongue from slander;
  because no secret word is without result,[a]
  and a lying mouth destroys the soul.

12 Do not invite death by the error of your
    life,
  or bring on destruction by the works of your
    hands;
13 because God did not make death,
  and he does not delight in the death of the
    living.
14 For he created all things so that they might
    exist;

---

a Or *will go unpunished*

733

the generative forces[b] of the world are
>wholesome,
and there is no destructive poison in them,
and the dominion[c] of Hades is not on earth.
15 For righteousness is immortal.

PRAY IT!

God Knows Our Heart

God, you know my heart (Wis 1.6) even
better than I do. This could scare me,
or it could give me peace—the peace of
knowing that despite my weakness and sin,
you still love me. I choose to feel peace! And
knowing that you see my heart truly and
still love me, I choose to do good. Give me
the courage to do the right thing. Help me
never to say a word meant to injure another
person. Give me too the wisdom of loving
justice, so that my heart might be a reflec-
tion of your own. Amen.

▸ **Wis 1.6–15**

Life as the Ungodly See It

16 But the ungodly by their words and deeds
>summoned death;[d]
considering him a friend, they pined away
and made a covenant with him,
because they are fit to belong to his
>company.

2 For they reasoned unsoundly, saying to
>themselves,
"Short and sorrowful is our life,
and there is no remedy when a life comes to its
>end,
and no one has been known to return from
>Hades.
2 For we were born by mere chance,
and hereafter we shall be as though we had
>never been,
for the breath in our nostrils is smoke,
and reason is a spark kindled by the beating of
>our hearts;
3 when it is extinguished, the body will turn to
>ashes,
and the spirit will dissolve like empty air.
4 Our name will be forgotten in time,
and no one will remember our works;
our life will pass away like the traces of a
>cloud,
and be scattered like mist
that is chased by the rays of the sun

and overcome by its heat.
5 For our allotted time is the passing of a
>shadow,
and there is no return from our death,
because it is sealed up and no one turns back.

6 "Come, therefore, let us enjoy the good things
>that exist,
and make use of the creation to the full as in
>youth.
7 Let us take our fill of costly wine and
>perfumes,
and let no flower of spring pass us by.
8 Let us crown ourselves with rosebuds before
>they wither.
9 Let none of us fail to share in our revelry;
everywhere let us leave signs of enjoyment,
because this is our portion, and this our lot.
10 Let us oppress the righteous poor man;
let us not spare the widow
or regard the gray hairs of the aged.
11 But let our might be our law of right,
for what is weak proves itself to be useless.

12 "Let us lie in wait for the righteous man,
because he is inconvenient to us and opposes
>our actions;
he reproaches us for sins against the law,
and accuses us of sins against our training.
13 He professes to have knowledge of God,
and calls himself a child[e] of the Lord.
14 He became to us a reproof of our
>thoughts;
15 the very sight of him is a burden to us,
because his manner of life is unlike that of
>others,
and his ways are strange.
16 We are considered by him as something
>base,
and he avoids our ways as unclean;
he calls the last end of the righteous happy,
and boasts that God is his father.
17 Let us see if his words are true,
and let us test what will happen at the end of
>his life;
18 for if the righteous man is God's child, he will
>help him,
and will deliver him from the hand of his
>adversaries.
19 Let us test him with insult and torture,
so that we may find out how gentle he is,
and make trial of his forbearance.
20 Let us condemn him to a shameful death,
for, according to what he says, he will be
>protected."

---

b Or *the creatures*   c Or *palace*   d Gk *him*   e Or *servant*

Error of the Wicked
(Cp Gen 1.26–27)

21 Thus they reasoned, but they were led astray,
for their wickedness blinded them,
22 and they did not know the secret purposes
of God,
nor hoped for the wages of holiness,
nor discerned the prize for blameless souls;
23 for God created us for incorruption,
and made us in the image of his own eternity,*f*
24 but through the devil's envy death entered the
world,
and those who belong to his company
experience it.

The Destiny of the Righteous
(Wis 4.17)

3 But the souls of the righteous are in the
hand of God,
and no torment will ever touch them.
2 In the eyes of the foolish they seemed to have
died,
and their departure was thought to be a
disaster,
3 and their going from us to be their destruction;
but they are at peace.
4 For though in the sight of others they were
punished,
their hope is full of immortality.
5 Having been disciplined a little, they will
receive great good,
because God tested them and found them
worthy of himself;
6 like gold in the furnace he tried them,
and like a sacrificial burnt offering he accepted
them.
7 In the time of their visitation they will shine
forth,
and will run like sparks through the stubble.
8 They will govern nations and rule over peoples,
and the Lord will reign over them forever.
9 Those who trust in him will understand truth,
and the faithful will abide with him in love,
because grace and mercy are upon his holy
ones,
and he watches over his elect.*g*

The Destiny of the Ungodly

10 But the ungodly will be punished as their
reasoning deserves,
those who disregarded the righteous*h*
and rebelled against the Lord;
11 for those who despise wisdom and instruction
are miserable.
Their hope is vain, their labors are
unprofitable,
and their works are useless.

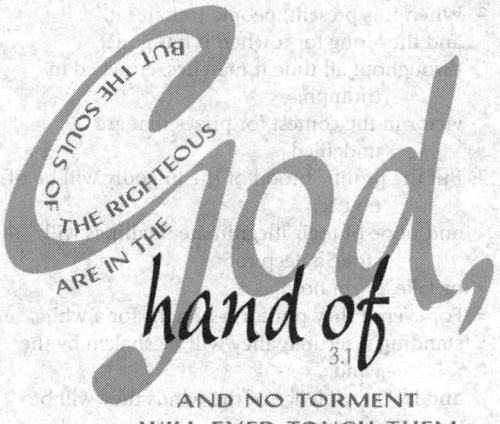

BUT THE SOULS OF THE RIGHTEOUS ARE IN THE God, hand of 3.1
AND NO TORMENT
WILL EVER TOUCH THEM

12 Their wives are foolish, and their children evil;
13 their offspring are accursed.

On Childlessness
(Sir 16.3)

For blessed is the barren woman who is
undefiled,
who has not entered into a sinful union;
she will have fruit when God examines souls.
14 Blessed also is the eunuch whose hands have
done no lawless deed,
and who has not devised wicked things against
the Lord;
for special favor will be shown him for his
faithfulness,
and a place of great delight in the temple of
the Lord.
15 For the fruit of good labors is renowned,
and the root of understanding does not fail.
16 But children of adulterers will not come to
maturity,
and the offspring of an unlawful union will
perish.
17 Even if they live long they will be held of no
account,
and finally their old age will be without
honor.
18 If they die young, they will have no hope
and no consolation on the day of judgment.
19 For the end of an unrighteous generation is
grievous.

4 Better than this is childlessness with virtue,
for in the memory of virtue*i* is immortality,
because it is known both by God and by
mortals.

---

f Other ancient authorities read *nature* *g* Text of this line
uncertain; omitted by some ancient authorities. Compare
4.15   *h* Or *what is right* *i* Gk *it*

WIS

2 When it is present, people imitate[j] it,
and they long for it when it has gone;
throughout all time it marches, crowned in
triumph,
victor in the contest for prizes that are
undefiled.

3 But the prolific brood of the ungodly will be of
no use,
and none of their illegitimate seedlings will
strike a deep root
or take a firm hold.

4 For even if they put forth boughs for a while,
standing insecurely they will be shaken by the
wind,
and by the violence of the winds they will be
uprooted.

5 The branches will be broken off before they
come to maturity,
and their fruit will be useless,
not ripe enough to eat, and good for nothing.

6 For children born of unlawful unions
are witnesses of evil against their parents when
God examines them.[k]

7 But the righteous, though they die early, will
be at rest.

8 For old age is not honored for length of time,
or measured by number of years;

9 but understanding is gray hair for anyone,
and a blameless life is ripe old age.

10 There were some who pleased God and were
loved by him,
and while living among sinners were taken up.

11 They were caught up so that evil might not
change their understanding
or guile deceive their souls.

12 For the fascination of wickedness obscures
what is good,
and roving desire perverts the innocent mind.

13 Being perfected in a short time, they fulfilled
long years;

14 for their souls were pleasing to the Lord,
therefore he took them quickly from the midst
of wickedness.

15 Yet the peoples saw and did not understand,
or take such a thing to heart,
that God's grace and mercy are with his
elect,
and that he watches over his holy ones.

The Triumph of the Righteous

16 The righteous who have died will condemn the
ungodly who are living,
and youth that is quickly perfected[l] will
condemn the prolonged old age of the
unrighteous.

17 For they will see the end of the wise,

and will not understand what the Lord
purposed for them,
and for what he kept them safe.

18 The unrighteous[m] will see, and will have
contempt for them,
but the Lord will laugh them to scorn.
After this they will become dishonored corpses,
and an outrage among the dead forever;

19 because he will dash them speechless to the
ground,
and shake them from the foundations;
they will be left utterly dry and barren,
and they will suffer anguish,
and the memory of them will perish.

The Final Judgment

20 They will come with dread when their sins are
reckoned up,
and their lawless deeds will convict them to
their face.

5 Then the righteous will stand with great
confidence
in the presence of those who have oppressed
them
and those who make light of their labors.

2 When the unrighteous[n] see them, they will be
shaken with dreadful fear,
and they will be amazed at the unexpected
salvation of the righteous.

3 They will speak to one another in repentance,
and in anguish of spirit they will groan, and
say,

4 "These are persons whom we once held in
derision
and made a byword of reproach—fools that
we were!
We thought that their lives were madness
and that their end was without honor.

5 Why have they been numbered among the
children of God?
And why is their lot among the saints?

6 So it was we who strayed from the way of
truth,
and the light of righteousness did not shine
on us,
and the sun did not rise upon us.

7 We took our fill of the paths of lawlessness and
destruction,
and we journeyed through trackless deserts,
but the way of the Lord we have not
known.

8 What has our arrogance profited us?
And what good has our boasted wealth
brought us?

---

j Other ancient authorities read *honor*   k Gk *at their
examination*   l Or *ended*   m Gk *They*   n Gk *they*

9 "All those things have vanished like a shadow,
and like a rumor that passes by;

10 like a ship that sails through the billowy water,
and when it has passed no trace can be found,
no track of its keel in the waves;

11 or as, when a bird flies through the air,
no evidence of its passage is found;
the light air, lashed by the beat of its pinions
and pierced by the force of its rushing flight,
is traversed by the movement of its wings,
and afterward no sign of its coming is found
there;

12 or as, when an arrow is shot at a target,
the air, thus divided, comes together at once,
so that no one knows its pathway.

13 So we also, as soon as we were born,
ceased to be,
and we had no sign of virtue to show,
but were consumed in our wickedness."

14 Because the hope of the ungodly is like
thistledown[o] carried by the wind,
and like a light frost[p] driven away by a storm;
it is dispersed like smoke before the wind,
and it passes like the remembrance of a guest
who stays but a day.

The Reward of the Righteous
(Eph 6.10–20)

15 But the righteous live forever,
and their reward is with the Lord;
the Most High takes care of them.

16 Therefore they will receive a glorious crown
and a beautiful diadem from the hand of the
Lord,
because with his right hand he will cover them,
and with his arm he will shield them.

17 The Lord[q] will take his zeal as his whole armor,
and will arm all creation to repel[r] his enemies;

18 he will put on righteousness as a breastplate,
and wear impartial justice as a helmet;

19 he will take holiness as an invincible shield,

20 and sharpen stern wrath for a sword,
and creation will join with him to fight against
his frenzied foes.

21 Shafts of lightning will fly with true aim,
and will leap from the clouds to the target, as
from a well-drawn bow,

22 and hailstones full of wrath will be hurled as
from a catapult;
the water of the sea will rage against them,
and rivers will relentlessly overwhelm them;

23 a mighty wind will rise against them,
and like a tempest it will winnow them
away.
Lawlessness will lay waste the whole earth,
and evildoing will overturn the thrones of
rulers.

Kings Should Seek Wisdom
(Rom 13.1)

6 Listen therefore, O kings, and understand;
learn, O judges of the ends of the earth.

2 Give ear, you that rule over multitudes,
and boast of many nations.

3 For your dominion was given you from the
Lord,
and your sovereignty from the Most High;
he will search out your works and inquire into
your plans.

4 Because as servants of his kingdom you did not
rule rightly,
or keep the law,
or walk according to the purpose of God,

5 he will come upon you terribly and swiftly,
because severe judgment falls on those in high
places.

6 For the lowliest may be pardoned in mercy,
but the mighty will be mightily tested.

7 For the Lord of all will not stand in awe of
anyone,
or show deference to greatness;
because he himself made both small and great,
and he takes thought for all alike.

8 But a strict inquiry is in store for the mighty.

9 To you then, O monarchs, my words are
directed,
so that you may learn wisdom and not
transgress.

10 For they will be made holy who observe holy
things in holiness,
and those who have been taught them will find
a defense.

11 Therefore set your desire on my words;
long for them, and you will be instructed.

Description of Wisdom
(Cp Prov 8.1–36)

12 Wisdom is radiant and unfading,
and she is easily discerned by those who love
her,
and is found by those who seek her.

13 She hastens to make herself known to those
who desire her.

14 One who rises early to seek her will have no
difficulty,
for she will be found sitting at the gate.

15 To fix one's thought on her is perfect
understanding,
and one who is vigilant on her account will
soon be free from care,

16 because she goes about seeking those worthy
of her,

WIS

---

o Other ancient authorities read *dust*   *p* Other ancient
authorities read *spider's web*   *q* Gk He   *r* Or *punish*

Wisdom Speaks

My name is Wisdom. In Greek, I am called Sophia. The Bible speaks of me as an aspect, or image, of God. I am sought after by many. I reveal myself to few. I appear many times in the Scriptures, yet I am elusive. What is it about me that is so attractive, so appealing? Solomon prayed for understanding, and I came to him. Indeed, wisdom is often associated with his name.

Those who seek me must desire deep in their heart to know me. That desire is the first step to finding me. The next is patience. Nothing of true and lasting importance comes quickly. Quiet time is essential. You must be willing to simply be present, with no agenda. Imagine a "radiant and unfading" flame (Wis 6.12). Let that be your focus.

Soon, I will come to you. I will seek you out. I will meet you in your thoughts, and we will become friends. We will dance together, you and I. You will be changed, transformed. You will grow deeper, quieter, and peace will begin to fill your soul.

My name is Wisdom. I want to be your friend. I wait for you.

---

and she graciously appears to them in their
   paths,
and meets them in every thought.

17 The beginning of wisdom[s] is the most sincere
   desire for instruction,
   and concern for instruction is love of her,
18 and love of her is the keeping of her laws,
   and giving heed to her laws is assurance of
   immortality,
19 and immortality brings one near to God;
20 so the desire for wisdom leads to a kingdom.

21 Therefore if you delight in thrones and
   scepters, O monarchs over the peoples,
   honor wisdom, so that you may reign forever.
22 I will tell you what wisdom is and how she
   came to be,
   and I will hide no secrets from you,
   but I will trace her course from the beginning
   of creation,
   and make knowledge of her clear,
   and I will not pass by the truth;
23 nor will I travel in the company of sickly
   envy,
   for envy[t] does not associate with wisdom.
24 The multitude of the wise is the salvation of
   the world,
   and a sensible king is the stability of any
   people.
25 Therefore be instructed by my words, and you
   will profit.

Solomon Like Other Mortals

7 I also am mortal, like everyone else,
   a descendant of the first-formed child of
   earth;

and in the womb of a mother I was molded
   into flesh,
2 within the period of ten months, compacted
   with blood,
   from the seed of a man and the pleasure of
   marriage.
3 And when I was born, I began to breathe the
   common air,
   and fell upon the kindred earth;
   my first sound was a cry, as is true of all.
4 I was nursed with care in swaddling cloths.
5 For no king has had a different beginning of
   existence;
6 there is for all one entrance into life, and one
   way out.

Solomon's Respect for Wisdom
(1 Kings 3.3–9; Wis 9.1–18)

7 Therefore I prayed, and understanding was
   given me;
   I called on God, and the spirit of wisdom came
   to me.
8 I preferred her to scepters and thrones,
   and I accounted wealth as nothing in
   comparison with her.
9 Neither did I liken to her any priceless gem,
   because all gold is but a little sand in her sight,
   and silver will be accounted as clay before her.
10 I loved her more than health and beauty,
   and I chose to have her rather than light,
   because her radiance never ceases.
11 All good things came to me along with her,
   and in her hands uncounted wealth.
12 I rejoiced in them all, because wisdom leads
   them;

---

s Gk *Her beginning*   t Gk *this*

but I did not know that she was their mother.

13 I learned without guile and I impart without
grudging;
I do not hide her wealth,

14 for it is an unfailing treasure for mortals;
those who get it obtain friendship with God,
commended for the gifts that come from
instruction.

Solomon Prays for Wisdom

15 May God grant me to speak with judgment,
and to have thoughts worthy of what I have
received;
for he is the guide even of wisdom
and the corrector of the wise.

16 For both we and our words are in his hand,
as are all understanding and skill in crafts.

17 For it is he who gave me unerring knowledge
of what exists,
to know the structure of the world and the
activity of the elements;

18 the beginning and end and middle of times,
the alternations of the solstices and the
changes of the seasons,

19 the cycles of the year and the constellations of
the stars,

20 the natures of animals and the tempers of wild
animals,
the powers of spirits[u] and the thoughts of
human beings,
the varieties of plants and the virtues of roots;

21 I learned both what is secret and what is
manifest,

22 for wisdom, the fashioner of all things,
taught me.

The Nature of Wisdom
(Jn 1.1–14; Heb 1.1–4)

There is in her a spirit that is intelligent, holy,
unique, manifold, subtle,

---

u Or *winds*

THE SOURCE OF WISDOM

Solomon valued wisdom above riches, authority, health, and beauty (Wis 7.7–10). All of God's
creation is seen as a potential source of wisdom. Notice how this is reflected in the following
prayer:

Oh Great Spirit, whose voice I hear in the winds
And whose breath gives life to everyone,
Hear me.
I come to you as one of your many children;
I am weak . . . I am small . . . I need your wisdom and your strength.
Let me walk in beauty, and make my eyes ever behold the red and purple sunsets.
Make my hands respect the things you have made, and make my ears sharp so I may hear your
    voice.
Make me wise, so that I may understand what you have taught my people and
The lessons you have hidden in each leaf and each rock.
I ask for wisdom and strength,
Not to be superior to my brothers, but to be able to fight my greatest enemy, myself.
Make me ever ready to come before you with clean hands and a straight eye,
So as life fades away as a fading sunset,
My spirit may come to you without shame.

(Author unknown, "Ojibwa Prayer")

▶ Wis 7.7–12

How Do You Image God?

Old Testament writers sometimes used attributes of God, such as spirit, word, and justice, as titles for God. Wisdom is another of these titles. Each title gives us some insight into God's nature, although no one of them, or even all of them together, can give us the whole picture. The author of the Book of Wisdom describes God's wisdom as a woman, which gives us insight into God's feminine dimension.

Read the qualities of wisdom given in Wis 7.23—8.1. This passage summarizes the author's understanding of God's nature. It was probably familiar to New Testament authors. Aspects of it show up in the Letter to the Hebrews (1.1–4) and in the Gospel of John (1.1–14).

Explore your images of God. Choose an attribute of God that is significant for you. It might be love, faithfulness, truth, or some other quality. Write a poem, like the one in Wis 8.2–8, that describes this quality as a person.

▸ **Wis 7.23—8.8**

mobile, clear, unpolluted,
distinct, invulnerable, loving the good, keen,
irresistible, 23 beneficent, humane,
steadfast, sure, free from anxiety,
all-powerful, overseeing all,
and penetrating through all spirits
that are intelligent, pure, and altogether subtle.
24 For wisdom is more mobile than any motion;
because of her pureness she pervades and
    penetrates all things.
25 For she is a breath of the power of God,
and a pure emanation of the glory of the
    Almighty;
therefore nothing defiled gains entrance into her.
26 For she is a reflection of eternal light,
a spotless mirror of the working of God,
and an image of his goodness.
27 Although she is but one, she can do all things,
and while remaining in herself, she renews all
    things;
in every generation she passes into holy souls
and makes them friends of God, and prophets;
28 for God loves nothing so much as the person
    who lives with wisdom.

29 She is more beautiful than the sun,
and excels every constellation of the stars.
Compared with the light she is found to be
    superior,
30 for it is succeeded by the night,
but against wisdom evil does not prevail.
8 She reaches mightily from one end of the
    earth to the other,
and she orders all things well.

Solomon's Love for Wisdom
(Cp Prov 8.22–31)

2 I loved her and sought her from my youth;
I desired to take her for my bride,
and became enamored of her beauty.
3 She glorifies her noble birth by living with
    God,
and the Lord of all loves her.
4 For she is an initiate in the knowledge of God,
and an associate in his works.
5 If riches are a desirable possession in life,
what is richer than wisdom, the active cause of
    all things?
6 And if understanding is effective,
who more than she is fashioner of what exists?
7 And if anyone loves righteousness,
her labors are virtues;
for she teaches self-control and prudence,
justice and courage;
nothing in life is more profitable for mortals
    than these.
8 And if anyone longs for wide experience,
she knows the things of old, and infers the
    things to come;
she understands turns of speech and the
    solutions of riddles;
she has foreknowledge of signs and wonders
and of the outcome of seasons and times.

Wisdom Indispensible to Rulers

9 Therefore I determined to take her to live
    with me,
knowing that she would give me good counsel
and encouragement in cares and grief.
10 Because of her I shall have glory among the
    multitudes
and honor in the presence of the elders,
    though I am young.
11 I shall be found keen in judgment,
and in the sight of rulers I shall be admired.
12 When I am silent they will wait for me,
and when I speak they will give heed;
if I speak at greater length,
they will put their hands on their mouths.
13 Because of her I shall have immortality,
and leave an everlasting remembrance to those
    who come after me.

14 I shall govern peoples,
and nations will be subject to me;
15 dread monarchs will be afraid of me when they
hear of me;
among the people I shall show myself capable,
and courageous in war.
16 When I enter my house, I shall find rest with
her;
for companionship with her has no bitterness,
and life with her has no pain, but gladness and
joy.
17 When I considered these things inwardly,
and pondered in my heart
that in kinship with wisdom there is
immortality,
18 and in friendship with her, pure delight,
and in the labors of her hands, unfailing
wealth,
and in the experience of her company,
understanding,
and renown in sharing her words,
I went about seeking how to get her for myself.
19 As a child I was naturally gifted,
and a good soul fell to my lot;
20 or rather, being good, I entered an undefiled
body.
21 But I perceived that I would not possess
wisdom unless God gave her to me—
and it was a mark of insight to know whose
gift she was—
so I appealed to the Lord and implored him,
and with my whole heart I said:

Solomon's Prayer for Wisdom
(1 Kings 3.3–9; Wis 7.7–22a)

9 "O God of my ancestors and Lord of mercy,
who have made all things by your word,
2 and by your wisdom have formed humankind
to have dominion over the creatures you have
made,
3 and rule the world in holiness and
righteousness,
and pronounce judgment in uprightness of
soul,
4 give me the wisdom that sits by your throne,
and do not reject me from among your servants.
5 For I am your servant[v] the son of your serving
girl,
a man who is weak and short-lived,
with little understanding of judgment and
laws;
6 for even one who is perfect among human
beings
will be regarded as nothing without the
wisdom that comes from you.
7 You have chosen me to be king of your people
and to be judge over your sons and daughters.

8 You have given command to build a temple on
your holy mountain,
and an altar in the city of your habitation,
a copy of the holy tent that you prepared from
the beginning.
9 With you is wisdom, she who knows your works
and was present when you made the world;
she understands what is pleasing in your sight
and what is right according to your
commandments.
10 Send her forth from the holy heavens,
and from the throne of your glory send her,
that she may labor at my side,
and that I may learn what is pleasing to you.
11 For she knows and understands all things,
and she will guide me wisely in my actions
and guard me with her glory.
12 Then my works will be acceptable,
and I shall judge your people justly,
and shall be worthy of the throne[w] of my
father.
13 For who can learn the counsel of God?
Or who can discern what the Lord wills?
14 For the reasoning of mortals is worthless,
and our designs are likely to fail;
15 for a perishable body weighs down the soul,
and this earthy tent burdens the thoughtful[x]
mind.
16 We can hardly guess at what is on earth,
and what is at hand we find with labor;
but who has traced out what is in the heavens?
17 Who has learned your counsel,
unless you have given wisdom
and sent your holy spirit from on high?
18 And thus the paths of those on earth were set
right,
and people were taught what pleases you, and
were saved by wisdom."

The Work of Wisdom from Adam to Moses

10 Wisdom[y] protected the first-formed
father of the world, when he
alone had been created;
she delivered him from his transgression,
2 and gave him strength to rule all things.
3 But when an unrighteous man departed from
her in his anger,
he perished because in rage he killed his brother.
4 When the earth was flooded because of him,
wisdom again saved it,
steering the righteous man by a paltry piece of
wood.
5 Wisdom[y] also, when the nations in wicked
agreement had been put to confusion,

---

v Gk *slave*   w Gk *thrones*   x Or *anxious*   y Gk *She*

recognized the righteous man and preserved
  him blameless before God,
and kept him strong in the face of his
  compassion for his child.

6 Wisdom[z] rescued a righteous man when the
    ungodly were perishing;
  he escaped the fire that descended on the Five
    Cities.[a]
7 Evidence of their wickedness still remains:
  a continually smoking wasteland,
  plants bearing fruit that does not ripen,
  and a pillar of salt standing as a monument to
    an unbelieving soul.
8 For because they passed wisdom by,
  they not only were hindered from recognizing
    the good,
  but also left for humankind a reminder of their
    folly,
  so that their failures could never go unnoticed.

9 Wisdom rescued from troubles those who
    served her.
10 When a righteous man fled from his brother's
    wrath,

she guided him on straight paths;
she showed him the kingdom of God,
and gave him knowledge of holy things;
she prospered him in his labors,
and increased the fruit of his toil.

11 When his oppressors were covetous,
  she stood by him and made him rich.
12 She protected him from his enemies,
  and kept him safe from those who lay in wait
    for him;
  in his arduous contest she gave him the
    victory,
  so that he might learn that godliness is more
    powerful than anything else.

13 When a righteous man was sold, wisdom[b] did
    not desert him,
  but delivered him from sin.
  She descended with him into the dungeon,
14 and when he was in prison she did not leave
    him,
  until she brought him the scepter of a kingdom
    and authority over his masters.

_z_ Gk She   _a_ Or on Pentapolis   _b_ Gk she

WORDS FROM A FATHER TO HIS SON!

The following translation of a text originally written in Nahuatl is the wisdom of a native father in
sixteenth-century Mexico. This spirit of wisdom still exists in many Mexican families.

My son, . . . my precious feather, you have come to life, been born, been blessed to come
into the world in the land of our LORD. The One for whom we live forged your life, gave you
shape. We, your mother and father, have watched over you; your aunts and uncles, all your
family, have watched over you, have cried for you, have suffered for you that you might be
born. (P. 49)

Love and serve others in holiness; respect and obey your mother and father, and do their
hearts' desire. Your gift of service, obedience, and respect will be the recompense they deserve. (P. 53)

Push away from you all that is not good: that which is wrong, all the things that dishonor
you. . . . Do no damage to the community, or the peace. Because if you do bad things, you
will not come away unscathed: you must eventually suffer for such actions. (P. 79)

With these words, I encourage and strengthen you; through them, I console you. Throw
away nothing I have told you, nothing you have heard. May all this be your inspiration, helping
you always to remember the LORD, our God. (P. 86)

(Miguel Léon-Portilla and Librado Silva Galeana,
Huehuehtlahtolli, as translated by Richard Wood)

Those who accused him she showed to be
false,
and she gave him everlasting honor.

Wisdom Led the Israelites out of Egypt
(Ex 13—15)

15 A holy people and blameless race
wisdom delivered from a nation of oppressors.

16 She entered the soul of a servant of the Lord,
and withstood dread kings with wonders and
signs.

17 She gave to holy people the reward of their
labors;
she guided them along a marvelous way,
and became a shelter to them by day,
and a starry flame through the night.

18 She brought them over the Red Sea,
and led them through deep waters;

19 but she drowned their enemies,
and cast them up from the depth of the sea.

20 Therefore the righteous plundered the ungodly;
they sang hymns, O Lord, to your holy name,
and praised with one accord your defending
hand;

21 for wisdom opened the mouths of those who
were mute,
and made the tongues of infants speak clearly.

Wisdom Led the Israelites through the Desert
(Ex 15—17)

11 Wisdom*c* prospered their works by the
hand of a holy prophet.

2 They journeyed through an uninhabited
wilderness,
and pitched their tents in untrodden places.

3 They withstood their enemies and fought off
their foes.

4 When they were thirsty, they called upon you,
and water was given them out of flinty rock,
and from hard stone a remedy for their thirst.

5 For through the very things by which their
enemies were punished,
they themselves received benefit in their need.

6 Instead of the fountain of an ever-flowing river,
stirred up and defiled with blood

7 in rebuke for the decree to kill the infants,
you gave them abundant water unexpectedly,

8 showing by their thirst at that time
how you punished their enemies.

9 For when they were tried, though they were
being disciplined in mercy,
they learned how the ungodly were tormented
when judged in wrath.

10 For you tested them as a parent*d* does in
warning,
but you examined the ungodly*e* as a stern king
does in condemnation.

11 Whether absent or present, they were equally
distressed,

12 for a twofold grief possessed them,
and a groaning at the memory of what had
occurred.

13 For when they heard that through their own
punishments
the righteous*f* had received benefit, they
perceived it was the Lord's doing.

14 For though they had mockingly rejected him
who long before had been cast out and
exposed,
at the end of the events they marveled at him,
when they felt thirst in a different way from the
righteous.

Punishment of the Wicked
(Ex 7—11)

15 In return for their foolish and wicked thoughts,
which led them astray to worship irrational
serpents and worthless animals,
you sent upon them a multitude of irrational
creatures to punish them,

16 so that they might learn that one is punished
by the very things by which one sins.

17 For your all-powerful hand,
which created the world out of formless matter,
did not lack the means to send upon them a
multitude of bears, or bold lions,

18 or newly-created unknown beasts full of rage,
or such as breathe out fiery breath,
or belch forth a thick pall of smoke,
or flash terrible sparks from their eyes;

19 not only could the harm they did destroy
people,*g*
but the mere sight of them could kill by fright.

20 Even apart from these, people*f* could fall at a
single breath
when pursued by justice
and scattered by the breath of your power.
But you have arranged all things by measure
and number and weight.

God Is Powerful and Merciful

21 For it is always in your power to show great
strength,
and who can withstand the might of your arm?

22 Because the whole world before you is like a
speck that tips the scales,
and like a drop of morning dew that falls on
the ground.

23 But you are merciful to all, for you can do all
things,
and you overlook people's sins, so that they
may repent.

W
I
S

---

c Gk *She*   *d* Gk *a father*   *e* Gk *those*   *f* Gk *they*   *g* Gk *them*

WORDS FROM A MOTHER TO HER DAUGHTER!

The following translation of a text originally written in Nahuatl is the wisdom of a native mother in sixteenth-century Mexico. This spirit of wisdom still exists in many Mexican families.

Now, my daughter, my turtledove, little woman: you have life, you are born. You have entered the world, emerged from my womb, nourished at my breast. Our LORD forged your life, shaped you, made you within me. . . . Our LORD makes each of us earn our reputation, our honor, our warmth, our passion, our sweetness, our savor. . . .

Sing well, speak well, converse deeply, respond to all, pray deeply; words are not to be bought and sold. Never allow the world to make you stupid, or silly. . . . In this way, you will live among the people, and you will be worthy of all you need . . . you will please our LORD and be worthy of our LORD's kindness and mercy. (Pp. 91–92)

Be not a friend to liars, to thieves, to evil women, to meddlers, to those who are lazy. . . . And if you have belongings or property, do not waste them; do not display them when you go out to the market. . . . Then you will leave what is yours to your children and grandchildren after you.

If you live in this way, as I have taught you, then in truth, you will live well among your own people, favored by all. (Pp. 95–97)

(Miguel Léon-Portilla and Librado Silva Galeana,
Huehuehtlahtolli, **as translated by Richard Wood)**

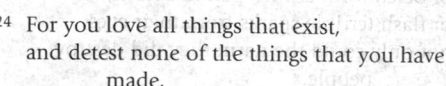

24 For you love all things that exist,
and detest none of the things that you have
made,
for you would not have made anything if you
had hated it.
25 How would anything have endured if you had
not willed it?
Or how would anything not called forth by
you have been preserved?
26 You spare all things, for they are yours,
O Lord, you who love the living.

12 For your immortal spirit is in all things.
2 Therefore you correct little by little
those who trespass,
and you remind and warn them of the things
through which they sin,
so that they may be freed from wickedness and
put their trust in you, O Lord.

The Sins of the Canaanites
(Ex 23.20–33; Deut 18.9–14)

3 Those who lived long ago in your holy land
4 you hated for their detestable practices,
their works of sorcery and unholy rites,
5 their merciless slaughter[h] of children,

and their sacrificial feasting on human flesh
and blood.
These initiates from the midst of a heathen
cult,[i]
6 these parents who murder helpless lives,
you willed to destroy by the hands of our
ancestors,
7 so that the land most precious of all to you
might receive a worthy colony of the servants[j]
of God.
8 But even these you spared, since they were but
mortals,
and sent wasps[k] as forerunners of your army
to destroy them little by little,
9 though you were not unable to give the
ungodly into the hands of the
righteous in battle,
or to destroy them at one blow by dread wild
animals or your stern word.
10 But judging them little by little you gave them
an opportunity to repent,

---

h Gk *slaughterers* i Meaning of Gk uncertain
j Or *children* k Or *hornets*

though you were not unaware that their origin[l]
was evil
and their wickedness inborn,
and that their way of thinking would never
change.
11 For they were an accursed race from the
beginning,
and it was not through fear of anyone that you
left them unpunished for their sins.

God Is Sovereign

12 For who will say, "What have you done?"
or will resist your judgment?
Who will accuse you for the destruction of
nations that you made?
Or who will come before you to plead as an
advocate for the unrighteous?
13 For neither is there any god besides you, whose
care is for all people,[m]
to whom you should prove that you have not
judged unjustly;
14 nor can any king or monarch confront you
about those whom you have punished.
15 You are righteous and you rule all things
righteously,
deeming it alien to your power
to condemn anyone who does not deserve to
be punished.
16 For your strength is the source of
righteousness,
and your sovereignty over all causes you to
spare all.
17 For you show your strength when people
doubt the completeness of your power,
and you rebuke any insolence among those
who know it.[n]
18 Although you are sovereign in strength, you
judge with mildness,
and with great forbearance you govern us;
for you have power to act whenever you
choose.

God's Lessons for Israel

19 Through such works you have taught your
people
that the righteous must be kind,
and you have filled your children with good
hope,
because you give repentance for sins.
20 For if you punished with such great care and
indulgence[o]
the enemies of your servants[p] and those
deserving of death,
granting them time and opportunity to give up
their wickedness,
21 with what strictness you have judged your
children,

to whose ancestors you gave oaths and
covenants full of good promises!
22 So while chastening us you scourge our
enemies ten thousand times more,
so that, when we judge, we may meditate upon
your goodness,
and when we are judged, we may expect mercy.

The Punishment of the Egyptians

23 Therefore those who lived unrighteously, in a
life of folly,
you tormented through their own
abominations.
24 For they went far astray on the paths of error,
accepting as gods those animals that even their
enemies[q] despised;
they were deceived like foolish infants.
25 Therefore, as though to children who cannot
reason,
you sent your judgment to mock them.
26 But those who have not heeded the warning of
mild rebukes
will experience the deserved judgment of God.
27 For when in their suffering they became
incensed
at those creatures that they had thought to be
gods, being punished by means of
them,
they saw and recognized as the true God the
one whom they had before refused to
know.
Therefore the utmost condemnation came
upon them.

The Foolishness of Nature Worship

13 For all people who were ignorant of
God were foolish by nature;
and they were unable from the good things
that are seen to know the one who
exists,
nor did they recognize the artisan while paying
heed to his works;
2 but they supposed that either fire or wind or
swift air,
or the circle of the stars, or turbulent water,
or the luminaries of heaven were the gods that
rule the world.
3 If through delight in the beauty of these things
people assumed them to be gods,
let them know how much better than these is
their Lord,
for the author of beauty created them.
4 And if people[q] were amazed at their power and
working,

---

[l] Or *nature*   [m] Or *all things*   [n] Meaning of Gk uncertain
[o] Other ancient authorities lack *and indulgence*; others read
and entreaty   [p] Or *children*   [q] Gk *they*

WIS

let them perceive from them
how much more powerful is the one who
    formed them.

5 For from the greatness and beauty of created
    things
comes a corresponding perception of their
    Creator.

6 Yet these people are little to be blamed,
for perhaps they go astray
while seeking God and desiring to find him.

7 For while they live among his works, they keep
    searching,
and they trust in what they see, because the
    things that are seen are beautiful.

8 Yet again, not even they are to be excused;

9 for if they had the power to know so much
that they could investigate the world,
how did they fail to find sooner the Lord of
    these things?

The Foolishness of Idolatry
(Isa 44.9–20; Jer 10.1–16; Let Jer 8–73)

10 But miserable, with their hopes set on dead
    things, are those
who give the name "gods" to the works of
    human hands,
gold and silver fashioned with skill,
and likenesses of animals,
or a useless stone, the work of an ancient hand.

11 A skilled woodcutter may saw down a tree easy
    to handle
and skillfully strip off all its bark,
and then with pleasing workmanship
make a useful vessel that serves life's needs,

12 and burn the cast-off pieces of his work
to prepare his food, and eat his fill.

13 But a cast-off piece from among them, useful
    for nothing,
a stick crooked and full of knots,
he takes and carves with care in his leisure,
and shapes it with skill gained in idleness;*r*
he forms it in the likeness of a human being,

14 or makes it like some worthless animal,
giving it a coat of red paint and coloring its
    surface red
and covering every blemish in it with paint;

15 then he makes a suitable niche for it,
and sets it in the wall, and fastens it there with
    iron.

16 He takes thought for it, so that it may not
    fall,
because he knows that it cannot help itself,
for it is only an image and has need of help.

17 When he prays about possessions and his
    marriage and children,
he is not ashamed to address a lifeless thing.

18 For health he appeals to a thing that is weak;

for life he prays to a thing that is dead;
for aid he entreats a thing that is utterly
    inexperienced;
for a prosperous journey, a thing that cannot
    take a step;

19 for money-making and work and success with
    his hands
he asks strength of a thing whose hands have
    no strength.

Folly of a Navigator Praying to an Idol

14 Again, one preparing to sail and about
    to voyage over raging waves
calls upon a piece of wood more fragile than
    the ship that carries him.

2 For it was desire for gain that planned that
    vessel,
and wisdom was the artisan who built it;

3 but it is your providence, O Father, that steers
    its course,
because you have given it a path in the sea,
and a safe way through the waves,

4 showing that you can save from every
    danger,
so that even a person who lacks skill may put
    to sea.

5 It is your will that works of your wisdom
    should not be without effect;
therefore people trust their lives even to the
    smallest piece of wood,
and passing through the billows on a raft they
    come safely to land.

6 For even in the beginning, when arrogant
    giants were perishing,
the hope of the world took refuge on a raft,
and guided by your hand left to the world the
    seed of a new generation.

7 For blessed is the wood by which righteousness
    comes.

8 But the idol made with hands is accursed, and
    so is the one who made it—
he for having made it, and the perishable thing
    because it was named a god.

9 For equally hateful to God are the ungodly and
    their ungodliness;

10 for what was done will be punished together
    with the one who did it.

11 Therefore there will be a visitation also upon
    the heathen idols,
because, though part of what God created, they
    became an abomination,
snares for human souls
and a trap for the feet of the foolish.

---

r Other ancient authorities read *with intelligent skill*

WIS

LIVE IT!

God Is My Copilot!

The message in Wis 14.3 seems to be saying, "Don't put your trust in a little idol made of wood; it is the one true God who helps you, who guides you, who sets your course!"

Your life has many challenges. One way to face those challenges is to take God along on the journey. When you feel like you can't go on, call on God. When you fail and stumble, call on God. When you succeed, call on God and celebrate. God is here to be your copilot, to help you navigate through life, so just let go and let God!

▸ **Wis 14.1–7**

The Origin and Evils of Idolatry

12 For the idea of making idols was the beginning
    of fornication,
and the invention of them was the corruption
    of life;
13 for they did not exist from the beginning,
nor will they last forever.
14 For through human vanity they entered the
    world,
and therefore their speedy end has been
    planned.

15 For a father, consumed with grief at an
    untimely bereavement,
made an image of his child, who had been
    suddenly taken from him;
he now honored as a god what was once a
    dead human being,
and handed on to his dependents secret rites
    and initiations.
16 Then the ungodly custom, grown strong with
    time, was kept as a law,
and at the command of monarchs carved
    images were worshiped.
17 When people could not honor monarchss in
    their presence, since they lived at a
    distance,
they imagined their appearance far away,
and made a visible image of the king whom
    they honored,
so that by their zeal they might flatter the
    absent one as though present.
18 Then the ambition of the artisan impelled
even those who did not know the king to
    intensify their worship.
19 For he, perhaps wishing to please his ruler,
skillfully forced the likeness to take more
    beautiful form,
20 and the multitude, attracted by the charm of
    his work,

now regarded as an object of worship the one
    whom shortly before they had
    honored as a human being.
21 And this became a hidden trap for humankind,
because people, in bondage to misfortune or to
    royal authority,
bestowed on objects of stone or wood the
    name that ought not to be shared.

22 Then it was not enough for them to err about
    the knowledge of God,
but though living in great strife due to
    ignorance,
they call such great evils peace.
23 For whether they kill children in their
    initiations, or celebrate secret
    mysteries,
or hold frenzied revels with strange customs,
24 they no longer keep either their lives or their
    marriages pure,
but they either treacherously kill one another,
    or grieve one another by adultery,
25 and all is a raging riot of blood and murder,
    theft and deceit, corruption,
    faithlessness, tumult, perjury,
26 confusion over what is good, forgetfulness of
    favors,
defiling of souls, sexual perversion,
disorder in marriages, adultery, and
    debauchery.
27 For the worship of idols not to be named
is the beginning and cause and end of every
    evil.
28 For their worshiperst either rave in exultation,
or prophesy lies, or live unrighteously, or
    readily commit perjury;
29 for because they trust in lifeless idols
they swear wicked oaths and expect to suffer
    no harm.

---

s Gk *them*　t Gk *they*

W
I
S

30 But just penalties will overtake them on two
     counts:
because they thought wrongly about God in
     devoting themselves to idols,
and because in deceit they swore unrighteously
     through contempt for holiness.
31 For it is not the power of the things by which
     people swear,*u*
but the just penalty for those who sin,
that always pursues the transgression of the
     unrighteous.

Benefits of Worshiping the True God

15 But you, our God, are kind and true,
     patient, and ruling all things*v* in mercy.
2 For even if we sin we are yours, knowing your
     power;
but we will not sin, because we know that you
     acknowledge us as yours.
3 For to know you is complete righteousness,
and to know your power is the root of
     immortality.
4 For neither has the evil intent of human art
     misled us,
nor the fruitless toil of painters,
a figure stained with varied colors,
5 whose appearance arouses yearning in fools,
so that they desire*w* the lifeless form of a dead
     image.
6 Lovers of evil things and fit for such objects of
     hope*x*
are those who either make or desire or worship
     them.

The Foolishness of Worshiping Clay Idols

7 A potter kneads the soft earth
and laboriously molds each vessel for our
     service,
fashioning out of the same clay
both the vessels that serve clean uses
and those for contrary uses, making all alike;
but which shall be the use of each of them
the worker in clay decides.
8 With misspent toil, these workers form a futile
     god from the same clay—
these mortals who were made of earth a short
     time before
and after a little while go to the earth from
     which all mortals are taken,
when the time comes to return the souls that
     were borrowed.
9 But the workers are not concerned that mortals
     are destined to die
or that their life is brief,
but they compete with workers in gold and
     silver,
and imitate workers in copper;

and they count it a glorious thing to mold
     counterfeit gods.
10 Their heart is ashes, their hope is cheaper than
     dirt,
and their lives are of less worth than clay,
11 because they failed to know the one who
     formed them
and inspired them with active souls
and breathed a living spirit into them.
12 But they considered our existence an idle
     game,
and life a festival held for profit,
for they say one must get money however one
     can, even by base means.
13 For these persons, more than all others, know
     that they sin
when they make from earthy matter fragile
     vessels and carved images.

14 But most foolish, and more miserable than an
     infant,
are all the enemies who oppressed your
     people.
15 For they thought that all their heathen idols
     were gods,
though these have neither the use of their eyes
     to see with,
nor nostrils with which to draw breath,
nor ears with which to hear,
nor fingers to feel with,
and their feet are of no use for walking.
16 For a human being made them,
and one whose spirit is borrowed formed
     them;
for none can form gods that are like
     themselves.
17 People are mortal, and what they make with
     lawless hands is dead;
for they are better than the objects they
     worship,
since*y* they have life, but the idols*z* never had.

Serpents in the Desert
(Num 11.31–35; 21.6–9)

18 Moreover, they worship even the most hateful
     animals,
which are worse than all others when judged
     by their lack of intelligence;
19 and even as animals they are not so beautiful
     in appearance that one would desire
     them,
but they have excaped both the praise of God
     and his blessing.

---

u Or *of the oaths people swear*   *v* Or *ruling the universe*   *w* Gk
and he desires   *x* Gk *such hopes*   *y* Other ancient authorities
read *of which*   *z* Gk *but they*

16

Therefore those people[a] were deservedly punished through such creatures,
and were tormented by a multitude of animals.

2 Instead of this punishment you showed kindness to your people,
and you prepared quails to eat,
a delicacy to satisfy the desire of appetite;

3 in order that those people, when they desired food,
might lose the least remnant of appetite[b]
because of the odious creatures sent to them,
while your people,[a] after suffering want a short time,
might partake of delicacies.

4 For it was necessary that upon those oppressors inescapable want should come,
while to these others it was merely shown how their enemies were being tormented.

5 For when the terrible rage of wild animals came upon your people[c]
and they were being destroyed by the bites of writhing serpents,
your wrath did not continue to the end;

6 they were troubled for a little while as a warning,
and received a symbol of deliverance to remind them of your law's command.

7 For the one who turned toward it was saved, not by the thing that was beheld,
but by you, the Savior of all.

8 And by this also you convinced our enemies that it is you who deliver from every evil.

9 For they were killed by the bites of locusts and flies,
and no healing was found for them,
because they deserved to be punished by such things.

10 But your children were not conquered even by the fangs of venomous serpents,
for your mercy came to their help and healed them.

11 To remind them of your oracles they were bitten,
and then were quickly delivered,
so that they would not fall into deep forgetfulness
and become unresponsive[d] to your kindness.

12 For neither herb nor poultice cured them,
but it was your word, O Lord, that heals all people.

13 For you have power over life and death;
you lead mortals down to the gates of Hades and back again.

14 A person in wickedness kills another,
but cannot bring back the departed spirit,
or set free the imprisoned soul.

Disastrous Storms Strike Egypt

15 To escape from your hand is impossible;

16 for the ungodly, refusing to know you,
were flogged by the strength of your arm,
pursued by unusual rains and hail and relentless storms,
and utterly consumed by fire.

17 For—most incredible of all—in water, which quenches all things,
the fire had still greater effect,
for the universe defends the righteous.

18 At one time the flame was restrained,
so that it might not consume the creatures sent against the ungodly,
but that seeing this they might know
that they were being pursued by the judgment of God;

19 and at another time even in the midst of water it burned more intensely than fire,
to destroy the crops of the unrighteous land.

The Israelites Receive Manna
(Ex 16.1–21)

20 Instead of these things you gave your people food of angels,
and without their toil you supplied them from heaven with bread ready to eat,
providing every pleasure and suited to every taste.

21 For your sustenance manifested your sweetness toward your children;
and the bread, ministering[e] to the desire of the one who took it,
was changed to suit everyone's liking.

22 Snow and ice withstood fire without melting,
so that they might know that the crops of their enemies
were being destroyed by the fire that blazed in the hail
and flashed in the showers of rain;

23 whereas the fire,[f] in order that the righteous might be fed,
even forgot its native power.

24 For creation, serving you who made it,
exerts itself to punish the unrighteous,
and in kindness relaxes on behalf of those who trust in you.

25 Therefore at that time also, changed into all forms,

---

a Gk they   b Gk loathed the necessary appetite   c Gk them
d Meaning of Gk uncertain   e Gk and it, ministering
f Gk this

it served your all-nourishing bounty,
according to the desire of those who had need,*g*

26 so that your children, whom you loved,
   O Lord, might learn
that it is not the production of crops that feeds
   humankind
but that your word sustains those who trust in
   you.

27 For what was not destroyed by fire
was melted when simply warmed by a fleeting
   ray of the sun,

28 to make it known that one must rise before the
   sun to give you thanks,
and must pray to you at the dawning of the
   light;

29 for the hope of an ungrateful person will melt
   like wintry frost,
and flow away like waste water.

Terror Strikes the Egyptians at Night
(Ex 10.21–23)

17 Great are your judgments and hard to
      describe;
therefore uninstructed souls have gone astray.

2 For when lawless people supposed that they
      held the holy nation in their power,
they themselves lay as captives of darkness and
   prisoners of long night,
shut in under their roofs, exiles from eternal
   providence.

3 For thinking that in their secret sins they were
   unobserved
behind a dark curtain of forgetfulness,
they were scattered, terribly *h* alarmed,
and appalled by specters.

4 For not even the inner chamber that held them
      protected them from fear,
but terrifying sounds rang out around them,
and dismal phantoms with gloomy faces
      appeared.

5 And no power of fire was able to give light,
nor did the brilliant flames of the stars
avail to illumine that hateful night.

6 Nothing was shining through to them
except a dreadful, self-kindled fire,
and in terror they deemed the things that they
   saw
to be worse than that unseen appearance.

7 The delusions of their magic art lay humbled,
and their boasted wisdom was scornfully
   rebuked.

8 For those who promised to drive off the fears
      and disorders of a sick soul
were sick themselves with ridiculous fear.

9 For even if nothing disturbing frightened them,
yet, scared by the passing of wild animals and
   the hissing of snakes

10 they perished in trembling fear,
refusing to look even at the air, though it
      nowhere could be avoided.

11 For wickedness is a cowardly thing,
      condemned by its own testimony;*i*
distressed by conscience, it has always
      exaggerated*j* the difficulties.

12 For fear is nothing but a giving up of the helps
      that come from reason;

13 and hope, defeated by this inward
      weakness,
prefers ignorance of what causes the
   torment.

14 But throughout the night, which was really
      powerless
and which came upon them from the recesses
      of powerless Hades,
they all slept the same sleep,

15 and now were driven by monstrous specters,
and now were paralyzed by their souls'
      surrender;
for sudden and unexpected fear overwhelmed
      them.

16 And whoever was there fell down,
and thus was kept shut up in a prison not
      made of iron;

17 for whether they were farmers or shepherds
or workers who toiled in the wilderness, they
      were seized, and endured the
      inescapable fate;
for with one chain of darkness they all were
      bound.

18 Whether there came a whistling wind,
or a melodious sound of birds in wide-
      spreading branches,
or the rhythm of violently rushing water,

19 or the harsh crash of rocks hurled down,
or the unseen running of leaping animals,
or the sound of the most savage roaring
      beasts,
or an echo thrown back from a hollow of the
      mountains,
it paralyzed them with terror.

20 For the whole world was illumined with
      brilliant light,
and went about its work unhindered,

21 while over those people alone heavy night was
      spread,
an image of the darkness that was destined to
      receive them;
but still heavier than darkness were they to
      themselves.

---

g Or *who made supplication*   *h* Other ancient authorities read
*unobserved, they were darkened behind a dark curtain of
forgetfulness, terribly*   *i* Meaning of Gk uncertain   *j* Other
ancient authorities read *anticipated*

The Exodus Pattern

The Exodus refers to all the events surrounding God's leading the formerly enslaved Israelites out of Egypt as recorded in the Books of Exodus, Leviticus, Numbers, and Deuteronomy. Because the Exodus was an important experience in the Israelites' religious history, later biblical writers began to see in it a pattern in which God rescued the just and punished the wicked.

The author of the Wisdom of Solomon applies the Exodus pattern to explain how the righteous will be rewarded and sinners will be punished in the author's time. Throughout chapters 11–19, the writer refers to the journey through the desert, the Egyptians, the plagues, the manna in the desert, the pillars of fire, and the Red Sea. The author even takes the liberty of adding details that were not recorded in the original books! In doing so, the writer reminds the people of that time that the pattern of the Exodus is being repeated in their life now, so they should not lose hope that God will be with them always.

▸ **Wis 11.1—19.22**

Light Shines on the Israelites
(Ex 13.17–22)

18 But for your holy ones there was very great light.

Their enemies[k] heard their voices but did not
see their forms,
and counted them happy for not having
suffered,

2 and were thankful that your holy ones,[l] though
previously wronged, were doing them
no injury;
and they begged their pardon for having been
at variance with them.[l]

3 Therefore you provided a flaming pillar of fire
as a guide for your people's[m] unknown
journey,
and a harmless sun for their glorious
wandering.

4 For their enemies[n] deserved to be deprived of
light and imprisoned in darkness,

those who had kept your children imprisoned,
through whom the imperishable light of the
law was to be given to the world.

The Death of the Egyptian Firstborn
(Ex 12.29–30; 14.26–31)

5 When they had resolved to kill the infants of
your holy ones,
and one child had been abandoned and
rescued,
you in punishment took away a multitude of
their children;
and you destroyed them all together by a
mighty flood.

6 That night was made known beforehand to our
ancestors,
so that they might rejoice in sure knowledge of
the oaths in which they trusted.

7 The deliverance of the righteous and the
destruction of their enemies
were expected by your people.

8 For by the same means by which you punished
our enemies
you called us to yourself and glorified us.

9 For in secret the holy children of good people
offered sacrifices,
and with one accord agreed to the divine law,
so that the saints would share alike the same
things,
both blessings and dangers;
and already they were singing the praises of the
ancestors.[o]

10 But the discordant cry of their enemies echoed
back,
and their piteous lament for their children was
spread abroad.

11 The slave was punished with the same penalty
as the master,
and the commoner suffered the same loss as
the king;

12 and they all together, by the one form[p] of
death,
had corpses too many to count.
For the living were not sufficient even to bury
them,
since in one instant their most valued children
had been destroyed.

13 For though they had disbelieved everything
because of their magic arts,
yet, when their firstborn were destroyed, they
acknowledged your people to be God's
child.

14 For while gentle silence enveloped all things,

---

k Gk *They*   *l* Meaning of Gk uncertain   *m* Gk *their*   *n* Gk
those persons   *o* Other ancient authorities read *dangers, the
ancestors already leading the songs of praise*   *p* Gk *name*

W
I
S

and night in its swift course was now half
  gone,
15 your all-powerful word leaped from heaven,
  from the royal throne,
into the midst of the land that was doomed,
a stern warrior
16 carrying the sharp sword of your authentic
  command,
and stood and filled all things with death,
and touched heaven while standing on the
  earth.
17 Then at once apparitions in dreadful dreams
  greatly troubled them,
and unexpected fears assailed them;
18 and one here and another there, hurled down
  half dead,
made known why they were dying;
19 for the dreams that disturbed them forewarned
  them of this,
so that they might not perish without knowing
  why they suffered.

Threat of Annihilation in the Desert
(Num 16.41–50)

20 The experience of death touched also the
  righteous,
and a plague came upon the multitude in the
  desert,
but the wrath did not long continue.
21 For a blameless man was quick to act as their
  champion;
he brought forward the shield of his
  ministry,
prayer and propitiation by incense;
he withstood the anger and put an end to the
  disaster,
showing that he was your servant.
22 He conquered the wrath^q not by strength of
  body,
not by force of arms,
but by his word he subdued the
  avenger,
appealing to the oaths and covenants given to
  our ancestors.
23 For when the dead had already fallen on one
  another in heaps,
he intervened and held back the wrath,
and cut off its way to the living.
24 For on his long robe the whole world was
  depicted,
and the glories of the ancestors were engraved
  on the four rows of stones,
and your majesty was on the diadem upon his
  head.
25 To these the destroyer yielded, these her^r
  feared;
for merely to test the wrath was enough.

The Red Sea

19 But the ungodly were assailed to the
  end by pitiless anger,
for God^s knew in advance even their future
  actions:
2 how, though they themselves had permitted^t
  your people to depart
and hastily sent them out,
they would change their minds and pursue
  them.
3 For while they were still engaged in mourning,
and were lamenting at the graves of their
  dead,
they reached another foolish decision,
and pursued as fugitives those whom they had
  begged and compelled to leave.
4 For the fate they deserved drew them on to this
  end,
and made them forget what had happened,
in order that they might fill up the punishment
  that their torments still lacked,
5 and that your people might experience^u an
  incredible journey,
but they themselves might meet a strange
  death.

God Guides and Protects His People
(Num 11.1–35)

6 For the whole creation in its nature was
  fashioned anew,
complying with your commands,
so that your children^v might be kept
  unharmed.
7 The cloud was seen overshadowing the camp,
and dry land emerging where water had stood
  before,
an unhindered way out of the Red Sea,
and a grassy plain out of the raging waves,
8 where those protected by your hand passed
  through as one nation,
after gazing on marvelous wonders.
9 For they ranged like horses,
and leaped like lambs,
praising you, O Lord, who delivered them.
10 For they still recalled the events of their
  sojourn,
how instead of producing animals the earth
  brought forth gnats,
and instead of fish the river spewed out vast
  numbers of frogs.
11 Afterward they saw also a new kind^w of birds,
when desire led them to ask for luxurious food;

---

q Cn: Gk *multitude*   r Other ancient authorities read *they*
s Gk *he*   t Other ancient authorities read *had changed their*
minds to permit   u Other ancient authorities read *accomplish*
v Or *servants*   w Or *production*

Supernatural Resources

The Book of Wisdom ends with an inspiring statement of faith:

> For in everything, O LORD! you have exalted and glorified your people;
> and you have not neglected to help them at all times and in all places.
> (19.22)

Could you say these words? Do you have the kind of faith that is able to see the hand of God at work through everything that happens?

So many times, we pray for God's help, especially if we are struggling or someone we love is suffering. Later, when that particular crisis is over, we quickly forget how God helped us through. The Bible's message is that God is at work through all the times in our life, even in ways that we do not realize at the moment. The church's word for God's help is *grace*. Unlike most of our natural resources, the supernatural resource of grace is never in danger of being used up. In fact, the more we use it, the more of it there is!

Find a way of keeping track of how God has helped you through life. Perhaps you can maintain a journal of the difficult times you've made it through and the people who have supported you. You might be surprised by this record of how God's grace has been active!

▶ **Wis 19.22**

---

12 for, to give them relief, quails came up from
  the sea.

The Punishment of the Egyptians

13 The punishments did not come upon the
  sinners
without prior signs in the violence of thunder,
for they justly suffered because of their wicked
  acts;
for they practiced a more bitter hatred of
  strangers.
14 Others had refused to receive strangers when
  they came to them,
but these made slaves of guests who were their
  benefactors.
15 And not only so—but, while punishment of
  some sort will come upon the former
for having received strangers with hostility,
16 the latter, having first received them with festal
  celebrations,
afterward afflicted with terrible sufferings
those who had already shared the same rights.
17 They were stricken also with loss of sight—
just as were those at the door of the righteous
  man—
when, surrounded by yawning darkness,
all of them tried to find the way through their
  own doors.

A New Harmony in Nature

18 For the elements changed[x] places with one
  another,
as on a harp the notes vary the nature of the
  rhythm,
while each note remains the same.[y]
This may be clearly inferred from the sight of
  what took place.
19 For land animals were transformed into water
  creatures,
and creatures that swim moved over to the
  land.
20 Fire even in water retained its normal power,
and water forgot its fire-quenching nature.
21 Flames, on the contrary, failed to consume
the flesh of perishable creatures that walked
  among them,
nor did they melt[z] the crystalline,
  quick-melting kind of heavenly food.

Conclusion

22 For in everything, O Lord, you have exalted
  and glorified your people,
and you have not neglected to help them at all
  times and in all places.

---

x Gk *changing*   y Meaning of Gk uncertain   z Cn: Gk *nor could be melted*

W
I
S

Imagine that many years ago, your grandfather—a learned and wise man—wrote a book summarizing all his wisdom. Recently, you read the book and discovered it has answers to many of the problems you and your friends are struggling with. But the book is written in your grandfather's native language, which your friends don't understand. So, what do you do? You translate the book! This is exactly what the grandson of Jesus Ben Sira did. He translated into Greek the book his grandfather had written in Hebrew.

At a Glance

- **Chapters 1–43.** praise of wisdom and general moral teaching

- **Chapters 44.1–50.24** praise of the heroes of Israel

- **Chapter 50.25.–51.30** a concluding prayer and poem

In-depth

The Book of Sirach is unique in the Old Testament because it clearly identifies its author: Jesus Ben Sira, a wise teacher who lived early in the second century B.C. Living in Jerusalem during a time of great change, he saw many of his people—especially those who were rich—deserting traditional Jewish beliefs in favor of more fashionable ideas coming from Greece. A book underlining the superiority of Jewish wisdom was needed, Ben Sira thought. So, he collected his class notes into a single volume and offered it to those who desired to learn the ways of living well. Though full of many different kinds of writing—sayings, hymns, prayers, and lists—the book is unified in its overall conviction: "All wisdom is from the Lord, / and with him it remains forever" (1.1).

The Book of Sirach holds fast to the long-standing belief that in this life, good is rewarded and evil is punished. Unlike Second Maccabees and Daniel—also written in the second century B.C.—Sirach never mentions the possibility of life after death. But like other wisdom books, it celebrates the glories of wisdom (chapter 1) and recalls the heroes of Jewish faith (chapters 44–50). Its view of women is harsher than that of most of the Old Testament, though. In interpreting Sirach, you must take special care not to conclude that women are the source of most of men's troubles!

Sometimes called Ecclesiasticus or Ben Sira (which is the short form for "son of Sirach"), the Book of Sirach was well known among the ancient Jews. It was popular in the early Christian church as well. Its influence can be found in the New Testament, especially in the Letter of James. Long after his death, Ben Sira continues to share the wisdom of the past and offers us trustworthy guidance for the present.

Quick Facts

Author
Jesus Ben Sira, writing around 180 B.C.

Theme
the superiority of Jewish wisdom over Greek wisdom

Of Note
Sirach is not found in every translation of the Old Testament (see "The Case of the Missing Books," Tob 1.16).

Sirach

THE PROLOGUE

Many great teachings have been given to us through the Law and the Prophets and the others[a] that followed them, and for these we should praise Israel for instruction and wisdom. Now, those who read the scriptures must not only themselves understand them, but must also as lovers of learning be able through the spoken and written word to help the outsiders. So my grandfather Jesus, who had devoted himself especially to the reading of the Law and the Prophets and the other books of our ancestors, and had acquired considerable proficiency in them, was himself also led to write something pertaining to instruction and wisdom so that by becoming familiar also with his book[b] those who love learning might make even greater progress in living according to the law.

You are invited therefore to read it with goodwill and attention, and to be indulgent in cases where, despite our diligent labor in translating, we may seem to have rendered some phrases imperfectly. For what was originally expressed in Hebrew does not have exactly the same sense when translated into another language. Not only this book, but even the Law itself, the Prophecies, and the rest of the books differ not a little when read in the original.

When I came to Egypt in the thirty-eighth year of the reign of Eū·er′ge·tēs and stayed for some time, I found opportunity for no little instruction.[c] It seemed highly necessary that I should myself devote some diligence and labor to the translation of this book. During that time I have applied my skill day and night to complete and publish the book for those living abroad who wished to gain learning and are disposed to live according to the law.

In Praise of Wisdom
(Cp Prov 3.13–20; 8.22–31; Rom 11.33)

1 All wisdom is from the Lord,
and with him it remains forever.
² The sand of the sea, the drops of rain,
and the days of eternity—who can count
them?
³ The height of heaven, the breadth of the
earth,
the abyss, and wisdom[d]—who can search
them out?
⁴ Wisdom was created before all other
things,
and prudent understanding from
eternity.[e]
⁶ The root of wisdom—to whom has it been
revealed?

---

a Or *other books*   *b* Gk *with these things*   *c* Other ancient authorities read *I found a copy affording no little instruction*   *d* Other ancient authorities read *the depth of the abyss*   *e* Other ancient authorities add as verse 5, *The source of wisdom is God's word in the highest heaven, and her ways are the eternal commandments.*

Her subtleties—who knows them?*f*

8 There is but one who is wise, greatly to be
feared,
seated upon his throne—the Lord.

9 It is he who created her;
he saw her and took her measure;
he poured her out upon all his works,

10 upon all the living according to his gift;
he lavished her upon those who love him.*g*

Fear of the Lord Is True Wisdom
(Job 28.28; Prov 1.7)

11 The fear of the Lord is glory and exultation,
and gladness and a crown of rejoicing.

12 The fear of the Lord delights the heart,
and gives gladness and joy and long life.*h*

13 Those who fear the Lord will have a happy
end;
on the day of their death they will be
blessed.

14 To fear the Lord is the beginning of wisdom;
she is created with the faithful in the
womb.

15 She made*i* among human beings an eternal
foundation,
and among their descendants she will abide
faithfully.

16 To fear the Lord is fullness of wisdom;
she inebriates mortals with her fruits;

17 she fills their*j* whole house with desirable
goods,
and their*j* storehouses with her produce.

18 The fear of the Lord is the crown of wisdom,
making peace and perfect health to
flourish.*k*

19 She rained down knowledge and discerning
comprehension,
and she heightened the glory of those who
held her fast.

20 To fear the Lord is the root of wisdom,
and her branches are long life.*l*

22 Unjust anger cannot be justified,
for anger tips the scale to one's ruin.

23 Those who are patient stay calm until the right
moment,
and then cheerfulness comes back to
them.

24 They hold back their words until the right
moment;
then the lips of many tell of their good
sense.

25 In the treasuries of wisdom are wise sayings,
but godliness is an abomination to a sinner.

26 If you desire wisdom, keep the
commandments,

and the Lord will lavish her upon you.

27 For the fear of the Lord is wisdom and
discipline,
fidelity and humility are his delight.

28 Do not disobey the fear of the Lord;
do not approach him with a divided mind.

29 Do not be a hypocrite before others,
and keep watch over your lips.

30 Do not exalt yourself, or you may fall
and bring dishonor upon yourself.
The Lord will reveal your secrets
and overthrow you before the whole
congregation,
because you did not come in the fear of the
Lord,
and your heart was full of deceit.

Duties toward God
(Jas 1.2–4, 12–16; Wis 3.1–9)

2 My child, when you come to serve the Lord,
prepare yourself for testing.*m*

2 Set your heart right and be steadfast,
and do not be impetuous in time of
calamity.

3 Cling to him and do not depart,
so that your last days may be prosperous.

4 Accept whatever befalls you,
and in times of humiliation be patient.

5 For gold is tested in the fire,
and those found acceptable, in the furnace
of humiliation.*n*

6 Trust in him, and he will help you;
make your ways straight, and hope in him.

7 You who fear the Lord, wait for his mercy;
do not stray, or else you may fall.

8 You who fear the Lord, trust in him,
and your reward will not be lost.

9 You who fear the Lord, hope for good things,
for lasting joy and mercy.*o*

10 Consider the generations of old and see:

---

f Other ancient authorities add as verse 7, *The knowledge of
wisdom—to whom was it manifested? And her abundant
experience—who has understood it?* *g* Other ancient
authorities add *Love of the Lord is glorious wisdom; to those to
whom he appears he apportions her, that they may see him.*
h Other ancient authorities add *The fear of the Lord is a gift
from the Lord; also for love he makes firm paths.* *i* Gk made as
a nest *j* Other ancient authorities read *her* *k* Other
ancient authorities add *Both are gifts of God for peace; glory
opens out for those who love him. He saw her and took her
measure.* *l* Other ancient authorities add as verse 21, *The
fear of the Lord drives away sins; and where it abides, it will
turn away all anger.* *m* Or *trials* *n* Other ancient
authorities add *in sickness and poverty put your trust in him*
o Other ancient authorities add *For his reward is an
everlasting gift with joy.*

has anyone trusted in the Lord and been
        disappointed?
Or has anyone persevered in the fear of the
        Lord[p] and been forsaken?
Or has anyone called upon him and been
        neglected?

11 For the Lord is compassionate and merciful;
        he forgives sins and saves in time of
        distress.

12 Woe to timid hearts and to slack hands,
        and to the sinner who walks a double
        path!

13 Woe to the fainthearted who have no trust!
        Therefore they will have no shelter.

14 Woe to you who have lost your nerve!
        What will you do when the Lord's
        reckoning comes?

15 Those who fear the Lord do not disobey his
        words,
        and those who love him keep his ways.

16 Those who fear the Lord seek to please him,
        and those who love him are filled with his
        law.

17 Those who fear the Lord prepare their hearts,
        and humble themselves before him.

18 Let us fall into the hands of the Lord,
        but not into the hands of mortals;
for equal to his majesty is his mercy,
        and equal to his name are his works.[q]

Duties toward Parents
(Ex 20.12; Deut 5.16; Eph 6.1–3)

3 Listen to me your father, O children;
        act accordingly, that you may be kept
        in safety.

2 For the Lord honors a father above his
        children,
        and he confirms a mother's right over her
        children.

3 Those who honor their father atone for sins,

4   and those who respect their mother are like
        those who lay up treasure.

5 Those who honor their father will have joy in
        their own children,
        and when they pray they will be heard.

6 Those who respect their father will have long
        life,
        and those who honor[r] their mother obey
        the Lord;

---

p Gk *of him*   q Syr: Gk lacks this line   r Heb: Other ancient
authorities read *comfort*

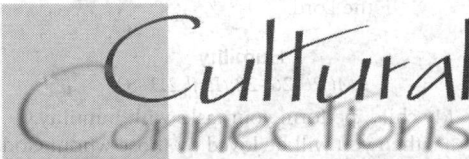

HONORING OUR PARENTS IN GOD'S WAY!

You hear Sir 3.1–7 every year on Holy Family Sunday, the weekend after Christmas. This reading calls us to honor our parents, because this is the way God established children's responsibilities toward parents. To honor our parents is to revere them (verse 6), to be kind to them (verse 14), to not dishonor them in order to feel superior (verse 10), and to take care of them and be considerate of them as they age (verses 12–13). According to Ben Sira, God assures many blessings to those who honor their parents, including safety, happiness, forgiveness of sins, the hearing of their prayers, and a long life.

Latin Americans have a long tradition of being parented not only by birth parents but by the extended family, including grandparents, godparents, aunts, and uncles. Today, many young people are also parented by foster parents, stepparents, and adoptive parents.

■ Take a moment to think of the adults who have parented you. In what specific ways do you honor and show your love to them? In what ways might you have failed to do so?

■ Thank God, our heavenly parent, for the love and sacrifices of all the people who have parented you. Ask God to give you love, understanding, strength, and patience to honor them in word and deed.

▶ Sir 3.1–16

S
I
R

Cultural Connections

CELEBRATING FAMILIES

Ben Sira holds family relationships in high esteem. In chapter 3, he emphasizes the importance of honor and respect among family members. Many cultures have special days honoring parents and children. In the United States, we celebrate Mother's Day, Father's Day, and Grandparent's Day.

Japan also has special days honoring family members. Girls' Festival (Hinamatsuri) is celebrated on 3 March with doll displays and peach blossoms. Boys' Festival (Kodomo No Hi) is celebrated on 5 May with streamers. Respect for the Aged Day (Keiro No Hi) is celebrated on 15 September. On 15 January, the Coming of Age Festival (Seigin No Hi) takes place. This day celebrates all young people who have turned twenty during the previous year—the age when young adults are permitted to vote, drink, and smoke.

If you have Japanese friends or acquaintances, consider marking these holidays on your calendar and sending a card or note with a prayer on the appropriate day.

▶ Sir 3.1–16

7 they will serve their parents as their masters.[s]

8 Honor your father by word and deed,
that his blessing may come upon you.

9 For a father's blessing strengthens the houses of the children,
but a mother's curse uproots their foundations.

10 Do not glorify yourself by dishonoring your father,
for your father's dishonor is no glory to you.

11 The glory of one's father is one's own glory,
and it is a disgrace for children not to respect their mother.

12 My child, help your father in his old age,
and do not grieve him as long as he lives;

13 even if his mind fails, be patient with him;
because you have all your faculties do not despise him.

14 For kindness to a father will not be forgotten,
and will be credited to you against your sins;

15 in the day of your distress it will be remembered in your favor;
like frost in fair weather, your sins will melt away.

16 Whoever forsakes a father is like a blasphemer,

and whoever angers a mother is cursed by the Lord.

Humility
(Mt 20.26–28; Phil 2.3–8)

17 My child, perform your tasks with humility;[t]
then you will be loved by those whom God accepts.

18 The greater you are, the more you must humble yourself;
so you will find favor in the sight of the Lord.[u]

20 For great is the might of the Lord;
but by the humble he is glorified.

21 Neither seek what is too difficult for you,
nor investigate what is beyond your power.

22 Reflect upon what you have been commanded,
for what is hidden is not your concern.

23 Do not meddle in matters that are beyond you,
for more than you can understand has been shown you.

24 For their conceit has led many astray,
and wrong opinion has impaired their judgment.

---

s In other ancient authorities this line is preceded by *Those who fear the Lord honor their father,*   t Heb: Gk *meekness*   u Other ancient authorities add as verse 19, *Many are lofty and renowned, but to the humble he reveals his secrets.*

25 Without eyes there is no light;
   without knowledge there is no wisdom.[v]
26 A stubborn mind will fare badly at the end,
   and whoever loves danger will perish in it.
27 A stubborn mind will be burdened by troubles,
   and the sinner adds sin to sins.
28 When calamity befalls the proud, there is no
      healing,
   for an evil plant has taken root in him.
29 The mind of the intelligent appreciates
      proverbs,
   and an attentive ear is the desire of the wise.

Alms for the Poor
(Tob 4.7–11)

30 As water extinguishes a blazing fire,
   so almsgiving atones for sin.
31 Those who repay favors give thought to the
      future;
   when they fall they will find support.

Duties toward the Poor and the Oppressed
(Deut 15.7–11)

4 My child, do not cheat the poor of their
      living,
   and do not keep needy eyes waiting.
2 Do not grieve the hungry,
   or anger one in need.
3 Do not add to the troubles of the desperate,
   or delay giving to the needy.
4 Do not reject a suppliant in distress,
   or turn your face away from the poor.
5 Do not avert your eye from the needy,
   and give no one reason to curse you;
6 for if in bitterness of soul some should curse
      you,
   their Creator will hear their prayer.

7 Endear yourself to the congregation;
   bow your head low to the great.
8 Give a hearing to the poor,
   and return their greeting politely.
9 Rescue the oppressed from the oppressor;
   and do not be hesitant in giving a verdict.
10 Be a father to orphans,
   and be like a husband to their mother;
   you will then be like a son of the Most High,
   and he will love you more than does your
      mother.

The Rewards of Wisdom
(Prov 3.13–18; Wis 8.17–18)

11 Wisdom teaches[w] her children
   and gives help to those who seek her.
12 Whoever loves her loves life,
   and those who seek her from early morning
      are filled with joy.

13 Whoever holds her fast inherits glory,
   and the Lord blesses the place she[x] enters.
14 Those who serve her minister to the
      Holy One;
   the Lord loves those who love her.
15 Those who obey her will judge the nations,
   and all who listen to her will live secure.
16 If they remain faithful, they will inherit her;
   their descendants will also obtain her.
17 For at first she will walk with them on tortuous
      paths;
   she will bring fear and dread upon them,
   and will torment them by her discipline
      until she trusts them,[y]
   and she will test them with her ordinances.
18 Then she will come straight back to them again
      and gladden them,
   and will reveal her secrets to them.
19 If they go astray she will forsake them,
   and hand them over to their ruin.

20 Watch for the opportune time, and beware of
      evil,
   and do not be ashamed to be yourself.
21 For there is a shame that leads to sin,
   and there is a shame that is glory and favor.
22 Do not show partiality, to your own harm,
   or deference, to your downfall.
23 Do not refrain from speaking at the proper
      moment,[z]
   and do not hide your wisdom.[a]
24 For wisdom becomes known through speech,
   and education through the words of the
      tongue.
25 Never speak against the truth,
   but be ashamed of your ignorance.
26 Do not be ashamed to confess your sins,
   and do not try to stop the current of a
      river.
27 Do not subject yourself to a fool,
   or show partiality to a ruler.
28 Fight to the death for truth,
   and the Lord God will fight for you.

29 Do not be reckless in your speech,
   or sluggish and remiss in your deeds.
30 Do not be like a lion in your home,
   or suspicious of your servants.
31 Do not let your hand be stretched out to
      receive
   and closed when it is time to give.

---

v Heb: Other ancient authorities lack verse 25   w Heb Syr:
Gk *exalts*   x Or *he*   y Or *until they remain faithful in their
heart*   z Heb: Gk *at a time of salvation*   a So some Gk Mss
and Heb Syr Lat: Other Gk Mss lack *and do not hide your
wisdom*

S
I
R

Precepts for Everyday Living

5 Do not rely on your wealth,
　　or say, "I have enough."
2 Do not follow your inclination and strength
　　in pursuing the desires of your heart.
3 Do not say, "Who can have power over me?"
　　for the Lord will surely punish you.

4 Do not say, "I sinned, yet what has happened
　　to me?"
　　for the Lord is slow to anger.
5 Do not be so confident of forgiveness[b]
　　that you add sin to sin.
6 Do not say, "His mercy is great,
　　he will forgive[c] the multitude of my sins,"
　　for both mercy and wrath are with him,
　　and his anger will rest on sinners.
7 Do not delay to turn back to the Lord,
　　and do not postpone it from day to day;
　　for suddenly the wrath of the Lord will come
　　upon you,
　　and at the time of punishment you will
　　perish.
8 Do not depend on dishonest wealth,
　　for it will not benefit you on the day of
　　calamity.

9 Do not winnow in every wind,
　　or follow every path.[d]
10 Stand firm for what you know,
　　and let your speech be consistent.
11 Be quick to hear,
　　but deliberate in answering.
12 If you know what to say, answer your
　　neighbor;
　　but if not, put your hand over your mouth.

13 Honor and dishonor come from speaking,
　　and the tongue of mortals may be their
　　downfall.
14 Do not be called double-tongued[e]
　　and do not lay traps with your tongue;
　　for shame comes to the thief,
　　and severe condemnation to the
　　double-tongued.
15 In great and small matters cause no harm,[f]

6 1 and do not become an enemy instead of
　　a friend;
　　for a bad name incurs shame and reproach;
　　so it is with the double-tongued sinner.

2 Do not fall into the grip of passion,[g]
　　or you may be torn apart as by a bull.[h]
3 Your leaves will be devoured and your fruit
　　destroyed,
　　and you will be left like a withered tree.
4 Evil passion destroys those who have it,
　　and makes them the laughingstock of their
　　enemies.

Friendship, False and True

5 Pleasant speech multiplies friends,
　　and a gracious tongue multiplies
　　courtesies.
6 Let those who are friendly with you be many,
　　but let your advisers be one in a thousand.
7 When you gain friends, gain them through
　　testing,
　　and do not trust them hastily.
8 For there are friends who are such when it suits
　　them,
　　but they will not stand by you in time of
　　trouble.
9 And there are friends who change into
　　enemies,
　　and tell of the quarrel to your disgrace.
10 And there are friends who sit at your table,
　　but they will not stand by you in time of
　　trouble.
11 When you are prosperous, they become your
　　second self,
　　and lord it over your servants;
12 but if you are brought low, they turn against
　　you,
　　and hide themselves from you.
13 Keep away from your enemies,
　　and be on guard with your friends.

---

b Heb: Gk *atonement*　c Heb: Gk *he (or it) will atone for*
d Gk adds *so it is with the double-tongued sinner* (see 6.1)
e Heb: Gk *a slanderer*　f Heb Syr: Gk *be ignorant*　g Heb:
Meaning of Gk uncertain　h Meaning of Gk uncertain

PRAY IT!
Friends

God of friendship,
　Thank you for my friends, especially
　for those who give me wise advice.
Thank you for my closest friends whom I see
　every day, who motivate me to grow and
　serve.
Thank you for all the good friends whom I
　used to see more often but don't see as
　much anymore.
LORD, continue to give me good friends
　throughout my life, and help me be a
　better friend to all. Amen.

▶ Sir 6.5–17

14 Faithful friends are a sturdy shelter:
  whoever finds one has found a treasure.
15 Faithful friends are beyond price;
  no amount can balance their worth.
16 Faithful friends are life-saving medicine;
  and those who fear the Lord will find
    them.
17 Those who fear the Lord direct their friendship
    aright,
  for as they are, so are their neighbors also.

Blessings of Wisdom

18 My child, from your youth choose discipline,
  and when you have gray hair you will still
    find wisdom.
19 Come to her like one who plows and sows,
  and wait for her good harvest.
  For when you cultivate her you will toil but
    little,
  and soon you will eat of her produce.
20 She seems very harsh to the undisciplined;
  fools cannot remain with her.
21 She will be like a heavy stone to test them,
  and they will not delay in casting her aside.
22 For wisdom is like her name;
  she is not readily perceived by many.

23 Listen, my child, and accept my judgment;
  do not reject my counsel.
24 Put your feet into her fetters,
  and your neck into her collar.
25 Bend your shoulders and carry her,
  and do not fret under her bonds.
26 Come to her with all your soul,
  and keep her ways with all your might.
27 Search out and seek, and she will become
    known to you;
  and when you get hold of her, do not let
    her go.
28 For at last you will find the rest she gives,
  and she will be changed into joy for you.
29 Then her fetters will become for you a strong
    defense,
  and her collar a glorious robe.
30 Her yoke[i] is a golden ornament,
  and her bonds a purple cord.
31 You will wear her like a glorious robe,
  and put her on like a splendid crown.[j]

32 If you are willing, my child, you can be
    disciplined,
  and if you apply yourself you will become
    clever.
33 If you love to listen you will gain knowledge,
  and if you pay attention you will become
    wise.
34 Stand in the company of the elders.

Who is wise? Attach yourself to such a one.
35 Be ready to listen to every godly discourse,
  and let no wise proverbs escape you.
36 If you see an intelligent person, rise early to
    visit him;
  let your foot wear out his doorstep.
37 Reflect on the statutes of the Lord,
  and meditate at all times on his
    commandments.
  It is he who will give insight to[k] your mind,
  and your desire for wisdom will be granted.

Miscellaneous Advice

7 Do no evil, and evil will never overtake you.
2   Stay away from wrong, and it will turn
    away from you.
3 Do[l] not sow in the furrows of injustice,
  and you will not reap a sevenfold crop.

4 Do not seek from the Lord high office,
  or the seat of honor from the king.
5 Do not assert your righteousness before the
    Lord,
  or display your wisdom before the king.
6 Do not seek to become a judge,
  or you may be unable to root out injustice;
  you may be partial to the powerful,
  and so mar your integrity.
7 Commit no offense against the public,
  and do not disgrace yourself among the
    people.

8 Do not commit a sin twice;
  not even for one will you go unpunished.
9 Do not say, "He will consider the great number
    of my gifts,
  and when I make an offering to the Most
    High God, he will accept it."
10 Do not grow weary when you pray;
  do not neglect to give alms.
11 Do not ridicule a person who is embittered in
    spirit,
  for there is One who humbles and exalts.
12 Do not devise[m] a lie against your brother,
  or do the same to a friend.
13 Refuse to utter any lie,
  for it is a habit that results in no good.
14 Do not babble in the assembly of the elders,
  and do not repeat yourself when you pray.
15 Do not hate hard labor
  or farm work, which was created by the
    Most High.
16 Do not enroll in the ranks of sinners;

---

i Heb: Gk *Upon her*   j Heb: Gk *crown of gladness*   k Heb: Gk
will confirm   l Gk *My child, do*   m Heb: Gk *plow*

remember that retribution does not delay.

17 Humble yourself to the utmost,
for the punishment of the ungodly is fire
and worms.[n]

Relations with Others

18 Do not exchange a friend for money,
or a real brother for the gold of O'phir.
19 Do not dismiss[o] a wise and good wife,
for her charm is worth more than gold.
20 Do not abuse slaves who work faithfully,
or hired laborers who devote themselves to
their task.
21 Let your soul love intelligent slaves;[p]
do not withhold from them their freedom.

22 Do you have cattle? Look after them;
if they are profitable to you, keep them.
23 Do you have children? Discipline them,
and make them obedient[q] from their youth.
24 Do you have daughters? Be concerned for their
chastity,[r]
and do not show yourself too indulgent
with them.
25 Give a daughter in marriage, and you complete
a great task;
but give her to a sensible man.
26 Do you have a wife who pleases you?[s] Do not
divorce her;
but do not trust yourself to one whom you
detest.

27 With all your heart honor your father,
and do not forget the birth pangs of your
mother.
28 Remember that it was of your parents[t] you
were born;
how can you repay what they have given to
you?

29 With all your soul fear the Lord,
and revere his priests.
30 With all your might love your Maker,
and do not neglect his ministers.
31 Fear the Lord and honor the priest,
and give him his portion, as you have been
commanded:
the first fruits, the guilt offering, the gift of the
shoulders,
the sacrifice of sanctification, and the first
fruits of the holy things.

32 Stretch out your hand to the poor,
so that your blessing may be complete.
33 Give graciously to all the living;
do not withhold kindness even from the
dead.

34 Do not avoid those who weep,
but mourn with those who mourn.
35 Do not hesitate to visit the sick,
because for such deeds you will be loved.
36 In all you do, remember the end of your life,
and then you will never sin.

Prudence and Common Sense

8 Do not contend with the powerful,
or you may fall into their hands.
2 Do not quarrel with the rich,
in case their resources outweigh yours;
for gold has ruined many,
and has perverted the minds of kings.
3 Do not argue with the loud of mouth,
and do not heap wood on their fire.

4 Do not make fun of one who is ill-bred,
or your ancestors may be insulted.
5 Do not reproach one who is turning away from
sin;
remember that we all deserve punishment.
6 Do not disdain one who is old,
for some of us are also growing old.
7 Do not rejoice over anyone's death;
remember that we must all die.

8 Do not slight the discourse of the sages,
but busy yourself with their maxims;
because from them you will learn discipline
and how to serve princes.
9 Do not ignore the discourse of the aged,
for they themselves learned from their
parents;[u]
from them you learn how to understand
and to give an answer when the need arises.

10 Do not kindle the coals of sinners,
or you may be burned in their flaming fire.
11 Do not let the insolent bring you to your feet,
or they may lie in ambush against your
words.
12 Do not lend to one who is stronger than you;
but if you do lend anything, count it as a
loss.
13 Do not give surety beyond your means;
but if you give surety, be prepared to pay.

14 Do not go to law against a judge,
for the decision will favor him because of
his standing.
15 Do not go traveling with the reckless,

---

n Heb *for the expectation of mortals is worms*   o Heb: Gk
deprive yourself of   p Heb *Love a wise slave as yourself*
q Gk *bend their necks*   r Gk *body*   s Heb Syr *lack who
pleases you*   t Gk *them*   u Or *ancestors*

S
I
R

or they will be burdensome to you;
  for they will act as they please,
    and through their folly you will perish with
      them.

16 Do not pick a fight with the quick-tempered,
    and do not journey with them through
      lonely country,
  because bloodshed means nothing to them,
    and where no help is at hand, they will
      strike you down.

17 Do not consult with fools,
    for they cannot keep a secret.

18 In the presence of strangers do nothing that is
      to be kept secret,
    for you do not know what they will
      divulge.ᵛ

19 Do not reveal your thoughts to anyone,
    or you may drive away your happiness.ʷ

Advice Concerning Women
(Cp Num 5.11–15)

9 Do not be jealous of the wife of your
      bosom,
    or you will teach her an evil lesson to your
      own hurt.

2 Do not give yourself to a woman
    and let her trample down your strength.

3 Do not go near a loose woman,
    or you will fall into her snares.

4 Do not dally with a singing girl,
    or you will be caught by her tricks.

5 Do not look intently at a virgin,
    or you may stumble and incur penalties
      for her.

6 Do not give yourself to prostitutes,

or you may lose your inheritance.

7 Do not look around in the streets of a city,
    or wander about in its deserted sections.

8 Turn away your eyes from a shapely woman,
    and do not gaze at beauty belonging to
      another;
  many have been seduced by a woman's beauty,
    and by it passion is kindled like a fire.

9 Never dine with another man's wife,
    or revel with her at wine;
  or your heart may turn aside to her,
    and in bloodˣ you may be plunged into
      destruction.

Choice of Friends

10 Do not abandon old friends,
    for new ones cannot equal them.
  A new friend is like new wine;
    when it has aged, you can drink it with
      pleasure.

11 Do not envy the success of sinners,
    for you do not know what their end will be
      like.

12 Do not delight in what pleases the ungodly;
    remember that they will not be held
      guiltless all their lives.

13 Keep far from those who have power to kill,
    and you will not be haunted by the fear of
      death.
  But if you approach them, make no misstep,

ᵛ Or *it will bring forth*   ʷ Heb: Gk *and let him not return a
favor to you*   ˣ Heb: Gk *by your spirit*

Friends, Old and New   **LIVE IT!**

Out there, somewhere, is a special person you have not yet met. He or she will
eventually become a key person in your life. In fact, a lot of such people are out
there, somewhere—including future classmates, coworkers, roommates, and
friends. The challenge is in finding the particular people who will become close to
you, your soul mates.

Ben Sira reminds us in Sir 9.10 that in the excitement that accompanies making new
friends, we should not forget the pleasure and comfort that an old friend brings us. A friend
we have known for a long time is someone to trust, someone who knows and accepts us,
warts and all. And when the circumstances of life cause separation from old friends, there is
value in reconnecting occasionally to share where life has taken us or even to seek direction
and support if life has become confusing or hard. We need to treasure our tried-and-true
friendships, as well as welcome new ones.

Spend some time reflecting on your friends, old and new, and their value in your life.

▶ Sir 9.10

S
I
R

or they may rob you of your life.
Know that you are stepping among snares,
  and that you are walking on the city
    battlements.

14 As much as you can, aim to know your
    neighbors,
  and consult with the wise.
15 Let your conversation be with intelligent
    people,
  and let all your discussion be about the law
    of the Most High.
16 Let the righteous be your dinner companions,
  and let your glory be in the fear of the Lord.

Concerning Rulers
(Prov 8.15–16; Wis 6.1–11)

17 A work is praised for the skill of the artisan;
  so a people's leader is proved wise by his
    words.
18 The loud of mouth are feared in their city,
  and the one who is reckless in speech is
    hated.

10
A wise magistrate educates his people,
  and the rule of an intelligent person
    is well ordered.
2 As the people's judge is, so are his officials;
  as the ruler of the city is, so are all its
    inhabitants.
3 An undisciplined king ruins his people,
  but a city becomes fit to live in through the
    understanding of its rulers.
4 The government of the earth is in the hand of
    the Lord,
  and over it he will raise up the right leader
    for the time.
5 Human success is in the hand of the Lord,
  and it is he who confers honor upon the
    lawgiver.*y*

The Sin of Pride

6 Do not get angry with your neighbor for every
    injury,
  and do not resort to acts of insolence.
7 Arrogance is hateful to the Lord and to mortals,
  and injustice is outrageous to both.
8 Sovereignty passes from nation to nation
  on account of injustice and insolence and
    wealth.*z*
9 How can dust and ashes be proud?
  Even in life the human body decays.*a*
10 A long illness baffles the physician;*b*
  the king of today will die tomorrow.
11 For when one is dead
  he inherits maggots and vermin*c* and worms.
12 The beginning of human pride is to forsake the
    Lord;

the heart has withdrawn from its Maker.
13 For the beginning of pride is sin,
  and the one who clings to it pours out
    abominations.
Therefore the Lord brings upon them
    unheard-of calamities,
  and destroys them completely.
14 The Lord overthrows the thrones of rulers,
  and enthrones the lowly in their place.
15 The Lord plucks up the roots of the
    nations,*d*
  and plants the humble in their place.
16 The Lord lays waste the lands of the nations,
  and destroys them to the foundations of the
    earth.
17 He removes some of them and destroys them,
  and erases the memory of them from the
    earth.
18 Pride was not created for human beings,
  or violent anger for those born of
    women.

Persons Deserving Honor
(Cp Jer 9.23–24; 1 Cor 1.26–31)

19 Whose offspring are worthy of honor?
    Human offspring.
  Whose offspring are worthy of honor?
    Those who fear the Lord.
  Whose offspring are unworthy of honor?
    Human offspring.
  Whose offspring are unworthy of honor?
    Those who break the commandments.
20 Among family members their leader is worthy
    of honor,
  but those who fear the Lord are worthy of
    honor in his eyes.*e*
22 The rich, and the eminent, and the poor—
  their glory is the fear of the Lord.
23 It is not right to despise one who is intelligent
    but poor,
  and it is not proper to honor one who is
    sinful.
24 The prince and the judge and the ruler are
    honored,
  but none of them is greater than the one
    who fears the Lord.
25 Free citizens will serve a wise servant,
  and an intelligent person will not
    complain.

---

y Heb: Gk *scribe*   *z* Other ancient authorities add here or
after verse 9a, *Nothing is more wicked than one who loves
money, for such a person puts his own soul up for sale.*   *a* Heb:
Meaning of Gk uncertain   *b* Heb Lat: Meaning of Gk
uncertain   *c* Heb: Gk *wild animals*   *d* Other ancient
authorities read *proud nations*   *e* Other ancient authorities
add as verse 21, *The fear of the Lord is the beginning of
acceptance; obduracy and pride are the beginning of rejection.*

Concerning Humility

26 Do not make a display of your wisdom when
        you do your work,
    and do not boast when you are in need.
27 Better is the worker who has goods in plenty
        than the boaster who lacks bread.

28 My child, honor yourself with humility,
    and give yourself the esteem you deserve.
29 Who will acquit those who condemn*f*
        themselves?
    And who will honor those who dishonor
        themselves?*g*
30 The poor are honored for their knowledge,
    while the rich are honored for their wealth.
31 One who is honored in poverty, how much
        more in wealth!
    And one dishonored in wealth, how much
        more in poverty!

The Deceptiveness of Appearances

11
The wisdom of the humble lifts their
        heads high,
    and seats them among the great.
2 Do not praise individuals for their good looks,
    or loathe anyone because of appearance
        alone.
3 The bee is small among flying creatures,
    but what it produces is the best of sweet
        things.
4 Do not boast about wearing fine clothes,
    and do not exalt yourself when you are
        honored;
    for the works of the Lord are wonderful,
    and his works are concealed from
        humankind.
5 Many kings have had to sit on the ground,
    but one who was never thought of has
        worn a crown.
6 Many rulers have been utterly disgraced,
    and the honored have been handed over to
        others.

Deliberation and Caution

(Prov 18.13)

7 Do not find fault before you investigate;
    examine first, and then criticize.
8 Do not answer before you listen,
    and do not interrupt when another is
        speaking.
9 Do not argue about a matter that does not
        concern you,
    and do not sit with sinners when they judge
        a case.

10 My child, do not busy yourself with many
        matters;

if you multiply activities, you will not be
        held blameless.
    If you pursue, you will not overtake,
    and by fleeing you will not escape.
11 There are those who work and struggle and
        hurry,
    but are so much the more in want.
12 There are others who are slow and need help,
    who lack strength and abound in poverty;
    but the eyes of the Lord look kindly upon them;
    he lifts them out of their lowly condition
13 and raises up their heads
    to the amazement of the many.

14 Good things and bad, life and death,
    poverty and wealth, come from the Lord.*h*
17 The Lord's gift remains with the devout,
    and his favor brings lasting success.
18 One becomes rich through diligence and
        self-denial,
    and the reward allotted to him is this:
19 when he says, "I have found rest,
    and now I shall feast on my goods!"
    he does not know how long it will be
    until he leaves them to others and dies.

20 Stand by your agreement and attend to it,
    and grow old in your work.
21 Do not wonder at the works of a sinner,
    but trust in the Lord and keep at your job;
    for it is easy in the sight of the Lord
    to make the poor rich suddenly, in an
        instant.
22 The blessing of the Lord is*i* the reward of the
        pious,
    and quickly God causes his blessing to
        flourish.
23 Do not say, "What do I need,
    and what further benefit can be mine?"
24 Do not say, "I have enough,
    and what harm can come to me now?"
25 In the day of prosperity, adversity is forgotten,
    and in the day of adversity, prosperity is not
        remembered.
26 For it is easy for the Lord on the day of death
    to reward individuals according to their
        conduct.
27 An hour's misery makes one forget past
        delights,
    and at the close of one's life one's deeds are
        revealed.

---

f Heb: Gk *sin against*   *g* Heb Lat: Gk *their own life*   *h* Other
ancient authorities add as verses 15 and 16, 15*Wisdom,
understanding, and knowledge of the law come from the Lord;
affection and the ways of good works come from him.* 16*Error
and darkness were created with sinners; evil grows old with those
who take pride in malice*   *i* Heb: Gk *is in*

S
I
R

28 Call no one happy before his death;
    by how he ends, a person becomes known.*j*

Care in Choosing Friends
(Prov 19.4, 6)

29 Do not invite everyone into your home,
    for many are the tricks of the crafty.
30 Like a decoy partridge in a cage, so is the mind
        of the proud,
    and like spies they observe your weakness;*k*
31 for they lie in wait, turning good into evil,
    and to worthy actions they attach blame.
32 From a spark many coals are kindled,
    and a sinner lies in wait to shed blood.
33 Beware of scoundrels, for they devise evil,
    and they may ruin your reputation forever.
34 Receive strangers into your home and they will
        stir up trouble for you,
    and will make you a stranger to your own
        family.

12

If you do good, know to whom you
        do it,
    and you will be thanked for your good
        deeds.
2 Do good to the devout, and you will be
        repaid—
    if not by them, certainly by the Most High.
3 No good comes to one who persists in evil
    or to one who does not give alms.
4 Give to the devout, but do not help the
        sinner.
5   Do good to the humble, but do not give to
        the ungodly;
    hold back their bread, and do not give it to
        them,
        for by means of it they might subdue you;
    then you will receive twice as much evil
        for all the good you have done to them.
6 For the Most High also hates sinners
    and will inflict punishment on the
        ungodly.*l*
7 Give to the one who is good, but do not help
        the sinner.
8 A friend is not known*m* in prosperity,
    nor is an enemy hidden in adversity.
9 One's enemies are friendly*n* when one
        prospers,
    but in adversity even one's friend
        disappears.
10 Never trust your enemy,
        for like corrosion in copper, so is his
        wickedness.
11 Even if he humbles himself and walks bowed
        down,
    take care to be on your guard against him.
Be to him like one who polishes a mirror,

to be sure it does not become completely
        tarnished.
12 Do not put him next to you,
    or he may overthrow you and take your
        place.
Do not let him sit at your right hand,
    or else he may try to take your own seat,
and at last you will realize the truth of my
        words,
    and be stung by what I have said.
13 Who pities a snake charmer when he is bitten,
    or all those who go near wild animals?
14 So no one pities a person who associates with a
        sinner
    and becomes involved in the other's sins.
15 He stands by you for a while,
    but if you falter, he will not be there.
16 An enemy speaks sweetly with his lips,
    but in his heart he plans to throw you into
        a pit;
an enemy may have tears in his eyes,
    but if he finds an opportunity he will never
        have enough of your blood.
17 If evil comes upon you, you will find him there
        ahead of you;
    pretending to help, he will trip you up.
18 Then he will shake his head, and clap his
        hands,
    and whisper much, and show his true face.

Caution Regarding Associates

13

Whoever touches pitch gets dirty,
    and whoever associates with a proud
        person becomes like him.
2 Do not lift a weight too heavy for you,
    or associate with one mightier and richer
        than you.
How can the clay pot associate with the iron
        kettle?
    The pot will strike against it and be
        smashed.
3 A rich person does wrong, and even adds
        insults;
    a poor person suffers wrong, and must add
        apologies.
4 A rich person*o* will exploit you if you can be of
        use to him,
    but if you are in need he will abandon you.
5 If you own something, he will live with you;
    he will drain your resources without a
        qualm.

---

j Heb: Gk *and through his children a person becomes known*
k Heb: Gk *downfall*   *l* Other ancient authorities add *and he
is keeping them for the day of their punishment*   *m* Other
ancient authorities read *punished*   *n* Heb: Gk *grieved*
o Gk *He*

6 When he needs you he will deceive you,
      and will smile at you and encourage you;
   he will speak to you kindly and say, "What
      do you need?"
7 He will embarrass you with his delicacies,
      until he has drained you two or three times,
      and finally he will laugh at you.
   Should he see you afterwards, he will pass
      you by
      and shake his head at you.

8 Take care not to be led astray
      and humiliated when you are enjoying
      yourself.*p*
9 When an influential person invites you, be
      reserved,
      and he will invite you more insistently.
10 Do not be forward, or you may be rebuffed;
      do not stand aloof, or you will be forgotten.
11 Do not try to treat him as an equal,
      or trust his lengthy conversations;
   for he will test you by prolonged talk,
      and while he smiles he will be examining
      you.
12 Cruel are those who do not keep your secrets;
      they will not spare you harm or
      imprisonment.
13 Be on your guard and very careful,
      for you are walking about with your own
      downfall.*q*

15 Every creature loves its like,
      and every person the neighbor.
16 All living beings associate with their own kind,
      and people stick close to those like
      themselves.
17 What does a wolf have in common with a
      lamb?
      No more has a sinner with the devout.
18 What peace is there between a hyena and a
      dog?
      And what peace between the rich and the
      poor?
19 Wild asses in the wilderness are the prey of
      lions;
      likewise the poor are feeding grounds for
      the rich.
20 Humility is an abomination to the proud;
      likewise the poor are an abomination to the
      rich.

21 When the rich person totters, he is supported
      by friends,
      but when the humble*r* falls, he is pushed
      away even by friends.
22 If the rich person slips, many come to the
      rescue;

he speaks unseemly words, but they justify
      him.
   If the humble person slips, they even criticize
      him;
      he talks sense, but is not given a hearing.
23 The rich person speaks and all are silent;
      they extol to the clouds what he says.
   The poor person speaks and they say, "Who is
      this fellow?"
   And should he stumble, they even push
      him down.
24 Riches are good if they are free from sin;
      poverty is evil only in the opinion of the
      ungodly.

25 The heart changes the countenance,
      either for good or for evil.*s*
26 The sign of a happy heart is a cheerful face,
      but to devise proverbs requires painful
      thinking.

14

Happy are those who do not blunder
      with their lips,
   and need not suffer remorse for sin.
2 Happy are those whose hearts do not condemn
      them,
      and who have not given up their hope.

Responsible Use of Wealth

3 Riches are inappropriate for a small-minded
      person;
      and of what use is wealth to a miser?
4 What he denies himself he collects for others;
      and others will live in luxury on his goods.
5 If one is mean to himself, to whom will he be
      generous?
      He will not enjoy his own riches.
6 No one is worse than one who is grudging to
      himself;
      this is the punishment for his meanness.
7 If ever he does good, it is by mistake;
      and in the end he reveals his meanness.
8 The miser is an evil person;
      he turns away and disregards people.
9 The eye of the greedy person is not satisfied
      with his share;
      greedy injustice withers the soul.
10 A miser begrudges bread,
      and it is lacking at his table.

11 My child, treat yourself well, according to your
      means,

S
I
R

---

p Other ancient authorities read *in your folly*   *q* Other
ancient authorities add as verse 14, *When you hear these
things in your sleep, wake up! During all your life love the Lord,
and call on him for your salvation.*   *r* Other ancient
authorities read *poor*   *s* Other ancient authorities add *and a
glad heart makes a cheerful countenance*

and present worthy offerings to the Lord.

12 Remember that death does not tarry,
    and the decree[t] of Hades has not been
        shown to you.

13 Do good to friends before you die,
    and reach out and give to them as much as
        you can.

14 Do not deprive yourself of a day's enjoyment;
    do not let your share of desired good pass
        by you.

15 Will you not leave the fruit of your labors to
        another,
    and what you acquired by toil to be divided
        by lot?

16 Give, and take, and indulge yourself,
    because in Hades one cannot look for
        luxury.

17 All living beings become old like a garment,
    for the decree[u] from of old is, "You must
        die!"

18 Like abundant leaves on a spreading tree
    that sheds some and puts forth others,
so are the generations of flesh and blood:
    one dies and another is born.

19 Every work decays and ceases to exist,
    and the one who made it will pass away
        with it.

The Happiness of Seeking Wisdom
(Prov 8.32–36)

20 Happy is the person who meditates on[v]
        wisdom
    and reasons intelligently,

21 who[w] reflects in his heart on her ways
    and ponders her secrets,

22 pursuing her like a hunter,
    and lying in wait on her paths;

23 who peers through her windows
    and listens at her doors;

24 who camps near her house
    and fastens his tent peg to her walls;

25 who pitches his tent near her,
    and so occupies an excellent lodging place;

26 who places his children under her shelter,
    and lodges under her boughs;

27 who is sheltered by her from the heat,
    and dwells in the midst of her glory.

15 Whoever fears the Lord will do this,
    and whoever holds to the law will
        obtain wisdom.[x]

2 She will come to meet him like a mother,
    and like a young bride she will welcome
        him.

3 She will feed him with the bread of learning,
    and give him the water of wisdom to drink.

4 He will lean on her and not fall,

and he will rely on her and not be put to
        shame.

5 She will exalt him above his neighbors,
    and will open his mouth in the midst of the
        assembly.

6 He will find gladness and a crown of rejoicing,
    and will inherit an everlasting name.

7 The foolish will not obtain her,
    and sinners will not see her.

8 She is far from arrogance,
    and liars will never think of her.

9 Praise is unseemly on the lips of a sinner,
    for it has not been sent from the Lord.

10 For in wisdom must praise be uttered,
    and the Lord will make it prosper.

Freedom of Choice
(Cp Sir 17.1–12)

11 Do not say, "It was the Lord's doing that I fell
        away";

---

[t] Heb Syr: Gk covenant [u] Heb: Gk covenant [v] Other
ancient authorities read dies in [w] The structure adopted in
verses 21–27 follows the Heb [x] Gk her

PRAY IT
Taking Responsibility

"It isn't my fault; she made me do it."
"He started it!" "The devil made me
do it!" We have lots of ways of blaming
others when bad things happen. Sir 15.11
tells of one way people in Ben Sira's time
tried to put the blame on someone else:
"It was the Lord's doing." Evidently, some
people blamed God when they fell into
sin. Ben Sira tells us it isn't God's will
when bad things happen as a result of
human choice (verses 14–17)—which is
why we need to stop the blame game and
take responsibility for our own actions.

In your prayer, take some time to
reflect or journal on the following questions:
- Do you tend to blame others when
  bad things happen?
- Have there been hurtful situations in
  which you would not accept your part
  of the responsibility? If so, describe one
  and explain how you could have
  owned up to your responsibility.

▶ Sir 15.11–20

for he does not do[y] what he hates.

12 Do not say, "It was he who led me astray";
  for he has no need of the sinful.

13 The Lord hates all abominations;
  such things are not loved by those who fear
    him.

14 It was he who created humankind in the
    beginning,
  and he left them in the power of their own
    free choice.

15 If you choose, you can keep the
    commandments,
  and to act faithfully is a matter of your own
    choice.

16 He has placed before you fire and water;
  stretch out your hand for whichever you
    choose.

17 Before each person are life and death,
  and whichever one chooses will be given.

18 For great is the wisdom of the Lord;
  he is mighty in power and sees everything;

19 his eyes are on those who fear him,
  and he knows every human action.

20 He has not commanded anyone to be wicked,
  and he has not given anyone permission to
    sin.

God's Punishment of Sinners

16 Do not desire a multitude of worthless[z]
    children,
  and do not rejoice in ungodly offspring.

2 If they multiply, do not rejoice in them,
  unless the fear of the Lord is in them.

3 Do not trust in their survival,
  or rely on their numbers;[a]
for one can be better than a thousand,
  and to die childless is better than to have
    ungodly children.

4 For through one intelligent person a city can be
    filled with people,
  but through a clan of outlaws it becomes
    desolate.

5 Many such things my eye has seen,
  and my ear has heard things more striking
    than these.

6 In an assembly of sinners a fire is kindled,
  and in a disobedient nation wrath
    blazes up.

7 He did not forgive the ancient giants
  who revolted in their might.

8 He did not spare the neighbors of Lot,
  whom he loathed on account of their
    arrogance.

9 He showed no pity on the doomed nation,
  on those dispossessed because of their sins;[b]

10 or on the six hundred thousand foot soldiers

who assembled in their stubbornness.[c]

11 Even if there were only one stiff-necked
    person,
  it would be a wonder if he remained
    unpunished.
For mercy and wrath are with the Lord;[d]
  he is mighty to forgive—but he also pours
    out wrath.

12 Great as is his mercy, so also is his
    chastisement;
  he judges a person according to his or her
    deeds.

13 The sinner will not escape with plunder,
  and the patience of the godly will not be
    frustrated.

14 He makes room for every act of mercy;
  everyone receives in accordance with his or
    her deeds.[e]

17 Do not say, "I am hidden from the Lord,
  and who from on high has me in mind?
Among so many people I am unknown,
  for what am I in a boundless creation?

18 Lo, heaven and the highest heaven,
  the abyss and the earth, tremble at his
    visitation![f]

19 The very mountains and the foundations of the
    earth
  quiver and quake when he looks upon
    them.

20 But no human mind can grasp this,
  and who can comprehend his ways?

21 Like a tempest that no one can see,
  so most of his works are concealed.[g]

22 Who is to announce his acts of justice?
  Or who can await them? For his decree[h] is
    far off."[i]

23 Such are the thoughts of one devoid of
    understanding;
  a senseless and misguided person thinks
    foolishly.

---

[y] Heb: Gk *you ought not to do*   [z] Heb: Gk *unprofitable*
[a] Other ancient authorities add *For you will groan in untimely
mourning, and will know of their sudden end.*   [b] Other
ancient authorities add *All these things he did to the
hard-hearted nations, and by the multitude of his holy ones he
was not appeased.*   [c] Other ancient authorities add
*Chastising, showing mercy, striking, healing, the Lord persisted
in mercy and discipline.*   [d] Gk *him*   [e] Other ancient
authorities add   15*The Lord hardened Pharaoh so that he did
not recognize him, in order that his works might be known under
heaven.* 16*His mercy is manifest to the whole of creation, and he
divided his light and darkness with a plumb line*   [f] Other
ancient authorities add *The whole world past and present is in
his will.*   [g] Meaning of Gk uncertain: Heb Syr *If I sin, no eye
can see me, and if I am disloyal in all secret, who is to know?*
[h] Heb *the decree*: Gk *the covenant*   [i] Other ancient
authorities add *and a scrutiny for all comes at the end*

God's Wisdom Seen in Creation
(Gen 1.1—2.4a)

24 Listen to me, my child, and acquire knowledge,
  and pay close attention to my words.
25 I will impart discipline precisely[j]
  and declare knowledge accurately.

26 When the Lord created[k] his works from the
    beginning,
  and, in making them, determined their
    boundaries,
27 he arranged his works in an eternal order,
  and their dominion[l] for all generations.
  They neither hunger nor grow weary,
  and they do not abandon their tasks.
28 They do not crowd one another,
  and they never disobey his word.
29 Then the Lord looked upon the earth,
  and filled it with his good things.
30 With all kinds of living beings he covered its
    surface,
  and into it they must return.

17 The Lord created human beings out of
    earth,
  and makes them return to it again.
2 He gave them a fixed number of days,
  but granted them authority over everything
    on the earth.[m]
3 He endowed them with strength like his own,[n]
  and made them in his own image.
4 He put the fear of them[o] in all living beings,
  and gave them dominion over beasts and
    birds. [p]
6 Discretion and tongue and eyes,
  ears and a mind for thinking he gave them.
7 He filled them with knowledge and
    understanding,
  and showed them good and evil.
8 He put the fear of him into[q] their hearts
  to show them the majesty of his works.[r]
10 And they will praise his holy name,
9   to proclaim the grandeur of his works.
11 He bestowed knowledge upon them,
  and allotted to them the law of life.[s]
12 He established with them an eternal covenant,
  and revealed to them his decrees.
13 Their eyes saw his glorious majesty,
  and their ears heard the glory of his voice.
14 He said to them, "Beware of all evil."
  And he gave commandment to each of
    them concerning the neighbor.
15 Their ways are always known to him;
  they will not be hid from his eyes.[t]
17 He appointed a ruler for every nation,
  but Israel is the Lord's own portion.[u]
19 All their works are as clear as the sun before him,

  and his eyes are ever upon their ways.
20 Their iniquities are not hidden from him,
  and all their sins are before the Lord.[v]
22 One's almsgiving is like a signet ring with the
    Lord,[w]
  and he will keep a person's kindness like
    the apple of his eye.[x]
23 Afterward he will rise up and repay them,
  and he will bring their recompense on their
    heads.
24 Yet to those who repent he grants a return,
  and he encourages those who are losing
    hope.

A Call to Repentance
25 Turn back to the Lord and forsake your sins;
  pray in his presence and lessen your
    offense.
26 Return to the Most High and turn away from
    iniquity,[y]
  and hate intensely what he abhors.
27 Who will sing praises to the Most High in
    Hades
  in place of the living who give thanks?
28 From the dead, as from one who does not exist,
    thanksgiving has ceased;
  those who are alive and well sing the Lord's
    praises.
29 How great is the mercy of the Lord,
  and his forgiveness for those who return to
    him!
30 For not everything is within human
    capability,
  since human beings are not immortal.
31 What is brighter than the sun? Yet it can be
    eclipsed.
  So flesh and blood devise evil.

j Gk *by weight*   k Heb: Gk *judged*   l Or *elements*   m Lat:
Gk *it*   n Lat: Gk *proper to them*   o Syr: Gk *him*   p Other
ancient authorities add as verse 5, *They obtained the use of
the five faculties of the Lord; as sixth he distributed to them the
gift of mind, and as seventh, reason, the interpreter of one's
faculties.*   q Other ancient authorities read *He set his eye
upon*   r Other ancient authorities add *and he gave them to
boast of his marvels forever*   s Other ancient authorities add
so that they may know that they who are alive now are mortal
t Other ancient authorities add 16*Their ways from youth tend
toward evil, and they are unable to make for themselves hearts of
flesh in place of their stony hearts.* 17*For in the division of the
nations of the whole earth, he appointed*   u Other ancient
authorities add as verse 18, *whom, being his firstborn, he
brings up with discipline, and allotting to him the light of his
love, he does not neglect him.*   v Other ancient authorities
add as verse 21, *But the Lord, who is gracious and knows how
they are formed, has neither left them nor abandoned them, but
has spared them.*   w Gk *him*   x Other ancient authorities
add *apportioning repentance to his sons and daughters*   y Other
ancient authorities add *for he will lead you out of darkness to
the light of health.*

32 He marshals the host of the height of heaven;
    but all human beings are dust and ashes.

The Majesty of God

18 He who lives forever created the whole
        universe;
2 the Lord alone is just.z
4 To none has he given power to proclaim his
    works;
    and who can search out his mighty deeds?
5 Who can measure his majestic power?
    And who can fully recount his mercies?
6 It is not possible to diminish or increase them,
    nor is it possible to fathom the wonders of
    the Lord.
7 When human beings have finished, they are
    just beginning,
    and when they stop, they are still
    perplexed.
8 What are human beings, and of what use are
    they?
    What is good in them, and what is evil?
9 The number of days in their life is great if they
    reach one hundred years.a
10 Like a drop of water from the sea and a grain
    of sand,
    so are a few years among the days of
    eternity.
11 That is why the Lord is patient with them
    and pours out his mercy upon them.
12 He sees and recognizes that their end is
    miserable;
    therefore he grants them forgiveness all the
    more.
13 The compassion of human beings is for their
    neighbors,
    but the compassion of the Lord is for every
    living thing.
He rebukes and trains and teaches them,
    and turns them back, as a shepherd his
    flock.
14 He has compassion on those who accept his
    discipline
    and who are eager for his precepts.

The Right Spirit in Giving Alms

15 My child, do not mix reproach with your good
    deeds,
    or spoil your gift by harsh words.
16 Does not the dew give relief from the scorching
    heat?
    So a word is better than a gift.
17 Indeed, does not a word surpass a good gift?
    Both are to be found in a gracious person.
18 A fool is ungracious and abusive,
    and the gift of a grudging giver makes the
    eyes dim.

The Need of Reflection and Self-control

19 Before you speak, learn;
    and before you fall ill, take care of your
    health.
20 Before judgment comes, examine yourself;
    and at the time of scrutiny you will find
    forgiveness.
21 Before falling ill, humble yourself;
    and when you have sinned, repent.
22 Let nothing hinder you from paying a vow
    promptly,
    and do not wait until death to be released
    from it.
23 Before making a vow, prepare yourself;
    do not be like one who puts the Lord to the
    test.
24 Think of his wrath on the day of death,
    and of the moment of vengeance when he
    turns away his face.
25 In the time of plenty think of the time of
    hunger;
    in days of wealth think of poverty and
    need.
26 From morning to evening conditions
    change;
    all things move swiftly before the Lord.

27 One who is wise is cautious in everything;
    when sin is all around, one guards against
    wrongdoing.
28 Every intelligent person knows wisdom,
    and praises the one who finds her.
29 Those who are skilled in words become wise
    themselves,
    and pour forth apt proverbs.b

SELF-CONTROLc

30 Do not follow your base desires,
    but restrain your appetites.
31 If you allow your soul to take pleasure in base
    desire,
    it will make you the laughingstock of your
    enemies.
32 Do not revel in great luxury,
    or you may become impoverished by its
    expense.
33 Do not become a beggar by feasting with
    borrowed money,

---

z Other ancient authorities add *and there is no other beside
him; 3he steers the world with the span of his hand, and all
things obey his will; for he is king of all things by his power,
separating among them the holy things from the profane.*
a Other ancient authorities add *but the death of each one is
beyond the calculation of all*   b Other ancient authorities add
*Better is confidence in the one Lord than clinging with a dead
heart to a dead one.*   c This heading is included in the
Gk text.

Don't Get Burned

It is easy to give in to temptation. Every day, we face decisions that can hurt our relationship with God. Ben Sira soundly advises us not to give in to our base desires (Sir 18.30). These are attitudes and practices that include laziness, drunkenness, and lust, which might bring some immediate pleasure but also lead to long-term problems. Self-control is the strength to resist the lusts that lead to lifelong problems.

An old saying—If you play with matches, you might get burned—is often used by people recovering from addictions. It reminds them that risky behaviors often end up hurting them. It helps them stay focused on their long-term goal of leading a healthy and happy life. If they follow Ben Sira's advice—practice self-control—they won't end up getting burned!

What base desires tempt you the most? What do you need to do to avoid getting burned by them?

▶ Sir 18.30—19.3

19 when you have nothing in your purse.*d*
The one who does this*e* will not become rich;
one who despises small things will fail little by little.

2 Wine and women lead intelligent men astray,
   and the man who consorts with prostitutes is reckless.

3 Decay and worms will take possession of him,
   and the reckless person will be snatched away.

Against Loose Talk

4 One who trusts others too quickly has a shallow mind,
   and one who sins does wrong to himself.

5 One who rejoices in wickedness*f* will be condemned,*g*

6   but one who hates gossip has less evil.

7 Never repeat a conversation,
   and you will lose nothing at all.

8 With friend or foe do not report it,
   and unless it would be a sin for you, do not reveal it;

9 for someone may have heard you and watched you,
   and in time will hate you.

10 Have you heard something? Let it die with you.
    Be brave, it will not make you burst!

11 Having heard something, the fool suffers birth pangs
    like a woman in labor with a child.

12 Like an arrow stuck in a person's thigh,
    so is gossip inside a fool.

13 Question a friend; perhaps he did not do it;
    or if he did, so that he may not do it again.

14 Question a neighbor; perhaps he did not say it;

or if he said it, so that he may not repeat it.

15 Question a friend, for often it is slander;
    so do not believe everything you hear.

16 A person may make a slip without intending it.
    Who has not sinned with his tongue?

17 Question your neighbor before you threaten him;
    and let the law of the Most High take its course.*h*

True and False Wisdom

20 The whole of wisdom is fear of the Lord,
    and in all wisdom there is the fulfillment of the law.*i*

22 The knowledge of wickedness is not wisdom,
    nor is there prudence in the counsel of sinners.

23 There is a cleverness that is detestable,
    and there is a fool who merely lacks wisdom.

24 Better are the God-fearing who lack understanding
    than the highly intelligent who transgress the law.

25 There is a cleverness that is exact but unjust,

---

d Other ancient authorities add *for you will be plotting against your own life*   *e* Heb: Gk *A worker who is a drunkard*   *f* Other ancient authorities read *heart*   *g* Other ancient authorities add *but one who withstands pleasures crowns his life.* *6One who controls the tongue will live without strife,*   *h* Other ancient authorities add *and do not be angry.* *18The fear of the Lord is the beginning of acceptance, and wisdom obtains his love.* *19The knowledge of the Lord's commandments is life-giving discipline; and those who do what is pleasing to him enjoy the fruit of the tree of immortality.*   *i* Other ancient authorities add *and the knowledge of his omnipotence.* *21When a slave says to his master, "I will not act as you wish," even if later he does it, he angers the one who supports him.*

and there are people who abuse favors to
  gain a verdict.
26 There is the villain bowed down in mourning,
  but inwardly he is full of deceit.
27 He hides his face and pretends not to hear,
  but when no one notices, he will take
    advantage of you.
28 Even if lack of strength keeps him from
    sinning,
  he will nevertheless do evil when he finds
    the opportunity.
29 A person is known by his appearance,
  and a sensible person is known when first
    met, face to face.
30 A person's attire and hearty laughter,
  and the way he walks, show what he is.

Silence and Speech

20 There is a rebuke that is untimely,
  and there is the person who is wise
    enough to keep silent.
2 How much better it is to rebuke than to fume!
3 And the one who admits his fault will be kept
    from failure.
4 Like a eunuch lusting to violate a girl
  is the person who does right under
    compulsion.
5 Some people keep silent and are thought to be
    wise,
  while others are detested for being talkative.
6 Some people keep silent because they have
    nothing to say,
  while others keep silent because they know
    when to speak.
7 The wise remain silent until the right moment,
  but a boasting fool misses the right
    moment.
8 Whoever talks too much is detested,
  and whoever pretends to authority is hated.j

Paradoxes

9 There may be good fortune for a person in
    adversity,
  and a windfall may result in a loss.
10 There is the gift that profits you nothing,
  and the gift to be paid back double.
11 There are losses for the sake of glory,
  and there are some who have raised their
    heads from humble circumstances.
12 Some buy much for little,
  but pay for it seven times over.
13 The wise make themselves beloved by only few
    words,k
  but the courtesies of fools are wasted.
14 A fool's gift will profit you nothing,l
  for he looks for recompense sevenfold.m
15 He gives little and upbraids much;

he opens his mouth like a town crier.
  Today he lends and tomorrow he asks it back;
    such a one is hateful to God and humans.n
16 The fool says, "I have no friends,
  and I get no thanks for my good deeds.
  Those who eat my bread are evil-tongued."
17 How many will ridicule him, and how often!o

Inappropriate Speech

18 A slip on the pavement is better than a slip of
    the tongue;
  the downfall of the wicked will occur just as
    speedily.
19 A coarse person is like an inappropriate story,
  continually on the lips of the ignorant.
20 A proverb from a fool's lips will be rejected,
  for he does not tell it at the proper time.
21 One may be prevented from sinning by
    poverty;
  so when he rests he feels no remorse.
22 One may lose his life through shame,
  or lose it because of human respect.p
23 Another out of shame makes promises to a
    friend,
  and so makes an enemy for nothing.

Lying

24 A lie is an ugly blot on a person;
  it is continually on the lips of the ignorant.
25 A thief is preferable to a habitual liar,
  but the lot of both is ruin.
26 A liar's way leads to disgrace,
  and his shame is ever with him.

Proverbial Sayingsq

27 The wise person advances himself by his
    words,
  and one who is sensible pleases the great.
28 Those who cultivate the soil heap up their
    harvest,
  and those who please the great atone for
    injustice.
29 Favors and gifts blind the eyes of the wise;
  like a muzzle on the mouth they stop
    reproofs.

---

j Other ancient authorities add *How good it is to show
repentance when you are reproved, for so you will escape
deliberate sin!*   k Heb: Gk *by words*   l Other ancient
authorities add *so it is with the envious who give under
compulsion*   m Syr: Gk *he has many eyes instead of one*
n Other ancient authorities lack *to God and humans*
o Other ancient authorities add *for he has not honestly
received what he has, and what he does not have is unimportant
to him*   p Other ancient authorities read *his foolish look*
q This heading is included in the Gk text.

30 Hidden wisdom and unseen treasure,
　　of what value is either?
31 Better are those who hide their folly
　　than those who hide their wisdom.ʳ

Various Sins

21 Have you sinned, my child? Do so no
　　more,
　　but ask forgiveness for your past sins.
2 Flee from sin as from a snake;
　　for if you approach sin, it will bite you.
　Its teeth are lion's teeth,
　　and can destroy human lives.
3 All lawlessness is like a two-edged sword;
　　there is no healing for the wound it inflicts.

4 Panic and insolence will waste away riches;
　　thus the house of the proud will be laid
　　waste.ˢ
5 The prayer of the poor goes from their lips to
　　the ears of God,ᵗ
　　and his judgment comes speedily.
6 Those who hate reproof walk in the sinner's
　　steps,
　　but those who fear the Lord repent in their
　　heart.
7 The mighty in speech are widely known;
　　when they slip, the sensible person
　　knows it.

8 Whoever builds his house with other people's
　　money
　　is like one who gathers stones for his burial
　　mound.ᵘ
9 An assembly of the wicked is like a bundle of
　　tow,
　　and their end is a blazing fire.
10 The way of sinners is paved with smooth
　　stones,
　　but at its end is the pit of Hades.

Wisdom and Foolishness

11 Whoever keeps the law controls his thoughts,
　　and the fulfillment of the fear of the Lord is
　　wisdom.
12 The one who is not clever cannot be taught,
　　but there is a cleverness that increases
　　bitterness.
13 The knowledge of the wise will increase like a
　　flood,
　　and their counsel like a life-giving spring.
14 The mindᵛ of a fool is like a broken jar;
　　it can hold no knowledge.

15 When an intelligent person hears a wise saying,
　　he praises it and adds to it;
　when a foolʷ hears it, he laughs atˣ it

PRAY IT?
Examine Your Conscience

An examination of conscience is a
moral inventory of one's life. When
we examine our conscience, we can recognize those we have hurt, make amends
where possible, and turn our life around
before a pattern of sin becomes a major
obstacle in our relationships with God
and with others. We can also recognize
the positive moral choices that we have
made. Chapters 19–22 of Sirach list some
of the sins from Ben Sira's time. Use
them as a guide for making your own
examination of conscience, as follows:

- **Have you broken a confidence (19.5–12)?**
- **Do you offend others with your language (20.18–19)?**
- **Have you lied (20.24–26)?**
- **Have you stolen from others (21.8)?**
- **Have you been lazy in your use of time (22.1–2)?**
- **Have you disobeyed your parents (22.3–5)?**

　　When you have finished this examination, read 22.27—23.6 as your own prayer
for God's help against sinning.

▶ Sir 19.5—23.6

and throws it behind his back.
16 A fool's chatter is like a burden on a journey,
　　but delight is found in the speech of the
　　intelligent.
17 The utterance of a sensible person is sought in
　　the assembly,
　　and they ponder his words in their minds.
18 Like a house in ruins is wisdom to a fool,
　　and to the ignorant, knowledge is talk that
　　has no meaning.
19 To a senseless person education is fetters on his
　　feet,
　　and like manacles on his right hand.

ʳ Other ancient authorities add ³²Unwearied endurance in
seeking the Lord is better than a masterless charioteer of one's
own life.　ˢ Other ancient authorities read uprooted　ᵗ Gk his
ears　ᵘ Other ancient authorities read for the winter　ᵛ Syr
Lat: Gk entrails　ʷ Syr: Gk reveler　ˣ Syr: Gk dislikes

S
I
R

20 A fool raises his voice when he laughs,
    but the wise[y] smile quietly.
21 To the sensible person education is like a
    golden ornament,
    and like a bracelet on the right arm.

22 The foot of a fool rushes into a house,
    but an experienced person waits respectfully
    outside.
23 A boor peers into the house from the door,
    but a cultivated person remains outside.
24 It is ill-mannered for a person to listen at a
    door;
    the discreet would be grieved by the
    disgrace.

25 The lips of babblers speak of what is not their
    concern,[z]
    but the words of the prudent are weighed in
    the balance.
26 The mind of fools is in their mouth,
    but the mouth of the wise is in[a] their mind.
27 When an ungodly person curses an adversary,[b]
    he curses himself.
28 A whisperer degrades himself
    and is hated in his neighborhood.

The Idler

22 The idler is like a filthy stone,
    and every one hisses at his disgrace.
2 The idler is like the filth of dunghills;
    anyone that picks it up will shake it off his
    hand.

Degenerate Children

3 It is a disgrace to be the father of an
    undisciplined son,
    and the birth of a daughter is a loss.
4 A sensible daughter obtains a husband of her
    own,
    but one who acts shamefully is a grief to
    her father.
5 An impudent daughter disgraces father and
    husband,
    and is despised by both.
6 Like music in time of mourning is ill-timed
    conversation,
    but a thrashing and discipline are at all
    times wisdom.[c]

Wisdom and Folly

9 Whoever teaches a fool is like one who glues
    potsherds together,
    or who rouses a sleeper from deep slumber.
10 Whoever tells a story to a fool tells it to a
    drowsy man;
    and at the end he will say, "What is it?"

11 Weep for the dead, for he has left the light
    behind;
    and weep for the fool, for he has left
    intelligence behind.
Weep less bitterly for the dead, for he is at rest;
    but the life of the fool is worse than death.
12 Mourning for the dead lasts seven days,
    but for the foolish or the ungodly it lasts all
    the days of their lives.

13 Do not talk much with a senseless person
    or visit an unintelligent person.[d]
Stay clear of him, or you may have trouble,
    and be spattered when he shakes himself
    off.
Avoid him and you will find rest,
    and you will never be wearied by his lack of
    sense.
14 What is heavier than lead?
    And what is its name except "Fool"?
15 Sand, salt, and a piece of iron
    are easier to bear than a stupid person.

16 A wooden beam firmly bonded into a
    building
    is not loosened by an earthquake;
so the mind firmly resolved after due reflection
    will not be afraid in a crisis.
17 A mind settled on an intelligent thought
    is like stucco decoration that makes a wall
    smooth.
18 Fences[e] set on a high place
    will not stand firm against the wind;
so a timid mind with a fool's resolve
    will not stand firm against any fear.

The Preservation of Friendship

19 One who pricks the eye brings tears,
    and one who pricks the heart makes clear
    its feelings.
20 One who throws a stone at birds scares them
    away,
    and one who reviles a friend destroys a
    friendship.
21 Even if you draw your sword against a friend,
    do not despair, for there is a way back.
22 If you open your mouth against your friend,
    do not worry, for reconciliation is possible.

---

y Syr Lat: Gk *clever*   z Other ancient authorities read *of
strangers speak of these things*   a Other ancient authorities
omit *in*   b Or *curses Satan*   c Other ancient authorities
add 7*Children who are brought up in a good life, conceal the
lowly birth of their parents.* 8*Children who are disdainfully and
boorishly haughty stain the nobility of their kindred.*   d Other
ancient authorities add *For being without sense he will despise
everything about you*   e Other ancient authorities read
Pebbles

S
I
R

But as for reviling, arrogance, disclosure of
secrets, or a treacherous blow—
in these cases any friend will take to flight.

23 Gain the trust of your neighbor in his poverty,
so that you may rejoice with him in his
prosperity.
Stand by him in time of distress,
so that you may share with him in his
inheritance.f

24 The vapor and smoke of the furnace precede
the fire;
so insults precede bloodshed.

25 I am not ashamed to shelter a friend,
and I will not hide from him.

26 But if harm should come to me because of
him,
whoever hears of it will beware of him.

A Prayer for Help against Sinning

27 Who will set a guard over my mouth,
and an effective seal upon my lips,
so that I may not fall because of them,
and my tongue may not destroy me?

23

O Lord, Father and Master of my life,
do not abandon me to their designs,
and do not let me fall because of them!

2 Who will set whips over my thoughts,
and the discipline of wisdom over my
mind,
so as not to spare me in my errors,
and not overlook myg sins?

3 Otherwise my mistakes may be multiplied,
and my sins may abound,
and I may fall before my adversaries,
and my enemy may rejoice over me.h

4 O Lord, Father and God of my life,
do not give me haughty eyes,

5 and remove evil desire from me.

6 Let neither gluttony nor lust overcome me,
and do not give me over to shameless
passion.

DISCIPLINE OF THE TONGUEi

7 Listen, my children, to instruction concerning
the mouth;
the one who observes it will never be
caught.

8 Sinners are overtaken through their lips;
by them the reviler and the arrogant are
tripped up.

9 Do not accustom your mouth to oaths,
nor habitually utter the name of the Holy
One;

10 for as a servant who is constantly under
scrutiny
will not lack bruises,

so also the person who always swears and
utters the Name
will never be cleansedj from sin.

11 The one who swears many oaths is full of
iniquity,
and the scourge will not leave his house.
If he swears in error, his sin remains on him,
and if he disregards it, he sins doubly;
if he swears a false oath, he will not be justified,
for his house will be filled with calamities.

Foul Language

12 There is a manner of speaking comparable to
death;k
may it never be found in the inheritance of
Jacob!
Such conduct will be far from the godly,
and they will not wallow in sins.

13 Do not accustom your mouth to coarse, foul
language,
for it involves sinful speech.

14 Remember your father and mother
when you sit among the great,
or you may forget yourself in their presence,
and behave like a fool through bad habit;
then you will wish that you had never been
born,
and you will curse the day of your birth.

15 Those who are accustomed to using abusive
language
will never become disciplined as long as
they live.

Concerning Sexual Sins

16 Two kinds of individuals multiply sins,
and a third incurs wrath.
Hot passion that blazes like a fire
will not be quenched until it burns itself out;
one who commits fornication with his near of
kin
will never cease until the fire burns him up.

17 To a fornicator all bread is sweet;
he will never weary until he dies.

18 The one who sins against his marriage bed
says to himself, "Who can see me?
Darkness surrounds me, the walls hide me,
and no one sees me. Why should I worry?
The Most High will not remember sins."

19 His fear is confined to human eyes
and he does not realize that the eyes of the
Lord

---

f Other ancient authorities add *For one should not always
despise restricted circumstances, or admire a rich person who is
stupid*   g Gk *their*   h Other ancient authorities add *From
them the hope of your mercy is remote*   i This heading is
included in the Gk text.   j Syr *be free*   k Other ancient
authorities read *clothed about with death*

Sinful Speech

LIVE IT!

You might wonder, So, what's the problem with foul language? Why does Ben Sira call it "sinful speech" (Sir 23.13)? Well, part of the problem is that using it easily becomes a habit. You become less aware of when you are using it. You can get yourself into trouble. Ben Sira warns that you may "behave like a fool through bad habit" (verse 14).

Maybe the worst part of the problem is that frequent use of foul language shows a lack of respect and reverence for others and certainly for God's name. Ben Sira reminds us, "Such conduct will be far from the godly" (verse 12).

Certainly, there are more creative ways to express emotion or frustration than relying on those all-too-familiar foul words. If you've developed the habit of using them, ask God and your friends to help you stop.

▶ Sir 23.12–15

are ten thousand times brighter than the
  sun;
they look upon every aspect of human
    behavior
  and see into hidden corners.
20 Before the universe was created, it was known
    to him,
  and so it is since its completion.
21 This man will be punished in the streets of the
    city,
  and where he least suspects it, he will be
    seized.

22 So it is with a woman who leaves her
    husband
  and presents him with an heir by another
    man.
23 For first of all, she has disobeyed the law of the
    Most High;
  second, she has committed an offense
    against her husband;
and third, through her fornication she has
    committed adultery
  and brought forth children by another man.
24 She herself will be brought before the
    assembly,
  and her punishment will extend to her
    children.
25 Her children will not take root,
  and her branches will not bear fruit.
26 She will leave behind an accursed memory
  and her disgrace will never be blotted out.
27 Those who survive her will recognize
  that nothing is better than the fear of the
    Lord,

and nothing sweeter than to heed the
    commandments of the Lord.*l*

THE PRAISE OF WISDOM*m*

24 Wisdom praises herself,
  and tells of her glory in the midst
    of her people.
2 In the assembly of the Most High she opens
    her mouth,
  and in the presence of his hosts she tells of
    her glory:
3 "I came forth from the mouth of the Most
    High,
  and covered the earth like a mist.
4 I dwelt in the highest heavens,
  and my throne was in a pillar of cloud.
5 Alone I compassed the vault of heaven
  and traversed the depths of the abyss.
6 Over waves of the sea, over all the earth,
  and over every people and nation I have
    held sway.*n*
7 Among all these I sought a resting place;
  in whose territory should I abide?
8 "Then the Creator of all things gave me a
    command,
  and my Creator chose the place for my
    tent.
He said, 'Make your dwelling in Jacob,
  and in Israel receive your inheritance.'

---

l Other ancient authorities add as verse 28, *It is a great honor to follow God, and to be received by him is long life.* *m* This heading is included in the Gk text. *n* Other ancient authorities read *I have acquired a possession*

S
I
R

9 Before the ages, in the beginning, he
        created me,
      and for all the ages I shall not cease to be.
10 In the holy tent I ministered before him,
      and so I was established in Zion.
11 Thus in the beloved city he gave me a resting
        place,
      and in Jerusalem was my domain.
12 I took root in an honored people,
      in the portion of the Lord, his heritage.

13 "I grew tall like a cedar in Lebanon,
      and like a cypress on the heights of
        Hermon.
14 I grew tall like a palm tree in En-ge'di,[o]
      and like rosebushes in Jericho;
    like a fair olive tree in the field,
      and like a plane tree beside water[p] I grew
        tall.
15 Like cassia and camel's thorn I gave forth
        perfume,
      and like choice myrrh I spread my
        fragrance,
    like galbanum, onycha, and stacte,
      and like the odor of incense in the tent.
16 Like a terebinth I spread out my branches,
      and my branches are glorious and graceful.
17 Like the vine I bud forth delights,
      and my blossoms become glorious and
        abundant fruit.[q]

19 "Come to me, you who desire me,
      and eat your fill of my fruits.
20 For the memory of me is sweeter than honey,
      and the possession of me sweeter than the
        honeycomb.
21 Those who eat of me will hunger for more,
      and those who drink of me will thirst for
        more.
22 Whoever obeys me will not be put to shame,
      and those who work with me will not sin."

Wisdom and the Law

23 All this is the book of the covenant of the Most
        High God,
      the law that Moses commanded us
      as an inheritance for the congregations of
        Jacob.[r]
25 It overflows, like the Pi'shon, with wisdom,
      and like the Tigris at the time of the first
        fruits.
26 It runs over, like the Euphrates, with
        understanding,
      and like the Jordan at harvest time.
27 It pours forth instruction like the Nile,[s]
      like the Gi'hon at the time of vintage.
28 The first man did not know wisdom[t] fully,

nor will the last one fathom her.
29 For her thoughts are more abundant than the
        sea,
      and her counsel deeper than the great abyss.

30 As for me, I was like a canal from a river,
      like a water channel into a garden.
31 I said, "I will water my garden
      and drench my flower-beds."
    And lo, my canal became a river,
      and my river a sea.
32 I will again make instruction shine forth like
        the dawn,
      and I will make it clear from far away.
33 I will again pour out teaching like prophecy,
      and leave it to all future generations.
34 Observe that I have not labored for myself
        alone,
      but for all who seek wisdom.[t]

Those Who Are Worthy of Praise

25 I take pleasure in three things,
        and they are beautiful in the sight of
          God and of mortals:[u]
    agreement among brothers and sisters,
        friendship among neighbors,
    and a wife and a husband who live in
        harmony.
2 I hate three kinds of people,
      and I loathe their manner of life:
    a pauper who boasts, a rich person who lies,
      and an old fool who commits adultery.

3 If you gathered nothing in your youth,
      how can you find anything in your old age?
4 How attractive is sound judgment in the
        gray-haired,
      and for the aged to possess good counsel!
5 How attractive is wisdom in the aged,
      and understanding and counsel in the
        venerable!
6 Rich experience is the crown of the aged,
      and their boast is the fear of the Lord.
7 I can think of nine whom I would call blessed,
      and a tenth my tongue proclaims:
    a man who can rejoice in his children;

---

o Other ancient authorities read *on the beaches*   p Other
ancient authorities omit *beside water*   q Other ancient
authorities add as verse 18, *I am the mother of beautiful love,
of fear, of knowledge, and of holy hope; being eternal, I am given
to all my children, to those who are named by him.*   r Other
ancient authorities add as verse 24, "*Do not cease to be strong
in the Lord, cling to him so that he may strengthen you; the
Lord Almighty alone is God, and besides him there is no savior.*"
s Syr: Gk *It makes instruction shine forth like light*   t Gk *her*
u Syr Lat: Gk *In three things I was beautiful and I stood in
beauty before the Lord and mortals.*

a man who lives to see the downfall of his
  foes.
8 Happy the man who lives with a sensible wife,
  and the one who does not plow with ox
    and ass together.[v]
Happy is the one who does not sin with the
    tongue,
  and the one who has not served an inferior.
9 Happy is the one who finds a friend,[w]
  and the one who speaks to attentive
    listeners.
10 How great is the one who finds wisdom!
  But none is superior to the one who fears
    the Lord.
11 Fear of the Lord surpasses everything;
  to whom can we compare the one who
    has it?[x]

Some Extreme Forms of Evil

13 Any wound, but not a wound of the heart!
  Any wickedness, but not the wickedness of
    a woman!
14 Any suffering, but not suffering from those
    who hate!
  And any vengeance, but not the vengeance
    of enemies!
15 There is no venom[y] worse than a snake's
    venom,[y]
  and no anger worse than a woman's[z] wrath.

The Evil of a Wicked Woman

16 I would rather live with a lion and a dragon
  than live with an evil woman.
17 A woman's wickedness changes her
    appearance,
  and darkens her face like that of a bear.
18 Her husband sits[a] among the neighbors,
  and he cannot help sighing[b] bitterly.
19 Any iniquity is small compared to a woman's
    iniquity;
  may a sinner's lot befall her!
20 A sandy ascent for the feet of the aged—
  such is a garrulous wife to a quiet husband.
21 Do not be ensnared by a woman's beauty,
  and do not desire a woman for her
    possessions.[c]
22 There is wrath and impudence and great
    disgrace
  when a wife supports her husband.
23 Dejected mind, gloomy face,
  and wounded heart come from an evil wife.
Drooping hands and weak knees
  come from the wife who does not make her
    husband happy.
24 From a woman sin had its beginning,
  and because of her we all die.
25 Allow no outlet to water,

and no boldness of speech to an evil wife.
26 If she does not go as you direct,
  separate her from yourself.

The Joy of a Good Wife

26 Happy is the husband of a good wife;
  the number of his days will be
    doubled.
2 A loyal wife brings joy to her husband,
  and he will complete his years in peace.
3 A good wife is a great blessing;
  she will be granted among the blessings of
    the man who fears the Lord.
4 Whether rich or poor, his heart is content,
  and at all times his face is cheerful.

The Worst of Evils: A Wicked Wife

5 Of three things my heart is frightened,
  and of a fourth I am in great fear:[d]
Slander in the city, the gathering of a mob,
  and false accusation—all these are worse
    than death.
6 But it is heartache and sorrow when a wife is
    jealous of a rival,
  and a tongue-lashing makes it known to all.
7 A bad wife is a chafing yoke;
  taking hold of her is like grasping a
    scorpion.
8 A drunken wife arouses great anger;
  she cannot hide her shame.
9 The haughty stare betrays an unchaste wife;
  her eyelids give her away.

10 Keep strict watch over a headstrong daughter,
  or else, when she finds liberty, she will
    make use of it.
11 Be on guard against her impudent eye,
  and do not be surprised if she sins against
    you.
12 As a thirsty traveler opens his mouth
  and drinks from any water near him,
so she will sit in front of every tent peg
  and open her quiver to the arrow.

The Blessing of a Good Wife

13 A wife's charm delights her husband,
  and her skill puts flesh on his bones.
14 A silent wife is a gift from the Lord,

---

v Heb Syr: Gk lacks *and the one who does not plow with ox and
ass together*   w Lat Syr: Gk *good sense*   x Other ancient
authorities add as verse 12, *The fear of the Lord is the
beginning of love for him, and faith is the beginning of clinging
to him.*   y Syr: Gk *head*   z Other ancient authorities read
an enemy's   a Heb Syr: Gk *loses heart*   b Other ancient
authorities read *and listening he sighs*   c Heb Syr: Other Gk
authorities read *for her beauty*   d Syr: Meaning of Gk
uncertain

and nothing is so precious as her
   self-discipline.
15 A modest wife adds charm to charm,
   and no scales can weigh the value of her
      chastity.
16 Like the sun rising in the heights of the Lord,
   so is the beauty of a good wife in her
      well-ordered home.
17 Like the shining lamp on the holy lampstand,
   so is a beautiful face on a stately figure.
18 Like golden pillars on silver bases,
   so are shapely legs and steadfast feet.

_____

Other ancient authorities add verses 19–27:

19 *My child, keep sound the bloom of your youth,*
   and do not give your strength to strangers.
20 *Seek a fertile field within the whole plain,*
   and sow it with your own seed, trusting in your
      fine stock.
21 *So your offspring will prosper,*
   and, having confidence in their good descent,
      will grow great.
22 *A prostitute is regarded as spittle,*
   and a married woman as a tower of death to
      her lovers.
23 *A godless wife is given as a portion to a lawless*
      man,
   but a pious wife is given to the man who fears
      the Lord.
24 *A shameless woman constantly acts disgracefully,*
   but a modest daughter will even be embarrassed
      before her husband.
25 *A headstrong wife is regarded as a dog,*
   but one who has a sense of shame will fear the
      Lord.
26 *A wife honoring her husband will seem wise to all,*
   but if she dishonors him in her pride she will be
      known to all as ungodly.
   Happy is the husband of a good wife;
   for the number of his years will be doubled.
27 *A loud-voiced and garrulous wife is like a trumpet*
      sounding the charge,
   and every person like this lives in the anarchy
      of war.

Three Depressing Things

28 At two things my heart is grieved,
   and because of a third anger comes
      over me:
   a warrior in want through poverty,
      intelligent men who are treated
         contemptuously,
   and a man who turns back from righteousness
      to sin—
   the Lord will prepare him for the sword!

The Temptations of Commerce

29 A merchant can hardly keep from wrongdoing,
   nor is a tradesman innocent of sin.

27 Many have committed sin for gain,[e]
   and those who seek to get rich will
      avert their eyes.
2 As a stake is driven firmly into a fissure
      between stones,
   so sin is wedged in between selling and
      buying.
3 If a person is not steadfast in the fear of the
      Lord,
   his house will be quickly overthrown.

Tests in Life

4 When a sieve is shaken, the refuse appears;
   so do a person's faults when he speaks.
5 The kiln tests the potter's vessels;
   so the test of a person is in his
      conversation.
6 Its fruit discloses the cultivation of a tree;
   so a person's speech discloses the
      cultivation of his mind.
7 Do not praise anyone before he speaks,
   for this is the way people are tested.

Reward and Retribution

8 If you pursue justice, you will attain it
   and wear it like a glorious robe.
9 Birds roost with their own kind,
   so honesty comes home to those who
      practice it.
10 A lion lies in wait for prey;
   so does sin for evildoers.

Varieties of Speech

11 The conversation of the godly is always
      wise,
   but the fool changes like the moon.
12 Among stupid people limit your time,
   but among thoughtful people linger on.
13 The talk of fools is offensive,
   and their laughter is wantonly sinful.
14 Their cursing and swearing make one's hair
      stand on end,
   and their quarrels make others stop their
      ears.
15 The strife of the proud leads to bloodshed,
   and their abuse is grievous to hear.

Betraying Secrets
(Prov 20.19; 25.9)

16 Whoever betrays secrets destroys confidence,
   and will never find a congenial friend.
17 Love your friend and keep faith with him;

_____

e Other ancient authorities read *a trifle*

S
I
R

but if you betray his secrets, do not follow
after him.

18 For as a person destroys his enemy,
so you have destroyed the friendship of
your neighbor.

19 And as you allow a bird to escape from your
hand,
so you have let your neighbor go, and will
not catch him again.

20 Do not go after him, for he is too far off,
and has escaped like a gazelle from a snare.

21 For a wound may be bandaged,
and there is reconciliation after abuse,
but whoever has betrayed secrets is without
hope.

Hypocrisy and Retribution

22 Whoever winks the eye plots mischief,
and those who know him will keep their
distance.

23 In your presence his mouth is all sweetness,
and he admires your words;
but later he will twist his speech
and with your own words he will trip you up.

24 I have hated many things, but him above all;
even the Lord hates him.

25 Whoever throws a stone straight up throws it
on his own head,
and a treacherous blow opens up many
wounds.

26 Whoever digs a pit will fall into it,
and whoever sets a snare will be caught
in it.

27 If a person does evil, it will roll back upon him,
and he will not know where it came from.

28 Mockery and abuse issue from the proud,
but vengeance lies in wait for them like a
lion.

29 Those who rejoice in the fall of the godly will
be caught in a snare,
and pain will consume them before their
death.

Anger and Vengeance

30 Anger and wrath, these also are abominations,
yet a sinner holds on to them.

28
The vengeful will face the Lord's
vengeance,
for he keeps a strict account of *f* their sins.

2 Forgive your neighbor the wrong he has done,
and then your sins will be pardoned when
you pray.

3 Does anyone harbor anger against another,
and expect healing from the Lord?

4 If one has no mercy toward another like
himself,
can he then seek pardon for his own sins?

5 If a mere mortal harbors wrath,
who will make an atoning sacrifice for his
sins?

6 Remember the end of your life, and set enmity
aside;
remember corruption and death, and be
true to the commandments.

7 Remember the commandments, and do not be
angry with your neighbor;
remember the covenant of the Most High,
and overlook faults.

8 Refrain from strife, and your sins will be fewer;
for the hot-tempered kindle strife,

9 and the sinner disrupts friendships
and sows discord among those who are at
peace.

10 In proportion to the fuel, so will the fire burn,
and in proportion to the obstinacy, so will
strife increase;*g*
in proportion to a person's strength will be his
anger,
and in proportion to his wealth he will
increase his wrath.

11 A hasty quarrel kindles a fire,
and a hasty dispute sheds blood.

The Evil Tongue
(Jas 3.1–12)

12 If you blow on a spark, it will glow;
if you spit on it, it will be put out;
yet both come out of your mouth.

13 Curse the gossips and the double-tongued,
for they destroy the peace of many.

14 Slander*h* has shaken many,
and scattered them from nation to nation;
it has destroyed strong cities,
and overturned the houses of the great.

15 Slander*h* has driven virtuous women from their
homes,
and deprived them of the fruit of their toil.

16 Those who pay heed to slander*i* will not find
rest,
nor will they settle down in peace.

17 The blow of a whip raises a welt,
but a blow of the tongue crushes the bones.

18 Many have fallen by the edge of the sword,
but not as many as have fallen because of
the tongue.

19 Happy is the one who is protected from it,
who has not been exposed to its anger,
who has not borne its yoke,

---

f Other ancient authorities read *for he firmly establishes*
g Other ancient authorities read *burn*   *h* Gk A *third tongue*
i Gk *it*

As you fence in your property with thorns,

so make a door and a bolt for your mouth.

As you lock up your silver and gold,

so make balances and scales for your words.

Take care not to err with your tongue,

and fall victim to one lying in wait.

and has not been bound with its fetters.

20 For its yoke is a yoke of iron,
    and its fetters are fetters of bronze;
21 its death is an evil death,
    and Hades is preferable to it.
22 It has no power over the godly;
    they will not be burned in its flame.
23 Those who forsake the Lord will fall into its
        power;
    it will burn among them and will not be
        put out.
    It will be sent out against them like a lion;
    like a leopard it will mangle them.
24a As you fence in your property with thorns,

25b   so make a door and a bolt for your mouth.
24b As you lock up your silver and gold,
25a   so make balances and scales for your words.
26 Take care not to err with your tongue,[j]
    and fall victim to one lying in wait.

On Lending and Borrowing
(Cp Ex 22.25; Lev 25.35–38)

29 The merciful lend to their neighbors;
    by holding out a helping hand they
        keep the commandments.
2 Lend to your neighbor in his time of need;

---

j Gk *with it*

repay your neighbor when a loan falls due.
3 Keep your promise and be honest with him,
  and on every occasion you will find what
    you need.
4 Many regard a loan as a windfall,
  and cause trouble to those who help them.
5 One kisses another's hands until he gets a loan,
  and is deferential in speaking of his
    neighbor's money;
  but at the time for repayment he delays,
  and pays back with empty promises,
  and finds fault with the time.
6 If he can pay, his creditor[k] will hardly get back
    half,
  and will regard that as a windfall.
  If he cannot pay, the borrower[k] has robbed the
    other of his money,
  and he has needlessly made him an enemy;
  he will repay him with curses and reproaches,
  and instead of glory will repay him with
    dishonor.
7 Many refuse to lend, not because of meanness,
  but from fear[l] of being defrauded
    needlessly.

8 Nevertheless, be patient with someone in
    humble circumstances,
  and do not keep him waiting for your alms.
9 Help the poor for the commandment's sake,
  and in their need do not send them away
    empty-handed.
10 Lose your silver for the sake of a brother or a
    friend,
  and do not let it rust under a stone and be
    lost.
11 Lay up your treasure according to the
    commandments of the Most High,
  and it will profit you more than gold.
12 Store up almsgiving in your treasury,
  and it will rescue you from every disaster;
13 better than a stout shield and a sturdy spear,
  it will fight for you against the enemy.

On Guaranteeing Debts

14 A good person will be surety for his neighbor,
  but the one who has lost all sense of shame
    will fail him.
15 Do not forget the kindness of your guarantor,
  for he has given his life for you.
16 A sinner wastes the property of his guarantor,
17   and the ungrateful person abandons his
    rescuer.
18 Being surety has ruined many who were
    prosperous,
  and has tossed them about like waves of the
    sea;
  it has driven the influential into exile,

and they have wandered among foreign
    nations.
19 The sinner comes to grief through surety;
  his pursuit of gain involves him in lawsuits.
20 Assist your neighbor to the best of your ability,
  but be careful not to fall yourself.

Home and Hospitality

21 The necessities of life are water, bread, and
    clothing,
  and also a house to assure privacy.
22 Better is the life of the poor under their own
    crude roof
  than sumptuous food in the house of
    others.
23 Be content with little or much,
  and you will hear no reproach for being a
    guest.[m]
24 It is a miserable life to go from house to house;
  as a guest you should not open your
    mouth;
25 you will play the host and provide drink
    without being thanked,
  and besides this you will hear rude words
    like these:
26 "Come here, stranger, prepare the table;
  let me eat what you have there."
27 "Be off, stranger, for an honored guest is here;
  my brother has come for a visit, and I need
    the guest-room."
28 It is hard for a sensible person to bear
  scolding about lodging[n] and the insults of
    the moneylender.

CONCERNING CHILDREN [o]

30
He who loves his son will whip him
    often,
  so that he may rejoice at the way he turns
    out.
2 He who disciplines his son will profit by him,
  and will boast of him among
    acquaintances.
3 He who teaches his son will make his enemies
    envious,
  and will glory in him among his friends.
4 When the father dies he will not seem to be
    dead,
  for he has left behind him one like himself,
5 whom in his life he looked upon with joy
  and at death, without grief.
6 He has left behind him an avenger against his
    enemies,

---

k Gk he l Other ancient authorities read *many refuse to
lend, therefore, because of such meanness; they are afraid*
m Lat: Gk *reproach from your family*; other ancient authorities
lack this line n Or *scolding from the household* o This
heading is included in the Gk text.

and one to repay the kindness of his
   friends.

7 Whoever spoils his son will bind up his
      wounds,
   and will suffer heartache at every cry.
8 An unbroken horse turns out stubborn,
   and an unchecked son turns out
      headstrong.
9 Pamper a child, and he will terrorize you;
   play with him, and he will grieve you.
10 Do not laugh with him, or you will have
      sorrow with him,
   and in the end you will gnash your teeth.
11 Give him no freedom in his youth,
   and do not ignore his errors.
12 Bow down his neck in his youth,[p]
   and beat his sides while he is young,
   or else he will become stubborn and disobey
      you,
   and you will have sorrow of soul from
      him.[q]
13 Discipline your son and make his yoke
      heavy,[r]
   so that you may not be offended by his
      shamelessness.

14 Better off poor, healthy, and fit
   than rich and afflicted in body.
15 Health and fitness are better than any gold,
   and a robust body than countless riches.
16 There is no wealth better than health of body,
   and no gladness above joy of heart.
17 Death is better than a life of misery,
   and eternal sleep[s] than chronic sickness.

CONCERNING FOODS[t]

18 Good things poured out upon a mouth that is
      closed
   are like offerings of food placed upon a
      grave.
19 Of what use to an idol is a sacrifice?
   For it can neither eat nor smell.
   So is the one punished by the Lord;
20 he sees with his eyes and groans
   as a eunuch groans when embracing a girl.[u]

21 Do not give yourself over to sorrow,
   and do not distress yourself deliberately.
22 A joyful heart is life itself,
   and rejoicing lengthens one's life span.
23 Indulge yourself[v] and take comfort,
   and remove sorrow far from you,
   for sorrow has destroyed many,
   and no advantage ever comes from it.
24 Jealousy and anger shorten life,
   and anxiety brings on premature old age.

25 Those who are cheerful and merry at table
   will benefit from their food.

Right Attitude toward Riches

31 Wakefulness over wealth wastes away
      one's flesh,
   and anxiety about it drives away sleep.
2 Wakeful anxiety prevents slumber,
   and a severe illness carries off sleep.[w]
3 The rich person toils to amass a fortune,
   and when he rests he fills himself with his
      dainties.
4 The poor person toils to make a meager living,
   and if ever he rests he becomes needy.

5 One who loves gold will not be justified;
   one who pursues money will be led astray[x]
      by it.
6 Many have come to ruin because of gold,
   and their destruction has met them face to
      face.
7 It is a stumbling block to those who are avid
      for it,
   and every fool will be taken captive by it.
8 Blessed is the rich person who is found
      blameless,
   and who does not go after gold.
9 Who is he, that we may praise him?
   For he has done wonders among his
      people.
10 Who has been tested by it and been found
      perfect?
   Let it be for him a ground for boasting.
   Who has had the power to transgress and did
      not transgress,
   and to do evil and did not do it?
11 His prosperity will be established,[y]
   and the assembly will proclaim his acts of
      charity.

Table Etiquette

12 Are you seated at the table of the great?[z]
   Do not be greedy at it,
   and do not say, "How much food there is
      here!"
13 Remember that a greedy eye is a bad thing.

---

p Other ancient authorities lack this line and the preceding
line q Other ancient authorities lack this line r Heb:
Gk take pains with him s Other ancient authorities lack
eternal sleep t This heading is included in the Gk text;
other ancient authorities place the heading before verse 16
u Other ancient authorities add So is the person who does
right under compulsion v Other ancient authorities read
Beguile yourself w Other ancient authorities read sleep
carries off a severe illness x Heb Syr: Gk pursues destruction
will be filled y Other ancient authorities add because
of this z Heb Syr: Gk at a great table

What has been created more greedy than
    the eye?
    Therefore it sheds tears for any reason.

14 Do not reach out your hand for everything you
    see,
    and do not crowd your neighbor[a] at the
    dish.

15 Judge your neighbor's feelings by your own,
    and in every matter be thoughtful.

16 Eat what is set before you like a well
    brought-up person,[b]
    and do not chew greedily, or you will give
    offense.

17 Be the first to stop, as befits good manners,
    and do not be insatiable, or you will give
    offense.

18 If you are seated among many persons,
    do not help yourself[c] before they do.

19 How ample a little is for a well-disciplined
    person!
    He does not breathe heavily when in bed.

20 Healthy sleep depends on moderate eating;
    he rises early, and feels fit.
The distress of sleeplessness and of nausea
    and colic are with the glutton.

21 If you are overstuffed with food,
    get up to vomit, and you will have relief.

22 Listen to me, my child, and do not
    disregard me,
    and in the end you will appreciate my
    words.

In everything you do be moderate,[d]
    and no sickness will overtake you.

23 People bless the one who is liberal with food,
    and their testimony to his generosity is
    trustworthy.

24 The city complains of the one who is stingy
    with food,
    and their testimony to his stinginess is
    accurate.

Temperance in Drinking Wine

25 Do not try to prove your strength by
    wine-drinking,
    for wine has destroyed many.

26 As the furnace tests the work of the smith,[e]
    so wine tests hearts when the insolent
    quarrel.

27 Wine is very life to human beings
    if taken in moderation.
What is life to one who is without wine?
    It has been created to make people
    happy.

28 Wine drunk at the proper time and in
    moderation
    is rejoicing of heart and gladness of soul.

29 Wine drunk to excess leads to bitterness of
    spirit,
    to quarrels and stumbling.

---

a Gk *him* *b* Heb: Gk *like a human being* *c* Gk *reach out your hand* *d* Heb Syr: Gk *industrious* *e* Heb: Gk *tests the hardening of steel by dipping*

DO NOT reach out your hand for everything you see, and DO NOT crowd your neighbor at the dish. Judge your neighbor's feelings by your own, and in every matter be thoughtful.

31.14–15

S
I
R

30 Drunkenness increases the anger of a fool to
      his own hurt,
    reducing his strength and adding wounds.
31 Do not reprove your neighbor at a banquet of
      wine,
    and do not despise him in his
      merrymaking;
  speak no word of reproach to him,
    and do not distress him by making
      demands of him.

Etiquette at a Banquet

32 If they make you master of the feast, do
      not exalt yourself;
  be among them as one of their number.
  Take care of them first and then sit down;
2   when you have fulfilled all your duties, take
      your place,
  so that you may be merry along with them
    and receive a wreath for your excellent
      leadership.

3 Speak, you who are older, for it is your right,
    but with accurate knowledge, and do not
      interrupt the music.
4 Where there is entertainment, do not pour out
      talk;
    do not display your cleverness at the wrong
      time.
5 A ruby seal in a setting of gold
    is a concert of music at a banquet of wine.
6 A seal of emerald in a rich setting of gold
    is the melody of music with good wine.

7 Speak, you who are young, if you are
      obliged to,
    but no more than twice, and only if asked.
8 Be brief; say much in few words;
    be as one who knows and can still hold his
      tongue.
9 Among the great do not act as their equal;
    and when another is speaking, do not
      babble.

10 Lightning travels ahead of the thunder,
    and approval goes before one who is
      modest.
11 Leave in good time and do not be the last;
    go home quickly and do not linger.
12 Amuse yourself there to your heart's content,
    but do not sin through proud speech.
13 But above all bless your Maker,
    who fills you with his good gifts.

The Providence of God

14 The one who seeks God *f* will accept his
      discipline,

and those who rise early to seek him*g* will
      find favor.
15 The one who seeks the law will be filled
      with it,
    but the hypocrite will stumble at it.
16 Those who fear the Lord will form true
      judgments,
    and they will kindle righteous deeds like a
      light.
17 The sinner will shun reproof,
    and will find a decision according to his
      liking.

18 A sensible person will not overlook a
      thoughtful suggestion;
  an insolent*h* and proud person will not be
      deterred by fear.*i*
19 Do nothing without deliberation,
    but when you have acted, do not regret it.
20 Do not go on a path full of hazards,
    and do not stumble at an obstacle twice.*j*
21 Do not be overconfident on a smooth*k* road,
22   and give good heed to your paths.*l*
23 Guard*m* yourself in every act,
    for this is the keeping of the
      commandments.

24 The one who keeps the law preserves himself,*n*
    and the one who trusts the Lord will not
      suffer loss.

33 No evil will befall the one who fears
      the Lord,
  but in trials such a one will be rescued
      again and again.
2 The wise will not hate the law,
    but the one who is hypocritical about it is
      like a boat in a storm.
3 The sensible person will trust in the law;
    for such a one the law is as dependable as a
      divine oracle.

4 Prepare what to say, and then you will be
      listened to;
    draw upon your training, and give your
      answer.
5 The heart of a fool is like a cart wheel,
    and his thoughts like a turning axle.
6 A mocking friend is like a stallion
    that neighs no matter who the rider is.

---

f Heb: Gk *who fears the Lord*   *g* Other ancient authorities
lack *to seek him*   *h* Heb: Gk *alien*   *i* Meaning of Gk
uncertain. Other ancient authorities add *and after acting,
with him, without deliberation*   *j* Heb: Gk *stumble on stony
ground*   *k* Or *an unexplored*   *l* Heb Syr: Gk *and beware of
your children*   *m* Heb Syr: Gk *Trust*   *n* Heb: Gk *who believes
the law heeds the commandments*

Differences in Nature and in Humankind

7 Why is one day more important than another,
  when all the daylight in the year is from the
  sun?
8 By the Lord's wisdom they were distinguished,
  and he appointed the different seasons and
  festivals.
9 Some days he exalted and hallowed,
  and some he made ordinary days.
10 All human beings come from the ground,
  and humankind° was created out of the
  dust.
11 In the fullness of his knowledge the Lord
  distinguished them
  and appointed their different ways.
12 Some he blessed and exalted,
  and some he made holy and brought near
  to himself;
  but some he cursed and brought low,
  and turned them out of their place.
13 Like clay in the hand of the potter,
  to be molded as he pleases,
  so all are in the hand of their Maker,
  to be given whatever he decides.

14 Good is the opposite of evil,
  and life the opposite of death;
  so the sinner is the opposite of the godly.
15 Look at all the works of the Most High;
  they come in pairs, one the opposite of the
  other.

16 Now I was the last to keep vigil;
  I was like a gleaner following the
  grape-pickers;
17 by the blessing of the Lord I arrived first,
  and like a grape-picker I filled my wine
  press.
18 Consider that I have not labored for myself
  alone,
  but for all who seek instruction.
19 Hear me, you who are great among the people,
  and you leaders of the congregation, pay
  heed!

The Advantage of Independence

20 To son or wife, to brother or friend,
  do not give power over yourself, as long as
  you live;
  and do not give your property to another,
  in case you change your mind and must ask
  for it.
21 While you are still alive and have breath in
  you,
  do not let anyone take your place.
22 For it is better that your children should ask
  from you

than that you should look to the hand of
  your children.
23 Excel in all that you do;
  bring no stain upon your honor.
24 At the time when you end the days of your life,
  in the hour of death, distribute your
  inheritance.

The Treatment of Slaves

25 Fodder and a stick and burdens for a donkey;
  bread and discipline and work for a slave.
26 Set your slave to work, and you will find rest;
  leave his hands idle, and he will seek
  liberty.
27 Yoke and thong will bow the neck,
  and for a wicked slave there are racks and
  tortures.
28 Put him to work, in order that he may not be
  idle,
29 for idleness teaches much evil.
30 Set him to work, as is fitting for him,
  and if he does not obey, make his fetters
  heavy.
  Do not be overbearing toward anyone,
  and do nothing unjust.

31 If you have but one slave, treat him like
  yourself,
  because you have bought him with blood.
  If you have but one slave, treat him like a
  brother,
  for you will need him as you need your life.
32 If you ill-treat him, and he leaves you and runs
  away,
33 which way will you go to seek him?

Dreams Mean Nothing
(Deut 13.1–5; 18.9–14)

34 The senseless have vain and false
  hopes,
  and dreams give wings to fools.
2 As one who catches at a shadow and pursues
  the wind,
  so is anyone who believes inᵖ dreams.
3 What is seen in dreams is but a reflection,
  the likeness of a face looking at itself.
4 From an unclean thing what can be clean?
  And from something false what can be true?
5 Divinations and omens and dreams are unreal,
  and like a woman in labor, the mind has
  fantasies.
6 Unless they are sent by intervention from the
  Most High,
  pay no attention to them.
7 For dreams have deceived many,

---

o Heb: Gk *Adam*   p Syr: Gk *pays heed to*

and those who put their hope in them have
     perished.

8 Without such deceptions the law will be
     fulfilled,
and wisdom is complete in the mouth of
     the faithful.

Experience as a Teacher

9 An educated[q] person knows many things,
and one with much experience knows what
     he is talking about.
10 An inexperienced person knows few things,
11   but he that has traveled acquires much
     cleverness.
12 I have seen many things in my travels,
and I understand more than I can express.
13 I have often been in danger of death,
but have escaped because of these
     experiences.

Fear the Lord

14 The spirit of those who fear the Lord will live,
15   for their hope is in him who saves them.
16 Those who fear the Lord will not be timid,
or play the coward, for he is their hope.
17 Happy is the soul that fears the Lord!
18   To whom does he look? And who is his
     support?
19 The eyes of the Lord are on those who love him,
a mighty shield and strong support,
a shelter from scorching wind and a shade
     from noonday sun,
a guard against stumbling and a help
     against falling.
20 He lifts up the soul and makes the eyes sparkle;
he gives health and life and blessing.

Offering Sacrifices

21 If one sacrifices ill-gotten goods, the offering is
     blemished;[r]
22   the gifts[s] of the lawless are not acceptable.
23 The Most High is not pleased with the offerings
     of the ungodly,
nor for a multitude of sacrifices does he
     forgive sins.
24 Like one who kills a son before his father's eyes
is the person who offers a sacrifice from the
     property of the poor.
25 The bread of the needy is the life of the poor;
whoever deprives them of it is a murderer.
26 To take away a neighbor's living is to commit
     murder;
27   to deprive an employee of wages is to shed
     blood.

28 When one builds and another tears down,
what do they gain but hard work?

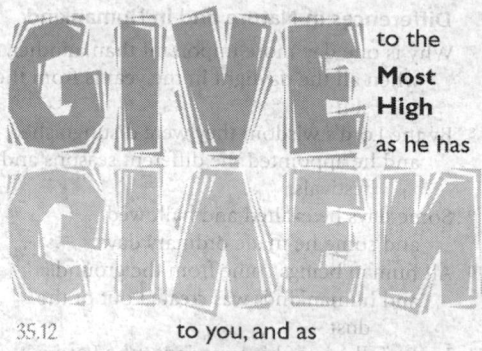

GIVE to the **Most High** as he has GIVEN
35.12   to you, and as **generously** as you can afford.

29 When one prays and another curses,
to whose voice will the Lord listen?
30 If one washes after touching a corpse, and
     touches it again,
what has been gained by washing?
31 So if one fasts for his sins,
and goes again and does the same things,
who will listen to his prayer?
And what has he gained by humbling
     himself?

The Law and Sacrifices
(Cp 2 Cor 9.7)

35 The one who keeps the law makes
     many offerings;
2   one who heeds the commandments makes
     an offering of well-being.
3 The one who returns a kindness offers choice
     flour,
4   and one who gives alms sacrifices a thank
     offering.
5 To keep from wickedness is pleasing to the
     Lord,
and to forsake unrighteousness is an
     atonement.
6 Do not appear before the Lord empty-handed,
7   for all that you offer is in fulfillment of the
     commandment.
8 The offering of the righteous enriches the altar,
and its pleasing odor rises before the Most
     High.
9 The sacrifice of the righteous is acceptable,
and it will never be forgotten.
10 Be generous when you worship the Lord,
and do not stint the first fruits of your
     hands.

---

q Other ancient authorities read *A traveled*   r Other ancient
authorities read *is made in mockery*   s Other ancient
authorities read *mockeries*

S
I
R

11 With every gift show a cheerful face,
    and dedicate your tithe with gladness.
12 Give to the Most High as he has given to you,
    and as generously as you can afford.
13 For the Lord is the one who repays,
    and he will repay you sevenfold.

Divine Justice

14 Do not offer him a bribe, for he will not
    accept it;
15 and do not rely on a dishonest sacrifice;
    for the Lord is the judge,
    and with him there is no partiality.
16 He will not show partiality to the poor;
    but he will listen to the prayer of one who
    is wronged.
17 He will not ignore the supplication of the
    orphan,
    or the widow when she pours out her
    complaint.
18 Do not the tears of the widow run down her
    cheek
19 as she cries out against the one who causes
    them to fall?
20 The one whose service is pleasing to the Lord
    will be accepted,
    and his prayer will reach to the clouds.
21 The prayer of the humble pierces the clouds,
    and it will not rest until it reaches its goal;
    it will not desist until the Most High responds
22 and does justice for the righteous, and
    executes judgment.
    Indeed, the Lord will not delay,
    and like a warrior^t will not be patient
    until he crushes the loins of the unmerciful
23 and repays vengeance on the nations;
    until he destroys the multitude of the insolent,
    and breaks the scepters of the unrighteous;
24 until he repays mortals according to their
    deeds,
    and the works of all according to their
    thoughts;
25 until he judges the case of his people
    and makes them rejoice in his mercy.
26 His mercy is as welcome in time of distress
    as clouds of rain in time of drought.

A Prayer for God's People

36 Have mercy upon us, O God^u of all,
2   and put all the nations in fear
    of you.
3 Lift up your hand against foreign nations
    and let them see your might.
4 As you have used us to show your holiness to
    them,
    so use them to show your glory to us.
5 Then they will know,^{v} as we have known,

that there is no God but you, O Lord.
6 Give new signs, and work other wonders;
7   make your hand and right arm glorious.
8 Rouse your anger and pour out your wrath;
9   destroy the adversary and wipe out the
    enemy.
10 Hasten the day, and remember the appointed
    time,^{w}
    and let people recount your mighty deeds.
11 Let survivors be consumed in the fiery wrath,
    and may those who harm your people meet
    destruction.
12 Crush the heads of hostile rulers
    who say, "There is no one but ourselves."
13 Gather all the tribes of Jacob,^{x}
16   and give them their inheritance, as at the
    beginning.
17 Have mercy, O Lord, on the people called by
    your name,
    on Israel, whom you have named^y your
    firstborn,
18 Have pity on the city of your sanctuary,^{z}
    Jerusalem, the place of your dwelling.^{a}
19 Fill Zion with your majesty,^{b}
    and your temple^c with your glory.
20 Bear witness to those whom you created in the
    beginning,
    and fulfill the prophecies spoken in your
    name.
21 Reward those who wait for you
    and let your prophets be found trustworthy.
22 Hear, O Lord, the prayer of your servants,
    according to your goodwill toward^d
    your people,
    and all who are on the earth will know
    that you are the Lord, the God of the ages.

Concerning Discrimination

23 The stomach will take any food,
    yet one food is better than another.
24 As the palate tastes the kinds of game,
    so an intelligent mind detects false words.
25 A perverse mind will cause grief,
    but a person with experience will pay him
    back.
26 A woman will accept any man as a husband,

---

^{t} Heb: Gk *and with them* ^{u} Heb: Gk *O Master, the God*
^{v} Heb: Gk *And let them know you* ^{w} Other ancient
authorities read *remember your oath* ^{x} Owing to a
dislocation in the Greek Mss of Sirach, the verse numbers
14 and 15 are not used in chapter 36, though no text is
missing. ^{y} Other ancient authorities read *you have
likened to* ^{z} Or *on your holy city* ^{a} Heb: Gk *your rest*
^{b} Heb Syr: Gk *the celebration of your wondrous deeds* ^{c} Heb
Syr: Gk Lat *people* ^{d} Heb and two Gk witnesses: Lat
and most Gk witnesses read *according to the blessing of
Aaron for*

but one girl is preferable to another.

27 A woman's beauty lights up a man's face,
and there is nothing he desires more.

28 If kindness and humility mark her speech,
her husband is more fortunate than other
men.

29 He who acquires a wife gets his best
possession,*e*
a helper fit for him and a pillar of support.*f*

30 Where there is no fence, the property will be
plundered;
and where there is no wife, a man will
become a fugitive and a wanderer.*g*

31 For who will trust a nimble robber
that skips from city to city?
So who will trust a man that has no nest,
but lodges wherever night overtakes him?

False Friends

37 Every friend says, "I too am a friend";
but some friends are friends only in
name.

2 Is it not a sorrow like that for death itself
when a dear friend turns into an enemy?

3 O inclination to evil, why were you formed
to cover the land with deceit?

4 Some companions rejoice in the happiness of a
friend,
but in time of trouble they are against him.

5 Some companions help a friend for their
stomachs' sake,
yet in battle they will carry his shield.

6 Do not forget a friend during the battle,*h*
and do not be unmindful of him when you
distribute your spoils.*i*

Caution in Taking Advice

7 All counselors praise the counsel they give,
but some give counsel in their own interest.

8 Be wary of a counselor,
and learn first what is his interest,
for he will take thought for himself.
He may cast the lot against you

9 and tell you, "Your way is good,"
and then stand aside to see what happens
to you.

10 Do not consult the one who regards you with
suspicion;
hide your intentions from those who are
jealous of you.

11 Do not consult with a woman about her rival
or with a coward about war,
with a merchant about business
or with a buyer about selling,
with a miser about generosity*j*
or with the merciless about kindness,
with an idler about any work

or with a seasonal laborer about completing
his work,
with a lazy servant about a big task—
pay no attention to any advice they give.

12 But associate with a godly person
whom you know to be a keeper of the
commandments,
who is like-minded with yourself,
and who will grieve with you if you fail.

13 And heed*k* the counsel of your own heart,
for no one is more faithful to you than it is.

14 For our own mind sometimes keeps us better
informed
than seven sentinels sitting high on a
watchtower.

15 But above all pray to the Most High
that he may direct your way in truth.

True and False Wisdom

16 Discussion is the beginning of every work,
and counsel precedes every undertaking.

17 The mind is the root of all conduct;

18 it sprouts four branches,*l*
good and evil, life and death;
and it is the tongue that continually rules
them.

19 Some people may be clever enough to teach
many,
and yet be useless to themselves.

20 A skillful speaker may be hated;
he will be destitute of all food,

21 for the Lord has withheld the gift of charm,
since he is lacking in all wisdom.

22 If a person is wise to his own advantage,
the fruits of his good sense will be
praiseworthy.*m*

23 A wise person instructs his own people,
and the fruits of his good sense will endure.

24 A wise person will have praise heaped upon
him,
and all who see him will call him happy.

25 The days of a person's life are numbered,
but the days of Israel are without number.

26 One who is wise among his people will inherit
honor,*n*
and his name will live forever.

Concerning Moderation

27 My child, test yourself while you live;
see what is bad for you and do not give in
to it.

---

e Heb: Gk *enters upon a possession*   *f* Heb: Gk *rest*   *g* Heb:
Gk *wander about and sigh*   *h* Heb: Gk *in your heart*   *i* Heb:
Gk *him in your wealth*   *j* Heb: Gk *gratitude*   *k* Heb: Gk
establish   *l* Heb: Gk *As a clue to changes of heart four kinds of
destiny appear*   *m* Other ancient witnesses read *trustworthy*
n Other ancient authorities read *confidence*

28 For not everything is good for everyone,
   and no one enjoys everything.
29 Do not be greedy for every delicacy,
   and do not eat without restraint;
30 for overeating brings sickness,
   and gluttony leads to nausea.
31 Many have died of gluttony,
   but the one who guards against it prolongs
   his life.

Concerning Physicians and Health

38 Honor physicians for their services,
   for the Lord created them;
2 for their gift of healing comes from the Most
   High,
   and they are rewarded by the king.
3 The skill of physicians makes them
   distinguished,
   and in the presence of the great they are
   admired.
4 The Lord created medicines out of the earth,
   and the sensible will not despise them.
5 Was not water made sweet with a tree
   in order that its° power might be known?
6 And he gave skill to human beings
   that he ᵖ might be glorified in his marvelous
   works.
7 By them the physician�q heals and takes away
   pain;
8 the pharmacist makes a mixture from them.
   God'sʳ works will never be finished;

PRAY IT
Health-Care Providers

When was the last time you went to
the doctor? How often do you take
medicine? Did you ever spend a night in a
hospital? It's humbling to realize that the
basic health care we take for granted is
not available to millions of people in this
country and throughout the world.

God gives the skill to heal to doctors,
nurses, dentists, pharmacists, therapists,
and medical technicians of every kind
(Sir 38.2). Their jobs often demand huge
amounts of time and energy. Take a moment to remember in prayer the health-
care providers you know personally, and
ask yourself if you have a vocation in the
medical profession.

▶ Sir 38.1–15

and from him healthˢ spreads over all the
   earth.

9 My child, when you are ill, do not delay,
   but pray to the Lord, and he will heal you.
10 Give up your faults and direct your hands
   rightly,
   and cleanse your heart from all sin.
11 Offer a sweet-smelling sacrifice, and a
   memorial portion of choice flour,
   and pour oil on your offering, as much as
   you can afford.ᵗ
12 Then give the physician his place, for the Lord
   created him;
   do not let him leave you, for you need him.
13 There may come a time when recovery lies in
   the hands of physicians,ᵘ
14 for they too pray to the Lord
   that he grant them success in diagnosisᵛ
   and in healing, for the sake of preserving
   life.
15 He who sins against his Maker,
   will be defiant toward the physician.ʷ

On Mourning for the Dead
(Cp Sir 22.11–12)

16 My child, let your tears fall for the dead,
   and as one in great pain begin the lament.
   Lay out the body with due ceremony,
   and do not neglect the burial.
17 Let your weeping be bitter and your wailing
   fervent;
   make your mourning worthy of the
   departed,
   for one day, or two, to avoid criticism;
   then be comforted for your grief.
18 For grief may result in death,
   and a sorrowful heart saps one's strength.
19 When a person is taken away, sorrow is over;
   but the life of the poor weighs down the
   heart.
20 Do not give your heart to grief;
   drive it away, and remember your own end.
21 Do not forget, there is no coming back;
   you do the deadˣ no good, and you injure
   yourself.
22 Remember hisʸ fate, for yours is like it;
   yesterday it was his,ᶻ and today it is yours.
23 When the dead is at rest, let his remembrance
   rest too,
   and be comforted for him when his spirit
   has departed.

---

o Or *his* p Or *they* q Heb: Gk *he* r Gk *His* s Or *peace*
t Heb: Lat lacks *as much as you can afford;* Meaning of Gk
uncertain u Gk *in their hands* v Heb: Gk *rest* w Heb: Gk
may he fall into the hands of the physician x Gk *him* y Heb:
Gk *my* z Heb: Gk *mine*

Trades and Crafts

24 The wisdom of the scribe depends on the
      opportunity of leisure;
    only the one who has little business can
      become wise.
25 How can one become wise who handles the
      plow,
    and who glories in the shaft of a goad,
  who drives oxen and is occupied with their
      work,
    and whose talk is about bulls?
26 He sets his heart on plowing furrows,
    and he is careful about fodder for the
      heifers.
27 So it is with every artisan and master artisan
    who labors by night as well as by day;
  those who cut the signets of seals,
    each is diligent in making a great variety;
  they set their heart on painting a lifelike
      image,
    and they are careful to finish their work.
28 So it is with the smith, sitting by the anvil,
    intent on his iron-work;
  the breath of the fire melts his flesh,
    and he struggles with the heat of the
      furnace;
  the sound of the hammer deafens his ears,*a*
    and his eyes are on the pattern of the
      object.
  He sets his heart on finishing his handiwork,
    and he is careful to complete its
      decoration.
29 So it is with the potter sitting at his work
    and turning the wheel with his feet;
  he is always deeply concerned over his
      products,
    and he produces them in quantity.
30 He molds the clay with his arm
    and makes it pliable with his feet;
  he sets his heart to finish the glazing,
    and he takes care in firing*b* the kiln.

31 All these rely on their hands,
    and all are skillful in their own work.
32 Without them no city can be inhabited,
    and wherever they live, they will not go
      hungry.*c*
  Yet they are not sought out for the council of
      the people,*d*
33   nor do they attain eminence in the public
      assembly.
  They do not sit in the judge's seat,
    nor do they understand the decisions of the
      courts;
  they cannot expound discipline or judgment,
    and they are not found among the rulers.*e*
34 But they maintain the fabric of the world,

and their concern is for*f* the exercise of
      their trade.

The Activity of the Scribe

How different the one who devotes himself
    to the study of the law of the Most High!

39 He seeks out the wisdom of all the
      ancients,
    and is concerned with prophecies;
2 he preserves the sayings of the famous
    and penetrates the subtleties of parables;
3 he seeks out the hidden meanings of proverbs
    and is at home with the obscurities of
      parables.
4 He serves among the great
    and appears before rulers;
  he travels in foreign lands
    and learns what is good and evil in the
      human lot.
5 He sets his heart to rise early
    to seek the Lord who made him,
    and to petition the Most High;
  he opens his mouth in prayer
    and asks pardon for his sins.

6 If the great Lord is willing,
    he will be filled with the spirit of
      understanding;
  he will pour forth words of wisdom of his own
    and give thanks to the Lord in prayer.
7 The Lord*g* will direct his counsel and
      knowledge,
    as he meditates on his mysteries.
8 He will show the wisdom of what he has
      learned,
    and will glory in the law of the Lord's
      covenant.
9 Many will praise his understanding;
    it will never be blotted out.
  His memory will not disappear,
    and his name will live through all
      generations.
10 Nations will speak of his wisdom,
    and the congregation will proclaim his
      praise.
11 If he lives long, he will leave a name greater
      than a thousand,
    and if he goes to rest, it is enough*h* for him.

A Hymn of Praise to God

12 I have more on my mind to express;
    I am full like the full moon.

---

a Cn: Gk *renews his ear*   *b* Cn: Gk *cleaning*   *c* Syr: Gk *and
people can neither live nor walk there*   *d* Most ancient
authorities lack this line   *e* Cn: Gk *among parables*
f Syr: Gk *prayer is in*   *g* Gk *He himself*   *h* Cn: Meaning of
Gk uncertain

13 Listen to me, my faithful children, and
> blossom
> like a rose growing by a stream of water.

14 Send out fragrance like incense,
> and put forth blossoms like a lily.
> Scatter the fragrance, and sing a hymn of
> praise;
> bless the Lord for all his works.

15 Ascribe majesty to his name
> and give thanks to him with praise,
> with songs on your lips, and with harps;
> this is what you shall say in thanksgiving:

16 "All the works of the Lord are very good,
> and whatever he commands will be done at
> the appointed time.

17 No one can say, 'What is this?' or 'Why is
> that?'—
> for at the appointed time all such questions
> will be answered.
> At his word the waters stood in a heap,
> and the reservoirs of water at the word of
> his mouth.

18 When he commands, his every purpose is
> fulfilled,
> and none can limit his saving power.

19 The works of all are before him,
> and nothing can be hidden from his eyes.

20 From the beginning to the end of time he can
> see everything,
> and nothing is too marvelous for him.

21 No one can say, 'What is this?' or 'Why is
> that?'—
> for everything has been created for its own
> purpose.

22 "His blessing covers the dry land like a river,
> and drenches it like a flood.

23 But his wrath drives out the nations,
> as when he turned a watered land into salt.

24 To the faithful his ways are straight,
> but full of pitfalls for the wicked.

25 From the beginning good things were created
> for the good,
> but for sinners good things and bad.[i]

26 The basic necessities of human life
> are water and fire and iron and salt
> and wheat flour and milk and honey,
> the blood of the grape and oil and clothing.

27 All these are good for the godly,
> but for sinners they turn into evils.

28 "There are winds created for vengeance,
> and in their anger they can dislodge
> mountains;[j]
> on the day of reckoning they will pour out
> their strength

and calm the anger of their Maker.

29 Fire and hail and famine and pestilence,
> all these have been created for vengeance;

30 the fangs of wild animals and scorpions and
> vipers,
> and the sword that punishes the ungodly
> with destruction.

31 They take delight in doing his bidding,
> always ready for his service on earth;
> and when their time comes they never
> disobey his command."

32 So from the beginning I have been convinced
> of all this
> and have thought it out and left it in
> writing:

33 All the works of the Lord are good,
> and he will supply every need in its time.

34 No one can say, "This is not as good as that,"
> for everything proves good in its appointed
> time.

35 So now sing praise with all your heart and
> voice,
> and bless the name of the Lord.

Human Wretchedness

40 Hard work was created for everyone,
> and a heavy yoke is laid on the
> children of Adam,
> from the day they come forth from their
> mother's womb
> until the day they return to[k] the mother of
> all the living.[l]

2 Perplexities and fear of heart are theirs,
> and anxious thought of the day of their
> death.

3 From the one who sits on a splendid throne
> to the one who grovels in dust and ashes,

4 from the one who wears purple and a crown
> to the one who is clothed in burlap,

5 there is anger and envy and trouble and unrest,
> and fear of death, and fury and strife.
> And when one rests upon his bed,
> his sleep at night confuses his mind.

6 He gets little or no rest;
> he struggles in his sleep as he did by day.[m]
> He is troubled by the visions of his mind
> like one who has escaped from the
> battlefield.

7 At the moment he reaches safety he wakes up,
> astonished that his fears were groundless.

8 To all creatures, human and animal,
> but to sinners seven times more,

---

i Heb Lat: Gk *sinners bad things*   *j* Heb Syr: Gk *can scourge
mightily*   *k* Other Gk and Lat authorities read *are buried in*
l Heb: Gk *of all*   *m* Arm: Meaning of Gk uncertain

3 of keeping accounts with a partner or with
    traveling companions,
  and of dividing the inheritance of friends;
4 of accuracy with scales and weights,
    and of acquiring much or little;
5 of profit from dealing with merchants,
    and of frequent disciplining of children,
    and of drawing blood from the back of a
    wicked slave.
6 Where there is an untrustworthy wife, a seal is
    a good thing;
  and where there are many hands, lock
    things up.
7 When you make a deposit, be sure it is counted
    and weighed,
  and when you give or receive, put it all in
    writing.
8 Do not be ashamed to correct the stupid or
    foolish
  or the aged who are guilty of sexual
    immorality.
Then you will show your sound training,
    and will be approved by all.

Daughters and Fathers
(Sir 7.24–25; 26.10–12)

9 A daughter is a secret anxiety to her father,
  and worry over her robs him of sleep;
when she is young, for fear she may not marry,
  or if married, for fear she may be disliked;
10 while a virgin, for fear she may be seduced
    and become pregnant in her father's house;
or having a husband, for fear she may go
    astray,
or, though married, for fear she may be
    barren.

11 Keep strict watch over a headstrong daughter,
  or she may make you a laughingstock to
    your enemies,
a byword in the city and the assembly of*w* the
    people,
  and put you to shame in public gatherings.*x*
See that there is no lattice in her room,
  no spot that overlooks the approaches to
    the house.*y*
12 Do not let her parade her beauty before any
    man,
  or spend her time among married women;*w*
13 for from garments comes the moth,
  and from a woman comes woman's
    wickedness.
14 Better is the wickedness of a man than a
    woman who does good;
  it is woman who brings shame and
    disgrace.

The Works of God in Nature

15 I will now call to mind the works of the Lord,
  and will declare what I have seen.
By the word of the Lord his works are made;
  and all his creatures do his will.*z*
16 The sun looks down on everything with its
    light,
  and the work of the Lord is full of his
    glory.
17 The Lord has not empowered even his holy
    ones
  to recount all his marvelous works,

---

w Heb: Meaning of Gk uncertain   *x* Heb: Gk *to shame before
the great multitude*   *y* Heb: Gk lacks *See . . . house*   *z* Syr
Compare Heb: most Gk witnesses lack *and all . . . will*

Equality

**As you read Sir 42.9–14, you probably think it's a curse to have a daughter! Verse
14 says, "Better is the wickedness of a man than a woman who does good; / it is
woman who brings shame and disgrace." Wow, with an attitude like that, Ben
Sira wouldn't be welcomed by many modern people.**
  Once again, we have to remember that the Bible was written by human beings and
reflects their cultural standards. Ben Sira's attitude was commonly accepted in his culture.
But the cultural standards in the Bible don't always reflect God's truth. That's why we need
the help of the larger church community to properly interpret the Bible. Today, the church
teaches that women and men are to be treated with equal dignity and respect. Let's work
together to continue making that vision a reality.

▶ Sir 42.9–14

which the Lord the Almighty has established
  so that the universe may stand firm in his
    glory.
18 He searches out the abyss and the human
    heart;
  he understands their innermost secrets.
For the Most High knows all that may be
    known;
  he sees from of old the things that are to
    come.*a*
19 He discloses what has been and what is to be,
  and he reveals the traces of hidden things.
20 No thought escapes him,
  and nothing is hidden from him.
21 He has set in order the splendors of his
    wisdom;
  he is from all eternity one and the same.
Nothing can be added or taken away,
  and he needs no one to be his counselor.
22 How desirable are all his works,
  and how sparkling they are to see!*b*
23 All these things live and remain forever;
  each creature is preserved to meet a
    particular need.*c*
24 All things come in pairs, one opposite the
    other,
  and he has made nothing incomplete.
25 Each supplements the virtues of the other.
  Who could ever tire of seeing his glory?

The Splendor of the Sun

43 The pride of the higher realms is the
    clear vault of the sky,
  as glorious to behold as the sight of the
    heavens.
2 The sun, when it appears, proclaims as it
    rises
  what a marvelous instrument it is, the work
    of the Most High.
3 At noon it parches the land,
  and who can withstand its burning heat?
4 A man tending*d* a furnace works in burning
    heat,
  but three times as hot is the sun scorching
    the mountains;
  it breathes out fiery vapors,
  and its bright rays blind the eyes.
5 Great is the Lord who made it;
  at his orders it hurries on its course.

The Splendor of the Moon

6 It is the moon that marks the changing
    seasons,*e*
  governing the times, their everlasting sign.
7 From the moon comes the sign for festal days,
  a light that wanes when it completes its
    course.

8 The new moon, as its name suggests, renews
    itself;*f*
  how marvelous it is in this change,
a beacon to the hosts on high,
  shining in the vault of the heavens!

The Glory of the Stars and the Rainbow

9 The glory of the stars is the beauty of heaven,
  a glittering array in the heights of the Lord.
10 On the orders of the Holy One they stand in
    their appointed places;
  they never relax in their watches.
11 Look at the rainbow, and praise him who
    made it;
  it is exceedingly beautiful in its brightness.
12 It encircles the sky with its glorious arc;
  the hands of the Most High have stretched
    it out.

The Marvels of Nature

13 By his command he sends the driving snow
  and speeds the lightnings of his judgment.
14 Therefore the storehouses are opened,
  and the clouds fly out like birds.
15 In his majesty he gives the clouds their
    strength,
  and the hailstones are broken in pieces.
17a The voice of his thunder rebukes the earth;
16   when he appears, the mountains shake.
At his will the south wind blows;
17b   so do the storm from the north and the
    whirlwind.
He scatters the snow like birds flying down,
  and its descent is like locusts alighting.
18 The eye is dazzled by the beauty of its
    whiteness,
  and the mind is amazed as it falls.
19 He pours frost over the earth like salt,
  and icicles form like pointed thorns.
20 The cold north wind blows,
  and ice freezes on the water;
  it settles on every pool of water,
  and the water puts it on like a breastplate.
21 He consumes the mountains and burns up the
    wilderness,
  and withers the tender grass like fire.
22 A mist quickly heals all things;
  the falling dew gives refreshment from the
    heat.
23 By his plan he stilled the deep
  and planted islands in it.

---

a Heb: Gk *he sees the sign(s) of the age*   *b* Meaning of Gk
uncertain   *c* Heb: Gk *forever for every need, and all are
obedient*   *d* Other ancient authorities read *blowing upon*
e Heb: Meaning of Gk uncertain   *f* Heb: Gk *The month is
named after the moon*

24 Those who sail the sea tell of its dangers,
   and we marvel at what we hear.
25 In it are strange and marvelous creatures,
   all kinds of living things, and huge
      sea-monsters.
26 Because of him each of his messengers
      succeeds,
   and by his word all things hold together.

27 We could say more but could never say
      enough;
   let the final word be: "He is the all."
28 Where can we find the strength to praise him?
   For he is greater than all his works.
29 Awesome is the Lord and very great,
   and marvelous is his power.
30 Glorify the Lord and exalt him as much as you
      can,
   for he surpasses even that.
   When you exalt him, summon all your
      strength,
   and do not grow weary, for you cannot
      praise him enough.
31 Who has seen him and can describe him?
   Or who can extol him as he is?
32 Many things greater than these lie hidden,
   for I*g* have seen but few of his works.
33 For the Lord has made all things,
   and to the godly he has given wisdom.

HYMN IN HONOR OF OUR ANCESTORS*h*

44 Let us now sing the praises of famous
      men,
   our ancestors in their generations.
2 The Lord apportioned to them*i* great glory,
   his majesty from the beginning.
3 There were those who ruled in their kingdoms,
   and made a name for themselves by their
      valor;
   those who gave counsel because they were
      intelligent;
   those who spoke in prophetic oracles;
4 those who led the people by their counsels
   and by their knowledge of the people's
      lore;
   they were wise in their words of instruction;
5 those who composed musical tunes,
   or put verses in writing;
6 rich men endowed with resources,
   living peacefully in their homes—
7 all these were honored in their generations,
   and were the pride of their times.
8 Some of them have left behind a name,
   so that others declare their praise.
9 But of others there is no memory;
   they have perished as though they had
      never existed;

they have become as though they had never
      been born,
   they and their children after them.
10 But these also were godly men,
   whose righteous deeds have not been
      forgotten;
11 their wealth will remain with their
      descendants,
   and their inheritance with their children's
      children.*j*
12 Their descendants stand by the covenants;
   their children also, for their sake.
13 Their offspring will continue forever,
   and their glory will never be blotted out.
14 Their bodies are buried in peace,
   but their name lives on generation after
      generation.
15 The assembly declares*k* their wisdom,
   and the congregation proclaims their
      praise.

Enoch
(Gen 5.24; Heb 11.5)

16 Ē'noch pleased the Lord and was taken up,
   an example of repentance to all generations.

Noah
(Gen 6.9—9.17)

17 Noah was found perfect and righteous;
   in the time of wrath he kept the race alive;*l*
   therefore a remnant was left on the earth
      when the flood came.
18 Everlasting covenants were made with him
   that all flesh should never again be blotted
      out by a flood.

Abraham
(Gen 15.1—17.27; 22.1-18)

19 Abraham was the great father of a multitude of
      nations,
   and no one has been found like him in
      glory.
20 He kept the law of the Most High,
   and entered into a covenant with him;
   he certified the covenant in his flesh,
   and when he was tested he proved faithful.
21 Therefore the Lord*m* assured him with an oath
   that the nations would be blessed through
      his offspring;
   that he would make him as numerous as the
      dust of the earth,
   and exalt his offspring like the stars,

S
I
R

---

g Heb: Gk *we*   *h* This title is included in the Gk text.
i Heb: Gk *created*   *j* Heb Compare Lat Syr: Meaning of Gk
uncertain   *k* Heb: Gk *Peoples declare*   *l* Heb: Gk *was taken
in exchange*   *m* Gk *he*

and give them an inheritance from sea to sea
    and from the Euphrates[n] to the ends of the
    earth.

Isaac and Jacob
(Gen 26.1–5; 27.1–29)

22 To Isaac also he gave the same assurance
    for the sake of his father Abraham.
The blessing of all people and the covenant
23   he made to rest on the head of Jacob;
he acknowledged him with his blessings,
    and gave him his inheritance;
he divided his portions,
    and distributed them among twelve tribes.

Moses
(Ex 6.28—11.10; 20.1–21)

From his descendants the Lord[o] brought forth a
    godly man,
    who found favor in the sight of all

45 ¹ and was beloved by God and
    people,
    Moses, whose memory is blessed.
2 He made him equal in glory to the holy ones,
    and made him great, to the terror of his
    enemies.
3 By his words he performed swift miracles;[p]
    the Lord[o] glorified him in the presence of
    kings.
He gave him commandments for his people,
    and revealed to him his glory.
4 For his faithfulness and meekness he
    consecrated him,
    choosing him out of all humankind.
5 He allowed him to hear his voice,
    and led him into the dark cloud,
and gave him the commandments face to face,
    the law of life and knowledge,
so that he might teach Jacob the covenant,
    and Israel his decrees.

Aaron
(Ex 28.1–43; Lev 8.1–36; Num 16.1–35)

6 He exalted Aaron, a holy man like Moses[q]
    who was his brother, of the tribe of Levi.
7 He made an everlasting covenant with him,
    and gave him the priesthood of the people.
He blessed him with stateliness,
    and put a glorious robe on him.
8 He clothed him in perfect splendor,
    and strengthened him with the symbols of
    authority,
    the linen undergarments, the long robe,
    and the ephod.
9 And he encircled him with pomegranates,
    with many golden bells all around,
to send forth a sound as he walked,

to make their ringing heard in the temple
    as a reminder to his people;
10 with the sacred vestment, of gold and violet
    and purple, the work of an embroiderer;
with the oracle of judgment, U′rim and
    Thum′mim;
11   with twisted crimson, the work of an
    artisan;
with precious stones engraved like seals,
    in a setting of gold, the work of a jeweler,
to commemorate in engraved letters
    each of the tribes of Israel;
12 with a gold crown upon his turban,
    inscribed like a seal with "Holiness,"
a distinction to be prized, the work of an
    expert,
    a delight to the eyes, richly adorned.
13 Before him such beautiful things did not exist.
    No outsider ever put them on,
but only his sons
    and his descendants in perpetuity.
14 His sacrifices shall be wholly burned
    twice every day continually.
15 Moses ordained him,
    and anointed him with holy oil;
it was an everlasting covenant for him
    and for his descendants as long as the
    heavens endure,
to minister to the Lord[q] and serve as priest
    and bless his people in his name.
16 He chose him out of all the living
    to offer sacrifice to the Lord,
incense and a pleasing odor as a memorial
    portion,
    to make atonement for the[r] people.
17 In his commandments he gave him
    authority and statutes and[s] judgments,
to teach Jacob the testimonies,
    and to enlighten Israel with his law.
18 Outsiders conspired against him,
    and envied him in the wilderness,
Da′than and A·bi′ram and their followers
    and the company of Ko′rah, in wrath and
    anger.
19 The Lord saw it and was not pleased,
    and in the heat of his anger they were
    destroyed;
he performed wonders against them
    to consume them in flaming fire.
20 He added glory to Aaron
    and gave him a heritage;
he allotted to him the best of the first fruits,
    and prepared bread of first fruits in
    abundance;

---

n Syr: Heb Gk River   o Gk he   p Heb: Gk caused signs
to cease   q Gk him   r Other ancient authorities read his
or your   s Heb: Gk authority in covenants of

Heroes

Who are your heroes? Maybe they include a teacher, a coach, a friend, or a parent. What sets them apart and makes them people you look up to? Their accomplishments? A cause they represent? Or a personal trait that only someone who knows them personally would be aware of?

Whom we look to as heroes says a lot about us. If our heroes are kind and generous, then maybe we value kindness and generosity. If our heroes are wealthy, perhaps we desire wealth.

Read the last section of Sirach, starting with chapter 44, which honors many Old Testament heroes. Ben Sira considered them heroes because their hearts were fixed on the Lord (49.3). What an awesome way to describe heroes!

Whom do you know who has his or her heart fixed on the Lord? What does your choice of heroes say about your dreams and values?

▶ **Sirach, chapters 44–49**

21 for they eat the sacrifices of the Lord,
  which he gave to him and his descendants.
22 But in the land of the people he has no
    inheritance,
  and he has no portion among the people;
  for the Lord*t* himself is his*u* portion and
    inheritance.

Phinehas
(Num 25.7-13)

23 Phin'e·has son of El·e·a'zar ranks third in
    glory
  for being zealous in the fear of the Lord,
  and standing firm, when the people turned
    away,
    in the noble courage of his soul;
  and he made atonement for Israel.
24 Therefore a covenant of friendship was
    established with him,
    that he should be leader of the sanctuary
      and of his people,
  that he and his descendants should have
    the dignity of the priesthood forever.
25 Just as a covenant was established with David
    son of Jesse of the tribe of Judah,
  that the king's heritage passes only from son to
    son,
    so the heritage of Aaron is for his
      descendants alone.

26 And now bless the Lord
    who has crowned you with glory.*v*
  May the Lord*t* grant you wisdom of mind
    to judge his people with justice,
  so that their prosperity may not vanish,
    and that their glory may endure through all
      their generations.

Joshua and Caleb
(Josh 6—11)

46 Joshua son of Nun was mighty in war,
    and was the successor of Moses in
      the prophetic office.
  He became, as his name implies,
    a great savior of God's*w* elect,
  to take vengeance on the enemies that rose
      against them,
    so that he might give Israel its inheritance.
2 How glorious he was when he lifted his hands
    and brandished his sword against the cities!
3 Who before him ever stood so firm?
    For he waged the wars of the Lord.
4 Was it not through him that the sun stood still
    and one day became as long as two?
5 He called upon the Most High, the Mighty
      One,
    when enemies pressed him on every side,
  and the great Lord answered him
    with hailstones of mighty power.
6 He overwhelmed that nation in battle,
    and on the slope he destroyed his
      opponents,
  so that the nations might know his armament,
    that he was fighting in the sight of the
      Lord;
    for he was a devoted follower of the Mighty
      One.
7 And in the days of Moses he proved his loyalty,
    he and Caleb son of Je·phun'neh:
  they opposed the congregation,*x*
    restrained the people from sin,

---

t Gk *he* *u* Other ancient authorities read *your* *v* Heb: Gk
lacks *And . . . glory* *w* Gk *his* *x* Other ancient authorities
read *the enemy*

S
I
R

and stilled their wicked grumbling.
8 And these two alone were spared
    out of six hundred thousand infantry,
  to lead the people[y] into their inheritance,
    the land flowing with milk and honey.
9 The Lord gave Caleb strength,
    which remained with him in his old age,
  so that he went up to the hill country,
    and his children obtained it for an
      inheritance,
10 so that all the Israelites might see
    how good it is to follow the Lord.

The Judges
(Judg 1—16; 1 Sam 3.19–20)

11 The judges also, with their respective names,
    whose hearts did not fall into idolatry
  and who did not turn away from the Lord—
    may their memory be blessed!
12 May their bones send forth new life from
      where they lie,
    and may the names of those who have been
      honored
    live again in their children!

13 Samuel was beloved by his Lord;
    a prophet of the Lord, he established the
      kingdom
    and anointed rulers over his people.
14 By the law of the Lord he judged the
      congregation,
    and the Lord watched over Jacob.
15 By his faithfulness he was proved to be a
      prophet,
    and by his words he became known as a
      trustworthy seer.
16 He called upon the Lord, the Mighty One,
    when his enemies pressed him on every
      side,
    and he offered in sacrifice a suckling lamb.
17 Then the Lord thundered from heaven,
    and made his voice heard with a mighty
      sound;
18 he subdued the leaders of the enemy[z]
    and all the rulers of the Phi·lis′tines.
19 Before the time of his eternal sleep,
    Samuel[a] bore witness before the Lord and
      his anointed:
  "No property, not so much as a pair of shoes,
    have I taken from anyone!"
    And no one accused him.
20 Even after he had fallen asleep, he
      prophesied
    and made known to the king his death,
  and lifted up his voice from the ground
    in prophecy, to blot out the wickedness of
      the people.

Nathan
(2 Sam 7.1–3; 12.1–14)

47 After him Nathan rose up
        to prophesy in the days of David.

David
(1 Sam 17.12—18.7)

2 As the fat is set apart from the offering of
      well-being,
    so David was set apart from the
      Israelites.
3 He played with lions as though they were
      young goats,
    and with bears as though they were lambs
      of the flock.
4 In his youth did he not kill a giant,
    and take away the people's disgrace,
  when he whirled the stone in the sling
    and struck down the boasting
      Goliath?
5 For he called on the Lord, the Most High,
    and he gave strength to his right arm
  to strike down a mighty warrior,
    and to exalt the power[b] of his people.
6 So they glorified him for the tens of thousands
      he conquered,
    and praised him for the blessings bestowed
      by the Lord,
    when the glorious diadem was given to
      him.
7 For he wiped out his enemies on every side,
    and annihilated his adversaries the
      Phi·lis′tines;
  he crushed their power[b] to our own
      day.
8 In all that he did he gave thanks
    to the Holy One, the Most High,
      proclaiming his glory;
  he sang praise with all his heart,
    and he loved his Maker.
9 He placed singers before the altar,
    to make sweet melody with their
      voices.[c]
10 He gave beauty to the festivals,
    and arranged their times throughout the
      year,[d]
  while they praised God's[e] holy name,
    and the sanctuary resounded from early
      morning.
11 The Lord took away his sins,
    and exalted his power[b] forever;
  he gave him a covenant of kingship
    and a glorious throne in Israel.

---

y Gk them   z Heb: Gk leaders of the people of Tyre   a Gk he
b Gk horn   c Other ancient authorities add and daily they
sing his praises   d Gk to completion   e Gk his

Solomon
(1 Kings 4.20–34)

12 After him a wise son rose up
  who because of him lived in security:[f]

13 Solomon reigned in an age of peace,
  because God made all his borders tranquil,
so that he might build a house in his name
  and provide a sanctuary to stand forever.

14 How wise you were when you were young!
  You overflowed like the Nile[g] with
    understanding.

15 Your influence spread throughout the earth,
  and you filled it with proverbs having deep
    meaning.

16 Your fame reached to far-off islands,
  and you were loved for your peaceful
    reign.

17 Your songs, proverbs, and parables,
  and the answers you gave astounded the
    nations.

18 In the name of the Lord God,
  who is called the God of Israel,
you gathered gold like tin
  and amassed silver like lead.

19 But you brought in women to lie at your side,
  and through your body you were brought
    into subjection.

20 You stained your honor,
  and defiled your family line,
so that you brought wrath upon your children,
  and they were grieved[h] at your folly,

21 because the sovereignty was divided
  and a rebel kingdom arose out of
    E'phra·im.

22 But the Lord will never give up his mercy,
  or cause any of his works to perish;
he will never blot out the descendants of his
    chosen one,
  or destroy the family line of him who loved
    him.
So he gave a remnant to Jacob,
  and to David a root from his own family.

Rehoboam and Jeroboam
(1 Kings 12.6–33)

23 Solomon rested with his ancestors,
  and left behind him one of his sons,
broad in[i] folly and lacking in sense,
  Rē·ho·bō'am, whose policy drove the
    people to revolt.
Then Jer·o·bō'am son of Nē'bat led Israel into
    sin
  and started E'phra·im on its sinful ways.

24 Their sins increased more and more,
  until they were exiled from their land.

25 For they sought out every kind of wickedness,
  until vengeance came upon them.

Elijah
(1 Kings 17.1—19.18)

48 Then E·li'jah arose, a prophet like fire,
    and his word burned like a torch.

2 He brought a famine upon them,
  and by his zeal he made them few in
    number.

3 By the word of the Lord he shut up the
    heavens,
  and also three times brought down fire.

4 How glorious you were, E·li'jah, in your
    wondrous deeds!
  Whose glory is equal to yours?

5 You raised a corpse from death
  and from Hades, by the word of the Most
    High.

6 You sent kings down to destruction,
  and famous men, from their sickbeds.

7 You heard rebuke at Sinai
  and judgments of vengeance at Hō'reb.

8 You anointed kings to inflict retribution,
  and prophets to succeed you.[j]

9 You were taken up by a whirlwind of fire,
  in a chariot with horses of fire.

10 At the appointed time, it is written, you are
    destined[k]
  to calm the wrath of God before it breaks
    out in fury,
to turn the hearts of parents to their
    children,
  and to restore the tribes of Jacob.

11 Happy are those who saw you
  and were adorned[l] with your love! For we
    also shall surely live.[m]

Elisha
(2 Kings 2.9–13)

12 When E·li'jah was enveloped in the
    whirlwind,
E·li'sha was filled with his spirit.
He performed twice as many signs,
  and marvels with every utterance of his
    mouth.[n]
Never in his lifetime did he tremble before any
    ruler,
  nor could anyone intimidate him at all.

13 Nothing was too hard for him,
  and when he was dead, his body
    prophesied.

14 In his life he did wonders,
  and in death his deeds were marvelous.

---

f Heb: Gk *in a broad place* g Heb: Gk *a river* h Other
ancient authorities read *I was grieved* i Heb (with a play
on the name Rehoboam) Syr: Gk *the people's* j Heb: Gk
him k Heb: Gk *are for reproofs* l Other ancient authorities
read *and have died* m Text and meaning of Gk uncertain
n Heb: Gk lacks *He performed . . . mouth*

15 Despite all this the people did not repent,
  nor did they forsake their sins,
until they were carried off as plunder from
    their land,
and were scattered over all the earth.
The people were left very few in number,
  but with a ruler from the house of David.
16 Some of them did what was right,
  but others sinned more and more.

Hezekiah
(2 Kings 18.1—20.21)

17 Hez·e·kī'ah fortified his city,
  and brought water into its midst;
he tunneled the rock with iron tools,
  and built cisterns for the water.
18 In his days Sen·nach'e·rib invaded the
    country;
he sent his commander ⁰ and departed;
he shook his fist against Zion,
  and made great boasts in his arrogance.
19 Then their hearts were shaken and their hands
    trembled,
  and they were in anguish, like women in
    labor.
20 But they called upon the Lord who is merciful,
  spreading out their hands toward him.
The Holy One quickly heard them from
    heaven,
  and delivered them through Ī·sāi'ah.
21 The Lordᵖ struck down the camp of the
    Assyrians,
  and his angel wiped them out.
22 For Hez·e·kī'ah did what was pleasing to the
    Lord,
  and he kept firmly to the ways of his
    ancestor David,
as he was commanded by the prophet
    Ī·sāi'ah,
  who was great and trustworthy in his
    visions.

Isaiah
(2 Kings 20.10–11)

23 In Ī·sāi'ah's�q days the sun went backward,
  and he prolonged the life of the king.
24 By his dauntless spirit he saw the future,
  and comforted the mourners in Zion.
25 He revealed what was to occur to the end of
    time,
  and the hidden things before they
    happened.

Josiah and Other Worthies

49 The nameʳ of Jō·sī'ah is like blended
    incense
prepared by the skill of the perfumer;

his memoryˢ is as sweet as honey to every
    mouth,
  and like music at a banquet of wine.
2 He did what was right by reforming the people,
  and removing the wicked abominations.
3 He kept his heart fixed on the Lord;
  in lawless times he made godliness prevail.

4 Except for David and Hez·e·kī'ah and Jō·sī'ah,
  all of them were great sinners,
for they abandoned the law of the Most High;
  the kings of Judah came to an end.
5 Theyᵗ gave their power to others,
  and their glory to a foreign nation,
6 who set fire to the chosen city of the sanctuary,
  and made its streets desolate,
  as Jer·e·mī'ah had foretold.ᵘ
7 For they had mistreated him,
  who even in the womb had been
    consecrated a prophet,
to pluck up and ruin and destroy,
  and likewise to build and to plant.

8 It was E·zēk'i·el who saw the vision of glory,
  which Godᵖ showed him above the chariot
    of the cherubim.
9 For Godᵛ also mentioned Jōb
  who held fast to all the ways of justice.ʷ
10 May the bones of the Twelve Prophets
  send forth new life from where they lie,
for they comforted the people of Jacob
  and delivered them with confident hope.

11 How shall we magnify Ze·rub'ba·bel?
  He was like a signet ring on the right
    hand,
12   and so was Jesh'ū·a son of Jō'za·dak;
in their days they built the house
  and raised a templeˣ holy to the Lord,
    destined for everlasting glory.
13 The memory of Nē·he·mī'ah also is lasting;
  he raised our fallen walls,
and set up gates and bars,
  and rebuilt our ruined houses.

Retrospect

14 Few haveʸ ever been created on earth like
    Ē'noch,
  for he was taken up from the earth.
15 Nor was anyone ever born like Joseph;ᶻ
  even his bones were cared for.

⁰ Other ancient authorities add *from Lachish*   ᵖ Gk *He*
�q Gk *his*   ʳ Heb: Gk *memory*   ˢ Heb: Gk *it*   ᵗ Heb *He*
ᵘ Gk *by the hand of Jeremiah*   ᵛ Gk *he*   ʷ Heb Compare Syr:
Meaning of Gk uncertain   ˣ Other ancient authorities read
people   ʸ Heb Syr: Gk *No one has*   ᶻ Heb Syr: Gk adds *the
leader of his brothers, the support of the people*

S
I
R

16 Shem and Seth and E'nosh were honored,[a]
   but above every other created living being
      was Adam.

Simon Son of Onias

50 The leader of his brothers and the pride
      of his people[b]
was the high priest, Simon son of O·ni'as,
   who in his life repaired the house,
   and in his time fortified the temple.
2 He laid the foundations for the high double
      walls,
   the high retaining walls for the temple
      enclosure.
3 In his days a water cistern was dug,[c]
   a reservoir like the sea in circumference.
4 He considered how to save his people from
      ruin,
   and fortified the city against siege.
5 How glorious he was, surrounded by the
      people,
   as he came out of the house of the curtain.
6 Like the morning star among the clouds,
   like the full moon at the festal season;[c]
7 like the sun shining on the temple of the Most
      High,
   like the rainbow gleaming in splendid
      clouds;
8 like roses in the days of first fruits,
   like lilies by a spring of water,
   like a green shoot on Lebanon on a
      summer day;
9 like fire and incense in the censer,
   like a vessel of hammered gold
   studded with all kinds of precious stones;
10 like an olive tree laden with fruit,
   and like a cypress towering in the clouds.
11 When he put on his glorious robe
   and clothed himself in perfect splendor,
when he went up to the holy altar,
   he made the court of the sanctuary glorious.

12 When he received the portions from the hands
      of the priests,
   as he stood by the hearth of the altar
with a garland of brothers around him,
   he was like a young cedar on Lebanon
   surrounded by the trunks of palm trees.
13 All the sons of Aaron in their splendor
   held the Lord's offering in their hands
   before the whole congregation of Israel.
14 Finishing the service at the altars,[d]
   and arranging the offering to the Most
      High, the Almighty,
15 he held out his hand for the cup
   and poured a drink offering of the blood of
      the grape;

he poured it out at the foot of the altar,
   a pleasing odor to the Most High, the king
      of all.
16 Then the sons of Aaron shouted;
   they blew their trumpets of hammered
      metal;
they sounded a mighty fanfare
   as a reminder before the Most High.
17 Then all the people together quickly
   fell to the ground on their faces
to worship their Lord,
   the Almighty, God Most High.
18 Then the singers praised him with their voices
   in sweet and full-toned melody.[e]
19 And the people of the Lord Most High
      offered
   their prayers before the Merciful One,
until the order of worship of the Lord was
      ended,
   and they completed his ritual.
20 Then Simon[f] came down and raised his
      hands
   over the whole congregation of Israelites,
to pronounce the blessing of the Lord with his
      lips,
   and to glory in his name;
21 and they bowed down in worship a second
      time,
   to receive the blessing from the Most High.

A Benediction

22 And now bless the God of all,
   who everywhere works great wonders,
who fosters our growth from birth,
   and deals with us according to his
      mercy.
23 May he give us[g] gladness of heart,
   and may there be peace in our[h] days
   in Israel, as in the days of old.
24 May he entrust to us his mercy,
   and may he deliver us in our[i] days!

Epilogue

25 Two nations my soul detests,
   and the third is not even a people:
26 Those who live in Se'ir,[j] and the Phi·lis'tines,
   and the foolish people that live in
      She'chem.

---

a Heb: Gk *Shem and Seth were honored by people*   b Heb Syr:
Gk lacks this line. Compare 49.15   c Heb: Meaning of Gk
uncertain   d Other ancient authorities read *altar*   e Other
ancient authorities read *in sweet melody throughout the
house*   f Gk *he*   g Other ancient authorities read *you*
h Other ancient authorities read *your*   i Other ancient
authorities read *his*   j Heb Compare Lat: Gk *on the
mountain of Samaria*

27 Instruction in understanding and knowledge
    I have written in this book,
Jesus son of El·e·a'zar son of Si'rach[k] of
      Jerusalem,
    whose mind poured forth wisdom.
28 Happy are those who concern themselves with
        these things,
    and those who lay them to heart will
        become wise.
29 For if they put them into practice, they will be
        equal to anything,
    for the fear[l] of the Lord is their path.

PRAYER OF JESUS SON OF SIRACH[m]

51 I give you thanks, O Lord and King,
        and praise you, O God my Savior.
I give thanks to your name,
2   for you have been my protector and helper
and have delivered me from destruction
    and from the trap laid by a slanderous
        tongue,
    from lips that fabricate lies.
In the face of my adversaries
    you have been my helper ³and
        delivered me,
    in the greatness of your mercy and of your
        name,
from grinding teeth about to devour me,
    from the hand of those seeking my life,
    from the many troubles I endured,
4 from choking fire on every side,
    and from the midst of fire that I had not
        kindled,
5 from the deep belly of Hades,
    from an unclean tongue and lying words—
6   the slander of an unrighteous tongue to the
        king.
My soul drew near to death,
    and my life was on the brink of Hades
        below.
7 They surrounded me on every side,
    and there was no one to help me;
I looked for human assistance,
    and there was none.
8 Then I remembered your mercy, O Lord,
    and your kindness[n] from of old,
for you rescue those who wait for you
    and save them from the hand of their
        enemies.
9 And I sent up my prayer from the earth,
    and begged for rescue from death.
10 I cried out, "Lord, you are my Father;[o]
    do not forsake me in the days of trouble,
    when there is no help against the proud.
11 I will praise your name continually,
    and will sing hymns of thanksgiving."
My prayer was heard,

12   for you saved me from destruction
    and rescued me in time of trouble.
For this reason I thank you and praise you,
    and I bless the name of the Lord.

Heb adds:
Give thanks to the LORD, for he is good,
    for his steadfast love endures forever;

Give thanks to the God of praises,
    for his steadfast love endures forever;

Give thanks to the guardian of Israel,
    for his steadfast love endures forever;

Give thanks to him who formed all things,
    for his steadfast love endures forever;

Give thanks to the redeemer of Israel,
    for his steadfast love endures forever;

Give thanks to him who gathers the dispersed of
    Israel,
    for his steadfast love endures forever;

Give thanks to him who rebuilt his city and his
    sanctuary,
    for his steadfast love endures forever;

Give thanks to him who makes a horn to sprout for
    the house of David,
    for his steadfast love endures forever;

Give thanks to him who has chosen the sons of
    Za'dok to be priests,
    for his steadfast love endures forever;

Give thanks to the shield of Abraham,
    for his steadfast love endures forever;

Give thanks to the rock of Isaac,
    for his steadfast love endures forever;

Give thanks to the mighty one of Jacob,
    for his steadfast love endures forever;

Give thanks to him who has chosen Zion,
    for his steadfast love endures forever;

Give thanks to the King of the kings of kings,
    for his steadfast love endures forever;

---

k Heb: Meaning of Gk uncertain l Heb: Other ancient
authorities read *light* m This title is included in the
Gk text. n Other ancient authorities read *work* o Heb: Gk
the Father of my lord

S
I
R

He has raised up a horn for his people,
  praise for all his loyal ones.

For the children of Israel, the people close to him.
  Praise the LORD!

Autobiographical Poem on Wisdom

13 While I was still young, before I went on my
      travels,
    I sought wisdom openly in my prayer.
14 Before the temple I asked for her,
    and I will search for her until the end.

15 From the first blossom to the ripening grape
    my heart delighted in her;
    my foot walked on the straight path;
    from my youth I followed her steps.

16 I inclined my ear a little and received her,
    and I found for myself much instruction.
17 I made progress in her;
    to him who gives wisdom I will give glory.

18 For I resolved to live according to wisdom,^{p}
    and I was zealous for the good,
    and I shall never be disappointed.
19 My soul grappled with wisdom,^{p}
    and in my conduct I was strict;^{q}

    I spread out my hands to the heavens,
    and lamented my ignorance of her.
20 I directed my soul to her,
    and in purity I found her.

    With her I gained understanding from the first;
    therefore I will never be forsaken.

21 My heart was stirred to seek her;
    therefore I have gained a prize possession.
22 The Lord gave me my tongue as a reward,
    and I will praise him with it.

23 Draw near to me, you who are uneducated,
    and lodge in the house of instruction.
24 Why do you say you are lacking in these
      things,^{r}
    and why do you endure such great thirst?
25 I opened my mouth and said,
    Acquire wisdom^s for yourselves without
      money.

26 Put your neck under her^t yoke,
    and let your souls receive instruction;
    it is to be found close by.

27 See with your own eyes that I have labored but
      little
    and found for myself much serenity.
28 Hear but a little of my instruction,
    and through me you will acquire silver and
      gold.^{u}

29 May your soul rejoice in God's^v mercy,
    and may you never be ashamed to praise
      him.
30 Do your work in good time,
    and in his own time God^w will give you
      your reward.

---

p Gk *her* q Meaning of Gk uncertain r Cn Compare Heb
Syr: Meaning of Gk uncertain s Heb: Gk lacks *wisdom*
t Heb: other ancient authorities read *the* u Syr Compare
Heb: Gk *Get instruction with a large sum of silver, and you will
gain by it much gold.* v Gk *his* w Gk *he*

Introduction to the

Prophets

Have you ever heard a speaker who seemed to be talking right to you? someone who could see past external appearances and into the hearts of people and events? someone committed to total honesty even if it hurt? someone who inspired you to make some needed changes and gave you hope for the future? If so, you've encountered a modern-day prophet—a person who names what God wants to say to us. In this section of books, you will meet the prophets of the Bible —unique and courageous people who did these things for ancient Israel.

In-depth

WHAT IS A PROPHET? FIRST AND FOREMOST, A prophet is a person—or sometimes a group—who speaks for God. The prophet's words spoken in God's name— usually called prophecies or oracles—are God's words. Some people think that prophets can predict the future, but this is not their role in the Bible. The biblical prophets were called by God during times of crisis to offer God's people challenge or comfort, depending on their circumstances. So, to properly understand biblical prophecies, we must try to understand the historical situation God was addressing through the prophets.

Through the prophets' inspired messages, God reminded the Israelites of the Covenant God had made with them (see "Introduction to the Pentateuch"). If the people or their leaders were not keeping their side of the Covenant, the prophets challenged them to do so. If the people were in despair that God was not keeping God's side of the Covenant, the prophets promised that God would. Here are some common Covenant themes the prophets emphasized:

- *Warnings against idolatry.* The Israelites were constantly tempted to worship the gods of other nations and cultures. The prophets had to keep reminding the kings and people of the first law of the Ten Commandments: "I, the LORD, am your God, who brought you out of the land of Egypt, that place of slavery. You shall not have other gods besides me" (Ex 20.2–3).

- *Warnings to act justly and to treat the poor fairly.* In their greed and struggle for power, the wealthy and the ruling class often cheated and oppressed other people. Operating as Israel's conscience, the prophets were unanimous in challenging Israel to act justly and to care for the poor and marginalized. This did not always make the prophets popular with the kings and the ruling class—they were often ridiculed and even threatened with violence.

- *Attempts to deepen the understanding of God's love and mercy.* Some Israelites felt God would not forgive them after Israel (the northern kingdom) and Judah (the southern kingdom) were conquered by foreign nations. The prophets assured them that they would receive God's forgiveness if they turned to God and kept the Covenant. In addition, some of the prophets began to teach that God was Lord over—and cared for—all nations, not just Israel.

- *Promises of hope for the future.* During these troubled and often violent times, it must have seemed to many Israelites that their world was coming to an end. The prophets responded to the people's despair with hope-filled promises that ultimately God's love and justice would prevail. These hopeful prophecies took different forms: the coming of the Ideal Ruler, the restoration of Jerusalem and the Temple, a time of judgment when good is rewarded and evil punished, and so on.

The stories of the earliest prophets—Samuel, Nathan, Elijah, and Elisha—are in the Bible's historical Books of 1 and 2 Samuel and 1 and 2 Kings. God's revelation through the later prophets is recorded in the books of this section of the Bible. The introduction to each book in this section gives background about the historical situation the prophet faced. The timeline in the back of this Bible identifies the time period for each prophet.

As you read these books, keep this in mind: the role of prophets has not died, only changed. In every age, there are people who challenge us to be faithful to God, and remind us about God's faithful love for us. In fact, Christians believe that through their Baptism, God calls them to be priest, prophet, and king. You can fulfill your prophetic calling by challenging others to live justly and reminding them of God's love. It's exciting and humbling to be called into such a proud tradition.

Other Background

- Isaiah, Jeremiah, and Ezekiel are sometimes called the major prophets because their books are long.

- Hosea, Amos, Jeremiah, First Isaiah, Obadiah, Micah, Nahum, Habakkuk, and Zephaniah prophesied before the Babylonian Exile.

- Ezekiel, Second Isaiah, and Lamentations wrote during the Exile.

- Joel, Haggai, Zechariah, Malachi, Third Isaiah, and Baruch wrote after the Exile.

- Jonah isn't a real prophet, but a fictional, reluctant prophet.

- Seven of the prophets talk about "the day of the Lord"—a final time of God's judgment when evil will be punished.

Once in a while, film studios release a new movie that is actually a remake of an older film. The new movie has a new director and new actors and actresses. It keeps the same basic plot as the original but is adapted to appeal to a modern audience. This is what happened with the prophet Isaiah. The original Isaiah was such a hit that years after he died, a second and even a third person or group adapted his ideas to their situation. The stories of the original Isaiah and his two "remakes" were collected into the single Book of Isaiah that we have today.

At a Glance

- **Chapters 1–39.** First Isaiah (before the Babylonian Exile)

- **Chapters 40–55.** Second Isaiah (during the Exile)

- **Chapters 56–66.** Third Isaiah (after the Exile)

In-depth

Prophets from three different periods in Israel's history contributed to the Book of Isaiah. Chapters 1–39 reflect the prophecies of the original Isaiah, called First Isaiah. His career began with his call in the Temple during the reign of Uzziah around 742 B.C. (see the timeline at the back of this Bible). First Isaiah advised the kings of Judah about the dangers of alliances with foreign nations and cautioned them to trust only in God. He cried out against the social injustices of the rich ruling class against the poor, and taught that God had a plan in which all, rich and poor, powerful and oppressed, would have a part. First Isaiah is responsible for the messianic prophecies, which tell of the coming of a perfect king.

Years later, when Israel was exiled in Babylon (587–538 B.C.), another prophet, Second Isaiah, reworked First Isaiah's prophecies to address his own people (chapters 40–55). Second Isaiah's people were struggling to understand why God allowed them to be captives in a strange land. The prophet comforted them with a hopeful message: They had been taken captive so that they would turn away from their sinful practices; now that they had learned their lesson, God would return them to rebuild Israel. Contained in this prophet's writings are the famous servant songs (see "The Servant Songs," 42.1–7).

After the Israelites returned from exile and resettled in Judah (537–500 B.C.), they once again fell into patterns of social injustice and religious apathy. Third Isaiah responded by demanding that they practice justice toward one another, and even toward the Gentiles, non-Jews (chapters 56–66). Realizing that Israel would never be a perfect community, he spoke of "new heavens / and a new earth" (65.17), where people would live according to God's plan.

Quick Facts

Period Covered
742–500 B.C.

Authors
the three Isaiahs or their followers

Themes
faithfulness to God, justice for the poor, hope for the future, messianic prophecies, God as lord over all nations

Isaiah

6.7

1 The vision of Ī·saī'ah son of Ā'moz, which he saw concerning Judah and Jerusalem in the days of Uz·zī'ah, Jō'tham, Ā'haz, and Hez·e·kī'ah, kings of Judah.

The Wickedness of Judah

2 Hear, O heavens, and listen, O earth;
    for the LORD has spoken:
I reared children and brought them up,
    but they have rebelled against me.
3 The ox knows its owner,
    and the donkey its master's crib;
but Israel does not know,
    my people do not understand.

4 Ah, sinful nation,
    people laden with iniquity,
offspring who do evil,
    children who deal corruptly,
who have forsaken the LORD,
    who have despised the Holy One of Israel,
    who are utterly estranged!

5 Why do you seek further beatings?
    Why do you continue to rebel?
The whole head is sick,
    and the whole heart faint.
6 From the sole of the foot even to the head,
    there is no soundness in it,
but bruises and sores
    and bleeding wounds;
they have not been drained, or bound up,
    or softened with oil.

7 Your country lies desolate,
    your cities are burned with fire;
in your very presence
    aliens devour your land;
    it is desolate, as overthrown by foreigners.
8 And daughter Zion is left
    like a booth in a vineyard,
like a shelter in a cucumber field,
    like a besieged city.
9 If the LORD of hosts
    had not left us a few survivors,
we would have been like Sod'om,
    and become like Go·mor'rah.

10 Hear the word of the LORD,
    you rulers of Sod'om!
Listen to the teaching of our God,
    you people of Go·mor'rah!
11 What to me is the multitude of your
        sacrifices?
    says the LORD;
I have had enough of burnt offerings of
        rams
    and the fat of fed beasts;
I do not delight in the blood of bulls,
    or of lambs, or of goats.

GOD WANTS JUSTICE, NOT EMPTY RITES!

First Isaiah denounces the hypocrisy of practicing empty religious rituals that are not grounded in justice, sincerity, and good deeds. Speaking for God, he calls the people to do good, seek justice, rescue the oppressed, and defend the orphans and the widows.

- How do you actively seek justice and take care of people in need?
- In your prayer, ask God's forgiveness for when you have not responded to God's call to practice justice or help people in need.

▶ Isa 1.10–20

12 When you come to appear before me,*
   who asked this from your hand?
   Trample my courts no more;
13 bringing offerings is futile;
   incense is an abomination to me.
   New moon and sabbath and calling of
      convocation—
   I cannot endure solemn assemblies with
      iniquity.
14 Your new moons and your appointed festivals
   my soul hates;
   they have become a burden to me,
   I am weary of bearing them.
15 When you stretch out your hands,
   I will hide my eyes from you;
   even though you make many prayers,
   I will not listen;
   your hands are full of blood.
16 Wash yourselves; make yourselves clean;
   remove the evil of your doings
   from before my eyes;
   cease to do evil,
17   learn to do good;
   seek justice,
   rescue the oppressed,
   defend the orphan,
      plead for the widow.

18 Come now, let us argue it out,
   says the LORD:
   though your sins are like scarlet,
      they shall be like snow;
   though they are red like crimson,
      they shall become like wool.
19 If you are willing and obedient,
   you shall eat the good of the land;

20 but if you refuse and rebel,
   you shall be devoured by the sword;
   for the mouth of the LORD has spoken.

The Degenerate City

21 How the faithful city
      has become a whore!
   She that was full of justice,
   righteousness lodged in her—
      but now murderers!
22 Your silver has become dross,
   your wine is mixed with water.
23 Your princes are rebels
      and companions of thieves.
   Everyone loves a bribe
      and runs after gifts.
   They do not defend the orphan,
      and the widow's cause does not come
         before them.

24 Therefore says the Sovereign, the LORD of
         hosts, the Mighty One of Israel:
   Ah, I will pour out my wrath on my enemies,
      and avenge myself on my foes!
25 I will turn my hand against you;
   I will smelt away your dross as with lye
      and remove all your alloy.
26 And I will restore your judges as at the
         first,
   and your counselors as at the beginning.
   Afterward you shall be called the city of
         righteousness,
      the faithful city.

---

a Or see my face

I
S
A

27 Zion shall be redeemed by justice,
    and those in her who repent, by
        righteousness.
28 But rebels and sinners shall be destroyed
        together,
    and those who forsake the LORD shall be
        consumed.
29 For you shall be ashamed of the oaks
    in which you delighted;
and you shall blush for the gardens
    that you have chosen.
30 For you shall be like an oak
    whose leaf withers,
    and like a garden without water.
31 The strong shall become like tinder,
    and their work[b] like a spark;

PRAY IT!
From Violence to Love

We hear Isa 2.1–5 read every three
years in church on the first Sunday
of Advent. Its "swords into plowshares"
theme is all about moving from violence
to nonviolence and ultimately to love in
our responses to conflict (see also Joel
4.10 and Mic 4.3).
    But what exactly is a plowshare? A
plowshare is a tool that helps a farmer
harvest the fields. The message is that
instead of tools of violence (swords), a
world of peace needs only tools to feed
and nourish its people (plowshares).
God's reign is present when swords are
turned into plowshares.
    Take a few minutes to pray, reflect, or
journal on the following questions:
- Why does our society glorify violence?
- As a member of society, do you
    support violence or nonviolence?
    How?
- What nonviolent actions can you take
    when you find yourself in conflict situ-
    ations? (For example, walking away
    from the situation, remaining calm, and
    counting to ten before responding.)
- How can we be people of love in a
    world that is all too often hateful?

▶ Isa 2.1–5

they and their work shall burn together,
    with no one to quench them.

The Future House of God
(Mic 4.1–5)

2 The word that Ĭ·sāi'ah son of Ā'moz saw concerning Judah and Jerusalem.

2 In days to come
    the mountain of the LORD's house
shall be established as the highest of the
        mountains,
    and shall be raised above the hills;
all the nations shall stream to it.
3   Many peoples shall come and say,
"Come, let us go up to the mountain of the
        LORD,
    to the house of the God of Jacob;
that he may teach us his ways
    and that we may walk in his paths."
For out of Zion shall go forth instruction,
    and the word of the LORD from Jerusalem.
4 He shall judge between the nations,
    and shall arbitrate for many peoples;
they shall beat their swords into plowshares,
    and their spears into pruning hooks;
nation shall not lift up sword against nation,
    neither shall they learn war any more.

Judgment Pronounced on Arrogance

5 O house of Jacob,
    come, let us walk
    in the light of the LORD!
6 For you have forsaken the ways of[c] your people,
    O house of Jacob.
Indeed they are full of diviners[d] from the east
    and of soothsayers like the Phi·lis'tines,
    and they clasp hands with foreigners.
7 Their land is filled with silver and gold,
    and there is no end to their treasures;
their land is filled with horses,
    and there is no end to their chariots.
8 Their land is filled with idols;
    they bow down to the work of their hands,
    to what their own fingers have made.
9 And so people are humbled,
    and everyone is brought low—
    do not forgive them!
10 Enter into the rock,
    and hide in the dust
from the terror of the LORD,
    and from the glory of his majesty.
11 The haughty eyes of people shall be brought
        low,

---

b Or its makers   c Heb lacks the ways of   d Cn: Heb lacks of
diviners

and the pride of everyone shall be
    humbled;
and the LORD alone will be exalted on that day.

12 For the LORD of hosts has a day
    against all that is proud and lofty,
    against all that is lifted up and high;*e*

13 against all the cedars of Lebanon,
    lofty and lifted up;
    and against all the oaks of Bā′shan;

14 against all the high mountains,
    and against all the lofty hills;

15 against every high tower,
    and against every fortified wall;

16 against all the ships of Tar′shish,
    and against all the beautiful craft.*f*

17 The haughtiness of people shall be humbled,
    and the pride of everyone shall be brought
      low;
    and the LORD alone will be exalted on that
      day.

18 The idols shall utterly pass away.

19 Enter the caves of the rocks
    and the holes of the ground,
from the terror of the LORD,
    and from the glory of his majesty,
    when he rises to terrify the earth.

20 On that day people will throw away
    to the moles and to the bats
their idols of silver and their idols of gold,
    which they made for themselves to
      worship,

21 to enter the caverns of the rocks
    and the clefts in the crags,
from the terror of the LORD,
    and from the glory of his majesty,
    when he rises to terrify the earth.

22 Turn away from mortals,
    who have only breath in their nostrils,
    for of what account are they?

3 For now the Sovereign, the LORD of hosts,
    is taking away from Jerusalem and from
      Judah
support and staff—
    all support of bread,
    and all support of water—

2 warrior and soldier,
    judge and prophet,
    diviner and elder,

3 captain of fifty
    and dignitary,
counselor and skillful magician
    and expert enchanter.

4 And I will make boys their princes,
    and babes shall rule over them.

5 The people will be oppressed,
    everyone by another
    and everyone by a neighbor;

the youth will be insolent to the elder,
    and the base to the honorable.

6 Someone will even seize a relative,
    a member of the clan, saying,
"You have a cloak;
    you shall be our leader,
and this heap of ruins
    shall be under your rule."

7 But the other will cry out on that day, saying,
"I will not be a healer;
    in my house there is neither bread nor
      cloak;
you shall not make me
    leader of the people."

8 For Jerusalem has stumbled
    and Judah has fallen,
because their speech and their deeds are
      against the LORD,
    defying his glorious presence.

9 The look on their faces bears witness against
      them;
    they proclaim their sin like Sod′om,
    they do not hide it.
Woe to them!
    For they have brought evil on themselves.

10 Tell the innocent how fortunate they are,
    for they shall eat the fruit of their labors.

11 Woe to the guilty! How unfortunate they are,
    for what their hands have done shall be
      done to them.

12 My people—children are their oppressors,
    and women rule over them.
O my people, your leaders mislead you,
    and confuse the course of your paths.

13 The LORD rises to argue his case;
    he stands to judge the peoples.

14 The LORD enters into judgment
    with the elders and princes of his people:
It is you who have devoured the vineyard;
    the spoil of the poor is in your houses.

15 What do you mean by crushing my people,
    by grinding the face of the poor? says the
      Lord GOD of hosts.

16 The LORD said:
Because the daughters of Zion are haughty
    and walk with outstretched necks,
    glancing wantonly with their eyes,
mincing along as they go,
    tinkling with their feet;

17 the Lord will afflict with scabs

---

e Cn Compare Gk: Heb *low* *f* Compare Gk: Meaning of
Heb uncertain

the heads of the daughters of Zion,
and the LORD will lay bare their secret parts.

18 In that day the Lord will take away the finery
of the anklets, the headbands, and the crescents;
19 the pendants, the bracelets, and the scarfs; 20 the
headdresses, the armlets, the sashes, the perfume
boxes, and the amulets; 21 the signet rings and nose
rings; 22 the festal robes, the mantles, the cloaks,
and the handbags; 23 the garments of gauze, the
linen garments, the turbans, and the veils.

24 Instead of perfume there will be a stench;
and instead of a sash, a rope;
and instead of well-set hair, baldness;
and instead of a rich robe, a binding of
sackcloth;
instead of beauty, shame.g

25 Your men shall fall by the sword
and your warriors in battle.

26 And her gates shall lament and mourn;
ravaged, she shall sit upon the ground.
Seven women shall take hold of one man in
that day, saying,
"We will eat our own bread and wear our own
clothes;
just let us be called by your name;
take away our disgrace."

The Future Glory of the Survivors in Zion

2 On that day the branch of the LORD shall be
beautiful and glorious, and the fruit of the land
shall be the pride and glory of the survivors of Israel. 3 Whoever is left in Zion and remains in
Jerusalem will be called holy, everyone who has
been recorded for life in Jerusalem, 4 once the Lord
has washed away the filth of the daughters of Zion
and cleansed the bloodstains of Jerusalem from its
midst by a spirit of judgment and by a spirit of
burning. 5 Then the LORD will create over the whole
site of Mount Zion and over its places of assembly
a cloud by day and smoke and the shining of a
flaming fire by night. Indeed over all the glory there
will be a canopy. 6 It will serve as a pavilion, a
shade by day from the heat, and a refuge and a shelter from the storm and rain.

The Song of the Unfruitful Vineyard

5 Let me sing for my beloved
my love-song concerning his vineyard:
My beloved had a vineyard
on a very fertile hill.

2 He dug it and cleared it of stones,
and planted it with choice vines;
he built a watchtower in the midst of it,
and hewed out a wine vat in it;
he expected it to yield grapes,
but it yielded wild grapes.

3 And now, inhabitants of Jerusalem
and people of Judah,
judge between me
and my vineyard.

4 What more was there to do for my vineyard
that I have not done in it?
When I expected it to yield grapes,
why did it yield wild grapes?

5 And now I will tell you
what I will do to my vineyard.
I will remove its hedge,
and it shall be devoured;
I will break down its wall,
and it shall be trampled down.

6 I will make it a waste;
it shall not be pruned or hoed,
and it shall be overgrown with briers and
thorns;
I will also command the clouds
that they rain no rain upon it.

7 For the vineyard of the LORD of hosts
is the house of Israel,
and the people of Judah
are his pleasant planting;
he expected justice,
but saw bloodshed;
righteousness,
but heard a cry!

Social Injustice Denounced

8 Ah, you who join house to house,
who add field to field,
until there is room for no one but you,
and you are left to live alone
in the midst of the land!

9 The LORD of hosts has sworn in my hearing:
Surely many houses shall be desolate,
large and beautiful houses, without
inhabitant.

10 For ten acres of vineyard shall yield but one
bath,
and a homer of seed shall yield a mere
ephah.h

11 Ah, you who rise early in the morning
in pursuit of strong drink,
who linger in the evening
to be inflamed by wine,

12 whose feasts consist of lyre and harp,
tambourine and flute and wine,
but who do not regard the deeds of the LORD,
or see the work of his hands!

---

g Q Ms: MT lacks shame   h The Heb bath, homer, and ephah
are measures of quantity

13 Therefore my people go into exile without
knowledge;
their nobles are dying of hunger,
and their multitude is parched with thirst.

14 Therefore Shē'ōl has enlarged its appetite
and opened its mouth beyond measure;
the nobility of Jerusalem[i] and her multitude go
down,
her throng and all who exult in her.

15 People are bowed down, everyone is brought
low,
and the eyes of the haughty are humbled.

16 But the LORD of hosts is exalted by justice,
and the Holy God shows himself holy by
righteousness.

17 Then the lambs shall graze as in their pasture,
fatlings and kids[j] shall feed among the ruins.

18 Ah, you who drag iniquity along with cords of
falsehood,
who drag sin along as with cart ropes,

19 who say, "Let him make haste,
let him speed his work
that we may see it;
let the plan of the Holy One of Israel hasten to
fulfillment,
that we may know it!"

20 Ah, you who call evil good
and good evil,
who put darkness for light
and light for darkness,
who put bitter for sweet
and sweet for bitter!

21 Ah, you who are wise in your own eyes,
and shrewd in your own sight!

22 Ah, you who are heroes in drinking wine
and valiant at mixing drink,

23 who acquit the guilty for a bribe,
and deprive the innocent of their rights!

Foreign Invasion Predicted

24 Therefore, as the tongue of fire devours the
stubble,
and as dry grass sinks down in the flame,
so their root will become rotten,
and their blossom go up like dust;
for they have rejected the instruction of the
LORD of hosts,
and have despised the word of the Holy
One of Israel.

25 Therefore the anger of the LORD was kindled
against his people,
and he stretched out his hand against them
and struck them;
the mountains quaked,
and their corpses were like refuse
in the streets.
For all this his anger has not turned away,
and his hand is stretched out still.

26 He will raise a signal for a nation far away,
and whistle for a people at the ends of the
earth;
Here they come, swiftly, speedily!

27 None of them is weary, none stumbles,
none slumbers or sleeps,

---

i Heb *her nobility*   j Cn Compare Gk: Heb *aliens*

Introducing ▶ FIRST ISAIAH

The name Isaiah means "God is salvation" in Hebrew, and First Isaiah's preaching certainly reflects that message. Born in Jerusalem, he prophesied there during the reigns of Kings Uzziah, Jotham, Ahaz, and Hezekiah, between 742 and 701 B.C. (see 2 Kings, chapters 15–20, and 2 Chronicles, chapters 26–32). He was married to a prophetess, and they had two sons whose names played a symbolic role in his prophecy: Shear-jashub, meaning "a remnant shall remain," and Maher-shalal-hash-baz, meaning "the spoil speeds,
the prey hastes." In his preaching, he emphasized the role of Jerusalem (Zion) as God's dwelling place and home to King David's dynasty. For this reason, he is also called Isaiah of Jerusalem.

First Isaiah had ready access to Judah's kings and was probably a member of an aristocratic family. His education shows in his use of language—he is responsible for some of the loftiest and most beautiful poetry in the Old Testament.

Here I Am, Lord!

Phrases from the sixth chapter of Isaiah may be familiar from the song "Here I Am, Lord." This chapter tells of First Isaiah's call, which follows a biblical pattern:

1. *The person has some experience of God.* Isaiah has a dramatic vision of God in the Temple.
2. *God gives the person a mission.* God sends Isaiah to speak to the people.
3. *The person may deny being worthy.* Isaiah knows he has unclean (or sinful) lips.
4. *God addresses the denial and reassures the person.* God purifies Isaiah with fire and words of forgiveness.

You can see the same pattern for Moses' call in Ex 3.1–12, Samuel's call in 1 Sam 3.1–14, Jeremiah's call in Jer 1.4–10, and Mary's call in Lk 1.26–38.

Christians are called by God to participate in Jesus' saving mission. They believe everyone needs to discover the way God wants them to live out that call. Do you believe that God has a mission for your life? How can you use your talents to create a more loving and just world?

▶ Isa 6.1–13

---

not a loincloth is loose,
  not a sandal-thong broken;
28 their arrows are sharp,
  all their bows bent,
their horses' hoofs seem like flint,
  and their wheels like the whirlwind.
29 Their roaring is like a lion,
  like young lions they roar;
they growl and seize their prey,
  they carry it off, and no one can
    rescue.
30 They will roar over it on that day,
  like the roaring of the sea.
And if one look to the land—
  only darkness and distress;
and the light grows dark with clouds.

A Vision of God in the Temple
(Cp Ezek 1.4–28)

6 In the year that King Uz·zi′ah died, I saw the Lord sitting on a throne, high and lofty; and the hem of his robe filled the temple. 2 Seraphs were in attendance above him; each had six wings: with two they covered their faces, and with two they covered their feet, and with two they flew. 3 And one called to another and said:

"Holy, holy, holy is the LORD of hosts;
  the whole earth is full of his glory."

4 The pivots[k] on the thresholds shook at the voices of those who called, and the house filled with smoke. 5 And I said: "Woe is me! I am lost, for I am a man of unclean lips, and I live among a people of unclean lips; yet my eyes have seen the King, the LORD of hosts!"

6 Then one of the seraphs flew to me, holding a live coal that had been taken from the altar with a pair of tongs. 7 The seraph[l] touched my mouth with it and said: "Now that this has touched your lips, your guilt has departed and your sin is blotted out." 8 Then I heard the voice of the Lord saying, "Whom shall I send, and who will go for us?" And I said, "Here am I; send me!" 9 And he said, "Go and say to this people:

'Keep listening, but do not comprehend;
  keep looking, but do not understand.'
10 Make the mind of this people dull,
  and stop their ears,
  and shut their eyes,
so that they may not look with their eyes,
  and listen with their ears,
and comprehend with their minds,
  and turn and be healed."

11 Then I said, "How long, O Lord?" And he said:

"Until cities lie waste
  without inhabitant,
and houses without people,
  and the land is utterly desolate;
12 until the LORD sends everyone far away,
  and vast is the emptiness in the midst of
    the land.
13 Even if a tenth part remain in it,
  it will be burned again,
like a terebinth or an oak
  whose stump remains standing
  when it is felled."[k]
The holy seed is its stump.

---

k Meaning of Heb uncertain   l Heb *He*

I
S
A

Isaiah Reassures King Ahaz
(2 Kings 16.5; 2 Chr 28.5–15)

7 In the days of Ă'haz son of Jŏ'tham son of Uz-zī'ah, king of Judah, King Rĕ'zin of Ar'am and King Pĕ'kah son of Rem•a•li'ah of Israel went up to attack Jerusalem, but could not mount an attack against it. 2 When the house of David heard that Ar'am had allied itself with Ĕ'phra•im, the heart of Ă'haz[m] and the heart of his people shook as the trees of the forest shake before the wind.

3 Then the LORD said to I•sāi'ah, Go out to meet Ă'haz, you and your son Shĕ'ar-jash'ub,[n] at the end of the conduit of the upper pool on the highway to the Fuller's Field, 4 and say to him, Take heed, be quiet, do not fear, and do not let your heart be faint because of these two smoldering stumps of firebrands, because of the fierce anger of Rĕ'zin and Ar'am and the son of Rem•a•li'ah. 5 Because Ar'am—with Ĕ'phra•im and the son of Rem•a•li'ah—has plotted evil against you, saying, 6 Let us go up against Judah and cut off Jerusalem[o]

and conquer it for ourselves and make the son of Tă'bĕ•el king in it; 7 therefore thus says the Lord GOD:

> It shall not stand,
> and it shall not come to pass.
> 8 For the head of Ar'am is Damascus,
> and the head of Damascus is Rĕ'zin.

(Within sixty-five years Ĕ'phra•im will be shattered, no longer a people.)

> 9 The head of Ĕ'phra•im is Sa•mār'i•a,
> and the head of Sa•mār'i•a is the son of Rem•a•li'ah.
> If you do not stand firm in faith,
> you shall not stand at all.

Isaiah Gives Ahaz the Sign of Immanuel

10 Again the LORD spoke to Ă'haz, saying, 11 Ask a sign of the LORD your God; let it be deep as

---

m Heb *his heart*   *n* That is *A remnant shall return*   *o* Heb *cut it off*

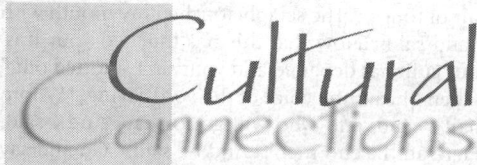

GOD-WITH-US!

Many Bibles refer to Isaiah, chapters 7–12, as the Book of Immanuel. In these chapters, First Isaiah announces that Israel's salvation will come from a child from the family of Jesse, the father of King David. This child will be named Immanuel (also spelled Emmanuel), which means "God-with-Us." With this message, Isaiah emphasizes that God is with the little ones who trust in God's saving power.

Biblical scholars agree that the child Isaiah is referring to is the son of King Ahaz—the future king Hezekiah. But the Gospel writers later see in this passage a reference to Jesus (Mt 1.23), the Son of God, who is truly Immanuel, God-with-Us.

For Latin American people, Immanuel is a constant reality. Latin Americans give witness of the nearness of God in daily affairs through the following expressions, which you may hear more than a dozen times a day in their communities: "God help you" (*Dios te ayude*), "Go with God" (*Ve con Dios*), "If God wants it" (*Si Dios quiere*), "With God's permission" (*Si Dios lo permite*), "Through the power of God" (*Dios mediante*), "Thanks to God" (*Gracias a Dios*), "For the love of God" (*Por el amor de Dios*), "God give you a good day" (*Buen día te dé Dios*), and "God bless you" (*Dios te bendiga*).

- ■ **If you come from a family or community tradition where these faith expressions are common, feel the presence of God each time they are voiced, and use them boldly yourself.**
- ■ **Think about what happened to you today. How many of these expressions could you have applied to different situations and felt God-with-You? Choose the expression that best fits the yearnings of your heart at this time, and pray with it, repeating it several times.**

▶ **Isaiah, chapters 7–12**

She'ŏl or high as heaven. 12 But Ā'haz said, I will not ask, and I will not put the LORD to the test. 13 Then I•sāi'ah[p] said: "Hear then, O house of David! Is it too little for you to weary mortals, that you weary my God also? 14 Therefore the Lord himself will give you a sign. Look, the young woman[q] is with child and shall bear a son, and shall name him Im•man'ū•el.[r] 15 He shall eat curds and honey by the time he knows how to refuse the evil and choose the good. 16 For before the child knows how to refuse the evil and choose the good, the land before whose two kings you are in dread will be deserted. 17 The LORD will bring on you and on your people and on your ancestral house such days as have not come since the day that Ē'phra•im departed from Judah—the king of Assyria."

18 On that day the LORD will whistle for the fly that is at the sources of the streams of Egypt, and for the bee that is in the land of Assyria. 19 And they will all come and settle in the steep ravines, and in the clefts of the rocks, and on all the thornbushes, and on all the pastures.

20 On that day the Lord will shave with a razor hired beyond the River—with the king of Assyria—the head and the hair of the feet, and it will take off the beard as well.

21 On that day one will keep alive a young cow and two sheep, 22 and will eat curds because of the abundance of milk that they give; for everyone that is left in the land shall eat curds and honey.

23 On that day every place where there used to be a thousand vines, worth a thousand shekels of silver, will become briers and thorns. 24 With bow and arrows one will go there, for all the land will be briers and thorns; 25 and as for all the hills that used to be hoed with a hoe, you will not go there for fear of briers and thorns; but they will become a place where cattle are let loose and where sheep tread.

Isaiah's Son a Sign of the Assyrian Invasion

8 Then the LORD said to me, Take a large tablet and write on it in common characters, "Belonging to Mā'her-shal'al-hash-baz,"[s] 2 and have it attested[t] for me by reliable witnesses, the priest Ū•rī'ah and Zech•a•rī'ah son of Je•ber•e•chī'ah. 3 And I went to the prophetess, and she conceived and bore a son. Then the LORD said to me, Name him Mā'her-shal'al-hash-baz; 4 for before the child knows how to call "My father" or "My mother," the wealth of Damascus and the spoil of Sa•mār'i•a will be carried away by the king of Assyria.

5 The LORD spoke to me again: 6 Because this people has refused the waters of Shī•lō'ah that flow gently, and melt in fear before[u] Rē'zin and the son of Rem•a•lī'ah; 7 therefore, the Lord is bringing up against it the mighty flood waters of the River, the king of Assyria and all his glory; it will rise above all

its channels and overflow all its banks; 8 it will sweep on into Judah as a flood, and, pouring over, it will reach up to the neck; and its outspread wings will fill the breadth of your land, O Im•man'ū•el.

9 Band together, you peoples, and be dismayed;
　　listen, all you far countries;
　gird yourselves and be dismayed;
　　gird yourselves and be dismayed!
10 Take counsel together, but it shall be brought
　　to naught;
　speak a word, but it will not stand,
　　for God is with us.[v]

11 For the LORD spoke thus to me while his hand was strong upon me, and warned me not to walk in the way of this people, saying: 12 Do not call conspiracy all that this people calls conspiracy, and do not fear what it fears, or be in dread. 13 But the LORD of hosts, him you shall regard as holy; let him be your fear, and let him be your dread. 14 He will become a sanctuary, a stone one strikes against; for both houses of Israel he will become a rock one stumbles over—a trap and a snare for the inhabitants of Jerusalem. 15 And many among them shall stumble; they shall fall and be broken; they shall be snared and taken.

Disciples of Isaiah

16 Bind up the testimony, seal the teaching among my disciples. 17 I will wait for the LORD, who is hiding his face from the house of Jacob, and I will hope in him. 18 See, I and the children whom the LORD has given me are signs and portents in Israel from the LORD of hosts, who dwells on Mount Zion. 19 Now if people say to you, "Consult the ghosts and the familiar spirits that chirp and mutter; should not a people consult their gods, the dead on behalf of the living, 20 for teaching and for instruction?" surely, those who speak like this will have no dawn! 21 They will pass through the land,[w] greatly distressed and hungry; when they are hungry, they will be enraged and will curse[x] their king and their gods. They will turn their faces upward, 22 or they will look to the earth, but will see only distress and darkness, the gloom of anguish; and they will be thrust into thick darkness.[y]

The Righteous Reign of the Coming King
(Isa 11.1–9)

9 [z]But there will be no gloom for those who were in anguish. In the former time he brought into contempt the land of Zeb'ū•lun and

---

p Heb he　q Gk the virgin　r That is God is with us　s That is The spoil speeds, the prey hastens　t Q Ms Gk Syr: MT and I caused to be attested　u Cn: Meaning of Heb uncertain　v Heb immanu el　w Heb it　x Or curse by　y Meaning of Heb uncertain　z Ch 8.23 in Heb

ISA

the land of Naph'ta•lī, but in the latter time he will make glorious the way of the sea, the land beyond the Jordan, Galilee of the nations.

2a The people who walked in darkness
        have seen a great light;
    those who lived in a land of deep darkness—
        on them light has shined.
3 You have multiplied the nation,
        you have increased its joy;
    they rejoice before you
        as with joy at the harvest,
        as people exult when dividing plunder.
4 For the yoke of their burden,
        and the bar across their shoulders,
        the rod of their oppressor,
    you have broken as on the day of Mid'i•an.
5 For all the boots of the tramping warriors
        and all the garments rolled in blood
        shall be burned as fuel for the fire.
6 For a child has been born for us,
        a son given to us;
    authority rests upon his shoulders;
        and he is named
    Wonderful Counselor, Mighty God,
        Everlasting Father, Prince of Peace.
7 His authority shall grow continually,
        and there shall be endless peace
    for the throne of David and his kingdom.
        He will establish and uphold it
    with justice and with righteousness
        from this time onward and forevermore.
    The zeal of the LORD of hosts will do this.

Judgment on Arrogance and Oppression

8 The Lord sent a word against Jacob,
        and it fell on Israel;
9 and all the people knew it—
        Ē'phra•im and the inhabitants of Sa•mār'i•a—
        but in pride and arrogance of heart they
            said:
10 "The bricks have fallen,
        but we will build with dressed stones;
    the sycamores have been cut down,
        but we will put cedars in their place."
11 So the LORD raised adversaries[b] against them,
        and stirred up their enemies,
12 the Ar•a•mē'ans on the east and the Phi•lis'tines
            on the west,
        and they devoured Israel with open mouth.
    For all this his anger has not turned away;
        his hand is stretched out still.

13 The people did not turn to him who struck
            them,
        or seek the LORD of hosts.
14 So the LORD cut off from Israel head and tail,
        palm branch and reed in one day—

PRAY IT!
Christmas Light

Isaiah 9.2–7 describes Immanuel as a wise, brave, courageous, virtuous, and righteous king. Here, First Isaiah may be referring to King Hezekiah, the reformer king of Judah (see 2 Chronicles, chapters 29–33). However, after Hezekiah's death, the passage came to be understood as predicting the coming of an ideal future savior or messiah. That's why the passage is called a messianic prophecy.

Christians see in these words a perfect description of Jesus. In fact, Catholics read these verses at Christmas during midnight Mass. On one of the longest nights of the year, they imagine Jesus' presence in the world as a light dispelling the darkness of sin.

This is the opening prayer for the Christmas Mass at midnight:

Father,
You make this holy night radiant
with the splendor of Jesus Christ our
    light.
We welcome him as Lord, the true light
    of the world.
Bring us to eternal joy in the kingdom of
    heaven,
where he lives and reigns with you and
    the Holy Spirit,
one God, for ever and ever.
                    (Sacramentary, p. 40)

▶ Isa 9.2–7

15 elders and dignitaries are the head,
        and prophets who teach lies are the tail;
16 for those who led this people led them astray,
        and those who were led by them were left
            in confusion.
17 That is why the Lord did not have pity on[c]
            their young people,
        or compassion on their orphans and
            widows;
    for everyone was godless and an evildoer,
        and every mouth spoke folly.
    For all this his anger has not turned away;
        his hand is stretched out still.

---

a Ch 9.1 in Heb   b Cn: Heb *the adversaries of Rezin*
c Q Ms: MT *rejoice over*

18 For wickedness burned like a fire,
     consuming briers and thorns;
   it kindled the thickets of the forest,
     and they swirled upward in a column of
       smoke.
19 Through the wrath of the LORD of hosts
     the land was burned,
   and the people became like fuel for the fire;
     no one spared another.
20 They gorged on the right, but still were hungry,
     and they devoured on the left, but were not
       satisfied;
   they devoured the flesh of their own kindred;*d*
21 Ma•nas′seh devoured Ē′phra•im, and Ē′phra•im
       Ma•nas′seh,
   and together they were against Judah.
   For all this his anger has not turned away;
     his hand is stretched out still.

10 Ah, you who make iniquitous decrees,
       who write oppressive statutes,
2 to turn aside the needy from justice
     and to rob the poor of my people of their
       right,
   that widows may be your spoil,
     and that you may make the orphans your
       prey!
3 What will you do on the day of punishment,
     in the calamity that will come from far
       away?
   To whom will you flee for help,
     and where will you leave your wealth,
4 so as not to crouch among the prisoners
     or fall among the slain?
   For all this his anger has not turned away;
     his hand is stretched out still.

Arrogant Assyria Also Judged

5 Ah, Assyria, the rod of my anger—
     the club in their hands is my fury!
6 Against a godless nation I send him,
     and against the people of my wrath I
       command him,
   to take spoil and seize plunder,
     and to tread them down like the mire of the
       streets.
7 But this is not what he intends,
     nor does he have this in mind;
   but it is in his heart to destroy,
     and to cut off nations not a few.
8 For he says:
   "Are not my commanders all kings?
9 Is not Cal′nō like Car′chem•ish?
     Is not Hā′math like Ar′pad?
     Is not Sa•mār′i•a like Damascus?
10 As my hand has reached to the kingdoms of
       the idols

whose images were greater than those of
     Jerusalem and Sa•mār′i•a,
11 shall I not do to Jerusalem and her idols
     what I have done to Sa•mār′i•a and her
       images?"

12 When the Lord has finished all his work on
Mount Zion and on Jerusalem, he*e* will punish the
arrogant boasting of the king of Assyria and his
haughty pride. 13 For he says:
   "By the strength of my hand I have done it,
     and by my wisdom, for I have
       understanding;
   I have removed the boundaries of peoples,
     and have plundered their treasures;
   like a bull I have brought down those who
       sat on thrones.
14 My hand has found, like a nest,
     the wealth of the peoples;
   and as one gathers eggs that have been
       forsaken,
     so I have gathered all the earth;
   and there was none that moved a wing,
     or opened its mouth, or chirped."

15 Shall the ax vaunt itself over the one who
       wields it,
     or the saw magnify itself against the one
       who handles it?
   As if a rod should raise the one who lifts it up,
     or as if a staff should lift the one who is not
       wood!
16 Therefore the Sovereign, the LORD of hosts,
     will send wasting sickness among his stout
       warriors,
   and under his glory a burning will be kindled,
     like the burning of fire.
17 The light of Israel will become a fire,
     and his Holy One a flame;
   and it will burn and devour
     his thorns and briers in one day.
18 The glory of his forest and his fruitful land
     the LORD will destroy, both soul and body,
   and it will be as when an invalid wastes
       away.
19 The remnant of the trees of his forest will be so
       few
     that a child can write them down.

The Repentant Remnant of Israel

20 On that day the remnant of Israel and the
survivors of the house of Jacob will no more lean
on the one who struck them, but will lean on the
LORD, the Holy One of Israel, in truth. 21 A remnant
will return, the remnant of Jacob, to the mighty

---

d Or *arm*   *e* Heb *I*

God. 22 For though your people Israel were like the sand of the sea, only a remnant of them will return. Destruction is decreed, overflowing with righteousness. 23 For the Lord GOD of hosts will make a full end, as decreed, in all the earth.*f*

24 Therefore thus says the Lord GOD of hosts: O my people, who live in Zion, do not be afraid of the Assyrians when they beat you with a rod and lift up their staff against you as the Egyptians did. 25 For in a very little while my indignation will come to an end, and my anger will be directed to their destruction. 26 The LORD of hosts will wield a whip against them, as when he struck Mid'i•an at the rock of Or'eb; his staff will be over the sea, and he will lift it as he did in Egypt. 27 On that day his burden will be removed from your shoulder, and his yoke will be destroyed from your neck.

He has gone up from Rim'mon,*g*
28   he has come to Ai'ath;
he has passed through Mig'ron,
        at Mich'mash he stores his baggage;
29 they have crossed over the pass,
        at Gē'ba they lodge for the night;
Rā'mah trembles,
        Gib•ē•ah of Saul has fled.
30 Cry aloud, O daughter Gal'lim!
        Listen, O Lā'i•shah!
        Answer her, O An'a•thoth!
31 Mad•mē'nah is in flight,
        the inhabitants of Gē'bim flee for safety.
32 This very day he will halt at Nob,
        he will shake his fist
        at the mount of daughter Zion,
        the hill of Jerusalem.

33 Look, the Sovereign, the LORD of hosts,
        will lop the boughs with terrifying
            power;
    the tallest trees will be cut down,
        and the lofty will be brought low.
34 He will hack down the thickets of the forest
            with an ax,
        and Lebanon with its majestic trees*h* will
            fall.

The Peaceful Kingdom
(Isa 9.1–7)

11 A shoot shall come out from the stump
            of Jesse,
        and a branch shall grow out of his roots.
2   The spirit of the LORD shall rest on him,
        the spirit of wisdom and understanding,
        the spirit of counsel and might,
        the spirit of knowledge and the fear of the
            LORD.
3   His delight shall be in the fear of the LORD.

He shall not judge by what his eyes see,
        or decide by what his ears hear;
4   but with righteousness he shall judge the poor,
        and decide with equity for the meek of the
            earth;
    he shall strike the earth with the rod of his
            mouth,
        and with the breath of his lips he shall kill
            the wicked.
5   Righteousness shall be the belt around his waist,
        and faithfulness the belt around his loins.

6   The wolf shall live with the lamb,
        the leopard shall lie down with the kid,
    the calf and the lion and the fatling together,
        and a little child shall lead them.

7   The cow and the bear shall graze,
        their young shall lie down together;
        and the lion shall eat straw like the ox.
8   The nursing child shall play over the hole of
            the asp,
        and the weaned child shall put its hand on
            the adder's den.
9   They will not hurt or destroy
        on all my holy mountain;
    for the earth will be full of the knowledge of
            the LORD
        as the waters cover the sea.

Return of the Remnant of Israel and Judah

10 On that day the root of Jesse shall stand as a signal to the peoples; the nations shall inquire of him, and his dwelling shall be glorious.

---

f Or *land* *g* Cn: Heb *and his yoke from your neck, and a yoke will be destroyed because of fatness* *h* Cn Compare Gk Vg: Heb *with a majestic one*

Lions and Lambs

There are so many troubled spots in the world. It seems that almost every week, violence and ethnic clashes occur somewhere. How easily we forget that we are all members of the human family.

Yet, we are drawn to the image of the peaceable kingdom in Isa 11.6–9. To imagine natural predators such as wolves and lions living together in harmony with lambs and calves, their natural prey, gives us an insight into the Reign of God. Harmony. Peace. Gentleness. No wonder this scene has been the inspiration for numerous artists.

It is a vision we must all aim for, while we do our best to resist all the things that pull us apart as a human family. We are all in this together. We need to work to make the peaceable Reign of God a reality. It is God's work we do.

It is inspiring that First Isaiah also uses the image of youth to express his vision of peace. What can you as a young person do to help bring about the peaceable kingdom?

▸ Isa 11.6–9

11 On that day the Lord will extend his hand yet a second time to recover the remnant that is left of his people, from Assyria, from Egypt, from Path′ros, from Ethiopia,[i] from E′lam, from Shi′nar, from Ha′math, and from the coastlands of the sea.
12 He will raise a signal for the nations,
 and will assemble the outcasts of Israel,
and gather the dispersed of Judah
 from the four corners of the earth.
13 The jealousy of E′phra·im shall depart,
 the hostility of Judah shall be cut off;
E′phra·im shall not be jealous of Judah,
 and Judah shall not be hostile towards
 E′phra·im.
14 But they shall swoop down on the backs of the
 Phi·lis′tines in the west,
 together they shall plunder the people of
 the east.
They shall put forth their hand against E′dom
 and Mo′ab,
 and the Am′mon·ites shall obey them.
15 And the LORD will utterly destroy
 the tongue of the sea of Egypt;
and will wave his hand over the River
 with his scorching wind;
and will split it into seven channels,
 and make a way to cross on foot;
16 so there shall be a highway from Assyria
 for the remnant that is left of his people,
as there was for Israel
 when they came up from the land of
 Egypt.

Thanksgiving and Praise

12 You will say in that day:
 I will give thanks to you, O LORD,
 for though you were angry with me,

your anger turned away,
 and you comforted me.

2 Surely God is my salvation;
 I will trust, and will not be afraid,
for the LORD GOD[j] is my strength and my
 might;
 he has become my salvation.

3 With joy you will draw water from the wells of salvation. 4 And you will say in that day:
 Give thanks to the LORD,
 call on his name;
 make known his deeds among the nations;
 proclaim that his name is exalted.

5 Sing praises to the LORD, for he has done
 gloriously;
 let this be known[k] in all the earth.
6 Shout aloud and sing for joy, O royal[l] Zion,
 for great in your midst is the Holy One of
 Israel.

Proclamation against Babylon

13 The oracle concerning Babylon that I·sai′ah son of A′moz saw.

2 On a bare hill raise a signal,
 cry aloud to them;
wave the hand for them to enter
 the gates of the nobles.
3 I myself have commanded my consecrated ones,
 have summoned my warriors, my proudly
 exulting ones,
 to execute my anger.

---

i Or Nubia; Heb Cush j Heb for Yah, the LORD k Or this is made known l Or O inhabitant of

In God We Trust

First Isaiah proclaims this message:

> **Surely God is my salvation;**
> **I will trust, and will not be afraid,**
> **for the LORD GOD is my strength and my might.**
> **(Isa 12.2)**

How often does fear keep us from trusting? How often does it keep us from being and doing what God is calling us to be and do? We need to reach out to God and to others in our life and trust that God is with us. Jesus came to tell us that love is more powerful than fear, and his life and death testified to his deep trust in his Father. Many times, he told his disciples, "Do not be afraid."

Let us truly live the words "In God we trust."

▶ Isa 12.1–6

---

4 Listen, a tumult on the mountains
  as of a great multitude!
Listen, an uproar of kingdoms,
  of nations gathering together!
The LORD of hosts is mustering
  an army for battle.
5 They come from a distant land,
  from the end of the heavens,
the LORD and the weapons of his indignation,
  to destroy the whole earth.

6 Wail, for the day of the LORD is near;
  it will come like destruction from the
    Almighty!m
7 Therefore all hands will be feeble,
  and every human heart will melt,
8 and they will be dismayed.
Pangs and agony will seize them;
  they will be in anguish like a woman in
    labor.
They will look aghast at one another;
  their faces will be aflame.
9 See, the day of the LORD comes,
  cruel, with wrath and fierce anger,
to make the earth a desolation,
  and to destroy its sinners from it.
10 For the stars of the heavens and their
    constellations
  will not give their light;
the sun will be dark at its rising,
  and the moon will not shed its light.
11 I will punish the world for its evil,
  and the wicked for their iniquity;
I will put an end to the pride of the
    arrogant,
  and lay low the insolence of tyrants.

12 I will make mortals more rare than fine gold,
  and humans than the gold of Ō'phir.
13 Therefore I will make the heavens tremble,
  and the earth will be shaken out of its
    place,
at the wrath of the LORD of hosts
  in the day of his fierce anger.
14 Like a hunted gazelle,
  or like sheep with no one to gather them,
all will turn to their own people,
  and all will flee to their own lands.
15 Whoever is found will be thrust through,
  and whoever is caught will fall by the
    sword.
16 Their infants will be dashed to pieces
  before their eyes;
  their houses will be plundered,
  and their wives ravished.
17 See, I am stirring up the Mēdes against them,
  who have no regard for silver
  and do not delight in gold.
18 Their bows will slaughter the young men;
  they will have no mercy on the fruit of the
    womb;
  their eyes will not pity children.
19 And Babylon, the glory of kingdoms,
  the splendor and pride of the Chal•dē'ans,
will be like Sod'om and Go•mor'rah
  when God overthrew them.
20 It will never be inhabited
  or lived in for all generations;
Arabs will not pitch their tents there,
  shepherds will not make their flocks lie
    down there.

---

m Traditional rendering of Heb *Shaddai*

21 But wild animals will lie down there,
   and its houses will be full of howling
      creatures;
there ostriches will live,
   and there goat-demons will dance.
22 Hyenas will cry in its towers,
   and jackals in the pleasant palaces;
its time is close at hand,
   and its days will not be prolonged.

Restoration of Judah

14 But the LORD will have compassion on
Jacob and will again choose Israel, and
will set them in their own land; and aliens will join
them and attach themselves to the house of Jacob.
2 And the nations will take them and bring them to
their place, and the house of Israel will possess the
nations[n] as male and female slaves in the LORD's
land; they will take captive those who were their
captors, and rule over those who oppressed them.

Downfall of the King of Babylon

3 When the LORD has given you rest from your
pain and turmoil and the hard service with which
you were made to serve, 4 you will take up this
taunt against the king of Babylon:
How the oppressor has ceased!
   How his insolence[o] has ceased!
5 The LORD has broken the staff of the wicked,
   the scepter of rulers,
6 that struck down the peoples in wrath
   with unceasing blows,
that ruled the nations in anger
   with unrelenting persecution.
7 The whole earth is at rest and quiet;
   they break forth into singing.
8 The cypresses exult over you,
   the cedars of Lebanon, saying,
"Since you were laid low,
   no one comes to cut us down."
9 Shē'ōl beneath is stirred up
   to meet you when you come;
it rouses the shades to greet you,
   all who were leaders of the earth;
it raises from their thrones
   all who were kings of the nations.
10 All of them will speak
   and say to you:
"You too have become as weak as we!
   You have become like us!"
11 Your pomp is brought down to Shē'ōl,
   and the sound of your harps;
maggots are the bed beneath you,
   and worms are your covering.

12 How you are fallen from heaven,
   O Day Star, son of Dawn!

How you are cut down to the ground,
   you who laid the nations low!
13 You said in your heart,
   "I will ascend to heaven;
I will raise my throne
   above the stars of God;
I will sit on the mount of assembly
   on the heights of Zā'phon;[p]
14 I will ascend to the tops of the clouds,
   I will make myself like the Most High."
15 But you are brought down to Shē'ōl,
   to the depths of the Pit.
16 Those who see you will stare at you,
   and ponder over you:
"Is this the man who made the earth tremble,
   who shook kingdoms,
17 who made the world like a desert
   and overthrew its cities,
   who would not let his prisoners go home?"
18 All the kings of the nations lie in glory,
   each in his own tomb;
19 but you are cast out, away from your grave,
   like loathsome carrion,[q]
clothed with the dead, those pierced by the
      sword,
who go down to the stones of the Pit,
   like a corpse trampled underfoot.
20 You will not be joined with them in burial,
   because you have destroyed your land,
   you have killed your people.

May the descendants of evildoers
   nevermore be named!
21 Prepare slaughter for his sons
   because of the guilt of their father.[r]
Let them never rise to possess the earth
   or cover the face of the world with cities.

22 I will rise up against them, says the LORD of
hosts, and will cut off from Babylon name and remnant, offspring and posterity, says the LORD. 23 And
I will make it a possession of the hedgehog, and
pools of water, and I will sweep it with the broom
of destruction, says the LORD of hosts.

An Oracle concerning Assyria

24 The LORD of hosts has sworn:
As I have designed,
   so shall it be;
and as I have planned,
   so shall it come to pass:
25 I will break the Assyrian in my land,

---

n Heb *them*   o Q Ms Compare Gk Syr Vg: Meaning of MT
uncertain   p Or *assembly in the far north*   q Cn Compare
Gk: Heb *like a loathed branch*   r Syr Compare Gk: Heb
fathers

ISA

and on my mountains trample him under
　　foot;
his yoke shall be removed from them,
　　and his burden from their shoulders.
26 This is the plan that is planned
　　concerning the whole earth;
and this is the hand that is stretched out
　　over all the nations.
27 For the LORD of hosts has planned,
　　and who will annul it?
His hand is stretched out,
　　and who will turn it back?

An Oracle concerning Philistia

28 In the year that King Ā′haz died this oracle
came:

29 Do not rejoice, all you Phi·lis′tines,
　　that the rod that struck you is broken,
for from the root of the snake will come forth
　　an adder,
　　and its fruit will be a flying fiery serpent.
30 The firstborn of the poor will graze,
　　and the needy lie down in safety;
but I will make your root die of famine,
　　and your remnant Iˢ will kill.
31 Wail, O gate; cry, O city;
　　melt in fear, O Phi·lis′ti·a, all of you!
For smoke comes out of the north,
　　and there is no straggler in its ranks.

32 What will one answer the messengers of the
　　nation?
"The LORD has founded Zion,
　　and the needy among his people
　　will find refuge in her."

An Oracle concerning Moab

15 An oracle concerning Mō′ab.

Because Ar is laid waste in a night,
　　Mō′ab is undone;
because Kir is laid waste in a night,
　　Mō′ab is undone.
2 Dī′bonᵗ has gone up to the temple,
　　to the high places to weep;
over Nē′bō and over Med′e·ba
　　Mō′ab wails.
On every head is baldness,
　　every beard is shorn;
3 in the streets they bind on sackcloth;
　　on the housetops and in the squares
everyone wails and melts in tears.
4 Hesh′bon and Ĕ·le·ā′leh cry out,
　　their voices are heard as far as Jā′haz;
therefore the loins of Mō′ab quiver;ᵘ
　　his soul trembles.

5 My heart cries out for Mō′ab;
　　his fugitives flee to Zō′ar,
　　to Eg′lath-she·lish′i·yah.
For at the ascent of Lū′hith
　　they go up weeping;
on the road to Hor·ō·nā′im
　　they raise a cry of destruction;
6 the waters of Nim′rim
　　are a desolation;
the grass is withered, the new growth fails,
　　the verdure is no more.
7 Therefore the abundance they have gained
　　and what they have laid up
they carry away
　　over the Wadi of the Willows.
8 For a cry has gone
　　around the land of Mō′ab;
the wailing reaches to Eg·lā′im,
　　the wailing reaches to Bē′er-ē′lim.
9 For the waters of Dī′bonᵛ are full of blood;
　　yet I will bring upon Dī′bonᵛ even more—
a lion for those of Mō′ab who escape,
　　for the remnant of the land.

16 Send lambs
　　to the ruler of the land,
from Sē′la, by way of the desert,
　　to the mount of daughter Zion.
2 Like fluttering birds,
　　like scattered nestlings,
so are the daughters of Mō′ab
　　at the fords of the Ar′non.
3 "Give counsel,
　　grant justice;
make your shade like night
　　at the height of noon;
hide the outcasts,
　　do not betray the fugitive;
4 let the outcasts of Mō′ab
　　settle among you;
be a refuge to them
　　from the destroyer."

When the oppressor is no more,
　　and destruction has ceased,
and marauders have vanished from the land,
5 then a throne shall be established in steadfast
　　love
　　in the tent of David,
　　and on it shall sit in faithfulness
a ruler who seeks justice
　　and is swift to do what is right.

6 We have heard of the pride of Mō′ab
　　—how proud he is!—

ˢ Q Ms Vg: MT *he*　ᵗ Cn: Heb *the house and Dibon*　ᵘ Cn
Compare Gk Syr: Heb *the armed men of Moab cry aloud*
ᵛ Q Ms Vg Compare Syr: MT *Dimon*

did you KNOW?

Oracles

In the ancient world, an oracle was understood as a communication of the gods. By means of oracles, First Isaiah presents God's judgment on Israel's enemies, including Egypt, Babylon, Assyria, Philistia, Moab, and Edom (Isaiah, chapters 13–23). When we read these oracles today, we can understand their angry and vengeful spirit if we recall the terrible suffering that these nations inflicted on Israel. Still, we should also keep in mind the New Testament commandment to avoid revenge in all its forms (Mt 5.38–48). Jesus calls us to be peacemakers in spite of our suffering.

▶ Isaiah, chapters 13–23

of his arrogance, his pride, and his insolence;
   his boasts are false.
7 Therefore let Mō′ab wail,
   let everyone wail for Mō′ab.
Mourn, utterly stricken,
   for the raisin cakes of Kir-har′e·seth.

8 For the fields of Hesh′bon languish,
   and the vines of Sib′mah,
whose clusters once made drunk
   the lords of the nations,
reached to Jā′zer
   and strayed to the desert;
their shoots once spread abroad
   and crossed over the sea.
9 Therefore I weep with the weeping of Jā′zer
   for the vines of Sib′mah;
I drench you with my tears,
   O Hesh′bon and Ē′le·ā′leh;
for the shout over your fruit harvest
   and your grain harvest has ceased.
10 Joy and gladness are taken away
   from the fruitful field;
and in the vineyards no songs are sung,
   no shouts are raised;
no treader treads out wine in the presses;
   the vintage-shout is hushed.[w]
11 Therefore my heart throbs like a harp for
   Mō′ab,
   and my very soul for Kir-hē′res.
12 When Mō′ab presents himself, when he wea-

ries himself upon the high place, when he comes to his sanctuary to pray, he will not prevail.

13 This was the word that the LORD spoke concerning Mō′ab in the past. 14 But now the LORD says, In three years, like the years of a hired worker, the glory of Mō′ab will be brought into contempt, in spite of all its great multitude; and those who survive will be very few and feeble.

An Oracle concerning Damascus

17 An oracle concerning Damascus.

See, Damascus will cease to be a city,
   and will become a heap of ruins.
2 Her towns will be deserted forever;[x]
   they will be places for flocks,
   which will lie down, and no one will make
      them afraid.
3 The fortress will disappear from Ē′phra·im,
   and the kingdom from Damascus;
and the remnant of Ar′am will be
   like the glory of the children of Israel,
                  says the LORD of hosts.

4 On that day
   the glory of Jacob will be brought low,
   and the fat of his flesh will grow lean.
5 And it shall be as when reapers gather standing
      grain
   and their arms harvest the ears,
and as when one gleans the ears of grain
   in the Valley of Reph′a·im.
6 Gleanings will be left in it,
   as when an olive tree is beaten—
two or three berries
   in the top of the highest bough,
four or five
   on the branches of a fruit tree,
                  says the LORD God of Israel.

7 On that day people will regard their Maker, and their eyes will look to the Holy One of Israel; 8 they will not have regard for the altars, the work of their hands, and they will not look to what their own fingers have made, either the sacred poles[y] or the altars of incense.

9 On that day their strong cities will be like the deserted places of the Hī′vītes and the Am′o·rītes,[z] which they deserted because of the children of Israel, and there will be desolation.

10 For you have forgotten the God of your
      salvation,

---
w Gk: Heb I have hushed   x Cn Compare Gk: Heb the cities of Aroer are deserted   y Heb Asherim   z Cn Compare Gk: Heb places of the wood and the highest bough

and have not remembered the Rock of your
    refuge;
therefore, though you plant pleasant plants
    and set out slips of an alien god,
11 though you make them grow on the day that
      you plant them,
    and make them blossom in the morning
      that you sow;
yet the harvest will flee away
    in a day of grief and incurable pain.
12 Ah, the thunder of many peoples,
    they thunder like the thundering of the sea!
Ah, the roar of nations,
    they roar like the roaring of mighty waters!
13 The nations roar like the roaring of many
      waters,
    but he will rebuke them, and they will flee
      far away,
chased like chaff on the mountains before the
      wind
    and whirling dust before the storm.
14 At evening time, lo, terror!
    Before morning, they are no more.
This is the fate of those who despoil us,
    and the lot of those who plunder us.

An Oracle concerning Ethiopia

18 Ah, land of whirring wings
      beyond the rivers of Ethiopia,[a]
2 sending ambassadors by the Nile
    in vessels of papyrus on the waters!
Go, you swift messengers,
    to a nation tall and smooth,
to a people feared near and far,
    a nation mighty and conquering,
    whose land the rivers divide.

3 All you inhabitants of the world,
    you who live on the earth,
when a signal is raised on the mountains,
    look!
When a trumpet is blown, listen!
4 For thus the LORD said to me:
I will quietly look from my dwelling
    like clear heat in sunshine,
    like a cloud of dew in the heat of harvest.
5 For before the harvest, when the blossom is
      over
    and the flower becomes a ripening grape,
he will cut off the shoots with pruning
      hooks,
    and the spreading branches he will hew
      away.
6 They shall all be left
    to the birds of prey of the mountains
    and to the animals of the earth.
And the birds of prey will summer on them,

and all the animals of the earth will winter
    on them.

7 At that time gifts will be brought to the LORD
of hosts from[b] a people tall and smooth, from a
people feared near and far, a nation mighty and
conquering, whose land the rivers divide, to Mount
Zion, the place of the name of the LORD of hosts.

An Oracle concerning Egypt

19 An oracle concerning Egypt.

See, the LORD is riding on a swift cloud
    and comes to Egypt;
the idols of Egypt will tremble at his presence,
    and the heart of the Egyptians will melt
      within them.
2 I will stir up Egyptians against Egyptians,
    and they will fight, one against the other,
      neighbor against neighbor,
      city against city, kingdom against kingdom;
3 the spirit of the Egyptians within them will be
      emptied out,
    and I will confound their plans;
they will consult the idols and the spirits of the
      dead
    and the ghosts and the familiar spirits;
4 I will deliver the Egyptians
    into the hand of a hard master;
a fierce king will rule over them,
    says the Sovereign, the LORD of hosts.

5 The waters of the Nile will be dried up,
    and the river will be parched and dry;
6 its canals will become foul,
    and the branches of Egypt's Nile will
      diminish and dry up,
    reeds and rushes will rot away.
7 There will be bare places by the Nile,
    on the brink of the Nile;
and all that is sown by the Nile will dry up,
    be driven away, and be no more.
8 Those who fish will mourn;
    all who cast hooks in the Nile will lament,
    and those who spread nets on the water
      will languish.
9 The workers in flax will be in despair,
    and the carders and those at the loom will
      grow pale.
10 Its weavers will be dismayed,
    and all who work for wages will be grieved.

11 The princes of Zō'an are utterly foolish;
    the wise counselors of Pharaoh give stupid
      counsel.

---

a Or Nubia; Heb Cush   b Q Ms Gk Vg: MT of

How can you say to Pharaoh,
  "I am one of the sages,
  a descendant of ancient kings"?
12 Where now are your sages?
  Let them tell you and make known
  what the LORD of hosts has planned against
    Egypt.
13 The princes of Zō'an have become fools,
  and the princes of Memphis are
    deluded;
  those who are the cornerstones of its
    tribes
  have led Egypt astray.
14 The LORD has poured into them[c]
  a spirit of confusion;
  and they have made Egypt stagger in all its
    doings
  as a drunkard staggers around in vomit.
15 Neither head nor tail, palm branch or reed,
  will be able to do anything for Egypt.

16 On that day the Egyptians will be like
women, and tremble with fear before the hand that
the LORD of hosts raises against them. 17 And the
land of Judah will become a terror to the Egyptians;
everyone to whom it is mentioned will fear because
of the plan that the LORD of hosts is planning
against them.

Egypt, Assyria, and Israel Blessed

18 On that day there will be five cities in the
land of Egypt that speak the language of Cā'naan
and swear allegiance to the LORD of hosts. One of
these will be called the City of the Sun.

19 On that day there will be an altar to the
LORD in the center of the land of Egypt, and a pillar
to the LORD at its border. 20 It will be a sign and a
witness to the LORD of hosts in the land of Egypt;
when they cry to the LORD because of oppressors,
he will send them a savior, and will defend and deliver them. 21 The LORD will make himself known
to the Egyptians; and the Egyptians will know the
LORD on that day, and will worship with sacrifice
and burnt offering, and they will make vows to the
LORD and perform them. 22 The LORD will strike
Egypt, striking and healing; they will return to the
LORD, and he will listen to their supplications and
heal them.

23 On that day there will be a highway from
Egypt to Assyria, and the Assyrian will come into
Egypt, and the Egyptian into Assyria, and the Egyp-
tians will worship with the Assyrians.

24 On that day Israel will be the third with
Egypt and Assyria, a blessing in the midst of the
earth, 25 whom the LORD of hosts has blessed, saying, "Blessed be Egypt my people, and Assyria the
work of my hands, and Israel my heritage."

Isaiah Dramatizes the Conquest of Egypt and Ethiopia

20 In the year that the commander-in-chief,
who was sent by King Sar'gon of Assyria,
came to Ash'dod and fought against it and took it—
2 at that time the LORD had spoken to Ī•sāi'ah son
of Ā'moz, saying, "Go, and loose the sackcloth from
your loins and take your sandals off your feet," and
he had done so, walking naked and barefoot.
3 Then the LORD said, "Just as my servant Ī•sāi'ah
has walked naked and barefoot for three years as a
sign and a portent against Egypt and Ethiopia,[d] 4 so
shall the king of Assyria lead away the Egyptians as
captives and the Ethiopians[e] as exiles, both the
young and the old, naked and barefoot, with but-
tocks uncovered, to the shame of Egypt. 5 And they
shall be dismayed and confounded because of
Ethiopia[d] their hope and of Egypt their boast. 6 In
that day the inhabitants of this coastland will say,
'See, this is what has happened to those in whom
we hoped and to whom we fled for help and deliverance from the king of Assyria! And we, how shall
we escape?' "

Oracles concerning Babylon, Edom, and Arabia

21 The oracle concerning the wilderness of
the sea.

As whirlwinds in the Neg'eb sweep on,
  it comes from the desert,
  from a terrible land.
2 A stern vision is told to me;
  the betrayer betrays,
  and the destroyer destroys.
Go up, O Ē'lam,
  lay siege, O Mēd'i•a;
all the sighing she has caused
  I bring to an end.
3 Therefore my loins are filled with anguish;
  pangs have seized me,
  like the pangs of a woman in labor;
I am bowed down so that I cannot hear,
  I am dismayed so that I cannot see.
4 My mind reels, horror has appalled me;
  the twilight I longed for
  has been turned for me into trembling.
5 They prepare the table,
  they spread the rugs,
  they eat, they drink.
Rise up, commanders,
  oil the shield!
6 For thus the Lord said to me:
  "Go, post a lookout,
  let him announce what he sees.

c Gk Compare Tg: Heb *it*   d Or *Nubia*; Heb *Cush*   e Or
Nubians; Heb *Cushites*

ISA

7 When he sees riders, horsemen in pairs,
    riders on donkeys, riders on camels,
let him listen diligently,
    very diligently."
8 Then the watcher*f* called out:
"Upon a watchtower I stand, O Lord,
    continually by day,
and at my post I am stationed
    throughout the night.
9 Look, there they come, riders,
    horsemen in pairs!"
Then he responded,
    "Fallen, fallen is Babylon;
and all the images of her gods
    lie shattered on the ground."
10 O my threshed and winnowed one,
    what I have heard from the LORD of hosts,
    the God of Israel, I announce to you.

11 The oracle concerning Dū'mah.

One is calling to me from Sē'ir,
"Sentinel, what of the night?
Sentinel, what of the night?"
12 The sentinel says:
"Morning comes, and also the night.
    If you will inquire, inquire;
    come back again."

13 The oracle concerning the desert plain.

In the scrub of the desert plain you will
        lodge,
    O caravans of Ded'an•ites.
14 Bring water to the thirsty,
    meet the fugitive with bread,
    O inhabitants of the land of Tē'ma.
15 For they have fled from the swords,
    from the drawn sword,
from the bent bow,
    and from the stress of battle.
16 For thus the Lord said to me: Within a year,
according to the years of a hired worker, all the glory of Kē'dar will come to an end; 17 and the remaining bows of Kē'dar's warriors will be few; for
the LORD, the God of Israel, has spoken.

A Warning of Destruction of Jerusalem

22 The oracle concerning the valley of vision.

What do you mean that you have gone up,
    all of you, to the housetops,
2 you that are full of shoutings,
    tumultuous city, exultant town?
Your slain are not slain by the sword,
    nor are they dead in battle.

3 Your rulers have all fled together;
    they were captured without the use of a
        bow.*g*
All of you who were found were captured,
    though they had fled far away.*h*
4 Therefore I said:
Look away from me,
    let me weep bitter tears;
do not try to comfort me
    for the destruction of my beloved people.

5 For the Lord GOD of hosts has a day
    of tumult and trampling and confusion
        in the valley of vision,
a battering down of walls
    and a cry for help to the mountains.
6 Ē'lam bore the quiver
    with chariots and cavalry,*i*
    and Kir uncovered the shield.
7 Your choicest valleys were full of chariots,
    and the cavalry took their stand at the gates.
8 He has taken away the covering of Judah.

On that day you looked to the weapons of the
House of the Forest, 9 and you saw that there were
many breaches in the city of David, and you
collected the waters of the lower pool. 10 You
counted the houses of Jerusalem, and you broke
down the houses to fortify the wall. 11 You made a
reservoir between the two walls for the water of the
old pool. But you did not look to him who did it,
or have regard for him who planned it long ago.

12 In that day the Lord GOD of hosts
    called to weeping and mourning,
        to baldness and putting on sackcloth;
13 but instead there was joy and festivity,
    killing oxen and slaughtering sheep,
        eating meat and drinking wine.
"Let us eat and drink,
    for tomorrow we die."
14 The LORD of hosts has revealed himself in my
        ears:
Surely this iniquity will not be forgiven you
        until you die,
    says the Lord GOD of hosts.

Denunciation of Self-Seeking Officials

15 Thus says the Lord GOD of hosts: Come, go
to this steward, to Sheb'na, who is master of the
household, and say to him: 16 What right do you
have here? Who are your relatives here, that you
have cut out a tomb here for yourself, cutting a
tomb on the height, and carving a habitation for

---

f Q Ms: MT *a lion*   *g* Or *without their bows*   *h* Gk Syr Vg:
Heb *fled from far away*   *i* Meaning of Heb uncertain

LIVE IT!

Faith and Politics

Every group that we belong to has a leader. And every leader might be corrupt. Like First Isaiah, we should demand integrity from our leaders as well as practicing it ourselves.

In Isa 22.15–25, the prophet denounces the steward Shebna for his self-seeking ways. Evidently, Shebna is using his position of leadership to prepare an expensive tomb for himself (verse 16) and to acquire ornate chariots (verse 18). Isaiah prefers Eliakim to take over his position. The prophet's interest in local politics points out a biblical truth: Our faith applies to our daily life, including our political choices.

We need to search out and endorse good leaders. Challenge your leaders to be people of integrity by avoiding corruption and seeking the best for the people they serve.

▶ Isa 22.15–25

---

yourself in the rock? 17 The LORD is about to hurl you away violently, my fellow. He will seize firm hold on you, 18 whirl you round and round, and throw you like a ball into a wide land; there you shall die, and there your splendid chariots shall lie, O you disgrace to your master's house! 19 I will thrust you from your office, and you will be pulled down from your post.

20 On that day I will call my servant E•li′a•kim son of Hil•ki′ah, 21 and will clothe him with your robe and bind your sash on him. I will commit your authority to his hand, and he shall be a father to the inhabitants of Jerusalem and to the house of Judah. 22 I will place on his shoulder the key of the house of David; he shall open, and no one shall shut; he shall shut, and no one shall open. 23 I will fasten him like a peg in a secure place, and he will become a throne of honor to his ancestral house. 24 And they will hang on him the whole weight of his ancestral house, the offspring and issue, every small vessel, from the cups to all the flagons. 25 On that day, says the LORD of hosts, the peg that was fastened in a secure place will give way; it will be cut down and fall, and the load that was on it will perish, for the LORD has spoken.

An Oracle concerning Tyre

23

The oracle concerning Tyre.

Wail, O ships of Tar′shish,
    for your fortress is destroyed.j
When they came in from Cyprus
    they learned of it.
2 Be still, O inhabitants of the coast,
    O merchants of Si′don,
your messengers crossed over the seak
3   and were on the mighty waters;
your revenue was the grain of Shi′hor,

the harvest of the Nile;
    you were the merchant of the nations.
4 Be ashamed, O Si′don, for the sea has
      spoken,
    the fortress of the sea, saying:
"I have neither labored nor given birth,
    I have neither reared young men
    nor brought up young women."
5 When the report comes to Egypt,
    they will be in anguish over the report
      about Tyre.
6 Cross over to Tar′shish—
    wail, O inhabitants of the coast!
7 Is this your exultant city
    whose origin is from days of old,
whose feet carried her
    to settle far away?
8 Who has planned this
    against Tyre, the bestower of crowns,
whose merchants were princes,
    whose traders were the honored of the
      earth?
9 The LORD of hosts has planned it—
    to defile the pride of all glory,
    to shame all the honored of the earth.
10 Cross over to your own land,
    O ships ofl Tar′shish;
    this is a harborm no more.
11 He has stretched out his hand over the sea,
    he has shaken the kingdoms;
the LORD has given command concerning
      Ca′naan
    to destroy its fortresses.

---

j Cn Compare verse 14: Heb *for it is destroyed, without houses*
k Q Ms: MT *crossing over the sea, they replenished you*   l Cn
Compare Gk: Heb *like the Nile, daughter*   m Cn: Heb
restraint

ISA

12 He said:
You will exult no longer,
  O oppressed virgin daughter Si′don;
rise, cross over to Cyprus—
  even there you will have no rest.

13 Look at the land of the Chal·de′ans! This is the people; it was not Assyria. They destined Tȳre for wild animals. They erected their siege towers, they tore down her palaces, they made her a ruin.[n]
14 Wail, O ships of Tar′shish,
  for your fortress is destroyed.
15 From that day Tȳre will be forgotten for seventy years, the lifetime of one king. At the end of seventy years, it will happen to Tȳre as in the song about the prostitute:
16 Take a harp,
  go about the city,
  you forgotten prostitute!
Make sweet melody,
  sing many songs,
  that you may be remembered.
17 At the end of seventy years, the Lord will visit Tȳre, and she will return to her trade, and will prostitute herself with all the kingdoms of the world on the face of the earth. 18 Her merchandise and her wages will be dedicated to the Lord; her profits[o] will not be stored or hoarded, but her merchandise will supply abundant food and fine clothing for those who live in the presence of the Lord.

Impending Judgment on the Earth

24 Now the Lord is about to lay waste the earth and make it desolate,
  and he will twist its surface and scatter its inhabitants.
2 And it shall be, as with the people, so with the priest;
  as with the slave, so with his master;
  as with the maid, so with her mistress;
as with the buyer, so with the seller;
  as with the lender, so with the borrower;
  as with the creditor, so with the debtor.
3 The earth shall be utterly laid waste and utterly despoiled;
  for the Lord has spoken this word.

4 The earth dries up and withers,
  the world languishes and withers;
  the heavens languish together with the earth.
5 The earth lies polluted
  under its inhabitants;
for they have transgressed laws,
  violated the statutes,
  broken the everlasting covenant.

6 Therefore a curse devours the earth,
  and its inhabitants suffer for their guilt;
therefore the inhabitants of the earth dwindled,
  and few people are left.
7 The wine dries up,
  the vine languishes,
  all the merry-hearted sigh.
8 The mirth of the timbrels is stilled,
  the noise of the jubilant has ceased,
  the mirth of the lyre is stilled.
9 No longer do they drink wine with singing;
  strong drink is bitter to those who drink it.
10 The city of chaos is broken down,
  every house is shut up so that no one can enter.
11 There is an outcry in the streets for lack of wine;
  all joy has reached its eventide;
  the gladness of the earth is banished.
12 Desolation is left in the city,
  the gates are battered into ruins.
13 For thus it shall be on the earth
  and among the nations,
as when an olive tree is beaten,
  as at the gleaning when the grape harvest is ended.

14 They lift up their voices, they sing for joy;
  they shout from the west over the majesty of the Lord.
15 Therefore in the east give glory to the Lord;
  in the coastlands of the sea glorify the name of the Lord, the God of Israel.
16 From the ends of the earth we hear songs of praise,
  of glory to the Righteous One.
But I say, I pine away,
  I pine away. Woe is me!
For the treacherous deal treacherously,
  the treacherous deal very treacherously.

17 Terror, and the pit, and the snare
  are upon you, O inhabitant of the earth!
18 Whoever flees at the sound of the terror
  shall fall into the pit;
and whoever climbs out of the pit
  shall be caught in the snare.
For the windows of heaven are opened,
  and the foundations of the earth tremble.
19 The earth is utterly broken,
  the earth is torn asunder,
  the earth is violently shaken.
20 The earth staggers like a drunkard,
  it sways like a hut;
its transgression lies heavy upon it,
  and it falls, and will not rise again.

---

[n] Meaning of Heb uncertain [o] Heb *it*

21 On that day the LORD will punish
        the host of heaven in heaven,
        and on earth the kings of the earth.
22 They will be gathered together
        like prisoners in a pit;
    they will be shut up in a prison,
        and after many days they will be punished.
23 Then the moon will be abashed,
        and the sun ashamed;
    for the LORD of hosts will reign
        on Mount Zion and in Jerusalem,
    and before his elders he will manifest his glory.

Praise for Deliverance from Oppression

25 O LORD, you are my God;
        I will exalt you, I will praise your
            name;
    for you have done wonderful things,
        plans formed of old, faithful and sure.
2 For you have made the city a heap,
        the fortified city a ruin;
    the palace of aliens is a city no more,
        it will never be rebuilt.
3 Therefore strong peoples will glorify you;
        cities of ruthless nations will fear you.
4 For you have been a refuge to the poor,
        a refuge to the needy in their distress,
        a shelter from the rainstorm and a shade
            from the heat.
    When the blast of the ruthless was like a winter
        rainstorm,
5   the noise of aliens like heat in a dry place,
    you subdued the heat with the shade of clouds;
        the song of the ruthless was stilled.

6 On this mountain the LORD of hosts will make
            for all peoples
        a feast of rich food, a feast of well-aged
            wines,
        of rich food filled with marrow, of
            well-aged wines strained clear.
7 And he will destroy on this mountain
        the shroud that is cast over all peoples,
        the sheet that is spread over all nations;
8   he will swallow up death forever.
    Then the Lord GOD will wipe away the tears
            from all faces,
        and the disgrace of his people he will take
            away from all the earth,
        for the LORD has spoken.
9 It will be said on that day,
        Lo, this is our God; we have waited for him,
            so that he might save us.
    This is the LORD for whom we have waited;
        let us be glad and rejoice in his salvation.
10 For the hand of the LORD will rest on this
        mountain.

The Mō′ab•ites shall be trodden down in their
            place
        as straw is trodden down in a dung-pit.
11 Though they spread out their hands in the
            midst of it,
        as swimmers spread out their hands to
            swim,
        their pride will be laid low despite the
            struggleᵖ of their hands.
12 The high fortifications of his walls will be
        brought down,
        laid low, cast to the ground, even to the
            dust.

Judah's Song of Victory

26 On that day this song will be sung in the
        land of Judah:
    We have a strong city;
        he sets up victory
        like walls and bulwarks.
2 Open the gates,
        so that the righteous nation that keeps faith
        may enter in.
3 Those of steadfast mind you keep in peace—
        in peace because they trust in you.
4 Trust in the LORD forever,
        for in the LORD GOD�q
        you have an everlasting rock.
5 For he has brought low
        the inhabitants of the height;
        the lofty city he lays low.
    He lays it low to the ground,
        casts it to the dust.
6 The foot tramples it,
        the feet of the poor,
        the steps of the needy.

7 The way of the righteous is level;
        O Just One, you make smooth the path of
            the righteous.
8 In the path of your judgments,
        O LORD, we wait for you;
    your name and your renown
        are the soul's desire.
9 My soul yearns for you in the night,
        my spirit within me earnestly seeks you.
    For when your judgments are in the earth,
        the inhabitants of the world learn
            righteousness.
10 If favor is shown to the wicked,
        they do not learn righteousness;
    in the land of uprightness they deal perversely
        and do not see the majesty of the LORD.
11 O LORD, your hand is lifted up,
        but they do not see it.

p Meaning of Heb uncertain   q Heb in Yah, the LORD

Let them see your zeal for your people, and be
    ashamed.
Let the fire for your adversaries consume
    them.
12 O LORD, you will ordain peace for us,
    for indeed, all that we have done, you have
      done for us.
13 O LORD our God,
    other lords besides you have ruled over us,
    but we acknowledge your name alone.
14 The dead do not live;
    shades do not rise—
because you have punished and destroyed them,
    and wiped out all memory of them.
15 But you have increased the nation, O LORD,
    you have increased the nation; you are
      glorified;
    you have enlarged all the borders of the
      land.

16 O LORD, in distress they sought you,
    they poured out a prayer[r]
    when your chastening was on them.
17 Like a woman with child,
    who writhes and cries out in her pangs
    when she is near her time,
so were we because of you, O LORD;
18   we were with child, we writhed,
    but we gave birth only to wind.
We have won no victories on earth,
    and no one is born to inhabit the world.
19 Your dead shall live, their corpses[s] shall rise.
    O dwellers in the dust, awake and sing for
      joy!
For your dew is a radiant dew,
    and the earth will give birth to those long
      dead.[t]

20 Come, my people, enter your chambers,
    and shut your doors behind you;
hide yourselves for a little while
    until the wrath is past.
21 For the LORD comes out from his place
    to punish the inhabitants of the earth for
      their iniquity;
the earth will disclose the blood shed on it,
    and will no longer cover its slain.

Israel's Redemption

27 On that day the LORD with his cruel and
great and strong sword will punish
Le·vi′a·than the fleeing serpent, Le·vi′a·than the
twisting serpent, and he will kill the dragon that is
in the sea.

2 On that day:
A pleasant vineyard, sing about it!

3   I, the LORD, am its keeper;
    every moment I water it.
I guard it night and day
    so that no one can harm it;
4   I have no wrath.
If it gives me thorns and briers,
    I will march to battle against it.
    I will burn it up.
5 Or else let it cling to me for protection,
    let it make peace with me,
    let it make peace with me.

6 In days to come[u] Jacob shall take root,
    Israel shall blossom and put forth shoots,
    and fill the whole world with fruit.

7 Has he struck them down as he struck down
    those who struck them?
    Or have they been killed as their killers
      were killed?
8 By expulsion,[r] by exile you struggled against
    them;
    with his fierce blast he removed them in the
      day of the east wind.
9 Therefore by this the guilt of Jacob will be
    expiated,
    and this will be the full fruit of the removal
      of his sin:
when he makes all the stones of the altars
    like chalkstones crushed to pieces,
    no sacred poles[v] or incense altars will
      remain standing.
10 For the fortified city is solitary,
    a habitation deserted and forsaken, like the
      wilderness;
the calves graze there,
    there they lie down, and strip its branches.
11 When its boughs are dry, they are broken;
    women come and make a fire of them.
For this is a people without understanding;
    therefore he that made them will not have
      compassion on them,
    he that formed them will show them no
      favor.

12 On that day the LORD will thresh from the
channel of the Euphrates to the Wadi of Egypt, and
you will be gathered one by one, O people of Israel.
13 And on that day a great trumpet will be blown,
and those who were lost in the land of Assyria and
those who were driven out to the land of Egypt will
come and worship the LORD on the holy mountain
at Jerusalem.

---

[r] Meaning of Heb uncertain   [s] Cn Compare Syr Tg: Heb
my corpse   [t] Heb *to the shades*   [u] Heb *Those to come*   [v] Heb
Asherim

Judgment on Corrupt Rulers, Priests, and Prophets

28 Ah, the proud garland of the drunkards
of Éʹphra•im,
and the fading flower of its glorious beauty,
which is on the head of those bloated with
rich food, of those overcome with
wine!
2 See, the Lord has one who is mighty and
strong;
like a storm of hail, a destroying tempest,
like a storm of mighty, overflowing waters;
with his hand he will hurl them down to
the earth.
3 Trampled under foot will be
the proud garland of the drunkards of
Éʹphra•im.
4 And the fading flower of its glorious beauty,
which is on the head of those bloated with
rich food,
will be like a first-ripe fig before the summer;
whoever sees it, eats it up
as soon as it comes to hand.

5 In that day the LORD of hosts will be a garland
of glory,
and a diadem of beauty, to the remnant of
his people;
6 and a spirit of justice to the one who sits in
judgment,
and strength to those who turn back the
battle at the gate.

7 These also reel with wine
and stagger with strong drink;
the priest and the prophet reel with strong
drink,
they are confused with wine,
they stagger with strong drink;
they err in vision,
they stumble in giving judgment.
8 All tables are covered with filthy vomit;
no place is clean.

9 "Whom will he teach knowledge,
and to whom will he explain the message?
Those who are weaned from milk,
those taken from the breast?
10 For it is precept upon precept, precept upon
precept,
line upon line, line upon line,
here a little, there a little."*w*

11 Truly, with stammering lip
and with alien tongue
he will speak to this people,
12 to whom he has said,

"This is rest;
give rest to the weary;
and this is repose";
yet they would not hear.
13 Therefore the word of the LORD will be to
them,
"Precept upon precept, precept upon
precept,
line upon line, line upon line,
here a little, there a little;"*w*
in order that they may go, and fall backward,
and be broken, and snared, and taken.

14 Therefore hear the word of the LORD, you
scoffers
who rule this people in Jerusalem.
15 Because you have said, "We have made a
covenant with death,
and with Shēʹōl we have an agreement;
when the overwhelming scourge passes
through
it will not come to us;
for we have made lies our refuge,
and in falsehood we have taken shelter";
16 therefore thus says the Lord GOD,
See, I am laying in Zion a foundation stone,
a tested stone,
a precious cornerstone, a sure foundation:
"One who trusts will not panic."
17 And I will make justice the line,
and righteousness the plummet;
hail will sweep away the refuge of lies,
and waters will overwhelm the shelter.
18 Then your covenant with death will be
annulled,
and your agreement with Shēʹōl will not
stand;
when the overwhelming scourge passes
through
you will be beaten down by it.
19 As often as it passes through, it will take you;
for morning by morning it will pass
through,
by day and by night;
and it will be sheer terror to understand the
message.
20 For the bed is too short to stretch oneself on it,
and the covering too narrow to wrap
oneself in it.
21 For the LORD will rise up as on Mount
Pe•rāʹzim,
he will rage as in the valley of Gibʹe•on
to do his deed—strange is his deed!—
and to work his work—alien is his work!
22 Now therefore do not scoff,

---

*w Meaning of Heb of this verse uncertain

or your bonds will be made stronger;
for I have heard a decree of destruction
   from the Lord GOD of hosts upon the
     whole land.

23 Listen, and hear my voice;
   Pay attention, and hear my speech.
24 Do those who plow for sowing plow
     continually?
   Do they continually open and harrow their
     ground?
25 When they have leveled its surface,
   do they not scatter dill, sow cummin,
and plant wheat in rows
   and barley in its proper place,
   and spelt as the border?
26 For they are well instructed;
   their God teaches them.

27 Dill is not threshed with a threshing sledge,
   nor is a cart wheel rolled over cummin;
but dill is beaten out with a stick,
   and cummin with a rod.
28 Grain is crushed for bread,
   but one does not thresh it forever;
one drives the cart wheel and horses over it,
   but does not pulverize it.
29 This also comes from the LORD of hosts;
   he is wonderful in counsel,
   and excellent in wisdom.

The Siege of Jerusalem

29 Ah, Ar′i•el, A′ri•el,
     the city where David encamped!
Add year to year;
   let the festivals run their round.
2 Yet I will distress Ar′i•el,
   and there shall be moaning and
     lamentation,
   and Jerusalem x shall be to me like an
     Ar′i•el.y
3 And like Davidz I will encamp against you;
   I will besiege you with towers
   and raise siegeworks against you.
4 Then deep from the earth you shall speak,
   from low in the dust your words shall
     come;
your voice shall come from the ground like the
     voice of a ghost,
   and your speech shall whisper out of the
     dust.

5 But the multitude of your foesa shall be like
     small dust,
   and the multitude of tyrants like flying
     chaff.
And in an instant, suddenly,

6   you will be visited by the LORD of hosts
with thunder and earthquake and great noise,
   with whirlwind and tempest, and the flame
     of a devouring fire.
7 And the multitude of all the nations that fight
     against Ar′i•el,
   all that fight against her and her stronghold,
     and who distress her,
   shall be like a dream, a vision of the night.
8 Just as when a hungry person dreams of
     eating
   and wakes up still hungry,
or a thirsty person dreams of drinking
   and wakes up faint, still thirsty,
so shall the multitude of all the nations be
   that fight against Mount Zion.

9 Stupefy yourselves and be in a stupor,
   blind yourselves and be blind!
Be drunk, but not from wine;
   stagger, but not from strong drink!
10 For the LORD has poured out upon you
   a spirit of deep sleep;
he has closed your eyes, you prophets,
   and covered your heads, you seers.

11 The vision of all this has become for you like
the words of a sealed document. If it is given to
those who can read, with the command, "Read
this," they say, "We cannot, for it is sealed." 12 And
if it is given to those who cannot read, saying,
"Read this," they say, "We cannot read."

13 The Lord said:
Because these people draw near with their
     mouths
   and honor me with their lips,
   while their hearts are far from me,
and their worship of me is a human
     commandment learned by rote;
14 so I will again do
   amazing things with this people,
   shocking and amazing.
The wisdom of their wise shall perish,
   and the discernment of the discerning shall
     be hidden.

15 Ha! You who hide a plan too deep for the
     LORD,
   whose deeds are in the dark,
   and who say, "Who sees us? Who knows us?"
16 You turn things upside down!
   Shall the potter be regarded as the clay?
Shall the thing made say of its maker,

---

x Heb *she* y Probable meaning, *altar hearth;* compare Ezek
43.15 z Gk: Meaning of Heb uncertain a Cn: Heb
strangers

"He did not make me";
or the thing formed say of the one who
        formed it,
"He has no understanding"?

Hope for the Future

17 Shall not Lebanon in a very little while
        become a fruitful field,
        and the fruitful field be regarded as a forest?
18 On that day the deaf shall hear
        the words of a scroll,
and out of their gloom and darkness
        the eyes of the blind shall see.
19 The meek shall obtain fresh joy in the LORD,
        and the neediest people shall exult in the
                Holy One of Israel.
20 For the tyrant shall be no more,
        and the scoffer shall cease to be;
        all those alert to do evil shall be cut off—
21 those who cause a person to lose a lawsuit,

PRAY IT!
Preference for the Poor

Isaiah 29.17–21 proclaims that God's
power will transform society: the deaf
will hear, the blind will see, the lowly will
know joy and the poor will rejoice. First
Isaiah's words are reflected in Jesus'
words in the Beatitudes (see Lk 6.20–26).
Both Jesus and Isaiah say that in God's
Reign, the rights and needs of the lowliest
and the weakest come first (see Isaiah,
chapters 58, 61).

The Catholic church refers to this
principle as the preferential option for the
poor. People who are poor and helpless
have a right to a just society where they
get what they need to live with dignity
and where they have a voice in the structures that govern their life. One can tell
how near a society is to the Reign of God
by seeing how it treats the most vulnerable members of the human family. Those
who are poor should never be ignored
when others have the resources to share.

Write your own prayer describing
God's vision for those who are poor.
Use Isaiah's words and the Beatitudes for
ideas. Share your prayer with your family
or youth group.

▶ Isa 29.17–21

who set a trap for the arbiter in the gate,
        and without grounds deny justice to the
                one in the right.

22 Therefore thus says the LORD, who redeemed
Abraham, concerning the house of Jacob:
        No longer shall Jacob be ashamed,
        no longer shall his face grow pale.
23 For when he sees his children,
        the work of my hands, in his midst,
        they will sanctify my name;
        they will sanctify the Holy One of Jacob,
        and will stand in awe of the God of Israel.
24 And those who err in spirit will come to
                understanding,
        and those who grumble will accept
                instruction.

The Futility of Reliance on Egypt

30 Oh, rebellious children, says the LORD,
        who carry out a plan, but not mine;
who make an alliance, but against my will,
        adding sin to sin;
2 who set out to go down to Egypt
        without asking for my counsel,
to take refuge in the protection of Pharaoh,
        and to seek shelter in the shadow of Egypt;
3 Therefore the protection of Pharaoh shall
                become your shame,
        and the shelter in the shadow of Egypt your
                humiliation.
4 For though his officials are at Zō′an
        and his envoys reach Hā′nēs,
5 everyone comes to shame
        through a people that cannot profit them,
that brings neither help nor profit,
        but shame and disgrace.

6 An oracle concerning the animals of the
Neg′eb.
        Through a land of trouble and distress,
                of lioness and roaring[b] lion,
                of viper and flying serpent,
        they carry their riches on the backs of donkeys,
                and their treasures on the humps of camels,
                to a people that cannot profit them.
7 For Egypt's help is worthless and empty,
        therefore I have called her,
        "Rā′hab who sits still."[c]

A Rebellious People

8 Go now, write it before them on a tablet,
        and inscribe it in a book,
so that it may be for the time to come
        as a witness forever.

---

b Cn: Heb *from them*   c Meaning of Heb uncertain

9 For they are a rebellious people,
    faithless children,
  children who will not hear
      the instruction of the LORD;
10 who say to the seers, "Do not see";
      and to the prophets, "Do not prophesy to
        us what is right;
  speak to us smooth things,
      prophesy illusions,
11 leave the way, turn aside from the path,
      let us hear no more about the Holy One of
        Israel."
12 Therefore thus says the Holy One of Israel:
  Because you reject this word,
      and put your trust in oppression and deceit,
      and rely on them;
13 therefore this iniquity shall become for you
      like a break in a high wall, bulging out, and
        about to collapse,
      whose crash comes suddenly, in an instant;
14 its breaking is like that of a potter's vessel
      that is smashed so ruthlessly
  that among its fragments not a sherd is
        found
      for taking fire from the hearth,
      or dipping water out of the cistern.

15 For thus said the Lord GOD, the Holy One of
      Israel:
  In returning and rest you shall be saved;
      in quietness and in trust shall be your
        strength.
  But you refused 16 and said,
  "No! We will flee upon horses"—
      therefore you shall flee!
  and, "We will ride upon swift steeds"—
      therefore your pursuers shall be swift!
17 A thousand shall flee at the threat of one,
      at the threat of five you shall flee,
  until you are left
      like a flagstaff on the top of a mountain,
      like a signal on a hill.

God's Promise to Zion

18 Therefore the LORD waits to be gracious to you;
      therefore he will rise up to show mercy to
        you.
  For the LORD is a God of justice;
      blessed are all those who wait for him.
19 Truly, O people in Zion, inhabitants of
Jerusalem, you shall weep no more. He will surely
be gracious to you at the sound of your cry; when
he hears it, he will answer you. 20 Though the Lord
may give you the bread of adversity and the water
of affliction, yet your Teacher will not hide himself
any more, but your eyes shall see your Teacher.
21 And when you turn to the right or when you turn

to the left, your ears shall hear a word behind you,
saying, "This is the way; walk in it." 22 Then you
will defile your silver-covered idols and your gold-
plated images. You will scatter them like filthy rags;
you will say to them, "Away with you!"

23 He will give rain for the seed with which you
sow the ground, and grain, the produce of the
ground, which will be rich and plenteous. On that
day your cattle will graze in broad pastures; 24 and
the oxen and donkeys that till the ground will eat
silage, which has been winnowed with shovel and
fork. 25 On every lofty mountain and every high hill
there will be brooks running with water—on a day
of the great slaughter, when the towers fall.
26 Moreover the light of the moon will be like the
light of the sun, and the light of the sun will be sevenfold, like the light of seven days, on the day when
the LORD binds up the injuries of his people, and
heals the wounds inflicted by his blow.

Judgment on Assyria

27 See, the name of the LORD comes from far away,
      burning with his anger, and in thick rising
        smoke;[d]
  his lips are full of indignation,
      and his tongue is like a devouring fire;
28 his breath is like an overflowing stream
      that reaches up to the neck—
  to sift the nations with the sieve of destruction,
      and to place on the jaws of the peoples a
        bridle that leads them astray.

29 You shall have a song as in the night when a
holy festival is kept; and gladness of heart, as when
one sets out to the sound of the flute to go to the
mountain of the LORD, to the Rock of Israel. 30 And
the LORD will cause his majestic voice to be heard
and the descending blow of his arm to be seen, in
furious anger and a flame of devouring fire, with a
cloudburst and tempest and hailstones. 31 The Assyrian will be terror-stricken at the voice of the
LORD, when he strikes with his rod. 32 And every
stroke of the staff of punishment that the LORD lays
upon him will be to the sound of timbrels and
lyres; battling with brandished arm he will fight
with him. 33 For his burning place[e] has long been
prepared; truly it is made ready for the king,[f] its
pyre made deep and wide, with fire and wood in
abundance; the breath of the LORD, like a stream of
sulfur, kindles it.

Alliance with Egypt Is Futile

31 Alas for those who go down to Egypt
      for help
  and who rely on horses,

---

d Meaning of Heb uncertain   e Or Topheth   f Or Molech

who trust in chariots because they are many
and in horsemen because they are very
strong,
but do not look to the Holy One of Israel
or consult the LORD!
2 Yet he too is wise and brings disaster;
he does not call back his words,
but will rise against the house of the evildoers,
and against the helpers of those who work
iniquity.
3 The Egyptians are human, and not God;
their horses are flesh, and not spirit.
When the LORD stretches out his hand,
the helper will stumble, and the one helped
will fall,
and they will all perish together.

4 For thus the LORD said to me,
As a lion or a young lion growls over its prey,
and—when a band of shepherds is called
out against it—
is not terrified by their shouting
or daunted at their noise,
so the LORD of hosts will come down
to fight upon Mount Zion and upon its hill.
5 Like birds hovering overhead, so the LORD of
hosts
will protect Jerusalem;
he will protect and deliver it,
he will spare and rescue it.

6 Turn back to him whom you*s* have deeply betrayed, O people of Israel. 7 For on that day all of
you shall throw away your idols of silver and idols
of gold, which your hands have sinfully made for
you.
8 "Then the Assyrian shall fall by a sword, not of
mortals;
and a sword, not of humans, shall devour
him;
he shall flee from the sword,
and his young men shall be put to forced
labor.
9 His rock shall pass away in terror,
and his officers desert the standard in
panic,"
says the LORD, whose fire is in Zion,
and whose furnace is in Jerusalem.

Government with Justice Predicted

32 See, a king will reign in righteousness,
and princes will rule with justice.
2 Each will be like a hiding place from the wind,
a covert from the tempest,
like streams of water in a dry place,
like the shade of a great rock in a weary
land.

3 Then the eyes of those who have sight will not
be closed,
and the ears of those who have hearing will
listen.
4 The minds of the rash will have good
judgment,
and the tongues of stammerers will speak
readily and distinctly.
5 A fool will no longer be called noble,
nor a villain said to be honorable.
6 For fools speak folly,
and their minds plot iniquity:
to practice ungodliness,
to utter error concerning the LORD,
to leave the craving of the hungry unsatisfied,
and to deprive the thirsty of drink.
7 The villainies of villains are evil;
they devise wicked devices
to ruin the poor with lying words,
even when the plea of the needy is right.
8 But those who are noble plan noble things,
and by noble things they stand.

Complacent Women Warned of Disaster

9 Rise up, you women who are at ease, hear my
voice;
you complacent daughters, listen to my
speech.
10 In little more than a year
you will shudder, you complacent ones;
for the vintage will fail,
the fruit harvest will not come.
11 Tremble, you women who are at ease,
shudder, you complacent ones;
strip, and make yourselves bare,
and put sackcloth on your loins.
12 Beat your breasts for the pleasant fields,
for the fruitful vine,
13 for the soil of my people
growing up in thorns and briers;
yes, for all the joyous houses
in the jubilant city.
14 For the palace will be forsaken,
the populous city deserted;
the hill and the watchtower
will become dens forever,
the joy of wild asses,
a pasture for flocks;
15 until a spirit from on high is poured out on us,
and the wilderness becomes a fruitful field,
and the fruitful field is deemed a forest.

The Peace of God's Reign

16 Then justice will dwell in the wilderness,
and righteousness abide in the fruitful field.

----
s Heb *they*

Shalom

In Israel, people greet one another by saying "Shalom." In the Bible, *shalom* means "peace" in its fullest sense (see Isa 32.16–20). Shalom is not just the absence of war and violence but also the presence of justice, righteousness, happiness, and fullness of life. What better way to greet your neighbors or friends than to wish them shalom.

In your own life, seek peace. Begin each day by praying for peace of mind and heart, and to act with justice in all that you do. The very prayer that you speak will become the way that you live. Peace can become a reality only when we become a shalom people. It begins with us. If we wait, it may never come.

▶ Isa 32.16–20

17 The effect of righteousness will be peace,
    and the result of righteousness, quietness
        and trust forever.
18 My people will abide in a peaceful habitation,
    in secure dwellings, and in quiet resting
        places.
19 The forest will disappear completely,*h*
    and the city will be utterly laid low.
20 Happy will you be who sow beside every stream,
    who let the ox and the donkey range freely.

A Prophecy of Deliverance from Foes

33 Ah, you destroyer,
        who yourself have not been
            destroyed;
you treacherous one,
    with whom no one has dealt treacherously!
When you have ceased to destroy,
    you will be destroyed;
and when you have stopped dealing
        treacherously,
    you will be dealt with treacherously.

2 O LORD, be gracious to us; we wait for you.
    Be our arm every morning,
    our salvation in the time of trouble.
3 At the sound of tumult, peoples fled;
    before your majesty, nations scattered.
4 Spoil was gathered as the caterpillar gathers;
    as locusts leap, they leaped*i* upon it.
5 The LORD is exalted, he dwells on high;
    he filled Zion with justice and
        righteousness;
6 he will be the stability of your times,
    abundance of salvation, wisdom, and
        knowledge;
    the fear of the LORD is Zion's treasure.*j*

7 Listen! the valiant*i* cry in the streets;
    the envoys of peace weep bitterly.

8 The highways are deserted,
    travelers have quit the road.
The treaty is broken,
    its oaths*k* are despised,
    its obligation*l* is disregarded.
9 The land mourns and languishes;
    Lebanon is confounded and withers away;
Sharon is like a desert;
    and Bā'shan and Car'mel shake off their
        leaves.

10 "Now I will arise," says the LORD,
    "now I will lift myself up;
    now I will be exalted.
11 You conceive chaff, you bring forth stubble;
    your breath is a fire that will consume you.
12 And the peoples will be as if burned to lime,
    like thorns cut down, that are burned in the
        fire."

13 Hear, you who are far away, what I have done;
    and you who are near, acknowledge my
        might.
14 The sinners in Zion are afraid;
    trembling has seized the godless:
"Who among us can live with the devouring
        fire?
    Who among us can live with everlasting
        flames?"
15 Those who walk righteously and speak uprightly,
    who despise the gain of oppression,
who wave away a bribe instead of accepting it,
    who stop their ears from hearing of
        bloodshed
    and shut their eyes from looking on evil,
16 they will live on the heights;

---

h Cn: Heb *And it will hail when the forest comes down*
i Meaning of Heb uncertain   *j* Heb *his treasure*; meaning of Heb uncertain   *k* Q Ms: MT *cities*   *l* Or *everyone*

their refuge will be the fortresses of rocks;
  their food will be supplied, their water
    assured.

The Land of the Majestic King

17 Your eyes will see the king in his beauty;
      they will behold a land that stretches far
        away.
18 Your mind will muse on the terror:
      "Where is the one who counted?
      Where is the one who weighed the tribute?
      Where is the one who counted the towers?"
19 No longer will you see the insolent people,
      the people of an obscure speech that you
          cannot comprehend,
        stammering in a language that you cannot
          understand.
20 Look on Zion, the city of our appointed
          festivals!
      Your eyes will see Jerusalem,
      a quiet habitation, an immovable tent,
  whose stakes will never be pulled up,
    and none of whose ropes will be broken.
21 But there the LORD in majesty will be for us
      a place of broad rivers and streams,
  where no galley with oars can go,
    nor stately ship can pass.
22 For the LORD is our judge, the LORD is our
          ruler,
      the LORD is our king; he will save us.

23 Your rigging hangs loose;
      it cannot hold the mast firm in its place,
      or keep the sail spread out.

  Then prey and spoil in abundance will be
          divided;
      even the lame will fall to plundering.
24 And no inhabitant will say, "I am sick";
      the people who live there will be forgiven
          their iniquity.

Judgment on the Nations

34 Draw near, O nations, to hear;
          O peoples, give heed!
  Let the earth hear, and all that fills it;
      the world, and all that comes from it.
2 For the LORD is enraged against all the nations,
      and furious against all their hordes;
      he has doomed them, has given them over
          for slaughter.
3 Their slain shall be cast out,
      and the stench of their corpses shall rise;
      the mountains shall flow with their blood.
4 All the host of heaven shall rot away,
      and the skies roll up like a scroll.
  All their host shall wither

like a leaf withering on a vine,
  or fruit withering on a fig tree.

5 When my sword has drunk its fill in the
          heavens,
      lo, it will descend upon É'dom,
      upon the people I have doomed to
          judgment.
6 The LORD has a sword; it is sated with blood,
      it is gorged with fat,
      with the blood of lambs and goats,
      with the fat of the kidneys of rams.
  For the LORD has a sacrifice in Boz'rah,
      a great slaughter in the land of É'dom.
7 Wild oxen shall fall with them,
      and young steers with the mighty bulls.
  Their land shall be soaked with blood,
      and their soil made rich with fat.

8 For the LORD has a day of vengeance,
      a year of vindication by Zion's cause.[m]
9 And the streams of É'dom[n] shall be turned into
          pitch,
      and her soil into sulfur;
      her land shall become burning pitch.
10 Night and day it shall not be quenched;
      its smoke shall go up forever.
  From generation to generation it shall lie
          waste;
      no one shall pass through it forever and
          ever.
11 But the hawk[o] and the hedgehog[o] shall
          possess it;
      the owl[o] and the raven shall live in it.
  He shall stretch the line of confusion over it,
      and the plummet of chaos over[p] its nobles.
12 They shall name it No Kingdom There,
      and all its princes shall be nothing.
13 Thorns shall grow over its strongholds,
      nettles and thistles in its fortresses.
  It shall be the haunt of jackals,
      an abode for ostriches.
14 Wildcats shall meet with hyenas,
      goat-demons shall call to each other;
  there too Lil'ith shall repose,
      and find a place to rest.
15 There shall the owl nest
      and lay and hatch and brood in its shadow;
  there too the buzzards shall gather,
      each one with its mate.
16 Seek and read from the book of the LORD:
      Not one of these shall be missing;
      none shall be without its mate.
  For the mouth of the LORD has commanded,

---

m Or of recompense by Zion's defender   n Heb her streams
o Identification uncertain   p Heb lacks over

ISA

and his spirit has gathered them.

17 He has cast the lot for them,
  his hand has portioned it out to them with
    the line;
they shall possess it forever,
  from generation to generation they shall
    live in it.

The Return of the Redeemed to Zion

35 The wilderness and the dry land shall
      be glad,
  the desert shall rejoice and blossom;
like the crocus 2 it shall blossom
    abundantly,
  and rejoice with joy and singing.
The glory of Lebanon shall be given to it,
  the majesty of Car'mel and Sharon.
They shall see the glory of the LORD,
  the majesty of our God.

3 Strengthen the weak hands,
  and make firm the feeble knees.
4 Say to those who are of a fearful heart,
  "Be strong, do not fear!
Here is your God.
  He will come with vengeance,
with terrible recompense.
  He will come and save you."

5 Then the eyes of the blind shall be opened,
  and the ears of the deaf unstopped;
6 then the lame shall leap like a deer,
  and the tongue of the speechless sing for
    joy.
For waters shall break forth in the wilderness,
  and streams in the desert;
7 the burning sand shall become a pool,
  and the thirsty ground springs of water;
the haunt of jackals shall become a swamp,*q*
  the grass shall become reeds and rushes.

8 A highway shall be there,
  and it shall be called the Holy Way;
the unclean shall not travel on it,*r*
  but it shall be for God's people;*s*
  no traveler, not even fools, shall go
    astray.
9 No lion shall be there,
  nor shall any ravenous beast come up
    on it;
they shall not be found there,
  but the redeemed shall walk there.
10 And the ransomed of the LORD shall return,
  and come to Zion with singing;
everlasting joy shall be upon their heads;
  they shall obtain joy and gladness,
  and sorrow and sighing shall flee away.

Catholic Connections

ADVENT REJOICING

Isaiah 35.1–10 is read at Mass on the third Sunday of Advent. The third candle of the Advent wreath and the vestments that priests wear on this Sunday are often the color rose, which is a symbol for rejoicing. Together, this passage from Isaiah and this color remind us that the coming of the Messiah is a joyful event.

▸ Isa 35.1–10

Sennacherib Threatens Jerusalem
(2 Kings 18.13–37; 2 Chr 32.1–19)

36 In the fourteenth year of King
      Hez·e·ki'ah, King Sen·nach'e·rib of As-
syria came up against all the fortified cities of Judah
and captured them. 2 The king of Assyria sent the
Rab'sha·keh from La'chish to King Hez·e·ki'ah at
Jerusalem, with a great army. He stood by the con-
duit of the upper pool on the highway to the
Fuller's Field. 3 And there came out to him
E·li'a·kim son of Hil·ki'ah, who was in charge of the
palace, and Sheb'na the secretary, and Jo'ah son of
A'saph, the recorder.

4 The Rab'sha·keh said to them, "Say to
Hez·e·ki'ah: Thus says the great king, the king of Assyria: On what do you base this confidence of
yours? 5 Do you think that mere words are strategy
and power for war? On whom do you now rely,
that you have rebelled against me? 6 See, you are relying on Egypt, that broken reed of a staff, which
will pierce the hand of anyone who leans on it.
Such is Pharaoh king of Egypt to all who rely on
him. 7 But if you say to me, 'We rely on the LORD
our God,' is it not he whose high places and altars
Hez·e·ki'ah has removed, saying to Judah and to
Jerusalem, 'You shall worship before this altar'?
8 Come now, make a wager with my master the
king of Assyria: I will give you two thousand

---

q Cn: Heb *in the haunt of jackals is her resting place*   *r* Or *pass it by*   *s* Cn: Heb *for them* horses, if you are able on your part to set riders on them. 9 How then can you repulse a single captain among the least of my master's servants, when you rely on Egypt for chariots and for horsemen? 10 Moreover, is it without the LORD that I have come up against this land to destroy it? The LORD said to me, Go up against this land, and destroy it."

11 Then E·li′a·kim, Sheb′na, and Jō′ah said to the Rab′sha·keh, "Please speak to your servants in Ar·a·mā′ic, for we understand it; do not speak to us in the language of Judah within the hearing of the people who are on the wall." 12 But the Rab′sha·keh said, "Has my master sent me to speak these words to your master and to you, and not to the people sitting on the wall, who are doomed with you to eat their own dung and drink their own urine?"

13 Then the Rab′sha·keh stood and called out in a loud voice in the language of Judah, "Hear the words of the great king, the king of Assyria! 14 Thus says the king: 'Do not let Hez·e·kī′ah deceive you, for he will not be able to deliver you. 15 Do not let Hez·e·kī′ah make you rely on the LORD by saying, The LORD will surely deliver us; this city will not be given into the hand of the king of Assyria.' 16 Do not listen to Hez·e·kī′ah; for thus says the king of Assyria: 'Make your peace with me and come out to me; then every one of you will eat from your own vine and your own fig tree and drink water from your own cistern, 17 until I come and take you away to a land like your own land, a land of grain and wine, a land of bread and vineyards. 18 Do not let Hez·e·kī′ah mislead you by saying, The LORD will save us. Has any of the gods of the nations saved their land out of the hand of the king of Assyria? 19 Where are the gods of Hā′math and Ar′pad? Where are the gods of Seph·ar·vā′im? Have they delivered Sa·mār′i·a out of my hand? 20 Who among all the gods of these countries have saved their countries out of my hand, that the LORD should save Jerusalem out of my hand?' "

21 But they were silent and answered him not a word, for the king's command was, "Do not answer him." 22 Then E·li′a·kim son of Hil·kī′ah, who was in charge of the palace, and Sheb′na the secretary, and Jō′ah son of Ā′saph, the recorder, came to Hez·e·kī′ah with their clothes torn, and told him the words of the Rab′sha·keh.

Hezekiah Consults Isaiah
(2 Kings 19.1–13)

37 When King Hez·e·kī′ah heard it, he tore his clothes, covered himself with sackcloth, and went into the house of the LORD. 2 And he sent E·li′a·kim, who was in charge of the palace, and Sheb′na the secretary, and the senior priests, covered with sackcloth, to the prophet Ī·sāi′ah son of Ā′moz. 3 They said to him, "Thus says Hez·e·

kī′ah, This day is a day of distress, of rebuke, and of disgrace; children have come to the birth, and there is no strength to bring them forth. 4 It may be that the LORD your God heard the words of the Rab′sha·keh, whom his master the king of Assyria has sent to mock the living God, and will rebuke the words that the LORD your God has heard; therefore lift up your prayer for the remnant that is left."

5 When the servants of King Hez·e·kī′ah came to Ī·sāi′ah, 6 Ī·sāi′ah said to them, "Say to your master, 'Thus says the LORD: Do not be afraid because of the words that you have heard, with which the servants of the king of Assyria have reviled me. 7 I myself will put a spirit in him, so that he shall hear a rumor, and return to his own land; I will cause him to fall by the sword in his own land.' "

8 The Rab′sha·keh returned, and found the king of Assyria fighting against Lib′nah; for he had heard that the king had left Lā′chish. 9 Now the king[t] heard concerning King Tir·hā′kah of Ethiopia,[u] "He has set out to fight against you." When he heard it, he sent messengers to Hez·e·kī′ah, saying, 10 "Thus shall you speak to King Hez·e·kī′ah of Judah: Do not let your God on whom you rely deceive you by promising that Jerusalem will not be given into the hand of the king of Assyria. 11 See, you have heard what the kings of Assyria have done to all lands, destroying them utterly. Shall you be delivered? 12 Have the gods of the nations delivered them, the nations that my predecessors destroyed, Gō′zan, Har′an, Rē′zeph, and the people of Eden who were in Te·las′sar? 13 Where is the king of Hā′math, the king of Ar′pad, the king of the city of Seph·ar·vā′im, the king of Hē′na, or the king of Iv′vah?"

Hezekiah's Prayer
(2 Kings 19.14–34)

14 Hez·e·kī′ah received the letter from the hand of the messengers and read it; then Hez·e·kī′ah went up to the house of the LORD and spread it before the LORD. 15 And Hez·e·kī′ah prayed to the LORD, saying: 16 "O LORD of hosts, God of Israel, who are enthroned above the cherubim, you are God, you alone, of all the kingdoms of the earth; you have made heaven and earth. 17 Incline your ear, O LORD, and hear; open your eyes, O LORD, and see; hear all the words of Sen·nach′e·rib, which he has sent to mock the living God. 18 Truly, O LORD, the kings of Assyria have laid waste all the nations and their lands, 19 and have hurled their gods into the fire, though they were no gods, but the work of human hands—wood and stone—and so they were destroyed. 20 So now, O LORD our God, save us from his hand, so that all the kingdoms of the earth may know that you alone are the LORD."

---

t Heb *he*   u Or *Nubia*; Heb *Cush*

I
S
A

21 Then Ī•sāi′ah son of Ā′moz sent to Hez•e-kī′ah, saying: "Thus says the LORD, the God of Israel: Because you have prayed to me concerning King Sen•nach′e•rib of Assyria, 22 this is the word that the LORD has spoken concerning him:

> She despises you, she scorns you—
> virgin daughter Zion;
> she tosses her head—behind your back,
> daughter Jerusalem.

23 "Whom have you mocked and reviled?
> Against whom have you raised your voice
> and haughtily lifted your eyes?
> Against the Holy One of Israel!
24 By your servants you have mocked the Lord,
> and you have said, 'With my many chariots
> I have gone up the heights of the mountains,
> to the far recesses of Lebanon;
> I felled its tallest cedars,
> its choicest cypresses;
> I came to its remotest height,
> its densest forest.
25 I dug wells
> and drank waters,
> I dried up with the sole of my foot
> all the streams of Egypt.'

26 "Have you not heard
> that I determined it long ago?
> I planned from days of old
> what now I bring to pass,
> that you should make fortified cities
> crash into heaps of ruins,
27 while their inhabitants, shorn of strength,
> are dismayed and confounded;
> they have become like plants of the field
> and like tender grass,
> like grass on the housetops,
> blighted[v] before it is grown.

28 "I know your rising up[w] and your sitting down,
> your going out and coming in,
> and your raging against me.
29 Because you have raged against me
> and your arrogance has come to my ears,
> I will put my hook in your nose
> and my bit in your mouth;
> I will turn you back on the way
> by which you came.

30 "And this shall be the sign for you: This year eat what grows of itself, and in the second year what springs from that; then in the third year sow, reap, plant vineyards, and eat their fruit. 31 The surviving remnant of the house of Judah shall again take root downward, and bear fruit upward; 32 for from Jerusalem a remnant shall go out, and from Mount Zion a band of survivors. The zeal of the LORD of hosts will do this.

33 "Therefore thus says the LORD concerning the king of Assyria: He shall not come into this city, shoot an arrow there, come before it with a shield, or cast up a siege ramp against it. 34 By the way that he came, by the same he shall return; he shall not come into this city, says the LORD. 35 For I will defend this city to save it, for my own sake and for the sake of my servant David."

Sennacherib's Defeat and Death
(2 Kings 19.35–37)

36 Then the angel of the LORD set out and struck down one hundred eighty-five thousand in the camp of the Assyrians; when morning dawned, they were all dead bodies. 37 Then King Sen•nach′-e•rib of Assyria left, went home, and lived at Nin′-e•veh. 38 As he was worshiping in the house of his god Nis′roch, his sons A•dram′me•lech and Sha•rē′-zer killed him with the sword, and they escaped into the land of Ar′a•rat. His son Ē′sar-had′don succeeded him.

Hezekiah's Illness
(2 Kings 20.1–11; 2 Chr 32.24–26)

38 In those days Hez•e•kī′ah became sick and was at the point of death. The prophet Ī•sāi′ah son of Ā′moz came to him, and said to him, "Thus says the LORD: Set your house in order, for you shall die; you shall not recover." 2 Then Hez•e•kī′ah turned his face to the wall, and prayed to the LORD: 3 "Remember now, O LORD, I implore you, how I have walked before you in faithfulness with a whole heart, and have done what is good in your sight." And Hez•e•kī′ah wept bitterly.

4 Then the word of the LORD came to Ī•sāi′ah: 5 "Go and say to Hez•e•kī′ah, Thus says the LORD, the God of your ancestor David: I have heard your prayer, I have seen your tears; I will add fifteen years to your life. 6 I will deliver you and this city out of the hand of the king of Assyria, and defend this city.

7 "This is the sign to you from the LORD, that the LORD will do this thing that he has promised: 8 See, I will make the shadow cast by the declining sun on the dial of Ā′haz turn back ten steps." So the sun turned back on the dial the ten steps by which it had declined.[x]

9 A writing of King Hez•e•kī′ah of Judah, after he had been sick and had recovered from his sickness:
10 I said: In the noontide of my days

---

v With 2 Kings 19.26: Heb *field*   w Q Ms Gk: MT lacks *your rising up*   x Meaning of Heb uncertain

I must depart;
I am consigned to the gates of Shĕ′ōl
    for the rest of my years.
11 I said, I shall not see the LORD
    in the land of the living;
I shall look upon mortals no more
    among the inhabitants of the world.
12 My dwelling is plucked up and removed
       from me
    like a shepherd's tent;
like a weaver I have rolled up my life;
    he cuts me off from the loom;
from day to night you bring me to an end;*y*
13   I cry for help*z* until morning;
like a lion he breaks all my bones;
    from day to night you bring me to an
    end.*y*

14 Like a swallow or a crane*y* I clamor,
    I moan like a dove.
My eyes are weary with looking upward.
    O Lord, I am oppressed; be my security!
15 But what can I say? For he has spoken to me,
    and he himself has done it.
All my sleep has fled*a*
    because of the bitterness of my soul.

16 O Lord, by these things people live,
    and in all these is the life of my spirit.*y*
    Oh, restore me to health and make
      me live!
17 Surely it was for my welfare
    that I had great bitterness;
but you have held back*b* my life
    from the pit of destruction,
for you have cast all my sins
    behind your back.
18 For Shĕ′ōl cannot thank you,
    death cannot praise you;
those who go down to the Pit cannot hope
    for your faithfulness.
19 The living, the living, they thank you,
    as I do this day;
fathers make known to children
    your faithfulness.

20 The LORD will save me,
    and we will sing to stringed
      instruments*c*
all the days of our lives,
    at the house of the LORD.

21 Now Ĭ•sāi′ah had said, "Let them take a lump of figs, and apply it to the boil, so that he may recover." 22 Hĕz•e•kī′ah also had said, "What is the sign that I shall go up to the house of the LORD?"

Envoys from Babylon Welcomed
(2 Kings 20.12–19)

39 At that time King Mer′o•dach-bal′a•dan son of Bal′a•dan of Babylon sent envoys with letters and a present to Hĕz•e•kī′ah, for he heard that he had been sick and had recovered. 2 Hĕz•e•kī′ah welcomed them; he showed them his treasure house, the silver, the gold, the spices, the precious oil, his whole armory, all that was found in his storehouses. There was nothing in his house or in all his realm that Hĕz•e•kī′ah did not show them. 3 Then the prophet Ĭ•sāi′ah came to King Hĕz•e•kī′ah and said to him, "What did these men say? From where did they come to you?" Hĕz•e•kī′ah answered, "They have come to me from a far country, from Babylon." 4 He said, "What have they seen in your house?" Hĕz•e•kī′ah answered, "They have seen all that is in my house; there is nothing in my storehouses that I did not show them."

5 Then Ĭ•sāi′ah said to Hĕz•e•kī′ah, "Hear the word of the LORD of hosts: 6 Days are coming when all that is in your house, and that which your ancestors have stored up until this day, shall be carried to Babylon; nothing shall be left, says the LORD. 7 Some of your own sons who are born to you shall be taken away; they shall be eunuchs in the palace of the king of Babylon." 8 Then Hĕz•e•kī′ah said to Ĭ•sāi′ah, "The word of the LORD that you have spoken is good." For he thought, "There will be peace and security in my days."

---

y Meaning of Heb uncertain   *z* Cn: Meaning of Heb uncertain   *a* Cn Compare Syr: Heb *I will walk slowly all my years*   *b* Cn Compare Gk Vg: Heb *loved*   *c* Heb *my stringed instruments*

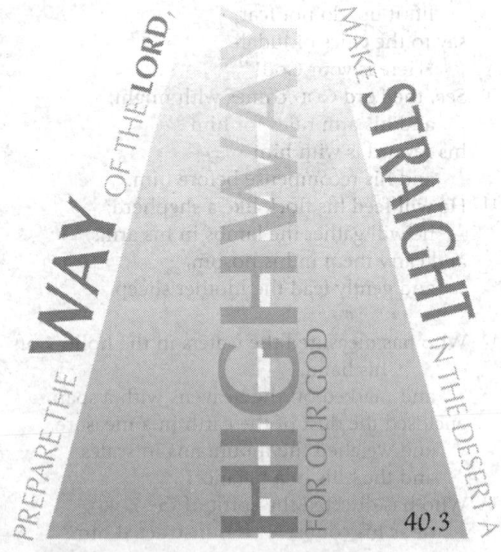

PREPARE THE WAY OF THE LORD, MAKE STRAIGHT IN THE DESERT A HIGHWAY FOR OUR GOD

40.3

God's People Are Comforted
(Cp Lk 3.4–6)

40 Comfort, O comfort my people,
          says your God.
2 Speak tenderly to Jerusalem,
     and cry to her
that she has served her term,
     that her penalty is paid,
that she has received from the LORD's hand
     double for all her sins.

3 A voice cries out:
"In the wilderness prepare the way of the LORD,
     make straight in the desert a highway for
          our God.
4 Every valley shall be lifted up,
     and every mountain and hill be made low;
the uneven ground shall become level,
     and the rough places a plain.
5 Then the glory of the LORD shall be revealed,
     and all people shall see it together,
for the mouth of the LORD has spoken."

6 A voice says, "Cry out!"
     And I said, "What shall I cry?"
All people are grass,
     their constancy is like the flower of the
          field.
7 The grass withers, the flower fades,
     when the breath of the LORD blows upon it;
     surely the people are grass.
8 The grass withers, the flower fades;
     but the word of our God will stand forever.
9 Get you up to a high mountain,
     O Zion, herald of good tidings;*d*
lift up your voice with strength,
     O Jerusalem, herald of good tidings,*e*
     lift it up, do not fear;
say to the cities of Judah,
     "Here is your God!"
10 See, the Lord GOD comes with might,
     and his arm rules for him;
his reward is with him,
     and his recompense before him.
11 He will feed his flock like a shepherd;
     he will gather the lambs in his arms,
and carry them in his bosom,
     and gently lead the mother sheep.

12 Who has measured the waters in the hollow of
          his hand
     and marked off the heavens with a span,
enclosed the dust of the earth in a measure,
     and weighed the mountains in scales
     and the hills in a balance?
13 Who has directed the spirit of the LORD,
     or as his counselor has instructed him?

PRAY IT!
The Hope
of Second Isaiah

Second Isaiah prophesies to the Israelites living in exile in Babylon with words full of love and hope: "Comfort, O comfort my people, / says your God" (Isa 40.1). Isaiah promises these Israelites a new liberation and the eventual restoration of Jerusalem and the Temple (44.26–28).

The author of the Gospel of Luke uses Isa 40.3–5 to describe the ministry of John the Baptist in announcing Jesus' arrival (Lk 3.4–6). This writer wants to make it clear that Isaiah's promises are answered by the coming of Jesus.

In your prayer, reflect or journal on the following questions:
- Is there hope for our society?
- What are some things that you are hopeful for?
- Imagine God is speaking words of hope to you. What is God saying?

▶ **Isa 40.1–5**

14 Whom did he consult for his enlightenment,
     and who taught him the path of justice?
Who taught him knowledge,
     and showed him the way of understanding?
15 Even the nations are like a drop from a bucket,
     and are accounted as dust on the scales;
     see, he takes up the isles like fine dust.
16 Lebanon would not provide fuel enough,
     nor are its animals enough for a burnt
          offering.
17 All the nations are as nothing before him;
     they are accounted by him as less than
          nothing and emptiness.

18 To whom then will you liken God,
     or what likeness compare with him?
19 An idol?—A workman casts it,
     and a goldsmith overlays it with gold,
     and casts for it silver chains.
20 As a gift one chooses mulberry wood*f*
     —wood that will not rot—

---

d Or *O herald of good tidings to Zion*   *e* Or *O herald of good tidings to Jerusalem*   *f* Meaning of Heb uncertain

then seeks out a skilled artisan
  to set up an image that will not topple.

21 Have you not known? Have you not heard?
    Has it not been told you from the
      beginning?
    Have you not understood from the
      foundations of the earth?
22 It is he who sits above the circle of the earth,
    and its inhabitants are like grasshoppers;
  who stretches out the heavens like a curtain,
    and spreads them like a tent to live in;
23 who brings princes to naught,
    and makes the rulers of the earth as
      nothing.

24 Scarcely are they planted, scarcely sown,
    scarcely has their stem taken root in the
      earth,
  when he blows upon them, and they wither,
    and the tempest carries them off like
      stubble.

25 To whom then will you compare me,
    or who is my equal? says the Holy One.
26 Lift up your eyes on high and see:
    Who created these?

He who brings out their host and numbers
  them,
    calling them all by name;
because he is great in strength,
  mighty in power,
    not one is missing.

27 Why do you say, O Jacob,
    and speak, O Israel,
  "My way is hidden from the LORD,
    and my right is disregarded by my God"?
28 Have you not known? Have you not
    heard?
  The LORD is the everlasting God,
    the Creator of the ends of the earth.
  He does not faint or grow weary;
    his understanding is unsearchable.
29 He gives power to the faint,
    and strengthens the powerless.
30 Even youths will faint and be weary,
    and the young will fall exhausted;
31 but those who wait for the LORD shall renew
      their strength,
    they shall mount up with wings like
      eagles,
  they shall run and not be weary,
    they shall walk and not faint.

Between a Rock and a Soft Place

Joe. Is God a rock or a pillow?

Valerie. A rock, I guess. God is strong and reliable. When I think of a rock, I think of something I can brace myself against when things are changing all around me.

Joe. For me, God is a pillow. God is someone I can come home to and be comfortable with. I can sit back and relax, leaning against God and feeling at ease.

Valerie. But a pillow is so ordinary and doesn't have any character. A rock is distinctive and doesn't change.

Joe. But a rock is so hard and unyielding. What kind of compassion can you get from a rock?

Valerie. What kind of strength can you draw from a pillow?

Joe. The strength that comes from relaxing and resting and being comforted. The strength that comes from being energized to go forward again.

Valerie. I'm sorry, but a pillow seems too soft to be like God.

Joe. And a rock seems much too hard.

Valerie. Isn't God both a pillow and a rock? In chapter 40 of Isaiah, it seems that the pillow image wins out. The picture of a comforting God gathering the lambs conveys a softness that is sometimes hard to find in the Old Testament.

Joe. That's true. There are times when we need a pillow to get comfortable. It is good to know that God is there waiting for us, helping us to feel at home.

Valerie. And it is also good to know that God the rock is there for the times when we need something to hold on to (see Ps 18.2).

▸ Isa 40.1–11

do not fear, for I am with you,
do not be afraid, for I am your God;

'You are
my servant,
I have chosen you
and not cast you off;

I will strengthen you, I will help you,
I will uphold you with my victorious right hand.

41.9–10

Israel Assured of God's Help

41 Listen to me in silence, O coastlands;
      let the peoples renew their strength;
let them approach, then let them speak;
   let us together draw near for judgment.

2 Who has roused a victor from the east,
      summoned him to his service?
He delivers up nations to him,
   and tramples kings under foot;
he makes them like dust with his sword,
   like driven stubble with his bow.

3 He pursues them and passes on safely,
      scarcely touching the path with his feet.

4 Who has performed and done this,
      calling the generations from the beginning?
I, the LORD, am first,
   and will be with the last.

5 The coastlands have seen and are afraid,
   the ends of the earth tremble;
   they have drawn near and come.

6 Each one helps the other,
   saying to one another, "Take courage!"

7 The artisan encourages the goldsmith,
   and the one who smooths with the hammer
      encourages the one who strikes the
         anvil,

saying of the soldering, "It is good";
   and they fasten it with nails so that it
      cannot be moved.

8 But you, Israel, my servant,
   Jacob, whom I have chosen,
   the offspring of Abraham, my friend;

9 you whom I took from the ends of the
         earth,
   and called from its farthest corners,
saying to you, "You are my servant,
   I have chosen you and not cast you off";

10 do not fear, for I am with you,
   do not be afraid, for I am your God;
I will strengthen you, I will help you,
   I will uphold you with my victorious right
      hand.

11 Yes, all who are incensed against you
   shall be ashamed and disgraced;
those who strive against you
   shall be as nothing and shall perish.

12 You shall seek those who contend with you,
   but you shall not find them;
those who war against you
   shall be as nothing at all.

13 For I, the LORD your God,
   hold your right hand;

it is I who say to you, "Do not fear,
    I will help you."

14 Do not fear, you worm Jacob,
        you insects Israel!
I will help you, says the LORD;
        your Redeemer is the Holy One of Israel.
15 Now, I will make of you a threshing sledge,
        sharp, new, and having teeth;
you shall thresh the mountains and crush them,
        and you shall make the hills like chaff.
16 You shall winnow them and the wind shall
            carry them away,
        and the tempest shall scatter them.
Then you shall rejoice in the LORD;
        in the Holy One of Israel you shall glory.

17 When the poor and needy seek water,
        and there is none,
        and their tongue is parched with thirst,
I the LORD will answer them,
        I the God of Israel will not forsake them.
18 I will open rivers on the bare heights,[h]
        and fountains in the midst of the valleys;
I will make the wilderness a pool of water,
        and the dry land springs of water.
19 I will put in the wilderness the cedar,
        the acacia, the myrtle, and the olive;
I will set in the desert the cypress,
        the plane and the pine together,
20 so that all may see and know,
        all may consider and understand,
that the hand of the LORD has done this,
        the Holy One of Israel has created it.

The Futility of Idols

21 Set forth your case, says the LORD;
        bring your proofs, says the King of Jacob.
22 Let them bring them, and tell us
        what is to happen.
Tell us the former things, what they are,
        so that we may consider them,
and that we may know their outcome;
        or declare to us the things to come.
23 Tell us what is to come hereafter,
        that we may know that you are gods;
do good, or do harm,
        that we may be afraid and terrified.
24 You, indeed, are nothing
        and your work is nothing at all;
        whoever chooses you is an abomination.

25 I stirred up one from the north, and he has
            come,
        from the rising of the sun he was
            summoned by name.[i]
He shall trample[j] on rulers as on mortar,

as the potter treads clay.
26 Who declared it from the beginning, so that we
            might know,
        and beforehand, so that we might say, "He
            is right"?
There was no one who declared it, none who
            proclaimed,
        none who heard your words.
27 I first have declared it to Zion,[k]
        and I give to Jerusalem a herald of good
            tidings.
28 But when I look there is no one;
        among these there is no counselor
        who, when I ask, gives an answer.
29 No, they are all a delusion;
        their works are nothing;
        their images are empty wind.

The Servant, a Light to the Nations

42 Here is my servant, whom I uphold,
        my chosen, in whom my soul
            delights;
I have put my spirit upon him;
        he will bring forth justice to the nations.
2 He will not cry or lift up his voice,
        or make it heard in the street;
3 a bruised reed he will not break,
        and a dimly burning wick he will not
            quench;
        he will faithfully bring forth justice.
4 He will not grow faint or be crushed
        until he has established justice in the
            earth;
        and the coastlands wait for his teaching.

---

g Syr: Heb *men of*   h Or *trails*   i Cn Compare Q Ms Gk: MT
and he shall call on my name   j Cn: Heb *come*   k Cn: Heb
First to Zion—Behold, behold them

PRAY IT!
The Servant's Mission

Read Isa 42.1–7 and then reflect or
journal on the following questions:
- What is the servant's mission from
  God?
- How does Jesus fulfill this mission
  (compare Isa 42.6–7 with Lk 4.18–19)?
- How do you participate in this
  mission?

▶ Isa 42.1–7

did you KNOW?

The Servant Songs

Second Isaiah's four songs of the servant (Isa 42.1–7; 49.1–6; 50.4–9; 52.13—53.12) have had an important place in Christian theology and worship. They portray the qualities of the ideal servant leader. Through these songs, the prophet speaks of hope: the faithful Israelites, though in exile, are still God's servants (42.1), chosen from the womb (49.1). Through their courageous suffering (50.7–8), Israel will be restored to bring salvation to all nations (53.5).

It is not surprising that the early Christians saw in the servant songs a remarkable similarity to Jesus' words and actions. The fourth song in particular—which talks of a suffering servant—helped the followers of Jesus understand his suffering and humiliating death on the cross. Because of this, these passages have become part of the Catholic church's formal worship during Holy Week (the week before Easter): Isa 42.1–7 on Monday, 49.1–6 on Tuesday, 50.4–9 on Wednesday, and 52.13—53.12 on Friday.

▶ Isa 42.1–7

5 Thus says God, the LORD,
   who created the heavens and stretched
      them out,
   who spread out the earth and what comes
      from it,
who gives breath to the people upon it
   and spirit to those who walk in it:
6 I am the LORD, I have called you in righteousness,
   I have taken you by the hand and kept you;
I have given you as a covenant to the people,[l]
   a light to the nations,
7   to open the eyes that are blind,
to bring out the prisoners from the dungeon,
   from the prison those who sit in darkness.
8 I am the LORD, that is my name;
   my glory I give to no other,
   nor my praise to idols.
9 See, the former things have come to pass,
   and new things I now declare;
before they spring forth,
   I tell you of them.

A Hymn of Praise

10 Sing to the LORD a new song,
   his praise from the end of the earth!
Let the sea roar[m] and all that fills it,
   the coastlands and their inhabitants.
11 Let the desert and its towns lift up their
      voice,
   the villages that Kē′dar inhabits;
let the inhabitants of Sē′la sing for joy,
   let them shout from the tops of the
      mountains.
12 Let them give glory to the LORD,
   and declare his praise in the coastlands.
13 The LORD goes forth like a soldier,
   like a warrior he stirs up his fury;
he cries out, he shouts aloud,
   he shows himself mighty against his foes.

14 For a long time I have held my peace,
   I have kept still and restrained myself;
now I will cry out like a woman in labor,
   I will gasp and pant.
15 I will lay waste mountains and hills,
   and dry up all their herbage;
I will turn the rivers into islands,
   and dry up the pools.
16 I will lead the blind
   by a road they do not know,
by paths they have not known
   I will guide them.
I will turn the darkness before them into light,
   the rough places into level ground.
These are the things I will do,
   and I will not forsake them.
17 They shall be turned back and utterly put to
      shame—
   those who trust in carved images,
who say to cast images,
   "You are our gods."

18 Listen, you that are deaf;
   and you that are blind, look up and see!
19 Who is blind but my servant,
   or deaf like my messenger whom I send?
Who is blind like my dedicated one,
   or blind like the servant of the LORD?
20 He sees many things, but does[n] not observe
      them;
   his ears are open, but he does not hear.

Israel's Disobedience

21 The LORD was pleased, for the sake of his
      righteousness,

---

l Meaning of Heb uncertain   m Cn Compare Ps 96.11;
98.7: Heb Those who go down to the sea   n Heb You see many
things but do

to magnify his teaching and make it
glorious.

22 But this is a people robbed and plundered,
all of them are trapped in holes
and hidden in prisons;
they have become a prey with no one to
rescue,
a spoil with no one to say, "Restore!"

23 Who among you will give heed to this,
who will attend and listen for the time to
come?

24 Who gave up Jacob to the spoiler,
and Israel to the robbers?
Was it not the LORD, against whom we have
sinned,
in whose ways they would not walk,
and whose law they would not obey?

25 So he poured upon him the heat of his
anger
and the fury of war;
it set him on fire all around, but he did not
understand;
it burned him, but he did not take it to
heart.

Restoration and Protection Promised

43 But now thus says the LORD,
he who created you, O Jacob,
he who formed you, O Israel:
Do not fear, for I have redeemed you;
I have called you by name, you are mine.

2 When you pass through the waters, I will be
with you;
and through the rivers, they shall not
overwhelm you;
when you walk through fire you shall not be
burned,
and the flame shall not consume you.

3 For I am the LORD your God,
the Holy One of Israel, your Savior.
I give Egypt as your ransom,
Ethiopia⁰ and Sē'ba in exchange for you.

4 Because you are precious in my sight,
and honored, and I love you,
I give people in return for you,
nations in exchange for your life.

5 Do not fear, for I am with you;
I will bring your offspring from the east,
and from the west I will gather you;

6 I will say to the north, "Give them up,"
and to the south, "Do not withhold;
bring my sons from far away
and my daughters from the end of the
earth—

7 everyone who is called by my name,
whom I created for my glory,
whom I formed and made."

8 Bring forth the people who are blind, yet have
eyes,
who are deaf, yet have ears!

9 Let all the nations gather together,
and let the peoples assemble.
Who among them declared this,
and foretold to us the former things?
Let them bring their witnesses to justify them,
and let them hear and say, "It is true."

10 You are my witnesses, says the LORD,
and my servant whom I have chosen,
so that you may know and believe me
and understand that I am he.
Before me no god was formed,
nor shall there be any after me.

11 I, I am the LORD,
and besides me there is no savior.

12 I declared and saved and proclaimed,
when there was no strange god among you;
and you are my witnesses, says the LORD.

13 I am God, and also henceforth I am He;
there is no one who can deliver from my
hand;
I work and who can hinder it?

PRAY IT!
Be Not Afraid

The words of Isa 43.1–5 might sound
familiar to you. Most of the song "Be
Not Afraid" is based on these verses.
    God calls us to be disciples and lead-
ers. God calls us from within our faith
community to serve others. How easy is
it for you to go forth and do God's work?
How easy is it to be not afraid?

    Be not afraid.
    I go before you always.
    Come follow me,
    and I will give you rest.
        (From Bob Dufford, "Be Not Afraid")

▶ Isa 43.1–5

14 Thus says the LORD,
your Redeemer, the Holy One of Israel:
For your sake I will send to Babylon
and break down all the bars,
and the shouting of the Chal·dē'ans will be
turned to lamentation.ᵖ

15 I am the LORD, your Holy One,

⁰ Or *Nubia*; Heb *Cush*   ᵖ Meaning of Heb uncertain

the Creator of Israel, your King.

16 Thus says the LORD,
   who makes a way in the sea,
   a path in the mighty waters,
17 who brings out chariot and horse,
   army and warrior;
 they lie down, they cannot rise,
   they are extinguished, quenched like a wick:
18 Do not remember the former things,
   or consider the things of old.
19 I am about to do a new thing;
   now it springs forth, do you not perceive it?
 I will make a way in the wilderness
   and rivers in the desert.
20 The wild animals will honor me,
   the jackals and the ostriches;
 for I give water in the wilderness,
   rivers in the desert,
 to give drink to my chosen people,
21   the people whom I formed for myself
 so that they might declare my praise.

22 Yet you did not call upon me, O Jacob;
   but you have been weary of me, O Israel!
23 You have not brought me your sheep for burnt
     offerings,
   or honored me with your sacrifices.
 I have not burdened you with offerings,
   or wearied you with frankincense.
24 You have not bought me sweet cane with
     money,
   or satisfied me with the fat of your
     sacrifices.
 But you have burdened me with your sins;
   you have wearied me with your iniquities.

25 I, I am He
   who blots out your transgressions for my
     own sake,
   and I will not remember your sins.
26 Accuse me, let us go to trial;
   set forth your case, so that you may be
     proved right.
27 Your first ancestor sinned,
   and your interpreters transgressed
     against me.
28 Therefore I profaned the princes of the
     sanctuary,
   I delivered Jacob to utter destruction,
   and Israel to reviling.

God's Blessing on Israel

44 But now hear, O Jacob my servant,
   Israel whom I have chosen!
2 Thus says the LORD who made you,
   who formed you in the womb and will help
     you:

Do not fear, O Jacob my servant,
   Jesh′ū•run whom I have chosen.
3 For I will pour water on the thirsty land,
   and streams on the dry ground;
 I will pour my spirit upon your descendants,
   and my blessing on your offspring.
4 They shall spring up like a green tamarisk,
   like willows by flowing streams.
5 This one will say, "I am the LORD's,"
   another will be called by the name of Jacob,
 yet another will write on the hand, "The
     LORD's,"
   and adopt the name of Israel.

6 Thus says the LORD, the King of Israel,
   and his Redeemer, the LORD of hosts:
 I am the first and I am the last;
   besides me there is no god.
7 Who is like me? Let them proclaim it,
   let them declare and set it forth before me.
 Who has announced from of old the things to
     come?^q
   Let them tell us^r what is yet to be.
8 Do not fear, or be afraid;
   have I not told you from of old and
     declared it?
   You are my witnesses!
 Is there any god besides me?
   There is no other rock; I know not one.

The Absurdity of Idol Worship

9 All who make idols are nothing, and the things they delight in do not profit; their witnesses neither see nor know. And so they will be put to shame. 10 Who would fashion a god or cast an image that can do no good? 11 Look, all its devotees shall be put to shame; the artisans too are merely human. Let them all assemble, let them stand up; they shall be terrified, they shall all be put to shame.

12 The ironsmith fashions it^s and works it over the coals, shaping it with hammers, and forging it with his strong arm; he becomes hungry and his strength fails, he drinks no water and is faint. 13 The carpenter stretches a line, marks it out with a stylus, fashions it with planes, and marks it with a compass; he makes it in human form, with human beauty, to be set up in a shrine. 14 He cuts down cedars or chooses a holm tree or an oak and lets it grow strong among the trees of the forest. He plants a cedar and the rain nourishes it. 15 Then it can be used as fuel. Part of it he takes and warms himself; he kindles a fire and bakes bread. Then he makes a god and worships it, makes it a carved image and

---

^q Cn: Heb *from my placing an eternal people and things to come*   ^r Tg: Heb *them*   ^s Cn: Heb *an ax*

bows down before it. 16 Half of it he burns in the fire; over this half he roasts meat, eats it and is satisfied. He also warms himself and says, "Ah, I am warm, I can feel the fire!" 17 The rest of it he makes into a god, his idol, bows down to it and worships it; he prays to it and says, "Save me, for you are my god!"

18 They do not know, nor do they comprehend; for their eyes are shut, so that they cannot see, and their minds as well, so that they cannot understand. 19 No one considers, nor is there knowledge or discernment to say, "Half of it I burned in the fire; I also baked bread on its coals, I roasted meat and have eaten. Now shall I make the rest of it an abomination? Shall I fall down before a block of wood?" 20 He feeds on ashes; a deluded mind has led him astray, and he cannot save himself or say, "Is not this thing in my right hand a fraud?"

Israel Is Not Forgotten

21 Remember these things, O Jacob,
    and Israel, for you are my servant;
I formed you, you are my servant;
    O Israel, you will not be forgotten by me.
22 I have swept away your transgressions like a
        cloud,
    and your sins like mist;
return to me, for I have redeemed you.

23 Sing, O heavens, for the LORD has done it;
    shout, O depths of the earth;
break forth into singing, O mountains,
    O forest, and every tree in it!
For the LORD has redeemed Jacob,
    and will be glorified in Israel.

24 Thus says the LORD, your Redeemer,
    who formed you in the womb:
I am the LORD, who made all things,
    who alone stretched out the heavens,
    who by myself spread out the earth;
25 who frustrates the omens of liars,
    and makes fools of diviners;
who turns back the wise,
    and makes their knowledge foolish;
26 who confirms the word of his servant,
    and fulfills the prediction of his
        messengers;
who says of Jerusalem, "It shall be inhabited,"
    and of the cities of Judah, "They shall be
        rebuilt,
    and I will raise up their ruins";
27 who says to the deep, "Be dry—
    I will dry up your rivers";
28 who says of Cyrus, "He is my shepherd,
    and he shall carry out all my purpose";
and who says of Jerusalem, "It shall be rebuilt,"

and of the temple, "Your foundation shall
    be laid."

Cyrus, God's Instrument

45 Thus says the LORD to his anointed, to
        Cyrus,
    whose right hand I have grasped
to subdue nations before him
    and strip kings of their robes,
to open doors before him—
    and the gates shall not be closed:
2 I will go before you
    and level the mountains,t
I will break in pieces the doors of bronze
    and cut through the bars of iron,
3 I will give you the treasures of darkness
    and riches hidden in secret places,
so that you may know that it is I, the LORD,
    the God of Israel, who call you by your
        name.
4 For the sake of my servant Jacob,
    and Israel my chosen,
I call you by your name,
    I surname you, though you do not
        know me.
5 I am the LORD, and there is no other;
    besides me there is no god.
I arm you, though you do not know me,
6 so that they may know, from the rising of the
        sun
    and from the west, that there is no one
        besides me;
I am the LORD, and there is no other.
7 I form light and create darkness,
    I make weal and create woe;
    I the LORD do all these things.

8 Shower, O heavens, from above,
    and let the skies rain down righteousness;
let the earth open, that salvation may
        spring up,u
    and let it cause righteousness to sprout up
        also;
    I the LORD have created it.

9 Woe to you who strive with your Maker,
    earthen vessels with the potter!v
Does the clay say to the one who fashions it,
    "What are you making"?
    or "Your work has no handles"?
10 Woe to anyone who says to a father, "What are
        you begetting?"
    or to a woman, "With what are you in
        labor?"

---

t Q Ms Gk: MT the swellings   u Q Ms: MT that they may bring
forth salvation   v Cn: Heb with the potsherds, or with the
potters

11 Thus says the LORD,
    the Holy One of Israel, and its Maker:
Will you question me[w] about my children,
    or command me concerning the work of
        my hands?
12 I made the earth,
    and created humankind upon it;
it was my hands that stretched out the heavens,
    and I commanded all their host.
13 I have aroused Cyrus[x] in righteousness,
    and I will make all his paths straight;
he shall build my city
    and set my exiles free,
not for price or reward,
    says the LORD of hosts.
14 Thus says the LORD:
The wealth of Egypt and the merchandise of
        Ethiopia,[y]
    and the Sa·bē′ans, tall of stature,
shall come over to you and be yours,
    they shall follow you;
    they shall come over in chains and bow
        down to you.
They will make supplication to you, saying,
    "God is with you alone, and there is no
        other;
    there is no god besides him."
15 Truly, you are a God who hides himself,
    O God of Israel, the Savior.
16 All of them are put to shame and confounded,
    the makers of idols go in confusion
        together.
17 But Israel is saved by the LORD
    with everlasting salvation;
you shall not be put to shame or confounded
    to all eternity.

18 For thus says the LORD,
who created the heavens
    (he is God!),
who formed the earth and made it
    (he established it;
he did not create it a chaos,
    he formed it to be inhabited!):
I am the LORD, and there is no other.
19 I did not speak in secret,
    in a land of darkness;
I did not say to the offspring of Jacob,
    "Seek me in chaos."
I the LORD speak the truth,
    I declare what is right.

Idols Cannot Save Babylon

20 Assemble yourselves and come together,
    draw near, you survivors of the nations!
They have no knowledge—
    those who carry about their wooden idols,

and keep on praying to a god
    that cannot save.
21 Declare and present your case;
    let them take counsel together!
Who told this long ago?
    Who declared it of old?
Was it not I, the LORD?
    There is no other god besides me,
a righteous God and a Savior;
    there is no one besides me.

22 Turn to me and be saved,
    all the ends of the earth!
For I am God, and there is no other.
23 By myself I have sworn,
    from my mouth has gone forth in
        righteousness
    a word that shall not return:
"To me every knee shall bow,
    every tongue shall swear."

24 Only in the LORD, it shall be said of me,
    are righteousness and strength;
all who were incensed against him
    shall come to him and be ashamed.
25 In the LORD all the offspring of Israel
    shall triumph and glory.

46 Bel bows down, Nē′bo stoops,
        their idols are on beasts and cattle;
these things you carry are loaded
    as burdens on weary animals.
2 They stoop, they bow down together;
    they cannot save the burden,
    but themselves go into captivity.

3 Listen to me, O house of Jacob,
    all the remnant of the house of Israel,
who have been borne by me from your birth,
    carried from the womb;
4 even to your old age I am he,
    even when you turn gray I will carry you.
I have made, and I will bear;
    I will carry and will save.

5 To whom will you liken me and make me
        equal,
    and compare me, as though we were
        alike?
6 Those who lavish gold from the purse,
    and weigh out silver in the scales—
they hire a goldsmith, who makes it into a god;
    then they fall down and worship!
7 They lift it to their shoulders, they carry it,

---

w Cn: Heb *Ask me of things to come*   x Heb *him*   y Or *Nubia*;
Heb *Cush*

they set it in its place, and it stands there;
　it cannot move from its place.
If one cries out to it, it does not answer
　or save anyone from trouble.

8 Remember this and consider,[z]
　　recall it to mind, you transgressors,
9 　remember the former things of old;
for I am God, and there is no other;
　I am God, and there is no one like me,
10 declaring the end from the beginning
　　and from ancient times things not yet done,
saying, "My purpose shall stand,
　and I will fulfill my intention,"
11 calling a bird of prey from the east,
　　the man for my purpose from a far
　　　country.
I have spoken, and I will bring it to pass;
　I have planned, and I will do it.

12 Listen to me, you stubborn of heart,
　　you who are far from deliverance:
13 I bring near my deliverance, it is not far off,
　　and my salvation will not tarry;
I will put salvation in Zion,
　for Israel my glory.

The Humiliation of Babylon

47 Come down and sit in the dust,
　　　virgin daughter Babylon!
Sit on the ground without a throne,
　daughter Chal·dē′a!
For you shall no more be called
　tender and delicate.
2 Take the millstones and grind meal,
　　remove your veil,
strip off your robe, uncover your legs,
　pass through the rivers.
3 Your nakedness shall be uncovered,
　　and your shame shall be seen.
I will take vengeance,
　and I will spare no one.
4 Our Redeemer—the LORD of hosts is his
　　name—
　is the Holy One of Israel.

5 Sit in silence, and go into darkness,
　　daughter Chal·dē′a!
For you shall no more be called
　the mistress of kingdoms.
6 I was angry with my people,
　　I profaned my heritage;
I gave them into your hand,
　you showed them no mercy;
on the aged you made your yoke
　exceedingly heavy.
7 You said, "I shall be mistress forever,"

so that you did not lay these things to heart
　or remember their end.

8 Now therefore hear this, you lover of pleasures,
　　who sit securely,
who say in your heart,
　"I am, and there is no one besides me;
I shall not sit as a widow
　or know the loss of children"—
9 both these things shall come you
　　in a moment, in one day:
the loss of children and widowhood
　shall come upon you in full measure,
in spite of your many sorceries
　and the great power of your enchantments.

10 You felt secure in your wickedness;
　　you said, "No one sees me."
Your wisdom and your knowledge
　led you astray,
and you said in your heart,
　"I am, and there is no one besides me."
11 But evil shall come upon you,
　　which you cannot charm away;
disaster shall fall upon you,
　which you will not be able to ward off;
and ruin shall come on you suddenly,
　of which you know nothing.

12 Stand fast in your enchantments
　　and your many sorceries,
　　with which you have labored from your
　　　youth;
perhaps you may be able to succeed,
　perhaps you may inspire terror.
13 You are wearied with your many consultations;
　　let those who study[z] the heavens
stand up and save you,
　those who gaze at the stars,
and at each new moon predict
　what[a] shall befall you.

14 See, they are like stubble,
　　the fire consumes them;
they cannot deliver themselves
　from the power of the flame.
No coal for warming oneself is this,
　no fire to sit before!
15 Such to you are those with whom you have
　　labored,
　　who have trafficked with you from your
　　　youth;
they all wander about in their own paths;
　there is no one to save you.

---

[z] Meaning of Heb uncertain   [a] Gk Syr Compare Vg: Heb
from what

ISA

God the Creator and Redeemer

48

Hear this, O house of Jacob,
  who are called by the name of Israel,
and who came forth from the loins[b] of
  Judah;
who swear by the name of the LORD,
  and invoke the God of Israel,
  but not in truth or right.
2 For they call themselves after the holy city,
  and lean on the God of Israel;
  the LORD of hosts is his name.

3 The former things I declared long ago,
  they went out from my mouth and I made
    them known;
  then suddenly I did them and they came to
    pass.
4 Because I know that you are obstinate,
  and your neck is an iron sinew
  and your forehead brass,
5 I declared them to you from long ago,
  before they came to pass I announced them
    to you,
so that you would not say, "My idol did them,
  my carved image and my cast image
    commanded them."

6 You have heard; now see all this;
  and will you not declare it?
From this time forward I make you hear new
    things,
  hidden things that you have not known.
7 They are created now, not long ago;
  before today you have never heard of them,
  so that you could not say, "I already knew
    them."
8 You have never heard, you have never known,
  from of old your ear has not been opened.
For I knew that you would deal very
    treacherously,
  and that from birth you were called a rebel.

9 For my name's sake I defer my anger,
  for the sake of my praise I restrain it for
    you,
  so that I may not cut you off.
10 See, I have refined you, but not like[c] silver;
  I have tested you in the furnace of adversity.
11 For my own sake, for my own sake, I do it,
  for why should my name[d] be profaned?
  My glory I will not give to another.

12 Listen to me, O Jacob,
  and Israel, whom I called:
I am He; I am the first,
  and I am the last.
13 My hand laid the foundation of the earth,

and my right hand spread out the heavens;
when I summon them,
  they stand at attention.

14 Assemble, all of you, and hear!
  Who among them has declared these
    things?
The LORD loves him;
  he shall perform his purpose on Babylon,
  and his arm shall be against the Chal•dē'ans.
15 I, even I, have spoken and called him,
  I have brought him, and he will prosper in
    his way.
16 Draw near to me, hear this!
  From the beginning I have not spoken in
    secret,
  from the time it came to be I have been
    there.
And now the Lord GOD has sent me and his
    spirit.

17 Thus says the LORD,
  your Redeemer, the Holy One of Israel:
I am the LORD your God,
  who teaches you for your own good,
  who leads you in the way you should go.
18 O that you had paid attention to my
    commandments!
  Then your prosperity would have been like
    a river,
  and your success like the waves of the sea;
19 your offspring would have been like the sand,
  and your descendants like its grains;
their name would never be cut off
  or destroyed from before me.

20 Go out from Babylon, flee from Chal•dē'a,
  declare this with a shout of joy, proclaim it,
send it forth to the end of the earth;
  say, "The LORD has redeemed his servant
    Jacob!"
21 They did not thirst when he led them through
    the deserts;
  he made water flow for them from the rock;
  he split open the rock and the water gushed
    out.

22 "There is no peace," says the LORD, "for the
    wicked."

The Servant's Mission

49

Listen to me, O coastlands,
  pay attention, you peoples from far
    away!

---

b Cn: Heb waters   c Cn: Heb with   d Gk Old Latin: Heb for
why should it

The LORD called me before I was born,
  while I was in my mother's womb he
    named me.
2 He made my mouth like a sharp sword,
  in the shadow of his hand he hid me;
he made me a polished arrow,
  in his quiver he hid me away.
3 And he said to me, "You are my servant,
  Israel, in whom I will be glorified."
4 But I said, "I have labored in vain,
  I have spent my strength for nothing and
    vanity;
yet surely my cause is with the LORD,
  and my reward with my God."

5 And now the LORD says,
  who formed me in the womb to be his
    servant,
to bring Jacob back to him,
  and that Israel might be gathered to him,
for I am honored in the sight of the LORD,
  and my God has become my strength—
6 he says,
"It is too light a thing that you should be my
    servant
  to raise up the tribes of Jacob
  and to restore the survivors of Israel;
I will give you as a light to the nations,
  that my salvation may reach to the end of
    the earth."

PRAY IT!
The Servant's Success

Isaiah 49.1–6 is the second of the four
servant songs (see "The Servant
Songs," Isa 42.1–7). In this passage, the
servant expresses a feeling of failure
(49.4). But God responds that the servant
will be a success, a "light to the nations"
(verse 6). In your prayer, reflect or journal on a time when you felt you failed, but
something good happened anyway. How
do you now see God's hand at work in the
situation?

▶ Isa 49.1–6

7 Thus says the LORD,
  the Redeemer of Israel and his Holy One,
to one deeply despised, abhorred by the
    nations,
  the slave of rulers,

"Kings shall see and stand up,
  princes, and they shall prostrate themselves,
because of the LORD, who is faithful,
  the Holy One of Israel, who has chosen
    you."

Zion's Children to Be Brought Home

8 Thus says the LORD:
In a time of favor I have answered you,
  on a day of salvation I have helped you;
I have kept you and given you
  as a covenant to the people,*e*
to establish the land,
  to apportion the desolate heritages;
9 saying to the prisoners, "Come out,"
  to those who are in darkness, "Show
    yourselves."
They shall feed along the ways,
  on all the bare heights*f* shall be their
    pasture;
10 they shall not hunger or thirst,
  neither scorching wind nor sun shall strike
    them down,
for he who has pity on them will lead them,
  and by springs of water will guide them.
11 And I will turn all my mountains into a road,
  and my highways shall be raised up.
12 Lo, these shall come from far away,
  and lo, these from the north and from the
    west,
  and these from the land of Sy̆·ē′nē.*g*

13 Sing for joy, O heavens, and exult, O earth;
  break forth, O mountains, into singing!
For the LORD has comforted his people,
  and will have compassion on his suffering
    ones.

14 But Zion said, "The LORD has forsaken me,
  my Lord has forgotten me."
15 Can a woman forget her nursing child,
  or show no compassion for the child of her
    womb?
Even these may forget,
  yet I will not forget you.
16 See, I have inscribed you on the palms of my
    hands;
  your walls are continually before me.
17 Your builders outdo your destroyers,*h*
  and those who laid you waste go away from
    you.
18 Lift up your eyes all around and see;
  they all gather, they come to you.
As I live, says the LORD,

---

e Meaning of Heb uncertain   *f* Or *the trails*   *g* Q Ms: MT
Sinim   *h* Or *Your children come swiftly; your destroyers*

I Will Never Forget You, My People

God is like a loving mother: forgiving, embracing, nurturing, tender, and gentle. The Hebrew root of the word _compassion_ means "womb." A God of compassion and love is by definition a God of the womb, a God of motherly tenderness.

Picture your mother figure: perhaps your birth mother, grandmother, adoptive mother, stepmother, or godmother. How do you see God's love reflected in her love?

▶ **Isa 49.13–16**

you shall put all of them on like an
    ornament,
and like a bride you shall bind them on.

19 Surely your waste and your desolate places
    and your devastated land—
surely now you will be too crowded for your
    inhabitants,
    and those who swallowed you up will be
    far away.
20 The children born in the time of your
    bereavement
    will yet say in your hearing:
"The place is too crowded for me;
    make room for me to settle."
21 Then you will say in your heart,
    "Who has borne me these?
I was bereaved and barren,
    exiled and put away—
so who has reared these?
I was left all alone—
    where then have these come from?"

22 Thus says the Lord GOD:
I will soon lift up my hand to the nations,
    and raise my signal to the peoples;
and they shall bring your sons in their bosom,
    and your daughters shall be carried on their
    shoulders.
23 Kings shall be your foster fathers,
    and their queens your nursing mothers.
With their faces to the ground they shall bow
    down to you,
    and lick the dust of your feet.
Then you will know that I am the LORD;
    those who wait for me shall not be put to
    shame.

24 Can the prey be taken from the mighty,
    or the captives of a tyrant[i] be rescued?
25 But thus says the LORD:
Even the captives of the mighty shall be
    taken,
    and the prey of the tyrant be rescued;

for I will contend with those who contend with
    you,
    and I will save your children.
26 I will make your oppressors eat their own flesh,
    and they shall be drunk with their own
    blood as with wine.
Then all flesh shall know
    that I am the LORD your Savior,
    and your Redeemer, the Mighty One of
    Jacob.

50 Thus says the LORD:
    Where is your mother's bill of divorce
    with which I put her away?
Or which of my creditors is it
    to whom I have sold you?
No, because of your sins you were sold,
    and for your transgressions your mother
    was put away.
2 Why was no one there when I came?
    Why did no one answer when I called?
Is my hand shortened, that it cannot redeem?
    Or have I no power to deliver?
By my rebuke I dry up the sea,
    I make the rivers a desert;
their fish stink for lack of water,
    and die of thirst.[j]
3 I clothe the heavens with blackness,
    and make sackcloth their covering.

The Servant's Humiliation and Vindication

4 The Lord GOD has given me
    the tongue of a teacher,[k]
that I may know how to sustain
    the weary with a word.
Morning by morning he wakens—
    wakens my ear
    to listen as those who are taught.
5 The Lord GOD has opened my ear,
    and I was not rebellious,
    I did not turn backward.

---

i Q Ms Syr Vg: MT _of a righteous person_　j Or _die on the thirsty ground_　k Cn: Heb _of those who are taught_

6 I gave my back to those who struck me,
    and my cheeks to those who pulled out the
        beard;
I did not hide my face
    from insult and spitting.

7 The Lord GOD helps me;
    therefore I have not been disgraced;
therefore I have set my face like flint,
    and I know that I shall not be put to shame;
8   he who vindicates me is near.
Who will contend with me?
    Let us stand up together.
Who are my adversaries?
    Let them confront me.
9 It is the Lord GOD who helps me;
    who will declare me guilty?
All of them will wear out like a garment;
    the moth will eat them up.

PRAY IT!
The Servant's Strength

Isaiah 50.4–9 is the third of the four servant songs (see "The Servant Songs," Isa 42.1–7). Read the song twice. The first time, think of how it reflects Jesus' relationship with his heavenly Father. The second time, meditate on the verses that inspire you and give you strength to be a prophet to other young people.

▶ Isa 50.4–9

10 Who among you fears the LORD
    and obeys the voice of his servant,
who walks in darkness
    and has no light,
yet trusts in the name of the LORD
    and relies upon his God?
11 But all of you are kindlers of fire,
    lighters of firebrands.*l*
Walk in the flame of your fire,
    and among the brands that you have
        kindled!
This is what you shall have from my hand:
    you shall lie down in torment.

Blessings in Store for God's People
(Cp Gen 12.1–3)

51
Listen to me, you that pursue
    righteousness,
you that seek the LORD.

Look to the rock from which you were hewn,
    and to the quarry from which you were
        dug.
2 Look to Abraham your father
    and to Sarah who bore you;
for he was but one when I called him,
    but I blessed him and made him many.
3 For the LORD will comfort Zion;
    he will comfort all her waste places,
and will make her wilderness like Eden,
    her desert like the garden of the LORD;
joy and gladness will be found in her,
    thanksgiving and the voice of song.

4 Listen to me, my people,
    and give heed to me, my nation;
for a teaching will go out from me,
    and my justice for a light to the peoples.
5 I will bring near my deliverance swiftly,
    my salvation has gone out
and my arms will rule the peoples;
    the coastlands wait for me,
    and for my arm they hope.
6 Lift up your eyes to the heavens,
    and look at the earth beneath;
for the heavens will vanish like smoke,
    the earth will wear out like a garment,
    and those who live on it will die like
        gnats;*m*
but my salvation will be forever,
    and my deliverance will never be ended.

7 Listen to me, you who know righteousness,
    you people who have my teaching in your
        hearts;
do not fear the reproach of others,
    and do not be dismayed when they revile
        you.
8 For the moth will eat them up like a garment,
    and the worm will eat them like wool;
but my deliverance will be forever,
    and my salvation to all generations.

9 Awake, awake, put on strength,
    O arm of the LORD!
Awake, as in days of old,
    the generations of long ago!
Was it not you who cut Ra′hab in pieces,
    who pierced the dragon?
10 Was it not you who dried up the sea,
    the waters of the great deep;
who made the depths of the sea a way
    for the redeemed to cross over?
11 So the ransomed of the LORD shall return,

---

l Syr: Heb *you gird yourselves with firebrands*   *m* Or *in like manner*

and come to Zion with singing;
   everlasting joy shall be upon their heads;
    they shall obtain joy and gladness,
    and sorrow and sighing shall flee away.

12 I, I am he who comforts you;
    why then are you afraid of a mere mortal
      who must die,
    a human being who fades like grass?
13 You have forgotten the LORD, your Maker,
    who stretched out the heavens
    and laid the foundations of the earth.
You fear continually all day long
    because of the fury of the oppressor,
who is bent on destruction.
    But where is the fury of the oppressor?
14 The oppressed shall speedily be released;
    they shall not die and go down to the Pit,
    nor shall they lack bread.
15 For I am the LORD your God,
    who stirs up the sea so that its waves roar—
    the LORD of hosts is his name.
16 I have put my words in your mouth,
    and hidden you in the shadow of my
      hand,
stretching out[n] the heavens
    and laying the foundations of the earth,
    and saying to Zion, "You are my people."

17 Rouse yourself, rouse yourself!
    Stand up, O Jerusalem,
you who have drunk at the hand of the LORD
    the cup of his wrath,
who have drunk to the dregs
    the bowl of staggering.
18 There is no one to guide her
    among all the children she has borne;
there is no one to take her by the hand
    among all the children she has brought up.
19 These two things have befallen you
    —who will grieve with you?—
devastation and destruction, famine and
      sword—
    who will comfort you?[o]
20 Your children have fainted,
    they lie at the head of every street
    like an antelope in a net;
they are full of the wrath of the LORD,
    the rebuke of your God.

21 Therefore hear this, you who are wounded,[p]
    who are drunk, but not with wine:
22 Thus says your Sovereign, the LORD,
    your God who pleads the cause of his
      people:
See, I have taken from your hand the cup of
      staggering;

you shall drink no more
    from the bowl of my wrath.
23 And I will put it into the hand of your
      tormentors,
    who have said to you,"
    Bow down, that we may walk on you";
and you have made your back like the
      ground
    and like the street for them to walk on.

Let Zion Rejoice

52 Awake, awake,
    put on your strength, O Zion!
Put on your beautiful garments,
    O Jerusalem, the holy city;
for the uncircumcised and the unclean
    shall enter you no more.
2 Shake yourself from the dust, rise up,
    O captive[q] Jerusalem;
loose the bonds from your neck,
    O captive daughter Zion!

3 For thus says the LORD: You were sold for nothing, and you shall be redeemed without money. 4 For thus says the Lord GOD: Long ago, my people went down into Egypt to reside there as aliens; the Assyrian, too, has oppressed them without cause. 5 Now therefore what am I doing here, says the LORD, seeing that my people are taken away without cause? Their rulers howl, says the LORD, and continually, all day long, my name is despised. 6 Therefore my people shall know my name; therefore in that day they shall know that it is I who speak; here am I.

7 How beautiful upon the mountains
    are the feet of the messenger who
      announces peace,
who brings good news,
    who announces salvation,
    who says to Zion, "Your God reigns."
8 Listen! Your sentinels lift up their voices,
    together they sing for joy;
for in plain sight they see
    the return of the LORD to Zion.
9 Break forth together into singing,
    you ruins of Jerusalem;
for the LORD has comforted his people,
    he has redeemed Jerusalem.
10 The LORD has bared his holy arm
    before the eyes of all the nations;
and all the ends of the earth shall see
    the salvation of our God.

---

n Syr: Heb *planting* o Q Ms Gk Syr Vg: MT *how may I
comfort you?* p Or *humbled* q Cn: Heb *rise up, sit*

I
S
A

11 Depart, depart, go out from there!
   Touch no unclean thing;
   go out from the midst of it, purify yourselves,
   you who carry the vessels of the LORD.
12 For you shall not go out in haste,
   and you shall not go in flight;
   for the LORD will go before you,
   and the God of Israel will be your rear
   guard.

The Suffering Servant

13 See, my servant shall prosper;
   he shall be exalted and lifted up,
   and shall be very high.
14 Just as there were many who were astonished
   at him[r]
   —so marred was his appearance, beyond
   human semblance,
   and his form beyond that of mortals—
15 so he shall startle[s] many nations;
   kings shall shut their mouths because of him;
   for that which had not been told them they
   shall see,
   and that which they had not heard they
   shall contemplate.

53
Who has believed what we have heard?
   And to whom has the arm of the
   LORD been revealed?
2 For he grew up before him like a young plant,
   and like a root out of dry ground;
   he had no form or majesty that we should look
   at him,
   nothing in his appearance that we should
   desire him.
3 He was despised and rejected by others;
   a man of suffering[t] and acquainted with
   infirmity;
   and as one from whom others hide their faces[u]
   he was despised, and we held him of no
   account.

4 Surely he has borne our infirmities
   and carried our diseases;
   yet we accounted him stricken,
   struck down by God, and afflicted.
5 But he was wounded for our transgressions,
   crushed for our iniquities;
   upon him was the punishment that made
   us whole,
   and by his bruises we are healed.
6 All we like sheep have gone astray;
   we have all turned to our own way,
   and the LORD has laid on him
   the iniquity of us all.

7 He was oppressed, and he was afflicted,
   yet he did not open his mouth;

like a lamb that is led to the slaughter,
   and like a sheep that before its shearers is
   silent,
   so he did not open his mouth.
8 By a perversion of justice he was taken away.
   Who could have imagined his future?
   For he was cut off from the land of the living,
   stricken for the transgression of my people.
9 They made his grave with the wicked
   and his tomb[v] with the rich,[w]
   although he had done no violence,
   and there was no deceit in his mouth.

10 Yet it was the will of the LORD to crush him
   with pain.[x]
   When you make his life an offering for sin,[s]
   he shall see his offspring, and shall prolong
   his days;
   through him the will of the LORD shall prosper.
11   Out of his anguish he shall see light;[y]
   he shall find satisfaction through his
   knowledge.
   The righteous one,[z] my servant, shall make
   many righteous,

---

r Syr Tg: Heb *you*   s Meaning of Heb uncertain   t Or *a man
of sorrows*   u Or *as one who hides his face from us*   v Q Ms:
MT *and in his death*   w Cn: Heb *with a rich person*   x Or *by
disease*; meaning of Heb uncertain   y Q Mss: MT lacks
light   z Or *and he shall find satisfaction. Through his
knowledge, the righteous one*

Catholic Connections

THE SUFFERING SERVANT

Isaiah 52.13—53.12 is the fourth of the four
servant songs (see "The Servant Songs,"
Isa 42.1–7). In it, the servant suffers for the
salvation of others. Can you see how this
description fits Jesus? Take a moment to say
your own prayer of thanksgiving to Jesus for
saving us from sin and death.

▶ Isa 52.13—53.12

and he shall bear their iniquities.
12 Therefore I will allot him a portion with the
        great,
    and he shall divide the spoil with the
        strong;
because he poured out himself to death,
    and was numbered with the transgressors;
yet he bore the sin of many,
    and made intercession for the transgressors.

The Eternal Covenant of Peace

54 Sing, O barren one who did not bear;
        burst into song and shout,
    you who have not been in labor!
For the children of the desolate woman will be
        more
    than the children of her that is married,
        says the LORD.
2 Enlarge the site of your tent,
    and let the curtains of your habitations be
        stretched out;
    do not hold back; lengthen your cords
        and strengthen your stakes.
3 For you will spread out to the right and to the
        left,
    and your descendants will possess the
        nations
    and will settle the desolate towns.

4 Do not fear, for you will not be ashamed;
    do not be discouraged, for you will not
        suffer disgrace;
for you will forget the shame of your youth,
    and the disgrace of your widowhood you
        will remember no more.
5 For your Maker is your husband,
    the LORD of hosts is his name;
the Holy One of Israel is your Redeemer,
    the God of the whole earth he is called.
6 For the LORD has called you
    like a wife forsaken and grieved in spirit,
like the wife of a man's youth when she is cast
        off,
    says your God.
7 For a brief moment I abandoned you,
    but with great compassion I will gather you.
8 In overflowing wrath for a moment
    I hid my face from you,
but with everlasting love I will have
        compassion on you,
    says the LORD, your Redeemer.

9 This is like the days of Noah to me:
    Just as I swore that the waters of Noah
    would never again go over the earth,
so I have sworn that I will not be angry with
        you

and will not rebuke you.
10 For the mountains may depart
    and the hills be removed,
but my steadfast love shall not depart from
        you,
    and my covenant of peace shall not be
        removed,
    says the LORD, who has compassion on you.

11 O afflicted one, storm-tossed, and not
        comforted,
    I am about to set your stones in antimony,
    and lay your foundations with sapphires.[a]
12 I will make your pinnacles of rubies,
    your gates of jewels,
    and all your wall of precious stones.
13 All your children shall be taught by the LORD,
    and great shall be the prosperity of your
        children.
14 In righteousness you shall be established;
    you shall be far from oppression, for you
        shall not fear;
    and from terror, for it shall not come near
        you.
15 If anyone stirs up strife,
    it is not from me;
whoever stirs up strife with you
    shall fall because of you.
16 See it is I who have created the smith
    who blows the fire of coals,
    and produces a weapon fit for its purpose;
I have also created the ravager to destroy.
17 No weapon that is fashioned against you
        shall prosper,
    and you shall confute every tongue that
        rises against you in judgment.
This is the heritage of the servants of the LORD
    and their vindication from me, says the
        LORD.

An Invitation to Abundant Life

55 Ho, everyone who thirsts,
        come to the waters;
and you that have no money,
    come, buy and eat!
Come, buy wine and milk
    without money and without price.
2 Why do you spend your money for that which
        is not bread,
    and your labor for that which does not
        satisfy?
Listen carefully to me, and eat what is good,
    and delight yourselves in rich food.
3 Incline your ear, and come to me;
    listen, so that you may live.

---

a Or *lapis lazuli*

I will make with you an everlasting covenant,
   my steadfast, sure love for David.
4 See, I made him a witness to the peoples,
   a leader and commander for the peoples.
5 See, you shall call nations that you do not
     know,
   and nations that do not know you shall run
     to you,
because of the LORD your God, the Holy One
   of Israel,
   for he has glorified you.

6 Seek the LORD while he may be found,
   call upon him while he is near;
7 let the wicked forsake their way,
   and the unrighteous their thoughts;
let them return to the LORD, that he may have
   mercy on them,
   and to our God, for he will abundantly
   pardon.
8 For my thoughts are not your thoughts,
   nor are your ways my ways, says the
   LORD.
9 For as the heavens are higher than the earth,
   so are my ways higher than your ways
   and my thoughts than your thoughts.

10 For as the rain and the snow come down from
    heaven,
   and do not return there until they have
    watered the earth,
making it bring forth and sprout,
   giving seed to the sower and bread to the
   eater,
11 so shall my word be that goes out from my
    mouth;
   it shall not return to me empty,
but it shall accomplish that which I purpose,
   and succeed in the thing for which I sent it.

12 For you shall go out in joy,
   and be led back in peace;
the mountains and the hills before you
   shall burst into song,
   and all the trees of the field shall clap their
   hands.
13 Instead of the thorn shall come up the cypress;
   instead of the brier shall come up the
   myrtle;
and it shall be to the LORD for a memorial,
   for an everlasting sign that shall not be cut
   off.

The Covenant Extended to All Who Obey

56 Thus says the LORD:
   Maintain justice, and do what is
    right,
for soon my salvation will come,
   and my deliverance be revealed.

2 Happy is the mortal who does this,
   the one who holds it fast,
who keeps the sabbath, not profaning it,
   and refrains from doing any evil.

3 Do not let the foreigner joined to the LORD say,
   "The LORD will surely separate me from his
    people";
and do not let the eunuch say,
   "I am just a dry tree."
4 For thus says the LORD:
To the eunuchs who keep my sabbaths,
   who choose the things that please me
   and hold fast my covenant,
5 I will give, in my house and within my walls,
   a monument and a name
   better than sons and daughters;
I will give them an everlasting name
   that shall not be cut off.

The Optimism of Third Isaiah

The last eleven chapters of Isaiah contain the messages of several prophets known collectively as Third Isaiah. The common element of these prophecies is optimism. They proclaim the hopeful message that God's Covenant will be extended to all nations and that Jerusalem will become God's holy city, the throne of the Eternal King.

Third Isaiah, in contrast to many of the other biblical prophets, proclaims joy as a sign of God's presence. Joy is absent in the life of many people today, as it was in the time of Isaiah. Let us remember all the wonderful things God has done for us, and we too will find cause for rejoicing!

▶ Isa 56.1—66.24

6 And the foreigners who join themselves to the
LORD,
to minister to him, to love the name of the
LORD,
and to be his servants,
all who keep the sabbath, and do not
profane it,
and hold fast my covenant—
7 these I will bring to my holy mountain,
and make them joyful in my house of
prayer;
their burnt offerings and their sacrifices
will be accepted on my altar;
for my house shall be called a house of prayer
for all peoples.
8 Thus says the Lord GOD,
who gathers the outcasts of Israel,
I will gather others to them
besides those already gathered.[b]

The Corruption of Israel's Rulers

9 All you wild animals,
all you wild animals in the forest, come to
devour!
10 Israel's[c] sentinels are blind,
they are all without knowledge;
they are all silent dogs
that cannot bark;
dreaming, lying down,
loving to slumber.
11 The dogs have a mighty appetite;
they never have enough.
The shepherds also have no understanding;
they have all turned to their own way,
to their own gain, one and all.
12 "Come," they say, "let us[d] get wine;
let us fill ourselves with strong drink.
And tomorrow will be like today,
great beyond measure."

Israel's Futile Idolatry

57 The righteous perish,
and no one takes it to heart;
the devout are taken away,
while no one understands.
For the righteous are taken away from
calamity,
2 and they enter into peace;
those who walk uprightly
will rest on their couches.
3 But as for you, come here,
you children of a sorceress,
you offspring of an adulterer and a whore.[e]
4 Whom are you mocking?
Against whom do you open your mouth
wide
and stick out your tongue?

Are you not children of transgression,
the offspring of deceit—
5 you that burn with lust among the oaks,
under every green tree;
you that slaughter your children in the
valleys,
under the clefts of the rocks?
6 Among the smooth stones of the valley is your
portion;
they, they, are your lot;
to them you have poured out a drink
offering,
you have brought a grain offering.
Shall I be appeased for these things?
7 Upon a high and lofty mountain
you have set your bed,
and there you went up to offer sacrifice.
8 Behind the door and the doorpost
you have set up your symbol;
for, in deserting me,[f] you have uncovered your
bed,
you have gone up to it,
you have made it wide;
and you have made a bargain for yourself with
them,
you have loved their bed,
you have gazed on their nakedness.[g]
9 You journeyed to Mō'lech[h] with oil,
and multiplied your perfumes;
you sent your envoys far away,
and sent down even to Shē'ōl.
10 You grew weary from your many wanderings,
but you did not say, "It is useless."
You found your desire rekindled,
and so you did not weaken.

11 Whom did you dread and fear
so that you lied,
and did not remember me
or give me a thought?
Have I not kept silent and closed my eyes,[i]
and so you do not fear me?
12 I will concede your righteousness and your
works,
but they will not help you.
13 When you cry out, let your collection of idols
deliver you!
The wind will carry them off,
a breath will take them away.
But whoever takes refuge in me shall possess
the land
and inherit my holy mountain.

---

b Heb *besides his gathered ones*   c Heb *His*   d Q Ms Syr Vg
Tg: MT *me*   e Heb *an adulterer and she plays the whore*
f Meaning of Heb uncertain   g Or *their phallus*; Heb
the hand   h Or *the king*   i Gk Vg: Heb *silent even for a
long time*

A Promise of Help and Healing

14 It shall be said,
  "Build up, build up, prepare the way,
    remove every obstruction from my people's
        way."
15 For thus says the high and lofty one
    who inhabits eternity, whose name is Holy:
  I dwell in the high and holy place,
    and also with those who are contrite and
        humble in spirit,
  to revive the spirit of the humble,
    and to revive the heart of the contrite.
16 For I will not continually accuse,
    nor will I always be angry;
  for then the spirits would grow faint before me,
    even the souls that I have made.
17 Because of their wicked covetousness I was
        angry;
  I struck them, I hid and was angry;
    but they kept turning back to their own ways.
18 I have seen their ways, but I will heal them;
  I will lead them and repay them with
        comfort,
    creating for their mourners the fruit of the
        lips. j
19 Peace, peace, to the far and the near, says the
        LORD;
    and I will heal them.
20 But the wicked are like the tossing sea
    that cannot keep still;
    its waters toss up mire and mud.
21 There is no peace, says my God, for the wicked.

False and True Worship

58 Shout out, do not hold back!
      Lift up your voice like a trumpet!
  Announce to my people their rebellion,
    to the house of Jacob their sins.
2 Yet day after day they seek me
    and delight to know my ways,
  as if they were a nation that practiced
        righteousness
    and did not forsake the ordinance of their
        God;
  they ask of me righteous judgments,
    they delight to draw near to God.
3 "Why do we fast, but you do not see?
    Why humble ourselves, but you do not
        notice?"
  Look, you serve your own interest on your fast
        day,
    and oppress all your workers.
4 Look, you fast only to quarrel and to fight
    and to strike with a wicked fist.
  Such fasting as you do today
    will not make your voice heard on high.
5 Is such the fast that I choose,

  a day to humble oneself?
  Is it to bow down the head like a bulrush,
    and to lie in sackcloth and ashes?
  Will you call this a fast,
    a day acceptable to the LORD?
6 Is not this the fast that I choose:
    to loose the bonds of injustice,
    to undo the thongs of the yoke,
  to let the oppressed go free,
    and to break every yoke?

58.6

7 Is it not to share your bread with the hungry,
    and bring the homeless poor into your
        house;
  when you see the naked, to cover them,
    and not to hide yourself from your own
        kin?
8 Then your light shall break forth like the dawn,
    and your healing shall spring up quickly;
  your vindicator k shall go before you,
    the glory of the LORD shall be your rear
        guard.
9 Then you shall call, and the LORD will answer;
    you shall cry for help, and he will say, Here
        I am.

  If you remove the yoke from among you,
    the pointing of the finger, the speaking of
        evil,
10 if you offer your food to the hungry
    and satisfy the needs of the afflicted,
  then your light shall rise in the darkness
    and your gloom be like the noonday.
11 The LORD will guide you continually,
    and satisfy your needs in parched places,

---

j Meaning of Heb uncertain   k Or *vindication*

ISA

"IF YOU WANT PEACE, WORK FOR JUSTICE"

"If you want peace, work for justice" is a famous quote of Pope Paul VI. We hear a similar message in Isa 56.1, and 58.6–14 gives us clear examples of works that create justice and peace.

At the core of justice is the understanding that life—all life—is precious. All people are to be honored, protected, and celebrated. Ensuring that this happens is our responsibility, even when it seems to be a burden. The following prayer by a worker of Peace Market in Korea reflects this passion:

> *Make us keep the sputtering lantern burning*
> *and not to break a wounded reed.*
> *Make us understand*
> *the secret of eternal life*
> *from the pulse of blood in our veins*
> *and realise the worth of a life*
> *from the movement of a warm heart.*
> *Make us not discriminate*
> *the rich and the poor,*
> *the high and the low,*
> *the learned and the ignorant*
> *those we know well and those we do not know.*
> *Oh!*
> *A human life can't be exchanged for the whole world*
> *this supreme task of keeping the lives*
> *of the sons and daughters of God.*
> *Let us realise how lovely it is*
> *to feel the burdens of responsibility.*
> *("Our Prayer" from Your Will Be Done)*

▶ Isa 58.6–14

---

and make your bones strong;
and you shall be like a watered garden,
  like a spring of water,
  whose waters never fail.
12 Your ancient ruins shall be rebuilt;
  you shall raise up the foundations of many
    generations;
you shall be called the repairer of the
    breach,
  the restorer of streets to live in.

13 If you refrain from trampling the sabbath,
  from pursuing your own interests on my
    holy day;
if you call the sabbath a delight
  and the holy day of the LORD honorable;
if you honor it, not going your own ways,

serving your own interests, or pursuing your
  own affairs;[1]
14 then you shall take delight in the LORD,
  and I will make you ride upon the heights
    of the earth;
I will feed you with the heritage of your
    ancestor Jacob,
  for the mouth of the LORD has spoken.

Injustice and Oppression to Be Punished

59 See, the LORD's hand is not too short to
    save,
  nor his ear too dull to hear.
2 Rather, your iniquities have been barriers
  between you and your God,

---

[1] Heb *or speaking words*

and your sins have hidden his face from you
    so that he does not hear.
3 For your hands are defiled with blood,
    and your fingers with iniquity;
your lips have spoken lies,
    your tongue mutters wickedness.
4 No one brings suit justly,
    no one goes to law honestly;
they rely on empty pleas, they speak lies,
    conceiving mischief and begetting iniquity.
5 They hatch adders' eggs,
    and weave the spider's web;
whoever eats their eggs dies,
    and the crushed egg hatches out a viper.
6 Their webs cannot serve as clothing;
    they cannot cover themselves with what
      they make.
Their works are works of iniquity,
    and deeds of violence are in their hands.
7 Their feet run to evil,
    and they rush to shed innocent blood;
their thoughts are thoughts of iniquity,
    desolation and destruction are in their
      highways.
8 The way of peace they do not know,
    and there is no justice in their paths.
Their roads they have made crooked;
    no one who walks in them knows peace.

9 Therefore justice is far from us,
    and righteousness does not reach us;
we wait for light, and lo! there is darkness;
    and for brightness, but we walk in gloom.
10 We grope like the blind along a wall,
    groping like those who have no eyes;
we stumble at noon as in the twilight,
    among the vigorous[m] as though we were
      dead.
11 We all growl like bears;
    like doves we moan mournfully.
We wait for justice, but there is none;
    for salvation, but it is far from us.
12 For our transgressions before you are many,
    and our sins testify against us.
Our transgressions indeed are with us,
    and we know our iniquities:
13 transgressing, and denying the LORD,
    and turning away from following our God,
talking oppression and revolt,
    conceiving lying words and uttering them
      from the heart.
14 Justice is turned back,
    and righteousness stands at a distance;
for truth stumbles in the public square,
    and uprightness cannot enter.
15 Truth is lacking,
    and whoever turns from evil is despoiled.

The LORD saw it, and it displeased him
    that there was no justice.
16 He saw that there was no one,
    and was appalled that there was no one to
      intervene;
so his own arm brought him victory,
    and his righteousness upheld him.
17 He put on righteousness like a breastplate,
    and a helmet of salvation on his head;
he put on garments of vengeance for clothing,
    and wrapped himself in fury as in a mantle.
18 According to their deeds, so will he repay;
    wrath to his adversaries, requital to his
      enemies;
    to the coastlands he will render requital.
19 So those in the west shall fear the name of the
      LORD,
    and those in the east, his glory;
for he will come like a pent-up stream
    that the wind of the LORD drives on.

20 And he will come to Zion as Redeemer,
    to those in Jacob who turn from
      transgression, says the LORD.
21 And as for me, this is my covenant with them,
says the LORD: my spirit that is upon you, and my
words that I have put in your mouth, shall not
depart out of your mouth, or out of the mouths of
your children, or out of the mouths of your
children's children, says the LORD, from now on
and forever.

The Ingathering of the Dispersed

60 Arise, shine; for your light has come,
    and the glory of the LORD has risen
      upon you.
2 For darkness shall cover the earth,
    and thick darkness the peoples;
but the LORD will arise upon you,
    and his glory will appear over you.
3 Nations shall come to your light,
    and kings to the brightness of your dawn.

4 Lift up your eyes and look around;
    they all gather together, they come to you;
your sons shall come from far away,
    and your daughters shall be carried on their
      nurses' arms.
5 Then you shall see and be radiant;
    your heart shall thrill and rejoice,[n]
because the abundance of the sea shall be
      brought to you,
    the wealth of the nations shall come to you.
6 A multitude of camels shall cover you,
    the young camels of Mid'i•an and E'phah;

---

m Meaning of Heb uncertain   n Heb *be enlarged*

all those from Shē′ba shall come.
They shall bring gold and frankincense,
and shall proclaim the praise of the LORD.
7 All the flocks of Kē′dar shall be gathered to you,
the rams of Ne•bā′i•oth shall minister to
you;
they shall be acceptable on my altar,
and I will glorify my glorious house.

8 Who are these that fly like a cloud,
and like doves to their windows?
9 For the coastlands shall wait for me,
the ships of Tar′shish first,
to bring your children from far away,
their silver and gold with them,
for the name of the LORD your God,
and for the Holy One of Israel,
because he has glorified you.
10 Foreigners shall build up your walls,
and their kings shall minister to you;
for in my wrath I struck you down,
but in my favor I have had mercy on you.
11 Your gates shall always be open;
day and night they shall not be shut,
so that nations shall bring you their wealth,
with their kings led in procession.
12 For the nation and kingdom
that will not serve you shall perish;
those nations shall be utterly laid waste.
13 The glory of Lebanon shall come to you,
the cypress, the plane, and the pine,
to beautify the place of my sanctuary;
and I will glorify where my feet rest.
14 The descendants of those who oppressed you
shall come bending low to you,
and all who despised you
shall bow down at your feet;
they shall call you the City of the LORD,
the Zion of the Holy One of Israel.
15 Whereas you have been forsaken and hated,
with no one passing through,
I will make you majestic forever,
a joy from age to age.
16 You shall suck the milk of nations,
you shall suck the breasts of kings;
and you shall know that I, the LORD, am your
Savior
and your Redeemer, the Mighty One of
Jacob.

17 Instead of bronze I will bring gold,
instead of iron I will bring silver;
instead of wood, bronze,
instead of stones, iron.
I will appoint Peace as your overseer
and Righteousness as your taskmaster.
18 Violence shall no more be heard in your land,

devastation or destruction within your
borders;
you shall call your walls Salvation,
and your gates Praise.

God the Glory of Zion

19 The sun shall no longer be
your light by day,
nor for brightness shall the moon
give light to you by night;[o]
but the LORD will be your everlasting light,
and your God will be your glory.
20 Your sun shall no more go down,
or your moon withdraw itself;
for the LORD will be your everlasting light,
and your days of mourning shall be ended.
21 Your people shall all be righteous;
they shall possess the land forever.
They are the shoot that I planted, the work of
my hands,
so that I might be glorified.
22 The least of them shall become a clan,
and the smallest one a mighty nation;
I am the LORD;
in its time I will accomplish it quickly.

The Good News of Deliverance

61 The spirit of the Lord GOD is upon me,
because the LORD has anointed me;
he has sent me to bring good news to the
oppressed,
to bind up the brokenhearted,
to proclaim liberty to the captives,
and release to the prisoners;
2 to proclaim the year of the LORD's favor,
and the day of vengeance of our God;
to comfort all who mourn;
3 to provide for those who mourn in Zion—
to give them a garland instead of ashes,
the oil of gladness instead of mourning,
the mantle of praise instead of a faint spirit.
They will be called oaks of righteousness,
the planting of the LORD, to display his
glory.
4 They shall build up the ancient ruins,
they shall raise up the former devastations;
they shall repair the ruined cities,
the devastations of many generations.

5 Strangers shall stand and feed your flocks,
foreigners shall till your land and dress your
vines;
6 but you shall be called priests of the LORD,
you shall be named ministers of our God;
you shall enjoy the wealth of the nations,

_____
o Q Ms Gk Old Latin Tg: MT lacks by night

and in their riches you shall glory.

7 Because their[p] shame was double,
 and dishonor was proclaimed as their lot,
therefore they shall possess a double portion;
 everlasting joy shall be theirs.

8 For I the LORD love justice,
 I hate robbery and wrongdoing;[q]
I will faithfully give them their recompense,
 and I will make an everlasting covenant
  with them.
9 Their descendants shall be known among the
  nations,
 and their offspring among the peoples;
all who see them shall acknowledge
 that they are a people whom the LORD has
  blessed.
10 I will greatly rejoice in the LORD,
 my whole being shall exult in my God;
for he has clothed me with the garments of
  salvation,
 he has covered me with the robe of
  righteousness,
as a bridegroom decks himself with a garland,
 and as a bride adorns herself with her
  jewels.

did you KNOW?

Bride and Bridegroom

In ancient Israel, the bride and bridegroom gradually became a metaphor, or symbol, for the relation between Israel and God as pictured in Isa 61.10 and 62.5. In these passages, Israel is the bride, and God is the faithful bridegroom, who loves her, lavishes her with blessings, and continues to be faithful to her. When Israel strays from the Covenant or goes after foreign gods, she is compared to an unfaithful lover, even a prostitute who pursues other partners (for a graphic example, see Ezek 16.1–43). The prophet Hosea even marries a prostitute as a living example of God's faithfulness (Hos 1.2)! The wonder of God's love is that through all of Israel's infidelity (and ours), God always remains willing to take it (and us) back.

▸ Isa 61.10

11 For as the earth brings forth its shoots,
 and as a garden causes what is sown in it to
  spring up,
so the Lord GOD will cause righteousness and
  praise
 to spring up before all the nations.

The Vindication and Salvation of Zion

62 For Zion's sake I will not keep silent,
 and for Jerusalem's sake I will not
  rest,
until her vindication shines out like the dawn,
 and her salvation like a burning torch.
2 The nations shall see your vindication,
 and all the kings your glory;
and you shall be called by a new name
 that the mouth of the LORD will give.
3 You shall be a crown of beauty in the hand of
  the LORD,
 and a royal diadem in the hand of your
  God.
4 You shall no more be termed Forsaken,[r]
 and your land shall no more be termed
  Desolate;[s]
but you shall be called My Delight Is in Her,[t]
 and your land Married;[u]
for the LORD delights in you,
 and your land shall be married.
5 For as a young man marries a young woman,
 so shall your builder[v] marry you,
and as the bridegroom rejoices over the
  bride,
 so shall your God rejoice over you.
6 Upon your walls, O Jerusalem,
 I have posted sentinels;
all day and all night
 they shall never be silent.
You who remind the LORD,
 take no rest,
7 and give him no rest
 until he establishes Jerusalem
 and makes it renowned throughout the
  earth.
8 The LORD has sworn by his right hand
 and by his mighty arm:
I will not again give your grain
 to be food for your enemies,
and foreigners shall not drink the wine
 for which you have labored;
9 but those who garner it shall eat it
 and praise the LORD,
and those who gather it shall drink it
 in my holy courts.

---

p Heb your q Or robbery with a burnt offering
r Heb Azubah s Heb Shemamah t Heb Hephzibah
u Heb Beulah v Cn: Heb your sons

10 Go through, go through the gates,
    prepare the way for the people;
build up, build up the highway,
    clear it of stones,
    lift up an ensign over the peoples.
11 The LORD has proclaimed
    to the end of the earth:
Say to daughter Zion,
    "See, your salvation comes;
his reward is with him,
    and his recompense before him."
12 They shall be called, "The Holy People,
    The Redeemed of the LORD";
and you shall be called, "Sought Out,
    A City Not Forsaken."

Vengeance on Edom

63
"Who is this that comes from E'dom,
    from Boz'rah in garments stained
        crimson?
Who is this so splendidly robed,
    marching in his great might?"

"It is I, announcing vindication,
    mighty to save."

2 "Why are your robes red,
    and your garments like theirs who tread the
        wine press?"

3 "I have trodden the wine press alone,
    and from the peoples no one was with me;
I trod them in my anger
    and trampled them in my wrath;
their juice spattered on my garments,
    and stained all my robes.
4 For the day of vengeance was in my heart,
    and the year for my redeeming work had
        come.
5 I looked, but there was no helper;
    I stared, but there was no one to sustain me;
so my own arm brought me victory,
    and my wrath sustained me.
6 I trampled down peoples in my anger,
    I crushed them in my wrath,
    and I poured out their lifeblood on the
        earth."

God's Mercy Remembered

7 I will recount the gracious deeds of the LORD,
    the praiseworthy acts of the LORD,
because of all that the LORD has done for us,
    and the great favor to the house of Israel
that he has shown them according to his
        mercy,
    according to the abundance of his steadfast
        love.

8 For he said, "Surely they are my people,
    children who will not deal falsely";
and he became their savior
9   in all their distress.
It was no messenger[w] or angel
    but his presence that saved them;[x]
in his love and in his pity he redeemed
        them;
    he lifted them up and carried them all the
        days of old.

10 But they rebelled
    and grieved his holy spirit;
therefore he became their enemy;
    he himself fought against them.
11 Then they[y] remembered the days of old,
    of Moses his servant.[z]
Where is the one who brought them up out of
        the sea
    with the shepherds of his flock?
Where is the one who put within them
    his holy spirit,
12 who caused his glorious arm
    to march at the right hand of Moses,
who divided the waters before them
    to make for himself an everlasting
        name,
13   who led them through the depths?
Like a horse in the desert,
    they did not stumble.
14 Like cattle that go down into the valley,
    the spirit of the LORD gave them rest.
Thus you led your people,
    to make for yourself a glorious name.

A Prayer of Penitence

15 Look down from heaven and see,
    from your holy and glorious habitation.
Where are your zeal and your might?
    The yearning of your heart and your
        compassion?
    They are withheld from me.
16 For you are our father,
    though Abraham does not know us
    and Israel does not acknowledge us;
you, O LORD, are our father;
    our Redeemer from of old is your name.
17 Why, O LORD, do you make us stray from your
        ways
    and harden our heart, so that we do not
        fear you?
Turn back for the sake of your servants,
    for the sake of the tribes that are your
        heritage.

---

w Gk: Heb anguish   x Or savior. 9In all their distress he was
distressed; the angel of his presence saved them;   y Heb he
z Cn: Heb his people

18 Your holy people took possession for a little
    while;
        but now our adversaries have trampled
        down your sanctuary.
19 We have long been like those whom you do
    not rule,
        like those not called by your name

64 O that you would tear open the
            heavens and come down,
        so that the mountains would quake at your
        presence—
2a as when fire kindles brushwood
        and the fire causes water to boil—
    to make your name known to your adversaries,
        so that the nations might tremble at your
        presence!
3 When you did awesome deeds that we did not
    expect,
        you came down, the mountains quaked at
        your presence.
4 From ages past no one has heard,
        no ear has perceived,
    no eye has seen any God besides you,
        who works for those who wait for him.
5 You meet those who gladly do right,
        those who remember you in your ways.
    But you were angry, and we sinned;
        because you hid yourself we transgressed.*b*
6 We have all become like one who is
            unclean,
        and all our righteous deeds are like a filthy
        cloth.
    We all fade like a leaf,
        and our iniquities, like the wind, take us
        away.
7 There is no one who calls on your name,
        or attempts to take hold of you;
    for you have hidden your face from us,
        and have delivered*c* us into the hand of our
        iniquity.
8 Yet, O LORD, you are our Father;
        we are the clay, and you are our potter;
        we are all the work of your hand.
9 Do not be exceedingly angry, O LORD,
        and do not remember iniquity forever.
        Now consider, we are all your people.
10 Your holy cities have become a wilderness,
        Zion has become a wilderness,
        Jerusalem a desolation.
11 Our holy and beautiful house,
        where our ancestors praised you,
    has been burned by fire,
        and all our pleasant places have become
        ruins.
12 After all this, will you restrain yourself,
        O LORD?

PRAY IT!
The Master Potter

Have you ever seen a potter at work?
Perhaps you have even made a pot
yourself. Pot making is still practiced
today much as it was at the time of Third
Isaiah: The potter takes a lump of moist
clay and begins to shape it by hand, with
an image in mind of what the finished
product will look like. The artisan then
puts the piece of clay on a potter's wheel
and spins the wheel, continuing to form
the pot with his or her hands. Because it
is designed by hand, rather than mass-
produced by machine, each work of the
potter is original; there is no other just
like it.

The image of God as a potter and
each of us as a clay pot reminds us of the
second Creation story, where God scoops
up clay from the earth and forms the
first human being and breathes life into
the being (Gen 2.7). It also reminds us of
Psalm 139's description of our being knit
together in our mother's womb.

The idea of God's hands shaping us
like clay is intimate and comforting. No
one but the potter knows how much time
and love went into the fashioning of a
particular pot. The potter gives each pot
its own special design and markings. The
potter also knows its flaws. The potter
and the pot share a bond that seems
much like the one between each of us and
God. Isaiah 64.8 indeed gives us a vivid
and beautiful image for God's relationship
with each of us (see also Jer 18.1–6).

In your prayer, reflect or journal on
the following questions:
- How has God molded you as a unique
  person?
- What are your special features and
  markings (gifts), and what are your
  flaws (weaknesses)?
- How is God still molding you?

▸ Isa 64.8

Will you keep silent, and punish us so
    severely?

---

a Ch 64.1 in Heb   *b* Meaning of Heb uncertain   *c* Gk Syr
Old Latin Tg: Heb *melted*

The Righteousness of God's Judgment

65 I was ready to be sought out by those
who did not ask,
to be found by those who did not seek me.
I said, "Here I am, here I am,"
to a nation that did not call on my name.
2 I held out my hands all day long
to a rebellious people,
who walk in a way that is not good,
following their own devices;
3 a people who provoke me
to my face continually,
sacrificing in gardens
and offering incense on bricks;
4 who sit inside tombs,
and spend the night in secret places;
who eat swine's flesh,
with broth of abominable things in their
vessels;
5 who say, "Keep to yourself,
do not come near me, for I am too holy for
you."
These are a smoke in my nostrils,
a fire that burns all day long.
6 See, it is written before me:
I will not keep silent, but I will repay;
I will indeed repay into their laps
7 their[d] iniquities and their[d] ancestors' iniquities
together,
　　　　　　　　　　　　says the LORD;
because they offered incense on the mountains
and reviled me on the hills,
I will measure into their laps
full payment for their actions.
8 Thus says the LORD:
As the wine is found in the cluster,
and they say, "Do not destroy it,
for there is a blessing in it,"
so I will do for my servants' sake,
and not destroy them all.
9 I will bring forth descendants[e] from Jacob,
and from Judah inheritors[f] of my
mountains;
my chosen shall inherit it,
and my servants shall settle there.
10 Sharon shall become a pasture for flocks,
and the Valley of Ā'chor a place for herds to
lie down,
for my people who have sought me.
11 But you who forsake the LORD,
who forget my holy mountain,
who set a table for Fortune
and fill cups of mixed wine for Destiny;
12 I will destine you to the sword,
and all of you shall bow down to the
slaughter;
because, when I called, you did not answer,

when I spoke, you did not listen,
but you did what was evil in my sight,
and chose what I did not delight in.
13 Therefore thus says the Lord GOD:
My servants shall eat,
but you shall be hungry;
my servants shall drink,
but you shall be thirsty;
my servants shall rejoice,
but you shall be put to shame;
14 my servants shall sing for gladness of heart,
but you shall cry out for pain of heart,
and shall wail for anguish of spirit.
15 You shall leave your name to my chosen to use
as a curse,
and the Lord GOD will put you to death;
but to his servants he will give a different
name.
16 Then whoever invokes a blessing in the
land
shall bless by the God of faithfulness,
and whoever takes an oath in the land
shall swear by the God of faithfulness;
because the former troubles are forgotten
and are hidden from my sight.

The Glorious New Creation

17 For I am about to create new heavens
and a new earth;
the former things shall not be remembered
or come to mind.
18 But be glad and rejoice forever
in what I am creating;
for I am about to create Jerusalem as a joy,
and its people as a delight.
19 I will rejoice in Jerusalem,
and delight in my people;
no more shall the sound of weeping be heard
in it,
or the cry of distress.
20 No more shall there be in it
an infant that lives but a few days,
or an old person who does not live out a
lifetime;
for one who dies at a hundred years will be
considered a youth,
and one who falls short of a hundred will
be considered accursed.
21 They shall build houses and inhabit them;
they shall plant vineyards and eat their
fruit.
22 They shall not build and another inhabit;
they shall not plant and another eat;
for like the days of a tree shall the days of my
people be,

---

d Gk Syr: Heb *your*　*e* Or *a descendant*　*f* Or *an inheritor*

and my chosen shall long enjoy the work of
    their hands.
23 They shall not labor in vain,
    or bear children for calamity;*g*
for they shall be offspring blessed by the
    LORD—
    and their descendants as well.
24 Before they call I will answer,
    while they are yet speaking I will hear.
25 The wolf and the lamb shall feed together,
    the lion shall eat straw like the ox;
    but the serpent—its food shall be dust!
They shall not hurt or destroy
    on all my holy mountain,
               says the LORD.

The Worship God Demands

66 Thus says the LORD:
    Heaven is my throne
  and the earth is my footstool;
what is the house that you would build
    for me,
  and what is my resting place?
2 All these things my hand has made,
  and so all these things are mine,*h*
               says the LORD.
But this is the one to whom I will look,
  to the humble and contrite in spirit,
  who trembles at my word.

3 Whoever slaughters an ox is like one who kills
    a human being;
  whoever sacrifices a lamb, like one who
    breaks a dog's neck;
whoever presents a grain offering, like one who
    offers swine's blood;*i*
  whoever makes a memorial offering of
    frankincense, like one who blesses an
    idol.
These have chosen their own ways,
  and in their abominations they take
    delight;
4 I also will choose to mock*j* them,
  and bring upon them what they fear;
because, when I called, no one answered,
  when I spoke, they did not listen;
but they did what was evil in my sight,
  and chose what did not please me.

The LORD Vindicates Zion

5 Hear the word of the LORD,
  you who tremble at his word:
Your own people who hate you
  and reject you for my name's sake
have said, "Let the LORD be glorified,
  so that we may see your joy";
but it is they who shall be put to shame.

6 Listen, an uproar from the city!
  A voice from the temple!
The voice of the LORD,
  dealing retribution to his enemies!

7 Before she was in labor
  she gave birth;
before her pain came upon her
  she delivered a son.
8 Who has heard of such a thing?
  Who has seen such things?
Shall a land be born in one day?
  Shall a nation be delivered in one moment?
Yet as soon as Zion was in labor
  she delivered her children.
9 Shall I open the womb and not deliver?
  says the LORD;
shall I, the one who delivers, shut the womb?
  says your God.

10 Rejoice with Jerusalem, and be glad for her,
  all you who love her;
rejoice with her in joy,
  all you who mourn over her—
11 that you may nurse and be satisfied
  from her consoling breast;
that you may drink deeply with delight
  from her glorious bosom.

12 For thus says the LORD:
I will extend prosperity to her like a river,
  and the wealth of the nations like an
    overflowing stream;
and you shall nurse and be carried on her
    arm,
  and dandled on her knees.
13 As a mother comforts her child,
  so I will comfort you;
  you shall be comforted in Jerusalem.

The Reign and Indignation of God

14 You shall see, and your heart shall rejoice;
  your bodies*k* shall flourish like the grass;
and it shall be known that the hand of the
    LORD is with his servants,
  and his indignation is against his
    enemies.
15 For the LORD will come in fire,
  and his chariots like the whirlwind,
to pay back his anger in fury,
  and his rebuke in flames of fire.
16 For by fire will the LORD execute judgment,
  and by his sword, on all flesh;
  and those slain by the LORD shall be many.

---

g Or *sudden terror*   *h* Gk Syr: Heb *these things came to be*
i Meaning of Heb uncertain   *j* Or *to punish*   *k* Heb *bones*

17 Those who sanctify and purify themselves to go into the gardens, following the one in the center, eating the flesh of pigs, vermin, and rodents, shall come to an end together, says the LORD.

18 For I know[l] their works and their thoughts, and I am[m] coming to gather all nations and tongues; and they shall come and shall see my glory, 19 and I will set a sign among them. From them I will send survivors to the nations, to Tar′shish, Put,[n] and Lud—which draw the bow—to Tū′bal and Jā′van, to the coastlands far away that have not heard of my fame or seen my glory; and they shall declare my glory among the nations. 20 They shall bring all your kindred from all the nations as an offering to the LORD, on horses, and in chariots, and in litters, and on mules, and on dromedaries, to my holy mountain Jerusalem, says the LORD, just as the Israelites bring a grain offering in a clean vessel to the house of the LORD. 21 And I will also take some of them as priests and as Lē′vītes, says the LORD.

22 For as the new heavens and the new earth,
    which I will make,
shall remain before me, says the LORD;
    so shall your descendants and your name
    remain.
23 From new moon to new moon,
    and from sabbath to sabbath,
all flesh shall come to worship before me,
    says the LORD.

24 And they shall go out and look at the dead bodies of the people who have rebelled against me; for their worm shall not die, their fire shall not be quenched, and they shall be an abhorrence to all flesh.

---

[l] Gk Syr: Heb lacks *know*   [m] Gk Syr Vg Tg: Heb *it is*   [n] Gk: Heb *Pul*

Imagine you're watching a movie. One of the leading characters imposes severe hardships on others and then goes off to dine in luxury. Immediately, you know the character is a villain. Another leading character calls for others to endure sacrifice and lives under the same conditions as they do. You know this is a hero, because heroes practice what they preach. Jeremiah the prophet was such a hero; he not only preached a hard message but accepted the trials that came with it.

In-depth

At the beginning of Jeremiah's prophetic ministry, King Josiah ruled the southern kingdom of Judah (2 Chronicles, chapters 34–35). He was a good king who expanded Judah's territory and started a religious reform. Jeremiah approved of Josiah and Josiah's reforms, but he was afraid they were too little, too late. Chapters 2–5 of his book contain his prophecies during Josiah's rule. In them, he speaks out against Israel's sin and corruption but hopes that things will improve if the people turn to God (4.1–2). Unfortunately, King Josiah was suddenly killed in battle, and things went from bad to worse.

Kings Jehoiakim and Zedekiah were the main rulers who followed Josiah, and they were Josiah's complete opposite (2 Chr 36.1–14). Both were ruthless, power hungry, and corrupt. During Jehoiakim's reign, Jeremiah had to go into hiding out of fear for his life. Chapters 7–20 of Jeremiah's book contain his prophecies during this time, when his preaching against the sins of Israel became stronger. Chapters 21–29 and 34–45 record his life and preaching during Zedekiah's reign—the last few years before the Babylonian Exile. While Zedekiah ruled, Jeremiah was imprisoned, beaten, and thrown into a well to die.

Jeremiah survived his experience in the well to see Jerusalem and the Temple destroyed by the Babylonians. To give the people hope that God was still on their side, he prophesied the destruction of all Israel's enemies, especially Babylon (see chapters 46–51).

Ultimately, Jeremiah realized that even a new king like David would not be enough to correct what was wrong. The people were unable to fulfill God's commandments because they had hearts of stone. In chapters 30–33, the Book of Consolation, Jeremiah said that the Lord would make a new Covenant with Israel in the future, and this time, the Law would be written on the people's hearts (31.33–34).

At a Glance

- **Chapter 1.** Jeremiah's call

- **Chapters 2–25.** prophecies against Judah and Jerusalem

- **Chapters 26–45.** biographical material and a discussion of the restoration of Israel

- **Chapters 46–52.** prophecies against other nations

Quick Facts

Period Covered
626–583 B.C.

Authors
Jeremiah and his disciples, including Baruch

Themes
Israel's need for repentance, Jeremiah's struggles, the New Covenant

The Book of *Jeremiah*

Jeremiah

Before I formed you in the womb I knew you.

1 The words of Jer·e·mī′ah son of Hil·kī′ah, of the priests who were in An′a·thoth in the land of Benjamin, 2 to whom the word of the LORD came in the days of King Jō·sī′ah son of Ā′mon of Judah, in the thirteenth year of his reign. 3 It came also in the days of King Je·hoi′a·kim son of Jō·sī′ah of Judah, and until the end of the eleventh year of King Zed·e·kī′ah son of Jō·sī′ah of Judah, until the captivity of Jerusalem in the fifth month.

Jeremiah's Call and Commission

4 Now the word of the LORD came to me saying,
5 "Before I formed you in the womb I
   knew you,
and before you were born I consecrated
   you;
I appointed you a prophet to the nations."
6 Then I said, "Ah, Lord GOD! Truly I do not know how to speak, for I am only a boy." 7 But the LORD said to me,
"Do not say, 'I am only a boy';
for you shall go to all to whom I send you,
and you shall speak whatever I
   command you.
8 Do not be afraid of them,
for I am with you to deliver you,
                    says the LORD."
9 Then the LORD put out his hand and touched my mouth; and the LORD said to me,
"Now I have put my words in your mouth.

10 See, today I appoint you over nations and over
   kingdoms,
to pluck up and to pull down,
to destroy and to overthrow,
to build and to plant."

11 The word of the LORD came to me, saying, "Jer·e·mī′ah, what do you see?" And I said, "I see a branch of an almond tree."*a* 12 Then the LORD said to me, "You have seen well, for I am watching*b* over my word to perform it." 13 The word of the LORD came to me a second time, saying, "What do you see?" And I said, "I see a boiling pot, tilted away from the north."

14 Then the LORD said to me: Out of the north disaster shall break out on all the inhabitants of the land. 15 For now I am calling all the tribes of the kingdoms of the north, says the LORD; and they shall come and all of them shall set their thrones at the entrance of the gates of Jerusalem, against all its surrounding walls and against all the cities of Judah. 16 And I will utter my judgments against them, for all their wickedness in forsaking me; they have made offerings to other gods, and worshiped the works of their own hands. 17 But you, gird up your loins; stand up and tell them everything that I command you. Do not break down before them, or I will break you before them. 18 And I for my part have made you today a fortified city, an iron pillar,

---

a Heb *shaqed* *b* Heb *shoqed*

and a bronze wall, against the whole land—against the kings of Judah, its princes, its priests, and the people of the land. [19] They will fight against you; but they shall not prevail against you, for I am with you, says the LORD, to deliver you.

God Pleads with Israel to Repent

2 The word of the LORD came to me, saying: [2] Go and proclaim in the hearing of Jerusalem, Thus says the LORD:

I remember the devotion of your youth,
> your love as a bride,
how you followed me in the wilderness,
> in a land not sown.
[3] Israel was holy to the LORD,
> the first fruits of his harvest.
All who ate of it were held guilty;
> disaster came upon them,
>> says the LORD.

4 Hear the word of the LORD, O house of Jacob, and all the families of the house of Israel. [5] Thus says the LORD:

What wrong did your ancestors find in me
> that they went far from me,
and went after worthless things, and became
> worthless themselves?
[6] They did not say, "Where is the LORD
> who brought us up from the land of Egypt,
who led us in the wilderness,
> in a land of deserts and pits,
in a land of drought and deep darkness,
> in a land that no one passes through,
> where no one lives?"
[7] I brought you into a plentiful land
> to eat its fruits and its good things.
But when you entered you defiled my land,
> and made my heritage an abomination.
[8] The priests did not say, "Where is the LORD?"
> Those who handle the law did not
>> know me;
the rulers[c] transgressed against me;

the prophets prophesied by Bā'al,
> and went after things that do not profit.

[9] Therefore once more I accuse you,
>> says the LORD,
and I accuse your children's children.
[10] Cross to the coasts of Cyprus and look,
> send to Kĕ'dar and examine with care;
> see if there has ever been such a thing.
[11] Has a nation changed its gods,
> even though they are no gods?
But my people have changed their glory
> for something that does not profit.
[12] Be appalled, O heavens, at this,
> be shocked, be utterly desolate,
>> says the LORD,
[13] for my people have committed two evils:
> they have forsaken me,
the fountain of living water,
> and dug out cisterns for themselves,
cracked cisterns
> that can hold no water.

[14] Is Israel a slave? Is he a homeborn servant?
> Why then has he become plunder?
[15] The lions have roared against him,
> they have roared loudly.
They have made his land a waste;
> his cities are in ruins, without inhabitant.
[16] Moreover, the people of Memphis and
> Tah'pan•hēs
> have broken the crown of your head.
[17] Have you not brought this upon yourself
> by forsaking the LORD your God,
> while he led you in the way?
[18] What then do you gain by going to Egypt,
> to drink the waters of the Nile?
Or what do you gain by going to Assyria,
> to drink the waters of the Euphrates?
[19] Your wickedness will punish you,

---
c Heb shepherds

You Are Not Too Young!

Jeremiah was a young man when God tapped him on the shoulder. In response to God, Jeremiah said, "Truly I do not know how to speak, for I am only a boy" (verse 6). But God gave Jeremiah the words and the ability to become a hero.

When you need to do something difficult but for the good of others, remember God's response to Jeremiah: "Do not say, 'I am only a boy'" (verse 7). God wants you to know that you too are capable of bringing about positive change in the world. God knows what you are able to do and say and be. Listen to God.

▶ Jer 1.4–10

and your apostasies will convict you.
Know and see that it is evil and bitter
    for you to forsake the LORD your God;
    the fear of me is not in you,
        says the Lord GOD of hosts.

20 For long ago you broke your yoke
    and burst your bonds,
    and you said, "I will not serve!"
On every high hill
    and under every green tree
    you sprawled and played the whore.
21 Yet I planted you as a choice vine,
    from the purest stock.
How then did you turn degenerate
    and become a wild vine?
22 Though you wash yourself with lye
    and use much soap,
    the stain of your guilt is still before me,
        says the Lord GOD.
23 How can you say, "I am not defiled,
    I have not gone after the Ba'als"?
Look at your way in the valley;
    know what you have done—
a restive young camel interlacing her tracks,

24   a wild ass at home in the wilderness,
in her heat sniffing the wind!
    Who can restrain her lust?
None who seek her need weary themselves;
    in her month they will find her.
25 Keep your feet from going unshod
    and your throat from thirst.
But you said, "It is hopeless,
    for I have loved strangers,
    and after them I will go."

26 As a thief is shamed when caught,
    so the house of Israel shall be shamed—
they, their kings, their officials,
    their priests, and their prophets,
27 who say to a tree, "You are my father,"
    and to a stone, "You gave me birth."
For they have turned their backs to me,
    and not their faces.
But in the time of their trouble they say,
    "Come and save us!"
28 But where are your gods
    that you made for yourself?
Let them come, if they can save you,
    in your time of trouble;

Introducing ►JEREMIAH

Have you ever felt ridiculed for defending your values or doing a good deed? If so, then you can probably relate to Jeremiah, who once told God:

> **You duped me, O LORD,**
>   **and I let myself be duped;**
>
> . . . .
>
> **All the day I am an object of laughter;**
>   **everyone mocks me.**
>
>   **(Jer 20, 7)**

Jeremiah knew what it was like to be rejected for delivering God's message.

    Jeremiah was born in 645 B.C. of a priestly family from a northern Israelite tribe. He was very young when he began his prophetic career. Like Isaiah, Jeremiah was a prophet for all seasons. He was both optimistic (chapter 31) and condemning (22, 18–23). He was courageous (chapter 37), enduring beatings, imprisonment, and even being thrown into a well to die (38, 1–6) for the sake of delivering God's message. He loved his people so much that he was sometimes called the weeping prophet because of his bitter tears for them and their fast-approaching doom (8, 23; 13, 7).

    The Book of Jeremiah gives us a fascinating inside look at the prophet's relationship with God. Several passages, called the Confessions of Jeremiah, are personal accounts of his struggles with God (12, 1–6; 15, 10–21; 17, 12–18; 18, 18–23; 20, 7–18). If you take the time to read these passages, you may find that your own doubts and struggles aren't all that different.

WHY do you complain against me**?**

YOU have all rebelled against me,
says the Lord.

O GENERATION, 2.29,31 **!**
behold the word of the Lord

for you have as many gods
   as you have towns, O Judah.
29 Why do you complain against me?
   You have all rebelled against me,
                                    says the LORD.
30 In vain I have struck down your children;
   they accepted no correction.
   Your own sword devoured your prophets
   like a ravening lion.
31 And you, O generation, behold the word of the
   LORD!*d*
   Have I been a wilderness to Israel,
   or a land of thick darkness?
   Why then do my people say, "We are free,
   we will come to you no more"?
32 Can a girl forget her ornaments,
   or a bride her attire?
   Yet my people have forgotten me,
   days without number.

33 How well you direct your course
   to seek lovers!
   So that even to wicked women
   you have taught your ways.
34 Also on your skirts is found
   the lifeblood of the innocent poor,
   though you did not catch them breaking in.
   Yet in spite of all these things*d*
35 you say, "I am innocent;

   surely his anger has turned from me."
   Now I am bringing you to judgment
   for saying, "I have not sinned."
36 How lightly you gad about,
   changing your ways!
   You shall be put to shame by Egypt
   as you were put to shame by Assyria.
37 From there also you will come away
   with your hands on your head;
   for the LORD has rejected those in whom you
      trust,
   and you will not prosper through them.

Unfaithful Israel

3 If*e* a man divorces his wife
   and she goes from him
and becomes another man's wife,
   will he return to her?
Would not such a land be greatly polluted?
You have played the whore with many lovers;
   and would you return to me?
                                    says the LORD.
2 Look up to the bare heights,*f* and see!
   Where have you not been lain with?
By the waysides you have sat waiting for lovers,
   like a nomad in the wilderness.
You have polluted the land

---

d Meaning of Heb uncertain   *e* Q Ms Gk Syr: MT
Saying, If   f Or *the trails*

with your whoring and wickedness.
3 Therefore the showers have been withheld,
    and the spring rain has not come;
yet you have the forehead of a whore,
    you refuse to be ashamed.
4 Have you not just now called to me,
    "My Father, you are the friend of my
        youth—
5 will he be angry forever,
    will he be indignant to the end?"
This is how you have spoken,
    but you have done all the evil that you
        could.

A Call to Repentance

6 The LORD said to me in the days of King
Jō·sī′ah: Have you seen what she did, that faithless
one, Israel, how she went up on every high hill and
under every green tree, and played the whore there?
7 And I thought, "After she has done all this she will
return to me"; but she did not return, and her false
sister Judah saw it. 8 She8 saw that for all the adulteries of that faithless one, Israel, I had sent her
away with a decree of divorce; yet her false sister Judah did not fear, but she too went and played the
whore. 9 Because she took her whoredom so lightly, she polluted the land, committing adultery with
stone and tree. 10 Yet for all this her false sister Judah did not return to me with her whole heart, but
only in pretense, says the LORD.

11 Then the LORD said to me: Faithless Israel
has shown herself less guilty than false Judah.
12 Go, and proclaim these words toward the north,
and say:
    Return, faithless Israel,

                        says the LORD.
    I will not look on you in anger,
        for I am merciful,

                        says the LORD;
    I will not be angry forever.
13 Only acknowledge your guilt,
        that you have rebelled against the LORD
            your God,
    and scattered your favors among strangers
            under every green tree,
        and have not obeyed my voice,

                        says the LORD.
14 Return, O faithless children,

                        says the LORD,
        for I am your master;
    I will take you, one from a city and two from a
        family,
        and I will bring you to Zion.

15 I will give you shepherds after my own heart,
who will feed you with knowledge and understanding. 16 And when you have multiplied and increased

CONTRITION

Jeremiah calls the people to acknowledge
their sin and return to God. In Catholic
Tradition, the word contrition describes
sorrow for sins and the commitment not
to sin again. Jeremiah is calling the people
to contrition with the promise that God
wants their return and is eager to welcome
them back.

An act of contrition is a prayer in
which you express your sorrow and hate
for your sin and your resolve not to sin
again. You may have learned an act of contrition to prepare to celebrate the sacrament of Reconciliation (or Penance). You
can use this prayer form any time you
need to acknowledge a sin and ask God's
forgiveness.

Try writing your own act of contrition.
Use it whenever sin has separated you
from God—knowing that God is merciful
and wants nothing to separate you from
God's love.

▶ Jer 3.12–14

in the land, in those days, says the LORD, they shall
no longer say, "The ark of the covenant of the
LORD." It shall not come to mind, or be remembered, or missed; nor shall another one be made.
17 At that time Jerusalem shall be called the throne
of the LORD, and all nations shall gather to it, to the
presence of the LORD in Jerusalem, and they shall
no longer stubbornly follow their own evil will.
18 In those days the house of Judah shall join the
house of Israel, and together they shall come from
the land of the north to the land that I gave your ancestors for a heritage.

19 I thought
    how I would set you among my children,
    and give you a pleasant land,

8 Q Ms Gk Mss Syr: MT I

the most beautiful heritage of all the
nations.
And I thought you would call me, My Father,
and would not turn from following me.
20 Instead, as a faithless wife leaves her husband,
so you have been faithless to me, O house
of Israel,

says the LORD.

21 A voice on the bare heights[h] is heard,
the plaintive weeping of Israel's children,
because they have perverted their way,
they have forgotten the LORD their God:
22 Return, O faithless children,
I will heal your faithlessness.

"Here we come to you;
for you are the LORD our God.
23 Truly the hills are[i] a delusion,
the orgies on the mountains.
Truly in the LORD our God
is the salvation of Israel.
24 "But from our youth the shameful thing has
devoured all for which our ancestors had labored,
their flocks and their herds, their sons and their
daughters. 25 Let us lie down in our shame, and let
our dishonor cover us; for we have sinned against
the LORD our God, we and our ancestors, from our
youth even to this day; and we have not obeyed the
voice of the LORD God."

4 If you return, O Israel,

says the LORD,

if you return to me,
if you remove your abominations from my
presence,
and do not waver,
2 and if you swear, "As the LORD lives!"
in truth, in justice, and in uprightness,
then nations shall be blessed[j] by him,
and by him they shall boast.
3 For thus says the LORD to the people of Judah
and to the inhabitants of Jerusalem:
Break up your fallow ground,
and do not sow among thorns.
4 Circumcise yourselves to the LORD,
remove the foreskin of your hearts,
O people of Judah and inhabitants of
Jerusalem,
or else my wrath will go forth like fire,
and burn with no one to quench it,
because of the evil of your doings.

Invasion and Desolation of Judah Threatened

5 Declare in Judah, and proclaim in Jerusalem,
and say:
Blow the trumpet through the land;

shout aloud[k] and say,
"Gather together, and let us go
into the fortified cities!"
6 Raise a standard toward Zion,
flee for safety, do not delay,
for I am bringing evil from the north,
and a great destruction.
7 A lion has gone up from its thicket,
a destroyer of nations has set out;
he has gone out from his place
to make your land a waste;
your cities will be ruins
without inhabitant.
8 Because of this put on sackcloth,
lament and wail:
"The fierce anger of the LORD
has not turned away from us."

9 On that day, says the LORD, courage shall fail the
king and the officials; the priests shall be appalled
and the prophets astounded. 10 Then I said, "Ah,
Lord GOD, how utterly you have deceived this
people and Jerusalem, saying, 'It shall be well with
you,' even while the sword is at the throat!"

11 At that time it will be said to this people and
to Jerusalem: A hot wind comes from me out of the
bare heights[h] in the desert toward my poor people,
not to winnow or cleanse— 12 a wind too strong for
that. Now it is I who speak in judgment against
them.
13 Look! He comes up like clouds,
his chariots like the whirlwind;
his horses are swifter than eagles—
woe to us, for we are ruined!
14 O Jerusalem, wash your heart clean of
wickedness
so that you may be saved.
How long shall your evil schemes
lodge within you?
15 For a voice declares from Dan
and proclaims disaster from Mount E'phra·im.
16 Tell the nations, "Here they are!"
Proclaim against Jerusalem,
"Besiegers come from a distant land;
they shout against the cities of Judah.
17 They have closed in around her like watchers
of a field,
because she has rebelled against me,

says the LORD.

18 Your ways and your doings
have brought this upon you.
This is your doom; how bitter it is!
It has reached your very heart."

---

h Or *the trails*   i Gk Syr Vg: Heb *Truly from the hills is*   j Or
shall bless themselves   k Or *shout, take your weapons*: Heb
shout, fill (your hand)

JER

Sorrow for a Doomed Nation

19 My anguish, my anguish! I writhe in pain!
　　Oh, the walls of my heart!
　My heart is beating wildly;
　　I cannot keep silent;
　for I[l] hear the sound of the trumpet,
　　the alarm of war.
20 Disaster overtakes disaster,
　　the whole land is laid waste.
　Suddenly my tents are destroyed,
　　my curtains in a moment.
21 How long must I see the standard,
　　and hear the sound of the trumpet?
22 "For my people are foolish,
　　they do not know me;
　they are stupid children,
　　they have no understanding.
　They are skilled in doing evil,
　　but do not know how to do good."

23 I looked on the earth, and lo, it was waste and
　　void;
　　and to the heavens, and they had no light.
24 I looked on the mountains, and lo, they were
　　quaking,
　　and all the hills moved to and fro.
25 I looked, and lo, there was no one at all,
　　and all the birds of the air had fled.
26 I looked, and lo, the fruitful land was a desert,
　　and all its cities were laid in ruins
　before the LORD, before his fierce anger.
　27 For thus says the LORD: The whole land shall
be a desolation; yet I will not make a full end.
28 Because of this the earth shall mourn,
　　and the heavens above grow black;
　for I have spoken, I have purposed;
　　I have not relented nor will I turn back.

29 At the noise of horseman and archer
　　every town takes to flight;
　they enter thickets; they climb among rocks;
　　all the towns are forsaken,
　　and no one lives in them.
30 And you, O desolate one,
　what do you mean that you dress in crimson,
　　that you deck yourself with ornaments of
　　gold,
　　that you enlarge your eyes with paint?
　In vain you beautify yourself.
　　Your lovers despise you;
　　they seek your life.
31 For I heard a cry as of a woman in labor,
　　anguish as of one bringing forth her first
　　child,
　the cry of daughter Zion gasping for breath,
　　stretching out her hands,
　"Woe is me! I am fainting before killers!"

The Utter Corruption of God's People

5 Run to and fro through the streets of
　　Jerusalem,
　　look around and take note!
　Search its squares and see
　　if you can find one person
　who acts justly
　　and seeks truth—
　so that I may pardon Jerusalem.[m]
2 Although they say, "As the LORD lives,"
　　yet they swear falsely.
3 O LORD, do your eyes not look for truth?
　You have struck them,
　　but they felt no anguish;
　you have consumed them,
　　but they refused to take correction.
　They have made their faces harder than rock;
　　they have refused to turn back.

4 Then I said, "These are only the poor,
　　they have no sense;
　for they do not know the way of the LORD,
　　the law of their God.
5 Let me go to the rich[n]
　　and speak to them;
　surely they know the way of the LORD,
　　the law of their God."
　But they all alike had broken the yoke,
　　they had burst the bonds.

6 Therefore a lion from the forest shall kill them,
　　a wolf from the desert shall destroy them.
　A leopard is watching against their cities;
　　everyone who goes out of them shall be
　　torn in pieces—
　because their transgressions are many,
　　their apostasies are great.

7 How can I pardon you?
　　Your children have forsaken me,
　　and have sworn by those who are no gods.
　When I fed them to the full,
　　they committed adultery
　　and trooped to the houses of prostitutes.
8 They were well-fed lusty stallions,
　　each neighing for his neighbor's wife.
9 Shall I not punish them for these things?
　　　　　　　　　　　　says the LORD;
　and shall I not bring retribution
　　on a nation such as this?

10 Go up through her vine-rows and destroy,
　　but do not make a full end;
　strip away her branches,

---

l Another reading is *for you, O my soul,*　m Heb *it*
n Or *the great*

for they are not the LORD's.

11 For the house of Israel and the house of Judah
  have been utterly faithless to me,
                                   says the LORD.
12 They have spoken falsely of the LORD,
    and have said, "He will do nothing.
No evil will come upon us,
    and we shall not see sword or famine."
13 The prophets are nothing but wind,
    for the word is not in them.
Thus shall it be done to them!

14 Therefore thus says the LORD, the God of
       hosts:
Because they[o] have spoken this word,
I am now making my words in your mouth a fire,
    and this people wood, and the fire shall
       devour them.
15 I am going to bring upon you
    a nation from far away, O house of Israel,
                                   says the LORD.
It is an enduring nation,
    it is an ancient nation,
a nation whose language you do not know,
    nor can you understand what they say.
16 Their quiver is like an open tomb;
    all of them are mighty warriors.
17 They shall eat up your harvest and your food;
    they shall eat up your sons and your
       daughters;
they shall eat up your flocks and your herds;
    they shall eat up your vines and your fig
       trees;
they shall destroy with the sword
    your fortified cities in which you trust.

18 But even in those days, says the LORD, I will
not make a full end of you. 19 And when your people say, "Why has the LORD our God done all these
things to us?" you shall say to them, "As you have
forsaken me and served foreign gods in your land,
so you shall serve strangers in a land that is not
yours."

20 Declare this in the house of Jacob,
    proclaim it in Judah:
21 Hear this, O foolish and senseless people,
    who have eyes, but do not see,
    who have ears, but do not hear.
22 Do you not fear me? says the LORD;
    Do you not tremble before me?
I placed the sand as a boundary for the sea,
    a perpetual barrier that it cannot pass;
though the waves toss, they cannot prevail,
    though they roar, they cannot pass over it.
23 But this people has a stubborn and rebellious
       heart;

they have turned aside and gone away.
24 They do not say in their hearts,
    "Let us fear the LORD our God,
who gives the rain in its season,
    the autumn rain and the spring rain,
and keeps for us
    the weeks appointed for the harvest."
25 Your iniquities have turned these away,
    and your sins have deprived you of good.
26 For scoundrels are found among my people;
    they take over the goods of others.
Like fowlers they set a trap;[p]
    they catch human beings.
27 Like a cage full of birds,
    their houses are full of treachery;
therefore they have become great and rich,
28   they have grown fat and sleek.
They know no limits in deeds of wickedness;
    they do not judge with justice
the cause of the orphan, to make it prosper,
    and they do not defend the rights of the
       needy.
29 Shall I not punish them for these things?
                                   says the LORD,
    and shall I not bring retribution
    on a nation such as this?

30 An appalling and horrible thing
    has happened in the land:
31 the prophets prophesy falsely,
    and the priests rule as the prophets
       direct;[q]
my people love to have it so,
    but what will you do when the end comes?

The Imminence and Horror of the Invasion

6 Flee for safety, O children of Benjamin,
    from the midst of Jerusalem!
Blow the trumpet in Te·ko′a,
    and raise a signal on Beth-hac·che′rem;
for evil looms out of the north,
    and great destruction.
2 I have likened daughter Zion
    to the loveliest pasture.[r]
3 Shepherds with their flocks shall come against
       her.
They shall pitch their tents around her;
    they shall pasture, all in their places.
4 "Prepare war against her;
    up, and let us attack at noon!"
"Woe to us, for the day declines,
    the shadows of evening lengthen!"
5 "Up, and let us attack by night,

---

o Heb *you*   p Meaning of Heb uncertain   q Or *rule by their
own authority*   r Or *I will destroy daughter Zion, the loveliest
pasture*

and destroy her palaces!"

6 For thus says the LORD of hosts:
Cut down her trees;
   cast up a siege ramp against Jerusalem.
This is the city that must be punished;ˢ
   there is nothing but oppression within her.
7 As a well keeps its water fresh,
   so she keeps fresh her wickedness;
violence and destruction are heard within her;
   sickness and wounds are ever before me.
8 Take warning, O Jerusalem,
   or I shall turn from you in disgust,
and make you a desolation,
   an uninhabited land.

9 Thus says the LORD of hosts:
Gleanᵗ thoroughly as a vine
   the remnant of Israel;
like a grape-gatherer, pass your hand again
   over its branches.

10 To whom shall I speak and give warning,
   that they may hear?
See, their ears are closed,ᵘ
   they cannot listen.
The word of the LORD is to them an object of
   scorn;
   they take no pleasure in it.
11 But I am full of the wrath of the LORD;
   I am weary of holding it in.

Pour it out on the children in the street,
   and on the gatherings of young men as well;
both husband and wife shall be taken,
   the old folk and the very aged.
12 Their houses shall be turned over to others,
   their fields and wives together;
for I will stretch out my hand
   against the inhabitants of the land,
             says the LORD.

13 For from the least to the greatest of them,
   everyone is greedy for unjust gain;
and from prophet to priest,
   everyone deals falsely.
14 They have treated the wound of my people
   carelessly,
saying, "Peace, peace,"
   when there is no peace.
15 They acted shamefully, they committed
   abomination;
yet they were not ashamed,
   they did not know how to blush.
Therefore they shall fall among those who fall;
   at the time that I punish them, they shall be
   overthrown,
             says the LORD.

16 Thus says the LORD:
Stand at the crossroads, and look,
   and ask for the ancient paths,
where the good way lies; and walk in it,
   and find rest for your souls.
But they said, "We will not walk in it."
17 Also I raised up sentinels for you:
   "Give heed to the sound of the trumpet!"
But they said, "We will not give heed."
18 Therefore hear, O nations,
   and know, O congregation, what will
      happen to them.
19 Hear, O earth; I am going to bring disaster on
   this people,
   the fruit of their schemes,
because they have not given heed to my words;
   and as for my teaching, they have rejected it.
20 Of what use to me is frankincense that comes
   from Shē'ba,
   or sweet cane from a distant land?
Your burnt offerings are not acceptable,
   nor are your sacrifices pleasing to me.
21 Therefore thus says the LORD:
See, I am laying before this people
   stumbling blocks against which they shall
     stumble;
parents and children together,
   neighbor and friend shall perish.

22 Thus says the LORD:
See, a people is coming from the land of the
     north,
   a great nation is stirring from the farthest
     parts of the earth.
23 They grasp the bow and the javelin,
   they are cruel and have no mercy,
   their sound is like the roaring sea;
they ride on horses,
   equipped like a warrior for battle,
   against you, O daughter Zion!

24 "We have heard news of them,
   our hands fall helpless;
anguish has taken hold of us,
   pain as of a woman in labor.
25 Do not go out into the field,
   or walk on the road;
for the enemy has a sword,
   terror is on every side."

26 O my poor people, put on sackcloth,
   and roll in ashes;
make mourning as for an only child,
   most bitter lamentation:

ˢ Or *the city of license* ᵗ Cn: Heb *They shall glean* ᵘ Heb *are uncircumcised*

for suddenly the destroyer
    will come upon us.

27 I have made you a tester and a refiner[v] among
       my people
    so that you may know and test their ways.
28 They are all stubbornly rebellious,
      going about with slanders;
    they are bronze and iron,
      all of them act corruptly.
29 The bellows blow fiercely,
      the lead is consumed by the fire;
    in vain the refining goes on,
      for the wicked are not removed.
30 They are called "rejected silver,"
      for the LORD has rejected them.

Jeremiah Proclaims God's Judgment on the Nation

(Cp Jer 26.4–6)

7 The word that came to Jer·e·mi′ah from the LORD: 2 Stand in the gate of the LORD's house, and proclaim there this word, and say, Hear the word of the LORD, all you people of Judah, you that enter these gates to worship the LORD. 3 Thus says the LORD of hosts, the God of Israel: Amend your ways and your doings, and let me dwell with you[w] in this place. 4 Do not trust in these deceptive words: "This is[x] the temple of the LORD, the temple of the LORD, the temple of the LORD."

5 For if you truly amend your ways and your doings, if you truly act justly one with another, 6 if you do not oppress the alien, the orphan, and the widow, or shed innocent blood in this place, and if you do not go after other gods to your own hurt, 7 then I will dwell with you in this place, in the land that I gave of old to your ancestors forever and ever.

8 Here you are, trusting in deceptive words to no avail. 9 Will you steal, murder, commit adultery, swear falsely, make offerings to Ba′al, and go after other gods that you have not known, 10 and then come and stand before me in this house, which is called by my name, and say, "We are safe!"—only to go on doing all these abominations? 11 Has this house, which is called by my name, become a den of robbers in your sight? You know, I too am watching, says the LORD. 12 Go now to my place that was in Shi′loh, where I made my name dwell at first, and see what I did to it for the wickedness of my people Israel. 13 And now, because you have done all these things, says the LORD, and when I spoke to you persistently, you did not listen, and when I called you, you did not answer, 14 therefore I will do to the house that is called by my name, in which you trust, and to the place that I gave to you and to your ancestors, just what I did to Shi′loh. 15 And I will cast you out of my sight, just as I cast out all your kinsfolk, all the offspring of E′phra·im.

The People's Disobedience

16 As for you, do not pray for this people, do not raise a cry or prayer on their behalf, and do not intercede with me, for I will not hear you. 17 Do you not see what they are doing in the towns of Judah and in the streets of Jerusalem? 18 The children gather wood, the fathers kindle fire, and the women knead dough, to make cakes for the queen of heaven; and they pour out drink offerings to other gods,

---

v Or a fortress   w Or and I will let you dwell   x Heb They are

did you KNOW?

The Prophet and the Temple

In ancient Israel, the Temple was considered the dwelling place of God. Most Israelites felt that as long as the Temple stood, God was keeping the Covenant promise to stay with Israel. They believed this because Jerusalem and Judea had been spared when the northern kingdom fell to Assyria (721 B.C.). The Israelites failed to remember that God's Covenant with them was a mutual one—that they in turn had to keep their commitment to worship God alone.

Speaking for God at the gates of the Temple, Jeremiah told the people the Temple would be destroyed if Israel continued to disobey the commandments of the Covenant (see how the sins he accused them of in Jer 7.8–9 reflect the Ten Commandments). The destruction of the Temple would be a visible sign that the Covenant had been broken—not by God, but by the people.

The Temple was destroyed, and then rebuilt. Centuries later, Jesus preached to a new generation who thought that the Temple was a guarantee of God's presence and favor. He predicted the Temple would be destroyed again (Mt 24.1–2).

▶ Jer 7.1–14

J
E
R

to provoke me to anger. 19 Is it I whom they provoke? says the LORD. Is it not themselves, to their own hurt? 20 Therefore thus says the Lord GOD: My anger and my wrath shall be poured out on this place, on human beings and animals, on the trees of the field and the fruit of the ground; it will burn and not be quenched.

21 Thus says the LORD of hosts, the God of Israel: Add your burnt offerings to your sacrifices, and eat the flesh. 22 For in the day that I brought your ancestors out of the land of Egypt, I did not speak to them or command them concerning burnt offerings and sacrifices. 23 But this command I gave them, "Obey my voice, and I will be your God, and you shall be my people; and walk only in the way that I command you, so that it may be well with you." 24 Yet they did not obey or incline their ear, but, in the stubbornness of their evil will, they walked in their own counsels, and looked backward rather than forward. 25 From the day that your ancestors came out of the land of Egypt until this day, I have persistently sent all my servants the prophets to them, day after day; 26 yet they did not listen to me, or pay attention, but they stiffened their necks. They did worse than their ancestors did.

27 So you shall speak all these words to them, but they will not listen to you. You shall call to them, but they will not answer you. 28 You shall say to them: This is the nation that did not obey the voice of the LORD their God, and did not accept discipline; truth has perished; it is cut off from their lips.

29 Cut off your hair and throw it away;
    raise a lamentation on the bare heights,y
   for the LORD has rejected and forsaken
    the generation that provoked his wrath.

30 For the people of Judah have done evil in my sight, says the LORD; they have set their abominations in the house that is called by my name, defiling it. 31 And they go on building the high placez of Tō'pheth, which is in the valley of the son of Hin'nom, to burn their sons and their daughters in the fire—which I did not command, nor did it come into my mind. 32 Therefore, the days are surely coming, says the LORD, when it will no more be called Tō'pheth, or the valley of the son of Hin'nom, but the valley of Slaughter: for they will bury in Tō'pheth until there is no more room. 33 The corpses of this people will be food for the birds of the air, and for the animals of the earth; and no one will frighten them away. 34 And I will bring to an end the sound of mirth and gladness, the voice of the bride and bridegroom in the cities of Judah and in the streets of Jerusalem; for the land shall become a waste.

8 At that time, says the LORD, the bones of the kings of Judah, the bones of its officials, the bones of the priests, the bones of the prophets, and the bones of the inhabitants of Jerusalem shall be brought out of their tombs; 2 and they shall be spread before the sun and the moon and all the host of heaven, which they have loved and served, which they have followed, and which they have inquired of and worshiped; and they shall not be gathered or buried; they shall be like dung on the surface of the ground. 3 Death shall be preferred to life by all the remnant that remains of this evil family in all the places where I have driven them, says the LORD of hosts.

The Blind Perversity of the Whole Nation

4 You shall say to them, Thus says the LORD:
   When people fall, do they not get up again?
    If they go astray, do they not turn back?
5 Why then has this peoplea turned away
    in perpetual backsliding?
   They have held fast to deceit,
    they have refused to return.
6 I have given heed and listened,
    but they do not speak honestly;
   no one repents of wickedness,
    saying, "What have I done!"
   All of them turn to their own course,
    like a horse plunging headlong into battle.
7 Even the stork in the heavens
    knows its times;
   and the turtledove, swallow, and craneb
    observe the time of their coming;
   but my people do not know
    the ordinance of the LORD.

8 How can you say, "We are wise,
    and the law of the LORD is with us,"
   when, in fact, the false pen of the scribes
    has made it into a lie?
9 The wise shall be put to shame,
    they shall be dismayed and taken;
   since they have rejected the word of the LORD,
    what wisdom is in them?
10 Therefore I will give their wives to others
    and their fields to conquerors,
   because from the least to the greatest
    everyone is greedy for unjust gain;
   from prophet to priest
    everyone deals falsely.
11 They have treated the wound of my people
     carelessly,
    saying, "Peace, peace,"
    when there is no peace.
12 They acted shamefully, they committed
     abomination;
    yet they were not at all ashamed,

---

y Or the trails   z Gk Tg: Heb high places   a One Ms Gk: MT
this people, Jerusalem,   b Meaning of Heb uncertain

they did not know how to blush.
Therefore they shall fall among those who fall;
at the time when I punish them, they shall
be overthrown,
says the LORD.
13 When I wanted to gather them, says the LORD,
there are[c] no grapes on the vine,
nor figs on the fig tree;
even the leaves are withered,
and what I gave them has passed away from
them.[d]

14 Why do we sit still?
Gather together, let us go into the fortified cities
and perish there;
for the LORD our God has doomed us to perish,
and has given us poisoned water to drink,
because we have sinned against the LORD.
15 We look for peace, but find no good,
for a time of healing, but there is terror
instead.

16 The snorting of their horses is heard from Dan;
at the sound of the neighing of their
stallions
the whole land quakes.
They come and devour the land and all that
fills it,
the city and those who live in it.
17 See, I am letting snakes loose among you,
adders that cannot be charmed,
and they shall bite you,
says the LORD.

The Prophet Mourns for the People

18 My joy is gone, grief is upon me,
my heart is sick.
19 Hark, the cry of my poor people
from far and wide in the land:
"Is the LORD not in Zion?
Is her King not in her?"
("Why have they provoked me to anger with
their images,
with their foreign idols?")
20 "The harvest is past, the summer is ended,
and we are not saved."
21 For the hurt of my poor people I am hurt,
I mourn, and dismay has taken hold of me.

22 Is there no balm in Gil'e•ad?
Is there no physician there?
Why then has the health of my poor people
not been restored?

9
[e] O that my head were a spring of water,
and my eyes a fountain of tears,
so that I might weep day and night
for the slain of my poor people!

2[f] O that I had in the desert
a traveler's lodging place,
that I might leave my people
and go away from them!
For they are all adulterers,
a band of traitors.
3 They bend their tongues like bows;
they have grown strong in the land for
falsehood, and not for truth;
for they proceed from evil to evil,
and they do not know me, says the LORD.

4 Beware of your neighbors,
and put no trust in any of your kin;[g]
for all your kin[h] are supplanters,
and every neighbor goes around like a
slanderer.
5 They all deceive their neighbors,
and no one speaks the truth;
they have taught their tongues to speak lies;
they commit iniquity and are too weary to
repent.[i]
6 Oppression upon oppression, deceit[j] upon
deceit!
They refuse to know me, says the LORD.

7 Therefore thus says the LORD of hosts:
I will now refine and test them,
for what else can I do with my sinful
people?[k]
8 Their tongue is a deadly arrow;
it speaks deceit through the mouth.
They all speak friendly words to their
neighbors,
but inwardly are planning to lay an
ambush.
9 Shall I not punish them for these things? says
the LORD;
and shall I not bring retribution
on a nation such as this?

10 Take up[l] weeping and wailing for the
mountains,
and a lamentation for the pastures of the
wilderness,
because they are laid waste so that no one
passes through,
and the lowing of cattle is not heard;
both the birds of the air and the animals
have fled and are gone.
11 I will make Jerusalem a heap of ruins,

---

[c] Or *I will make an end of them, says the* LORD. *There are*
[d] Meaning of Heb uncertain   [e] Ch 8.23 in Heb   [f] Ch 9.1
in Heb   [g] Heb *in a brother*   [h] Heb *for every brother*   [i] Cn
Compare Gk: Heb *they weary themselves with iniquity.* 6*Your
dwelling*   [j] Cn: Heb *Your dwelling in the midst of deceit*   [k] Or
my poor people   [l] Gk Syr: Heb *I will take up*

have broken the covenant that I made with their ancestors. 11 Therefore, thus says the LORD, assuredly I am going to bring disaster upon them that they cannot escape; though they cry out to me, I will not listen to them. 12 Then the cities of Judah and the inhabitants of Jerusalem will go and cry out to the gods to whom they make offerings, but they will never save them in the time of their trouble. 13 For your gods have become as many as your towns, O Judah; and as many as the streets of Jerusalem are the altars to shame you have set up, altars to make offerings to Bā'al.

14 As for you, do not pray for this people, or lift up a cry or prayer on their behalf, for I will not listen when they call to me in the time of their trouble. 15 What right has my beloved in my house, when she has done vile deeds? Can vows*q* and sacrificial flesh avert your doom? Can you then exult? 16 The LORD once called you, "A green olive tree, fair with goodly fruit"; but with the roar of a great tempest he will set fire to it, and its branches will be consumed. 17 The LORD of hosts, who planted you, has pronounced evil against you, because of the evil that the house of Israel and the house of Judah have done, provoking me to anger by making offerings to Bā'al.

Jeremiah's Life Threatened

18 It was the LORD who made it known to me,
        and I knew;
    then you showed me their evil deeds.
19 But I was like a gentle lamb
        led to the slaughter.
    And I did not know it was against me
        that they devised schemes, saying,
    "Let us destroy the tree with its fruit,
        let us cut him off from the land of the
            living,
        so that his name will no longer be
            remembered!"
20 But you, O LORD of hosts, who judge
        righteously,
    who try the heart and the mind,
    let me see your retribution upon
            them,
        for to you I have committed my
            cause.

21 Therefore thus says the LORD concerning the people of An'a•thoth, who seek your life, and say, "You shall not prophesy in the name of the LORD, or you will die by our hand"— 22 therefore thus says the LORD of hosts: I am going to punish them; the young men shall die by the sword; their sons and their daughters shall die by famine; 23 and not even a remnant shall be left of them. For I will bring disaster upon the people of An'a•thoth, the year of their punishment.

Jeremiah's First Confession

12 You will be in the right, O LORD,
        when I lay charges against you;
    but let me put my case to you.
    Why does the way of the guilty prosper?
        Why do all who are treacherous thrive?
2   You plant them, and they take root;
        they grow and bring forth fruit;
    you are near in their mouths
        yet far from their hearts.
3   But you, O LORD, know me;
        You see me and test me—my heart is with
            you.
    Pull them out like sheep for the slaughter,
        and set them apart for the day of slaughter.
4   How long will the land mourn,
        and the grass of every field wither?
    For the wickedness of those who live in it
        the animals and the birds are swept away,
        and because people said, "He is blind to
            our ways."*r*

5   If you have raced with foot-runners and they
            have wearied you,
        how will you compete with horses?
    And if in a safe land you fall down,
        how will you fare in the thickets of the
            Jordan?
6   For even your kinsfolk and your own family,
        even they have dealt treacherously with you;
        they are in full cry after you;
    do not believe them,
        though they speak friendly words to you.

God Replies to Jeremiah

7   I have forsaken my house,
        I have abandoned my heritage;
    I have given the beloved of my heart
        into the hands of her enemies.
8   My heritage has become to me
        like a lion in the forest;
    she hass lifted up her voice against me—
        therefore I hate her.
9   Is the hyena greedy*s* for my heritage at my
            command?
        Are the birds of prey all around her?
    Go, assemble all the wild animals;
        bring them to devour her.
10 Many shepherds have destroyed my vineyard,
        they have trampled down my portion,
    they have made my pleasant portion
        a desolate wilderness.
11 They have made it a desolation;
        desolate, it mourns to me.

---

q Gk: Heb *Can many*   *r* Gk: Heb *to our future*   *s* Cn: Heb *Is the hyena, the bird of prey*

did you KNOW?

The Confessions of Jeremiah

Jeremiah 12.1–6 is the first of five passages that are sometimes called the Confessions of Jeremiah (12.1–6; 15.10–21; 17.12–18; 18.18–23; 20.7–18). In the confessions, Jeremiah speaks to God in a very personal, very direct way. He complains to God about the people's stubbornness, he complains about his treatment, and he accuses God of deceiving him. Some scholars believe the confessions are a private journal kept by Jeremiah that he never intended to be made public.

In 12.1–4, Jeremiah asks God why God lets evil people prosper—why doesn't God just slaughter them like sheep? God's reply in verses 5–6 is that things are going to get worse before they get better and that even Jeremiah's own family will turn against him. God never answers Jeremiah directly in any of the confessions—although in 15.19–21, God does promise to support Jeremiah.

If this famous prophet shared his anger, doubts, and fears with God honestly, so can we. Jeremiah's confessions are a good reminder that God wants to share everything with us—not just our happy thoughts.

▸ Jer 12.1–6

---

them up from their land, and I will pluck up the house of Judah from among them. 15 And after I have plucked them up, I will again have compassion on them, and I will bring them again to their heritage and to their land, every one of them. 16 And then, if they will diligently learn the ways of my people, to swear by my name, "As the LORD lives," as they taught my people to swear by Bā′al, then they shall be built up in the midst of my people. 17 But if any nation will not listen, then I will completely uproot it and destroy it, says the LORD.

The Linen Loincloth

13 Thus said the LORD to me, "Go and buy yourself a linen loincloth, and put it on your loins, but do not dip it in water." 2 So I bought a loincloth according to the word of the LORD, and put it on my loins. 3 And the word of the LORD came to me a second time, saying, 4 "Take the loincloth that you bought and are wearing, and go now to the Euphrates,*v* and hide it there in a cleft of the rock." 5 So I went, and hid it by the Euphrates,*w* as the LORD commanded me. 6 And after many days the LORD said to me, "Go now to the Euphrates,*v* and take from there the loincloth that I commanded you to hide there." 7 Then I went to the Euphrates,*v* and dug, and I took the loincloth from the place where I had hidden it. But now the loincloth was ruined; it was good for nothing.

8 Then the word of the LORD came to me: 9 Thus says the LORD: Just so I will ruin the pride of Judah and the great pride of Jerusalem. 10 This evil people, who refuse to hear my words, who stubbornly follow their own will and have gone after other gods to serve them and worship them, shall be like this loincloth, which is good for nothing. 11 For as the loincloth clings to one's loins, so I made the whole house of Israel and the whole house of Judah cling to me, says the LORD, in order that they might be for me a people, a name, a praise, and a glory. But they would not listen.

Symbol of the Wine-Jars

12 You shall speak to them this word: Thus says the LORD, the God of Israel: Every wine-jar should be filled with wine. And they will say to you, "Do you think we do not know that every wine-jar should be filled with wine?" 13 Then you shall say to them: Thus says the LORD: I am about to fill all the inhabitants of this land—the kings who sit on David's throne, the priests, the prophets, and all the inhabitants of Jerusalem—with drunkenness. 14 And I will dash them one against another, parents and children together, says the LORD. I will not

---

The whole land is made desolate,
   but no one lays it to heart.
12 Upon all the bare heights*t* in the desert
   spoilers have come;
for the sword of the LORD devours
   from one end of the land to the other;
   no one shall be safe.
13 They have sown wheat and have reaped thorns,
   they have tired themselves out but profit
      nothing.
They shall be ashamed of their*u* harvests
   because of the fierce anger of the LORD.

14 Thus says the LORD concerning all my evil neighbors who touch the heritage that I have given my people Israel to inherit: I am about to pluck

---

t Or *the trails*   *u* Heb *your*   *v* Or *to Parah;* Heb *perath*   *w* Or *by Parah;* Heb *perath* pity or spare or have compassion when I destroy them.

Exile Threatened

15 Hear and give ear; do not be haughty,
  for the LORD has spoken.
16 Give glory to the LORD your God
    before he brings darkness,
and before your feet stumble
    on the mountains at twilight;
while you look for light,
  he turns it into gloom
  and makes it deep darkness.
17 But if you will not listen,
    my soul will weep in secret for your pride;
my eyes will weep bitterly and run down with
      tears,
    because the LORD's flock has been taken
      captive.

18 Say to the king and the queen mother:
    "Take a lowly seat,
for your beautiful crown
  has come down from your head."*x*
19 The towns of the Neg'eb are shut up
    with no one to open them;
all Judah is taken into exile,
  wholly taken into exile.

20 Lift up your eyes and see
    those who come from the north.
Where is the flock that was given you,
    your beautiful flock?
21 What will you say when they set as head over
      you
    those whom you have trained
    to be your allies?
Will not pangs take hold of you,
  like those of a woman in labor?
22 And if you say in your heart,
    "Why have these things come upon me?"
it is for the greatness of your iniquity
    that your skirts are lifted up,
    and you are violated.
23 Can Ethiopians*y* change their skin
    or leopards their spots?
Then also you can do good
    who are accustomed to do evil.
24 I will scatter you*z* like chaff
    driven by the wind from the desert.
25 This is your lot,
    the portion I have measured out to you,
      says the LORD,
because you have forgotten me
    and trusted in lies.
26 I myself will lift up your skirts over your face,
    and your shame will be seen.

27 I have seen your abominations,
    your adulteries and neighings, your
      shameless prostitutions
  on the hills of the countryside.
Woe to you, O Jerusalem!
  How long will it be
  before you are made clean?

The Great Drought

14 The word of the LORD that came to
Jer·e·mī'ah concerning the drought:
2 Judah mourns
    and her gates languish;
they lie in gloom on the ground,
    and the cry of Jerusalem goes up.
3 Her nobles send their servants for water;
    they come to the cisterns,
they find no water,
    they return with their vessels empty.
They are ashamed and dismayed
    and cover their heads,
4 because the ground is cracked.
    Because there has been no rain on the land
the farmers are dismayed;
    they cover their heads.
5 Even the doe in the field forsakes her newborn
      fawn
    because there is no grass.
6 The wild asses stand on the bare heights,*a*
    they pant for air like jackals;
their eyes fail
    because there is no herbage.

7 Although our iniquities testify against us,
    act, O LORD, for your name's sake;
our apostasies indeed are many,
    and we have sinned against you.
8 O hope of Israel,
    its savior in time of trouble,
why should you be like a stranger in the land,
    like a traveler turning aside for the night?
9 Why should you be like someone confused,
    like a mighty warrior who cannot give
      help?
Yet you, O LORD, are in the midst of us,
    and we are called by your name;
    do not forsake us!

10 Thus says the LORD concerning this people:
Truly they have loved to wander,
    they have not restrained their feet;
therefore the LORD does not accept them,
    now he will remember their iniquity
    and punish their sins.

---

x Gk Syr Vg: Meaning of Heb uncertain   *y* Or *Nubians*; Heb
Cushites   *z* Heb *them*   *a* Or *the trails*

11 The LORD said to me: Do not pray for the welfare of this people. 12 Although they fast, I do not hear their cry, and although they offer burnt offering and grain offering, I do not accept them; but by the sword, by famine, and by pestilence I consume them.

Denunciation of Lying Prophets

13 Then I said: "Ah, Lord GOD! Here are the prophets saying to them, 'You shall not see the sword, nor shall you have famine, but I will give you true peace in this place.' " 14 And the LORD said to me: The prophets are prophesying lies in my name; I did not send them, nor did I command them or speak to them. They are prophesying to you a lying vision, worthless divination, and the deceit of their own minds. 15 Therefore thus says the LORD concerning the prophets who prophesy in my name though I did not send them, and who say, "Sword and famine shall not come on this land": By sword and famine those prophets shall be consumed. 16 And the people to whom they prophesy shall be thrown out into the streets of Jerusalem, victims of famine and sword. There shall be no one to bury them—themselves, their wives, their sons,

and their daughters. For I will pour out their wickedness upon them.

17 You shall say to them this word:
Let my eyes run down with tears night and day,
   and let them not cease,
for the virgin daughter—my people—is struck
   down with a crushing blow,
   with a very grievous wound.
18 If I go out into the field,
   look—those killed by the sword!
And if I enter the city,
   look—those sick with[b] famine!
For both prophet and priest ply their trade
   throughout the land,
   and have no knowledge.

The People Plead for Mercy

19 Have you completely rejected Judah?
   Does your heart loathe Zion?
Why have you struck us down
   so that there is no healing for us?
We look for peace, but find no good;
   for a time of healing, but there is terror
     instead.
20 We acknowledge our wickedness, O LORD,
   the iniquity of our ancestors,
   for we have sinned against you.
21 Do not spurn us, for your name's sake;
   do not dishonor your glorious throne;
   remember and do not break your covenant
     with us.
22 Can any idols of the nations bring rain?
   Or can the heavens give showers?
Is it not you, O LORD our God?
   We set our hope on you,
   for it is you who do all this.

Punishment Is Inevitable

15 Then the LORD said to me: Though Moses and Samuel stood before me, yet my heart would not turn toward this people. Send them out of my sight, and let them go! 2 And when they say to you, "Where shall we go?" you shall say to them: Thus says the LORD:
Those destined for pestilence, to pestilence,
   and those destined for the sword, to the
     sword;
those destined for famine, to famine,
   and those destined for captivity, to captivity.
3 And I will appoint over them four kinds of destroyers, says the LORD: the sword to kill, the dogs to drag away, and the birds of the air and the wild animals of the earth to devour and destroy. 4 I will make them a horror to all the kingdoms of the

---

PRAY IT!

The Empty Promises of False Prophets

In Jer 14.13–16, Jeremiah attacks prophets who preach what the people want to hear. The people want peace and plenty, so that is what the false prophets preach. They offer false and dangerous security.

People deceive themselves when they listen only to what they want to hear. Sometimes, God tells us things that are hard to hear or asks us to do things that are hard to do.

In your prayer, reflect or journal on the following questions:

- When have you tried to ignore God's message for you?
- When have you heard and responded to God even if God's message was difficult?
- What are the hardest things for you to hear or do?

▸ Jer 14.13–16

---

b Heb look—the sicknesses of

earth because of what King Ma•nas′seh son of Hez•e•ki′ah of Judah did in Jerusalem.

5 Who will have pity on you, O Jerusalem,
     or who will bemoan you?
   Who will turn aside
     to ask about your welfare?
6 You have rejected me, says the LORD,
     you are going backward;
   so I have stretched out my hand against you
          and destroyed you—
     I am weary of relenting.
7 I have winnowed them with a winnowing fork
     in the gates of the land;
   I have bereaved them, I have destroyed my
          people;
     they did not turn from their ways.
8 Their widows became more numerous
     than the sand of the seas;
   I have brought against the mothers of youths
     a destroyer at noonday;
   I have made anguish and terror
     fall upon her suddenly.
9 She who bore seven has languished;
     she has swooned away;
   her sun went down while it was yet day;
     she has been shamed and disgraced.
   And the rest of them I will give to the sword
     before their enemies,
                    says the LORD.

Jeremiah's Second Confession

10 Woe is me, my mother, that you ever bore me, a man of strife and contention to the whole land! I have not lent, nor have I borrowed, yet all of them curse me. 11 The LORD said: Surely I have intervened in your life[c] for good, surely I have imposed enemies on you in a time of trouble and in a time of distress.[d] 12 Can iron and bronze break iron from the north?

13 Your wealth and your treasures I will give as plunder, without price, for all your sins, throughout all your territory. 14 I will make you serve your enemies in a land that you do not know, for in my anger a fire is kindled that shall burn forever.

15 O LORD, you know;
     remember me and visit me,
       and bring down retribution for me on my
          persecutors.
   In your forbearance do not take me away;
     know that on your account I suffer insult.
16 Your words were found, and I ate them,
     and your words became to me a joy
       and the delight of my heart;
   for I am called by your name,
     O LORD, God of hosts.
17 I did not sit in the company of merrymakers,

     nor did I rejoice;
   under the weight of your hand I sat alone,
     for you had filled me with indignation.
18 Why is my pain unceasing,
     my wound incurable,
       refusing to be healed?
   Truly, you are to me like a deceitful brook,
     like waters that fail.

19 Therefore thus says the LORD:
   If you turn back, I will take you back,
     and you shall stand before me.
   If you utter what is precious, and not what is
          worthless,
     you shall serve as my mouth.
   It is they who will turn to you,
     not you who will turn to them.
20 And I will make you to this people
     a fortified wall of bronze;
   they will fight against you,
     but they shall not prevail over you,
   for I am with you
     to save you and deliver you,
                    says the LORD.
21 I will deliver you out of the hand of the
          wicked,
     and redeem you from the grasp of the
          ruthless.

Jeremiah's Celibacy and Message

16 The word of the LORD came to me: 2 You shall not take a wife, nor shall you have sons or daughters in this place. 3 For thus says the LORD concerning the sons and daughters who are born in this place, and concerning the mothers who bear them and the fathers who beget them in this land: 4 They shall die of deadly diseases. They shall not be lamented, nor shall they be buried; they shall become like dung on the surface of the ground. They shall perish by the sword and by famine, and their dead bodies shall become food for the birds of the air and for the wild animals of the earth.

5 For thus says the LORD: Do not enter the house of mourning, or go to lament, or bemoan them; for I have taken away my peace from this people, says the LORD, my steadfast love and mercy. 6 Both great and small shall die in this land; they shall not be buried, and no one shall lament for them; there shall be no gashing, no shaving of the head for them. 7 No one shall break bread[e] for the mourner, to offer comfort for the dead; nor shall anyone give them the cup of consolation to drink for their fathers or their mothers. 8 You shall not go

---

c Heb *intervened with you*   d Meaning of Heb uncertain
e Two Mss Gk: MT *break for them*

into the house of feasting to sit with them, to eat and drink. 9 For thus says the LORD of hosts, the God of Israel: I am going to banish from this place, in your days and before your eyes, the voice of mirth and the voice of gladness, the voice of the bridegroom and the voice of the bride.

10 And when you tell this people all these words, and they say to you, "Why has the LORD pronounced all this great evil against us? What is our iniquity? What is the sin that we have committed against the LORD our God?" 11 then you shall say to them: It is because your ancestors have forsaken me, says the LORD, and have gone after other gods and have served and worshiped them, and have forsaken me and have not kept my law; 12 and because you have behaved worse than your ancestors, for here you are, every one of you, following your stubborn evil will, refusing to listen to me. 13 Therefore I will hurl you out of this land into a land that neither you nor your ancestors have known, and there you shall serve other gods day and night, for I will show you no favor.

God Will Restore Israel
(Cp Jer 23.7–8)

14 Therefore, the days are surely coming, says the LORD, when it shall no longer be said, "As the LORD lives who brought the people of Israel up out of the land of Egypt," 15 but "As the LORD lives who brought the people of Israel up out of the land of the north and out of all the lands where he had driven them." For I will bring them back to their own land that I gave to their ancestors.

16 I am now sending for many fishermen, says the LORD, and they shall catch them; and afterward I will send for many hunters, and they shall hunt them from every mountain and every hill, and out of the clefts of the rocks. 17 For my eyes are on all their ways; they are not hidden from my presence, nor is their iniquity concealed from my sight. 18 And*f* I will doubly repay their iniquity and their sin, because they have polluted my land with the carcasses of their detestable idols, and have filled my inheritance with their abominations.

19 O LORD, my strength and my stronghold,
   my refuge in the day of trouble,
to you shall the nations come
   from the ends of the earth and say:
Our ancestors have inherited nothing but lies,
   worthlesss things in which there is no
      profit.
20 Can mortals make for themselves gods?
   Such are no gods!

21 "Therefore I am surely going to teach them, this time I am going to teach them my power and my might, and they shall know that my name is the LORD."

Judah's Sin and Punishment

17 The sin of Judah is written with an iron pen; with a diamond point it is engraved on the tablet of their hearts, and on the horns of their altars, 2 while their children remember their altars and their sacred poles,*g* beside every green tree, and on the high hills, 3 on the mountains in the open country. Your wealth and all your treasures I will give for spoil as the price of your sin*h* throughout all your territory. 4 By your own act you shall lose the heritage that I gave you, and I will make you serve your enemies in a land that you do not know, for in my anger a fire is kindled*i* that shall burn forever.

5 Thus says the LORD:
   Cursed are those who trust in mere mortals
      and make mere flesh their strength,
      whose hearts turn away from the LORD.
6 They shall be like a shrub in the desert,
      and shall not see when relief comes.
   They shall live in the parched places of the
         wilderness,
      in an uninhabited salt land.

7 Blessed are those who trust in the LORD,
      whose trust is the LORD.
8 They shall be like a tree planted by water,
      sending out its roots by the stream.
   It shall not fear when heat comes,
      and its leaves shall stay green;
   in the year of drought it is not anxious,
      and it does not cease to bear fruit.

9 The heart is devious above all else;
      it is perverse—
      who can understand it?
10 I the LORD test the mind
      and search the heart,
   to give to all according to their ways,
      according to the fruit of their doings.

11 Like the partridge hatching what it did not lay,
      so are all who amass wealth unjustly;
   in mid-life it will leave them,
      and at their end they will prove to be fools.

12 O glorious throne, exalted from the
         beginning,
      shrine of our sanctuary!
13 O hope of Israel! O LORD!

---

f Gk: Heb *And first*   *g* Heb *Asherim*   *h* Cn: Heb *spoil your high places for sin*   *i* Two Mss Theodotion: *you kindled*

J
E
R

CHILDREN AND GREEN TREES

The land is very important in Native American spirituality; trees, grass, and flowers are given reverence similar to that afforded people because all are connected. It is the greatest wish of the elders that the children learn this lesson and carry it on to their own children. Native Americans would view the loss and destruction of the land described in Jer 17.1–3 as a horrible punishment. See how their value for the land is reflected in this prayer from the Mohawk tradition:

> *Oh Great Spirit, Creator of all things;*
> *Human Beings, trees, grass, berries.*
> *Help us, be kind to us.*
> *Let us be happy on earth.*
> *Let us lead our children*
> *To a good life and old age.*
> *These our people; give them good minds*
> *To love one another.*
> *Oh Great Spirit,*
> *Be kind to us.*
> *Give these people the favour*
> *To see green trees,*
> *Green grass, flowers, and berries*
> *This next spring;*
> *So we all meet again.*
> *Oh Great Spirit,*
> *We ask of you.*
> **(Author unknown, "Mohawk Indian Prayer")**

▸ Jer 17.1–3

All who forsake you shall be put to shame;
those who turn away from you*ʲ* shall be
  recorded in the underworld,*ᵏ*
for they have forsaken the fountain of living
  water, the LORD.

Jeremiah's Third Confession

14 Heal me, O LORD, and I shall be healed;
  save me, and I shall be saved;
  for you are my praise.
15 See how they say to me,
  "Where is the word of the LORD?
  Let it come!"
16 But I have not run away from being a
    shepherd*ˡ* in your service,
  nor have I desired the fatal day.
  You know what came from my lips;
  it was before your face.
17 Do not become a terror to me;

you are my refuge in the day of disaster;
18 Let my persecutors be shamed,
  but do not let me be shamed;
let them be dismayed,
  but do not let me be dismayed;
bring on them the day of disaster;
  destroy them with double destruction!

Hallow the Sabbath Day

19 Thus said the LORD to me: Go and stand in the People's Gate, by which the kings of Judah enter and by which they go out, and in all the gates of Jerusalem, 20 and say to them: Hear the word of the LORD, you kings of Judah, and all Judah, and all the inhabitants of Jerusalem, who enter by these gates. 21 Thus says the LORD: For the sake of your lives, take care that you do not bear a burden on the sab-

---

ʲ Heb *me*   *ᵏ* Or *in the earth*   *ˡ* Meaning of Heb uncertain bath day or bring it in by the gates of Jerusalem. 22 And do not carry a burden out of your houses on the sabbath or do any work, but keep the sabbath day holy, as I commanded your ancestors. 23 Yet they did not listen or incline their ear; they stiffened their necks and would not hear or receive instruction.

24 But if you listen to me, says the LORD, and bring in no burden by the gates of this city on the sabbath day, but keep the sabbath day holy and do no work on it, 25 then there shall enter by the gates of this city kings*m* who sit on the throne of David, riding in chariots and on horses, they and their officials, the people of Judah and the inhabitants of Jerusalem; and this city shall be inhabited forever. 26 And people shall come from the towns of Judah and the places around Jerusalem, from the land of Benjamin, from the She•phe'lah, from the hill country, and from the Neg'eb, bringing burnt offerings and sacrifices, grain offerings and frankincense, and bringing thank offerings to the house of the LORD. 27 But if you do not listen to me, to keep the sabbath day holy, and to carry in no burden through the gates of Jerusalem on the sabbath day, then I will kindle a fire in its gates; it shall devour the palaces of Jerusalem and shall not be quenched.

The Potter and the Clay

18 The word that came to Jer•e•mi'ah from the LORD: 2 "Come, go down to the potter's house, and there I will let you hear my words." 3 So I went down to the potter's house, and there he was working at his wheel. 4 The vessel he was making of clay was spoiled in the potter's hand, and he reworked it into another vessel, as seemed good to him.

5 Then the word of the LORD came to me: 6 Can I not do with you, O house of Israel, just as this potter has done? says the LORD. Just like the clay in the potter's hand, so are you in my hand, O house of Israel. 7 At one moment I may declare concerning a nation or a kingdom, that I will pluck up and break down and destroy it, 8 but if that nation, concerning which I have spoken, turns from its evil, I will change my mind about the disaster that I intended to bring on it. 9 And at another moment I may declare concerning a nation or a kingdom that I will build and plant it, 10 but if it does evil in my sight, not listening to my voice, then I will change my mind about the good that I had intended to do to it. 11 Now, therefore, say to the people of Judah and the inhabitants of Jerusalem: Thus says the LORD: Look, I am a potter shaping evil against you and devising a plan against you. Turn now, all of you from your evil way, and amend your ways and your doings.

Israel's Stubborn Idolatry

12 But they say, "It is no use! We will follow our own plans, and each of us will act according to the stubbornness of our evil will."

13 Therefore thus says the LORD:
  Ask among the nations:
      Who has heard the like of this?
  The virgin Israel has done
      a most horrible thing.
14 Does the snow of Lebanon leave
      the crags of Sir'i•on?*n*
  Do the mountain*o* waters run dry,*p*
      the cold flowing streams?
15 But my people have forgotten me,
      they burn offerings to a delusion;
  they have stumbled*q* in their ways,
      in the ancient roads,
  and have gone into bypaths,
      not the highway,
16 making their land a horror,
      a thing to be hissed at forever.
  All who pass by it are horrified
      and shake their heads.
17 Like the wind from the east,
      I will scatter them before the enemy.
  I will show them my back, not my face,
      in the day of their calamity.

Jeremiah's Fourth Confession

18 Then they said, "Come, let us make plots against Jer•e•mi'ah—for instruction shall not perish from the priest, nor counsel from the wise, nor the word from the prophet. Come, let us bring charges against him,*r* and let us not heed any of his words."

19 Give heed to me, O LORD,
      and listen to what my adversaries say!
20 Is evil a recompense for good?
      Yet they have dug a pit for my life.
  Remember how I stood before you
      to speak good for them,
      to turn away your wrath from them.
21 Therefore give their children over to famine;
      hurl them out to the power of the sword,
  let their wives become childless and widowed.
      May their men meet death by pestilence,
      their youths be slain by the sword in battle.
22 May a cry be heard from their houses,
      when you bring the marauder suddenly
          upon them!
  For they have dug a pit to catch me,

---

m Cn: Heb *kings and officials*   *n* Cn: Heb *of the field*   *o* Cn: Heb *foreign*   *p* Cn: Heb *Are . . . plucked up?*   *q* Gk Syr Vg: Heb *they made them stumble*   *r* Heb *strike him with the tongue*

and laid snares for my feet.
23 Yet you, O LORD, know
all their plotting to kill me.
Do not forgive their iniquity,
do not blot out their sin from your sight.
Let them be tripped up before you;
deal with them while you are angry.

The Broken Earthenware Jug

19 Thus said the LORD: Go and buy a potter's earthenware jug. Take with you[s] some of the elders of the people and some of the senior priests, 2 and go out to the valley of the son of Hin'nom at the entry of the Potsherd Gate, and proclaim there the words that I tell you. 3 You shall say: Hear the word of the LORD, O kings of Judah and inhabitants of Jerusalem. Thus says the LORD of hosts, the God of Israel: I am going to bring such disaster upon this place that the ears of everyone who hears of it will tingle. 4 Because the people have forsaken me, and have profaned this place by making offerings in it to other gods whom neither they nor their ancestors nor the kings of Judah have known, and because they have filled this place with the blood of the innocent, 5 and gone on building the high places of Ba'al to burn their children in the fire as burnt offerings to Ba'al, which I did not command or decree, nor did it enter my mind; 6 therefore the days are surely coming, says the LORD, when this place shall no more be called Tō'pheth, or the valley of the son of Hin'nom, but the valley of Slaughter. 7 And in this place I will make void the plans of Judah and Jerusalem, and will make them fall by the sword before their enemies, and by the hand of those who seek their life. I will give their dead bodies for food to the birds of the air and to the wild animals of the earth. 8 And I will make this city a horror, a thing to be hissed at; everyone who passes by it will be horrified and will hiss because of all its disasters. 9 And I will make them eat the flesh of their sons and the flesh of their daughters, and all shall eat the flesh of their neighbors in the siege, and in the distress with which their enemies and those who seek their life afflict them.

10 Then you shall break the jug in the sight of those who go with you, 11 and shall say to them: Thus says the LORD of hosts: So will I break this people and this city, as one breaks a potter's vessel, so that it can never be mended. In Tō'pheth they shall bury until there is no more room to bury. 12 Thus will I do to this place, says the LORD, and to its inhabitants, making this city like Tō'pheth. 13 And the houses of Jerusalem and the houses of the kings of Judah shall be defiled like the place of Tō'pheth—all the houses upon whose roofs offerings have been made to the whole host of heaven, and libations have been poured out to other gods.

14 When Jer•e•mi'ah came from Tō'pheth, where the LORD had sent him to prophesy, he stood in the court of the LORD's house and said to all the people: 15 Thus says the LORD of hosts, the God of Israel: I am now bringing upon this city and upon all its towns all the disaster that I have pronounced against it, because they have stiffened their necks, refusing to hear my words.

Jeremiah Persecuted by Pashhur

20 Now the priest Pash'hur son of Im'mer, who was chief officer in the house of the LORD, heard Jer•e•mi'ah prophesying these things. 2 Then Pash'hur struck the prophet Jer•e•mi'ah, and put him in the stocks that were in the upper Benjamin Gate of the house of the LORD. 3 The next morning when Pash'hur released Jer•e•mi'ah from the stocks, Jer•e•mi'ah said to him, The LORD has named you not Pash'hur but "Terror-all-around." 4 For thus says the LORD: I am making you a terror to yourself and to all your friends; and they shall fall by the sword of their enemies while you look on. And I will give all Judah into the hand of the king of Babylon; he shall carry them captive to Babylon, and shall kill them with the sword. 5 I will give all the wealth of this city, all its gains, all its prized belongings, and all the treasures of the kings of Judah into the hand of their enemies, who shall plunder them, and seize them, and carry them to Babylon. 6 And you, Pash'hur, and all who live in your house, shall go into captivity, and to Babylon you shall go; there you shall die, and there you shall be buried, you and all your friends, to whom you have prophesied falsely.

Jeremiah's Fifth Confession

7 O LORD, you have enticed me,
and I was enticed;
you have overpowered me,
and you have prevailed.
I have become a laughingstock all day long;
everyone mocks me.
8 For whenever I speak, I must cry out,
I must shout, "Violence and destruction!"
For the word of the LORD has become for me
a reproach and derision all day long.
9 If I say, "I will not mention him,
or speak any more in his name,"
then within me there is something like a
burning fire
shut up in my bones;
I am weary with holding it in,
and I cannot.
10 For I hear many whispering:
"Terror is all around!

---

s Syr Tg Compare Gk: Heb lacks *take with you*

Denounce him! Let us denounce him!"
   All my close friends
   are watching for me to stumble.
"Perhaps he can be enticed,
   and we can prevail against him,
   and take our revenge on him."
11 But the LORD is with me like a dread warrior;
   therefore my persecutors will stumble,
   and they will not prevail.
They will be greatly shamed,
   for they will not succeed.
Their eternal dishonor
   will never be forgotten.
12 O LORD of hosts, you test the righteous,
   you see the heart and the mind;
let me see your retribution upon them,
   for to you I have committed my cause.

13 Sing to the LORD;
   praise the LORD!
For he has delivered the life of the needy
   from the hands of evildoers.

14 Cursed be the day
   on which I was born!
The day when my mother bore me,
   let it not be blessed!
15 Cursed be the man
   who brought the news to my father, saying,
"A child is born to you, a son,"
   making him very glad.
16 Let that man be like the cities
   that the LORD overthrew without pity;
let him hear a cry in the morning
   and an alarm at noon,
17 because he did not kill me in the womb;
   so my mother would have been my grave,
   and her womb forever great.
18 Why did I come forth from the womb
   to see toil and sorrow,
   and spend my days in shame?

Jerusalem Will Fall to Nebuchadrezzar

21 This is the word that came to Jer·e·mi′ah from the LORD, when King Zed·e·ki′ah sent to him Pash′hur son of Mal·chi′ah and the priest Zeph·a·ni′ah son of Mā·a·sēi′ah, saying, 2 "Please inquire of the LORD on our behalf, for King Ne·bū·chad·rez′zar of Babylon is making war against us; perhaps the LORD will perform a wonderful deed for us, as he has often done, and will make him withdraw from us."

3 Then Jer·e·mi′ah said to them: 4 Thus you shall say to Zed·e·ki′ah: Thus says the LORD, the God of Israel: I am going to turn back the weapons of war that are in your hands and with which you are fighting against the king of Babylon and against

the Chal·dē′ans who are besieging you outside the walls; and I will bring them together into the center of this city. 5 I myself will fight against you with outstretched hand and mighty arm, in anger, in fury, and in great wrath. 6 And I will strike down the inhabitants of this city, both human beings and animals; they shall die of a great pestilence. 7 Afterward, says the LORD, I will give King Zed·e·ki′ah of Judah, and his servants, and the people in this city—those who survive the pestilence, sword, and famine—into the hands of King Ne·bū·chad·rez′zar of Babylon, into the hands of their enemies, into the hands of those who seek their lives. He shall strike them down with the edge of the sword; he shall not pity them, or spare them, or have compassion.

8 And to this people you shall say: Thus says the LORD: See, I am setting before you the way of life and the way of death. 9 Those who stay in this city shall die by the sword, by famine, and by pestilence; but those who go out and surrender to the Chal·dē′ans who are besieging you shall live and shall have their lives as a prize of war. 10 For I have set my face against this city for evil and not for good, says the LORD: it shall be given into the hands of the king of Babylon, and he shall burn it with fire.

Message to the House of David

11 To the house of the king of Judah say: Hear the word of the LORD, 12 O house of David! Thus says the LORD:
   Execute justice in the morning,
      and deliver from the hand of the oppressor
      anyone who has been robbed,
   or else my wrath will go forth like fire,
      and burn, with no one to quench it,
      because of your evil doings.

13 See, I am against you, O inhabitant of the
      valley,
   O rock of the plain,
                     says the LORD;
you who say, "Who can come down against us,
   or who can enter our places of refuge?"
14 I will punish you according to the fruit of your
      doings,
                     says the LORD;
I will kindle a fire in its forest,
   and it shall devour all that is around it.

Exhortation to Repent

22 Thus says the LORD: Go down to the house of the king of Judah, and speak there this word, 2 and say: Hear the word of the LORD, O King of Judah sitting on the throne of David—you, and your servants, and your people

J
E
R

who enter these gates. 3 Thus says the LORD: Act with justice and righteousness, and deliver from the hand of the oppressor anyone who has been robbed. And do no wrong or violence to the alien, the orphan, and the widow, or shed innocent blood in this place. 4 For if you will indeed obey this word, then through the gates of this house shall enter kings who sit on the throne of David, riding in chariots and on horses, they, and their servants, and their people. 5 But if you will not heed these words, I swear by myself, says the LORD, that this house shall become a desolation. 6 For thus says the LORD concerning the house of the king of Judah:

You are like Gil'e•ad to me,
     like the summit of Lebanon;
but I swear that I will make you a desert,
     an uninhabited city.ᵗ
7 I will prepare destroyers against you,
     all with their weapons;
they shall cut down your choicest cedars
     and cast them into the fire.

8 And many nations will pass by this city, and all of them will say one to another, "Why has the LORD dealt in this way with that great city?" 9 And they will answer, "Because they abandoned the covenant of the LORD their God, and worshiped other gods and served them."

10 Do not weep for him who is dead,
     nor bemoan him;
weep rather for him who goes away,
     for he shall return no more
     to see his native land.

Message to the Sons of Josiah

11 For thus says the LORD concerning Shal'lum son of King Jō•sī'ah of Judah, who succeeded his father Jō•sī'ah, and who went away from this place: He shall return here no more, 12 but in the place where they have carried him captive he shall die, and he shall never see this land again.

13 Woe to him who builds his house by
          unrighteousness,
     and his upper rooms by injustice;
who makes his neighbors work for nothing,
     and does not give them their wages;
14 who says, "I will build myself a spacious house
     with large upper rooms,"
and who cuts out windows for it,
     paneling it with cedar,
     and painting it with vermilion.
15 Are you a king
     because you compete in cedar?
Did not your father eat and drink
     and do justice and righteousness?
     Then it was well with him.

16 He judged the cause of the poor and needy;
     then it was well.
Is not this to know me?
     says the LORD.
17 But your eyes and heart
     are only on your dishonest gain,
for shedding innocent blood,
     and for practicing oppression and violence.

18 Therefore thus says the LORD concerning King Je•hoi'a•kim son of Jō•sī'ah of Judah:
They shall not lament for him, saying,
     "Alas, my brother!" or "Alas, sister!"
They shall not lament for him, saying,
     "Alas, lord!" or "Alas, his majesty!"
19 With the burial of a donkey he shall be
          buried—
     dragged off and thrown out beyond the
          gates of Jerusalem.
20 Go up to Lebanon, and cry out,
     and lift up your voice in Bā'shan;
cry out from Ab'a•rim,
     for all your lovers are crushed.

ᵗ Cn: Heb *uninhabited cities*

PRAY IT?
Admit It!

Jeremiah's words against King Jehoiakim in Jer 22.21–23 are harsh. Jehoiakim is guilty of some serious sin and is leading the nation to destruction. But he doesn't want to hear about it. In fact, when Jehoiakim is presented with a scroll of Jeremiah's prophecies, he burns it (36.23)!

Forgiving God,
Help us to hear the prophets in today's
     world who call us to own our sin.
The prophets who call us to end
     discrimination,
     who call us to care for the needy,
     who call us to care for the earth,
     who call us to end violence,
     who call us to healthy relationships,
     who call us to be people of integrity,
          avoiding sin in all its forms.
May we be humble enough to admit our
     faults
and courageous enough to do something
     about them.

▸ Jer 22.18–23

21 I spoke to you in your prosperity,
        but you said, "I will not listen."
    This has been your way from your youth,
        for you have not obeyed my voice.
22 The wind shall shepherd all your
        shepherds,
        and your lovers shall go into captivity;
    then you will be ashamed and dismayed
        because of all your wickedness.
23 O inhabitant of Lebanon,
        nested among the cedars,
    how you will groanᵘ when pangs come upon
        you,
        pain as of a woman in labor!

Judgment on Coniah (Jehoiachin)

24 As I live, says the LORD, even if King
Cō·ni'ah son of Je·hoi'a·kim of Judah were the
signet ring on my right hand, even from there I
would tear you off 25 and give you into the hands
of those who seek your life, into the hands of those
of whom you are afraid, even into the hands of
King Ne·bū·chad·rez'zar of Babylon and into the
hands of the Chal·dē'ans. 26 I will hurl you and the
mother who bore you into another country, where
you were not born, and there you shall die. 27 But
they shall not return to the land to which they long
to return.
28 Is this man Cō·ni'ah a despised broken pot,
        a vessel no one wants?
    Why are he and his offspring hurled out
        and cast away in a land that they do not
            know?
29 O land, land, land,
        hear the word of the LORD!
30 Thus says the LORD:
    Record this man as childless,
        a man who shall not succeed in his days;
    for none of his offspring shall succeed
        in sitting on the throne of David,
        and ruling again in Judah.

Restoration after Exile

23 Woe to the shepherds who destroy and
scatter the sheep of my pasture! says the
LORD. 2 Therefore thus says the LORD, the God of Israel, concerning the shepherds who shepherd my
people: It is you who have scattered my flock, and
have driven them away, and you have not attended
to them. So I will attend to you for your evil doings,
says the LORD. 3 Then I myself will gather the remnant of my flock out of all the lands where I have
driven them, and I will bring them back to their
fold, and they shall be fruitful and multiply. 4 I will
raise up shepherds over them who will shepherd
them, and they shall not fear any longer, or be dismayed, nor shall any be missing, says the LORD.

The Righteous Branch of David
(Cp Jer 16.14–15)

5 The days are surely coming, says the LORD,
when I will raise up for David a righteous Branch,
and he shall reign as king and deal wisely, and shall
execute justice and righteousness in the land. 6 In
his days Judah will be saved and Israel will live in
safety. And this is the name by which he will be
called: "The LORD is our righteousness."

7 Therefore, the days are surely coming, says the
LORD, when it shall no longer be said, "As the LORD
lives who brought the people of Israel up out of
the land of Egypt," 8 but "As the LORD lives who
brought out and led the offspring of the house of Israel out of the land of the north and out of all the
lands where heᵛ had driven them." Then they shall
live in their own land.

False Prophets of Hope Denounced

9 Concerning the prophets:
    My heart is crushed within me,
        all my bones shake;
    I have become like a drunkard,
        like one overcome by wine,
    because of the LORD
        and because of his holy words.
10 For the land is full of adulterers;
        because of the curse the land mourns,
        and the pastures of the wilderness are
            dried up.
    Their course has been evil,
        and their might is not right.
11 Both prophet and priest are ungodly;
        even in my house I have found their
            wickedness,
                                            says the LORD.
12 Therefore their way shall be to them
        like slippery paths in the darkness,
        into which they shall be driven and fall;
    for I will bring disaster upon them
        in the year of their punishment,
                                            says the LORD.
13 In the prophets of Sa·mār'i·a
        I saw a disgusting thing:
    they prophesied by Bā'al
        and led my people Israel astray.
14 But in the prophets of Jerusalem
        I have seen a more shocking thing:
    they commit adultery and walk in lies;
        they strengthen the hands of evildoers,
        so that no one turns from wickedness;
    all of them have become like Sod'om to me,
        and its inhabitants like Go·mor'rah.
15 Therefore thus says the LORD of hosts
        concerning the prophets:

ᵘ Gk Vg Syr: Heb *will be pitied*   ᵛ Gk: Heb *I*

"I am going to make them eat wormwood,
  and give them poisoned water to drink;
for from the prophets of Jerusalem
  ungodliness has spread throughout the land."

16 Thus says the LORD of hosts: Do not listen to the words of the prophets who prophesy to you; they are deluding you. They speak visions of their own minds, not from the mouth of the LORD. 17 They keep saying to those who despise the word of the LORD, "It shall be well with you"; and to all who stubbornly follow their own stubborn hearts, they say, "No calamity shall come upon you."

18 For who has stood in the council of the LORD
    so as to see and to hear his word?
  Who has given heed to his word so as to
    proclaim it?
19 Look, the storm of the LORD!
    Wrath has gone forth,
  a whirling tempest;
    it will burst upon the head of the wicked.
20 The anger of the LORD will not turn back
    until he has executed and accomplished
    the intents of his mind.
  In the latter days you will understand it clearly.

21 I did not send the prophets,
    yet they ran;
  I did not speak to them,
    yet they prophesied.
22 But if they had stood in my council,
    then they would have proclaimed my words
      to my people,
  and they would have turned them from their
      evil way,
    and from the evil of their doings.

23 Am I a God near by, says the LORD, and not a God far off? 24 Who can hide in secret places so that I cannot see them? says the LORD. Do I not fill heaven and earth? says the LORD. 25 I have heard what the prophets have said who prophesy lies in my name, saying, "I have dreamed, I have dreamed!" 26 How long? Will the hearts of the prophets ever turn back—those who prophesy lies, and who prophesy the deceit of their own heart? 27 They plan to make my people forget my name by their dreams that they tell one another, just as their ancestors forgot my name for Ba′al. 28 Let the prophet who has a dream tell the dream, but let the one who has my word speak my word faithfully. What has straw in common with wheat? says the LORD. 29 Is not my word like fire, says the LORD, and like a hammer that breaks a rock in pieces? 30 See, therefore, I am against the prophets, says the LORD, who steal my words from one another.

31 See, I am against the prophets, says the LORD, who use their own tongues and say, "Says the LORD." 32 See, I am against those who prophesy lying dreams, says the LORD, and who tell them, and who lead my people astray by their lies and their recklessness, when I did not send them or appoint them; so they do not profit this people at all, says the LORD.

33 When this people, or a prophet, or a priest asks you, "What is the burden of the LORD?" you shall say to them, "You are the burden,w and I will cast you off, says the LORD." 34 And as for the prophet, priest, or the people who say, "The burden of the LORD," I will punish them and their households. 35 Thus shall you say to one another, among yourselves, "What has the LORD answered?" or "What has the LORD spoken?" 36 But "the burden of the LORD" you shall mention no more, for the burden is everyone's own word, and so you pervert the words of the living God, the LORD of hosts, our God. 37 Thus you shall ask the prophet, "What has the LORD answered you?" or "What has the LORD spoken?" 38 But if you say, "the burden of the LORD," thus says the LORD: Because you have said these words, "the burden of the LORD," when I sent to you, saying, You shall not say, "the burden of the LORD," 39 therefore, I will surely lift you upx and cast you away from my presence, you and the city that I gave to you and your ancestors. 40 And I will bring upon you everlasting disgrace and perpetual shame, which shall not be forgotten.

The Good and the Bad Figs

24 The LORD showed me two baskets of figs placed before the temple of the LORD. This was after King Ne·bu·chad·rez′zar of Babylon had taken into exile from Jerusalem King Jec·o·ni′ah son of Je·hoi′a·kim of Judah, together with the officials of Judah, the artisans, and the smiths, and had brought them to Babylon. 2 One basket had very good figs, like first-ripe figs, but the other basket had very bad figs, so bad that they could not be eaten. 3 And the LORD said to me, "What do you see, Jer·e·mi′ah?" I said, "Figs, the good figs very good, and the bad figs very bad, so bad that they cannot be eaten."

4 Then the word of the LORD came to me: 5 Thus says the LORD, the God of Israel: Like these good figs, so I will regard as good the exiles from Judah, whom I have sent away from this place to the land of the Chal·de′ans. 6 I will set my eyes upon them for good, and I will bring them back to this land. I will build them up, and not tear them down; I will plant them, and not pluck them up. 7 I will give them a heart to know that I am the LORD; and

---

w Gk Vg: Heb *What burden* x Heb Mss Gk Vg: MT *forget you* they shall be my people and I will be their God, for they shall return to me with their whole heart.

8 But thus says the LORD: Like the bad figs that are so bad they cannot be eaten, so will I treat King Zed·e·ki'ah of Judah, his officials, the remnant of Jerusalem who remain in this land, and those who live in the land of Egypt. 9 I will make them a horror, an evil thing, to all the kingdoms of the earth— a disgrace, a byword, a taunt, and a curse in all the places where I shall drive them. 10 And I will send sword, famine, and pestilence upon them, until they are utterly destroyed from the land that I gave to them and their ancestors.

did you KNOW?

Fig Trees

The fig tree was widely cultivated in the ancient Near East. Its sweet fruit was a delight to taste, and its broad leaves offered welcome shade from the scorching summer sun. In Jer 24.5–7, ripe figs are presented as an image of the faithful exiles in Babylon. In I Kings 4.25, fig leaves symbolize protection and safety. Jesus tells a parable about a fig tree in Lk 13.6–9. Think about it the next time you eat a Fig Newton!

▸ Jer 24.1–10

The Babylonian Captivity Foretold

25 The word that came to Jer·e·mi'ah concerning all the people of Judah, in the fourth year of King Je·hoi'a·kim son of Jō·si'ah of Judah (that was the first year of King Ne·bū·chad·rez'zar of Babylon), 2 which the prophet Jer·e·mi'ah spoke to all the people of Judah and all the inhabitants of Jerusalem: 3 For twenty-three years, from the thirteenth year of King Jō·si'ah son of Ā'mon of Judah, to this day, the word of the LORD has come to me, and I have spoken persistently to you, but you have not listened. 4 And though the LORD persistently sent you all his servants the prophets, you have neither listened nor inclined your ears to hear 5 when they said, "Turn now, every one of you, from your evil way and wicked doings, and you will remain upon the land that the LORD has given to you and your ancestors from of old and forever; 6 do not go after other gods to serve and worship them, and do not provoke me to anger with the work of your hands. Then I will do you no harm." 7 Yet you

did not listen to me, says the LORD, and so you have provoked me to anger with the work of your hands to your own harm.

8 Therefore thus says the LORD of hosts: Because you have not obeyed my words, 9 I am going to send for all the tribes of the north, says the LORD, even for King Ne·bū·chad·rez'zar of Babylon, my servant, and I will bring them against this land and its inhabitants, and against all these nations around; I will utterly destroy them, and make them an object of horror and of hissing, and an everlasting disgrace.y 10 And I will banish from them the sound of mirth and the sound of gladness, the voice of the bridegroom and the voice of the bride, the sound of the millstones and the light of the lamp. 11 This whole land shall become a ruin and a waste, and these nations shall serve the king of Babylon seventy years. 12 Then after seventy years are completed, I will punish the king of Babylon and that nation, the land of the Chal·dē'ans, for their iniquity, says the LORD, making the land an everlasting waste. 13 I will bring upon that land all the words that I have uttered against it, everything written in this book, which Jer·e·mi'ah prophesied against all the nations. 14 For many nations and great kings shall make slaves of them also; and I will repay them according to their deeds and the work of their hands.

The Cup of God's Wrath

15 For thus the LORD, the God of Israel, said to me: Take from my hand this cup of the wine of wrath, and make all the nations to whom I send you drink it. 16 They shall drink and stagger and go out of their minds because of the sword that I am sending among them.

17 So I took the cup from the LORD's hand, and made all the nations to whom the LORD sent me drink it: 18 Jerusalem and the towns of Judah, its kings and officials, to make them a desolation and a waste, an object of hissing and of cursing, as they are today; 19 Pharaoh king of Egypt, his servants, his officials, and all his people; 20 all the mixed people;z all the kings of the land of Uz; all the kings of the land of the Phi·lis'tines—Ash'ke·lon, Gā'za, Ek'ron, and the remnant of Ash'dod; 21 Ē'dom, Mō'ab, and the Am'mon·ites; 22 all the kings of Tyre, all the kings of Si'don, and the kings of the coastland across the sea; 23 Dē'dan, Tē'ma, Buz, and all who have shaven temples; 24 all the kings of Arabia and all the kings of the mixed peoplesz that live in the desert; 25 all the kings of Zim'ri, all the kings of Ē'lam, and all the kings of Mēd'i·a; 26 all the kings of the north, far and near, one after another,

---

y Gk Compare Syr: Heb *and everlasting desolations*
z Meaning of Heb uncertain

and all the kingdoms of the world that are on the face of the earth. And after them the king of Shē′-shach[a] shall drink.

27 Then you shall say to them, Thus says the LORD of hosts, the God of Israel: Drink, get drunk and vomit, fall and rise no more, because of the sword that I am sending among you.

28 And if they refuse to accept the cup from your hand to drink, then you shall say to them: Thus says the LORD of hosts: You must drink! 29 See, I am beginning to bring disaster on the city that is called by my name, and how can you possibly avoid punishment? You shall not go unpunished, for I am summoning a sword against all the inhabitants of the earth, says the LORD of hosts.

30 You, therefore, shall prophesy against them all these words, and say to them:

The LORD will roar from on high,
    and from his holy habitation utter his
        voice;
he will roar mightily against his fold,
    and shout, like those who tread grapes,
    against all the inhabitants of the earth.
31 The clamor will resound to the ends of the
       earth,
    for the LORD has an indictment against the
       nations;
he is entering into judgment with all flesh,
    and the guilty he will put to the sword,
                     says the LORD.

32 Thus says the LORD of hosts:
    See, disaster is spreading
       from nation to nation,
    and a great tempest is stirring
       from the farthest parts of the earth!

33 Those slain by the LORD on that day shall extend from one end of the earth to the other. They shall not be lamented, or gathered, or buried; they shall become dung on the surface of the ground.
34 Wail, you shepherds, and cry out;
    roll in ashes, you lords of the flock,
for the days of your slaughter have come—and
       your dispersions,[b]
    and you shall fall like a choice vessel.
35 Flight shall fail the shepherds,
    and there shall be no escape for the lords of
       the flock.
36 Hark! the cry of the shepherds,
    and the wail of the lords of the flock!
For the LORD is despoiling their pasture,
37   and the peaceful folds are devastated,
       because of the fierce anger of the LORD.
38 Like a lion he has left his covert;
    for their land has become a waste
because of the cruel sword,
    and because of his fierce anger.

Jeremiah's Prophecies in the Temple
(Cp Jer 7.1–15)

26 At the beginning of the reign of King Je•hoi′a•kim son of Jō•sī′ah of Judah, this word came from the LORD: 2 Thus says the LORD: Stand in the court of the LORD's house, and speak to all the cities of Judah that come to worship in the house of the LORD; speak to them all the words that I command you; do not hold back a word. 3 It may be that they will listen, all of them, and will turn from their evil way, that I may change my mind about the disaster that I intend to bring on them because of their evil doings. 4 You shall say to them: Thus says the LORD: If you will not listen to me, to walk in my law that I have set before you, 5 and to heed the words of my servants the prophets whom I send to you urgently—though you have not heeded— 6 then I will make this house like Shi′lōh, and I will make this city a curse for all the nations of the earth.

7 The priests and the prophets and all the people heard Jer•e•mi′ah speaking these words in the house of the LORD. 8 And when Jer•e•mi′ah had finished speaking all that the LORD had commanded him to speak to all the people, then the priests and the prophets and all the people laid hold of him, saying, "You shall die! 9 Why have you prophesied in the name of the LORD, saying, 'This house shall be like Shi′lōh, and this city shall be desolate, without inhabitant'?" And all the people gathered around Jer•e•mi′ah in the house of the LORD.

10 When the officials of Judah heard these things, they came up from the king's house to the house of the LORD and took their seat in the entry of the New Gate of the house of the LORD. 11 Then the priests and the prophets said to the officials and to all the people, "This man deserves the sentence of death because he has prophesied against this city, as you have heard with your own ears."

12 Then Jer•e•mi′ah spoke to all the officials and all the people, saying, "It is the LORD who sent me to prophesy against this house and this city all the words you have heard. 13 Now therefore amend your ways and your doings, and obey the voice of the LORD your God, and the LORD will change his mind about the disaster that he has pronounced against you. 14 But as for me, here I am in your hands. Do with me as seems good and right to you. 15 Only know for certain that if you put me to death, you will be bringing innocent blood upon yourselves and upon this city and its inhabitants, for in truth the LORD sent me to you to speak all these words in your ears."

16 Then the officials and all the people said to

---

a *Sheshach* is a cryptogram for *Babel*, Babylon   b Meaning of Heb uncertain the priests and the prophets, "This man does not deserve the sentence of death, for he has spoken to us in the name of the LORD our God." 17 And some of the elders of the land arose and said to all the assembled people, 18 "Mĭ′cah of Mō′re·sheth, who prophesied during the days of King Hez·e·kĭ′ah of Judah, said to all the people of Judah: 'Thus says the LORD of hosts,

Zion shall be plowed as a field;
> Jerusalem shall become a heap of ruins,
> and the mountain of the house a wooded
> height.'

19 Did King Hez·e·kĭ′ah of Judah and all Judah actually put him to death? Did he not fear the LORD and entreat the favor of the LORD, and did not the LORD change his mind about the disaster that he had pronounced against them? But we are about to bring great disaster on ourselves!"

20 There was another man prophesying in the name of the LORD, Ū·rĭ′ah son of She·māi′ah from Kir′i·ath-jē′a·rim. He prophesied against this city and against this land in words exactly like those of Jer·e·mĭ′ah. 21 And when King Je·hoi′a·kim, with all his warriors and all the officials, heard his words, the king sought to put him to death; but when Ū·rĭ′ah heard of it, he was afraid and fled and escaped to Egypt. 22 Then King Je·hoi′a·kim sent[c] El·nā′than son of Ach′bor and men with him to Egypt, 23 and they took Ū·rĭ′ah from Egypt and brought him to King Je·hoi′a·kim, who struck him down with the sword and threw his dead body into the burial place of the common people.

24 But the hand of A·hĭ′kam son of Shā′phan was with Jer·e·mĭ′ah so that he was not given over into the hands of the people to be put to death.

The Sign of the Yoke

27 In the beginning of the reign of King Zed·e·kĭ′ah[d] son of Jō·sĭ′ah of Judah, this word came to Jer·e·mĭ′ah from the LORD. 2 Thus the LORD said to me: Make yourself a yoke of straps and bars, and put them on your neck. 3 Send word[e] to the king of E′dom, the king of Mō′ab, the king of the Am′mon·ītes, the king of Tȳre, and the king of Sĭ′don by the hand of the envoys who have come to Jerusalem to King Zed·e·kĭ′ah of Judah. 4 Give them this charge for their masters: Thus says the LORD of hosts, the God of Israel: This is what you shall say to your masters: 5 It is I who by my great power and my outstretched arm have made the earth, with the people and animals that are on the earth, and I give it to whomever I please. 6 Now I have given all these lands into the hand of King Ne·bū·chad·nez′-zar of Babylon, my servant, and I have given him even the wild animals of the field to serve him. 7 All the nations shall serve him and his son and his grandson, until the time of his own land comes;

then many nations and great kings shall make him their slave.

8 But if any nation or kingdom will not serve this king, Ne·bū·chad·nez′zar of Babylon, and put its neck under the yoke of the king of Babylon, then I will punish that nation with the sword, with famine, and with pestilence, says the LORD, until I have completed its[f] destruction by his hand. 9 You, therefore, must not listen to your prophets, your diviners, your dreamers,[g] your soothsayers, or your sorcerers, who are saying to you, "You shall not serve the king of Babylon." 10 For they are prophesying a lie to you, with the result that you will be removed far from your land; I will drive you out, and you will perish. 11 But any nation that will bring its neck under the yoke of the king of Babylon and serve him, I will leave on its own land, says the LORD, to till it and live there.

12 I spoke to King Zed·e·kĭ′ah of Judah in the same way: Bring your necks under the yoke of the king of Babylon, and serve him and his people, and live. 13 Why should you and your people die by the sword, by famine, and by pestilence, as the LORD has spoken concerning any nation that will not serve the king of Babylon? 14 Do not listen to the words of the prophets who are telling you not to serve the king of Babylon, for they are prophesying a lie to you. 15 I have not sent them, says the LORD, but they are prophesying falsely in my name, with the result that I will drive you out and you will perish, you and the prophets who are prophesying to you.

16 Then I spoke to the priests and to all this

---

c Heb adds *men to Egypt*   d Another reading is *Jehoiakim*
e Cn: Heb *send them*   f Heb *their*   g Gk Syr Vg: Heb *dreams*

27.2

people, saying, Thus says the LORD: Do not listen to the words of your prophets who are prophesying to you, saying, "The vessels of the LORD's house will soon be brought back from Babylon," for they are prophesying a lie to you. 17 Do not listen to them; serve the king of Babylon and live. Why should this city become a desolation? 18 If indeed they are prophets, and if the word of the LORD is with them, then let them intercede with the LORD of hosts, that the vessels left in the house of the LORD, in the house of the king of Judah, and in Jerusalem may not go to Babylon. 19 For thus says the LORD of hosts concerning the pillars, the sea, the stands, and the rest of the vessels that are left in this city, 20 which King Ne•bū•chad•nez′zar of Babylon did not take away when he took into exile from Jerusalem to Babylon King Jec•o•nī′ah son of Je•hoi′a•kim of Judah, and all the nobles of Judah and Jerusalem— 21 thus says the LORD of hosts, the God of Israel, concerning the vessels left in the house of the LORD, in the house of the king of Judah, and in Jerusalem: 22 They shall be carried to Babylon, and there they shall stay, until the day when I give attention to them, says the LORD. Then I will bring them up and restore them to this place.

Hananiah Opposes Jeremiah and Dies

28 In that same year, at the beginning of the reign of King Zed•e•kī′ah of Judah, in the fifth month of the fourth year, the prophet Han•a•nī′ah son of Az′zur, from Gib′ē•on, spoke to me in the house of the LORD, in the presence of the priests and all the people, saying, 2 "Thus says the LORD of hosts, the God of Israel: I have broken the yoke of the king of Babylon. 3 Within two years I will bring back to this place all the vessels of the LORD's house, which King Ne•bū•chad•nez′zar of Babylon took away from this place and carried to Babylon. 4 I will also bring back to this place King Jec•o•nī′ah son of Je•hoi′a•kim of Judah, and all the exiles from Judah who went to Babylon, says the LORD, for I will break the yoke of the king of Babylon."

5 Then the prophet Jer•e•mī′ah spoke to the prophet Han•a•nī′ah in the presence of the priests and all the people who were standing in the house of the LORD; 6 and the prophet Jer•e•mī′ah said, "Amen! May the LORD do so; may the LORD fulfill the words that you have prophesied, and bring back to this place from Babylon the vessels of the house of the LORD, and all the exiles. 7 But listen now to this word that I speak in your hearing and in the hearing of all the people. 8 The prophets who preceded you and me from ancient times prophesied war, famine, and pestilence against many countries and great kingdoms. 9 As for the prophet who prophesies peace, when the word of that prophet comes true, then it will be known that the LORD has truly sent the prophet."

10 Then the prophet Han•a•nī′ah took the yoke from the neck of the prophet Jer•e•mī′ah, and broke it. 11 And Han•a•nī′ah spoke in the presence of all the people, saying, "Thus says the LORD: This is how I will break the yoke of King Ne•bū•chad•nez′zar of Babylon from the neck of all the nations within two years." At this, the prophet Jer•e•mī′ah went his way.

12 Sometime after the prophet Han•a•nī′ah had broken the yoke from the neck of the prophet Jer•e•mī′ah, the word of the LORD came to Jer•e•mī′ah: 13 Go, tell Han•a•nī′ah, Thus says the LORD: You have broken wooden bars only to forge iron bars in place of them! 14 For thus says the LORD of hosts, the God of Israel: I have put an iron yoke on the neck of all these nations so that they may serve King Ne•bū•chad•nez′zar of Babylon, and they shall indeed serve him; I have even given him the wild animals. 15 And the prophet Jer•e•mī′ah said to the prophet Han•a•nī′ah, "Listen, Han•a•nī′ah, the LORD has not sent you, and you made this people trust in a lie. 16 Therefore thus says the LORD: I am going to send you off the face of the earth. Within this year you will be dead, because you have spoken rebellion against the LORD."

17 In that same year, in the seventh month, the prophet Han•a•nī′ah died.

Jeremiah's Letter to the Exiles in Babylon

29 These are the words of the letter that the prophet Jer•e•mī′ah sent from Jerusalem to the remaining elders among the exiles, and to the priests, the prophets, and all the people, whom Ne•bū•chad•nez′zar had taken into exile from Jerusalem to Babylon. 2 This was after King Jec•o•nī′ah, and the queen mother, the court officials, the leaders of Judah and Jerusalem, the artisans, and the smiths had departed from Jerusalem. 3 The letter was sent by the hand of El•ā′sah son of Shā′phan and Gem•a•rī′ah son of Hil•kī′ah, whom King Zed•e•kī′ah of Judah sent to Babylon to King Ne•bū•chad•nez′zar of Babylon. It said: 4 Thus says the LORD of hosts, the God of Israel, to all the exiles whom I have sent into exile from Jerusalem to Babylon: 5 Build houses and live in them; plant gardens and eat what they produce. 6 Take wives and have sons and daughters; take wives for your sons, and give your daughters in marriage, that they may bear sons and daughters; multiply there, and do not decrease. 7 But seek the welfare of the city where I have sent you into exile, and pray to the LORD on its behalf, for in its welfare you will find your welfare. 8 For thus says the LORD of hosts, the God of Israel: Do not let the prophets and the diviners who are among you deceive you, and do not listen to the dreams that they dream,[h] 9 for it is a lie that they are prophesying to you in my name; I did not send them, says the LORD.

10 For thus says the LORD: Only when Babylon's seventy years are completed will I visit you, and I will fulfill to you my promise and bring you back to this place. 11 For surely I know the plans I have for you, says the LORD, plans for your welfare and not for harm, to give you a future with hope. 12 Then when you call upon me and come and pray to me, I will hear you. 13 When you search for me, you will find me; if you seek me with all your heart, 14 I will let you find me, says the LORD, and I will restore your fortunes and gather you from all the nations and all the places where I have driven you, says the LORD, and I will bring you back to the place from which I sent you into exile.

15 Because you have said, "The LORD has raised up prophets for us in Babylon,"— 16 Thus says the LORD concerning the king who sits on the throne of David, and concerning all the people who live in this city, your kinsfolk who did not go out with you into exile: 17 Thus says the LORD of hosts, I am going to let loose on them sword, famine, and pestilence, and I will make them like rotten figs that are so bad they cannot be eaten. 18 I will pursue them with the sword, with famine, and with pestilence, and will make them a horror to all the kingdoms of the earth, to be an object of cursing, and horror, and hissing, and a derision among all the nations where I have driven them, 19 because they did not heed my words, says the LORD, when I persistently sent to you my servants the prophets, but they[i] would not listen, says the LORD. 20 But now, all you exiles whom I sent away from Jerusalem to Babylon, hear the word of the LORD: 21 Thus says the LORD of hosts, the God of Israel, concerning Ā'hab son of Kō·laī'ah and Zed·e·kī'ah son of Mā·a·sēī'ah, who are prophesying a lie to you in my name: I am going to deliver them into the hand of King Ne·bū·chad·rez'zar of Babylon, and he shall kill them before your eyes. 22 And on account of them this curse shall be used by all the exiles from Judah in Babylon: "The LORD make you like Zed·e·kī'ah and Ā'hab, whom the king of Babylon roasted in the fire," 23 because they have perpetrated outrage in Israel and have committed adultery with their neighbors' wives, and have spoken in my name lying words that I did not command them; I am the one who knows and bears witness, says the LORD.

The Letter of Shemaiah

24 To She·māi'ah of Ne·hel'am you shall say: 25 Thus says the LORD of hosts, the God of Israel: In your own name you sent a letter to all the people who are in Jerusalem, and to the priest Zeph·a·nī'ah son of Mā·a·sēī'ah, and to all the priests, saying, 26 The LORD himself has made you priest instead of the priest Je·hoi'a·da, so that there may be officers in the house of the LORD to control any madman who plays the prophet, to put him in the stocks and the collar. 27 So now why have you not rebuked Jer·e·mī'ah of An'a·thoth who plays the prophet for you? 28 For he has actually sent to us in Babylon, saying, "It will be a long time; build houses and live in them, and plant gardens and eat what they produce."

29 The priest Zeph·a·nī'ah read this letter in the hearing of the prophet Jer·e·mī'ah. 30 Then the word of the LORD came to Jer·e·mī'ah: 31 Send to all the exiles, saying, Thus says the LORD concerning She·māi'ah of Ne·hel'am: Because She·māi'ah has prophesied to you, though I did not send him, and has led you to trust in a lie, 32 therefore thus says the LORD: I am going to punish She·māi'ah of Ne·hel'am and his descendants; he shall not have anyone living among this people to see[j] the good that I am going to do to my people, says the LORD, for he has spoken rebellion against the LORD.

Restoration Promised for Israel and Judah

30 The word that came to Jer·e·mī'ah from the LORD: 2 Thus says the LORD, the God of Israel: Write in a book all the words that I have spoken to you. 3 For the days are surely coming, says the LORD, when I will restore the fortunes of my people, Israel and Judah, says the LORD, and I will bring them back to the land that I gave to their ancestors and they shall take possession of it.

4 These are the words that the LORD spoke concerning Israel and Judah:

5 Thus says the LORD:
We have heard a cry of panic,
    of terror, and no peace.
6 Ask now, and see,
    can a man bear a child?
Why then do I see every man
    with his hands on his loins like a woman in labor?
    Why has every face turned pale?
7 Alas! that day is so great
    there is none like it;
it is a time of distress for Jacob;
    yet he shall be rescued from it.

8 On that day, says the LORD of hosts, I will break the yoke from off his[k] neck, and I will burst his[k] bonds, and strangers shall no more make a servant of him. 9 But they shall serve the LORD their God and David their king, whom I will raise up for them.

---

h Cn: Heb *your dreams that you cause to dream*   i Syr:
Heb *you*   j Gk: Heb *and he shall not see*   k Cn: Heb *your*

J
E
R

10 But as for you, have no fear, my servant Jacob,
       says the LORD,
   and do not be dismayed, O Israel;
for I am going to save you from far away,
       and your offspring from the land of their
            captivity.
Jacob shall return and have quiet and ease,
   and no one shall make him afraid.
11 For I am with you, says the LORD, to save you;
I will make an end of all the nations
       among which I scattered you,
   but of you I will not make an end.
I will chastise you in just measure,
   and I will by no means leave you
            unpunished.

12 For thus says the LORD:
Your hurt is incurable,
   your wound is grievous.
13 There is no one to uphold your cause,
   no medicine for your wound,
   no healing for you.
14 All your lovers have forgotten you;
   they care nothing for you;
for I have dealt you the blow of an enemy,
   the punishment of a merciless foe,
because your guilt is great,
   because your sins are so numerous.
15 Why do you cry out over your hurt?
   Your pain is incurable.
Because your guilt is great,
   because your sins are so numerous,
   I have done these things to you.
16 Therefore all who devour you shall be
            devoured,
   and all your foes, every one of them, shall
            go into captivity;
those who plunder you shall be plundered,
   and all who prey on you I will make a prey.
17 For I will restore health to you,
   and your wounds I will heal,
                         says the LORD,
because they have called you an outcast:
   "It is Zion; no one cares for her!"

18 Thus says the LORD:
I am going to restore the fortunes of the tents
            of Jacob,
   and have compassion on his dwellings;
the city shall be rebuilt upon its mound,
   and the citadel set on its rightful site.
19 Out of them shall come thanksgiving,
   and the sound of merrymakers.
I will make them many, and they shall not be
            few;
   I will make them honored, and they shall
            not be disdained.

20 Their children shall be as of old,
   their congregation shall be established
            before me;
   and I will punish all who oppress them.
21 Their prince shall be one of their own,
   their ruler shall come from their midst;
I will bring him near, and he shall
            approach me,
   for who would otherwise dare to
            approach me?
                         says the LORD.
22 And you shall be my people,
   and I will be your God.

23 Look, the storm of the LORD!
   Wrath has gone forth,
a whirling*l* tempest;
   it will burst upon the head of the wicked.
24 The fierce anger of the LORD will not turn back
   until he has executed and accomplished
   the intents of his mind.
In the latter days you will understand this.

The Joyful Return of the Exiles

31 At that time, says the LORD, I will be the
God of all the families of Israel, and they
shall be my people.
2 Thus says the LORD:
The people who survived the sword
   found grace in the wilderness;
when Israel sought for rest,
3   the LORD appeared to him *m* from far away.*n*
I have loved you with an everlasting love;
   therefore I have continued my faithfulness
            to you.
4 Again I will build you, and you shall be built,
   O virgin Israel!
Again you shall take*o* your tambourines,
   and go forth in the dance of the merrymakers.
5 Again you shall plant vineyards
   on the mountains of Sa·mar'i·a;
the planters shall plant,
   and shall enjoy the fruit.
6 For there shall be a day when sentinels will call
   in the hill country of E'phra·im:
"Come, let us go up to Zion,
   to the LORD our God."

7 For thus says the LORD:
Sing aloud with gladness for Jacob,
   and raise shouts for the chief of the nations;
proclaim, give praise, and say,
   "Save, O LORD, your people,
   the remnant of Israel."

---

l One Ms: Meaning of MT uncertain   *m* Gk: Heb *me*   *n* Or
to him long ago   *o* Or *adorn yourself with*

8 See, I am going to bring them from the land of
the north,
and gather them from the farthest parts of
the earth,
among them the blind and the lame,
those with child and those in labor,
together;
a great company, they shall return here.
9 With weeping they shall come,
and with consolations*p* I will lead them
back,
I will let them walk by brooks of water,
in a straight path in which they shall not
stumble;
for I have become a father to Israel,
and Ē′phra·im is my firstborn.

10 Hear the word of the LORD, O nations,
and declare it in the coastlands far away;
say, "He who scattered Israel will gather him,
and will keep him as a shepherd a flock."

PRAY IT!
Rachel Weeps

Rachel was the "mother of Israel," the
favored wife of Jacob (Gen 29.28–30)—
the patriarch whose twelve sons formed
the twelve tribes of Israel. In Jer 31.15–17,
she is symbolically weeping over the
death and captivity of her children—the
Israelites—after the Babylonian invasion.

Rachel weeping has become an image
of trauma and unrelenting grief over
violence, death, and slaughter, especially
when children are involved. For example,
Mt 2.16–18 quotes Jer 31.15–17 in a story
about the massacre of infants in Bethlehem. Rachel Weeps is a holocaust exhibi-
tion recalling the murder of millions of
Jewish men, women, and children.

Jeremiah goes on in verses 16–17 with
words of hope. God promises that the
scattered children will be brought back.
We can trust that God is with the victims of senseless violence and those who
grieve for them. Let us pray for Rachel's
grief to end.

▶ Jer 31.15–17

11 For the LORD has ransomed Jacob,
and has redeemed him from hands too
strong for him.
12 They shall come and sing aloud on the height
of Zion,
and they shall be radiant over the goodness
of the LORD,
over the grain, the wine, and the oil,
and over the young of the flock and the
herd;
their life shall become like a watered garden,
and they shall never languish again.
13 Then shall the young women rejoice in the
dance,
and the young men and the old shall be
merry.
I will turn their mourning into joy,
I will comfort them, and give them gladness
for sorrow.
14 I will give the priests their fill of fatness,
and my people shall be satisfied with my
bounty,
         says the LORD.

15 Thus says the LORD:
A voice is heard in Rā′mah,
lamentation and bitter weeping.
Rachel is weeping for her children;
she refuses to be comforted for her
children,
because they are no more.
16 Thus says the LORD:
Keep your voice from weeping,
and your eyes from tears;
for there is a reward for your work,
         says the LORD:
they shall come back from the land of the
enemy;
17 there is hope for your future,
         says the LORD:
your children shall come back to their own
country.

18 Indeed I heard Ē′phra·im pleading:
"You disciplined me, and I took the discipline;
I was like a calf untrained.
Bring me back, let me come back,
for you are the LORD my God.
19 For after I had turned away I repented;
and after I was discovered, I struck my
thigh;
I was ashamed, and I was dismayed
because I bore the disgrace of my youth."
20 Is Ē′phra·im my dear son?
Is he the child I delight in?
As often as I speak against him,

---

p Gk Compare Vg Tg: Heb *supplications*

JER

I still remember him.
Therefore I am deeply moved for him;
I will surely have mercy on him,
                              says the LORD.

21 Set up road markers for yourself,
        make yourself signposts;
    consider well the highway,
        the road by which you went.
    Return, O virgin Israel,
        return to these your cities.
22 How long will you waver,
        O faithless daughter?
    For the LORD has created a new thing on the
        earth:
        a woman encompasses*q* a man.

23 Thus says the LORD of hosts, the God of Israel: Once more they shall use these words in the land of Judah and in its towns when I restore their fortunes:
    "The LORD bless you, O abode of
            righteousness,
        O holy hill!"
24 And Judah and all its towns shall live there together, and the farmers and those who wander*r* with their flocks. 25 I will satisfy the weary,
        and all who are faint I will replenish.
26 Thereupon I awoke and looked, and my sleep was pleasant to me.

Individual Retribution

27 The days are surely coming, says the LORD, when I will sow the house of Israel and the house of Judah with the seed of humans and the seed of animals. 28 And just as I have watched over them to pluck up and break down, to overthrow, destroy, and bring evil, so I will watch over them to build

and to plant, says the LORD. 29 In those days they shall no longer say:
    "The parents have eaten sour grapes,
        and the children's teeth are set on edge."
30 But all shall die for their own sins; the teeth of everyone who eats sour grapes shall be set on edge.

A New Covenant

31 The days are surely coming, says the LORD, when I will make a new covenant with the house of Israel and the house of Judah. 32 It will not be like the covenant that I made with their ancestors when I took them by the hand to bring them out of the land of Egypt—a covenant that they broke, though I was their husband,*s* says the LORD. 33 But this is the covenant that I will make with the house of Israel after those days, says the LORD: I will put my law within them, and I will write it on their hearts; and I will be their God, and they shall be my people. 34 No longer shall they teach one another, or say to each other, "Know the LORD," for they shall all know me, from the least of them to the greatest, says the LORD; for I will forgive their iniquity, and remember their sin no more.

35 Thus says the LORD,
    who gives the sun for light by day
        and the fixed order of the moon and the
            stars for light by night,
    who stirs up the sea so that its waves roar—
        the LORD of hosts is his name:
36 If this fixed order were ever to cease
        from my presence, says the LORD,
    then also the offspring of Israel would cease
        to be a nation before me forever.

---

q Meaning of Heb uncertain   *r* Cn Compare Syr Vg Tg: Heb *and they shall wander*   *s* Or *master*

The Heart of the Matter

LIVE IT!

The Ten Commandments. The stone tablets on which they were written are the most famous stone tablets in the world, and yet no one knows where they are. The ark of the Covenant, in which they were once kept, was taken during a raid on the Temple (Jer 52.17–23). What a find they would be today! Imagine all the people flocking to see the original Ten Commandments.

But perhaps their absence makes Jeremiah's beautiful words about the new Covenant in Jer 31.31–34 even more fitting. What was etched in stone on those tablets needs to be etched in our heart. We keep in our heart what is most valuable to us. If we keep God's law there, we have no need for it written in stone.

When you look into your heart, what do you find written there?

▶ Jer 31.31–34

37 Thus says the LORD:
> If the heavens above can be measured,
>> and the foundations of the earth below can
>> be explored,
> then I will reject all the offspring of Israel
>> because of all they have done,
>>>> says the LORD.

Jerusalem to Be Enlarged

38 The days are surely coming, says the LORD, when the city shall be rebuilt for the LORD from the tower of Ha·nan′el to the Corner Gate. 39 And the measuring line shall go out farther, straight to the hill Gā′reb, and shall then turn to Gō′ah. 40 The whole valley of the dead bodies and the ashes, and all the fields as far as the Wadi Kid′ron, to the corner of the Horse Gate toward the east, shall be sacred to the LORD. It shall never again be uprooted or overthrown.

Jeremiah Buys a Field During the Siege

32 The word that came to Jer·e·mi′ah from the LORD in the tenth year of King Zed·e·ki′ah of Judah, which was the eighteenth year of Ne·bū·chad·rez′zar. 2 At that time the army of the king of Babylon was besieging Jerusalem, and the prophet Jer·e·mi′ah was confined in the court of the guard that was in the palace of the king of Judah, 3 where King Zed·e·ki′ah of Judah had confined him. Zed·e·ki′ah had said, "Why do you prophesy and say: Thus says the LORD: I am going to give this city into the hand of the king of Babylon, and he shall take it; 4 King Zed·e·ki′ah of Judah shall not escape out of the hands of the Chal·dē′ans, but shall surely be given into the hands of the king of Babylon, and shall speak with him face to face and see him eye to eye; 5 and he shall take Zed·e·ki′ah to Babylon, and there he shall remain until I attend to him, says the LORD; though you fight against the Chal·dē′ans, you shall not succeed?"

6 Jer·e·mi′ah said, The word of the LORD came to me: 7 Han′a·mel son of your uncle Shal′lum is going to come to you and say, "Buy my field that is at An′a·thoth, for the right of redemption by purchase is yours." 8 Then my cousin Han′a·mel came to me in the court of the guard, in accordance with the word of the LORD, and said to me, "Buy my field that is at An′a·thoth in the land of Benjamin, for the right of possession and redemption is yours; buy it for yourself." Then I knew that this was the word of the LORD.

9 And I bought the field at An′a·thoth from my cousin Han′a·mel, and weighed out the money to him, seventeen shekels of silver. 10 I signed the deed, sealed it, got witnesses, and weighed the money on scales. 11 Then I took the sealed deed of purchase, containing the terms and conditions, and the open copy; 12 and I gave the deed of purchase to Bar′uch son of Ne·rī′ah son of Mah′sēi·ah, in the presence of my cousin Han′a·mel, in the presence of the witnesses who signed the deed of purchase, and in the presence of all the Judeans who were sitting in the court of the guard. 13 In their presence I charged Bar′uch, saying, 14 Thus says the LORD of hosts, the God of Israel: Take these deeds, both this sealed deed of purchase and this open deed, and put them in an earthenware jar, in order that they may last for a long time. 15 For thus says the LORD of hosts, the God of Israel: Houses and fields and vineyards shall again be bought in this land.

Jeremiah Prays for Understanding

16 After I had given the deed of purchase to Bar′uch son of Ne·rī′ah, I prayed to the LORD, saying: 17 Ah Lord GOD! It is you who made the heavens and the earth by your great power and by your outstretched arm! Nothing is too hard for you. 18 You show steadfast love to the thousandth generation,[t] but repay the guilt of parents into the laps of their children after them, O great and mighty God whose name is the LORD of hosts, 19 great in counsel and mighty in deed; whose eyes are open to all the ways of mortals, rewarding all according to their ways and according to the fruit of their doings. 20 You showed signs and wonders in the land of Egypt, and to this day in Israel and among all humankind, and have made yourself a name that continues to this very day. 21 You brought your people Israel out of the land of Egypt with signs and wonders, with a strong hand and outstretched arm, and with great terror; 22 and you gave them this land, which you swore to their ancestors to give them, a land flowing with milk and honey; 23 and they entered and took possession of it. But they did not obey your voice or follow your law; of all you commanded them to do, they did nothing. Therefore you have made all these disasters come upon them. 24 See, the siege ramps have been cast up against the city to take it, and the city, faced with sword, famine, and pestilence, has been given into the hands of the Chal·dē′ans who are fighting against it. What you spoke has happened, as you yourself can see. 25 Yet you, O Lord GOD, have said to me, "Buy the field for money and get witnesses"— though the city has been given into the hands of the Chal·dē′ans.

God's Assurance of the People's Return

26 The word of the LORD came to Jer·e·mi′ah: 27 See, I am the LORD, the God of all flesh; is anything too hard for me? 28 Therefore, thus says the

---

t Or *to thousands*

LORD: I am going to give this city into the hands of the Chal·dē′ans and into the hand of King Ne·bū·chad·rez′zar of Babylon, and he shall take it. 29 The Chal·dē′ans who are fighting against this city shall come, set it on fire, and burn it, with the houses on whose roofs offerings have been made to Bā′al and libations have been poured out to other gods, to provoke me to anger. 30 For the people of Israel and the people of Judah have done nothing but evil in my sight from their youth; the people of Israel have done nothing but provoke me to anger by the work of their hands, says the LORD. 31 This city has aroused my anger and wrath, from the day it was built until this day, so that I will remove it from my sight 32 because of all the evil of the people of Israel and the people of Judah that they did to provoke me to anger—they, their kings and their officials, their priests and their prophets, the citizens of Judah and the inhabitants of Jerusalem. 33 They have turned their backs to me, not their faces; though I have taught them persistently, they would not listen and accept correction. 34 They set up their abominations in the house that bears my name, and defiled it. 35 They built the high places of Bā′al in the valley of the son of Hin′nom, to offer up their sons and daughters to Mō′lech, though I did not command them, nor did it enter my mind that they should do this abomination, causing Judah to sin.

36 Now therefore thus says the LORD, the God of Israel, concerning this city of which you say, "It is being given into the hand of the king of Babylon by the sword, by famine, and by pestilence": 37 See, I am going to gather them from all the lands to which I drove them in my anger and my wrath and in great indignation; I will bring them back to this place, and I will settle them in safety. 38 They shall be my people, and I will be their God. 39 I will give them one heart and one way, that they may fear me for all time, for their own good and the good of their children after them. 40 I will make an everlasting covenant with them, never to draw back from doing good to them; and I will put the fear of me in their hearts, so that they may not turn from me. 41 I will rejoice in doing good to them, and I will plant them in this land in faithfulness, with all my heart and all my soul.

42 For thus says the LORD: Just as I have brought all this great disaster upon this people, so I will bring upon them all the good fortune that I now promise them. 43 Fields shall be bought in this land of which you are saying, It is a desolation, without human beings or animals; it has been given into the hands of the Chal·dē′ans. 44 Fields shall be bought for money, and deeds shall be signed and sealed and witnessed, in the land of Benjamin, in the places around Jerusalem, and in the cities of

Judah, of the hill country, of the She·phē′lah, and of the Neg′eb; for I will restore their fortunes, says the LORD.

Healing after Punishment

33 The word of the LORD came to Jer·e·mī′ah a second time, while he was still confined in the court of the guard: 2 Thus says the LORD who made the earth,[u] the LORD who formed it to establish it—the LORD is his name: 3 Call to me and I will answer you, and will tell you great and hidden things that you have not known. 4 For thus says the LORD, the God of Israel, concerning the houses of this city and the houses of the kings of Judah that were torn down to make a defense against the siege ramps and before the sword:[v] 5 The Chal·dē′ans are coming in to fight[w] and to fill them with the dead bodies of those whom I shall strike down in my anger and my wrath, for I have hidden my face from this city because of all their wickedness. 6 I am going to bring it recovery and healing; I will heal them and reveal to them abundance[v] of prosperity and security. 7 I will restore the fortunes of Judah and the fortunes of Israel, and rebuild them as they were at first. 8 I will cleanse them from all the guilt of their sin against me, and I will forgive all the guilt of their sin and rebellion against me. 9 And this city[x] shall be to me a name of joy, a praise and a glory before all the nations of the earth who shall hear of all the good that I do for them; they shall fear and tremble because of all the good and all the prosperity I provide for it.

10 Thus says the LORD: In this place of which you say, "It is a waste without human beings or animals," in the towns of Judah and the streets of Jerusalem that are desolate, without inhabitants, human or animal, there shall once more be heard 11 the voice of mirth and the voice of gladness, the voice of the bridegroom and the voice of the bride, the voices of those who sing, as they bring thank offerings to the house of the LORD:

"Give thanks to the LORD of hosts,
　for the LORD is good,
　　for his steadfast love endures forever!"
For I will restore the fortunes of the land as at first, says the LORD.

12 Thus says the LORD of hosts: In this place that is waste, without human beings or animals, and in all its towns there shall again be pasture for shepherds resting their flocks. 13 In the towns of the hill country, of the She·phē′lah, and of the Neg′eb, in the land of Benjamin, the places around Jerusalem, and in the towns of Judah, flocks shall

---

u Gk: Heb it　v Meaning of Heb uncertain　w Cn: Heb *They are coming in to fight against the Chaldeans*　x Heb *And it* again pass under the hands of the one who counts them, says the LORD.

The Righteous Branch and the Covenant with David

14 The days are surely coming, says the LORD, when I will fulfill the promise I made to the house of Israel and the house of Judah. 15 In those days and at that time I will cause a righteous Branch to spring up for David; and he shall execute justice and righteousness in the land. 16 In those days Judah will be saved and Jerusalem will live in safety. And this is the name by which it will be called: "The LORD is our righteousness."

17 For thus says the LORD: David shall never lack a man to sit on the throne of the house of Israel, 18 and the levitical priests shall never lack a man in my presence to offer burnt offerings, to make grain offerings, and to make sacrifices for all time.

19 The word of the LORD came to Jer•e•mi′ah: 20 Thus says the LORD: If any of you could break my covenant with the day and my covenant with the night, so that day and night would not come at their appointed time, 21 only then could my covenant with my servant David be broken, so that he would not have a son to reign on his throne, and my covenant with my ministers the Lĕ′vītes. 22 Just as the host of heaven cannot be numbered and the sands of the sea cannot be measured, so I will increase the offspring of my servant David, and the Lĕ′vītes who minister to me.

23 The word of the LORD came to Jer•e•mi′ah: 24 Have you not observed how these people say, "The two families that the LORD chose have been rejected by him," and how they hold my people in such contempt that they no longer regard them as a nation? 25 Thus says the LORD: Only if I had not established my covenant with day and night and the ordinances of heaven and earth, 26 would I reject the offspring of Jacob and of my servant David and not choose any of his descendants as rulers over the offspring of Abraham, Isaac, and Jacob. For I will restore their fortunes, and will have mercy upon them.

Death in Captivity Predicted for Zedekiah

34 The word that came to Jer•e•mi′ah from the LORD, when King Ne•bū•chad•rez′zar of Babylon and all his army and all the kingdoms of the earth and all the peoples under his dominion were fighting against Jerusalem and all its cities: 2 Thus says the LORD, the God of Israel: Go and speak to King Zed•e•ki′ah of Judah and say to him: Thus says the LORD: I am going to give this city into the hand of the king of Babylon, and he shall burn it with fire. 3 And you yourself shall not escape

from his hand, but shall surely be captured and handed over to him; you shall see the king of Babylon eye to eye and speak with him face to face; and you shall go to Babylon. 4 Yet hear the word of the LORD, O King Zed•e•ki′ah of Judah! Thus says the LORD concerning you: You shall not die by the sword; 5 you shall die in peace. And as spices were burned*y* for your ancestors, the earlier kings who preceded you, so they shall burn spices*z* for you and lament for you, saying, "Alas, lord!" For I have spoken the word, says the LORD.

6 Then the prophet Jer•e•mi′ah spoke all these words to Zed•e•ki′ah king of Judah, in Jerusalem, 7 when the army of the king of Babylon was fighting against Jerusalem and against all the cities of Judah that were left, Lā′chish and A•zē′kah; for these were the only fortified cities of Judah that remained.

Treacherous Treatment of Slaves

8 The word that came to Jer•e•mi′ah from the LORD, after King Zed•e•ki′ah had made a covenant with all the people in Jerusalem to make a proclamation of liberty to them— 9 that all should set free their Hebrew slaves, male and female, so that no one should hold another Judean in slavery. 10 And they obeyed, all the officials and all the people who had entered into the covenant that all would set free their slaves, male or female, so that they would not be enslaved again; they obeyed and set them free. 11 But afterward they turned around and took back the male and female slaves they had set free, and brought them again into subjection as slaves. 12 The word of the LORD came to Jer•e•mi′ah from the LORD: 13 Thus says the LORD, the God of Israel: I myself made a covenant with your ancestors when I brought them out of the land of Egypt, out of the house of slavery, saying, 14 "Every seventh year each of you must set free any Hebrews who have been sold to you and have served you six years; you must set them free from your service." But your ancestors did not listen to me or incline their ears to me. 15 You yourselves recently repented and did what was right in my sight by proclaiming liberty to one another, and you made a covenant before me in the house that is called by my name; 16 but then you turned around and profaned my name when each of you took back your male and female slaves, whom you had set free according to their desire, and you brought them again into subjection to be your slaves. 17 Therefore, thus says the LORD: You have not obeyed me by granting a release to your neighbors and friends; I am going to grant a release to you, says the LORD—a release to the sword, to pestilence, and to famine. I will make you a horror

---

y Heb *as there was burning*   *z* Heb *shall burn*

to all the kingdoms of the earth. 18 And those who transgressed my covenant and did not keep the terms of the covenant that they made before me, I will make like*a* the calf when they cut it in two and passed between its parts: 19 the officials of Judah, the officials of Jerusalem, the eunuchs, the priests, and all the people of the land who passed between the parts of the calf 20 shall be handed over to their enemies and to those who seek their lives. Their corpses shall become food for the birds of the air and the wild animals of the earth. 21 And as for King Zed•e•kī'ah of Judah and his officials, I will hand them over to their enemies and to those who seek their lives, to the army of the king of Babylon, which has withdrawn from you. 22 I am going to command, says the LORD, and will bring them back to this city; and they will fight against it, and take it, and burn it with fire. The towns of Judah I will make a desolation without inhabitant.

The Rechabites Commended

35 The word that came to Jer•e•mī'ah from the LORD in the days of King Je•hoi'-a•kim son of Jō•sī'ah of Judah: 2 Go to the house of the Rē'chab•ites, and speak with them, and bring them to the house of the LORD, into one of the chambers; then offer them wine to drink. 3 So I took Jā•az•a•nī'ah son of Jer•e•mī'ah son of Ha•baz•zi•nī'ah, and his brothers, and all his sons, and the whole house of the Rē'chab•ites. 4 I brought them to the house of the LORD into the chamber of the sons of Hā'nan son of Ig•da•lī'ah, the man of God, which was near the chamber of the officials, above the chamber of Mā•a•sēī'ah son of Shal'lum, keeper of the threshold. 5 Then I set before the Rē'chab•ites pitchers full of wine, and cups; and I said to them, "Have some wine." 6 But they answered, "We will drink no wine, for our ancestor Jon'a•dab son of Rē'chab commanded us, 'You shall never drink wine, neither you nor your children; 7 nor shall you ever build a house, or sow seed; nor shall you plant a vineyard, or even own one; but you shall live in tents all your days, that you may live many days in the land where you reside.' 8 We have obeyed the charge of our ancestor Jon'a•dab son of Rē'chab in all that he commanded us, to drink no wine all our days, ourselves, our wives, our sons, or our daughters, 9 and not to build houses to live in. We have no vineyard or field or seed; 10 but we have lived in tents, and have obeyed and done all that our ancestor Jon'a•dab commanded us. 11 But when King Ne•bū•chad•rez'zar of Babylon came up against the land, we said, 'Come, and let us go to Jerusalem for fear of the army of the Chal•dē'ans and the army of the Ar•a•mē'ans.' That is why we are living in Jerusalem."

12 Then the word of the LORD came to Jer•e•mī'ah: 13 Thus says the LORD of hosts, the God of Israel: Go and say to the people of Judah and the inhabitants of Jerusalem, Can you not learn a lesson and obey my words? says the LORD. 14 The command has been carried out that Jon'a•dab son of Rē'chab gave to his descendants to drink no wine; and they drink none to this day, for they have obeyed their ancestor's command. But I myself have spoken to you persistently, and you have not obeyed me. 15 I have sent to you all my servants the prophets, sending them persistently, saying, "Turn now every one of you from your evil way, and amend your doings, and do not go after other gods to serve them, and then you shall live in the land that I gave to you and your ancestors." But you did not incline your ear or obey me. 16 The descendants of Jon'a•dab son of Rē'chab have carried out the command that their ancestor gave them, but this people has not obeyed me. 17 Therefore, thus says the LORD, the God of hosts, the God of Israel: I am going to bring on Judah and on all the inhabitants of Jerusalem every disaster that I have pronounced against them; because I have spoken to them and they have not listened, I have called to them and they have not answered.

18 But to the house of the Rē'chab•ites Jer•e•mī'ah said: Thus says the LORD of hosts, the God of Israel: Because you have obeyed the command of your ancestor Jon'a•dab, and kept all his precepts, and done all that he commanded you, 19 therefore thus says the LORD of hosts, the God of Israel: Jon'a•dab son of Rē'chab shall not lack a descendant to stand before me for all time.

The Scroll Read in the Temple

36 In the fourth year of King Je•hoi'a•kim son of Jō•sī'ah of Judah, this word came to Jer•e•mī'ah from the LORD: 2 Take a scroll and write on it all the words that I have spoken to you against Israel and Judah and all the nations, from the day I spoke to you, from the days of Jō•sī'ah until today. 3 It may be that when the house of Judah hears of all the disasters that I intend to do to them, all of them may turn from their evil ways, so that I may forgive their iniquity and their sin.

4 Then Jer•e•mī'ah called Bar'uch son of Ne•rī'ah, and Bar'uch wrote on a scroll at Jer•e•mī'-ah's dictation all the words of the LORD that he had spoken to him. 5 And Jer•e•mī'ah ordered Bar'uch, saying, "I am prevented from entering the house of the LORD; 6 so you go yourself, and on a fast day in the hearing of the people in the LORD's house you shall read the words of the LORD from the scroll that you have written at my dictation. You shall

---

a Cn: Heb lacks *like*

read them also in the hearing of all the people of Judah who come up from their towns. 7 It may be that their plea will come before the LORD, and that all of them will turn from their evil ways, for great is the anger and wrath that the LORD has pronounced against this people." 8 And Bar′uch son of Ne·rī′ah did all that the prophet Jer·e·mī′ah ordered him about reading from the scroll the words of the LORD in the LORD's house.

9 In the fifth year of King Je·hoi′a·kim son of Jō·sī′ah of Judah, in the ninth month, all the people in Jerusalem and all the people who came from the towns of Judah to Jerusalem proclaimed a fast before the LORD. 10 Then, in the hearing of all the people, Bar′uch read the words of Jer·e·mī′ah from the scroll, in the house of the LORD, in the chamber of Gem·a·rī′ah son of Shā′phan the secretary, which was in the upper court, at the entry of the New Gate of the LORD's house.

The Scroll Read in the Palace

11 When Mī·cāi′ah son of Gem·a·rī′ah son of Shā′phan heard all the words of the LORD from the scroll, 12 he went down to the king's house, into the secretary's chamber; and all the officials were sitting there: E·lish′a·ma the secretary, De·lai′ah son of She·māi′ah, El·nā′than son of Ach′bor, Gem·a·rī′ah son of Shā′phan, Zed·e·kī′ah son of Han·a·nī′ah, and all the officials. 13 And Mī·cāi′ah told them all the words that he had heard, when Bar′uch read the scroll in the hearing of the people. 14 Then all the officials sent Je·hū′dī son of Neth·a·nī′ah son of Shel·e·mī′ah son of Cū′shī to say to Bar′uch, "Bring the scroll that you read in the hearing of the people, and come." So Bar′uch son of Ne·rī′ah took the scroll in his hand and came to them. 15 And they said to him, "Sit down and read it to us." So Bar′uch read it to them. 16 When they heard all the words, they turned to one another in alarm, and said to Bar′uch, "We certainly must report all these words to the king." 17 Then they questioned Bar′uch, "Tell us now, how did you write all these words? Was it at his dictation?" 18 Bar′uch answered them, "He dictated all these words to me, and I wrote them with ink on the scroll." 19 Then the officials said to Bar′uch, "Go and hide, you and Jer·e·mī′ah, and let no one know where you are."

Jehoiakim Burns the Scroll

20 Leaving the scroll in the chamber of E·lish′a·ma the secretary, they went to the court of the king; and they reported all the words to the king. 21 Then the king sent Je·hū′dī to get the scroll, and he took it from the chamber of E·lish′a·ma the secretary; and Je·hū′dī read it to the king and all the officials who stood beside the king. 22 Now the king was sitting in his winter apartment (it was the ninth month), and there was a fire burning in the brazier before him. 23 As Je·hū′dī read three or four columns, the king[b] would cut them off with a penknife and throw them into the fire in the brazier, until the entire scroll was consumed in the fire that was in the brazier. 24 Yet neither the king, nor any of his servants who heard all these words, was alarmed, nor did they tear their garments. 25 Even when El·nā′than and De·lai′ah and Gem·a·rī′ah urged the king not to burn the scroll, he would not listen to them. 26 And the king commanded Je·rah′mē·el the king's son and Se·rāi′ah son of Az′ri·el and Shel·e·mī′ah son of Ab·dě′el to arrest the secretary Bar′uch and the prophet Jer·e·mī′ah. But the LORD hid them.

Jeremiah Dictates Another

27 Now, after the king had burned the scroll with the words that Bar′uch wrote at Jer·e·mī′ah's dictation, the word of the LORD came to Jer·e·mī′ah: 28 Take another scroll and write on it all the former words that were in the first scroll, which King Je·hoi′a·kim of Judah has burned. 29 And concerning King Je·hoi′a·kim of Judah you shall say: Thus says the LORD, You have dared to burn this scroll, saying, Why have you written in it that the king of Babylon will certainly come and destroy this land, and will cut off from it human beings and animals? 30 Therefore thus says the LORD concerning King Je·hoi′a·kim of Judah: He shall have no one to sit upon the throne of David, and his dead body shall be cast out to the heat by day and the frost by night. 31 And I will punish him and his offspring and his servants for their iniquity; I will bring on them, and on the inhabitants of Jerusalem, and on the people of Judah, all the disasters with which I have threatened them—but they would not listen.

32 Then Jer·e·mī′ah took another scroll and gave it to the secretary Bar′uch son of Ne·rī′ah, who wrote on it at Jer·e·mī′ah's dictation all the words of the scroll that King Je·hoi′a·kim of Judah had burned in the fire; and many similar words were added to them.

Zedekiah's Vain Hope
(2 Kings 24.17; 2 Chr 36.10)

37 Zed·e·kī′ah son of Jō·sī′ah, whom King Ne·bū·chad·rez′zar of Babylon made king in the land of Judah, succeeded Cō·nī′ah son of Je·hoi′a·kim. 2 But neither he nor his servants nor the people of the land listened to the words of the LORD that he spoke through the prophet Jer·e·mī′ah.

3 King Zed·e·kī′ah sent Je·hū′cal son of Shel·e·mī′ah and the priest Zeph·a·nī′ah son of

---

b Heb he

Mă·a·sēi′ah to the prophet Jer·e·mī′ah saying, "Please pray for us to the LORD our God." 4 Now Jer·e·mī′ah was still going in and out among the people, for he had not yet been put in prison. 5 Meanwhile, the army of Pharaoh had come out of Egypt; and when the Chal·dē′ans who were besieging Jerusalem heard news of them, they withdrew from Jerusalem.

6 Then the word of the LORD came to the prophet Jer·e·mī′ah: 7 Thus says the LORD, God of Israel: This is what the two of you shall say to the king of Judah, who sent you to me to inquire of me: Pharaoh's army, which set out to help you, is going to return to its own land, to Egypt. 8 And the Chal·dē′ans shall return and fight against this city; they shall take it and burn it with fire. 9 Thus says the LORD: Do not deceive yourselves, saying, "The Chal·dē′ans will surely go away from us," for they will not go away. 10 Even if you defeated the whole army of Chal·dē′ans who are fighting against you,

and there remained of them only wounded men in their tents, they would rise up and burn this city with fire.

Jeremiah Is Imprisoned

11 Now when the Chal·dē′an army had withdrawn from Jerusalem at the approach of Pharaoh's army, 12 Jer·e·mī′ah set out from Jerusalem to go to the land of Benjamin to receive his share of property*c* among the people there. 13 When he reached the Benjamin Gate, a sentinel there named I·rī′jah son of Shel·e·mī′ah son of Han·a·nī′ah arrested the prophet Jer·e·mī′ah saying, "You are deserting to the Chal·dē′ans." 14 And Jer·e·mī′ah said, "That is a lie; I am not deserting to the Chal·dē′ans." But I·rī′jah would not listen to him, and arrested Jer·e·mī′ah and brought him to the officials. 15 The officials were enraged at Jer·e·mī′ah, and they beat him and imprisoned him in the house of the secretary Jonathan, for it had been made a prison. 16 Thus Jer·e·mī′ah was put in the cistern house, in the cells, and remained there many days.

17 Then King Zed·e·kī′ah sent for him, and received him. The king questioned him secretly in his house, and said, "Is there any word from the LORD?" Jer·e·mī′ah said, "There is!" Then he said, "You shall be handed over to the king of Babylon." 18 Jer·e·mī′ah also said to King Zed·e·kī′ah, "What wrong have I done to you or your servants or this people, that you have put me in prison? 19 Where are your prophets who prophesied to you, saying, 'The king of Babylon will not come against you and against this land'? 20 Now please hear me, my lord king: be good enough to listen to my plea, and do not send me back to the house of the secretary Jonathan to die there." 21 So King Zed·e·kī′ah gave orders, and they committed Jer·e·mī′ah to the court of the guard; and a loaf of bread was given him daily from the bakers' street, until all the bread of the city was gone. So Jer·e·mī′ah remained in the court of the guard.

Jeremiah in the Cistern

38 Now Sheph·a·tī′ah son of Mat′tan, Ged·a·lī′ah son of Pash′hur, Jū′cal son of Shel·e·mī′ah, and Pash′hur son of Mal·chī′ah heard the words that Jer·e·mī′ah was saying to all the people, 2 Thus says the LORD, Those who stay in this city shall die by the sword, by famine, and by pestilence; but those who go out to the Chal·dē′ans shall live; they shall have their lives as a prize of war, and live. 3 Thus says the LORD, This city shall surely be handed over to the army of the king of Babylon and be taken. 4 Then the officials said to the king, "This man ought to be put to death, because he is dis-

PRAY IT?

Facing Fear

You can bet Jeremiah felt fear at times. For example, in Jer 37.17, King Zedekiah asks the prophet if he has had any word from God. Jeremiah has just been beaten and imprisoned (verse 15). Surely, he has some fear for what will happen to him if he delivers a message that angers the king. But Jeremiah courageously tells Zedekiah that he, Zedekiah, will be handed over to the king of Babylon (verse 17).

Throughout our life, when trying to do God's will, we will face situations that cause us to fear for our safety, for our reputation, or even that our friends will abandon us. This fear is an anxiety that can cause us to shut down and quit trying. We need to offer up that fear to God and ask the LORD to calm our heart.

Quiet your mind and pray:

LORD, give me the courage I need to be faithful to you. Let my love for you and for other people be so great that my fears will never be able to keep me from doing what is right. Amen!

▶ Jer 37.11–21

---

c Meaning of Heb uncertain

PRAY IT!

Prayer from the Cistern

Almighty Creator of ups and downs, like Jeremiah, I often find myself at the bottom. Sometimes, I just fall there; other times, I am thrown there. It's cold, dark, and lonely there.

Bless me with friends like Ebed-melech to care for me and pull me out. And make me an Ebed-melech for others—a friend who is loyal enough to get the rope and tug until they are up again, who is considerate enough to get rags for their armpits so that the process won't be so painful. Amen.

▸ Jer 38.1–13

couraging the soldiers who are left in this city, and all the people, by speaking such words to them. For this man is not seeking the welfare of this people, but their harm." 5 King Zed·e·kī'ah said, "Here he is; he is in your hands; for the king is powerless against you." 6 So they took Jer·e·mī'ah and threw him into the cistern of Mal·chī'ah, the king's son, which was in the court of the guard, letting Jer·e·mī'ah down by ropes. Now there was no water in the cistern, but only mud, and Jer·e·mī'ah sank in the mud.

Jeremiah Is Rescued by Ebed-melech

7 Ē'bed-mē'lech the Ethiopian,*d* a eunuch in the king's house, heard that they had put Jer·e·mī'ah into the cistern. The king happened to be sitting at the Benjamin Gate, 8 So Ē'bed-mē'lech left the king's house and spoke to the king, 9 "My lord king, these men have acted wickedly in all they did to the prophet Jer·e·mī'ah by throwing him into the cistern to die there of hunger, for there is no bread left in the city." 10 Then the king commanded Ē'bed-mē'lech the Ethiopian,*d* "Take three men with you from here, and pull the prophet Jer·e·mī'ah up from the cistern before he dies." 11 So Ē'bed-mē'lech took the men with him and went to the house of the king, to a wardrobe of*e* the storehouse, and took from there old rags and worn-out clothes, which he let down to Jer·e·mī'ah in the cistern by ropes. 12 Then Ē'bed-mē'lech the Ethiopian*d* said to Jer·e·mī'ah, "Just put the rags and clothes between your armpits and the ropes." Jer·e·mī'ah did so. 13 Then they drew Jer·e·mī'ah up by the ropes and pulled him out of the cistern. And Jer·e·mī'ah remained in the court of the guard.

Zedekiah Consults Jeremiah Again

14 King Zed·e·kī'ah sent for the prophet Jer·e·mī'ah and received him at the third entrance of the temple of the LORD. The king said to Jer·e·mī'ah, "I have something to ask you; do not hide anything from me." 15 Jer·e·mī'ah said to Zed·e·kī'ah, "If I tell you, you will put me to death, will you not? And if I give you advice, you will not listen to me." 16 So King Zed·e·kī'ah swore an oath in secret to Jer·e·mī'ah, "As the LORD lives, who gave us our lives, I will not put you to death or hand you over to these men who seek your life."

17 Then Jer·e·mī'ah said to Zed·e·kī'ah, "Thus says the LORD, the God of hosts, the God of Israel, If you will only surrender to the officials of the king of Babylon, then your life shall be spared, and this city shall not be burned with fire, and you and your house shall live. 18 But if you do not surrender to the officials of the king of Babylon, then this city shall be handed over to the Chal·dē'ans, and they shall burn it with fire, and you yourself shall not escape from their hand." 19 King Zed·e·kī'ah said to Jer·e·mī'ah, "I am afraid of the Judeans who have deserted to the Chal·dē'ans, for I might be handed over to them and they would abuse me." 20 Jer·e·mī'ah said, "That will not happen. Just obey the voice of the LORD in what I say to you, and it shall go well with you, and your life shall be spared. 21 But if you are determined not to surrender, this is what the LORD has shown me— 22 a vision of all the women remaining in the house of the king of Judah being led out to the officials of the king of Babylon and saying,

'Your trusted friends have seduced you
    and have overcome you;
Now that your feet are stuck in the mud,
    they desert you.'

23 All your wives and your children shall be led out to the Chal·dē'ans, and you yourself shall not escape from their hand, but shall be seized by the king of Babylon; and this city shall be burned with fire."

24 Then Zed·e·kī'ah said to Jer·e·mī'ah, "Do not let anyone else know of this conversation, or you will die. 25 If the officials should hear that I have spoken with you, and they should come and say to you, 'Just tell us what you said to the king; do not conceal it from us, or we will put you to death. What did the king say to you?' 26 then you shall say to them, 'I was presenting my plea to the king not to send me back to the house of Jonathan to die there.'" 27 All the officials did come to Jer·e·mī'ah and questioned him; and he answered them in the very words the king had commanded. So they stopped questioning him, for the conversation had

d Or Nubian; Heb Cushite   *e* Cn: Heb to under

not been overheard. 28 And Jer•e•mī′ah remained in the court of the guard until the day that Jerusalem was taken.

The Fall of Jerusalem
(2 Kings 25.1–12; Jer 52.4–16)

39 In the ninth year of King Zed•e•kī′ah of Judah, in the tenth month, King Ne•bū•chad•rez′zar of Babylon and all his army came against Jerusalem and besieged it; 2 in the eleventh year of Zed•e•kī′ah, in the fourth month, on the ninth day of the month, a breach was made in the city. 3 When Jerusalem was taken,*f* all the officials of the king of Babylon came and sat in the middle gate: Ner′gal-sha•rē′zer, Sam′gar-nē′bō, Sar′se•chim the Rab•sar′is, Ner′gal-sha•rē′zer the Rab′mag, with all the rest of the officials of the king of Babylon. 4 When King Zed•e•kī′ah of Judah and all the soldiers saw them, they fled, going out of the city at night by way of the king's garden through the gate between the two walls; and they went toward the Ar′a•bah. 5 But the army of the Chal•dē′ans pursued them, and overtook Zed•e•kī′ah in the plains of Jericho; and when they had taken him, they brought him up to King Ne•bū•chad•rez′zar of

Babylon, at Rib′lah, in the land of Hā′math; and he passed sentence on him. 6 The king of Babylon slaughtered the sons of Zed•e•kī′ah at Rib′lah before his eyes; also the king of Babylon slaughtered all the nobles of Judah. 7 He put out the eyes of Zed•e•kī′ah, and bound him in fetters to take him to Babylon. 8 The Chal•dē′ans burned the king's house and the houses of the people, and broke down the walls of Jerusalem. 9 Then Ne•bū•za-rad′an the captain of the guard exiled to Babylon the rest of the people who were left in the city, those who had deserted to him, and the people who remained. 10 Ne•bū•za•rad′an the captain of the guard left in the land of Judah some of the poor people who owned nothing, and gave them vineyards and fields at the same time.

Jeremiah, Set Free, Remembers Ebed-melech

11 King Ne•bū•chad•rez′zar of Babylon gave command concerning Jer•e•mī′ah through Ne•bū-za•rad′an, the captain of the guard, saying, 12 "Take him, look after him well and do him no harm, but deal with him as he may ask you." 13 So

---

f This clause has been transposed from 38.28

RISKY BUSINESS

Ebed-melech is a biblical character we do not hear too much about. But he played a significant role in Jeremiah's life. The Bible refers to him as the Ethiopian.

Ebed-melech is important because he was available to God and he was willing to risk his neck. Although Ebed-melech had the king's permission to rescue Jeremiah, he would have lost his life if his plan to do so had been discovered by the king's generals and counselors (Jer 38.7–13). Ebed-melech shows us that being a servant of God is risky business. We cannot do God's will without taking risks. There is just no such thing as playing it safe and doing what God wants us to do.

Ebed-melech is also important because he was willing to help his "brother." Jeremiah was a Jew, and Ebed-melech was an Ethiopian, but still they were brothers in the LORD. Ebed-melech knew that he had to act when he saw his brother in trouble. When destruction finally came upon Jerusalem, God rewarded Ebed-melech by keeping him safe (39.18) because he had trusted in God enough to help his brother Jeremiah.

LORD, grant me a large portion of trust in you, that I might step out at your bidding and not be afraid of the outcome. Amen.

▶ Jer 39.15–18

Ne•bū•za•rad′an the captain of the guard, Ne•bū•shaz′ban the Rab•sar′is, Ner′gal-sha•rē′zer the Rab′-mag, and all the chief officers of the king of Babylon sent [14] and took Jer•e•mī′ah from the court of the guard. They entrusted him to Ged•a•lī′ah son of A•hī′kam son of Shā′phan to be brought home. So he stayed with his own people.

15 The word of the LORD came to Jer•e•mī′ah while he was confined in the court of the guard: [16] Go and say to Ē′bed-mē′lech the Ethiopian:[g] Thus says the LORD of hosts, the God of Israel: I am going to fulfill my words against this city for evil and not for good, and they shall be accomplished in your presence on that day. [17] But I will save you on that day, says the LORD, and you shall not be handed over to those whom you dread. [18] For I will surely save you, and you shall not fall by the sword; but you shall have your life as a prize of war, because you have trusted in me, says the LORD.

Jeremiah with Gedaliah the Governor
(2 Kings 25.22–26)

40 The word that came to Jer•e•mī′ah from the LORD after Ne•bū•za•rad′an the captain of the guard had let him go from Rā′mah, when he took him bound in fetters along with all the captives of Jerusalem and Judah who were being exiled to Babylon. 2 The captain of the guard took Jer•e•mī′ah and said to him, "The LORD your God threatened this place with this disaster; 3 and now the LORD has brought it about, and has done as he said, because all of you sinned against the LORD and did not obey his voice. Therefore this thing has come upon you. 4 Now look, I have just released you today from the fetters on your hands. If you wish to come with me to Babylon, come, and I will take good care of you; but if you do not wish to come with me to Babylon, you need not come. See, the whole land is before you; go wherever you think it good and right to go. 5 If you remain,[h] then return to Ged•a•lī′ah son of A•hī′kam son of Shā′phan, whom the king of Babylon appointed governor of the towns of Judah, and stay with him among the people; or go wherever you think it right to go." So the captain of the guard gave him an allowance of food and a present, and let him go. 6 Then Jer•e•mī′ah went to Ged•a•lī′ah son of A•hī′kam at Miz′pah, and stayed with him among the people who were left in the land.

7 When all the leaders of the forces in the open country and their troops heard that the king of Babylon had appointed Ged•a•lī′ah son of A•hī′kam governor in the land, and had committed to him men, women, and children, those of the poorest of the land who had not been taken into exile to Babylon, 8 they went to Ged•a•lī′ah at Miz′pah—Ish′ma•el son of Neth•a•nī′ah, Jō•hā′nan son of

Ka•rē′ah, Se•rāi′ah son of Tan′hu•meth, the sons of Ē′phai the Ne•toph′a•thīte, Jez•a•nī′ah son of the Mā′a•ca•thīte, they and their troops. 9 Ged•a•lī′ah son of A•hī′kam son of Shā′phan swore to them and their troops, saying, "Do not be afraid to serve the Chal•dē′ans. Stay in the land and serve the king of Babylon, and it shall go well with you. 10 As for me, I am staying at Miz′pah to represent you before the Chal•dē′ans who come to us; but as for you, gather wine and summer fruits and oil, and store them in your vessels, and live in the towns that you have taken over." 11 Likewise, when all the Judeans who were in Mō′ab and among the Am′mon•ites and in Ē′dom and in other lands heard that the king of Babylon had left a remnant in Judah and had appointed Ged•a•lī′ah son of A•hī′kam son of Shā′-phan as governor over them, 12 then all the Judeans returned from all the places to which they had been scattered and came to the land of Judah, to Ged•a•lī′ah at Miz′pah; and they gathered wine and summer fruits in great abundance.

13 Now Jō•hā′nan son of Ka•rē′ah and all the leaders of the forces in the open country came to Ged•a•lī′ah at Miz′pah [14] and said to him, "Are you at all aware that Bā′a•lis king of the Am′mon•ites has sent Ish′ma•el son of Neth•a•nī′ah to take your life?" But Ged•a•lī′ah son of A•hī′kam would not believe them. 15 Then Jō•hā′nan son of Ka•rē′ah spoke secretly to Ged•a•lī′ah at Miz′pah, "Please let me go and kill Ish′ma•el son of Neth•a•nī′ah, and no one else will know. Why should he take your life, so that all the Judeans who are gathered around you would be scattered, and the remnant of Judah would perish?" 16 But Ged•a•lī′ah son of A•hī′kam said to Jō•hā′nan son of Ka•rē′ah, "Do not do such a thing, for you are telling a lie about Ish′ma•el."

Insurrection against Gedaliah

41 In the seventh month, Ish′ma•el son of Neth•a•nī′ah son of E•lish′a•ma, of the royal family, one of the chief officers of the king, came with ten men to Ged•a•lī′ah son of A•hī′kam, at Miz′pah. As they ate bread together there at Miz′-pah, 2 Ish′ma•el son of Neth•a•nī′ah and the ten men with him got up and struck down Ged•a•lī′ah son of A•hī′kam son of Shā′phan with the sword and killed him, because the king of Babylon had appointed him governor in the land. 3 Ish′ma•el also killed all the Judeans who were with Ged•a•lī′-ah at Miz′pah, and the Chal•dē′an soldiers who happened to be there.

4 On the day after the murder of Ged•a•lī′ah, before anyone knew of it, 5 eighty men arrived from Shē′chem and Shī′lōh and Sa•mār′i•a, with their beards shaved and their clothes torn, and their

---

g Or *Nubian;* Heb *Cushite*   *h* Syr: Meaning of Heb uncertain bodies gashed, bringing grain offerings and incense to present at the temple of the LORD. 6 And Ish′ma·el son of Neth·a·ni′ah came out from Miz′pah to meet them, weeping as he came. As he met them, he said to them, "Come to Ged·a·li′ah son of A·hi′kam." 7 When they reached the middle of the city, Ish′ma·el son of Neth·a·ni′ah and the men with him slaughtered them, and threw them[i] into a cistern. 8 But there were ten men among them who said to Ish′ma·el, "Do not kill us, for we have stores of wheat, barley, oil, and honey hidden in the fields." So he refrained, and did not kill them along with their companions.

9 Now the cistern into which Ish′ma·el had thrown all the bodies of the men whom he had struck down was the large cistern[j] that King Asa had made for defense against King Bā′a·sha of Israel; Ish′ma·el son of Neth·a·ni′ah filled that cistern with those whom he had killed. 10 Then Ish′ma·el took captive all the rest of the people who were in Miz′pah, the king's daughters and all the people who were left at Miz′pah, whom Ne·bū·za·rad′an, the captain of the guard, had committed to Ged·a·li′ah son of A·hi′kam. Ish′ma·el son of Neth·a·ni′ah took them captive and set out to cross over to the Am′mon·ites.

11 But when Jō·hā′nan son of Ka·rē′ah and all the leaders of the forces with him heard of all the crimes that Ish′ma·el son of Neth·a·ni′ah had done, 12 they took all their men and went to fight against Ish′ma·el son of Neth·a·ni′ah. They came upon him at the great pool that is in Gib′ē·on. 13 And when all the people who were with Ish′ma·el saw Jō·hā′nan son of Ka·rē′ah and all the leaders of the forces with him, they were glad. 14 So all the people whom Ish′ma·el had carried away captive from Miz′pah turned around and came back, and went to Jō·hā′nan son of Ka·rē′ah. 15 But Ish′ma·el son of Neth·a·ni′ah escaped from Jō·hā′nan with eight men, and went to the Am′mon·ites. 16 Then Jō·hā′nan son of Ka·rē′ah and all the leaders of the forces with him took all the rest of the people whom Ish′ma·el son of Neth·a·ni′ah had carried away captive[k] from Miz′pah after he had slain Ged·a·li′ah son of A·hi′kam—soldiers, women, children, and eunuchs, whom Jō·hā′nan brought back from Gib′ē·on.[l] 17 And they set out, and stopped at Gē′rūth Chim′ham near Bethlehem, intending to go to Egypt 18 because of the Chal·dē′ans; for they were afraid of them, because Ish′ma·el son of Neth·a·ni′ah had killed Ged·a·li′ah son of A·hi′kam, whom the king of Babylon had made governor over the land.

Jeremiah Advises Survivors Not to Migrate

42 Then all the commanders of the forces, and Jō·hā′nan son of Ka·rē′ah and Az·a·rī′ah[m] son of Hō·shaī′ah, and all the people from the least to the greatest, approached 2 the prophet Jer·e·mī′ah and said, "Be good enough to listen to our plea, and pray to the LORD your God for us—for all this remnant. For there are only a few of us left out of many, as your eyes can see. 3 Let the LORD your God show us where we should go and what we should do." 4 The prophet Jer·e·mī′ah said to them, "Very well: I am going to pray to the LORD your God as you request, and whatever the LORD answers you I will tell you; I will keep nothing back from you." 5 They in their turn said to Jer·e·mī′ah, "May the LORD be a true and faithful witness against us if we do not act according to everything that the LORD your God sends us through you. 6 Whether it is good or bad, we will obey the voice of the LORD our God to whom we are sending you, in order that it may go well with us when we obey the voice of the LORD our God."

7 At the end of ten days the word of the LORD came to Jer·e·mī′ah. 8 Then he summoned Jō·hā′nan son of Ka·rē′ah and all the commanders of the forces who were with him, and all the people from the least to the greatest, 9 and said to them, "Thus says the LORD, the God of Israel, to whom you sent me to present your plea before him: 10 If you will only remain in this land, then I will build you up and not pull you down; I will plant you, and not pluck you up; for I am sorry for the disaster that I have brought upon you. 11 Do not be afraid of the king of Babylon, as you have been; do not be afraid of him, says the LORD, for I am with you, to save you and to rescue you from his hand. 12 I will grant you mercy, and he will have mercy on you and restore you to your native soil. 13 But if you continue to say, 'We will not stay in this land,' thus disobeying the voice of the LORD your God 14 and saying, 'No, we will go to the land of Egypt, where we shall not see war, or hear the sound of the trumpet, or be hungry for bread, and there we will stay,' 15 then hear the word of the LORD, O remnant of Judah. Thus says the LORD of hosts, the God of Israel: If you are determined to enter Egypt and go to settle there, 16 then the sword that you fear shall overtake you there, in the land of Egypt; and the famine that you dread shall follow close after you into Egypt; and there you shall die. 17 All the people who have determined to go to Egypt to settle there shall die by the sword, by famine, and by pestilence; they shall have no remnant or survivor from the disaster that I am bringing upon them.

18 "For thus says the LORD of hosts, the God of

---

i Syr: Heb lacks *and threw them*; compare verse 9   *j* Gk: Heb *whom he had killed by the hand of Gedaliah*   *k* Cn: Heb *whom he recovered from Ishmael son of Nethaniah*   *l* Meaning of Heb uncertain   *m* Gk: Heb *Jezaniah*

Israel: Just as my anger and my wrath were poured out on the inhabitants of Jerusalem, so my wrath will be poured out on you when you go to Egypt. You shall become an object of execration and horror, of cursing and ridicule. You shall see this place no more. 19 The LORD has said to you, O remnant of Judah, Do not go to Egypt. Be well aware that I have warned you today 20 that you have made a fatal mistake. For you yourselves sent me to the LORD your God, saying, 'Pray for us to the LORD our God, and whatever the LORD our God says, tell us and we will do it.' 21 So I have told you today, but you have not obeyed the voice of the LORD your God in anything that he sent me to tell you. 22 Be well aware, then, that you shall die by the sword, by famine, and by pestilence in the place where you desire to go and settle."

Taken to Egypt, Jeremiah Warns of Judgment

43 When Jer•e•mi′ah finished speaking to all the people all these words of the LORD their God, with which the LORD their God had sent him to them, 2 Az•a•ri′ah son of Hō•shaī′-ah and Jō•hā′nan son of Ka•rē′ah and all the other insolent men said to Jer•e•mi′ah, "You are telling a lie. The LORD our God did not send you to say, 'Do not go to Egypt to settle there'; 3 but Bar′uch son of Ne•ri′ah is inciting you against us, to hand us over to the Chal•dē′ans, in order that they may kill us or take us into exile in Babylon." 4 So Jō•hā′nan son of Ka•rē′ah and all the commanders of the forces and all the people did not obey the voice of the LORD, to stay in the land of Judah. 5 But Jō•hā′nan son of Ka•rē′ah and all the commanders of the forces took all the remnant of Judah who had returned to settle in the land of Judah from all the nations to which they had been driven— 6 the men, the women, the children, the princesses, and everyone whom Ne•bū•za•rad′an the captain of the guard had left with Ged•a•li′ah son of A•hī′kam son of Shā′phan; also the prophet Jer•e•mi′ah and Bar′uch son of Ne•ri′ah. 7 And they came into the land of Egypt, for they did not obey the voice of the LORD. And they arrived at Tah′pan•hēs.

8 Then the word of the LORD came to Jer•e•mi′-ah in Tah′pan•hēs: 9 Take some large stones in your hands, and bury them in the clay pavement*n* that is at the entrance to Pharaoh's palace in Tah′pan•hēs. Let the Judeans see you do it, 10 and say to them, Thus says the LORD of hosts, the God of Israel: I am going to send and take my servant King Ne•bū-chad•rez′zar of Babylon, and he*o* will set his throne above these stones that I have buried, and he will spread his royal canopy over them. 11 He shall come and ravage the land of Egypt, giving

those who are destined for pestilence, to
    pestilence,

and those who are destined for captivity, to
    captivity,
and those who are destined for the sword,
    to the sword.

12 He*p* shall kindle a fire in the temples of the gods of Egypt; and he shall burn them and carry them away captive; and he shall pick clean the land of Egypt, as a shepherd picks his cloak clean of vermin; and he shall depart from there safely. 13 He shall break the obelisks of Hē•li•op′o•lis, which is in the land of Egypt; and the temples of the gods of Egypt he shall burn with fire.

Denunciation of Persistent Idolatry

44 The word that came to Jer•e•mi′ah for all the Judeans living in the land of Egypt, at Mig′dōl, at Tah′pan•hēs, at Memphis, and in the land of Path′ros, 2 Thus says the LORD of hosts, the God of Israel: You yourselves have seen all the disaster that I have brought on Jerusalem and on all the towns of Judah. Look at them; today they are a desolation, without an inhabitant in them, 3 because of the wickedness that they committed, provoking me to anger, in that they went to make offerings and serve other gods that they had not known, neither they, nor you, nor your ancestors. 4 Yet I persistently sent to you all my servants the prophets, saying, "I beg you not to do this abominable thing that I hate!" 5 But they did not listen or incline their ear, to turn from their wickedness and make no offerings to other gods. 6 So my wrath and my anger were poured out and kindled in the towns of Judah and in the streets of Jerusalem; and they became a waste and a desolation, as they still are today. 7 And now thus says the LORD God of hosts, the God of Israel: Why are you doing such great harm to yourselves, to cut off man and woman, child and infant, from the midst of Judah, leaving yourselves without a remnant? 8 Why do you provoke me to anger with the works of your hands, making offerings to other gods in the land of Egypt where you have come to settle? Will you be cut off and become an object of cursing and ridicule among all the nations of the earth? 9 Have you forgotten the crimes of your ancestors, of the kings of Judah, of their*q* wives, your own crimes and those of your wives, which they committed in the land of Judah and in the streets of Jerusalem? 10 They have shown no contrition or fear to this day, nor have they walked in my law and my statutes that I set before you and before your ancestors.

11 Therefore thus says the LORD of hosts, the God of Israel: I am determined to bring disaster on you, to bring all Judah to an end. 12 I will take the

---

n Meaning of Heb uncertain   *o* Gk Syr: Heb I   *p* Gk Syr Vg: Heb I   *q* Heb *his* remnant of Judah who are determined to come to the land of Egypt to settle, and they shall perish, everyone; in the land of Egypt they shall fall; by the sword and by famine they shall perish; from the least to the greatest, they shall die by the sword and by famine; and they shall become an object of execration and horror, of cursing and ridicule. 13 I will punish those who live in the land of Egypt, as I have punished Jerusalem, with the sword, with famine, and with pestilence, 14 so that none of the remnant of Judah who have come to settle in the land of Egypt shall escape or survive or return to the land of Judah. Although they long to go back to live there, they shall not go back, except some fugitives.

15 Then all the men who were aware that their wives had been making offerings to other gods, and all the women who stood by, a great assembly, all the people who lived in Path'ros in the land of Egypt, answered Jer·e·mi'ah: 16 "As for the word that you have spoken to us in the name of the LORD, we are not going to listen to you. 17 Instead, we will do everything that we have vowed, make offerings to the queen of heaven and pour out libations to her, just as we and our ancestors, our kings and our officials, used to do in the towns of Judah and in the streets of Jerusalem. We used to have plenty of food, and prospered, and saw no misfortune. 18 But from the time we stopped making offerings to the queen of heaven and pouring out libations to her, we have lacked everything and have perished by the sword and by famine." 19 And the women said,ʳ "Indeed we will go on making offerings to the queen of heaven and pouring out libations to her; do you think that we made cakes for her, marked with her image, and poured out libations to her without our husbands' being involved?"

20 Then Jer·e·mi'ah said to all the people, men and women, all the people who were giving him this answer: 21 "As for the offerings that you made in the towns of Judah and in the streets of Jerusalem, you and your ancestors, your kings and your officials, and the people of the land, did not the LORD remember them? Did it not come into his mind? 22 The LORD could no longer bear the sight of your evil doings, the abominations that you committed; therefore your land became a desolation and a waste and a curse, without inhabitant, as it is to this day. 23 It is because you burned offerings, and because you sinned against the LORD and did not obey the voice of the LORD or walk in his law and in his statutes and in his decrees, that this disaster has befallen you, as is still evident today."

24 Jer·e·mi'ah said to all the people and all the women, "Hear the word of the LORD, all you Judeans who are in the land of Egypt, 25 Thus says the LORD of hosts, the God of Israel: You and your

wives have accomplished in deeds what you declared in words, saying, 'We are determined to perform the vows that we have made, to make offerings to the queen of heaven and to pour out libations to her.' By all means, keep your vows and make your libations! 26 Therefore hear the word of the LORD, all you Judeans who live in the land of Egypt: Lo, I swear by my great name, says the LORD, that my name shall no longer be pronounced on the lips of any of the people of Judah in all the land of Egypt, saying, 'As the Lord GOD lives.' 27 I am going to watch over them for harm and not for good; all the people of Judah who are in the land of Egypt shall perish by the sword and by famine, until not one is left. 28 And those who escape the sword shall return from the land of Egypt to the land of Judah, few in number; and all the remnant of Judah, who have come to the land of Egypt to settle, shall know whose words will stand, mine or theirs! 29 This shall be the sign to you, says the LORD, that I am going to punish you in this place, in order that you may know that my words against you will surely be carried out: 30 Thus says the LORD, I am going to give Pharaoh Hoph'ra, king of Egypt, into the hands of his enemies, those who seek his life, just as I gave King Zed·e·ki'ah of Judah into the hand of King Ne·bu·chad·rez'zar of Babylon, his enemy who sought his life."

A Word of Comfort to Baruch

45 The word that the prophet Jer·e·mi'ah spoke to Bar'uch son of Ne·ri'ah, when he wrote these words in a scroll at the dictation of Jer·e·mi'ah, in the fourth year of King Je·hoi'a·kim son of Jo·si'ah of Judah: 2 Thus says the LORD, the God of Israel, to you, O Bar'uch: 3 You said, "Woe is me! The LORD has added sorrow to my pain; I am weary with my groaning, and I find no rest." 4 Thus you shall say to him, "Thus says the LORD: I am going to break down what I have built, and pluck up what I have planted—that is, the whole land. 5 And you, do you seek great things for yourself? Do not seek them; for I am going to bring disaster upon all flesh, says the LORD; but I will give you your life as a prize of war in every place to which you may go."

Judgment on Egypt

46 The word of the LORD that came to the prophet Jer·e·mi'ah concerning the nations.

2 Concerning Egypt, about the army of Pharaoh Ne'co, king of Egypt, which was by the river Euphrates at Car'chem·ish and which King Ne·bu·chad·rez'zar of Babylon defeated in the fourth year of King Je·hoi'a·kim son of Jo·si'ah of Judah:

ʳ Compare Syr: Heb lacks *And the women said*

3 Prepare buckler and shield,
    and advance for battle!
4 Harness the horses;
    mount the steeds!
Take your stations with your helmets,
    whet your lances,
    put on your coats of mail!
5 Why do I see them terrified?
    They have fallen back;
their warriors are beaten down,
    and have fled in haste.
They do not look back—
    terror is all around!
                              says the LORD.

6 The swift cannot flee away,
    nor can the warrior escape;
in the north by the river Euphrates
    they have stumbled and fallen.

7 Who is this, rising like the Nile,
    like rivers whose waters surge?

did you KNOW?

Oracles against the Nations

The Oracles against the Nations, in Jeremiah, chapters 46–51, resemble the oracles in chapters 13–23 of Isaiah. In both, God's threats to destroy the enemies of Israel, as proclaimed by a prophet, reflect the bitterness that has welled up in the nation's heart during its long history of suffering.

Is God really as vengeful as the prophecies from Jeremiah suggest? We must balance our understanding of God's vengeance with Jesus' teachings—for example, Jesus' claim that God makes the "sun rise on the evil and on the good" (Mt 5.45). The God whom Jesus called Abba is the parent of all nations, who wants enemies to be reconciled with one another. The Oracles against the Nations challenge Christians to be the first to offer the handshake of forgiveness and break the cycle of violence.

▶ Jeremiah, chapters 46–51

8 Egypt rises like the Nile,
    like rivers whose waters surge.
It said, Let me rise, let me cover the earth,
    let me destroy cities and their inhabitants.
9 Advance, O horses,
    and dash madly, O chariots!
Let the warriors go forth:
    Ethiopia[s] and Put who carry the shield,
    the Lu'dim, who draw[t] the bow.
10 That day is the day of the Lord GOD of hosts,
    a day of retribution,
    to gain vindication from his foes.
The sword shall devour and be sated,
    and drink its fill of their blood.
For the Lord GOD of hosts holds a sacrifice
    in the land of the north by the river
        Euphrates.
11 Go up to Gil'e·ad, and take balm,
    O virgin daughter Egypt!
In vain you have used many medicines;
    there is no healing for you.
12 The nations have heard of your shame,
    and the earth is full of your cry;
for warrior has stumbled against warrior;
    both have fallen together.

Babylonia Will Strike Egypt

13 The word that the LORD spoke to the prophet Jer·e·mi'ah about the coming of King Ne·bu·chad·rez'zar of Babylon to attack the land of Egypt:
14 Declare in Egypt, and proclaim in Mig'dol;
    proclaim in Memphis and Tah'pan·hes;
Say, "Take your stations and be ready,
    for the sword shall devour those around
        you."
15 Why has A'pis fled?[u]
    Why did your bull not stand?
    —because the LORD thrust him down.
16 Your multitude stumbled[v] and fell,
    and one said to another,[w]
"Come, let us go back to our own people
    and to the land of our birth,
    because of the destroying sword."
17 Give Pharaoh, king of Egypt, the name
    "Braggart who missed his chance."

18 As I live, says the King,
    whose name is the LORD of hosts,
one is coming
    like Ta'bor among the mountains,
    and like Car'mel by the sea.
19 Pack your bags for exile,

---

s Or Nubia; Heb Cush   t Cn: Heb who grasp, who draw
u Gk: Heb Why was it swept away   v Gk: Meaning of Heb
uncertain   w Gk: Heb and fell one to another and they said

JER

sheltered daughter Egypt!
For Memphis shall become a waste,
　　a ruin, without inhabitant.

20 A beautiful heifer is Egypt—
　　a gadfly from the north lights upon her.
21 Even her mercenaries in her midst
　　are like fatted calves;
they too have turned and fled together,
　　they did not stand;
for the day of their calamity has come upon
　　　　them,
　　the time of their punishment.

22 She makes a sound like a snake gliding away;
　　for her enemies march in force,
and come against her with axes,
　　like those who fell trees.
23 They shall cut down her forest,
　　　　　　　　　　　says the LORD,
　　though it is impenetrable,
because they are more numerous
　　than locusts;
　　they are without number.
24 Daughter Egypt shall be put to shame;
　　she shall be handed over to a people from
　　　　the north.

25 The LORD of hosts, the God of Israel, said:
See, I am bringing punishment upon Ā′mon of
Thēbes, and Pharaoh, and Egypt and her gods and
her kings, upon Pharaoh and those who trust in
him. 26 I will hand them over to those who seek
their life, to King Ne·bū·chad·rez′zar of Babylon
and his officers. Afterward Egypt shall be inhabited
as in the days of old, says the LORD.

God Will Save Israel
(Cp Jer 30.10–11)

27 But as for you, have no fear, my servant
　　　　Jacob,
　　and do not be dismayed, O Israel;
for I am going to save you from far away,
　　and your offspring from the land of their
　　　　captivity.
Jacob shall return and have quiet and
　　　　ease,
　　and no one shall make him afraid.
28 As for you, have no fear, my servant Jacob,
　　　　　　　　　　　says the LORD,
　　for I am with you.
I will make an end of all the nations
　　among which I have banished you,
　　but I will not make an end of you!
I will chastise you in just measure,
　　and I will by no means leave you
　　　　unpunished.

Judgment on the Philistines

47 The word of the LORD that came to the
prophet Jer·e·mī′ah concerning the
Phi·lis′tines, before Pharaoh attacked Gā′za:
2 Thus says the LORD:
See, waters are rising out of the north
　　and shall become an overflowing torrent;
they shall overflow the land and all that fills it,
　　the city and those who live in it.
People shall cry out,
　　and all the inhabitants of the land shall
　　　　wail.
3 At the noise of the stamping of the hoofs of his
　　　　stallions,
　　at the clatter of his chariots, at the rumbling
　　　　of their wheels,
parents do not turn back for children,
　　so feeble are their hands,
4 because of the day that is coming
　　to destroy all the Phi·lis′tines,
to cut off from Tyre and Si′don
　　every helper that remains.
For the LORD is destroying the Phi·lis′tines,
　　the remnant of the coastland of Caph′tor.
5 Baldness has come upon Gā′za,
　　Ash′ke·lon is silenced.
O remnant of their power!x
　　How long will you gash yourselves?
6 Ah, sword of the LORD!
　　How long until you are quiet?
Put yourself into your scabbard,
　　rest and be still!
7 How can ity be quiet,
　　when the LORD has given it an order?
Against Ash′ke·lon and against the seashore—
　　there he has appointed it.

Judgment on Moab

48 Concerning Mō′ab.
Thus says the LORD of hosts, the God of Israel:
Alas for Ne′bō, it is laid waste!
　　Kir·i·a·tha′im is put to shame, it is taken;
the fortress is put to shame and broken down;
2 　　the renown of Mō′ab is no more.
In Hesh′bon they planned evil against her:
　　"Come, let us cut her off from being a
　　　　nation!"
You also, O Madmen, shall be brought to
　　silence;z
　　the sword shall pursue you.

3 Hark! a cry from Hor·o·na′im,
　　"Desolation and great destruction!"

---

x Gk: Heb *their valley*　y Gk Vg: Heb *you*　z The place-name
Madmen sounds like the Hebrew verb *to be silent*

4 "Mō′ab is destroyed!"
  her little ones cry out.
5 For at the ascent of Lū′hith
  they go^a up weeping bitterly;
for at the descent of Hor•ō•nā′im
  they have heard the distressing cry of
    anguish.
6 Flee! Save yourselves!
  Be like a wild ass^b in the desert!

7 Surely, because you trusted in your
    strongholds^c and your treasures,
  you also shall be taken;
Chē′mosh shall go out into exile,
  with his priests and his attendants.
8 The destroyer shall come upon every town,
  and no town shall escape;
the valley shall perish,
  and the plain shall be destroyed,
    as the LORD has spoken.

9 Set aside salt for Mō′ab,
  for she will surely fall;
her towns shall become a desolation,
  with no inhabitant in them.

10 Accursed is the one who is slack in doing the work of the LORD; and accursed is the one who keeps back the sword from bloodshed.

11 Mō′ab has been at ease from his youth,
  settled like wine^d on its dregs;
he has not been emptied from vessel to vessel,
  nor has he gone into exile;
therefore his flavor has remained
  and his aroma is unspoiled.
12 Therefore, the time is surely coming, says the LORD, when I shall send to him decanters to decant him, and empty his vessels, and break his^e jars in pieces. 13 Then Mō′ab shall be ashamed of Chē′-mosh, as the house of Israel was ashamed of Beth′el, their confidence.

14 How can you say, "We are heroes
  and mighty warriors"?
15 The destroyer of Mō′ab and his towns has
    come up,
  and the choicest of his young men have
    gone down to slaughter,
  says the King, whose name is the LORD of
    hosts.
16 The calamity of Mō′ab is near at hand
  and his doom approaches swiftly.
17 Mourn over him, all you his neighbors,
  and all who know his name;
say, "How the mighty scepter is broken,
  the glorious staff!"

18 Come down from glory,
  and sit on the parched ground,
    enthroned daughter Dī′bon!
For the destroyer of Mō′ab has come up against
    you;
  he has destroyed your strongholds.
19 Stand by the road and watch,
  you inhabitant of A•rō′er!
Ask the man fleeing and the woman
    escaping;
  say, "What has happened?"
20 Mō′ab is put to shame, for it is broken down;
  wail and cry!
Tell it by the Ar′non,
  that Mō′ab is laid waste.

21 Judgment has come upon the tableland, upon Hō′lon, and Jah′zah, and Meph′a•ath, 22 and Dī′bon, and Nē′bō, and Beth-dib•la•thā′im, 23 and Kir-i•a•thā′im, and Beth-gā′mul, and Beth-mē′on, 24 and Ker′i•oth, and Boz′rah, and all the towns of the land of Mō′ab, far and near. 25 The horn of Mō′ab is cut off, and his arm is broken, says the LORD.

26 Make him drunk, because he magnified himself against the LORD; let Mō′ab wallow in his vomit; he too shall become a laughingstock. 27 Israel was a laughingstock for you, though he was not caught among thieves; but whenever you spoke of him you shook your head!

28 Leave the towns, and live on the rock,
  O inhabitants of Mō′ab!
Be like the dove that nests
  on the sides of the mouth of a gorge.
29 We have heard of the pride of Mō′ab—
  he is very proud—
of his loftiness, his pride, and his arrogance,
  and the haughtiness of his heart.
30 I myself know his insolence, says the LORD;
  his boasts are false,
  his deeds are false.
31 Therefore I wail for Mō′ab;
  I cry out for all Mō′ab;
  for the people of Kir-hē′res I mourn.
32 More than for Jā′zer I weep for you,
  O vine of Sib′mah!
Your branches crossed over the sea,
  reached as far as Jā′zer;^f
upon your summer fruits and your vintage
  the destroyer has fallen.
33 Gladness and joy have been taken away
  from the fruitful land of Mō′ab;
  I have stopped the wine from the wine presses;

---

^a Cn: Heb *he goes*   ^b Gk Aquila: Heb *like Aroer*   ^c Gk: Heb *works*   ^d Heb lacks *like wine*   ^e Gk Aquila: Heb *their*   ^f Two Mss and Isa 16.8: MT *the sea of Jazer*

no one treads them with shouts of joy;
the shouting is not the shout of joy.

34 Hesh'bon and Ê•le•ā'leh cry out;*s* as far as Jā'-
haz they utter their voice, from Zō'ar to Hor•ō-
nā'im and Eg'lath-she•lish'i•yah. For even the
waters of Nim'rim have become desolate. 35 And I
will bring to an end in Mō'ab, says the LORD, those
who offer sacrifice at a high place and make offerings to their gods. 36 Therefore my heart moans for
Mō'ab like a flute, and my heart moans like a flute
for the people of Kir-hē'res; for the riches they
gained have perished.

37 For every head is shaved and every beard cut
off; on all the hands there are gashes, and on the
loins sackcloth. 38 On all the housetops of Mō'ab
and in the squares there is nothing but lamentation; for I have broken Mō'ab like a vessel that no
one wants, says the LORD. 39 How it is broken! How
they wail! How Mō'ab has turned his back in
shame! So Mō'ab has become a derision and a horror to all his neighbors.

40 For thus says the LORD:
    Look, he shall swoop down like an eagle,
        and spread his wings against Mō'ab;
41 the towns*h* shall be taken
        and the strongholds seized.
    The hearts of the warriors of Mō'ab, on that
        day,
    shall be like the heart of a woman in labor.

42 Mō'ab shall be destroyed as a people,
    because he magnified himself against the
        LORD.
43 Terror, pit, and trap
    are before you, O inhabitants of Mō'ab!
                says the LORD.
44 Everyone who flees from the terror
    shall fall into the pit,
and everyone who climbs out of the pit
    shall be caught in the trap.
For I will bring these things*i* upon Mō'ab
    in the year of their punishment,
                says the LORD.

45 In the shadow of Hesh'bon
    fugitives stop exhausted;
for a fire has gone out from Hesh'bon,
    a flame from the house of Sī'hon;
it has destroyed the forehead of Mō'ab,
    the scalp of the people of tumult.*j*
46 Woe to you, O Mō'ab!
    The people of Chē'mosh have perished,
for your sons have been taken captive,
    and your daughters into captivity.
47 Yet I will restore the fortunes of Mō'ab
    in the latter days, says the LORD.
Thus far is the judgment on Mō'ab.

---

s Cn: Heb *From the cry of Heshbon to Elealeh*   *h* Or *Kerioth*
i Gk Syr: Heb *bring upon it*   *j* Or *of Shaon*

THUS SAYS THE LORD

Look,
he shall swoop down
like an eagle,
and spread his wings
against Mō'ab;

the towns shall be taken

and the strongholds seized.

48.40–41

Judgment on the Ammonites

49 Concerning the Am′mon•ites.

Thus says the LORD:
Has Israel no sons?
    Has he no heir?
Why then has Mil′com dispossessed Gad,
    and his people settled in its towns?
2 Therefore, the time is surely coming,
    says the LORD,
when I will sound the battle alarm
    against Rab′bah of the Am′mon•ites;
it shall become a desolate mound,
    and its villages shall be burned with fire;
then Israel shall dispossess those who
            dispossessed him,
    says the LORD.

3 Wail, O Hesh′bon, for Aī is laid waste!
    Cry out, O daughters*k* of Rab′bah!
Put on sackcloth,
    lament, and slash yourselves with
            whips!*l*
For Mil′com shall go into exile,
    with his priests and his attendants.
4 Why do you boast in your strength?
    Your strength is ebbing,
O faithless daughter.
    You trusted in your treasures, saying,
    "Who will attack me?"
5 I am going to bring terror upon you,
    says the Lord GOD of hosts,
    from all your neighbors,
and you will be scattered, each headlong,
    with no one to gather the fugitives.

6 But afterward I will restore the fortunes of the Am′mon•ites, says the LORD.

Judgment on Edom

7 Concerning Ē′dom.

Thus says the LORD of hosts:
Is there no longer wisdom in Tē′man?
    Has counsel perished from the
            prudent?
    Has their wisdom vanished?
8 Flee, turn back, get down low,
    inhabitants of Dē′dan!
For I will bring the calamity of Esau upon
            him,
    the time when I punish him.
9 If grape-gatherers came to you,
    would they not leave gleanings?
If thieves came by night,
    even they would pillage only what they
            wanted.
10 But as for me, I have stripped Esau bare,

I have uncovered his hiding places,
    and he is not able to conceal himself.
His offspring are destroyed, his kinsfolk
    and his neighbors; and he is no more.
11 Leave your orphans, I will keep them alive;
    and let your widows trust in me.

12 For thus says the LORD: If those who do not deserve to drink the cup still have to drink it, shall you be the one to go unpunished? You shall not go unpunished; you must drink it. 13 For by myself I have sworn, says the LORD, that Boz′rah shall become an object of horror and ridicule, a waste, and an object of cursing; and all her towns shall be perpetual wastes.
14 I have heard tidings from the LORD,
        and a messenger has been sent among the
                nations:
    "Gather yourselves together and come against
                her,
        and rise up for battle!"
15 For I will make you least among the nations,
        despised by humankind.
16 The terror you inspire
        and the pride of your heart have deceived
                you,
    you who live in the clefts of the rock,*m*
        who hold the height of the hill.
    Although you make your nest as high as the
                eagle's,
        from there I will bring you down,
                        says the LORD.

17 Ē′dom shall become an object of horror; everyone who passes by it will be horrified and will hiss because of all its disasters. 18 As when Sod′om and Go•mor′rah and their neighbors were overthrown, says the LORD, no one shall live there, nor shall anyone settle in it. 19 Like a lion coming up from the thickets of the Jordan against a perennial pasture, I will suddenly chase Ē′dom*n* away from it; and I will appoint over it whomever I choose.*o* For who is like me? Who can summon me? Who is the shepherd who can stand before me? 20 Therefore hear the plan that the LORD has made against Ē′dom and the purposes that he has formed against the inhabitants of Tē′man: Surely the little ones of the flock shall be dragged away; surely their fold shall be appalled at their fate. 21 At the sound of their fall the earth shall tremble; the sound of their cry shall be heard at the Red Sea.*p* 22 Look, he shall mount up and swoop down like an eagle, and spread his wings against Boz′rah, and the heart of the warriors of Ē′dom in that day shall be like the heart of a woman in labor.

---

k Or *villages*   *l* Cn: Meaning of Heb uncertain   *m* Or *of Sela*   *n* Heb *him*   *o* Or *and I will single out the choicest of his rams:* Meaning of Heb uncertain   *p* Or *Sea of Reeds*

Judgment on Damascus

23 Concerning Damascus.

Hā′math and Ar′pad are confounded,
    for they have heard bad news;
they melt in fear, they are troubled like the sea*q*
    that cannot be quiet.
24 Damascus has become feeble, she turned to
      flee,
    and panic seized her;
anguish and sorrows have taken hold of her,
    as of a woman in labor.
25 How the famous city is forsaken,*r*
    the joyful town!*s*
26 Therefore her young men shall fall in her
      squares,
    and all her soldiers shall be destroyed in
      that day,
                says the LORD of hosts.
27 And I will kindle a fire at the wall of
      Damascus,
    and it shall devour the strongholds of
      Ben-hā′dad.

Judgment on Kedar and Hazor

28 Concerning Kē′dar and the kingdoms of
Hā′zor that King Ne•bū•chad•rez′zar of Babylon defeated.

Thus says the LORD:
Rise up, advance against Kē′dar!
Destroy the people of the east!
29 Take their tents and their flocks,
    their curtains and all their goods;
carry off their camels for yourselves,
    and a cry shall go up: "Terror is all around!"
30 Flee, wander far away, hide in deep places,
    O inhabitants of Hā′zor!
                says the LORD.
For King Ne•bū•chad•rez′zar of Babylon
    has made a plan against you
    and formed a purpose against you.

31 Rise up, advance against a nation at ease,
    that lives secure,
              says the LORD,
that has no gates or bars,
    that lives alone.
32 Their camels shall become booty,
    their herds of cattle a spoil.
I will scatter to every wind
    those who have shaven temples,
and I will bring calamity
    against them from every side,
             says the LORD.
33 Hā′zor shall become a lair of jackals,
    an everlasting waste;

no one shall live there,
    nor shall anyone settle in it.

Judgment on Elam

34 The word of the LORD that came to the
prophet Jer•e•mi′ah concerning Ē′lam, at the beginning of the reign of King Zed•e•ki′ah of Judah.

35 Thus says the LORD of hosts: I am going to
break the bow of Ē′lam, the mainstay of their
might; 36 and I will bring upon Ē′lam the four
winds from the four quarters of heaven; and I will
scatter them to all these winds, and there shall be
no nation to which the exiles from Ē′lam shall not
come. 37 I will terrify Ē′lam before their enemies,
and before those who seek their life; I will bring disaster upon them, my fierce anger, says the LORD. I
will send the sword after them, until I have consumed them; 38 and I will set my throne in Ē′lam,
and destroy their king and officials, says the LORD.

39 But in the latter days I will restore the fortunes of Ē′lam, says the LORD.

Judgment on Babylon

50 The word that the LORD spoke concerning Babylon, concerning the land of the
Chal•dē′ans, by the prophet Jer•e•mi′ah:
2 Declare among the nations and proclaim,
    set up a banner and proclaim,
    do not conceal it, say:
Babylon is taken,
    Bel is put to shame,
    Mer′o•dach is dismayed.
Her images are put to shame,
    her idols are dismayed.
3 For out of the north a nation has come up
against her; it shall make her land a desolation, and
no one shall live in it; both human beings and animals shall flee away.

4 In those days and in that time, says the LORD,
the people of Israel shall come, they and the people
of Judah together; they shall come weeping as they
seek the LORD their God. 5 They shall ask the way to
Zion, with faces turned toward it, and they shall
come and join*t* themselves to the LORD by an everlasting covenant that will never be forgotten.

6 My people have been lost sheep; their shepherds have led them astray, turning them away on
the mountains; from mountain to hill they have
gone, they have forgotten their fold. 7 All who
found them have devoured them, and their enemies have said, "We are not guilty, because they

---

q Cn: Heb *there is trouble in the sea*   *r* Vg: Heb *is not*
forsaken   *s* Syr Vg Tg: Heb *the town of my joy*   *t* Gk: Heb
toward it. Come! They shall join

have sinned against the LORD, the true pasture, the LORD, the hope of their ancestors."

8 Flee from Babylon, and go out of the land of the Chal·dē'ans, and be like male goats leading the flock. 9 For I am going to stir up and bring against Babylon a company of great nations from the land of the north; and they shall array themselves against her; from there she shall be taken. Their arrows are like the arrows of a skilled warrior who does not return empty-handed. 10 Chal·dē'a shall be plundered; all who plunder her shall be sated, says the LORD.

11 Though you rejoice, though you exult,
    O plunderers of my heritage,
though you frisk about like a heifer on the
        grass,
    and neigh like stallions,
12 your mother shall be utterly shamed,
    and she who bore you shall be disgraced.
Lo, she shall be the last of the nations,
    a wilderness, dry land, and a desert.
13 Because of the wrath of the LORD she shall not
        be inhabited,
    but shall be an utter desolation;
everyone who passes by Babylon shall be
        appalled
    and hiss because of all her wounds.
14 Take up your positions around Babylon,
    all you that bend the bow;
shoot at her, spare no arrows,
    for she has sinned against the LORD.
15 Raise a shout against her from all sides,
    "She has surrendered;
her bulwarks have fallen,
    her walls are thrown down."
For this is the vengeance of the LORD:
    take vengeance on her,
    do to her as she has done.
16 Cut off from Babylon the sower,
    and the wielder of the sickle in time of
        harvest;
because of the destroying sword
    all of them shall return to their own people,
    and all of them shall flee to their own land.

17 Israel is a hunted sheep driven away by lions. First the king of Assyria devoured it, and now at the end King Ne·bū·chad·rez'zar of Babylon has gnawed its bones. 18 Therefore, thus says the LORD of hosts, the God of Israel: I am going to punish the king of Babylon and his land, as I punished the king of Assyria. 19 I will restore Israel to its pasture, and it shall feed on Car'mel and in Ba'shan, and on the hills of E'phra·im and in Gil'e·ad its hunger shall be satisfied. 20 In those days and at that time,

says the LORD, the iniquity of Israel shall be sought, and there shall be none; and the sins of Judah, and none shall be found; for I will pardon the remnant that I have spared.

21 Go up to the land of Mer·a·thā'im;[u]
    go up against her,
    and attack the inhabitants of Pe'kod[v]
    and utterly destroy the last of them,[w]
                        says the LORD;
    do all that I have commanded you.
22 The noise of battle is in the land,
    and great destruction!
23 How the hammer of the whole earth
    is cut down and broken!
How Babylon has become
    a horror among the nations!
24 You set a snare for yourself and you were
        caught, O Babylon,
    but you did not know it;
you were discovered and seized,
    because you challenged the LORD.
25 The LORD has opened his armory,
    and brought out the weapons of his wrath,
for the Lord GOD of hosts has a task to do
    in the land of the Chal·dē'ans.
26 Come against her from every quarter;
    open her granaries;
pile her up like heaps of grain, and destroy her
        utterly;
    let nothing be left of her.
27 Kill all her bulls,
    let them go down to the slaughter.
Alas for them, their day has come,
    the time of their punishment!

28 Listen! Fugitives and refugees from the land of Babylon are coming to declare in Zion the vengeance of the LORD our God, vengeance for his temple.

29 Summon archers against Babylon, all who bend the bow. Encamp all around her; let no one escape. Repay her according to her deeds; just as she has done, do to her—for she has arrogantly defied the LORD, the Holy One of Israel. 30 Therefore her young men shall fall in her squares, and all her soldiers shall be destroyed on that day, says the LORD.

31 I am against you, O arrogant one,
    says the Lord GOD of hosts;
for your day has come,
    the time when I will punish you.
32 The arrogant one shall stumble and fall,

---

u Or of Double Rebellion   v Or of Punishment   w Tg: Heb destroy after them

with no one to raise him up,
and I will kindle a fire in his cities,
and it will devour everything around him.

33 Thus says the LORD of hosts: The people of Israel are oppressed, and so too are the people of Judah; all their captors have held them fast and refuse to let them go. 34 Their Redeemer is strong; the LORD of hosts is his name. He will surely plead their cause, that he may give rest to the earth, but unrest to the inhabitants of Babylon.

35 A sword against the Chal·dē′ans, says the LORD,
and against the inhabitants of Babylon,
and against her officials and her sages!
36 A sword against the diviners,
so that they may become fools!
A sword against her warriors,
so that they may be destroyed!
37 A sword against her ˣ horses and against her ˣ
chariots,
and against all the foreign troops in her
midst,
so that they may become women!
A sword against all her treasures,
that they may be plundered!
38 A drought ʸ against her waters,
that they may be dried up!
For it is a land of images,
and they go mad over idols.

39 Therefore wild animals shall live with hyenas in Babylon, ᶻ and ostriches shall inhabit her; she shall never again be peopled, or inhabited for all generations. 40 As when God overthrew Sod′om and Go·mor′rah and their neighbors, says the LORD, so no one shall live there, nor shall anyone settle in her.

41 Look, a people is coming from the north;
a mighty nation and many kings
are stirring from the farthest parts of the
earth.
42 They wield bow and spear,
they are cruel and have no mercy.
The sound of them is like the roaring sea;
they ride upon horses,
set in array as a warrior for battle,
against you, O daughter Babylon!

43 The king of Babylon heard news of them,
and his hands fell helpless;
anguish seized him,
pain like that of a woman in labor.

44 Like a lion coming up from the thickets of the Jordan against a perennial pasture, I will sud-

denly chase them away from her; and I will appoint over her whomever I choose.ᵃ For who is like me? Who can summon me? Who is the shepherd who can stand before me? 45 Therefore hear the plan that the LORD has made against Babylon, and the purposes that he has formed against the land of the Chal·dē′ans: Surely the little ones of the flock shall be dragged away; surely their ᵇ fold shall be appalled at their fate. 46 At the sound of the capture of Babylon the earth shall tremble, and her cry shall be heard among the nations.

51 Thus says the LORD:
I am going to stir up a destructive
wind ᶜ
against Babylon
and against the inhabitants of Leb-qā′mai; ᵈ
2 and I will send winnowers to Babylon,
and they shall winnow her.
They shall empty her land
when they come against her from every side
on the day of trouble.
3 Let not the archer bend his bow,
and let him not array himself in his coat of
mail.
Do not spare her young men;
utterly destroy her entire army.
4 They shall fall down slain in the land of the
Chal·dē′ans,
and wounded in her streets.
5 Israel and Judah have not been forsaken
by their God, the LORD of hosts,
though their land is full of guilt
before the Holy One of Israel.

6 Flee from the midst of Babylon,
save your lives, each of you!
Do not perish because of her guilt,
for this is the time of the LORD's vengeance;
he is repaying her what is due.
7 Babylon was a golden cup in the LORD's hand,
making all the earth drunken;
the nations drank of her wine,
and so the nations went mad.
8 Suddenly Babylon has fallen and is shattered;
wail for her!
Bring balm for her wound;
perhaps she may be healed.
9 We tried to heal Babylon,
but she could not be healed.
Forsake her, and let each of us go
to our own country;

ˣ Cn: Heb *his*   ʸ Another reading is *A sword*   ᶻ Heb lacks *in Babylon*   ᵃ Or *and I will single out the choicest of her rams:* Meaning of Heb uncertain   ᵇ Syr Gk Tg Compare 49.20: Heb lacks *their*   ᶜ Or *stir up the spirit of a destroyer*   ᵈ *Leb-qamai* is a cryptogram for *Kasdim,* Chaldea

for her judgment has reached up to heaven
and has been lifted up even to the skies.
10 The LORD has brought forth our vindication;
come, let us declare in Zion
the work of the LORD our God.

11 Sharpen the arrows!
Fill the quivers!
The LORD has stirred up the spirit of the kings of the
Mēdes, because his purpose concerning Babylon is
to destroy it, for that is the vengeance of the LORD,
vengeance for his temple.
12 Raise a standard against the walls of Babylon;
make the watch strong;
post sentinels;
prepare the ambushes;
for the LORD has both planned and done
what he spoke concerning the inhabitants
of Babylon.
13 You who live by mighty waters,
rich in treasures,
your end has come,
the thread of your life is cut.
14 The LORD of hosts has sworn by himself:
Surely I will fill you with troops like a swarm
of locusts,
and they shall raise a shout of victory over
you.

15 It is he who made the earth by his power,
who established the world by his wisdom,
and by his understanding stretched out the
heavens.
16 When he utters his voice there is a tumult of
waters in the heavens,
and he makes the mist rise from the ends of
the earth.
He makes lightnings for the rain,
and he brings out the wind from his
storehouses.
17 Everyone is stupid and without knowledge;
goldsmiths are all put to shame by their
idols;
for their images are false,
and there is no breath in them.
18 They are worthless, a work of delusion;
at the time of their punishment they shall
perish.
19 Not like these is the LORD,*e* the portion of Jacob,
for he is the one who formed all things,
and Israel is the tribe of his inheritance;
the LORD of hosts is his name.

Israel the Creator's Instrument

20 You are my war club, my weapon of battle:
with you I smash nations;
with you I destroy kingdoms;

21 with you I smash the horse and its rider;
with you I smash the chariot and the
charioteer;
22 with you I smash man and woman;
with you I smash the old man and the boy;
with you I smash the young man and the girl;
23 with you I smash shepherds and their
flocks;
with you I smash farmers and their teams;
with you I smash governors and deputies.

The Doom of Babylon

24 I will repay Babylon and all the inhabitants
of Chal·dē′a before your very eyes for all the wrong
that they have done in Zion, says the LORD.

25 I am against you, O destroying mountain,
says the LORD,
that destroys the whole earth;
I will stretch out my hand against you,
and roll you down from the crags,
and make you a burned-out mountain.
26 No stone shall be taken from you for a corner
and no stone for a foundation,
but you shall be a perpetual waste,
says the LORD.

27 Raise a standard in the land,
blow the trumpet among the nations;
prepare the nations for war against her,
summon against her the kingdoms,
Ar′a·rat, Min′nī, and Ash′ke·naz;
appoint a marshal against her,
bring up horses like bristling locusts.
28 Prepare the nations for war against her,
the kings of the Mēdes, with their governors
and deputies,
and every land under their dominion.
29 The land trembles and writhes,
for the LORD's purposes against Babylon
stand,
to make the land of Babylon a desolation,
without inhabitant.
30 The warriors of Babylon have given up fighting,
they remain in their strongholds;
their strength has failed,
they have become women;
her buildings are set on fire,
her bars are broken.
31 One runner runs to meet another,
and one messenger to meet another,
to tell the king of Babylon
that his city is taken from end to end:
32 the fords have been seized,
the marshes have been burned with fire,

J
E
R

---

e Heb lacks *the LORD*

and the soldiers are in panic.

33 For thus says the LORD of hosts, the God of
      Israel:
Daughter Babylon is like a threshing floor
      at the time when it is trodden;
yet a little while
      and the time of her harvest will come.

34 "King Ne•bū•chad•rez′zar of Babylon has
            devoured me,
      he has crushed me;
he has made me an empty vessel,
      he has swallowed me like a monster;
he has filled his belly with my delicacies,
      he has spewed me out.
35 May my torn flesh be avenged on Babylon,"
      the inhabitants of Zion shall say.
"May my blood be avenged on the inhabitants
            of Chal•dē′a,"
      Jerusalem shall say.

36 Therefore thus says the LORD:
I am going to defend your cause
      and take vengeance for you.
I will dry up her sea
      and make her fountain dry;
37 and Babylon shall become a heap of ruins,
      a den of jackals,
an object of horror and of hissing,
      without inhabitant.

38 Like lions they shall roar together;
      they shall growl like lions' whelps.
39 When they are inflamed, I will set out their
            drink
      and make them drunk, until they become
            merry
and then sleep a perpetual sleep
      and never wake, says the LORD.
40 I will bring them down like lambs to the
            slaughter,
      like rams and goats.
41 How Shē′shach⨍ is taken,
      the pride of the whole earth seized!
How Babylon has become
      an object of horror among the nations!
42 The sea has risen over Babylon;
      she has been covered by its tumultuous
            waves.
43 Her cities have become an object of horror,
      a land of drought and a desert,
a land in which no one lives,
      and through which no mortal passes.
44 I will punish Bel in Babylon,
      and make him disgorge what he has
            swallowed.
The nations shall no longer stream to him;
      the wall of Babylon has fallen.

45 Come out of her, my people!
      Save your lives, each of you,
      from the fierce anger of the LORD!
46 Do not be fainthearted or fearful
      at the rumors heard in the land—
one year one rumor comes,
      the next year another,
rumors of violence in the land
      and of ruler against ruler.

47 Assuredly, the days are coming
      when I will punish the images of Babylon;
her whole land shall be put to shame,
      and all her slain shall fall in her midst.
48 Then the heavens and the earth,
      and all that is in them,
shall shout for joy over Babylon;
      for the destroyers shall come against them
            out of the north,
                              says the LORD.
49 Babylon must fall for the slain of Israel,
      as the slain of all the earth have fallen
            because of Babylon.

50 You survivors of the sword,
      go, do not linger!
Remember the LORD in a distant land,
      and let Jerusalem come into your mind:
51 We are put to shame, for we have heard insults;
      dishonor has covered our face,
for aliens have come
      into the holy places of the LORD's house.

52 Therefore the time is surely coming, says the
            LORD,
      when I will punish her idols,
and through all her land
      the wounded shall groan.
53 Though Babylon should mount up to heaven,
      and though she should fortify her strong
            height,
from me destroyers would come upon her,
      says the LORD.

54 Listen!—a cry from Babylon!
      A great crashing from the land of the
            Chal•dē′ans!
55 For the LORD is laying Babylon waste,
      and stilling her loud clamor.
Their waves roar like mighty waters,
      the sound of their clamor resounds;
56 for a destroyer has come against her,
      against Babylon;
her warriors are taken,
      their bows are broken;

⨍ Sheshach is a cryptogram for Babel, Babylon

did you **KNOW?**

Whatever Happened to Babylon?

In his time, Jeremiah prophesied about the destruction of Babylon, the powerful empire with the most glamorous and glittering capital in the Middle East (see Jeremiah, chapters 50–51). Not long afterward, in 587 B.C., King Nebuchadrezzar (also called Nebuchadnezzar) of Babylon destroyed Jerusalem, blinded the king of Judah, and led the leaders of Judah off to exile. This seemed to be the end of Jerusalem and perhaps even the Israelites. However, the captives were eventually released when Persia defeated Babylon. Today, Jerusalem is a thriving city, and Judaism—as it emerged after the Exile—is a great religion. Babylon is long gone, and no one worships its chief god, Marduk.

Jeremiah saw past the immediate destruction of Jerusalem to the eventual doom of Babylon. He had a much broader vision of the future. Great cities come and go, but God is forever, and the people of God live on through all the ebbs and flows of history.

▶ Jeremiah, chapter 51

for the LORD is a God of recompense,
 he will repay in full.
57 I will make her officials and her sages
  drunk,
  also her governors, her deputies, and her
   warriors;
 they shall sleep a perpetual sleep and never
  wake,
 says the King, whose name is the LORD of
  hosts.

58 Thus says the LORD of hosts:
 The broad wall of Babylon
  shall be leveled to the ground,
 and her high gates
  shall be burned with fire.
 The peoples exhaust themselves for nothing,
  and the nations weary themselves only for
   fire.*g*

Jeremiah's Command to Seraiah

59 The word that the prophet Jer·e·mi′ah commanded Se·rāi′ah son of Ne·rī′ah son of Mah′sēi·ah, when he went with King Zed·e·kī′ah of Judah to Babylon, in the fourth year of his reign. Se·rāi′ah was the quartermaster. 60 Jer·e·mi′ah wrote in a*h* scroll all the disasters that would come on Babylon, all these words that are written concerning Babylon. 61 And Jer·e·mi′ah said to Se·rāi′ah: "When you come to Babylon, see that you read all these words, 62 and say, 'O LORD, you yourself threatened to destroy this place so that neither human beings nor animals shall live in it, and it shall be desolate forever.' 63 When you finish reading this scroll, tie a stone to it, and throw it into the middle of the Euphrates, 64 and say, 'Thus shall Babylon sink, to rise no more, because of the disasters that I am bringing on her.' "*i*

Thus far are the words of Jer·e·mi′ah.

The Destruction of Jerusalem Reviewed
(2 Kings 24.18—25.26; 2 Chr 36.11–20;
Jer 39.1–10)

52 Zed·e·kī′ah was twenty-one years old when he began to reign; he reigned eleven years in Jerusalem. His mother's name was Ha·mū′tal daughter of Jer·e·mi′ah of Lib′nah. 2 He did what was evil in the sight of the LORD, just as Je·hoi′a·kim had done. 3 Indeed, Jerusalem and Judah so angered the LORD that he expelled them from his presence.

Zed·e·kī′ah rebelled against the king of Babylon. 4 And in the ninth year of his reign, in the tenth month, on the tenth day of the month, King Ne·bū·chad·rez′zar of Babylon came with all his army against Jerusalem, and they laid siege to it; they built siegeworks against it all around. 5 So the city was besieged until the eleventh year of King Zed·e·kī′ah. 6 On the ninth day of the fourth month the famine became so severe in the city that there was no food for the people of the land. 7 Then a breach was made in the city wall;*j* and all the soldiers fled and went out from the city by night by the way of the gate between the two walls, by the king's garden, though the Chal·dē′ans were all around the city. They went in the direction of the Ar′a·bah. 8 But the army of the Chal·dē′ans pursued the king, and overtook Zed·e·kī′ah in the plains of Jericho; and all his army was scattered, deserting him. 9 Then they captured the king, and brought him up to the king of Babylon at Rib′lah in the land of Hā′math, and he passed sentence on him. 10 The king of Babylon killed the sons of Zed·e·kī′ah before his

J E R

---

g Gk Syr Compare Hab 2.13: Heb *and the nations for fire, and they are weary*   *h* Or *one*   *i* Gk: Heb *on her. And they shall weary themselves*   *j* Heb lacks *wall* eyes, and also killed all the officers of Judah at Rib'lah. 11 He put out the eyes of Zed·e·kī'ah, and bound him in fetters, and the king of Babylon took him to Babylon, and put him in prison until the day of his death.

12 In the fifth month, on the tenth day of the month—which was the nineteenth year of King Ne·bū·chad·rez'zar, king of Babylon—Ne·bū·za·rad'an the captain of the bodyguard who served the king of Babylon, entered Jerusalem. 13 He burned the house of the LORD, the king's house, and all the houses of Jerusalem; every great house he burned down. 14 All the army of the Chal·dē'ans, who were with the captain of the guard, broke down all the walls around Jerusalem. 15 Ne·bū·za·rad'an the captain of the guard carried into exile some of the poorest of the people and the rest of the people who were left in the city and the deserters who had defected to the king of Babylon, together with the rest of the artisans. 16 But Ne·bū·za·rad'an the captain of the guard left some of the poorest people of the land to be vinedressers and tillers of the soil.

17 The pillars of bronze that were in the house of the LORD, and the stands and the bronze sea that were in the house of the LORD, the Chal·dē'ans broke in pieces, and carried all the bronze to Babylon. 18 They took away the pots, the shovels, the snuffers, the basins, the ladles, and all the vessels of bronze used in the temple service. 19 The captain of the guard took away the small bowls also, the firepans, the basins, the pots, the lampstands, the ladles, and the bowls for libation, both those of gold and those of silver. 20 As for the two pillars, the one sea, the twelve bronze bulls that were under the sea, and the stands,*k* which King Solomon had made for the house of the LORD, the bronze of all these vessels was beyond weighing. 21 As for the pillars, the height of the one pillar was eighteen cubits, its circumference was twelve cubits; it was hollow and its thickness was four fingers. 22 Upon it was a capital of bronze; the height of the capital was five cubits; latticework and pomegranates, all of bronze, encircled the top of the capital. And the second pillar had the same, with pomegranates. 23 There were ninety-six pomegranates on the sides; all the pome-

granates encircling the latticework numbered one hundred.

24 The captain of the guard took the chief priest Se·rāi'ah, the second priest Zeph·a·nī'ah, and the three guardians of the threshold; 25 and from the city he took an officer who had been in command of the soldiers, and seven men of the king's council who were found in the city; the secretary of the commander of the army who mustered the people of the land; and sixty men of the people of the land who were found inside the city. 26 Then Ne·bū·za·rad'an the captain of the guard took them, and brought them to the king of Babylon at Rib'lah. 27 And the king of Babylon struck them down, and put them to death at Rib'lah in the land of Hā'-math. So Judah went into exile out of its land.

28 This is the number of the people whom Nebū·chad·rez'zar took into exile: in the seventh year, three thousand twenty-three Judeans; 29 in the eighteenth year of Ne·bū·chad·rez'zar he took into exile from Jerusalem eight hundred thirty-two persons; 30 in the twenty-third year of Ne·bū·chad-rez'zar, Ne·bū·za·rad'an the captain of the guard took into exile of the Judeans seven hundred forty-five persons; all the persons were four thousand six hundred.

Jehoiachin Favored in Captivity
(2 Kings 25.27–30)

31 In the thirty-seventh year of the exile of King Je·hoi'a·chin of Judah, in the twelfth month, on the twenty-fifth day of the month, King Ê'vil-me·rō'dach of Babylon, in the year he began to reign, showed favor to King Je·hoi'a·chin of Judah and brought him out of prison; 32 he spoke kindly to him, and gave him a seat above the seats of the other kings who were with him in Babylon. 33 So Je·hoi'a·chin put aside his prison clothes, and every day of his life he dined regularly at the king's table. 34 For his allowance, a regular daily allowance was given him by the king of Babylon, as long as he lived, up to the day of his death.

---

k Cn: Heb *that were under the stands*

If someone close to you has died, you know that the grief and sadness can be almost too much for words. At such times of deep emotion, many people resort to poetry or song to try to express their feelings. Written during the Babylonian Exile, the Book of Lamentations poetically expresses the overwhelming grief the Israelites felt over the loss of their homes, their freedom, their capital, and their Temple. Through its passages, we get an insight into how devastating and destructive those days actually were.

In-depth

The Book of Lamentations is a collection of five poem songs, each a separate chapter in the book. If you take a quick look, you will notice that each poem has twenty-two verses, except the third, which has sixty-six. This is not an accident. In the original Hebrew language, each verse of the first, second, fourth, and fifth poems begins with a different letter of the Hebrew alphabet, which has twenty-two letters. In the third poem, every set of three verses begins with a different letter of the alphabet. This poetic structure, called acrostic, cannot be successfully translated into English. It is found in several poetic sections of the Old Testament, including Psalm 119.

We are not sure why the Lamentation poems were written in this fashion. It may be because the structure made them easier to memorize. Some scholars believe that it may have been a mystical sign of order and completeness. Another possibility is that the poem's structure helped to give form to the people's grief, which is important because uncontrollable grief can keep people from moving on in life. Knowing that the poem had a definite end may have reminded them that their sorrow would also come to an end.

Through these beautiful poems, Israelites were able to grieve and acknowledge the sin that led to their destruction. By recalling their experience of the goodness of God in the past, they were also able to hope for the day when God would lead them back to their land to rebuild their lives in faithfulness to the Covenant.

At a Glance

- **Chapter 1.** a description of the desolation of Mount Zion and Jerusalem
- **Chapter 2.** a discussion of God's wrath upon Jerusalem
- **Chapter 3.** an account moving from grief to memory to hope
- **Chapter 4.** a revisitation of Jerusalem
- **Chapter 5.** a prayer of the people

Quick Facts

Period Covered
the Babylonian Exile, 587–538 B.C.

Authors
unknown

Theme
poems of grief over the destruction of Jerusalem and the hardships of the Exile

The Book of *Lamentations*

Lamentations

The Deserted City

1 How lonely sits the city
    that once was full of people!
How like a widow she has become,
    she that was great among the nations!
She that was a princess among the provinces
    has become a vassal.

2 She weeps bitterly in the night,
    with tears on her cheeks;
among all her lovers
    she has no one to comfort her;
all her friends have dealt treacherously with
      her,
    they have become her enemies.

3 Judah has gone into exile with suffering
    and hard servitude;
she lives now among the nations,
    and finds no resting place;
her pursuers have all overtaken her
    in the midst of her distress.

4 The roads to Zion mourn,
    for no one comes to the festivals;
all her gates are desolate,
    her priests groan;
her young girls grieve,*a*
    and her lot is bitter.

5 Her foes have become the masters,
    her enemies prosper,
because the LORD has made her suffer
    for the multitude of her transgressions;
her children have gone away,
    captives before the foe.

6 From daughter Zion has departed
    all her majesty.
Her princes have become like stags
    that find no pasture;
they fled without strength
    before the pursuer.

7 Jerusalem remembers,
    in the days of her affliction and wandering,
all the precious things
    that were hers in days of old.
When her people fell into the hand of the foe,
    and there was no one to help her,
the foe looked on mocking
    over her downfall.

8 Jerusalem sinned grievously,
    so she has become a mockery;
all who honored her despise her,
    for they have seen her nakedness;
she herself groans,
    and turns her face away.

9 Her uncleanness was in her skirts;
    she took no thought of her future;

---

a Meaning of Heb uncertain

her downfall was appalling,
 with none to comfort her.
"O LORD, look at my affliction,
 for the enemy has triumphed!"

10 Enemies have stretched out their hands
 over all her precious things;
she has even seen the nations
 invade her sanctuary,
those whom you forbade
 to enter your congregation.

11 All her people groan
 as they search for bread;
they trade their treasures for food
 to revive their strength.
Look, O LORD, and see
 how worthless I have become.

12 Is it nothing to you,[b] all you who pass by?
 Look and see
if there is any sorrow like my sorrow,
 which was brought upon me,
which the LORD inflicted
 on the day of his fierce anger.

13 From on high he sent fire;
 it went deep into my bones;
he spread a net for my feet;
 he turned me back;
he has left me stunned,
 faint all day long.

14 My transgressions were bound[b] into a yoke;
 by his hand they were fastened together;
they weigh on my neck,
 sapping my strength;
the Lord handed me over
 to those whom I cannot withstand.

15 The LORD has rejected
 all my warriors in the midst of me;
he proclaimed a time against me
 to crush my young men;
the Lord has trodden as in a wine press
 the virgin daughter Judah.

16 For these things I weep;
 my eyes flow with tears;
for a comforter is far from me,
 one to revive my courage;
my children are desolate,
 for the enemy has prevailed.

17 Zion stretches out her hands,
 but there is no one to comfort her;
the LORD has commanded against Jacob

that his neighbors should become his
 foes;
Jerusalem has become
 a filthy thing among them.

18 The LORD is in the right,
 for I have rebelled against his word;
but hear, all you peoples,
 and behold my suffering;
my young women and young men
 have gone into captivity.

19 I called to my lovers
 but they deceived me;
my priests and elders
 perished in the city
while seeking food
 to revive their strength.

20 See, O LORD, how distressed I am;
 my stomach churns,
my heart is wrung within me,
 because I have been very rebellious.
In the street the sword bereaves;
 in the house it is like death.

21 They heard how I was groaning,
 with no one to comfort me.
All my enemies heard of my trouble;
 they are glad that you have done it.
Bring on the day you have announced,
 and let them be as I am.

22 Let all their evil doing come before you;
 and deal with them
as you have dealt with me
 because of all my transgressions;
for my groans are many
 and my heart is faint.

God's Warnings Fulfilled

2 How the Lord in his anger
 has humiliated[b] daughter Zion!
He has thrown down from heaven to earth
 the splendor of Israel;
he has not remembered his footstool
 in the day of his anger.

2 The Lord has destroyed without mercy
 all the dwellings of Jacob;
in his wrath he has broken down
 the strongholds of daughter Judah;
he has brought down to the ground in
  dishonor
 the kingdom and its rulers.

---

b Meaning of Heb uncertain

3 He has cut down in fierce anger
    all the might of Israel;
he has withdrawn his right hand from
    them
    in the face of the enemy;
he has burned like a flaming fire in Jacob,
    consuming all around.

4 He has bent his bow like an enemy,
    with his right hand set like a foe;
he has killed all in whom we took pride
    in the tent of daughter Zion;
he has poured out his fury like fire.

5 The Lord has become like an enemy;
    he has destroyed Israel.
He has destroyed all its palaces,
    laid in ruins its strongholds,
and multiplied in daughter Judah
    mourning and lamentation.

6 He has broken down his booth like a
    garden,
    he has destroyed his tabernacle;
the LORD has abolished in Zion
    festival and sabbath,
and in his fierce indignation has spurned
    king and priest.

7 The Lord has scorned his altar,
    disowned his sanctuary;
he has delivered into the hand of the enemy
    the walls of her palaces;
a clamor was raised in the house of the LORD
    as on a day of festival.

8 The LORD determined to lay in ruins
    the wall of daughter Zion;
he stretched the line;
    he did not withhold his hand from
    destroying;
he caused rampart and wall to lament;
    they languish together.

9 Her gates have sunk into the ground;
    he has ruined and broken her bars;
her king and princes are among the nations;
    guidance is no more,
and her prophets obtain
    no vision from the LORD.

10 The elders of daughter Zion
    sit on the ground in silence;
they have thrown dust on their heads
    and put on sackcloth;
the young girls of Jerusalem
    have bowed their heads to the ground.

PRAY IT! Violence in Our City Streets

Poetic language is often used in the Bible to express the depth of human emotion that either the author feels or the author is trying to convey. When reading the Scriptures, we should be aware that poetic language often does not lend itself to a literal interpretation. Instead, we should open ourselves up to the spiritual and emotional truth this poetry contains.

The Book of Lamentations is a book of poetry that helps us reflect on the feelings and thoughts of the Jewish people in exile, who were suffering from the loss of their homes, freedom, security, and so much more. Verses 12 and 19 of the poem in chapter 2 of Lamentations both mention hunger and violence in the streets. Are things much different in our streets? In our own time, children are hungry, and people are being killed and violated. Our voice echoes the voice of this ancient prayer, calling out for God's mercy.

When will the violence stop, Lord?
How many will die today from drug over-
*   dose and domestic abuse?*
How many children will go hungry because
*   nobody took the time to care for them?*
Have mercy on your people, Lord!

▸ **Lamentations, chapter 2**

11 My eyes are spent with weeping;
    my stomach churns;
my bile is poured out on the ground
    because of the destruction of my
    people,
because infants and babes faint
    in the streets of the city.

12 They cry to their mothers,
    "Where is bread and wine?"
as they faint like the wounded
    in the streets of the city,
as their life is poured out
    on their mothers' bosom.

13 What can I say for you, to what compare you,
    O daughter Jerusalem?
To what can I liken you, that I may comfort
    you,
    O virgin daughter Zion?
For vast as the sea is your ruin;
    who can heal you?

14 Your prophets have seen for you
    false and deceptive visions;
they have not exposed your iniquity
    to restore your fortunes,
but have seen oracles for you
    that are false and misleading.

15 All who pass along the way
    clap their hands at you;
they hiss and wag their heads
    at daughter Jerusalem;
"Is this the city that was called
    the perfection of beauty,
    the joy of all the earth?"

16 All your enemies
    open their mouths against you;
they hiss, they gnash their teeth,
    they cry: "We have devoured her!
Ah, this is the day we longed for;
    at last we have seen it!"

17 The LORD has done what he purposed,
    he has carried out his threat;
as he ordained long ago,
    he has demolished without pity;
he has made the enemy rejoice over you,
    and exalted the might of your foes.

18 Cry aloud[c] to the Lord!
    O wall of daughter Zion!
Let tears stream down like a torrent
    day and night!
Give yourself no rest,
    your eyes no respite!

19 Arise, cry out in the night,
    at the beginning of the watches!
Pour out your heart like water
    before the presence of the Lord!
Lift your hands to him
    for the lives of your children,
who faint for hunger
    at the head of every street.

20 Look, O LORD, and consider!
    To whom have you done this?
Should women eat their offspring,
    the children they have borne?

Should priest and prophet be killed
    in the sanctuary of the Lord?

21 The young and the old are lying
    on the ground in the streets;
my young women and my young men
    have fallen by the sword;
in the day of your anger you have killed them,
    slaughtering without mercy.

22 You invited my enemies from all around
    as if for a day of festival;
and on the day of the anger of the LORD
    no one escaped or survived;
those whom I bore and reared
    my enemy has destroyed.

God's Steadfast Love Endures

3 I am one who has seen affliction
    under the rod of God's[d] wrath;
2 he has driven and brought me
    into darkness without any light;
3 against me alone he turns his hand,
    again and again, all day long.

4 He has made my flesh and my skin waste
    away,
    and broken my bones;
5 he has besieged and enveloped me
    with bitterness and tribulation;
6 he has made me sit in darkness
    like the dead of long ago.

7 He has walled me about so that I cannot
    escape;
    he has put heavy chains on me;
8 though I call and cry for help,
    he shuts out my prayer;
9 he has blocked my ways with hewn stones,
    he has made my paths crooked.

10 He is a bear lying in wait for me,
    a lion in hiding;
11 he led me off my way and tore me to pieces;
    he has made me desolate;
12 he bent his bow and set me
    as a mark for his arrow.

13 He shot into my vitals
    the arrows of his quiver;
14 I have become the laughingstock of all my
    people,
    the object of their taunt-songs all day long.
15 He has filled me with bitterness,
    he has sated me with wormwood.

---

c Cn: Heb *Their heart cried*   d Heb *his*

L A M

16 He has made my teeth grind on gravel,
    and made me cower in ashes;
17 my soul is bereft of peace;
    I have forgotten what happiness is;
18 so I say, "Gone is my glory,
    and all that I had hoped for from the LORD."

19 The thought of my affliction and my
        homelessness
    is wormwood and gall!
20 My soul continually thinks of it
    and is bowed down within me.
21 But this I call to mind,
    and therefore I have hope:

22 The steadfast love of the LORD never ceases,*e*
    his mercies never come to an end;
23 they are new every morning;
    great is your faithfulness.
24 "The LORD is my portion," says my soul,
    "therefore I will hope in him."
25 The LORD is good to those who wait for
        him,
    to the soul that seeks him.
26 It is good that one should wait quietly
    for the salvation of the LORD.

27 It is good for one to bear
    the yoke in youth,
28 to sit alone in silence
    when the Lord has imposed it,
29 to put one's mouth to the dust
    (there may yet be hope),
30 to give one's cheek to the smiter,
    and be filled with insults.

31 For the Lord will not
    reject forever.
32 Although he causes grief, he will have
        compassion
    according to the abundance of his steadfast
        love;
33 for he does not willingly afflict
    or grieve anyone.

34 When all the prisoners of the land
    are crushed under foot,
35 when human rights are perverted
    in the presence of the Most High,
36 when one's case is subverted
    —does the Lord not see it?

37 Who can command and have it done,
    if the Lord has not ordained it?
38 Is it not from the mouth of the Most High
    that good and bad come?
39 Why should any who draw breath complain
    about the punishment of their sins?

40 Let us test and examine our ways,
    and return to the LORD.
41 Let us lift up our hearts as well as our hands
    to God in heaven.
42 We have transgressed and rebelled,
    and you have not forgiven.

43 You have wrapped yourself with anger and
        pursued us,
    killing without pity;
44 you have wrapped yourself with a cloud
    so that no prayer can pass through.
45 You have made us filth and rubbish
    among the peoples.

46 All our enemies
    have opened their mouths against us;
47 panic and pitfall have come upon us,
    devastation and destruction.

---

e Syr Tg: Heb LORD, we are not cut off

Each New Day

LIVE IT!

The poems in Lamentations also have their hopeful side. They acknowledge that God's love never ceases (3.22) and that the Israelites will not experience God's rejection forever (verse 31). Verse 23 reminds the people that God's love is there each new day.

God gives you 86,400 seconds every day to use however you like. Try making a one-day budget of the best ways to spend your 86,400 seconds. Remember, each day is a new gift filled with God's love. Make the most of it, and do so for God!

▶ **Lam 3.22–33**

48 My eyes flow with rivers of tears
    because of the destruction of my people.

49 My eyes will flow without ceasing,
    without respite,
50 until the LORD from heaven
    looks down and sees.
51 My eyes cause me grief
    at the fate of all the young women in my
      city.

52 Those who were my enemies without cause
    have hunted me like a bird;
53 they flung me alive into a pit
    and hurled stones on me;
54 water closed over my head;
    I said, "I am lost."

55 I called on your name, O LORD,
    from the depths of the pit;
56 you heard my plea, "Do not close your ear
    to my cry for help, but give me relief!"
57 You came near when I called on you;
    you said, "Do not fear!"

58 You have taken up my cause, O Lord,
    you have redeemed my life.
59 You have seen the wrong done to me,
      O LORD;
    judge my cause.
60 You have seen all their malice,
    all their plots against me.

61 You have heard their taunts, O LORD,
    all their plots against me.
62 The whispers and murmurs of my assailants
    are against me all day long.
63 Whether they sit or rise—see,
    I am the object of their taunt-songs.

64 Pay them back for their deeds, O LORD,
    according to the work of their hands!
65 Give them anguish of heart;
    your curse be on them!
66 Pursue them in anger and destroy them
    from under the LORD's heavens.

The Punishment of Zion

4 How the gold has grown dim,
    how the pure gold is changed!
The sacred stones lie scattered
    at the head of every street.

2 The precious children of Zion,
    worth their weight in fine gold—
how they are reckoned as earthen pots,
    the work of a potter's hands!

3 Even the jackals offer the breast
    and nurse their young,
but my people has become cruel,
    like the ostriches in the wilderness.

4 The tongue of the infant sticks
    to the roof of its mouth for thirst;
the children beg for food,
    but no one gives them anything.

5 Those who feasted on delicacies
    perish in the streets;
those who were brought up in purple
    cling to ash heaps.

6 For the chastisement^f of my people has been
      greater
    than the punishment^g of Sod'om,
which was overthrown in a moment,
    though no hand was laid on it.^{h}

7 Her princes were purer than snow,
    whiter than milk;
their bodies were more ruddy than coral,
    their hair^h like sapphire.^{i}

8 Now their visage is blacker than soot;
    they are not recognized in the streets.
Their skin has shriveled on their bones;
    it has become as dry as wood.

9 Happier were those pierced by the sword
    than those pierced by hunger,
whose life drains away, deprived
    of the produce of the field.

10 The hands of compassionate women
    have boiled their own children;
they became their food
    in the destruction of my people.

11 The LORD gave full vent to his wrath;
    he poured out his hot anger,
and kindled a fire in Zion
    that consumed its foundations.

12 The kings of the earth did not believe,
    nor did any of the inhabitants of the
      world,
that foe or enemy could enter
    the gates of Jerusalem.

13 It was for the sins of her prophets
    and the iniquities of her priests,

_____

f Or *iniquity* g Or *sin* h Meaning of Heb uncertain i Or
lapis lazuli

LAM

who shed the blood of the righteous
in the midst of her.

14 Blindly they wandered through the streets,
so defiled with blood
that no one was able
to touch their garments.

15 "Away! Unclean!" people shouted at them;
"Away! Away! Do not touch!"
So they became fugitives and wanderers;
it was said among the nations,
"They shall stay here no longer."

16 The LORD himself has scattered them,
he will regard them no more;
no honor was shown to the priests,
no favor to the elders.

17 Our eyes failed, ever watching
vainly for help;
we were watching eagerly
for a nation that could not save.

18 They dogged our steps
so that we could not walk in our
streets;
our end drew near; our days were numbered;
for our end had come.

19 Our pursuers were swifter
than the eagles in the heavens;
they chased us on the mountains,
they lay in wait for us in the wilderness.

20 The LORD's anointed, the breath of our life,
was taken in their pits—

the one of whom we said, "Under his
shadow
we shall live among the nations."

21 Rejoice and be glad, O daughter Ē'dom,
you that live in the land of Uz;
but to you also the cup shall pass;
you shall become drunk and strip yourself
bare.

22 The punishment of your iniquity, O daughter
Zion, is accomplished,
he will keep you in exile no longer;
but your iniquity, O daughter Ē'dom, he will
punish,
he will uncover your sins.

A Plea for Mercy

5 Remember, O LORD, what has befallen us;
look, and see our disgrace!
2 Our inheritance has been turned over to
strangers,
our homes to aliens.
3 We have become orphans, fatherless;
our mothers are like widows.
4 We must pay for the water we drink;
the wood we get must be bought.
5 With a yoke*j* on our necks we are hard driven;
we are weary, we are given no rest.
6 We have made a pact with*k* Egypt and Assyria,
to get enough bread.
7 Our ancestors sinned; they are no more,
and we bear their iniquities.
8 Slaves rule over us;

---

j Symmachus: Heb lacks *With a yoke*   *k* Heb *have given the
hand to*

Growing Through Loss

LIVE IT!

One purpose of the poems in Lamentations is to help the ancient Israelites heal
from the horrible tragedy of their loss. The poems accomplish this in three ways.
First, in describing Israel's present loss and tragedy, they acknowledge that grief
and mourning are needed. Second, they challenge Israel to look at its past, both to
accept responsibility for its sin and to remember its great blessings from God. Finally, they
encourage Israel to have hope for the future. In image after image, Israel is assured that the
door to God's mercy is still open, in spite of great pain and loss.

So too must we allow ourselves to grieve when we have experienced the loss of someone we love. If we wall up our grief—and perhaps our guilt, because guilt often accompanies
such a loss—we may at the same time shut out those who can help us heal. We must also
reclaim our memories of the person we lost, celebrating those of good times and healing
those of hurtful times. Finally, as difficult as it may seem, we must open ourselves to the
future, for God's love continues to be there for us, calling us to new life.

there is no one to deliver us from their
    hand.
9 We get our bread at the peril of our lives,
    because of the sword in the wilderness.
10 Our skin is black as an oven
    from the scorching heat of famine.
11 Women are raped in Zion,
    virgins in the towns of Judah.
12 Princes are hung up by their hands;
    no respect is shown to the elders.
13 Young men are compelled to grind,
    and boys stagger under loads of wood.
14 The old men have left the city gate,
    the young men their music.
15 The joy of our hearts has ceased;
    our dancing has been turned to mourning.
16 The crown has fallen from our head;

    woe to us, for we have sinned!
17 Because of this our hearts are sick,
    because of these things our eyes have grown
        dim:
18 because of Mount Zion, which lies desolate;
    jackals prowl over it.

19 But you, O LORD, reign forever;
    your throne endures to all generations.
20 Why have you forgotten us completely?
    Why have you forsaken us these many
        days?
21 Restore us to yourself, O LORD, that we may be
        restored;
    renew our days as of old—
22 unless you have utterly rejected us,
    and are angry with us beyond measure.

L
A
M

The Book of Baruch

Perhaps you've seen or heard of long lines of refugees leaving war-torn countries. Or the camps where they set up temporary homes, waiting to return to their homeland. The sad truth is many of them can never return home. They are faced with the difficult task of building new homes in a foreign land. The Book of Baruch was written in such a situation—after many Israelites were forced to relocate following the Babylonian invasion in 587 B.C.

In-depth

In the ancient world, it was not uncommon for people to write books and letters in the name of famous ancestors or historical figures. Several Old and New Testament books, including Baruch, were written in this manner. An anonymous person collected a variety of independent writings and named them for Baruch, the famous secretary of the prophet Jeremiah, in order to emphasize their link with Jeremiah's tradition of prophecy.

The short Book of Baruch recalls the Babylonian conquest of Jerusalem in the sixth century B.C. In doing so, it points out these lessons to be learned from the painful past:

- We do not gain anything when we sin. Instead, we invite suffering into our life.
- No matter how difficult life gets, we can always rely on God's goodness.
- Believers can always approach God in prayer, even when their situation seems impossibly painful.
- The traditions we have inherited from our ancestors are a reliable guide in facing life's challenges.
- We should resist all cultural pressures to act in violation of God's will.

The core truth Baruch addresses is that no matter where they are, God's people can lead a happy and holy life by admitting their sinfulness and committing themselves to the Lord. This is an important lesson for all believers to learn. Unless we learn from history, we will repeat its mistakes.

At a Glance

- **1.1—3.8.** an introduction and a penitential prayer
- **3.9—4.4.** a poem on wisdom
- **4.5—5.9.** words of comfort for believers
- **Chapter 6.** a letter from Jeremiah against idolatry

Quick Facts

Period Covered
after the Babylonian Exile, probably 500–300 B.C.

Author
an unknown compiler who attributed the book to Baruch, Jeremiah's secretary

Theme
Even in foreign lands, God's people can live a faithful life and find hope in God's promises.

Of Note
Baruch is not found in every translation of the Old Testament (see "The Case of the Missing Books" Tob 1.16).

Baruch

Chap. 6

Baruch and the Jews in Babylon
(Cp 2 Kings 24.8–17; Ezra 1.7–11; Jer 36.4)

1 These are the words of the book that Bar′uch son of Ne·rī′ah son of Mah·sēi·ah son of Zed·e·kī′ah son of Has·a·dī′ah son of Hil·kī′ah wrote in Babylon, **2** in the fifth year, on the seventh day of the month, at the time when the Chal·dē′ans took Jerusalem and burned it with fire.

3 Bar′uch read the words of this book to Jec·o·nī′ah son of Je·hoi′a·kim, king of Judah, and to all the people who came to hear the book, **4** and to the nobles and the princes, and to the elders, and to all the people, small and great, all who lived in Babylon by the river Sud.

5 Then they wept, and fasted, and prayed before the Lord; **6** they collected as much money as each could give, **7** and sent it to Jerusalem to the high priest*ᵃ* Je·hoi′a·kim son of Hil·kī′ah son of Shal′lum, and to the priests, and to all the people who were present with him in Jerusalem. **8** At the same time, on the tenth day of Sī′van, Bar′uch*ᵇ* took the vessels of the house of the Lord, which had been carried away from the temple, to return them to the land of Judah—the silver vessels that Zed·e·kī′ah son of Jō·sī′ah, king of Judah, had made, **9** after King Ne·bū·chad·nez′zar of Babylon had carried away from Jerusalem Jec·o·nī′ah and the princes and the prisoners and the nobles and the people of the land, and brought them to Babylon.

A Letter to Jerusalem

10 They said: Here we send you money; so buy with the money burnt offerings and sin offerings and incense, and prepare a grain offering, and offer them on the altar of the Lord our God; **11** and pray for the life of King Ne·bū·chad·nez′zar of Babylon, and for the life of his son Bel·shaz′zar, so that their days on earth may be like the days of heaven. **12** The Lord will give us strength, and light to our eyes; we shall live under the protection*ᶜ* of King Ne·bū·chad·nez′zar of Babylon, and under the protection of his son Bel·shaz′zar, and we shall serve them many days and find favor in their sight. **13** Pray also for us to the Lord our God, for we have sinned against the Lord our God, and to this day the anger of the Lord and his wrath have not turned away from us. **14** And you shall read aloud this scroll that we are sending you, to make your confession in the house of the Lord on the days of the festivals and at appointed seasons.

Confession of Sins
(Cp Deut 28.15–68; Jer 11.3–5)

15 And you shall say: The Lord our God is in the right, but there is open shame on us today, on the people of Judah, on the inhabitants of Jerusalem, **16** and on our kings, our rulers, our

---

a Gk *the priest* *b* Gk *he* *c* Gk *in the shadow*

945

priests, our prophets, and our ancestors, 17 because we have sinned before the Lord. 18 We have disobeyed him, and have not heeded the voice of the Lord our God, to walk in the statutes of the Lord that he set before us. 19 From the time when the Lord brought our ancestors out of the land of Egypt until today, we have been disobedient to the Lord our God, and we have been negligent, in not heeding his voice. 20 So to this day there have clung to us the calamities and the curse that the Lord declared through his servant Moses at the time when he brought our ancestors out of the land of Egypt to give to us a land flowing with milk and honey. 21 We did not listen to the voice of the Lord our God in all the words of the prophets whom he sent to us, 22 but all of us followed the intent of our own wicked hearts by serving other gods and doing what is evil in the sight of the Lord our God.

2 So the Lord carried out the threat he spoke against us: against our judges who ruled Israel, and against our kings and our rulers and the people of Israel and Judah. 2 Under the whole heaven there has not been done the like of what he has done in Jerusalem, in accordance with the threats that were[d] written in the law of Moses. 3 Some of us ate the flesh of their sons and others the flesh of their daughters. 4 He made them subject to all the kingdoms around us, to be an object of scorn and a desolation among all the surrounding peoples, where the Lord has scattered them. 5 They were brought down and not raised up, because our nation[e] sinned against the Lord our God, in not heeding his voice.

6 The Lord our God is in the right, but there is open shame on us and our ancestors this very day. 7 All those calamities with which the Lord threatened us have come upon us. 8 Yet we have not entreated the favor of the Lord by turning away, each of us, from the thoughts of our wicked hearts. 9 And the Lord has kept the calamities ready, and the Lord has brought them upon us, for the Lord is just in all the works that he has commanded us to do. 10 Yet we have not obeyed his voice, to walk in the statutes of the Lord that he set before us.

Prayer for Deliverance
(Cp Dan 9.15–17)

11 And now, O Lord God of Israel, who brought your people out of the land of Egypt with a mighty hand and with signs and wonders and with great power and outstretched arm, and made yourself a name that continues to this day, 12 we have sinned, we have been ungodly, we have done wrong, O Lord our God, against all your ordinances. 13 Let your anger turn away from us, for we are left, few in number, among the nations where you have scattered us. 14 Hear, O Lord, our prayer

and our supplication, and for your own sake deliver us, and grant us favor in the sight of those who have carried us into exile; 15 so that all the earth may know that you are the Lord our God, for Israel and his descendants are called by your name.

16 O Lord, look down from your holy dwelling, and consider us. Incline your ear, O Lord, and hear; 17 open your eyes, O Lord, and see, for the dead who are in Hades, whose spirit has been taken from their bodies, will not ascribe glory or justice to the Lord; 18 but the person who is deeply grieved, who walks bowed and feeble, with failing eyes and famished soul, will declare your glory and righteousness, O Lord.

19 For it is not because of any righteous deeds of our ancestors or our kings that we bring before you our prayer for mercy, O Lord our God. 20 For you have sent your anger and your wrath upon us, as you declared by your servants the prophets, saying: 21 Thus says the Lord: Bend your shoulders and serve the king of Babylon, and you will remain in the land that I gave to your ancestors. 22 But if you will not obey the voice of the Lord and will not serve the king of Babylon, 23 I will make to cease from the towns of Judah and from the region around Jerusalem the voice of mirth and the voice of gladness, the voice of the bridegroom and the voice of the bride, and the whole land will be a desolation without inhabitants.

24 But we did not obey your voice, to serve the king of Babylon; and you have carried out your threats, which you spoke by your servants the prophets, that the bones of our kings and the bones of our ancestors would be brought out of their resting place; 25 and indeed they have been thrown out to the heat of day and the frost of night. They perished in great misery, by famine and sword and pestilence. 26 And the house that is called by your name you have made as it is today, because of the wickedness of the house of Israel and the house of Judah.

God's Promise Recalled
(Deut 28.58–62; Cp Jer 32.38–40)

27 Yet you have dealt with us, O Lord our God, in all your kindness and in all your great compassion, 28 as you spoke by your servant Moses on the day when you commanded him to write your law in the presence of the people of Israel, saying, 29 "If you will not obey my voice, this very great multitude will surely turn into a small number among the nations, where I will scatter them. 30 For I know that they will not obey me, for they are a stiff-necked people. But in the land of their exile they will come to themselves 31 and know that I am the

---

d Gk in accordance with what is e Gk because we

Lord their God. I will give them a heart that obeys and ears that hear; 32 they will praise me in the land of their exile, and will remember my name 33 and turn from their stubbornness and their wicked deeds; for they will remember the ways of their ancestors, who sinned before the Lord. 34 I will bring them again into the land that I swore to give to their ancestors, to Abraham, Isaac, and Jacob, and they will rule over it; and I will increase them, and they will not be diminished. 35 I will make an everlasting covenant with them to be their God and they shall be my people; and I will never again remove my people Israel from the land that I have given them."

3 O Lord Almighty, God of Israel, the soul in anguish and the wearied spirit cry out to you. 2 Hear, O Lord, and have mercy, for we have sinned before you. 3 For you are enthroned forever, and we are perishing forever. 4 O Lord Almighty, God of Israel, hear now the prayer of the people*f* of Israel, the children of those who sinned before you, who did not heed the voice of the Lord their God, so that calamities have clung to us. 5 Do not remember the iniquities of our ancestors, but in this crisis remember your power and your name. 6 For you are the Lord our God, and it is you, O Lord, whom we will praise. 7 For you have put the fear of you in our hearts so that we would call upon your name; and we will praise you in our exile, for we have put away from our hearts all the iniquity of our ancestors who sinned against you. 8 See, we are today in our exile where you have scattered us, to be reproached and cursed and punished for all the iniquities of our ancestors, who forsook the Lord our God.

In Praise of Wisdom
(Cp Job 28.23–28; Prov 8.22–31; Sir 24.1–22)

9 Hear the commandments of life, O Israel;
　　give ear, and learn wisdom!
10 Why is it, O Israel, why is it that you are in the
　　　　land of your enemies,
　　that you are growing old in a foreign
　　　　country,
　　that you are defiled with the dead,
11 　　that you are counted among those in
　　　　Hades?
12 You have forsaken the fountain of
　　wisdom.
13 If you had walked in the way of God,
　　you would be living in peace forever.
14 Learn where there is wisdom,
　　where there is strength,
　　where there is understanding,
　　so that you may at the same time discern
　　where there is length of days, and life,
　　where there is light for the eyes, and
　　　　peace.

15 Who has found her place?
　　And who has entered her storehouses?
16 Where are the rulers of the nations,
　　and those who lorded it over the animals
　　　　on earth;
17 those who made sport of the birds of the air,
　　and who hoarded up silver and gold
　　in which people trust,
　　and there is no end to their getting;
18 those who schemed to get silver, and were
　　　　anxious,
　　but there is no trace of their works?
19 They have vanished and gone down to Hades,
　　and others have arisen in their place.

20 Later generations have seen the light of day,
　　and have lived upon the earth;
　　but they have not learned the way to
　　　　knowledge,
　　nor understood her paths,
　　nor laid hold of her.
21 Their descendants have strayed far from her*g*
　　way.
22 She has not been heard of in Cā′naan,
　　or seen in Tĕ′man;
23 the descendants of Hā′gar, who seek for
　　　　understanding on the earth,
　　the merchants of Mer′ran and Tĕ′man,
　　the story-tellers and the seekers for
　　　　understanding,
　　have not learned the way to wisdom,
　　or given thought to her paths.

24 O Israel, how great is the house of God,
　　how vast the territory that he possesses!
25 It is great and has no bounds;
　　it is high and immeasurable.
26 The giants were born there, who were famous
　　　　of old,
　　great in stature, expert in war.
27 God did not choose them,
　　or give them the way to knowledge;
28 so they perished because they had no wisdom,
　　they perished through their folly.

29 Who has gone up into heaven, and taken her,
　　and brought her down from the clouds?
30 Who has gone over the sea, and found her,
　　and will buy her for pure gold?
31 No one knows the way to her,
　　or is concerned about the path to her.
32 But the one who knows all things knows her,
　　he found her by his understanding.
　　The one who prepared the earth for all time
　　filled it with four-footed creatures;

---

f Gk *dead*　*g* Other ancient authorities read *their*

The House of God

It is a warm, clear night. You and a good friend are sitting outside talking about the struggles both of you have been having with parents. Suddenly, you see a shooting star. Both of you spend a few moments gazing at the sky and marveling at how many stars there are and how clear the night is. The problems you were just discussing seem to pale in significance next to the vastness of the universe. And you realize that the two of you are seeing only one corner of the universe, "the house of God" (Bar 3.24). You both feel a connection with the stars and the sky and with the God who created it all.

The author of Bar 3.24–34 seems to be having a similar moment. This writer describes God's wisdom as vast and endless (verse 25) and beyond any person's grasp (verse 29), but given to Israel for salvation (verse 36). The author is saying: "Be at ease. God is bigger than your problems and in control."

When struggling with life's problems, recall the beauty of the night sky in order to put them in perspective. Spend a few moments gazing at the stars, and remember who's really in control.

▶ Bar 3.24–34

33 the one who sends forth the light, and it goes;
　　he called it, and it obeyed him, trembling;
34 the stars shone in their watches, and were glad;
　　he called them, and they said, "Here we
　　　　are!"
　　They shone with gladness for him who
　　　　made them.
35 This is our God;
　　no other can be compared to him.
36 He found the whole way to knowledge,
　　and gave her to his servant Jacob
　　and to Israel, whom he loved.
37 Afterward she appeared on earth
　　and lived with humankind.

4 She is the book of the commandments
　　　　of God,
　　the law that endures forever.
All who hold her fast will live,
　　and those who forsake her will die.
2 Turn, O Jacob, and take her;
　　walk toward the shining of her light.
3 Do not give your glory to another,
　　or your advantages to an alien people.
4 Happy are we, O Israel,
　　for we know what is pleasing to God.

Encouragement for Israel

5 Take courage, my people,
　　who perpetuate Israel's name!
6 It was not for destruction
　　that you were sold to the nations,
but you were handed over to your enemies
　　because you angered God.

7 For you provoked the one who made you
　　by sacrificing to demons and not to God.
8 You forgot the everlasting God, who brought
　　　　you up,
　　and you grieved Jerusalem, who reared you.
9 For she saw the wrath that came upon you
　　　　　　from God,
　　and she said:
Listen, you neighbors of Zion,
　　God has brought great sorrow upon me;
10 for I have seen the exile of my sons and
　　　　　　daughters,
　　which the Everlasting brought upon them.
11 With joy I nurtured them,
　　but I sent them away with weeping and
　　　　sorrow.
12 Let no one rejoice over me, a widow
　　and bereaved of many;
I was left desolate because of the sins of my
　　　　children,
　　because they turned away from the law of
　　　　　　God.
13 They had no regard for his statutes;
　　they did not walk in the ways of God's
　　　　commandments,
　　or tread the paths his righteousness showed
　　　　them.
14 Let the neighbors of Zion come;
　　remember the capture of my sons and
　　　　daughters,
　　which the Everlasting brought upon them.
15 For he brought a distant nation against them,
　　a nation ruthless and of a strange language,
which had no respect for the aged

and no pity for a child.

16 They led away the widow's beloved sons,
    and bereaved the lonely woman of her
      daughters.

17 But I, how can I help you?

18 For he who brought these calamities upon you
    will deliver you from the hand of your
      enemies.

19 Go, my children, go;
    for I have been left desolate.

20 I have taken off the robe of peace
    and put on sackcloth for my supplication;
    I will cry to the Everlasting all my days.

21 Take courage, my children, cry to God,
    and he will deliver you from the power and
      hand of the enemy.

22 For I have put my hope in the Everlasting to
      save you,
    and joy has come to me from the Holy One,
because of the mercy that will soon come to
      you
    from your everlasting savior.[h]

23 For I sent you out with sorrow and weeping,
    but God will give you back to me with joy
      and gladness forever.

24 For as the neighbors of Zion have now seen
      your capture,
    so they soon will see your salvation by God,
which will come to you with great glory
    and with the splendor of the Everlasting.

25 My children, endure with patience the wrath
      that has come upon you from God.
Your enemy has overtaken you,
    but you will soon see their destruction
    and will tread upon their necks.

26 My pampered children have traveled rough roads;
    they were taken away like a flock carried off
      by the enemy.

27 Take courage, my children, and cry to God,
    for you will be remembered by the one who
      brought this upon you.

28 For just as you were disposed to go astray from
      God,
    return with tenfold zeal to seek him.

29 For the one who brought these calamities upon
      you
    will bring you everlasting joy with your
      salvation.

Jerusalem Is Assured of Help
(Cp Isa 52.1–10)

30 Take courage, O Jerusalem,
    for the one who named you will comfort
      you.

31 Wretched will be those who mistreated you
    and who rejoiced at your fall.

32 Wretched will be the cities that your children
      served as slaves;
    wretched will be the city that received your
      offspring.

33 For just as she rejoiced at your fall
    and was glad for your ruin,
    so she will be grieved at her own
      desolation.

34 I will take away her pride in her great
      population,
    and her insolence will be turned to
      grief.

35 For fire will come upon her from the
      Everlasting for many days,
    and for a long time she will be inhabited by
      demons.

36 Look toward the east, O Jerusalem,
    and see the joy that is coming to you from
      God.

---

h Or *from the Everlasting, your savior*

Stand Up!

LIVE IT!

The poem that begins with Bar 4.5 has the nation of Israel speaking to the Jews in exile. After recalling that their disobedience brought on the exile, the author of the poem calls them to conversion. Worried that they may start worshiping the false gods of their new neighbors, the writer reminds them that if they are faithful to God, God will not abandon them.

It can be said that as Christians, we too live in a culture that is in some ways foreign to our values and beliefs. How easy is it to stand up against the pressures of peers, media values, and social standards that go against Christian values and beliefs? Are you confident enough to do what's right if others do not?

▶ Bar 4.17–19

³⁷ Look, your children are coming, whom you
      sent away;
  they are coming, gathered from east and
      west,
at the word of the Holy One,
  rejoicing in the glory of God.

5 Take off the garment of your sorrow and
      affliction, O Jerusalem,
  and put on forever the beauty of the glory
      from God.
² Put on the robe of the righteousness that
      comes from God;
  put on your head the diadem of the glory of
      the Everlasting;
³ for God will show your splendor everywhere
      under heaven.
⁴ For God will give you evermore the name,
  "Righteous Peace, Godly Glory."

⁵ Arise, O Jerusalem, stand upon the height;
      look toward the east,
and see your children gathered from west and
      east
  at the word of the Holy One,
  rejoicing that God has remembered them.
⁶ For they went out from you on foot,
      led away by their enemies;
but God will bring them back to you,
  carried in glory, as on a royal throne.
⁷ For God has ordered that every high mountain
      and the everlasting hills be made low
and the valleys filled up, to make level
      ground,
  so that Israel may walk safely in the glory of
      God.
⁸ The woods and every fragrant tree
  have shaded Israel at God's command.
⁹ For God will lead Israel with joy,
  in the light of his glory,
  with the mercy and righteousness that come
      from him.

The Letter of Jeremiah

6 ⁱ A copy of a letter that Jer·e·mi′ah sent to
those who were to be taken to Babylon as ex-
iles by the king of the Babylonians, to give them the
message that God had commanded him.

The People Face a Long Captivity
(Cp Jer 29.1–23)

² Because of the sins that you have committed
before God, you will be taken to Babylon as exiles
by Ne·bu·chad·nez′zar, king of the Babylonians.
³ Therefore when you have come to Babylon you
will remain there for many years, for a long time,
up to seven generations; after that I will bring you

away from there in peace. ⁴ Now in Babylon you
will see gods made of silver and gold and wood,
which people carry on their shoulders, and which
cause the heathen to fear. ⁵ So beware of becoming
at all like the foreigners or of letting fear for these
gods^j possess you ⁶ when you see the multitude before and behind them worshiping them. But say in
your heart, "It is you, O Lord, whom we must worship." ⁷ For my angel is with you, and he is watching over your lives.

The Helplessness of Idols

⁸ Their tongues are smoothed by the carpenter,
and they themselves are overlaid with gold and sil-
ver; but they are false and cannot speak. ⁹ People^k
take gold and make crowns for the heads of their
gods, as they might for a girl who loves ornaments.
¹⁰ Sometimes the priests secretly take gold and sil-
ver from their gods and spend it on themselves,
¹¹ or even give some of it to the prostitutes on the
terrace. They deck their gods^l out with garments like
human beings—these gods of silver and gold and
wood ¹² that cannot save themselves from rust and
corrosion. When they have been dressed in purple
robes, ¹³ their faces are wiped because of the dust
from the temple, which is thick upon them. ¹⁴ One
of them holds a scepter, like a district judge, but is
unable to destroy anyone who offends it. ¹⁵ Another has a dagger in its right hand, and an ax, but cannot defend itself from war and robbers. ¹⁶ From this
it is evident that they are not gods; so do not fear
them.

¹⁷ For just as someone's dish is useless when it
is broken, ¹⁸ so are their gods when they have been
set up in the temples. Their eyes are full of the dust
raised by the feet of those who enter. And just as the
gates are shut on every side against anyone who has
offended a king, as though under sentence of death,
so the priests make their temples secure with doors
and locks and bars, in order that they may not be
plundered by robbers. ¹⁹ They light more lamps for
them than they light for themselves, though their
gods^m can see none of them. ²⁰ They areⁿ just like a
beam of the temple, but their hearts, it is said, are
eaten away when crawling creatures from the earth
devour them and their robes. They do not notice
²¹ when their faces have been blackened by the
smoke of the temple. ²² Bats, swallows, and birds
alight on their bodies and heads; and so do cats.
²³ From this you will know that they are not gods;
so do not fear them.

ⁱ The King James Version (like the Latin Vulgate) prints The
Letter of Jeremiah as Chapter 6 of the Book of Baruch, and
the chapter and verse numbers are here retained. In the
Greek Septuagint, the Letter is separated from Baruch by the
Book of Lamentations.   *j* Gk *for them*   *k* Gk *They*   *l* Gk
them   *m* Gk *they*   *n* Gk *It is*

PRAY IT
Lucky Charms?

The whole sixth chapter of Baruch points out the foolishness of people who worship statues of gods and goddesses. Some ancient peoples felt these images gave them luck or fertility or health. The author of this chapter is warning, "Just because you are in a foreign land, don't take up silly superstitions!"

Sometimes, modern people like to carry a special lucky charm in the belief that it will protect them or bring them good luck. Do you carry a good luck charm? If so, why?

Dear LORD, sometimes, when I feel like I can use every bit of luck I can get, a "lucky" object can be a comfort. Help me to remember, though, the true power over my life that comes from you.

▸ Baruch, chapter 6

---

24 As for the gold that they wear for beauty—it*o* will not shine unless someone wipes off the tarnish; for even when they were being cast, they did not feel it. 25 They are bought without regard to cost, but there is no breath in them. 26 Having no feet, they are carried on the shoulders of others, revealing to humankind their worthlessness. And those who serve them are put to shame 27 because, if any of these gods falls*p* to the ground, they themselves must pick it up. If anyone sets it upright, it cannot move itself; and if it is tipped over, it cannot straighten itself. Gifts are placed before them just as before the dead. 28 The priests sell the sacrifices that are offered to these gods*q* and use the money themselves. Likewise their wives preserve some of the meat*r* with salt, but give none to the poor or helpless. 29 Sacrifices to them may even be touched by women in their periods or at childbirth. Since you know by these things that they are not gods, do not fear them.

30 For how can they be called gods? Women serve meals for gods of silver and gold and wood; 31 and in their temples the priests sit with their clothes torn, their heads and beards shaved, and their heads uncovered. 32 They howl and shout before their gods as some do at a funeral banquet. 33 The priests take some of the clothing of their gods*s* to clothe their wives and children. 34 Whether one does evil to them or good, they will not be able to repay it. They cannot set up a king or depose one. 35 Likewise they are not able to give either wealth or money; if one makes a vow to them and does not keep it, they will not require it. 36 They cannot save anyone from death or rescue the weak from the strong. 37 They cannot restore sight to the blind; they cannot rescue one who is in distress. 38 They cannot take pity on a widow or do good to an orphan. 39 These things that are made of wood and overlaid with gold and silver are like stones from the mountain, and those who serve them will be put to shame. 40 Why then must anyone think that they are gods, or call them gods?

The Foolishness of Worshiping Idols
(Cp Isa 46.1–13)

Besides, even the Chal·dē'ans themselves dishonor them; for when they see someone who cannot speak, they bring Bel and pray that the mute may speak, as though Bel*t* were able to understand! 41 Yet they themselves cannot perceive this and abandon them, for they have no sense. 42 And the women, with cords around them, sit along the passageways, burning bran for incense. 43 When one of them is led off by one of the passers-by and is taken to bed by him, she derides the woman next to her, because she was not as attractive as herself and her cord was not broken. 44 Whatever is done for these idols*u* is false. Why then must anyone think that they are gods, or call them gods?

45 They are made by carpenters and goldsmiths; they can be nothing but what the artisans wish them to be. 46 Those who make them will certainly not live very long themselves; 47 how then can the things that are made by them be gods? They have left only lies and reproach for those who come after. 48 For when war or calamity comes upon them, the priests consult together as to where they can hide themselves and their gods.*u* 49 How then can one fail to see that these are not gods, for they cannot save themselves from war or calamity? 50 Since they are made of wood and overlaid with gold and silver, it will afterward be known that they are false. 51 It will be manifest to all the nations and kings that they are not gods but the work of human hands, and that there is no work of God in them. 52 Who then can fail to know that they are not gods?*v*

53 For they cannot set up a king over a country or give rain to people. 54 They cannot judge their own cause or deliver one who is wronged, for they have no power; 55 they are like crows between

o Lat Syr: Gk *they*   *p* Gk *if they fall*   *q* Gk *to them*   *r* Gk *of them*   *s* Gk *some of their clothing*   *t* Gk *he*   *u* Gk *them*
v Meaning of Gk uncertain

B
A
R

heaven and earth. When fire breaks out in a temple of wooden gods overlaid with gold or silver, their priests will flee and escape, but the gods[w] will be burned up like timbers. 56 Besides, they can offer no resistance to king or enemy. Why then must anyone admit or think that they are gods?

57 Gods made of wood and overlaid with silver and gold are unable to save themselves from thieves or robbers. 58 Anyone who can will strip them of their gold and silver and of the robes they wear, and go off with this booty, and they will not be able to help themselves. 59 So it is better to be a king who shows his courage, or a household utensil that serves its owner's need, than to be these false gods; better even the door of a house that protects its contents, than these false gods; better also a wooden pillar in a palace, than these false gods.

60 For sun and moon and stars are bright, and when sent to do a service, they are obedient. 61 So also the lightning, when it flashes, is widely seen; and the wind likewise blows in every land. 62 When God commands the clouds to go over the whole world, they carry out his command. 63 And the fire sent from above to consume mountains and woods does what it is ordered. But these idols[x] are not to be compared with them in appearance or power.

64 Therefore one must not think that they are gods, nor call them gods, for they are not able either to decide a case or to do good to anyone. 65 Since you know then that they are not gods, do not fear them.

66 They can neither curse nor bless kings; 67 they cannot show signs in the heavens for the nations, or shine like the sun or give light like the moon. 68 The wild animals are better than they are, for they can flee to shelter and help themselves. 69 So we have no evidence whatever that they are gods; therefore do not fear them.

70 Like a scarecrow in a cucumber bed, which guards nothing, so are their gods of wood, overlaid with gold and silver. 71 In the same way, their gods of wood, overlaid with gold and silver, are like a thornbush in a garden on which every bird perches; or like a corpse thrown out in the darkness. 72 From the purple and linen[y] that rot upon them you will know that they are not gods; and they will finally be consumed themselves, and be a reproach in the land. 73 Better, therefore, is someone upright who has no idols; such a person will be far above reproach.

---

w Gk *they* *x* Gk *these things* *y* Cn: Gk *marble*, Syr *silk*

Four-headed creatures, a strange craft made up of wheels within wheels, a being of light that appears out of the sky—the first chapter of the Book of Ezekiel sounds like a preview for a science fiction movie. Ezekiel, more than any other prophet, proclaims astonishing visions that are filled with bizarre images, symbols, and creatures.

In-depth

Ezekiel lived during the last days of Judah, just before it was destroyed by the Babylonians. He was probably among an early group of captives sent into exile in Babylon before Judah and the city of Jerusalem were demolished in 587 B.C. (see the timeline at the back of this Bible). He began his prophetic ministry in 593 B.C., when he received a fantastic vision and call, described in chapters 1–3 of his book. We know that Ezekiel came from a priestly family (1.3) and that he was married (24.16–18).

Ezekiel preached many of the traditional themes of the other prophets but in a unique way. Note these examples:

- *The Lord's presence in the Temple.* Possibly because of Ezekiel's priestly heritage, he gave God's presence—or lack of presence—in the Temple a more central role than did the other prophets. In his vision, the Temple will be the center of the new Israel, and a great priest will rule instead of a king.

- *The awesomeness of God.* For Ezekiel, the Lord did not appear as a parent or someone to be argued with. Rather, God was awesome and overpowering, beyond human explanations. Ezekiel often spoke of God's glory and holiness.

- *Personal responsibility.* Ezekiel did not condemn the previous generation for the destruction of Judah, but preached that every generation is responsible for its own acts. Each individual can direct his or her life according to God's will.

- *Apocalyptic prophecy.* Some of Ezekiel's prophecies take the form of symbolic images. The images are so mysterious they require special explanation by heavenly beings. The Books of Daniel and Revelation continue this type of writing, which is called apocalyptic literature.

At a Glance

- **Chapters 1–3.** Ezekiel's call

- **Chapters 4–24.** visions and prophecies about Jerusalem

- **Chapters 25–32.** oracles against foreign nations

- **Chapters 33–39.** oracles of the restoration of Judah and Jerusalem

- **Chapters 40–48.** visions of a new Temple and a new worship

Quick Facts

Period Covered
593–573 B.C.

Authors
Ezekiel, and the scribes who recorded his words and actions

Themes
Jerusalem is being punished for its sin. God's glory will be known to all the nations. God will restore the Temple.

The Book of *Ezekiel*

Ezekiel

The Vision of the Chariot

1 In the thirtieth year, in the fourth month, on the fifth day of the month, as I was among the exiles by the river Chĕʹbar, the heavens were opened, and I saw visions of God. 2 On the fifth day of the month (it was the fifth year of the exile of King Je•hoiʹa•chin), 3 the word of the LORD came to the priest E•zĕkʹi•el son of Būʹzī, in the land of the Chal•dĕʹans by the river Chĕʹbar; and the hand of the LORD was on him there.

4 As I looked, a stormy wind came out of the north: a great cloud with brightness around it and fire flashing forth continually, and in the middle of the fire, something like gleaming amber. 5 In the middle of it was something like four living creatures. This was their appearance: they were of human form. 6 Each had four faces, and each of them had four wings. 7 Their legs were straight, and the soles of their feet were like the sole of a calf's foot; and they sparkled like burnished bronze. 8 Under their wings on their four sides they had human hands. And the four had their faces and their wings thus: 9 their wings touched one another; each of them moved straight ahead, without turning as they moved. 10 As for the appearance of their faces: the four had the face of a human being, the face of a lion on the right side, the face of an ox on the left side, and the face of an eagle; 11 such were their faces. Their wings were spread out above; each creature had two wings, each of which touched the wing of another, while two covered their bodies.

12 Each moved straight ahead; wherever the spirit would go, they went, without turning as they went. 13 In the middle of *a* the living creatures there was something that looked like burning coals of fire, like torches moving to and fro among the living creatures; the fire was bright, and lightning issued from the fire. 14 The living creatures darted to and fro, like a flash of lightning.

15 As I looked at the living creatures, I saw a wheel on the earth beside the living creatures, one for each of the four of them.*b* 16 As for the appearance of the wheels and their construction: their appearance was like the gleaming of beryl; and the four had the same form, their construction being something like a wheel within a wheel. 17 When they moved, they moved in any of the four directions without veering as they moved. 18 Their rims were tall and awesome, for the rims of all four were full of eyes all around. 19 When the living creatures moved, the wheels moved beside them; and when the living creatures rose from the earth, the wheels rose. 20 Wherever the spirit would go, they went, and the wheels rose along with them; for the spirit of the living creatures was in the wheels. 21 When they moved, the others moved; when they stopped, the others stopped; and when they rose from the earth, the wheels rose along with them; for the spirit of the living creatures was in the wheels.

22 Over the heads of the living creatures there

---

a Gk OL: Heb *And the appearance of*   *b* Heb *of their faces* was something like a dome, shining like crystal,[c] spread out above their heads. 23 Under the dome their wings were stretched out straight, one toward another; and each of the creatures had two wings covering its body. 24 When they moved, I heard the sound of their wings like the sound of mighty waters, like the thunder of the Almighty,[d] a sound of tumult like the sound of an army; when they stopped, they let down their wings. 25 And there came a voice from above the dome over their heads; when they stopped, they let down their wings.

26 And above the dome over their heads there was something like a throne, in appearance like sapphire;[e] and seated above the likeness of a throne was something that seemed like a human form. 27 Upward from what appeared like the loins I saw something like gleaming amber, something that looked like fire enclosed all around; and downward from what looked like the loins I saw something that looked like fire, and there was a splendor all around. 28 Like the bow in a cloud on a rainy day, such was the appearance of the splendor all around. This was the appearance of the likeness of the glory of the LORD. When I saw it, I fell on my face, and I heard the voice of someone speaking.

The Vision of the Scroll

2 He said to me: O mortal,[f] stand up on your feet, and I will speak with you. 2 And when he spoke to me, a spirit entered into me and set me on my feet; and I heard him speaking to me. 3 He said to me, Mortal, I am sending you to the people of Israel, to a nation[g] of rebels who have rebelled against me; they and their ancestors have trans-

gressed against me to this very day. 4 The descendants are impudent and stubborn. I am sending you to them, and you shall say to them, "Thus says the Lord GOD." 5 Whether they hear or refuse to hear (for they are a rebellious house), they shall know that there has been a prophet among them. 6 And you, O mortal, do not be afraid of them, and do not be afraid of their words, though briers and thorns surround you and you live among scorpions; do not be afraid of their words, and do not be dismayed at their looks, for they are a rebellious house. 7 You shall speak my words to them, whether they hear or refuse to hear; for they are a rebellious house.

8 But you, mortal, hear what I say to you; do not be rebellious like that rebellious house; open your mouth and eat what I give you. 9 I looked, and a hand was stretched out to me, and a written scroll was in it. 10 He spread it before me; it had writing on the front and on the back, and written on it were words of lamentation and mourning and woe.

3 He said to me, O mortal, eat what is offered to you; eat this scroll, and go, speak to the house of Israel. 2 So I opened my mouth, and he gave me the scroll to eat. 3 He said to me, Mortal, eat this scroll that I give you and fill your stomach with it. Then I ate it; and in my mouth it was as sweet as honey.

4 He said to me: Mortal, go to the house of

---

c Gk: Heb *like the awesome crystal*   d Traditional rendering of Heb *Shaddai*   e Or *lapis lazuli*   f Or *son of man*; Heb *ben adam* (and so throughout the book when Ezekiel is addressed)   g Syr: Heb *to nations*

Introducing ▶ EZEKIEL

Ezekiel's name means "God strengthens." He was a complex person: priest and prophet, poet and teacher, tender and angry. He experienced God in mysterious ways, often through visions that greatly influenced his life and prophetic ministry.

Ezekiel's vision of creatures from heaven in chapters 1–3 of his book was the basis for his call and prophetic ministry. His vision of the defilement of the Temple in chapters 8–11 was a major conversion experience. He, along with most of Israel, believed that God's glory resided in the Temple and that nothing could ever change that. The vision revealed corruption in Jerusalem and that the glory of God had left the Temple and had come to Babylon. His vision of dry bones coming to life in chapter 37 helped him understand that God would breathe new life into Israel. His final visions of a new Temple in chapters 40, 43, and 47 told him that God would restore Jerusalem and the Temple.

Besides having symbolic visions, Ezekiel also performed many dramatic, symbolic actions (see "Street Theater," Ezek 4.1—5.4). These were designed to catch people's attention and transmit God's message.

The Word Is Sweet

God called Ezekiel to speak God's Word to the people. It was a tough job; those people were rebellious. But Ezekiel opened his mouth to receive the scroll containing God's Word, and the scroll was sweet (see Ezek 3.3).

God gave Ezekiel words to eat. God nourished Ezekiel so that Ezekiel could carry out his calling. In the same way, God gives us the Word to eat and nourishes us to carry out our calling. Jesus is often called the Word of God (see "The 'Cosmic Christ,'" Jn 1.1–18).

At the Eucharist, we receive not only the Word of God when the Scriptures are proclaimed but also the body of Christ when we come forward for Communion. With both Word and nourishment, we are called to share the Good News of our faith with others.

What are some ways we can bring this Good News to others? What are some things we might say or do to share our faith with the people we know?

▶ Ezek 2.1—3.11

Israel and speak my very words to them. 5 For you are not sent to a people of obscure speech and difficult language, but to the house of Israel— 6 not to many peoples of obscure speech and difficult language, whose words you cannot understand. Surely, if I sent you to them, they would listen to you. 7 But the house of Israel will not listen to you, for they are not willing to listen to me; because all the house of Israel have a hard forehead and a stubborn heart. 8 See, I have made your face hard against their faces, and your forehead hard against their foreheads. 9 Like the hardest stone, harder than flint, I have made your forehead; do not fear them or be dismayed at their looks, for they are a rebellious house. 10 He said to me: Mortal, all my words that I shall speak to you receive in your heart and hear with your ears; 11 then go to the exiles, to your people, and speak to them. Say to them, "Thus says the Lord GOD"; whether they hear or refuse to hear.

Ezekiel at the River Chebar

12 Then the spirit lifted me up, and as the glory of the LORD rose[h] from its place, I heard behind me the sound of loud rumbling; 13 it was the sound of the wings of the living creatures brushing against one another, and the sound of the wheels beside them, that sounded like a loud rumbling. 14 The spirit lifted me up and bore me away; I went in bitterness in the heat of my spirit, the hand of the LORD being strong upon me. 15 I came to the exiles at Tel-a·bib', who lived by the river Chē'bar.[i] And I sat there among them, stunned, for seven days.

16 At the end of seven days, the word of the LORD came to me: 17 Mortal, I have made you a sentinel for the house of Israel; whenever you hear a word from my mouth, you shall give them warning from me. 18 If I say to the wicked, "You shall surely die," and you give them no warning, or speak to warn the wicked from their wicked way, in order to save their life, those wicked persons shall die for their iniquity; but their blood I will require at your hand. 19 But if you warn the wicked, and they do not turn from their wickedness, or from their wicked way, they shall die for their iniquity; but you will have saved your life. 20 Again, if the righteous turn from their righteousness and commit iniquity, and I lay a stumbling block before them, they shall die; because you have not warned them, they shall die for their sin, and their righteous deeds that they have done shall not be remembered; but their blood I will require at your hand. 21 If, however, you warn the righteous not to sin, and they do not sin, they shall surely live, because they took warning; and you will have saved your life.

Ezekiel Isolated and Silenced

22 Then the hand of the LORD was upon me there; and he said to me, Rise up, go out into the valley, and there I will speak with you. 23 So I rose up and went out into the valley; and the glory of the LORD stood there, like the glory that I had seen by the river Chē'bar; and I fell on my face. 24 The spirit entered into me, and set me on my feet; and he spoke with me and said to me: Go, shut yourself inside your house. 25 As for you, mortal, cords shall be placed on you, and you shall be bound with them, so that you cannot go out among the people; 26 and I will make your tongue cling to the roof of your mouth, so that you shall be speechless and unable to reprove them; for they are a rebellious

---

h Cn: Heb *and blessed be the glory of the LORD*   i Two Mss Syr: Heb *Chebar, and to where they lived.* Another reading is *Chebar, and I sat where they sat* house. 27 But when I speak with you, I will open your mouth, and you shall say to them, "Thus says the Lord GOD"; let those who will hear, hear; and let those who refuse to hear, refuse; for they are a rebellious house.

The Siege of Jerusalem Portrayed

4 And you, O mortal, take a brick and set it before you. On it portray a city, Jerusalem; 2 and put siegeworks against it, and build a siege wall against it, and cast up a ramp against it; set camps also against it, and plant battering rams against it all around. 3 Then take an iron plate and place it as an iron wall between you and the city; set your face toward it, and let it be in a state of siege, and press the siege against it. This is a sign for the house of Israel.

4 Then lie on your left side, and place the punishment of the house of Israel upon it; you shall bear their punishment for the number of the days that you lie there. 5 For I assign to you a number of days, three hundred ninety days, equal to the number of the years of their punishment; and so you shall bear the punishment of the house of Israel. 6 When you have completed these, you shall lie down a second time, but on your right side, and bear the punishment of the house of Judah; forty days I assign you, one day for each year. 7 You shall set your face toward the siege of Jerusalem, and with your arm bared you shall prophesy against it. 8 See, I am putting cords on you so that you cannot turn from one side to the other until you have completed the days of your siege.

9 And you, take wheat and barley, beans and lentils, millet and spelt; put them into one vessel, and make bread for yourself. During the number of days that you lie on your side, three hundred ninety days, you shall eat it. 10 The food that you eat shall be twenty shekels a day by weight; at fixed times you shall eat it. 11 And you shall drink water by measure, one-sixth of a hin; at fixed times you shall drink. 12 You shall eat it as a barley-cake, baking it in their sight on human dung. 13 The LORD said, "Thus shall the people of Israel eat their bread, unclean, among the nations to which I will drive them." 14 Then I said, "Ah Lord GOD! I have never defiled myself; from my youth up until now I have never eaten what died of itself or was torn by animals, nor has carrion flesh come into my mouth." 15 Then he said to me, "See, I will let you have cow's dung instead of human dung, on which you may prepare your bread."

16 Then he said to me, Mortal, I am going to break the staff of bread in Jerusalem; they shall eat bread by weight and with fearfulness; and they shall drink water by measure and in dismay. 17 Lacking bread and water, they will look at one another in dismay, and waste away under their punishment.

A Sword against Jerusalem

5 And you, O mortal, take a sharp sword; use it as a barber's razor and run it over your head and your beard; then take balances for weighing, and divide the hair. 2 One third of the hair you shall burn in the fire inside the city, when the days of the siege are completed; one third you shall take and strike with the sword all around the city;j and one third you shall scatter to the wind, and I will unsheathe the sword after them. 3 Then you shall take from these a small number, and bind them in the skirts of your robe. 4 From these, again, you shall take some, throw them into the fire and burn them up; from there a fire will come out against all the house of Israel.

j Heb it

EZEK

Street Theater

Look over what the prophet does in Ezekiel, chapters 3–5, to get people's attention before the fall of Jerusalem in 587 B.C. He is speechless (3.22–27) as a sign that the people are rebellious and unwilling to hear God's word. He lies on his left side for days, and then his right (4.4–5), as a sign of the number of years the two kingdoms Israel and Judah will be in exile. He eats small amounts of food cooked on dung (verses 10–15) as a sign of the shortage of food during the siege of the city. Ezekiel's "street theater" is a good way of making a point that everyone can understand.

Christians today need to use creative means to raise consciousness about the ways society violates human life and harms our world. Radio and television, public prayer services, and rallies all help people get the message out. What does your church do to raise consciousness and move people to change their ways? What can you do?

▶ Ezek 4.1—5.4

5 Thus says the Lord GOD: This is Jerusalem; I have set her in the center of the nations, with countries all around her. 6 But she has rebelled against my ordinances and my statutes, becoming more wicked than the nations and the countries all around her, rejecting my ordinances and not following my statutes. 7 Therefore thus says the Lord GOD: Because you are more turbulent than the nations that are all around you, and have not followed my statutes or kept my ordinances, but have acted according to the ordinances of the nations that are all around you; 8 therefore thus says the Lord GOD: I, I myself, am coming against you; I will execute judgments among you in the sight of the nations. 9 And because of all your abominations, I will do to you what I have never yet done, and the like of which I will never do again. 10 Surely, parents shall eat their children in your midst, and children shall eat their parents; I will execute judgments on you, and any of you who survive I will scatter to every wind. 11 Therefore, as I live, says the Lord GOD, surely, because you have defiled my sanctuary with all your detestable things and with all your abominations—therefore I will cut you down;*k* my eye will not spare, and I will have no pity. 12 One third of you shall die of pestilence or be consumed by famine among you; one third shall fall by the sword around you; and one third I will scatter to every wind and will unsheathe the sword after them.

13 My anger shall spend itself, and I will vent my fury on them and satisfy myself; and they shall know that I, the LORD, have spoken in my jealousy, when I spend my fury on them. 14 Moreover I will make you a desolation and an object of mocking among the nations around you, in the sight of all that pass by. 15 You shall be*l* a mockery and a taunt, a warning and a horror, to the nations around you, when I execute judgments on you in anger and fury, and with furious punishments—I, the LORD, have spoken— 16 when I loose against you*m* my deadly arrows of famine, arrows for destruction, which I will let loose to destroy you, and when I bring more and more famine upon you, and break your staff of bread. 17 I will send famine and wild animals against you, and they will rob you of your children; pestilence and bloodshed shall pass through you; and I will bring the sword upon you. I, the LORD, have spoken.

Judgment on Idolatrous Israel

6 The word of the LORD came to me: 2 O mortal, set your face toward the mountains of Israel, and prophesy against them, 3 and say, You mountains of Israel, hear the word of the Lord GOD! Thus says the Lord GOD to the mountains and the hills, to the ravines and the valleys: I, I my-

self will bring a sword upon you, and I will destroy your high places. 4 Your altars shall become desolate, and your incense stands shall be broken; and I will throw down your slain in front of your idols. 5 I will lay the corpses of the people of Israel in front of their idols; and I will scatter your bones around your altars. 6 Wherever you live, your towns shall be waste and your high places ruined, so that your altars will be waste and ruined,*n* your idols broken and destroyed, your incense stands cut down, and your works wiped out. 7 The slain shall fall in your midst; then you shall know that I am the LORD.

8 But I will spare some. Some of you shall escape the sword among the nations and be scattered through the countries. 9 Those of you who escape shall remember me among the nations where they are carried captive, how I was crushed by their wanton heart that turned away from me, and their wanton eyes that turned after their idols. Then they will be loathsome in their own sight for the evils that they have committed, for all their abominations. 10 And they shall know that I am the LORD; I did not threaten in vain to bring this disaster upon them.

11 Thus says the Lord GOD: Clap your hands and stamp your foot, and say, Alas for all the vile abominations of the house of Israel! For they shall fall by the sword, by famine, and by pestilence. 12 Those far off shall die of pestilence; those nearby shall fall by the sword; and any who are left and are spared shall die of famine. Thus I will spend my fury upon them. 13 And you shall know that I am the LORD, when their slain lie among their idols around their altars, on every high hill, on all the mountain tops, under every green tree, and under every leafy oak, wherever they offered pleasing odor to all their idols. 14 I will stretch out my hand against them, and make the land desolate and waste, throughout all their settlements, from the wilderness to Rib'lah.*o* Then they shall know that I am the LORD.

Impending Disaster

7 The word of the LORD came to me: 2 You, O mortal, thus says the Lord GOD to the land of Israel:

An end! The end has come
    upon the four corners of the land.
3 Now the end is upon you,
    I will let loose my anger upon you;
I will judge you according to your ways,
    I will punish you for all your abominations.

---

k Another reading is *I will withdraw*   l Gk Syr Vg Tg: Heb *It shall be*   m Heb *them*   n Syr Vg Tg: Heb *and be made guilty*   o Another reading is *Diblah*

⁴ My eye will not spare you, I will have no pity.
  I will punish you for your ways,
    while your abominations are among you.
Then you shall know that I am the LORD.
  5 Thus says the Lord GOD:
Disaster after disaster! See, it comes.
⁶   An end has come, the end has come.
It has awakened against you; see, it comes!
⁷ Your doom ᵖ has come to you,
    O inhabitant of the land.
The time has come, the day is near—
    of tumult, not of reveling on the
      mountains.
⁸ Soon now I will pour out my wrath upon
      you;
  I will spend my anger against you.
I will judge you according to your ways,
    and punish you for all your abominations.
⁹ My eye will not spare; I will have no pity.
    I will punish you according to your ways,
    while your abominations are among you.
Then you shall know that it is I the LORD who
strike.
¹⁰ See, the day! See, it comes!
    Your doom ᵖ has gone out.
The rod has blossomed; pride has budded.
¹¹   Violence has grown into a rod of
      wickedness.
  None of them shall remain,
    not their abundance, not their wealth;
    no pre-eminence among them.ᵖ
¹² The time has come, the day draws near;
    let not the buyer rejoice, nor the seller
      mourn,
    for wrath is upon all their multitude.
¹³ For the sellers shall not return to what has been
sold as long as they remain alive. For the vision
concerns all their multitude; it shall not be revoked.
Because of their iniquity, they cannot maintain
their lives.ᵖ
¹⁴ They have blown the horn and made
      everything ready;
    but no one goes to battle,
    for my wrath is upon all their multitude.
¹⁵ The sword is outside, pestilence and famine are
      inside;
    those in the field die by the sword;
    those in the city—famine and pestilence
      devour them.
¹⁶ If any survivors escape,
    they shall be found on the mountains
    like doves of the valleys,
  all of them moaning over their iniquity.
¹⁷ All hands shall grow feeble,
    all knees turn to water.
¹⁸ They shall put on sackcloth,
    horror shall cover them.

Shame shall be on all faces,
    baldness on all their heads.
¹⁹ They shall fling their silver into the streets,
    their gold shall be treated as unclean.
Their silver and gold cannot save them on the day
of the wrath of the LORD. They shall not satisfy their
hunger or fill their stomachs with it. For it was the
stumbling block of their iniquity. ²⁰ From their�q
beautiful ornament, in which they took pride, they
made their abominable images, their detestable
things; therefore I will make of it an unclean thing
to them.
²¹ I will hand it over to strangers as booty,
    to the wicked of the earth as plunder;
    they shall profane it.
²² I will avert my face from them,
    so that they may profane my treasuredʳ
      place;
  the violent shall enter it,
    they shall profane it.
²³ Make a chain!ᵖ
For the land is full of bloody crimes;
    the city is full of violence.
²⁴ I will bring the worst of the nations
    to take possession of their houses.
I will put an end to the arrogance of the
      strong,
    and their holy places shall be profaned.
²⁵ When anguish comes, they will seek peace,
    but there shall be none.
²⁶ Disaster comes upon disaster,
    rumor follows rumor;
  they shall keep seeking a vision from the
      prophet;
  instruction shall perish from the priest,
    and counsel from the elders.
²⁷ The king shall mourn,
    the prince shall be wrapped in despair,
    and the hands of the people of the land
      shall tremble.
According to their way I will deal with them;
    according to their own judgments I will
      judge them.
And they shall know that I am the LORD.

Abominations in the Temple

8 In the sixth year, in the sixth month, on the
fifth day of the month, as I sat in my house,
with the elders of Judah sitting before me there, the hand
of the Lord GOD fell upon me there. ² I looked, and
there was a figure that looked like a human being;ˢ
below what appeared to be its loins it was fire, and
above the loins it was like the appearance of brightness, like gleaming amber. ³ It stretched out the

EZEK

ᵖ Meaning of Heb uncertain   q Syr Symmachus: Heb *its*
ʳ Or *secret*   ˢ Gk: Heb *like fire*

form of a hand, and took me by a lock of my head; and the spirit lifted me up between earth and heaven, and brought me in visions of God to Jerusalem, to the entrance of the gateway of the inner court that faces north, to the seat of the image of jealousy, which provokes to jealousy. 4 And the glory of the God of Israel was there, like the vision that I had seen in the valley.

5 Then God[t] said to me, "O mortal, lift up your eyes now in the direction of the north." So I lifted up my eyes toward the north, and there, north of the altar gate, in the entrance, was this image of jealousy. 6 He said to me, "Mortal, do you see what they are doing, the great abominations that the house of Israel are committing here, to drive me far from my sanctuary? Yet you will see still greater abominations."

7 And he brought me to the entrance of the court; I looked, and there was a hole in the wall. 8 Then he said to me, "Mortal, dig through the wall"; and when I dug through the wall, there was an entrance. 9 He said to me, "Go in, and see the vile abominations that they are committing here." 10 So I went in and looked; there, portrayed on the wall all around, were all kinds of creeping things, and loathsome animals, and all the idols of the house of Israel. 11 Before them stood seventy of the elders of the house of Israel, with Ja·az·a·ni′ah son of Sha′phan standing among them. Each had his censer in his hand, and the fragrant cloud of incense was ascending. 12 Then he said to me, "Mortal, have you seen what the elders of the house of Israel are doing in the dark, each in his room of images? For they say, 'The LORD does not see us, the LORD has forsaken the land.' " 13 He said also to me, "You will see still greater abominations that they are committing."

14 Then he brought me to the entrance of the north gate of the house of the LORD; women were sitting there weeping for Tam′muz. 15 Then he said to me, "Have you seen this, O mortal? You will see still greater abominations than these."

16 And he brought me into the inner court of the house of the LORD; there, at the entrance of the temple of the LORD, between the porch and the altar, were about twenty-five men, with their backs to the temple of the LORD, and their faces toward the east, prostrating themselves to the sun toward the east. 17 Then he said to me, "Have you seen this, O mortal? Is it not bad enough that the house of Judah commits the abominations done here? Must they fill the land with violence, and provoke my anger still further? See, they are putting the branch to their nose! 18 Therefore I will act in wrath; my eye will not spare, nor will I have pity; and though they cry in my hearing with a loud voice, I will not listen to them."

The Slaughter of the Idolaters

9 Then he cried in my hearing with a loud voice, saying, "Draw near, you executioners of the city, each with his destroying weapon in his hand." 2 And six men came from the direction of the upper gate, which faces north, each with his weapon for slaughter in his hand; among them was a man clothed in linen, with a writing case at his side. They went in and stood beside the bronze altar.

3 Now the glory of the God of Israel had gone up from the cherub on which it rested to the threshold of the house. The LORD called to the man clothed in linen, who had the writing case at his side; 4 and said to him, "Go through the city, through Jerusalem, and put a mark on the foreheads of those who sigh and groan over all the abominations that are committed in it." 5 To the others he said in my hearing, "Pass through the city after him, and kill; your eye shall not spare, and you shall show no pity. 6 Cut down old men, young men and young women, little children and women, but touch no one who has the mark. And begin at my sanctuary." So they began with the elders who were in front of the house. 7 Then he said to them, "Defile the house, and fill the courts with the slain. Go!" So they went out and killed in the city. 8 While they were killing, and I was left alone, I fell prostrate on my face and cried out, "Ah Lord GOD! will you destroy all who remain of Israel as you pour out your wrath upon Jerusalem?" 9 He said to me, "The guilt of the house of Israel and Judah is exceedingly great; the land is full of bloodshed and the city full of perversity; for they say, 'The LORD has forsaken the land, and the LORD does not see.' 10 As for me, my eye will not spare, nor will I have pity, but I will bring down their deeds upon their heads."

11 Then the man clothed in linen, with the writing case at his side, brought back word, saying, "I have done as you commanded me."

God's Glory Leaves Jerusalem

10 Then I looked, and above the dome that was over the heads of the cherubim there appeared above them something like a sapphire,[u] in form resembling a throne. 2 He said to the man clothed in linen, "Go within the wheelwork underneath the cherubim; fill your hands with burning coals from among the cherubim, and scatter them over the city." He went in as I looked on. 3 Now the cherubim were standing on the south side of the house when the man went in; and a cloud filled the inner court. 4 Then the glory of the LORD rose up from the cherub to the threshold of the house;

---

t Heb *he* u Or *lapis lazuli*

the house was filled with the cloud, and the court was full of the brightness of the glory of the LORD. 5 The sound of the wings of the cherubim was heard as far as the outer court, like the voice of God Almighty[v] when he speaks.

6 When he commanded the man clothed in linen, "Take fire from within the wheelwork, from among the cherubim," he went in and stood beside a wheel. 7 And a cherub stretched out his hand from among the cherubim to the fire that was among the cherubim, took some of it and put it into the hands of the man clothed in linen, who took it and went out. 8 The cherubim appeared to have the form of a human hand under their wings.

9 I looked, and there were four wheels beside the cherubim, one beside each cherub; and the appearance of the wheels was like gleaming beryl. 10 And as for their appearance, the four looked alike, something like a wheel within a wheel. 11 When they moved, they moved in any of the four directions without veering as they moved; but in whatever direction the front wheel faced, the others followed without veering as they moved. 12 Their entire body, their rims, their spokes, their wings, and the wheels—the wheels of the four of them— were full of eyes all around. 13 As for the wheels, they were called in my hearing "the wheelwork." 14 Each one had four faces: the first face was that of the cherub, the second face was that of a human being, the third that of a lion, and the fourth that of an eagle.

15 The cherubim rose up. These were the living creatures that I saw by the river Chě′bar. 16 When the cherubim moved, the wheels moved beside them; and when the cherubim lifted up their wings to rise up from the earth, the wheels at their side did not veer. 17 When they stopped, the others stopped, and when they rose up, the others rose up with them; for the spirit of the living creatures was in them.

18 Then the glory of the LORD went out from the threshold of the house and stopped above the cherubim. 19 The cherubim lifted up their wings and rose up from the earth in my sight as they went out with the wheels beside them. They stopped at the entrance of the east gate of the house of the LORD; and the glory of the God of Israel was above them.

20 These were the living creatures that I saw underneath the God of Israel by the river Chě′bar; and I knew that they were cherubim. 21 Each had four faces, each four wings, and underneath their wings something like human hands. 22 As for what their faces were like, they were the same faces whose appearance I had seen by the river Chě′bar. Each one moved straight ahead.

Judgment on Wicked Counselors

11 The spirit lifted me up and brought me to the east gate of the house of the LORD, which faces east. There, at the entrance of the gateway, were twenty-five men; among them I saw Jǎ·az·a·ni′ah son of Az′zur, and Pel·a·ti′ah son of Be·nā′i·ah, officials of the people. 2 He said to me, "Mortal, these are the men who devise iniquity and who give wicked counsel in this city; 3 they say, 'The time is not near to build houses; this city is the pot, and we are the meat.' 4 Therefore prophesy against them; prophesy, O mortal."

5 Then the spirit of the LORD fell upon me, and he said to me, "Say, Thus says the LORD: This is what you think, O house of Israel; I know the things that come into your mind. 6 You have killed many in this city, and have filled its streets with the slain. 7 Therefore thus says the Lord GOD: The slain whom you have placed within it are the meat, and this city is the pot; but you shall be taken out of it. 8 You have feared the sword; and I will bring the sword upon you, says the Lord GOD. 9 I will take you out of it and give you over to the hands of foreigners, and execute judgments upon you. 10 You shall fall by the sword; I will judge you at the border of Israel. And you shall know that I am the LORD. 11 This city shall not be your pot, and you shall not be the meat inside it; I will judge you at the border of Israel. 12 Then you shall know that I am the LORD, whose statutes you have not followed, and whose ordinances you have not kept, but you have acted according to the ordinances of the nations that are around you."

13 Now, while I was prophesying, Pel·a·ti′ah son of Be·nā′i·ah died. Then I fell down on my face, cried with a loud voice, and said, "Ah Lord GOD! will you make a full end of the remnant of Israel?"

God Will Restore Israel

14 Then the word of the LORD came to me: 15 Mortal, your kinsfolk, your own kin, your fellow exiles,[w] the whole house of Israel, all of them, are those of whom the inhabitants of Jerusalem have said, "They have gone far from the LORD; to us this land is given for a possession." 16 Therefore say: Thus says the Lord GOD: Though I removed them far away among the nations, and though I scattered them among the countries, yet I have been a sanctuary to them for a little while[x] in the countries where they have gone. 17 Therefore say: Thus says the Lord GOD: I will gather you from the peoples, and assemble you out of the countries where you have been scattered, and I will give you the land of Israel. 18 When they come there, they will remove

---

v Traditional rendering of Heb *El Shaddai* w Gk Syr: Heb *people of your kindred* x Or *to some extent* from it all its detestable things and all its abominations. 19 I will give them one[y] heart, and put a new spirit within them; I will remove the heart of stone from their flesh and give them a heart of flesh, 20 so that they may follow my statutes and keep my ordinances and obey them. Then they shall be my people, and I will be their God. 21 But as for those whose heart goes after their detestable things and their abominations,[z] I will bring their deeds upon their own heads, says the Lord GOD.

PRAY IT!
Have a Heart!

The Old Testament prophets are concerned about people's hearts. The ancient Israelites understood the heart as the center of intelligence, feelings, and human will. Jeremiah says the new Covenant will be written on people's hearts (Jer 31.33), and Ezekiel says God will take away their stony hearts and give them natural hearts (Ezek 11.19).

In your prayer, reflect or journal on the following questions:

- What's the difference between having a natural, fleshy heart and a cold, stony heart?
- Why would a natural heart lead to obeying God (verse 20)?
- When does your heart feel natural? When does it feel stony?

▶ Ezek 11.19–20

22 Then the cherubim lifted up their wings, with the wheels beside them; and the glory of the God of Israel was above them. 23 And the glory of the LORD ascended from the middle of the city, and stopped on the mountain east of the city. 24 The spirit lifted me up and brought me in a vision by the spirit of God into Chal·dē′a, to the exiles. Then the vision that I had seen left me. 25 And I told the exiles all the things that the LORD had shown me.

Judah's Captivity Portrayed

12 The word of the LORD came to me: 2 Mortal, you are living in the midst of a rebellious house, who have eyes to see but do not see, who have ears to hear but do not hear; 3 for they are a rebellious house. Therefore, mortal, prepare for yourself an exile's baggage, and go into exile by day in their sight; you shall go like an exile from your place to another place in their sight. Perhaps they will understand, though they are a rebellious house. 4 You shall bring out your baggage by day in their sight, as baggage for exile; and you shall go out yourself at evening in their sight, as those do who go into exile. 5 Dig through the wall in their sight, and carry the baggage through it. 6 In their sight you shall lift the baggage on your shoulder, and carry it out in the dark; you shall cover your face, so that you may not see the land; for I have made you a sign for the house of Israel.

7 I did just as I was commanded. I brought out my baggage by day, as baggage for exile, and in the evening I dug through the wall with my own hands; I brought it out in the dark, carrying it on my shoulder in their sight.

8 In the morning the word of the LORD came to me: 9 Mortal, has not the house of Israel, the rebellious house, said to you, "What are you doing?" 10 Say to them, "Thus says the Lord GOD: This oracle concerns the prince in Jerusalem and all the house of Israel in it." 11 Say, "I am a sign for you: as I have done, so shall it be done to them; they shall go into exile, into captivity." 12 And the prince who is among them shall lift his baggage on his shoulder in the dark, and shall go out; he[a] shall dig through the wall and carry it through; he shall cover his face, so that he may not see the land with his eyes. 13 I will spread my net over him, and he shall be caught in my snare; and I will bring him to Babylon, the land of the Chal·dē′ans, yet he shall not see it; and he shall die there. 14 I will scatter to every wind all who are around him, his helpers and all his troops; and I will unsheathe the sword behind them. 15 And they shall know that I am the LORD, when I disperse them among the nations and scatter them through the countries. 16 But I will let a few of them escape from the sword, from famine and pestilence, so that they may tell of all their abominations among the nations where they go; then they shall know that I am the LORD.

Judgment Not Postponed

17 The word of the LORD came to me: 18 Mortal, eat your bread with quaking, and drink your water with trembling and with fearfulness; 19 and say to the people of the land, Thus says the Lord GOD concerning the inhabitants of Jerusalem in the land of Israel: They shall eat their bread with fearfulness, and drink their water in dismay, because their land shall be stripped of all it contains, on account of the violence of all those who live in it. 20 The inhabited cities shall be laid waste, and the land shall become a desolation; and you shall know that I am the LORD.

21 The word of the LORD came to me: 22 Mortal, what is this proverb of yours about the land of Israel, which says, "The days are prolonged, and every vision comes to nothing"? 23 Tell them therefore, "Thus says the Lord GOD: I will put an end to this proverb, and they shall use it no more as a proverb in Israel." But say to them, The days are near, and the fulfillment of every vision. 24 For there shall no longer be any false vision or flattering divination within the house of Israel. 25 But I the LORD will speak the word that I speak, and it will be fulfilled. It will no longer be delayed; but in your days, O rebellious house, I will speak the word and fulfill it, says the Lord GOD.

26 The word of the LORD came to me: 27 Mortal, the house of Israel is saying, "The vision that he sees is for many years ahead; he prophesies for distant times." 28 Therefore say to them, Thus says the Lord GOD: None of my words will be delayed any longer, but the word that I speak will be fulfilled, says the Lord GOD.

False Prophets Condemned

13 The word of the LORD came to me: 2 Mortal, prophesy against the prophets of Israel who are prophesying; say to those who prophesy out of their own imagination: "Hear the word of the LORD!" 3 Thus says the Lord GOD, Alas for the senseless prophets who follow their own spirit, and have seen nothing! 4 Your prophets have been like jackals among ruins, O Israel. 5 You have not gone up into the breaches, or repaired a wall for the house of Israel, so that it might stand in battle on the day of the LORD. 6 They have envisioned falsehood and lying divination; they say, "Says the LORD," when the LORD has not sent them, and yet they wait for the fulfillment of their word! 7 Have you not seen a false vision or uttered a lying divination, when you have said, "Says the LORD," even though I did not speak?

8 Therefore thus says the Lord GOD: Because you have uttered falsehood and envisioned lies, I am against you, says the Lord GOD. 9 My hand will be against the prophets who see false visions and utter lying divinations; they shall not be in the council of my people, nor be enrolled in the register of the house of Israel, nor shall they enter the land of Israel; and you shall know that I am the Lord GOD. 10 Because, in truth, because they have misled my people, saying, "Peace," when there is no peace; and because, when the people build a wall, these prophets*b* smear whitewash on it. 11 Say to those who smear whitewash on it that it shall fall. There will be a deluge of rain,*c* great hailstones will fall, and a stormy wind will break out. 12 When the wall falls, will it not be said to you, "Where is the whitewash you smeared on it?" 13 Therefore

thus says the Lord GOD: In my wrath I will make a stormy wind break out, and in my anger there shall be a deluge of rain, and hailstones in wrath to destroy it. 14 I will break down the wall that you have smeared with whitewash, and bring it to the ground, so that its foundation will be laid bare; when it falls, you shall perish within it; and you shall know that I am the LORD. 15 Thus I will spend my wrath upon the wall, and upon those who have smeared it with whitewash; and I will say to you, The wall is no more, nor those who smeared it— 16 the prophets of Israel who prophesied concerning Jerusalem and saw visions of peace for it, when there was no peace, says the Lord GOD.

17 As for you, mortal, set your face against the daughters of your people, who prophesy out of their own imagination; prophesy against them 18 and say, Thus says the Lord GOD: Woe to the women who sew bands on all wrists, and make veils for the heads of persons of every height, in the hunt for human lives! Will you hunt down lives among my people, and maintain your own lives? 19 You have profaned me among my people for handfuls of barley and for pieces of bread, putting to death persons who should not die and keeping alive persons who should not live, by your lies to my people, who listen to lies.

20 Therefore thus says the Lord GOD: I am against your bands with which you hunt lives;*d* I will tear them from your arms, and let the lives go free, the lives that you hunt down like birds. 21 I will tear off your veils, and save my people from your hands; they shall no longer be prey in your hands; and you shall know that I am the LORD. 22 Because you have disheartened the righteous falsely, although I have not disheartened them, and you have encouraged the wicked not to turn from their wicked way and save their lives; 23 therefore you shall no longer see false visions or practice divination; I will save my people from your hand. Then you will know that I am the LORD.

God's Judgments Justified

14 Certain elders of Israel came to me and sat down before me. 2 And the word of the LORD came to me: 3 Mortal, these men have taken their idols into their hearts, and placed their iniquity as a stumbling block before them; shall I let myself be consulted by them? 4 Therefore speak to them, and say to them, Thus says the Lord GOD: Any of those of the house of Israel who take their idols into their hearts and place their iniquity as a stumbling block before them, and yet come to the prophet—I the LORD will answer those who come

---

b Heb *they*   *c* Heb *rain and you*   *d* Gk Syr: Heb *lives for birds* with the multitude of their idols, 5 in order that I may take hold of the hearts of the house of Israel, all of whom are estranged from me through their idols.

6 Therefore say to the house of Israel, Thus says the Lord GOD: Repent and turn away from your idols; and turn away your faces from all your abominations. 7 For any of those of the house of Israel, or of the aliens who reside in Israel, who separate themselves from me, taking their idols into their hearts and placing their iniquity as a stumbling block before them, and yet come to a prophet to inquire of me by him, I the LORD will answer them myself. 8 I will set my face against them; I will make them a sign and a byword and cut them off from the midst of my people; and you shall know that I am the LORD.

9 If a prophet is deceived and speaks a word, I, the LORD, have deceived that prophet, and I will stretch out my hand against him, and will destroy him from the midst of my people Israel. 10 And they shall bear their punishment—the punishment of the inquirer and the punishment of the prophet shall be the same— 11 so that the house of Israel may no longer go astray from me, nor defile themselves any more with all their transgressions. Then they shall be my people, and I will be their God, says the Lord GOD.

12 The word of the LORD came to me: 13 Mortal, when a land sins against me by acting faithlessly, and I stretch out my hand against it, and break its staff of bread and send famine upon it, and cut off from it human beings and animals, 14 even if Noah, Daniel,*e* and Job, these three, were in it, they would save only their own lives by their righteousness, says the Lord GOD. 15 If I send wild animals through the land to ravage it, so that it is made desolate, and no one may pass through because of the animals; 16 even if these three men were in it, as I live, says the Lord GOD, they would save neither sons nor daughters; they alone would be saved, but the land would be desolate. 17 Or if I bring a sword upon that land and say, "Let a sword pass through the land," and I cut off human beings and animals from it; 18 though these three men were in it, as I live, says the Lord GOD, they would save neither sons nor daughters, but they alone would be saved. 19 Or if I send a pestilence into that land, and pour out my wrath upon it with blood, to cut off humans and animals from it; 20 even if Noah, Daniel,*e* and Job were in it, as I live, says the Lord GOD, they would save neither son nor daughter; they would save only their own lives by their righteousness.

21 For thus says the Lord GOD: How much more when I send upon Jerusalem my four deadly acts of judgment, sword, famine, wild animals, and pestilence, to cut off humans and animals from it!

22 Yet, survivors shall be left in it, sons and daughters who will be brought out; they will come out to you. When you see their ways and their deeds, you will be consoled for the evil that I have brought upon Jerusalem, for all that I have brought upon it. 23 They shall console you, when you see their ways and their deeds; and you shall know that it was not without cause that I did all that I have done in it, says the Lord GOD.

The Useless Vine

15 The word of the LORD came to me: 2 O mortal, how does the wood of the
 vine surpass all other wood—
the vine branch that is among the trees of
 the forest?
3 Is wood taken from it to make anything?
 Does one take a peg from it on which to
  hang any object?
4 It is put in the fire for fuel;
 when the fire has consumed both ends
  of it
and the middle of it is charred,
 is it useful for anything?
5 When it was whole it was used for nothing;
 how much less—when the fire has
  consumed it,
 and it is charred—
 can it ever be used for anything!

6 Therefore thus says the Lord GOD: Like the wood of the vine among the trees of the forest, which I have given to the fire for fuel, so I will give up the inhabitants of Jerusalem. 7 I will set my face against them; although they escape from the fire, the fire shall still consume them; and you shall know that I am the LORD, when I set my face against them. 8 And I will make the land desolate, because they have acted faithlessly, says the Lord GOD.

God's Faithless Bride

16 The word of the LORD came to me: 2 Mortal, make known to Jerusalem her abominations, 3 and say, Thus says the Lord GOD to Jerusalem: Your origin and your birth were in the land of the Cā'naan•ites; your father was an Am'o•rīte, and your mother a Hit'tīte. 4 As for your birth, on the day you were born your navel cord was not cut, nor were you washed with water to cleanse you, nor rubbed with salt, nor wrapped in cloths. 5 No eye pitied you, to do any of these things for you out of compassion for you; but you were thrown out in the open field, for you were abhorred on the day you were born.

6 I passed by you, and saw you flailing about in your blood. As you lay in your blood, I said to you,

---

e Or, as otherwise read, *Danel*

"Live! [7] and grow up [f] like a plant of the field." You grew up and became tall and arrived at full womanhood; [g] your breasts were formed, and your hair had grown; yet you were naked and bare.

8 I passed by you again and looked on you; you were at the age for love. I spread the edge of my cloak over you, and covered your nakedness: I pledged myself to you and entered into a covenant with you, says the Lord GOD, and you became mine. [9] Then I bathed you with water and washed off the blood from you, and anointed you with oil. [10] I clothed you with embroidered cloth and with sandals of fine leather; I bound you in fine linen and covered you with rich fabric. [h] [11] I adorned you with ornaments: I put bracelets on your arms, a chain on your neck, [12] a ring on your nose, earrings in your ears, and a beautiful crown upon your head. [13] You were adorned with gold and silver, while your clothing was of fine linen, rich fabric, [h] and embroidered cloth. You had choice flour and honey and oil for food. You grew exceedingly beautiful, fit to be a queen. [14] Your fame spread among the nations on account of your beauty, for it was perfect because of my splendor that I had bestowed on you, says the Lord GOD.

15 But you trusted in your beauty, and played the whore because of your fame, and lavished your whorings on any passer-by. [i] [16] You took some of your garments, and made for yourself colorful shrines, and on them played the whore; nothing like this has ever been or ever shall be. [h] [17] You also took your beautiful jewels of my gold and my silver that I had given you, and made for yourself male images, and with them played the whore; [18] and you took your embroidered garments to cover them, and set my oil and my incense before them. [19] Also my bread that I gave you—I fed you with choice flour and oil and honey—you set it before them as a pleasing odor; and so it was, says the Lord GOD. [20] You took your sons and your daughters, whom you had borne to me, and these you sacrificed to them to be devoured. As if your whorings were not enough! [21] You slaughtered my children and delivered them up as an offering to them. [22] And in all your abominations and your whorings you did not remember the days of your youth, when you were naked and bare, flailing about in your blood.

23 After all your wickedness (woe, woe to you! says the Lord GOD), [24] you built yourself a platform and made yourself a lofty place in every square; [25] at the head of every street you built your lofty place and prostituted your beauty, offering yourself to every passer-by, and multiplying your whoring. [26] You played the whore with the Egyptians, your lustful neighbors, multiplying your whoring, to provoke me to anger. [27] Therefore I stretched out my hand against you, reduced your rations, and gave you up to the will of your enemies, the daughters of the Phi·lis'tines, who were ashamed of your lewd behavior. [28] You played the whore with the Assyrians, because you were insatiable; you played the whore with them, and still you were not satisfied. [29] You multiplied your whoring with Chaldē'a, the land of merchants; and even with this you were not satisfied.

30 How sick is your heart, says the Lord GOD, that you did all these things, the deeds of a brazen whore; [31] building your platform at the head of every street, and making your lofty place in every square! Yet you were not like a whore, because you scorned payment. [32] Adulterous wife, who receives strangers instead of her husband! [33] Gifts are given to all whores; but you gave your gifts to all your lovers, bribing them to come to you from all around for your whorings. [34] So you were different from other women in your whorings: no one solicited you to play the whore; and you gave payment, while no payment was given to you; you were different.

35 Therefore, O whore, hear the word of the LORD: [36] Thus says the Lord GOD, Because your lust was poured out and your nakedness uncovered in your whoring with your lovers, and because of all your abominable idols, and because of the blood of your children that you gave to them, [37] therefore, I will gather all your lovers, with whom you took pleasure, all those you loved and all those you hated; I will gather them against you from all around, and will uncover your nakedness to them, so that they may see all your nakedness. [38] I will judge you as women who commit adultery and shed blood are judged, and bring blood upon you in wrath and jealousy. [39] I will deliver you into their hands, and they shall throw down your platform and break down your lofty places; they shall strip you of your clothes and take your beautiful objects and leave you naked and bare. [40] They shall bring up a mob against you, and they shall stone you and cut you to pieces with their swords. [41] They shall burn your houses and execute judgments on you in the sight of many women; I will stop you from playing the whore, and you shall also make no more payments. [42] So I will satisfy my fury on you, and my jealousy shall turn away from you; I will be calm, and will be angry no longer. [43] Because you have not remembered the days of your youth, but have enraged me with all these things; therefore, I have returned your deeds upon your head, says the Lord GOD.

---

[f] Gk Syr: Heb *Live! I made you a myriad*   [g] Cn: Heb *ornament of ornaments*   [h] Meaning of Heb uncertain   [i] Heb adds *let it be his*

Have you not committed lewdness beyond all your abominations? 44 See, everyone who uses proverbs will use this proverb about you, "Like mother, like daughter." 45 You are the daughter of your mother, who loathed her husband and her children; and you are the sister of your sisters, who loathed their husbands and their children. Your mother was a Hit'tīte and your father an Am'o•rite. 46 Your elder sister is Sa•mār'i•a, who lived with her daughters to the north of you; and your younger sister, who lived to the south of you, is Sod'om with her daughters. 47 You not only followed their ways, and acted according to their abominations; within a very little time you were more corrupt than they in all your ways. 48 As I live, says the Lord GOD, your sister Sod'om and her daughters have not done as you and your daughters have done. 49 This was the guilt of your sister Sod'om: she and her daughters had pride, excess of food, and prosperous ease, but did not aid the poor and needy. 50 They were haughty, and did abominable things before me; therefore I removed them when I saw it. 51 Sa•mār'i•a has not committed half your sins; you have committed more abominations than they, and have made your sisters appear righteous by all the abominations that you have committed. 52 Bear your disgrace, you also, for you have brought about for your sisters a more favorable judgment; because of your sins in which you acted more abominably than they, they are more in the right than you. So be ashamed, you also, and bear your disgrace, for you have made your sisters appear righteous.

53 I will restore their fortunes, the fortunes of Sod'om and her daughters and the fortunes of Sa•mār'i•a and her daughters, and I will restore your own fortunes along with theirs, 54 in order that you may bear your disgrace and be ashamed of all that you have done, becoming a consolation to them. 55 As for your sisters, Sod'om and her daughters shall return to their former state, Sa•mār'i•a and her daughters shall return to their former state, and you and your daughters shall return to your former state. 56 Was not your sister Sod'om a byword in your mouth in the day of your pride, 57 before your wickedness was uncovered? Now you are a mockery to the daughters of Ar'am j and all her neighbors, and to the daughters of the Phi•lis'tines, those all around who despise you. 58 You must bear the penalty of your lewdness and your abominations, says the LORD.

An Everlasting Covenant

59 Yes, thus says the Lord GOD: I will deal with you as you have done, you who have despised the oath, breaking the covenant; 60 yet I will remember my covenant with you in the days of your youth, and I will establish with you an everlasting covenant. 61 Then you will remember your ways, and be ashamed when I k take your sisters, both your elder and your younger, and give them to you as daughters, but not on account of my l covenant with you. 62 I will establish my covenant with you, and you shall know that I am the LORD, 63 in order that you may remember and be confounded, and never open your mouth again because of your shame, when I forgive you all that you have done, says the Lord GOD.

The Two Eagles and the Vine

17 The word of the LORD came to me: 2 O mortal, propound a riddle, and speak an allegory to the house of Israel. 3 Say: Thus says the Lord GOD:

A great eagle, with great wings and long pinions,
   rich in plumage of many colors,
   came to the Lebanon.
He took the top of the cedar,
4   broke off its topmost shoot;
he carried it to a land of trade,
   set it in a city of merchants.
5 Then he took a seed from the land,
   placed it in fertile soil;
a plant m by abundant waters,
   he set it like a willow twig.
6 It sprouted and became a vine
   spreading out, but low;
its branches turned toward him,
   its roots remained where it stood.
So it became a vine;
   it brought forth branches,
   put forth foliage.

7 There was another great eagle,
   with great wings and much plumage.
And see! This vine stretched out
   its roots toward him;
it shot out its branches toward him,
   so that he might water it.
From the bed where it was planted
8   it was transplanted
to good soil by abundant waters,
   so that it might produce branches
   and bear fruit
   and become a noble vine.
9 Say: Thus says the Lord GOD:
Will it prosper?
Will he not pull up its roots,
   cause its fruit to rot m and wither,
   its fresh sprouting leaves to fade?
No strong arm or mighty army will be needed
   to pull it from its roots.

---

j Another reading is *Edom* k Syr: Heb *you* l Heb lacks *my*
m Meaning of Heb uncertain

10 When it is transplanted, will it thrive?
When the east wind strikes it,
will it not utterly wither,
wither on the bed where it grew?

11 Then the word of the LORD came to me:
12 Say now to the rebellious house: Do you not know what these things mean? Tell them: The king of Babylon came to Jerusalem, took its king and its officials, and brought them back with him to Babylon. 13 He took one of the royal offspring and made a covenant with him, putting him under oath (he had taken away the chief men of the land), 14 so that the kingdom might be humble and not lift itself up, and that by keeping his covenant it might stand. 15 But he rebelled against him by sending ambassadors to Egypt, in order that they might give him horses and a large army. Will he succeed? Can one escape who does such things? Can he break the covenant and yet escape? 16 As I live, says the Lord GOD, surely in the place where the king resides who made him king, whose oath he despised, and whose covenant with him he broke—in Babylon he shall die. 17 Pharaoh with his mighty army and great company will not help him in war, when ramps are cast up and siege walls built to cut off many lives. 18 Because he despised the oath and broke the covenant, because he gave his hand and yet did all these things, he shall not escape. 19 Therefore thus says the Lord GOD: As I live, I will surely return upon his head my oath that he despised, and my covenant that he broke. 20 I will spread my net over him, and he shall be caught in my snare; I will bring him to Babylon and enter into judgment with him there for the treason he has committed against me. 21 All the pick*n* of his troops shall fall by the sword, and the survivors shall be scattered to every wind; and you shall know that I, the LORD, have spoken.

Israel Exalted at Last
(Cp Ezek 31.1–9)

22 Thus says the Lord GOD:
I myself will take a sprig
from the lofty top of a cedar;
I will set it out.
I will break off a tender one
from the topmost of its young twigs;
I myself will plant it
on a high and lofty mountain.
23 On the mountain height of Israel
I will plant it,
in order that it may produce boughs and bear
fruit,
and become a noble cedar.
Under it every kind of bird will live;
in the shade of its branches will nest
winged creatures of every kind.
24 All the trees of the field shall know

that I am the LORD.
I bring low the high tree,
I make high the low tree;
I dry up the green tree
and make the dry tree flourish.
I the LORD have spoken;
I will accomplish it.

Individual Retribution

18 The word of the LORD came to me: 2 What do you mean by repeating this proverb concerning the land of Israel, "The parents have eaten sour grapes, and the children's teeth are set on edge"? 3 As I live, says the Lord GOD, this proverb shall no more be used by you in Israel. 4 Know that all lives are mine; the life of the parent as well as the life of the child is mine: it is only the person who sins that shall die.

5 If a man is righteous and does what is lawful and right— 6 if he does not eat upon the mountains or lift up his eyes to the idols of the house of Israel, does not defile his neighbor's wife or approach a woman during her menstrual period, 7 does not oppress anyone, but restores to the debtor his pledge, commits no robbery, gives his bread to the hungry and covers the naked with a garment, 8 does not take advance or accrued interest, withholds his hand from iniquity, executes true justice between contending parties, 9 follows my statutes, and is careful to observe my ordinances, acting faithfully—such a one is righteous; he shall surely live, says the Lord GOD.

10 If he has a son who is violent, a shedder of blood, 11 who does any of these things (though his father*o* does none of them), who eats upon the mountains, defiles his neighbor's wife, 12 oppresses the poor and needy, commits robbery, does not restore the pledge, lifts up his eyes to the idols, commits abomination, 13 takes advance or accrued interest; shall he then live? He shall not. He has done all these abominable things; he shall surely die; his blood shall be upon himself.

14 But if this man has a son who sees all the sins that his father has done, considers, and does not do likewise, 15 who does not eat upon the mountains or lift up his eyes to the idols of the house of Israel, does not defile his neighbor's wife, 16 does not wrong anyone, exacts no pledge, commits no robbery, but gives his bread to the hungry and covers the naked with a garment, 17 withholds his hand from iniquity,*p* takes no advance or accrued interest, observes my ordinances, and follows my statutes; he shall not die for his father's iniquity; he shall surely live. 18 As for his father, because he practiced extortion, robbed his brother, and did

EZEK

---

n Another reading is *fugitives*   *o* Heb *he*   *p* Gk: Heb *the poor*

INDIVIDUALS ARE RESPONSIBLE FOR THEIR BEHAVIOR!

Ezekiel, chapter 18, begins with a popular proverb from Ezekiel's time that implies that children are destined to bear the burden of their parents' actions. Ezekiel goes on to explain how this is not so. He emphasizes individual responsibility for our actions. He discourages fatalistic beliefs that we will somehow suffer for the sins of our ancestors (verse 20) and that parents are responsible for the sins of their children. Ezekiel calls the people of his time—and us—to overcome immature attitudes that blame God or others for our personal faults and sins.
- **In what areas do you need to assume responsibility for your actions?**
- **Pray for God's help in abandoning immature attitudes that blame others and prevent you from assuming personal responsibility for your actions.**

▶ **Ezek 18.1–32**

what is not good among his people, he dies for his iniquity.

19 Yet you say, "Why should not the son suffer for the iniquity of the father?" When the son has done what is lawful and right, and has been careful to observe all my statutes, he shall surely live. 20 The person who sins shall die. A child shall not suffer for the iniquity of a parent, nor a parent suffer for the iniquity of a child; the righteousness of the righteous shall be his own, and the wickedness of the wicked shall be his own.

21 But if the wicked turn away from all their sins that they have committed and keep all my statutes and do what is lawful and right, they shall surely live; they shall not die. 22 None of the transgressions that they have committed shall be remembered against them; for the righteousness that they have done they shall live. 23 Have I any pleasure in the death of the wicked, says the Lord GOD, and not rather that they should turn from their ways and live? 24 But when the righteous turn away from their righteousness and commit iniquity and do the same abominable things that the wicked do, shall they live? None of the righteous deeds that they have done shall be remembered; for the treachery of which they are guilty and the sin they have committed, they shall die.

25 Yet you say, "The way of the Lord is unfair." Hear now, O house of Israel: Is my way unfair? Is it not your ways that are unfair? 26 When the righteous turn away from their righteousness and commit iniquity, they shall die for it; for the iniquity that they have committed they shall die. 27 Again,

when the wicked turn away from the wickedness they have committed and do what is lawful and right, they shall save their life. 28 Because they considered and turned away from all the transgressions that they had committed, they shall surely live; they shall not die. 29 Yet the house of Israel says, "The way of the Lord is unfair." O house of Israel, are my ways unfair? Is it not your ways that are unfair?

30 Therefore I will judge you, O house of Israel, all of you according to your ways, says the Lord GOD. Repent and turn from all your transgressions; otherwise iniquity will be your ruin.*q* 31 Cast away from you all the transgressions that you have committed against me, and get yourselves a new heart and a new spirit! Why will you die, O house of Israel? 32 For I have no pleasure in the death of anyone, says the Lord GOD. Turn, then, and live.

Israel Degraded

19 As for you, raise up a lamentation for the princes of Israel, 2 and say:
What a lioness was your mother
    among lions!
She lay down among young lions,
    rearing her cubs.
3 She raised up one of her cubs;
    he became a young lion,
and he learned to catch prey;
    he devoured humans.
4 The nations sounded an alarm against him;

---

q Or so that they shall not be a stumbling block of iniquity to you

EZEK

he was caught in their pit;
   and they brought him with hooks
      to the land of Egypt.
5 When she saw that she was thwarted,
     that her hope was lost,
she took another of her cubs
    and made him a young lion.
6 He prowled among the lions;
    he became a young lion,
and he learned to catch prey;
    he devoured people.
7 And he ravaged their strongholds,[r]
    and laid waste their towns;
the land was appalled, and all in it,
    at the sound of his roaring.
8 The nations set upon him
   from the provinces all around;
they spread their net over him;
    he was caught in their pit.
9 With hooks they put him in a cage,
   and brought him to the king of Babylon;
    they brought him into custody,
so that his voice should be heard no more
    on the mountains of Israel.
10 Your mother was like a vine in a vineyard[s]
    transplanted by the water,
fruitful and full of branches
    from abundant water.
11 Its strongest stem became
    a ruler's scepter;[t]
it towered aloft
    among the thick boughs;
it stood out in its height
    with its mass of branches.
12 But it was plucked up in fury,
    cast down to the ground;
the east wind dried it up;
    its fruit was stripped off,
its strong stem was withered;
    the fire consumed it.
13 Now it is transplanted into the wilderness,
    into a dry and thirsty land.
14 And fire has gone out from its stem,
   has consumed its branches and fruit,
so that there remains in it no strong stem,
    no scepter for ruling.

This is a lamentation, and it is used as a lamentation.

Israel's Continuing Rebellion

20 In the seventh year, in the fifth month, on the tenth day of the month, certain elders of Israel came to consult the LORD, and sat down before me. 2 And the word of the LORD came to me: 3 Mortal, speak to the elders of Israel, and say to them: Thus says the Lord GOD: Why are you coming? To consult me? As I live, says the Lord GOD, I will not be consulted by you. 4 Will you judge them, mortal, will you judge them? Then let them know the abominations of their ancestors, 5 and say to them: Thus says the Lord GOD: On the day when I chose Israel, I swore to the offspring of the house of Jacob—making myself known to them in the land of Egypt—I swore to them, saying, I am the LORD your God. 6 On that day I swore to them that I would bring them out of the land of Egypt into a land that I had searched out for them, a land flowing with milk and honey, the most glorious of all lands. 7 And I said to them, Cast away the detestable things your eyes feast on, every one of you, and do not defile yourselves with the idols of Egypt; I am the LORD your God. 8 But they rebelled against me and would not listen to me; not one of them cast away the detestable things their eyes feasted on, nor did they forsake the idols of Egypt.

Then I thought I would pour out my wrath upon them and spend my anger against them in the midst of the land of Egypt. 9 But I acted for the sake of my name, that it should not be profaned in the sight of the nations among whom they lived, in whose sight I made myself known to them in bringing them out of the land of Egypt. 10 So I led them out of the land of Egypt and brought them into the wilderness. 11 I gave them my statutes and showed them my ordinances, by whose observance everyone shall live. 12 Moreover I gave them my sabbaths, as a sign between me and them, so that they might know that I the LORD sanctify them. 13 But the house of Israel rebelled against me in the wilderness; they did not observe my statutes but rejected my ordinances, by whose observance everyone shall live; and my sabbaths they greatly profaned.

Then I thought I would pour out my wrath upon them in the wilderness, to make an end of them. 14 But I acted for the sake of my name, so that it should not be profaned in the sight of the nations, in whose sight I had brought them out. 15 Moreover I swore to them in the wilderness that I would not bring them into the land that I had given them, a land flowing with milk and honey, the most glorious of all lands, 16 because they rejected my ordinances and did not observe my statutes, and profaned my sabbaths; for their heart went after their idols. 17 Nevertheless my eye spared them, and I did not destroy them or make an end of them in the wilderness.

18 I said to their children in the wilderness, Do not follow the statutes of your parents, nor observe their ordinances, nor defile yourselves with their

---

r Heb *his widows*   s Cn: Heb *in your blood*   t Heb *Its strongest stems became rulers' scepters* idols. 19 I the LORD am your God; follow my statutes, and be careful to observe my ordinances, 20 and hallow my sabbaths that they may be a sign between me and you, so that you may know that I the LORD am your God. 21 But the children rebelled against me; they did not follow my statutes, and were not careful to observe my ordinances, by whose observance everyone shall live; they profaned my sabbaths.

Then I thought I would pour out my wrath upon them and spend my anger against them in the wilderness. 22 But I withheld my hand, and acted for the sake of my name, so that it should not be profaned in the sight of the nations, in whose sight I had brought them out. 23 Moreover I swore to them in the wilderness that I would scatter them among the nations and disperse them through the countries, 24 because they had not executed my ordinances, but had rejected my statutes and profaned my sabbaths, and their eyes were set on their ancestors' idols. 25 Moreover I gave them statutes that were not good and ordinances by which they could not live. 26 I defiled them through their very gifts, in their offering up all their firstborn, in order that I might horrify them, so that they might know that I am the LORD.

27 Therefore, mortal, speak to the house of Israel and say to them, Thus says the Lord GOD: In this again your ancestors blasphemed me, by dealing treacherously with me. 28 For when I had brought them into the land that I swore to give them, then wherever they saw any high hill or any leafy tree, there they offered their sacrifices and presented the provocation of their offering; there they sent up their pleasing odors, and there they poured out their drink offerings. 29 (I said to them, What is the high place to which you go? So it is called Bā′mahᵘ to this day.) 30 Therefore say to the house of Israel, Thus says the Lord GOD: Will you defile yourselves after the manner of your ancestors and go astray after their detestable things? 31 When you offer your gifts and make your children pass through the fire, you defile yourselves with all your idols to this day. And shall I be consulted by you, O house of Israel? As I live, says the Lord GOD, I will not be consulted by you.

32 What is in your mind shall never happen— the thought, "Let us be like the nations, like the tribes of the countries, and worship wood and stone."

God Will Restore Israel

33 As I live, says the Lord GOD, surely with a mighty hand and an outstretched arm, and with wrath poured out, I will be king over you. 34 I will bring you out from the peoples and gather you out of the countries where you are scattered, with a mighty hand and an outstretched arm, and with wrath poured out; 35 and I will bring you into the wilderness of the peoples, and there I will enter into judgment with you face to face. 36 As I entered into judgment with your ancestors in the wilderness of the land of Egypt, so I will enter into judgment with you, says the Lord GOD. 37 I will make you pass under the staff, and will bring you within the bond of the covenant. 38 I will purge out the rebels among you, and those who transgress against me; I will bring them out of the land where they reside as aliens, but they shall not enter the land of Israel. Then you shall know that I am the LORD.

39 As for you, O house of Israel, thus says the Lord GOD: Go serve your idols, every one of you now and hereafter, if you will not listen to me; but my holy name you shall no more profane with your gifts and your idols.

40 For on my holy mountain, the mountain height of Israel, says the Lord GOD, there all the house of Israel, all of them, shall serve me in the land; there I will accept them, and there I will require your contributions and the choicest of your gifts, with all your sacred things. 41 As a pleasing odor I will accept you, when I bring you out from the peoples, and gather you out of the countries where you have been scattered; and I will manifest my holiness among you in the sight of the nations. 42 You shall know that I am the LORD, when I bring you into the land of Israel, the country that I swore to give to your ancestors. 43 There you shall remember your ways and all the deeds by which you have polluted yourselves; and you shall loathe yourselves for all the evils that you have committed. 44 And you shall know that I am the LORD, when I deal with you for my name's sake, not according to your evil ways, or corrupt deeds, O house of Israel, says the Lord GOD.

A Prophecy against the Negeb

45ᵛ The word of the LORD came to me: 46 Mortal, set your face toward the south, preach against the south, and prophesy against the forest land in the Neg′eb; 47 say to the forest of the Neg′eb, Hear the word of the LORD: Thus says the Lord GOD, I will kindle a fire in you, and it shall devour every green tree in you and every dry tree; the blazing flame shall not be quenched, and all faces from south to north shall be scorched by it. 48 All flesh shall see that I the LORD have kindled it; it shall not be quenched. 49 Then I said, "Ah Lord GOD! they are saying of me, 'Is he not a maker of allegories?'"

ᵘ That is *High Place*   ᵛ Ch 21.1 in Heb

The Drawn Sword of God

21 *w* The word of the LORD came to me: ² Mortal, set your face toward Jerusalem and preach against the sanctuaries; prophesy against the land of Israel ³ and say to the land of Israel, Thus says the LORD: I am coming against you, and will draw my sword out of its sheath, and will cut off from you both righteous and wicked. ⁴ Because I will cut off from you both righteous and wicked, therefore my sword shall go out of its sheath against all flesh from south to north; ⁵ and all flesh shall know that I the LORD have drawn my sword out of its sheath; it shall not be sheathed again. ⁶ Moan therefore, mortal; moan with breaking heart and bitter grief before their eyes. ⁷ And when they say to you, "Why do you moan?" you shall say, "Because of the news that has come. Every heart will melt and all hands will be feeble, every spirit will faint and all knees will turn to water. See, it comes and it will be fulfilled," says the Lord GOD.

8 And the word of the LORD came to me: ⁹ Mortal, prophesy and say: Thus says the Lord; Say:

A sword, a sword is sharpened,
    it is also polished;
¹⁰ it is sharpened for slaughter,
    honed to flash like lightning!
How can we make merry?
    You have despised the rod,
    and all discipline.ˣ
¹¹ The sword ʸ is given to be polished,
    to be grasped in the hand;
it is sharpened, the sword is polished,
    to be placed in the slayer's hand.
¹² Cry and wail, O mortal,
    for it is against my people;
it is against all Israel's princes;
    they are thrown to the sword,
    together with my people.
    Ah! Strike the thigh!
¹³ For consider: What! If you despise the rod, will it not happen?ˣ says the Lord GOD.
¹⁴ And you, mortal, prophesy;
    strike hand to hand.
Let the sword fall twice, thrice;
    it is a sword for killing.
A sword for great slaughter—
    it surrounds them;
¹⁵ therefore hearts melt
    and many stumble.
At all their gates I have set
    the pointˣ of the sword.
Ah! It is made for flashing,
    it is polishedᶻ for slaughter.
¹⁶ Attack to the right!
    Engage to the left!
    —wherever your edge is directed.
¹⁷ I too will strike hand to hand,

I will satisfy my fury;
    I the LORD have spoken.

18 The word of the LORD came to me: ¹⁹ Mortal, mark out two roads for the sword of the king of Babylon to come; both of them shall issue from the same land. And make a signpost, make it for a fork in the road leading to a city; ²⁰ mark out the road for the sword to come to Rab'bah of the Am'monites or to Judah and toᵃ Jerusalem the fortified. ²¹ For the king of Babylon stands at the parting of the way, at the fork in the two roads, to use divination; he shakes the arrows, he consults the teraphim,ᵇ he inspects the liver. ²² Into his right hand comes the lot for Jerusalem, to set battering rams, to call out for slaughter, for raising the battle cry, to set battering rams against the gates, to cast up ramps, to build siege towers. ²³ But to them it will seem like a false divination; they have sworn solemn oaths; but he brings their guilt to remembrance, bringing about their capture.

24 Therefore thus says the Lord GOD: Because you have brought your guilt to remembrance, in that your transgressions are uncovered, so that in all your deeds your sins appear—because you have come to remembrance, you shall be taken in hand.ᶜ
²⁵ As for you, vile, wicked prince of Israel,
    you whose day has come,
    the time of final punishment,
²⁶ thus says the Lord GOD:
Remove the turban, take off the crown;
    things shall not remain as they are.
Exalt that which is low,
    abase that which is high.
²⁷ A ruin, a ruin, a ruin—
    I will make it!
    (Such has never occurred.)
Until he comes whose right it is;
    to him I will give it.

28 As for you, mortal, prophesy, and say, Thus says the Lord GOD concerning the Am'mon•ites, and concerning their reproach; say:

A sword, a sword! Drawn for slaughter,
    polished to consume,ᵈ to flash like
       lightning.
²⁹ Offering false visions for you,
    divining lies for you,
they place you over the necks
    of the vile, wicked ones—
those whose day has come,
    the time of final punishment.
³⁰ Return it to its sheath!
In the place where you were created,
    in the land of your origin,

EZEK

---

w Ch 21.6 in Heb   *x* Meaning of Heb uncertain   *y* Heb *It*
z Tg: Heb *wrapped up*   *a* Gk Syr: Heb *Judah in*   *b* Or *the household gods*   *c* Or *be taken captive*   *d* Cn: Heb *to contain*

I will judge you.
31 I will pour out my indignation upon you,
   with the fire of my wrath
   I will blow upon you.
I will deliver you into brutish hands,
   those skillful to destroy.
32 You shall be fuel for the fire,
   your blood shall enter the earth;
you shall be remembered no more,
   for I the LORD have spoken.

The Bloody City

22 The word of the LORD came to me: 2 You, mortal, will you judge, will you judge the bloody city? Then declare to it all its abominable deeds. 3 You shall say, Thus says the Lord GOD: A city! Shedding blood within itself; its time has come; making its idols, defiling itself. 4 You have become guilty by the blood that you have shed, and defiled by the idols that you have made; you have brought your day near, the appointed time of your years has come. Therefore I have made you a disgrace before the nations, and a mockery to all the countries. 5 Those who are near and those who are far from you will mock you, you infamous one, full of tumult.

6 The princes of Israel in you, everyone according to his power, have been bent on shedding blood. 7 Father and mother are treated with contempt in you; the alien residing within you suffers extortion; the orphan and the widow are wronged in you. 8 You have despised my holy things, and profaned my sabbaths. 9 In you are those who slander to shed blood, those in you who eat upon the mountains, who commit lewdness in your midst. 10 In you they uncover their fathers' nakedness; in you they violate women in their menstrual periods. 11 One commits abomination with his neighbor's wife; another lewdly defiles his daughter-in-law; another in you defiles his sister, his father's daughter. 12 In you, they take bribes to shed blood; you take both advance interest and accrued interest, and make gain of your neighbors by extortion; and you have forgotten me, says the Lord GOD.

13 See, I strike my hands together at the dishonest gain you have made, and at the blood that has been shed within you. 14 Can your courage endure, or can your hands remain strong in the days when I shall deal with you? I the LORD have spoken, and I will do it. 15 I will scatter you among the nations and disperse you through the countries, and I will purge your filthiness out of you. 16 And I[e] shall be profaned through you in the sight of the nations; and you shall know that I am the LORD.

17 The word of the LORD came to me: 18 Mortal, the house of Israel has become dross to me; all of them, silver,[f] bronze, tin, iron, and lead. In the smelter they have become dross. 19 Therefore thus says the Lord GOD: Because you have all become dross, I will gather you into the midst of Jerusalem. 20 As one gathers silver, bronze, iron, lead, and tin into a smelter, to blow the fire upon them in order to melt them; so I will gather you in my anger and in my wrath, and I will put you in and melt you. 21 I will gather you and blow upon you with the fire of my wrath, and you shall be melted within it. 22 As silver is melted in a smelter, so you shall be melted in it; and you shall know that I the LORD have poured out my wrath upon you.

23 The word of the LORD came to me: 24 Mortal, say to it: You are a land that is not cleansed, not rained upon in the day of indignation. 25 Its princes[g] within it are like a roaring lion tearing the prey; they have devoured human lives; they have taken treasure and precious things; they have made many widows within it. 26 Its priests have done violence to my teaching and have profaned my holy things; they have made no distinction between the holy and the common, neither have they taught the difference between the unclean and the clean, and they have disregarded my sabbaths, so that I am profaned among them. 27 Its officials within it are like wolves tearing the prey, shedding blood, destroying lives to get dishonest gain. 28 Its prophets have smeared whitewash on their behalf, seeing false visions and divining lies for them, saying, "Thus says the Lord GOD," when the LORD has not spoken. 29 The people of the land have practiced extortion and committed robbery; they have oppressed the poor and needy, and have extorted from the alien without redress. 30 And I sought for anyone among them who would repair the wall and stand in the breach before me on behalf of the land, so that I would not destroy it; but I found no one. 31 Therefore I have poured out my indignation upon them; I have consumed them with the fire of my wrath; I have returned their conduct upon their heads, says the Lord GOD.

Oholah and Oholibah

23 The word of the LORD came to me: 2 Mortal, there were two women, the daughters of one mother; 3 they played the whore in Egypt; they played the whore in their youth; their breasts were caressed there, and their virgin bosoms were fondled. 4 Ō•hō'lah was the name of the elder and Ō•hol'i•bah the name of her sister. They became mine, and they bore sons and daughters. As for their names, Ō•hō'lah is Sa•mār'i•a, and Ō•hol'i•bah is Jerusalem.

---

e Gk Syr Vg: Heb *you*   f Transposed from the end of the verse; compare verse 20   g Gk: Heb *indignation*. 25A *conspiracy of its prophets*

5 Ō•hō′lah played the whore while she was mine; she lusted after her lovers the Assyrians, warriors[h] 6 clothed in blue, governors and commanders, all of them handsome young men, mounted horsemen. 7 She bestowed her favors upon them, the choicest men of Assyria all of them; and she defiled herself with all the idols of everyone for whom she lusted. 8 She did not give up her whorings that she had practiced since Egypt; for in her youth men had lain with her and fondled her virgin bosom and poured out their lust upon her. 9 Therefore I delivered her into the hands of her lovers, into the hands of the Assyrians, for whom she lusted. 10 These uncovered her nakedness; they seized her sons and her daughters; and they killed her with the sword. Judgment was executed upon her, and she became a byword among women.

11 Her sister Ō•hol′i•bah saw this, yet she was more corrupt than she in her lusting and in her whorings, which were worse than those of her sister. 12 She lusted after the Assyrians, governors and commanders, warriors[h] clothed in full armor, mounted horsemen, all of them handsome young men. 13 And I saw that she was defiled; they both took the same way. 14 But she carried her whorings further; she saw male figures carved on the wall, images of the Chal•dē′ans portrayed in vermilion, 15 with belts around their waists, with flowing turbans on their heads, all of them looking like officers—a picture of Babylonians whose native land was Chal•dē′a. 16 When she saw them she lusted after them, and sent messengers to them in Chal•dē′a. 17 And the Babylonians came to her into the bed of love, and they defiled her with their lust; and after she defiled herself with them, she turned from them in disgust. 18 When she carried on her whorings so openly and flaunted her nakedness, I turned in disgust from her, as I had turned from her sister. 19 Yet she increased her whorings, remembering the days of her youth, when she played the whore in the land of Egypt 20 and lusted after her paramours there, whose members were like those of donkeys, and whose emission was like that of stallions. 21 Thus you longed for the lewdness of your youth, when the Egyptians[i] fondled your bosom and caressed[j] your young breasts.

22 Therefore, O Ō•hol′i•bah, thus says the Lord GOD: I will rouse against you your lovers from whom you turned in disgust, and I will bring them against you from every side: 23 the Babylonians and all the Chal•dē′ans, Pē′kod and Shō′a and Kō′a, and all the Assyrians with them, handsome young men, governors and commanders all of them, officers and warriors,[k] all of them riding on horses. 24 They shall come against you from the north[l] with chariots and wagons and a host of peoples; they shall set themselves against you on every side with buckler, shield, and helmet, and I will commit the judgment to them, and they shall judge you according to their ordinances. 25 I will direct my indignation against you, in order that they may deal with you in fury. They shall cut off your nose and your ears, and your survivors shall fall by the sword. They shall seize your sons and your daughters, and your survivors

---

h Meaning of Heb uncertain   i Two Mss: MT *from Egypt*   j Cn: Heb *for the sake of*   k Compare verses 6 and 12: Heb *officers and called ones*   l Gk: Meaning of Heb uncertain

EZEK

Irresponsible Children

LIVE IT!

Raising children is a demanding job. In teaching their children about life, parents try to help them be responsible—to accept the consequences of their actions. For example, a parent might say: "You threw the ball and broke the window. The wind had nothing to do with it! Now, what are you going to do about it?"

Chapters 13–24 of Ezekiel contain prophecies, allegories, fables, and symbolic actions, all intended to encourage the people of Judah to take responsibility for their sinful actions. In a graphic allegory in chapter 23, the northern and southern kingdoms are compared to promiscuous daughters who will sleep with almost anyone who comes their way. God is using just about every possible means to say, "Take responsibility for your actions, my children, and live with the consequences!"

We are all like little children in that we are often tempted to ignore the consequences of our actions. For instance, we may think of cheating on homework as just a little wrong. But that wrong will catch up with us. It will lead to more cheating, in bigger things. By then, our "little" wrong could mean losing a job or destroying a relationship. If you want to please God, be honest in looking at the consequences of your actions and choose responsibly!

▶ Ezek 23.1–21

shall be devoured by fire. 26 They shall also strip you of your clothes and take away your fine jewels. 27 So I will put an end to your lewdness and your whoring brought from the land of Egypt; you shall not long for them, or remember Egypt any more. 28 For thus says the Lord GOD: I will deliver you into the hands of those whom you hate, into the hands of those from whom you turned in disgust; 29 and they shall deal with you in hatred, and take away all the fruit of your labor, and leave you naked and bare, and the nakedness of your whorings shall be exposed. Your lewdness and your whorings 30 have brought this upon you, because you played the whore with the nations, and polluted yourself with their idols. 31 You have gone the way of your sister; therefore I will give her cup into your hand. 32 Thus says the Lord GOD:

You shall drink your sister's cup,
    deep and wide;
you shall be scorned and derided,
    it holds so much.
33 You shall be filled with drunkenness and
        sorrow.
A cup of horror and desolation
    is the cup of your sister Sa•mār'i•a;
34 you shall drink it and drain it out,
    and gnaw its sherds,
    and tear out your breasts;
for I have spoken, says the Lord GOD. 35 Therefore thus says the Lord GOD: Because you have forgotten me and cast me behind your back, therefore bear the consequences of your lewdness and whorings.

36 The LORD said to me: Mortal, will you judge Ō•hō'lah and Ō•hol'i•bah? Then declare to them their abominable deeds. 37 For they have committed adultery, and blood is on their hands; with their idols they have committed adultery; and they have even offered up to them for food the children whom they had borne to me. 38 Moreover this they have done to me: they have defiled my sanctuary on the same day and profaned my sabbaths. 39 For when they had slaughtered their children for their idols, on the same day they came into my sanctuary to profane it. This is what they did in my house. 40 They even sent for men to come from far away, to whom a messenger was sent, and they came. For them you bathed yourself, painted your eyes, and decked yourself with ornaments; 41 you sat on a stately couch, with a table spread before it on which you had placed my incense and my oil. 42 The sound of a raucous multitude was around her, with many of the rabble brought in drunken from the wilderness; and they put bracelets on the arms[m] of the women, and beautiful crowns upon their heads.

43 Then I said, Ah, she is worn out with adulteries, but they carry on their sexual acts with her.

44 For they have gone in to her, as one goes in to a whore. Thus they went in to Ō•hō'lah and to Ō•hol'i•bah, wanton women. 45 But righteous judges shall declare them guilty of adultery and of bloodshed; because they are adulteresses and blood is on their hands.

46 For thus says the Lord GOD: Bring up an assembly against them, and make them an object of terror and of plunder. 47 The assembly shall stone them and with their swords they shall cut them down; they shall kill their sons and their daughters, and burn up their houses. 48 Thus will I put an end to lewdness in the land, so that all women may take warning and not commit lewdness as you have done. 49 They shall repay you for your lewdness, and you shall bear the penalty for your sinful idolatry; and you shall know that I am the Lord GOD.

The Boiling Pot
(Cp Jer 1.13–19)

24 In the ninth year, in the tenth month, on the tenth day of the month, the word of the LORD came to me: 2 Mortal, write down the name of this day, this very day. The king of Babylon has laid siege to Jerusalem this very day. 3 And utter an allegory to the rebellious house and say to them, Thus says the Lord GOD:

Set on the pot, set it on,
    pour in water also;
4 put in it the pieces,
    all the good pieces, the thigh and the
        shoulder;
    fill it with choice bones.
5 Take the choicest one of the flock,
    pile the logs[n] under it;
boil its pieces,[o]
    seethe[p] also its bones in it.

6 Therefore thus says the Lord GOD:
Woe to the bloody city,
    the pot whose rust is in it,
    whose rust has not gone out of it!
Empty it piece by piece,
    making no choice at all.[q]
7 For the blood she shed is inside it;
    she placed it on a bare rock;
she did not pour it out on the ground,
    to cover it with earth.
8 To rouse my wrath, to take vengeance,
    I have placed the blood she shed
    on a bare rock,
    so that it may not be covered.
9 Therefore thus says the Lord GOD:

---

m Heb *hands*   n Compare verse 10: Heb *the bones*   o Two Mss: Heb *its boilings*   p Cn: Heb *its bones seethe*   q Heb *piece, no lot has fallen on it*

Woe to the bloody city!
    I will even make the pile great.
10 Heap up the logs, kindle the fire;
    boil the meat well, mix in the spices,
    let the bones be burned.
11 Stand it empty upon the coals,
    so that it may become hot, its copper glow,
    its filth melt in it, its rust be consumed.
12 In vain I have wearied myself;r
    its thick rust does not depart.
    To the fire with its rust!s
13 Yet, when I cleansed you in your filthy
      lewdness,
    you did not become clean from your
      filth;
    you shall not again be cleansed
    until I have satisfied my fury upon you.
14 I the LORD have spoken; the time is coming, I will act. I will not refrain, I will not spare, I will not relent. According to your ways and your doings I will judge you, says the Lord GOD.

Ezekiel's Bereavement

15 The word of the LORD came to me: 16 Mortal, with one blow I am about to take away from you the delight of your eyes; yet you shall not mourn or weep, nor shall your tears run down. 17 Sigh, but not aloud; make no mourning for the dead. Bind on your turban, and put your sandals on your feet; do not cover your upper lip or eat the bread of mourners.t 18 So I spoke to the people in the morning, and at evening my wife died. And on the next morning I did as I was commanded.

19 Then the people said to me, "Will you not tell us what these things mean for us, that you are acting this way?" 20 Then I said to them: The word of the LORD came to me: 21 Say to the house of Israel, Thus says the Lord GOD: I will profane my sanctuary, the pride of your power, the delight of your eyes, and your heart's desire; and your sons and your daughters whom you left behind shall fall by the sword. 22 And you shall do as I have done; you shall not cover your upper lip or eat the bread of mourners.t 23 Your turbans shall be on your heads and your sandals on your feet; you shall not mourn or weep, but you shall pine away in your iniquities and groan to one another. 24 Thus E·zek'i·el shall be a sign to you; you shall do just as he has done. When this comes, then you shall know that I am the Lord GOD.

25 And you, mortal, on the day when I take from them their stronghold, their joy and glory, the delight of their eyes and their heart's affection, and alsou their sons and their daughters, 26 on that day, one who has escaped will come to you to report to you the news. 27 On that day your mouth shall be opened to the one who has escaped, and you shall speak and no longer be silent. So you shall be a sign to them; and they shall know that I am the LORD.

Proclamation against Ammon

25 The word of the LORD came to me: 2 Mortal, set your face toward the Am'mon•ites and prophesy against them. 3 Say to the Am'mon•ites, Hear the word of the Lord GOD: Thus says the Lord GOD, Because you said, "Aha!" over my sanctuary when it was profaned, and over the land of Israel when it was made desolate, and over the house of Judah when it went into exile; 4 therefore I am handing you over to the people of the east for a possession. They shall set their encampments among you and pitch their tents in your midst; they shall eat your fruit, and they shall drink your milk. 5 I will make Rab'bah a pasture for camels and Am'mon a fold for flocks. Then you shall know that I am the LORD. 6 For thus says the Lord GOD: Because you have clapped your hands and stamped your feet and rejoiced with all the malice within you against the land of Israel, 7 therefore I have stretched out my hand against you, and will hand you over as plunder to the nations. I will cut you off from the peoples and will make you perish out of the countries; I will destroy you. Then you shall know that I am the LORD.

Proclamation against Moab

8 Thus says the Lord GOD: Because Mō'abv said, The house of Judah is like all the other nations, 9 therefore I will lay open the flank of Mō'ab from the townsw on its frontier, the glory of the country, Beth-jesh'i·moth, Bā'al-mē'on, and Kir·i·a·thā'im. 10 I will give it along with Am'mon to the people of the east as a possession. Thus Am'mon shall be remembered no more among the nations, 11 and I will execute judgments upon Mō'ab. Then they shall know that I am the LORD.

Proclamation against Edom

12 Thus says the Lord GOD: Because Ē'dom acted revengefully against the house of Judah and has grievously offended in taking vengeance upon them, 13 therefore thus says the Lord GOD, I will stretch out my hand against Ē'dom, and cut off from it humans and animals, and I will make it desolate; from Tē'man even to Dē'dan they shall fall by the sword. 14 I will lay my vengeance upon Ē'dom by the hand of my people Israel; and they shall act in Ē'dom according to my anger and according to my wrath; and they shall know my vengeance, says the Lord GOD.

---

r Cn: Meaning of Heb uncertain   s Meaning of Heb uncertain   t Vg Tg: Heb *of men*   u Heb lacks *and also*   v Gk Old Latin: Heb *Moab and Seir*   w Heb *towns from its towns*

Proclamation against Philistia

15 Thus says the Lord GOD: Because with unending hostilities the Phi·lis'tines acted in vengeance, and with malice of heart took revenge in destruction; 16 therefore thus says the Lord GOD, I will stretch out my hand against the Phi·lis'tines, cut off the Cher'e·thites, and destroy the rest of the seacoast. 17 I will execute great vengeance on them with wrathful punishments. Then they shall know that I am the LORD, when I lay my vengeance on them.

Proclamation against Tyre

26 In the eleventh year, on the first day of the month, the word of the LORD came to me: 2 Mortal, because Tyre said concerning Jerusalem,

"Aha, broken is the gateway of the peoples;
　it has swung open to me;
I shall be replenished,
　now that it is wasted,"

3 therefore, thus says the Lord GOD:
See, I am against you, O Tyre!
　I will hurl many nations against you,
　as the sea hurls its waves.
4 They shall destroy the walls of Tyre
　and break down its towers.
I will scrape its soil from it
　and make it a bare rock.
5 It shall become, in the midst of the sea,
　a place for spreading nets.
I have spoken, says the Lord GOD.
　It shall become plunder for the nations,
6 　and its daughter-towns in the country
　shall be killed by the sword.
Then they shall know that I am the LORD.

7 For thus says the Lord GOD: I will bring against Tyre from the north King Ne·bu·chad·rez'zar of Babylon, king of kings, together with horses, chariots, cavalry, and a great and powerful army. 8 Your daughter-towns in the country
　he shall put to the sword.
He shall set up a siege wall against you,
　cast up a ramp against you,
　and raise a roof of shields against you.
9 He shall direct the shock of his battering rams
　　against your walls
　and break down your towers with his axes.
10 His horses shall be so many
　that their dust shall cover you.
At the noise of cavalry, wheels, and chariots
　your very walls shall shake,
when he enters your gates
　like those entering a breached city.
11 With the hoofs of his horses
　he shall trample all your streets.
He shall put your people to the sword,

and your strong pillars shall fall to the
　ground.
12 They will plunder your riches
　and loot your merchandise;
they shall break down your walls
　and destroy your fine houses.
Your stones and timber and soil
　they shall cast into the water.
13 I will silence the music of your songs;
　the sound of your lyres shall be heard no
　　more.
14 I will make you a bare rock;
　you shall be a place for spreading nets.
You shall never again be rebuilt,
　for I the LORD have spoken,
　says the Lord GOD.

15 Thus says the Lord GOD to Tyre: Shall not the coastlands shake at the sound of your fall, when the wounded groan, when slaughter goes on within you? 16 Then all the princes of the sea shall step down from their thrones; they shall remove their robes and strip off their embroidered garments. They shall clothe themselves with trembling, and shall sit on the ground; they shall tremble every moment, and be appalled at you. 17 And they shall raise a lamentation over you, and say to you:
How you have vanished[x] from the seas,
　O city renowned,
once mighty on the sea,
　you and your inhabitants,[y]
who imposed your[z] terror
　on all the mainland![a]
18 Now the coastlands tremble
　on the day of your fall;
the coastlands by the sea
　are dismayed at your passing.

19 For thus says the Lord GOD: When I make you a city laid waste, like cities that are not inhabited, when I bring up the deep over you, and the great waters cover you, 20 then I will thrust you down with those who descend into the Pit, to the people of long ago, and I will make you live in the world below, among primeval ruins, with those who go down to the Pit, so that you will not be inhabited or have a place[b] in the land of the living. 21 I will bring you to a dreadful end, and you shall be no more; though sought for, you will never be found again, says the Lord GOD.

Lamentation over Tyre

27 The word of the LORD came to me: 2 Now you, mortal, raise a lamentation over Tyre, 3 and say to Tyre, which sits at the en-

---

x Gk OL Aquila: Heb *have vanished, O inhabited one*,　y Heb *it and its inhabitants*　z Heb *their*　a Cn: Heb *its inhabitants*　b Gk: Heb *I will give beauty* trance to the sea, merchant of the peoples on many coastlands, Thus says the Lord GOD:

O Tȳre, you have said,
  "I am perfect in beauty."
4 Your borders are in the heart of the seas;
  your builders made perfect your beauty.
5 They made all your planks
  of fir trees from Sē'nir;
they took a cedar from Lebanon
  to make a mast for you.
6 From oaks of Bā'shan
  they made your oars;
they made your deck of pines*c*
  from the coasts of Cyprus,
  inlaid with ivory.
7 Of fine embroidered linen from Egypt
  was your sail,
  serving as your ensign;
blue and purple from the coasts of E•li'shah
  was your awning.
8 The inhabitants of Sī'don and Ar'vad
  were your rowers;
skilled men of Zē'mer*d* were within you,
  they were your pilots.
9 The elders of Gē'bal and its artisans were
    within you,
  caulking your seams;
all the ships of the sea with their mariners were
    within you,
  to barter for your wares.
10 Par'as*e* and Lud and Put
  were in your army,
  your mighty warriors;
they hung shield and helmet in you;
  they gave you splendor.
11 Men of Ar'vad and Hē'lech*f*
  were on your walls all around;
  men of Gā'mad were at your towers.
They hung their quivers all around your walls;
  they made perfect your beauty.

12 Tar'shish did business with you out of the abundance of your great wealth; silver, iron, tin, and lead they exchanged for your wares. 13 Jā'van, Tū'bal, and Mē'shech traded with you; they exchanged human beings and vessels of bronze for your merchandise. 14 Beth-tō•gar'mah exchanged for your wares horses, war horses, and mules. 15 The Rhō'di•ans*g* traded with you; many coastlands were your own special markets; they brought you in payment ivory tusks and ebony. 16 Ē'dom*h* did business with you because of your abundant goods; they exchanged for your wares turquoise, purple, embroidered work, fine linen, coral, and rubies. 17 Judah and the land of Israel traded with you; they exchanged for your merchandise wheat from Min'nith, millet,*i* honey, oil, and balm. 18 Damascus traded with you for your abundant

goods—because of your great wealth of every kind—wine of Hel'bon, and white wool. 19 Vē'dan and Jā'van from Ū'zal*i* entered into trade for your wares; wrought iron, cassia, and sweet cane were bartered for your merchandise. 20 Dē'dan traded with you in saddlecloths for riding. 21 Arabia and all the princes of Kē'dar were your favored dealers in lambs, rams, and goats; in these they did business with you. 22 The merchants of Shē'ba and Rā'a•mah traded with you; they exchanged for your wares the best of all kinds of spices, and all precious stones, and gold. 23 Har'an, Can'neh, Eden, the merchants of Shē'ba, As'shur, and Chil'mad traded with you. 24 These traded with you in choice garments, in clothes of blue and embroidered work, and in carpets of colored material, bound with cords and made secure; in these they traded with you.*j* 25 The ships of Tar'shish traveled for you in your trade.

So you were filled and heavily laden
  in the heart of the seas.
26 Your rowers have brought you
  into the high seas.
The east wind has wrecked you
  in the heart of the seas.
27 Your riches, your wares, your merchandise,
  your mariners and your pilots,
your caulkers, your dealers in merchandise,
  and all your warriors within you,
with all the company
  that is with you,
sink into the heart of the seas
  on the day of your ruin.
28 At the sound of the cry of your pilots
  the countryside shakes,
29 and down from their ships
  come all that handle the oar.
The mariners and all the pilots of the sea
  stand on the shore
30 and wail aloud over you,
  and cry bitterly.
They throw dust on their heads
  and wallow in ashes;
31 they make themselves bald for you,
  and put on sackcloth,
and they weep over you in bitterness of soul,
  with bitter mourning.
32 In their wailing they raise a lamentation for
    you,
  and lament over you:
"Who was ever destroyed*k* like Tȳre
  in the midst of the sea?

---

c Or *boxwood*   *d* Cn Compare Gen 10.18: Heb *your skilled men, O Tyre*   *e* Or *Persia*   *f* Or *and your army*   *g* Gk: Heb *The Dedanites*   *h* Another reading is *Aram*   *i* Meaning of Heb uncertain   *j* Cn: Heb *in your market*   *k* Tg Vg: Heb *like silence*

33 When your wares came from the seas,
    you satisfied many peoples;
with your abundant wealth and merchandise
    you enriched the kings of the earth.
34 Now you are wrecked by the seas,
    in the depths of the waters;
your merchandise and all your crew
    have sunk with you.

27.34

35 All the inhabitants of the coastlands
    are appalled at you;
and their kings are horribly afraid,
    their faces are convulsed.
36 The merchants among the peoples hiss at you;
    you have come to a dreadful end
    and shall be no more forever."

Proclamation against the King of Tyre

28 The word of the LORD came to me:
2 Mortal, say to the prince of Tyre, Thus
says the Lord GOD:
Because your heart is proud
    and you have said, "I am a god;
I sit in the seat of the gods,
    in the heart of the seas,"
yet you are but a mortal, and no god,
    though you compare your mind
    with the mind of a god.
3 You are indeed wiser than Daniel;*l*
    no secret is hidden from you;
4 by your wisdom and your understanding
    you have amassed wealth for yourself,
and have gathered gold and silver
    into your treasuries.
5 By your great wisdom in trade
    you have increased your wealth,
    and your heart has become proud in your
        wealth.

6 Therefore thus says the Lord GOD:
Because you compare your mind
    with the mind of a god,
7 therefore, I will bring strangers against you,
    the most terrible of the nations;
they shall draw their swords against the beauty
        of your wisdom
    and defile your splendor.
8 They shall thrust you down to the Pit,
    and you shall die a violent death
    in the heart of the seas.
9 Will you still say, "I am a god,"
    in the presence of those who kill you,
though you are but a mortal, and no god,
    in the hands of those who wound you?
10 You shall die the death of the uncircumcised
    by the hand of foreigners;
    for I have spoken, says the Lord GOD.

Lamentation over the King of Tyre

11 Moreover the word of the LORD came to me:
12 Mortal, raise a lamentation over the king of Tyre,
and say to him, Thus says the Lord GOD:
You were the signet of perfection,*m*
    full of wisdom and perfect in beauty.
13 You were in Eden, the garden of God;
    every precious stone was your covering,
carnelian, chrysolite, and moonstone,
    beryl, onyx, and jasper,
sapphire,*n* turquoise, and emerald;
    and worked in gold were your settings
    and your engravings.*m*
On the day that you were created
    they were prepared.
14 With an anointed cherub as guardian I placed
        you;*m*
    you were on the holy mountain of God;
    you walked among the stones of fire.
15 You were blameless in your ways
    from the day that you were created,
    until iniquity was found in you.
16 In the abundance of your trade
    you were filled with violence, and you
        sinned;
so I cast you as a profane thing from the
        mountain of God,
    and the guardian cherub drove you out
    from among the stones of fire.
17 Your heart was proud because of your beauty;
    you corrupted your wisdom for the sake of
        your splendor.
I cast you to the ground;
    I exposed you before kings,
    to feast their eyes on you.

l Or, as otherwise read, *Danel*   *m* Meaning of Heb
uncertain   *n* Or *lapis lazuli*

EZEK

18 By the multitude of your iniquities,
   in the unrighteousness of your trade,
   you profaned your sanctuaries.
So I brought out fire from within you;
   it consumed you,
and I turned you to ashes on the earth
   in the sight of all who saw you.
19 All who know you among the peoples
   are appalled at you;
you have come to a dreadful end
   and shall be no more forever.

Proclamation against Sidon

20 The word of the LORD came to me: 21 Mortal, set your face toward Si′don, and prophesy against it, 22 and say, Thus says the Lord GOD:
   I am against you, O Si′don,
   and I will gain glory in your midst.
They shall know that I am the LORD
   when I execute judgments in it,
   and manifest my holiness in it;
23 for I will send pestilence into it,
   and bloodshed into its streets;
and the dead shall fall in its midst,
   by the sword that is against it on every side.
And they shall know that I am the LORD.

24 The house of Israel shall no longer find a pricking brier or a piercing thorn among all their neighbors who have treated them with contempt. And they shall know that I am the Lord GOD.

Future Blessing for Israel

25 Thus says the Lord GOD: When I gather the house of Israel from the peoples among whom they are scattered, and manifest my holiness in them in the sight of the nations, then they shall settle on their own soil that I gave to my servant Jacob. 26 They shall live in safety in it, and shall build houses and plant vineyards. They shall live in safety, when I execute judgments upon all their neighbors who have treated them with contempt. And they shall know that I am the LORD their God.

Proclamation against Egypt

29 In the tenth year, in the tenth month, on the twelfth day of the month, the word of the LORD came to me: 2 Mortal, set your face against Pharaoh king of Egypt, and prophesy against him and against all Egypt; 3 speak, and say, Thus says the Lord GOD:
   I am against you,
      Pharaoh king of Egypt,
   the great dragon sprawling
      in the midst of its channels,
   saying, "My Nile is my own;
      I made it for myself."
4 I will put hooks in your jaws,

and make the fish of your channels stick to
   your scales.
I will draw you up from your channels,
   with all the fish of your channels
   sticking to your scales.
5 I will fling you into the wilderness,
   you and all the fish of your channels;
you shall fall in the open field,
   and not be gathered and buried.
To the animals of the earth and to the birds of
   the air
   I have given you as food.
6 Then all the inhabitants of Egypt shall know
   that I am the LORD
because youᵒ were a staff of reed
   to the house of Israel;
7 when they grasped you with the hand, you broke,
   and tore all their shoulders;
and when they leaned on you, you broke,
   and made all their legs unsteady.ᵖ

8 Therefore, thus says the Lord GOD: I will bring a sword upon you, and will cut off from you human being and animal; 9 and the land of Egypt shall be a desolation and a waste. Then they shall know that I am the LORD.

Because you�q said, "The Nile is mine, and I made it," 10 therefore, I am against you, and against your channels, and I will make the land of Egypt an utter waste and desolation, from Mig′dōl to Sȳ•e′nē, as far as the border of Ethiopia.ʳ 11 No human foot shall pass through it, and no animal foot shall pass through it; it shall be uninhabited forty years. 12 I will make the land of Egypt a desolation among desolated countries; and her cities shall be a desolation forty years among cities that are laid waste. I will scatter the Egyptians among the nations, and disperse them among the countries.

13 Further, thus says the Lord GOD: At the end of forty years I will gather the Egyptians from the peoples among whom they were scattered; 14 and I will restore the fortunes of Egypt, and bring them back to the land of Path′ros, the land of their origin; and there they shall be a lowly kingdom. 15 It shall be the most lowly of the kingdoms, and never again exalt itself above the nations; and I will make them so small that they will never again rule over the nations. 16 The Egyptiansˢ shall never again be the reliance of the house of Israel; they will recall their iniquity, when they turned to them for aid. Then they shall know that I am the Lord GOD.

Babylonia Will Plunder Egypt

17 In the twenty-seventh year, in the first month, on the first day of the month, the word of

---

ᵒ Gk Syr Vg: Heb *they*   ᵖ Syr: Heb *stand*   �q Gk Syr Vg: Heb *he*   ʳ Or *Nubia*; Heb *Cush*   ˢ Heb *It* the LORD came to me: 18 Mortal, King Ne•bu•chad-rez′zar of Babylon made his army labor hard against Tȳre; every head was made bald and every shoulder was rubbed bare; yet neither he nor his army got anything from Tȳre to pay for the labor that he had expended against it. 19 Therefore thus says the Lord GOD: I will give the land of Egypt to King Ne•bu•chad•rez′zar of Babylon; and he shall carry off its wealth and despoil it and plunder it; and it shall be the wages for his army. 20 I have given him the land of Egypt as his payment for which he labored, because they worked for me, says the Lord GOD.

21 On that day I will cause a horn to sprout up for the house of Israel, and I will open your lips among them. Then they shall know that I am the LORD.

Lamentation for Egypt

30 The word of the LORD came to me: 2 Mortal, prophesy, and say, Thus says the Lord GOD:
Wail, "Alas for the day!"
3   For a day is near,
     the day of the LORD is near;
it will be a day of clouds,
     a time of doom[t] for the nations.
4 A sword shall come upon Egypt,
     and anguish shall be in Ethiopia,[u]
when the slain fall in Egypt,
     and its wealth is carried away,
     and its foundations are torn down.
5 Ethiopia,[u] and Put, and Lud, and all Arabia, and Lib′ya,[v] and the people of the allied land[w] shall fall with them by the sword.

6   Thus says the LORD:
Those who support Egypt shall fall,
     and its proud might shall come down;
from Mig′dōl to Sȳ•ē′nē
     they shall fall within it by the sword,
says the Lord GOD.
7 They shall be desolated among other desolated
     countries,
     and their cities shall lie among cities laid
       waste.
8 Then they shall know that I am the
     LORD,
     when I have set fire to Egypt,
     and all who help it are broken.
9 On that day, messengers shall go out from me in ships to terrify the unsuspecting Ethiopians;[x] and anguish shall come upon them on the day of Egypt's doom;[y] for it is coming!

10 Thus says the Lord GOD:
I will put an end to the hordes of Egypt,

by the hand of King Ne•bu•chad•rez′zar of Babylon.
11 He and his people with him, the most terrible
     of the nations,
     shall be brought in to destroy the land;
and they shall draw their swords against Egypt,
     and fill the land with the slain.
12 I will dry up the channels,
     and will sell the land into the hand of
       evildoers;
I will bring desolation upon the land and
     everything in it
     by the hand of foreigners;
I the LORD have spoken.

13 Thus says the Lord GOD:
I will destroy the idols
     and put an end to the images in Memphis;
there shall no longer be a prince in the land of
     Egypt;
     so I will put fear in the land of Egypt.
14 I will make Path′ros a desolation,
     and will set fire to Zō′an,
     and will execute acts of judgment on
       Thēbes.
15 I will pour my wrath upon Pe•lū′si•um,
     the stronghold of Egypt,
     and cut off the hordes of Thēbes.
16 I will set fire to Egypt;
     Pe•lū′si•um shall be in great agony;
Thēbes shall be breached,
     and Memphis face adversaries by day.
17 The young men of On and of Pī•bē′seth shall
     fall by the sword;
     and the cities themselves[z] shall go into
       captivity.
18 At Te•haph′ne•hēs the day shall be dark,
     when I break there the dominion of Egypt,
and its proud might shall come to an end;
     the city[a] shall be covered by a cloud,
     and its daughter-towns shall go into
       captivity.
19 Thus I will execute acts of judgment on Egypt.
     Then they shall know that I am the LORD.

Proclamation against Pharaoh

20 In the eleventh year, in the first month, on the seventh day of the month, the word of the LORD came to me: 21 Mortal, I have broken the arm of Pharaoh king of Egypt; it has not been bound up for healing or wrapped with a bandage, so that it may become strong to wield the sword. 22 There-

---

t Heb lacks *of doom* u Or *Nubia*; Heb *Cush* v Compare Gk Syr Vg: Heb *Cub* w Meaning of Heb uncertain x Or *Nubians*; Heb *Cush* y Heb *the day of Egypt* z Heb *and they* a Heb *she* fore thus says the Lord GOD: I am against Pharaoh king of Egypt, and will break his arms, both the strong arm and the one that was broken; and I will make the sword fall from his hand. 23 I will scatter the Egyptians among the nations, and disperse them throughout the lands. 24 I will strengthen the arms of the king of Babylon, and put my sword in his hand; but I will break the arms of Pharaoh, and he will groan before him with the groans of one mortally wounded. 25 I will strengthen the arms of the king of Babylon, but the arms of Pharaoh shall fall. And they shall know that I am the LORD, when I put my sword into the hand of the king of Babylon. He shall stretch it out against the land of Egypt, 26 and I will scatter the Egyptians among the nations and disperse them throughout the countries. Then they shall know that I am the LORD.

The Lofty Cedar
(Cp Ezek 17.22–24)

31 In the eleventh year, in the third month, on the first day of the month, the word of the LORD came to me: 2 Mortal, say to Pharaoh king of Egypt and to his hordes:

Whom are you like in your greatness?
3   Consider Assyria, a cedar of Lebanon,
  with fair branches and forest shade,
        and of great height,
          its top among the clouds.*b*
4 The waters nourished it,
        the deep made it grow tall,
  making its rivers flow*c*
        around the place it was planted,
  sending forth its streams
        to all the trees of the field.
5 So it towered high
        above all the trees of the field;
  its boughs grew large
        and its branches long,
  from abundant water in its shoots.
6 All the birds of the air
        made their nests in its boughs;
  under its branches all the animals of the field
        gave birth to their young;
  and in its shade
        all great nations lived.
7 It was beautiful in its greatness,
        in the length of its branches;
  for its roots went down
        to abundant water.
8 The cedars in the garden of God could not
            rival it,
        nor the fir trees equal its boughs;
  the plane trees were as nothing
        compared with its branches;
  no tree in the garden of God
        was like it in beauty.

9 I made it beautiful
        with its mass of branches,
  the envy of all the trees of Eden
        that were in the garden of God.
10 Therefore thus says the Lord GOD: Because it*d* towered high and set its top among the clouds,*b* and its heart was proud of its height, 11 I gave it into the hand of the prince of the nations; he has dealt with it as its wickedness deserves. I have cast it out. 12 Foreigners from the most terrible of the nations have cut it down and left it. On the mountains and in all the valleys its branches have fallen, and its boughs lie broken in all the watercourses of the land; and all the peoples of the earth went away from its shade and left it.
13 On its fallen trunk settle
        all the birds of the air,
  and among its boughs lodge
        all the wild animals.
14 All this is in order that no trees by the waters may grow to lofty height or set their tops among the clouds,*b* and that no trees that drink water may reach up to them in height.

  For all of them are handed over to death,
        to the world below;
  along with all mortals,
        with those who go down to the Pit.
15 Thus says the Lord GOD: On the day it went down to Shē′ōl I closed the deep over it and covered it; I restrained its rivers, and its mighty waters were checked. I clothed Lebanon in gloom for it, and all the trees of the field fainted because of it. 16 I made the nations quake at the sound of its fall, when I cast it down to Shē′ōl with those who go down to the Pit; and all the trees of Eden, the choice and best of Lebanon, all that were well watered, were consoled in the world below. 17 They also went down to Shē′ōl with it, to those killed by the sword, along with its allies,*e* those who lived in its shade among the nations.
18 Which among the trees of Eden was like you in glory and in greatness? Now you shall be brought down with the trees of Eden to the world below; you shall lie among the uncircumcised, with those who are killed by the sword. This is Pharaoh and all his horde, says the Lord GOD.

Lamentation over Pharaoh and Egypt

32 In the twelfth year, in the twelfth month, on the first day of the month, the word of the LORD came to me: 2 Mortal, raise a lamentation over Pharaoh king of Egypt, and say to him:
  You consider yourself a lion among the
            nations,

---

b Gk: Heb *thick boughs*   *c* Gk: Heb *rivers going*   *d* Syr Vg: Heb *you*   *e* Heb *its arms*

but you are like a dragon in the seas;
 you thrash about in your streams,
  trouble the water with your feet,
  and foul your *f* streams.
3 Thus says the Lord GOD:
  In an assembly of many peoples
  I will throw my net over you;
  and I *g* will haul you up in my dragnet.
4 I will throw you on the ground,
  on the open field I will fling you,
 and will cause all the birds of the air to settle
    on you,
   and I will let the wild animals of the whole
    earth gorge themselves with you.
5 I will strew your flesh on the mountains,
  and fill the valleys with your carcass. *h*
6 I will drench the land with your flowing blood
  up to the mountains,
  and the watercourses will be filled with you.
7 When I blot you out, I will cover the heavens,
  and make their stars dark;
 I will cover the sun with a cloud,
  and the moon shall not give its light.
8 All the shining lights of the heavens
  I will darken above you,
  and put darkness on your land,
                 says the Lord GOD.
9 I will trouble the hearts of many peoples,
  as I carry you captive *i* among the nations,
  into countries you have not known.
10 I will make many peoples appalled at you;
  their kings shall shudder because of you.
 When I brandish my sword before them,
  they shall tremble every moment
 for their lives, each one of them,
  on the day of your downfall.
11 For thus says the Lord GOD:
 The sword of the king of Babylon shall come
    against you.
12 I will cause your hordes to fall
  by the swords of mighty ones,
  all of them most terrible among the
    nations.
 They shall bring to ruin the pride of Egypt,
  and all its hordes shall perish.
13 I will destroy all its livestock
  from beside abundant waters;
 and no human foot shall trouble them any
    more,
  nor shall the hoofs of cattle trouble them.
14 Then I will make their waters clear,
  and cause their streams to run like oil, says
    the Lord GOD.
15 When I make the land of Egypt desolate
  and when the land is stripped of all that
    fills it,
 when I strike down all who live in it,

then they shall know that I am the LORD.
16 This is a lamentation; it shall be chanted.
 The women of the nations shall chant it.
 Over Egypt and all its hordes they shall
    chant it,
  says the Lord GOD.

Dirge over Egypt

17 In the twelfth year, in the first month, *j* on
the fifteenth day of the month, the word of the
LORD came to me:
18 Mortal, wail over the hordes of Egypt,
  and send them down,
 with Egypt *k* and the daughters of majestic
    nations,
  to the world below,
  with those who go down to the Pit.
19 "Whom do you surpass in beauty?
  Go down! Be laid to rest with the
    uncircumcised!"
20 They shall fall among those who are killed by the
sword. Egypt *l* has been handed over to the sword;
carry away both it and its hordes. 21 The mighty
chiefs shall speak of them, with their helpers, out of
the midst of Shĕ'ōl: "They have come down, they lie
still, the uncircumcised, killed by the sword."

22 Assyria is there, and all its company, their
graves all around it, all of them killed, fallen by the
sword. 23 Their graves are set in the uttermost parts
of the Pit. Its company is all around its grave, all of
them killed, fallen by the sword, who spread terror
in the land of the living.

24 Ē'lam is there, and all its hordes around its
grave; all of them killed, fallen by the sword, who
went down uncircumcised into the world below,
who spread terror in the land of the living. They
bear their shame with those who go down to the
Pit. 25 They have made Ē'lam *k* a bed among the
slain with all its hordes, their graves all around it,
all of them uncircumcised, killed by the sword; for
terror of them was spread in the land of the living,
and they bear their shame with those who go down
to the Pit; they are placed among the slain.

26 Mĕ'shech and Tū'bal are there, and all their
multitude, their graves all around them, all of them
uncircumcised, killed by the sword; for they spread
terror in the land of the living. 27 And they do not
lie with the fallen warriors of long ago *m* who went
down to Shĕ'ōl with their weapons of war, whose
swords were laid under their heads, and whose
shields *n* are upon their bones; for the terror of the
warriors was in the land of the living. 28 So you

---

f Heb *their*   *g* Gk Vg: Heb *they*   *h* Symmachus Syr Vg: Heb
your height   *i* Gk: Heb *bring your destruction*   *j* Gk: Heb
lacks *in the first month*   *k* Heb *it*   *l* Heb *It*   *m* Gk Old Latin:
Heb *of the uncircumcised*   *n* Cn: Heb *iniquities*

shall be broken and lie among the uncircumcised, with those who are killed by the sword.

29 É'dom is there, its kings and all its princes, who for all their might are laid with those who are killed by the sword; they lie with the uncircumcised, with those who go down to the Pit.

30 The princes of the north are there, all of them, and all the Sī•dō'ni•ans, who have gone down in shame with the slain, for all the terror that they caused by their might; they lie uncircumcised with those who are killed by the sword, and bear their shame with those who go down to the Pit.

31 When Pharaoh sees them, he will be consoled for all his hordes—Pharaoh and all his army, killed by the sword, says the Lord GOD. 32 For he*o* spread terror in the land of the living; therefore he shall be laid to rest among the uncircumcised, with those who are slain by the sword—Pharaoh and all his multitude, says the Lord GOD.

Ezekiel Israel's Sentry

33 The word of the LORD came to me: 2 O Mortal, speak to your people and say to them, If I bring the sword upon a land, and the people of the land take one of their number as their sentinel; 3 and if the sentinel sees the sword coming upon the land and blows the trumpet and warns the people; 4 then if any who hear the sound of the trumpet do not take warning, and the sword comes and takes them away, their blood shall be upon their own heads. 5 They heard the sound of the trumpet and did not take warning; their blood shall be upon themselves. But if they had taken warning, they would have saved their lives. 6 But if the sentinel sees the sword coming and does not blow the trumpet, so that the people are not warned, and the sword comes and takes any of them, they are taken away in their iniquity, but their blood I will require at the sentinel's hand.

7 So you, mortal, I have made a sentinel for the house of Israel; whenever you hear a word from my mouth, you shall give them warning from me. 8 If I say to the wicked, "O wicked ones, you shall surely die," and you do not speak to warn the wicked to turn from their ways, the wicked shall die in their iniquity, but their blood I will require at your hand. 9 But if you warn the wicked to turn from their ways, and they do not turn from their ways, the wicked shall die in their iniquity, but you will have saved your life.

God's Justice and Mercy

10 Now you, mortal, say to the house of Israel, Thus you have said: "Our transgressions and our sins weigh upon us, and we waste away because of them; how then can we live?" 11 Say to them, As I live, says the Lord GOD, I have no pleasure in the death of the wicked, but that the wicked turn from their ways and live; turn back, turn back from your evil ways; for why will you die, O house of Israel? 12 And you, mortal, say to your people, The righteousness of the righteous shall not save them when they transgress; and as for the wickedness of the wicked, it shall not make them stumble when they turn from their wickedness; and the righteous shall not be able to live by their righteousness*p* when they sin. 13 Though I say to the righteous that they shall surely live, yet if they trust in their righteousness and commit iniquity, none of their righteous deeds shall be remembered; but in the iniquity that they have committed they shall die. 14 Again, though I say to the wicked, "You shall surely die," yet if they turn from their sin and do what is lawful and right— 15 if the wicked restore the pledge, give back what they have taken by robbery, and walk in the statutes of life, committing no iniquity—they shall surely live, they shall not die. 16 None of the sins that they have committed shall be remembered against them; they have done what is lawful and right, they shall surely live.

17 Yet your people say, "The way of the Lord is not just," when it is their own way that is not just. 18 When the righteous turn from their righteousness, and commit iniquity, they shall die for it.*q* 19 And when the wicked turn from their wickedness, and do what is lawful and right, they shall live by it.*q* 20 Yet you say, "The way of the Lord is not just." O house of Israel, I will judge all of you according to your ways!

The Fall of Jerusalem

21 In the twelfth year of our exile, in the tenth month, on the fifth day of the month, someone who had escaped from Jerusalem came to me and said, "The city has fallen." 22 Now the hand of the LORD had been upon me the evening before the fugitive came; but he had opened my mouth by the time the fugitive came to me in the morning; so my mouth was opened, and I was no longer unable to speak.

The Survivors in Judah

23 The word of the LORD came to me: 24 Mortal, the inhabitants of these waste places in the land of Israel keep saying, "Abraham was only one man, yet he got possession of the land; but we are many; the land is surely given us to possess." 25 Therefore say to them, Thus says the Lord GOD: You eat flesh with the blood, and lift up your eyes to your idols, and shed blood; shall you then possess the land? 26 You depend on your swords, you commit abominations, and each of you defiles his neighbor's wife;

---

o Cn: Heb *I*   *p* Heb *by it*   *q* Heb *them*

shall you then possess the land? 27 Say this to them, Thus says the Lord GOD: As I live, surely those who are in the waste places shall fall by the sword; and those who are in the open field I will give to the wild animals to be devoured; and those who are in strongholds and in caves shall die by pestilence. 28 I will make the land a desolation and a waste, and its proud might shall come to an end; and the mountains of Israel shall be so desolate that no one will pass through. 29 Then they shall know that I am the LORD, when I have made the land a desolation and a waste because of all their abominations that they have committed.

30 As for you, mortal, your people who talk together about you by the walls, and at the doors of the houses, say to one another, each to a neighbor, "Come and hear what the word is that comes from the LORD." 31 They come to you as people come, and they sit before you as my people, and they hear your words, but they will not obey them. For flattery is on their lips, but their heart is set on their gain. 32 To them you are like a singer of love songs,r one who has a beautiful voice and plays well on an instrument; they hear what you say, but they will not do it. 33 When this comes—and come it will!—then they shall know that a prophet has been among them.

Israel's False Shepherds

34 The word of the LORD came to me: 2 Mortal, prophesy against the shepherds of Israel: prophesy, and say to them—to the shepherds: Thus says the Lord GOD: Ah, you shepherds of Israel who have been feeding yourselves! Should not shepherds feed the sheep? 3 You eat the fat, you clothe yourselves with the wool, you slaughter the fatlings; but you do not feed the sheep. 4 You have not strengthened the weak, you have not healed the sick, you have not bound up the injured, you have not brought back the strayed, you have not sought the lost, but with force and harshness you have ruled them. 5 So they were scattered, because there was no shepherd; and scattered, they became food for all the wild animals. 6 My sheep were scattered, they wandered over all the mountains and on every high hill; my sheep were scattered over all the face of the earth, with no one to search or seek for them.

7 Therefore, you shepherds, hear the word of the LORD: 8 As I live, says the Lord GOD, because my sheep have become a prey, and my sheep have become food for all the wild animals, since there was no shepherd; and because my shepherds have not searched for my sheep, but the shepherds have fed themselves, and have not fed my sheep; 9 therefore, you shepherds, hear the word of the LORD: 10 Thus says the Lord GOD, I am against the shep-

herds; and I will demand my sheep at their hand, and put a stop to their feeding the sheep; no longer shall the shepherds feed themselves. I will rescue my sheep from their mouths, so that they may not be food for them.

God, the True Shepherd

11 For thus says the Lord GOD: I myself will search for my sheep, and will seek them out. 12 As shepherds seek out their flocks when they are among their scattered sheep, so I will seek out my sheep. I will rescue them from all the places to which they have been scattered on a day of clouds and thick darkness. 13 I will bring them out from the peoples and gather them from the countries, and will bring them into their own land; and I will feed them on the mountains of Israel, by the watercourses, and in all the inhabited parts of the land. 14 I will feed them with good pasture, and the mountain heights of Israel shall be their pasture; there they shall lie down in good grazing land, and they shall feed on rich pasture on the mountains of Israel. 15 I myself will be the shepherd of my sheep, and I will make them lie down, says the Lord GOD. 16 I will seek the lost, and I will bring back the strayed, and I will bind up the injured, and I will

---

r Cn: Heb *like a love song*

PRAY IT!
The Good Shepherd

The theme of the good shepherd is common in the Bible. Psalm 23 compares God to a protective shepherd. Ezekiel, chapter 34, describes bad shepherds and contrasts them with God, the true shepherd, who feeds the flock with justice. In Jn 10.1–18, Jesus compares himself to a good shepherd.

God, the true shepherd, thank you for your care and protection. Today, I will do what I can to help your work. Make me aware of the people in my life who are weak, injured, straying, or lost. With your help, I will do what I can to strengthen them, heal them, and bring them back to you. Maybe I too can be more like a shepherd than like a sheep that merely follows!

▶ **Ezekiel, chapter 34**

strengthen the weak, but the fat and the strong I will destroy. I will feed them with justice.

17 As for you, my flock, thus says the Lord GOD: I shall judge between sheep and sheep, between rams and goats: 18 Is it not enough for you to feed on the good pasture, but you must tread down with your feet the rest of your pasture? When you drink of clear water, must you foul the rest with your feet? 19 And must my sheep eat what you have trodden with your feet, and drink what you have fouled with your feet?

20 Therefore, thus says the Lord GOD to them: I myself will judge between the fat sheep and the lean sheep. 21 Because you pushed with flank and shoulder, and butted at all the weak animals with your horns until you scattered them far and wide, 22 I will save my flock, and they shall no longer be ravaged; and I will judge between sheep and sheep.

23 I will set up over them one shepherd, my servant David, and he shall feed them: he shall feed them and be their shepherd. 24 And I, the LORD, will be their God, and my servant David shall be prince among them; I, the LORD, have spoken.

25 I will make with them a covenant of peace and banish wild animals from the land, so that they may live in the wild and sleep in the woods securely. 26 I will make them and the region around my hill a blessing; and I will send down the showers in their season; they shall be showers of blessing. 27 The trees of the field shall yield their fruit, and the earth shall yield its increase. They shall be secure on their soil; and they shall know that I am the LORD, when I break the bars of their yoke, and save them from the hands of those who enslaved them. 28 They shall no more be plunder for the nations, nor shall the animals of the land devour them; they shall live in safety, and no one shall make them afraid. 29 I will provide for them a splendid vegetation so that they shall no more be consumed with hunger in the land, and no longer suffer the insults of the nations. 30 They shall know that I, the LORD their God, am with them, and that they, the house of Israel, are my people, says the Lord GOD. 31 You are my sheep, the sheep of my pasture[s] and I am your God, says the Lord GOD.

Judgment on Mount Seir

35 The word of the LORD came to me: 2 Mortal, set your face against Mount Sē'ir, and prophesy against it, 3 and say to it, Thus says the Lord GOD:

I am against you, Mount Sē'ir;
    I stretch out my hand against you
       to make you a desolation and a waste.
4 I lay your towns in ruins;
    you shall become a desolation,
    and you shall know that I am the LORD.

5 Because you cherished an ancient enmity, and gave over the people of Israel to the power of the sword at the time of their calamity, at the time of their final punishment; 6 therefore, as I live, says the Lord GOD, I will prepare you for blood, and blood shall pursue you; since you did not hate bloodshed, bloodshed shall pursue you. 7 I will make Mount Sē'ir a waste and a desolation; and I will cut off from it all who come and go. 8 I will fill its mountains with the slain; on your hills and in your valleys and in all your watercourses those killed with the sword shall fall. 9 I will make you a perpetual desolation, and your cities shall never be inhabited. Then you shall know that I am the LORD.

10 Because you said, "These two nations and these two countries shall be mine, and we will take possession of them,"—although the LORD was there— 11 therefore, as I live, says the Lord GOD, I will deal with you according to the anger and envy that you showed because of your hatred against them; and I will make myself known among you,[t] when I judge you. 12 You shall know that I, the LORD, have heard all the abusive speech that you uttered against the mountains of Israel, saying, "They are laid desolate, they are given us to devour." 13 And you magnified yourselves against me with your mouth, and multiplied your words against me; I heard it. 14 Thus says the Lord GOD: As the whole earth rejoices, I will make you desolate. 15 As you rejoiced over the inheritance of the house of Israel, because it was desolate, so I will deal with you; you shall be desolate, Mount Sē'ir, and all E'dom, all of it. Then they shall know that I am the LORD.

Blessing on Israel

36 And you, mortal, prophesy to the mountains of Israel, and say: O mountains of Israel, hear the word of the LORD. 2 Thus says the Lord GOD: Because the enemy said of you, "Aha!" and, "The ancient heights have become our possession," 3 therefore prophesy, and say: Thus says the Lord GOD: Because they made you desolate indeed, and crushed you from all sides, so that you became the possession of the rest of the nations, and you became an object of gossip and slander among the people; 4 therefore, O mountains of Israel, hear the word of the Lord GOD: Thus says the Lord GOD to the mountains and the hills, the watercourses and the valleys, the desolate wastes and the deserted towns, which have become a source of plunder and an object of derision to the rest of the nations all around; 5 therefore thus says the Lord GOD: I am speaking in my hot jealousy against the rest of the nations, and against all E'dom, who, with wholehearted joy and utter contempt, took my land as

---

[s] Gk OL: Heb *pasture, you are people*   [t] Gk: Heb *them*

their possession, because of its pasture, to plunder it. 6 Therefore prophesy concerning the land of Israel, and say to the mountains and hills, to the watercourses and valleys, Thus says the Lord GOD: I am speaking in my jealous wrath, because you have suffered the insults of the nations; 7 therefore thus says the Lord GOD: I swear that the nations that are all around you shall themselves suffer insults.

8 But you, O mountains of Israel, shall shoot out your branches, and yield your fruit to my people Israel; for they shall soon come home. 9 See now, I am for you; I will turn to you, and you shall be tilled and sown; 10 and I will multiply your population, the whole house of Israel, all of it; the towns shall be inhabited and the waste places rebuilt; 11 and I will multiply human beings and animals upon you. They shall increase and be fruitful; and I will cause you to be inhabited as in your former times, and will do more good to you than ever before. Then you shall know that I am the LORD. 12 I will lead people upon you—my people Israel—and they shall possess you, and you shall be their inheritance. No longer shall you bereave them of children.

13 Thus says the Lord GOD: Because they say to you, "You devour people, and you bereave your nation of children," 14 therefore you shall no longer devour people and no longer bereave your nation of children, says the Lord GOD; 15 and no longer will I let you hear the insults of the nations, no longer shall you bear the disgrace of the peoples;

and no longer shall you cause your nation to stumble, says the Lord GOD.

The Renewal of Israel

16 The word of the LORD came to me: 17 Mortal, when the house of Israel lived on their own soil, they defiled it with their ways and their deeds; their conduct in my sight was like the uncleanness of a woman in her menstrual period. 18 So I poured out my wrath upon them for the blood that they had shed upon the land, and for the idols with which they had defiled it. 19 I scattered them among the nations, and they were dispersed through the countries; in accordance with their conduct and their deeds I judged them. 20 But when they came to the nations, wherever they came, they profaned my holy name, in that it was said of them, "These are the people of the LORD, and yet they had to go out of his land." 21 But I had concern for my holy name, which the house of Israel had profaned among the nations to which they came.

22 Therefore say to the house of Israel, Thus says the Lord GOD: It is not for your sake, O house of Israel, that I am about to act, but for the sake of my holy name, which you have profaned among the nations to which you came. 23 I will sanctify my great name, which has been profaned among the nations, and which you have profaned among them; and the nations shall know that I am the LORD, says the Lord GOD, when through you I display my holiness before their eyes. 24 I will take you

EZEK

Therefore say to the house of Israel,

Thus says the LORD GOD:

It is not for your sake,

O house of Israel,

that I am about to act,

but for the sake of my holy name

36.22

from the nations, and gather you from all the countries, and bring you into your own land. 25 I will sprinkle clean water upon you, and you shall be clean from all your uncleannesses, and from all your idols I will cleanse you. 26 A new heart I will give you, and a new spirit I will put within you; and I will remove from your body the heart of stone and give you a heart of flesh. 27 I will put my spirit within you, and make you follow my statutes and be careful to observe my ordinances. 28 Then you shall live in the land that I gave to your ancestors; and you shall be my people, and I will be your God. 29 I will save you from all your uncleannesses, and I will summon the grain and make it abundant and lay no famine upon you. 30 I will make the fruit of the tree and the produce of the field abundant, so that you may never again suffer the disgrace of famine among the nations. 31 Then you shall remember your evil ways, and your dealings that were not good; and you shall loathe yourselves for your iniquities and your abominable deeds. 32 It is not for your sake that I will act, says the Lord GOD; let that be known to you. Be ashamed and dismayed for your ways, O house of Israel.

33 Thus says the Lord GOD: On the day that I cleanse you from all your iniquities, I will cause the towns to be inhabited, and the waste places shall be rebuilt. 34 The land that was desolate shall be tilled, instead of being the desolation that it was in the sight of all who passed by. 35 And they will say, "This land that was desolate has become like the garden of Eden; and the waste and desolate and ruined towns are now inhabited and fortified." 36 Then the nations that are left all around you shall know that I, the LORD, have rebuilt the ruined places, and replanted that which was desolate; I, the LORD, have spoken, and I will do it.

37 Thus says the Lord GOD: I will also let the house of Israel ask me to do this for them: to increase their population like a flock. 38 Like the flock for sacrifices,u like the flock at Jerusalem during her appointed festivals, so shall the ruined towns be filled with flocks of people. Then they shall know that I am the LORD.

The Valley of Dry Bones

37 The hand of the LORD came upon me, and he brought me out by the spirit of the LORD and set me down in the middle of a valley; it was full of bones. 2 He led me all around them; there were very many lying in the valley, and they were very dry. 3 He said to me, "Mortal, can these bones live?" I answered, "O Lord GOD, you know." 4 Then he said to me, "Prophesy to these bones, and say to them: O dry bones, hear the word of the LORD. 5 Thus says the Lord GOD to these bones: I will cause breathv to enter you, and you

did you KNOW?

Wind, Breath, and Spirit

English has the words *wind, breath,* and *spirit,* with three different meanings. Hebrew has only one word for all three meanings: *ruah.* The "wind from God [that] swept over the face of the waters" at Creation (Gen 1.2) is *ruah.* The "breath of life" that God blows into the lifeless clay of the first human (Gen 2.7) is *ruah.* And the "spirit of the LORD [that] came mightily upon David" at his anointing (1 Sam 16.13) is *ruah.*

In Ezek 37.1–14, all three meanings of the word *ruah* come into play. Ezekiel cries out, "Thus says the Lord GOD: Come from the four winds, O breath [or spirit], and breathe upon these slain, that they may live" (verse 9). In the prophet's vision, the bones scattered across the battlefield are the exiled people of God, who have experienced the "death" of defeat and humiliation. God promises that the spirit (*ruah*) of God (verse 14) will bring the people of Israel back from the Exile and restore them to their land.

▶ Ezek 37.1–14

shall live. 6 I will lay sinews on you, and will cause flesh to come upon you, and cover you with skin, and put breathv in you, and you shall live; and you shall know that I am the LORD."

7 So I prophesied as I had been commanded; and as I prophesied, suddenly there was a noise, a rattling, and the bones came together, bone to its bone. 8 I looked, and there were sinews on them, and flesh had come upon them, and skin had covered them; but there was no breath in them. 9 Then he said to me, "Prophesy to the breath, prophesy, mortal, and say to the breath:w Thus says the Lord GOD: Come from the four winds, O breath,w and breathe upon these slain, that they may live." 10 I prophesied as he commanded me, and the breath came into them, and they lived, and stood on their feet, a vast multitude.

11 Then he said to me, "Mortal, these bones are the whole house of Israel. They say, 'Our bones are

---

u Heb *flock of holy things*   v Or *spirit*   w Or *wind* or *spirit*

Bone Dry

When have you felt dry and lifeless, like the collection of dry bones Ezekiel sees in his vision in Ezek 37.1–2? What helps you to re-energize, to put muscle and flesh back on your tired bones? What winds blow life through you to give you breath again, to make you new again?

Bones are our body's support structure, and prayer is our soul's support structure. In verse 14, God's spirit brings life. We need to pray for God's spirit—the Holy Spirit—to fill us in order to avoid shriveling up and becoming parched and lifeless. And we need to share God's spirit with others, to breathe life into the dry bones around us—the people who seem to have no energy or hope.

What are the dry bones in your life? What can you do to be re-energized by God when you feel like dry bones? How can you help to energize others who seem dry and lifeless?

▸ **Ezekiel, chapter 37**

---

dried up, and our hope is lost; we are cut off completely.' 12 Therefore prophesy, and say to them, Thus says the Lord GOD: I am going to open your graves, and bring you up from your graves, O my people; and I will bring you back to the land of Israel. 13 And you shall know that I am the LORD, when I open your graves, and bring you up from your graves, O my people. 14 I will put my spirit within you, and you shall live, and I will place you on your own soil; then you shall know that I, the LORD, have spoken and will act, says the LORD."

The Two Sticks

15 The word of the LORD came to me: 16 Mortal, take a stick and write on it, "For Judah, and the Israelites associated with it"; then take another stick and write on it, "For Joseph (the stick of Ē'phra•im) and all the house of Israel associated with it"; 17 and join them together into one stick, so that they may become one in your hand. 18 And when your people say to you, "Will you not show us what you mean by these?" 19 say to them, Thus says the Lord GOD: I am about to take the stick of Joseph (which is in the hand of Ē'phra•im) and the tribes of Israel associated with it; and I will put the stick of Judah upon it,ˣ and make them one stick, in order that they may be one in my hand. 20 When the sticks on which you write are in your hand before their eyes, 21 then say to them, Thus says the Lord GOD: I will take the people of Israel from the nations among which they have gone, and will gather them from every quarter, and bring them to their own land. 22 I will make them one nation in the land, on the mountains of Israel; and one king shall be king over them all. Never again shall they be two nations, and never again shall they be divided into two kingdoms. 23 They shall never again defile themselves with their idols and their detestable

things, or with any of their transgressions. I will save them from all the apostasies into which they have fallen,ʸ and will cleanse them. Then they shall be my people, and I will be their God.

24 My servant David shall be king over them; and they shall all have one shepherd. They shall follow my ordinances and be careful to observe my statutes. 25 They shall live in the land that I gave to my servant Jacob, in which your ancestors lived; they and their children and their children's children shall live there forever; and my servant David shall be their prince forever. 26 I will make a covenant of peace with them; it shall be an everlasting covenant with them; and I will blessᶻ them and multiply them, and will set my sanctuary among them forevermore. 27 My dwelling place shall be with them; and I will be their God, and they shall be my people. 28 Then the nations shall know that I the LORD sanctify Israel, when my sanctuary is among them forevermore.

Invasion by Gog

38 The word of the LORD came to me: 2 Mortal, set your face toward Gog, of the land of Mā'gog, the chief prince of Mē'shech and Tū'bal. Prophesy against him 3 and say: Thus says the Lord GOD: I am against you, O Gog, chief prince of Mē'shech and Tū'bal; 4 I will turn you around and put hooks into your jaws, and I will lead you out with all your army, horses and horsemen, all of them clothed in full armor, a great company, all of them with shield and buckler, wielding swords. 5 Persia, Ethiopia,ᵃ and Put are with them, all of them with buckler and helmet; 6 Gō'mer and

---

x Heb *I will put them upon it* y Another reading is *from all the settlements in which they have sinned* z Tg: Heb *give*
a Or *Nubia*; Heb *Cush*

all its troops; Beth-tō·gar′mah from the remotest parts of the north with all its troops—many peoples are with you.

7 Be ready and keep ready, you and all the companies that are assembled around you, and hold yourselves in reserve for them. 8 After many days you shall be mustered; in the latter years you shall go against a land restored from war, a land where people were gathered from many nations on the mountains of Israel, which had long lain waste; its people were brought out from the nations and now are living in safety, all of them. 9 You shall advance, coming on like a storm; you shall be like a cloud covering the land, you and all your troops, and many peoples with you.

10 Thus says the Lord GOD: On that day thoughts will come into your mind, and you will devise an evil scheme. 11 You will say, "I will go up against the land of unwalled villages; I will fall upon the quiet people who live in safety, all of them living without walls, and having no bars or gates"; 12 to seize spoil and carry off plunder; to assail the waste places that are now inhabited, and the people who were gathered from the nations, who are acquiring cattle and goods, who live at the center*b* of the earth. 13 Shē′ba and Dē′dan and the merchants of Tar′shish and all its young warriors*c* will say to you, "Have you come to seize spoil? Have you assembled your horde to carry off plunder, to carry away silver and gold, to take away cattle and goods, to seize a great amount of booty?"

14 Therefore, mortal, prophesy, and say to Gog: Thus says the Lord GOD: On that day when my people Israel are living securely, you will rouse yourself*d* 15 and come from your place out of the remotest parts of the north, you and many peoples with you, all of them riding on horses, a great horde, a mighty army; 16 you will come up against my people Israel, like a cloud covering the earth. In the latter days I will bring you against my land, so that the nations may know me, when through you, O Gog, I display my holiness before their eyes.

Judgment on Gog

17 Thus says the Lord GOD: Are you he of whom I spoke in former days by my servants the prophets of Israel, who in those days prophesied for years that I would bring you against them? 18 On that day, when Gog comes against the land of Israel, says the Lord GOD, my wrath shall be aroused. 19 For in my jealousy and in my blazing wrath I declare: On that day there shall be a great shaking in the land of Israel; 20 the fish of the sea, and the birds of the air, and the animals of the field, and all creeping things that creep on the ground, and all human beings that are on the face of the earth, shall quake at my presence, and the mountains

shall be thrown down, and the cliffs shall fall, and every wall shall tumble to the ground. 21 I will summon the sword against Gog*e* in*f* all my mountains, says the Lord GOD; the swords of all will be against their comrades. 22 With pestilence and bloodshed I will enter into judgment with him; and I will pour down torrential rains and hailstones, fire and sulfur, upon him and his troops and the many peoples that are with him. 23 So I will display my greatness and my holiness and make myself known in the eyes of many nations. Then they shall know that I am the LORD.

Gog's Armies Destroyed

39 And you, mortal, prophesy against Gog, and say: Thus says the Lord GOD: I am against you, O Gog, chief prince of Mē′shech and Tū′bal! 2 I will turn you around and drive you forward, and bring you up from the remotest parts of the north, and lead you against the mountains of Israel. 3 I will strike your bow from your left hand, and will make your arrows drop out of your right hand. 4 You shall fall on the mountains of Israel, you and all your troops and the peoples that are with you; I will give you to birds of prey of every kind and to the wild animals to be devoured. 5 You shall fall in the open field; for I have spoken, says the Lord GOD. 6 I will send fire on Mā′gog and on those who live securely in the coastlands; and they shall know that I am the LORD.

7 My holy name I will make known among my people Israel; and I will not let my holy name be profaned any more; and the nations shall know that I am the LORD, the Holy One in Israel. 8 It has come! It has happened, says the Lord GOD. This is the day of which I have spoken.

9 Then those who live in the towns of Israel will go out and make fires of the weapons and burn them—bucklers and shields, bows and arrows, handpikes and spears—and they will make fires of them for seven years. 10 They will not need to take wood out of the field or cut down any trees in the forests, for they will make their fires of the weapons; they will despoil those who despoiled them, and plunder those who plundered them, says the Lord GOD.

The Burial of Gog

11 On that day I will give to Gog a place for burial in Israel, the Valley of the Travelers*g* east of the sea; it shall block the path of the travelers, for there Gog and all his horde will be buried; it shall be called the Valley of Hā′mon-gog.*h* 12 Seven

---

b Heb *navel*   *c* Heb *young lions*   *d* Gk: Heb *will you not know?*   *e* Heb *him*   *f* Heb *to* or *for*   *g* Or *of the Abarim*   *h* That is, *the Horde of Gog* months the house of Israel shall spend burying them, in order to cleanse the land. 13 All the people of the land shall bury them; and it will bring them honor on the day that I show my glory, says the Lord GOD. 14 They will set apart men to pass through the land regularly and bury any invaders[i] who remain on the face of the land, so as to cleanse it; for seven months they shall make their search. 15 As the searchers[i] pass through the land, anyone who sees a human bone shall set up a sign by it, until the buriers have buried it in the Valley of Hā'mon-gog.[j] 16 (A city Ha•mō'nah[k] is there also.) Thus they shall cleanse the land.

17 As for you, mortal, thus says the Lord GOD: Speak to the birds of every kind and to all the wild animals: Assemble and come, gather from all around to the sacrificial feast that I am preparing for you, a great sacrificial feast on the mountains of Israel, and you shall eat flesh and drink blood. 18 You shall eat the flesh of the mighty, and drink the blood of the princes of the earth—of rams, of lambs, and of goats, of bulls, all of them fatlings of Bā'shan. 19 You shall eat fat until you are filled, and drink blood until you are drunk, at the sacrificial feast that I am preparing for you. 20 And you shall be filled at my table with horses and charioteers,[l] with warriors and all kinds of soldiers, says the Lord GOD.

Israel Restored to the Land

21 I will display my glory among the nations; and all the nations shall see my judgment that I have executed, and my hand that I have laid on them. 22 The house of Israel shall know that I am the LORD their God, from that day forward. 23 And the nations shall know that the house of Israel went into captivity for their iniquity, because they dealt treacherously with me. So I hid my face from them and gave them into the hand of their adversaries, and they all fell by the sword. 24 I dealt with them according to their uncleanness and their transgressions, and hid my face from them.

25 Therefore thus says the Lord GOD: Now I will restore the fortunes of Jacob, and have mercy on the whole house of Israel; and I will be jealous for my holy name. 26 They shall forget[m] their shame, and all the treachery they have practiced against me, when they live securely in their land with no one to make them afraid, 27 when I have brought them back from the peoples and gathered them from their enemies' lands, and through them have displayed my holiness in the sight of many nations. 28 Then they shall know that I am the LORD their God because I sent them into exile among the nations, and then gathered them into their own land. I will leave none of them behind; 29 and I will never again hide my face from them, when I pour out my spirit upon the house of Israel, says the Lord GOD.

The Vision of the New Temple

40 In the twenty-fifth year of our exile, at the beginning of the year, on the tenth day of the month, in the fourteenth year after the city was struck down, on that very day, the hand of the LORD was upon me, and he brought me there. 2 He brought me, in visions of God, to the land of Israel, and set me down upon a very high mountain, on which was a structure like a city to the south. 3 When he brought me there, a man was there, whose appearance shone like bronze, with a linen cord and a measuring reed in his hand; and he was standing in the gateway. 4 The man said to me, "Mortal, look closely and listen attentively, and set your mind upon all that I shall show you, for you were brought here in order that I might show it to you; declare all that you see to the house of Israel."

5 Now there was a wall all around the outside of the temple area. The length of the measuring reed in the man's hand was six long cubits, each being a cubit and a handbreadth in length; so he measured the thickness of the wall, one reed; and the height, one reed. 6 Then he went into the gateway facing east, going up its steps, and measured the threshold of the gate, one reed deep.[n] There were 7 recesses, and each recess was one reed wide and one reed deep; and the space between the recesses, five cubits; and the threshold of the gate by the vestibule of the gate at the inner end was one reed deep. 8 Then he measured the inner vestibule of the gateway, one cubit. 9 Then he measured the vestibule of the gateway, eight cubits; and its pilasters, two cubits; and the vestibule of the gate was at the inner end. 10 There were three recesses on either side of the east gate; the three were of the same size; and the pilasters on either side were of the same size. 11 Then he measured the width of the opening of the gateway, ten cubits; and the width of the gateway, thirteen cubits. 12 There was a barrier before the recesses, one cubit on either side; and the recesses were six cubits on either side. 13 Then he measured the gate from the back[o] of the one recess to the back[o] of the other, a width of twenty-five cubits, from wall to wall.[p] 14 He measured[q] also the vestibule, twenty cubits; and the gate next to the pilaster on every side of the court.[r] 15 From the front of the gate at the entrance to the end of the inner vestibule of the gate was fifty cubits. 16 The recesses and their pilasters had windows, with shutters[r] on

---

[i] Heb travelers   [j] That is, the Horde of Gog   [k] That is The Horde   [l] Heb chariots   [m] Another reading is They shall bear   [n] Heb deep, and one threshold, one reed deep   [o] Gk: Heb roof   [p] Heb opening facing opening   [q] Heb made   [r] Meaning of Heb uncertain

the inside of the gateway all around, and the vestibules also had windows on the inside all around; and on the pilasters were palm trees.

17 Then he brought me into the outer court; there were chambers there, and a pavement, all around the court; thirty chambers fronted on the pavement. 18 The pavement ran along the side of the gates, corresponding to the length of the gates; this was the lower pavement. 19 Then he measured the distance from the inner front of*s* the lower gate to the outer front of the inner court, one hundred cubits.*t*

20 Then he measured the gate of the outer court that faced north—its depth and width. 21 Its recesses, three on either side, and its pilasters and its vestibule were of the same size as those of the first gate; its depth was fifty cubits, and its width twenty-five cubits. 22 Its windows, its vestibule, and its palm trees were of the same size as those of the gate that faced toward the east. Seven steps led up to it; and its vestibule was on the inside.*u* 23 Opposite the gate on the north, as on the east, was a gate to the inner court; he measured from gate to gate, one hundred cubits.

24 Then he led me toward the south, and there was a gate on the south; and he measured its pilasters and its vestibule; they had the same dimensions as the others. 25 There were windows all around in it and in its vestibule, like the windows of the others; its depth was fifty cubits, and its width twenty-five cubits. 26 There were seven steps leading up to it; its vestibule was on the inside.*u* It had palm trees on its pilasters, one on either side. 27 There was a gate on the south of the inner court; and he measured from gate to gate toward the south, one hundred cubits.

28 Then he brought me to the inner court by the south gate, and he measured the south gate; it was of the same dimensions as the others. 29 Its recesses, its pilasters, and its vestibule were of the same size as the others; and there were windows all around in it and in its vestibule; its depth was fifty cubits, and its width twenty-five cubits. 30 There were vestibules all around, twenty-five cubits deep and five cubits wide. 31 Its vestibule faced the outer court, and palm trees were on its pilasters, and its stairway had eight steps.

32 Then he brought me to the inner court on the east side, and he measured the gate; it was of the same size as the others. 33 Its recesses, its pilasters, and its vestibule were of the same dimensions as the others; and there were windows all around it and in its vestibule; its depth was fifty cubits, and its width twenty-five cubits. 34 Its vestibule faced the outer court, and it had palm trees on its pilasters, on either side; and its stairway had eight steps.

35 Then he brought me to the north gate, and he measured it; it had the same dimensions as the others. 36 Its recesses, its pilasters, and its vestibule were of the same size as the others;*v* and it had windows all around. Its depth was fifty cubits, and its width twenty-five cubits. 37 Its vestibule*w* faced the outer court, and it had palm trees on its pilasters, on either side; and its stairway had eight steps.

38 There was a chamber with its door in the vestibule of the gate,*x* where the burnt offering was to be washed. 39 And in the vestibule of the gate were two tables on either side, on which the burnt offering and the sin offering and the guilt offering were to be slaughtered. 40 On the outside of the vestibule*y* at the entrance of the north gate were two tables; and on the other side of the vestibule of the gate were two tables. 41 Four tables were on the inside, and four tables on the outside of the side of the gate, eight tables, on which the sacrifices were to be slaughtered. 42 There were also four tables of hewn stone for the burnt offering, a cubit and a half long, and one cubit and a half wide, and one cubit high, on which the instruments were to be laid with which the burnt offerings and the sacrifices were slaughtered. 43 There were pegs, one handbreadth long, fastened all around the inside. And on the tables the flesh of the offering was to be laid.

44 On the outside of the inner gateway there were chambers for the singers in the inner court, one*z* at the side of the north gate facing south, the other at the side of the east gate facing north. 45 He said to me, "This chamber that faces south is for the priests who have charge of the temple, 46 and the chamber that faces north is for the priests who have charge of the altar; these are the descendants of Zā'-dok, who alone among the descendants of Levi may come near to the LORD to minister to him." 47 He measured the court, one hundred cubits deep, and one hundred cubits wide, a square; and the altar was in front of the temple.

The Temple
(Cp 1 Kings 7.14–22)

48 Then he brought me to the vestibule of the temple and measured the pilasters of the vestibule, five cubits on either side; and the width of the gate was fourteen cubits; and the sidewalls of the gate were three cubits*a* on either side. 49 The depth of the vestibule was twenty cubits, and the width twelve*b* cubits; ten steps led up*c* to it; and there were pillars beside the pilasters on either side.

---

s Compare Gk: Heb *from before*   *t* Heb adds *the east and the north*   *u* Gk: Heb *before them*   *v* One Ms: Compare verses 29 and 33: MT lacks *were of the same size as the others*   *w* Gk Vg Compare verses 26, 31, 34: Heb *pilasters*   *x* Cn: Heb *at the pilasters of the gates*   *y* Cn: Heb *to him who goes up*   *z* Heb lacks *one*   *a* Gk: Heb *and the width of the gate was three cubits*   *b* Gk: Heb *eleven*   *c* Gk: Heb *and by steps that went up*

41 Then he brought me to the nave, and measured the pilasters; on each side six cubits was the width of the pilasters.*d* 2 The width of the entrance was ten cubits; and the sidewalls of the entrance were five cubits on either side. He measured the length of the nave, forty cubits, and its width, twenty cubits. 3 Then he went into the inner room and measured the pilasters of the entrance, two cubits; and the width of the entrance, six cubits; and the sidewalls*e* of the entrance, seven cubits. 4 He measured the depth of the room, twenty cubits, and its width, twenty cubits, beyond the nave. And he said to me, This is the most holy place.

5 Then he measured the wall of the temple, six cubits thick; and the width of the side chambers, four cubits, all around the temple. 6 The side chambers were in three stories, one over another, thirty in each story. There were offsets*f* all around the wall of the temple to serve as supports for the side chambers, so that they should not be supported by the wall of the temple. 7 The passageways*g* of the side chambers widened from story to story; for the structure was supplied with a stairway all around the temple. For this reason the structure became wider from story to story. One ascended from the bottom story to the uppermost story by way of the middle one. 8 I saw also that the temple had a raised platform all around; the foundations of the side chambers measured a full reed of six long cubits. 9 The thickness of the outer wall of the side chambers was five cubits; and the free space between the side chambers of the temple 10 and the chambers of the court was a width of twenty cubits all around the temple on every side. 11 The side chambers opened onto the area left free, one door toward the north, and another door toward the south; and the width of the part that was left free was five cubits all around.

12 The building that was facing the temple yard on the west side was seventy cubits wide; and the wall of the building was five cubits thick all around, and its depth ninety cubits.

13 Then he measured the temple, one hundred cubits deep; and the yard and the building with its walls, one hundred cubits deep; 14 also the width of the east front of the temple and the yard, one hundred cubits.

15 Then he measured the depth of the building facing the yard at the west, together with its galleries*h* on either side, one hundred cubits.

The nave of the temple and the inner room and the outer*i* vestibule 16 were paneled,*j* and, all around, all three had windows with recessed*k* frames. Facing the threshold the temple was paneled with wood all around, from the floor up to the windows (now the windows were covered), 17 to the space above the door, even to the inner room, and on the out-

side. And on all the walls all around in the inner room and the nave there was a pattern.*l* 18 It was formed of cherubim and palm trees, a palm tree between cherub and cherub. Each cherub had two faces: 19 a human face turned toward the palm tree on the one side, and the face of a young lion turned toward the palm tree on the other side. They were carved on the whole temple all around; 20 from the floor to the area above the door, cherubim and palm trees were carved on the wall.*m*

41.18–21

21 The doorposts of the nave were square. In front of the holy place was something resembling 22 an altar of wood, three cubits high, two cubits long, and two cubits wide;*n* its corners, its base,*o* and its walls were of wood. He said to me, "This is the table that stands before the LORD." 23 The nave and the holy place had each a double door. 24 The doors had two leaves apiece, two swinging leaves for each door. 25 On the doors of the nave were carved cherubim and palm trees, such as were carved on the walls; and there was a canopy of wood in front of the vestibule outside. 26 And there were recessed windows and palm trees on either side, on the sidewalls of the vestibule.*p*

The Holy Chambers and the Outer Wall

42 Then he led me out into the outer court, toward the north, and he brought me to the chambers that were opposite the temple yard

---

d Compare Gk: Heb *tent*   *e* Gk: Heb *width*   *f* Gk Compare 1 Kings 6.6: Heb *they entered*   *g* Cn: Heb *it was surrounded*   *h* Cn: Meaning of Heb uncertain   *i* Gk: Heb *of the court*   *j* Gk: Heb *the thresholds*   *k* Cn Compare Gk 1 Kings 6.4: Meaning of Heb uncertain   *l* Heb *measures*   *m* Cn Compare verse 25: Heb *and the wall*   *n* Gk: Heb lacks *two cubits wide*   *o* Gk: Heb *length*   *p* Cn: Heb *vestibule. And the side chambers of the temple and the canopies* and opposite the building on the north. [2] The length of the building that was on the north side[q] was[r] one hundred cubits, and the width fifty cubits. [3] Across the twenty cubits that belonged to the inner court, and facing the pavement that belonged to the outer court, the chambers rose[s] gallery[t] by gallery[t] in three stories. [4] In front of the chambers was a passage on the inner side, ten cubits wide and one hundred cubits deep,[u] and its[v] entrances were on the north. [5] Now the upper chambers were narrower, for the galleries[t] took more away from them than from the lower and middle chambers in the building. [6] For they were in three stories, and they had no pillars like the pillars of the outer[w] court; for this reason the upper chambers were set back from the ground more than the lower and the middle ones. [7] There was a wall outside parallel to the chambers, toward the outer court, opposite the chambers, fifty cubits long. [8] For the chambers on the outer court were fifty cubits long, while those opposite the temple were one hundred cubits long. [9] At the foot of these chambers ran a passage that one entered from the east in order to enter them from the outer court. [10] The width of the passage[x] was fixed by the wall of the court.

On the south[y] also, opposite the vacant area and opposite the building, there were chambers [11] with a passage in front of them; they were similar to the chambers on the north, of the same length and width, with the same exits[z] and arrangements and doors. [12] So the entrances of the chambers to the south were entered through the entrance at the head of the corresponding passage, from the east, along the matching wall.[t]

[13] Then he said to me, "The north chambers and the south chambers opposite the vacant area are the holy chambers, where the priests who approach the LORD shall eat the most holy offerings; there they shall deposit the most holy offerings—the grain offering, the sin offering, and the guilt offering—for the place is holy. [14] When the priests enter the holy place, they shall not go out of it into the outer court without laying there the vestments in which they minister, for these are holy; they shall put on other garments before they go near to the area open to the people."

[15] When he had finished measuring the interior of the temple area, he led me out by the gate that faces east, and measured the temple area all around. [16] He measured the east side with the measuring reed, five hundred cubits by the measuring reed. [17] Then he turned and measured[a] the north side, five hundred cubits by the measuring reed. [18] Then he turned and measured[a] the south side, five hundred cubits by the measuring reed. [19] Then he turned to the west side and measured, five hundred cubits by the measuring reed. [20] He measured it on the four sides. It had a wall around it, five hundred cubits long and five hundred cubits wide, to make a separation between the holy and the common.

The Divine Glory Returns to the Temple

43 Then he brought me to the gate, the gate facing east. [2] And there, the glory of the God of Israel was coming from the east; the sound was like the sound of mighty waters; and the earth shone with his glory. [3] The[b] vision I saw was like

---

[q] Gk: Heb door   [r] Gk: Heb before the length   [s] Heb lacks the chambers rose   [t] Meaning of Heb uncertain   [u] Gk Syr: Heb a way of one cubit   [v] Heb their   [w] Gk: Heb lacks outer   [x] Heb lacks of the passage   [y] Gk: Heb east   [z] Heb and all their exits   [a] Gk: Heb measuring reed all around. He measured   [b] Gk: Heb Like the vision

E
Z
E
K

God's Dwelling Place

LIVE IT!

Ezekiel's vision of God returning to the Temple in Ezek 43.1–5 completes the circle of his prophecy. Earlier, as described in chapter 10, he had a unique vision of God's glory leaving the Temple and coming to rest in Babylon. For Ezekiel, the Temple represents the heart of Israel's relationship with God, and it is important that God's presence will return to it. This probably explains why Ezekiel carefully records the specifics of the new Temple in the remaining chapters of his book—to help make it more real.

The early Christians learned from Jesus that God's presence isn't limited to the Temple. The good news is that God is present in every person! First Corinthians 3.16 says, "Do you not know that you are God's temple and that God's Spirit dwells in you?" The basis for our self-worth should be knowing that God's spirit dwells within us. If that doesn't make us special, what will?

▶ Ezek 43.1–5

the vision that I had seen when he came to destroy the city, and*c* like the vision that I had seen by the river Chĕ′bar; and I fell upon my face. 4 As the glory of the LORD entered the temple by the gate facing east, 5 the spirit lifted me up, and brought me into the inner court; and the glory of the LORD filled the temple.

6 While the man was standing beside me, I heard someone speaking to me out of the temple. 7 He said to me: Mortal, this is the place of my throne and the place for the soles of my feet, where I will reside among the people of Israel forever. The house of Israel shall no more defile my holy name, neither they nor their kings, by their whoring, and by the corpses of their kings at their death.*d* 8 When they placed their threshold by my threshold and their doorposts beside my doorposts, with only a wall between me and them, they were defiling my holy name by their abominations that they committed; therefore I have consumed them in my anger. 9 Now let them put away their idolatry and the corpses of their kings far from me, and I will reside among them forever.

10 As for you, mortal, describe the temple to the house of Israel, and let them measure the pattern; and let them be ashamed of their iniquities. 11 When they are ashamed of all that they have done, make known to them the plan of the temple, its arrangement, its exits and its entrances, and its whole form—all its ordinances and its entire plan and all its laws; and write it down in their sight, so that they may observe and follow the entire plan and all its ordinances. 12 This is the law of the temple: the whole territory on the top of the mountain all around shall be most holy. This is the law of the temple.

The Altar

13 These are the dimensions of the altar by cubits (the cubit being one cubit and a handbreadth): its base shall be one cubit high,*e* and one cubit wide, with a rim of one span around its edge. This shall be the height of the altar: 14 From the base on the ground to the lower ledge, two cubits, with a width of one cubit; and from the smaller ledge to the larger ledge, four cubits, with a width of one cubit; 15 and the altar hearth, four cubits; and from the altar hearth projecting upward, four horns. 16 The altar hearth shall be square, twelve cubits long by twelve wide. 17 The ledge also shall be square, fourteen cubits long by fourteen wide, with a rim around it half a cubit wide, and its surrounding base, one cubit. Its steps shall face east.

18 Then he said to me: Mortal, thus says the Lord GOD: These are the ordinances for the altar: On the day when it is erected for offering burnt offerings upon it and for dashing blood against it,

19 you shall give to the levitical priests of the family of Zā′dok, who draw near to me to minister to me, says the Lord GOD, a bull for a sin offering. 20 And you shall take some of its blood, and put it on the four horns of the altar, and on the four corners of the ledge, and upon the rim all around; thus you shall purify it and make atonement for it. 21 You shall also take the bull of the sin offering, and it shall be burnt in the appointed place belonging to the temple, outside the sacred area.

22 On the second day you shall offer a male goat without blemish for a sin offering; and the altar shall be purified, as it was purified with the bull. 23 When you have finished purifying it, you shall offer a bull without blemish and a ram from the flock without blemish. 24 You shall present them before the LORD, and the priests shall throw salt on them and offer them up as a burnt offering to the LORD. 25 For seven days you shall provide daily a goat for a sin offering; also a bull and a ram from the flock, without blemish, shall be provided. 26 Seven days shall they make atonement for the altar and cleanse it, and so consecrate it. 27 When these days are over, then from the eighth day onward the priests shall offer upon the altar your burnt offerings and your offerings of well-being; and I will accept you, says the Lord GOD.

The Closed Gate

44 Then he brought me back to the outer gate of the sanctuary, which faces east; and it was shut. 2 The LORD said to me: This gate shall remain shut; it shall not be opened, and no one shall enter by it; for the LORD, the God of Israel, has entered by it; therefore it shall remain shut. 3 Only the prince, because he is a prince, may sit in it to eat food before the LORD; he shall enter by way of the vestibule of the gate, and shall go out by the same way.

Admission to the Temple

4 Then he brought me by way of the north gate to the front of the temple; and I looked, and lo! the glory of the LORD filled the temple of the LORD; and I fell upon my face. 5 The LORD said to me: Mortal, mark well, look closely, and listen attentively to all that I shall tell you concerning all the ordinances of the temple of the LORD and all its laws; and mark well those who may be admitted to*f* the temple and all those who are to be excluded from the sanctuary. 6 Say to the rebellious house,*g* to the house of Israel, Thus says the Lord GOD: O house of Israel, let there be an end to all your abominations 7 in

---

c Syr: Heb *and the visions*   *d* Or *on their high places*   *e* Gk: Heb lacks *high*   *f* Cn: Heb *the entrance of*   *g* Gk: Heb lacks *house* admitting foreigners, uncircumcised in heart and flesh, to be in my sanctuary, profaning my temple when you offer to me my food, the fat and the blood. You[h] have broken my covenant with all your abominations. 8 And you have not kept charge of my sacred offerings; but you have appointed foreigners[i] to act for you in keeping my charge in my sanctuary.

9 Thus says the Lord GOD: No foreigner, uncircumcised in heart and flesh, of all the foreigners who are among the people of Israel, shall enter my sanctuary. 10 But the Lē'vites who went far from me, going astray from me after their idols when Israel went astray, shall bear their punishment. 11 They shall be ministers in my sanctuary, having oversight at the gates of the temple, and serving in the temple; they shall slaughter the burnt offering and the sacrifice for the people, and they shall attend on them and serve them. 12 Because they ministered to them before their idols and made the house of Israel stumble into iniquity, therefore I have sworn concerning them, says the Lord GOD, that they shall bear their punishment. 13 They shall not come near to me, to serve me as priest, nor come near any of my sacred offerings, the things that are most sacred; but they shall bear their shame, and the consequences of the abominations that they have committed. 14 Yet I will appoint them to keep charge of the temple, to do all its chores, all that is to be done in it.

The Levitical Priests

15 But the levitical priests, the descendants of Zā'dok, who kept the charge of my sanctuary when the people of Israel went astray from me, shall come near to me to minister to me; and they shall attend me to offer me the fat and the blood, says the Lord GOD. 16 It is they who shall enter my sanctuary, it is they who shall approach my table, to minister to me, and they shall keep my charge. 17 When they enter the gates of the inner court, they shall wear linen vestments; they shall have nothing of wool on them, while they minister at the gates of the inner court, and within. 18 They shall have linen turbans on their heads, and linen undergarments on their loins; they shall not bind themselves with anything that causes sweat. 19 When they go out into the outer court to the people, they shall remove the vestments in which they have been ministering, and lay them in the holy chambers; and they shall put on other garments, so that they may not communicate holiness to the people with their vestments. 20 They shall not shave their heads or let their locks grow long; they shall only trim the hair of their heads. 21 No priest shall drink wine when he enters the inner court. 22 They shall not marry a widow, or a divorced woman, but only a virgin of the stock of the house of Israel, or a widow who is the widow of a priest. 23 They shall teach my people the difference between the holy and the common, and show them how to distinguish between the unclean and the clean. 24 In a controversy they shall act as judges, and they shall decide it according to my judgments. They shall keep my laws and my statutes regarding all my appointed festivals, and they shall keep my sabbaths holy. 25 They shall not defile themselves by going near to a dead person; for father or mother, however, and for son or daughter, and for brother or unmarried sister they may defile themselves. 26 After he has become clean, they shall count seven days for him. 27 On the day that he goes into the holy place, into the inner court, to minister in the holy place, he shall offer his sin offering, says the Lord GOD.

28 This shall be their inheritance: I am their inheritance; and you shall give them no holding in Israel; I am their holding. 29 They shall eat the grain offering, the sin offering, and the guilt offering; and every devoted thing in Israel shall be theirs. 30 The first of all the first fruits of all kinds, and every offering of all kinds from all your offerings, shall belong to the priests; you shall also give to the priests the first of your dough, in order that a blessing may rest on your house. 31 The priests shall not eat of anything, whether bird or animal, that died of itself or was torn by animals.

The Holy District

45 When you allot the land as an inheritance, you shall set aside for the LORD a portion of the land as a holy district, twenty-five thousand cubits long and twenty[j] thousand cubits wide; it shall be holy throughout its entire extent. 2 Of this, a square plot of five hundred by five hundred cubits shall be for the sanctuary, with fifty cubits for an open space around it. 3 In the holy district you shall measure off a section twenty-five thousand cubits long and ten thousand wide, in which shall be the sanctuary, the most holy place. 4 It shall be a holy portion of the land; it shall be for the priests, who minister in the sanctuary and approach the LORD to minister to him; and it shall be both a place for their houses and a holy place for the sanctuary. 5 Another section, twenty-five thousand cubits long and ten thousand cubits wide, shall be for the Lē'vites who minister at the temple, as their holding for cities to live in.[k]

6 Alongside the portion set apart as the holy district you shall assign as a holding for the city an area five thousand cubits wide, and twenty-five thousand cubits long; it shall belong to the whole house of Israel.

---

h Gk Syr Vg: Heb *They*   i Heb lacks *foreigners*   j Gk:
Heb *ten*   k Gk: Heb *as their holding, twenty chambers*

7 And to the prince shall belong the land on both sides of the holy district and the holding of the city, alongside the holy district and the holding of the city, on the west and on the east, corresponding in length to one of the tribal portions, and extending from the western to the eastern boundary 8 of the land. It is to be his property in Israel. And my princes shall no longer oppress my people; but they shall let the house of Israel have the land according to their tribes.

9 Thus says the Lord GOD: Enough, O princes of Israel! Put away violence and oppression, and do what is just and right. Cease your evictions of my people, says the Lord GOD.

Weights and Measures

10 You shall have honest balances, an honest ephah, and an honest bath.^{l} 11 The ephah and the bath shall be of the same measure, the bath containing one-tenth of a homer, and the ephah one-tenth of a homer; the homer shall be the standard measure. 12 The shekel shall be twenty gerahs. Twenty shekels, twenty-five shekels, and fifteen shekels shall make a mina for you.

Offerings

13 This is the offering that you shall make: one-sixth of an ephah from each homer of wheat, and one-sixth of an ephah from each homer of barley, 14 and as the fixed portion of oil,^{m} one-tenth of a bath from each cor (the cor,^{n} like the homer, contains ten baths); 15 and one sheep from every flock of two hundred, from the pastures of Israel. This is the offering for grain offerings, burnt offerings, and offerings of well-being, to make atonement for them, says the Lord GOD. 16 All the people of the land shall join with the prince in Israel in making this offering. 17 But this shall be the obligation of the prince regarding the burnt offerings, grain offerings, and drink offerings, at the festivals, the new moons, and the sabbaths, all the appointed festivals of the house of Israel: he shall provide the sin offerings, grain offerings, the burnt offerings, and the offerings of well-being, to make atonement for the house of Israel.

Festivals

(Ex 12.1–20; Lev 23.33–43)

18 Thus says the Lord GOD: In the first month, on the first day of the month, you shall take a young bull without blemish, and purify the sanctuary. 19 The priest shall take some of the blood of the sin offering and put it on the doorposts of the temple, the four corners of the ledge of the altar, and the posts of the gate of the inner court. 20 You shall do the same on the seventh day of the month for anyone who has sinned through error or igno-

rance; so you shall make atonement for the temple.

21 In the first month, on the fourteenth day of the month, you shall celebrate the festival of the passover, and for seven days unleavened bread shall be eaten. 22 On that day the prince shall provide for himself and all the people of the land a young bull for a sin offering. 23 And during the seven days of the festival he shall provide as a burnt offering to the LORD seven young bulls and seven rams without blemish, on each of the seven days; and a male goat daily for a sin offering. 24 He shall provide as a grain offering an ephah for each bull, an ephah for each ram, and a hin of oil to each ephah. 25 In the seventh month, on the fifteenth day of the month and for the seven days of the festival, he shall make the same provision for sin offerings, burnt offerings, and grain offerings, and for the oil.

Miscellaneous Regulations

46 Thus says the Lord GOD: The gate of the inner court that faces east shall remain closed on the six working days; but on the sabbath day it shall be opened and on the day of the new moon it shall be opened. 2 The prince shall enter by the vestibule of the gate from outside, and shall take his stand by the post of the gate. The priests shall offer his burnt offering and his offerings of well-being, and he shall bow down at the threshold of the gate. Then he shall go out, but the gate shall not be closed until evening. 3 The people of the land shall bow down at the entrance of that gate before the LORD on the sabbaths and on the new moons. 4 The burnt offering that the prince offers to the LORD on the sabbath day shall be six lambs without blemish and a ram without blemish; 5 and the grain offering with the ram shall be an ephah, and the grain offering with the lambs shall be as much as he wishes to give, together with a hin of oil to each ephah. 6 On the day of the new moon he shall offer a young bull without blemish, and six lambs and a ram, which shall be without blemish; 7 as a grain offering he shall provide an ephah with the bull and an ephah with the ram, and with the lambs as much as he wishes, together with a hin of oil to each ephah. 8 When the prince enters, he shall come in by the vestibule of the gate, and he shall go out by the same way.

9 When the people of the land come before the LORD at the appointed festivals, whoever enters by the north gate to worship shall go out by the south gate; and whoever enters by the south gate shall go out by the north gate: they shall not return by way of the gate by which they entered, but shall go out

^{l} A Heb measure of volume ^{m} Cn: Heb oil, the bath the oil ^{n} Vg: Heb homer straight ahead. 10 When they come in, the prince shall come in with them; and when they go out, he shall go out.

11 At the festivals and the appointed seasons the grain offering with a young bull shall be an ephah, and with a ram an ephah, and with the lambs as much as one wishes to give, together with a hin of oil to an ephah. 12 When the prince provides a freewill offering, either a burnt offering or offerings of well-being as a freewill offering to the LORD, the gate facing east shall be opened for him; and he shall offer his burnt offering or his offerings of well-being as he does on the sabbath day. Then he shall go out, and after he has gone out the gate shall be closed.

13 He shall provide a lamb, a yearling, without blemish, for a burnt offering to the LORD daily; morning by morning he shall provide it. 14 And he shall provide a grain offering with it morning by morning regularly, one-sixth of an ephah, and one-third of a hin of oil to moisten the choice flour, as a grain offering to the LORD; this is the ordinance for all time. 15 Thus the lamb and the grain offering and the oil shall be provided, morning by morning, as a regular burnt offering.

16 Thus says the Lord GOD: If the prince makes a gift to any of his sons out of his inheritance,*o* it shall belong to his sons, it is their holding by inheritance. 17 But if he makes a gift out of his inheritance to one of his servants, it shall be his to the year of liberty; then it shall revert to the prince; only his sons may keep a gift from his inheritance. 18 The prince shall not take any of the inheritance of the people, thrusting them out of their holding; he shall give his sons their inheritance out of his own holding, so that none of my people shall be dispossessed of their holding.

19 Then he brought me through the entrance, which was at the side of the gate, to the north row of the holy chambers for the priests; and there I saw a place at the extreme western end of them. 20 He said to me, "This is the place where the priests shall boil the guilt offering and the sin offering, and where they shall bake the grain offering, in order not to bring them out into the outer court and so communicate holiness to the people."

21 Then he brought me out to the outer court, and led me past the four corners of the court; and in each corner of the court there was a court— 22 in the four corners of the court were small*p* courts, forty cubits long and thirty wide; the four were of the same size. 23 On the inside, around each of the four courts*q* was a row of masonry, with hearths made at the bottom of the rows all around. 24 Then he said to me, "These are the kitchens where those who serve at the temple shall boil the sacrifices of the people."

Water Flowing from the Temple

47 Then he brought me back to the entrance of the temple; there, water was flowing from below the threshold of the temple toward the east (for the temple faced east); and the water was flowing down from below the south end of the threshold of the temple, south of the altar. 2 Then he brought me out by way of the north gate, and led me around on the outside to the outer gate that faces toward the east;*r* and the water was coming out on the south side.

3 Going on eastward with a cord in his hand, the man measured one thousand cubits, and then led me through the water; and it was ankle-deep. 4 Again he measured one thousand, and led me through the water; and it was knee-deep. Again he measured one thousand, and led me through the water; and it was up to the waist. 5 Again he measured one thousand, and it was a river that I could not cross, for the water had risen; it was deep enough to swim in, a river that could not be crossed. 6 He said to me, "Mortal, have you seen this?"

Then he led me back along the bank of the river. 7 As I came back, I saw on the bank of the river a great many trees on the one side and on the other. 8 He said to me, "This water flows toward the eastern region and goes down into the Ar′a·bah; and when it enters the sea, the sea of stagnant waters, the water will become fresh. 9 Wherever the river goes,*s* every living creature that swarms will live, and there will be very many fish, once these waters reach there. It will become fresh; and everything will live where the river goes. 10 People will stand fishing beside the sea*t* from En-ge′di to En-eg′lā·im; it will be a place for the spreading of nets; its fish will be of a great many kinds, like the fish of the Great Sea. 11 But its swamps and marshes will not become fresh; they are to be left for salt. 12 On the banks, on both sides of the river, there will grow all kinds of trees for food. Their leaves will not wither nor their fruit fail, but they will bear fresh fruit every month, because the water for them flows from the sanctuary. Their fruit will be for food, and their leaves for healing."

The New Boundaries of the Land
(Cp Num 34.1–12)

13 Thus says the Lord GOD: These are the boundaries by which you shall divide the land for inheritance among the twelve tribes of Israel. Joseph shall have two portions. 14 You shall divide it equally; I swore to give it to your ancestors, and this land shall fall to you as your inheritance.

EZEK

---

o Gk: Heb *it is his inheritance* *p* Gk Syr Vg: Meaning of Heb uncertain *q* Heb *the four of them* *r* Meaning of Heb uncertain *s* Gk Syr Vg Tg: Heb *the two rivers go* *t* Heb *it*

15 This shall be the boundary of the land: On the north side, from the Great Sea by way of Heth′-lon to Lĕ′bō-hā′math, and on to Zē′dad,*u* 16 Be•rō′-thah, Sib′rā•im (which lies between the border of Damascus and the border of Hā′math), as far as Hā′zer-hat′ti•con, which is on the border of Hau′ran. 17 So the boundary shall run from the sea to Hā′zar- ĕ′non, which is north of the border of Damascus, with the border of Hā′math to the north.*v* This shall be the north side.

18 On the east side, between Hau′ran and Damascus; along the Jordan between Gil′e•ad and the land of Israel; to the eastern sea and as far as Tā-mar.*w* This shall be the east side.

19 On the south side, it shall run from Tā′mar as far as the waters of Mer′i•bath-kā′desh, from there along the Wadi of Egypt*x* to the Great Sea. This shall be the south side.

20 On the west side, the Great Sea shall be the boundary to a point opposite Lĕ′bō-hā′math. This shall be the west side.

21 So you shall divide this land among you according to the tribes of Israel. 22 You shall allot it as an inheritance for yourselves and for the aliens who reside among you and have begotten children among you. They shall be to you as citizens of Israel; with you they shall be allotted an inheritance among the tribes of Israel. 23 In whatever tribe aliens reside, there you shall assign them their inheritance, says the Lord GOD.

The Tribal Portions

48 These are the names of the tribes: Beginning at the northern border, on the Heth′lon road,*y* from Lĕ′bō-hā′math, as far as Hā′-zar-ĕ′non (which is on the border of Damascus, with Hā′math to the north), and*z* extending from the east side to the west,*a* Dan, one portion. 2 Adjoining the territory of Dan, from the east side to the west, Ash′er, one portion. 3 Adjoining the territory of Ash′er, from the east side to the west, Naph′ta•lī, one portion. 4 Adjoining the territory of Naph′ta•lī, from the east side to the west, Ma•nas′-seh, one portion. 5 Adjoining the territory of Ma•nas′seh, from the east side to the west, Ē′phra-im, one portion. 6 Adjoining the territory of Ē′phra•im, from the east side to the west, Reuben, one portion. 7 Adjoining the territory of Reuben, from the east side to the west, Judah, one portion.

8 Adjoining the territory of Judah, from the east side to the west, shall be the portion that you shall set apart, twenty-five thousand cubits in width, and in length equal to one of the tribal portions, from the east side to the west, with the sanctuary in the middle of it. 9 The portion that you shall set apart for the LORD shall be twenty-five thousand cubits in length, and twenty*b* thousand in width. 10 These shall be the allotments of the holy portion: the priests shall have an allotment measuring twenty-five thousand cubits on the northern side, ten thousand cubits in width on the western side, ten thousand in width on the eastern side, and twenty-five thousand in length on the southern side, with the sanctuary of the LORD in the middle of it. 11 This shall be for the consecrated priests, the descendants*c* of Zā′dok, who kept my charge, who did not go astray when the people of Israel went astray, as the Lĕ′vītes did. 12 It shall belong to them as a special portion from the holy portion of the land, a most holy place, adjoining the territory of the Lĕ′vītes. 13 Alongside the territory of the priests, the Lĕ′vītes shall have an allotment twenty-five thousand cubits in length and ten thousand in width. The whole length shall be twenty-five thousand cubits and the width twenty*d* thousand. 14 They shall not sell or exchange any of it; they shall not transfer this choice portion of the land, for it is holy to the LORD.

15 The remainder, five thousand cubits in width and twenty-five thousand in length, shall be for ordinary use for the city, for dwellings and for open country. In the middle of it shall be the city; 16 and these shall be its dimensions: the north side four thousand five hundred cubits, the south side four thousand five hundred, the east side four thousand five hundred, and the west side four thousand five hundred. 17 The city shall have open land: on the north two hundred fifty cubits, on the south two hundred fifty, on the east two hundred fifty, on the west two hundred fifty. 18 The remainder of the length alongside the holy portion shall be ten thousand cubits to the east, and ten thousand to the west, and it shall be alongside the holy portion. Its produce shall be food for the workers of the city. 19 The workers of the city, from all the tribes of Israel, shall cultivate it. 20 The whole portion that you shall set apart shall be twenty-five thousand cubits square, that is, the holy portion together with the property of the city.

21 What remains on both sides of the holy portion and of the property of the city shall belong to the prince. Extending from the twenty-five thousand cubits of the holy portion to the east border, and westward from the twenty-five thousand cubits to the west border, parallel to the tribal portions, it shall belong to the prince. The holy portion with the sanctuary of the temple in the middle of it, 22 and the property of the Lĕ′vītes and of the city,

---

u Gk: Heb *Lebo-zedad,* 16*Hamath*   *v* Meaning of Heb uncertain   *w* Compare Syr: Heb *you shall measure*   *x* Heb lacks *of Egypt*   *y* Compare 47.15: Heb *by the side of the way*   *z* Cn: Heb *and they shall be his*   *a* Gk Compare verses 2-8: Heb *the east side the west*   *b* Compare 45.1: Heb *ten*   *c* One Ms Gk: Heb *of the descendants*   *d* Gk: Heb *ten* shall be in the middle of that which belongs to the prince. The portion of the prince shall lie between the territory of Judah and the territory of Benjamin.

23 As for the rest of the tribes: from the east side to the west, Benjamin, one portion. 24 Adjoining the territory of Benjamin, from the east side to the west, Sim′e·on, one portion. 25 Adjoining the territory of Sim′e·on, from the east side to the west, Is′sa·char, one portion. 26 Adjoining the territory of Is′sa·char, from the east side to the west, Zeb′u·lun, one portion. 27 Adjoining the territory of Zeb′u·lun, from the east side to the west, Gad, one portion. 28 And adjoining the territory of Gad to the south, the boundary shall run from Ta′mar to the waters of Mer′i·bath-ka′desh, from there along the Wadi of Egypt*e* to the Great Sea. 29 This is the land that you shall allot as an inheritance among the tribes of Israel, and these are their portions, says the Lord GOD.

30 These shall be the exits of the city: On the north side, which is to be four thousand five hundred cubits by measure, 31 three gates, the gate of Reuben, the gate of Judah, and the gate of Levi, the gates of the city being named after the tribes of Israel. 32 On the east side, which is to be four thousand five hundred cubits, three gates, the gate of Joseph, the gate of Benjamin, and the gate of Dan. 33 On the south side, which is to be four thousand five hundred cubits by measure, three gates, the gate of Sim′e·on, the gate of Is′sa·char, and the gate of Zeb′u·lun. 34 On the west side, which is to be four thousand five hundred cubits, three gates,*f* the gate of Gad, the gate of Ash′er, and the gate of Naph′ta·li. 35 The circumference of the city shall be eighteen thousand cubits. And the name of the city from that time on shall be, The LORD is There.

---

e Heb lacks *of Egypt* *f* One Ms Gk Syr: MT *their gates three*

The Book of Daniel

Do you have a favorite superhero? One characteristic of these larger-than-life heroes is their commitment to their own values and to saving victims of injustice. The Book of Daniel portrays just such a hero. Daniel's powers are his courage to remain faithful to God despite the threat of punishment, and his special visions, which foresee how things will turn out good even though the present situation seems far from hopeful. These powers enable him to lead his people on the right path in a foreign land filled with persecution and idolatry.

At a Glance

- **Chapters 1–6.** stories of Daniel at the Babylonian court

- **Chapters 7–12.** apocalyptic visions of Daniel

- **Chapters 13–14.** stories about Daniel that were added later

In-depth

Daniel represents the ideal leader with the spiritual and prophetic insight to lead people through troubled times. Scholars question whether he was an actual person. If he was, he lived in the sixth century B.C.—but the Book of Daniel was written four hundred years later, during the reign of an evil Greek-Syrian king, Antiochus IV Epiphanes. This was also the time of the Maccabean revolt told about in 1 and 2 Maccabees (see the timeline at the back of this Bible). King Antiochus desecrated the Temple and attempted to erase many of Israel's religious practices. To many in Israel, this seemed like the end of the world.

The author of the Book of Daniel writes about the great hero Daniel to give the people hope during this persecution. Chapters 1–6 present six stories of Daniel and three friends living their faith during the Babylonian Exile. Chapters 7–12 tell of Daniel's four visions about the empires that dominated Israel after the Exile: Media, Persia, and Greece. The visions are full of strange symbols meant to be understood by the Israelites but not the Greek rulers of the author's time.

Quick Facts

Period Covered
before the Babylonian Exile, the sixth century B.C.

Author
unknown, writing around 164 B.C., during the persecution of Israel by Antiochus IV Epiphanes

Theme
to give hope to those experiencing oppression and persecution

As you read the Book of Daniel, you will find themes familiar from other biblical books. Like Baruch, it describes living faithfully in a strange land. Like 1 and 2 Maccabees, the book shows the courage of Israelites willing to die for their beliefs. And it declares even more clearly than 2 Maccabees and the Wisdom of Solomon the belief in life after death. Daniel is shown as the ideal Jew—the embodiment of all the best of the people in exile. In the face of unjust persecution and oppression, he leads his people in faithfulness to God, even through death itself.

Daniel

Chap. 6

Four Young Israelites at the Babylonian Court
(Cp. 2 Kings 24.10–17)

1 In the third year of the reign of King Je•hoi′a•kim of Judah, King Ne•bū•chad•nez′zar of Babylon came to Jerusalem and besieged it. ² The Lord let King Je•hoi′a•kim of Judah fall into his power, as well as some of the vessels of the house of God. These he brought to the land of Shi′nar,ᵃ and placed the vessels in the treasury of his gods.

3 Then the king commanded his palace master Ash′pe•naz to bring some of the Israelites of the royal family and of the nobility, ⁴ young men without physical defect and handsome, versed in every branch of wisdom, endowed with knowledge and insight, and competent to serve in the king's palace; they were to be taught the literature and language of the Chal•dē′ans. ⁵ The king assigned them a daily portion of the royal rations of food and wine. They were to be educated for three years, so that at the end of that time they could be stationed in the king's court. ⁶ Among them were Daniel, Han•a•nī′ah, Mish′a•el, and Az•a•rī′ah, from the tribe of Judah. ⁷ The palace master gave them other names: Daniel he called Bel•te•shaz′zar, Han•a•nī′ah he called Shad′rach, Mish′a•el he called Mē′shach, and Az•a•rī′ah he called A•bed′ne•gō.

8 But Daniel resolved that he would not defile himself with the royal rations of food and wine; so he asked the palace master to allow him not to defile himself. ⁹ Now God allowed Daniel to receive favor and compassion from the palace master. ¹⁰ The palace master said to Daniel, "I am afraid of my lord the king; he has appointed your food and your drink. If he should see you in poorer condition than the other young men of your own age, you would endanger my head with the king." ¹¹ Then Daniel asked the guard whom the palace master had appointed over Daniel, Han•a•nī′ah, Mish′a•el, and Az•a•rī′ah: ¹² "Please test your servants for ten days. Let us be given vegetables to eat and water to drink. ¹³ You can then compare our appearance with the appearance of the young men who eat the royal rations, and deal with your servants according to what you observe." ¹⁴ So he agreed to this proposal and tested them for ten days. ¹⁵ At the end of ten days it was observed that they appeared better and fatter than all the young men who had been eating the royal rations. ¹⁶ So the guard continued to withdraw their royal rations and the wine they were to drink, and gave them vegetables. ¹⁷ To these four young men God gave knowledge and skill in every aspect of literature and wisdom; Daniel also had insight into all visions and dreams.

18 At the end of the time that the king had set for them to be brought in, the palace master brought them into the presence of Ne•bū•chad•nez′zar, ¹⁹ and the king spoke with them. And

---

ᵃ Gk Theodotion: Heb adds *to the house of his own gods*

1001

among them all, no one was found to compare with Daniel, Han•a•nī′ah, Mish′a•el, and Az•a•rī′ah; therefore they were stationed in the king's court. 20 In every matter of wisdom and understanding concerning which the king inquired of them, he found them ten times better than all the magicians and enchanters in his whole kingdom. 21 And Daniel continued there until the first year of King Cyrus.

Nebuchadnezzar's Dream

2 In the second year of Ne•bū•chad•nez′zar's reign, Ne•bū•chad•nez′zar dreamed such dreams that his spirit was troubled and his sleep left him. 2 So the king commanded that the magicians, the enchanters, the sorcerers, and the Chal•dē′ans be summoned to tell the king his dreams. When they came in and stood before the king, 3 he said to them, "I have had such a dream that my spirit is troubled by the desire to understand it." 4 The Chal•dē′ans said to the king (in Ar•a•mā′ic),b "O king, live forever! Tell your servants the dream, and we will reveal the interpretation." 5 The king answered the Chal•dē′ans, "This is a public decree: if you do not tell me both the dream and its interpretation, you shall be torn limb from limb, and your houses shall be laid in ruins. 6 But if you do tell me the dream and its interpretation, you shall receive from me gifts and rewards and great honor. Therefore tell me the dream and its interpretation." 7 They answered a second time, "Let the king first tell his servants the dream, then we can give its interpretation." 8 The king answered, "I know with certainty that you are trying to gain time, because you see I have firmly decreed: 9 if you do not tell me the dream, there is but one verdict for you. You have agreed to speak lying and misleading words to me until things take a turn. Therefore, tell me the dream, and I shall know that you can give me its interpretation." 10 The Chal•dē′ans answered the king, "There is no one on earth who can reveal what the king demands! In fact no king, however great and powerful, has ever asked such a thing of any magician or enchanter or Chal•dē′an. 11 The thing that the king is asking is too difficult, and no one can reveal it to the king except the gods, whose dwelling is not with mortals."

12 Because of this the king flew into a violent rage and commanded that all the wise men of Babylon be destroyed. 13 The decree was issued, and the wise men were about to be executed; and they looked for Daniel and his companions, to execute them. 14 Then Daniel responded with prudence and discretion to Ar′i•och, the king's chief executioner, who had gone out to execute the wise men of Babylon; 15 he asked Ar′i•och, the royal official, "Why is the decree of the king so urgent?" Ar′i•och then ex-

plained the matter to Daniel. 16 So Daniel went in and requested that the king give him time and he would tell the king the interpretation.

God Reveals Nebuchadnezzar's Dream

17 Then Daniel went to his home and informed his companions, Han•a•nī′ah, Mish′a•el, and Az•a•rī′ah, 18 and told them to seek mercy from the God of heaven concerning this mystery, so that Daniel and his companions with the rest of the wise men of Babylon might not perish. 19 Then the mystery was revealed to Daniel in a vision of the night, and Daniel blessed the God of heaven.
20 Daniel said:

"Blessed be the name of God from age
       to age,
    for wisdom and power are his.
21 He changes times and seasons,
       deposes kings and sets up kings;
he gives wisdom to the wise
       and knowledge to those who have
          understanding.
22 He reveals deep and hidden things;
       he knows what is in the darkness,
       and light dwells with him.
23 To you, O God of my ancestors,
       I give thanks and praise,
for you have given me wisdom and
          power,
    and have now revealed to me what we
          asked of you,
for you have revealed to us what the king
          ordered."

Daniel Interprets the Dream

24 Therefore Daniel went to Ar′i•och, whom the king had appointed to destroy the wise men of Babylon, and said to him, "Do not destroy the wise men of Babylon; bring me in before the king, and I will give the king the interpretation."

25 Then Ar′i•och quickly brought Daniel before the king and said to him: "I have found among the exiles from Judah a man who can tell the king the interpretation." 26 The king said to Daniel, whose name was Bel•te•shaz′zar, "Are you able to tell me the dream that I have seen and its interpretation?" 27 Daniel answered the king, "No wise men, enchanters, magicians, or diviners can show to the king the mystery that the king is asking, 28 but there is a God in heaven who reveals mysteries, and he has disclosed to King Ne•bū•chad•nez′zar what will happen at the end of days. Your dream and the visions of your head as you lay in bed were these: 29 To you, O king, as you lay in bed, came thoughts

b The text from this point to the end of chapter 7 is in Aramaic, except for 3.24-91a, the text of which is in Greek of what would be hereafter, and the revealer of mysteries disclosed to you what is to be. 30 But as for me, this mystery has not been revealed to me because of any wisdom that I have more than any other living being, but in order that the interpretation may be known to the king and that you may understand the thoughts of your mind.

31 "You were looking, O king, and lo! there was a great statue. This statue was huge, its brilliance extraordinary; it was standing before you, and its appearance was frightening. 32 The head of that statue was of fine gold, its chest and arms of silver, its middle and thighs of bronze, 33 its legs of iron, its feet partly of iron and partly of clay. 34 As you looked on, a stone was cut out, not by human hands, and it struck the statue on its feet of iron and clay and broke them in pieces. 35 Then the iron, the clay, the bronze, the silver, and the gold, were all broken in pieces and became like the chaff of the summer threshing floors; and the wind carried them away, so that not a trace of them could be found. But the stone that struck the statue became a great mountain and filled the whole earth.

36 "This was the dream; now we will tell the king its interpretation. 37 You, O king, the king of kings—to whom the God of heaven has given the kingdom, the power, the might, and the glory, 38 into whose hand he has given human beings, wherever they live, the wild animals of the field, and the birds of the air, and whom he has established as ruler over them all—you are the head of gold. 39 After you shall arise another kingdom inferior to yours, and yet a third kingdom of bronze, which shall rule over the whole earth. 40 And there shall be a fourth kingdom, strong as iron; just as iron crushes and smashes everything,c it shall crush and shatter all these. 41 As you saw the feet and toes partly of potter's clay and partly of iron, it shall be a divided kingdom; but some of the strength of iron shall be in it, as you saw the iron mixed with the clay. 42 As the toes of the feet were part iron and part clay, so the kingdom shall be partly strong and partly brittle. 43 As you saw the iron mixed with clay, so will they mix with one another in marriage,d but they will not hold together, just as iron does not mix with clay. 44 And in the days of those kings the God of heaven will set up a kingdom that shall never be destroyed, nor shall this kingdom be left to another people. It shall crush all these kingdoms and bring them to an end, and it shall stand forever; 45 just as you saw that a stone was cut from the mountain not by hands, and that it crushed the iron, the bronze, the clay, the silver, and the gold. The great God has informed the king what shall be hereafter. The dream is certain, and its interpretation trustworthy."

Daniel and His Friends Promoted

46 Then King Ne•bu•chad•nez'zar fell on his face, worshiped Daniel, and commanded that a grain offering and incense be offered to him. 47 The king said to Daniel, "Truly, your God is God of gods and Lord of kings and a revealer of mysteries, for you have been able to reveal this mystery!" 48 Then the king promoted Daniel, gave him many great gifts, and made him ruler over the whole province of Babylon and chief prefect over all the wise men of Babylon. 49 Daniel made a request of the king, and he appointed Shad'rach, Me'shach, and A•bed'ne•go over the affairs of the province of Babylon. But Daniel remained at the king's court.

The Golden Image

3 King Ne•bu•chad•nez'zar made a golden statue whose height was sixty cubits and whose width was six cubits; he set it up on the plain of Du'ra in the province of Babylon. 2 Then King Ne•bu•chad•nez'zar sent for the satraps, the prefects, and the governors, the counselors, the treasurers, the justices, the magistrates, and all the officials of the provinces, to assemble and come to the dedication of the statue that King Ne•bu•chad•nez'zar had set up. 3 So the satraps, the prefects, and the governors, the counselors, the treasurers, the justices, the magistrates, and all the officials of the provinces, assembled for the dedication of the statue that King Ne•bu•chad•nez'zar had set up. When they were standing before the statue that Ne•bu•chad•nez'zar had set up, 4 the herald proclaimed aloud, "You are commanded, O peoples, nations, and languages, 5 that when you hear the sound of the horn, pipe, lyre, trigon, harp, drum, and entire musical ensemble, you are to fall down and worship the golden statue that King Ne•bu•chad•nez'zar has set up. 6 Whoever does not fall down and worship shall immediately be thrown into a furnace of blazing fire." 7 Therefore, as soon as all the peoples heard the sound of the horn, pipe, lyre, trigon, harp, drum, and entire musical ensemble, all the peoples, nations, and languages fell down and worshiped the golden statue that King Ne•bu•chad•nez'zar had set up.

8 Accordingly, at this time certain Chal•de'ans came forward and denounced the Jews. 9 They said to King Ne•bu•chad•nez'zar, "O king, live forever! 10 You, O king, have made a decree, that everyone who hears the sound of the horn, pipe, lyre, trigon, harp, drum, and entire musical ensemble, shall fall down and worship the golden statue, 11 and whoever does not fall down and worship shall be thrown into a furnace of blazing fire. 12 There are

D
A
N

---

c Gk Theodotion Syr Vg: Aram adds and like iron that crushes   d Aram by human seed certain Jews whom you have appointed over the affairs of the province of Babylon: Shad'rach, Mē'-shach, and A·bed'ne·gō. These pay no heed to you, O king. They do not serve your gods and they do not worship the golden statue that you have set up."

13 Then Ne·bū·chad·nez'zar in furious rage commanded that Shad'rach, Mē'shach, and A·bed'-ne·gō be brought in; so they brought those men before the king. 14 Ne·bū·chad·nez'zar said to them, "Is it true, O Shad'rach, Mē'shach, and A·bed'ne·gō, that you do not serve my gods and you do not worship the golden statue that I have set up? 15 Now if you are ready when you hear the sound of the horn, pipe, lyre, trigon, harp, drum, and entire musical ensemble to fall down and worship the statue that I have made, well and good.ᵉ But if you do not worship, you shall immediately be thrown into a furnace of blazing fire, and who is the god that will deliver you out of my hands?"

16 Shad'rach, Mē'shach, and A·bed'ne·gō answered the king, "O Ne·bū·chad·nez'zar, we have no need to present a defense to you in this matter. 17 If our God whom we serve is able to deliver us from the furnace of blazing fire and out of your hand, O king, let him deliver us.ᶠ 18 But if not, be it known to you, O king, that we will not serve your gods and we will not worship the golden statue that you have set up."

The Fiery Furnace

19 Then Ne·bū·chad·nez'zar was so filled with rage against Shad'rach, Mē'shach, and A·bed'ne·gō that his face was distorted. He ordered the furnace heated up seven times more than was customary, 20 and ordered some of the strongest guards in his army to bind Shad'rach, Mē'shach, and A·bed'ne·gō and to throw them into the furnace of blazing fire.

21 So the men were bound, still wearing their tunics,ᵍ their trousers,ᵍ their hats, and their other garments, and they were thrown into the furnace of blazing fire. 22 Because the king's command was urgent and the furnace was so overheated, the raging flames killed the men who lifted Shad'rach, Mē'shach, and A·bed'ne·gō. 23 But the three men, Shad'rach, Mē'shach, and A·bed'ne·gō, fell down, bound, into the furnace of blazing fire.

The Prayer of Azariah in the Furnace

24 They walked around in the midst of the flames, singing hymns to God and blessing the Lord. 25 Then Az·a·rī'ah stood still in the fire and prayed aloud:

26 "Blessed are you, O Lord, God of our ancestors,
   and worthy of praise;
   and glorious is your name forever!
27 For you are just in all you have done;
   all your works are true and your ways right,
   and all your judgments are true.
28 You have executed true judgments in all you
      have brought upon us
   and upon Jerusalem, the holy city of our
      ancestors;
   by a true judgment you have brought all
      this upon us because of our sins.
29 For we have sinned and broken your law in
      turning away from you;
   in all matters we have sinned grievously.
30 We have not obeyed your commandments,
   we have not kept them or done what you
      have commanded us for our own
      good.

ᵉ Aram lacks *well and good* ᶠ Or *If our God whom we serve is able to deliver us, he will deliver us from the furnace of blazing fire and out of your hand, O king.* ᵍ Meaning of Aram word uncertain

Doing the Right Thing

Chapter 3 of Daniel tells us of Shadrach, Meshach, and Abednego, three companions of Daniel's who refuse to compromise their religious beliefs. Even in the face of death, they will not denounce the Lord and worship the god of Nebuchadnezzar (also called Nebuchadrezzar).

The pressure to do what we know is wrong takes many forms. Caving in to that pressure leads many people to suffering, because by definition, sin leads to unhappy and unhealthy consequences. It may offer some short-term satisfaction, but denying what we know is right is ultimately denying God and the fullness of life God has planned for us.

Follow Shadrach, Meshach, and Abednego's example and stand up for what is right, stand up for God!

▶ Dan 3.1–24

31 So all that you have brought upon us,
    and all that you have done to us,
    you have done by a true judgment.
32 You have handed us over to our enemies,
      lawless and hateful rebels,
    and to an unjust king, the most wicked in
      all the world.
33 And now we cannot open our mouths;
    we, your servants who worship you, have
      become a shame and a reproach.
34 For your name's sake do not give us up
      forever,
    and do not annul your covenant.
35 Do not withdraw your mercy from us,
  for the sake of Abraham your beloved
    and for the sake of your servant Isaac
    and Israel your holy one,
36 to whom you promised
    to multiply their descendants like the stars
      of heaven
    and like the sand on the shore of the sea.
37 For we, O Lord, have become fewer than any
      other nation,
    and are brought low this day in all the
      world because of our sins.
38 In our day we have no ruler, or prophet, or
      leader,
    no burnt offering, or sacrifice, or oblation,
      or incense,
    no place to make an offering before you
      and to find mercy.
39 Yet with a contrite heart and a humble spirit
      may we be accepted,
40   as though it were with burnt offerings of
      rams and bulls,
    or with tens of thousands of fat lambs;
    such may our sacrifice be in your sight
      today,
    and may we unreservedly follow you,*h*
    for no shame will come to those who trust
      in you.
41 And now with all our heart we follow you;
    we fear you and seek your presence.
42 Do not put us to shame,
    but deal with us in your patience
    and in your abundant mercy.
43 Deliver us in accordance with your marvelous
      works,
    and bring glory to your name, O Lord.
44 Let all who do harm to your servants be put to
      shame;
    let them be disgraced and deprived of all
      power,
    and let their strength be broken.
45 Let them know that you alone are the Lord
      God,
    glorious over the whole world."

The Song of the Three Jews

46 Now the king's servants who threw them in
kept stoking the furnace with naphtha, pitch, tow,
and brushwood. 47 And the flames poured out
above the furnace forty-nine cubits, 48 and spread
out and burned those Chal·dē′ans who were caught
near the furnace. 49 But the angel of the Lord came
down into the furnace to be with Az·a·ri′ah and his
companions, and drove the fiery flame out of the
furnace, 50 and made the inside of the furnace as
though a moist wind were whistling through it. The
fire did not touch them at all and caused them no
pain or distress.

51 Then the three with one voice praised and
glorified and blessed God in the furnace:
52 "Blessed are you, O Lord, God of our ancestors,
    and to be praised and highly exalted
      forever;
  And blessed is your glorious, holy name,
    and to be highly praised and highly exalted
      forever.
53 Blessed are you in the temple of your holy
      glory,
    and to be extolled and highly glorified
      forever.
54 Blessed are you who look into the depths from
      your throne on the cherubim,
    and to be praised and highly exalted
      forever.
55 Blessed are you on the throne of your
      kingdom,
    and to be extolled and highly exalted
      forever.
56 Blessed are you in the firmament of heaven,
    and to be sung and glorified forever.

57 "Bless the Lord, all you works of the Lord;
    sing praise to him and highly exalt him
      forever.
58 Bless the Lord, you heavens;
    sing praise to him and highly exalt him
      forever.
59 Bless the Lord, you angels of the Lord;
    sing praise to him and highly exalt him
      forever.
60 Bless the Lord, all you waters above the
      heavens;
    sing praise to him and highly exalt him
      forever.
61 Bless the Lord, all you powers of the Lord;
    sing praise to him and highly exalt him
      forever.
62 Bless the Lord, sun and moon;
    sing praise to him and highly exalt him
      forever.

h Meaning of Gk uncertain

D
A
N

63 Bless the Lord, stars of heaven;
      sing praise to him and highly exalt him
          forever.

64 "Bless the Lord, all rain and dew;
      sing praise to him and highly exalt him
          forever.
65 Bless the Lord, all you winds;
      sing praise to him and highly exalt him
          forever.
66 Bless the Lord, fire and heat;
      sing praise to him and highly exalt him
          forever.
67 Bless the Lord, winter cold and summer heat;
      sing praise to him and highly exalt him
          forever.
68 Bless the Lord, dews and falling snow;
      sing praise to him and highly exalt him
          forever.
69 Bless the Lord, ice and cold;
      sing praise to him and highly exalt him
          forever.
70 Bless the Lord, frosts and snows;
      sing praise to him and highly exalt him
          forever.
71 Bless the Lord, nights and days;
      sing praise to him and highly exalt him
          forever.
72 Bless the Lord, light and darkness;
      sing praise to him and highly exalt him
          forever.
73 Bless the Lord, lightnings and clouds;
      sing praise to him and highly exalt him
          forever.

74 "Let the earth bless the Lord;
      let it sing praise to him and highly exalt
          him forever.
75 Bless the Lord, mountains and hills;
      sing praise to him and highly exalt him
          forever.
76 Bless the Lord, all that grows in the ground;
      sing praise to him and highly exalt him
          forever.
77 Bless the Lord, you springs;
      sing praise to him and highly exalt him
          forever.
78 Bless the Lord, seas and rivers;
      sing praise to him and highly exalt him
          forever.
79 Bless the Lord, you whales and all that swim in
          the waters;
      sing praise to him and highly exalt him
          forever.
80 Bless the Lord, all birds of the air;
      sing praise to him and highly exalt him
          forever.

3.19–97

81 Bless the Lord, all wild animals and cattle;
      sing praise to him and highly exalt him
          forever.

82 "Bless the Lord, all people on earth;
      sing praise to him and highly exalt him
          forever.
83 Bless the Lord, O Israel;
      sing praise to him and highly exalt him
          forever.
84 Bless the Lord, you priests of the Lord;
      sing praise to him and highly exalt him
          forever.
85 Bless the Lord, you servants of the Lord;
      sing praise to him and highly exalt him
          forever.
86 Bless the Lord, spirits and souls of the
          righteous;
      sing praise to him and highly exalt him
          forever.
87 Bless the Lord, you who are holy and humble
          in heart;
      sing praise to him and highly exalt him
          forever.

88 "Bless the Lord, Han·a·ni′ah, Az·a·ri′ah, and
          Mish′a·el;
      sing praise to him and highly exalt him
          forever.
    For he has rescued us from Hades and saved us
          from the power[i] of death,
      and delivered us from the midst of the
          burning fiery furnace;
      from the midst of the fire he has
          delivered us.

---

i Gk *hand*

89 Give thanks to the Lord, for he is good,
  for his mercy endures forever.
90 All who worship the Lord, bless the God of
    gods,
  sing praise to him and give thanks to him,
  for his mercy endures forever."

91 Hearing them sing, and amazed at seeing
them alive, King Ne·bū·chad·nez′zar rose up quickly. He said to his counselors, "Was it not three men
that we threw bound into the fire?" They answered
the king, "True, O king." 92 He replied, "But I see
four men unbound, walking in the middle of the
fire, and they are not hurt; and the fourth has the
appearance of a god."ʲ 93 Ne·bū·chad·nez′zar then
approached the door of the furnace of blazing fire
and said, "Shad′rach, Mē′shach, and A·bed′ne·gō,
servants of the Most High God, come out! Come
here!" So Shad′rach, Mē′shach, and A·bed′ne·gō
came out from the fire. 94 And the satraps, the prefects, the governors, and the king's counselors gathered together and saw that the fire had not had any
power over the bodies of those men; the hair of
their heads was not singed, their tunicsᵏ were not
harmed, and not even the smell of fire came from
them. 95 Ne·bū·chad·nez′zar said, "Blessed be the
God of Shad′rach, Mē′shach, and A·bed′ne·gō, who
has sent his angel and delivered his servants who
trusted in him. They disobeyed the king's command and yielded up their bodies rather than serve
and worship any god except their own God.
96 Therefore I make a decree: Any people, nation, or
language that utters blasphemy against the God of
Shad′rach, Mē′shach, and A·bed′ne·gō shall be torn
limb from limb, and their houses laid in ruins; for
there is no other god who is able to deliver in this
way." 97 Then the king promoted Shad′rach,
Mē′shach, and A·bed′ne·gō in the province of
Babylon.

Nebuchadnezzar's Second Dream

4 ˡ King Ne·bū·chad·nez′zar to all peoples, nations, and languages that live throughout the
earth: May you have abundant prosperity! 2 The
signs and wonders that the Most High God has
worked for me I am pleased to recount.
3 How great are his signs,
    how mighty his wonders!
  His kingdom is an everlasting kingdom,
    and his sovereignty is from generation to
      generation.
4ᵐ I, Ne·bū·chad·nez′zar, was living at ease in
my home and prospering in my palace. 5 I saw a
dream that frightened me; my fantasies in bed and
the visions of my head terrified me. 6 So I made a
decree that all the wise men of Babylon should be
brought before me, in order that they might tell me
the interpretation of the dream. 7 Then the magi-

cians, the enchanters, the Chal·dē′ans, and the diviners came in, and I told them the dream, but they
could not tell me its interpretation. 8 At last Daniel
came in before me—he who was named Bel·te-
shaz′zar after the name of my god, and who is endowed with a spirit of the holy godsⁿ—and I told
him the dream: 9 "O Bel·te·shaz′zar, chief of the
magicians, I know that you are endowed with a
spirit of the holy godsⁿ and that no mystery is too
difficult for you. Hearᵒ the dream that I saw; tell me
its interpretation.

ʲ Aram *a son of the gods*   ᵏ Meaning of Aram word
uncertain   ˡ Ch 3.31 in Aram   ᵐ Ch 4.1 in Aram   ⁿ Or *a
holy, divine spirit*   ᵒ Theodotion: Aram *The visions of*

PRAY IT!
King Nebuchadnezzar's Conversion

Sometimes, it seems God has to go to
extremes to get our attention. In Daniel, chapter 4 (written like a letter from
the king to his subjects), King Nebuchadnezzar tells how he had to go through
some pretty intense humiliation—acting
like a wild animal (verses 32–33)—before
God got his attention. Even Daniel's prior
warning didn't rein in his ego and bring
him to his senses (see verses 26–27).
After Nebuchadnezzar's reason returned,
he realized the power of God and turned
to praise and honor God.

   Many people go through a conversion
—a turning toward God—after they have
suffered the consequences of their sinful
actions. For others, the catalyst might be
an illness or the death of a close friend or
family member. Why does it take a crisis
for us to realize our need for God? Maybe
because during such a time, we realize
that we cannot control life and that we
need God's loving presence.

   In your prayer, reflect or journal on
the following questions:
■ Where do you recognize your need
  for God?
■ Is a conversion toward God in a crisis
  only a temporary thing, or can it lead
  to a lifelong commitment? Why?

▸ Daniel, chapter 4

DAN

10*p* Upon my bed this is what I saw;
　　there was a tree at the center of the earth,
　　and its height was great.
11 The tree grew great and strong,
　　its top reached to heaven,
　　and it was visible to the ends of the whole
　　　earth.
12 Its foliage was beautiful,
　　its fruit abundant,
　　and it provided food for all.
The animals of the field found shade under it,
　　the birds of the air nested in its branches,
　　and from it all living beings were fed.

13 "I continued looking, in the visions of my head as I lay in bed, and there was a holy watcher, coming down from heaven. 14 He cried aloud and said:

'Cut down the tree and chop off its branches,
　　strip off its foliage and scatter its fruit.
Let the animals flee from beneath it
　　and the birds from its branches.
15 But leave its stump and roots in the ground,
　　with a band of iron and bronze,
　　in the tender grass of the field.
Let him be bathed with the dew of heaven,
　　and let his lot be with the animals of the
　　　field
　　in the grass of the earth.
16 Let his mind be changed from that of a human,
　　and let the mind of an animal be given to
　　　him.
And let seven times pass over him.
17 The sentence is rendered by decree of the
　　　watchers,
　　the decision is given by order of the holy
　　　ones,
in order that all who live may know
　　that the Most High is sovereign over the
　　　kingdom of mortals;
he gives it to whom he will
　　and sets over it the lowliest of human
　　　beings.'

18 "This is the dream that I, King Ne·bu·chad·nez'zar, saw. Now you, Bel·te·shaz'zar, declare the interpretation, since all the wise men of my kingdom are unable to tell me the interpretation. You are able, however, for you are endowed with a spirit of the holy gods."*q*

Daniel Interprets the Second Dream

19 Then Daniel, who was called Bel·te·shaz'zar, was severely distressed for a while. His thoughts terrified him. The king said, "Bel·te·shaz'zar, do not let the dream or the interpretation terrify you." Bel·te·shaz'zar answered, "My lord, may the dream be for those who hate you, and its interpretation for your enemies! 20 The tree that you saw, which grew great and strong, so that its top reached to heaven and was visible to the end of the whole earth, 21 whose foliage was beautiful and its fruit abundant, and which provided food for all, under which animals of the field lived, and in whose branches the birds of the air had nests— 22 it is you, O king! You have grown great and strong. Your greatness has increased and reaches to heaven, and your sovereignty to the ends of the earth. 23 And whereas the king saw a holy watcher coming down from heaven and saying, 'Cut down the tree and destroy it, but leave its stump and roots in the ground, with a band of iron and bronze, in the grass of the field; and let him be bathed with the dew of heaven, and let his lot be with the animals of the field, until seven times pass over him'— 24 this is the interpretation, O king, and it is a decree of the Most High that has come upon my lord the king: 25 You shall be driven away from human society, and your dwelling shall be with the wild animals. You shall be made to eat grass like oxen, you shall be bathed with the dew of heaven, and seven times shall pass over you, until you have learned that the Most High has sovereignty over the kingdom of mortals, and gives it to whom he will. 26 As it was commanded to leave the stump and roots of the tree, your kingdom shall be re-established for you from the time that you learn that Heaven is sovereign. 27 Therefore, O king, may my counsel be acceptable to you: atone for*r* your sins with righteousness, and your iniquities with mercy to the oppressed, so that your prosperity may be prolonged."

Nebuchadnezzar's Humiliation

28 All this came upon King Ne·bu·chad·nez'zar. 29 At the end of twelve months he was walking on the roof of the royal palace of Babylon, 30 and the king said, "Is this not magnificent Babylon, which I have built as a royal capital by my mighty power and for my glorious majesty?" 31 While the words were still in the king's mouth, a voice came from heaven: "O King Ne·bu·chad·nez'zar, to you it is declared: The kingdom has departed from you! 32 You shall be driven away from human society, and your dwelling shall be with the animals of the field. You shall be made to eat grass like oxen, and seven times shall pass over you, until you have learned that the Most High has sovereignty over the kingdom of mortals and gives it to whom he will." 33 Immediately the sentence was fulfilled against Ne·bu·chad·nez'zar. He was driven away from human society, ate grass like oxen, and his body was

---

p Theodotion Syr Compare Gk: Aram adds *The visions of my head*　　*q* Or *a holy, divine spirit*　　*r* Aram *break off* bathed with the dew of heaven, until his hair grew as long as eagles' feathers and his nails became like birds' claws.

Nebuchadnezzar Praises God

34 When that period was over, I, Ne•bū•chad-nez′zar, lifted my eyes to heaven, and my reason returned to me.

I blessed the Most High,
>   and praised and honored the one who lives
>   forever.

For his sovereignty is an everlasting
>   sovereignty,
>   and his kingdom endures from generation
>   to generation.

35 All the inhabitants of the earth are accounted
>   as nothing,
>   and he does what he wills with the host of
>   heaven
>   and the inhabitants of the earth.

There is no one who can stay his hand
>   or say to him, "What are you doing?"

36 At that time my reason returned to me; and my majesty and splendor were restored to me for the glory of my kingdom. My counselors and my lords sought me out, I was re-established over my kingdom, and still more greatness was added to me. 37 Now I, Ne•bū•chad•nez′zar, praise and extol and honor the King of heaven,
>   for all his works are truth,
>   and his ways are justice;
>   and he is able to bring low
>   those who walk in pride.

Belshazzar's Feast

5 King Bel•shaz′zar made a great festival for a thousand of his lords, and he was drinking wine in the presence of the thousand.

2 Under the influence of the wine, Bel•shaz′zar commanded that they bring in the vessels of gold and silver that his father Ne•bū•chad•nez′zar had taken out of the temple in Jerusalem, so that the king and his lords, his wives, and his concubines might drink from them. 3 So they brought in the vessels of gold and silver[s] that had been taken out of the temple, the house of God in Jerusalem, and the king and his lords, his wives, and his concubines drank from them. 4 They drank the wine and praised the gods of gold and silver, bronze, iron, wood, and stone.

The Writing on the Wall

5 Immediately the fingers of a human hand appeared and began writing on the plaster of the wall of the royal palace, next to the lampstand. The king was watching the hand as it wrote. 6 Then the king's face turned pale, and his thoughts terrified him. His limbs gave way, and his knees knocked together. 7 The king cried aloud to bring in the enchanters, the Chal•dē′ans, and the diviners; and the king said to the wise men of Babylon, "Whoever can read this writing and tell me its interpretation shall be clothed in purple, have a chain of gold around his neck, and rank third in the kingdom." 8 Then all the king's wise men came in, but they could not read the writing or tell the king the interpretation. 9 Then King Bel•shaz′zar became greatly terrified and his face turned pale, and his lords were perplexed.

10 The queen, when she heard the discussion of the king and his lords, came into the banqueting hall. The queen said, "O king, live forever! Do not let your thoughts terrify you or your face grow pale. 11 There is a man in your kingdom who is endowed with a spirit of the holy gods.[t] In the days of your father he was found to have enlightenment, understanding, and wisdom like the wisdom of the gods. Your father, King Ne•bū•chad•nez′zar, made him chief of the magicians, enchanters, Chal•dē′ans, and diviners,[u] 12 because an excellent spirit, knowledge, and understanding to interpret dreams, explain riddles, and solve problems were found in this Daniel, whom the king named Bel•te•shaz′zar. Now let Daniel be called, and he will give the interpretation."

The Writing on the Wall Interpreted

13 Then Daniel was brought in before the king. The king said to Daniel, "So you are Daniel, one of the exiles of Judah, whom my father the king brought from Judah? 14 I have heard of you that a spirit of the gods[v] is in you, and that enlightenment, understanding, and excellent wisdom are found in you. 15 Now the wise men, the enchanters, have been brought in before me to read this writing and tell me its interpretation, but they were not able to give the interpretation of the matter. 16 But I have heard that you can give interpretations and solve problems. Now if you are able to read the writing and tell me its interpretation, you shall be clothed in purple, have a chain of gold around your neck, and rank third in the kingdom."

17 Then Daniel answered in the presence of the king, "Let your gifts be for yourself, or give your rewards to someone else! Nevertheless I will read the writing to the king and let him know the interpretation. 18 O king, the Most High God gave your father Ne•bū•chad•nez′zar kingship, greatness, glory, and majesty. 19 And because of the greatness that he gave him, all peoples, nations, and languages

---

s Theodotion Vg: Aram lacks *and silver*   t Or *a holy,*
divine spirit   u Aram adds *the king your father*   v Or *a*
divine spirit

trembled and feared before him. He killed those he wanted to kill, kept alive those he wanted to keep alive, honored those he wanted to honor, and degraded those he wanted to degrade. 20 But when his heart was lifted up and his spirit was hardened so that he acted proudly, he was deposed from his kingly throne, and his glory was stripped from him. 21 He was driven from human society, and his mind was made like that of an animal. His dwelling was with the wild asses, he was fed grass like oxen, and his body was bathed with the dew of heaven, until he learned that the Most High God has sovereignty over the kingdom of mortals, and sets over it whomever he will. 22 And you, Bel·shaz′zar his son, have not humbled your heart, even though you knew all this! 23 You have exalted yourself against the Lord of heaven! The vessels of his temple have been brought in before you, and you and your lords, your wives and your concubines have been drinking wine from them. You have praised the gods of silver and gold, of bronze, iron, wood, and stone, which do not see or hear or know; but the God in whose power is your very breath, and to whom belong all your ways, you have not honored.

24 "So from his presence the hand was sent and this writing was inscribed. 25 And this is the writing that was inscribed: MENE, MENE, TEKEL, and PARSIN. 26 This is the interpretation of the matter: MENE, God has numbered the days of[w] your kingdom and brought it to an end; 27 TEKEL, you have been weighed on the scales and found wanting; 28 PERES,[x] your kingdom is divided and given to the Mēdes and Persians."

29 Then Bel·shaz′zar gave the command, and Daniel was clothed in purple, a chain of gold was put around his neck, and a proclamation was made concerning him that he should rank third in the kingdom.

30 That very night Bel·shaz′zar, the Chal·dē′an king, was killed. 31[y] And Da·rī′us the Mēde received the kingdom, being about sixty-two years old.

The Plot against Daniel

6 It pleased Da·rī′us to set over the kingdom one hundred twenty satraps, stationed throughout the whole kingdom, 2 and over them three presidents, including Daniel; to these the satraps gave account, so that the king might suffer no loss. 3 Soon Daniel distinguished himself above all the other presidents and satraps because an excellent spirit was in him, and the king planned to appoint him over the whole kingdom. 4 So the presidents and the satraps tried to find grounds for complaint against Daniel in connection with the kingdom. But they could find no grounds for complaint or any corruption, because he was faithful, and no negligence or corruption could be found in

him. 5 The men said, "We shall not find any ground for complaint against this Daniel unless we find it in connection with the law of his God."

6 So the presidents and satraps conspired and came to the king and said to him, "O King Da·rī′us, live forever! 7 All the presidents of the kingdom, the prefects and the satraps, the counselors and the governors are agreed that the king should establish an ordinance and enforce an interdict, that whoever prays to anyone, divine or human, for thirty days, except to you, O king, shall be thrown into a den of lions. 8 Now, O king, establish the interdict and sign the document, so that it cannot be changed, according to the law of the Mēdes and the Persians, which cannot be revoked." 9 Therefore King Da·rī′us signed the document and interdict.

Daniel in the Lions' Den

10 Although Daniel knew that the document had been signed, he continued to go to his house, which had windows in its upper room open toward Jerusalem, and to get down on his knees three times a day to pray to his God and praise him, just as he had done previously. 11 The conspirators came and found Daniel praying and seeking mercy before his God. 12 Then they approached the king and said concerning the interdict, "O king! Did you not sign an interdict, that anyone who prays to anyone, divine or human, within thirty days except to you, O king, shall be thrown into a den of lions?" The king answered, "The thing stands fast, according to the law of the Mēdes and Persians, which cannot be revoked." 13 Then they responded to the king, "Daniel, one of the exiles from Judah, pays no attention to you, O king, or to the interdict you have signed, but he is saying his prayers three times a day."

14 When the king heard the charge, he was very much distressed. He was determined to save Daniel, and until the sun went down he made every effort to rescue him. 15 Then the conspirators came to the king and said to him, "Know, O king, that it is a law of the Mēdes and Persians that no interdict or ordinance that the king establishes can be changed."

16 Then the king gave the command, and Daniel was brought and thrown into the den of lions. The king said to Daniel, "May your God, whom you faithfully serve, deliver you!" 17 A stone was brought and laid on the mouth of the den, and the king sealed it with his own signet and with the signet of his lords, so that nothing might be changed concerning Daniel. 18 Then the king went to his palace and spent the night fasting; no food was brought to him, and sleep fled from him.

---

w Aram lacks *the days of*   x The singular of *Parsin*   y Ch 6.1 in Aram

Daniel Saved from the Lions

19 Then, at break of day, the king got up and hurried to the den of lions. 20 When he came near the den where Daniel was, he cried out anxiously to Daniel, "O Daniel, servant of the living God, has your God whom you faithfully serve been able to deliver you from the lions?" 21 Daniel then said to the king, "O king, live forever! 22 My God sent his angel and shut the lions' mouths so that they would not hurt me, because I was found blameless before him; and also before you, O king, I have done no wrong." 23 Then the king was exceedingly glad and commanded that Daniel be taken up out of the den. So Daniel was taken up out of the den, and no kind of harm was found on him, because he had trusted in his God. 24 The king gave a command, and those who had accused Daniel were brought and thrown into the den of lions—they, their children, and their wives. Before they reached the bottom of the den the lions overpowered them and broke all their bones in pieces.

25 Then King Da•ri′us wrote to all peoples and nations of every language throughout the whole world: "May you have abundant prosperity! 26 I make a decree, that in all my royal dominion people should tremble and fear before the God of Daniel:

For he is the living God,
    enduring forever.
His kingdom shall never be destroyed,
    and his dominion has no end.
27 He delivers and rescues,
    he works signs and wonders in heaven and
        on earth;
for he has saved Daniel
    from the power of the lions."

28 So this Daniel prospered during the reign of Da•ri′us and the reign of Cyrus the Persian.

Visions of the Four Beasts

7 In the first year of King Bel•shaz′zar of Babylon, Daniel had a dream and visions of his head as he lay in bed. Then he wrote down the dream:ᶻ 2 I,ᵃ Daniel, saw in my vision by night the four winds of heaven stirring up the great sea, 3 and four great beasts came up out of the sea, different from one another. 4 The first was like a lion and had eagles' wings. Then, as I watched, its wings were plucked off, and it was lifted up from the ground and made to stand on two feet like a human being; and a human mind was given to it. 5 Another beast appeared, a second one, that looked like a bear. It was raised up on one side, had three tusksᵇ in its mouth among its teeth and was told, "Arise, devour many bodies!" 6 After this, as I watched, another appeared, like a leopard. The beast had four wings of a bird on its back and four heads; and do-

minion was given to it. 7 After this I saw in the visions by night a fourth beast, terrifying and dreadful and exceedingly strong. It had great iron teeth and was devouring, breaking in pieces, and stamping what was left with its feet. It was different from all the beasts that preceded it, and it had ten horns. 8 I was considering the horns, when another horn appeared, a little one coming up among them; to make room for it, three of the earlier horns were plucked up by the roots. There were eyes like human eyes in this horn, and a mouth speaking arrogantly.

Judgment before the Ancient One

9 As I watched,
thrones were set in place,
    and an Ancient Oneᶜ took his throne,
his clothing was white as snow,
    and the hair of his head like pure wool;
his throne was fiery flames,
    and its wheels were burning fire.
10 A stream of fire issued
    and flowed out from his presence.
A thousand thousands served him,
    and ten thousand times ten thousand stood
        attending him.
The court sat in judgment,
    and the books were opened.

11 I watched then because of the noise of the arrogant words that the horn was speaking. And as I watched, the beast was put to death, and its body destroyed and given over to be burned with fire. 12 As for the rest of the beasts, their dominion was taken away, but their lives were prolonged for a season and a time. 13 As I watched in the night visions,

I saw one like a human beingᵈ
    coming with the clouds of heaven.
And he came to the Ancient Oneᵉ
    and was presented before him.
14 To him was given dominion
    and glory and kingship,
that all peoples, nations, and languages
    should serve him.
His dominion is an everlasting dominion
    that shall not pass away,
and his kingship is one
    that shall never be destroyed.

Daniel's Visions Interpreted

15 As for me, Daniel, my spirit was troubled within me,ᶠ and the visions of my head terrified me.

ᶻ Q Ms Theodotion: MT adds *the beginning of the words; he said*   ᵃ Theodotion: Aram *Daniel answered and said, I*   ᵇ Or *ribs*   ᶜ Aram *an Ancient of Days*   ᵈ Aram *one like a son of man*   ᵉ Aram *the Ancient of Days*   ᶠ Aram *troubled in its sheath*

did you KNOW?

Apocalyptic Literature

As you read chapters 7–10 of Daniel, you might ask, What's with the four beasts in chapter 7, and the goat with the horn in chapter 8, and the man with a face like lightning in chapter 10? These are all examples of apocalyptic literature. *Apocalypse* is a Greek word meaning "to uncover or reveal." Apocalyptic literature is written to sound like an attempt to foretell the future by using symbols and visions. But the symbols are often codes for people and events in the present. This type of literature frequently is produced during a time of persecution, when using real names could get a person into trouble or even killed. Apocalyptic literature developed in Israel around 200 B.C. when the country was enduring great persecution and suffering. The Book of Revelation in the New Testament is another example of apocalyptic literature.

The Book of Daniel contains some explanation of the visions it describes. But sometimes, you will have to consult a good Bible commentary (a book that gives additional background on Bible passages) to completely understand the symbols. For instance, you might need help recognizing that the four beasts in chapter 7 are symbols for Babylon, Media, Persia, and Greece—the four nations that ruled over Israel but would pass away. Or that the arrogant eleventh horn on the fourth beast's head is a symbol for Antiochus IV Epiphanes, the king who persecuted the Jews during the time Daniel was written.

Apocalyptic literature assured the people of Israel that God would triumph and the present evil would eventually pass away. It was one more way to reinforce the belief that evil would be punished and good rewarded, even when it didn't look that way at the moment.

▸ Daniel, chapters 7–10

16 I approached one of the attendants to ask him the truth concerning all this. So he said that he would disclose to me the interpretation of the mat-

ter: 17 "As for these four great beasts, four kings shall arise out of the earth. 18 But the holy ones of the Most High shall receive the kingdom and possess the kingdom forever—forever and ever."

19 Then I desired to know the truth concerning the fourth beast, which was different from all the rest, exceedingly terrifying, with its teeth of iron and claws of bronze, and which devoured and broke in pieces, and stamped what was left with its feet; 20 and concerning the ten horns that were on its head, and concerning the other horn, which came up and to make room for which three of them fell out—the horn that had eyes and a mouth that spoke arrogantly, and that seemed greater than the others. 21 As I looked, this horn made war with the holy ones and was prevailing over them, 22 until the Ancient One*g* came; then judgment was given for the holy ones of the Most High, and the time arrived when the holy ones gained possession of the kingdom.

23 This is what he said: "As for the fourth beast,
   there shall be a fourth kingdom on earth
      that shall be different from all the other
         kingdoms;
   it shall devour the whole earth,
      and trample it down, and break it to
         pieces.
24 As for the ten horns,
   out of this kingdom ten kings shall arise,
      and another shall arise after them.
   This one shall be different from the former
         ones,
      and shall put down three kings.
25 He shall speak words against the Most High,
      shall wear out the holy ones of the Most
         High,
   and shall attempt to change the sacred
         seasons and the law;
   and they shall be given into his power
      for a time, two times,*h* and half a time.
26 Then the court shall sit in judgment,
      and his dominion shall be taken away,
      to be consumed and totally destroyed.
27 The kingship and dominion
   and the greatness of the kingdoms under
         the whole heaven
   shall be given to the people of the holy
         ones of the Most High;
   their kingdom shall be an everlasting
         kingdom,
      and all dominions shall serve and obey
         them."

28 Here the account ends. As for me, Daniel, my thoughts greatly terrified me, and my face turned pale; but I kept the matter in my mind.

g Aram *the Ancient of Days*   *h* Aram *a time, times*

Vision of a Ram and a Goat

8 In the third year of the reign of King Bel•shaz′zar a vision appeared to me, Daniel, after the one that had appeared to me at first. 2 In the vision I was looking and saw myself in Su′sa the capital, in the province of E′lam,[i] and I was by the river U′lai.[j] 3 I looked up and saw a ram standing beside the river.[k] It had two horns. Both horns were long, but one was longer than the other, and the longer one came up second. 4 I saw the ram charging westward and northward and southward. All beasts were powerless to withstand it, and no one could rescue from its power; it did as it pleased and became strong.

5 As I was watching, a male goat appeared from the west, coming across the face of the whole earth without touching the ground. The goat had a horn[l] between its eyes. 6 It came toward the ram with the two horns that I had seen standing beside the river,[k] and it ran at it with savage force. 7 I saw it approaching the ram. It was enraged against it and struck the ram, breaking its two horns. The ram did not have power to withstand it; it threw the ram down to the ground and trampled upon it, and there was no one who could rescue the ram from its power. 8 Then the male goat grew exceedingly great; but at the height of its power, the great horn was broken, and in its place there came up four prominent horns toward the four winds of heaven.

9 Out of one of them came another[m] horn, a little one, which grew exceedingly great toward the south, toward the east, and toward the beautiful land. 10 It grew as high as the host of heaven. It threw down to the earth some of the host and some of the stars, and trampled on them. 11 Even against the prince of the host it acted arrogantly; it took the regular burnt offering away from him and overthrew the place of his sanctuary. 12 Because of wickedness, the host was given over to it together with the regular burnt offering;[n] it cast truth to the ground, and kept prospering in what it did. 13 Then I heard a holy one speaking, and another holy one said to the one that spoke, "For how long is this vision concerning the regular burnt offering, the transgression that makes desolate, and the giving over of the sanctuary and host to be trampled?"[n] 14 And he answered him,[o] "For two thousand three hundred evenings and mornings; then the sanctuary shall be restored to its rightful state."

Gabriel Interprets the Vision

15 When I, Daniel, had seen the vision, I tried to understand it. Then someone appeared standing before me, having the appearance of a man, 16 and I heard a human voice by the U′lai, calling, "Gabriel, help this man understand the vision." 17 So he came near where I stood; and when he

came, I became frightened and fell prostrate. But he said to me, "Understand, O mortal,[p] that the vision is for the time of the end."

18 As he was speaking to me, I fell into a trance, face to the ground; then he touched me and set me on my feet. 19 He said, "Listen, and I will tell you what will take place later in the period of wrath; for it refers to the appointed time of the end. 20 As for the ram that you saw with the two horns, these are the kings of Med′i•a and Persia. 21 The male goat[q] is the king of Greece, and the great horn between its eyes is the first king. 22 As for the horn that was broken, in place of which four others arose, four kingdoms shall arise from his[r] nation, but not with his power.

23 At the end of their rule,
when the transgressions have reached their
full measure,
a king of bold countenance shall arise,
skilled in intrigue.
24 He shall grow strong in power,[s]
shall cause fearful destruction,
and shall succeed in what he does.
He shall destroy the powerful
and the people of the holy ones.
25 By his cunning
he shall make deceit prosper under his
hand,
and in his own mind he shall be
great.
Without warning he shall destroy many
and shall even rise up against the Prince of
princes.
But he shall be broken, and not by human
hands.

26 The vision of the evenings and the mornings that has been told is true. As for you, seal up the vision, for it refers to many days from now."

27 So I, Daniel, was overcome and lay sick for some days; then I arose and went about the king's business. But I was dismayed by the vision and did not understand it.

Daniel's Prayer for the People

9 In the first year of Da•ri′us son of A•has-u•e′rus, by birth a Mede, who became king over the realm of the Chal•de′ans— 2 in the first year of his reign, I, Daniel, perceived in the books the number of years that, according to the word of the LORD to the prophet Jer•e•mi′ah, must be

---

[i] Gk Theodotion: MT Q Ms repeat *in the vision I was looking*   [j] Or *the Ulai Gate*   [k] Or *gate*   [l] Theodotion: Gk *one horn;* Heb *a horn of vision*   [m] Cn Compare 7.8: Heb *one*   [n] Meaning of Heb uncertain   [o] Gk Theodotion Syr Vg: Heb *me*   [p] Heb *son of man*   [q] Or *shaggy male goat*   [r] Gk Theodotion Vg: Heb *the*   [s] Theodotion and one Gk Ms: Heb repeats (from 8.22) *but not with his power*

fulfilled for the devastation of Jerusalem, namely, seventy years.

3 Then I turned to the Lord God, to seek an answer by prayer and supplication with fasting and sackcloth and ashes. 4 I prayed to the LORD my God and made confession, saying,

"Ah, Lord, great and awesome God, keeping covenant and steadfast love with those who love you and keep your commandments, 5 we have sinned and done wrong, acted wickedly and rebelled, turning aside from your commandments and ordinances. 6 We have not listened to your servants the prophets, who spoke in your name to our kings, our princes, and our ancestors, and to all the people of the land.

7 "Righteousness is on your side, O Lord, but open shame, as at this day, falls on us, the people of Judah, the inhabitants of Jerusalem, and all Israel, those who are near and those who are far away, in all the lands to which you have driven them, because of the treachery that they have committed against you. 8 Open shame, O LORD, falls on us, our kings, our officials, and our ancestors, because we have sinned against you. 9 To the Lord our God belong mercy and forgiveness, for we have rebelled against him, 10 and have not obeyed the voice of the LORD our God by following his laws, which he set before us by his servants the prophets.

11 "All Israel has transgressed your law and turned aside, refusing to obey your voice. So the curse and the oath written in the law of Moses, the servant of God, have been poured out upon us, because we have sinned against you. 12 He has confirmed his words, which he spoke against us and against our rulers, by bringing upon us a calamity so great that what has been done against Jerusalem has never before been done under the whole heaven. 13 Just as it is written in the law of Moses, all this calamity has come upon us. We did not entreat the favor of the LORD our God, turning from our iniquities and reflecting on his^t fidelity. 14 So the LORD kept watch over this calamity until he brought it upon us. Indeed, the LORD our God is right in all that he has done; for we have disobeyed his voice.

15 "And now, O Lord our God, who brought your people out of the land of Egypt with a mighty hand and made your name renowned even to this day—we have sinned, we have done wickedly. 16 O Lord, in view of all your righteous acts, let your anger and wrath, we pray, turn away from your city Jerusalem, your holy mountain; because of our sins and the iniquities of our ancestors, Jerusalem and your people have become a disgrace among all our neighbors. 17 Now therefore, O our God, listen to the prayer of your servant and to his supplication, and for your own sake, Lord,^u let your face shine upon your desolated sanctuary. 18 Incline your ear, O my God, and hear. Open your eyes and look at our desolation and the city that bears your name. We do not present our supplication before you on the ground of our righteousness, but on the ground of your great mercies. 19 O Lord, hear; O Lord, forgive; O Lord, listen and act and do not delay! For your own sake, O my God, because your city and your people bear your name!"

The Seventy Weeks

20 While I was speaking, and was praying and confessing my sin and the sin of my people Israel, and presenting my supplication before the LORD my God on behalf of the holy mountain of my God— 21 while I was speaking in prayer, the man Gabriel, whom I had seen before in a vision, came to me in swift flight at the time of the evening sacrifice. 22 He came^v and said to me, "Daniel, I have now come out to give you wisdom and understanding. 23 At the beginning of your supplications a word went out, and I have come to declare it, for you are greatly beloved. So consider the word and understand the vision:

24 "Seventy weeks are decreed for your people and your holy city: to finish the transgression, to put an end to sin, and to atone for iniquity, to bring in everlasting righteousness, to seal both vision and prophet, and to anoint a most holy place.^w 25 Know

PRAY IT!
A Closer Look

Let's look closely at the prayer in chapter 9 of Daniel. Here, the prophet uses four types of prayer:

- *intercession*, because he prays on behalf of the people
- *praise*, because he proclaims God to be awesome and great
- *sorrow*, because he expresses sadness for past sinfulness and asks for forgiveness
- *petition*, because he asks God for help

Try creating a personal prayer that includes three or all four of these types of prayer.

▶ Daniel, chapter 9

---

t Heb *your*   u Theodotion Vg Compare Syr: Heb *for the Lord's sake*   v Gk Syr: Heb *He made to understand*
w Or *thing* or *one*

therefore and understand: from the time that the word went out to restore and rebuild Jerusalem until the time of an anointed prince, there shall be seven weeks; and for sixty-two weeks it shall be built again with streets and moat, but in a troubled time. 26 After the sixty-two weeks, an anointed one shall be cut off and shall have nothing, and the troops of the prince who is to come shall destroy the city and the sanctuary. Its*x* end shall come with a flood, and to the end there shall be war. Desolations are decreed. 27 He shall make a strong covenant with many for one week, and for half of the week he shall make sacrifice and offering cease; and in their place*y* shall be an abomination that desolates, until the decreed end is poured out upon the desolator."

Conflict of Nations and Heavenly Powers

10 In the third year of King Cyrus of Persia a word was revealed to Daniel, who was named Bel·te·shaz'zar. The word was true, and it concerned a great conflict. He understood the word, having received understanding in the vision.

2 At that time I, Daniel, had been mourning for three weeks. 3 I had eaten no rich food, no meat or wine had entered my mouth, and I had not anointed myself at all, for the full three weeks. 4 On the twenty-fourth day of the first month, as I was standing on the bank of the great river (that is, the Tigris), 5 I looked up and saw a man clothed in linen, with a belt of gold from U'phaz around his waist. 6 His body was like beryl, his face like lightning, his eyes like flaming torches, his arms and legs like the gleam of burnished bronze, and the sound of his words like the roar of a multitude. 7 I, Daniel, alone saw the vision; the people who were with me did not see the vision, though a great trembling fell upon them, and they fled and hid themselves. 8 So I was left alone to see this great vision. My strength left me, and my complexion grew deathly pale, and I retained no strength. 9 Then I heard the sound of his words; and when I heard the sound of his words, I fell into a trance, face to the ground.

10 But then a hand touched me and roused me to my hands and knees. 11 He said to me, "Daniel, greatly beloved, pay attention to the words that I am going to speak to you. Stand on your feet, for I have now been sent to you." So while he was speaking this word to me, I stood up trembling. 12 He said to me, "Do not fear, Daniel, for from the first day that you set your mind to gain understanding and to humble yourself before your God, your words have been heard, and I have come because of your words. 13 But the prince of the kingdom of Persia opposed me twenty-one days. So Michael, one of the chief princes, came to help me, and I left

him there with the prince of the kingdom of Persia,*z* 14 and have come to help you understand what is to happen to your people at the end of days. For there is a further vision for those days."

15 While he was speaking these words to me, I turned my face toward the ground and was speechless. 16 Then one in human form touched my lips, and I opened my mouth to speak, and said to the one who stood before me, "My lord, because of the vision such pains have come upon me that I retain no strength. 17 How can my lord's servant talk with my lord? For I am shaking,*a* no strength remains in me, and no breath is left in me."

18 Again one in human form touched me and strengthened me. 19 He said, "Do not fear, greatly beloved, you are safe. Be strong and courageous!" When he spoke to me, I was strengthened and said, "Let my lord speak, for you have strengthened me." 20 Then he said, "Do you know why I have come to you? Now I must return to fight against the prince of Persia, and when I am through with him, the prince of Greece will come. 21 But I am to tell you what is inscribed in the book of truth. There is no one with me who contends against these princes

11 except Michael, your prince. 1 As for me, in the first year of Da·ri'us the Mēde, I stood up to support and strengthen him.

2 "Now I will announce the truth to you. Three more kings shall arise in Persia. The fourth shall be far richer than all of them, and when he has become strong through his riches, he shall stir up all against the kingdom of Greece. 3 Then a warrior king shall arise, who shall rule with great dominion and take action as he pleases. 4 And while still rising in power, his kingdom shall be broken and divided toward the four winds of heaven, but not to his posterity, nor according to the dominion with which he ruled; for his kingdom shall be uprooted and go to others besides these.

5 "Then the king of the south shall grow strong, but one of his officers shall grow stronger than he and shall rule a realm greater than his own realm. 6 After some years they shall make an alliance, and the daughter of the king of the south shall come to the king of the north to ratify the agreement. But she shall not retain her power, and his offspring shall not endure. She shall be given up, she and her attendants and her child and the one who supported her.

"In those times 7 a branch from her roots shall rise up in his place. He shall come against the army and enter the fortress of the king of the north, and he shall take action against them and prevail.

---

x Or *His*   *y* Cn: Meaning of Heb uncertain   *z* Gk
Theodotion: Heb *I was left there with the kings of Persia*
a Gk: Heb *from now*

8 Even their gods, with their idols and with their precious vessels of silver and gold, he shall carry off to Egypt as spoils of war. For some years he shall refrain from attacking the king of the north; 9 then the latter shall invade the realm of the king of the south, but will return to his own land.

10 "His sons shall wage war and assemble a multitude of great forces, which shall advance like a flood and pass through, and again shall carry the war as far as his fortress. 11 Moved with rage, the king of the south shall go out and do battle against the king of the north, who shall muster a great multitude, which shall, however, be defeated by his enemy. 12 When the multitude has been carried off, his heart shall be exalted, and he shall overthrow tens of thousands, but he shall not prevail. 13 For the king of the north shall again raise a multitude, larger than the former, and after some years[b] he shall advance with a great army and abundant supplies.

14 "In those times many shall rise against the king of the south. The lawless among your own people shall lift themselves up in order to fulfill the vision, but they shall fail. 15 Then the king of the north shall come and throw up siegeworks, and take a well-fortified city. And the forces of the south shall not stand, not even his picked troops, for there shall be no strength to resist. 16 But he who comes against him shall take the actions he pleases, and no one shall withstand him. He shall take a position in the beautiful land, and all of it shall be in his power. 17 He shall set his mind to come with the strength of his whole kingdom, and he shall bring terms of peace[c] and perform them. In order to destroy the kingdom,[d] he shall give him a woman in marriage; but it shall not succeed or be to his advantage. 18 Afterward he shall turn to the coastlands, and shall capture many. But a commander shall put an end to his insolence; indeed,[e] he shall turn his insolence back upon him. 19 Then he shall turn back toward the fortresses of his own land, but he shall stumble and fall, and shall not be found.

20 "Then shall arise in his place one who shall send an official for the glory of the kingdom; but within a few days he shall be broken, though not in anger or in battle. 21 In his place shall arise a contemptible person on whom royal majesty had not been conferred; he shall come in without warning and obtain the kingdom through intrigue. 22 Armies shall be utterly swept away and broken before him, and the prince of the covenant as well. 23 And after an alliance is made with him, he shall act deceitfully and become strong with a small party. 24 Without warning he shall come into the richest parts[f] of the province and do what none of his predecessors had ever done, lavishing plunder, spoil, and wealth on them. He shall devise plans against strongholds, but only for a time. 25 He shall stir up his power and determination against the king of the south with a great army, and the king of the south shall wage war with a much greater and stronger army. But he shall not succeed, for plots shall be devised against him 26 by those who eat of the royal rations. They shall break him, his army shall be swept away, and many shall fall slain. 27 The two kings, their minds bent on evil, shall sit at one table and exchange lies. But it shall not succeed, for there remains an end at the time appointed. 28 He shall return to his land with great wealth, but his heart shall be set against the holy covenant. He shall work his will, and return to his own land.

29 "At the time appointed he shall return and come into the south, but this time it shall not be as it was before. 30 For ships of Kit'tim shall come against him, and he shall lose heart and withdraw. He shall be enraged and take action against the holy covenant. He shall turn back and pay heed to those who forsake the holy covenant. 31 Forces sent by him shall occupy and profane the temple and fortress. They shall abolish the regular burnt offering and set up the abomination that makes desolate. 32 He shall seduce with intrigue those who violate the covenant; but the people who are loyal to their God shall stand firm and take action. 33 The wise among the people shall give understanding to many; for some days, however, they shall fall by sword and flame, and suffer captivity and plunder. 34 When they fall victim, they shall receive a little help, and many shall join them insincerely. 35 Some of the wise shall fall, so that they may be refined, purified, and cleansed,[g] until the time of the end, for there is still an interval until the time appointed.

36 "The king shall act as he pleases. He shall exalt himself and consider himself greater than any god, and shall speak horrendous things against the God of gods. He shall prosper until the period of wrath is completed, for what is determined shall be done. 37 He shall pay no respect to the gods of his ancestors, or to the one beloved by women; he shall pay no respect to any other god, for he shall consider himself greater than all. 38 He shall honor the god of fortresses instead of these; a god whom his ancestors did not know he shall honor with gold and silver, with precious stones and costly gifts. 39 He shall deal with the strongest fortresses by the help of a foreign god. Those who acknowledge him he shall make more wealthy, and shall appoint them as rulers over many, and shall distribute the land for a price.

---

b Heb *and at the end of the times years*   c Gk: Heb *kingdom, and upright ones with him*   d Heb *it*   e Meaning of Heb uncertain   f Or *among the richest men*   g Heb *made them white*

The Time of the End

40 "At the time of the end the king of the south shall attack him. But the king of the north shall rush upon him like a whirlwind, with chariots and horsemen, and with many ships. He shall advance against countries and pass through like a flood. 41 He shall come into the beautiful land, and tens of thousands shall fall victim, but Ē′dom and Mō′ab and the main part of the Am′mon·ītes shall escape from his power. 42 He shall stretch out his hand against the countries, and the land of Egypt shall not escape. 43 He shall become ruler of the treasures of gold and of silver, and all the riches of Egypt; and the Libyans and the Ethiopians[h] shall follow in his train. 44 But reports from the east and the north shall alarm him, and he shall go out with great fury to bring ruin and complete destruction to many. 45 He shall pitch his palatial tents between the sea and the beautiful holy mountain. Yet he shall come to his end, with no one to help him.

The Resurrection of the Dead

12 "At that time Michael, the great prince, the protector of your people, shall arise. There shall be a time of anguish, such as has never occurred since nations first came into existence. But at that time your people shall be delivered, everyone who is found written in the book. 2 Many of those who sleep in the dust of the earth[i] shall awake, some to everlasting life, and some to shame

and everlasting contempt. 3 Those who are wise shall shine like the brightness of the sky,[j] and those who lead many to righteousness, like the stars forever and ever. 4 But you, Daniel, keep the words secret and the book sealed until the time of the end. Many shall be running back and forth, and evil[k] shall increase."

5 Then I, Daniel, looked, and two others appeared, one standing on this bank of the stream and one on the other. 6 One of them said to the man clothed in linen, who was upstream, "How long shall it be until the end of these wonders?" 7 The man clothed in linen, who was upstream, raised his right hand and his left hand toward heaven. And I heard him swear by the one who lives forever that it would be for a time, two times, and half a time,[l] and that when the shattering of the power of the holy people comes to an end, all these things would be accomplished. 8 I heard but could not understand; so I said, "My lord, what shall be the outcome of these things?" 9 He said, "Go your way, Daniel, for the words are to remain secret and sealed until the time of the end. 10 Many shall be purified, cleansed, and refined, but the wicked shall continue to act wickedly. None of the wicked shall understand, but those who are wise shall understand. 11 From the time that the regular burnt offering is taken away and the abomination that desolates is set up, there shall be one thousand two hundred ninety days. 12 Happy are those who persevere and attain the thousand three hundred thirty-five days. 13 But you, go your way,[m] and rest; you shall rise for your reward at the end of the days."

Susanna's Beauty Attracts Two Elders

13 There was a man living in Babylon whose name was Jō′a·kim. 2 He married the daughter of Hil·kī′ah, named Susanna, a very beautiful woman and one who feared the Lord. 3 Her parents were righteous, and had trained their daughter according to the law of Moses. 4 Jō′a·kim was very rich, and had a fine garden adjoining his house; the Jews used to come to him because he was the most honored of them all.

5 That year two elders from the people were appointed as judges. Concerning them the Lord had said: "Wickedness came forth from Babylon, from elders who were judges, who were supposed to govern the people." 6 These men were frequently at Jō′a·kim's house, and all who had a case to be tried came to them there.

7 When the people left at noon, Susanna would go into her husband's garden to walk. 8 Every day

---

[h] Or *Nubians*; Heb *Cushites*   [i] Or *the land of dust*   [j] Or *dome*   [k] Cn Compare Gk: Heb *knowledge*   [l] Heb *a time, times, and a half*   [m] Gk Theodotion: Heb adds *to the end*

D
A
N

the two elders used to see her, going in and walking about, and they began to lust for her. 9 They suppressed their consciences and turned away their eyes from looking to Heaven or remembering their duty to administer justice. 10 Both were overwhelmed with passion for her, but they did not tell each other of their distress, 11 for they were ashamed to disclose their lustful desire to seduce her. 12 Day after day they watched eagerly to see her.

13 One day they said to each other, "Let us go home, for it is time for lunch." So they both left and parted from each other. 14 But turning back, they met again; and when each pressed the other for the reason, they confessed their lust. Then together they arranged for a time when they could find her alone.

The Elders Attempt to Seduce Susanna

15 Once, while they were watching for an opportune day, she went in as before with only two maids, and wished to bathe in the garden, for it was a hot day. 16 No one was there except the two elders, who had hidden themselves and were watching her. 17 She said to her maids, "Bring me olive oil and ointments, and shut the garden doors so that I can bathe." 18 They did as she told them: they shut the doors of the garden and went out by the side doors to bring what they had been commanded; they did not see the elders, because they were hiding.

19 When the maids had gone out, the two elders got up and ran to her. 20 They said, "Look, the garden doors are shut, and no one can see us. We are burning with desire for you; so give your consent, and lie with us. 21 If you refuse, we will testify against you that a young man was with you, and this was why you sent your maids away."

22 Susanna groaned and said, "I am completely trapped. For if I do this, it will mean death for me; if I do not, I cannot escape your hands. 23 I choose not to do it; I will fall into your hands, rather than sin in the sight of the Lord."

24 Then Susanna cried out with a loud voice, and the two elders shouted against her. 25 And one of them ran and opened the garden doors. 26 When the people in the house heard the shouting in the garden, they rushed in at the side door to see what had happened to her. 27 And when the elders told their story, the servants felt very much ashamed, for nothing like this had ever been said about Susanna.

The Elders Testify against Susanna

28 The next day, when the people gathered at the house of her husband Jō'a·kim, the two elders came, full of their wicked plot to have Susanna put to death. In the presence of the people they said,

PRAY IT!
Susanna

Daniel is called the hero of chapter 13 of his book. But don't forget Susanna. A real hero, Susanna chooses to risk death rather than submitting to sin. Her prayer demanding God's justice causes the Holy Spirit to stir Daniel into action. Prayer can challenge and inspire us. What injustices might you pray about? Whose attention do you need to get?

▸ **Daniel, chapter 13**

29 "Send for Susanna daughter of Hil·kī'ah, the wife of Jō'a·kim." So they sent for her. 30 And she came with her parents, her children, and all her relatives.

31 Now Susanna was a woman of great refinement and beautiful in appearance. 32 As she was veiled, the scoundrels ordered her to be unveiled, so that they might feast their eyes on her beauty. 33 Those who were with her and all who saw her were weeping.

34 Then the two elders stood up before the people and laid their hands on her head. 35 Through her tears she looked up toward Heaven, for her heart trusted in the Lord. 36 The elders said, "While we were walking in the garden alone, this woman came in with two maids, shut the garden doors, and dismissed the maids. 37 Then a young man, who was hiding there, came to her and lay with her. 38 We were in a corner of the garden, and when we saw this wickedness we ran to them. 39 Although we saw them embracing, we could not hold the man, because he was stronger than we, and he opened the doors and got away. 40 We did, however, seize this woman and asked who the young man was, 41 but she would not tell us. These things we testify."

Because they were elders of the people and judges, the assembly believed them and condemned her to death.

42 Then Susanna cried out with a loud voice, and said, "O eternal God, you know what is secret and are aware of all things before they come to be; 43 you know that these men have given false evidence against me. And now I am to die, though I have done none of the wicked things that the have charged against me!"

44 The Lord heard her cry. 45 Just as she was being led off to execution, God stirred up the holy spirit of a young lad named Daniel, 46 and he

shouted with a loud voice, "I want no part in shedding this woman's blood!"

Daniel Rescues Susanna

47 All the people turned to him and asked, "What is this you are saying?" 48 Taking his stand among them he said, "Are you such fools, O Israelites, as to condemn a daughter of Israel without examination and without learning the facts? 49 Return to court, for these men have given false evidence against her."

50 So all the people hurried back. And the rest of the[n] elders said to him, "Come, sit among us and inform us, for God has given you the standing of an elder." 51 Daniel said to them, "Separate them far from each other, and I will examine them."

52 When they were separated from each other, he summoned one of them and said to him, "You old relic of wicked days, your sins have now come home, which you have committed in the past, 53 pronouncing unjust judgments, condemning the innocent and acquitting the guilty, though the Lord said, 'You shall not put an innocent and righteous person to death.' 54 Now then, if you really saw this woman, tell me this: Under what tree did you see them being intimate with each other?" He answered, "Under a mastic tree."[o] 55 And Daniel said, "Very well! This lie has cost you your head, for the angel of God has received the sentence from God and will immediately cut[o] you in two."

56 Then, putting him to one side, he ordered them to bring the other. And he said to him, "You offspring of Ca'naan and not of Judah, beauty has beguiled you and lust has perverted your heart. 57 This is how you have been treating the daughters of Israel, and they were intimate with you through fear; but a daughter of Judah would not tolerate your wickedness. 58 Now then, tell me: Under what tree did you catch them being intimate with each other?" He answered, "Under an evergreen oak."[p] 59 Daniel said to him, "Very well! This lie has cost you also your head, for the angel of God is waiting with his sword to split[p] you in two, so as to destroy you both."

60 Then the whole assembly raised a great shout and blessed God, who saves those who hope in him. 61 And they took action against the two elders, because out of their own mouths Daniel had convicted them of bearing false witness; they did to them as they had wickedly planned to do to their neighbor. 62 Acting in accordance with the law of Moses, they put them to death. Thus innocent blood was spared that day.

63 Hil·ki'ah and his wife praised God for their daughter Susanna, and so did her husband Jō'a·kim and all her relatives, because she was found innocent of a shameful deed. 64 And from that day on-

ward Daniel had a great reputation among the people.

Daniel and the Priests of Bel

14 When King As·tȳ'a·gēs was laid to rest with his ancestors, Cyrus the Persian succeeded to his kingdom. 2 Daniel was a companion of the king, and was the most honored of all his Friends.

3 Now the Babylonians had an idol called Bel, and every day they provided for it twelve bushels of choice flour and forty sheep and six measures[q] of wine. 4 The king revered it and went every day to worship it. But Daniel worshiped his own God.

So the king said to him, "Why do you not worship Bel?" 5 He answered, "Because I do not revere idols made with hands, but the living God, who created heaven and earth and has dominion over all living creatures."

6 The king said to him, "Do you not think that Bel is a living god? Do you not see how much he eats and drinks every day?" 7 And Daniel laughed, and said, "Do not be deceived, O king, for this thing is only clay inside and bronze outside, and it never ate or drank anything."

8 Then the king was angry and called the priests of Bel[r] and said to them, "If you do not tell me who is eating these provisions, you shall die. 9 But if you prove that Bel is eating them, Daniel shall die, because he has spoken blasphemy against Bel." Daniel said to the king, "Let it be done as you have said."

10 Now there were seventy priests of Bel, besides their wives and children. So the king went with Daniel into the temple of Bel. 11 The priests of Bel said, "See, we are now going outside; you yourself, O king, set out the food and prepare the wine, and shut the door and seal it with your signet. 12 When you return in the morning, if you do not find that Bel has eaten it all, we will die; otherwise Daniel will, who is telling lies about us." 13 They were unconcerned, for beneath the table they had made a hidden entrance, through which they used to go in regularly and consume the provisions. 14 After they had gone out, the king set out the food for Bel. Then Daniel ordered his servants to bring ashes, and they scattered them throughout the whole temple in the presence of the king alone. Then they went out, shut the door and sealed it with the king's signet, and departed. 15 During the night the priests came as usual, with their wives and children, and they ate and drank everything.

---

n Gk lacks *rest of the*   o The Greek words for *mastic tree* and *cut* are similar, thus forming an ironic wordplay   p The Greek words for *evergreen oak* and *split* are similar, thus forming an ironic wordplay   q A little more than fifty gallons   r Gk *his priests*

DAN

16 Early in the morning the king rose and came, and Daniel with him. 17 The king said, "Are the seals unbroken, Daniel?" He answered, "They are unbroken, O king." 18 As soon as the doors were opened, the king looked at the table, and shouted in a loud voice, "You are great, O Bel, and in you there is no deceit at all!"

19 But Daniel laughed and restrained the king from going in. "Look at the floor," he said, "and notice whose footprints these are." 20 The king said, "I see the footprints of men and women and children."

21 Then the king was enraged, and he arrested the priests and their wives and children. They showed him the secret doors through which they used to enter to consume what was on the table. 22 Therefore the king put them to death, and gave Bel over to Daniel, who destroyed it and its temple.

Daniel Kills the Dragon

23 Now in that place[s] there was a great dragon, which the Babylonians revered. 24 The king said to Daniel, "You cannot deny that this is a living god; so worship him." 25 Daniel said, "I worship the Lord my God, for he is the living God. 26 But give me permission, O king, and I will kill the dragon without sword or club." The king said, "I give you permission."

27 Then Daniel took pitch, fat, and hair, and boiled them together and made cakes, which he fed to the dragon. The dragon ate them, and burst open. Then Daniel said, "See what you have been worshiping!"

28 When the Babylonians heard about it, they were very indignant and conspired against the king, saying, "The king has become a Jew; he has destroyed Bel, and killed the dragon, and slaughtered the priests." 29 Going to the king, they said, "Hand Daniel over to us, or else we will kill you and your household." 30 The king saw that they were pressing him hard, and under compulsion he handed Daniel over to them.

---

s Other ancient authorities lack *in that place*

NOW IN THAT PLACE THERE WAS A GREAT DRAGON, WHICH THE BABYLONIANS REVERED. THE KING SAID TO DANIEL, "YOU CANNOT DENY THAT THIS IS A LIVING GOD; SO WORSHIP HIM."

DANIEL SAID,

"I WORSHIP THE LORD MY GOD, FOR HE IS THE LIVING GOD."

14.23–25

DAN

Daniel in the Lions' Den

31 They threw Daniel into the lions' den, and he was there for six days. 32 There were seven lions in the den, and every day they had been given two human bodies and two sheep; but now they were given nothing, so that they would devour Daniel.

33 Now the prophet Ha·bak′kuk was in Judea; he had made a stew and had broken bread into a bowl, and was going into the field to take it to the reapers. 34 But the angel of the Lord said to Ha·bak′kuk, "Take the food that you have to Babylon, to Daniel, in the lions' den." 35 Ha·bak′kuk said, "Sir, I have never seen Babylon, and I know nothing about the den." 36 Then the angel of the Lord took him by the crown of his head and carried him by his hair; with the speed of the wind*t* he set him down in Babylon, right over the den.

37 Then Ha·bak′kuk shouted, "Daniel, Daniel! Take the food that God has sent you." 38 Daniel said, "You have remembered me, O God, and have not forsaken those who love you." 39 So Daniel got up and ate. And the angel of God immediately returned Ha·bak′kuk to his own place.

40 On the seventh day the king came to mourn for Daniel. When he came to the den he looked in, and there sat Daniel! 41 The king shouted with a loud voice, "You are great, O Lord, the God of Daniel, and there is no other besides you!" 42 Then he pulled Daniel*u* out, and threw into the den those who had attempted his destruction, and they were instantly eaten before his eyes.

---

t Or by the power of his spirit   u Gk him

Go marry a prostitute." Say what, God? A picture is worth a thousand words, and Hosea's family life was a living picture of Israel's infidelity and God's continuing faithfulness. The Book of Hosea captures this faithful prophet's commitment to God and his loving faithfulness to his straying wife.

In-depth

Hosea preached to the northern kingdom of Israel before it was conquered by the Assyrians in 721 B.C. As we learn from Hosea's speeches, the situation in the northern kingdom was not good. Over twenty-five years, Hosea saw seven kings come and go, most of them corrupt (see the timeline at the back of this Bible, and 2 Kings 14.23—17.23). Pursuing their own greedy ends and trying to play power politics, the ruling class overlooked the poor and the needy in their midst and led the people into idolatry. Through Hosea, God proclaimed, "I have been the LORD your God / ever since the land of Egypt" (Hos 13.4).

Even more powerful than Hosea's words was the living symbol of his marriage. Early in Hosea's preaching, God commanded him to marry a prostitute and have children by her. Hosea remained faithful to her, loving her even when she wandered to other men. Hosea used the image of his own marriage to preach his message to Israel. As Hosea's wife was unfaithful to him, so too was Israel unfaithful to God, wandering off in worship of other gods. However, just as Hosea was faithful to his wife and awaited her return, so too God was faithful to Israel and awaited its return from the distractions of power, wealth, and other gods.

Hosea and Amos were prophets in the northern kingdom at about the same time. But Amos had come from the southern kingdom and was more distant and cynical in describing the sins of the ruling class (see his description of well-off women in Am 4.1–3). Hosea was from the northern kingdom—these people were his people! He took their sins personally and passionately. Initially, he had hopes that the people would repent and return to God (see Hos 2.14–23). But after a succession of selfish and violent rulers, he prophesied against his people with all the passion of a scorned lover (see 13.7–11). Still, at the end, he hoped for Israel's return to God (14.1–2).

At a Glance

- **Chapters 1–3.** descriptions of Hosea's marriage and family
- **Chapters 4–14.** Hosea's speeches

Quick Facts

Period Covered
786–746 B.C.

Authors
Hosea and later scribes

Themes
God's faithful love for Israel, the image of God as a loving parent

Hosea

3.1

1 The word of the LORD that came to Hō•sē′a
son of Be•ē′rī, in the days of Kings Uz•zī′ah,
Jō′tham, Ā′haz, and Hez•e•kī′ah of Judah, and in
the days of King Jer•o•bō′am son of Jō′ash of Israel.

The Family of Hosea
(Cp 2 Kings 24.10–17)

2 When the LORD first spoke through Hō•sē′a,
the LORD said to Hō•sē′a, "Go, take for yourself a
wife of whoredom and have children of whoredom,
for the land commits great whoredom by forsaking
the LORD." 3 So he went and took Gō′mer daughter
of Dib•lā′im, and she conceived and bore him a
son.

4 And the LORD said to him, "Name him
Jez′rē•el;*a* for in a little while I will punish the house
of Jē′hū for the blood of Jez′rē•el, and I will put an
end to the kingdom of the house of Israel. 5 On that
day I will break the bow of Israel in the valley of
Jez′rē•el."

6 She conceived again and bore a daughter.
Then the LORD said to him, "Name her Lō-
rū•ha′mah,*b* for I will no longer have pity on the
house of Israel or forgive them. 7 But I will have
pity on the house of Judah, and I will save them by
the LORD their God; I will not save them by bow, or
by sword, or by war, or by horses, or by horsemen."

8 When she had weaned Lō-rū•ha′mah, she
conceived and bore a son. 9 Then the LORD said,
"Name him Lō-am′mī,*c* for you are not my people
and I am not your God."*d*

The Restoration of Israel

10*e* Yet the number of the people of Israel shall
be like the sand of the sea, which can be neither
measured nor numbered; and in the place where it
was said to them, "You are not my people," it shall
be said to them, "Children of the living God."
11 The people of Judah and the people of Israel shall
be gathered together, and they shall appoint for
themselves one head; and they shall take possession of*f* the land, for great shall be the day of
Jez′rē•el.

2*g* Say to your brother,*h* Am′mī,*i* and to your sister,*j* Rū•ha′mah.*k*

Israel's Infidelity, Punishment, and Redemption

2 Plead with your mother, plead—
   for she is not my wife,
   and I am not her husband—
that she put away her whoring from her face,
   and her adultery from between her breasts,
3 or I will strip her naked
   and expose her as in the day she was born,
and make her like a wilderness,
   and turn her into a parched land,
   and kill her with thirst.
4 Upon her children also I will have no pity,

---

a That is *God sows* *b* That is *Not pitied* *c* That is *Not my
people* *d* Heb *I am not yours* *e* Ch 2.1 in Heb *f* Heb *rise
up from* *g* Ch 2.3 in Heb *h* Gk: Heb *brothers* *i* That is *My
people* *j* Gk Vg: Heb *sisters* *k* That is *Pitied*

because they are children of whoredom.
5 For their mother has played the whore;
  she who conceived them has acted
    shamefully.
For she said, "I will go after my lovers;
  they give me my bread and my water,
  my wool and my flax, my oil and my
    drink."
6 Therefore I will hedge up her[j] way with thorns;
  and I will build a wall against her,
  so that she cannot find her paths.
7 She shall pursue her lovers,
  but not overtake them;
and she shall seek them,
  but shall not find them.
Then she shall say, "I will go
  and return to my first husband,
  for it was better with me then than now."
8 She did not know
  that it was I who gave her the grain,
  the wine, and the oil,
and who lavished upon her silver
  and gold that they used for Bā'al.
9 Therefore I will take back
  my grain in its time,
  and my wine in its season;
and I will take away my wool and my flax,
  which were to cover her nakedness.
10 Now I will uncover her shame
  in the sight of her lovers,
  and no one shall rescue her out of my hand.
11 I will put an end to all her mirth,
  her festivals, her new moons, her sabbaths,
  and all her appointed festivals.
12 I will lay waste her vines and her fig trees,
  of which she said,
"These are my pay,
  which my lovers have given me."
I will make them a forest,
  and the wild animals shall devour them.
13 I will punish her for the festival days of the
    Bā'als,
  when she offered incense to them
and decked herself with her ring and jewelry,
  and went after her lovers,
  and forgot me, says the LORD.

14 Therefore, I will now allure her,
  and bring her into the wilderness,
  and speak tenderly to her.
15 From there I will give her her vineyards,
  and make the Valley of Ā'chor a door of
    hope.
There she shall respond as in the days of her
    youth,
  as at the time when she came out of the
    land of Egypt.

16 On that day, says the LORD, you will call me, "My husband," and no longer will you call me, "My Bā'al."[m] 17 For I will remove the names of the Bā'als from her mouth, and they shall be mentioned by name no more. 18 I will make for you[n] a covenant on that day with the wild animals, the birds of the air, and the creeping things of the ground; and I will abolish[o] the bow, the sword, and war from the land; and I will make you lie down in safety. 19 And I will take you for my wife forever; I will take you for my wife in righteousness and in justice, in steadfast love, and in mercy. 20 I will take you for my wife in faithfulness; and you shall know the LORD.

21 On that day I will answer, says the LORD,
  I will answer the heavens
  and they shall answer the earth;
22 and the earth shall answer the grain, the wine,
    and the oil,
  and they shall answer Jez're·el; [p]
23 and I will sow him[q] for myself in the land.
And I will have pity on Lō-rū·ha'mah,[r]
  and I will say to Lō-am'mī,[s] "You are my
    people";
  and he shall say, "You are my God."

Further Assurances of God's Redeeming Love

3 The LORD said to me again, "Go, love a woman who has a lover and is an adulteress, just as the LORD loves the people of Israel, though they turn to other gods and love raisin cakes." 2 So I bought her for fifteen shekels of silver and a homer of barley and a measure of wine.[t] 3 And I said to her, "You must remain as mine for many days; you shall not play the whore, you shall not have intercourse with a man, nor I with you." 4 For the Israelites shall remain many days without king or prince, without sacrifice or pillar, without ephod or teraphim. 5 Afterward the Israelites shall return and seek the LORD their God, and David their king; they shall come in awe to the LORD and to his goodness in the latter days.

God Accuses Israel

4 Hear the word of the LORD, O people of
    Israel;
  for the LORD has an indictment against the
    inhabitants of the land.
There is no faithfulness or loyalty,
  and no knowledge of God in the land.
2 Swearing, lying, and murder,
  and stealing and adultery break out;

---

[j] Gk Syr: Heb *your*   [m] That is, *"My master"*   [n] Heb *them*   [o] Heb *break*   [p] That is *God sows*   [q] Cn: Heb *her*   [r] That is *Not pitied*   [s] That is *Not my people*   [t] Gk: Heb *a homer of barley and a lethech of barley*

Unconditional Faithfulness

We don't know all the details of Hosea's relationship with his wife, Gomer. But most people understand Hos 3.1–3 to mean that Hosea accepted her back after she was unfaithful to him. We can only hope that Gomer was so touched by Hosea's unconditional forgiveness that she turned her life around and was faithful to him in return.

It is hard to be faithful to someone who is unfaithful to you. The other person doesn't have to be an adulterous spouse. She or he can be a friend who starts spending time with someone else instead of you, or a family member who keeps breaking promises to be with you. A natural reaction is to return the hurt in some way. How much harder—and more Christlike—it is to keep being faithful and friendly.

Have you ever been hurt by someone's unfaithful behavior? If so, how did you react? How can you address a friend's or family member's unfaithful behavior and still remain faithful and loving yourself?

▶ Hos 3.1–3

bloodshed follows bloodshed.

3 Therefore the land mourns,
    and all who live in it languish;
together with the wild animals
    and the birds of the air,
    even the fish of the sea are perishing.

4 Yet let no one contend,
    and let none accuse,
    for with you is my contention, O priest.[u]

5 You shall stumble by day;
    the prophet also shall stumble with you by
        night,
    and I will destroy your mother.

6 My people are destroyed for lack of knowledge;
    because you have rejected knowledge,
    I reject you from being a priest to me.
And since you have forgotten the law of your God,
    I also will forget your children.

7 The more they increased,
    the more they sinned against me;
    they changed[v] their glory into shame.

8 They feed on the sin of my people;
    they are greedy for their iniquity.

9 And it shall be like people, like priest;
    I will punish them for their ways,
    and repay them for their deeds.

10 They shall eat, but not be satisfied;
    they shall play the whore, but not multiply;
because they have forsaken the LORD
    to devote themselves to 11 whoredom.

The Idolatry of Israel

Wine and new wine
    take away the understanding.

12 My people consult a piece of wood,
    and their divining rod gives them oracles.
For a spirit of whoredom has led them astray,
    and they have played the whore, forsaking
        their God.

13 They sacrifice on the tops of the mountains,
    and make offerings upon the hills,
under oak, poplar, and terebinth,
    because their shade is good.

Therefore your daughters play the whore,
    and your daughters-in-law commit adultery.

14 I will not punish your daughters when they
        play the whore,
    nor your daughters-in-law when they
        commit adultery;
for the men themselves go aside with whores,
    and sacrifice with temple prostitutes;
thus a people without understanding comes to
        ruin.

15 Though you play the whore, O Israel,
    do not let Judah become guilty.
Do not enter into Gil'gal,
    or go up to Beth-a'ven,
    and do not swear, "As the LORD lives."

16 Like a stubborn heifer,
    Israel is stubborn;
can the LORD now feed them
    like a lamb in a broad pasture?

17 E'phra·im is joined to idols—
    let him alone.

---

u Cn: Meaning of Heb uncertain   v Ancient Heb tradition:
MT *I will change*

HOS

18 When their drinking is ended, they indulge in
      sexual orgies;
   they love lewdness more than their glory.*w*

19 A wind has wrapped them*x* in its wings,
      and they shall be ashamed because of their
      altars.*y*

Impending Judgment on Israel and Judah

5 Hear this, O priests!
      Give heed, O house of Israel!
   Listen, O house of the king!
      For the judgment pertains to you;
   for you have been a snare at Miz′pah,
      and a net spread upon Tā′bor,
2 and a pit dug deep in Shit′tim;*z*
      but I will punish all of them.

3 I know Ē′phra·im,
      and Israel is not hidden from me;
   for now, O Ē′phra·im, you have played the
      whore;
   Israel is defiled.
4 Their deeds do not permit them
      to return to their God.
   For the spirit of whoredom is within them,
      and they do not know the LORD.

5 Israel's pride testifies against him;
      Ē′phra·im*a* stumbles in his guilt;
   Judah also stumbles with them.
6 With their flocks and herds they shall go
      to seek the LORD,
   but they will not find him;
      he has withdrawn from them.
7 They have dealt faithlessly with the LORD;
      for they have borne illegitimate children.
   Now the new moon shall devour them
      along with their fields.

8 Blow the horn in Gib′e·ah,
      the trumpet in Rā′mah.
   Sound the alarm at Beth-ā′ven;
      look behind you, Benjamin!
9 Ē′phra·im shall become a desolation
      in the day of punishment;
   among the tribes of Israel
      I declare what is sure.
10 The princes of Judah have become
      like those who remove the landmark;
   on them I will pour out
      my wrath like water.
11 Ē′phra·im is oppressed, crushed in judgment,
      because he was determined to go after
      vanity.*b*
12 Therefore I am like maggots to Ē′phra·im,
      and like rottenness to the house of Judah.
13 When Ē′phra·im saw his sickness,

   and Judah his wound,
      then Ē′phra·im went to Assyria,
      and sent to the great king.*c*
   But he is not able to cure you
      or heal your wound.
14 For I will be like a lion to Ē′phra·im,
      and like a young lion to the house of Judah.
   I myself will tear and go away;
      I will carry off, and no one shall rescue.
15 I will return again to my place
      until they acknowledge their guilt and seek
      my face.
   In their distress they will beg my favor:

A Call to Repentance

6 "Come, let us return to the LORD;
      for it is he who has torn, and he will
      heal us;
   he has struck down, and he will bind us up.
2 After two days he will revive us;
      on the third day he will raise us up,
      that we may live before him.
3 Let us know, let us press on to know the LORD;
      his appearing is as sure as the dawn;
   he will come to us like the showers,
      like the spring rains that water the earth."

Impenitence of Israel and Judah

4 What shall I do with you, O Ē′phra·im?
      What shall I do with you, O Judah?
   Your love is like a morning cloud,
      like the dew that goes away early.
5 Therefore I have hewn them by the prophets,
      I have killed them by the words of my
      mouth,
   and my*d* judgment goes forth as the light.
6 For I desire steadfast love and not sacrifice,
      the knowledge of God rather than burnt
      offerings.

7 But at*e* Adam they transgressed the covenant;
      there they dealt faithlessly with me.
8 Gil′e·ad is a city of evildoers,
      tracked with blood.
9 As robbers lie in wait*z* for someone,
      so the priests are banded together;*f*
   they murder on the road to Shē′chem,
      they commit a monstrous crime.
10 In the house of Israel I have seen a horrible
      thing;
   Ē′phra·im's whoredom is there, Israel is
      defiled.

----

w Cn Compare Gk: Meaning of Heb uncertain   *x* Heb *her*
y Gk Syr: Heb *sacrifices*   *z* Cn: Meaning of Heb uncertain
a Heb *Israel and Ephraim*   *b* Gk: Meaning of Heb
uncertain   *c* Cn: Heb *to a king who will contend*   *d* Gk Syr:
Heb *your*   *e* Cn: Heb *like*   *f* Syr: Heb *are a company*

11 For you also, O Judah, a harvest is
  appointed.

When I would restore the fortunes of my
  people,

7 1 when I would heal Israel,
  the corruption of Ē′phra•im is revealed,
 and the wicked deeds of Sa•mār′i•a;
for they deal falsely,
 the thief breaks in,
 and the bandits raid outside.
2 But they do not consider
 that I remember all their wickedness.
Now their deeds surround them,
 they are before my face.
3 By their wickedness they make the king glad,
 and the officials by their treachery.
4 They are all adulterers;
  they are like a heated oven,
whose baker does not need to stir the fire,
 from the kneading of the dough until it is
  leavened.
5 On the day of our king the officials
 became sick with the heat of wine;
 he stretched out his hand with mockers.
6 For they are kindled*g* like an oven, their heart
  burns within them;
 all night their anger smolders;
 in the morning it blazes like a flaming fire.
7 All of them are hot as an oven,
 and they devour their rulers.
All their kings have fallen;
 none of them calls upon me.

8 Ē′phra•im mixes himself with the peoples;
 Ē′phra•im is a cake not turned.
9 Foreigners devour his strength,
 but he does not know it;
gray hairs are sprinkled upon him,
 but he does not know it.
10 Israel's pride testifies against*h* him;
 yet they do not return to the LORD their God,
 or seek him, for all this.

Futile Reliance on the Nations

11 Ē′phra•im has become like a dove,
 silly and without sense;
 they call upon Egypt, they go to Assyria.
12 As they go, I will cast my net over them;
 I will bring them down like birds of the air;
 I will discipline them according to the
  report made to their assembly.*i*
13 Woe to them, for they have strayed from me!
 Destruction to them, for they have rebelled
  against me!
I would redeem them,
 but they speak lies against me.

14 They do not cry to me from the heart,
 but they wail upon their beds;
they gash themselves for grain and wine;
 they rebel against me.
15 It was I who trained and strengthened their
  arms,
 yet they plot evil against me.
16 They turn to that which does not profit;*j*
 they have become like a defective bow;
their officials shall fall by the sword
 because of the rage of their tongue.
So much for their babbling in the land of
 Egypt.

Israel's Apostasy

8 Set the trumpet to your lips!
 One like a vulture *i* is over the house of
  the LORD,
because they have broken my covenant,
 and transgressed my law.
2 Israel cries to me,
 "My God, we—Israel—know you!"
3 Israel has spurned the good;
 the enemy shall pursue him.

4 They made kings, but not through me;
 they set up princes, but without my
  knowledge.
With their silver and gold they made idols
 for their own destruction.
5 Your calf is rejected, O Sa•mār′i•a.
 My anger burns against them.
How long will they be incapable of
 innocence?
6 For it is from Israel,
an artisan made it;
 it is not God.
The calf of Sa•mār′i•a
 shall be broken to pieces.*k*

7 For they sow the wind,
 and they shall reap the whirlwind.
The standing grain has no heads,
 it shall yield no meal;
if it were to yield,
 foreigners would devour it.
8 Israel is swallowed up;
 now they are among the nations
 as a useless vessel.
9 For they have gone up to Assyria,
 a wild ass wandering alone;
 Ē′phra•im has bargained for lovers.
10 Though they bargain with the nations,

---

g Gk Syr: Heb *brought near*   *h* Or *humbles*   *i* Meaning of
Heb uncertain   *j* Cn: Meaning of Heb uncertain   *k* Or *shall
go up in flames*

PRAY IT?

Reaping the Whirlwind

Hosea uses lots of metaphors, or symbols, in describing Israel's relationship with God. Hosea 8.7 gives one of those metaphors, saying the Israelites have sowed the wind and will reap the whirlwind. The wind is their political scheming, injustice, and idolatry; the whirlwind is violence and injustice that will destroy the whole country.

Like Israel, we are free to reject or accept God, but will have to reap the consequences of our choices.

In your prayer, reflect or journal on the following questions:

- What significant decisions have you made recently?
- What consequences are likely to follow as a result of each decision?
- Were your choices the ones that God wanted you to make?

▶ Hos 8.7

I will now gather them up.
They shall soon writhe
　　under the burden of kings and princes.

11 When Ē′phra·im multiplied altars to expiate sin,
　　they became to him altars for sinning.
12 Though I write for him the multitude of my
　　　　instructions,
　　they are regarded as a strange thing.
13 Though they offer choice sacrifices,[l]
　　though they eat flesh,
　　　　the LORD does not accept them.
Now he will remember their iniquity,
　　and punish their sins;
　　they shall return to Egypt.
14 Israel has forgotten his Maker,
　　and built palaces;
and Judah has multiplied fortified cities;
　　but I will send a fire upon his cities,
　　and it shall devour his strongholds.

Punishment for Israel's Sin

9 Do not rejoice, O Israel!
　　Do not exult[m] as other nations do;
for you have played the whore, departing from
　　　　your God.
You have loved a prostitute's pay

on all threshing floors.
2 Threshing floor and wine vat shall not feed
　　them,
　　and the new wine shall fail them.
3 They shall not remain in the land of the LORD;
　　but Ē′phra·im shall return to Egypt,
　　and in Assyria they shall eat unclean food.

4 They shall not pour drink offerings of wine to
　　　　the LORD,
　　and their sacrifices shall not please him.
Such sacrifices shall be like mourners' bread;
　　all who eat of it shall be defiled;
for their bread shall be for their hunger only;
　　it shall not come to the house of the LORD.

5 What will you do on the day of appointed
　　　　festival,
　　and on the day of the festival of the LORD?
6 For even if they escape destruction,
　　Egypt shall gather them,
　　Memphis shall bury them.
Nettles shall possess their precious things of
　　　　silver;[n]
　　thorns shall be in their tents.

7 The days of punishment have come,
　　the days of recompense have come;
　　Israel cries,[o]
"The prophet is a fool,
　　the man of the spirit is mad!"
Because of your great iniquity,
　　your hostility is great.
8 The prophet is a sentinel for my God over
　　　　Ē′phra·im,
yet a fowler's snare is on all his ways,
　　and hostility in the house of his God.
9 They have deeply corrupted themselves
　　as in the days of Gib′e·ah;
he will remember their iniquity,
　　he will punish their sins.

10 Like grapes in the wilderness,
　　I found Israel.
Like the first fruit on the fig tree,
　　in its first season,
　　I saw your ancestors.
But they came to Bā′al-pē′or,
　　and consecrated themselves to a thing of
　　　　shame,
　　and became detestable like the thing they
　　　　loved.
11 Ē′phra·im's glory shall fly away like a bird—

---

l Cn: Meaning of Heb uncertain　m Gk: Heb *To exultation*
n Meaning of Heb uncertain　o Cn Compare Gk: Heb
shall know

no birth, no pregnancy, no conception!

12 Even if they bring up children,
    I will bereave them until no one is left.
Woe to them indeed
    when I depart from them!

13 Once I saw Ēʹphra·im as a young palm planted
    in a lovely meadow,ᵖ
but now Ēʹphra·im must lead out his
    children for slaughter.

14 Give them, O LORD—
    what will you give?
Give them a miscarrying womb
    and dry breasts.

15 Every evil of theirs began at Gilʹgal;
    there I came to hate them.
Because of the wickedness of their deeds
    I will drive them out of my house.
I will love them no more;
    all their officials are rebels.

16 Ēʹphra·im is stricken,
    their root is dried up,
    they shall bear no fruit.
Even though they give birth,
    I will kill the cherished offspring of their
      womb.

17 Because they have not listened to him,
    my God will reject them;
they shall become wanderers among the
    nations.

Israel's Sin and Captivity

10 Israel is a luxuriant vine
    that yields its fruit.
The more his fruit increased
    the more altars he built;
as his country improved,
    he improved his pillars.

2 Their heart is false;
    now they must bear their guilt.
The LORD�q will break down their altars,
    and destroy their pillars.

3 For now they will say:
    "We have no king,
for we do not fear the LORD,
    and a king—what could he do for us?"

4 They utter mere words;
    with empty oaths they make covenants;
so litigation springs up like poisonous weeds
    in the furrows of the field.

5 The inhabitants of Sa·mārʹi·a tremble
    for the calfʳ of Beth-āʹven.
Its people shall mourn for it,
    and its idolatrous priests shall wailˢ over it,
    over its glory that has departed from it.

6 The thing itself shall be carried to Assyria
    as tribute to the great king.ᵗ
Ēʹphra·im shall be put to shame,
    and Israel shall be ashamed of his idol.ᵘ

7 Sa·mārʹi·a's king shall perish
    like a chip on the face of the waters.

8 The high places of Āʹven, the sin of Israel,
    shall be destroyed.
Thorn and thistle shall grow up
    on their altars.
They shall say to the mountains, Cover us,
    and to the hills, Fall on us.

9 Since the days of Gibʹe·ah you have sinned,
    O Israel;
there they have continued.
    Shall not war overtake them in Gibʹe·ah?

10 I will comeᵛ against the wayward people to
    punish them;
and nations shall be gathered against them
when they are punishedʷ for their double
    iniquity.

11 Ēʹphra·im was a trained heifer
    that loved to thresh,
    and I spared her fair neck;
but I will make Ēʹphra·im break the ground;
    Judah must plow;
    Jacob must harrow for himself.

12 Sow for yourselves righteousness;
    reap steadfast love;
    break up your fallow ground;
for it is time to seek the LORD,
    that he may come and rain righteousness
      upon you.

13 You have plowed wickedness,
    you have reaped injustice,
    you have eaten the fruit of lies.
Because you have trusted in your power
    and in the multitude of your warriors,

14 therefore the tumult of war shall rise against
    your people,
    and all your fortresses shall be destroyed,
as Shalʹman destroyed Beth-arʹbel on the day
    of battle
    when mothers were dashed in pieces with
      their children.

15 Thus it shall be done to you, O Bethʹel,
    because of your great wickedness.
At dawn the king of Israel
    shall be utterly cut off.

---

p Meaning of Heb uncertain   q Heb *he*   r Gk Syr: Heb
calves   s Cn: Heb *exult*   t Cn: Heb *to a king who will
contend*   u Cn: Heb *counsel*   v Cn Compare Gk: Heb *In my
desire*   w Gk: Heb *bound*

God's Compassion Despite Israel's Ingratitude

11 When Israel was a child, I loved him,
and out of Egypt I called my son.
2 The more I[x] called them,
the more they went from me;[y]
they kept sacrificing to the Ba′als,
and offering incense to idols.

3 Yet it was I who taught E′phra·im to walk,
I took them up in my[z] arms;
but they did not know that I healed them.
4 I led them with cords of human kindness,
with bands of love.
I was to them like those
who lift infants to their cheeks.[a]
I bent down to them and fed them.

5 They shall return to the land of Egypt,
and Assyria shall be their king,
because they have refused to return to me.
6 The sword rages in their cities,
it consumes their oracle-priests,
and devours because of their schemes.
7 My people are bent on turning away from me.
To the Most High they call,
but he does not raise them up at all.[b]

A Parent's Love

Hosea, chapter 11, describes God as a loving parent. This is one of the most touching passages of the Old Testament. Despite God's tenderness and care, Israel behaves as a rebellious child. God is heartbroken by Israel's rejection, but is compassionate in calling for its return.

God, loving father and mother, thank you for your generous and unconditional love. Let me remember that you always love me even when I have done something wrong. Help me to return your love by living in a way that is pleasing to you. Amen.

▶ Hos 11.1–7

8 How can I give you up, E′phra·im?
How can I hand you over, O Israel?
How can I make you like Ad′mah?
How can I treat you like Ze·boi′im?
My heart recoils within me;
my compassion grows warm and tender.
9 I will not execute my fierce anger;

I will not again destroy E′phra·im;
for I am God and no mortal,
the Holy One in your midst,
and I will not come in wrath.[b]

10 They shall go after the LORD,
who roars like a lion;
when he roars,
his children shall come trembling from the
west.
11 They shall come trembling like birds from
Egypt,
and like doves from the land of
Assyria;
and I will return them to their homes, says
the LORD.

12c E′phra·im has surrounded me with lies,
and the house of Israel with deceit;
but Judah still walks[d] with God,
and is faithful to the Holy One.

12 E′phra·im herds the wind,
and pursues the east wind all day
long;
they multiply falsehood and violence;
they make a treaty with Assyria,
and oil is carried to Egypt.

The Long History of Rebellion
(Cp Gen 25—32)

2 The LORD has an indictment against Judah,
and will punish Jacob according to his
ways,
and repay him according to his deeds.
3 In the womb he tried to supplant his
brother,
and in his manhood he strove with God.
4 He strove with the angel and prevailed,
he wept and sought his favor;
he met him at Beth′el,
and there he spoke with him.[e]
5 The LORD the God of hosts,
the LORD is his name!
6 But as for you, return to your God,
hold fast to love and justice,
and wait continually for your God.

7 A trader, in whose hands are false balances,
he loves to oppress.
8 E′phra·im has said, "Ah, I am rich,
I have gained wealth for myself;
in all of my gain
no offense has been found in me

---

x Gk: Heb *they*   y Gk: Heb *them*   z Gk Syr Vg: Heb *his*
a Or *who ease the yoke on their jaws*   b Meaning of Heb
uncertain   c Ch 12.1 in Heb   d Heb *roams* or *rules*   e Gk
Syr: Heb *us*

I THEREFORE COMMIT

This prayer from Elizabeth S. Tapia of the Philippines could have been written in response to Hosea's call to live justly, to live the spirit of being a holy people of God:

We should not oppress children, indigenous people,
women, the homeless, refugees and victims of war.
We need to live in defense of peoples and creation.
For I believe in the interwovenness of life.
Creator and Creatures. Cosmic and Individual.
West, North, East, South. Rest and Prayer.
Food and Freedom. Theology and Ecology.
I therefore commit myself, together with you,
to take care of mother earth.
To advocate for peace and justice.
To choose and celebrate life!
These things I believe. Amen.

("Earth Credo," from *A Time to Speak*)

▶ Hos 12.3–7

that would be sin."*f*

9 I am the LORD your God
   from the land of Egypt;
 I will make you live in tents again,
   as in the days of the appointed festival.

10 I spoke to the prophets;
   it was I who multiplied visions,
   and through the prophets I will bring
      destruction.
11 In Gil'e•ad*g* there is iniquity,
   they shall surely come to nothing.
 In Gil'gal they sacrifice bulls,
   so their altars shall be like stone heaps
   on the furrows of the field.
12 Jacob fled to the land of Ar'am,
   there Israel served for a wife,
   and for a wife he guarded sheep.*h*
13 By a prophet the LORD brought Israel up from
      Egypt,
   and by a prophet he was guarded.
14 É'phra•im has given bitter offense,
   so his Lord will bring his crimes down on
      him
   and pay him back for his insults.

Relentless Judgment on Israel

13 When É'phra•im spoke, there was
   trembling;
 he was exalted in Israel;
 but he incurred guilt through Bā'al and
      died.
2 And now they keep on sinning
   and make a cast image for themselves,
 idols of silver made according to their
      understanding,
 all of them the work of artisans.
 "Sacrifice to these," they say.*i*
   People are kissing calves!
3 Therefore they shall be like the morning mist
   or like the dew that goes away early,
 like chaff that swirls from the threshing floor
   or like smoke from a window.

4 Yet I have been the LORD your God
   ever since the land of Egypt;
 you know no God but me,

HOS

---

f Meaning of Heb uncertain   *g* Compare Syr: Heb *Gilead*
h Heb lacks *sheep*   *i* Cn Compare Gk: Heb *To these they say*
sacrifices of people

and besides me there is no savior.
5 It was I who fed[j] you in the wilderness,
   in the land of drought.
6 When I fed[k] them, they were satisfied;
   they were satisfied, and their heart was
      proud;
   therefore they forgot me.
7 So I will become like a lion to them,
   like a leopard I will lurk beside the way.
8 I will fall upon them like a bear robbed of her
      cubs,
   and will tear open the covering of their
      heart;
there I will devour them like a lion,
   as a wild animal would mangle them.

9 I will destroy you, O Israel;
   who can help you?[l]
10 Where now is[m] your king, that he may save you?
   Where in all your cities are your rulers,
of whom you said,
   "Give me a king and rulers"?
11 I gave you a king in my anger,
   and I took him away in my wrath.

12 E'phra·im's iniquity is bound up;
   his sin is kept in store.
13 The pangs of childbirth come for him,
   but he is an unwise son;
for at the proper time he does not present
      himself
   at the mouth of the womb.

14 Shall I ransom them from the power of She'ōl?
   Shall I redeem them from Death?
   O Death, where are[n] your plagues?
   O She'ōl, where is[n] your destruction?
   Compassion is hidden from my eyes.

15 Although he may flourish among rushes,[o]
   the east wind shall come, a blast from the
      LORD,
   rising from the wilderness;
and his fountain shall dry up,
   his spring shall be parched.
It shall strip his treasury
   of every precious thing.
16p Sa·mār'i·a shall bear her guilt,
   because she has rebelled against her God;
they shall fall by the sword,
   their little ones shall be dashed in pieces,
   and their pregnant women ripped open.

A Plea for Repentance

14 Return, O Israel, to the LORD your God,
for you have stumbled because of
your iniquity.

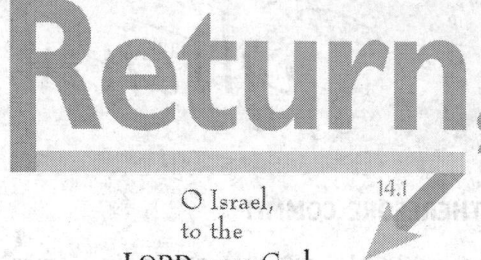

Return, O Israel,
to the
LORD your God,
for you have
stumbled
because of your iniquity. 14.1

2 Take words with you
   and return to the LORD;
say to him,
   "Take away all guilt;
accept that which is good,
   and we will offer
   the fruit[q] of our lips.
3 Assyria shall not save us;
   we will not ride upon horses;
we will say no more, 'Our God,'
   to the work of our hands.
In you the orphan finds mercy."

Assurance of Forgiveness

4 I will heal their disloyalty;
   I will love them freely,
   for my anger has turned from them.
5 I will be like the dew to Israel;
   he shall blossom like the lily,
   he shall strike root like the forests of
      Lebanon.[r]
6 His shoots shall spread out;
   his beauty shall be like the olive tree,
   and his fragrance like that of Lebanon.
7 They shall again live beneath my[s] shadow,
   they shall flourish as a garden;[t]
they shall blossom like the vine,
   their fragrance shall be like the wine of
      Lebanon.

8 O E'phra·im, what have I[u] to do with idols?
   It is I who answer and look after you.[v]

---

j Gk Syr: Heb *knew*   k Cn: Heb *according to their pasture*
l Gk Syr: Heb *for in me is your help*   m Gk Syr Vg: Heb *I will be*   n Gk Syr: Heb *I will be*   o Or *among brothers*
p Ch 14.1 in Heb   q Gk Syr: Heb *bulls*   r Cn: Heb *like Lebanon*   s Heb *his*   t Cn: Heb *they shall grow grain*
u Or *What more has Ephraim*   v Heb *him*

HOS

I am like an evergreen cypress;
  your faithfulness[w] comes from me.
9 Those who are wise understand these things;
  those who are discerning know them.
For the ways of the LORD are right,

and the upright walk in them,
  but transgressors stumble in them.

_____

w Heb *your fruit*

You're just cruising along, in the groove, and everything is going your way. Then, it happens. You hit a major bump in the road, and everything starts falling apart. This appears to have been the situation in Joel's time, when a major plague of locusts was causing widespread destruction. Joel took it as a wake-up sign, calling Israel to rely totally on God no matter what happened.

At a Glance

- **1.1—2.17.** a discussion of a plague of locusts and the day of the Lord

- **2.18—3.21.** several prophecies promising God's salvation for Israel

In-depth

The Book of Joel does not state clearly when it was written, but it gives several clues that lead biblical scholars to believe it was written after the Babylonian Exile. During this time, Israel was ruled by the Greeks and did not have a king. The Temple and Jerusalem had been rebuilt, and Israel enjoyed relative peace, along with a growing expectancy for the coming of a messiah, a savior.

In this period, a natural disaster, perhaps a plague of locusts, occurred. In the first part of the book, Joel uses this tragedy to call Israel's attention toward God and renew its faith. He compares the plague of locusts to an invading army that brings devastation to a city. Eventually, prayer and penance end the plague and bring rain for new crops. More important, the gift of the Spirit renews the people of God (Joel 2.28–29).

A major element of this book is a warrior-type song in which Joel speaks of the coming of the day of the Lord (2.1–17). He describes this as the day when judgment will be delivered against the nations that have destroyed Israel. The day of the Lord is a theme that runs throughout the Bible. It is sometimes described as a joyful time of celebration (Isa 9.3), and other times as a day of punishment and destruction (Am 5.18–24). Initially, writers of the Scriptures applied the term *day of the Lord* only to Israel; Joel applied it to all nations. Gradually, it became connected to the final judgment (Mt 25.31–46).

The Book of Joel ends by affirming that the Lord dwells in Zion (Jerusalem) and the land will be fruitful once more. This is Joel's central message: Despite plagues and even war, God is present in Judah, and there is reason for hope.

Quick Facts

Period Covered
after the rebuilding of the Temple (515 B.C.) and before the destruction of Sidon (343 B.C.)

Authors
Joel and scribes, writing around 400 B.C.

Theme
a plague of locusts as an occasion to call for Israel to repent and turn to the Lord

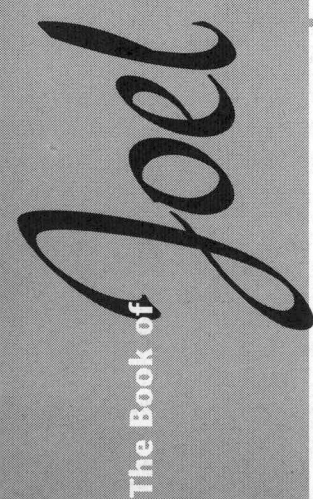

The Book of Joel

Joel

1 The word of the LORD that came to Jō'el son of Pe•thū'el:

Lament over the Ruin of the Country
(Ex 10.1–20)

2 Hear this, O elders,
    give ear, all inhabitants of the land!
Has such a thing happened in your days,
    or in the days of your ancestors?
3 Tell your children of it,
    and let your children tell their
        children,
    and their children another generation.

4 What the cutting locust left,
    the swarming locust has eaten.
What the swarming locust left,
    the hopping locust has eaten,
and what the hopping locust left,
    the destroying locust has eaten.

5 Wake up, you drunkards, and weep;
    and wail, all you wine-drinkers,
over the sweet wine,
    for it is cut off from your mouth.
6 For a nation has invaded my land,
    powerful and innumerable;
its teeth are lions' teeth,
    and it has the fangs of a lioness.

7 It has laid waste my vines,
    and splintered my fig trees;
it has stripped off their bark and thrown it
        down;
    their branches have turned white.

8 Lament like a virgin dressed in sackcloth
    for the husband of her youth.
9 The grain offering and the drink offering are
        cut off
    from the house of the LORD.
The priests mourn,
    the ministers of the LORD.
10 The fields are devastated,
    the ground mourns;
for the grain is destroyed,
    the wine dries up,
    the oil fails.

11 Be dismayed, you farmers,
    wail, you vinedressers,
over the wheat and the barley;
    for the crops of the field are ruined.
12 The vine withers,
    the fig tree droops.
Pomegranate, palm, and apple—
    all the trees of the field are dried up;
surely, joy withers away
    among the people.

A Call to Repentance and Prayer

13 Put on sackcloth and lament, you priests;
    wail, you ministers of the altar.
Come, pass the night in sackcloth,
    you ministers of my God!
Grain offering and drink offering
    are withheld from the house of your God.

14 Sanctify a fast,
    call a solemn assembly.
Gather the elders
    and all the inhabitants of the land
to the house of the LORD your God,
    and cry out to the LORD.

15 Alas for the day!
For the day of the LORD is near,
    and as destruction from the Almighty[a]
        it comes.
16 Is not the food cut off
    before our eyes,
joy and gladness
    from the house of our God?

17 The seed shrivels under the clods,[b]
    the storehouses are desolate;
the granaries are ruined
    because the grain has failed.
18 How the animals groan!
    The herds of cattle wander about
because there is no pasture for them;
    even the flocks of sheep are dazed.[c]

19 To you, O LORD, I cry.
For fire has devoured
    the pastures of the wilderness,
and flames have burned
    all the trees of the field.
20 Even the wild animals cry to you
    because the watercourses are dried up,
and fire has devoured
    the pastures of the wilderness.

2 Blow the trumpet in Zion;
    sound the alarm on my holy mountain!
Let all the inhabitants of the land tremble,
    for the day of the LORD is coming, it is near—
2 a day of darkness and gloom,
    a day of clouds and thick darkness!
Like blackness spread upon the mountains
    a great and powerful army comes;
their like has never been from of old,
    nor will be again after them
        in ages to come.

3 Fire devours in front of them,
    and behind them a flame burns.

Catholic Connections

ASH WEDNESDAY

Joel 2.12–18 is the first reading Catholics hear every year on Ash Wednesday. On that day, Catholics gather to receive ashes and to be reminded at the beginning of the Lenten season of the importance of prayer fasting, and almsgiving. Why?

We pray to renew our connection to God.

We fast to remind ourselves how it feels to be hungry, and to empty ourselves so that God can fill us up spiritually.

We give alms (money for those who are less fortunate) as an act of penance, mercy, and charity (to remind ourselves of the need to share our wealth with those in greater need).

▶ Joel 2.12–18

Before them the land is like the garden of
    Eden,
but after them a desolate wilderness,
    and nothing escapes them.

4 They have the appearance of horses,
    and like war-horses they charge.
5 As with the rumbling of chariots,
    they leap on the tops of the mountains,
like the crackling of a flame of fire
    devouring the stubble,
like a powerful army
    drawn up for battle.

6 Before them peoples are in anguish,
    all faces grow pale.[b]
7 Like warriors they charge,
    like soldiers they scale the wall.
Each keeps to its own course,

---

a Traditional rendering of Heb Shaddai   b Meaning of Heb uncertain   c Compare Gk Syr Vg: Meaning of Heb uncertain

they do not swerve from[d] their paths.
8 They do not jostle one another,
    each keeps to its own track;
they burst through the weapons
    and are not halted.
9 They leap upon the city,
    they run upon the walls;
they climb up into the houses,
    they enter through the windows like a
        thief.

10 The earth quakes before them,
    the heavens tremble.
The sun and the moon are darkened,
    and the stars withdraw their shining.
11 The LORD utters his voice
    at the head of his army;
how vast is his host!
    Numberless are those who obey his
        command.
Truly the day of the LORD is great;
    terrible indeed—who can endure it?

12 Yet even now, says the LORD,
    return to me with all your heart,
with fasting, with weeping, and with
        mourning;
13   rend your hearts and not your clothing.
Return to the LORD, your God,
    for he is gracious and merciful,
slow to anger, and abounding in steadfast love,
    and relents from punishing.
14 Who knows whether he will not turn and
        relent,
    and leave a blessing behind him,
a grain offering and a drink offering
    for the LORD, your God?

15 Blow the trumpet in Zion;
    sanctify a fast;
call a solemn assembly;
16   gather the people.
Sanctify the congregation;
    assemble the aged;
gather the children,
    even infants at the breast.
Let the bridegroom leave his room,
    and the bride her canopy.

17 Between the vestibule and the altar
    let the priests, the ministers of the LORD,
        weep.
Let them say, "Spare your people, O LORD,
    and do not make your heritage a mockery,
    a byword among the nations.
Why should it be said among the peoples,
    'Where is their God?'"

God's Response and Promise
(Acts 2.17)

18 Then the LORD became jealous for his land,
    and had pity on his people.
19 In response to his people the LORD said:
I am sending you
    grain, wine, and oil,
    and you will be satisfied;
and I will no more make you
    a mockery among the nations.

20 I will remove the northern army far from you,
    and drive it into a parched and desolate
        land,
its front into the eastern sea,
    and its rear into the western sea;
its stench and foul smell will rise up.
    Surely he has done great things!

21 Do not fear, O soil;
    be glad and rejoice,
    for the LORD has done great things!
22 Do not fear, you animals of the field,
    for the pastures of the wilderness are green;
the tree bears its fruit,
    the fig tree and vine give their full yield.

23 O children of Zion, be glad
    and rejoice in the LORD your God;
for he has given the early rain[e] for your
        vindication,
    he has poured down for you abundant
        rain,
    the early and the later rain, as before.
24 The threshing floors shall be full of grain,
    the vats shall overflow with wine and oil.

25 I will repay you for the years
    that the swarming locust has eaten,
the hopper, the destroyer, and the cutter,
    my great army, which I sent against you.

26 You shall eat in plenty and be satisfied,
    and praise the name of the LORD your
        God,
    who has dealt wondrously with you.
And my people shall never again be put to
        shame.
27 You shall know that I am in the midst of
        Israel,
    and that I, the LORD, am your God and
        there is no other.
And my people shall never again be put to
        shame.

---

[d] Gk Syr Vg: Heb *they do not take a pledge along*   [e] Meaning of Heb uncertain

VISION QUEST

Joel 2.28 mentions young men having visions. Vision quests are an indigenous tradition. A young man with only a blanket is led by a holy person to a hill to be on his own for several days. During that time, he refrains from eating and drinking and tries to focus on being very still, believing that he will receive a personal vision. That vision will give shape to his life and help him know his place in the world. The key is in the waiting. When the young man returns from his vision quest, he is considered a man and can become the person he is destined to become. He now has a vision to live out.

Jesus went on something like a vision quest before he began his public ministry. He went into the wilderness, fasted, and wrestled with the demons.

Joel 2.28–29 is read at Pentecost—the church feast day that celebrates the coming of the Holy Spirit. You can let the Holy Spirit help you discern the path for your life through a personal retreat, guided by a spiritual director in the Christian tradition.

▶ Joel 2.28–29

God's Spirit Poured Out

28*f* Then afterward
 I will pour out my spirit on all flesh;
 your sons and your daughters shall prophesy,
 your old men shall dream dreams,
 and your young men shall see visions.
29 Even on the male and female slaves,
 in those days, I will pour out my spirit.

30 I will show portents in the heavens and on the earth, blood and fire and columns of smoke. 31 The sun shall be turned to darkness, and the moon to blood, before the great and terrible day of the LORD comes. 32 Then everyone who calls on the name of the LORD shall be saved; for in Mount Zion and in Jerusalem there shall be those who escape, as the LORD has said, and among the survivors shall be those whom the LORD calls.

3 *g* For then, in those days and at that time, when I restore the fortunes of Judah and Jerusalem, 2 I will gather all the nations and bring them down to the valley of Je•hosh′a•phat, and I will enter into judgment with them there, on account of my people and my heritage Israel, because they have scattered them among the nations. They have divided my land, 3 and cast lots for my people, and traded boys for prostitutes, and sold girls for wine, and drunk it down.

4 What are you to me, O Tȳre and Si′don, and all the regions of Phi•lis′ti•a? Are you paying me

back for something? If you are paying me back, I will turn your deeds back upon your own heads swiftly and speedily. 5 For you have taken my silver and my gold, and have carried my rich treasures into your temples.*h* 6 You have sold the people of Judah and Jerusalem to the Greeks, removing them far from their own border. 7 But now I will rouse them to leave the places to which you have sold them, and I will turn your deeds back upon your own heads. 8 I will sell your sons and your daughters into the hand of the people of Judah, and they will sell them to the Sa•bē′ans, to a nation far away; for the LORD has spoken.

Judgment in the Valley of Jehoshaphat
(Cp Isa 2.4; Mic 4.3)

9 Proclaim this among the nations:
 Prepare war,*i*
  stir up the warriors.
 Let all the soldiers draw near,
  let them come up.
10 Beat your plowshares into swords,
  and your pruning hooks into spears;
  let the weakling say, "I am a warrior."

11 Come quickly,*j*
  all you nations all around,

---

f Ch 3.1 in Heb   *g* Ch 4.1 in Heb   *h* Or *palaces*   *i* Heb *sanctify war*   *j* Meaning of Heb uncertain

gather yourselves there.
Bring down your warriors, O LORD.
12 Let the nations rouse themselves,
and come up to the valley of
Je•hosh′a•phat;
for there I will sit to judge
all the neighboring nations.

13 Put in the sickle,
for the harvest is ripe.
Go in, tread,
for the wine press is full.
The vats overflow,
for their wickedness is great.

14 Multitudes, multitudes,
in the valley of decision!
For the day of the LORD is near
in the valley of decision.
15 The sun and the moon are darkened,
and the stars withdraw their shining.

16 The LORD roars from Zion,
and utters his voice from
Jerusalem,
and the heavens and the earth
shake.
But the LORD is a refuge for his people,
a stronghold for the people of
Israel.

The Glorious Future of Judah

17 So you shall know that I, the LORD your God,
dwell in Zion, my holy mountain.
And Jerusalem shall be holy,
and strangers shall never again pass
through it.

18 In that day
the mountains shall drip sweet wine,
the hills shall flow with milk,
and all the stream beds of Judah
shall flow with water;
a fountain shall come forth from the house of
the LORD
and water the Wadi Shit′tim.

19 Egypt shall become a desolation
and Ê′dom a desolate wilderness,
because of the violence done to the people of
Judah,
in whose land they have shed innocent
blood.
20 But Judah shall be inhabited forever,
and Jerusalem to all generations.
21 I will avenge their blood, and I will not clear
the guilty,^{k}
for the LORD dwells in Zion.

---

k Gk Syr: Heb *I will hold innocent their blood that I have not
held innocent*

JOEL

You've probably run across people who bluntly state what they see going on. They don't seem to care too much about what other people think. They say, "I just tell it like it is." The prophet Amos was like that. He didn't pull any punches in describing the wealthy class's sins or the destruction that God had planned for it. He was a powerful voice calling for justice in God's plan of salvation.

At a Glance

- **1.1—2.3.** a condemnation of Israel's neighbors
- **2.4—9.8.** a proclamation of the destruction of the northern kingdom, Israel
- **9.9–15.** a word of hope, probably added by a later editor

In-depth

Amos lived when there were two separate kingdoms of Israelites: a northern kingdom, named Israel, and a southern kingdom, named Judah. He was born in the southern kingdom and worked as a shepherd and tree trimmer (Am 7.14). But God called him to preach to the northern kingdom. Amos was not an official prophet of the king's court, so he was free to speak against the king and the court and to be brutally honest in delivering God's message.

Among the Old Testament prophecies, Amos's are the least hopeful. Amos stresses that Israel's destruction, complete and total, is certain. He condemns Israel for its failure to be faithful to the Covenant, but he has a special anger toward the king, the priests, and the wealthy class. He accuses them of being hypocrites who lead the people of Israel astray while pretending to be faithful themselves.

What was Amos's evidence? First, the Covenant demanded special care for the poor, the outcast, and the marginalized. The king, the wealthy, and some of the priests were ignoring this demand. Instead of caring for the poor and the lowly, the wealthy were cheating them and treating them unjustly (2.6–8).

Second, with the monies they cheated out of the poor, the ruling class and the wealthy staged lavish ceremonies to God that were modeled on ceremonies honoring foreign gods. They went through the motions of worshiping God, but they ignored the demand to care for their neighbor (5.21–24). For Amos, this was the heart of Israel's hypocrisy—its sinful habit of separating its religious rituals from concern for its citizens. This phoniness was repulsive to God, and because of Israel's sin, God would bring it to destruction. Amos is rightly called the prophet of the Lord's justice.

Quick Facts

Period Covered
786–746 B.C.

Authors
Amos and later scribes

Theme
God's destruction of Israel because of the injustice and hypocrisy of the wealthy and the ruling class

The Book of *Amos*

Amos

5.24

1 The words of Ā′mos, who was among the shepherds of Te•kō′a, which he saw concerning Israel in the days of King Uz•zī′ah of Judah and in the days of King Jer•o•bō′am son of Jō′ash of Israel, two years[a] before the earthquake.

Judgment on Israel's Neighbors

2 And he said:
The LORD roars from Zion,
  and utters his voice from Jerusalem;
the pastures of the shepherds wither,
  and the top of Car′mel dries up.

3 Thus says the LORD:
For three transgressions of Damascus,
  and for four, I will not revoke the
    punishment;[b]
because they have threshed Gil′e•ad
  with threshing sledges of iron.
4 So I will send a fire on the house of Haz′a•el,
  and it shall devour the strongholds of
    Ben-hā′dad.
5 I will break the gate bars of Damascus,
  and cut off the inhabitants from the Valley
    of Ā′ven,
and the one who holds the scepter from
    Beth-e′den;
  and the people of Ar′am shall go into exile
    to Kir,
                        says the LORD.

6 Thus says the LORD:
For three transgressions of Gā′za,
  and for four, I will not revoke the
    punishment;[b]
because they carried into exile entire
    communities,
  to hand them over to E′dom.
7 So I will send a fire on the wall of Gā′za,
  fire that shall devour its strongholds.
8 I will cut off the inhabitants from Ash′dod,
  and the one who holds the scepter from
    Ash′ke•lon;
I will turn my hand against Ek′ron,
  and the remnant of the Phi•lis′tines shall
    perish,
                        says the Lord GOD.

9 Thus says the LORD:
For three transgressions of Tȳre,
  and for four, I will not revoke the
    punishment;[b]
because they delivered entire communities over
    to E′dom,
  and did not remember the covenant of
    kinship.
10 So I will send a fire on the wall of Tȳre,
  fire that shall devour its strongholds.

---

a Or *during two years* b Heb *cause it to return*

1041

11 Thus says the LORD:
For three transgressions of Ê'dom,
     and for four, I will not revoke the
          punishment;*c*
because he pursued his brother with the sword
     and cast off all pity;
he maintained his anger perpetually,*d*
     and kept his wrath*e* forever.
12 So I will send a fire on Tê'man,
     and it shall devour the strongholds of
          Boz'rah.

13 Thus says the LORD:
For three transgressions of the Am'mon•ites,
     and for four, I will not revoke the
          punishment;*c*
because they have ripped open pregnant
     women in Gil'e•ad
in order to enlarge their territory.
14 So I will kindle a fire against the wall of
     Rab'bah,
fire that shall devour its strongholds,
with shouting on the day of battle,
     with a storm on the day of the whirlwind;
15 then their king shall go into exile,
     he and his officials together,
                              says the LORD.

2 Thus says the LORD:
For three transgressions of Mô'ab,
     and for four, I will not revoke the
          punishment;*c*
because he burned to lime
     the bones of the king of Ê'dom.
2 So I will send a fire on Mô'ab,
     and it shall devour the strongholds of
          Ker'i•oth,
and Mô'ab shall die amid uproar,
     amid shouting and the sound of the
          trumpet;
3 I will cut off the ruler from its midst,
     and will kill all its officials with him,
                              says the LORD.

Judgment on Judah

4 Thus says the LORD:
For three transgressions of Judah,
     and for four, I will not revoke the
          punishment;*c*
because they have rejected the law of the LORD,
     and have not kept his statutes,
but they have been led astray by the same
     lies
after which their ancestors walked.
5 So I will send a fire on Judah,
     and it shall devour the strongholds of
          Jerusalem.

Judgment on Israel

6 Thus says the LORD:
For three transgressions of Israel,
     and for four, I will not revoke the
          punishment;*c*
because they sell the righteous for silver,
     and the needy for a pair of sandals—
7 they who trample the head of the poor into the
     dust of the earth,
     and push the afflicted out of the way;
father and son go in to the same girl,
     so that my holy name is profaned;
8 they lay themselves down beside every altar
     on garments taken in pledge;
and in the house of their God they drink
     wine bought with fines they imposed.

9 Yet I destroyed the Am'o•rīte before them,
     whose height was like the height of cedars,
     and who was as strong as oaks;
I destroyed his fruit above,
     and his roots beneath.
10 Also I brought you up out of the land of
     Egypt,
     and led you forty years in the wilderness,
     to possess the land of the Am'o•rīte.
11 And I raised up some of your children to be
     prophets
     and some of your youths to be nazirites.*f*
     Is it not indeed so, O people of Israel?
                              says the LORD.

12 But you made the nazirites*f* drink wine,
     and commanded the prophets,
     saying, "You shall not prophesy."

13 So, I will press you down in your place,
     just as a cart presses down
     when it is full of sheaves.*g*
14 Flight shall perish from the swift,
     and the strong shall not retain their
          strength,
     nor shall the mighty save their lives;
15 those who handle the bow shall not stand,
     and those who are swift of foot shall not
          save themselves,
     nor shall those who ride horses save their
          lives;
16 and those who are stout of heart among the
     mighty
     shall flee away naked in that day,
                              says the LORD.

---

c Heb *cause it to return*   *d* Syr Vg: Heb *and his anger tore
perpetually*   *e* Gk Syr Vg: Heb *and his wrath kept*   *f* That is,
those separated or *those consecrated*   *g* Meaning of Heb
uncertain

Israel's Guilt and Punishment

3 Hear this word that the LORD has spoken against you, O people of Israel, against the whole family that I brought up out of the land of Egypt:

2 You only have I known
   of all the families of the earth;
   therefore I will punish you
   for all your iniquities.

3 Do two walk together
   unless they have made an appointment?
4 Does a lion roar in the forest,
   when it has no prey?
   Does a young lion cry out from its den,
   if it has caught nothing?
5 Does a bird fall into a snare on the earth,
   when there is no trap for it?
   Does a snare spring up from the ground,
   when it has taken nothing?
6 Is a trumpet blown in a city,
   and the people are not afraid?
   Does disaster befall a city,
   unless the LORD has done it?
7 Surely the Lord GOD does nothing,
   without revealing his secret
   to his servants the prophets.
8 The lion has roared;
   who will not fear?
   The Lord GOD has spoken;
   who can but prophesy?

9 Proclaim to the strongholds in Ash'dod,
   and to the strongholds in the land of Egypt,
   and say, "Assemble yourselves on Mount^h
      Sa•mār'i•a,
   and see what great tumults are within it,
   and what oppressions are in its midst."
10 They do not know how to do right, says the
      LORD,
   those who store up violence and robbery in
      their strongholds.
11 Therefore thus says the Lord GOD:
   An adversary shall surround the land,
   and strip you of your defense;
   and your strongholds shall be plundered.

12 Thus says the LORD: As the shepherd rescues from the mouth of the lion two legs, or a piece of an ear, so shall the people of Israel who live in Sa•mār'i•a be rescued, with the corner of a couch and part^i of a bed.

13 Hear, and testify against the house of Jacob,
   says the Lord GOD, the God of hosts:
14 On the day I punish Israel for its
      transgressions,

I will punish the altars of Beth'el,
   and the horns of the altar shall be cut off
   and fall to the ground.
15 I will tear down the winter house as well as the
      summer house;
   and the houses of ivory shall perish,
   and the great houses^j shall come to an end,
                           says the LORD.

4 Hear this word, you cows of Bā'shan
      who are on Mount Sa•mār'i•a,
   who oppress the poor, who crush the needy,
   who say to their husbands, "Bring
      something to drink!"
2 The Lord GOD has sworn by his holiness:
   The time is surely coming upon you,
   when they shall take you away with hooks,
   even the last of you with fishhooks.
3 Through breaches in the wall you shall leave,
   each one straight ahead;
   and you shall be flung out into Har'mon,^i
                           says the LORD.
4 Come to Beth'el—and transgress;
   to Gil'gal—and multiply transgression;
   bring your sacrifices every morning,
   your tithes every three days;
5 bring a thank offering of leavened bread,
   and proclaim freewill offerings, publish them;

---

h Gk Syr: Heb *the mountains of*   i Meaning of Heb
uncertain   j Or *many houses*

did you KNOW?

The Remnant

Does Amos feel that Israel is so corrupt that God will destroy it entirely? Apparently not, because he refers in several places to a tiny portion that will be saved (Am 3.12). The idea that God will save a remnant—a small part—of the Jewish people gets picked up by others who prophesy after Amos (see Isa 10.20–22; Jer 23.3; Mic 5.7–8; Zeph 3.13).

The remnant that will be saved becomes an important biblical symbol of God's plan not to let Israel be completely destroyed. It will be known as a holy group because of its faith, repentance, purification, and willingness to be God's servant.

▶ **Am 3.12**

A
M

for so you love to do, O people of Israel!
                    says the Lord GOD.

Israel Rejects Correction

6 I gave you cleanness of teeth in all your cities,
    and lack of bread in all your places,
yet you did not return to me,
                    says the LORD.

7 And I also withheld the rain from you
    when there were still three months to the
        harvest;
I would send rain on one city,
    and send no rain on another city;
one field would be rained upon,
    and the field on which it did not rain
        withered;
8 so two or three towns wandered to one town
    to drink water, and were not satisfied;
yet you did not return to me,
                    says the LORD.

9 I struck you with blight and mildew;
    I laid waste[k] your gardens and your vineyards;
    the locust devoured your fig trees and your
        olive trees;
yet you did not return to me,
                    says the LORD.

10 I sent among you a pestilence after the manner
        of Egypt;
    I killed your young men with the sword;
I carried away your horses;[l]
    and I made the stench of your camp go up
        into your nostrils;
yet you did not return to me,
                    says the LORD.

11 I overthrew some of you,
    as when God overthrew Sod'om and
        Go•mor'rah,
    and you were like a brand snatched from
        the fire;
yet you did not return to me,
                    says the LORD.

12 Therefore thus I will do to you, O Israel;
    because I will do this to you,
    prepare to meet your God, O Israel!

13 For lo, the one who forms the mountains,
        creates the wind,
    reveals his thoughts to mortals,
makes the morning darkness,
    and treads on the heights of the earth—
    the LORD, the God of hosts, is his
        name!

A Lament for Israel's Sin

5 Hear this word that I take up over you in
    lamentation, O house of Israel:
2 Fallen, no more to rise,
    is maiden Israel;
forsaken on her land,
    with no one to raise her up.

3 For thus says the Lord GOD:
The city that marched out a thousand
    shall have a hundred left,
and that which marched out a hundred
    shall have ten left.[m]

4 For thus says the LORD to the house of Israel:
Seek me and live;
5   but do not seek Beth'el,
and do not enter into Gil'gal
    or cross over to Bē'er-shē'ba;
for Gil'gal shall surely go into exile,
    and Beth'el shall come to nothing.

6 Seek the LORD and live,
    or he will break out against the house of
        Joseph like fire,
    and it will devour Beth'el, with no one to
        quench it.
7 Ah, you that turn justice to wormwood,
    and bring righteousness to the ground!

8 The one who made the Plēi'a•dēs and Ō•rī'on,
    and turns deep darkness into the morning,

---

k Cn: Heb the multitude of   l Heb with the captivity of your
horses   m Heb adds to the house of Israel

PRAY IT?
Prayer That Does Justice

In 5.21–24, Amos again has harsh words,
this time for the people who attend
lavish religious ceremonies but don't
practice justice in their life. Amos says
that their worship is meaningless noise to
God—just so many empty words.
    Amos's harsh words challenge us too.
The next time you attend Mass or pray,
think about the words you say and hear.
How are they challenging you to act more
justly? How would trying to act more justly change the way you pray?

▶ Am 5.21–24

and darkens the day into night,
who calls for the waters of the sea,
  and pours them out on the surface of the
    earth,
the LORD is his name,
⁹ who makes destruction flash out against the
    strong,
  so that destruction comes upon the fortress.

¹⁰ They hate the one who reproves in the gate,
  and they abhor the one who speaks the
    truth.
¹¹ Therefore because you trample on the poor
  and take from them levies of grain,
you have built houses of hewn stone,
  but you shall not live in them;
you have planted pleasant vineyards,
  but you shall not drink their wine.
¹² For I know how many are your transgressions,
  and how great are your sins—
you who afflict the righteous, who take a bribe,
  and push aside the needy in the gate.
¹³ Therefore the prudent will keep silent in such a
    time;
  for it is an evil time.

¹⁴ Seek good and not evil,
  that you may live;
and so the LORD, the God of hosts, will be with
    you,
  just as you have said.
¹⁵ Hate evil and love good,
  and establish justice in the gate;
it may be that the LORD, the God of hosts,
  will be gracious to the remnant of Joseph.

¹⁶ Therefore thus says the LORD, the God of hosts,
    the Lord:
In all the squares there shall be wailing;
  and in all the streets they shall say, "Alas!
    alas!"
They shall call the farmers to mourning,
  and those skilled in lamentation, to
    wailing;
¹⁷ in all the vineyards there shall be wailing,
  for I will pass through the midst of you,
                              says the LORD.

The Day of the LORD a Dark Day

¹⁸ Alas for you who desire the day of the LORD!
  Why do you want the day of the LORD?
It is darkness, not light;
¹⁹   as if someone fled from a lion,
  and was met by a bear;
or went into the house and rested a hand
    against the wall,
  and was bitten by a snake.

²⁰ Is not the day of the LORD darkness, not light,
  and gloom with no brightness in it?

²¹ I hate, I despise your festivals,
  and I take no delight in your solemn
    assemblies.
²² Even though you offer me your burnt offerings
  and grain offerings,
  I will not accept them;
and the offerings of well-being of your fatted
    animals
  I will not look upon.
²³ Take away from me the noise of your songs;
  I will not listen to the melody of your
    harps.
²⁴ But let justice roll down like waters,
  and righteousness like an ever-flowing
    stream.

Let Justice roll down like waters, and righteousness like an ever-flowing stream. 5.24

²⁵ Did you bring to me sacrifices and offerings the forty years in the wilderness, O house of Israel? ²⁶ You shall take up Sak'kuth your king, and Kai'wan your star-god, your images,ⁿ which you made for yourselves; ²⁷ therefore I will take you into exile beyond Damascus, says the LORD, whose name is the God of hosts.

Complacent Self-Indulgence Will Be Punished

6 Alas for those who are at ease in Zion,
  and for those who feel secure on Mount
    Sa•mār'i•a,
the notables of the first of the nations,
  to whom the house of Israel resorts!
² Cross over to Cal'neh, and see;
  from there go to Hā'math the great;
then go down to Gath of the
    Phi•lis'tines.

ⁿ Heb *your images, your star-god*

Are you better *o* than these kingdoms?
     Or is your*p* territory greater than their *q*
         territory,
3   O you that put far away the evil day,
     and bring near a reign of violence?

4   Alas for those who lie on beds of ivory,
     and lounge on their couches,
and eat lambs from the flock,
     and calves from the stall;
5   who sing idle songs to the sound of the harp,
     and like David improvise on instruments of
         music;
6   who drink wine from bowls,
     and anoint themselves with the finest oils,
     but are not grieved over the ruin of Joseph!
7   Therefore they shall now be the first to go
         into exile,
     and the revelry of the loungers shall pass
         away.

8   The Lord GOD has sworn by himself
(says the LORD, the God of hosts):
I abhor the pride of Jacob
     and hate his strongholds;
     and I will deliver up the city and all that is
         in it.

9   If ten people remain in one house, they shall die. 10And if a relative, one who burns the dead,*r* shall take up the body to bring it out of the house, and shall say to someone in the innermost parts of the house, "Is anyone else with you?" the answer will come, "No." Then the relative*s* shall say, "Hush! We must not mention the name of the LORD."

11   See, the LORD commands,
     and the great house shall be shattered to bits,
     and the little house to pieces.
12   Do horses run on rocks?
     Does one plow the sea with oxen?*t*
But you have turned justice into poison
     and the fruit of righteousness into
         wormwood—
13   you who rejoice in Lō-dĕʹbar,*u*
     who say, "Have we not by our own strength
     taken Kar•nāʹim*v* for ourselves?"
14   Indeed, I am raising up against you a nation,
     O house of Israel, says the Lord, the God of
         hosts,
and they shall oppress you from Lĕʹbo-hăʹmath
     to the Wadi Arʹa•bah.

Locusts, Fire, and a Plumb Line

7   This is what the Lord GOD showed me: he was forming locusts at the time the latter growth began to sprout (it was the latter growth after the

king's mowings). 2When they had finished eating the grass of the land, I said,
     "O Lord GOD, forgive, I beg you!
         How can Jacob stand?
         He is so small!"
3   The LORD relented concerning this;
     "It shall not be," said the LORD.

4   This is what the Lord GOD showed me: the Lord GOD was calling for a shower of fire,*w* and it devoured the great deep and was eating up the land. 5Then I said,
     "O Lord God, cease, I beg you!
         How can Jacob stand?
         He is so small!"
6   The LORD relented concerning this;
     "This also shall not be," said the
         Lord GOD.

7   This is what he showed me: the Lord was standing beside a wall built with a plumb line, with a plumb line in his hand. 8And the LORD said to me, "Āʹmos, what do you see?" And I said, "A plumb line." Then the Lord said,
     "See, I am setting a plumb line
         in the midst of my people Israel;
     I will never again pass them by;
9   the high places of Isaac shall be made desolate,
     and the sanctuaries of Israel shall be laid
         waste,
and I will rise against the house of
     Jer•o•bōʹam with the sword."

Amaziah Complains to the King

10   Then Am•a•zīʹah, the priest of Bethʹel, sent to King Jer•o•bōʹam of Israel, saying, "Āʹmos has conspired against you in the very center of the house of Israel; the land is not able to bear all his words. 11For thus Āʹmos has said,
     'Jer•o•bōʹam shall die by the sword,
     and Israel must go into exile
         away from his land.' "
12 And Am•a•zīʹah said to Āʹmos, "O seer, go, flee away to the land of Judah, earn your bread there, and prophesy there; 13but never again prophesy at Bethʹel, for it is the king's sanctuary, and it is a temple of the kingdom."
14 Then Āʹmos answered Am•a•zīʹah, "I am*x* no prophet, nor a prophet's son; but I am*x* a herdsman, and a dresser of sycamore trees, 15and the LORD took me from following the flock, and the LORD said to me, 'Go, prophesy to my people Israel.'

---

o Or Are they better   *p Heb their*   *q Heb your*   *r Or who makes a burning for him*   *s Heb he*   *t Or Does one plow them with oxen*   *u Or in a thing of nothingness*   *v Or horns*   *w Or for a judgment by fire*   *x Or was*

16 "Now therefore hear the word of the LORD.
You say, 'Do not prophesy against Israel,
 and do not preach against the house of
 Isaac.'
17 Therefore thus says the LORD:
'Your wife shall become a prostitute in the city,
 and your sons and your daughters shall fall
 by the sword,
 and your land shall be parceled out by line;
you yourself shall die in an unclean land,
 and Israel shall surely go into exile away
 from its land.' "

The Basket of Fruit

8 This is what the Lord GOD showed me—a
basket of summer fruit.*y* 2 He said, "Ā'mos,
what do you see?" And I said, "A basket of summer
fruit."*y* Then the LORD said to me,
"The end*z* has come upon my people Israel;
 I will never again pass them by.
3 The songs of the temple*a* shall become
 wailings in that day,"
                              says the Lord GOD;
"the dead bodies shall be many,
 cast out in every place. Be silent!"

4 Hear this, you that trample on the needy,
 and bring to ruin the poor of the land,
5 saying, "When will the new moon be over
 so that we may sell grain;
and the sabbath,
 so that we may offer wheat for sale?
We will make the ephah small and the shekel
 great,
 and practice deceit with false balances,

6 buying the poor for silver
 and the needy for a pair of sandals,
 and selling the sweepings of the wheat."

7 The LORD has sworn by the pride of Jacob:
Surely I will never forget any of their deeds.
8 Shall not the land tremble on this account,
 and everyone mourn who lives in it,
and all of it rise like the Nile,
 and be tossed about and sink again, like the
 Nile of Egypt?

9 On that day, says the Lord GOD,
 I will make the sun go down at noon,
 and darken the earth in broad daylight.
10 I will turn your feasts into mourning,
 and all your songs into lamentation;
I will bring sackcloth on all loins,
 and baldness on every head;
I will make it like the mourning for an only
 son,
 and the end of it like a bitter day.

11 The time is surely coming, says the
 Lord GOD,
 when I will send a famine on the land;
not a famine of bread, or a thirst for water,
 but of hearing the words of the LORD.
12 They shall wander from sea to sea,
 and from north to east;
they shall run to and fro, seeking the word of
 the LORD,
 but they shall not find it.

---

y Heb *qayits*   *z* Heb *qets*   *a* Or *palace*

Stand Up and Be Counted!

Read 8.4–10 for his words condemning the people of his time who had no care or thought for the poor. Amos says that the more we choose to think of ourselves, rather than those who are needy, the closer we come to our own destruction.
 Jesus later echoes Amos in teaching that God's reign of peace and justice will come through our efforts to support the weaker and less fortunate people in our world (see "Jesus' Preference for the Poor!" Lk 6.17–49).
 Let's be examples of God's care for those who are poor, until all opinion-page letters read, "Stand up and be counted—let's work to end poverty.

▶ Am 8.4–10

13 In that day the beautiful young women and the
        young men
    shall faint for thirst.
14 Those who swear by Ash'i•mah of Sa•mār'i•a,
    and say, "As your god lives, O Dan,"
    and, "As the way of Bē'er-shē'ba lives"—
    they shall fall, and never rise again.

The Destruction of Israel

9 I saw the LORD standing beside[b] the altar, and
    he said:
    Strike the capitals until the thresholds shake,
        and shatter them on the heads of all the
            people;[c]
    and those who are left I will kill with the
            sword;
        not one of them shall flee away,
        not one of them shall escape.

2 Though they dig into Shē'ōl,
        from there shall my hand take them;
    though they climb up to heaven,
        from there I will bring them down.
3 Though they hide themselves on the top of
            Car'mel,
        from there I will search out and take them;
    and though they hide from my sight at the
            bottom of the sea,
        there I will command the sea-serpent, and it
            shall bite them.
4 And though they go into captivity in front of
            their enemies,
        there I will command the sword, and it
            shall kill them;
    and I will fix my eyes on them
        for harm and not for good.

5 The Lord, GOD of hosts,
    he who touches the earth and it melts,
        and all who live in it mourn,
    and all of it rises like the Nile,
        and sinks again, like the Nile of Egypt;
6 who builds his upper chambers in the heavens,
        and founds his vault upon the earth;
    who calls for the waters of the sea,
        and pours them out upon the surface of the
            earth—
    the LORD is his name.

7 Are you not like the Ethiopians[d] to me,
        O people of Israel? says the LORD.
    Did I not bring Israel up from the land of
            Egypt,

and the Phi•lis'tines from Caph'tor and the
            Ar•a•mē'ans from Kir?
8 The eyes of the Lord GOD are upon the sinful
            kingdom,
    and I will destroy it from the face of the
            earth
    —except that I will not utterly destroy the
            house of Jacob,
                                        says the LORD.

9 For lo, I will command,
    and shake the house of Israel among all the
            nations
    as one shakes with a sieve,
        but no pebble shall fall to the ground.
10 All the sinners of my people shall die by the
            sword,
        who say, "Evil shall not overtake or
            meet us."

The Restoration of David's Kingdom
(Cp Acts 15.16–17)

11 On that day I will raise up
        the booth of David that is fallen,
    and repair its[e] breaches,
        and raise up its[f] ruins,
        and rebuild it as in the days of old;
12 in order that they may possess the remnant of
            Ē'dom
    and all the nations who are called by my
            name,
        says the LORD who does this.

13 The time is surely coming, says the LORD,
        when the one who plows shall overtake the
            one who reaps,
        and the treader of grapes the one who sows
            the seed;
    the mountains shall drip sweet wine,
        and all the hills shall flow with it.
14 I will restore the fortunes of my people Israel,
        and they shall rebuild the ruined cities and
            inhabit them;
    they shall plant vineyards and drink their wine,
        and they shall make gardens and eat their
            fruit.
15 I will plant them upon their land,
        and they shall never again be plucked up
        out of the land that I have given them,
                                says the LORD your God.

---

b Or on   c Heb all of them   d Or Nubians; Heb Cushites
e Gk: Heb their   f Gk: Heb his

A betrayal is always difficult, and a betrayal by someone who is related to you is a particularly hard pill to swallow. The Book of Obadiah has angry words against the nation of Edom, whose people were related to the Israelites. It should remind us that when the people we expect to care for us actually take advantage of us, the wound is especially painful.

At a Glance

- **Verses 1–9.** prophecies of Edom's destruction

- **Verses 10–14.** a discussion of Edom's cruelty to the Israelites

- **Verses 15–21.** a message about the day of the Lord

In-depth

The Book of Genesis records a conflict between Jacob (the father of the nation of Israel) and his brother Esau (the father of the nation of Edom, later called Idumea). Hundreds of years later, the Israelites still fought with the Edomites (see map 3, "The Kingdom Years"). In the Book of Obadiah, the bitterness deepens.

In 587 B.C., Jerusalem was destroyed by the Babylonians. Apparently, the Edomites not only did not aid their "brother" (Obadiah, verse 10) but took advantage of Israel's situation by gloating (verse 12), looting (verse 13), and raiding its territory (verse 14). Because of the Edomites' cruelty, the prophet Obadiah foretold the destruction of Edom by another country (verse 15).

Like many of the Old Testament prophets, Obadiah ultimately saw a hopeful future for Israel. All Israel's enemies would whither before the strong arm of the Lord. And there would come a day—"the day of the LORD" (verse 15)—when all Jews would unite and return to Mount Zion (the place where the Temple stood in Jerusalem). Mount Zion would "rule Mount Esau" and that new "kingdom shall be the LORD's" (verse 21).

We are given no clues about the identity or life of the prophet Obadiah. We know only that he wrote the shortest book in the Old Testament—just one chapter long.

Quick Facts

Period Covered
after the Babylonian Exile, sometime in the fifth century B.C.

Author
Obadiah

Theme
God will punish Edom for its abuse of Judah.

Of Note
Obadiah means "servant" or "worshiper of the Lord."

The Book of Obadiah

Obadiah

Proud Edom Will Be Brought Low

1 The vision of Ò·ba·dǐ'ah.

Thus says the Lord GOD concerning Ê'dom:
We have heard a report from the LORD,
   and a messenger has been sent among the
      nations:
"Rise up! Let us rise against it for battle!"
2 I will surely make you least among the
      nations;
   you shall be utterly despised.
3 Your proud heart has deceived you,
   you that live in the clefts of the rock,[a]
   whose dwelling is in the heights.
You say in your heart,
   "Who will bring me down to the
      ground?"
4 Though you soar aloft like the eagle,
   though your nest is set among the stars,
   from there I will bring you down,
              says the LORD.

Pillage and Slaughter Will Repay Edom's Cruelty

5 If thieves came to you,
   if plunderers by night
   —how you have been destroyed!—
   would they not steal only what they
      wanted?
If grape-gatherers came to you,

   would they not leave gleanings?
6 How Esau has been pillaged,
   his treasures searched out!
7 All your allies have deceived you,
   they have driven you to the border;
your confederates have prevailed
      against you;
   those who ate[b] your bread have set a trap
      for you—
   there is no understanding of it.
8 On that day, says the LORD,
   I will destroy the wise out of Ê'dom,
   and understanding out of Mount Esau.
9 Your warriors shall be shattered, O Tĕ'man,
   so that everyone from Mount Esau will be
      cut off.

Edom Mistreated His Brother

10 For the slaughter and violence done to your
      brother Jacob,
   shame shall cover you,
   and you shall be cut off forever.
11 On the day that you stood aside,
   on the day that strangers carried off his
      wealth,
and foreigners entered his gates
   and cast lots for Jerusalem,
   you too were like one of them.

---

a Or *clefts of Sela* *b* Cn: Heb lacks *those who ate*

you should not have handed over his survivors
    on the day of distress.

15 For the day of the LORD is near against all the
        nations.
    As you have done, it shall be done to you;
        your deeds shall return on your own head.
16 For as you have drunk on my holy mountain,
        all the nations around you shall drink;
    they shall drink and gulp down, *f*
        and shall be as though they had never been.

Israel's Final Triumph

17 But on Mount Zion there shall be those that
        escape,
        and it shall be holy;
    and the house of Jacob shall take possession of
        those who dispossessed them.
18 The house of Jacob shall be a fire,
        the house of Joseph a flame,
        and the house of Esau stubble;
    they shall burn them and consume them,
        and there shall be no survivor of the house
            of Esau;
                    for the LORD has spoken.
19 Those of the Neg'eb shall possess Mount Esau,
        and those of the She•phē'lah the land of the
            Phi•lis'tines;
    they shall possess the land of E'phra•im and
            the land of Sa•mār'i•a,
    and Benjamin shall possess Gil'e•ad.
20 The exiles of the Israelites who are in Hā'lah *g*
        shall possess *h* Phoe•ni'ci•a as far as
            Zar'e•phath;
    and the exiles of Jerusalem who are in
        Se•phar'ad
    shall possess the towns of the Neg'eb.
21 Those who have been saved *i* shall go up to
        Mount Zion
        to rule Mount Esau;
    and the kingdom shall be the LORD's.

---

c Heb *But do not gloat* (and similarly through verse 14)
d Heb *on the day of*   *e* Heb *his*   *f* Meaning of Heb
uncertain   *g* Cn: Heb *in this army*   *h* Cn: Meaning of
Heb uncertain   *i* Or *Saviors*

PRAY IT!
What Goes Around

What goes around comes around.
    Have you ever heard that saying?
Isn't that exactly what Obadiah is saying
in verse 15?
    Whatever you do comes back to
affect you eventually. If you are honest,
people will trust you and tell you the
truth. If you lie, cheat, and steal, people
will deceive you. If you respect the earth,
it will take care of you. If you litter, pollute, and destroy, you ruin your home,
your country, and your world.
    Pray that all people take this lesson to
heart. Pray that we learn to respect all
living things. The results of our actions
will come back to us eventually—if not to
us personally, to other people and future
generations.

▶ **Obadiah, verse 15**

12 But you should not have gloated *c* over *d* your
        brother
        on the day of his misfortune;
    you should not have rejoiced over the people
        of Judah
        on the day of their ruin;
    you should not have boasted
        on the day of distress.
13 You should not have entered the gate of my
        people
        on the day of their calamity;
    you should not have joined in the gloating
        over Judah's *e* disaster
        on the day of his calamity;
    you should not have looted his goods
        on the day of his calamity.
14 You should not have stood at the crossings
        to cut off his fugitives;

O
B

The basis of satire is that someone or something that is supposed to act one way acts another way. You're about to read a biblical satire about Jonah the prophet. The Book of Jonah uses humor to make an important point—God is the God of all people, even those we consider our enemies.

The Book of **Jonah**

At a Glance

- **1.1–16.** Jonah being sent by God to Nineveh

- **1.17—2.10.** Jonah in the belly of a large fish

- **Chapter 3.** the Ninevites' conversion

- **Chapter 4.** Jonah's anger outside of Nineveh

In-depth

This story was written after the Jews returned from their exile in Babylon. Jewish leaders encouraged Jewish people to stay away from non-Jewish people (see Ezra, chapter 9) in order to avoid falling into idolatry again. A result was a religious bigotry against other nations—a belief that God was against every nation that opposed Israel. The Book of Jonah was written to correct that narrow attitude. Through satire, this fictional short story gently pokes fun at Israel's religious self-righteousness.

How is the book funny? Well, right off the bat, Jonah is called by God and immediately takes off in the opposite direction (1.1–3). What kind of prophet is this? When God tries to get his attention with a storm, it's the non-Jewish sailors who get the point (verse 14). Just as the reader is probably wondering how God is going to get Jonah to Nineveh, along comes a taxi in the form of a large fish's stomach (verse 17).

There's more. Readers from the author's time would have expected Jonah to be ignored at best, more likely beaten or killed by the people of Nineveh. After all, these were Israel's mortal enemies. Instead, the Ninevites immediately respond to Jonah's message and repent, even the animals (3.8)! At this point, the reader is giggling at the goofiness of pigs and sheep in sackcloth, but getting the message about God's salvation being for all nations.

Quick Facts

Period Covered
the eighth century B.C.
Author
unknown, probably writing in the fifth century B.C.
Theme
a fictional short story showing that God cares for all people, including Israel's enemies

Jonah's angry and upset. He didn't expect the Ninevites to convert—he wanted them punished. He goes outside the city to mope, and his favorite tree dies. The book ends with God chiding Jonah for his bigoted anger. If Jonah is so concerned for his little tree (4.6–8), shouldn't God be concerned for the great city of Nineveh with its thousands of people (verse 11)? The point is driven home, and the humor has helped to make a challenging message easier to accept.

Jonah

Jonah Tries to Run Away from God

1 Now the word of the LORD came to Jonah son of A·mit′taī, saying, 2 "Go at once to Nin′-e·veh, that great city, and cry out against it; for their wickedness has come up before me." 3 But Jonah set out to flee to Tar′shish from the presence of the LORD. He went down to Jop′pa and found a ship going to Tar′shish; so he paid his fare and went on board, to go with them to Tar′shish, away from the presence of the LORD.

4 But the LORD hurled a great wind upon the sea, and such a mighty storm came upon the sea that the ship threatened to break up. 5 Then the mariners were afraid, and each cried to his god. They threw the cargo that was in the ship into the sea, to lighten it for them. Jonah, meanwhile, had gone down into the hold of the ship and had lain down, and was fast asleep. 6 The captain came and said to him, "What are you doing sound asleep? Get up, call on your god! Perhaps the god will spare us a thought so that we do not perish."

7 The sailors*a* said to one another, "Come, let us cast lots, so that we may know on whose account this calamity has come upon us." So they cast lots, and the lot fell on Jonah. 8 Then they said to him, "Tell us why this calamity has come upon us. What is your occupation? Where do you come from? What is your country? And of what people are you?" 9 "I am a Hebrew," he replied. "I worship the LORD, the God of heaven, who made the sea and the dry land." 10 Then the men were even more afraid, and said to him, "What is this that you have done!" For the men knew that he was fleeing from the presence of the LORD, because he had told them so.

11 Then they said to him, "What shall we do to you, that the sea may quiet down for us?" For the sea was growing more and more tempestuous. 12 He said to them, "Pick me up and throw me into the sea; then the sea will quiet down for you; for I know it is because of me that this great storm has come upon you." 13 Nevertheless the men rowed hard to bring the ship back to land, but they could not, for the sea grew more and more stormy against them. 14 Then they cried out to the LORD, "Please, O LORD, we pray, do not let us perish on account of this man's life. Do not make us guilty of innocent blood; for you, O LORD, have done as it pleased you." 15 So they picked Jonah up and threw him into the sea; and the sea ceased from its raging. 16 Then the men feared the LORD even more, and they offered a sacrifice to the LORD and made vows.

17*b* But the LORD provided a large fish to swallow up Jonah; and Jonah was in the belly of the fish three days and three nights.

---

a Heb *They* *b* Ch 2.1 in Heb

A Psalm of Thanksgiving

2 Then Jonah prayed to the LORD his God from the belly of the fish, 2 saying,

"I called to the LORD out of my distress,
and he answered me;
out of the belly of Shě′ōl I cried,
and you heard my voice.
3 You cast me into the deep,
into the heart of the seas,
and the flood surrounded me;
all your waves and your billows
passed over me.
4 Then I said, 'I am driven away
from your sight;
howᶜ shall I look again
upon your holy temple?'
5 The waters closed in over me;
the deep surrounded me;
weeds were wrapped around my head
6   at the roots of the mountains.
I went down to the land
whose bars closed upon me forever;
yet you brought up my life from the Pit,
O LORD my God.

PRAY IT
Jesus and Jonah

Do you see any similarities between Jonah and Jesus? Jonah is in the darkness of a fish's belly for three days before the LORD commands the fish to spit him out. Jesus experiences the darkness of death for three days before he bursts from the tomb in resurrected glory. In Mt 16.4 and Lk 11.29, Jesus even refers to "the sign of Jonah" in relation to his own ministry.

Jonah's prayer in Jon 2.2–10 could well have been Jesus' prayer before his death. It reminds us that salvation comes from God when we are experiencing dark times. When you are going through a difficult time, use Jonah's prayer as a model for writing your own prayer of trust. Describe your difficulties and your situation, and end by expressing your ultimate trust in God. Then say your prayer until the difficulty passes. It could make a difference!

▶ Jon 2.2–10

7 As my life was ebbing away,
I remembered the LORD;
and my prayer came to you,
into your holy temple.
8 Those who worship vain idols
forsake their true loyalty.
9 But I with the voice of thanksgiving
will sacrifice to you;
what I have vowed I will pay.
Deliverance belongs to the LORD!"

10 Then the LORD spoke to the fish, and it spewed Jonah out upon the dry land.

Conversion of Nineveh

3 The word of the LORD came to Jonah a second time, saying, 2 "Get up, go to Nin′e•veh, that great city, and proclaim to it the message that I tell you." 3 So Jonah set out and went to Nin′e•veh, according to the word of the LORD. Now Nin′e•veh was an exceedingly large city, a three days' walk across. 4 Jonah began to go into the city, going a day's walk. And he cried out, "Forty days more, and Nin′e•veh shall be overthrown!" 5 And the people of Nin′e•veh believed God; they proclaimed a fast, and everyone, great and small, put on sackcloth.

6 When the news reached the king of Nin′e•veh, he rose from his throne, removed his robe, covered himself with sackcloth, and sat in ashes. 7 Then he had a proclamation made in Nin′e•veh: "By the decree of the king and his nobles: No human being or animal, no herd or flock, shall taste anything. They shall not feed, nor shall they drink water. 8 Human beings and animals shall be covered with sackcloth, and they shall cry mightily to God. All shall turn from their evil ways and from the violence that is in their hands. 9 Who knows? God may relent and change his mind; he may turn from his fierce anger, so that we do not perish."

10 When God saw what they did, how they turned from their evil ways, God changed his mind about the calamity that he had said he would bring upon them; and he did not do it.

Jonah's Anger

4 But this was very displeasing to Jonah, and he became angry. 2 He prayed to the LORD and said, "O LORD! Is not this what I said while I was still in my own country? That is why I fled to Tar′shish at the beginning; for I knew that you are a gracious God and merciful, slow to anger, and abounding in steadfast love, and ready to relent from punishing. 3 And now, O LORD, please take my life from me, for it is better for me to die than to live." 4 And the LORD said, "Is it right for you to be angry?" 5 Then Jonah went out of the city and sat

ᶜ Theodotion: Heb *surely*

Mistaken Loyalties

When God spares Nineveh, Jonah is angry! He is so angry he is willing to let his anger destroy him. And all because of mistaken loyalty. Jonah thought he was loyal to God (which is funny because at first, he tried to run away from God), and he feels that God is being disloyal to him by not destroying Nineveh. Jonah does not— or will not—understand that God's loyalty is to the whole human race, not just to Jonah's desires.

Are you ever angry with God because things don't go your way? Maybe your anger is about mistaken loyalties. If you didn't get picked for the lead part, that doesn't mean God is being disloyal to you. God is God over everyone—which sometimes means you will not get what you want so that other people can receive what they need.

The next time you are angry at God, ask yourself: Am I willing to see things from a large enough perspective? Am I expecting to receive God's favor at someone else's expense?

▸ Jon 4.1–8

J
O
N

down east of the city, and made a booth for himself there. He sat under it in the shade, waiting to see what would become of the city.

6 The LORD God appointed a bush,*d* and made it come up over Jonah, to give shade over his head, to save him from his discomfort; so Jonah was very happy about the bush. 7 But when dawn came up the next day, God appointed a worm that attacked the bush, so that it withered. 8 When the sun rose, God prepared a sultry east wind, and the sun beat down on the head of Jonah so that he was faint and asked that he might die. He said, "It is better for me to die than to live."

Jonah Is Reproved

9 But God said to Jonah, "Is it right for you to be angry about the bush?" And he said, "Yes, angry enough to die." 10 Then the LORD said, "You are concerned about the bush, for which you did not labor and which you did not grow; it came into being in a night and perished in a night. 11 And should I not be concerned about Nin′e·veh, that great city, in which there are more than a hundred and twenty thousand persons who do not know their right hand from their left, and also many animals?"

---

d Heb *qiqayon*, possibly *the castor bean plant*

The Book of Micah

There is a story about a country mouse and a city mouse who visit each other on separate occasions. For each, the visit is a discovery of new experiences and a different way of life. Indeed, people who visit the places we live in often see things that we have overlooked or taken for granted. The prophet Micah was like such a visitor. His home was a small village, but he prophesied in the big capital city of Jerusalem. God uses Micah's unique perspective to communicate warnings and promises to the people of Israel and to us.

At a Glance

- **Chapters 1–2.** a judgment against Israel and Judah, and promise

- **3.1—5.9.** a judgment against rulers, prophets, and priests, and promise

- **5.10—6.8.** a judgment against foreign religions, and a plea for justice

- **6.9—7.20.** a judgment against the people, and message of God's compassion

In-depth

The Book of Micah is a collection of oracles (poemlike prophetic messages) taking different forms. Some of the oracles are harsh judgments (see 1.8—2.11), some are comforting promises that God will not desert the people (see chapter 4), and some are the prophet's own confessions of faith (3.8; 7.7). The Book of Micah shows us a God who is passionate for justice and fairness (3.9).

Perhaps because of his rural background, the prophet Micah had a special connection to the land and the people who work it. He speaks against those who covet and seize fields and homes (2.2). He describes the destruction of Zion (Jerusalem) as plowing a field (3.12). He represents the Ideal Kingdom as a place where all the people have their own grapevines and fig trees (4.3–4).

The Book of Micah shows signs of being extensively edited and revised to keep the prophet's message relevant during changing times. This is particularly true in chapters 4 and 5, which were added after the Babylonian Exile to give hope following the nation's great tragedy. In 4.3, the prophet envisions a day when nations will "beat their swords into plowshares" and "nation shall not lift up sword against nation, / neither shall they learn war any more."

Micah prophesied at about the same time as First Isaiah (see the timeline at the back of this Bible), during the days of Kings Jotham, Ahaz, and Hezekiah (see 2 Chr 27.1—31.21). But whereas Isaiah was a member of the upper class, defending the rights of the poor, Micah was a poor person, suffering with the poor. That is why he speaks so passionately about their mistreatment (see Mic 3.1–3). Even though his message went unheeded at the time, he models for us trust in the Lord's saving power (7.7).

Quick Facts

Period Covered
the late eighth century B.C.

Authors
Micah and later editors

Themes
warnings against injustice and idolatry, promises of a new future

Micah

1 The word of the LORD that came to Mĭ′cah of Mō′re·sheth in the days of Kings Jō′tham, Ā′haz, and Hez·e·kī′ah of Judah, which he saw concerning Samār′i·a and Jerusalem.

Judgment Pronounced against Samaria

2 Hear, you peoples, all of you;
    listen, O earth, and all that is in it;
and let the Lord GOD be a witness
        against you,
    the Lord from his holy temple.
3 For lo, the LORD is coming out of his place,
    and will come down and tread upon the
        high places of the earth.
4 Then the mountains will melt under him
    and the valleys will burst open,
like wax near the fire,
    like waters poured down a steep place.
5 All this is for the transgression of Jacob
    and for the sins of the house of Israel.
What is the transgression of Jacob?
    Is it not Sa·mār′i·a?
And what is the high place[a] of Judah?
    Is it not Jerusalem?
6 Therefore I will make Sa·mār′i·a a heap in the
        open country,
    a place for planting vineyards.
I will pour down her stones into the valley,
    and uncover her foundations.
7 All her images shall be beaten to pieces,

all her wages shall be burned with fire,
    and all her idols I will lay waste;
for as the wages of a prostitute she gathered
        them,
    and as the wages of a prostitute they shall
        again be used.

The Doom of the Cities of Judah

8 For this I will lament and wail;
    I will go barefoot and naked;
I will make lamentation like the jackals,
    and mourning like the ostriches.
9 For her wound[b] is incurable.
    It has come to Judah;
it has reached to the gate of my people,
    to Jerusalem.

10 Tell it not in Gath,
    weep not at all;
in Beth-le·aph′rah
    roll yourselves in the dust.
11 Pass on your way,
    inhabitants of Shā′phir,
    in nakedness and shame;
the inhabitants of Zā′a·nan
    do not come forth;
Beth-ē′zel is wailing
    and shall remove its support from you.

---

a Heb *what are the high places*   b Gk Syr Vg: Heb *wounds*

12 For the inhabitants of Mā′roth
      wait anxiously for good,
   yet disaster has come down from the LORD
      to the gate of Jerusalem.
13 Harness the steeds to the chariots,
      inhabitants of Lā′chish;
   it was the beginning of sin
      to daughter Zion,
   for in you were found
      the transgressions of Israel.
14 Therefore you shall give parting gifts
      to Mō′re·sheth-gath;
   the houses of Ach′zib shall be a deception
      to the kings of Israel.
15 I will again bring a conqueror upon you,
      inhabitants of Ma·rē′shah;
   the glory of Israel
      shall come to A·dul′lam.
16 Make yourselves bald and cut off your hair
      for your pampered children;
   make yourselves as bald as the eagle,
      for they have gone from you into exile.

Social Evils Denounced

2 Alas for those who devise wickedness
      and evil deeds*c* on their beds!
   When the morning dawns, they perform it,
      because it is in their power.
2 They covet fields, and seize them;
      houses, and take them away;
   they oppress householder and house,
      people and their inheritance.
3 Therefore thus says the LORD:
   Now, I am devising against this family an evil
      from which you cannot remove your necks;
   and you shall not walk haughtily,
      for it will be an evil time.
4 On that day they shall take up a taunt song
         against you,
      and wail with bitter lamentation,
   and say, "We are utterly ruined;
      the LORD*d* alters the inheritance of my
         people;
   how he removes it from me!
      Among our captors*e* he parcels out our
         fields."
5 Therefore you will have no one to cast the line
      by lot
   in the assembly of the LORD.

6 "Do not preach"—thus they preach—
      "one should not preach of such things;
   disgrace will not overtake us."
7 Should this be said, O house of Jacob?
      Is the LORD's patience exhausted?
   Are these his doings?
   Do not my words do good

did you KNOW?

Micah Challenges Us to Fight Injustice

In chapter 2, the prophet Micah challenges the people to take an honest look at their behavior. In harsh images and language, he articulates how greed and injustice have destroyed the well-being of the nation. In verse 3, Micah implies that because of their injustice, the people will be like oxen whose necks are confined to yokes that hold their heads down in shame. Micah's message is that injustice forces all in the community and nation to carry a heavy burden.

This theme of examining injustices in the world has been repeated numerous times throughout the Scriptures. And to this very day, we continue to hear similar teachings coming out of the church. What are we doing in our communities and in our country to fight against modern instances of injustice, such as racism, hunger, poverty, abortion, capital punishment, violence, and destruction of the natural environment? What injustices do you see in your own actions and in your own community? What can you do to stop injustices from happening so that our communities and nation can live freely in peace?

▶ Micah, chapter 2

      to one who walks uprightly?
8 But you rise up against my people*f* as an
         enemy;
      you strip the robe from the peaceful,*g*
   from those who pass by trustingly
      with no thought of war.
9 The women of my people you drive out
      from their pleasant houses;
   from their young children you take away
      my glory forever.
10 Arise and go;
      for this is no place to rest,
   because of uncleanness that destroys

c Cn: Heb *work evil*   *d* Heb *he*   *e* Cn: Heb *the rebellious*
f Cn: Heb *But yesterday my people rose*   *g* Cn: Heb *from before a garment*

with a grievous destruction.ʰ

11 If someone were to go about uttering empty
falsehoods,
saying, "I will preach to you of wine and
strong drink,"
such a one would be the preacher for this
people!

A Promise for the Remnant of Israel

12 I will surely gather all of you, O Jacob,
I will gather the survivors of Israel;
I will set them together
like sheep in a fold,
like a flock in its pasture;
it will resound with people.
13 The one who breaks out will go up before
them;
they will break through and pass the gate,
going out by it.
Their king will pass on before them,
the Lord at their head.

Wicked Rulers and Prophets

3 And I said:
Listen, you heads of Jacob
and rulers of the house of Israel!
Should you not know justice?—
2 you who hate the good and love the evil,
who tear the skin off my people,ⁱ
and the flesh off their bones;
3 who eat the flesh of my people,
flay their skin off them,
break their bones in pieces,
and chop them up like meatʲ in a kettle,
like flesh in a caldron.

4 Then they will cry to the Lord,
but he will not answer them;
he will hide his face from them at that time,
because they have acted wickedly.

5 Thus says the Lord concerning the prophets
who lead my people astray,
who cry "Peace"
when they have something to eat,
but declare war against those
who put nothing into their mouths.
6 Therefore it shall be night to you, without
vision,
and darkness to you, without revelation.
The sun shall go down upon the prophets,
and the day shall be black over them;
7 the seers shall be disgraced,
and the diviners put to shame;
they shall all cover their lips,
for there is no answer from God.
8 But as for me, I am filled with power,

with the spirit of the Lord,
and with justice and might,
to declare to Jacob his transgression
and to Israel his sin.

9 Hear this, you rulers of the house of Jacob
and chiefs of the house of Israel,
who abhor justice
and pervert all equity,
10 who build Zion with blood
and Jerusalem with wrong!
11 Its rulers give judgment for a bribe,
its priests teach for a price,
its prophets give oracles for money;
yet they lean upon the Lord and say,
"Surely the Lord is with us!
No harm shall come upon us."
12 Therefore because of you
Zion shall be plowed as a field;
Jerusalem shall become a heap of ruins,
and the mountain of the house a wooded
height.

Peace and Security through Obedience
(Cp Isa 2.2–4)

4 In days to come
the mountain of the Lord's house
shall be established as the highest of the
mountains,
and shall be raised up above the hills.
Peoples shall stream to it,
2 and many nations shall come and say:
"Come, let us go up to the mountain of the
Lord,
to the house of the God of Jacob;
that he may teach us his ways
and that we may walk in his paths."
For out of Zion shall go forth instruction,
and the word of the Lord from Jerusalem.
3 He shall judge between many peoples,
and shall arbitrate between strong nations
far away;
they shall beat their swords into plowshares,
and their spears into pruning hooks;
nation shall not lift up sword against nation,
neither shall they learn war any more;
4 but they shall all sit under their own vines and
under their own fig trees,
and no one shall make them afraid;
for the mouth of the Lord of hosts has
spoken.

5 For all the peoples walk,
each in the name of its god,

ʰ Meaning of Heb uncertain　ⁱ Heb *from them*
ʲ Gk: Heb *as*

but we will walk in the name of the LORD our
        God
    forever and ever.

Restoration Promised after Exile

6 In that day, says the LORD,
    I will assemble the lame
and gather those who have been driven away,
    and those whom I have afflicted.
7 The lame I will make the remnant,
    and those who were cast off, a strong
        nation;
and the LORD will reign over them in Mount
        Zion
    now and forevermore.

8 And you, O tower of the flock,
    hill of daughter Zion,
to you it shall come,
    the former dominion shall come,
    the sovereignty of daughter Jerusalem.

9 Now why do you cry aloud?
    Is there no king in you?
Has your counselor perished,
    that pangs have seized you like a woman in
        labor?
10 Writhe and groan,[k] O daughter Zion,
    like a woman in labor;
for now you shall go forth from the city
    and camp in the open country;
    you shall go to Babylon.
There you shall be rescued,
    there the LORD will redeem you
    from the hands of your enemies.

11 Now many nations
    are assembled against you,
saying, "Let her be profaned,
    and let our eyes gaze upon Zion."
12 But they do not know
    the thoughts of the LORD;
they do not understand his plan,
    that he has gathered them as sheaves to the
        threshing floor.
13 Arise and thresh,
    O daughter Zion,
for I will make your horn iron
    and your hoofs bronze;
you shall beat in pieces many peoples,
    and shall[l] devote their gain to the LORD,
    their wealth to the Lord of the whole earth.

5 [m] Now you are walled around with a wall;[n]
        siege is laid against us;
with a rod they strike the ruler of Israel
    upon the cheek.

The Ruler from Bethlehem

2 [o] But you, O Bethlehem of Eph′ra·thah,
    who are one of the little clans of Judah,
from you shall come forth for me
    one who is to rule in Israel,
whose origin is from of old,
    from ancient days.
3 Therefore he shall give them up until the
        time
    when she who is in labor has brought forth;
then the rest of his kindred shall return
    to the people of Israel.
4 And he shall stand and feed his flock in the
        strength of the LORD,
    in the majesty of the name of the LORD his
        God.
And they shall live secure, for now he shall be
        great
    to the ends of the earth;
5 and he shall be the one of peace.

---

k Meaning of Heb uncertain   l Gk Syr Tg: Heb and I will
m Ch 4.14 in Heb   n Cn Compare Gk: Meaning of Heb
uncertain   o Ch 5.1 in Heb

PRAY IT!
From Humble Beginnings

As a country boy, Micah has a different
vision than do some of the other
prophets. He doesn't see the Ideal Ruler
coming out of a big city like Jerusalem.
No, he sees this great person coming
from Bethlehem—a tiny, insignificant
city, but also a place free from political
corruption. The Gospel of Matthew shows
Micah's prophecy being fulfilled in the
birth of Jesus (Mt 2.5–6).

   Often in the Bible, we hear of God's
accomplishing huge feats with small and
humble people and things. In your prayer,
reflect or journal on the following questions:
■ **What famous people started from
   humble beginnings?**
■ **Why does God often use small and
   hidden people or things to accomplish
   God's purposes?**
■ **What small or hidden gifts do you
   have to offer God to work with?**

▸ Mic 5.2–5

If the Assyrians come into our land
　and tread upon our soil, *p*
we will raise against them seven shepherds
　and eight installed as rulers.
6 They shall rule the land of Assyria with the
　　sword,
　and the land of Nim'rod with the drawn
　　sword;*q*
they*r* shall rescue us from the Assyrians
　if they come into our land
　or tread within our border.

The Future Role of the Remnant

7 Then the remnant of Jacob,
　surrounded by many peoples,
shall be like dew from the LORD,
　like showers on the grass,
which do not depend upon people
　or wait for any mortal.
8 And among the nations the remnant of Jacob,
　surrounded by many peoples,
shall be like a lion among the animals of the
　　forest,
　like a young lion among the flocks of
　　sheep,
which, when it goes through, treads down
　and tears in pieces, with no one to deliver.
9 Your hand shall be lifted up over your
　　adversaries,
　and all your enemies shall be cut off.

10 In that day, says the LORD,
　I will cut off your horses from among you
　and will destroy your chariots;
11 and I will cut off the cities of your land
　and throw down all your strongholds;
12 and I will cut off sorceries from your hand,
　and you shall have no more soothsayers;
13 and I will cut off your images
　and your pillars from among you,
and you shall bow down no more
　to the work of your hands;
14 and I will uproot your sacred poles*s* from
　　among you
　and destroy your towns.
15 And in anger and wrath I will execute
　　vengeance
　on the nations that did not obey.

God Challenges Israel

6 Hear what the LORD says:
　Rise, plead your case before the
　　mountains,
　and let the hills hear your voice.
2 Hear, you mountains, the controversy of the
　　LORD,
　and you enduring foundations of the earth;

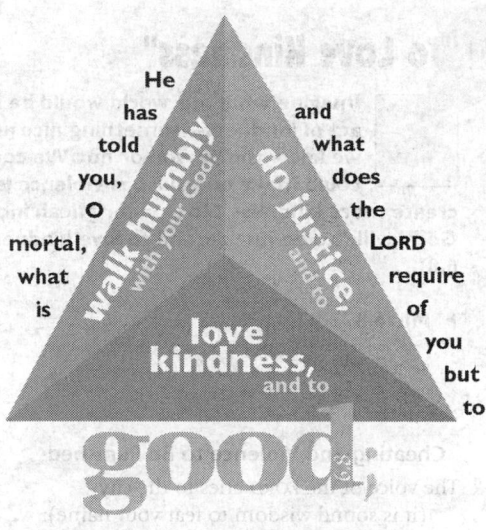

He has told you, O mortal, what is good; and what does the LORD require of you but to do justice, and to love kindness, and to walk humbly with your God?

for the LORD has a controversy with his people,
　and he will contend with Israel.

3 "O my people, what have I done to you?
　In what have I wearied you? Answer me!
4 For I brought you up from the land of Egypt,
　and redeemed you from the house of
　　slavery;
and I sent before you Moses,
　Aaron, and Miriam.
5 O my people, remember now what King Bā'lak
　　of Mō'ab devised,
　what Bā'laam son of Bē'or answered him,
and what happened from Shit'tim to Gil'gal,
　that you may know the saving acts of the
　　LORD."

What God Requires
(Cp Am 5.24)

6 "With what shall I come before the LORD,
　and bow myself before God on high?
Shall I come before him with burnt offerings,
　with calves a year old?
7 Will the LORD be pleased with thousands of
　　rams,
　with ten thousands of rivers of oil?
Shall I give my firstborn for my transgression,
　the fruit of my body for the sin of my
　　soul?"
8 He has told you, O mortal, what is good;
　and what does the LORD require of you
but to do justice, and to love kindness,
　and to walk humbly with your God?

---

p Gk: Heb *in our palaces*　*q* Cn: Heb *in its entrances*
r Heb *he*　*s* Heb *Asherim*

MIC

"To Love Kindness"

Imagine what our world would be like if each day, each of us performed a random act of kindness—something nice and unexpected for someone, anyone, whether we knew the person or not. We could make someone's day. And in turn, someone could make ours. Just as violence leads to more violence, so also can kindness create more kindness. No wonder Micah includes kindness in his simple formula for doing God's will: "to do justice, and to love kindness, / and to walk humbly with your God" (Mic 6.8).

▶ Mic 6.8

Cheating and Violence to Be Punished

9 The voice of the LORD cries to the city
  (it is sound wisdom to fear your name):
Hear, O tribe and **assembly** of the city!^{t}

10   Can I forget^u the treasures of wickedness in
    the house of the wicked,
  and the scant measure that is accursed?

11 Can I tolerate wicked scales
    and a bag of dishonest weights?

12 Your^v wealthy are full of violence;
    your^w inhabitants speak lies,
  with tongues of deceit in their mouths.

13 Therefore I have begun^x to strike you down,
    making you desolate because of your sins.

14 You shall eat, but not be satisfied,
    and there shall be a gnawing hunger within
      you;
  you shall put away, but not save,
    and what you save, I will hand over to the
      sword.

15 You shall sow, but not reap;
    you shall tread olives, but not anoint
      yourselves with oil;
    you shall tread grapes, but not drink wine.

16 For you have kept the statutes of Om′ri^y
    and all the works of the house of A′hab,
    and you have followed their counsels.
  Therefore I will make you a desolation, and
      your^z inhabitants an object of hissing;
    so you shall bear the scorn of my people.

The Total Corruption of the People

7 Woe is me! For I have become like one who,
    after the summer fruit has been gathered,
    after the vintage has been gleaned,
  finds no cluster to eat;
    there is no first-ripe fig for which I hunger.

2 The faithful have disappeared from the land,
    and there is no one left who is upright;
  they all lie in wait for blood,
    and they hunt each other with nets.

3 Their hands are skilled to do evil;
    the official and the judge ask for a bribe,
  and the powerful dictate what they desire;
    thus they pervert justice.^{a}

4 The best of them is like a brier,
    the most upright of them a thorn hedge.
  The day of their^b sentinels, of their^b
      punishment, has come;
    now their confusion is at hand.

5 Put no trust in a friend,
    have no confidence in a loved one;
  guard the doors of your mouth
    from her who lies in your embrace;

6 for the son treats the father with contempt,
    the daughter rises up against her mother,
  the daughter-in-law against her mother-in-law;
    your enemies are members of your own
      household.

7 But as for me, I will look to the LORD,
    I will wait for the God of my salvation;
    my God will hear me.

Penitence and Trust in God

8 Do not rejoice over me, O my enemy;
    when I fall, I shall rise;
  when I sit in darkness,
    the LORD will be a light to me.

9 I must bear the indignation of the LORD,
    because I have sinned against him,
  until he takes my side
    and executes judgment for me.
  He will bring me out to the light;
    I shall see his vindication.

10 Then my enemy will see,
    and shame will cover her who said to me,
    "Where is the LORD your God?"

---

^{t} Cn Compare Gk: Heb *tribe, and who has appointed it yet?*
^{u} Cn: Meaning of Heb uncertain ^{v} Heb *Whose* ^{w} Heb
whose ^{x} Gk Syr Vg: Heb *have made sick* ^{y} Gk Syr Vg Tg:
Heb *the statutes of Omri are kept* ^{z} Heb *its* ^{a} Cn: Heb *they
weave it* ^{b} Heb *your*

My eyes will see her downfall;[c]
  now she will be trodden down
  like the mire of the streets.

A Prophecy of Restoration

11 A day for the building of your walls!
  In that day the boundary shall be far
    extended.
12 In that day they will come to you
    from Assyria to[d] Egypt,
  and from Egypt to the River,
    from sea to sea and from mountain to
      mountain.
13 But the earth will be desolate
    because of its inhabitants,
  for the fruit of their doings.

14 Shepherd your people with your staff,
    the flock that belongs to you,
  which lives alone in a forest
    in the midst of a garden land;
  let them feed in Bā′shan and Gil′e•ad
    as in the days of old.
15 As in the days when you came out of the land
      of Egypt,
    show us[e] marvelous things.
16 The nations shall see and be ashamed
    of all their might;

they shall lay their hands on their mouths;
    their ears shall be deaf;
17 they shall lick dust like a snake,
    like the crawling things of the earth;
  they shall come trembling out of their
      fortresses;
    they shall turn in dread to the LORD our
        God,
    and they shall stand in fear of you.

God's Compassion and Steadfast Love

18 Who is a God like you, pardoning iniquity
    and passing over the transgression
    of the remnant of your[f] possession?
  He does not retain his anger forever,
    because he delights in showing clemency.
19 He will again have compassion upon us;
    he will tread our iniquities under foot.
  You will cast all our[g] sins
    into the depths of the sea.
20 You will show faithfulness to Jacob
    and unswerving loyalty to Abraham,
  as you have sworn to our ancestors
    from the days of old.

---

c Heb lacks *downfall*   d One Ms: MT *Assyria and cities of*
e Cn: Heb *I will show him*   f Heb *his*   g Gk Syr Vg Tg:
Heb *their*

M
I
C

Devastation, desolation, and destruction! You are about to read some angry words. They portray a vengeful God bringing destruction upon Israel's enemies. What could make the prophet Nahum so angry? What could make God so angry?

In-depth

At the time Nahum was written, the Assyrian Empire had been the terror of the Middle East for several centuries. In 721 B.C., it destroyed the northern part of Israel, called Israel. In 701 B.C., it invaded the southern part of Israel, called Judah, and laid siege to Jerusalem (see the timeline and map 4, "The Assyrian Empire," at the back of this Bible). The siege broke off, and Jerusalem did not fall, but the chosen people of God got a gruesome taste of Assyria's savage cruelty.

The sole concern of the prophet Nahum is the destruction of this evil world power. In the first chapter of his book, he declares the coming wrath of God, and in chapters 2–3, he describes the destruction of Nineveh (the Assyrian capital). We shouldn't be too surprised that when Assyria falls in 612 B.C., Nahum sees the justice of God being worked out: the Assyrians are finally getting a taste of their own medicine! Nahum seems almost to be gloating in 3.19:

> All who hear the news about you
> clap their hands over you.
> For who has ever escaped
> your endless cruelty?

Hidden among the threats and violence against Assyria, we also find words of comfort for God's chosen people: the awesome war with which God will avenge them because their enemies are God's enemies (1.2); good news and peace are coming for Judah (1.15); the Lord will restore Israel to its original majesty (2.2). We even find some wonderful reminders of God's love and protection, which balance the image of the God of vengeance and destruction: "the LORD is slow to anger but great in power" (1.3); "the LORD is good" (1.7); God is "a stronghold in a day of trouble" (1.7); God "protects those who take refuge in him" (1.7). Nahum reminds us that God has many sides and is always more than we can imagine.

At a Glance

- **1.1–11.** the coming of the Lord in judgment
- **1.12–15.** good news for Judah
- **Chapters 2–3.** the destruction of Nineveh

Quick Facts

Period Covered
663–612 B.C.

Author
Nahum

Theme
God will avenge Israel and destroy its cruel enemies, the Assyrians.

The Book of *Nahum*

Nahum

1 An oracle concerning Nin'e•veh. The book of the vision of Nā'hum of El'kosh.

The Consuming Wrath of God

2 A jealous and avenging God is the LORD,
    the LORD is avenging and wrathful;
the LORD takes vengeance on his adversaries
    and rages against his enemies.
3 The LORD is slow to anger but great in power,
    and the LORD will by no means clear the
        guilty.

His way is in whirlwind and storm,
    and the clouds are the dust of his feet.
4 He rebukes the sea and makes it dry,
    and he dries up all the rivers;
Bā'shan and Car'mel wither,
    and the bloom of Lebanon fades.
5 The mountains quake before him,
    and the hills melt;
the earth heaves before him,
    the world and all who live in it.
6 Who can stand before his indignation?
    Who can endure the heat of his anger?
His wrath is poured out like fire,
    and by him the rocks are broken in pieces.
7 The LORD is good,
    a stronghold in a day of trouble;
he protects those who take refuge in him,
8   even in a rushing flood.
He will make a full end of his adversaries,*a*

and will pursue his enemies into darkness.
9 Why do you plot against the LORD?
    He will make an end;
    no adversary will rise up twice.
10 Like thorns they are entangled,
    like drunkards they are drunk;
    they are consumed like dry straw.
11 From you one has gone out
    who plots evil against the LORD,
    one who counsels wickedness.

Good News for Judah

12 Thus says the LORD,
"Though they are at full strength and many,*b*
    they will be cut off and pass away.
Though I have afflicted you,
    I will afflict you no more.
13 And now I will break off his yoke from you
    and snap the bonds that bind you."

14 The LORD has commanded concerning you:
    "Your name shall be perpetuated no
        longer;
from the house of your gods I will cut off
    the carved image and the cast image.
I will make your grave, for you are worthless."

15*c* Look! On the mountains the feet of one
    who brings good tidings,

---

a Gk: Heb *of her place*   *b* Meaning of Heb uncertain
c Ch 2.1 in Heb

who proclaims peace!
Celebrate your festivals, O Judah,
fulfill your vows,
for never again shall the wicked invade you;
they are utterly cut off.

The Destruction of the Wicked City

2 A shatterer[d] has come up against you.
Guard the ramparts;
watch the road;
gird your loins;
collect all your strength.

2 (For the LORD is restoring the majesty of
Jacob,
as well as the majesty of Israel,
though ravagers have ravaged them
and ruined their branches.)

3 The shields of his warriors are red;
his soldiers are clothed in crimson.
The metal on the chariots flashes
on the day when he musters them;
the chargers[e] prance.
4 The chariots race madly through the streets,
they rush to and fro through the squares;
their appearance is like torches,
they dart like lightning.

5 He calls his officers;
they stumble as they come forward;
they hasten to the wall,
and the mantelet[f] is set up.
6 The river gates are opened,
the palace trembles.
7 It is decreed[f] that the city[g] be exiled,
its slave women led away,
moaning like doves
and beating their breasts.
8 Nin'e•veh is like a pool
whose waters[h] run away.
"Halt! Halt!"—
but no one turns back.
9 "Plunder the silver,
plunder the gold!
There is no end of treasure!
An abundance of every precious thing!"

10 Devastation, desolation, and destruction!
Hearts faint and knees tremble,
all loins quake,
all faces grow pale!
11 What became of the lions' den,

---

d Cn: Heb *scatterer* e Cn Compare Gk Syr: Heb *cypresses*
f Meaning of Heb uncertain g Heb *it* h Cn Compare Gk:
Heb *a pool, from the days that she has become, and they*

Images of God

> Piles of dead,
>   heaps of corpses,
>   dead bodies without end ...
>   (Nah 3.3)

The descriptions of God's vengeance on the Assyrians throughout chapters 2 and 3 of Nahum seem contradictory to Jesus' command to love one's enemies (Mt 5.43–48). Was God different back in Old Testament times? Or was Nahum just mistaken? These are difficult but important questions!

In understanding Nahum's message, it helps to keep in mind three things. First, throughout the Bible, there is a strong theme of divine hatred for all sin. In the New Testament, though, a distinction emerges that although God hates the sin, God still loves the sinner. Nahum doesn't make that distinction.

Second, Christians today make a distinction between God's directly causing something to happen and God's allowing something to occur—usually as a result of human limitations, people's poor choices, or natural phenomena. Again, Nahum doesn't make this distinction —for Nahum, if something happens, God is its direct cause.

Finally, we have to keep in mind that all our attempts to understand God will fall short. God is beyond human understanding. That is why the Bible's authors, including Nahum, describe God in many different—and often seemingly contradictory—ways.

How do you see God? as a vengeful fire (Nah 1.6) or as a stronghold of protection (verse 7)? Are you comfortable imagining God in different—even opposite—ways?

▶ Nah 2.1—3.3

the cave[i] of the young lions,
where the lion goes,
and the lion's cubs, with no one to disturb
them?
12 The lion has torn enough for his whelps
and strangled prey for his lionesses;
he has filled his caves with prey
and his dens with torn flesh.

13 See, I am against you, says the LORD of hosts,
and I will burn your[j] chariots in smoke, and the
sword shall devour your young lions; I will cut off
your prey from the earth, and the voice of your
messengers shall be heard no more.

Ruin Imminent and Inevitable

3 Ah! City of bloodshed,
utterly deceitful, full of booty—
no end to the plunder!
2 The crack of whip and rumble of wheel,
galloping horse and bounding chariot!
3 Horsemen charging,
flashing sword and glittering spear,
piles of dead,
heaps of corpses,
dead bodies without end—
they stumble over the bodies!
4 Because of the countless debaucheries of the
prostitute,
gracefully alluring, mistress of sorcery,
who enslaves[k] nations through her
debaucheries,
and peoples through her sorcery,
5 I am against you,
says the LORD of hosts,
and will lift up your skirts over your face;
and I will let nations look on your
nakedness
and kingdoms on your shame.
6 I will throw filth at you
and treat you with contempt,
and make you a spectacle.
7 Then all who see you will shrink from you and
say,
"Nin'e•veh is devastated; who will bemoan
her?"
Where shall I seek comforters for you?

8 Are you better than Thēbes[l]
that sat by the Nile,
with water around her,
her rampart a sea, water her wall?
9 Ethiopia[m] was her strength,
Egypt too, and that without limit;
Put and the Libyans were her[n] helpers.

10 Yet she became an exile,
she went into captivity;
even her infants were dashed in pieces
at the head of every street;
lots were cast for her nobles,
all her dignitaries were bound in fetters.
11 You also will be drunken,
you will go into hiding;[o]
you will seek
a refuge from the enemy.
12 All your fortresses are like fig trees
with first-ripe figs—
if shaken they fall
into the mouth of the eater.
13 Look at your troops:
they are women in your midst.
The gates of your land
are wide open to your foes;
fire has devoured the bars of your gates.

14 Draw water for the siege,
strengthen your forts;
trample the clay,
tread the mortar,
take hold of the brick mold!
15 There the fire will devour you,
the sword will cut you off.
It will devour you like the locust.

Multiply yourselves like the locust,
multiply like the grasshopper!
16 You increased your merchants
more than the stars of the heavens.
The locust sheds its skin and flies away.
17 Your guards are like grasshoppers,
your scribes like swarms[o] of locusts
settling on the fences
on a cold day—
when the sun rises, they fly away;
no one knows where they have gone.

18 Your shepherds are asleep,
O king of Assyria;
your nobles slumber.
Your people are scattered on the mountains
with no one to gather them.
19 There is no assuaging your hurt,
your wound is mortal.
All who hear the news about you
clap their hands over you.
For who has ever escaped
your endless cruelty?

---

i Cn: Heb *pasture*   j Heb *her*   k Heb *sells*
l Heb *No-amon*   m Or *Nubia*; Heb *Cush*   n Gk: Heb *your*
o Meaning of Heb uncertain

N
A
H

God, why aren't you answering our cries for help? How long must we endure this trial?" Most people have wondered this at times. Why does our good, all-powerful God let suffering or injustice go on? The prophet Habakkuk struggled with these same painful and disturbing questions. His hope in God's justice is a model of faith amid doubt.

At a Glance

- **1.1—2.5.** Habakkuk's complaints and God's responses
- **2.6—20.** five warnings against wicked people
- **Chapter 3.** Habakkuk's prayer of confidence

In-depth

Habakkuk was the first prophet who dared to ask God about God's behavior. He looked around at all the terrible things that were happening to his people and cried out: "God, where are you? Do you even care about us? Why do you allow evil people to oppress us?"

We know little about Habakkuk except that he was a prophet in the southern kingdom of Judah in the late seventh century B.C. The Chaldeans (another name for the Babylonians) and the corrupt king of Judah, Jehoiakim, were causing so much trouble that Habakkuk was ready to despair. God answered him in a most surprising way, saying that the Chaldeans—as bad as they were—were chosen as God's instrument to punish the wicked all over the earth. Habakkuk was not satisfied. He asked why God was silent while the wicked destroyed the righteous. God then spoke to him in a vision (Hab 2.2), saying that justice would come to the wicked in its own time, but "the righteous live by their faith" (verse 4). Later, Paul would use these same words to describe the Christians (Rom 1.17; Gal 3.11). For Habakkuk, faith in God and hope in God's justice were the same thing.

The short Book of Habakkuk is unique among the prophetic books in the variety of its writings. Its reflections about the problem of evil in the world resemble the wisdom literature. Its dialogs with God (see 1.2) are similar to Jeremiah's confessions (see Jer 12.6). Chapter 3 is a canticle (song).

The prophet's concluding canticle is a prayer of confidence in God's power to save the people. We too can pray in confidence because God is just and will save us in our time of need.

Quick Facts

Period Covered
probably the reign of King Jehoiakim, 605–597 B.C. (see 2 Kings 23.36—24.7)

Author
Habakkuk

Theme
The answer to evil is faith in God's justice.

The Book of Habakkuk

Habakkuk

1.8

1 The oracle that the prophet Ha·bak'kuk saw.

The Prophet's First Complaint

2 O LORD, how long shall I cry for help,
  and you will not listen?
Or cry to you "Violence!"
  and you will not save?
3 Why do you make me see wrongdoing
  and look at trouble?
Destruction and violence are before me;
  strife and contention arise.
4 So the law becomes slack
  and justice never prevails.
The wicked surround the righteous—
  therefore judgment comes forth perverted.

God' Reply to the Prophet's Complaint

5 Look at the nations, and see!
  Be astonished! Be astounded!
For a work is being done in your days
  that you would not believe if you were
    told.
6 For I am rousing the Chal·dē'ans,
  that fierce and impetuous nation,
who march through the breadth of the earth
  to seize dwellings not their own.
7 Dread and fearsome are they;
  their justice and dignity proceed from
    themselves.
8 Their horses are swifter than leopards,
  more menacing than wolves at dusk;
    their horses charge.
Their horsemen come from far away;
  they fly like an eagle swift to devour.
9 They all come for violence,
  with faces pressing*a* forward;
  they gather captives like sand.
10 At kings they scoff,
  and of rulers they make sport.
They laugh at every fortress,
  and heap up earth to take it.
11 Then they sweep by like the wind;
  they transgress and become guilty;
  their own might is their god!

The Prophet's Second Complaint

12 Are you not from of old,
  O LORD my God, my Holy One?
You*b* shall not die.
O LORD, you have marked them for
    judgment;
  and you, O Rock, have established them for
    punishment.
13 Your eyes are too pure to behold evil,
  and you cannot look on wrongdoing;
why do you look on the treacherous,
  and are silent when the wicked swallow

---

a Meaning of Heb uncertain   *b* Ancient Heb tradition:
MT *We*

those more righteous than they?

14 You have made people like the fish of the sea,
      like crawling things that have no ruler.

15 The enemy[c] brings all of them up with a hook;
      he drags them out with his net,
   he gathers them in his seine;
      so he rejoices and exults.
16 Therefore he sacrifices to his net
      and makes offerings to his seine;
   for by them his portion is lavish,
      and his food is rich.
17 Is he then to keep on emptying his net,
      and destroying nations without mercy?

God's Reply to the Prophet's Complaint

2 I will stand at my watchpost,
      and station myself on the rampart;
   I will keep watch to see what he will say to me,
      and what he[d] will answer concerning my
         complaint.
2 Then the LORD answered me and said:
   Write the vision;
      make it plain on tablets,
      so that a runner may read it.
3 For there is still a vision for the appointed
         time;
      it speaks of the end, and does not lie.
   If it seems to tarry, wait for it;
      it will surely come, it will not delay.
4 Look at the proud!
      Their spirit is not right in them,
      but the righteous live by their faith.[e]
5 Moreover, wealth[f] is treacherous;
      the arrogant do not endure.

They open their throats wide as Shĕ'ōl;
      like Death they never have enough.
   They gather all nations for themselves,
      and collect all peoples as their own.

The Woes of the Wicked

6 Shall not everyone taunt such people and,
with mocking riddles, say about them,
   "Alas for you who heap up what is not your
         own!"
      How long will you load yourselves with
         goods taken in pledge?
7 Will not your own creditors suddenly rise,
      and those who make you tremble wake up?
      Then you will be booty for them.
8 Because you have plundered many nations,
      all that survive of the peoples shall plunder
         you—
   because of human bloodshed, and violence to
         the earth,
      to cities and all who live in them.

9 "Alas for you who get evil gain for your
         house,
      setting your nest on high
      to be safe from the reach of harm!"
10 You have devised shame for your house
      by cutting off many peoples;
      you have forfeited your life.
11 The very stones will cry out from the wall,
      and the plaster[g] will respond from the
         woodwork.

---

c Heb He   d Syr: Heb I   e Or *faithfulness*   f Other Heb Mss
read *wine*   g Or *beam*

Now!

"I want it all, and I want it now!"
      **That statement could sum up the ambitions of a lot of people. It is how they
define success. The key word in their goal is now. They don't like to wait in lines;
they want instant service and immediate gratification.**
      **There is a temptation to apply this goal to our spiritual life. We want to grow closer to
God—now! But the spiritual life does not work that way. Recall these words from the Book
of Ecclesiastes: "For everything there is a season, and a time for every matter under heav-
en" (3.1). We have to remind ourselves that many valuable things take time. Our growth in
faith will take time. We need to be open, patient, and trusting. As God reminds Habakkuk
in his vision in Hab 2.3, "If it seems to tarry, wait for it, / it will surely come, it will not delay."**
      Consider these questions:
- **What are your goals for your relationship with God?**
- **How patient are you with your spiritual growth? How do you nurture it day by day?**

▶ **Hab 2.3**

12 "Alas for you who build a town by bloodshed,
  and found a city on iniquity!"
13 Is it not from the LORD of hosts
  that peoples labor only to feed the flames,
  and nations weary themselves for nothing?
14 But the earth will be filled
  with the knowledge of the glory of the
    LORD,
  as the waters cover the sea.

15 "Alas for you who make your neighbors
    drink,
  pouring out your wrath[h] until they are
    drunk,
  in order to gaze on their nakedness!"
16 You will be sated with contempt instead of
    glory.
  Drink, you yourself, and stagger![i]
  The cup in the LORD's right hand
  will come around to you,
  and shame will come upon your glory!
17 For the violence done to Lebanon will
    overwhelm you;
  the destruction of the animals will terrify
    you—[j]
  because of human bloodshed and violence to
    the earth,
  to cities and all who live in them.

18 What use is an idol
  once its maker has shaped it—
  a cast image, a teacher of lies?
  For its maker trusts in what has been made,
  though the product is only an idol that
    cannot speak!
19 Alas for you who say to the wood, "Wake up!"
  to silent stone, "Rouse yourself!"
  Can it teach?
  See, it is gold and silver plated,
  and there is no breath in it at all.

20 But the LORD is in his holy temple;
  let all the earth keep silence before him!

3 A prayer of the prophet Ha·bak'kuk according
  to Shig·i·ōn'oth.

The Prophet's Prayer

2 O LORD, I have heard of your renown,
  and I stand in awe, O LORD, of your work.
  In our own time revive it;
  in our own time make it known;
  in wrath may you remember mercy.
3 God came from Tē'man,
  the Holy One from Mount Par'an.   Sē'lah
  His glory covered the heavens,
  and the earth was full of his praise.

4 The brightness was like the sun;
  rays came forth from his hand,
  where his power lay hidden.
5 Before him went pestilence,
  and plague followed close behind.
6 He stopped and shook the earth;
  he looked and made the nations tremble.
  The eternal mountains were shattered;
  along his ancient pathways
  the everlasting hills sank low.
7 I saw the tents of Cūsh'an under affliction;
  the tent-curtains of the land of Mid'i·an
    trembled.
8 Was your wrath against the rivers,[k] O LORD?
  Or your anger against the rivers,[k]
  or your rage against the sea,[l]
  when you drove your horses,
  your chariots to victory?
9 You brandished your naked bow,
  sated[m] were the arrows at your
    command.[n]   Sē'lah
  You split the earth with rivers.
10 The mountains saw you, and writhed;
  a torrent of water swept by;
  the deep gave forth its voice.
  The sun[o] raised high its hands;
11 the moon[p] stood still in its exalted place,
  at the light of your arrows speeding by,
  at the gleam of your flashing spear.
12 In fury you trod the earth,
  in anger you trampled nations.
13 You came forth to save your people,
  to save your anointed.
  You crushed the head of the wicked
    house,
  laying it bare from foundation to
    roof.[n]   Sē'lah
14 You pierced with their[q] own arrows the head[r]
    of his warriors,[s]
  who came like a whirlwind to scatter us,[t]
  gloating as if ready to devour the poor who
    were in hiding.
15 You trampled the sea with your horses,
  churning the mighty waters.

16 I hear, and I tremble within;
  my lips quiver at the sound.
  Rottenness enters into my bones,
  and my steps tremble[u] beneath me.
  I wait quietly for the day of calamity
  to come upon the people who attack us.

---

h Or poison i Q Ms Gk: MT be uncircumcised j Gk Syr:
Meaning of Heb uncertain k Or against River l Or against
Sea m Cn: Heb oaths n Meaning of Heb uncertain o Heb
It p Heb sun, moon q Heb his r Or leader s Vg Compare
Gk Syr: Meaning of Heb uncertain t Heb me u Cn
Compare Gk: Meaning of Heb uncertain

Trust and Joy in the Midst of Trouble

17 Though the fig tree does not blossom,
    and no fruit is on the vines;
though the produce of the olive fails,
    and the fields yield no food;
though the flock is cut off from the fold,
    and there is no herd in the stalls,
18 yet I will rejoice in the LORD;

I will exult in the God of my salvation.
19 GOD, the Lord, is my strength;
    he makes my feet like the feet of a deer,
    and makes me tread upon the heights.[v]

To the leader: with stringed[w] instruments.

---

v Heb *my heights*   *w* Heb *my stringed*

During childhood, we usually have to clean up messes, or lose privileges as consequences for poor choices we have made. As we get older, we learn that our wrongdoing has more personal and painful consequences: perhaps a parent's refusal to trust us, a friend's anger, or pain after hurting someone we love. The prophet Zephaniah warned the people of Judah of the severe consequences of their sin against the Lord.

At a Glance

- **Chapter 1.** a warning about Judah's idolatry

- **2.1—3.7.** a discussion of the destruction of the nations and the corrupt nature of Jerusalem

- **3.8–20.** a message about the conversion of the nations and salvation for Jerusalem

In-depth

The Book of Zephaniah gives us few clues about the prophet Zephaniah's identity. We do know that he preached in the southern kingdom of Judah during the reign of King Josiah (see 2 Chronicles, chapters 34–35), around 630 B.C. He followed First Isaiah and Micah, and came a little before Habakkuk and during the time of Nahum.

Zephaniah follows the footsteps of the classical Old Testament prophets in denouncing the wrongdoing of society. His main contribution is considering pride (1.6; 2.10; 3.11) as the source of problems such as smugness (1.12), rebellion (3.2), and treachery (3.11). All these attitudes toward God lead to idolatry and social sin. Although all people sin, leaders have a greater responsibility, and their sins will provoke a harsh judgment during the coming day of the Lord (1.14). Only those who worship God humbly and who seek justice will be spared. Zephaniah calls them the remnant (3.12–13), meaning "a little piece that is left over." They are the ones who will stay faithful to God through both good times and bad.

The book ends with a song of joy reassuring the people of Jerusalem that God still loves them and will save them in the end. We are not sure whether the song is from Zephaniah himself or is the addition of a later editor. It is as if the writer knows that when people are experiencing the negative results of sinful actions, they need to be reassured that they are still loved. God's punishment is to teach us, not to destroy us. Therefore, God's people should not despair but keep their trust in God.

Quick Facts

Period Covered
approximately 630 B.C.

Author
Zephaniah (and perhaps a later editor)

Theme
Judah and its neighbors will experience the consequences of their sinfulness.

Zephaniah

1 The word of the LORD that came to Zeph·a-nī′ah son of Cū′shī son of Ged·a·lī′ah son of Am·a·rī′ah son of Hez·e·kī′ah, in the days of King Jō·sī′ah son of Ā′mon of Judah.

The Coming Judgment on Judah

2 I will utterly sweep away everything
    from the face of the earth, says the LORD.
3 I will sweep away humans and animals;
    I will sweep away the birds of the air
    and the fish of the sea.
I will make the wicked stumble.*a*
    I will cut off humanity
    from the face of the earth, says the LORD.
4 I will stretch out my hand against Judah,
    and against all the inhabitants of Jerusalem;
and I will cut off from this place every remnant
        of Bā′al
    and the name of the idolatrous priests;*b*
5 those who bow down on the roofs
    to the host of the heavens;
those who bow down and swear to the LORD,
    but also swear by Mil′com;*c*
6 those who have turned back from following
        the LORD,
    who have not sought the LORD or inquired
        of him.

7 Be silent before the Lord GOD!
    For the day of the LORD is at hand;

the LORD has prepared a sacrifice,
    he has consecrated his guests.
8 And on the day of the LORD's sacrifice
    I will punish the officials and the king's
        sons
    and all who dress themselves in foreign
        attire.
9 On that day I will punish
    all who leap over the threshold,
who fill their master's house
    with violence and fraud.

10 On that day, says the LORD,
    a cry will be heard from the Fish Gate,
a wail from the Second Quarter,
    a loud crash from the hills.
11 The inhabitants of the Mortar wail,
    for all the traders have perished;
    all who weigh out silver are cut off.
12 At that time I will search Jerusalem with
        lamps,
    and I will punish the people
who rest complacently*d* on their dregs,
    those who say in their hearts,
"The LORD will not do good,

---

a Cn: Heb *sea, and those who cause the wicked to stumble*
b Compare Gk: Heb *the idolatrous priests with the priests*
c Gk Mss Syr Vg: Heb *Malcam* (or, *their king*)   *d* Heb *who thicken*

nor will he do harm."

13 Their wealth shall be plundered,
    and their houses laid waste.
Though they build houses,
    they shall not inhabit them;
though they plant vineyards,
    they shall not drink wine from them.

The Great Day of the LORD
(Cp Am 5.18–20)

14 The great day of the LORD is near,
    near and hastening fast;
the sound of the day of the LORD is bitter,
    the warrior cries aloud there.
15 That day will be a day of wrath,
    a day of distress and anguish,
a day of ruin and devastation,
    a day of darkness and gloom,
a day of clouds and thick darkness,
16   a day of trumpet blast and battle cry
against the fortified cities
    and against the lofty battlements.

17 I will bring such distress upon people
    that they shall walk like the blind;
    because they have sinned against the LORD,
their blood shall be poured out like dust,
    and their flesh like dung.
18 Neither their silver nor their gold
    will be able to save them
    on the day of the LORD's wrath;
in the fire of his passion
    the whole earth shall be consumed;
for a full, a terrible end
    he will make of all the inhabitants of the
        earth.

Judgment on Israel's Enemies

2 Gather together, gather,
    O shameless nation,
2 before you are driven away
    like the drifting chaff,*e*
before there comes upon you
    the fierce anger of the LORD,
before there comes upon you
    the day of the LORD's wrath.
3 Seek the LORD, all you humble of the land,
    who do his commands;
seek righteousness, seek humility;
    perhaps you may be hidden
    on the day of the LORD's wrath.
4 For Gā'za shall be deserted,
    and Ash'ke·lon shall become a
        desolation;
Ash'dod's people shall be driven out at
        noon,
    and Ek'ron shall be uprooted.

5 Ah, inhabitants of the seacoast,
    you nation of the Cher'e·thītes!
The word of the LORD is against you,
    O Cā'naan, land of the Phi·lis'tines;
    and I will destroy you until no inhabitant is
        left.
6 And you, O seacoast, shall be pastures,
    meadows for shepherds
    and folds for flocks.
7 The seacoast shall become the possession
    of the remnant of the house of Judah,
    on which they shall pasture,
and in the houses of Ash'ke·lon
    they shall lie down at evening.
For the LORD their God will be mindful of
        them
    and restore their fortunes.

8 I have heard the taunts of Mō'ab
    and the revilings of the Am'mon·ites,
how they have taunted my people
    and made boasts against their territory.
9 Therefore, as I live, says the LORD of hosts,
    the God of Israel,
Mō'ab shall become like Sod'om
    and the Am'mon·ites like Go·mor'rah,
a land possessed by nettles and salt pits,
    and a waste forever.
The remnant of my people shall plunder them,
    and the survivors of my nation shall possess
        them.
10 This shall be their lot in return for their pride,
    because they scoffed and boasted
    against the people of the LORD of hosts.
11 The LORD will be terrible against them;
    he will shrivel all the gods of the earth,
and to him shall bow down,
    each in its place,
    all the coasts and islands of the nations.

12 You also, O Ethiopians,*f*
    shall be killed by my sword.

13 And he will stretch out his hand against the
        north,
    and destroy Assyria;
and he will make Nin'e·veh a desolation,
    a dry waste like the desert.
14 Herds shall lie down in it,
    every wild animal;*g*
the desert owl*h* and the screech owl*h*
    shall lodge on its capitals;

---

e Cn Compare Gk Syr: Heb *before a decree is born; like
chaff a day has passed away*   *f* Or *Nubians;* Heb *Cushites*
g Tg Compare Gk: Heb *nation*   *h* Meaning of Heb
uncertain

the owl[i] shall hoot at the window,
  the raven[j] croak on the threshold;
  for its cedar work will be laid bare.
15 Is this the exultant city
  that lived secure,
that said to itself,
  "I am, and there is no one else"?
What a desolation it has become,
  a lair for wild animals!
Everyone who passes by it
  hisses and shakes the fist.

The Wickedness of Jerusalem

3 Ah, soiled, defiled,
    oppressing city!
2 It has listened to no voice;
  it has accepted no correction.
It has not trusted in the LORD;
  it has not drawn near to its God.

3 The officials within it
  are roaring lions;
its judges are evening wolves
  that leave nothing until the morning.
4 Its prophets are reckless,
  faithless persons;
its priests have profaned what is sacred,
  they have done violence to the law.
5 The LORD within it is righteous;
  he does no wrong.
Every morning he renders his judgment,
  each dawn without fail;
  but the unjust knows no shame.

6 I have cut off nations;
  their battlements are in ruins;
I have laid waste their streets
  so that no one walks in them;
their cities have been made desolate,
  without people, without inhabitants.
7 I said, "Surely the city[k] will fear me,
  it will accept correction;
it will not lose sight[l]
  of all that I have brought upon it."
But they were the more eager
  to make all their deeds corrupt.

Punishment and Conversion of the Nations
(Cp Gen 11.1–9; Acts 2.1–11)

8 Therefore wait for me, says the LORD,
  for the day when I arise as a witness.
For my decision is to gather nations,
  to assemble kingdoms,
to pour out upon them my indignation,
  all the heat of my anger;
for in the fire of my passion
  all the earth shall be consumed.

9 At that time I will change the speech of the
    peoples
  to a pure speech,
that all of them may call on the name of the
    LORD
  and serve him with one accord.
10 From beyond the rivers of Ethiopia[m]
  my suppliants, my scattered ones,
  shall bring my offering.

11 On that day you shall not be put to shame
  because of all the deeds by which you have
    rebelled against me;
for then I will remove from your midst
  your proudly exultant ones,
and you shall no longer be haughty
  in my holy mountain.
12 For I will leave in the midst of you
  a people humble and lowly.
They shall seek refuge in the name of the
  LORD—
13 the remnant of Israel;
they shall do no wrong
  and utter no lies,
nor shall a deceitful tongue
  be found in their mouths.
Then they will pasture and lie down,
  and no one shall make them afraid.

A Song of Joy

14 Sing aloud, O daughter Zion;
  shout, O Israel!
Rejoice and exult with all your heart,
  O daughter Jerusalem!
15 The LORD has taken away the judgments
    against you,
  he has turned away your enemies.
The king of Israel, the LORD, is in your
    midst;
  you shall fear disaster no more.
16 On that day it shall be said to Jerusalem:
Do not fear, O Zion;
  do not let your hands grow weak.
17 The LORD, your God, is in your midst,
  a warrior who gives victory;
he will rejoice over you with gladness,
  he will renew you[n] in his love;
he will exult over you with loud singing
18   as on a day of festival.[o]
  I will remove disaster from you, [p]
    so that you will not bear reproach for it.

---

i Cn: Heb *a voice*   j Gk Vg: Heb *desolation*   k Heb *it*
l Gk Syr: Heb *its dwelling will not be cut off*   m Or *Nubia*;
Heb *Cush*   n Gk Syr: Heb *he will be silent*   o Gk Syr:
Meaning of Heb uncertain   p Cn: Heb *I will remove from
you; they were*

MATERIAL POVERTY AND SPIRITUAL POVERTY!

In the Bible, God is always opposed to material poverty and misery. Over and over in the Old Testament, wealth is called a blessing and poverty a curse. The laws of the Covenant assert that poverty should not exist in Israel. Rich people are commanded to periodically forgive the debts of the poor and return land taken as payment of debt to the land's original owners (see Lev 25.8). Selfishness leads to injustice, and injustice leads to tragedy, violence, and despair.

Zephaniah gives a spiritual connotation to the word *poor* (translated as "lowly" in Zeph 3.12). He relates poverty to humility. In this sense, to be poor is to be empty of egoism and pride, and therefore open to God's action in us. Zephaniah believes a small group of spiritually poor people, known as the remnant of Israel or the poor of God, will keep the Covenant alive.

Latin American spirituality is deeply rooted in this concept of the poor, and the Virgin Mary is the culture's supreme example of it. To be spiritually poor is to be receptive to the Holy Spirit, to be generous with others, to trust in God's providence, and to accept suffering without losing hope.

■ How will you live out the call to be spiritually poor, free of material goods beyond what is necessary to live?

■ Ask God to give you the strength to respond to this call, which is so necessary in this world of pride, injustice, and materialism.

▶ **Zeph 3.11–13**

19 I will deal with all your oppressors
     at that time.
   And I will save the lame
     and gather the outcast,
   and I will change their shame into praise
     and renown in all the earth.

20 At that time I will bring you home,
     at the time when I gather you;
   for I will make you renowned and praised
     among all the peoples of the earth,
   when I restore your fortunes
     before your eyes, says the LORD.

ZEPH

The Jews at the time of the prophet Haggai faced a difficult decision when they returned to Jerusalem after the Babylonian Exile: which would they rebuild first—their homes or God's Temple?

At a Glance

- **Chapter 1.** a command to rebuild the Temple

- **2.1–19.** a description of the future glory of God's Temple and the future prosperity of God's people

- **2.20–23.** a message about the future nation of Judah and its king

In-depth

When the people of ancient Judah lost their Temple in 587 B.C. and were deported to a strange land, they experienced a crisis in faith. Had God abandoned them? Were they no longer God's people? Was God punishing them for their sins? Some of them dreamed of a time when they could return to their land and rebuild God's Temple. However, when they finally were able to return in 538 B.C., things weren't as easy as they had hoped. Suffering from poverty, droughts, and crop failures (Hag 1.10–11), they put off rebuilding the Temple. Into this scene came the prophet Haggai. He told the people that God was still with them, and life was so difficult because they didn't seem to care that God's house was in ruins (verse 9). They had to get their priorities in order!

The people heard God's word spoken through Haggai, and immediately began working on the Temple. In their minds, they knew the new Temple would never be as beautiful as the original one (2.3). Haggai used this opportunity to prophesy about a future Temple that would be filled with God's splendor (verse 7), a time when God would again bless these people and make their offerings holy. God would establish Judah as a powerful nation, and Zerubbabel (a descendant of David) would be its anointed king.

Quick Facts

Period Covered
approximately 520 B.C.

Author
Haggai

Theme
rebuilding God's Temple

Haggai

The Command to Rebuild the Temple
(Ezra 5.1)

1 In the second year of King Da·ri′us, in the sixth month, on the first day of the month, the word of the LORD came by the prophet Hag′gai to Ze·rub′ba·bel son of She·al′ti·el, governor of Judah, and to Joshua son of Je·hoz′a·dak, the high priest: 2 Thus says the LORD of hosts: These people say the time has not yet come to rebuild the LORD's house. 3 Then the word of the LORD came by the prophet Hag′gai, saying: 4 Is it a time for you yourselves to live in your paneled houses, while this house lies in ruins? 5 Now therefore thus says the LORD of hosts: Consider how you have fared. 6 You have sown much, and harvested little; you eat, but you never have enough; you drink, but you never have your fill; you clothe yourselves, but no one is warm; and you that earn wages earn wages to put them into a bag with holes.

7 Thus says the LORD of hosts: Consider how you have fared. 8 Go up to the hills and bring wood and build the house, so that I may take pleasure in it and be honored, says the LORD. 9 You have looked for much, and, lo, it came to little; and when you brought it home, I blew it away. Why? says the LORD of hosts. Because my house lies in ruins, while all of you hurry off to your own houses. 10 Therefore the heavens above you have withheld the dew, and the earth has withheld its produce.

11 And I have called for a drought on the land and the hills, on the grain, the new wine, the oil, on what the soil produces, on human beings and animals, and on all their labors.

12 Then Ze·rub′ba·bel son of She·al′ti·el, and Joshua son of Je·hoz′a·dak, the high priest, with all the remnant of the people, obeyed the voice of the LORD their God, and the words of the prophet Hag′gai, as the LORD their God had sent him; and the people feared the LORD. 13 Then Hag′gai, the messenger of the LORD, spoke to the people with the LORD's message, saying, I am with you, says the LORD. 14 And the LORD stirred up the spirit of Zer·ub′ba·bel son of She·al′ti·el, governor of Judah, and the spirit of Joshua son of Je·hoz′a·dak, the high priest, and the spirit of all the remnant of the people; and they came and worked on the house of the LORD of hosts, their God, 15 on the twenty-fourth day of the month, in the sixth month.

The Future Glory of the Temple

2 In the second year of King Da·ri′us, 1 in the seventh month, on the twenty-first day of the month, the word of the LORD came by the prophet Hag′gai, saying: 2 Speak now to Ze·rub′ba·bel son of She·al′ti·el, governor of Judah, and to Joshua son of Je·hoz′a·dak, the high priest, and to the remnant of the people, and say, 3 Who is left among you that saw this house in its former glory? How does it look

On that day,
says the LORD of hosts,

I will take you,

O Ze·rub'ba·bel

my servant...

and make you like

a signet ring;

for I have

chosen you,

says the LORD of hosts.

to you now? Is it not in your sight as nothing? 4 Yet now take courage, O Ze·rub'ba·bel, says the LORD; take courage, O Joshua, son of Je·hoz'a·dak, the high priest; take courage, all you people of the land, says the LORD; work, for I am with you, says the LORD of hosts, 5 according to the promise that I made you when you came out of Egypt. My spirit abides among you; do not fear. 6 For thus says the LORD of hosts: Once again, in a little while, I will shake the heavens and the earth and the sea and the dry land; 7 and I will shake all the nations, so that the treasure of all nations shall come, and I will fill this house with splendor, says the LORD of hosts. 8 The silver is mine, and the gold is mine, says the LORD of hosts. 9 The latter splendor of this house shall be greater than the former, says the LORD of hosts; and

in this place I will give prosperity, says the LORD of hosts.

A Rebuke and a Promise

10 On the twenty-fourth day of the ninth month, in the second year of Da·ri'us, the word of the LORD came by the prophet Hag'gai, saying: 11 Thus says the LORD of hosts: Ask the priests for a ruling: 12 If one carries consecrated meat in the fold of one's garment, and with the fold touches bread, or stew, or wine, or oil, or any kind of food, does it become holy? The priests answered, "No." 13 Then Hag'gai said, "If one who is unclean by contact with a dead body touches any of these, does it become unclean?" The priests answered, "Yes, it becomes unclean." 14 Hag'gai then said, So is it with this people, and with this nation before me, says the LORD; and so with every work of their hands; and what they offer there is unclean. 15 But now, consider what will come to pass from this day on. Before a stone was placed upon a stone in the LORD's temple, 16 how did you fare?ᵃ When one came to a heap of twenty measures, there were but ten; when one came to the wine vat to draw fifty measures, there were but twenty. 17 I struck you and all the products of your toil with blight and mildew and hail; yet you did not return to me, says the LORD. 18 Consider from this day on, from the twenty-fourth day of the ninth month. Since the day that the foundation of the LORD's temple was laid, consider: 19 Is there any seed left in the barn? Do the vine, the fig tree, the pomegranate, and the olive tree still yield nothing? From this day on I will bless you.

God's Promise to Zerubbabel

20 The word of the LORD came a second time to Hag'gai on the twenty-fourth day of the month: 21 Speak to Ze·rub'ba·bel, governor of Judah, saying, I am about to shake the heavens and the earth, 22 and to overthrow the throne of kingdoms; I am about to destroy the strength of the kingdoms of the nations, and overthrow the chariots and their riders; and the horses and their riders shall fall, every one by the sword of a comrade. 23 On that day, says the LORD of hosts, I will take you, O Ze·rub'ba·bel my servant, son of She·al'ti·el, says the LORD, and make you like a signet ring; for I have chosen you, says the LORD of hosts.

ᵃ Gk: Heb *since they were*

What do you do when life is difficult and things only seem to be getting worse? Some people dream about the future. They imagine a time when all their troubles have ended and life is happy again. If their trouble is caused by certain people, they may imagine how these people eventually pay for their wrongdoing. The Book of Zechariah looks at Israel's future in exactly these two ways.

In-depth

Like the Book of Isaiah, the Book of Zechariah was written by at least two prophets. The original Zechariah—we'll call him First Zechariah—lived around the same time as Haggai, after the exiled Israelites returned to Jerusalem from Babylon (see the timeline at the back of this Bible). Second Zechariah, who may have been one or more prophets, wrote about two hundred years later.

The optimistic message of the first prophet in chapters 1–8 of Zechariah is centered on two concerns: the rebuilding of the Temple and the end of time. First Zechariah saw that a rebuilt Temple was needed to restore the people's unity, identity, and relationship with God. Through a series of visions (see "Apocalyptic Literature," Daniel, chapters 7–10), he announced his message: under the guidance of the priest Joshua and the prince Zerubbabel (a descendant of King David), Israel would be restored. It would become a nation of justice, faith, love, mercy, and truth where the Lord would dwell. Even the Gentiles (non-Jews) would come from faraway lands to worship God.

Second Zechariah wrote later, when Israel was under Greek domination (see the timeline). He preached not through visions, but through oracles (prophetic speeches) of warning, violence, and also promise. He talked about a great battle that was about to take place between the forces of good and the forces of evil. This was the final war, which would bring an end to the present-day evil and corrupt world. But Second Zechariah also proclaimed the coming of a humble king who would bring peace to all nations. Jerusalem would be purified and would become victorious as the city where God reigns as the highest power for good.

Quick Facts

Period Covered
First Zechariah around 520 B.C., Second Zechariah sometime after 333 B.C.

Authors
the original Zechariah, and an unknown prophet or prophets writing much later

Themes
a command to rebuild the Temple, the message that God will win the final victory

Of Note
The prophecies of Zechariah are quoted in the New Testament as proof that Jesus was the promised Messiah.

The Book of Zechariah

Zechariah

Chap. 11

Israel Urged to Repent

1 In the eighth month, in the second year of Da·rī'us, the word of the LORD came to the prophet Zech·a·rī'ah son of Ber·e·chī'ah son of Id'dō, saying: 2 The LORD was very angry with your ancestors. 3 Therefore say to them, Thus says the LORD of hosts: Return to me, says the LORD of hosts, and I will return to you, says the LORD of hosts. 4 Do not be like your ancestors, to whom the former prophets proclaimed, "Thus says the LORD of hosts, Return from your evil ways and from your evil deeds." But they did not hear or heed me, says the LORD. 5 Your ancestors, where are they? And the prophets, do they live forever? 6 But my words and my statutes, which I commanded my servants the prophets, did they not overtake your ancestors? So they repented and said, "The LORD of hosts has dealt with us according to our ways and deeds, just as he planned to do."

First Vision: The Horsemen

7 On the twenty-fourth day of the eleventh month, the month of She·bat', in the second year of Da·rī'us, the word of the LORD came to the prophet Zech·a·rī'ah son of Ber·e·chī'ah son of Id'dō; and Zech·a·rī'ah*a* said, 8 In the night I saw a man riding on a red horse! He was standing among the myrtle trees in the glen; and behind him were red, sorrel, and white horses. 9 Then I said, "What are these, my lord?" The angel who talked with me said to me, "I will show you what they are." 10 So the man who was standing among the myrtle trees answered, "They are those whom the LORD has sent to patrol the earth." 11 Then they spoke to the angel of the LORD who was standing among the myrtle trees, "We have patrolled the earth, and lo, the whole earth remains at peace." 12 Then the angel of the LORD said, "O LORD of hosts, how long will you withhold mercy from Jerusalem and the cities of Judah, with which you have been angry these seventy years?" 13 Then the LORD replied with gracious and comforting words to the angel who talked with me. 14 So the angel who talked with me said to me, Proclaim this message: Thus says the LORD of hosts; I am very jealous for Jerusalem and for Zion. 15 And I am extremely angry with the nations that are at ease; for while I was only a little angry, they made the disaster worse. 16 Therefore, thus says the LORD, I have returned to Jerusalem with compassion; my house shall be built in it, says the LORD of hosts, and the measuring line shall be stretched out over Jerusalem. 17 Proclaim further: Thus says the LORD of hosts: My cities shall again overflow with prosperity; the LORD will again comfort Zion and again choose Jerusalem.

---

a Heb *and he*

1082

Up, up! Flee from the land of the north, says the LORD;
for I have spread you abroad like the four winds of heaven,
says the LORD.

Up! Escape to Zion, you that live with daughter Babylon.

Be silent, all people, before the LORD;
for he has roused himself from his holy dwelling.

Second Vision: The Horns and the Smiths

18b And I looked up and saw four horns. 19 I asked the angel who talked with me, "What are these?" And he answered me, "These are the horns that have scattered Judah, Israel, and Jerusalem." 20 Then the LORD showed me four blacksmiths. 21 And I asked, "What are they coming to do?" He answered, "These are the horns that scattered Judah, so that no head could be raised; but these have come to terrify them, to strike down the horns of the nations that lifted up their horns against the land of Judah to scatter its people."c

Third Vision: The Man with a Measuring Line

2d I looked up and saw a man with a measuring line in his hand. 2 Then I asked, "Where are you going?" He answered me, "To measure Jerusalem, to see what is its width and what is its length." 3 Then the angel who talked with me came forward, and another angel came forward to meet him, 4 and said to him, "Run, say to that young man: Jerusalem shall be inhabited like villages without walls, because of the multitude of people and animals in it. 5 For I will be a wall of fire all around it, says the LORD, and I will be the glory within it."

Interlude: An Appeal to the Exiles

6 Up, up! Flee from the land of the north, says the LORD; for I have spread you abroad like the four winds of heaven, says the LORD. 7 Up! Escape to Zion, you that live with daughter Babylon. 8 For thus said the LORD of hosts (after his glorye sent me) regarding the nations that plundered you: Truly, one who touches you touches the apple of my eye.f 9 See now, I am going to raiseg my hand against them, and they shall become plunder for their own slaves. Then you will know that the LORD of hosts has sent me. 10 Sing and rejoice, O daughter Zion! For lo, I will come and dwell in your midst, says the LORD. 11 Many nations shall join themselves to the LORD on that day, and shall be my people; and I will dwell in your midst. And you shall know that the LORD of hosts has sent me to you. 12 The LORD will inherit Judah as his portion in the holy land, and will again choose Jerusalem.

13 Be silent, all people, before the LORD; for he has roused himself from his holy dwelling.

---

b Ch 2.1 in Heb   c Heb it   d Ch 2.5 in Heb   e Cn: Heb after glory he   f Heb his eye   g Or wave

ZECH

Fourth Vision: Joshua and Satan

3 Then he showed me the high priest Joshua standing before the angel of the LORD, and Satan[h] standing at his right hand to accuse him. 2 And the LORD said to Satan,[h] "The LORD rebuke you, O Satan![h] The LORD who has chosen Jerusalem rebuke you! Is not this man a brand plucked from the fire?" 3 Now Joshua was dressed with filthy clothes as he stood before the angel. 4 The angel said to those who were standing before him, "Take off his filthy clothes." And to him he said, "See, I have taken your guilt away from you, and I will clothe you with festal apparel." 5 And I said, "Let them put a clean turban on his head." So they put a clean turban on his head and clothed him with the apparel; and the angel of the LORD was standing by.

6 Then the angel of the LORD assured Joshua, saying 7 "Thus says the LORD of hosts: If you will walk in my ways and keep my requirements, then you shall rule my house and have charge of my courts, and I will give you the right of access among those who are standing here. 8 Now listen, Joshua, high priest, you and your colleagues who sit before you! For they are an omen of things to come: I am going to bring my servant the Branch. 9 For on the stone that I have set before Joshua, on a single stone with seven facets, I will engrave its inscription, says the LORD of hosts, and I will remove the guilt of this land in a single day. 10 On that day, says the LORD of hosts, you shall invite each other to come under your vine and fig tree."

Fifth Vision: The Lampstand and Olive Trees

4 The angel who talked with me came again, and wakened me, as one is wakened from sleep. 2 He said to me, "What do you see?" And I said, "I see a lampstand all of gold, with a bowl on the top of it; there are seven lamps on it, with seven lips on each of the lamps that are on the top of it. 3 And by it there are two olive trees, one on the right of the bowl and the other on its left." 4 I said to the angel who talked with me, "What are these, my lord?" 5 Then the angel who talked with me answered me, "Do you not know what these are?" I said, "No, my lord." 6 He said to me, "This is the word of the LORD to Ze•rub′ba•bel: Not by might, nor by power, but by my spirit, says the LORD of hosts. 7 What are you, O great mountain? Before Ze•rub′ba•bel you shall become a plain; and he shall bring out the top stone amid shouts of 'Grace, grace to it!'"

8 Moreover the word of the LORD came to me, saying, 9 "The hands of Ze•rub′ba•bel have laid the foundation of this house; his hands shall also complete it. Then you shall know that the LORD of hosts has sent me to you. 10 For whoever has despised the day of small things shall rejoice, and shall see the plummet in the hand of Ze•rub′ba•bel.

"These seven are the eyes of the LORD, which range through the whole earth." 11 Then I said to him, "What are these two olive trees on the right and the left of the lampstand?" 12 And a second time I said to him, "What are these two branches of the olive trees, which pour out the oil[i] through the two golden pipes?" 13 He said to me, "Do you not know what these are?" I said, "No, my lord." 14 Then he said, "These are the two anointed ones who stand by the Lord of the whole earth."

Sixth Vision: The Flying Scroll

5 Again I looked up and saw a flying scroll. 2 And he said to me, "What do you see?" I answered, "I see a flying scroll; its length is twenty cubits, and its width ten cubits." 3 Then he said to me, "This is the curse that goes out over the face of the whole land; for everyone who steals shall be cut off according to the writing on one side, and everyone who swears falsely[j] shall be cut off according to the writing on the other side. 4 I have sent it out, says the LORD of hosts, and it shall enter the house of the thief, and the house of anyone who swears falsely by my name; and it shall abide in that house and consume it, both timber and stones."

Seventh Vision: The Woman in a Basket

5 Then the angel who talked with me came forward and said to me, "Look up and see what this is that is coming out." 6 I said, "What is it?" He said, "This is a basket[k] coming out." And he said, "This is their iniquity[l] in all the land." 7 Then a leaden cover was lifted, and there was a woman sitting in the basket![k] 8 And he said, "This is Wickedness." So he thrust her back into the basket,[k] and pressed the leaden weight down on its mouth. 9 Then I looked up and saw two women coming forward. The wind was in their wings; they had wings like the wings of a stork, and they lifted up the basket[k] between earth and sky. 10 Then I said to the angel who talked with me, "Where are they taking the basket?"[k] 11 He said to me, "To the land of Shi′nar, to build a house for it; and when this is prepared, they will set the basket[k] down there on its base."

Eighth Vision: Four Chariots

6 And again I looked up and saw four chariots coming out from between two mountains— mountains of bronze. 2 The first chariot had red horses, the second chariot black horses, 3 the third

---

h Or the Accuser; Heb the Adversary i Cn: Heb gold j The word falsely added from verse 4 k Heb ephah l Gk Compare Syr: Heb their eye m Compare Gk: Meaning of Heb uncertain

6.1

chariot white horses, and the fourth chariot dappled gray[m] horses. 4 Then I said to the angel who talked with me, "What are these, my lord?" 5 The angel answered me, "These are the four winds[n] of heaven going out, after presenting themselves before the LORD of all the earth. 6 The chariot with the black horses goes toward the north country, the white ones go toward the west country,[o] and the dappled ones go toward the south country." 7 When the steeds came out, they were impatient to get off and patrol the earth. And he said, "Go, patrol the earth." So they patrolled the earth. 8 Then he cried out to me, "Lo, those who go toward the north country have set my spirit at rest in the north country."

The Coronation of the Branch

9 The word of the LORD came to me: 10 Collect silver and gold[p] from the exiles—from Hel'daī, Tō·bī'jah, and Je·daī'ah—who have arrived from Babylon; and go the same day to the house of Jō·sī'ah son of Zeph·a·nī'ah. 11 Take the silver and gold and make a crown,[q] and set it on the head of the high priest Joshua son of Je·hoz'a·dak; 12 say to him: Thus says the LORD of hosts: Here is a man whose name is Branch: for he shall branch out in his place, and he shall build the temple of the LORD. 13 It is he that shall build the temple of the LORD; he shall bear royal honor, and shall sit upon his throne and rule. There shall be a priest by his throne, with peaceful understanding between the two of them. 14 And the crown[r] shall be in the care of Hel'daī,[s] Tō·bī'jah, Je·daī'ah, and Jō·sī'ah[t] son of Zeph·a·nī'ah, as a memorial in the temple of the LORD.

15 Those who are far off shall come and help to build the temple of the LORD; and you shall know

that the LORD of hosts has sent me to you. This will happen if you diligently obey the voice of the LORD your God.

Hypocritical Fasting Condemned

7 In the fourth year of King Da·rī'us, the word of the LORD came to Zech·a·rī'ah on the fourth day of the ninth month, which is Chis'lev. 2 Now the people of Beth'el had sent Sha·rē'zer and Reg'em-mel'ech and their men, to entreat the favor of the LORD, 3 and to ask the priests of the house of the LORD of hosts and the prophets, "Should I mourn and practice abstinence in the fifth month, as I have done for so many years?" 4 Then the word of the LORD of hosts came to me: 5 Say to all the people of the land and the priests: When you fasted and lamented in the fifth month and in the seventh, for these seventy years, was it for me that you fasted? 6 And when you eat and when you drink, do you not eat and drink only for yourselves? 7 Were not these the words that the LORD proclaimed by the former prophets, when Jerusalem was inhabited and in prosperity, along with the towns around it, and when the Neg'eb and the She·phē'lah were inhabited?

Punishment for Rejecting God's Demands

8 The word of the LORD came to Zech·a·rī'ah, saying: 9 Thus says the LORD of hosts: Render true judgments, show kindness and mercy to one another; 10 do not oppress the widow, the orphan, the alien, or the poor; and do not devise evil in your hearts against one another. 11 But they refused to listen, and turned a stubborn shoulder, and stopped their ears in order not to hear. 12 They made their hearts adamant in order not to hear the law and the words that the LORD of hosts had sent by his spirit through the former prophets. Therefore great wrath came from the LORD of hosts. 13 Just as, when I[u] called, they would not hear, so, when they called, I would not hear, says the LORD of hosts, 14 and I scattered them with a whirlwind among all the nations that they had not known. Thus the land they left was desolate, so that no one went to and fro, and a pleasant land was made desolate.

God's Promises to Zion

8 The word of the LORD of hosts came to me, saying: 2 Thus says the LORD of hosts: I am jealous for Zion with great jealousy, and I am jealous for her with great wrath. 3 Thus says the LORD: I will return to Zion, and will dwell in the midst of Jerusalem; Jerusalem shall be called the faithful

---

n Or *spirits*   o Cn: Heb *go after them*   p Cn Compare verse 11: Heb lacks *silver and gold*   q Gk Mss Syr Tg: Heb *crowns*   r Gk Syr: Heb *crowns*   s Syr Compare verse 10: Heb *Helem*   t Syr Compare verse 10: Heb *Hen*   u Heb *he*

ZECH

city, and the mountain of the LORD of hosts shall be called the holy mountain. 4 Thus says the LORD of hosts: Old men and old women shall again sit in the streets of Jerusalem, each with staff in hand because of their great age. 5 And the streets of the city shall be full of boys and girls playing in its streets. 6 Thus says the LORD of hosts: Even though it seems impossible to the remnant of this people in these days, should it also seem impossible to me, says the LORD of hosts? 7 Thus says the LORD of hosts: I will save my people from the east country and from the west country; 8 and I will bring them to live in Jerusalem. They shall be my people and I will be their God, in faithfulness and in righteousness.

9 Thus says the LORD of hosts: Let your hands be strong—you that have recently been hearing these words from the mouths of the prophets who were present when the foundation was laid for the rebuilding of the temple, the house of the LORD of hosts. 10 For before those days there were no wages for people or for animals, nor was there any safety from the foe for those who went out or came in, and I set them all against one another. 11 But now I will not deal with the remnant of this people as in the former days, says the LORD of hosts. 12 For there shall be a sowing of peace; the vine shall yield its fruit, the ground shall give its produce, and the skies shall give their dew; and I will cause the remnant of this people to possess all these things. 13 Just as you have been a cursing among the nations, O house of Judah and house of Israel, so I will save you and you shall be a blessing. Do not be afraid, but let your hands be strong.

14 For thus says the LORD of hosts: Just as I purposed to bring disaster upon you, when your ancestors provoked me to wrath, and I did not relent, says the LORD of hosts, 15 so again I have purposed in these days to do good to Jerusalem and to the house of Judah; do not be afraid. 16 These are the things that you shall do: Speak the truth to one another, render in your gates judgments that are true and make for peace, 17 do not devise evil in your hearts against one another, and love no false oath; for all these are things that I hate, says the LORD.

Joyful Fasting

18 The word of the LORD of hosts came to me, saying: 19 Thus says the LORD of hosts: The fast of the fourth month, and the fast of the fifth, and the fast of the seventh, and the fast of the tenth, shall be seasons of joy and gladness, and cheerful festivals for the house of Judah: therefore love truth and peace.

Many Peoples Drawn to Jerusalem

20 Thus says the LORD of hosts: Peoples shall yet come, the inhabitants of many cities; 21 the inhabitants of one city shall go to another, saying, "Come, let us go to entreat the favor of the LORD, and to seek the LORD of hosts; I myself am going." 22 Many peoples and strong nations shall come to seek the LORD of hosts in Jerusalem, and to entreat the favor of the LORD. 23 Thus says the LORD of hosts: In those days ten men from nations of every language shall take hold of a Jew, grasping his garment and saying, "Let us go with you, for we have heard that God is with you."

Judgment on Israel's Enemies

9   An Oracle.

The word of the LORD is against the land of Had'rach
    and will rest upon Damascus.

Thumbs Up!

LIVE IT!

"I will save you and you shall be a blessing. Do not be afraid, but let your hands be strong" (Zech 8.13). These words are a promise that God will bring the people of Israel out of hard times into good times. They are also an encouragement to us.

A young woman named Ana was in a car accident in which the driver lost control and three people were killed. Ana was severely hurt and faced months of rehabilitation. Ana now needed to learn to walk and talk again.

Ana knew that for some reason, God spared her life. She knew that it was not going to be easy and would take hard work. She was motivated by her faith and the feeling that God was there helping her. Her attitude and ambition came out every time she was asked how she was doing. She raised her hand and lifted her thumb and said faintly, "Thumbs up."

How might you say, "Thumbs up," when faced with a personal challenge?

 Zech 8.9–17

For to the LORD belongs the capital[v] of Ar'am,[w]
   as do all the tribes of Israel;
2 Hā'math also, which borders on it,
   Tyre and Sī'don, though they are very wise.
3 Tyre has built itself a rampart,
   and heaped up silver like dust,
   and gold like the dirt of the streets.
4 But now, the Lord will strip it of its possessions
   and hurl its wealth into the sea,
   and it shall be devoured by fire.

5 Ash'ke•lon shall see it and be afraid;
   Gā'za too, and shall writhe in anguish;
   Ek'ron also, because its hopes are
      withered.
The king shall perish from Gā'za;
   Ash'ke•lon shall be uninhabited;
6 a mongrel people shall settle in Ash'dod,
   and I will make an end of the pride of
      Phi•lis'ti•a.
7 I will take away its blood from its mouth,
   and its abominations from between its
      teeth;
it too shall be a remnant for our God;
   it shall be like a clan in Judah,
   and Ek'ron shall be like the Jeb'ū•sītes.
8 Then I will encamp at my house as a guard,
   so that no one shall march to and fro;
no oppressor shall again overrun them,
   for now I have seen with my own eyes.

The Coming Ruler of God's People
(Mt 21.5; Jn 12.14–15)

9 Rejoice greatly, O daughter Zion!
   Shout aloud, O daughter Jerusalem!
Lo, your king comes to you;
   triumphant and victorious is he,
humble and riding on a donkey,
   on a colt, the foal of a donkey.
10 He[x] will cut off the chariot from Ē'phra•im
   and the war-horse from Jerusalem;
and the battle bow shall be cut off,
   and he shall command peace to the
      nations;
his dominion shall be from sea to sea,
   and from the River to the ends of the earth.
11 As for you also, because of the blood of my
      covenant with you,
   I will set your prisoners free from the
      waterless pit.
12 Return to your stronghold, O prisoners of
      hope;
   today I declare that I will restore to you
      double.
13 For I have bent Judah as my bow;
   I have made Ē'phra•im its arrow.
I will arouse your sons, O Zion,

against your sons, O Greece,
   and wield you like a warrior's sword.
14 Then the LORD will appear over them,
   and his arrow go forth like lightning;
the Lord GOD will sound the trumpet
   and march forth in the whirlwinds of the
      south.
15 The LORD of hosts will protect them,
   and they shall devour and tread down the
      slingers;[y]
they shall drink their blood[z] like wine,
   and be full like a bowl,
   drenched like the corners of the altar.

16 On that day the LORD their God will save them
   for they are the flock of his people;
for like the jewels of a crown
   they shall shine on his land.
17 For what goodness and beauty are his!
   Grain shall make the young men flourish,
   and new wine the young women.

Restoration of Judah and Israel

10 Ask rain from the LORD
   in the season of the spring rain,
from the LORD who makes the storm clouds,
   who gives showers of rain to you,[a]
   the vegetation in the field to everyone.
2 For the teraphim[b] utter nonsense,
   and the diviners see lies;
the dreamers tell false dreams,
   and give empty consolation.
Therefore the people wander like sheep;
   they suffer for lack of a shepherd.

3 My anger is hot against the shepherds,
   and I will punish the leaders;[c]
for the LORD of hosts cares for his flock, the
      house of Judah,
   and will make them like his proud war-horse.
4 Out of them shall come the cornerstone,
   out of them the tent peg,
out of them the battle bow,
   out of them every commander.
5 Together they shall be like warriors in battle,
   trampling the foe in the mud of the streets;
they shall fight, for the LORD is with them,
   and they shall put to shame the riders on
      horses.

6 I will strengthen the house of Judah,
   and I will save the house of Joseph.

---

v Heb *eye* *w* Cn: Heb *of Adam* (or *of humankind*)
x Gk: Heb *I* *y* Cn: Heb *the slingstones* *z* Gk: Heb *shall drink* *a* Heb *them* *b* Or *household gods* *c* Or *male goats*

I will bring them back because I have
 compassion on them,
and they shall be as though I had not
 rejected them;
for I am the LORD their God and I will
 answer them.
7 Then the people of E′phra•im shall become like
 warriors,
 and their hearts shall be glad as with
  wine.
Their children shall see it and rejoice,
 their hearts shall exult in the LORD.

8 I will signal for them and gather them in,
 for I have redeemed them,
 and they shall be as numerous as they were
  before.
9 Though I scattered them among the nations,
 yet in far countries they shall remember me,
 and they shall rear their children and
  return.
10 I will bring them home from the land of
 Egypt,
 and gather them from Assyria;
I will bring them to the land of Gil′e•ad and to
 Lebanon,
 until there is no room for them.
11 They[d] shall pass through the sea of distress,
 and the waves of the sea shall be struck
  down,
 and all the depths of the Nile dried up.
The pride of Assyria shall be laid low,
 and the scepter of Egypt shall depart.
12 I will make them strong in the LORD,
 and they shall walk in his name,
      says the LORD.

11

Open your doors, O Lebanon,
 so that fire may devour your cedars!
2 Wail, O cypress, for the cedar has fallen,
 for the glorious trees are ruined!
Wail, oaks of Ba′shan,
 for the thick forest has been felled!
3 Listen, the wail of the shepherds,
 for their glory is despoiled!
Listen, the roar of the lions,
 for the thickets of the Jordan are
  destroyed!

Two Kinds of Shepherds

4 Thus said the LORD my God: Be a shepherd of
the flock doomed to slaughter. 5 Those who buy
them kill them and go unpunished; and those who
sell them say, "Blessed be the LORD, for I have become rich"; and their own shepherds have no pity
on them. 6 For I will no longer have pity on the inhabitants of the earth, says the LORD. I will cause

them, every one, to fall each into the hand of a
neighbor, and each into the hand of the king; and
they shall devastate the earth, and I will deliver no
one from their hand.

7 So, on behalf of the sheep merchants, I became the shepherd of the flock doomed to
slaughter. I took two staffs; one I named Favor,
the other I named Unity, and I tended the sheep.
8 In one month I disposed of the three shepherds,
for I had become impatient with them, and they
also detested me. 9 So I said, "I will not be your
shepherd. What is to die, let it die; what is to be
destroyed, let it be destroyed; and let those that
are left devour the flesh of one another!" 10 I took
my staff Favor and broke it, annulling the
covenant that I had made with all the peoples.
11 So it was annulled on that day, and the sheep
merchants, who were watching me, knew that it
was the word of the LORD. 12 I then said to them,
"If it seems right to you, give me my wages; but if
not, keep them." So they weighed out as my wages
thirty shekels of silver. 13 Then the LORD said to
me, "Throw it into the treasury"[e]—this lordly price
at which I was valued by them. So I took the thirty shekels of silver and threw them into the treasury[e] in the house of the LORD. 14 Then I broke my
second staff Unity, annulling the family ties between Judah and Israel.

15 Then the LORD said to me: Take once more
the implements of a worthless shepherd. 16 For I
am now raising up in the land a shepherd who does
not care for the perishing, or seek the wandering,[f]
or heal the maimed, or nourish the healthy,[g] but
devours the flesh of the fat ones, tearing off even
their hoofs.
17 Oh, my worthless shepherd,
 who deserts the flock!
May the sword strike his arm
 and his right eye!
Let his arm be completely withered,
 his right eye utterly blinded!

Jerusalem's Victory

12

An Oracle.

The word of the LORD concerning Israel: Thus
says the LORD, who stretched out the heavens and
founded the earth and formed the human spirit
within: 2 See, I am about to make Jerusalem a cup
of reeling for all the surrounding peoples; it will be
against Judah also in the siege against Jerusalem.
3 On that day I will make Jerusalem a heavy stone
for all the peoples; all who lift it shall grievously
hurt themselves. And all the nations of the earth

---

d Gk: Heb He e Syr: Heb it to the potter f Syr Compare Gk
Vg: Heb the youth g Meaning of Heb uncertain

THE PRINCIPLE OF *UMOJA*

Chapter 11 of Zechariah contains several allegorical images that represent the breakdown of the Israelite nation. In one, a shepherd's staff named Unity, or Bonds, is broken—symbolizing that the people have lost the unity that bound them together.

Unity is vital to the success of any people. For example, Africans rely on the Kwanzaa principle of unity, called umoja (see "Kwanzaa as a Way of Life," Deut 10.12–22). *Umoja* signifies unity in the family, community, nation, and race. This unity keeps brothers from killing brothers and sisters from killing sisters. This unity keeps families together even when the going gets tough.

Any race or culture can and often does experience difficulty maintaining and promoting *umoja,* especially a race or culture facing injustice, racism, or prejudice. With these elements present, a race or culture can be negatively affected; positive unity can become negative as individuals, young and old, are tempted to come together in attitudes and behaviors that are selfish and destructive.

All of us are called to live in unity. All of us are called to foster unity and to direct our efforts toward bringing our families, communities, races, and nations together.

Keep the Kwanzaa principle of *umoja* alive! Be united in making the honor roll. Be united in respecting and protecting one another. Be united in putting an end to the problems that plague our cities and nation. Be united in being the best you can be!

▶ Zech 11.4–17

shall come together against it. 4 On that day, says the LORD, I will strike every horse with panic, and its rider with madness. But on the house of Judah I will keep a watchful eye, when I strike every horse of the peoples with blindness. 5 Then the clans of Judah shall say to themselves, "The inhabitants of Jerusalem have strength through the LORD of hosts, their God."

6 On that day I will make the clans of Judah like a blazing pot on a pile of wood, like a flaming torch among sheaves; and they shall devour to the right and to the left all the surrounding peoples, while Jerusalem shall again be inhabited in its place, in Jerusalem.

7 And the LORD will give victory to the tents of Judah first, that the glory of the house of David and the glory of the inhabitants of Jerusalem may not be exalted over that of Judah. 8 On that day the LORD will shield the inhabitants of Jerusalem so that the feeblest among them on that day shall be like David, and the house of David shall be like God, like the angel of the LORD, at their head. 9 And on that day I will seek to destroy all the nations that come against Jerusalem.

Mourning for the Pierced One

10 And I will pour out a spirit of compassion and supplication on the house of David and the inhabitants of Jerusalem, so that, when they look on the one[h] whom they have pierced, they shall mourn for him, as one mourns for an only child, and weep bitterly over him, as one weeps over a firstborn. 11 On that day the mourning in Jerusalem will be as great as the mourning for Hā'dad-rim'-mon in the plain of Me•gid'dō. 12 The land shall mourn, each family by itself; the family of the house of David by itself, and their wives by themselves; the family of the house of Nathan by itself, and their wives by themselves; 13 the family of the house of Levi by itself, and their wives by themselves; the family of the Shim'ē•ites by itself, and their wives by themselves; 14 and all the families that are left, each by itself, and their wives by themselves.

13 On that day a fountain shall be opened for the house of David and the inhabitants of Jerusalem, to cleanse them from sin and impurity.

---

h Heb *on me*

did you KNOW?

Prophecies of God's Victory

Zechariah, chapters 12–14, has several of Second Zechariah's prophecies on the final judgment, the restoration of Israel, and the Reign of God. Many of these prophecies were applied to Jesus by the first Christians.

For example: Zechariah foretells a time of mourning for "one whom they have pierced" (Zech 12.10); the Gospel of John applies this verse to Jesus' death on the cross (Jn 19.37). Zechariah says the sheep will be dispersed when the shepherd is struck (Zech 13.7); the Gospel of Matthew uses this verse to describe the disciples deserting Jesus (Mt 26.31). And passages from Zechariah's description of the day of the LORD (Zech 14.6–9) show up in the Book of Revelation's description of the new Jerusalem (Rev 11.15; 21.23)

These beautiful prophecies assured Israel's people of God's love and mercy. For Christians, they have additional meaning. They also describe Jesus Christ, whose death is our salvation and whose Resurrection is the promise of the fullness of God's Reign!

▶ Zechariah, chapters 12–14

Idolatry Cut Off

2 On that day, says the LORD of hosts, I will cut off the names of the idols from the land, so that they shall be remembered no more; and also I will remove from the land the prophets and the unclean spirit. 3 And if any prophets appear again, their fathers and mothers who bore them will say to them, "You shall not live, for you speak lies in the name of the LORD"; and their fathers and their mothers who bore them shall pierce them through when they prophesy. 4 On that day the prophets will be ashamed, every one, of their visions when they prophesy; they will not put on a hairy mantle in order to deceive, 5 but each of them will say, "I am no prophet, I am a tiller of the soil; for the land has been my possession[i] since my youth." 6 And if anyone asks them, "What are these wounds on your

chest?"[j] the answer will be "The wounds I received in the house of my friends."

The Shepherd Struck, the Flock Scattered

7 "Awake, O sword, against my shepherd,
    against the man who is my associate,"
                    says the LORD of hosts.
Strike the shepherd, that the sheep may be
    scattered;
    I will turn my hand against the little ones.
8 In the whole land, says the LORD,
    two-thirds shall be cut off and perish,
    and one-third shall be left alive.
9 And I will put this third into the fire,
    refine them as one refines silver,
    and test them as gold is tested.
They will call on my name,
    and I will answer them.
I will say, "They are my people";
    and they will say, "The LORD is our God."

Future Warfare and Final Victory
(Cp Ezek 38–39; Mk 13; Rev 20–22)

14 See, a day is coming for the LORD, when the plunder taken from you will be divided in your midst. 2 For I will gather all the nations against Jerusalem to battle, and the city shall be taken and the houses looted and the women raped; half the city shall go into exile, but the rest of the people shall not be cut off from the city. 3 Then the LORD will go forth and fight against those nations as when he fights on a day of battle. 4 On that day his feet shall stand on the Mount of Olives, which lies before Jerusalem on the east; and the Mount of Olives shall be split in two from east to west by a very wide valley; so that one half of the Mount shall withdraw northward, and the other half southward. 5 And you shall flee by the valley of the LORD's mountain,[k] for the valley between the mountains shall reach to Ā'zal;[l] and you shall flee as you fled from the earthquake in the days of King Uz•zi'ah of Judah. Then the LORD my God will come, and all the holy ones with him.

6 On that day there shall not be[m] either cold or frost.[n] 7 And there shall be continuous day (it is known to the LORD), not day and not night, for at evening time there shall be light.

8 On that day living waters shall flow out from Jerusalem, half of them to the eastern sea and half of them to the western sea; it shall continue in summer as in winter.

9 And the LORD will become king over all the

---

i Cn: Heb for humankind has caused me to possess
j Heb wounds between your hands   k Heb my mountains
l Meaning of Heb uncertain   m Cn: Heb there shall not
be light   n Compare Gk Syr Vg Tg: Meaning of Heb
uncertain

earth; on that day the LORD will be one and his name one.

10 The whole land shall be turned into a plain from Ge'ba to Rim'mon south of Jerusalem. But Jerusalem shall remain aloft on its site from the Gate of Benjamin to the place of the former gate, to the Corner Gate, and from the Tower of Ha·nan'el to the king's wine presses. 11 And it shall be inhabited, for never again shall it be doomed to destruction; Jerusalem shall abide in security.

12 This shall be the plague with which the LORD will strike all the peoples that wage war against Jerusalem: their flesh shall rot while they are still on their feet; their eyes shall rot in their sockets, and their tongues shall rot in their mouths. 13 On that day a great panic from the LORD shall fall on them, so that each will seize the hand of a neighbor, and the hand of the one will be raised against the hand of the other; 14 even Judah will fight at Jerusalem. And the wealth of all the surrounding nations shall be collected—gold, silver, and garments in great abundance. 15 And a plague like this plague shall fall on the horses, the mules, the camels, the donkeys, and whatever animals may be in those camps.

16 Then all who survive of the nations that have come against Jerusalem shall go up year after year to worship the King, the LORD of hosts, and to keep the festival of booths.*o* 17 If any of the families of the earth do not go up to Jerusalem to worship the King, the LORD of hosts, there will be no rain upon them. 18 And if the family of Egypt do not go up and present themselves, then on them shall*p* come the plague that the LORD inflicts on the nations that do not go up to keep the festival of booths.*o* 19 Such shall be the punishment of Egypt and the punishment of all the nations that do not go up to keep the festival of booths.*o*

20 On that day there shall be inscribed on the bells of the horses, "Holy to the LORD." And the cooking pots in the house of the LORD shall be as holy as*q* the bowls in front of the altar; 21 and every cooking pot in Jerusalem and Judah shall be sacred to the LORD of hosts, so that all who sacrifice may come and use them to boil the flesh of the sacrifice. And there shall no longer be traders*r* in the house of the LORD of hosts on that day.

---

o Or *tabernacles;* Heb *succoth*   *p* Gk Syr: Heb *shall not*
q Heb *shall be like*   *r* Or *Canaanites*

Malachi

You promised me!" These three words speak volumes when they're used against us. A promise is a sacred thing, and breaking promises hurts and destroys relationships. The last book of the Old Testament, Malachi, focuses on promises with God that have been broken. At the time of its writing, priests had broken the Covenant by offering inferior sacrifices, and men had broken the Covenant by marrying foreign women and divorcing their Jewish wives. The prophet Malachi predicts that someone is coming who will purify the people, punishing the wicked and rewarding the righteous.

At a Glance

- **1.1—2.9.** a message of God's love for Israel and of the sins of the priests
- **2.10–16.** call for faithfulness in marriage
- **2.17—4.3.** prophecies about God's messenger and God's judgment
- **4.4–6.** God's promise to send the prophet Elijah

In-depth

The author of the Book of Malachi wrote just before the reforms of Ezra and Nehemiah, starting around 458 B.C. (see the timeline at the back of this Bible). The Temple had been rebuilt (see the Books of Haggai and Zechariah), and Temple worship had been restored, but serious violations of the covenantal law existed.

The Book of Malachi addresses two main problems. The first is the failure of Israel's priests to provide good leadership. Through a series of questions and answers, the prophet Malachi speaks harsh words against the priests of the Temple for failing to live up to their calling to honor God. They offer inferior sacrifices on the altar of the Temple, thinking that God won't notice. The prophet compares these priests with their ancestor Levi, who offered only the finest gifts to God. Levi was a good and honest man who kept God's Covenant; these priests are not.

The second problem has to do with marriage and divorce. Evidently, many men are marrying non-Jewish women and divorcing their Jewish wives. It's not clear why they are doing this, but maybe they are trying to climb the social ladder. The prophet challenges the people to be faithful to one another because their marriages are a reminder of God's Covenant with the people of Judah.

The book ends with a prophecy that forms a bridge to the New Testament and the coming of Jesus. It says that God will send a messenger, the prophet Elijah, before the day of judgment. His job will be to prepare the way for God. Those who repent will enjoy God's blessings; those who do not will be punished by God. New Testament writers saw this prophecy fulfilled by John the Baptist, who prepared the way for the coming of the Messiah, Jesus of Nazareth.

Quick Facts

Period Covered
around 455 B.C.
Author
unknown
Theme
calls for priestly reform and faithfulness in marriage

Malachi

3.1–5

1 An oracle. The word of the LORD to Israel by Mal'a·chi.[a]

Israel Preferred to Edom

2 I have loved you, says the LORD. But you say, "How have you loved us?" Is not Esau Jacob's brother? says the LORD. Yet I have loved Jacob 3 but I have hated Esau; I have made his hill country a desolation and his heritage a desert for jackals. 4 If Ē'dom says, "We are shattered but we will rebuild the ruins," the LORD of hosts says: They may build, but I will tear down, until they are called the wicked country, the people with whom the LORD is angry forever. 5 Your own eyes shall see this, and you shall say, "Great is the LORD beyond the borders of Israel!"

Corruption of the Priesthood

6 A son honors his father, and servants their master. If then I am a father, where is the honor due me? And if I am a master, where is the respect due me? says the LORD of hosts to you, O priests, who despise my name. You say, "How have we despised your name?" 7 By offering polluted food on my altar. And you say, "How have we polluted it?"[b] By thinking that the LORD's table may be despised. 8 When you offer blind animals in sacrifice, is that not wrong? And when you offer those that are lame or sick, is that not wrong? Try presenting that to your governor; will he be pleased with you or show you favor? says the LORD of hosts. 9 And now implore the favor of God, that he may be gracious to us. The fault is yours. Will he show favor to any of you? says the LORD of hosts. 10 Oh, that someone among you would shut the temple[c] doors, so that you would not kindle fire on my altar in vain! I have no pleasure in you, says the LORD of hosts, and I will not accept an offering from your hands. 11 For from the rising of the sun to its setting my name is great among the nations, and in every place incense is offered to my name, and a pure offering; for my name is great among the nations, says the LORD of hosts. 12 But you profane it when you say that the Lord's table is polluted, and the food for it[d] may be despised. 13 "What a weariness this is," you say, and you sniff at me,[e] says the LORD of hosts. You bring what has been taken by violence or is lame or sick, and this you bring as your offering! Shall I accept that from your hand? says the LORD. 14 Cursed be the cheat who has a male in the flock and vows to give it, and yet sacrifices to the Lord what is blemished; for I am a great King, says the LORD of hosts, and my name is reverenced among the nations.

---

a Or by my messenger b Gk: Heb you c Heb lacks temple
d Compare Syr Tg: Heb its fruit, its food e Another reading is at it

2 And now, O priests, this command is for you.
² If you will not listen, if you will not lay it to
heart to give glory to my name, says the LORD of
hosts, then I will send the curse on you and I will
curse your blessings; indeed I have already cursed
them,ᶠ because you do not lay it to heart. ³ I will rebuke your offspring, and spread dung on your
faces, the dung of your offerings, and I will put you
out of my presence.ᵍ

4 Know, then, that I have sent this command to
you, that my covenant with Levi may hold, says the
LORD of hosts. ⁵ My covenant with him was a
covenant of life and well-being, which I gave him;
this called for reverence, and he revered me and
stood in awe of my name. ⁶ True instruction was in
his mouth, and no wrong was found on his lips. He
walked with me in integrity and uprightness, and
he turned many from iniquity. ⁷ For the lips of a
priest should guard knowledge, and people should
seek instruction from his mouth, for he is the messenger of the LORD of hosts. ⁸ But you have turned
aside from the way; you have caused many to stumble by your instruction; you have corrupted the
covenant of Levi, says the LORD of hosts, ⁹ and so I
make you despised and abased before all the people, inasmuch as you have not kept my ways but
have shown partiality in your instruction.

The Covenant Profaned by Judah

10 Have we not all one father? Has not one God
created us? Why then are we faithless to one another, profaning the covenant of our ancestors? ¹¹ Judah has been faithless, and abomination has been
committed in Israel and in Jerusalem; for Judah has
profaned the sanctuary of the LORD, which he loves,
and has married the daughter of a foreign god.
¹² May the LORD cut off from the tents of Jacob anyone who does this—any to witnessʰ or answer, or to
bring an offering to the LORD of hosts.

13 And this you do as well: You cover the
LORD's altar with tears, with weeping and groaning
because he no longer regards the offering or accepts
it with favor at your hand. ¹⁴ You ask, "Why does
he not?" Because the LORD was a witness between
you and the wife of your youth, to whom you have
been faithless, though she is your companion and
your wife by covenant. ¹⁵ Did not one God make
her?ⁱ Both flesh and spirit are his.ʲ And what does
the one Godᵏ desire? Godly offspring. So look to
yourselves, and do not let anyone be faithless to the
wife of his youth. ¹⁶ For I hateˡ divorce, says the
LORD, the God of Israel, and covering one's garment
with violence, says the LORD of hosts. So take heed
to yourselves and do not be faithless.

17 You have wearied the LORD with your words.
Yet you say, "How have we wearied him?" By saying, "All who do evil are good in the sight of the

LORD, and he delights in them." Or by asking,
"Where is the God of justice?"

The Coming Messenger

3 See, I am sending my messenger to prepare
the way before me, and the Lord whom you
seek will suddenly come to his temple. The messenger of the covenant in whom you delight—indeed, he is coming, says the LORD of hosts. ² But
who can endure the day of his coming, and who
can stand when he appears?

For he is like a refiner's fire and like fullers' soap;
³ he will sit as a refiner and purifier of silver, and he
will purify the descendants of Levi and refine them
like gold and silver, until they present offerings to
the LORD in righteousness.ᵐ ⁴ Then the offering of
Judah and Jerusalem will be pleasing to the LORD as
in the days of old and as in former years.

ᶠ Heb it   ᵍ Cn Compare Gk Syr: Heb *and he shall bear you
to it*   ʰ Cn Compare Gk: Heb *arouse*   ⁱ Or *Has he not
made one?*   ʲ Cn: Heb *and a remnant of spirit was his*
ᵏ Heb *he*   ˡ Cn: Heb *he hates*   ᵐ Or *right offerings to
the LORD*

5 Then I will draw near to you for judgment; I will be swift to bear witness against the sorcerers, against the adulterers, against those who swear falsely, against those who oppress the hired workers in their wages, the widow and the orphan, against those who thrust aside the alien, and do not fear me, says the LORD of hosts.

6 For I the LORD do not change; therefore you, O children of Jacob, have not perished. 7 Ever since the days of your ancestors you have turned aside from my statutes and have not kept them. Return to me, and I will return to you, says the LORD of hosts. But you say, "How shall we return?"

Do Not Rob God

8 Will anyone rob God? Yet you are robbing me! But you say, "How are we robbing you?" In your tithes and offerings! 9 You are cursed with a curse, for you are robbing me—the whole nation of you! 10 Bring the full tithe into the storehouse, so that there may be food in my house, and thus put me to the test, says the LORD of hosts; see if I will not open the windows of heaven for you and pour down for you an overflowing blessing. 11 I will rebuke the locust[n] for you, so that it will not destroy the produce of your soil; and your vine in the field shall not be barren, says the LORD of hosts. 12 Then all nations will count you happy, for you will be a land of delight, says the LORD of hosts.

13 You have spoken harsh words against me, says the LORD. Yet you say, "How have we spoken against you?" 14 You have said, "It is vain to serve God. What do we profit by keeping his command or by going about as mourners before the LORD of hosts? 15 Now we count the arrogant happy; evildoers not only prosper, but when they put God to the test they escape."

The Reward of the Faithful

16 Then those who revered the LORD spoke with one another. The LORD took note and listened, and a book of remembrance was written before him of those who revered the LORD and thought on his name. 17 They shall be mine, says the LORD of hosts, my special possession on the day when I act, and I will spare them as parents spare their children who serve them. 18 Then once more you shall see the difference between the righteous and the wicked, between one who serves God and one who does not serve him.

The Great Day of the LORD

4 [o] See, the day is coming, burning like an oven, when all the arrogant and all evildoers will be stubble; the day that comes shall burn them up, says the LORD of hosts, so that it will leave them neither root nor branch. 2 But for you who revere my name the sun of righteousness shall rise, with

---

[n] Heb *devourer*   [o] Ch 4.1-6 are Ch 3.19-24 in Heb

Prepare the Way

LIVE IT!

Malachi 3.1–2 talks about the sending of a messenger to prepare for God's coming. That arrival will mark a day of purification, when anything that isn't of value will be burnt away. What does that have to do with you? Take a few moments to reflect on the following dialog:

Prophet. **Prepare the way of the LORD!**
Listener. **Who, me?**
Prophet. **Yes, of course, you!**
Listener. **But that's John the Baptist's job.**
Prophet. **Was. That *was* John the Baptist's job. Now, it belongs to you, as a follower of Christ.**
Listener. **So, what do I do? Where do I start?**
Prophet. **Listen to Jesus. Nurture your relationship with God through prayer and the sacraments. Live a happy, holy, and healthy life in order to be a light for others. Share what you believe with others so that they can also find their way. By the way, you are not alone.**
Listener. **You mean there are a lot of us preparing the way?**
Prophet. **That's right.**
Listener. **Well, then, I'm on my way—or rather, we are on *God's* way.**

▶ Mal 3.1–7

healing in its wings. You shall go out leaping like calves from the stall. 3 And you shall tread down the wicked, for they will be ashes under the soles of your feet, on the day when I act, says the LORD of hosts.

4 Remember the teaching of my servant Moses, the statutes and ordinances that I commanded him at Hō′reb for all Israel.

5 Lo, I will send you the prophet E·lī′jah before the great and terrible day of the LORD comes. 6 He will turn the hearts of parents to their children and the hearts of children to their parents, so that I will not come and strike the land with a curse.*p*

p Or *a ban of utter destruction*

See, I am sending my **messenger...** WHO can endure the **day of his coming?** 3.1–2

THE *New Testament*

Introduction to the

Gospels

and the Acts of the Apostles

If you have ever written a research paper for a class project, you know how important it is to have good sources. You want sources that have the most insight into your chosen topic, sources that provide inspiration. The books of the New Testament are those sources for the Christian faith. The Gospels of Matthew, Mark, Luke, and John lay the foundation for understanding the message and the mission of Jesus, the center of the Christian faith. The Acts of the Apostles continues with an inspiring account of how the earliest Christians continued Jesus' mission despite conflicts and persecution. The Good News in these books invites a response from us: to accept Jesus as the promised Messiah, the Son of God, the savior of the world.

In-depth

THE BOOKS OF THE NEW TESTAMENT CONTINUE the Old Testament's revelation of God's saving work in the world. Their focus is on Jesus Christ—the hoped-for Messiah, the savior. Jesus Christ is revealed as God's Son, being both fully human and fully divine. In Jesus, God's promises to Abraham, Moses, and David were fulfilled. In Jesus, a New Covenant is available to all people, not just the Jews. In Jesus, lie the forgiveness of sins and a new life of love and freedom for anyone who believes.

The New Testament tells of this Good News through four different types of books: (1) four similar but unique views of Jesus' life and teaching in books called Gospels, (2) stories on how the Apostles spread the Good News of Jesus in the Acts of the Apostles, (3) letters from early Christian leaders to the first Christians and Christian communities, and (4) apocalyptic writings in the Book of Revelation. This introduction is on the four Gospels and the Acts of the Apostles; another introduction will give further background on the letters and Revelation.

The Gospels of Matthew, Mark, Luke, and John tell the story of Jesus from four different perspectives. They are not historical biographies or documentaries like you might read today. They grew out of the teaching and preaching about Jesus in different early Christian communities. They reflect these early Christian communities' beliefs about Jesus, but they do not tell us exactly what Jesus said and did in his life on earth. Inspired by God, the authors of the Gospels arranged the stories to bring out a particular understanding of Jesus that had great importance in their Christian communities.

The Gospels of Matthew, Mark, and Luke are similar in their style and share much of the same content. They are called synoptic (from a Greek word that means "seeing the whole together") Gospels. It is likely that Mark was written first and the authors of Matthew and Luke used Mark as a source in creating their own Gospels (Lk 1.1 mentions other accounts of Jesus). The Gospel of John is quite different from the synoptic Gospels. It was written later than them and is more symbolic in its expression of who Jesus is.

The Acts of the Apostles is a continuation of Luke's Gospel (see Acts 1.1). However, it is not itself a Gospel. It picks up where the Gospel of Luke ends, telling the story of the origins of Christianity after the death and Resurrection of Jesus, covering the period from about A.D. 30 to 64. Although Acts gives us a good deal of information about early church leaders like Peter and Paul, its purpose is not to tell us their biographies. Rather, it gives us an interpretation of the events of the beginnings of Christianity that emphasizes God's saving purpose. The Book of Acts explains how Christianity, which began as an offshoot of the Jewish faith, gradually spread beyond Judaism into the Gentile, or non-Jewish, world.

The original Greek word for *gospel* is *euangelion*, which means "big or important news" (sometimes translated as "good news"). The authors of the Gospels wanted to share with others the important news of Jesus Christ. When you read these powerful stories of faith, let God use them to inspire and strengthen your faith in Jesus.

Other Background

- **The Gospel of Matthew emphasizes Jesus as the promised Messiah of the Jewish people. Jesus is portrayed as the greatest prophet, teaching the New Law and calling people to be faithful to God.**

- **The Gospel of Mark was probably the first of the four Gospels to be written. It portrays Jesus as an active healer and miracle worker who accepts loneliness and suffering as the cost of obedience to God's will.**

- **The Gospel of Luke is a clear, orderly presentation of Jesus' mission to all people, Jews and Gentiles. This Gospel emphasizes Jesus' mercy, compassion, and concern for poor people.**

- **The Gospel of John was the last Gospel written and seeks to show Jesus as the fully divine Son of God. This Gospel portrays Jesus as noble and powerful, fully in control of his own destiny.**

- **The Acts of the Apostles was written by the author of the Gospel of Luke. It shows God at work in the growth of the early Christian communities, particularly through the efforts of Peter and Paul.**

Does your family have a traditional way of celebrating a holiday? Family traditions are usually handed down from one generation to the next. They give meaning to our special celebrations and help us know where we came from. The author of the Gospel of Matthew presents Jesus as the promised Messiah and highlights Jesus' Jewish origins. The author wanted Jewish-Christian readers to know that believing in Jesus was not a break with their tradition but a continuation of it.

In-depth

The author of Matthew was probably a Christian convert from Judaism in a community of Jewish Christians. This community was feeling the sting of being rejected by other Jews. In defense of the community's belief in Jesus, the Gospel of Matthew links Jesus to important Jewish traditions and gives them new meanings. The Gospel begins with a list of Jesus' Jewish ancestors, connecting Jesus to Abraham, the father of Judaism, and David, Israel's greatest king. Then it makes frequent references to Old Testament laws, prophecies, and events that Jesus fulfills or completes.

The author of Matthew also wanted to show how Jesus broke with certain Jewish beliefs—no doubt to help explain why his community of Jewish Christians was rejected by other Jews. So in the Sermon on the Mount (5.1—7.29), the Gospel has Jesus giving new interpretation to Jewish laws. And Jesus is frequently in conflict with the scribes and Pharisees over things like healing on the Sabbath (12.9–14). Such incidents probably reflect the experience of the author's community with Jewish leaders as much as Jesus' own conflicts.

Gradually, the Gospel of Matthew paints a picture of Jesus as the promised son of David who would reign as king forever. He is the Messiah, the fulfillment of all that the Jewish people have been waiting for, the one who will bring their liberation and salvation. This good news should be proclaimed to Jews and non-Jews alike. And so the Gospel ends with the risen Jesus telling his disciples, "Go therefore and make disciples of all nations" (28.19).

At a Glance

- **1.1—4.17.** the birth of Jesus and the beginning of Jesus' ministry

- **4.18—9.38.** the Sermon on the Mount and miracles in Galilee

- **10.1—12.50.** teaching on mission and rejection

- **13.1—17.27.** parables on the Kingdom of God, the disciples' acknowledging Jesus as the Messiah

- **18.1—20.34.** teaching about community and forgiveness

- **21.1—25.46.** teaching about coming destruction, conflicts with Jewish leaders in Jerusalem

- **26.1—28.20.** Jesus' death and Resurrection

Quick Facts

Author
unknown; traditionally associated with the Apostle Matthew

Date Written
approximately A.D. 85

Audience
Christian Jews

Image of Jesus
the greatest prophet, who brings the New Law

The Gospel According to **Matthew**

Matthew

The Genealogy of Jesus the Messiah
(Ruth 4.18–22; 1 Chr 2.1–15; Lk 3.23–38)

1 An account of the genealogy[a] of Jesus the Messiah,[b] the son of David, the son of Abraham.

2 Abraham was the father of Isaac, and Isaac the father of Jacob, and Jacob the father of Judah and his brothers, 3 and Judah the father of Per'ez and Zē'rah by Tā'mar, and Per'ez the father of Hez'ron, and Hez'ron the father of Ar'am, 4 and Ar'am the father of A·min'a·dab, and A·min'a·dab the father of Nah'shon, and Nah'shon the father of Sal'mon, 5 and Sal'mon the father of Bō'az by Rā'hab, and Bō'az the father of Ō'bed by Ruth, and Ō'bed the father of Jesse, 6 and Jesse the father of King David.

And David was the father of Solomon by the wife of Ū·rī'ah, 7 and Solomon the father of Rē·ho·bō'am, and Rē·ho·bō'am the father of A·bī'jah, and A·bī'jah the father of Ā'saph,[c] 8 and Ā'saph[c] the father of Je·hosh'a·phat, and Je·hosh'a·phat the father of Jō'ram, and Jō'ram the father of Uz·zī'ah, 9 and Uz·zī'ah the father of Jō'tham, and Jō'tham the father of Ā'haz, and Ā'haz the father of Hez·e·kī'ah, 10 and Hez·e·kī'ah the father of Ma·nas'seh, and Ma·nas'seh the father of Ā'mos,[d] and Ā'mos[d] the father of Jō·sī'ah, 11 and Jō·sī'ah the father of Jech·o·nī'ah and his brothers, at the time of the deportation to Babylon.

12 And after the deportation to Babylon: Jech·o·nī'ah was the father of Sa·lā'thi·el, and Sa·lā'thi·el the father of Ze·rub'ba·bel, 13 and Ze·rub'-ba·bel the father of A·bī'ud, and A·bī'ud the father of E·lī'a·kim, and E·lī'a·kim the father of Ā'zor, 14 and Ā'zor the father of Zā'dok, and Zā'dok the father of Ā'chim, and Ā'chim the father of E·lī'ud, 15 and E·lī'ud the father of El·e·ā'zar, and El·e·ā'zar the father of Mat'than, and Mat'than the father of Jacob, 16 and Jacob the father of Joseph the husband of Mary, of whom Jesus was born, who is called the Messiah.[e]

17 So all the generations from Abraham to David are fourteen generations; and from David to the deportation to Babylon, fourteen generations; and from the deportation to Babylon to the Messiah,[e] fourteen generations.

The Birth of Jesus the Messiah
(Lk 2.1–7)

18 Now the birth of Jesus the Messiah[b] took place in this way. When his mother Mary had been engaged to Joseph, but before they lived together, she was found to be with child from the Holy Spirit. 19 Her husband Joseph, being a righteous man and unwilling to expose her to public disgrace, planned to dismiss her quietly. 20 But just when he had resolved to do this, an angel of the Lord appeared to him in a dream and said, "Joseph, son of David, do not be afraid to take Mary as your wife,

---

a Or *birth*   *b* Or *Jesus Christ*   *c* Other ancient authorities read *Asa*   *d* Other ancient authorities read *Amon*   *e* Or *the Christ*

did you KNOW?

Jesus' Family Tree

In the first two chapters of Matthew, the author begins to reveal the unique focus of the Gospel. He starts by tracing Jesus' family tree, making his case that Jesus was the Messiah who would restore the Covenant promised to Abraham, the father of the Jewish people. He also traces Jesus' ancestry back to David to show that Jesus is the fulfillment of the promises made to David (2 Samuel, chapter 7).

Things get even more interesting with a closer look at all the people mentioned in the list. There is a wide assortment of groups and social classes: patriarchs and slaves, kings and peasants, men and women, Jews and non-Jews. Matthew is planting the seed that Jesus has come for the salvation of all people.

▸ Mt 1.1–17

for the child conceived in her is from the Holy Spirit. 21 She will bear a son, and you are to name him Jesus, for he will save his people from their sins." 22 All this took place to fulfill what had been spoken by the Lord through the prophet:

23 "Look, the virgin shall conceive and bear a son,
and they shall name him Em•man'ū•el,"

which means, "God is with us." 24 When Joseph awoke from sleep, he did as the angel of the Lord commanded him; he took her as his wife, 25 but had no marital relations with her until she had borne a son;*f* and he named him Jesus.

The Visit of the Wise Men

2 In the time of King Her'od, after Jesus was born in Bethlehem of Judea, wise men*g* from the East came to Jerusalem, 2 asking, "Where is the child who has been born king of the Jews? For we observed his star at its rising,*h* and have come to pay him homage." 3 When King Her'od heard this, he was frightened, and all Jerusalem with him; 4 and calling together all the chief priests and scribes of the people, he inquired of them where the Messiah*i* was to be born. 5 They told him, "In Bethlehem of Judea; for so it has been written by the prophet:

---

f Other ancient authorities read *her firstborn son* *g* Or *astrologers*; Gk *magi* *h* Or *in the East* *i* Or *the Christ*

Cultural Connections

JESUS BROUGHT THE GOOD NEWS OF SALVATION TO PEOPLE OF ALL RACES!

The Wise Men from another culture, who came to offer Jesus gifts for a royal messiah, symbolize that Jesus came as the savior of all races and cultures. Matthew 2.1–12 is the biblical basis for the religious feast day of Epiphany, which officially is 6 January but is celebrated on the first Sunday after the New Year.

In some Latin American traditions, children receive gifts on Epiphany, in remembrance of the gifts the Wise Men offered to Jesus. The evening before, at parties celebrated in homes and offices, a special bread is shared that has a figure of the baby Jesus baked inside of it. Whoever finds the figure of the baby Jesus in a piece of bread has to sponsor a party to celebrate Jesus' presentation in the Temple (Lk 2.22–24). The church celebrates this feast on 2 February.

■ How do you accept and celebrate people of different cultures?
■ Think of spiritual gifts that you have received from other people. Express your gratitude to God for those gifts.

▸ Mt 2.1–12

did you KNOW?

Jesus, Emmanuel

In announcing Jesus' birth, the Gospel of Matthew quotes Isa 7.14, in which Isaiah tells King Ahaz that his young wife will conceive a son and they will name him Emmanuel, which means "God is with us" (see Mt 1.23). This is the perfect description for Jesus, the Son of God, who fully shares our humanity. The Gospel ends with the same promise, when the risen Jesus tells his disciples, "I am with you always" (28.20).

▶ Mt 1.23

6 'And you, Bethlehem, in the land of Judah,
    are by no means least among the rulers of
       Judah;
   for from you shall come a ruler
      who is to shepherd^j my people Israel.' "
7 Then Her'od secretly called for the wise men^k and learned from them the exact time when the star had appeared. 8 Then he sent them to Bethlehem, saying, "Go and search diligently for the child; and when you have found him, bring me word so that I may also go and pay him homage." 9 When they had heard the king, they set out; and there, ahead of them, went the star that they had seen at its rising,^l until it stopped over the place where the child was. 10 When they saw that the star had stopped,^m they were overwhelmed with joy. 11 On entering the house, they saw the child with Mary his mother; and they knelt down and paid him homage. Then, opening their treasure chests, they offered him gifts of gold, frankincense, and myrrh. 12 And having been warned in a dream not to return to Her'od, they left for their own country by another road.

The Escape to Egypt

13 Now after they had left, an angel of the Lord appeared to Joseph in a dream and said, "Get up, take the child and his mother, and flee to Egypt, and remain there until I tell you; for Her'od is about to search for the child, to destroy him." 14 Then Josephⁿ got up, took the child and his mother by night, and went to Egypt, 15 and remained there until the death of Her'od. This was to fulfill what had been spoken by the Lord through the prophet, "Out of Egypt I have called my son."

---

j Or rule   k Or astrologers; Gk magi   l Or in the East
m Gk saw the star   n Gk he

JESUS' FAMILY LIVES AS IMMIGRANTS!

Following an angel's order and facing the massacre of all boys under two years old, Joseph takes Mary and Jesus to Egypt to protect them from Herod's threats. They become immigrants to avoid persecution.

Every year, millions of people in the world become immigrants, fleeing their countries because of hunger, poverty, or persecution. Often, they find themselves unwelcomed strangers, not able to communicate in the language of their new land and even persecuted by its inhabitants. But Christians should have a special compassion for immigrants because Jesus told us to love everyone, especially those who suffer.
- Imagine Jesus, Mary, and Joseph exiled in this country. How would you treat them?
- What is your attitude toward refugees and immigrants in our country?
- Ask God to bless legislators with the love and wisdom to welcome immigrants, and to give your generation a courageous heart to seek justice and peace in the world.

▶ Mt 2.13

The Slaughter of the Innocents

The event described in Mt 2.16–18 is often called the Slaughter of the Innocents. In many circumstances in history, innocent people, including infants and young children, have been massacred in the name of war or convenience (see "Rachel Weeps," Jer 31.15–17).

Today, abortion is one of those circumstances. To many people, it seems to be a simple solution to the inconvenience of an unwanted pregnancy. But what of the innocent lives that are destroyed? With abortion, "they were no more" (Mt 2.18). Our church teaching is clear: All human life is sacred, and abortion is wrong. How might we as individuals or communities support pregnant women to ensure they do not choose abortion?

▸ Mt 2.16–18

did you KNOW?

Pharisees, Sadducees, and Scribes

In Jesus' day, several groups of Jews held positions of status or leadership. The *Pharisees* were devoted laymen who believed that salvation was achieved by rigorously following the Jewish Law. People looked up to them for guidance about how they should live as good Jews. The *Sadducees* were associated with the Temple and the ruling class. They did not believe in life after death. They did believe that wealth was a sign of being blessed by God. The *scribes* were skilled at reading and writing, and performed those services for the majority of the population, who were unable to read and write for themselves. Scribes probably were involved in writing some of the Old Testament books.

The negative reaction of John the Baptist to the Pharisees and Sadducees is typical in Matthew. But in general, Pharisees, Sadducees, and scribes were respected leaders during Jesus' time. The persecution later experienced by the community in which the author of Matthew lived probably affected his portrayal of them. (See "Jewish Sects," near the end of 2 Maccabees, for more information on these groups.)

▸ Mt 3.7

The Massacre of the Infants

16 When Her′od saw that he had been tricked by the wise men,[o] he was infuriated, and he sent and killed all the children in and around Bethlehem who were two years old or under, according to the time that he had learned from the wise men.[o] 17 Then was fulfilled what had been spoken through the prophet Jer•e•mi′ah:

18 "A voice was heard in Rā′mah,
    wailing and loud lamentation,
Rachel weeping for her children;
    she refused to be consoled, because they are no more."

The Return from Egypt
(Lk 2.39)

19 When Her′od died, an angel of the Lord suddenly appeared in a dream to Joseph in Egypt and said, 20 "Get up, take the child and his mother, and go to the land of Israel, for those who were seeking the child's life are dead." 21 Then Joseph[p] got up, took the child and his mother, and went to the land of Israel. 22 But when he heard that Ar•che•lā′us was ruling over Judea in place of his father Her′od, he was afraid to go there. And after being warned in a dream, he went away to the district of Galilee. 23 There he made his home in a town called Nazareth, so that what had been spoken through the prophets might be fulfilled, "He will be called a Naz•o•rē′an."

The Proclamation of John the Baptist
(Mk 1.2–8; Lk 3.1–20)

3 In those days John the Baptist appeared in the wilderness of Judea, proclaiming, 2 "Repent, for the kingdom of heaven has come near."[q] 3 This is the one of whom the prophet Ī•sāi′ah spoke when he said,

---

[o] Or *astrologers*; Gk *magi*   [p] Gk *he*   [q] Or *is at hand*

"The voice of one crying out in the wilderness:
'Prepare the way of the Lord,
        make his paths straight.' "
4 Now John wore clothing of camel's hair with a
leather belt around his waist, and his food was
locusts and wild honey. 5 Then the people of
Jerusalem and all Judea were going out to him, and
all the region along the Jordan, 6 and they were
baptized by him in the river Jordan, confessing
their sins.

7 But when he saw many Phar'i•sees and
Sad'du•cees coming for baptism, he said to them,
"You brood of vipers! Who warned you to flee from
the wrath to come? 8 Bear fruit worthy of repentance. 9 Do not presume to say to yourselves, 'We
have Abraham as our ancestor'; for I tell you, God
is able from these stones to raise up children to
Abraham. 10 Even now the ax is lying at the root of
the trees; every tree therefore that does not bear
good fruit is cut down and thrown into the fire.

11 "I baptize you with^r water for repentance,
but one who is more powerful than I is coming after me; I am not worthy to carry his sandals. He will
baptize you with^r the Holy Spirit and fire. 12 His
winnowing fork is in his hand, and he will clear his
threshing floor and will gather his wheat into the
granary; but the chaff he will burn with unquenchable fire."

The Baptism of Jesus
(Mk 1.9–11; Lk 3.21–22; Jn 1.29–34)

13 Then Jesus came from Galilee to John at the
Jordan, to be baptized by him. 14 John would have
prevented him, saying, "I need to be baptized by
you, and do you come to me?" 15 But Jesus answered him, "Let it be so now; for it is proper for us
in this way to fulfill all righteousness." Then he
consented. 16 And when Jesus had been baptized,
just as he came up from the water, suddenly the
heavens were opened to him and he saw the Spirit
of God descending like a dove and alighting on
him. 17 And a voice from heaven said, "This is my
Son, the Beloved,^s with whom I am well pleased."

The Temptation of Jesus
(Mk 1.12–13; Lk 4.1–13)

4 Then Jesus was led up by the Spirit into the
wilderness to be tempted by the devil. 2 He
fasted forty days and forty nights, and afterwards he
was famished. 3 The tempter came and said to him,
"If you are the Son of God, command these stones
to become loaves of bread." 4 But he answered, "It
is written,

'One does not live by bread alone,
    but by every word that comes from the
        mouth of God.' "

5 Then the devil took him to the holy city and

Catholic Connections

BAPTISM

John the Baptist was the last great prophet
before Jesus. John may have belonged to a
religious group that initiated new members
through a rite of immersion in water (baptism). The rite used by John symbolized the
moral conversion—through repentance,
confession of sins, and change of heart—
required for receiving God's salvation. Although Jesus was without sin, his willingness
to be baptized is a sign of how fully he embraced his humanity.

Baptism is also one of the seven sacraments that Catholics celebrate. Although
many Catholics are baptized as infants, some
young people and adults, called catechu-
mens, are baptized at the Easter Vigil on
Holy Saturday each year. During the Baptism ritual, the baptized person is marked
with chrism, a special oil. (In the Old Testament, such an oil was used to anoint priests,
prophets, and kings for service.) The person
then has water poured over her or him or is
immersed in water. This is a sign of dying to
sin and rising anew in the presence of God.
The Holy Trinity is called upon, baptizing
her or him in the name of the Father, the
Son, and the Holy Spirit. A candle is given
to the newly baptized person to symbolize
the light of Christ that now burns within her
or him, and a white garment or stole is put
on the person to signify her or his new life
in Christ.

The sacraments of Baptism, Confirmation, and the Eucharist are a person's initiation into the Christian community. They call
Christians to continual conversion in following Jesus.

▶ **Mt 3.13–17**

placed him on the pinnacle of the temple, 6 saying
to him, "If you are the Son of God, throw yourself
down; for it is written,

---

^r Or *in*   ^s Or *my beloved Son*

MT

PRAY IT!

Jesus' Temptations, My Temptations

Command that these stones become loaves of bread." (Mt 4.3)

Jesus, you trusted God to provide your material needs. Help me to avoid placing my priorities on material things.

"Throw yourself down; for it is written, . . .
'you will not dash your foot against a stone.' "

(Verse 6)

Jesus, you resisted using your power for vain and foolish reasons. Help me to resist doing foolish things only to impress others.

"All these I will give you, if you will fall down and worship me." (Verse 9)

Jesus, you refused to cooperate with the devil to achieve status and power. Help me to refuse to cooperate with evil and injustice in achieving my life's goals.

▶ Mt 4.1–11

'He will command his angels
          concerning you,'
     and 'On their hands they will bear
          you up,
     so that you will not dash your foot against a
          stone.' "
7 Jesus said to him, "Again it is written, 'Do not put the Lord your God to the test.' "
8 Again, the devil took him to a very high mountain and showed him all the kingdoms of the world and their splendor; 9 and he said to him, "All these I will give you, if you will fall down and worship me." 10 Jesus said to him, "Away with you, Satan! for it is written,
     'Worship the Lord your God,
          and serve only him.' "
11 Then the devil left him, and suddenly angels came and waited on him.

Jesus Begins His Ministry in Galilee
(Mk 1.14–15; Lk 4.14–15)

12 Now when Jesus[t] heard that John had been arrested, he withdrew to Galilee. 13 He left Nazareth and made his home in Ca·per′na·um by the sea, in the territory of Zeb′u·lun and Naph′ta·li, 14 so that

what had been spoken through the prophet I·sāi′ah might be fulfilled:
15 "Land of Zeb′u·lun, land of Naph′ta·li,
          on the road by the sea, across the Jordan,
               Galilee of the Gentiles—
16 the people who sat in darkness
          have seen a great light,
     and for those who sat in the region and
               shadow of death
          light has dawned."
17 From that time Jesus began to proclaim, "Repent, for the kingdom of heaven has come near."[u]

Jesus Calls the First Disciples
(Mk 1.16–20; Lk 5.1–11)

18 As he walked by the Sea of Galilee, he saw two brothers, Simon, who is called Peter, and Andrew his brother, casting a net into the sea—for they were fishermen. 19 And he said to them, "Follow me, and I will make you fish for people." 20 Immediately they left their nets and followed him. 21 As he went from there, he saw two other brothers, James son of Zeb′e·dee and his brother John, in the boat with their father Zeb′e·dee, mending their nets, and he called them. 22 Immediately they left the boat and their father, and followed him.

Follow Me

As the first disciples chose to follow Jesus, what did they leave behind? Nets, boats, even parents. The very things they depended on for life and security! Knowing what you know of Jesus, what are you ready to "leave behind" in order to follow him and continue his mission?

▶ Mt 4.18–22

Jesus Ministers to Crowds of People
(Mk 1.35–39; Lk 4.44; 6.17–19)

23 Jesus[v] went throughout Galilee, teaching in their synagogues and proclaiming the good news[w] of the kingdom and curing every disease and every sickness among the people. 24 So his fame spread throughout all Syria, and they brought to him all the sick, those who were afflicted with various diseases and pains, demoniacs, epileptics, and paralytics, and he cured them. 25 And great crowds followed him from Galilee, the De·cap′o·lis, Jerusalem, Judea, and from beyond the Jordan.

---

t Gk *he*   u Or *is at hand*   v Gk *He*   w Gk *gospel*

The Sermon on the Mount

5 When Jesus[x] saw the crowds, he went up the mountain; and after he sat down, his disciples came to him. 2 Then he began to speak, and taught them, saying:

The Beatitudes
(Lk 6.20–26)

3 "Blessed are the poor in spirit, for theirs is the kingdom of heaven.

4 "Blessed are those who mourn, for they will be comforted.

5 "Blessed are the meek, for they will inherit the earth.

6 "Blessed are those who hunger and thirst for righteousness, for they will be filled.

7 "Blessed are the merciful, for they will receive mercy.

8 "Blessed are the pure in heart, for they will see God.

9 "Blessed are the peacemakers, for they will be called children of God.

10 "Blessed are those who are persecuted for righteousness' sake, for theirs is the kingdom of heaven.

11 "Blessed are you when people revile you and persecute you and utter all kinds of evil against you falsely[y] on my account. 12 Rejoice and be glad, for your reward is great in heaven, for in the same way they persecuted the prophets who were before you.

Salt and Light
(Mk 9.50; Lk 14.34–35)

13 "You are the salt of the earth; but if salt has lost its taste, how can its saltiness be restored? It is no longer good for anything, but is thrown out and trampled under foot.

14 "You are the light of the world. A city built on a hill cannot be hid. 15 No one after lighting a lamp puts it under the bushel basket, but on the lampstand, and it gives light to all in the house. 16 In the same way, let your light shine before others, so that they may see your good works and give glory to your Father in heaven.

The Law and the Prophets

17 "Do not think that I have come to abolish the law or the prophets; I have come not to abolish but to fulfill. 18 For truly I tell you, until heaven and earth pass away, not one letter,[z] not one stroke of a letter, will pass from the law until all is accomplished. 19 Therefore, whoever breaks[a] one of the least of these commandments, and teaches others to do the same, will be called least in the kingdom of heaven; but whoever does them and teaches them will be called great in the kingdom of heaven. 20 For I tell you, unless your righteousness exceeds that of the scribes and Phar'i•sees, you will never enter the kingdom of heaven.

Concerning Anger
(Lk 12.57–59)

21 "You have heard that it was said to those of ancient times, 'You shall not murder'; and 'whoever murders shall be liable to judgment.' 22 But I say to you that if you are angry with a brother or sister[b] you will be liable to judgment; and if you insult[c] a brother or sister,[d] you will be liable to the council; and if you say, 'You fool,' you will be liable to the hell[e] of fire. 23 So when you are offering your gift at the altar, if you remember that your brother or sister[f] has something against you, 24 leave your gift there before the altar and go; first be reconciled to your brother or sister,[f] and then come and offer

---

[x] Gk *he* [y] Other ancient authorities lack *falsely* [z] Gk *one iota* [a] Or *annuls* [b] Gk *a brother*; other ancient authorities add *without cause* [c] Gk *say Raca to* (an obscure term of abuse) [d] Gk *a brother* [e] Gk *Gehenna* [f] Gk *your brother*

An Upside-Down Kingdom

Read Mt 5.1–12. These familiar words of Jesus, called the Beatitudes, begin what is called the Sermon on the Mount. In chapters 5–7, Jesus speaks about life in a way that startled his listeners. Many thought it was a sign of God's blessing to be rich, powerful, and content. They thought it was justified to respond to violence and oppression with violence and oppression.

Jesus' words continue to challenge us today. Pay attention to these hard words of Jesus. Christianity is not always easy, but it is the only way for all people to live as sons and daughters of God. The challenge for us is to see life more and more the way God does, and then to live that vision!

▶ Mt 5.1–12

MT

your gift. 25 Come to terms quickly with your accuser while you are on the way to court*g* with him, or your accuser may hand you over to the judge, and the judge to the guard, and you will be thrown into prison. 26 Truly I tell you, you will never get out until you have paid the last penny.

Concerning Adultery

27 "You have heard that it was said, 'You shall not commit adultery.' 28 But I say to you that everyone who looks at a woman with lust has already committed adultery with her in his heart. 29 If your right eye causes you to sin, tear it out and throw it away; it is better for you to lose one of your members than for your whole body to be thrown into hell.*h* 30 And if your right hand causes you to sin, cut it off and throw it away; it is better for you to lose one of your members than for your whole body to go into hell.*h*

Concerning Divorce
(Mt 19.9; Mk 10.11–12; Lk 16.18)

31 "It was also said, 'Whoever divorces his wife, let him give her a certificate of divorce.' 32 But I say to you that anyone who divorces his wife, except on the ground of unchastity, causes her to commit adultery; and whoever marries a divorced woman commits adultery.

Concerning Oaths

33 "Again, you have heard that it was said to those of ancient times, 'You shall not swear falsely, but carry out the vows you have made to the Lord.' 34 But I say to you, Do not swear at all, either by heaven, for it is the throne of God, 35 or by the earth, for it is his footstool, or by Jerusalem, for it is the city of the great King. 36 And do not swear by your head, for you cannot make one hair white or black. 37 Let your word be 'Yes, Yes' or 'No, No'; anything more than this comes from the evil one.*i*

Concerning Retaliation
(Lk 6.29–31)

38 "You have heard that it was said, 'An eye for an eye and a tooth for a tooth.' 39 But I say to you, Do not resist an evildoer. But if anyone strikes you on the right cheek, turn the other also; 40 and if anyone wants to sue you and take your coat, give your cloak as well; 41 and if anyone forces you to go one mile, go also the second mile. 42 Give to everyone who begs from you, and do not refuse anyone who wants to borrow from you.

Love for Enemies
(Lk 6.27–28, 32–36)

43 "You have heard that it was said, 'You shall love your neighbor and hate your enemy.' 44 But I

PRAY IT?
Christians and Revenge

For Jesus, one way to love our enemies is to refuse to take revenge on those who have wronged us. Is this really possible to do?

Consider the case of a young woman named Julie Welch who was killed by a terrorist bombing in Oklahoma City. Julie's father worked unceasingly against the death penalty for the man responsible for the bombing. He knew that revenge would not bring his daughter back or make him feel better. He believed that Christians are obligated to always assume that for even the most heinous criminal, reconciliation and remorse are possible. Although his stance was not easy or popular, it illustrates what this passage teaches.

In your prayer, reflect or journal on the following questions:
- Who are your enemies?
- When they or someone else hurts you, what is your usual reaction?
- What is the greatest challenge for you in living out this teaching from Jesus?

▶ Mt 5.38–48

say to you, Love your enemies and pray for those who persecute you, 45 so that you may be children of your Father in heaven; for he makes his sun rise on the evil and on the good, and sends rain on the righteous and on the unrighteous. 46 For if you love those who love you, what reward do you have? Do not even the tax collectors do the same? 47 And if you greet only your brothers and sisters,*j* what more are you doing than others? Do not even the Gentiles do the same? 48 Be perfect, therefore, as your heavenly Father is perfect.

Concerning Almsgiving

6 "Beware of practicing your piety before others in order to be seen by them; for then you have no reward from your Father in heaven.

2 "So whenever you give alms, do not sound a trumpet before you, as the hypocrites do in the synagogues and in the streets, so that they may be

g Gk lacks *to court*   *h* Gk *Gehenna*   *i* Or *evil*
j Gk *your brothers*

praised by others. Truly I tell you, they have received their reward. 3 But when you give alms, do not let your left hand know what your right hand is doing, 4 so that your alms may be done in secret; and your Father who sees in secret will reward you.*k*

Concerning Prayer
(Lk 11.2–4)

5 "And whenever you pray, do not be like the hypocrites; for they love to stand and pray in the synagogues and at the street corners, so that they may be seen by others. Truly I tell you, they have received their reward. 6 But whenever you pray, go into your room and shut the door and pray to your Father who is in secret; and your Father who sees in secret will reward you.*k*

7 "When you are praying, do not heap up empty phrases as the Gentiles do; for they think that they will be heard because of their many words.

PRAY IT!
Ash Wednesday

Matthew 6.1–18 is read on Ash Wednesday, the beginning of Lent. Lent is traditionally a forty-day period to examine and renew our spiritual life. It is a time of prayer, service, and fasting. The forty days recall the forty years that the people of Israel wandered in the wilderness before arriving at the Promised Land and the forty days that Jesus spent in the wilderness after being baptized.

On Ash Wednesday, we receive ashes that remind us of our nature as created beings (Gen 3.19). This practice echoes the Old Testament tradition of wearing ashes as a sign of anguish and repentance (Jdt 4.11). As the ash cross is made on our forehead, we hear words that echo John the Baptist's call to conversion, "Turn away from sin and be faithful to the gospel" (*Sacramentary*, p. 77). We respond "Amen," meaning "So be it."

When Lent begins again, how will you use the forty days to strengthen your spiritual life? Make a special commitment and ask God for the grace to grow from it.

▶ Mt 6.1–18

8 Do not be like them, for your Father knows what you need before you ask him.

9 "Pray then in this way:
Our Father in heaven,
    hallowed be your name.
10   Your kingdom come.
    Your will be done,
        on earth as it is in heaven.
11   Give us this day our daily bread.*l*
12   And forgive us our debts,
        as we also have forgiven our debtors.
13   And do not bring us to the time of trial,*m*
        but rescue us from the evil one.*n*

14 For if you forgive others their trespasses, your heavenly Father will also forgive you; 15 but if you do not forgive others, neither will your Father forgive your trespasses.

Concerning Fasting

16 "And whenever you fast, do not look dismal, like the hypocrites, for they disfigure their faces so as to show others that they are fasting. Truly I tell you, they have received their reward. 17 But when you fast, put oil on your head and wash your face, 18 so that your fasting may be seen not by others but by your Father who is in secret; and your Father who sees in secret will reward you.*k*

Concerning Treasures
(Lk 12.33–34)

19 "Do not store up for yourselves treasures on earth, where moth and rust*o* consume and where thieves break in and steal; 20 but store up for yourselves treasures in heaven, where neither moth nor rust*o* consumes and where thieves do not break in and steal. 21 For where your treasure is, there your heart will be also.

The Sound Eye
(Lk 11.34–36)

22 "The eye is the lamp of the body. So, if your eye is healthy, your whole body will be full of light; 23 but if your eye is unhealthy, your whole body will be full of darkness. If then the light in you is darkness, how great is the darkness!

Serving Two Masters

24 "No one can serve two masters; for a slave will either hate the one and love the other, or be devoted to the one and despise the other. You cannot serve God and wealth.*p*

---

k Other ancient authorities add *openly*   *l* Or *our bread for tomorrow*   *m* Or *us into temptation*   *n* Or *from evil*. Other ancient authorities add, in some form, *For the kingdom and the power and the glory are yours forever. Amen.*   *o* Gk *eating*   *p* Gk *mammon*

PRAY IT!
A Lord's Prayer Reflection

In Matthew, Jesus teaches his followers the Lord's Prayer as an alternative to hypocritical and empty prayer. Most of us have memorized the Lord's Prayer. But although we know it by heart, we do not always pray it from the heart. It can easily become "empty phrases" (6.7). Let this reflection help you to pray the Lord's Prayer thoughtfully:

Our Father in heaven,
   hallowed be your name.
                              (Verse 9)

How do I honor God as creator of all things? How do I honor God in my thoughts, my words, and my actions?

Your kingdom come.
Your will be done,
   on earth as it is in heaven.
                              (Verse 10)

How does my life reflect God's reign of love, justice, and peace? Am I putting too much emphasis on the material things I have?

Give us this day our daily bread.
                              (Verse 11)

Can I trust God to provide for my daily physical, emotional, and spiritual needs?

And forgive us our debts,
   as we also have forgiven our debtors.
                              (Verse 12)

When I have sinned, do I admit my wrong, ask God's forgiveness, and start anew? When people have wronged me, do I hold a grudge? Am I able to forgive them as God forgives me?

And do not bring us to the time of trial,
   but rescue us from the evil one.
                              (Verse 13)

What are the temptations I face in life? How do I rely on God for the strength to resist them?

▶ Mt 6.5–15

Do Not Worry
(Lk 12.22–31)

25 "Therefore I tell you, do not worry about your life, what you will eat or what you will drink,[q] or about your body, what you will wear. Is not life more than food, and the body more than clothing? 26 Look at the birds of the air; they neither sow nor reap nor gather into barns, and yet your heavenly Father feeds them. Are you not of more value than they? 27 And can any of you by worrying add a single hour to your span of life?[r] 28 And why do you worry about clothing? Consider the lilies of the field, how they grow; they neither toil nor spin, 29 yet I tell you, even Solomon in all his glory was not clothed like one of these. 30 But if God so clothes the grass of the field, which is alive today and tomorrow is thrown into the oven, will he not much more clothe you—you of little faith? 31 Therefore do not worry, saying, 'What will we eat?' or 'What will we drink?' or 'What will we wear?' 32 For it is the Gentiles who strive for all these things; and indeed your heavenly Father knows that you need all these things. 33 But strive first for the kingdom of God[s] and his[t] righteousness, and all these things will be given to you as well.

34 "So do not worry about tomorrow, for tomorrow will bring worries of its own. Today's trouble is enough for today.

Judging Others
(Lk 6.37–42)

7 "Do not judge, so that you may not be judged. 2 For with the judgment you make you will be judged, and the measure you give will be the measure you get. 3 Why do you see the speck in your neighbor's[u] eye, but do not notice the log in your own eye? 4 Or how can you say to your neighbor,[v] Let me take the speck out of your eye,' while the log is in your own eye? 5 You hypocrite, first take the log out of your own eye, and then you will see clearly to take the speck out of your neighbor's[u] eye.

Profaning the Holy

6 "Do not give what is holy to dogs; and do not throw your pearls before swine, or they will trample them under foot and turn and maul you.

Ask, Search, Knock
(Lk 11.9–13)

7 "Ask, and it will be given you; search, and you will find; knock, and the door will be opened for you. 8 For everyone who asks receives, and every-

---

q Other ancient authorities lack *or what you will drink*   r Or *add one cubit to your height*   s Other ancient authorities lack *of God*   t Or *its*   u Gk *brother's*   v Gk *brother* one who searches finds, and for everyone who knocks, the door will be opened. 9 Is there anyone among you who, if your child asks for bread, will give a stone? 10 Or if the child asks for a fish, will give a snake? 11 If you then, who are evil, know how to give good gifts to your children, how much more will your Father in heaven give good things to those who ask him!

The Golden Rule
(Lk 6.31)

12 "In everything do to others as you would have them do to you; for this is the law and the prophets.

The Narrow Gate
(Lk 13.24)

13 "Enter through the narrow gate; for the gate is wide and the road is easy*w* that leads to destruction, and there are many who take it. 14 For the gate is narrow and the road is hard that leads to life, and there are few who find it.

A Tree and Its Fruit
(Mt 12.33; Lk 6.43–45)

15 "Beware of false prophets, who come to you in sheep's clothing but inwardly are ravenous wolves. 16 You will know them by their fruits. Are grapes gathered from thorns, or figs from thistles? 17 In the same way, every good tree bears good fruit, but the bad tree bears bad fruit. 18 A good tree cannot bear bad fruit, nor can a bad tree bear good fruit. 19 Every tree that does not bear good fruit is cut down and thrown into the fire. 20 Thus you will know them by their fruits.

Concerning Self-Deception
(Lk 6.46; 13.26–27)

21 "Not everyone who says to me, 'Lord, Lord,' will enter the kingdom of heaven, but only the one who does the will of my Father in heaven. 22 On that day many will say to me, 'Lord, Lord, did we not prophesy in your name, and cast out demons in your name, and do many deeds of power in your name?' 23 Then I will declare to them, 'I never knew you; go away from me, you evildoers.'

Hearers and Doers
(Lk 6.47–49)

24 "Everyone then who hears these words of mine and acts on them will be like a wise man who built his house on rock. 25 The rain fell, the floods came, and the winds blew and beat on that house, but it did not fall, because it had been founded on rock. 26 And everyone who hears these words of mine and does not act on them will be like a foolish man who built his house on sand. 27 The rain fell, and the floods came, and the winds blew and

PRAY IT!
The Gospel Call to Conversion

In closing the Sermon on the Mount, Jesus calls people to conversion. It is not enough to talk the talk; you must also walk the walk. To make present the Reign of God, Jesus teaches the following:

- **Rich people need to share their wealth with poor people.**
- **Powerful people need to serve those without power.**
- **Priests need to serve all people without prejudice.**
- **Politicians need to govern with justice, taking into account the needs of people, especially people in want.**
- **Wise people need to express their knowledge in ways everyone can understand.**
- **Pharisees need to leave their hypocrisy behind and remove the weight of the Law through which they oppressed the people.**

In your prayer, reflect or journal on the following questions:

- **In the above list, what are some of the most needed areas of conversion in society today? in your local community? in your life?**
- **List some concrete ways you can make those conversions real.**

▶ **Mt 7.21–27**

beat against that house, and it fell—and great was its fall!"

28 Now when Jesus had finished saying these things, the crowds were astounded at his teaching, 29 for he taught them as one having authority, and not as their scribes.

Jesus Cleanses a Leper
(Mk 1.40–45; Lk 5.12–16)

8 When Jesus*x* had come down from the mountain, great crowds followed him; 2 and there was a leper*y* who came to him and knelt before

---

w Other ancient authorities read *for the road is wide and easy*
x Gk *he*   *y* The terms *leper* and *leprosy* can refer to several diseases

him, saying, "Lord, if you choose, you can make me clean." 3 He stretched out his hand and touched him, saying, "I do choose. Be made clean!" Immediately his leprosy[z] was cleansed. 4 Then Jesus said to him, "See that you say nothing to anyone; but go, show yourself to the priest, and offer the gift that Moses commanded, as a testimony to them."

Jesus Heals a Centurion's Servant
(Lk 7.1–10)

5 When he entered Ca·per'na·um, a centurion came to him, appealing to him 6 and saying, "Lord, my servant is lying at home paralyzed, in terrible distress." 7 And he said to him, "I will come and cure him." 8 The centurion answered, "Lord, I am not worthy to have you come under my roof; but only speak the word, and my servant will be healed. 9 For I also am a man under authority, with soldiers under me; and I say to one, 'Go,' and he goes, and to another, 'Come,' and he comes, and to my slave, 'Do this,' and the slave does it." 10 When Jesus heard him, he was amazed and said to those who followed him, "Truly I tell you, in no one[a] in Israel have I found such faith. 11 I tell you, many will come from east and west and will eat with Abraham and Isaac and Jacob in the kingdom of heaven, 12 while the heirs of the kingdom will be thrown into the outer darkness, where there will be weeping and gnashing of teeth." 13 And to the centurion Jesus said, "Go; let it be done for you according to your faith." And the servant was healed in that hour.

Jesus Heals Many at Peter's House
(Mk 1.29–34; Lk 4.38–41)

14 When Jesus entered Peter's house, he saw his mother-in-law lying in bed with a fever; 15 he touched her hand, and the fever left her, and she got up and began to serve him. 16 That evening they brought to him many who were possessed with demons; and he cast out the spirits with a word, and cured all who were sick. 17 This was to fulfill what had been spoken through the prophet I·sai'ah, "He took our infirmities and bore our diseases."

Would-Be Followers of Jesus
(Lk 9.57–62)

18 Now when Jesus saw great crowds around him, he gave orders to go over to the other side. 19 A scribe then approached and said, "Teacher, I will follow you wherever you go." 20 And Jesus said to him, "Foxes have holes, and birds of the air have nests; but the Son of Man has nowhere to lay his head." 21 Another of his disciples said to him, "Lord, first let me go and bury my father." 22 But Jesus said to him, "Follow me, and let the dead bury their own dead."

Jesus Stills the Storm
(Mk 4.35–41; Lk 8.22–25)

23 And when he got into the boat, his disciples followed him. 24 A windstorm arose on the sea, so great that the boat was being swamped by the waves; but he was asleep. 25 And they went and woke him up, saying, "Lord, save us! We are perishing!" 26 And he said to them, "Why are you afraid, you of little faith?" Then he got up and rebuked the winds and the sea; and there was a dead calm. 27 They were amazed, saying, "What sort of man is this, that even the winds and the sea obey him?"

Jesus Heals the Gadarene Demoniacs
(Mk 5.1–20; Lk 8.26–39)

28 When he came to the other side, to the country of the Gad'a·renes,[b] two demoniacs coming out of the tombs met him. They were so fierce that no one could pass that way. 29 Suddenly they shouted, "What have you to do with us, Son of God? Have you come here to torment us before the time?" 30 Now a large herd of swine was feeding at some distance from them. 31 The demons begged him, "If

---

z The terms *leper* and *leprosy* can refer to several diseases
a Other ancient authorities read *Truly I tell you, not even*
b Other ancient authorities read *Gergesenes*; others, *Gerasenes*.

LORD, I AM NOT WORTHY

Those words of the centurion are similar to the ones Catholics say at Mass just before receiving the body and blood of Christ. We say these words not to emphasize our sinfulness but in humble recognition of God's awesome gift of Jesus, whom we are about to receive in the bread and wine of the Eucharist. The next time you receive the Eucharist, think about these words and pray for the faith it takes to believe in what you are saying.

▶ Mt 8.8

MT

you cast us out, send us into the herd of swine."
32 And he said to them, "Go!" So they came out and
entered the swine; and suddenly, the whole herd
rushed down the steep bank into the sea and perished in the water. 33 The swineherds ran off, and
on going into the town, they told the whole story
about what had happened to the demoniacs.
34 Then the whole town came out to meet Jesus;
and when they saw him, they begged him to leave
their neighborhood. 1 And after getting into a
boat he crossed the sea and came to his own
town.

9

Jesus Heals a Paralytic
(Mk 2.1–12; Lk 5.17–26)

2 And just then some people were carrying a
paralyzed man lying on a bed. When Jesus saw their
faith, he said to the paralytic, "Take heart, son; your
sins are forgiven." 3 Then some of the scribes said to
themselves, "This man is blaspheming." 4 But Jesus,
perceiving their thoughts, said, "Why do you think
evil in your hearts? 5 For which is easier, to say,
'Your sins are forgiven,' or to say, 'Stand up and
walk'? 6 But so that you may know that the Son of
Man has authority on earth to forgive sins"—he
then said to the paralytic—"Stand up, take your bed
and go to your home." 7 And he stood up and went
to his home. 8 When the crowds saw it, they were
filled with awe, and they glorified God, who had
given such authority to human beings.

The Call of Matthew
(Mk 2.13–17; Lk 5.27–32)

9 As Jesus was walking along, he saw a man
called Matthew sitting at the tax booth; and he said
to him, "Follow me." And he got up and followed
him.

10 And as he sat at dinner[c] in the house, many
tax collectors and sinners came and were sitting[d]
with him and his disciples. 11 When the Phar'i·sees
saw this, they said to his disciples, "Why does your
teacher eat with tax collectors and sinners?" 12 But
when he heard this, he said, "Those who are well
have no need of a physician, but those who are sick.
13 Go and learn what this means, 'I desire mercy,
not sacrifice.' For I have come to call not the righteous but sinners."

The Question about Fasting
(Mk 2.18–22; Lk 5.33–39)

14 Then the disciples of John came to him, saying, "Why do we and the Phar'i·sees fast often,[e] but
your disciples do not fast?" 15 And Jesus said to
them, "The wedding guests cannot mourn as long
as the bridegroom is with them, can they? The days
will come when the bridegroom is taken away from
them, and then they will fast. 16 No one sews a

piece of unshrunk cloth on an old cloak, for the
patch pulls away from the cloak, and a worse
tear is made. 17 Neither is new wine put into old

---

c Gk *reclined*   d Gk *were reclining*   e Other ancient
authorities lack *often*

did you KNOW?

Miracles and the Reign of God

Matthew, chapters 8–9, describes ten miracles of Jesus intended as signs of the
coming of the Reign of God. Most of Jesus'
miracles are healings, but some also show
his power over demons and nature. The
Gospel of Mark records the most miracles, twenty-one, and the Gospel of John,
the least, eight.

People today tend to view reports of
miracles with suspicion. That's because
our scientific mind wants to believe everything has a rational explanation. Because
of this, we miss the point. People in Jesus'
time were more concerned about what
the miracle revealed than in the miracle
itself or even the miracle worker. Other
people besides Jesus were known to perform miracles. In fact, Jesus' healing miracles were not taken as proof of his divinity
(although this seemed to be the purpose
of his nature miracles).

In curing people of their illnesses and
driving out demons, Jesus was revealing
that the Reign of God is a place where
suffering and evil are banished. By curing sinners, women, and foreigners, he
showed that the Reign of God is also open
to all, especially outcasts.

Miracles—then and now—point to
God. Whether they are easily explained
or beyond reasonable explanation does
not matter. What matters is that they
make us aware of God's loving presence in
our life. If we look at the events in our life
and ask: "What do they point to? What
do they tell us about God's presence in
the world?" we might find ourselves utterly surrounded by miracles.

▶ Mt 8.1—9.34

MT

PRAY IT!

Spiritual Paralysis

Jesus, healer, like the man you healed spiritually and physically, I too have experienced paralysis. Not a physical paralysis, but a spiritual paralysis that keeps me from walking with you.

This paralysis happens at times in school and in my neighborhood when I know what the right thing to do is, but I am afraid to do it. I see someone discriminating against or abusing another person, but I stand by and do nothing. By my silence, I give my approval, but I am afraid to risk ridicule and rejection.

Forgive me of my sin of silence, Lord. Help me to overcome my fears so that I can stand up for what is right. Heal me of my spiritual paralysis so that I may walk with you. Amen.

▶ Mt 9.1–8

wineskins; otherwise, the skins burst, and the wine is spilled, and the skins are destroyed; but new wine is put into fresh wineskins, and so both are preserved."

A Girl Restored to Life and a Woman Healed
(Mk 5.21–43; Lk 8.40–56)

18 While he was saying these things to them, suddenly a leader of the synagogue*f* came in and knelt before him, saying, "My daughter has just died; but come and lay your hand on her, and she will live." 19 And Jesus got up and followed him, with his disciples. 20 Then suddenly a woman who had been suffering from hemorrhages for twelve years came up behind him and touched the fringe of his cloak, 21 for she said to herself, "If I only touch his cloak, I will be made well." 22 Jesus turned, and seeing her he said, "Take heart, daughter; your faith has made you well." And instantly the woman was made well. 23 When Jesus came to the leader's house and saw the flute players and the crowd making a commotion, 24 he said, "Go away; for the girl is not dead but sleeping." And they laughed at him. 25 But when the crowd had been put outside, he went in and took her by the hand, and the girl got up. 26 And the report of this spread throughout that district.

Jesus Heals Two Blind Men

27 As Jesus went on from there, two blind men followed him, crying loudly, "Have mercy on us, Son of David!" 28 When he entered the house, the blind men came to him; and Jesus said to them, "Do you believe that I am able to do this?" They said to him, "Yes, Lord." 29 Then he touched their eyes and said, "According to your faith let it be done to you." 30 And their eyes were opened. Then Jesus sternly ordered them, "See that no one knows of this." 31 But they went away and spread the news about him throughout that district.

Jesus Heals One Who Was Mute

32 After they had gone away, a demoniac who was mute was brought to him. 33 And when the demon had been cast out, the one who had been mute spoke; and the crowds were amazed and said, "Never has anything like this been seen in Israel." 34 But the Phar′i·sees said, "By the ruler of the demons he casts out the demons."*g*

The Harvest Is Great, the Laborers Few
(Lk 10.2–3)

35 Then Jesus went about all the cities and villages, teaching in their synagogues, and proclaiming the good news of the kingdom, and curing every disease and every sickness. 36 When he saw the crowds, he had compassion for them, because they were harassed and helpless, like sheep without a shepherd. 37 Then he said to his disciples, "The harvest is plentiful, but the laborers are few; 38 therefore ask the Lord of the harvest to send out laborers into his harvest."

---

f Gk lacks *of the synagogue*   *g* Other ancient authorities lack this verse

9.25

The Twelve Apostles
(Mk 3.13–19a; Lk 6.12–16)

10 Then Jesus[h] summoned his twelve disciples and gave them authority over unclean spirits, to cast them out, and to cure every disease and every sickness. 2 These are the names of the twelve apostles: first, Simon, also known as Peter, and his brother Andrew; James son of Zeb'e·dee, and his brother John; 3 Philip and Bartholomew; Thomas and Matthew the tax collector; James son of Al·phae'us, and Thad·dae'us;[i] 4 Simon the Ca·na·nae'an, and Judas Is·car'i·ot, the one who betrayed him.

The Mission of the Twelve
(Mk 6.6b–13; Lk 9.1–6)

5 These twelve Jesus sent out with the following instructions: "Go nowhere among the Gentiles, and enter no town of the Sa·mar'i·tans, 6 but go rather to the lost sheep of the house of Israel. 7 As you go, proclaim the good news, 'The kingdom of heaven has come near.'[j] 8 Cure the sick, raise the dead, cleanse the lepers,[k] cast out demons. You received without payment; give without payment. 9 Take no gold, or silver, or copper in your belts, 10 no bag for your journey, or two tunics, or sandals, or a staff; for laborers deserve their food. 11 Whatever town or village you enter, find out who in it is worthy, and stay there until you leave. 12 As you enter the house, greet it. 13 If the house is worthy, let your peace come upon it; but if it is not worthy, let your peace return to you. 14 If anyone will not welcome you or listen to your words, shake off the dust from your feet as you leave that house or town. 15 Truly I tell you, it will be more tolerable for the land of Sod'om and Go·mor'rah on the day of judgment than for that town.

Coming Persecutions
(Mk 13.9–13; Lk 21.12–17)

16 "See, I am sending you out like sheep into the midst of wolves; so be wise as serpents and innocent as doves. 17 Beware of them, for they will hand you over to councils and flog you in their synagogues; 18 and you will be dragged before governors and kings because of me, as a testimony to them and the Gentiles. 19 When they hand you over, do not worry about how you are to speak or what you are to say; for what you are to say will be given to you at that time; 20 for it is not you who speak, but the Spirit of your Father speaking through you. 21 Brother will betray brother to death, and a father his child, and children will rise against parents and have them put to death; 22 and you will be hated by all because of my name. But the one who endures to the end will be saved. 23 When they persecute you in one town, flee to the next; for truly I tell you, you will not have gone through all the towns of Israel before the Son of Man comes.

24 "A disciple is not above the teacher, nor a slave above the master; 25 it is enough for the disciple to be like the teacher, and the slave like the master. If they have called the master of the house Be·el'ze·bul, how much more will they malign those of his household!

Whom to Fear
(Lk 12.2–7)

26 "So have no fear of them; for nothing is covered up that will not be uncovered, and nothing secret that will not become known. 27 What I say to you in the dark, tell in the light; and what you hear whispered, proclaim from the housetops. 28 Do not fear those who kill the body but cannot kill the soul; rather fear him who can destroy both soul and body in hell.[l] 29 Are not two sparrows sold for a penny? Yet not one of them will fall to the ground apart from your Father. 30 And even the hairs of your head are all counted. 31 So do not be afraid; you are of more value than many sparrows.

32 "Everyone therefore who acknowledges me before others, I also will acknowledge before my Father in heaven; 33 but whoever denies me before others, I also will deny before my Father in heaven.

Not Peace, but a Sword
(Lk 12.51–53; 14.26–27)

34 "Do not think that I have come to bring peace to the earth; I have not come to bring peace, but a sword.
35 For I have come to set a man against his father,
and a daughter against her mother,
and a daughter-in-law against her
mother-in-law;
36 and one's foes will be members of one's own household.

37 Whoever loves father or mother more than me is not worthy of me; and whoever loves son or daughter more than me is not worthy of me; 38 and whoever does not take up the cross and follow me is not worthy of me. 39 Those who find their life will lose it, and those who lose their life for my sake will find it.

Rewards
(Mk 9.41)

40 "Whoever welcomes you welcomes me, and whoever welcomes me welcomes the one who sent me. 41 Whoever welcomes a prophet in the name of

---

h Gk *he* i Other ancient authorities read *Lebbaeus*, or *Lebbaeus called Thaddaeus* j Or *is at hand* k The terms *leper* and *leprosy* can refer to several diseases l Gk *Gehenna*

A Violent Jesus?

Jesus says a curious thing as he prepares the Twelve for their mission, "I have not come to bring peace, but a sword" (Mt 10.34). This is one of the many hard sayings attributed to Jesus in the Gospels. Jesus is speaking metaphorically to emphasize the extreme demands of discipleship. He is not advocating violence but simply predicting how people will react to the new values and way of life of his followers. The author of Matthew lived in a community that knew living as Jesus' disciples is not always simple or easy. The people wished for peace, but living by Jesus' words brought them hatred and conflict with people in power. At the time Matthew was written, Christians needed to be able to give up everything, including family attachments, in order to follow Jesus. Is it any different today? Are you up to the challenge?

▶ Mt 10.34–39

a prophet will receive a prophet's reward; and whoever welcomes a righteous person in the name of a righteous person will receive the reward of the righteous; 42 and whoever gives even a cup of cold water to one of these little ones in the name of a disciple—truly I tell you, none of these will lose their reward."

11 Now when Jesus had finished instructing his twelve disciples, he went on from there to teach and proclaim his message in their cities.

Messengers from John the Baptist
(Lk 7.18–23)

2 When John heard in prison what the Messiah[m] was doing, he sent word by his[n] disciples 3 and said to him, "Are you the one who is to come, or are we to wait for another?" 4 Jesus answered them, "Go and tell John what you hear and see: 5 the blind receive their sight, the lame walk, the lepers[o] are cleansed, the deaf hear, the dead are raised, and the poor have good news brought to them. 6 And blessed is anyone who takes no offense at me."

Jesus Praises John the Baptist
(Lk 7.24–35)

7 As they went away, Jesus began to speak to the crowds about John: "What did you go out into the wilderness to look at? A reed shaken by the wind? 8 What then did you go out to see? Someone[p] dressed in soft robes? Look, those who wear soft robes are in royal palaces. 9 What then did you go out to see? A prophet?[q] Yes, I tell you, and more than a prophet. 10 This is the one about whom it is written,

'See, I am sending my messenger ahead of you,
who will prepare your way before you.'

11 Truly I tell you, among those born of women no one has arisen greater than John the Baptist; yet the least in the kingdom of heaven is greater than he. 12 From the days of John the Baptist until now the kingdom of heaven has suffered violence,[r] and the violent take it by force. 13 For all the prophets and the law prophesied until John came; 14 and if you are willing to accept it, he is E·li'jah who is to come. 15 Let anyone with ears[s] listen!

16 "But to what will I compare this generation? It is like children sitting in the marketplaces and calling to one another,

17 'We played the flute for you, and you did not
dance;
we wailed, and you did not mourn.'

18 For John came neither eating nor drinking, and they say, 'He has a demon'; 19 the Son of Man came eating and drinking, and they say, 'Look, a glutton and a drunkard, a friend of tax collectors and sinners!' Yet wisdom is vindicated by her deeds."[t]

Woes to Unrepentant Cities
(Gen 19.12–14; Lk 10.13–15)

20 Then he began to reproach the cities in which most of his deeds of power had been done, because they did not repent. 21 "Woe to you, Chō·ra'zin! Woe to you, Beth·sā'i·da! For if the deeds of power done in you had been done in Tyre and Si'don, they would have repented long ago in sackcloth and ashes. 22 But I tell you, on the day of judgment it will be more tolerable for Tyre and Si'don than for you. 23 And you, Ca·per'na·um,

m Or the Christ   n Other ancient authorities read two of his   o The terms leper and leprosy can refer to several diseases   p Or Why then did you go out? To see someone   q Other ancient authorities read Why then did you go out? To see a prophet?   r Or has been coming violently   s Other ancient authorities add to hear   t Other ancient authorities read children will you be exalted to heaven?

No, you will be brought down to Hades. For if the deeds of power done in you had been done in Sod′om, it would have remained until this day. 24 But I tell you that on the day of judgment it will be more tolerable for the land of Sod′om than for you."

Jesus Thanks His Father
(Lk 10.21–22)

25 At that time Jesus said, "I thank[u] you, Father, Lord of heaven and earth, because you have hidden these things from the wise and the intelligent and have revealed them to infants; 26 yes, Father, for such was your gracious will.[v] 27 All things have been handed over to me by my Father; and no one knows the Son except the Father, and no one knows the Father except the Son and anyone to whom the Son chooses to reveal him.

28 "Come to me, all you that are weary and are carrying heavy burdens, and I will give you rest. 29 Take my yoke upon you, and learn from me; for I am gentle and humble in heart, and you will find rest for your souls. 30 For my yoke is easy, and my burden is light."

Plucking Grain on the Sabbath
(Mk 2.23–28; Lk 6.1–5)

12 At that time Jesus went through the grainfields on the sabbath; his disciples were hungry, and they began to pluck heads of grain and to eat. 2 When the Phar′i•sees saw it, they said to him, "Look, your disciples are doing what is not lawful to do on the sabbath." 3 He said to them, "Have you not read what David did when he and his companions were hungry? 4 He entered the house of God and ate the bread of the Presence, which it was not lawful for him or his companions to eat, but only for the priests. 5 Or have you not read in the law that on the sabbath the priests in the temple break the sabbath and yet are guiltless? 6 I tell you, something greater than the temple is here. 7 But if you had known what this means, 'I desire mercy and not sacrifice,' you would not have condemned the guiltless. 8 For the Son of Man is lord of the sabbath."

The Man with a Withered Hand
(Mk 3.1–6; Lk 6.6–11)

9 He left that place and entered their synagogue; 10 a man was there with a withered hand, and they asked him, "Is it lawful to cure on the sabbath?" so that they might accuse him. 11 He said to them, "Suppose one of you has only one sheep and it falls into a pit on the sabbath; will you not lay hold of it and lift it out? 12 How much more valuable is a human being than a sheep! So it is lawful

to do good on the sabbath." 13 Then he said to the man, "Stretch out your hand." He stretched it out, and it was restored, as sound as the other. 14 But the Phar′i•sees went out and conspired against him, how to destroy him.

God's Chosen Servant

15 When Jesus became aware of this, he departed. Many crowds[w] followed him, and he cured all of them, 16 and he ordered them not to make him known. 17 This was to fulfill what had been spoken through the prophet Ī•sāi′ah:

18 "Here is my servant, whom I have chosen,
    my beloved, with whom my soul is well
        pleased.
I will put my Spirit upon him,
    and he will proclaim justice to the Gentiles.
19 He will not wrangle or cry aloud,
    nor will anyone hear his voice in the streets.
20 He will not break a bruised reed
    or quench a smoldering wick
until he brings justice to victory.
21   And in his name the Gentiles will hope."

Jesus and Beelzebul
(Mk 3.19b–30; Lk 11.14–23)

22 Then they brought to him a demoniac who was blind and mute; and he cured him, so that the one who had been mute could speak and see. 23 All the crowds were amazed and said, "Can this be the Son of David?" 24 But when the Phar′i•sees heard it, they said, "It is only by Bē•el′ze•bul, the ruler of the demons, that this fellow casts out the demons." 25 He knew what they were thinking and said to them, "Every kingdom divided against itself is laid waste, and no city or house divided against itself will stand. 26 If Satan casts out Satan, he is divided against himself; how then will his kingdom stand? 27 If I cast out demons by Bē•el′ze•bul, by whom do your own exorcists[x] cast them out? Therefore they will be your judges. 28 But if it is by the Spirit of God that I cast out demons, then the kingdom of God has come to you. 29 Or how can one enter a strong man's house and plunder his property, without first tying up the strong man? Then indeed the house can be plundered. 30 Whoever is not with me is against me, and whoever does not gather with me scatters. 31 Therefore I tell you, people will be forgiven for every sin and blasphemy, but blasphemy against the Spirit will not be forgiven. 32 Whoever speaks a word against the Son of Man will be forgiven, but whoever speaks against the Holy Spirit will not be forgiven, either in this age or in the age to come.

---

u Or *praise*   v Or *for so it was well-pleasing in your sight*
w Other ancient authorities lack *crowds*   x Gk *sons*

A Tree and Its Fruit
(Mt 7.15–20)

33 "Either make the tree good, and its fruit good; or make the tree bad, and its fruit bad; for the tree is known by its fruit. 34 You brood of vipers! How can you speak good things, when you are evil? For out of the abundance of the heart the mouth speaks. 35 The good person brings good things out of a good treasure, and the evil person brings evil things out of an evil treasure. 36 I tell you, on the day of judgment you will have to give an account for every careless word you utter; 37 for by your words you will be justified, and by your words you will be condemned."

PRAY IT?
Tripping Over My Tongue

Watch what you say! Jesus is telling us that our words will ultimately reveal the intentions of our heart—just as a tree's fruit reveals whether the tree is good or bad. So let us tend to our heart as a gardener tends the trees in an orchard.

God, help me tend to the goodness of my heart. Let my words reflect my heart's goodness in building other people up—not tearing them down. Let me be careful in choosing my words so that they serve only to honor you. Amen.

▶ Mt 12.33–37

The Sign of Jonah
(Lk 11.29–32)

38 Then some of the scribes and Phar'i·sees said to him, "Teacher, we wish to see a sign from you." 39 But he answered them, "An evil and adulterous generation asks for a sign, but no sign will be given to it except the sign of the prophet Jonah. 40 For just as Jonah was three days and three nights in the belly of the sea monster, so for three days and three nights the Son of Man will be in the heart of the earth. 41 The people of Nin'e·veh will rise up at the judgment with this generation and condemn it, because they repented at the proclamation of Jonah, and see, something greater than Jonah is here! 42 The queen of the South will rise up at the judgment with this generation and condemn it, because she came from the ends of the earth to listen to the wisdom of Solomon, and see, something greater than Solomon is here!

The Return of the Unclean Spirit
(Lk 11.24–26)

43 "When the unclean spirit has gone out of a person, it wanders through waterless regions looking for a resting place, but it finds none. 44 Then it says, 'I will return to my house from which I came.' When it comes, it finds it empty, swept, and put in order. 45 Then it goes and brings along seven other spirits more evil than itself, and they enter and live there; and the last state of that person is worse than the first. So will it be also with this evil generation."

The True Kindred of Jesus
(Mk 3.31–35; Lk 8.19–21)

46 While he was still speaking to the crowds, his mother and his brothers were standing outside, wanting to speak to him. 47 Someone told him, "Look, your mother and your brothers are standing outside, wanting to speak to you."*y* 48 But to the one who had told him this, Jesus*z* replied, "Who is my mother, and who are my brothers?" 49 And pointing to his disciples, he said, "Here are my mother and my brothers! 50 For whoever does the will of my Father in heaven is my brother and sister and mother."

The Parable of the Sower
(Mk 4.1–9, 13–20; Lk 8.4–8, 11–15)

13 That same day Jesus went out of the house and sat beside the sea. 2 Such great crowds gathered around him that he got into a boat and sat there, while the whole crowd stood on the beach. 3 And he told them many things in parables, saying: "Listen! A sower went out to sow. 4 And as he sowed, some seeds fell on the path, and the birds came and ate them up. 5 Other seeds fell on rocky ground, where they did not have much soil, and they sprang up quickly, since they had no depth of soil. 6 But when the sun rose, they were scorched; and since they had no root, they withered away. 7 Other seeds fell among thorns, and the thorns grew up and choked them. 8 Other seeds fell on good soil and brought forth grain, some a hundredfold, some sixty, some thirty. 9 Let anyone with ears*a* listen!"

The Purpose of the Parables
(Mk 4.10–12; Lk 8.9–10)

10 Then the disciples came and asked him, "Why do you speak to them in parables?" 11 He answered, "To you it has been given to know the

---

y Other ancient authorities lack verse 47   *z* Gk *he*
a Other ancient authorities add *to hear*

secrets[b] of the kingdom of heaven, but to them it has not been given. 12 For to those who have, more will be given, and they will have an abundance; but from those who have nothing, even what they have will be taken away. 13 The reason I speak to them in parables is that 'seeing they do not perceive, and hearing they do not listen, nor do they understand.' 14 With them indeed is fulfilled the prophecy of I·sāi'ah that says:

'You will indeed listen, but never understand,
    and you will indeed look, but never
        perceive.
15 For this people's heart has grown dull,
    and their ears are hard of hearing,
        and they have shut their eyes;
        so that they might not look with their
           eyes,
    and listen with their ears,
and understand with their heart and turn—
    and I would heal them.'

did you KNOW?

Parables

The Gospels frequently describe Jesus teaching in parables. A parable is a literary form that uses a fictional story to make a point.

Many of Jesus' parables are like riddles. They have surprising or shocking endings designed to tease the people of his time into examining certain beliefs they took for granted. Unfortunately, the surprise of Jesus' parables is hard for some of us to understand today because we may be unfamiliar with the examples he used: baking bread, planting crops, herding sheep, or fishing for our supper.

Jesus also used parables to teach about God's Reign. These were often in the form of analogies comparing God's Reign to common things or events: "The kingdom of heaven is like . . .". Using parables, Jesus challenged powerful and educated people but was also understood by common people.

▸ Mt 13.10

16 But blessed are your eyes, for they see, and your ears, for they hear. 17 Truly I tell you, many prophets and righteous people longed to see what you see, but did not see it, and to hear what you hear, but did not hear it.

The Parable of the Sower Explained

18 "Hear then the parable of the sower. 19 When anyone hears the word of the kingdom and does not understand it, the evil one comes and snatches away what is sown in the heart; this is what was sown on the path. 20 As for what was sown on rocky ground, this is the one who hears the word and immediately receives it with joy; 21 yet such a person has no root, but endures only for a while, and when trouble or persecution arises on account of the word, that person immediately falls away.[c] 22 As for what was sown among thorns, this is the one who hears the word, but the cares of the world and the lure of wealth choke the word, and it yields nothing. 23 But as for what was sown on good soil, this is the one who hears the word and understands it, who indeed bears fruit and yields, in one case a hundredfold, in another sixty, and in another thirty."

The Parable of Weeds among the Wheat

24 He put before them another parable: "The kingdom of heaven may be compared to someone who sowed good seed in his field; 25 but while everybody was asleep, an enemy came and sowed weeds among the wheat, and then went away. 26 So when the plants came up and bore grain, then the weeds appeared as well. 27 And the slaves of the householder came and said to him, 'Master, did you not sow good seed in your field? Where, then, did these weeds come from?' 28 He answered, 'An enemy has done this.' The slaves said to him, 'Then do you want us to go and gather them?' 29 But he replied, 'No; for in gathering the weeds you would uproot the wheat along with them. 30 Let both of them grow together until the harvest; and at harvest time I will tell the reapers, Collect the weeds first and bind them in bundles to be burned, but gather the wheat into my barn.' "

The Parable of the Mustard Seed
(Mk 4.30–32; Lk 13.18–19)

31 He put before them another parable: "The kingdom of heaven is like a mustard seed that someone took and sowed in his field; 32 it is the smallest of all the seeds, but when it has grown it is the greatest of shrubs and becomes a tree, so that the birds of the air come and make nests in its branches."

---

b Or mysteries   c Gk stumbles

MT

PRAY IT!
The Kingdom Is Like . . .

In trying to get people to understand something as mystifying and overwhelming as the kingdom of heaven, Jesus used ordinary objects like seeds and light, salt and yeast. He chose everyday actions like farming, fishing, and baking. And in doing so, he helped the people of his time understand the new life that comes with the kingdom of heaven.

What is the kingdom like to you? Take a walk outside, or look around the room you are in right now. Pick any object that catches your attention. Try to imagine how Jesus, the master teacher, would use that object to describe the kingdom of heaven. For example, he might say: "The kingdom of heaven is like this telephone. It connects you to everyone else in the world no matter who or where they are."

End your meditation with a prayer that your life will be a living sign to help others understand what the kingdom of heaven is all about.

▸ Mt 13.10–53

The Parable of the Yeast
(Lk 13.20–21)

33 He told them another parable: "The kingdom of heaven is like yeast that a woman took and mixed in with*d* three measures of flour until all of it was leavened."

The Use of Parables

34 Jesus told the crowds all these things in parables; without a parable he told them nothing. 35 This was to fulfill what had been spoken through the prophet:*e*

"I will open my mouth to speak in parables;
    I will proclaim what has been hidden from
        the foundation of the world."*f*

Jesus Explains the Parable of the Weeds

36 Then he left the crowds and went into the house. And his disciples approached him, saying, "Explain to us the parable of the weeds of the field."

37 He answered, "The one who sows the good seed is the Son of Man; 38 the field is the world, and the good seed are the children of the kingdom; the weeds are the children of the evil one, 39 and the enemy who sowed them is the devil; the harvest is the end of the age, and the reapers are angels. 40 Just as the weeds are collected and burned up with fire, so will it be at the end of the age. 41 The Son of Man will send his angels, and they will collect out of his kingdom all causes of sin and all evildoers, 42 and they will throw them into the furnace of fire, where there will be weeping and gnashing of teeth. 43 Then the righteous will shine like the sun in the kingdom of their Father. Let anyone with ears*g* listen!

Three Parables

44 "The kingdom of heaven is like treasure hidden in a field, which someone found and hid; then in his joy he goes and sells all that he has and buys that field.

45 "Again, the kingdom of heaven is like a merchant in search of fine pearls; 46 on finding one pearl of great value, he went and sold all that he had and bought it.

47 "Again, the kingdom of heaven is like a net that was thrown into the sea and caught fish of every kind; 48 when it was full, they drew it ashore, sat down, and put the good into baskets but threw out the bad. 49 So it will be at the end of the age. The angels will come out and separate the evil from the righteous 50 and throw them into the furnace of fire, where there will be weeping and gnashing of teeth.

Treasures New and Old

51 "Have you understood all this?" They answered, "Yes." 52 And he said to them, "Therefore every scribe who has been trained for the kingdom of heaven is like the master of a household who brings out of his treasure what is new and what is old." 53 When Jesus had finished these parables, he left that place.

The Rejection of Jesus at Nazareth
(Mk 6.1–6; Lk 4.16–30)

54 He came to his hometown and began to teach the people*h* in their synagogue, so that they were astounded and said, "Where did this man get this wisdom and these deeds of power? 55 Is not this the carpenter's son? Is not his mother called Mary? And are not his brothers James and Joseph and Simon and Judas? 56 And are not all his sisters

---

d Gk *hid in*   *e* Other ancient authorities read *the prophet Isaiah*   *f* Other ancient authorities lack *of the world*   *g* Other ancient authorities add *to hear*   *h* Gk *them*

THE CARPENTER'S SON

In Mt 13.55, Jesus is called the carpenter's son. The carpenter is Saint Joseph, who has two feast days attributed to him. In Sicily, there is a custom called Saint Joseph's Altar. The custom began during a time of severe drought and famine in the Middle Ages. The Sicilian people offered intercessory prayers to Saint Joseph for rain so that their crops would grow. Eventually, their prayers were answered, the crops grew, and they harvested grains, fruits, and vegetables in abundance. In thanksgiving to Saint Joseph, the people gathered to share their harvest with the poor people of the area. Bread, wine, vegetables, fruits, eggs, and fish were placed on an altar and then distributed to those in need. The altar filled with the harvest came to be known as Saint Joseph's Altar.

This event is now celebrated annually in Sicily on 19 March. Throughout the year, Sicilians also direct many other intercessions toward Saint Joseph, their patron saint. The Sicilians pray not only for good weather and crops but also for health, for family members and friends, and for all kinds of other personal intentions. On 19 March, they show their gratitude to Saint Joseph by preparing a Saint Joseph's Altar and by celebrating their good fortune with one another and the community.

▶ Mt 13.55

with us? Where then did this man get all this?" 57 And they took offense at him. But Jesus said to them, "Prophets are not without honor except in their own country and in their own house." 58 And he did not do many deeds of power there, because of their unbelief.

The Death of John the Baptist
(Lk 9.7–9; Mk 6.14–29)

14 At that time Her′od the ruler[i] heard reports about Jesus; 2 and he said to his servants, "This is John the Baptist; he has been raised from the dead, and for this reason these powers are at work in him." 3 For Her′od had arrested John, bound him, and put him in prison on account of He·rō′di·as, his brother Philip's wife,[j] 4 because John had been telling him, "It is not lawful for you to have her." 5 Though Her′od[k] wanted to put him to death, he feared the crowd, because they regarded him as a prophet. 6 But when Her′od's birthday came, the daughter of He·rō′di·as danced before the company, and she pleased Her′od 7 so much that he promised on oath to grant her whatever she might ask. 8 Prompted by her mother, she said, "Give me the head of John the Baptist here on a platter." 9 The king was grieved, yet out of regard for his oaths and for the guests, he commanded it

to be given; 10 he sent and had John beheaded in the prison. 11 The head was brought on a platter and given to the girl, who brought it to her mother. 12 His disciples came and took the body and buried it; then they went and told Jesus.

Feeding the Five Thousand
(Mk 6.30–44; Lk 9.10–17; Jn 6.1–14)

13 Now when Jesus heard this, he withdrew from there in a boat to a deserted place by himself. But when the crowds heard it, they followed him on foot from the towns. 14 When he went ashore, he saw a great crowd; and he had compassion for them and cured their sick. 15 When it was evening, the disciples came to him and said, "This is a deserted place, and the hour is now late; send the crowds away so that they may go into the villages and buy food for themselves." 16 Jesus said to them, "They need not go away; you give them something to eat." 17 They replied, "We have nothing here but five loaves and two fish." 18 And he said, "Bring them here to me." 19 Then he ordered the crowds to sit down on the grass. Taking the five loaves and the two fish, he looked up to heaven, and blessed and

---

i Gk tetrarch   j Other ancient authorities read his brother's wife   k Gk he broke the loaves, and gave them to the disciples, and the disciples gave them to the crowds. 20 And all ate and were filled; and they took up what was left over of the broken pieces, twelve baskets full. 21 And those who ate were about five thousand men, besides women and children.

Jesus Walks on the Water
(Mk 6.45–52; Jn 6.15–21)

22 Immediately he made the disciples get into the boat and go on ahead to the other side, while he dismissed the crowds. 23 And after he had dismissed the crowds, he went up the mountain by himself to pray. When evening came, he was there alone, 24 but by this time the boat, battered by the waves, was far from the land,[l] for the wind was against them. 25 And early in the morning he came walking toward them on the sea. 26 But when the disciples saw him walking on the sea, they were terrified, saying, "It is a ghost!" And they cried out in fear. 27 But immediately Jesus spoke to them and said, "Take heart, it is I; do not be afraid."

28 Peter answered him, "Lord, if it is you, command me to come to you on the water." 29 He said, "Come." So Peter got out of the boat, started walking on the water, and came toward Jesus. 30 But when he noticed the strong wind,[m] he became frightened, and beginning to sink, he cried out, "Lord, save me!" 31 Jesus immediately reached out his hand and caught him, saying to him, "You of little faith, why did you doubt?" 32 When they got into the boat, the wind ceased. 33 And those in the boat worshiped him, saying, "Truly you are the Son of God."

Jesus Heals the Sick in Gennesaret
(Mk 6.53–56)

34 When they had crossed over, they came to land at Gen·nes'a·ret. 35 After the people of that place recognized him, they sent word throughout the region and brought all who were sick to him, 36 and begged him that they might touch even the fringe of his cloak; and all who touched it were healed.

The Tradition of the Elders
(Mk 7.1–13)

15 Then Phar'i·sees and scribes came to Jesus from Jerusalem and said, 2 "Why do your disciples break the tradition of the elders? For they do not wash their hands before they eat." 3 He answered them, "And why do you break the commandment of God for the sake of your tradition? 4 For God said,[n] 'Honor your father and your mother,' and, 'Whoever speaks evil of father or mother must surely die.' 5 But you say that whoever tells father or mother, 'Whatever support you might have had from me is given to God,'[o] then that person need not honor the father.[p] 6 So, for the sake of your tradition, you make void the word[q] of God. 7 You hypocrites! I·sai'ah prophesied rightly about you when he said:

8 'This people honors me with their lips,
    but their hearts are far from me;

---

[l] Other ancient authorities read *was out on the sea*
[m] Other ancient authorities read *the wind*   [n] Other ancient authorities read *commanded, saying*   [o] Or *is an offering*
[p] Other ancient authorities add *or the mother*   [q] Other ancient authorities read *law*; others, *commandment*

Do You Trust Jesus?

LIVE IT!

At this point in the Gospel of Matthew, different groups are beginning to line up for or against Jesus. The Pharisees, Sadducees, and scribes do not trust him. The disciples still follow Jesus, but they do not yet understand who he really is. In chapters 14–17, through several signs and wonders, the true identity of Jesus is revealed to the disciples. Peter in particular is being prepared for his role as leader.

Of the four Gospels, only Matthew includes the story of Peter walking on the water. If you have gotten acquainted with Peter (see "Peter the Rock," Mt 16.13–20), it will not surprise you that he was willing to take the risk. But why does Peter start to sink? When he is focused on Jesus, everything is fine. It is when he takes his eyes off Jesus, noticing the fierce wind, that he begins to sink.

Jesus invites you to risk a relationship with him. You have to step out in faith, maybe leaving some old ways of life behind. Learn from Peter to keep your focus on Jesus. As the disciples learned, this is no ordinary man but the Son of God! Following Jesus might get scary or difficult at times, but all great adventures involve some risks.

▶ Mt 14.22–33

A PRAYER FOR HEALING HUMANKIND

In Mt 15.1–20, Jesus addresses the hypocrisy of the Jewish leaders who manipulate the Law to their own good. They and the people who follow them are blind to the results. In this prayer, the Native American Ojibwa (or Anishinabe) recognize the need for humans to overcome their blindness to the results of evil intentions:

> Grandfather,
> Look at our brokenness.
> We know that in all creation
> Only the human family
> Has strayed from the Sacred Way.
> We know that we are the ones
> Who must come back together
> To walk in the Sacred Way.
> Grandfather,
> Sacred One,
> Teach us love, compassion, and honor
> That we may heal the earth
> And heal each other.
> (David Schiller, editor, The Little Book of Prayers, pp. 328–329)

▸ Mt 15.1–20

---

9 in vain do they worship me,
   teaching human precepts as doctrines.' "

Things That Defile
(Mk 7.14–23)

10 Then he called the crowd to him and said to them, "Listen and understand: 11 it is not what goes into the mouth that defiles a person, but it is what comes out of the mouth that defiles." 12 Then the disciples approached and said to him, "Do you know that the Phar'i·sees took offense when they heard what you said?" 13 He answered, "Every plant that my heavenly Father has not planted will be uprooted. 14 Let them alone; they are blind guides of the blind.ʳ And if one blind person guides another, both will fall into a pit." 15 But Peter said to him, "Explain this parable to us." 16 Then he said, "Are you also still without understanding? 17 Do you not see that whatever goes into the mouth enters the stomach, and goes out into the sewer? 18 But what comes out of the mouth proceeds from the heart, and this is what defiles. 19 For out of the heart come evil intentions, murder, adultery, fornication, theft,

false witness, slander. 20 These are what defile a person, but to eat with unwashed hands does not defile."

The Canaanite Woman's Faith
(Mk 7.24–30)

21 Jesus left that place and went away to the district of Tyre and Si'don. 22 Just then a Cā'naan·ite woman from that region came out and started shouting, "Have mercy on me, Lord, Son of David; my daughter is tormented by a demon." 23 But he did not answer her at all. And his disciples came and urged him, saying, "Send her away, for she keeps shouting after us." 24 He answered, "I was sent only to the lost sheep of the house of Israel." 25 But she came and knelt before him, saying, "Lord, help me." 26 He answered, "It is not fair to take the children's food and throw it to the dogs." 27 She said, "Yes, Lord, yet even the dogs eat the crumbs that fall from their masters' table." 28 Then Jesus answered her, "Woman, great is your faith!

ʳ Other ancient authorities lack *of the blind*

M
T

Let it be done for you as you wish." And her daughter was healed instantly.

Jesus Cures Many People
(Mk 7.31–37)

29 After Jesus had left that place, he passed along the Sea of Galilee, and he went up the mountain, where he sat down. 30 Great crowds came to him, bringing with them the lame, the maimed, the blind, the mute, and many others. They put them at his feet, and he cured them, 31 so that the crowd was amazed when they saw the mute speaking, the maimed whole, the lame walking, and the blind seeing. And they praised the God of Israel.

Feeding the Four Thousand
(Mk 8.1–10)

32 Then Jesus called his disciples to him and said, "I have compassion for the crowd, because they have been with me now for three days and have nothing to eat; and I do not want to send them away hungry, for they might faint on the way." 33 The disciples said to him, "Where are we to get enough bread in the desert to feed so great a crowd?" 34 Jesus asked them, "How many loaves have you?" They said, "Seven, and a few small fish." 35 Then ordering the crowd to sit down on the ground, 36 he took the seven loaves and the fish; and after giving thanks he broke them and gave them to the disciples, and the disciples gave them to the crowds. 37 And all of them ate and were filled; and they took up the broken pieces left over, seven baskets full. 38 Those who had eaten were four thousand men, besides women and children. 39 After sending away the crowds, he got into the boat and went to the region of Mag'a•dan.^{s}

The Demand for a Sign
(Mk 8.11–13; Lk 12.54–56)

16 The Phar'i•sees and Sad'du•cees came, and to test Jesus^t they asked him to show them a sign from heaven. 2 He answered them, "When it is evening, you say, 'It will be fair weather, for the sky is red.' 3 And in the morning, 'It will be stormy today, for the sky is red and threatening.' You know how to interpret the appearance of the sky, but you cannot interpret the signs of the times.^{u} 4 An evil and adulterous generation asks for a sign, but no sign will be given to it except the sign of Jonah." Then he left them and went away.

The Yeast of the Pharisees and Sadducees
(Mk 8.14–21)

5 When the disciples reached the other side, they had forgotten to bring any bread. 6 Jesus said to them, "Watch out, and beware of the yeast of the Phar'i•sees and Sad'du•cees." 7 They said to one another, "It is because we have brought no bread."

---

^{s} Other ancient authorities read *Magdala* or *Magdalan*
^{t} Gk *him* ^{u} Other ancient authorities lack *2When it is . . . of the times*

Introducing... ▶PETER THE ROCK

What images does the name Saint Peter bring to your mind? The simple fisherman named Simon who was among the first disciples called by Jesus (Mt 4.18; Mk 1.16; Lk 5.10)? The hopeful believer who first recognized Jesus as the Messiah (Mt 16.16; Mk 8.29; Lk 9.20)? The fearful friend who denied Jesus three times (Mt 26.69–74; Mk 14.66–72; Lk 22.54–61; Jn 18.15–27)? The leader of the early church whom we recognize as the first pope (Jn 21.15; Acts 2.14)? Peter is all these things and more. The Bible paints a picture of a very human leader with sins and weaknesses along with many gifts and great faith.

The author of Matthew uses a play on words to make a statement about Peter as the foundation of the church. The new name that Jesus gives him—Peter—means "rock." So Jesus is saying, "You are a rock, and on this rock I will build my church" (Mt 16.18). The Catholic church uses this Scripture passage as support for its teaching on the pope's position as the spiritual leader and highest authority of the church. Peter's primacy as the first of Jesus' Apostles is understood to be passed on to the current pope, through the succession of popes who go back to the beginnings of the church at Rome.

Mt 16.13–20

THE PRINCIPLE OF *UJAMAA*

Jesus tells us that we need to leave behind our old life of selfishness and embrace a new way of life marked by caring about the needs of others. Only then can the spirit of the Lord abound.

The African Kwanzaa principle of *ujamaa*, or cooperative economics, requires this kind of selfless love for others. To practice *ujamaa* means sharing resources with our brothers and sisters, supporting one another's businesses, and living so that everybody receives what they need to prosper. Jesus' words challenge us to build up our communities, preserving the gains we have made and laying foundations for the success of those who come after us. The cost is our me-first attitudes, but the reward is a new life of justice and freedom.

Dear God, my humanness wants to hoard myself; my spirit wants to give!

▸ Mt 16.25

---

8 And becoming aware of it, Jesus said, "You of little faith, why are you talking about having no bread? 9 Do you still not perceive? Do you not remember the five loaves for the five thousand, and how many baskets you gathered? 10 Or the seven loaves for the four thousand, and how many baskets you gathered? 11 How could you fail to perceive that I was not speaking about bread? Beware of the yeast of the Phar'i•sees and Sad'du•cees!" 12 Then they understood that he had not told them to beware of the yeast of bread, but of the teaching of the Phar'i•sees and Sad'du•cees.

Peter's Declaration about Jesus
(Mk 8.27–30; Lk 9.18–20)

13 Now when Jesus came into the district of Caes•a•re'a Phi•lip'pi, he asked his disciples, "Who do people say that the Son of Man is?" 14 And they said, "Some say John the Baptist, but others E•li'jah, and still others Jer•e•mi'ah or one of the prophets." 15 He said to them, "But who do you say that I am?" 16 Simon Peter answered, "You are the Messiah,[v] the Son of the living God." 17 And Jesus answered him, "Blessed are you, Simon son of Jonah! For flesh and blood has not revealed this to you, but my Father in heaven. 18 And I tell you, you are Peter,[w] and on this rock[x] I will build my church, and the gates of Hades will not prevail against it. 19 I will give you the keys of the kingdom of heaven,

and whatever you bind on earth will be bound in heaven, and whatever you loose on earth will be loosed in heaven." 20 Then he sternly ordered the disciples not to tell anyone that he was[y] the Messiah.[v]

Jesus Foretells His Death and Resurrection
(Mk 8.31–33; Lk 9.21–22)

21 From that time on, Jesus began to show his disciples that he must go to Jerusalem and undergo great suffering at the hands of the elders and chief priests and scribes, and be killed, and on the third day be raised. 22 And Peter took him aside and began to rebuke him, saying, "God forbid it, Lord! This must never happen to you." 23 But he turned and said to Peter, "Get behind me, Satan! You are a stumbling block to me; for you are setting your mind not on divine things but on human things."

The Cross and Self-Denial
(Mk 8.34—9.1; Lk 9.23–27)

24 Then Jesus told his disciples, "If any want to become my followers, let them deny themselves and take up their cross and follow me. 25 For those who want to save their life will lose it, and those who lose their life for my sake will find it. 26 For what will it profit them if they gain the whole world

---

v Or the Christ   *w* Gk Petros   *x* Gk petra   *y* Other ancient authorities add Jesus

MT

but forfeit their life? Or what will they give in return for their life?

27 "For the Son of Man is to come with his angels in the glory of his Father, and then he will repay everyone for what has been done. 28 Truly I tell you, there are some standing here who will not taste death before they see the Son of Man coming in his kingdom."

The Transfiguration
(Mk 9.2–13; Lk 9.28–36; 2 Pet 1.16–18)

17 Six days later, Jesus took with him Peter and James and his brother John and led them up a high mountain, by themselves. 2 And he was transfigured before them, and his face shone like the sun, and his clothes became dazzling white. 3 Suddenly there appeared to them Moses and E•li′jah, talking with him. 4 Then Peter said to Jesus, "Lord, it is good for us to be here; if you wish, I*z* will make three dwellings*a* here, one for you, one for Moses, and one for E•li′jah." 5 While he was still speaking, suddenly a bright cloud overshadowed them, and from the cloud a voice said, "This is my Son, the Beloved;*b* with him I am well pleased; listen to him!" 6 When the disciples heard this, they fell to the ground and were overcome by fear. 7 But Jesus came and touched them, saying, "Get up and do not be afraid." 8 And when they looked up, they saw no one except Jesus himself alone.

9 As they were coming down the mountain, Jesus ordered them, "Tell no one about the vision until after the Son of Man has been raised from the dead." 10 And the disciples asked him, "Why, then, do the scribes say that E•li′jah must come first?" 11 He replied, "E•li′jah is indeed coming and will restore all things; 12 but I tell you that E•li′jah has already come, and they did not recognize him, but they did to him whatever they pleased. So also the Son of Man is about to suffer at their hands." 13 Then the disciples understood that he was speaking to them about John the Baptist.

Jesus Cures a Boy with a Demon
(Mk 9.14–29; Lk 9.37–43a)

14 When they came to the crowd, a man came to him, knelt before him, 15 and said, "Lord, have mercy on my son, for he is an epileptic and he suffers terribly; he often falls into the fire and often into the water. 16 And I brought him to your disciples, but they could not cure him." 17 Jesus answered, "You faithless and perverse generation, how much longer must I be with you? How much longer must I put up with you? Bring him here to me." 18 And Jesus rebuked the demon,*c* and it*d* came out of him, and the boy was cured instantly. 19 Then the disciples came to Jesus privately and said, "Why could we not cast it out?" 20 He said to

Catholic Connections

THE TRANSFIGURATION

The Gospels of Matthew, Mark, and Luke each include the story in Mt 17.1–13, called the Transfiguration. Jesus goes up a mountain with his select disciples, who get to see him in his full glory, as brilliant as the sun. In the Old Testament, mountains are sacred places where people encounter God. The same is true here. God's voice comes from a cloud overshadowing the mountain, and God reveals to the disciples that Jesus is God's beloved Son. Moses (see "Moses," Ex 2.1), representing the Law, and Elijah (see "Elijah and Elisha," 1 Kings 17.1), representing the prophets, also appear with Jesus. The appearance of these two Old Testament heroes confirms that Jesus is the fulfillment of both the Law and the prophets—a key point for the author of Matthew.

The Catholic church celebrates the Transfiguration of Jesus in its liturgical year on 6 August.

▶ Mt 17.1–13

them, "Because of your little faith. For truly I tell you, if you have faith the size of a*e* mustard seed, you will say to this mountain, 'Move from here to there,' and it will move; and nothing will be impossible for you."*f*

Jesus Again Foretells His Death and Resurrection
(Mk 9.30–32; Lk 9.43b–45)

22 As they were gathering*g* in Galilee, Jesus said to them, "The Son of Man is going to be betrayed into human hands, 23 and they will kill him, and on the third day he will be raised." And they were greatly distressed.

---

z Other ancient authorities read *we* *a* Or *tents* *b* Or *my beloved Son* *c* Gk *it* or *him* *d* Gk *the demon* *e* Gk *faith as a grain of* *f* Other ancient authorities add verse 21, *But this kind does not come out except by prayer and fasting* *g* Other ancient authorities read *living*

Jesus and the Temple Tax

24 When they reached Ca•per′na•um, the collectors of the temple tax[h] came to Peter and said, "Does your teacher not pay the temple tax?"[h] 25 He said, "Yes, he does." And when he came home, Jesus spoke of it first, asking, "What do you think, Simon? From whom do kings of the earth take toll or tribute? From their children or from others?" 26 When Peter[i] said, "From others," Jesus said to him, "Then the children are free. 27 However, so that we do not give offense to them, go to the sea and cast a hook; take the first fish that comes up; and when you open its mouth, you will find a coin;[j] take that and give it to them for you and me."

True Greatness
(Mk 9.33–37; Lk 9.46–48)

18 At that time the disciples came to Jesus and asked, "Who is the greatest in the kingdom of heaven?" 2 He called a child, whom he put among them, 3 and said, "Truly I tell you, unless you change and become like children, you will never enter the kingdom of heaven. 4 Whoever becomes humble like this child is the greatest in the kingdom of heaven. 5 Whoever welcomes one such child in my name welcomes me.

Temptations to Sin
(Mk 9.42–48; Lk 17.1–2)

6 "If any of you put a stumbling block before one of these little ones who believe in me, it would be better for you if a great millstone were fastened around your neck and you were drowned in the depth of the sea. 7 Woe to the world because of stumbling blocks! Occasions for stumbling are bound to come, but woe to the one by whom the stumbling block comes!

8 "If your hand or your foot causes you to stumble, cut it off and throw it away; it is better for you to enter life maimed or lame than to have two hands or two feet and to be thrown into the eternal fire. 9 And if your eye causes you to stumble, tear it out and throw it away; it is better for you to enter life with one eye than to have two eyes and to be thrown into the hell[k] of fire.

The Parable of the Lost Sheep
(Lk 15.1–7)

10 "Take care that you do not despise one of these little ones; for, I tell you, in heaven their angels continually see the face of my Father in

h Gk didrachma   i Gk he   j Gk stater; the stater was worth two didrachmas   k Gk Gehenna

SANTO NINO

The feast of Santo Nino, which means "Holy Child," is celebrated in the Philippines on the Sunday after the feast of the baptism of the Lord. The beginning of chapter 18 of Matthew is one of the readings you might hear at Mass that day. The feast of Santo Nino celebrates Jesus as a child and is associated with a special statue. The statue portrays the child Jesus wearing a crown, red pants, and a white robe with a large triangular red collar flaring out from the shoulders. The statue can be found in many Philippine churches and car windows.

The original Santo Nino statue was made in Belgium and sent to a girl in the Philippines as a gift for her Baptism. Then it was lost for twenty-four years, until, during a battle, a soldier found it unharmed in the flaming ruins of a house. Folklore says that the statue once hid the island of Cebu from English invaders and that when the statue was placed in the sea during a drought, it miraculously began to rain.

The devotion to Santo Nino can help us remember that Jesus was once a child who was taught and cared for by loving parents. In the spirit of Santo Nino, why not surprise a parent or grandparent with a love letter thanking him or her for all he or she has done for you?

▸ Mt 18.1–11

heaven.*l* 12 What do you think? If a shepherd has a hundred sheep, and one of them has gone astray, does he not leave the ninety-nine on the mountains and go in search of the one that went astray? 13 And if he finds it, truly I tell you, he rejoices over it more than over the ninety-nine that never went astray. 14 So it is not the will of your*m* Father in heaven that one of these little ones should be lost.

Reproving Another Who Sins

15 "If another member of the church*n* sins against you,*o* go and point out the fault when the two of you are alone. If the member listens to you, you have regained that one.*p* 16 But if you are not listened to, take one or two others along with you, so that every word may be confirmed by the evidence of two or three witnesses. 17 If the member refuses to listen to them, tell it to the church; and if the offender refuses to listen even to the church, let such a one be to you as a Gentile and a tax collector. 18 Truly I tell you, whatever you bind on earth will be bound in heaven, and whatever you loose on earth will be loosed in heaven. 19 Again, truly I tell you, if two of you agree on earth about anything you ask, it will be done for you by my Father in heaven. 20 For where two or three are gathered in my name, I am there among them."

Forgiveness

21 Then Peter came and said to him, "Lord, if another member of the church*q* sins against me, how often should I forgive? As many as seven times?" 22 Jesus said to him, "Not seven times, but, I tell you, seventy-seven*r* times.

The Parable of the Unforgiving Servant

23 "For this reason the kingdom of heaven may be compared to a king who wished to settle accounts with his slaves. 24 When he began the reckoning, one who owed him ten thousand talents*s* was brought to him; 25 and, as he could not pay, his lord ordered him to be sold, together with his wife and children and all his possessions, and payment to be made. 26 So the slave fell on his knees before him, saying, 'Have patience with me, and I will pay you everything.' 27 And out of pity for him, the lord of that slave released him and forgave him the debt. 28 But that same slave, as he went out, came upon one of his fellow slaves who owed him a hundred denarii;*t* and seizing him by the throat, he said, 'Pay what you owe.' 29 Then his fellow slave fell down and pleaded with him, 'Have patience with me, and I will pay you.' 30 But he refused; then he went and threw him into prison until he would pay the debt. 31 When his fellow slaves saw what had happened, they were greatly distressed, and they went and reported to their lord all that had taken place. 32 Then

his lord summoned him and said to him, 'You wicked slave! I forgave you all that debt because you pleaded with me. 33 Should you not have had mercy on your fellow slave, as I had mercy on you?' 34 And in anger his lord handed him over to be tortured until he would pay his entire debt. 35 So my heavenly Father will also do to every one of you, if you do not forgive your brother or sister*u* from your heart."

PRAY IT?
Forgive Us Our Debts

The parable of the unforgiving servant spells out clearly (and a bit harshly) what it means to ask God to "forgive us our debts, / as we also have forgiven our debtors" (Mt 6.12).

Bring to mind a person who has hurt you or made you angry lately. Hold this person's image in your thoughts, and realize that Jesus is calling you to forgive her or him. Now, tell this person in your thoughts how she or he has hurt you. Finally, offer your forgiveness to the person so that you can let go of the burden of your hurt.

When you are done, imagine Jesus in your prayer and share with him something you have done that has hurt another person. Let Jesus forgive you in the same way you just forgave.

▶ Mt 18.21–35

Teaching about Divorce
(Mk 10.1–12)

19 When Jesus had finished saying these things, he left Galilee and went to the region of Judea beyond the Jordan. 2 Large crowds followed him, and he cured them there.

3 Some Phar'i·sees came to him, and to test him they asked, "Is it lawful for a man to divorce his wife for any cause?" 4 He answered, "Have you not read that the one who made them at the beginning 'made them male and female,' 5 and said, 'For this

---

l Other ancient authorities add verse 11, *For the Son of Man came to save the lost*　*m* Other ancient authorities read *my*　*n* Gk *If your brother*　*o* Other ancient authorities lack *against you*　*p* Gk *the brother*　*q* Gk *if my brother*　*r* Or *seventy times seven*　*s* A talent was worth more than fifteen years' wages of a laborer　*t* The denarius was the usual day's wage for a laborer　*u* Gk *brother* reason a man shall leave his father and mother and be joined to his wife, and the two shall become one flesh'? 6 So they are no longer two, but one flesh. Therefore what God has joined together, let no one separate." 7 They said to him, "Why then did Moses command us to give a certificate of dismissal and to divorce her?" 8 He said to them, "It was because you were so hard-hearted that Moses allowed you to divorce your wives, but from the beginning it was not so. 9 And I say to you, whoever divorces his wife, except for unchastity, and marries another commits adultery."v

10 His disciples said to him, "If such is the case of a man with his wife, it is better not to marry." 11 But he said to them, "Not everyone can accept this teaching, but only those to whom it is given. 12 For there are eunuchs who have been so from birth, and there are eunuchs who have been made eunuchs by others, and there are eunuchs who have made themselves eunuchs for the sake of the kingdom of heaven. Let anyone accept this who can."

Jesus Blesses Little Children
(Mk 10.13–16; Lk 18.15–17)

13 Then little children were being brought to him in order that he might lay his hands on them and pray. The disciples spoke sternly to those who brought them; 14 but Jesus said, "Let the little children come to me, and do not stop them; for it is to such as these that the kingdom of heaven belongs." 15 And he laid his hands on them and went on his way.

The Rich Young Man
(Mk 10.17–31; Lk 18.18–30)

16 Then someone came to him and said, "Teacher, what good deed must I do to have eternal life?" 17 And he said to him, "Why do you ask me about what is good? There is only one who is good. If you wish to enter into life, keep the commandments." 18 He said to him, "Which ones?" And Jesus said, "You shall not murder; You shall not commit adultery; You shall not steal; You shall not bear false witness; 19 Honor your father and mother; also, You shall love your neighbor as yourself." 20 The young man said to him, "I have kept all these;w what do I still lack?" 21 Jesus said to him, "If you wish to be perfect, go, sell your possessions, and give the moneyx to the poor, and you will have treasure in heaven; then come, follow me." 22 When the young man heard this word, he went away grieving, for he had many possessions.

23 Then Jesus said to his disciples, "Truly I tell you, it will be hard for a rich person to enter the kingdom of heaven. 24 Again I tell you, it is easier for a camel to go through the eye of a needle than for someone who is rich to enter the kingdom of

Catholic Connections

MARRIAGE

When the Pharisees try to test Jesus with a question about divorce, Jesus speaks about marriage. Rather than focus on the negative, Jesus turns everyone's attention to the positive—the beauty of two people who "are no longer two, but one flesh" (Mt 19.6). Catholics celebrate Jesus' positive view in the sacrament of Marriage, one of the seven official sacraments of the church. The church believes that in a Christian marriage, God's love and grace are present in a special way (see Eph 5.21–33).

The vows exchanged by the bride and groom and received by the church's official witness are the sacramental experience of marriage. It is the married couple's love, commitment, and faith that make God's love real and present to the community.

▶ Mt 19.1–9

God." 25 When the disciples heard this, they were greatly astounded and said, "Then who can be saved?" 26 But Jesus looked at them and said, "For mortals it is impossible, but for God all things are possible."

27 Then Peter said in reply, "Look, we have left everything and followed you. What then will we have?" 28 Jesus said to them, "Truly I tell you, at the renewal of all things, when the Son of Man is seated on the throne of his glory, you who have followed me will also sit on twelve thrones, judging the twelve tribes of Israel. 29 And everyone who has left houses or brothers or sisters or father or mother or children or fields, for my name's sake, will receive a hundredfold,y and will inherit eternal life. 30 But many who are first will be last, and the last will be first.

---

v Other ancient authorities read *except on the ground of unchastity, causes her to commit adultery*; others add at the end of the verse *and he who marries a divorced woman commits adultery*   w Other ancient authorities add *from my youth*   x Gk lacks *the money*   y Other ancient authorities read *manifold*

The Laborers in the Vineyard

20 "For the kingdom of heaven is like a landowner who went out early in the morning to hire laborers for his vineyard. 2 After agreeing with the laborers for the usual daily wage,*z* he sent them into his vineyard. 3 When he went out about nine o'clock, he saw others standing idle in the marketplace; 4 and he said to them, 'You also go into the vineyard, and I will pay you whatever is right.' So they went. 5 When he went out again about noon and about three o'clock, he did the same. 6 And about five o'clock he went out and found others standing around; and he said to them, 'Why are you standing here idle all day?' 7 They said to him, 'Because no one has hired us.' He said to them, 'You also go into the vineyard.' 8 When evening came, the owner of the vineyard said to his manager, 'Call the laborers and give them their pay, beginning with the last and then going to the first.' 9 When those hired about five o'clock came, each of them received the usual daily wage.*z* 10 Now when the first came, they thought they would receive more; but each of them also received the usual daily wage.*z* 11 And when they received it, they grumbled against the landowner, 12 saying, 'These last worked only one hour, and you have made them equal to us who have borne the burden of the day and the scorching heat.' 13 But he replied to one of them, 'Friend, I am doing you no wrong; did you not agree with me for the usual daily wage?*z* 14 Take what belongs to you and go; I choose to give to this last the same as I give to you. 15 Am I not allowed to do what I choose with what belongs to me? Or are you envious because I am generous?'*a* 16 So the last will be first, and the first will be last."*b*

A Third Time Jesus Foretells His Death and Resurrection
(Mk 10.32–34; Lk 18.31–34)

17 While Jesus was going up to Jerusalem, he took the twelve disciples aside by themselves, and said to them on the way, 18 "See, we are going up to Jerusalem, and the Son of Man will be handed over to the chief priests and scribes, and they will condemn him to death; 19 then they will hand him over to the Gentiles to be mocked and flogged and crucified; and on the third day he will be raised."

The Request of the Mother of James and John
(Mk 10.35–45)

20 Then the mother of the sons of Zeb′e•dee came to him with her sons, and kneeling before him, she asked a favor of him. 21 And he said to her, "What do you want?" She said to him, "Declare that these two sons of mine will sit, one at your right hand and one at your left, in your kingdom." 22 But Jesus answered, "You do not know what you are asking. Are you able to drink the cup that I am about to drink?"*c* They said to him, "We are able." 23 He said to them, "You will indeed drink my cup, but to sit at my right hand and at my left, this is not mine to grant, but it is for those for whom it has been prepared by my Father."

24 When the ten heard it, they were angry with the two brothers. 25 But Jesus called them to him and said, "You know that the rulers of the Gentiles lord it over them, and their great ones are tyrants over them. 26 It will not be so among you; but whoever wishes to be great among you must be your servant, 27 and whoever wishes to be first among

---

z Gk *a denarius*   *a* Gk *is your eye evil because I am good?*
b Other ancient authorities add *for many are called but few are chosen*   *c* Other ancient authorities add *or to be baptized with the baptism that I am baptized with?*

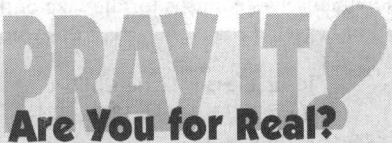

Are You for Real?

Read Mt 20.1–16 as an introduction to this prayer:

Lord, could you really be such a generous God? I have heard that you offer the same welcome to the sinner as to the saint. That you walk with the angry as well as the joyful, and can embrace the hurtful as well as the helpful. That you even offer the exact same love for the last to turn to you as you do for the first.

That's just not the way it is done around here, God, so excuse me if I have a hard time believing. But then, I've heard it said that you are as patient with the doubtful as you are with the faithful.

If you are this type of God, then please be with me right now. I need to talk to someone who understands and loves me in spite of my doubts and sin. I need a God who breaks the rules to let me know how much I am loved.

If you are indeed this kind of God, thanks! Thanks for being so crazy with your love that you would allow someone like me to hang around you. Promise to stay with me as I learn to trust in you and your acceptance of all people. Amen.

▸ Mt 20.1–16

LIVE IT!

True Greatness

What good parent does not want his or her son or daughter to find success in life? Like most people at the time of Jesus, the mother of James and John is confused about the Kingdom that Jesus had come to establish. She lobbies for her sons (see verse 21), hoping they might be made "senior vice presidents" of the new "firm."

The resulting confusion and anger among the disciples allows Jesus the opportunity to remind them of how God defined true greatness. Jesus turns the tables on them by asking in a veiled way, "Are you able to drink the cup that I am about to drink?" (verse 22). He reminds them—and reminds us today—that true greatness is gained in serving others (see verses 26–27).

When you are in a position of leadership, do you see it as a chance to control others in order to gain power or social status, or do you see it as a chance to serve others and help them obtain what they need to live full and healthy lives? Why is it that wanting power for ourselves so often gets in the way of our wanting to serve the needs of others?

▸ Mt 20.20–28

---

you must be your slave; 28 just as the Son of Man came not to be served but to serve, and to give his life a ransom for many."

Jesus Heals Two Blind Men
(Mk 10.46–52; Lk 18.35–43)

29 As they were leaving Jericho, a large crowd followed him. 30 There were two blind men sitting by the roadside. When they heard that Jesus was passing by, they shouted, "Lord,*d* have mercy on us, Son of David!" 31 The crowd sternly ordered them to be quiet; but they shouted even more loudly, "Have mercy on us, Lord, Son of David!" 32 Jesus stood still and called them, saying, "What do you want me to do for you?" 33 They said to him, "Lord, let our eyes be opened." 34 Moved with compassion, Jesus touched their eyes. Immediately they regained their sight and followed him.

Jesus' Triumphal Entry into Jerusalem
(Mk 11.1–10; Lk 19.28–40; Jn 12.12–19)

21 When they had come near Jerusalem and had reached Beth'pha·gē, at the Mount of Olives, Jesus sent two disciples, 2 saying to them, "Go into the village ahead of you, and immediately you will find a donkey tied, and a colt with her; untie them and bring them to me. 3 If anyone says anything to you, just say this, 'The Lord needs them.' And he will send them immediately.*e*"
4 This took place to fulfill what had been spoken through the prophet, saying,

5 "Tell the daughter of Zion,
   Look, your king is coming to you,
      humble, and mounted on a donkey,
         and on a colt, the foal of a donkey."

6 The disciples went and did as Jesus had directed them; 7 they brought the donkey and the colt, and put their cloaks on them, and he sat on them. 8 A very large crowd*f* spread their cloaks on the road, and others cut branches from the trees and spread them on the road. 9 The crowds that went ahead of him and that followed were shouting,

"Hosanna to the Son of David!
   Blessed is the one who comes in the name
      of the Lord!
   Hosanna in the highest heaven!"

---

a Other ancient authorities lack *Lord*   *e* Or *'The Lord needs them and will send them back immediately.'*   *f* Or *Most of the crowd*

21.8

10 When he entered Jerusalem, the whole city was in turmoil, asking, "Who is this?" 11 The crowds were saying, "This is the prophet Jesus from Nazareth in Galilee."

Jesus Cleanses the Temple
(Mk 11.15–19; Lk 19.45–48; Jn 2.13–25)

12 Then Jesus entered the temple*g* and drove out all who were selling and buying in the temple, and he overturned the tables of the money changers and the seats of those who sold doves. 13 He said to them, "It is written,

'My house shall be called a house of prayer';
      but you are making it a den of robbers."

14 The blind and the lame came to him in the temple, and he cured them. 15 But when the chief priests and the scribes saw the amazing things that he did, and heard*h* the children crying out in the temple, "Hosanna to the Son of David," they became angry 16 and said to him, "Do you hear what these are saying?" Jesus said to them, "Yes; have you never read,

'Out of the mouths of infants and nursing
      babies
you have prepared praise for yourself'?"

17 He left them, went out of the city to Beth'a·ny, and spent the night there.

Jesus Curses the Fig Tree
(Mk 11.12–14, 20–25)

18 In the morning, when he returned to the city, he was hungry. 19 And seeing a fig tree by the side of the road, he went to it and found nothing at all on it but leaves. Then he said to it, "May no fruit ever come from you again!" And the fig tree withered at once. 20 When the disciples saw it, they were amazed, saying, "How did the fig tree wither at once?" 21 Jesus answered them, "Truly I tell you, if you have faith and do not doubt, not only will you do what has been done to the fig tree, but even if you say to this mountain, 'Be lifted up and thrown into the sea,' it will be done. 22 Whatever you ask for in prayer with faith, you will receive."

The Authority of Jesus Questioned
(Mk 11.27–33; Lk 20.1–8)

23 When he entered the temple, the chief priests and the elders of the people came to him as he was teaching, and said, "By what authority are you doing these things, and who gave you this authority?" 24 Jesus said to them, "I will also ask you one question; if you tell me the answer, then I will also tell you by what authority I do these things. 25 Did the baptism of John come from heaven, or was it of human origin?" And they argued with one another, "If we say, 'From heaven,' he will say to us, 'Why then did you not believe him?' 26 But if we say, 'Of human origin,' we are afraid of the crowd; for all regard John as a prophet." 27 So they answered Jesus, "We do not know." And he said to them, "Neither will I tell you by what authority I am doing these things.

The Parable of the Two Sons

28 "What do you think? A man had two sons; he went to the first and said, 'Son, go and work in the vineyard today.' 29 He answered, 'I will not'; but

did you KNOW?

Jesus and Civil Disobedience

The cleansing of the Temple is one of the few stories that occur in all four Gospels. To fully understand Jesus' anger in this situation, we need to remember that the Jews were required to offer sacrificial animals as part of their religious obligation. Herod the Great had turned the sale of sacrificial animals into a money-making enterprise. Money changers were needed because Roman coins had images of pagan gods on them and could not be used to purchase animals for this religious purpose; therefore, religious and civil leaders were becoming wealthy, charging people a fee for this necessary exchange of coins. Because this was not an appropriate Temple activity, it upset many people, including Jesus.

Jesus' clearing of the Temple was an act of religious and civil disobedience, challenging the highest members of Jewish society. The Gospels of Luke and Mark both say that immediately after this event, Jewish leaders began looking for a way to kill Jesus. They waited because Jesus was so popular with the people (see Mk 11.18–19 and Lk 19.47–48). Jesus knew that his actions and teachings made these corrupt leaders angry and would ultimately lead to his death (see Mt 20.17–19).

▶ Mt 21.12–13

---

g Other ancient authorities add *of God*   *h* Gk lacks *heard* later he changed his mind and went. 30 The father[i] went to the second and said the same; and he answered, 'I go, sir'; but he did not go. 31 Which of the two did the will of his father?" They said, "The first." Jesus said to them, "Truly I tell you, the tax collectors and the prostitutes are going into the kingdom of God ahead of you. 32 For John came to you in the way of righteousness and you did not believe him, but the tax collectors and the prostitutes believed him; and even after you saw it, you did not change your minds and believe him.

The Parable of the Wicked Tenants
(Mk 12.1–12; Lk 20.9–19)

33 "Listen to another parable. There was a landowner who planted a vineyard, put a fence around it, dug a wine press in it, and built a watchtower. Then he leased it to tenants and went to another country. 34 When the harvest time had come, he sent his slaves to the tenants to collect his produce. 35 But the tenants seized his slaves and beat one, killed another, and stoned another. 36 Again he sent other slaves, more than the first; and they treated them in the same way. 37 Finally he sent his son to them, saying, 'They will respect my son.' 38 But when the tenants saw the son, they said to themselves, 'This is the heir; come, let us kill him and get his inheritance.' 39 So they seized him, threw him out of the vineyard, and killed him. 40 Now when the owner of the vineyard comes, what will he do to those tenants?" 41 They said to him, "He will put those wretches to a miserable death, and lease the vineyard to other tenants who will give him the produce at the harvest time."

42 Jesus said to them, "Have you never read in the scriptures:

'The stone that the builders rejected
    has become the cornerstone;[j]
this was the Lord's doing,
    and it is amazing in our eyes'?

43 Therefore I tell you, the kingdom of God will be taken away from you and given to a people that produces the fruits of the kingdom.[k] 44 The one who falls on this stone will be broken to pieces; and it will crush anyone on whom it falls."[l]

45 When the chief priests and the Phar'i•sees heard his parables, they realized that he was speaking about them. 46 They wanted to arrest him, but they feared the crowds, because they regarded him as a prophet.

The Parable of the Wedding Banquet
(Lk 14.15–24)

22 Once more Jesus spoke to them in parables, saying: 2 "The kingdom of heaven may be compared to a king who gave a wedding banquet for his son. 3 He sent his slaves to call those who had been invited to the wedding banquet, but they would not come. 4 Again he sent other slaves, saying, 'Tell those who have been invited: Look, I have prepared my dinner, my oxen and my fat calves have been slaughtered, and everything is ready; come to the wedding banquet.' 5 But they made light of it and went away, one to his farm, another to his business, 6 while the rest seized his slaves, mistreated them, and killed them. 7 The king was enraged. He sent his troops, destroyed those murderers, and burned their city. 8 Then he said to his slaves, 'The wedding is ready, but those invited were not worthy. 9 Go therefore into the main streets, and invite everyone you find to the wedding banquet.' 10 Those slaves went out into the streets and gathered all whom they found, both good and bad; so the wedding hall was filled with guests.

11 "But when the king came in to see the guests, he noticed a man there who was not wearing a wedding robe, 12 and he said to him, 'Friend, how did you get in here without a wedding robe?' And he was speechless. 13 Then the king said to the attendants, 'Bind him hand and foot, and throw him into the outer darkness, where there will be weeping and gnashing of teeth.' 14 For many are called, but few are chosen."

The Question about Paying Taxes
(Mk 12.13–17; Lk 20.20–26)

15 Then the Phar'i•sees went and plotted to entrap him in what he said. 16 So they sent their disciples to him, along with the He•rō'di•ans, saying, "Teacher, we know that you are sincere, and teach the way of God in accordance with truth, and show deference to no one; for you do not regard people with partiality. 17 Tell us, then, what you think. Is it lawful to pay taxes to the emperor, or not?" 18 But Jesus, aware of their malice, said, "Why are you putting me to the test, you hypocrites? 19 Show me the coin used for the tax." And they brought him a denarius. 20 Then he said to them, "Whose head is this, and whose title?" 21 They answered, "The emperor's." Then he said to them, "Give therefore to the emperor the things that are the emperor's, and to God the things that are God's." 22 When they heard this, they were amazed; and they left him and went away.

The Question about the Resurrection
(Mk 12.18–27; Lk 20.27–40)

23 The same day some Sad'du•cees came to him, saying there is no resurrection;[m] and they

---

i Gk *He*   j Or *keystone*   k Gk *the fruits of it*   l Other ancient authorities lack verse 44   m Other ancient authorities read *who say that there is no resurrection* asked him a question, saying, 24 "Teacher, Moses said, 'If a man dies childless, his brother shall marry the widow, and raise up children for his brother.' 25 Now there were seven brothers among us; the first married, and died childless, leaving the widow to his brother. 26 The second did the same, so also the third, down to the seventh. 27 Last of all, the woman herself died. 28 In the resurrection, then, whose wife of the seven will she be? For all of them had married her."

29 Jesus answered them, "You are wrong, because you know neither the scriptures nor the power of God. 30 For in the resurrection they neither marry nor are given in marriage, but are like angels[n] in heaven. 31 And as for the resurrection of the dead, have you not read what was said to you by God, 32 'I am the God of Abraham, the God of Isaac, and the God of Jacob'? He is God not of the dead, but of the living." 33 And when the crowd heard it, they were astounded at his teaching.

The Greatest Commandment
(Mk 12.28–34; Lk 10.25–28)

34 When the Phar'i·sees heard that he had silenced the Sad'du·cees, they gathered together, 35 and one of them, a lawyer, asked him a question to test him. 36 "Teacher, which commandment in the law is the greatest?" 37 He said to him, " 'You shall love the Lord your God with all your heart, and with all your soul, and with all your mind.' 38 This is the greatest and first commandment. 39 And a second is like it: 'You shall love your neighbor as yourself.' 40 On these two commandments hang all the law and the prophets."

The Question about David's Son
(Mk 12.35–37; Lk 20.41–44)

41 Now while the Phar'i·sees were gathered together, Jesus asked them this question: 42 "What do you think of the Messiah?[o] Whose son is he?" They said to him, "The son of David." 43 He said to them, "How is it then that David by the Spirit[p] calls him Lord, saying,

44 'The Lord said to my Lord,
  "Sit at my right hand,
    until I put your enemies under your
      feet" '?

45 If David thus calls him Lord, how can he be his son?" 46 No one was able to give him an answer, nor from that day did anyone dare to ask him any more questions.

Jesus Denounces Scribes and Pharisees
(Mk 12.38–40; Lk 20.45–47)

23 Then Jesus said to the crowds and to his disciples, 2 "The scribes and the Phar'i·sees sit on Moses' seat; 3 therefore, do whatever they teach you and follow it; but do not do as they do, for they do not practice what they teach. 4 They tie up heavy burdens, hard to bear,[q] and lay them on the shoulders of others; but they themselves are unwilling to lift a finger to move them. 5 They do all their deeds to be seen by others; for they make their phylacteries broad and their fringes long. 6 They love to have the place of honor at banquets and the best seats in the synagogues, 7 and to be greeted with respect in the marketplaces, and to have people call them rabbi. 8 But you are not to be called rabbi, for you have one teacher, and you are all students.[r] 9 And call no one your father on earth, for you have one Father—the one in heaven. 10 Nor are you to be called instructors, for you have one instructor, the Messiah.[s] 11 The greatest among you will be your servant. 12 All who exalt them-

---

[n] Other ancient authorities add *of God*   [o] Or *Christ*
[p] Gk *in spirit*   [q] Other ancient authorities lack *hard to bear*   [r] Gk *brothers*   [s] Or *the Christ*

The Miniature Gospel

LIVE IT!

Can you imagine a world where every person lives according to the two commandments Jesus gives in Mt 22.34–40? Where every word, thought, and action are motivated by a deep love for God and by a desire for the well-being of others? Sounds a bit like the Garden of Eden! Libraries are filled with volumes describing philosophies for achieving the ideal human society, yet Jesus articulates the perfect plan in a few short sentences. These two great commandments remain for us as a kind of miniature Gospel.

Why not take the time to memorize verses 37–39? Let this miniature Gospel become such a part of you that you become a living, breathing example for others.

▶ Mt 22.34–40

selves will be humbled, and all who humble themselves will be exalted.

13 "But woe to you, scribes and Phar'i•sees, hypocrites! For you lock people out of the kingdom

PRAY IT!
No Respect

The "woe" statements of Jesus in Mt 23.1–24 are his harshest words in all the Gospels. The community in which the author of Matthew lived had negative experiences with Jewish leaders (see "Pharisees, Sadducees, and Scribes," Mt 3.7), and their hard feelings are reflected in Jesus' words. We should take Mt 23.3–4 not as a condemnation of Jewish people but as a call to do the following:

- practice what we preach (verse 3)
- show compassion; don't burden others (verse 4)
- practice religion not to look important but as an expression of faith (verses 8–15)
- humbly respect the people who follow us (verses 8–15)
- be guided by mercy and justice in our understanding of law (verses 23–24)

Jesus' sharpest criticism here and in many other places in the Gospels is directed towards hypocrisy—the act of pretending to be holy and just while actually doing sinful things. In your prayer, reflect or journal on the following questions:

- How have I expressed my faith in my spoken words as well as in my inner thoughts?
- When has my life demonstrated what my faith is all about?
- When have I asked others to do something that I was not willing to do myself? Why did I do that?
- When have I used any power or influence I might have in a way that was humble and served the needs of others? How did I do that?

Try looking at these same questions each week or month, and see if your answers change over time.

▶ Mt 23.1–36

of heaven. For you do not go in yourselves, and when others are going in, you stop them.[t] 15 Woe to you, scribes and Phar'i•sees, hypocrites! For you cross sea and land to make a single convert, and you make the new convert twice as much a child of hell[u] as yourselves.

16 "Woe to you, blind guides, who say, 'Whoever swears by the sanctuary is bound by nothing, but whoever swears by the gold of the sanctuary is bound by the oath.' 17 You blind fools! For which is greater, the gold or the sanctuary that has made the gold sacred? 18 And you say, 'Whoever swears by the altar is bound by nothing, but whoever swears by the gift that is on the altar is bound by the oath.' 19 How blind you are! For which is greater, the gift or the altar that makes the gift sacred? 20 So whoever swears by the altar, swears by it and by everything on it; 21 and whoever swears by the sanctuary, swears by it and by the one who dwells in it; 22 and whoever swears by heaven, swears by the throne of God and by the one who is seated upon it.

23 "Woe to you, scribes and Phar'i•sees, hypocrites! For you tithe mint, dill, and cummin, and have neglected the weightier matters of the law: justice and mercy and faith. It is these you ought to have practiced without neglecting the others. 24 You blind guides! You strain out a gnat but swallow a camel!

25 "Woe to you, scribes and Phar'i•sees, hypocrites! For you clean the outside of the cup and of the plate, but inside they are full of greed and self-indulgence. 26 You blind Phar'i•see! First clean the inside of the cup,[v] so that the outside also may become clean.

27 "Woe to you, scribes and Phar'i•sees, hypocrites! For you are like whitewashed tombs, which on the outside look beautiful, but inside they are full of the bones of the dead and of all kinds of filth. 28 So you also on the outside look righteous to others, but inside you are full of hypocrisy and lawlessness.

29 "Woe to you, scribes and Phar'i•sees, hypocrites! For you build the tombs of the prophets and decorate the graves of the righteous, 30 and you say, 'If we had lived in the days of our ancestors, we would not have taken part with them in shedding the blood of the prophets.' 31 Thus you testify against yourselves that you are descendants of those who murdered the prophets. 32 Fill up, then, the measure of your ancestors. 33 You snakes, you brood of vipers! How can you escape being sentenced to hell?[u] 34 Therefore I send you prophets,

---

t Other authorities add here (or after verse 12) verse 14, *Woe to you, scribes and Pharisees, hypocrites! For you devour widows' houses and for the sake of appearance you make long prayers; therefore you will receive the greater condemnation* *u* Gk *Gehenna*   *v* Other ancient authorities add *and of the plate* sages, and scribes, some of whom you will kill and crucify, and some you will flog in your synagogues and pursue from town to town, 35 so that upon you may come all the righteous blood shed on earth, from the blood of righteous Abel to the blood of Zech•a•ri′ah son of Bar•a•chi′ah, whom you murdered between the sanctuary and the altar. 36 Truly I tell you, all this will come upon this generation.

The Lament over Jerusalem
(Lk 13.34–35)

37 "Jerusalem, Jerusalem, the city that kills the prophets and stones those who are sent to it! How often have I desired to gather your children together as a hen gathers her brood under her wings, and you were not willing! 38 See, your house is left to you, desolate.ʷ 39 For I tell you, you will not see me again until you say, 'Blessed is the one who comes in the name of the Lord.' "

The Destruction of the Temple Foretold
(Mk 13.1–2; Lk 21.5–6)

24 As Jesus came out of the temple and was going away, his disciples came to point out to him the buildings of the temple. 2 Then he asked them, "You see all these, do you not? Truly I tell you, not one stone will be left here upon another; all will be thrown down."

Signs of the End of the Age
(Mk 13.3–8; Lk 21.7–11)

3 When he was sitting on the Mount of Olives, the disciples came to him privately, saying, "Tell us, when will this be, and what will be the sign of your coming and of the end of the age?" 4 Jesus answered them, "Beware that no one leads you astray. 5 For many will come in my name, saying, 'I am the Messiah!'ˣ and they will lead many astray. 6 And you will hear of wars and rumors of wars; see that you are not alarmed; for this must take place, but the end is not yet. 7 For nation will rise against nation, and kingdom against kingdom, and there will be faminesʸ and earthquakes in various places: 8 all this is but the beginning of the birth pangs.

Persecutions Foretold
(Mk 13.9–13; Lk 21.12–19)

9 "Then they will hand you over to be tortured and will put you to death, and you will be hated by all nations because of my name. 10 Then many will fall away,ᶻ and they will betray one another and hate one another. 11 And many false prophets will arise and lead many astray. 12 And because of the increase of lawlessness, the love of many will grow cold. 13 But the one who endures to the end will be saved. 14 And this good newsᵃ of the kingdom will be proclaimed throughout the world, as a testimony to all the nations; and then the end will come.

The Desolating Sacrilege
(Mk 13.14–23; Lk 17.23–24, 37; 21.20–24)

15 "So when you see the desolating sacrilege standing in the holy place, as was spoken of by the prophet Daniel (let the reader understand), 16 then those in Judea must flee to the mountains; 17 the one on the housetop must not go down to take what is in the house; 18 the one in the field must not turn back to get a coat. 19 Woe to those who are pregnant and to those who are nursing infants in those days! 20 Pray that your flight may not be in winter or on a sabbath. 21 For at that time there will be great suffering, such as has not been from the be-

---

w Other ancient authorities lack *desolate*   x Or *the Christ*
y Other ancient authorities add *and pestilences*
z Or *stumble*   a Or *gospel*

Be Ready

Have you ever been asked questions like these: If you knew you only had one week to live, what would you do in that time? If you knew you were going to see a loved one for the last time, what would you say to him or her? Faced with those scenarios, many people imagine themselves acting more lovingly and generously than they ordinarily do.

Jesus sets up a similar scenario when he warns his followers to stay awake (Mt 24.42). In this final teaching in Matthew, Jesus is speaking of the final coming of God. The Gospel reminds us that no one knows when Christ will come for us. It is foolish and dangerous to put off living a life committed to Christ.

If you knew you were to stand before God tomorrow, how would you live your life today?

▶ Mt 24.36–44

ginning of the world until now, no, and never will be. 22 And if those days had not been cut short, no one would be saved; but for the sake of the elect those days will be cut short. 23 Then if anyone says to you, 'Look! Here is the Messiah!'*b* or 'There he is!'—do not believe it. 24 For false messiahs*c* and false prophets will appear and produce great signs and omens, to lead astray, if possible, even the elect. 25 Take note, I have told you beforehand. 26 So, if they say to you, 'Look! He is in the wilderness,' do not go out. If they say, 'Look! He is in the inner rooms,' do not believe it. 27 For as the lightning comes from the east and flashes as far as the west, so will be the coming of the Son of Man. 28 Wherever the corpse is, there the vultures will gather.

The Coming of the Son of Man
(Mk 13.24–27; Lk 21.25–28)

29 "Immediately after the suffering of those days

the sun will be darkened,
   and the moon will not give its light;
the stars will fall from heaven,
   and the powers of heaven will be shaken.

30 Then the sign of the Son of Man will appear in heaven, and then all the tribes of the earth will mourn, and they will see 'the Son of Man coming on the clouds of heaven' with power and great glory. 31 And he will send out his angels with a loud trumpet call, and they will gather his elect from the four winds, from one end of heaven to the other.

The Lesson of the Fig Tree
(Mk 13.28–31; Lk 21.29–33)

32 "From the fig tree learn its lesson: as soon as its branch becomes tender and puts forth its leaves, you know that summer is near. 33 So also, when you see all these things, you know that he*d* is near, at the very gates. 34 Truly I tell you, this generation will not pass away until all these things have taken place. 35 Heaven and earth will pass away, but my words will not pass away.

The Necessity for Watchfulness
(Mk 13.32–37; Lk 17.26–27, 34–35; 21.34–36)

36 "But about that day and hour no one knows, neither the angels of heaven, nor the Son,*e* but only the Father. 37 For as the days of Noah were, so will be the coming of the Son of Man. 38 For as in those days before the flood they were eating and drinking, marrying and giving in marriage, until the day Noah entered the ark, 39 and they knew nothing until the flood came and swept them all away, so too will be the coming of the Son of Man. 40 Then two will be in the field; one will be taken and one will be left. 41 Two women will be grinding meal to-

gether; one will be taken and one will be left. 42 Keep awake therefore, for you do not know on what day*f* your Lord is coming. 43 But understand this: if the owner of the house had known in what part of the night the thief was coming, he would have stayed awake and would not have let his house be broken into. 44 Therefore you also must be ready, for the Son of Man is coming at an unexpected hour.

The Faithful or the Unfaithful Slave
(Lk 12.41–48)

45 "Who then is the faithful and wise slave, whom his master has put in charge of his household, to give the other slaves*g* their allowance of food at the proper time? 46 Blessed is that slave whom his master will find at work when he arrives. 47 Truly I tell you, he will put that one in charge of all his possessions. 48 But if that wicked slave says to himself, 'My master is delayed,' 49 and he begins to beat his fellow slaves, and eats and drinks with drunkards, 50 the master of that slave will come on a day when he does not expect him and at an hour that he does not know. 51 He will cut him in pieces*h* and put him with the hypocrites, where there will be weeping and gnashing of teeth.

PRAY IT!
When Are You Coming?

I have accepted your invitation, Lord.
   But when are you coming?
I need to be ready, Lord.
   But when are you coming?
I want to share your love with others, Lord.
   But when are you coming?
I will be prepared, Lord.
   No matter when you are coming.

▶ **Mt 25.1–13**

The Parable of the Ten Bridesmaids

25 "Then the kingdom of heaven will be like this. Ten bridesmaids*i* took their lamps and went to meet the bridegroom.*j* 2 Five of them were foolish, and five were wise. 3 When the foolish took their lamps, they took no oil with them; 4 but the wise took flasks of oil with their

---

b Or *the Christ*   *c* Or *christs*   *d* Or *it*   *e* Other ancient authorities lack *nor the Son*   *f* Other ancient authorities read *at what hour*   *g* Gk *to give them*   *h* Or *cut him off*   *i* Gk *virgins*   *j* Other ancient authorities add *and the bride* lamps. 5 As the bridegroom was delayed, all of them became drowsy and slept. 6 But at midnight there was a shout, 'Look! Here is the bridegroom! Come out to meet him.' 7 Then all those bridesmaids*k* got up and trimmed their lamps. 8 The foolish said to the wise, 'Give us some of your oil, for our lamps are going out.' 9 But the wise replied, 'No! there will not be enough for you and for us; you had better go to the dealers and buy some for yourselves.' 10 And while they went to buy it, the bridegroom came, and those who were ready went with him into the wedding banquet; and the door was shut. 11 Later the other bridesmaids*k* came also, saying, 'Lord, lord, open to us.' 12 But he replied, 'Truly I tell you, I do not know you.' 13 Keep awake therefore, for you know neither the day nor the hour.*l*

The Parable of the Talents
(Lk 19.11–27)

14 "For it is as if a man, going on a journey, summoned his slaves and entrusted his property to them; 15 to one he gave five talents,*m* to another two, to another one, to each according to his ability. Then he went away. 16 The one who had received the five talents went off at once and traded with them, and made five more talents. 17 In the same way, the one who had the two talents made

two more talents. 18 But the one who had received the one talent went off and dug a hole in the ground and hid his master's money. 19 After a long time the master of those slaves came and settled accounts with them. 20 Then the one who had received the five talents came forward, bringing five more talents, saying, 'Master, you handed over to me five talents; see, I have made five more talents.' 21 His master said to him, 'Well done, good and trustworthy slave; you have been trustworthy in a few things, I will put you in charge of many things; enter into the joy of your master.' 22 And the one with the two talents also came forward, saying, 'Master, you handed over to me two talents; see, I have made two more talents.' 23 His master said to him, 'Well done, good and trustworthy slave; you have been trustworthy in a few things, I will put you in charge of many things; enter into the joy of your master.' 24 Then the one who had received the one talent also came forward, saying, 'Master, I knew that you were a harsh man, reaping where you did not sow, and gathering where you did not scatter seed; 25 so I was afraid, and I went and hid your talent in the ground. Here you have what is yours.'

---

k Gk *virgins*   *l* Other ancient authorities add *in which the Son of Man is coming*   *m* A talent was worth more than fifteen years' wages of a laborer

THE PRINCIPLE OF *KUUMBA*

Sometimes I wish I had a great singing voice. I often daydream about belting out songs with the vocal power of a great artist. Sure, I have other gifts, but more than anything else, I wish I could sing. Here I go again, neglecting what I do have as I yearn for what I lack. Why do I do that?

This attitude sounds a bit like that of the ungrateful servant Jesus speaks of in Mt 25.14–30, the parable of the talents, doesn't it? In the parable, the master gives the third servant a talent, but the servant keeps it hidden. And precisely because he keeps it hidden, the timid servant loses the one talent he does have.

God has given us our talents and abilities. The African Kwanzaa principle of *kuumba* (creativity) calls us to use our talents creatively and boldly in the service of God. Don't second-guess the Lord by wanting something you do not have. Trust that God has blessed you with the gifts you need, and use them!

Dear God, thank you for what I have. Help me to use it to your glory. Amen.

▸ Mt 25.14–30

26 But his master replied, 'You wicked and lazy slave! You knew, did you, that I reap where I did not sow, and gather where I did not scatter? 27 Then you ought to have invested my money with the bankers, and on my return I would have received what was my own with interest. 28 So take the talent from him, and give it to the one with the ten talents. 29 For to all those who have, more will be given, and they will have an abundance; but from those who have nothing, even what they have will be taken away. 30 As for this worthless slave, throw him into the outer darkness, where there will be weeping and gnashing of teeth.'

The Judgment of the Nations

31 "When the Son of Man comes in his glory, and all the angels with him, then he will sit on the throne of his glory. 32 All the nations will be gathered before him, and he will separate people one from another as a shepherd separates the sheep from the goats, 33 and he will put the sheep at his right hand and the goats at the left. 34 Then the king will say to those at his right hand, 'Come, you that are blessed by my Father, inherit the kingdom prepared for you from the foundation of the world; 35 for I was hungry and you gave me food, I was thirsty and you gave me something to drink, I was a stranger and you welcomed me, 36 I was naked and you gave me clothing, I was sick and you took care of me, I was in prison and you visited me.' 37 Then the righteous will answer him, 'Lord, when

was it that we saw you hungry and gave you food, or thirsty and gave you something to drink? 38 And when was it that we saw you a stranger and welcomed you, or naked and gave you clothing? 39 And when was it that we saw you sick or in prison and visited you?' 40 And the king will answer them, 'Truly I tell you, just as you did it to one of the least of these who are members of my family,[n] you did it to me.' 41 Then he will say to those at his left hand, 'You that are accursed, depart from me into the eternal fire prepared for the devil and his angels; 42 for I was hungry and you gave me no food, I was thirsty and you gave me nothing to drink, 43 I was a stranger and you did not welcome me, naked and you did not give me clothing, sick and in prison and you did not visit me.' 44 Then they also will answer, 'Lord, when was it that we saw you hungry or thirsty or a stranger or naked or sick or in prison, and did not take care of you?' 45 Then he will answer them, 'Truly I tell you, just as you did not do it to one of the least of these, you did not do it to me.' 46 And these will go away into eternal punishment, but the righteous into eternal life."

The Plot to Kill Jesus
(Mk 14.1–2; Lk 22.1–2; Jn 11.45–53)

26 When Jesus had finished saying all these things, he said to his disciples, 2 "You know that after two days the Passover is coming,

---

n Gk *these my brothers*

'For to all those who **have**, **more** will be given, and they will have an **abundance**; but from those who have nothing, even what they have will be taken away

25.29

MT

and the Son of Man will be handed over to be crucified."

3 Then the chief priests and the elders of the people gathered in the palace of the high priest, who was called Cā'i•a•phas, 4 and they conspired to arrest Jesus by stealth and kill him. 5 But they said, "Not during the festival, or there may be a riot among the people."

The Anointing at Bethany
(Mk 14.3–9; Jn 12.1–8)

6 Now while Jesus was at Beth'a•ny in the house of Simon the leper,⁰ 7 a woman came to him with an alabaster jar of very costly ointment, and she poured it on his head as he sat at the table. 8 But when the disciples saw it, they were angry and said, "Why this waste? 9 For this ointment could have been sold for a large sum, and the money given to the poor." 10 But Jesus, aware of this, said to them, "Why do you trouble the woman? She has performed a good service for me. 11 For you always have the poor with you, but you will not always have me. 12 By pouring this ointment on my body she has prepared me for burial. 13 Truly I tell you, wherever this good newsᵖ is proclaimed in the whole world, what she has done will be told in remembrance of her."

Judas Agrees to Betray Jesus
(Mk 14.10–11; Lk 22.3–6)

14 Then one of the twelve, who was called Ju-das Is•car'i•ot, went to the chief priests 15 and said, "What will you give me if I betray him to you?" They paid him thirty pieces of silver. 16 And from that moment he began to look for an opportunity to betray him.

The Passover with the Disciples
(Mk 14.12–21; Lk 22.7–13)

17 On the first day of Unleavened Bread the disciples came to Jesus, saying, "Where do you want us to make the preparations for you to eat the Passover?" 18 He said, "Go into the city to a certain man, and say to him, 'The Teacher says, My time is near; I will keep the Passover at your house with my disciples.' " 19 So the disciples did as Jesus had directed them, and they prepared the Passover meal.

20 When it was evening, he took his place with the twelve;�q 21 and while they were eating, he said, "Truly I tell you, one of you will betray me." 22 And they became greatly distressed and began to say to him one after another, "Surely not I, Lord?" 23 He answered, "The one who has dipped his hand into the bowl with me will betray me. 24 The Son of Man goes as it is written of him, but woe to that one by whom the Son of Man is betrayed! It would have been better for that one not to have been born."

Catholic Connections

THE NEW COVENANT

In the Old Testament, the word *covenant* is used to express the special relationship between God and the people of Israel. Covenant relationships are rooted in mutual and freely made promises. The laws and worship practices in the Old Testament were signs of this special relationship. But during the Last Supper, Jesus establishes a New Covenant, one sealed with his blood, his very life.

Christians believe that through the paschal mystery—Jesus' life, death, and Resurrection—the New Covenant is established and the Old Covenant is fulfilled. We enter into this new and eternal Covenant through our Baptism. We keep the Covenant by remaining faithful to Christ. The Holy Spirit, God's loving presence in our life, gives us power to live the New Covenant.

In the Eucharist, as we share in the consecrated bread and wine, it is the New Covenant that we celebrate and renew. So the next time you respond "Amen" at a eucharistic celebration, know that you are saying "Yes!" to a special and life-giving relationship with God.

For more on the Eucharist, see the articles for Mk 14.22–25; Lk 22.14–20; Jn 13.1–17.

▶ Mt 26.26–29

25 Judas, who betrayed him, said, "Surely not I, Rabbi?" He replied, "You have said so."

The Institution of the Lord's Supper
(Mk 14.22–26; Lk 22.14–23; 1 Cor 11.23–26)

26 While they were eating, Jesus took a loaf of bread, and after blessing it he broke it, gave it to the disciples, and said, "Take, eat; this is my body." 27 Then he took a cup, and after giving thanks

---

o The terms *leper* and *leprosy* can refer to several diseases
p Or *gospel*   q Other ancient authorities add *disciples*

26.26

he gave it to them, saying, "Drink from it, all of you; 28 for this is my blood of the[r] covenant, which is poured out for many for the forgiveness of sins. 29 I tell you, I will never again drink of this fruit of the vine until that day when I drink it new with you in my Father's kingdom."

30 When they had sung the hymn, they went out to the Mount of Olives.

Peter's Denial Foretold
(Mk 14.27–31; Lk 22.31–34; Jn 13.36–38)

31 Then Jesus said to them, "You will all become deserters because of me this night; for it is written,

'I will strike the shepherd,
and the sheep of the flock will be scattered.'

32 But after I am raised up, I will go ahead of you to Galilee." 33 Peter said to him, "Though all become deserters because of you, I will never desert you." 34 Jesus said to him, "Truly I tell you, this very night, before the cock crows, you will deny me three times." 35 Peter said to him, "Even though I must die with you, I will not deny you." And so said all the disciples.

Jesus Prays in Gethsemane
(Mk 14.32–42; Lk 22.39–46)

36 Then Jesus went with them to a place called Geth·sem'a·nē; and he said to his disciples, "Sit here while I go over there and pray." 37 He took with him Peter and the two sons of Zeb'e·dee, and began to be grieved and agitated. 38 Then he said to them, "I am deeply grieved, even to death; remain here, and stay awake with me." 39 And going a little farther, he threw himself on the ground and prayed, "My Father, if it is possible, let this cup pass from me; yet not what I want but what you want." 40 Then he came to the disciples and found them sleeping; and he said to Peter, "So, could you not stay awake with me one hour? 41 Stay awake and pray that you may not come into the time of trial;[s] the spirit indeed is willing, but the flesh is weak." 42 Again he went away for the second time and prayed, "My Father, if this cannot pass unless I drink it, your will be done." 43 Again he came and found them sleeping, for their eyes were heavy. 44 So leaving them again, he went away and prayed for the third time, saying the same words. 45 Then he came to the disciples and said to them, "Are you still sleeping and taking your rest? See, the hour is

---

r Other ancient authorities add *new*   s Or *into temptation*

Jesus' Imperfect Friends

LIVE IT!

Imagine that you are in the middle of a crisis and ask your best friends to stay with you while you prepare to face the situation. They all promise to be there for you. But one friend after another fails to come through, and you are left to face the trauma alone.

The friends of Jesus were no different. They were well-intentioned and meant to stay awake with him. But in their tiredness, they let him down.

We recognize that the friends of Jesus, the Apostles in particular, were special and holy, but they were also human and had their own weaknesses. Even Peter, one of the greatest heroes of Christianity, lacked the courage to admit he knew Jesus, as we read in Mt 26.69–75. Yet Jesus loved them despite their failings and even when they were disloyal.

Is it easy for you to stay friends with those who let you down? Can you follow the example of Jesus?

▶ Mt 26.36–45

at hand, and the Son of Man is betrayed into the hands of sinners. 46 Get up, let us be going. See, my betrayer is at hand."

The Betrayal and Arrest of Jesus
(Mk 14.43–52; Lk 22.47–53; Jn 18.1–11)

47 While he was still speaking, Judas, one of the twelve, arrived; with him was a large crowd with swords and clubs, from the chief priests and the elders of the people. 48 Now the betrayer had given them a sign, saying, "The one I will kiss is the man; arrest him." 49 At once he came up to Jesus and said, "Greetings, Rabbi!" and kissed him. 50 Jesus said to him, "Friend, do what you are here to do." Then they came and laid hands on Jesus and arrested him. 51 Suddenly, one of those with Jesus put his hand on his sword, drew it, and struck the slave of the high priest, cutting off his ear. 52 Then Jesus said to him, "Put your sword back into its place; for all who take the sword will perish by the sword. 53 Do you think that I cannot appeal to my Father, and he will at once send me more than twelve legions of angels? 54 But how then would the scriptures be fulfilled, which say it must happen in this way?" 55 At that hour Jesus said to the crowds, "Have you come out with swords and clubs to arrest me as though I were a bandit? Day after day I sat in the temple teaching, and you did not arrest me. 56 But all this has taken place, so that the scriptures of the prophets may be fulfilled." Then all the disciples deserted him and fled.

Jesus before the High Priest
(Mk 14.53–65; Lk 22.66–71;
Jn 18.12–14, 19–24)

57 Those who had arrested Jesus took him to Cā'i•a•phas the high priest, in whose house the scribes and the elders had gathered. 58 But Peter was following him at a distance, as far as the courtyard of the high priest; and going inside, he sat with the guards in order to see how this would end. 59 Now the chief priests and the whole council were looking for false testimony against Jesus so that they might put him to death, 60 but they found none, though many false witnesses came forward. At last two came forward 61 and said, "This fellow said, 'I am able to destroy the temple of God and to build it in three days.' " 62 The high priest stood up and said, "Have you no answer? What is it that they testify against you?" 63 But Jesus was silent. Then the high priest said to him, "I put you under oath before the living God, tell us if you are the Messiah,*t* the Son of God." 64 Jesus said to him, "You have said so. But I tell you,

From now on you will see the Son of Man
    seated at the right hand of Power
    and coming on the clouds of heaven."

65 Then the high priest tore his clothes and said, "He has blasphemed! Why do we still need witnesses? You have now heard his blasphemy. 66 What is your verdict?" They answered, "He deserves death." 67 Then they spat in his face and struck him; and some slapped him, 68 saying, "Prophesy to us, you Messiah!*t* Who is it that struck you?"

Peter's Denial of Jesus
(Mk 14.66–72; Lk 22.54–62; Jn 18.15–18, 25–27)

69 Now Peter was sitting outside in the courtyard. A servant-girl came to him and said, "You also were with Jesus the Galilean." 70 But he denied it before all of them, saying, "I do not know what you are talking about." 71 When he went out to the porch, another servant-girl saw him, and she said to the bystanders, "This man was with Jesus of Nazareth."*u* 72 Again he denied it with an oath, "I do not know the man." 73 After a little while the bystanders came up and said to Peter, "Certainly you are also one of them, for your accent betrays you." 74 Then he began to curse, and he swore an oath, "I do not know the man!" At that moment the cock crowed. 75 Then Peter remembered what Jesus had said: "Before the cock crows, you will deny me three times." And he went out and wept bitterly.

Jesus Brought before Pilate
(Mk 15.1; Lk 23.1; Jn 18.28)

27 When morning came, all the chief priests and the elders of the people conferred together against Jesus in order to bring about his death. 2 They bound him, led him away, and handed him over to Pilate the governor.

The Suicide of Judas
(Acts 1.18–19)

3 When Judas, his betrayer, saw that Jesus*v* was condemned, he repented and brought back the thirty pieces of silver to the chief priests and the elders. 4 He said, "I have sinned by betraying innocent*w* blood." But they said, "What is that to us? See to it yourself." 5 Throwing down the pieces of silver in the temple, he departed; and he went and hanged himself. 6 But the chief priests, taking the pieces of silver, said, "It is not lawful to put them into the treasury, since they are blood money." 7 After conferring together, they used them to buy the potter's field as a place to bury foreigners. 8 For this reason that field has been called the Field of Blood to this day. 9 Then was fulfilled what had been spoken through the prophet Jer•e•mi'ah,*x* "And they took*y*

---

t Or *Christ*   *u* Gk *the Nazorean*   *v* Gk *he*   *w* Other ancient authorities read *righteous*   *x* Other ancient authorities read *Zechariah* or *Isaiah*   *y* Or *I took*

did you KNOW?

Judas's Suicide

The Gospel of Matthew presents Judas's suicide as the fulfillment of an Old Testament prophecy from Jeremiah, but it does not tell us why Judas killed himself. Did he kill himself because he felt guilty and could not face the other disciples? Did he feel that the only way he could pay for his sin was with his own life? Whatever his reason, Judas did not believe that he could make up for his mistake—but suicide didn't solve his problem.

Some teenagers think suicide will end their pain, and use it as a way out. Unfortunately, suicide ends everything; not just the current pain but future possibilities for healing, for growth, for new relationships and good times. Consider that both Judas and Peter betrayed Jesus. But whereas Judas ended his life, Peter trusted in God's love and forgiveness and went on to become a great hero. Nothing you can do is so terrible that your only option is taking your life.

Do you ever have thoughts of suicide? If so, talk about them with someone you trust. Speak with a priest, a parent, a youth minister, a school counselor, a coach, or a trusted friend. Caring people will help you. Seeking their help is a better way out.

For more on suicide, see "Suicide Is Not an Answer," 1 Sam 31.1–6.

▶ Mt 27.3–10

the thirty pieces of silver, the price of the one on whom a price had been set,[z] on whom some of the people of Israel had set a price, 10 and they gave[a] them for the potter's field, as the Lord commanded me."

Pilate Questions Jesus
(Mk 15.2–5; Lk 23.2–5; Jn 18.29–38a)

11 Now Jesus stood before the governor; and the governor asked him, "Are you the King of the Jews?" Jesus said, "You say so." 12 But when he was accused by the chief priests and elders, he did not answer. 13 Then Pilate said to him, "Do you not hear how many accusations they make against you?" 14 But he gave him no answer, not even to a single charge, so that the governor was greatly amazed.

Barabbas or Jesus?
(Mk 15.6–14; Lk 23.13–24; Jn 18.39–40)

15 Now at the festival the governor was accustomed to release a prisoner for the crowd, anyone whom they wanted. 16 At that time they had a notorious prisoner, called Jesus[b] Ba·rab′bas. 17 So after they had gathered, Pilate said to them, "Whom do you want me to release for you, Jesus[b] Ba·rab′bas or Jesus who is called the Messiah?"[c] 18 For he realized that it was out of jealousy that they had handed him over. 19 While he was sitting on the judgment seat, his wife sent word to him, "Have nothing to do with that innocent man, for today I have suffered a great deal because of a dream about him." 20 Now the chief priests and the elders persuaded the crowds to ask for Ba·rab′bas and to have Jesus killed. 21 The governor again said to them, "Which of the two do you want me to release for you?" And they said, "Ba·rab′bas." 22 Pilate said to them, "Then what should I do with Jesus who is called the Messiah?"[c] All of them said, "Let him be crucified!" 23 Then he asked, "Why, what evil has he done?" But they shouted all the more, "Let him be crucified!"

Pilate Hands Jesus over to Be Crucified
(Mk 15.15; Lk 23.25; Jn 19.16)

24 So when Pilate saw that he could do nothing, but rather that a riot was beginning, he took some water and washed his hands before the crowd, saying, "I am innocent of this man's blood;[d] see to it yourselves." 25 Then the people as a whole answered, "His blood be on us and on our children!" 26 So he released Ba·rab′bas for them; and after flogging Jesus, he handed him over to be crucified.

The Soldiers Mock Jesus
(Mk 15.16–20)

27 Then the soldiers of the governor took Jesus into the governor's headquarters,[e] and they gathered the whole cohort around him. 28 They stripped him and put a scarlet robe on him, 29 and after twisting some thorns into a crown, they put it on his head. They put a reed in his right hand and knelt before him and mocked him, saying, "Hail, King of the Jews!" 30 They spat on him, and took

---

z Or *the price of the precious One*   a Other ancient authorities read *I gave*   b Other ancient authorities lack *Jesus*   c Or *the Christ*   d Other ancient authorities read *this righteous blood*, or *this righteous man's blood*   e Gk *the praetorium*

MT

PRAY IT?
Suffering Prayer

Jesus, anointed one, everyone endures some suffering in their life. Some suffer in silence. Some loudly complain, making it known to all. Some bitterly blame everyone around them. You suffered ridicule, betrayal, persecution, crucifixion, and death. Your burden was so great, yet you endured. Glorifying God, your sacrifice gives us the hope of eternal life.

Strengthen me to withstand the suffering I must face in my life. When I feel that I have more than I can take, fortify me with the endurance of Job. Give me the patience to suffer injustices without lashing out at others. Fill me with mercy to forgive those who persecute me. Fill me with your loving presence to be a faithful witness to the glory of God and to the promise of eternal life. Amen.

▶ Mt 27.27–44

the reed and struck him on the head. 31 After mocking him, they stripped him of the robe and put his own clothes on him. Then they led him away to crucify him.

The Crucifixion of Jesus
(Mk 15.21–32; Lk 23.26–43; Jn 19.16b–27)

32 As they went out, they came upon a man from Cȳ•rē′nē named Simon; they compelled this man to carry his cross. 33 And when they came to a place called Gol′go•tha (which means Place of a Skull), 34 they offered him wine to drink, mixed with gall; but when he tasted it, he would not drink it. 35 And when they had crucified him, they divided his clothes among themselves by casting lots;*f* 36 then they sat down there and kept watch over him. 37 Over his head they put the charge against him, which read, "This is Jesus, the King of the Jews."

38 Then two bandits were crucified with him, one on his right and one on his left. 39 Those who passed by derided*g* him, shaking their heads 40 and saying, "You who would destroy the temple and build it in three days, save yourself! If you are the Son of God, come down from the cross." 41 In the same way the chief priests also, along with the scribes and elders, were mocking him, saying, 42 "He saved others; he cannot save himself.*h* He is

the King of Israel; let him come down from the cross now, and we will believe in him. 43 He trusts in God; let God deliver him now, if he wants to; for he said, 'I am God's Son.' " 44 The bandits who were crucified with him also taunted him in the same way.

The Death of Jesus
(Mk 15.33–41; Lk 23.44–49; Jn 19.28–30)

45 From noon on, darkness came over the whole land*i* until three in the afternoon. 46 And about three o'clock Jesus cried with a loud voice, "Ē′lī, Ē′lī, le•ma′ sa•bach′tha•nī?" that is, "My God, my God, why have you forsaken me?" 47 When some of the bystanders heard it, they said, "This man is calling for E•lī′jah." 48 At once one of them ran and got a sponge, filled it with sour wine, put it on a stick, and gave it to him to drink. 49 But the others said, "Wait, let us see whether E•lī′jah will

---

f Other ancient authorities add *in order that what had been spoken through the prophet might be fulfilled, "They divided my clothes among themselves, and for my clothing they cast lots."*
g Or *blasphemed*   h Or *is he unable to save himself?*
i Or *earth*

did you KNOW?
The Dawn of a New Age

According to the Gospel of Matthew, some strange things happened when Jesus died. Each event tells us something about Jesus. The darkness that covered the land (27.45) and the earthquake (verse 51) show that all creation was aware that something significant had happened, a new age was dawning. The splitting of the sanctuary veil (verse 51), which is the barrier that separated the holiest part of the Temple (where God was thought to dwell) from the rest of the Temple area, symbolizes that now God would be directly accessible to the people. And what do the dead saints who came out of their tombs to walk in the city symbolize? They are the fulfillment of Ezekiel's vision (Ezekiel, chapter 37). The dried bones had come to life—God had triumphed over death!

▶ Mt 27.45–54

did you KNOW?

Jesus Prays Psalm 22

The Gospel writer tells us that before Jesus gave up his spirit and breathed his last breath, he cried out, "My God, my God, why have you forsaken me?" Jesus was actually reciting and praying the opening lines to Psalm 22. This Psalm begins in despair but ends in triumph and confidence through God's saving help. With this prayer to God, Jesus invites all people gathered at the crucifixion to pray the entire psalm, not just the first words of despair but also the concluding words of hope.

Read also "Hope in Despair," Psalm 22.

▶ Mt 27.46

come to save him."[j] 50 Then Jesus cried again with a loud voice and breathed his last.[k] 51 At that moment the curtain of the temple was torn in two, from top to bottom. The earth shook, and the rocks were split. 52 The tombs also were opened, and many bodies of the saints who had fallen asleep were raised. 53 After his resurrection they came out of the tombs and entered the holy city and appeared to many. 54 Now when the centurion and those with him, who were keeping watch over Jesus, saw the earthquake and what took place, they were terrified and said, "Truly this man was God's Son!"[l]

55 Many women were also there, looking on from a distance; they had followed Jesus from Galilee and had provided for him. 56 Among them were Mary Mag'da•lēne, and Mary the mother of James and Joseph, and the mother of the sons of Zeb'e•dee.

The Burial of Jesus
(Mk 15.42–47; Lk 23.50–56; Jn 19.38–42)

57 When it was evening, there came a rich man from Ar•i•ma•thē'a, named Joseph, who was also a

---

j Other ancient authorities add *And another took a spear and pierced his side, and out came water and blood*   k Or *gave up his spirit*   l Or *a son of God*

JESUS DIED ON THE CROSS BECAUSE HE LOVES US!

In some cultures, people often identify more with the suffering and crucified Christ than with the risen Christ. In the cross is a redemptive love, one that brings peace and the strength to accept what cannot be changed and to continue the struggle out of poverty and oppression.

There is always suffering in life. When this suffering is not accepted, it is even worse. In contrast, when we accept suffering, it is bearable, and we have the inner peace needed to continue living and working for a better life. Suffering achieves its highest meaning when it is accepted out of love. That Jesus is capable of suffering gives witness to God's special love for those who suffer.

Finding God's life in the midst of suffering leads to generous sacrifices that are a source of life for those we love. Let's pray:

Jesus, help us to always remember that your commitment to your mission led to your death. Help us to understand that true life is always achieved through love. Help us to have love at the core of all we think and do. And help us to share your love, especially with those who need it the most, the poor and marginalized people. Amen.

▶ Mt 27.24–56

MT

disciple of Jesus. 58 He went to Pilate and asked for the body of Jesus; then Pilate ordered it to be given to him. 59 So Joseph took the body and wrapped it in a clean linen cloth 60 and laid it in his own new tomb, which he had hewn in the rock. He then rolled a great stone to the door of the tomb and went away. 61 Mary Mag'da·lēne and the other Mary were there, sitting opposite the tomb.

The Guard at the Tomb

62 The next day, that is, after the day of Preparation, the chief priests and the Phar'i·sees gathered before Pilate 63 and said, "Sir, we remember what that impostor said while he was still alive, 'After three days I will rise again.' 64 Therefore command the tomb to be made secure until the third day; otherwise his disciples may go and steal him away, and tell the people, 'He has been raised from the dead,' and the last deception would be worse than the first." 65 Pilate said to them, "You have a guard *m* of soldiers; go, make it as secure as you can."*n* 66 So they went with the guard and made the tomb secure by sealing the stone.

The Resurrection of Jesus
(Mk 16.1–8; Lk 24.1–12; Jn 20.1–10)

28 After the sabbath, as the first day of the week was dawning, Mary Mag'da·lēne and the other Mary went to see the tomb. 2 And suddenly there was a great earthquake; for an angel of the Lord, descending from heaven, came and rolled back the stone and sat on it. 3 His appearance

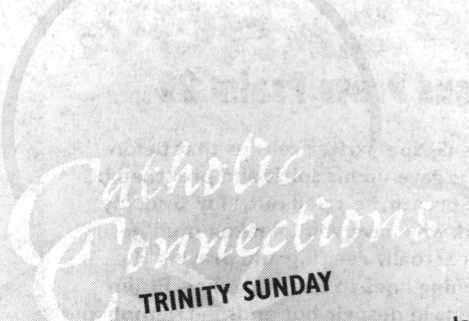

was like lightning, and his clothing white as snow. 4 For fear of him the guards shook and became like dead men. 5 But the angel said to the women, "Do not be afraid; I know that you are looking for Jesus who was crucified. 6 He is not here; for he has been raised, as he said. Come, see the place where he*o* lay. 7 Then go quickly and tell his disciples, 'He has been raised from the dead,*p* and indeed he is going ahead of you to Galilee; there you will see him.' This is my message for you." 8 So they left the tomb quickly with fear and great joy, and ran to tell his disciples. 9 Suddenly Jesus met them and said, "Greetings!" And they came to him, took hold of his feet, and worshiped him. 10 Then Jesus said to them, "Do not be afraid; go and tell my brothers to go to Galilee; there they will see me."

The Report of the Guard

11 While they were going, some of the guard went into the city and told the chief priests everything that had happened. 12 After the priests*q* had assembled with the elders, they devised a plan to give a large sum of money to the soldiers, 13 telling them, "You must say, 'His disciples came by night and stole him away while we were asleep.' 14 If this comes to the governor's ears, we will satisfy him and keep you out of trouble." 15 So they took the money and did as they were directed. And this story is still told among the Jews to this day.

PRAY IT
I Will Follow

If you lead me to travel to other nations,
  I will follow, Lord.
If you lead me to write to glorify your name,
  I will follow, Lord.
If you lead me to preach of your heavenly
    Kingdom,
  I will follow, Lord.
If you lead me to show others your way,
  I will follow, Lord.
If you lead me to use my actions to declare
    your Gospel,
  I will follow, Lord.
Because you are always with me,
  so I will follow, Lord.

▶ Mt 28.16–20

---

m Or *Take a guard* *n* Gk *you know how* *o* Other ancient authorities read *the Lord* *p* Other ancient authorities lack *from the dead* *q* Gk *they*

The Commissioning of the Disciples
(Mk 16.14–18; Lk 24.36–49; Jn 20.19–23;
Acts 1.6–8)

16 Now the eleven disciples went to Galilee, to the mountain to which Jesus had directed them. 17 When they saw him, they worshiped him; but some doubted. 18 And Jesus came and said to them, "All authority in heaven and on earth has been given to me. 19 Go therefore and make disciples of all nations, baptizing them in the name of the Father and of the Son and of the Holy Spirit, 20 and teaching them to obey everything that I have commanded you. And remember, I am with you always, to the end of the age."ʳ

ʳ Other ancient authorities add *Amen*

Have you ever been ridiculed or rejected by others—maybe even your friends—for trying to do something good? Jesus would understand your feelings. In the Gospel of Mark, Jesus is misunderstood and abandoned by those closest to him. This Gospel was written for early Christians experiencing persecution or death for their faith. The author is reminding them and us to put our total trust in God as Jesus did, despite whatever difficulties we encounter in being a Christian.

At a Glance

- **1.1–15.** John the Baptist's announcement of Jesus' ministry

- **1.16—8.21.** Jesus' preaching and miracles in Galilee

- **8.22—10.52.** Jesus' teaching and healing on the way to Jerusalem

- **Chapters 11–13.** Jesus' teaching in Jerusalem

- **Chapters 14–16.** Jesus' death and Resurrection

In-depth

The Gospel of Mark is the shortest of the four Gospels and can be easily read in one sitting. It portrays Jesus as a man of action—human in his feelings, and always on the move fulfilling his mission. This Gospel answers two fundamental questions: Who is this Jesus called the Christ? and What does it mean to be his disciple? Because the people hearing this Gospel were in danger of losing their life for what they believed, those questions were a matter of life and death.

To answer the first question, the Gospel of Mark tells stories about Jesus' power to heal and about his compassion for suffering people. It tells about his conflicts with demons and with religious and civil authorities and how he was misunderstood by his own disciples. Through these stories comes the realization that Jesus is the Messiah, the promised savior. But he did not come as the victorious king many Jews expected. Instead, he accepted the suffering that comes with doing God's will. His painful and shameful death was needed before his glory could be seen. Can we believe in a very human, suffering Messiah?

Mark answers the second question in surprising ways. The disciples Jesus called were initially fearful and hard-hearted. They wanted to be powerful and important, and they wanted the approval of their peers. But gradually, they came to believe that Jesus was the Messiah, and to understand his mission. The Gospel of Mark also tells stories about a blind man, a leper, and Gentiles (non-Jews), all of whom were Jesus' disciples because they placed their total trust in him. Whether gradually or quickly, can we place our complete faith in Jesus, becoming his disciples?

Quick Facts

Author
a Gentile Christian, possibly a disciple of Peter named John Mark

Date Written
approximately A.D. 65 to 70; this was the first written Gospel

Audience
non-Jewish Christians (in Rome?) who were experiencing persecution because of their belief in Jesus

Image of Jesus
healer and miracle worker who accepts suffering as the cost for following God's will

Mark

1.9

The Proclamation of John the Baptist
(Mt 3.1–12; Lk 3.1–20; Jn 1.19–28)

1 The beginning of the good news[a] of Jesus Christ, the Son of God.[b]

2 As it is written in the prophet I•sāi'ah,[c]
"See, I am sending my messenger ahead of
you,[d]
who will prepare your way;

3 the voice of one crying out in the
wilderness:
'Prepare the way of the Lord,
make his paths straight,' "

4 John the baptizer appeared[e] in the wilderness, proclaiming a baptism of repentance for the forgiveness of sins. 5 And people from the whole Judean countryside and all the people of Jerusalem were going out to him, and were baptized by him in the river Jordan, confessing their sins. 6 Now John was clothed with camel's hair, with a leather belt around his waist, and he ate locusts and wild honey. 7 He proclaimed, "The one who is more powerful than I is coming after me; I am not worthy to stoop down and untie the thong of his sandals. 8 I have baptized you with[f] water; but he will baptize you with[f] the Holy Spirit."

The Baptism of Jesus
(Mt 3.13–17; Lk 3.21–22; Jn 1.29–34)

9 In those days Jesus came from Nazareth of Galilee and was baptized by John in the Jordan. 10 And just as he was coming up out of the water, he saw the heavens torn apart and the Spirit descending like a dove on him. 11 And a voice came from heaven, "You are my Son, the Beloved;[g] with you I am well pleased."

The Temptation of Jesus
(Mt 4.1–11; Lk 4.1–13)

12 And the Spirit immediately drove him out into the wilderness. 13 He was in the wilderness forty days, tempted by Satan; and he was with the wild beasts; and the angels waited on him.

The Beginning of the Galilean Ministry
(Mt 4.12–17; Lk 4.14–15)

14 Now after John was arrested, Jesus came to Galilee, proclaiming the good news[a] of God,[h] 15 and saying, "The time is fulfilled, and the kingdom of God has come near;[i] repent, and believe in the good news."[a]

Jesus Calls the First Disciples
(Mt 4.18–22; Lk 5.1–11)

16 As Jesus passed along the Sea of Galilee, he saw Simon and his brother Andrew casting a net into the sea—for they were fishermen. 17 And Jesus said to them, "Follow me and I will make you fish

---

a Or *gospel*   *b* Other ancient authorities lack *the Son of God*   *c* Other ancient authorities read *in the prophets*   *d* Gk *before your face*   *e* Other ancient authorities read *John was baptizing*   *f* Or *in*   *g* Or *my beloved Son*   *h* Other ancient authorities read *of the kingdom*   *i* Or *is at hand* for people." 18 And immediately they left their nets and followed him. 19 As he went a little farther, he saw James son of Zeb′e•dee and his brother John, who were in their boat mending the nets. 20 Immediately he called them; and they left their father Zeb′e•dee in the boat with the hired men, and followed him.

The Man with an Unclean Spirit
(Lk 4.31–37)

21 They went to Ca•per′na•um; and when the sabbath came, he entered the synagogue and taught. 22 They were astounded at his teaching, for he taught them as one having authority, and not as the scribes. 23 Just then there was in their synagogue a man with an unclean spirit, 24 and he cried out, "What have you to do with us, Jesus of Nazareth? Have you come to destroy us? I know who you are, the Holy One of God." 25 But Jesus rebuked him, saying, "Be silent, and come out of him!" 26 And the unclean spirit, convulsing him and crying with a loud voice, came out of him. 27 They were all amazed, and they kept on asking one another, "What is this? A new teaching—with authority! He*j* commands even the unclean spirits, and they obey him." 28 At once his fame began to spread throughout the surrounding region of Galilee.

Jesus Heals Many at Simon's House
(Mt. 8.14–17; Lk 4.38–41)

29 As soon as they*k* left the synagogue, they entered the house of Simon and Andrew, with James and John. 30 Now Simon's mother-in-law was in bed with a fever, and they told him about her at once. 31 He came and took her by the hand and lifted her up. Then the fever left her, and she began to serve them.

32 That evening, at sunset, they brought to him all who were sick or possessed with demons. 33 And the whole city was gathered around the door. 34 And he cured many who were sick with various diseases, and cast out many demons; and he would not permit the demons to speak, because they knew him.

A Preaching Tour in Galilee
(Mt 4.23–25; Lk 4.42–44)

35 In the morning, while it was still very dark, he got up and went out to a deserted place, and there he prayed. 36 And Simon and his companions hunted for him. 37 When they found him, they said to him, "Everyone is searching for you." 38 He answered, "Let us go on to the neighboring towns, so that I may proclaim the message there also; for that is what I came out to do." 39 And he went throughout Galilee, proclaiming the message in their synagogues and casting out demons.

Jesus Cleanses a Leper
(Mt 8.1–4; Lk 5.12–16)

40 A leper*l* came to him begging him, and kneeling*m* he said to him, "If you choose, you can

---

j Or A *new teaching! With authority he*   *k* Other ancient authorities read *he*   *l* The terms *leper* and *leprosy* can refer to several diseases   *m* Other ancient authorities lack *kneeling*

LIVE IT!

Called to Follow Jesus

The response of Peter, Andrew, James, and John to Jesus is an example of obedience to God's call. Jesus calls them because he loves them and trusts them to share in his mission.

    The Catholic church believes that through Baptism, all Christians are called to be Jesus' disciples (followers) in whatever path their life takes. Most people are called to mission as a layperson. A few are called to serve through the priesthood, diaconate, or religious life. So whether you end up a priest or a plumber, married or single, poor or rich, faithfulness to God's call is the most important loyalty you can have.

    It might be hard to imagine how school or work is part of your call to follow Jesus. But attitude is everything! Do you see school as only necessary to get a job that makes lots of money? Or do you see it as preparation for a career that will allow you to serve others and contribute to society? If you work, do you approach your job halfheartedly, or are you enthusiastic, always giving your best effort? Do you treat coworkers and customers with warmth and respect? Jesus is calling you to be his disciple wherever you are and whatever you might be doing.

▸ Mk 1.16–20

Moved with pity,
     Jesus stretched out his hand
          and touched him, and said to him,

"I do choose.
Be made clean!"

1.41–42

Immediately the leprosy left him,
and he was made clean.

make me clean." [41] Moved with pity,[n] Jesus[o] stretched out his hand and touched him, and said to him, "I do choose. Be made clean!" [42] Immediately the leprosy[p] left him, and he was made clean. [43] After sternly warning him he sent him away at once, [44] saying to him, "See that you say nothing to anyone; but go, show yourself to the priest, and offer for your cleansing what Moses commanded, as a testimony to them." [45] But he went out and began to proclaim it freely, and to spread the word, so that Jesus[o] could no longer go into a town openly, but stayed out in the country; and people came to him from every quarter.

Jesus Heals a Paralytic
(Mt 9.2–8; Lk 5.17–26)

2 When he returned to Ca·per'na·um after some days, it was reported that he was at home. [2] So many gathered around that there was no longer room for them, not even in front of the door; and he was speaking the word to them. [3] Then some people[q] came, bringing to him a paralyzed man, carried by four of them. [4] And when

---

[n] Other ancient authorities read *anger*   [o] Gk *he*
[p] The terms *leper* and *leprosy* can refer to several diseases
[q] Gk *they*

Faithful Friends

We are not given many details about the paralyzed man in the story in Mk 2.1–12, but we might conclude one thing: he had at least four good friends! The main point of this story is that Jesus has the authority to forgive sins, a power that belongs only to God. But what can be said about the four friends who carried the paralyzed man to Jesus?

First, their actions show that they were convinced that Jesus could do something for their paralyzed friend. Second, they were committed to their friend. And last, they didn't let a seemingly insurmountable obstacle—the crowded doorway—prevent them from getting their friend to the feet of Jesus.

What faithful people in your life have helped you come to know Jesus? For whom might you currently have the opportunity to be that kind of faithful friend?

▶ Mk 2.1–12

M
K

they could not bring him to Jesus because of the crowd, they removed the roof above him; and after having dug through it, they let down the mat on which the paralytic lay. 5 When Jesus saw their faith, he said to the paralytic, "Son, your sins are forgiven." 6 Now some of the scribes were sitting there, questioning in their hearts, 7 "Why does this fellow speak in this way? It is blasphemy! Who can forgive sins but God alone?" 8 At once Jesus perceived in his spirit that they were discussing these questions among themselves; and he said to them, "Why do you raise such questions in your hearts? 9 Which is easier, to say to the paralytic, 'Your sins are forgiven,' or to say, 'Stand up and take your mat and walk'? 10 But so that you may know that the Son of Man has authority on earth to forgive sins"—he said to the paralytic— 11 "I say to you, stand up, take your mat and go to your home." 12 And he stood up, and immediately took the mat and went out before all of them; so that they were all amazed and glorified God, saying, "We have never seen anything like this!"

Jesus Calls Levi
(Mt 9.9–13; Lk 5.27–32)

13 Jesus[r] went out again beside the sea; the whole crowd gathered around him, and he taught them. 14 As he was walking along, he saw Levi son of Al•phae'us sitting at the tax booth, and he said to him, "Follow me." And he got up and followed him.

15 And as he sat at dinner[s] in Levi's[t] house, many tax collectors and sinners were also sitting[u] with Jesus and his disciples—for there were many who followed him. 16 When the scribes of[v] the Phar'i•sees saw that he was eating with sinners and tax collectors, they said to his disciples, "Why does he

eat[w] with tax collectors and sinners?" 17 When Jesus heard this, he said to them, "Those who are well have no need of a physician, but those who are sick; I have come to call not the righteous but sinners."

The Question about Fasting
(Mt 9.14–17; Lk 5.33–39)

18 Now John's disciples and the Phar'i•sees were fasting; and people[x] came and said to him, "Why do John's disciples and the disciples of the Phar'i•sees fast, but your disciples do not fast?" 19 Jesus said to them, "The wedding guests cannot fast while the bridegroom is with them, can they? As long as they have the bridegroom with them, they cannot fast. 20 The days will come when the bridegroom is taken away from them, and then they will fast on that day.

21 "No one sews a piece of unshrunk cloth on an old cloak; otherwise, the patch pulls away from it, the new from the old, and a worse tear is made. 22 And no one puts new wine into old wineskins; otherwise, the wine will burst the skins, and the wine is lost, and so are the skins; but one puts new wine into fresh wineskins."[y]

Pronouncement about the Sabbath
(Mt 12.1–8; Lk 6.1–5)

23 One sabbath he was going through the grainfields; and as they made their way his disciples began to pluck heads of grain. 24 The Phar'isees said to him, "Look, why are they doing what is not lawful on the sabbath?" 25 And he said to them, "Have

---

r Gk He s Gk reclined t Gk his u Gk reclining v Other ancient authorities read and w Other ancient authorities add and drink x Gk they y Other ancient authorities lack but one puts new wine into fresh wineskins

---

Getting Personal

It is one thing to be seen associating with certain groups of people, but it is another to be seen eating with them. Jesus was often criticized for eating with the wrong kind of people, a charge he answers in Mk 2.13–17. He knew that the only way to help someone grow was to get to know him or her—personally.

It did not matter to Jesus whether the person was rich or poor, well known or unknown, regarded as a saint or as a sinner. It did not matter to him whether the person was black or white, male or female, young or old. What did matter to Jesus was whether the person he approached was interested in getting to know him—and his heavenly Father—personally.

Are you ready to get to know Jesus personally? If so, take a few minutes to close your eyes and think about what it says in this passage. Talk to Jesus about what is going on in your life and in your family's life. When you are done talking, spend some time quietly listening for what Jesus has to say to you—personally.

▶ Mk 2.13–17

you never read what David did when he and his companions were hungry and in need of food? 26 He entered the house of God, when A•bī′a•thar was high priest, and ate the bread of the Presence, which it is not lawful for any but the priests to eat, and he gave some to his companions." 27 Then he said to them, "The sabbath was made for humankind, and not humankind for the sabbath; 28 so the Son of Man is lord even of the sabbath."

beyond the Jordan, and the region around Tȳre and Si′don. 9 He told his disciples to have a boat ready for him because of the crowd, so that they would not crush him; 10 for he had cured many, so that all who had diseases pressed upon him to touch him. 11 Whenever the unclean spirits saw him, they fell down before him and shouted, "You are the Son of God!" 12 But he sternly ordered them not to make him known.

Trusting God

In the book *Johnny Tremain*, the main character is a boy whose hand is severely burned, and the story is about how he learns to live with a disfigured limb. At many points in the story, Johnny hides his hand from others to avoid feeling embarrassed.

In Mk 3.1–6, among those gathered in the synagogue is a man with a "withered hand." There is no indication that he is seeking out Jesus or that he commands any special attention. Jesus notices him and invites him to come forward. Jesus then asks the man to stretch out his disfigured hand for all to see.

Like Johnny Tremain, the man, we might guess, probably did not feel proud of his hand. It certainly would be understandable if, when invited by Jesus to stretch out his hand for all to see, the man had stormed out of the synagogue in anger and shame. Instead, he did what Jesus asked, and through his trust in Jesus, his hand was restored to wholeness.

Whether physically, emotionally, or spiritually, we are all "disfigured" in some ways. What source of pain or shame in your own life might Jesus be inviting you to share with him? Can you risk becoming vulnerable and trusting him with it?

▶ Mk 3.1–6

The Man with a Withered Hand
(Mt 12.9–14; Lk 6.6–11)

3 Again he entered the synagogue, and a man was there who had a withered hand. 2 They watched him to see whether he would cure him on the sabbath, so that they might accuse him. 3 And he said to the man who had the withered hand, "Come forward." 4 Then he said to them, "Is it lawful to do good or to do harm on the sabbath, to save life or to kill?" But they were silent. 5 He looked around at them with anger; he was grieved at their hardness of heart and said to the man, "Stretch out your hand." He stretched it out, and his hand was restored. 6 The Phar′i•sees went out and immediately conspired with the He•rō′di•ans against him, how to destroy him.

A Multitude at the Seaside
(Mt 12.15–21)

7 Jesus departed with his disciples to the sea, and a great multitude from Galilee followed him; 8 hearing all that he was doing, they came to him in great numbers from Judea, Jerusalem, Id•u•mē′a,

Jesus Appoints the Twelve
(Mt 10.1–4; Lk 6.12–16)

13 He went up the mountain and called to him those whom he wanted, and they came to him. 14 And he appointed twelve, whom he also named apostles,z to be with him, and to be sent out to proclaim the message, 15 and to have authority to cast out demons. 16 So he appointed the twelve:a Simon (to whom he gave the name Peter); 17 James son of Zeb′e•dee and John the brother of James (to whom he gave the name Bō•a•ner′gēs, that is, Sons of Thunder); 18 and Andrew, and Philip, and Bartholomew, and Matthew, and Thomas, and James son of Al•phaē′us, and Thad•daē′us, and Simon the Cā•na•naē′an, 19 and Judas Is•car′i•ot, who betrayed him.

Jesus and Beelzebul
(Mt 12.22–32; Lk 11.14–23)

Then he went home; 20 and the crowd came together again, so that they could not even eat.

---

z Other ancient authorities lack *whom he also named apostles*
a Other ancient authorities lack *So he appointed the twelve*

21 When his family heard it, they went out to restrain him, for people were saying, "He has gone out of his mind." 22 And the scribes who came down from Jerusalem said, "He has Bē·el′ze·bul, and by the ruler of the demons he casts out demons." 23 And he called them to him, and spoke to them in parables, "How can Satan cast out Satan? 24 If a kingdom is divided against itself, that kingdom cannot stand. 25 And if a house is divided against itself, that house will not be able to stand. 26 And if Satan has risen up against himself and is divided, he cannot stand, but his end has come. 27 But no one can enter a strong man's house and plunder his property without first tying up the strong man; then indeed the house can be plundered.

28 "Truly I tell you, people will be forgiven for their sins and whatever blasphemies they utter; 29 but whoever blasphemes against the Holy Spirit can never have forgiveness, but is guilty of an eternal sin"— 30 for they had said, "He has an unclean spirit."

The True Kindred of Jesus
(Mt 12.46–50; Lk 8.19–21)

31 Then his mother and his brothers came; and standing outside, they sent to him and called him. 32 A crowd was sitting around him; and they said to him, "Your mother and your brothers and sisters[b] are outside, asking for you." 33 And he replied, "Who are my mother and my brothers?" 34 And looking at those who sat around him, he said, "Here are my mother and my brothers! 35 Whoever does the will of God is my brother and sister and mother."

The Parable of the Sower
(Mt 13.1–23; Lk 8.4–15)

4 Again he began to teach beside the sea. Such a very large crowd gathered around him that he got into a boat on the sea and sat there, while the whole crowd was beside the sea on the land. 2 He began to teach them many things in parables, and in his teaching he said to them: 3 "Listen! A sower went out to sow. 4 And as he sowed, some seed fell on the path, and the birds came and ate it up. 5 Other seed fell on rocky ground, where it did not have much soil, and it sprang up quickly, since it had no depth of soil. 6 And when the sun rose, it was scorched; and since it had no root, it withered away. 7 Other seed fell among thorns, and the thorns grew up and choked it, and it yielded no grain. 8 Other seed fell into good soil and brought forth grain, growing up and increasing and yielding thirty and sixty and a hundredfold." 9 And he said, "Let anyone with ears to hear listen!"

Catholic Connections

HOLY ORDERS

Jesus appoints twelve men as the Apostles (the word *apostle* means "sent out"). Their mission—to preach the Good News, drive out demons, and cure the sick—is an extension of Jesus' mission. The Catholic church considers bishops as the successors of the Apostles. Bishops are responsible for the church's mission, for its organization, and for seeing that Jesus' message is taught and lived faithfully from generation to generation.

Bishops are ordained by other bishops as a sign of their unbroken connection with the first Apostles. Bishops also ordain priests and deacons for service in the church, especially for sacramental ministry. These ordinations happen in the sacrament of Holy Orders, one of the seven sacraments of the church. In the sacrament of Holy Orders, the bishop places his hands on the head of the man being ordained and prays for a special outpouring of the Holy Spirit.

▶ Mk 3.13–19

The Purpose of the Parables
(Mt 13.10–17; Lk 8.9–10)

10 When he was alone, those who were around him along with the twelve asked him about the parables. 11 And he said to them, "To you has been given the secret[c] of the kingdom of God, but for those outside, everything comes in parables; 12 in order that

'they may indeed look, but not perceive,
   and may indeed listen, but not understand;
so that they may not turn again and be
   forgiven.' "

13 And he said to them, "Do you not understand this parable? Then how will you understand all the parables? 14 The sower sows the word. 15 These are the ones on the path where the word is sown: when they hear, Satan immediately comes

---

b Other ancient authorities lack *and sisters*   c Or *mystery* and takes away the word that is sown in them. 16 And these are the ones sown on rocky ground: when they hear the word, they immediately receive it with joy. 17 But they have no root, and endure only for a while; then, when trouble or persecution arises on account of the word, immediately they fall away.*d* 18 And others are those sown among the thorns: these are the ones who hear the word, 19 but the cares of the world, and the lure of wealth, and the desire for other things come in and choke the word, and it yields nothing. 20 And these are the ones sown on the good soil: they hear the word and accept it and bear fruit, thirty and sixty and a hundredfold."

A Lamp under a Bushel Basket
(Lk 8.16–18)

21 He said to them, "Is a lamp brought in to be put under the bushel basket, or under the bed, and not on the lampstand? 22 For there is nothing hidden, except to be disclosed; nor is anything secret, except to come to light. 23 Let anyone with ears to hear listen!" 24 And he said to them, "Pay attention to what you hear; the measure you give will be the measure you get, and still more will be given you. 25 For to those who have, more will be given; and

from those who have nothing, even what they have will be taken away."

The Parable of the Growing Seed

26 He also said, "The kingdom of God is as if someone would scatter seed on the ground, 27 and would sleep and rise night and day, and the seed would sprout and grow, he does not know how. 28 The earth produces of itself, first the stalk, then the head, then the full grain in the head. 29 But when the grain is ripe, at once he goes in with his sickle, because the harvest has come."

The Parable of the Mustard Seed
(Mt 13.31–32; Lk 13.18–19)

30 He also said, "With what can we compare the kingdom of God, or what parable will we use for it? 31 It is like a mustard seed, which, when sown upon the ground, is the smallest of all the seeds on earth; 32 yet when it is sown it grows up and becomes the greatest of all shrubs, and puts forth large branches, so that the birds of the air can make nests in its shade."

---

d Or *stumble*

JESUS TEACHES US THROUGH STORIES!

In Mark, chapter 4, Jesus teaches about God's Reign through parables (see "Parables," Mt 13.10). In some cultures, it is customary for young people to hear their grandmother tell stories about their family history, traditions, and faith. Many of the stories are true, others may be created to give a moral teaching, like the parables. Here is a true story:

A little girl's father died, leaving her family in extreme poverty. Her mother never lost faith in God, daily prayed to the Divine Providence, and asked other people to pray with her. Her prayers were always answered: food appeared miraculously in front of the family's door, and her six children were accepted free in Catholic schools.

Eventually, the mother married a creative businessman. When the business prospered, she remembered the way God had moved the hearts of people so that her family could have food and education, and with great confidence in God, she started a boarding school for boys. Whenever there was not enough food, she prayed and invited other people to pray. The Divine Providence always responded. The school has sheltered and educated two hundred boys each year for the last seventy years.

■ Which stories of faith, love, and service have marked the history of your family?
■ How are you honoring your family's tradition of bringing the Gospel to people in need?

▸ Mk 4.1–34

The Use of Parables

33 With many such parables he spoke the word to them, as they were able to hear it; 34 he did not speak to them except in parables, but he explained everything in private to his disciples.

Jesus Stills a Storm
(Mt 8.23–27; Lk 8.22–25)

35 On that day, when evening had come, he said to them, "Let us go across to the other side." 36 And leaving the crowd behind, they took him with them in the boat, just as he was. Other boats were with him. 37 A great windstorm arose, and the waves beat into the boat, so that the boat was already being swamped. 38 But he was in the stern, asleep on the cushion; and they woke him up and said to him, "Teacher, do you not care that we are perishing?" 39 He woke up and rebuked the wind, and said to the sea, "Peace! Be still!" Then the wind ceased, and there was a dead calm. 40 He said to them, "Why are you afraid? Have you still no faith?" 41 And they were filled with great awe and said to one another, "Who then is this, that even the wind and the sea obey him?"

PRAY IT!
Everyone's Welcome!

In Mark, chapters 5–8, Jesus expands his mission into Gentile territory, the region on the eastern side of the Sea of Galilee. Three miraculous healings of Gentiles—the Gerasene demoniac (5.1–13), the Syrophoenician's daughter (7.24–30), and the deaf man from Tyre (7.31–37)—extend the promises of the Reign of God to all who have faith in Jesus. In arranging these stories, the author of the Gospel emphasizes that God's salvation is available to everyone, not just to the Jews.

In your prayer, reflect or journal on the following questions:
- How do you treat people from a different race, culture, or religion?
- How could you be more welcoming toward them, more like Jesus?

Write a prayer expressing your desire.

▸ Mk 5.1—8.30

PRAY IT!
Life's Storms

Storms on the Sea of Galilee are a common occurrence. They are a fisher's nightmare, and the one described in Mk 4.35–41 was really bad! It is no wonder the Apostles felt fearful and powerless. As part of your prayer, try this meditation:

Begin by closing your eyes and relaxing. Then visualize yourself standing on the beach with Jesus and the disciples. Join them as they board the boat. When the squall comes, experience the rocking of the boat, the waves crashing on deck, and the winds blowing. Feel the disciples' anxiety and fear as the boat is tossed and water pours into the boat. Go with the disciples to wake Jesus, and watch as Jesus calms the storm. Now, experience the peacefulness and tranquility of the miracle you have witnessed.

All of us have storms we must face, that is, parts of our life that are filled with anxiety or fear. Think about your life. What are the storms that batter and rock your world? Who in your family or in your community can calm your fears? How would you respond to Jesus' question, "Have you still no faith?" (Mk 4.40).

▸ Mk 4.35—41

Jesus Heals the Gerasene Demoniac
(Mt 8.28—9.1; Lk 8.26–39)

5 They came to the other side of the sea, to the country of the Ger'a·sēnes.*e* 2 And when he had stepped out of the boat, immediately a man out of the tombs with an unclean spirit met him. 3 He lived among the tombs; and no one could restrain him any more, even with a chain; 4 for he had often been restrained with shackles and chains, but the chains he wrenched apart, and the shackles he broke in pieces; and no one had the strength to subdue him. 5 Night and day among the tombs and on the mountains he was always howling and bruising himself with stones. 6 When he saw Jesus from a distance, he ran and bowed down before him; 7 and he shouted at the top of his voice, "What have you to do with me, Jesus, Son of the Most High God? I adjure you by God, do not torment me." 8 For he had said to him, "Come out of the

---

e Other ancient authorities read *Gergesenes*; others, *Gadarenes* man, you unclean spirit!" [9] Then Jesus[f] asked him, "What is your name?" He replied, "My name is Legion; for we are many." [10] He begged him earnestly not to send them out of the country. [11] Now there on the hillside a great herd of swine was feeding; [12] and the unclean spirits[g] begged him, "Send us into the swine; let us enter them." [13] So he gave them permission. And the unclean spirits came out and entered the swine; and the herd, numbering about two thousand, rushed down the steep bank into the sea, and were drowned in the sea.

[14] The swineherds ran off and told it in the city and in the country. Then people came to see what it was that had happened. [15] They came to Jesus and saw the demoniac sitting there, clothed and in his right mind, the very man who had had the legion; and they were afraid. [16] Those who had seen what had happened to the demoniac and to the swine reported it. [17] Then they began to beg Jesus[h] to leave their neighborhood. [18] As he was getting into the boat, the man who had been possessed by demons begged him that he might be with him. [19] But Jesus[f] refused, and said to him, "Go home to your friends, and tell them how much the Lord has done for you, and what mercy he has shown you." [20] And he went away and began to proclaim in the De·cap'o·lis how much Jesus had done for him; and everyone was amazed.

A Girl Restored to Life and a Woman Healed
(Mt 9.18–26; Lk 8.40–56)

[21] When Jesus had crossed again in the boat[i] to the other side, a great crowd gathered around him; and he was by the sea. [22] Then one of the leaders of the synagogue named Jā·i'rus came and, when he saw him, fell at his feet [23] and begged him repeatedly, "My little daughter is at the point of death. Come and lay your hands on her, so that she may be made well, and live." [24] So he went with him.

And a large crowd followed him and pressed in on him. [25] Now there was a woman who had been suffering from hemorrhages for twelve years. [26] She had endured much under many physicians, and had spent all that she had; and she was no better, but rather grew worse. [27] She had heard about Jesus, and came up behind him in the crowd and touched his cloak, [28] for she said, "If I but touch his clothes, I will be made well." [29] Immediately her hemorrhage stopped; and she felt in her body that she was healed of her disease. [30] Immediately aware that power had gone forth from him, Jesus turned about in the crowd and said, "Who touched my clothes?" [31] And his disciples said to him, "You see the crowd pressing in on you; how can you say, 'Who touched me?'" [32] He looked all around to see who had done it. [33] But the woman, knowing what had happened to her, came in fear and trembling,

did you KNOW?

Demon Possession

The Gospels of Matthew, Mark, and Luke all have stories about Jesus curing people of unclean spirits, or demons. Many cultures believe in spirits, both good and bad, that can influence or even control people's decisions and actions. In the Bible, a demon is first mentioned in the Book of Tobit, which was written about two hundred years before Jesus' birth. Demons represented evil—mysterious powers hostile to God, health, and goodness. Jesus' ability to free people of demonic influence was a sign of the arrival of the Reign of God (see "Miracles and the Reign of God," Mt 8.1—9.34).

Over time, the explanation for evil or illness shifted from unclean spirits to Satan (see "Satan," Job 1.6—2.10), the leader of all demonic forces. The Gospel of John does not mention unclean spirits at all but instead refers to Satan's influence in the evil leading to Jesus' death (see Jn 13.2).

What the Bible calls demon possession, Western culture might call mental or physical illness. But many people are becoming aware of what the ancient people already knew: that illness and evil are part of the spiritual reality that can affect our life.

▶ Mk 1.23–34; 5.1–20

M
K

fell down before him, and told him the whole truth. [34] He said to her, "Daughter, your faith has made you well; go in peace, and be healed of your disease."

[35] While he was still speaking, some people came from the leader's house to say, "Your daughter is dead. Why trouble the teacher any further?" [36] But overhearing[j] what they said, Jesus said to the leader of the synagogue, "Do not fear, only believe." [37] He allowed no one to follow him except Peter, James, and John, the brother of James.

---

f Gk *he*   *g* Gk *they*   *h* Gk *him*   *i* Other ancient authorities lack *in the boat*   *j* Or *ignoring;* other ancient authorities read *hearing*

38 When they came to the house of the leader of the synagogue, he saw a commotion, people weeping and wailing loudly. 39 When he had entered, he said to them, "Why do you make a commotion and weep? The child is not dead but sleeping." 40 And they laughed at him. Then he put them all outside, and took the child's father and mother and those who were with him, and went in where the child was. 41 He took her by the hand and said to her, "Tal'i•tha cūm," which means, "Little girl, get up!" 42 And immediately the girl got up and began to walk about (she was twelve years of age). At this they were overcome with amazement. 43 He strictly ordered them that no one should know this, and told them to give her something to eat.

The Rejection of Jesus at Nazareth
(Mt 13.54–58; Lk 4.16–30)

6 He left that place and came to his hometown, and his disciples followed him. 2 On the sabbath he began to teach in the synagogue, and many who heard him were astounded. They said, "Where did this man get all this? What is this wisdom that has been given to him? What deeds of power are being done by his hands! 3 Is not this the carpenter, the son of Mary[k] and brother of James and Jō'sēs and Judas and Simon, and are not his sisters here with us?" And they took offense[l] at him. 4 Then Jesus said to them, "Prophets are not without honor, except in their hometown, and among their own

kin, and in their own house." 5 And he could do no deed of power there, except that he laid his hands on a few sick people and cured them. 6 And he was amazed at their unbelief.

The Mission of the Twelve
(Mt 10.5–15; Lk 9.1–6)

Then he went about among the villages teaching. 7 He called the twelve and began to send them out two by two, and gave them authority over the unclean spirits. 8 He ordered them to take nothing for their journey except a staff; no bread, no bag, no money in their belts; 9 but to wear sandals and not to put on two tunics. 10 He said to them, "Wherever you enter a house, stay there until you leave the place. 11 If any place will not welcome you and they refuse to hear you, as you leave, shake off the dust that is on your feet as a testimony against them." 12 So they went out and proclaimed that all should repent. 13 They cast out many demons, and anointed with oil many who were sick and cured them.

The Death of John the Baptist
(Mt 14.1–12; Lk 9.7–9)

14 King Her'od heard of it, for Jesus'[m] name had become known. Some were[n] saying, "John the baptizer has been raised from the dead; and for this reason these powers are at work in him." 15 But others said, "It is E•li'jah." And others said, "It is a prophet, like one of the prophets of old." 16 But when Her'od heard of it, he said, "John, whom I beheaded, has been raised."

17 For Her'od himself had sent men who arrested John, bound him, and put him in prison on account of He•rō'di•as, his brother Philip's wife, because Her'od[o] had married her. 18 For John had been telling Her'od, "It is not lawful for you to have your brother's wife." 19 And He•rō'di•as had a grudge against him, and wanted to kill him. But she could not, 20 for Her'od feared John, knowing that he was a righteous and holy man, and he protected him. When he heard him, he was greatly perplexed;[p] and yet he liked to listen to him. 21 But an opportunity came when Her'od on his birthday gave a banquet for his courtiers and officers and for the leaders of Galilee. 22 When his daughter He•rō'di•as[q] came in and danced, she pleased Her'od and his guests; and the king said to the girl, "Ask me for whatever you wish, and I will give it." 23 And he solemnly swore to her, "Whatever you ask me, I will give you, even half of my kingdom." 24 She went

PRAY IT!
When the Good News Comes Calling

We often can choose whether to allow into our life the people bearing the Good News of Jesus, just as the people to whom the disciples were sent in Mk 6.6–13 could. Why might we turn away such guests? Perhaps their message is too challenging or upsetting to our lifestyle. Maybe we are not ready to accept what God is offering to us through them. Maybe we are too busy to realize that they have something to offer us.

Open your hands as if to receive a gift, and offer a prayer to God for the openness to welcome God's messengers and to receive the Good News they bring.

▸ Mk 6.6–13

---

k Other ancient authorities read *son of the carpenter and of Mary* l Or *stumbled* m Gk *his* n Other ancient authorities read *He was* o Gk *he* p Other ancient authorities read *he did many things* q Other ancient authorities read *the daughter of Herodias herself* out and said to her mother, "What should I ask for?" She replied, "The head of John the baptizer." 25 Immediately she rushed back to the king and requested, "I want you to give me at once the head of John the Baptist on a platter." 26 The king was deeply grieved; yet out of regard for his oaths and for the guests, he did not want to refuse her. 27 Immediately the king sent a soldier of the guard with orders to bring John'sʳ head. He went and beheaded him in the prison, 28 brought his head on a platter, and gave it to the girl. Then the girl gave it to her mother. 29 When his disciples heard about it, they came and took his body, and laid it in a tomb.

Feeding the Five Thousand
(Mt 14.13–21; Lk 9.10–17; Jn 6.1–14)

30 The apostles gathered around Jesus, and told him all that they had done and taught. 31 He said to them, "Come away to a deserted place all by yourselves and rest a while." For many were coming and going, and they had no leisure even to eat. 32 And they went away in the boat to a deserted place by themselves. 33 Now many saw them going and recognized them, and they hurried there on foot from all the towns and arrived ahead of them. 34 As he went ashore, he saw a great crowd; and he had compassion for them, because they were like sheep without a shepherd; and he began to teach them many things. 35 When it grew late, his disciples came to him and said, "This is a deserted place, and the hour is now very late; 36 send them away so that they may go into the surrounding country and villages and buy something for themselves to eat." 37 But he answered them, "You give them something to eat." They said to him, "Are we to go and buy two hundred denariiˢ worth of bread, and give it to them to eat?" 38 And he said to them, "How many loaves have you? Go and see." When they had found out, they said, "Five, and two fish." 39 Then he ordered them to get all the people to sit down in groups on the green grass. 40 So they sat down in groups of hundreds and of fifties. 41 Taking the five loaves and the two fish, he looked up to heaven, and blessed and broke the loaves, and gave them to his disciples to set before the people; and he divided the two fish among them all. 42 And all ate and were filled; 43 and they took up twelve baskets full of broken pieces and of the fish. 44 Those who had eaten the loaves numbered five thousand men.

Jesus Walks on the Water
(Mt 14.22–33; Jn 6.15–21)

45 Immediately he made his disciples get into the boat and go on ahead to the other side, to Beth·sa'i·da, while he dismissed the crowd. 46 After saying farewell to them, he went up on the mountain to pray.

did you KNOW?

Those Thickheaded Disciples

The disciples in the Gospel of Mark seem unable to do anything right. During a storm at sea, they fail to put their trust in Jesus (4.35–41). Then they cannot understand about the miracle of the bread because their hearts are hardened (6.52). When Jesus gives them private tutoring sessions, they still fail to understand his teachings. Later, Peter proclaims that Jesus is the Messiah, but he ends up arguing with him after Jesus predicts that he will be a suffering Messiah (8.27–33). Finally, when Jesus is arrested, the disciples all desert him (14.50).

The author of Mark intentionally emphasizes the lack of faith of the original disciples in order to contrast it with the unexpected faith of people like the Syrophoenician woman in 7.24–30. The Gospel makes the point that Jesus' true disciples are the ones who hear Jesus and place their faith in him. But don't count out the original disciples. Their journey is like most of ours, a lifelong experience of growing in faith and understanding. The Acts of the Apostles tells how they fearlessly preached the news about the risen Christ. Despite their human weakness, God works through them. That goes for us too!

► **Mk 6.30–52**

47 When evening came, the boat was out on the sea, and he was alone on the land. 48 When he saw that they were straining at the oars against an adverse wind, he came towards them early in the morning, walking on the sea. He intended to pass them by. 49 But when they saw him walking on the sea, they thought it was a ghost and cried out; 50 for

---

ʳ Gk *his*   ˢ The denarius was the usual day's wage for a laborer they all saw him and were terrified. But immediately he spoke to them and said, "Take heart, it is I; do not be afraid." 51 Then he got into the boat with them and the wind ceased. And they were utterly astounded, 52 for they did not understand about the loaves, but their hearts were hardened.

Healing the Sick in Gennesaret
(Mt 14.34–36)

53 When they had crossed over, they came to land at Gen·nes′a·ret and moored the boat. 54 When they got out of the boat, people at once recognized him, 55 and rushed about that whole region and began to bring the sick on mats to wherever they heard he was. 56 And wherever he went, into villages or cities or farms, they laid the sick in the marketplaces, and begged him that they might touch even the fringe of his cloak; and all who touched it were healed.

The Tradition of the Elders
(Mt 15.1–20)

7 Now when the Phar′i·sees and some of the scribes who had come from Jerusalem gathered around him, 2 they noticed that some of his disciples were eating with defiled hands, that is, without washing them. 3 (For the Phar′i·sees, and all the Jews, do not eat unless they thoroughly wash their hands,*t* thus observing the tradition of the elders; 4 and they do not eat anything from the market unless they wash it;*u* and there are also many other traditions that they observe, the washing of cups, pots, and bronze kettles.*v*) 5 So the Phar′i·sees and the scribes asked him, "Why do your disciples not live*w* according to the tradition of the elders, but eat with defiled hands?" 6 He said to them, "I·sāi′ah prophesied rightly about you hypocrites, as it is written,

'This people honors me with their lips,
    but their hearts are far from me;
7 in vain do they worship me,
    teaching human precepts as doctrines.'

8 You abandon the commandment of God and hold to human tradition."

9 Then he said to them, "You have a fine way of rejecting the commandment of God in order to keep your tradition! 10 For Moses said, 'Honor your father and your mother'; and, 'Whoever speaks evil of father or mother must surely die.' 11 But you say that if anyone tells father or mother, 'Whatever support you might have had from me is Cor′ban' (that is, an offering to God*x*)— 12 then you no longer permit doing anything for a father or mother, 13 thus making void the word of God through your tradition that you have handed on. And you do many things like this."

14 Then he called the crowd again and said to them, "Listen to me, all of you, and understand: 15 there is nothing outside a person that by going in can defile, but the things that come out are what defile."*y*

17 When he had left the crowd and entered the house, his disciples asked him about the parable. 18 He said to them, "Then do you also fail to understand? Do you not see that whatever goes into a person from outside cannot defile, 19 since it enters, not the heart but the stomach, and goes out into the sewer?" (Thus he declared all foods clean.) 20 And he said, "It is what comes out of a person that defiles. 21 For it is from within, from the human heart, that evil intentions come: fornication, theft, murder, 22 adultery, avarice, wickedness, deceit, licentiousness, envy, slander, pride, folly. 23 All these evil things come from within, and they defile a person."

The Syrophoenician Woman's Faith
(Mt 15.21–28)

24 From there he set out and went away to the region of Tyre.*z* He entered a house and did not want anyone to know he was there. Yet he could not escape notice, 25 but a woman whose little daughter had an unclean spirit immediately heard

---

t Meaning of Gk uncertain   *u* Other ancient authorities read *and when they come from the marketplace, they do not eat unless they purify themselves*   *v* Other ancient authorities add *and beds*   *w* Gk *walk*   *x* Gk lacks *to God*   *y* Other ancient authorities add verse 16, *"Let anyone with ears to hear listen"*   *z* Other ancient authorities add *and Sidon*

Sin's Source

LIVE IT!

Some people believe that spiritual depth is measured by how well certain rules or religious practices are followed. Jesus reminds us in Mk 7.14–15 that our greater concern ought to be with what is in our heart. What is in our heart should have a greater effect on our spiritual life than do outside sources.

▶ Mk 7.14–23

about him, and she came and bowed down at his feet. 26 Now the woman was a Gentile, of Sȳ•rō-phoe•ni′ci•an origin. She begged him to cast the demon out of her daughter. 27 He said to her, "Let the children be fed first, for it is not fair to take the children's food and throw it to the dogs." 28 But she answered him, "Sir,ᵃ even the dogs under the table eat the children's crumbs." 29 Then he said to her, "For saying that, you may go—the demon has left your daughter." 30 So she went home, found the child lying on the bed, and the demon gone.

8.8

Jesus Cures a Deaf Man
(Mt 15.29–31)

31 Then he returned from the region of Tȳre, and went by way of Si′don towards the Sea of Galilee, in the region of the De•cap′o•lis. 32 They brought to him a deaf man who had an impediment in his speech; and they begged him to lay his hand on him. 33 He took him aside in private, away from the crowd, and put his fingers into his ears, and he spat and touched his tongue. 34 Then looking up to heaven, he sighed and said to him, "Eph′pha•tha," that is, "Be opened." 35 And immediately his ears were opened, his tongue was released, and he spoke plainly. 36 Then Jesusᵇ ordered them to tell no one; but the more he ordered them, the more zealously they proclaimed it. 37 They were astounded beyond measure, saying, "He has done everything well; he even makes the deaf to hear and the mute to speak."

Feeding the Four Thousand
(Mt 15.32–39)

8 In those days when there was again a great crowd without anything to eat, he called his disciples and said to them, 2 "I have compassion for the crowd, because they have been with me now for three days and have nothing to eat. 3 If I send them away hungry to their homes, they will faint on the way—and some of them have come from a great distance." 4 His disciples replied, "How can one feed these people with bread here in the desert?" 5 He asked them, "How many loaves do you have?" They said, "Seven." 6 Then he ordered the crowd to sit down on the ground; and he took the seven loaves, and after giving thanks he broke them and gave them to his disciples to distribute; and they distributed them to the crowd. 7 They had also a few small fish; and after blessing them, he ordered that these too should be distributed. 8 They ate and were filled; and they took up the broken pieces left over, seven baskets full. 9 Now there were about four thousand people. And he sent them away. 10 And immediately he got into the boat with his disciples and went to the district of Dal•ma•nu′tha.ᶜ

The Demand for a Sign
(Mt 16.1–4)

11 The Phar′i•sees came and began to argue with him, asking him for a sign from heaven, to test him. 12 And he sighed deeply in his spirit and said, "Why does this generation ask for a sign? Truly I tell you, no sign will be given to this generation." 13 And he left them, and getting into the boat again, he went across to the other side.

The Yeast of the Pharisees and of Herod
(Mt 16.5–12)

14 Now the disciplesᵈ had forgotten to bring any bread; and they had only one loaf with them in the boat. 15 And he cautioned them, saying, "Watch out—beware of the yeast of the Phar′i•sees and the yeast of Her′od."ᵉ 16 They said to one another, "It is because we have no bread." 17 And becoming aware of it, Jesus said to them, "Why are you talking about having no bread? Do you still not perceive or understand? Are your hearts hardened? 18 Do you have eyes, and fail to see? Do you have ears, and fail to hear? And do you not remember? 19 When I broke the five loaves for the five thousand, how many baskets full of broken pieces did you collect?" They said to him, "Twelve." 20 "And the seven for the four thousand, how many baskets full of broken pieces did you collect?" And they said to him, "Seven." 21 Then he said to them, "Do you not yet understand?"

---

a Or *Lord*; other ancient authorities prefix *Yes*   *b* Gk *he*
c Other ancient authorities read *Mageda* or *Magdala*
d Gk *they*   *e* Other ancient authorities read *the Herodians*

MK

Total Commitment

In Mk 8.34–38, Jesus calls for a total commitment requiring great sacrifice. He tells the disciples that to be truly alive, they must be willing to deny themselves and take up their own crosses. The cross symbolizes denying the way of the world and embracing the way of Jesus. It means tough self-sacrifice and, at times, a willingness to suffer for what is right.

But what does it mean to deny ourselves and take up our own crosses?

When we deny ourselves, it means that we cannot be fooled by what the world says about being truly alive. The world tells us to buy our happiness with wealth, power, prestige, or selfish pleasure. But those things actually make us feel less alive and more anxious.

Taking up our own crosses means that we need to be willing to cling to the right things—forgiveness, justice, service, and compassion for the poor and unpopular—even if it brings us suffering and pain. Being committed to Jesus and these virtues or "right things" will bring us real life, true freedom, joy, and inner peace.

The way of the cross is the path to resurrection and eternal life.

▸ Mk 8.34–38

Jesus Cures a Blind Man at Bethsaida

22 They came to Beth·sa'i·da. Some people*f* brought a blind man to him and begged him to touch him. 23 He took the blind man by the hand and led him out of the village; and when he had put saliva on his eyes and laid his hands on him, he asked him, "Can you see anything?" 24 And the man*g* looked up and said, "I can see people, but they look like trees, walking." 25 Then Jesus*g* laid his hands on his eyes again; and he looked intently and his sight was restored, and he saw everything clearly. 26 Then he sent him away to his home, saying, "Do not even go into the village."*h*

Peter's Declaration about Jesus
(Mt 16.13–20; Lk 9.18–20)

27 Jesus went on with his disciples to the villages of Caes·a·re'a Phi·lip'pi; and on the way he asked his disciples, "Who do people say that I am?" 28 And they answered him, "John the Baptist; and others, E·li'jah; and still others, one of the prophets." 29 He asked them, "But who do you say that I am?" Peter answered him, "You are the Messiah."*i* 30 And he sternly ordered them not to tell anyone about him.

Jesus Foretells His Death and Resurrection
(Mt 16.21–28; Lk 9.21–27)

31 Then he began to teach them that the Son of Man must undergo great suffering, and be rejected by the elders, the chief priests, and the scribes, and be killed, and after three days rise again. 32 He said all this quite openly. And Peter took him aside and began to rebuke him. 33 But turning and looking at his disciples, he rebuked Peter and said, "Get be-

hind me, Satan! For you are setting your mind not on divine things but on human things."

34 He called the crowd with his disciples, and said to them, "If any want to become my followers, let them deny themselves and take up their cross and follow me. 35 For those who want to save their life will lose it, and those who lose their life for my sake, and for the sake of the gospel,*j* will save it. 36 For what will it profit them to gain the whole world and forfeit their life? 37 Indeed, what can they give in return for their life? 38 Those who are ashamed of me and of my words*k* in this adulterous and sinful generation, of them the Son of Man will also be ashamed when he comes in the glory of his Father with the holy angels." 1 And he said to them, "Truly I tell you, there are some standing here who will not taste death until they see that the kingdom of God has come with*l* power."

The Transfiguration
(Mt 17.1–8; Lk 9.28–36; 2 Pet 1.16–18)

2 Six days later, Jesus took with him Peter and James and John, and led them up a high mountain apart, by themselves. And he was transfigured before them, 3 and his clothes became dazzling white, such as no one*m* on earth could bleach them. 4 And there appeared to them E·li'jah with Moses, who were talking with Jesus. 5 Then Peter said to Jesus, "Rabbi, it is good for us to be here; let us make

---

f Gk They *g* Gk he *h* Other ancient authorities add *or tell anyone in the village* *i* Or *the Christ* *j* Other ancient authorities read *lose their life for the sake of the gospel* *k* Other ancient authorities read *and of mine* *l* Or *in* *m* Gk *no fuller* three dwellings,[n] one for you, one for Moses, and one for E•li'jah." [6] He did not know what to say, for they were terrified. [7] Then a cloud overshadowed them, and from the cloud there came a voice, "This is my Son, the Beloved;[o] listen to him!" [8] Suddenly when they looked around, they saw no one with them any more, but only Jesus.

The Coming of Elijah
(Mt 17.9–13)

[9] As they were coming down the mountain, he ordered them to tell no one about what they had seen, until after the Son of Man had risen from the dead. [10] So they kept the matter to themselves, questioning what this rising from the dead could mean. [11] Then they asked him, "Why do the scribes say that E•li'jah must come first?" [12] He said to them, "E•li'jah is indeed coming first to restore all things. How then is it written about the Son of Man, that he is to go through many sufferings and be treated with contempt? [13] But I tell you that E•li'jah has come, and they did to him whatever they pleased, as it is written about him."

The Healing of a Boy with a Spirit
(Mt 17.14–21; Lk 9.37–43a)

[14] When they came to the disciples, they saw a great crowd around them, and some scribes arguing with them. [15] When the whole crowd saw him, they were immediately overcome with awe, and they ran forward to greet him. [16] He asked them, "What are you arguing about with them?" [17] Someone from the crowd answered him, "Teacher, I brought you my son; he has a spirit that makes him unable to speak; [18] and whenever it seizes him, it dashes him down; and he foams and grinds his teeth and becomes rigid; and I asked your disciples to cast it out, but they could not do so." [19] He answered them, "You faithless generation, how much longer must I be among you? How much longer must I put up with you? Bring him to me." [20] And they brought the boy[p] to him. When the spirit saw him, immediately it convulsed the boy,[p] and he fell on the ground and rolled about, foaming at the mouth. [21] Jesus[q] asked the father, "How long has this been happening to him?" And he said, "From childhood. [22] It has often cast him into the fire and into the water, to destroy him; but if you are able to do anything, have pity on us and help us." [23] Jesus said to him, "If you are able!—All things can be done for the one who believes." [24] Immediately the father of the child cried out,[r] "I believe; help my unbelief!" [25] When Jesus saw that a crowd came running together, he rebuked the unclean spirit, saying to it, "You spirit that keeps this boy from speaking and hearing, I command you, come out of him, and never enter him again!" [26] After crying out and convulsing him terribly, it came out, and the boy was like a corpse, so that most of them said, "He is dead." [27] But Jesus took him by the hand and lifted him up, and he was able to stand. [28] When he had entered the house, his disciples asked him privately, "Why could we not cast it out?" [29] He said to them, "This kind can come out only through prayer."[s]

MK

---

[n] Or tents   [o] Or my beloved Son   [p] Gk him   [q] Gk He
[r] Other ancient authorities add with tears   [s] Other ancient authorities add and fasting

---

The Transfiguration: On Top of the World — LIVE IT!

The story of the Transfiguration takes place after Jesus tells his disciples about his coming suffering, death, and Resurrection (Mk 8.31). They need hope and a boost of faith. Jesus takes three disciples to a mountaintop to see the Kingdom of God coming in power. The three disciples see Jesus in a glorious state talking with Moses and Elijah.

God revealed the secret about Jesus to three of his disciples. The two Old Testament figures are key symbols: Moses represents the Law, and Elijah, the prophets. The message is clear: Jesus is the person who fulfills the Law and who realizes God's promises to the prophets. It was a profound religious experience. The disciples glimpsed Jesus' glory, but they could not understand it. Understanding came only after Jesus' Resurrection.

It is understandable to want to found our faith on mountaintop experiences (see "Spiritual Highs," Lk 9.28–36). But though profound religious experiences enliven our faith, listening and following Jesus' words daily are what really fortify our faith and give us a new life.

▶ Mk 9.2–8

"I Believe, Help My Unbelief!"

Saying that we believe in something may not be enough to prove that we truly believe. Faith in God means knowing that God is totally with us even when it doesn't seem that way!

When we have nagging doubts whether even God can help us in a particular situation—like the father in Mk 9.24—we can turn to God by praying for faith. We don't have to have our faith or our life perfectly together before we ask God for help. The test of faith is trusting that God cares for us and provides what we need, even when our prayers are not answered in the way we desire.

▶ Mk 9.14–29

Jesus Again Foretells His Death and Resurrection
(Mt 17.22–23; Lk 9.43b–45)

30 They went on from there and passed through Galilee. He did not want anyone to know it; 31 for he was teaching his disciples, saying to them, "The Son of Man is to be betrayed into human hands, and they will kill him, and three days after being killed, he will rise again." 32 But they did not understand what he was saying and were afraid to ask him.

Who Is the Greatest?
(Mt 18.1–5; Lk 9.46–48)

33 Then they came to Ca·per'na·um; and when he was in the house he asked them, "What were you arguing about on the way?" 34 But they were silent, for on the way they had argued with one another who was the greatest. 35 He sat down, called the twelve, and said to them, "Whoever wants to be first must be last of all and servant of all." 36 Then he took a little child and put it among them; and taking it in his arms, he said to them, 37 "Whoever welcomes one such child in my name welcomes me, and whoever welcomes me welcomes not me but the one who sent me."

Another Exorcist
(Mt 10.40–42; Lk 9.49–50)

38 John said to him, "Teacher, we saw some-one[t] casting out demons in your name, and we tried to stop him, because he was not following us." 39 But Jesus said, "Do not stop him; for no one who does a deed of power in my name will be able soon afterward to speak evil of me. 40 Whoever is not against us is for us. 41 For truly I tell you, whoever gives you a cup of water to drink because you bear the name of Christ will by no means lose the reward.

Temptations to Sin
(Mt 18.6–9; Lk 17.1–2)

42 "If any of you put a stumbling block before one of these little ones who believe in me,[u] it would be better for you if a great millstone were hung around your neck and you were thrown into the sea. 43 If your hand causes you to stumble, cut it off; it is better for you to enter life maimed than to have two hands and to go to hell,[v] to the unquenchable fire.[w] 45 And if your foot causes you to stumble, cut it off; it is better for you to enter life lame than to have two feet and to be thrown into hell.[v,w] 47 And if your eye causes you to stumble, tear it out; it is better for you to enter the kingdom of God with one eye than to have two eyes and to be thrown into hell,[v] 48 where their worm never dies, and the fire is never quenched.

49 "For everyone will be salted with fire.[x] 50 Salt is good; but if salt has lost its saltiness, how can you season it?[y] Have salt in yourselves, and be at peace with one another."

Teaching about Divorce
(Mt 19.1–9)

10 He left that place and went to the region of Judea and[z] beyond the Jordan. And crowds again gathered around him; and, as was his custom, he again taught them.

2 Some Phar'i·sees came, and to test him they asked, "Is it lawful for a man to divorce his wife?" 3 He answered them, "What did Moses command you?" 4 They said, "Moses allowed a man to write a certificate of dismissal and to divorce her." 5 But Jesus said to them, "Because of your hardness of heart he wrote this commandment for you. 6 But from the beginning of creation, 'God made them male and female.' 7 'For this reason a man shall leave his father and mother and be joined to his wife,[a] 8 and the two shall become one flesh.' So they are no longer two, but one flesh. 9 Therefore what God has joined together, let no one separate."

---

[t] Other ancient authorities add *who does not follow us*
[u] Other ancient authorities lack *in me*   [v] Gk *Gehenna*
[w] Verses 44 and 46 (which are identical with verse 48) are lacking in the best ancient authorities   [x] Other ancient authorities either add or substitute *and every sacrifice will be salted with salt*   [y] Or *how can you restore its saltiness?*
[z] Other ancient authorities lack *and*   [a] Other ancient authorities lack *and be joined to his wife*

10 Then in the house the disciples asked him again about this matter. 11 He said to them, "Whoever divorces his wife and marries another commits adultery against her; 12 and if she divorces her husband and marries another, she commits adultery."

Jesus Blesses Little Children
(Mt 19.13–15; Lk 18.15–17)

13 People were bringing little children to him in order that he might touch them; and the disciples spoke sternly to them. 14 But when Jesus saw this, he was indignant and said to them, "Let the little children come to me; do not stop them; for it is to such as these that the kingdom of God belongs. 15 Truly I tell you, whoever does not receive the kingdom of God as a little child will never enter it." 16 And he took them up in his arms, laid his hands on them, and blessed them.

The Rich Man
(Mt 19.16–30; Lk 18.18–30)

17 As he was setting out on a journey, a man ran up and knelt before him, and asked him, "Good Teacher, what must I do to inherit eternal life?" 18 Jesus said to him, "Why do you call me good? No one is good but God alone. 19 You know the commandments: 'You shall not murder; You shall not commit adultery; You shall not steal; You shall not bear false witness; You shall not defraud; Honor your father and mother.' " 20 He said to him, "Teacher, I have kept all these since my youth." 21 Jesus, looking at him, loved him and said, "You lack one thing; go, sell what you own, and give the money*b* to the poor, and you will have treasure in heaven; then come, follow me." 22 When he heard this, he was shocked and went away grieving, for he had many possessions.

23 Then Jesus looked around and said to his disciples, "How hard it will be for those who have wealth to enter the kingdom of God!" 24 And the disciples were perplexed at these words. But Jesus said to them again, "Children, how hard it is*c* to enter the kingdom of God! 25 It is easier for a camel to go through the eye of a needle than for someone who is rich to enter the kingdom of God." 26 They were greatly astounded and said to one another,*d* "Then who can be saved?" 27 Jesus looked at them and said, "For mortals it is impossible, but not for God; for God all things are possible."

28 Peter began to say to him, "Look, we have left everything and followed you." 29 Jesus said, "Truly I tell you, there is no one who has left house or brothers or sisters or mother or father or children or fields, for my sake and for the sake of the good news,*e* 30 who will not receive a hundredfold now in this age—houses, brothers and sisters, mothers and children, and fields, with persecutions—and in

the age to come eternal life. 31 But many who are first will be last, and the last will be first."

A Third Time Jesus Foretells His Death and Resurrection
(Mt 20.17–19; Lk 18.31–34)

32 They were on the road, going up to Jerusalem, and Jesus was walking ahead of them; they were amazed, and those who followed were afraid. He took the twelve aside again and began to tell them what was to happen to him, 33 saying, "See, we are going up to Jerusalem, and the Son of Man will be handed over to the chief priests and the scribes, and they will condemn him to death; then they will hand him over to the Gentiles; 34 they will mock him, and spit upon him, and flog him, and kill him; and after three days he will rise again."

The Request of James and John
(Mt 20.20–28)

35 James and John, the sons of Zeb'e·dee, came forward to him and said to him, "Teacher, we want you to do for us whatever we ask of you." 36 And he said to them, "What is it you want me to do for you?" 37 And they said to him, "Grant us to sit, one

---

b Gk lacks *the money*   *c* Other ancient authorities add *for those who trust in riches*   *d* Other ancient authorities read *to him*   *e* Or *gospel*

TRUE GREATNESS

The disciples think that Jesus is going to be a great king, and they want to share in his power and glory. Instead, Jesus tells them that they must be servants. Servanthood is the true mark of greatness. That is why the pope is sometimes called the servant of the servants of God. Jesus not only taught true servanthood but lived it by giving up his life as a ransom for all.

▶ Mk 10.35–45

at your right hand and one at your left, in your glory." 38 But Jesus said to them, "You do not know what you are asking. Are you able to drink the cup that I drink, or be baptized with the baptism that I am baptized with?" 39 They replied, "We are able." Then Jesus said to them, "The cup that I drink you will drink; and with the baptism with which I am baptized, you will be baptized; 40 but to sit at my right hand or at my left is not mine to grant, but it is for those for whom it has been prepared."

41 When the ten heard this, they began to be angry with James and John. 42 So Jesus called them and said to them, "You know that among the Gentiles those whom they recognize as their rulers lord it over them, and their great ones are tyrants over them. 43 But it is not so among you; but whoever wishes to become great among you must be your servant, 44 and whoever wishes to be first among you must be slave of all. 45 For the Son of Man came not to be served but to serve, and to give his life a ransom for many."

The Healing of Blind Bartimaeus
(Mt 20.29–34; Lk 18.35–43)

46 They came to Jericho. As he and his disciples and a large crowd were leaving Jericho, Bar·ti·mae͂͂us son of Ti·mae͂us, a blind beggar, was sitting by the roadside. 47 When he heard that it was Jesus of Nazareth, he began to shout out and say, "Jesus, Son of David, have mercy on me!" 48 Many sternly ordered him to be quiet, but he cried out even more loudly, "Son of David, have mercy on me!" 49 Jesus stood still and said, "Call him here." And they called the blind man, saying to him, "Take heart; get up, he is calling you." 50 So throwing off his cloak, he sprang up and came to Jesus. 51 Then Jesus said to him, "What do you want me to do for you?" The blind man said to him, "My teacher,ƒ let me see again." 52 Jesus said to him, "Go; your faith has made you well." Immediately he regained his sight and followed him on the way.

Jesus' Triumphal Entry into Jerusalem
(Mt 21.1–11; Lk 19.28–40; Jn 12.12–19)

11 When they were approaching Jerusalem, at Beth'pha·ge and Beth'a·ny, near the Mount of Olives, he sent two of his disciples 2 and said to them, "Go into the village ahead of you, and immediately as you enter it, you will find tied there a colt that has never been ridden; untie it and bring it. 3 If anyone says to you, 'Why are you doing this?' just say this, 'The Lord needs it and will send it back here immediately.' " 4 They went away and found a colt tied near a door, outside in the street. As they were untying it, 5 some of the bystanders said to them, "What are you doing, untying the colt?" 6 They told them what Jesus had said; and they allowed them to take it. 7 Then they brought the colt to Jesus and threw their cloaks on it; and he sat on it. 8 Many people spread their cloaks on the road, and others spread leafy branches that they had cut in the fields. 9 Then those who went ahead and those who followed were shouting,

"Hosanna!
    Blessed is the one who comes in the name
        of the Lord!
10   Blessed is the coming kingdom of our
        ancestor David!
Hosanna in the highest heaven!"

11 Then he entered Jerusalem and went into the temple; and when he had looked around at everything, as it was already late, he went out to Beth'-a·ny with the twelve.

Jesus Curses the Fig Tree
(Mt 21.18–19)

12 On the following day, when they came from Beth'a·ny, he was hungry. 13 Seeing in the distance a fig tree in leaf, he went to see whether perhaps he would find anything on it. When he came to it, he found nothing but leaves, for it was not the season for figs. 14 He said to it, "May no one ever eat fruit from you again." And his disciples heard it.

Jesus Cleanses the Temple
(Mt 21.12–17; Lk 19.45–48; Jn 2.13–22)

15 Then they came to Jerusalem. And he entered the temple and began to drive out those who were selling and those who were buying in the temple, and he overturned the tables of the money changers and the seats of those who sold doves; 16 and he would not allow anyone to carry anything through the temple. 17 He was teaching and saying, "Is it not written,
    'My house shall be called a house of prayer for
        all the nations'?
    But you have made it a den of robbers."
18 And when the chief priests and the scribes heard it, they kept looking for a way to kill him; for they were afraid of him, because the whole crowd was spellbound by his teaching. 19 And when evening came, Jesus and his disciplesg went out of the city.

The Lesson from the Withered Fig Tree
(Mt 21.20–22)

20 In the morning as they passed by, they saw the fig tree withered away to its roots. 21 Then Peter remembered and said to him, "Rabbi, look! The fig tree that you cursed has withered." 22 Jesus answered them, "Haveh faith in God. 23 Truly I tell you, if you say to this mountain, 'Be taken up and

---

ƒ Aramaic *Rabbouni*   g Gk *they*: other ancient authorities read *he*   h Other ancient authorities read *"If you have* thrown into the sea,' and if you do not doubt in your heart, but believe that what you say will come to pass, it will be done for you. 24 So I tell you, whatever you ask for in prayer, believe that you have received[i] it, and it will be yours.

25 "Whenever you stand praying, forgive, if you have anything against anyone; so that your Father in heaven may also forgive you your trespasses."[j]

Jesus' Authority Is Questioned
(Mt 21.23–27; Lk 20.1–8)

27 Again they came to Jerusalem. As he was walking in the temple, the chief priests, the scribes, and the elders came to him 28 and said, "By what authority are you doing these things? Who gave you this authority to do them?" 29 Jesus said to them, "I will ask you one question; answer me, and I will tell you by what authority I do these things. 30 Did the baptism of John come from heaven, or was it of human origin? Answer me." 31 They argued with one another, "If we say, 'From heaven,' he will say, 'Why then did you not believe him?' 32 But shall we say, 'Of human origin'?"—they were afraid of the crowd, for all regarded John as truly a prophet. 33 So they answered Jesus, "We do not know." And Jesus said to them, "Neither will I tell you by what authority I am doing these things."

The Parable of the Wicked Tenants
(Mt 21.33–46; Lk 20.9–19)

12 Then he began to speak to them in parables. "A man planted a vineyard, put a fence around it, dug a pit for the wine press, and built a watchtower; then he leased it to tenants and went to another country. 2 When the season came, he sent a slave to the tenants to collect from them his share of the produce of the vineyard. 3 But they seized him, and beat him, and sent him away empty-handed. 4 And again he sent another slave to them; this one they beat over the head and insulted. 5 Then he sent another, and that one they killed. And so it was with many others; some they beat, and others they killed. 6 He had still one other, a beloved son. Finally he sent him to them, saying, 'They will respect my son.' 7 But those tenants said to one another, 'This is the heir; come, let us kill him, and the inheritance will be ours.' 8 So they seized him, killed him, and threw him out of the vineyard. 9 What then will the owner of the vineyard do? He will come and destroy the tenants and give the vineyard to others. 10 Have you not read this scripture:

'The stone that the builders rejected
　　has become the cornerstone;[k]
11　this was the Lord's doing,
　　and it is amazing in our eyes'?"

12 When they realized that he had told this parable against them, they wanted to arrest him, but they feared the crowd. So they left him and went away.

The Question about Paying Taxes
(Mt 22.15–22; Lk 20.20–26)

13 Then they sent to him some Phar'i·sees and some He·rō'di·ans to trap him in what he said. 14 And they came and said to him, "Teacher, we know that you are sincere, and show deference to no one; for you do not regard people with partiality, but teach the way of God in accordance with truth. Is it lawful to pay taxes to the emperor, or not? 15 Should we pay them, or should we not?"

PRAY IT?
Unanswered Prayer

Did you ever want something so badly that you prayed for it?

Sometimes when things turn out the way we want, we say that God has answered our prayers. But when things don't turn out the way we want, we say that God didn't answer our prayers.

In Mk 11.24, it seems that we have the power to obtain what we want from God—just by stating our wishes. This is a dangerous thought, though, especially when someone else might be praying for the exact opposite of what we're praying for. Why should God answer our prayers and not someone else's? In addition, when something horrible happens, despite all our prayers, it is dangerous to think that God willed such pain and suffering. For example, sometimes we hear people saying, "God must have wanted me to learn some lesson from this tragedy." God never causes tragedy. Tragedy just happens.

People often ask, and we may be asking ourselves, "Why pray at all if it isn't going to change anything?"

Here's a good response: "Prayer doesn't change things. Prayer changes people, and people change things."

▶ Mk 11.24

---

i Other ancient authorities read *are receiving*   j Other ancient authorities add verse 26, *"But if you do not forgive, neither will your Father in heaven forgive your trespasses."*   k Or *keystone*

But knowing their hypocrisy, he said to them, "Why are you putting me to the test? Bring me a denarius and let me see it." 16 And they brought one. Then he said to them, "Whose head is this, and whose title?" They answered, "The emperor's." 17 Jesus said to them, "Give to the emperor the things that are the emperor's, and to God the things that are God's." And they were utterly amazed at him.

PRAY IT?

What Do You Want from Me?

Dear God, Jesus tells us to give to you what is yours. What do you want from me, God? What can I give to you?

As a young person still growing and developing, I don't have much to offer financially. I can make a small financial contribution to the church, to poor people, . . . but is it enough, Lord? What more can I give?

I can offer my time and talents to serve my faith community. I can sing, play an instrument, draw posters, greet visitors, clean, decorate, organize, cook, bake, and telephone. I can help teach children, lector, or usher, . . . but is it enough, Lord? What more can I give?

I can reach out to serve and share your love at home, in my neighborhood, my school, my community, . . . but is it enough, Lord? What more can I give?

I want to serve you better, Lord. Speak to me, and I will listen. Amen.

▸ Mk 12.13–17

The Question about the Resurrection
(Mt 22.23–33; Lk 20.27–40)

18 Some Sad′du·cees, who say there is no resurrection, came to him and asked him a question, saying, 19 "Teacher, Moses wrote for us that if a man's brother dies, leaving a wife but no child, the man[l] shall marry the widow and raise up children for his brother. 20 There were seven brothers; the first married and, when he died, left no children; 21 and the second married the widow[m] and died, leaving no children; and the third likewise; 22 none of the seven left children. Last of all the woman herself died. 23 In the resurrection[n] whose wife will she be? For the seven had married her."

24 Jesus said to them, "Is not this the reason you are wrong, that you know neither the scriptures nor the power of God? 25 For when they rise from the dead, they neither marry nor are given in marriage, but are like angels in heaven. 26 And as for the dead being raised, have you not read in the book of Moses, in the story about the bush, how God said to him, 'I am the God of Abraham, the God of Isaac, and the God of Jacob'? 27 He is God not of the dead, but of the living; you are quite wrong."

The First Commandment
(Mt 22.34–40; Lk 10.25–28)

28 One of the scribes came near and heard them disputing with one another, and seeing that he answered them well, he asked him, "Which commandment is the first of all?" 29 Jesus answered, "The first is, 'Hear, O Israel: the Lord our God, the Lord is one; 30 you shall love the Lord your God with all your heart, and with all your soul, and with all your mind, and with all your strength.' 31 The second is this, 'You shall love your neighbor as yourself.' There is no other commandment greater than these." 32 Then the scribe said to him, "You are right, Teacher; you have truly said that 'he is one, and besides him there is no other'; 33 and 'to love him with all the heart, and with all the understanding, and with all the strength,' and 'to love one's neighbor as oneself,'—this is much more important than all whole burnt offerings and sacrifices." 34 When Jesus saw that he answered wisely, he said to him, "You are not far from the kingdom of God." After that no one dared to ask him any question.

The Question about David's Son
(Mt 22.41–46; Lk 20.41–44)

35 While Jesus was teaching in the temple, he said, "How can the scribes say that the Messiah[o] is the son of David? 36 David himself, by the Holy Spirit, declared,

'The Lord said to my Lord,
    "Sit at my right hand,
       until I put your enemies under your feet." '

37 David himself calls him Lord; so how can he be his son?" And the large crowd was listening to him with delight.

Jesus Denounces the Scribes
(Mt 23.1–7; Lk 20.45–47)

38 As he taught, he said, "Beware of the scribes, who like to walk around in long robes, and to be greeted with respect in the marketplaces, 39 and to have the best seats in the synagogues and places of

---

l Gk *his brother*   *m* Gk *her*   *n* Other ancient authorities add *when they rise*   *o* Or *the Christ*

MK

honor at banquets! 40 They devour widows' houses and for the sake of appearance say long prayers. They will receive the greater condemnation."

The Widow's Offering
(Lk 21.1–4)

41 He sat down opposite the treasury, and watched the crowd putting money into the treasury. Many rich people put in large sums. 42 A poor widow came and put in two small copper coins, which are worth a penny. 43 Then he called his disciples and said to them, "Truly I tell you, this poor widow has put in more than all those who are contributing to the treasury. 44 For all of them have contributed out of their abundance; but she out of her poverty has put in everything she had, all she had to live on."

The Destruction of the Temple Foretold
(Mt 24.1–8; Lk 21.5–11)

13 As he came out of the temple, one of his disciples said to him, "Look, Teacher, what large stones and what large buildings!" 2 Then Jesus asked him, "Do you see these great buildings? Not one stone will be left here upon another; all will be thrown down."

3 When he was sitting on the Mount of Olives opposite the temple, Peter, James, John, and Andrew asked him privately, 4 "Tell us, when will this be, and what will be the sign that all these things are about to be accomplished?" 5 Then Jesus began to say to them, "Beware that no one leads you astray. 6 Many will come in my name and say, 'I am he!'p and they will lead many astray. 7 When you hear of wars and rumors of wars, do not be alarmed; this must take place, but the end is still to come. 8 For nation will rise against nation, and kingdom against kingdom; there will be earthquakes in various places; there will be famines. This is but the beginning of the birth pangs.

Persecution Foretold
(Mt 24.9–14; Lk 21.12–19)

9 "As for yourselves, beware; for they will hand you over to councils; and you will be beaten in synagogues; and you will stand before governors and kings because of me, as a testimony to them. 10 And the good newsq must first be proclaimed to all nations. 11 When they bring you to trial and hand you over, do not worry beforehand about what you are to say; but say whatever is given you at that time, for it is not you who speak, but the Holy Spirit. 12 Brother will betray brother to death, and a father his child, and children will rise against parents and have them put to death; 13 and you will be hated by all because of my name. But the one who endures to the end will be saved.

The Desolating Sacrilege
(Mt 24.15–28; Lk 21.20–24)

14 "But when you see the desolating sacrilege set up where it ought not to be (let the reader understand), then those in Judea must flee to the mountains; 15 the one on the housetop must not go

p Gk I am q Gk gospel

12.42–44

A poor widow came and put in two small copper coins, which are worth a penny.

Then he called his disciples and said to them,

"Truly I tell you, this poor widow has put in more than all those who are contributing to the treasury. For all of them have contributed out of their abundance; but she out of her poverty has put in everything she had, all she had to live on."

MK

down or enter the house to take anything away; 16 the one in the field must not turn back to get a coat. 17 Woe to those who are pregnant and to those who are nursing infants in those days! 18 Pray that it may not be in winter. 19 For in those days there will be suffering, such as has not been from the beginning of the creation that God created until now, no, and never will be. 20 And if the Lord had not cut short those days, no one would be saved; but for the sake of the elect, whom he chose, he has cut short those days. 21 And if anyone says to you at that time, 'Look! Here is the Messiah!'[r] or 'Look! There he is!'—do not believe it. 22 False messiahs[s] and false prophets will appear and produce signs and omens, to lead astray, if possible, the elect. 23 But be alert; I have already told you everything.

The Coming of the Son of Man
(Mt 24.29–31; Lk 21.25–28)

24 "But in those days, after that suffering,
the sun will be darkened,
and the moon will not give its light,
25 and the stars will be falling from heaven,

did you KNOW?
Signs and Omens

The community for which the author of Mark's Gospel wrote saw its sufferings as part of the troubles that would come with the end time. However, the author didn't intend that his readers take Jesus' signs and omens of wars and earthquakes literally to mean that the end of the world was at hand. Rather, these descriptions were used symbolically (see "Apocalyptic Literature," Daniel, chapters 7–10) to help the community make sense of its persecutions. The message of this Gospel is that Christians who were getting beaten up and thrown in jail would be saved by God. And ultimately, human history would climax in the perfect Reign of God. It was their job to hang on and endure to the end. All they had to worry about was spreading the Good News of Jesus Christ, and God would take care of the rest.

▶ **Mark, chapter 13**

and the powers in the heavens will be
shaken.
26 Then they will see 'the Son of Man coming in clouds' with great power and glory. 27 Then he will send out the angels, and gather his elect from the four winds, from the ends of the earth to the ends of heaven.

The Lesson of the Fig Tree
(Mt 24.32–35; Lk 21.29–33)

28 "From the fig tree learn its lesson: as soon as its branch becomes tender and puts forth its leaves, you know that summer is near. 29 So also, when you see these things taking place, you know that he[t] is near, at the very gates. 30 Truly I tell you, this generation will not pass away until all these things have taken place. 31 Heaven and earth will pass away, but my words will not pass away.

The Necessity for Watchfulness
(Mt 24.36–44; Lk 21.34–36)

32 "But about that day or hour no one knows, neither the angels in heaven, nor the Son, but only the Father. 33 Beware, keep alert;[u] for you do not know when the time will come. 34 It is like a man going on a journey, when he leaves home and puts his slaves in charge, each with his work, and commands the doorkeeper to be on the watch. 35 Therefore, keep awake—for you do not know when the master of the house will come, in the evening, or at midnight, or at cockcrow, or at dawn, 36 or else he may find you asleep when he comes suddenly. 37 And what I say to you I say to all: Keep awake."

The Plot to Kill Jesus
(Mt 26.1–5; Lk 22.1–2; Jn 11.45–53)

14 It was two days before the Passover and the festival of Unleavened Bread. The chief priests and the scribes were looking for a way to arrest Jesus[v] by stealth and kill him; 2 for they said, "Not during the festival, or there may be a riot among the people."

The Anointing at Bethany
(Mt 26.6–13; Jn 12.1–8)

3 While he was at Beth'a·ny in the house of Simon the leper,[w] as he sat at the table, a woman came with an alabaster jar of very costly ointment of nard, and she broke open the jar and poured the ointment on his head. 4 But some were there who said to one another in anger, "Why was the ointment wasted in this way? 5 For this ointment could have been sold for more than three hundred

---

[r] Or *the Christ* [s] Or *christs* [t] Or *it* [u] Other ancient authorities add *and pray* [v] Gk *him* [w] The terms *leper* and *leprosy* can refer to several diseases

denarii,[x] and the money given to the poor." And they scolded her. [6] But Jesus said, "Let her alone; why do you trouble her? She has performed a good service for me. [7] For you always have the poor with you, and you can show kindness to them whenever you wish; but you will not always have me. [8] She has done what she could; she has anointed my body beforehand for its burial. [9] Truly I tell you, wherever the good news[y] is proclaimed in the whole world, what she has done will be told in remembrance of her."

Judas Agrees to Betray Jesus
(Mt 26.14–16; Lk 22.3–6)

[10] Then Judas Is·car'i·ot, who was one of the twelve, went to the chief priests in order to betray him to them. [11] When they heard it, they were greatly pleased, and promised to give him money. So he began to look for an opportunity to betray him.

The Passover with the Disciples
(Mt 26.17–25; Lk 22.7–13; Jn 13.21–30)

[12] On the first day of Unleavened Bread, when the Passover lamb is sacrificed, his disciples said to him, "Where do you want us to go and make the preparations for you to eat the Passover?" [13] So he sent two of his disciples, saying to them, "Go into the city, and a man carrying a jar of water will meet you; follow him, [14] and wherever he enters, say to the owner of the house, 'The Teacher asks, Where is my guest room where I may eat the Passover with my disciples?' [15] He will show you a large room upstairs, furnished and ready. Make preparations for us there." [16] So the disciples set out and went to the city, and found everything as he had told them; and they prepared the Passover meal.

[17] When it was evening, he came with the twelve. [18] And when they had taken their places and were eating, Jesus said, "Truly I tell you, one of you will betray me, one who is eating with me." [19] They began to be distressed and to say to him one after another, "Surely, not I?" [20] He said to them, "It is one of the twelve, one who is dipping bread[z] into the bowl[a] with me. [21] For the Son of Man goes as it is written of him, but woe to that one by whom the Son of Man is betrayed! It would have been better for that one not to have been born."

The Institution of the Lord's Supper
(Mt 26.26–29; Lk 22.14–23; 1 Cor 11.23–26)

[22] While they were eating, he took a loaf of bread, and after blessing it he broke it, gave it to them, and said, "Take; this is my body." [23] Then he took a cup, and after giving thanks he gave it to them, and all of them drank from it. [24] He said to them, "This is my blood of the[b] covenant, which is

---

PRAY IT?
Mass Prayer

Dear Jesus, "Take it; this is my body. . . . This is my blood." Those words make me feel guilty because I should be hearing them at Mass. And you know I often find excuses not to go to Mass. The church pews are uncomfortable; I'd rather sleep late; I don't like the music or the homily; it is too nice outside; it's boring. My parents have even quit trying to get me to go.

Why is it so easy to forget that you gave us this special invitation to share in the eucharistic meal? It is a way of participating in your death and Resurrection and strengthening our faith and renewing our hope until you come again in glory. It is a privilege to be invited to the eucharistic table and to connect with both the present church and all the saints of the past who have shared this sacred meal.

Thank you for your invitation, Lord. Help me to value the Eucharist more, and give me the desire to meet you there. Amen.

For more on the Eucharist, see the articles for Mt 26.26–29; Lk 22.14–20; Jn 13.1–17.

▶ Mk 14.22–25

---

poured out for many. [25] Truly I tell you, I will never again drink of the fruit of the vine until that day when I drink it new in the kingdom of God."

Peter's Denial Foretold
(Mt 26.30–35; Lk 22.31–34; Jn 13.36–38)

[26] When they had sung the hymn, they went out to the Mount of Olives. [27] And Jesus said to them, "You will all become deserters; for it is written,

'I will strike the shepherd,
    and the sheep will be scattered.'

[28] But after I am raised up, I will go before you to Galilee." [29] Peter said to him, "Even though all become deserters, I will not." [30] Jesus said to him, "Truly I tell you, this day, this very night, before the cock crows twice, you will deny me three times." [31] But he said vehemently, "Even though I must die

---

x The denarius was the usual day's wage for a laborer *y* Or *gospel*   *z* Gk lacks *bread*   *a* Other ancient authorities read *same bowl*   *b* Other ancient authorities add *new* with you, I will not deny you." And all of them said the same.

Jesus Prays in Gethsemane
(Mt 26.36–46; Lk 22.39–46)

32 They went to a place called Geth·sem'a·nē; and he said to his disciples, "Sit here while I pray." 33 He took with him Peter and James and John, and began to be distressed and agitated. 34 And he said to them, "I am deeply grieved, even to death; remain here, and keep awake." 35 And going a little farther, he threw himself on the ground and prayed that, if it were possible, the hour might pass from him. 36 He said, "Abba,c Father, for you all things are possible; remove this cup from me; yet, not what I want, but what you want." 37 He came and found them sleeping; and he said to Peter, "Simon, are you asleep? Could you not keep awake one hour? 38 Keep awake and pray that you may not come into the time of trial;d the spirit indeed is willing, but the flesh is weak." 39 And again he went away and prayed, saying the same words. 40 And once more he came and found them sleeping, for their eyes were very heavy; and they did not know what to say to him. 41 He came a third time and said to them, "Are you still sleeping and taking your rest? Enough! The hour has come; the Son of Man is betrayed into the hands of sinners. 42 Get up, let us be going. See, my betrayer is at hand."

The Betrayal and Arrest of Jesus
(Mt 26.47–56; Lk 22.47–53; Jn 18.1–11)

43 Immediately, while he was still speaking, Judas, one of the twelve, arrived; and with him there was a crowd with swords and clubs, from the chief priests, the scribes, and the elders. 44 Now the betrayer had given them a sign, saying, "The one I will kiss is the man; arrest him and lead him away under guard." 45 So when he came, he went up to him at once and said, "Rabbi!" and kissed him. 46 Then they laid hands on him and arrested him. 47 But one of those who stood near drew his sword and struck the slave of the high priest, cutting off his ear. 48 Then Jesus said to them, "Have you come out with swords and clubs to arrest me as though I were a bandit? 49 Day after day I was with you in the temple teaching, and you did not arrest me. But let the scriptures be fulfilled." 50 All of them deserted him and fled.

51 A certain young man was following him, wearing nothing but a linen cloth. They caught hold of him, 52 but he left the linen cloth and ran off naked.

Jesus before the Council
(Mt 26.57–68; Lk 22.66–71; Jn 18.12–14, 19–24)

53 They took Jesus to the high priest; and all the chief priests, the elders, and the scribes were assembled. 54 Peter had followed him at a distance, right into the courtyard of the high priest; and he was sitting with the guards, warming himself at the fire. 55 Now the chief priests and the whole council were looking for testimony against Jesus to put him to death; but they found none. 56 For many gave false testimony against him, and their testimony did not agree. 57 Some stood up and gave false testimony against him, saying, 58 "We heard him say, 'I will destroy this temple that is made with hands, and in

---

c Aramaic for *Father*   d Or *into temptation*

A Friend's Betrayal

LIVE IT!

Imagine that you are facing a difficult time. Your best friend promises to be with you no matter what. This is the one person you rely on, who has been there for you and has been the most loyal and faithful of all your friends. You have spent the last three years together . . . working, studying, enjoying holidays, traveling, and sharing countless meals and discussions. Now, imagine that this friend completely lets you down.

Peter was one of Jesus' best friends. As the story is told in the Gospel of Mark, the relationship has its difficult times, but Jesus continuously tries to reach Peter. Knowing Peter is going to deny him, Jesus even tries warning Peter that things would happen this way (14.30).

Probably just like some of your friends, Peter had good intentions but could not follow through with his assurances to Jesus (verses 66–72). But Jesus did not give up on Peter (Jn 21.15–19), and Peter became one of the greatest heroes of our church. Don't give up on your friends either.

▶ Mk 14.66–72

three days I will build another, not made with hands.' " 59 But even on this point their testimony did not agree. 60 Then the high priest stood up before them and asked Jesus, "Have you no answer? What is it that they testify against you?" 61 But he was silent and did not answer. Again the high priest asked him, "Are you the Messiah,*e* the Son of the Blessed One?" 62 Jesus said, "I am; and

'you will see the Son of Man
     seated at the right hand of the Power,'
and 'coming with the clouds of heaven.' "

63 Then the high priest tore his clothes and said, "Why do we still need witnesses? 64 You have heard his blasphemy! What is your decision?" All of them condemned him as deserving death. 65 Some began to spit on him, to blindfold him, and to strike him, saying to him, "Prophesy!" The guards also took him over and beat him.

Peter Denies Jesus
(Mt 26.69–75; Lk 22.54–62; Jn 18.15–18, 25–27)

66 While Peter was below in the courtyard, one of the servant-girls of the high priest came by. 67 When she saw Peter warming himself, she stared at him and said, "You also were with Jesus, the man from Nazareth." 68 But he denied it, saying, "I do not know or understand what you are talking about." And he went out into the forecourt.*f* Then the cock crowed.*g* 69 And the servant-girl, on seeing him, began again to say to the bystanders, "This man is one of them." 70 But again he denied it. Then after a little while the bystanders again said to Peter, "Certainly you are one of them; for you are a Galilean." 71 But he began to curse, and he swore an oath, "I do not know this man you are talking about." 72 At that moment the cock crowed for the second time. Then Peter remembered that Jesus had said to him, "Before the cock crows twice, you will deny me three times." And he broke down and wept.

Jesus before Pilate
(Mt 27.1–2, 11–14; Lk 23.1–5, 13–16;
Jn 18.28–38a)

15 As soon as it was morning, the chief priests held a consultation with the elders and scribes and the whole council. They bound Jesus, led him away, and handed him over to Pilate. 2 Pilate asked him, "Are you the King of the Jews?" He answered him, "You say so." 3 Then the chief priests accused him of many things. 4 Pilate asked him again, "Have you no answer? See how many charges they bring against you." 5 But Jesus made no further reply, so that Pilate was amazed.

Pilate Hands Jesus over to Be Crucified
(Mt 27.15–26; Lk 23.18–25; Jn 18.38b—19.16)

6 Now at the festival he used to release a pris-oner for them, anyone for whom they asked. 7 Now a man called Ba•rab'bas was in prison with the rebels who had committed murder during the insurrection. 8 So the crowd came and began to ask Pilate to do for them according to his custom. 9 Then he answered them, "Do you want me to release for you the King of the Jews?" 10 For he realized that it was out of jealousy that the chief priests had handed him over. 11 But the chief priests stirred up the crowd to have him release Ba•rab'bas for them instead. 12 Pilate spoke to them again, "Then what do you wish me to do*h* with the man you call*i* the King of the Jews?" 13 They shouted back, "Crucify him!" 14 Pilate asked them, "Why, what evil has he done?" But they shouted all the more, "Crucify him!" 15 So Pilate, wishing to satisfy the crowd, released Ba•rab'bas for them; and after flogging Jesus, he handed him over to be crucified.

---

e Or *the Christ* *f* Or *gateway* *g* Other ancient authorities lack *Then the cock crowed* *h* Other ancient authorities read *what should I do* *i* Other ancient authorities lack *the man you call*

PRAY IT!
Facing the Hard Times

Lord, you really do know what it is like to be beaten, teased, pushed around, and rejected.

If you could put up with this torment, then maybe there is hope for others who feel the same way at times. Like when we are made fun of or rejected because of the way we look or act or for what we believe in. Or when we feel all alone or that no one understands what we are feeling.

But now, I know that you understand, Lord. You took these difficult steps even before we did. You have been there. You show us a way through these tough times.

Teach me to pray as you did: "Abba, Father, for you all things are possible; remove this cup [suffering] from me, yet, not what I want, but what you want" (Mk 14.36). Give me the strength to overcome my despair. Give me faith to abandon myself in God's hands as you did. Give me hope to see a new life beyond these moments of pain and hopelessness. Amen.

▸ Mk 15.16–20

MK

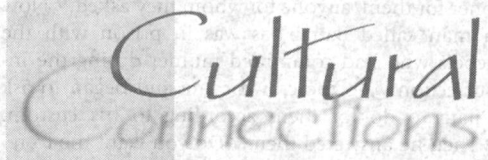

WE WERE THERE

According to Mk 15.21, the Roman soldiers compelled a North African black man from Cyrene by the name of Simon, a passerby, to carry the cross of Jesus. We do not know anything more about Simon of Cyrene, except that Mark identifies him as the father of Alexander and Rufus. The reference to Simon's sons by name and the possibility that Rufus is the same person Paul greets in Rom 16.13 indicate that they were known among the early Christians. This is significant for Africans because it is evidence of the prominence and influence of African people in the early Christian church.

African people were there from the beginning of Christianity (see also Acts 8.26–40). They were not latecomers to the Christian faith. Thank God, somebody always remembers! Africans and other people who have experienced oppression are in danger of forgetting who they are and where they come from. Not because they are forgetful peoples, but because the oppressors have tried to erase their culture and identity in order to cripple and control them.
Yet despite all of this, somebody always remembers.

We praise you, God, for having African people there from the beginning of your plan of salvation. We praise you in knowing that people of all races will be with you at the end. Hallelujah. Amen!

▸ Mk 15.21

The Soldiers Mock Jesus
(Mt 27.27–31)

16 Then the soldiers led him into the courtyard of the palace (that is, the governor's headquarters*j*); and they called together the whole cohort. 17 And they clothed him in a purple cloak; and after twisting some thorns into a crown, they put it on him. 18 And they began saluting him, "Hail, King of the Jews!" 19 They struck his head with a reed, spat upon him, and knelt down in homage to him. 20 After mocking him, they stripped him of the purple cloak and put his own clothes on him. Then they led him out to crucify him.

The Crucifixion of Jesus
(Mt 27.32–44; Lk 23.26–43; Jn 19.16b–27)

21 They compelled a passer-by, who was coming in from the country, to carry his cross; it was Simon of Cy·re′nē, the father of Alexander and Rufus. 22 Then they brought Jesus*k* to the place called Gol′go·tha (which means the place of a skull). 23 And they offered him wine mixed with myrrh; but he did not take it. 24 And they crucified him, and divided his clothes among them, casting lots to decide what each should take.

25 It was nine o'clock in the morning when they crucified him. 26 The inscription of the charge

against him read, "The King of the Jews." 27 And with him they crucified two bandits, one on his right and one on his left.*l* 29 Those who passed by derided*m* him, shaking their heads and saying, "Aha! You who would destroy the temple and build it in three days, 30 save yourself, and come down from the cross!" 31 In the same way the chief priests, along with the scribes, were also mocking him among themselves and saying, "He saved others; he cannot save himself. 32 Let the Messiah,*n* the King of Israel, come down from the cross now, so that we may see and believe." Those who were crucified with him also taunted him.

The Death of Jesus
(Mt 27.45–56; Lk 23.44–49; Jn 19.28–30)

33 When it was noon, darkness came over the whole land*o* until three in the afternoon. 34 At three o'clock Jesus cried out with a loud voice, "Ē′lō·ī, Ē′lō·ī, le·ma′ sa·bach′tha·nī?" which means, "My God, my God, why have you forsaken me?"*p* 35 When some of the bystanders heard it, they said, "Listen, he is calling

---

j Gk *the praetorium*   *k* Gk *him*   *l* Other ancient authorities add verse 28, *And the scripture was fulfilled that says, "And he was counted among the lawless."*   *m* Or *blasphemed*   *n* Or *the Christ*   *o* Or *earth*   *p* Other ancient authorities read *made me a reproach*

15

for E·li′jah." 36 And someone ran, filled a sponge with sour wine, put it on a stick, and gave it to him to drink, saying, "Wait, let us see whether E·li′jah will come to take him down." 37 Then Jesus gave a loud cry and breathed his last. 38 And the curtain of the temple was torn in two, from top to bottom. 39 Now when the centurion, who stood facing him, saw that in this way he*q* breathed his last, he said, "Truly this man was God's Son!"*r*

40 There were also women looking on from a distance; among them were Mary Mag′da·lēne, and Mary the mother of James the younger and of Jō′sēs, and Sa·lō′mē. 41 These used to follow him and provided for him when he was in Galilee; and there were many other women who had come up with him to Jerusalem.

The Burial of Jesus
(Mt 27.57–61; Lk 23.50–56; Jn 19.38–42)

42 When evening had come, and since it was the day of Preparation, that is, the day before the sabbath, 43 Joseph of Ar·i·ma·thē′a, a respected member of the council, who was also himself waiting expectantly for the kingdom of God, went boldly to Pilate and asked for the body of Jesus. 44 Then Pilate wondered if he were already dead; and summoning the centurion, he asked him whether he had been dead for some time. 45 When he learned from the centurion that he was dead, he granted the body to Joseph. 46 Then Joseph*s* bought a linen cloth, and taking down the body,*t* wrapped it in the linen cloth, and laid it in a tomb that had been hewn out of the rock. He then rolled a stone against the door of the tomb. 47 Mary Mag′da·lēne and Mary the mother of Jō′sēs saw where the body*t* was laid.

The Resurrection of Jesus
(Mt 28.1–10; Lk 24.1–12; Jn 20.1–10)

16 When the sabbath was over, Mary Mag′-da·lēne, and Mary the mother of James, and Sa·lō′mē bought spices, so that they might go

---

q Other ancient authorities add *cried out and*   *r* Or *a son of God*   *s* Gk *he*   *t* Gk *it*

Alone!

One summer weekend several years ago, eight teenagers went on a hiking trip to the mountains. After an argument, one of the girls wandered off by herself and became separated from the group. When her absence was discovered, a search party quickly formed. Everyone was worried and anxious.

Afraid! Vulnerable! Lost and alone! She later described her feelings as the worst she had ever had in her life. She had no way of changing the situation. She even screamed at the sky and begged God to save her! All she could do was just pray and wait and hope.

Jesus may have had similar feelings. He may have felt lost, and he may have felt completely abandoned by his friends and even by God. He had to face his death alone. Can you imagine anything more lonely? His prayers did not change his circumstances but gave him a way to lament, to cry out to God to express his distress.

What makes you the most lonely and afraid? Have you ever felt abandoned? It is always okay to lament. When do you most feel the need to do so? Crying out does not always change our circumstances, but it can help remind us that we are not truly alone—God is with us.

▶ Mk 15.33–34

Jesus Strengthens Our Faith

A group of faithful women accompany Jesus from afar when he dies on the cross, and they look to see where he is buried (Mk 15.40–47). They are witnesses to the terrible violence of Jesus' death. Two days later, after the Sabbath, three of the women go to the tomb to anoint Jesus' body, giving him a proper burial. When they receive the good news that Jesus is alive, they flee from the tomb terrified and amazed.

This is where the original Gospel of Mark ends. Immediately, we want to ask lots of questions. What happened to the disciples? Did they go to Galilee? How did the word get out that Jesus had risen from the dead? Apparently, early Christians found this abrupt ending troublesome, and so they added other endings similar to those of the other Gospels.

These additions, starting at Mk 16.9, emphasize the surprise of the disciples. It seems as if they are paralyzed. Only a strong scolding by Jesus and being commissioned to proclaim the Good News to the whole creation brings them around.

How do doubts and confusion paralyze you in living your faith? Pay attention to Jesus! Hear his voice! He is telling you to carry his message of love to other people. By doing so, you will strengthen your faith, and your life will be full of joy!

▶ Mk 16.1–20

---

and anoint him. 2 And very early on the first day of the week, when the sun had risen, they went to the tomb. 3 They had been saying to one another, "Who will roll away the stone for us from the entrance to the tomb?" 4 When they looked up, they saw that the stone, which was very large, had already been rolled back. 5 As they entered the tomb, they saw a young man, dressed in a white robe, sitting on the right side; and they were alarmed. 6 But he said to them, "Do not be alarmed; you are looking for Jesus of Nazareth, who was crucified. He has been raised; he is not here. Look, there is the place they laid him. 7 But go, tell his disciples and Peter that he is going ahead of you to Galilee; there you will see him, just as he told you." 8 So they went out and fled from the tomb, for terror and amazement had seized them; and they said nothing to anyone, for they were afraid.[u]

THE SHORTER ENDING OF MARK

[And all that had been commanded them they told briefly to those around Peter. And afterward Jesus himself sent out through them, from east to west, the sacred and imperishable proclamation of eternal salvation.[v]]

THE LONGER ENDING OF MARK

Jesus Appears to Mary Magdalene
(Jn 20.11–18)

9 [Now after he rose early on the first day of the week, he appeared first to Mary Mag'da·lēne, from whom he had cast out seven demons. 10 She went out and told those who had been with him, while they were mourning and weeping. 11 But when they

heard that he was alive and had been seen by her, they would not believe it.

Jesus Appears to Two Disciples
(Lk 24.13–43; Jn 20.19–23)

12 After this he appeared in another form to two of them, as they were walking into the country. 13 And they went back and told the rest, but they did not believe them.

Jesus Commissions the Disciples
(Mt 28.16–20; Lk 24.44–49; Jn 20.19–23; Acts 1.6–8)

14 Later he appeared to the eleven themselves as they were sitting at the table; and he upbraided them for their lack of faith and stubbornness, because they had not believed those who saw him after he had risen.[w] 15 And he said to them, "Go into

---

u Some of the most ancient authorities bring the book to a close at the end of verse 8. One authority concludes the book with the shorter ending; others include the shorter ending and then continue with verses 9-20. In most authorities verses 9-20 follow immediately after verse 8, though in some of these authorities the passage is marked as being doubtful.   v Other ancient authorities add *Amen*
w Other ancient authorities add, in whole or in part, *And they excused themselves, saying, "This age of lawlessness and unbelief is under Satan, who does not allow the truth and power of God to prevail over the unclean things of the spirits. Therefore reveal your righteousness now"—thus they spoke to Christ. And Christ replied to them, "The term of years of Satan's power has been fulfilled, but other terrible things draw near. And for those who have sinned I was handed over to death, that they may return to the truth and sin no more, that they may inherit the spiritual and imperishable glory of righteousness that is in heaven."*

all the world and proclaim the good news*x* to the whole creation. 16 The one who believes and is baptized will be saved; but the one who does not believe will be condemned. 17 And these signs will accompany those who believe: by using my name they will cast out demons; they will speak in new tongues; 18 they will pick up snakes in their hands,*y* and if they drink any deadly thing, it will not hurt them; they will lay their hands on the sick, and they will recover."

The Ascension of Jesus
(Lk 24.50–53)

19 So then the Lord Jesus, after he had spoken to them, was taken up into heaven and sat down at the right hand of God. 20 And they went out and proclaimed the good news everywhere, while the Lord worked with them and confirmed the message by the signs that accompanied it.*z*]

x Or *gospel*   *y* Other ancient authorities lack *in their hands*
z Other ancient authorities add *Amen*

M
K

Perhaps one of the most discouraging moments in life is the first time you realize that you are in the "out"-group. Children, youth, and adults all have ways of marking who's "in" and who's "out." For people who find themselves frequently in the out-group, life can be painful. The good news in the Gospel of Luke is that there is no out-group any-more. In the Reign of God, every-one is part of the in-group.

In-depth

The author of the Gospel of Luke was a Gen-tile (non-Jewish) convert to Christianity. So one of Luke's important concerns is to show that both Gentiles and Jews are seen as part of Jesus' in-group. In Luke, Jesus praises the faith of a centurion (7.1–10), who is a Gentile and a hated symbol of the Roman occupation. Jesus also makes a Samaritan (Samaritans were con-sidered foreigners by other Jews) the hero of a parable (10.25–37).

Other in-groups for Jesus in Luke's Gospel are women and poor people. Women had little status in society at the time. But Luke includes many stories about women, including Mary's visit to her cousin Elizabeth before the births of their sons, Jesus and John the Baptist (1.39–66). This Gospel also shows how Jesus loved the poor and scolded the rich for their lack of concern for the poor. For example, it includes a story about a poor man named Lazarus, who begged for food at a rich man's door. God honored Lazarus with a special place in Abraham's bosom (heaven) when he died (16.19–31), whereas the rich man suffered in Hades.

Finally, Luke's Gospel shows Jesus' com-passion and forgiveness for outcasts and sinners. It includes stories about the tax collector Zac-chaeus, who climbs a tree to see Jesus (19.1–10), the good Samaritan (10.25–37), and the pen-itent sinner who was crucified beside Jesus (23.39–43). The Gospel presents a vivid picture of how Jesus made the Reign of God present, in-spiring his disciples to take the Gospel message to other lands and cultures.

At a Glance

- **Chapters 1–2.** introduc-tion; stories about Jesus' birth and early child-hood

- **3.1—9.50.** Jesus' minis-try in Galilee

- **9.51—19.27.** parables and miracles on the way to Jerusalem

- **19.28—21.38.** Jesus in Jerusalem: conflict with the religious authorities

- **Chapters 22–24.** stories about Jesus' death, Res-urrection, and Ascension

Quick Facts

Author
a Gentile Christian named Luke, who may have been a disciple of Paul (Col 4.14)

Date Written
approximately A.D. 80–90

Audience
Gentile (Greek) Christians represented by Theophilus (see Lk 1.3)

Of Note
Luke also wrote the Acts of the Apostles.

Image of Jesus
merciful, compassionate, with a special concern for poor people, women, and non-Jews

The Gospel According to **Luke**

Luke

2.8

Dedication to Theophilus

1 Since many have undertaken to set down an orderly account of the events that have been fulfilled among us, 2 just as they were handed on to us by those who from the beginning were eyewitnesses and servants of the word, 3 I too decided, after investigating everything carefully from the very first,[a] to write an orderly account for you, most excellent Thē·oph'i·lus, 4 so that you may know the truth concerning the things about which you have been instructed.

The Birth of John the Baptist Foretold

5 In the days of King Her'od of Judea, there was a priest named Zech·a·rī'ah, who belonged to the priestly order of A·bī'jah. His wife was a descendant of Aaron, and her name was Elizabeth. 6 Both of them were righteous before God, living blamelessly according to all the commandments and regulations of the Lord. 7 But they had no children, because Elizabeth was barren, and both were getting on in years.

8 Once when he was serving as priest before God and his section was on duty, 9 he was chosen by lot, according to the custom of the priesthood, to enter the sanctuary of the Lord and offer incense. 10 Now at the time of the incense offering, the whole assembly of the people was praying outside. 11 Then there appeared to him an angel of the Lord, standing at the right side of the altar of incense.

12 When Zech·a·rī'ah saw him, he was terrified; and fear overwhelmed him. 13 But the angel said to him, "Do not be afraid, Zech·a·rī'ah, for your prayer has been heard. Your wife Elizabeth will bear you a son, and you will name him John. 14 You will have joy and gladness, and many will rejoice at his birth, 15 for he will be great in the sight of the Lord. He must never drink wine or strong drink; even before his birth he will be filled with the Holy Spirit. 16 He will turn many of the people of Israel to the Lord their God. 17 With the spirit and power of E·lī'jah he will go before him, to turn the hearts of parents to their children, and the disobedient to the wisdom of the righteous, to make ready a people prepared for the Lord." 18 Zech·a·rī'ah said to the angel, "How will I know that this is so? For I am an old man, and my wife is getting on in years." 19 The angel replied, "I am Gabriel. I stand in the presence of God, and I have been sent to speak to you and to bring you this good news. 20 But now, because you did not believe my words, which will be fulfilled in their time, you will become mute, unable to speak, until the day these things occur."

21 Meanwhile the people were waiting for Zech·a·rī'ah, and wondered at his delay in the sanctuary. 22 When he did come out, he could not speak to them, and they realized that he had seen a vision in the sanctuary. He kept motioning to them and

---

a Or *for a long time*

remained unable to speak. 23 When his time of service was ended, he went to his home.

24 After those days his wife Elizabeth conceived, and for five months she remained in seclusion. She said, 25 "This is what the Lord has done for me when he looked favorably on me and took away the disgrace I have endured among my people."

The Birth of Jesus Foretold

26 In the sixth month the angel Gabriel was sent by God to a town in Galilee called Nazareth, 27 to a virgin engaged to a man whose name was Joseph, of the house of David. The virgin's name was Mary. 28 And he came to her and said, "Greetings, favored one! The Lord is with you."b 29 But she was much perplexed by his words and pondered what sort of greeting this might be. 30 The angel said to her, "Do not be afraid, Mary, for you have found favor with God. 31 And now, you will conceive in your womb and bear a son, and you will name him Jesus. 32 He will be great, and will be called the Son of the Most High, and the Lord God will give to him the throne of his ancestor David. 33 He will reign over the house of Jacob forever, and of his kingdom there will be no end." 34 Mary said to the angel, "How can this be, since I am a virgin?"c

35 The angel said to her, "The Holy Spirit will come upon you, and the power of the Most High will overshadow you; therefore the child to be bornd will be holy; he will be called Son of God. 36 And now, your relative Elizabeth in her old age has also conceived a son; and this is the sixth month for her who was said to be barren. 37 For nothing will be impossible with God." 38 Then Mary said, "Here am I, the servant of the Lord; let it be with me according to your word." Then the angel departed from her.

Mary Visits Elizabeth

39 In those days Mary set out and went with haste to a Judean town in the hill country, 40 where she entered the house of Zech·a·ri'ah and greeted Elizabeth. 41 When Elizabeth heard Mary's greeting, the child leaped in her womb. And Elizabeth was filled with the Holy Spirit 42 and exclaimed with a loud cry, "Blessed are you among women, and blessed is the fruit of your womb. 43 And why has this happened to me, that the mother of my Lord comes to me? 44 For as soon as I heard the sound of

---

b Other ancient authorities add *Blessed are you among women* c Gk *I do not know a man* d Other ancient authorities add *of you*

Introducing

▶ MARY OF NAZARETH

Luke's Gospel makes it clear that Mary of Nazareth has a special place in God's plan of salvation. Beginning with Mary's humble acceptance of God's will revealed by the angel Gabriel (1.26–38), Mary is presented as the true, first disciple who does the will of God. Her yes to God leads to Jesus' presence among us. She follows Jesus to the cross and is with the disciples in the upper room during the coming of the Holy Spirit (Acts 1.14). Mary reveals to us the meaning of true faith—a willingness to accept God's call and to gradually discover the full meaning of God's will.

In choosing Mary to be the mother of Jesus, God selected not a rich queen, but a poor young girl open to the action of the Holy Spirit in her life. In Mary, Luke emphasizes God's preference for the poor and the little ones (see "The Magnificat, the Prayer of the Poor!" Lk 1.39–56).

Besides being the mother of Jesus, Mary is presented in the Bible as the mother of the church (Jn 19.25–27). For this reason, Catholic Christians have a special devotion to Mary. They celebrate her virginal conception of Jesus on the feast of the Annunciation (25 March). They believe that Mary was born free from original sin, and celebrate this on the feast of the Immaculate Conception (8 December). They also believe that she was taken into heaven, body and soul, at the end of her life, and celebrate this on the feast of the Assumption (15 August). Catholics also have a special prayer form honoring Mary, called the rosary.

Lk 1.26–56

THE MAGNIFICAT, THE PRAYER OF THE POOR!

Mary gives a testimony of her faith right after she receives the news that she will be the mother of God. During her visit to her cousin Elizabeth, she sings of God's salvation in a song known as the Magnificat, which means "[my soul] praises." This prayer is mainly made up of verses taken from the Psalms and the Prophets. Mary first sings of her salvation; then she sings of God's salvation brought to the humble, the poor, and the hungry; and she finishes by singing of the salvation brought to all the people of God as promised to Abraham.

The Magnificat is an important prayer. It is the song of the poor of God, those who expected salvation from God, not from people in power or through wars and conquests. The social consequences of God's salvation are clearly revealed in Mary's song. The Magnificat is like a summary of Jesus' life on earth, which raised up the lowly and brought down the powerful to build the Reign of God.

- In a world marked by huge gaps between rich people and poor people, is it clear that Christians are in solidarity with the poor?
- How are you helping the poor now, and how are you planning to do so as an adult?
- Pray the Magnificat slowly, savoring what it says, letting it move to the core of your heart.

▶ Lk 1.39–56

your greeting, the child in my womb leaped for joy. ⁴⁵ And blessed is she who believed that there would be^e a fulfillment of what was spoken to her by the Lord."

Mary's Magnificat

46 And Mary^f said,
"My soul magnifies the Lord,
⁴⁷   and my spirit rejoices in God my Savior,
⁴⁸ for he has looked with favor on the lowliness
         of his servant.
         Surely, from now on all generations will
            call me blessed;
⁴⁹ for the Mighty One has done great things for me,
         and holy is his name.
⁵⁰ His mercy is for those who fear him
         from generation to generation.
⁵¹ He has shown strength with his arm;
         he has scattered the proud in the thoughts
            of their hearts.
⁵² He has brought down the powerful from their
            thrones,
         and lifted up the lowly;
⁵³ he has filled the hungry with good things,
         and sent the rich away empty.
⁵⁴ He has helped his servant Israel,
         in remembrance of his mercy,

55   according to the promise he made to our
            ancestors,
         to Abraham and to his descendants forever."
56 And Mary remained with her about three months and then returned to her home.

The Birth of John the Baptist

57 Now the time came for Elizabeth to give birth, and she bore a son. ⁵⁸ Her neighbors and relatives heard that the Lord had shown his great mercy to her, and they rejoiced with her.

59 On the eighth day they came to circumcise the child, and they were going to name him Zech·a·ri′ah after his father. ⁶⁰ But his mother said, "No; he is to be called John." ⁶¹ They said to her, "None of your relatives has this name." ⁶² Then they began motioning to his father to find out what name he wanted to give him. ⁶³ He asked for a writing tablet and wrote, "His name is John." And all of them were amazed. ⁶⁴ Immediately his mouth was opened and his tongue freed, and he began to speak, praising God. ⁶⁵ Fear came over all their neighbors, and all these things were talked about throughout the entire hill country of Judea. ⁶⁶ All

_____

e Or believed, for there will be   f Other ancient authorities read Elizabeth who heard them pondered them and said, "What then will this child become?" For, indeed, the hand of the Lord was with him.

The Canticle of Zechariah

67 Then his father Zech·a·ri'ah was filled with the Holy Spirit and spoke this prophecy:
68 "Blessed be the Lord God of Israel,
    for he has looked favorably on his people
        and redeemed them.
69 He has raised up a mighty savior[g] for us
    in the house of his servant David,
70 as he spoke through the mouth of his holy
        prophets from of old,
71   that we would be saved from our enemies
        and from the hand of all who hate us.
72 Thus he has shown the mercy promised to our
        ancestors,
    and has remembered his holy covenant,
73 the oath that he swore to our ancestor Abraham,
    to grant us 74 that we, being rescued from
        the hands of our enemies,
    might serve him without fear, 75 in holiness
        and righteousness
    before him all our days.
76 And you, child, will be called the prophet of
        the Most High;
    for you will go before the Lord to prepare
        his ways,
77 to give knowledge of salvation to his people
    by the forgiveness of their sins.
78 By the tender mercy of our God,
    the dawn from on high will break upon[h] us,
79 to give light to those who sit in darkness and
        in the shadow of death,
    to guide our feet into the way of peace."

80 The child grew and became strong in spirit, and he was in the wilderness until the day he appeared publicly to Israel.

The Birth of Jesus
(Mt 1.18–25)

2 In those days a decree went out from Emperor Augustus that all the world should be registered. 2 This was the first registration and was taken while Qui·rin'i·us was governor of Syria. 3 All went to their own towns to be registered. 4 Joseph also went from the town of Nazareth in Galilee to Judea, to the city of David called Bethlehem, because he was descended from the house and family of David. 5 He went to be registered with Mary, to whom he was engaged and who was expecting a child. 6 While they were there, the time came for her to deliver her child. 7 And she gave birth to her firstborn son and wrapped him in bands of cloth, and laid him in a manger, because there was no place for them in the inn.

Catholic Connections

THE BENEDICTUS

Zechariah's prayer in Lk 1.68–79 is called the Benedictus (which means "blessed") or the Canticle of Zechariah. After Zechariah regains his voice, he praises God for sending a savior from the line of David. The savior he sings of is not a warrior king but someone bringing salvation through the forgiveness of sins and leading people into the way of peace.

The Benedictus is recited during morning prayer, and the Magnificat (see Lk 1.46–55) is recited during evening prayer in the Liturgy of the Hours. Why not make the Magnificat and the Benedictus part of your prayer life too? Place a bookmark in this chapter and turn to it when you want to praise God and express your faith in God's saving power.

▶ Lk 1.46–80

The Shepherds and the Angels

8 In that region there were shepherds living in the fields, keeping watch over their flock by night. 9 Then an angel of the Lord stood before them, and the glory of the Lord shone around them, and they were terrified. 10 But the angel said to them, "Do not be afraid; for see—I am bringing you good news of great joy for all the people: 11 to you is born this day in the city of David a Savior, who is the Messiah,[i] the Lord. 12 This will be a sign for you: you will find a child wrapped in bands of cloth and lying in a manger." 13 And suddenly there was with the angel a multitude of the heavenly host,[j] praising God and saying,
14 "Glory to God in the highest heaven,
        and on earth peace among those whom he
            favors!"[k]
15 When the angels had left them and gone

---

[g] Gk *a horn of salvation*   [h] Other ancient authorities read *has broken upon*   [i] Or *the Christ*   [j] Gk *army*   [k] Other ancient authorities read *peace, goodwill among people*

into heaven, the shepherds said to one another, "Let us go now to Bethlehem and see this thing that has taken place, which the Lord has made known to us." 16 So they went with haste and found Mary and Joseph, and the child lying in the manger. 17 When they saw this, they made known what had been told them about this child; 18 and all who heard it were amazed at what the shepherds told them. 19 But Mary treasured all these words and pondered them in her heart. 20 The shepherds returned, glorifying and praising God for all they had heard and seen, as it had been told them.

Jesus Is Named

21 When eight days had passed, it was time to circumcise the child; and he was called Jesus, the name given by the angel before he was conceived in the womb.

Jesus Is Presented in the Temple

22 When the time came for their purification according to the law of Moses, they brought him up to Jerusalem to present him to the Lord 23 (as it is written in the law of the Lord, "Every firstborn male shall be designated as holy to the Lord"), 24 and they offered a sacrifice according to what is stated in the law of the Lord, "a pair of turtledoves or two young pigeons."

25 Now there was a man in Jerusalem whose name was Sim′e·on;*l* this man was righteous and devout, looking forward to the consolation of Israel, and the Holy Spirit rested on him. 26 It had been revealed to him by the Holy Spirit that he would not see death before he had seen the Lord's Messiah.*m* 27 Guided by the Spirit, Sim′e·on*n* came into the temple; and when the parents brought in the child Jesus, to do for him what was customary under the law, 28 Sim′e·on*o* took him in his arms and praised God, saying,

29 "Master, now you are dismissing your servant*p*
        in peace,
    according to your word;
30 for my eyes have seen your salvation,
31   which you have prepared in the presence of
        all peoples,
32 a light for revelation to the Gentiles
    and for glory to your people Israel."

33 And the child's father and mother were amazed at what was being said about him. 34 Then Sim′e·on*l* blessed them and said to his mother Mary, "This child is destined for the falling and the rising of many in Israel, and to be a sign that will be opposed 35 so that the inner thoughts of many will

---

l Gk Symeon   *m* Or the Lord's Christ   *n* Gk In the Spirit, he
o Gk he   *p* Gk slave

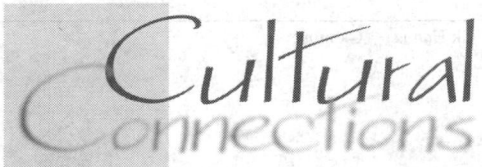

O CHRISTMAS TREE

Did you ever wonder where the tradition of the Christmas tree came from? It began in Germany, the country that also gave us the beautiful song "Silent Night." For hundreds of years, the Christmas tree has been the focal point and symbol of the Christmas season for the people of Germany.

In the year A.D. 350, Pope Julius declared 25 December, which had been the day of the pagan feast of the sun god, a feast day in observance of the birth of the Son of God. Prior to A.D. 350, the German people had a tradition of keeping evergreen branches in the house to ward off evil spirits. This pagan tradition was exchanged for a Christian tradition of having branches in the house to symbolize the life that Jesus brought to the world. After some time, the branches themselves were exchanged for entire trees, which were brought into homes and decorated with candles.

Today, the Christmas tree is a central symbol of Christmas in many countries. Adding lights and decorations helps us to celebrate the birth of Jesus, the light of the world.

▸ Lk 2.1–14

Jesus' Birth: Good News to the Poor

On 25 December, we celebrate Christmas, the birth of Jesus. We recall the moment of God's entering our world—a defining moment in the history of salvation. As Luke records the moment of the birth of the Messiah, who are the stars of the show? To whom do the angels appear to announce this remarkable event, this "good news of great joy for all the people"? the high priest? the rich and important residents of Bethlehem? No. The announcement is made to shepherds, poor workers living in the fields nearby.

Like Mary, the shepherds are people of little power and significance. Luke makes the point that sometimes what the world sees as unimportant, God honors. This is the justice of God. It is the same today. The poorest in our world, the most hidden people who have no power, hold a special place in the heart of God. And, like the shepherds, poor people often know God better than those who are rich or powerful by this world's standards.

This truth is a challenge but also good news for all of us, rich and poor alike. How do your attitudes and actions—even the way you celebrate Christmas—reflect God's special attention to poor people?

▶ Lk 2.8–20

be revealed—and a sword will pierce your own soul too."

36 There was also a prophet, Anna[q] the daughter of Phan′ū•el, of the tribe of Ash′er. She was of a great age, having lived with her husband seven years after her marriage, 37 then as a widow to the age of eighty-four. She never left the temple but worshiped there with fasting and prayer night and day. 38 At that moment she came, and began to praise God and to speak about the child[r] to all who were looking for the redemption of Jerusalem.

The Return to Nazareth

39 When they had finished everything required by the law of the Lord, they returned to Galilee, to their own town of Nazareth. 40 The child grew and

q Gk Hanna   r Gk him

Introducing ▶ THE HOLY FAMILY

On the first Sunday after Christmas, the Catholic church celebrates the feast of the Holy Family: Jesus, Mary, and Joseph. The Bible does not tell us a lot about the Holy Family. We know that Joseph was a kind and compassionate man, eager to do God's will. He raised Jesus as his own son, even though he was not Jesus' biological father. Jesus was raised in a home in which love and faith were the norm.

We can be sure that the Holy Family had their moments of conflict and crisis—all families do. Luke's story of Jesus' getting separated from his parents demonstrates that. But we can also be sure that their love and faith helped them to survive such conflicts and grow stronger because of them. The church holds the Holy Family up as a model of respect, compassion, love, and faith in family life.

How does your family express love and respect for one another? What crises and conflicts have you and your family survived? What can you do to bring the qualities of the Holy Family more fully into your family's life?

Lk 2.41–52

Jesus Grows in Age and Wisdom

Luke is the only Gospel that has any stories of Jesus' childhood. When Jesus was twelve, he left his family to stay in the Temple in Jerusalem. At the Temple, Jesus listened to and questioned the teachers, trying to understand his faith better. His questions and his understanding—and we can presume his sincerity—amazed all who heard him.

Adolescence is an important time for exploring life's questions—including life's religious questions. Sometimes, young people are led to believe that they shouldn't have any questions—which is a sad statement about adult leaders and teachers. Wise teachers—like those the boy Jesus met in the Temple—welcome and encourage your questions, even your religious questions. So ask yourself: How well do I know my faith? What are my main questions? Who are the wise teachers I can go to for help in searching out the answers?

▸ Lk 2.41–52

became strong, filled with wisdom; and the favor of God was upon him.

The Boy Jesus in the Temple

41 Now every year his parents went to Jerusalem for the festival of the Passover. 42 And when he was twelve years old, they went up as usual for the festival. 43 When the festival was ended and they started to return, the boy Jesus stayed behind in Jerusalem, but his parents did not know it. 44 Assuming that he was in the group of travelers, they went a day's journey. Then they started to look for him among their relatives and friends. 45 When they did not find him, they returned to Jerusalem to search for him. 46 After three days they found him in the temple, sitting among the teachers, listening to them and asking them questions. 47 And all who heard him were amazed at his understanding and his answers. 48 When his parents[s] saw him they were astonished; and his mother said to him, "Child, why have you treated us like this? Look, your father and I have been searching for you in great anxiety." 49 He said to them, "Why were you searching for me? Did you not know that I must be in my Father's house?"[t] 50 But they did not understand what he said to them. 51 Then he went down with them and came to Nazareth, and was obedient to them. His mother treasured all these things in her heart. 52 And Jesus increased in wisdom and in years,[u] and in divine and human favor.

The Proclamation of John the Baptist
(Mt 3.1–12; Mk 1.1–8; Jn 1.19–28)

3 In the fifteenth year of the reign of Emperor Tī·bē′ri·us, when Pon′ti·us Pilate was governor of Judea, and Her′od was ruler[v] of Galilee, and his brother Philip ruler[v] of the region of Ī·tu·raē′a

and Trach·o·nī′tis, and Lȳ·sā′ni·as ruler[v] of Ab·i·lē′nē, 2 during the high priesthood of An′nas and Cā′i·a·phas, the word of God came to John son of Zech·a·rī′ah in the wilderness. 3 He went into all the region around the Jordan, proclaiming a baptism of repentance for the forgiveness of sins, 4 as it is written in the book of the words of the prophet Ī·sāi′ah,

"The voice of one crying out in the
    wilderness:
'Prepare the way of the Lord,
    make his paths straight.
5 Every valley shall be filled,
    and every mountain and hill shall be made
      low,
and the crooked shall be made straight,
    and the rough ways made smooth;
6 and all flesh shall see the salvation of God.' "

7 John said to the crowds that came out to be baptized by him, "You brood of vipers! Who warned you to flee from the wrath to come? 8 Bear fruits worthy of repentance. Do not begin to say to yourselves, 'We have Abraham as our ancestor'; for I tell you, God is able from these stones to raise up children to Abraham. 9 Even now the ax is lying at the root of the trees; every tree therefore that does not bear good fruit is cut down and thrown into the fire."

10 And the crowds asked him, "What then should we do?" 11 In reply he said to them, "Whoever has two coats must share with anyone who has none; and whoever has food must do likewise." 12 Even tax collectors came to be baptized, and they asked him, "Teacher, what should we do?" 13 He said to them, "Collect no more than the amount prescribed for you." 14 Soldiers also asked him,

---

[s] Gk they   [t] Or be about my Father's interests?   [u] Or in stature   [v] Gk tetrarch

"And we, what should we do?" He said to them, "Do not extort money from anyone by threats or false accusation, and be satisfied with your wages."

15 As the people were filled with expectation, and all were questioning in their hearts concerning John, whether he might be the Messiah,*w* 16 John answered all of them by saying, "I baptize you with water; but one who is more powerful than I is coming; I am not worthy to untie the thong of his sandals. He will baptize you with*x* the Holy Spirit and fire. 17 His winnowing fork is in his hand, to clear his threshing floor and to gather the wheat into his granary; but the chaff he will burn with unquenchable fire."

18 So, with many other exhortations, he proclaimed the good news to the people. 19 But Her′od the ruler,*y* who had been rebuked by him because of He·rō′di·as, his brother's wife, and because of all the evil things that Her′od had done, 20 added to them all by shutting up John in prison.

The Baptism of Jesus
(Mt 3.13–17; Mk 1.9–11; Jn 1.29–34)

21 Now when all the people were baptized, and when Jesus also had been baptized and was praying, the heaven was opened, 22 and the Holy Spirit descended upon him in bodily form like a dove. And a voice came from heaven, "You are my Son, the Beloved;*z* with you I am well pleased."*a*

The Ancestors of Jesus
(Gen 5.1–32; 11.10–26; Ruth 4.18–22;
1 Chr 1.1–4, 24–27, 34; 2.1–15; Mt 1.2–16)

23 Jesus was about thirty years old when he began his work. He was the son (as was thought) of Joseph son of Hē′lī, 24 son of Mat′that, son of Levi, son of Mel′chī, son of Jan′naī, son of Joseph, 25 son of Mat·ta·thī′as, son of Ā′mos, son of Nā′hum, son of Es′lī, son of Nag′ga·ī, 26 son of Mā′ath, son of Mat·ta·thī′as, son of Sem′ē·in, son of Jō′sech, son of Jō′da, 27 son of Jō·an′an, son of Rhē′sa, son of Ze·rub′ba·bel, son of She·al′ti·el,*b* son of Nē′rī, 28 son of Mel′chī, son of Ad′dī, son of Cō′sam, son of El·mā′dam, son of Er, 29 son of Joshua, son of El·i·ē′zer, son of Jō′rim, son of Mat′that, son of Levi, 30 son of Sim′ē·on, son of Judah, son of Joseph, son of Jō′nam, son of E·li′a·kim, 31 son of Mē′le·a, son of Men′na, son of Mat′ta·tha, son of Nathan, son of David, 32 son of Jesse, son of Ō′bed, son of Bō′az, son of Sā′la,*c* son of Nah′shon, 33 son of Am·min′a·dab, son of Ad·min, son of Ar′nī,*d* son of Hez′ron, son of Per′ez, son of Judah, 34 son of Jacob, son of Isaac, son of Abraham, son of Tē′rah, son of Nā′hor,

---

w Or *the Christ*   *x* Or *in*   *y* Gk *tetrarch*   *z* Or *my beloved Son* *a* Other ancient authorities read *You are my Son, today I have begotten you*   *b* Gk *Salathiel*   *c* Other ancient authorities read *Salmon*   *d* Other ancient authorities read *Amminadab, son of Aram*; others vary widely

Introducing

▶ JOHN THE BAPTIST

Picture a man living in the desert, eating grasshoppers and wild honey, and wearing a camel hair coat. Does this sound like the person Jesus described as "among those born of women no one is greater than John" (Lk 7.28)? The person Jesus is talking about is John the Baptist, and he plays an important role in all four Gospels. John is portrayed like an Old Testament prophet, calling people to repentance for their sins. Indeed, his ministry was so similar to Jesus' ministry that after Herod had John killed (Mt 14.1–12), he thought that Jesus might have been John raised from the dead (Lk 9.7–9). The power of John's preaching is demonstrated by Jesus' disciples' still encountering John's followers years after John's death (Acts 19.1–7).

John the Baptist was Jesus' cousin, and the Gospel of Luke presents many parallels between the two men. John's preaching gives us a preview into Jesus' message. John was preparing the way for Jesus. He was a humble servant "not worthy to untie the thong of [Jesus'] sandals" (Lk 3.16). He described his baptism as a baptism of water in contrast with Jesus' baptism with "the Holy Spirit and fire" (verse 16).

John the Baptist is the model of how Christians should perform their prophetic mission, pointing others toward Jesus with passion and humility.

Lk 3.1–20

35 son of Sē′rug, son of Rē′ū, son of Pē′leg, son of Ē′ber, son of Shē′lah, 36 son of Cā•ī′nan, son of Ar-phā′xad, son of Shem, son of Noah, son of Lā′mech, 37 son of Me•thū′se•lah, son of Ē′noch, son of Jar′ed, son of Ma•hā′la•lē•el, son of Cā•ī′nan, 38 son of Ē′nos, son of Seth, son of Adam, son of God.

The Temptation of Jesus
(Mt 4.1–11; Mk 1.12–13)

4 Jesus, full of the Holy Spirit, returned from the Jordan and was led by the Spirit in the wilderness, 2 where for forty days he was tempted by the devil. He ate nothing at all during those days, and when they were over, he was famished. 3 The devil said to him, "If you are the Son of God, command this stone to become a loaf of bread." 4 Jesus answered him, "It is written, 'One does not live by bread alone.'"

5 Then the devil*e* led him up and showed him in an instant all the kingdoms of the world. 6 And the devil*e* said to him, "To you I will give their glory and all this authority; for it has been given over to me, and I give it to anyone I please. 7 If you, then, will worship me, it will all be yours." 8 Jesus answered him, "It is written,

'Worship the Lord your God,
    and serve only him.' "

9 Then the devil*e* took him to Jerusalem, and placed him on the pinnacle of the temple, saying to him, "If you are the Son of God, throw yourself down from here, 10 for it is written,

'He will command his angels concerning you,
    to protect you,'

did you KNOW?
The Liturgical Year

The story of Jesus' baptism is one of the readings for the feast of the Baptism of the Lord. The feast days and holy days celebrated by Catholics and other Christians follow a yearly pattern. This pattern is called the liturgical year; it is not the same as the calendar year. You can read more about church feast days and see a diagram of the church year on pages xvi–xvii.

▶ Lk 3.15–22

Catholic Connections
THE BIBLE, TRADITION, AND THE MAGISTERIUM

Notice that each time Jesus is tempted, he uses phrases from the Bible as a defense against the devil (Lk 4.4, 8, 12). But also notice that the devil knows the Scriptures and uses them to try to tempt Jesus (verses 10–11)!

We should always be careful about mis-interpreting the Bible. That is why the Catholic church teaches that our faith is based on both the Bible and the sacred Tradition handed down by the Apostles. The apostolic Tradition provides direction for understanding the Bible, and the Bible provides background for understanding the Tradition. The Magisterium—the pope and bishops—ensures that the Bible and Tradition are correctly taught and misinterpretations are corrected. That is why the Bible, Tradition, and the Magisterium are considered the three pillars of the Catholic church.

The Bible is a reliable guide and companion as long as we take care not to misuse it!

▶ Lk 4.1–13

11 and

'On their hands they will bear you up,
    so that you will not dash your foot against
    a stone.' "

12 Jesus answered him, "It is said, 'Do not put the Lord your God to the test.' " 13 When the devil had finished every test, he departed from him until an opportune time.

The Beginning of the Galilean Ministry
(Mt 4.17; Mk 1.14–15)

14 Then Jesus, filled with the power of the Spirit, returned to Galilee, and a report about him spread through all the surrounding country. 15 He began to teach in their synagogues and was praised by everyone.

e Gk *he*

"THE SPIRIT OF THE LORD is upon me,
because he has annointed me
to bring good news to the poor.

HE HAS SENT ME
to proclaim release to the captives
and recovery of sight to the blind,
to let the oppressed go free,
to proclaim the year of the Lord's favor."

LK

The Rejection of Jesus at Nazareth
(Mt 13.54–58; Mk 6.1–6)

16 When he came to Nazareth, where he had been brought up, he went to the synagogue on the sabbath day, as was his custom. He stood up to read, 17 and the scroll of the prophet Ī•sāi′ah was given to him. He unrolled the scroll and found the place where it was written:
18 "The Spirit of the Lord is upon me,
    because he has anointed me
        to bring good news to the poor.
    He has sent me to proclaim release to the captives
        and recovery of sight to the blind,
            to let the oppressed go free,
19 to proclaim the year of the Lord's favor."
20 And he rolled up the scroll, gave it back to the attendant, and sat down. The eyes of all in the synagogue were fixed on him. 21 Then he began to say to them, "Today this scripture has been fulfilled in your hearing." 22 All spoke well of him and were amazed at the gracious words that came from his mouth. They said, "Is not this Joseph's son?" 23 He said to them, "Doubtless you will quote to me this proverb, 'Doctor, cure yourself!' And you will say, 'Do here also in your hometown the things that we

have heard you did at Ca•per′na•um.' " 24 And he said, "Truly I tell you, no prophet is accepted in the prophet's hometown. 25 But the truth is, there were many widows in Israel in the time of E•lī′jah, when the heaven was shut up three years and six months, and there was a severe famine over all the land; 26 yet E•lī′jah was sent to none of them except to a widow at Zar′e•phath in Sī′don. 27 There were also many lepers[f] in Israel in the time of the prophet E•lī′sha, and none of them was cleansed except Nā′-a•man the Syrian." 28 When they heard this, all in the synagogue were filled with rage. 29 They got up, drove him out of the town, and led him to the brow of the hill on which their town was built, so that they might hurl him off the cliff. 30 But he passed through the midst of them and went on his way.

The Man with an Unclean Spirit
(Mk 1.21–28)

31 He went down to Ca•per′na•um, a city in Galilee, and was teaching them on the sabbath. 32 They were astounded at his teaching, because he spoke with authority. 33 In the synagogue there was a man who had the spirit of an unclean demon, and

---

f The terms *leper* and *leprosy* can refer to several diseases he cried out with a loud voice, 34 "Let us alone! What have you to do with us, Jesus of Nazareth? Have you come to destroy us? I know who you are, the Holy One of God." 35 But Jesus rebuked him, saying, "Be silent, and come out of him!" When the demon had thrown him down before them, he came out of him without having done him any harm. 36 They were all amazed and kept saying to one another, "What kind of utterance is this? For with authority and power he commands the unclean spirits, and out they come!" 37 And a report about him began to reach every place in the region.

Healings at Simon's House
(Mt 8.14–17; Mk 1.29–34)

38 After leaving the synagogue he entered Simon's house. Now Simon's mother-in-law was suffering from a high fever, and they asked him about her. 39 Then he stood over her and rebuked the fever, and it left her. Immediately she got up and began to serve them.

40 As the sun was setting, all those who had any who were sick with various kinds of diseases brought them to him; and he laid his hands on each

of them and cured them. 41 Demons also came out of many, shouting, "You are the Son of God!" But he rebuked them and would not allow them to speak, because they knew that he was the Messiah.g

Jesus Preaches in the Synagogues
(Mt 4.23–25; Mk 1.35–39)

42 At daybreak he departed and went into a deserted place. And the crowds were looking for him; and when they reached him, they wanted to prevent him from leaving them. 43 But he said to them, "I must proclaim the good news of the kingdom of God to the other cities also; for I was sent for this purpose." 44 So he continued proclaiming the message in the synagogues of Judea.h

Jesus Calls the First Disciples
(Mt 4.18–22; Mk 1.16–20)

5 Once while Jesusi was standing beside the lake of Gen•nes'a•ret, and the crowd was pressing in on him to hear the word of God, 2 he

---

g Or *the Christ*   h Other ancient authorities read *Galilee*
i Gk *he*

JESUS LIBERATES PEOPLE FROM OPPRESSION!

In Luke, Jesus begins his mission by referring to Isaiah's prophecy (Isa 61.1). In the Gospel, we see Jesus fulfilling this prophecy by acting in the following ways:

- healing the sick, whose sickness is viewed as God's punishment for their sinfulness
- touching and curing lepers, who are separated from the rest of society
- speaking and spending time with Samaritans, who are looked down upon and rejected by the Jews
- accepting as disciples women, who are generally not accepted as equals, socially and religiously
- responding to the request of the Roman centurion, a foreigner who represents social domination
- forgiving and eating with sinners, who are put down and discriminated against by leaders of the Temple
- liberating those possessed by demons, whom all avoid because they are believed to be under the power of Satan

     Consider these questions:
- What types of oppression in society do Christians need to respond to today?
- Are you suffering from oppression? If so, how and from whom?

Ask God for help in responding to oppression in your life and in society with truth and love.

▶ Lk 4.14–30

saw two boats there at the shore of the lake; the fishermen had gone out of them and were washing their nets. 3 He got into one of the boats, the one belonging to Simon, and asked him to put out a little way from the shore. Then he sat down and taught the crowds from the boat. 4 When he had finished speaking, he said to Simon, "Put out into the deep water and let down your nets for a catch." 5 Simon answered, "Master, we have worked all night long but have caught nothing. Yet if you say so, I will let down the nets." 6 When they had done this, they caught so many fish that their nets were beginning to break. 7 So they signaled their partners in the other boat to come and help them. And they came and filled both boats, so that they began to sink. 8 But when Simon Peter saw it, he fell down at Jesus' knees, saying, "Go away from me, Lord, for I am a sinful man!" 9 For he and all who were with him were amazed at the catch of fish that they had taken; 10 and so also were James and John, sons of Zeb'e•dee, who were partners with Simon. Then Jesus said to Simon, "Do not be afraid; from now on you will be catching people." 11 When they had brought their boats to shore, they left everything and followed him.

Jesus Cleanses a Leper
(Mt 8.1–4; Mk 1.40–45)

12 Once, when he was in one of the cities, there was a man covered with leprosy.j When he saw Jesus, he bowed with his face to the ground and begged him, "Lord, if you choose, you can make me clean." 13 Then Jesusk stretched out his hand, touched him, and said, "I do choose. Be made clean." Immediately the leprosyj left him. 14 And he

ordered him to tell no one. "Go," he said, "and show yourself to the priest, and, as Moses commanded, make an offering for your cleansing, for a testimony to them." 15 But now more than ever the word about Jesusl spread abroad; many crowds would gather to hear him and to be cured of their diseases. 16 But he would withdraw to deserted places and pray.

Jesus Heals a Paralytic
(Mt 9.2–8; Mk 2.1–12)

17 One day, while he was teaching, Phar'i•sees and teachers of the law were sitting near by (they had come from every village of Galilee and Judea and from Jerusalem); and the power of the Lord was with him to heal.m 18 Just then some men came, carrying a paralyzed man on a bed. They were trying to bring him in and lay him before Jesus;l 19 but finding no way to bring him in because of the crowd, they went up on the roof and let him down with his bed through the tiles into the middle of the crowdn in front of Jesus. 20 When he saw their faith, he said, "Friend,o your sins are forgiven you." 21 Then the scribes and the Phar'i•sees began to question, "Who is this who is speaking blasphemies? Who can forgive sins but God alone?" 22 When Jesus perceived their questionings, he answered them, "Why do you raise such questions in your hearts? 23 Which is easier, to say, 'Your sins are forgiven you,' or to say, 'Stand up and walk'? 24 But so that you may know that the Son of Man has au-

j The terms *leper* and *leprosy* can refer to several diseases
k Gk *he*   l Gk *him*   m Other ancient authorities read *was present to heal them*   n Gk *into the midst*   o Gk *Man*

Do Not Be Afraid   LIVE IT!

How would you respond if someone walked into the room right now and announced that God wanted to see you in the next room in five minutes? As astonishing as that would be, few of us would probably be anxious to run right in to see God. We would probably want a little more time to get some things in our life "straightened out"!

The Gospel of Luke reveals something interesting when it describes a miraculous catch of fish and the call of the first disciples. Upon seeing the miraculous catch, Peter knows he is in the presence of a holy person and asks Jesus to leave because he is overwhelmed by his own sinfulness and feels unworthy in Jesus' presence (5.8).

If we found ourselves in a boat with God, we might respond the same way. Jesus reassures Peter, uttering words so important that they are repeated six times in Luke: "Do not be afraid." God knows we are sinners too. Jesus came not to condemn us but to save us and to make God's love known to us. Jesus is also saying to us: "Do not be afraid. Come, follow me!"

▶ Lk 5.1–11

thority on earth to forgive sins"—he said to the one who was paralyzed—"I say to you, stand up and take your bed and go to your home." 25 Immediately he stood up before them, took what he had been lying on, and went to his home, glorifying God. 26 Amazement seized all of them, and they glorified God and were filled with awe, saying, "We have seen strange things today."

Jesus Calls Levi
(Mt 9.9–13; Mk 2.13–17)

27 After this he went out and saw a tax collector named Levi, sitting at the tax booth; and he said to him, "Follow me." 28 And he got up, left everything, and followed him.

29 Then Levi gave a great banquet for him in his house; and there was a large crowd of tax collectors and others sitting at the table*p* with them. 30 The Phar'i•sees and their scribes were complaining to his disciples, saying, "Why do you eat and drink with tax collectors and sinners?" 31 Jesus answered, "Those who are well have no need of a physician, but those who are sick; 32 I have come to call not the righteous but sinners to repentance."

The Question about Fasting
(Mt 9.14–17; Mk 2.18–22)

33 Then they said to him, "John's disciples, like the disciples of the Phar'i•sees, frequently fast and pray, but your disciples eat and drink." 34 Jesus said to them, "You cannot make wedding guests fast while the bridegroom is with them, can you? 35 The days will come when the bridegroom will be taken away from them, and then they will fast in those days." 36 He also told them a parable: "No one tears a piece from a new garment and sews it on an old

garment; otherwise the new will be torn, and the piece from the new will not match the old. 37 And no one puts new wine into old wineskins; otherwise the new wine will burst the skins and will be spilled, and the skins will be destroyed. 38 But new wine must be put into fresh wineskins. 39 And no one after drinking old wine desires new wine, but says, 'The old is good.' "*q*

The Question about the Sabbath
(Mt 12.1–8; Mk 2.23–28)

6 One sabbath*r* while Jesus*s* was going through the grainfields, his disciples plucked some heads of grain, rubbed them in their hands, and ate them. 2 But some of the Phar'i•sees said, "Why are you doing what is not lawful*t* on the sabbath?" 3 Jesus answered, "Have you not read what David did when he and his companions were hungry? 4 He entered the house of God and took and ate the bread of the Presence, which it is not lawful for any but the priests to eat, and gave some to his companions?" 5 Then he said to them, "The Son of Man is lord of the sabbath."

The Man with a Withered Hand
(Mt 12.9–14; Mk 3.1–6)

6 On another sabbath he entered the synagogue and taught, and there was a man there whose right hand was withered. 7 The scribes and the Phar'i•sees watched him to see whether he would cure on the sabbath, so that they might find an accusation against him. 8 Even though he knew what they were thinking, he said to the man who had the withered hand, "Come and stand here." He got up and stood there. 9 Then Jesus said to them, "I ask you, is it lawful to do good or to do harm on the sabbath, to save life or to destroy it?" 10 After looking around at all of them, he said to him, "Stretch out your hand." He did so, and his hand was restored. 11 But they were filled with fury and discussed with one another what they might do to Jesus.

Jesus Chooses the Twelve Apostles
(Mt 10.1–4; Mk 3.13–19a)

12 Now during those days he went out to the mountain to pray; and he spent the night in prayer to God. 13 And when day came, he called his disciples and chose twelve of them, whom he also named apostles: 14 Simon, whom he named Peter, and his brother Andrew, and James, and John, and Philip, and Bartholomew, 15 and Matthew, and Thomas, and James son of Al•phae'us, and Simon,

---

p Gk *reclining* *q* Other ancient authorities read *better;* others lack verse 39 *r* Other ancient authorities read *On the second first sabbath* *s* Gk *he* *t* Other ancient authorities add *to do* who was called the Zealot, 16 and Judas son of James, and Judas Is•car'i•ot, who became a traitor.

Sermon on the Plain
(Mt 4.23–25; Mk 1.35–39; Lk 4.44)

17 He came down with them and stood on a level place, with a great crowd of his disciples and a great multitude of people from all Judea, Jerusalem, and the coast of Tyre and Si'don. 18 They had come to hear him and to be healed of their diseases; and those who were troubled with unclean spirits were cured. 19 And all in the crowd were trying to touch him, for power came out from him and healed all of them.

Blessings and Woes
(Mt 5.1–12)

20 Then he looked up at his disciples and said:
"Blessed are you who are poor,
　　for yours is the kingdom of God.
21 "Blessed are you who are hungry now,
　　for you will be filled.
"Blessed are you who weep now,
　　for you will laugh.
22 "Blessed are you when people hate you, and when they exclude you, revile you, and defame you[u] on account of the Son of Man. 23 Rejoice in that day and leap for joy, for surely your reward is great in heaven; for that is what their ancestors did to the prophets.
24 "But woe to you who are rich,
　　for you have received your consolation.
25 "Woe to you who are full now,
　　for you will be hungry.
"Woe to you who are laughing now,
　　for you will mourn and weep.
26 "Woe to you when all speak well of you, for that is what their ancestors did to the false prophets.

Love for Enemies
(Mt 5.33–48)

27 "But I say to you that listen, Love your enemies, do good to those who hate you, 28 bless those who curse you, pray for those who abuse you. 29 If anyone strikes you on the cheek, offer the other also; and from anyone who takes away your coat do not withhold even your shirt. 30 Give to everyone who begs from you; and if anyone takes away your goods, do not ask for them again. 31 Do to others as you would have them do to you. 32 "If you love those who love you, what credit is that to you? For even sinners love those who love them. 33 If you do good to those who do good to you, what credit is that to you? For even sinners do the same. 34 If you lend to those from whom you hope to receive, what credit is that to you? Even sin-

ners lend to sinners, to receive as much again. 35 But love your enemies, do good, and lend, expecting nothing in return.[v] Your reward will be great, and you will be children of the Most High; for he is kind to the ungrateful and the wicked. 36 Be merciful, just as your Father is merciful.

Judging Others
(Mt 7.1–5)

37 "Do not judge, and you will not be judged; do not condemn, and you will not be condemned. Forgive, and you will be forgiven; 38 give, and it will

---

u Gk cast out your name as evil　v Other ancient authorities read despairing of no one

PRAY IT!
Jesus' Preference for the Poor

In the Gospel of Luke, Jesus gives the Sermon on the Plain, which parallels the Sermon on the Mount in Matthew. Even more clearly than Matthew, Luke makes the point that God's justice has a preference for the poor and the little ones. So it's not surprising that the four beatitudes (blessings) in Luke are balanced by four woes ("Woe!" is like saying, "Trouble ahead!"). For example, "Blessed are you who are poor" (6.20) is countered by "Woe to you who are rich" (verse 24). Jesus shows his care for both rich people and poor people by calling the rich to practice justice and the poor to have hope.

Unlike Matthew, Luke does not "spiritualize" the Beatitudes. Matthew says, "Blessed are the poor in spirit" (5.3), but Luke simply says, "Blessed are you who are poor" (6.20), meaning materially poor. Matthew is concerned for people's salvation; Luke is concerned about their salvation and their material needs.

How do you show special concern for poor people? Pray that God helps us to share God's love with those caught in the struggles of life.

▶ Lk 6.17–49

be given to you. A good measure, pressed down, shaken together, running over, will be put into your lap; for the measure you give will be the measure you get back."

39 He also told them a parable: "Can a blind person guide a blind person? Will not both fall into a pit? 40 A disciple is not above the teacher, but everyone who is fully qualified will be like the teacher. 41 Why do you see the speck in your neighbor's[w] eye, but do not notice the log in your own eye? 42 Or how can you say to your neighbor,[x] 'Friend,[x] let me take out the speck in your eye,' when you yourself do not see the log in your own eye? You hypocrite, first take the log out of your own eye, and then you will see clearly to take the speck out of your neighbor's[w] eye.

A Tree and Its Fruit
(Mt 7.15–20)

43 "No good tree bears bad fruit, nor again does a bad tree bear good fruit; 44 for each tree is known by its own fruit. Figs are not gathered from thorns, nor are grapes picked from a bramble bush. 45 The good person out of the good treasure of the heart produces good, and the evil person out of evil treasure produces evil; for it is out of the abundance of the heart that the mouth speaks.

The Two Foundations
(Mt 7.21–27)

46 "Why do you call me 'Lord, Lord,' and do not do what I tell you? 47 I will show you what someone is like who comes to me, hears my words,

and acts on them. 48 That one is like a man building a house, who dug deeply and laid the foundation on rock; when a flood arose, the river burst against that house but could not shake it, because it had been well built.[y] 49 But the one who hears and does not act is like a man who built a house on the ground without a foundation. When the river burst against it, immediately it fell, and great was the ruin of that house."

Jesus Heals a Centurion's Servant
(Mt 8.5–13)

7 After Jesus[z] had finished all his sayings in the hearing of the people, he entered Ca·per'-na·um. 2 A centurion there had a slave whom he valued highly, and who was ill and close to death. 3 When he heard about Jesus, he sent some Jewish elders to him, asking him to come and heal his slave. 4 When they came to Jesus, they appealed to him earnestly, saying, "He is worthy of having you do this for him, 5 for he loves our people, and it is he who built our synagogue for us." 6 And Jesus went with them, but when he was not far from the house, the centurion sent friends to say to him, "Lord, do not trouble yourself, for I am not worthy to have you come under my roof; 7 therefore I did not presume to come to you. But only speak the word, and let my servant be healed. 8 For I also am a man set under authority, with soldiers under me; and I say to one, 'Go,' and he goes, and to another,

L
K

---

w Gk *brother's*   x Gk *brother*   y Other ancient authorities read *founded upon the rock*   z Gk *he*

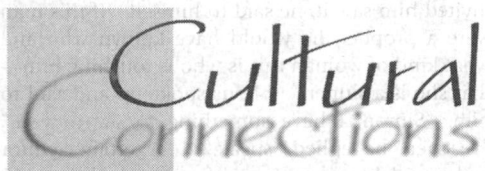

THE REUNION DINNER

The words of the centurion in Lk 7.6–7 are the basis for the words Catholics say before receiving the Holy Eucharist, "Lord, I am not worthy to receive you, but only say the word and I shall be healed." These words indicate our humility and our willingness to accept God's forgiveness and healing in our life. They remind us to receive Jesus in a state of peace with God and one another, especially by seeking reconciliation with family and friends.

The Chinese New Year's celebration includes a "reunion dinner." The whole family gathers at the home of the eldest family member. People travel from faraway cities, and even from other countries, to be together. The meal is not eaten until everyone is present, and no one eats until any disagreement or hurt is forgiven, and the family is at peace.

▶ Lk 7.1–10

'Come,' and he comes, and to my slave, 'Do this,' and the slave does it." 9 When Jesus heard this he was amazed at him, and turning to the crowd that followed him, he said, "I tell you, not even in Israel have I found such faith." 10 When those who had been sent returned to the house, they found the slave in good health.

Jesus Raises the Widow's Son at Nain

11 Soon afterwards*a* he went to a town called Na'in, and his disciples and a large crowd went with him. 12 As he approached the gate of the town, a man who had died was being carried out. He was his mother's only son, and she was a widow; and with her was a large crowd from the town. 13 When the Lord saw her, he had compassion for her and said to her, "Do not weep." 14 Then he came forward and touched the bier, and the bearers stood still. And he said, "Young man, I say to you, rise!" 15 The dead man sat up and began to speak, and Jesus*b* gave him to his mother. 16 Fear seized all of them; and they glorified God, saying, "A great prophet has risen among us!" and "God has looked favorably on his people!" 17 This word about him spread throughout Judea and all the surrounding country.

Messengers from John the Baptist
(Mt 11.2–19)

18 The disciples of John reported all these things to him. So John summoned two of his disciples 19 and sent them to the Lord to ask, "Are you the one who is to come, or are we to wait for another?" 20 When the men had come to him, they said, "John the Baptist has sent us to you to ask, 'Are you the one who is to come, or are we to wait for another?' " 21 Jesus*c* had just then cured many people of diseases, plagues, and evil spirits, and had given sight to many who were blind. 22 And he answered them, "Go and tell John what you have seen and heard: the blind receive their sight, the lame walk, the lepers*d* are cleansed, the deaf hear, the dead are raised, the poor have good news brought to them. 23 And blessed is anyone who takes no offense at me."

24 When John's messengers had gone, Jesus*b* began to speak to the crowds about John:*e* "What did you go out into the wilderness to look at? A reed shaken by the wind? 25 What then did you go out to see? Someone*f* dressed in soft robes? Look, those who put on fine clothing and live in luxury are in royal palaces. 26 What then did you go out to see? A prophet? Yes, I tell you, and more than a prophet. 27 This is the one about whom it is written,

'See, I am sending my messenger ahead of you,
  who will prepare your way before you.'

28 I tell you, among those born of women no one is greater than John; yet the least in the kingdom of God is greater than he." 29 (And all the people who heard this, including the tax collectors, acknowledged the justice of God,*g* because they had been baptized with John's baptism. 30 But by refusing to be baptized by him, the Phar'i•sees and the lawyers rejected God's purpose for themselves.)

31 "To what then will I compare the people of this generation, and what are they like? 32 They are like children sitting in the marketplace and calling to one another,

'We played the flute for you, and you did not
      dance;
  we wailed, and you did not weep.'

33 For John the Baptist has come eating no bread and drinking no wine, and you say, 'He has a demon'; 34 the Son of Man has come eating and drinking, and you say, 'Look, a glutton and a drunkard, a friend of tax collectors and sinners!' 35 Nevertheless, wisdom is vindicated by all her children."

A Sinful Woman Forgiven

36 One of the Phar'i•sees asked Jesus*e* to eat with him, and he went into the Phar'i•see's house and took his place at the table. 37 And a woman in the city, who was a sinner, having learned that he was eating in the Phar'i•see's house, brought an alabaster jar of ointment. 38 She stood behind him at his feet, weeping, and began to bathe his feet with her tears and to dry them with her hair. Then she continued kissing his feet and anointing them with the ointment. 39 Now when the Phar'i•see who had invited him saw it, he said to himself, "If this man were a prophet, he would have known who and what kind of woman this is who is touching him— that she is a sinner." 40 Jesus spoke up and said to him, "Simon, I have something to say to you." "Teacher," he replied, "speak." 41 "A certain creditor had two debtors; one owed five hundred denarii,*h* and the other fifty. 42 When they could not pay, he canceled the debts for both of them. Now which of them will love him more?" 43 Simon answered, "I suppose the one for whom he canceled the greater debt." And Jesus*b* said to him, "You have judged rightly." 44 Then turning toward the woman, he said to Simon, "Do you see this woman? I entered your house; you gave me no water for my feet, but she has bathed my feet with her tears and dried them with her hair. 45 You gave me no kiss, but

---

a Other ancient authorities read *Next day*   *b* Gk *he*
c Gk *He*   *d* The terms *leper* and *leprosy* can refer to several diseases   *e* Gk *him*   *f* Or *Why then did you go out? To see someone*   *g* Or *praised God*   *h* The denarius was the usual day's wage for a laborer

from the time I came in she has not stopped kissing my feet. 46 You did not anoint my head with oil, but she has anointed my feet with ointment. 47 Therefore, I tell you, her sins, which were many, have been forgiven; hence she has shown great love. But the one to whom little is forgiven, loves little." 48 Then he said to her, "Your sins are forgiven." 49 But those who were at the table with him began to say among themselves, "Who is this who even forgives sins?" 50 And he said to the woman, "Your faith has saved you; go in peace."

Some Women Accompany Jesus

8 Soon afterwards he went on through cities and villages, proclaiming and bringing the good news of the kingdom of God. The twelve were with him, 2 as well as some women who had been cured of evil spirits and infirmities: Mary, called Mag′da•lēne, from whom seven demons had gone out, 3 and Jō•an′na, the wife of Her′od's steward Chū′za, and Susanna, and many others, who provided for them[i] out of their resources.

The Parable of the Sower
(Mt 13.1–9; Mk 4.1–9)

4 When a great crowd gathered and people from town after town came to him, he said in a parable: 5 "A sower went out to sow his seed; and as he sowed, some fell on the path and was trampled on, and the birds of the air ate it up. 6 Some fell on the rock; and as it grew up, it withered for lack of moisture. 7 Some fell among thorns, and the thorns grew with it and choked it. 8 Some fell into good soil, and when it grew, it produced a hundredfold." As he said this, he called out, "Let anyone with ears to hear listen!"

The Purpose of the Parables
(Mt 13.10–17; Mk 4.10–12)

9 Then his disciples asked him what this parable meant. 10 He said, "To you it has been given to know the secrets[j] of the kingdom of God; but to others I speak[k] in parables, so that

'looking they may not perceive,
   and listening they may not understand.'

The Parable of the Sower Explained
(Mt 13.18–23; Mk 4.13–20)

11 "Now the parable is this: The seed is the word of God. 12 The ones on the path are those who have heard; then the devil comes and takes away the word from their hearts, so that they may not believe and be saved. 13 The ones on the rock are those who, when they hear the word, receive it with joy. But these have no root; they believe only for a while and in a time of testing fall away. 14 As for what fell among the thorns, these are the ones

who hear; but as they go on their way, they are choked by the cares and riches and pleasures of life, and their fruit does not mature. 15 But as for that in the good soil, these are the ones who, when they hear the word, hold it fast in an honest and good heart, and bear fruit with patient endurance.

A Lamp under a Jar
(Mt 4.21–25)

16 "No one after lighting a lamp hides it under a jar, or puts it under a bed, but puts it on a lampstand, so that those who enter may see the light. 17 For nothing is hidden that will not be disclosed, nor is anything secret that will not become known and come to light. 18 Then pay attention to how you listen; for to those who have, more will be given; and from those who do not have, even what they seem to have will be taken away."

The True Kindred of Jesus
(Mt 12.46–50; Mk 3.31–35)

19 Then his mother and his brothers came to him, but they could not reach him because of the crowd. 20 And he was told, "Your mother and your brothers are standing outside, wanting to see you." 21 But he said to them, "My mother and my brothers are those who hear the word of God and do it."

Jesus Calms a Storm
(Mt 8.23–27; Mk 4.35–41)

22 One day he got into a boat with his disciples, and he said to them, "Let us go across to the other side of the lake." So they put out, 23 and while they were sailing he fell asleep. A windstorm swept down on the lake, and the boat was filling with water, and they were in danger. 24 They went to him and woke him up, shouting, "Master, Master, we are perishing!" And he woke up and rebuked the wind and the raging waves; they ceased, and there was a calm. 25 He said to them, "Where is your faith?" They were afraid and amazed, and said to one another, "Who then is this, that he commands even the winds and the water, and they obey him?"

Jesus Heals the Gerasene Demoniac
(Mt 8.28—9.1; Mk 5.1–20)

26 Then they arrived at the country of the Ger′a•sēnes,[l] which is opposite Galilee. 27 As he stepped out on land, a man of the city who had demons met him. For a long time he had worn[m] no clothes, and he did not live in a house but in the

---

i Other ancient authorities read him   j Or mysteries
k Gk lacks I speak   l Other ancient authorities read
Gadarenes; others, Gergesenes   m Other ancient authorities
read a man of the city who had had demons for a long time
met him. He wore

tombs. 28 When he saw Jesus, he fell down before him and shouted at the top of his voice, "What have you to do with me, Jesus, Son of the Most High God? I beg you, do not torment me"— 29 for Jesus*n* had commanded the unclean spirit to come out of the man. (For many times it had seized him; he was kept under guard and bound with chains and shackles, but he would break the bonds and be driven by the demon into the wilds.) 30 Jesus then asked him, "What is your name?" He said, "Legion"; for many demons had entered him. 31 They begged him not to order them to go back into the abyss.

32 Now there on the hillside a large herd of swine was feeding; and the demons*o* begged Jesus*p* to let them enter these. So he gave them permission. 33 Then the demons came out of the man and entered the swine, and the herd rushed down the steep bank into the lake and was drowned.

34 When the swineherds saw what had happened, they ran off and told it in the city and in the country. 35 Then people came out to see what had happened, and when they came to Jesus, they found the man from whom the demons had gone sitting at the feet of Jesus, clothed and in his right mind. And they were afraid. 36 Those who had seen it told them how the one who had been possessed by demons had been healed. 37 Then all the people of the surrounding country of the Ger′a•sēnes*q* asked Jesus*p* to leave them; for they were seized with great fear. So he got into the boat and returned. 38 The man from whom the demons had gone begged that he might be with him; but Jesus*n* sent him away, saying, 39 "Return to your home, and declare how much God has done for you." So he went away, proclaiming throughout the city how much Jesus had done for him.

A Girl Restored to Life and a Woman Healed
(Mt 9.18–26; Mk 5.21–43)

40 Now when Jesus returned, the crowd welcomed him, for they were all waiting for him. 41 Just then there came a man named Jā•ī′rus, a leader of the synagogue. He fell at Jesus' feet and begged him to come to his house, 42 for he had an only daughter, about twelve years old, who was dying.

As he went, the crowds pressed in on him. 43 Now there was a woman who had been suffering from hemorrhages for twelve years; and though she had spent all she had on physicians,*r* no one could cure her. 44 She came up behind him and touched the fringe of his clothes, and immediately her hemorrhage stopped. 45 Then Jesus asked, "Who touched me?" When all denied it, Peter*s* said, "Master, the crowds surround you and press in on you." 46 But Jesus said, "Someone touched me; for I noticed that power had gone out from me." 47 When

the woman saw that she could not remain hidden, she came trembling; and falling down before him, she declared in the presence of all the people why she had touched him, and how she had been immediately healed. 48 He said to her, "Daughter, your faith has made you well; go in peace."

49 While he was still speaking, someone came from the leader's house to say, "Your daughter is dead; do not trouble the teacher any longer." 50 When Jesus heard this, he replied, "Do not fear. Only believe, and she will be saved." 51 When he came to the house, he did not allow anyone to enter with him, except Peter, John, and James, and the child's father and mother. 52 They were all weeping and wailing for her; but he said, "Do not weep; for she is not dead but sleeping." 53 And they laughed at him, knowing that she was dead. 54 But he took her by the hand and called out, "Child, get up!" 55 Her spirit returned, and she got up at once. Then he directed them to give her something to eat. 56 Her parents were astounded; but he ordered them to tell no one what had happened.

The Mission of the Twelve
(Mt 10.5–15)

9 Then Jesus*n* called the twelve together and gave them power and authority over all demons and to cure diseases, 2 and he sent them out to proclaim the kingdom of God and to heal. 3 He said to them, "Take nothing for your journey, no staff, nor bag, nor bread, nor money—not even an extra tunic. 4 Whatever house you enter, stay there, and leave from there. 5 Wherever they do not welcome you, as you are leaving that town shake the dust off your feet as a testimony against them." 6 They departed and went through the villages, bringing the good news and curing diseases everywhere.

Herod's Perplexity
(Mt 14.1–12; Mk 6.14–29)

7 Now Her′od the ruler*t* heard about all that had taken place, and he was perplexed, because it was said by some that John had been raised from the dead, 8 by some that E•lī′jah had appeared, and by others that one of the ancient prophets had arisen. 9 Her′od said, "John I beheaded; but who is this about whom I hear such things?" And he tried to see him.

Feeding the Five Thousand
(Mt 14.13–21; Mk 6.30–44; Jn 6.1–15)

10 On their return the apostles told Jesus*p* all they had done. He took them with him and withdrew pri-

---

n Gk he   *o* Gk they   *p* Gk him   *q* Other ancient authorities read *Gadarenes*; others, *Gergesenes*   *r* Other ancient authorities lack *and though she had spent all she had on physicians*   *s* Other ancient authorities add *and those who were with him*   *t* Gk tetrarch vately to a city called Beth•sā'i•da. 11 When the crowds found out about it, they followed him; and he welcomed them, and spoke to them about the kingdom of God, and healed those who needed to be cured.

12 The day was drawing to a close, and the twelve came to him and said, "Send the crowd away, so that they may go into the surrounding villages and countryside, to lodge and get provisions; for we are here in a deserted place." 13 But he said to them, "You give them something to eat." They said, "We have no more than five loaves and two fish—unless we are to go and buy food for all these people." 14 For there were about five thousand men. And he said to his disciples, "Make them sit down in groups of about fifty each." 15 They did so and made them all sit down. 16 And taking the five loaves and the two fish, he looked up to heaven, and blessed and broke them, and gave them to the disciples to set before the crowd. 17 And all ate and were filled. What was left over was gathered up, twelve baskets of broken pieces.

23 Then he said to them all, "If any want to become my followers, let them deny themselves and take up their cross daily and follow me. 24 For those who want to save their life will lose it, and those who lose their life for my sake will save it. 25 What does it profit them if they gain the whole world, but lose or forfeit themselves? 26 Those who are ashamed of me and of my words, of them the Son of Man will be ashamed when he comes in his glory and the glory of the Father and of the holy angels. 27 But truly I tell you, there are some standing here who will not taste death before they see the kingdom of God."

The Transfiguration
(Mt 17.1–8; Mk 9.2–8; 2 Pet 1.16–18)

28 Now about eight days after these sayings Jesus[u] took with him Peter and John and James, and went up on the mountain to pray. 29 And while he was praying, the appearance of his face changed, and his clothes became dazzling white. 30 Sudden-

He said to them,

"BUT WHO DO YOU SAY THAT I AM?"

Peter answered,

"THE MESSIAH OF GOD."

Peter's Declaration about Jesus
(Mt 16.13–20; Mk 8.27–30)

18 Once when Jesus[u] was praying alone, with only the disciples near him, he asked them, "Who do the crowds say that I am?" 19 They answered, "John the Baptist; but others, E•li'jah; and still others, that one of the ancient prophets has arisen." 20 He said to them, "But who do you say that I am?" Peter answered, "The Messiah[v] of God."

Jesus Foretells His Death and Resurrection
(Mt 16.24–28; Mk 8.31—9.1)

21 He sternly ordered and commanded them not to tell anyone, 22 saying, "The Son of Man must undergo great suffering, and be rejected by the elders, chief priests, and scribes, and be killed, and on the third day be raised."

ly they saw two men, Moses and E•li'jah, talking to him. 31 They appeared in glory and were speaking of his departure, which he was about to accomplish at Jerusalem. 32 Now Peter and his companions were weighed down with sleep; but since they had stayed awake,[w] they saw his glory and the two men who stood with him. 33 Just as they were leaving him, Peter said to Jesus, "Master, it is good for us to be here; let us make three dwellings,[x] one for you, one for Moses, and one for E•li'jah"—not knowing what he said. 34 While he was saying this, a cloud came and overshadowed them; and they were terrified as they entered the cloud. 35 Then from the cloud came a voice that said, "This is my Son, my Chosen;[y]

---

u Gk he   v Or *The Christ*   w Or *but when they were fully awake*   x Or *tents*   y Other ancient authorities read *my Beloved*

Spiritual Highs

Have you ever had an experience where you felt really close to God and to others who shared that experience with you? You may have even wished the experience did not have to end.

Peter, James, and John must have felt that way when they saw Jesus in his glory talking with Moses and Elijah on the mountaintop. Peter wanted to stay up on the mountain, but it quickly became clear that he could not do so.

Faith has its high moments as well as its low moments. It is unrealistic to think that we can maintain some kind of spiritual high all the time—doing so may even be dangerous. The faith of those who depend on mountaintop experiences often fizzles out. The better challenge is to learn what it means to live as a Christian down in the thick of life. Remember: Our faith is more than feelings. God's love and mercy do not depend on our ability to feel "warm fuzzies," as nice as those can be.

Recall a special time in your life when you felt on top of the world. Relive the moment in your mind, this time looking for how God was present in that experience. What direction was God inviting you to go after it was over? Are you there yet?

▶ Lk 9.28–36

listen to him!" 36 When the voice had spoken, Jesus was found alone. And they kept silent and in those days told no one any of the things they had seen.

Jesus Heals a Boy with a Demon
(Mt 17.14–21; Mk 9.14–29)

37 On the next day, when they had come down from the mountain, a great crowd met him. 38 Just then a man from the crowd shouted, "Teacher, I beg you to look at my son; he is my only child. 39 Suddenly a spirit seizes him, and all at once he[z] shrieks. It convulses him until he foams at the mouth; it mauls him and will scarcely leave him. 40 I begged your disciples to cast it out, but they could not." 41 Jesus answered, "You faithless and perverse generation, how much longer must I be with you and bear with you? Bring your son here." 42 While he was coming, the demon dashed him to the ground in convulsions. But Jesus rebuked the unclean spirit, healed the boy, and gave him back to his father. 43 And all were astounded at the greatness of God.

Jesus Again Foretells His Death
(Mt 17.22–23; Mk 9.30–32)

While everyone was amazed at all that he was doing, he said to his disciples, 44 "Let these words sink into your ears: The Son of Man is going to be betrayed into human hands." 45 But they did not understand this saying; its meaning was concealed from them, so that they could not perceive it. And they were afraid to ask him about this saying.

True Greatness
(Mt 18.1–5; Mk 9.33–37)

46 An argument arose among them as to which one of them was the greatest. 47 But Jesus, aware of their inner thoughts, took a little child and put it by his side, 48 and said to them, "Whoever welcomes this child in my name welcomes me, and whoever welcomes me welcomes the one who sent me; for the least among all of you is the greatest."

Another Exorcist
(Mk 9.38–41)

49 John answered, "Master, we saw someone casting out demons in your name, and we tried to stop him, because he does not follow with us." 50 But Jesus said to him, "Do not stop him; for whoever is not against you is for you."

A Samaritan Village Refuses to Receive Jesus

51 When the days drew near for him to be taken up, he set his face to go to Jerusalem. 52 And he sent messengers ahead of him. On their way they entered a village of the Sa•mār'i•tans to make ready for him; 53 but they did not receive him, because his face was set toward Jerusalem. 54 When his disciples James and John saw it, they said, "Lord, do you want us to command fire to come down from heaven and consume them?"[a] 55 But he turned and rebuked them. 56 Then[b] they went on to another village.

z Or it   a Other ancient authorities add as Elijah did
b Other ancient authorities read rebuked them, and said, "You do not know what spirit you are of, 56for the Son of Man has not come to destroy the lives of human beings but to save them." Then

Would-Be Followers of Jesus
(Mt 8.18–22)

57 As they were going along the road, someone said to him, "I will follow you wherever you go." 58 And Jesus said to him, "Foxes have holes, and birds of the air have nests; but the Son of Man has nowhere to lay his head." 59 To another he said, "Follow me." But he said, "Lord, first let me go and bury my father." 60 But Jesus*c* said to him, "Let the dead bury their own dead; but as for you, go and proclaim the kingdom of God." 61 Another said, "I will follow you, Lord; but let me first say farewell to those at my home." 62 Jesus said to him, "No one who puts a hand to the plow and looks back is fit for the kingdom of God."

The Mission of the Seventy

10 After this the Lord appointed seventy*d* others and sent them on ahead of him in pairs to every town and place where he himself intended to go. 2 He said to them, "The harvest is plentiful, but the laborers are few; therefore ask the Lord of the harvest to send out laborers into his harvest. 3 Go on your way. See, I am sending you out like lambs into the midst of wolves. 4 Carry no purse, no bag, no sandals; and greet no one on the road. 5 Whatever house you enter, first say, 'Peace to this house!' 6 And if anyone is there who shares in peace, your peace will rest on that person; but if not, it will return to you. 7 Remain in the same house, eating and drinking whatever they provide, for the laborer deserves to be paid. Do not move about from house to house. 8 Whenever you enter a town and its people welcome you, eat what is set before you; 9 cure the sick who are there, and say to them, 'The kingdom of God has come near to you.'*e* 10 But whenever you enter a town and they do not welcome you, go out into its streets and say, 11 'Even the dust of your town that clings to our feet, we wipe off in protest against you. Yet know this: the kingdom of God has come near.'*f* 12 I tell you, on that day it will be more tolerable for Sod'om than for that town.

Woes to Unrepentant Cities
(Mt 11.20–24)

13 "Woe to you, Chō•rā'zin! Woe to you, Beth-sā'i•da! For if the deeds of power done in you had been done in Tȳre and Sī'don, they would have repented long ago, sitting in sackcloth and ashes. 14 But at the judgment it will be more tolerable for Tȳre and Sī'don than for you. 15 And you, Ca•per'na•um,

> will you be exalted to heaven?
> No, you will be brought down to
> Hades.

16 "Whoever listens to you listens to me, and whoever rejects you rejects me, and whoever rejects me rejects the one who sent me."

The Return of the Seventy

17 The seventy*d* returned with joy, saying, "Lord, in your name even the demons submit to us!" 18 He said to them, "I watched Satan fall from heaven like a flash of lightning. 19 See, I have given you authority to tread on snakes and scorpions, and over all the power of the enemy; and nothing will hurt you. 20 Nevertheless, do not rejoice at this, that the spirits submit to you, but rejoice that your names are written in heaven."

Jesus Rejoices
(Mt 11.25–27)

21 At that same hour Jesus*c* rejoiced in the Holy Spirit*g* and said, "I thank*h* you, Father, Lord of heaven and earth, because you have hidden these things from the wise and the intelligent and have revealed them to infants; yes, Father, for such was your gracious will.*i* 22 All things have been handed over to me by my Father; and no one knows who the Son is except the Father, or who the Father is except the Son and anyone to whom the Son chooses to reveal him."

23 Then turning to the disciples, Jesus*c* said to them privately, "Blessed are the eyes that see what you see! 24 For I tell you that many prophets and kings desired to see what you see, but did not see it, and to hear what you hear, but did not hear it."

The Parable of the Good Samaritan
(Mt 22.34–40; Mk 12.28–34)

25 Just then a lawyer stood up to test Jesus.*j* "Teacher," he said, "what must I do to inherit eternal life?" 26 He said to him, "What is written in the law? What do you read there?" 27 He answered, "You shall love the Lord your God with all your heart, and with all your soul, and with all your strength, and with all your mind; and your neighbor as yourself." 28 And he said to him, "You have given the right answer; do this, and you will live."

29 But wanting to justify himself, he asked Jesus, "And who is my neighbor?" 30 Jesus replied, "A man was going down from Jerusalem to Jericho, and fell into the hands of robbers, who stripped him, beat him, and went away, leaving him half dead. 31 Now by chance a priest was going down that road; and when he saw him, he passed by on the other side. 32 So likewise a Lē'vite, when he

L
K

---

c Gk *he*   *d* Other ancient authorities read *seventy-two*
e Or *is at hand for you*   *f* Or *is at hand*   *g* Other authorities read *in the spirit*   *h* Or *praise*   *i* Or *for so it was well-pleasing in your sight*   *j* Gk *him*

Discrimination in Jesus' Time

The good Samaritan is a popular Bible story with an obvious message: We must help others. But did you know it is also a story about prejudice and discrimination? In Jesus' day, the Samaritans were despised by Jews, even though Abraham was the father of faith for both groups. Jesus' making a Samaritan the hero of the story would have given the lawyer and other people listening to Jesus something to think about.

Imagine that this story takes place in your community. Who are the Samaritans, that is, the culture or race that other people judge and reject? How does this reflection affect your understanding of discrimination and racism?

It seems that when we have a real relationship with others—even with those who are different from us—we are less likely to be prejudiced or to discriminate. Maybe we should work in our communities to invite all people to get to know one another better so that all "Samaritans" are regarded as good. What do you think?

▶ Lk 10.25–37

came to the place and saw him, passed by on the other side. 33 But a Sa•măr′i•tan while traveling came near him; and when he saw him, he was moved with pity. 34 He went to him and bandaged his wounds, having poured oil and wine on them. Then he put him on his own animal, brought him to an inn, and took care of him. 35 The next day he took out two denarii,k gave them to the innkeeper, and said, 'Take care of him; and when I come back, I will repay you whatever more you spend.' 36 Which of these three, do you think, was a neighbor to the man who fell into the hands of the robbers?" 37 He said, "The one who showed him mercy." Jesus said to him, "Go and do likewise."

Jesus Visits Martha and Mary

38 Now as they went on their way, he entered a certain village, where a woman named Martha welcomed him into her home. 39 She had a sister named Mary, who sat at the Lord's feet and listened to what he was saying. 40 But Martha was distracted by her many tasks; so she came to him and asked, "Lord, do you not care that my sister has left me to do all the work by myself? Tell her then to help me." 41 But the Lord answered her, "Martha, Martha, you are worried and distracted by many things; 42 there is need of only one thing.l Mary has chosen the better part, which will not be taken away from her."

The Lord's Prayer
(Mt 6.9–15)

11 He was praying in a certain place, and after he had finished, one of his disciples said to him, "Lord, teach us to pray, as John taught his disciples." 2 He said to them, "When you pray, say:

Father,m hallowed be your name.
    Your kingdom come.n
3   Give us each day our daily bread.o
4   And forgive us our sins,
        for we ourselves forgive everyone
        indebted to us.
    And do not bring us to the time of trial."p

PRAY IT!
Too Busy to Be Still

Help me slow down, Lord, right now, before I think of something else that I should be doing—as if it really is more important than you. Let me sit in the quiet peace of your presence and soak up all that you have to say to me. Give me the patience and perception to do nothing else for these next few moments except to be totally, completely, and wonderfully centered on you!

▶ Lk 10.38–42

---

k The denarius was the usual day's wage for a laborer
l Other ancient authorities read *few things are necessary, or only one*   m Other ancient authorities read *Our Father in heaven*   n A few ancient authorities read *Your Holy Spirit come upon us and cleanse us.* Other ancient authorities add *Your will be done, on earth as in heaven*   o Or *our bread for tomorrow*   p Or *us into temptation.* Other ancient authorities add *but rescue us from the evil one* (or *from evil*)

Perseverance in Prayer
(Mt 7.7–11)

5 And he said to them, "Suppose one of you has a friend, and you go to him at midnight and say to him, 'Friend, lend me three loaves of bread; 6 for a friend of mine has arrived, and I have nothing to set before him.' 7 And he answers from within, 'Do not bother me; the door has already been locked, and my children are with me in bed; I cannot get up and give you anything.' 8 I tell you, even though he will not get up and give him anything because he is his friend, at least because of his persistence he will get up and give him whatever he needs.

9 "So I say to you, Ask, and it will be given you; search, and you will find; knock, and the door will be opened for you. 10 For everyone who asks receives, and everyone who searches finds, and for everyone who knocks, the door will be opened. 11 Is there anyone among you who, if your child asks for[q] a fish, will give a snake instead of a fish? 12 Or if the child asks for an egg, will give a scorpion? 13 If you then, who are evil, know how to give good gifts to your children, how much more will the heavenly Father give the Holy Spirit[r] to those who ask him!"

Jesus and Beelzebul
(Mt 12.22–32; Mk 3.19b–30)

14 Now he was casting out a demon that was mute; when the demon had gone out, the one who had been mute spoke, and the crowds were amazed. 15 But some of them said, "He casts out demons by Be·el′ze·bul, the ruler of the demons." 16 Others, to test him, kept demanding from him a sign from heaven. 17 But he knew what they were thinking and said to them, "Every kingdom divided against itself becomes a desert, and house falls on house. 18 If Satan also is divided against himself, how will his kingdom stand? —for you say that I cast out the demons by Be·el′ze·bul. 19 Now if I cast out the demons by Be·el′ze·bul, by whom do your exorcists[s] cast them out? Therefore they will be your judges. 20 But if it is by the finger of God that I cast out the demons, then the kingdom of God has come to you. 21 When a strong man, fully armed, guards his castle, his property is safe. 22 But when one stronger than he attacks him and overpowers him, he takes away his armor in which he trusted and divides his plunder. 23 Whoever is not with me is against me, and whoever does not gather with me scatters.

The Return of the Unclean Spirit
(Mt 12.43–45)

24 "When the unclean spirit has gone out of a person, it wanders through waterless regions looking for a resting place, but not finding any, it says, 'I will return to my house from which I came.' 25 When it comes, it finds it swept and put in order. 26 Then it goes and brings seven other spirits more evil than itself, and they enter and live there; and the last state of that person is worse than the first."

True Blessedness

27 While he was saying this, a woman in the crowd raised her voice and said to him, "Blessed is the womb that bore you and the breasts that nursed you!" 28 But he said, "Blessed rather are those who hear the word of God and obey it!"

The Sign of Jonah
(Mt 12.38–42)

29 When the crowds were increasing, he began to say, "This generation is an evil generation; it asks for a sign, but no sign will be given to it except the sign of Jonah. 30 For just as Jonah became a sign to

---

q Other ancient authorities add bread, will give a stone; or if your child asks for   r Other ancient authorities read the Father give the Holy Spirit from heaven   s Gk sons

L
K

Nagging God

LIVE IT!

Have you ever nagged your parents for something? They may have replied, "Will you stop nagging me?!"

This is one response you will never hear from God. In fact, Jesus tells us to be persistent with God, to nag God. God wants to be nagged by us! Too often we hesitate to bring everything inside of us to God. We sort through what we think God wants to hear. Don't be selective! Bring it all to God—the big stuff as well as the little stuff. Be a nag. God doesn't mind at all.

Go ahead, nag God right now!

▶ Lk 11.5–13

the people of Nin′e•veh, so the Son of Man will be to this generation. 31 The queen of the South will rise at the judgment with the people of this generation and condemn them, because she came from the ends of the earth to listen to the wisdom of Solomon, and see, something greater than Solomon is here! 32 The people of Nin′e•veh will rise up at the judgment with this generation and condemn it, because they repented at the proclamation of Jonah, and see, something greater than Jonah is here!

The Light of the Body
(Mt 6.22–23)

33 "No one after lighting a lamp puts it in a cellar,[t] but on the lampstand so that those who enter may see the light. 34 Your eye is the lamp of your body. If your eye is healthy, your whole body is full of light; but if it is not healthy, your body is full of darkness. 35 Therefore consider whether the light in you is not darkness. 36 If then your whole body is full of light, with no part of it in darkness, it will be as full of light as when a lamp gives you light with its rays."

Jesus Denounces Pharisees and Lawyers

37 While he was speaking, a Phar′i•see invited him to dine with him; so he went in and took his place at the table. 38 The Phar′i•see was amazed to see that he did not first wash before dinner. 39 Then the Lord said to him, "Now you Phar′i•sees clean the outside of the cup and of the dish, but inside you are full of greed and wickedness. 40 You fools! Did not the one who made the outside make the inside also? 41 So give for alms those things that are within; and see, everything will be clean for you.

42 "But woe to you Phar′i•sees! For you tithe mint and rue and herbs of all kinds, and neglect justice and the love of God; it is these you ought to have practiced, without neglecting the others. 43 Woe to you Phar′i•sees! For you love to have the seat of honor in the synagogues and to be greeted with respect in the marketplaces. 44 Woe to you! For you are like unmarked graves, and people walk over them without realizing it."

45 One of the lawyers answered him, "Teacher, when you say these things, you insult us too." 46 And he said, "Woe also to you lawyers! For you load people with burdens hard to bear, and you yourselves do not lift a finger to ease them. 47 Woe to you! For you build the tombs of the prophets whom your ancestors killed. 48 So you are witnesses and approve of the deeds of your ancestors; for they killed them, and you build their tombs. 49 Therefore also the Wisdom of God said, 'I will send them prophets and apostles, some of whom they will kill and persecute,' 50 so that this generation may be charged with the blood of all the prophets shed since the foundation of the world, 51 from the blood of Abel to the blood of Zech•a•ri′ah, who perished between the altar and the sanctuary. Yes, I tell you, it will be charged against this generation. 52 Woe to you lawyers! For you have taken away the key of knowledge; you did not enter yourselves, and you hindered those who were entering."

53 When he went outside, the scribes and the Phar′i•sees began to be very hostile toward him and to cross-examine him about many things, 54 lying in wait for him, to catch him in something he might say.

A Warning against Hypocrisy

12 Meanwhile, when the crowd gathered by the thousands, so that they trampled on one another, he began to speak first to his disciples, "Beware of the yeast of the Phar′i•sees, that is, their hypocrisy. 2 Nothing is covered up that will not be uncovered, and nothing secret that will not become known. 3 Therefore whatever you have said in the dark will be heard in the light, and what you have whispered behind closed doors will be proclaimed from the housetops.

Exhortation to Fearless Confession
(Mt 10.26–33)

4 "I tell you, my friends, do not fear those who kill the body, and after that can do nothing more. 5 But I will warn you whom to fear: fear him who, after he has killed, has authority[u] to cast into hell.[v] Yes, I tell you, fear him! 6 Are not five sparrows sold for two pennies? Yet not one of them is forgotten in God's sight. 7 But even the hairs of your head are all counted. Do not be afraid; you are of more value than many sparrows.

8 "And I tell you, everyone who acknowledges me before others, the Son of Man also will acknowledge before the angels of God; 9 but whoever denies me before others will be denied before the angels of God. 10 And everyone who speaks a word against the Son of Man will be forgiven; but whoever blasphemes against the Holy Spirit will not be forgiven. 11 When they bring you before the synagogues, the rulers, and the authorities, do not worry about how[w] you are to defend yourselves or what you are to say; 12 for the Holy Spirit will teach you at that very hour what you ought to say."

The Parable of the Rich Fool

13 Someone in the crowd said to him, "Teacher, tell my brother to divide the family in-

---

t Other ancient authorities add or under the bushel basket
u Or power   v Gk Gehenna   w Other ancient authorities add or what

heritance with me." 14 But he said to him, "Friend, who set me to be a judge or arbitrator over you?" 15 And he said to them, "Take care! Be on your guard against all kinds of greed; for one's life does not consist in the abundance of possessions." 16 Then he told them a parable: "The land of a rich man produced abundantly. 17 And he thought to himself, 'What should I do, for I have no place to store my crops?' 18 Then he said, 'I will do this: I will pull down my barns and build larger ones, and there I will store all my grain and my goods. 19 And I will say to my soul, Soul, you have ample goods laid up for many years; relax, eat, drink, be merry.' 20 But God said to him, 'You fool! This very night your life is being demanded of you. And the things you have prepared, whose will they be?' 21 So it is with those who store up treasures for themselves but are not rich toward God."

clothe you—you of little faith! 29 And do not keep striving for what you are to eat and what you are to drink, and do not keep worrying. 30 For it is the nations of the world that strive after all these things, and your Father knows that you need them. 31 Instead, strive for hisz kingdom, and these things will be given to you as well.

32 "Do not be afraid, little flock, for it is your Father's good pleasure to give you the kingdom. 33 Sell your possessions, and give alms. Make purses for yourselves that do not wear out, an unfailing treasure in heaven, where no thief comes near and no moth destroys. 34 For where your treasure is, there your heart will be also.

Watchful Slaves

35 "Be dressed for action and have your lamps lit; 36 be like those who are waiting for their master

LIVE IT!

The Greed Trap

It is easy to regard possessions as treasures and to find so much pleasure in them that we want more and more. This is the greed trap Jesus warns against in Lk 12.13–21. How do we let ourselves fall into this trap? Certainly, advertisements play a role in convincing us that we need to own everything that is new and improved (see "New and Improved!" Eccl 1.1–11). Our own insecurities also play a role—the more we possess, the more important we tend to think we are. But as Lk 12.18 indicates, greed is a sin that is addictive. Instead of feeling fulfilled by attaining the thing we crave, we feel that what we have still isn't enough. It is a vicious cycle.

The solution to greed is simple. It's sharing—that value that we learned when we were very small. Sharing our time and possessions makes us "rich toward God" (verse 21). Where do you see the sin of greed at work in your world? Where and when could you, your friends, and your family share more? Don't fall into the greed trap. Share!

▶ Lk 12.13–21

Do Not Worry
(Mt 6.19–21, 25–34)

22 He said to his disciples, "Therefore I tell you, do not worry about your life, what you will eat, or about your body, what you will wear. 23 For life is more than food, and the body more than clothing. 24 Consider the ravens: they neither sow nor reap, they have neither storehouse nor barn, and yet God feeds them. Of how much more value are you than the birds! 25 And can any of you by worrying add a single hour to your span of life?x 26 If then you are not able to do so small a thing as that, why do you worry about the rest? 27 Consider the lilies, how they grow: they neither toil nor spin;y yet I tell you, even Solomon in all his glory was not clothed like one of these. 28 But if God so clothes the grass of the field, which is alive today and tomorrow is thrown into the oven, how much more will he

to return from the wedding banquet, so that they may open the door for him as soon as he comes and knocks. 37 Blessed are those slaves whom the master finds alert when he comes; truly I tell you, he will fasten his belt and have them sit down to eat, and he will come and serve them. 38 If he comes during the middle of the night, or near dawn, and finds them so, blessed are those slaves.

39 "But know this: if the owner of the house had known at what hour the thief was coming, hea would not have let his house be broken into. 40 You also must be ready, for the Son of Man is coming at an unexpected hour."

---

x Or *add a cubit to your stature*   y Other ancient authorities read *Consider the lilies; they neither spin nor weave*   z Other ancient authorities read *God's*   a Other ancient authorities add *would have watched and*

The Anxiety Trap

Doesn't it seem a little naive to assume that if we just trust God, we will get what we need; that we shouldn't worry about the everyday things like clothing, food, and shelter? Seems pretty risky and yet . . .

Lakeesha and Miguel were best friends. Miguel had a big problem. He worried all the time. He sometimes made himself sick with worrying. He worried that his parents would lose their jobs. He worried that he wouldn't find a job. He worried about doing poorly in school. When it was stormy out, he worried about tornadoes. He drove his friends crazy with his worrying.

Lakeesha, on the other hand, never worried. One day, Miguel asked her for her secret to staying calm. She told him: "Miguel, if you keep focused on the negative things that could happen and worry about them, you will not see all the good things happening around you. Did you know that your mom just got a raise? You didn't notice that our band teacher said you had the best fingering technique he had ever seen. And I bet you didn't even look at the want ads for new summer jobs. Right? You spend too much time worrying and not enough time noticing."

Jesus says the same thing. Don't worry so much about everyday needs. Look for the simple signs that God cares for you. Some people even keep a journal of the good things that happen to them every day. Life will be so much calmer and less stressful if you heed Jesus' message. Try it!

▶ Lk 12.22–34

The Faithful or the Unfaithful Slave
(Mt 24.45–51)

41 Peter said, "Lord, are you telling this parable for us or for everyone?" 42 And the Lord said, "Who then is the faithful and prudent manager whom his master will put in charge of his slaves, to give them their allowance of food at the proper time? 43 Blessed is that slave whom his master will find at work when he arrives. 44 Truly I tell you, he will put that one in charge of all his possessions. 45 But if that slave says to himself, 'My master is delayed in coming,' and if he begins to beat the other slaves, men and women, and to eat and drink and get drunk, 46 the master of that slave will come on a day when he does not expect him and at an hour that he does not know, and will cut him in pieces,[b] and put him with the unfaithful. 47 That slave who knew what his master wanted, but did not prepare himself or do what was wanted, will receive a severe beating. 48 But the one who did not know and did what deserved a beating will receive a light beating. From everyone to whom much has been given, much will be required; and from the one to whom much has been entrusted, even more will be demanded.

Jesus the Cause of Division
(Mt 10.34–39)

49 "I came to bring fire to the earth, and how I wish it were already kindled! 50 I have a baptism with which to be baptized, and what stress I am under until it is completed! 51 Do you think that I have come to bring peace to the earth? No, I tell you, but rather division! 52 From now on five in one household will be divided, three against two and two against three; 53 they will be divided:
father against son
    and son against father,
mother against daughter
    and daughter against mother,
mother-in-law against her daughter-in-law
    and daughter-in-law against
        mother-in-law."

Interpreting the Time
(Mt 16.1–4)

54 He also said to the crowds, "When you see a cloud rising in the west, you immediately say, 'It is going to rain'; and so it happens. 55 And when you see the south wind blowing, you say, 'There will be scorching heat'; and it happens. 56 You hypocrites! You know how to interpret the appearance of earth and sky, but why do you not know how to interpret the present time?

Settling with Your Opponent

57 "And why do you not judge for yourselves what is right? 58 Thus, when you go with your ac-

---

b Or cut him off

cuser before a magistrate, on the way make an effort to settle the case,*c* or you may be dragged before the judge, and the judge hand you over to the officer, and the officer throw you in prison. 59 I tell you, you will never get out until you have paid the very last penny."

Repent or Perish

13 At that very time there were some present who told him about the Galileans whose blood Pilate had mingled with their sacrifices. 2 He asked them, "Do you think that because these Galileans suffered in this way they were worse sinners than all other Galileans? 3 No, I tell you; but unless you repent, you will all perish as they did. 4 Or those eighteen who were killed when the tower of Sī•lō′am fell on them—do you think that they were worse offenders than all the others living in Jerusalem? 5 No, I tell you; but unless you repent, you will all perish just as they did."

The Parable of the Barren Fig Tree

6 Then he told this parable: "A man had a fig tree planted in his vineyard; and he came looking for fruit on it and found none. 7 So he said to the gardener, 'See here! For three years I have come looking for fruit on this fig tree, and still I find none. Cut it down! Why should it be wasting the soil?' 8 He replied, 'Sir, let it alone for one more year, until I dig around it and put manure on it. 9 If it bears fruit next year, well and good; but if not, you can cut it down.' "

Jesus Heals a Crippled Woman

10 Now he was teaching in one of the synagogues on the sabbath. 11 And just then there appeared a woman with a spirit that had crippled her for eighteen years. She was bent over and was quite unable to stand up straight. 12 When Jesus saw her, he called her over and said, "Woman, you are set free from your ailment." 13 When he laid his hands on her, immediately she stood up straight and began praising God. 14 But the leader of the synagogue, indignant because Jesus had cured on the sabbath, kept saying to the crowd, "There are six days on which work ought to be done; come on those days and be cured, and not on the sabbath day." 15 But the Lord answered him and said, "You hypocrites! Does not each of you on the sabbath untie his ox or his donkey from the manger, and lead it away to give it water? 16 And ought not this woman, a daughter of Abraham whom Satan bound for eighteen long years, be set free from this bondage on the sabbath day?" 17 When he said this, all his opponents were put to shame; and the entire crowd was rejoicing at all the wonderful things that he was doing.

The Parable of the Mustard Seed
(Mt 13.31–32; Mk 4.30–32)

18 He said therefore, "What is the kingdom of God like? And to what should I compare it? 19 It is like a mustard seed that someone took and sowed in the garden; it grew and became a tree, and the birds of the air made nests in its branches."

The Parable of the Yeast
(Mt 13.33)

20 And again he said, "To what should I compare the kingdom of God? 21 It is like yeast that a woman took and mixed in with*d* three measures of flour until all of it was leavened."

The Narrow Door
(Mt 7.13–14)

22 Jesus*e* went through one town and village after another, teaching as he made his way to Jerusalem. 23 Someone asked him, "Lord, will only a few be saved?" He said to them, 24 "Strive to enter

---

c Gk *settle with him*   *d* Gk *hid in*   *e* Gk *He*

L
k

Catholic Connections

ANOINTING OF THE SICK

The crippled woman in Lk 13.10–17 is just one of many people Jesus heals in Luke. Much of Jesus' ministry was spent healing people with a variety of illnesses. Through the sacrament of Anointing of the Sick, one of the seven sacraments of the Catholic church, Jesus' ministry of extending God's healing love is continued.

In this sacrament, people young and old are anointed with sacred oil and prayed over by a priest. The sacrament is often given to people who are struggling with a serious illness, going into surgery, or dying. The sacrament is not a guarantee of physical healing but a way of receiving in a special way God's love and strength during those times of trial.

▶ Lk 13.10–17

through the narrow door; for many, I tell you, will try to enter and will not be able. 25 When once the owner of the house has got up and shut the door, and you begin to stand outside and to knock at the door, saying, 'Lord, open to us,' then in reply he will say to you, 'I do not know where you come from.' 26 Then you will begin to say, 'We ate and drank with you, and you taught in our streets.' 27 But he will say, 'I do not know where you come from; go away from me, all you evildoers!' 28 There will be weeping and gnashing of teeth when you see Abraham and Isaac and Jacob and all the prophets in the kingdom of God, and you yourselves thrown out. 29 Then people will come from east and west, from north and south, and will eat in the kingdom of God. 30 Indeed, some are last who will be first, and some are first who will be last."

The Lament over Jerusalem
(Mt 23.37–39)

31 At that very hour some Phar′i•sees came and said to him, "Get away from here, for Her′od wants to kill you." 32 He said to them, "Go and tell that fox for me,ƒ 'Listen, I am casting out demons and performing cures today and tomorrow, and on the third day I finish my work. 33 Yet today, tomorrow, and the next day I must be on my way, because it is impossible for a prophet to be killed outside of Jerusalem.' 34 Jerusalem, Jerusalem, the city that kills the prophets and stones those who are sent to it! How often have I desired to gather your children together as a hen gathers her brood under her wings, and you were not willing! 35 See, your house is left to you. And I tell you, you will not see me until the time comes wheng you say, 'Blessed is the one who comes in the name of the Lord.' "

Jesus Heals the Man with Dropsy

14 On one occasion when Jesush was going to the house of a leader of the Phar′i•sees to eat a meal on the sabbath, they were watching him closely. 2 Just then, in front of him, there was a man who had dropsy. 3 And Jesus asked the lawyers and Phar′i•sees, "Is it lawful to cure people on the sabbath, or not?" 4 But they were silent. So Jesush took him and healed him, and sent him away. 5 Then he said to them, "If one of you has a childi or an ox that has fallen into a well, will you not immediately pull it out on a sabbath day?" 6 And they could not reply to this.

Humility and Hospitality

7 When he noticed how the guests chose the places of honor, he told them a parable. 8 "When you are invited by someone to a wedding banquet, do not sit down at the place of honor, in case someone more distinguished than you has been invited

by your host; 9 and the host who invited both of you may come and say to you, 'Give this person your place,' and then in disgrace you would start to take the lowest place. 10 But when you are invited, go and sit down at the lowest place, so that when your host comes, he may say to you, 'Friend, move up higher'; then you will be honored in the presence of all who sit at the table with you. 11 For all who exalt themselves will be humbled, and those who humble themselves will be exalted."

12 He said also to the one who had invited him, "When you give a luncheon or a dinner, do not invite your friends or your brothers or your relatives or rich neighbors, in case they may invite you in return, and you would be repaid. 13 But when you give a banquet, invite the poor, the crippled, the lame, and the blind. 14 And you will be blessed, because they cannot repay you, for you will be repaid at the resurrection of the righteous."

The Parable of the Great Dinner
(Mt 22.1–14)

15 One of the dinner guests, on hearing this, said to him, "Blessed is anyone who will eat bread in the kingdom of God!" 16 Then Jesush said to him, "Someone gave a great dinner and invited many. 17 At the time for the dinner he sent his slave to say to those who had been invited, 'Come; for everything is ready now.' 18 But they all alike began to make excuses. The first said to him, 'I have bought a piece of land, and I must go out and see it; please accept my regrets.' 19 Another said, 'I have bought five yoke of oxen, and I am going to try them out; please accept my regrets.' 20 Another said, 'I have just been married, and therefore I cannot come.' 21 So the slave returned and reported this to

---

ƒ Gk lacks *for me* g Other ancient authorities lack *the time comes when* h Gk *he* i Other ancient authorities read *a donkey*

God's Invitation List

Jesus uses the image of a banquet to describe the Kingdom of God. Jesus' point is not about what is on the menu but who is on the invitation list: the weak, the poor, and the little ones. Who is on your "invitation list"—who are the people you reach out to and serve?

▸ Lk 14.7–24

PRAY IT!

Spice Me Up, Lord

Lord, I want to be where I can make a difference, where I can spice up another person's life by bringing him or her the good news of your love and justice.

Help me discover all the gifts you have graced me with so that I can help turn this world around—starting with my own life! Show me how to keep fresh in my commitment to serve you each day. Amen.

▶ Lk 14.34–35

his master. Then the owner of the house became angry and said to his slave, 'Go out at once into the streets and lanes of the town and bring in the poor, the crippled, the blind, and the lame.' 22 And the slave said, 'Sir, what you ordered has been done, and there is still room.' 23 Then the master said to the slave, 'Go out into the roads and lanes, and compel people to come in, so that my house may be filled. 24 For I tell you,ʲ none of those who were invited will taste my dinner.' "

The Cost of Discipleship
(Mt 10.34–39)

25 Now large crowds were traveling with him; and he turned and said to them, 26 "Whoever comes to me and does not hate father and mother, wife and children, brothers and sisters, yes, and even life itself, cannot be my disciple. 27 Whoever does not carry the cross and follow me cannot be

my disciple. 28 For which of you, intending to build a tower, does not first sit down and estimate the cost, to see whether he has enough to complete it? 29 Otherwise, when he has laid a foundation and is not able to finish, all who see it will begin to ridicule him, 30 saying, 'This fellow began to build and was not able to finish.' 31 Or what king, going out to wage war against another king, will not sit down first and consider whether he is able with ten thousand to oppose the one who comes against him with twenty thousand? 32 If he cannot, then, while the other is still far away, he sends a delegation and asks for the terms of peace. 33 So therefore, none of you can become my disciple if you do not give up all your possessions.

About Salt
(Mt 5.13; Mk 9.50)

34 "Salt is good; but if salt has lost its taste, how can its saltiness be restored?ᵏ 35 It is fit neither for the soil nor for the manure pile; they throw it away. Let anyone with ears to hear listen!"

The Parable of the Lost Sheep
(Mt 18.10–14)

15 Now all the tax collectors and sinners were coming near to listen to him. 2 And the Phar′i·sees and the scribes were grumbling and saying, "This fellow welcomes sinners and eats with them."

3 So he told them this parable: 4 "Which one of you, having a hundred sheep and losing one of them, does not leave the ninety-nine in the wilderness and go after the one that is lost until he finds it? 5 When he has found it, he lays it on his shoulders

---

ʲ The Greek word for *you* here is plural   ᵏ Or *how can it be used for seasoning?*

Lost and Found

LIVE IT!

Who hasn't been lost at some point in life? Everyone can identify with the frustration, fear, and loneliness that come with being lost. Which means that everyone can also identify with being found! What a wonderful feeling it is to finally see the familiar landmark or to make the right turn to the main road or to have someone help you get your life back on track.

If you identify with that lone sheep who strayed from the flock (Lk 15.1–7), remember that God never stops looking for you. Maybe all you need to do is stop and listen for God's call so that God can embrace you and celebrate your return.

Talk to God now about the recent experiences that have led you astray and have made you feel lost. Let God hold you tight and lift you high as the divine shepherd celebrates your return.

▶ Lk 15.1–7

and rejoices. 6 And when he comes home, he calls together his friends and neighbors, saying to them, 'Rejoice with me, for I have found my sheep that was lost.' 7 Just so, I tell you, there will be more joy in heaven over one sinner who repents than over ninety-nine righteous persons who need no repentance.

The Parable of the Lost Coin

8 "Or what woman having ten silver coins,[l] if she loses one of them, does not light a lamp, sweep the house, and search carefully until she finds it? 9 When she has found it, she calls together her friends and neighbors, saying, 'Rejoice with me, for I have found the coin that I had lost.' 10 Just so, I tell you, there is joy in the presence of the angels of God over one sinner who repents."

The Parable of the Prodigal and His Brother

11 Then Jesus[m] said, "There was a man who had two sons. 12 The younger of them said to his father, 'Father, give me the share of the property that will belong to me.' So he divided his property between them. 13 A few days later the younger son gathered all he had and traveled to a distant country, and there he squandered his property in dissolute living. 14 When he had spent everything, a severe famine took place throughout that country, and he

15.20

began to be in need. 15 So he went and hired himself out to one of the citizens of that country, who sent him to his fields to feed the pigs. 16 He would gladly have filled himself with[n] the pods that the

---

[l] Gk drachmas, each worth about a day's wage for a laborer   [m] Gk he   [n] Other ancient authorities read filled his stomach with

God's Limitless Love

We have all heard the story of the lost son (prodigal son). We have all heard about the older brother's envious reaction to his father's generosity. And it seems clear that the forgiving father represents God and that the sons represent each of us at different points in our life.

On second thought, perhaps there is more to this familiar parable than meets the eye. Think about the story for a moment. What does it really say about God? Not only is the father not upset about his son wasting all his money, but the father is incredibly happy to see his son return home. He runs to meet him! Picture it—this man so eager to welcome his son that he runs down the road toward him and then hugs and kisses him. Doesn't this seem a bit excessive?

But it doesn't end there. Despite the son's apology, which the father ignores, the father tells his servants to throw a huge party, to go all out for his son. This seems almost too much to believe, doesn't it? Music, dancing, expensive robes and rings, and a feast for everyone! What's going on here?

Luke is trying to show us, in the most visual way possible, that there is simply no limit to God's love for us. It is not a conditional love. It is an extravagant, outrageous love. God doesn't hold back. How can we refuse such boundless love? How can we hold back from such divine eagerness? The next time you think you have separated yourself from God's love, picture yourself walking down a road and God running toward you with open arms. What is your response?

▶ Lk 15.11–32

pigs were eating; and no one gave him anything.
17 But when he came to himself he said, 'How
many of my father's hired hands have bread
enough and to spare, but here I am dying of
hunger! 18 I will get up and go to my father, and I
will say to him, "Father, I have sinned against heav-
en and before you; 19 I am no longer worthy to be
called your son; treat me like one of your hired
hands." ' 20 So he set off and went to his father. But
while he was still far off, his father saw him and was
filled with compassion; he ran and put his arms
around him and kissed him. 21 Then the son said to
him, 'Father, I have sinned against heaven and before you; I am no longer worthy to be called your
son.'n 22 But the father said to his slaves, 'Quickly,
bring out a robe—the best one—and put it on him;
put a ring on his finger and sandals on his feet.
23 And get the fatted calf and kill it, and let us eat
and celebrate; 24 for this son of mine was dead and
is alive again; he was lost and is found!' And they
began to celebrate.

25 "Now his elder son was in the field; and
when he came and approached the house, he heard
music and dancing. 26 He called one of the slaves
and asked what was going on. 27 He replied, 'Your
brother has come, and your father has killed the fatted calf, because he has got him back safe and
sound.' 28 Then he became angry and refused to go
in. His father came out and began to plead with
him. 29 But he answered his father, 'Listen! For all
these years I have been working like a slave for you,
and I have never disobeyed your command; yet you
have never given me even a young goat so that I
might celebrate with my friends. 30 But when this
son of yours came back, who has devoured your
property with prostitutes, you killed the fatted calf
for him!' 31 Then the fathero said to him, 'Son, you
are always with me, and all that is mine is yours.
32 But we had to celebrate and rejoice, because this
brother of yours was dead and has come to life; he
was lost and has been found.' "

The Parable of the Dishonest Manager

16 Then Jesuso said to the disciples, "There
was a rich man who had a manager, and
charges were brought to him that this man was
squandering his property. 2 So he summoned him
and said to him, 'What is this that I hear about you?
Give me an accounting of your management, because you cannot be my manager any longer.'
3 Then the manager said to himself, 'What will I do,
now that my master is taking the position away
from me? I am not strong enough to dig, and I am
ashamed to beg. 4 I have decided what to do so
that, when I am dismissed as manager, people may
welcome me into their homes.' 5 So, summoning
his master's debtors one by one, he asked the first,

'How much do you owe my master?' 6 He answered, 'A hundred jugs of olive oil.' He said to
him, 'Take your bill, sit down quickly, and make it
fifty.' 7 Then he asked another, 'And how much do
you owe?' He replied, 'A hundred containers of
wheat.' He said to him, 'Take your bill and make it
eighty.' 8 And his master commended the dishonest
manager because he had acted shrewdly; for the
children of this age are more shrewd in dealing with
their own generation than are the children of light.
9 And I tell you, make friends for yourselves by
means of dishonest wealthp so that when it is gone,
they may welcome you into the eternal homes.q

10 "Whoever is faithful in a very little is faithful
also in much; and whoever is dishonest in a very little is dishonest also in much. 11 If then you have
not been faithful with the dishonest wealth,p who
will entrust to you the true riches? 12 And if you
have not been faithful with what belongs to another, who will give you what is your own? 13 No slave

---

n Other ancient authorities add *Treat me like one of your
hired servants*   o Gk *he*   p Gk *mammon*   q Gk *tents*

can serve two masters; for a slave will either hate the one and love the other, or be devoted to the one and despise the other. You cannot serve God and wealth."ʳ

The Law and the Kingdom of God

14 The Phar′i•sees, who were lovers of money, heard all this, and they ridiculed him. 15 So he said to them, "You are those who justify yourselves in the sight of others; but God knows your hearts; for what is prized by human beings is an abomination in the sight of God.

16 "The law and the prophets were in effect until John came; since then the good news of the kingdom of God is proclaimed, and everyone tries to enter it by force.ˢ 17 But it is easier for heaven and earth to pass away, than for one stroke of a letter in the law to be dropped.

18 "Anyone who divorces his wife and marries another commits adultery, and whoever marries a woman divorced from her husband commits adultery.

The Rich Man and Lazarus

19 "There was a rich man who was dressed in purple and fine linen and who feasted sumptuously every day. 20 And at his gate lay a poor man named Laz′a•rus, covered with sores, 21 who longed to satisfy his hunger with what fell from the rich man's table; even the dogs would come and lick his sores. 22 The poor man died and was carried away by the angels to be with Abraham.ᵗ The rich man also died and was buried. 23 In Hades, where he

was being tormented, he looked up and saw Abraham far away with Laz′a•rus by his side.ᵘ 24 He called out, 'Father Abraham, have mercy on me, and send Laz′a•rus to dip the tip of his finger in water and cool my tongue; for I am in agony in these flames.' 25 But Abraham said, 'Child, remember that during your lifetime you received your good things, and Laz′a•rus in like manner evil things; but now he is comforted here, and you are in agony. 26 Besides all this, between you and us a great chasm has been fixed, so that those who might want to pass from here to you cannot do so, and no one can cross from there to us.' 27 He said, 'Then, father, I beg you to send him to my father's house— 28 for I have five brothers—that he may warn them, so that they will not also come into this place of torment.' 29 Abraham replied, 'They have Moses and the prophets; they should listen to them.' 30 He said, 'No, father Abraham; but if someone goes to them from the dead, they will repent.' 31 He said to him, 'If they do not listen to Moses and the prophets, neither will they be convinced even if someone rises from the dead.' "

Some Sayings of Jesus
(Mt 18.6–9; Mk 9.42–48)

17 Jesusᵛ said to his disciples, "Occasions for stumbling are bound to come, but woe to anyone by whom they come! 2 It would be better for you if a millstone were hung around your

---

ʳ Gk *mammon*   ˢ Or *everyone is strongly urged to enter it*
ᵗ Gk *to Abraham's bosom*   ᵘ Gk *in his bosom*   ᵛ Gk *He*

The Great Chasm

In this famous parable about the rich man and poor Lazarus, Luke puts the following words in the mouth of Abraham: "Between you and us a great chasm has been fixed, so that those who might want to pass from here to you cannot do so, and no one can cross from there to us" (verse 26). Abraham is speaking metaphorically about heaven and hell, but he could just as easily be speaking about the gap between the "haves" and the "have-nots."

Across the globe, the gap between those who are wealthy and those who are poor is indeed becoming a great chasm. It grows more and more difficult for those who are poor and destitute to improve their lot in life. And yet, we hear about the rich becoming richer, many of whom seem to have little or no regard for the millions of people who go without in the world.

This parable speaks volumes to the inequities in our world and to our responsibility to be concerned for all the Lazaruses at our door. What are we doing now for those who are poor? What more could we be doing? How can we become more sensitive to the needs of those who are poor?

▶ Lk 16.19–31

neck and you were thrown into the sea than for you to cause one of these little ones to stumble. 3 Be on your guard! If another disciple*w* sins, you must rebuke the offender, and if there is repentance, you must forgive. 4 And if the same person sins against you seven times a day, and turns back to you seven times and says, 'I repent,' you must forgive."

5 The apostles said to the Lord, "Increase our faith!" 6 The Lord replied, "If you had faith the size of a*x* mustard seed, you could say to this mulberry tree, 'Be uprooted and planted in the sea,' and it would obey you.

7 "Who among you would say to your slave who has just come in from plowing or tending sheep in the field, 'Come here at once and take your place at the table'? 8 Would you not rather say to him, 'Prepare supper for me, put on your apron and serve me while I eat and drink; later you may eat and drink'? 9 Do you thank the slave for doing what was commanded? 10 So you also, when you have done all that you were ordered to do, say, 'We are worthless slaves; we have done only what we ought to have done!' "

Jesus Cleanses Ten Lepers

11 On the way to Jerusalem Jesus*y* was going through the region between Sa•mār'i•a and Galilee. 12 As he entered a village, ten lepers*z* approached him. Keeping their distance, 13 they called out, saying, "Jesus, Master, have mercy on us!" 14 When he saw them, he said to them, "Go and show yourselves to the priests." And as they went, they were made clean. 15 Then one of them, when he saw that he was healed, turned back, praising God with a loud voice. 16 He prostrated himself at Jesus'*a* feet and thanked him. And he was a Sa•mār'i•tan. 17 Then Jesus asked, "Were not ten made clean? But the other nine, where are they? 18 Was none of them found to return and give praise to God except this foreigner?" 19 Then he said to him, "Get up and go on your way; your faith has made you well."

The Coming of the Kingdom
(Gen 6.5—8.22; 19.12–14)

20 Once Jesus*y* was asked by the Phar'i•sees when the kingdom of God was coming, and he answered, "The kingdom of God is not coming with things that can be observed; 21 nor will they say, 'Look, here it is!' or 'There it is!' For, in fact, the kingdom of God is among*b* you."

22 Then he said to the disciples, "The days are coming when you will long to see one of the days of the Son of Man, and you will not see it. 23 They will say to you, 'Look there!' or 'Look here!' Do not go, do not set off in pursuit. 24 For as the lightning flashes and lights up the sky from one side to the other, so will the Son of Man be in his day.*c* 25 But

first he must endure much suffering and be rejected by this generation. 26 Just as it was in the days of Noah, so too it will be in the days of the Son of Man. 27 They were eating and drinking, and marrying and being given in marriage, until the day Noah entered the ark, and the flood came and destroyed all of them. 28 Likewise, just as it was in the days of Lot: they were eating and drinking, buying and selling, planting and building, 29 but on the day that Lot left Sod'om, it rained fire and sulfur from heaven and destroyed all of them 30 —it will be like that on the day that the Son of Man is revealed. 31 On that day, anyone on the housetop who has belongings in the house must not come down to take them away; and likewise anyone in the field must not turn back. 32 Remember Lot's wife. 33 Those who try to make their life secure will lose it, but those who lose their life will keep it. 34 I tell you, on that night there will be two in one bed; one will be taken and the other left. 35 There will be two women grinding meal together; one will be taken and the other left."*d* 37 Then they asked him, "Where, Lord?" He said to them, "Where the corpse is, there the vultures will gather."

L
K

PRAY IT?
Can You Hear Me, Lord?

Dear God, Jesus had to remind people to pray always and not to lose hope when faced with injustice. I need to hear that too. Sometimes it seems like I pray and pray, but you are not answering.

I know that I have to be willing to look and listen for your response. I know that I have to pray always, not just in times of need. I know I need to share my daily life with you. Help me to do these things I know I need to do. Help me to pray, Lord. Amen.

▶ Lk 18.1–8

The Parable of the Widow and
the Unjust Judge

18 Then Jesus*y* told them a parable about their need to pray always and not to lose heart. 2 He said, "In a certain city there was a judge

---

w Gk *your brother*   *x* Gk *faith as a grain of*   *y* Gk *he*
z The terms *leper* and *leprosy* can refer to several diseases
a Gk *his*   *b* Or *within*   *c* Other ancient authorities lack *in his day*   *d* Other ancient authorities add verse 36, *"Two will be in the field; one will be taken and the other left."*

who neither feared God nor had respect for people. 3 In that city there was a widow who kept coming to him and saying, 'Grant me justice against my opponent.' 4 For a while he refused; but later he said to himself, 'Though I have no fear of God and no respect for anyone, 5 yet because this widow keeps bothering me, I will grant her justice, so that she may not wear me out by continually coming.' "*e* 6 And the Lord said, "Listen to what the unjust judge says. 7 And will not God grant justice to his chosen ones who cry to him day and night? Will he delay long in helping them? 8 I tell you, he will quickly grant justice to them. And yet, when the Son of Man comes, will he find faith on earth?"

The Parable of the Pharisee and the Tax Collector

9 He also told this parable to some who trusted in themselves that they were righteous and regarded others with contempt: 10 "Two men went up to the temple to pray, one a Phar'i•see and the other a tax collector. 11 The Phar'i•see, standing by himself, was praying thus, 'God, I thank you that I am not like other people: thieves, rogues, adulterers, or even like this tax collector. 12 I fast twice a week; I give a tenth of all my income.' 13 But the tax collector, standing far off, would not even look up to heaven, but was beating his breast and saying, 'God, be merciful to me, a sinner!' 14 I tell you, this man went down to his home justified rather than the other; for all who exalt themselves will be humbled, but all who humble themselves will be exalted."

Jesus Blesses Little Children
(Mt 19.13–15; Mk 10.13–16)

15 People were bringing even infants to him that he might touch them; and when the disciples saw it, they sternly ordered them not to do it. 16 But Jesus called for them and said, "Let the little children come to me, and do not stop them; for it is to such as these that the kingdom of God belongs. 17 Truly I tell you, whoever does not receive the kingdom of God as a little child will never enter it."

The Rich Ruler
(Mt 19.16–30; Mk 10.17–31)

18 A certain ruler asked him, "Good Teacher, what must I do to inherit eternal life?" 19 Jesus said to him, "Why do you call me good? No one is good but God alone. 20 You know the commandments: 'You shall not commit adultery; You shall not murder; You shall not steal; You shall not bear false witness; Honor your father and mother.' " 21 He replied, "I have kept all these since my youth." 22 When Jesus heard this, he said to him, "There is still one thing lacking. Sell all that you own and distribute the money*f* to the poor, and you will have treasure in heaven; then come, follow me." 23 But when he heard this, he became sad; for he was very rich. 24 Jesus looked at him and said, "How hard it is for those who have wealth to enter the kingdom of God! 25 Indeed, it is easier for a camel to go through the eye of a needle than for someone who is rich to enter the kingdom of God." 26 Those who heard it said, "Then who can be saved?" 27 He replied, "What is impossible for mortals is possible for God." 28 Then Peter said, "Look, we have left our homes and followed you." 29 And he said to them, "Truly I tell you, there is no one who has left house or wife or brothers or parents or children, for the sake of the kingdom of God, 30 who will not get

---

e Or *so that she may not finally come and slap me in the face*
f Gk lacks *the money*

What Must I Do?

LIVE IT!

Picture the rich ruler in Lk 18.18–30, proud that he has closely and devoutly followed the Commandments all his life. Is it eagerness or conceit that makes him ask Jesus, "What must I do?"

Jesus' answer, "Sell all that you own and distribute the money to the poor," must have been like a blow. Jesus asked a radical commitment from this rich ruler, just as Jesus asks a radical commitment from us. As often happens in Luke's portrayal of Jesus, that radical commitment has something to do with wealth and the poor (verse 22). If we dare to ask the loaded question, "What must I do?" we must be prepared to *unload* something too. Our human tendency is to hoard our money and our material goods. But with God's help (verse 27), we can become generous with those in need.

▶ Lk 18.18–30

Noticed by Jesus

Why would Jesus choose Zacchaeus, who was hated and despised as a tax collector, to become a disciple? Besides that, he was pretty short and did not stand out in a crowd. Perhaps Luke is trying to tell us that our physical attributes, our past history, and other people's perceptions do not figure into God's equation.

When Jesus notices Zacchaeus, Zacchaeus ends up not only believing in Jesus but also doing something surprising. He gives away half of his money and possessions, perhaps to make up for all the times he cheated people. This is what conversion is—a change of heart and behavior. Conversion calls us to act in ways we would not have acted before.

Jesus has been with you from the moment of your conception. How have you tried to know him better? How do you feel knowing that he sees past externals and loves you for who you truly are?

▶ Lk 19.1–10

L
K

back very much more in this age, and in the age to come eternal life."

A Third Time Jesus Foretells His Death and Resurrection

(Mt 20.17–19; Mk 10.32–34)

31 Then he took the twelve aside and said to them, "See, we are going up to Jerusalem, and everything that is written about the Son of Man by the prophets will be accomplished. 32 For he will be handed over to the Gentiles; and he will be mocked and insulted and spat upon. 33 After they have flogged him, they will kill him, and on the third day he will rise again." 34 But they understood nothing about all these things; in fact, what he said was hidden from them, and they did not grasp what was said.

Jesus Heals a Blind Beggar Near Jericho

(Mt 20.29–34; Mk 10.46–52)

35 As he approached Jericho, a blind man was sitting by the roadside begging. 36 When he heard a crowd going by, he asked what was happening. 37 They told him, "Jesus of Nazareth *g* is passing by." 38 Then he shouted, "Jesus, Son of David, have mercy on me!" 39 Those who were in front sternly ordered him to be quiet; but he shouted even more loudly, "Son of David, have mercy on me!" 40 Jesus stood still and ordered the man to be brought to him; and when he came near, he asked him, 41 "What do you want me to do for you?" He said, "Lord, let me see again." 42 Jesus said to him, "Receive your sight; your faith has saved you." 43 Immediately he regained his sight and followed him, glorifying God; and all the people, when they saw it, praised God.

Jesus and Zacchaeus

19 He entered Jericho and was passing through it. 2 A man was there named Zac·chae'us; he was a chief tax collector and was rich. 3 He was trying to see who Jesus was, but on account of the crowd he could not, because he was short in stature. 4 So he ran ahead and climbed a sycamore tree to see him, because he was going to pass that way. 5 When Jesus came to the place, he looked up and said to him, "Zac·chae'us, hurry and come down; for I must stay at your house today." 6 So he hurried down and was happy to welcome him. 7 All who saw it began to grumble and said, "He has gone to be the guest of one who is a sinner." 8 Zac·chae'us stood there and said to the Lord, "Look, half of my possessions, Lord, I will give to the poor; and if I have defrauded anyone of anything, I will pay back four times as much." 9 Then Jesus said to him, "Today salvation has come to this house, because he too is a son of Abraham. 10 For the Son of Man came to seek out and to save the lost."

The Parable of the Ten Pounds

(Mt 25.14–30)

11 As they were listening to this, he went on to tell a parable, because he was near Jerusalem, and because they supposed that the kingdom of God was to appear immediately. 12 So he said, "A nobleman went to a distant country to get royal power for himself and then return. 13 He summoned ten of his slaves, and gave them ten pounds,*h* and said to them, 'Do business with these until I come back.' 14 But the citizens of his

---

g Gk *the Nazorean*   *h* The mina, rendered here by *pound*, was about three months' wages for a laborer

JESUS GOES TO JERUSALEM AS THE MESSIAH!

As Jesus enters Jerusalem to celebrate the Passover, the crowd joyfully hails him as the king and Messiah returning to the City of David. He is the prophet who brings new hope and calls people to conversion.

On Palm Sunday—also known as Passion Sunday—we begin our preparation for Holy Week. At Mass, we receive blessed branches of palms to symbolize our profession of Jesus as the Messiah, king of peace. In some cultures, the palms are woven into beautiful braids, crosses, and flowers. In others, people receive a small donkey made of palm leaves, as a remembrance of Jesus' riding the donkey into Jerusalem. Often, his entrance into Jerusalem is re-enacted. Hispanics use art, song, and drama to celebrate and express their faith.

■ **Picture yourself in the crowd welcoming Jesus. Does Jesus' coming fill you with joy and hope?**
■ **Next Palm Sunday, find a special place for your palm. Think of a concrete way you will live out your calling as a disciple of Jesus in the coming year. Each time you see the palm, remember your call, and pray for help to respond to it.**

▶ Lk 19.28–40

country hated him and sent a delegation after him, saying, 'We do not want this man to rule over us.' 15 When he returned, having received royal power, he ordered these slaves, to whom he had given the money, to be summoned so that he might find out what they had gained by trading. 16 The first came forward and said, 'Lord, your pound has made ten more pounds.' 17 He said to him, 'Well done, good slave! Because you have been trustworthy in a very small thing, take charge of ten cities.' 18 Then the second came, saying, 'Lord, your pound has made five pounds.' 19 He said to him, 'And you, rule over five cities.' 20 Then the other came, saying, 'Lord, here is your pound. I wrapped it up in a piece of cloth, 21 for I was afraid of you, because you are a harsh man; you take what you did not deposit, and reap what you did not sow.' 22 He said to him, 'I will judge you by your own words, you wicked slave! You knew, did you, that I was a harsh man, taking what I did not deposit and reaping what I did not sow? 23 Why then did you not put my money into the bank? Then when I returned, I could have collected it with interest.' 24 He said to the bystanders, 'Take the pound from him and give it to the one who has ten pounds.' 25 (And they said to him, 'Lord, he has ten pounds!') 26 'I tell you, to all those who have, more will be given; but from those who have nothing, even what they have will be taken away. 27 But as for these enemies of

mine who did not want me to be king over them— bring them here and slaughter them in my presence.' "

Jesus' Triumphal Entry into Jerusalem
(Mt 21.1–11; Mk 11.1–11; Jn 12.12–19)

28 After he had said this, he went on ahead, going up to Jerusalem.

29 When he had come near Beth'pha•gē and Beth'a•ny, at the place called the Mount of Olives, he sent two of the disciples, 30 saying, "Go into the village ahead of you, and as you enter it you will find tied there a colt that has never been ridden. Untie it and bring it here. 31 If anyone asks you, 'Why are you untying it?' just say this, 'The Lord needs it.' " 32 So those who were sent departed and found it as he had told them. 33 As they were untying the colt, its owners asked them, "Why are you untying the colt?" 34 They said, "The Lord needs it." 35 Then they brought it to Jesus; and after throwing their cloaks on the colt, they set Jesus on it. 36 As he rode along, people kept spreading their cloaks on the road. 37 As he was now approaching the path down from the Mount of Olives, the whole multitude of the disciples began to praise God joyfully with a loud voice for all the deeds of power that they had seen, 38 saying,

"Blessed is the king
    who comes in the name of the Lord!

Peace in heaven,
    and glory in the highest heaven!"
39 Some of the Phar'i•sees in the crowd said to him, "Teacher, order your disciples to stop." 40 He answered, "I tell you, if these were silent, the stones would shout out."

Jesus Weeps over Jerusalem

41 As he came near and saw the city, he wept over it, 42 saying, "If you, even you, had only recognized on this day the things that make for peace! But now they are hidden from your eyes. 43 Indeed, the days will come upon you, when your enemies will set up ramparts around you and surround you, and hem you in on every side. 44 They will crush you to the ground, you and your children within you, and they will not leave within you one stone upon another; because you did not recognize the time of your visitation from God."[i]

Jesus Cleanses the Temple
(Mt 21.12–17; Mk 11.15–19; Jn 2.12–25)

45 Then he entered the temple and began to drive out those who were selling things there;

46 and he said, "It is written,
    'My house shall be a house of prayer';
        but you have made it a den of
            robbers."

47 Every day he was teaching in the temple. The chief priests, the scribes, and the leaders of the people kept looking for a way to kill him; 48 but they did not find anything they could do, for all the people were spellbound by what they heard.

The Authority of Jesus Questioned
(Mt 21.23–27; Mk 11.27–33)

20 One day, as he was teaching the people in the temple and telling the good news, the chief priests and the scribes came with the elders 2 and said to him, "Tell us, by what authority are you doing these things? Who is it who gave you this authority?" 3 He answered them, "I will also ask you a question, and you tell me: 4 Did the baptism of John come from heaven, or was it of human origin?" 5 They discussed it with one another, saying, "If we say, 'From heaven,' he

---

i Gk lacks *from God*

As he came near and saw the city, he wept over it, saying,

"If you, even you, had only **recognized** on this day the things that make for **peace!** But now they are **hidden** from your eyes."

20.41–42

did you KNOW?

The Human Jesus

Have you ever been so disappointed in something that you just sat down and wept? That's what happened to Jesus. In Lk 19.41–42, we hear of his great disappointment and frustration that he cannot help Jerusalem and its people. The people of Jerusalem do not accept his message of justice and peace, so the Temple and Jerusalem are to be destroyed again. Jesus is so upset that he weeps.

We often forget that although Jesus is fully God, he is also fully human and experienced all the things that normal people experience. He enjoyed excitement, laughter, and fun times with friends. He also experienced fear, sadness, and frustration. He was completely human in all things but sin.

What does it mean to you that Jesus shares our humanity? Why is Jesus' humanity an important part of the Christian message?

▸ Lk 19.41–42

will say, 'Why did you not believe him?' 6 But if we say, 'Of human origin,' all the people will stone us; for they are convinced that John was a prophet." 7 So they answered that they did not know where it came from. 8 Then Jesus said to them, "Neither will I tell you by what authority I am doing these things."

The Parable of the Wicked Tenants
(Mt 21.33–46; Mk 12.1–12)

9 He began to tell the people this parable: "A man planted a vineyard, and leased it to tenants, and went to another country for a long time. 10 When the season came, he sent a slave to the tenants in order that they might give him his share of the produce of the vineyard; but the tenants beat him and sent him away empty-handed. 11 Next he sent another slave; that one also they beat and insulted and sent away empty-handed. 12 And he sent still a third; this one also they wounded and threw out. 13 Then the owner of the vineyard said, 'What shall I do? I will send my beloved son; perhaps they will respect him.' 14 But when the tenants saw him,

they discussed it among themselves and said, 'This is the heir; let us kill him so that the inheritance may be ours.' 15 So they threw him out of the vineyard and killed him. What then will the owner of the vineyard do to them? 16 He will come and destroy those tenants and give the vineyard to others." When they heard this, they said, "Heaven forbid!" 17 But he looked at them and said, "What then does this text mean:

'The stone that the builders rejected
has become the cornerstone'?j

18 Everyone who falls on that stone will be broken to pieces; and it will crush anyone on whom it falls." 19 When the scribes and chief priests realized that he had told this parable against them, they wanted to lay hands on him at that very hour, but they feared the people.

The Question about Paying Taxes
(Mt 22.15–22; Mk 12.13–17)

20 So they watched him and sent spies who pretended to be honest, in order to trap him by what he said, so as to hand him over to the jurisdiction and authority of the governor. 21 So they asked him, "Teacher, we know that you are right in what you say and teach, and you show deference to no one, but teach the way of God in accordance with truth. 22 Is it lawful for us to pay taxes to the emperor, or not?" 23 But he perceived their craftiness and said to them, 24 "Show me a denarius. Whose head and whose title does it bear?" They said, "The emperor's." 25 He said to them, "Then give to the emperor the things that are the emperor's, and to God the things that are God's." 26 And they were not able in the presence of the people to trap him by what he said; and being amazed by his answer, they became silent.

The Question about the Resurrection
(Mt 22.23–33; Mk 12.18–27)

27 Some Sad'du·cees, those who say there is no resurrection, came to him 28 and asked him a question, "Teacher, Moses wrote for us that if a man's brother dies, leaving a wife but no children, the mank shall marry the widow and raise up children for his brother. 29 Now there were seven brothers; the first married, and died childless; 30 then the second 31 and the third married her, and so in the same way all seven died childless. 32 Finally the woman also died. 33 In the resurrection, therefore, whose wife will the woman be? For the seven had married her."

34 Jesus said to them, "Those who belong to this age marry and are given in marriage; 35 but

---

j Or keystone   k Gk his brother

those who are considered worthy of a place in that age and in the resurrection from the dead neither marry nor are given in marriage. 36 Indeed they cannot die anymore, because they are like angels and are children of God, being children of the resurrection. 37 And the fact that the dead are raised Moses himself showed, in the story about the bush, where he speaks of the Lord as the God of Abraham, the God of Isaac, and the God of Jacob. 38 Now he is God not of the dead, but of the living; for to him all of them are alive." 39 Then some of the scribes answered, "Teacher, you have spoken well." 40 For they no longer dared to ask him another question.

The Question about David's Son
(Mt 22.41–46; Mk 12.35–37)

41 Then he said to them, "How can they say that the Messiah*l* is David's son? 42 For David himself says in the book of Psalms,

'The Lord said to my Lord,
"Sit at my right hand,
43   until I make your enemies your footstool." '
44 David thus calls him Lord; so how can he be his son?"

Jesus Denounces the Scribes
(Mt 23.1–7; Mk 12.38–40)

45 In the hearing of all the people he said to the*m* disciples, 46 "Beware of the scribes, who like to walk around in long robes, and love to be greeted with respect in the marketplaces, and to have the best seats in the synagogues and places of honor at banquets. 47 They devour widows' houses and for the sake of appearance say long prayers. They will receive the greater condemnation."

The Widow's Offering
(Mk 12.41–44)

21 He looked up and saw rich people putting their gifts into the treasury; 2 he also saw a poor widow put in two small copper coins. 3 He said, "Truly I tell you, this poor widow has put in more than all of them; 4 for all of them have contributed out of their abundance, but she out of her poverty has put in all she had to live on."

The Destruction of the Temple Foretold
(Mt 24.1–2; Mk 13.1–2)

5 When some were speaking about the temple, how it was adorned with beautiful stones and gifts dedicated to God, he said, 6 "As for these things that you see, the days will come when not one stone will be left upon another; all will be thrown down."

Signs and Persecutions
(Mt 24.3–14; Mk 13.3–13)

7 They asked him, "Teacher, when will this be, and what will be the sign that this is about to take place?" 8 And he said, "Beware that you are not led astray; for many will come in my name and say, 'I am he!'*n* and, 'The time is near!'*o* Do not go after them.

9 "When you hear of wars and insurrections, do not be terrified; for these things must take place first, but the end will not follow immediately." 10 Then he said to them, "Nation will rise against nation, and kingdom against kingdom; 11 there will be great earthquakes, and in various places famines and plagues; and there will be dreadful portents and great signs from heaven.

---

l Or *the Christ* *m* Other ancient authorities read *his*
n Gk I am *o* Or *at hand*

Stewardship: Making a Contribution

LIVE IT!

In Lk 21.1–4, Jesus notices that the rich people gave from their excess wealth, but the widow gave from her limited budget. She actually contributed more meaningfully because she gave from what little she had.

   God calls us to be contributing members of the faith community and the human family—even to the point of sacrifice. We are called to support the church's mission to spread the Good News of Jesus Christ. We should also support other organizations that contribute to the positive welfare of all people in need.

   How are you responding to God's call to give? Pray for the generosity of the poor widow as you discern how much of your time, talents, and treasure you are being called to give.

▶ Lk 21.1–4

12 "But before all this occurs, they will arrest you and persecute you; they will hand you over to synagogues and prisons, and you will be brought before kings and governors because of my name. 13 This will give you an opportunity to testify. 14 So make up your minds not to prepare your defense in advance; 15 for I will give you words*p* and a wisdom that none of your opponents will be able to withstand or contradict. 16 You will be betrayed even by parents and brothers, by relatives and friends; and they will put some of you to death. 17 You will be hated by all because of my name. 18 But not a hair of your head will perish. 19 By your endurance you will gain your souls.

The Destruction of Jerusalem Foretold
(Mt 24.15–28; Mk 13.14–23)

20 "When you see Jerusalem surrounded by armies, then know that its desolation has come near.*q* 21 Then those in Judea must flee to the mountains, and those inside the city must leave it, and those out in the country must not enter it; 22 for these are days of vengeance, as a fulfillment of all that is written. 23 Woe to those who are pregnant and to those who are nursing infants in those days! For there will be great distress on the earth and wrath against this people; 24 they will fall by the edge of the sword and be taken away as captives among all nations; and Jerusalem will be trampled on by the Gentiles, until the times of the Gentiles are fulfilled.

The Coming of the Son of Man
(Mt 24.29–31; Mk 13.24–27)

25 "There will be signs in the sun, the moon, and the stars, and on the earth distress among nations confused by the roaring of the sea and the waves. 26 People will faint from fear and foreboding of what is coming upon the world, for the powers of the heavens will be shaken. 27 Then they will see 'the Son of Man coming in a cloud' with power and great glory. 28 Now when these things begin to take place, stand up and raise your heads, because your redemption is drawing near."

The Lesson of the Fig Tree
(Mt 24.32–35; Mk 13.28–31)

29 Then he told them a parable: "Look at the fig tree and all the trees; 30 as soon as they sprout leaves you can see for yourselves and know that summer is already near. 31 So also, when you see these things taking place, you know that the kingdom of God is near. 32 Truly I tell you, this generation will not pass away until all things have taken place. 33 Heaven and earth will pass away, but my words will not pass away.

Exhortation to Watch
(Mt 24.36–44; Mk 13.32–37)

34 "Be on guard so that your hearts are not weighed down with dissipation and drunkenness and the worries of this life, and that day does not catch you unexpectedly, 35 like a trap. For it will come upon all who live on the face of the whole earth. 36 Be alert at all times, praying that you may have the strength to escape all these things that will take place, and to stand before the Son of Man."

37 Every day he was teaching in the temple, and at night he would go out and spend the night on the Mount of Olives, as it was called. 38 And all the people would get up early in the morning to listen to him in the temple.

The Plot to Kill Jesus
(Mt 26.1–5, 14–16; Mk 14.1–2, 10–11; Jn 11.45–53)

22 Now the festival of Unleavened Bread, which is called the Passover, was near. 2 The chief priests and the scribes were looking for a way to put Jesus*r* to death, for they were afraid of the people.

3 Then Satan entered into Judas called Is·car'i·ot, who was one of the twelve; 4 he went away and conferred with the chief priests and officers of the temple police about how he might betray him to them. 5 They were greatly pleased and agreed to give him money. 6 So he consented and began to look for an opportunity to betray him to them when no crowd was present.

The Preparation of the Passover
(Mt 26.17–19; Mk 14.12–16)

7 Then came the day of Unleavened Bread, on which the Passover lamb had to be sacrificed. 8 So Jesus*s* sent Peter and John, saying, "Go and prepare the Passover meal for us that we may eat it." 9 They asked him, "Where do you want us to make preparations for it?" 10 "Listen," he said to them "when you have entered the city, a man carrying a jar of water will meet you; follow him into the house he enters 11 and say to the owner of the house, 'The teacher asks you, "Where is the guest room, where I may eat the Passover with my disciples?"' 12 He will show you a large room upstairs, already furnished. Make preparations for us there." 13 So they went and found everything as he had told them; and they prepared the Passover meal.

The Institution of the Lord's Supper
(Mt 26.20–30; Mk 14.17–26; Jn 13.21–30)

14 When the hour came, he took his place at the table, and the apostles with him. 15 He said to

---

p Gk *a mouth*   *q* Or *is at hand*   *r* Gk *him*   *s* Gk *he* them, "I have eagerly desired to eat this Passover with you before I suffer; [16] for I tell you, I will not eat it[t] until it is fulfilled in the kingdom of God." [17] Then he took a cup, and after giving thanks he said, "Take this and divide it among yourselves; [18] for I tell you that from now on I will not drink of the fruit of the vine until the kingdom of God comes." [19] Then he took a loaf of bread, and when he had given thanks, he broke it and gave it to them, saying, "This is my body, which is given for you. Do this in remembrance of me." [20] And he did the same with the cup after supper, saying, "This cup that is poured out for you is the new covenant in my blood.[u] [21] But see, the one who betrays me is with me, and his hand is on the table. [22] For the Son of Man is going as it has been determined, but woe to that one by whom he is betrayed!" [23] Then they began to ask one another which one of them it could be who would do this.

The Dispute about Greatness

[24] A dispute also arose among them as to which one of them was to be regarded as the greatest. [25] But he said to them, "The kings of the Gentiles lord it over them; and those in authority over them are called benefactors. [26] But not so with you; rather the greatest among you must become like the youngest, and the leader like one who serves. [27] For who is greater, the one who is at the table or the one who serves? Is it not the one at the table? But I am among you as one who serves.

[28] "You are those who have stood by me in my trials; [29] and I confer on you, just as my Father has conferred on me, a kingdom, [30] so that you may eat

Catholic Connections

THE EUCHARIST

In Luke's account of the Last Supper, Jesus asks his disciples to remember him and all that he did, as they share the loaf of bread that he identified as his body given for us and the cup of wine that he identified with the New Covenant sealed by his blood. The celebration of this great mystery, along with its awesome meaning, is at the center of the Eucharistic celebration.

The Eucharist is one of the seven Catholic sacraments, and it is the heart and soul of what it means to be Catholic. It serves as the common celebration of our faith, and it brings together all Catholics—young and old, rich and poor, male and female, and people of all colors, nationalities, and walks of life—to participate in the death and Resurrection of Jesus. In the Eucharist, we are all members of the one Body of Christ. No matter where you go in the world, you can join in celebrating the Eucharist as a member of the Catholic church.

For more on the Eucharist, see the articles for Mt 26.26–29; Mk 14.22–25; Jn 13.1–17.

▶ Lk 22.14–20

PRAY IT
Prayer of a Servant Leader

Dear Jesus, you made it clear that those who are greatest are the ones who serve, not the ones who have fame, fortune, or authority. Help me adjust my priorities to put others first. Place within me a genuine desire to serve. Enable me to recognize the daily opportunities I have to reach out to those in need in my family, in my school, and in my community. Guide me as I strive to follow your example to become a servant leader. Amen.

▶ Lk 22.24–27

and drink at my table in my kingdom, and you will sit on thrones judging the twelve tribes of Israel.

Jesus Predicts Peter's Denial
(Mt 26.31–35; Mk 14.27–31; Jn 13.36–38)

[31] "Simon, Simon, listen! Satan has demanded[v] to sift all of you like wheat, [32] but I have prayed for you that your own faith may not fail; and you, when once you have turned back, strengthen your brothers." [33] And he said to him, "Lord, I am ready to go with you to prison and to death!" [34] Jesus[w] said, "I tell you, Peter, the cock will not crow this

---

[t] Other ancient authorities read *never eat it again*   [u] Other ancient authorities lack, in whole or in part, verses 19b-20 (*which is given . . . in my blood*)   [v] Or *has obtained permission*   [w] Gk *He*

day, until you have denied three times that you know me."

Purse, Bag, and Sword

35 He said to them, "When I sent you out without a purse, bag, or sandals, did you lack anything?" They said, "No, not a thing." 36 He said to them, "But now, the one who has a purse must take it, and likewise a bag. And the one who has no sword must sell his cloak and buy one. 37 For I tell you, this scripture must be fulfilled in me, 'And he was counted among the lawless'; and indeed what is written about me is being fulfilled." 38 They said, "Lord, look, here are two swords." He replied, "It is enough."

22.39

Jesus Prays on the Mount of Olives
(Mt 26.36–46; Mk 14.32–42; Jn 18.1)

39 He came out and went, as was his custom, to the Mount of Olives; and the disciples followed him. 40 When he reached the place, he said to them, "Pray that you may not come into the time of trial."ˣ 41 Then he withdrew from them about a stone's throw, knelt down, and prayed, 42 "Father if you are willing, remove this cup from me; yet, not my will but yours be done." [43 Then an angel from heaven appeared to him and gave him strength. 44 In his anguish he prayed more earnestly, and his sweat became like great drops of blood falling down on the ground.]ʸ 45 When he got up from prayer, he came to the disciples and found them sleeping because of grief, 46 and he said to them, "Why are you sleeping? Get up and pray that you may not come into the time of trial."ˣ

The Betrayal and Arrest of Jesus
(Mt 26.47–56; Mk 14.43–52; Jn 18.1–11)

47 While he was still speaking, suddenly a crowd came, and the one called Judas, one of the twelve, was leading them. He approached Jesus to kiss him; 48 but Jesus said to him, "Judas, is it with a kiss that you are betraying the Son of Man?" 49 When those who were around him saw what was coming, they asked, "Lord, should we strike with the sword?" 50 Then one of them struck the slave of the high priest and cut off his right ear. 51 But Jesus said, "No more of this!" And he touched his ear and healed him. 52 Then Jesus said to the chief priests, the officers of the temple police, and the elders who had come for him, "Have you come out with swords and clubs as if I were a bandit? 53 When I was with you day after day in the temple, you did not lay hands on me. But this is your hour, and the power of darkness!"

Peter Denies Jesus
(Mt 25.69–75; Mk 14.66–72; Jn 18.15–18, 25–27)

54 Then they seized him and led him away, bringing him into the high priest's house. But Peter was following at a distance. 55 When they had kindled a fire in the middle of the courtyard and sat down together, Peter sat among them. 56 Then a servant-girl, seeing him in the firelight, stared at him and said, "This man also was with him." 57 But he denied it, saying, "Woman, I do not know him." 58 A little later someone else, on seeing him, said, "You also are one of them." But Peter said, "Man, I am not!" 59 Then about an hour later still another kept insisting, "Surely this man also was with him; for he is a Galilean." 60 But Peter said, "Man, I do not know what you are talking about!" At that moment, while he was still speaking, the cock crowed. 61 The Lord turned and looked at Peter. Then Peter remembered the word of the Lord, how he had said to him, "Before the cock crows today, you will deny me three times." 62 And he went out and wept bitterly.

The Mocking and Beating of Jesus
(Mt 26.67–68; Mk 14.65)

63 Now the men who were holding Jesus began to mock him and beat him; 64 they also blindfolded him and kept asking him, "Prophesy! Who is it that struck you?" 65 They kept heaping many other insults on him.

Jesus before the Council
(Mt 26.57–68; Mk 14.61–64; Jn 18.12–14, 19–24)

66 When day came, the assembly of the elders of the people, both chief priests and scribes, gath-

---

ˣ Or *into temptation* ʸ Other ancient authorities lack verses 43 and 44

did you KNOW?

Luke's Account of Jesus' Death

The stories of Jesus' Passion—the name Christians use to describe his suffering and death—differ in all four Gospels. By comparing these stories, we get insight into the authors' portrayal of Jesus. Let's take a closer look at the perspective in the Gospel of Luke.

First, in Jesus' Passion, Luke describes the openness of Gentiles to Jesus' message of salvation. For example, Pilate finds Jesus innocent three times in Luke (23.4,14,22) and hands him over to be crucified only at the insistence of the Jewish leaders (verse 24). Later, it is a Roman centurion who praises God at the moment of Jesus' death (verse 47).

Second, Luke emphasizes Jesus' compassion and forgiveness, even during his greatest suffering. While carrying the cross, Jesus shows his concern for the women who are following him (verses 28–31). As he is nailed to the cross, he forgives those responsible (verse 34). And when one of the criminals asks for Jesus to remember him, Jesus goes beyond that to promise him the first place in Paradise (verse 43).

Third, Luke emphasizes Jesus' glory and divinity. Whereas Mark portrays Jesus abandoned in his Passion (Mk 15.34), Luke surrounds Jesus with sympathetic people: a crowd including the women of Jerusalem (Lk 23.27), the good thief (verses 40–41), and the centurion (verse 47). In Mark, Jesus feels God's absence (Mk 15.34), but Luke presents Jesus in control even at his death, handing his spirit over to God (Lk 23.46). Luke is making it clear in his portrayal of Jesus' Passion that Jesus is the loving, forgiving savior of all humankind.

▸ Lk 22.47—23.56

from now on the Son of Man will be seated at the right hand of the power of God." 70 All of them asked, "Are you, then, the Son of God?" He said to them, "You say that I am." 71 Then they said, "What further testimony do we need? We have heard it ourselves from his own lips!"

Jesus before Pilate
(Mt 27.1–2, 11–14; Mk 15.1–5; Jn 18.28–38)

23 Then the assembly rose as a body and brought Jesus[a] before Pilate. 2 They began to accuse him, saying, "We found this man perverting our nation, forbidding us to pay taxes to the emperor, and saying that he himself is the Messiah, a king."[b] 3 Then Pilate asked him, "Are you the king of the Jews?" He answered, "You say so." 4 Then Pilate said to the chief priests and the crowds, "I find no basis for an accusation against this man." 5 But they were insistent and said, "He stirs up the people by teaching throughout all Judea, from Galilee where he began even to this place."

Jesus before Herod

6 When Pilate heard this, he asked whether the man was a Galilean. 7 And when he learned that he was under Her'od's jurisdiction, he sent him off to Her'od, who was himself in Jerusalem at that time. 8 When Her'od saw Jesus, he was very glad, for he had been wanting to see him for a long time, because he had heard about him and was hoping to see him perform some sign. 9 He questioned him at some length, but Jesus[c] gave him no answer. 10 The chief priests and the scribes stood by, vehemently accusing him. 11 Even Her'od with his soldiers treated him with contempt and mocked him; then he put an elegant robe on him, and sent him back to Pilate. 12 That same day Her'od and Pilate became friends with each other; before this they had been enemies.

Jesus Sentenced to Death
(Mt 27.15–26; Mk 15.6–15; Jn 18.38b—19.16a)

13 Pilate then called together the chief priests, the leaders, and the people, 14 and said to them, "You brought me this man as one who was perverting the people; and here I have examined him in your presence and have not found this man guilty of any of your charges against him. 15 Neither has Her'od, for he sent him back to us. Indeed, he has done nothing to deserve death. 16 I will therefore have him flogged and release him."[d]

17 Then they all shouted out together, "Away

ered together, and they brought him to their council. 67 They said, "If you are the Messiah,[z] tell us." He replied, "If I tell you, you will not believe; 68 and if I question you, you will not answer. 69 But

---

[z] Or *the Christ* [a] Gk *him* [b] Or *is an anointed king*
[c] Gk *he* [d] Here, or after verse 19, other ancient authorities add verse 17, *Now he was obliged to release someone for them at the festival*

with this fellow! Release Ba·rab′bas for us!" ¹⁹ (This was a man who had been put in prison for an insurrection that had taken place in the city, and for murder.) ²⁰ Pilate, wanting to release Jesus, addressed them again; ²¹ but they kept shouting, "Crucify, crucify him!" ²² A third time he said to them, "Why, what evil has he done? I have found in him no ground for the sentence of death; I will therefore have him flogged and then release him." ²³ But they kept urgently demanding with loud shouts that he should be crucified; and their voices prevailed. ²⁴ So Pilate gave his verdict that their demand should be granted. ²⁵ He released the man they asked for, the one who had been put in prison for insurrection and murder, and he handed Jesus over as they wished.

The Crucifixion of Jesus
(Mt 27.32–44; Mk 15.21–32; Jn 19.16b–24)

26 As they led him away, they seized a man, Simon of Cy·rē′nē, who was coming from the country, and they laid the cross on him, and made him carry it behind Jesus. ²⁷ A great number of the people followed him, and among them were women who were beating their breasts and wailing for him. ²⁸ But Jesus turned to them and said, "Daughters of Jerusalem, do not weep for me, but weep for yourselves and for your children. ²⁹ For the days are surely coming when they will say, 'Blessed are the barren, and the wombs that never bore, and the breasts that never nursed.' ³⁰ Then they will begin to say to the mountains, 'Fall on us'; and to the hills, 'Cover us.' ³¹ For if they do this when the wood is green, what will happen when it is dry?"

32 Two others also, who were criminals, were led away to be put to death with him. ³³ When they came to the place that is called The Skull, they crucified Jesus*e* there with the criminals, one on his right and one on his left. [³⁴ Then Jesus said, "Father, forgive them; for they do not know what they are doing."]*f* And they cast lots to divide his clothing. ³⁵ And the people stood by, watching; but the leaders scoffed at him, saying, "He saved others; let him save himself if he is the Messiah*g* of God, his chosen one!" ³⁶ The soldiers also mocked him, coming up and offering him sour wine, ³⁷ and saying, "If you are the King of the Jews, save yourself!" ³⁸ There was also an inscription over him,*h* "This is the King of the Jews."

39 One of the criminals who were hanged there kept deriding*i* him and saying, "Are you not the Messiah?*g* Save yourself and us!" ⁴⁰ But the other rebuked him, saying, "Do you not fear God, since you are under the same sentence of condemnation? ⁴¹ And we indeed have been condemned justly, for we are getting what we deserve for our deeds, but this man has done nothing wrong." ⁴² Then he said, "Jesus, remember me when you come into*j* your kingdom." ⁴³ He replied, "Truly I tell you, today you will be with me in Paradise."

---

e Gk *him* *f* Other ancient authorities lack the sentence *Then Jesus . . . what they are doing* *g* Or *the Christ* *h* Other ancient authorities add *written in Greek and Latin and Hebrew* (that is, *Aramaic*) *i* Or *blaspheming* *j* Other ancient authorities read *in*

SALUBONG

In the Philippines, Catholics celebrate the Salubong—meaning the encounter between the risen Jesus and his sorrowful mother on Easter morning. This is based on a tradition that Mary was with the women mentioned in Lk 23.27.

On the day of Salubong, at dawn, two groups of worshipers begin walking in two different directions. One group carries a statue of Jesus, and the other group, a statue of Mary. Both statues are draped in black capes. The people walk through the town and meet on a main street, usually under an arch. A little robed "angel" (a small girl or boy) then removes the sorrowful black capes to reveal joyful white or golden robes on each statue, symbolizing the joy and glory of the Resurrection. Then the entire assembly returns to the church, and Easter Mass begins.

▶ Lk 23.26–31

Cultural Connections

WAITING IN DARKNESS

The darkness before Jesus died symbolizes the coming of the day of the Lord (see the introduction to Joel). This prayer expresses the feeling of that moment:

> *We wait in the darkness!*
> *Come, all ye who listen,*
> *Help in our night journey:*
> *Now no sun is shining;*
> *Now no star is glowing;*
> *Come show us the pathway:*
> *The night is not friendly;*
> *The moon has forgot us,*
> *We wait in the darkness!*
> (David Schiller, editor, The Little Book of Prayers, p. 322)

▶ Lk 23.44–46

L
K

The Death of Jesus
(Mt 27.45–56; Mk 15.33–41; Jn 19.25–30)

44 It was now about noon, and darkness came over the whole land*k* until three in the afternoon, 45 while the sun's light failed;*l* and the curtain of the temple was torn in two. 46 Then Jesus, crying with a loud voice, said, "Father, into your hands I commend my spirit." Having said this, he breathed his last. 47 When the centurion saw what had taken place, he praised God and said, "Certainly this man was innocent."*m* 48 And when all the crowds who had gathered there for this spectacle saw what had taken place, they returned home, beating their breasts. 49 But all his acquaintances, including the women who had followed him from Galilee, stood at a distance, watching these things.

The Burial of Jesus
(Mt 27.57–61; Mk 15.42–47; Jn 19.38–42)

50 Now there was a good and righteous man named Joseph, who, though a member of the council, 51 had not agreed to their plan and action. He came from the Jewish town of Ar·i·ma·the′a, and he was waiting expectantly for the kingdom of God. 52 This man went to Pilate and asked for the body of Jesus. 53 Then he took it down, wrapped it in a linen cloth, and laid it in a rock-hewn tomb where no one had ever been laid. 54 It was the day of Preparation, and the sabbath was beginning.*n* 55 The women who had come with him from Galilee followed, and they saw the tomb and how his body was laid. 56 Then they returned, and prepared spices and ointments.

On the sabbath they rested according to the commandment.

The Resurrection of Jesus
(Mt 28.1–10; Mk 16.1–8; Jn 20.1–10)

24 But on the first day of the week, at early dawn, they came to the tomb, taking the spices that they had prepared. 2 They found the stone rolled away from the tomb, 3 but when they went in, they did not find the body.*o* 4 While they were perplexed about this, suddenly two men in dazzling clothes stood beside them. 5 The women*p* were terrified and bowed their faces to the ground, but the men*q* said to them, "Why do you look for the living among the dead? He is not here, but has risen.*r* 6 Remember how he told you, while he was still in Galilee, 7 that the Son of Man must be handed over to sinners, and be crucified, and on the

k Or *earth* *l* Or *the sun was eclipsed.* Other ancient authorities read *the sun was darkened* *m* Or *righteous* *n* Gk *was dawning* *o* Other ancient authorities add *of the Lord Jesus* *p* Gk *They* *q* Gk *but they* *r* Other ancient authorities lack *He is not here, but has risen* third day rise again." 8 Then they remembered his words, 9 and returning from the tomb, they told all this to the eleven and to all the rest. 10 Now it was Mary Mag'da•lēne, Jō•an'na, Mary the mother of James, and the other women with them who told this to the apostles. 11 But these words seemed to them an idle tale, and they did not believe them. 12 But Peter got up and ran to the tomb; stooping and looking in, he saw the linen cloths by themselves; then he went home, amazed at what had happened.ʳ

did you KNOW?

Resurrection Hope

Think about a time when you felt hopeless. Were you depressed? lonely? angry? afraid? These were probably some of the feelings of the women who approached Jesus' tomb on the Sunday morning after his death. Their leader, their teacher, their Lord had just been horribly executed before a huge crowd, and his wonderful vision of love, justice, and forgiveness had been shattered.

But what they encountered in that tomb changed their lives forever. The tomb was empty. Two dazzling men appeared and spoke to them. Jesus had indeed risen!

When you think that a situation is hopeless, that no end is in sight, that evil is winning out, remember this story. Along with the Resurrection stories in the other three Gospels, this story is proof that despair and death do not win, that God is at work in the most hopeless situations!

▸ Lk 24.1–12

The Walk to Emmaus
(Mt 16.12–13)

13 Now on that same day two of them were going to a village called Em•ma'us, about seven milesˢ from Jerusalem, 14 and talking with each other about all these things that had happened. 15 While they were talking and discussing, Jesus himself came near and went with them, 16 but their eyes were kept from recognizing him. 17 And he said to them, "What are you discussing with each other while you walk along?" They stood still, looking sad.ᵗ 18 Then one of them, whose name was Clē'o•pas, answered him, "Are you the only stranger

in Jerusalem who does not know the things that have taken place there in these days?" 19 He asked them, "What things?" They replied, "The things about Jesus of Nazareth,ᵘ who was a prophet mighty in deed and word before God and all the people, 20 and how our chief priests and leaders handed him over to be condemned to death and crucified him. 21 But we had hoped that he was the one to redeem Israel.ᵛ Yes, and besides all this, it is now the third day since these things took place. 22 Moreover, some women of our group astounded us. They were at the tomb early this morning, 23 and when they did not find his body there, they came back and told us that they had indeed seen a vision of angels who said that he was alive. 24 Some of those who were with us went to the tomb and found it just as the women had said; but they did not see him." 25 Then he said to them, "Oh, how foolish you are, and how slow of heart to believe all that the prophets have declared! 26 Was it not necessary that the Messiahʷ should suffer these things and then enter into his glory?" 27 Then beginning with Moses and all the prophets, he interpreted to them the things about himself in all the scriptures.

28 As they came near the village to which they were going, he walked ahead as if he were going on. 29 But they urged him strongly, saying, "Stay with us, because it is almost evening and the day is now nearly over." So he went in to stay with them. 30 When he was at the table with them, he took bread, blessed and broke it, and gave it to them. 31 Then their eyes were opened, and they recognized him; and he vanished from their sight. 32 They said to each other, "Were not our hearts burning within usˣ while he was talking to us on the road, while he was opening the scriptures to us?" 33 That same hour they got up and returned to Jerusalem; and they found the eleven and their companions gathered together. 34 They were saying, "The Lord has risen indeed, and he has appeared to Simon!" 35 Then they told what had happened on the road, and how he had been made known to them in the breaking of the bread.

Jesus Appears to His Disciples
(Jn 20.19–23; Acts 1.3–5; 1 Cor 15.5)

36 While they were talking about this, Jesus himself stood among them and said to them, "Peace be with you."ʸ 37 They were startled and terrified, and thought that they were seeing a ghost.

ʳ Other ancient authorities lack verse 12   ˢ Gk sixty stadia; other ancient authorities read a hundred sixty stadia
ᵗ Other ancient authorities read walk along, looking sad?"
ᵘ Other ancient authorities read Jesus the Nazorean   ᵛ Or to set Israel free   ʷ Or the Christ   ˣ Other ancient authorities lack within us   ʸ Other ancient authorities lack and said to them, "Peace be with you."

LIVE IT!

Jesus Is with Us!

A young man was at Mass when he heard Lk 24.13–35. "Pretty strange!" he thought. "Those two guys did not recognize Jesus after they had been with him for three years. I wonder if he looked different after the Resurrection. If I had been walking on the road to Emmaus, I wonder if I would have recognized him. I wonder if people would recognize him today if he came among us." He continued to ponder these thoughts as the Mass continued. He remembered his mother saying that Jesus is present among us every day—in the people we meet, when we gather to pray, and in the Eucharist.

Suddenly, the young man was aware of what the priest was saying: "This is my body which will be given up for you. This is the cup of my blood . . . it will be shed for you and for all. Do this in memory of me."

He looked around the church, noticing people he had not paid attention to before: the Amouri family, who were refugees from a war-torn country; the little Tucker baby, who had been born with severe disabilities; an elderly man who lived alone at ninety-six years old; some other youth who were sitting together in the front of church. Somehow, all these different people found love and acceptance in the parish family. "I think I understand now," he thought. "Jesus does look different, but he is here!"

When Jesus joined the disciples at their table and broke the bread, they recognized him. It was at the Eucharist that the young man recognized the presence of Jesus alive today. How about you? When and where do you recognize Jesus? Who in your community reminds you of him the most? Why?

▶ Lk 24.13–35

38 He said to them, "Why are you frightened, and why do doubts arise in your hearts? 39 Look at my hands and my feet; see that it is I myself. Touch me and see; for a ghost does not have flesh and bones as you see that I have." 40 And when he had said this, he showed them his hands and his feet.[z] 41 While in their joy they were disbelieving and still wondering, he said to them, "Have you anything here to eat?" 42 They gave him a piece of broiled fish, 43 and he took it and ate in their presence.

44 Then he said to them, "These are my words that I spoke to you while I was still with you—that everything written about me in the law of Moses, the prophets, and the psalms must be fulfilled." 45 Then he opened their minds to understand the scriptures, 46 and he said to them, "Thus it is written, that the Messiah[a] is to suffer and to rise from the dead on the third day, 47 and that repentance and forgiveness of sins is to be proclaimed in his name to all nations, beginning from Jerusalem.

48 You are witnesses[b] of these things. 49 And see, I am sending upon you what my Father promised; so stay here in the city until you have been clothed with power from on high."

The Ascension of Jesus
(Mk 16.19–20; Acts 1.9)

50 Then he led them out as far as Beth·a·ny, and, lifting up his hands, he blessed them. 51 While he was blessing them, he withdrew from them and was carried up into heaven.[c] 52 And they worshiped him, and[d] returned to Jerusalem with great joy; 53 and they were continually in the temple blessing God.[e]

---

z Other ancient authorities lack verse 40   a Or the Christ
b Or nations. Beginning from Jerusalem 48you are witnesses
c Other ancient authorities lack and was carried up into
heaven   d Other ancient authorities lack worshiped
him, and   e Other ancient authorities add Amen

People often use analogies or symbolic images in describing their closest relationships. The author of the Gospel of John does this. Through-out the Gospel, symbolic imagery is used to describe the Christian believer's relationship with Jesus. Very different in style from the other Gospels, John also gives us the clearest picture of the divinity of Jesus.

At a Glance

- **1.1–18.** prologue: a poem about the Word of God

- **1.19—12.50.** the Book of Signs: Jesus' miracles and teachings, disputes with "the Jews"

- **Chapters 13–20.** the Book of Glory: the Last Supper, and Jesus' suffering, death, and Resurrection

- **Chapter 21.** epilogue: the appearance of the risen Jesus

In-depth

The Gospel of John begins with symbolic language describing Jesus as the Word, who was with God in the beginning of creation and who became flesh to live among us. The author goes on to describe Jesus as the light that overcomes darkness. Those who believe in Jesus walk in the light—their lives have meaning and direction. Those who do not believe stumble in the darkness of confusion and sin. John is clear that Jesus is the divine Son of God and that to belong to God, we have to follow Jesus.

In addition to its symbolic language and stress on Jesus' divinity, John's Gospel differs from the synoptic Gospels—Matthew, Mark, and Luke—in other ways:

- In the synoptic Gospels, Jesus' teaching focuses on the Kingdom (or Reign) of God. In John, Jesus' teaching stresses relationships: Jesus' relationship with God the Father and our relationship with Jesus.

- In the synoptic Gospels, Jesus teaches with parables and performs many healings and miracles. In John, Jesus does not teach by parables. Instead, Jesus performs seven miraculous signs and explains their meaning.

- John has several passages about the role of the Holy Spirit. The synoptic Gospels hardly mention the Holy Spirit.

John's story of Jesus climaxes with the coming of Jesus' "hour," a symbol for Jesus' death. But in John, Jesus' death is not tragic at all—it is his glorious return to the Father. This Gospel assures us that trust in God will pay off in the end. "I will come again and will take you to myself," says Jesus, "so that where I am, there you may be also" (14.3).

Quick Facts

Author
a member of a Christian community possibly founded by the Beloved Disciple

Date Written
most likely from A.D. 90 to 100

Audience
all the Christians of the world

Image of Jesus
noble, powerful, and divine; fully in control of his destiny

The Gospel According to John

John

The Word Became Flesh
(Gen 1.1—2.4a)

1 In the beginning was the Word, and the Word was with God, and the Word was God. 2 He was in the beginning with God. 3 All things came into being through him, and without him not one thing came into being. What has come into being 4 in him was life,*a* and the life was the light of all people. 5 The light shines in the darkness, and the darkness did not overcome it.

6 There was a man sent from God, whose name was John. 7 He came as a witness to testify to the light, so that all might believe through him. 8 He himself was not the light, but he came to testify to the light. 9 The true light, which enlightens everyone, was coming into the world.*b*

10 He was in the world, and the world came into being through him; yet the world did not know him. 11 He came to what was his own,*c* and his own people did not accept him. 12 But to all who received him, who believed in his name, he gave power to become children of God, 13 who were born, not of blood or of the will of the flesh or of the will of man, but of God.

14 And the Word became flesh and lived among us, and we have seen his glory, the glory as of a father's only son,*d* full of grace and truth. 15 (John testified to him and cried out, "This was he of whom I said, 'He who comes after me ranks ahead of me because he was before me.' ") 16 From his fullness we have all received, grace upon grace.

17 The law indeed was given through Moses; grace and truth came through Jesus Christ. 18 No one has ever seen God. It is God the only Son,*e* who is close to the Father's heart,*f* who has made him known.

The Testimony of John the Baptist
(Mt 3.1–12; Mk 1.1–8; Lk 3.1–20)

19 This is the testimony given by John when the Jews sent priests and Lē'vītes from Jerusalem to ask him, "Who are you?" 20 He confessed and did not deny it, but confessed, "I am not the Messiah."*g* 21 And they asked him, "What then? Are you E•lī'-jah?" He said, "I am not." "Are you the prophet?" He answered, "No." 22 Then they said to him, "Who are you? Let us have an answer for those who sent us. What do you say about yourself?" 23 He said,

"I am the voice of one crying out in the
wilderness,
'Make straight the way of the Lord,' "
as the prophet Ī•sāi'ah said.

24 Now they had been sent from the Phar'i•sees. 25 They asked him, "Why then are you baptizing if you are neither the Messiah,*g* nor E•lī'jah, nor the prophet?" 26 John answered them, "I baptize with

---

a Or 3*through him. And without him not one thing came into being that has come into being.* 4*In him was life* *b* Or *He was the true light that enlightens everyone coming into the world* *c* Or *to his own home* *d* Or *the Father's only Son* *e* Other ancient authorities read *It is an only Son, God,* or *It is the only Son* *f* Gk *bosom* *g* Or *the Christ*

The "Cosmic Christ"

Science fiction or fantasy movies and books often include important eternal beings or powers. The *Star Wars* series has "the Force." *The Chronicles of Narnia,* a fantasy series by C. S. Lewis, has Aslan, the noble lion who is the creator and savior of Narnia.

The poem that begins the Gospel of John reads like something from a great science fiction classic. Only, in this case, the story is not fiction but God's revelation! The poem presents Jesus as the Word, who has existed from all time, the one through whom all things came into being. The Scriptures tell us a great mystery here: the man named Jesus, who lived in Nazareth some two thousand years ago, is the eternal God, who "became flesh and lived among us" (Jn 1.14). No one has ever seen God. But Jesus, the perfect image of God, "has made him known" (verse 18) in flesh and blood.

Many people in the Gospel of John do not recognize or accept Jesus, and many people still do not today. What does it mean for you to accept Jesus?

▶ Jn 1.1–18

---

water. Among you stands one whom you do not know, 27 the one who is coming after me; I am not worthy to untie the thong of his sandal." 28 This took place in Beth′a•ny across the Jordan where John was baptizing.

The Lamb of God
(Mt 3.13–17; Mk 1.9–11; Lk 3.21–22)

29 The next day he saw Jesus coming toward him and declared, "Here is the Lamb of God who takes away the sin of the world! 30 This is he of whom I said, 'After me comes a man who ranks ahead of me because he was before me.' 31 I myself did not know him; but I came baptizing with water for this reason, that he might be revealed to Israel." 32 And John testified, "I saw the Spirit descending from heaven like a dove, and it remained on him. 33 I myself did not know him, but the one who sent me to baptize with water said to me, 'He on whom you see the Spirit descend and remain is the one who baptizes with the Holy Spirit.' 34 And I myself have seen and have testified that this is the Son of God."[h]

The First Disciples of Jesus

35 The next day John again was standing with two of his disciples, 36 and as he watched Jesus walk by, he exclaimed, "Look, here is the Lamb of God!" 37 The two disciples heard him say this, and they followed Jesus. 38 When Jesus turned and saw them following, he said to them, "What are you looking for?" They said to him, "Rabbi" (which translated means Teacher), "where are you staying?" 39 He said to them, "Come and see." They came and saw where he was staying, and they remained with him that day. It was about four o'clock in the afternoon.

40 One of the two who heard John speak and followed him was Andrew, Simon Peter's brother. 41 He first found his brother Simon and said to him, "We have found the Messiah" (which is translated Anointed[i]). 42 He brought Simon[j] to Jesus, who looked at him and said, "You are Simon son of John. You are to be called Ce′phas" (which is translated Peter[k]).

Jesus Calls Philip and Nathanael

43 The next day Jesus decided to go to Galilee. He found Philip and said to him, "Follow me." 44 Now Philip was from Beth•sa′i•da, the city of Andrew and Peter. 45 Philip found Na•than′a•el and said to him, "We have found him about whom Moses in the law and also the prophets wrote, Jesus son of Joseph from Nazareth." 46 Na•than′a•el said to him, "Can anything good come out of Nazareth?" Philip said to him, "Come and see." 47 When Jesus saw Na•than′a•el coming toward him, he said of him, "Here is truly an Israelite in whom there is no deceit!" 48 Na•than′a•el asked him, "Where did you get to know me?" Jesus answered, "I saw you under the fig tree before Philip called you." 49 Na•than′a•el replied, "Rabbi, you are the Son of God! You are the King of Israel!" 50 Jesus answered, "Do you believe because I told you that I saw you under the fig tree? You will see greater things than these." 51 And he said to him, "Very truly, I tell you,[l] you will see heaven opened and the angels of God ascending and descending upon the Son of Man."

---

h Other ancient authorities read *is God's chosen one*
i Or *Christ*   j Gk *him*   k From the word for *rock* in Aramaic (*kepha*) and Greek (*petra*), respectively   l Both instances of the Greek word for *you* in this verse are plural

The Wedding at Cana

2 On the third day there was a wedding in Cā́na of Galilee, and the mother of Jesus was there. ² Jesus and his disciples had also been invited to the wedding. ³ When the wine gave out, the mother of Jesus said to him, "They have no wine." ⁴ And Jesus said to her, "Woman, what concern is that to you and to me? My hour has not yet come." ⁵ His mother said to the servants, "Do whatever he tells you." ⁶ Now standing there were six stone water jars for the Jewish rites of purification, each holding twenty or thirty gallons. ⁷ Jesus said to them, "Fill the jars with water." And they filled them up to the brim. ⁸ He said to them, "Now draw some out, and take it to the chief steward." So they took it. ⁹ When the steward tasted the water that had become wine, and did not know where it came from (though the servants who had drawn the water knew), the steward called the bridegroom ¹⁰ and said to him, "Everyone serves the good wine first, and then the inferior wine after the guests have become drunk. But you have kept the good wine until now." ¹¹ Jesus did this, the first of his signs, in Cā́na of Galilee, and revealed his glory; and his disciples believed in him.

12 After this he went down to Ca·per′na·um with his mother, his brothers, and his disciples; and they remained there a few days.

Jesus Cleanses the Temple
(Mt 21.12–17; Mk 11.15–19; Lk 19.45–48)

13 The Passover of the Jews was near, and Jesus went up to Jerusalem. ¹⁴ In the temple he found people selling cattle, sheep, and doves, and the

---

did you KNOW?

Righteous Anger

Shouting! Tipping over tables! These are signs of anger. Some people might even label this behavior as out of control. But Jesus does not strike anyone with the whip; he only drives out the animals. He is not out of control, but he certainly is angry!

Even though we are often told that we should not show anger, sometimes it is appropriate to do so. Righteous anger is a reaction to an injustice or something that is not right. Jesus is upset because the greedy merchants and Temple officials have made the Temple a marketplace and have defiled the sacred space. He controls his righteous anger and channels it in a civil and religious challenge against the corrupt and greedy leaders. Righteous anger should be expressed in ways that challenge evil and unjust situations but never in ways that cause violence or injury to another person.

What situations in your life or in the world might call for a response of righteous anger? How might you express your anger without going out of control?

▶ Jn 2.13–17

J
N

The First Sign

LIVE IT!

If there is one day that people want to go exactly as planned, it's usually a wedding day. Months of planning, and usually lots of money, go into ensuring that the big day will go smoothly. Imagine if there wasn't enough food to feed everyone! How embarrassing! Imagine if the cake never arrived, or if there wasn't enough wine for all the guests!

This is exactly what happens at the wedding at Cana. Jesus is there, along with his followers and his mother, Mary. Mary mentions to Jesus that they are running out of wine. Take a moment to study Jesus' reaction to his mother's comment. Does it seem a bit strange? Why do you think Jesus hesitates? Why does Mary persist?

In the Gospel of John, this is the first of seven miracles, or as John calls them, signs, that Jesus performs. How is this miracle different from all the others that Jesus performs? Why do you think this one is first? What happens because of this miracle? What might it be a sign of? Take a few moments to ponder these questions about this intriguing incident in the life of Jesus.

▶ Jn 2.1–11

did you KNOW?

"The Jews" in the Gospel of John

When you read the Gospel of John, you may notice that the Gospel writer often makes negative references to "the Jews." They are often portrayed questioning (2.18) or challenging Jesus. When the Gospel was being written, many Jews were persecuting Christian Jews who still worshiped in the synagogues. As a result, the Gospel writer lumps all Jews together, portraying them as the "bad guys." Christian churches teach that we should not take John's references to "the Jews" as a basis for prejudice or anger against Jewish people.

▶ Jn 2.18–20

money changers seated at their tables. 15 Making a whip of cords, he drove all of them out of the temple, both the sheep and the cattle. He also poured out the coins of the money changers and overturned their tables. 16 He told those who were selling the doves, "Take these things out of here! Stop making my Father's house a marketplace!" 17 His disciples remembered that it was written, "Zeal for your house will consume me." 18 The Jews then said to him, "What sign can you show us for doing this?" 19 Jesus answered them, "Destroy this tem-

ple, and in three days I will raise it up." 20 The Jews then said, "This temple has been under construction for forty-six years, and will you raise it up in three days?" 21 But he was speaking of the temple of his body. 22 After he was raised from the dead, his disciples remembered that he had said this; and they believed the scripture and the word that Jesus had spoken.

23 When he was in Jerusalem during the Passover festival, many believed in his name because they saw the signs that he was doing. 24 But Jesus on his part would not entrust himself to them, because he knew all people 25 and needed no one to testify about anyone; for he himself knew what was in everyone.

Nicodemus Visits Jesus

3 Now there was a Phar'i·see named Nic·o·dē'-mus, a leader of the Jews. 2 He came to Jesus[m] by night and said to him, "Rabbi, we know that you are a teacher who has come from God; for no one can do these signs that you do apart from the presence of God." 3 Jesus answered him, "Very truly, I tell you, no one can see the kingdom of God without being born from above."[n] 4 Nic·o·dē'mus said to him, "How can anyone be born after having grown old? Can one enter a second time into the mother's womb and be born?" 5 Jesus answered, "Very truly, I tell you, no one can enter the kingdom of God without being born of water and Spirit. 6 What is born of the flesh is flesh, and what is born of the Spirit is spirit.[o] 7 Do not be astonished that I said to you, 'You[p] must be born from above.'[q] 8 The wind[o] blows where it chooses, and you hear

---

m Gk *him* n Or *born anew* o The same Greek word means both *wind* and *spirit* p The Greek word for *you* here is plural q Or *anew*

Nic at Night

LIVE IT!

Nicodemus, a Jewish teacher with a high position of leadership, is meeting secretly with Jesus. Nicodemus has been waiting for a sign that God's promise of salvation through a savior will happen in his lifetime. He senses that maybe Jesus is this savior. But he does not yet believe in Jesus, as is emphasized by his coming to Jesus "by night" (Jn 3.2). Speaking symbolically, Jesus outlines what it takes for salvation: to believe in Jesus as the one sent by God and to be born again through Baptism and the Holy Spirit. The same is true for people today.

Nicodemus knew that to accept Jesus publicly would put him in bad standing with the other Jewish leaders. Sometimes, we must make choices that might make us look foolish to others. How hard would it be for you to express belief in Jesus publicly? Will you be a believer in the night or in the light?

▶ Jn 3.1–21

the sound of it, but you do not know where it comes from or where it goes. So it is with everyone who is born of the Spirit." 9 Nic•o•de′mus said to him, "How can these things be?" 10 Jesus answered him, "Are you a teacher of Israel, and yet you do not understand these things?

11 "Very truly, I tell you, we speak of what we know and testify to what we have seen; yet you[r] do not receive our testimony. 12 If I have told you about earthly things and you do not believe, how can you believe if I tell you about heavenly things? 13 No one has ascended into heaven except the one who descended from heaven, the Son of Man.[s] 14 And just as Moses lifted up the serpent in the wilderness, so must the Son of Man be lifted up, 15 that whoever believes in him may have eternal life.[t]

16 "For God so loved the world that he gave his only Son, so that everyone who believes in him may not perish but may have eternal life.

17 "Indeed, God did not send the Son into the world to condemn the world, but in order that the world might be saved through him. 18 Those who believe in him are not condemned; but those who do not believe are condemned already, because they have not believed in the name of the only Son of God. 19 And this is the judgment, that the light has come into the world, and people loved darkness rather than light because their deeds were evil. 20 For all who do evil hate the light and do not come to the light, so that their deeds may not be exposed. 21 But those who do what is true come to the light, so that it may be clearly seen that their deeds have been done in God."[t]

Jesus and John the Baptist

22 After this Jesus and his disciples went into the Judean countryside, and he spent some time there with them and baptized. 23 John also was baptizing at Ae′non near Sā′lim because water was abundant there; and people kept coming and were being baptized 24 —John, of course, had not yet been thrown into prison.

25 Now a discussion about purification arose between John's disciples and a Jew.[u] 26 They came to John and said to him, "Rabbi, the one who was with you across the Jordan, to whom you testified, here he is baptizing, and all are going to him." 27 John answered, "No one can receive anything except what has been given from heaven. 28 You yourselves are my witnesses that I said, 'I am not the Messiah,[v] but I have been sent ahead of him.' 29 He

---

[r] The Greek word for *you* here and in verse 12 is plural
[s] Other ancient authorities add *who is in heaven*   [t] Some interpreters hold that the quotation concludes with verse 15
[u] Other ancient authorities read *the Jews*   [v] Or *the Christ*

Catholic Connections

ARE YOU BORN AGAIN?

Rani was confused. Some of her Christian friends from school had approached her and asked if she had been saved and born again. She told them that she was Catholic and went to Mass every Sunday. Her friends told her that in order to be saved, she had to claim Jesus as her personal Lord and Savior and be baptized in the Holy Spirit. Her friends' claims caused her to worry that she might somehow not be okay with God.

In the Gospel of John, chapter 3, Jesus tells Nicodemus that no one can enter the kingdom of God unless born of water and the Holy Spirit. Some Christian churches interpret this passage to mean that one must make a conscious decision to be baptized (Baptism as an infant doesn't count) and make a public witness, or altar call, acknowledging the lordship of Jesus in one's life.

The Catholic church teaches that Baptism is a sacrament that brings us into special relationship with God. Through Baptism, we become temples of the Holy Spirit, members of the church, and God's adopted daughters and sons, through Christ. We may not have asked to be baptized, but each day we choose to be in relationship with Jesus. We renew our baptismal grace every day of our life when we live as Jesus calls us to live. And when, as disciples of Jesus, we celebrate the Eucharist and Penance and Reconciliation, we proclaim that Jesus is our Lord and Savior, whose saving death and Resurrection have brought us new life.

So how should Rani and the rest of us respond the next time someone asks if we are born again? We should say: "Yes—every day! I was baptized in the name of the Father and the Son and the Holy Spirit, and I try to live in the Spirit of Christ each and every day."

▶ Jn 3.3–8

J
N

who has the bride is the bridegroom. The friend of the bridegroom, who stands and hears him, rejoices greatly at the bridegroom's voice. For this reason my joy has been fulfilled. 30 He must increase, but I must decrease."w

The One Who Comes from Heaven

31 The one who comes from above is above all; the one who is of the earth belongs to the earth and speaks about earthly things. The one who comes from heaven is above all. 32 He testifies to what he has seen and heard, yet no one accepts his testimony. 33 Whoever has accepted his testimony has certifiedx this, that God is true. 34 He whom God has sent speaks the words of God, for he gives the Spirit without measure. 35 The Father loves the Son and has placed all things in his hands. 36 Whoever believes in the Son has eternal life; whoever disobeys the Son will not see life, but must endure God's wrath.

Jesus and the Woman of Samaria

4 Now when Jesusy learned that the Phar'i·sees had heard, "Jesus is making and baptizing more disciples than John" 2—although it was not Jesus himself but his disciples who baptized— 3 he left Judea and started back to Galilee. 4 But he had

did you KNOW?

Why Are the Disciples Surprised?

The disciples "were astonished that he [Jesus] was speaking with a woman" (Jn 4.27). For several reasons, it was unusual for Jesus to be talking to her. First, in first-century Israel, men did not talk to women, especially strangers, in public places. Second, Jews did not talk to Samaritans (see "Who Belongs, and Who Does Not?" Ezra, chapters 9–10, and "Discrimination in Jesus' Time," Lk 10.25–37), who were considered guilty of false worship (Jn 4.20). And finally, the woman with whom Jesus was speaking was a known sinner, having married far too many times.

This episode is one more example in the Gospel of John that shows Jesus is not bound by customs and stereotypes when the message of the Gospel is at stake.

▸ Jn 4.1–42

PRAY IT

How Deep Is Your Well?

In Jn 4.1–42, Jesus engages a Samaritan woman in conversation. She has no idea who Jesus is and what living water he is referring to, but she stands and listens. She is changed as a result. She comes to believe in Jesus and goes to tell others about the Messiah. John uses her as a role model for those who believe.

Look inside the well of faith within you. How deep is that well? Do you thirst for a deeper relationship with Jesus? Are you ready to share the Good News with others? Jesus invites each of us to join with him in a personal relationship. All we have to do is ask. Begin your relationship with Jesus by praying:

Jesus, you are the Messiah, the anointed one. I am thirsty. . . . Quench my thirst.

▸ Jn 4.1–42

to go through Sa·mar'i·a. 5 So he came to a Sa·mar'i·tan city called Sy'char, near the plot of ground that Jacob had given to his son Joseph. 6 Jacob's well was there, and Jesus, tired out by his journey, was sitting by the well. It was about noon.

7 A Sa·mar'i·tan woman came to draw water, and Jesus said to her, "Give me a drink." 8 (His disciples had gone to the city to buy food.) 9 The Sa·mar'i·tan woman said to him, "How is it that you, a Jew, ask a drink of me, a woman of Sa·mar'i·a?" (Jews do not share things in common with Sa·mar'i·tans.)z 10 Jesus answered her, "If you knew the gift of God, and who it is that is saying to you, 'Give me a drink,' you would have asked him, and he would have given you living water." 11 The woman said to him, "Sir, you have no bucket, and the well is deep. Where do you get that living water? 12 Are you greater than our ancestor Jacob, who gave us the well, and with his sons and his flocks drank from it?" 13 Jesus said to her, "Everyone who

w Some interpreters hold that the quotation continues through verse 36   x Gk set a seal to   y Other ancient authorities read the Lord   z Other ancient authorities lack this sentence

THIS IS CHRISTMAS

This poem, by Masao and Fumiko Takenaka of Japan, is a reflection on Jesus as "living water" (Jn 4.10):

> One who said I am the eternal water
> Dwelt among us
> Living with us
> Sustaining us
> This is Christmas.
>
> To receive a cup of living water
> Is not only to cleanse ourselves
> But also to cleanse all the waters.
> River and well, lake and ocean,
> And to share them with all.
> This is Christmas.

(From Maren C. Tirabassi and Kathy Wonson Eddy, editors,
Gifts of Many Cultures, p. 144)

▶ Jn 4.1–15

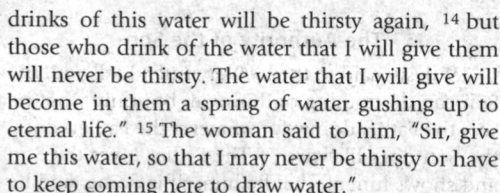

drinks of this water will be thirsty again, 14 but those who drink of the water that I will give them will never be thirsty. The water that I will give will become in them a spring of water gushing up to eternal life." 15 The woman said to him, "Sir, give me this water, so that I may never be thirsty or have to keep coming here to draw water."

16 Jesus said to her, "Go, call your husband, and come back." 17 The woman answered him, "I have no husband." Jesus said to her, "You are right in saying, 'I have no husband'; 18 for you have had five husbands, and the one you have now is not your husband. What you have said is true!" 19 The woman said to him, "Sir, I see that you are a prophet. 20 Our ancestors worshiped on this mountain, but you*a* say that the place where people must worship is in Jerusalem." 21 Jesus said to her, "Woman, believe me, the hour is coming when you will worship the Father neither on this mountain nor in Jerusalem. 22 You worship what you do not know; we worship what we know, for salvation is from the Jews. 23 But the hour is coming, and is now here, when the true worshipers will worship the Father in spirit and truth, for the Father seeks such as these to worship him. 24 God is spirit, and those who worship him must worship in spirit and

truth." 25 The woman said to him, "I know that Messiah is coming" (who is called Christ). "When he comes, he will proclaim all things to us." 26 Jesus said to her, "I am he,*b* the one who is speaking to you."

27 Just then his disciples came. They were astonished that he was speaking with a woman, but no one said, "What do you want?" or, "Why are you speaking with her?" 28 Then the woman left her water jar and went back to the city. She said to the people, 29 "Come and see a man who told me everything I have ever done! He cannot be the Messiah,*c* can he?" 30 They left the city and were on their way to him.

31 Meanwhile the disciples were urging him, "Rabbi, eat something." 32 But he said to them, "I have food to eat that you do not know about." 33 So the disciples said to one another, "Surely no one has brought him something to eat?" 34 Jesus said to them, "My food is to do the will of him who sent me and to complete his work. 35 Do you not say, 'Four months more, then comes the harvest'? But I tell you, look around you, and see how the fields

---

a The Greek word for *you* here and in verses 21 and 22 is plural   *b* Gk *I am*   *c* Or *the Christ* are ripe for harvesting. 36 The reaper is already receiving[d] wages and is gathering fruit for eternal life, so that sower and reaper may rejoice together. 37 For here the saying holds true, 'One sows and another reaps.' 38 I sent you to reap that for which you did not labor. Others have labored, and you have entered into their labor."

39 Many Sa•mār′i•tans from that city believed in him because of the woman's testimony, "He told me everything I have ever done." 40 So when the Sa•mār′i•tans came to him, they asked him to stay with them; and he stayed there two days. 41 And many more believed because of his word. 42 They said to the woman, "It is no longer because of what you said that we believe, for we have heard for ourselves, and we know that this is truly the Savior of the world."

Jesus Returns to Galilee

43 When the two days were over, he went from that place to Galilee 44 (for Jesus himself had testified that a prophet has no honor in the prophet's own country). 45 When he came to Galilee, the Galileans welcomed him, since they had seen all that he had done in Jerusalem at the festival; for they too had gone to the festival.

Jesus Heals an Official's Son

46 Then he came again to Cā′na in Galilee where he had changed the water into wine. Now there was a royal official whose son lay ill in Ca•per′na•um. 47 When he heard that Jesus had come from Judea to Galilee, he went and begged him to come down and heal his son, for he was at the point of death. 48 Then Jesus said to him, "Unless you[e] see signs and wonders you will not believe." 49 The official said to him, "Sir, come down before my little boy dies." 50 Jesus said to him, "Go; your son will live." The man believed the word that Jesus spoke to him and started on his way. 51 As he was going down, his slaves met him and told him that his child was alive. 52 So he asked them the hour when he began to recover, and they said to him, "Yesterday at one in the afternoon the fever left him." 53 The father realized that this was the hour when Jesus had said to him, "Your son will live." So he himself believed, along with his whole household. 54 Now this was the second sign that Jesus did after coming from Judea to Galilee.

Jesus Heals on the Sabbath

5 After this there was a festival of the Jews, and Jesus went up to Jerusalem.

2 Now in Jerusalem by the Sheep Gate there is a pool, called in Hebrew[f] Beth-zā′tha,[g] which has five porticoes. 3 In these lay many invalids—blind, lame, and paralyzed.[h] 5 One man was there who had been ill for thirty-eight years. 6 When Jesus saw him lying there and knew that he had been there a long time, he said to him, "Do you want to be made well?" 7 The sick man answered him, "Sir, I have no one to put me into the pool when the water is stirred up; and while I am making my way, someone else steps down ahead of me." 8 Jesus said to him, "Stand up, take your mat and walk." 9 At once the man was made well, and he took up his mat and began to walk.

Now that day was a sabbath. 10 So the Jews said to the man who had been cured, "It is the sabbath; it is not lawful for you to carry your mat." 11 But he answered them, "The man who made me well said to me, 'Take up your mat and walk.' " 12 They asked him, "Who is the man who said to you, 'Take it up and walk'?" 13 Now the man who had been healed did not know who it was, for Jesus had disappeared in[i] the crowd that was there. 14 Later Jesus found him in the temple and said to him, "See, you have been made well! Do not sin any more, so that nothing worse happens to you." 15 The man went away and told the Jews that it was Jesus who had made him well. 16 Therefore the Jews started persecuting Jesus, because he was doing such things on the sabbath. 17 But Jesus answered them, "My Father is still working, and I also am working." 18 For this reason the Jews were seeking all the more to kill him, because he was not only breaking the sabbath, but was also calling God his own Father, thereby making himself equal to God.

The Authority of the Son

19 Jesus said to them, "Very truly, I tell you, the Son can do nothing on his own, but only what he sees the Father doing; for whatever the Father[j] does, the Son does likewise. 20 The Father loves the Son and shows him all that he himself is doing; and he will show him greater works than these, so that you will be astonished. 21 Indeed, just as the Father raises the dead and gives them life, so also the Son gives life to whomever he wishes. 22 The Father judges no one but has given all judgment to the Son, 23 so that all may honor the Son just as they honor the Father. Anyone who does not honor the Son does not honor the Father who sent him. 24 Very truly, I tell you, anyone who hears my word

---

d Or 35. . . . the fields are already ripe for harvesting. 36 The reaper is receiving   e Both instances of the Greek word for you in this verse are plural   f That is, Aramaic   g Other ancient authorities read Bethesda, others Bethsaida   h Other ancient authorities add, wholly or in part, waiting for the stirring of the water; 4 for an angel of the Lord went down at certain seasons into the pool, and stirred up the water; whoever stepped in first after the stirring of the water was made well from whatever disease that person had.   i Or had left because of j Gk that one and believes him who sent me has eternal life, and does not come under judgment, but has passed from death to life.

25 "Very truly, I tell you, the hour is coming, and is now here, when the dead will hear the voice of the Son of God, and those who hear will live. 26 For just as the Father has life in himself, so he has granted the Son also to have life in himself; 27 and he has given him authority to execute judgment, because he is the Son of Man. 28 Do not be astonished at this; for the hour is coming when all who are in their graves will hear his voice 29 and will come out—those who have done good, to the resurrection of life, and those who have done evil, to the resurrection of condemnation.

Witnesses to Jesus

30 "I can do nothing on my own. As I hear, I judge; and my judgment is just, because I seek to do not my own will but the will of him who sent me.

31 "If I testify about myself, my testimony is not true. 32 There is another who testifies on my behalf, and I know that his testimony to me is true. 33 You sent messengers to John, and he testified to the truth. 34 Not that I accept such human testimony, but I say these things so that you may be saved. 35 He was a burning and shining lamp, and you were willing to rejoice for a while in his light. 36 But I have a testimony greater than John's. The works that the Father has given me to complete, the very works that I am doing, testify on my behalf that the Father has sent me. 37 And the Father who sent me has himself testified on my behalf. You have never heard his voice or seen his form, 38 and you do not have his word abiding in you, because you do not believe him whom he has sent.

39 "You search the scriptures because you think that in them you have eternal life; and it is they that testify on my behalf. 40 Yet you refuse to come to me to have life. 41 I do not accept glory from human beings. 42 But I know that you do not have the love of God in[k] you. 43 I have come in my Father's name, and you do not accept me; if another comes in his own name, you will accept him. 44 How can you believe when you accept glory from one another and do not seek the glory that comes from the one who alone is God? 45 Do not think that I will accuse you before the Father; your accuser is Moses, on whom you have set your hope. 46 If you believed Moses, you would believe me, for he wrote about me. 47 But if you do not believe what he wrote, how will you believe what I say?"

did you KNOW?

"I Am" Sayings of Jesus

The Gospel of John contains a whole series of "I am" sayings as a way for Jesus to explain his role as the Messiah. For example:

- **"I am the bread of life" (6.35).**
- **"I am the light of the world" (8.12).**
- **"I am the gate for the sheep" (10.7).**
- **"I am the good shepherd" (10.11).**
- **"I am the resurrection and the life" (11.25).**
- **"I am the way, and the truth, and the life" (14.6).**
- **"I am the vine, you are the branches" (15.5).**

The "I am" sayings are also a means of establishing the divine nature of Jesus. Jesus' use of "I am" is similar to the revelation of God's name to Moses at the burning bush (Ex 3.14). Ironically, in John, the Jewish leaders are correct in thinking that Jesus is equating himself with God (5.18). But they are wrong in not recognizing that Jesus is right!

▶ Jn 5.16–18

Feeding the Five Thousand
(Mt 14.13–21; Mk 6.30–44; Lk 9.10–17)

6 After this Jesus went to the other side of the Sea of Galilee, also called the Sea of Tĭ·bē'-ri·as.[l] 2 A large crowd kept following him, because they saw the signs that he was doing for the sick. 3 Jesus went up the mountain and sat down there with his disciples. 4 Now the Passover, the festival of the Jews, was near. 5 When he looked up and saw a large crowd coming toward him, Jesus said to Philip, "Where are we to buy bread for these people to eat?" 6 He said this to test him, for he himself knew what he was going to do. 7 Philip answered him, "Six months' wages[m] would not buy enough bread for each of them to get a little." 8 One of his disciples, Andrew, Simon Peter's brother, said to him, 9 "There is a boy here who has five barley loaves and two fish. But what are they among so many people?" 10 Jesus said, "Make the people sit down." Now there was a great deal of grass in the

---

k Or *among*   *l* Gk *of Galilee of Tiberias*   *m* Gk *Two hundred denarii; the denarius was the usual day's wage for a laborer* place; so they[n] sat down, about five thousand in all. [11] Then Jesus took the loaves, and when he had given thanks, he distributed them to those who were seated; so also the fish, as much as they wanted. [12] When they were satisfied, he told his disciples, "Gather up the fragments left over, so that nothing may be lost." [13] So they gathered them up, and from the fragments of the five barley loaves, left by those who had eaten, they filled twelve baskets. [14] When the people saw the sign that he had done, they began to say, "This is indeed the prophet who is to come into the world."

[15] When Jesus realized that they were about to come and take him by force to make him king, he withdrew again to the mountain by himself.

Jesus Walks on the Water
(Mt 14.22–33; Mk 6.45–52)

[16] When evening came, his disciples went down to the sea, [17] got into a boat, and started across the sea to Ca·per'na·um. It was now dark, and Jesus had not yet come to them. [18] The sea became rough because a strong wind was blowing. [19] When they had rowed about three or four miles,[o] they saw Jesus walking on the sea and coming near the boat, and they were terrified. [20] But he said to them, "It is I;[p] do not be afraid." [21] Then they wanted to take him into the boat, and immediately the boat reached the land toward which they were going.

The Bread from Heaven

[22] The next day the crowd that had stayed on the other side of the sea saw that there had been only one boat there. They also saw that Jesus had not got into the boat with his disciples, but that his disciples had gone away alone. [23] Then some boats from Ti·be'ri·as came near the place where they had eaten the bread after the Lord had given thanks.[q] [24] So when the crowd saw that neither Jesus nor his disciples were there, they themselves got into the boats and went to Ca·per'na·um looking for Jesus.

[25] When they found him on the other side of the sea, they said to him, "Rabbi, when did you come here?" [26] Jesus answered them, "Very truly, I tell you, you are looking for me, not because you saw signs, but because you ate your fill of the loaves. [27] Do not work for the food that perishes, but for the food that endures for eternal life, which the Son of Man will give you. For it is on him that God the Father has set his seal." [28] Then they said to him, "What must we do to perform the works of God?" [29] Jesus answered them, "This is the work of God, that you believe in him whom he has sent." [30] So they said to him, "What sign are you going to give us then, so that we may see it and believe you? What work are you performing? [31] Our ancestors ate the manna in the wilderness; as it is written, 'He gave them bread from heaven to eat.' " [32] Then Jesus said to them, "Very truly, I tell you, it was not Moses who gave you the bread from heaven, but it is my Father who gives you the true bread from heaven. [33] For the bread of God is that which[r] comes down from heaven and gives life to the world." [34] They said to him, "Sir, give us this bread always."

[35] Jesus said to them, "I am the bread of life. Whoever comes to me will never be hungry, and whoever believes in me will never be thirsty. [36] But I said to you that you have seen me and yet do not believe. [37] Everything that the Father gives me will come to me, and anyone who comes to me I will never drive away; [38] for I have come down from heaven, not to do my own will, but the will of him

JN

PRAY IT!
A Little Gift Goes a Long Way

God, could you use me like the boy who helped feed the five thousand? Out of the thousands of people gathered to see you, you chose a young person, took his five loaves and two fish, and made sure thousands had more than their fill to eat (Jn 6.1–13).

I wonder how those people felt when that little bit of food was offered by a youth? Were they embarrassed by the boy's foolishness? Or did they feel guilty that they had not offered their own food? Regardless, you accepted the gift and did fantastic things with it.

Could you do the same with me? Could you take my simple gifts and do wondrous things with them? I'm just afraid that my gifts will be rejected. It is risky, Lord, and I do not do well with risks, remember?

Help me to take the risk and let you use the gifts I have, trusting that it doesn't matter what other people think. Even if things don't work out as I plan, I'll trust that you are in charge and know better than I do. Thanks, God—and wish me luck! Amen.

▶ Jn 6.1–14

---

[n] Gk *the men*   [o] Gk *about twenty-five or thirty stadia*
[p] Gk *I am*   [q] Other ancient authorities lack *after the Lord had given thanks*   [r] Or *he who*

PRAY IT
The Eucharist

Jesus calls himself the "bread of life" (Jn 6.35). Some type of bread is part of the basic diet of almost every culture. Thus, in a symbolic way, Jesus is telling us that he is part of the basic diet for spiritual life. And just as bread is shared and valued in every culture, Jesus shares himself with all people who are willing to believe.

Many of Jesus' early followers were troubled when he taught that they must eat his flesh and drink his blood in order to have true life (verses 56–60). The confusion and arguing among his listeners are understandable; his words must have sounded strange. Yet this teaching about the body and blood of Christ (which is portrayed in the Last Supper in Matthew, Mark, and Luke) is central to the Catholic faith. Catholics believe that Jesus is really present with us and nourishes us when we celebrate the Eucharist together, the bread and wine being changed into the body and blood of Christ.

In your prayer, reflect or journal on the following questions:

- How is Jesus a source of nourishment for you?
- How does celebrating the Eucharist help you recognize more clearly Jesus' presence?
- How are you called to be the body and blood of Christ to the world around you?

▸ John, chapter 6

I will raise that person up on the last day. 45 It is written in the prophets, 'And they shall all be taught by God.' Everyone who has heard and learned from the Father comes to me. 46 Not that anyone has seen the Father except the one who is from God; he has seen the Father. 47 Very truly, I tell you, whoever believes has eternal life. 48 I am the bread of life. 49 Your ancestors ate the manna in the wilderness, and they died. 50 This is the bread that comes down from heaven, so that one may eat of it and not die. 51 I am the living bread that came down from heaven. Whoever eats of this bread will live forever; and the bread that I will give for the life of the world is my flesh."

52 The Jews then disputed among themselves, saying, "How can this man give us his flesh to eat?" 53 So Jesus said to them, "Very truly, I tell you, unless you eat the flesh of the Son of Man and drink his blood, you have no life in you. 54 Those who eat my flesh and drink my blood have eternal life, and I will raise them up on the last day; 55 for my flesh is true food and my blood is true drink. 56 Those who eat my flesh and drink my blood abide in me, and I in them. 57 Just as the living Father sent me, and I live because of the Father, so whoever eats me will live because of me. 58 This is the bread that came down from heaven, not like that which your ancestors ate, and they died. But the one who eats this bread will live forever." 59 He said these things while he was teaching in the synagogue at Ca·per·na·um.

The Words of Eternal Life

60 When many of his disciples heard it, they said, "This teaching is difficult; who can accept it?" 61 But Jesus, being aware that his disciples were complaining about it, said to them, "Does this offend you? 62 Then what if you were to see the Son of Man ascending to where he was before? 63 It is the spirit that gives life; the flesh is useless. The words that I have spoken to you are spirit and life. 64 But among you there are some who do not believe." For Jesus knew from the first who were the ones that did not believe, and who was the one that would betray him. 65 And he said, "For this reason I have told you that no one can come to me unless it is granted by the Father."

66 Because of this many of his disciples turned back and no longer went about with him. 67 So Jesus asked the twelve, "Do you also wish to go away?" 68 Simon Peter answered him, "Lord, to whom can we go? You have the words of eternal life. 69 We have come to believe and know that you are the Holy One of God."s 70 Jesus answered them,

who sent me. 39 And this is the will of him who sent me, that I should lose nothing of all that he has given me, but raise it up on the last day. 40 This is indeed the will of my Father, that all who see the Son and believe in him may have eternal life; and I will raise them up on the last day."

41 Then the Jews began to complain about him because he said, "I am the bread that came down from heaven." 42 They were saying, "Is not this Jesus, the son of Joseph, whose father and mother we know? How can he now say, 'I have come down from heaven'?" 43 Jesus answered them, "Do not complain among yourselves. 44 No one can come to me unless drawn by the Father who sent me; and

s Other ancient authorities read *the Christ, the Son of the living God*

"Did I not choose you, the twelve? Yet one of you is a devil." 71 He was speaking of Judas son of Simon Is•car'i•ot,[t] for he, though one of the twelve, was going to betray him.

The Unbelief of Jesus' Brothers

7 After this Jesus went about in Galilee. He did not wish[u] to go about in Judea because the Jews were looking for an opportunity to kill him. 2 Now the Jewish festival of Booths[v] was near. 3 So his brothers said to him, "Leave here and go to Judea so that your disciples also may see the works you are doing; 4 for no one who wants[w] to be widely known acts in secret. If you do these things, show yourself to the world." 5 (For not even his brothers believed in him.) 6 Jesus said to them, "My time has not yet come, but your time is always here. 7 The world cannot hate you, but it hates me because I testify against it that its works are evil. 8 Go to the festival yourselves. I am not[x] going to this festival, for my time has not yet fully come." 9 After saying this, he remained in Galilee.

Jesus at the Festival of Booths

10 But after his brothers had gone to the festival, then he also went, not publicly but as it were[y] in secret. 11 The Jews were looking for him at the festival and saying, "Where is he?" 12 And there was considerable complaining about him among the crowds. While some were saying, "He is a good man," others were saying, "No, he is deceiving the crowd." 13 Yet no one would speak openly about him for fear of the Jews.

14 About the middle of the festival Jesus went up into the temple and began to teach. 15 The Jews were astonished at it, saying, "How does this man have such learning,[z] when he has never been taught?" 16 Then Jesus answered them, "My teaching is not mine but his who sent me. 17 Anyone who resolves to do the will of God will know whether the teaching is from God or whether I am speaking on my own. 18 Those who speak on their own seek their own glory; but the one who seeks the glory of him who sent him is true, and there is nothing false in him.

19 "Did not Moses give you the law? Yet none of you keeps the law. Why are you looking for an opportunity to kill me?" 20 The crowd answered, "You have a demon! Who is trying to kill you?" 21 Jesus answered them, "I performed one work, and all of you are astonished. 22 Moses gave you circumcision (it is, of course, not from Moses, but from the patriarchs), and you circumcise a man on the sabbath. 23 If a man receives circumcision on the sabbath in order that the law of Moses may not be broken, are you angry with me because I healed a man's whole body on the sabbath? 24 Do not judge by appearances, but judge with right judgment."

Is This the Christ?

25 Now some of the people of Jerusalem were saying, "Is not this the man whom they are trying to kill? 26 And here he is, speaking openly, but they say nothing to him! Can it be that the authorities really know that this is the Messiah?[a] 27 Yet we know where this man is from; but when the Messiah[a] comes, no one will know where he is from." 28 Then Jesus cried out as he was teaching in the temple, "You know me, and you know where I am from. I have not come on my own. But the one who sent me is true, and you do not know him. 29 I know him, because I am from him, and he sent me." 30 Then they tried to arrest him, but no one laid hands on him, because his hour had not yet come. 31 Yet many in the crowd believed in him and were saying, "When the Messiah[a] comes, will he do more signs than this man has done?"[b]

Officers Are Sent to Arrest Jesus

32 The Phar'i•sees heard the crowd muttering such things about him, and the chief priests and Phar'i•sees sent temple police to arrest him. 33 Jesus then said, "I will be with you a little while longer, and then I am going to him who sent me. 34 You will search for me, but you will not find me; and where I am, you cannot come." 35 The Jews said to one another, "Where does this man intend to go that we will not find him? Does he intend to go to the Dispersion among the Greeks and teach the Greeks? 36 What does he mean by saying, 'You will search for me and you will not find me' and 'Where I am, you cannot come'?"

Rivers of Living Water

37 On the last day of the festival, the great day, while Jesus was standing there, he cried out, "Let anyone who is thirsty come to me, 38 and let the one who believes in me drink. As[c] the scripture has said, 'Out of the believer's heart[d] shall flow rivers of living water.' " 39 Now he said this about the Spirit, which believers in him were to receive; for as yet there was no Spirit,[e] because Jesus was not yet glorified.

---

[t] Other ancient authorities read *Judas Iscariot son of Simon;* others, *Judas son of Simon from Karyot* (Kerioth)　[u] Other ancient authorities read *was not at liberty*　[v] Or *Tabernacles*　[w] Other ancient authorities read *wants it*　[x] Other ancient authorities add *yet*　[y] Other ancient authorities lack *as it were*　[z] Or *this man know his letters*　[a] Or *the Christ*　[b] Other ancient authorities read *is doing*　[c] Or *come to me and drink.* 38*The one who believes in me, as*　[d] Gk *out of his belly*　[e] Other ancient authorities read *for as yet the Spirit* (others, *Holy Spirit*) *had not been given*

did you KNOW?

Jesus Fulfills Jewish Feasts

In John, chapters 5–10, several references are made to four Old Testament feasts, which are also called festivals. On each feast, the author of John has Jesus say or do something that cleverly indicates he is the fulfillment of the feast's intent.

In chapter 5, after healing on the *Sabbath*, Jesus says, "My Father is still working, and I also am working" (verse 17). Essentially, he is declaring himself equal to God. In chapter 6, near the feast of the *Passover* (see "The Passover," Ex 12.14–28), Jesus feeds five thousand people and teaches that he is the bread of life. The implication is that the Eucharist, symbolizing Jesus' own sacrifice, has taken over the Passover meal and the sacrifice of the lamb.

Chapters 7–9 of John refer to the *feast of Booths*, also called tabernacles. This is a harvest festival that lasts for a whole week. Two of the main symbols of the feast of Booths are water and light. Jesus proclaims himself living water (7.38) and the light of the world (8.12).

Finally, the *feast of the Dedication*, sometimes called Hanukkah (see "Hanukkah," 1 Macc 4.52–59), is mentioned in chapter 10. During this festival, which celebrates the dedication of the Temple, Jesus claims to be the one who is consecrated and sent into the world (verse 26). In fulfilling these feasts, Jesus' divinity and his saving mission are made clear. But his actions also lead to continued conflicts with the Jewish leaders.

▸ John, chapters 5–10

Division among the People

40 When they heard these words, some in the crowd said, "This is really the prophet." 41 Others said, "This is the Messiah."*f* But some asked, "Surely the Messiah*f* does not come from Galilee, does he? 42 Has not the scripture said that the Messiah*f* is descended from David and comes from Bethlehem, the village where David lived?" 43 So there was a division in the crowd because of him. 44 Some of them wanted to arrest him, but no one laid hands on him.

The Unbelief of Those in Authority

45 Then the temple police went back to the chief priests and Phar'i•sees, who asked them, "Why did you not arrest him?" 46 The police answered, "Never has anyone spoken like this!" 47 Then the Phar'i•sees replied, "Surely you have not been deceived too, have you? 48 Has any one of the authorities or of the Phar'i•sees believed in him? 49 But this crowd, which does not know the law—they are accursed." 50 Nic•o•dē'mus, who had gone to Jesus*g* before, and who was one of them, asked, 51 "Our law does not judge people without first giving them a hearing to find out what they are doing, does it?" 52 They replied, "Surely you are not also from Galilee, are you? Search and you will see that no prophet is to arise from Galilee."

The Woman Caught in Adultery

8 ⟦53 Then each of them went home, 1 while Jesus went to the Mount of Olives. 2 Early in the morning he came again to the temple. All the people came to him and he sat down and began to teach them. 3 The scribes and the Phar'i•sees brought a woman who had been caught in adultery; and making her stand before all of them, 4 they said to him, "Teacher, this woman was caught in the very act of committing adultery. 5 Now in the law Moses commanded us to stone such women. Now what do you say?" 6 They said this to test him, so that they might have some charge to bring against him. Jesus bent down and wrote with his finger on the ground. 7 When they kept on questioning him, he straightened up and said to them, "Let anyone among you who is without sin be the first to throw a stone at her." 8 And once again he bent down and wrote on the ground.*h* 9 When they heard it, they went away, one by one, beginning with the elders; and Jesus was left alone with the woman standing before him. 10 Jesus straightened up and said to her, "Woman, where are they? Has no one condemned you?" 11 She said, "No one, sir."*i* And Jesus said, "Neither do I condemn you. Go your way, and from now on do not sin again."⟧*j*

Jesus the Light of the World

12 Again Jesus spoke to them, saying, "I am the light of the world. Whoever follows me will never walk in darkness but will have the light of life."

f Or *the Christ*   *g* Gk *him*   *h* Other ancient authorities add *the sins of each of them*   *i* Or *Lord*   *j* The most ancient authorities lack 7.53—8.11; other authorities add the passage here or after 7.36 or after 21.25 or after Luke 21.38, with variations of text; some mark the passage as doubtful.

Divine Compassion

Jesus was great at turning the tables on his enemies. In Jn 8.2–11, the scribes and Pharisees think they have come up with a perfect trap. He will have to either abandon his teaching on forgiveness and have a woman caught in adultery stoned to death according to the Law of Moses, or set himself up as being above the law. Either way, it will make him unpopular with the people. They know they have him!

With one amazing sentence, Jesus redefines the game. The focus moves away from the woman and onto the accusers, who cannot deny that they too are guilty of sin. The trap fails miserably, and the humbled religious leaders leave in silence.

We are often quick to notice the sinfulness of others while minimizing our own guilt. Jesus reminds us to be compassionate toward the sins of others. And notice how tenderly Christ dealt with the woman, whose dignity and reputation had been trampled upon. When you recognize your own guilt and stand exposed and shamed before God and others, remember that God is just as tender and compassionate toward you.

▸ Jn 8.2–11

13 Then the Phar′i·sees said to him, "You are testifying on your own behalf; your testimony is not valid." 14 Jesus answered, "Even if I testify on my own behalf, my testimony is valid because I know where I have come from and where I am going, but you do not know where I come from or where I am going. 15 You judge by human standards;*k* I judge no one. 16 Yet even if I do judge, my judgment is valid; for it is not I alone who judge, but I and the Father*l* who sent me. 17 In your law it is written that the testimony of two witnesses is valid. 18 I testify on my own behalf, and the Father who sent me testifies on my behalf." 19 Then they said to him,

---

k Gk *according to the flesh* *l* Other ancient authorities read *he*

THE SUN GIVES LIFE

The Sun, the Light of the world,
I hear Him coming,
I see His Face as He comes.
He makes the beings on earth happy,
And they rejoice.
O Wakan-Tanka, I offer to You this world of light . . .
I offer all to You. . . .
May all be attentive and behold! . . . that they may live.
                    (Black Elk, "The Sun Dance")

For many Native Americans, the sun is a symbol of the Great Spirit, or Wakan-Tanka. Black Elk's poem prayer has a strong parallel in the Gospel of John, when Jesus reveals his divinity by saying, "I am the light of the world" (8.12). In Christian spirituality, Jesus is sometimes called the Sun (or Son) of Righteousness.

▸ Jn 8.12–20

"Where is your Father?" Jesus answered, "You know neither me nor my Father. If you knew me, you would know my Father also." 20 He spoke these words while he was teaching in the treasury of the temple, but no one arrested him, because his hour had not yet come.

Jesus Foretells His Death

21 Again he said to them, "I am going away, and you will search for me, but you will die in your sin. Where I am going, you cannot come." 22 Then the Jews said, "Is he going to kill himself? Is that what he means by saying, 'Where I am going, you cannot come'?" 23 He said to them, "You are from below, I am from above; you are of this world, I am not of this world. 24 I told you that you would die in your sins, for you will die in your sins unless you believe that I am he."*m* 25 They said to him, "Who are you?" Jesus said to them, "Why do I speak to you at all?*n* 26 I have much to say about you and much to condemn; but the one who sent me is true, and I declare to the world what I have heard from him." 27 They did not understand that he was speaking to them about the Father. 28 So Jesus said, "When you have lifted up the Son of Man, then you will realize that I am he,*m* and that I do nothing on my own, but I speak these things as the Father instructed me. 29 And the one who sent me is with me; he has not left me alone, for I always do what

is pleasing to him." 30 As he was saying these things, many believed in him.

True Disciples

31 Then Jesus said to the Jews who had believed in him, "If you continue in my word, you are truly my disciples; 32 and you will know the truth, and the truth will make you free." 33 They answered him, "We are descendants of Abraham and have never been slaves to anyone. What do you mean by saying, 'You will be made free'?"

34 Jesus answered them, "Very truly, I tell you, everyone who commits sin is a slave to sin. 35 The slave does not have a permanent place in the household; the son has a place there forever. 36 So if the Son makes you free, you will be free indeed. 37 I know that you are descendants of Abraham; yet you look for an opportunity to kill me, because there is no place in you for my word. 38 I declare what I have seen in the Father's presence; as for you, you should do what you have heard from the Father."*o*

Jesus and Abraham

39 They answered him, "Abraham is our father." Jesus said to them, "If you were Abraham's

---

m Gk I am   *n* Or *What I have told you from the beginning*
o Other ancient authorities read *you do what you have heard from your father*

J
N

JESUS IS THE LIGHT OF LIFE!

Once again, the Gospel of John creates a sharp distinction between light and darkness, good and evil. Those who follow Jesus will never walk in darkness but will have the light of life. Light is a symbol of life, happiness, justice, and the joy of salvation and liberation in Christ. Darkness is a symbol of death, disgrace, tears, and imprisonment.

Certain cultures have a long tradition of lighting candles in church, at home, and at their job site. The candles symbolize the light that comes from Christ and guides us to true life.

We need the light of Christ to live with wholeness and integrity, and to give a proper value and place to material things and human activities. The light of Christ can direct us in our journey to God. Religious symbols and rituals are privileged means to help us remember the Gospel, give witness of the Gospel with our own life, and radiate God's love to those around us.

■ How do you transmit the light of Christ to others today?
■ Where in your life do you need the light of Christ?
■ Give thanks to Jesus for inviting you to share in the life of God.

▶ Jn 8.12–59

children, you would be doing[p] what Abraham did, [40] but now you are trying to kill me, a man who has told you the truth that I heard from God. This is not what Abraham did. [41] You are indeed doing what your father does." They said to him, "We are not illegitimate children; we have one father, God himself." [42] Jesus said to them, "If God were your Father, you would love me, for I came from God and now I am here. I did not come on my own, but he sent me. [43] Why do you not understand what I say? It is because you cannot accept my word. [44] You are from your father the devil, and you choose to do your father's desires. He was a murderer from the beginning and does not stand in the truth, because there is no truth in him. When he lies, he speaks according to his own nature, for he is a liar and the father of lies. [45] But because I tell the truth, you do not believe me. [46] Which of you convicts me of sin? If I tell the truth, why do you not believe me? [47] Whoever is from God hears the words of God. The reason you do not hear them is that you are not from God."

[48] The Jews answered him, "Are we not right in saying that you are a Sa•mar'i•tan and have a demon?" [49] Jesus answered, "I do not have a demon; but I honor my Father, and you dishonor me. [50] Yet I do not seek my own glory; there is one who seeks it and he is the judge. [51] Very truly, I tell you, whoever keeps my word will never see death." [52] The Jews said to him, "Now we know that you have a demon. Abraham died, and so did the prophets; yet you say, 'Whoever keeps my word will never taste death.' [53] Are you greater than our father Abraham, who died? The prophets also died. Who do you claim to be?" [54] Jesus answered, "If I glorify myself, my glory is nothing. It is my Father who glorifies me, he of whom you say, 'He is our God,' [55] though you do not know him. But I know him; if I would say that I do not know him, I would be a liar like you. But I do know him and I keep his word. [56] Your ancestor Abraham rejoiced that he would see my day; he saw it and was glad." [57] Then the Jews said to him, "You are not yet fifty years old, and have you seen Abraham?"[q] [58] Jesus said to them, "Very truly, I tell you, before Abraham was, I am." [59] So they picked up stones to throw at him, but Jesus hid himself and went out of the temple.

A Man Born Blind Receives Sight

9 As he walked along, he saw a man blind from birth. [2] His disciples asked him, "Rabbi, who sinned, this man or his parents, that he was born blind?" [3] Jesus answered, "Neither this man nor his parents sinned; he was born blind so that God's works might be revealed in him. [4] We[r] must work the works of him who sent me[s] while it is day; night is coming when no one can work. [5] As long as I am in the world, I am the light of the world." [6] When he had said this, he spat on the ground and made mud with the saliva and spread the mud on the man's eyes, [7] saying to him, "Go, wash in the pool of Si•lo'am" (which means Sent). Then he went and washed and came back able to see. [8] The neighbors and those who had seen him before as a beggar began to ask, "Is this not the man who used to sit and beg?" [9] Some were saying, "It is he." Others were saying, "No, but it is someone like him." He kept saying, "I am the man." [10] But they kept asking him, "Then how were your eyes opened?" [11] He answered, "The man called Jesus made mud, spread it on my eyes, and said to me, 'Go to Si•lo'am and wash.' Then I went and washed and received my sight." [12] They said to him, "Where is he?" He said, "I do not know."

The Pharisees Investigate the Healing

[13] They brought to the Phar'i•sees the man who had formerly been blind. [14] Now it was a sabbath day when Jesus made the mud and opened his eyes. [15] Then the Phar'i•sees also began to ask him how he had received his sight. He said to them, "He put mud on my eyes. Then I washed, and now I see." [16] Some of the Phar'i•sees said, "This man is not from God, for he does not observe the sabbath." But others said, "How can a man who is a sinner perform such signs?" And they were divided. [17] So they said again to the blind man, "What do you say about him? It was your eyes he opened." He said, "He is a prophet."

[18] The Jews did not believe that he had been blind and had received his sight until they called the parents of the man who had received his sight [19] and asked them, "Is this your son, who you say was born blind? How then does he now see?" [20] His parents answered, "We know that this is our son, and that he was born blind; [21] but we do not know how it is that now he sees, nor do we know who opened his eyes. Ask him; he is of age. He will speak for himself." [22] His parents said this because they were afraid of the Jews; for the Jews had already agreed that anyone who confessed Jesus[t] to be the Messiah[u] would be put out of the synagogue. [23] Therefore his parents said, "He is of age; ask him."

[24] So for the second time they called the man who had been blind, and they said to him, "Give glory to God! We know that this man is a sinner." [25] He answered, "I do not know whether he is a sin-

---

p Other ancient authorities read *If you are Abraham's children, then do*   q Other ancient authorities read *has Abraham seen you?*   r Other ancient authorities read *I*
s Other ancient authorities read *us*   t Gk *him*   u Or *the Christ*

ner. One thing I do know, that though I was blind, now I see." 26 They said to him, "What did he do to you? How did he open your eyes?" 27 He answered them, "I have told you already, and you would not listen. Why do you want to hear it again? Do you also want to become his disciples?" 28 Then they reviled him, saying, "You are his disciple, but we are disciples of Moses. 29 We know that God has spoken to Moses, but as for this man, we do not know where he comes from." 30 The man answered, "Here is an astonishing thing! You do not know where he comes from, and yet he opened my eyes. 31 We know that God does not listen to sinners, but he does listen to one who worships him and obeys his will. 32 Never since the world began has it been heard that anyone opened the eyes of a person born blind. 33 If this man were not from God, he could do nothing." 34 They answered him, "You were born entirely in sins, and are you trying to teach us?" And they drove him out.

Spiritual Blindness

35 Jesus heard that they had driven him out, and when he found him, he said, "Do you believe

PRAY IT!

Seeing with God's Eyes

Lord, can you fix my eyesight like you did for the blind man?

I want to see with your eyes those who are teased for being different at school.

I want to see with your eyes the homeless person on a park bench.

I want to see with your eyes people from other races and cultures.

I want to see more than people who think that being thinner or stronger makes you more lovable.

I want to see more than people who look at wealth and think that's what life is all about.

Help me to see with your eyes, Lord! Blind me to the way the world sees so that I won't give in to judging people on their looks or skin color or possessions or personality.

Help me to see, and to love, as you love, Lord—with eyes so wide open that they see past the outside and right into the heart of another.

▸ John, chapter 9

in the Son of Man?"[v] 36 He answered, "And who is he, sir?[w] Tell me, so that I may believe in him." 37 Jesus said to him, "You have seen him, and the one speaking with you is he." 38 He said, "Lord,[w] I believe." And he worshiped him. 39 Jesus said, "I came into this world for judgment so that those who do not see may see, and those who do see may become blind." 40 Some of the Phar′i•sees near him heard this and said to him, "Surely we are not blind, are we?" 41 Jesus said to them, "If you were blind, you would not have sin. But now that you say, 'We see,' your sin remains.

Jesus the Good Shepherd

10 "Very truly, I tell you, anyone who does not enter the sheepfold by the gate but climbs in by another way is a thief and a bandit. 2 The one who enters by the gate is the shepherd of the sheep. 3 The gatekeeper opens the gate for him, and the sheep hear his voice. He calls his own sheep by name and leads them out. 4 When he has brought out all his own, he goes ahead of them, and the sheep follow him because they know his voice. 5 They will not follow a stranger, but they will run from him because they do not know the voice of strangers." 6 Jesus used this figure of speech with them, but they did not understand what he was saying to them.

7 So again Jesus said to them, "Very truly, I tell you, I am the gate for the sheep. 8 All who came before me are thieves and bandits; but the sheep did not listen to them. 9 I am the gate. Whoever enters by me will be saved, and will come in and go out and find pasture. 10 The thief comes only to steal and kill and destroy. I came that they may have life, and have it abundantly.

11 "I am the good shepherd. The good shepherd lays down his life for the sheep. 12 The hired hand, who is not the shepherd and does not own the sheep, sees the wolf coming and leaves the sheep and runs away—and the wolf snatches them and scatters them. 13 The hired hand runs away because a hired hand does not care for the sheep. 14 I am the good shepherd. I know my own and my own know me, 15 just as the Father knows me and I know the Father. And I lay down my life for the sheep. 16 I have other sheep that do not belong to this fold. I must bring them also, and they will listen to my voice. So there will be one flock, one shepherd. 17 For this reason the Father loves me, because I lay down my life in order to take it up again. 18 No one takes[x] it from me, but I lay it down of my own accord. I have power to lay it down, and

---

v Other ancient authorities read *the Son of God*   w *Sir* and *Lord* translate the same Greek word   x Other ancient authorities read *has taken*

I have power to take it up again. I have received this command from my Father."

19 Again the Jews were divided because of these words. 20 Many of them were saying, "He has a demon and is out of his mind. Why listen to him?" 21 Others were saying, "These are not the words of one who has a demon. Can a demon open the eyes of the blind?"

PRAY IT!

Jesus, the Good Shepherd

The theme of shepherds and sheep is a recurring one in the Bible. In the Old Testament, God is often portrayed as a shepherd. For example, see Psalm 23 and Ezekiel, chapter 34. David, the greatest king of Israel, is also portrayed as a shepherd in Ps 78.70–72. In passages like Jer 23.1–6, God promises to raise up new shepherds who will follow in David's legacy. So it is natural that Jesus compares himself to a shepherd in Jn 10.1–18.

Being a shepherd is not an easy job. Sheep are pretty defenseless creatures, and shepherds have to protect them from predators like lions and wolves. Sheep also have a tendency to stray from the flock, making them especially vulnerable. Shepherds endure the hardships of being away from their homes and putting up with simple food and harsh weather while pasturing sheep. Their lives can be endangered when confronted by desperate predators. Sheep learn to recognize their shepherd's voice, which makes it easier to separate different flocks when flocks are mixed together for grazing or protection.

In your prayer, reflect or journal on the following questions:

- How do you relate to Jesus as the good shepherd?
- When is it reassuring to know that Jesus is watching out for you? How do you see yourself helping to "shepherd" other people as a follower of Jesus?

▶ Jn 10.1–18

Jesus Is Rejected by the Jews

22 At that time the festival of the Dedication took place in Jerusalem. It was winter, 23 and Jesus was walking in the temple, in the portico of Solomon. 24 So the Jews gathered around him and said to him, "How long will you keep us in suspense? If you are the Messiah,ʸ tell us plainly." 25 Jesus answered, "I have told you, and you do not believe. The works that I do in my Father's name testify to me; 26 but you do not believe, because you do not belong to my sheep. 27 My sheep hear my voice. I know them, and they follow me. 28 I give them eternal life, and they will never perish. No one will snatch them out of my hand. 29 What my Father has given me is greater than all else, and no one can snatch it out of the Father's hand.ᶻ 30 The Father and I are one."

31 The Jews took up stones again to stone him. 32 Jesus replied, "I have shown you many good works from the Father. For which of these are you going to stone me?" 33 The Jews answered, "It is not for a good work that we are going to stone you, but for blasphemy, because you, though only a human being, are making yourself God." 34 Jesus answered, "Is it not written in your law,ᵃ 'I said, you are gods'? 35 If those to whom the word of God came were called 'gods'—and the scripture cannot be annulled— 36 can you say that the one whom the Father has sanctified and sent into the world is blaspheming because I said, 'I am God's Son'? 37 If I am not doing the works of my Father, then do not believe me. 38 But if I do them, even though you do not believe me, believe the works, so that you may know and understandᵇ that the Father is in me and I am in the Father." 39 Then they tried to arrest him again, but he escaped from their hands.

40 He went away again across the Jordan to the place where John had been baptizing earlier, and he remained there. 41 Many came to him, and they were saying, "John performed no sign, but everything that John said about this man was true." 42 And many believed in him there.

The Death of Lazarus

11 Now a certain man was ill, Laz'a·rus of Beth'a·ny, the village of Mary and her sister Martha. 2 Mary was the one who anointed the Lord with perfume and wiped his feet with her hair; her brother Laz'a·rus was ill. 3 So the sisters sent a message to Jesus,ᶜ "Lord, he whom you love is ill." 4 But when Jesus heard it, he said, "This illness does

---

ʸ Or *the Christ*   ᶻ Other ancient authorities read *My Father who has given them to me is greater than all, and no one can snatch them out of the Father's hand*   ᵃ Other ancient authorities read *in the law*   ᵇ Other ancient authorities lack *and understand*; others read *and believe*   ᶜ Gk *him*

Alive Again!

"Jesus began to weep" (Jn 11.35). This is the shortest verse in the Bible and also the most telling. Why does Jesus weep? He sees his dear friend Mary crying because of the death of her brother Lazarus, and Jesus cannot help himself. He cries too, expressing both compassion for Mary and his own grief at the loss of his friend Lazarus. What a beautiful, powerful expression of Jesus' humanity!

What follows next is a powerful expression of the divinity of Jesus. It is the seventh and final sign in John's Gospel. What a dramatic moment, as Jesus steps into the tomb of a man who has been dead for four days. He says three words—"Lazarus, come out!"—and Lazarus, bound in burial cloth, indeed comes out! He is alive again. Imagine how astonished the onlookers must have been and how grateful Martha and Mary would have been to have their brother alive again.

It does make one wonder what it would feel like to be alive again after being in the grave for four days. How do people react to this man who is alive once again? Why do you think John chose this as the last sign of Jesus' power? Notice that this event occurs about a week before the last days of Jesus' life. Why is this sign such a threat to the ruling officials of Jerusalem?

▶ Jn 11.1–44

---

not lead to death; rather it is for God's glory, so that the Son of God may be glorified through it." 5 Accordingly, though Jesus loved Martha and her sister and Laz′a•rus, 6 after having heard that Laz′a•rus[d] was ill, he stayed two days longer in the place where he was.

7 Then after this he said to the disciples, "Let us go to Judea again." 8 The disciples said to him, "Rabbi, the Jews were just now trying to stone you, and are you going there again?" 9 Jesus answered, "Are there not twelve hours of daylight? Those who walk during the day do not stumble, because they see the light of this world. 10 But those who walk at night stumble, because the light is not in them." 11 After saying this, he told them, "Our friend Laz′a•rus has fallen asleep, but I am going there to awaken him." 12 The disciples said to him, "Lord, if he has fallen asleep, he will be all right." 13 Jesus, however, had been speaking about his death, but they thought that he was referring merely to sleep. 14 Then Jesus told them plainly, "Laz′a•rus is dead. 15 For your sake I am glad I was not there, so that you may believe. But let us go to him." 16 Thomas, who was called the Twin,[e] said to his fellow disciples, "Let us also go, that we may die with him."

Jesus the Resurrection and the Life

17 When Jesus arrived, he found that Laz′a•rus[d] had already been in the tomb four days. 18 Now Beth′a•ny was near Jerusalem, some two miles[f] away, 19 and many of the Jews had come to Martha and Mary to console them about their brother. 20 When Martha heard that Jesus was coming, she

went and met him, while Mary stayed at home. 21 Martha said to Jesus, "Lord, if you had been here, my brother would not have died. 22 But even now I know that God will give you whatever you ask of him." 23 Jesus said to her, "Your brother will rise again." 24 Martha said to him, "I know that he will rise again in the resurrection on the last day." 25 Jesus said to her, "I am the resurrection and the life.[g] Those who believe in me, even though they die, will live, 26 and everyone who lives and believes in me will never die. Do you believe this?" 27 She said to him, "Yes, Lord, I believe that you are the Messiah,[h] the Son of God, the one coming into the world."

Jesus Weeps

28 When she had said this, she went back and called her sister Mary, and told her privately, "The Teacher is here and is calling for you." 29 And when she heard it, she got up quickly and went to him. 30 Now Jesus had not yet come to the village, but was still at the place where Martha had met him. 31 The Jews who were with her in the house, consoling her, saw Mary get up quickly and go out. They followed her because they thought that she was going to the tomb to weep there. 32 When Mary came where Jesus was and saw him, she knelt at his feet and said to him, "Lord, if you had been here, my brother would not have died." 33 When Jesus saw her weeping, and the Jews who came with her

---

d Gk he   e Gk Didymus   f Gk fifteen stadia   g Other ancient authorities lack and the life   h Or the Christ also weeping, he was greatly disturbed in spirit and deeply moved. 34 He said, "Where have you laid him?" They said to him, "Lord, come and see." 35 Jesus began to weep. 36 So the Jews said, "See how he loved him!" 37 But some of them said, "Could not he who opened the eyes of the blind man have kept this man from dying?"

PRAY IT!
A God Who Cries

Lord, have I ever made you cry? angry enough to yell? tickled enough to laugh? proud enough to burst? I hope so. I hope you know me so well that my every movement, my every breath, is noticed by you. I want to believe that about you, Jesus, because that is the image of you I can talk to, a God who can relate to me and accept me in all that I do. Amen.

▸ Jn 11.35

Jesus Raises Lazarus to Life

38 Then Jesus, again greatly disturbed, came to the tomb. It was a cave, and a stone was lying against it. 39 Jesus said, "Take away the stone." Martha, the sister of the dead man, said to him, "Lord, already there is a stench because he has been dead four days." 40 Jesus said to her, "Did I not tell you that if you believed, you would see the glory of God?" 41 So they took away the stone. And Jesus looked upward and said, "Father, I thank you for having heard me. 42 I knew that you always hear me, but I have said this for the sake of the crowd standing here, so that they may believe that you sent me." 43 When he had said this, he cried with a loud voice, "Laz'a·rus, come out!" 44 The dead man came out, his hands and feet bound with strips of cloth, and his face wrapped in a cloth. Jesus said to them, "Unbind him, and let him go."

The Plot to Kill Jesus
(Mt 26.1–5; Mk 14.1–2; Lk 22.1–2)

45 Many of the Jews therefore, who had come with Mary and had seen what Jesus did, believed in him. 46 But some of them went to the Phar'i·sees and told them what he had done. 47 So the chief priests and the Phar'i·sees called a meeting of the council, and said, "What are we to do? This man is performing many signs. 48 If we let him go on like this, everyone will believe in him, and the Romans

will come and destroy both our holy place[i] and our nation." 49 But one of them, Ca'ia·phas, who was high priest that year, said to them, "You know nothing at all! 50 You do not understand that it is better for you to have one man die for the people than to have the whole nation destroyed." 51 He did not say this on his own, but being high priest that year he prophesied that Jesus was about to die for the nation, 52 and not for the nation only, but to gather into one the dispersed children of God. 53 So from that day on they planned to put him to death.

54 Jesus therefore no longer walked about openly among the Jews, but went from there to a town called E'phra·im in the region near the wilderness; and he remained there with the disciples.

55 Now the Passover of the Jews was near, and many went up from the country to Jerusalem before the Passover to purify themselves. 56 They were looking for Jesus and were asking one another as they stood in the temple, "What do you think? Surely he will not come to the festival, will he?" 57 Now the chief priests and the Phar'i·sees had given orders that anyone who knew where Jesus[j] was should let them know, so that they might arrest him.

Mary Anoints Jesus
(Mt 26.6–13; Mk 14.3–9)

12 Six days before the Passover Jesus came to Beth'a·ny, the home of Laz'a·rus, whom he had raised from the dead. 2 There they gave a dinner for him. Martha served, and Laz'a·rus was one of those at the table with him. 3 Mary took a pound of costly perfume made of pure nard, anointed Jesus' feet, and wiped them[k] with her hair. The house was filled with the fragrance of the perfume. 4 But Judas Is·car'i·ot, one of his disciples (the one who was about to betray him), said, 5 "Why was this perfume not sold for three hundred denarii[l] and the money given to the poor?" 6 (He said this not because he cared about the poor, but because he was a thief; he kept the common purse and used to steal what was put into it.) 7 Jesus said, "Leave her alone. She bought it[m] so that she might keep it for the day of my burial. 8 You always have the poor with you, but you do not always have me."

The Plot to Kill Lazarus

9 When the great crowd of the Jews learned that he was there, they came not only because of Jesus but also to see Laz'a·rus, whom he had raised from the dead. 10 So the chief priests planned to put

---

i Or *our temple*; Greek *our place*   *j* Gk *he*   *k* Gk *his feet*
l Three hundred denarii would be nearly a year's wages for a laborer   *m* Gk lacks *She bought it*

Laz'a•rus to death as well, 11 since it was on account of him that many of the Jews were deserting and were believing in Jesus.

Jesus' Triumphal Entry into Jerusalem
(Mt 21.1–11; Mk 11.1–11; Lk 19.28–40)

12 The next day the great crowd that had come to the festival heard that Jesus was coming to Jerusalem. 13 So they took branches of palm trees and went out to meet him, shouting,

"Hosanna!
Blessed is the one who comes in the name
        of the Lord—
    the King of Israel!"

14 Jesus found a young donkey and sat on it; as it is written:

15 "Do not be afraid, daughter of Zion.
Look, your king is coming,
    sitting on a donkey's colt!"

16 His disciples did not understand these things at first; but when Jesus was glorified, then they remembered that these things had been written of him and had been done to him. 17 So the crowd that had been with him when he called Laz'a•rus out of the tomb and raised him from the dead continued to testify.ⁿ 18 It was also because they heard that he had performed this sign that the crowd went to meet him. 19 The Phar'i•sees then said to one another, "You see, you can do nothing. Look, the world has gone after him!"

Some Greeks Wish to See Jesus

20 Now among those who went up to worship at the festival were some Greeks. 21 They came to Philip, who was from Beth•sā'i•da in Galilee, and said to him, "Sir, we wish to see Jesus." 22 Philip went and told Andrew; then Andrew and Philip went and told Jesus. 23 Jesus answered them, "The hour has come for the Son of Man to be glorified. 24 Very truly, I tell you, unless a grain of wheat falls into the earth and dies, it remains just a single grain; but if it dies, it bears much fruit. 25 Those who love their life lose it, and those who hate their life in this world will keep it for eternal life. 26 Whoever serves me must follow me, and where I am, there will my servant be also. Whoever serves me, the Father will honor.

Jesus Speaks about His Death

27 "Now my soul is troubled. And what should I say—'Father, save me from this hour'? No, it is for this reason that I have come to this hour. 28 Father, glorify your name." Then a voice came from heaven, "I have glorified it, and I will glorify it again." 29 The crowd standing there heard it and said that it was thunder. Others said, "An angel has spoken to him." 30 Jesus answered, "This voice has come for your sake, not for mine. 31 Now is the judgment of this world; now the ruler of this world will be driven out. 32 And I, when I am lifted up from the earth, will draw all peopleᵒ to myself." 33 He said this to indicate the kind of death he was to die. 34 The crowd answered him, "We have heard from the law that the Messiahᵖ remains forever. How can you say that the Son of Man must be lifted up? Who is this Son of Man?" 35 Jesus said to them, "The light is with you for a little longer. Walk while you have the light, so that the darkness may not overtake you. If you walk in the darkness, you do not know where you are going. 36 While you have the light, believe in the light, so that you may become children of light."

---

n Other ancient authorities read *with him began to testify that he had called. . .from the dead* o Other ancient authorities read *all things* p Or *the Christ*

PRAY IT!
Dying for New Life

In Jn 12.24–26, Jesus is describing what Christians call the *paschal mystery*. It is the belief that God brings new life out of suffering and death. The first and ultimate expression of the paschal mystery is Jesus' own death and Resurrection. God used Christ's sacrifice to free us from the bonds of sin, and Christ's Resurrection to open the path to new life. It is a mystery that no one can fully explain, but the Gospels and experience tell us it is so.

Like the grain of wheat in this Gospel passage, in death we bear the fruit of new life. The path to new life is through sacrifice and death. By dying to our selfishness and focusing on loving others, we experience the fullness of life in Christ Jesus.

In your prayer, reflect or journal on the following questions:
- What does the paschal mystery mean to you?
- What kinds of attitudes, desires, or actions must you "die to"?

Write a prayer asking God to give you the courage to let go of the things that keep you from fullness of life.

▶ Jn 12.24–26

JN

The Unbelief of the People

After Jesus had said this, he departed and hid from them. 37 Although he had performed so many signs in their presence, they did not believe in him. 38 This was to fulfill the word spoken by the prophet Ī·sāi′ah:

"Lord, who has believed our message,
  and to whom has the arm of the Lord been revealed?"

39 And so they could not believe, because Ī·sāi′ah also said,

40 "He has blinded their eyes
  and hardened their heart,
 so that they might not look with their eyes,
  and understand with their heart and turn—
  and I would heal them."

41 Ī·sāi′ah said this because[q] he saw his glory and spoke about him. 42 Nevertheless many, even of the authorities, believed in him. But because of the Phar′i·sees they did not confess it, for fear that they would be put out of the synagogue; 43 for they loved human glory more than the glory that comes from God.

13.5

Summary of Jesus' Teaching

44 Then Jesus cried aloud: "Whoever believes in me believes not in me but in him who sent me. 45 And whoever sees me sees him who sent me. 46 I have come as light into the world, so that everyone who believes in me should not remain in the darkness. 47 I do not judge anyone who hears my words and does not keep them, for I came not to judge the world, but to save the world. 48 The one who rejects me and does not receive my word has a judge; on the last day the word that I have spoken will serve as judge, 49 for I have not spoken on my own, but the Father who sent me has himself given me a commandment about what to say and what to speak. 50 And I know that his commandment is

eternal life. What I speak, therefore, I speak just as the Father has told me."

Jesus Washes the Disciples' Feet

13 Now before the festival of the Passover, Jesus knew that his hour had come to depart from this world and go to the Father. Having loved his own who were in the world, he loved them to the end. 2 The devil had already put it into the heart of Judas son of Simon Is·car′i·ot to betray him. And during supper 3 Jesus, knowing that the Father had given all things into his hands, and that he had come from God and was going to God, 4 got up from the table,[r] took off his outer robe, and tied a towel around himself. 5 Then he poured water into a basin and began to wash the disciples' feet and to

---

[q] Other ancient witnesses read *when* [r] Gk *from supper*

Jesus Models Service to Others

In Matthew, Mark, and Luke, the focus of the Last Supper is on the institution of the Eucharist. But in John, the focus is on Jesus' cleaning his disciples' feet (13.1–17). John makes the point that serving others is at the heart of being a follower of Jesus. In Holy Thursday Mass, we celebrate both traditions, indicating that service is a necessary part of living the paschal mystery that we celebrate in the Eucharist.

■ The washing of the feet is a symbol of service, humility, and purification. Have you ever felt honored and humbled at the same time?

■ Read Jn 13.1–17. Reflect on and listen to Jesus' message to you.

For more on the Eucharist, see the articles for Mt 26.26–29; Mk 14.22–25; Lk 22.14–20.

▶ Jn 13.1–17

THE *INDRIAPPAM*

In the province of Kerala, in India, about 80 percent of the population is Catholic and celebrates the Lord's Passion with special time-honored customs. One such custom takes place on Holy Thursday. On that day, nearly all the villagers or townspeople attend morning Mass. During the Eucharist, the ritual of foot washing occurs, the priest washing the feet of twelve children chosen from among those who are poor. Then, after dinner that evening, the people gather again for the stations of the cross and prayers. They return home around nine or ten o'clock for a special Passover meal.

The Passover meal consists of bread baked only on Holy Thursday and a special drink of coconut milk mixed with brown sugar and spices. This Passover bread, or *indriappam,* is baked with a cross of palm on top, which is placed there by the oldest woman of the family. At the meal, the oldest man cuts the bread and passes a piece to each person, beginning with the oldest and working down to the youngest. Often families visit one another and share this tradition throughout the evening. And if a death has occurred in any family that year, the other households of the village provide the *indriappam* for them.

On Good Friday, which is a national holiday in India despite the fact that it is a primarily Hindu country, the leftover bread and milk are served to the servants and those of the village who are poor and needy. This custom of *indriappam* combines devotion to Christ in the Eucharist with a reminder of the service we are obliged to offer to those who are needy and poor.

What customs and traditions does your family or parish take part in to commemorate the gift of the Eucharist given at the Last Supper?

▶ Jn 13.1–13

wipe them with the towel that was tied around him. [6] He came to Simon Peter, who said to him, "Lord, are you going to wash my feet?" [7] Jesus answered, "You do not know now what I am doing, but later you will understand." [8] Peter said to him, "You will never wash my feet." Jesus answered, "Unless I wash you, you have no share with me." [9] Simon Peter said to him, "Lord, not my feet only but also my hands and my head!" [10] Jesus said to him, "One who has bathed does not need to wash, except for the feet,[s] but is entirely clean. And you[t] are clean, though not all of you." [11] For he knew who was to betray him; for this reason he said, "Not all of you are clean."

[12] After he had washed their feet, had put on his robe, and had returned to the table, he said to them, "Do you know what I have done to you? [13] You call me Teacher and Lord—and you are right, for that is what I am. [14] So if I, your Lord and Teacher, have washed your feet, you also ought to wash one another's feet. [15] For I have set you an example, that you also should do as I have done to

you. [16] Very truly, I tell you, servants[u] are not greater than their master, nor are messengers greater than the one who sent them. [17] If you know these things, you are blessed if you do them. [18] I am not speaking of all of you; I know whom I have chosen. But it is to fulfill the scripture, 'The one who ate my bread[v] has lifted his heel against me.' [19] I tell you this now, before it occurs, so that when it does occur, you may believe that I am he.[w] [20] Very truly, I tell you, whoever receives one whom I send receives me; and whoever receives me receives him who sent me."

Jesus Foretells His Betrayal
(Mt 26.21–25; Mk 14.18–19; Lk 22.21–23)

[21] After saying this Jesus was troubled in spirit, and declared, "Very truly, I tell you, one of you will

---

[s] Other ancient authorities lack *except for the feet*   [t] The Greek word for *you* here is plural   [u] Gk *slaves*   [v] Other ancient authorities read *ate bread with me*   [w] Gk *I am*

did you KNOW?

Feast of the Passover

Chapter 13 is the beginning of the second part of the Gospel of John, sometimes called the Book of Glory. Its central theme is how Jesus is glorified through his Passion, death, and Resurrection. It begins with Jesus' washing the disciples' feet at the Last Supper, before the Passover.

The Jewish feast of Passover, also called the feast of Unleavened Bread, reminds us of how God rescued the Israelites from slavery in Egypt by killing the firstborn Egyptians and "passing over" the homes of the Israelites (about 1250 B.C.). The feast was traditionally celebrated with a meal of lamb, bitter herbs, and unleavened bread (see "The Passover," Ex 12.14–28). It was the blood of a lamb, smeared on the doorposts of the Israelites' houses, that signaled the angel of death to spare the firstborn of God's people.

In the other Gospels, the last meal that Jesus shares with his disciples is the Passover meal. However, in the Gospel of John, Jesus is arrested before Passover. He is crucified on the preparation day of the feast of Unleavened Bread, at the same time that the lambs are being sacrificed in the Temple. The symbolism would not be missed by the readers of John: Jesus is the new and perfect Passover lamb.

▶ Jn 13.1–20

you are going to do." 28 Now no one at the table knew why he said this to him. 29 Some thought that, because Judas had the common purse, Jesus was telling him, "Buy what we need for the festival"; or, that he should give something to the poor. 30 So, after receiving the piece of bread, he immediately went out. And it was night.

The New Commandment

31 When he had gone out, Jesus said, "Now the Son of Man has been glorified, and God has been glorified in him. 32 If God has been glorified in him,[a] God will also glorify him in himself and will glorify him at once. 33 Little children, I am with you only a little longer. You will look for me; and as I said to the Jews so now I say to you, 'Where I am going, you cannot come.' 34 I give you a new commandment, that you love one another. Just as I have loved you, you also should love one another. 35 By this everyone will know that you are my disciples, if you have love for one another."

Jesus Foretells Peter's Denial

36 Simon Peter said to him, "Lord, where are you going?" Jesus answered, "Where I am going, you cannot follow me now; but you will follow afterward." 37 Peter said to him, "Lord, why can I not follow you now? I will lay down my life for you." 38 Jesus answered, "Will you lay down your life for me? Very truly, I tell you, before the cock crows, you will have denied me three times.

Jesus the Way to the Father

14 "Do not let your hearts be troubled. Believe[b] in God, believe also in me. 2 In my Father's house there are many dwelling places. If it were not so, would I have told you that I go to prepare a place for you?[c] 3 And if I go and prepare a place for you, I will come again and will take you to myself, so that where I am, there you may be also. 4 And you know the way to the place where I am going."[d] 5 Thomas said to him, "Lord, we do not know where you are going. How can we know the way?" 6 Jesus said to him, "I am the way, and the truth, and the life. No one comes to the Father except through me. 7 If you know me, you will know[e] my Father also. From now on you do know him and have seen him."

betray me." 22 The disciples looked at one another, uncertain of whom he was speaking. 23 One of his disciples—the one whom Jesus loved—was reclining next to him; 24 Simon Peter therefore motioned to him to ask Jesus of whom he was speaking. 25 So while reclining next to Jesus, he asked him, "Lord, who is it?" 26 Jesus answered, "It is the one to whom I give this piece of bread when I have dipped it in the dish."[x] So when he had dipped the piece of bread, he gave it to Judas son of Simon Is·car'i·ot.[y] 27 After he received the piece of bread,[z] Satan entered into him. Jesus said to him, "Do quickly what

---

x Gk *dipped it*   y Other ancient authorities read *Judas Iscariot son of Simon*; others, *Judas son of Simon from Karyot* (Kerioth)   z Gk *After the piece of bread*   a Other ancient authorities lack *If God has been glorified in him*   b Or *You believe*   c Or *If it were not so, I would have told you; for I go to prepare a place for you*   d Other ancient authorities read *Where I am going you know, and the way you know*   e Other ancient authorities read *If you had known me, you would have known*

J
N

Introducing
▶ THE BELOVED DISCIPLE

In the Last Supper scene, we are introduced to a mysterious character found only in the Gospel of John, described as the disciple "whom Jesus loved" (Jn 13.23). He is mentioned several more times in John: at the foot of the cross with Jesus' mother (19.25–27), on Easter morning when he enters the empty tomb with Peter (20.2–12), and after the Resurrection when he identifies Jesus from the boat (21.7,20). He is always with Peter or where Peter should be (at the cross).

So who is the mystery man? Traditionally, he has been identified as John, the son of Zebedee and one of the twelve Apostles, and as the writer of the Gospel of John. But if that is true, why does he refer to himself so strangely? Many scholars today believe that the Beloved Disciple was a lesser-known follower of Jesus who was the founder of the Christian community that ultimately produced the Gospel of John. They think that his eyewitness accounts (see 21.24) were passed on and are the basis for the Gospel we have today.

Jn 13.23–25

8 Philip said to him, "Lord, show us the Father, and we will be satisfied." 9 Jesus said to him, "Have I been with you all this time, Philip, and you still do not know me? Whoever has seen me has seen the Father. How can you say, 'Show us the Father'? 10 Do you not believe that I am in the Father and the Father is in me? The words that I say to you I do not speak on my own; but the Father who dwells in me does his works. 11 Believe me that I am in the Father and the Father is in me; but if you do not, then believe me because of the works themselves. 12 Very truly, I tell you, the one who believes in me will also do the works that I do and, in fact, will do greater works than these, because I am going to the Father. 13 I will do whatever you ask in my name, so that the Father may be glorified in the Son. 14 If in my name you ask me*f* for anything, I will do it.

The Promise of the Holy Spirit

15 "If you love me, you will keep*g* my commandments. 16 And I will ask the Father, and he will give you another Advocate,*h* to be with you forever. 17 This is the Spirit of truth, whom the world cannot receive, because it neither sees him nor

---

f Other ancient authorities lack *me*   *g* Other ancient authorities read *me, keep*   *h* Or Helper

Cultural Connections

THE WAY AND THE TRUTH AND THE LIFE

Laotian Catholics often point to Jn 14.6 as a significant connection between the Buddhist faith and their Catholic faith. There is a Buddhist tradition of honoring the way and the truth. Becoming a Catholic and knowing the risen Christ bring a deeper appreciation of everlasting life. This completes the triangle of "the way, and the truth, and the life."

▶ Jn 14.6–7

JN

knows him. You know him, because he abides with you, and he will be in[i] you.

18 "I will not leave you orphaned; I am coming to you. 19 In a little while the world will no longer see me, but you will see me; because I live, you also will live. 20 On that day you will know that I am in my Father, and you in me, and I in you. 21 They who have my commandments and keep them are those who love me; and those who love me will be loved by my Father, and I will love them and reveal myself to them." 22 Judas (not Is•car'i•ot) said to him, "Lord, how is it that you will reveal yourself to us, and not to the world?" 23 Jesus answered him, "Those who love me will keep my word, and my Father will love them, and we will come to them and make our home with them. 24 Whoever does not love me does not keep my words; and the word that you hear is not mine, but is from the Father who sent me.

25 "I have said these things to you while I am still with you. 26 But the Advocate,[j] the Holy Spirit, whom the Father will send in my name, will teach you everything, and remind you of all that I have said to you. 27 Peace I leave with you; my peace I give to you. I do not give to you as the world gives. Do not let your hearts be troubled, and do not let them be afraid. 28 You heard me say to you, 'I am going away, and I am coming to you.' If you loved me, you would rejoice that I am going to the Father, because the Father is greater than I. 29 And now I have told you this before it occurs, so that when it does occur, you may believe. 30 I will no longer talk much with you, for the ruler of this world is coming. He has no power over me; 31 but I do as the Fa-

Catholic Connections

THE PEACE OF CHRIST

John 14.27 is the passage the priest recites during Mass just before he invites the community to share a sign of peace. This is no ordinary peace, however. It is the peace of Christ. It is a peace that is not of this world. It has allowed Christians to endure hardships, oppression, war, sickness, and death with dignity and hope. The next time you are at Mass, think about the awesome power in the peace of Christ that you are extending to the people around you.

▶ Jn 14.27

ther has commanded me, so that the world may know that I love the Father. Rise, let us be on our way.

_____

i Or among   j Or Helper

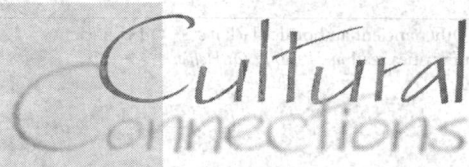

Cultural Connections

THE HOLY SPIRIT GUIDES US INTO ALL TRUTH!

Jesus told his disciples that after his death, God would send the Spirit of Truth to be with them forever. Jesus calls the Holy Spirit the Advocate (Jn 16.7), the one who defends us from evil and sin. The Holy Spirit also guides us into all Truth, by helping us to grasp the meaning of Jesus' words, actions, and miracles.

■ Jesus promises his followers that the Holy Spirit will abide in us (14.17). How are you aware of the Holy Spirit's presence in your life?
■ Place yourself in the hands of the Most Holy Trinity and call upon the Holy Spirit to protect you from all sin and evil and to bring you peace.

▶ Jn 14.15–31; 16.5–15

Jesus the True Vine

15 "I am the true vine, and my Father is the vinegrower. 2 He removes every branch in me that bears no fruit. Every branch that bears fruit he prunes[k] to make it bear more fruit. 3 You have already been cleansed[k] by the word that I have spoken to you. 4 Abide in me as I abide in you. Just as the branch cannot bear fruit by itself unless it abides in the vine, neither can you unless you abide in me. 5 I am the vine, you are the branches. Those who abide in me and I in them bear much fruit, because apart from me you can do nothing. 6 Whoever does not abide in me is thrown away like a branch and withers; such branches are gathered, thrown into the fire, and burned. 7 If you abide in me, and my words abide in you, ask for whatever you wish, and it will be done for you. 8 My Father is glorified by this, that you bear much fruit and become[l] my disciples. 9 As the Father has loved me, so I have loved you; abide in my love. 10 If you keep

MAKE YOUR HOME WITH JESUS

Jesus calls himself the true vine, and us the branches (Jn 15.5). What does this mean for us? First, it means that apart from Jesus, we can produce no fruit. That is, we have nothing of ultimate value to offer others. It also means that to stay alive, we must "remain" in Jesus (verse 4). To remain, in this sense, means to stay or make our home with. How at home are you with Jesus?

▶ Jn 15.1–11

my commandments, you will abide in my love, just as I have kept my Father's commandments and abide in his love. 11 I have said these things to you so that my joy may be in you, and that your joy may be complete.

12 "This is my commandment, that you love one another as I have loved you. 13 No one has greater love than this, to lay down one's life for one's friends. 14 You are my friends if you do what I command you. 15 I do not call you servants[m] any longer, because the servant[n] does not know what the master is doing; but I have called you friends, because I have made known to you everything that I have heard from my Father. 16 You did not choose me but I chose you. And I appointed you to go and bear fruit, fruit that will last, so that the Father will give you whatever you ask him in my name. 17 I am giving you these commands so that you may love one another.

PRAY IT
Not of This World

It is easy to get caught up in the pressures put on us by our society. It seems that we have to dress a certain way, have certain possessions, and live in a certain kind of house just to be considered average. People who resist those pressures are often labeled weird or different. They often feel out of place, not of this world.

The community from which the Gospel of John emerged did not feel at home in the world either. Their message of the divine Jesus had been rejected by Jews, Gentiles, and perhaps even other early Christians. No wonder the author has Jesus emphasize, "because you do not belong to the world, . . . therefore the world hates you" (15.19).

In your prayer, reflect or journal on the following questions:
- How might Christians today be considered not of this world?
- What societal pressures do you need to resist?
- How does Jesus' warning to his disciples about the world's hatred (verses 18–25) apply to Christians today?

▶ Jn 15.18–25

The World's Hatred

18 "If the world hates you, be aware that it hated me before it hated you. 19 If you belonged to the world,[o] the world would love you as its own. Because you do not belong to the world, but I have chosen you out of the world—therefore the world hates you. 20 Remember the word that I said to you, 'Servants[p] are not greater than their master.' If they persecuted me, they will persecute you; if they kept my word, they will keep yours also. 21 But they will do all these things to you on account of my name, because they do not know him who sent me. 22 If I

---

k The same Greek root refers to pruning and cleansing
l Or be   m Gk slaves   n Gk slave   o Gk were of the world
p Gk Slaves

CHRIST LIVES IN US THROUGH THE HOLY SPIRIT!

In his farewell speech to his Apostles, Jesus tells them that he will return to the Father, but will not leave them orphaned (Jn 14.18). The Father will give them another Advocate—the Holy Spirit. We also receive the Holy Spirit, through our Baptism and our Confirmation. Certain Latin American spirituality emphasizes the Spirit's gifts of love, freedom, truth, life, and hope.

- *Love* lets us find joy in the midst of suffering and pain. Christ did not end human suffering; instead, he showed how suffering for those we love can bring new life to them.
- *Freedom* from material goods, false gratification, and addictions nurtures the lifestyle we adopt as disciples of Jesus.
- *Truth* about God, us, and history can be achieved only through God's revelation. The Spirit gives us the light to discover this truth and the strength to direct our life by it.
- *God's life* in us helps us overcome prejudices, promote reconciliation, foster unity in diversity, and work for justice and peace.
- *Hope* in being forever with God and the people we love is continuously nourished by the Spirit, who gives us a glimpse of the glory to come despite our earthly limitations.

▶ Jn 14.12–21; 16.12–15

had not come and spoken to them, they would not have sin; but now they have no excuse for their sin. 23 Whoever hates me hates my Father also. 24 If I had not done among them the works that no one else did, they would not have sin. But now they have seen and hated both me and my Father. 25 It was to fulfill the word that is written in their law, 'They hated me without a cause.'

26 "When the Advocate^q comes, whom I will send to you from the Father, the Spirit of truth who comes from the Father, he will testify on my behalf. 27 You also are to testify because you have been with me from the beginning.

16 "I have said these things to you to keep you from stumbling. 2 They will put you out of the synagogues. Indeed, an hour is coming when those who kill you will think that by doing so they are offering worship to God. 3 And they will do this because they have not known the Father or me. 4 But I have said these things to you so that when their hour comes you may remember that I told you about them.

The Work of the Spirit

"I did not say these things to you from the beginning, because I was with you. 5 But now I am going to him who sent me; yet none of you asks me, 'Where are you going?' 6 But because I have said these things to you, sorrow has filled your hearts. 7 Nevertheless I tell you the truth: it is to your advantage that I go away, for if I do not go away, the Advocate^q will not come to you; but if I go, I will send him to you. 8 And when he comes, he will prove the world wrong about^r sin and righteousness and judgment; 9 about sin, because they do not believe in me; 10 about righteousness, because I am going to the Father and you will see me no longer; 11 about judgment, because the ruler of this world has been condemned.

12 "I still have many things to say to you, but you cannot bear them now. 13 When the Spirit of truth comes, he will guide you into all the truth; for he will not speak on his own, but will speak whatever he hears, and he will declare to you the things that are to come. 14 He will glorify me, because he will take what is mine and declare it to you. 15 All that the Father has is mine. For this reason I said that he will take what is mine and declare it to you.

Sorrow Will Turn into Joy

16 "A little while, and you will no longer see me, and again a little while, and you will see me." 17 Then some of his disciples said to one another, "What does he mean by saying to us, 'A little while,

---

q Or *Helper*   r Or *convict the world of*

and you will no longer see me, and again a little while, and you will see me'; and 'Because I am going to the Father'?" 18 They said, "What does he mean by this 'a little while'? We do not know what he is talking about." 19 Jesus knew that they wanted to ask him, so he said to them, "Are you discussing among yourselves what I meant when I said, 'A little while, and you will no longer see me, and again a little while, and you will see me'? 20 Very truly, I tell you, you will weep and mourn, but the world will rejoice; you will have pain, but your pain will turn into joy. 21 When a woman is in labor, she has pain, because her hour has come. But when her child is born, she no longer remembers the anguish because of the joy of having brought a human being into the world. 22 So you have pain now; but I will see you again, and your hearts will rejoice, and no one will take your joy from you. 23 On that day you will ask nothing of me.*s* Very truly, I tell you, if you ask anything of the Father in my name, he will give it to you.*t* 24 Until now you have not asked for anything in my name. Ask and you will receive, so that your joy may be complete.

Peace for the Disciples

25 "I have said these things to you in figures of speech. The hour is coming when I will no longer speak to you in figures, but will tell you plainly of the Father. 26 On that day you will ask in my name. I do not say to you that I will ask the Father on your behalf; 27 for the Father himself loves you, because you have loved me and have believed that I came from God.*u* 28 I came from the Father and have come into the world; again, I am leaving the world and am going to the Father."

29 His disciples said, "Yes, now you are speaking plainly, not in any figure of speech! 30 Now we know that you know all things, and do not need to have anyone question you; by this we believe that you came from God." 31 Jesus answered them, "Do you now believe? 32 The hour is coming, indeed it has come, when you will be scattered, each one to his home, and you will leave me alone. Yet I am not alone because the Father is with me. 33 I have said this to you, so that in me you may have peace. In the world you face persecution. But take courage; I have conquered the world!"

Jesus Prays for His Disciples

17 After Jesus had spoken these words, he looked up to heaven and said, "Father, the hour has come; glorify your Son so that the Son may glorify you, 2 since you have given him authority over all people,*v* to give eternal life to all whom you have given him. 3 And this is eternal life, that they may know you, the only true God, and Jesus Christ whom you have sent. 4 I glorified you

on earth by finishing the work that you gave me to do. 5 So now, Father, glorify me in your own presence with the glory that I had in your presence before the world existed.

6 "I have made your name known to those whom you gave me from the world. They were yours, and you gave them to me, and they have kept your word. 7 Now they know that everything you have given me is from you; 8 for the words that you gave to me I have given to them, and they have received them and know in truth that I came from you; and they have believed that you sent me. 9 I am asking on their behalf; I am not asking on behalf of the world, but on behalf of those whom you

---

s Or *will ask me no question*   *t* Other ancient authorities read *Father, he will give it to you in my name*   *u* Other ancient authorities read *the Father*   *v* Gk *flesh*

Catholic Connections

RACE RELATIONS

On 4 April 2001, the thirty-third anniversary of the death of Martin Luther King Jr., Cardinal George of the Archdiocese of Chicago published a letter to the faithful titled "Dwell in My Love." In it, Cardinal George challenges us to look at Jn 17.7–10, in which Jesus invites us to dwell in his love. Cardinal George makes the point that all people, races, cultures, and nationalities are part of the human family and that Jesus invites us to be unified in his love.

Race is a gift from God that underscores our uniqueness. It is important for us to celebrate our differences in a way that brings us together as followers of Jesus. The main point of Cardinal George's letter is that our diversity enriches us, making life more full and interesting.

Think of all the ways in which people of different races, cultures, and nationalities have brought richness to your community, family, parish, and school.

▸ Jn 17.7–10

gave me, because they are yours. 10 All mine are yours, and yours are mine; and I have been glorified in them. 11 And now I am no longer in the world, but they are in the world, and I am coming to you. Holy Father, protect them in your name that you have given me, so that they may be one, as we are one. 12 While I was with them, I protected them in your name that*w* you have given me. I guarded them, and not one of them was lost except the one destined to be lost,*x* so that the scripture might be fulfilled. 13 But now I am coming to you, and I speak these things in the world so that they may have my joy made complete in themselves.*y* 14 I have given them your word, and the world has hated them because they do not belong to the world, just as I do not belong to the world. 15 I am not asking you to take them out of the world, but I ask you to protect them from the evil one.*z* 16 They do not belong to the world, just as I do not belong to the world. 17 Sanctify them in the truth; your word is truth. 18 As you have sent me into the world, so I have sent them into the world. 19 And for their sakes I sanctify myself, so that they also may be sanctified in truth.

JN

PRAY IT
A Prayer for Friends

In John, chapter 17, Jesus prays for his friends, the disciples. And he also prays for us, his future disciples (verse 20)! Here is a prayer you can say for your friends:

Dear Jesus, thank you for my true friends. They accept me for who I am. With them, I don't have to pretend to be someone else. They support me when I feel that the world is crumbling around me. They are honest with me even if what they say is not what I want to hear. They offer their sense of humor so that we can laugh together.

Spirit of Jesus, watch over these friends just as you watch over me. Show them your loving acceptance and support. Help them to honestly look at themselves and the decisions they are making. If they experience pain, frustration, or failure, give them strength to lean on you. Fill their days with laughter and love. Protect them and keep them safe all the days of their lives. Amen.

▶ John, chapter 17

Catholic Connections
THE WORK OF THE TRINITY

Have you ever wondered who forgives us when we confess our sins? Sometimes you hear that it is Jesus who forgives, like in the sacrament of Penance and Reconciliation; other times you may hear it is God the Father who forgives sin. Whose job is it anyway?

There is a bit of confusion about how the three persons of the Trinity work in our lives, in general, and in the sacraments, in particular. The answer is simple: God the Father, and the Son, and the Holy Spirit forgive our sins, and together they are responsible for all the things that bring us grace and salvation.

In Jn 14.9–11, Jesus says to Philip: "Whoever has seen me has seen the Father. How can you say, 'Show us the Father'?" In fact, throughout chapters 14–17, Jesus alludes to the unity of the Father, the Son, and the Holy Spirit (see Jn 15.18–27 and 17.10–11, 21–23a). When the Father or the Son or the Holy Spirit acts, the whole Trinity acts. The three persons of the Holy Trinity are inseparable in who they are and in what they do.

So what is the best way to deal with the Holy Trinity? Again, the answer is rather simple—pray. Pray to the one God, the Father and the Son and the Holy Spirit, who will draw you ever closer to the one Divine Presence.

O Blessed Trinity, one and three, fill me with your presence that I may live and love with you, Father, Son, and Holy Spirit, forever and ever. Amen

▶ Jn 17.21–23

---

w Other ancient authorities read *protected in your name those whom*   *x* Gk *except the son of destruction*   *y* Or *among themselves*   *z* Or *from evil*

20 "I ask not only on behalf of these, but also on behalf of those who will believe in me through their word, 21 that they may all be one. As you, Father, are in me and I am in you, may they also be in us,*a* so that the world may believe that you have sent me. 22 The glory that you have given me I have given them, so that they may be one, as we are one, 23 I in them and you in me, that they may become completely one, so that the world may know that you have sent me and have loved them even as you have loved me. 24 Father, I desire that those also, whom you have given me, may be with me where I am, to see my glory, which you have given me because you loved me before the foundation of the world.

25 "Righteous Father, the world does not know you, but I know you; and these know that you have sent me. 26 I made your name known to them, and I will make it known, so that the love with which you have loved me may be in them, and I in them."

The Betrayal and Arrest of Jesus
(Mt 26.47–56; Mk 14.43–52; Lk 22.47–53)

18 After Jesus had spoken these words, he went out with his disciples across the Kid'ron valley to a place where there was a garden, which he and his disciples entered. 2 Now Judas, who betrayed him, also knew the place, because Jesus often met there with his disciples. 3 So Judas brought a detachment of soldiers together with police from the chief priests and the Phar'i•sees, and they came there with lanterns and torches and weapons. 4 Then Jesus, knowing all that was to happen to him, came forward and asked them, "Whom are you looking for?" 5 They answered, "Jesus of Nazareth."*b* Jesus replied, "I am he."*c* Judas, who betrayed him, was standing with them. 6 When Jesus*d* said to them, "I am he,"*c* they stepped back and fell to the ground. 7 Again he asked them, "Whom are you looking for?" And they said, "Jesus of Nazareth."*b* 8 Jesus answered, "I told you that I am he.*c* So if you are looking for me, let these men go." 9 This was to fulfill the word that he had spoken, "I did not lose a single one of those whom you gave me." 10 Then Simon Peter, who had a sword, drew it, struck the high priest's slave, and cut off his right ear. The slave's name was Mal'chus. 11 Jesus said to Peter, "Put your sword back into its sheath. Am I not to drink the cup that the Father has given me?"

Jesus before the High Priest

12 So the soldiers, their officer, and the Jewish police arrested Jesus and bound him. 13 First they took him to An'nas, who was the father-in-law of Cā'i•a•phas, the high priest that year. 14 Cā'i•a•phas was the one who had advised the Jews that it was better to have one person die for the people.

did you KNOW?
The Triumph of Jesus

The Gospel of John most closely resembles the other three Gospels in its stories of Jesus' trial, death, and Resurrection. But even here, John's unique portrayal of Jesus is seen. The most obvious difference is that in John, Jesus is clearly in charge and in his glory from the moment he is arrested. There is no agony in the garden. When the soldiers and police come to arrest Jesus, they fall to the ground as he speaks (18.6). He teaches Pilate about his identity and mission, in essence putting Pilate on trial (verses 33–38). Jesus brings together his mother and the Beloved Disciple (19.26–27). Jesus is not killed but decides the moment of his death when he gives up his spirit (verse 30).

John is also careful to show in detail the ways Jesus' Crucifixion fulfills Old Testament prophecies of the Messiah. He identifies Jesus with the just man who was persecuted in Psalms 22 and 69. He does this by connecting the gambling for Jesus' seamless tunic (Jn 19.24) with Ps 22.18, and the offering of sour wine (Jn 19.29) with Ps 69.21. Jesus' unbroken legs (Jn 19.33) are a reference to the paschal lamb in Ex 12.46, and his pierced side (Jn 19.34) is seen as the fulfillment of Zech 12.10.

John wants us to know that these events are the central "Hour" in the world's history and the time of Jesus' triumph. For the author of John, Jesus is clearly the divine Son of God, and by Jesus' self-sacrifice, God brings salvation to the entire world. The author of John wants to focus us not on the tragedy but on God's power at work in Jesus.

▸ John, chapters 18–19

Peter Denies Jesus
(Mt 26.69–75; Mk 14.66–72; Lk 22.54–62)

15 Simon Peter and another disciple followed Jesus. Since that disciple was known to the high priest, he went with Jesus into the courtyard of the

---

a Other ancient authorities read *be one in us*   *b* Gk *the Nazorean*   *c* Gk *I am*   *d* Gk *he*

J
N

high priest, 16 but Peter was standing outside at the gate. So the other disciple, who was known to the high priest, went out, spoke to the woman who guarded the gate, and brought Peter in. 17 The woman said to Peter, "You are not also one of this man's disciples, are you?" He said, "I am not." 18 Now the slaves and the police had made a charcoal fire because it was cold, and they were standing around it and warming themselves. Peter also was standing with them and warming himself.

The High Priest Questions Jesus

19 Then the high priest questioned Jesus about his disciples and about his teaching. 20 Jesus answered, "I have spoken openly to the world; I have always taught in synagogues and in the temple, where all the Jews come together. I have said nothing in secret. 21 Why do you ask me? Ask those who heard what I said to them; they know what I said." 22 When he had said this, one of the police standing nearby struck Jesus on the face, saying, "Is that how you answer the high priest?" 23 Jesus answered, "If I have spoken wrongly, testify to the wrong. But if I have spoken rightly, why do you strike me?" 24 Then An′nas sent him bound to Cā′i·a·phas the high priest.

Peter Denies Jesus Again

25 Now Simon Peter was standing and warming himself. They asked him, "You are not also one of his disciples, are you?" He denied it and said, "I am not." 26 One of the slaves of the high priest, a relative of the man whose ear Peter had cut off, asked, "Did I not see you in the garden with him?" 27 Again Peter denied it, and at that moment the cock crowed.

Jesus before Pilate
(Mt 27.1–2, 11–14; Mk 15.1–5; Lk 23.1–5)

28 Then they took Jesus from Cā′i·a·phas to Pilate's headquarters.ᵉ It was early in the morning. They themselves did not enter the headquarters,ᵉ so as to avoid ritual defilement and to be able to eat the Passover. 29 So Pilate went out to them and said, "What accusation do you bring against this man?" 30 They answered, "If this man were not a criminal, we would not have handed him over to you." 31 Pilate said to them, "Take him yourselves and judge him according to your law." The Jews replied, "We are not permitted to put anyone to death." 32 (This was to fulfill what Jesus had said when he indicated the kind of death he was to die.)

33 Then Pilate entered the headquartersᵉ again, summoned Jesus, and asked him, "Are you the King of the Jews?" 34 Jesus answered, "Do you ask this on your own, or did others tell you about me?" 35 Pilate replied, "I am not a Jew, am I? Your own nation

Catholic Connections
EASTER TRIDUUM

For Catholics, the center of the liturgical year is the Easter Triduum, the three holy days that celebrate Jesus' death and Resurrection. The Triduum begins on Holy Thursday, the Thursday before Easter. The reading for the day, Jn 13.1–15, recounts the Last Supper and Christ's humility when washing the feet of the disciples.

Holy Thursday is followed by Good Friday, during which John's account of Jesus' Passion (chapters 18–19) is read. During the service, Catholics venerate (honor) the cross, recalling Jesus' painful sacrifice that God used for our salvation.

The climax to the Triduum is the Easter Vigil held on Saturday evening, beginning after nightfall. This celebration incorporates a dramatic ceremony of light in which the Easter fire is lit, followed by the lighting of the paschal (Jesus) candle and of a candle for every person in the church. Then those who have been preparing to join the church are baptized, confirmed, and welcomed to receive the Eucharist.

The Easter Triduum, although celebrated over three days, is actually one celebration, from the opening song on Holy Thursday to the closing song of the Easter Vigil.

▶ Jn 13.1—20.18

and the chief priests have handed you over to me. What have you done?" 36 Jesus answered, "My kingdom is not from this world. If my kingdom were from this world, my followers would be fighting to keep me from being handed over to the Jews. But as it is, my kingdom is not from here." 37 Pilate asked him, "So you are a king?" Jesus answered, "You say that I am a king. For this I was born, and for this I came into the world, to testify to the truth. Everyone who belongs to the truth listens to my voice." 38 Pilate asked him, "What is truth?"

ᵉ Gk *the praetorium*

Jesus Sentenced to Death
(Mt 27.15–31; Mk 15.6–20; Lk 23.13–25)

After he had said this, he went out to the Jews again and told them, "I find no case against him. 39 But you have a custom that I release someone for you at the Passover. Do you want me to release for you the King of the Jews?" 40 They shouted in reply, "Not this man, but Ba·rab′bas!" Now Ba·rab′bas was a bandit.

19 Then Pilate took Jesus and had him flogged. 2 And the soldiers wove a crown of thorns and put it on his head, and they dressed him in a purple robe. 3 They kept coming up to him, saying, "Hail, King of the Jews!" and striking him on the face. 4 Pilate went out again and said to them, "Look, I am bringing him out to you to let you know that I find no case against him." 5 So Jesus came out, wearing the crown of thorns and the purple robe. Pilate said to them, "Here is the man!" 6 When the chief priests and the police saw him, they shouted, "Crucify him! Crucify him!" Pilate said to them, "Take him yourselves and crucify him; I find no case against him." 7 The Jews answered him, "We have a law, and according to that law he ought to die because he has claimed to be the Son of God."

8 Now when Pilate heard this, he was more afraid than ever. 9 He entered his headquarters*f* again and asked Jesus, "Where are you from?" But Jesus gave him no answer. 10 Pilate therefore said to him, "Do you refuse to speak to me? Do you not know that I have power to release you, and power to crucify you?" 11 Jesus answered him, "You would have no power over me unless it had been given you from above; therefore the one who handed me over to you is guilty of a greater sin." 12 From then on Pilate tried to release him, but the Jews cried out, "If you release this man, you are no friend of the emperor. Everyone who claims to be a king sets himself against the emperor."

13 When Pilate heard these words, he brought Jesus outside and sat*g* on the judge's bench at a place called The Stone Pavement, or in Hebrew*h* Gab′ba·tha. 14 Now it was the day of Preparation for the Passover; and it was about noon. He said to the Jews, "Here is your King!" 15 They cried out, "Away with him! Away with him! Crucify him!" Pilate asked them, "Shall I crucify your King?" The chief priests answered, "We have no king but the emperor." 16 Then he handed him over to them to be crucified.

The Crucifixion of Jesus
(Mt 27.32–56; Mk 15.21–41; Lk 23.26–49)

So they took Jesus; 17 and carrying the cross by himself, he went out to what is called The Place of the Skull, which in Hebrew*h* is called Gol′go·tha.

18 There they crucified him, and with him two others, one on either side, with Jesus between them. 19 Pilate also had an inscription written and put on the cross. It read, "Jesus of Nazareth,*i* the King of the Jews." 20 Many of the Jews read this inscription, because the place where Jesus was crucified was near the city; and it was written in Hebrew,*h* in Latin, and in Greek. 21 Then the chief priests of the Jews said to Pilate, "Do not write, 'The King of the

---

f Gk *the praetorium*   *g* Or *seated him*   *h* That is, *Aramaic*
i Gk *the Nazorean*

did you KNOW?
The Words on the Cross

In the Gospel of John, Pontius Pilate acts as a mediator between two worlds—the outside world of darkness and unbelief and the inner world of light and truth. During Jesus' trial, Pilate goes back and forth between the Jewish religious authorities who are outside (in the dark) and Jesus, who is inside Pilate's headquarters (in the light).

Does Pilate know the truth about Jesus? When he writes out the charges to be placed on the cross, "the Jews" (see "'The Jews' in the Gospel of John," Jn 2.18–20) argue with him about the wording. He answers by saying, "What I have written I have written" (19.22), that is, "These words are the truth about Jesus." The words he writes are "Jesus of Nazareth, the King of the Jews" (verse 19). In Latin, they read, *"Iesus Nazarenus Rex Iudaeorum."* When artists draw or sculpt the Crucifixion scene, they often include this Latin phrase in abbreviated form above the cross—*INRI.*

In another of the Gospel's ironies, Pilate recognizes what the Jewish leaders rejected—Jesus Christ is a king. Christians believe a deeper truth—Christ is king not only of the Jews but of all creation! On the last Sunday of the liturgical year, the Catholic church celebrates this in the feast of Christ the King.

▶ Jn 19.19–22

Jews,' but, 'This man said, I am King of the Jews.' " 22 Pilate answered, "What I have written I have written." 23 When the soldiers had crucified Jesus, they took his clothes and divided them into four parts, one for each soldier. They also took his tunic; now the tunic was seamless, woven in one piece from the top. 24 So they said to one another, "Let us not tear it, but cast lots for it to see who will get it." This was to fulfill what the scripture says,

"They divided my clothes among
        themselves,
    and for my clothing they cast lots."
25 And that is what the soldiers did.

Meanwhile, standing near the cross of Jesus were his mother, and his mother's sister, Mary the wife of Clō'pas, and Mary Mag'da·lēne. 26 When Jesus saw his mother and the disciple whom he loved standing beside her, he said to his mother, "Woman, here is your son." 27 Then he said to the disciple, "Here is your mother." And from that hour the disciple took her into his own home.

28 After this, when Jesus knew that all was now finished, he said (in order to fulfill the scripture), "I am thirsty." 29 A jar full of sour wine was standing there. So they put a sponge full of the wine on a branch of hyssop and held it to his mouth. 30 When Jesus had received the wine, he said, "It is finished." Then he bowed his head and gave up his spirit.

Jesus' Side Is Pierced

31 Since it was the day of Preparation, the Jews did not want the bodies left on the cross during the sabbath, especially because that sabbath was a day of great solemnity. So they asked Pilate to have the legs of the crucified men broken and the bodies removed. 32 Then the soldiers came and broke the legs of the first and of the other who had been crucified with him. 33 But when they came to Jesus and

OUR MOTHER OF GUADALUPE, A GIFT FROM GOD!

Devotion to Mary as mother of God and mother of the church has been a consistent dimension of Christian faith. From Jesus' words on the cross in Jn 19.25–27, Christians have identified with the Beloved Disciple and seen Mary as their mother. This experience has led Catholics of many countries to name Mary as their patroness (advocate, protector, supporter, mother): for instance, they call her Virgin of the Immaculate Conception in the United States and Chile, Virgin of Lourdes in France, and Virgin of Fátima in Portugal. The strong devotion of Latin American countries to Mary as a mother who protects and assists her children is revealed in their titles for her: Our Lady of Mercy in the Dominican Republic, Our Lady of Caridad del Cobre (charity) in Cuba, Our Lady of Divine Providence in Puerto Rico, and Our Lady of Help in Guatemala, to name a few.

But Mexico developed the strongest devotion to Mary as mother of a nation. The Virgin of Guadalupe appeared to Saint Juan Diego, a humble native from Tenochtitlán, near Mexico City. She had the face of the mestizo people (the descendants of native and Spanish peoples), and her words to Juan Diego were those of a caring mother, especially for her children who are suffering, poor, or oppressed:

Here I wish to hear and help you, and all who dwell in this land and all those who love me, and invoke and place their confidence in me; and to hear your complaints and remedy all your sorrows, hardships, and suffering. . . .

Listen and understand well my son, smallest of all, that you have no cause to be frightened. . . . Is this not your mother here next to you? Are you not here in the shelter of my loving shadow? . . . Let nothing worry or afflict you further. . . . (Office of Religious Education, *A Handbook on Guadalupe*, pp. 148, 152)

▸ Jn 19.25–27

saw that he was already dead, they did not break his legs. 34 Instead, one of the soldiers pierced his side with a spear, and at once blood and water came out. 35 (He who saw this has testified so that you also may believe. His testimony is true, and he knows*j* that he tells the truth.) 36 These things occurred so that the scripture might be fulfilled, "None of his bones shall be broken." 37 And again another passage of scripture says, "They will look on the one whom they have pierced."

The Burial of Jesus
(Mt 27.57–61; Mk 15.42–47; Lk 23.50–56)

38 After these things, Joseph of Ar·i·ma·thē′a, who was a disciple of Jesus, though a secret one because of his fear of the Jews, asked Pilate to let him take away the body of Jesus. Pilate gave him permission; so he came and removed his body. 39 Nic·o·dē′mus, who had at first come to Jesus by night, also came, bringing a mixture of myrrh and aloes, weighing about a hundred pounds. 40 They took the body of Jesus and wrapped it with the spices in linen cloths, according to the burial custom of the Jews. 41 Now there was a garden in the place where he was crucified, and in the garden there was a new tomb in which no one had ever been laid. 42 And so, because it was the Jewish day of Preparation, and the tomb was nearby, they laid Jesus there.

The Resurrection of Jesus
(Mt 28.1–10; Mk 16.1–8; Lk 24.1–12)

20 Early on the first day of the week, while it was still dark, Mary Mag′da·lēne came to the tomb and saw that the stone had been removed from the tomb. 2 So she ran and went to Simon Peter and the other disciple, the one whom

Catholic Connections

RECONCILIATION

In Jn 20.21–23, Jesus empowers his disciples to forgive the sins of others in his name. This is one of the Bible passages that the Catholic church teaches is the basis for the sacrament of Reconciliation (or Penance). Some may know this sacrament by the term confession, because we confess our sins to a priest. The priest serves as a representative of both God and the community in the sacrament. But confessing our sins is only one step in the reconciliation process. We must also be truly sorry and attempt to repair the damage our sin has done. By seeking true reconciliation through the sacrament, we restore the peace of the risen Christ.

▶ Jn 20.21–23

j Or there is one who knows

Introducing ▶ MARY MAGDALENE

Like the Samaritan woman, who is the first to spread the word that Jesus is the Messiah (Jn 4.1–42), Mary Magdalene is the first to announce that Jesus has been raised from the dead. She comes to the tomb while it is still dark (symbolizing unbelief). Later, she encounters the risen Jesus and begins to see with eyes of faith. Belief prompts her to action, and so she goes to tell the others, "I have seen the Lord" (verse 18).

Mary Magdalene is first in every listing of Jesus' female disciples (Mt 27.55–56; Mk 15.40–41; Lk 8.2–3). She seems to have been the leader of a group of women who followed Jesus from the beginning of his ministry, through his death and beyond. Luke indicates that Jesus cured her of seven demons (8.2). All four Gospels name her as one of the first eyewitnesses of Jesus' Resurrection. From all this, we can presume that she was a special friend and disciple of Jesus and an important leader among the first Christians.

Jn 20.1–18

Jesus loved, and said to them, "They have taken the Lord out of the tomb, and we do not know where they have laid him." 3 Then Peter and the other disciple set out and went toward the tomb. 4 The two were running together, but the other disciple outran Peter and reached the tomb first. 5 He bent down to look in and saw the linen wrappings lying there, but he did not go in. 6 Then Simon Peter came, following him, and went into the tomb. He saw the linen wrappings lying there, 7 and the cloth that had been on Jesus' head, not lying with the linen wrappings but rolled up in a place by itself. 8 Then the other disciple, who reached the tomb first, also went in, and he saw and believed; 9 for as yet they did not understand the scripture, that he must rise from the dead. 10 Then the disciples returned to their homes.

Jesus Appears to Mary Magdalene

11 But Mary stood weeping outside the tomb. As she wept, she bent over to lookᵏ into the tomb; 12 and she saw two angels in white, sitting where the body of Jesus had been lying, one at the head and the other at the feet. 13 They said to her, "Woman, why are you weeping?" She said to them, "They have taken away my Lord, and I do not know where they have laid him." 14 When she had said this, she turned around and saw Jesus standing there, but she did not know that it was Jesus. 15 Jesus said to her, "Woman, why are you weeping? Whom are you looking for?" Supposing him to be the gardener, she said to him, "Sir, if you have carried him away, tell me where you have laid him, and I will take him away." 16 Jesus said to her, "Mary!" She turned and said to him in Hebrew,ˡ "Rab·boū'ni!" (which means Teacher). 17 Jesus said to her, "Do not hold on to me, because I have not yet ascended to the Father. But go to my brothers and say to them, 'I am ascending to my Father and your Father, to my God and your God.'" 18 Mary Mag'da·lēne went and announced to the disciples, "I have seen the Lord"; and she told them that he had said these things to her.

Jesus Appears to the Disciples
(Lk 24.36–43; 1 Cor 15.5)

19 When it was evening on that day, the first day of the week, and the doors of the house where the disciples had met were locked for fear of the Jews, Jesus came and stood among them and said, "Peace be with you." 20 After he said this, he showed them his hands and his side. Then the disciples rejoiced when they saw the Lord. 21 Jesus said to them again, "Peace be with you. As the Father

---

k Gk lacks *to look*   l That is, *Aramaic*

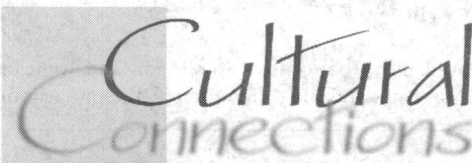

THE BLESSING OF BASKETS

It's early Holy Saturday morning, and the priest of the parish arrives to open the church for a special event. As he draws near the front door, the smell of eggs, sausages, freshly baked bread, and other breakfast foods wafts from the baskets of those already gathered. As people enter the church, they place their baskets on a table before the altar. The priest begins Mass with a prayer and then blesses the baskets of food with holy water and the sign of the cross:

"Blessed are you, O God! In your bounty you provide for your people. As we prepare to celebrate the Resurrection of your Son, bless these Easter foods, and strengthen your people that they may be true witnesses to the new life offered in Christ Jesus, our Lord. Amen."

This custom originated in Eastern Europe and can be found today in many churches around the world. The blessing of baskets reminds us that Jesus' death and Resurrection should touch every aspect of the life of the faithful. Especially after a long Lent of fasting and self-denial, the rich foods of the Easter table call to mind that Good Friday's sacrifice culminated in Easter glory—a time for celebration and feasting.

▸ Jn 21.1–14

has sent me, so I send you." 22 When he had said this, he breathed on them and said to them, "Receive the Holy Spirit. 23 If you forgive the sins of any, they are forgiven them; if you retain the sins of any, they are retained."

Jesus and Thomas

24 But Thomas (who was called the Twin*m*), one of the twelve, was not with them when Jesus came. 25 So the other disciples told him, "We have seen the Lord." But he said to them, "Unless I see the mark of the nails in his hands, and put my finger in the mark of the nails and my hand in his side, I will not believe."

26 A week later his disciples were again in the house, and Thomas was with them. Although the doors were shut, Jesus came and stood among them and said, "Peace be with you." 27 Then he said to Thomas, "Put your finger here and see my hands. Reach out your hand and put it in my side. Do not doubt but believe." 28 Thomas answered him, "My Lord and my God!" 29 Jesus said to him, "Have you believed because you have seen me? Blessed are those who have not seen and yet have come to believe."

The Purpose of This Book

30 Now Jesus did many other signs in the presence of his disciples, which are not written in this book. 31 But these are written so that you may come to believe*n* that Jesus is the Messiah,*o* the Son of God, and that through believing you may have life in his name.

Jesus Appears to Seven Disciples

21 After these things Jesus showed himself again to the disciples by the Sea of Ti·bēr'i·as; and he showed himself in this way. 2 Gathered there together were Simon Peter, Thomas called the Twin,*m* Na·than'a·el of Cā'na in Galilee, the sons of Zeb'e·dee, and two others of his disciples. 3 Simon Peter said to them, "I am going fishing." They said to him, "We will go with you." They went out and got into the boat, but that night they caught nothing.

4 Just after daybreak, Jesus stood on the beach; but the disciples did not know that it was Jesus. 5 Jesus said to them, "Children, you have no fish, have you?" They answered him, "No." 6 He said to them, "Cast the net to the right side of the boat, and you will find some." So they cast it, and now they were not able to haul it in because there were so many fish. 7 That disciple whom Jesus loved said to Peter, "It is the Lord!" When Simon Peter heard that it was the Lord, he put on some clothes, for he was naked, and jumped into the sea. 8 But the other disciples came in the boat, dragging the net full of fish,

for they were not far from the land, only about a hundred yards*p* off.

9 When they had gone ashore, they saw a charcoal fire there, with fish on it, and bread. 10 Jesus said to them, "Bring some of the fish that you have just caught." 11 So Simon Peter went aboard and hauled the net ashore, full of large fish, a hundred fifty-three of them; and though there were so many, the net was not torn. 12 Jesus said to them, "Come and have breakfast." Now none of the disciples dared to ask him, "Who are you?" because they knew it was the Lord. 13 Jesus came and took the bread and gave it to them, and did the same with the fish. 14 This was now the third time that Jesus appeared to the disciples after he was raised from the dead.

Jesus and Peter

15 When they had finished breakfast, Jesus said to Simon Peter, "Simon son of John, do you love me more than these?" He said to him, "Yes, Lord; you know that I love you." Jesus said to him, "Feed my lambs." 16 A second time he said to him,

---

m Gk *Didymus*   *n* Other ancient authorities read *may continue to believe*   *o* Or *the Christ*   *p* Gk *two hundred cubits*

THE HUMBLE CHURCH

Peter must have felt terribly guilty about denying Jesus three times. When the risen Jesus appears to Peter, Jesus offers him three opportunities to reaffirm his love and be reconciled.

The Catholic church also believes that this passage establishes Peter as the leader of the early church and as the first pope, indicated by Jesus' commands to Peter to "feed my lambs," "tend my sheep," and "feed my sheep." By linking Peter's reconciliation to Peter's authority, John seems to be reminding the church to be humble and forgiving.

▶ Jn 21.15–19

did you KNOW?

Resurrection Stories

There are fourteen stories about Jesus' Resurrection in the four Gospels. None of the stories describes the actual Resurrection or the physical appearance of the resurrected Christ. Matthew emphasizes God's power with dramatic symbols like earthquakes and lightning (see 28.2–3). Mark, in its original ending, focuses on the empty tomb (see 16.1–8). Luke emphasizes the living presence of Jesus in the Scriptures and the Eucharist (see 24.13–35). John brings out the authority of the leaders of the early church, especially Peter's role as head of the Apostles (see Jn 20.19–23; 21.15–19).

Together, all these stories convey the faith of the disciples that Jesus is alive. Through God's power, life has triumphed over death. The disciples' mission is to communicate this Good News. And that's our mission too!

▶ Jn 21.15–19

had reclined next to Jesus at the supper and had said, "Lord, who is it that is going to betray you?" 21 When Peter saw him, he said to Jesus, "Lord, what about him?" 22 Jesus said to him, "If it is my will that he remain until I come, what is that to you? Follow me!" 23 So the rumor spread in the community*q* that this disciple would not die. Yet Jesus did not say to him that he would not die, but, "If it is my will that he remain until I come, what is that to you?"*r*

24 This is the disciple who is testifying to these things and has written them, and we know that his testimony is true. 25 But there are also many other things that Jesus did; if every one of them were written down, I suppose that the world itself could not contain the books that would be written.

---

q Gk *among the brothers*   *r* Other ancient authorities lack *what is that to you*

"Simon son of John, do you love me?" He said to him, "Yes, Lord; you know that I love you." Jesus said to him, "Tend my sheep." 17 He said to him the third time, "Simon son of John, do you love me?" Peter felt hurt because he said to him the third time, "Do you love me?" And he said to him, "Lord, you know everything; you know that I love you." Jesus said to him, "Feed my sheep. 18 Very truly, I tell you, when you were younger, you used to fasten your own belt and to go wherever you wished. But when you grow old, you will stretch out your hands, and someone else will fasten a belt around you and take you where you do not wish to go." 19 (He said this to indicate the kind of death by which he would glorify God.) After this he said to him, "Follow me."

Jesus and the Beloved Disciple

20 Peter turned and saw the disciple whom Jesus loved following them; he was the one who

THE GOSPEL ACCORDING TO . . .

The Gospel of John ends by saying that if everything Jesus did were to be written down, the entire world could not contain it. Sounds like a challenge, doesn't it? Perhaps the author was thinking of all the things the risen Christ continues to do in the lives of believers. If you were to write your own Gospel story, one based on the risen Jesus at work in your life, what marvelous stories would it hold? What messages and teachings would you offer to the people of today? How has your life revealed and reflected the Good News of Jesus?

As you think about these things, why not take out some paper and a pen and begin to write your Gospel story? Keep your paper near this Bible so that you can add more good news each time you read it and reflect on where the risen Christ is alive in your life and in the world.

▶ Jn 21.24–25

Stories about famous people are an important part of national identity. The Acts of the Apostles is a book containing stories like these. It continues the account of salvation history by telling about the beginnings of the Christian movement, primarily through stories about two of its most important missionaries, Peter and Paul.

At a Glance

- **1.1—6.7.** the new Pentecost, the mission in Jerusalem

- **6.8—9.43.** the martyrdom of Stephen, the spread of the mission outside Jerusalem, Paul's conversion

- **10.1—15.35.** the spread of the mission to the Gentiles, the Council of Jerusalem

- **15.36—28.31.** Paul's mission to the ends of the earth

In-depth

The Acts of the Apostles—sometimes simply called Acts—was written by the same author as the Gospel of Luke. So Acts is really the second volume of a two-volume history. Like the Gospels, it is not a history in the sense of an eyewitness account of the beginnings of Christianity. Rather, it is an interpretation of this history, explaining how Christianity spread outside of Judaism to the Gentile world under the direction of the Holy Spirit.

Lots of great stories are in the Acts of the Apostles. We read about the descent of the Holy Spirit on the Apostles (2.1–42), Paul's conversion to the Christian way (9.1–19), and some miraculous escapes from prisons and riots (12.6–11; 16.16–40). We learn about the first church council in Jerusalem, where a decision was made to accept Gentiles (non-Jews) as Christians without requiring that they also become practicing Jews (15.1–35). Acts continuously emphasizes how faith in Christ is shared and supported through Christian community.

The Acts of the Apostles gives us information about how Christians lived in the years after Jesus' Resurrection and Ascension. We learn how the believers celebrated the Eucharist together and shared their belongings (2.43–47). We learn how the Gospel message was preached, first to Jews in the synagogues and later to Gentiles. We learn how traveling missionaries like Paul went on long journeys and suffered many hardships to form new groups of believers across the Roman Empire. Under the guidance of the Holy Spirit, the church miraculously went from a small group of disciples in Jerusalem to a movement spreading across the entire Roman Empire, even to Rome itself.

Quick Facts

Author
often identified as Luke, who also wrote the Gospel of Luke

Date Written
approximately A.D. 80

Audience
Gentile (Greek) Christians represented by Theophilus (see Acts 1.1)

Acts

The Promise of the Holy Spirit

1 In the first book, Thē·oph'i·lus, I wrote about all that Jesus did and taught from the beginning 2 until the day when he was taken up to heaven, after giving instructions through the Holy Spirit to the apostles whom he had chosen. 3 After his suffering he presented himself alive to them by many convincing proofs, appearing to them during forty days and speaking about the kingdom of God. 4 While staying*a* with them, he ordered them not to leave Jerusalem, but to wait there for the promise of the Father. "This," he said, "is what you have heard from me; 5 for John baptized with water, but you will be baptized with*b* the Holy Spirit not many days from now."

The Ascension of Jesus
(Mk 16.19–20; Lk 24.50–53)

6 So when they had come together, they asked him, "Lord, is this the time when you will restore the kingdom to Israel?" 7 He replied, "It is not for you to know the times or periods that the Father has set by his own authority. 8 But you will receive power when the Holy Spirit has come upon you; and you will be my witnesses in Jerusalem, in all Judea and Sa·mār'i·a, and to the ends of the earth." 9 When he had said this, as they were watching, he was lifted up, and a cloud took him out of their sight. 10 While he was going and they were gazing up toward heaven, suddenly two men in white robes stood by them. 11 They said, "Men of Gali-

lee, why do you stand looking up toward heaven? This Jesus, who has been taken up from you into heaven, will come in the same way as you saw him go into heaven."

Matthias Chosen to Replace Judas
(Cp Ps 109.8)

12 Then they returned to Jerusalem from the mount called Ol'i·vet, which is near Jerusalem, a sabbath day's journey away. 13 When they had entered the city, they went to the room upstairs where they were staying, Peter, and John, and James, and Andrew, Philip and Thomas, Bartholomew and Matthew, James son of Al·phae'us, and Simon the Zealot, and Judas son of*c* James. 14 All these were constantly devoting themselves to prayer, together with certain women, including Mary the mother of Jesus, as well as his brothers.

15 In those days Peter stood up among the believers*d* (together the crowd numbered about one hundred twenty persons) and said, 16 "Friends,*e* the scripture had to be fulfilled, which the Holy Spirit through David foretold concerning Judas, who became a guide for those who arrested Jesus— 17 for he was numbered among us and was allotted his share in this ministry." 18 (Now this man acquired a field with the reward of his wickedness; and falling headlong,*f* he burst open in the middle and

---

a Or *eating*   *b* Or *by*   *c* Or *the brother of*   *d* Gk *brothers*
e Gk *Men, brothers*   *f* Or *swelling up*

SEND US YOUR SPIRIT!

After Jesus was taken up to heaven, the Apostles, Mary, and other women and men gathered to pray together. They knew that they needed the Holy Spirit, promised by Jesus, to begin the difficult task of giving witness to the Reign of God. Today, we continue to pray:

Jesus, send us your Spirit, and renew the face of the earth. You know our strengths and weaknesses. Transform us into messengers of your Gospel for those who yearn for you.

Jesus, send us your Spirit, and renew the face of the earth. You know our history, with its beautiful and painful experiences. Help us to be untiring promoters of a society based on love, justice, and peace.

Jesus, send us your Spirit, and renew the face of the earth. You know our longing for love and community. Make us instruments of unity and service, especially for those who are weak and those who are lonely. Amen.

▶ **Acts 1.1–11**

all his bowels gushed out. 19 This became known to all the residents of Jerusalem, so that the field was called in their language Ha•kel′da•ma, that is, Field of Blood.) 20 "For it is written in the book of Psalms,

'Let his homestead become desolate,
      and let there be no one to live in it';
and
'Let another take his position of overseer.'
21 So one of the men who have accompanied us during all the time that the Lord Jesus went in and out among us, 22 beginning from the baptism of John until the day when he was taken up from us— one of these must become a witness with us to his resurrection." 23 So they proposed two, Joseph, called Bar•sab′bas, who was also known as Justus, and Mat•thi′as. 24 Then they prayed and said, "Lord, you know everyone's heart. Show us which one of these two you have chosen 25 to take the place in this ministry and apostleship from which Judas turned aside to go to his own place." 26 And they cast lots for them, and the lot fell on Mat•thi′as; and he was added to the eleven apostles.

The Coming of the Holy Spirit

2 When the day of Pentecost had come, they were all together in one place. 2 And suddenly from heaven there came a sound like the rush of a violent wind, and it filled the entire house where they were sitting. 3 Divided tongues, as of fire, appeared among them, and a tongue rested on each of

them. 4 All of them were filled with the Holy Spirit and began to speak in other languages, as the Spirit gave them ability.

5 Now there were devout Jews from every nation under heaven living in Jerusalem. 6 And at this sound the crowd gathered and was bewildered, because each one heard them speaking in the native language of each. 7 Amazed and astonished, they asked, "Are not all these who are speaking Galileans? 8 And how is it that we hear, each of us, in our own native language? 9 Par′thi•ans, Mēdes, Ē′lam•ites, and residents of Mes•o•po•tā′mi•a, Judea and Cap•pa•dō′ci•a, Pon′tus and Asia, 10 Phryg′i•a and Pam•phyl′i•a, Egypt and the parts of Lib′ya belonging to Cȳ•rē′nē, and visitors from Rome, both Jews and proselytes, 11 Crē′tans and Arabs—in our own languages we hear them speaking about God's deeds of power." 12 All were amazed and perplexed, saying to one another, "What does this mean?" 13 But others sneered and said, "They are filled with new wine."

Peter Addresses the Crowd
(Joel 2.28–32)

14 But Peter, standing with the eleven, raised his voice and addressed them, "Men of Judea and all who live in Jerusalem, let this be known to you, and listen to what I say. 15 Indeed, these are not drunk, as you suppose, for it is only nine o'clock in

ACTS

---

8 Other ancient authorities read *the share*

the morning. 16 No, this is what was spoken
through the prophet Jō'el:
17 'In the last days it will be, God declares,
      that I will pour out my Spirit upon all flesh,
         and your sons and your daughters shall
               prophesy,
      and your young men shall see visions,
         and your old men shall dream dreams.
18 Even upon my slaves, both men and
            women,
         in those days I will pour out my Spirit;
            and they shall prophesy.
19 And I will show portents in the heaven
            above
         and signs on the earth below,
            blood, and fire, and smoky mist.
20 The sun shall be turned to darkness
         and the moon to blood,
            before the coming of the Lord's great
               and glorious day.
21 Then everyone who calls on the name of the
            Lord shall be saved.'

22 "You that are Israelites,[h] listen to what I have
to say: Jesus of Nazareth,[i] a man attested to you by
God with deeds of power, wonders, and signs that
God did through him among you, as you yourselves know— 23 this man, handed over to you according to the definite plan and foreknowledge of
God, you crucified and killed by the hands of those
outside the law. 24 But God raised him up, having
freed him from death,[j] because it was impossible
for him to be held in its power. 25 For David says
concerning him,
   'I saw the Lord always before me,
      for he is at my right hand so that I will not
            be shaken;
26 therefore my heart was glad, and my tongue
            rejoiced;
      moreover my flesh will live in hope.
27 For you will not abandon my soul to Hades,
      or let your Holy One experience
            corruption.
28 You have made known to me the ways of
            life;
      you will make me full of gladness with your
            presence.'
29 "Fellow Israelites,[k] I may say to you confidently of our ancestor David that he both died and
was buried, and his tomb is with us to this day.
30 Since he was a prophet, he knew that God had
sworn with an oath to him that he would put one
of his descendants on his throne. 31 Foreseeing this,
David[l] spoke of the resurrection of the Messiah,[m]
saying,
   'He was not abandoned to Hades,
      nor did his flesh experience corruption.'
32 This Jesus God raised up, and of that all of us are

CONFIRMATION

The first verses of the Acts of the Apostles,
chapter 2, are a biblical story associated
with the sacrament of Confirmation, one of
the seven sacraments celebrated within the
Catholic church. As one of the three sacraments of initiation—along with Baptism and
the Eucharist—Confirmation celebrates a
person's membership in the church. But in a
special way, Confirmation is associated with
the gift of the Holy Spirit.

During the Confirmation ceremony,
the bishop or priest anoints with blessed
oil, called chrism, the foreheads of those
being confirmed and signs them with the
gift of the Holy Spirit. We pray that the
Holy Spirit strengthen those who have been
confirmed to live the Gospel and share the
Good News of Jesus Christ, just as the Apostles did at the first Pentecost.

If you have been confirmed, what was
your experience of receiving the sacrament?
How are you aware of the presence and
guidance of the Holy Spirit? How do you
participate in the life of your church community? If you have not been confirmed, what
would you hope for in Confirmation?

▶ Acts 2.1–13

witnesses. 33 Being therefore exalted at[n] the right
hand of God, and having received from the Father
the promise of the Holy Spirit, he has poured out
this that you both see and hear. 34 For David did
not ascend into the heavens, but he himself says,
   'The Lord said to my Lord,
   "Sit at my right hand,
35   until I make your enemies your footstool." '

---

[h] Gk Men, Israelites   [i] Gk the Nazorean   [j] Gk the pains
of death   [k] Gk Men, brothers   [l] Gk he   [m] Or the Christ
[n] Or by

36 Therefore let the entire house of Israel know with certainty that God has made him both Lord and Messiah,o this Jesus whom you crucified."

The First Converts

37 Now when they heard this, they were cut to the heart and said to Peter and to the other apostles, "Brothers,p what should we do?" 38 Peter said to them, "Repent, and be baptized every one of you in the name of Jesus Christ so that your sins may be forgiven; and you will receive the gift of the Holy Spirit. 39 For the promise is for you, for your children, and for all who are far away, everyone whom the Lord our God calls to him." 40 And he testified with many other arguments and exhorted them, saying, "Save yourselves from this corrupt generation." 41 So those who welcomed his message were baptized, and that day about three thousand persons were added. 42 They devoted themselves to the apostles' teaching and fellowship, to the breaking of bread and the prayers.

Life among the Believers

43 Awe came upon everyone, because many wonders and signs were being done by the apostles. 44 All who believed were together and had all things in common; 45 they would sell their possessions and goods and distribute the proceedsq to all, as any had need. 46 Day by day, as they spent much time together in the temple, they broke bread at homer and ate their food with glad and generouss hearts, 47 praising God and having the goodwill of all the people. And day by day the Lord added to their number those who were being saved.

Peter Heals a Crippled Beggar

3 One day Peter and John were going up to the temple at the hour of prayer, at three o'clock in the afternoon. 2 And a man lame from birth was being carried in. People would lay him daily at the gate of the temple called the Beautiful Gate so that he could ask for alms from those entering the temple. 3 When he saw Peter and John about to go into the temple, he asked them for alms. 4 Peter looked intently at him, as did John, and said, "Look at us." 5 And he fixed his attention on them, expecting to receive something from them. 6 But Peter said, "I have no silver or gold, but what I have I give you; in the name of Jesus Christ of Nazareth,t stand up and walk." 7 And he took him by the right hand and raised him up; and immediately his feet and ankles were made strong. 8 Jumping up, he stood and began to walk, and he entered the temple with them, walking and leaping and praising God. 9 All the people saw him walking and praising God, 10 and they recognized him as the one who used to sit and ask for alms at the Beautiful Gate of the temple;

Catholic Connections

PENTECOST

Genesis, chapter 11, is the story of arrogant workers who tried to build the tower of Babel to reach up to heaven. God confused their languages so they couldn't understand one another. Building was impossible.

Pentecost was just the reverse! Heaven came down as the Holy Spirit descended upon the Apostles. The Jewish feast of Pentecost had celebrated the wheat harvest. Now the Apostles received the harvest of the Holy Spirit: the courage, confidence, and zeal to go out into the world and proclaim God's salvation in Jesus Christ. No matter what their language, everyone present could understand the Apostles' message. It was a holy day. It was a day to build God's people up.

Pentecost is considered the birthday of the Christian church. The Catholic church traditionally celebrates the feast of Pentecost on the second Sunday after Ascension Thursday, which is approximately fifty days after Easter (the term pente means "fifty"). It continues to be an important feast to celebrate the unity of all Christians. In the United States alone, the Gospel is preached in more than a hundred languages to people of many different cultures.

▶ Acts 2.1–13

and they were filled with wonder and amazement at what had happened to him.

Peter Speaks in Solomon's Portico

11 While he clung to Peter and John, all the people ran together to them in the portico called Solomon's Portico, utterly astonished. 12 When Peter saw it, he addressed the people, "You Israelites,u

---

o Or Christ   p Gk Men, brothers   q Gk them   r Or from house to house   s Or sincere   t Gk the Nazorean   u Gk Men, Israelites

Christian Community

In the famous passage of Acts 2.43–47, the ideal Christian community is portrayed as open to the Holy Spirit. They shared everything in common, including prayer, meals, and possessions. No one went in need. Sound impossible?

Across the world, groups of people live together in intentional Christian communities similar to that among the believers described in Acts. Some of them pool their finances and possessions to provide for their food and housing. They commit themselves to building caring relationships of trust and respect with one another. They spend time praying together. They perform works of service together in the community. Many Christian families strive for this vision in their life together.

Is living like this attractive to you? What would be hard for you in living like this? What do you think society would be like today if this were everyone's lifestyle? Intentional Christian communities are attractive to many Christians today. As you grow older, you might look for such a community when you leave home—or even start one yourself. It is a wonderful experience of the Christian way of life.

▶ **Acts 2.43–47**

why do you wonder at this, or why do you stare at us, as though by our own power or piety we had made him walk? 13 The God of Abraham, the God of Isaac, and the God of Jacob, the God of our ancestors has glorified his servant*v* Jesus, whom you handed over and rejected in the presence of Pilate, though he had decided to release him. 14 But you rejected the Holy and Righteous One and asked to have a murderer given to you, 15 and you killed the Author of life, whom God raised from the dead. To this we are witnesses. 16 And by faith in his name, his name itself has made this man strong, whom you see and know; and the faith that is through Jesus*w* has given him this perfect health in the presence of all of you.

17 "And now, friends,*x* I know that you acted in ignorance, as did also your rulers. 18 In this way God fulfilled what he had foretold through all the prophets, that his Messiah*y* would suffer. 19 Repent therefore, and turn to God so that your sins may be wiped out, 20 so that times of refreshing may come from the presence of the Lord, and that he may send the Messiah*z* appointed for you, that is, Jesus, 21 who must remain in heaven until the time of universal restoration that God announced long ago through his holy prophets. 22 Moses said, 'The Lord your God will raise up for you from your own people*x* a prophet like me. You must listen to whatever he tells you. 23 And it will be that everyone who

---

v Or *child*   *w* Gk *him*   *x* Gk *brothers*   *y* Or *his Christ*   *z* Or *the Christ*

A
C
T
S

Share Christ

As is true in our own cities today, in Jerusalem during the first century, it was not uncommon to encounter beggars on the streets. And probably, like today, some people averted their eyes and walked by while others stopped to offer a few coins.

When Peter and John encounter a beggar in Acts 3.3, they don't have a whole lot of money to share with him, but they stop just the same. Looking him in the eye, Peter offers the lame man the one thing of value he does have: the powerful gift of healing found in the name of Jesus Christ.

You may not have the gift of healing or lots of extra money to give to those in need. But Peter and John remind us that knowing Jesus is the greatest treasure one can acquire in life, and that this treasure has been given to us freely. Don't forget to share it with others!

▶ **Acts 3.1–10**

does not listen to that prophet will be utterly rooted out of the people.' 24 And all the prophets, as
many as have spoken, from Samuel and those after
him, also predicted these days. 25 You are the descendants of the prophets and of the covenant that
God gave to your ancestors, saying to Abraham,
'And in your descendants all the families of the
earth shall be blessed.' 26 When God raised up his
servant,*a* he sent him first to you, to bless you by
turning each of you from your wicked ways."

Peter and John before the Council

4 While Peter and John*b* were speaking to the
people, the priests, the captain of the temple,
and the Sad'du·cees came to them, 2 much annoyed
because they were teaching the people and proclaiming that in Jesus there is the resurrection of the
dead. 3 So they arrested them and put them in custody until the next day, for it was already evening.
4 But many of those who heard the word believed;
and they numbered about five thousand.

5 The next day their rulers, elders, and scribes
assembled in Jerusalem, 6 with An'nas the high
priest, Cā'i·a·phas, John,*c* and Alexander, and all
who were of the high-priestly family. 7 When they
had made the prisoners*d* stand in their midst, they
inquired, "By what power or by what name did you
do this?" 8 Then Peter, filled with the Holy Spirit,
said to them, "Rulers of the people and elders, 9 if
we are questioned today because of a good deed
done to someone who was sick and are asked how
this man has been healed, 10 let it be known to all
of you, and to all the people of Israel, that this man
is standing before you in good health by the name
of Jesus Christ of Nazareth,*e* whom you crucified,
whom God raised from the dead. 11 This Jesus*f* is

'the stone that was rejected by you, the
builders;
it has become the cornerstone.'*g*

12 There is salvation in no one else, for there is no
other name under heaven given among mortals by
which we must be saved."

13 Now when they saw the boldness of Peter
and John and realized that they were uneducated
and ordinary men, they were amazed and recognized them as companions of Jesus. 14 When they
saw the man who had been cured standing beside
them, they had nothing to say in opposition. 15 So
they ordered them to leave the council while they
discussed the matter with one another. 16 They said,
"What will we do with them? For it is obvious to all
who live in Jerusalem that a notable sign has been
done through them; we cannot deny it. 17 But to
keep it from spreading further among the people,
let us warn them to speak no more to anyone in
this name." 18 So they called them and ordered
them not to speak or teach at all in the name of

PRAY IT!

I Believe!
The Apostles' Creed

In Acts 4.5–12, Peter stands up before
the unbelieving rulers and elders and
boldly proclaims his faith in Jesus as healer and Messiah. Every Sunday at Mass,
Catholic Christians profess the same
faith when they pray the Nicene Creed.
(A creed is a type of prayer that expresses faith beliefs.) Did you know there is
also a shorter creed called the Apostles'
Creed? The Apostles' Creed is based on
the teachings and beliefs of the earliest
Christians.

Take a moment to pray the Apostles'
Creed:

*I believe in God, the Father almighty,
creator of heaven and earth. I believe in
Jesus Christ, his only Son, our Lord. He
was conceived by the power of the Holy
Spirit and born of the Virgin Mary. He
suffered under Pontius Pilate, was crucified, died, and was buried. He descended
into hell. On the third day he rose again.
He ascended into heaven and is seated at
the right hand of the Father. He will come
again to judge the living and the dead. I
believe in the Holy Spirit, the holy
catholic Church, the communion of
saints, the forgiveness of sins, the resurrection of the body, and the life everlasting. Amen.* (Catechism of the Catholic
Church, pp. 49–50)

Then reflect or journal on the following
questions:
- **Which statements of the creed do you
  have questions about?**
- **How hard would it be for you to express your faith beliefs to people who
  don't believe in Jesus?**

▸ **Acts 4.5–12**

Jesus. 19 But Peter and John answered them,
"Whether it is right in God's sight to listen to you
rather than to God, you must judge; 20 for we

ACTS

---

a Or *child*   *b* Gk *While they*   *c* Other ancient authorities
read *Jonathan*   *d* Gk *them*   *e* Gk *the Nazorean*   *f* Gk *This*
g Or *keystone*

cannot keep from speaking about what we have seen and heard." 21 After threatening them again, they let them go, finding no way to punish them because of the people, for all of them praised God for what had happened. 22 For the man on whom this sign of healing had been performed was more than forty years old.

The Believers Pray for Boldness
(Cp Ps 2.1–2)

23 After they were released, they went to their friends[h] and reported what the chief priests and the elders had said to them. 24 When they heard it, they raised their voices together to God and said, "Sovereign Lord, who made the heaven and the earth, the sea, and everything in them, 25 it is you who said by the Holy Spirit through our ancestor David, your servant:[i]

'Why did the Gentiles rage,
　　and the peoples imagine vain things?
26 The kings of the earth took their stand,
　　and the rulers have gathered together
　　　　against the Lord and against his
　　　　　　Messiah.'[j]

27 For in this city, in fact, both Her'od and Pon'ti·us Pilate, with the Gentiles and the peoples of Israel, gathered together against your holy servant[i] Jesus, whom you anointed, 28 to do whatever your hand and your plan had predestined to take place. 29 And now, Lord, look at their threats, and grant to your servants[k] to speak your word with all boldness, 30 while you stretch out your hand to heal, and signs and wonders are performed through the name of your holy servant[i] Jesus." 31 When they had prayed, the place in which they were gathered together was shaken; and they were all filled with the Holy Spirit and spoke the word of God with boldness.

The Believers Share Their Possessions

32 Now the whole group of those who believed were of one heart and soul, and no one claimed private ownership of any possessions, but everything they owned was held in common. 33 With great power the apostles gave their testimony to the resurrection of the Lord Jesus, and great grace was upon them all. 34 There was not a needy person among them, for as many as owned lands or houses sold them and brought the proceeds of what was sold. 35 They laid it at the apostles' feet, and it was distributed to each as any had need. 36 There was a Le'vite, a native of Cyprus, Joseph, to whom the apostles gave the name Bar'na·bas (which means "son of encouragement"). 37 He sold a field that belonged to him, then brought the money, and laid it at the apostles' feet.

did you KNOW?

Stewardship

Acts 4.32–37 describes a Christian behavior called stewardship. Stewardship involves sharing the gifts of time, talent, and treasure that God has placed in your care (see "Stewardship: Making a Contribution," Lk 21.1–4). It is key to the life of any Christian community.

Sharing our treasure and giving money are the most obvious ways of sharing. Consider the disciple named in the passage, Joseph Barnabas. How did he share? Can you think of things you spend money on—a CD, new jeans, a movie—and make a commitment to give some of that money to a charitable organization?

But giving money isn't the only way to share with others. Think about your own gifts. What are you good at that you could share with your parish, school, or community? Do not discount even the simplest ability. For example, maybe you are persistent; this talent can help any project to be successful. Or perhaps you love children and can baby-sit for overwhelmed parents.

How are you a good steward of your time, talent, and treasure? Think about it!

▶ Acts 4.32–37

Ananias and Sapphira

5 But a man named An·a·ni'as, with the consent of his wife Sap·phi'ra, sold a piece of property; 2 with his wife's knowledge, he kept back some of the proceeds, and brought only a part and laid it at the apostles' feet. 3 "An·a·ni'as," Peter asked, "why has Satan filled your heart to lie to the Holy Spirit and to keep back part of the proceeds of the land? 4 While it remained unsold, did it not remain your own? And after it was sold, were not the proceeds at your disposal? How is it that you have contrived this deed in your heart? You did not lie to us[l] but to God!" 5 Now when An·a·ni'as heard these words, he fell down and died. And great fear seized all who heard of it. 6 The young men came and wrapped up his body,[m] then carried him out and buried him.

---

h Gk *their own*　i Or *child*　j Or *his Christ*　k Gk *slaves*
l Gk *to men*　m Meaning of Gk uncertain

7 After an interval of about three hours his wife came in, not knowing what had happened. 8 Peter said to her, "Tell me whether you and your husband sold the land for such and such a price." And she said, "Yes, that was the price." 9 Then Peter said to her, "How is it that you have agreed together to put the Spirit of the Lord to the test? Look, the feet of those who have buried your husband are at the door, and they will carry you out." 10 Immediately she fell down at his feet and died. When the young men came in they found her dead, so they carried her out and buried her beside her husband. 11 And great fear seized the whole church and all who heard of these things.

The Apostles Heal Many

12 Now many signs and wonders were done among the people through the apostles. And they were all together in Solomon's Portico. 13 None of the rest dared to join them, but the people held them in high esteem. 14 Yet more than ever believers were added to the Lord, great numbers of both men and women, 15 so that they even carried out the sick into the streets, and laid them on cots and mats, in order that Peter's shadow might fall on some of them as he came by. 16 A great number of people would also gather from the towns around Jerusalem, bringing the sick and those tormented by unclean spirits, and they were all cured.

The Apostles Are Persecuted

17 Then the high priest took action; he and all who were with him (that is, the sect of the Sad·du·cees), being filled with jealousy, 18 arrested the apostles and put them in the public prison. 19 But during the night an angel of the Lord opened the prison doors, brought them out, and said, 20 "Go, stand in the temple and tell the people the whole message about this life." 21 When they heard this, they entered the temple at daybreak and went on with their teaching.

When the high priest and those with him arrived, they called together the council and the whole body of the elders of Israel, and sent to the prison to have them brought. 22 But when the temple police went there, they did not find them in the prison; so they returned and reported, 23 "We found the prison securely locked and the guards standing at the doors, but when we opened them, we found no one inside." 24 Now when the captain of the temple and the chief priests heard these words, they were perplexed about them, wondering what might be going on. 25 Then someone arrived and announced, "Look, the men whom you put in prison are standing in the temple and teaching the people!" 26 Then the captain went with the temple police and brought them, but without violence, for they were afraid of being stoned by the people.

27 When they had brought them, they had them stand before the council. The high priest questioned them, 28 saying, "We gave you strict orders not to teach in this name,[n] yet here you have filled Jerusalem with your teaching and you are determined to bring this man's blood on us." 29 But Peter and the apostles answered, "We must obey God rather than any human authority.[o] 30 The God of our ancestors raised up Jesus, whom you had killed by hanging him on a tree. 31 God exalted him at his right hand as Leader and Savior that he might

---

n Other ancient authorities read *Did we not give you strict orders not to teach in this name?*   o Gk *than men*

A
C
T
S

LIVE IT!

Pop Quiz

The scene. The disciples, who are spreading the Good News of Jesus Christ, are taken before the Jewish council to explain their motives and reasons for this work.

The test. Gamaliel, a wise Jewish leader, talks the rest of the council out of killing the disciples, by using the following reasoning: If the disciples' mission is from God, it will succeed despite anything the council does. But if it is not of God's design, it will fail and the Christians will eventually disappear anyway.

The question. If you were brought before a similar council, would your life's mission pass or fail this test? That is, would your words and actions in the past week reflect Jesus' attitudes, actions, and mission?

Your answer.

▶ Acts 5.27–39

give repentance to Israel and forgiveness of sins. [32] And we are witnesses to these things, and so is the Holy Spirit whom God has given to those who obey him."

33 When they heard this, they were enraged and wanted to kill them. [34] But a Phar'i·see in the council named Ga·ma'li·el, a teacher of the law, respected by all the people, stood up and ordered the men to be put outside for a short time. [35] Then he said to them, "Fellow Israelites,[p] consider carefully what you propose to do to these men. [36] For some time ago Theu'das rose up, claiming to be somebody, and a number of men, about four hundred, joined him; but he was killed, and all who followed him were dispersed and disappeared. [37] After him Judas the Galilean rose up at the time of the census and got people to follow him; he also perished, and all who followed him were scattered. [38] So in the present case, I tell you, keep away from these men and let them alone; because if this plan or this undertaking is of human origin, it will fail; [39] but if it is of God, you will not be able to overthrow them— in that case you may even be found fighting against God!"

They were convinced by him, [40] and when they had called in the apostles, they had them flogged. Then they ordered them not to speak in the name of Jesus, and let them go. [41] As they left the council, they rejoiced that they were considered worthy to suffer dishonor for the sake of the name. [42] And every day in the temple and at home[q] they did not cease to teach and proclaim Jesus as the Messiah.[r]

Seven Chosen to Serve

6 Now during those days, when the disciples were increasing in number, the Hellenists complained against the Hebrews because their widows were being neglected in the daily distribution of food. [2] And the twelve called together the whole community of the disciples and said, "It is not right that we should neglect the word of God in order to wait on tables.[s] [3] Therefore, friends,[t] select from among yourselves seven men of good standing, full of the Spirit and of wisdom, whom we may appoint to this task, [4] while we, for our part, will devote ourselves to prayer and to serving the word." [5] What they said pleased the whole community, and they chose Stephen, a man full of faith and the Holy Spirit, together with Philip, Proch'o·rus, Ni·ca'nor, Ti'mon, Par'me·nas, and Nic·o·la'us, a proselyte of An'ti·och. [6] They had these men stand before the apostles, who prayed and laid their hands on them.

7 The word of God continued to spread; the number of the disciples increased greatly in Jerusalem, and a great many of the priests became obedient to the faith.

The Arrest of Stephen

8 Stephen, full of grace and power, did great wonders and signs among the people. [9] Then some of those who belonged to the synagogue of the Freedmen (as it was called), Cy·re'ni·ans, Alexandrians, and others of those from Ci·li'ci·a and Asia, stood up and argued with Stephen. [10] But they could not withstand the wisdom and the Spirit[u] with which he spoke. [11] Then they secretly instigated some men to say, "We have heard him speak blasphemous words against Moses and God." [12] They stirred up the people as well as the elders and the scribes; then they suddenly confronted him, seized him, and brought him before the council. [13] They set up false witnesses who said, "This man never stops saying things against this holy place and the law; [14] for we have heard him say that this Jesus of Nazareth[v] will destroy this place and will change the customs that Moses handed on to us." [15] And all who sat in the council looked intently at him, and they saw that his face was like the face of an angel.

Stephen's Speech to the Council
(Gen 12.1—50.26)

7 Then the high priest asked him, "Are these things so?" [2] And Stephen replied:

"Brothers[w] and fathers, listen to me. The God of glory appeared to our ancestor Abraham when he was in Mes·o·po·ta'mi·a, before he lived in Har'an, [3] and said to him, 'Leave your country and your relatives and go to the land that I will show you.' [4] Then he left the country of the Chal·de'ans and settled in Har'an. After his father died, God had him move from there to this country in which you are now living. [5] He did not give him any of it as a heritage, not even a foot's length, but promised to give it to him as his possession and to his descendants after him, even though he had no child. [6] And God spoke in these terms, that his descendants would be resident aliens in a country belonging to others, who would enslave them and mistreat them during four hundred years. [7] 'But I will judge the nation that they serve,' said God, 'and after that they shall come out and worship me in this place.' [8] Then he gave him the covenant of circumcision. And so Abraham[x] became the father of Isaac and circumcised him on the eighth day; and Isaac became the father of Jacob, and Jacob of the twelve patriarchs.

9 "The patriarchs, jealous of Joseph, sold him into Egypt; but God was with him, [10] and rescued him from all his afflictions, and enabled him to win

---

p Gk *Men, Israelites*   q Or *from house to house*   r Or *the Christ*   s Or *keep accounts*   t Gk *brothers*   u Or *spirit*   v Gk *the Nazorean*   w Gk *Men, brothers*   x Gk *he*

did you KNOW?

Martyrs

The stoning of Stephen is a turning point in Luke's account of the first Christians. Stephen was the first Christian martyr—someone who dies for his or her faith. His death marked the beginning of a period of persecution of the early Christians. Up to then, Christians had been imprisoned but not put to death. Would the Christian movement fall apart now that the stakes were higher? Luke makes it clear that Stephen's death actually strengthened the church. His heroic sacrifice is even presented as a model for Christians—notice all the similarities between his death and Jesus'.

All around the world, including places close to home, people are mistreated, and even killed, because of their religious beliefs.

For example, Archbishop Oscar Romero of El Salvador was shot to death because he challenged the wealthy and powerful people in his country to change their ways so the poor people could have a better quality of life. Archbishop Romero, like Stephen, was killed for being a faithful Christian.

Stephen was young just like you. He was convinced that following the teachings of Jesus was the most important way to live. He died for his beliefs, and the church became stronger because of his faith and heroism. What would you die for?

▶ Acts 6.8—8.1

favor and to show wisdom when he stood before Pharaoh, king of Egypt, who appointed him ruler over Egypt and over all his household. 11 Now there came a famine throughout Egypt and Cā'naan, and great suffering, and our ancestors could find no food. 12 But when Jacob heard that there was grain in Egypt, he sent our ancestors there on their first visit. 13 On the second visit Joseph made himself known to his brothers, and Joseph's family became known to Pharaoh. 14 Then Joseph sent and invited his father Jacob and all his relatives to come to him, seventy-five in all; 15 so Jacob went down to Egypt. He himself died there as well as our ancestors, 16 and their bodies were brought back to Shē'chem and laid in the tomb that Abraham had bought for a sum of silver from the sons of Hā'mor in Shē'chem.

17 "But as the time drew near for the fulfillment of the promise that God had made to Abraham, our people in Egypt increased and multiplied 18 until another king who had not known Joseph ruled over Egypt. 19 He dealt craftily with our race and forced our ancestors to abandon their infants so that they would die. 20 At this time Moses was born, and he was beautiful before God. For three months he was brought up in his father's house; 21 and when he was abandoned, Pharaoh's daughter adopted him and brought him up as her own son. 22 So Moses was instructed in all the wisdom of the Egyptians and was powerful in his words and deeds.

23 "When he was forty years old, it came into his heart to visit his relatives, the Israelites.z 24 When he saw one of them being wronged, he defended the oppressed man and avenged him by striking down the Egyptian. 25 He supposed that his kinsfolk would understand that God through him was rescuing them, but they did not understand. 26 The next day he came to some of them as they were quarreling and tried to reconcile them, saying, 'Men, you are brothers; why do you wrong each other?' 27 But the man who was wronging his neighbor pushed Mosesa aside, saying, 'Who made you a ruler and a judge over us? 28 Do you want to kill me as you killed the Egyptian yesterday?' 29 When he heard this, Moses fled and became a resident alien in the land of Mid'i•an. There he became the father of two sons.

30 "Now when forty years had passed, an angel appeared to him in the wilderness of Mount Sinai, in the flame of a burning bush. 31 When Moses saw it, he was amazed at the sight; and as he approached to look, there came the voice of the Lord: 32 'I am the God of your ancestors, the God of Abraham, Isaac, and Jacob.' Moses began to tremble and did not dare to look. 33 Then the Lord said to him, 'Take off the sandals from your feet, for the place where you are standing is holy ground. 34 I have surely seen the mistreatment of my people who are in Egypt and have heard their groaning, and I have come down to rescue them. Come now, I will send you to Egypt.'

35 "It was this Moses whom they rejected when

ACTS

---

y Gk they   z Gk his brothers, the sons of Israel   a Gk him

'God will raise up
a prophet for you
from your own people
as he raised me up.'

He is the one who was in the congregation

in the wilderness with the angel

who spoke to him at Mount Sinai,

and with our ancestors;

and he received living oracles to give to us.

THIS IS THE MOSES WHO SAID TO THE ISRAELITES,

they said, 'Who made you a ruler and a judge?' and whom God now sent as both ruler and liberator through the angel who appeared to him in the bush. 36 He led them out, having performed wonders and signs in Egypt, at the Red Sea, and in the wilderness for forty years. 37 This is the Moses who said to the Israelites, 'God will raise up a prophet for you from your own people[b] as he raised me up.' 38 He is the one who was in the congregation in the wilderness with the angel who spoke to him at Mount Sinai, and with our ancestors; and he received living oracles to give to us. 39 Our ancestors were unwilling to obey him; instead, they pushed him aside, and in their hearts they turned back to Egypt, 40 saying to Aaron, 'Make gods for us who will lead the way for us; as for this Moses who led us out from the land of Egypt, we do not know what has happened to him.' 41 At that time they made a calf, offered a sacrifice to the idol, and reveled in the works of their hands. 42 But God turned away from them and handed them over to worship the host of heaven, as it is written in the book of the prophets:

'Did you offer to me slain victims and sacrifices
forty years in the wilderness, O house of
Israel?

43 No; you took along the tent of Mō′loch,
and the star of your god Rē′phan,
the images that you made to worship;
so I will remove you beyond Babylon.'

44 "Our ancestors had the tent of testimony in the wilderness, as God[c] directed when he spoke to Moses, ordering him to make it according to the pattern he had seen. 45 Our ancestors in turn brought it in with Joshua when they dispossessed the nations that God drove out before our ancestors. And it was there until the time of David, 46 who found favor with God and asked that he might find a dwelling place for the house of Jacob.[d] 47 But it was Solomon who built a house for him. 48 Yet the Most High does not dwell in houses made with human hands;[e] as the prophet says,

49 'Heaven is my throne,
and the earth is my footstool.
What kind of house will you build for me, says
the Lord,
or what is the place of my rest?
50 Did not my hand make all these things?'
51 "You stiff-necked people, uncircumcised in

b Gk your brothers   c Gk he   d Other ancient authorities read for the God of Jacob   e Gk with hands heart and ears, you are forever opposing the Holy Spirit, just as your ancestors used to do. 52 Which of the prophets did your ancestors not persecute? They killed those who foretold the coming of the Righteous One, and now you have become his betrayers and murderers. 53 You are the ones that received the law as ordained by angels, and yet you have not kept it."

The Stoning of Stephen

54 When they heard these things, they became enraged and ground their teeth at Stephen.*f* 55 But filled with the Holy Spirit, he gazed into heaven and saw the glory of God and Jesus standing at the right hand of God. 56 "Look," he said, "I see the heavens opened and the Son of Man standing at the right hand of God!" 57 But they covered their ears, and with a loud shout all rushed together against him. 58 Then they dragged him out of the city and began to stone him; and the witnesses laid their coats at the feet of a young man named Saul. 59 While they were stoning Stephen, he prayed, "Lord Jesus, receive my spirit." 60 Then he knelt down and cried out in a loud voice, "Lord, do not hold this sin against them." When he had said this,

8 he died.*g* 1 And Saul approved of their killing him.

Saul Persecutes the Church

That day a severe persecution began against the church in Jerusalem, and all except the apostles were scattered throughout the countryside of Judea and Sa•mār′i•a. 2 Devout men buried Stephen and made loud lamentation over him. 3 But Saul was ravaging the church by entering house after house; dragging off both men and women, he committed them to prison.

Philip Preaches in Samaria

4 Now those who were scattered went from place to place, proclaiming the word. 5 Philip went down to the city*h* of Sa•mār′i•a and proclaimed the Messiah*i* to them. 6 The crowds with one accord listened eagerly to what was said by Philip, hearing and seeing the signs that he did, 7 for unclean

---

f Gk *him*   *g* Gk *fell asleep*   *h* Other ancient authorities read *a city*   *i* Or *the Christ*

Introducing ▶ SAINT PAUL

As Stephen is stoned to death, Acts introduces a person who will become the major character in the second half of the book, Saul of Tarsus, also known as Paul. Paul begins as a persecutor of the early Christians. He is a member of the Pharisees, a group that holds to a rigid interpretation of Jewish Law (26.4–5). He probably sees the Christians as a threat to the Jewish faith. But after a profound experience of the risen Christ, Paul is converted to the Christian faith. Paul is initially distrusted by other Christians who remember his persecution of them. However, another early Christian leader, Barnabas, becomes Paul's companion and advocate (9.27).

Paul's major insight is that God has made salvation available to everyone, Jews and Gentiles alike. He also knows that God's offer of salvation is a free gift, that no one could do anything to actually earn it. But many of the early Christians, who are former Jews, disagree with him. This conflict comes to a head at the Council of Jerusalem (Acts of the Apostles, chapter 15), where Paul stands toe-to-toe with Peter and James (Gal 2.1–10) and argues that the Gentiles can become Christians without following Jewish laws and customs, including circumcision.

Paul took it upon himself to spread the good news of God's salvation in Jesus to the Gentiles. During three different missionary journeys, he was instrumental in founding new Christian communities in what is now the Middle East and western Europe. He stayed in touch with those communities through letters, some of which are included as books in the New Testament. Paul's impact in spreading Christianity was so great that he is sometimes called the second founder of Christianity.

spirits, crying with loud shrieks, came out of many who were possessed; and many others who were paralyzed or lame were cured. 8 So there was great joy in that city.

9 Now a certain man named Simon had previously practiced magic in the city and amazed the people of Sa•mār′i•a, saying that he was someone great. 10 All of them, from the least to the greatest, listened to him eagerly, saying, "This man is the power of God that is called Great." 11 And they listened eagerly to him because for a long time he had amazed them with his magic. 12 But when they believed Philip, who was proclaiming the good news about the kingdom of God and the name of Jesus Christ, they were baptized, both men and women. 13 Even Simon himself believed. After being baptized, he stayed constantly with Philip and was amazed when he saw the signs and great miracles that took place.

14 Now when the apostles at Jerusalem heard that Sa•mār′i•a had accepted the word of God, they sent Peter and John to them. 15 The two went down and prayed for them that they might receive the Holy Spirit 16 (for as yet the Spirit had not come*j* upon any of them; they had only been baptized in the name of the Lord Jesus). 17 Then Peter and John*k* laid their hands on them, and they received the Holy Spirit. 18 Now when Simon saw that the Spirit was given through the laying on of the apostles' hands, he offered them money, 19 saying, "Give me also this power so that anyone on whom I lay my hands may receive the Holy Spirit." 20 But Peter said to him, "May your silver perish with you,

because you thought you could obtain God's gift with money! 21 You have no part or share in this, for your heart is not right before God. 22 Repent therefore of this wickedness of yours, and pray to the Lord that, if possible, the intent of your heart may be forgiven you. 23 For I see that you are in the gall of bitterness and the chains of wickedness." 24 Simon answered, "Pray for me to the Lord, that nothing of what you*l* have said may happen to me."

25 Now after Peter and John*m* had testified and spoken the word of the Lord, they returned to Jerusalem, proclaiming the good news to many villages of the Sa•mār′i•tans.

Philip and the Ethiopian Eunuch
(Cp Isa 53.7–8)

26 Then an angel of the Lord said to Philip, "Get up and go toward the south*n* to the road that goes down from Jerusalem to Gă′za." (This is a wilderness road.) 27 So he got up and went. Now there was an Ethiopian eunuch, a court official of the Can•dă′cē, queen of the Ethiopians, in charge of her entire treasury. He had come to Jerusalem to worship 28 and was returning home; seated in his chariot, he was reading the prophet I•sāi′ah. 29 Then the Spirit said to Philip, "Go over to this chariot and join it." 30 So Philip ran up to it and heard him reading the prophet I•sāi′ah. He asked, "Do you understand what you are reading?" 31 He replied, "How can I, unless someone guides me?" And he

---

j Gk *fallen*   *k* Gk *they*   *l* The Greek word for *you* and the verb *pray* are plural   *m* Gk *after they*   *n* Or *go at noon*

Bearing Good News

Acts 8.26–40 tells the story of an Ethiopian eunuch. A eunuch is a man who has been castrated, either by accident or by design. Eunuchs often served as guards of the harems of kings. This eunuch was reading a text from Isaiah while returning from a visit to Jerusalem. The Holy Spirit moved the missionary Philip to explain to him how Isaiah's prophecies pointed to Jesus. And the eunuch believed and was baptized. His baptism signals the beginning acceptance of Gentile believers.

The eunuch's faith was dependent on the interaction of three characters: himself, the searching eunuch; Philip, bearing the Good News; and the Holy Spirit, who brought them together. Reflect for a moment on the following questions:

- How are you like the Ethiopian? What are you searching for in your faith?
- How are you like Philip? How do you share the Good News with others?
- How can you share in the work of the Holy Spirit? How can you motivate other young people to become bearers of the Good News?

As Philip baptized the eunuch, geographical, ethnic, and legal barriers were washed away. Praise God for the salvation brought by Jesus to all people!

▶ Acts 8.26–40

invited Philip to get in and sit beside him. 32 Now the passage of the scripture that he was reading was this:

> "Like a sheep he was led to the slaughter,
>   and like a lamb silent before its shearer,
>   so he does not open his mouth.
> 33 In his humiliation justice was denied him.
>   Who can describe his generation?
>   For his life is taken away from the
>   earth."

34 The eunuch asked Philip, "About whom, may I ask you, does the prophet say this, about himself or about someone else?" 35 Then Philip began to speak, and starting with this scripture, he proclaimed to him the good news about Jesus. 36 As they were going along the road, they came to some water; and the eunuch said, "Look, here is water! What is to prevent me from being baptized?"[o] 38 He commanded the chariot to stop, and both of them, Philip and the eunuch, went down into the water, and Philip[p] baptized him. 39 When they came up out of the water, the Spirit of the Lord snatched Philip away; the eunuch saw him no more, and went on his way rejoicing. 40 But Philip found himself at A·zō'tus, and as he was passing through the region, he proclaimed the good news to all the towns until he came to Caes·a·rē'a.

The Conversion of Saul
(Acts 22.6–16; 26.12–18)

9 Meanwhile Saul, still breathing threats and murder against the disciples of the Lord, went to the high priest 2 and asked him for letters to the synagogues at Damascus, so that if he found any who belonged to the Way, men or women, he might bring them bound to Jerusalem. 3 Now as he was going along and approaching Damascus, suddenly a light from heaven flashed around him. 4 He fell to the ground and heard a voice saying to him, "Saul, Saul, why do you persecute me?" 5 He asked, "Who are you, Lord?" The reply came, "I am Jesus, whom you are persecuting. 6 But get up and enter the city, and you will be told what you are to do." 7 The men who were traveling with him stood speechless because they heard the voice but saw no one. 8 Saul got up from the ground, and though his eyes were open, he could see nothing; so they led him by the hand and brought him into Damascus. 9 For three days he was without sight, and neither ate nor drank.

10 Now there was a disciple in Damascus named An·a·ni'as. The Lord said to him in a vision, "An·a·ni'as." He answered, "Here I am, Lord." 11 The Lord said to him, "Get up and go to the street called Straight, and at the house of Judas look for a man of Tar'sus named Saul. At this moment he is praying, 12 and he has seen in a vision[q] a man named An·a·ni'as come in and lay his hands on him so that he might regain his sight." 13 But An·a·ni'as answered, "Lord, I have heard from many about this man, how much evil he has done to your saints in Jerusalem; 14 and here he has authority from the chief priests to bind all who invoke your name." 15 But the Lord said to him, "Go, for he is an instrument whom I have chosen to bring my name before Gentiles and kings and before the people of Israel; 16 I myself will show him how much he must suffer for the sake of my name." 17 So An·a·ni'as went and entered the house. He laid his hands on Saul[r] and said, "Brother Saul, the Lord Jesus, who appeared to you on your way here, has sent me so that you may regain your sight and be filled with the Holy Spirit." 18 And immediately something like scales fell from his eyes, and his sight was restored. Then he got up and was baptized, 19 and after taking some food, he regained his strength.

9.4

Saul Preaches in Damascus

For several days he was with the disciples in Damascus, 20 and immediately he began to proclaim Jesus in the synagogues, saying, "He is the Son of God." 21 All who heard him were amazed and said, "Is not this the man who made havoc in Jerusalem among those who invoked this name? And has he not come here for the purpose of bringing them bound before the chief priests?" 22 Saul

---

o Other ancient authorities add all or most of verse 37, *And Philip said, "If you believe with all your heart, you may." And he replied, "I believe that Jesus Christ is the Son of God."*
p Gk *he*   q Other ancient authorities lack *in a vision*
r Gk *him*

PRAY IT!
Conversion

Saul (or Paul) experienced some dramatic events that converted him from a persecutor of Christians to a believer in Jesus Christ. He had a powerful experience of the risen Christ during which he was blinded. His physical blindness is symbolic of his previous spiritual blindness. For three days, Paul was practically lifeless—not seeing, not eating, not drinking. This period reminds us of Jesus' three days in the tomb. In many ways, going through a conversion is like dying—dying to old ways of thinking and acting. But after three days, Paul's blindness was lifted, and he was filled with the Holy Spirit, as the other Apostles were at Pentecost.

No longer a persecutor of Christians, Paul was a new person. He now felt compelled to learn more about Jesus and to share the Good News with other people. Paul's conversion told the early Christians that even the most hard-hearted person can be called by God and radically changed.

In your prayer, reflect or journal on the following questions:
- Have you ever been suddenly aware of God's presence and calling in your life?
- What mission is God calling you for?
- How will you respond?

Then close with these words:

Dear Jesus, following you is an unending journey in which we must turn our back to sin and focus on living out Christ's message. Sometimes, it is an easy journey; sometimes, it is a struggle. Help me to find your light in the Scriptures, in others, and within myself. Amen.

▶ Acts 9.1–19

became increasingly more powerful and confounded the Jews who lived in Damascus by proving that Jesus^s was the Messiah.^t

Saul Escapes from the Jews

23 After some time had passed, the Jews plotted to kill him, 24 but their plot became known to Saul. They were watching the gates day and night so that they might kill him; 25 but his disciples took him by night and let him down through an opening in the wall,^u lowering him in a basket.

Saul in Jerusalem

26 When he had come to Jerusalem, he attempted to join the disciples; and they were all afraid of him, for they did not believe that he was a disciple. 27 But Bar'na•bas took him, brought him to the apostles, and described for them how on the road he had seen the Lord, who had spoken to him, and how in Damascus he had spoken boldly in the name of Jesus. 28 So he went in and out among them in Jerusalem, speaking boldly in the name of the Lord. 29 He spoke and argued with the Hellenists; but they were attempting to kill him. 30 When the believers^v learned of it, they brought him down to Caes•a•re′a and sent him off to Tar′sus.

31 Meanwhile the church throughout Judea, Galilee, and Sa•mar′i•a had peace and was built up. Living in the fear of the Lord and in the comfort of the Holy Spirit, it increased in numbers.

The Healing of Aeneas

32 Now as Peter went here and there among all the believers,^w he came down also to the saints living in Lyd′da. 33 There he found a man named Aē•nē′as, who had been bedridden for eight years, for he was paralyzed. 34 Peter said to him, "Aē•nē′as, Jesus Christ heals you; get up and make your bed!" And immediately he got up. 35 And all the residents of Lyd′da and Sharon saw him and turned to the Lord.

Peter in Lydda and Joppa

36 Now in Jop′pa there was a disciple whose name was Tab′i•tha, which in Greek is Dor′cas.^x She was devoted to good works and acts of charity. 37 At that time she became ill and died. When they had washed her, they laid her in a room upstairs. 38 Since Lyd′da was near Jop′pa, the disciples, who heard that Peter was there, sent two men to him with the request, "Please come to us without delay." 39 So Peter got up and went with them; and when he arrived, they took him to the room upstairs. All the widows stood beside him, weeping and showing tunics and other clothing that Dor′cas had made while she was with them. 40 Peter put all of them outside, and then he knelt down and prayed. He turned to the body and said, "Tab′i•tha, get up." Then she opened her eyes, and seeing Peter, she sat up. 41 He gave her his hand and helped her up.

---

^s Gk *that this*   ^t Or *the Christ*   ^u Gk *through the wall*
^v Gk *brothers*   ^w Gk *all of them*   ^x The name Tabitha in Aramaic and the name Dorcas in Greek mean *a gazelle*

ACTS

Then calling the saints and widows, he showed her to be alive. 42 This became known throughout Jop'pa, and many believed in the Lord. 43 Meanwhile he stayed in Jop'pa for some time with a certain Simon, a tanner.

Peter and Cornelius

10 In Caes•a•rē'a there was a man named Cornelius, a centurion of the Italian Cohort, as it was called. 2 He was a devout man who feared God with all his household; he gave alms generously to the people and prayed constantly to God. 3 One afternoon at about three o'clock he had a vision in which he clearly saw an angel of God coming in and saying to him, "Cornelius." 4 He stared at him in terror and said, "What is it, Lord?" He answered, "Your prayers and your alms have ascended as a memorial before God. 5 Now send men to Jop'pa for a certain Simon who is called Peter; 6 he is lodging with Simon, a tanner, whose house is by the seaside." 7 When the angel who spoke to him had left, he called two of his slaves and a devout soldier from the ranks of those who served him, 8 and after telling them everything, he sent them to Jop'pa.

9 About noon the next day, as they were on their journey and approaching the city, Peter went up on the roof to pray. 10 He became hungry and wanted something to eat; and while it was being prepared, he fell into a trance. 11 He saw the heaven opened and something like a large sheet coming down, being lowered to the ground by its four corners. 12 In it were all kinds of four-footed creatures and reptiles and birds of the air. 13 Then he heard a voice saying, "Get up, Peter; kill and eat." 14 But Peter said, "By no means, Lord; for I have never eaten anything that is profane or unclean." 15 The voice said to him again, a second time, "What God has made clean, you must not call profane." 16 This happened three times, and the thing was suddenly taken up to heaven.

17 Now while Peter was greatly puzzled about what to make of the vision that he had seen, suddenly the men sent by Cornelius appeared. They were asking for Simon's house and were standing by the gate. 18 They called out to ask whether Simon, who was called Peter, was staying there. 19 While Peter was still thinking about the vision, the Spirit said to him, "Look, three*y* men are searching for you. 20 Now get up, go down, and go with them without hesitation; for I have sent them." 21 So Peter went down to the men and said, "I am the one you are looking for; what is the reason for your coming?" 22 They answered, "Cornelius, a centurion, an upright and God-fearing man, who is well spoken of by the whole Jewish nation, was directed by a holy angel to send for you to come to

his house and to hear what you have to say." 23 So Peter*z* invited them in and gave them lodging.

The next day he got up and went with them, and some of the believers*a* from Jop'pa accompanied him. 24 The following day they came to Caes•a•rē'a. Cornelius was expecting them and had called together his relatives and close friends. 25 On Peter's arrival Cornelius met him, and falling at his feet, worshiped him. 26 But Peter made him get up, saying, "Stand up; I am only a mortal." 27 And as he talked with him, he went in and found that many had assembled; 28 and he said to them, "You yourselves know that it is unlawful for a Jew to associate with or to visit a Gentile; but God has shown me that I should not call anyone profane or unclean. 29 So when I was sent for, I came without objection. Now may I ask why you sent for me?"

30 Cornelius replied, "Four days ago at this very hour, at three o'clock, I was praying in my house when suddenly a man in dazzling clothes stood before me. 31 He said, 'Cornelius, your prayer has been heard and your alms have been remembered before God. 32 Send therefore to Jop'pa and ask for Simon, who is called Peter; he is staying in the home of Simon, a tanner, by the sea.' 33 Therefore I sent for you immediately, and you have been kind enough to come. So now all of us are here in the presence of God to listen to all that the Lord has commanded you to say."

Gentiles Hear the Good News

34 Then Peter began to speak to them: "I truly understand that God shows no partiality, 35 but in every nation anyone who fears him and does what is right is acceptable to him. 36 You know the message he sent to the people of Israel, preaching peace by Jesus Christ—he is Lord of all. 37 That message spread throughout Judea, beginning in Galilee after the baptism that John announced: 38 how God anointed Jesus of Nazareth with the Holy Spirit and with power; how he went about doing good and healing all who were oppressed by the devil, for God was with him. 39 We are witnesses to all that he did both in Judea and in Jerusalem. They put him to death by hanging him on a tree; 40 but God raised him on the third day and allowed him to appear, 41 not to all the people but to us who were chosen by God as witnesses, and who ate and drank with him after he rose from the dead. 42 He commanded us to preach to the people and to testify that he is the one ordained by God as judge of the living and the dead. 43 All the prophets testify about him that everyone who believes in him receives forgiveness of sins through his name."

---

y One ancient authority reads *two*; others lack the word
z Gk *he*   *a* Gk *brothers*

HERE COMES EVERYBODY

The word *catholic* means "universal." Someone once described being Catholic as, "Here comes everybody!"

In Acts 10.34–36, we hear that because God shows no partiality, neither should we. Even so, it is sometimes easier to stick with people who are similar to us. They understand us and know where we are coming from. There's less explaining to do. Right?

But being catholic means reaching out of our familiar circle of friends and including in our group people of different cultures and religions.

Have you ever seen a handwoven blanket? Threads of various colors are woven together to form an intricate, new pattern. Each blanket is completely different from every other blanket. By building relationships with people of different cultures and embracing their diversity, we become like one of the threads in such a blanket, weaving our uniquenesses in a new and beautiful pattern. The result is different and enriching, and then we become truly catholic.

▶ Acts 10.34–36

Gentiles Receive the Holy Spirit

44 While Peter was still speaking, the Holy Spirit fell upon all who heard the word. 45 The circumcised believers who had come with Peter were astounded that the gift of the Holy Spirit had been poured out even on the Gentiles, 46 for they heard them speaking in tongues and extolling God. Then Peter said, 47 "Can anyone withhold the water for baptizing these people who have received the Holy Spirit just as we have?" 48 So he ordered them to be baptized in the name of Jesus Christ. Then they invited him to stay for several days.

Peter's Report to the Church at Jerusalem

11 Now the apostles and the believers[b] who were in Judea heard that the Gentiles had also accepted the word of God. 2 So when Peter went up to Jerusalem, the circumcised believers[c] criticized him, 3 saying, "Why did you go to uncircumcised men and eat with them?" 4 Then Peter began to explain it to them, step by step, saying, 5 "I was in the city of Jop'pa praying, and in a trance I saw a vision. There was something like a large sheet coming down from heaven, being lowered by its four corners; and it came close to me. 6 As I looked at it closely I saw four-footed animals, beasts of prey, reptiles, and birds of the air. 7 I also heard a voice saying to me, 'Get up, Peter; kill and eat.' 8 But I replied, 'By no means, Lord; for nothing profane or unclean has ever entered my mouth.' 9 But

a second time the voice answered from heaven, 'What God has made clean, you must not call profane.' 10 This happened three times; then everything was pulled up again to heaven. 11 At that very moment three men, sent to me from Caes•a•rē'a, arrived at the house where we were. 12 The Spirit told me to go with them and not to make a distinction between them and us.[d] These six brothers also accompanied me, and we entered the man's house. 13 He told us how he had seen the angel standing in his house and saying, 'Send to Jop'pa and bring Simon, who is called Peter; 14 he will give you a message by which you and your entire household will be saved.' 15 And as I began to speak, the Holy Spirit fell upon them just as it had upon us at the beginning. 16 And I remembered the word of the Lord, how he had said, 'John baptized with water, but you will be baptized with the Holy Spirit.' 17 If then God gave them the same gift that he gave us when we believed in the Lord Jesus Christ, who was I that I could hinder God?" 18 When they heard this, they were silenced. And they praised God, saying, "Then God has given even to the Gentiles the repentance that leads to life."

The Church in Antioch

19 Now those who were scattered because of the persecution that took place over Stephen trav-

---

b Gk *brothers*   *c* Gk lacks *believers*   *d* Or *not to hesitate* eled as far as Phoe•ni'ci•a, Cyprus, and An'ti•och, and they spoke the word to no one except Jews. 20 But among them were some men of Cyprus and Cȳ•rē'nē who, on coming to An'ti•och, spoke to the Hellenists*e* also, proclaiming the Lord Jesus. 21 The hand of the Lord was with them, and a great number became believers and turned to the Lord. 22 News of this came to the ears of the church in Jerusalem, and they sent Bar'na•bas to An'ti•och. 23 When he came and saw the grace of God, he rejoiced, and he exhorted them all to remain faithful to the Lord with steadfast devotion; 24 for he was a good man, full of the Holy Spirit and of faith. And a great many people were brought to the Lord. 25 Then Bar'na•bas went to Tar'sus to look for Saul, 26 and when he had found him, he brought him to An'ti•och. So it was that for an entire year they met with*f* the church and taught a great many people, and it was in An'ti•och that the disciples were first called "Christians."

27 At that time prophets came down from Jerusalem to An'ti•och. 28 One of them named Ag'a•bus stood up and predicted by the Spirit that there would be a severe famine over all the world; and this took place during the reign of Clau'di•us. 29 The disciples determined that according to their ability, each would send relief to the believers*g* living in Judea; 30 this they did, sending it to the elders by Bar'na•bas and Saul.

James Killed and Peter Imprisoned

12 About that time King Her'od laid violent hands upon some who belonged to the church. 2 He had James, the brother of John, killed with the sword. 3 After he saw that it pleased the

Jews, he proceeded to arrest Peter also. (This was during the festival of Unleavened Bread.) 4 When he had seized him, he put him in prison and handed him over to four squads of soldiers to guard him, intending to bring him out to the people after the Passover. 5 While Peter was kept in prison, the church prayed fervently to God for him.

Peter Delivered from Prison

6 The very night before Her'od was going to bring him out, Peter, bound with two chains, was sleeping between two soldiers, while guards in front of the door were keeping watch over the prison. 7 Suddenly an angel of the Lord appeared and a light shone in the cell. He tapped Peter on the side and woke him, saying, "Get up quickly." And the chains fell off his wrists. 8 The angel said to him, "Fasten your belt and put on your sandals." He did so. Then he said to him, "Wrap your cloak around you and follow me." 9 Peter*h* went out and followed him; he did not realize that what was happening with the angel's help was real; he thought he was seeing a vision. 10 After they had passed the first and the second guard, they came before the iron gate leading into the city. It opened for them of its own accord, and they went outside and walked along a lane, when suddenly the angel left him. 11 Then Peter came to himself and said, "Now I am sure that the Lord has sent his angel and rescued me from the hands of Her'od and from all that the Jewish people were expecting."

12 As soon as he realized this, he went to the

---

e Other ancient authorities read *Greeks* *f* Or *were guests of* *g* Gk *brothers* *h* Gk *He*

Introducing ▶BARNABAS

We first met Barnabas defending Paul after Paul's conversion in Acts of the Apostles, chapter 9. Now, in chapter 11, we are told that Barnabas "was a good man, full of the Holy Spirit and of faith." Barnabas's name literally means "son of encouragement." And encouraging others seemed to be Barnabas's gift. He recognized Paul's gifts and brought Paul to Antioch to minister to the new Christians there when no one else trusted Paul. Later, Barnabas reached out to Mark, disagreeing with Paul on whether to give Mark a second chance to travel with them (15.36–39). Barnabas sounds like the friend we would all like to have, someone who would believe in us through good times and bad.

Have you had a Barnabas in your life, someone who encouraged you and believed in you even after you made mistakes? Can you be that kind of encouraging friend to others?

•

Acts 11.19–26

house of Mary, the mother of John whose other name was Mark, where many had gathered and were praying. 13 When he knocked at the outer gate, a maid named Rhō′da came to answer. 14 On recognizing Peter's voice, she was so overjoyed that, instead of opening the gate, she ran in and announced that Peter was standing at the gate. 15 They said to her, "You are out of your mind!" But she insisted that it was so. They said, "It is his angel." 16 Meanwhile Peter continued knocking; and when they opened the gate, they saw him and were amazed. 17 He motioned to them with his hand to be silent, and described for them how the Lord had brought him out of the prison. And he added, "Tell this to James and to the believers."*i* Then he left and went to another place.

18 When morning came, there was no small commotion among the soldiers over what had become of Peter. 19 When Her′od had searched for him and could not find him, he examined the guards and ordered them to be put to death. Then he went down from Judea to Caes·a·rē′a and stayed there.

What Imprisons You?

*H*oly Spirit, come! Open my mind to seek the truth. Break down the barriers that imprison me. Empower me to overcome any guilt by asking for forgiveness. Enable me to forgive others and release my past hurt and anger. Open my eyes to vices, habits, and attitudes that are destructive to me and to others. Guide me to true freedom with your Word. Amen.

▸ Acts 12.6–19

The Death of Herod

20 Now Her′od*i* was angry with the people of Tȳre and Sī′don. So they came to him in a body; and after winning over Blas′tus, the king's chamberlain, they asked for a reconciliation, because their country depended on the king's country for food. 21 On an appointed day Her′od put on his royal robes, took his seat on the platform, and delivered a public address to them. 22 The people kept shouting, "The voice of a god, and not of a mortal!" 23 And immediately, because he had not given the glory to God, an angel of the Lord struck him down, and he was eaten by worms and died.

24 But the word of God continued to advance and gain adherents. 25 Then after completing their mission Bar′na·bas and Saul returned to*k* Jerusalem and brought with them John, whose other name was Mark.

Barnabas and Saul Commissioned

13 Now in the church at An′ti·och there were prophets and teachers: Bar′na·bas, Sim′ē·on who was called Nī′ger, Lucius of Cȳ·rē′nē, Man′a·en a member of the court of Her′od the ruler,*l* and Saul. 2 While they were worshiping the Lord and fasting, the Holy Spirit said, "Set apart for me Bar′na·bas and Saul for the work to which I have called them." 3 Then after fasting and praying they laid their hands on them and sent them off.

The Apostles Preach in Cyprus

4 So, being sent out by the Holy Spirit, they went down to Se·leū′ci·a; and from there they sailed to Cyprus. 5 When they arrived at Sal′a·mis, they proclaimed the word of God in the synagogues of the Jews. And they had John also to assist them. 6 When they had gone through the whole island as far as Pā′phos, they met a certain magician, a Jewish false prophet, named Bar-Jesus. 7 He was with the proconsul, Ser′gi·us Paul′us, an intelligent man, who summoned Bar′na·bas and Saul and wanted to hear the word of God. 8 But the magician El′y·mas (for that is the translation of his name) opposed them and tried to turn the proconsul away from the faith. 9 But Saul, also known as Paul, filled with the Holy Spirit, looked intently at him 10 and said, "You son of the devil, you enemy of all righteousness, full of all deceit and villainy, will you not stop making crooked the straight paths of the Lord? 11 And now listen—the hand of the Lord is against you, and you will be blind for a while, unable to see the sun." Immediately mist and darkness came over him, and he went about groping for someone to lead him by the hand. 12 When the proconsul saw what had happened, he believed, for he was astonished at the teaching about the Lord.

Paul and Barnabas in Antioch of Pisidia

13 Then Paul and his companions set sail from Pā′phos and came to Per′ga in Pam·phyl′i·a. John, however, left them and returned to Jerusalem; 14 but they went on from Per′ga and came to An′ti·och in Pi·sid′i·a. And on the sabbath day they went into the synagogue and sat down. 15 After the reading of the law and the prophets, the officials of the synagogue sent them a message, saying, "Brothers, if you have any word of exhortation for the people, give it." 16 So Paul stood up and with a gesture began to speak:

---

i Gk *brothers*   *j* Gk *he*   *k* Other ancient authorities read *from*   *l* Gk *tetrarch*

"You Israelites,[m] and others who fear God, listen. [17] The God of this people Israel chose our ancestors and made the people great during their stay in the land of Egypt, and with uplifted arm he led them out of it. [18] For about forty years he put up with[n] them in the wilderness. [19] After he had destroyed seven nations in the land of Ca′naan, he gave them their land as an inheritance [20] for about four hundred fifty years. After that he gave them judges until the time of the prophet Samuel. [21] Then they asked for a king; and God gave them Saul son of Kish, a man of the tribe of Benjamin, who reigned for forty years. [22] When he had removed him, he made David their king. In his testimony about him he said, 'I have found David, son of Jesse, to be a man after my heart, who will carry out all my wishes.' [23] Of this man's posterity God has brought to Israel a Savior, Jesus, as he promised; [24] before his coming John had already proclaimed a baptism of repentance to all the people of Israel. [25] And as John was finishing his work, he said, 'What do you suppose that I am? I am not he. No, but one is coming after me; I am not worthy to untie the thong of the sandals[o] on his feet.'

26 "My brothers, you descendants of Abraham's family, and others who fear God, to us[p] the message of this salvation has been sent. [27] Because the residents of Jerusalem and their leaders did not recognize him or understand the words of the prophets that are read every sabbath, they fulfilled those words by condemning him. [28] Even though they found no cause for a sentence of death, they asked Pilate to have him killed. [29] When they had carried out everything that was written about him, they took him down from the tree and laid him in a tomb. [30] But God raised him from the dead; [31] and for many days he appeared to those who came up with him from Galilee to Jerusalem, and they are now his witnesses to the people. [32] And we bring you the good news that what God promised to our ancestors [33] he has fulfilled for us, their children, by raising Jesus; as also it is written in the second psalm,

'You are my Son;
    today I have begotten you.'

[34] As to his raising him from the dead, no more to return to corruption, he has spoken in this way,
'I will give you the holy promises made to
    David.'

[35] Therefore he has also said in another psalm,
'You will not let your Holy One experience
    corruption.'

[36] For David, after he had served the purpose of God in his own generation, died,[q] was laid beside his ancestors, and experienced corruption; [37] but he whom God raised up experienced no corruption. [38] Let it be known to you therefore, my brothers,

did you KNOW?

The Journeys of Paul

According to most interpretations of Acts, Paul made three missionary journeys over a ten-year period to spread the Gospel message. The details of his first journey are covered in chapters 13–14. The second journey is reported in chapters 16–18. The third journey is described in chapters 19–21. Paul himself may have seen these not as three separate journeys but as one continuous missionary activity. On these journeys, Paul made converts and started Christian communities. On the second and third journeys, he also visited established communities to give them guidance and support. See maps 7 and 8 for the routes of Paul's journeys.

Paul's third journey landed him back in Jerusalem, where some Jews had him arrested. On the basis of his Roman citizenship, Paul appealed to the emperor. So he was transported to Rome (this trip is referred to as his fourth journey). He probably died there as a martyr around A.D. 65. Some traditions say that Paul wasn't martyred there but went on to evangelize in Spain.

▶ **Acts of the Apostles, chapters 13–21**

ACTS

that through this man forgiveness of sins is proclaimed to you; [39] by this Jesus[r] everyone who believes is set free from all those sins[s] from which you could not be freed by the law of Moses. [40] Beware, therefore, that what the prophets said does not happen to you:
[41] 'Look, you scoffers!
        Be amazed and perish,
    for in your days I am doing a work,
        a work that you will never believe, even if
            someone tells you.' "

42 As Paul and Bar′na·bas[t] were going out, the people urged them to speak about these things again the next sabbath. [43] When the meeting of the synagogue broke up, many Jews and devout con-

---

[m] Gk Men, Israelites   [n] Other ancient authorities read *cared for*   [o] Gk *untie the sandals*   [p] Other ancient authorities read *you*   [q] Gk *fell asleep*   [r] Gk *this*   [s] Gk *all*   [t] Gk *they*

verts to Jū′da•ism followed Paul and Bar′na•bas, who spoke to them and urged them to continue in the grace of God.

44 The next sabbath almost the whole city gathered to hear the word of the Lord.ᵘ 45 But when the Jews saw the crowds, they were filled with jealousy; and blaspheming, they contradicted what was spoken by Paul. 46 Then both Paul and Bar′na•bas spoke out boldly, saying, "It was necessary that the word of God should be spoken first to you. Since you reject it and judge yourselves to be unworthy of eternal life, we are now turning to the Gentiles. 47 For so the Lord has commanded us, saying,

'I have set you to be a light for the Gentiles,
    so that you may bring salvation to the ends
        of the earth.' "

48 When the Gentiles heard this, they were glad and praised the word of the Lord; and as many as had been destined for eternal life became believers. 49 Thus the word of the Lord spread throughout the region. 50 But the Jews incited the devout women of high standing and the leading men of the city, and stirred up persecution against Paul and Bar′na•bas, and drove them out of their region. 51 So they shook the dust off their feet in protest against them, and went to I•cō′ni•um. 52 And the disciples were filled with joy and with the Holy Spirit.

Paul and Barnabas in Iconium

14 The same thing occurred in I•cō′ni•um, where Paul and Bar′na•basᵛ went into the Jewish synagogue and spoke in such a way that a great number of both Jews and Greeks became believers. 2 But the unbelieving Jews stirred up the Gentiles and poisoned their minds against the brothers. 3 So they remained for a long time, speaking boldly for the Lord, who testified to the word of his grace by granting signs and wonders to be done through them. 4 But the residents of the city were divided; some sided with the Jews, and some with the apostles. 5 And when an attempt was made by both Gentiles and Jews, with their rulers, to mistreat them and to stone them, 6 the apostlesᵛ learned of it and fled to Lys′tra and Der′bē, cities of Lyc•ā•ō′ni•a, and to the surrounding country; 7 and there they continued proclaiming the good news.

Paul and Barnabas in Lystra and Derbe

8 In Lys′tra there was a man sitting who could not use his feet and had never walked, for he had been crippled from birth. 9 He listened to Paul as he was speaking. And Paul, looking at him intently and seeing that he had faith to be healed, 10 said in a loud voice, "Stand upright on your feet." And the manʷ sprang up and began to walk. 11 When the crowds saw what Paul had done, they shouted in the Lyc•ā•ō′ni•an language, "The gods have come down to us in human form!" 12 Bar′na•bas they called Zeūs, and Paul they called Her′mēs, because he was the chief speaker. 13 The priest of Zeūs, whose temple was just outside the city,ˣ brought oxen and garlands to the gates; he and the crowds wanted to offer sacrifice. 14 When the apostles Bar′na•bas and Paul heard of it, they tore their clothes and rushed out into the crowd, shouting, 15 "Friends,ʸ why are you doing this? We are mortals just like you, and we bring you good news, that you should turn from these worthless things to the living God, who made the heaven and the earth and the sea and all that is in them. 16 In past generations he allowed all the nations to follow their own ways; 17 yet he has not left himself without a witness in doing good—giving you rains from heaven and fruitful seasons, and filling you with food and your hearts with joy." 18 Even with these words, they scarcely restrained the crowds from offering sacrifice to them.

19 But Jews came there from An′ti•och and I•cō′ni•um and won over the crowds. Then they

---

ᵘ Other ancient authorities read *God*   ᵛ Gk *they*   ʷ Gk *he*
ˣ Or *The priest of Zeus-Outside-the-City*   ʸ Gk *Men*

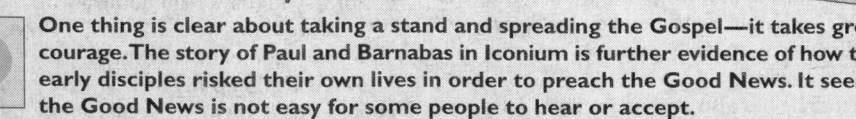

A Courageous Stance

One thing is clear about taking a stand and spreading the Gospel—it takes great courage. The story of Paul and Barnabas in Iconium is further evidence of how the early disciples risked their own lives in order to preach the Good News. It seems the Good News is not easy for some people to hear or accept.

In your prayer, reflect or journal on the following questions:
- In what ways is God inviting you to live a little more courageously in order to spread the Good News in your school? your home? your neighborhood and community?
- What keeps you from responding?

▶ Acts 14.1–7

stoned Paul and dragged him out of the city, supposing that he was dead. 20 But when the disciples surrounded him, he got up and went into the city. The next day he went on with Bar′na•bas to Der′bē.

The Return to Antioch in Syria

21 After they had proclaimed the good news to that city and had made many disciples, they returned to Lys′tra, then on to Ī•cō′ni•um and An′ti•och. 22 There they strengthened the souls of the disciples and encouraged them to continue in the faith, saying, "It is through many persecutions that we must enter the kingdom of God." 23 And after they had appointed elders for them in each church, with prayer and fasting they entrusted them to the Lord in whom they had come to believe.

24 Then they passed through Pi•sid′i•a and came to Pam•phyl′i•a. 25 When they had spoken the word in Per′ga, they went down to At•ta•lī′a. 26 From there they sailed back to An′ti•och, where they had been commended to the grace of God for the workz that they had completed. 27 When they arrived, they called the church together and related all that God had done with them, and how he had opened a door of faith for the Gentiles. 28 And they stayed there with the disciples for some time.

The Council at Jerusalem

15 Then certain individuals came down from Judea and were teaching the brothers, "Unless you are circumcised according to the custom of Moses, you cannot be saved." 2 And after Paul and Bar′na•bas had no small dissension and debate with them, Paul and Bar′na•bas and some of the others were appointed to go up to Jerusalem to discuss this question with the apostles and the elders. 3 So they were sent on their way by the church, and as they passed through both Phoe•ni′ci•a and Sa•mār′i•a, they reported the conversion of the Gentiles, and brought great joy to all the believers.a 4 When they came to Jerusalem, they were welcomed by the church and the apostles and the elders, and they reported all that God had done with them. 5 But some believers who belonged to the sect of the Phar′i•sees stood up and said, "It is necessary for them to be circumcised and ordered to keep the law of Moses."

6 The apostles and the elders met together to consider this matter. 7 After there had been much debate, Peter stood up and said to them, "My brothers,b you know that in the early days God made a choice among you, that I should be the one through whom the Gentiles would hear the message of the good news and become believers. 8 And God, who knows the human heart, testified to them by giving them the Holy Spirit, just as he did to us; 9 and in cleansing their hearts by faith he has made

Catholic Connections

MINISTRY IN THE CHURCH

The Acts of the Apostles gives us some clues about how positions of ministry developed in the first Christian communities. One of the first ministries that developed was the ministry of service. Acts 6.1–7 tells how seven people were chosen for a special ministry of service. Eventually, people with special roles of service were called deacons (see 1 Tim 3.8–13). Today, deacons continue to have service to the community as their primary goal.

Acts 14.21–28 tells how Paul and Barnabas appointed leaders, or "presbyters," in the communities they formed. These leaders watched over the community and guarded against those who would distort the true faith (20.28–32). Over time, the chief leaders in this role became known as bishops (see 1 Tim 3.1–7) and were recognized as the successors of the Apostles. The leaders who assisted the bishops became known as priests, or presbyters.

Many other ministries are listed in the New Testament, including the ministries of evangelization, of teaching, of interpreting the Scriptures, of prophecy, and of healing (see 1 Cor 12.7–11 for one list). Many of these ministries required no special office. Today, parish ministers such as youth ministers, religious educators, liturgical ministers, outreach ministers, and many others, continue this practice of sharing their gifts with the Christian community.

no distinction between them and us. 10 Now therefore why are you putting God to the test by placing on the neck of the disciples a yoke that neither our ancestors nor we have been able to bear? 11 On the contrary, we believe that we will be saved through the grace of the Lord Jesus, just as they will."

---

z Or *committed in the grace of God to the work*
a Gk *brothers*   b Gk *Men, brothers*

12 The whole assembly kept silence, and listened to Bar′na•bas and Paul as they told of all the signs and wonders that God had done through them among the Gentiles. 13 After they finished speaking, James replied, "My brothers,*c* listen to me. 14 Sim′ē•on has related how God first looked favorably on the Gentiles, to take from among them a people for his name. 15 This agrees with the words of the prophets, as it is written,

16 'After this I will return,
     and I will rebuild the dwelling of David, which
          has fallen;
     from its ruins I will rebuild it,
          and I will set it up,
17 so that all other peoples may seek the Lord—
     even all the Gentiles over whom my name
          has been called.
     Thus says the Lord, who has been
          making these things 18 known from
          long ago.'*d*

19 Therefore I have reached the decision that we should not trouble those Gentiles who are turning to God, 20 but we should write to them to abstain only from things polluted by idols and from fornication and from whatever has been strangled*e* and from blood. 21 For in every city, for generations past, Moses has had those who proclaim him, for he has been read aloud every sabbath in the synagogues."

The Council's Letter to Gentile Believers

22 Then the apostles and the elders, with the consent of the whole church, decided to choose men from among their members*f* and to send them to An′ti•och with Paul and Bar′na•bas. They sent Judas called Bar•sab′bas, and Silas, leaders among the brothers, 23 with the following letter: "The brothers, both the apostles and the elders, to the believers*g* of Gentile origin in An′ti•och and Syria and Ci•li′ci•a, greetings. 24 Since we have heard that certain persons who have gone out from us, though with no instructions from us, have said things to disturb you and have unsettled your minds,*h* 25 we have decided unanimously to choose representatives*i* and send them to you, along with our beloved Bar′na•bas and Paul, 26 who have risked their lives for the sake of our Lord Jesus Christ. 27 We have therefore sent Judas and Silas, who themselves will tell you the same things by word of mouth. 28 For it has seemed good to the Holy Spirit and to us to impose on you no further burden than these essentials: 29 that you abstain from what has been sacrificed to idols and from blood and from what is strangled*j* and from fornication. If you keep yourselves from these, you will do well. Farewell."

30 So they were sent off and went down to An′ti•och. When they gathered the congregation together, they delivered the letter. 31 When its members*k* read it, they rejoiced at the exhortation.

---

c Gk Men, brothers   *d* Other ancient authorities read *things.* *18Known to God from of old are all his works.'*   *e* Other ancient authorities lack *and from whatever has been strangled*   *f* Gk *from among them*   *g* Gk brothers   *h* Other ancient authorities add *saying, 'You must be circumcised and keep the law,'*   *i* Gk men   *j* Other ancient authorities lack *and from what is strangled*   *k* Gk When they

Unity in Faith and Love

LIVE IT!

When Paul and Barnabas were in Antioch, a controversy arose regarding the need for Gentiles to be circumcised and to follow certain Jewish laws and holidays. The earliest Christians were Jews. They believed in Jesus and continued to follow the rules of the Jewish faith as a sign that they were a Covenant people. But with Gentiles becoming Christians, new questions were raised, like: Do Gentiles have to follow all the Jewish rules? Do Gentiles need to be circumcised as a sign of the Covenant? Circumcision is the surgical removal of the foreskin from a penis, and the Gentile converts did not see the need for it.

Paul and Barnabas insisted that Christians were free from such Jewish laws; they went to Jerusalem to meet with the other Apostles to defend their position. With Peter's support, Paul and Barnabas's view won the day. This meeting of the Apostles is called the Council of Jerusalem and was a pivotal point in the history of the church. At it the Apostles decided that the center of the Christian faith was believing in the risen Christ, not conforming to a Jewish ritual.

▶ Acts 15.1–35

32 Judas and Silas, who were themselves prophets, said much to encourage and strengthen the believers.[l] 33 After they had been there for some time, they were sent off in peace by the believers[l] to those who had sent them.[m] 35 But Paul and Bar′na·bas remained in An′ti·och, and there, with many others, they taught and proclaimed the word of the Lord.

Paul and Barnabas Separate

36 After some days Paul said to Bar′na·bas, "Come, let us return and visit the believers[l] in every city where we proclaimed the word of the Lord and see how they are doing." 37 Bar′na·bas wanted to take with them John called Mark. 38 But Paul decided not to take with them one who had deserted them in Pam·phyl′i·a and had not accompanied them in the work. 39 The disagreement became so sharp that they parted company; Bar′na·bas took Mark with him and sailed away to Cyprus. 40 But Paul chose Silas and set out, the believers[l] commending him to the grace of the Lord. 41 He went through Syria and Ci·li′ci·a, strengthening the churches.

Timothy Joins Paul and Silas

16 Paul[n] went on also to Der′bē and to Lys′tra, where there was a disciple named Timothy, the son of a Jewish woman who was a believer; but his father was a Greek. 2 He was well spoken of by the believers[l] in Lys′tra and I·cō′ni·um. 3 Paul wanted Timothy to accompany him; and he took him and had him circumcised because of the Jews who were in those places, for they all knew that his father was a Greek. 4 As they went from town to town, they delivered to them for observance the decisions that had been reached by the apostles and elders who were in Jerusalem. 5 So the churches were strengthened in the faith and increased in numbers daily.

Paul's Vision of the Man of Macedonia

6 They went through the region of Phryg′i·a and Galatia, having been forbidden by the Holy Spirit to speak the word in Asia. 7 When they had come opposite My′si·a, they attempted to go into Bi·thyn′i·a, but the Spirit of Jesus did not allow them; 8 so, passing by My′si·a, they went down to Trō′as. 9 During the night Paul had a vision: there stood a man of Mac·e·dō′ni·a pleading with him and saying, "Come over to Mac·e·dō′ni·a and help us." 10 When he had seen the vision, we immediately tried to cross over to Mac·e·dō′ni·a, being convinced that God had called us to proclaim the good news to them.

The Conversion of Lydia

11 We set sail from Trō′as and took a straight course to Sam′o·thrāce, the following day to Ne·ap′o·lis, 12 and from there to Phi·lip′pī, which is a leading city of the district[o] of Mac·e·dō′ni·a and a Roman colony. We remained in this city for some days. 13 On the sabbath day we went outside the gate by the river, where we supposed there was a place of prayer; and we sat down and spoke to the women who had gathered there. 14 A certain woman named Lyd′i·a, a worshiper of God, was listening to us; she was from the city of Thȳ·a·tī′ra and a dealer in purple cloth. The Lord opened her heart to listen eagerly to what was said by Paul. 15 When she and her household were baptized, she urged us, saying, "If you have judged me to be faithful to the Lord, come and stay at my home." And she prevailed upon us.

Paul and Silas in Prison

16 One day, as we were going to the place of prayer, we met a slave-girl who had a spirit of divination and brought her owners a great deal of money by fortune-telling. 17 While she followed Paul and us, she would cry out, "These men are slaves of the Most High God, who proclaim to you[p] a way of salvation." 18 She kept doing this for many days. But Paul, very much annoyed, turned and said to the spirit, "I order you in the name of Jesus Christ to come out of her." And it came out that very hour.

19 But when her owners saw that their hope of making money was gone, they seized Paul and Silas and dragged them into the marketplace before the authorities. 20 When they had brought them before the magistrates, they said, "These men are disturbing our city; they are Jews 21 and are advocating customs that are not lawful for us as Romans to adopt or observe." 22 The crowd joined in attacking them, and the magistrates had them stripped of their clothing and ordered them to be beaten with rods. 23 After they had given them a severe flogging, they threw them into prison and ordered the jailer to keep them securely. 24 Following these instructions, he put them in the innermost cell and fastened their feet in the stocks.

25 About midnight Paul and Silas were praying and singing hymns to God, and the prisoners were listening to them. 26 Suddenly there was an earthquake, so violent that the foundations of the prison were shaken; and immediately all the doors were opened and everyone's chains were unfastened. 27 When the jailer woke up and saw the prison doors wide open, he drew his sword and was about to kill himself, since he supposed

A
C
T
S

---

[l] Gk brothers   [m] Other ancient authorities add verse 34, *But it seemed good to Silas to remain there*   [n] Gk He   [o] Other authorities read *a city of the first district*   [p] Other ancient authorities read *to us*

that the prisoners had escaped. 28 But Paul shouted in a loud voice, "Do not harm yourself, for we are all here." 29 The jailer*q* called for lights, and rushing in, he fell down trembling before Paul and Silas. 30 Then he brought them outside and said, "Sirs, what must I do to be saved?" 31 They answered, "Believe on the Lord Jesus, and you will be saved, you and your household." 32 They spoke the word of the Lord*r* to him and to all who were in his house. 33 At the same hour of the night he took them and washed their wounds; then he and his entire family were baptized without delay. 34 He brought them up into the house and set food before them; and he and his entire household rejoiced that he had become a believer in God.

35 When morning came, the magistrates sent the police, saying, "Let those men go." 36 And the jailer reported the message to Paul, saying, "The magistrates sent word to let you go; therefore come out now and go in peace." 37 But Paul replied, "They have beaten us in public, uncondemned, men who are Roman citizens, and have thrown us into prison; and now are they going to discharge us in secret? Certainly not! Let them come and take us out themselves." 38 The police reported these words to the magistrates, and they were afraid when they heard that they were Roman citizens; 39 so they came and apologized to them. And they took them out and asked them to leave the city. 40 After leaving the prison they went to Lyd'i•a's home; and when they had seen and encouraged the brothers and sisters*s* there, they departed.

The Uproar in Thessalonica

17 After Paul and Silas*t* had passed through Am•phip'o•lis and Ap•ol•lō'ni•a, they came to Thes•sa•lo•ni'ca, where there was a synagogue of the Jews. 2 And Paul went in, as was his custom, and on three sabbath days argued with them from the scriptures, 3 explaining and proving that it was necessary for the Messiah*u* to suffer and to rise from the dead, and saying, "This is the Messiah,*u* Jesus whom I am proclaiming to you." 4 Some of them were persuaded and joined Paul and Silas, as did a great many of the devout Greeks and not a few of the leading women. 5 But the Jews became jealous, and with the help of some ruffians in the marketplaces they formed a mob and set the city in an uproar. While they were searching for Paul and Silas to bring them out to the assembly, they attacked Jason's house. 6 When they could not find them, they dragged Jason and some believers*s* before the city authorities,*v* shouting, "These people who have been turning the world upside down have come here also, 7 and Jason has entertained them as guests. They are all acting contrary to the decrees of the emperor, saying that there is another king named Jesus." 8 The people and the city officials were disturbed when they heard this, 9 and after they had taken bail from Jason and the others, they let them go.

---

q Gk *He*   *r* Other ancient authorities read *word of God*
s Gk *brothers*   *t* Gk *they*   *u* Or *the Christ*   *v* Gk *politarchs*

ACTS

Introducing ▶LYDIA AND PRISCILLA

Women were a crucial part of Christianity from its beginnings. The Acts of the Apostles names two women who were instrumental in Paul's missionary journeys: Lydia and Priscilla. Lydia (16.11–15) was Paul's first convert in Philippi, which is part of modern-day Europe. She was a textile merchant and was wealthy enough to support a household and open her home to Paul and Silas to stay for an extended time.

In chapter 18, we meet Priscilla and her husband, Aquila. This family hosted Paul in Corinth. Later, they accompanied him from Corinth to Antioch. While there, they instructed Apollos in the "Way of God" (18.26). Luke's inclusion of these women indicates that women were active in the early church, not only supporting the missionary work of Paul but also leading and teaching. For more on the women in the Bible, see the chapter titled "Suggested Reading Plans," near the beginning of this Bible.

Acts 16.14–15; 18.1–26

PRAY IT

Help Us Evangelize

Paul was wonderfully gifted for his work as an evangelist. He had the ability to communicate with both common people and intellectuals. He was familiar with three cultures—Jewish, Greek, and Roman—and proclaimed the Gospel message in ways all three could understand. He was skilled at building Christian communities. And he was absolutely fearless in preaching about Jesus Christ. Let's pray for these gifts in ourselves so that we can continue the church's mission of evangelization, particularly to young people.

O God, how I admire Paul! I too want to share your Good News with my generation. So let your Holy Spirit bless me with the gift of evangelization. Help me reach out to other young people no matter what clique or group they belong to. Help me to bring out the best in our culture and to challenge that which is wrong or misleading. Give me courage to speak fearlessly about my faith in Jesus when it is right to do so. And let me be your instrument in building communities of faith, hope, and love. Amen.

▶ **Acts of the Apostles, chapter 17**

Paul and Silas in Beroea

10 That very night the believers[w] sent Paul and Silas off to Be•roe'a; and when they arrived, they went to the Jewish synagogue. 11 These Jews were more receptive than those in Thes•sa•lo•ni'ca, for they welcomed the message very eagerly and examined the scriptures every day to see whether these things were so. 12 Many of them therefore believed, including not a few Greek women and men of high standing. 13 But when the Jews of Thes•sa•lo•ni'ca learned that the word of God had been proclaimed by Paul in Be•roe'a as well, they came there too, to stir up and incite the crowds. 14 Then the believers[w] immediately sent Paul away to the coast, but Silas and Timothy remained behind. 15 Those who conducted Paul brought him as far as Athens; and after receiving instructions to have Silas and Timothy join him as soon as possible, they left him.

Paul in Athens

16 While Paul was waiting for them in Athens, he was deeply distressed to see that the city was full of idols. 17 So he argued in the synagogue with the Jews and the devout persons, and also in the marketplace[x] every day with those who happened to be there. 18 Also some Ep•i•cu•re'an and Stoic philosophers debated with him. Some said, "What does this babbler want to say?" Others said, "He seems to be a proclaimer of foreign divinities." (This was because he was telling the good news about Jesus and the resurrection.) 19 So they took him and brought him to the Ar•e•op'a•gus and asked him, "May we know what this new teaching is that you are presenting? 20 It sounds rather strange to us, so we would like to know what it means." 21 Now all the Athenians and the foreigners living there would spend their time in nothing but telling or hearing something new.

22 Then Paul stood in front of the Ar•e•op'a•gus and said, "Athenians, I see how extremely religious you are in every way. 23 For as I went through the city and looked carefully at the objects of your worship, I found among them an altar with the inscription, 'To an unknown god.' What therefore you worship as unknown, this I proclaim to you. 24 The God who made the world and everything in it, he who is Lord of heaven and earth, does not live in shrines made by human hands, 25 nor is he served by human hands, as though he needed anything, since he himself gives to all mortals life and breath and all things. 26 From one ancestor[y] he made all nations to inhabit the whole earth, and he allotted the times of their existence and the boundaries of the places where they would live, 27 so that they would search for God[z] and perhaps grope for him and find him—though indeed he is not far from each one of us. 28 For 'In him we live and move and have our being'; as even some of your own poets have said,

'For we too are his offspring.'

29 Since we are God's offspring, we ought not to think that the deity is like gold, or silver, or stone, an image formed by the art and imagination of mortals. 30 While God has overlooked the times of human ignorance, now he commands all people everywhere to repent, 31 because he has fixed a day on which he will have the world judged in righteousness by a man whom he has appointed, and of this he has given assurance to all by raising him from the dead."

32 When they heard of the resurrection of the dead, some scoffed; but others said, "We will hear you again about this." 33 At that point Paul left them. 34 But some of them joined him and became believers, including Di•o•nys'i•us the Ar•e•op'a•gite

---

w Gk *brothers*　*x* Or *civic center;* Gk *agora*　*y* Gk *From one;* other ancient authorities read *From one blood*　*z* Other ancient authorities read *the Lord* and a woman named Dam′a•ris, and others with them.

Paul in Corinth

18 After this Paul[a] left Athens and went to Corinth. 2 There he found a Jew named A•qui′la, a native of Pon′tus, who had recently come from Italy with his wife Priscilla, because Clau′di•us had ordered all Jews to leave Rome. Paul[b] went to see them, 3 and, because he was of the same trade, he stayed with them, and they worked together—by trade they were tentmakers. 4 Every sabbath he would argue in the synagogue and would try to convince Jews and Greeks.

5 When Silas and Timothy arrived from Mac•e•dō′ni•a, Paul was occupied with proclaiming the word,[c] testifying to the Jews that the Messiah[d] was Jesus. 6 When they opposed and reviled him, in protest he shook the dust from his clothes[e] and said to them, "Your blood be on your own heads! I am innocent. From now on I will go to the Gentiles." 7 Then he left the synagogue[f] and went to the house of a man named Tit′i•us[g] Justus, a worshiper of God; his house was next door to the synagogue. 8 Cris′pus, the official of the synagogue, became a believer in the Lord, together with all his household; and many of the Corinthians who heard Paul became believers and were baptized. 9 One night the Lord said to Paul in a vision, "Do not be afraid, but speak and do not be silent; 10 for I am with you, and no one will lay a hand on you to harm you, for there are many in this city who are my people." 11 He stayed there a year and six months, teaching the word of God among them.

12 But when Gal′li•ō was proconsul of A•chā′-i•a, the Jews made a united attack on Paul and brought him before the tribunal. 13 They said, "This man is persuading people to worship God in ways that are contrary to the law." 14 Just as Paul was about to speak, Gal′li•ō said to the Jews, "If it were a matter of crime or serious villainy, I would be justified in accepting the complaint of you Jews; 15 but since it is a matter of questions about words and names and your own law, see to it yourselves; I do not wish to be a judge of these matters." 16 And he dismissed them from the tribunal. 17 Then all of them[h] seized Sos′the•nēs, the official of the synagogue, and beat him in front of the tribunal. But Gal′li•ō paid no attention to any of these things.

Paul's Return to Antioch

18 After staying there for a considerable time, Paul said farewell to the believers[i] and sailed for Syria, accompanied by Priscilla and A•qui′la. At Cen′chrē•ae he had his hair cut, for he was under a vow. 19 When they reached Eph′e•sus, he left them there, but first he himself went into the synagogue

18.18

and had a discussion with the Jews. 20 When they asked him to stay longer, he declined; 21 but on taking leave of them, he said, "I[j] will return to you, if God wills." Then he set sail from Eph′e•sus.

22 When he had landed at Caes•a•rē′a, he went up to Jerusalem[k] and greeted the church, and then went down to An′ti•och. 23 After spending some time there he departed and went from place to place through the region of Galatia[l] and Phryg′i•a, strengthening all the disciples.

Ministry of Apollos

24 Now there came to Eph′e•sus a Jew named A•pol′los, a native of Alexandria. He was an eloquent man, well-versed in the scriptures. 25 He had been instructed in the Way of the Lord; and he spoke with burning enthusiasm and taught accurately the things concerning Jesus, though he knew only the baptism of John. 26 He began to speak boldly in the synagogue; but when Priscilla and A•qui′la heard him, they took him aside and explained the Way of God to him more accurately. 27 And when he wished to cross over to A•chā′i•a, the believers[i] encouraged him and wrote to the disciples to welcome him. On his arrival he greatly helped those who through grace had become believers, 28 for he powerfully refuted the Jews in public, showing by the scriptures that the Messiah[d] is Jesus.

---

a Gk *he*   *b* Gk *He*   *c* Gk *with the word*   *d* Or *the Christ*
e Gk *reviled him, he shook out his clothes*   *f* Gk *left there*
g Other ancient authorities read *Titus*   *h* Other ancient
authorities read *all the Greeks*   *i* Gk *brothers*   *j* Other
ancient authorities read *I must at all costs keep the*
approaching festival in Jerusalem, but I   *k* Gk *went up*
l Gk *the Galatian region*

Paul in Ephesus

19 While A•pol'los was in Corinth, Paul passed through the interior regions and came to Eph'e•sus, where he found some disciples. 2 He said to them, "Did you receive the Holy Spirit when you became believers?" They replied, "No, we have not even heard that there is a Holy Spirit." 3 Then he said, "Into what then were you baptized?" They answered, "Into John's baptism." 4 Paul said, "John baptized with the baptism of repentance, telling the people to believe in the one who was to come after him, that is, in Jesus." 5 On hearing this, they were baptized in the name of the Lord Jesus. 6 When Paul had laid his hands on them, the Holy Spirit came upon them, and they spoke in tongues and prophesied— 7 altogether there were about twelve of them.

8 He entered the synagogue and for three months spoke out boldly, and argued persuasively about the kingdom of God. 9 When some stubbornly refused to believe and spoke evil of the Way before the congregation, he left them, taking the disciples with him, and argued daily in the lecture hall of Ty̅•ran'nus.*m* 10 This continued for two years, so that all the residents of Asia, both Jews and Greeks, heard the word of the Lord.

The Sons of Sceva

11 God did extraordinary miracles through Paul, 12 so that when the handkerchiefs or aprons that had touched his skin were brought to the sick, their diseases left them, and the evil spirits came out of them. 13 Then some itinerant Jewish exorcists tried to use the name of the Lord Jesus over those who had evil spirits, saying, "I adjure you by the Jesus whom Paul proclaims." 14 Seven sons of a Jewish high priest named Scē'va were doing this. 15 But the evil spirit said to them in reply, "Jesus I know, and Paul I know; but who are you?" 16 Then the man with the evil spirit leaped on them, mastered them all, and so overpowered them that they fled out of the house naked and wounded. 17 When this became known to all residents of Eph'e•sus, both Jews and Greeks, everyone was awestruck; and the name of the Lord Jesus was praised. 18 Also many of those who became believers confessed and disclosed their practices. 19 A number of those who practiced magic collected their books and burned them publicly; when the value of these books*n* was calculated, it was found to come to fifty thousand silver coins. 20 So the word of the Lord grew mightily and prevailed.

The Riot in Ephesus

21 Now after these things had been accomplished, Paul resolved in the Spirit to go through Mac•e•dō'ni•a and A•chā'i•a, and then to go on to Jerusalem. He said, "After I have gone there, I must also see Rome." 22 So he sent two of his helpers, Timothy and E•ras'tus, to Mac•e•dō'ni•a, while he himself stayed for some time longer in Asia.

23 About that time no little disturbance broke out concerning the Way. 24 A man named De•mē'tri•us, a silversmith who made silver shrines of Ar'te•mis, brought no little business to the artisans. 25 These he gathered together, with the workers of the same trade, and said, "Men, you know that we get our wealth from this business. 26 You also see and hear that not only in Eph'e•sus but in almost the whole of Asia this Paul has persuaded and drawn away a considerable number of people by saying that gods made with hands are not gods. 27 And there is danger not only that this trade of ours may come into disrepute but also that the temple of the great goddess Ar'te•mis will be scorned, and she will be deprived of her majesty that brought all Asia and the world to worship her."

28 When they heard this, they were enraged and shouted, "Great is Ar'te•mis of the E•phē'si•ans!" 29 The city was filled with the confusion; and people*o* rushed together to the theater, dragging with them Gā'i•us and Ar•is•tar'chus, Mac•e•dō'ni•ans who were Paul's travel companions. 30 Paul wished to go into the crowd, but the disciples would not let him; 31 even some officials of the province of Asia,*p* who were friendly to him, sent him a message urging him not to venture into the theater. 32 Meanwhile, some were shouting one thing, some another; for the assembly was in confusion, and most of them did not know why they had come together. 33 Some of the crowd gave instructions to Alexander, whom the Jews had pushed forward. And Alexander motioned for silence and tried to make a defense before the people. 34 But when they recognized that he was a Jew, for about two hours all of them shouted in unison, "Great is Ar'te•mis of the E•phē'si•ans!" 35 But when the town clerk had quieted the crowd, he said, "Citizens of Eph'e•sus, who is there that does not know that the city of the E•phē'si•ans is the temple keeper of the great Ar'te•mis and of the statue that fell from heaven?*q* 36 Since these things cannot be denied, you ought to be quiet and do nothing rash. 37 You have brought these men here who are neither temple robbers nor blasphemers of our*r* goddess. 38 If therefore De•mē'tri•us and the artisans with him have a complaint against anyone, the courts are open, and there are proconsuls; let them bring charges there against one another. 39 If there is

---

m Other ancient authorities read *of a certain Tyrannus, from eleven o'clock in the morning to four in the afternoon*
n Gk *them*   *o* Gk *they*   *p* Gk *some of the Asiarchs*   *q* Meaning of Gk uncertain   *r* Other ancient authorities read *your*

anything further[s] you want to know, it must be settled in the regular assembly. 40 For we are in danger of being charged with rioting today, since there is no cause that we can give to justify this commotion." 41 When he had said this, he dismissed the assembly.

Paul Goes to Macedonia and Greece

20 After the uproar had ceased, Paul sent for the disciples; and after encouraging them and saying farewell, he left for Mac·e·dō′ni·a. 2 When he had gone through those regions and had given the believers[t] much encouragement, he came to Greece, 3 where he stayed for three months. He was about to set sail for Syria when a plot was made against him by the Jews, and so he decided to return through Mac·e·dō′ni·a. 4 He was accompanied by Sop′a·ter son of Pyr′rhus from Be·roē′a, by Ar·is·tar′chus and Se·cun′dus from Thes·sa·lo·nī′ca, by Gā′i·us from Der′bē, and by Timothy, as well as by Tych′i·cus and Troph′i·mus from Asia. 5 They went ahead and were waiting for us in Trō′as; 6 but we sailed from Phi·lip′pī after the days of Unleavened Bread, and in five days we joined them in Trō′as, where we stayed for seven days.

Paul's Farewell Visit to Troas

7 On the first day of the week, when we met to break bread, Paul was holding a discussion with them; since he intended to leave the next day, he continued speaking until midnight. 8 There were many lamps in the room upstairs where we were meeting. 9 A young man named Eū′ty·chus, who was sitting in the window, began to sink off into a deep sleep while Paul talked still longer. Overcome by sleep, he fell to the ground three floors below and was picked up dead. 10 But Paul went down, and bending over him took him in his arms, and said, "Do not be alarmed, for his life is in him." 11 Then Paul went upstairs, and after he had broken bread and eaten, he continued to converse with them until dawn; then he left. 12 Meanwhile they had taken the boy away alive and were not a little comforted.

The Voyage from Troas to Miletus

13 We went ahead to the ship and set sail for As′sos, intending to take Paul on board there; for he had made this arrangement, intending to go by land himself. 14 When he met us in As′sos, we took him on board and went to Mit·y·lē′nē. 15 We sailed from there, and on the following day we arrived opposite Chī′os. The next day we touched at Sā′mos, and[u] the day after that we came to Mī·lē′tus. 16 For Paul had decided to sail past Eph′e·sus, so that he might not have to spend time in Asia; he was eager to be in Jerusalem, if possible, on the day of Pentecost.

Paul Speaks to the Ephesian Elders

17 From Mī·lē′tus he sent a message to Eph′e·sus, asking the elders of the church to meet him. 18 When they came to him, he said to them:

"You yourselves know how I lived among you the entire time from the first day that I set foot in Asia, 19 serving the Lord with all humility and with tears, enduring the trials that came to me through the plots of the Jews. 20 I did not shrink from doing anything helpful, proclaiming the message to you and teaching you publicly and from house to house, 21 as I testified to both Jews and Greeks about repentance toward God and faith toward our Lord Jesus. 22 And now, as a captive to the Spirit,[v] I am on my way to Jerusalem, not knowing what will happen to me there, 23 except that the Holy Spirit testifies to me in every city that imprisonment and persecutions are waiting for me. 24 But I do not count my life of any value to myself, if only I may finish my course and the ministry that I received from the Lord Jesus, to testify to the good news of God's grace.

25 "And now I know that none of you, among whom I have gone about proclaiming the kingdom, will ever see my face again. 26 Therefore I declare to you this day that I am not responsible for the blood of any of you, 27 for I did not shrink from declaring to you the whole purpose of God. 28 Keep watch over yourselves and over all the flock, of which the Holy Spirit has made you overseers, to shepherd the church of God[w] that he obtained with the blood of his own Son.[x] 29 I know that after I have gone, savage wolves will come in among you, not sparing the flock. 30 Some even from your own group will come distorting the truth in order to entice the disciples to follow them. 31 Therefore be alert, remembering that for three years I did not cease night or day to warn everyone with tears. 32 And now I commend you to God and to the message of his grace, a message that is able to build you up and to give you the inheritance among all who are sanctified. 33 I coveted no one's silver or gold or clothing. 34 You know for yourselves that I worked with my own hands to support myself and my companions. 35 In all this I have given you an example that by such work we must support the weak, remembering the words of the Lord Jesus, for he himself said, 'It is more blessed to give than to receive.' "

36 When he had finished speaking, he knelt down with them all and prayed. 37 There was much weeping among them all; they embraced Paul and

---

s Other ancient authorities read *about other matters*　t Gk *given them*　u Other ancient authorities add *after remaining at Trogyllium*　v Or *And now, bound in the spirit*　w Other ancient authorities read *of the Lord*　x Or *with his own blood*; Gk *with the blood of his Own*

PRAY IT!

Good-bye to a Friend

As Paul sadly says good-bye in Acts 20.36–38, we hear that the Christian community is experiencing similar feelings as they prepare to say good-bye to Paul. He has been an important person in their lives, and they have come to depend on him. Their grief overwhelms them, and they all experience great pain over his departure.

When we have to say good-bye to someone we care for deeply, we go through a grieving process. We feel sad and mad at the same time. Even after our friend has been gone for a long time, our heart has an empty space that our friend used to fill.

Lord, it is so difficult to say good-bye to my friend. We have shared so much together. I thank you for blessing me with this friendship. As we depart in separate directions, be our constant guardian and companion. Guide each of us safely to our destination. And until our paths cross again, surround my dear friend in your loving and protective embrace. Amen.

▸ Acts 20.36–38

kissed him, [38] grieving especially because of what he had said, that they would not see him again. Then they brought him to the ship.

Paul's Journey to Jerusalem

21 When we had parted from them and set sail, we came by a straight course to Cōs, and the next day to Rhōdes, and from there to Pat′a·ra.[y] [2] When we found a ship bound for Phoe·ni′ci·a, we went on board and set sail. [3] We came in sight of Cyprus; and leaving it on our left, we sailed to Syria and landed at Tȳre, because the ship was to unload its cargo there. [4] We looked up the disciples and stayed there for seven days. Through the Spirit they told Paul not to go on to Jerusalem. [5] When our days there were ended, we left and proceeded on our journey; and all of them, with wives and children, escorted us outside the city. There we knelt down on the beach and prayed [6] and said farewell to one another. Then we went on board the ship, and they returned home.

[7] When we had finished[z] the voyage from Tȳre,

we arrived at Ptol·e·mā′is; and we greeted the believers[a] and stayed with them for one day. [8] The next day we left and came to Caes·a·rē′a; and we went into the house of Philip the evangelist, one of the seven, and stayed with him. [9] He had four unmarried daughters[b] who had the gift of prophecy. [10] While we were staying there for several days, a prophet named Ag′a·bus came down from Judea. [11] He came to us and took Paul's belt, bound his own feet and hands with it, and said, "Thus says the Holy Spirit, 'This is the way the Jews in Jerusalem will bind the man who owns this belt and will hand him over to the Gentiles.' " [12] When we heard this, we and the people there urged him not to go up to Jerusalem. [13] Then Paul answered, "What are you doing, weeping and breaking my heart? For I am ready not only to be bound but even to die in Jerusalem for the name of the Lord Jesus." [14] Since he would not be persuaded, we remained silent except to say, "The Lord's will be done."

[15] After these days we got ready and started to go up to Jerusalem. [16] Some of the disciples from Caes·a·rē′a also came along and brought us to the house of Mnā′son of Cyprus, an early disciple, with whom we were to stay.

Paul Visits James at Jerusalem

[17] When we arrived in Jerusalem, the brothers welcomed us warmly. [18] The next day Paul went with us to visit James; and all the elders were present. [19] After greeting them, he related one by one the things that God had done among the Gentiles through his ministry. [20] When they heard it, they praised God. Then they said to him, "You see, brother, how many thousands of believers there are among the Jews, and they are all zealous for the law. [21] They have been told about you that you teach all the Jews living among the Gentiles to forsake Moses, and that you tell them not to circumcise their children or observe the customs. [22] What then is to be done? They will certainly hear that you have come. [23] So do what we tell you. We have four men who are under a vow. [24] Join these men, go through the rite of purification with them, and pay for the shaving of their heads. Thus all will know that there is nothing in what they have been told about you, but that you yourself observe and guard the law. [25] But as for the Gentiles who have become believers, we have sent a letter with our judgment that they should abstain from what has been sacrificed to idols and from blood and from what is strangled[c] and from fornication." [26] Then Paul took the men, and the next day, having purified himself,

---

[y] Other ancient authorities add *and Myra*   [z] Or *continued*
[a] Gk *brothers*   [b] Gk *four daughters, virgins,*   [c] Other ancient authorities lack *and from what is strangled*

did you KNOW?

Who Are Paul's Opponents?

As you read about Paul's return to Jerusalem, it may become confusing keeping track of the main characters. To help you keep it straight, here are some clues:

■ One group is the Jewish Christians, represented by James and the elders (Acts 21.17–26). Although the Jewish Christians might be suspicious of Paul's defense of the Gentile Christians, they support Paul and come up with a plan for him to try to prove his Jewish loyalty.

■ Another group is the Jews who don't believe in Jesus. These Jews see the rise of the Christian faith as a threat to Judaism, and Paul as the most well-known representative of Christians. They attempt to arrest him and have him killed in a mob scene (verses 27–36).

■ The third group is the Roman rulers. The Romans probably have no interest in this conflict except to keep the peace. The Roman tribune (governor) thinks he can keep the Jews happy by having Paul flogged (22.22–29). But surprise! Paul is a Roman citizen and has civil rights that the tribune must honor.

So who are Paul's—and Christianity's—opponents? Luke tells us that at first they are the Jewish Christians. Later, they are the Jews who don't believe in Jesus. Still later—after this story occurs—they will be the Romans. Luke knows all this in hindsight and brings all three opponents into play in describing Paul's arrest and imprisonment.

▶ Acts 21.17–26

he entered the temple with them, making public the completion of the days of purification when the sacrifice would be made for each of them.

Paul Arrested in the Temple

27 When the seven days were almost completed, the Jews from Asia, who had seen him in the temple, stirred up the whole crowd. They seized him, 28 shouting, "Fellow Israelites, help! This is the man who is teaching everyone everywhere against our people, our law, and this place; more than that, he has actually brought Greeks into the temple and has defiled this holy place." 29 For they had previously seen Troph'i·mus the E·phe'si·an with him in the city, and they supposed that Paul had brought him into the temple. 30 Then all the city was aroused, and the people rushed together. They seized Paul and dragged him out of the temple, and immediately the doors were shut. 31 While they were trying to kill him, word came to the tribune of the cohort that all Jerusalem was in an uproar. 32 Immediately he took soldiers and centurions and ran down to them. When they saw the tribune and the soldiers, they stopped beating Paul. 33 Then the tribune came, arrested him, and ordered him to be bound with two chains; he inquired who he was and what he had done. 34 Some in the crowd shouted one thing, some another; and as he could not learn the facts because of the uproar, he ordered him to be brought into the barracks. 35 When Paul[d] came to the steps, the violence of the mob was so great that he had to be carried by the soldiers. 36 The crowd that followed kept shouting, "Away with him!"

Paul Defends Himself

37 Just as Paul was about to be brought into the barracks, he said to the tribune, "May I say something to you?" The tribune[e] replied, "Do you know Greek? 38 Then you are not the Egyptian who recently stirred up a revolt and led the four thousand assassins out into the wilderness?" 39 Paul replied, "I am a Jew, from Tar'sus in Ci·li'ci·a, a citizen of an important city; I beg you, let me speak to the people." 40 When he had given him permission, Paul stood on the steps and motioned to the people for silence; and when there was a great hush, he addressed them in the Hebrew[f] language, saying:

22 "Brothers and fathers, listen to the defense that I now make before you."

2 When they heard him addressing them in Hebrew,[f] they became even more quiet. Then he said:

3 "I am a Jew, born in Tar'sus in Ci·li'ci·a, but brought up in this city at the feet of Ga·ma'li·el, educated strictly according to our ancestral law, being zealous for God, just as all of you are today. 4 I persecuted this Way up to the point of death by binding both men and women and putting them in prison, 5 as the high priest and the whole council of elders can testify about me. From them I also received letters to the brothers in Damascus, and I went there in order to bind those who were there

d Gk he e Gk He f That is, Aramaic

and to bring them back to Jerusalem for punishment.

Paul Tells of His Conversion
(Acts 9.1–19a; 26.12–18)

6 "While I was on my way and approaching Damascus, about noon a great light from heaven suddenly shone about me. 7 I fell to the ground and heard a voice saying to me, 'Saul, Saul, why are you persecuting me?' 8 I answered, 'Who are you, Lord?' Then he said to me, 'I am Jesus of Nazareth*g* whom you are persecuting.' 9 Now those who were with me saw the light but did not hear the voice of the one who was speaking to me. 10 I asked, 'What am I to do, Lord?' The Lord said to me, 'Get up and go to Damascus; there you will be told everything that has been assigned to you to do.' 11 Since I could not see because of the brightness of that light, those who were with me took my hand and led me to Damascus.

12 "A certain An·a·ni'as, who was a devout man according to the law and well spoken of by all the Jews living there, 13 came to me; and standing beside me, he said, 'Brother Saul, regain your sight!' In that very hour I regained my sight and saw him. 14 Then he said, 'The God of our ancestors has chosen you to know his will, to see the Righteous One and to hear his own voice; 15 for you will be his witness to all the world of what you have seen and heard. 16 And now why do you delay? Get up, be baptized, and have your sins washed away, calling on his name.'

Paul Sent to the Gentiles

17 "After I had returned to Jerusalem and while I was praying in the temple, I fell into a trance 18 and saw Jesus*h* saying to me, 'Hurry and get out of Jerusalem quickly, because they will not accept your testimony about me.' 19 And I said, 'Lord, they themselves know that in every synagogue I imprisoned and beat those who believed in you. 20 And while the blood of your witness Stephen was shed, I myself was standing by, approving and keeping the coats of those who killed him.' 21 Then he said to me, 'Go, for I will send you far away to the Gentiles.'"

Paul and the Roman Tribune

22 Up to this point they listened to him, but then they shouted, "Away with such a fellow from the earth! For he should not be allowed to live." 23 And while they were shouting, throwing off their cloaks, and tossing dust into the air, 24 the tribune directed that he was to be brought into the barracks, and ordered him to be examined by flogging, to find out the reason for this outcry against him. 25 But when they had tied him up with thongs,*i* Paul said to the centurion who was standing by, "Is it legal for you to flog a Roman citizen who is uncondemned?" 26 When the centurion heard that, he went to the tribune and said to him, "What are you about to do? This man is a Roman citizen." 27 The tribune came and asked Paul,*j* "Tell me, are you a Roman citizen?" And he said, "Yes." 28 The tribune answered, "It cost me a large sum of money to get my citizenship." Paul said, "But I was born a citizen." 29 Immediately those who were about to examine him drew back from him; and the tribune also was afraid, for he realized that Paul was a Roman citizen and that he had bound him.

Paul before the Council

30 Since he wanted to find out what Paul*j* was being accused of by the Jews, the next day he

---

g Gk *the Nazorean*   *h* Gk *him*   *i* Or *up for the lashes*   *j* Gk *he*

Sharing Your Story

Have you ever heard a dramatic conversion story? Sometimes on religious television programs or at large youth rallies, individuals share personal stories of overcoming addictions, terrible problems, or a great sin by believing in God. Or they tell of how they came to recognize and accept God in their life as a result of a serious illness or the death of a close friend or family member. Listening to these dramatic stories may make us feel that our own journey as a follower of Jesus—our own story—does not quite measure up. Nothing could be further from the truth in God's eyes.

We all have our own conversion stories—those moments of turning to God, of receiving a special call to serve others. And though our personal story might not be as dramatic as other people's stories, God will use it to encourage others to put their faith in Christ and dedicate their life to his mission. Are you willing to share your story of faith with others?

▶ Acts 22.6–16

released him and ordered the chief priests and the entire council to meet. He brought Paul down and had him stand before them.

23 While Paul was looking intently at the council he said, "Brothers,*k* up to this day I have lived my life with a clear conscience before God." 2 Then the high priest An·a·ni'as ordered those standing near him to strike him on the mouth. 3 At this Paul said to him, "God will strike you, you whitewashed wall! Are you sitting there to judge me according to the law, and yet in violation of the law you order me to be struck?" 4 Those standing nearby said, "Do you dare to insult God's high priest?" 5 And Paul said, "I did not realize, brothers, that he was high priest; for it is written, 'You shall not speak evil of a leader of your people.' "

6 When Paul noticed that some were Sad'du·cees and others were Phar'i·sees, he called out in the council, "Brothers, I am a Phar'i·see, a son of Phar'i·sees. I am on trial concerning the hope of the resurrection*l* of the dead." 7 When he said this, a dissension began between the Phar'i·sees and the Sad'du·cees, and the assembly was divided. 8 (The Sad'du·cees say that there is no resurrection, or angel, or spirit; but the Phar'i·sees acknowledge all three.) 9 Then a great clamor arose, and certain scribes of the Phar'i·sees' group stood up and contended, "We find nothing wrong with this man. What if a spirit or an angel has spoken to him?" 10 When the dissension became violent, the tribune, fearing that they would tear Paul to pieces, ordered the soldiers to go down, take him by force, and bring him into the barracks.

11 That night the Lord stood near him and said, "Keep up your courage! For just as you have testified for me in Jerusalem, so you must bear witness also in Rome."

The Plot to Kill Paul

12 In the morning the Jews joined in a conspiracy and bound themselves by an oath neither to eat nor drink until they had killed Paul. 13 There were more than forty who joined in this conspiracy. 14 They went to the chief priests and elders and said, "We have strictly bound ourselves by an oath to taste no food until we have killed Paul. 15 Now then, you and the council must notify the tribune to bring him down to you, on the pretext that you want to make a more thorough examination of his case. And we are ready to do away with him before he arrives."

16 Now the son of Paul's sister heard about the ambush; so he went and gained entrance to the barracks and told Paul. 17 Paul called one of the centurions and said, "Take this young man to the tribune, for he has something to report to him." 18 So he took him, brought him to the tribune, and

said, "The prisoner Paul called me and asked me to bring this young man to you; he has something to tell you." 19 The tribune took him by the hand, drew him aside privately, and asked, "What is it that you have to report to me?" 20 He answered, "The Jews have agreed to ask you to bring Paul down to the council tomorrow, as though they were going to inquire more thoroughly into his case. 21 But do not be persuaded by them, for more than forty of their men are lying in ambush for him. They have bound themselves by an oath neither to eat nor drink until they kill him. They are ready now and are waiting for your consent." 22 So the tribune dismissed the young man, ordering him, "Tell no one that you have informed me of this."

Paul Sent to Felix the Governor

23 Then he summoned two of the centurions and said, "Get ready to leave by nine o'clock tonight for Caes·a·re'a with two hundred soldiers, seventy horsemen, and two hundred spearmen. 24 Also provide mounts for Paul to ride, and take him safely to Felix the governor." 25 He wrote a letter to this effect:

26 "Clau'di·us Lys'i·as to his Excellency the governor Felix, greetings. 27 This man was seized by the Jews and was about to be killed by them, but when I had learned that he was a Roman citizen, I came with the guard and rescued him. 28 Since I wanted to know the charge for which they accused him, I had him brought to their council. 29 I found that he was accused concerning questions of their law, but was charged with nothing deserving death or imprisonment. 30 When I was informed that there would be a plot against the man, I sent him to you at once, ordering his accusers also to state before you what they have against him.*m*"

31 So the soldiers, according to their instructions, took Paul and brought him during the night to An·tip'a·tris. 32 The next day they let the horsemen go on with him, while they returned to the barracks. 33 When they came to Caes·a·re'a and delivered the letter to the governor, they presented Paul also before him. 34 On reading the letter, he asked what province he belonged to, and when he learned that he was from Ci·li'ci·a, 35 he said, "I will give you a hearing when your accusers arrive." Then he ordered that he be kept under guard in Her'od's headquarters.*n*

Paul before Felix at Caesarea

24 Five days later the high priest An·a·ni'as came down with some elders and an attorney, a certain Ter·tul'lus, and they reported their

---

k Gk Men, brothers   *l* Gk concerning hope and resurrection   *m* Other ancient authorities add Farewell   *n* Gk praetorium case against Paul to the governor. 2 When Paul[o] had been summoned, Ter·tul′lus began to accuse him, saying:

"Your Excellency,[p] because of you we have long enjoyed peace, and reforms have been made for this people because of your foresight. 3 We welcome this in every way and everywhere with utmost gratitude. 4 But, to detain you no further, I beg you to hear us briefly with your customary graciousness. 5 We have, in fact, found this man a pestilent fellow, an agitator among all the Jews throughout the world, and a ringleader of the sect of the Naz′-a·rēnes.[q] 6 He even tried to profane the temple, and so we seized him.[r] 8 By examining him yourself you will be able to learn from him concerning everything of which we accuse him."

9 The Jews also joined in the charge by asserting that all this was true.

Paul's Defense before Felix

10 When the governor motioned to him to speak, Paul replied:

"I cheerfully make my defense, knowing that for many years you have been a judge over this nation. 11 As you can find out, it is not more than twelve days since I went up to worship in Jerusalem. 12 They did not find me disputing with anyone in the temple or stirring up a crowd either in the synagogues or throughout the city. 13 Neither can they prove to you the charge that they now bring against me. 14 But this I admit to you, that according to the Way, which they call a sect, I worship the God of our ancestors, believing everything laid down according to the law or written in the prophets. 15 I have a hope in God—a hope that they themselves also accept—that there will be a resurrection of both[s] the righteous and the unrighteous. 16 Therefore I do my best always to have a clear conscience toward God and all people. 17 Now after some years I came to bring alms to my nation and to offer sacrifices. 18 While I was doing this, they found me in the temple, completing the rite of purification, without any crowd or disturbance. 19 But there were some Jews from Asia—they ought to be here before you to make an accusation, if they have anything against me. 20 Or let these men here tell what crime they had found when I stood before the council, 21 unless it was this one sentence that I called out while standing before them, 'It is about the resurrection of the dead that I am on trial before you today.' "

22 But Felix, who was rather well informed about the Way, adjourned the hearing with the comment, "When Lys′i·as the tribune comes down, I will decide your case." 23 Then he ordered the centurion to keep him in custody, but to let him have some liberty and not to prevent any of his friends from taking care of his needs.

Paul Held in Custody

24 Some days later when Felix came with his wife Drū·sil′la, who was Jewish, he sent for Paul and heard him speak concerning faith in Christ Jesus. 25 And as he discussed justice, self-control, and the coming judgment, Felix became frightened and said, "Go away for the present; when I have an opportunity, I will send for you." 26 At the same time he hoped that money would be given him by Paul, and for that reason he used to send for him very often and converse with him.

27 After two years had passed, Felix was succeeded by Por′ci·us Fes′tus; and since he wanted to grant the Jews a favor, Felix left Paul in prison.

Paul Appeals to the Emperor

25 Three days after Fes′tus had arrived in the province, he went up from Caes-a·rē′a to Jerusalem 2 where the chief priests and the leaders of the Jews gave him a report against Paul. They appealed to him 3 and requested, as a favor to them against Paul,[t] to have him transferred to Jerusalem. They were, in fact, planning an ambush to kill him along the way. 4 Fes′tus replied that Paul was being kept at Caes·a·rē′a, and that he himself intended to go there shortly. 5 "So," he said, "let those of you who have the authority come down with me, and if there is anything wrong about the man, let them accuse him."

6 After he had stayed among them not more than eight or ten days, he went down to Caes·a·rē′a; the next day he took his seat on the tribunal and ordered Paul to be brought. 7 When he arrived, the Jews who had gone down from Jerusalem surrounded him, bringing many serious charges against him, which they could not prove. 8 Paul said in his defense, "I have in no way committed an offense against the law of the Jews, or against the temple, or against the emperor." 9 But Fes′tus, wishing to do the Jews a favor, asked Paul, "Do you wish to go up to Jerusalem and be tried there before me on these charges?" 10 Paul said, "I am appealing to the emperor's tribunal; this is where I should be tried. I have done no wrong to the Jews, as you very well know. 11 Now if I am in the wrong and have committed something for which I deserve to die, I am not trying to escape death; but if there is nothing to their charges against me, no one can turn me over to them. I appeal to the emperor." 12 Then Fes′tus, after he had conferred with his council,

ACTS

---

o Gk he   p Gk lacks *Your Excellency*   q Gk *Nazoreans*
r Other ancient authorities add *and we would have judged him according to our law.* 7*But the chief captain Lysias came and with great violence took him out of our hands,* 8*commanding his accusers to come before you.*   s Other ancient authorities read *of the dead, both of*   t Gk *him*

replied, "You have appealed to the emperor; to the emperor you will go."

Festus Consults King Agrippa

13 After several days had passed, King A·grip'pa and Ber·ni'cē arrived at Caes·a·rē'a to welcome Fes'tus. 14 Since they were staying there several days, Fes'tus laid Paul's case before the king, saying, "There is a man here who was left in prison by Felix. 15 When I was in Jerusalem, the chief priests and the elders of the Jews informed me about him and asked for a sentence against him. 16 I told them that it was not the custom of the Romans to hand over anyone before the accused had met the accusers face to face and had been given an opportunity to make a defense against the charge. 17 So when they met here, I lost no time, but on the next day took my seat on the tribunal and ordered the man to be brought. 18 When the accusers stood up, they did not charge him with any of the crimesᵘ that I was expecting. 19 Instead they had certain points of disagreement with him about their own religion and about a certain Jesus, who had died, but whom Paul asserted to be alive. 20 Since I was at a loss how to investigate these questions, I asked whether he wished to go to Jerusalem and be tried there on these charges.ᵛ 21 But when Paul had appealed to be kept in custody for the decision of his Imperial Majesty, I ordered him to be held until I could send him to the emperor." 22 A·grip'pa said to Fes'tus, "I would like to hear the man myself." "Tomorrow," he said, "you will hear him."

Paul Brought before Agrippa

23 So on the next day A·grip'pa and Ber·ni'cē came with great pomp, and they entered the audience hall with the military tribunes and the prominent men of the city. Then Fes'tus gave the order and Paul was brought in. 24 And Fes'tus said, "King A·grip'pa and all here present with us, you see this man about whom the whole Jewish community petitioned me, both in Jerusalem and here, shouting that he ought not to live any longer. 25 But I found that he had done nothing deserving death; and when he appealed to his Imperial Majesty, I decided to send him. 26 But I have nothing definite to write to our sovereign about him. Therefore I have brought him before all of you, and especially before you, King A·grip'pa, so that, after we have examined him, I may have something to write— 27 for it seems to me unreasonable to send a prisoner without indicating the charges against him."

Paul Defends Himself before Agrippa

26 A·grip'pa said to Paul, "You have permission to speak for yourself." Then Paul stretched out his hand and began to defend himself:

2 "I consider myself fortunate that it is before you, King A·grip'pa, I am to make my defense today against all the accusations of the Jews, 3 because you are especially familiar with all the customs and controversies of the Jews; therefore I beg of you to listen to me patiently.

4 "All the Jews know my way of life from my youth, a life spent from the beginning among my own people and in Jerusalem. 5 They have known for a long time, if they are willing to testify, that I have belonged to the strictest sect of our religion and lived as a Phar'i·see. 6 And now I stand here on trial on account of my hope in the promise made by God to our ancestors, 7 a promise that our twelve tribes hope to attain, as they earnestly worship day and night. It is for this hope, your Excellency,ʷ that I am accused by Jews! 8 Why is it thought incredible by any of you that God raises the dead?

9 "Indeed, I myself was convinced that I ought to do many things against the name of Jesus of Nazareth.ˣ 10 And that is what I did in Jerusalem; with authority received from the chief priests, I not only locked up many of the saints in prison, but I

_____

u Other ancient authorities read *with anything*   v Gk *on them*   w Gk *O king*   x Gk *the Nazorean* also cast my vote against them when they were being condemned to death. ¹¹ By punishing them often in all the synagogues I tried to force them to blaspheme; and since I was so furiously enraged at them, I pursued them even to foreign cities.

Paul Tells of His Conversion
(Acts 9.1–19; 22.6–16)

12 "With this in mind, I was traveling to Damascus with the authority and commission of the chief priests, ¹³ when at midday along the road, your Excellency,ʸ I saw a light from heaven, brighter than the sun, shining around me and my companions. ¹⁴ When we had all fallen to the ground, I heard a voice saying to me in the Hebrewᶻ language, 'Saul, Saul, why are you persecuting me? It hurts you to kick against the goads.' ¹⁵ I asked, 'Who are you, Lord?' The Lord answered, 'I am Jesus whom you are persecuting. ¹⁶ But get up and stand on your feet; for I have appeared to you for this pur-

pose, to appoint you to serve and testify to the things in which you have seen meᵃ and to those in which I will appear to you. ¹⁷ I will rescue you from your people and from the Gentiles—to whom I am sending you ¹⁸ to open their eyes so that they may turn from darkness to light and from the power of Satan to God, so that they may receive forgiveness of sins and a place among those who are sanctified by faith in me.'

Paul Tells of His Preaching

19 "After that, King A·grip′pa, I was not disobedient to the heavenly vision, ²⁰ but declared first to those in Damascus, then in Jerusalem and throughout the countryside of Judea, and also to the Gentiles, that they should repent and turn to God and do deeds consistent with repentance. ²¹ For this

---

ʸ Gk *O king*   ᶻ That is, *Aramaic*   ᵃ Other ancient authorities read *the things that you have seen*

PAUL TEACHES US HOW TO LIVE OUR FAITH!

Reporters Marisa and Ricardo. [Speaking into their microphones] **We're here, live, in Caesarea, where Paul of Tarsus has just spoken with King Agrippa and Governor Festus. Here comes Paul now. Let's see what he has to say. Paul, why has your message caused so much controversy?**

Paul. **It was never my intention to cause strife or conflict. But I must speak the truth, and the truth is that God has revealed his salvation for us in Jesus Christ. In Jesus, salvation is available to everyone—Jews and Gentiles, slaves and free people, men and women—and we are all equal as sons and daughters of God. Unfortunately, this truth is upsetting to some people, and they have gone to great lengths to try to get rid of me.**

Marisa and Ricardo. **But hasn't your message been well received by many people—including many different types of people?**

Paul. **Yes it has. I think this is because Jesus taught us always to respect every person as a son or daughter of God regardless of his or her culture or social class. Under the guidance of the Holy Spirit, Christian communities allow for diversity while keeping a common unity in Jesus Christ. I think people are hungry for this.**

Marisa and Ricardo. **Soon you will be heading for Rome, where you will be on trial for alleged crimes against the empire. Are you worried?**

Paul. [Smiling] **Why be worried? No one has ultimate power over me except my Lord Jesus Christ. I only need to be faithful to my calling, and I will receive my prize—eternal life with God. Plus I have the prayers and support of many close friends. But thank you for your concern. God's grace and peace be with you.**

Marisa and Ricardo. **And thank you, Paul.**

▸ **Acts of the Apostles, chapter 26**

reason the Jews seized me in the temple and tried to kill me. 22 To this day I have had help from God, and so I stand here, testifying to both small and great, saying nothing but what the prophets and Moses said would take place: 23 that the Messiah[b] must suffer, and that, by being the first to rise from the dead, he would proclaim light both to our people and to the Gentiles."

Paul Appeals to Agrippa to Believe

24 While he was making this defense, Fes'tus exclaimed, "You are out of your mind, Paul! Too much learning is driving you insane!" 25 But Paul said, "I am not out of my mind, most excellent Fes'tus, but I am speaking the sober truth. 26 Indeed the king knows about these things, and to him I speak freely; for I am certain that none of these things has escaped his notice, for this was not done in a corner. 27 King A•grip'pa, do you believe the prophets? I know that you believe." 28 A•grip'pa said to Paul, "Are you so quickly persuading me to become a Christian?"[c] 29 Paul replied, "Whether quickly or not, I pray to God that not only you but also all who are listening to me today might become such as I am—except for these chains."

30 Then the king got up, and with him the governor and Ber•ni'ce and those who had been seated with them; 31 and as they were leaving, they said to one another, "This man is doing nothing to deserve death or imprisonment." 32 A•grip'pa said to Fes'tus, "This man could have been set free if he had not appealed to the emperor."

Paul Sails for Rome

27 When it was decided that we were to sail for Italy, they transferred Paul and some other prisoners to a centurion of the Augustan Cohort, named Julius. 2 Embarking on a ship of Ad•ra•myt'ti•um that was about to set sail to the ports along the coast of Asia, we put to sea, accompanied by Ar•is•tar'chus, a Mac•e•do'ni•an from Thes•sa•lo•ni'ca. 3 The next day we put in at Si'don; and Julius treated Paul kindly, and allowed him to go to his friends to be cared for. 4 Putting out to sea from there, we sailed under the lee of Cyprus, because the winds were against us. 5 After we had sailed across the sea that is off Ci•li'ci•a and Pam•phyl'i•a, we came to My'ra in Ly'ci•a. 6 There the centurion found an Alexandrian ship bound for Italy and put us on board. 7 We sailed slowly for a number of days and arrived with difficulty off Cni'dus, and as the wind was against us, we sailed under the lee of Crete off Sal•mo'ne. 8 Sailing past it with difficulty, we came to a place called Fair Havens, near the city of La•se'a.

9 Since much time had been lost and sailing was now dangerous, because even the Fast had al-

ready gone by, Paul advised them, 10 saying, "Sirs, I can see that the voyage will be with danger and much heavy loss, not only of the cargo and the ship, but also of our lives." 11 But the centurion paid more attention to the pilot and to the owner of the ship than to what Paul said. 12 Since the harbor was not suitable for spending the winter, the majority was in favor of putting to sea from there, on the chance that somehow they could reach Phoenix, where they could spend the winter. It was a harbor of Crete, facing southwest and northwest.

The Storm at Sea

13 When a moderate south wind began to blow, they thought they could achieve their purpose; so they weighed anchor and began to sail past Crete, close to the shore. 14 But soon a violent wind, called the northeaster, rushed down from Crete.[d] 15 Since the ship was caught and could not be turned head-on into the wind, we gave way to it and were driven. 16 By running under the lee of a small island called Cau'da[e] we were scarcely able to get the ship's boat under control. 17 After hoisting it up they took measures[f] to undergird the ship; then, fearing that they would run on the Syr'tis, they lowered the sea anchor and so were driven. 18 We were being pounded by the storm so violently that on the next day they began to throw the cargo overboard, 19 and on the third day with their own hands they threw the ship's tackle overboard. 20 When neither sun nor stars appeared for many days, and no small tempest raged, all hope of our being saved was at last abandoned.

21 Since they had been without food for a long time, Paul then stood up among them and said, "Men, you should have listened to me and not have set sail from Crete and thereby avoided this damage and loss. 22 I urge you now to keep up your courage, for there will be no loss of life among you, but only of the ship. 23 For last night there stood by me an angel of the God to whom I belong and whom I worship, 24 and he said, 'Do not be afraid, Paul; you must stand before the emperor; and indeed, God has granted safety to all those who are sailing with you.' 25 So keep up your courage, men, for I have faith in God that it will be exactly as I have been told. 26 But we will have to run aground on some island."

27 When the fourteenth night had come, as we were drifting across the sea of A'dri•a, about midnight the sailors suspected that they were nearing land. 28 So they took soundings and found twenty fathoms; a little farther on they took soundings

---

[b] Or *the Christ* [c] Or *Quickly you will persuade me to play the Christian* [d] Gk *it* [e] Other ancient authorities read *Clauda* [f] Gk *helps*

PRAY IT!

When the Waves Get Too Rough

It is not easy to be courageous when you face danger. When you find yourself in situations where things are beyond your control, like the storm that endangered the ship Paul was on, turn to God. After all, isn't faith for the times when you feel the most helpless and out of control?

Help, Lord, I'm lost at sea! When I started this journey of life, I thought I knew where I was headed, but then a few waves started to rock the boat, and I became frightened.

Next, the wind picked up, and my fear turned into confusion. Then the night fell, and my confusion turned into despair. And now, I am lost and need you to help calm the waves in my life and stand beside me until the night turns into day.

Help me to find my bearings again, Lord. And when this storm is over, gift me with the wisdom to learn from this experience—to go back and make right what was wrong, not to lose hope at the first sign of trouble, and to hang on to you, my anchor, when life gets rough. Amen.

▶ **Acts 27.21–25**

again and found fifteen fathoms. 29 Fearing that we might run on the rocks, they let down four anchors from the stern and prayed for day to come. 30 But when the sailors tried to escape from the ship and had lowered the boat into the sea, on the pretext of putting out anchors from the bow, 31 Paul said to the centurion and the soldiers, "Unless these men stay in the ship, you cannot be saved." 32 Then the soldiers cut away the ropes of the boat and set it adrift.

33 Just before daybreak, Paul urged all of them to take some food, saying, "Today is the fourteenth day that you have been in suspense and remaining without food, having eaten nothing. 34 Therefore I urge you to take some food, for it will help you survive; for none of you will lose a hair from your heads." 35 After he had said this, he took bread; and giving thanks to God in the presence of all, he broke it and began to eat. 36 Then all of them were encouraged and took food for themselves. 37 (We were in all two hundred seventy-six[g] persons in the ship.) 38 After they had satisfied their hunger, they lightened the ship by throwing the wheat into the sea.

The Shipwreck

39 In the morning they did not recognize the land, but they noticed a bay with a beach, on which they planned to run the ship ashore, if they could. 40 So they cast off the anchors and left them in the sea. At the same time they loosened the ropes that tied the steering-oars; then hoisting the foresail to the wind, they made for the beach. 41 But striking a reef,[h] they ran the ship aground; the bow stuck and remained immovable, but the stern was being broken up by the force of the waves. 42 The soldiers' plan was to kill the prisoners, so that none might swim away and escape; 43 but the centurion, wishing to save Paul, kept them from carrying out their plan. He ordered those who could swim to jump overboard first and make for the land, 44 and the rest to follow, some on planks and others on pieces of the ship. And so it was that all were brought safely to land.

Paul on the Island of Malta

28 After we had reached safety, we then learned that the island was called Malta. 2 The natives showed us unusual kindness. Since it had begun to rain and was cold, they kindled a fire and welcomed all of us around it. 3 Paul had gathered a bundle of brushwood and was putting it on the fire, when a viper, driven out by the heat, fastened itself on his hand. 4 When the natives saw the creature hanging from his hand, they said to one another, "This man must be a murderer; though he has escaped from the sea, justice has not allowed him to live." 5 He, however, shook off the creature into the fire and suffered no harm. 6 They were expecting him to swell up or drop dead, but after they had waited a long time and saw that nothing unusual had happened to him, they changed their minds and began to say that he was a god.

7 Now in the neighborhood of that place were lands belonging to the leading man of the island, named Pub'li•us, who received us and entertained us hospitably for three days. 8 It so happened that the father of Pub'li•us lay sick in bed with fever and dysentery. Paul visited him and cured him by praying and putting his hands on him. 9 After this happened, the rest of the people on the island who had diseases also came and were cured. 10 They bestowed many honors on us, and when we were about to sail, they put on board all the provisions we needed.

---

g Other ancient authorities read *seventy-six*; others, *about seventy-six*   h Gk *place of two seas*

ACTS

Paul Arrives at Rome

11 Three months later we set sail on a ship that had wintered at the island, an Alexandrian ship with the Twin Brothers as its figurehead. 12 We put in at Syracuse and stayed there for three days; 13 then we weighed anchor and came to Rhē′gi•um. After one day there a south wind sprang up, and on the second day we came to Pū•tē′o•li. 14 There we found believers[i] and were invited to stay with them for seven days. And so we came to Rome. 15 The believers[i] from there, when they heard of us, came as far as the Forum of Ap′pi•us and Three Taverns to meet us. On seeing them, Paul thanked God and took courage.

16 When we came into Rome, Paul was allowed to live by himself, with the soldier who was guarding him.

Paul and Jewish Leaders in Rome

17 Three days later he called together the local leaders of the Jews. When they had assembled, he said to them, "Brothers, though I had done nothing against our people or the customs of our ancestors, yet I was arrested in Jerusalem and handed over to the Romans. 18 When they had examined me, the Romans[j] wanted to release me, because there was no reason for the death penalty in my case. 19 But when the Jews objected, I was compelled to appeal to the emperor—even though I had no charge to bring against my nation. 20 For this reason therefore I have asked to see you and speak with you,[k] since it is for the sake of the hope of Israel that I am bound with this chain." 21 They replied, "We have received no letters from Judea about you, and none of the brothers coming here has reported or spoken anything evil about you. 22 But we would like to hear from you what you think, for with regard to this sect we know that everywhere it is spoken against."

Paul Preaches in Rome
(Isa 6.9–10)

23 After they had set a day to meet with him, they came to him at his lodgings in great numbers. From morning until evening he explained the matter to them, testifying to the kingdom of God and trying to convince them about Jesus both from the law of Moses and from the prophets. 24 Some were convinced by what he had said, while others refused to believe. 25 So they disagreed with each other; and as they were leaving, Paul made one further statement: "The Holy Spirit was right in saying to your ancestors through the prophet Ī•sāi′ah,

26 'Go to this people and say,
You will indeed listen, but never
    understand,
and you will indeed look, but never
    perceive.
27 For this people's heart has grown dull,
    and their ears are hard of hearing,
        and they have shut their eyes;
    so that they might not look with their
        eyes,
    and listen with their ears,
  and understand with their heart and turn—
    and I would heal them.'

28 Let it be known to you then that this salvation of God has been sent to the Gentiles; they will listen."[l]

30 He lived there two whole years at his own expense[m] and welcomed all who came to him, 31 proclaiming the kingdom of God and teaching about the Lord Jesus Christ with all boldness and without hindrance.

---

i Gk brothers   j Gk they   k Or I have asked you to see me and speak with me   l Other ancient authorities add verse 29, And when he had said these words, the Jews departed, arguing vigorously among themselves   m Or in his own hired dwelling

Introduction to the

Letters

and Revelation

Despite the popularity of e-mailing, writing letters with pen and paper is still alive today. In letters, people often express themselves more clearly than they do in person, and say things that are difficult to say face-to-face. Perhaps you've been lucky enough to receive some special letters. Letters between parents and children, engaged couples, and even pen pals are often saved to be read again and again. They are treasured for their stories, their advice, and their expressions of love. The next twenty-one books of the New Testament are also treasured letters. Their stories, their advice, and their confidence in God's loving guidance have inspired generations of Christians.

In-depth

WHEN YOU READ SOMEONE ELSE'S MAIL, YOU see only one side of the conversation. So you have to do some reading between the lines to understand the issues being addressed. This is also true of the New Testament letters. But when you do this, they give you a firsthand look at the first Christian communities and what they believed. In fact, the letters written by Paul are the oldest Christian documents that we have, written even before the four Gospels. Paul's earliest letter, 1 Thessalonians, was probably written around A.D. 50. That's just a little over twenty years after the death and Resurrection of Jesus!

These letters follow a common pattern. They usually begin with (1) a greeting from the sender to the receiver or receivers. Next is (2) a prayer, most often of thanksgiving. This is followed by (3) the body of the letter, which addresses whatever issues the author wants to discuss; often, it includes general advice about Christian living. The letters close with (4) greetings and instructions to specific people and a final blessing.

There are exceptions to this pattern. Hebrews and 1 John do not have all four of these features, and are more like essays about faith. James has more of the features, but reads like a good sermon rather than a letter.

Saint Paul was the most prolific writer of the letters. At one time, it was thought that he produced thirteen of the twenty-one. However, modern scholars believe that some of the letters traditionally attributed to Paul were actually written by associates or later followers. Scholars have reached this conclusion because of differences in writing style, vocabulary, and thought. Those associates or followers of Paul applied his teaching to new situations faced by the early Christian communities. Similarly, the letters bearing the names of James, Peter, and John were probably written by associates or later followers of those men.

To a modern person, that might seem like forgery. But in the ancient world, it was not uncommon for followers of an important person to write in the person's name after her or his death. It was a way of honoring the person and keeping her or his traditions alive.

Although the Book of Revelation is grouped together with the letters in this introduction, it really is not a letter at all. Revelation was written as a series of visions to a disciple named John. The visions are filled with dramatic imagery and events. Some people interpret them as prophecies about the way the world will end, but for the most part, they are really coded messages about events happening in John's own time. Ultimately, the Book of Revelation is a hopeful message to persecuted Christians that God is in control and that goodness and justice will triumph.

As you explore these letters and the Book of Revelation, you'll see the church at its best: the miraculous growth, the Spirit-filled enthusiasm, and the deep love the early Christians had for one another and for Jesus. You'll also see how the early church was threatened by intense disagreements, jealousy, and scandals. Through it all, the authors reveal a deep faith and missionary spirit. They focus again and again on the death and Resurrection of Jesus and on the mystery of the church as the living Body of Christ acting in the world through the power of the Holy Spirit. These letters had a specific audience in the first century A.D., but because God inspired them, their words are for you too!

Other Background

- There are nine letters by Paul or his followers named for the communities in which the recipient churches were located: Romans, I and 2 Corinthians, Galatians, Ephesians (called a captivity letter because it is attributed to Paul writing from jail), Philippians (also a captivity letter), Colossians (also a captivity letter), and I and 2 Thessalonians.

- There are four letters by Paul or his followers named for the individuals to whom they were sent: I and 2 Timothy and Titus (called pastoral letters), and Philemon (a captivity letter).

- Hebrews is named for the Christian Jews for whom it was intended.

- There are seven catholic letters named after their stated authors: James; I and 2 Peter; I, 2, and 3 John; and Jude. They are called catholic because they are general letters to all Christians.

- The Book of Revelation is not a letter. It is a collection of the prophecies and visions of John of Patmos, a Christian prophet.

Romans

Have you ever wondered if you're good enough to deserve someone's unconditional love? Has it ever puzzled you that sometimes it is easier to do the wrong thing than the right thing? If you have, you're not alone. Saint Paul felt the same way. In his Letter to the Romans, he addresses some important questions of life and faith. But at its core, the message of the letter is simple: We are justified—made right with God—by faith in Jesus Christ.

At a Glance

- **1.1–15.** a greeting and thanks
- **1.16—7.25.** the lesson that humanity is lost, but saved through faith in Christ
- **Chapter 8.** a description of our life in the spirit of Christ
- **Chapters 9–11.** a discussion of Judaism and Christianity
- **Chapters 12–16.** moral advice, personal notes, and blessings

In-depth

Many people consider the Letter to the Romans to be the deepest expression of Paul's thinking. This was the only letter Paul wrote to a community he had not yet visited. At the time, he was planning to go to Rome and was trying to prepare the way by explaining his teaching on salvation and faith. His ideas are summed up in a verse from the first chapter: "I am not ashamed of the gospel; it is the power of God for salvation to everyone who has faith" (verse 16).

Romans is not easy reading. Paul often makes his case by using arguments that might seem strange to us today. Some of his main points are these:

- Salvation is available to both Jews and Gentiles (non-Jews).
- Because all people have sinned, no one has "earned" salvation.
- Salvation comes through faith in Jesus Christ, not through following the Jewish religious Law.
- Even though salvation has come to the Gentiles, God has not abandoned the Jews.

The Letter to the Romans contains many wonderfully comforting words. It tells us that when we don't know how to pray, God prays for us "with sighs too deep for words" (8.26)! And it says that "all things work together for good for those who love God" (verse 28). And it asks, "If God is for us, who is against us?" (verse 31).

So as you read this powerful letter, let go of your fears. Even though you're not perfect, God will never leave you. As Paul says, "I am convinced that neither death, nor life . . . nor anything else in all creation, will be able to separate us from the love of God in Christ Jesus our Lord" (verses 38–39).

Quick Facts

Author
Paul

Date Written
A.D. 56–58

Audience
Jewish and Gentile Christians in Rome

Romans

6.4

Salutation

1 Paul, a servant[a] of Jesus Christ, called to be an apostle, set apart for the gospel of God, [2] which he promised beforehand through his prophets in the holy scriptures, [3] the gospel concerning his Son, who was descended from David according to the flesh [4] and was declared to be Son of God with power according to the spirit[b] of holiness by resurrection from the dead, Jesus Christ our Lord, [5] through whom we have received grace and apostleship to bring about the obedience of faith among all the Gentiles for the sake of his name, [6] including yourselves who are called to belong to Jesus Christ,

[7] To all God's beloved in Rome, who are called to be saints:

Grace to you and peace from God our Father and the Lord Jesus Christ.

Prayer of Thanksgiving

[8] First, I thank my God through Jesus Christ for all of you, because your faith is proclaimed throughout the world. [9] For God, whom I serve with my spirit by announcing the gospel[c] of his Son, is my witness that without ceasing I remember you always in my prayers, [10] asking that by God's will I may somehow at last succeed in coming to you. [11] For I am longing to see you so that I may share with you some spiritual gift to strengthen you— [12] or rather so that we may be mutually encouraged by each other's faith, both yours and mine. [13] I want you to know, brothers and sisters,[d] that I have often intended to come to you (but thus far have been prevented), in order that I may reap some harvest among you as I have among the rest of the Gentiles. [14] I am a debtor both to Greeks and to barbarians, both to the wise and to the foolish [15]—hence my eagerness to proclaim the gospel to you also who are in Rome.

The Power of the Gospel

[16] For I am not ashamed of the gospel; it is the power of God for salvation to everyone who has faith, to the Jew first and also to the Greek. [17] For in it the righteousness of God is revealed through faith for faith; as it is written, "The one who is righteous will live by faith."[e]

The Guilt of Humankind

[18] For the wrath of God is revealed from heaven against all ungodliness and wickedness of those who by their wickedness suppress the truth. [19] For what can be known about God is plain to them, because God has shown it to them. [20] Ever since the creation of the world his eternal power and divine nature, invisible though they are, have been understood and seen through the things he has made. So they are without excuse; [21] for though they knew

---

a Gk *slave*   *b* Or *Spirit*   *c* Gk *my spirit in the gospel*
d Gk *brothers*   *e* Or *The one who is righteous through faith will live*

did you KNOW?

The Many Meanings of Gospel

The word *gospel* is the best translation of the Greek word *euangelion*, which was used in Rom 1.16. *Gospel* comes from the old English word *godspel*, which means "good news." From *euangelion*, we get the word *evangelize*, which means "to share the good news."

In the New Testament, the meaning of the word *Gospel* goes through an evolution. For Paul, whose writings are the earliest in the New Testament, *Gospel* referred to the good news of salvation for all who believe. Paul associated the Gospel directly with Jesus himself, centering on his death and Resurrection.

As Christian faith developed, the understanding of *Gospel* expanded to include the Reign (Kingdom) of God that Jesus preached. The Gospel was not just associated with Jesus' saving death and Resurrection, but included all his teachings, miracles, promises, and demands. After the original Apostles died or were killed, Christian communities desired a record of their teachings about Jesus, and the Gospel message was written down. So *Gospel* came also to refer to the writings named for Matthew, Mark, Luke, and John.

▸ Rom 1.16

God, they did not honor him as God or give thanks to him, but they became futile in their thinking, and their senseless minds were darkened. 22 Claiming to be wise, they became fools; 23 and they exchanged the glory of the immortal God for images resembling a mortal human being or birds or four-footed animals or reptiles.

24 Therefore God gave them up in the lusts of their hearts to impurity, to the degrading of their bodies among themselves, 25 because they exchanged the truth about God for a lie and worshiped and served the creature rather than the Creator, who is blessed forever! Amen.

26 For this reason God gave them up to degrading passions. Their women exchanged natural intercourse for unnatural, 27 and in the same way also the men, giving up natural intercourse with women, were consumed with passion for one another. Men committed shameless acts with men and received in their own persons the due penalty for their error.

28 And since they did not see fit to acknowledge God, God gave them up to a debased mind and to things that should not be done. 29 They were filled with every kind of wickedness, evil, covetousness, malice. Full of envy, murder, strife, deceit, craftiness, they are gossips, 30 slanderers,

did you KNOW?

Homosexuality and AIDS

In making his case that all people are in need of salvation, Paul talks about the sinfulness of humankind in Rom 1.18–32. As a specific example of what happens when people turn from God's truth, he discusses homosexual activity in verses 26–27.

Some people interpret these verses to mean Paul is condemning homosexual persons. But this is a serious misinterpretation of Paul's words. Why? First, look at the context. After this specific example in verses 26–27, Paul lists all kinds of sinful behaviors in verses 28–32. He is not picking on homosexuals—rather, he is showing that all people are guilty of sin.

Most important, notice that Paul never condemns people; he condemns sinful behavior. The Catholic church does the same. The church teaches that homosexual orientation is not sinful, but it also states that any sexual activity outside of marriage is wrong.

Romans 1.18–32 has also been used wrongly against AIDS victims. Some of them have been told that their horrible disease is a result of God's vengeance against homosexual behavior. Our loving God would never use AIDS, or any other disease, to punish people.

▸ Rom 1.18–32

God-haters,f insolent, haughty, boastful, inventors of evil, rebellious toward parents, 31 foolish, faithless, heartless, ruthless. 32 They know God's decree, that those who practice such things deserve to die—yet they not only do them but even applaud others who practice them.

PRAY IT!

Examination of Conscience

Lord, knock me off my pedestal whenever I begin to think I've earned the right to judge others. Paul reminds us that we are all guilty of sin. I have no right to judge others.

Direct me to turn my attention to examining my own conscience:

Have I been patient with those around me?

Have I offered forgiveness to those who have hurt me?

Have I had the courage to admit when I am wrong?

Have I treated my parents and siblings with respect?

Have I been sensitive to the feelings and needs of those around me?

Forgive me, God, for I have sinned. Bathe me in your mercy and love. Deliver me from evil as I continue to grow in Christ. Amen.

▶ Rom 2.1–4

The Righteous Judgment of God

2 Therefore you have no excuse, whoever you are, when you judge others; for in passing judgment on another you condemn yourself, because you, the judge, are doing the very same things. 2 You say,g "We know that God's judgment on those who do such things is in accordance with truth." 3 Do you imagine, whoever you are, that when you judge those who do such things and yet do them yourself, you will escape the judgment of God? 4 Or do you despise the riches of his kindness and forbearance and patience? Do you not realize that God's kindness is meant to lead you to repentance? 5 But by your hard and impenitent heart you are storing up wrath for yourself on the day of wrath, when God's righteous judgment will be revealed. 6 For he will repay according to each one's

deeds: 7 to those who by patiently doing good seek for glory and honor and immortality, he will give eternal life; 8 while for those who are self-seeking and who obey not the truth but wickedness, there will be wrath and fury. 9 There will be anguish and distress for everyone who does evil, the Jew first and also the Greek, 10 but glory and honor and peace for everyone who does good, the Jew first and also the Greek. 11 For God shows no partiality.

12 All who have sinned apart from the law will also perish apart from the law, and all who have sinned under the law will be judged by the law. 13 For it is not the hearers of the law who are righteous in God's sight, but the doers of the law who will be justified. 14 When Gentiles, who do not possess the law, do instinctively what the law requires, these, though not having the law, are a law to themselves. 15 They show that what the law requires is written on their hearts, to which their own conscience also bears witness; and their conflicting thoughts will accuse or perhaps excuse them 16 on the day when, according to my gospel, God, through Jesus Christ, will judge the secret thoughts of all.

The Jews and the Law

17 But if you call yourself a Jew and rely on the law and boast of your relation to God 18 and know his will and determine what is best because you are instructed in the law, 19 and if you are sure that you are a guide to the blind, a light to those who are in darkness, 20 a corrector of the foolish, a teacher of children, having in the law the embodiment of knowledge and truth, 21 you, then, that teach others, will you not teach yourself? While you preach against stealing, do you steal? 22 You that forbid adultery, do you commit adultery? You that abhor idols, do you rob temples? 23 You that boast in the law, do you dishonor God by breaking the law? 24 For, as it is written, "The name of God is blasphemed among the Gentiles because of you."

25 Circumcision indeed is of value if you obey the law; but if you break the law, your circumcision has become uncircumcision. 26 So, if those who are uncircumcised keep the requirements of the law, will not their uncircumcision be regarded as circumcision? 27 Then those who are physically uncircumcised but keep the law will condemn you that have the written code and circumcision but break the law. 28 For a person is not a Jew who is one outwardly, nor is true circumcision something external and physical. 29 Rather, a person is a Jew who is one inwardly, and real circumcision is a matter of the heart—it is spiritual and not literal. Such a person receives praise not from others but from God.

ROM

---

f Or *God-hated*   g Gk lacks *You say*

did you KNOW?

Circumcision, the Law, and Faith

Circumcision is the surgical removal of the foreskin from a male's penis. It was the sign of the Covenant (agreement) between Israel and God (Gen 17.2). As Gentiles became Christians, many Jewish Christians claimed they had to live by Jewish religious laws, including circumcision.

Paul consistently insists that such rituals are not necessary. He says that "real circumcision is a matter of the heart" (Rom 2.29), which leads to "faith working through love" (Gal 5.6). In Romans, chapter 4, Paul sheds further light on this by considering the case of Abraham. Abraham was considered the father of the Jewish faith. He was made righteous by God before he was circumcised (verse 10). Why? Because of his strong and heroic faith in God. Christians are called to this kind of faith in God, whose plan of salvation is now fully revealed in Jesus Christ.

▶ Rom 2.25–29

None Is Righteous
(Ps 14.1–3; 53.1–4)

9 What then? Are we any better off? *j* No, not at all; for we have already charged that all, both Jews and Greeks, are under the power of sin, 10 as it is written:

"There is no one who is righteous, not even one;
11   there is no one who has understanding,
        there is no one who seeks God.
12 All have turned aside, together they have become worthless;
        there is no one who shows kindness,
        there is not even one."
13 "Their throats are opened graves;
        they use their tongues to deceive."
    "The venom of vipers is under their lips."
14   "Their mouths are full of cursing and bitterness."
15 "Their feet are swift to shed blood;
16   ruin and misery are in their paths,
17 and the way of peace they have not known."
18   "There is no fear of God before their eyes."

19 Now we know that whatever the law says, it speaks to those who are under the law, so that every mouth may be silenced, and the whole world may be held accountable to God. 20 For "no human being will be justified in his sight" by deeds prescribed by the law, for through the law comes the knowledge of sin.

Righteousness through Faith

21 But now, apart from law, the righteousness of God has been disclosed, and is attested by the law and the prophets, 22 the righteousness of God through faith in Jesus Christ*k* for all who believe. For there is no distinction, 23 since all have sinned and fall short of the glory of God; 24 they are now justified by his grace as a gift, through the redemption that is in Christ Jesus, 25 whom God put forward as a sacrifice of atonement*l* by his blood, effective through faith. He did this to show his righteousness, because in his divine forbearance he had passed over the sins previously committed; 26 it was to prove at the present time that he himself is righteous and that he justifies the one who has faith in Jesus.*m*

27 Then what becomes of boasting? It is excluded. By what law? By that of works? No, but by the law of faith. 28 For we hold that a person is justified by faith apart from works prescribed by the law. 29 Or is God the God of Jews only? Is he not the God of Gentiles also? Yes, of Gentiles also,

3 Then what advantage has the Jew? Or what is the value of circumcision? 2 Much, in every way. For in the first place the Jews*h* were entrusted with the oracles of God. 3 What if some were unfaithful? Will their faithlessness nullify the faithfulness of God? 4 By no means! Although everyone is a liar, let God be proved true, as it is written,

"So that you may be justified in your words,
    and prevail in your judging."*i*

5 But if our injustice serves to confirm the justice of God, what should we say? That God is unjust to inflict wrath on us? (I speak in a human way.) 6 By no means! For then how could God judge the world? 7 But if through my falsehood God's truthfulness abounds to his glory, why am I still being condemned as a sinner? 8 And why not say (as some people slander us by saying that we say), "Let us do evil so that good may come"? Their condemnation is deserved!

h Gk they   i Gk when you are being judged   j Or at any disadvantage?   k Or through the faith of Jesus Christ   l Or a place of atonement   m Or who has the faith of Jesus

The Law, Faith, and Salvation

Throughout much of Romans, Paul is explaining the relationship between the Law, faith, and salvation. At the end of chapter 2 and the beginning of chapter 3, he shows that the Jewish Law of the Old Testament cannot save us from the effect of sin. But he recognizes the value of the Law (see 3.31). The Law was the expression of the Jewish people's response of faith to God's Covenant. It protected their relationships with God and one another.

We often think of sin as breaking God's law. But at its core, sin is really breaking our relationship with God and distancing ourselves from God. Remember what Adam and Eve did after their first sin? They hid from God, ashamed of their action. Paul is clear that we are all guilty of sin. Separated from God, the source of all life, we would eventually perish without God's help. But God is always seeking us out. In the ultimate act of love, God sent Jesus to restore the break in our relationship caused by sin. Jesus' death and Resurrection show us that God's great love is far more powerful than any sin we can commit.

Paul uses two key words to explain all of this. He talks about *justification*, which is the process that brings us back into a good relationship with God. And he talks about *righteousness* as the state of being right with God, of not being separated from God.

How are we justified? How are we considered righteous? Not by our ability to keep any laws but by our faith in Jesus Christ. And the effect of faith is opposite that of sin. Where sin creates distance, faith draws us close. Where sin kills, faith gives life. Where sin shrivels in hate, faith is active in love.

▶ Rom 3.21–31

---

30 since God is one; and he will justify the circumcised on the ground of faith and the uncircumcised through that same faith. 31 Do we then overthrow the law by this faith? By no means! On the contrary, we uphold the law.

The Example of Abraham
(Gen 17.10)

4 What then are we to say was gained by[n] Abraham, our ancestor according to the flesh? 2 For if Abraham was justified by works, he has something to boast about, but not before God. 3 For what does the scripture say? "Abraham believed God, and it was reckoned to him as righteousness." 4 Now to one who works, wages are not reckoned as a gift but as something due. 5 But to one who without works trusts him who justifies the ungodly, such faith is reckoned as righteousness. 6 So also David speaks of the blessedness of those to whom God reckons righteousness apart from works:

7 "Blessed are those whose iniquities are
        forgiven,
    and whose sins are covered;
8 blessed is the one against whom the Lord will
        not reckon sin."

9 Is this blessedness, then, pronounced only on the circumcised, or also on the uncircumcised? We say, "Faith was reckoned to Abraham as righteousness." 10 How then was it reckoned to him? Was it before or after he had been circumcised? It was not after, but before he was circumcised. 11 He received the sign of circumcision as a seal of the righteousness that he had by faith while he was still uncircumcised. The purpose was to make him the ancestor of all who believe without being circumcised and who thus have righteousness reckoned to them, 12 and likewise the ancestor of the circumcised who are not only circumcised but who also follow the example of the faith that our ancestor Abraham had before he was circumcised.

God's Promise Realized through Faith

13 For the promise that he would inherit the world did not come to Abraham or to his descendants through the law but through the righteousness of faith. 14 If it is the adherents of the law who are to be the heirs, faith is null and the promise is void. 15 For the law brings wrath; but where there is no law, neither is there violation.

16 For this reason it depends on faith, in order that the promise may rest on grace and be guaranteed to all his descendants, not only to the adherents of the law but also to those who share the faith of Abraham (for he is the father of all of us, 17 as it is written, "I have made you the father of many

R
O
M

---

n Other ancient authorities read *say about*

nations")—in the presence of the God in whom he believed, who gives life to the dead and calls into existence the things that do not exist. 18 Hoping against hope, he believed that he would become "the father of many nations," according to what was said, "So numerous shall your descendants be." 19 He did not weaken in faith when he considered his own body, which was already[o] as good as dead (for he was about a hundred years old), or when he considered the barrenness of Sarah's womb. 20 No distrust made him waver concerning the promise of God, but he grew strong in his faith as he gave glory to God, 21 being fully convinced that God was able to do what he had promised. 22 Therefore his faith[p] "was reckoned to him as righteousness." 23 Now the words, "it was reckoned to him," were written not for his sake alone, 24 but for ours also. It will be reckoned to us who believe in him who raised Jesus our Lord from the dead, 25 who was handed over to death for our trespasses and was raised for our justification.

Results of Justification

5 Therefore, since we are justified by faith, we[q] have peace with God through our Lord Jesus Christ, 2 through whom we have obtained access[r] to this grace in which we stand; and we[s] boast in our hope of sharing the glory of God. 3 And not only that, but we[s] also boast in our sufferings, knowing that suffering produces endurance, 4 and endurance produces character, and character produces hope, 5 and hope does not disappoint us, because God's love has been poured into our hearts through the Holy Spirit that has been given to us.

6 For while we were still weak, at the right time Christ died for the ungodly. 7 Indeed, rarely will anyone die for a righteous person—though perhaps for a good person someone might actually dare to

die. 8 But God proves his love for us in that while we still were sinners Christ died for us. 9 Much more surely then, now that we have been justified by his blood, will we be saved through him from the wrath of God.[t] 10 For if while we were enemies, we were reconciled to God through the death of his Son, much more surely, having been reconciled, will we be saved by his life. 11 But more than that, we even boast in God through our Lord Jesus Christ, through whom we have now received reconciliation.

Adam and Christ
(Gen 3.1–19)

12 Therefore, just as sin came into the world through one man, and death came through sin, and so death spread to all because all have sinned— 13 sin was indeed in the world before the law, but sin is not reckoned when there is no law. 14 Yet death exercised dominion from Adam to Moses, even over those whose sins were not like the transgression of Adam, who is a type of the one who was to come.

15 But the free gift is not like the trespass. For if the many died through the one man's trespass, much more surely have the grace of God and the free gift in the grace of the one man, Jesus Christ, abounded for the many. 16 And the free gift is not like the effect of the one man's sin. For the judgment following one trespass brought condemnation, but the free gift following many trespasses brings justification. 17 If, because of the one man's trespass, death exercised dominion through that one, much more surely will those who receive the

---

o Other ancient authorities lack *already*   *p* Gk *Therefore it*
q Other ancient authorities read *let us*   *r* Other ancient
authorities add *by faith*   *s* Or *let us*   *t* Gk *the wrath*

Trusting the Grace of God

A grandmother pushes her grandson out of the path of a speeding car, and is hit by the car and dies. A stranger jumps into a surging river to save a young girl, and loses his own life. A firefighter is killed battling a blaze to rescue three trapped people. Their concern for others leads these real-life heroes to make the ultimate sacrifice.

Like the grandson, the young girl, and the three trapped people, we too have been saved from death at a great cost—Jesus' loving sacrifice in obedience to God's will. Paul reminds us that our justification—our reconciliation and peace with God—is not a reward we deserve for being good. It is God's free gift of love and salvation despite our weakness and sin. And that is grace. Put your faith not in your own ability to please God, but in God's abundant grace.

▶ Rom 5.1–11

abundance of grace and the free gift of righteousness exercise dominion in life through the one man, Jesus Christ.

18 Therefore just as one man's trespass led to condemnation for all, so one man's act of righteousness leads to justification and life for all. 19 For just as by the one man's disobedience the many were made sinners, so by the one man's obedience the many will be made righteous. 20 But law came in, with the result that the trespass multiplied; but where sin increased, grace abounded all the more, 21 so that, just as sin exercised dominion in death, so grace might also exercise dominion through justification[u] leading to eternal life through Jesus Christ our Lord.

Dying and Rising with Christ

6 What then are we to say? Should we continue in sin in order that grace may abound? 2 By no means! How can we who died to sin go on living in it? 3 Do you not know that all of us who have been baptized into Christ Jesus were baptized into his death? 4 Therefore we have been buried with him by baptism into death, so that, just as Christ was raised from the dead by the glory of the Father, so we too might walk in newness of life.

5 For if we have been united with him in a death like his, we will certainly be united with him in a resurrection like his. 6 We know that our old self was crucified with him so that the body of sin might be destroyed, and we might no longer be enslaved to sin. 7 For whoever has died is freed from sin. 8 But if we have died with Christ, we believe that we will also live with him. 9 We know that Christ, being raised from the dead, will never die again; death no longer has dominion over him. 10 The death he died, he died to sin, once for all; but the life he lives, he lives to God. 11 So you also must consider yourselves dead to sin and alive to God in Christ Jesus.

12 Therefore, do not let sin exercise dominion in your mortal bodies, to make you obey their passions. 13 No longer present your members to sin as instruments[v] of wickedness, but present yourselves to God as those who have been brought from death to life, and present your members to God as instruments[v] of righteousness. 14 For sin will have no dominion over you, since you are not under law but under grace.

Slaves of Righteousness

15 What then? Should we sin because we are not under law but under grace? By no means! 16 Do you not know that if you present yourselves to anyone as obedient slaves, you are slaves of the one whom you obey, either of sin, which leads to death, or of obedience, which leads to righteousness?

PRAY IT!
In Christ, We Receive New Life!

In chapter 6 of Romans, Paul tells us that we die to sin and receive a new life in Jesus Christ—who died for the forgiveness of all sin and overcame death with his Resurrection. By participating in the paschal mystery (see "Dying for New Life," Jn 12.24–26) through Baptism, we are no longer enslaved to sin.

"The end is eternal life. For the wages of sin is death, but the free gift of God is eternal life in Christ Jesus our Lord" (Rom 6.22–23). Let the message of this passage fill you. Feel God's liberating grace in you. Never forget that Christ has already saved you, and God's mercy is there for you as soon as you repent, pray for forgiveness, and are willing to sin no more.

▶ **Rom 6.1–23**

17 But thanks be to God that you, having once been slaves of sin, have become obedient from the heart to the form of teaching to which you were entrusted, 18 and that you, having been set free from sin, have become slaves of righteousness. 19 I am speaking in human terms because of your natural limitations.[w] For just as you once presented your members as slaves to impurity and to greater and greater iniquity, so now present your members as slaves to righteousness for sanctification.

20 When you were slaves of sin, you were free in regard to righteousness. 21 So what advantage did you then get from the things of which you now are ashamed? The end of those things is death. 22 But now that you have been freed from sin and enslaved to God, the advantage you get is sanctification. The end is eternal life. 23 For the wages of sin is death, but the free gift of God is eternal life in Christ Jesus our Lord.

An Analogy from Marriage

7 Do you not know, brothers and sisters[x]—for I am speaking to those who know the law—that the law is binding on a person only during that

R
O
M

---

u Or *righteousness*   v Or *weapons*   w Gk *the weakness of your flesh*   x Gk *brothers*

PRAY IT!

I'm Not Perfect

Some people today think, "If God is always willing to forgive me, why should I be concerned about sinning?" Evidently, some people in Paul's time thought that too (see Rom 6.15). Paul reminds them, and us, that faith in Christ should be a matter of the heart, not simply a mechanical commitment. Like a married couple's love calls them to commit to each other (7.2), so our love for Christ should make us want to live in the light, free from sin. Why would we want to return to the things that bring death to the soul (6.21)?

But even when we commit to follow Christ, sin is a constant challenge. Paul encourages us, in the face of temptation, to maintain our focus on God and refrain from sin.

Jesus, you experienced temptation throughout your ministry. Yet you always made the decision to avoid sin and live in the light.

I have made the commitment to follow you. Give me the strength to overcome temptations and avoid sin. If in my weaknesses I allow my sin and passions to steer me in the wrong direction, please forgive me and help me regain control. Amen.

▶ Rom 6.15—7.6

person's lifetime? 2 Thus a married woman is bound by the law to her husband as long as he lives; but if her husband dies, she is discharged from the law concerning the husband. 3 Accordingly, she will be called an adulteress if she lives with another man while her husband is alive. But if her husband dies, she is free from that law, and if she marries another man, she is not an adulteress.

4 In the same way, my friends,*y* you have died to the law through the body of Christ, so that you may belong to another, to him who has been raised from the dead in order that we may bear fruit for God. 5 While we were living in the flesh, our sinful passions, aroused by the law, were at work in our members to bear fruit for death. 6 But now we are discharged from the law, dead to that which held us captive, so that we are slaves not under the old written code but in the new life of the Spirit.

The Law and Sin

7 What then should we say? That the law is sin? By no means! Yet, if it had not been for the law, I would not have known sin. I would not have known what it is to covet if the law had not said, "You shall not covet." 8 But sin, seizing an opportunity in the commandment, produced in me all kinds of covetousness. Apart from the law sin lies dead. 9 I was once alive apart from the law, but when the commandment came, sin revived 10 and I died, and the very commandment that promised life proved to be death to me. 11 For sin, seizing an opportunity in the commandment, deceived me and through it killed me. 12 So the law is holy, and the commandment is holy and just and good.

13 Did what is good, then, bring death to me?

---

y Gk *brothers*

Our Inner Struggle

In Rom 7.15–16, Paul reveals his own struggle to do what is right. It seems there's a part of us that wants to do right, and another part that wants to do wrong. Even when we try to be good, "evil lies close at hand" (verse 21), ready to have its way.

Paul uses the words *spirit* and *flesh* to describe this struggle. In his time, people thought passions and strong emotions originated in the body. So Paul says our flesh tempts us to do wrong, and our spirit wants us to do right. Paul does not mean that our physical bodies are evil and the source of sin. He means that we are all at war with ourselves.

Sin is hard to resist at times. To do what is right requires us to stop and think clearly about our choices and actively select good over sin. The good news is that God, the understanding forgiver, is on our side in the struggle. Thanks be to God!

▶ Rom 7.13–25

By no means! It was sin, working death in me through what is good, in order that sin might be shown to be sin, and through the commandment might become sinful beyond measure.

The Inner Conflict

14 For we know that the law is spiritual; but I am of the flesh, sold into slavery under sin.[z] 15 I do not understand my own actions. For I do not do what I want, but I do the very thing I hate. 16 Now if I do what I do not want, I agree that the law is good. 17 But in fact it is no longer I that do it, but sin that dwells within me. 18 For I know that nothing good dwells within me, that is, in my flesh. I can will what is right, but I cannot do it. 19 For I do not do the good I want, but the evil I do not want is what I do. 20 Now if I do what I do not want, it is no longer I that do it, but sin that dwells within me.

21 So I find it to be a law that when I want to do what is good, evil lies close at hand. 22 For I delight in the law of God in my inmost self, 23 but I see in my members another law at war with the law of my mind, making me captive to the law of sin that dwells in my members. 24 Wretched man that I am! Who will rescue me from this body of death? 25 Thanks be to God through Jesus Christ our Lord!

So then, with my mind I am a slave to the law of God, but with my flesh I am a slave to the law of sin.

Life in the Spirit

8 There is therefore now no condemnation for those who are in Christ Jesus. 2 For the law of the Spirit[a] of life in Christ Jesus has set you[b] free from the law of sin and of death. 3 For God has done what the law, weakened by the flesh, could not do: by sending his own Son in the likeness of sinful flesh, and to deal with sin,[c] he condemned sin in the flesh, 4 so that the just requirement of the law might be fulfilled in us, who walk not according to the flesh but according to the Spirit.[a] 5 For those who live according to the flesh set their minds on the things of the flesh, but those who live according to the Spirit[a] set their minds on the things of the Spirit.[a] 6 To set the mind on the flesh is death, but to set the mind on the Spirit[a] is life and peace. 7 For this reason the mind that is set on the flesh is hostile to God; it does not submit to God's law—indeed it cannot, 8 and those who are in the flesh cannot please God.

9 But you are not in the flesh; you are in the Spirit,[a] since the Spirit of God dwells in you. Anyone who does not have the Spirit of Christ does not belong to him. 10 But if Christ is in you, though the body is dead because of sin, the Spirit[a] is life because of righteousness. 11 If the Spirit of him who raised Jesus from the dead dwells in you, he who

Catholic Connections

LED BY THE SPIRIT

Do we allow the Spirit of God to lead us through life?

At Baptism, we receive the Holy Spirit and become temples, or homes, for that Spirit. As a result, we are God's adopted daughters and sons, and Jesus is our brother! The life of Christ has been given to us as daughters and sons and to all those who are baptized.

Jesus lived in the Spirit of compassion, justice, and love. His disciples, who heard his words and witnessed his deeds, discovered that they were encountering God's Holy Presence—God's Spirit.

Do our friends and family recognize and experience the Spirit of Christ in us? If we were to take an honest look at the kind of spirit we manifest every day, what would we see? Do we see justice and compassion guiding our hearts? Are our daily activities directed by faith in Christ and Christian values? Do we face opposition, even unpopularity, as we make choices to do the right thing?

▶ Rom 8.1–17

raised Christ[d] from the dead will give life to your mortal bodies also through[e] his Spirit that dwells in you.

12 So then, brothers and sisters,[f] we are debtors, not to the flesh, to live according to the flesh— 13 for if you live according to the flesh, you will die; but if by the Spirit you put to death the deeds of the body, you will live. 14 For all who are led by the Spirit of God are children of God. 15 For you did not receive a spirit of slavery to fall back into fear, but you have received a spirit of adoption. When

R
O
M

---

z Gk sold under sin   a Or spirit   b Here the Greek word you is singular number; other ancient authorities read me or us   c Or and as a sin offering   d Other ancient authorities read the Christ or Christ Jesus or Jesus Christ   e Other ancient authorities read on account of   f Gk brothers we cry, "Abba!$ Father!" 16 it is that very Spirit bearing witness^h with our spirit that we are children of God, 17 and if children, then heirs, heirs of God and joint heirs with Christ—if, in fact, we suffer with him so that we may also be glorified with him.

Future Glory

18 I consider that the sufferings of this present time are not worth comparing with the glory about to be revealed to us. 19 For the creation waits with eager longing for the revealing of the children of God; 20 for the creation was subjected to futility, not of its own will but by the will of the one who subjected it, in hope 21 that the creation itself will be set free from its bondage to decay and will obtain the freedom of the glory of the children of God. 22 We know that the whole creation has been groaning in labor pains until now; 23 and not only the creation, but we ourselves, who have the first fruits of the Spirit, groan inwardly while we wait for adoption, the redemption of our bodies. 24 For in^i hope we were saved. Now hope that is seen is not hope. For who hopes^j for what is seen? 25 But if we hope for what we do not see, we wait for it with patience.

26 Likewise the Spirit helps us in our weakness; for we do not know how to pray as we ought, but that very Spirit intercedes^k with sighs too deep for words. 27 And God,^{l} who searches the heart, knows what is the mind of the Spirit, because the Spirit^m intercedes for the saints according to the will of God.^{n}

28 We know that all things work together for good^o for those who love God, who are called according to his purpose. 29 For those whom he foreknew he also predestined to be conformed to the image of his Son, in order that he might be the firstborn within a large family.^{p} 30 And those whom

he predestined he also called; and those whom he called he also justified; and those whom he justified he also glorified.

God's Love in Christ Jesus

31 What then are we to say about these things? If God is for us, who is against us? 32 He who did not withhold his own Son, but gave him up for all of us, will he not with him also give us everything else? 33 Who will bring any charge against God's elect? It is God who justifies. 34 Who is to condemn? It is Christ Jesus, who died, yes, who was raised, who is at the right hand of God, who indeed intercedes for us.^{q} 35 Who will separate us from the love of Christ? Will hardship, or distress, or persecution, or famine, or nakedness, or peril, or sword? 36 As it is written,

> "For your sake we are being killed all day
> long;
> we are accounted as sheep to be
> slaughtered."

37 No, in all these things we are more than conquerors through him who loved us. 38 For I am convinced that neither death, nor life, nor angels, nor rulers, nor things present, nor things to come, nor powers, 39 nor height, nor depth, nor anything else in all creation, will be able to separate us from the love of God in Christ Jesus our Lord.

God's Election of Israel
(Gen 25.19–23)

9 I am speaking the truth in Christ—I am not lying; my conscience confirms it by the Holy Spirit— 2 I have great sorrow and unceasing anguish in my heart. 3 For I could wish that I myself were accursed and cut off from Christ for the sake of my own people,^{r} my kindred according to the flesh. 4 They are Israelites, and to them belong the adoption, the glory, the covenants, the giving of the law, the worship, and the promises; 5 to them belong the patriarchs, and from them, according to the flesh, comes the Messiah,^{s} who is over all, God blessed forever.^{t} Amen.

6 It is not as though the word of God had failed. For not all Israelites truly belong to Israel, 7 and not all of Abraham's children are his true descendants; but "It is through Isaac that descendants shall be

We know that *all things work together* **for good for those who** love God, who are called *according to his purpose*

8.28

---

g Aramaic for *Father* h Or 15*a spirit of adoption, by which we cry, "Abba! Father!"* 16*The Spirit itself bears witness* i Or *by* j Other ancient authorities read *awaits* k Other ancient authorities add *for us* l Gk *the one* m Gk *he or it* n Gk *according to God* o Other ancient authorities read *God makes all things work together for good,* or *in all things God works for good* p Gk *among many brothers* q Or *Is it Christ Jesus . . . for us?* r Gk *my brothers* s Or *the Christ* t Or *Messiah, who is God over all, blessed forever;* or *Messiah. May he who is God over all be blessed forever*

PRAY IT

Absolutely Nothing!

*G**od, what could separate me from your
love?*

*Not a failed test, or a broken promise, or a
hurtful word.*

What could tear you from me?

*Not the lure of power, or immediate
gratification, or unnatural highs.*

*If you, God, are on my side, who could be
against me?*

*Not a vengeful peer, or an uncaring date, or
someone whose relationship with me has
gone sour.*

*What situation could divide you and me,
God?*

*Not depression over a loss, or anger over
being laughed at, or guilt from being
caught red-handed.*

*No, in all these things, I know that I am
never alone, because you, God, conquered
sin, despair, and even death itself through
your endless love, a love that showed itself
through your Son. I am convinced, Lord,
that nothing, absolutely nothing, will ever
separate me from your love . . . ever!
Amen.*

▶ **Rom 8.31–39**

named for you." 8 This means that it is not the children of the flesh who are the children of God, but the children of the promise are counted as descendants. 9 For this is what the promise said, "About this time I will return and Sarah shall have a son." 10 Nor is that all; something similar happened to Rebecca when she had conceived children by one husband, our ancestor Isaac. 11 Even before they had been born or had done anything good or bad (so that God's purpose of election might continue, 12 not by works but by his call) she was told, "The elder shall serve the younger." 13 As it is written,

"I have loved Jacob,
but I have hated Esau."

14 What then are we to say? Is there injustice on God's part? By no means! 15 For he says to Moses,

"I will have mercy on whom I have mercy,
and I will have compassion on whom I
have compassion."

16 So it depends not on human will or exertion, but on God who shows mercy. 17 For the scripture says to Pharaoh, "I have raised you up for the very purpose of showing my power in you, so that my name may be proclaimed in all the earth." 18 So then he has mercy on whomever he chooses, and he hardens the heart of whomever he chooses.

God's Wrath and Mercy

19 You will say to me then, "Why then does he still find fault? For who can resist his will?" 20 But who indeed are you, a human being, to argue with God? Will what is molded say to the one who molds it, "Why have you made me like this?" 21 Has the potter no right over the clay, to make out of the same lump one object for special use and another for ordinary use? 22 What if God, desiring to show his wrath and to make known his power, has endured with much patience the objects of wrath that are made for destruction; 23 and what if he has done so in order to make known the riches of his glory for the objects of mercy, which he has prepared beforehand for glory— 24 including us whom he has called, not from the Jews only but also from the Gentiles? 25 As indeed he says in Hō•sē'a,

"Those who were not my people I will call 'my
people,'
and her who was not beloved I will call
'beloved.' "

26 "And in the very place where it was said to
them, 'You are not my people,'
there they shall be called children of the
living God."

27 And Ī•sāi'ah cries out concerning Israel, "Though the number of the children of Israel were like the sand of the sea, only a remnant of them will be saved; 28 for the Lord will execute his sentence on the earth quickly and decisively."u 29 And as Ī•sāi'ah predicted,

"If the Lord of hosts had not left survivorsv
to us,
we would have fared like Sod'om
and been made like Go•mor'rah."

Israel's Unbelief

30 What then are we to say? Gentiles, who did not strive for righteousness, have attained it, that is, righteousness through faith; 31 but Israel, who did strive for the righteousness that is based on the law, did not succeed in fulfilling that law. 32 Why not? Because they did not strive for it on the basis of faith, but as if it were based on works. They have stumbled over the stumbling stone, 33 as it is written,

"See, I am laying in Zion a stone that will
make people stumble, a rock that will
make them fall,

ROM

---

u Other ancient authorities read *for he will finish his work
and cut it short in righteousness, because the Lord will make the
sentence shortened on the earth*   v Or *descendants; Gk seed*

?did you KNOW?

The Fate of Israel

In Romans, chapters 9–11, Paul takes on a difficult question: What will happen to Israel (the Jews), God's chosen people, if they reject Jesus? For the early Jewish Christians, who probably had friends and maybe had family members who didn't believe in Jesus, this was an important question.

To respond, Paul makes several points. In the beginning of chapter 9, he affirms Israel's special place in God's plan of salvation. But the people's righteousness (see "The Law, Faith, and Salvation," Rom 3.21–31) is based on faith, not on fulfilling the Law. In chapter 10, Paul notes that salvation is available for all. The Jewish people are not left out if they call on the name of the Lord. But Israel's rejection of Jesus is good news for the Gentiles who have come to believe.

In chapter 11, Paul uses the analogy of grafting branches onto a tree. The Gentiles were grafted onto the original tree, which is Israel. Paul says the Jews can be grafted back onto that tree (verse 23). In fact, he ends with the hopeful promise that after the salvation of the Gentiles, all Israel will be saved (verse 26)!

Christians recognize Jewish people as their spiritual ancestors. Christians have inherited from the Jews part of their Scriptures and a rich spiritual tradition. They respect the Jews' faith and their relationship with God. They pray for the Jews' salvation and their own, in the hope that Paul's promise will come to pass.

▸ Romans, chapters 9–11

and whoever believes in him[w] will not be put to shame."

10 Brothers and sisters,[x] my heart's desire and prayer to God for them is that they may be saved. 2 I can testify that they have a zeal for God, but it is not enlightened. 3 For, being ignorant of the righteousness that comes from God, and seeking to establish their own, they have not submitted to God's righteousness. 4 For Christ is the end of the law so that there may be righteousness for everyone who believes.

Salvation Is for All

5 Moses writes concerning the righteousness that comes from the law, that "the person who does these things will live by them." 6 But the righteousness that comes from faith says, "Do not say in your heart, 'Who will ascend into heaven?'" (that is, to bring Christ down) 7 "or 'Who will descend into the abyss?'" (that is, to bring Christ up from the dead). 8 But what does it say?

"The word is near you,
    on your lips and in your heart"
(that is, the word of faith that we proclaim); 9 because[y] if you confess with your lips that Jesus is Lord and believe in your heart that God raised him from the dead, you will be saved. 10 For one believes with the heart and so is justified, and one confesses with the mouth and so is saved. 11 The scripture says, "No one who believes in him will be put to shame." 12 For there is no distinction between Jew and Greek; the same Lord is Lord of all and is generous to all who call on him. 13 For, "Everyone who calls on the name of the Lord shall be saved."

14 But how are they to call on one in whom they have not believed? And how are they to believe in one of whom they have never heard? And how are they to hear without someone to proclaim him? 15 And how are they to proclaim him unless they are sent? As it is written, "How beautiful are the feet of those who bring good news!" 16 But not all have obeyed the good news;[z] for I•saiʹah says, "Lord, who has believed our message?" 17 So faith comes from what is heard, and what is heard comes through the word of Christ.[a]

18 But I ask, have they not heard? Indeed they have; for

"Their voice has gone out to all the earth,
    and their words to the ends of the
        world."
19 Again I ask, did Israel not understand? First Moses says,

"I will make you jealous of those who are not a
        nation;
    with a foolish nation I will make you
        angry."
20 Then I•saiʹah is so bold as to say,

"I have been found by those who did not
        seek me;
    I have shown myself to those who did not
        ask for me."
21 But of Israel he says, "All day long I have held out my hands to a disobedient and contrary people."

---

w Or *trusts in it*   x Gk *Brothers*   y Or *namely, that*   z Or *gospel*   a Or *about Christ*; other ancient authorities read *of God*

Israel's Rejection Is Not Final

(Cp Ps 69.22–23; Isa 29.10)

11 I ask, then, has God rejected his people? By no means! I myself am an Israelite, a descendant of Abraham, a member of the tribe of Benjamin. 2 God has not rejected his people whom he foreknew. Do you not know what the scripture says of E•li'jah, how he pleads with God against Israel? 3 "Lord, they have killed your prophets, they have demolished your altars; I alone am left, and they are seeking my life." 4 But what is the divine reply to him? "I have kept for myself seven thousand who have not bowed the knee to Bā'al." 5 So too at the present time there is a remnant, chosen by grace. 6 But if it is by grace, it is no longer on the basis of works, otherwise grace would no longer be grace.*b*

7 What then? Israel failed to obtain what it was seeking. The elect obtained it, but the rest were hardened, 8 as it is written,

"God gave them a sluggish spirit,
    eyes that would not see
        and ears that would not hear,
down to this very day."

9 And David says,

"Let their table become a snare and a trap,
    a stumbling block and a retribution for
        them;
10 let their eyes be darkened so that they cannot
        see,
    and keep their backs forever bent."

The Salvation of the Gentiles

11 So I ask, have they stumbled so as to fall? By no means! But through their stumbling*c* salvation has come to the Gentiles, so as to make Israel*d* jealous. 12 Now if their stumbling*c* means riches for the world, and if their defeat means riches for Gentiles, how much more will their full inclusion mean!

13 Now I am speaking to you Gentiles. Inasmuch then as I am an apostle to the Gentiles, I glorify my ministry 14 in order to make my own people*e* jealous, and thus save some of them. 15 For if their rejection is the reconciliation of the world, what will their acceptance be but life from the dead! 16 If the part of the dough offered as first fruits is holy, then the whole batch is holy; and if the root is holy, then the branches also are holy.

17 But if some of the branches were broken off, and you, a wild olive shoot, were grafted in their place to share the rich root*f* of the olive tree, 18 do not boast over the branches. If you do boast, remember that it is not you that support the root, but the root that supports you. 19 You will say, "Branches were broken off so that I might be grafted in." 20 That is true. They were broken off because of their unbelief, but you stand only through faith. So do not become proud, but stand in awe. 21 For if God did not spare the natural branches, perhaps he will not spare you.*g* 22 Note then the kindness and the severity of God: severity toward those who have fallen, but God's kindness toward you, provided you continue in his kindness; otherwise you also will be cut off. 23 And even those of Israel,*h* if they do not persist in unbelief, will be grafted in, for God has the power to graft them in again. 24 For if you have been cut from what is by nature a wild

---

PRAY IT

Are Your Feet Beautiful?

Spread the word!" "Attention all shoppers!" "Special announcement!" Companies trying to sell a product and organizations trying to attract new members go to great lengths and expense to get their message out. Without this effort, they will reach few people and fail in their mission.

The church has undoubtedly the most important mission of all—to share with others the saving power that comes from faith in Jesus Christ. The promise in Rom 10.11–15 is that all who know and call on the name of Jesus will be saved. God is great!

How do others hear about this Good News? Paul says only through us. And he adds, "How beautiful are the feet of those who bring good news!" (verse 15). In your prayer, reflect or journal on the following questions:

- Who brought the Good News to you? What made you trust what they had to tell you about Jesus?
- Which of your friends need to hear this Good News about Jesus? How can you share your faith with them, perhaps through a message of hope, forgiveness, healing, or encouragement?

▶ Rom 10.11–15

---

b Other ancient authorities add *But if it is by works, it is no longer on the basis of grace, otherwise work would no longer be work*   *c* Gk *transgression*   *d* Gk *them*   *e* Gk *my flesh*   *f* Other ancient authorities read *the richness*   *g* Other ancient authorities read *neither will he spare you*   *h* Gk lacks *of Israel* olive tree and grafted, contrary to nature, into a cultivated olive tree, how much more will these natural branches be grafted back into their own olive tree.

All Israel Will Be Saved

25 So that you may not claim to be wiser than you are, brothers and sisters,[i] I want you to under stand this mystery: a hardening has come upon part of Israel, until the full number of the Gentiles has come in. 26 And so all Israel will be saved; as it is written,

"Out of Zion will come the Deliverer;
    he will banish ungodliness from Jacob."
27 "And this is my covenant with them,
    when I take away their sins."

28 As regards the gospel they are enemies of God[j] for your sake; but as regards election they are beloved, for the sake of their ancestors; 29 for the gifts and the calling of God are irrevocable. 30 Just as you were once disobedient to God but have now received mercy because of their disobedience, 31 so they have now been disobedient in order that, by the mercy shown to you, they too may now[k] receive mercy. 32 For God has imprisoned all in disobedience so that he may be merciful to all.

The New Life in Christ

12 I appeal to you therefore, brothers and sisters,[i] by the mercies of God, to present your bodies as a living sacrifice, holy and acceptable to God, which is your spiritual[l] worship. 2 Do not be conformed to this world,[m] but be transformed by the renewing of your minds, so that you may discern what is the will of God—what is good and acceptable and perfect.[n]

3 For by the grace given to me I say to everyone among you not to think of yourself more highly than you ought to think, but to think with sober judgment, each according to the measure of faith that God has assigned. 4 For as in one body we have many members, and not all the members have the same function, 5 so we, who are many, are one body in Christ, and individually we are members one of another. 6 We have gifts that differ according to the grace given to us: prophecy, in proportion to faith; 7 ministry, in ministering; the teacher, in teaching; 8 the exhorter, in exhortation; the giver, in generosity; the leader, in diligence; the compassionate, in cheerfulness.

I appeal to you therefore, brothers and sisters, by the mercies of God, to present your bodies as a living sacrifice, holy and acceptable to God, which is your spiritual worship.

Do not be conformed to this world, but be transformed by the renewing of your minds, so that you may discern what is the will of God— what is good and acceptable and perfect.

33 O the depth of the riches and wisdom and knowledge of God! How unsearchable are his judgments and how inscrutable his ways!
34 "For who has known the mind of the
    Lord?
    Or who has been his counselor?"
35 "Or who has given a gift to him,
    to receive a gift in return?"
36 For from him and through him and to him are all things. To him be the glory forever. Amen.

Marks of the True Christian

9 Let love be genuine; hate what is evil, hold fast to what is good; 10 love one another with mutual affection; outdo one another in showing honor. 11 Do not lag in zeal, be ardent in spirit, serve the Lord.[o] 12 Rejoice in hope, be patient in suffer-

i Gk brothers j Gk lacks of God k Other ancient authorities lack now l Or reasonable m Gk age n Or what is the good and acceptable and perfect will of God o Other ancient authorities read serve the opportune time

WE ARE THE BODY OF CHRIST!

According to Rom 12.1–8, we are the Body of Christ! Just thinking about this beautiful and powerful belief fills us with energy. Imagine the power if all Christians really behaved as the living Body of Christ in their home, church, neighborhood, country, and planet.

In verse 1, Paul calls us to present our body to God as a living, holy, and acceptable sacrifice. The best thing that we can offer to God is our whole life—all we are and all we do. When we worship God by doing this, our prayer and rituals are real and meaningful.

In verse 2, Paul calls us not to be conformed to this world but to be transformed. We are transformed by renewing our mind. We are intelligent people. God gave us the power to discern what is good and evil, true and false, in agreement with or against God's loving plan for humanity.

We must think and act according to the measure of faith and the different gifts that we have received for the service of others (charisms). So we, who are many, may become one Body in Christ and be better collaborators in Jesus' mission.

▸ Rom 12.1–8

---

ing, persevere in prayer. 13 Contribute to the needs of the saints; extend hospitality to strangers.

14 Bless those who persecute you; bless and do not curse them. 15 Rejoice with those who rejoice, weep with those who weep. 16 Live in harmony with one another; do not be haughty, but associate with the lowly;*p* do not claim to be wiser than you are. 17 Do not repay anyone evil for evil, but take thought for what is noble in the sight of all. 18 If it is possible, so far as it depends on you, live peaceably with all. 19 Beloved, never avenge yourselves, but leave room for the wrath of God;*q* for it is written, "Vengeance is mine, I will repay, says the

Lord." 20 No, "if your enemies are hungry, feed them; if they are thirsty, give them something to drink; for by doing this you will heap burning coals on their heads." 21 Do not be overcome by evil, but overcome evil with good.

Being Subject to Authorities

13 Let every person be subject to the governing authorities; for there is no authority except from God, and those authorities that exist have been instituted by God. 2 Therefore

---

p Or give yourselves to humble tasks   q Gk the wrath

Becoming a Peacemaker

A common response when someone mistreats us is to seek revenge. But in Rom 12.17–19, Paul tells us that only God should be the avenger. He goes on to remind us of Jesus' teaching to treat our enemies with kindness. That is certainly easier said than done! It is difficult to respond with goodwill when we are hurt.

Nevertheless, people have tried to live by this teaching. Perhaps you know people who have made similar commitments in your own community.

Think of the people you know. Who is a peacemaker in your life? What can you do to be a peacemaker in your family, school, or community?

▸ Rom 12.17–19

whoever resists authority resists what God has appointed, and those who resist will incur judgment. 3 For rulers are not a terror to good conduct, but to bad. Do you wish to have no fear of the authority? Then do what is good, and you will receive its approval; 4 for it is God's servant for your good. But if you do what is wrong, you should be afraid, for the authority*r* does not bear the sword in vain! It is the servant of God to execute wrath on the wrongdoer. 5 Therefore one must be subject, not only because of wrath but also because of conscience. 6 For the same reason you also pay taxes, for the authorities are God's servants, busy with this very thing. 7 Pay to all what is due them—taxes to whom taxes are due, revenue to whom revenue is due, respect to whom respect is due, honor to whom honor is due.

Love for One Another
(Cp Mk 12.31; Jas 2.8)

8 Owe no one anything, except to love one another; for the one who loves another has fulfilled the law. 9 The commandments, "You shall not commit adultery; You shall not murder; You shall not steal; You shall not covet"; and any other commandment, are summed up in this word, "Love your neighbor as yourself." 10 Love does no wrong to a neighbor; therefore, love is the fulfilling of the law.

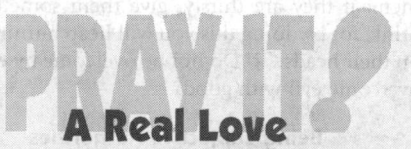

A Real Love

Lord, why is it so hard to love? Love is mentioned so much in the Bible that it makes me wonder why we don't get it. It seems that we do a good job of talking love and a poor job of doing love. We can point out where there is no love, but it sure is hard to bring love to where it is needed.

Jesus, fill me with your love to share with others. The kind of love that changes people forever. The kind of love that breaks down barriers and overcomes fears. The love that gives without counting the costs. Amen.

▸ Rom 13.8–10

An Urgent Appeal

11 Besides this, you know what time it is, how it is now the moment for you to wake from sleep. For salvation is nearer to us now than when we became believers; 12 the night is far gone, the day is near. Let us then lay aside the works of darkness and put on the armor of light; 13 let us live honorably as in the day, not in reveling and drunkenness, not in debauchery and licentiousness, not in quarreling and jealousy. 14 Instead, put on the Lord Jesus Christ, and make no provision for the flesh, to gratify its desires.

Do Not Judge Another

14 Welcome those who are weak in faith,*s* but not for the purpose of quarreling over opinions. 2 Some believe in eating anything, while the weak eat only vegetables. 3 Those who eat must not despise those who abstain, and those who abstain must not pass judgment on those who eat; for God has welcomed them. 4 Who are you to pass judgment on servants of another? It is before their own lord that they stand or fall. And they will be upheld, for the Lord*t* is able to make them stand.

5 Some judge one day to be better than another, while others judge all days to be alike. Let all be fully convinced in their own minds. 6 Those who observe the day, observe it in honor of the Lord. Also those who eat, eat in honor of the Lord, since they give thanks to God; while those who abstain, abstain in honor of the Lord and give thanks to God.

7 We do not live to ourselves, and we do not die to ourselves. 8 If we live, we live to the Lord, and if we die, we die to the Lord; so then, whether we live or whether we die, we are the Lord's. 9 For to this end Christ died and lived again, so that he might be Lord of both the dead and the living.

10 Why do you pass judgment on your brother or sister?*u* Or you, why do you despise your brother or sister?*u* For we will all stand before the judgment seat of God.*v* 11 For it is written,

"As I live, says the Lord, every knee shall bow
    to me,
and every tongue shall give praise
    to*w* God."

12 So then, each of us will be accountable to God.*x*

Do Not Make Another Stumble

13 Let us therefore no longer pass judgment on one another, but resolve instead never to put a stumbling block or hindrance in the way of another.*y* 14 I know and am persuaded in the Lord Jesus that nothing is unclean in itself; but it is unclean for anyone who thinks it unclean. 15 If your brother or sister*u* is being injured by what you eat, you are no longer walking in love. Do not let what you eat

---

r Gk it   *s* Or *conviction*   *t* Other ancient authorities read *for God*   *u* Gk *brother*   *v* Other ancient authorities read *of Christ*   *w* Or *confess*   *x* Other ancient authorities lack *to God*   *y* Gk *of a brother*

Respecting Differences

Christians have different ideas about what to believe and how to act. It seems Paul has heard that the Christians in Rome disagree about what to eat (Rom 14.2) and what days to hold holy (verse 5). He tells them not to quarrel over these differences. Whatever they do, they should do it "in honor of the Lord" (verse 6). The church would be shamed if these minor differences became a stumbling block to someone's faith.

A healthy respect for differences pulls together Christians from various religious denominations or traditions. Christians of all denominations should rejoice in their common faith, respect and learn from their differences, and work together "in honor of the Lord."

▶ Rom 14.1–23

---

cause the ruin of one for whom Christ died. ¹⁶ So do not let your good be spoken of as evil. ¹⁷ For the kingdom of God is not food and drink but righteousness and peace and joy in the Holy Spirit. ¹⁸ The one who thus serves Christ is acceptable to God and has human approval. ¹⁹ Let us then pursue what makes for peace and for mutual upbuilding. ²⁰ Do not, for the sake of food, destroy the work of God. Everything is indeed clean, but it is wrong for you to make others fall by what you eat; ²¹ it is good not to eat meat or drink wine or do anything that makes your brother or sister*z* stumble.*a* ²² The faith that you have, have as your own conviction before God. Blessed are those who have no reason to condemn themselves because of what they approve. ²³ But those who have doubts are condemned if they eat, because they do not act from faith;*b* for whatever does not proceed from faith*b* is sin.*c*

Please Others, Not Yourselves

15 We who are strong ought to put up with the failings of the weak, and not to please ourselves. ² Each of us must please our neighbor for the good purpose of building up the neighbor. ³ For Christ did not please himself; but, as it is written, "The insults of those who insult you have fallen on me." ⁴ For whatever was written in former days was written for our instruction, so that by steadfastness and by the encouragement of the scriptures we might have hope. ⁵ May the God of steadfastness and encouragement grant you to live in harmony with one another, in accordance with Christ Jesus, ⁶ so that together you may with one voice glorify the God and Father of our Lord Jesus Christ.

The Gospel for Jews and Gentiles Alike

7 Welcome one another, therefore, just as Christ has welcomed you, for the glory of God. ⁸ For I tell you that Christ has become a servant of the circumcised on behalf of the truth of God in order that he might confirm the promises given to the patriarchs, ⁹ and in order that the Gentiles might glorify God for his mercy. As it is written,

"Therefore I will confess*d* you among the
        Gentiles,
    and sing praises to your name";
¹⁰ and again he says,
    "Rejoice, O Gentiles, with his people";
¹¹ and again,
    "Praise the Lord, all you Gentiles,
    and let all the peoples praise him";
¹² and again I•sāi′ah says,
    "The root of Jesse shall come,
        the one who rises to rule the Gentiles;
    in him the Gentiles shall hope."

¹³ May the God of hope fill you with all joy and peace in believing, so that you may abound in hope by the power of the Holy Spirit.

Paul's Reason for Writing So Boldly

14 I myself feel confident about you, my brothers and sisters,*e* that you yourselves are full of goodness, filled with all knowledge, and able to instruct one another. ¹⁵ Nevertheless on some points I have written to you rather boldly by way of reminder, because of the grace given me by God ¹⁶ to be a minister of Christ Jesus to the Gentiles in the priestly

R
O
M

---

z Gk *brother*   *a* Other ancient authorities add *or be upset or be weakened*   *b* Or *conviction*   *c* Other authorities, some ancient, add here 16.25-27   *d* Or *thank*   *e* Gk *brothers* service of the gospel of God, so that the offering of the Gentiles may be acceptable, sanctified by the Holy Spirit. 17 In Christ Jesus, then, I have reason to boast of my work for God. 18 For I will not venture to speak of anything except what Christ has accomplished *f* through me to win obedience from the Gentiles, by word and deed, 19 by the power of signs and wonders, by the power of the Spirit of God,*g* so that from Jerusalem and as far around as Il·lyr'i·cum I have fully proclaimed the good news *h* of Christ. 20 Thus I make it my ambition to proclaim the good news,*h* not where Christ has already been named, so that I do not build on someone else's foundation, 21 but as it is written,

"Those who have never been told of him shall see,
and those who have never heard of him shall understand."

Paul's Plan to Visit Rome

22 This is the reason that I have so often been hindered from coming to you. 23 But now, with no further place for me in these regions, I desire, as I have for many years, to come to you 24 when I go to Spain. For I do hope to see you on my journey and to be sent on by you, once I have enjoyed your company for a little while. 25 At present, however, I am going to Jerusalem in a ministry to the saints; 26 for Mac·e·dō'ni·a and A·chā'i·a have been pleased to share their resources with the poor among the saints at Jerusalem. 27 They were pleased to do this, and indeed they owe it to them; for if the Gentiles have come to share in their spiritual blessings, they ought also to be of service to them in material things. 28 So, when I have completed this, and have delivered to them what has been collected,*i* I will set out by way of you to Spain; 29 and I know that when I come to you, I will come in the fullness of the blessing*j* of Christ.

30 I appeal to you, brothers and sisters,*k* by our Lord Jesus Christ and by the love of the Spirit, to join me in earnest prayer to God on my behalf, 31 that I may be rescued from the unbelievers in Judea, and that my ministry*l* to Jerusalem may be acceptable to the saints, 32 so that by God's will I may come to you with joy and be refreshed in your company. 33 The God of peace be with all of you.*m* Amen.

Personal Greetings

16 I commend to you our sister Phoē'bē, a deacon*n* of the church at Cen'chrē·ae, 2 so that you may welcome her in the Lord as is fitting for the saints, and help her in whatever she may require from you, for she has been a benefactor of many and of myself as well.

3 Greet Pris'ca and A·qui'la, who work with me in Christ Jesus, 4 and who risked their necks for my life, to whom not only I give thanks, but also all the churches of the Gentiles. 5 Greet also the church in their house. Greet my beloved E·paē'ne·tus, who

---

f Gk *speak of those things that Christ has not accomplished*
g Other ancient authorities read *of the Spirit* or *of the Holy Spirit*   *h* Or *gospel*   *i* Gk *have sealed to them this fruit*
j Other ancient authorities add *of the gospel*   *k* Gk *brothers*
l Other ancient authorities read *my bringing of a gift*   *m* One ancient authority adds 16.25-27 here   *n* Or *minister*

Introducing ▶ PHOEBE AND JUNIA

In Rom 16.1–16, Paul greets almost thirty people and their families in Rome—more people than he greets in any of his other letters. It is thought that perhaps he is trying to establish a connection among the Christians in Rome by mentioning mutual acquaintances. About a third of the people he greets are women, highlighting the important role women played in Paul's ministry and in the leadership of the early church.

Of particular interest are Paul's comments about Phoebe, whom he calls a deacon, and Junia (also called Julia), whom he declares "prominent among the apostles" (verse 7). In Paul's time, deacons were usually associated with a ministry of service, and apostles with a ministry of leadership. Even though women were not allowed to fill official positions in government or society, the early church recognized them as being as important as men in service, leadership, and bringing the Gospel to others.

Rom 16.1–16

was the first convert*o* in Asia for Christ. 6 Greet Mary, who has worked very hard among you. 7 Greet An·dron'i·cus and Ju̅'ni·a,*p* my relatives*q* who were in prison with me; they are prominent among the apostles, and they were in Christ before I was. 8 Greet Am·pli·a̅'tus, my beloved in the Lord. 9 Greet Ur·ba̅'nus, our co-worker in Christ, and my beloved Sta̅'chys. 10 Greet A·pel'le̅s, who is approved in Christ. Greet those who belong to the family of Ar·is·tob'u̅·lus. 11 Greet my relative*r* He·ro̅'di·on. Greet those in the Lord who belong to the family of Nar·cis'sus. 12 Greet those workers in the Lord, Try̅·phae̅'na and Try̅·pho̅'sa. Greet the beloved Per'sis, who has worked hard in the Lord. 13 Greet Rufus, chosen in the Lord; and greet his mother—a mother to me also. 14 Greet A·syn'cri·tus, Phle̅'gon, Her'me̅s, Pat'ro·bas, Her'mas, and the brothers and sisters*s* who are with them. 15 Greet Phi·lol'o·gus, Julia, Ne̅'re·us and his sister, and O̅·lym'pas, and all the saints who are with them. 16 Greet one another with a holy kiss. All the churches of Christ greet you.

Final Instructions

17 I urge you, brothers and sisters,*s* to keep an eye on those who cause dissensions and offenses, in opposition to the teaching that you have learned; avoid them. 18 For such people do not serve our Lord Christ, but their own appetites,*t* and by smooth talk and flattery they deceive the hearts of the simple-minded. 19 For while your obedience is known to all, so that I rejoice over you, I want you to be wise in what is good and guileless in what is evil. 20 The God of peace will shortly crush Satan under your feet. The grace of our Lord Jesus Christ be with you.*u*

21 Timothy, my co-worker, greets you; so do Lucius and Jason and So̅·sip'a·ter, my relatives.*q*

22 I Ter'ti·us, the writer of this letter, greet you in the Lord.*v*

23 Ga̅'i·us, who is host to me and to the whole church, greets you. E·ras'tus, the city treasurer, and our brother Quar'tus, greet you.*w*

Final Doxology

25 Now to God*x* who is able to strengthen you according to my gospel and the proclamation of Jesus Christ, according to the revelation of the mystery that was kept secret for long ages 26 but is now disclosed, and through the prophetic writings is made known to all the Gentiles, according to the command of the eternal God, to bring about the obedience of faith— 27 to the only wise God, through Jesus Christ, to whom*y* be the glory forever! Amen.*z*

---

o Gk *first fruits*   *p* Or *Junias;* other ancient authorities read *Julia*   *q* Or *compatriots*   *r* Or *compatriot*   *s* Gk *brothers*   *t* Gk *their own belly*   *u* Other ancient authorities lack this sentence   *v* Or *I Tertius, writing this letter in the Lord, greet you*   *w* Other ancient authorities add verse 24, *The grace of our Lord Jesus Christ be with all of you. Amen.*   *x* Gk *the one*   *y* Other ancient authorities lack *to whom.* The verse then reads, *to the only wise God be the glory through Jesus Christ forever. Amen.*   *z* Other ancient authorities lack 16.25-27 or include it after 14.23 or 15.33; others put verse 24 after verse 27

The First Letter to the Corinthians

Corinthians

Churches have problems. Sometimes, parishes harbor power struggles, scandals, troubled mariages, bitter disagreements, alcohol abuse, and even disorderly worship. Maybe you know Christian communities that have had some of these difficulties. The early church in Corinth had them all. In his first letter to the Corinthians, Paul gave them guidance and encouragement. This letter can teach churches in all times to more faithfully follow Christ.

In-depth

Corinth was an important seaport city in what is now southern Greece. It was a center of commerce for people from many cultures. It also had quite a reputation for sexual immorality. Paul established the Christian church there around A.D. 51 and spent about eighteen months with its converts. After Paul left, a man named Apollos came to help the young church grow.

Later, when Paul was in Ephesus, he got a letter (1 Cor 7.1) and visitors (1.11; 16.17) from Corinth. The church there was having problems. The problems were natural in a young Christian community whose members included both Jewish Christians and Gentile (non-Jewish) converts. The community was divided into groups with different leaders. There were some disagreements on how to worship properly. And there were different opinions about eating meat that had been sacrificed to pagan idols. In addition, some of the wealthy Christians were ignoring those who were poorer. And those with certain spiritual gifts were claiming to be more important than other people.

In response to all these divisions and various questions, Paul gives the Corinthians good, practical advice. At the same time, he reminds them of what is truly important for Christian believers: the Resurrection is central to faith; human wisdom is foolish when measured against God's wisdom; others' needs and concerns must always be put before their own; and love should be the primary focus in everything they do and say.

To this divided, confused community, Paul offers a picture of unity: we are all different parts of the same Body of Christ (12.12–26). Paul celebrates our diversity and insists on our unity. The advice and teaching he gives in this letter are good for Christians of any time or place to take to heart.

At a Glance

- **1.1–9.** a greeting and thanks

- **1.10—4.21.** a discussion of divisions in the church

- **Chapters 5–11.** advice and answers to some questions

- **Chapters 12–14.** an explanation of spiritual gifts and the primacy of love

- **Chapter 15.** Paul's teaching about the Resurrection

- **Chapter 16.** Paul's plans and final blessing

Quick Facts

Author
Paul

Date Written
A.D. 56

Audience
the mainly Gentile church at Corinth

1 Corinthians

Salutation

1 Paul, called to be an apostle of Christ Jesus by the will of God, and our brother Sos'the•nēs,

2 To the church of God that is in Corinth, to those who are sanctified in Christ Jesus, called to be saints, together with all those who in every place call on the name of our Lord Jesus Christ, both their Lord[a] and ours:

3 Grace to you and peace from God our Father and the Lord Jesus Christ.

4 I give thanks to my[b] God always for you because of the grace of God that has been given you in Christ Jesus, 5 for in every way you have been enriched in him, in speech and knowledge of every kind— 6 just as the testimony of[c] Christ has been strengthened among you— 7 so that you are not lacking in any spiritual gift as you wait for the revealing of our Lord Jesus Christ. 8 He will also strengthen you to the end, so that you may be blameless on the day of our Lord Jesus Christ. 9 God is faithful; by him you were called into the fellowship of his Son, Jesus Christ our Lord.

Divisions in the Church

10 Now I appeal to you, brothers and sisters,[d] by the name of our Lord Jesus Christ, that all of you be in agreement and that there be no divisions among you, but that you be united in the same mind and the same purpose. 11 For it has been reported to me by Chlō'ē's people that there are quar-

rels among you, my brothers and sisters.[e] 12 What I mean is that each of you says, "I belong to Paul," or "I belong to A•pol'los," or "I belong to Cē'phas," or "I belong to Christ." 13 Has Christ been divided? Was Paul crucified for you? Or were you baptized in the name of Paul? 14 I thank God[f] that I baptized none of you except Cris'pus and Gā'i•us, 15 so that no one can say that you were baptized in my name. 16 (I did baptize also the household of Steph'a•nas; beyond that, I do not know whether I baptized anyone else.) 17 For Christ did not send me to baptize but to proclaim the gospel, and not with eloquent wisdom, so that the cross of Christ might not be emptied of its power.

Christ the Power and Wisdom of God
(Cp Isa 29.14)

18 For the message about the cross is foolishness to those who are perishing, but to us who are being saved it is the power of God. 19 For it is written,

"I will destroy the wisdom of the wise,
    and the discernment of the discerning I will
        thwart."

20 Where is the one who is wise? Where is the scribe? Where is the debater of this age? Has not

---

a Gk *theirs*   *b* Other ancient authorities lack *my*   *c* Or *to*
d Gk *brothers*   *e* Gk *my brothers*   *f* Other ancient authorities read *I am thankful*

Divisions in the Church

The Christians in Corinth held a common belief in Jesus but spent useless energy arguing over which leaders to follow. Paul challenges them to get over this foolish division and focus on the important thing they share—the love of God and their salvation through the cross of Christ.

Today, Christians face similar challenges. Strong divisions in the past have created different Christian churches. Even within the Catholic church, divisions distract people from their central mission.

What causes division in your family, your school, and your church? How can you help people focus on the important things you hold in common?

▶ 1 Cor 1.10–17

God made foolish the wisdom of the world? 21 For since, in the wisdom of God, the world did not know God through wisdom, God decided, through the foolishness of our proclamation, to save those who believe. 22 For Jews demand signs and Greeks desire wisdom, 23 but we proclaim Christ crucified, a stumbling block to Jews and foolishness to Gentiles, 24 but to those who are the called, both Jews and Greeks, Christ the power of God and the wisdom of God. 25 For God's foolishness is wiser than human wisdom, and God's weakness is stronger than human strength.

26 Consider your own call, brothers and sisters:*g* not many of you were wise by human standards,*h* not many were powerful, not many were of noble birth. 27 But God chose what is foolish in the world to shame the wise; God chose what is weak in the world to shame the strong; 28 God chose what is low and despised in the world, things that are not, to reduce to nothing things that are, 29 so that no one*i* might boast in the presence of God. 30 He is the source of your life in Christ Jesus, who

---

g Gk brothers   *h* Gk according to the flesh   *i* Gk no flesh

God's Wisdom and Ours

What is the difference between a smart person and a wise person? Many smart people excel in a subject in school or a skill at work. But being smart in these ways does not make a person wise in the ways of God.

Paul reminds the Corinthians that the central Christian message—that Christ was crucified for our salvation—seems foolish to many wise people of their time. The Jews and Greeks of this period pride themselves on their wisdom. But the Jews hope for a kingly messiah who will make the nation strong. And the Greeks believe that their gods are strong. Both Jews and Greeks think the idea of a crucified messiah, or a god who can suffer and die, is foolish.

There is great mystery here: the foolishness of God is wiser than the greatest wisdom of the world. Our ways are not God's ways. Christ hanging on a cross turns upside down the world's ideas of success and failure, of victory and defeat, of power and weakness. Many people in Paul's time—and many people in our time—are not able to accept this "foolish" way of seeing the world as God sees it.

▶ 1 Cor 1.18–31

became for us wisdom from God, and righteousness and sanctification and redemption, 31 in order that, as it is written, "Let the one who boasts, boast in*j* the Lord."

Proclaiming Christ Crucified

2 When I came to you, brothers and sisters,*k* I did not come proclaiming the mystery*l* of God to you in lofty words or wisdom. 2 For I decided to know nothing among you except Jesus Christ, and him crucified. 3 And I came to you in weakness and in fear and in much trembling. 4 My speech and my proclamation were not with plausible words of wisdom,*m* but with a demonstration of the Spirit and of power, 5 so that your faith might rest not on human wisdom but on the power of God.

The True Wisdom of God

6 Yet among the mature we do speak wisdom, though it is not a wisdom of this age or of the rulers of this age, who are doomed to perish. 7 But we speak God's wisdom, secret and hidden, which God decreed before the ages for our glory. 8 None of the rulers of this age understood this; for if they had, they would not have crucified the Lord of glory. 9 But, as it is written,

"What no eye has seen,
      nor ear heard, nor the human heart conceived,
   what God has prepared for those who love him"—
10 these things God has revealed to us through the Spirit; for the Spirit searches everything, even the depths of God. 11 For what human being knows what is truly human except the human spirit that is within? So also no one comprehends what is truly God's except the Spirit of God. 12 Now we have received not the spirit of the world, but the Spirit that is from God, so that we may understand the gifts bestowed on us by God. 13 And we speak of these things in words not taught by human wisdom but taught by the Spirit, interpreting spiritual things to those who are spiritual.*n*

14 Those who are unspiritual*o* do not receive the gifts of God's Spirit, for they are foolishness to them, and they are unable to understand them because they are spiritually discerned. 15 Those who are spiritual discern all things, and they are themselves subject to no one else's scrutiny.
16 "For who has known the mind of the Lord
          so as to instruct him?"
But we have the mind of Christ.

On Divisions in the Corinthian Church

3 And so, brothers and sisters,*k* I could not speak to you as spiritual people, but rather as people of the flesh, as infants in Christ. 2 I fed you

---

j Or *of*   *k* Gk *brothers*   *l* Other ancient authorities read *testimony*   *m* Other ancient authorities read *the persuasiveness of wisdom*   *n* Or *interpreting spiritual things in spiritual language,* or *comparing spiritual things with spiritual*   *o* Or *natural*

WE ARE GOD'S SERVANTS, WHO SHARE A COMMON MISSION!

Sometimes, Christians engage in destructive competition or are motivated by personal pride. Paul says clearly that all Christians are God's servants, should work together, and should have a common purpose. Whatever we do for the Gospel is part of Jesus' mission and has the same value for God. Paul uses two images to tell us this: "So neither the one who plants nor the one who waters is anything, but only God who gives the growth" (3.7) and "Like a skilled master builder I laid a foundation, and someone else is building on it. . . . That foundation is Jesus Christ" (verses 10–11).

■ As a young person, how can you work cooperatively with other young people and with the adult community?

■ Express your gratitude for the building of the church done by previous generations of Christians. Pray that young Christians will embrace Jesus' mission with passion and with the global perspective needed at this time in history.

▶ 1 Cor 3.1–15

with milk, not solid food, for you were not ready for solid food. Even now you are still not ready, 3 for you are still of the flesh. For as long as there is jealousy and quarreling among you, are you not of the flesh, and behaving according to human inclinations? 4 For when one says, "I belong to Paul," and another, "I belong to A•pol'los," are you not merely human?

5 What then is A•pol'los? What is Paul? Servants through whom you came to believe, as the Lord assigned to each. 6 I planted, A•pol'los watered, but God gave the growth. 7 So neither the one who plants nor the one who waters is anything, but only God who gives the growth. 8 The one who plants and the one who waters have a common purpose, and each will receive wages according to the labor of each. 9 For we are God's servants, working together; you are God's field, God's building.

10 According to the grace of God given to me, like a skilled master builder I laid a foundation, and someone else is building on it. Each builder must choose with care how to build on it. 11 For no one can lay any foundation other than the one that has been laid; that foundation is Jesus Christ. 12 Now if anyone builds on the foundation with gold, silver, precious stones, wood, hay, straw— 13 the work of each builder will become visible, for the Day will disclose it, because it will be revealed with fire, and the fire will test what sort of work each has done. 14 If what has been built on the foundation survives, the builder will receive a reward. 15 If the work is burned up, the builder will suffer loss; the builder will be saved, but only as through fire.

16 Do you not know that you are God's temple and that God's Spirit dwells in you?p 17 If anyone destroys God's temple, God will destroy that person. For God's temple is holy, and you are that temple.

18 Do not deceive yourselves. If you think that you are wise in this age, you should become fools so that you may become wise. 19 For the wisdom of this world is foolishness with God. For it is written,
"He catches the wise in their craftiness,"
20 and again,
"The Lord knows the thoughts of the wise,
    that they are futile."
21 So let no one boast about human leaders. For all things are yours, 22 whether Paul or A•pol'los or Cĕ'phas or the world or life or death or the present or the future—all belong to you, 23 and you belong to Christ, and Christ belongs to God.

The Ministry of the Apostles

4 Think of us in this way, as servants of Christ and stewards of God's mysteries. 2 Moreover, it is required of stewards that they be found trustworthy. 3 But with me it is a very small thing that I should be judged by you or by any human court. I do not even judge myself. 4 I am not aware of anything against myself, but I am not thereby acquitted. It is the Lord who judges me. 5 Therefore do not pronounce judgment before the time, before the Lord comes, who will bring to light the things now hidden in darkness and will disclose the purposes of the heart. Then each one will receive commendation from God.

6 I have applied all this to A•pol'los and myself for your benefit, brothers and sisters,q so that you may learn through us the meaning of the saying,

---

p In verses 16 and 17 the Greek word for you is plural
q Gk brothers

PRAY IT?
From the Bottom Up

The most important part of a building is its foundation. If the foundation is built well and with care, what is placed on it will last. And so it is with people. We all have before us a wide variety of construction materials—values, beliefs, and principles—to use in building the foundation of our life. Initially, our foundation is built through our family, using the values taught in schools and churches. In our adolescent years, most of us discover that other materials are available and that we must choose which ones to add to our foundation.

In 1 Cor 3.10–17, Paul tells the people of Corinth that whatever they choose to use in building their foundation will show itself in the end. A poor foundation will lead to a poor end. He also reminds them that they are living temples of God, to be filled with the Holy Spirit.

In your prayer, reflect or journal on the following questions:
- On what foundation do you want to build your life?
- What kind of person do you want to be remembered as when you are gone?
- What qualities, values, and virtues do you want to have? How can these be a sign of the Holy Spirit living within you?

▶ 1 Cor 3.10–17

PRAY IT!

We Are God's Temple

We are God's temple.
We are rich, we are poor,
We are young, we are old,
We are male, we are female,
We are disabled, we are sick, we are healthy,
We are unborn,
We are all races and cultures.
O God,
Fill us with your spirit of unity.
Abolish the destructive forces of hate:
prejudice, racism, physical and verbal
abuse, abortion, murder, and euthanasia.
Break down the barriers that divide us.
Fill us with your loving spirit and an
appreciation for the value of each and
every life. Amen.

▸ I Cor 3.16–17

"Nothing beyond what is written," so that none of you will be puffed up in favor of one against another. 7 For who sees anything different in you?r What do you have that you did not receive? And if you received it, why do you boast as if it were not a gift?

8 Already you have all you want! Already you have become rich! Quite apart from us you have become kings! Indeed, I wish that you had become kings, so that we might be kings with you! 9 For I think that God has exhibited us apostles as last of all, as though sentenced to death, because we have become a spectacle to the world, to angels and to mortals. 10 We are fools for the sake of Christ, but you are wise in Christ. We are weak, but you are strong. You are held in honor, but we in disrepute. 11 To the present hour we are hungry and thirsty, we are poorly clothed and beaten and homeless, 12 and we grow weary from the work of our own hands. When reviled, we bless; when persecuted, we endure; 13 when slandered, we speak kindly. We have become like the rubbish of the world, the dregs of all things, to this very day.

Fatherly Admonition

14 I am not writing this to make you ashamed, but to admonish you as my beloved children. 15 For though you might have ten thousand guardians in Christ, you do not have many fathers. Indeed, in Christ Jesus I became your father through the gospel. 16 I appeal to you, then, be imitators of me.

17 For this reason I sents you Timothy, who is my beloved and faithful child in the Lord, to remind you of my ways in Christ Jesus, as I teach them everywhere in every church. 18 But some of you, thinking that I am not coming to you, have become arrogant. 19 But I will come to you soon, if the Lord wills, and I will find out not the talk of these arrogant people but their power. 20 For the kingdom of God depends not on talk but on power. 21 What would you prefer? Am I to come to you with a stick, or with love in a spirit of gentleness?

Sexual Immorality Defiles the Church

5 It is actually reported that there is sexual immorality among you, and of a kind that is not found even among pagans; for a man is living with his father's wife. 2 And you are arrogant! Should you not rather have mourned, so that he who has done this would have been removed from among you?

3 For though absent in body, I am present in spirit; and as if present I have already pronounced judgment 4 in the name of the Lord Jesus on the man who has done such a thing.t When you are assembled, and my spirit is present with the power of our Lord Jesus, 5 you are to hand this man over to Satan for the destruction of the flesh, so that his spirit may be saved in the day of the Lord.u

6 Your boasting is not a good thing. Do you not know that a little yeast leavens the whole batch of dough? 7 Clean out the old yeast so that you may be a new batch, as you really are unleavened. For our paschal lamb, Christ, has been sacrificed. 8 Therefore, let us celebrate the festival, not with the old yeast, the yeast of malice and evil, but with the unleavened bread of sincerity and truth.

Sexual Immorality Must Be Judged

9 I wrote to you in my letter not to associate with sexually immoral persons— 10 not at all meaning the immoral of this world, or the greedy and robbers, or idolaters, since you would then need to go out of the world. 11 But now I am writing to you not to associate with anyone who bears the name of brother or sisterv who is sexually immoral or greedy, or is an idolater, reviler, drunkard, or robber. Do not even eat with such a one. 12 For what have I to do with judging those outside? Is it not those who are inside that you are to judge? 13 God will judge those outside. "Drive out the wicked person from among you."

---

r Or *Who makes you different from another?*   s Or *am sending*   t Or *on the man who has done such a thing in the name of the Lord Jesus*   u Other ancient authorities add *Jesus*   v Gk *brother*

Lawsuits among Believers

6 When any of you has a grievance against another, do you dare to take it to court before the unrighteous, instead of taking it before the saints? 2 Do you not know that the saints will judge the world? And if the world is to be judged by you, are you incompetent to try trivial cases? 3 Do you not know that we are to judge angels—to say nothing of ordinary matters? 4 If you have ordinary cases, then, do you appoint as judges those who have no standing in the church? 5 I say this to your shame. Can it be that there is no one among you wise enough to decide between one believer*w* and another, 6 but a believer*w* goes to court against a believer*w*—and before unbelievers at that?

7 In fact, to have lawsuits at all with one another is already a defeat for you. Why not rather be wronged? Why not rather be defrauded? 8 But you yourselves wrong and defraud—and believers*x* at that.

9 Do you not know that wrongdoers will not inherit the kingdom of God? Do not be deceived! Fornicators, idolaters, adulterers, male prostitutes, sodomites, 10 thieves, the greedy, drunkards, revilers, robbers—none of these will inherit the kingdom of God. 11 And this is what some of you used to be. But you were washed, you were sanctified, you were justified in the name of the Lord Jesus Christ and in the Spirit of our God.

Glorify God in Body and Spirit

12 "All things are lawful for me," but not all things are beneficial. "All things are lawful for me," but I will not be dominated by anything. 13 "Food is meant for the stomach and the stomach for food,"*y* and God will destroy both one and the other. The body is meant not for fornication but for the Lord, and the Lord for the body. 14 And God raised the Lord and will also raise us by his power. 15 Do you not know that your bodies are members of Christ? Should I therefore take the members of Christ and make them members of a prostitute? Never! 16 Do you not know that whoever is united to a prostitute becomes one body with her? For it is said, "The two shall be one flesh." 17 But anyone united to the Lord becomes one spirit with him. 18 Shun fornication! Every sin that a person commits is outside the body; but the fornicator sins against the body itself. 19 Or do you not know that your body is a temple*z* of the Holy Spirit within you, which you have from God, and that you are not your own? 20 For you were bought with a price; therefore glorify God in your body.

Directions concerning Marriage

7 Now concerning the matters about which you wrote: "It is well for a man not to touch a woman." 2 But because of cases of sexual immorality, each man should have his own wife and each woman her own husband. 3 The husband should give to his wife her conjugal rights, and likewise the wife to her husband. 4 For the wife does not have authority over her own body, but the husband does; likewise the husband does not have authority over his own body, but the wife does. 5 Do not deprive one another except perhaps by agreement for a set time, to devote yourselves to prayer, and then come together again, so that Satan may not tempt

---

w Gk *brother*   *x* Gk *brothers*   *y* The quotation may extend to the word *other*   *z* Or *sanctuary*

Living Well

LIVE IT!

Some people think that God or the Christian religion is primarily interested in preventing us from doing fun things. They imagine the Bible as a book of thou-shalt-nots, and the church as a place where they are told to avoid enjoying themselves!

Paul helps us understand that God's desire is for us to live well. All good gifts from God, including food and sexuality, are meant to be enjoyed to the fullest. But they also can be misused, and if they are, we miss out on the joy and purpose intended by God.

For example, in 1 Cor 6.12–20, Paul affirms that sexual intercourse is meant to bond a man and a woman for life. Fornication—sexual intercourse between people who are not married—defeats its true purpose. Fornication diminishes the full joy and beauty of sexual intimacy as intended by God.

God created our sexuality. Our sexual desires—felt keenly during adolescence!—are not sinful but a normal part of being human. As the author of our sexuality, God wants us not to be hurt by this gift but instead to experience its fullness in marriage.

▶ 1 Cor 6.12–20

you because of your lack of self-control. 6 This I say by way of concession, not of command. 7 I wish that all were as I myself am. But each has a particular gift from God, one having one kind and another a different kind.

8 To the unmarried and the widows I say that it is well for them to remain unmarried as I am. 9 But if they are not practicing self-control, they should marry. For it is better to marry than to be aflame with passion.

10 To the married I give this command—not I but the Lord—that the wife should not separate from her husband 11 (but if she does separate, let her remain unmarried or else be reconciled to her husband), and that the husband should not divorce his wife.

12 To the rest I say—I and not the Lord—that if any believer[a] has a wife who is an unbeliever, and she consents to live with him, he should not divorce her. 13 And if any woman has a husband who is an unbeliever, and he consents to live with her, she should not divorce him. 14 For the unbelieving husband is made holy through his wife, and the unbelieving wife is made holy through her husband. Otherwise, your children would be unclean, but as it is, they are holy. 15 But if the unbelieving partner separates, let it be so; in such a case the brother or sister is not bound. It is to peace that God has called you.[b] 16 Wife, for all you know, you might save your husband. Husband, for all you know, you might save your wife.

The Life That the Lord Has Assigned

17 However that may be, let each of you lead the life that the Lord has assigned, to which God called you. This is my rule in all the churches. 18 Was anyone at the time of his call already circumcised? Let him not seek to remove the marks of circumcision. Was anyone at the time of his call uncircumcised? Let him not seek circumcision. 19 Circumcision is nothing, and uncircumcision is nothing; but obeying the commandments of God is everything. 20 Let each of you remain in the condition in which you were called.

21 Were you a slave when called? Do not be concerned about it. Even if you can gain your freedom, make use of your present condition now more than ever.[c] 22 For whoever was called in the Lord as a slave is a freed person belonging to the Lord, just as whoever was free when called is a slave of Christ. 23 You were bought with a price; do not become slaves of human masters. 24 In whatever condition you were called, brothers and sisters,[d] there remain with God.

The Unmarried and the Widows

25 Now concerning virgins, I have no command of the Lord, but I give my opinion as one

did you KNOW?

Strange Advice!?

First Corinthians, chapter 7, says people shouldn't marry, uncircumcised people shouldn't get circumcised, and slaves should remain slaves.

Why is Paul giving such strange advice? Because Paul thinks that Jesus will be returning soon to establish God's Reign for all time (verse 31). So he advises the Corinthians to remain in whatever condition they were called, in order to avoid the confusion that comes when making big life changes.

But Jesus didn't come back during Paul's time. In fact, we are still waiting for his return. When is Jesus going to come again? Don't try to figure it out. Jesus told us we will never know (Mt 24.36–44). But whatever our state of life is or will become, we would be wise to follow Paul's intent "to promote good order and unhindered devotion to the Lord" (1 Cor 7.35).

▶ **1 Corinthians, chapter 7**

who by the Lord's mercy is trustworthy. 26 I think that, in view of the impending[e] crisis, it is well for you to remain as you are. 27 Are you bound to a wife? Do not seek to be free. Are you free from a wife? Do not seek a wife. 28 But if you marry, you do not sin, and if a virgin marries, she does not sin. Yet those who marry will experience distress in this life,[f] and I would spare you that. 29 I mean, brothers and sisters,[d] the appointed time has grown short; from now on, let even those who have wives be as though they had none, 30 and those who mourn as though they were not mourning, and those who rejoice as though they were not rejoicing, and those who buy as though they had no possessions, 31 and those who deal with the world as though they had no dealings with it. For the present form of this world is passing away.

32 I want you to be free from anxieties. The unmarried man is anxious about the affairs of the Lord, how to please the Lord; 33 but the married man is

---

a Gk *brother*   b Other ancient authorities read *us*   c Or *avail yourself of the opportunity*   d Gk *brothers*   e Or *present*   f Gk *in the flesh* anxious about the affairs of the world, how to please his wife, 34 and his interests are divided. And the unmarried woman and the virgin are anxious about the affairs of the Lord, so that they may be holy in body and spirit; but the married woman is anxious about the affairs of the world, how to please her husband. 35 I say this for your own benefit, not to put any restraint upon you, but to promote good order and unhindered devotion to the Lord.

36 If anyone thinks that he is not behaving properly toward his fiancée,*g* if his passions are strong, and so it has to be, let him marry as he wishes; it is no sin. Let them marry. 37 But if someone stands firm in his resolve, being under no necessity but having his own desire under control, and has determined in his own mind to keep her as his fiancée,*g* he will do well. 38 So then, he who marries his fiancée*g* does well; and he who refrains from marriage will do better.

39 A wife is bound as long as her husband lives. But if the husband dies,*h* she is free to marry anyone she wishes, only in the Lord. 40 But in my judgment she is more blessed if she remains as she is. And I think that I too have the Spirit of God.

Food Offered to Idols

8 Now concerning food sacrificed to idols: we know that "all of us possess knowledge." Knowledge puffs up, but love builds up. 2 Anyone who claims to know something does not yet have the necessary knowledge; 3 but anyone who loves God is known by him.

4 Hence, as to the eating of food offered to idols, we know that "no idol in the world really exists," and that "there is no God but one." 5 Indeed, even though there may be so-called gods in heaven or on earth—as in fact there are many gods and many lords— 6 yet for us there is one God, the Father, from whom are all things and for whom we exist, and one Lord, Jesus Christ, through whom are all things and through whom we exist.

7 It is not everyone, however, who has this knowledge. Since some have become so accustomed to idols until now, they still think of the food they eat as food offered to an idol; and their conscience, being weak, is defiled. 8 "Food will not bring us close to God."*i* We are no worse off if we do not eat, and no better off if we do. 9 But take care that this liberty of yours does not somehow become a stumbling block to the weak. 10 For if others see you, who possess knowledge, eating in the temple of an idol, might they not, since their conscience is weak, be encouraged to the point of eating food sacrificed to idols? 11 So by your knowledge those weak believers for whom Christ died are destroyed.*j* 12 But when you thus sin against members of your family,*k* and wound their conscience when it is weak, you sin against Christ. 13 Therefore, if food is a cause of their falling,*l* I will never eat meat, so that I may not cause one of them*m* to fall.

---

g Gk *virgin*   *h* Gk *falls asleep*   *i* The quotation may extend to the end of the verse   *j* Gk *the weak brother . . . is destroyed*   *k* Gk *against the brothers*   *l* Gk *my brother's falling*   *m* Gk *cause my brother*

Restrain Your Ego!

LIVE IT!

Paul recognizes that it is not necessarily wrong for the community of Christians in Corinth to eat meat sacrificed to idols, or pagan gods, because they don't believe in those gods. Still, he recommends that they not do it, because some members of the community find it upsetting. For Paul, keeping unity is more important than always "being right."

Do you ever do things that aren't necessarily wrong just because it's your right? like whistle around a sibling who cannot stand it? or pick a sweater for the family picture that doesn't match anyone else's? or, when your younger brothers and sisters are around, watch a television show that's okay for you but not for them? When you find yourself doing something like this, think about Paul's advice. Are you making your ego more important than other people's feelings?

▶ 1 Cor 8.1–13

The Rights of an Apostle

9 Am I not free? Am I not an apostle? Have I not seen Jesus our Lord? Are you not my work in the Lord? 2 If I am not an apostle to others, at least I am to you; for you are the seal of my apostleship in the Lord.

3 This is my defense to those who would examine me. 4 Do we not have the right to our food and drink? 5 Do we not have the right to be accompanied by a believing wife,[n] as do the other apostles and the brothers of the Lord and Cē′phas? 6 Or is it only Bar′na·bas and I who have no right to refrain from working for a living? 7 Who at any time pays the expenses for doing military service? Who plants a vineyard and does not eat any of its fruit? Or who tends a flock and does not get any of its milk?

8 Do I say this on human authority? Does not the law also say the same? 9 For it is written in the law of Moses, "You shall not muzzle an ox while it is treading out the grain." Is it for oxen that God is concerned? 10 Or does he not speak entirely for our sake? It was indeed written for our sake, for whoever plows should plow in hope and whoever threshes should thresh in hope of a share in the crop. 11 If we have sown spiritual good among you, is it too much if we reap your material benefits? 12 If others share this rightful claim on you, do not we still more?

Nevertheless, we have not made use of this right, but we endure anything rather than put an obstacle in the way of the gospel of Christ. 13 Do you not know that those who are employed in the temple service get their food from the temple, and those who serve at the altar share in what is sacrificed on the altar? 14 In the same way, the Lord commanded that those who proclaim the gospel should get their living by the gospel.

15 But I have made no use of any of these rights, nor am I writing this so that they may be applied in my case. Indeed, I would rather die than that—no one will deprive me of my ground for boasting! 16 If I proclaim the gospel, this gives me no ground for boasting, for an obligation is laid on me, and woe to me if I do not proclaim the gospel! 17 For if I do this of my own will, I have a reward; but if not of my own will, I am entrusted with a commission. 18 What then is my reward? Just this: that in my proclamation I may make the gospel free of charge, so as not to make full use of my rights in the gospel.

19 For though I am free with respect to all, I have made myself a slave to all, so that I might win more of them. 20 To the Jews I became as a Jew, in order to win Jews. To those under the law I became as one under the law (though I myself am not under the law) so that I might win those under the law. 21 To those outside the law I became as one outside the law (though I am not free from God's law but am under Christ's law) so that I might win those outside the law. 22 To the weak I became weak, so that I might win the weak. I have become all things to all people, that I might by all means save some. 23 I do it all for the sake of the gospel, so that I may share in its blessings.

24 Do you not know that in a race the runners all compete, but only one receives the prize? Run in such a way that you may win it. 25 Athletes exercise self-control in all things; they do it to receive a perishable wreath, but we an imperishable one. 26 So I do not run aimlessly, nor do I box as though beating the air; 27 but I punish my body and enslave it, so that after proclaiming to others I myself should not be disqualified.

---

n Gk a sister as wife

Spiritual Perseverance

LIVE IT!

Persevering means setting priorities, sticking to them even when you get discouraged, and trying over and over to accomplish your goals. For the next six months, set yourself a goal that will help you grow closer to God. What will you have to do to accomplish it? What priorities must you establish? As 1 Cor 9.24–27 says, run your race by staying focused on your goal!

▶ 1 Cor 9.24–27

Warnings from Israel's History

10 I do not want you to be unaware, brothers and sisters,[o] that our ancestors were all under the cloud, and all passed through the sea, 2 and all were baptized into Moses in the cloud and in the sea, 3 and all ate the same spiritual food, 4 and all drank the same spiritual drink. For they drank from the spiritual rock that followed them, and the rock was Christ. 5 Nevertheless, God was not pleased with most of them, and they were struck down in the wilderness.

6 Now these things occurred as examples for us, so that we might not desire evil as they did. 7 Do not become idolaters as some of them did; as it is written, "The people sat down to eat and drink, and they rose up to play." 8 We must not indulge in sexual immorality as some of them did, and twenty-three thousand fell in a single day. 9 We must not put Christ[p] to the test, as some of them did, and were destroyed by serpents. 10 And do not complain as some of them did, and were destroyed by the destroyer. 11 These things happened to them to serve as an example, and they were written down to instruct us, on whom the ends of the ages have come. 12 So if you think you are standing, watch out that you do not fall. 13 No testing has overtaken you that is not common to everyone. God is faithful, and he will not let you be tested beyond your strength, but with the testing he will also provide the way out so that you may be able to endure it.

14 Therefore, my dear friends,[q] flee from the worship of idols. 15 I speak as to sensible people; judge for yourselves what I say. 16 The cup of blessing that we bless, is it not a sharing in the blood of Christ? The bread that we break, is it not a sharing in the body of Christ? 17 Because there is one bread, we who are many are one body, for we all partake of the one bread. 18 Consider the people of Israel;[r] are not those who eat the sacrifices partners in the altar? 19 What do I imply then? That food sacrificed to idols is anything, or that an idol is anything? 20 No, I imply that what pagans sacrifice, they sacrifice to demons and not to God. I do not want you to be partners with demons. 21 You cannot drink the cup of the Lord and the cup of demons. You cannot partake of the table of the Lord and the table of demons. 22 Or are we provoking the Lord to jealousy? Are we stronger than he?

Do All to the Glory of God
(Cp Ps 24.1)

23 "All things are lawful," but not all things are beneficial. "All things are lawful," but not all things build up. 24 Do not seek your own advantage, but that of the other. 25 Eat whatever is sold in the meat market without raising any question on the ground of conscience, 26 for "the earth and its fullness are the Lord's." 27 If an unbeliever invites you to a meal and you are disposed to go, eat whatever is set before you without raising any question on the ground of conscience. 28 But if someone says to you, "This has been offered in sacrifice," then do

---

o Gk *brothers*   *p* Other ancient authorities read *the Lord*
q Gk *my beloved*   *r* Gk *Israel according to the flesh*

Addictive Behavior

How do you spend the bulk of your free time? talking with your friends on the phone? playing video games? listening to your favorite music? If you discover that you have become obsessed with that activity, maybe it has become addictive. Perhaps your obsession might have more control over your life than it should have.

Paul reminds the Corinthians that they should put God at the center of their life. He points out that they will always be tempted to replace God with something else—which is called idolatry—like the ancient Israelites were tempted.

How about us today? We may not worship foreign gods or eat meat sacrificed to idols. But in many ways, our addictive behaviors are like idolatry. They consume our thoughts and time and can even lead us away from God.

Addictive behaviors are hard to break. And true addictions are very difficult to control. But you have the promise that God "will not let you be tested beyond your strength" (1 Cor 10.13). If you think you may have an addiction, talk to a parent or school counselor or minister.

▶ 1 Cor 10.6–14

1
C
O
R

I WANT YOU TO UNDERSTAND THAT CHRIST IS THE HEAD OF EVERY MAN, AND GOD IS THE HEAD OF CHRIST.

11.3

not eat it, out of consideration for the one who informed you, and for the sake of conscience— 29 I mean the other's conscience, not your own. For why should my liberty be subject to the judgment of someone else's conscience? 30 If I partake with thankfulness, why should I be denounced because of that for which I give thanks?

31 So, whether you eat or drink, or whatever you do, do everything for the glory of God. 32 Give no offense to Jews or to Greeks or to the church of God, 33 just as I try to please everyone in everything I do, not seeking my own advantage, but that of **11** many, so that they may be saved. 1 Be imitators of me, as I am of Christ.

Head Coverings

2 I commend you because you remember me in everything and maintain the traditions just as I handed them on to you. 3 But I want you to understand that Christ is the head of every man, and the husband[s] is the head of his wife,[t] and God is the head of Christ. 4 Any man who prays or prophesies with something on his head disgraces his head, 5 but any woman who prays or prophesies with her head unveiled disgraces her head—it is one and the same thing as having her head shaved. 6 For if a woman will not veil herself, then she should cut off her hair; but if it is disgraceful for a woman to have her hair cut off or to be shaved, she should wear a veil. 7 For a man ought not to have his head veiled, since he is the image and reflection[u] of God; but woman is the reflection[u] of man. 8 Indeed, man was

Whatever you do, do everything

for the glory of God

10.31

1 C O R

---

[s] The same Greek word means *man* or *husband*   [t] Or *head of the woman*   [u] Or *glory*

not made from woman, but woman from man. [9] Neither was man created for the sake of woman, but woman for the sake of man. [10] For this reason a woman ought to have a symbol of[v] authority on her head,[w] because of the angels. [11] Nevertheless, in the Lord woman is not independent of man or man independent of woman. [12] For just as woman came from man, so man comes through woman; but all things come from God. [13] Judge for yourselves: is it proper for a woman to pray to God with her head unveiled? [14] Does not nature itself teach you that if a man wears long hair, it is degrading to him, [15] but if a woman has long hair, it is her glory? For her hair is given to her for a covering. [16] But if anyone is disposed to be contentious—we have no such custom, nor do the churches of God.

Abuses at the Lord's Supper

[17] Now in the following instructions I do not commend you, because when you come together it is not for the better but for the worse. [18] For, to begin with, when you come together as a church, I hear that there are divisions among you; and to some extent I believe it. [19] Indeed, there have to be factions among you, for only so will it become clear who among you are genuine. [20] When you come to-

gether, it is not really to eat the Lord's supper. [21] For when the time comes to eat, each of you goes ahead with your own supper, and one goes hungry and another becomes drunk. [22] What! Do you not have homes to eat and drink in? Or do you show contempt for the church of God and humiliate those who have nothing? What should I say to you? Should I commend you? In this matter I do not commend you!

The Institution of the Lord's Supper
(Mt 26.26–29; Mk 14.22–25; Lk 22.14–23)

[23] For I received from the Lord what I also handed on to you, that the Lord Jesus on the night when he was betrayed took a loaf of bread, [24] and when he had given thanks, he broke it and said, "This is my body that is for[x] you. Do this in remembrance of me." [25] In the same way he took the cup also, after supper, saying, "This cup is the new covenant in my blood. Do this, as often as you drink it, in remembrance of me." [26] For as often as you eat this bread and drink the cup, you proclaim the Lord's death until he comes.

---

v Gk lacks *a symbol of*   *w* Or *have freedom of choice regarding her head*   *x* Other ancient authorities read *is broken for*

CALLED TO SHARE

In China and Singapore, when people meet up with friends, they ask whether the friends have eaten a meal yet. This custom dates back to the great famine of China in the 1950s, when there was so little food that people were starving and a friend's last meal might have been a day or two ago. So whatever food someone had was shared with their friends. Such generosity is truly a sign of God's love and justice.

Paul had to remind the Corinthians about God's love and justice when they gathered in their homes to talk about their faith, share a meal, and celebrate the Eucharist. In 1 Cor 11.17–22, Paul tells the Corinthians that when the wealthy humiliate the poor by not inviting them to share the meal, they are abusing the purpose of the Lord's Supper. To celebrate the Lord's Supper is to partake in the body and blood of Christ, and it is impossible to do this if they do not live out the values of Christ.

In your prayer, journal or reflect on the following questions:
- What might Paul say to your church community if he sat with you during Sunday Mass?
- How do you share with people who have little or nothing?
- What can you do in your community so that the celebration of the Lord's Supper is more truly a sign of generosity, justice, and love?

▶ 1 Cor 11.17–33

Partaking of the Supper Unworthily

27 Whoever, therefore, eats the bread or drinks the cup of the Lord in an unworthy manner will be answerable for the body and blood of the Lord. 28 Examine yourselves, and only then eat of the bread and drink of the cup. 29 For all who eat and drink[y] without discerning the body,[z] eat and drink judgment against themselves. 30 For this reason many of you are weak and ill, and some have died.[a] 31 But if we judged ourselves, we would not be judged. 32 But when we are judged by the Lord, we are disciplined[b] so that we may not be condemned along with the world.

33 So then, my brothers and sisters,[c] when you come together to eat, wait for one another. 34 If you are hungry, eat at home, so that when you come together, it will not be for your condemnation. About the other things I will give instructions when I come.

Spiritual Gifts

12 Now concerning spiritual gifts,[d] brothers and sisters,[c] I do not want you to be uninformed. 2 You know that when you were pagans, you were enticed and led astray to idols that could not speak. 3 Therefore I want you to understand that no one speaking by the Spirit of God ever says "Let Jesus be cursed!" and no one can say "Jesus is Lord" except by the Holy Spirit.

4 Now there are varieties of gifts, but the same Spirit; 5 and there are varieties of services, but the same Lord; 6 and there are varieties of activities, but it is the same God who activates all of them in everyone. 7 To each is given the manifestation of the Spirit for the common good. 8 To one is given through the Spirit the utterance of wisdom, and to another the utterance of knowledge according to the same Spirit, 9 to another faith by the same Spirit, to another gifts of healing by the one Spirit, 10 to another the working of miracles, to another prophecy, to another the discernment of spirits, to another various kinds of tongues, to another the interpretation of tongues. 11 All these are activated by one and the same Spirit, who allots to each one individually just as the Spirit chooses.

One Body with Many Members
(Cp Eph 4.1–16)

12 For just as the body is one and has many members, and all the members of the body, though many, are one body, so it is with Christ. 13 For in the one Spirit we were all baptized into one body— Jews or Greeks, slaves or free—and we were all made to drink of one Spirit.

14 Indeed, the body does not consist of one member but of many. 15 If the foot would say, "Because I am not a hand, I do not belong to the

Catholic Connections

THE CONSECRATION

First Corinthians 11.23–26 contains the earliest recorded words of the Christian celebration of the Last Supper. These words are at the heart of the celebration of the Catholic Mass, or Eucharist. They are known as the words of consecration and are said by the priest just before he holds up the bread and wine. Catholics believe that the bread and wine are changed (or transubstantiated) into the real body and blood of Jesus Christ.

▶ 1 Cor 11.23–26

body," that would not make it any less a part of the body. 16 And if the ear would say, "Because I am not an eye, I do not belong to the body," that would not make it any less a part of the body. 17 If the whole body were an eye, where would the hearing be? If the whole body were hearing, where would the sense of smell be? 18 But as it is, God arranged the members in the body, each one of them, as he chose. 19 If all were a single member, where would the body be? 20 As it is, there are many members, yet one body. 21 The eye cannot say to the hand, "I have no need of you," nor again the head to the feet, "I have no need of you." 22 On the contrary, the members of the body that seem to be weaker are indispensable, 23 and those members of the body that we think less honorable we clothe with greater honor, and our less respectable members are treated with greater respect; 24 whereas our more respectable members do not need this. But God has so arranged the body, giving the greater honor to the inferior member, 25 that there may be no dissension within the body, but the members may have the same care for one another. 26 If one member suffers, all suffer together with it; if one member is honored, all rejoice together with it.

1 COR

y Other ancient authorities add *in an unworthy manner,* z Other ancient authorities read *the Lord's body* a Gk *fallen asleep* b Or *When we are judged, we are being disciplined by the Lord* c Gk *brothers* d Or *spiritual persons*

THE BODY OF CHRIST

As Christians, we are called to work together within the Body of Christ. Read 1 Cor 12.12–31.
Here, Paul says that God has given us different gifts precisely so that we need one another.

Everyone can make a contribution to the world, regardless of status or possessions.

Paul proclaims that each part of the Body of Christ—not only each person, but each diverse
culture and race—is needed for the church to function properly. Many look at the most visible
people in the church and conclude that they are more important than others. Remember that
God sees differently. Often, important things are done by quiet people with little fanfare, but God
always notices.

Can you focus on the success of the whole, rather than on what you have or do not have?

*Dear God, free me from excessive worry about what someone else has or is able to do. Place my mind
on unity and community. Amen.*

▶ 1 Cor 12.12–31

27 Now you are the body of Christ and individually members of it. 28 And God has appointed in the church first apostles, second prophets, third teachers; then deeds of power, then gifts of healing, forms of assistance, forms of leadership, various kinds of tongues. 29 Are all apostles? Are all prophets? Are all teachers? Do all work miracles? 30 Do all possess gifts of healing? Do all speak in tongues? Do all interpret? 31 But strive for the greater gifts. And I will show you a still more excellent way.

The Gift of Love

13 If I speak in the tongues of mortals and of angels, but do not have love, I am a noisy gong or a clanging cymbal. 2 And if I have prophetic powers, and understand all mysteries and all knowledge, and if I have all faith, so as to remove mountains, but do not have love, I am nothing. 3 If I give away all my possessions, and if I hand over my body so that I may boast,*e* but do not have love, I gain nothing.

4 Love is patient; love is kind; love is not envious or boastful or arrogant 5 or rude. It does not insist on its own way; it is not irritable or resentful; 6 it does not rejoice in wrongdoing, but rejoices in

the truth. 7 It bears all things, believes all things, hopes all things, endures all things.

8 Love never ends. But as for prophecies, they will come to an end; as for tongues, they will cease; as for knowledge, it will come to an end. 9 For we know only in part, and we prophesy only in part; 10 but when the complete comes, the partial will come to an end. 11 When I was a child, I spoke like a child, I thought like a child, I reasoned like a child; when I became an adult, I put an end to childish ways. 12 For now we see in a mirror, dimly,*f* but then we will see face to face. Now I know only in part; then I will know fully, even as I have been fully known. 13 And now faith, hope, and love abide, these three; and the greatest of these is love.

Gifts of Prophecy and Tongues

14 Pursue love and strive for the spiritual gifts, and especially that you may prophesy. 2 For those who speak in a tongue do not speak to other people but to God; for nobody understands them, since they are speaking mysteries in the Spirit. 3 On the other hand, those who proph-

---

e Other ancient authorities read *body to be burned*
f Gk *in a riddle*

1
C
O
R

esy speak to other people for their upbuilding and encouragement and consolation. 4 Those who speak in a tongue build up themselves, but those who prophesy build up the church. 5 Now I would like all of you to speak in tongues, but even more to prophesy. One who prophesies is greater than one who speaks in tongues, unless someone interprets, so that the church may be built up.

6 Now, brothers and sisters,g if I come to you speaking in tongues, how will I benefit you unless I speak to you in some revelation or knowledge or prophecy or teaching? 7 It is the same way with lifeless instruments that produce sound, such as the flute or the harp. If they do not give distinct notes, how will anyone know what is being played? 8 And if the bugle gives an indistinct sound, who will get ready for battle? 9 So with yourselves; if in a tongue you utter speech that is not intelligible, how will anyone know what is being said? For you will be speaking into the air. 10 There are doubtless many different kinds of sounds in the world, and nothing is without sound. 11 If then I do not know the

---

g Gk brothers

did you KNOW?

God's Love

Greek, the language of the New Testament, has several words for love. There are words for parental love, romantic love, and love between friends or relatives. The rare Greek word Paul uses in First Corinthians, chapter 13—agape—is reserved for a special kind of love.

Agape (ah-GAH-pay) is love without conditions or motivations. It is there no matter who you are or what you do. It willingly chooses to serve without expectation of service in return. The Bible tells us that God is agape (1 Jn 4.16). The source of agape is the unconditional love of God. God's agape is revealed to us in Jesus Christ. Through our faith in Christ, we become a channel for communicating this wonderful love to others.

We are created in God's image. God wants us to love one another with the agape that Paul describes in chapter 13. It's a wonderful challenge!

▸ 1 Corinthians, chapter 13

PRAY IT?

Loving Others

Read 1 Cor 13.1–13. It is a beautiful description of how the love we receive from God translates into multiple and delicate details for the people we love.

The following statements can help you see how to express God's love to others. Think about that love as you complete the statements. Repeat each statement as many times as necessary to include all the people and situations it applies to in your life. You might want to record your responses on a sheet of paper or in your journal.

1. I show love to _____ by being patient when _____.
2. I need to show kindness to _____, especially when _____.
3. I should not envy _____, especially about _____.
4. I should not act arrogantly with _____ when _____.
5. I should not be rude with _____, especially when _____.
6. I must not force my way on _____, particularly in regard to _____.
7. When _____ does _____ to me, I should not become irritated or resentful.
8. When _____ does _____ to me, I should forgive and seek reconciliation.
9. When _____ suffers or experiences something bad, I should show empathy.
10. I should rejoice in the truth whenever _____.
11. I must bear the behaviors that bother me, especially _____.
12. I must believe when I am told _____.
13. I must hope that my relationship with _____ will be _____.
14. I would endure hard times with _____ even though _____.

Now, pray to God to give you enough love to share in the ways you have described.

▸ 1 Corinthians, chapter 13

meaning of a sound, I will be a foreigner to the speaker and the speaker a foreigner to me. 12 So with yourselves; since you are eager for spiritual gifts, strive to excel in them for building up the church.

13 Therefore, one who speaks in a tongue should pray for the power to interpret. 14 For if I pray in a tongue, my spirit prays but my mind is unproductive. 15 What should I do then? I will pray with the spirit, but I will pray with the mind also; I will sing praise with the spirit, but I will sing praise with the mind also. 16 Otherwise, if you say a blessing with the spirit, how can anyone in the position of an outsider say the "Amen" to your thanksgiving, since the outsider does not know what you are saying? 17 For you may give thanks well enough, but the other person is not built up. 18 I thank God that I speak in tongues more than all of you; 19 nevertheless, in church I would rather speak five words with my mind, in order to instruct others also, than ten thousand words in a tongue.

20 Brothers and sisters,*h* do not be children in your thinking; rather, be infants in evil, but in thinking be adults. 21 In the law it is written,

"By people of strange tongues
and by the lips of foreigners
I will speak to this people;
yet even then they will not listen to me,"

says the Lord. 22 Tongues, then, are a sign not for believers but for unbelievers, while prophecy is not for unbelievers but for believers. 23 If, therefore, the whole church comes together and all speak in tongues, and outsiders or unbelievers enter, will they not say that you are out of your mind? 24 But if all prophesy, an unbeliever or outsider who enters is reproved by all and called to account by all. 25 After the secrets of the unbeliever's heart are disclosed, that person will bow down before God and worship him, declaring, "God is really among you."

Orderly Worship

26 What should be done then, my friends?*h* When you come together, each one has a hymn, a lesson, a revelation, a tongue, or an interpretation. Let all things be done for building up. 27 If anyone speaks in a tongue, let there be only two or at most three, and each in turn; and let one interpret. 28 But if there is no one to interpret, let them be silent in church and speak to themselves and to God. 29 Let two or three prophets speak, and let the others weigh what is said. 30 If a revelation is made to someone else sitting nearby, let the first person be silent. 31 For you can all prophesy one by one, so that all may learn and all be encouraged. 32 And the spirits of prophets are subject to the prophets, 33 for God is a God not of disorder but of peace.

(As in all the churches of the saints, 34 women should be silent in the churches. For they are not permitted to speak, but should be subordinate, as the law also says. 35 If there is anything they desire to know, let them ask their husbands at home. For it is shameful for a woman to speak in church.*i* 36 Or did the word of God originate with you? Or are you the only ones it has reached?)

did you KNOW?
What's Going On?

In 1 Cor 14.34, Paul says women should be silent in church. Yet, in 11.5, he implies that women can pray and prophesy in church, and throughout his life, he supported and worked closely with many different women (see "Lydia and Priscilla," Acts 16.14–15; 18.1–26 and "Phoebe and Junia," Rom 16.1–16).

What explains Paul's turnaround? It appears that 1 Cor 14.34–36, which is set in parentheses, was added to Paul's original letter by a later writer. Perhaps someone copying Paul's letters needed to show that Christianity was not a movement that would disrupt the social order by allowing women to speak in public.

Like Paul, the Catholic church today values women's participation in worship. Women are cantors, musicians, lectors, and eucharistic ministers. But like the later editor of 1 Corinthians, chapter 14, the church insists on a certain order in worship. Only those who are ordained can read the Gospel during Mass and preach the homily.

▶ 1 Cor 14.34–36

37 Anyone who claims to be a prophet, or to have spiritual powers, must acknowledge that what I am writing to you is a command of the Lord. 38 Anyone who does not recognize this is not to be recognized. 39 So, my friends,*j* be eager to prophesy, and do not forbid speaking in tongues; 40 but all things should be done decently and in order.

The Resurrection of Christ
(Cp Mk 16.9–20)

15 Now I would remind you, brothers and sisters,*h* of the good news*k* that I proclaimed to you, which you in turn received, in

---

h Gk *brothers*   *i* Other ancient authorities put verses 34-35 after verse 40   *j* Gk *my brothers*   *k* Or *gospel* which also you stand, 2 through which also you are being saved, if you hold firmly to the message that I proclaimed to you—unless you have come to believe in vain.

3 For I handed on to you as of first importance what I in turn had received: that Christ died for our sins in accordance with the scriptures, 4 and that he was buried, and that he was raised on the third day in accordance with the scriptures, 5 and that he appeared to Cē′phas, then to the twelve. 6 Then he appeared to more than five hundred brothers and sisters[l] at one time, most of whom are still alive, though some have died.[m] 7 Then he appeared to James, then to all the apostles. 8 Last of all, as to one untimely born, he appeared also to me. 9 For I am the least of the apostles, unfit to be called an apostle, because I persecuted the church of God. 10 But by the grace of God I am what I am, and his grace toward me has not been in vain. On the contrary, I worked harder than any of them—though it was not I, but the grace of God that is with me. 11 Whether then it was I or they, so we proclaim and so you have come to believe.

The Resurrection of the Dead
(Cp 1 Thess 4.13–18)

12 Now if Christ is proclaimed as raised from the dead, how can some of you say there is no

---

l Gk brothers   m Gk fallen asleep

FOR I HANDED ON TO YOU AS OF FIRST IMPORTANCE WHAT I IN TURN HAD RECEIVED:

that Christ died for our sins
in accordance with the scriptures,

and that he was buried,

and that he was raised on the third day
in accordance with the scriptures,

and that he appeared to Cē′phas,
then to the twelve.

Then he appeared to more than five hundred
brothers and sisters at one time,
most of whom are still alive, though some have died.

Then he appeared to James,
then to all the apostles.

Last of all, as to one untimely born,
he appeared also to me.

resurrection of the dead? 13 If there is no resurrection of the dead, then Christ has not been raised; 14 and if Christ has not been raised, then our proclamation has been in vain and your faith has been in vain. 15 We are even found to be misrepresenting God, because we testified of God that he raised Christ—whom he did not raise if it is true that the dead are not raised. 16 For if the dead are not raised, then Christ has not been raised. 17 If Christ has not been raised, your faith is futile and you are still in your sins. 18 Then those also who have died[n] in Christ have perished. 19 If for this life only we have hoped in Christ, we are of all people most to be pitied.

20 But in fact Christ has been raised from the dead, the first fruits of those who have died.[n] 21 For since death came through a human being, the resurrection of the dead has also come through a human being; 22 for as all die in Adam, so all will be made alive in Christ. 23 But each in his own order: Christ the first fruits, then at his coming those who belong to Christ. 24 Then comes the end,[o] when he hands over the kingdom to God the Father, after he has destroyed every ruler and every authority and power. 25 For he must reign until he has put all his enemies under his feet. 26 The last enemy to be destroyed is death. 27 For "God[p] has put all things in subjection under his feet." But when it says, "All things are put in subjection," it is plain that this does not include the one who put all things in subjection under him. 28 When all things are subjected to him, then the Son himself will also be subjected to the one who put all things in subjection under him, so that God may be all in all.

29 Otherwise, what will those people do who receive baptism on behalf of the dead? If the dead are not raised at all, why are people baptized on their behalf?

30 And why are we putting ourselves in danger every hour? 31 I die every day! That is as certain, brothers and sisters,[q] as my boasting of you—a boast that I make in Christ Jesus our Lord. 32 If with merely human hopes I fought with wild animals at Eph′e•sus, what would I have gained by it? If the dead are not raised,

"Let us eat and drink,
    for tomorrow we die."

33 Do not be deceived:

"Bad company ruins good morals."

34 Come to a sober and right mind, and sin no more; for some people have no knowledge of God. I say this to your shame.

The Resurrection Body

35 But someone will ask, "How are the dead raised? With what kind of body do they come?" 36 Fool! What you sow does not come to life unless it dies. 37 And as for what you sow, you do not sow the body that is to be, but a bare seed, perhaps of wheat or of some other grain. 38 But God gives it a body as he has chosen, and to each kind of seed its own body. 39 Not all flesh is alike, but there is one flesh for human beings, another for animals, another for birds, and another for fish. 40 There are both heavenly bodies and earthly bodies, but the glory of the heavenly is one thing, and that of the earthly is another. 41 There is one glory of the sun, and another glory of the moon, and another glory of the stars; indeed, star differs from star in glory.

42 So it is with the resurrection of the dead. What is sown is perishable, what is raised is imperishable. 43 It is sown in dishonor, it is raised in glory. It is sown in weakness, it is raised in power. 44 It is sown a physical body, it is raised a spiritual body. If there is a physical body, there is also a spiritual body. 45 Thus it is written, "The first man, Adam, became a living being"; the last Adam became a life-giving spirit. 46 But it is not the spiritual that is first, but the physical, and then the spiritual. 47 The first man was from the earth, a man of dust; the second man is[r] from heaven. 48 As was the man of dust, so are those who are of the dust; and as is the man of heaven, so are those who are of heaven. 49 Just as we have borne the image of the man of dust, we will[s] also bear the image of the man of heaven.

50 What I am saying, brothers and sisters,[q] is this: flesh and blood cannot inherit the kingdom of God, nor does the perishable inherit the imperishable. 51 Listen, I will tell you a mystery! We will not all die,[t] but we will all be changed, 52 in a moment, in the twinkling of an eye, at the last trumpet. For the trumpet will sound, and the dead will be raised imperishable, and we will be changed. 53 For this perishable body must put on imperishability, and this mortal body must put on immortality. 54 When this perishable body puts on imperishability, and this mortal body puts on immortality, then the saying that is written will be fulfilled:

"Death has been swallowed up in victory."
55 "Where, O death, is your victory?
    Where, O death, is your sting?"

56 The sting of death is sin, and the power of sin is the law. 57 But thanks be to God, who gives us the victory through our Lord Jesus Christ.

58 Therefore, my beloved,[u] be steadfast, immovable, always excelling in the work of the Lord, because you know that in the Lord your labor is not in vain.

---

n Gk *fallen asleep*   o Or *Then come the rest*   p Gk *he*
q Gk *brothers*   r Other ancient authorities add *the Lord*
s Other ancient authorities read *let us*   t Gk *fall asleep*
u Gk *beloved brothers*

Life After Death

During childhood, reality and fantasy are often confused. We may imagine heaven as having pearly gates, golden streets, and angels flying with harps. As we grow older, some of us exchange this fantastic image for a more mature belief in the mystery of the Resurrection. But many adult Christians simply do not know what to believe about life after death.

Christians from Corinth also had problems with the concept of human resurrection. Common ideas influenced by Greek philosophy made it difficult for them to think of a body returning to life after death. For them, the body and soul were separate. The soul was immortal and continued living after the body died.

In contrast, the Hebrews saw a unity between the spiritual and material aspects of the human person. When the prophets, such as Daniel, envisaged a blessed life after death, they did not think in terms of a soul freed from the body but in terms of a body filled once more with life. (See "Resurrection," Dan 12.1–3.)

Believing in the Resurrection is essential in the Christian faith. The Gospel writers describe the risen Jesus as different from the Jesus who died on the cross; the disciples did not recognize him at first sight; they knew him only through their faith.

Paul gets right to the point: our faith depends on the fact that Christ was raised from death. He explains that in the resurrection our earthly body will be transformed—it will become a glorious, imperishable, and immortal body. We will not be disembodied spirits or souls when we have eternal life in communion with God. And we will be made alive in Christ, whether our mind can comprehend that idea or not. Our end is not death, but eternal life with Christ!

▸ 1 Cor 15.35–58

The Collection for the Saints

16 Now concerning the collection for the saints: you should follow the directions I gave to the churches of Galatia. 2 On the first day of every week, each of you is to put aside and save whatever extra you earn, so that collections need not be taken when I come. 3 And when I arrive, I will send any whom you approve with letters to take your gift to Jerusalem. 4 If it seems advisable that I should go also, they will accompany me.

Plans for Travel
(Cp Acts 19.21)

5 I will visit you after passing through Mac·e·dō′ni·a—for I intend to pass through Mac·e·dō′ni·a— 6 and perhaps I will stay with you or even spend the winter, so that you may send me on my way, wherever I go. 7 I do not want to see you now just in passing, for I hope to spend some time with you, if the Lord permits. 8 But I will stay in Eph′e·sus until Pentecost, 9 for a wide door for effective work has opened to me, and there are many adversaries.

10 If Timothy comes, see that he has nothing to fear among you, for he is doing the work of the Lord just as I am; 11 therefore let no one despise him. Send him on his way in peace, so that he may come to me; for I am expecting him with the brothers.

12 Now concerning our brother A·pol′los, I strongly urged him to visit you with the other brothers, but he was not at all willing*ᵛ* to come now. He will come when he has the opportunity.

Final Messages and Greetings

13 Keep alert, stand firm in your faith, be courageous, be strong. 14 Let all that you do be done in love.

15 Now, brothers and sisters,*ʷ* you know that members of the household of Steph′a·nas were the first converts in A·chā′i·a, and they have devoted themselves to the service of the saints; 16 I urge you to put yourselves at the service of such people, and of everyone who works and toils with them. 17 I rejoice at the coming of Steph′a·nas and For·tu·nā′tus and A·chā′i·cus, because they have made up for your absence; 18 for they refreshed my spirit as well as yours. So give recognition to such persons.

19 The churches of Asia send greetings. A·qui′la and Pris′ca, together with the church in their house,

---

v Or it was not at all God's will for him   *w Gk brothers* greet you warmly in the Lord. 20 All the brothers and sisters[x] send greetings. Greet one another with a holy kiss.

21 I, Paul, write this greeting with my own hand. 22 Let anyone be accursed who has no love for the Lord. Our Lord, come![y] 23 The grace of the Lord Jesus be with you. 24 My love be with all of you in Christ Jesus.[z]

---

[x] Gk *brothers*   [y] Gk *Marana tha.* These Aramaic words can also be read *Maran atha,* meaning *Our Lord has come*   [z] Other ancient authorities add *Amen*

Unfortunately, you probably know all too well what it's like to be criticized. It's no fun to be under attack. Our instinct is to get defensive and strike back. But in his Second Letter to the Corinthians, Paul shows us how God helps us rise above our instincts. Paul responds to personal attacks with directness and honesty. He demonstrates how to witness to Jesus—even when we are in the middle of conflict.

In-depth

The relationship between Paul and the Corinthians deteriorated after he wrote 1 Corinthians. Apparently, some other traveling missionaries came to Corinth and undermined Paul's credibility. They attacked him as a person (2 Cor 10.10), implied that he was mentally imbalanced (5.13), and criticized him as a speaker (10.10). They even suggested that Paul was not trustworthy about money (8.20–21).

As part of these attacks, some people claimed that Paul couldn't make up his mind about returning to visit Corinth; they said he kept changing between yes and no. In defending himself, Paul skillfully changes the focus and says that in Jesus, we always find a yes. For in Jesus, every one of God's promises is a yes (1.19–20). And whereas Paul's opponents make boastful claims for themselves, Paul realizes that God's grace is all he needs. In fact, he says, "I will boast . . . of my weaknesses, so that the power of Christ may dwell in me" (12.9).

With breathtaking insight, Paul puts all the conflict into perspective. "From now on, . . . we regard no one from a human point of view. . . . So if anyone is in Christ, there is a new creation" (5.16–17). Knowing Christ changes everything! Through Christ, we are reconciled with God—meaning, God overcomes the sin and weakness that separate us from God's love. We should also become ambassadors for Christ, reconciling with one another and announcing to all that they are reconciled with God.

Scholars see evidence that several original letters were combined to form 2 Corinthians. For example, Paul's concerns seem to be resolved in chapter 7, but then, chapters 10–13 pick up those concerns again. And chapters 8 and 9 each describe a collection being taken up for the Christians in Jerusalem without making any connection between the two collections. Despite its uneven flow, the letter reveals a very personal look into Paul's life and ministry.

At a Glance

- **1.1–11.** greetings
- **1.12—7.16.** a description of how Paul and the Corinthians resolve their conflict
- **Chapters 8–9.** a discussion of a collection for the church at Jerusalem
- **10.1—13.10.** a defense of Paul's ministry as an Apostle
- **13.11–13.** a final greeting and a blessing

Quick Facts

Author
Paul

Date Written
around A.D. 57

Audience
the mainly Gentile (non-Jewish) church in Corinth

Corinthians

The Second Letter to the

2 Corinthians

Salutation

1 Paul, an apostle of Christ Jesus by the will of God, and Timothy our brother,

To the church of God that is in Corinth, including all the saints throughout A•chā′i•a:

2 Grace to you and peace from God our Father and the Lord Jesus Christ.

Paul's Thanksgiving after Affliction

3 Blessed be the God and Father of our Lord Jesus Christ, the Father of mercies and the God of all consolation, 4 who consoles us in all our affliction, so that we may be able to console those who are in any affliction with the consolation with which we ourselves are consoled by God. 5 For just as the sufferings of Christ are abundant for us, so also our consolation is abundant through Christ. 6 If we are being afflicted, it is for your consolation and salvation; if we are being consoled, it is for your consolation, which you experience when you patiently endure the same sufferings that we are also suffering. 7 Our hope for you is unshaken; for we know that as you share in our sufferings, so also you share in our consolation.

8 We do not want you to be unaware, brothers and sisters,[a] of the affliction we experienced in Asia; for we were so utterly, unbearably crushed that we despaired of life itself. 9 Indeed, we felt that we had received the sentence of death so that we would rely not on ourselves but on God who raises the dead.

10 He who rescued us from so deadly a peril will continue to rescue us; on him we have set our hope that he will rescue us again, 11 as you also join in helping us by your prayers, so that many will give thanks on our[b] behalf for the blessing granted us through the prayers of many.

The Postponement of Paul's Visit

12 Indeed, this is our boast, the testimony of our conscience: we have behaved in the world with frankness[c] and godly sincerity, not by earthly wisdom but by the grace of God—and all the more toward you. 13 For we write you nothing other than what you can read and also understand; I hope you will understand until the end— 14 as you have already understood us in part—that on the day of the Lord Jesus we are your boast even as you are our boast.

15 Since I was sure of this, I wanted to come to you first, so that you might have a double favor;[d] 16 I wanted to visit you on my way to Mac•e•dō′ni•a, and to come back to you from Mac•e•dō′ni•a and have you send me on to Judea. 17 Was I vacillating when I wanted to do this? Do I make my plans according to ordinary human standards,[e] ready to say "Yes, yes" and "No, no" at the same time? 18 As

---

a Gk *brothers*   b Other ancient authorities read *your*
c Other ancient authorities read *holiness*   d Other ancient authorities read *pleasure*   e Gk *according to the flesh*

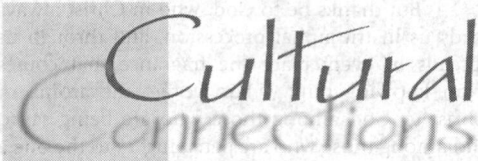

YES, YES, MAY WE NOT FAIL

Paul ensures the people of Corinth that he has not wavered in his commitment to them. In a similar manner, Saint Andrew Dung-Lac and the Vietnamese martyrs were unwavering in their commitment to the Gospels. These martyrs consisted of 117 people who died for their faith in nineteenth-century Vietnam. Saint Andrew was a priest in Vietnam, and many of the other 117 martyrs were Catholic laypeople. Pope John Paul II made them all saints of the church on 19 June, 1988.

Vietnam is a country that has been rocked by many bloody wars, run by ruthless dictators, and overrun by rampant violence through many of the years of its history as a country. Despite such extreme social conditions, and in the midst of such horrible violence, these martyrs and many like them had the courage to preach the Gospel and live as disciples of Christ.

Take a few moments to reflect on the life of these martyrs.

▶ 2 Cor 1.15–22

surely as God is faithful, our word to you has not been "Yes and No." 19 For the Son of God, Jesus Christ, whom we proclaimed among you, Sil•vā′-nus and Timothy and I, was not "Yes and No"; but in him it is always "Yes." 20 For in him every one of God's promises is a "Yes." For this reason it is through him that we say the "Amen," to the glory of God. 21 But it is God who establishes us with you in Christ and has anointed us, 22 by putting his seal on us and giving us his Spirit in our hearts as a first installment.

23 But I call on God as witness against me: it was to spare you that I did not come again to Corinth. 24 I do not mean to imply that we lord it over

The Presence of God

The prisoners of war are cold, and it takes every bit of their energy to stay warm. The conversation this night centers on the discouragement the men feel and their frustration about being abandoned and being left alone. Captain Valdez listens to the conversation for a long time, and then he interrupts: "We are not alone, and we have not been abandoned. God has been with us every minute through this ordeal. I pray every morning and every night in thanksgiving for that presence. It is on the worst days that I most strongly feel the presence of God."

When we are suffering, we often feel alone and abandoned—sometimes even by God. But Paul indicates that God is present, consoling us in our affliction. It is sometimes difficult to feel this presence because we are caught up in the pain and hurt of the situation, as are the prisoners of war in this story. How do you experience God's presence or absence during times of pain and suffering?

Paul also says that the support of the Christian community can help us get through our pain. The comfort of friends and relatives during difficult times can help us recognize the action of God. Is there someone you can comfort who is going through a hard time?

▶ 2 Cor 1.3–11

your faith; rather, we are workers with you for your joy, because you stand firm in the faith. 1 So I made up my mind not to make you another painful visit. 2 For if I cause you pain, who is there to make me glad but the one whom I have pained? 3 And I wrote as I did, so that when I came, I might not suffer pain from those who should have made me rejoice; for I am confident about all of you, that my joy would be the joy of all of you. 4 For I wrote you out of much distress and anguish of heart and with many tears, not to cause you pain, but to let you know the abundant love that I have for you.

Forgiveness for the Offender

5 But if anyone has caused pain, he has caused it not to me, but to some extent—not to exaggerate it—to all of you. 6 This punishment by the majority is enough for such a person; 7 so now instead you should forgive and console him, so that he may not be overwhelmed by excessive sorrow. 8 So I urge you to reaffirm your love for him. 9 I wrote for this reason: to test you and to know whether you are obedient in everything. 10 Anyone whom you forgive, I also forgive. What I have forgiven, if I have forgiven anything, has been for your sake in the presence of Christ. 11 And we do this so that we may not be outwitted by Satan; for we are not ignorant of his designs.

Paul's Anxiety in Troas

12 When I came to Trō′as to proclaim the good news of Christ, a door was opened for me in the Lord; 13 but my mind could not rest because I did not find my brother Titus there. So I said farewell to them and went on to Mac·e·dō′ni·a.

14 But thanks be to God, who in Christ always leads us in triumphal procession, and through us spreads in every place the fragrance that comes from knowing him. 15 For we are the aroma of Christ to God among those who are being saved and among those who are perishing; 16 to the one a fragrance from death to death, to the other a fragrance from life to life. Who is sufficient for these things? 17 For we are not peddlers of God's word like so many;f but in Christ we speak as persons of sincerity, as persons sent from God and standing in his presence.

Ministers of the New Covenant
(Cp Jer 31.31–34)

3 Are we beginning to commend ourselves again? Surely we do not need, as some do, letters of recommendation to you or from you, do we? 2 You yourselves are our letter, written on oursg hearts, to be known and read by all; 3 and you show that you are a letter of Christ, prepared by us, written not with ink but with the Spirit of the living God, not on tablets of stone but on tablets of human hearts.

4 Such is the confidence that we have through Christ toward God. 5 Not that we are competent of ourselves to claim anything as coming from us; our competence is from God, 6 who has made us competent to be ministers of a new covenant, not of letter but of spirit; for the letter kills, but the Spirit gives life.

7 Now if the ministry of death, chiseled in let-

---

f Other ancient authorities read *like the others*   g Other ancient authorities read *your*

Ministers of the New Covenant

LIVE IT!

Sometimes we get caught up in the notion that faith is all about following the rules. We want so badly to win the "great prize" that we structure our life as a list of do's and don'ts.

Paul recalls God's words from Jer 31.33: "I will put my law within them, and I will write it on their hearts" to emphasize that Christ enables us to be ministers of this new covenant—not of the old written law but of the law of the New Covenant, "for the letter [of the law] kills, but the Spirit gives life" (2 Cor 3.6). Because Paul's ministry comes from the Spirit, the Spirit is the only letter of recommendation he needs.

The same is true for us. With the law of the New Covenant written on our heart, we give witness to it in our lifestyle. In promoting reconciliation, fostering peace and hope, and passing Christ on to others, we are a living letter of recommendation for the Gospel, to be known and read by all people.

Think of the great honor of having been called by God to be a minister of the New Covenant. How are you doing your job? How can you do it better?

▶ 2 Cor 3.1–11

Christz in Us

LIVE IT!

It is sometimes tempting to take ourselves a bit too seriously, to feel too self-important. When given a particular responsibility at school, home, or church, we may begin to act as though we are what is important, rather than the task.

The same is true when we accept our calling as a disciple of Christ. Feelings of self-righteousness or pride can creep in, leading to what friends might call a holier-than-thou attitude. Paul reminds us that "we do not proclaim ourselves; we proclaim Jesus Christ as Lord" (2 Cor 4.5). We are simply ordinary clay jars that hold a great treasure to be shared with all. What a wonderful and awesome responsibility we have been given: to share, with our life and our words, what Jesus has done in us, giving him the glory and not seeking it for ourselves.

▶ 2 Cor 4.5–10

---

ters on stone tablets,^{h} came in glory so that the people of Israel could not gaze at Moses' face because of the glory of his face, a glory now set aside, 8 how much more will the ministry of the Spirit come in glory? 9 For if there was glory in the ministry of condemnation, much more does the ministry of justification abound in glory! 10 Indeed, what once had glory has lost its glory because of the greater glory; 11 for if what was set aside came through glory, much more has the permanent come in glory!

12 Since, then, we have such a hope, we act with great boldness, 13 not like Moses, who put a veil over his face to keep the people of Israel from gazing at the end of the glory that^i was being set aside. 14 But their minds were hardened. Indeed, to this very day, when they hear the reading of the old covenant, that same veil is still there, since only in Christ is it set aside. 15 Indeed, to this very day whenever Moses is read, a veil lies over their minds; 16 but when one turns to the Lord, the veil is removed. 17 Now the Lord is the Spirit, and where the Spirit of the Lord is, there is freedom. 18 And all of us, with unveiled faces, seeing the glory of the Lord as though reflected in a mirror, are being transformed into the same image from one degree of glory to another; for this comes from the Lord, the Spirit.

Treasure in Clay Jars

4 Therefore, since it is by God's mercy that we are engaged in this ministry, we do not lose heart. 2 We have renounced the shameful things that one hides; we refuse to practice cunning or to falsify God's word; but by the open statement of the truth we commend ourselves to the conscience of everyone in the sight of God. 3 And even if our gospel is veiled, it is veiled to those who are perishing. 4 In their case the god of this world has blinded the minds of the unbelievers, to keep them from seeing the light of the gospel of the glory of Christ, who is

the image of God. 5 For we do not proclaim ourselves; we proclaim Jesus Christ as Lord and ourselves as your slaves for Jesus' sake. 6 For it is the God who said, "Let light shine out of darkness," who has shone in our hearts to give the light of the knowledge of the glory of God in the face of Jesus Christ.

7 But we have this treasure in clay jars, so that it may be made clear that this extraordinary power belongs to God and does not come from us. 8 We are afflicted in every way, but not crushed; perplexed, but not driven to despair; 9 persecuted, but not forsaken; struck down, but not destroyed; 10 always carrying in the body the death of Jesus, so that the life of Jesus may also be made visible in our bodies. 11 For while we live, we are always being given up to death for Jesus' sake, so that the life of Jesus may be made visible in our mortal flesh. 12 So death is at work in us, but life in you.

13 But just as we have the same spirit of faith that is in accordance with scripture—"I believed, and so I spoke"—we also believe, and so we speak, 14 because we know that the one who raised the Lord Jesus will raise us also with Jesus, and will bring us with you into his presence. 15 Yes, everything is for your sake, so that grace, as it extends to more and more people, may increase thanksgiving, to the glory of God.

Living by Faith

16 So we do not lose heart. Even though our outer nature is wasting away, our inner nature is being renewed day by day. 17 For this slight momentary affliction is preparing us for an eternal weight of glory beyond all measure, 18 because we look not at what can be seen but at what cannot be seen; for what can be seen is temporary, but what cannot be seen is eternal.

---

^{h} Gk on stones ^{i} Gk of what

PRAY IT!
Hopeless and Hurting

Sometimes life can be filled with despair and discouragement. We can get down in the dumps and feel like everything is a waste of our time and energy. Paul encourages us not to lose hope but to keep our hearts and minds very much alive. Paul connects our moments of despair to Jesus' suffering on the cross. Jesus never lost hope. He believed to the end and then was raised from the dead to new life to show the world that his suffering and death had a hopeful outcome. God promises us this same hopeful outcome of being raised up.

Try this exercise: Re-read 2 Cor 4.7–18 in a prayerful way, perhaps with some reflective music in the background. Then write a few thoughts of your own in a journal, or write your own prayer about suffering and despair. Don't forget to mention hope at the end of your prayer, because, ultimately, that was Jesus' message.

▶ 2 Cor 4.7–18

5 For we know that if the earthly tent we live in is destroyed, we have a building from God, a house not made with hands, eternal in the heavens. 2 For in this tent we groan, longing to be clothed with our heavenly dwelling— 3 if indeed, when we have taken it off ʲ we will not be found naked. 4 For while we are still in this tent, we groan under our burden, because we wish not to be unclothed but to be further clothed, so that what is mortal may be swallowed up by life. 5 He who has prepared us for this very thing is God, who has given us the Spirit as a guarantee.

6 So we are always confident; even though we know that while we are at home in the body we are away from the Lord— 7 for we walk by faith, not by sight. 8 Yes, we do have confidence, and we would rather be away from the body and at home with the Lord. 9 So whether we are at home or away, we make it our aim to please him. 10 For all of us must appear before the judgment seat of Christ, so that each may receive recompense for what has been done in the body, whether good or evil.

The Ministry of Reconciliation

11 Therefore, knowing the fear of the Lord, we try to persuade others; but we ourselves are well known to God, and I hope that we are also well known to your consciences. 12 We are not commending ourselves to you again, but giving you an opportunity to boast about us, so that you may be able to answer those who boast in outward appearance and not in the heart. 13 For if we are beside ourselves, it is for God; if we are in our right mind, it is for you. 14 For the love of Christ urges us on, because we are convinced that one has died for all; therefore all have died. 15 And he died for all, so

---

ʲ Other ancient authorities read *put it on*

PRAY IT!
It's What's Inside That Counts

Television, magazines, and advertising show images of the ideal person. Very few people fit that image. Many of those who don't fit that image feel insecure and inadequate. Some people try desperately to measure up to that standard.

In 2 Cor 5.1–5, Paul reminds us that our earthly body is a temporary dwelling. It is important for us to take care of this earthly "tent" with a healthy diet and regular exercise. But our desire for our heavenly dwelling should cause us to focus on our inner appearance more than our outer appearance.

In your prayer, reflect on the following questions:
■ Are you satisfied with your physical appearance? Why or why not?
■ Do you spend as much time working on your inner appearance—by developing virtues like compassion, generosity, mercy, and patience—as you do on your outer appearance?

Write a prayer asking God for the grace (gift) to feel secure in your outward appearance. Listen for God's response.

▶ 2 Cor 5.1–5

So if anyone is in Christ there is a new creation

5.17

knew no sin, so that in him we might become the righteousness of God.

6 As we work together with him,[m] we urge you also not to accept the grace of God in vain. 2 For he says,

> "At an acceptable time I have listened to you,
> and on a day of salvation I have helped you."

See, now is the acceptable time; see, now is the day of salvation! 3 We are putting no obstacle in anyone's way, so that no fault may be found with our ministry, 4 but as servants of God we have commended ourselves in every way: through great endurance, in afflictions, hardships, calamities, 5 beatings, imprisonments, riots, labors, sleepless nights, hunger; 6 by purity, knowledge, patience, kindness, holiness of spirit, genuine love, 7 truthful speech, and the power of God; with the weapons of righteousness for the right hand and for the left; 8 in honor and dishonor, in ill repute and good repute. We are treated as impostors, and yet are true; 9 as unknown, and yet are well known; as dying, and see—we are alive; as punished, and yet not killed; 10 as sorrowful, yet always rejoicing; as poor, yet making many rich; as having nothing, and yet possessing everything.

11 We have spoken frankly to you Corinthians; our heart is wide open to you. 12 There is no restriction in our affections, but only in yours. 13 In return—I speak as to children—open wide your hearts also.

that those who live might live no longer for themselves, but for him who died and was raised for them.

16 From now on, therefore, we regard no one from a human point of view;[k] even though we once knew Christ from a human point of view,[k] we know him no longer in that way. 17 So if anyone is in Christ, there is a new creation: everything old has passed away; see, everything has become new! 18 All this is from God, who reconciled us to himself through Christ, and has given us the ministry of reconciliation; 19 that is, in Christ God was reconciling the world to himself,[l] not counting their trespasses against them, and entrusting the message of reconciliation to us. 20 So we are ambassadors for Christ, since God is making his appeal through us; we entreat you on behalf of Christ, be reconciled to God. 21 For our sake he made him to be sin who

---

[k] Gk *according to the flesh*   [l] Or *God was in Christ reconciling the world to himself*   [m] Gk *As we work together*

Ambassadors for Christ

The title ambassador is usually used by people who are authorized to represent their country while living as a resident in a foreign nation.

Paul tells us that we are reconciled—that is, united—with God through Christ, and that God has now entrusted us with the ministry of helping others to be reconciled through Christ. Imagine that; we are called ambassadors for Christ! Of all the ways God could be made known in the world, God chooses to use us. We are "authorized representatives." We are God's messengers.

That might sound a bit intimidating! We might naturally wonder how we, broken and imperfect people, are supposed to represent God, who is completely holy and just. The reality is that God wants to use us, flaws and all. God does not need perfect people—just willing people! Spend some time in prayer, and share with God your thoughts, feelings, and fears about being invited to take on this great role of ambassador for Christ.

▶ 2 Cor 5.17–21

2 COR

"I will live in them and walk among them, and I will be their God, and they shall be my people.
I will welcome you, and I will be your father, and you shall be my sons and daughters
says the Lord Almighty."

The Temple of the Living God

14 Do not be mismatched with unbelievers. For what partnership is there between righteousness and lawlessness? Or what fellowship is there between light and darkness? 15 What agreement does Christ have with Bē′li•ar? Or what does a believer share with an unbeliever? 16 What agreement has the temple of God with idols? For we[n] are the temple of the living God; as God said,

"I will live in them and walk among them,
    and I will be their God,
    and they shall be my people.
17 Therefore come out from them,
    and be separate from them, says the Lord,
    and touch nothing unclean;
        then I will welcome you,
18 and I will be your father,
    and you shall be my sons and daughters,
says the Lord Almighty."

7 Since we have these promises, beloved, let us cleanse ourselves from every defilement of body and of spirit, making holiness perfect in the fear of God.

Paul's Joy at the Church's Repentance

2 Make room in your hearts[o] for us; we have wronged no one, we have corrupted no one, we have taken advantage of no one. 3 I do not say this to condemn you, for I said before that you are in our hearts, to die together and to live together. 4 I often boast about you; I have great pride in you; I am filled with consolation; I am overjoyed in all our affliction.

5 For even when we came into Mac•e•dō′ni•a, our bodies had no rest, but we were afflicted in every way—disputes without and fears within. 6 But God, who consoles the downcast, consoled us by the arrival of Titus, 7 and not only by his coming, but also by the consolation with which he was consoled about you, as he told us of your longing, your mourning, your zeal for me, so that I rejoiced still more. 8 For even if I made you sorry with my letter, I do not regret it (though I did regret it, for I see that I grieved you with that letter, though only briefly). 9 Now I rejoice, not because you were grieved, but because your grief led to repentance; for you felt a godly grief, so that you were not harmed in any way by us. 10 For godly grief produces a repentance that leads to salvation and brings no regret, but worldly grief produces death. 11 For see what earnestness this godly grief has produced in you, what eagerness to clear yourselves, what indignation, what alarm, what longing, what zeal, what punishment! At every point you have proved yourselves guiltless in the matter. 12 So although I wrote to you, it was not on account of the one who did the wrong, nor

---

n Other ancient authorities read *you* o Gk lacks *in your hearts* on account of the one who was wronged, but in order that your zeal for us might be made known to you before God. 13 In this we find comfort.

In addition to our own consolation, we rejoiced still more at the joy of Titus, because his mind has been set at rest by all of you. 14 For if I have been somewhat boastful about you to him, I was not disgraced; but just as everything we said to you was true, so our boasting to Titus has proved true as well. 15 And his heart goes out all the more to you, as he remembers the obedience of all of you, and how you welcomed him with fear and trembling. 16 I rejoice, because I have complete confidence in you.

Encouragement to Be Generous

8 We want you to know, brothers and sisters,p about the grace of God that has been granted to the churches of Mac·e·dō'ni·a; 2 for during a severe ordeal of affliction, their abundant joy and their extreme poverty have overflowed in a wealth of generosity on their part. 3 For, as I can testify, they voluntarily gave according to their means, and even beyond their means, 4 begging us earnestly for the privilegeq of sharing in this ministry to the saints— 5 and this, not merely as we expected; they gave themselves first to the Lord and, by the will of God, to us, 6 so that we might urge Titus that, as he had already made a beginning, so he should also complete this generous undertakingr among you. 7 Now as you excel in everything—in faith, in speech, in knowledge, in utmost eagerness, and in our love for yous—so we want you to excel also in this generous undertaking.r

8 I do not say this as a command, but I am testing the genuineness of your love against the earnestness of others. 9 For you know the generous actt of our Lord Jesus Christ, that though he was rich, yet for your sakes he became poor, so that by his poverty you might become rich. 10 And in this matter I am giving my advice: it is appropriate for you who began last year not only to do something but even to desire to do something— 11 now finish doing it, so that your eagerness may be matched by completing it according to your means. 12 For if the eagerness is there, the gift is acceptable according to what one has—not according to what one does not have. 13 I do not mean that there should be relief for others and pressure on you, but it is a question of a fair balance between 14 your present abundance and their need, so that their abundance may be for your need, in order that there may be a fair balance. 15 As it is written,

"The one who had much did not have too
> much,
and the one who had little did not have too
> little."

Commendation of Titus

16 But thanks be to God who put in the heart of Titus the same eagerness for you that I myself have. 17 For he not only accepted our appeal, but since he is more eager than ever, he is going to you of his own accord. 18 With him we are sending the brother who is famous among all the churches for his proclaiming the good news;u 19 and not only that, but he has also been appointed by the churches to travel with us while we are administering this

---

p Gk brothers   q Gk grace   r Gk this grace   s Other ancient authorities read your love for us   t Gk the grace   u Or the gospel.

Shine Like a Star   LIVE IT!

Second Corinthians 6.14 makes a sudden transition; 6.14—7.1 may even be a fragment from another letter. We are not sure what kind of behavior or problem Paul is talking about here. But it does seem clear that Paul is cautioning the Corinthians against being too closely influenced by non-Christians—unbelievers. Paul doesn't want the Corinthians to return to sinful behaviors.

We are often surrounded by many unhealthy and unholy choices. Our words and behaviors should show that "we are the temple of the living God" (6.16). We must be careful of friendships and media influences that might tempt us to start thinking that wrong is right. This doesn't mean we should be arrogant and separate ourselves from others. Remember that Jesus sometimes hung around with sinners. But he didn't share in their sins. He was a light for them.

As Paul says in Phil 2.15, we are "children of God" in a "perverse generation," where we shine "like stars in the world."

▶ 2 Cor 6.14–18

The one who sows sparingly
will also reap sparingly,
and the one who sows bountifully
will also reap bountifully.

Each of you must give
as you have made up your mind,
not reluctantly or under compulsion,
for God loves a cheerful giver.

9.6–7

generous undertaking[v] for the glory of the Lord himself[w] and to show our goodwill. 20 We intend that no one should blame us about this generous gift that we are administering, 21 for we intend to do what is right not only in the Lord's sight but also in the sight of others. 22 And with them we are sending our brother whom we have often tested and found eager in many matters, but who is now more eager than ever because of his great confidence in you. 23 As for Titus, he is my partner and co-worker in your service; as for our brothers, they are messengers[x] of the churches, the glory of Christ. 24 Therefore openly before the churches, show them the proof of your love and of our reason for boasting about you.

The Collection for Christians at Jerusalem

9 Now it is not necessary for me to write you about the ministry to the saints, 2 for I know your eagerness, which is the subject of my boasting about you to the people of Mac·e·dō′ni·a, saying that A·chā′i·a has been ready since last year; and your zeal has stirred up most of them. 3 But I am sending the brothers in order that our boasting about you may not prove to have been empty in this case, so that you may be ready, as I said you would be; 4 otherwise, if some Mac·e·dō′ni·ans come with me and find that you are not ready, we

would be humiliated—to say nothing of you—in this undertaking.[y] 5 So I thought it necessary to urge the brothers to go on ahead to you, and arrange in advance for this bountiful gift that you have promised, so that it may be ready as a voluntary gift and not as an extortion.

6 The point is this: the one who sows sparingly will also reap sparingly, and the one who sows bountifully will also reap bountifully. 7 Each of you must give as you have made up your mind, not reluctantly or under compulsion, for God loves a cheerful giver. 8 And God is able to provide you with every blessing in abundance, so that by always having enough of everything, you may share abundantly in every good work. 9 As it is written,

"He scatters abroad, he gives to the poor;
    his righteousness[z] endures forever."

10 He who supplies seed to the sower and bread for food will supply and multiply your seed for sowing and increase the harvest of your righteousness.[z] 11 You will be enriched in every way for your great generosity, which will produce thanksgiving to God through us; 12 for the rendering of this ministry not only supplies the needs of the saints but also

---

v Gk *this grace*   *w* Other ancient authorities lack *himself*
x Gk *apostles*   *y* Other ancient authorities add *of boasting*
z Or *benevolence*

overflows with many thanksgivings to God. [13] Through the testing of this ministry you glorify God by your obedience to the confession of the gospel of Christ and by the generosity of your sharing with them and with all others, [14] while they long for you and pray for you because of the surpassing grace of God that he has given you. [15] Thanks be to God for his indescribable gift!

Paul Defends His Ministry

10 I myself, Paul, appeal to you by the meekness and gentleness of Christ—I who am humble when face to face with you, but bold toward you when I am away!— [2] I ask that when I am present I need not show boldness by daring to oppose those who think we are acting according to human standards.[a] [3] Indeed, we live as human beings,[b] but we do not wage war according to human standards;[a] [4] for the weapons of our warfare are not merely human,[c] but they have divine power to destroy strongholds. We destroy arguments [5] and every proud obstacle raised up against the knowledge of God, and we take every thought captive to obey Christ. [6] We are ready to punish every disobedience when your obedience is complete.

[7] Look at what is before your eyes. If you are confident that you belong to Christ, remind yourself of this, that just as you belong to Christ, so also do we. [8] Now, even if I boast a little too much of our authority, which the Lord gave for building you up and not for tearing you down, I will not be ashamed of it. [9] I do not want to seem as though I am trying to frighten you with my letters. [10] For they say, "His letters are weighty and strong, but his bodily presence is weak, and his speech contemptible." [11] Let such people understand that what we say by letter when absent, we will also do when present.

[12] We do not dare to classify or compare ourselves with some of those who commend themselves. But when they measure themselves by one another, and compare themselves with one another, they do not show good sense. [13] We, however, will not boast beyond limits, but will keep within the field that God has assigned to us, to reach out even as far as you. [14] For we were not overstepping our limits when we reached you; we were the first to come all the way to you with the good news[d] of Christ. [15] We do not boast beyond limits, that is, in the labors of others; but our hope is that, as your faith increases, our sphere of action among you may be greatly enlarged, [16] so that we may proclaim the good news[d] in lands beyond you, without boasting of work already done in someone else's sphere of action. [17] "Let the one who boasts, boast in the Lord." [18] For it is not those who commend themselves that are approved, but those whom the Lord commends.

Paul and the False Apostles

11 I wish you would bear with me in a little foolishness. Do bear with me! [2] I feel a divine jealousy for you, for I promised you in marriage to one husband, to present you as a chaste virgin to Christ. [3] But I am afraid that as the serpent deceived Eve by its cunning, your thoughts will be led astray from a sincere and pure[e] devotion to Christ. [4] For if someone comes and proclaims another Jesus than the one we proclaimed, or if you receive a different spirit from the one you received, or a different gospel from the one you accepted, you submit to it readily enough. [5] I think that I am not in the least inferior to these super-apostles. [6] I may be untrained in speech, but not in knowledge; certainly in every way and in all things we have made this evident to you.

[7] Did I commit a sin by humbling myself so that you might be exalted, because I proclaimed God's good news[f] to you free of charge? [8] I robbed other churches by accepting support from them in order to serve you. [9] And when I was with you and was in need, I did not burden anyone, for my needs were supplied by the friends[g] who came from Mac·e·dō'ni·a. So I refrained and will continue to refrain from burdening you in any way. [10] As the truth of Christ is in me, this boast of mine will not be silenced in the regions of A·chā'i·a. [11] And why? Because I do not love you? God knows I do!

[12] And what I do I will also continue to do, in order to deny an opportunity to those who want an opportunity to be recognized as our equals in what they boast about. [13] For such boasters are false apostles, deceitful workers, disguising themselves as apostles of Christ. [14] And no wonder! Even Satan disguises himself as an angel of light. [15] So it is not strange if his ministers also disguise themselves as ministers of righteousness. Their end will match their deeds.

Paul's Sufferings as an Apostle

[16] I repeat, let no one think that I am a fool; but if you do, then accept me as a fool, so that I too may boast a little. [17] What I am saying in regard to this boastful confidence, I am saying not with the Lord's authority, but as a fool; [18] since many boast according to human standards,[a] I will also boast. [19] For you gladly put up with fools, being wise yourselves! [20] For you put up with it when someone makes slaves of you, or preys upon you, or

---

[a] Gk *according to the flesh*   [b] Gk *in the flesh*   [c] Gk *fleshly*
[d] Or *the gospel*   [e] Other ancient authorities lack *and pure*
[f] Gk *the gospel of God*   [g] Gk *brothers*

takes advantage of you, or puts on airs, or gives you a slap in the face. 21 To my shame, I must say, we were too weak for that!

But whatever anyone dares to boast of—I am speaking as a fool—I also dare to boast of that. 22 Are they Hebrews? So am I. Are they Israelites? So am I. Are they descendants of Abraham? So am I. 23 Are they ministers of Christ? I am talking like a madman—I am a better one: with far greater labors, far more imprisonments, with countless floggings, and often near death. 24 Five times I have received from the Jews the forty lashes minus one. 25 Three times I was beaten with rods. Once I received a stoning. Three times I was shipwrecked; for a night and a day I was adrift at sea; 26 on frequent journeys, in danger from rivers, danger from bandits, danger from my own people, danger from Gentiles, danger in the city, danger in the wilderness, danger at sea, danger from false brothers and sisters;*h* 27 in toil and hardship, through many a sleepless night, hungry and thirsty, often without food, cold and naked. 28 And, besides other things, I am under daily pressure because of my anxiety for all the churches. 29 Who is weak, and I am not weak? Who is made to stumble, and I am not indignant?

30 If I must boast, I will boast of the things that show my weakness. 31 The God and Father of the Lord Jesus (blessed be he forever!) knows that I do not lie. 32 In Damascus, the governor*i* under King Ar·e·tas guarded the city of Damascus in order to*j* seize me, 33 but I was let down in a basket through a window in the wall,*k* and escaped from his hands.

Paul's Visions and Revelations

12 It is necessary to boast; nothing is to be gained by it, but I will go on to visions and revelations of the Lord. 2 I know a person in Christ who fourteen years ago was caught up to the third heaven—whether in the body or out of the body I do not know; God knows. 3 And I know that such a person—whether in the body or out of the body I do not know; God knows— 4 was caught up into Paradise and heard things that are not to be told, that no mortal is permitted to repeat. 5 On behalf of such a one I will boast, but on my own behalf I will not boast, except of my weaknesses. 6 But if I wish to boast, I will not be a fool, for I will be speaking the truth. But I refrain from it, so that no one may think better of me than what is seen in me or heard from me, 7 even considering the exceptional character of the revelations. Therefore, to keep*l* me from being too elated, a thorn was given me in the flesh, a messenger of Satan to torment me, to keep me from being too elated.*m* 8 Three times I appealed to the Lord about this, that it would leave me, 9 but he said to me, "My grace is sufficient for you, for power*n* is made perfect in weakness." So, I will boast all the more gladly of my weaknesses, so that the power of Christ may dwell in me. 10 Therefore I am content with weaknesses, insults, hardships, persecutions, and calamities for the sake of Christ; for whenever I am weak, then I am strong.

Paul's Concern for the Corinthian Church

11 I have been a fool! You forced me to it. Indeed you should have been the ones commending me, for I am not at all inferior to these super-apostles, even though I am nothing. 12 The signs of a true apostle were performed among you with ut-

---

h Gk *brothers*　*i* Gk *ethnarch*　*j* Other ancient authorities read *and wanted to*　*k* Gk *through the wall*　*l* Other ancient authorities read *To keep*　*m* Other ancient authorities lack *to keep me from being too elated*　*n* Other ancient authorities read *my power*

When I Am Weak, Then I Am Strong!

Sensible people go to a physician when they are suffering from an illness or injury. Smart students seek help from a teacher when they are stumped by an assigned project. Honest people admit when they have failed. Humble people are not afraid to apologize. Admitting that we are sick, or need help with a problem, or have failed or been wrong is a sign not of weakness but of wisdom and maturity.

Paul mentions a mysterious affliction he had to suffer—a "thorn . . . in the flesh" (2 Cor 12.7)—and how desperately he wanted to be rid of it. When he asked God to remove the "thorn," God chose to let it remain in Paul's life.

Paul wanted to be strong on his own, but his experience of struggling with this thorn reminded him that he needed to depend completely on the grace of God. Recognizing that we need God, admitting that we cannot make it on our own—that is a sign of true strength!

▶ 2 Cor 12.1–10

A Spiritual Checkup

LIVE IT!

STOP!

How often do you take a break from all the activities in your life to do a spiritual checkup on your relationships with God, other people, and yourself? In 2 Cor 13.5–7, Paul suggests that the Corinthians give themselves a spiritual self-check. This is good advice for us today as well.

A STOP sign is a good guiding image for a spiritual checkup. It signals you to interrupt the motion of life and look at what's going on around you. Each letter of the sign can be a reminder to check a different area of your spiritual life:

- *S* can stand for "seek." Do you seek information, counsel, and help when facing difficult or confusing situations and choices?
- *T* can stand for "think." Do you honestly think about how your actions and behaviors affect you, others, and your relationship with God?
- *O* can stand for "others." Do you make it a priority to reach out and support others— particularly those in great need? Are you there for your family and friends?
- *P* can stand for "pray." Do you turn to God for guidance in your life? for the strength to do what is right? Do you thank God for your blessings and the struggles that make you stronger?

▶ 2 Cor 13.5–7

most patience, signs and wonders and mighty works. 13 How have you been worse off than the other churches, except that I myself did not burden you? Forgive me this wrong!

14 Here I am, ready to come to you this third time. And I will not be a burden, because I do not want what is yours but you; for children ought not to lay up for their parents, but parents for their children. 15 I will most gladly spend and be spent for you. If I love you more, am I to be loved less? 16 Let it be assumed that I did not burden you. Nevertheless (you say) since I was crafty, I took you in by deceit. 17 Did I take advantage of you through any of those whom I sent to you? 18 I urged Titus to go, and sent the brother with him. Titus did not take advantage of you, did he? Did we not conduct ourselves with the same spirit? Did we not take the same steps?

19 Have you been thinking all along that we have been defending ourselves before you? We are speaking in Christ before God. Everything we do, beloved, is for the sake of building you up. 20 For I fear that when I come, I may find you not as I wish, and that you may find me not as you wish; I fear that there may perhaps be quarreling, jealousy, anger, selfishness, slander, gossip, conceit, and disorder. 21 I fear that when I come again, my God may humble me before you, and that I may have to mourn over many who previously sinned and have not repented of the impurity, sexual immorality, and licentiousness that they have practiced.

Further Warning

13 This is the third time I am coming to you. "Any charge must be sustained by the evidence of two or three witnesses." 2 I warned those who sinned previously and all the others, and I warn them now while absent, as I did when present on my second visit, that if I come again, I will not be lenient— 3 since you desire proof that Christ is speaking in me. He is not weak in dealing with you, but is powerful in you. 4 For he was crucified in weakness, but lives by the power of God. For we are weak in him,* but in dealing with you we will live with him by the power of God.

5 Examine yourselves to see whether you are living in the faith. Test yourselves. Do you not realize that Jesus Christ is in you?—unless, indeed, you fail to meet the test! 6 I hope you will find out that we have not failed. 7 But we pray to God that you may not do anything wrong—not that we may appear to have met the test, but that you may do what is right, though we may seem to have failed. 8 For we cannot do anything against the truth, but only for the truth. 9 For we rejoice when we are weak and you are strong. This is what we pray for, that you may become perfect. 10 So I write these things while I am away from you, so that when I come, I may not have to be severe in using the authority that the Lord has given me for building up and not for tearing down.

---

* Other ancient authorities read *with him*

2
COR

Final Greetings and Benediction

11 Finally, brothers and sisters,*p* farewell.*q* Put things in order, listen to my appeal,*r* agree with one another, live in peace; and the God of love and peace will be with you. 12 Greet one another with a holy kiss. All the saints greet you.

13 The grace of the Lord Jesus Christ, the love of God, and the communion of*s* the Holy Spirit be with all of you.

---

p Gk *brothers*   *q* Or *rejoice*   *r* Or *encourage one another*   *s* Or *and the sharing in*

Do you ever scan a letter before you start to read, to see what mood the writer was in? Try it with Galatians. Notice that Paul is angry and upset. He was weak and sick when he founded the church in Galatia. Now, everything is falling apart. He feels like a mother who has to give birth to her children all over again (4.12–20). Why? Paul is afraid the Galatians are trading in the true Gospel, based on faith in Jesus, for a false gospel based on Jewish rules and customs.

At a Glance

- **1.1–5.** a greeting
- **1.6—2.21.** the work of Paul and the other Apostles
- **3.1—5.1.** the message that salvation is by faith, not works
- **5.2—6.10.** advice on Christian living
- **6.11–18.** final words and a blessing

In-depth

Jesus, the disciples, and most of the first Christians were Jewish. When Gentiles (non-Jews) started to become Christians, a question came up that almost split the early Christian community: Do Gentiles have to become Jewish before they can become Christian? The whole debate soon centered around the Jewish law of circumcision. (Circumcision is the surgical removal of the foreskin of a male's penis.)

Paul insisted that circumcision—and all the other Jewish ceremonial laws—had nothing to do with faith in Jesus and was unnecessary for Gentile Christians. At the Council of Jerusalem (see Acts of the Apostles, chapter 15), the other Apostles reluctantly agreed with Paul. But the argument wasn't over. Other Christian missionaries came to Galatia after Paul left the Christian community there. They implied that faith in Christ wasn't enough and insisted that Gentile Christians must be circumcised. They attacked Paul's credibility by saying he wasn't a true Apostle.

When Paul heard of this, he was mad! In his Letter to the Galatians, he doesn't even include his typical thanksgiving at the end of his greeting but launches right into his concern. He starts by defending his apostlehood. He goes on to tell how the other Apostles at the Council of Jerusalem had agreed with him that the Gentiles do not need to be circumcised. He states how he later challenged Peter personally when Peter allowed himself to be influenced by missionaries preaching something else.

In his passion, Paul confronts the Galatians: "I am afraid that my work for you may have been wasted" (4.11). He condemns the false missionaries: "If anyone proclaims to you a gospel contrary to what you received, let that one be accursed!" (1.9). Paul is defending the freedom of Christians from the old Jewish religious laws. He is writing the Christians' declaration of independence: "Christ has set us free" (5.1).

Quick Facts

Author
Paul

Date
A.D. 54–55

Audience
Gentile Christian churches in northern Galatia

Galatians

Galatians

Salutation

1 Paul an apostle—sent neither by human commission nor from human authorities, but through Jesus Christ and God the Father, who raised him from the dead— 2 and all the members of God's family*a* who are with me,

To the churches of Galatia:

3 Grace to you and peace from God our Father and the Lord Jesus Christ, 4 who gave himself for our sins to set us free from the present evil age, according to the will of our God and Father, 5 to whom be the glory forever and ever. Amen.

There Is No Other Gospel

6 I am astonished that you are so quickly deserting the one who called you in the grace of Christ and are turning to a different gospel— 7 not that there is another gospel, but there are some who are confusing you and want to pervert the gospel of Christ. 8 But even if we or an angel*b* from heaven should proclaim to you a gospel contrary to what we proclaimed to you, let that one be accursed! 9 As we have said before, so now I repeat, if anyone proclaims to you a gospel contrary to what you received, let that one be accursed!

10 Am I now seeking human approval, or God's approval? Or am I trying to please people? If I were still pleasing people, I would not be a servant*c* of Christ.

Paul's Vindication of His Apostleship
(Cp Acts 9)

11 For I want you to know, brothers and sisters,*d* that the gospel that was proclaimed by me is not of human origin; 12 for I did not receive it from a human source, nor was I taught it, but I received it through a revelation of Jesus Christ.

13 You have heard, no doubt, of my earlier life in Jū′da•ism. I was violently persecuting the church of God and was trying to destroy it. 14 I advanced in Jū′da•ism beyond many among my people of the same age, for I was far more zealous for the traditions of my ancestors. 15 But when God, who had set me apart before I was born and called me through his grace, was pleased 16 to reveal his Son to me,*e* so that I might proclaim him among the Gentiles, I did not confer with any human being, 17 nor did I go up to Jerusalem to those who were already apostles before me, but I went away at once into Arabia, and afterwards I returned to Damascus.

18 Then after three years I did go up to Jerusalem to visit Cē′phas and stayed with him fifteen days; 19 but I did not see any other apostle except James the Lord's brother. 20 In what I am writing to you, before God, I do not lie! 21 Then I went into the regions of Syria and Ci•li′ci•a, 22 and I was still

---

a Gk *all the brothers*   *b* Or *a messenger*   *c* Gk *slave*
d Gk *brothers*   *e* Gk *in me*

unknown by sight to the churches of Judea that are in Christ; 23 they only heard it said, "The one who formerly was persecuting us is now proclaiming the faith he once tried to destroy." 24 And they glorified God because of me.

Paul and the Other Apostles
(Cp Acts 15.1–21)

2 Then after fourteen years I went up again to Jerusalem with Bar′na•bas, taking Titus along with me. 2 I went up in response to a revelation. Then I laid before them (though only in a private meeting with the acknowledged leaders) the gospel that I proclaim among the Gentiles, in order to make sure that I was not running, or had not run, in vain. 3 But even Titus, who was with me, was not compelled to be circumcised, though he was a Greek. 4 But because of false believers*f* secretly brought in, who slipped in to spy on the freedom we have in Christ Jesus, so that they might enslave us— 5 we did not submit to them even for a moment, so that the truth of the gospel might always remain with you. 6 And from those who were supposed to be acknowledged leaders (what they actually were makes no difference to me; God shows no partiality)—those leaders contributed nothing to me. 7 On the contrary, when they saw that I had been entrusted with the gospel for the uncircumcised, just as Peter had been entrusted with the gospel for the circumcised 8 (for he who worked through Peter making him an apostle to the circumcised also worked through me in sending me to the Gentiles), 9 and when James and Cē′phas and John, who were acknowledged pillars, recognized the grace that had been given to me, they gave to Bar′na•bas and me the right hand of fellowship, agreeing that we should go to the Gentiles and they to the circumcised. 10 They asked only one thing, that we remember the poor, which was actually what I was*g* eager to do.

Paul Rebukes Peter at Antioch

11 But when Cē′phas came to An′ti•och, I opposed him to his face, because he stood self-condemned; 12 for until certain people came from James, he used to eat with the Gentiles. But after they came, he drew back and kept himself separate for fear of the circumcision faction. 13 And the other Jews joined him in this hypocrisy, so that even Bar′na•bas was led astray by their hypocrisy. 14 But when I saw that they were not acting consistently with the truth of the gospel, I said to Cē′phas before them all, "If you, though a Jew, live like a Gentile and not like a Jew, how can you compel the Gentiles to live like Jews?"*h*

Jews and Gentiles Are Saved by Faith

15 We ourselves are Jews by birth and not Gentile sinners; 16 yet we know that a person is justified*i* not by the works of the law but through faith in

f Gk *false brothers*   *g* Or *had been*   *h* Some interpreters hold that the quotation extends into the following paragraph   *i* Or *reckoned as righteous*; and so elsewhere

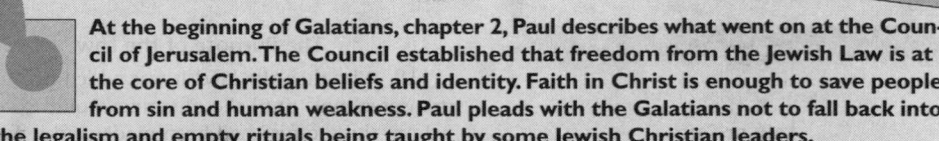

Consistent and Trustworthy

At the beginning of Galatians, chapter 2, Paul describes what went on at the Council of Jerusalem. The Council established that freedom from the Jewish Law is at the core of Christian beliefs and identity. Faith in Christ is enough to save people from sin and human weakness. Paul pleads with the Galatians not to fall back into the legalism and empty rituals being taught by some Jewish Christian leaders.

So when Peter stops eating with Gentile Christians under pressure from some Jewish Christians, Paul challenges him. He points out that Peter's behavior is not consistent with the truth of the Gospel and that this inconsistency is misleading and confusing to the Christian community.

To be a credible Christian demands that you stay consistent in your words and actions. Remember, your actions speak louder than your words. Furthermore, when your actions do not match your words, people lose their trust in you. And you begin to feel like a hypocrite and lose your self-esteem.

Take some time to reflect on how consistently your actions reflect your words. Consider ways you can improve. When your actions match your words, people will recognize you as a person of integrity and place their trust in you.

▶ Gal 2.11–14

Jesus Christ.*j* And we have come to believe in Christ Jesus, so that we might be justified by faith in Christ,*k* and not by doing the works of the law, because no one will be justified by the works of the law. 17 But if, in our effort to be justified in Christ, we ourselves have been found to be sinners, is Christ then a servant of sin? Certainly not! 18 But if I build up again the very things that I once tore down, then I demonstrate that I am a transgressor. 19 For through the law I died to the law, so that I might live to God. I have been crucified with Christ; 20 and it is no longer I who live, but it is Christ who lives in me. And the life I now live in the flesh I live by faith in the Son of God,*l* who loved me and gave himself for me. 21 I do not nullify the grace of God; for if justification*m* comes through the law, then Christ died for nothing.

did you KNOW?

Saved by Christ

Throughout Galatians, Paul speaks about the difference between being saved by faith and being saved through the Law. Christians believe that they are justified— made right with God—not through a perfect keeping of religious laws, but through faith in Christ. Christ's saving sacrifice alone will set them free from their sin. Their trust must be in him and not in their own ability to please God.

▸ **Gal 3.1—4.7**

Law or Faith
(Cp Rom 4.1–25)

3 You foolish Galatians! Who has bewitched you? It was before your eyes that Jesus Christ was publicly exhibited as crucified! 2 The only thing I want to learn from you is this: Did you receive the Spirit by doing the works of the law or by believing what you heard? 3 Are you so foolish? Having started with the Spirit, are you now ending with the flesh? 4 Did you experience so much for nothing?— if it really was for nothing. 5 Well then, does God*n* supply you with the Spirit and work miracles among you by your doing the works of the law, or by your believing what you heard?

6 Just as Abraham "believed God, and it was

reckoned to him as righteousness," 7 so, you see, those who believe are the descendants of Abraham. 8 And the scripture, foreseeing that God would justify the Gentiles by faith, declared the gospel beforehand to Abraham, saying, "All the Gentiles shall be blessed in you." 9 For this reason, those who believe are blessed with Abraham who believed.

10 For all who rely on the works of the law are under a curse; for it is written, "Cursed is everyone who does not observe and obey all the things written in the book of the law." 11 Now it is evident that no one is justified before God by the law; for "The one who is righteous will live by faith."*o* 12 But the law does not rest on faith; on the contrary, "Whoever does the works of the law*p* will live by them." 13 Christ redeemed us from the curse of the law by becoming a curse for us—for it is written, "Cursed is everyone who hangs on a tree"— 14 in order that in Christ Jesus the blessing of Abraham might come to the Gentiles, so that we might receive the promise of the Spirit through faith.

The Promise to Abraham
(Cp Gen 12.1–3)

15 Brothers and sisters,*q* I give an example from daily life: once a person's will*r* has been ratified, no one adds to it or annuls it. 16 Now the promises were made to Abraham and to his offspring;*s* it does not say, "And to offsprings,"*t* as of many; but it says, "And to your offspring,"*s* that is, to one person, who is Christ. 17 My point is this: the law, which came four hundred thirty years later, does not annul a covenant previously ratified by God, so as to nullify the promise. 18 For if the inheritance comes from the law, it no longer comes from the promise; but God granted it to Abraham through the promise.

The Purpose of the Law

19 Why then the law? It was added because of transgressions, until the offspring*s* would come to whom the promise had been made; and it was ordained through angels by a mediator. 20 Now a mediator involves more than one party; but God is one.

21 Is the law then opposed to the promises of God? Certainly not! For if a law had been given that could make alive, then righteousness would indeed come through the law. 22 But the scripture has imprisoned all things under the power of sin, so that

---

j Or *the faith of Jesus Christ*   *k* Or *the faith of Christ*   *l* Or *by the faith of the Son of God*   *m* Or *righteousness*   *n* Gk *he*
o Or *The one who is righteous through faith will live*
p Gk *does them*   *q* Gk *Brothers*   *r* Or *covenant* (as in verse 17)   *s* Gk *seed*   *t* Gk *seeds*

There is no longer
Jew or **Greek**,
there is no longer
slave *or free*,
there is no longer
male and **female**;
for all of you are one in
Christ Jesus
3.28

what was promised through faith in Jesus Christ[u] might be given to those who believe.

23 Now before faith came, we were imprisoned and guarded under the law until faith would be revealed. 24 Therefore the law was our disciplinarian until Christ came, so that we might be justified by faith. 25 But now that faith has come, we are no longer subject to a disciplinarian, 26 for in Christ Jesus you are all children of God through faith. 27 As many of you as were baptized into Christ have clothed yourselves with Christ. 28 There is no longer Jew or Greek, there is no longer slave or free, there is no longer male and female; for all of you are one in Christ Jesus. 29 And if you belong to Christ, then you are Abraham's offspring,[v] heirs according to the promise.

4 My point is this: heirs, as long as they are minors, are no better than slaves, though they are the owners of all the property; 2 but they remain under guardians and trustees until the date set by the father. 3 So with us; while we were minors, we were enslaved to the elemental spirits[w] of the world. 4 But when the fullness of time had come,

God sent his Son, born of a woman, born under the law, 5 in order to redeem those who were under the law, so that we might receive adoption as children. 6 And because you are children, God has sent the Spirit of his Son into our[x] hearts, crying, "Abba![y] Father!" 7 So you are no longer a slave but a child, and if a child then also an heir, through God.[z]

Paul Reproves the Galatians

8 Formerly, when you did not know God, you were enslaved to beings that by nature are not gods. 9 Now, however, that you have come to know God, or rather to be known by God, how can you turn back again to the weak and beggarly elemental spirits?[a] How can you want to be enslaved to them again? 10 You are observing special days, and months, and seasons, and years. 11 I am afraid that my work for you may have been wasted.

12 Friends,[b] I beg you, become as I am, for I also have become as you are. You have done me no wrong. 13 You know that it was because of a physical infirmity that I first announced the gospel to you; 14 though my condition put you to the test, you did not scorn or despise me, but welcomed me as an angel of God, as Christ Jesus. 15 What has become of the goodwill you felt? For I testify that, had it been possible, you would have torn out your eyes and given them to me. 16 Have I now become your enemy by telling you the truth? 17 They make much of you, but for no good purpose; they want to exclude you, so that you may make much of them. 18 It is good to be made much of for a good purpose at all times, and not only when I am present with you. 19 My little children, for whom I am again in the pain of childbirth until Christ is formed in you, 20 I wish I were present with you

---

u Or *through the faith of Jesus Christ*   v Gk *seed*   w Or *the rudiments*   x Other ancient authorities read *your*   y Aramaic for *Father*   z Other ancient authorities read *an heir of God through Christ*   a Or *beggarly rudiments*   b Gk *Brothers*

Radical Equality

LIVE IT!

Galatians 3.28 may have been an early baptismal formula. In it, Paul makes a radical statement: The source of our equality as humans is Jesus Christ! (Note that the word *radical* means both "root" and "extreme"—and that Paul's statement is both fundamental to Christian belief and a great expression of that belief.)

Think about what Paul says: Everyone is equal! But is this the reality in the world around you? Are all the people in your school regarded as equally valuable? Consider the equality of women in work, church, and society. What about those who are poor, how are they regarded? It is clear that we still need to work toward Paul's vision!

▶ **Gal 3.28**

now and could change my tone, for I am perplexed about you.

The Allegory of Hagar and Sarah
(Gen 21.8–21; Isa 54.1)

21 Tell me, you who desire to be subject to the law, will you not listen to the law? 22 For it is written that Abraham had two sons, one by a slave woman and the other by a free woman. 23 One, the child of the slave, was born according to the flesh; the other, the child of the free woman, was born through the promise. 24 Now this is an allegory: these women are two covenants. One woman, in fact, is Hā′gar, from Mount Sinai, bearing children for slavery. 25 Now Hā′gar is Mount Sinai in Arabia*c* and corresponds to the present Jerusalem, for she is in slavery with her children. 26 But the other woman corresponds to the Jerusalem above; she is free, and she is our mother. 27 For it is written,

"Rejoice, you childless one, you who bear no
          children,
     burst into song and shout, you who endure
          no birth pangs;
for the children of the desolate woman are
          more numerous
     than the children of the one who is
          married."

28 Now you,*d* my friends,*e* are children of the promise, like Isaac. 29 But just as at that time the child who was born according to the flesh persecuted the child who was born according to the Spirit, so it is now also. 30 But what does the scripture say? "Drive out the slave and her child; for the child of the slave will not share the inheritance with the child of the free woman." 31 So then, friends,*e* we are children, not of the slave but of the free woman. 1 For freedom Christ has set us free. Stand firm, therefore, and do not submit again to a yoke of slavery.

The Nature of Christian Freedom

2 Listen! I, Paul, am telling you that if you let yourselves be circumcised, Christ will be of no benefit to you. 3 Once again I testify to every man who lets himself be circumcised that he is obliged to obey the entire law. 4 You who want to be justified by the law have cut yourselves off from Christ; you have fallen away from grace. 5 For through the Spirit, by faith, we eagerly wait for the hope of righteousness. 6 For in Christ Jesus neither circumcision nor uncircumcision counts for anything; the only thing that counts is faith working*f* through love.

7 You were running well; who prevented you from obeying the truth? 8 Such persuasion does not come from the one who calls you. 9 A little yeast leavens the whole batch of dough. 10 I am confident about you in the Lord that you will not think

otherwise. But whoever it is that is confusing you will pay the penalty. 11 But my friends,*e* why am I still being persecuted if I am still preaching circumcision? In that case the offense of the cross has been removed. 12 I wish those who unsettle you would castrate themselves!

13 For you were called to freedom, brothers and sisters;*e* only do not use your freedom as an opportunity for self-indulgence,*g* but through love become slaves to one another. 14 For the whole law is

---

c Other ancient authorities read *For Sinai is a mountain in Arabia*   *d* Other ancient authorities read *we*
e Gk *brothers*   *f* Or *made effective*   *g* Gk *the flesh*

summed up in a single commandment, "You shall love your neighbor as yourself." 15 If, however, you bite and devour one another, take care that you are not consumed by one another.

The Works of the Flesh

16 Live by the Spirit, I say, and do not gratify the desires of the flesh. 17 For what the flesh desires is opposed to the Spirit, and what the Spirit desires is opposed to the flesh; for these are opposed to each other, to prevent you from doing what you want. 18 But if you are led by the Spirit, you are not subject to the law. 19 Now the works of the flesh are obvious: fornication, impurity, licentiousness, 20 idolatry, sorcery, enmities, strife, jealousy, anger, quarrels, dissensions, factions, 21 envy,[h] drunkenness, carousing, and things like these. I am warning you, as I warned you before: those who do such things will not inherit the kingdom of God.

The Fruit of the Spirit
(Cp Col 3.12–13)

22 By contrast, the fruit of the Spirit is love, joy, peace, patience, kindness, generosity, faithfulness, 23 gentleness, and self-control. There is no law against such things. 24 And those who belong to Christ Jesus have crucified the flesh with its passions and desires. 25 If we live by the Spirit, let us

also be guided by the Spirit. 26 Let us not become conceited, competing against one another, envying one another.

Bear One Another's Burdens

6 My friends,[i] if anyone is detected in a transgression, you who have received the Spirit should restore such a one in a spirit of gentleness. Take care that you yourselves are not tempted. 2 Bear one another's burdens, and in this way you will fulfill[j] the law of Christ. 3 For if those who are nothing think they are something, they deceive themselves. 4 All must test their own work; then that work, rather than their neighbor's work, will become a cause for pride. 5 For all must carry their own loads.

6 Those who are taught the word must share in all good things with their teacher.

7 Do not be deceived; God is not mocked, for you reap whatever you sow. 8 If you sow to your own flesh, you will reap corruption from the flesh; but if you sow to the Spirit, you will reap eternal life from the Spirit. 9 So let us not grow weary in doing what is right, for we will reap at harvest time, if we do not give up. 10 So then, whenever we have an

---

h Other ancient authorities add *murder*   i Gk *Brothers*
j Other ancient authorities read *in this way fulfill*

THE PRINCIPLE OF *IMANI*

Be not discouraged. There is a future for you. . . . The resistance encountered now predicates hope. . . . Only as we rise . . . do we encounter opposition.

These words by Frederick Douglass in 1892 encouraged the descendants of African slaves in North America not to abandon their struggle for equality. It seemed that the more they struggled, the more pain was inflicted on them. In the face of certain suffering, Douglass urged them to look toward the promise of living as equals under the law.

They knew that God was their liberator and justice giver. God made them brave in the face of danger and capable of dying for the cause they embraced. They looked to God and saw their future. They took the words of Gal 6.9 seriously: "Let us not grow weary in doing what is right."

Today, we don't face slave masters and live on plantations as servants in fetters, but we do endure other situations equally as perilous. Let us not grow weary or lose heart. Our God is still in the saving business.

Dear God, my future is in your hands. Lead me to it with your power. Amen.

▶ **Gal 6.9**

opportunity, let us work for the good of all, and especially for those of the family of faith.

Final Admonitions and Benediction

11 See what large letters I make when I am writing in my own hand! 12 It is those who want to make a good showing in the flesh that try to compel you to be circumcised—only that they may not be persecuted for the cross of Christ. 13 Even the circumcised do not themselves obey the law, but they want you to be circumcised so that they may boast about your flesh. 14 May I never boast of anything except the cross of our Lord Jesus Christ, by which[k] the world has been crucified to me, and I to the world. 15 For[l] neither circumcision nor uncircumcision is anything; but a new creation is everything! 16 As for those who will follow this rule—peace be upon them, and mercy, and upon the Israel of God.

17 From now on, let no one make trouble for me; for I carry the marks of Jesus branded on my body.

18 May the grace of our Lord Jesus Christ be with your spirit, brothers and sisters.[m] Amen.

---

k Or *through whom* l Other ancient authorities add *in Christ Jesus* m Gk *brothers*

What's the purpose to life? Why am I alive? What's the point of it all anyway? You may have asked questions like these out of simple curiosity, or during a time when life wasn't going so well. In either case, God has an answer for you tucked away inside the Letter to the Ephesians. This letter talks about God's plan to save us for a life in union with God and one another, both now and for all eternity!

In-depth

Three times in the poetic opening chapter, the writer of Ephesians tells us that we are here because we have been chosen by God! In this beautiful trinity of praise for the Father (verses 3–6), the Son (verse 12), and the Holy Spirit (verses 13–14), we are told that that's why we're alive!

This letter has hardly any of the personal greeting you'd expect in a communication to a specific group of people. Also, the reference to the saints in the first verse doesn't appear in many of the earliest copies we have of the letter. For these reasons, most scholars believe that this letter was intended to be read by several Christian communities and has a universal message for the early church.

Ephesians emphasizes unity among Christians. It especially emphasizes that Gentile (non-Jewish) Christians are one with Jewish Christians, for Christ "has made both groups into one" (2.14). It explains that it is the early Christians' job—as it is our job—to treat one another with love, "making every effort to maintain the unity" (4.3). The image of the body is used here, as it is in 1 Corinthians, chapter 12, to emphasize our unity (4.15–16).

Ephesians also talks about the place of good works in the life of a Christian. Good works can be thought of as living a moral life, or as following moral rules, such as the Jewish Law. Paul has made clear that we are not saved by the Law. So, what is the point of living a moral life? The letter explains that we are saved not *by doing* good works but *in order to do* good works.

The letter ends with some practical advice for living out the faith on a daily basis. There are rules for moral living. There are instructions for Christian family life. There is an analogy for putting on the "armor of God" to resist evil in all its forms. If we keep in mind that this letter is written for a culture that was different from ours, the advice will serve us well too!

At a Glance

- **1.1–2.** a greeting
- **1.3–23.** a benediction, and thanksgiving for salvation
- **Chapters 2–3.** a discussion of unity in Christ
- **4.1—6.20.** advice for Christian living
- **6.21–24.** a final message and a blessing

Quick Facts

Author
a follower of Paul (see "Introduction to the Letters and Revelation")

Date Written
after Paul's death, A.D. 70–95

Audience
Gentile churches, possibly in Asia Minor

Ephesians

The Letter to the

Ephesians

2.20

Salutation

1 Paul, an apostle of Christ Jesus by the will of God,

To the saints who are in Eph′e•sus and are faithful*a* in Christ Jesus:

2 Grace to you and peace from God our Father and the Lord Jesus Christ.

Spiritual Blessings in Christ

3 Blessed be the God and Father of our Lord Jesus Christ, who has blessed us in Christ with every spiritual blessing in the heavenly places, 4 just as he chose us in Christ*b* before the foundation of the world to be holy and blameless before him in love. 5 He destined us for adoption as his children through Jesus Christ, according to the good pleasure of his will, 6 to the praise of his glorious grace that he freely bestowed on us in the Beloved. 7 In him we have redemption through his blood, the forgiveness of our trespasses, according to the riches of his grace 8 that he lavished on us. With all wisdom and insight 9 he has made known to us the mystery of his will, according to his good pleasure that he set forth in Christ, 10 as a plan for the fullness of time, to gather up all things in him, things in heaven and things on earth. 11 In Christ we have also obtained an inheritance,*c* having been destined according to the purpose of him who accomplishes all things according to his counsel and will, 12 so

that we, who were the first to set our hope on Christ, might live for the praise of his glory. 13 In him you also, when you had heard the word of truth, the gospel of your salvation, and had believed in him, were marked with the seal of the promised Holy Spirit; 14 this*d* is the pledge of our inheritance toward redemption as God's own people, to the praise of his glory.

Paul's Prayer

15 I have heard of your faith in the Lord Jesus and your love*e* toward all the saints, and for this reason 16 I do not cease to give thanks for you as I remember you in my prayers. 17 I pray that the God of our Lord Jesus Christ, the Father of glory, may give you a spirit of wisdom and revelation as you come to know him, 18 so that, with the eyes of your heart enlightened, you may know what is the hope to which he has called you, what are the riches of his glorious inheritance among the saints, 19 and what is the immeasurable greatness of his power for us who believe, according to the working of his great power. 20 God*f* put this power to work in Christ when he raised him from the dead and

---

a Other ancient authorities lack *in Ephesus*, reading *saints who are also faithful* *b* Gk *in him* *c* Or *been made a heritage* *d* Other ancient authorities read *who* *e* Other ancient authorities lack *and your love* *f* Gk *He* seated him at his right hand in the heavenly places, 21 far above all rule and authority and power and dominion, and above every name that is named, not only in this age but also in the age to come. 22 And he has put all things under his feet and has made him the head over all things for the church, 23 which is his body, the fullness of him who fills all in all.

I Give God Thanks for You!

Think of people in your family, community, school, and church who are living out the Gospel message. Who is honestly striving to live her or his Christian faith? a parent or guardian? a friend? a neighbor? a teacher? a minister?

Hold this person in your heart as you read Eph 1.15–23. Meditate on how this person has influenced you as a Christian. How has he or she helped you on your faith journey? Consider writing your own prayer of thanks to God for this person's example. If it seems appropriate, share your prayer with this person.

▸ Eph 1.15–23

From Death to Life

2 You were dead through the trespasses and sins 2 in which you once lived, following the course of this world, following the ruler of the power of the air, the spirit that is now at work among those who are disobedient. 3 All of us once lived among them in the passions of our flesh, following the desires of flesh and senses, and we were by nature children of wrath, like everyone else. 4 But God, who is rich in mercy, out of the great love with which he loved us 5 even when we were dead through our trespasses, made us alive together with Christ*g*—by grace you have been saved— 6 and raised us up with him and seated us with him in the heavenly places in Christ Jesus, 7 so that in the ages to come he might show the immeasurable riches of his grace in kindness toward us in Christ Jesus. 8 For by grace you have been saved through faith, and this is not your own doing; it is the gift of God— 9 not the result of works, so that no one may boast. 10 For we are what he has made us, created in Christ Jesus for good works, which God prepared beforehand to be our way of life.

One in Christ

11 So then, remember that at one time you Gentiles by birth,*h* called "the uncircumcision" by those who are called "the circumcision"—a physical circumcision made in the flesh by human hands— 12 remember that you were at that time without Christ, being aliens from the commonwealth of Israel, and strangers to the covenants of promise, having no hope and without God in the world. 13 But now in Christ Jesus you who once were far off have been brought near by the blood of Christ. 14 For he is our peace; in his flesh he has made both groups into one and has broken down the dividing wall, that is, the hostility between us. 15 He has abolished the law with its commandments and ordinances, that he might create in himself one new humanity in place of the two, thus making peace, 16 and might reconcile both groups to God in one body*i* through the cross, thus putting to death that

g Other ancient authorities read *in Christ*   *h* Gk *in the flesh*   *i* Or *reconcile both of us in one body for God*

did you KNOW?
Faith Versus Good Works

Ephesians 2.1–10 deals with the question of faith versus good works (good works are moral living and Gospel-motivated works of service, justice, courage, and so on). This issue has divided Christians since the early church and was a major issue at the time of the Protestant Reformation. Some say that we are saved by our good works. Others say that good works are irrelevant and that we are saved only through our faith in Christ.

The writer of Ephesians makes it clear that both those statements are incomplete. The core Christian belief is this: We are saved by God's grace through faith in Jesus Christ. We were saved not *by doing* good works but *in order to do* good works. Our salvation is God's gift to us; how we live is our gift to God.

▸ Eph 2.1–10

EPH

hostility through it.[j] 17 So he came and proclaimed peace to you who were far off and peace to those who were near; 18 for through him both of us have access in one Spirit to the Father. 19 So then you are no longer strangers and aliens, but you are citizens with the saints and also members of the household of God, 20 built upon the foundation of the apostles and prophets, with Christ Jesus himself as the cornerstone.[k] 21 In him the whole structure is joined together and grows into a holy temple in the Lord; 22 in whom you also are built together spiritually[l] into a dwelling place for God.

Paul's Ministry to the Gentiles

3 This is the reason that I Paul am a prisoner for[m] Christ Jesus for the sake of you Gentiles— 2 for surely you have already heard of the commission of God's grace that was given me for you, 3 and how the mystery was made known to me by revelation, as I wrote above in a few words, 4 a reading of which will enable you to perceive my understanding of the mystery of Christ. 5 In former generations this mystery[n] was not made known to humankind, as it has now been revealed to his holy apostles and prophets by the Spirit: 6 that is, the Gentiles have become fellow heirs, members of the same body, and sharers in the promise in Christ Jesus through the gospel.

7 Of this gospel I have become a servant according to the gift of God's grace that was given me by the working of his power. 8 Although I am the very least of all the saints, this grace was given to me to bring to the Gentiles the news of the boundless riches of Christ, 9 and to make everyone see[o] what is the plan of the mystery hidden for ages in[p] God who created all things; 10 so that through the church the wisdom of God in its rich variety might now be made known to the rulers and authorities in the heavenly places. 11 This was in accordance with the eternal purpose that he has carried out in Christ Jesus our Lord, 12 in whom we have access to God in boldness and confidence through faith in him.[q] 13 I pray therefore that you[r] may not lose heart over my sufferings for you; they are your glory.

---

[j] Or in him, or in himself   [k] Or keystone   [l] Gk in the Spirit   [m] Or of   [n] Gk it   [o] Other ancient authorities read to bring to light   [p] Or by   [q] Or the faith of him   [r] Or I

ROOTED IN LOVE

Read the prayer in Eph 3.14–21. Then reflect on the prayer below from the Philippines, which also talks about roots and love.

> Lord,
> make us realise that our Christianity is like a rice field:
> when it is newly planted the paddies are prominent,
> but as the plants take root and grow taller,
> these divided paddies gradually vanish,
> and soon there appears only one vast continuous field.
> So give us roots that love,
> and help us grow in Christian fellowship and service,
> that thy will be done in our lives,
> through our Savior, Jesus Christ.
>
> **(From Your Will Be Done)**

Finally, personalize the prayer in 3.14–21 by changing you to I or we, and your to my or our. Kneel and pray this prayer, knowing that God is indeed listening to you at this very moment.

▸ Eph 3.14–21

I pray that,

according to the riches of his glory,

he may grant that you may be strengthened

in your inner being with power through his Spirit,

and that Christ may dwell in your hearts through faith,

as you are being rooted and grounded in love.

3.16–17

Prayer for the Readers

14 For this reason I bow my knees before the Father,[s] 15 from whom every family[t] in heaven and on earth takes its name. 16 I pray that, according to the riches of his glory, he may grant that you may be strengthened in your inner being with power through his Spirit, 17 and that Christ may dwell in your hearts through faith, as you are being rooted and grounded in love. 18 I pray that you may have the power to comprehend, with all the saints, what is the breadth and length and height and depth, 19 and to know the love of Christ that surpasses knowledge, so that you may be filled with all the fullness of God.

20 Now to him who by the power at work within us is able to accomplish abundantly far more than all we can ask or imagine, 21 to him be glory in the church and in Christ Jesus to all generations, forever and ever. Amen.

Unity in the Body of Christ

4 I therefore, the prisoner in the Lord, beg you to lead a life worthy of the calling to which you have been called, 2 with all humility and

There is *one* body and *one* Spirit, just as you were called to the *one* hope of your calling, *one* Lord, *one* faith, *one* baptism, *one* God and Father of all

---

[s] Other ancient authorities add *of our Lord Jesus Christ*
[t] Gk *fatherhood*

4.4–6

PROPHETS OF HOPE, YOUTH ON A MISSION!

Ephesians 4.17–32 has some teachings that were probably used in the preparation for Baptism. In some cultures young people have been baptized as Catholics but have not had an opportunity to live their faith in a vital church community. Those who are trying to follow Jesus want to be prophets of hope, as expressed in this song:

> We're Prophets of Hope, youth on a mission,
> spreading the Gospel of Christ.
> We're Prophets of Hope, issuing the challenge:
> to build the Reign of God.
>
> Pilgrims on a journey, marching towards our goal.
> Led by the Spirit, strengthened by the Lord.
> We bear each other's burdens and give each other hope.
> Following our savior we press on towards our goal.
>
> We come from towns and cities.
> We are immigrants and natives,
> laborers and students who want a better life.
> We want to be successful, but not at any cost.
> Unless we work for justice humanity is lost.
>
> We face discrimination, poverty and drugs.
> The values of our culture are all under attack.
> But we have faith in Jesus; he will give us strength.
> Together we will struggle to build a better world.
>
> The Gospel is our road map, the Church is our guide.
> We're Catholic Latinos, youth who take a stand.
> Leaders in our churches, reflecting as we go.
> Learning from our set-backs, we never give up hope.
>
> (Jose Antonio Rubio)

▶ Eph 4.17–32

gentleness, with patience, bearing with one another in love, 3 making every effort to maintain the unity of the Spirit in the bond of peace. 4 There is one body and one Spirit, just as you were called to the one hope of your calling, 5 one Lord, one faith, one baptism, 6 one God and Father of all, who is above all and through all and in all.

7 But each of us was given grace according to the measure of Christ's gift. 8 Therefore it is said,

"When he ascended on high he made captivity
    itself a captive;
he gave gifts to his people."

9 (When it says, "He ascended," what does it mean

but that he had also descended[u] into the lower parts of the earth? 10 He who descended is the same one who ascended far above all the heavens, so that he might fill all things.) 11 The gifts he gave were that some would be apostles, some prophets, some evangelists, some pastors and teachers, 12 to equip the saints for the work of ministry, for building up the body of Christ, 13 until all of us come to the unity of the faith and of the knowledge of the Son of God, to maturity, to the measure of the full stature of Christ. 14 We must no longer be children,

---

u Other ancient authorities add *first*

tossed to and fro and blown about by every wind of doctrine, by people's trickery, by their craftiness in deceitful scheming. 15 But speaking the truth in love, we must grow up in every way into him who is the head, into Christ, 16 from whom the whole body, joined and knit together by every ligament with which it is equipped, as each part is working properly, promotes the body's growth in building itself up in love.

The Old Life and the New

17 Now this I affirm and insist on in the Lord: you must no longer live as the Gentiles live, in the futility of their minds. 18 They are darkened in their understanding, alienated from the life of God because of their ignorance and hardness of heart. 19 They have lost all sensitivity and have abandoned themselves to licentiousness, greedy to practice every kind of impurity. 20 That is not the way you learned Christ! 21 For surely you have heard about him and were taught in him, as truth is in Jesus. 22 You were taught to put away your former way of life, your old self, corrupt and deluded by its lusts, 23 and to be renewed in the spirit of your minds, 24 and to clothe yourselves with the new self, created according to the likeness of God in true righteousness and holiness.

Rules for the New Life

25 So then, putting away falsehood, let all of us speak the truth to our neighbors, for we are members of one another. 26 Be angry but do not sin; do not let the sun go down on your anger, 27 and do not make room for the devil. 28 Thieves must give up stealing; rather let them labor and work honestly with their own hands, so as to have something to share with the needy. 29 Let no evil talk come out of your mouths, but only what is useful for building up,ᵛ as there is need, so that your words may give grace to those who hear. 30 And do not grieve the Holy Spirit of God, with which you were marked with a seal for the day of redemption. 31 Put away from you all bitterness and wrath and anger and wrangling and slander, together with all malice, 32 and be kind to one another, tenderhearted, forgiving one another, as God in Christ has forgiven you.ʷ 1 Therefore be imitators of God, as beloved children, 2 and live in love, as Christ loved usˣ and gave himself up for us, a fragrant offering and sacrifice to God.

Renounce Pagan Ways

3 But fornication and impurity of any kind, or greed, must not even be mentioned among you, as is proper among saints. 4 Entirely out of place is obscene, silly, and vulgar talk; but instead, let there be thanksgiving. 5 Be sure of this, that no fornicator or impure person, or one who is greedy (that is, an idolater), has any inheritance in the kingdom of Christ and of God.

6 Let no one deceive you with empty words, for because of these things the wrath of God comes on those who are disobedient. 7 Therefore do not be associated with them. 8 For once you were darkness, but now in the Lord you are light. Live as children of light— 9 for the fruit of the light is found in

---

ᵛ Other ancient authorities read *building up faith*
ʷ Other ancient authorities read *us* ˣ Other ancient authorities read *you*

Alcohol

LIVE IT!

The author of Eph 5.10-20 does not mince words. This passage encourages the early Christians, and us, to wake up and find out what pleases God. It calls them to avoid participating in actions they would be ashamed of if the actions were exposed in the light. Its tone is not of scolding but rather of passionate encouragement, wanting the best for each of us.

Although the use of alcohol is singled out in this passage, drinking is not the only substance abuse issue young people face during adolescence. Many young people have to choose whether to participate in drinking, smoking, and using drugs. Abuse of these substances prevents us from being filled with the Spirit. As the author of Ephesians advises, making wise choices about these substances is important.

Take some time to reflect on your own life. What temptations do you face in this regard? What choices can you make that would please God and allow you to enjoy the fullness of life in the Spirit? Who can help you make the correct decisions and help you stick to them?

▶ Eph 5.10–20

all that is good and right and true. 10 Try to find out what is pleasing to the Lord. 11 Take no part in the unfruitful works of darkness, but instead expose them. 12 For it is shameful even to mention what such people do secretly; 13 but everything exposed by the light becomes visible, 14 for everything that becomes visible is light. Therefore it says,

"Sleeper, awake!
Rise from the dead,
and Christ will shine on you."

15 Be careful then how you live, not as unwise people but as wise, 16 making the most of the time, because the days are evil. 17 So do not be foolish, but understand what the will of the Lord is. 18 Do not get drunk with wine, for that is debauchery; but be filled with the Spirit, 19 as you sing psalms and hymns and spiritual songs among yourselves, singing and making melody to the Lord in your hearts, 20 giving thanks to God the Father at all times and for everything in the name of our Lord Jesus Christ.

The Christian Household
(Cp Col 3.18–19)

21 Be subject to one another out of reverence for Christ.

22 Wives, be subject to your husbands as you are to the Lord. 23 For the husband is the head of the wife just as Christ is the head of the church, the body of which he is the Savior. 24 Just as the church is subject to Christ, so also wives ought to be, in everything, to their husbands.

25 Husbands, love your wives, just as Christ loved the church and gave himself up for her, 26 in order to make her holy by cleansing her with the washing of water by the word, 27 so as to present the church to himself in splendor, without a spot or wrinkle or anything of the kind—yes, so that she may be holy and without blemish. 28 In the same way, husbands should love their wives as they do their own bodies. He who loves his wife loves himself. 29 For no one ever hates his own body, but he nourishes and tenderly cares for it, just as Christ does for the church, 30 because we are members of his body.*y* 31 "For this reason a man will leave his father and mother and be joined to his wife, and the two will become one flesh." 32 This is a great mystery, and I am applying it to Christ and the church. 33 Each of you, however, should love his wife as himself, and a wife should respect her husband.

Children and Parents
(Ex 20.12; Deut 5.16)

6 Children, obey your parents in the Lord,*z* for this is right. 2 "Honor your father and mother" —this is the first commandment with a promise: 3 "so that it may be well with you and you may live long on the earth."

4 And, fathers, do not provoke your children to anger, but bring them up in the discipline and instruction of the Lord.

---

y Other ancient authorities add *of his flesh and of his bones*
z Other ancient authorities lack *in the Lord*

Family Relationships

LIVE IT!

When Eph 5.21—6.4 comes up in the Sunday readings, it sometimes causes confusion. People ask, "How can the Bible teach that a wife should be subject to her husband?" This is another case where we must take into account the cultural context in order to properly interpret the passage. At the time the Letter to the Ephesians was written, the male gender was dominant in society. Wives and children were considered men's property. The letter's challenge to a man to love his wife and to treat his children respectfully was probably viewed as a radical statement by people at the time.

Just as we should not interpret 6.5–9 as giving permission to own slaves, we should not interpret 5.21—6.4 as commanding submissive behavior of married women today. Understanding this, we can appreciate the passage as it was intended: a practical guide for a family life where love is the rule (see "The Christian Family," Col 3.18—4.1).

Read Eph 5.21—6.4 and then reflect on these questions:
■ How does 6.1–4 indicate that honoring is a two-way street?
■ What does it mean to live in a family where love is the rule?
■ How do you love and honor your parents and siblings?

▶ Eph 5.21—6.4

Slaves and Masters

5 Slaves, obey your earthly masters with fear and trembling, in singleness of heart, as you obey Christ; 6 not only while being watched, and in order to please them, but as slaves of Christ, doing the will of God from the heart. 7 Render service with enthusiasm, as to the Lord and not to men and women, 8 knowing that whatever good we do, we will receive the same again from the Lord, whether we are slaves or free.

9 And, masters, do the same to them. Stop threatening them, for you know that both of you have the same Master in heaven, and with him there is no partiality.

The Whole Armor of God

10 Finally, be strong in the Lord and in the strength of his power. 11 Put on the whole armor of God, so that you may be able to stand against the wiles of the devil. 12 For our[a] struggle is not against enemies of blood and flesh, but against the rulers, against the authorities, against the cosmic powers of this present darkness, against the spiritual forces of evil in the heavenly places. 13 Therefore take up the whole armor of God, so that you may be able to withstand on that evil day, and having done everything, to stand firm. 14 Stand therefore, and fasten the belt of truth around your waist, and put on the breastplate of righteousness. 15 As shoes for your feet put on whatever will make you ready to proclaim the gospel of peace. 16 With all of these,[b] take the shield of faith, with which you will be able to quench all the flaming arrows of the evil one. 17 Take the helmet of salvation, and the sword of the Spirit, which is the word of God.

18 Pray in the Spirit at all times in every prayer and supplication. To that end keep alert and always persevere in supplication for all the saints. 19 Pray also for me, so that when I speak, a message may be given to me to make known with boldness the mystery of the gospel,[c] 20 for which I am an ambassador in chains. Pray that I may declare it boldly, as I must speak.

Personal Matters and Benediction

21 So that you also may know how I am and what I am doing, Tych'i•cus will tell you everything. He is a dear brother and a faithful minister in the

PRAY IT!

The Peace Prayer of Saint Francis of Assisi

Ephesians 6.10–17 is a poetic passage encouraging us to resist evil. The Peace Prayer of Saint Francis of Assisi tells us how to do this—without using the imagery of warfare. After you read each line of this powerful prayer, close your eyes to meditate on its meaning for your life. What is one way you can live out each line of this prayer?

Lord, make me an instrument of your peace;
where there is hatred, let me sow love;
where there is injury, pardon;
where there is doubt, faith;
where there is despair, hope;
where there is darkness, light;
and where there is sadness, joy.
Grant that I may not so much seek
to be consoled as to console;
to be understood as to understand,
to be loved as to love;
for it is in giving that we receive,
it is in pardoning that we are pardoned,
and it is in dying that we are born to eternal life.

▸ **Eph 6.10–17**

Lord. 22 I am sending him to you for this very purpose, to let you know how we are, and to encourage your hearts.

23 Peace be to the whole community,[d] and love with faith, from God the Father and the Lord Jesus Christ. 24 Grace be with all who have an undying love for our Lord Jesus Christ.[e]

---

[a] Other ancient authorities read *your*   [b] Or *In all circumstances*   [c] Other ancient authorities lack *of the gospel*   [d] Gk *to the brothers*   [e] Other ancient authorities add *Amen*

EPH

To be, or not to be: that is the question." In this line from Shakespeare's play *Hamlet,* Hamlet wonders which is better for him—to live or to die. He doesn't want to live and suffer, but he's afraid the "sleep of death" may be worse. Either way, he loses. In the Letter to the Philippians, Paul struggles with a similar question.

At a Glance

- **1.1–26.** a greeting, thanks, and a discussion of Paul's imprisonment

- **1.27—2.18.** advice to imitate Christ

- **2.19—3.1.** plans for Timothy and Epaphroditus

- **3.2—4.9.** advice for Christian living

- **4.10–23.** thanks, a final greeting, and a blessing

In-depth

When Paul wrote this letter, he was imprisoned facing a charge that might end in his death. He wrote it either near the end of his life when he was under house arrest in Rome or, more likely, during an earlier imprisonment in Ephesus (see 1 Cor 15.32, 2 Cor 1.8).

Like Hamlet, Paul is torn: "I am hard pressed between" life and death (Phil 1.23). But unlike Hamlet, Paul feels he'll win either way: "For to me, living is Christ and dying is gain" (verse 21). In addition, Paul believes that this imprisonment will not end with his death, because he is still needed to support the new churches he helped start.

Incredibly, even in prison, Paul exhibits a spirit of hope and encouragement. In this short letter, he uses the words *joy, rejoice, be glad,* and *be cheered* seventeen times! Living in Christ doesn't mean everything will always go wonderfully. But it does mean that God can get you through the good times and the difficult times with joy.

In this letter, Paul asks the Philippians—and us—to imitate Christ. Imitating Christ is the way to keep a positive attitude even when things aren't going our way. Paul quotes an early Christian song (2.6–11) to the Philippians to show what imitating Christ means. The song praises our Lord Jesus, who chose to humble himself, chose to become a servant, and was "obedient to the point of death" (verse 8).

It is clear from this letter that Paul had a close relationship with the Philippians. No doubt, they were upset for him. Paul wanted them to rejoice and stop worrying (4.4–6). He encouraged them to present their concerns—all of them—to God in prayer. And he pointed out that if they did so, "the peace of God, which surpasses all understanding, will guard your hearts and your minds in Christ Jesus" (verse 7). What marvelous advice and comfort for people of all times and ages.

Quick Facts

Author
Paul

Date Written
A.D. 55 if from Ephesus,
A.D. 59–63 if from Rome

Audience
the church in Philippi

Philippians

Salutation

1 Paul and Timothy, servants[a] of Christ Jesus,
To all the saints in Christ Jesus who are in Phi·lip′pi, with the bishops[b] and deacons:[c]

2 Grace to you and peace from God our Father and the Lord Jesus Christ.

Paul's Prayer for the Philippians

3 I thank my God every time I remember you, 4 constantly praying with joy in every one of my prayers for all of you, 5 because of your sharing in the gospel from the first day until now. 6 I am confident of this, that the one who began a good work among you will bring it to completion by the day of Jesus Christ. 7 It is right for me to think this way about all of you, because you hold me in your heart,[d] for all of you share in God's grace[e] with me, both in my imprisonment and in the defense and confirmation of the gospel. 8 For God is my witness, how I long for all of you with the compassion of Christ Jesus. 9 And this is my prayer, that your love may overflow more and more with knowledge and full insight 10 to help you to determine what is best, so that in the day of Christ you may be pure and blameless, 11 having produced the harvest of righteousness that comes through Jesus Christ for the glory and praise of God.

Paul's Present Circumstances

12 I want you to know, beloved,[f] that what has happened to me has actually helped to spread the gospel, 13 so that it has become known throughout the whole imperial guard[g] and to everyone else that my imprisonment is for Christ; 14 and most of the brothers and sisters,[f] having been made confident in the Lord by my imprisonment, dare to speak the word[h] with greater boldness and without fear.

15 Some proclaim Christ from envy and rivalry, but others from goodwill. 16 These proclaim Christ out of love, knowing that I have been put here for the defense of the gospel; 17 the others proclaim Christ out of selfish ambition, not sincerely but intending to increase my suffering in my imprisonment. 18 What does it matter? Just this, that Christ is proclaimed in every way, whether out of false motives or true; and in that I rejoice.

Yes, and I will continue to rejoice, 19 for I know that through your prayers and the help of the Spirit of Jesus Christ this will turn out for my deliverance. 20 It is my eager expectation and hope that I will not be put to shame in any way, but that by my

---

a Gk slaves b Or overseers c Or overseers and helpers
d Or because I hold you in my heart e Gk in grace
f Gk brothers g Gk whole praetorium h Other ancient authorities read word of God

PHIL

speaking with all boldness, Christ will be exalted now as always in my body, whether by life or by death. 21 For to me, living is Christ and dying is gain. 22 If I am to live in the flesh, that means fruitful labor for me; and I do not know which I prefer. 23 I am hard pressed between the two: my desire is to depart and be with Christ, for that is far better; 24 but to remain in the flesh is more necessary for you. 25 Since I am convinced of this, I know that I will remain and continue with all of you for your progress and joy in faith, 26 so that I may share abundantly in your boasting in Christ Jesus when I come to you again.

27 Only, live your life in a manner worthy of the gospel of Christ, so that, whether I come and see you or am absent and hear about you, I will know that you are standing firm in one spirit, striving side by side with one mind for the faith of the gospel, 28 and are in no way intimidated by your opponents. For them this is evidence of their destruction, but of your salvation. And this is God's doing. 29 For he has graciously granted you the privilege not only of believing in Christ, but of suffering for him as well— 30 since you are having the same struggle that you saw I had and now hear that I still have.

Imitating Christ's Humility

2 If then there is any encouragement in Christ, any consolation from love, any sharing in the Spirit, any compassion and sympathy, 2 make my joy complete: be of the same mind, having the same love, being in full accord and of one mind. 3 Do nothing from selfish ambition or conceit, but in humility regard others as better than yourselves. 4 Let each of you look not to your own interests, but

FRIENDSHIP

In Phil 1.3–11, Paul writes beautifully of his love for and friendship with the people living in Philippi. We need to remember that Paul—and the other people who wrote the inspired words of the Scriptures—was a real person with problems and needs. He had some dear friends in Philippi, and his words to them provide a great model of true friendship: sharing the ups and downs, being committed to one another, being thankful for one another, and wanting the best for one another. Friendship in Christ is like that!

Who are true friends for you? How can you keep Christ at the center of your friendships?

▶ Phil 1.3–11

to the interests of others. 5 Let the same mind be in you that was[i] in Christ Jesus,

6 who, though he was in the form of God,
did not regard equality with God
as something to be exploited,
7 but emptied himself,
taking the form of a slave,
being born in human likeness.
And being found in human form,
8 he humbled himself
and became obedient to the point of
death—

---

i Or *that you have*

Divine Humility, Cosmic Glory   LIVE IT!

Mention the name Jesus, or the title Christ, and many images spring to mind. That is good, because no single image can capture Jesus' true nature completely.

In Phil 2.6–11, borrowing from a hymn sung in the earliest days of the church, Paul describes the mystery of Jesus Christ. Jesus willingly gave up the right to remain "in the form of God" (verse 6) and entered our world as a human being. He lived in utter humility, from his simple birth to his Crucifixion. Because of his humility and obedience, Jesus' name is exalted by God so that Jesus Christ is now Lord of all creation. Because of Jesus' humility, creation achieves cosmic harmony!

To be the loving people God calls us to be, we must imitate Christ's humility in our love for one another. Most of us are used to seeing those who are "powerful" in this world being served by others. But Paul reminds us it is the nature of Jesus to serve. Christians are called to be powerful in a radically different way—to see humble service as their basic call and the path to true glory—with the "same mind . . . that was in Christ Jesus" (verse 5).

▶ Phil 2.1–11

even death on a cross.
9 Therefore God also highly exalted him
and gave him the name
that is above every name,
10 so that at the name of Jesus
every knee should bend,
in heaven and on earth and under the
earth,
11 and every tongue should confess
that Jesus Christ is Lord,
to the glory of God the Father.

Shining as Lights in the World

12 Therefore, my beloved, just as you have always obeyed me, not only in my presence, but much more now in my absence, work out your own salvation with fear and trembling; 13 for it is God who is at work in you, enabling you both to will and to work for his good pleasure.

14 Do all things without murmuring and arguing, 15 so that you may be blameless and innocent, children of God without blemish in the midst of a crooked and perverse generation, in which you shine like stars in the world. 16 It is by your holding fast to the word of life that I can boast on the day of Christ that I did not run in vain or labor in vain. 17 But even if I am being poured out as a libation over the sacrifice and the offering of your faith, I am glad and rejoice with all of you— 18 and in the same way you also must be glad and rejoice with me.

Timothy and Epaphroditus

19 I hope in the Lord Jesus to send Timothy to you soon, so that I may be cheered by news of you. 20 I have no one like him who will be genuinely concerned for your welfare. 21 All of them are seeking their own interests, not those of Jesus Christ. 22 But Timothy's[j] worth you know, how like a son with a father he has served with me in the work of the gospel. 23 I hope therefore to send him as soon as I see how things go with me; 24 and I trust in the Lord that I will also come soon.

25 Still, I think it necessary to send to you E•paph•ro•di′tus—my brother and co-worker and fellow soldier, your messenger[k] and minister to my need; 26 for he has been longing for[l] all of you, and has been distressed because you heard that he was ill. 27 He was indeed so ill that he nearly died. But God had mercy on him, and not only on him but on me also, so that I would not have one sorrow after another. 28 I am the more eager to send him, therefore, in order that you may rejoice at seeing him again, and that I may be less anxious. 29 Welcome him then in the Lord with all joy, and honor such people, 30 because he came close to death for the work of Christ,[m] risking his life to make up for those services that you could not give me.

3 Finally, my brothers and sisters,[n] rejoice[o] in the Lord.

Breaking with the Past

To write the same things to you is not troublesome to me, and for you it is a safeguard.

2 Beware of the dogs, beware of the evil workers, beware of those who mutilate the flesh![p] 3 For it is we who are the circumcision, who worship in the Spirit of God[q] and boast in Christ Jesus and have no confidence in the flesh— 4 even though I, too, have reason for confidence in the flesh.

If anyone else has reason to be confident in the flesh, I have more: 5 circumcised on the eighth day, a member of the people of Israel, of the tribe of Benjamin, a Hebrew born of Hebrews; as to the law, a Phar′i•see; 6 as to zeal, a persecutor of the church; as to righteousness under the law, blameless.

7 Yet whatever gains I had, these I have come to regard as loss because of Christ. 8 More than that, I regard everything as loss because of the surpassing value of knowing Christ Jesus my Lord. For his sake I have suffered the loss of all things, and I regard them as rubbish, in order that I may gain Christ 9 and be found in him, not having a righteousness of my own that comes from the law, but one that comes through faith in Christ,[r] the righteousness from God based on faith. 10 I want to know Christ[s] and the power of his resurrection and the sharing of his sufferings by becoming like him in his death, 11 if somehow I may attain the resurrection from the dead.

Pressing toward the Goal

12 Not that I have already obtained this or have already reached the goal;[t] but I press on to make it my own, because Christ Jesus has made me his own. 13 Beloved,[u] I do not consider that I have made it my own;[v] but this one thing I do: forgetting what lies behind and straining forward to what lies ahead, 14 I press on toward the goal for the prize of the heavenly[w] call of God in Christ Jesus. 15 Let those of us then who are mature be of the same mind; and if you think differently about anything, this too God will reveal to you. 16 Only let us hold fast to what we have attained.

17 Brothers and sisters,[u] join in imitating me, and observe those who live according to the example you have in us. 18 For many live as enemies of the cross of Christ; I have often told you of them,

P
H
I
L

---

j Gk *his*   *k* Gk *apostle*   *l* Other ancient authorities read *longing to see*   *m* Other ancient authorities read *of the Lord*   *n* Gk *my brothers*   *o* Or *farewell*   *p* Gk *the mutilation*   *q* Other ancient authorities read *worship God in spirit*   *r* Or *through the faith of Christ*   *s* Gk *him*   *t* Or *have already been made perfect*   *u* Gk *Brothers*   *v* Other ancient authorities read *my own yet*   *w* Gk *upward*

Commitment to Your Goal

In what ways have you become more mature in the last five years? How do other people recognize that you are maturing?

In Phil 3.12–16, Paul describes one measure of maturity—the ability to keep a commitment to an ultimate goal. Mature people—whether sixteen or sixty—are always striving to perfect themselves in pursuit of their goals.

Paul says the goal that guides his life is "to know [Christ] and the power of his resurrection" (verse 10). What is the goal that guides your life? How hard is it for you to stay focused on your goal?

▶ Phil 3.12–16

P H I L

and now I tell you even with tears. 19 Their end is destruction; their god is the belly; and their glory is in their shame; their minds are set on earthly things. 20 But our citizenship[x] is in heaven, and it is from there that we are expecting a Savior, the Lord Jesus Christ. 21 He will transform the body of our humiliation[y] that it may be conformed to the body of his glory,[z] by the power that also enables him to make all things subject to himself. 1 Therefore, my brothers and sisters,[a] whom I love and long for, my joy and crown, stand firm in the Lord in this way, my beloved.

Exhortations

2 I urge Eū·ō′di·a and I urge Syn′ty·chē to be of the same mind in the Lord. 3 Yes, and I ask you also, my loyal companion,[b] help these women, for they have struggled beside me in the work of the gospel, together with Clement and the rest of my co-workers, whose names are in the book of life.

4 Rejoice[c] in the Lord always; again I will say, Rejoice.[c] 5 Let your gentleness be known to everyone. The Lord is near. 6 Do not worry about anything, but in everything by prayer and supplication with thanksgiving let your requests be made known to God. 7 And the peace of God, which surpasses all understanding, will guard your hearts and your minds in Christ Jesus.

8 Finally, beloved,[d] whatever is true, whatever is honorable, whatever is just, whatever is pure, whatever is pleasing, whatever is commendable, if there is any excellence and if there is anything worthy of praise, think about[e] these things. 9 Keep on doing the things that you have learned and received and heard and seen in me, and the God of peace will be with you.

Acknowledgment of the Philippians' Gift

10 I rejoice[f] in the Lord greatly that now at last you have revived your concern for me; indeed, you were concerned for me, but had no opportunity to show it.[g] 11 Not that I am referring to being in need; for I have learned to be content with whatever I have. 12 I know what it is to have little, and I know what it is to have plenty. In any and all circumstances I have learned the secret of being well-fed and of going hungry, of having plenty and of being in need. 13 I can do all things through him who strengthens me. 14 In any case, it was kind of you to share my distress.

15 You Phi·lip′pi·ans indeed know that in the early days of the gospel, when I left Mac·e·dō′ni·a, no church shared with me in the matter of giving and receiving, except you alone. 16 For even when I was in Thes·sa·lo·ni′ca, you sent me help for my needs more than once. 17 Not that I seek the gift,

4.4

x Or commonwealth   y Or our humble bodies   z Or his glorious body   a Gk my brothers   b Or loyal Syzygus   c Or Farewell   d Gk brothers   e Gk take account of   f Gk I rejoiced   g Gk lacks to show it

THE BEAUTY OF CREATION

Paul ends his message to the Philippians by encouraging them to keep their minds on anything that is of excellence and worthy of praise. This would certainly include the wonder and beauty of creation. Let this Native American Navajo prayer in praise of creation inspire you to keep focused on the beauty God has provided in the world around us:

> *I walk with beauty before me*
> *I walk with beauty behind me*
> *I walk with beauty above me*
> *I walk with beauty below me*
> *Beauty has been restored from the East*
> *Beauty has been restored from the South*
> *Beauty has been restored from the West*
> *Beauty has been restored from the North*
> *Beauty has been restored from the sky-top*
> *Beauty has been restored from the earth-bottom*
> *Beauty has been restored from all around me*
> **(From Michael F. Steltenkamp, The Sacred Vision, p. 92)**

▸ Phil 4.8–9

but I seek the profit that accumulates to your account. 18 I have been paid in full and have more than enough; I am fully satisfied, now that I have received from E·paph·ro·di′tus the gifts you sent, a fragrant offering, a sacrifice acceptable and pleasing to God. 19 And my God will fully satisfy every need of yours according to his riches in glory in Christ Jesus. 20 To our God and Father be glory forever and ever. Amen.

Final Greetings and Benediction

21 Greet every saint in Christ Jesus. The friends[h] who are with me greet you. 22 All the saints greet you, especially those of the emperor's household.

23 The grace of the Lord Jesus Christ be with your spirit.[i]

---

[h] Gk *brothers*   [i] Other ancient authorities add *Amen*

Every now and then, we hear about some cult on the news. All cults tend to have the same characteristics: strict rules, strange ideas, and total obedience to the leader. Cults have been around a long time. In fact, some strange things that sounded pretty cultish were going on in the early Christian community at Colossae. The author's advice in the Letter to the Colossians is pretty direct: Let Christ be the one and only ruler in your heart!

At a Glance

- **1.1–14.** a greeting
- **1.15—2.3.** a description of Christ as the First, the Creator, the One
- **2.4–23.** warnings against false teachers
- **3.1—4.6.** advice for Christian living
- **4.7–18.** final greetings

In-depth

This letter attacks a group that was teaching a weird mixture of ideas. It insisted on rituals (2.16), plenty of regulations (verse 22), severe treatment of one's own body (verse 23), special festivals (verse 16), and a fancy philosophy that included "the elemental spirits of the universe" (verse 8). This strange group might have had Jewish roots, because it observed the Sabbath (verse 16). The biggest concern was that it was teaching that faith in Christ's death and Resurrection was not enough for salvation.

Against the backdrop of all this mysterious thinking, the author—who may not have been Paul but a disciple of Paul—declares the supreme mystery of Christ. Quoting a Christian hymn (1.15–20), the writer says Christ is lifted up not only as the firstborn of creation, but also as the one through whom everything was created and who holds everything together. Christ is all we need!

Christians believe that Jesus is more than just a great teacher; they believe Jesus is God, who chose to become human and live with us. This letter gives us an early statement of that belief: "In [Christ] the whole fullness of deity dwells bodily" (2.9).

The Letter to the Colossians also offers comforting words about our God. God has given us life and forgiveness. God erased the record of our sins, and set it aside, "nailing it to the cross" (verse 14). Unlike cults that burden their followers with guilt and impossible rules, our God frees us from guilt and gives us life! As you read this letter, you will find these and many other words to live by: "God's chosen ones . . . forgive each other . . . clothe yourselves with love . . . And let the peace of Christ rule in your hearts" (3.12–15).

Quick Facts

Author
Paul or equally likely a follower of Paul (see "Introduction to the Letters and Revelation")

Date Written
around A.D. 61 if by Paul, after A.D. 61 if by a follower

Audience
the Christian community at Colossae

Colossians

3.12

Salutation

1 Paul, an apostle of Christ Jesus by the will of God, and Timothy our brother,

2 To the saints and faithful brothers and sisters[a] in Christ in Co·los'saē:

Grace to you and peace from God our Father.

Paul Thanks God for the Colossians

3 In our prayers for you we always thank God, the Father of our Lord Jesus Christ, 4 for we have heard of your faith in Christ Jesus and of the love that you have for all the saints, 5 because of the hope laid up for you in heaven. You have heard of this hope before in the word of the truth, the gospel 6 that has come to you. Just as it is bearing fruit and growing in the whole world, so it has been bearing fruit among yourselves from the day you heard it and truly comprehended the grace of God. 7 This you learned from Ep'a·phras, our beloved fellow servant.[b] He is a faithful minister of Christ on your[c] behalf, 8 and he has made known to us your love in the Spirit.

9 For this reason, since the day we heard it, we have not ceased praying for you and asking that you may be filled with the knowledge of God's[d] will in all spiritual wisdom and understanding, 10 so that you may lead lives worthy of the Lord, fully pleasing to him, as you bear fruit in every good work and as you grow in the knowledge of God. 11 May you be made strong with all the strength that comes from his glorious power, and may you be prepared to endure everything with patience, while joyfully 12 giving thanks to the Father, who has enabled[e] you[f] to share in the inheritance of the saints in the light. 13 He has rescued us from the power of darkness and transferred us into the kingdom of his beloved Son, 14 in whom we have redemption, the forgiveness of sins.[g]

The Supremacy of Christ
(Cp Jn 1.1–5)

15 He is the image of the invisible God, the firstborn of all creation; 16 for in[h] him all things in heaven and on earth were created, things visible and invisible, whether thrones or dominions or rulers or powers—all things have been created through him and for him. 17 He himself is before all things, and in[h] him all things hold together. 18 He is the head of the body, the church; he is the beginning, the firstborn from the dead, so that he might come to have first place in everything. 19 For in him all the fullness of God was pleased to dwell, 20 and through him God was pleased to reconcile to himself all things, whether on earth or in heaven, by making peace through the blood of his cross.

---

a Gk *brothers* *b* Gk *slave* *c* Other ancient authorities read *our* *d* Gk *his* *e* Other ancient authorities read *called* *f* Other ancient authorities read *us* *g* Other ancient authorities add *through his blood* *h* Or *by*

The Image of God

It is possible to describe God by naming certain characteristics. We can say God is all-powerful, all-knowing, and eternal. But knowing about God is not the same as knowing God. So how can we really understand the mysterious, invisible, eternal God?

The author of Colossians gives us a clue. This writer calls Jesus "the image of the invisible God" (Col 1.15). If we want to know about God, who is hidden from us in mystery, we look at Christ. God has existed for all eternity; through God, all things were created; and in God, all things continue to "hold together." But God also appeared on our earth as a real human being, Jesus.

Is there still mystery? Yes. We still cannot comprehend God completely. But we can understand more about God by getting to know more about Jesus Christ.

▸ Col 1.15–20

---

21 And you who were once estranged and hostile in mind, doing evil deeds, 22 he has now reconciled[i] in his fleshly body[j] through death, so as to present you holy and blameless and irreproachable before him— 23 provided that you continue securely established and steadfast in the faith, without shifting from the hope promised by the gospel that you heard, which has been proclaimed to every creature under heaven. I, Paul, became a servant of this gospel.

Paul's Interest in the Colossians

24 I am now rejoicing in my sufferings for your sake, and in my flesh I am completing what is lacking in Christ's afflictions for the sake of his body, that is, the church. 25 I became its servant according to God's commission that was given to me for you, to make the word of God fully known, 26 the mystery that has been hidden throughout the ages and generations but has now been revealed to his saints. 27 To them God chose to make known how great among the Gentiles are the riches of the glory of this mystery, which is Christ in you, the hope of glory. 28 It is he whom we proclaim, warning everyone and teaching everyone in all wisdom, so that we may present everyone mature in Christ. 29 For this I toil and struggle with all the energy that he powerfully inspires within me.

2 For I want you to know how much I am struggling for you, and for those in La·o·di·cē'a, and for all who have not seen me face to face. 2 I want their hearts to be encouraged and united in love, so that they may have all the riches of assured understanding and have the knowledge of God's mystery, that is, Christ himself,[k] 3 in whom are hidden all the treasures of wisdom and knowledge. 4 I am saying this so that no one may deceive you with plausible arguments. 5 For though I am absent in body, yet I am with you in spirit, and I rejoice to see your morale and the firmness of your faith in Christ.

---

i Other ancient authorities read *you have now been reconciled*   j Gk *in the body of his flesh*   k Other ancient authorities read *of the mystery of God, both of the Father and of Christ*

Where Are Your Roots?

What is one thing that motivates you, that keeps you going? Is it a special friendship or a close family? the drive to succeed or to be the best? Maybe it's having a car or holding down a job.

Colossians 2.7 says that we should be "rooted and built up in[Christ]." Where you have your roots is where you get your nourishment to keep going. Think again about what motivates you. Is it enough to nourish a full, rich life?

In your prayer, journal or reflect on the following questions:

■ What things are most important in your life right now? Where is God in each of those things?

■ What do you need to reorder so that God "might come to have first place" in your life (1.18)?

▸ Col 2.6–7

Fullness of Life in Christ

6 As you therefore have received Christ Jesus the Lord, continue to live your lives[l] in him, 7 rooted and built up in him and established in the faith, just as you were taught, abounding in thanksgiving.

8 See to it that no one takes you captive through philosophy and empty deceit, according to human tradition, according to the elemental spirits of the universe,[m] and not according to Christ. 9 For in him the whole fullness of deity dwells bodily, 10 and you have come to fullness in him, who is the head of every ruler and authority. 11 In him also you were circumcised with a spiritual circumcision,[n] by putting off the body of the flesh in the circumcision of Christ; 12 when you were buried with him in baptism, you were also raised with him through faith in the power of God, who raised him from the dead. 13 And when you were dead in trespasses and the uncircumcision of your flesh, God[o] made you[p] alive together with him, when he forgave us all our trespasses, 14 erasing the record that stood against us with its legal demands. He set this aside, nailing it to the cross. 15 He disarmed[q] the rulers and authorities and made a public example of them, triumphing over them in it.

16 Therefore do not let anyone condemn you in matters of food and drink or of observing festivals, new moons, or sabbaths. 17 These are only a shadow of what is to come, but the substance belongs to Christ. 18 Do not let anyone disqualify you, insisting on self-abasement and worship of angels, dwelling[r] on visions,[s] puffed up without cause by a human way of thinking,[t] 19 and not holding fast to the head, from whom the whole body, nourished and held together by its ligaments and sinews, grows with a growth that is from God.

Warnings against False Teachers

20 If with Christ you died to the elemental spirits of the universe,[m] why do you live as if you still belonged to the world? Why do you submit to regulations, 21 "Do not handle, Do not taste, Do not touch"? 22 All these regulations refer to things that perish with use; they are simply human commands and teachings. 23 These have indeed an appearance of wisdom in promoting self-imposed piety, humility, and severe treatment of the body, but they are of no value in checking self" indulgence.[u]

The New Life in Christ

3 So if you have been raised with Christ, seek the things that are above, where Christ is, seated at the right hand of God. 2 Set your minds on things that are above, not on things that are on earth, 3 for you have died, and your life is hidden with Christ in God. 4 When Christ who is your[v] life is revealed, then you also will be revealed with him in glory.

5 Put to death, therefore, whatever in you is earthly: fornication, impurity, passion, evil desire,

C
O
L

l Gk to walk   m Or the rudiments of the world   n Gk a circumcision made without hands   o Gk he   p Other ancient authorities read made us; others, made   q Or divested himself of   r Other ancient authorities read not dwelling   s Meaning of Gk uncertain   t Gk by the mind of his flesh   u Or are of no value, serving only to indulge the flesh   v Other authorities read our

A Top-Shelf Life

LIVE IT!

In stores, the best product is often put on the top shelf, for all to see. It is also usually priced higher than other products, and therefore is not purchased by everyone. Colossians 3.1 calls us to "seek the things that are above, where Christ is"—in other words, a top-shelf life.

Living a top-shelf life means living a moral life, free from sin. It means ridding ourselves of "anger, wrath, malice, slander, and abusive language" (verse 8). It means avoiding "fornication, impurity, . . . strife, jealousy, anger, quarrels, dissensions, factions, envy, drunkenness, carousing" (Gal 5.19–21). It also means living with "compassion, kindness, humility, meekness, and patience," and forgiving one another and clothing ourselves with love (Col 3.12–14). Paul and the other authors of the letters focus on moral living because it is what God wants for us. How could we claim to have faith in Jesus Christ and choose to live in sin?

Living a moral life, a top-shelf life, isn't always easy. But it is the way to true happiness, holiness, and health. This is the witness of the church and generations of Christian believers. Why settle for less?

▸ Col 3.1–4

Thessalonians

The First Letter to the

You're about to read what is probably the oldest book in the New Testament. It was written a little over twenty years after Jesus' death and Resurrection, by a man named Paul. It is the very first Christian letter that we still have! In it, Paul answers some questions that were on people's minds back then. Even though it was written so long ago, you might have some of the same questions.

In-depth

Thessalonica was the capital of a Roman province called Macedonia. Today, that area is in northern Greece (see map 7, "Paul's First and Second Journeys"). Acts of the Apostles, chapter 17, tells us that Paul spent three weeks in Thessalonica preaching about Jesus Christ. Because of his preaching, many people, mainly Gentiles (non-Jews), became Christians. Paul was forced to leave the city by the non-Christians there. After he left, he worried about the new Christian community, so he sent his coworker Timothy back to check things out. When Timothy rejoined Paul, he had some great news. Even though the Thessalonians were being persecuted, they were staying strong in their "faith and love" (1 Thess 3.6).

When you read this letter, you can tell that Paul is thankful that the church is thriving! Four different times he expresses his gratitude. But he also apparently feels the need to defend himself against some critics. So he reminds everyone that he has been genuine and "like a nurse tenderly caring for her own children" (2.7).

After reassuring the Thessalonians that the persecution they are suffering is to be expected (3.3–4), Paul takes the time to answer some questions about the coming of the Lord at the end of time. Apparently, some of the Thessalonians are concerned about their friends who have already died. Will they join the living when Christ returns again?

Paul tells them that they don't have to worry about those who die before Jesus returns; the dead will be raised first and join the living, to "be with the Lord forever" (4.17). When will that happen? they ask. No one knows, Paul says, but Christians don't have to be afraid of that day. Their job is to stay alert and clothe themselves with "faith and love, and . . . hope" (5.8).

At a Glance

- **Chapter 1.** a greeting
- **Chapters 2–3.** a discussion of Paul's ministry and Timothy's trip
- **4.1—5.11.** advice about life now and the life to come
- **5.12–28.** final advice and a blessing

Quick Facts

Author
Paul

Date Written
A.D. 51

Audience
the mainly Gentile church in Thessalonica

1 Thessalonians

5.4-6

Salutation

1 Paul, Sil•vā′nus, and Timothy,
To the church of the Thes•sa•lō′ni•ans in God the Father and the Lord Jesus Christ:
Grace to you and peace.

The Thessalonians' Faith and Example

2 We always give thanks to God for all of you and mention you in our prayers, constantly 3 remembering before our God and Father your work of faith and labor of love and steadfastness of hope in our Lord Jesus Christ. 4 For we know, brothers and sisters[a] beloved by God, that he has chosen you, 5 because our message of the gospel came to you not in word only, but also in power and in the Holy Spirit and with full conviction; just as you know what kind of persons we proved to be among you for your sake. 6 And you became imitators of us and of the Lord, for in spite of persecution you received the word with joy inspired by the Holy Spirit, 7 so that you became an example to all the believers in Mac•e•dō′ni•a and in A•chā′i•a. 8 For the word of the Lord has sounded forth from you not only in Mac•e•dō′ni•a and A•chā′i•a, but in every place your faith in God has become known, so that we have no need to speak about it. 9 For the people of those regions[b] report about us what kind of welcome we had among you, and how you turned to God from idols, to serve a living and true God, 10 and to wait for his Son from heaven, whom he raised from the dead—Jesus, who rescues us from the wrath that is coming.

Paul's Ministry in Thessalonica
(Cp Acts 17.1–9)

2 You yourselves know, brothers and sisters,[a] that our coming to you was not in vain, 2 but though we had already suffered and been shamefully mistreated at Phi•lip′pī, as you know, we had courage in our God to declare to you the gospel of God in spite of great opposition. 3 For our appeal does not spring from deceit or impure motives or trickery, 4 but just as we have been approved by God to be entrusted with the message of the gospel, even so we speak, not to please mortals, but to please God who tests our hearts. 5 As you know and as God is our witness, we never came with words of flattery or with a pretext for greed; 6 nor did we seek praise from mortals, whether from you or from others, 7 though we might have made demands as apostles of Christ. But we were gentle[c] among you, like a nurse tenderly caring for her own children. 8 So deeply do we care for you that we are determined to share with you not only the gospel of God but also our own selves, because you have become very dear to us.

9 You remember our labor and toil, brothers

---

a Gk *brothers*   *b* Gk *For they*   *c* Other ancient authorities read *infants*

PRAY IT!
Doing the Right Thing

Angela normally keeps to herself. But the three girls teasing Nicole have her almost in tears. Angela hesitates to say anything. But then, she looks at her WWJD ("What would Jesus do?") bracelet and speaks up: "Stop it, you guys. Can't you see you are hurting Nicole's feelings?" The three girls are quiet for a second. Then, they start in on Angela. "Hey, this isn't your business. Who do you think you are telling us what to do?" The comments sting, but despite them, Angela experiences a growing sense of peace, almost as if she can feel Jesus smiling at her.

Lord, make me stronger. Stronger to do the right thing—the Christlike thing—the next time I'm in a hurtful situation. Stronger to declare my faith in you as the reason for my actions. Stronger even to forgive those who insult me.

Jesus, give me the courage to live out what I believe in my heart, and allow me the wisdom to know that it comes from you. Amen.

▶ 1 Thess 2.1–2

and sisters,[d] we worked night and day, so that we might not burden any of you while we proclaimed to you the gospel of God. 10 You are witnesses, and God also, how pure, upright, and blameless our conduct was toward you believers. 11 As you know, we dealt with each one of you like a father with his children, 12 urging and encouraging you and pleading that you lead a life worthy of God, who calls you into his own kingdom and glory.

13 We also constantly give thanks to God for this, that when you received the word of God that you heard from us, you accepted it not as a human word but as what it really is, God's word, which is also at work in you believers. 14 For you, brothers and sisters,[d] became imitators of the churches of God in Christ Jesus that are in Judea, for you suffered the same things from your own compatriots as they did from the Jews, 15 who killed both the Lord Jesus and the prophets,[e] and drove us out; they displease God and oppose everyone 16 by hindering us from speaking to the Gentiles so that they may

be saved. Thus they have constantly been filling up the measure of their sins; but God's wrath has overtaken them at last.[f]

Paul's Desire to Visit the Thessalonians Again

17 As for us, brothers and sisters,[d] when, for a short time, we were made orphans by being separated from you—in person, not in heart—we longed with great eagerness to see you face to face. 18 For we wanted to come to you—certainly I, Paul, wanted to again and again—but Satan blocked our way. 19 For what is our hope or joy or crown of boasting before our Lord Jesus at his coming? Is it not you? 20 Yes, you are our glory and joy!

3 Therefore when we could bear it no longer, we decided to be left alone in Athens; 2 and we sent Timothy, our brother and co-worker for God in proclaiming[g] the gospel of Christ, to strengthen and encourage you for the sake of your faith, 3 so that no one would be shaken by these

---

d Gk *brothers*   *e* Other ancient authorities read *their own prophets*   *f* Or *completely* or *forever*   *g* Gk lacks *proclaiming*

PRAY IT!
Encouragement

Sometimes, we feel alone in our faith. We wonder if anyone feels, thinks, or prays the way we do. As a first missionary of the faith, Paul must have experienced his share of dark days when he wondered if the people would really accept the Good News. He must have been so encouraged when Timothy returned to tell him of the "faith and love" of the Thessalonians (1 Thess 3.6).

The Christian faith is never meant to be held privately. We don't grow in our faith, hope, and love by being isolated from other people. Like Paul, we need the encouragement and challenge of other people: our family, friends, and the entire Christian community.

In your prayer, reflect or journal on the following questions:
- How do you encourage others to grow in Christ?
- How do others encourage or challenge you to grow in faith, hope, and love?

▶ 1 Thess 3.6–13

1 THESS

persecutions. Indeed, you yourselves know that this is what we are destined for. 4 In fact, when we were with you, we told you beforehand that we were to suffer persecution; so it turned out, as you know. 5 For this reason, when I could bear it no longer, I sent to find out about your faith; I was afraid that somehow the tempter had tempted you and that our labor had been in vain.

Timothy's Encouraging Report

6 But Timothy has just now come to us from you, and has brought us the good news of your faith and love. He has told us also that you always remember us kindly and long to see us—just as we long to see you. 7 For this reason, brothers and sisters,*h* during all our distress and persecution we have been encouraged about you through your faith. 8 For we now live, if you continue to stand firm in the Lord. 9 How can we thank God enough for you in return for all the joy that we feel before our God because of you? 10 Night and day we pray most earnestly that we may see you face to face and restore whatever is lacking in your faith.

11 Now may our God and Father himself and our Lord Jesus direct our way to you. 12 And may the Lord make you increase and abound in love for one another and for all, just as we abound in love for you. 13 And may he so strengthen your hearts in holiness that you may be blameless before our God and Father at the coming of our Lord Jesus with all his saints.

h Gk *brothers*

Catholic Connections

THE COMMUNION OF SAINTS

Many early Christians thought the world would end during their lifetime. So when people started to die before Jesus returned and the world was made new, they were concerned. Paul didn't want his Thessalonian friends to worry about their dead friends and family. He assured them that just as Jesus died and rose again, so the "dead in Christ will rise" (1 Thess 4.16). A time would come when those who were alive would meet the Lord along with the risen dead.

Grief always comes with the death of someone we love. But for Christians, there is also the joy of knowing that the person will rise again to be with God. Those who believe have God's promise that they will someday be together again in the communion of saints—which is the whole church, including the Christians who are alive and those who have died.

▶ 1 Thess 4.13–18

True Love Waits

LIVE IT!

The church has taught from its beginning that fornication, including pre-marital sex, is wrong. Paul's teaching in 1 Thess 4.1–8 clearly explains why. If we get involved in a sexual relationship outside of marriage, we are exploiting another person (verse 6)—even if that person is a willing partner. God intends sexual intercourse to create a lifelong bond between a man and a woman for the creation of a family. Sexual expression outside of marriage diminishes the beautiful purpose of sexual intimacy.

Paul reminds the Thessalonians to live in ways pleasing to God. To behave contrary to God's purpose is to say no to the gift of the Holy Spirit and to the holiness God wants for us. In our culture, sex is often portrayed as a recreational activity, violating the gift of sexuality God created within us! God's message in the Bible and the church calls us to take a stand that is unpopular with some people—to support sexual abstinence until marriage.

Valuing our gift of sexuality and expressing it as God intended is not always easy. Think about it!

▶ 1 Thess 4.1–8

ANCIENT PRAYER OF THANKSGIVING

This ancient prayer—although clearly not addressed to the one God who is creator of all—is still a beautiful expression of thankfulness for the wonders of the natural world. It can remind us of Paul's instruction to the Thessalonians (5.16–24) to give thanks without ceasing.

We return thanks to our mother,
the earth, which sustains us.
We return thanks to the rivers and streams,
which supply us with water.
We return thanks to all herbs,
which furnish medicines for the cure to our diseases.
We return thanks to the corn, and to her sisters,
the beans and squashes,
which give us life.
We return thanks to the bushes and trees,
which provide us with fruit.
We return thanks to the wind,
which, moving in the air, has banished diseases.
We return thanks to the moon and stars,
which have given to us their light
when the sun was gone.
We return thanks to our grandfather Hé-no,
that he has protected his grandchildren
from witches and reptiles,
and has given to us his rain.
We return thanks to the sun,
that he has looked upon the earth
with a beneficent eye.
Lastly, we return thanks to the Great Spirit,
in whom is embodied all goodness,
and who directs all things
for the good of his children.
(From David Schiller, editor, The Little Book of Prayers, pp. 154–155)

▶ I Thess 5.16–24

A Life Pleasing to God

4 Finally, brothers and sisters,[i] we ask and urge you in the Lord Jesus that, as you learned from us how you ought to live and to please God (as, in fact, you are doing), you should do so more and more. 2 For you know what instructions we gave you through the Lord Jesus. 3 For this is the will of God, your sanctification: that you abstain from fornication; 4 that each one of you know how to control your own body[j] in holiness and honor, 5 not with lustful passion, like the Gentiles who do not know God; 6 that no one wrong or exploit a brother or sister[k] in this matter, because the Lord is an avenger in all these things, just as we have already told you beforehand and solemnly warned you. 7 For God did not call us to impurity but in holiness. 8 Therefore whoever rejects this rejects not

---

i Gk brothers   j Or how to take a wife for himself
k Gk brother

human authority but God, who also gives his Holy Spirit to you.

9 Now concerning love of the brothers and sisters,[l] you do not need to have anyone write to you, for you yourselves have been taught by God to love one another; 10 and indeed you do love all the brothers and sisters[l] throughout Mac•e•dō'ni•a. But we urge you, beloved,[l] to do so more and more, 11 to aspire to live quietly, to mind your own affairs, and to work with your hands, as we directed you, 12 so that you may behave properly toward outsiders and be dependent on no one.

The Coming of the Lord

13 But we do not want you to be uninformed, brothers and sisters,[l] about those who have died,[m] so that you may not grieve as others do who have no hope. 14 For since we believe that Jesus died and rose again, even so, through Jesus, God will bring with him those who have died.[m] 15 For this we declare to you by the word of the Lord, that we who are alive, who are left until the coming of the Lord, will by no means precede those who have died.[m] 16 For the Lord himself, with a cry of command, with the archangel's call and with the sound of

God's trumpet, will descend from heaven, and the dead in Christ will rise first. 17 Then we who are alive, who are left, will be caught up in the clouds together with them to meet the Lord in the air; and so we will be with the Lord forever. 18 Therefore encourage one another with these words.

5 Now concerning the times and the seasons, brothers and sisters,[l] you do not need to have anything written to you. 2 For you yourselves know very well that the day of the Lord will come like a thief in the night. 3 When they say, "There is peace and security," then sudden destruction will come upon them, as labor pains come upon a pregnant woman, and there will be no escape! 4 But you, beloved,[l] are not in darkness, for that day to surprise you like a thief; 5 for you are all children of light and children of the day; we are not of the night or of darkness. 6 So then let us not fall asleep as others do, but let us keep awake and be sober; 7 for those who sleep sleep at night, and those who are drunk get drunk at night. 8 But since we belong to the day, let us be sober, and put on the breastplate of faith and love, and for a helmet the hope of

---

[l] Gk brothers   [m] Gk fallen asleep

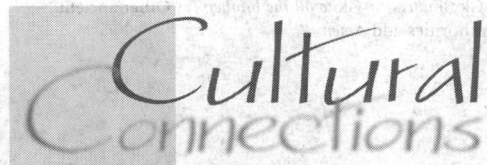

GIVE THANKS AT ALL TIMES!

Gratitude is an essential element of the Christian faith for Mexican people. We turn to the Scriptures and Tradition for examples of gratitude in all things. Mary, the mother of Jesus, personified this gratitude when she accepted the responsibility of bearing the Son of God in her womb. Paul continually promoted gratitude in his letters to the first Christians.

To be grateful, we must humbly open up to receiving and acknowledging God's many gifts to us. When we do this, we express our gratitude for God's gifts by loving God and neighbor. Expressing love is an automatic response for someone who is grateful.

Juan Diego, a sixteenth-century Mexican man, opened up to the love and message of Our Lady of Guadalupe, who appeared to him on Tepeyac Hill, today located within Mexico City. In the spirit of gratitude, Juan Diego wanted to share the news of this loving appearance. After persistently speaking about it and eventually providing proof of the appearance to his local bishop, he was finally listened to and believed. For hundreds of years, a church, which is now a basilica, has stood on Tepeyac Hill. Mary had asked Juan Diego to see that a church was built there.

Juan Diego's message and Mary's message to him continue to be spread today in the lives of Mexicans. Because Juan Diego's gratitude was so great and because he shared his gratitude with so many others, Pope John Paul II declared him a saint on 31 July 2002.

▸ 1 Thess 5.18

salvation. 9 For God has destined us not for wrath but for obtaining salvation through our Lord Jesus Christ, 10 who died for us, so that whether we are awake or asleep we may live with him. 11 Therefore encourage one another and build up each other, as indeed you are doing.

Final Exhortations, Greetings, and Benediction

12 But we appeal to you, brothers and sisters,n to respect those who labor among you, and have charge of you in the Lord and admonish you; 13 esteem them very highly in love because of their work. Be at peace among yourselves. 14 And we urge you, beloved,n to admonish the idlers, encourage the fainthearted, help the weak, be patient with all of them. 15 See that none of you repays evil for evil, but always seek to do good to one another and to all. 16 Rejoice always, 17 pray without ceasing, 18 give thanks in all circumstances; for this is the will of God in Christ Jesus for you. 19 Do not quench the Spirit. 20 Do not despise the words of prophets,o 21 but test everything; hold fast to what is good; 22 abstain from every form of evil.

23 May the God of peace himself sanctify you entirely; and may your spirit and soul and body be kept soundp and blameless at the coming of our Lord Jesus Christ. 24 The one who calls you is faithful, and he will do this.

> # Test everything;
>
> ☑ hold fast   ☑ abstain from
> to what is   every form
> good;   of evil
>
> 5.21–22

25 Beloved,q pray for us.
26 Greet all the brothers and sistersn with a holy kiss. 27 I solemnly command you by the Lord that this letter be read to all of them.r
28 The grace of our Lord Jesus Christ be with you.s

---

n Gk brothers   o Gk despise prophecies   p Or complete
q Gk Brothers   r Gk to all the brothers   s Other ancient authorities add Amen

Has a parent or another adult ever said to you, "You know, when I was your age," and launched into some story about how hard it was in the "good old days"? It seems all past generations, including those who lived in biblical times, had their struggles and challenges. When the Thessalonians were going through some really tough times, Paul's second letter to them promised that if they continued to trust God, everything would come out right.

At a Glance

- **Chapter 1.** a greeting
- **Chapter 2.** information about the day of the Lord
- **3.1–14.** a prayer request, and warning against idleness
- **3.16–18.** a final blessing

In-depth

From the short Second Letter to the Thessalonians, it appears the Thessalonians were experiencing two problems. First, they were being persecuted by non-Christians. Second, some of them were becoming confused over "the coming of our Lord Jesus Christ" (2.1), sometimes called the Second Coming. Word was being spread that Jesus had already come again (verse 2)! And some believers may have been using that as an excuse not to work and earn their keep (3.6).

This letter speaks to the Thessalonians using apocalyptic language (see "Apocalyptic Literature," Daniel, chapters 7–10; and the introduction to Revelation). It tells the Thessalonians to have peace and not let themselves be deceived, "for that day will not come unless the rebellion comes first and the lawless one is revealed, the one destined for destruction" (2.3). It also tells them to have hope because at the end time, Christ will overcome all evil and will destroy the lawless one.

This letter is not as warm and personal as 1 Thessalonians. Perhaps that's because it's filled with the sobering awareness that persecution is here to stay, and that evil and deception are all around. In such an environment, the letter advises the Thessalonians—and us—to "stand firm and hold fast to the traditions that you were taught" (verse 15).

Quick Facts

Author
possibly Paul, but more likely a disciple of Paul

Date Written
around A.D. 51 if by Paul, A.D. 70–90 if by a disciple

Audience
the mainly Gentile (non-Jewish) church in Thessalonica

Thessalonians

The Second Letter to the

2 Thessalonians

Salutation

1 Paul, Sil·vā′nus, and Timothy,

To the church of the Thes·sa·lō′ni·ans in God our Father and the Lord Jesus Christ:

2 Grace to you and peace from God our*a* Father and the Lord Jesus Christ.

Thanksgiving

3 We must always give thanks to God for you, brothers and sisters,*b* as is right, because your faith is growing abundantly, and the love of every one of you for one another is increasing. 4 Therefore we ourselves boast of you among the churches of God for your steadfastness and faith during all your persecutions and the afflictions that you are enduring.

The Judgment at Christ's Coming

5 This is evidence of the righteous judgment of God, and is intended to make you worthy of the kingdom of God, for which you are also suffering. 6 For it is indeed just of God to repay with affliction those who afflict you, 7 and to give relief to the afflicted as well as to us, when the Lord Jesus is revealed from heaven with his mighty angels 8 in flaming fire, inflicting vengeance on those who do not know God and on those who do not obey the gospel of our Lord Jesus. 9 These will suffer the punishment of eternal destruction, separated from the presence of the Lord and from the glory of his might, 10 when he comes to be glorified by his saints and to be marveled at on that day among all who have believed, because our testimony to you was believed. 11 To this end we always pray for you, asking that our God will make you worthy of his call and will fulfill by his power every good resolve and work of faith, 12 so that the name of our Lord Jesus may be glorified in you, and you in him, according to the grace of our God and the Lord Jesus Christ.

The Man of Lawlessness

2 As to the coming of our Lord Jesus Christ and our being gathered together to him, we beg you, brothers and sisters,*b* 2 not to be quickly shaken in mind or alarmed, either by spirit or by word or by letter, as though from us, to the effect that the day of the Lord is already here. 3 Let no one deceive you in any way; for that day will not come unless the rebellion comes first and the lawless one*c* is revealed, the one destined for destruction.*d* 4 He opposes and exalts himself above every so-called god or object of worship, so that he takes his seat in the temple of God, declaring himself to be God. 5 Do you not remember that I told you these things when I was still with you? 6 And you know what is now restraining him, so that he may be revealed

---

a Other ancient authorities read *the* *b* Gk *brothers*
c Gk *the man of lawlessness*; other ancient authorities read *the man of sin* *d* Gk *the son of destruction*

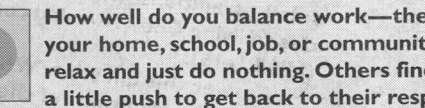

The Parousia

After Jesus' death and Resurrection, the early Christians start to wait for his Second Coming, also called the Parousia. They think Jesus will return soon in glory to judge the living and the dead and to bring to complete fulfillment the Reign of God. They even see some signs of his imminent arrival and express an urgent call to be prepared. Paul seems to expect Christ's return in the near future but insists that nobody can predict when. He emphasizes the importance of living the Gospel and always being prepared for "our being gathered together to him" (2 Thess 2.1).

The important message for us today is that our history has meaning and purpose and that Christ ultimately triumphs over sin and death. The various descriptions of the signs preceding the end time are intended not to predict the future but rather to encourage us to live the Gospel as we wait in hope for Christ's glorious return.

▸ **2 Thess 1.5—2.17**

when his time comes. 7 For the mystery of lawlessness is already at work, but only until the one who now restrains it is removed. 8 And then the lawless one will be revealed, whom the Lord Jesus*e* will destroy*f* with the breath of his mouth, annihilating him by the manifestation of his coming. 9 The coming of the lawless one is apparent in the working of Satan, who uses all power, signs, lying wonders, 10 and every kind of wicked deception for those who are perishing, because they refused to love the truth and so be saved. 11 For this reason God sends them a powerful delusion, leading them to believe what is false, 12 so that all who have not believed the truth but took pleasure in unrighteousness will be condemned.

Chosen for Salvation

13 But we must always give thanks to God for you, brothers and sisters*g* beloved by the Lord, because God chose you as the first fruits*h* for salvation through sanctification by the Spirit and through belief in the truth. 14 For this purpose he called you through our proclamation of the good news,*i* so that you may obtain the glory of our Lord Jesus Christ. 15 So then, brothers and sisters,*g* stand firm and hold fast to the traditions that you were taught by us, either by word of mouth or by our letter.

16 Now may our Lord Jesus Christ himself and God our Father, who loved us and through grace gave us eternal comfort and good hope, 17 comfort your hearts and strengthen them in every good work and word.

---

e Other ancient authorities lack *Jesus*   *f* Other ancient authorities read *consume*   *g* Gk *brothers*   *h* Other ancient authorities read *from the beginning*   *i* Or *through our gospel*

Laziness

LIVE IT!

How well do you balance work—the things you are expected to do in your home, school, job, or community—with leisure? Workaholics find it hard to relax and just do nothing. Others find it easy to loosen up and recreate, and need a little push to get back to their responsibilities.

Evidently, some of the early Thessalonians are determined to avoid work altogether (2 Thess 3.6), presuming they can depend on the Christian community to feed and take care of them. Perhaps they feel that if the Second Coming is close, there is no need to work. The author of 2 Thessalonians sees this idleness as destructive for the church. His answer is simple: no work, no food (verse 10).

Christ invites us not to a life of laziness, where we take advantage of the kindness of others, but to an active life. Our work ought to be an expression of who we are and should contribute something meaningful and positive to the world.

▸ **2 Thess 3.6—13**

Request for Prayer

3 Finally, brothers and sisters,*ʲ* pray for us, so that the word of the Lord may spread rapidly and be glorified everywhere, just as it is among you, 2 and that we may be rescued from wicked and evil people; for not all have faith. 3 But the Lord is faithful; he will strengthen you and guard you from the evil one.*ᵏ* 4 And we have confidence in the Lord concerning you, that you are doing and will go on doing the things that we command. 5 May the Lord direct your hearts to the love of God and to the steadfastness of Christ.

Warning against Idleness

6 Now we command you, beloved,*ʲ* in the name of our Lord Jesus Christ, to keep away from believers who are*ˡ* living in idleness and not according to the tradition that they*ᵐ* received from us. 7 For you yourselves know how you ought to imitate us; we were not idle when we were with you, 8 and we did not eat anyone's bread without paying for it; but with toil and labor we worked night and day, so that we might not burden any of you. 9 This was not because we do not have that right, but in order to give you an example to imitate. 10 For even when we were with you, we gave you this command: Anyone unwilling to work should not eat. 11 For we hear that some of you are living in idleness, mere busybodies, not doing any work. 12 Now such persons we command and exhort in the Lord Jesus Christ to do their work quietly and to earn their own living. 13 Brothers and sisters,*ⁿ* do not be weary in doing what is right.

14 Take note of those who do not obey what we say in this letter; have nothing to do with them, so that they may be ashamed. 15 Do not regard them as enemies, but warn them as believers.*ᵒ*

Final Greetings and Benediction

16 Now may the Lord of peace himself give you peace at all times in all ways. The Lord be with all of you.

17 I, Paul, write this greeting with my own hand. This is the mark in every letter of mine; it is the way I write. 18 The grace of our Lord Jesus Christ be with all of you.*ᵖ*

ʲ Gk *brothers*   *ᵏ* Or *from evil*   *ˡ* Gk *from every brother who is*   *ᵐ* Other ancient authorities read *you*   *ⁿ* Gk *Brothers*
ᵒ Gk *a brother*   *ᵖ* Other ancient authorities add *Amen*

TRADITIONS

Second Thessalonians 2.15 directs the Thessalonians to "stand firm and hold fast to the traditions that" they were taught (this message is repeated somewhat differently in 3.6). Traditions are an important part of the Catholic church. They give Catholics their identity and also keep them faithful to the mission and teachings of Jesus Christ.

It's important to understand the difference between traditions with a small t and Tradition with a large T. Large-T Tradition is the core truths of the Christian faith as taught by the Apostles (see "The Bible, Tradition, and the Magisterium," Lk 4.1–13). Like the Bible, it is a primary source of God's revelation for us. The truths of Tradition are unchanging and the same for every age.

Small-t traditions are the customs and rituals that help Catholics and other Christians live out their faith. These traditions are influenced by history and culture. They can differ between cultures and times, and they account for the rich variety of faith expressions in the universal church. These traditions are also important, and they are good as long as they help us live out the mission and teachings of Jesus embodied in the Scriptures and Tradition. But Jesus condemns the exaggerated importance of small-t traditions when they present obstacles to living God's revealed commandments (Mk 7.1–15).

Answer this question: What from the Tradition or traditions of the church has been important to you? Then ask the same question of a parent, a grandparent, or another person from a previous generation and compare the answers.

▶ 2 Thess 2.15

I magine you are a bishop writing a letter to the new priests, deacons, and lay ministers in your diocese. How do you encourage them? What do you warn them about? The two Letters to Timothy and the Letter to Titus are such letters, written to give good, practical advice to the leaders of the early church.

In-depth

The Letters to Timothy and Titus are called the pastoral letters because they were written to church leaders, or pastors. These letters sound as if they were written by Paul. But a great deal of evidence suggests they may have been written by later disciples of Paul, adapting Paul's teaching and advice to the situation of the churches a generation later.

The First Letter to Timothy addresses practical issues the churches needed to deal with in order to achieve stability and respond to new challenges as Christianity became more visible in society: How should the churches deal with people teaching false beliefs? What qualities should church leaders have? Who deserves financial help from the community? How should Christians view success?

The Second Letter to Timothy presents Paul as being close to his execution. As you read this letter, you will experience his sadness at death, hear his reflections on his life and ministry, and see a man who feels deserted by many. This letter tells Timothy—who stands for all faithful Christians—that he needs to endure suffering. Doing the right thing often means more pain than popularity. But even when other people desert us, God "remains faithful— / for he cannot deny himself" (2.13).

The Letter to Titus gives advice for elders, bishops, older men, older women, slaves, younger men, and younger women. It also offers repeated warnings to guard against temptations and false teachings and to be self-controlled.

The pastoral letters give us a picture of the church moving into a new phase. The church seems to have more structure, leadership roles are becoming more defined, and the people are more concerned about its public appearance. Like Christians today, the early Christians struggled to be faithful in applying the Gospel of Jesus Christ to their culture and time.

At a Glance

- **1 Tim 1.1–2.** a greeting
- **1 Tim 1.3—2.15.** advice for Timothy
- **1 Tim 3.1—6.21.** rules for God's people, final advice, and a blessing
- **2 Tim 1.1–5.** a greeting and thanks
- **2 Tim 1.6—4.8.** advice to Timothy
- **2 Tim 4.9–22.** final instructions, greetings, and a blessing
- **Titus 1.1–4.** a greeting
- **Titus 1.5—3.15.** advice for the community of faith and a final blessing

Quick Facts

Author
Paul or followers of Paul (see "Introduction to the Letters and Revelation")

Date Written
around A.D. 65 if by Paul, around A.D. 100 if by followers

Audience
leaders of the early churches

The Pastoral Letters

1 Timothy

Salutation

1 Paul, an apostle of Christ Jesus by the command of God our Savior and of Christ Jesus our hope,

2 To Timothy, my loyal child in the faith:

Grace, mercy, and peace from God the Father and Christ Jesus our Lord.

Warning against False Teachers

3 I urge you, as I did when I was on my way to Mac•e•dō′ni•a, to remain in Eph′e•sus so that you may instruct certain people not to teach any different doctrine, 4 and not to occupy themselves with myths and endless genealogies that promote speculations rather than the divine training*a* that is known by faith. 5 But the aim of such instruction is love that comes from a pure heart, a good conscience, and sincere faith. 6 Some people have deviated from these and turned to meaningless talk, 7 desiring to be teachers of the law, without understanding either what they are saying or the things about which they make assertions.

8 Now we know that the law is good, if one uses it legitimately. 9 This means understanding that the law is laid down not for the innocent but for the lawless and disobedient, for the godless and sinful, for the unholy and profane, for those who kill their father or mother, for murderers, 10 fornicators, sodomites, slave traders, liars, perjurers, and whatever else is contrary to the sound teaching 11 that

conforms to the glorious gospel of the blessed God, which he entrusted to me.

Gratitude for Mercy
(Cp Acts 8.1–3; 9.1–19)

12 I am grateful to Christ Jesus our Lord, who has strengthened me, because he judged me faithful and appointed me to his service, 13 even though I was formerly a blasphemer, a persecutor, and a man of violence. But I received mercy because I had acted ignorantly in unbelief, 14 and the grace of our Lord overflowed for me with the faith and love that are in Christ Jesus. 15 The saying is sure and worthy of full acceptance, that Christ Jesus came into the world to save sinners—of whom I am the foremost. 16 But for that very reason I received mercy, so that in me, as the foremost, Jesus Christ might display the utmost patience, making me an example to those who would come to believe in him for eternal life. 17 To the King of the ages, immortal, invisible, the only God, be honor and glory forever and ever.*b* Amen.

18 I am giving you these instructions, Timothy, my child, in accordance with the prophecies made earlier about you, so that by following them you may fight the good fight, 19 having faith and a good conscience. By rejecting conscience, certain persons have suffered shipwreck in the faith; 20 among

---

a Or *plan* *b* Gk *to the ages of the ages*

Conscience: God in the Gut

Do you ever wonder where God is during those really difficult moments of decision? Like when you're with some friends and someone proposes you all do something exciting but dangerous, and you feel caught in the middle. Or when an entire group is taking advantage of a teacher who has left the room during a test, or when a new kid trips and falls in the cafeteria and no one makes a move to help.

One of the best places to look for God's direction is that feeling in the center of your stomach when you are faced with life's dilemmas. That feeling may be a sign of your conscience prompting you to act.

In I Tim 1.19, Timothy is told to have "faith and a good conscience." A good conscience is based on reason and love and is developed through a commitment to make good and thoughtful moral decisions. Take time to develop your conscience by studying moral issues and the church's teaching on them. The more you develop your conscience, the more you will experience God speaking to you through those gut feelings.

▶ I Tim 1.18–19.

them are Hy•me•naē′us and Alexander, whom I have turned over to Satan, so that they may learn not to blaspheme.

Instructions concerning Prayer

2 First of all, then, I urge that supplications, prayers, intercessions, and thanksgivings be made for everyone, 2 for kings and all who are in high positions, so that we may lead a quiet and peaceable life in all godliness and dignity. 3 This is right and is acceptable in the sight of God our Savior, 4 who desires everyone to be saved and to come to the knowledge of the truth. 5 For

there is one God;
     there is also one mediator between God
          and humankind,
     Christ Jesus, himself human,
6   who gave himself a ransom for all
—this was attested at the right time. 7 For this I was appointed a herald and an apostle (I am telling the truth,[c] I am not lying), a teacher of the Gentiles in faith and truth.

8 I desire, then, that in every place the men should pray, lifting up holy hands without anger or argument; 9 also that the women should dress themselves modestly and decently in suitable clothing, not with their hair braided, or with gold, pearls, or expensive clothes, 10 but with good works, as is proper for women who profess reverence for God. 11 Let a woman[d] learn in silence with full submission. 12 I permit no woman[d] to teach or to have authority over a man;[e] she is to keep silent. 13 For Adam was formed first, then Eve; 14 and Adam was not deceived, but the woman was deceived and became a transgressor. 15 Yet she will be saved through childbearing, pro-

vided they continue in faith and love and holiness, with modesty.

Qualifications of Bishops

3 The saying is sure:[f] whoever aspires to the office of bishop[g] desires a noble task. 2 Now a bishop[h] must be above reproach, married only once,[i] temperate, sensible, respectable, hospitable, an apt teacher, 3 not a drunkard, not violent but gentle, not quarrelsome, and not a lover of money. 4 He must manage his own household well, keeping his children submissive and respectful in every way— 5 for if someone does not know how to manage his own household, how can he take care of God's church? 6 He must not be a recent convert, or he may be puffed up with conceit and fall into the condemnation of the devil. 7 Moreover, he must be well thought of by outsiders, so that he may not fall into disgrace and the snare of the devil.

Qualifications of Deacons

8 Deacons likewise must be serious, not double-tongued, not indulging in much wine, not greedy for money; 9 they must hold fast to the mystery of the faith with a clear conscience. 10 And let them first be tested; then, if they prove themselves blameless, let them serve as deacons. 11 Women[j] likewise must be serious, not slanderers, but temperate, faithful in all things. 12 Let deacons be married

---

c Other ancient authorities add in Christ   d Or wife
e Or her husband   f Some interpreters place these words at
the end of the previous paragraph. Other ancient
authorities read The saying is commonly accepted   g Or
overseer   h Or an overseer   i Gk the husband of one wife
j Or Their wives, or Women deacons

1
T
I
M

▶ 1 Tim 2.8–15

did you KNOW?
Women and Cultural Roles

A modern person reading 1 Tim 2.8–15 may be shocked by the teaching there. A passage like this can be easily misunderstood and even misused against women. It is very important to realize that it is a reflection of women's roles in the ancient world. Whatever her religious background—Jewish, Christian, or pagan—a woman's place was in the home. Women generally married young, had no education, and were not allowed to hold a position of public authority.

The earliest Christian communities gathered in members' homes. In this less public arena, women taught and performed other ministries. As Christianity became more widely accepted, concern for how the church appeared to outsiders grew—including concern about drunken bishops, immodest dress, and women teaching in public. That is probably why the author of First Timothy says, "I permit no woman to teach" (2.12).

Are things different for women in contemporary Christianity? Think of women you know who are involved in church life. In your own parish or community, for example, there are probably women who are religious education directors, coordinators of youth ministry, or pastoral ministers.

The Mystery of Our Religion

14 I hope to come to you soon, but I am writing these instructions to you so that, 15 if I am delayed, you may know how one ought to behave in the household of God, which is the church of the living God, the pillar and bulwark of the truth. 16 Without any doubt, the mystery of our religion is great:

He^l was revealed in flesh,
　　vindicated^m in spirit,^{n}
　　　　seen by angels,
　　proclaimed among Gentiles,
　　　　believed in throughout the world,
　　　　　　taken up in glory.

False Asceticism

4 Now the Spirit expressly says that in later^o times some will renounce the faith by paying attention to deceitful spirits and teachings of demons, 2 through the hypocrisy of liars whose consciences are seared with a hot iron. 3 They forbid marriage and demand abstinence from foods, which God created to be received with thanksgiving by those who believe and know the truth. 4 For everything created by God is good, and nothing is to be rejected, provided it is received with thanksgiving; 5 for it is sanctified by God's word and by prayer.

A Good Minister of Jesus Christ

6 If you put these instructions before the brothers and sisters,^{p} you will be a good servant^q of Christ Jesus, nourished on the words of the faith and of the sound teaching that you have followed. 7 Have nothing to do with profane myths and old wives' tales. Train yourself in godliness, 8 for, while physical training is of some value, godliness is valuable in every way, holding promise for both the present life and the life to come. 9 The saying is sure and worthy of full acceptance. 10 For to this end we toil and struggle,^{r} because we have our hope set on the living God, who is the Savior of all people, especially of those who believe.

11 These are the things you must insist on and teach. 12 Let no one despise your youth, but set the believers an example in speech and conduct, in love, in faith, in purity. 13 Until I arrive, give attention to the public reading of scripture,^{s} to exhorting, to teaching. 14 Do not neglect the gift that is in you, which was given to you through prophecy with the laying on of hands by the council of

only once,^{k} and let them manage their children and their households well; 13 for those who serve well as deacons gain a good standing for themselves and great boldness in the faith that is in Christ Jesus.

---

^{k} Gk *be husbands of one wife* ^{l} Gk *Who*; other ancient authorities read *God*; others, *Which* ^{m} Or *justified* ^{n} Or *by the Spirit* ^{o} Or *the last* ^{p} Gk *brothers* ^{q} Or *deacon* ^{r} Other ancient authorities read *suffer reproach* ^{s} Gk *to the reading*

Training for Christ

We spend countless hours in training to become better athletes, musicians, scientists, teachers, electricians; you name it, we train for it if we want to be good at it. Paul says the soul needs that same kind of training.

In your journal or on a piece of paper, make two columns, one to list the ways you train for your sporting event or other activity and the other to list ways you might train your soul to become a more loving person, in the image of Jesus. Once you have completed your lists, put them in a place where you can see them every day. Use them as a guide and as a reminder to continue in your efforts to train for Christ. You may also find that you need to keep adding to your soul-training list as your training starts to pay off!

▸ **I Tim 4.7–10**

elders.*t* 15 Put these things into practice, devote yourself to them, so that all may see your progress. 16 Pay close attention to yourself and to your teaching; continue in these things, for in doing this you will save both yourself and your hearers.

Duties toward Believers

5 Do not speak harshly to an older man,*u* but speak to him as to a father, to younger men as brothers, 2 to older women as mothers, to younger women as sisters—with absolute purity.

3 Honor widows who are really widows. 4 If a widow has children or grandchildren, they should first learn their religious duty to their own family and make some repayment to their parents; for this is pleasing in God's sight. 5 The real widow, left alone, has set her hope on God and continues in supplications and prayers night and day; 6 but the widow*v* who lives for pleasure is dead even while

she lives. 7 Give these commands as well, so that they may be above reproach. 8 And whoever does not provide for relatives, and especially for family members, has denied the faith and is worse than an unbeliever.

9 Let a widow be put on the list if she is not less than sixty years old and has been married only once;*w* 10 she must be well attested for her good works, as one who has brought up children, shown hospitality, washed the saints' feet, helped the afflicted, and devoted herself to doing good in every way. 11 But refuse to put younger widows on the list; for when their sensual desires alienate them from Christ, they want to marry, 12 and so they incur condemnation for having violated their first pledge. 13 Besides that, they learn to be idle, gadding about from house to house; and they are not merely idle, but also gossips and busybodies, saying what they should not say. 14 So I would have younger widows marry, bear children, and manage their households, so as to give the adversary no occasion to revile us. 15 For some have already turned away to follow Satan. 16 If any believing woman*x* has relatives who are really widows, let her assist them; let the church not be burdened, so that it can assist those who are real widows.

17 Let the elders who rule well be considered worthy of double honor,*y* especially those who labor in preaching and teaching; 18 for the scripture says, "You shall not muzzle an ox while it is treading out the grain," and, "The laborer deserves to be paid." 19 Never accept any accusation against an elder except on the evidence of two or three witnesses. 20 As for those who persist in sin, rebuke them in the presence of all, so that the rest also may

Let no one despise your **youth,** *but set the believers an example in speech and conduct*

4.12

t Gk by the presbytery   *u* Or an elder, or a presbyter
v Gk she   *w* Gk the wife of one husband   *x* Other ancient authorities read believing man or woman; others, believing man   *y* Or compensation

1
T
I
M

stand in fear. 21 In the presence of God and of Christ Jesus and of the elect angels, I warn you to keep these instructions without prejudice, doing nothing on the basis of partiality. 22 Do not ordainᶻ anyone hastily, and do not participate in the sins of others; keep yourself pure.

23 No longer drink only water, but take a little wine for the sake of your stomach and your frequent ailments.

24 The sins of some people are conspicuous and precede them to judgment, while the sins of others follow them there. 25 So also good works are conspicuous; and even when they are not, they cannot remain hidden.

6 Let all who are under the yoke of slavery regard their masters as worthy of all honor, so that the name of God and the teaching may not be blasphemed. 2 Those who have believing masters must not be disrespectful to them on the ground that they are members of the church;ᵃ rather they must serve them all the more, since those who benefit by their service are believers and beloved.ᵇ

False Teaching and True Riches

Teach and urge these duties. 3 Whoever teaches otherwise and does not agree with the sound words of our Lord Jesus Christ and the teaching that is in accordance with godliness, 4 is conceited, understanding nothing, and has a morbid craving for controversy and for disputes about words. From these come envy, dissension, slander, base suspicions, 5 and wrangling among those who are depraved in mind and bereft of the truth, imagining that godliness is a means of gain.ᶜ 6 Of course, there is great gain in godliness combined with content-

ment; 7 for we brought nothing into the world, so thatᵈ we can take nothing out of it; 8 but if we have food and clothing, we will be content with these. 9 But those who want to be rich fall into temptation and are trapped by many senseless and harmful desires that plunge people into ruin and destruction. 10 For the love of money is a root of all kinds of evil, and in their eagerness to be rich some have wandered away from the faith and pierced themselves with many pains.

The Good Fight of Faith

11 But as for you, man of God, shun all this; pursue righteousness, godliness, faith, love, endurance, gentleness. 12 Fight the good fight of the faith; take hold of the eternal life, to which you were called and for which you madeᵉ the good confession in the presence of many witnesses. 13 In the presence of God, who gives life to all things, and of Christ Jesus, who in his testimony before Pon'ti•us Pilate made the good confession, I charge you 14 to keep the commandment without spot or blame until the manifestation of our Lord Jesus Christ, 15 which he will bring about at the right time—he who is the blessed and only Sovereign, the King of kings and Lord of lords. 16 It is he alone who has immortality and dwells in unapproachable light, whom no one has ever seen or can see; to him be honor and eternal dominion. Amen.

ᶻ Gk Do not lay hands on   ᵃ Gk are brothers   ᵇ Or since they are believers and beloved, who devote themselves to good deeds   ᶜ Other ancient authorities add Withdraw yourself from such people   ᵈ Other ancient authorities read world—it is certain that   ᵉ Gk confessed

But as for you, man of God, pursue *righteousness, godliness, faith, love, endurance, gentleness.* Fight the good fight of the faith; take hold of the eternal life, to which you were called and for which you made the good confession in the presence of many witnesses.

17 As for those who in the present age are rich, command them not to be haughty, or to set their hopes on the uncertainty of riches, but rather on God who richly provides us with everything for our enjoyment. 18 They are to do good, to be rich in good works, generous, and ready to share, 19 thus storing up for themselves the treasure of a good foundation for the future, so that they may take hold of the life that really is life.

Personal Instructions and Benediction

20 Timothy, guard what has been entrusted to you. Avoid the profane chatter and contradictions of what is falsely called knowledge; 21 by professing it some have missed the mark as regards the faith.

Grace be with you.*f*

---

f The Greek word for *you* here is plural; in other ancient authorities it is singular. Other ancient authorities add *Amen*

2 Timothy

1.8

Salutation

1 Paul, an apostle of Christ Jesus by the will of God, for the sake of the promise of life that is in Christ Jesus,

2 To Timothy, my beloved child:

Grace, mercy, and peace from God the Father and Christ Jesus our Lord.

Thanksgiving and Encouragement

3 I am grateful to God—whom I worship with a clear conscience, as my ancestors did—when I remember you constantly in my prayers night and day. 4 Recalling your tears, I long to see you so that I may be filled with joy. 5 I am reminded of your sincere faith, a faith that lived first in your grandmother Lō'is and your mother Eū'nice and now, I am sure, lives in you. 6 For this reason I remind you to rekindle the gift of God that is within you through the laying on of my hands; 7 for God did not give us a spirit of cowardice, but rather a spirit of power and of love and of self-discipline.

8 Do not be ashamed, then, of the testimony about our Lord or of me his prisoner, but join with me in suffering for the gospel, relying on the power of God, 9 who saved us and called us with a holy calling, not according to our works but according to his own purpose and grace. This grace was given to us in Christ Jesus before the ages began, 10 but it has now been revealed through the appearing of our Savior Christ Jesus, who abolished death and brought life and immortality to light through the gospel. 11 For this gospel I was appointed a herald and an apostle and a teacher,*a* 12 and for this reason I suffer as I do. But I am not ashamed, for I know the one in whom I have put my trust, and I am sure that he is able to guard until that day what I have entrusted to him.*b* 13 Hold to the standard of sound teaching that you have heard from me, in the faith and love that are in Christ Jesus. 14 Guard the good treasure entrusted to you, with the help of the Holy Spirit living in us.

15 You are aware that all who are in Asia have turned away from me, including Phy̆'ge·lus and Her·mog'e·nēs. 16 May the Lord grant mercy to the household of On·e·siph'o·rus, because he often refreshed me and was not ashamed of my chain; 17 when he arrived in Rome, he eagerly*c* searched for me and found me 18—may the Lord grant that he will find mercy from the Lord on that day! And you know very well how much service he rendered in Eph'e·sus.

---

a Other ancient authorities add *of the Gentiles*   *b* Or *what has been entrusted to me*   *c* Or *promptly*

If we have died with him, we will also live with him;

if we endure, we will also reign with him;

if we deny him, he will also deny us;

if we are faithless, he remains faithful—

for he cannot deny himself.

A Good Soldier of Christ Jesus

2 You then, my child, be strong in the grace that is in Christ Jesus; 2 and what you have heard from me through many witnesses entrust to faithful people who will be able to teach others as well. 3 Share in suffering like a good soldier of Christ Jesus. 4 No one serving in the army gets entangled in everyday affairs; the soldier's aim is to please the enlisting officer. 5 And in the case of an athlete, no one is crowned without competing according to the rules. 6 It is the farmer who does the work who ought to have the first share of the crops. 7 Think over what I say, for the Lord will give you understanding in all things.

8 Remember Jesus Christ, raised from the dead, a descendant of David—that is my gospel, 9 for which I suffer hardship, even to the point of being chained like a criminal. But the word of God is not chained. 10 Therefore I endure everything for the sake of the elect, so that they may also obtain the salvation that is in Christ Jesus, with eternal glory. 11 The saying is sure:

If we have died with him, we will also live with
him;
12 if we endure, we will also reign with him;
if we deny him, he will also deny us;
13 if we are faithless, he remains faithful—
for he cannot deny himself.

A Worker Approved by God

14 Remind them of this, and warn them before God[d] that they are to avoid wrangling over words, which does no good but only ruins those who are listening. 15 Do your best to present yourself to God as one approved by him, a worker who has no need to be ashamed, rightly explaining the word of truth. 16 Avoid profane chatter, for it will lead people into more and more impiety, 17 and their talk will spread like gangrene. Among them are Hy·me-naē'us and Phi·lē'tus, 18 who have swerved from the truth by claiming that the resurrection has already taken place. They are upsetting the faith of some. 19 But God's firm foundation stands, bearing this inscription: "The Lord knows those who are his," and, "Let everyone who calls on the name of the Lord turn away from wickedness."

20 In a large house there are utensils not only of gold and silver but also of wood and clay, some for special use, some for ordinary. 21 All who cleanse themselves of the things I have mentioned[e] will become special utensils, dedicated and useful to the owner of the house, ready for every good work. 22 Shun youthful passions and pursue righteousness, faith, love, and peace, along with those who call on the Lord from a pure heart. 23 Have nothing to do with stupid and senseless controversies; you know that they breed quarrels. 24 And the Lord's servant[f] must not be quarrelsome but kindly to everyone, an apt teacher, patient, 25 correcting opponents with gentleness. God may perhaps grant that they will repent and come to know the truth, 26 and that they may escape from the snare of the devil, having been held captive by him to do his will.[g]

Godlessness in the Last Days

3 You must understand this, that in the last days distressing times will come. 2 For people will be lovers of themselves, lovers of money, boasters, arrogant, abusive, disobedient to their parents, ungrateful, unholy, 3 inhuman, implacable, slanderers, profligates, brutes, haters of good, 4 treacherous, reckless, swollen with conceit, lovers of pleasure rather than lovers of God, 5 holding to the outward form of godliness but denying its

---

d Other ancient authorities read *the Lord*   e Gk *of these things*   f Gk *slave*   g Or *by him, to do his* (that is, God's) *will*

Teaching Others

Have you ever tried to explain to someone something about your faith? That can be challenging. Second Timothy 2.22–26 contains some tips on sharing faith with others: Avoid senseless controversies. Be kind, patient, and gentle. And be an apt teacher, that is, someone who is qualified or prepared.

Imagine that you are helping to teach a group of younger people about their faith. What do you want to say about God? How do you explain Jesus' love? How do you show your patience and gentleness? If you can answer these questions, maybe you should volunteer to help with your church's religious education program!

▶ 2 Tim 2.22–26

power. Avoid them! 6 For among them are those who make their way into households and captivate silly women, overwhelmed by their sins and swayed by all kinds of desires, 7 who are always being instructed and can never arrive at a knowledge of the truth. 8 As Jan′nēs and Jam′brēs opposed Moses, so these people, of corrupt mind and counterfeit faith, also oppose the truth. 9 But they will not make much progress, because, as in the case of those two men,[h] their folly will become plain to everyone.

Paul's Charge to Timothy

10 Now you have observed my teaching, my conduct, my aim in life, my faith, my patience, my love, my steadfastness, 11 my persecutions, and my suffering the things that happened to me in An′ti·och, Ī·cō′ni·um, and Lys′tra. What persecutions I endured! Yet the Lord rescued me from all of them. 12 Indeed, all who want to live a godly life in Christ Jesus will be persecuted. 13 But wicked people and impostors will go from bad to worse, deceiving others and being deceived. 14 But as for you, continue in what you have learned and firmly believed, knowing from whom you learned it, 15 and how from childhood you have known the sacred writings that are able to instruct you for salvation through faith in Christ Jesus. 16 All scripture is inspired by God and is[i] useful for teaching, for reproof, for correction, and for training in righteousness, 17 so that everyone who belongs to God may be proficient, equipped for every good work.

4 In the presence of God and of Christ Jesus, who is to judge the living and the dead, and in view of his appearing and his kingdom, I solemnly urge you: 2 proclaim the message; be persistent whether the time is favorable or unfavorable; convince, rebuke, and encourage, with the utmost patience in teaching. 3 For the time is coming when people will not put up with sound doctrine, but having itching ears, they will accumulate

for themselves teachers to suit their own desires, 4 and will turn away from listening to the truth and wander away to myths. 5 As for you, always be sober, endure suffering, do the work of an evangelist, carry out your ministry fully.

6 As for me, I am already being poured out as a libation, and the time of my departure has come. 7 I have fought the good fight, I have finished the race,

---

h Gk lacks *two men*   i Or *Every scripture inspired by God is also*

PRAY IT! For Those Who Walk with Us

We pray, Lord, for those who formed us in our faith.

We pray for our families who first spoke your name to us and shared our journey of faith from the beginning.

We pray for our friends who shared their faith and continue to walk with us in our journey.

We pray for the teachers, priests, youth ministers, and other members of our church who took the time to recognize us as individuals and who showed us that faith can be both fun and challenging.

Thank you, God, for sending these people into our lives and for their gifts of faith, love, and patience. May we honor them by sharing our faith with a new generation of believers. We pray this in Jesus' name. Amen.

▶ 2 Tim 3.12–14

All scripture is (inspired) by God and is useful for teaching, for reproof, for correction, and for training in righteousness

3.16

me. Get Mark and bring him with you, for he is useful in my ministry. 12 I have sent Tych′i•cus to Eph′e•sus. 13 When you come, bring the cloak that I left with Car′pus at Trō′as, also the books, and above all the parchments. 14 Alexander the coppersmith did me great harm; the Lord will pay him back for his deeds. 15 You also must beware of him, for he strongly opposed our message.

16 At my first defense no one came to my support, but all deserted me. May it not be counted against them! 17 But the Lord stood by me and gave me strength, so that through me the message might be fully proclaimed and all the Gentiles might hear it. So I was rescued from the lion's mouth. 18 The Lord will rescue me from every evil attack and save me for his heavenly kingdom. To him be the glory forever and ever. Amen.

Final Greetings and Benediction

19 Greet Pris′ca and A•qui′la, and the household of On•e•siph′o•rus. 20 E•ras′tus remained in Corinth; Troph′i•mus I left ill in Mi•lē′tus. 21 Do your best to come before winter. Eū•bū′lus sends greetings to you, as do Pū′dens and Li′nus and Clau′di•a and all the brothers and sisters.*k*

22 The Lord be with your spirit. Grace be with you.*l*

I have kept the faith. 8 From now on there is reserved for me the crown of righteousness, which the Lord, the righteous judge, will give me on that day, and not only to me but also to all who have longed for his appearing.

Personal Instructions

9 Do your best to come to me soon, 10 for Dē′mas, in love with this present world, has deserted me and gone to Thes•sa•lo•nī′ca; Cres′cens has gone to Galatia,*j* Titus to Dal•mā′tia. 11 Only Luke is with

j Other ancient authorities read *Gaul*   *k* Gk *all the brothers*
l The Greek word for *you* here is plural. Other ancient authorities add *Amen*

Misleading Messages

LIVE IT!

Sticking with something can be difficult. When things get tough, many people are tempted to quit or walk away. We are surrounded by messages like "If it feels good, do it," and "You should have whatever your heart desires," and "Life will be great if you wear these clothes" or "drink this beverage" or "hang out with these people."

But reaching a worthy goal often requires hard choices and hard work. Second Timothy 4.1–5 warns us against being taken in by deceptive teachers or messages—like cultural teachings that life should always be easy and pleasurable. Such teachings water down the real challenge of living as a follower of Jesus Christ! If we are not finding life to be challenging, maybe we have tuned in to these misleading messages.

▶ **2 Tim 4.1–5**

Titus

Salutation

1 Paul, a servant[a] of God and an apostle of Jesus Christ, for the sake of the faith of God's elect and the knowledge of the truth that is in accordance with godliness, 2 in the hope of eternal life that God, who never lies, promised before the ages began— 3 in due time he revealed his word through the proclamation with which I have been entrusted by the command of God our Savior,

4 To Titus, my loyal child in the faith we share:

Grace[b] and peace from God the Father and Christ Jesus our Savior.

Titus in Crete

5 I left you behind in Crete for this reason, so that you should put in order what remained to be done, and should appoint elders in every town, as I directed you: 6 someone who is blameless, married only once,[c] whose children are believers, not accused of debauchery and not rebellious. 7 For a bishop,[d] as God's steward, must be blameless; he must not be arrogant or quick-tempered or addicted to wine or violent or greedy for gain; 8 but he must be hospitable, a lover of goodness, prudent, upright, devout, and self-controlled. 9 He must have a firm grasp of the word that is trustworthy in accordance with the teaching, so that he may be able both to preach with sound doctrine and to refute those who contradict it.

10 There are also many rebellious people, idle talkers and deceivers, especially those of the circumcision; 11 they must be silenced, since they are upsetting whole families by teaching for sordid gain what it is not right to teach. 12 It was one of them, their very own prophet, who said,

"Cre'tans are always liars, vicious brutes, lazy gluttons."

13 That testimony is true. For this reason rebuke them sharply, so that they may become sound in the faith, 14 not paying attention to Jewish myths or to commandments of those who reject the truth. 15 To the pure all things are pure, but to the corrupt and unbelieving nothing is pure. Their very minds and consciences are corrupted. 16 They profess to know God, but they deny him by their actions. They are detestable, disobedient, unfit for any good work.

Teach Sound Doctrine

2 But as for you, teach what is consistent with sound doctrine. 2 Tell the older men to be temperate, serious, prudent, and sound in faith, in love, and in endurance.

3 Likewise, tell the older women to be reverent in behavior, not to be slanderers or slaves to drink; they are to teach what is good, 4 so that they may encourage the young women to love their hus-

---

a Gk *slave*   *b* Other ancient authorities read *Grace, mercy,*   *c* Gk *husband of one wife*   *d* Or *an overseer*

Christian Leadership

Leadership is an esteemed but difficult calling. Church leaders in particular must earn the respect of others through the integrity of their lifestyle and their commitment and service to the values of Jesus Christ. Good leaders also know how to motivate others to grow and to serve.

Maybe you too possess leadership qualities and wish to pursue a leadership position in the church or in another field. Make a list of the values you think a leader should have. How closely does your list match the characteristics of a good leader in verses 5–9? When you are ready to lead, review the list from verses 5–9, and remember the importance of living a life of character and leading others to positions of leadership.

As you discern your own leadership potential, look to others who you feel possess good leadership qualities. Which leaders in your school or youth program do you admire the most? What qualities make them good leaders? How do these leaders manifest the good-leader characteristics you listed?

▸ Titus 1.5–9

bands, to love their children, 5 to be self-controlled, chaste, good managers of the household, kind, being submissive to their husbands, so that the word of God may not be discredited.

6 Likewise, urge the younger men to be self-controlled. 7 Show yourself in all respects a model of good works, and in your teaching show integrity, gravity, 8 and sound speech that cannot be censured; then any opponent will be put to shame, having nothing evil to say of us.

9 Tell slaves to be submissive to their masters and to give satisfaction in every respect; they are not to talk back, 10 not to pilfer, but to show complete and perfect fidelity, so that in everything they may be an ornament to the doctrine of God our Savior.

11 For the grace of God has appeared, bringing salvation to all,*e* 12 training us to renounce impiety and worldly passions, and in the present age to live lives that are self-controlled, upright, and godly, 13 while we wait for the blessed hope and the manifestation of the glory of our great God and Savior,*f* Jesus Christ. 14 He it is who gave himself for us that he might redeem us from all iniquity and purify for himself a people of his own who are zealous for good deeds.

15 Declare these things; exhort and reprove with all authority.*g* Let no one look down on you.

Maintain Good Deeds

3 Remind them to be subject to rulers and authorities, to be obedient, to be ready for every good work, 2 to speak evil of no one, to avoid quarreling, to be gentle, and to show every courtesy to everyone. 3 For we ourselves were once foolish, disobedient, led astray, slaves to various passions and pleasures, passing our days in malice and envy, despicable, hating one another. 4 But when the good-

ness and loving kindness of God our Savior appeared, 5 he saved us, not because of any works of righteousness that we had done, but according to his mercy, through the water*h* of rebirth and renewal by the Holy Spirit. 6 This Spirit he poured out on us richly through Jesus Christ our Savior, 7 so that, having been justified by his grace, we might become heirs according to the hope of eternal life. 8 The saying is sure.

I desire that you insist on these things, so that those who have come to believe in God may be careful to devote themselves to good works; these things are excellent and profitable to everyone. 9 But avoid stupid controversies, genealogies, dissensions, and quarrels about the law, for they are unprofitable and worthless. 10 After a first and second admonition, have nothing more to do with anyone who causes divisions, 11 since you know that such a person is perverted and sinful, being self-condemned.

Final Messages and Benediction

12 When I send Ar'te•mas to you, or Tych'i•cus, do your best to come to me at Ni•cop'o•lis, for I have decided to spend the winter there. 13 Make every effort to send Zē'nas the lawyer and A•pol'los on their way, and see that they lack nothing. 14 And let people learn to devote themselves to good works in order to meet urgent needs, so that they may not be unproductive.

15 All who are with me send greetings to you. Greet those who love us in the faith.

Grace be with all of you.*i*

---

e Or *has appeared to all, bringing salvation*   *f* Or *of the great God and our Savior*   *g* Gk *commandment*   *h* Gk *washing*
i Other ancient authorities add *Amen*

When the goodness

and loving kindess

of God our Savior appeared,

he saved us,

not because of any works of

righteousness that we had done,

but according to his mercy,

through the water of rebirth

and renewal by the Holy Spirit.

3.4–5

The brief Letter to Philemon is about slavery. It may surprise you that it doesn't condemn slavery outright. In fact, other parts of the Bible take the idea of human slavery for granted! How can the Bible not challenge something we think is wrong? Seeking to understand this puzzling question gives us a key to understanding God's revelation in the Bible.

In-depth

One key to understanding God's message in the Bible is to understand the beliefs of the authors and the first readers. The Letter to Philemon is addressed to a slave owner named Philemon, a woman named Apphia, and a soldier named Archippus, who all lived in Colossae. Philemon's slave, Onesimus, ran away, wound up in prison with Paul, and became a Christian. Now, Paul is sending him back to Philemon, as the law requires. That same law gives Philemon the right to punish Onesimus for escaping. But Paul asks—indirectly, but clearly enough—for Onesimus's freedom. Paul also asks for something far more challenging—that Philemon, Apphia, and Archippus accept Onesimus as "a beloved brother" (verse 16) in Christ.

It is safe to believe that Paul did not agree with slavery. Recall his basic statement on Christian freedom in Gal 3.28: "There is no longer slave or free, there is no longer male and female; for all of you are one in Christ Jesus." However, Paul expected slavery would pass away very soon with the Second Coming of Jesus Christ (see "Strange Advice!?" 1 Corinthians, chapter 7). This is probably why he never directly challenged the institution of slavery.

Although Paul may not have been a social revolutionary by our standards, he consistently challenged social institutions to reflect Gospel values. This letter is a masterpiece of persuasion as it urges the church community in Colossae to accept Onesimus as a beloved brother in Christ. It uses flattery (verses 4–7), a veiled reference to Paul's authority (verses 8–9), Paul's personal relationship with everyone involved (verses 12–17), and maybe even a little guilt in Paul's offer to pay for anything Onesimus stole (verses 18–19). Paul's message to the household of Philemon and to us is this: We must get beyond whatever cultural boundaries prevent us from treating one another as equals in Christ!

At a Glance

- **Verses 1–7.** a greeting and gratitude for Philemon

- **Verses 8–22.** Paul's request

- **Verses 23–25.** final greetings and a blessing

Quick Facts

Author
Paul

Date Written
A.D. 54–56 if from Ephesus, A.D. 61–63 if from Rome

Audience
Philemon and his household

The Letter to Philemon

Philemon

Salutation

1 Paul, a prisoner of Christ Jesus, and Timothy our brother,[a]

To Phi·lē′mon our dear friend and co-worker, [2] to Ap′phi·a our sister,[b] to Ar·chip′pus our fellow soldier, and to the church in your house:

3 Grace to you and peace from God our Father and the Lord Jesus Christ.

Philemon's Love and Faith

4 When I remember you[c] in my prayers, I always thank my God [5] because I hear of your love for all the saints and your faith toward the Lord Jesus. [6] I pray that the sharing of your faith may become effective when you perceive all the good that we[d] may do for Christ. [7] I have indeed received much joy and encouragement from your love, because the hearts of the saints have been refreshed through you, my brother.

Paul's Plea for Onesimus

8 For this reason, though I am bold enough in Christ to command you to do your duty, [9] yet I would rather appeal to you on the basis of love— and I, Paul, do this as an old man, and now also as a prisoner of Christ Jesus.[e] [10] I am appealing to you for my child, O·nes′i·mus, whose father I have become during my imprisonment. [11] Formerly he was useless to you, but now he is indeed useful[f] both to

you and to me. [12] I am sending him, that is, my own heart, back to you. [13] I wanted to keep him with me, so that he might be of service to me in your place during my imprisonment for the gospel; [14] but I preferred to do nothing without your consent, in order that your good deed might be voluntary and not something forced. [15] Perhaps this is the reason he was separated from you for a while, so that you might have him back forever, [16] no longer as a slave but more than a slave, a beloved brother—especially to me but how much more to you, both in the flesh and in the Lord.

17 So if you consider me your partner, welcome him as you would welcome me. [18] If he has wronged you in any way, or owes you anything, charge that to my account. [19] I, Paul, am writing this with my own hand: I will repay it. I say nothing about your owing me even your own self. [20] Yes, brother, let me have this benefit from you in the Lord! Refresh my heart in Christ. [21] Confident of your obedience, I am writing to you, knowing that you will do even more than I say.

22 One thing more—prepare a guest room for

---

a Gk *the brother*   b Gk *the sister*   c From verse 4 through verse 21, *you* is singular   d Other ancient authorities read *you* (plural)   e Or *as an ambassador of Christ Jesus, and now also his prisoner*   f The name Onesimus means *useful* or (compare verse 20) *beneficial*

Rethinking Social Structures

In sending Onesimus back to Philemon, Paul asked Philemon not only to forgive his runaway slave but to rethink his relationship with him. Paul's plea to Philemon and the church in Colossae to look on Onesimus as a brother in Christ was radical for the time. People expected runaway slaves to be punished severely. Accepting Onesimus as a Christian would be a sign that the church truly believed in baptismal forgiveness and new life.

What commonly accepted social structures in our day might need a fresh look? Might any privileges that we take for granted actually prevent true equality in Christ?

▸ Philemon, verses 8–21

me, for I am hoping through your prayers to be restored to you.

Final Greetings and Benediction

23 Ep′a·phras, my fellow prisoner in Christ Jesus, sends greetings to you,g 24 and so do Mark,

Ar·is·tar′chus, De̅′mas, and Luke, my fellow workers.

25 The grace of the Lord Jesus Christ be with your spirit.h

---

g Here *you* is singular   h Other ancient authorities add *Amen*

Have you ever wondered why it makes sense to believe that Jesus is the savior of all humanity? It's an honest question. Evidently, some early Christians asked it. The Letter to the Hebrews is a sermon—to them and to us—to strengthen our faith and belief in Jesus Christ, the Son of God and our "great high priest" (4.14).

In-depth

The Letter to the Hebrews gives us almost no information about its author and the community it is addressed to. But it appears that some members of the community are in danger of giving up their faith—and this is happening after the group has already survived a period of persecution. The letter encourages them to be strong in their faith and seeks to give a sound foundation for believing in Jesus Christ. It is a statement on Christ's divinity and the saving power of Christ's sacrificial death.

The letter presents Christ as the divine Son of God, through whom the world was created, superior to any angel, and the culmination of all the promises and expectations of the Old Testament. In explaining Christ's importance, the letter uses a type of argument called "from the lesser to the greater." This type of argument is based on the idea that if you accept something as true in a lesser situation, then it is certainly true in a greater situation. The author uses it to show that Christ's sacrifice is far greater than the sacrifices offered by the priests in the Temple. As the perfect high priest, Christ offers the perfect sacrifice—his death on the cross—through which God saves us once and for all from sin.

This letter reads like one long sermon made up of interconnecting parts. Begin by reading the whole thing out loud to truly appreciate its power and wording. Then, look up some of its references to people and events in the Old Testament to better appreciate its inspired explanation of Christ's nature and mission.

At a Glance

- **Chapters 1–2.** an introduction, and a message that Christ is greater than the angels

- **Chapters 3–7.** a message that Christ is greater than Moses, and a discussion of Melchizedek and the priests of the Temple

- **8.1—10.18.** a message that Christ offers the sacrifice of the New Covenant

- **10.19—12.29.** exhortations and warnings, and a list of the heroes of the Christian faith

- **Chapter 13.** a conclusion

Quick Facts

Author
unknown

Date Written
approximately A.D. 80–90

Audience
Hellenistic (Greek-speaking) Christians and possibly Jewish Christians

Hebrews

God Has Spoken by His Son
(Cp Jn 1.1–4)

1 Long ago God spoke to our ancestors in many and various ways by the prophets, 2 but in these last days he has spoken to us by a Son,[a] whom he appointed heir of all things, through whom he also created the worlds. 3 He is the reflection of God's glory and the exact imprint of God's very being, and he sustains[b] all things by his powerful word. When he had made purification for sins, he sat down at the right hand of the Majesty on high, 4 having become as much superior to angels as the name he has inherited is more excellent than theirs.

The Son Is Superior to Angels

5 For to which of the angels did God ever say,
"You are my Son;
  today I have begotten you"?
Or again,
"I will be his Father,
  and he will be my Son"?
6 And again, when he brings the firstborn into the world, he says,
"Let all God's angels worship him."
7 Of the angels he says,
"He makes his angels winds,
  and his servants flames of fire."
8 But of the Son he says,
"Your throne, O God, is[c] forever and ever,

and the righteous scepter is the scepter of
  your[d] kingdom.
9 You have loved righteousness and hated
    wickedness;
therefore God, your God, has anointed you
  with the oil of gladness beyond your
    companions."
10 And,
"In the beginning, Lord, you founded the
    earth,
  and the heavens are the work of your
    hands;
11 they will perish, but you remain;
  they will all wear out like clothing;
12 like a cloak you will roll them up,
  and like clothing[e] they will be changed.
But you are the same,
  and your years will never end."
13 But to which of the angels has he ever said,
"Sit at my right hand
  until I make your enemies a footstool for
    your feet"?
14 Are not all angels[f] spirits in the divine service, sent to serve for the sake of those who are to inherit salvation?

---

a Or *the Son* b Or *bears along* c Or *God is your throne*
d Other ancient authorities read *his* e Other ancient
authorities lack *like clothing* f Gk *all of them*

1421

"The Exact Imprint"

Throughout history, there have been many opinions about who Jesus of Nazareth was. Some have called him a great teacher, some a prophet, some a charismatic preacher, and others a worker of miracles. Christians believe Jesus was all of these and more—much more.

The New Testament makes a bold claim about Jesus. It says the historical human being from Nazareth named Jesus is the perfect human image of God. Jesus reflects God's glory and is "the exact imprint of God's very being" (1.3). In other words, although a human being like us, Jesus is God.

This astonishing claim is central to the Christian faith. If you accept it as true, it will change your life. And if you are to believe it, you need to know the whole story behind it and all the evidence that supports it. The best place to start is with the book in your hands right now. Read on!

▶ Heb 1.1–14

H
E
B

Warning to Pay Attention

2 Therefore we must pay greater attention to what we have heard, so that we do not drift away from it. ² For if the message declared through

So Great a Salvation!

It is easy for us humans to rationalize why we do certain things. Even if our actions hurt other people and separate us from God, we can come up with a way to justify them. Though this way of thinking may seem to work for us, Heb 2.1–4 says quite clearly that it never works with God.

We cannot hide from our "just penalty" (verse 2). But the good news is that God offers us salvation from our sins through Jesus Christ. In your prayer, journal or reflect on the following questions:

- Do you believe that you will receive a just penalty for the things you have done wrong?
- If we can be saved from our just penalty by placing our faith in Jesus Christ, why would anyone want to "neglect so great a salvation" (verse 3)?
- How can you avoid being carried away (verse 1) from the good news of salvation?

▶ Heb 2.1–4

angels was valid, and every transgression or disobedience received a just penalty, ³ how can we escape if we neglect so great a salvation? It was declared at first through the Lord, and it was attested to us by those who heard him, ⁴ while God added his testimony by signs and wonders and various miracles, and by gifts of the Holy Spirit, distributed according to his will.

Exaltation through Abasement
(Cp Ps 8.1–9)

5 Now God*g* did not subject the coming world, about which we are speaking, to angels. ⁶ But someone has testified somewhere,

"What are human beings that you are mindful
    of them,*h*
  or mortals, that you care for them?*i*
⁷ You have made them for a little while lower*j*
    than the angels;
  you have crowned them with glory and
    honor,*k*
⁸   subjecting all things under their feet."
Now in subjecting all things to them, God*g* left nothing outside their control. As it is, we do not yet see everything in subjection to them, ⁹ but we do see Jesus, who for a little while was made lower*l* than the angels, now crowned with glory and honor because of the suffering of death, so that by the grace of God*m* he might taste death for everyone.

10 It was fitting that God,*g* for whom and

---

g Gk he   *h* Gk What is man that you are mindful of him?
i Gk or the son of man that you care for him? In the Hebrew of Psalm 8.4-6 both man and son of man refer to all humankind   *j* Or them only a little lower   *k* Other ancient authorities add and set them over the works of your hands
l Or who was made a little lower   *m* Other ancient authorities read apart from God

through whom all things exist, in bringing many children to glory, should make the pioneer of their salvation perfect through sufferings. 11 For the one who sanctifies and those who are sanctified all have one Father.[n] For this reason Jesus[o] is not ashamed to call them brothers and sisters,[p] 12 saying,

"I will proclaim your name to my brothers and
        sisters,[p]
    in the midst of the congregation I will
        praise you."

13 And again,

"I will put my trust in him."

And again,

"Here am I and the children whom God has
        given me."

14 Since, therefore, the children share flesh and blood, he himself likewise shared the same things, so that through death he might destroy the one who has the power of death, that is, the devil, 15 and free those who all their lives were held in slavery by the fear of death. 16 For it is clear that he did not come to help angels, but the descendants of Abraham. 17 Therefore he had to become like his brothers and sisters[p] in every respect, so that he might be a merciful and faithful high priest in the service of God, to make a sacrifice of atonement for the sins of the people. 18 Because he himself was tested by what he suffered, he is able to help those who are being tested.

Moses a Servant, Christ a Son

3 Therefore, brothers and sisters,[p] holy partners in a heavenly calling, consider that Jesus, the apostle and high priest of our confession, 2 was faithful to the one who appointed him, just as Moses also "was faithful in all[q] God's[r] house." 3 Yet Jesus[s] is worthy of more glory than Moses, just as the builder of a house has more honor than the house itself. 4 (For every house is built by someone, but the builder of all things is God.) 5 Now Moses was faithful in all God's[r] house as a servant, to testify to the things that would be spoken later. 6 Christ, however, was faithful over God's[r] house as a son, and we are his house if we hold firm[t] the confidence and the pride that belong to hope.

Warning against Unbelief
(Ps 95.7b–11)

7 Therefore, as the Holy Spirit says,

"Today, if you hear his voice,
8   do not harden your hearts as in the rebellion,
        as on the day of testing in the
        wilderness,
9   where your ancestors put me to the test,
        though they had seen my works 10 for forty
        years.
Therefore I was angry with that generation,

and I said, 'They always go astray in their
        hearts,
    and they have not known my ways.'
11 As in my anger I swore,
    'They will not enter my rest.' "

12 Take care, brothers and sisters,[p] that none of you may have an evil, unbelieving heart that turns away from the living God. 13 But exhort one another every day, as long as it is called "today," so that none of you may be hardened by the deceitfulness of sin. 14 For we have become partners of Christ, if only we hold our first confidence firm to the end. 15 As it is said,

"Today, if you hear his voice,
    do not harden your hearts as in the rebellion."

16 Now who were they who heard and yet were rebellious? Was it not all those who left Egypt under the leadership of Moses? 17 But with whom was he angry forty years? Was it not those who sinned, whose bodies fell in the wilderness? 18 And to whom did he swear that they would not enter his rest, if not to those who were disobedient? 19 So we see that they were unable to enter because of unbelief.

The Rest That God Promised

4 Therefore, while the promise of entering his rest is still open, let us take care that none of you should seem to have failed to reach it. 2 For indeed the good news came to us just as to them; but the message they heard did not benefit them, because they were not united by faith with those who listened.[u] 3 For we who have believed enter that rest, just as God[o] has said,

"As in my anger I swore,
    'They shall not enter my rest,' "

though his works were finished at the foundation of the world. 4 For in one place it speaks about the seventh day as follows, "And God rested on the seventh day from all his works." 5 And again in this place it says, "They shall not enter my rest." 6 Since therefore it remains open for some to enter it, and those who formerly received the good news failed to enter because of disobedience, 7 again he sets a certain day—"today"—saying through David much later, in the words already quoted,

"Today, if you hear his voice,
    do not harden your hearts."

8 For if Joshua had given them rest, God[o] would not speak later about another day. 9 So then, a sabbath rest still remains for the people of God; 10 for those who enter God's rest also cease from their labors as

---

n Gk *are all of one*   o Gk *he*   p Gk *brothers*   q Other ancient authorities lack *all*   r Gk *his*   s Gk *this one*   t Other ancient authorities add *to the end*   u Other ancient authorities read *it did not meet with faith in those who listened*

The **word** of **God** is *living* and *active,* **sharper than any two-edged** sword

4.12

God did from his. 11 Let us therefore make every effort to enter that rest, so that no one may fall through such disobedience as theirs.

12 Indeed, the word of God is living and active, sharper than any two-edged sword, piercing until it divides soul from spirit, joints from marrow; it is able to judge the thoughts and intentions of the heart. 13 And before him no creature is hidden, but all are naked and laid bare to the eyes of the one to whom we must render an account.

Jesus the Great High Priest

14 Since, then, we have a great high priest who has passed through the heavens, Jesus, the Son of God, let us hold fast to our confession. 15 For we do not have a high priest who is unable to sympathize with our weaknesses, but we have one who in every respect has been tested*v* as we are, yet without sin.

16 Let us therefore approach the throne of grace with boldness, so that we may receive mercy and find grace to help in time of need.

5 Every high priest chosen from among mortals is put in charge of things pertaining to God on their behalf, to offer gifts and sacrifices for sins. 2 He is able to deal gently with the ignorant and wayward, since he himself is subject to weakness; 3 and because of this he must offer sacrifice for his own sins as well as for those of the people. 4 And one does not presume to take this honor, but takes it only when called by God, just as Aaron was.

5 So also Christ did not glorify himself in becoming a high priest, but was appointed by the one who said to him,

"You are my Son,
today I have begotten you";
6 as he says also in another place,
"You are a priest forever,
according to the order of Mel•chiz'e•dek."

7 In the days of his flesh, Jesus*w* offered up prayers and supplications, with loud cries and tears, to the one who was able to save him from death, and he was heard because of his reverent submission. 8 Although he was a Son, he learned obedience through what he suffered; 9 and having been made perfect, he became the source of eternal salvation for all who obey him, 10 having been designated by God a high priest according to the order of Mel•chiz'e•dek.

Warning against Falling Away

11 About this*x* we have much to say that is hard to explain, since you have become dull in understanding. 12 For though by this time you ought to be teachers, you need someone to teach you again

---

v Or *tempted*   *w* Gk *he*   *x* Or *him*

LIVE IT!

Approach God Boldly!

Have you ever believed that you did something that God could never forgive? Or do you ever have thoughts that make you feel so ashamed that you do not dare talk with God about them?

Hebrews 4.14–16 reminds us of a remarkable truth: Jesus, while fully divine, was also fully human. And though he never sinned, this Scripture passage tells us that he was tempted as we are in every respect. Think about that! Jesus was once fourteen years old. He was once seventeen. He was once twenty-two. There is no temptation that you have considered that Jesus cannot understand. And that is why you can approach him in any circumstance—even your deepest trouble—and find compassion and grace.

Remember: (1) you cannot hide from God, and (2) you don't have to!

▶ Heb 4.14–16

did you KNOW?

The Priesthood and Christ's Sacrifice

In the Old Testament, the priesthood evolved after Israel became a nation, and it underwent a long process of development. Priests were not ordained; the priesthood was considered hereditary within the tribe of Levi. After the Exile, three classes of clergy emerged: high priests, priests, and Levites. Priestly functions included maintaining religion as the center of Israel's life, taking care of the Temple of Jerusalem, and interpreting and teaching the Scriptures. In a special way, the priests of Israel represented the people before God by offering prayer and sacrifices for the forgiveness of sin. Their sacrifices foreshadowed the sacrifice of Jesus, the only sacrifice truly capable of reconciling a broken relationship with God caused by sin.

In the New Testament, Christ made the Apostles co-ministers in his saving mission, including a special participation in his high priesthood—the high priesthood described in Heb 4.14—5.10. Today, the bishops, as successors of the Apostles, continue the apostolic tradition. They ordain priests to assist in their responsibilities as pastors of the faithful, preachers of God's word, and celebrants of Christian worship (see "Holy Orders," Mk 3.13–19).

Catholic bishops and priests exercise their special participation in Christ's priesthood while presiding at the Eucharist. Acting in Christ's name and in communion with the assembly, they celebrate a memorial of Jesus' life, death, and Resurrection. In the celebration of the Eucharist, Christ's sacrifice on the cross is "re-presented," that is, Jesus' sacrifice for the forgiveness of sins is made real and present.

▸ Heb 4.14—5.10

of righteousness. 14 But solid food is for the mature, for those whose faculties have been trained by practice to distinguish good from evil.

The Peril of Falling Away

6 Therefore let us go on toward perfection,[y] leaving behind the basic teaching about Christ, and not laying again the foundation: repentance from dead works and faith toward God, 2 instruction about baptisms, laying on of hands, resurrection of the dead, and eternal judgment. 3 And we will do[z] this, if God permits. 4 For it is impossible to restore again to repentance those who have once been enlightened, and have tasted the heavenly gift, and have shared in the Holy Spirit, 5 and have tasted the goodness of the word of God and the powers of the age to come, 6 and then have fallen away, since on their own they are crucifying again the Son of God and are holding him up to contempt. 7 Ground that drinks up the rain falling on it repeatedly, and that produces a crop useful to those for whom it is cultivated, receives a blessing from God. 8 But if it produces thorns and thistles, it is worthless and on the verge of being cursed; its end is to be burned over.

9 Even though we speak in this way, beloved, we are confident of better things in your case, things that belong to salvation. 10 For God is not unjust; he will not overlook your work and the love that you showed for his sake[a] in serving the saints, as you still do. 11 And we want each one of you to show the same diligence so as to realize the full assurance of hope to the very end, 12 so that you may not become sluggish, but imitators of those who through faith and patience inherit the promises.

The Certainty of God's Promise
(Cp Gen 12.1–3)

13 When God made a promise to Abraham, because he had no one greater by whom to swear, he swore by himself, 14 saying, "I will surely bless you and multiply you." 15 And thus Abraham,[b] having patiently endured, obtained the promise. 16 Human beings, of course, swear by someone greater than themselves, and an oath given as confirmation puts an end to all dispute. 17 In the same way, when God desired to show even more clearly to the heirs of the promise the unchangeable character of his purpose, he guaranteed it by an oath, 18 so that through two unchangeable things, in which it is impossible that God would prove false, we who have taken refuge might be strongly encouraged to seize the hope set before us. 19 We have this hope, a sure and steadfast anchor of the soul, a hope that enters

the basic elements of the oracles of God. You need milk, not solid food; 13 for everyone who lives on milk, being still an infant, is unskilled in the word

---

[y] Or *toward maturity*   [z] Other ancient authorities read *let us do*   [a] Gk *for his name*   [b] Gk *he*

H
E
B

ANCHOR OF THE SOUL

Something mighty powerful kept a smile on my mother's face every day when I was a little girl. I never knew she was in pain. All I saw was a woman with a demeanor of hope and a purpose in life.

I did not know it back then, but she was enduring racial harassment on her job. There was unceasing verbal hate toward her. As I have matured, I have learned that her harassment was not unique. It was a common experience for many people.

When faced with oppressive situations, let us be thankful for a God who continuously fills us with hope. Without hope, oppression is lethal. Hope keeps us moving forward when we'd just as soon give up. Hope makes us smile at tomorrow, even though today is a bitter pill.

Hope is "a sure and steadfast anchor of the soul" (Heb 6.19). A hopeless soul is a major threat to the body. Is your hope anchored in the Lord?

Dear God, give me hope when I face oppression. Amen.

▶ Heb 6.19–20

---

the inner shrine behind the curtain, 20 where Jesus, a forerunner on our behalf, has entered, having become a high priest forever according to the order of Mel•chiz′e•dek.

The Priestly Order of Melchizedek
(Gen 14.17–20)

7 This "King Mel•chiz′e•dek of Salem, priest of the Most High God, met Abraham as he was returning from defeating the kings and blessed him"; 2 and to him Abraham apportioned "one-tenth of everything." His name, in the first place, means "king of righteousness"; next he is also king of Salem, that is, "king of peace." 3 Without father, without mother, without genealogy, having neither beginning of days nor end of life, but resembling the Son of God, he remains a priest forever.

4 See how great he is! Even*c* Abraham the patriarch gave him a tenth of the spoils. 5 And those descendants of Levi who receive the priestly office have a commandment in the law to collect tithes*d* from the people, that is, from their kindred,*e* though these also are descended from Abraham. 6 But this man, who does not belong to their ancestry, collected tithes*d* from Abraham and blessed him who had received the promises. 7 It is beyond dispute that the inferior is blessed by the superior. 8 In the one case, tithes are received by those who

are mortal; in the other, by one of whom it is testified that he lives. 9 One might even say that Levi himself, who receives tithes, paid tithes through Abraham, 10 for he was still in the loins of his ancestor when Mel•chiz′e•dek met him.

Another Priest, Like Melchizedek
(Ps 110.4)

11 Now if perfection had been attainable through the levitical priesthood—for the people received the law under this priesthood—what further need would there have been to speak of another priest arising according to the order of Mel•chiz′e•dek, rather than one according to the order of Aaron? 12 For when there is a change in the priesthood, there is necessarily a change in the law as well. 13 Now the one of whom these things are spoken belonged to another tribe, from which no one has ever served at the altar. 14 For it is evident that our Lord was descended from Judah, and in connection with that tribe Moses said nothing about priests.

15 It is even more obvious when another priest arises, resembling Mel•chiz′e•dek, 16 one who has become a priest, not through a legal requirement

---

c Other ancient authorities lack *Even*   *d* Or *a tenth*
e Gk *brothers*

concerning physical descent, but through the power of an indestructible life. 17 For it is attested of him,

"You are a priest forever,
    according to the order of Mel•chiz'e•dek."

18 There is, on the one hand, the abrogation of an earlier commandment because it was weak and ineffectual 19 (for the law made nothing perfect); there is, on the other hand, the introduction of a better hope, through which we approach God.

20 This was confirmed with an oath; for others who became priests took their office without an oath, 21 but this one became a priest with an oath, because of the one who said to him,

"The Lord has sworn
    and will not change his mind,
'You are a priest forever' "—

22 accordingly Jesus has also become the guarantee of a better covenant.

23 Furthermore, the former priests were many in number, because they were prevented by death from continuing in office; 24 but he holds his priesthood permanently, because he continues forever. 25 Consequently he is able for all time to save/ those who approach God through him, since he always lives to make intercession for them.

26 For it was fitting that we should have such a high priest, holy, blameless, undefiled, separated from sinners, and exalted above the heavens. 27 Unlike the others high priests, he has no need to offer sacrifices day after day, first for his own sins, and then for those of the people; this he did once for all when he offered himself. 28 For the law appoints as high priests those who are subject to weakness, but the word of the oath, which came later than the law, appoints a Son who has been made perfect forever.

Mediator of a Better Covenant
(Jer 31.31–34)

8 Now the main point in what we are saying is this: we have such a high priest, one who is seated at the right hand of the throne of the Majesty in the heavens, 2 a minister in the sanctuary and the true tent/ that the Lord, and not any mortal, has set up. 3 For every high priest is appointed to offer gifts and sacrifices; hence it is necessary for this priest also to have something to offer. 4 Now if he were on earth, he would not be a priest at all, since there are priests who offer gifts according to the law. 5 They offer worship in a sanctuary that is a sketch and shadow of the heavenly one; for Moses, when he was about to erect the tent,/ was warned, "See that you make everything according to the pattern that was shown you on the mountain." 6 But Jesus/ has now obtained a more excellent ministry, and to that degree he is the mediator of a better covenant,

Catholic Connections

MELCHIZEDEK

Look with favor on these offerings and accept them as once you accepted the gifts of your servant Abel, the sacrifice of Abraham, our father in faith, and the bread and wine offered by your priest Melchisedech.
(Sacramentary, p. 546)

This quote is from the first Eucharistic prayer in the Catholic Mass. Who is Melchisedech (also spelled Melchizedek)? In the Book of Genesis, after Abraham successfully conquers the enemies of his nephew Lot, Melchizedek, a priest and king, offers a sacrifice of bread and wine to God on Abraham's behalf (14.17–20). In this way, he becomes Abraham's priest. Early Christians saw parallels to Jesus in the story of Melchizedek, and even in his name, which means "king of righteousness." Thus, Melchizedek's life came to be viewed as an early but incomplete example of Jesus' high priesthood.

▶ Heb 7.1–10

which has been enacted through better promises. 7 For if that first covenant had been faultless, there would have been no need to look for a second one. 8 God/ finds fault with them when he says:

"The days are surely coming, says the Lord,
    when I will establish a new covenant with
        the house of Israel
    and with the house of Judah;
9 not like the covenant that I made with their
        ancestors,
    on the day when I took them by the hand
        to lead them out of the land of Egypt;
for they did not continue in my covenant,
    and so I had no concern for them, says the
        Lord.

---

*f Or able to save completely g Gk lacks other
h Or tabernacle i Gk he j Gk He*

10 This is the covenant that I will make with the
            house of Israel
      after those days, says the Lord:
   I will put my laws in their minds,
         and write them on their hearts,
   and I will be their God,
         and they shall be my people.
11 And they shall not teach one another
         or say to each other, 'Know the Lord,'
      for they shall all know me,
         from the least of them to the greatest.
12 For I will be merciful toward their iniquities,
         and I will remember their sins no more."
13 In speaking of "a new covenant," he has made
the first one obsolete. And what is obsolete and
growing old will soon disappear.

The Earthly and the Heavenly Sanctuaries
(Cp Ex 25.10–40)

9 Now even the first covenant had regulations
for worship and an earthly sanctuary. 2 For a
tent[k] was constructed, the first one, in which were
the lampstand, the table, and the bread of the Presence;[l] this is called the Holy Place. 3 Behind the second curtain was a tent[k] called the Holy of Holies.
4 In it stood the golden altar of incense and the ark
of the covenant overlaid on all sides with gold, in
which there were a golden urn holding the manna,
and Aaron's rod that budded, and the tablets of the
covenant; 5 above it were the cherubim of glory
overshadowing the mercy seat.[m] Of these things we
cannot speak now in detail.

6 Such preparations having been made, the
priests go continually into the first tent[k] to carry out
their ritual duties; 7 but only the high priest goes
into the second, and he but once a year, and not
without taking the blood that he offers for himself
and for the sins committed unintentionally by the
people. 8 By this the Holy Spirit indicates that the
way into the sanctuary has not yet been disclosed as
long as the first tent[k] is still standing. 9 This is a symbol[n] of the present time, during which gifts and sacrifices are offered that cannot perfect the conscience
of the worshiper, 10 but deal only with food and
drink and various baptisms, regulations for the body
imposed until the time comes to set things right.

11 But when Christ came as a high priest of the
good things that have come,[o] then through the
greater and perfect[p] tent[k] (not made with hands,
that is, not of this creation), 12 he entered once for
all into the Holy Place, not with the blood of goats
and calves, but with his own blood, thus obtaining
eternal redemption. 13 For if the blood of goats and
bulls, with the sprinkling of the ashes of a heifer,
sanctifies those who have been defiled so that their
flesh is purified, 14 how much more will the blood
of Christ, who through the eternal Spirit[q] offered

himself without blemish to God, purify our[r] conscience from dead works to worship the living God!

15 For this reason he is the mediator of a new
covenant, so that those who are called may receive
the promised eternal inheritance, because a death
has occurred that redeems them from the transgressions under the first covenant.[s] 16 Where a will[s] is
involved, the death of the one who made it must be
established. 17 For a will[s] takes effect only at death,
since it is not in force as long as the one who made
it is alive. 18 Hence not even the first covenant was
inaugurated without blood. 19 For when every commandment had been told to all the people by
Moses in accordance with the law, he took the
blood of calves and goats,[t] with water and scarlet
wool and hyssop, and sprinkled both the scroll itself and all the people, 20 saying, "This is the blood
of the covenant that God has ordained for you."
21 And in the same way he sprinkled with the blood
both the tent[k] and all the vessels used in worship.
22 Indeed, under the law almost everything is purified with blood, and without the shedding of blood
there is no forgiveness of sins.

Christ's Sacrifice Takes Away Sin

23 Thus it was necessary for the sketches of the
heavenly things to be purified with these rites, but
the heavenly things themselves need better sacrifices than these. 24 For Christ did not enter a sanctuary made by human hands, a mere copy of the
true one, but he entered into heaven itself, now to
appear in the presence of God on our behalf. 25 Nor
was it to offer himself again and again, as the high
priest enters the Holy Place year after year with
blood that is not his own; 26 for then he would
have had to suffer again and again since the foundation of the world. But as it is, he has appeared
once for all at the end of the age to remove sin by
the sacrifice of himself. 27 And just as it is appointed for mortals to die once, and after that the judgment, 28 so Christ, having been offered once to bear
the sins of many, will appear a second time, not to
deal with sin, but to save those who are eagerly
waiting for him.

Christ's Sacrifice Once for All
(Cp Ps 40.6–8)

10 Since the law has only a shadow of the
good things to come and not the true
form of these realities, it[u] can never, by the same

---

k Or *tabernacle* l Gk *the presentation of the loaves*
m Or *the place of atonement* n Gk *parable* o Other ancient
authorities read *good things to come* p Gk *more perfect*
q Other ancient authorities read *Holy Spirit* r Other ancient
authorities read *your* s The Greek word used here means
both *covenant* and *will* t Other ancient authorities lack
and goats u Other ancient authorities read *they*

did you KNOW?

The Perfect Sacrifice

The author of the Letter to the Hebrews uses the "from the lesser to the greater" argument again to explain that Christ's sacrifice on the cross is greater than any sacrifice that could ever be offered in the Temple. Even though perfect animals are offered over and over, they never take away sins (10.1–4). The sacrifice of Christ takes away sins because it is the perfect sacrifice, offered only once for the sins of all (verses 12–14). After Christ's death, there is no longer any need for anyone else to offer a sacrifice for the forgiveness of sins.

▶ Heb 10.1–18

sacrifices that are continually offered year after year, make perfect those who approach. 2 Otherwise, would they not have ceased being offered, since the worshipers, cleansed once for all, would no longer have any consciousness of sin? 3 But in these sacrifices there is a reminder of sin year after year. 4 For it is impossible for the blood of bulls and goats to take away sins. 5 Consequently, when Christ*v* came into the world, he said,

"Sacrifices and offerings you have not desired,
　　but a body you have prepared for me;
6 　in burnt offerings and sin offerings
　　you have taken no pleasure.
7 Then I said, 'See, God, I have come to do your
　　will, O God'
　　(in the scroll of the book*w* it is written
　　　of me)."

8 When he said above, "You have neither desired nor taken pleasure in sacrifices and offerings and burnt offerings and sin offerings" (these are offered according to the law), 9 then he added, "See, I have come to do your will." He abolishes the first in order to establish the second. 10 And it is by God's will*x* that we have been sanctified through the offering of the body of Jesus Christ once for all.

11 And every priest stands day after day at his service, offering again and again the same sacrifices that can never take away sins. 12 But when Christ*y* had offered for all time a single sacrifice for sins, "he sat down at the right hand of God," 13 and since then has been waiting "until his enemies

would be made a footstool for his feet." 14 For by a single offering he has perfected for all time those who are sanctified. 15 And the Holy Spirit also testifies to us, for after saying,

16 "This is the covenant that I will make with
　　them
　　after those days, says the Lord:
　I will put my laws in their hearts,
　　and I will write them on their minds,"
17 he also adds,
　"I will remember*z* their sins and their lawless
　　　deeds no more."
18 Where there is forgiveness of these, there is no longer any offering for sin.

A Call to Persevere

19 Therefore, my friends,*a* since we have confidence to enter the sanctuary by the blood of Jesus, 20 by the new and living way that he opened for us through the curtain (that is, through his flesh), 21 and since we have a great priest over the house of God, 22 let us approach with a true heart in full assurance of faith, with our hearts sprinkled clean from an evil conscience and our bodies washed with pure water. 23 Let us hold fast to the confession of our hope without wavering, for he who has promised is faithful. 24 And let us consider how to provoke one another to love and good deeds, 25 not neglecting to meet together, as is the habit of some, but encouraging one another, and all the more as you see the Day approaching.

26 For if we willfully persist in sin after having received the knowledge of the truth, there no longer remains a sacrifice for sins, 27 but a fearful prospect of judgment, and a fury of fire that will consume the adversaries. 28 Anyone who has violated the law of Moses dies without mercy "on the testimony of two or three witnesses." 29 How much worse punishment do you think will be deserved by those who have spurned the Son of God, profaned the blood of the covenant by which they were sanctified, and outraged the Spirit of grace? 30 For we know the one who said, "Vengeance is mine, I will repay." And again, "The Lord will judge his people." 31 It is a fearful thing to fall into the hands of the living God.

32 But recall those earlier days when, after you had been enlightened, you endured a hard struggle with sufferings, 33 sometimes being publicly exposed to abuse and persecution, and sometimes being partners with those so treated. 34 For you had compassion for those who were in prison, and you cheerfully accepted the plundering of your

---

v Gk he   *w* Meaning of Gk uncertain   *x* Gk by that will
y Gk this one   *z* Gk on their minds and I will remember
a Gk Therefore, brothers

H
E
B

possessions, knowing that you yourselves possessed something better and more lasting. 35 Do not, therefore, abandon that confidence of yours; it brings a great reward. 36 For you need endurance, so that when you have done the will of God, you may receive what was promised. 37 For yet

> "in a very little while,
>> the one who is coming will come and will not delay;
> 38 but my righteous one will live by faith.
>> My soul takes no pleasure in anyone who shrinks back."

39 But we are not among those who shrink back and so are lost, but among those who have faith and so are saved.

The Meaning of Faith

11 Now faith is the assurance of things hoped for, the conviction of things not seen. 2 Indeed, by faith[b] our ancestors received approval. 3 By faith we understand that the worlds were prepared by the word of God, so that what is seen was made from things that are not visible.[c]

The Examples of Abel, Enoch, and Noah
(Gen 4.1–16; 6.5—8.22)

4 By faith Abel offered to God a more acceptable[d] sacrifice than Cain's. Through this he received approval as righteous, God himself giving approval to his gifts; he died, but through his faith[e] he still speaks. 5 By faith Énoch was taken so that he did not experience death; and "he was not found, because God had taken him." For it was attested before he was taken away that "he had pleased God." 6 And without faith it is impossible to please God, for whoever would approach him must believe that he exists and that he rewards those who seek him. 7 By faith Noah, warned by God about events as yet unseen, respected the warning and built an ark to save his household; by this he condemned the world and became an heir to the righteousness that is in accordance with faith.

The Faith of Abraham
(Gen 15.1–6; 21.1–7; 22.1–14; 48.8–16; 50.22–25)

8 By faith Abraham obeyed when he was called to set out for a place that he was to receive as an inheritance; and he set out, not knowing where he was going. 9 By faith he stayed for a time in the land he had been promised, as in a foreign land, living in tents, as did Isaac and Jacob, who were heirs with him of the same promise. 10 For he looked forward to the city that has foundations, whose architect and builder is God. 11 By faith he received power of procreation, even though he was too old—and Sarah herself was barren—because he considered him faithful who had promised.[f] 12 Therefore from

Catholic Connections
THE CLOUD OF WITNESS

In chapters 11 and 12 of The Letter to the Hebrews, the author reminds his audience of the great legacy of men and women who have served as examples of faith and virtue. Their faith in God and their fidelity to the Covenant stand as compelling witnesses to those who seek to follow Christ. From Abel to Abraham and Sarah and from Moses up through the ages, the word of God attests to how women and men have lived their lives for God.

Jesus, however, is the one upon whom we are urged to "fix" our eyes so that we see the leader and perfecter of such faith. Christ and his sacrifice stand as the ultimate example of faith and fidelity.

The cloud of witnesses has grown as Christ has called people of all ages to holiness. From Mary, his mother, to Peter and the Apostles and martyrs, from Augustine and Aquinas to Francis and Theresa, men and women of every age, in every corner of the earth, have lived their lives for God. The cloud grows ever larger as these saints continue to forge a legacy, a witness to God's love and salvation offered in Jesus the Son.

We too are called to resist sin and offer our lives to God, even if it means facing the discipline of suffering. We are called to be the new generation of witnesses—the saints of our day whose example calls and strengthens others on the journey.

▶ Hebrews, chapters 11 and 12

one person, and this one as good as dead, descendants were born, "as many as the stars of heaven and as the innumerable grains of sand by the seashore."

---

b Gk by this   c Or was not made out of visible things
d Gk greater   e Gk through it   f Or By faith Sarah herself, though barren, received power to conceive, even when she was too old, because she considered him faithful who had promised.

13 All of these died in faith without having received the promises, but from a distance they saw and greeted them. They confessed that they were strangers and foreigners on the earth, 14 for people who speak in this way make it clear that they are seeking a homeland. 15 If they had been thinking of the land that they had left behind, they would have had opportunity to return. 16 But as it is, they desire a better country, that is, a heavenly one. Therefore God is not ashamed to be called their God; indeed, he has prepared a city for them.

17 By faith Abraham, when put to the test, offered up Isaac. He who had received the promises was ready to offer up his only son, 18 of whom he had been told, "It is through Isaac that descendants shall be named for you." 19 He considered the fact that God is able even to raise someone from the dead—and figuratively speaking, he did receive him back. 20 By faith Isaac invoked blessings for the future on Jacob and Esau. 21 By faith Jacob, when dying, blessed each of the sons of Joseph, "bowing in worship over the top of his staff." 22 By faith Joseph, at the end of his life, made mention of the exodus of the Israelites and gave instructions about his burial.g

The Faith of Moses
(Ex 2.1–10; 12.31–51)

23 By faith Moses was hidden by his parents for three months after his birth, because they saw that the child was beautiful; and they were not afraid of the king's edict.h 24 By faith Moses, when he was grown up, refused to be called a son of Pharaoh's daughter, 25 choosing rather to share ill-treatment with the people of God than to enjoy the fleeting pleasures of sin. 26 He considered abuse suffered for the Christi to be greater wealth than the treasures of Egypt, for he was looking ahead to the reward. 27 By faith he left Egypt, unafraid of the king's anger; for he persevered as thoughj he saw him who is invisible. 28 By faith he kept the Passover and the sprinkling of blood, so that the destroyer of the firstborn would not touch the firstborn of Israel.k

The Faith of Other Israelite Heroes

29 By faith the people passed through the Red Sea as if it were dry land, but when the Egyptians attempted to do so they were drowned. 30 By faith the walls of Jericho fell after they had been encircled for seven days. 31 By faith Ra'hab the prostitute did not perish with those who were disobedient,l because she had received the spies in peace.

32 And what more should I say? For time would fail me to tell of Gideon, Bar'ak, Samson, Jeph'thah, of David and Samuel and the prophets— 33 who through faith conquered kingdoms, administered justice, obtained promises, shut the mouths

of lions, 34 quenched raging fire, escaped the edge of the sword, won strength out of weakness, became mighty in war, put foreign armies to flight. 35 Women received their dead by resurrection. Others were tortured, refusing to accept release, in order to obtain a better resurrection. 36 Others suffered mocking and flogging, and even chains and imprisonment. 37 They were stoned to death, they were sawn in two,m they were killed by the sword; they went about in skins of sheep and goats, destitute, persecuted, tormented— 38 of whom the world was not worthy. They wandered in deserts and mountains, and in caves and holes in the ground.

39 Yet all these, though they were commended for their faith, did not receive what was promised, 40 since God had provided something better so that they would not, apart from us, be made perfect.

The Example of Jesus
(Prov 3.11–12)

12 Therefore, since we are surrounded by so great a cloud of witnesses, let us also lay aside every weight and the sin that clings so closely,n and let us run with perseverance the race that is set before us, 2 looking to Jesus the pioneer and perfecter of our faith, who for the sake ofo the joy that was set before him endured the cross, disregarding its shame, and has taken his seat at the right hand of the throne of God.

3 Consider him who endured such hostility against himself from sinners,p so that you may not grow weary or lose heart. 4 In your struggle against sin you have not yet resisted to the point of shedding your blood. 5 And you have forgotten the exhortation that addresses you as children—

"My child, do not regard lightly the discipline
   of the Lord,
      or lose heart when you are punished by
         him;
 6 for the Lord disciplines those whom he loves,
      and chastises every child whom he accepts."
7 Endure trials for the sake of discipline. God is treating you as children; for what child is there whom a parent does not discipline? 8 If you do not have that discipline in which all children share, then you are illegitimate and not his children. 9 Moreover, we had human parents to discipline us, and we respected them. Should we not be even more willing to be subject to the Father of spirits

---

g Gk his bones h Other ancient authorities add By faith Moses, when he was grown up, killed the Egyptian, because he observed the humiliation of his people (Gk brothers) i Or the Messiah j Or because k Gk would not touch them l Or unbelieving m Other ancient authorities add they were tempted n Other ancient authorities read sin that easily distracts o Or who instead of p Other ancient authorities read such hostility from sinners against themselves and live? 10 For they disciplined us for a short time as seemed best to them, but he disciplines us for our good, in order that we may share his holiness. 11 Now, discipline always seems painful rather than pleasant at the time, but later it yields the peaceful fruit of righteousness to those who have been trained by it.

12 Therefore lift your drooping hands and strengthen your weak knees, 13 and make straight paths for your feet, so that what is lame may not be put out of joint, but rather be healed.

Warnings against Rejecting God's Grace
(Gen 25.29–34; 27.30–40)

14 Pursue peace with everyone, and the holiness without which no one will see the Lord. 15 See to it that no one fails to obtain the grace of God; that no root of bitterness springs up and causes trouble, and through it many become defiled. 16 See to it that no one becomes like Esau, an immoral and godless person, who sold his birthright for a single meal. 17 You know that later, when he wanted to inherit the blessing, he was rejected, for he found no chance to repent,*q* even though he sought the blessing*r* with tears.

18 You have not come to something*s* that can be touched, a blazing fire, and darkness, and gloom, and a tempest, 19 and the sound of a trumpet, and a voice whose words made the hearers beg that not another word be spoken to them. 20 (For they could not endure the order that was given, "If even an animal touches the mountain, it shall be stoned to death." 21 Indeed, so terrifying was the sight that Moses said, "I tremble with fear.") 22 But you have come to Mount Zion and to the city of the living God, the heavenly Jerusalem, and to innumerable angels in festal gathering, 23 and to the assembly*t* of the firstborn who are enrolled in heaven, and to God the judge of all, and to the spirits of the righteous made perfect, 24 and to Jesus, the mediator of a new covenant, and to the sprinkled blood that speaks a better word than the blood of Abel.

25 See that you do not refuse the one who is speaking; for if they did not escape when they refused the one who warned them on earth, how much less will we escape if we reject the one who warns from heaven! 26 At that time his voice shook the earth; but now he has promised, "Yet once more I will shake not only the earth but also the heaven." 27 This phrase, "Yet once more," indicates the removal of what is shaken—that is, created things—so that what cannot be shaken may remain. 28 Therefore, since we are receiving a kingdom that cannot be shaken, let us give thanks, by which we offer to God an acceptable worship with reverence and awe; 29 for indeed our God is a consuming fire.

Service Well-Pleasing to God

13 Let mutual love continue. 2 Do not neglect to show hospitality to strangers, for by doing that some have entertained angels without knowing it. 3 Remember those who are in prison, as though you were in prison with them; those who are being tortured, as though you yourselves were being tortured.*u* 4 Let marriage be held in honor by all, and let the marriage bed be kept undefiled; for God will judge fornicators and adulterers. 5 Keep your lives free from the love of money, and be content with what you have; for he has said, "I will never leave you or forsake you." 6 So we can say with confidence,

"The Lord is my helper;
    I will not be afraid.
What can anyone do to me?"

7 Remember your leaders, those who spoke the word of God to you; consider the outcome of their way of life, and imitate their faith. 8 Jesus Christ is the same yesterday and today and forever. 9 Do not be carried away by all kinds of strange teachings; for it is well for the heart to be strengthened by grace, not by regulations about food,*v* which have not benefited those who observe them. 10 We have an altar from which those who officiate in the tent*w* have no right to eat. 11 For the bodies of those animals whose blood is brought into the sanctuary by the high priest as a sacrifice for sin are burned outside the camp. 12 Therefore Jesus also suffered outside the city gate in order to sanctify the people by his own blood. 13 Let us then go to him outside the camp and bear the abuse he endured. 14 For here we have no lasting city, but we are looking for the city that is to come. 15 Through him, then, let us continually offer a sacrifice of praise to God, that is, the fruit of lips that confess his name. 16 Do not neglect to do good and to share what you have, for such sacrifices are pleasing to God.

17 Obey your leaders and submit to them, for they are keeping watch over your souls and will give an account. Let them do this with joy and not with sighing—for that would be harmful to you.

18 Pray for us; we are sure that we have a clear conscience, desiring to act honorably in all things. 19 I urge you all the more to do this, so that I may be restored to you very soon.

Benediction

20 Now may the God of peace, who brought back from the dead our Lord Jesus, the great shepherd of the sheep, by the blood of the eternal

---

q Or no chance to change his father's *mind*   *r* Gk *it*
s Other ancient authorities read a *mountain*   *t* Or *angels,*
and to the festal gathering 23and assembly   *u* Gk *were in the*
body   *v* Gk *not by foods*   *w* Or *tabernacle*

Entertaining Angels

The subject of angels has always fascinated the media, especially filmmakers and television show producers. They often develop stories around the idea from The Letter to the Hebrews that people sometimes encounter angels and that angels are sent to rescue people caught in dire or tragic circumstances.

We know that God has created a category of beings that is made up of pure spirits without bodies. These beings act as God's messengers and serve as spiritual guardians for humans. Their mission is to bring God's word to those who are open to hear it and respond to it with faith and humility.

Will we ever be "touched by an angel" or have the opportunity to entertain angels in human disguise? We may never know the answer to these questions, but we should entertain this truth in our hearts and minds: God guides the world and has sent messengers and guardians, angels, whose mysterious presence offers support, protection, and intercession for those who believe in God and seek the face of God.

▸ Heb 13.1–5

H
E
B

covenant, 21 make you complete in everything good so that you may do his will, working among us[x] that which is pleasing in his sight, through Jesus Christ, to whom be the glory forever and ever. Amen.

Final Exhortation and Greetings

22 I appeal to you, brothers and sisters,[y] bear with my word of exhortation, for I have written to you briefly. 23 I want you to know that our brother Timothy has been set free; and if he comes in time, he will be with me when I see you. 24 Greet all your leaders and all the saints. Those from Italy send you greetings. 25 Grace be with all of you.[z]

---

x Other ancient authorities read *you*   y Gk *brothers*
z Other ancient authorities add *Amen*

Have you ever noticed how a kite strains at the string as it soars in the sky? It seems to want to be free of the string that ties it down, free to fly on its own. But if that string does break, the kite flounders and crashes. The kite only has the freedom to fly as long as it's tied to something. That's the way we are under the New Covenant in Christ. We may think we're free to do whatever we want. But if we break from a faithful response to God's love for us, we flounder and crash. The Letter of James provides guidance for living "the law of liberty" (1.25), which leads to real freedom.

At a Glance

- **Chapter 1.** proverbs for Christian living

- **2.1–13.** a discussion of discrimination within the Christian community

- **2.14–26.** a message that faith without works is dead

- **3.1–12.** warnings about controlling the tongue

- **3.13—5.20.** more advice for Christian living

In-depth

Defining the literary style of James is a little difficult. It opens like the other letters but lacks the typical closing. In ways, it is similar to the wisdom literature of the Old Testament. It provides practical advice for how wise people ought to live. It is also similar to Greek moral teaching, which used famous people as models for how we ought to live. This has led scholars to think the book might have been written by an educated Jewish Christian, possibly living in Jerusalem. The author could have been an admirer of James, the first leader of the early church in Jerusalem.

The letter addresses several issues in Christian living. It warns that rich people should not discriminate against poor people. It insists that Christians' actions must reflect their beliefs. It cautions against careless speech and a poorly controlled tongue. It encourages believers to patiently endure suffering.

James also addresses a misunderstanding of Paul's teaching that "a person is justified by faith apart from works prescribed by the law" (Rom 3.28). Using Abraham and Rahab as examples, the author of James declares, "A person is justified by works and not by faith alone" (Jas 2.24). After all, "faith by itself, if it has no works, is dead" (verse 17). To say you love Jesus, and then do unloving things, makes no sense; it's just plain hypocritical.

So here is God's message of freedom for you: Soar like a kite by staying connected to the law of liberty!

Quick Facts

Author
possibly James the relative of Jesus, but more likely a later admirer of James

Date Written
A.D. 57–62 if by James, A.D. 70–150 if by a later admirer

Audience
Christians in Palestine, Syria, or Rome

James

Salutation

1 James, a servant[a] of God and of the Lord Jesus Christ,

To the twelve tribes in the Dispersion:

Greetings.

Faith and Wisdom

2 My brothers and sisters,[b] whenever you face trials of any kind, consider it nothing but joy, 3 because you know that the testing of your faith produces endurance; 4 and let endurance have its full effect, so that you may be mature and complete, lacking in nothing.

5 If any of you is lacking in wisdom, ask God, who gives to all generously and ungrudgingly, and it will be given you. 6 But ask in faith, never doubting, for the one who doubts is like a wave of the sea, driven and tossed by the wind; 7, 8 for the doubter, being double-minded and unstable in every way, must not expect to receive anything from the Lord.

Poverty and Riches

9 Let the believer[c] who is lowly boast in being raised up, 10 and the rich in being brought low, because the rich will disappear like a flower in the field. 11 For the sun rises with its scorching heat and withers the field; its flower falls, and its beauty perishes. It is the same way with the rich; in the midst of a busy life, they will wither away.

Trial and Temptation

12 Blessed is anyone who endures temptation. Such a one has stood the test and will receive the crown of life that the Lord[d] has promised to those who love him. 13 No one, when tempted, should say, "I am being tempted by God"; for God cannot be tempted by evil and he himself tempts no one. 14 But one is tempted by one's own desire, being lured and enticed by it; 15 then, when that desire has conceived, it gives birth to sin, and that sin, when it is fully grown, gives birth to death. 16 Do not be deceived, my beloved.[e]

17 Every generous act of giving, with every perfect gift, is from above, coming down from the Father of lights, with whom there is no variation or shadow due to change.[f] 18 In fulfillment of his own purpose he gave us birth by the word of truth, so that we would become a kind of first fruits of his creatures.

Hearing and Doing the Word

19 You must understand this, my beloved:[e] let everyone be quick to listen, slow to speak, slow to anger; 20 for your anger does not produce God's righteousness. 21 Therefore rid yourselves of all

---

a Gk slave b Gk brothers c Gk brother d Gk he; other ancient authorities read God e Gk my beloved brothers
f Other ancient authorities read variation due to a shadow of turning

PRAY IT!

Meditation on the Walk of Faith

Relax. Clear your mind. Read and reflect on this meditation:

Imagine yourself on your favorite stretch of road. Look back along the road as if it represents your life so far. You have traveled this road all your life to get to where you are standing right now. What obstacles and temptations to your faith have you encountered? Which ones have you stumbled over? Which ones have you overcome?

You see a figure approaching. You strain to see who it is. It gets close enough to recognize. It is Jesus! Jesus sits down with you and asks about the trials you have encountered on your journey. Talk to Jesus about how they have given you the opportunity to grow. Talk to him about the many choices you have made, the good and the bad.

Leave with Jesus to continue forward on the journey. With Jesus, you can joyfully accept the tests of faith that lie ahead, knowing that each is an opportunity to build endurance "so that you may be mature and complete, lacking in nothing" (Jas 1.4).

▸ Jas 1.2–18

JAS

sordidness and rank growth of wickedness, and welcome with meekness the implanted word that has the power to save your souls.

22 But be doers of the word, and not merely hearers who deceive themselves. 23 For if any are hearers of the word and not doers, they are like those who look at themselves in a mirror; 24 for they look at themselves and, on going away, immediately forget what they were like. 25 But those who look into the perfect law, the law of liberty, and persevere, being not hearers who forget but doers who act—they will be blessed in their doing.

26 If any think they are religious, and do not bridle their tongues but deceive their hearts, their religion is worthless. 27 Religion that is pure and undefiled before God, the Father, is this: to care for orphans and widows in their distress, and to keep oneself unstained by the world.

Warning against Partiality

2 My brothers and sisters,[h] do you with your acts of favoritism really believe in our glorious Lord Jesus Christ?[i] 2 For if a person with gold rings and in fine clothes comes into your assembly, and if a poor person in dirty clothes also comes in, 3 and if you take notice of the one wearing the fine clothes and say, "Have a seat here, please," while to the one who is poor you say, "Stand there," or, "Sit at my feet,"[j] 4 have you not made distinctions among yourselves, and become judges with evil thoughts? 5 Listen, my beloved brothers and sisters.[k] Has not God chosen the poor in the world to be rich in faith and to be heirs of the kingdom that he has promised to those who love him? 6 But you have dishonored the poor. Is it not the rich who oppress you? Is it not they who drag you into court? 7 Is it not they who blaspheme the excellent name that was invoked over you?

8 You do well if you really fulfill the royal law according to the scripture, "You shall love your neighbor as yourself." 9 But if you show partiality, you commit sin and are convicted by the law as transgressors. 10 For whoever keeps the whole law but fails in one point has become accountable for all of it. 11 For the one who said, "You shall not commit adultery," also said, "You shall not murder." Now if you do not commit adultery but if you murder, you have become a transgressor of the law. 12 So speak and so act as those who are to be judged by the law of liberty. 13 For judgment will be without mercy to anyone who has shown no mercy; mercy triumphs over judgment.

Faith without Works Is Dead
(Cp Gen 22; Josh 2)

14 What good is it, my brothers and sisters,[k] if you say you have faith but do not have works? Can faith save you? 15 If a brother or sister is naked and lacks daily food, 16 and one of you says to them, "Go in peace; keep warm and eat your fill," and yet you do not supply their bodily needs, what is the good of that? 17 So faith by itself, if it has no works, is dead.

18 But someone will say, "You have faith and I have works." Show me your faith apart from your works, and I by my works will show you my faith. 19 You believe that God is one; you do well. Even the demons believe—and shudder. 20 Do you want to be shown, you senseless person, that faith apart from works is barren? 21 Was not our ancestor Abraham justified by works when he offered his son Isaac on the altar? 22 You see that faith was active

---

g Gk at the face of his birth   h Gk My brothers   i Or hold the faith of our glorious Lord Jesus Christ without acts of favoritism   j Gk Sit under my footstool   k Gk brothers

The Favorite

We all know people we label as "the favorite." We also call these people teacher's pet, brown nose, and so on. Whatever name we use, when we raise a person or a group above others because of money, personality, or power, it seems unfair; yet we all play favorites. We often want to hang out with the most popular students at school, and we usually don't want the most unpopular students to become our friends. We play favorites so that we might become the favorite. And we hate it when others—and not us!—are the favorites.

This is the situation in Jas 2.1–13. The author clearly spells out where God stands on the issue of favoritism and partiality. God's response is to turn things upside down by raising up the poor and the lowly (verse 5). The Catholic church refers to this response as the "preferential option for the poor," which means always keeping in mind the needs of those who are poor when setting policies, providing benefits, and so on.

In our world, there is a big difference between rich and poor, top and bottom, included and excluded. God needs us to carry out the divine response to this injustice. If we do not give poor people real opportunities to rise up, and if we do not challenge the people in power to live according to God's justice, who will? And if we don't reach out to those students at school who seem to be the least popular or least favorite, who will?

▸ Jas 2.1–13

along with his works, and faith was brought to completion by the works. 23 Thus the scripture was fulfilled that says, "Abraham believed God, and it was reckoned to him as righteousness," and he was called the friend of God. 24 You see that a person is justified by works and not by faith alone. 25 Likewise, was not Rā'hab the prostitute also justified by works when she welcomed the messengers and sent them out by another road? 26 For just as the body without the spirit is dead, so faith without works is also dead.

Taming the Tongue

3 Not many of you should become teachers, my brothers and sisters,[1] for you know that we who teach will be judged with greater strictness. 2 For all of us make many mistakes. Anyone who makes no mistakes in speaking is perfect, able to keep the whole body in check with a bridle. 3 If we put bits into the mouths of horses to make them obey us, we guide their whole bodies. 4 Or look at

---

[1] Gk brothers

Faith and Works

A person who insists that faith alone is necessary for our salvation might think: "I don't have to demonstrate my faith with action at all. I just have to believe in Jesus, and then I can do anything I want." Such an attitude isn't very faithful, mature, or helpful.

Yet a person who insists that particular actions alone are necessary for our salvation might think: "I don't have to really believe in what I'm doing. I'll just go through the motions of faith, and that way I'll play it safe." This attitude is not very faithful, mature, or helpful either.

James is nearly saying the same thing—show me a person who has real faith, and I will show you a person doing good works.

Faith and works are discussed at length in two other letters from Paul: Rom 3.21–31 (see also "The Law, Faith, and Salvation," Rom 3.21–31) and Gal 2.15—3.14 (see also "Saved by Christ," Gal 3.1—4.7).

▸ Jas 2.14–26

The Tongue: Friend or Foe?

Sometimes, we are advised to hold it. Other times, we are ordered to bite it. Try as we might to keep this counsel, our tongue often proves to be much stronger than our will to control it.

All of us have said things that we later regretted. Frequently against our better judgment, we find ourselves speaking in ways that hurt or offend others and God. People are injured by what others say to—or about—them far more often than by physical attack. The scars left by hurtful words can last a lifetime, destroying families and ruining friendships.

Have you spoken words that are hurtful to another person, directly or behind the person's back? How might you use your tongue to begin to heal someone's hurts? Apologies, compliments, and affirmations—the tongue can utter these things too! It is a mark of maturity and confidence when we are able to ask forgiveness or affirm others. Christians are called to this kind of courage and maturity.

Use your tongue to speak positively to others today!

▶ Jas 3.1–12

ships: though they are so large that it takes strong winds to drive them, yet they are guided by a very small rudder wherever the will of the pilot directs. 5 So also the tongue is a small member, yet it boasts of great exploits.

How great a forest is set ablaze by a small fire! 6 And the tongue is a fire. The tongue is placed among our members as a world of iniquity; it stains the whole body, sets on fire the cycle of nature,*m* and is itself set on fire by hell.*n* 7 For every species of beast and bird, of reptile and sea creature, can be tamed and has been tamed by the human species, 8 but no one can tame the tongue—a restless evil, full of deadly poison. 9 With it we bless the Lord and Father, and with it we curse those who are made in the likeness of God. 10 From the same mouth come blessing and cursing. My brothers and sisters,*o* this ought not to be so. 11 Does a spring pour forth from the same opening both fresh and brackish water? 12 Can a fig tree, my brothers and sisters,*p* yield olives, or a grapevine figs? No more can salt water yield fresh.

Two Kinds of Wisdom

13 Who is wise and understanding among you? Show by your good life that your works are done with gentleness born of wisdom. 14 But if you have bitter envy and selfish ambition in your hearts, do not be boastful and false to the truth. 15 Such wisdom does not come down from above, but is earthly, unspiritual, devilish. 16 For where there is envy and selfish ambition, there will also be disorder and wickedness of every kind. 17 But the wisdom from above is first pure, then peaceable, gentle, willing to yield, full of mercy and good fruits, without a trace of partiality or hypocrisy. 18 And a har-

vest of righteousness is sown in peace for*q* those who make peace.

Friendship with the World

4 Those conflicts and disputes among you, where do they come from? Do they not come from your cravings that are at war within you? 2 You want something and do not have it; so you commit murder. And you covet*r* something and cannot obtain it; so you engage in disputes and conflicts. You do not have, because you do not ask. 3 You ask and do not receive, because you ask wrongly, in order to spend what you get on your pleasures. 4 Adulterers! Do you not know that friendship with the world is enmity with God? Therefore whoever wishes to be a friend of the world becomes an enemy of God. 5 Or do you suppose that it is for nothing that the scripture says, "God*s* yearns jealously for the spirit that he has made to dwell in us"? 6 But he gives all the more grace; therefore it says,

"God opposes the proud,
    but gives grace to the humble."

7 Submit yourselves therefore to God. Resist the devil, and he will flee from you. 8 Draw near, to God, and he will draw near to you. Cleanse your hands, you sinners, and purify your hearts, you double-minded. 9 Lament and mourn and weep. Let your laughter be turned into mourning and your joy into dejection. 10 Humble yourselves before the Lord, and he will exalt you.

---

m Or *wheel of birth*   *n* Gk *Gehenna*   *o* Gk *My brothers*
p Gk *my brothers*   *q* Or *by*   *r* Or *you murder and you covet*
s Gk *He*

Draw near to God, and he will draw near to you 4.8

Warning against Judging Another

11 Do not speak evil against one another, brothers and sisters.[t] Whoever speaks evil against another or judges another, speaks evil against the law and judges the law; but if you judge the law, you are not a doer of the law but a judge. 12 There is one lawgiver and judge who is able to save and to destroy. So who, then, are you to judge your neighbor?

Boasting about Tomorrow

13 Come now, you who say, "Today or tomorrow we will go to such and such a town and spend a year there, doing business and making money." 14 Yet you do not even know what tomorrow will bring. What is your life? For you are a mist that appears for a little while and then vanishes. 15 Instead you ought to say, "If the Lord wishes, we will live and do this or that." 16 As it is, you boast in your arrogance; all such boasting is evil. 17 Anyone, then, who knows the right thing to do and fails to do it, commits sin.

Warning to Rich Oppressors

5 Come now, you rich people, weep and wail for the miseries that are coming to you. 2 Your riches have rotted, and your clothes are moth-eaten. 3 Your gold and silver have rusted, and their rust will be evidence against you, and it will eat your flesh like fire. You have laid up treasure[u] for the last days. 4 Listen! The wages of the laborers who mowed your fields, which you kept back by fraud, cry out, and the cries of the harvesters have reached the ears of the Lord of hosts. 5 You have lived on the earth in luxury and in pleasure; you have fattened your hearts in a day of slaughter. 6 You have condemned and murdered the righteous one, who does not resist you.

---

t Gk brothers   u Or will eat your flesh, since you have stored up fire

J A S

Justice for Those Who Are Poor

LIVE IT!

Warnings to the rich are common in the Bible, and should be of concern for Christians living in a wealthy nation. Here are two tough questions to consider: First, in what do we put our trust—the comfort and pleasure that can be had in wealth and material possessions, or God? And second, how does our lifestyle—including the way we spend money, the choices we make about our future work, and the way we use our time—affect the poor people of this world?

God's justice requires that Christians care about the abuse of poor people for the benefit of rich people. God does not want us to become paralyzed with guilt because we are wealthy compared with the rest of the earth. But the Scriptures remind us that the life choices we make matter, and that those choices may either contribute to a more just world, or support a status quo that keeps rich people comfortable and poor people down. To make good life choices, we must educate ourselves about the situations that cause poverty, and examine how our own lifestyle or beliefs might unintentionally contribute to the misery of those who are poor. That is hard work—perhaps work we would rather avoid. But ignoring the plight of poor people is exactly what the Scriptures warn us against!

5.1-6

PRAY IT

The Making of a Prayer

Have you ever been in a prayer rut? It happens when you get stuck on saying the same prayer every time, no matter what the situation. It becomes a habit, and like all habits, after a while, you may stop thinking about why you are even doing it.

James offers some advice in 5.13 that can help you to get out of such a rut and back on track with your prayer life. This passage says to think about the needs and feelings you have at any given moment of the day and turn them into a prayer. Feeling down? Tell God about it. Just had the best day of your life? Share it with God. Want to get even with a person who hurt you? Let God know about it. In fact, there is nothing you can't tell God—even if you are mad and God is the one you are mad at.

Get in touch with what is occupying your mind the most right now—good, bad, or ordinary—and turn it into a prayer by sharing it with the God who is always ready to hear what you have to say.

▸ **Jas 5.13**

Patience in Suffering

7 Be patient, therefore, beloved,ᵛ until the coming of the Lord. The farmer waits for the precious crop from the earth, being patient with it until it receives the early and the late rains. 8 You also must be patient. Strengthen your hearts, for the coming of the Lord is near.ʷ 9 Beloved,ˣ do not grumble against one another, so that you may not be judged. See, the Judge is standing at the doors! 10 As an example of suffering and patience, beloved,ᵛ take the prophets who spoke in the name of the Lord. 11 Indeed we call blessed those who showed endurance. You have heard of the endurance of Jōb, and you have seen the purpose of the Lord, how the Lord is compassionate and merciful.

12 Above all, my beloved,ᵛ do not swear, either by heaven or by earth or by any other oath, but let your "Yes" be yes and your "No" be no, so that you may not fall under condemnation.

The Prayer of Faith
(Cp 1 Kings 18.41–46)

13 Are any among you suffering? They should pray. Are any cheerful? They should sing songs of praise. 14 Are any among you sick? They should call for the elders of the church and have them pray over them, anointing them with oil in the name of the Lord. 15 The prayer of faith will save the sick, and the Lord will raise them up; and anyone who has committed sins will be forgiven. 16 Therefore confess your sins to one another, and pray for one another, so that you may be healed. The prayer of the righteous is powerful and effective. 17 E·lī'jah was a human being like us, and he prayed fervently that it might not rain, and for three years and six months it did not rain on the earth. 18 Then he prayed again, and the heaven gave rain and the earth yielded its harvest.

19 My brothers and sisters,ʸ if anyone among you wanders from the truth and is brought back by another, 20 you should know that whoever brings back a sinner from wandering will save the sinner'sᶻ soul from death and will cover a multitude of sins.

ᵛ Gk *brothers* ʷ Or is *at* hand ˣ Gk *Brothers* ʸ Gk *My brothers* ᶻ Gk his

Close friends refuse to speak to you. Students make fun of classmates. Citizens break windows in the homes of Christian leaders who have spoken out publicly. It's enough to make some Christians ask, Is living our faith worth this persecution and separation? This is a major concern addressed by the First Letter of Peter.

At a Glance

- **1.1–2.** a greeting and thanksgiving
- **1.3—2.10.** the message that Christians are called to be a chosen race and a royal priest-hood
- **2.11—3.12.** a description of the Christian way of life
- **3.13—5.11.** a discussion of Christian suffering
- **5.12–14.** a closing

In-depth

The First Letter of Peter was written to a Christian community that was alienated and persecuted because of its Christian lifestyle. Its members were ridiculed, treated as evildoers, and insulted by unbelieving neighbors who did not understand their faith or their moral code of behavior. The author—who may have been Peter but was more likely a later disciple of his—wants to console them and help them make sense of what they're going through.

The author of Peter says that Christ suffered, and therefore we should expect to suffer too. The writer also says that suffering purifies our faith and makes it more genuine (1 Pet 1.7). When we suffer, we are united with all the world's people who are suffering (5.9). And no matter how great our suffering is, we should be hopeful, and we should be willing to witness to our hope. Then, our persecutors will be ashamed and will repent of their wrongdoing (3.14–16). We cannot avoid suffering, but when we follow in the footsteps of Jesus, we can make it result in something good.

Despite all this attention to suffering, 1 Peter is a hope-filled letter. It offers constant reminders of the wonderful things God has done—and will do—for us. When you are going through a hard time, turn to this letter for hope and encouragement. "And after you have suffered for a little while, the God of all grace, who has called you to his eternal glory in Christ, will himself restore, support, strengthen, and establish you" (5.10).

Quick Facts

Author
possibly Peter, but most likely a later disciple of Peter

Date Written
A.D. 60–63 if by Peter, A.D. 70–90 if by a later disciple

Audience
a Gentile (non-Jewish) Christian community

The First Letter of **Peter**

1 Peter

Salutation

1 Peter, an apostle of Jesus Christ,

To the exiles of the Dispersion in Pon′tus, Galatia, Cap•pa•dō′ci•a, Asia, and Bi•thyn′i•a, 2 who have been chosen and destined by God the Father and sanctified by the Spirit to be obedient to Jesus Christ and to be sprinkled with his blood:

May grace and peace be yours in abundance.

A Living Hope

3 Blessed be the God and Father of our Lord Jesus Christ! By his great mercy he has given us a new birth into a living hope through the resurrection of Jesus Christ from the dead, 4 and into an inheritance that is imperishable, undefiled, and unfading, kept in heaven for you, 5 who are being protected by the power of God through faith for a salvation ready to be revealed in the last time. 6 In this you rejoice,*a* even if now for a little while you have had to suffer various trials, 7 so that the genuineness of your faith—being more precious than gold that, though perishable, is tested by fire—may be found to result in praise and glory and honor when Jesus Christ is revealed. 8 Although you have not seen*b* him, you love him; and even though you do not see him now, you believe in him and rejoice with an indescribable and glorious joy, 9 for you are receiving the outcome of your faith, the salvation of your souls.

10 Concerning this salvation, the prophets who prophesied of the grace that was to be yours made careful search and inquiry, 11 inquiring about the person or time that the Spirit of Christ within them indicated when it testified in advance to the sufferings destined for Christ and the subsequent glory. 12 It was revealed to them that they were serving not themselves but you, in regard to the things that have now been announced to you through those who brought you good news by the Holy Spirit sent from heaven—things into which angels long to look!

A Call to Holy Living

13 Therefore prepare your minds for action;*c* discipline yourselves; set all your hope on the grace that Jesus Christ will bring you when he is revealed. 14 Like obedient children, do not be conformed to the desires that you formerly had in ignorance. 15 Instead, as he who called you is holy, be holy yourselves in all your conduct; 16 for it is written, "You shall be holy, for I am holy."

17 If you invoke as Father the one who judges all people impartially according to their deeds, live in reverent fear during the time of your exile. 18 You know that you were ransomed from the futile ways

---

a Or *Rejoice in this* *b* Other ancient authorities read *known*
c Gk *gird up the loins of your mind*

Cultural Connections

SAINT LUCY

December 13 marks the feast day of Saint Lucy. Little is known about Saint Lucy except that she was martyred in Sicily early in the fourth century.

In Scandinavia, however, Saint Lucy is a very important part of the Christmas celebration. By tradition, the feast of Santa Lucia marks the longest night of the year. And keep in mind that winter nights are very long there because of the northern location.

The tradition goes that the oldest daughter in each home dresses in white with a red ribbon tied around her waist and wears on her head a wreath with candles. She then rises early in the morning to serve the family hot chocolate and cinnamon rolls. This is done in commemoration of the legend that Saint Lucy brought food and water to the early Christians who were hiding from their Roman persecutors.

This Scandinavian tradition is a beautiful reminder of how, even in the midst of darkness, Christians can bring the light of hope and nourishment to one another. To whom can you bring the light of hope today?

▶ 1 Pet 1.3–9

---

inherited from your ancestors, not with perishable things like silver or gold, 19 but with the precious blood of Christ, like that of a lamb without defect or blemish. 20 He was destined before the foundation of the world, but was revealed at the end of the ages for your sake. 21 Through him you have come to trust in God, who raised him from the dead and gave him glory, so that your faith and hope are set on God.

22 Now that you have purified your souls by your obedience to the truth*d* so that you have genuine mutual love, love one another deeply*e* from the heart.*f* 23 You have been born anew, not of perishable but of imperishable seed, through the living and enduring word of God.*g* 24 For

"All flesh is like grass
    and all its glory like the flower of grass.
The grass withers,
    and the flower falls,
25 but the word of the Lord endures forever."
That word is the good news that was announced to you.

The Living Stone and a Chosen People
(Ps 118.22; Isa 28.16)

2 Rid yourselves, therefore, of all malice, and all guile, insincerity, envy, and all slander. 2 Like newborn infants, long for the pure, spiritual

---

d Other ancient authorities add *through the Spirit*
e Or *constantly* *f* Other ancient authorities read *a pure heart* *g* Or *through the word of the living and enduring God*

PRAY IT
Live the Belief

Holy God,
You invite me to live the Gospel
    message, not just hear and accept it. It
    is not enough to say I believe. I need to
    live that belief.
I need to lovingly serve you, God, and all my
    brothers and sisters.
I need to seek knowledge of your word and
    follow it faithfully.
I need to exercise self-control and avoid
    temptations.
I need to build endurance to stand firm
    against life's trials.
I need to value truth and goodness.
Provide me with the fruits of your spirit to
    sustain me for my journey, as I work to
    imitate your Son, Jesus Christ. Amen.

▶ 1 Pet 1.13–25

did you KNOW?

The Priesthood of the Faithful

In the New Testament, the only person, other than the Jewish priests, who is actually called a priest is Jesus. In The Letter to the Hebrews, the efficacy, or effectiveness, of Jesus as High Priest is proclaimed—a new priesthood has been born in Christ, one that surpasses the priesthood of the Old Testament. The church has always understood that Christ also commissioned the Apostles to share his priesthood and to ordain others to do the same.

But did you know that every baptized Christian shares in Christ's priesthood as well? Although it is different from hierarchical or ordained priesthood, the priesthood of each baptized person is recognized in their participating in the priestly work of offering sacrifice to God. Every Christian is to offer his or her life as a living sacrifice and to intercede on behalf of the church and the world with the Father.

The priesthood of the faithful is part of our baptismal responsibility to proclaim what God has done for his people and to live a life consecrated by faith and hope in Christ crucified and risen. Because we share in the priesthood of the Son through Baptism, we have access to the divine through him. We are consecrated, put aside for the work of salvation.

We live this priesthood by offering ourselves to God. When we do so, we align ourselves to the way of Christ and live as lights for the world. We live for others and thus become instruments in the hand of God. Remember the words of 1 Pet 2.9: "You are a chosen race, a royal priesthood, a holy nation, God's own people."

▶ 1 Pet 2.1–10

spiritual sacrifices acceptable to God through Jesus Christ. 6 For it stands in scripture:

"See, I am laying in Zion a stone,
    a cornerstone chosen and precious;
and whoever believes in him[i] will not be put to shame."

7 To you then who believe, he is precious; but for those who do not believe,

"The stone that the builders rejected
    has become the very head of the corner,"

8 and

"A stone that makes them stumble,
    and a rock that makes them fall."

They stumble because they disobey the word, as they were destined to do.

> **You are a chosen race, a royal priesthood, God's own a holy nation, people** 2.9

9 But you are a chosen race, a royal priesthood, a holy nation, God's own people,[j] in order that you may proclaim the mighty acts of him who called you out of darkness into his marvelous light.
10 Once you were not a people,
    but now you are God's people;
once you had not received mercy,
    but now you have received mercy.

Live as Servants of God
(Cp Rom 13.1–5)

11 Beloved, I urge you as aliens and exiles to abstain from the desires of the flesh that wage war against the soul. 12 Conduct yourselves honorably among the Gentiles, so that, though they malign you as evildoers, they may see your honorable deeds and glorify God when he comes to judge.[k]
13 For the Lord's sake accept the authority of every human institution,[l] whether of the emperor

milk, so that by it you may grow into salvation—
3 if indeed you have tasted that the Lord is good.
4 Come to him, a living stone, though rejected by mortals yet chosen and precious in God's sight, and 5 like living stones, let yourselves be built[h] into a spiritual house, to be a holy priesthood, to offer

---

h Or you yourselves are being built   i Or it   j Gk a people for his possession   k Gk God on the day of visitation   l Or every institution ordained for human beings

1
P
E
T

PRAY IT!
Part of the Family

All of us come from and belong to a family. Some families are large and some small, some have two parents and others one, and some include aunts, uncles, or grandparents. Every family is unique.

Christians belong to a family that extends well beyond the relationships of blood or adoption. As followers of Christ, they make up a "royal priesthood" and a "holy nation," and are called "God's own people" (1 Pet 2.9). That is pretty lofty language! What does it mean?

First, it means that our faith is not just between us and God but also shared with others. Yes, there is something personal about our relationship with the Lord, but in addition, we are called by God into a community of disciples who share a common faith. Second, God has chosen us to live together in such a way that others who see our example will see something so good that they want to be a part of it.

In your prayer, reflect or journal on the following questions:
- How connected do you feel to the Christian family?
- What kind of support would you like to receive from other believers? What kind of support can you give?

▶ 1 Pet 2.9–17

as supreme, 14 or of governors, as sent by him to punish those who do wrong and to praise those who do right. 15 For it is God's will that by doing right you should silence the ignorance of the foolish. 16 As servants[m] of God, live as free people, yet do not use your freedom as a pretext for evil. 17 Honor everyone. Love the family of believers.[n] Fear God. Honor the emperor.

Advice for Slaves
(Isa 53.7–9)

18 Slaves, accept the authority of your masters with all deference, not only those who are kind and gentle but also those who are harsh. 19 For it is a credit to you if, being aware of God, you endure pain while suffering unjustly. 20 If you endure when you are beaten for doing wrong, what credit is that?

But if you endure when you do right and suffer for it, you have God's approval. 21 For to this you have been called, because Christ also suffered for you, leaving you an example, so that you should follow in his steps.
22 "He committed no sin,
    and no deceit was found in his mouth."
23 When he was abused, he did not return abuse; when he suffered, he did not threaten; but he entrusted himself to the one who judges justly. 24 He himself bore our sins in his body on the cross,[o] so that, free from sins, we might live for righteousness; by his wounds[p] you have been healed. 25 For you were going astray like sheep, but now you have returned to the shepherd and guardian of your souls.

Advice for Wives and Husbands

3 Wives, in the same way, accept the authority of your husbands, so that, even if some of them do not obey the word, they may be won over without a word by their wives' conduct, 2 when they see the purity and reverence of your lives. 3 Do not adorn yourselves outwardly by braiding your hair, and by wearing gold ornaments or fine clothing; 4 rather, let your adornment be the inner self with the lasting beauty of a gentle and quiet spirit, which is very precious in God's sight. 5 It was in this way long ago that the holy women who hoped in God used to adorn themselves by accepting the authority of their husbands. 6 Thus Sarah obeyed Abraham and called him lord. You have become her daughters as long as you do what is good and never let fears alarm you.

7 Husbands, in the same way, show consideration for your wives in your life together, paying honor to the woman as the weaker sex,[q] since they too are also heirs of the gracious gift of life—so that nothing may hinder your prayers.

Advice for All

8 Finally, all of you, have unity of spirit, sympathy, love for one another, a tender heart, and a humble mind. 9 Do not repay evil for evil or abuse for abuse; but, on the contrary, repay with a blessing. It is for this that you were called—that you might inherit a blessing. 10 For
"Those who desire life
    and desire to see good days,
let them keep their tongues from evil
    and their lips from speaking deceit;
11 let them turn away from evil and do good;
    let them seek peace and pursue it.
12 For the eyes of the Lord are on the righteous,

---

m Gk slaves   n Gk Love the brotherhood   o Or carried up our sins in his body to the tree   p Gk bruise   q Gk vessel

and his ears are open to their prayer.
But the face of the Lord is against those who
    do evil."

Suffering for Doing Right

13 Now who will harm you if you are eager to do what is good? 14 But even if you do suffer for doing what is right, you are blessed. Do not fear what they fear,*r* and do not be intimidated, 15 but in your hearts sanctify Christ as Lord. Always be ready to make your defense to anyone who demands from you an accounting for the hope that is in you; 16 yet do it with gentleness and reverence.*s* Keep your conscience clear, so that, when you are maligned, those who abuse you for your good conduct in Christ may be put to shame. 17 For it is better to suffer for doing good, if suffering should be God's will, than to suffer for doing evil. 18 For Christ also suffered*t* for sins once for all, the righteous for the unrighteous, in order to bring you*u* to God. He was put to death in the flesh, but made alive in the spirit, 19 in which also he went and made a proclamation to the spirits in prison, 20 who in former times did not obey, when God waited patiently in the days of Noah, during the building of the ark, in which a few, that is, eight persons, were saved through water. 21 And baptism, which this prefigured, now saves you—not as a removal of dirt from the body, but as an appeal to God for*v* a good conscience, through the resurrection of Jesus Christ, 22 who has gone into heaven and is at the right hand of God, with angels, authorities, and powers made subject to him.

Good Stewards of God's Grace

4 Since therefore Christ suffered in the flesh,*w* arm yourselves also with the same intention (for whoever has suffered in the flesh has finished with sin), 2 so as to live for the rest of your earthly life*x* no longer by human desires but by the will of God. 3 You have already spent enough time in doing what the Gentiles like to do, living in licentiousness, passions, drunkenness, revels, carousing, and lawless idolatry. 4 They are surprised that you no longer join them in the same excesses of dissipation, and so they blaspheme.*y* 5 But they will have to give an accounting to him who stands ready to judge the living and the dead. 6 For this is the reason the gospel was proclaimed even to the dead, so that, though they had been judged in the flesh as

---

r Gk *their fear*   *s* Or *respect*   *t* Other ancient authorities read *died*   *u* Other ancient authorities read *us*   *v* Or *a pledge to God from*   *w* Other ancient authorities add *for us; others, for you*   *x* Gk *rest of the time in the flesh*   *y* Or *they malign you*

LIVING GOSPEL VALUES EVEN IF IT DEMANDS SUFFERING!

Young people of many cultures suffer for living the Gospel. Those who want to leave a gang are harassed by gang members. Young women and men who want to maintain their virginity are made fun of. Young people who start participating in church programs are not understood by their friends. The commitment of young leaders sometimes is misinterpreted by their parents as a way of escaping their duties at home.

    These behaviors cause suffering because Gospel values are conflicting with society's values.
- How does a true Christian lifestyle cause conflict with mainstream society? How can young Hispanics keep their values of love, generosity, and solidarity with their family while continuing their own personal development?
- Think of Peter's advice to the early Christian communities. Remember Jesus' suffering, and offer yours together with his so that you and all young people may share Christ's new life.

▶ 1 Pet 3.13–22

everyone is judged, they might live in the spirit as God does.

7 The end of all things is near;[z] therefore be serious and discipline yourselves for the sake of your prayers. 8 Above all, maintain constant love for one another, for love covers a multitude of sins. 9 Be hospitable to one another without complaining. 10 Like good stewards of the manifold grace of God, serve one another with whatever gift each of you has received. 11 Whoever speaks must do so as one speaking the very words of God; whoever serves must do so with the strength that God supplies, so that God may be glorified in all things through Jesus Christ. To him belong the glory and the power forever and ever. Amen.

Suffering as a Christian

12 Beloved, do not be surprised at the fiery ordeal that is taking place among you to test you, as though something strange were happening to you. 13 But rejoice insofar as you are sharing Christ's sufferings, so that you may also be glad and shout for joy when his glory is revealed. 14 If you are reviled for the name of Christ, you are blessed, because the spirit of glory,[a] which is the Spirit of God, is resting on you.[b] 15 But let none of you suffer as a murderer, a thief, a criminal, or even as a mischief maker. 16 Yet if any of you suffers as a Christian, do not consider it a disgrace, but glorify God because you bear this name. 17 For the time has come for judgment to begin with the household of God; if it begins with us, what will be the end for those who do not obey the gospel of God? 18 And

"If it is hard for the righteous to be saved,
    what will become of the ungodly and the
        sinners?"

19 Therefore, let those suffering in accordance with God's will entrust themselves to a faithful Creator, while continuing to do good.

Tending the Flock of God

5 Now as an elder myself and a witness of the sufferings of Christ, as well as one who shares in the glory to be revealed, I exhort the elders among you 2 to tend the flock of God that is in your charge, exercising the oversight,[c] not under compulsion but willingly, as God would have you do it[d]—not for sordid gain but eagerly. 3 Do not lord it over those in your charge, but be examples to the flock. 4 And when the chief shepherd appears, you will win the crown of glory that never fades away. 5 In the same way, you who are younger must accept the authority of the elders.[e] And all of you must clothe yourselves with humility in your dealings with one another, for

"God opposes the proud,
    but gives grace to the humble."

SHOUT FOR JOY!

No healthy person likes to suffer. Yet, when we suffer for something good—like being identified as a follower of Christ or defending someone who is under attack by others—First Peter calls us blessed. God notices when we are mocked or ridiculed for our faith. We are challenged to rejoice when we experience such treatment, rather than take it as a sign of failure. For didn't Christ suffer for doing good? And won't he be with us when we suffer for his name? The Gospel has a strange way of turning things upside down—it says that what would cause others sorrow should cause us joy!

The Bible has a lot of other things to say on the topic of suffering. You can use reading plan 7, "Why Do We Suffer?" to locate other passages.

▶ 1 Pet 4.12–19

6 Humble yourselves therefore under the mighty hand of God, so that he may exalt you in due time. 7 Cast all your anxiety on him, because he cares for you. 8 Discipline yourselves, keep alert.[f] Like a roaring lion your adversary the devil prowls around, looking for someone to devour. 9 Resist him, steadfast in your faith, for you know that your brothers and sisters[g] in all the world are undergoing the same kinds of suffering. 10 And after you have suffered for a little while, the God of all grace, who has called you to his eternal glory in Christ, will himself restore, support, strengthen, and establish you. 11 To him be the power forever and ever. Amen.

Final Greetings and Benediction

12 Through Sil·va'nus, whom I consider a faithful brother, I have written this short letter to encourage you and to testify that this is the true grace of God. Stand fast in it. 13 Your sister church[h] in Babylon, chosen together with you, sends you greetings; and so does my son Mark. 14 Greet one another with a kiss of love. Peace to all of you who are in Christ.[i]

---

z Or is at hand   a Other ancient authorities add and of power   b Other ancient authorities add On their part he is blasphemed, but on your part he is glorified   c Other ancient authorities lack exercising the oversight   d Other ancient authorities lack as God would have you do it   e Or of those who are older   f Or be vigilant   g Gk your brotherhood   h Gk She who is   i Other ancient authorities add Amen

1
P
E
T

What happens to us when we die? What is heaven like? Does God even care what happens to us? Many people believe there is no heaven, no hell, and no God. Some say that when we die, our bodies simply decay and we no longer exist in any form. They say that there is no life after death, no punishment, and no reward. But the Bible tells us differently. Second Peter was written to reassure believers that God does indeed care, and that they will be rewarded for leading a faithful and virtuous life.

At a Glance

- **Chapter 1.** a greeting, and encouragement to lead a holy life

- **Chapter 2.** a warning to beware of false teachers

- **Chapter 3.** a message that the day of God's judgment is coming

In-depth

Bible scholars have convincing evidence that 2 Peter is one of the latest books in the New Testament. The letter appears to have been written by someone who is appealing to the authority of the dead Apostle Peter (see "Introduction to the Letters and Revelation"). At the time of its writing—perhaps as much as one hundred years after Jesus' death and Resurrection—some Christians were starting to wonder if what they believed was true. People were even teaching that there would be no reward or punishment after death. So why not live any way you wanted to?

The author of the Second Letter of Peter is arguing against these false teachers. This writer uses famous examples from the Old Testament to remind readers how God has acted through history. And the author promises that those who have chosen to separate themselves from God in their lifetime will experience the fullness of separation from God in death—a separation that Christians call hell. Those who have stayed faithful to God's calling will enjoy eternal life in union with God—a life that Christians call heaven. Why? Because God is good and just.

Tied in to this argument is another concern. Many of the earliest Christians believed that Christ would return soon after his Resurrection, probably within their lifetime, to establish God's Reign once and for all (see "The Parousia," 2 Thess 1.5—2.17). When generations had passed and Christ had not yet returned, false teachers claimed that he would never return. The author of 2 Peter reminds readers that God's time is not our time—Christ is simply waiting so that more people have a chance to repent of their sins before he comes for judgment (2 Pet 3.9).

Quick Facts

Author
an unknown person writing in Peter's name

Date Written
approximately A.D. 130

Audience
a community of both Jewish and Gentile (non-Jewish) Christians

The Second Letter of *Peter*

2 Peter

We wait for New Heavens and a new earth. 3.13

Salutation

1 Sim′e·on*a* Peter, a servant*b* and apostle of Jesus Christ,

To those who have received a faith as precious as ours through the righteousness of our God and Savior Jesus Christ:*c*

2 May grace and peace be yours in abundance in the knowledge of God and of Jesus our Lord.

The Christian's Call and Election

3 His divine power has given us everything needed for life and godliness, through the knowledge of him who called us by*d* his own glory and goodness. 4 Thus he has given us, through these things, his precious and very great promises, so that through them you may escape from the corruption that is in the world because of lust, and may become participants of the divine nature. 5 For this very reason, you must make every effort to support your faith with goodness, and goodness with knowledge, 6 and knowledge with self-control, and self-control with endurance, and endurance with godliness, 7 and godliness with mutual*e* affection, and mutual*e* affection with love. 8 For if these things are yours and are increasing among you, they keep you from being ineffective and unfruitful in the knowledge of our Lord Jesus Christ. 9 For anyone who lacks these things is short-sighted and blind, and is forgetful of the cleansing of past sins. 10 Therefore, brothers and sisters,*f* be all the more

eager to confirm your call and election, for if you do this, you will never stumble. 11 For in this way, entry into the eternal kingdom of our Lord and Savior Jesus Christ will be richly provided for you.

12 Therefore I intend to keep on reminding you of these things, though you know them already and are established in the truth that has come to you. 13 I think it right, as long as I am in this body,*g* to refresh your memory, 14 since I know that my death*h* will come soon, as indeed our Lord Jesus Christ has made clear to me. 15 And I will make every effort so that after my departure you may be able at any time to recall these things.

Eyewitnesses of Christ's Glory
(Mt 17.5; Mk 9.7; Lk 9.35)

16 For we did not follow cleverly devised myths when we made known to you the power and coming of our Lord Jesus Christ, but we had been eyewitnesses of his majesty. 17 For he received honor and glory from God the Father when that voice was conveyed to him by the Majestic Glory, saying, "This is my Son, my Beloved,*i* with whom I am well pleased." 18 We ourselves heard this voice come

---

a Other ancient authorities read *Simon*   *b* Gk *slave*
c Or *of our God and the Savior Jesus Christ*   *d* Other ancient authorities read *through*   *e* Gk *brotherly*   *f* Gk *brothers*
g Gk *tent*   *h* Gk *the putting off of my tent*   *i* Other ancient authorities read *my beloved Son*

from heaven, while we were with him on the holy mountain.

19 So we have the prophetic message more fully confirmed. You will do well to be attentive to this as to a lamp shining in a dark place, until the day dawns and the morning star rises in your hearts. 20 First of all you must understand this, that no prophecy of scripture is a matter of one's own interpretation, 21 because no prophecy ever came by human will, but men and women moved by the Holy Spirit spoke from God.[j]

False Prophets and Their Punishment

2 But false prophets also arose among the people, just as there will be false teachers among you, who will secretly bring in destructive opinions. They will even deny the Master who bought them—bringing swift destruction on themselves. 2 Even so, many will follow their licentious ways, and because of these teachers[k] the way of truth will be maligned. 3 And in their greed they will exploit you with deceptive words. Their condemnation, pronounced against them long ago, has not been idle, and their destruction is not asleep.

4 For if God did not spare the angels when they sinned, but cast them into hell[l] and committed them to chains[m] of deepest darkness to be kept until the judgment; 5 and if he did not spare the ancient world, even though he saved Noah, a herald of righteousness, with seven others, when he brought a flood on a world of the ungodly; 6 and if by turning the cities of Sod'om and Go•mor'rah to ashes he condemned them to extinction[n] and made them an example of what is coming to the ungodly;[o] 7 and if he rescued Lot, a righteous man greatly distressed by the licentiousness of the lawless 8 (for that righteous man, living among them day after day, was tormented in his righteous soul by their lawless deeds that he saw and heard), 9 then the Lord knows how to rescue the godly from trial, and to keep the unrighteous under punishment until the day of judgment 10—especially those who indulge their flesh in depraved lust, and who despise authority.

Bold and willful, they are not afraid to slander the glorious ones,[p] 11 whereas angels, though greater in might and power, do not bring against them a slanderous judgment from the Lord.[q] 12 These people, however, are like irrational animals, mere creatures of instinct, born to be caught and killed. They slander what they do not understand, and when those creatures are destroyed,[r] they also will be destroyed, 13 suffering[s] the penalty for doing wrong. They count it a pleasure to revel in the daytime. They are blots and blemishes, reveling in their dissipation[t] while they feast with you. 14 They have eyes full of adultery, insatiable for sin. They

did you KNOW?
Identifying False Prophets

Many times throughout history, people have misled others in the name of God. Adolf Hitler is probably the best-known such leader in the twentieth century. Some of these leaders have even convinced their followers to commit mass suicide as part of their beliefs. These extreme examples show how people can be misguided by false prophets.

Second Peter 2.1–3 gives guidelines for identifying false prophets. The author says false prophets use secrets, propose destructive opinions, deny God's teachings, twist the truth to their needs, and exploit their followers. Beware of any leader, religious or nonreligious, who uses these techniques. As 2 Peter says, they malign the way of truth.

▶ **2 Pet 2.1–3**

entice unsteady souls. They have hearts trained in greed. Accursed children! 15 They have left the straight road and have gone astray, following the road of Bā'laam son of Bō'sor,[u] who loved the wages of doing wrong, 16 but was rebuked for his own transgression; a speechless donkey spoke with a human voice and restrained the prophet's madness.

17 These are waterless springs and mists driven by a storm; for them the deepest darkness has been reserved. 18 For they speak bombastic nonsense, and with licentious desires of the flesh they entice people who have just[v] escaped from those who live in error. 19 They promise them freedom, but they themselves are slaves of corruption; for people are slaves to whatever masters them. 20 For if, after they have escaped the defilements of the world through the knowledge of our Lord and Savior Jesus Christ,

---

[j] Other ancient authorities read *but moved by the Holy Spirit saints of God spoke*   [k] Gk *because of them*   [l] Gk *Tartaros*   [m] Other ancient authorities read *pits*   [n] Other ancient authorities lack *to extinction*   [o] Other ancient authorities read *an example to those who were to be ungodly*   [p] Or *angels*; Gk *glories*   [q] Other ancient authorities read *before the Lord*; others lack the phrase   [r] Gk *in their destruction*   [s] Other ancient authorities read *receiving*   [t] Other ancient authorities read *love-feasts*   [u] Other ancient authorities read *Beor*   [v] Other ancient authorities read *actually*

they are again entangled in them and overpowered, the last state has become worse for them than the first. 21 For it would have been better for them never to have known the way of righteousness than, after knowing it, to turn back from the holy commandment that was passed on to them. 22 It has happened to them according to the true proverb,

"The dog turns back to its own vomit,"

and,

"The sow is washed only to wallow in the mud."

The Promise of the Lord's Coming
(Gen 6.5—8.22)

3 This is now, beloved, the second letter I am writing to you; in them I am trying to arouse your sincere intention by reminding you 2 that you should remember the words spoken in the past by the holy prophets, and the commandment of the Lord and Savior spoken through your apostles. 3 First of all you must understand this, that in the last days scoffers will come, scoffing and indulging their own lusts 4 and saying, "Where is the promise of his coming? For ever since our ancestors died,ʷ all things continue as they were from the beginning of creation!" 5 They deliberately ignore this fact, that by the word of God heavens existed long ago and an earth was formed out of water and by means of water, 6 through which the world of that time was deluged with water and perished. 7 But by the same word the present heavens and earth have been reserved for fire, being kept until the day of judgment and destruction of the godless.

8 But do not ignore this one fact, beloved, that with the Lord one day is like a thousand years, and a thousand years are like one day. 9 The Lord is not slow about his promise, as some think of slowness, but is patient with you,ˣ not wanting any to perish, but all to come to repentance. 10 But the day of the Lord will come like a thief, and then the heavens will pass away with a loud noise, and the elements will be dissolved with fire, and the earth and everything that is done on it will be disclosed.ʸ

11 Since all these things are to be dissolved in this way, what sort of persons ought you to be in leading lives of holiness and godliness, 12 waiting for and hasteningᶻ the coming of the day of God, because of which the heavens will be set ablaze and dissolved, and the elements will melt with fire? 13 But, in accordance with his promise, we wait for new heavens and a new earth, where righteousness is at home.

Final Exhortation and Doxology

14 Therefore, beloved, while you are waiting for these things, strive to be found by him at peace, without spot or blemish; 15 and regard the patience of our Lord as salvation. So also our beloved brother Paul wrote to you according to the wisdom given him, 16 speaking of this as he does in all his letters. There are some things in them hard to understand, which the ignorant and unstable twist to their own destruction, as they do the other scriptures. 17 You therefore, beloved, since you are forewarned, beware that you are not carried away with the error of the lawless and lose your own stability. 18 But grow in the grace and knowledge of our Lord and Savior Jesus Christ. To him be the glory both now and to the day of eternity. Amen.ᵃ

ʷ Gk our fathers fell asleep   ˣ Other ancient authorities read on your account   ʸ Other ancient authorities read will be burned up   ᶻ Or earnestly desiring   ᵃ Other ancient authorities lack Amen

Where Is God?

LIVE IT!

A frustrated and frazzled tour guide is trying to get her group through a maze of homeless people and panhandlers outside the great cathedral. After the group has safely entered the cathedral, she exclaims, with arms outstretched, "God is definitely here!" A young girl whose gaze lingers on the people outside asks, with all seriousness, "Why won't they let him out?"

The early readers of 2 Peter were confused that Jesus Christ had not yet returned again (see "The Parousia," 2 Thess 1.5—2.17). They wondered, "Where is God?" The author reminds them not to apply human limits to God's response.

Sometimes, when we pray for something, it seems like God keeps us waiting for an eternity. We want something to happen quickly—but God is on a different schedule. You might say the only limits we have in seeing God's actions are the ones we establish. Where are *you* not seeing God these days?

▶ 2 Pet 3.9

John

Betrayal is painful. Unfortunately, most of us have experienced it at one time or another. It often begins with a misunderstanding. Sometimes, harsh words are exchanged, and people part ways feeling sad and bitter. The community addressed by the three Letters of John had experienced sharp division and conflict. It is impossible to avoid the author's feeling of betrayal as you read these letters.

In-depth

All three Letters of John were probably written by the same person, the elder referred to in the second and third letters. This writer had, perhaps a decade earlier, belonged to the community for which the Gospel of John was written. He saw himself and his community as being faithful to the true meaning of John's Gospel. Now, others who had once belonged to this community had abandoned it in its time of need. They too read the Gospel of John, but they interpreted it very differently. The disagreement between these two groups resulted in a bitter conflict.

The First Letter of John really isn't a letter at all but is more like a teaching homily. The second letter tells the community not to associate with the "deceivers" who have broken off from the group. The third letter asks the community to welcome a representative or missionary sent by the elder.

Even after careful study of the first letter, it is difficult to determine exactly what the disagreement was about. One issue seems to have been the proper understanding of Jesus' humanity. Apparently, the deceivers did not fully believe in Jesus' humanity and its connection to salvation through Jesus' death and Resurrection. To emphasize Jesus' humanity, the author several times mentions that Jesus came "in the flesh" and comments on the saving power of the "blood of Jesus."

The author also challenges the deceivers' claims that they were free to do anything they wanted and still love God. If they truly loved God, they would also love their brothers and sisters and would not have abandoned the community.

Through this letter, God reminds today's Christians that believers can have profoundly different understandings about what they believe. Conflict and disagreement will occur even within the Christian community. Can Christians handle such discord with love and respect?

At a Glance

- **1 Jn 1.1–4.** an introduction
- **1 Jn 1.5—3.10.** a message that God is light, and we must walk in the light
- **1 Jn 3.11—5.12.** a message that those who are God's children show it by their love
- **1 Jn 5.13–21.** a conclusion
- **2 Jn.** a second letter of John
- **3 Jn.** a third letter of John

Quick Facts

Author
an unknown person associated with the community that produced the Gospel of John

Date Written
approximately A.D. 100

Audience
Christians who were suffering from a split in their community

1 John

Love one another

4.7

The Word of Life

(Jn 1.1–5)

1 We declare to you what was from the beginning, what we have heard, what we have seen with our eyes, what we have looked at and touched with our hands, concerning the word of life— 2 this life was revealed, and we have seen it and testify to it, and declare to you the eternal life that was with the Father and was revealed to us— 3 we declare to you what we have seen and heard so that you also may have fellowship with us; and truly our fellowship is with the Father and with his Son Jesus Christ. 4 We are writing these things so that our*a* joy may be complete.

God Is Light

5 This is the message we have heard from him and proclaim to you, that God is light and in him there is no darkness at all. 6 If we say that we have fellowship with him while we are walking in darkness, we lie and do not do what is true; 7 but if we walk in the light as he himself is in the light, we have fellowship with one another, and the blood of Jesus his Son cleanses us from all sin. 8 If we say that we have no sin, we deceive ourselves, and the truth is not in us. 9 If we confess our sins, he who is faithful and just will forgive us our sins and cleanse us from all unrighteousness. 10 If we say that we have not sinned, we make him a liar, and his word is not in us.

Christ Our Advocate

2 My little children, I am writing these things to you so that you may not sin. But if anyone does sin, we have an advocate with the Father, Jesus Christ the righteous; 2 and he is the atoning sacrifice for our sins, and not for ours only but also for the sins of the whole world.

3 Now by this we may be sure that we know him, if we obey his commandments. 4 Whoever says, "I have come to know him," but does not obey his commandments, is a liar, and in such a person the truth does not exist; 5 but whoever obeys his word, truly in this person the love of God has reached perfection. By this we may be sure that we are in him: 6 whoever says, "I abide in him," ought to walk just as he walked.

A New Commandment

7 Beloved, I am writing you no new commandment, but an old commandment that you have had from the beginning; the old commandment is the word that you have heard. 8 Yet I am writing you a new commandment that is true in him and in you, because*b* the darkness is passing away and the true light is already shining. 9 Whoever says, "I am in the light," while hating a brother or sister,*c* is still in the darkness. 10 Whoever loves a brother or sister*d*

---

a Other ancient authorities read *your*   *b* Or *that*
c Gk *hating a brother*   *d* Gk *loves a brother*

Live in the Light

Do you ever find it hard to decide whether something is right or wrong? Instead of the sharp distinction between light and darkness described in 1 John, you might see a lot of shades of gray. But be careful; you might simply be seeing what you want to see! Remember, "If we say that we have no sin, we deceive ourselves" (1 Jn 1.8). There are times when our choices aren't clear—but usually they are. Listen to your inner voice of honesty and integrity, and courageously choose to live in the light!

▶ 1 Jn 1.5–10

lives in the light, and in such a person*e* there is no cause for stumbling. 11 But whoever hates another believer*f* is in the darkness, walks in the darkness, and does not know the way to go, because the darkness has brought on blindness.
12 I am writing to you, little children,
    because your sins are forgiven on account
        of his name.
13 I am writing to you, fathers,
    because you know him who is from the
        beginning.
I am writing to you, young people,
    because you have conquered the evil one.
14 I write to you, children,
    because you know the Father.

I write to you, fathers,
    because you know him who is from the
        beginning.
I write to you, young people,
    because you are strong
    and the word of God abides in you,
        and you have overcome the evil one.
15 Do not love the world or the things in the world. The love of the Father is not in those who love the world; 16 for all that is in the world—the desire of the flesh, the desire of the eyes, the pride in riches—comes not from the Father but from the world. 17 And the world and its desire*g* are passing

---

e Or *in it*   *f* Gk *hates a brother*   *g* Or *the desire for it*

Cultural Connections

BE RECONCILED

Sometimes, it's hardest to show your love to the people you are closest to. Maybe you get along great with all your friends but are always arguing with your brother or sister. Or in your youth group, you are always tense around that one person with whom you had angry words several months ago.

The author of 1 John tells us that we cannot ignore a relationship with a brother or sister in the Lord who has been upset. The Hmong culture has the same tradition. If you frighten or hurt or offend someone, you have created an imbalance of spirits. It is your responsibility to go back and seek to re-establish harmony. It is the Hmong custom to go to a shaman (an elder of the community, a holy person) for advice and to perform a ritual for reconciliation.

The Catholic Tradition has the sacrament of Reconciliation for the same purpose: to admit the imbalance in a relationship caused by sin, discuss ways to make things right, express sorrow, and celebrate God's forgiveness and love.

▶ 1 Jn 2.7–11

away, but those who do the will of God live forever.

Warning against Antichrists

18 Children, it is the last hour! As you have heard that antichrist is coming, so now many antichrists have come. From this we know that it is the last hour. 19 They went out from us, but they did not belong to us; for if they had belonged to us, they would have remained with us. But by going out they made it plain that none of them belongs to us. 20 But you have been anointed by the Holy One, and all of you have knowledge.*h* 21 I write to you, not because you do not know the truth, but because you know it, and you know that no lie comes from the truth. 22 Who is the liar but the one who denies that Jesus is the Christ?*i* This is the antichrist, the one who denies the Father and the Son. 23 No one who denies the Son has the Father; everyone who confesses the Son has the Father also. 24 Let what you heard from the beginning abide in you. If what you heard from the beginning abides in you, then you will abide in the Son and in the Father. 25 And this is what he has promised us,*j* eternal life.

26 I write these things to you concerning those who would deceive you. 27 As for you, the anointing that you received from him abides in you, and so you do not need anyone to teach you. But as his anointing teaches you about all things, and is true and is not a lie, and just as it has taught you, abide in him.*k*

28 And now, little children, abide in him, so that when he is revealed we may have confidence and not be put to shame before him at his coming.

Children of God

29 If you know that he is righteous, you may be sure that everyone who does right has been born of him. 1 See what love the Father has given us, that we should be called children of God; and that is what we are. The reason the world does not know us is that it did not know him. 2 Beloved, we are God's children now; what we will be has not yet been revealed. What we do know is this: when he*k* is revealed, we will be like him, for we will see him as he is. 3 And all who have this hope in him purify themselves, just as he is pure.

4 Everyone who commits sin is guilty of lawlessness; sin is lawlessness. 5 You know that he was revealed to take away sins, and in him there is no sin. 6 No one who abides in him sins; no one who sins has either seen him or known him. 7 Little children, let no one deceive you. Everyone who does what is right is righteous, just as he is righteous. 8 Everyone who commits sin is a child of the devil; for the devil has been sinning from the beginning. The Son of God was revealed for this pur-

pose, to destroy the works of the devil. 9 Those who have been born of God do not sin, because God's seed abides in them;*l* they cannot sin, because they have been born of God. 10 The children of God and the children of the devil are revealed in this way: all who do not do what is right are not from God, nor are those who do not love their brothers and sisters.*m*

Love One Another
(Mt 22.39)

11 For this is the message you have heard from the beginning, that we should love one another. 12 We must not be like Cain who was from the evil one and murdered his brother. And why did he murder him? Because his own deeds were evil and his brother's righteous. 13 Do not be astonished, brothers and sisters,*n* that the world hates you. 14 We know that we have passed from death to life because we love one another. Whoever does not love abides in death. 15 All who hate a brother or sister*m* are murderers, and you know that murderers do not have eternal life abiding in them. 16 We know love by this, that he laid down his life for us—and we ought to lay down our lives for one another. 17 How does God's love abide in anyone who has the world's goods and sees a brother or sister*o* in need and yet refuses help?

---

h Other ancient authorities read *you know all things*
i Or *the Messiah*   *j* Other ancient authorities read *you*
k Or it   *l* Or *because the children of God abide in him*   *m* Gk *his brother*   *n* Gk *brothers*   *o* Gk *brother*

PRAY IT!
Love in Action

Clear your mind of all thoughts and concerns. Help your body and mind relax with some deep breaths. Now, read 1 Jn 3.18 several times until you can say it by heart. Reflect on its meaning. Think about how you have lived and acted during this past week. Have you shown love in truth and action? by word or speech?

Ask God to forgive you for any situations in which you failed to act lovingly. Pray for the gift of being able to put your love in action in your daily life. Throughout the remainder of this day, remind yourself of this prayer by calling to mind verse 18.

▶ 1 Jn 3.18

1
J
N

Let us love,

not in word or speech,

but in truth and action

3.18

18 Little children, let us love, not in word or speech, but in truth and action. 19 And by this we will know that we are from the truth and will reassure our hearts before him 20 whenever our hearts condemn us; for God is greater than our hearts, and he knows everything. 21 Beloved, if our hearts do not condemn us, we have boldness before God; 22 and we receive from him whatever we ask, because we obey his commandments and do what pleases him.

23 And this is his commandment, that we should believe in the name of his Son Jesus Christ and love one another, just as he has commanded us. 24 All who obey his commandments abide in him, and he abides in them. And by this we know that he abides in us, by the Spirit that he has given us.

Testing the Spirits

4 Beloved, do not believe every spirit, but test the spirits to see whether they are from God; for many false prophets have gone out into the world. 2 By this you know the Spirit of God: every spirit that confesses that Jesus Christ has come in the flesh is from God, 3 and every spirit that does not confess Jesus*p* is not from God. And this is the spirit of the antichrist, of which you have heard that it is coming; and now it is already in the world. 4 Little children, you are from God, and have conquered them; for the one who is in you is greater than the one who is in the world. 5 They are from

p Other ancient authorities read *does away with Jesus* (Gk *dissolves Jesus*)

LIVE IT!

Testing Spirits

The spirit is the primary essence of a person or a belief. The First Letter of John talks about two kinds of spirit: that which comes from God and that which does not come from God. This letter gives us two ways for testing whether our spirit comes from God: The first has to do with whether our actions reflect love for God and love for our brothers and sisters (3.18). The second has to do with our beliefs about Jesus Christ. To understand this, let's look closer at the controversy that prompted the author of this letter to offer these two tests.

The controversy in the community addressed by 1 John seems to revolve around what Christians call the Incarnation—the belief that Jesus Christ is both fully God and fully human. The "false prophets" deny Christ's humanity, saying Jesus only appeared to be human. The author insists that the spirits who come from God will confess, "Jesus Christ has come in the flesh" (4.2)—that is, he is fully human. Believing in the Incarnation is the foundation for understanding "that the Father has sent his Son as the Savior of the world" (verse 14).

You can apply this letter's two tests to just about any spiritual idea or practice you come across, whether it has to do with different religious traditions, New Age spirituality, or magic or the occult. Ask yourself: Does this help me love God and other people? Does this support the Christian belief that Jesus Christ is fully God and fully human, and that faith in him is necessary for salvation? If you cannot answer yes to both these questions, stay away!

▸ 1 Jn 4.1–21

the world; therefore what they say is from the world, and the world listens to them. 6 We are from God. Whoever knows God listens to us, and whoever is not from God does not listen to us. From this we know the spirit of truth and the spirit of error.

God Is Love
(Cp Jn 3.16)

7 Beloved, let us love one another, because love is from God; everyone who loves is born of God and knows God. 8 Whoever does not love does not know God, for God is love. 9 God's love was revealed among us in this way: God sent his only Son into the world so that we might live through him. 10 In this is love, not that we loved God but that he loved us and sent his Son to be the atoning sacrifice for our sins. 11 Beloved, since God loved us so much, we also ought to love one another. 12 No one has ever seen God; if we love one another, God lives in us, and his love is perfected in us.

13 By this we know that we abide in him and he in us, because he has given us of his Spirit. 14 And we have seen and do testify that the Father has sent his Son as the Savior of the world. 15 God abides in those who confess that Jesus is the Son of God, and they abide in God. 16 So we have known and believe the love that God has for us.

God is love, and those who abide in love abide in God, and God abides in them. 17 Love has been perfected among us in this: that we may have boldness on the day of judgment, because as he is, so are we in this world. 18 There is no fear in love, but perfect love casts out fear; for fear has to do with punishment, and whoever fears has not reached perfection in love. 19 We love^q because he first loved us. 20 Those who say, "I love God," and hate their brothers or sisters,^{r} are liars; for those who do not love a brother or sister^s whom they have seen,

cannot love God whom they have not seen. 21 The commandment we have from him is this: those who love God must love their brothers and sisters^r also.

Faith Conquers the World

5 Everyone who believes that Jesus is the Christ^t has been born of God, and everyone who loves the parent loves the child. 2 By this we know that we love the children of God, when we love God and obey his commandments. 3 For the love of God is this, that we obey his commandments. And his commandments are not burdensome, 4 for whatever is born of God conquers the world. And this is the victory that conquers the world, our faith. 5 Who is it that conquers the world but the one who believes that Jesus is the Son of God?

Testimony concerning the Son of God

6 This is the one who came by water and blood, Jesus Christ, not with the water only but with the water and the blood. And the Spirit is the one that testifies, for the Spirit is the truth. 7 There are three that testify:^{u} 8 the Spirit and the water and the blood, and these three agree. 9 If we receive human testimony, the testimony of God is greater; for this is the testimony of God that he has testified to his Son. 10 Those who believe in the Son of God have the testimony in their hearts. Those who do not believe in God^v have made him a liar by not believing in the testimony that God has given concerning his Son. 11 And this is the testimony: God gave us

---

q Other ancient authorities add *him*; others add *God*
r Gk *brothers* s Gk *brother* t Or *the Messiah* u A few other authorities read (with variations) 7*There are three that testify in heaven, the Father, the Word, and the Holy Spirit, and these three are one.* 8*And there are three that testify on earth:*
v Other ancient authorities read *in the Son*

Understanding Love

LIVE IT!

Some of the most beautiful prose and poetry about love are contained in the Bible. First John 4.7–21 is a particularly eloquent piece that captures the heart of the Good News: God has loved us in Christ Jesus, who came as the Savior of the world. Now, we have been given God and Jesus' spirit, and we are commanded to love others as we have been loved by God.

It is easy to say, "I love God." But 1 John tells us that our love for God is shown in our love for one another. Loving one another is much harder than simply saying, "I love God." What does this love for God look like? It is not the romantic love or sentimental affection the world usually presents to us. Read Mt 25.31–36 or 1 Corinthians, chapter 13, for some ideas.

▶ 1 Jn 4.7–21

eternal life, and this life is in his Son. 12 Whoever has the Son has life; whoever does not have the Son of God does not have life.

Epilogue

13 I write these things to you who believe in the name of the Son of God, so that you may know that you have eternal life.

14 And this is the boldness we have in him, that if we ask anything according to his will, he hears us. 15 And if we know that he hears us in whatever we ask, we know that we have obtained the requests made of him. 16 If you see your brother or sister*w* committing what is not a mortal sin, you will ask, and God*x* will give life to such a one—to those whose sin is not mortal. There is sin that is mortal; I do not say that you should pray about that. 17 All wrongdoing is sin, but there is sin that is not mortal.

18 We know that those who are born of God do not sin, but the one who was born of God protects them, and the evil one does not touch them. 19 We know that we are God's children, and that the whole world lies under the power of the evil one. 20 And we know that the Son of God has come and has given us understanding so that we may know him who is true;*y* and we are in him who is true, in his Son Jesus Christ. He is the true God and eternal life.

21 Little children, keep yourselves from idols.*z*

---

w Gk *your brother*   *x* Gk *he*   *y* Other ancient authorities read *know the true God*   *z* Other ancient authorities add *Amen*

2 John

For background on this letter, see the introduction to 1, 2, and 3 John, before 1 John.

Salutation

1 The elder to the elect lady and her children, whom I love in the truth, and not only I but also all who know the truth, 2 because of the truth that abides in us and will be with us forever:

3 Grace, mercy, and peace will be with us from God the Father and from*a* Jesus Christ, the Father's Son, in truth and love.

Truth and Love

4 I was overjoyed to find some of your children walking in the truth, just as we have been commanded by the Father. 5 But now, dear lady, I ask you, not as though I were writing you a new commandment, but one we have had from the beginning, let

---

a Other ancient authorities add *the Lord*

Unwelcome Guests

The author of 2 John is warning a Christian community—called elect lady and dear lady—about the false message of some "deceivers" (see the introduction to 1, 2, and 3 John, before 1 John). The author cautions the community not to have anything to do with such people, not even to let them into their homes (verses 10–11). Although the words sound harsh, the reasoning is sound.

Every day, we could be letting people with false messages into our home "virtually" through television, books, music, the Internet, and even magazines. Their false messages promote values and behaviors that are contrary to a healthy and holy way of life. Can these "guests" affect our attitudes and choices? They sure can, especially if we welcome them blindly without thinking about the impact of their messages.

On a piece of paper or in your journal, identify the television shows, magazines, radio stations, and Internet sites that regularly visit your home. List the positive values and behaviors these guests display. Now, list the negative ones. How do the lists compare? How can you manage your media exposure wisely in order to resist its negative influence?

1459

us love one another. 6 And this is love, that we walk according to his commandments; this is the commandment just as you have heard it from the beginning—you must walk in it.

7 Many deceivers have gone out into the world, those who do not confess that Jesus Christ has come in the flesh; any such person is the deceiver and the antichrist! 8 Be on your guard, so that you do not lose what we[b] have worked for, but may receive a full reward. 9 Everyone who does not abide in the teaching of Christ, but goes beyond it, does not have God; whoever abides in the teaching has both the Father and the Son. 10 Do not receive into the house or welcome anyone who comes to you and does not bring this teaching; 11 for to welcome is to participate in the evil deeds of such a person.

Final Greetings

12 Although I have much to write to you, I would rather not use paper and ink; instead I hope to come to you and talk with you face to face, so that our joy may be complete.

13 The children of your elect sister send you their greetings.[c]

---

[b] Other ancient authorities read *you*   [c] Other ancient authorities add *Amen*

3 John

Salutation

1 The elder to the beloved Gā'i•us, whom I love in truth.

Gaius Commended for His Hospitality

2 Beloved, I pray that all may go well with you and that you may be in good health, just as it is well with your soul. 3 I was overjoyed when some of the friends*a* arrived and testified to your faithfulness to the truth, namely how you walk in the truth. 4 I have no greater joy than this, to hear that my children are walking in the truth.

5 Beloved, you do faithfully whatever you do for the friends,*a* even though they are strangers to you; 6 they have testified to your love before the church. You will do well to send them on in a manner worthy of God; 7 for they began their journey for the sake of Christ,*b* accepting no support from non-believers.*c* 8 Therefore we ought to support such people, so that we may become co-workers with the truth.

---

a Gk *brothers*   *b* Gk *for the sake of the name*   *c* Gk *the Gentiles*

Supporting the Ministry of Others

Gaius was a man of faith who opened his home to missionaries who were passing through his city. Though Gaius did not personally know these missionaries, he provided hospitality for them because he knew that they were helping spread the Good News. In 3 John, the elder appeals to him to welcome his messenger, Demetrius, even when others refuse to do so.

Christians find many needs that they cannot respond to by themselves. The story of Gaius shows how you can become a co-missionary with Christians who are ministering in some way that you cannot. These may be ministers in your own parish or diocese, or a religious group that sends missionaries to other countries. You can offer them your hospitality, support them financially, or promote their work in your parish or community. Consider talking with your family about a specific ministry or missionary activity you can support together.

Diotrephes and Demetrius

9 I have written something to the church; but Di·ot′re·phēs, who likes to put himself first, does not acknowledge our authority. 10 So if I come, I will call attention to what he is doing in spreading false charges against us. And not content with those charges, he refuses to welcome the friends,*d* and even prevents those who want to do so and expels them from the church.

11 Beloved, do not imitate what is evil but imitate what is good. Whoever does good is from God; whoever does evil has not seen God. 12 Everyone has testified favorably about De·mē′tri·us, and so has the truth itself. We also testify for him,*e* and you know that our testimony is true.

Final Greetings

13 I have much to write to you, but I would rather not write with pen and ink; 14 instead I hope to see you soon, and we will talk together face to face.

15 Peace to you. The friends send you their greetings. Greet the friends there, each by name.

---

d Gk *brothers*   *e* Gk lacks *for him*

They pretend to be part of your group, but all they really do is cause trouble. They claim to have all the right answers, but they won't listen to other people's opinions. They flatter people to get what they want, but then they grumble and complain behind people's backs. They cause division wherever they go. Do you know people like this? Maybe you even find yourself acting like them sometimes. The Letter of Jude has some things to say about "these people."

At a Glance

- **Verses 1–2.** an opening
- **Verses 3–23.** warnings about judgment
- **Verses 24–25.** a closing

In-depth

The purpose of The Letter of Jude is to warn churches about false teachers who come into the Christian community with lies and tricks, making trouble wherever they go. The author recalls stories from the past in which God punished such people: stories about the Egyptians who opposed God's plan to bring the Hebrew people to the Promised Land; the immoral people of Sodom and Gomorrah; the angels who revolted against God; and Cain, who killed his brother. The author also encourages people to build themselves in the faith. Finally, the author cautions Christians to ignore ungodly people—unless those people truly want to change, in which case, Christians should be examples of the mercy of Jesus Christ.

Notice that this letter includes some words that are unfamiliar to modern Christians or that have different meanings today. For instance, the word *saints* refers to the members of the Christian community, and a *love feast* is a celebration of the Eucharist.

The message of The Letter of Jude is difficult to understand for many reasons. We know almost nothing about who wrote it, to whom it was written, when it was written, and what it is really addressing—except from hints in the letter itself. Tradition says that the author is Jude, the brother of James and Jesus (see Mk 6.3; the name Jude is a form of Judas).

Quick Facts

Author
unknown, or possibly
Jude, the brother of
James

Date Written
maybe A.D. 80–90

Audience
unknown

The Letter of Jude

Jude

Salutation

1 Jude,[a] a servant[b] of Jesus Christ and brother of James,

To those who are called, who are beloved[c] in[d] God the Father and kept safe for[d] Jesus Christ:

2 May mercy, peace, and love be yours in abundance.

Occasion of the Letter

3 Beloved, while eagerly preparing to write to you about the salvation we share, I find it necessary to write and appeal to you to contend for the faith that was once for all entrusted to the saints. 4 For certain intruders have stolen in among you, people who long ago were designated for this condemnation as ungodly, who pervert the grace of our God into licentiousness and deny our only Master and Lord, Jesus Christ.[e]

Judgment on False Teachers

5 Now I desire to remind you, though you are fully informed, that the Lord, who once for all saved[f] a people out of the land of Egypt, afterward destroyed those who did not believe. 6 And the angels who did not keep their own position, but left their proper dwelling, he has kept in eternal chains in deepest darkness for the judgment of the great day. 7 Likewise, Sod'om and Go·mor'rah and the surrounding cities, which, in the same manner as they, indulged in sexual immorality and pursued

unnatural lust,[g] serve as an example by undergoing a punishment of eternal fire.

8 Yet in the same way these dreamers also defile the flesh, reject authority, and slander the glorious ones.[h] 9 But when the archangel Michael contended with the devil and disputed about the body of Moses, he did not dare to bring a condemnation of slander[i] against him, but said, "The Lord rebuke you!" 10 But these people slander whatever they do not understand, and they are destroyed by those things that, like irrational animals, they know by instinct. 11 Woe to them! For they go the way of Cain, and abandon themselves to Ba'laam's error for the sake of gain, and perish in Kō'rah's rebellion. 12 These are blemishes[j] on your love-feasts, while they feast with you without fear, feeding themselves.[k] They are waterless clouds carried along by the winds; autumn trees without fruit, twice dead, uprooted; 13 wild waves of the sea, casting up the foam of their own shame; wandering stars, for whom the deepest darkness has been reserved forever.

14 It was also about these that Ē'noch, in the

---

a Gk Judas   b Gk slave   c Other ancient authorities read
  sanctified   d Or by   e Or the only Master and our Lord Jesus
  Christ   f Other ancient authorities read though you were once
  for all fully informed, that Jesus (or Joshua) who saved
g Gk went after other flesh   h Or angels; Gk glories
i Or condemnation for blasphemy   j Or reefs   k Or without
fear. They are shepherds who care only for themselves

seventh generation from Adam, prophesied, saying, "See, the Lord is coming*l* with ten thousands of his holy ones, 15 to execute judgment on all, and to convict everyone of all the deeds of ungodliness that they have committed in such an ungodly way, and of all the harsh things that ungodly sinners have spoken against him." 16 These are grumblers and malcontents; they indulge their own lusts; they are bombastic in speech, flattering people to their own advantage.

Warnings and Exhortations

17 But you, beloved, must remember the predictions of the apostles of our Lord Jesus Christ; 18 for they said to you, "In the last time there will be scoffers, indulging their own ungodly lusts." 19 It is these worldly people, devoid of the Spirit, who are causing divisions. 20 But you, beloved, build yourselves up on your most holy faith; pray in the Holy Spirit; 21 keep yourselves in the love of God; look forward to the mercy of our Lord Jesus Christ that leads to*m* eternal life. 22 And have mercy on some who are wavering; 23 save others by snatching them out of the fire; and have mercy on still others with fear, hating even the tunic defiled by their bodies.*n*

Benediction

24 Now to him who is able to keep you from falling, and to make you stand without blemish in the presence of his glory with rejoicing, 25 to the only God our Savior, through Jesus Christ our Lord, be glory, majesty, power, and authority, before all time and now and forever. Amen.

---

l Gk *came*   *m* Gk *Christ to*   *n* Gk *by the flesh*. The Greek text of verses 22-23 is uncertain at several points

The Revelation to John

What do you think about when someone mentions the Book of Revelation? Many people immediately think of its bizarre descriptions of monstrous beasts and its warnings about the terrible things that will happen at the end of the world. Some people believe it proves that the end of the world is about to take place very soon. In fact, the Book of Revelation does not predict when the world will end, but brings us hope in proclaiming God's ultimate triumph over evil in history.

In-depth

This book is unique in that the author—who calls himself John—received a series of visions from God that form most of the content. The recorded visions take the form of apocalyptic literature (see "Apocalyptic Literature," Daniel, chapters 7–10) and are full of symbols. These symbols are like the language of a secret club. You use it when you want to keep people who do not belong to your club from understanding what you are saying.

Why was it important that the meaning of the visions be known only to the Christian communities addressed by the letter? Because the Christians still remembered their persecution under the Roman emperor Nero Caesar (A.D. 54–68) and were suffering a new persecution under the Roman emperor Domitian (A.D. 81–96). This "coded language" allowed John to criticize the Roman emperor and empire without necessarily putting his readers at risk of persecution or even death. John himself was exiled to an island off Asia Minor for preaching the Gospel (Rev 1.9).

Once the symbols are understood, it is clear that the Book of Revelation offers hope to a church under persecution. It expresses belief in God's justice and God's victory over evil—an evil that at John's time was embodied in the Roman Empire. But it also expresses the great Christian belief that God will ultimately be victorious, at the end of time, when Christ will come again in his full glory and power. It is a mistake for Christians to try to decipher Revelation as a prediction as to when and how that final coming will occur. But they can take great joy and hope in the promise of a new world where God will wipe away every tear, and suffering and death will be no more (21.4).

At a Glance

- **Chapters 1–3.** an introduction, and letters to the seven churches
- **Chapters 4–11.** visions of God's throne, the Lamb, the seven seals, and the seven trumpets
- **Chapters 12–14.** visions of the dragon and the two beasts
- **Chapters 15–18.** visions of the seven plagues, and the fall of Babylon (Rome)
- **Chapters 19–22.** visions of the victory of Christ and the end of history

Quick Facts

Author
a Jewish-Christian prophet named John

Date
probably A.D. 92–96

Audience
Christian churches in Asia Minor during a time of Roman persecution

Revelation

22.1-5

Introduction and Salutation

1 The revelation of Jesus Christ, which God gave him to show his servants[a] what must soon take place; he made[b] it known by sending his angel to his servant[c] John, 2 who testified to the word of God and to the testimony of Jesus Christ, even to all that he saw.

3 Blessed is the one who reads aloud the words of the prophecy, and blessed are those who hear and who keep what is written in it; for the time is near.

4 John to the seven churches that are in Asia: Grace to you and peace from him who is and who was and who is to come, and from the seven spirits who are before his throne, 5 and from Jesus Christ, the faithful witness, the firstborn of the dead, and the ruler of the kings of the earth.

To him who loves us and freed[d] us from our sins by his blood, 6 and made[b] us to be a kingdom, priests serving[e] his God and Father, to him be glory and dominion forever and ever. Amen.

7 Look! He is coming with the clouds;
  every eye will see him,
 even those who pierced him;
   and on his account all the tribes of the
     earth will wail.
So it is to be. Amen.

8 "I am the Alpha and the Omega," says the Lord God, who is and who was and who is to come, the Almighty.

A Vision of Christ

9 I, John, your brother who share with you in Jesus the persecution and the kingdom and the patient endurance, was on the island called Pat'mos because of the word of God and the testimony of Jesus.[f] 10 I was in the spirit[g] on the Lord's day, and I heard behind me a loud voice like a trumpet 11 saying, "Write in a book what you see and send it to the seven churches, to Eph'e·sus, to Smyrna, to Per'ga·mum, to Thy̆·a·ti'ra, to Sar'dis, to Philadel-phia, and to Lā·o·di·cē'a."

12 Then I turned to see whose voice it was that spoke to me, and on turning I saw seven golden lampstands, 13 and in the midst of the lampstands I saw one like the Son of Man, clothed with a long robe and with a golden sash across his chest. 14 His head and his hair were white as white wool, white as snow; his eyes were like a flame of fire, 15 his feet were like burnished bronze, refined as in a furnace, and his voice was like the sound of many waters. 16 In his right hand he held seven stars, and from his mouth came a sharp, two-edged sword, and his face was like the sun shining with full force.

17 When I saw him, I fell at his feet as though dead. But he placed his right hand on me, saying, "Do not be afraid; I am the first and the last, 18 and the living one. I was dead, and see, I am alive

---

a Gk *slaves* *b* Gk *and he made* *c* Gk *slave* *d* Other ancient authorities read *washed* *e* Gk *priests to* *f* Or *testimony to Jesus* *g* Or *in the Spirit*

PRAY IT!

The Alpha and the Omega

In the first chapter of Revelation, John introduces God's message to the seven churches in Asia. After explaining that he received the message through a vision and that an angel instructed him to communicate it to them, John describes a vision of Christ.

A vision is like a dream. It cannot be interpreted literally; we must seek its deep meaning and be open to its message. For example, in the vision of Rev 1.12–16, a magnificently robed Jesus stands amid seven lampstands. The deeper meaning is that the resurrected Jesus in all his glory and power is watching over the seven churches. Here's another example: Rev 1.8 has Jesus (or God) saying, "I am the Alpha and the Omega." In the Greek alphabet, *alpha* is the first letter, and *omega* is the last letter. This passage is telling us that God and Jesus are in control of all history, from its beginning to its end.

In your prayer, think of any current event that frightens you or harassments that you experience because of your faith or moral principles. See the image of the risen Christ described by John. Feel Jesus lovingly touching your head. Hear Jesus telling you that history is always in God's hands. Let God strengthen your faith and renew your hope with this wonderful revelation of God's love.

▸ Rev 1.7–20

forever and ever; and I have the keys of Death and of Hades. 19 Now write what you have seen, what is, and what is to take place after this. 20 As for the mystery of the seven stars that you saw in my right hand, and the seven golden lampstands: the seven stars are the angels of the seven churches, and the seven lampstands are the seven churches.

The Message to Ephesus

2 "To the angel of the church in Eph'e•sus write: These are the words of him who holds the seven stars in his right hand, who walks among the seven golden lampstands:

2 "I know your works, your toil and your patient endurance. I know that you cannot tolerate evildoers; you have tested those who claim to be apostles but are not, and have found them to be false. 3 I also know that you are enduring patiently and bearing up for the sake of my name, and that you have not grown weary. 4 But I have this against you, that you have abandoned the love you had at first. 5 Remember then from what you have fallen; repent, and do the works you did at first. If not, I will come to you and remove your lampstand from its place, unless you repent. 6 Yet this is to your credit: you hate the works of the Nic•ō•lā'i•tans, which I also hate. 7 Let anyone who has an ear listen to what the Spirit is saying to the churches. To everyone who conquers, I will give permission to eat from the tree of life that is in the paradise of God.

The Message to Smyrna

8 "And to the angel of the church in Smyrna write: These are the words of the first and the last, who was dead and came to life:

9 "I know your affliction and your poverty, even though you are rich. I know the slander on the part of those who say that they are Jews and are not, but are a synagogue of Satan. 10 Do not fear what you are about to suffer. Beware, the devil is about to throw some of you into prison so that you may be tested, and for ten days you will have affliction. Be faithful until death, and I will give you the crown of life. 11 Let anyone who has an ear listen to what the Spirit is saying to the churches. Whoever conquers will not be harmed by the second death.

The Message to Pergamum

12 "And to the angel of the church in Per'ga-mum write: These are the words of him who has the sharp two-edged sword:

13 "I know where you are living, where Satan's throne is. Yet you are holding fast to my name, and you did not deny your faith in me[h] even in the days of An'ti•pas my witness, my faithful one, who was killed among you, where Satan lives. 14 But I have a few things against you: you have some there who hold to the teaching of Bā'laam, who taught Bā'lak to put a stumbling block before the people of Israel, so that they would eat food sacrificed to idols and practice fornication. 15 So you also have some who hold to the teaching of the Nic•ō•lā'i•tans. 16 Repent then. If not, I will come to you soon and make war against them with the sword of my mouth. 17 Let anyone who has an ear listen to what the Spirit is saying to the churches. To everyone who conquers I will give some of the hidden manna, and I will give

h Or deny my faith

did you KNOW?

The Seven Churches

The messages addressed to the seven churches in Asia Minor (modern Greece and Turkey) are not predictions of the future. Like the prophets of the Old Testament who called Israel to return to the Covenant, John calls these communities to deeper faith. Two churches (Smyrna and Philadelphia) are praised, two (Sardis and Laodicea) are scolded, and the remaining three receive both praise and criticism. The churches are scolded because they have tolerated leaders whose teaching contradicts the true Gospel message and because their faith has become "lukewarm," lacking the devotion it had when they first became Christians.

, If the author of Revelation wrote such a prophecy to your local church, what would he praise and what would he criticize? Is your community on fire in living the Gospel, or is it lukewarm in its commitment?

▶ Rev 2.1—3.22

a white stone, and on the white stone is written a new name that no one knows except the one who receives it.

The Message to Thyatira

18 "And to the angel of the church in Thў•a•tī′ra write: These are the words of the Son of God, who has eyes like a flame of fire, and whose feet are like burnished bronze:

19 "I know your works—your love, faith, service, and patient endurance. I know that your last works are greater than the first. 20 But I have this against you: you tolerate that woman Jez′e•bel, who calls herself a prophet and is teaching and beguiling my servants[i] to practice fornication and to eat food sacrificed to idols. 21 I gave her time to repent, but she refuses to repent of her fornication. 22 Beware, I am throwing her on a bed, and those who commit adultery with her I am throwing into great distress, unless they repent of her doings; 23 and I will strike her children dead. And all the churches will know that I am the one who searches minds and hearts, and I will give to each of you as your works deserve. 24 But to the rest of you in Thў•a•tī′ra, who do not

hold this teaching, who have not learned what some call 'the deep things of Satan,' to you I say, I do not lay on you any other burden; 25 only hold fast to what you have until I come. 26 To everyone who conquers and continues to do my works to the end,

I will give authority over the nations;
27 to rule[j] them with an iron rod,
    as when clay pots are shattered—
28 even as I also received authority from my Father. To the one who conquers I will also give the morning star. 29 Let anyone who has an ear listen to what the Spirit is saying to the churches.

The Message to Sardis

3 "And to the angel of the church in Sar′dis write: These are the words of him who has the seven spirits of God and the seven stars:

"I know your works; you have a name of being alive, but you are dead. 2 Wake up, and strengthen what remains and is on the point of death, for I have not found your works perfect in the sight of my God. 3 Remember then what you received and heard; obey it, and repent. If you do not wake up, I will come like a thief, and you will not know at what hour I will come to you. 4 Yet you have still a few persons in Sar′dis who have not soiled their clothes; they will walk with me, dressed in white, for they are worthy. 5 If you conquer, you will be clothed like them in white robes, and I will not blot your name out of the book of life; I will confess your name before my Father and before his angels. 6 Let anyone who has an ear listen to what the Spirit is saying to the churches.

The Message to Philadelphia

7 "And to the angel of the church in Philadelphia write:

These are the words of the holy one, the true one,
    who has the key of David,
    who opens and no one will shut,
    who shuts and no one opens:

8 "I know your works. Look, I have set before you an open door, which no one is able to shut. I know that you have but little power, and yet you have kept my word and have not denied my name. 9 I will make those of the synagogue of Satan who say that they are Jews and are not, but are lying—I will make them come and bow down before your feet, and they will learn that I have loved you. 10 Because you have kept my word of patient endurance, I will keep you from the hour of trial that is coming on the whole world to test the inhabitants of the earth. 11 I am coming soon; hold fast to what you have, so that no one may seize your crown. 12 If you

---

i Gk slaves   j Or to shepherd

Opening the Door

The image in Rev 3.20 inspired an artist to depict our relationship with Christ in a popular painting. The painting shows a door overgrown with vines. The door obviously has not been opened in a long time. As you examine it, you realize that it has no outside latch or knob—it can be opened only from the inside. At the door stands Jesus, knocking—not pounding, just knocking patiently.

What is your relationship with Christ like right now? Is the door of your life open to let Christ in? Or has it been closed for a while? Jesus will not force his way into your life. Jesus seeks a close friendship with you, and real friendship—real love—always involves a free choice. No one can choose to open the door but you.

▶ Rev 3.14–22

conquer, I will make you a pillar in the temple of my God; you will never go out of it. I will write on you the name of my God, and the name of the city of my God, the new Jerusalem that comes down from my God out of heaven, and my own new name. 13 Let anyone who has an ear listen to what the Spirit is saying to the churches.

The Message to Laodicea

14 "And to the angel of the church in Lā·o·di·cē'a write: The words of the Amen, the faithful and true witness, the origin[k] of God's creation:

15 "I know your works; you are neither cold nor hot. I wish that you were either cold or hot.

16 So, because you are lukewarm, and neither cold nor hot, I am about to spit you out of my mouth. 17 For you say, 'I am rich, I have prospered, and I need nothing.' You do not realize that you are wretched, pitiable, poor, blind, and naked. 18 Therefore I counsel you to buy from me gold refined by fire so that you may be rich; and white robes to clothe you and to keep the shame of your nakedness from being seen; and salve to anoint your eyes so that you may see. 19 I reprove and discipline those whom I love. Be earnest, therefore, and repent. 20 Listen! I am standing at the door, knock-

_____
k Or beginning

Jesus Christ Is the Lord of History

After the messages to the churches in Asia, John presents several visions that reveal God's action in history. Read Rev 4.1–11. The vision of God's throne is the background of the whole Book of Revelation. It symbolizes God's authority over history. The vision is enhanced by a heavenly liturgy proclaiming and praising God's name:

"Holy, holy, holy,
the Lord God the Almighty,
   who was and is and is to come."
                    (4.8)

Read 5.1–14. The vision continues. Two symbols stand out: a sealed scroll and a lamb. God holds a scroll containing the history of Israel, whose meaning was hidden to the Christian communities in their persecution. A slain lamb appears. It's the risen Jesus, carrying in his body the signs of his Passion. He receives the scroll from God. He is the only one who can open the scroll and reveal the mystery of death and life.

Read both passages again and experience the honor, glory, and power of Christ. Let these visions reinforce your faith and renew your hope every time that you wonder about the meaning of an event you cannot make sense of.

▶ Revelation, chapters 4–5

ing; if you hear my voice and open the door, I will come in to you and eat with you, and you with me. 21 To the one who conquers I will give a place with me on my throne, just as I myself conquered and sat down with my Father on his throne. 22 Let anyone who has an ear listen to what the Spirit is saying to the churches."

The Heavenly Worship
(Isa 6.1–3)

4 After this I looked, and there in heaven a door stood open! And the first voice, which I had heard speaking to me like a trumpet, said, "Come up here, and I will show you what must take place after this." 2 At once I was in the spirit,[l] and there in heaven stood a throne, with one seated on the throne! 3 And the one seated there looks like jasper and carnelian, and around the throne is a rainbow that looks like an emerald. 4 Around the throne are twenty-four thrones, and seated on the thrones are twenty-four elders, dressed in white robes, with golden crowns on their heads. 5 Coming from the throne are flashes of lightning, and rumblings and peals of thunder, and in front of the throne burn seven flaming torches, which are the seven spirits of God; 6 and in front of the throne there is something like a sea of glass, like crystal.

Around the throne, and on each side of the throne, are four living creatures, full of eyes in front and behind: 7 the first living creature like a lion, the second living creature like an ox, the third living creature with a face like a human face, and the fourth living creature like a flying eagle. 8 And the four living creatures, each of them with six wings, are full of eyes all around and inside. Day and night without ceasing they sing,

"Holy, holy, holy,
　the Lord God the Almighty,
　　who was and is and is to come."

9 And whenever the living creatures give glory and honor and thanks to the one who is seated on the throne, who lives forever and ever, 10 the twenty-four elders fall before the one who is seated on the throne and worship the one who lives forever and ever; they cast their crowns before the throne, singing,

11 "You are worthy, our Lord and God,
　　to receive glory and honor and
　　　power,
　for you created all things,
　　and by your will they existed and were
　　　created."

The Scroll and the Lamb

5 Then I saw in the right hand of the one seated on the throne a scroll written on the inside and on the back, sealed[m] with seven seals; 2 and I saw a mighty angel proclaiming with a loud voice, "Who is worthy to open the scroll and break its seals?" 3 And no one in heaven or on earth or under the earth was able to open the scroll or to look into it. 4 And I began to weep bitterly because no one was found worthy to open the scroll or to look into it. 5 Then one of the elders said to me, "Do not weep. See, the Lion of the tribe of Judah, the Root of David, has conquered, so that he can open the scroll and its seven seals."

6 Then I saw between the throne and the four living creatures and among the elders a Lamb standing as if it had been slaughtered, having seven horns and seven eyes, which are the seven spirits of

---

l Or in the Spirit　m Or written on the inside, and sealed on the back

PRAY IT?
Enthusiastic Praise!

O ver and over in John's vision of heaven, we find enthusiastic praise being offered to God, or to the Lamb of God, who is Christ Jesus. There are angels, incense, fantastic creatures, jewels, gold, elders, white-robed martyrs, and a crowd too great to number. The scenes of this vision inspire us to add our voice to theirs, to praise the majesty of God and the saving sacrifice of Jesus Christ.

In some Christian traditions, including some Catholic traditions, loud, spontaneous praise of God is common. However, most Catholics and many Christians from other denominations usually express their praise through softer types of songs and more solemn prayers. Whatever our expression, we should be enthusiastic with our praise!

How does the vision of the "countless in number, and they cried out in a loud voice" in Rev 5.11–12 encourage you to be more bold in your praise of God? Can you sing out more loudly in Mass? Can you participate more from your heart in saying common prayers with others? In your private prayer, can you praise God without asking for anything or using memorized prayers?

▶ Rev 4.1—5.14

did you KNOW?

Symbolic Numbers and Colors

To understand the Book of Revelation, we need to understand the symbolism of its numbers and colors. The numbers seven and twelve symbolize fullness or perfection. The number four symbolizes universalism (as in the four compass directions). The number one thousand symbolizes a multitude or a quantity too big to count. Thus, the twenty-four elders (4.4) represent the perfection of the twelve tribes of Israel and the twelve Apostles. The Lamb with horns and eyes (5.6) represents the risen Christ, who has the fullness of power (seven horns) and perfect knowledge (seven eyes). The 144,000 who will be saved (7.4) represent a chosen multitude from the twelve tribes of Israel, because 144,000 equals 12 times 12 times 1,000.

The color white symbolizes victory, and red symbolizes bloodshed. Thus, the people who are slaughtered and given white robes (6.9–11) are the martyrs, who gave up their life for their faith. They are victorious in martyrdom because God raised them to eternal life.

▶ Rev 4.1—7.17

God sent out into all the earth. 7 He went and took the scroll from the right hand of the one who was seated on the throne. 8 When he had taken the scroll, the four living creatures and the twenty-four elders fell before the Lamb, each holding a harp and golden bowls full of incense, which are the prayers of the saints. 9 They sing a new song:

"You are worthy to take the scroll
    and to open its seals,
for you were slaughtered and by your blood
        you ransomed for God
    saints from^n every tribe and language and
        people and nation;
10 you have made them to be a kingdom and
        priests serving^o our God,
    and they will reign on earth."

11 Then I looked, and I heard the voice of many angels surrounding the throne and the living creatures and the elders; they numbered myriads of

myriads and thousands of thousands, 12 singing with full voice,

"Worthy is the Lamb that was slaughtered
to receive power and wealth and wisdom and
        might
and honor and glory and blessing!"

13 Then I heard every creature in heaven and on earth and under the earth and in the sea, and all that is in them, singing,

"To the one seated on the throne and to the
        Lamb
be blessing and honor and glory and might
    forever and ever!"

14 And the four living creatures said, "Amen!" And the elders fell down and worshiped.

The Seven Seals

6 Then I saw the Lamb open one of the seven seals, and I heard one of the four living creatures call out, as with a voice of thunder, "Come!"^{p} 2 I looked, and there was a white horse! Its rider had a bow; a crown was given to him, and he came out conquering and to conquer.

3 When he opened the second seal, I heard the second living creature call out, "Come!"^{p} 4 And out came^q another horse, bright red; its rider was permitted to take peace from the earth, so that people would slaughter one another; and he was given a great sword.

5 When he opened the third seal, I heard the third living creature call out, "Come!"^{p} I looked, and there was a black horse! Its rider held a pair of scales in his hand, 6 and I heard what seemed to be a voice in the midst of the four living creatures saying, "A quart of wheat for a day's pay,^{r} and three quarts of barley for a day's pay,^{r} but do not damage the olive oil and the wine!"

7 When he opened the fourth seal, I heard the voice of the fourth living creature call out, "Come!"^{p} 8 I looked and there was a pale green horse! Its rider's name was Death, and Hades followed with him; they were given authority over a fourth of the earth, to kill with sword, famine, and pestilence, and by the wild animals of the earth.

9 When he opened the fifth seal, I saw under the altar the souls of those who had been slaughtered for the word of God and for the testimony they had given; 10 they cried out with a loud voice, "Sovereign Lord, holy and true, how long will it be before you judge and avenge our blood on the inhabitants of the earth?" 11 They were each given a white robe and told to rest a little longer, until the number would be complete both of their fellow servants^s and of their brothers and sisters,^{t} who were soon to be killed as they themselves had been killed.

^{n} Gk ransomed for God from ^{o} Gk priests to ^{p} Or "Go!"
^{q} Or went ^{r} Gk a denarius ^{s} Gk slaves ^{t} Gk brothers

12 When he opened the sixth seal, I looked, and there came a great earthquake; the sun became black as sackcloth, the full moon became like blood, 13 and the stars of the sky fell to the earth as the fig tree drops its winter fruit when shaken by a gale. 14 The sky vanished like a scroll rolling itself up, and every mountain and island was removed from its place. 15 Then the kings of the earth and the magnates and the generals and the rich and the powerful, and everyone, slave and free, hid in the caves and among the rocks of the mountains, 16 calling to the mountains and rocks, "Fall on us and hide us from the face of the one seated on the throne and from the wrath of the Lamb; 17 for the great day of their wrath has come, and who is able to stand?"

The 144,000 of Israel Sealed

7 After this I saw four angels standing at the four corners of the earth, holding back the four winds of the earth so that no wind could blow on earth or sea or against any tree. 2 I saw another angel ascending from the rising of the sun, having the seal of the living God, and he called with a loud voice to the four angels who had been given power to damage earth and sea, 3 saying, "Do not damage the earth or the sea or the trees, until we have marked the servantsᵘ of our God with a seal on their foreheads."

4 And I heard the number of those who were sealed, one hundred forty-four thousand, sealed out of every tribe of the people of Israel:

5 From the tribe of Judah twelve thousand sealed,
from the tribe of Reuben twelve thousand,
from the tribe of Gad twelve thousand,
6 from the tribe of Ash'er twelve thousand,
from the tribe of Naph'ta·li twelve thousand,
from the tribe of Ma·nas'seh twelve thousand,
7 from the tribe of Sim'e·on twelve thousand,
from the tribe of Levi twelve thousand,
from the tribe of Is'sa·char twelve thousand,
8 from the tribe of Zeb'u·lun twelve thousand,
from the tribe of Joseph twelve thousand,
from the tribe of Benjamin twelve thousand sealed.

The Multitude from Every Nation

9 After this I looked, and there was a great multitude that no one could count, from every nation, from all tribes and peoples and languages, standing before the throne and before the Lamb, robed in white, with palm branches in their hands. 10 They cried out in a loud voice, saying,

"Salvation belongs to our God who is seated on the throne, and to the Lamb!"

11 And all the angels stood around the throne and around the elders and the four living creatures, and

---

did you KNOW?

The Seven Seals and Seven Trumpets

The vision continues. In chapters 6–8 of Revelation, the Lamb opens the seven seals on the scroll and thus reveals the great forces in salvation history. The opening of the first four seals reveals the four horses of the apocalypse that bring conquest, strife, famine, and plagues. These are the things that throughout history have made people yearn for God's salvation.

The opening of the fifth seal reveals the souls of the martyrs, who demand justice. Their white robes indicate that they are already with the risen Christ. They are waiting for other martyrs, but this stage will end soon.

The opening of the sixth seal reveals the future. History will change, and all people, even the powerful, will suffer. The visions of the census and of the great crowd in 7.1–17 reveal the destiny of Christians. As in the Exodus, 144,000 people from all the tribes of Israel will be saved. After this, a multitude that cannot be counted, from all nations, tribes, peoples, and languages, will experience God's salvation and sing of God's glory.

Finally, the Lamb opens the last seal. Seven more trumpets are revealed. When they are played by angels, a new series of plagues is released (8.6—9.21). One-third of the people are destroyed by these plagues so that those remaining might repent. But in spite of these warnings, many people do not change.

This vision tells us that no matter what evil besets us, God saves the faithful.

▶ Revelation, chapters 6–9

ᵘ Gk slaves

R
E
V

they fell on their faces before the throne and worshiped God, 12 singing,

> "Amen! Blessing and glory and wisdom
> and thanksgiving and honor
> and power and might
> be to our God forever and ever!
>   Amen."

13 Then one of the elders addressed me, saying, "Who are these, robed in white, and where have they come from?" 14 I said to him, "Sir, you are the one that knows." Then he said to me, "These are they who have come out of the great ordeal; they have washed their robes and made them white in the blood of the Lamb.

15 For this reason they are before the throne of
      God,
      and worship him day and night within his
          temple,
      and the one who is seated on the throne
          will shelter them.
16 They will hunger no more, and thirst no
          more;
      the sun will not strike them,
      nor any scorching heat;
17 for the Lamb at the center of the throne will be
          their shepherd,
      and he will guide them to springs of the
          water of life,
      and God will wipe away every tear from their
          eyes."

PRAY IT

Sing God's Glory

The Book of Revelation contains beautiful prayers of praise. Among them are the hymn to the Lamb (5.9–14), the hymn of the multitude from every nation (7.10–17), the song of the Lamb (15.3–4), and the victory song (19.1–8).

In your prayer, read these prayers slowly and carefully. Imagine the awe-inspiring scenes of God's glory they describe. Quietly reflect on how you have experienced the glory and power of God in your life. Look at the events you experience day to day; can you find the extraordinary in the ordinary? End your reflection by letting these songs inspire your own prayer of praise to God.

▶ Rev 7.10–17

The Seventh Seal and the Golden Censer

8 When the Lamb opened the seventh seal, there was silence in heaven for about half an hour. 2 And I saw the seven angels who stand before God, and seven trumpets were given to them.

3 Another angel with a golden censer came and stood at the altar; he was given a great quantity of incense to offer with the prayers of all the saints on the golden altar that is before the throne. 4 And the smoke of the incense, with the prayers of the saints, rose before God from the hand of the angel. 5 Then the angel took the censer and filled it with fire from the altar and threw it on the earth; and there were peals of thunder, rumblings, flashes of lightning, and an earthquake.

The Seven Trumpets

6 Now the seven angels who had the seven trumpets made ready to blow them.

7 The first angel blew his trumpet, and there came hail and fire, mixed with blood, and they were hurled to the earth; and a third of the earth was burned up, and a third of the trees were burned up, and all green grass was burned up.

8 The second angel blew his trumpet, and something like a great mountain, burning with fire, was thrown into the sea. 9 A third of the sea became blood, a third of the living creatures in the sea died, and a third of the ships were destroyed.

10 The third angel blew his trumpet, and a great star fell from heaven, blazing like a torch, and it fell on a third of the rivers and on the springs of water. 11 The name of the star is Wormwood. A third of the waters became wormwood, and many died from the water, because it was made bitter.

12 The fourth angel blew his trumpet, and a third of the sun was struck, and a third of the moon, and a third of the stars, so that a third of their light was darkened; a third of the day was kept from shining, and likewise the night.

13 Then I looked, and I heard an eagle crying with a loud voice as it flew in midheaven, "Woe, woe, woe to the inhabitants of the earth, at the blasts of the other trumpets that the three angels are about to blow!"

9 And the fifth angel blew his trumpet, and I saw a star that had fallen from heaven to earth, and he was given the key to the shaft of the bottomless pit; 2 he opened the shaft of the bottomless pit, and from the shaft rose smoke like the smoke of a great furnace, and the sun and the air were darkened with the smoke from the shaft. 3 Then from the smoke came locusts on the earth, and they were given authority like the authority of scorpions of the earth. 4 They were told not to damage the grass of the earth or any green growth or any tree, but only those people who do not have the seal of God on their foreheads. 5 They were allowed to torture them for five months, but not to kill them, and their torture was like the torture of a scorpion when it stings someone. 6 And in those days people will seek death but will not find it; they will long to die, but death will flee from them.

7 In appearance the locusts were like horses equipped for battle. On their heads were what looked like crowns of gold; their faces were like human faces, 8 their hair like women's hair, and their teeth like lions' teeth; 9 they had scales like iron breastplates, and the noise of their wings was like the noise of many chariots with horses rushing into battle. 10 They have tails like scorpions, with stingers, and in their tails is their power to harm people for five months. 11 They have as king over them the angel of the bottomless pit; his name in Hebrew is A·bad'don,*v* and in Greek he is called A·pol'lyon.*w*

12 The first woe has passed. There are still two woes to come.

13 Then the sixth angel blew his trumpet, and I heard a voice from the four *x* horns of the golden altar before God, 14 saying to the sixth angel who had the trumpet, "Release the four angels who are bound at the great river Euphrates." 15 So the four angels were released, who had been held ready for the hour, the day, the month, and the year, to kill a third of humankind. 16 The number of the troops of cavalry was two hundred million; I heard their number. 17 And this was how I saw the horses in my vision: the riders wore breastplates the color of fire and of sapphire*y* and of sulfur; the heads of the horses were like lions' heads, and fire and smoke and sulfur came out of their mouths. 18 By these three plagues a third of humankind was killed, by the fire and smoke and sulfur coming out of their mouths. 19 For the power of the horses is in their mouths and in their tails; their tails are like serpents, having heads; and with them they inflict harm.

20 The rest of humankind, who were not killed by these plagues, did not repent of the works of their hands or give up worshiping demons and idols of gold and silver and bronze and stone and wood, which cannot see or hear or walk. 21 And they did not repent of their murders or their sorceries or their fornication or their thefts.

The Angel with the Little Scroll

10 And I saw another mighty angel coming down from heaven, wrapped in a cloud, with a rainbow over his head; his face was like the sun, and his legs like pillars of fire. 2 He held a little scroll open in his hand. Setting his right foot on the sea and his left foot on the land, 3 he gave a great shout, like a lion roaring. And when he

shouted, the seven thunders sounded. 4 And when the seven thunders had sounded, I was about to write, but I heard a voice from heaven saying, "Seal up what the seven thunders have said, and do not write it down." 5 Then the angel whom I saw standing on the sea and the land

   raised his right hand to heaven
6   and swore by him who lives forever and
       ever,

who created heaven and what is in it, the earth and what is in it, and the sea and what is in it: "There will be no more delay, 7 but in the days when the seventh angel is to blow his trumpet, the mystery of God will be fulfilled, as he announced to his servants*z* the prophets."

8 Then the voice that I had heard from heaven spoke to me again, saying, "Go, take the scroll that is open in the hand of the angel who is standing on the sea and on the land." 9 So I went to the angel and told him to give me the little scroll; and he said to me, "Take it, and eat; it will be bitter to your stomach, but sweet as honey in your mouth." 10 So I took the little scroll from the hand of the angel and ate it; it was sweet as honey in my mouth, but when I had eaten it, my stomach was made bitter.

11 Then they said to me, "You must prophesy again about many peoples and nations and languages and kings."

The Two Witnesses

11 Then I was given a measuring rod like a staff, and I was told, "Come and measure the temple of God and the altar and those who worship there, 2 but do not measure the court outside the temple; leave that out, for it is given over to the nations, and they will trample over the holy city for forty-two months. 3 And I will grant my two witnesses authority to prophesy for one thousand two hundred sixty days, wearing sackcloth."

4 These are the two olive trees and the two lampstands that stand before the Lord of the earth. 5 And if anyone wants to harm them, fire pours from their mouth and consumes their foes; anyone who wants to harm them must be killed in this manner. 6 They have authority to shut the sky, so that no rain may fall during the days of their prophesying, and they have authority over the waters to turn them into blood, and to strike the earth with every kind of plague, as often as they desire.

7 When they have finished their testimony, the beast that comes up from the bottomless pit will make war on them and conquer them and kill them, 8 and their dead bodies will lie in the street

v That is, *Destruction* *w* That is, *Destroyer* *x* Other ancient authorities lack *four* *y* Gk *hyacinth* *z* Gk *slaves* of the great city that is prophetically[a] called Sod'om and Egypt, where also their Lord was crucified. 9 For three and a half days members of the peoples and tribes and languages and nations will gaze at their dead bodies and refuse to let them be placed in a tomb; 10 and the inhabitants of the earth will gloat over them and celebrate and exchange presents, because these two prophets had been a torment to the inhabitants of the earth.

11 But after the three and a half days, the breath[b] of life from God entered them, and they stood on their feet, and those who saw them were terrified. 12 Then they[c] heard a loud voice from heaven saying to them, "Come up here!" And they went up to heaven in a cloud while their enemies watched them. 13 At that moment there was a great earthquake, and a tenth of the city fell; seven thousand people were killed in the earthquake, and the rest were terrified and gave glory to the God of heaven.

14 The second woe has passed. The third woe is coming very soon.

The Seventh Trumpet

15 Then the seventh angel blew his trumpet, and there were loud voices in heaven, saying,

"The kingdom of the world has become the
kingdom of our Lord
and of his Messiah,[d]
and he will reign forever and ever."

16 Then the twenty-four elders who sit on their thrones before God fell on their faces and worshiped God, 17 singing,

"We give you thanks, Lord God Almighty,
who are and who were,
for you have taken your great power
and begun to reign.
18 The nations raged,

but your wrath has come,
and the time for judging the dead,
for rewarding your servants,[e] the
prophets
and saints and all who fear your name,
both small and great,
and for destroying those who destroy the
earth."

19 Then God's temple in heaven was opened, and the ark of his covenant was seen within his temple; and there were flashes of lightning, rumblings, peals of thunder, an earthquake, and heavy hail.

The Woman and the Dragon

12 A great portent appeared in heaven: a woman clothed with the sun, with the moon under her feet, and on her head a crown of twelve stars. 2 She was pregnant and was crying out in birth pangs, in the agony of giving birth. 3 Then another portent appeared in heaven: a great red dragon, with seven heads and ten horns, and seven diadems on his heads. 4 His tail swept down a third of the stars of heaven and threw them to the earth. Then the dragon stood before the woman who was about to bear a child, so that he might devour her child as soon as it was born. 5 And she gave birth to a son, a male child, who is to rule[f] all the nations with a rod of iron. But her child was snatched away and taken to God and to his throne; 6 and the woman fled into the wilderness, where she has a place prepared by God, so that there she can be nourished for one thousand two hundred sixty days.

---

[a] Or *allegorically*; Gk *spiritually*   [b] Or *the spirit*   [c] Other ancient authorities read *I*   [d] Gk *Christ*   [e] Gk *slaves*   [f] Or *to shepherd*

God in Control

LIVE IT!

The world is a wonderful place, full of life and hope. At the same time, it is full of pain and suffering, illness and death. It can seem frightening and out of control. Wars break out, a drought threatens the lives of millions, a friend dies in a senseless car accident, terrorists attack and kill innocent people; we can be left wondering why God allows such things.

The Book of Revelation was written to encourage the people of John's time that despite the evil that happens, God is in control. It can do the same for us too. The song in 11.15–18 reminds us that there will come a time when the just will be rewarded and the wicked punished. And although God's Reign is not yet fully realized, as members of that Reign, we are called to be people of justice, peace, and hope to a world desperately seeking these things.

▶ Rev 11.15–18

so that she could fly from the serpent into the wilderness, to her place where she is nourished for a time, and times, and half a time. ¹⁵ Then from his mouth the serpent poured water like a river after the woman, to sweep her away with the flood. ¹⁶ But the earth came to the help of the woman; it opened its mouth and swallowed the river that the dragon had poured from his mouth. ¹⁷ Then the dragon was angry with the woman, and went off to make war on the rest of her children, those who keep the commandments of God and hold the testimony of Jesus.

did you KNOW?

The Woman and the Dragon

The vision in chapter 12 of Revelation symbolizes the great battle between Christ and Satan. In the opening scene, the pregnant woman represents Israel, from which the Messiah will come. The dragon waiting to devour her child is a symbol for Satan (verse 9). This child, who will rule all the nations, is the Messiah, Jesus Christ.

The conflict moves from heaven to earth when Satan fails to devour the child and is thrown down from his place in heaven. The dragon continues his pursuit of the woman on earth. The woman now represents the Christian churches, which the dragon angrily persecutes because he did not succeed in devouring her child. In this vision, John is telling the persecuted Christians of his time to have hope because in the end, Christ will totally and completely destroy Satan (see also 20.1–10).

▸ **Rev 12.1–18**

Michael Defeats the Dragon

7 And war broke out in heaven; Michael and his angels fought against the dragon. The dragon and his angels fought back, ⁸ but they were defeated, and there was no longer any place for them in heaven. ⁹ The great dragon was thrown down, that ancient serpent, who is called the Devil and Satan, the deceiver of the whole world—he was thrown down to the earth, and his angels were thrown down with him.

10 Then I heard a loud voice in heaven, proclaiming,

"Now have come the salvation and the power
      and the kingdom of our God
      and the authority of his Messiah,ᵍ
for the accuser of our comradesʰ has been
            thrown down,
      who accuses them day and night before our
            God.
¹¹ But they have conquered him by the blood of
            the Lamb
      and by the word of their testimony,
      for they did not cling to life even in the face of
            death.
¹² Rejoice then, you heavens
      and those who dwell in them!
But woe to the earth and the sea,
      for the devil has come down to you
with great wrath,
      because he knows that his time is short!"

The Dragon Fights Again on Earth

13 So when the dragon saw that he had been thrown down to the earth, he pursuedⁱ the woman who had given birth to the male child. ¹⁴ But the woman was given the two wings of the great eagle,

The First Beast

13 18 Then the dragonʲ took his stand on the sand of the seashore. ¹ And I saw a beast rising out of the sea, having ten horns and seven heads; and on its horns were ten diadems, and on its heads were blasphemous names. ² And

---

g Gk *Christ* h Gk *brothers* i Or *persecuted* j Gk *Then he;* other ancient authorities read *Then I stood*

REV

Cultural Connections

MARY HAS A VITAL MISSION IN SALVATION HISTORY!

The New Testament links Mary's mission intimately to the mystery of Christ. In Lk 1.38, Mary's yes to the angel Gabriel allows God to enter the world as a human being. At a wedding in Cana (Jn 2.1–11), Mary is a model for the church as she intercedes before Jesus, has faith in him, points to him as the source of life, and leads others to follow his words. Jesus' words to Mary and the Beloved Disciple at the cross (Jn 19.26–27) name Mary mother of the universal church, which is symbolized by the Beloved Disciple.

Over the centuries, some Catholics have seen in the unnamed woman mentioned in chapter 12 of Revelation representations of Mary and the church, who both share in Jesus' messianic mission. In the feast of the Assumption, this passage is one of the readings that celebrate Mary's entrance into heaven as the first disciple. Mary is a symbol of the triumphant church that awaits and intercedes for us, the pilgrim church.

Reflect on the ways Mary teaches us to be servants of the Reign of God. Pray that we are as willing to fulfill our mission in salvation history as she is.

▶ Revelation, chapter 12

the beast that I saw was like a leopard, its feet were like a bear's, and its mouth was like a lion's mouth. And the dragon gave it his power and his throne and great authority. ³ One of its heads seemed to have received a death-blow, but its mortal wound[k] had been healed. In amazement the whole earth followed the beast. ⁴ They worshiped the dragon, for he had given his authority to the beast, and they worshiped the beast, saying, "Who is like the beast, and who can fight against it?"

5 The beast was given a mouth uttering haughty and blasphemous words, and it was allowed to exercise authority for forty-two months. ⁶ It opened its mouth to utter blasphemies against God, blaspheming his name and his dwelling, that is, those who dwell in heaven. ⁷ Also it was allowed to make war on the saints and to conquer them.[l] It was given authority over every tribe and people and language and nation, ⁸ and all the inhabitants of the earth will worship it, everyone whose name has not been written from the foundation of the world in the book of life of the Lamb that was slaughtered.[m]

9 Let anyone who has an ear listen:
¹⁰ If you are to be taken captive,

into captivity you go;
if you kill with the sword,
with the sword you must be killed.
Here is a call for the endurance and faith of the saints.

The Second Beast

11 Then I saw another beast that rose out of the earth; it had two horns like a lamb and it spoke like a dragon. ¹² It exercises all the authority of the first beast on its behalf, and it makes the earth and its inhabitants worship the first beast, whose mortal wound[n] had been healed. ¹³ It performs great signs, even making fire come down from heaven to earth in the sight of all; ¹⁴ and by the signs that it is allowed to perform on behalf of the beast, it deceives the inhabitants of earth, telling them to make an image for the beast that had been wounded by the sword[o] and yet lived; ¹⁵ and it was allowed to give

---

k Gk *the plague of its death* l Other ancient authorities lack this sentence m Or *written in the book of life of the Lamb that was slaughtered from the foundation of the world* n Gk *whose plague of its death* o Or *that had received the plague of the sword* breath^p to the image of the beast so that the image of the beast could even speak and cause those who would not worship the image of the beast to be killed. 16 Also it causes all, both small and great, both rich and poor, both free and slave, to be marked on the right hand or the forehead, 17 so that no one can buy or sell who does not have the mark, that is, the name of the beast or the number of its name. 18 This calls for wisdom: let anyone with understanding calculate the number of the beast, for it is the number of a person. Its number is six hundred sixty-six.^{q}

did you **KNOW?**

The Number of the Beast

The vision of the two beasts in chapter 13 of Revelation is a continuation of the vision about the woman and the dragon in chapter 12. The beasts represent the Roman Empire and its emperor, which at the time threatened the true practice of Christianity. Roman leaders expected all citizens, including Christians, to offer sacrifices to the Roman gods and to worship the emperor as though he were a god. This may have been especially true in the cities in Asia Minor, which were trying to prove their loyalty to the Roman emperor.

In verse 18, we are told that the number of the second beast is 666. Most scholars believe that this stands for Nero Caesar, who was the emperor of Rome from A.D. 54 to 68. Their reasoning is that when you convert the Hebrew letters for Nero's name to Hebrew numbers, you get the number 666. Nero was responsible for some especially vicious attacks on Christians in Rome. The Book of Revelation was written after Nero committed suicide, but many people thought that he had not died and had come out of hiding in the East to lead this new wave of persecution against Christians (verse 3).

▶ **Revelation, chapter 13**

The Lamb and the 144,000

14 Then I looked, and there was the Lamb, standing on Mount Zion! And with him were one hundred forty-four thousand who had his name and his Father's name written on their foreheads. 2 And I heard a voice from heaven like the sound of many waters and like the sound of loud thunder; the voice I heard was like the sound of harpists playing on their harps, 3 and they sing a new song before the throne and before the four living creatures and before the elders. No one could learn that song except the one hundred forty-four thousand who have been redeemed from the earth. 4 It is these who have not defiled themselves with women, for they are virgins; these follow the Lamb wherever he goes. They have been redeemed from humankind as first fruits for God and the Lamb, 5 and in their mouth no lie was found; they are blameless.

The Messages of the Three Angels

6 Then I saw another angel flying in midheaven, with an eternal gospel to proclaim to those who live^r on the earth—to every nation and tribe and language and people. 7 He said in a loud voice, "Fear God and give him glory, for the hour of his judgment has come; and worship him who made heaven and earth, the sea and the springs of water."

8 Then another angel, a second, followed, saying, "Fallen, fallen is Babylon the great! She has made all nations drink of the wine of the wrath of her fornication."

9 Then another angel, a third, followed them, crying with a loud voice, "Those who worship the beast and its image, and receive a mark on their foreheads or on their hands, 10 they will also drink the wine of God's wrath, poured unmixed into the cup of his anger, and they will be tormented with fire and sulfur in the presence of the holy angels and in the presence of the Lamb. 11 And the smoke of their torment goes up forever and ever. There is no rest day or night for those who worship the beast and its image and for anyone who receives the mark of its name."

12 Here is a call for the endurance of the saints, those who keep the commandments of God and hold fast to the faith of^s Jesus.

13 And I heard a voice from heaven saying, "Write this: Blessed are the dead who from now on die in the Lord." "Yes," says the Spirit, "they will rest from their labors, for their deeds follow them."

R E V

---

^{p} Or *spirit* ^{q} Other ancient authorities read *six hundred sixteen* ^{r} Gk *sit* ^{s} Or *to their faith in*

Reaping the Earth's Harvest

14 Then I looked, and there was a white cloud, and seated on the cloud was one like the Son of Man, with a golden crown on his head, and a sharp sickle in his hand! 15 Another angel came out of the temple, calling with a loud voice to the one who sat on the cloud, "Use your sickle and reap, for the hour to reap has come, because the harvest of the earth is fully ripe." 16 So the one who sat on the cloud swung his sickle over the earth, and the earth was reaped.

17 Then another angel came out of the temple in heaven, and he too had a sharp sickle. 18 Then another angel came out from the altar, the angel who has authority over fire, and he called with a loud voice to him who had the sharp sickle, "Use your sharp sickle and gather the clusters of the vine of the earth, for its grapes are ripe." 19 So the angel swung his sickle over the earth and gathered the vintage of the earth, and he threw it into the great wine press of the wrath of God. 20 And the wine press was trodden outside the city, and blood flowed from the wine press, as high as a horse's bridle, for a distance of about two hundred miles.[t]

The Angels with the Seven Last Plagues

15 Then I saw another portent in heaven, great and amazing: seven angels with seven plagues, which are the last, for with them the wrath of God is ended.

2 And I saw what appeared to be a sea of glass mixed with fire, and those who had conquered the beast and its image and the number of its name, standing beside the sea of glass with harps of God in their hands. 3 And they sing the song of Moses, the servant[u] of God, and the song of the Lamb:

"Great and amazing are your deeds,
     Lord God the Almighty!
Just and true are your ways,
     King of the nations![v]
4 Lord, who will not fear
     and glorify your name?
For you alone are holy.
     All nations will come
     and worship before you,
for your judgments have been revealed."

5 After this I looked, and the temple of the tent[w] of witness in heaven was opened, 6 and out of the temple came the seven angels with the seven plagues, robed in pure bright linen,[x] with golden sashes across their chests. 7 Then one of the four living creatures gave the seven angels seven golden bowls full of the wrath of God, who lives forever and ever; 8 and the temple was filled with smoke from the glory of God and from his power, and no one could enter the temple until the seven plagues of the seven angels were ended.

The Bowls of God's Wrath

16 Then I heard a loud voice from the temple telling the seven angels, "Go and pour out on the earth the seven bowls of the wrath of God."

2 So the first angel went and poured his bowl on the earth, and a foul and painful sore came on those who had the mark of the beast and who worshiped its image.

3 The second angel poured his bowl into the sea, and it became like the blood of a corpse, and every living thing in the sea died.

4 The third angel poured his bowl into the rivers and the springs of water, and they became blood. 5 And I heard the angel of the waters say,

"You are just, O Holy One, who are and were,
     for you have judged these things;
6 because they shed the blood of saints and
          prophets,
     you have given them blood to drink.
It is what they deserve!"
7 And I heard the altar respond,
"Yes, O Lord God, the Almighty,
     your judgments are true and just!"

8 The fourth angel poured his bowl on the sun, and it was allowed to scorch people with fire; 9 they were scorched by the fierce heat, but they cursed the name of God, who had authority over these plagues, and they did not repent and give him glory.

10 The fifth angel poured his bowl on the throne of the beast, and its kingdom was plunged into darkness; people gnawed their tongues in agony, 11 and cursed the God of heaven because of their pains and sores, and they did not repent of their deeds.

12 The sixth angel poured his bowl on the great river Euphrates, and its water was dried up in order to prepare the way for the kings from the east. 13 And I saw three foul spirits like frogs coming from the mouth of the dragon, from the mouth of the beast, and from the mouth of the false prophet. 14 These are demonic spirits, performing signs, who go abroad to the kings of the whole world, to assemble them for battle on the great day of God the Almighty. 15 ("See, I am coming like a thief! Blessed is the one who stays awake and is clothed,[y] not going about naked and exposed to shame.") 16 And they assembled them at the place that in Hebrew is called Har·ma·ged'on.

---

t Gk *one thousand six hundred stadia*   u Gk *slave*   v Other ancient authorities read *the ages*   w Or *tabernacle*   x Other ancient authorities read *stone*   y Gk *and keeps his robes*

17 The seventh angel poured his bowl into the air, and a loud voice came out of the temple, from the throne, saying, "It is done!" 18 And there came flashes of lightning, rumblings, peals of thunder, and a violent earthquake, such as had not occurred since people were upon the earth, so violent was that earthquake. 19 The great city was split into three parts, and the cities of the nations fell. God remembered great Babylon and gave her the winecup of the fury of his wrath. 20 And every island fled away, and no mountains were to be found; 21 and huge hailstones, each weighing about a hundred pounds,z dropped from heaven on people, until they cursed God for the plague of the hail, so fearful was that plague.

The Great Whore and the Beast

17 Then one of the seven angels who had the seven bowls came and said to me, "Come, I will show you the judgment of the great whore who is seated on many waters, 2 with whom the kings of the earth have committed fornication, and with the wine of whose fornication the inhabitants of the earth have become drunk." 3 So he carried me away in the spirita into a wilderness, and I saw a woman sitting on a scarlet beast that was full of blasphemous names, and it had seven heads and ten horns. 4 The woman was clothed in purple and scarlet, and adorned with gold and jewels and pearls, holding in her hand a golden cup full of abominations and the impurities of her fornica-

tion; 5 and on her forehead was written a name, a mystery: "Babylon the great, mother of whores and of earth's abominations." 6 And I saw that the woman was drunk with the blood of the saints and the blood of the witnesses to Jesus.

When I saw her, I was greatly amazed. 7 But the angel said to me, "Why are you so amazed? I will tell you the mystery of the woman, and of the beast with seven heads and ten horns that carries her. 8 The beast that you saw was, and is not, and is about to ascend from the bottomless pit and go to destruction. And the inhabitants of the earth, whose names have not been written in the book of life from the foundation of the world, will be amazed when they see the beast, because it was and is not and is to come.

9 "This calls for a mind that has wisdom: the seven heads are seven mountains on which the woman is seated; also, they are seven kings, 10 of whom five have fallen, one is living, and the other has not yet come; and when he comes, he must remain only a little while. 11 As for the beast that was and is not, it is an eighth but it belongs to the seven, and it goes to destruction. 12 And the ten horns that you saw are ten kings who have not yet received a kingdom, but they are to receive authority as kings for one hour, together with the beast. 13 These are united in yielding their power and authority to the beast; 14 they will make war on the

z Gk weighing about a talent   a Or in the Spirit

The Sins of Empires

LIVE IT!

In John's coded language, the whore called Babylon in chapter 17 is Rome, a city built on seven hills. She is dressed in colors that symbolize her royalty (purple) and her obscene and immoral behavior (scarlet). Her gold and pearls are signs of her wealth and excessive luxury. The blasphemous names on her forehead are the titles that should be given to God but are given to the emperor instead. By calling her Babylon, John is creating a tie with the capital of another evil empire from the Old Testament (see "The Fall of Jerusalem," 2 Kings 25.1–21).

The whore is drunk on the blood of the saints who have been killed for their faith. John indicates that her evil is caused by her unrestrained desire for wealth and luxury and her abuse of power (Rev 18.3–19). He tells his Christian readers that they can be hopeful, even amid so much suffering, because in the end, the Lamb (Christ) will conquer the beast (17.14).

Since Revelation was written, many other empires have abused their power.

Reflect for a moment. In what areas does your country need to take more responsibility to ensure justice for all people? Where has the desire for wealth and luxury gone too far? What can you do locally to take greater responsibility in these areas?

▶ **Revelation, chapter 17**

Lamb, and the Lamb will conquer them, for he is Lord of lords and King of kings, and those with him are called and chosen and faithful."

15 And he said to me, "The waters that you saw, where the whore is seated, are peoples and multitudes and nations and languages. 16 And the ten horns that you saw, they and the beast will hate the whore; they will make her desolate and naked; they will devour her flesh and burn her up with fire. 17 For God has put it into their hearts to carry out his purpose by agreeing to give their kingdom to the beast, until the words of God will be fulfilled. 18 The woman you saw is the great city that rules over the kings of the earth."

The Fall of Babylon

18 After this I saw another angel coming down from heaven, having great authority; and the earth was made bright with his splendor. 2 He called out with a mighty voice,

"Fallen, fallen is Babylon the great!
It has become a dwelling place of demons,
a haunt of every foul spirit,
a haunt of every foul bird,
a haunt of every foul and hateful beast.*b*
3 For all the nations have drunk*c*
of the wine of the wrath of her fornication,
and the kings of the earth have committed
fornication with her,
and the merchants of the earth have grown
rich from the power*d* of her luxury."

4 Then I heard another voice from heaven saying,

"Come out of her, my people,
so that you do not take part in her sins,
and so that you do not share in her plagues;
5 for her sins are heaped high as heaven,
and God has remembered her iniquities.
6 Render to her as she herself has rendered,
and repay her double for her deeds;
mix a double draught for her in the cup she
mixed.
7 As she glorified herself and lived luxuriously,
so give her a like measure of torment and
grief.
Since in her heart she says,
'I rule as a queen;
I am no widow,
and I will never see grief,'
8 therefore her plagues will come in a single
day—
pestilence and mourning and famine—
and she will be burned with fire;
for mighty is the Lord God who judges her."

9 And the kings of the earth, who committed fornication and lived in luxury with her, will weep and wail over her when they see the smoke of her burning; 10 they will stand far off, in fear of her torment, and say,

"Alas, alas, the great city,
Babylon, the mighty city!
For in one hour your judgment has come."

11 And the merchants of the earth weep and mourn for her, since no one buys their cargo anymore, 12 cargo of gold, silver, jewels and pearls, fine linen, purple, silk and scarlet, all kinds of scented wood, all articles of ivory, all articles of costly wood, bronze, iron, and marble, 13 cinnamon, spice, incense, myrrh, frankincense, wine, olive oil, choice flour and wheat, cattle and sheep, horses and chariots, slaves—and human lives.*e*

14 "The fruit for which your soul longed
has gone from you,
and all your dainties and your splendor
are lost to you,
never to be found again!"

15 The merchants of these wares, who gained wealth from her, will stand far off, in fear of her torment, weeping and mourning aloud,

16 "Alas, alas, the great city,
clothed in fine linen,
in purple and scarlet,
adorned with gold,
with jewels, and with pearls!
17 For in one hour all this wealth has been laid
waste!"

And all shipmasters and seafarers, sailors and all whose trade is on the sea, stood far off 18 and cried out as they saw the smoke of her burning,

"What city was like the great city?"

19 And they threw dust on their heads, as they wept and mourned, crying out,

"Alas, alas, the great city,
where all who had ships at sea
grew rich by her wealth!
For in one hour she has been laid waste."

20 Rejoice over her, O heaven, you saints and apostles and prophets! For God has given judgment for you against her.

21 Then a mighty angel took up a stone like a great millstone and threw it into the sea, saying,

"With such violence Babylon the great city
will be thrown down,
and will be found no more;
22 and the sound of harpists and minstrels and of
flutists and trumpeters
will be heard in you no more;
and an artisan of any trade
will be found in you no more;

---

b Other ancient authorities lack the words *a haunt of every foul beast* and attach the words *and hateful* to the previous line so as to read *a haunt of every foul and hateful bird*   *c* Other ancient authorities read *She has made all nations drink*   *d* Or *resources*   *e* Or *chariots, and human bodies and souls*

and the sound of the millstone
    will be heard in you no more;
23 and the light of a lamp
    will shine in you no more;
and the voice of bridegroom and bride
    will be heard in you no more;
for your merchants were the magnates of the
        earth,
    and all nations were deceived by your
        sorcery.
24 And in you*f* was found the blood of prophets
        and of saints,
    and of all who have been slaughtered on
        earth."

The Rejoicing in Heaven

19 After this I heard what seemed to be the loud voice of a great multitude in heaven, saying,
"Hallelujah!
Salvation and glory and power to our God,
2   for his judgments are true and just;
he has judged the great whore
    who corrupted the earth with her
        fornication,
and he has avenged on her the blood of his
    servants."*g*
3 Once more they said,
"Hallelujah!
The smoke goes up from her forever and ever."
4 And the twenty-four elders and the four living creatures fell down and worshiped God who is seated on the throne, saying,
"Amen. Hallelujah!"
5 And from the throne came a voice saying,
"Praise our God,
    all you his servants,*g*
and all who fear him,
    small and great."
6 Then I heard what seemed to be the voice of a great multitude, like the sound of many waters and like the sound of mighty thunderpeals, crying out,
"Hallelujah!
For the Lord our God
    the Almighty reigns.
7 Let us rejoice and exult
    and give him the glory,
for the marriage of the Lamb has come,
    and his bride has made herself ready;
8 to her it has been granted to be clothed
    with fine linen, bright and pure"—
for the fine linen is the righteous deeds of the saints.
9 And the angel said*h* to me, "Write this: Blessed are those who are invited to the marriage supper of the Lamb." And he said to me, "These are true words of God." 10 Then I fell down at his feet to worship him, but he said to me, "You must not do that! I am a fellow servant*i* with you and your comrades*j* who hold the testimony of Jesus.*k* Worship God! For the testimony of Jesus*k* is the spirit of prophecy."

The Rider on the White Horse

11 Then I saw heaven opened, and there was a white horse! Its rider is called Faithful and True, and in righteousness he judges and makes war. 12 His eyes are like a flame of fire, and on his head are many diadems; and he has a name inscribed that no one knows but himself. 13 He is clothed in a robe dipped in*l* blood, and his name is called The Word of God. 14 And the armies of heaven, wearing fine linen, white and pure, were following him on white horses. 15 From his mouth comes a sharp sword with which to strike down the nations, and he will rule*m* them with a rod of iron; he will tread the wine press of the fury of the wrath of God the Almighty. 16 On his robe and on his thigh he has a name inscribed, "King of kings and Lord of lords."

The Beast and Its Armies Defeated

17 Then I saw an angel standing in the sun, and with a loud voice he called to all the birds that fly in midheaven, "Come, gather for the great supper of God, 18 to eat the flesh of kings, the flesh of captains, the flesh of the mighty, the flesh of horses and their riders—flesh of all, both free and slave, both small and great." 19 Then I saw the beast and the kings of the earth with their armies gathered to make war against the rider on the horse and against his army. 20 And the beast was captured, and with it the false prophet who had performed in its presence the signs by which he deceived those who had received the mark of the beast and those who worshiped its image. These two were thrown alive into the lake of fire that burns with sulfur. 21 And the rest were killed by the sword of the rider on the horse, the sword that came from his mouth; and all the birds were gorged with their flesh.

The Thousand Years

20 Then I saw an angel coming down from heaven, holding in his hand the key to the bottomless pit and a great chain. 2 He seized the dragon, that ancient serpent, who is the Devil and Satan, and bound him for a thousand years, 3 and threw him into the pit, and locked and sealed it over him, so that he would deceive the nations no more, until the thousand years were ended. After that he must be let out for a little while.

---

f Gk *her*   *g* Gk *slaves*   *h* Gk *he said*   *i* Gk *slave*
j Gk *brothers*   *k* Or *to Jesus*   *l* Other ancient authorities read *sprinkled with*   *m* Or *will shepherd*

20.2

4 Then I saw thrones, and those seated on them were given authority to judge. I also saw the souls of those who had been beheaded for their testimony to Jesus[n] and for the word of God. They had not worshiped the beast or its image and had not received its mark on their foreheads or their hands. They came to life and reigned with Christ a thousand years. 5 (The rest of the dead did not come to life until the thousand years were ended.) This is the first resurrection. 6 Blessed and holy are those who share in the first resurrection. Over these the second death has no power, but they will be priests of God and of Christ, and they will reign with him a thousand years.

Satan's Doom
(Cp Ezek 38–39)

7 When the thousand years are ended, Satan will be released from his prison 8 and will come out to deceive the nations at the four corners of the earth, Gog and Māʹgog, in order to gather them for battle; they are as numerous as the sands of the sea. 9 They marched up over the breadth of the earth and surrounded the camp of the saints and the beloved city. And fire came down from heaven[o] and consumed them. 10 And the devil who had deceived them was thrown into the lake of fire and sulfur, where the beast and the false prophet were, and they will be tormented day and night forever and ever.

The Dead Are Judged

11 Then I saw a great white throne and the one who sat on it; the earth and the heaven fled from his presence, and no place was found for them. 12 And I saw the dead, great and small, standing before the throne, and books were opened. Also an-

other book was opened, the book of life. And the dead were judged according to their works, as recorded in the books. 13 And the sea gave up the dead that were in it, Death and Hades gave up the dead that were in them, and all were judged according to what they had done. 14 Then Death and Hades were thrown into the lake of fire. This is the second death, the lake of fire; 15 and anyone whose name was not found written in the book of life was thrown into the lake of fire.

The New Heaven and the New Earth

21 Then I saw a new heaven and a new earth; for the first heaven and the first earth had passed away, and the sea was no more. 2 And I saw the holy city, the new Jerusalem, coming down out of heaven from God, prepared as a bride adorned for her husband. 3 And I heard a loud voice from the throne saying,

"See, the home[p] of God is among mortals.
He will dwell[q] with them;
they will be his peoples,[r]
and God himself will be with them;[s]
4   he will wipe every tear from their eyes.
Death will be no more;
mourning and crying and pain will be no
      more,
for the first things have passed away."

5 And the one who was seated on the throne said, "See, I am making all things new." Also he said, "Write this, for these words are trustworthy and true." 6 Then he said to me, "It is done! I am the Alpha and the Omega, the beginning and the end. To the thirsty I will give water as a gift from the spring of the water of life. 7 Those who conquer will inherit these things, and I will be their God and they will be my children. 8 But as for the cowardly, the faithless,[t] the polluted, the murderers, the fornicators, the sorcerers, the idolaters, and all liars, their place will be in the lake that burns with fire and sulfur, which is the second death."

Vision of the New Jerusalem
(Cp Ezek 48.30–35)

9 Then one of the seven angels who had the seven bowls full of the seven last plagues came and said to me, "Come, I will show you the bride, the wife of the Lamb." 10 And in the spirit[u] he carried me away to a great, high mountain and showed me the holy city Jerusalem coming down out of heaven from God. 11 It has the glory of God and a radiance like a very rare jewel, like jasper, clear as crystal. 12 It

---

[n] Or *for the testimony of Jesus*   [o] Other ancient authorities read *from God, out of heaven*, or *out of heaven from God*   [p] Gk *the tabernacle*   [q] Gk *will tabernacle*   [r] Other ancient authorities read *people*   [s] Other ancient authorities add *and be their God*   [t] Or *the unbelieving*   [u] Or *in the Spirit*

has a great, high wall with twelve gates, and at the gates twelve angels, and on the gates are inscribed the names of the twelve tribes of the Israelites; 13 on the east three gates, on the north three gates, on the south three gates, and on the west three gates. 14 And the wall of the city has twelve foundations, and on them are the twelve names of the twelve apostles of the Lamb.

15 The angel^v who talked to me had a measuring rod of gold to measure the city and its gates and walls. 16 The city lies foursquare, its length the same as its width; and he measured the city with his rod, fifteen hundred miles;^w its length and width and height are equal. 17 He also measured its wall, one hundred forty-four cubits^x by human measurement, which the angel was using. 18 The wall is built of jasper, while the city is pure gold, clear as glass. 19 The foundations of the wall of the city are adorned with every jewel; the first was jasper, the second sapphire, the third agate, the fourth emerald, 20 the fifth onyx, the sixth carnelian, the seventh chrysolite, the eighth beryl, the ninth topaz, the tenth chrysoprase, the eleventh jacinth, the twelfth amethyst. 21 And the twelve gates are twelve pearls, each of the gates is a single pearl, and the street of the city is pure gold, transparent as glass.

22 I saw no temple in the city, for its temple is the Lord God the Almighty and the Lamb. 23 And the city has no need of sun or moon to shine on it, for the glory of God is its light, and its lamp is the Lamb. 24 The nations will walk by its light, and the kings of the earth will bring their glory into it. 25 Its gates will never be shut by day—and there will be no night there. 26 People will bring into it the glory and the honor of the nations. 27 But nothing unclean will enter it, nor anyone who practices abomination or falsehood, but only those who are written in the Lamb's book of life.

The River of Life

22 Then the angel^y showed me the river of the water of life, bright as crystal, flowing from the throne of God and of the Lamb 2 through the middle of the street of the city. On either side of the river is the tree of life^z with its twelve kinds of fruit, producing its fruit each month; and the leaves of the tree are for the healing of the nations. 3 Nothing accursed will be found there any more. But the throne of God and of the

---

v Gk *He*   *w* Gk *twelve thousand stadia*   *x* That is, almost seventy-five yards   *y* Gk *he*   *z* Or *the Lamb.* 2*In the middle of the street of the city, and on either side of the river, is the tree of life*

The New Jerusalem

LIVE IT!

The last three chapters of Revelation contain John's visions of the Reign of God, the end of history, and eternal life. In chapter 20, Satan is alive but has limited power. This is symbolized by the dragon's thousand-year imprisonment, during which the martyrs reign with Christ. The thousand-year reign has been interpreted in many different ways over the centuries, but no one knows its true significance. At the end of the thousand years, Satan is defeated, and Christ sits in final judgment over all the dead.

In chapter 21, John describes a new heaven and a new earth. The Bible begins in Genesis with the story of the creation of a world in which everything is good. It ends in Revelation with a new creation where God's goodness again overflows. A holy city, the new Jerusalem, comes down out of heaven. The new Jerusalem is described as a beautiful bride who is preparing to marry Jesus Christ. John tells his Christian readers that they should look forward to the time of this new city with joy, because when it comes, God and Christ will live in their midst. The whole city will be God's temple. The sun will always shine, a river of living water will flow from God's throne, and the trees will produce fruit year-round. The new Jerusalem is a symbol for the new world that God will establish when evil is destroyed and suffering is banished.

These visions helped Christians at the end of the first century to maintain their hope by focusing on the glorious victory of God in history. They can also help us to renew our commitment to Christ and keep our hope alive, especially when we are misunderstood or harassed because of our faith.

▶ Rev 20.1—22.5

Lamb will be in it, and his servants[a] will worship him; 4 they will see his face, and his name will be on their foreheads. 5 And there will be no more night; they need no light of lamp or sun, for the Lord God will be their light, and they will reign forever and ever.

Epilogue and Benediction

6 And he said to me, "These words are trustworthy and true, for the Lord, the God of the spirits of the prophets, has sent his angel to show his servants[b] what must soon take place."

7 "See, I am coming soon! Blessed is the one who keeps the words of the prophecy of this book."

8 I, John, am the one who heard and saw these things. And when I heard and saw them, I fell down to worship at the feet of the angel who showed them to me; 9 but he said to me, "You must not do that! I am a fellow servant[b] with you and your comrades[c] the prophets, and with those who keep the words of this book. Worship God!"

10 And he said to me, "Do not seal up the words of the prophecy of this book, for the time is near. 11 Let the evildoer still do evil, and the filthy still be filthy, and the righteous still do right, and the holy still be holy."

12 "See, I am coming soon; my reward is with me, to repay according to everyone's work. 13 I am the Alpha and the Omega, the first and the last, the beginning and the end."

14 Blessed are those who wash their robes,[d] so that they will have the right to the tree of life and may enter the city by the gates. 15 Outside are the

AMEN!

In Hebrew, *amen* means "so be it" or "yes, it is true." So saying "Amen" in your prayers is the same as saying, "Yes, I believe!" It is an appropriate way to conclude the last book of the Bible, and it should not be said lightly. Are you able to say "Amen" to all that you have read, prayed, and reflected on in this Bible? Have the stories and the poems, the teachings and the parables, the songs and the sayings led you to believe in a God who is with you every step of your journey, every minute of the day and night?

Each of us is invited to join the great Amen, to say: "Yes, I believe in a loving God who is father and mother to us all! Yes, I believe in God's Son, Jesus Christ, who is my Lord and Savior! Yes, I believe in the Holy Spirit, who will help me continue Jesus' mission of justice, reconciliation, and love!" But these words remain just words until people with courage an conviction take the risk to live them out in their own corner of the world. Take the risk; heaven awaits you! Amen!

▸ **Rev 22.20**

---

[a] Gk *slaves*   [b] Gk *slave*   [c] Gk *brothers*   [d] Other ancient authorities read *do his commandments*

LIVE IT!

Come, Lord Jesus!

Most young children want immediate gratification. Waiting for Christmas or a birthday is nearly impossible. Saving a piece of candy for after dinner is downright torture.

The Bible tells us that Jesus will return. In the creed, Christians proclaim, "He will come again in glory to judge the living and the dead, / and his kingdom will have no end" (*Sacramentary*, p. 368). When will this happen? Like impatient children, some people have tried to predict the Lord's Second Coming. "But about that day and hour no one knows, . . . only the Father" (Mt 24.36).

Can we say, with John, "Amen! Come, Lord Jesus!" (Rev 22.20) and really hope that Jesus will come today? We may hesitate, wanting to hang on to the life we know here and now. Yet, the coming of Christ will be the most glorious event imaginable for those who have put their trust in God. So keep preparing and praying for the return of Christ!

▸ **Rev 22.7–21**

dogs and sorcerers and fornicators and murderers and idolaters, and everyone who loves and practices falsehood.

16 "It is I, Jesus, who sent my angel to you with this testimony for the churches. I am the root and the descendant of David, the bright morning star."

17 The Spirit and the bride say, "Come."
And let everyone who hears say, "Come."
And let everyone who is thirsty come.
Let anyone who wishes take the water of life as
    a gift.

18 I warn everyone who hears the words of the prophecy of this book: if anyone adds to them, God will add to that person the plagues described in this book; 19 if anyone takes away from the words of the book of this prophecy, God will take away that person's share in the tree of life and in the holy city, which are described in this book.

20 The one who testifies to these things says, "Surely I am coming soon."
Amen. Come, Lord Jesus!

21 The grace of the Lord Jesus be with all the saints. Amen.*

---

e Other ancient authorities lack *all*; others lack *the saints*; others lack *Amen*

REV

Where Do I Find It?

EVENTS, PEOPLE, AND TEACHINGS ?

OLD TESTAMENT STORIES

These stories are listed in the order in which they first appear in the Bible.

Creation, *Gen, chs 1–2*
original sin and its punishment, *Gen, ch 3*
Cain and Abel, *Gen 4.1–16*
Noah and the Great Flood, *Gen, chs 6–9*
God's covenant with Abraham,
Gen 17.1—18.15
God's command to sacrifice Isaac,
Gen 22.1–19
Isaac's blessing of Jacob, *Gen 27.1–29*
Jacob's dream, *Gen 28.10–22*
Joseph and his brothers, *Gen, chs 37–46*
birth and youth of Moses, *Ex 2.1–10*
Moses at the burning bush, *Ex 3.1–12*
plagues on Egypt, *Ex, chs 7–12*
Passover and the Exodus, *Ex, chs 12–14*
Ten Commandments, *Ex 20.1–17*
destruction of Jericho, *Josh 5.13—6.27*
Gideon and the sign of the fleece,
Judg 6.36–40
Samson, *Judg, chs 13–16*
Samuel's birth and calling, *1 Sam, chs 1–3*
David and Goliath, *1 Sam, ch 17*
David and Bathsheba, *2 Sam, ch 11*
Solomon's wisdom, *1 Kings, ch 3*
Elijah's triumph over the priests of Baal,
1 Kings 18.20–40
miracles of Elisha, *2 Kings 4.1—6.23*
end of the Babylonian captivity, *Ezra, ch 1*
battles of Judas Maccabeus, *1 Macc, chs 3–5*
Ezekiel and the valley of dry bones,
Ezek 37.1–14
Daniel, *Dan, chs 1–6*
Jonah and the Ninevites, *Jon, chs 1–3*

NEW TESTAMENT STORIES

These stories are listed in the order in which they first appear in the Bible.

birth of Jesus, *Mt 1.18—2.12; Lk, chs 1–2*
baptism of Jesus, *Mt 3.13–17; Mk 1.9–11;*
Lk 3.21–22
temptation of Jesus, *Mt 4.1–11; Mk 1.12–13;*
Lk 4.1–13
Peter's declaration about Jesus, *Mt 16.13–20;*
Mk 8.27–30; Lk 9.18–20
Transfiguration of Jesus, *Mt 17.1–13;*
Mk 9.2–13; Lk 9.28–36
Jesus' triumphal entry into Jerusalem,
Mt 21.1–11; Mk 11.1–11; Lk 19.28–40;
Jn 12.12–19
Jesus in the Temple, *Mt 21.12–17;*
Mk 11.15–19; Lk 19.45–48; Jn 2.13–16
Judas's betrayal of Jesus, *Mt 26.14–16,47–56;*
Mk 14.10–11,43–52; Lk 22.1–53;
Jn 13.21–30; Jn 18.1–5
Last Supper, *Mt 26.17–30; Mk 14.12–25;*
Lk 22.7–38; 1 Cor 11.23–26
Jesus at Gethsemane, *Mt 26.36–56;*
Mk 14.32–51; Lk 22.39–53
Peter's denial of Christ, *Mt 26.69–75; Mk*
14.66–72; Lk 22.54–62; Jn 18.15–18,25–27
Crucifixion, *Mt 27.32–56; Mk 15.21–41;*
Lk 23.26–49; Jn 19.16–30
Resurrection and appearances, *Mt, ch 28; Mk,*
ch 16; Lk, ch 24; Jn, chs 20–21; Acts 1.1–11
Jesus washing his disciples' feet, *Jn 13.1–17*
Holy Spirit at Pentecost, *Acts 2.1–42*
stoning of Stephen, *Acts, chs 6–7*
conversion of Saul, *Acts 9.1–31*
Peter's escape from prison, *Acts 12.1–19*
Paul and Silas's escape from prison,
Acts 16.16–40
Paul's journey to Rome for his trial,
Acts, chs 27–28

PEOPLE

Each person entry is followed by a page number or numbers that lead you to an "Introducing . . ." article or other articles in which the person is featured.

Abraham, *18, 23, 28*
Barnabas, *1283*
Beloved Disciple, *1251*
David, *281, 282, 297, 305, 306*
Elijah, *344, 353*
Elisha, *344*
Ezekiel, *955*
First Isaiah, *816*
Holy Family, *1103*
Jacob, *33, 34, 36, 37, 40, 41*
Jeremiah, *878, 891*
John the Baptist, *1105, 1186*
Joseph, *45*
Junia, *1326*
Lady Wisdom, *690*
Lydia, *1290*
Mary, the mother of Jesus, *1180, 1181, 1260, 1478*
Mary Magdalene, *1261*
Moses, *62, 67, 81, 96, 208*
Nicodemus, *1230*
Paul, *1277, 1280, 1285, 1291, 1296, 1300, 1301, 1349, 1363, 1380*
Peter, *1124, 1141, 1172, 1190, 1251, 1263*
Phoebe, *1326*
Priscilla, *1290*
Samson, *250, 253*
Sarah, *18*
Satan, *560, 1157, 1477, 1485*
Solomon, *324, 327, 337, 406*
Stephen, *1275, 1276*

PRAYERS

These prayers are listed in the order in which they first appear in the Bible.

The Lord bless you and keep you,
   Num 6.24–27
Hannah's prayer, *1 Sam 2.1–10*
Speak, Lord, for your servant is listening,
   1 Sam 3.9–10
Blessed be the Lord, *1 Kings 8.56–61*
Tobit's thanksgiving, *Tob, ch 13*
Judith's hymn of praise, *Jdt 16.1–17*

The Lord is my shepherd, *Ps 23*
Have mercy on me, O God, *Ps 51*
O Lord, you have searched me and known me,
   Ps 139
Holy, Holy, Holy (Hosanna), *Isa 6.3; Mt 21.9;
   Mk 11.9–10; Lk 19.38; Jn 12.13; Rev 4.8*
Lord's Prayer, *Mt 6.9–15; Lk 11.2–4*
Lord, I am not worthy, *Mt 8.8*
Jesus' prayer for deliverance, *Mt 26.39;
   Mk 14.36; Lk 22.42*
Mary's song of praise, *Lk 1.46–55*
Zechariah's prophecy, *Lk 1.68–79*
Glory to God in the highest, *Lk 2.14*
Simeon's prayer, *Lk 2.29–32*
God, be merciful to me, a sinner!, *Lk 18.13*
Lamb of God, *Jn 1.29*
Jesus' prayer for his disciples, *Jn, ch 17*
Paul's prayer for the Ephesians, *Eph 3.14–21*
Amen, *1 Pet 5.11; Jude, v 25; Rev 1.6–7; 3.14*

MIRACLES OF JESUS

These miracle stories are listed in the order in which they first appear in the Bible.

Healing Individuals

leper, *Mt 8.1–4; Mk 1.40–45; Lk 5.12–16*
centurion's servant, *Mt 8.5–13; Lk 7.1–10*
many at Peter's house, *Mt 8.14–17;
   Mk 1.29–34; Lk 4.38–41*
Gadarene (Gerasene) demoniacs, *Mt 8.28–34;
   Mk 5.1–20; Lk 8.26–39*
paralytic, *Mt 9.1–8; Mk 2.1–12; Lk 5.17–26*
woman with bleeding, *Mt 9.20–22;
   Mk 5.25–34; Lk 8.43–48*
two blind men, *Mt 9.27–31*
mute man, *Mt 9.32–34*
man with a withered hand, *Mt 12.9–13;
   Mk 3.1–5; Lk 6.6–11*
blind, mute, and possessed man, *Mt 12.22*
Canaanite woman's daughter, *Mt 15.21–28;
   Mk 7.24–30*
boy with a demon, *Mt 17.14–21; Mk 9.14–29;
   Lk 9.37–43*
blind Bartimaeus, *Mt 20.29–34; Mk 10.46–52;
   Lk 18.35–43*
man with an unclean spirit, *Mk 1.21–28;
   Lk 4.31–37*
deaf man, *Mk 7.31–37*
blind man at Bethsaida, *Mk 8.22–26*
crippled woman, *Lk 13.11–13*

MIRACLES OF JESUS (continued)

man with dropsy, *Lk 14.1–4*
ten lepers, *Lk 17.11–19*
high priest's servant, *Lk 22.50–51*
official's son, *Jn 4.46–54*
man at the pool of Beth-zatha, *Jn 5.1–9*

Controlling Nature
stilling the storm, *Mt 8.23–27; Mk 4.35–41;*
    Lk 8.22–25
feeding five thousand, *Mt 14.13–21;*
    Mk 6.30–44; Lk 9.10–17; Jn 6.1–15
walking on water, *Mt 14.22–33; Mk 6.45–52;*
    Jn 6.16–21
feeding four thousand, *Mt 15.32–39;*
    Mk 8.1–10
fish with a coin, *Mt 17.24–27*
fig tree withers, *Mt 21.18–22;*
    Mk 11.12–14,20–25
huge catch of fish, *Lk 5.1–11; Jn 21.1–11*
turning water into wine, *Jn 2.1–11*

Raising the Dead
Jairus's daughter, *Mt 9.18–19,23–26;*
    Mk 5.21–24,35–43; Lk 8.40–42,49–56
widow's son at Nain, *Lk 7.11–17*
Lazarus, *Jn 11.1–44*

PARABLES OF JESUS

These parables are listed in alphabetical order.

barren fig tree, *Lk 13.6–9*
canceled debts, *Lk 7.41–43*
cost of discipleship, *Lk 14.25–33*
dishonest manager, *Lk 16.1–8*
faithful or unfaithful slave, *Mt 24.45–51;*
    Lk 12.42–48
fig tree, *Mt 24.32–35; Mk 13.28–31;*
    Lk 21.29–33
good Samaritan, *Lk 10.30–37*
great dinner, *Lk 14.16–24*
growing seed, *Mk 4.26–29*
hidden treasure and pearl, *Mt 13.44–46*
honor at a banquet, *Lk 14.7–14*
laborers in the vineyard, *Mt 20.1–16*
light of the world, *Mt 5.14–16*
lost coin, *Lk 15.8–10*
lost sheep, *Mt 18.12–14; Lk 15.3–7*
mustard seed, *Mt 13.31–32; Mk 4.30–32;*
    Lk 13.18–19
net, *Mt 13.47–50*

new wine in old wineskins, *Mt 9.16–17;*
    Mk 2.21–22; Lk 5.36–39
persistent friend, *Lk 11.5–8*
persistent widow, *Lk 18.2–8*
Pharisee and the tax collector, *Lk 18.10–14*
prodigal son, *Lk 15.11–32*
rich fool, *Lk 12.16–21*
rich man and Lazarus, *Lk 16.19–31*
salt, *Mt 5.13; Mk 9.50; Lk 14.34–35*
sheep and the goats, *Mt 25.31–46*
sower, *Mt 13.3–8,18–23; Mk 4.3–9,14–20;*
    Lk 8.5–8,11–15
talents, *Mt 25.14–30*
ten bridesmaids, *Mt 25.1–13*
ten pounds, *Lk 19.11–27*
two sons, *Mt 21.28–31*
unforgiving servant, *Mt 18.23–35*
watchful slaves, *Lk 12.35–40*
wedding banquet, *Mt 22.1–14*
weeds among the wheat, *Mt 13.24–30,36–43*
wicked tenants, *Mt 21.33–44; Mk 12.1–12;*
    Lk 20.9–18
wise and foolish builders, *Mt 7.24–27;*
    Lk 6.47–49
worthless slaves, *Lk 17.7–10*
yeast, *Mt 13.33; Lk 13.20–21*

TEACHINGS OF JESUS

These teachings are listed in alphabetical order.

Beatitudes, *Mt 5.1–12; Lk 6.20–26*
born from above, *Jn 3.1–21*
bread of life, *Jn 6.25–59*
children, *Mk 10.13–16*
discipleship, *Lk 14.25–33*
do not worry, *Mt 6.19–21,25–34; Lk 12.22–34*
golden rule, *Mt 7.12; Lk 6.31*
good shepherd, *Jn 10.1–21*
greatest commandment, *Mt 22.34–40;*
    Mk 12.28–34; Lk 10.25–28
living water, *Jn 4.1–26*
Lord's Prayer, *Mt 6.9–13; Lk 11.2–4*
mission of the twelve Apostles, *Mt 10.1–15*
paying taxes, *Mt 22.15–22; Mk 12.13–17;*
    Lk 20.20–26
rich young man, *Mt 19.16–30; Mk 10.17–31;*
    Lk 18.18–30
Sermon on the Mount, *Mt, chs 5–7*
Sermon on the Plain, *Lk 6.17–49*
vine and branches, *Jn 15.1–17*
"the way, the truth, and the life," *Jn 14.1–14*
"where two or three are gathered," *Mt 18.20*

SACRAMENT CONNECTIONS

BAPTISM

Isa 43.1
Mt 3.13–17; 28.19–20
Mk 1.9–11
Lk 3.21–22
Jn 1.29–34; 3.5
Acts 2.37–41
Rom 6.3–4

CONFIRMATION

Isa 11.2; 61.1
Mt 3.13–17
Jn 1.33–34; 14.15–31;
    16.5–15
Acts 2.1–4; 8.14–17
2 Cor 1.21–22
Gal 5.22–23

EUCHARIST

Gen 14.17–20
Ex 12.1–28; 24.1–8
Mt 14.13–21; 26.17–29
Mk 6.30–44; 14.12–25
Lk 9.10–17; 22.7–20;
    24.13–35
Jn 6.1–13,25–59
1 Cor 11.17–34

RECONCILIATION (PENANCE)

Gen 45.1–15
Joel 2.12–13
Mt 5.21–26,38–48; 18.23–35
Mk 2.1–12
Lk 15.11–32
Jn 20.19–23
Rom, ch 6

ANOINTING

Ps 23
Mk 6.7–13
Lk 13.10–13
2 Tim 2.11–12
Jas 5.14–16

HOLY ORDERS

Deut 18.1–5
Ps 110.1–4
Mt 10.1–4
Mk 3.14–19
Lk 6.12–16
Jn 13.1–14
Rom 12.1–8
1 Tim 3.1–13
Titus 1.5–9
Heb 4.14—5.10

MARRIAGE

Gen 2.18–25
Song 8.6–7
Mt 19.1–12
Mk 10.2–12
Jn 2.1–11
1 Cor, ch 13
Eph 5.21–33
1 Jn 4.4–16

LIFE AND FAITH ISSUES

PROMISES OF GOD
Ex 6.1–9
Jer 29.11
Lk 4.14–30

REPENTANCE
1 Chr 21.1–17
Joel 2.12–18
Lk 15.11–32

RESPONSIBILITY
Sir 15.11–20
Ezek, ch 18

SERVICE
Isa 42.1–6
Mt 20.20–28;
    25.31–46
Mk 10.35–45
Jn 13.1–17

SEXUALITY
Gen 1.26–31
Tob 8.4–9
Song
Eph 5.1–14
1 Thess 4.3–8

SUFFERING
Job 1.13–21
Ps 22
Mt 5.1–12
1 Pet 3.13–18

TEMPTATION
Gen, ch 3
Mt 4.1–11
Mk 1.12–13;
    7.14–23
Lk 4.1–13

TRUST IN GOD
Ps 62
Isa 43.1–5
Mt 11.28–30
Mk 10.46–52

VOCATION (See
call; discipleship)

WISDOM
2 Chr 1.7–13
Prov 8.1–21
Wis, ch 7

ANGER
Mt 5.21–24
Jn 2.13–17
Eph 4.25–27,31–32
Jas 1.19–21

CALL
Gen 12.1–9
1 Sam, chs 1–3
Isa 6.1–8
Jer 1.4–10
Mt 4.18–22;
    28.16–20
Mk 1.16–20
Lk 5.1–11

COMMITMENT
Num 30.2–4
Deut 6.1–9; 11.8–9
Josh 24.14–15
Mk 8.34–38

COURAGE
Josh 1.9
1 Sam, ch 17
Ps 31

DISCIPLESHIP
Mk 8.34–38
Lk 9.1–6
Jn 4.1–42

FAMILY
Gen 4.9; 12.10–20
Sir 3.1–16
Eph 5.21—6.4

FEAR
Ps 27, 91
Zeph 3.14–20
Mt 14.22–33
Mk 4.35–41
Lk 22.54–62

FORGIVENESS
Gen 33.1–17
Ps 51
Mt 18.21–35
Lk 6.27–36; 23.34
Jn 8.2–11

FRIENDSHIP
Ruth 1.1–19
1 Sam, ch 20
Sir 6.5–17
Jn 15.12–17

FRIENDSHIP WITH GOD
Gen 28.10–22
Mic 6.8
Jn 15.12–17

GIVING
2 Chr 31.2–10
Ezra 1.6–11
Mk 12.41–44
Lk 21.1–4

HAPPINESS
Sir 25.1–11
Lk 12.22–34
Phil 4.4–9

HONESTY WITH GOD
Gen 18.22–33
Jer 12.1–16
Mk 14.32–42

HOPE
Eccl 3.1–8
Lam 3.22–26
Rom 8.18–30

HYPOCRISY
Mt 6.1–6; 23.1–36
Lk 18.9–14
Jas 1.22—2.4

IMAGES OF GOD
Gen 1.26–27;
    32.22–32
Ps 23
Jer 18.1–11

JUDGMENT OF OTHERS
Mt 7.1–5
Rom 14.1–12
Gal 3.26–28

LONELINESS AND ABANDONMENT
Ps 22.1–12
Mk 15.33–34
2 Tim 4.9–18

LOVE
Song 8.6–7
Mt 5.43–48
Mk 12.28–34
1 Cor, ch 13

PEACE
Isa 11.1–9
Mic 4.1–5
Jn 14.25–31

PERSISTENCE
Lk 11.5–8; 18.1–8

POPULARITY
Mk 9.33–37
1 Cor 3.1–9
Phil 2.1–11

PRESENCE OF GOD
Gen 15.7
Ex 3.1–6; 33.17–23
Mt 18.20

ARTICLE SUBJECT INDEX ?

This subject index is not an index to the Bible itself (sometimes called a concordance). Rather, it is an index to the subjects covered in the various articles in The Catholic Youth Bible. *But because most articles are based on a Bible passage, this index will also help you find Bible passages related to these topics.*

A

abandonment
1175. *See also* despair; loneliness

abortion
62, 674, 909, 1104

Abraham
18, 23, 28

abuse
21, 27

acceptance
1130

addiction
1203, 1338

Advent
842

advertising
714

Advocate
1252

afterlife
719, 1017, 1347. *See also* Resurrection

agape
1343

aging
722

AIDS
641, 1310

alcohol
487, 1377

altars
219

ancestors
22, 58, 129

angels
470, 1433

anger
560, 617, 652, 698, 1055, 1229

Anointing, sacrament of
1205

anxiety
721, 916, 1200, 1204

apocalyptic literature
1012, 1466

apocryphal books
463

Apostles
1141, 1150, 1154, 1156, 1159

Apostles' Creed
1271

ark of the Covenant
102, 105, 910

arrogance
537

Ash Wednesday
1036, 1109

Assyrian Empire
368, 1064

atheism
597

authority
238

awe
63, 601, 607, 700

B

baals
223, 344

Babylon
933, 1481

Babylonian Exile
377

balance
716

Baptism, sacrament of
1105, 1315

Barnabas
1283

Beatitudes
1107, 1192

beauty
725, 1385

beliefs
1271

faith
18, 28, 357, 450, 473, 560,
592, 597, 824, 1122, 1156,
1159, 1164, 1176, 1181, 1232,
1275, 1303, 1312, 1313, 1319,
1347, 1366, 1368, 1369,
1373, 1412, 1430, 1436

faith sharing
1270, 1297, 1355, 1412

false prophets
893, 1450

families
129, 657, 709, 757, 758, 1184,
1193, 1336, 1378, 1390

fasting
448

fatalism
968

fear
214, 700, 824, 857, 916, 1156,
1173, 1303

festivals (feasts)
73, 99, 129, 165, 502, 511,
1102, 1127, 1180, 1193, 1239,
1250. See also individual
names of

fidelity
869

fighting
698

fire
20

First Isaiah
816

flood
12, 13, 14

food
73, 80, 115, 466

forgiveness
41, 45, 248, 652, 1025, 1108,
1128, 1193, 1207, 1221. See
also Reconciliation, sacrament
of

fornication
1334, 1395

foundation, God as life's
318, 1332

friendship
263, 285, 695, 760, 763, 917,
1025, 1141, 1151, 1172, 1256,
1295, 1382. See also God,
closeness with

fruits of the Spirit
1368, 1443

G

genealogies
58, 382, 1102

generosity
429, 466, 1168

genocide
495

Gentiles
1156, 1221, 1278, 1312, 1320

gifts
689, 716, 940, 1138, 1168,
1207, 1217, 1236, 1254,
1342, 1397

giving, sacrificial
429, 605, 1217, 1272

God
587, 588; closeness with, 24,
36, 97, 564, 728, 734, 818,
858, 1131, 1200, 1319; glory
of, 953, 1474; help of, 27;
604, 668, 675, 753, 1086;
holiness of, 20; name of, 64,
403, 818, 1228; need for, 347;
power of, 601, 607, 948;
struggling with, 40, 878; will
of, 34, 53, 67, 191, 685, 1055,
1470. See also compassion of
God; images of God; presence
of God; Reign of God; trust in
God

gods
13, 223, 344

golden calf
96

Good Friday
603, 1258

goodness
6, 8, 53, 473. See also right
living

Good News
1098–1099, 1158, 1278, 1310,
1321

good shepherd
604, 984, 1244

good works
812, 1371, 1373, 1415

gospel, meaning of term
1099, 1310

gossip
693, 1118, 1438

grace
753, 1314, 1373

gratitude
See thanksgiving

greatness, true
1131

greed
717, 1132, 1203

grief
561, 909, 942, 1246, 1295

H

Hail Mary
199, 1180

Hanukkah
511

harassment
21

hard times
753, 1173

healing
315, 662, 791, 942, 1123, 1153

heart
734, 962

helping others
86, 466, 470, 561, 604, 918,
1155, 1461

heroes
519, 800, 1314

holiness
63, 106, 126

Holocaust
495, 909

Holy Family
1103

Holy Orders, sacrament of
1154

holy places
333, 395, 993

Holy Spirit
987, 1038, 1252, 1254, 1267,
1269, 1278, 1352

Holy Thursday
1248, 1258

Holy Trinity
143, 1146, 1252

holy war
138

Holy Week
850, 1258. See also liturgical
year

homosexuality
1310

honesty
692, 891

hope
473, 397, 603, 808–809, 846,
863, 940, 1224, 1318, 1354,
1376, 1426, 1476

hopelessness
See despair

hospitality
25, 1433, 1461

humiliation
617, 623

humility
484, 900, 1060, 1077, 1135,
1263, 1353, 1382

humor
23, 1052

hunger
451, 466, 938

hypocrisy
812, 1044, 1123, 1132

I

....

idolatry
96, 344, 661, 747, 808–809,
951, 1338

images of God
6, 8, 318, 488, 604, 607, 670,
730, 738, 740, 847, 858, 869,
871, 984, 1030, 1066, 1246,
1343, 1388

immigrants
1103

imprisonment
1284

Incarnation
1216, 1424, 1456

injustice
27, 37, 497, 1132, 1211

integrity
606, 688, 707, 831, 1365. See
also honesty; right living

Islam
31

Israel (kingdom)
322, 339, 360, 368

Israel (people)
58

J

....

Jacob
33, 34, 36, 37, 40, 41

jealousy
21, 149

Jeremiah
878, 891

Jerusalem
322, 377, 671, 1485

Jesus Christ
73, 88, 1190, 1098–1099,
1148, 1225, 1228, 1240, 1241,
1388, 1422, 1429, 1468;
baptism of, 1105; childhood
of, 1185; death and Resurrection of, 1145, 1176, 1221,
1247, 1250, 1259; divinity
of, 1221, 1235, 1257; as
Emmanuel (Immanuel), 818,
1103; family tree of, 1102;
humanity of, 1103, 1216,
1388, 1424; humility of,
1382; personal relationship
with, 1152, 1232, 1246, 1253,
1470; suffering of, 1173; trust
in, 1122, 1153; understanding,
1159, 1422. See also Messiah;
Second Coming

Jewish Christians
1100, 1288, 1296, 1300, 1312,
1320, 1365

Jewish sects
554, 1104

Jews
31, 494, 1296, 1300, 1320

John the Baptist
1105, 1186

Joseph
45

joy
15, 23, 717, 842, 863, 1447

Jubilee
131

Judah (kingdom)
322, 339, 360, 368, 377

Judas
1143

judgment of others
1311

praise
77, 302, 490, 590, 630, 1471, 1474. *See also* celebration

prayer
81, 159, 180, 267, 269, 394, 426, 448, 465, 473, 484, 564, 592, 685, 697, 729, 753, 988, 1014, 1018, 1109, 1164, 1167, 1192, 1201, 1211, 1440

preferential option for the poor
837, 1047, 1184, 1192, 1206, 1437

prejudice
215, 445, 495, 1200, 1230, 1243

preparedness
See readiness

presence of God
20, 36, 63, 97, 333, 347, 395, 470, 601, 607, 637, 953, 993, 1351, 1451

pride
16, 337, 1077, 1353

priests
See ministry in the church

Priscilla
1290

prodigal son
1208

profanity
777

promiscuity
124

promises of God
68. *See also* covenant; New Covenant; Sinai Covenant

prophetic themes
944, 953, 1090, 1468

prophets
49, 62, 65, 159, 353, 420, 808–809, 810, 859, 957, 1376

protection
984, 1244

Purim, feast of
502

purity
108, 1095

R

race
262

Rachel
909

racism
1200, 1426. *See also* prejudice

rainbow
15

readiness
1095, 1136, 1337, 1335, 1401

reading plans
xviii–xxiii

Reconciliation, sacrament of
397, 1261, 1454

redeemer
109, 1145. *See* Jesus Christ; Messiah

reflection time
302, 637, 774, 1436

reforms, religious
374

Reign of God
832, 1111, 1113, 1120, 1206, 1476, 1485

remnant
1043, 1077

repentance
397, 1109, 1186. *See also* Reconciliation, sacrament of

respect
700, 1325

responsibility
10, 81, 96, 122, 182, 306, 768, 900, 953, 968, 973, 1028

Resurrection
1017, 1054, 1176, 1224, 1258, 1347

revenge
827, 923, 1066, 1108

rice
80

ridicule
617

right living
126, 406, 606, 609, 661, 682, 690, 742, 744, 949, 1004, 1031, 1051, 1134, 1371, 1389, 1443, 1446. *See also* values

risk taking
918, 1114

role models
1373

Romans
1296, 1479, 1481

Rome
1481

S

Sabbath
7

sabbatical year
131

sacraments
See individual names of

sacrifice
28, 88, 541, 1275, 1429

Sadducees
554, 1104

saints
214, 328, 1395

salvation
109, 861, 1102, 1156, 1221, 1230, 1308, 1313, 1314, 1315, 1320, 1366, 1373, 1422

salvation history
8, 204, 1470, 1473, 1478

Samaritans
1200, 1232

Samson
250, 253

Sarah
18

Satan
560, 1157, 1477, 1485

scapegoats
122, 165

scribes
1104

Second Coming
1335, 1399, 1401, 1485

security
670, 686

self-control
772, 1377

self-deception
893, 1454

self-determination
482

self-image
6, 7, 725, 1354

Sermon on the Mount
1107, 1192

Sermon on the Plain
1192

service
851, 1131, 1150, 1155, 1165,
1168, 1206, 1219, 1248, 1326,
1382

sexism
497, 796

sexuality
124, 305, 723, 726, 728, 730,
1334, 1395

shalom
840

Shema
180

sibling rivalry
32

Simon of Cyrene
1174

sin
9, 12, 13, 96, 109, 248, 305,
337, 448, 774, 900, 973,
1240, 1261, 1313, 1316,
1389, 1481

Sinai Covenant
2–3, 83, 85, 108, 233,
808–809, 855, 910, 1077,
1313

sin offering
109

slavery
76, 1417

social action
448, 451

social justice
See justice

Solomon
324, 328, 337, 406

songs
77, 490, 647, 680, 850

sons
742

speaking
777, 1118, 1438. See also
gossip; language

spirits
1157, 1456

spiritual growth
357, 1070, 1160, 1184, 1253,
1332, 1361

spiritual poverty
1360

spiritual writings
374

status
1342

Stephen
1275

stereotypes
1232

stewardship
429, 1217, 1272

stories
306, 1156. See also parables

strangers
25, 86, 196, 1433

street theater
957

strength
859, 1394

strength in God
450, 1361

submissiveness
1406

success
857

suffering
465, 558, 560, 561, 564, 575,
588, 593, 1144, 1145, 1173,
1319, 1351, 1441, 1446, 1447

suffering servant
109, 849, 850, 859, 861

suicide
294, 465, 1143

superstition
951

symbols, biblical
6, 14, 15, 20, 102, 557, 869,
903, 953, 955, 957, 987, 1012,
1028, 1105, 1120, 1170, 1214,
1226, 1240, 1466, 1472

T

teaching
1412

temper
96, 698

Temple
440, 511, 605, 885, 953, 993,
1132

temptation
9, 305, 772, 1106, 1187, 1316,
1357, 1424

Acknowledgments *(continued)*

Consultants: Barbara Allaire, Mary Lee Becker, Philip J. Calderone, Brian K. Johnson, Carl Koch, Stephan Nagel, Pheme Perkins, and Kevin Schneider

Publishing team: Brian Singer-Towns, general editor; Carmen María Cervantes, Shirley Kelter, and Robert P. Stamschror, consulting editors; Lynn Riska Dahdal, production editor; Cheryl Drivdahl and Mary Duerson, copy editors; Hollace Storkel, article typesetter; Auto-Graphics, Scripture typesetters; Peachtree Editorial and Proofreading Service, Scripture proofreaders; Maurine R. Twait, art director; Stephan Nagel, art director and cover designer; Sue Campbell, Carol Evans-Smith, Kent Linder, and Cindi Ramm, designers; Alan S. Hanson, pre-press specialist; Gary J. Boisvert and Alan S. Hanson, illustration colorizers; Michael O. McGrath, illustrator

International edition, publishing team: Steven Roe, development editor; Heather Sutton, marketing director; Bill Northam, printing coordinator; Genevieve Nagel, production editor; Brian Singer-Towns, consulting editor; Andy Palmer, designer; Lynn Riska, consultant for typesetting; Brooke E. Saron, copy editor; Jim Koenig, technical consultant; Alan S. Hanson, pre-press specialist; The Livingstone Corporation, article and Scripture typesetter and project management; Peachtree Editorial and Proofreading Service, Scripture proofreaders. We extend a special thank-you to our student article reviewers for their time, enthusiasm, invaluable comments, and recommendations. The student article reviewer team included Renea Carlson, Neal Frantzen, Joshua Hamann, Aubrey Hollnagel, William Jaspers, Benjamin Leist, Megan Leopold, Kendall Marsden, and Brenda Maurer.

A special thank-you to the members of the original *Catholic Youth Bible* focus group: Catherine Cory; Carole Goodwin; Maryann Hakowski; Shirley Kelter; Marilyn Kielbasa; Joseph A. Morris, CM; Daniel Ponsetto; Pat Rinker; Virginia Smith; Carleen Suttman; and especially Robert P. Stamschror for his work in starting this project.

Finally, we are very grateful for the many young people, youth leaders, and teachers who helped as reviewers and consultants through the duration of this project.

The Old Testament
The quotation on page 67 is from *He Is Risen*, by Thomas Merton (Allen, TX: Tabor Publishing, 1975), page 22. Copyright © 1975 by RCL Enterprises. Used by permission.

The poem on page 80, Masao and Fumilko Takenaka's "God is Rice," and on page 1233, Masao and Fumilko Takenaka's "Living Waters," are from *Gifts of Many Cultures: Worship Resources for the Global Community,* edited by Maren C. Tirabassi and Kathy Wonson Eddy (Cleveland: United Church Press, 1995), pages 186 and 144. Copyright © 1995 by United Church Press. Used by permission.

The prayer on page 116 is from *Amen: Prayers and Blessings from Around the World,* compiled by Suzanne Slesin and Emily Gwathmey (New York: Penguin Books, 1998). Copyright © 1995 by Suzanne Slesin, Emily Gwathmey, and Stafford Cliff.

The quotation on page 179 is from *Sacred Ground: Reflections on Lakota Spirituality and the Gospel,* by Ron Zeilinger (Chamberlain, SD: Tipi Press, no date), pages 74–75. Used by permission.

The quotation on page 204 is from *Prophetic Voices: The Document on the Process of the Third Encuentro Nacional Hispano de Pastoral,* by the Secretariat for Hispanic Affairs of the

Image Credits

Vernon Sigl: gift page, pages iv–v, throughout (background art of Pray It! articles)

The icon on page 1533 was created by Sam Thiewes.

Maps.com grants no license or rights, expressly or otherwise, beyond the rights of Saint Mary's Press and Thomas Nelson Publishers. Maps.com revised the maps on pages 1581, 1582, 1583, 1585, 1586, and 1587. Contact www.maps.com for all your mapping needs.

Study Aids

ESSENTIAL CONCORDANCE

TO THE NRSV: CATHOLIC EDITION

A

ABANDON (ED)
Num	32:15	he will again **a** them
Deut	4:31	he will neither **a** you nor
Josh	10: 6	"Do not **a** your servants;
Judg	2:13	They **a** the LORD
1 Chr	28: 9	he will **a** you forever.
2 Chr	12: 5	You **a** me, so I have **a**
Tob	4: 3	your mother and do not **a** her
Ps	94:14	he will not **a** his heritage;
Sir	9:10	Do not **a** old friends,
Isa	54: 7	I **a** you, but with great
Mk	7: 8	You **a** the commandment
Acts	2:27	not **a** my soul to Hades,
Heb	10:35	therefore, **a** that confidence
Rev	2: 4	you have **a** the love you had at

ABBA
Mk	14:36	"**A**, Father, for you all things
Rom	8:15	When we cry, "**A**! Father!"
Gal	4: 6	our hearts, crying, "**A**! Father!"

ABIDE (S) (ABODE)
Gen	6: 3	shall not **a** in mortals forever,
Ex	15:17	your **a**, the sanctuary, O LORD,
Ps	26: 8	the place where your glory **a**.
	91: 1	Most High, who **a** in the
Prov	2:21	the upright will **a** in the land,
Wis	3:9	faithful will **a** with him in
Jer	31:23	bless you, O **a** of righteousness,
Hag	2: 5	My spirit **a** among you;
Jn	15: 4	**A** in me as I **a**
1 Cor	13:13	faith, hope, and love **a**, these
1 Jn	3:24	**a** in him, and he **a**
2 Jn	1: 9	not **a** in the teaching of Christ

ABILITY (ABLE)
Gen	15: 5	if you are **a** to count them."
Ex	18:25	Moses chose **a** men from all
Num	1: 3	Israel **a** to go to war. You
Josh	1: 5	shall be **a** to stand against you
1 Sam	7:33	"You are not **a** to go against
1 Kings	3: 9	your people, **a** to discern
1 Chr	29:14	we should be **a** to make this
2 Chr	25: 9	"The LORD is **a** to give you
Prov	27: 4	but who is **a** to stand before
Isa	36:14	he will not be **a** to deliver you.

Dan	2:26	you **a** to tell me the dream
Hos	5:13	he is not **a** to cure you or heal
Mt	9:28	I am **a** to do this?"
Mk	10:38	Are you **a** to drink the cup that
Lk	13:24	enter and will not be **a**.
Jn	9: 7	and came back **a** to see.
	18:28	defilement and to be **a** to eat
Acts	2: 4	as the Spirit gave them **a**.
Rom	4:21	convinced that God was **a** to do
2 Cor	1: 4	may be **a** to console those
	9: 8	And God is **a** to provide you
Eph	3:20	within us is **a** to accomplish
2 Tim	1:12	that he is **a** to guard until that
Heb	2:18	he is **a** to help those who are
	7:25	he is **a** for all time to save
Jas	3: 2	perfect, **a** to keep the whole
2 Pet	1:15	you may be **a** at any time to
Jude	1:24	to him who is **a** to keep you
Rev	6:17	and who is **a** to stand?"

ABOLISH (ED)
1 Macc	6:59	account of their laws that we **a**
2 Macc	2:22	laws that were about to be **a**,
Lam	2: 6	the LORD has **a** in Zion
Dan	11:31	They shall **a** the regular burnt
Hos	2:18	I will **a** the bow, the sword,
Mt	5:17	not to **a** but to fulfill.
Eph	2:15	He has **a** the law with its
2 Tim	1:10	who **a** death and brought life

ABOMINATION (S) (ABOMINABLE)
Gen	43:32	for that is an **a** to the Egyptians.
Lev	18:27	committed all of these **a**,
1 Kings	14:24	They committed all the **a** of
2 Chr	28: 3	according to the **a** practices of
Ezra	9: 1	their **a**, from the Canaanites
Ps	14: 1	they do **a** deeds; there is no
Prov	6:16	seven that are an **a** to him:
	26:25	there are seven **a** concealed
Sir	1:25	godliness is an **a** to a sinner
	13:20	poor are an **a** to the rich
Isa	6: 3	in their **a** they take delight;
Jer	4: 1	remove your **a** from my
Ezek	7:20	their **a** images, their detestable
	44: 7	my covenant with all your **a**.
Dan	9:27	shall be an **a** that desolates,
Lk	16:15	is an **a** in the sight of God
Rev	21:27	who practices **a** or falsehood,

ABOVE
Deut	4:39	LORD is God in heaven **a** and

Jdt	13:18	**a** all other women on earth;
Ps	8: 1	You have set your glory **a** the
	57: 5	O God, **a** the heavens.
Sir	32:13	But **a** all bless your Maker.
Isa	40:22	It is he who sits **a** the circle of
Ezek	1:26	seated **a** the likeness of a
	11:22	the God of Israel was **a** them.
Mt	10:24	"A disciple is not **a** the teacher,
Jn	3: 7	'You must be born from **a**.'
Eph	1:21	**a** every name that is named
Phil	2: 9	the name that is **a** every name,
Col	3: 2	things that are **a**, not on things
2 Thess	2: 4	exalts himself **a** every so-called
1 Tim	5: 7	they may be **a** reproach.
Heb	7:26	and exalted **a** the heavens.
Jas	1:17	every perfect gift, is from **a**,
1 Pet	4: 8	**A** all, maintain constant love

ABOUND (ED) (ING)
Ex	34: 6	and **a** in steadfast love and
Deut	28:11	LORD will make you **a** in
Neh	9:17	slow to anger and **a** in
Ps	103: 8	slow to anger and **a** in
Prov	8:24	were no springs **a** with water.
Joel	2:13	slow to anger, and **a** in
Rom	5:20	grace **a** all the more,
	6: 1	in order that grace may **a**?
2 Cor	3: 9	ministry of justification **a** in
Col	2: 7	were taught, **a** in thanksgiving.
1 Thess	3:12	increase and **a** in love for one

ABSTAIN
Acts	15:20	to **a** only from things polluted
Rom	14: 3	who **a**, and those who **a** must
1 Thess	5:22	**a** from every form of evil
1 Pet	2:11	exiles to **a** from the desires of

ABUNDANCE (ABUNDANTLY)
Deut	33:15	and the **a** of the everlasting
Job	36:31	peoples; he gives food in **a**.
Ps	36: 8	on the **a** of your house, and
Prov	11:14	but in an **a** of counselors there
Isa	33: 6	**a** of salvation, wisdom, and
Lam	3:32	according to the **a** of his
Mt	25:29	they will have an **a**;
Lk	6:45	out of the **a** of the heart
Jn	10:10	have life, and have it **a**.
2 Cor	9: 8	every blessing in **a**, so that by
Eph	3:20	to accomplish **a** far more than
1 Pet	1: 2	and peace be yours in **a**.
Jude	1: 2	and love be yours in **a**.

ABUSE (ABUSIVE)

Ex	22:22	not **a** any widow or orphan.
Prov	9: 7	corrects a scoffer wins **a**;
Sir	23:15	to using **a** language
Lk	6:28	pray for those who **a** you.
Col	3: 8	slander, and **a** language
2 Tim	3: 2	money, boasters, arrogant, **a**,
Heb	11:26	considered **a** suffered for the
1 Pet	3: 9	repay evil for evil or **a** for **a**;

ACCEPT (ED) (ACCEPTABLE)

Gen	4: 7	well, will you not be **a**?
Deut	16:19	you must not **a** bribes, for a
Job	42: 8	for I will **a** his prayer not to
Ps	19:14	meditation of my heart be **a** to
	119:108	**A** my offerings of praise, O
Prov	19:20	advice and **a** instruction,
	21: 3	justice is more **a** to the LORD
Isa	58: 5	a fast, a day **a** to the LORD?
Jer	6:20	Your burnt offerings are not **a**,
Ezek	43:27	and I will **a** you, says the Lord
Mal	1:10	and I will not **a** an offering
Mt	19:11	everyone can **a** this teaching,
Mk	4:20	hear the word and **a** it and
Lk	4:24	no prophet is **a** in the
Jn	1:11	his own people did not **a** him.
	5:43	you do not **a** me; if another
Acts	22:18	they will not **a** your testimony
Rom	12: 1	holy and **a** to God, which is
2 Cor	6: 2	"See, now is the **a** time;
Phil	4:18	a sacrifice **a** and pleasing to
Col	3:20	this is your **a** duty in the Lord.
1 Thess	2:13	you **a** it not as a human
1 Pet	2: 5	spiritual sacrifices **a** to God

ACCESS

Rom	5: 2	have obtained **a** to this grace
Eph	3;12	in whom we have **a** to God

ACCOMPLISH (ED)

Isa	55:11	shall **a** that which I purpose,
Ezek	17:24	LORD have spoken; I will **a** it.
Mt	5:18	the law until all is **a**.
Mk	13: 4	things are about to be **a**?"
Lk	18:31	by the prophets will be **a**.
Rom	15:18	what Christ has **a** through me
Eph	3:20	is able to **a** abundantly far

ACCOUNT (ABLE)

Mt	12:36	to give an **a** for every careless
Lk	1: 1	an orderly **a** of the events that
Rom	14:12	each of us will be **a** to God.
Col	3: 6	On **a** of these the wrath of
Heb	4:13	whom we must render an **a**.
1 Jn	2:12	sins are forgiven on **a** of his

ACKNOWLEDGE

Deut	4:35	you would **a** that the LORD is
Tob	12: 6	Do not be slow to **a** him.
Prov	3: 6	In all your ways **a** him, and he
Isa	26:13	but we **a** your name alone.
Jer	3:13	Only **a** your guilt, that you
Hos	5:15	until they **a** their guilt and
Mt	10:32	I also will **a** before my Father
Lk	12: 8	Son of Man also will **a** before
Rom	1:28	did not see fit to **a** God, God
3 Jn	1: 9	does not **a** our authority.

ACT (S) (ED)

Gen	19: 7	brothers, do not **a** so wickedly.

Ex	6: 6	with mighty **a** of judgment.
Josh	1: 8	be careful to **a** in accordance
Judg	19:23	do not **a** so wickedly.
2 Chr	6:37	we have **a** wickedly';
Neh	9:29	Yet they **a** presumptuously
Job	40:19	the great **a** of God— only its
Ps	31:23	repays the one who **a**
	71:15	your righteous **a**, of your
Prov	14:35	falls on one who **a** shamefully.
Eccl	7:16	and do not **a** too wise;
Sir	32:23	Guard yourself in every **a**,
Jer	9:24	the LORD; I **a** with steadfast
Ezek	20: 9	But I **a** for the sake of my
Dan	9:19	O Lord, listen and **a** and do
Mic	3: 4	because they have **a** wickedly.
Mt	7:24	words of mine and **a** on them
Jn	8: 4	very **a** of committing adultery.
Acts	3:17	you **a** in ignorance, as did also
Rom	1:27	shameless **a** with men and
Jas	1:25	doers who **a**—they will be

ADOPTION

Rom	9: 4	the **a**, the glory, the covenants,
Gal	4: 5	we might receive **a** as children.
Eph	1: 5	He destined us for **a** as his

ADORN (S) (ED) (MENT)

Ex	28: 2	the glorious **a** of your brother
2 Kings	9:30	and **a** her head, and looked
Ps	149: 4	he **a** the humble with victory.
Prov	3:22	your soul and **a** for your neck.
Isa	61:10	as a bride **a** herself with her
Ezek	16:11	I **a** you with ornaments: I put
Lk	21: 5	how it was **a** with beautiful
1 Pet	3: 4	let your **a** be the inner self
Rev	21: 2	prepared as a bride **a** for her

ADULTERY (ADULTRESS) (ADULTER-ER) (ADULTERERS)

Ex	20:14	You shall not commit **a**.
Lev	20:10	the **a** and the **a** shall be put to
Deut	5:18	Neither shall you commit **a**.
Prov	6:32	he who commits **a** has no
Sir	25: 2	an old fool who commits **a**.
Ezek	23:37	idols they have committed **a**;
Hos	3: 1	is an **a**, just as the LORD loves
Mal	3: 5	against the **a**, against those
Mt	5:27	'You shall not commit **a**.'
	15:19	murder, **a**, fornication,
Mk	10:11	commits **a** against her;
Lk	16:18	her husband commits **a**.
Jn	8: 3	caught in **a**; and making her
Rom	2:22	forbid **a**, do you commit **a**?
	7: 3	called an **a** if she lives with
1 Cor	6: 9	idolaters, **a**, male prostitutes,
Heb	13: 4	judge fornicators and **a**.
Jas	2:11	do not commit **a** but if you
2 Pet	2:14	They have eyes full of **a**,

ADVOCATE

Jn	14:16	another **A**, to be with you
	14:26	But the **A**, the Holy Spirit,
1 Jn	2: 1	we have an **a** with the Father,

AFFLICT (S) (ED) (ION) (IONS)

Gen	12:17	the LORD **a** Pharaoh and his
	16:11	has given heed to your **a**.
Deut	26: 7	saw our **a**, our toil, and our
2 Sam	7:10	evildoers shall **a** them no

Job	36:15	He delivers the **a** by their **a**,
Ps	25:16	for I am lonely and **a**.
	44:24	Why do you forget our **a** and
Isa	53: 7	he was **a**, yet he did not open
Lam	3:33	does not willingly **a** or grieve
Nah	1:12	have **a** you, I will **a** you no
2 Cor	1: 4	in all our **a**, so that we may be
	4:17	momentary **a** is preparing us
Col	1:24	lacking in Christ's **a** for the
2 Thess	1: 6	repay with **a** those who **a** you,
1 Tim	5:10	helped the **a**, and devoted
Rev	2: 9	your **a** and your poverty, even

AFRAID

Gen	3:10	I was **a**, because I was naked;
Ex	3: 6	for he was **a** to look at God.
	14:13	"Do not be **a**, stand firm, and
Deut	28:10	and they shall be **a** of you.
Josh	10:25	"Do not be **a** or dismayed;
Ruth	3:11	my daughter, do not be **a**, I
1 Sam	3:15	Samuel was **a** to tell the vision
1 Kings	19: 3	Then he was **a**; he got up and
1 Chr	13:12	David was **a** of God that day;
Ezra	4: 4	and made them **a** to build,
Ps	27: 1	of whom shall I be **a**?
	56: 3	when I am **a**, I put my trust in
Prov	3:24	you will not be **a**; when you
Isa	12: 2	and will not be **a**, for the LORD
	44: 8	Do not fear, or be **a**; have I not
Jer	1: 8	Do not be **a** of them, for I am
Ezek	34:28	no one shall make them **a**.
Mt	8:26	are you **a**, you of little faith?"
	14:27	is I; do not be **a**."
	28:10	"Do not be **a**; go and tell my
Lk	2:10	"Do not be **a**; for see—I am
	12:32	"Do not be **a**, little flock, for
Jn	14:27	do not let them be **a**.
Acts	27:24	'Do not be **a**, Paul; you must
Rom	13: 4	should be **a**, for the authority
Heb	13: 6	I will not be **a**. What can
2 Pet	2:10	they are not **a** to slander the

AGREE

Job	22:21	**A** with God, and be at
Mt	18:19	if two of you **a** on earth about
Mk	14:56	and their testimony did not **a**.
Rom	7:16	I do not want, I **a** that the law
2 Cor	13:11	**a** with one another, live in
1 Tim	6: 3	does not **a** with the sound
1 Jn	5: 8	and these three **a**.

ALIEN (S)

Gen	12:10	reside there as an **a**, for the
Ex	2:22	"I have been an **a** residing in a
	23: 9	**a**, for you were **a** in the land of
Lev	19:34	love the **a** as yourself, for you
Deut	24:17	not deprive a resident **a** or an
1 Macc	2: 7	the sanctuary given over to **a**?
Ps	144:11	the hand of **a**, whose mouths
Lam	5: 2	to strangers, our homes to **a**.
Eph	2:19	strangers and **a**, but you are
1 Pet	2:11	Beloved, I urge you as **a** and

ALIVE

Gen	16:13	remained **a** after seeing him?"
Num	16:30	they go down **a** into Sheol,
Deut	5:26	as we have, and remained **a**?
2 Sam	12:18	"While the child was still **a**, we
1 Kings	3:23	my son that is **a**, and your son
Ps	55:15	let them go down **a** to Sheol;

Prov	1:12	Sheol let us swallow them **a**
Zech	13:8	one-third shall be left **a**.
Lk	15:24	mine was dead and is **a** again;
	24:23	who said that he was **a**.
Jn	4:51	him that his child was **a**.
Acts	1:3	presented himself **a** to them
Rom	6:11	dead to sin and **a** to God in
	7:9	I was once **a** apart from the
1 Cor	15:22	so all will be made **a** in Christ.
2 Cor	6:9	and see—we are **a**; as punished,
Eph	2:5	us **a** together with Christ—by
Col	2:13	God made you **a** together with
1 Thess	4:17	Then we who are **a**, who are
1 Pet	3:18	but made **a** in the spirit,
Rev	1:18	see, I am **a** forever and ever;

ALMIGHTY

Gen	17:1	"I am God **A**; walk before me,
Ex	6:3	Jacob as God **A**, but by my
Num	24:4	sees the vision of the **A**, who
Ruth	1:20	for the **A** has dealt bitterly
Jdt	16:5	Lord **A** has foiled them by the
Job	6:4	the arrows of the **A** are in me;
	21:15	What is the **A**, that we should
Ps	91:1	in the shadow of the **A**,
Isa	13:6	like destruction from the **A**!
Bar	3:1	O Lord **A**, God of Israel,
Joel	1:15	as destruction from the **A** it
Rev	4:8	God the **A**, who was and is
	21:22	Lord God the **A** and the Lamb.

ALMS

Mt	6:2	give **a**, do not sound a trumpet
Lk	12:33	your possessions, and give **a**.
Acts	3:2	ask for **a** from those entering
Tob	4:16	Give all your surplus as **a**
	12:8	better to give **a** than to
Sir	7:10	do not neglect to give **a**.

ALONE

Gen	2:18	the man should be **a**; I will
Ex	18:18	you cannot do it **a**.
Deut	8:3	by bread **a**, but by every word
1 Kings	19:10	with the sword. I **a** am left,
Neh	9:6	"You are the LORD, you **a**;
Ps	51:4	you, you **a**, have I sinned, and
	148:13	for his name **a** is exalted;
Prov	16:33	decision is the LORD's **a**.
Eccl	4:11	how can one keep warm **a**?
Isa	2:11	and the LORD **a** will be exalted
Mt	4:4	by bread **a**, but by every word
Mk	2:7	can forgive sins but God **a**?"
	10:18	one is good but God **a**.
Jn	16:32	will leave me **a**. Yet I am not **a**
Rom	11:3	your altars; I **a** am left,
Jas	2:24	works and not by faith **a**.
Rev	15:4	For you **a** are holy.

ALPHA

Rev	1:8	"I am the **A** and the Omega,"
	21:6	the **A** and the Omega, the
	22:13	I am the **A** and the Omega, the

ALTAR (S)

Gen	8:20	Noah built an **a** to the LORD,
	22:9	laid him on the **a**, on top of
Ex	17:15	Moses built an **a** and called it,
	30:1	You shall make an **a** on which
	37:25	the **a** of incense of acacia
Lev	8:11	anointed the **a** and all its

Deut	27:5	build an **a** there to the LORD
Josh	8:30	built on Mount Ebal an **a** to
Judg	6:24	Gideon built an **a** there to the
1 Sam	14:35	Saul built an **a** to the LORD;
2 Sam	24:25	David built there an **a** to the
1 Kings	12:33	He went up to the **a** that he
	18:30	First he repaired the **a** of the
2 Kings	23:20	He slaughtered on the **a** all the
1 Chr	21:26	fire from heaven on the **a** of
2 Chr	32:12	one **a** you shall worship,
	33:16	restored the **a** of the LORD and
Ezra	3:2	build the **a** of the God of
Neh	10:34	to burn on the **a** of the LORD
1 Macc	2:24	and killed him on the **a**.
2 Macc	1:32	light from the **a** shone back.
Ps	43:4	go to the **a** of God, to God
	51:19	will be offered on your **a**.
Sir	35:8	of the righteous enriches the **a**,
Isa	6:6	taken from the **a** with a pair of
	60:7	shall be acceptable on my **a**,
Lam	2:7	The Lord has scorned his **a**,
Ezek	6:5	bones around your **a**.
Hos	8:11	became to him **a** for sinning.
Joel	1:13	ministers of the **a**. Come, pass
Am	9:1	standing beside the **a**, and he
Mal	1:7	polluted food on my **a**.
Mt	5:24	gift there before the **a** and go;
Lk	11:51	perished between the **a** and
Acts	17:23	an **a** with the inscription, 'To
1 Cor	10:18	the sacrifices partners in the **a**?
Heb	13:10	We have an **a** from which
Jas	2:21	his son Isaac on the **a**?
Rev	6:9	under the **a** the souls of those
	11:1	temple of God and the **a** and
	16:7	the **a** respond, "Yes, O Lord

AMAZED (AMAZING)

Mt	8:27	were **a**, saying, "What sort of
	9:33	the crowds were **a** and said,
Mk	6:6	And he was **a** at their unbelief.
	12:11	and it is **a** in our eyes'?"
Acts	2:7	**A** and astonished, they asked,
Rev	15:3	"Great and **a** are your deeds,
	17:8	be **a** when they see the beast

AMBASSADORS

2 Cor	5:20	we are **a** for Christ, since God

AMEN

Deut	27:15	shall respond, saying, "**A**!"
1 Chr	16:36	Then all the people said "**A**!"
Tob	8:8	they both said, "**A, A**."
Jdt	13:20	all the people said, "**A. A**."
Ps	89:52	be the LORD forever. **A** and **A**.
Rom	1:25	who is blessed forever! **A**.
Rom	11:36	him be the glory forever. **A**.
1 Cor	14:16	the "**A**" to your thanksgiving,
2 Cor	1:20	we say the "**A**," to the glory of
Rev	3:14	The words of the **A**, the
	5:14	living creatures said, "**A**!"
	22:20	coming soon." **A**. Come, Lord

ANCESTOR (S)

Gen	17:4	be the **a** of a multitude of
Ex	3:13	'The God of your **a** has sent
Deut	1:8	I swore to your **a**, to Abraham,
1 Kings	19:4	am no better than my **a**."
Ps	22:4	In you our **a** trusted; they
	106:6	we and our **a** have sinned; we
Lam	5:7	Our **a** sinned; they are no

Tob	8:5	are you, O God of our **a**,
Am	2:4	lies after which their **a** walked.
Zech	1:4	like your **a**, to whom the
Mt	3:9	'We have Abraham as our **a**;
Lk	11:48	deeds of your **a**; for they killed
Jn	4:20	Our **a** worshiped on this
Acts	5:30	God of our **a** raised up Jesus
Rom	4:1	by Abraham, our **a** according
1 Cor	10:1	our **a** were all under the cloud
Heb	11:2	faith our **a** received approval.

ANGEL (S)

Gen	16:7	The **a** of the LORD found her
	28:12	the **a** of God were ascending
Job	4:18	his **a** he charges with error;
Ps	91:11	command his **a** concerning
	148:2	Praise him, all his **a**; praise
Mt	4:6	command his **a** concerning
	18:10	their **a** continually see the face
Mk	8:38	his Father with the holy **a**."
	12:25	marriage, but are like **a** in
	13:27	the **a**, and gather his elect
Lk	2:15	When the **a** had left them and
	15:10	the presence of the **a** of God
Jn	20:12	she saw two **a** in white, sitting
Acts	7:53	law as ordained by **a**, and yet
Rom	8:38	nor life, nor **a**, nor rulers,
1 Cor	4:9	world, to **a** and to mortals.
	6:3	we are to judge **a**—to say
Gal	3:19	ordained through **a** by a
Col	2:18	worship of **a**, dwelling on
2 Thess	1:7	from heaven with his mighty **a**
1 Tim	3:16	seen by **a**, proclaimed among
Heb	1:4	become as much superior to **a**
	1:14	Are not all **a** spirits in the
	2:9	was made lower than the **a**,
1 Pet	3:22	right hand of God, with **a**,
2 Pet	2:4	God did not spare the **a** when
Jude	1:6	And the **a** who did not keep
Rev	5:11	voice of many **a** surrounding
	7:1	After this I saw four **a** standing
	8:2	the seven **a** who stand before

ANGER (ANGRY)

Gen	18:30	the LORD be **a** if I speak.
	27:45	your brother's **a** against you
Ex	4:14	the **a** of the LORD was kindled
	34:6	slow to **a**, and abounding in
Num	12:9	the **a** of the LORD was kindled
	14:18	'The LORD is slow to **a**, and
Deut	6:15	The **a** of the LORD your God
	9:19	I was afraid that the **a** that the
Josh	7:1	and the **a** of the LORD burned
Judg	2:12	they provoked the LORD to **a**.
1 Sam	20:30	Then Saul's **a** was kindled
2 Sam	12:5	David's **a** was greatly kindled
1 Kings	11:9	the LORD was **a** with Solomon,
Ps	30:5	For his **a** is but for a moment
	37:8	Refrain from **a**, and forsake
	90:7	we are consumed by your **a**;
Prov	12:16	Fools show their **a** at once, and
	19:11	good sense are slow to **a**, and
Eccl	7:9	not be quick to **a**, for **a** lodges
Sir	30:24	Jealousy and **a** shorten life.
Isa	5:25	the **a** of the LORD was kindled
Jer	3:12	I will not be **a** forever.
Lam	4:11	he poured out his hot **a**, and
Ezek	43:8	have consumed them in my **a**.
Dan	9:16	let your **a** and wrath, we pray,
Hos	11:9	will not execute my fierce **a**;

Jon	3: 9	may turn from his fierce **a**, so
Mic	7:18	does not retain his **a** forever,
Mt	5:22	if you are **a** with a brother or
Mk	3: 5	looked around at them with **a**;
Lk	15:28	Then he became **a** and refused
Jn	7:23	you **a** with me because I healed
2 Cor	12:20	quarreling, jealousy, **a**,
Gal	5:20	strife, jealousy, **a**, quarrels,
Eph	4:26	Be **a** but do not sin; do
	6: 4	provoke your children to **a**,
Col	3: 8	such things—**a**, wrath, malice,
1 Tim	2: 8	holy hands without **a** or
Heb	3:11	As in my **a** I swore, 'They will
Jas	1:19	slow to speak, slow to **a**;
Rev	12:17	dragon was **a** with the woman,
	14:10	into the cup of his **a**, and they

ANIMAL (S)

Gen	1:25	made the wild **a** of the earth
	3:14	cursed are you among all **a**
Ex	20:15	has sexual relations with an **a**,
	26:22	I will let loose wild **a** against
Deut	14: 4	These are the **a** you may eat:
2 Chr	25:18	but a **a** of Lebanon
Job	12: 7	"But ask the **a**, and they will
Ps	36: 6	you save humans and **a** alike,
	50:10	For every wild **a** of the forest is
Eccl	3:19	humans and the fate of **a** is
Wis	11:15	serpents and worthless **a**,
Isa	43:20	The wild **a** will honor me,
Ezek	14:21	sword, famine, wild **a**, and
Dan	4:15	be with the **a** of the field
Joel	2:22	Do not fear, you **a** of the field,
Hab	2:17	destruction of the **a** will terrify
Mal	1: 8	you offer blind **a** in sacrifice, is
Lk	10:34	own **a**, brought him to an inn
Acts	11: 6	closely I saw four-footed **a**,
Heb	12:20	an **a** touches the mountain, it
Jude	1:10	like irrational **a**, they know by

ANNOUNCE (D) (S) (ANNOUNCING)

Deut	17: 9	shall **a** to you the decision
Isa	48: 5	I **a** them to you, so that
	52: 7	messenger who **a** peace, who
Rom	1: 9	my spirit by **a** the gospel of his
Gal	4:13	that I first **a** the gospel to you;
1 Pet	1:25	good news that was **a** to you.
Rev	10: 7	fulfilled, as he **a** to his servants

ANOINT (ED) (ING)

Gen	31:13	God of Bethel, where you **a**
Ex	30:25	it shall be a holy **a** oil.
	30:30	You shall **a** Aaron and his
Lev	4: 3	If it is the **a** priest who sins,
Deut	28:40	but you shall not **a** yourself
1 Sam	2:10	exalt the power of his **a**."
	15: 1	LORD sent me to **a** you king
	26: 9	against the LORD's **a**, and be
2 Sam	1:14	hand to destroy the LORD's **a**?"
	19:21	he cursed the LORD's **a**?"
1 Kings	19:16	shall **a** Jehu son of Nimshi
	19:16	and you shall **a** Elisha son of
2 Kings	9: 3	I **a** you king over Israel.'
1 Chr	16:22	"Do not touch my **a** ones;
2 Chr	6:42	do not reject your **a** one.
Ps	18:50	shows steadfast love to his **a**,
	23: 5	my enemies; you **a** my head
	105:15	"Do not touch my **a** ones; do
Isa	61: 1	because the LORD has **a** me;
Ezek	28:14	With an **a** cherub as guardian I

Dan	9:24	and to **a** a most holy place.
Hab	3:13	to save your **a**. You crushed
Zech	4:14	"These are the two **a** ones who
Mk	6:13	many demons, and **a** with oil
Lk	4:18	because he has **a** me to bring
	7:46	You did not **a** my head with
Jn	12: 3	of pure nard, **a** Jesus' feet,
Acts	10:38	how God **a** Jesus of Nazareth
2 Cor	1:21	you in Christ and has **a** us,
Heb	1: 9	your God, has **a** you with the
1 Jn	2:20	have been **a** by the Holy One,
Rev	3:18	and salve to **a** your eyes so

ANSWER (ED)

1 Kings	18:26	"O Baal, **a** us!" But there was
	18:37	**A** me, O LORD, **a** me
1 Chr	21:26	and he **a** him with fire from
Job	30:20	you and you do not **a** me;
Ps	20: 9	O LORD; **a** us when we call.
	38:15	LORD my God, who will **a**.
	118:21	thank you that you have **a** me
Prov	15: 1	A soft **a** turns away wrath,
	18:13	If one gives **a** before hearing,
Isa	58: 9	call, and the LORD will **a**;
	65:24	Before they call I will **a**, while
Hos	14: 8	It is I who **a** and look after
Mt	27:14	But he gave him no **a**, not
Lk	23: 9	but Jesus gave him no **a**.

ANTICHRIST

1 Jn	2:18	have heard that **a** is coming,
	4: 3	is the spirit of the **a**, of which
2 Jn	1: 7	is the deceiver and the **a**!

APART

Ps	4: 3	the LORD has set **a** the faithful
Jn	15: 5	because **a** from me you can do
Rom	1: 1	an apostle, set **a** for the gospel
	3:21	But now, **a** from law, the
Jas	2:20	faith **a** from works is barren?

APOSTLE (S)

Mt	10: 2	of the twelve **a**: first, Simon,
Mk	3:14	whom he also named **a**, to be
Lk	11:49	prophets and **a**, some of
Acts	2:43	were being done by the **a**.
	4:33	With great power the gave
	8: 1	except the **a** were scattered
Rom	1: 1	called to be an **a**, set apart for
	11:13	I am an **a** to the Gentiles,
1 Cor	9: 1	Am I not an **a**? Have I not seen
	15: 9	be called an **a**, because I
2 Cor	11:13	For such boasters are false **a**,
Gal	2: 8	Peter making him an **a** to the
Eph	2:20	of the **a** and prophets,
	4:11	some would be **a**, some
2 Tim	1:11	herald and an **a** and a teacher,
Heb	3: 1	Jesus, the **a** and high priest of
Jude	1:17	the predictions of the **a** of our
Rev	2: 2	claim to be **a** but are not,
	21:14	of the twelve **a** of the Lamb.

APPEAR (ED) (ING) (S) (ANCE) (ANCES)

Gen	1: 9	and let the dry land **a**."
	12: 7	Then the LORD **a** to Abram,
Ex	3: 2	the angel of the LORD **a** to him
	16:10	the glory of the LORD **a** in the
Lev	16: 2	he will die; for I **a** in the cloud
Num	9:15	having the **a** of fire.
Num	16:19	the glory of the LORD **a** to the

Judg	6:12	The angel of the LORD **a** to
1 Sam	16: 7	"Do not look on his **a** or on
1 Kings	9: 2	the LORD **a** to Solomon a
2 Chr	1: 7	That night God **a** to Solomon,
Ps	21: 9	a fiery furnace when you **a**.
	102:16	he will **a** in his glory.
Sir	35: 6	not **a** before the Lord empty-
Isa	53: 2	nothing in his **a** that we
Ezek	10:22	were the same faces whose **a**
Dan	5: 5	fingers of a human hand **a**
Hos	6: 3	his **a** is as sure as the
Joel	2: 4	They have the **a** of horses, and
Mt	1:20	an angel of the Lord **a** to him
Mk	12:40	the sake of **a** say long prayers.
	13:22	false prophets will **a** and
Lk	1:11	Then there **a** to him an angel
	19:11	kingdom of God was to **a**
Jn	7:24	Do not judge by **a**, but judge
	21:14	the third time that Jesus **a** to
Acts	2: 3	tongues, as of fire, **a** among
	12: 7	an angel of the Lord **a** and a
1 Cor	15: 5	and that he **a** to Cephas, then
2 Cor	5:10	must **a** before the judgment
Col	2:23	indeed an **a** of wisdom in
Titus	2:11	the grace of God has **a**,
Heb	9:24	to **a** in the presence of God
	9:26	as it is, he has **a** once for all at
Rev	12: 1	A great portent **a** in heaven: a

APPOINT (ED)

Ex	18:25	all Israel and **a** them as heads
Lev	23: 2	These are the **a** festivals of the
1 Sam	8: 5	**a** for us, then, a king
1 Kings	1:35	for I have **a** him to be ruler
1 Chr	24: 3	according to the **a** duties in
Neh	5:14	I was **a** to be their governor in
	10:33	the new moons, the **a** festivals,
Esth	9:31	observed at their **a** seasons, as
Job	14: 5	you have **a** the bounds that
Ps	7: 6	you have **a** a judgment.
	75: 2	the set time that I **a** I will
Eccl	3:17	for he has **a** a time for every
Isa	60:17	I will **a** Peace as your overseer
Jer	33:20	not come at their **a** time,
Dan	2:49	he **a** Shadrach, Meshach, and
	8:19	for it refers to the **a** time of the
Hos	1:11	they shall **a** for themselves one
Hab	2: 3	still a vision for the **a** time;
Mk	3:16	So he **a** the twelve: Simon (to
Lk	10: 1	After this the Lord **a** seventy
Jn	15:16	I chose you. And I **a** you to go
Acts	3:20	send the Messiah **a** for you,
	15: 2	others were **a** to go up to
1 Cor	6: 4	do you **a** as judges those who
	12:28	God has **a** in the church first
1 Tim	1:12	and **a** me to his service,
Titus	1: 5	and should **a** elders in every
Heb	1: 2	whom he **a** heir of all things,
	9:27	it is **a** for mortals to die once

APPROVAL (APPROVED)

Sir	32:10	**a** goes before one who is
Acts	8: 1	And Saul **a** of their killing
2 Cor	10:18	themselves that are **a**, but
Gal	1:10	seeking human **a**, or God's **a**?
1 Thess	2: 4	just as we have been **a** by God
2 Tim	2:15	as one **a** by him, a worker who
Heb	11: 2	faith our ancestors received **a**.
1 Pet	2:20	suffer for it, you have God's **a**.

ARGUE (ARGUMENT) (ARGUMENTS)

Job	13:3	I desire to **a** my case with God.
Prov	25:9	**A** your case with your
Isa	3:13	The LORD rises to **a** his case;
Mk	8:11	Pharisees came and began to **a**
Lk	9:46	An **a** arose among them as to
Acts	18:4	Every sabbath he would **a** in
Rom	9:20	human being, to **a** with God?
2 Cor	10:4	strongholds. We destroy **a**
Col	2:4	deceive you with plausible **a**.
1 Tim	2:8	hands without anger or **a**;

ARISE

Num	10:35	"**A**, O LORD, let your enemies
1 Kings	3:12	one like you shall **a** after you.
2 Kings	23:25	did any like him **a** after him.
1 Macc	14:41	trustworthy prophet should **a**,
Song	2:10	and says to me: "**A**, my love,
Isa	60:1	**A**, shine; for your light has
Dan	7:17	four kings shall **a** out of the
Mic	4:13	**A** and thresh, O daughter Zion
Mt	24:11	false prophets will **a** and lead .

ARK

Gen	6:14	Make yourself an **a** of cypress
Ex	25:16	into the **a** the covenant that I
Num	3:31	to be the **a**, the table,
Deut	10:5	put the tablets in the **a** that I
Josh	3:3	you see the **a** of the covenant
Judg	20:27	for the **a** of the covenant of
1 Sam	4:11	The **a** of God was captured;
2 Sam	6:17	brought in the **a** of the LORD,
1 Kings	8:9	nothing in the **a** except the
1 Chr	13:9	to hold the **a**, for the oxen
2 Chr	35:3	"Put the holy **a** in the house
Ps	132:8	you and the **a** of your might.
Jer	3:16	say, "The **a** of the covenant
Lk	17:27	Noah entered the **a**, and the
Heb	9:4	incense and the **a** of the
1 Pet	3:20	during the building of the **a**,
Rev	11:19	and the **a** of his covenant was

ASCEND (ED) (ING)

Gen	28:12	the angels of God were **a** and
Judg	13:20	the angel of the LORD **a** in the
2 Kings	2:11	and Elijah **a** in a whirlwind
Tob	12:20	I am **a** to him who sent me
Ps	24:3	shall **a** the hill of the LORD
	139:8	If I **a** to heaven, you are there
Isa	14:13	"I will **a** to heaven; I will raise
Ezek	11:23	glory of the LORD **a** from the
Jn	6:62	see the Son of Man **a** to where
	20:17	I have not yet **a** to the Father.
Acts	2:34	For David did not **a** into the
Rom	10:6	'Who will **a** into heaven?'
Eph	4:8	"When he **a** on high he made
Rev	7:2	I saw another angel **a** from the
	17:8	to **a** from the bottomless pit

ASK (ED)

Ex	3:13	they **a** me, 'What is his name?'
	12:26	And when your children **a**
Deut	32:7	long past; **a** your father,
Judg	13:18	"Why do you **a** my name?
1 Kings	3:10	Solomon had **a** this.
1 Chr	4:10	And God granted what he **a**
Ps	2:8	**A** of me, and I will
	27:4	One thing I **a** of the LORD, that
Prov	30:7	Two things I **a** of you; do not
Isa	7:11	**A** a sign of the LORD

Jer	6:16	look, and **a** for the ancient
Mt	6:8	you need before you **a** him.
	7:7	**A**, and it will be given
Mk	6:23	"Whatever you **a** me, I will
	11:24	whatever you **a** for in prayer,
Lk	11:13	Holy Spirit to those who **a**
Jn	16:23	I tell you, if you **a** anything of
	16:24	you have not **a** for anything in
Rom	10:20	to those who did not **a** for me."
1 Cor	14:35	let them **a** their husbands at
Eph	3:20	all we can **a** or imagine,
Jas	1:5	lacking in wisdom, **a** God,
	4:3	You **a** and do not receive,
1 Jn	3:22	from him whatever we **a**,
	5:14	if we **a** anything according to

ASSEMBLY (ASSEMBLE)

Ex	12:16	you shall hold a solemn **a**,
Lev	4:21	the sin offering for the **a**.
Num	10:3	congregation shall **a** before
Deut	23:1	admitted to the **a** of the LORD.
1 Kings	18:19	Israel **a** for me at Mount
2 Chr	29:28	The whole **a** worshiped, the
Neh	8:2	brought the law before the **a**,
Ps	149:1	praise in the **a** of the faithful.
Isa	48:14	**A**, all of you, and hear
Joel	1:14	call a solemn **a**. Gather the
	2:15	a fast; call a solemn **a**;
Zeph	3:8	nations, to **a** kingdoms,
Lk	23:1	Then the **a** rose as a body and
Heb	12:23	the **a** of the firstborn who are
Jas	2:2	into your **a**, and if a poor
Rev	16:14	world, to **a** them for battle

ASSURANCE

Deut	28:66	dread, with no **a** of your life.
Heb	10:22	a true heart in full **a** of faith,
	11:1	Now faith is the **a** of things

ASSYRIA (ASSYRIANS)

Gen	10:11	into **A**, and built Nineveh,
2 Kings	15:19	King Pul of **A** came against the
	18:11	The king of **A** carried the
Tob	1:10	carried way captive to **A**
Isa	10:5	Ah, **A**, the rod of my anger
	10:24	not be afraid of the **A** when
Jer	50:18	I punished the king of **A**.
Ezek	23:5	lusted after her lovers the **A**,
Hos	14:3	**A** shall not save us; we
Nah	3:18	O king of **A**; your nobles
Zech	10:10	gather them from **A**; I will

ASTRAY

Num	5:12	wife goes **a** and is unfaithful
Deut	30:17	but are led **a** to bow down to
Ps	14:3	They have all gone **a**, they are
	119:176	I have gone **a** like a lost sheep;
Prov	10:17	who rejects a rebuke goes **a**.
	20:1	whoever is led **a** by it is not
Sir	31:5	pursues money will be led **a**
Isa	53:6	we like sheep have gone **a**;
Jer	23:13	and led my people Israel **a**.
	50:6	shepherds have led them **a**,
Ezek	14:11	Israel may no longer go **a**
Am	2:4	they have been led **a** by the
Mt	18:12	one of them has gone **a**,
	24:5	and they will lead many **a**.
Mk	13:5	that no one leads you **a**.
1 Cor	12:2	were enticed and led **a** to idols
2 Cor	11:3	your thoughts will be led **a**

1 Pet	2:25	you were going **a** like sheep,
2 Pet	2:15	straight road and have gone **a**,

ATONE (D) (ATONING)

Prov	16:6	iniquity is **a** for, and by the
Dan	4:27	**a** for your sins with
	9:24	and to **a** for iniquity,
1 Jn	2:2	and he is the **a** sacrifice for our
	4:10	the **a** sacrifice for our sins.

ATONEMENT

Ex	29:36	as a sin offering for **a**.
	32:30	I can make **a** for your sin."
Lev	4:35	priest shall make **a** on your
Num	8:21	and Aaron made **a** for them to
	25:13	and made **a** for the Israelites.'
1 Chr	6:49	to make **a** for Israel, according
Neh	10:33	offerings to make **a** for Israel,
Rom	3:25	as a sacrifice of **a** by his blood,
Heb	2:17	sacrifice of **a** for the sins of the

AUTHORITY (AUTHORITIES)

Gen	41:45	Thus Joseph gained **a** over the
Prov	29:2	When the righteous are in **a**,
Sir	20:8	pretends to **a** is hated.
Isa	9:6	a son given to us; **a** rests upon
Mt	9:6	the Son of Man has **a** on earth
	28:18	"All **a** in heaven and on earth
Mk	1:27	A new teaching—with **a**! He
	11:28	"By what **a** are you doing
Lk	5:24	the Son of Man has **a** on earth
	12:11	and the **a**, do not worry about
Jn	5:27	has given him **a** to execute
	12:42	many, even of the **a**, believed
Acts	1:7	has set by his own **a**.
	5:29	God rather than any human **a**.
Rom	13:1	be subject to the governing **a**;
	13:2	whoever resists **a** resists what
1 Cor	7:4	wife does not have **a** over her
	15:24	every ruler and every **a** and
2 Cor	10:8	our **a**, which the Lord gave
Eph	1:21	far above all rule and **a** and
	3:10	rulers and **a** in the heavenly
Col	2:10	head of every ruler and **a**.
	2:15	the rulers and **a** and made a
1 Tim	2:12	to teach or to have **a** over a
Titus	2:15	exhort and reprove with all **a**.
	3:1	be subject to rulers and **a**, to
1 Pet	2:13	accept the **a** of every human
	3:5	the **a** of their husbands.
	5:5	accept the **a** of the elders.
2 Pet	2:10	lust, and who despise **a**.
3 Jn	1:9	does not acknowledge our **a**.
Jude	1:8	defile the flesh, reject **a**, and
Rev	2:26	I will give **a** over the nations;
	13:4	given his **a** to the beast,
	20:4	on them were given **a** to judge.

AWAKE

Judg	5:12	**A**, **a**, Deborah!**a**, **a**, utter
Ps	44:23	O LORD? **A**, do not cast us off
	57:8	**A**, my soul! **A**, O harp and
Prov	6:22	and when you **a**, they will talk
Song	5:2	slept, but my heart was **a**.
Isa	51:9	**A**, **a**, put on strength, O
	52:1	**A**, **a**, put on your strength
Dan	12:2	dust of the earth shall **a**,
Zech	13:7	**A**, O sword, against my
Mt	24:42	Keep **a** therefore, for you do
	26:38	and stay **a** with me."

Mk 14:37 Could you not keep **a** one
Eph 5:14 "Sleeper, **a**! Rise from the
1 Thess 5: 6 but let us keep **a** and be sober;
5:10 whether we are **a** or asleep
Rev 16:15 who stays **a** and is clothed,

AWE (SOME)

Gen 28:17 "How **a** is this place! This is
Ex 15:11 in holiness, **a** in splendor,
34:10 for it is an **a** thing that I will
Deut 6:22 great and **a** signs and wonders
10:17 the great God, mighty and **a**, l
Josh 4:14 and they stood in **a** of him, as
2 Sam 7:23 doing great and **a** things for
1 Kings 3:28 they stood in **a** of the king,
Neh 1: 5 the great and **a** God who
9:32 mighty and **a** God, keeping
Job 37:22 around God is **a** majesty.
Ps 47: 2 the Most High, is **a**, a great
66: 3 Say to God, "How **a** are your
76: 7 But you indeed are **a**! Who
Sir 43:29 **A** is the Lord and very great,
Isa 29:23 and will stand in **a** of the God
64: 3 When you did **a** deeds that we
Ezek 1:18 Their rims were tall and **a**, for
Dan 9: 4 "Ah, LORD, great and **a** God,
Hos 3: 5 come in **a** to the LORD and to
Hab 3: 2 and I stand in **a**, O LORD, of
Mal 2: 5 and stood in **a** of my name.
Mt 9: 8 they were filled with **a**, and
Lk 5:26 God and were filled with **a**,
Acts 2:43 **A** came upon everyone,
Rom 11:20 become proud, but stand in **a**.
Heb 12:28 worship with reverence and **a**;

B

BAAL (S)

Num 25: 3 Israel yoked itself to the **B** of
Deut 4: 3 with regard to the **B** of Peor—
Judg 2:13 the LORD, and worshiped **B**
6:31 "Will you contend for **B**? Or
1 Sam 7: 4 So Israel put away the **B** and
1 Kings 16:32 altar for **B** in the house of **B**
18:25 said to the prophets of **B**,
2 Kings 3: 2 he removed the pillar of **B** that
10:28 Thus Jehu wiped out **B** from
2 Chr 17: 3 he did not seek the **B**,
23:17 killed Mattan, the priest of **B**,
Ps 106:28 themselves to the **B** of Peor,
Jer 2: 8 the prophets prophesied by **B**,
19: 5 the high places of **B** to burn
Hos 2:17 names of the **B** from her
13: 1 incurred guilt through **B** and
Rom 11: 4 not bowed the knee to **B**."

BABYLON

2 Kings 24:15 captivity from Jerusalem to **B**.
1 Chr 9: 1 into exile in **B** because of
2 Chr 36:18 all these he brought to **B**.
36:20 took into exile in **B** those who
Ps 137: 1 By the rivers of **B**—there we
137: 8 O daughter **B**, you devastator!
Isa 13: 1 concerning **B** that Isaiah son
21: 9 "Fallen, fallen is **B**; and all the
Jer 25:11 serve the king of **B** seventy

Jer 51:37 and **B** shall become a heap of
Bar 2:24 to serve the king of **B**;
Dan 2:48 whole province of **B** and chief
4:30 "Is this not magnificent **B**,
1 Pet 5:13 Your sister church in **B**, chosen
Rev 14: 8 "Fallen, fallen is **B** the great!
17: 5 "**B** the great, mother of whores
18: 2 "Fallen, fallen is **B** the great!

BAPTISM (S)

Mt 3: 7 Sadducees coming for **b**,
21:25 Did the **b** of John come from
Mk 1: 4 proclaiming a **b** of repentance
10:38 or be baptized with the **b** that
Lk 7:29 been baptized with John's **b**.
12:50 I have a **b** with which to be
Acts 13:24 proclaimed a **b** of repentance
18:25 knew only the **b** of John.
Rom 6: 4 with him by **b** into death,
1 Cor 15:29 receive **b** on behalf of the dead
Eph 4: 5 one Lord, one faith, one **b**,
Col 2:12 buried with him in **b**, you
Heb 6: 2 instruction about **b**, laying on
9:10 drink and various **b**, regulations
1 Pet 3:21 And **b**, which this prefigured,

BAPTIZE (D) (BAPTIZING)

Mt 3:11 "I **b** you with water for
3:16 And when Jesus had been **b**,
28:19 of all nations, **b** them in the
Mk 1: 8 **b** you with water; but he will **b**
1: 9 Galilee and was **b** by John in
16:16 one who believes and is **b** will
Lk 3: 7 that came out to be **b** by him,
3:16 He will **b** you with the Holy
Jn 3:23 kept coming and were being **b**
4: 2 but his disciples who **b**—
Acts 2:38 "Repent, and be **b** every one of
8:12 they were **b**, both men and
10:48 to be **b** in the name of Jesus
16:33 and his entire family were **b**
Rom 6: 3 **b** into Christ Jesus were **b**
1 Cor 1:13 were you **b** in the name of Paul
10: 2 and all were **b** into Moses in
12:13 we were all **b** into one body—
Gal 3:27 you as were **b** into Christ

BARREN (NESS)

Gen 11:30 Now Sarai was **b**; she had no
29:31 her womb; but Rachel was **b**.
Ex 23:26 miscarry or be **b** in your land;
Deut 7:14 neither sterility nor **b** among
Judg 13: 2 His wife was **b**, having borne
1 Sam 2: 5 The **b** has borne seven, but she
Ps 113: 9 He gives the **b** woman a home,
Prov 30:16 the **b** womb, the earth ever
Isa 49:21 I was bereaved and **b**, exiled
Lk 1: 7 because Elizabeth was **b**, and
23:29 'Blessed are the **b**, and the
Rom 4:19 considered the **b** of Sarah's
Heb 11:11 and Sarah herself was **b**—
Jas 2:20 faith apart from works is **b**?

BATTLE

Ex 13:18 land of Egypt prepared for **b**.
Josh 4:13 the plains of Jericho for **b**.
1 Sam 17:47 for the **b** is the LORD's
2 Sam 1:25 midst of the **b**! Jonathan lies
1 Kings 22:30 disguise myself and go into **b**,
2 Chr 20:15 the **b** is not yours but God's.

1 Macc 3:19 the army that victory in **b**
Ps 24: 8 mighty, the LORD, mighty in **b**.
Eccl 9:11 swift, nor the **b** to the strong,
Ezek 13: 5 it might stand in **b** on the day
1 Cor 14: 8 who will get ready for **b**?
Rev 16:14 assemble them for **b** on the
20: 8 to gather them for **b**; they are

BEAR (S) (BORE)

Gen 4:13 is greater than I can **b**!
17:19 your wife Sarah shall **b** you a
Ex 19: 4 how I **b** you on eagles' wings
23: 2 when you **b** witness in a
Josh 3:17 the priests who **b** the ark of
Judg 13: 3 shall conceive and **b** a son.
1 Sam 17:36 has killed both lions and **b**;
Job 9: 9 who made the **B** and Orion,
Ps 68:19 be the Lord, who daily **b**
Isa 7:14 and shall **b** a son, and shall
11: 7 The cow and the **b** shall graze,
Jer 30: 6 can a man **b** a child? Why
Ezek 3:14 spirit lifted me up and **b** me
14:10 they shall **b** their punishment
Dan 7: 5 that looked like a **b**.
Am 5:19 and was met by a **b**; or went
Mt 1:23 the virgin shall conceive and **b**
7:18 A good tree cannot **b** bad fruit,
8:17 "He took our infirmities and **b**
Lk 1:13 Elizabeth will **b** you a son,
11:46 with burdens hard to **b**,
Jn 15: 2 he prunes to make it **b** more
15: 8 that you **b** much fruit and
Acts 15:10 we have been able to **b**?
Rom 7: 4 that we may **b** fruit for God.
1 Cor 15:49 we will also **b** the image of the
Gal 6: 2 **B** one another's burdens,
Col 1:10 as you **b** fruit in every good
3:13 **B** with one another and, if
Heb 9:28 offered once to **b** the sins of
1 Pet 2:24 himself **b** our sins in his body
4:16 glorify God because you **b** this
Rev 12: 4 woman who was about to **b** a

BEAT (EN) (ING)

Ex 2:11 an Egyptian **b** a Hebrew, one
5:16 Look how your servants are **b**!
Deut 24:20 When you **b** your olive trees,
Neh 13:25 cursed them and **b** some of
Prov 23:35 they **b** me, but I did not
Song 5: 7 they **b** me, they wounded me,
Isa 2: 4 they shall **b** their swords into
Joel 3:10 **B** your plowshares into
Mic 4: 3 they shall **b** their spears into
Mt 7:25 winds blew and **b** on that
Mk 14:65 also took him over and **b** him.
Lk 10:30 who stripped him, **b** him, and
22:63 began to mock him and **b**
Acts 22:19 and **b** those who believed in
1 Cor 9:26 do I box as though **b** the air;
2 Cor 11:25 Three times I was **b** with rods.
1 Pet 2:20 endure when you are **b** for

BEAUTIFUL (BEAUTY)

Gen 12:11 a woman **b** in appearance;
Deut 21:11 among the captives a **b**
Josh 7:21 among the spoil a **b** mantle
1 Sam 16:12 he was ruddy, and had **b** eyes,
25: 3 The woman was clever and **b**,
2 Sam 11: 2 the woman was very **b**.
14:25 so much for his **b** as Absalom;

1 Kings	1: 3	they searched for a **b** girl
Jdt	10: 7	greatly astounded at her **b**
Esth	1:11	peoples and the officials her **b**;
	2: 7	the girl was fair and **b**, and
Job	42:15	no women so **b** as Job's
Ps	27: 4	to behold the **b** of the LORD,
	48: 2	**b** in elevation, is the joy
Prov	6:25	Do not desire her **b** in your
	31:30	Charm is deceitful, and **b** is
Song	1:15	Ah, you are **b**, my love; ah,
	4: 7	You are altogether **b**, my love;
Wis	13:3	If through delight in the **b** of
Isa	28: 1	fading flower of its glorious **b**,
	52: 7	How **b** upon the mountains
Jer	13:18	for your **b** crown has come
	13:20	was given you, your **b** flock?
Lam	2:15	was called the perfection of **b**,
Bar	5:1	the **b** of the glory from God.
Ezek	16:17	You also took your **b** jewels of
	28:12	of wisdom and perfect in **b**.
Dan	4:12	Its foliage was **b**, its fruit
	11:41	He shall come into the **b** land,
Hos	14: 6	his **b** shall be like the olive
Am	8:13	day the **b** young women
Zech	9:17	For what goodness and **b** are
Mt	23:27	on the outside look **b**, but
Lk	21: 5	it was adorned with **b** stones
Acts	3: 2	temple called the **B** Gate
	7:20	and he was **b** before God.
Rom	10:15	"How **b** are the feet of those
Heb	11:23	the child was **b**; and they were
Jas	1:11	flower falls, and its **b** perishes.
1 Pet	3: 4	with the lasting **b** of a gentle

BEFORE

Gen	18:22	remained standing **b** the
	45: 5	for God sent me **b** you to
Ex	20: 3	shall have no other gods **b** me.
	33: 2	I will send an angel **b** you,
Lev	10: 2	and they died **b** the LORD.
Num	17: 7	So Moses placed the staffs **b**
Deut	1:30	LORD your God, who goes **b**
	11:26	See, I am setting **b** you today a
1 Sam	4: 7	like this has happened **b**.
Job	4:17	righteous **b** God? Can human
Ps	16: 8	I keep the LORD always **b** me;
	37: 7	Be still **b** the LORD, and wait
	139: 4	Even **b** a word is on my
Prov	16:18	Pride goes **b** destruction, and
	18:13	If one gives answer **b** hearing,
Isa	49: 1	The LORD called me **b** I was
	65:24	**B** they call I will answer
Jer	1: 5	**B** I formed you in the womb
Zeph	1: 7	Be silent **b** the Lord GOD!
Zech	2:13	Be silent, all people, **b** the
Mal	3: 1	to prepare the way **b** me,
Mt	6: 8	Father knows what you need **b**
	11:10	who will prepare your way **b**
Lk	12: 8	who acknowledges me **b**
	22:61	"**B** the cock crows today, you
Jn	8:58	**b** Abraham was, I am."
	13:19	I tell you this now, **b** it occurs,
Acts	2:25	'I saw the Lord always **b** me,
	8:32	and like a lamb silent **b** its
Rom	4:10	but **b** he was circumcised.
	14:10	all stand **b** the judgment seat
Gal	1:15	had set me apart **b** I was born
Col	1:17	He himself is **b** all things,
Titus	1: 2	who never lies, promised **b** the
Heb	12: 2	the joy that was set **b** him

1 Pet	1:20	destined **b** the foundation of
Rev	7: 9	standing **b** the throne and **b**

BEG (BEGGED) (BEGGAR)

Sir	40:28	do not lead the life of a **b**;
Lam	4: 4	the children **b** for food, but no
Mt	8:31	The demons **b** him, "If you
Mk	6:56	and **b** him that they might
	10:46	a blind **b**, was sitting by the
Lk	16: 3	and I am ashamed to **b**.
Jn	9: 8	who used to sit and **b**?"
	9: 8	before as a **b** began to ask,

BEGINNING

Gen	1: 1	In the **b** when God created the
Ps	111:10	of the LORD is the **b** of wisdom;
Prov	8:22	LORD created me at the **b** of
	9:10	fear of the LORD is the **b** of
Eccl	3:11	God has done from the **b** to
Wis	6:17	The **b** of wisdom is the most
Sir	1:14	the Lord is the **b** of wisdom;
Isa	46:10	declaring the end from the **b**
Mt	24: 8	is but the **b** of the birth pangs.
	24:21	been from the **b** of the world
Mk	1: 1	The **b** of the good news of
Lk	1: 2	from the **b** were eyewitnesses
Jn	1: 1	In the **b** was the Word, and
	15:27	been with me from the **b**.
Acts	1: 1	did and taught from the **b**
Col	1:18	he is the **b**, the firstborn from
Heb	7: 3	having neither **b** of days nor
1 Jn	1: 1	what was from the **b**, what we
2 Jn	1: 6	have heard it from the **b**—you
Rev	21: 6	Alpha and the Omega, the **b**

BEHIND

Ps	50:17	and you cast my words **b** you.
	139: 5	You hem me in, **b** and before,
Isa	38:17	cast all my sins **b** your back.
Ezek	3:12	I heard **b** me the sound of
Mt	16:23	"Get **b** me, Satan! You are a
Lk	2:43	the boy Jesus stayed **b** in
	8:44	She came up **b** him and
Phil	3:13	forgetting what lies **b** and
Heb	6: 1	leaving **b** the basic teaching
Rev	1:10	and I heard **b** me a loud voice
	4: 6	of eyes in front and **b**:

BELIEVE (D) (S) (BELIEVING)

Gen	45:26	he could not **b** them.
Ex	4: 5	they may **b** that the LORD,
	14:31	people feared the LORD and **b**
Num	14:11	long will they refuse to **b** in
1 Kings	10: 7	but I did not **b** the reports
2 Kings	17:14	who did not **b** in the LORD
2 Chr	20:20	**B** in the LORD your God
Tob	2:14	But I did not **b** her
Job	9:16	I do not **b** that he would listen
Ps	78:32	they did not **b** in his wonders.
	106:12	Then they **b** his words; they
Prov	14:15	The simple **b** everything, but
Sir	19:15	do not **b** everything you hear
Isa	53: 1	Who has **b** what we have
Jer	12: 6	do not **b** them, though they
Jon	3: 5	And the people of Nineveh **b**
Hab	1: 5	that you would not **b** if you
Mt	9:28	"Do you **b** that I am able to
	21:32	and the prostitutes **b** him;
Mk	9:42	these little ones who **b** in me,
	11:24	in prayer, **b** that you have

Lk	1:45	And blessed is she who **b** that
	20: 5	'Why did you not **b** him?'
Jn	1: 7	so that all might **b** through
	11:40	if you **b**, you would see the
	20:31	through **b** you may have life
Acts	2:44	All who **b** were together and
	15:11	we **b** that we will be saved
	24:14	**b** everything laid down
Rom	4:11	who **b** without being
	10: 9	and **b** in your heart that God
1 Cor	13: 7	bears all things, **b** all things,
2 Cor	4:13	—we also **b**, and so we
Gal	3: 2	law or by **b** what you heard?
	3:22	be given to those who **b**.
Eph	1:19	his power for us who **b**,
Phil	1:29	not only of **b** in Christ,
1 Thess	4:14	For since we **b** that Jesus died
2 Thess	2:11	leading them to **b** what is
1 Tim	1:16	who would come to **b** in him
2 Tim	3:14	you have learned and firmly **b**,
Titus	3: 8	who have come to **b** in God
Heb	11: 6	must **b** that he exists and that
Jas	2:19	You **b** that God is one;
1 Pet	2: 7	who do not **b**, "The stone
1 Jn	4: 1	Beloved, do not **b** every spirit,
	5: 1	Everyone who **b** that Jesus is
Jude	1: 5	those who did not **b**.

BELIEVER (S)

Jn	7:39	about the Spirit, which **b** in
Acts	11:21	and a great number became **b**
	16:34	that he had become a **b** in
	18:27	through grace had become **b**,
Rom	13:11	now than when we became **b**;
1 Cor	6: 6	but a **b** goes to court against a
2 Cor	6:15	a **b** share with an unbeliever?
Gal	2: 4	because of false **b** secretly
1 Thess	2:13	also at work in you **b**.
2 Thess	3: 6	away from **b** who are living in
1 Tim	4:12	but set the **b** an example in
Jas	1: 9	Let the **b** who is lowly boast in
1 Pet	2:17	Love the family of **b**.
1 Jn	2:11	whoever hates another **b** is

BELONG (S)

Gen	40: 8	"Do not interpretations **b** to
Deut	29:29	The secret things **b** to the
Ps	3: 8	Deliverance **b** to the LORD;
	89:18	For our shield **b** to the LORD,
Prov	16: 1	The plans of the mind **b** to
Dan	9: 9	To the Lord our God **b** mercy
Jon	2: 9	Deliverance **b** to the LORD!"
Mt	19:14	the kingdom of heaven **b**.
Jn	10:16	sheep that do not **b** to this
	18:37	Everyone who **b** to the truth
Rom	8: 9	Spirit of Christ does not **b** to
1 Cor	1:12	"I **b** to Paul," or "I **b** to
2 Cor	10: 7	confident that you **b** to Christ,
Gal	3:29	And if you **b** to Christ, then
Col	2:17	but the substance **b** to Christ.
1 Thess	5: 8	But since we **b** to the day,
1 Jn	2:19	but they did not **b** to us; for if
Rev	7:10	"Salvation **b** to our God

BELOVED

Deut	33:12	The **b** of the LORD rests in
2 Sam	1:26	Jonathan; greatly **b** were you
Neh	13:26	and he was **b** by his God, and
Jdt	9:4	divided among your **b**
Ps	127: 2	he gives sleep to his **b**.

Song	2:16	My **b** is mine and I am
	7:11	Come, my **b**, let us go forth
Sir	20:13	The wise make themselves **b**
Isa	5: 1	My **b** had a vineyard on a
Jer	12: 7	I have given the **b** of my heart
Bar	4:16	led away the widow's **b** sons
Dan	9:23	for you are greatly **b**.
Mt	17: 5	"This is my Son, the **B**; with
Mk	9: 7	"This is my Son, the **B**; listen
Lk	20:13	I will send my **b** son;
Rom	12:19	**B**, never avenge yourselves,
1 Cor	15:58	Therefore, my **b**, be steadfast,
2 Cor	12:19	Everything we do, **b**, is for the
Eph	5: 1	be imitators of God, as **b**
Phil	4: 8	Finally, **b**, whatever is true,
Col	3:12	chosen ones, holy and **b**,
1 Thess	5:14	And we urge you, **b**, to
2 Thess	2:13	brothers and sisters **b** by the
1 Tim	6: 2	service are believers and **b**.
Philem	1:16	more than a slave, a **b**
Heb	6: 9	in this way, **b**, we are confident
Jas	5: 9	**B**, do not grumble against one
1 Pet	2:11	**B**, I urge you as aliens
2 Pet	3: 8	one fact, **b**, that with the Lord
1 Jn	4: 1	**B**, do not believe every spirit
3 Jn	1:11	**B**, do not imitate what is
Jude	1:20	But you, **b**, build yourselves
Rev	20: 9	of the saints and the **b** city.

BESIDES

Deut	32:39	there is no god **b** me.
1 Sam	2: 2	no one **b** you; there is no Rock
1 Chr	17:20	and there is no God **b** you,
Ps	18:31	who is a rock **b** our God?—
Isa	45:21	There is no other god **b** me, a

BETHLEHEM

Gen	35:19	way to Ephrath (that is, **B**),
Ruth	4:11	and bestow a name in **B**;
1 Sam	17:12	son of an Ephrathite of **B** in
2 Sam	23:15	drink from the well of **B**
Mic	5: 2	But you, O **B** of Ephrathah,
Mt	2: 1	after Jesus was born in **B** of
Lk	2:15	"Let us go now to **B** and see
Jn	7:42	David and comes from **B**,

BETRAY (ED)

Mt	26:21	one of you will **b** me."
Mk	14:11	look for an opportunity to **b**
Lk	21:16	You will be **b** even by parents
Jn	13:11	he knew who was to **b** him;
1 Cor	11:23	the night when he was **b** took

BETTER

Num	11:18	Surely it was **b** for us in Egypt.'
Ruth	3:10	instance of your loyalty is **b**
1 Sam	15:22	Surely, to obey is **b** than
Tob	12:8	A little with righteousness is **b**
Ps	63: 3	your steadfast love is **b** than
Prov	16: 8	**B** is a little with righteousness
	16:19	It is **b** to be of a lowly
	19: 1	**B** the poor walking in integrity
	22: 1	favor is **b** than silver or gold.
Eccl	3:22	saw that there is nothing **b**
	5: 5	It is **b** that you should not vow
	7: 8	the patient in spirit are **b** than
Song	1: 2	For your love is **b** than wine,
Sir	23:27	is **b** than the fear of the Lord.
Jer	10: 8	given by idols is no **b** than
Dan	1:20	times **b** than all the magicians

Jon	4: 3	for it is **b** for me to die than
Mt	18: 6	it would be **b** for you if a great
Mk	14:21	It would have been **b** for that
Lk	10:42	Mary has chosen the **b** part,
Jn	11:50	it is **b** for you to have one
Rom	14: 5	judge one day to be **b** than
1 Cor	7: 9	For it is **b** to marry than to be
Phil	2: 3	regard others as **b** than
Heb	7:22	the guarantee of a **b** covenant.
	10:34	possessed something **b** and
1 Pet	3:17	For it is **b** to suffer for doing
2 Pet	2:21	would have been **b** for them

BEWARE

Job	36:21	**B**! Do not turn to iniquity
Eccl	12:12	beyond these, my child, **b**.
Jer	9: 4	**B** of your neighbors, and
Mt	7:15	**B** of false prophets, who come
Mk	13: 5	"**B** that no one leads you
Lk	20:46	**B** of the scribes, who like
Phil	3: 2	**B** of the dogs, **b** of
Rev	2:10	**B**, the devil is about to

BEYOND

Gen	31:52	I will not pass **b** this heap to
Num	22:18	I could not go **b** the command
Ps	147: 5	his understanding is **b**
Eccl	12:12	anything **b** these, my child,
Sir	3:23	meddle in matters that are **b**
	6:15	Faithful friends are **b** price
Isa	52:14	and his form **b** that of
Lam	5:22	and are angry with us **b**
1 Cor	10:13	not let you be tested **b** your
2 Cor	4:17	eternal weight of glory **b** all
2 Jn	1: 9	teaching of Christ, but goes **b**

BIND (S)

Deut	6: 8	**B** them as a sign on
Judg	15:10	"We have come up to **b**
Job	5:18	For he wounds, but he **b** up;
Ps	147: 3	and **b** up their wounds.
Prov	6:21	**B** them upon your heart
Isa	30:26	the LORD **b** up the injuries of
Ezek	34:16	I will **b** up the injured,
Mt	16:19	whatever you **b** on earth will
Col	3:14	love, which **b** everything

BIRTH

Deut	32:18	the God who gave you **b**.
Judg	13: 5	a nazirite to God from **b**.
Job	3: 1	cursed the day of his **b**.
Ps	22:10	I was cast from my **b**, and
Eccl	7: 1	death, than the day of **b**.
Isa	26:18	we writhed, but we gave **b**
Jer	2:27	a stone, "You gave me **b**."
Mt	1:18	Now the **b** of Jesus the
Lk	1:14	many will rejoice at his **b**,
Jn	9: 1	saw a man blind from **b**.
Acts	3: 2	a man lame from **b** was being
1 Cor	1:26	not many were of noble **b**.
Eph	2:11	one time you Gentiles by **b**,
Jas	1:18	own purpose he gave us **b** by
1 Pet	1: 3	given us a new **b** into a living
Rev	12: 5	And she gave **b** to a son, a

BIRTHRIGHT

Gen	25:34	Thus Esau despised his **b**.
1 Chr	5: 2	yet the **b** belonged to Joseph.)
Heb	12:16	who sold his **b** for a single

BISHOP

1 Tim	3: 1	aspires to the office of **b**
	3: 2	Now a **b** must be above
Titus	1: 7	For a **b**, as God's steward,

BITTER (NESS)

Ex	12: 8	with unleavened bread and **b**
Num	5:18	shall have the water of **b** that
	5:24	shall enter her and cause **b**
Ruth	1:13	it has been far more **b** for me
Prov	14:10	The heart knows its own **b**,
	27: 7	a ravenous appetite even the **b**
Eccl	7:26	more **b** than death the woman
Isa	5:20	who put **b** for sweet and sweet
Zeph	1:14	day of the LORD is **b**,
Rom	3:14	are full of cursing and **b**."
Eph	4:31	Put away from you all **b** and
Heb	12:15	that no root of **b** springs up
Rev	10: 9	it will be **b** to your stomach,

BLAMELESS

Gen	6: 9	Noah was a righteous man, **b**
1 Sam	29: 9	know that you are as **b** in my
2 Sam	22:24	I was **b** before him, and I kept
Job	2: 3	a **b** and upright man who
	9:22	he destroys both the **b** and the
Ps	18:23	I was **b** before him, and I kept
	119: 1	those whose way is **b**.
Prov	11:20	but those of **b** ways are his
Wis	4:9	and a **b** life is ripe old age.
	18:21	For a **b** man was quick to
Sir	11:10	you will not be held **b**.
Ezek	28:15	You were **b** in your ways from
Dan	6:22	because I was found **b** before
1 Cor	1: 8	so that you may be **b** on the
Eph	1: 4	to be holy and **b** before him
Phil	2:15	so that you may be **b** and
Col	1:22	to present you holy and **b** and
1 Thess	5:23	sound and **b** at the coming of
1 Tim	3:10	prove themselves **b**, let them
Titus	1: 6	someone who is **b**, married
Heb	7:26	such a high priest, holy, **b**,
Rev	14: 5	lie was found; they are **b**.

BLASPHEME (D) (S)

Lev	24:11	woman's son **b** the Name in a
	24:16	who **b** the name of the LORD
Ezek	20:27	In this again your ancestors **b**
Mt	26:65	said, "He has **b**! Why do we
Mk	3:29	against the Holy
Lk	12:10	whoever **b** against the Holy
Acts	26:11	tried to force them to **b**;
Rom	2:24	"The name of God is **b** among
1 Tim	6: 1	the teaching may not be **b**.
Jas	2: 7	they who **b** the excellent name
1 Pet	4: 4	of dissipation, and so they **b**.

BLASPHEMIES (BLASPHEMER)

Lev	24:16	congregation shall stone the **b**.
Neh	9:18	and had committed great **b**,
Mk	3:28	their sins and whatever **b** they
Lk	5:21	who is speaking **b**?
1 Tim	1:13	though I was formerly a **b**,
Rev	13: 6	mouth to utter **b** against God,

BLESS (ED)

Gen	1:22	God **b** them, saying, "Be
	22:17	I will indeed **b** you, and I will
Ex	20:11	the LORD **b** the sabbath day
	23:25	I will **b** your bread and your

Lev	9:22	the people and **b** them; and
Num	6:24	The Lord **b** you and keep you;
	22: 6	whomever you **b** is **b**, and
Deut	7:14	hall be the most **b** of peoples,
	28: 8	he will **b** you in the land that
Josh	8:33	should **b** the people of Israel.
Judg	13:24	boy grew, and the LORD **b** him.
Ruth	2: 4	They answered, "The LORD **b**
1 Sam	25:33	**B** be your good sense, and
2 Sam	7:29	you to **b** the house of your
1 Kings	1:48	on to pray thus, **B** be the
1 Chr	4:10	that you would **b** me and
2 Chr	31:10	for the Lord has **b** his people,
Neh	9: 5	**B** be your glorious name,
Tob	8:15	Let them **b** you forever
Job	42:12	The LORD **b** the latter days of
Ps	89:52	**B** be the LORD forever. Amen
	104: 1	**B** the LORD, O my soul
Prov	22: 9	Those who are generous are **b**,
Sir	39:35	and **b** the name of the Lord.
Isa	30:18	**b** are all those who wait
Jer	31:23	"The LORD **b** you, O abode of
Ezek	37:26	and I will **b** them and
Dan	2:20	Daniel said: "**B** be the name of
Mt	5: 3	**B** are the poor in spirit
Mk	6:41	**b** and broke the loaves,
Lk	1:42	"**B** are you among women,
	6:28	**b** those who curse you, pray
Jn	20:29	**B** are those who have not
Acts	3:26	to you, to **b** you by turning
	20:35	'It is more **b** to give than to
Rom	4: 7	**B** are those whose iniquities
1 Cor	4:12	When reviled, we **b**; when
Gal	3: 8	"All the Gentiles shall be **b** in
Eph	1: 3	**B** be the God and Father
Titus	2:13	while we wait for the **b** hope
Heb	6:14	"I will surely **b** you and
	7: 7	that the inferior is **b** by the
Jas	1:12	**B** is anyone who endures
1 Pet	3:14	what is right, you are **b**.
Rev	22: 7	**B** is the one who keeps

BLESSING (S)

Gen	12: 2	that you will be a **b**.
Ex	32:29	have brought a **b** on
Lev	25:21	I will order my **b** for you in
Deut	11:26	setting before you today a **b**
	28: 2	all these **b** shall come upon
Josh	8:34	the words of the law, **b** and
2 Sam	7:29	with your **b** shall the house of
1 Chr	23:13	and pronounce **b** in his name
Neh	13: 2	turned the curse into a **b**.
Ps	24: 5	They will receive **b** from the
	144:15	the people to whom such **b**
Prov	10:22	The **b** of the LORD makes rich
Isa	44: 3	and my **b** on your offspring.
Ezek	34:26	they shall be showers of **b**.
Joel	2:14	and leave a **b** behind him, a
Zech	8:13	you shall be a **b**. Do not be
Mal	2: 2	and I will curse your **b**;
	3:10	for you an overflowing **b**.
Mk	14:22	and after **b** it he broke it, gave
Lk	24:51	While he was **b** them, he
Rom	15:29	in the fullness of the **b** of
1 Cor	14:16	if you say a **b** with the spirit,
Gal	3:14	in Christ Jesus the **b** of
Eph	1: 3	with every spiritual **b** in the
Heb	12:17	he wanted to inherit the **b**, he
Jas	3:10	From the same mouth come **b**
1 Pet	3: 9	the contrary, repay with a **b**.

Rev	5:12	and honor and glory and **b**!"

BLIND (ED) (NESS)

Gen	19:11	And they struck with **b** the
Ex	4:11	mute or deaf, seeing or **b**?
Lev	19:14	block before the **b**;
Deut	27:18	be anyone who misleads a **b**
	28:28	you with madness, **b**, and
2 Sam	5: 8	attack the lame and the **b**,
2 Kings	6:18	this people, please, with **b**."
Tob	2:10	until I became completely **b**
Job	29:15	I was eyes to the **b**, and feet to
Ps	146: 8	opens the eyes of the **b**.
Isa	35: 5	Then the eyes of the **b** shall be
Zech	11:17	his right eye utterly **b**!
	12: 4	horse of the peoples with **b**.
Mal	1: 8	When you offer **b** animals in
Mt	11: 5	the **b** receive their sight, the
Mk	10:46	a **b** beggar, was sitting by the
Lk	6:39	"Can a **b** person guide a **b**
Jn	9:25	though I was **b**, now I see."
Rom	2:19	a guide to the **b**, a light to
2 Pet	1: 9	things is nearsighted and **b**,
1 Jn	2:11	darkness has brought on **b**.
Rev	3:17	are wretched, pitiable, poor, **b**,

BLOOD (SHED)

Gen	4:10	your brother's **b** is crying out
Ex	12:13	when I see the **b**, I will pass
Lev	17: 4	shall be held guilty of **b**;
Num	35:19	The avenger of **b** is the one
Deut	12:23	not eat the **b**; for the **b** is
1 Sam	14:32	troops ate them with the **b**.
1 Kings	21:19	will also lick up your **b**."
2 Kings	9:33	some of her **b** spattered on the
Ps	51:14	Deliver me from **b**, O God,
	72:14	precious is their **b** in his sight.
Prov	6:17	hands that shed innocent **b**,
Isa	5: 7	he expected justice, but saw **b**;
	34: 6	it is sated with **b**, it is gorged
Jer	48:10	keeps back the sword from **b**.
Ezek	33: 4	their **b** shall be upon their
Hos	4: 2	**b** follows **b**.
Joel	2:31	darkness, and the moon to **b**,
Hab	2: 8	because of human **b**, and
Zech	9:11	because of the **b** of my
Mt	27:24	innocent of this man's **b**;
Mk	14:24	"This is my **b** of the covenant,
Lk	22:20	the new covenant in my **b**.
Jn	1:13	who were born, not of **b** or of
Acts	18: 6	"Your **b** be on your own heads
Rom	3:25	of atonement by his **b**,
1 Cor	10:16	not a sharing in the **b** of
Eph	6:12	against enemies of **b** and flesh,
Col	1:20	making peace through the **b** of
Heb	9:22	without the shedding of **b**
	13:20	by the **b** of the eternal
1 Pet	1:19	but with the precious **b** of
1 Jn	5: 6	who came by water and **b**,
Rev	6:12	the full moon became like **b**,
	19:13	in a robe dipped in **b**,

BOAST (ING)

Ps	34: 2	My soul makes its **b** in the
Prov	27: 1	Do not **b** about tomorrow, for
Sir	25:6	and their **b** is the fear of the
Jer	9:24	but let those who **b** in this,
Rom	11:18	do not **b** over the branches.
1 Cor	1:31	"Let the one who **b**, in the

1 Cor	5: 6	Your **b** is not a good thing
2 Cor	11:30	If I must **b**, I will **b** of the
Gal	6:14	never **b** of anything except the
Eph	2: 9	so that no one may **b**.
Phil	2:16	that I can **b** on the day of
1 Thess	2:19	or crown of **b** before our Lord
Jas	1: 9	the believer who is lowly **b** in
	4:16	in your arrogance; all such **b** is

BOASTFUL

Ps	5: 5	The **b** will not stand before
Rom	1:30	haughty, **b**, inventors of evil,
1 Cor	13: 4	love is not envious or **b** or
Jas	3:14	do not be **b** and false to the

BODY (BODIES)

Num	14:29	your dead **b** shall fall in this
2 Sam	7:12	shall come forth from your **b**,
Ps	16: 9	my **b** also rests secure.
Prov	15:30	good news refreshes the **b**.
Isa	66:14	your **b** shall flourish like the
Ezek	1:23	had two wings covering its **b**.
Dan	3:27	any power over the **b** of those
Mic	6: 7	the fruit of my **b** for the sin of
Mt	6:22	is the lamp of the **b**. So, if
	27:52	and many **b** of the saints
Mk	14:22	said, "Take; this is my **b**."
Lk	12: 4	those who kill the **b**, and after
Jn	2:21	the temple of his **b**.
Rom	7:24	will rescue me from this **b** of
	12: 1	to present your **b** as a living
1 Cor	5: 3	For though absent in **b**, I am
	6:15	your **b** are members of Christ?
2 Cor	5: 8	rather be away from the **b** and
Gal	6:17	of Jesus branded on my **b**.
Eph	4: 4	There is one **b** and one Spirit,
Phil	3:21	transform the **b** of our
Col	2: 5	though I am absent in **b**, yet
1 Thess	4: 4	how to control your own **b**
Heb	10: 5	but a **b** you have prepared
	10:22	and our **b** washed with pure
Jas	2:26	just as the **b** without the
1 Pet	2:24	bore our sins in his **b** on the
2 Pet	1:13	as I am in this **b**, to refresh
Jude	1: 9	disputed about the **b** of Moses,
Rev	11: 8	their dead **b** will lie in the

BOLD (NESS)

Deut	31: 6	Be strong and **b**; have no fear
Prov	21:29	The wicked put on a **b** face,
	28: 1	the righteous are as **b** as a
Acts	4:29	speak your word with all **b**,
2 Cor	10: 1	but **b** toward you when I am
Eph	3:12	have access to God in **b** and
Phil	1:14	speak the word with greater **b**
Philem	1: 8	though I am **b** enough in
Heb	4:16	the throne of grace with **b**,
1 Jn	4:17	we may have **b** on the day of

BONE (S)

Gen	2:23	"This at last is **b** of my **b** and
	50:25	you shall carry up my **b** from
Ex	12:46	not break any of its **b**.
Josh	24:32	The **b** of Joseph, which the
2 Kings	13:21	as the man touched the **b** of
Ps	22:14	and all my **b** are out of joint;
Prov	25:15	a soft tongue can break **b**.
Sir	28:17	of the tongue crushes the **b**.
Jer	20: 9	fire shut up in my **b**;

Ezek	37: 4	O dry **b**, hear the word of the
	37: 7	**b** came together, **b** to its **b**.
Mt	23:27	they are full of the **b** of the
Jn	19:36	"None of his **b** shall be

BOOK (S)

Ex	24: 7	Then he took the **b** of the
Deut	29:20	the curses written in this **b** will
Josh	1: 8	This **b** of the law shall not
2 Kings	22: 8	"I have found the **b** of the law
Neh	8: 8	So they read from the **b**, from
Ps	69:28	out of the **b** of the living;
Eccl	12:12	Of making many **b** there is no
Isa	34:16	Seek and read from the **b** of
Dan	7:10	sat in judgment, and the **b**
	12: 1	is found written in the **b**.
Mk	12:26	you not read in the **b** of
Jn	20:30	are not written in this **b**.
	21:25	could not contain the **b** that
Phil	4: 3	names are in the **b** of life.
Heb	10: 7	(in the scroll of the **b** it is
Rev	3: 5	your name out of the **b** of life;
	20:12	before the throne, and **b** were

BORN

Gen	17:17	"Can a child be **b** to a man
Ex	1:22	"Every boy that is **b** to the
Job	14: 1	"A mortal, **b** of woman, few of
Prov	17:17	and kinsfolk are **b** to share
Eccl	3: 2	a time to be **b**, and a time to
Isa	9: 6	a child has been **b** for us, a
Jer	1: 5	before you were **b** I consecrated
Mt	1:16	Jesus was **b**, who is called the
Mk	14:21	one not to have been **b**."
Lk	2:11	to you is **b** this day in the city
Jn	3: 5	without being **b** of water
Rom	9:11	Even before they had been **b**
1 Cor	15: 8	as to one untimely **b**, he
Gal	4: 4	Son, **b** of a woman, **b** under
Phil	2: 7	being **b** in human likeness.
1 Pet	1:23	You have been **b** anew, not of
1 Jn	4: 7	who loves is **b** of God
Rev	12: 4	as soon as it was **b**.

BRANCH (ES)

Gen	40:10	the vine there were three **b**.
Num	13:23	cut down from there a **b** with
2 Sam	18: 9	mule went under the thick **b**
Sir	1:20	and her **b** are long life.
Isa	4: 2	On that day the **b** of the LORD
Jer	33:15	I will cause a righteous **B** to
Ezek	17: 6	Its **b** turned toward him, its
Dan	11: 7	a **b** from her roots shall rise
Zech	6:12	name is **B**: for he shall **b** out
Mal	4: 1	leave them neither root nor **b**.
Jn	15: 2	He removes every **b** in me that
Rom	11:21	did not spare the natural **b**,

BREAD

Gen	3:19	you shall eat **b** until you
Ex	16: 4	"I am going to rain **b** from
Lev	7:13	cakes of leavened **b**.
Deut	8: 3	one does not live by **b** alone,
Judg	7:13	a cake of barley **b** tumbled
1 Sam	21: 4	"I have no ordinary **b** at hand,
1 Kings	17: 6	ravens brought him **b** and
2 Chr	4:19	the tables for the **b** of the
Neh	9:15	you gave them **b** from heaven,
Ps	78:25	Mortals ate of the **b** of angels;
Prov	9:17	and **b** eaten in secret is

Eccl	11: 1	Send out your **b** upon the
Wis	16:20	from heaven with **b** ready to
Sir	15:3	will feed him with the **b** of
Isa	55: 2	that which is not **b**, and your
Ezek	18: 7	gives his **b** to the hungry and
Am	8:11	not a famine of **b**, or a thirst
Ob	1: 7	those who ate your **b** have set
Mt	6:11	Give us this day our daily **b**.
Mk	14:20	who is dipping **b** into the
Lk	4: 4	'One does not live by **b** alone.'
Jn	6:35	"I am the **b** of life. Whoever
Acts	2:42	to the breaking of **b** and the
1 Cor	11:26	often as you eat this **b** and

BREAK (ING) (BROKEN)

Gen	17:14	he has **b** my covenant."
Ex	12:46	shall not **b** any of its bones.
Lev	26:44	utterly and **b** my covenant
Num	30: 2	he shall not **b** his word; he
Deut	7: 5	deal with them: **b** down their
	31:20	despising me and **b** my
Judg	2: 1	will never **b** my covenant with
Ezra	9:14	shall we **b** your
Neh	1: 3	the wall of Jerusalem is **b**
Ps	2: 9	You shall **b** them with a rod of
	51:17	a **b** spirit; a **b** and contrite
Prov	18:14	endure sickness; but a **b** spirit
	25:15	and a soft tongue can **b** bones.
Eccl	3: 3	a time to **b** down, and a time
Sir	10:19	Those who **b** the
Isa	42: 3	bruised reed he will not **b**,
Ezek	16:59	the oath, **b** the covenant;
	44: 7	You have **b** my covenant with
Mt	12:20	He will not **b** a bruised reed
	14:20	left over of the **b** pieces, twelve
Lk	5: 6	their nets were beginning to **b**.
	20:18	on that stone will be **b** to
Jn	19:33	they did not **b** his legs.
Acts	2:42	to the **b** of bread and the
Rom	2:23	do you dishonor God by **b** the
1 Cor	10:16	The bread that we **b**, is it not a
Rev	5: 2	to open the scroll and **b** its

BREASTPLATE

1 Kings	22:34	the scale armor and the **b**;
Isa	59:17	put on righteousness like a **b**,
Eph	6:14	on the **b** of righteousness.
1 Thess	5: 8	and put on the **b** of faith and

BREATH

Gen	1:30	that has the **b** of life, I have
2 Sam	22:16	blast of the **b** of his nostrils.
Job	27: 3	as long as my **b** is in me
Ps	39:11	surely everyone is a mere **b**.
Eccl	12: 7	and the **b** returns to God who
Isa	40: 7	when the **b** of the LORD blows
Jer	10:14	and there is no **b** in them.
Lam	4:20	The LORD's anointed, the **b** of
Ezek	37: 9	"Prophesy to the **b**, prophesy,
Acts	17:25	to all mortals life and **b**
2 Thess	2: 8	Jesus will destroy with the **b** of
Rev	11:11	the **b** of life from God entered

BRIDE

Song	4: 8	me from Lebanon, my **b**;
Isa	62: 5	rejoices over the **b**,
Jer	2: 2	your love as a **b**, how you
Jn	3:29	He who has the **b** is the
Rev	21: 9	the **b**, the wife of the Lamb

BRIDEGROOM

Ex	4:25	"Truly you are a **b** of blood to
Ps	19: 5	comes out like a **b** from his
Jer	25:10	the voice of the **b** and the
Bar	2:23	the voice of the **b** and the
Mt	25: 1	and went to meet the **b**.
Mk	2:20	days will come when the **b** is
Jn	3:29	the **b**. The friend of the **b**
Rev	18:23	the voice of **b** and bride will

BRING (S) (ING)

Gen	6:19	you shall **b** two of every kind
Ex	36: 3	They still kept **b** him freewill
Lev	1: 2	When any of you **b** an offering
Num	14: 3	Why is the LORD **b** us into this
	20: 5	to **b** us to this wretched place
Deut	8: 7	your God is **b** you into a good
	24: 4	you shall not **b** guilt on the
1 Sam	2: 6	The LORD kills and **b** to life;
2 Sam	12:23	Can I **b** him back again?
1 Kings	21:21	I will **b** disaster on you;
Ps	25:17	and **b** me out of my distress
	34:21	Evil **b** death to the wicked,
Prov	18: 6	A fool's lips **b** strife, and a
	19: 4	Wealth **b** many friends, but
Eccl	12:14	For God will **b** every deed into
Isa	52: 7	announces peace, who **b** good
Jer	24: 6	I will **b** them back to this land
Dan	9:24	to **b** in everlasting
Mt	10:34	I have come to **b** peace to the
	12:35	The good person **b** good
Mk	15: 4	See how many charges they **b**
Lk	4:18	he has anointed me to **b** good
	11:26	goes and **b** seven other spirits
Jn	10:16	to this fold. I must **b** them
Rom	4:15	For the law **b** wrath; but where
	10:15	of those who **b** good news!"
1 Cor	8: 8	"Food will not **b** us close to
2 Cor	7:10	leads to salvation and **b** no
Titus	2:11	has appeared, **b** salvation to
Heb	1: 6	he **b** the firstborn into the
	2:10	in **b** many children to glory,
1 Pet	3:18	in order to **b** you to God.
2 Jn	1:10	and does not **b** this teaching;
Rev	21:24	kings of the earth will **b** their

BROKENHEARTED

Ps	34:18	LORD is near to the **b**, and
Isa	61: 1	to bind up the **b**, to proclaim

BROTHER (S)

Gen	4: 9	am I my **b** keeper?"
	27:29	Be lord over your **b**, and may
Deut	13: 6	even if it is your **b**, your
2 Sam	13:12	She answered him, "No, my **b**,
1 Macc	3:25	Judas and his **b** began to be
Ps	22:22	of your name to my **b** and
Song	8: 1	you were like a **b** to me, who
Wis	10:3	because in rage he killed his **b**.
Am	1:11	he pursued his **b** with the
Ob	1:10	violence done to your **b** Jacob,
Mal	1: 2	Is not Esau Jacob's **b**? says the
Mt	5:24	first be reconciled to your **b**
	12:49	are my mother and my **b**!
Mk	3:33	are my mother and my **b**?"
	3:35	will of God is my **b** and sister
Lk	22:32	back, strengthen your **b**."
Jn	7: 5	(For not even his **b** believed in
Rom	14:21	that makes your **b** or sister

1 Cor	5:11	bears the name of **b** or sister
2 Cor	11:26	from false **b** and sisters;
1 Tim	5: 1	father, to younger men as **b**,
Philem	1:16	than a slave, a beloved **b**—
Heb	2:11	ashamed to call them **b** and
Jas	2:15	If a **b** or sister is naked and
1 Jn	3:10	who do not love their **b** and
	3:17	and sees a **b** or sister in need

BUILD (S) (ER) (ERS) (BUILT)

Gen	8:20	Then Noah **b** an altar to the
	11: 4	"Come, let us **b** ourselves a
Ex	20:25	do not **b** it of hewn stones;
Deut	27: 5	And you shall **b** an altar there
Judg	6:24	Then Gideon **b** an altar there
1 Sam	7:17	and **b** there an altar to the
2 Sam	7: 5	Are you the one to **b** me a
1 Kings	6: 1	he began to **b** the house of the
Neh	7: 1	when the wall had been **b** and
Ps	118:22	The stone that the **b** rejected
	127: 1	Unless the LORD **b** the house,
Prov	24: 3	By wisdom a house is **b**,
Eccl	3: 3	and a time to **b** up;
Isa	5: 2	he **b** a watchtower in the
	62:10	**b** up, **b** up the highway
Jer	22:13	Woe to him who **b** his house
	31: 4	Again I will **b** you, and you
Dan	9:25	sixty-two weeks it shall be **b**
Mic	3:10	who **b** Zion with blood and
Zech	6:12	he shall **b** the temple of the
Mt	7:24	a wise man who **b** his house
	16:18	on this rock I will **b** my
Mk	12:10	The stone that the **b** rejected
	14:58	in three days I will **b** another,
Acts	20:32	message that is able to **b**
1 Cor	8: 1	puffs up, but love **b** up.
	14:17	the other person is not **b** up.
Eph	2:20	**b** upon the foundation of the
1 Thess	5:11	one another and **b** up each
Heb	3: 4	but the **b** of all things is God
Jude	1:20	But you, beloved, **b** yourselves
Rev	21:18	The wall is **b** of jasper, while

BUILDING

Josh	22:16	by **b** yourselves an altar today
1 Kings	6:12	this house that you are **b**,
Ezra	4: 1	exiles were **b** a temple to the
Neh	2:18	"Let us start **b**!" So they
Mic	7:11	A day for the **b** of your walls!
Lk	6:48	one is like a man **b** a house,
Rom	15: 2	good purpose of **b** up the
1 Cor	14:26	all things be done for **b** up.
2 Cor	10: 8	the Lord gave for **b** you up
Eph	4:12	for **b** up the body of Christ

BURDEN (S)

Gen	49:15	bowed his shoulder to the **b**,
Ex	18:22	and they will bear the **b** with
Num	11:11	you lay the **b** of all this people
Ps	55:22	Cast your **b** on the LORD,
Isa	10:27	On that day his **b** will be
Jer	23:33	"What is the **b** of the LORD?"
Mt	11:30	yoke is easy, and my **b** is
Lk	11:46	load people with **b** hard to
Acts	15:28	no further **b** than these
2 Cor	12:14	I will not be a **b**, because
2 Thess	3: 8	so that we might not **b** any of
Rev	2:24	lay on you any other **b**;

BURN (ED) (ING) (BURNT)

Gen	38:24	and let her be **b**."
Ex	3: 3	why the bush is not **b** up."
	32:10	my wrath may **b** hot against
Lev	6: 9	the altar shall be kept **b**.
	20:14	they shall be **b** to death,
Num	11: 3	the fire of the LORD **b** against
1 Sam	15:22	LORD as great delight in **b**
1 Kings	3: 4	offer a thousand **b** offerings
2 Kings	23:20	and **b** human bones on them.
2 Chr	36:19	They **b** the house of God,
Ezra	8:35	exiles, offered **b** offerings
Ps	89:46	long will your wrath **b** like
	140:10	Let **b** coals fall on them!
Prov	6:27	the bosom without **b** one's
Isa	1:11	had enough of **b** offerings of
Jer	6:20	Your **b** offerings are not
	36:29	You have dared to **b** this scroll,
Ezek	46:13	for a **b** offering to the LORD
Dan	7: 9	and its wheels were **b** fire.
Hos	6: 6	of God rather than **b** offerings.
Mal	4: 1	that comes shall **b** them up,
Mt	13:40	are collected and **b** up with
Mk	12:33	important than all whole **b**
Lk	3:17	he will **b** with unquenchable
	24:32	"Were not our hearts **b** within
Jn	15: 6	thrown into the fire, and **b**.
Acts	7:30	in the flame of a **b** bush.
Rom	12:20	you will heap **b** coals on their
1 Cor	3:15	If the work is **b** up, the builder
Heb	6: 8	its end is to be **b** over.
	10: 6	in **b** offerings and sin offerings
Rev	18: 8	she will be **b** with fire; for

C

CALL (ED) (ING)

Gen	3: 9	But the LORD God **c** to the
	22:11	the angel of the LORD **c** to him
Ex	3: 4	God **c** to him out of the
Deut	4:26	I **c** heaven and earth to witness
Ruth	1:20	"**C** me no longer Naomi, **c** me
1 Sam	3: 4	"I did not **c**; lie down again."
2 Sam	22: 4	I **c** upon the LORD, who is
1 Kings	18:24	Then you **c** on the name of
1 Chr	16: 8	**c** on his name, make known
2 Chr	7:14	if my people who are **c** by my
Ps	50:15	**C** on me in the day
	145:18	is near to all who **c** on him,
Prov	1:24	I have **c** and you refused,
	31:28	children rise up and **c** her
Sir	42:15	**c** to mind the works of the
Isa	43: 1	I have **c** you by name,
	55: 6	**c** upon him while he is
Jer	7:10	this house, which is **c** by my
	33: 3	**C** to me and I will
Lam	3:55	I **c** on your name, O LORD
Jon	1: 6	Get up, **c** on your god!
Zeph	3: 9	all of them may **c** on the name
Zech	13: 9	They will **c** on my name, and I
Mt	5: 9	they will be **c** children of God.
	27:47	"This man is **c** for Elijah."
Mk	10:18	"Why do you **c** me good?
	10:49	get up, he is **c** you."
Lk	6:46	"Why do you **c** me 'Lord,
	15:19	longer worthy to be **c** your

Jn	13:13	You **c** me Teacher and Lord—
Jn	15:15	I do not **c** you servants any
Acts	10:15	you must not **c** profane."
Rom	9:25	was not beloved I will **c**
	11:29	for the gifts and the **c** of God
1 Cor	1:26	Consider your own **c**, brothers
	7:24	condition you were **c**,
Gal	5:13	For you were **c** to freedom,
Eph	4: 1	worthy of the **c** to which you
Phil	3:14	the prize of the heavenly **c** of
Col	3:15	to which indeed you were **c** in
1 Thess	4: 7	For God did not **c** us to
2 Thess	2:14	For this purpose he **c** you
1 Tim	6:12	to which you were **c** and for
2 Tim	2:22	along with those who **c** on the
Heb	2:11	not ashamed to **c** them
Heb	9:15	those who are **c** may receive
Jas	2:23	and he was **c** the friend of
	5:14	They should **c** for the elders of
1 Pet	2: 9	him who **c** you out of
2 Pet	1:10	more eager to confirm your **c**
1 Jn	3: 1	that we should be **c** children
Rev	19:13	and his name is **c** The Word of

CAPTIVE (CAPTIVITY)

Gen	14:14	his nephew had been taken **c**,
Deut	28:41	for they shall go into **c**.
2 Kings	24:16	king of Babylon brought **c** to
2 Chr	6:38	in the land of their **c**, to which
Ezra	8:35	those who had come from **c**,
Neh	1: 2	those who had escaped the **c**,
Ps	106:46	by all who held them **c**.
Song	7: 5	a king is held in the tresses.
Isa	52: 2	rise up, O **c** Jerusalem;
Jer	13:17	flock has been taken **c**.
Acts	20:22	And now, as a **c** to the Spirit,
Rom	7:23	making me **c** to the law of sin
2 Cor	10: 5	every thought **c** to obey Christ.
Eph	4: 8	he made captivity itself a **c**;
Col	2: 8	that no one takes you **c**
2 Tim	2:26	the devil, having been held **c**
Rev	13:10	taken captive, into **c** you go;

CARE (S) (FUL) (CARING)

Gen	39:22	committed to Joseph's **c** all
Ex	19:12	'Be **c** not to go up the
Deut	6:12	take **c** that you do not forget
	15: 9	Be **c** that you do not entertain
Josh	23:11	Be very **c**, therefore, to love the
2 Kings	21: 8	if only they will be **c** to do
Ps	8: 4	that you **c** for them?
	94:19	When the **c** of my heart are
Sir	38:27	and they are **c** to finish their
Jer	30:17	"It is Zion; no one **c** for her!"
Mt	13:22	hears the word, but the **c** of
	25:36	was sick and you took **c** of me,
Lk	10:34	to an inn, and took **c** of him.
1 Cor	12:25	have the same **c** for one
Eph	5:15	Be **c** then how you live, not
	5:29	he nourishes and tenderly **c**
1 Thess	2: 7	like a nurse tenderly **c** for her
1 Tim	3: 5	how can he take **c** of God's
Titus	3: 8	believe in God may be **c** to
Heb	2: 6	mortals, that you **c** for them?
Jas	1:27	**c** for orphans and widows in
1 Pet	1:10	to be yours made **c** search and
	5: 7	because he **c** for you.

CAST

Gen	21:10	"**C** out this slave woman with

Ex	32: 4	in a mold, and **c** an image of a
Lev	16: 8	and Aaron shall **c** lots on the
Josh	18: 6	and I will **c** lots for you here
1 Sam	14:42	"**C** the lot between me and
1 Kings	7:15	He **c** two pillars of bronze.
2 Kings	17:16	made for themselves **c** images
Neh	10:34	We have also **c** lots among the
Ps	42: 5	Why are you **c** down, O my
	55:22	**C** your burden on the LORD
Prov	16:33	The lot is **c** into the lap,
Isa	38:17	for you have **c** all my sins
Jer	7:15	And I will **c** you out of my
Joel	3: 3	and **c** lots for my people,
Ob	1:11	entered his gates and **c** lots
Jon	1: 7	So they **c** lots, and the lot fell
Hab	2:18	a **c** image, a teacher of lies
Mt	12:27	If I **c** out demons by Beelzebul,
Mk	3:23	"How can Satan **c** out Satan?
Jn	19:24	and for my clothing they **c**
Acts	1:26	And they **c** lots for them,
1 Pet	5: 7	**C** all your anxiety on him
Rev	4:10	they **c** their crowns before the

CELEBRATE

Ex	12:14	You shall **c** it as a festival to
Lev	23: 4	you shall **c** at the time
Num	29:12	You shall **c** a festival to the
Deut	26:11	shall **c** with all the bounty that
Neh	12:27	to Jerusalem to **c** the
Ps	145: 7	They shall **c** the fame of your
Ezek	45:21	you shall **c** the festival of the
Nah	1:15	**C** your festivals, O Judah,
Lk	15:24	And they began to **c**.
1 Cor	5: 8	Therefore, let us **c** the festival,
Rev	11:10	will gloat over them and **c** and

CHAINS (CHAINED)

Ex	28:14	and two **c** of pure gold, twisted
1 Kings	6:21	then he drew **c** of gold across,
Lam	3: 7	he has put heavy **c** on me;
Mk	5: 4	restrained with shackles and **c**,
Acts	12: 7	And the **c** fell off his wrists.
Eph	6:20	I am an ambassador in **c**.
Col	4:18	Remember my **c**. Grace be
2 Tim	2: 9	to the point of being **c** like a
Heb	11:36	and flogging, and even **c** and
2 Pet	2: 4	committed them to **c** of
Jude	1: 6	kept in eternal **c** in deepest

CHANGE (D) (CHANGERS)

Gen	31: 7	has cheated me and **c** my
Ex	32:14	the LORD **c** his mind about the
Num	23:19	that he should **c** his mind.
1 Sam	15:29	Israel will not recant or **c** his
Ps	110: 4	sworn and will not **c** his mind,
Jer	2:11	Has a nation **c** its gods, even
Dan	4:16	Let his mind be **c** from that of
Jon	3: 9	God may relent and **c** his
Mal	3: 6	I the LORD do not **c**;
Mt	18: 3	unless you **c** and become like
Mk	11:15	the tables of the money **c** and
Lk	9:29	the appearance of his face **c**,
Jn	2:15	the coins of the money **c** and
1 Cor	15:51	but we will all be **c**,
Heb	1:12	like clothing they will be **c**.
Jas	1:17	variation or shadow due to **c**.

CHARGE

Gen	39: 4	and put him in **c** of all that he
Ex	23: 7	Keep far from a false **c**, and do

Num	4:16	Aaron the priest shall have **c**
Deut	23:19	You shall not **c** interest on
Job	34:13	Who gave him **c** over the earth
Ps	50:21	rebuke you, and lay the **c**
Mt	25:21	I will put you in **c** of many
Mk	15:26	The inscription of the **c**
Rom	8:33	Who will bring any **c** against
1 Cor	9:18	make the gospel free of **c**,
2 Cor	11: 7	news to you free of **c**?
Philem	1:18	anything, **c** that to my account.
1 Pet	5: 3	it over those in your **c**, but be

CHARIOT (S)

Gen	41:43	ride in the **c** of his second-in-
Ex	14:25	He clogged their **c** wheels so
Josh	11: 4	with very many horses and **c**
Judg	4:15	Sisera got down from his **c**
2 Sam	8: 4	David hamstrung all the **c**
1 Kings	7:33	wheels were made like a **c**
2 Kings	2:11	a **c** of fire and horses of
1 Chr	28:18	plan for the golden **c** of the
2 Chr	1:14	Solomon gathered together **c**
Ps	104: 3	you make the clouds your **c**,
Song	6:12	fancy set me in a **c** beside my
Sir	48:9	in a **c** with horses of fire.
Isa	36: 9	you rely on Egypt for **c** and for
Joel	2: 5	As with the rumbling of **c**,
Nah	2: 3	The metal on the **c** flashes on
Hag	2:22	and overthrow the **c** and their
Zech	6: 2	The first **c** had red horses, the
Acts	8:28	seated in his **c**, he was reading
Rev	9: 9	like the noise of many **c** with

CHEERFUL

Prov	17:22	A **c** heart is a good medicine
Sir	13:26	The sign of a happy heart is a **c**
Zech	8:19	and gladness, and **c** festivals
2 Cor	9: 7	for God loves a **c** giver.
Jas	5:13	Are any **c**? They should sing

CHIEF PRIEST

2 Kings	25:18	the guard took the **c** Seraiah,
2 Chr	24:11	the officer of the **c** would
Ezra	7: 5	Eleazar, son of the **c** Aaron—
Jer	52:24	the guard took the **c** Seraiah,

CHILD (REN)

Gen	3:16	in pain you shall bring forth **c**,
Ex	2: 3	she put the **c** in it and
	12:26	And when your **c** ask you,
Deut	6: 7	Recite them to your **c** and talk
Josh	4: 6	When your **c** ask in time to
Judg	11:34	She was his only **c**; he had no
Ruth	4:16	Then Naomi took the **c** and
1 Sam	1:27	For this **c** I prayed; and the
2 Sam	12:16	pleaded with God for the **c**;
1 Kings	3: 7	I am only a little **c**; I do not
Ezra	10:44	sent them away with their **c**.
Neh	13:24	and half of their **c** spoke the
Job	3:16	not buried like a stillborn **c**,
Ps	34:11	Come, O **c**, listen to me; I will
Prov	1: 8	Hear, my **c**, your father's
Eccl	6: 3	a stillborn **c** is better off than
Isa	9: 6	For a **c** has been born for us
Jer	31:15	Rachel is weeping for her **c**;
Ezek	18:20	A **c** shall not suffer for the
Hos	11: 1	When Israel was a **c**, I loved
Joel	1: 3	Tell your **c** of it, and let your
Zech	12:10	one mourns for an only **c**,
Mal	4: 6	hearts of parents to their **c** and

Mt	2:11	they saw the **c** with Mary his
	5: 9	they will be called **c** of God.
Mk	10:15	kingdom of God as a little **c**
	13:12	and **c** will rise against parents
Lk	1:80	The **c** grew and became
	18:16	"Let the little **c** come to me,
Jn	1:12	power to become **c** of God,
Acts	2:39	is for you, for your **c**, and
Rom	8:14	the Spirit of God are **c** of God.
1 Cor	13:11	I was a **c**, I spoke like a **c**
Gal	4: 7	but a **c**, and if a **c** then
Eph	5: 8	you are light. Live as **c** of
Phil	2:15	blameless and innocent, **c** of
Col	3:21	do not provoke your **c**,
1 Tim	3:12	and let them manage their **c**
Titus	1: 6	once, whose **c** are believers,
Heb	12: 6	and chastises every **c** whom he
1 Pet	1:14	Like obedient **c**, do not be
1 Jn	3: 8	commits sin is a **c** of the devil,
3 Jn	1: 4	to hear that my **c** are walking
Rev	12: 4	that he might devour her **c** as

CHOOSE (S) (CHOSE) (CHOSEN)

Gen	13:11	So Lot **c** for himself all the
	18:19	for I have **c** him, that he may
Num	17: 5	of the man whom I **c** shall
Deut	7: 6	your God has **c** you out of all
	30:19	blessings and curses. **C** life so
Josh	24:15	**c** this day whom you will
	24:22	you have the LORD, to serve
Judg	10:14	the gods whom you have **c**;
1 Sam	17:40	and **c** five smooth stones from
Neh	1: 9	I have **c** to establish my name.'
Ps	65: 4	those whom you **c** and bring
	119:30	I have **c** the way of faithfulness;
Prov	3:31	and do not **c** any of their ways;
Isa	7:15	to refuse the evil and **c** the
	42: 1	whom I uphold, my **c**, in
Ezek	20: 5	On the day when I **c** Israel, I
Zech	3: 2	The LORD who has **c** Jerusalem
Mt	11:27	anyone to whom the Son **c** to
	22:14	are called, but few are **c**."
Mk	13:20	of the elect, whom he **c**, he
Lk	6:13	he called his disciples and **c**
	10:22	to whom the Son **c** to reveal
Jn	3: 8	The wind blows where it **c**,
	15:16	You did not **c** me but I chose
Acts	9:15	an instrument whom I have **c**
Rom	9:18	has mercy on whomever he **c**,
	11: 5	time there is a remnant, **c** by
1 Cor	1:27	But God **c** what is foolish in
	12:11	just as the Spirit **c**.
Eph	1: 4	just as he **c** us in Christ
Col	3:12	As God's **c** ones, holy and
1 Thess	1: 4	by God, that he has **c** you,
2 Thess	2:13	because God **c** you as the first
Jas	2: 5	Has not God **c** the poor in the
1 Pet	2: 9	But you are a **c** race, a royal
Rev	17:14	with him are called and **c** and

CHRIST ('S)

Mk	1: 1	the good news of Jesus **C**, the
Jn	4:25	is coming" (who is called **C**).
Acts	3: 6	in the name of Jesus **C** of
Rom	5: 8	while we still were sinners **C**
	8:35	separate us from the love of **C**?
1 Cor	1:23	we proclaim **C** crucified, a
	9:21	God's law but am under **C**
	15:14	and if **C** has not been raised,
2 Cor	5:14	For the love of **C** urges us on,

2 Cor 10: 1 and gentleness of **C**—
Gal 3:28 all of you are one in **C** Jesus.
Eph 4:15 who is the head, into **C**,
5:23 wife just as **C** is the head of
Phil 1:21 living is **C** and dying is gain.
2: 5 in you that was in **C** Jesus,
Col 1:27 which is **C** in you, the hope of
3:15 let the peace of **C** rule in your
1 Thess 4:16 and the dead in **C** will rise
2 Thess 2: 1 coming of our Lord Jesus **C**
1 Tim 2: 5 God and humankind, **C** Jesus,
2 Tim 1: 1 was given to us in **C** Jesus
Titus 2:13 great God and Savior, Jesus **C**.
Philem 1:20 Refresh my heart in **C**.
Heb 5: 5 So also **C** did not glorify
13: 8 Jesus **C** is the same yesterday
1 Pet 3:18 For **C** also suffered for sins
4:13 you are sharing **C** sufferings,
1 Jn 2:22 denies that Jesus is the **C**?
5: 6 by water and blood, Jesus **C**,
2 Jn 1: 7 do not confess that Jesus **C** has
Jude 1: 4 only Master and Lord, Jesus **C**.
Rev 20: 4 and reigned with **C** a

CHRISTIAN (S)
Acts 11:26 disciples were first called "**C**."
26:28 me to become a **C**?"
1 Pet 4:16 of you suffers as a **C**, do not

CHURCH (ES)
Mt 16:18 rock I will build my **c**, and the
Acts 5:11 great fear seized the whole **c**
16: 5 So the **c** were strengthened in
Rom 16: 5 Greet also the **c** in their house.
1 Cor 11:18 you come together as a **c**,
14:34 should be silent in the **c**.
2 Cor 11: 8 I robbed other **c** by accepting
Gal 1:13 violently persecuting the **c** of
Eph 5:23 is the head of the **c**, the body
Phil 3: 6 a persecutor of the **c**; as to
Col 1:18 head of the body, the **c**; he is
1 Thess 2:14 imitators of the **c** of God in
2 Thess 1: 4 boast of you among the **c** of
1 Tim 3:15 the **c** of the living God,
Jas 5:14 for the elders of the **c** and have
3 Jn 1: 9 written something to the **c**;
Rev 1: 4 John to the seven **c** that are in
22:16 with this testimony for the **c**.

CIRCUMCISE (D)
Gen 17:11 You shall **c** the flesh
Deut 10:16 **C**, then, the foreskin of
Josh 5: 2 flint knives and **c** the Israelites
Jdt 14:10 he was **c**, and joined the house
Lk 1:59 eighth day they came to the **c**
Acts 21:21 not to **c** their children or
Rom 3:30 justify the **c** on the ground of
Col 3:11 and Jew, **c** and uncircumcised,

CIRCUMCISION
Ex 4:26 "A bridegroom of blood by **c**."
Acts 7: 8 covenant of **c**. And so
Rom 2:25 **C** indeed is of value if
1 Cor 7:19 **C** is nothing
Col 2:11 of the flesh in the **c** of Christ;

CLAY
Job 10: 9 you fashioned me like **c**; and
Wis 15:7 same **c** both the vessels that
Sir 33:13 Like **c** in the hand of the

Isa 45: 9 Does the **c** say to the one who
Jer 18: 4 **c** was spoiled in the potter's
Rom 9:21 potter no right over the **c**,
2 Tim 2:20 but also of wood and **c**,

CLEAN (CLEANSED) (CLEANSING)
Gen 7: 2 seven pairs of all **c** animals,
Lev 20:25 the unclean bird and the **c**;
Job 15:14 mortals, that they can be **c**?
Ps 51: 7 shall be **c**; wash me, and I
Prov 20: 9 "I have made my heart **c**;
Jer 4:14 wash your heart **c** of
Mk 1:40 you can make me **c**."
Jn 13:10 is entirely **c**. And you are **c**,
Rom 14:20 of God. Everything is indeed **c**,
Heb 10: 2 worshipers, **c** once for all,

CLOTHE (S) (CLOTHED) (CLOTHING)
Gen 37:29 the pit, he tore his **c**.
Lev 8: 7 **c** him with the robe,
1 Kings 21:27 he tore his **c** and put sackcloth
Neh 9:21 their **c** did not wear out and
Ps 22:18 and for my **c** they cast lots.
Prov 6:27 without burning one's **c**?
Jer 52:33 put aside his prison **c**, and
Mk 15:24 and divided his **c** among
Acts 10:30 suddenly a man in dazzling **c**
1 Tim 2: 9 and decently in suitable **c**,
Jas 2: 2 in fine **c** comes into your
Rev 3: 4 who have not soiled their **c**;

CLOUD (S)
Ex 13:21 them in a pillar of **c** by day,
1 Kings 18:45 black with **c** and wind; there
Job 38:37 the wisdom to number the **c**?
Ps 57:10 faithfulness extends to the **c**.
Prov 25:14 Like **c** and wind without rain
Joel 2: 2 a day of **c** and thick darkness!
Mt 24:30 of Man coming on the **c** of
1 Thess 4:17 up in the **c** together with them
Jude 1:12 waterless **c** carried along
Rev 1: 7 He is coming with the **c**;

COIN (S)
Mt 17:27 you will find a **c**; take that
Lk 15: 8 woman having ten silver **c**,
Jn 2:15 poured out the **c** of the money

COME (S) (COMING)
Ex 19:11 the LORD will **c** down upon
Deut 28:45 All these curses shall **c** upon
2 Sam 7:12 who shall **c** forth from your
Ps 96:13 for he is **c**, for he is **c** to
Prov 24:34 poverty will **c** upon you
Isa 1:18 **C** now, let us argue it
Jer 51:45 **C** out of her, my people
Hos 3: 5 they shall **c** in awe to the LORD
Mic 6: 6 what shall I **c** before the LORD,
Zech 10: 4 them shall **c** the cornerstone,
Lk 7:20 When the men had **c** to him,
Jn 6:37 and anyone who **c** to me I will
Acts 1:11 will **c** in the same way as
Gal 4: 4 the fullness of time had **c**,
Heb 12:22 you have **c** to Mount Zion
2 Pet 3: 9 but all to **c** to repentance.
Rev 4: 1 like a trumpet, said, "**C** up

COMFORT
Gen 37:35 daughters sought to **c** him;
1 Chr 7:22 his brothers came to **c** him.

Job 2:11 to go and console and **c** him.
Ps 71:21 and **c** me once again.
Eccl 4: 1 with no one to **c** them!
Jer 31:13 I will **c** them, and give
Lam 1: 9 with none to **c** her.
Acts 9:31 in the **c** of the Holy Spirit,
Col 4:11 they have been a **c** to me.
2 Thess 2:16 gave us eternal **c** and good ,

COMMAND (ED)
Gen 2:16 God **c** the man, "You may
Deut 12:32 everything that I **c** you;
Josh 1: 9 I hereby **c** you: Be strong
Ps 33: 9 he **c**, and it stood firm.
Eccl 8: 2 king's **c** because of your sacred
Isa 13: 3 have **c** my consecrated ones,
Dan 3:28 the king's **c** and yielded up
Mt 4: 3 **c** these stones to become
1 Cor 7:25 I have no **c** of the Lord, but I
1 Tim 6:17 are rich, **c** them not to be

COMMANDMENT (S)
Ex 34:28 of the covenant, the ten **c**.
Josh 22: 5 to keep his **c**, and to hold
1 Sam 12:14 rebel against the **c** of the LORD,
Tob 3: 4 and disobeyed your **c**.
Ps 119:98 Your **c** makes me wiser than my
Prov 2: 1 and treasure up my **c** within
Sir 15:15 choose, you can keep the **c**,
Jn 13:34 I give you a new **c**,
Gal 5:14 single **c**, "You shall love your
Heb 7:18 an earlier **c** because it was
2 Jn 1: 6 his **c**; this is the **c** just as
Rev 14:12 those who keep the **c** of God

COMMIT (S)
Ex 20:14 You shall not **c** adultery.
Lev 18:29 whoever **c** any of these
2 Kings 17:21 and made them **c** great sin.
Ps 22: 8 **C** your cause to the LORD
Prov 6:32 he who **c** adultery has no
Mt 5:27 'You shall not **c** adultery.'
1 Cor 6:18 Every sin that a person **c** is
Rev 2:22 and those who **c** adultery with

COMMON
Lev 10:10 between the holy and the **c**,
2 Chr 9:27 as **c** in Jerusalem as stone,
Prov 22: 2 the poor have this in **c**:
Ezek 22:26 between the holy and the **c**,
Acts 2:44 and had all things in **c**;
1 Cor 12: 7 of the Spirit for the **c** good.

COMPASSION
Deut 13: 8 Show them no pity or **c**
Judg 21:15 The people had **c** on Benjamin
1 Sam 23:21 the LORD for showing me **c**!
Tob 8:17 you had **c** on two only
1 Macc 3:44 pray and ask for mercy and **c**.
2 Macc 7:6 he will have **c** on his
Ps 77: 9 in anger shut up his **c**?"
Wis 10:5 him strong in the face of his **c**
Sir 18:14 **c** on those who accept his
Isa 49:13 and will have **c** on his
Jer 21: 7 or spare them, or have **c**.
Mic 7:19 He will again have **c** upon us;
Mk 6:34 and he had **c** for them,
Rom 9:15 I will have **c** on whom I have **c**
Col 3:12 clothe yourselves with **c**,

CONCEIT (ED)
Job	37:24	are wise in their own **c**."
Phil	2: 3	from selfish ambition or **c**,
2 Tim	3: 4	swollen with **c**, lovers of

CONDEMN (ATION) (ED)
Job	9:20	my own mouth would **c** me;
Ps	94:21	and **c** the innocent to death.
Prov	19:29	**C** is ready for scoffers,
Jn	8:11	"Neither do I **c** you. Go your
Acts	26:10	they were being **c** to death.
Rom	2:27	but keep the law will **c** you
1 Cor	11:34	will not be for your **c**.
1 Jn	3:20	whenever our hearts **c** us;
Jude	1: 9	dare to bring a **c** of slander

CONDUCT
Tob	4:14	yourself in all your **c**.
Ps	112: 5	who **c** their affairs with justice.
Prov	21: 8	but the **c** of the pure is right
Eccl	8:14	to the **c** of the wicked, and
Sir	11:26	according to their **c**.
Rom	13: 3	not a terror to good **c**,
1 Pet	3: 1	a word by their wives' **c**,

CONFESS (ES)
Lev	5: 5	you shall **c** the sin that you
1 Kings	8:33	**c** your name, pray and plead
Ps	38:18	I **c** my iniquity; I am sorry
Jn	12:42	they did not **c** it, for fear
Rom	10: 9	you **c** with your lips that Jesus
Phil	2:11	every tongue should **c** that
Jas	5:16	**c** your sins to one another
1 Jn	4:15	in those who **c** that Jesus
Rev	3: 5	I will **c** your name before my

CONFIDENCE (CONFIDENT)
Judg	9:26	of Shechem put **c** in him.
2 Kings	18:19	you base this **c** of yours?
Job	4: 6	fear of God your **c**, and the
Sir	5:5	not be so **c** of forgiveness
	27:16	betrays secrets destroys **c**,
Ps	118: 8	than to put **c** in mortals.
Prov	11:13	trustworthy in spirit keeps a **c**.
Mic	7: 5	have no **c** in a loved one;
2 Cor	3: 4	the **c** that we have through
Eph	3:12	in boldness and **c** through
Heb	3: 6	hold firm the **c** and the pride
1 Jn	2:28	we may have **c** and not be

CONQUER (ED)
Jn	16:33	I have **c** the world!"
Heb	11:33	through faith **c** kingdoms,
1 Jn	2:13	because you have **c** the evil
Rev	12:11	they have **c** him by the

CONSCIENCE
1 Sam	25:31	or pangs of **c**, for having shed
Wis	17:11	distressed by **c**, it has always
Acts	24:16	have a clear **c** toward God
Rom	2:15	to which their own **c** also
1 Cor	10:28	and for the sake of **c**—
1 Tim	3: 9	the faith with a clear **c**.
Heb	10:22	clean from an evil **c** and our
1 Pet	3:16	Keep your **c** clear,

CONSECRATE (D)
Ex	13: 2	**C** to me all the firstborn
Lev	8:15	Thus he **c** it, to make
1 Kings	9: 3	I have **c** this house that you

Neh	3: 1	Sheep Gate. They **c** it and set
Jer	1: 5	you were born I **c** you; I

CONSIDER (ED)
Ex	33:13	**C** too that this nation is
Deut	32: 7	**c** the years long past; ask
1 Sam	12:24	for **c** what great things he has
Ps	13: 3	**C** and answer me, O LORD
Prov	6: 6	**c** its ways, and be wise
Eccl	7:13	**C** the work of God;
Dan	11:36	and **c** himself greater than
Lk	12:27	**C** the lilies, how they grow
Rom	6:11	must **c** yourselves dead to sin
Heb	10:24	let us **c** how to provoke
1 Pet	4:16	do not **c** it a disgrace,

CONSUME (D) (CONSUMING)
Lev	9:24	and **c** the burnt offering and
2 Chr	7: 1	and **c** the burnt offering
Ps	69: 9	house that has **c** me; the
Lam	4:11	that **c** its foundations.
Rom	1:27	were **c** with passion for one
Rev	20: 9	down from heaven and **c**

CONTEMPT
Gen	16: 4	looked with **c** on her mistress.
1 Sam	2:17	offerings of the LORD with **c**.
1 Macc	1:39	reproach, her honor into **c**.
Ps	107:40	he pours **c** on princes
Dan	12: 2	shame and everlasting **c**.
Mk	9:12	and be treated with **c**?
1 Cor	11:22	you show **c** for the church
Heb	6: 6	are holding him up to **c**.

CONTRITE
Ps	51:17	a broken and **c** heart,
Isa	57:15	those who are **c** and humble

CONVINCE (D) (CONVINCING)
Lk	16:31	will they be **c** even if someone
Acts	18: 4	try to **c** Jews and Greeks.
Rom	14: 5	fully **c** in their own minds.
Phil	1:25	I am **c** of this, I know that

CORNERSTONE
Job	38: 6	or who laid its **c**
Isa	28:16	a precious **c**, a sure foundation:
Mt	21:42	has become the **c**;
Eph	2:20	Christ Jesus himself as the **c**.

CORRUPT (ION)
Gen	6:11	Now the earth was **c**
Ps	14: 1	They are **c**, they
Dan	6: 4	and no negligence or **c** could
Acts	2:40	from this **c** generation."
Eph	4:22	your old self, **c** and deluded

COUNSEL (OR) (ORS)
2 Sam	15:34	will defeat for me the **c**
Job	38: 2	darkens **c** by words without
Ps	33:11	The **c** of the LORD stands
Prov	15:22	Without **c**, plans go wrong,
Sir	37:7	All **c** praise the **c** they
Isa	11: 2	the spirit of **c** and might,
Rom	11:34	Or who has been his **c**?"
Rev	3:18	Therefore I **c** you to buy

COURAGE
Josh	2:11	and there was no **c** left in any
2 Sam	7:27	servant has found **c** to pray

---

2 Chr	15: 7	take **c**! Do not let your hands
Ezra	7:28	I took **c**, for the hand of the
Tob	5:10	young man said, "Take **c**;
Ps	107:26	**c** melted away in their
Hag	2: 4	take **c**, O Zerubbabel,
Jn	16:33	But take **c**; I have conquered
Acts	23:11	"Keep up your **c**! For just as

COVENANT (S)
Gen	6:18	establish my **c** with you;
Deut	4:13	He declared to you his **c**,
Josh	3: 6	up the ark of the **c**,
1 Sam	20:16	Jonathan made a **c** with
Ezra	10: 3	let us make a **c** with our
Job	31: 1	"I have made a **c** with my eyes;
Ps	78:37	were not true to his **c**.
Jer	11: 2	Hear the words of this **c**,
Mal	2: 4	that my **c** with Levi may hold,
Mt	26:28	is my blood of the **c**,
Acts	7: 8	him the **c** of circumcision.
1 Cor	11:25	cup is the new **c** in my blood.
Heb	7:22	the guarantee of a better **c**.
Rev	11:19	ark of his **c** was seen

COVET
Ex	20:17	not **c** your neighbor's house;
Prov	21:26	the wicked **c**, but the righteous
Rom	13: 9	You shall not **c**";
Jas	4: 2	And you **c** something and

CREATE (D)
Gen	1: 1	when God **c** the heavens and
Jdt	13:18	who **c** the heavens and the
Ps	148: 5	commanded and they were **c**.
Prov	8:22	The LORD **c** me at the
Wis	2:23	for God **c** us for incorruption
Sir	33:10	humankind was **c** out of the
Jer	31:22	For the LORD has **c** a new
Mk	13:19	creation that God **c** until now,
Eph	4:24	**c** according to the likeness
Heb	12:27	**c** things—so that what cannot
Rev	10: 6	who **c** heaven and what is in

CREATION
Gen	2: 3	that he had done in **c**.
Tob	8:5	and the whole **c** bless you
Jdt	9:12	King of all your **c**.
Sir	16:17	for what am I in a boundless **c**?
Mk	10: 6	from the beginning of **c**,
Rom	1:20	Ever since the **c** of the world
2 Cor	5:17	there is a new **c**: everything
2 Pet	3: 4	from the beginning of **c**!"

CREATOR
2 Macc	13:14	the decision to the **C** of
Eccl	12: 1	Remember your **c** in the days
Sir	24:8	my **C** chose the place for my
Isa	40:28	everlasting God, the **C** of the
Col	3:10	to the image of its **c**.

CREATURE (S)
Gen	2:19	the man called every living **c**,
Rom	1:25	the **c** rather than the Creator,
Jas	1:18	of first fruits of his **c**.
Rev	5:13	I heard every **c** in heaven

CROOKED
Deut	32: 5	a perverse and **c** generation.
Ps	125: 5	turn aside to their own **c** ways
Prov	17:20	The **c** of mind do not prosper

Eccl 7:13 straight what he has made **c**?
Lam 3:9 he has made my paths **c**.
Acts 13:10 will you not stop making **c**
Phil 2:15 of a **c** and perverse generation,

CRY (CRIED)
Ex 2:23 slavery their **c** for help
Josh 24:7 When they **c** out to the LORD,
1 Macc 4:10 Let us **c** to Heaven.
Ps 130:1 Out of the depths I **c** to you,
Prov 21:13 you will **c** out and not be
Jer 14:12 I do not hear their **c**,
Hos 7:14 They do not **c** to me
Mk 15:37 Then Jesus gave a loud **c**
Rom 8:15 When we **c**, "Abba! Father!"
1 Thess 4:16 with a **c** of command,

CROSS
Num 32:5 do not make us **c** the Jordan."
Mt 10:38 does not take up the **c**
Lk 14:27 not carry the **c** and follow me
Gal 6:14 boast of anything except the **c**
Heb 12:2 endured the **c**, disregarding its
1 Pet 2:24 on the **c**, so that, free from sins

CROWN (ED)
Lev 8:9 holy **c**, as the LORD
Job 31:36 it on me like a **c**;
Ps 8:5 and **c** them with glory and
Prov 14:18 clever are **c** with knowledge.
Song 3:11 **c** with which his mother **c** him
Mt 27:29 twisting some thorns into a **c**,
1 Thess 2:19 hope or joy or **c** of boasting
Jas 1:12 receive the **c** of life that
Rev 12:1 on her head a **c** of twelve stars.

CRUCIFY (CRUCIFIED)
Lk 24:7 and be **c**, and on the third day
Acts 2:36 this Jesus whom you **c**."
Rom 6:6 old self was **c** with him so
Gal 5:24 Christ Jesus have **c** the flesh
Rev 11:8 where also their Lord was **c**.

CRUSH (ED)
Num 24:17 it shall **c** the borderlands of
Job 6:9 would please God to **c** me,
Ps 89:23 I will **c** his foes before him
Isa 53:5 transgressions, **c** for our
Mt 21:44 and it will **c** anyone on whom
Rom 16:20 will shortly **c** Satan under your
2 Cor 4:8 but not **c**; perplexed,

CRY (ING) (CRIED)
Ex 2:23 the slavery their **c** for help
Judg 10:14 Go and **c** to the gods whom
1 Kings 18:27 "**C** aloud! Surely he is a
Ps 130:1 Out of the depths I **c** to you,
Prov 21:13 your ear to the **c** of the poor,
Lam 2:18 **C** aloud to the Lord!
Mk 15:37 Jesus gave a loud **c** and
Rom 8:15 When we **c**, "Abba! Father!"
1 Thess 4:16 Lord himself, with a **c** of
Jas 5:4 **c** out, and the cries of

CUP
Gen 40:11 **c** was in my hand;
2 Sam 12:3 and drink from his **c**, and
Ps 23:5 my head with oil; my **c**
Prov 23:31 sparkles in the **c** and goes
Jer 25:15 my hand this **c** of the wine

Lam 4:21 you also the **c** shall pass;
Ezek 23:31 I will give her **c** into your
Mk 14:36 remove this **c** from me; yet,
1 Cor 11:27 drinks the **c** of the Lord
Rev 16:19 the wine-**c** of the fury of his

CURE (D)
2 Kings 5:3 He would **c** him of his
Tob 12:3 to you safely, he **c** my wife,
Hos 5:13 he is not able to **c** you
Mt 8:7 him, "I will come and **c** him."
Acts 28:9 also came and were **c**.

CURSE
Num 22:6 **c** this people for me,
Josh 24:9 Balaam son of Beor to **c** you,
2 Sam 16:9 "Why should this dead dog **c**
Job 2:9 integrity? **C** God, and die."
Ps 109:28 Let them **c**, but you will bless.
Prov 30:11 those who **c** their fathers
Jer 23:10 because of the **c** the land
Mt 26:74 Then he began to **c**, and
Gal 3:10 the law are under a **c**;
Jas 3:9 and with it we **c** those who

D

DANCE (S)
Judg 21:21 Shiloh come out to **d** in the **d**,
Ps 150:4 him with tambourine and **d**;
Jer 31:4 in the **d** of the merrymakers.
Mt 11:17 and you did not **d**; we wailed,

DARK (NESS)
Gen 1:2 a formless void and **d** covered
Ex 10:21 there may be **d** over the land
Josh 24:7 **d** between you and the
Tob 5:10 but I lie in **d** like the dead
Job 12:22 out of **d**, and brings deep **d**
Ps 139:12 even the **d** is not **d** to you;
Prov 4:19 the wicked is like deep **d**
Eccl 2:13 excels folly as light excels **d**.
Isa 5:20 who put **d** for light
Joel 2:31 sun shall be turned to **d**,
Jn 1:5 The light shines in the **d**,
Acts 2:20 to **d** and the moon to blood
Rom 2:19 to those who are in **d**,
Eph 5:8 For once you were **d**, but now
Heb 12:18 a blazing fire, and **d**, and
1 Jn 1:5 in him there is no **d** at all.
Rev 16:10 kingdom was plunged into **d**;

DAUGHTER
Ex 2:5 The **d** of Pharaoh came
Judg 11:34 and there was his **d** coming
Ruth 2:2 said to her, "Go, my **d**."
2 Sam 6:16 the city of David, Michal **d** of
Jdt 10:12 replied, "I am a **d** of the
Esth 2:7 adopted her as his own **d**.
Ps 9:14 in the gates of **d** Zion,
Isa 62:11 Say to **d** Zion, "See, your
Zech 9:9 Rejoice greatly, O **d** Zion!
Mk 7:29 —the demon has left your **d**."
Heb 11:24 be called a son of Pharaoh's **d**,

DAY (S)
Ex 34:28 the LORD forty **d** and forty

Num 14:34 forty **d**, for every day a year
Judg 17:6 In those **d** there was no
1 Kings 19:8 food forty **d** and forty nights
Ps 21:4 length of **d** forever and ever.
Prov 31:12 all the **d** of her life.
Eccl 12:1 before the **d** of trouble come,
Dan 12:12 three hundred thirty-five **d**.
Lk 4:2 where for forty **d** he was
Acts 2:17 'In the last **d** it will be,
2 Tim 3:1 that in the last **d** distressing
2 Pet 3:3 that in the last **d** scoffers will
Rev 12:6 thousand two hundred sixty **d**.
Tob 12:18 Bless him each and every **d**;
Sir 5:8 you on the **d** of calamity

DEAD
Ex 12:30 a house without someone **d**.
Ruth 4:5 the widow of the **d** man,
Ps 115:17 The **d** do not praise the LORD
Eccl 9:4 dog is better than a **d** lion.
Isa 26:19 give birth to those long **d**
Jn 20:9 he must rise from the **d**.
Eph 5:14 Rise from the **d**, and Christ
2 Tim 4:1 judge the living and the **d**,
Jas 2:26 body without the spirit is **d**,
Rev 14:13 Blessed are the **d** who from

DECEIT
Deut 32:4 A faithful God, without **d**,
Job 27:4 my tongue will not utter **d**.
Ps 101:7 No one who practices **d** shall
Dan 8:25 he shall make **d** prosper under
Mk 7:22 wickedness, **d**, licentiousness,
Rom 1:29 Full of envy, murder, strife, **d**,
1 Pet 2:22 no **d** was found in his mouth

DECEIVE (S)
Josh 9:22 "Why did you **d** us, saying,
Job 13:9 you **d** him, as one person **d**
Jer 37:9 Do not **d** yourselves,
Zech 13:4 hairy mantle in order to **d**,
1 Cor 3:18 Do not **d** yourselves.
Col 2:4 so that no one may **d** you
1 Jn 3:7 let no one **d** you. Everyone
Rev 20:8 and will come out to **d** the

DECLARE
Deut 5:5 you to **d** to you the words of
1 Chr 16:24 **D** his glory among the nations
Job 38:18 **D**, if you know all this
Ps 50:6 heavens **d** his righteousness,
Sir 16:25 and knowledge accurately
Isa 66:19 and they shall **d** my glory
Jn 16:14 what is mine and **d** it to you.
Col 4:3 may **d** the mystery of Christ,
1 Jn 1:3 we **d** to you what we have

DEDICATED
Num 18:6 as a gift, **d** to the LORD,
1 Kings 7:51 that his father David had **d**,
Lk 21:5 stones and gifts **d** to God,

DEED (S)
Deut 3:24 earth can perform **d** and
Ezra 9:13 for our evil **d** and for
Ps 66:3 "How awesome are your **d**!
Eccl 1:14 I saw all the **d** that
Sir 16:12 a person according to one's **d**.
Isa 63:7 recount the gracious **d** of the
Hos 5:4 Their **d** do not permit them

Mt	13:58	he did not do many **d** of
Lk	10:13	For if the **d** of power
Acts	26:20	turn to God and do **d**
Rom	8:13	you put to death the **d** of the
Col	1:21	hostile in mind, doing evil **d**,
Titus	2:14	who are zealous for good **d**.
1 Pet	2:12	see your honorable **d**
Rev	18: 6	repay her double for her **d**;

DELIGHT

Gen	3: 6	that it was a **d** to the eyes,
1 Sam	15:22	Has the LORD as great **d** in
Job	27:10	Will they take **d** in the
Ps	147:10	His **d** is not in the strength
Prov	2:14	in doing evil and **d** in the
Sir	1:27	fidelity and humility are his **d**.
Isa	1:11	I do not **d** in the blood of
Jer	9:24	for in these things I **d**,
Ezek	24:16	from you the **d** of your eyes;
Mk	12:37	was listening to him with **d**.

DELIVER

Ex	3: 8	to **d** them from the Egyptians,
Deut	32:39	no one can **d** from my hand.
Ps	109:21	steadfast love is good, **d** me.
Eccl	8: 8	nor does wickedness **d** those
Isa	50: 2	have I no power to **d**?
Dan	3:17	is able to **d** us from the
Mt	27:43	let God **d** him now,

DELIVERANCE

Ex	14:13	and see the **d** that the LORD
Ps	53: 6	O that for Israel would
	72: 4	give **d** to the needy,
Jon	2: 9	**D** belongs to the LORD!"

DEMON (S)

Deut	32:17	They sacrificed to **d**, not God,
Ps	106:37	and their daughters to the **d**;
Mt	7:22	and cast out **d** in your name,
Mk	16:17	name they will cast out **d**;
Lk	4:33	the spirit of an unclean **d**,
Jn	10:21	has a **d**. Can a **d** open
1 Cor	10:20	sacrifice to **d** and not to God.
Jas	2:19	Even the **d** believe—and
Rev	18: 2	become a dwelling place of **d**,

DENY (DENIES)

Lev	16:29	you shall **d** yourselves, and
Num	29: 7	and **d** yourselves; you shall do
Sir	14:4	What he **d** himself he collects
Mt	16:24	let them **d** themselves and
Lk	12: 9	but whoever **d** me before
Acts	4:16	we cannot **d** it.
2 Tim	2:13	for he cannot **d** himself.
2 Pet	2: 1	They will even **d** the Master
Jude	1: 4	licentiousness and **d** our only

DESCENDANTS

Gen	9: 9	with you and your **d** after you,
Ex	28:43	for him and for his **d** after
2 Sam	22:51	to David and his **d** forever.
Ps	112: 2	Their **d** will be mighty in the
Isa	44: 3	pour my spirit upon your **d**,
Lk	1:55	Abraham and to his **d**
Rom	9: 7	children are his true **d**;
Gal	3: 7	believe are the **d** of Abraham.

DESCENDED

Ex	19:18	the LORD had **d** upon it in fire;
Lk	3:22	Holy Spirit **d** upon him in
Rom	1: 3	who was **d** from David
Heb	7:14	our Lord was **d** from Judah,

DESIRE (D) (S)

Gen	3:16	**d** shall be for your husband
Deut	5:21	Neither shall you **d** your
2 Sam	19:38	and all that you **d** of me I will
Job	13: 3	and I **d** to argue my case with
Ps	73:25	nothing on earth that I **d**
Prov	3:15	nothing you **d** can compare
Eccl	12: 5	drags itself along and **d** fails;
Isa	53: 2	appearance that we should **d**
Hos	6: 6	For I **d** steadfast love and not
Mal	2:15	what does the one God **d**?
Mt	9:13	I **d** mercy, not sacrifice.
Rom	10: 1	my heart's **d** and prayer to
2 Cor	8:10	even to **d** to do something—
Heb	11:16	they **d** a better country, that is
Jas	1:14	tempted by one's own **d**,
1 Jn	2:16	the **d** of the flesh, the **d**

DESPISE (D)

Num	14:11	long will this people **d** me?
Job	5:17	do not **d** the discipline
Ps	102:17	and will not **d** their prayer.
Prov	1: 7	fools **d** wisdom and
Mt	6:24	devoted to the one and **d** the
Rom	2: 4	Or do you **d** the riches of his
2 Pet	2:10	who **d** authority.

DESTROY (ED) (ING) (S)

Gen	6:13	I am going to **d** them along
Deut	6:15	you and he would **d** you from
1 Sam	15: 9	would not utterly **d** them;
Esth	3: 6	Haman plotted to **d** all the
1 Macc	3: 8	he **d** the ungodly out of the
Ps	145:20	all the wicked he will **d**.
Isa	11: 9	They will not hurt or **d** on all
Jer	1:10	to **d** and to overthrow,
Lk	4:34	Have you come to **d** us?
Jn	10:10	to steal and kill and **d**.
1 Cor	3:17	anyone **d** God's temple,
Jas	4:12	able to save and to **d**.
Rev	11:18	for **d** those who **d** the earth."

DESTRUCTION

Josh	6:17	devoted to the LORD for **d**.
Ps	107:20	and delivered them from **d**.
Prov	16:18	Pride goes before **d**, and a
Sir	36:11	harm your people meet **d**.
Isa	14:23	it with the broom of **d**,
Hos	13:14	O Sheol, where is your **d**?
Hab	2:17	the **d** of the animals will
Mt	7:13	is easy that leads to **d**,
1 Cor	5: 5	to Satan for the **d** of the flesh,
1 Thess	5: 3	then sudden **d** will come
2 Pet	2: 1	bringing swift **d** on themselves.
Rev	17:11	and it goes to **d**.

DEVIL

Mt	4:11	Then the **d** left him,
Lk	8:12	then the **d** comes and takes
Jn	13: 2	The **d** had already put it into
Acts	13:10	"You son of the **d**, you enemy
Eph	6:11	against the wiles of the **d**.
1 Tim	3: 7	and the snare of the **d**.
Jas	4: 7	Resist the **d**, and he

1 Pet	5: 8	adversary the **d** prowls
1 Jn	3:10	children of the **d** are revealed
Rev	20: 2	who is the **D** and Satan,

DIE (D) (DEAD)

Gen	2:17	eat of it you shall **d**."
Ex	14:11	away to **d** in the wilderness?
Num	23:10	the death of the upright
Tob	3: 6	For it is better for me to **d**
Job	14:14	If mortals **d**, will they live
Ps	118:17	I shall not **d**, but I shall live,
Prov	5:23	They **d** for lack of discipline,
Eccl	3: 2	and a time to **d**; a time to
Sir	40:28	it is better to **d** than to beg.
Isa	66:24	look at the **d** bodies of the
Ezek	3:18	"You shall surely **d**," and you
Jon	4: 8	and asked that he might **d**.
Jn	6:50	eat of it and not **d**.
Rom	5: 7	rarely will anyone **d** for a
1 Cor	15:22	for as all **d** in Adam,
Heb	9:27	appointed for mortals to **d**
Rev	14:13	from now on **d** in the Lord.

DISCIPLE (S)

Isa	8:16	seal the teaching among my **d**.
Mt	26:56	Then all the **d** deserted him
Mk	3: 7	Jesus departed with his **d** to
Lk	6:13	he called his **d** and chose
Jn	2:11	and his **d** believed
Acts	14:20	But when the **d** surrounded

DISCIPLINE

Deut	4:36	you hear his voice to **d** you.
1 Kings	12:11	will **d** you with scorpions.'
Job	5:17	despise the **d** of the Almighty.
Ps	6: 1	or **d** me in your wrath.
Prov	3:11	do not despise the LORD's **d**
Sir	6:18	from your youth choose **d**.
Jer	31:18	I took the **d**; I was like a calf
Eph	6: 4	in the **d** and instruction
Heb	12:11	**d** always seems painful rather
1 Pet	5: 8	**D** yourselves, keep alert.

DISEASE (S)

Ex	15:26	any of the **d** that I brought
Deut	28:60	you all the **d** of Egypt,
2 Chr	16:12	and his **d** became severe;
Ps	103: 3	who heals all your **d**,
Isa	53: 4	carried our **d**;
Mt	10: 1	and to cure every **d** and every
Mk	1:34	who were sick with various **d**,
Lk	6:18	to be healed of their **d**;
Acts	28: 9	**d** also came and were cured

DISHONEST

Ex	18:21	trustworthy, and hate **d** gain;
Sir	5:8	Do not depend on **d** wealth.
Ezek	22:27	destroying lives to get **d** gain.
Mic	6:11	and a bag of **d** weights?
Lk	16:10	little is **d** also in much.

DISOBEY (DISOBEDIENT)

Lev	26:27	despite this, you **d** me, and
Esth	3: 3	"Why do you **d** the king's
Rom	11:31	have now been **d** in order
Eph	5: 6	comes on those who are **d**.
1 Tim	1: 9	but for the lawless and **d**,
Titus	3: 3	were once foolish, **d**,
Heb	3:18	not to those who were **d**?

DISTRESS (ED)

Deut	4:30	In your **d**, when all these
Judg	2:15	and they were in great **d**.
2 Sam	22:7	In my **d** I called upon the
Ps	119:50	is my comfort in my **d**,
Prov	1:27	when **d** and anguish come
Sir	2:11	and saves in time of **d**.
Isa	37:3	day is a day of **d**, of rebuke,
Jon	2:2	the LORD out of my **d**, and he
Lk	21:23	For there will be great **d** on
Rom	8:35	hardship, or **d**, or persecution,
Jas	1:27	and widows in their **d**,
2 Pet	2:7	a righteous man greatly **d** by

DISTRIBUTED

Josh	13:32	Moses **d** in the plains of Moab
Ps	112:9	They have **d** freely, they have
Acts	4:35	and it was **d** to each as any

DIVORCE

Deut	22:19	permitted to **d** her as long
Sir	7:26	Do not **d** her;
Isa	50:1	your mother's bill of **d**
Mt	5:31	give her a certificate of **d**.'
Mk	10:4	of dismissal and to **d**
1 Cor	7:13	she should not **d** him.

DOCTRINE

Eph	4:14	about by every wind of **d**,
2 Tim	4:3	not put up with sound **d**,
Titus	2:10	to the **d** of God our Savior.

DOMINION

Gen	1:26	them have **d** over the fish of
Job	25:2	**D** and fear are with God
Ps	22:28	For **d** belongs to the LORD,
Sir	17:4	gave them **d** over beasts and
Dan	7:14	His **d** is an everlasting **d**
Rom	5:17	exercise **d** in life
Eph	1:21	authority and power and **d**,
Rev	1:6	glory and **d** forever and ever.

DREAM (S) (ER)

Gen	40:5	each his own **d**, and each **d**
Judg	7:13	man telling a **d** to his
1 Kings	3:5	Solomon in a **d** by night;
Jer	23:27	forget my name by their **d**
Dan	7:1	Then he wrote down the **d**:
Mt	2:13	appeared to Joseph in a **d** and
Acts	2:17	and your old men shall **d d**.

DRINK (DRANK)

Gen	19:33	their father **d** wine that night;
Ex	32:20	and made the Israelites **d** it.
Num	4:7	flagons for the **d** offering;
Judg	7:5	those who kneel down to **d**,
2 Sam	23:15	would give me water to **d**
Tob	4:15	Do not **d** wine to excess
Jdt	12:17	"Have a **d** and be merry
Ps	50:13	or **d** the blood of goats?
Prov	5:15	**D** water from your own cistern
Eccl	9:7	and **d** your wine with a merry
Sir	15:3	him the water of wisdom to **d**
Jer	35:2	then offer them wine to **d**.
Dan	1:12	to eat and water to **d**.
Hab	2:15	make your neighbors **d**,
Mt	27:34	they offered him wine to **d**,
Lk	22:18	I will not **d** of the fruit
Jn	7:38	one who believes in me **d**.
Rom	14:17	food and **d** but righteousness

1 Cor	12:13	all made to **d** of one Spirit.
1 Tim	5:23	No longer **d** only water,
Rev	16:6	have given them blood to **d**.

DRUNK

Gen	9:21	of the wine and became **d**,
Ruth	3:7	When Boaz had eaten and **d**,
1 Sam	25:36	him, for he was very **d**;
1 Kings	16:9	drinking himself **d** in the
Song	5:1	drink, and be **d** with love.
Sir	31:28	Wine **d** at the proper time
Isa	29:9	Be **d**, but not from wine;
Jn	2:10	guests have become **d**.
1 Cor	11:21	and another becomes **d**.
1 Thess	5:7	and those who are **d** get **d** at
Rev	18:3	the nations have **d** of the wine

DUST

Gen	13:16	count the **d** of the earth,
Num	23:10	Who can count the **d** of Jacob,
1 Sam	2:8	up the poor from the **d**;
Ps	90:3	You turn us back to **d**,
Eccl	3:20	from the **d**, and all turn to **d**
Sir	17:32	all human beings are **d** and
Isa	65:25	serpent—its food shall be **d**!
Mic	7:17	they shall lick **d** like a snake,
Mt	10:14	shake off the **d** from your
Acts	18:6	he shook the **d** from his
Rev	18:19	And they threw **d** on their

DWELL (ING) (S)

Ex	25:8	so that I may **d** among them.
1 Kings	6:13	I will **d** among the children
1 Macc	1:38	she became a **d** of strangers;
Ps	23:6	and I shall **d** in the house
Isa	57:15	I **d** in the high and holy
Joel	3:17	the LORD your God, **d** in Zion,
Zech	2:11	and I will **d** in your midst.
Acts	7:48	not **d** in houses made with
2 Cor	12:9	power of Christ may **d**
Col	3:16	word of Christ **d** in you richly;
Rev	21:3	He will **d** with them;

E

EAGLE

Deut	14:12	you shall not eat: the **e**,
Prov	30:19	the way of an **e** in the sky,
Ezek	17:3	A great **e**, with great wings
Rev	12:14	two wings of the great **e**,

EAR (S)

Ex	21:6	shall pierce his **e** with an awl;
2 Kings	19:16	Incline your **e**, O LORD, and
Neh	1:11	let your **e** be attentive
Ps	116:2	he inclined his **e** to me,
Prov	25:12	wise rebuke to a listening **e**.
Eccl	1:8	or the **e** filled with hearing.
Wis	15:15	nor **e** with which to hear
Bar	3:9	give **e**, and learn wisdom
Dan	9:18	Incline your **e**, O my God, and
Lk	22:51	touched his **e** and healed him.
1 Cor	2:9	nor **e** heard, nor the human
Rev	13:9	Let anyone who has an **e**

EARTH

Gen	1:1	created the heavens and the **e**,
Deut	5:8	in the water under the **e**.
Josh	3:13	the LORD of all the **e**,
1 Kings	8:27	God indeed dwell on the **e**?
1 Chr	16:23	to the Lord, all the **e**.
Job	26:7	and hangs the **e** upon nothing.
Ps	97:1	Let the **e** rejoice;
Isa	37:16	all the kingdoms of the **e**;
Jer	33:25	ordinances of heaven and **e**,
Dan	12:2	in the dust of the **e** shall
Joel	2:30	the heavens and on the **e**,
Am	9:5	he who touches the **e** and it
Hab	2:20	the **e** keep silence before him!
Hag	2:21	shake the heavens and the **e**,
Mt	5:18	until heaven and **e** pass away,
Lk	5:24	authority on **e** to forgive sins"
Jn	12:32	am lifted up from the **e**,
Acts	7:49	and the **e** is my footstool.
1 Cor	15:47	first man was from the **e**,
Eph	3:15	family in heaven and on **e**
Heb	12:26	time his voice shook the **e**;
2 Pet	3:13	new heavens and a new **e**,
Rev	20:11	the **e** and the heaven fled

EAT (ER) (ING)

Gen	2:16	"You may freely **e** of every tree
Ex	32:6	people sat down to **e** and
Lev	11:4	you shall not **e** the following:
Num	11:13	and say, 'Give us meat to **e**!'
Deut	14:4	are the animals you may **e**:
Judg	14:14	the **e** came something to **e**.
2 Sam	9:7	yourself shall **e** at my table
2 Kings	9:10	The dogs shall **e** Jezebel
Tob	1:11	from **e** the food of the
1 Macc	1:62	not to **e** unclean food.
Ps	22:26	The poor shall **e** and be
Eccl	5:18	it is fitting to **e** and drink
Isa	65:25	lion shall **e** straw like the ox;
Jer	19:9	and all shall **e** the flesh of
Ezek	3:1	O mortal, **e** what is offered
Hag	1:6	you **e**, but you never
Mt	15:2	their hands before they **e**."
Lk	10:8	**e** what is set before you
Acts	10:13	"Get up, Peter; kill and **e**."
Rom	14:20	others fall by what you **e**;
1 Cor	10:31	whether you **e** or drink,
2 Thess	3:10	to work should not **e**.
Rev	10:9	"Take it, and **e**; it will be

EGYPT

Gen	12:10	So Abram went down to **E**
Ex	32:1	out of the land of **E**,
Num	24:8	who brings him out of **E**,
Deut	16:12	you were a slave in **E**,
Josh	15:47	villages; to the Wadi of **E**,
1 Kings	14:25	King Shishak of **E** came up
2 Chr	36:3	Then the king of **E** deposed
Neh	9:18	brought you up out of **E**,
Ps	78:51	struck all the firstborn in **E**,
Isa	19:1	An oracle concerning **E**.
Jer	46:2	of Pharaoh Neco, king of **E**,
Ezek	29:2	against Pharaoh king of **E**,
Hos	11:1	and out of **E** I called my son.
Mt	2:15	"Out of **E** I have called my son
Heb	11:27	By faith he left **E**, unafraid
Rev	11:8	called Sodom and **E**, where

ELDER (S)

Gen	25:23	the **e** shall serve the younger."

Ex   24: 1 and seventy of the **e** of Israel,
Deut   25: 7 shall go up to the **e** at the gate
Josh   24: 1 and summoned the **e**, the
Judg   2: 7 the **e** who outlived Joshua,
Ruth   4: 2 took ten men of the **e** of the
Ps   105:22 and to teach his **e** wisdom.
Isa   3:14 with the **e** and princes of his
Mt   15: 2 break the tradition of the **e**?
Mk   7: 3 the tradition of the **e**;
Acts   21:18 and all the **e** were present.
1 Tim   5:17 Let the **e** who rule well be
Titus   1: 5 appoint **e** in every town,
1 Pet   5: 5 accept the authority of the **e**.
Rev   19: 4 twenty-four **e** and the four

ELECT

Wis   4:15 grace and mercy are with his **e**.
Sir   46:1   a great savior of God's **e**.
Mt   24:31 gather his **e** from the four
Mk   13:22 lead astray, if possible, the **e**.
Rom   11: 7 The **e** obtained it, but the rest
2 Tim   2:10 for the sake of the **e**,
2 Jn   1:13 The children of your **e** sister

EMPEROR

Mk   12:17 "Give to the **e** the things that
Jn   19:12 are no friend of the **e**.
Acts   25:11 them. I appeal to the **e**."
1 Pet   2:17 Fear God. Honor the **e**.

ENCOURAGE (MENT)

Deut   1:38 shall enter there; **e** him,
2 Sam   11:25 and overthrow it.' And **e** him."
1 Macc   12:9   we have as **e** the holy books
Acts   4:36 (which means "son of **e**").
Rom   15: 4 steadfastness and by the **e** of
1 Cor   14: 3 upbuilding and **e** and
Philem   1: 7 much joy and **e** from your

ENDURE (D) (S)

Gen   8:22 As long as the earth **e**,
Job   20:21 their prosperity will not **e**.
Ps   72:17 May his name **e** forever,
Jer   10:10 cannot **e** his indignation.
Lam   5:19 throne **e** to all generations.
Joel   2:11 terrible indeed—who can **e** it?
Lk   17:25 first he must **e** much suffering
Jn   6:27 food that **e** for eternal life,
Rom   9:22 has **e** with much patience the
1 Cor   10:13 you may be able to **e** it.
2 Cor   9: 9 his righteousness **e** forever."
2 Tim   2:10 I **e** everything for the sake of
Heb   12: 7 **E** trials for the sake of
1 Pet   2:19 you **e** pain while suffering

ENEMY (ENEMIES)

Ex   1:10 join our **e** and fight against us
Deut   6:19 thrusting out all your **e** from
Josh   21:44 had given all their **e** into
Judg   2:14 power of their **e** all around,
2 Sam   8:35 from all his **e** around him,
Jdt   8:35 to take vengeance on our **e**."
Esth   9: 5 all their **e** with the sword,
1 Macc   4:36 said, "See, our **e** are crushed;
Ps   74:10 Is the **e** to revile your name
Prov   16: 7 even their **e** to be at peace
Sir   6:9   friends who change into **e**.
Isa   59:18 requital to his **e**;
Dan   4:19 interpretation for your **e**!
Mt   5:44 Love your **e** and pray for those

Acts   2:35 make your **e** your footstool."
Rom   12:20 "if your **e** are hungry, feed
1 Cor   15:25 put all his **e** under his feet.
Heb   10:13 "until his **e** would be made a
Jas   4: 4 becomes an **e** of God.

ENTER

Ex   40:35 not able to **e** the tent of
Num   20:24 For he shall not **e** the land
Ps   118:19 that I may **e** through them
Isa   26: 2 keeps faith may **e** in.
Joel   3: 2 and I will **e** into judgment
Mt   5:20 you will never **e** the kingdom
Mk   10:15 a little child will never **e** it."
Jn   3: 5 no one can **e** the kingdom of
Acts   14:22 that we must **e** the kingdom of
Heb   4:11 every effort to **e** that rest,
Rev   21:27 But nothing unclean will **e** it,

ENVY

Prov   24: 1 Do not **e** the wicked, nor
Eccl   4: 4 one person's **e** of another.
Wis   2:24 through the devil's **e** death
Sir   9:11 Do not **e** the success of
Mk   7:22 deceit, licentiousness, **e**,
Rom   1:29 Full of **e**, murder, strife, deceit,
Phil   1:15 proclaim Christ from **e** and
Titus   3: 3 our days in malice and **e**,
Jas   3:16 there is **e** and selfish
1 Pet   2: 1 and all guile, insincerity, **e**,

ESCAPE

Gen   7: 1 the ark to **e** the waters
1 Sam   23:28 was called the Rock of **E**.
Job   11:20 all way of **e** will be lost
Ps   89:48 can **e** the power of Sheol?
Prov   12:13 but the righteous **e** from
Jer   11:11 upon them that they cannot **e**;
Joel   2:32 there shall be those who **e**,
Mt   23:33 How can you **e** being
Rom   2: 3 you will **e** the judgment of
2 Tim   2:26 and that they may **e** from the
Heb   12:25 not **e** when they refused
2 Pet   1: 4 may **e** from the corruption

ETERNAL (ETERNITY)

Gen   49:26 blessings of the **e** mountains,
Eccl   12: 5 go to their **e** home,
Jer   20:11 Their **e** dishonor will never
Hab   3: 6 The **e** mountains were
Mt   25:41 depart from me into the **e** fire
Mk   3:29 but is guilty of an **e** sin"—
Jn   3:16 not perish but may have **e** life.
Acts   13:46 unworthy of **e** life,
Rom   2: 7 he will give **e** life;
2 Cor   5: 1 **e** in the heavens.
Eph   3:11 accordance with the **e** purpose
2 Thess   2:16 gave us **e** comfort and good
1 Tim   6:16 honor and **e** dominion.
Titus   3: 7 according to the hope of **e** life.
Heb   13:20 the blood of the **e** covenant,
1 Pet   5:10 called you to his **e** glory in
1 Jn   3:15 murderers do not have **e** life
Jude   1:21 that leads to **e** life.
Rev   14: 6 with an **e** gospel to proclaim

EVERLASTING

Gen   9:16 remember the **e** covenant
2 Sam   23: 5 with me an **e** covenant,
1 Chr   16:17 to Israel as an **e** covenant,

Ps   119:142 righteousness is an **e**
Isa   24: 5 broken the **e** covenant.
Ezek   37:26 shall be an **e** covenant with
Dan   12: 2 some to **e** life,

EVERYTHING

Gen   6:17 **e** that is on the earth
Deut   29: 9 you may succeed in **e** that
Ps   150: 6 Let **e** that breathes praise the
Eccl   3:11 made **e** suitable for its time;
Sir   15:18 mighty in power and sees **e**;
          19:15 so do not believe **e** you hear
Mt   28:20 teaching them to obey **e**
Lk   1: 3 after investigating **e** carefully
Jn   14:26 will teach you **e**, and remind
Rom   14:20 **E** is indeed clean, but it
1 Cor   10:31 do **e** for the glory of God
Gal   6:15 but a new creation is **e**!
1 Thess   5:21 but test **e**; hold fast
1 Tim   4: 4 For **e** created by God is good
2 Pet   1: 3 power has given us **e** needed

EVIL

Gen   44: 4 'Why have you returned **e** for
Num   32:13 had done **e** in the sight of
Deut   28:20 account of the **e** of your deeds,
Judg   4: 1 what was **e** in the sight of
1 Sam   19: 9 Then an **e** spirit from the LORD
1 Kings   11: 6 Solomon did what was **e**
Job   2: 3 turns away from **e**. He
Ps   141: 4 turn my heart to any **e**,
Prov   3: 7 and turn away from **e**.
Eccl   12:14 whether good or **e**.
Isa   13:11 punish the world for its **e**,
Jer   18:10 if it does **e** in my sight,
Am   5:14 Seek good and not **e**,
Mic   3: 2 love the **e**, who tear
Mt   12:35 the **e** person brings **e** things
Lk   11:13 If you then, who are **e**, know
Jn   3:20 For all who do **e** hate the light
Rom   16:19 and guileless in what is **e**.
1 Cor   14:20 be infants in **e**, but in thinking
Eph   6:12 spiritual forces of **e** in
1 Thess   5:22 abstain from every form of **e**.
1 Tim   6:10 root of all kinds of **e**,
Heb   5:14 distinguish good from **e**.
Jas   4:16 all such boasting is **e**.
1 Pet   3:10 their tongues from **e** and their
1 Jn   2:13 you have conquered the **e** one.
2 Jn   1:11 participate in the **e** deeds of

EVILDOER (S)

2 Sam   7:10 and **e** shall afflict them no
Job   34:22 where **e** may hide themselves.
Ps   34:16 of the Lord is against **e**,
Prov   24:19 Do not fret because of **e**.
Jer   23:14 strengthen the hands of **e**,
Mt   7:23 go away from me, you **e**!'
1 Pet   2:12 though they malign you as **e**,

EXALT (ED)

Ex   15: 2 and I will **e** him.
Josh   3: 7 I will begin to **e** you in the
1 Sam   2:10 and **e** the power of his anointed
1 Chr   25: 5 the promise of God to **e** him;
Ps   66: 7 rebellious not **e** themselves.
Isa   25: 1 I will **e** you, I will praise your
Dan   11:36 He shall **e** himself and
Lk   14:11 humble themselves will be **e**."

Jas	4:10	the Lord, and he will **e** you.

EXIST (S) (ED)

Ps	119:89	The Lord **e** forever;
Rom	4:17	the things that do not **e**.
1 Cor	8:6	for whom we **e**, and one Lord,
Heb	2:10	through whom all things **e**,
Rev	4:11	will they **e** and were created."

EYE (S)

Gen	3:7	Then the **e** of both were
Num	33:55	as barbs in your **e** and thorns
Deut	11:12	The **e** of the Lord your God
Josh	23:13	and thorns in your **e**, until you
Judg	16:28	the Philistines for my two **e**."
1 Kings	10:7	I came and my own **e** had
2 Chr	16:9	For the **e** of the Lord range
Tob	6:9	and the **e** will be healed."
Job	36:7	He does not withdraw his **e**
Ps	119:37	Turn my **e** from looking at
Prov	15:3	The **e** of the Lord are in
Sir	23:4	do not give me haughty **e**.
Isa	42:7	to open the **e** that are blind,
Jer	24:6	set my **e** upon them for good,
Ezek	24:16	you the delight of your **e**;
Dan	10:6	his **e** like flaming torches,
Zech	4:10	"These seven are the **e** of the
Mt	9:30	And their **e** were opened.
Jn	9:10	"Then how were your **e**
Acts	28:27	might not look with their **e**,
Rom	11:10	let their **e** be darkened
Eph	1:18	with the **e** of your heart
1 Jn	2:16	the desire of the **e**, the pride in
Rev	7:17	away every tear from their **e**."

F

FACE

Gen	32:20	I shall see his **f**; perhaps he
Num	14:14	are seen **f** to **f**, and your cloud
Deut	5:4	you **f** to **f** at the mountain
2 Kings	14:8	look one another in the **f**."
Esth	7:8	they covered Haman's **f**.
Ps	27:8	my heart says, "seek his **f**!"
Song	2:14	and your **f** is lovely.
Isa	8:17	who is hiding his **f** from the
Jer	32:4	speak with him **f** to **f** and see
Ezek	39:29	never again hide my **f** from
Dan	10:6	his **f** like lightning,
Hos	5:15	their guilt and seek my **f**.
Mt	17:2	before them, and his **f** shone
Lk	9:29	appearance of his **f** changed,
Jn	19:3	and striking him on the **f**.
Acts	6:15	that his **f** was like the **f** of
1 Cor	13:12	we will see **f** to **f**. Now I know
2 Cor	10:1	I who am humble when **f** to **f**
3 Jn	1:14	talk together **f** to **f**. Peace to
Rev	22:4	see his **f**, and his name will be
Jdt	10:23	at the beauty of her **f**.
Sir	13:26	happy heart is a cheerful **f**,

FAIL

Num	15:22	unintentionally **f** to observe
Josh	1:5	I will not **f** you
1 Chr	28:20	He will not **f** you or forsake
Tob	14:4	none of all their words will **f**.
Isa	58:11	whose waters never **f**.

Zeph	3:5	each dawn without **f**;
Lk	22:32	your own faith may not **f**;
2 Cor	13:5	unless, indeed, you **f**

FAITH

Num	5:6	breaking **f** with the Lord,
Deut	32:51	you broke **f** with me
Josh	2:12	a sign of good **f**
	22:20	break **f** in the matter
Judg	9:15	in good **f** you are anointing
Ezra	10:2	We have broken **f**
1 Macc	10:27	Now continue still to keep **f**
Job	39:12	Do you have **f** in it
Ps	78:22	they had no **f** in God,
	116:10	I kept my **f**,
Sir	27:17	your friend and keep **f** with
Isa	7:9	stand firm in **f**.
Hab	2:4	the righteous live by their **f**.
Mt	6:30	you of little **f**?
	21:21	if you have **f**
Mk	2:5	When Jesus saw their **f**,
	11:22	Have **f** in God.
Lk	5:20	When he saw their **f**,
	18:42	your **f** has saved you.
Acts	3:16	by **f** in his name,
	14:9	seeing that he had **f**
	24:24	concerning **f** in Christ Jesus.
Rom	1:5	**f** among all the Gentiles
	16:26	the obedience of **f**—
1 Cor	2:5	your **f** might rest not on
	16:13	stand firm in your **f**,
2 Cor	1:24	lord it over your **f**;
	13:5	you are living in the **f**.
Gal	1:23	the **f** he once tried to destroy
	6:10	those of the family of **f**.
Eph	1:15	I have heard of your **f**
	6:16	the shield of **f**,
Phil	1:25	progress and joy in **f**,
	3:9	from God based on **f**.
Col	1:4	your **f** in Christ Jesus
	1:23	steadfast in the **f**,
1 Thess	1:3	your work of **f**
	3:10	whatever is lacking in your **f**.
2 Thess	1:3	your **f** is growing abundantly,
	1:11	good resolve and work of **f**,
1 Tim	1:2	my loyal child in the **f**:
	3:9	to the mystery of the **f**
	6:12	the good fight of the **f**;
2 Tim	1:5	your sincere **f**, a **f** that lived
	3:15	through **f** in Christ Jesus.
Titus	1:1	for the sake of the **f**
	1:13	may become sound in the **f**,
Philem	1:5	your **f** toward the Lord Jesus.
Heb	4:2	united by **f**
	11:1	**f** is the assurance of things
	11:13	these died in **f**
	12:2	pioneer and perfecter of our **f**,
Jas	1:3	**f** produces endurance;
	2:26	**f** without works is also dead
1 Pet	1:5	the power of God through **f**
	5:9	steadfast in your **f**,
2 Pet	1:1	a **f** as precious as ours
1 Jn	5:4	conquers the world, our **f**.
Jude	1:3	contend for the **f**
Rev	2:13	you did not deny your **f**

FAITHFUL (NESS)

Deut	7:9	the **f** God who maintains
Judg	5:15	and Issachar **f** to Barak;
1 Sam	2:9	guard the feet of his **f** ones,

1 Sam	20:14	show me the **f** love
2 Sam	2:6	steadfast love and **f**
2 Chr	6:41	your **f** rejoice in your
	31:20	**f** before the Lord his God
Neh	7:2	he was a **f** man
Ps	4:3	Lord has set apart the **f**
	16:10	let your **f** one see the Pit.
	116:15	the death of his **f** ones.
Prov	2:8	the way of his **f** ones.
	28:20	The **f** will abound with
Wis	3:9	the **f** will abide with him in
Sir	6:15	**f** friends are beyond price;
Isa	1:21	How the **f** city has become a
	25:1	formed of old, **f** and sure.
Jer	31:3	I have continued my **f** to you.
Dan	6:4	because he was **f**,
Hos	2:20	my wife in **f**;
Mic	7:2	The **f** have disappeared from
Zech	8:3	Jerusalem shall be called the **f**
Mt	24:45	"Who then is the **f** and wise
Lk	12:42	Who then is the **f** and prudent
	16:11	you have not been **f**
Acts	11:23	to remain **f** to the Lord
1 Cor	1:9	God is **f**;
2 Cor	1:18	As surely as God is **f**,
Eph	1:1	**f** in Christ Jesus:
	6:21	a dear brother and a **f** minister
Col	1:2	**f** brothers and sisters in Christ
	4:7	a **f** minister, and a fellow
1 Thess	5:24	one who calls you is **f**,
1 Tim	1:12	because he judged me **f**
2 Tim	2:2	many witnesses entrust to **f**
Heb	2:17	a merciful and **f** high priest
	11:11	he considered him **f**
1 Pet	4:19	entrust themselves to a **f**
1 Jn	1:9	he who is **f** and just will
Rev	1:5	Jesus Christ, the **f** witness,
	2:13	of Antipas my witness, my **f**
	17:14	are called and chosen and **f**."

FALL (S) (EN)

Gen	2:21	caused a deep sleep to **f**
Ex	5:3	our God, or he will **f** upon us
Lev	19:10	gather the **f** grapes of your
Num	11:9	the manna would **f** with it.
1 Sam	3:19	of his words **f** to the ground.
1 Chr	10:8	found Saul and his sons **f** on
Ps	5:10	let them **f** by their own
	91:7	A thousand may **f** at your side,
Prov	16:18	a haughty spirit before a **f**.
Eccl	4:10	For if they **f**, one will lift up
Sir	28:23	who forsake the Lord will **f**
Isa	40:30	and the young will **f**
Jer	6:15	shall **f** among those who **f**;
Dan	11:35	Some of the wise shall **f**,
Hos	10:8	to the hills, **f** on us.
Mt	7:25	but it did not **f**, because it had
Mk	4:17	immediately they **f** away.
Lk	10:18	I watched Satan **f** from heaven
Acts	5:15	Peter's shadow might **f** on
Rom	3:23	all have sinned and **f** short of
	11:11	they stumbled so as to **f**?
1 Cor	8:13	cause one of them to **f**.
1 Tim	6:9	who want to be rich **f** into
Heb	10:31	a fearful thing to **f** into the
1 Pet	2:8	a rock that makes them **f**.
Rev	6:16	**F** on us and hide us

FAMILY (FAMILIES)

Gen	8:19	out of the ark by **f**.

Ex	1:21	feared God, he gave them **f**.
Ps	107:41	and makes their **f** like flocks.
Am	3: 2	known of all the **f** of the earth;
Titus	1:11	they are upsetting whole **f**

FAMINE

Gen	12:10	Now there was a **f** in the land.
	43: 1	Now the **f** was severe in the
Ruth	1: 1	there was a **f** in the land,
1 Kings	8:37	If there is **f** in the land,
2 Kings	4:38	to Gilgal, there was a **f** in the
Job	5:20	In **f** he will redeem you from
Ps	37:19	in the days of **f** they have
Jer	14:15	Sword and **f** shall not come
Am	8:11	when I will send a **f** on the
Acts	11:28	there would be a severe **f**
Rom	8:35	distress, or persecution, or **f**,
Rev	18: 8	pestilence and mourning and **f**

FAST (ED)

Deut	10:20	you shall hold **f**, and by his
Josh	22: 5	his commandments, and to
		hold **f** to him, and to serve
2 Kings	18: 6	For he held **f** to the LORD; he
1 Chr	10:12	the oak in Jabesh, and **f** seven
2 Chr	20: 3	and proclaimed a **f** throughout
Ezra	8:21	Then I proclaimed a **f** there, at
Esth	4:16	in Susa, and hold a **f** on my
Ps	17: 5	My steps have held **f** to your
Prov	4: 4	me, "Let your heart hold **f** my
Sir	49:9	Job who held **f** to all the ways
Isa	56: 4	that please me and hold **f** my
Mt	6:16	"And whenever you **f**, do not
Lk	18:12	I **f** twice a week; I give
Rom	12: 9	hate what is evil, hold **f** to
Col	2:19	and not holding **f** to the head,
1 Thess	5:21	but test everything; hold **f** to
1 Tim	3: 9	they must hold **f** to the
Heb	4:14	of God, let us hold **f** to our
Rev	14:12	hold **f** to the faith of Jesus

FATHER

Gen	2:24	Therefore a man leaves his **f**
	26:24	am the God of your **f**
Ex	20:12	Honor your **f** and your
	21:17	Whoever curses **f** or mother
Deut	5:16	Honor your **f** and your
Judg	17:10	and be to me a **f** and a priest,
1 Kings	2:12	on the throne of his **f** David;
1 Chr	17:13	I will be a **f** to him, and he
Job	38:28	"Has the rain a **f**, or who has
Ps	27:10	If my **f** and mother forsake
	109:14	May the iniquity of his **f** be
Prov	3:12	one he loves, as a **f** the son in
	20:20	If you curse **f** or mother, your
Wis	2:16	and boasts that God is his **f**.
Sir	3:3	who honor their **f** atone for
Isa	8: 4	knows how to call "My **f**" or
	9: 6	Everlasting **F**, Prince of Peace.
Jer	2:27	"You are my **f**," and to a stone,
Ezek	16: 3	your **f** was an Amorite, and
Mic	7: 6	for the son treats the **f** with
Mal	1: 6	A son honors his **f**, and
Mt	5:16	and give glory to your **F** in
	11:27	over to me by my **F**; and no
	23: 9	And call no one your **f** on
Lk	6:36	Be merciful, just as your **F** is
	11: 2	you pray, say: **F**, hallowed be
	18:20	Honor your **f** and mother.' "
Jn	3:35	The **F** loves the Son and has

Jn	6:46	that anyone has seen the **F**
	14: 9	can you say, 'Show us the **F**?
Rom	4:16	Abraham (for he is the **f** of all
2 Cor	6:18	and I will be your **f**, and you
Eph	6: 2	"Honor your **f** and mother"—
1 Thess	2:11	like a **f** with his children,
1 Tim	5: 1	to him as to a **f**, to younger
Heb	1: 5	again, "I will be his **F**, and he
Jas	1:17	**F** of lights, with whom there
1 Jn	1: 3	our fellowship is with the **F**
Rev	3: 5	before my **F** and before his

FAVOR

Gen	6: 8	But Noah found **f** in the sight
Ex	33:12	and you have also found **f** in
Lev	26: 9	I will look with **f** upon you
Judg	6:17	"If now I have found **f** with
2 Chr	33:12	in distress he entreated the **f** of
1 Macc	4:10	to see whether he will **f** us
Ps	5:12	you cover them with **f** as with
Prov	3:34	to the humble he shows **f**.
	13:15	Good sense wins **f**, but the
Sir	32:14	to seek him will find **f**.
Isa	49: 8	LORD: In a time of **f** I have
Zech	11: 7	two staffs; one I named **F**, the
Lk	1:30	Mary, for you have found **f**
Acts	7:10	and enabled him to win **f** and

FEAR (S)

Gen	9: 2	The **f** and dread of you shall
Ex	9:30	that you do not yet **f** the LORD
Deut	2:25	to put the dread and **f** of you
	10:12	Only to **f** the LORD your God,
Josh	2:24	of the land melt in **f**
1 Sam	12:14	If you will **f** the LORD and
2 Chr	19: 7	Now, let the **f** of the LORD be
Job	1: 9	"Does Job **f** God for nothing?
Ps	2:11	Serve the LORD with **f**, with
	46: 2	Therefore we will not **f**,
	147:11	those who **f** him, in those who
Prov	1: 7	The **f** of the LORD is the
	10:27	The **f** of the LORD prolongs life
Eccl	8:12	be well with those who **f** God,
Sir	7:29	With all your soul **f** the Lord,
Isa	8:12	and do not **f** what it **f**,
	51: 7	do not **f** the reproach of
Jer	5:22	Do you not **f** me? says the
Mk	5:36	"Do not **f**, only believe."
Lk	12: 5	you whom to **f**: **f** him
Jn	7:13	for **f** of the Jews.
Rom	8:15	slavery to fall back into **f**,
2 Cor	5:11	knowing the **f** of the Lord,
Phil	2:12	with **f** and trembling;
Heb	2:15	slavery by the **f** of death.
1 Pet	1:17	live in reverent **f** during the
1 Jn	4:18	There is no **f** in love,
Rev	2:10	Do not **f** what you are about

FEET

Ex	3: 5	the sandals from your **f**,
	24:10	Under his **f** there was
Ruth	3: 8	lying at his **f**, was a woman!
1 Sam	2: 9	guard the **f** of his faithful
Ps	8: 6	put all things under their **f**,
	40: 2	and set my **f** upon a rock,
Prov	1:16	for their **f** run to evil,
Isa	6: 2	with two they covered their **f**,
Dan	2:33	its **f** partly of iron and partly
Nah	1: 3	are the dust of his **f**.
Zech	14: 4	his **f** shall stand on the Mount

Mt	10:14	the dust from your **f**
Lk	1:79	to guide our **f** into the way of
	8:35	sitting at the **f** of Jesus,
Acts	5: 2	and laid it at the apostles' **f**.
Rom	3:15	Their **f** are swift to shed blood
1 Cor	12:21	the head to the **f**,
Eph	1:22	put all things under his **f**
Heb	1:13	a footstool for your **f**"?
Rev	1:15	his **f** were like burnished

FIELD (S)

Gen	4: 8	us go out to the **f**.
	23:17	So the **f** of Ephron
Lev	19: 9	the very edges of your **f**,
Ruth	2: 3	came and gleaned in the **f**
Ps	50:11	all that moves in the **f**
Prov	24:30	I passed by the **f** of one
Isa	1: 8	a shelter in a cucumber **f**,
	40: 6	like the flower of the **f**.
Mt	6:28	Consider the lilies of the **f**,
	13:38	the **f** is the world,
2 Cor	10:13	but will keep within the **f**

FIGHT

Ex	14:14	The LORD will **f** for you,
Deut	1:30	is the one who will **f** for you,
Judg	1: 1	to **f** against them?
Neh	4:20	Our God will **f** for us."
1 Macc	2:40	and refuse to **f** with the
Sir	4:28	**F** to the death for truth, and
Jer	21: 5	I myself will **f** against you
1 Tim	1:18	you may **f** the good **f**,

FILL (ED)

Gen	1:28	**f** the earth and subdue it
Ps	72:19	may his glory **f** the whole
Jer	23:24	Do I not **f** heaven and earth?
Ezek	10: 2	**f** your hands with burning
Hag	2: 7	and I will **f** this house with
Jn	6:26	you ate your **f** of the loaves.
Rom	15:13	May the God of hope **f** you
Eph	4:10	so that he might **f** all things.)

FIND

Gen	18:26	If I **f** at Sodom fifty righteous
Num	32:23	be sure your sin will **f** you out.
Job	37:23	The Almighty—we cannot **f**
Ps	61: 4	**f** refuge under the shelter of
	132: 5	until I **f** a place for the LORD
Prov	2: 5	**f** the knowledge of God.
	8:17	who seek me diligently **f** me.
Eccl	12:10	sought to **f** pleasing words,
Jer	6:16	and **f** rest for your souls.
Mt	7: 7	search, and you will **f**;
Lk	23: 4	I **f** no basis for an accusation
Eph	5:10	Try to **f** out what is pleasing to

FIRE

Gen	15:17	a smoking **f** pot and a flaming
Ex	3: 2	a flame of **f** out of a bush; he
	40:38	and **f** was in the cloud by
Lev	9:24	**F** came out from the LORD
Num	16:35	And **f** came out from the LORD
Deut	4:24	your God is a devouring **f**,
Judg	6:21	and sprang up from the rock
1 Kings	18:38	Then the **f** of the LORD fell
2 Kings	1:10	let **f** come down from heaven
	6:17	horses and chariots of **f**
2 Chr	7: 1	**f** came down from heaven
Ps	11: 6	he will rain coals of **f**

Sir	7:17	of the ungodly is **f**
Isa	5:24	the tongue of **f** devours the
Jer	23:29	Is not my word like **f**,
Dan	3:25	in the middle of the **f**,
Zech	3: 2	a brand plucked from the **f**?"
Mt	3:11	with the Holy Spirit and **f**.
	18: 8	be thrown into the eternal **f**.
Mk	9:43	to hell, to the unquenchable **f**.
Lk	3:16	with the Holy Spirit and **f**.
Heb	10:27	judgment, and a fury of **f**
Jas	3: 6	And the tongue is a **f**,
Jude	1:23	snatching them out of the **f**;
Rev	1:14	were like a flame of **f**,
	20:14	thrown into the lake of **f**.

FIRST

Gen	1: 5	and there was morning, the **f**
	13: 4	made an altar at the **f**;
Ex	12: 2	the **f** month of the year
	34:19	All that **f** opens the womb is
Prov	3: 9	with the **f** fruits of all your
Sir	11:7	examine **f**, and then criticize.
Isa	41: 4	I, the LORD, am **f**,
Dan	7: 4	The **f** was like a lion
Mt	5:24	**f** be reconciled to your brother
	19:30	many who are **f** will be last,
Mk	9:11	that Elijah must come **f**?"
	13:10	good news must **f** be
Jn	2:11	Jesus did this, the **f** of his
Rom	1:16	to the Jew **f** and also to the
1 Cor	15:45	The **f** man, Adam, became a
Eph	1:12	we, who were the **f** to set our
Heb	3:14	we hold our **f** confidence
	10: 9	He abolishes the **f**
1 Jn	4:19	We love because he **f** loved us.
Rev	1:17	I am the **f** and the last,
	20: 5	This is the **f** resurrection.

FIRSTBORN

Gen	27:19	I am Esau your **f**.
Ex	4:22	Israel is my **f** son.
	34:20	All of your sons you shall
Josh	6:26	At the cost of his **f**
1 Kings	16:34	the cost of Abiram his **f**,
Ps	78:51	He struck all the **f** in Egypt,
Ezek	20:26	their offering up all their **f**,
Zech	12:10	as one weeps over a **f**.
Lk	2: 7	she gave birth to her **f** son
Col	1:15	the **f** of all creation;
Heb	1: 6	when he brings the **f** into the

FISH

Gen	1:26	dominion over the **f** of the
Ex	7:18	The **f** in the river shall die
Num	11: 5	We remember the **f** we used to
Tob	8:3	odor of the **f** so repelled the
Jon	1:17	a large **f** to swallow up Jonah;
Mt	7:10	for a **f**, will give a snake?
Lk	5: 6	so many **f** that their nets
Jn	6: 9	five barley loaves and two **f**.

FLESH

Gen	2:23	my bones and **f** of my **f**;
	17:13	in your **f** an everlasting
1 Sam	17:44	your **f** to the birds of the
2 Chr	32: 8	an arm of **f**, but with us
Ps	50:13	Do I eat the **f** of bulls,
Mal	2:15	Both **f** and spirit are his.
Mt	16:17	For **f** and blood has not
	26:41	willing, but the **f** is weak."

Lk	24:39	a ghost does not have **f** and
Jn	1:14	And the Word became **f**
Acts	2:17	my Spirit upon all **f**,
Rom	7: 5	we were living in the **f**,
	8:13	you live according to the **f**,
1 Cor	6:16	The two shall be one **f**.
	15:39	but there is one **f** for human
2 Cor	12: 7	was given me in the **f**,
Gal	3: 3	you now ending with the **f**?
Eph	2: 3	in the passions of our **f**,
	6:12	enemies of blood and **f**,
1 Pet	1:24	All **f** is like grass
1 Jn	2:16	the desire of the **f**,
Jude	1: 8	dreamers also defile the **f**,
Rev	19:18	to eat the **f** of kings, the **f** of

FLOCK

Gen	4: 4	of the firstlings of his **f**,
Ex	2:17	defense and watered their **f**.
Ps	77:20	led your people like a **f**
	80: 1	who lead Joseph like a **f**!
Song	4: 1	Your hair is like a **f** of goats,
Isa	40:11	He will feed his **f** like a
Jer	10:21	and all their **f** is scattered.
Zech	11: 7	the shepherd of the **f**,
Mal	1:14	has a male in the **f**
Lk	2: 8	watch over their **f** by night.
Acts	20:28	over all the **f**,
1 Pet	5: 2	to tend the **f** of God

FLOOD

Gen	9:15	a **f** to destroy all flesh.
Ps	29:10	LORD sits enthroned over the **f**;
Sir	40:10	on their account the **f** came
Mt	24:38	in those days before the **f**
2 Pet	2: 5	when he brought a **f** on a

FOLLOW

Ex	16: 4	they will **f** my instruction
Judg	2:17	they did not **f** their example.
1 Kings	11:10	he should not **f** other gods;
1 Macc	1:44	to **f** customs strange to the
Prov	20: 7	happy are the children who **f**
Sir	18:30	self-control. Do not **f** your
Mt	4:19	"**F** me, and I will make
Lk	9:23	their cross daily and **f** me.
Jn	10: 4	and the sheep **f** him because
	21:19	this he said to him, "**F** me."
1 Tim	5:15	already turned away to **f** Satan.
2 Pet	2: 2	many will **f** their licentious

FOOD

Gen	1:30	given every green plant for **f**.
Gen	9: 3	shall be **f** for you;
Num	21: 5	For there is no **f** and no water,
Ps	42: 3	My tears have been my **f** day
	104:27	to give them their **f** in due
Prov	12: 9	be self-important and lack **f**.
	23: 3	for they are deceptive **f**.
Mt	3: 4	and his **f** was locusts and wild
Jn	4:32	I have **f** to eat that you do
	6:27	the **f** that endures for eternal
1 Cor	3: 2	you with milk, not solid **f**,
	8: 1	Now concerning **f** sacrificed to
2 Cor	11:27	often without **f**, cold and
Heb	5:14	But solid **f** is for the mature,

FOOL

Ps	49:10	**f** and dolt perish together
Prov	10:18	whoever utters slander is a **f**.

Prov	20: 3	but every **f** is quick to quarrel.
Hos	9: 7	The prophet is a **f**,
Mt	5:22	You **f**, you will be liable to
2 Cor	11:21	I am speaking as a **f**

FOREVER

Gen	3:22	eat, and live **f**"—
Ex	3:15	This is my name **f**,
2 Sam	7:13	the throne of his kingdom **f**.
1 Kings	2:33	the head of his descendants **f**;
	9: 3	and put my name there **f**,
1 Chr	16:15	Remember his covenant **f**,
2 Chr	5:13	steadfast love endures **f**,
	33: 7	I will put my name **f**;
Tob	3:11	Blessed is your name **f**,
Ps	9: 7	But the LORD sits enthroned **f**,
	44: 8	give thanks to your name **f**.
	77: 8	Has his steadfast love ceased **f**?
	111: 3	righteousness endures **f**.
Prov	10:25	righteous are established **f**.
Eccl	3:14	whatever God does endures **f**,
Wis	5:15	But the righteous live **f**,
Sir	51:12	for his mercy endures **f**;
Isa	26: 4	Trust in the LORD **f**
	51: 8	but my deliverance will be **f**,
Jer	3: 5	will he be angry **f**,
Bar	3:3	For you are enthroned **f**,
Ezek	27:36	and shall be no more **f**.
Dan	2:44	and it shall stand **f**.
Jn	6:51	of this bread will live **f**;
Rom	9: 5	over all, God blessed **f**.
Heb	5: 6	You are a priest **f**,
	7:24	because he continues **f**.
1 Pet	1:25	word of the Lord endures **f**.
1 Jn	2:17	the will of God live **f**.
Rev	1:18	I am alive **f** and ever;
	22: 5	and they will reign **f** and ever.

FORGIVE

Gen	18:24	not **f** it for the fifty righteous
	50:17	I beg you, **f** the crime of your
Ex	10:17	Do **f** my sin just this once
Num	14:19	**F** the iniquity of this people
	30:12	and the LORD will **f** her.
1 Sam	25:28	Please **f** the trespass of your
1 Kings	8:30	heed and **f**.
	8:50	and **f** your people who have
2 Chr	6:21	hear and **f**.
	6:27	**f** the sin of your servants
Ps	25:18	and **f** all my sins.
Jer	18:23	Do not **f** their iniquity,
	33: 8	and I will **f** all the guilt
Hos	1: 6	the house of Israel or **f** them.
Mt	6:12	And **f** us our debts,
	18:35	if you do not **f** your brother
Mk	2: 7	Who can **f** sins but God
	11:25	**f**, if you have anything against
Lk	5:21	Who can **f** sins but God
	23:34	Father, **f** them; for they do not
2 Cor	2: 7	you should **f** and console him,
	12:13	**F** me this wrong!
Col	3:13	**f** each other; just as the

FORGIVENESS

Ps	130: 4	But there is **f** with you,
Dan	9: 9	our God belong mercy and **f**,
Mt	26:28	for many for the **f** of sins.
Mk	1: 4	repentance for the **f** of sins.
Lk	1:77	by the **f** of their sins.
Acts	5:31	repentance to Israel and **f** of

Col 1:14 redemption, the **f** of sins.
Heb 9:22 there is no **f** of sins.

FORNICATION
Mk 7:21 **f**, theft, murder,
1 Cor 6:13 body is meant not for **f**
Col 3: 5 whatever in you is earthly: **f**,
Rev 14: 8 of the wrath of her **f**.

FORSAKE (N)
Deut 31: 6 will not fail you or **f** you."
Josh 1: 5 will not fail you or **f** you.
1 Chr 28: 9 but if you **f** him, he will
Jdt 9:11 protector of the **f**,
Ps 27:10 If my father and mother **f** me,
Prov 4: 6 Do not **f** her, and she will
Sir 17:25 to the Lord and **f** your sins;
Isa 1:28 and those who **f** the LORD
 shall be consumed
Heb 13: 5 will never leave you or **f** you."

FORTY
Gen 7: 4 earth for **f** days and **f** nights;
Ex 16:35 The Israelites ate manna **f**
Deut 25: 3 **F** lashes may be given
1 Sam 4:18 He had judged Israel **f** years.
Neh 9:21 **F** years you sustained them in
Jon 3: 4 **F** days more, and Nineveh
Mt 4: 2 He fasted **f** days and **f** nights,

FOUNDATION
1 Kings 6:37 In the fourth year the **f** of the
Ezra 3: 6 But the **f** of the temple of the
Ps 97: 2 and justice are the **f**
Isa 28:16 am laying in Zion a **f** stone,
Lk 14:29 when he has laid a **f**
1 Cor 3:10 master builder I laid a **f**,
2 Tim 2:19 But God's firm **f** stands,
Heb 6: 1 and not laying again the **f**:

FOUNTAIN
Ps 36: 9 For with you is the **f** of life;
Prov 5:18 Let your **f** be blessed,
Jer 9: 1 and my eyes a **f** of tears,
Zech 13: 1 On that day a **f** shall be

FREE
Ex 21: 2 he shall go out a **f** person,
Lk 13:12 you are set **f** from your
Jn 8:32 the truth will make you **f**.
Rom 5:15 But the **f** gift is not like the
1 Cor 9:21 I am not **f** from God's law but
Gal 3:28 is no longer slave or **f**,
Heb 13: 5 **f** from the love of money

FRIEND
Ex 33:11 as one speaks to a **f**.
2 Sam 16:17 this your loyalty to your **f**?
2 Chr 20: 7 of your **f** Abraham?
Ps 41: 9 Even my bosom **f** in whom I
Prov 17:17 A **f** loves at all times,
Song 5:16 beloved and this is my **f**,
Mt 11:19 a **f** of tax collectors and
Jn 3:29 for the bridegroom,
Jas 2:23 he was called the **f** of God.

FRUIT
Gen 1:11 and **f** trees of every kind
Deut 28: 4 and the **f** of your livestock,
Ps 1: 3 yield their **f** in its season,

Prov 8:19 My **f** is better than gold,
Isa 27: 6 fill the whole world with **f**.
Ezek 47:12 will not wither nor their **f** fail,
Hos 9:10 Like the first **f** on the fig tree,
Am 8: 1 a basket of summer **f**.
Mt 3: 8 Bear **f** worthy of repentance.
 7:17 every good tree bears good **f**,
Lk 6:44 is known by its own **f**.
Jn 15: 2 to make it bear more **f**.
Acts 14:17 from heaven and **f** seasons,
Eph 5: 9 the **f** of the light is found
Heb 13:15 the **f** of lips that confess his
Rev 22: 2 with its twelve kinds of **f**,

FULFILL
Gen 26: 3 and I will **f** the oath that I
2 Chr 10:15 the LORD might **f** his word,
Ps 20: 5 May the LORD **f** all your
Jer 33:14 when I will **f** the promise I
 11:14 in order to **f** the vision,
Mt 1:22 to **f** what had been spoken by
 8:17 This was to **f** what had been
Jn 12:38 This was to **f** the word spoken
 15:25 It was to **f** the word
Gal 6: 2 you will **f** the law of Christ.
Jas 2: 8 if you really **f** the royal law

FULL (NESS)
Ruth 1:21 I went away **f**,
2 Chr 24:10 the chest until it was **f**.
Job 14: 1 few of days and **f** of trouble,
Ps 33: 5 the earth is **f** of the steadfast
Sir 42:16 work of the Lord is **f** of his
Isa 1:15 your hands are **f** of blood.
Mal 3:10 Bring the **f** tithe into the
Mt 6:22 your whole body will be **f** of
Jn 1:14 **f** of grace and truth.
Acts 6: 3 **f** of the Spirit and of
Eph 1:10 as a plan for the **f** of time,
Jas 3:17 **f** of mercy and good fruits.
Rev 4: 6 **f** of eyes in front and

FUTURE
Ex 13:14 When in the **f** your child asks
Ps 22:30 **f** generations will be told
Jer 29:11 to give you a **f** with hope.
1 Cor 3:22 or the present or the **f**

G

GAIN
Gen 24:60 your offspring **g** possession
1 Sam 8: 3 but turned aside after **g**;
Prov 1: 5 the wise also hear and **g** in
 28:16 hates unjust **g** will enjoy a
Ezek 28:22 and I will **g** glory in your
Mk 8:36 profit them to **g** the whole
Lk 9:25 if they **g** the whole world,
1 Cor 13: 3 do not have love, I **g** nothing.
Phil 1:21 is Christ and dying is **g**.
1 Tim 3:13 deacons **g** a good standing
Titus 1: 7 or violent or greedy for **g**;
1 Pet 5: 2 not for sordid **g** but eagerly.

GATE (S)
Gen 24:60 of the **g** of their foes."

Neh 1: 3 and its **g** have been destroyed
Ps 24: 7 Lift up your heads, O **g**!
Isa 60:11 Your **g** shall always be open;
Mt 16:18 and the **g** of Hades will not
Rev 21:12 high wall with twelve **g**,
1 Macc 4:38 profaned, and the **g** burned

GATHER
Ex 16: 4 go out and **g** enough for that
Ruth 2: 7 let me glean and **g** among the
Neh 1: 9 I will **g** them from there and
Ps 106:47 O LORD our God, and **g** us
Isa 11:12 and **g** the dispersed of Judah
Jer 3:17 all nations shall **g** to it,
Joel 3: 2 I will **g** all the nations
Mt 12:30 whoever does not **g** with me
 23:37 I desired to **g** your children
Lk 3:17 his threshing floor and to **g**
 17:37 there the vultures will **g**.
Jn 11:52 but to **g** into one the dispersed
Rev 14:18 sickle and **g** the clusters of the

GAVE
Gen 2:20 The man **g** names to all cattle,
 35:12 The land that I **g** to Abraham
Ex 31:18 he **g** him the two tablets of
Deut 2:12 the land that the LORD **g** them
 26: 9 this place and **g** us this land,
Josh 11:23 Joshua **g** it for an inheritance
 15:13 he **g** to Caleb son of
1 Sam 1: 5 but to Hannah he **g** a double
2 Sam 8: 6 The LORD **g** victory to David
1 Kings 4:29 God **g** Solomon very great
Neh 9:15 you **g** them bread from heaven,
 9:34 and the warnings that you **g**
Job 1:21 I return there; the LORD **g**.
Ps 69:21 They **g** me poison for food,
Ezek 3: 2 and he **g** me the scroll to eat
Dan 1: 7 The palace master **g** them
Mt 25:35 I was hungry and you **g** me
 25:42 I was hungry and you **g** me no
Mk 6: 7 out two by two, and **g** them
Jn 1:12 in his name, he **g** power
 17: 4 finishing the work that you **g**
 19:30 he bowed his head and **g** up
Rom 1:24 Therefore God **g** them up in
 1:28 God **g** them up to a debased
2 Cor 8: 3 they voluntarily **g** according to
Eph 4: 8 he **g** gifts to his people."
 5: 2 loved us and **g** himself up for
2 Thess 2:16 through grace **g** us eternal
Titus 2:14 He it is who **g** himself for us
1 Jn 5:11 God **g** us eternal life, and this
Rev 11:13 and **g** glory to the God of
 16:19 great Babylon and **g**

GENERATION (S)
Gen 7: 1 righteous before me in this **g**.
Ex 1: 6 his brothers, and that whole **g**.
Deut 1:35 —not one of this evil **g**
Tob 13:11 **G** after **g** will give joyful praise
1 Macc 2:61 "And so observe, from **g** to **g**
Ps 48:13 you may tell the next **g**
 102:18 this be recorded for a **g** to
Sir 44:1 our ancestors in their **g**.
Dan 4: 3 his sovereignty is from **g** to **g**.
Joel 1: 3 and their children another **g**.
Mt 12:39 An evil and adulterous **g** asks
 23:36 this will come upon this **g**.
Mk 9:19 You faithless **g**, how much

Lk 1:50 who fear him from **g** to **g**.
21:32 this **g** will not pass away until
Phil 2:15 of a crooked and perverse **g**.

GENEROUS

Tob 9:6 and noble, upright and **g**!
Prov 11:25 A **g** person will be enriched,
Sir 35:10 Be **g** when you worship the
Mt 20:15 you envious because I am **g**?
Rom 10:12 Lord of all and is **g** to all
1 Tim 6:18 be rich in good works, **g**,
Jas 1:17 Every **g** act of giving,

GENTILE (S)

Mt 4:15 the Jordan, Galilee of the **G**
Lk 2:32 light for revelation to the **G**
21:24 until the times of the **G** are
Acts 9:15 to bring my name before **G**
18:6 I will go to the **G**.
Rom 2:14 When **G**, who do not possess
15:9 will confess you among the **G**,
1 Cor 1:23 to Jews and foolishness to **G**,
Gal 1:16 proclaim him among the **G**,
Eph 3:6 the **G** have become fellow
1 Tim 2:7 teacher of the **G** in faith and

GENTLE

Deut 28:54 refined and **g** of men among
Prov 15:4 A **g** tongue is a tree of
Mt 11:29 for I am **g** and humble in
1 Tim 3:3 violent but **g**, not quarrelsome,
Jas 3:17 first pure, then peaceable, **g**,
1 Pet 2:18 those who are kind and **g**

GIFT

Num 18:7 give your priesthood as a **g**;
Prov 18:16 A **g** opens doors; it gives
Eccl 3:13 it is God's **g** that all should eat
Mt 5:23 when you are offering your **g**
Jn 4:10 If you knew the **g** of God,
Acts 2:38 receive the **g** of the Holy
Rom 1:11 you some spiritual **g**
5:15 of God and the free **g** in the
1 Cor 7:7 But each has a particular **g**
2 Cor 8:12 the **g** is acceptable
Eph 2:8 it is the **g** of God
1 Tim 4:14 Do not neglect the **g** that is in
Heb 6:4 have tasted the heavenly **g**,
1 Pet 3:7 also heirs of the gracious **g** of
Rev 21:6 will give water as a **g** from the

GLAD

Ex 4:14 you his heart will be **g**.
Job 22:19 righteous see it and are **g**;
Ps 9:2 I will be **g** and exult in you;
48:11 Let Mount Zion be **g**;
118:24 let us rejoice and be **g** in it.
Prov 10:1 A wise child makes a **g** father,
15:20 A wise child makes a **g** father,
Isa 25:9 let us be **g** and rejoice
65:18 But be **g** and rejoice forever
Jer 20:15 a son," making him very **g**,
Joel 2:21 be **g** and rejoice, for the LORD
Zech 10:7 hearts shall be **g** as with wine.
Mt 5:12 Rejoice and be **g**,
Jn 8:56 he saw it and was **g**."
Acts 2:26 therefore my heart was **g**,
Phil 2:17 I am **g** and rejoice with all of

GLORIFY (GLORIFIED)

Lev 10:3 I will be **g**' " And Aaron was
Isa 44:23 Jacob, and will be **g** in Israel.
Mk 2:12 were all amazed and **g** God,
Lk 5:26 all of them, and they **g** God
Jn 7:39 because Jesus was not yet **g**.
13:31 Son of Man has been **g**
Rom 8:17 that we may also be **g**
Gal 1:24 And they **g** God because
2 Thess 1:10 he comes to be **g** by his saints
1 Pet 4:11 so that God may be **g** in all

GLORY (GLORIOUS)

Ex 14:4 so that I will gain **g** for myself
16:10 and the **g** of the LORD
33:18 Moses said, "Show me your **g**."
Lev 9:6 so that the **g** of the LORD may
Num 14:10 Then the **g** of the LORD
16:42 and the **g** of the LORD
Deut 5:24 God has shown us his **g** and
1 Sam 4:21 "The **g** has departed from
1 Kings 8:11 for the **g** of the LORD filled the
1 Chr 16:10 **G** in his holy name;
2 Chr 5:14 for the **g** of the LORD filled
Tob 12:15 and enter before the **g** of the
Jdt 15:9 "You are the **g** of Jerusalem,
1 Macc 1:40 now grew as great as her **g**
Ps 3:3 a shield around me, my **g**.
63:2 beholding your power and **g**.
108:5 let your **g** be over all the earth
Prov 19:11 their **g** to overlook an offense.
25:2 It is the **g** of God to conceal
Wis 7:25 emanation of the **g** of the
Isa 2:10 and from the **g** of his majesty.
48:11 My **g** I will not give to
Ezek 1:28 likeness of the **g** of the LORD.
8:4 And the **g** of the God of Israel
11:23 the **g** of the LORD ascended
Dan 2:37 power, the might, and the **g**,
Hab 2:14 of the **g** of the LORD,
Zech 2:5 and I will be the **g** within it."
Mal 2:2 heart to give **g** to my name,
Mt 16:27 angels in the **g** of his Father,
25:31 on the throne of his **g**.
Mk 8:38 he comes in the **g** of his Father
Lk 2:9 and the **g** of the Lord shone
9:32 they saw his **g** and the two
Jn 1:14 and we have seen his **g**,
8:50 do not seek my own **g**;
17:5 with the **g** that I had in your
Acts 7:55 saw the **g** of God and Jesus
Rom 1:23 exchanged the **g** of the
16:27 to whom be the **g** forever!
1 Cor 2:7 before the ages for our **g**.
10:31 everything for the **g** of God.
2 Cor 1:20 say the "Amen," to the **g** of
4:17 for an eternal weight of **g**
Eph 1:12 for the praise of his **g**.
3:21 to him be **g** in the church
Phil 1:11 for the **g** and praise of God.
3:19 and their **g** is in their shame;
Col 1:27 are the riches of the **g** of this
1 Thess 2:12 into his own kingdom and **g**.
2 Thess 2:14 the **g** of our Lord Jesus Christ
1 Tim 1:11 that conforms to the **g** gospel
2 Tim 2:10 in Christ Jesus, with eternal **g**.
Heb 1:3 He is the reflection of God's **g**
3:3 Jesus is worthy of more **g** than
1 Pet 1:7 to result in praise and **g** and
4:11 To him belong the **g** and the

2 Pet 1:3 called us by his own **g** and
Rev 1:6 to him be **g** and dominion
19:7 and give him the **g**.

GODLY

Ps 12:1 no longer anyone who is **g**;
Mal 2:15 **G** offspring. So look to
2 Cor 1:12 with frankness and **g** sincerity,
7:11 what earnestness this **g** grief
Titus 2:12 self-controlled, upright, and **g**.

GODS

Gen 31:19 stole her father's household **g**.
Ex 12:12 animals; on all the **g** of Egypt
Deut 5:7 you shall have no other **g**
Josh 24:14 the **g** that your ancestors
1 Sam 17:43 cursed David by his **g**.
1 Kings 20:23 "Their **g** are **g** of the hills
2 Kings 17:7 They had worshiped other **g**
1 Chr 16:26 For all the **g** of the peoples are
2 Chr 2:5 God is greater than other **g**.
Jdt 3:8 to dstroy all the **g** of the land,
1 Macc 5:68 images of their **g** he burned
Ps 82:6 You are **g**, children of the
Wis 12:24 accepting as **g** those animals
Jer 2:11 Has a nation changed its **g**,
Zeph 2:11 he will shrivel all the **g** of the
Jn 10:34 your law, 'I said, you are **g**';
1 Cor 8:5 there may be so-called **g**

OLD

Ex 3:22 jewelry of silver and of **g**,
20:23 make for yourselves gods of **g**.
Josh 7:21 bar of **g** weighing fifty shekels,
1 Sam 6:4 Five **g** tumors and five **g** mice
1 Kings 6:21 of the house with pure **g**,
2 Chr 9:13 The weight of **g** that came to
Ezra 1:6 with silver vessels, with **g**,
Job 22:25 if the Almighty is your **g**
28:15 It cannot be gotten for **g**,
Ps 19:10 be desired are they than **g**,
Prov 3:14 and her revenue better than **g**,
Isa 60:17 of bronze I will bring **g**,
Dan 2:32 that statue was of fine **g**,
Zech 4:2 see a lampstand all of **g**,
Mt 2:11 they offered him gifts of **g**,
Rev 3:18 **g** refined by fire so that
21:18 while the city is pure **g**.

GOOD

Gen 1:4 saw that the light was **g**;
3:5 knowing **g** and evil."
41:26 The seven **g** cows are seven
Ex 3:8 of that land to a **g** and broad
Num 10:29 LORD has promised **g** to Israel."
Josh 21:45 the **g** promises that the LORD
2 Sam 14:17 discerning **g** and evil.
1 Kings 8:56 has failed of all his **g** promise,
2 Chr 7:3 For he is **g**, for his steadfast
Neh 2:18 themselves to the common **g**.
Job 2:10 Shall we receive the **g** at the
Ps 14:1 is no one who does **g**.
73:1 Truly God is **g** to the upright,
147:1 How **g** it is to sing praises
Prov 3:4 will find favor and **g** repute
19:2 without knowledge is not **g**,
Isa 5:20 you who call evil **g** and **g** evil,
Jer 6:16 ancient paths, where the **g** way
24:2 One basket had very **g** figs,
Am 5:14 Seek **g** and not evil,

Nah	1:15	who brings **g** tidings,
Zech	8:15	days to do **g** to Jerusalem
Mt	5:13	It is no longer **g** for anything,
	25:21	Well done, **g** and trustworthy
Mk	1:15	and believe in the **g** news."
	4:8	Other seed fell into **g** soil
Lk	2:10	I am bringing you **g** news of
	8:8	Some fell into **g** soil,
Jn	1:46	**g** come out of Nazareth?"
	10:11	"I am the **g** shepherd.
Acts	8:12	was proclaiming the **g** news
Rom	7:12	is holy and just and **g**
	16:19	be wise in what is **g**
2 Cor	9:8	share abundantly in every **g**
Gal	6:10	let us work for the **g** of all,
Eph	2:10	in Christ Jesus for **g** works,
Phil	1:6	the one who began a **g** work
1 Thess	5:21	hold fast to what is **g**;
1 Tim	1:5	a **g** conscience, and sincere
	6:18	They are to do **g**,
2 Tim	2:3	in suffering like a **g** soldier
	4:7	I have fought the **g** fight,
Titus	2:3	are to teach what is **g**,
	2:7	respects a model of **g** works,
Heb	5:14	to distinguish **g** from evil.
	13:16	Do not neglect to do **g**
1 Pet	2:3	tasted that the Lord is **g**.
3 Jn	1:2	that you may be in **g** health,

GOSPEL

Mk	8:35	for the sake of the **g**.
Rom	1:1	set apart for the **g** of God,
	1:16	am not ashamed of the **g**;
1 Cor	1:17	baptize but to proclaim the **g**,
	9:14	get their living by the **g**.
Gal	1:6	are turning to a different **g**
Eph	1:13	the **g** of your salvation,
Phil	1:5	of your sharing in the **g**
Col	1:23	hope promised by the **g** that
2 Thess	1:8	do not obey the **g** of our Lord
Philem	1:13	my imprisonment for the **g**;
1 Pet	4:6	reason the **g** was proclaimed
Rev	14:6	with an eternal **g** to proclaim

GOSSIP

Prov	11:13	A **g** goes about telling secrets,
Sir	19:6	one who hates **g** has less evil
2 Cor	12:20	selfishness, slander, **g**, conceit,

GRACE

Ps	45:2	**g** is poured upon your lips
Zech	4:7	**g** to it!' "
Jn	1:14	full of **g** and truth.
Acts	4:33	great **g** was upon them all.
	15:11	through the **g** of the Lord.
Rom	1:5	whom we have received **g**
	5:21	so **g** might also exercise
1 Cor	1:3	**G** to you and peace from
	3:10	According to the **g** of God
2 Cor	1:2	**G** to you and peace from
	9:14	of the surpassing **g** of God
Gal	1:3	**G** to you and peace from
	1:15	called me through his **g**
Eph	1:2	**G** to you and peace
	3:2	of the commission of God's **g**
Phil	1:2	**G** to you and peace
Col	1:2	**G** to you and peace
1 Thess	1:1	**G** to you and peace.
2 Thess	1:2	**G** to you and peace
	2:16	through **g** gave us eternal

1 Tim	1:2	**G**, mercy, and peace from God
2 Tim	1:2	**G**, mercy, and peace from God
	2:1	be strong in the **g** that is in
Titus	1:4	**G** and peace from God
	3:15	**G** be with all of you
Philem	1:3	**G** to you and peace from
Heb	2:9	so that by the **g** of God
	13:25	**G** be with all of you
Jas	4:6	he gives all the more **g**;
1 Pet	1:2	May **g** and peace be yours in
	5:12	that this is the true **g** of God.
2 Pet	1:2	May **g** and peace be yours
Jude	1:4	who pervert the **g** of our God
Rev	1:4	**G** to you and peace from

GRACIOUS

Ex	33:19	'The LORD'; and I will be **g** to
2 Sam	12:22	The LORD may be **g** to me,
2 Chr	30:9	the LORD your God is **g** and
Ezra	7:9	for the **g** hand of his God was
Neh	2:8	for the **g** hand of my God was
	9:17	**g** and merciful, slow to anger
Ps	4:1	Be **g** to me, and hear my
	41:4	O LORD, be **g** to me; heal me,
Prov	11:16	A **g** woman gets honor,
Isa	30:18	the LORD waits to be **g** to you;
	33:2	be **g** to us; we wait for
Joel	2:13	he is **g** and merciful, slow to
Jon	4:2	knew that you are a **g** God
Mal	1:9	that he may be **g** to us.
Lk	4:22	were amazed at the **g** words
1 Pet	3:7	are also heirs of the **g** gift of

GRAPES

Gen	40:11	the **g** and pressed them
Ezek	18:2	parents have eaten sour **g**.
Mic	6:15	shall tread **g**, but not drink
Mt	7:16	Are **g** gathered from thorns, or

GREAT (ER) (LY)

Gen	1:16	God made the two **g** lights—
	18:20	How **g** is the outcry against
Ex	32:10	you I will make a **g** nation."
Deut	4:32	has anything so **g** as this ever
	10:17	the **g** God, mighty and
Judg	16:5	what makes his strength so **g**
2 Sam	7:9	of the **g** ones of the earth.
	22:36	your help has made me **g**.
1 Chr	16:25	For **g** is the LORD, and **g**
Neh	1:5	the **g** and awesome God who
Ps	18:35	your help has made me **g**.
	77:13	What god is so **g** as our God?
Jer	10:6	you are **g**, and your name is **g**
	32:19	**g** in counsel and mighty in
Lam	3:23	**g** is your faithfulness.
Dan	2:31	there was a **g** statue.
	7:3	and four **g** beasts came up
Joel	2:11	day of the LORD is **g**;
Zeph	1:14	The **g** day of the LORD is
Mal	1:11	is **g** among the nations,
	4:5	Elijah before the **g** and terrible
Mt	4:16	have seen a **g** light,
	20:26	whoever wishes to be **g** among
Lk	2:10	bringing you good news of **g**
	6:35	Your reward will be **g**,
Eph	1:19	to the working of his **g** power.
1 Tim	3:16	mystery of our religion is **g**:
Heb	2:3	if we neglect so **g** a salvation?
	12:1	by so **g** a cloud of witnesses,
Jude	1:6	for the judgment of the **g** Day.

Rev	6:17	for the **g** day of their wrath
	20:11	Then I saw a **g** white throne

GREED (Y)

Prov	15:27	Those who are **g** for unjust
Sir	14:9	eye of the **g** person is not
1 Cor	5:11	who is sexually immoral or **g**,
Eph	4:19	to licentiousness, **g**
Titus	1:7	wine or violent or **g** for gain;

GREEK

2 Macc	4:10	over to the **G** way of life.
Jn	19:20	Hebrew, in Latin, and in **G**.
Acts	16:1	but his father was a **G**.
Gal	3:28	is no longer Jew or **G**,

GUARD

Gen	3:24	flaming and turning to **g**
Neh	4:9	and set a **g** as a protection
Ps	17:8	**G** me as the apple of
	91:11	angels concerning you to **g**
Prov	2:11	and understanding will **g** you.
Mt	27:66	So they went with the **g**
Phil	4:7	will **g** your hearts
1 Tim	6:20	**g** what has been entrusted to
2 Tim	1:12	that he is able to **g**
2 Jn	1:8	Be on your **g**.

GUIDE

Ps	31:3	name's sake lead me and **g** me,
	67:4	**g** the nations upon earth.
Isa	58:11	The LORD will **g** you
Lk	1:79	to **g** our feet into the way
Rev	7:17	and he will **g** them to

GUILT

Gen	44:16	out the **g** of your servants;
Lev	4:3	thus bringing **g** on the people,
	5:15	as your **g** offering to the LORD,
Ezra	9:6	and our **g** has mounted up to
Ps	32:5	and you forgave the **g** of my
Prov	14:9	Fools mock at the **g** offering,
Jer	2:22	stain of your **g** is still before
Hos	5:5	Ephraim stumbles in his **g**;
Zech	3:9	I will remove the **g** of this land

H

HADES

Mt	16:18	gates of **H** will not prevail
Rev	1:18	keys of Death and of **H**.
	20:13	Death and **H** gave up the dead

HAND

Gen	3:22	he might reach out his **h**
	16:12	with his **h** against everyone,
Ex	3:19	compelled by a mighty **h**.
	33:22	cover you with my **h** until I
Deut	4:34	by a mighty **h** and an
Josh	8:7	will give it into your **h**.
1 Sam	17:50	no sword in David's **h**.
2 Sam	1:14	your **h** to destroy the LORD's
1 Kings	8:24	this day fulfilled with your **h**
	13:4	Jeroboam stretched out his **h**
1 Chr	21:17	Let your **h**, I pray,
2 Chr	6:15	day have fulfilled with your **h**.

Neh	2: 8	for the gracious **h** of my God
Ps	10:12	lift up your **h**; do not forget
	32: 4	your **h** was heavy upon me;
	110: 1	"Sit at my right **h**
Prov	3:16	life is in her right **h**;
	21: 1	of water in the **h** of the LORD;
Eccl	2:24	I saw, is from the **h** of God;
	9:10	Whatever your **h** finds to do,
Isa	1:25	I will turn my **h** against you;
	11: 8	put its **h** on the adder's den.
Jer	22:24	signet ring on my right **h**,
Ezek	1: 3	and the **h** of the LORD was on
Dan	3:17	fire and out of your **h**,
Jon	4:11	their right **h** from their left,
Hab	2:16	The cup in the LORD's right **h**
Mt	3:12	winnowing fork is in his **h**,
	22:44	"Sit at my right **h**,
Mk	1:31	and took her by the **h**
	5:41	He took her by the **h**
Lk	5:13	Then Jesus stretched out his **h**,
	22:69	right **h** of the power of God
Jn	10:28	snatch them out of my **h**.
Acts	2:34	"Sit at my right **h**,
Rom	8:34	who is at the right **h** of God,
Eph	1:20	seated him at his right **h**
Heb	1:13	"Sit at my right **h** until I
Jas	4: 8	Cleanse your **h**, you sinners,
1 Pet	3:22	and is at the right **h** of God,
Rev	1:16	In his right **h** he held seven

HAPPY

Gen	30:13	And Leah said, "**H** am I!
1 Kings	4:20	ate and drank and were **h**.
Job	5:17	"How **h** is the one whom God
Ps	1: 1	**H** are those who do not
	32: 1	**H** are those whose
	112: 1	**H** are those who fear the
Prov	3:13	**H** are those who find wisdom
	31:28	rise up and call her **h**;
Eccl	3:12	for them than to be **h**
Sir	14:20	**H** is the person who meditates
Bar	4:4	**H** are we, O Israel, for we
Jon	4: 6	Jonah was very **h** about the

HARM

Gen	31: 7	did not permit him to **h** me.
	48:16	has redeemed me from all **h**,
1 Sam	26:21	for I will never **h** you again,
Neh	6: 2	they intended to do me **h**.
Prov	3:29	Do not plan **h** against your
	13:20	companion of fools suffers **h**.
Am	9: 4	for **h** and not for good.
Lk	6: 9	to do **h** on the sabbath,
Rev	9:19	and with them they inflict **h**.

HATE

Ex	18:21	and **h** dishonest gain;
2 Chr	18: 7	I **h** him, for he never
Ps	5: 5	you **h** all evildoers.
	97:10	LORD loves those who **h** evil;
	139:21	Do I not **h** those who **h** you,
Prov	1:22	and fools **h** knowledge?
	9: 8	is rebuked will only **h** you;
Isa	61: 8	I **h** robbery and wrongdoing;
Jer	44: 4	abominable thing that I **h**!"
Ezek	35: 6	you did not **h** bloodshed,
Mal	2:16	For I **h** divorce, says the LORD,
Mt	5:43	neighbor and **h** your enemy.'
Lk	6:22	are you when people **h** you,
	14:26	and does not **h** father and

Jn	7: 7	The world cannot **h** you,
Rom	7:15	do the very thing I **h**.

HEAD

Gen	3:15	he will strike your **h**,
Num	6: 5	razor shall come upon the **h**;
1 Sam	1:11	no razor shall touch his **h**."
Ps	23: 5	you anoint my **h** with oil;
Prov	1: 9	a fair garland for your **h**,
Isa	59:17	helmet of salvation on his **h**;
Ezek	8: 3	by a lock of my **h**;
Dan	2:32	The **h** of that statue was of
Mt	8:20	has nowhere to lay his **h**."
1 Cor	11: 3	Christ is the **h** of every man,
	11: 5	**h** unveiled disgraces her **h**—
Eph	1:22	and has made him the **h** over
Rev	1:14	His **h** and his hair were white

HEAL (ED) (ING)

Num	12:13	"O God, please **h** her."
Deut	32:39	I wound and I **h**; and no
2 Kings	20: 8	that the LORD will **h** me,
Ps	6: 2	O LORD, **h** me, for my
	30: 2	and you have **h** me.
Wis	16:10	came to their help and **h** them
Sir	38:9	pray to the Lord, and he will **h**
Isa	19:22	striking and **h**; they will return
Jer	3:22	I will **h** your faithlessness.
	30:17	and your wounds I will **h**,
Lam	2:13	is your ruin; who can **h** you?
Ezek	30:21	not been bound up for **h**
	34: 4	the weak, you have not **h**
Hos	5:13	or **h** your wound.
	7: 1	when I would **h** Israel,
Lk	5:17	Lord was with him to **h**.
Jn	4:47	to come down and **h** his son,
Acts	4:30	stretch out your hand to **h**,

HEAR

Num	14:13	"Then the Egyptians will **h**
Deut	1:17	**h** out the small and the
	20: 3	say to them: "**H**, O Israel!
1 Kings	8:30	O **h** in heaven your dwelling
2 Kings	19:16	O LORD, and **h**; open your
2 Chr	7:14	then I will **h** from heaven,
Job	5:27	**H**, and know it for yourself
	26:14	a whisper do we **h** of him!
Ps	30:10	**H**, O LORD, and be gracious
	94: 9	the ear, does he not **h**?
Eccl	7:21	may **h** your servant cursing
Sir	5:11	Be quick to **h**, but deliberate in
Isa	1:10	**H** the word of the LORD
	21: 3	I cannot **h**, I am dismayed
	65:24	are yet speaking I will **h**.
Bar	1:3	who came to **h** the book,
Ezek	33: 7	you **h** a word from my mouth
Mt	11: 5	the deaf **h**, the dead are raised,
Jn	5:25	when the dead will **h** the voice
Acts	13: 7	wanted to **h** the word of God.
Heb	3: 7	"Today, if you **h** his voice,
Rev	1: 3	blessed are those who **h**

HEART

Gen	6: 6	it grieved him to his **h**.
Ex	4:21	but I will harden his **h**,
	10:27	LORD hardened Pharaoh's **h**,
Deut	4:29	him with all your **h** and soul.
	10:12	your God with all your **h** and
	30: 6	your God with all your **h** and
1 Sam	10: 9	God gave him another **h**;

1 Sam	12:24	him faithfully with all your **h**;
1 Kings	2: 4	with all their **h** and
	11: 4	and his **h** was not true to the
2 Kings	22:19	because your **h** was penitent,
2 Chr	6:38	they repent with all their **h**
	17: 6	His **h** was courageous in the
Tob	1:12	mindful of God with all my **h**,
1 Macc	2:24	and his **h** was stirred.
Job	19:27	My **h** faints within me!
	31: 7	and my **h** has followed my
Ps	7:10	who saves the upright in **h**.
	37: 4	you the desires of your **h**.
	86:11	give me an undivided **h** to
	119:111	are the joy of my **h**.
Prov	2: 2	and inclining your **h** to
	13:12	Hope deferred makes the **h**
	23:17	Do not let your **h** envy
Eccl	2:10	I kept my **h** from no pleasure,
	7: 7	and a bribe corrupts the **h**.
Song	4: 9	You have ravished my **h**,
Sir	2:2	Set your **h** right and be
Isa	57:15	revive the **h** of the contrite.
Jer	3:10	to me with her whole **h**,
	17: 9	**h** is devious above all else
	29:13	seek me with all your **h**,
Bar	2:31	I will give them a **h** that obeys
Ezek	36:26	the **h** of stone and give you
Joel	2:12	with all your **h**, with fasting,
Mal	2: 2	do not lay it to **h**.
Mt	5: 8	"Blessed are the pure in **h**,
	15:19	For out of the **h** come evil
Lk	2:19	and pondered them in her **h**.
	24:25	and how slow of **h** to believe
Acts	1:24	"Lord, you know everyone's **h**.
	28:27	with their **h** and turn—
Rom	2:29	is a matter of the **h**—
2 Cor	2: 4	distress and anguish of **h**
Eph	1:18	eyes of your **h** enlightened,
Phil	1: 7	you hold me in your **h**,
1 Tim	1: 5	that comes from a pure **h**,
2 Tim	2:22	the Lord from a pure **h**.
Heb	3:12	unbelieving **h** that turns away
	10:22	with a true **h** in full assurance
Rev	18: 7	Since in her **h** she says,

HEAVEN

Gen	14:19	maker of **h** and earth;
	22:11	LORD called to him from **h**,
Ex	16: 4	to rain bread from **h** for you,
Deut	3:24	what god in **h** or on earth can
	26:15	from **h**, and bless your people
1 Kings	8:23	no God like you in **h** above
	8:30	O hear in **h** your dwelling
2 Kings	1:10	let fire come down from **h**
2 Chr	6:14	in **h** or on earth, keeping
Job	16:19	my witness is in **h**,
Ps	73:25	Whom have I in **h** but you?
Isa	66: 1	**H** is my throne and the
Dan	2:19	Daniel blessed the God of **h**.
Mt	3: 2	for the kingdom of **h**
	7:21	will of my Father in **h**
Mk	8:11	him for a sign from **h**,
	13:31	**H** and earth will pass away
Lk	3:21	the **h** was opened,
	12:33	an unfailing treasure in **h**,
	19:38	and glory in the highest **h**!"
Jn	3:13	No one has ascended into **h**
	12:28	Then a voice came from **h**,
Acts	2: 2	And suddenly from **h**
	11:10	was pulled up again to **h**.

Phil 2:10 in **h** and on earth and under
3:14 for the prize of the **h** call
Col 1: 5 laid up for you in **h**.
1 Thess 1:10 wait for his Son from **h**,
Heb 1:10 the **h** are the work of your
12:26 the earth but also the **h**."
1 Pet 1: 4 unfading, kept in **h** for you,
Rev 4: 1 there in **h** a door stood open!
12: 3 portent appeared in **h**:

HELL
Mt 5:22 will be liable to the **h** of fire.
23:33 escape being sentenced to **h**?
Mk 9:43 hands and to go to **h**,
2 Pet 2: 4 into **h** and committed them to

HELP
Gen 4: 1 with the **h** of the LORD."
Ex 2:23 cry for **h** rose up to God.
1 Chr 12:22 David to **h** him, until there
2 Chr 16:12 but sought **h** from physicians.
Neh 6:16 with the **h** of our God.
Ps 18: 6 my God I cried for **h**.
115:11 He is their **h** and their shield.
Lam 1: 7 there was no one to **h** her,
Acts 16: 9 over to Macedonia and **h** us."
1 Thess 5:14 **h** the weak, be patient with
Heb 2:18 he is able to **h** those who are

HID
Gen 4:14 I shall be **h** from your face;
Josh 2: 6 and **h** them with the stalks of
1 Sam 10:22 "See, he has **h** himself among
2 Kings 11: 3 **h** in the house of the
Job 28:11 **h** things they bring to light
Ps 19:12 Clear me from **h** faults.
142: 3 they have **h** a trap for me.
Prov 2: 4 search for it as for **h** treasures—
Isa 40:27 "My way is **h** from the LORD,
Dan 2:22 He reveals deep and **h** things;
Mt 13:35 **h** from the foundation of the
Lk 10:21 because you have **h** these
1 Cor 2: 7 secret and **h**, which God
Eph 3: 9 the mystery **h** for ages in God
Col 1:26 the mystery that has been **h**
Heb 4:13 before him no creature is **h**,
Rev 2:17 give some of the **h** manna,

HIGH
Gen 14:18 was priest of God Most **H**.
1 Kings 3: 2 sacrificing at the **h** places,
Ps 7: 7 it take your seat on **h**.
91: 1 the shelter of the Most **H**,
113: 5 God, who is seated on **h**,
Prov 24: 7 Wisdom is too **h** for fools;
Eccl 10: 6 folly is set in many **h** places,
Jer 2:20 On every **h** hill
Dan 4:17 that the Most **H** is sovereign
Mt 4: 8 took him to a very **h** mountain
Mk 5: 7 Son of the Most **H** God?
Jn 18:22 how you answer the **h** priest?"
Acts 23: 4 dare to insult God's **h** priest?"
Eph 4: 8 "When he ascended on **h** he

HOLY
Ex 3: 5 you are standing is **h** ground."
40: 9 so that it shall become **h**.
Lev 11:44 and be **h**, for I am **h**.
Num 4:15 they must not touch the **h**
Deut 5:12 sabbath day and keep it **h**.

Deut 26:19 you to be a people **h**
Josh 5:15 place where you stand is **h**."
1 Sam 2: 2 "There is no **H** One like the
2 Kings 4: 9 our way is a **h** man of God.
1 Chr 6:49 the work of the most **h** place,
2 Chr 3: 8 He made the most **h** place;
Ezra 9: 2 Thus the **h** seed has mixed
Tob 11:14 and blessed be all his **h** angels
1 Macc 1:15 abandoned the **h** covenant
Job 6:10 denied the words of the **H**
Ps 2: 6 my king on Zion, my **h** hill."
77:13 Your way, O God, is **h**.
89:18 king to the **H** One of Israel.
Prov 9:10 knowledge of the **H** One is
Isa 1: 4 who have despised the **H** One
58:13 the **h** day of the LORD
Jer 2: 3 Israel was **h** to the Lord,
Ezek 22:26 have profaned my **h** things;
Dan 4:13 and there was a **h** watcher,
9:24 your people and your **h** city:
Jon 2: 4 again upon your **h** temple?'
Zech 8: 3 be called the **h** mountain.
14:20 the LORD shall be as **h**
Mt 1:18 with child from the **H** Spirit,
28:19 the Son and of the **H** Spirit,
Mk 1:24 are, the **H** One of God."
Lk 1:15 will be filled with the **H** Spirit.
3:22 the **H** Spirit descended upon
11:13 Father give the **H** Spirit to
Jn 6:69 you are the **H** One of God."
20:22 "Receive the **H** Spirit.
Acts 1: 5 be baptized with the **H** Spirit
13:35 let your **H** One experience
19: 2 heard that there is a **H** Spirit."
Rom 1: 2 prophets in the **h** scriptures,
12: 1 sacrifice, **h** and acceptable
1 Cor 7:14 husband is made **h**
Eph 1: 4 to be **h** and blameless before
4:30 not grieve the **H** Spirit of God,
Col 1:22 present you **h** and blameless
1 Tim 2: 8 lifting up **h** hands without
2 Tim 1: 9 called us with a **h** calling,
Titus 3: 5 renewal by the **H** Spirit.
Heb 2: 4 and by gifts of the **H** Spirit,
Heb 9: 2 this is called the **H** Place.
1 Pet 1:15 he who called you is **h**,
3: 5 the **h** women who hoped in
1 Jn 2:20 been anointed by the **H** One,
Rev 3: 7 are the words of the **h** one,
21: 2 the **h** city, the new Jerusalem,

HOME (LESS)
Isa 58: 7 the **h** poor into your house;

HONEY
Ex 3: 8 flowing with milk and **h**,
Judg 14: 8 body of the lion, and **h**.
Ps 19:10 sweeter also than **h**,
Prov 5: 3 of a loose woman drip **h**,
Isa 7:15 He shall eat curds and **h**
Mt 3: 4 food was locusts and wild **h**.

HONOR
Ex 20:12 **H** your father and your
1 Sam 2: 8 and inherit a seat of **h**.
2 Chr 1:11 for possessions, wealth, **h**,
Ps 8: 5 them with glory and **h**.
Prov 3: 9 **H** the LORD with your
15:33 and humility goes before **h**.
29:23 lowly in spirit will obtain **h**.

Isa 29:13 and **h** me with their lips,
Mt 13:57 "Prophets are not without **h**
19:19 **H** your father and mother;
Lk 14: 8 at the place of **h**, in case
Jn 4:44 a prophet has no **h** in the
Rom 12:10 one another in showing **h**.
Eph 6: 2 **H** your father and mother"—
Heb 2: 7 them with glory and **h**,
2 Pet 1:17 For he received **h** and glory
Rev 4: 9 give glory and **h** and thanks

HOPE
Ruth 1:12 I thought there was **h** for me,
Ezra 10: 2 even now there is **h** for Israel
Jdt 9:11 savior of those without **h**.
Esth 9: 1 enemies of the Jews **h**
Job 13:15 I have no **h**; but I will
Ps 9:18 nor the **h** of the poor
39: 7 My **h** is in you.
130: 7 **h** in the LORD!
Prov 11: 7 their **h** perishes,
24:14 your **h** will not be cut off
Sir 34:15 their **h** is in him who saves
Isa 8:17 and I will **h** in him.
Jer 14: 8 O **h** of Israel,
Ezek 37:11 and our **h** is lost;
Mt 12:21 his name the Gentiles will **h**."
Jn 5:45 whom you have set your **h**.
Acts 2:26 my flesh will live in **h**.
Rom 4:18 Hoping against **h**, he believed
15:13 that you may abound in **h**
1 Cor 13:13 **h**, and love abide,
2 Cor 1:10 our **h** that he will rescue us
Eph 1:12 to set our **h** on Christ,
Col 1: 5 because of the **h** laid up
1 Thess 1: 3 steadfastness of **h** in our Lord
1 Tim 1: 1 and of Christ Jesus our **h**,
Titus 1: 2 in the **h** of eternal life
Heb 3: 6 the pride that belong to **h**.
1 Pet 1: 3 a living **h** through the
1 Jn 3: 3 And all who have this **h** in

HORN (S)
Gen 22:13 in a thicket by its **h**.
Josh 6: 4 seven trumpets of rams' **h**
Dan 7: 7 and it had ten **h**.
Zech 1:18 looked up and saw four **h**.
Rev 5: 6 having seven **h** and seven eyes,

HOSPITABLE
1 Tim 3: 2 respectable, **h**, an apt teacher,
Titus 1: 8 but he must be **h**, a lover
1 Pet 4: 9 Be **h** to one another

HOUR
Mt 6:27 add a single **h** to your span
Mk 14:35 the **h** might pass from him.
Jn 2: 4 My **h** has not yet come."
12:23 "The **h** has come for the Son
1 Jn 2:18 Children, it is the last **h**!
Rev 3:10 will keep you from the **h**

HOUSE
Gen 19: 2 turn aside to your servant's **h**
Ex 12:22 door of your **h** until morning.
Num 12: 7 is entrusted with all my **h**.
Josh 2: 1 entered the **h** of a prostitute
1 Sam 1: 7 went up to the **h** of the LORD,
2 Sam 2:10 But the **h** of Judah followed
7:11 LORD will make you a **h**.

1 Kings	8:43	has been invoked on this **h**
1 Chr	22:1	Here shall be the **h** of the LORD
Ezra	1:5	rebuild the **h** of the LORD
Jdt	9:13	and against your sacred **h**,
1 Macc	7:37	"You chose this **h** to be called
Ps	23:6	dwell in the **h** of the LORD
	69:9	zeal for your **h** that has
Prov	7:27	Her **h** is the way to Sheol
	14:11	The **h** of the wicked is
Eccl	10:18	through indolence the **h** leaks.
Jer	18:2	go down to the potter's **h**,
	32:34	the **h** that bears my name,
Joel	3:18	forth from the **h** of the LORD
Hag	1:4	while this **h** lies in ruins?
Mt	7:24	built his **h** on rock.
	13:57	country and in their own **h**."
Mk	3:25	that **h** will not be able
Lk	6:48	like a man building a **h**,
	19:9	salvation has come to this **h**,
Jn	2:16	my Father's **h** a marketplace!"
Rom	16:5	church in their **h**.
Heb	3:2	was faithful in all God's **h**."
2 Jn	1:10	receive into the **h** or welcome

HUMAN (KIND)

Gen	1:26	"Let us make **h** in our image,
	6:7	from the earth the **h** beings
Num	19:16	or a **h** bone, or a grave,
1 Kings	13:2	and **h** bones shall be burned
Ps	8:4	what are **h** beings that
	33:13	from heaven; he sees all **h**.
Dan	2:34	, not by **h** hands, and it struck
	8:25	broken, and not by **h** hands.
Hos	11:4	with cords of **h** kindness,
Mt	9:8	such authority to **h** beings.
Lk	20:6	'Of **h** origin,' all the people
Jn	5:34	I accept such **h** testimony,
Acts	5:29	obey God rather than any **h**
1 Cor	1:26	wise by **h** standards,
Phil	2:7	being born in **h** likeness.
1 Thess	4:8	not **h** authority but God,
Heb	12:9	we had **h** parents to discipline
Rev	4:7	with a face like a **h** face,

HUMBLE

Ex	10:3	refuse to **h** yourself before me?
Deut	8:2	in order to **h** you, testing you
2 Sam	22:28	You deliver a **h** people,
2 Chr	7:14	by my name **h** themselves,
Job	22:29	pride; for he saves the **h**.
Ps	18:27	For you deliver a **h** people,
	55:19	hear, and will **h** them—
Prov	3:34	but to the **h** he shows favor.
Isa	57:15	those who are contrite and **h**
Zeph	2:3	all you **h** of the land,
Mt	11:29	for I am gentle and **h** in heart,
2 Cor	12:21	my God may **h** me before you,
Jas	4:6	but gives grace to the **h**."
1 Pet	3:8	a tender heart, and a **h** mind.

HUNGER (HUNGRY)

Ex	16:3	this whole assembly with **h**."
Deut	8:3	humbled you by letting you **h**,
Neh	9:15	their **h** you gave them bread
Ps	50:12	"If I were **h**, I would not tell
Prov	10:3	the righteous go **h**, but he
Isa	29:8	as when a **h** person dreams
Mt	12:1	his disciples were **h**, and they
	25:42	for I was **h** and you gave me
Mk	11:12	came from Bethany, he was **h**.

Rom	12:20	"if your enemies are **h**,
1 Cor	4:11	present hour we are **h** and

HUSBAND (S)

Gen	3:6	also gave some to her **h**,
Num	30:8	time that her **h** hears of it,
Deut	24:4	her first **h**, who sent her away,
Prov	7:19	For my **h** is not at home;
	31:28	call her happy; her **h** too,
Isa	54:5	your Maker is your **h**, the
Jer	3:20	faithless wife leaves her **h**,
Mt	1:19	Her **h** Joseph, being a
Jn	4:17	"I have no **h**." Jesus said to
Rom	7:2	by the law to her **h** as long
1 Cor	7:2	and each woman her own **h**.
	7:39	bound as long as her **h** lives.
2 Cor	11:2	you in marriage to one **h**,
Eph	5:22	subject to your **h** as you are
	5:23	For the **h** is the head of the
Rev	21:2	a bride adorned for her **h**.

HYPOCRISY

Mt	23:28	are full of **h** and lawlessness.
Lk	12:1	Pharisees, that is, their **h**.
Jas	3:17	a trace of partiality or **h**.

HYPOCRITE (S)

Ps	26:4	nor do I consort with **h**;
Mt	6:2	as the **h** do in the synagogues
	15:7	You **h**! Isaiah prophesied
	23:27	and Pharisees, **h**! For you are
Mk	7:6	rightly about you **h**,
Lk	12:56	You **h**! You know how to

I

IDOL (S)

Ex	34:17	You shall not make cast **i**.
Deut	7:5	and burn their **i** with fire.
2 Kings	17:15	They went after false **i** and
Ps	31:6	who pay regard to worthless **i**,
Isa	2:8	Their land is filled with **i**;
Ezek	14:3	taken their **i** into their hearts,
Acts	15:20	from things polluted by **i** and
1 Cor	8:1	food sacrificed to **i**;
1 Jn	5:21	keep yourselves from **i**.
Rev	9:20	and **i** of gold and silver and

IMAGE

Gen	1:26	us make humankind in our **i**,
Ex	32:4	and cast an **i** of a calf;
Ps	106:19	Horeb and worshiped a cast **i**.
Wis	2:23	us in the **i** of his own eternity,
Sir	17:3	and made them in his own **i**.
Rom	8:29	conformed to the **i** of his Son,
1 Cor	11:7	the **i** and reflection of God;
Col	1:15	the **i** of the invisible God,
Rev	13:14	them to make an **i** for the

IMMANUEL (EMMANUEL)

Isa	7:14	son, and shall name him **I**.

IMMORALITY

Sir	41:17	Be ashamed of sexual **i**,
1 Cor	5:1	there is sexual **i** among you,
Jude	1:7	indulged in sexual **i** and

IMPOSSIBLE

Gen	11:6	to do will now be **i** for them.
Zech	8:6	Even though it seems **i** to
Mt	17:20	and nothing will be **i** for you."
Heb	6:4	For it is **i** to restore again

IMPURE (IMPURITY)

Zech	13:1	cleanse them from sin and **i**.
Rom	1:24	lusts of their hearts to **i**,
Eph	4:19	to practice every kind of **i**.
Col	3:5	fornication, **i**, passion, evil

INHERIT (ANCE)

Lev	20:24	You shall **i** their land, and I
Deut	10:9	no allotment or **i** with his
2 Kings	2:9	Please let me **i** a double share
Ps	37:11	But the meek shall **i** the land,
Prov	13:22	good leave an **i** to their
Eccl	7:11	is as good as an **i**,
Mt	5:5	for they will **i** the earth.
Lk	10:25	"what must I do to **i** eternal
1 Cor	6:9	not **i** the kingdom of God?
Heb	1:14	who are to **i** salvation?
Rev	21:7	who conquer will **i** these

INNOCENT

Ex	23:7	and do not kill the **i** and
Deut	19:10	blood of an **i** person may not
1 Macc	1:37	they shed **i** blood;
Job	34:5	'I am **i**, and God has taken
Ps	19:13	and **i** of great transgression.
Prov	6:17	and hands that shed **i** blood,
Mt	10:16	be wise as serpents and **i** as
Lk	23:47	"Certainly this man was **i**."
Phil	2:15	blameless and **i**, children of

ISRAEL

Gen	49:24	the Shepherd, the Rock of **I**,
Ex	28:11	names of the sons of **I**;
Num	19:13	shall be cut off from **I**.
Deut	10:12	O **I**, what does the LORD your
Judg	17:6	there was no king in **I**; all
Ruth	4:14	his name be renowned in **I**!
1 Sam	3:20	And all **I** from Dan to
	18:16	all **I** and Judah loved David;
2 Sam	5:2	who shall be ruler over **I**."
	14:25	in all **I** there was no one
1 Kings	1:35	to be ruler over **I** and
	19:18	leave seven thousand in **I**,
2 Kings	5:8	king of **I** had torn his clothes,
1 Chr	17:22	made your people **I** to be your
Ps	22:3	enthroned on the praises of **I**
	125:5	evildoers. Peace be upon **I**!
Isa	1:3	master's crib; but **I** does not
	44:21	you are my servant; O **I**,
Jer	2:3	**I** was holy to the LORD
	31:31	covenant with the house of **I**
Ezek	34:2	shepherds of **I** who have
	37:28	that I the LORD sanctify **I**,
Dan	9:20	the sin of my people **I**,
Hos	11:1	When **I** was a child,
Mic	5:2	who is to rule in **I**,
Mal	1:5	beyond the borders of **I**!"
Mt	2:6	shepherd my people **I**.' "
Mk	12:29	'Hear, O **I**: the Lord our God,
Lk	22:30	judging the twelve tribes of **I**.
Acts	9:15	and before the people of **I**;
Rom	11:7	**I** failed to obtain what it
Eph	2:12	commonwealth of **I**, and
Rev	7:4	tribe of the people of **I**:

J

JEALOUS (JEALOUSY)

Gen	37:11	his brothers were **j** of him,
Ex	20: 5	LORD your God am a **j** God,
Num	5:14	a spirit of **j** comes on him,
	5:30	and he is **j** of his wife;
Deut	4:24	is a devouring fire, a **j** God.
1 Kings	14:22	provoked him to **j** with their
Prov	6:34	For **j** arouses a husband's fury,
	27: 4	is able to stand before **j**?
Ezek	36: 6	I am speaking in my **j** wrath,
	39:25	I will be **j** for my holy name.
Joel	2:18	the LORD became **j** for his land,
Mt	27:18	out of **j** that they had handed
1 Cor	3: 3	there is **j** and quarreling
	10:22	provoking the Lord to **j**?
2 Cor	11: 2	I feel a divine **j** for you,
Gal	5:20	enmities, strife, **j**, anger,

JERUSALEM

Josh	10: 1	**J** heard how Joshua had taken
Judg	1: 8	fought against **J** and took it.
1 Sam	17:54	Philistine and brought it to **J**;
2 Sam	11: 1	But David remained at **J**.
	15:29	the ark of God back to **J**,
1 Kings	9:19	desired to build, in **J**,
	11:13	sake of **J**, which I have chosen."
2 Kings	19:31	from **J** a remnant shall go out
	25:10	down the walls around **J**.
1 Chr	6:15	LORD sent Judah and **J** into
	21:15	sent an angel to **J** to destroy it;
2 Chr	6: 6	I have chosen **J** in order that
	20:27	returned to **J** with joy,
Ezra	1: 2	build him a house at **J**
	10: 7	that they should assemble at **J**,
Neh	2:17	rebuild the wall of **J**, so that
	12:27	dedication of the wall of **J**
Tob	13:8	and acknowledge him in **J**.
Jdt	15:9	"You are the glory of **J**.
Esth	2: 6	had been carried away from **J**
1 Macc	6:7	had erected on the altar in **J**;
Ps	79: 1	they have laid **J** in ruins.
	147:12	Praise the LORD, O **J**!
Eccl	1:16	surpassing all who were over **J**
Isa	52: 2	rise up, O captive **J**;
	62: 7	no rest until he establishes **J**
Jer	3:17	**J** shall be called the throne
	4:14	O **J**, wash your heart clean of
	13:27	Woe to you, O **J**! How long
Lam	1: 8	**J** sinned grievously, so she has
Ezek	14:21	send upon **J** my four deadly
Dan	5: 3	the house of God in **J**,
	9:12	what has been done against **J**
Joel	3:17	And **J** shall be holy, and
Am	2: 5	devour the strongholds of **J**.
Ob	1:11	gates and cast lots for **J**,
Mic	4: 2	word of the LORD from **J**.
Zeph	3:16	said to **J**: Do not fear, O Zion
Zech	1:14	I am very jealous for **J** and for
	14: 2	the nations against **J** to battle,
Mal	3: 4	offering of Judah and **J** will be
Mt	21:10	When he entered **J**, the whole
Lk	4: 9	the devil took him to **J**,
	23:28	"Daughters of **J**, do not weep
Jn	5: 1	and Jesus went up to **J**.
	10:22	the Dedication took place in **J**.

Acts	1: 8	witnesses in **J**, in all Judea
	6: 7	increased greatly in **J**, and
Rom	15:19	so that from **J** and as far
1 Cor	16: 3	to take your gift to **J**.
Heb	12:22	the living God, the heavenly **J**,
Rev	3:12	the new **J** that comes down

JEW(S)

Ezra	5: 5	upon the elders of the **J**, and
Neh	4: 1	enraged, and he mocked the **J**.
Esth	3:13	to annihilate all **J**, young and
	4:14	deliverance will rise for the **J**
Dan	3: 8	forward and denounced the **J**.
Zech	8:23	take hold of a **J**, grasping
Mt	2: 2	been born king of the **J**?
	27:37	Jesus, the King of the **J**."
Jn	4:22	for salvation is from the **J**.
Acts	13:43	many **J** and devout converts
	20:21	both **J** and Greeks about
Rom	3:29	is God the God of **J** only?
1 Cor	9:20	To the **J** I became as a **J**
Gal	1:13	of my earlier life in **J**.
	3:28	There is no longer **J** or Greek,

JOY (FUL)

Judg	19: 3	and came with **j** to meet him.
1 Sam	18: 6	tambourines, with songs of **j**,
1 Kings	1:40	great **j**, so that the earth
1 Chr	16:27	strength and **j** are in his place.
2 Chr	30:26	There was great **j** in Jerusalem,
Ezra	6:22	the LORD had made them **j**,
Neh	8:10	not be grieved, for the **j** of the
Tob	13:17	Jerusalem will sing hymns of **j**,
Esth	8:17	there was gladness and **j**
1 Macc	4:58	very great **j** among the people,
Job	8:21	your lips with shouts of **j**.
	33:26	into his presence with **j**.
Ps	51:12	Restore to me the **j** of your
	71:23	My lips will shout for **j** when I
	98: 4	Make a **j** noise to the LORD,
	119:111	they are the **j** of my heart.
Prov	12:20	who counsel peace have **j**.
	15:23	an apt answer is a **j** to anyone,
Eccl	5:20	occupied with the **j** of their
Sir	26:2	loyal wife brings **j** to her
Isa	29:19	The meek shall obtain fresh **j**
	55:12	you shall go out in **j**, and be
	61: 7	everlasting **j** shall be theirs.
Jer	31:13	turn their mourning into **j**,
	33: 9	a name of **j**, a praise and a
Lam	5:15	The **j** of our hearts has ceased
Bar	5:9	For God will lead Israel with **j**,
Ezek	24:25	their **j** and glory, the delight of
Joel	1:12	surely, **j** withers away among
Mt	13:44	in his **j** he goes and sells all
	28: 8	with fear and great **j**, and ran
Mk	4:16	immediately receive it with **j**.
Lk	1:44	in my womb leaped for **j**.
	2:10	good news of great **j** for all
	24:41	in their **j** they were
Jn	3:29	my **j** has been fulfilled.
	15:11	that your **j** may be complete.
	16:20	your pain will turn into **j**.
Acts	8: 8	So there was great **j** in that
	13:52	the disciples were filled with **j**
Rom	14:17	righteousness and peace and **j**
	15:13	fill you with all **j** and peace
2 Cor	2: 3	my **j** would be the **j** of all of
Gal	5:22	love, **j**, peace, patience,
Phil	1: 4	constantly praying with **j** in

Phil	4: 1	my **j** and crown,
1 Thess	1: 6	you received the word with **j**
	2:19	what is our hope or **j** or crown
2 Tim	1: 4	I may be filled with **j**.
Philem	1: 7	I have indeed received much **j**
Heb	13:17	Let them do this with **j** and
Jas	1: 2	consider it nothing but **j**,
1 Pet	1: 8	indescribable and glorious **j**,
1 Jn	1: 4	our **j** may be complete.
2 Jn	1:12	so that our **j** may be complete.
3 Jn	1: 4	I have no greater **j** than this,

JUDEA

Mt	2: 1	was born in Bethlehem of **J**,
Lk	7:17	him spread throughout **J**
Jn	7: 3	"Leave here and go to **J**
Acts	9:31	the church throughout **J**,
Rom	15:31	from the unbelievers in **J**,
Gal	1:22	churches of **J** that are in

JUDGE (D) (S)

Gen	16: 5	May the LORD **j** between you
	18:25	Shall not the **J** of all the earth
Ex	18:26	they **j** the people at all times
Lev	19:15	with justice you shall **j** your
Num	35:24	then the congregation shall **j**
Deut	1:16	**j** rightly between one person
Judg	2:16	Then the LORD raised up **j**,
	11:27	Let the LORD, who is **j**, decide
Ruth	1: 1	In the days when the **j** ruled,
1 Sam	2:10	LORD will **j** the ends of the
1 Chr	16:33	for he comes to **j** the earth.
Job	21:22	he **j** those that are on high
	31:28	to be punished by the **j**,
Ps	7:11	God is a righteous **j**,
	75: 2	I will **j** with equity.
Prov	31: 9	Speak out, **j** righteously,
Eccl	3:17	God will **j** the righteous and
Isa	11: 3	He shall not **j** by what his eyes
	33:22	For the LORD is our **j**,
Jer	11:20	of hosts, who **j** righteously,
Ezek	7: 3	will **j** you according to your
	33:20	house of Israel, I will **j** all
Joel	3:12	there I will sit to **j** all
Mic	4: 3	He shall **j** between many
Lk	6:37	"Do not **j**, and you will not be
	19:22	'I will **j** you by your own
Jn	7:24	Do not **j** by appearances, but **j**
	12:47	for I came not to **j** the world,
Acts	10:42	ordained by God as **j** of the
Rom	2:16	through Jesus Christ, will **j**
	3: 6	then how could God **j** the
1 Cor	4: 4	It is the Lord who **j** me.
	11:31	But if we **j** ourselves, we would
1 Tim	1:12	he **j** me faithful and appointed
2 Tim	4: 8	the Lord, the righteous **j**,
Heb	10:30	"The Lord will **j** his people."
	13: 4	for God will **j** fornicators and
Jas	4:12	are you to **j** your neighbor?
1 Pet	4: 5	who stands ready to **j** the
Rev	20: 4	were given authority to **j**.

JUDGMENT (S)

Ex	6: 6	and with mighty acts of **j**.
Deut	1:17	for the **j** is God's.
1 Chr	16:14	his **j** are in all the earth
Ps	76: 8	the heavens you uttered **j**;
	119:66	me good **j** and knowledge,
Prov	18: 1	for all who have sound **j**.
Eccl	11: 9	God will bring you into **j**.

Wis	12:12	Or will resist your **j**?
Sir	6:23	my child, and accept my **j**;
Isa	66:16	by fire will the LORD execute **j**,
Jer	25:31	he is entering into **j** with all
Ezek	20:35	I will enter into **j** with you
Dan	7:22	then **j** was given for the holy
Joel	3: 2	I will enter into **j** with them
Hab	1:12	you have marked them for **j**;
Zeph	3: 5	morning he renders his **j**,
Mal	3: 5	draw near to you for **j**;
Mt	5:22	you will be liable to **j**; and if
	12:36	day of **j** you will have to give
Jn	5:30	and my **j** is just, because I seek
	12:31	Now is the **j** of this world;
Rom	11:33	How unsearchable are his **j**
	14:13	no longer pass **j** on one
1 Cor	7:40	in my **j** she is more blessed if
2 Cor	5:10	before the **j** seat of Christ,
2 Thess	1: 5	of the righteous **j** of God,
Heb	10:27	but a fearful prospect of **j**,
Jas	2:13	mercy triumphs over **j**.
1 Pet	4:17	the time has come for **j**
2 Pet	3: 7	the day of **j** and destruction
1 Jn	4:17	boldness on the day of **j**,
Jude	1: 6	in deepest darkness for the **j**
Rev	14: 7	for the hour of his **j** has come;
	16: 7	your **j** are true and just!"

JUST (ICE)

Ex	23: 6	You shall not pervert the **j** due
Deut	16:19	You must not distort **j**; you
	32: 4	and all his ways are **j**.
1 Sam	8: 3	took bribes and perverted **j**.
2 Sam	15: 4	and I would give them **j**."
2 Chr	9: 8	execute **j** and righteousness."
Neh	9:33	You have been **j** in all that has
Tob	3: 2	and all your deeds are **j**;
Job	9:19	it is a matter of **j**,
	19: 7	but there is no **j**.
	34:12	the Almighty will not pervert **j**.
Ps	82: 3	Give **j** to the weak and the
	119:121	I have done what is **j** and
	145:17	The LORD is **j** in all his ways,
Prov	12: 5	thoughts of the righteous are **j**;
	28: 5	The evil do not understand **j**,
Eccl	3:16	the place of **j**, wickedness was
Sir	18:2	the Lord alone is **j**.
Isa	1:17	learn to do good; seek **j**,
	26: 7	O **J** One, you make smooth
	59: 9	Therefore **j** is far from us, and
Jer	9:24	I act with steadfast love, **j**,
Ezek	45: 9	and do what is **j** and right.
Hos	12: 6	hold fast to love and **j**, and
Am	5: 7	Ah, you that turn **j** to
	5:24	But let **j** roll down like waters,
Mic	3: 1	Israel! Should you not know **j**?
Hab	1: 4	law becomes slack and **j** never
Mal	2:17	"Where is the God of **j**?"
Mt	12:18	will proclaim **j** to the Gentiles.
Lk	11:42	and neglect **j** and the love of
	18: 7	will not God grant **j** to his
Jn	5:30	I judge; and my judgment is **j**,
Acts	8:33	In his humiliation **j** was
2 Thess	1: 6	it is indeed **j** of God to repay
Heb	11:33	administered **j**, obtained
1 Jn	1: 9	he who is faithful and **j** will
Rev	16: 7	judgments are true and **j**!"

JUSTIFY (JUSTIFIED) (JUSTIFICATION)

Job	32: 2	he **j** himself rather than God;

Ps	51: 4	so that you are **j** in your
Sir	23:11	false oath, he will not be **j**,
Mt	12:37	your words you will be **j**,
Lk	10:29	But wanting to **j** himself, he
Lk	16:15	"You are those who **j**
Rom	5:18	act of righteousness leads to **j**
	8:30	whom he called he also **j**;
1 Cor	6:11	were **j** in the name of the Lord
2 Cor	3: 9	more does the ministry of **j**
Gal	2:16	a person is **j** not by the works
	2:21	for if **j** comes through the law,
Titus	3: 7	having been **j** by his grace,

K

KEEP (S) (KEPT) (KEEPER)

Gen	4: 9	am I my brother's **k**?"
	17: 9	you shall **k** my covenant,
Ex	19: 5	voice and **k** my covenant,
	20: 6	those who love me and **k** my
Num	6:24	The LORD bless you and **k** you;
Deut	6:17	diligently **k** the
	7: 8	the Lord loved you and **k** the
Josh	6:18	**k** away from the things
	14:10	the LORD has **k** me alive,
2 Sam	22:22	For I have **k** the ways of the
2 Kings	17:19	Judah also did not **k** the
1 Chr	29:18	**k** forever such purposes and
Neh	1: 5	those who love him and **k** his
Job	14:16	you would not **k** watch over
Ps	37:28	The righteous shall be **k** safe
	103: 9	nor will he **k** his anger forever.
Prov	7: 5	may **k** you from the loose
Eccl	3: 6	a time to **k**, and a time to
Mt	19:20	"I have **k** all these; what do I
Mk	7: 9	in order to **k** your tradition!
Lk	17:33	who lose their life will **k** it.
Jn	8:51	whoever **k** my word will never
Rom	16:17	to **k** an eye on those who
1 Cor	16:13	**K** alert, stand firm in your
2 Cor	12: 7	to **k** me from being too elated
2 Thess	3: 6	to **k** away from believers who
1 Tim	5:22	**k** yourself pure.
2 Tim	4: 7	I have **k** the faith.
Heb	13: 5	**K** your lives free from the love
Jas	2:10	whoever **k** the whole law but
1 Pet	3:10	let them **k** their tongues from
2 Pet	1: 8	they **k** you from being
1 Jn	5:21	**k** yourselves from idols
Jude	1:24	who is able to **k** you from
Rev	3:10	Because you have **k** my word

KEY (S)

Isa	22:22	on his shoulder the **k** of the
Mt	16:19	you the **k** of the kingdom
Lk	11:52	taken away the **k** of knowledge;
Rev	1:18	and I have the **k** of Death and
	20: 1	the **k** to the bottomless pit

KILL (ED)

Gen	4:14	who meets me may **k** me."
	37:18	they conspired to **k** him.
Ex	2:15	he sought to **k** Moses. But
	4:23	I will **k** your firstborn son.' "
1 Kings	11:40	sought therefore to **k**
1 Macc	2:24	he ran and **k** him on the altar

Eccl	3: 3	a time to **k**, and a time to heal
Mt	10:28	Do not fear those who **k** the
	17:23	they will **k** him, and on the
Mk	14: 1	arrest Jesus by stealth and **k**
Jn	10:10	comes only to steal and **k** and

KIND (NESS)

Gen	1:24	living creatures of every **k**;
Ruth	2:20	whose **k** has not forsaken
2 Sam	9: 3	I may show the **k** of God?"
2 Chr	10: 7	"If you will be **k** to this people
Ps	145:17	and **k** in all his doings.
Prov	11:17	Those who are **k** reward
	31:26	teaching of **k** is on her tongue.
Hos	11: 4	with cords of human **k**, with
Lk	6:35	for he is **k** to the ungrateful
Jn	21:19	the **k** of death by which he
Rom	11:22	Note then the **k** and the
1 Cor	13: 4	Love is patient; love is **k**;
2 Cor	6: 6	knowledge, patience, **k**,
Gal	5:22	love, joy, peace, patience, **k**,
Eph	2: 7	riches of his grace in **k**
	4:32	and be **k** to one another,
Col	3:12	with compassion, **k**, humility,
Titus	3: 4	goodness and loving **k** of God
Sir	3:14	to a father will not be

KING (S) ('S)

Gen	35:11	and **k** shall spring from you.
Ex	1: 8	Now a new **k** arose over Egypt,
Num	23:21	acclaimed as a **k** among them.
Deut	17:14	"I will set a **k** over me, like all
Judg	9: 8	to anoint a **k** over themselves.
	17: 6	there was no **k** in Israel;
1 Sam	11:15	made Saul **k** before the LORD
	12:12	LORD your God was your **k**.
2 Sam	2: 4	they anointed David **k**
1 Kings	1:30	shall succeed me as **k**,
Tob	10:13	Lord of heaven and earth, **K**
Jdt	9:12	**K** of all your creation,
Ps	33:16	A **k** is not saved by his
	44: 7	You are my **K** and my God;
Prov	21: 1	The **k** heart is a stream of
Eccl	8: 2	Keep the **k** command because
Sir	51:12	to the **K** of the kings of kings,
Isa	6: 5	my eyes have seen the **K**, the
	32: 1	a **k** will reign in righteousness,
Jer	10:10	God and the everlasting **K**.
Ezek	37:24	My servant David shall be **k**
Mic	2:13	Their **k** will pass on before
Zeph	3:15	The **k** of Israel, the LORD, is
Zech	9: 9	Lo, your **k** comes to you;
	14: 9	the LORD will become **k** over
Mal	1:14	for I am a great **K**, says the
Mt	2: 2	child who has been born **k** of
	27:37	"This is Jesus, the **K** of the
Mk	15:32	Let the Messiah, the **K** of
Lk	19:38	"Blessed is the **k** who comes
	23: 3	"Are you the **K** of the Jews?"
Jn	1:49	You are the **K** of Israel!"
	19:15	"We have no **k** but the
Acts	17: 7	another **k** named Jesus."
1 Tim	1:17	To the **K** of the ages,
Rev	15: 3	true are your ways, **K** of the
	19:16	"King of **k** and Lord of lords."

KINGDOM

Ex	19: 6	a priestly **k** and a holy nation.
Deut	17:18	taken the throne of his **k**,
1 Sam	13:14	now your **k** will not continue;

2 Sam 7:12 and I will establish his **k**.
1 Kings 11:31 tear the **k** from the hand of
1 Chr 29:11 yours is the **k**, O LORD, and
Ps 145:13 Your **k** is an everlasting **k**, and
Wis 10:10 she showed him the **k** of God,
Isa 9:7 throne of David and his **k**.
Jer 18:7 concerning a nation or a **k**,
Ezek 29:14 they shall be a lowly **k**.
Dan 2:39 After you shall arise another **k**
4:3 His **k** is an everlasting **k**, and
Mt 5:3 for theirs is the **k** of heaven.
6:33 But strive first for the **k** of God
25:34 inherit the **k** prepared for you
Mk 1:15 the **k** of God has come near
3:24 If a **k** is divided against itself,
10:15 whoever does not receive the **k**
12:34 are not far from the **k** of God."
Lk 7:28 the least in the **k** of God is
13:18 "What is the **k** of God like?
17:21 the **k** of God is among you
23:42 when you come into your **k**."
Jn 3:3 no one can see the **k** of God
18:36 "My **k** is not from this world
Acts 1:6 will restore the **k** to Israel?"
14:22 we must enter the **k** of God."
19:8 persuasively about the **k**
Rom 14:17 For the **k** of God is not food
1 Cor 4:20 For the **k** of God depends
6:9 will not inherit the **k** of God?
Eph 5:5 inheritance in the **k** of Christ
Col 1:13 transferred us into the **k** of his
4:11 co-workers for the **k** of God,
1 Thess 2:12 calls you into his own **k**
2 Thess 1:5 you worthy of the **k** of God,
2 Tim 4:18 save me for his heavenly **k**.
Heb 12:28 a **k** that cannot be shaken,
Jas 2:5 heirs of the **k** that he has
2 Pet 1:11 entry into the eternal **k** of
Rev 1:6 made us to be a **k**, priests
11:15 has become the **k** of our Lord

KISS (ED)

Gen 27:26 "Come near and **k** me, my
45:15 he **k** all his brothers and wept
Ex 18:7 he bowed down and **k** him;
Ruth 1:9 Then she **k** them, and they
1 Kings 19:20 "Let me **k** my father and my
Job 31:27 my mouth has **k** my hand;
Ps 85:10 righteousness and peace will **k**
Prov 24:26 an honest answer gives a **k** on
Song 1:2 Let him **k** me with the kisses
Mt 26:48 "The one I will **k** is the man;
Lk 7:45 gave me no **k**, but from the
22:48 "Judas, is it with a **k** that you
Acts 20:37 they embraced Paul and **k**
Rom 16:16 one another with a holy **k**.
1 Cor 16:20 one another with a holy **k**.
1 Thess 5:26 and sisters with a holy **k**.
1 Pet 5:14 Greet one another with a **k**

KNOW (ING) (KNEW)

Gen 3:5 be like God, **k** good and evil."
22:12 for now I **k** that you fear God,
Ex 6:7 You shall **k** that I am the LORD
33:12 'I **k** you by name, and you
Num 16:28 "This is how you shall **k** that
Deut 7:9 **K** therefore that the LORD your
8:2 testing you to **k** what was in
Josh 3:7 so that they may **k** that I will
23:14 you **k** in your hearts and souls

1 Sam 17:46 earth may **k** that there is a
1 Kings 8:39 **k** what is in every human
2 Chr 33:13 Then Manasseh **k** that the
Job 19:25 For I **k** that my Redeemer
42:2 "I **k** that you can do all
Ps 36:10 steadfast love to those who **k**
46:10 "Be still, and **k** that I am God!
139:23 Search me, O God, and **k** my
Prov 27:1 you do not **k** what a day may
Eccl 8:16 I applied my mind to **k**
Sir 5:10 Stand firm for what you **k**,
Isa 44:8 no other rock; I **k** not one.
Jer 1:5 in the womb I **k** you, and
29:11 surely I **k** the plans I have for
Ezek 6:10 they shall **k** that I am the LORD
Mt 7:23 'I never **k** you; go away from
12:25 He **k** what they were thinking
24:42 not **k** on what day your Lord
Mk 12:24 you **k** neither the scriptures
Lk 1:4 so that you may **k** the truth
4:41 they **k** that he was the Messiah
23:34 do not **k** what they are doing."
Jn 10:14 I **k** my own and my own **k**
13:1 Jesus **k** that his hour had
21:15 "Yes, Lord; you **k** that I love
Acts 1:7 is not for you to **k** the times
1:24 "Lord, you **k** everyone's heart.
Rom 6:6 We **k** that our old self was
8:28 We **k** that all things work
1 Cor 1:21 world did not **k** God through
3:16 **k** that you are God's temple
13:12 then I will **k** fully, even as I
2 Cor 4:14 we **k** that the one who raised
8:9 For you **k** the generous act of
Eph 1:17 as you come to **k** him,
3:19 and to **k** the love of Christ
Phil 3:10 I want to **k** Christ and the
4:12 I **k** what it is to have little
Col 4:1 **k** that you also have a Master
1 Thess 5:2 For you yourselves **k** very well
2 Thess 1:8 on those who do not **k** God
1 Tim 3:15 you may **k** how one ought to
2 Tim 1:12 am not ashamed, for I **k** the
Titus 1:16 profess to **k** God, but they
Heb 8:11 **'K** the Lord,' for they shall all **k**
Jas 1:3 because you **k** that the testing
4:4 Do you not **k** that friendship
1 Pet 1:18 You **k** that you were ransomed
2 Pet 1:12 though you **k** them already
1 Jn 2:3 we **k** him, if we obey his
3:24 by this we **k** that he abides
5:13 may **k** that you have eternal
3 Jn 1:12 **k** that our testimony is true
Rev 2:2 "I **k** your works, your toil and
3:3 you will not **k** at what hour I

KNOWLEDGE

Gen 2:9 tree of the **k** of good and evil.
Num 24:16 and knows the **k** of the Most
2 Chr 1:10 Give me now wisdom and **k**
Job 21:22 Will any teach God **k**,
Ps 119:66 good judgment and **k**,
139:6 Such **k** is too wonderful
Prov 1:7 LORD is the beginning of **k**;
15:7 lips of the wise spread **k**;
18:15 intelligent mind acquires **k**,
Eccl 2:26 God gives wisdom and **k** and
7:12 the advantage of **k** is that
Sir 6:33 love to listen you will gain **k**
Isa 11:9 full of the **k** of the LORD

53:11 find satisfaction through his **k**.
Jer 3:15 with **k** and understanding.
Dan 1:17 God gave **k** and skill in every
Hos 4:6 are destroyed for lack of **k**;
Hab 2:14 will be filled with the **k** of the
Mal 2:7 a priest should guard **k**,
Lk 1:77 give **k** of salvation to his
Rom 11:33 riches and wisdom and **k** of
15:14 filled with all **k**, and able to
1 Cor 8:1 **K** puffs up, but love
2 Cor 8:7 in faith, in speech, in **k**,
11:6 in speech, but not in **k**;
Eph 3:19 love of Christ that surpasses **k**,
Phil 1:9 more and more with **k**
Col 1:10 as you grow in the **k** of God.
2:3 the treasures of wisdom and **k**.
1 Tim 2:4 and to come to the **k** of the
Heb 10:26 sin after having received the **k**
2 Pet 1:3 the **k** of him who called us
3:18 grow in the grace and **k** of
1 Jn 2:20 and all of you have **k**.

L

LABOR (ER)

Ex 20:9 Six days you shall **l** and do all
Lev 19:13 the wages of a **l** until morning.
Judg 1:28 put the Canaanites to forced **l**,
Ps 107:12 were bowed down with hard **l**;
127:1 those who build it **l** in vain.
Prov 12:24 will be put to forced **l**.
Isa 55:2 **l** for that which does not
Hab 2:13 **l** only to feed the flames
Lk 10:7 for the **l** deserves to be paid.
1 Cor 3:8 wages according to the **l**
15:58 in the Lord your **l** is not in
Phil 2:16 not run in vain or **l** in vain.
1 Thess 1:3 your work of faith and **l** of

LAMB (S) ('S)

Gen 22:8 himself will provide the **l**
Ex 12:21 and slaughter the passover **l**.
2 Sam 12:6 he shall restore the **l** fourfold,
Sir 13:17 have in common with a **l**?
Isa 40:11 he will gather the **l** in his
65:25 wolf and the **l** shall feed
Jer 11:19 a gentle **l** led to the slaughter.
Mk 14:12 when the Passover **l** is
Lk 10:3 sending you out like **l** into
Jn 1:29 "Here is the **L** of God who
21:15 "Feed my **l**
1 Cor 5:7 our paschal **l**, Christ, has been
1 Pet 1:19 like that of a **l** without defect
Rev 5:12 "Worthy is the **L** that was
21:27 written in the **L** book of life.

LAMP (S)

1 Sam 3:3 the **l** of God had not yet
2 Sam 22:29 Indeed, you are my **l**, O LORD,
1 Kings 15:4 his God gave him a **l** in
2 Kings 8:19 had promised to give a **l** to
Ps 18:28 you who light my **l**; the LORD,
119:105 Your word is a **l** to my feet
Prov 6:23 For the commandment is a **l**
20:27 human spirit is the **l** of the
Mt 5:15 No one after lighting a **l** puts it

Mt 6:22 "The eye is the **l** of the body.
Lk 12:35 and have your **l** lit;
Jn 5:35 was a burning and shining **l**,
Rev 18:23 the light of a **l** will shine in
22:5 they need no light of **l** or sun,

LAND
Gen 1:10 God called the dry **l** Earth,
13:15 the **l** that you see I will give
Ex 3:8 a **l** flowing with milk and
8:22 the LORD am in this **l**.
Num 13:2 to spy out the **l** of Canaan,
35:33 shall not pollute the **l** in the
Deut 8:7 bringing you into a good **l**,
29:24 LORD done thus to this **l**?
Josh 2:1 "Go, view the **l**, especially
11:23 So Joshua took the whole **l**
Judg 1:27 continued to live in that **l**.
Ruth 1:1 was a famine in the **l**,
2 Sam 21:14 heeded supplications for the **l**.
1 Kings 8:34 bring them again to the **l** that
2 Kings 17:5 of Assyria invaded all the **l**
2 Chr 7:14 their sin and heal their **l**.
Neh 10:31 if the peoples of the **l** bring
Tob 14:7 forever in the **l** of Abraham
1 Macc 14:11 He established peace in the **l**,
Ps 25:13 children shall possess the **l**.
37:11 the meek shall inherit the **l**,
Prov 12:11 Those who till their **l** will have
Sir 46:8 the **l** flowing with milk and
Isa 2:8 Their **l** is filled with idols;
53:8 cut off from the **l** of the living,
Jer 2:7 you entered you defiled my **l**,
22:29 O **l**, **l**, **l**, hear the word
Ezek 7:23 For the **l** is full of bloody
Dan 11:41 shall come into the beautiful **l**,
Zech 3:9 remove the guilt of this **l**
Mal 4:6 come and strike the **l** with a
Mk 15:33 came over the whole **l**
Rev 10:2 his left foot on the **l**,

LAST
Ruth 3:10 this **l** instance of your loyalty
2 Sam 23:1 these are the **l** words of David:
Isa 41:4 and will be with the **l**,
48:12 I am the first, and I am the **l**.
Mt 19:30 first will be **l**, and the **l**
27:64 and the **l** deception would be
Mk 9:35 to be first must be **l** of all
15:37 loud cry and breathed his **l**.
Jn 6:40 raise them up on the **l** day."
15:16 bear fruit, fruit that will **l**,
Acts 2:17 'In the **l** days it will be,
1 Cor 15:26 The **l** enemy to be destroyed is
15:45 the **l** Adam became a
2 Tim 3:1 in the **l** days distressing times
Heb 1:2 in these **l** days he has spoken
Jas 5:3 laid up treasure for the **l** days.
1 Pet 1:5 to be revealed in the **l** time.
2 Pet 2:20 the **l** state has become worse
1 Jn 2:18 Children, it is the **l** hour!
Jude 1:18 "In the **l** time there will be
Rev 1:17 I am the first and the **l**,
21:9 bowls full of the seven **l**

LAUGH (INGSTOCK) (LAUGHTER)
Gen 21:6 who hears will **l** with me."
Job 12:4 I am a **l** to my friends;
Ps 59:8 But you **l** at them, O LORD;
126:2 our mouth was filled with **l**,

Prov 14:13 Even in **l** the heart is sad,
Eccl 3:4 time to weep, and a time to **l**;
7:3 Sorrow is better than **l**,
Lam 3:14 I have become the **l** of all my
Lk 6:21 weep now, for you will **l**.

LAY (LAID)
Gen 22:12 "Do not **l** your hand on the
Ex 7:4 I will **l** my hand upon Egypt
Num 27:18 and **l** your hand upon him;
Deut 9:25 I **l** prostrate before the LORD
34:9 Moses had **l** his hands on
Job 38:4 "Where were you when I **l** the
Ps 139:5 and **l** your hand upon me.
Prov 10:14 The wise **l** up knowledge, but
Mt 8:20 Man has nowhere to **l** his
28:6 see the place where he **l**.
Mk 6:29 took his body, and **l** it in a
Lk 6:48 and **l** the foundation on rock;
Jn 10:15 I **l** down my life for the sheep.
13:37 I will **l** down my life for you
Acts 6:6 prayed and **l** their hands on
8:19 on whom I **l** my hands may
1 Cor 3:11 no one can **l** any foundation
Col 1:5 the hope **l** up for you in
Heb 4:13 all are naked and **l** bare to the
12:1 let us also **l** aside every weight
1 Jn 3:16 we ought to **l** down our lives

LAW (FUL)
Num 5:29 is the **l** in cases of jealousy,
Deut 17:18 have a copy of this **l** written
27:26 uphold the words of this **l** by
Josh 1:8 book of the **l** shall not depart
2 Kings 22:8 found the book of the **l**
2 Chr 6:16 to walk in my **l** as you have
17:9 the book of the **l** of the LORD
Ezra 7:6 a scribe skilled in the **l** of
Neh 8:2 Ezra brought the **l** before the
Ps 1:2 on his **l** they meditate day and
40:8 your **l** is within my heart."
119:142 and your **l** is the truth.
Prov 28:9 will not listen to the **l**,
29:18 are those who keep the **l**.
Jer 8:8 and the **l** of the LORD is
31:33 I will put my **l** within them,
Dan 9:11 Israel has transgressed your **l**
Hos 4:6 you have forgotten the **l** of
Hab 1:4 the **l** becomes slack and justice
Zech 7:12 not to hear the **l** and the
Mt 5:17 have come to abolish the **l**
19:3 "Is it **l** for a man to divorce
Lk 14:3 "Is it **l** to cure people on the
20:22 Is it **l** for us to pay taxes
Jn 7:19 none of you keeps the **l**.
18:31 him according to your **l**."
Acts 6:13 this holy place and the **l**;
13:39 you could not be freed by the **l**
Rom 6:14 not under **l** but under grace.
7:4 you have died to the **l** through
8:4 the **l** might be fulfilled in us
1 Cor 9:20 I might win those under the **l**
10:23 "All things are **l**," but not all
Gal 2:19 through the **l** I died to the **l**
3:11 justified before God by the **l**;
Eph 2:15 He has abolished the **l**
Phil 3:9 own that comes from the **l**,
1 Tim 1:8 Now we know that the **l** is
Titus 3:9 and quarrels about the **l**,
Heb 7:19 (for the **l** made nothing

Heb 10:1 Since the **l** has only a shadow of
Jas 1:25 who look into the perfect **l**,
2:10 whoever keeps the whole **l** but

LEAD (S) (ER) (ERS)
Ex 15:10 they sank like **l** in the mighty
32:34 **l** the people to the place
1 Chr 28:4 for he chose Judah as **l**,
Ps 23:2 he **l** me beside still waters;
139:24 and **l** me in the way
Prov 2:18 for her way **l** down to death,
21:5 plans of the diligent **l** surely
Eccl 5:6 Do not let your mouth **l** you
Sir 19:2 and women **l** intelligent men
20:26 A liar's way **l** to disgrace
Isa 11:6 and a little child shall **l** them.
Jer 31:9 I will **l** them back,
Dan 12:3 those who **l** many to
Mt 7:14 the road is hard that **l** to life,
Mk 13:22 signs and omens, to **l** astray,
Lk 19:47 the **l** of the people kept
23:35 but the **l** scoffed at him,
Jn 11:4 "This illness does not **l** to
Rom 2:4 God's kindness is meant to **l**
6:16 either of sin, which **l** to death,
1 Cor 7:17 let each of you **l** the life that
2 Cor 2:14 in Christ always **l** us in
7:10 a repentance that **l** to salvation
Col 1:10 **l** lives worthy of the Lord
1 Tim 2:2 so that we may **l** a quiet and

LEARN (ED) (ING)
Deut 5:1 you shall **l** them and observe
18:9 you must not **l** to imitate the
Ps 119:152 Long ago I **l** from your decrees
Prov 1:2 **l** about wisdom and
9:9 and they will gain in **l**.
Isa 1:17 **l** to do good; seek justice
Jer 35:13 Can you not **l** a lesson and
Bar 3:9 give ear, and **l** wisdom!
Mt 11:29 my yoke upon you, and **l** from
Mk 13:28 "From the fig tree **l** its lesson:
Jn 6:45 Everyone who has heard and **l**
Eph 4:20 That is not the way you **l**
Phil 4:9 the things that you have **l**
4:11 for I have **l** to be content with
1 Tim 5:4 first **l** their religious duty
2 Tim 3:14 you have **l** and firmly
Titus 3:14 let people **l** to devote
Rev 14:3 No one could **l** that song

LEFT (LEAVE)
Gen 7:23 Only Noah was **l**,
Ex 11:8 '**L** us, you and all the people
Num 10:31 "Do not **l** us, for you know
11:20 'Why did we ever **l** Egypt?' "
Deut 28:14 either to the right or to the **l**,
Prov 14:7 **L** the presence of a fool
Isa 30:21 when you turn to the **l**, your
Joel 2:14 and **l** a blessing behind him,
Mt 5:24 **l** your gift there before the
6:3 do not let your **l** hand know
Mk 8:8 took up the broken pieces **l**
10:28 "Look, we have **l** everything
Lk 17:34 will be taken and the other **l**.
Jn 14:18 "I will not **l** you orphaned;
14:27 Peace I **l** with you;
Eph 5:31 a man will **l** his father and
2 Pet 2:15 They have **l** the straight road
Jude 1:6 but **l** their proper dwelling,

LIAR (LIE) (LYING)

Gen	19:32	drink wine, and we will **l** with
Deut	6: 7	when you **l** down and when
Ruth	3: 4	uncover his feet and **l** down;
2 Kings	9:12	They said, "**L**! Come on, tell
Job	24:25	who will prove me a **l**, and
Ps	23: 2	me **l** down in green pastures;
	120: 2	"Deliver me, O Lord, from **l**
Prov	12:22	**L** lips are an abomination to
	14: 5	A faithful witness does not **l**,
Hos	4: 2	Swearing, **l**, and murder,
Mk	7:30	found the child **l** on the bed,
Lk	2:12	of cloth and **l** in a manger."
Jn	5: 6	Jesus saw him **l** there and
	8:44	for he is a **l** and the father of
Acts	5: 3	Satan filled your heart to **l**
Rom	3: 4	everyone is a **l**, let
Col	3: 9	Do not **l** to one another,
1 Jn	1: 6	we **l** and do not do what is
	2:21	no **l** comes from the truth.

LIFE (LIVE)

Gen	2: 7	his nostrils the breath of **l**;
	3:22	of life, and eat, and **l** forever"
Ex	21: 6	he shall serve him for **l**.
	33:20	no one shall see me and **l**."
Num	35:31	accept no ransom for the **l** of a
Deut	8: 3	one does not **l** by bread alone,
	30:19	Choose **l** so that you and your
1 Sam	19: 5	for he took his **l** in his hand
Neh	9: 6	all of them you give **l**,
Jdt	13:20	because you risked your own **l**
Job	10: 1	"I loathe my **l**; I will give
	14:14	If mortals die, will they **l** again?
Ps	16:11	show me the path of **l**.
	63: 3	steadfast love is better than **l**,
	119:175	Let me **l** that I may praise you
Prov	8:35	For whoever finds me finds **l**
	16:22	Wisdom is a fountain of **l** to
Eccl	2:17	So I hated **l**, because what is
	7:12	is that wisdom gives **l**
Sir	30:22	A joyful hart is **l** itself.
Isa	11: 6	The wolf shall **l** with the lamb,
	53:10	When you make his **l** an
Lam	3:58	Lord, you have redeemed my **l**.
Ezek	18:27	they shall save their **l**.
Jon	2: 6	you brought up my **l** from the
Mal	2: 5	a covenant of **l** and well-
Mt	6:25	do not worry about your **l**,
	19:29	and will inherit eternal **l**.
	20:28	to give his **l** a ransom for
Mk	9:43	for you to enter **l** maimed
	10:30	the age to come eternal **l**.
Lk	6: 9	to save **l** or to destroy it?"
	10:28	do this, and you will **l**."
Jn	10:10	I came that they may have **l**,
	12:25	Those who love their **l** lose it,
	14: 6	way, and the truth, and the **l**.
	20:31	believing you may have **l**
Acts	2:28	known to me the ways of **l**;
	11:18	the repentance that leads to **l**."
Rom	6:23	God is eternal **l** in Christ
	8:38	neither death, nor **l**, nor
	14: 8	If we **l**, we **l** to the Lord
1 Cor	15:19	If for this **l** only we have
2 Cor	3: 6	but the Spirit gives **l**.
	6:16	"I will **l** in them and walk
Gal	2:20	no longer I who **l**, but it is
	5:25	If we **l** by the Spirit, let us
Eph	4: 1	to lead a **l** worthy of the

Eph	5: 8	**L** as children of light
Phil	1:20	whether by **l** or by death.
	2:16	to the word of **l** that I can
Col	3: 3	your **l** is hidden with Christ
1 Tim	1:16	believe in him for eternal **l**.
	4: 8	for both the present and the **l**
2 Tim	3:12	all who want to **l** a godly life
Titus	1: 2	in the hope of eternal **l** that
Heb	7:16	power of an indestructible **l**.
	10:38	my righteous one will **l** by
Jas	1:12	will receive the crown of **l**
	3:13	Show by your good **l** that your
1 Pet	3: 7	heirs of the gracious gift of **l**
2 Pet	1: 3	needed for **l** and godliness,
1 Jn	2:17	who do the will of God **l**
	3:16	that he laid down his **l** for us
Rev	2:10	give you the crown of **l**.
	20: 4	They came to **l** and reigned

LIKE (NESS)

Gen	1:26	our image, according to our **l**;
	3: 5	you will be **l** God, knowing
	28:14	your offspring shall be **l** the
Ex	8:10	no one **l** the LORD our God,
	24:17	glory of the LORD was **l**
Num	11: 7	the manna was **l** coriander
Deut	18:15	prophet **l** me from among
	32:31	their rock is not **l** our Rock;
1 Sam	2: 2	"There is no Holy One **l** the
2 Sam	7:22	for there is no one **l** you,
1 Kings	22:13	let your word be **l** the word of
1 Chr	17:21	Who is **l** your people Israel,
Job	40: 9	Have you an arm **l** God, and
Ps	1: 3	They are **l** trees planted by
	90: 4	years in your sight are **l**
	103:15	mortals, their days are **l** grass;
Prov	7:22	he follows her, and goes **l**
	25:11	A word fitly spoken is **l** apples
Eccl	2:16	can the wise die just **l** fools?
Isa	1:18	though your sins are **l** scarlet,
	40: 6	their constancy is **l** the flower
	53: 6	All we **l** sheep have gone
	64: 6	our righteous deeds are **l** a
Jer	23:29	Is not my word **l** fire,
Lam	1:12	if there is any sorrow **l** my
	2: 5	The Lord has become **l** an
Ezek	1: 4	something **l** gleaming amber.
Dan	7: 4	a lion and had eagles' wings
	10: 6	His body was **l** beryl, his face **l**
Hos	6: 4	Your love is **l** a morning cloud,
	14: 5	I will be **l** the dew to Israel;
Mic	7:18	Who is a God **l** you, pardoning
Nah	1: 6	His wrath is poured out **l** fire,
Zech	1: 4	Do not be **l** your ancestors.
Mt	10:16	I am sending you out **l** sheep
Lk	6:48	**l** a man building a house
Rom	5:15	free gift is not **l** the trespass.
Phil	2: 7	being born in human **l**.
Jas	1:24	forget what they were **l**.
	3: 9	who are made in the **l** of God.
1 Pet	1:24	"All flesh is **l** grass and all its
2 Pet	3:10	the Lord will come **l** a thief,
Rev	4: 7	first living creature **l** a lion,
	10: 1	his face was **l** the sun,

LION ('S) (S)

Gen	49: 9	he stretches out like a **l**,
Judg	14: 6	he tore the **l** apart barehanded
1 Sam	17:34	and whenever a **l** or a bear
Ps	91:13	You will tread on the **l** and

Song	4: 8	from the dens of **l**,
Sir	27:28	lies in wait for them like a **l**.
Isa	11: 7	and the **l** shall eat straw like
Jer	25:38	Like a **l** he has left his covert
Ezek	1:10	the face of a **l** on the right
Dan	6:20	to deliver you from the **l**?"
	7: 4	like a **l** and had eagles' wings.
Hos	13: 7	I will become like a **l** to them,
2 Tim	4:17	I was rescued from the **l**
1 Pet	5: 8	Like a roaring **l** your adversary
Rev	4: 7	first living creature like a **l**,

LIPS

Deut	23:23	Whatever your **l** utter you
Job	27: 4	my **l** will not speak falsehood,
Ps	12: 3	LORD cut off all flattering **l**,
	40: 9	I have not restrained my **l**,
	63: 3	my **l** will praise you.
Prov	10:21	The **l** of the righteous feed
	12:22	Lying **l** are an abomination to
	15: 7	**l** of the wise spread knowledge
Eccl	10:12	the **l** of fools consume them.
Song	4:11	Your **l** distill nectar, my bride;
Isa	6: 5	I am a man of unclean **l**,
	29:13	honor me with their **l**, while
Hos	14: 2	offer the fruit of our **l**.
Mal	2: 7	For the **l** of a priest should
Mt	15: 8	honors me with their **l**, but
Rom	3:13	of vipers is under their **l**."
1 Cor	14:21	the **l** of foreigners I will speak
Heb	13:15	fruit of **l** that confess his
1 Pet	3:10	and their **l** from speaking

LISTEN (S)

Ex	6:30	why would Pharaoh **l** to me?"
	23:22	if you **l** attentively to his voice
2 Kings	17:40	They would not **l**, however,
Ps	5: 2	**L** to the sound of my cry,
	34:11	Come, O children, **l** to me;
Prov	4: 1	**L**, children, to a father's
	8:34	Happy is the one who **l** to me,
Eccl	5: 1	to draw near to **l** is better than
Song	5: 2	**L**! my beloved is knocking.
Sir	11:8	Do not answer before you **l**,
Isa	1:10	**L** to the teaching of our God,
Mt	12:42	**l** to the wisdom of Solomon
Mk	4:23	anyone with ears to hear **l**!"
	9: 7	my Son, the Beloved; **l** to
Lk	10:16	"Whoever **l** to you **l** to me
	16:31	'If they do not **l** to Moses and
Jn	10:16	and they will **l** to my voice.
Acts	3:22	You must **l** to whatever he tells
Jas	1:19	let everyone be quick to **l**,
1 Jn	4: 6	Whoever knows God **l** to us,
Rev	2: 7	anyone who has an ear to **l** to

LITTLE

Ex	16:18	who gathered **l** had no
	23:30	**L** by **l** I will drive
1 Kings	17:12	and a **l** oil in a jug;
Ps	8: 5	them a **l** lower than God,
Prov	6:10	A **l** sleep, a **l** slumber,
	16: 8	Better is a **l** with righteousness
Eccl	10: 1	**l** folly outweighs wisdom and
Sir	51:28	Hear but a **l** of my instruction,
Isa	11: 6	and a **l** child shall lead them.
Mt	14:31	"You of **l** faith, why did you
	19:14	"Let the **l** children come to
Lk	7:47	to whom **l** is forgiven, loves **l**."
	18:17	kingdom of God as a **l** child

1 Cor	5: 6	a **l** yeast leavens the whole
2 Cor	8:15	who had **l** did not have too **l**
Gal	5: 9	A **l** yeast leavens the whole
1 Tim	5:23	but take a **l** wine for the sake
Heb	2: 7	made them for a **l** while lower
1 Pet	5:10	you have suffered for a **l** while,
1 Jn	4: 4	**L** children, you are from God
Rev	3: 8	know that you have but **l**

LIVING

Gen	2: 7	and the man became a **l** being.
Deut	5:26	heard the voice of the **l** God
Josh	3:10	among you is the **l** God who
1 Sam	17:26	defy the armies of the **l** God?"
2 Kings	19: 4	has sent to mock the **l** God,
Ps	84: 2	sing for joy to the **l** God.
Eccl	9: 4	is joined with all the **l** has
Isa	53: 8	from the land of the **l**,
Jer	10:10	he is the **l** God and the
	17:13	forsaken the fountain of **l**
Ezek	1: 5	something like four **l**
	10:17	for the spirit of the **l** creatures
Dan	6:26	he is the **l** God, enduring
Hos	1:10	"Children of the **l** God."
Zech	14: 8	On that day **l** waters shall flow
Mt	16:16	the Son of the **l** God."
	22:32	not of the dead, but of the **l**."
Jn	4:10	would have given you **l** water."
	6:51	I am the **l** bread that came
Rom	9:26	called children of the **l** God."
	12: 1	present your bodies as a **l**
1 Cor	9:14	get their **l** by the gospel.
2 Cor	6:16	are the temple of the **l** God;
1 Tim	4:10	our hope set on the **l** God,
2 Tim	4: 1	to judge the **l** and the dead,
Heb	4:12	word of God is **l** and active,
	10:20	new and **l** way that he opened
1 Pet	1:23	**l** and enduring word of God
	2: 4	Come to him, a **l** stone,
Rev	1:18	and the **l** one. I was dead,
	4: 6	are four **l** creatures, full of eyes

LOOK (ED) (S)

Gen	15: 5	"**L** toward heaven and count
	19:17	do not **l** back or stop
Ex	3: 6	for he was afraid to **l** at God.
Num	21: 8	who is bitten shall **l** at it
Deut	3:27	**L** well, for you shall not
	26:15	**L** down from your holy
1 Sam	16: 7	"Do not **l** on his appearance
Ps	14: 2	The LORD **l** down from heaven
	123: 2	eyes **l** to the LORD our God
Prov	4:25	Let your eyes **l** directly
	31:27	She **l** well to the ways of
Isa	3: 9	**l** on their faces bears witness
	17: 7	eyes will **l** to the Holy One
Jer	6:16	Stand at the crossroads, and **l**,
Hab	1:13	you cannot **l** on wrongdoing;
Zech	12:10	they **l** on the one whom they
Mal	2:15	So **l** to yourselves, and do not
Mt	5:28	who **l** at a woman with lust
	23:27	on the outside **l** beautiful, but
Mk	13:21	'**L**! Here is the Messiah!'
	16: 6	**L**, there is the place they laid
Lk	9:16	he **l** up to heaven, and blessed
	24:39	**L** at my hands and my feet;
Jn	4:35	I tell you, **l** around you, and
	13:33	You will **l** for me;
Phil	2: 4	Let each of you **l** not to your
1 Pet	1:12	into which angels long to **l**!

1 Jn	1: 1	what we have **l** at and touched
Rev	5:11	I **l**, and I heard the voice
	14: 1	I **l**, and there was the Lamb

LOSE (LOSS) (LOST)

Num	17:12	we are **l**, all of us are **l**
Ps	119:176	have gone astray like a **l** sheep;
Sir	9: 6	or you may **l** your inheritance.
Jer	50: 6	My people have been **l** sheep;
Ezek	34:16	I will seek the **l**, and I will
Mk	8:35	to save their life will **l** it,
Lk	15:24	he was **l** and is found!'
	19:10	to seek out and to save the **l**."
Jn	6:39	that I should **l** nothing of all
	12:25	Those who love their life **l** it,
1 Cor	3:15	the builder will suffer **l**;
2 Cor	4: 1	we do not **l** heart.
Phil	3: 8	I regard everything as **l**
Heb	12: 3	may not grow weary or **l** heart.
	12: 5	**l** heart when you are punished
2 Pet	3:17	and **l** your own stability.
2 Jn	1: 8	do not **l** what we have worked

LOVE (D) (S)

Gen	24:67	became his wife; and he **l** her.
Ex	15:13	"In your steadfast **l** you led the
Lev	19:18	**l** your neighbor as yourself:
Num	14:18	abounding in steadfast **l**,
Deut	5:10	who **l** me and keep my
	6: 5	You shall **l** the LORD your God
Josh	22: 5	to **l** the LORD your God,
Judg	16:15	"How can you say, 'I **l** you,'
Ru	4:15	for your daughter-in-law **l** you
1 Sam	16:21	Saul **l** him greatly, and he
	20:14	the faithful **l** of the LORD;
2 Sam	1:26	your **l** to me was wonderful,
	22:51	steadfast **l** to his anointed,
1 Kings	3: 3	Solomon **l** the LORD, walking
	11: 2	Solomon clung to these in **l**
1 Chr	16:34	his steadfast **l** endures forever.
2 Chr	6:14	keeping covenant in steadfast **l**
Ezra	3:11	steadfast **l** endures forever
Tob	14:7	sincerely **l** God will rejoice
Esth	2:17	the king **l** Esther more than all
1 Macc	4:33	the sword of those who **l** you,
Job	10:12	granted me life and steadfast **l**,
	37:13	or for **l**, he causes it to happen
Ps	33: 5	He **l** righteousness and justice;
	69:36	who **l** his name shall live
	97:10	**l** those who hate evil;
	119:97	Oh, how I **l** your law!
Prov	7:18	let us delight ourselves with **l**.
	10:12	but **l** covers all offenses.
	13: 1	A wise child **l** discipline,
	19: 8	To get wisdom is to **l** oneself;
Eccl	3: 8	a time to **l**, and a time to hate
Song	3: 5	not stir up or awaken **l** until it
	8: 6	for **l** is strong as death,
Wis	6:18	**l** of her is the keeping of her
Sir	7:30	all your might **l** your Maker,
Isa	54:10	I shall not depart from my **l**
	61: 8	For I the LORD **l** justice, I hate
Jer	9:24	I act with steadfast **l**, justice,
	31: 3	**l** you with an everlasting **l**;
Lam	3:22	The steadfast **l** of the LORD
Ezek	33:32	are like a singer of **l** songs,
Dan	9: 4	covenant and steadfast **l**
Hos	3: 1	"Go, **l** a woman who has a
	14: 4	I will **l** them freely, for my
Joel	2:13	and abounding in steadfast **l**,

Am	5:15	Hate evil and **l** good,
Jon	4: 2	and abounding in steadfast **l**,
Mic	6: 8	to **l** kindness, and to walk
Zeph	3:17	will renew you in his **l**;
Zech	8:17	and **l** no false oath;
Mal	1: 2	I have **l** you, says the LORD.
Mt	5:44	**L** your enemies and pray for
	22:37	" 'You shall **l** the Lord your
Mk	10:21	Jesus, looking at him, **l** him
Lk	7:42	of them will **l** him more?"
	16:13	hate the one and **l** the other,
Jn	3:16	"For God so **l** the world that
	15:13	No one has greater **l** than this,
	21:15	do you **l** me more than these?"
Rom	5: 8	God proves his **l** for us in that
	8:28	for good for those who **l** God,
	8:35	us from the **l** of Christ?
1 Cor	13: 4	**L** is patient; **l** is kind;
	14: 1	Pursue **l** and strive for the
2 Cor	5:14	For the **l** of Christ urges us on
	9: 7	for God **l** a cheerful giver.
Gal	2:20	who **l** me and give himself
	5:22	fruit of the Spirit is **l**, joy,
Eph	3:17	rooted and grounded in **l**.
	5: 2	as Christ **l** us and gave himself
Phil	1: 9	that your **l** may overflow more
	2: 2	same **l**, being in full accord
Col	2: 2	be encouraged and united in **l**,
	3:14	clothe yourselves with **l**,
1 Thess	3:12	increase and abound in **l** for
	5: 8	the breastplate of faith and **l**,
2 Thess	2:10	they refused to **l** the truth
	3: 5	your hearts to the **l** of God
1 Tim	1: 5	**l** that comes from a pure
	6:10	For the **l** of money is a root
2 Tim	3: 4	**l** of pleasure rather than **l** of
Titus	2: 4	the young women to **l**
Philem	1: 7	encouragement from your **l**,
Heb	13: 1	Let mutual **l** continue.
	13: 5	free from the **l** of money,
Jas	1:12	promised to those who **l** him.
1 Pet	1: 8	have not seen him, you **l** him;
	2:17	**L** the family of believers.
2 Pet	1: 7	and mutual affection with **l**.
1 Jn	2:15	Do not **l** the world or the
	4:16	God is **l**, and those who
	5: 2	**l** God and obey his
2 Jn	1: 5	let us **l** one another.
3 Jn	1: 6	they have testified to your **l**
Jude	1: 2	May mercy, peace, and **l** be
Rev	2: 4	you have abandoned the **l** you
	3:19	and discipline those whom I **l**.

LOW (ER) (LY)

Deut	28:43	you shall descend **l** and **l**.
Job	5:11	on high those who are **l**,
Ps	8: 5	made them a little **l** than God,
	116: 6	I was brought **l**, he saved me.
Prov	16:19	better to be of a **l** spirit
	29:23	who is **l** in spirit will obtain
Isa	40: 4	mountain and hill be made **l**;
Lk	1:52	and lifted up the **l**;
Rom	12:16	but associate with the **l**;
Eph	4: 9	descended into the **l** parts of
Heb	2: 7	a little while **l** than the angels;
Jas	1:10	the rich in being brought **l**,

LUST (S)

Ezek	23: 8	poured out their **l** upon her.
Mt	5:28	looks at a woman with **l** has

Rom	1:24	in the **l** of their hearts
Eph	4:22	corrupt and deluded by its **l**,
2 Pet	3: 3	and indulging their own **l**

M

MADE

Gen	1:31	saw everything that he had **m**,
	6: 6	sorry that he had **m**
	45: 9	God has **m** me lord of all
Ex	1:14	**m** their lives bitter with hard
Ex	15:25	the LORD **m** for them a statute
	36: 8	the workers **m** the tabernacle
Num	14:36	**m** all the congregation
	21: 2	Israel **m** a vow to the LORD
Deut	5: 2	LORD our God **m** a covenant
	32: 6	**m** you and established you?
Josh	24:25	So Joshua **m** a covenant with
Judg	11:30	And Jephthah **m** a vow to the
1 Sam	15:11	"I regret that I **m** Saul king,
	20:16	Jonathan **m** a covenant with
2 Sam	23: 5	he has **m** with me an
1 Kings	12:28	the king took counsel, and **m**
2 Kings	18: 4	serpent that Moses had **m**,
	19:15	you have **m** heaven and earth.
2 Chr	3:10	holy place he **m** two carved
	4:19	Solomon **m** all the things that
Neh	9:10	You **m** a name for yourself,
	12:43	God had **m** them rejoice with
Tob	8:6	You **m** Adam, and for him
1 Macc	4:49	They **m** new holy vessels,
Job	7:20	Why have you **m** me your
	33: 4	The spirit of God has **m** me,
Ps	73:28	I have **m** the Lord GOD my
	100: 3	It is he that **m** us, and we are
	118:24	the day that the LORD has **m**;
	139:14	fearfully and wonder-fully **m**,
Prov	8:26	when he had not yet **m** earth
Eccl	3:11	He has **m** everything suitable
	7:13	what he has **m** crooked?
Sir	43:33	For the Lord has **m** all things,
Wis	14:8	the idol **m** with hands is
Isa	66: 2	these things my hand has **m**,
Jer	10:12	It is he who **m** the earth
	31:32	covenant that I **m** with their
Ezek	3:17	Mortal, I have **m** you a
Dan	3: 1	King Nebuchadnezzar **m** a
Am	5: 8	**m** the Pleiades and Orion,
Jon	1: 9	God of heaven, who **m** the sea
Mt	5:33	vows you have **m** to the Lord.'
Mk	2:27	"The sabbath was **m** for
	15: 5	But Jesus **m** no further reply,
Lk	17:19	your faith has **m** you well."
	19:46	you have **m** it a den of robbers
Jn	1:18	who has **m** him known.
	9: 6	and **m** mud with the saliva
Acts	2:36	**m** him both Lord and Messiah
	10:15	"What God has **m** clean, you
1 Cor	1:20	Has not God **m** foolish the
	15:22	so all will be **m** alive in Christ.
2 Cor	5:21	our sake he **m** him to be sin
	12: 9	is **m** perfect in weakness."
Eph	2: 5	**m** us alive together with Christ
	2:14	he has **m** both groups into
Heb	2: 7	have **m** them for a little while
Heb	8: 9	like the covenant that I **m** with

MAJESTY (MAJESTIC)

Ex	15: 7	In the greatness of your **m** you
1 Chr	16:27	Honor and **m** are before him;
Esth	1: 4	splendor and pomp of his **m**
Job	37:22	around God is awesome **m**.
	40:10	yourself with **m** and dignity;
Ps	96: 6	Honor and **m** are before him;
	145: 5	glorious splendor of your **m**
Isa	26:10	do not see the **m** of the LORD.
	53: 2	he had no form or **m** that we
Dan	4:30	power and for my glorious **m**?"
Mic	5: 4	in the **m** of the name of the
Acts	19:27	will be deprived of her **m** that
Heb	1: 3	right hand of the **M** on high,
2 Pet	1:16	been eyewitnesses of his **m**.
Jude	1:25	our Lord, be glory, **m**, power,

MAKE (R)

Gen	1:26	"Let us **m** humankind in our
	24:40	and **m** your way successful.
Ex	6: 3	I did not **m** myself known to
	20: 4	not **m** for yourself an idol,
	32: 1	"Come, **m** gods for us, who
Num	6:25	LORD **m** his face to shine upon
	21: 8	"**M** a poisonous serpent,
Deut	7: 2	**M** no covenant with them and
	30: 9	**m** you abundantly prosperous
Josh	9: 7	can we **m** a treaty with you?"
2 Sam	7: 9	I will **m** for you a great name
Ezra	10: 3	us **m** a covenant with our God
	10:11	Now **m** confession to the LORD
Job	7:17	that you **m** so much of them,
	35:10	'Where is God my **M**, who
Ps	4: 8	O LORD, **m** me lie down in
	95: 6	kneel before the LORD, our **M**!
	110: 1	**m** your enemies your
Prov	3: 6	he will **m** straight your paths.
	22: 2	the LORD is the **m** of them all.
Eccl	5: 4	When you **m** a vow to God, do
Isa	29:16	say of its **m**, "He did not
Isa	40: 3	**m** straight in the desert a
	44: 9	All who **m** idols are nothing,
Jer	16:20	mortals **m** for themselves gods?
	30:10	no one shall **m** him afraid.
Ezek	37:26	I will **m** a covenant of peace
	39: 7	My holy name I will **m** known
Hos	2:18	I will **m** for you a covenant on
	8:14	Israel has forgotten his **M**,
Hab	2:18	idol once its **m** has shaped it
Mt	27:65	go, **m** it as secure as you
	28:19	**m** disciples of all nations,
Mk	1:17	I will **m** you fish for people."
Lk	1:17	to **m** ready a people prepared
Jn	1:23	'**M** straight the way of the
Acts	2:35	**m** your enemies your
Rom	14: 1	Lord is able to **m** them stand.
2 Cor	5: 9	we **m** it our aim to please
Heb	2:17	to **m** a sacrifice of atonement
	4:11	Let us therefore **m** every effort
2 Pet	1: 5	you must **m** every effort to
1 Jn	1:10	we **m** him a liar, and his
Rev	17:14	they will **m** war on the Lamb,
	19:19	gathered to **m** war against the

MAN ('S) (MEN)

Gen	2: 7	God formed **m** from the dust
Lev	20:10	If a **m** commits adultery with
Num	13: 2	"Send **m** to spy out the land
Deut	22: 5	shall not wear a **m** apparel,
Judg	8:21	as the **m** is, so is his strength
	15:15	it he killed a thousand **m**.
1 Sam	13:14	a **m** after his own heart;
1 Kings	12:10	The young **m** who had grown
Esth	6: 7	"For the **m** whom the king
Job	38: 3	Gird up your loins like a **m**,
Ps	90: 1	A Prayer of Moses, the **m** of
	127: 5	is the **m** who has his quiver
Prov	30:19	and the way of a **m** with a girl.
Sir	25:8	**m** who lives with a sensible
Isa	53: 3	**m** of suffering and acquainted
Jer	30: 6	see every **m** with his hands
Dan	1:17	four young **m** God gave
Zech	6:12	is a **m** whose name is Branch:
Mt	9: 6	the Son of **M** has authority
	19: 5	a **m** shall leave his father and
Lk	6: 5	Son of **M** is lord of the
	9:30	saw two **m**, Moses and Elijah,
Jn	3:14	so must the Son of **M** be lifted
	9:35	believe in the Son of **M**?"
Acts	4:13	uneducated and ordinary **m**,
	7:56	Son of **M** standing at the
Rom	1:27	**M** committed shameless acts
	5:12	into the world through one **m**,
1 Cor	7: 2	**m** should have his own wife
	11:14	that if a **m** wears long hair,
Eph	5:31	"For this reason a **m** will leave
1 Tim	2: 8	**m** should pray, lifting up holy
Titus	2: 2	Tell the older **m** to be
	2: 6	urge the younger **m** to be
Rev	14:14	the Son of **M**, with a golden

MANNA

Ex	16:31	house of Israel called it **m**;
Num	11: 6	nothing at all but this **m**
Deut	8:16	in the wilderness with **m** that
Josh	5:12	The **m** ceased on the day they
Ps	78:24	rained down on them **m** to eat,
Jn	6:49	ate the **m** in the wilderness,
Heb	9: 4	a golden urn holding the **m**,
Rev	2:17	give some of the hidden **m**,

MARRIAGE (MARRIED) (MARRIES)

Gen	20: 3	for she is a **m** woman."
Deut	24: 5	When a man is newly **m**, he
Sir	23:18	who sins against his **m** bed
Isa	62: 4	and your land shall be **m**.
Mt	5:32	whoever **m** a divorced woman
	19: 9	another commits adultery."
Mk	12:23	For the seven had **m** her."
Lk	17:27	marrying and being given in **m**,
Rom	7: 2	Thus a **m** woman is bound by
1 Cor	7:10	To the **m** I give this command
	7:38	who **m** his fiancee does well;
Gal	4:27	of the one who is **m**."
1 Tim	3:12	Let deacons be **m** only once,
Titus	1: 6	is blameless, **m** only once,
Heb	13: 4	Let **m** be held in honor by
Rev	19: 7	the **m** of the Lamb has come

MASTER (S)

Gen	4: 7	but you must **m** it."
Ex	21: 5	"I love my **m**, my wife, and my
Ps	12: 4	who is our **m**?"
Prov	25:13	refresh the spirit of their **m**.
Eccl	2:19	Yet they will be **m** of all

Mal	1: 6	And if I am a **m**, where is the
Mt	6:24	"No one can serve two **m**;
	25:23	**m** said to him, 'Well done,
Lk	16:13	No slave can serve two **m**;
Jn	13:16	are not greater than their **m**,
Eph	6: 5	obey your earthly **m** with fear
	6: 9	And, **m**, do the same to them
Col	3:22	obey your earthly **m** in
	4: 1	you also have a **M** in heaven.
1 Tim	6: 1	regard their **m** as worthy of all
Titus	2: 9	to be submissive to their **m**
1 Pet	2:18	accept the authority of your **m**
2 Pet	2: 1	even deny the **M** who bought

MATURE (MATURITY)

1 Macc	16:3	Heaven's mercy in years.
Lk	8:14	and their fruit does not **m**.
1 Cor	2: 6	the **m** we do speak wisdom,
Eph	4:13	to **m**, to the measure
Phil	3:15	are **m** be of the same mind
Col	1:28	present everyone **m** in Christ.
	4:12	may stand **m** and fully assured
Heb	5:14	solid food is for the **m**,
Jas	1: 4	you may be **m** and complete,

MEDITATE (MEDITATION)

Josh	1: 8	you shall **m** on it day and
Job	15: 4	and hindering **m** before God.
Ps	1: 2	his law they **m** day and night.
	19:14	**m** of my heart be acceptable
	143:5	I **m** on the works of your

MEEK (NESS)

Ps	10:17	hear the desire of the **m**;
	37:11	the **m** shall inherit the land,
Isa	29:19	The **m** shall obtain fresh joy in
Mt	5: 5	"Blessed are the **m**, for they
2 Cor	10: 1	the **m** and gentleness of Christ
Col	3:12	kindness, humility, **m**, and
Jas	1:21	with **m** the implanted word

MERCY (MERCIES) (MERCIFUL)

Gen	19:16	the LORD being **m** to him,
	43:14	God Almighty grant you **m**
Ex	25:17	make a **m** seat of pure gold;
	33:19	show **m** on whom I will show
Deut	4:31	LORD your God is a **m** God,
Josh	11:20	might receive no **m**, but be
1 Kings	20:31	house of Israel are **m** kings;
1 Chr	21:13	LORD, for his **m** is very great;
Neh	9:19	your great **m** did not forsake
	9:31	you are a gracious and **m** God.
Job	9:15	I must appeal for **m** to my
Ps	51: 1	Have **m** on me, O God,
	119:156	Great is your **m**, O LORD;
	145: 8	The LORD is gracious and **m**,
Prov	12:10	the **m** of the wicked is cruel
	21:10	find no **m** in their eyes.
Isa	47: 6	you showed them no **m**;
	55: 7	that he may have **m** on them,
Jer	3:12	for I am **m**, says the LORD;
	50:42	are cruel and have no **m**.
Dan	2:18	told them to seek **m** from the
	9: 9	God belong **m** and forgiveness,
Hab	1:17	destroying nations without **m**?
	3: 2	wrath may you remember **m**.
Zech	1:12	how long will you withhold **m**
	7: 9	kindness and **m** to one another;
Mt	5: 7	"Blessed are the **m**, for they
	9:13	'I desire **m**, not sacrifice.'

Mk	5:19	what **m** he has shown you."
	10:47	Son of David, have **m** on
Lk	1:50	His **m** is for those who fear
	6:36	Be **m**, just as your Father is
	18:13	'God, be **m** to me, a sinner!'
Rom	9:15	have **m** on whom I have **m**
	11:32	so that he may be **m** to all.
1 Cor	7:25	by the Lord's **m** is trustworthy.
2 Cor	1: 3	the Father of **m** and the God
	4: 1	since it is by God's **m** that we
Eph	2: 4	God, who is rich in **m**, out of
Phil	2:27	But God had **m** on him,
1 Tim	1:13	I received **m** because I had
2 Tim	1:18	grant that he will find **m**
Titus	3: 5	according to his **m**,
Heb	2:17	he might be a **m** and faithful
	4:16	we may receive **m** and find
Jas	2:13	**m** triumphs over judgment.
	3:17	full of **m** and good fruits,
1 Pet	1: 3	By his great **m** he has given
2 Jn	1: 3	Grace, **m**, and peace will be
Jude	1:21	the **m** of our Lord Jesus Christ

MESSAGE (MESSENGER)

Judg	3:20	"I have a **m** from God for
Prov	26: 6	to send a **m** by a fool.
Isa	28: 9	whom will he explain the **m**?
Hag	1:13	Haggai, the **m** of the LORD,
Mal	2: 7	he is the **m** of the LORD of
	3: 1	See, I am sending my **m** to
Mt	11:10	'See, I am sending my **m**
Jn	12:38	who has believed our **m**,
Acts	2:41	welcomed his **m** were baptized,
	10:36	You know the **m** he sent to
Rom	10:16	who has believed our **m**?"
1 Cor	1:18	**m** about the cross is foolishness
2 Cor	5:19	the **m** of reconciliation
	12: 7	a **m** of Satan to torment me
Heb	4: 2	**m** they heard did not benefit
1 Jn	1: 5	**m** we have heard from him

MESSIAH

Mt	1: 1	the genealogy of Jesus the **M**,
	16:16	Peter answered, "You are the **M**,
Mk	13:21	'Look! Here is the **M**!'
Lk	2:11	Savior, who is the **M**, the Lord.
	23:35	is the **M** of God, his chosen
Jn	1:41	"We have found the **M**"
	10:24	If you are the **M**, tell us
Acts	2:36	made him both Lord and **M**,
	3:20	may send the **M** appointed for
Rom	9: 5	the **M**, who is over all,
Rev	11:15	our Lord and of his **M**,

MIGHT (Y)

Gen	10: 9	a **m** hunter before the LORD."
	49:24	hands of the **M** One of Jacob,
Ex	6: 1	by a **m** hand he will let them
Deut	7: 8	you out with a **m** hand,
	10:17	great God, **m** and awesome,
Judg	16:30	He strained with all his **m**;
2 Sam	1:19	How the **m** have fallen!
	6: 5	the LORD with all their **m**,
2 Chr	6:41	and the ark of your **m**.
2 Chr	14:11	helping the **m** and the weak.
Neh	9:32	great and **m** and awesome God,
Job	36: 5	"Surely God is **m** and does not
Ps	71:16	come praising the **m** deeds
	89: 8	who is as **m** as you, O LORD?
	150: 1	him in his **m** firmament!

Sir	15:8	is **m** in power and sees
Isa	9: 6	Wonderful Counselor, **M** God,
Jer	32:19	in counsel and **m** in deed;
Bar	2:11	Egypt with a **m** hand and with
Ezek	20:33	**m** hand and an outstretched
Dan	4: 3	how **m** his wonders!
Mic	3: 8	with justice and **m**, to declare
Zech	4: 6	Not by **m**, nor by power,
Mt	13:15	they **m** not look with their
Mk	14:35	the hour **m** pass from him.
Lk	1:49	**M** One has done great things
	22: 4	about how he **m** betray him to
Jn	1: 7	that all **m** believe through him.
Acts	28:27	they **m** not look with their
1 Cor	9:22	I **m** by all means save some
	10: 6	so that we **m** not desire evil
2 Cor	8: 9	his poverty you **m** become rich.
1 Pet	2:24	we **m** live for righteousness;
1 Jn	4: 9	that we **m** live through him.
Rev	18: 8	for **m** is the Lord God who

MIND (FUL) (S)

Gen	37:11	father kept the matter in **m**.
Num	23:19	that he should change his **m**.
Deut	29: 4	given you a **m** to understand,
1 Sam	15:29	not recant or change his **m**;
1 Chr	28: 9	for the LORD searches every **m**,
	29: 9	with single **m** they had offered
Ps	7: 9	you who test the **m** and hearts,
	110: 4	and will not change his **m**,
Eccl	2: 3	my **m** still guiding me with
	3:11	past and future into their **m**,
Isa	26: 3	steadfast **m** you keep in peace
Jer	17:10	I the LORD test the **m** and
	23:16	speak visions of their own **m**,
Lam	3:21	But this I call to **m**,
Ezek	28: 2	compare your **m** with the **m** of
Dan	4:16	Let his **m** be changed from
Jon	3: 9	may relent and change his **m**;
Mt	22:37	soul, and with all your **m**.'
Mk	3:21	has gone out of his **m**."
	5:15	clothed and in his right **m**.
Lk	10:27	and with all your **m**;
	24:45	opened their **m** to understand
Rom	8: 5	set their **m** on the things of
	11:34	has known the **m** of the Lord?
1 Cor	1:10	united in the same **m** and the
	2:16	But we have the **m** of Christ.
2 Cor	3:14	But their **m** were hardened.
	4: 4	world has blinded the **m** of
Eph	4:23	in the spirit of your **m**,
Phil	2: 5	Let the same **m** be in you that
	4: 7	guard your hearts and your **m**
Col	3: 2	Set your **m** on things that are
1 Thess	4:11	live quietly, to **m** your own
2 Tim	3: 8	corrupt **m** and counterfeit
Heb	8:10	my laws in their **m**, and write
1 Pet	1:13	prepare your **m** for action;
Rev	2:23	who searches **m** and hearts,
	17; 9	calls for a **m** that has wisdom:

MINISTRY

Acts	1:17	allotted his share in this **m**."
Rom	11:13	to the Gentiles, I glorify my **m**
2 Cor	4: 1	we are engaged in this **m**,
	5:18	the **m** of reconciliation;
Eph	4:12	for the work of **m**, for building
2 Tim	4: 5	carry out your **m** fully.
Heb	8: 6	obtained a more excellent **m**,

MIRACLES

1 Chr	16:12	works he has done, his **m**, and
Ps	78:11	the **m** that he had shown them
	105:5	works he has done, his **m**, and
Acts	8:13	signs and great **m** that took
	19:11	extraordinary **m** through Paul,
1 Cor	12:10	to another the working of **m**,
Gal	3:5	work **m** among you by your
Heb	2:4	and wonders and various **m**,

MONEY

Ex	22:25	If you lend **m** to my people,
	30:16	take the atonement **m** from
2 Kings	12:4	**m** offered as sacred donations
Ps	15:5	who do not lend **m** at interest,
Eccl	5:10	lover of **m** will not be satisfied
	10:19	and **m** meets every need.
Isa	55:1	buy wine and milk without **m**
Mic	3:11	its prophets give oracles for **m**;
Mk	11:15	the tables of the **m** changers
Lk	3:14	"Do not extort **m** from anyone
	9:3	nor bag, nor bread, nor **m**
Jn	2:14	**m** changers seated at their
1 Tim	3:3	and not a lover of **m**.
	6:10	For the love of **m** is a root of
2 Tim	3:2	of themselves, lovers of **m**,
Heb	13:5	free from the love of **m**,

MOON (S)

Gen	37:9	sun, the **m**, and eleven stars
Deut	17:3	the sun or the **m** or any
Josh	10:13	stood still, and the **m** stopped,
2 Chr	8:13	for the sabbaths, the new **m**,
Ps	8:3	**m** and the stars that you have
	148:3	Praise him, sun and **m**; praise
Song	6:10	fair as the **m**, bright as the sun,
Isa	13:10	the **m** will not shed its light
Jer	31:35	order of the **m** and the stars
Ezek	32:7	the **m** shall not give its light
Joel	2:31	darkness, and the **m** to blood,
Hab	3:11	the **m** stood still in its exalted
Mt	24:29	the **m** will not give its light
Acts	2:20	darkness and the **m** to blood,
1 Cor	15:41	and another glory of the **m**,
Col	2:16	observing festivals, new **m**, or
Rev	6:12	the full **m** became like blood,
	21:23	no need of sun or **m** to shine

MORNING

Gen	1:5	and there was **m**, the first day.
Ex	12:10	that remains until the **m**
	16:12	the **m** you shall have your fill
Deut	28:67	shall say, "If only it were **m**!"
2 Sam	23:4	like the light of **m**, like the sun
Job	38:7	the **m** stars sang together
Ps	5:3	LORD, in the **m** you hear my
	30:5	but joy comes with the **m**.
Prov	27:14	early in the **m**, will be counted
Eccl	11:6	In the **m** sow your seed,
Isa	50:4	**M** by **m** he wakens
Lam	3:23	they are new every **m**; great is
Hos	6:4	Your love is like a **m** cloud,
	13:3	like the **m** mist or like the dew
Zeph	3:5	he renders his judgment,
Lk	24:22	at the tomb early this **m**,
Acts	2:15	is only nine o'clock in the **m**.
2 Pet	1:19	day dawns and the **m** star rises
Rev	2:28	I will also give the **m** star.
	22:16	the bright **m** star."

MORTAL (S)

Num	23:19	or a **m**, that he should change
1 Sam	15:29	**m**, that he should change his
Job	9:2	can a **m** be just before God?
	22:2	"Can a **m** be of use to God
Ps	56:11	What can a mere **m** do to me?
Sir	35:24	repays **m** according to their
Isa	51:12	afraid of a mere **m** who must
Rom	1:23	resembling a **m** human being
	8:11	will give life to your **m** bodies
2 Cor	5:4	what is **m** may be swallowed
1 Jn	5:16	There is sin that is **m**;
Rev	13:3	its **m** wound had been healed.

MOTHER ('S) (S)

Gen	2:24	leaves his father and his **m**
	3:20	she was the **m** of all living.
Ex	20:12	your father and your **m**,
	21:15	Whoever strikes father or **m**
Deut	5:16	your father and your **m**,
	27:16	who dishonors father or **m**."
Judg	5:7	Deborah, arose as a **m** in
1 Sam	2:19	His **m** used to make for him
2 Sam	20:19	a city that is a **m** in Israel;
1 Kings	19:20	kiss my father and my **m**,
Job	1:21	"Naked I came from my **m**
Ps	27:10	If my father and **m** forsake me,
	51:5	a sinner when my **m**
Prov	1:8	do not reject your **m** teaching;
	23:25	Let your father and **m** be glad;
Song	6:9	darling of her **m**, flawless to
Isa	66:13	As a **m** comforts her child, so I
Jer	20:17	**m** would have been my grave
Hos	2:2	Plead with your **m**, plead
	10:14	when **m** were dashed in pieces
Mic	7:6	rises up against her **m**,
Mt	10:37	Whoever loves father or **m**
	12:48	Jesus replied, "Who is my **m**,
Mk	7:10	your father and your **m**;
Lk	14:26	not hate father and **m**, wife
Jn	3:4	time into the **m** womb and
	19:27	disciple, "Here is your **m**."
Eph	5:31	leave his father and **m** and be
1 Tim	5:2	older women as **m**, to younger
Heb	7:3	Without father, without **m**,
Rev	17:5	"Babylon the great, **m** of

MOUNT (AIN) (AINS)

Gen	7:20	waters swelled above the **m**,
	8:4	to rest on the **m** of Ararat.
Ex	3:1	came to Horeb, the **m** of God.
Deut	5:4	face to face at the **m**,
Job	14:18	the **m** falls and crumbles away,
Ps	36:6	is like the mighty **m**,
	90:2	Before the **m** were brought
Isa	40:4	every **m** and hill be made low
	52:7	beautiful upon the **m** are the
Ezek	34:6	all the **m** and on every high
	39:4	shall fall upon the **m** of Israel,
Dan	2:45	stone was cut from the **m**
Hos	10:8	shall say to the **m**, Cover us,
Nah	1:15	Look! On the **m** the feet of
Mt	4:8	very high **m** and showed him
	17:20	say to this **m**, 'Move from here
Mk	13:14	Judea must flee to the **m**;
Lk	3:5	every **m** and hill shall be made
	23:30	say to the **m**, 'Fall on us';
Jn	4:21	neither on this **m** nor in
1 Cor	13:2	remove **m**, but do not have love
2 Pet	1:18	with him on the holy **m**.

Rev	16:20	and no **m** were to be found;

MOURN (ING)

Gen	23:2	Abraham went in to **m** for
Neh	8:9	do not **m** or weep."
Esth	4:3	was great **m** among the Jews,
	9:22	and from **m** into a holiday;
1 Macc	1:39	her feasts were turned into **m**,
Ps	30:11	You have turned my **m** into
Eccl	3:4	time to **m**, and a time to dance
Sir	7:34	but **m** with those who **m**.
Isa	61:2	to comfort all who **m**;
Jer	6:26	make **m** as for an only child
	31:13	I will turn their **m** into joy,
Lam	5:15	dancing has been turned to **m**.
Zech	12:10	they shall **m** for him,
Mt	5:4	"Blessed are those who **m**,
	9:15	wedding guests cannot **m** as
Lk	6:25	for you will **m** and weep.
1 Cor	7:30	who **m** as though they were
Rev	21:4	**m** and crying and pain will

MOUTH (S)

Ex	4:12	will be with your **m** and teach
Num	16:30	ground opens its **m** and
	22:38	word God puts in my **m**,
Deut	8:3	comes from the **m** of the LORD.
	30:14	in your **m** and in your heart
Josh	1:8	not depart out of your **m**;
2 Kings	4:34	putting his **m** upon his **m**,
Job	23:12	my bosom the words of his **m**.
	40:4	lay my hand on my **m**.
Ps	19:14	Let the words of my **m** and the
	119:103	sweeter than honey to my **m**!
	141:3	Set a guard over my **m**, O LORD;
Prov	8:7	for my **m** will utter truth;
	15:2	the **m** of fools pour out folly
	26:28	a flattering **m** works ruin.
Eccl	5:2	Never be rash with your **m**,
Song	1:2	with the kisses of his **m**!
Wis	1:11	lying **m** destroys the soul.
Sir	28:25	and a bolt for your **m**.
Isa	40:5	the **m** of the LORD has spoken
	49:2	my **m** like a sharp sword,
	53:7	he did not open his **m**.
Jer	1:9	put my words in your **m**.
Ezek	3:2	So I opened my **m**, and he
Dan	6:22	and shut the lions' **m**.
	7:8	a **m** speaking arrogantly.
Hos	6:5	them by the words of my **m**,
Mal	2:7	seek instruction from his **m**,
Mt	4:4	comes from the **m** of God.' "
Lk	6:45	of the heart that the **m** speaks.
Acts	8:32	he does not open his **m**.
Rom	3:14	"Their **m** are full of cursing
Eph	4:29	evil talk come out of your **m**,
2 Thess	2:8	with the breath of his **m**,
Heb	11:33	shut the **m** of lions,
Jas	3:10	same **m** come blessing and
1 Pet	2:22	deceit was found in his **m**."
Rev	3:16	spit you out of my **m**.
	10:10	sweet as honey in my **m**,

MURDER (ER) (ERS)

Ex	20:13	You shall not **m**.
Num	35:31	**m** must be put to death
Deut	5:17	You shall not **m**.
Hos	4:2	Swearing, lying, and **m**, and
Mt	5:21	'You shall not **m**;
	15:19	evil intentions, **m**, adultery,

Mk	10:19	'You shall not **m**; You shall not
Lk	23:25	prison for insurrection and **m**,
Jn	8:44	was a **m** from the beginning
Acts	3:14	asked to have a **m** given to
Rom	1:29	Full of envy, **m**, strife, deceit,
Jas	2:11	"You shall not **m**."
1 Jn	3:12	And why did he **m** him?
Rev	21: 8	faithless, the polluted, the **m**,

MYSTERY

Dan	2:19	the **m** was revealed to Daniel
	4: 9	no **m** is too difficult for you
Rom	16:25	of the **m** that was kept secret
1 Cor	2: 1	proclaiming the **m** of God
	15:51	I will tell you a **m**!
Eph	1: 9	known to us the **m** of his will,
	6:19	boldness the **m** of the gospel,
Col	1:26	the **m** that has been hidden
	2: 2	the knowledge of God's **m**,
	4: 3	may declare the **m** of Christ,
2 Thess	2: 7	the **m** of lawlessness is already
1 Tim	3: 9	hold fast to the **m** of the faith
	3:16	the **m** of our religion is great
Rev	1:20	As for the **m** of the seven stars
	10: 7	the **m** of God will be fulfilled

N

NAKED

Gen	2:25	man and his wife were both **n**,
Job	1:21	**N** I came from my mother's

NAME

Gen	2:19	living creature, that was its **n**.
Num	17: 2	Write each man's **n** on his
Judg	13:17	the the LORD, "What is your **n**,
2 Sam	7: 9	I will make for you a great **n**,
1 Kings	8:29	My **n** shall be there,'
Ezra	6:12	God who has established his **n**
Prov	10: 7	the **n** of the wicked will rot
Eccl	7: 1	A good **n** is better than
Song	1: 3	your **n** is perfume poured out;
Lam	3:55	I called on your **n**, O LORD,
Ezek	20: 9	acted for the sake of my **n**,
Dan	2:20	Blessed be the **n** of God from
Joel	2:32	who calls on the **n** of the LORD
Mic	5: 4	majesty of the **n** of the LORD
Zech	13: 9	my **n**, and I will answer them
Mal	1: 6	O priests, who despise my **n**.
Mt	6: 9	heaven, hallowed be your **n**.
Mk	11: 9	comes in the **n** of the Lord!
Lk	1:31	and you will **n** him Jesus.
Jn	1:12	him, who believed in his **n**,
Acts	2:21	who calls on the **n** of the Lord
1 Cor	6:11	you were justified in the **n** of
Phil	2: 9	the **n** that is above every **n**
Col	3:17	do everything in the **n** of the
Heb	1: 4	**n** he has inherited is more
Jas	5:14	them with oil in the **n** of

NATION (S)

Ex	34:24	I will cast out **n** before you,
Deut	15: 6	you will lend to many **n**, but
1 Kings	4:34	from all the **n** to hear the
Ps	2: 1	Why do the **n** conspire, and
Joel	3: 2	I will gather all the **n** and

NEAR

Deut	30:14	No, the word is very **n** to you;
Ps	69:18	Draw **n** to me, redeem me,
Isa	55: 6	call upon him while he is **n**;
Joel	1:15	for the day of the LORD is **n**,
Mal	3: 5	I will draw **n** to you for
Mk	1:15	kingdom of God has come **n**;
Rom	10: 8	The word is **n** you, on your
Jas	4: 8	**n** to God, and he will draw **n**
Rev	1: 3	written in it; for the time is **n**.

NEED (Y)

1 Sam	2: 8	lifts the **n** from the ash heap,
Ps	9:18	For the **n** shall not always be
Prov	14:31	are kind to the **n** honor him.
Sir	4:3	or delay giving to the **n**.

NEIGHBOR

Ex	3:22	each woman shall ask her **n**
Deut	5:20	false witness against your **n**.
Prov	24:28	against your **n** without cause
Isa	19: 2	against the other, **n** against **n**,
Mt	19:19	shall love your **n** as yourself."
Lk	10:29	Jesus, "And who is my **n**?"

NEVER

Gen	8:21	I will **n** again curse the ground
2 Chr	18: 7	he **n** prophesies anything
Prov	10:30	righteous will **n** be removed,
Isa	51: 6	deliverance will **n** be ended.
Jer	33:17	David shall **n** lack a man to sit
Dan	6:26	kingdom shall **n** be destroyed,
Joel	2:26	people shall **n** again be put to
Mt	7:23	declare to them, 'I **n** knew
Mk	3:29	the Holy Spirit can **n** have
Jn	6:35	comes to me will **n** be hungry,
1 Cor	13: 8	**n** ends. But as for prophecies
Heb	13: 5	I will **n** leave you or forsake
1 Pet	5: 4	crown of glory that **n** fades

NEW

Ex	1: 8	a **n** king arose over Egypt,
Jdt	16:1	Raise to him a **n** psalm;
1 Macc	4:47	built a **n** altar like the former
Ps	33: 3	Sing to him a **n** song;
Eccl	1: 9	is nothing **n** under the sun.
Sir	9:10	for **n** ones cannot equal them.
Jer	31:31	I will make a **n** covenant with
Lam	3:23	they are **n** every morning;
Mt	9:17	**n** wine put into old wineskins
Mk	1:27	A **n** teaching—with authority!
Lk	22:20	is the **n** covenant in my blood.
Jn	13:34	I give you a **n** commandment,
Acts	17:19	know what this **n** teaching
1 Cor	11:25	This cup is the **n** covenant in
2 Cor	5:17	Christ, there is a **n** creation:
1 Pet	1: 3	he has given us a **n** birth into
2 Pet	3:13	we wait for **n** heavens and a **n**

NIGHT

Gen	1: 5	and the darkness he called **N**.
Ex	13:21	a pillar of fire by **n**, to give
Josh	1: 8	shall meditate on it day and **n**,

NEAR

Zeph	3: 8	for my decision is to gather **n**,
Hag	2: 7	I will shake all the **n**,
Mal	3:12	Then all **n** will count you
Mt	24: 9	hated by all **n** because of my
Mk	11:17	a house of prayer for all the **n**?
Rev	2:26	I will give authority over the **n**;

NOTHING

2 Sam	24:24	Lord my God that cost me **n**.
2 Chr	9: 2	was **n** hidden from Solomon
Job	1: 9	Does Job fear God for **n**?
Ps	73:25	there is **n** on earth that I desire
Prov	13: 4	the lazy craves, and gets **n**,
Eccl	1: 9	there is **n** new under the sun.
Sir	39:20	**n** is too marvelous for him.
Isa	53: 2	**n** in his appearance that we
Mt	17:20	will be impossible for you
Lk	1:37	**n** will be impossible with God
Jn	5:30	I can do **n** on my own.
Rom	7:18	For I know that **n** good dwells
1 Cor	13: 2	but do not have love, I am **n**.

NUMEROUS

Gen	17: 2	will make you exceedingly **n**."
Ex	1: 9	Israelite people are more **n**
Zech	10: 8	be as **n** as they were before.

O

OBEY

Ex	19: 5	if you **o** my voice and keep my
Deut	12:28	Be careful to **o** all these words
Josh	24:24	will serve, and him we will **o**."
1 Sam	15:22	to **o** is better than sacrifice,
Mt	8:27	the winds and the sea **o** him?"
Lk	11:28	the word of God and **o** it!"
Acts	5:29	**o** God rather than any human
2 Cor	10: 5	thought captive to **o** Christ.
Eph	6: 1	Children, **o** your parents in
Col	3:22	Slaves, **o** your earthly masters
Heb	13:17	**O** your leaders and submit to
1 Jn	3:24	All who **o** his commandments

OFFER (ING) (INGS)

Gen	22: 2	**o** him there as a burnt **o**
Ex	29:38	what you shall **o** on the altar:
Deut	12:14	you shall **o** your burnt **o**
Ps	4: 5	**O** right sacrifices,
Hos	14: 2	we will **o** the fruit of our lips
Mt	5:24	then come and **o** your gift.
Heb	9:25	Nor was it to **o** himself again

OIL

Ex	29: 7	You shall take the anointing **o**,
1 Sam	16:13	Samuel took the horn of **o**,
1 Kings	17:16	neither did the jug of **o** fail,
2 Kings	4: 6	Then the **o** stopped flowing.
Ps	23: 5	you anoint my head with **o**;
Prov	5: 3	her speech is smoother than **o**;
Mt	25: 3	they took no **o** with them;
Jas	5:14	anointing them with **o** in the

OLD

Gen	17:12	when he is eight days **o**,
Num	1: 3	twenty years **o** and upward,
Deut	32: 7	Remember the days of **o**,

Ps	74:12	Yet God my King is from of **o**,
Sir	9:10	Do not abandon **o** friends,
Joel	2:28	**o** men shall dream dreams,
Mk	2:22	new wine into **o** wineskins;
Jn	3: 4	be born after having grown **o**?
Acts	2:17	**o** men shall dream dreams.
1 Cor	5: 7	Clean out the **o** yeast
2 Cor	5:17	everything **o** has passed away;

ONE
Gen	2:24	and they become **o** flesh.
Ps	14: 3	there is no **o** who does good,
Eccl	4: 9	Two are better than **o**,
Sir	1:8	There is but **o** who is wise,
Ezek	37:22	I will make them **o** nation
Mal	2:10	Have we not all **o** father?
Mk	10: 8	the two shall become **o** flesh.'
Lk	10:42	there is need of only **o** thing.
Jn	1:18	No **o** has ever seen God.
Rom	3:10	There is no **o** who is righteous,
1 Cor	8: 4	there is no God but **o**."
Eph	4: 5	**o** Lord, **o** faith, **o** baptism
1 Tim	2: 5	**o** God; there is also **o** mediator
2 Pet	3: 8	But do not ignore this **o** fact,

ONLY
Gen	7:23	**O** Noah was left,
Num	11: 4	If **o** we had meat to eat
Deut	15: 5	if **o** you will obey the LORD
1 Kings	18:22	I, even I **o**, am left a prophet
Ps	37: 8	Do not fret—it leads **o** to evil.
Mt	4:10	Lord your God, and serve **o**
Mk	13:32	Son, but **o** the Father.
Jn	1:18	It is God the **o** Son,
Rom	3:29	Or is God the God of Jews **o**?
1 Tim	1:17	the **o** God, be honor and glory
1 Jn	4: 9	God sent his **o** Son into the

OPEN (ED)
Deut	28:12	The LORD will **o** for you his
1 Macc	3:48	they **o** the book of the law
Ps	78: 2	I will **o** my mouth in a parable
Song	5: 2	**O** to me, my sister, my love
Isa	53: 7	yet he did not **o** his mouth
Mt	13:35	I will **o** my mouth to speak in

OPPRESS (OPPRESSED)
Ex	22:21	shall not wrong or **o** a resident
Ps	105:14	he allowed no one to **o** them
Sir	4:9	Rescue the **o** from the
Zech	7:10	not **o** the widow, the orphan
Jas	2: 6	is it not the rich who **o** you?
Jdt	9:11	of the lowly, helper of the **o**,

ORPHAN
Ex	22:22	not abuse any widow or **o**.
Isa	1:17	defend the **o**, plead for the
Hos	14: 3	In you the **o** finds mercy."

OTHER (S)
Ex	20: 3	you shall have no **o** gods
Deut	4:35	there is no **o** besides him.
Judg	2:19	following **o** gods,
1 Sam	8:20	we also may be like **o** nations,
2 Kings	17: 7	They had worshiped **o** gods
2 Chr	2: 5	God is greater than **o** gods.
Sir	1:4	was created before all **o**
Isa	44: 8	There is no **o** rock
Dan	3:29	**o** god who is able to deliver
Mt	6:24	to the one and love the **o**,

Lk	17:34	will be taken and the **o** left.
Jn	20:30	Now Jesus did many **o** signs

OX
Deut	25: 4	You shall not muzzle an **o**
1 Cor	9: 9	You shall not muzzle an **o**

P

PAIN
Gen	3:16	**p** you shall bring forth children
Job	33:19	chastened with **p** upon their
Jer	15:18	Why is my **p** unceasing,
Jn	16:21	woman is in labor, she has **p**,
1 Pet	2:19	endure **p** while suffering
Rev	21: 4	crying and **p** will be no more,

PARABLE (S)
Ps	78: 2	I will open my mouth in a **p**;
Sir	39:2	penetrates the subtleties of **p**;
Mt	13:18	Hear then the **p** of the sower.
Lk	20:19	had told this **p** against them,

PARADISE
Lk	23:43	you will be with me in **P**."
Rev	2: 7	of life that is in the **p** of God.

PARENT
Deut	8: 5	that as a **p** disciplines a child
Ezek	18:20	nor a **p** suffer for the iniquity

PARTIALITY
Deut	16:19	you must not show **p**
Job	13: 8	Will you show **p** toward him,
Prov	28:21	To show **p** is not good
Sir	35:15	and with him there is no **p**.
Mt	22:16	do not regard people with **p**.
Rom	2:11	For God shows no **p**.
Eph	6: 9	with him there is no **p**.
Jas	3:17	a trace of **p** or hypocrisy.

PASSOVER
Ex	12:11	It is the **p** of the LORD.
Num	9: 2	Let the Israelites keep the **p**
Josh	5:10	**p** in the evening on the
2 Kings	23:21	Keep the **p** to the LORD your
Ezra	6:19	the returned exiles kept the **p**.
Mk	14:12	when the **P** lamb is sacrificed,
Lk	22: 8	Go and prepare the **P** meal for
Heb	11:28	By faith he kept the **P**

PATH
Ps	16:11	You show me the **p** of life.
Prov	12:28	the **p** of righteousness there is
Mt	13: 4	some seeds fell on the **p**,

PATIENT
Neh	9:30	years you were **p** with them,
Job	6:11	is my end, that I should be **p**?
Wis	15:1	our God, are kind and true, **p**,
Sir	1:23	Those who are **p** stay calm
Lk	8:15	bear fruit with **p** endurance.
Rom	12:12	in hope, be **p** in suffering,
1 Cor	13: 4	Love is **p**; love is kind;
1 Thess	5:14	help the weak, be **p** with all of
Jas	5: 7	Be **p**, therefore, beloved

PAY
Lev	25:51	shall **p** for their redemption
Num	16:15	**P** no attention to their
Deut	24:15	You shall **p** them their wages
1 Macc	2:68	**P** back the Gentiles in full,
Prov	19:19	tempered person will **p** the
Mt	22:17	to **p** taxes to the emperor,
Lk	19: 8	I will **p** back four times as
Rom	13: 7	**P** to all what is due

PEACE
Lev	26: 6	And I will grant **p** in the land,
Num	6:26	upon you, and give you **p**.
1 Sam	1:17	Then Eli answered, "Go in **p**;
1 Kings	2:33	shall be **p** from the LORD
1 Chr	19:19	they made **p** with David,
Job	22:21	Agree with God, and be at **p**
Ps	34:14	evil, and do good; seek **p**,
Prov	12:20	those who counsel **p** have joy.
Eccl	3: 8	time for war, and a time for **p**.
Isa	9: 6	Everlasting Father, Prince of **P**.
Jer	6:14	"**P**, **p**," when there is no **p**
Lam	3:17	my soul is bereft of **p**
Zech	8:19	therefore love truth and **p**.
Mt	10:34	I have come to bring **p** to the
Mk	9:50	and be at **p** with one another."
Lk	2:14	on earth **p** among those
Jn	14:27	**P** I leave with you
Gal	5:22	of the Spirit is love, joy, **p**,
Phil	4: 7	the **p** of God, which surpasses
Col	3:15	And let the **p** of Christ rule in
1 Thess	5: 3	say, "There is **p** and security,"
2 Thess	3:16	Lord of **p** himself give you **p**
2 Tim	2:22	righteousness, faith, love, and **p**
Heb	12:14	Pursue **p** with everyone,
1 Pet	3:11	let them seek **p** and pursue it.

PEOPLE
Gen	11: 6	Look, they are one **p**
Ex	5: 1	the God of Israel, 'Let my **p** go
Num	14:11	How long will this **p** despise
Deut	4:20	to become a **p** of his very own
Josh	3:16	Then the **p** crossed over
Ruth	1:16	your **p** shall be my **p**
2 Kings	23: 3	**p** joined in the covenant.
1 Chr	29:17	and now I have seen your **p**,
2 Chr	7: 5	**p** dedicated the house of God
Ezra	3:.1	the **p** gathered together as
Neh	4: 6	for the **p** had a mind to work
Jdt	13:17	the enemies of your **p**."
Esth	3: 6	been told who Mordecai's **p**
1 Macc	3:43	us restore the ruins of our **p**,
Ps	29:11	LORD give strength to his **p**!
Isa	1: 3	my **p** do not understand.
Ezek	13:23	I will save my **p** from your
Zech	8: 7	I will save my **p** from the east
Mt	1:21	will save his **p** from their sins."
Mk	8:27	Who do **p** say that I am?"
Lk	1:17	a **p** prepared for the Lord."
Jn	18:14	have one person die for the **p**.
Acts	3:22	your own **p** a prophet like me.
Rom	9:25	were not my **p** I will call 'my **p**,'
2 Cor	6:16	and they shall be my **p**.
Titus	1:10	also many rebellious **p**,
1 Pet	2:10	Once you were not a **p**,
Rev	18: 4	Come out of her, my **p**,

PERFECT
2 Sam	22:31	This God—his way is **p**;
Ps	19: 7	law of the LORD is **p**,

Song	6: 9	My dove, my **p** one,
Wis	6:15	thought on her is **p**
Ezek	27: 3	said, "I am **p** in beauty."
Mt	5:48	Be **p**, therefore, as your
2 Cor	12: 9	for power is made **p** in
Col	3:14	everything together in **p**
1 Jn	4:18	but **p** love casts out fear;

PERISH

Lev	26:38	You shall **p** among the nations,
Esth	4:16	and if I **p**, I **p**."
Ps	37:20	But the wicked **p**,
Prov	11:10	when the wicked **p**, there is
Lk	13: 3	you will all **p** as they did.
Jn	10:28	never **p**. No one will snatch
Acts	8:20	May your silver **p** with you,
Heb	1:11	they will **p**, but you remain;
2 Pet	3: 9	not wanting any to **p**,

PERSECUTE (D)

Ps	119:84	will you judge those who **p** me?
Mt	5:44	and pray for those who **p** you,
Lk	21:12	they will arrest you and **p** you;
Jn	15:20	they **p** me, they will **p** you;
Acts	9: 4	Saul, Saul, why do you **p** me?"
Rom	12:14	Bless those who **p** you;

PHARAOH

Gen	41:14	Then **P** sent for Joseph,
Ex	1:22	Then **P** commanded all his
Rom	9:17	For the scripture says to **P**,

PHARISEE (S)

Lk	11:37	a **P** invited him to dine with
Jn	3: 1	was a **P** named Nicodemus,
Acts	23: 6	Brothers, I am a **P**, a son of **P**.

PHILISTINE (S)

Gen	21:34	in the land of the **P**.
1 Sam	14: 1	let us go over to the **P** garrison

PIERCED

Zech	12:10	the one whom they have **p**,
Rev	1: 7	even those who **p** him;

PILLAR

Gen	19:26	and she became a **p** of salt.
Ex	13:21	in a **p** of cloud by day,
Rev	3:12	I will make you a **p** in the

PLAGUE

Ex	11: 1	one more **p** upon Pharaoh
Num	14:37	died by a **p** before the LORD.
Rev	16:21	cursed God for the **p** of the

PLANT

Gen	1:29	given you every **p** yielding
Eccl	3: 2	a time to die; a time to **p**,
Am	9:15	I will **p** them upon their land,
Mt	15:13	Every **p** that my heavenly

PLEASE (D) (PLEASING)

Ps	69:31	This will **p** the LORD more
Sir	44:16	Enoch **p** the Lord and was
Rom	8: 8	are in the flesh cannot **p** God.
1 Thess	2: 4	not to **p** mortals, but to **p** God
1 Tim	5: 4	for this is **p** in God's sight.
Heb	11: 6	faith it is impossible to **p** God,

PLEASURE

Prov	18: 2	takes no **p** in understanding,
Eccl	2: 2	and of **p**, "What use is it?"
Ezek	18:32	For I have no **p** in the death of
2 Tim	3: 4	lovers of **p** rather than lovers

POOR

Deut	15:11	Open your hand to the **p** and
1 Sam	2: 8	He raises up the **p** from the
Job	5:16	So the **p** have hope,
Ps	34: 6	This **p** soul cried, and was
Prov	13: 7	others pretend to be **p**,
Eccl	4:13	Better is a **p** but wise youth
Mt	5: 3	Blessed are the **p** in spirit,
Mk	12:42	A **p** widow came
Lk	4:18	bring good news to the **p**.
Jn	12: 8	You always have the **p** with
2 Cor	8: 9	for your sakes he became **p**,
Jas	2: 5	Has not God chosen the **p** in

POSSESS

Deut	28:21	that you are entering to **p**.
1 Sam	10: 6	spirit of the LORD will **p** you,
Ps	25:13	and their children shall **p** the
Isa	60:21	they shall **p** the land forever.

POUR

Deut	12:16	shall **p** it out on the ground
Ps	62: 8	O people; **p** out your heart
Isa	44: 3	For I will **p** water on the
Joel	2:28	Then afterward I will **p** out my
Acts	2:17	that I will **p** out my Spirit

POWER

Ex	15: 6	O LORD, glorious in **p**
1 Sam	11: 6	God came upon Saul in **p**
Jdt	9:14	the God of all **p** and might,
Job	36:22	God is exalted in his **p**;
Ps	66: 3	Because of your great **p**,
Eccl	8: 8	No one has **p** over the wind
Sir	39:18	can limit his saving **p**.
Isa	40:29	He gives **p** to the faint,
Jer	27: 5	by my great **p** and my
Dan	6:27	from the **p** of the lions."
Zech	4: 6	Not by might, nor by **p**,
Mt	22:29	the scriptures nor the **p** of
Mk	9: 1	God has come with **p**."
Lk	1:17	With the spirit and **p** of Elijah
Jn	19:11	You would have no **p** over me
Acts	1: 8	receive **p** when the Holy Spirit
1 Cor	1:18	being saved it is the **p** of God.
Phil	3:10	know Christ and the **p** of his
2 Pet	1: 3	His divine **p** has given us
Jude	1:25	our Lord, be glory, majesty, **p**,

PRAISE

Ex	15: 2	and I will **p** him,
2 Chr	20:21	sing to the LORD and **p** him
Ps	22:23	You who fear the LORD, **p** him!
Prov	31:31	and let her works **p** her
Isa	38:18	death cannot **p** you;
Mt	21:16	prepared **p** for yourself
Lk	19:37	disciples began to **p** God
Rom	15:11	"**P** the Lord, all you Gentiles
1 Cor	14:15	I will sing **p** with the spirit,
Jas	5:13	They should sing songs of **p**.
Rev	19: 5	"**P** our God, all you his

PRAY

1 Sam	12:23	by ceasing to **p** for you;

1 Kings	8:30	when they **p** toward this place;
Job	42: 8	my servant Job shall **p** for you,
Ps	122: 6	**P** for the peace of Jerusalem
Jer	7:16	do not **p** for this people,
Mt	6: 5	And whenever you **p**,
Lk	6:28	**p** for those who abuse you
1 Thess	5:17	**p** without ceasing,
2 Thess	1:11	To this end we always **p** for
Jas	5:16	**p** for one another,

PRECEPT (S)

Ps	19: 8	the **p** of the LORD are right
Sir	18:14	and who are eager for his **p**.
Isa	28:10	For it is **p** upon **p**,

PRECIOUS

1 Sam	26:21	because my life was **p** in your
Ps	116:15	**P** in the sight of the LORD
Prov	3:15	She is more **p** than jewels,
1 Pet	1:19	but with the **p** blood of Christ,

PREPARE

Ps	23: 5	You **p** a table before me
Isa	40: 3	wilderness **p** the way of the
Mal	3: 1	my messenger to **p** the way
Mt	3: 3	**p** the way of the Lord
Jn	14: 2	I go to **p** a place for you?

PRESENCE

1 Sam	2:21	Samuel grew up in the **p** of
Job	1:12	Satan went out from the **p** of
Ps	16:11	In your **p** there is fullness of
Jn	17: 5	me in your own **p** with the
Heb	9:24	to appear in the **p** of God on
Rev	20:11	the heaven fled from his **p**,

PRIDE

2 Chr	32:26	himself for the **p** of his heart,
Ps	20: 7	Some take **p** in chariots,
Prov	11: 2	When **p** comes, then comes
Sir	10:13	For the beginnng of **p** is sin,
Isa	2:11	the **p** of everyone shall be
2 Cor	7: 4	I have great **p** in you;

PRIEST (HOOD)

Gen	14:18	he was **p** of God Most High.
Ex	18: 1	Jethro, the **p** of Midian,
Num	5:10	anyone gives to the **p** shall be
1 Sam	2:11	in the presence of the **p** Eli.
2 Macc	11:3	the high **p** for sale every year.
Ps	110: 4	"You are a **p** forever
Jer	23:11	Both prophet and **p** are
Ezek	1: 3	the Lord came to the **p** Ezekiel
Mk	14:63	high **p** tore his clothes
Heb	3: 1	Jesus, the apostle and high **p**

PRISON

Ps	142: 7	Bring me out of **p**,
Isa	42: 7	**p** those who sit in darkness
Mt	25:36	I was in **p** and you visited me.'
Lk	22:33	I am ready to go with you to **p**
Acts	12: 5	While Peter was kept in **p**,
Heb	13: 3	those who are in **p**,
Rev	20: 7	will be released from his **p**

PROCLAIM (ED)

Deut	32: 3	For I will **p** the name of the
Ps	22:31	and **p** his deliverance to a
Isa	61: 1	to **p** liberty to the captives,
Jon	3: 2	Nineveh, that great city, and **p**

Mt	10:27	**p** from the housetops.
Lk	4:19	to **p** the year of the Lord's favor
1 Cor	11:26	you **p** the Lord's death until he
Phil	1:15	Some **p** Christ from envy and

PROMISE

1 Kings	8:20	Lord has upheld the **p** that he
Neh	9: 8	and you have fulfilled your **p**,
Ps	105:42	For he remembered his holy **p**,
Acts	2:39	For the **p** is for you,
Eph	6: 2	first commandment with a **p**:
2 Pet	3: 9	Lord is not slow about his **p**,

PROPHECY (NOUN)

Prov	29:18	Where there is no **p**,
Acts	21: 9	who had the gift of **p**.
Rev	19:10	Jesus is the spirit of **p**."

PROPHESY (VERB)

Isa	30:10	Do not **p** to us what is right
Jer	5:31	the prophets **p** falsely,
Ezek	13: 2	**p** against the prophets of Israel
Am	7:16	Do not **p** against Israel,
Mt	7:22	Lord, did we not **p** in your
Lk	22:64	**P**! Who is it that struck you?

PROPHET (NOUN)

Ex	7: 1	brother Aaron shall be your **p**.
Deut	18:18	I will raise up for them a **p**
1 Sam	3:20	trustworthy **p** of the LORD.
1 Kings	18:36	the **p** Elijah came near
2 Kings	6:12	It is Elisha, the **p** in Israel,
2 Chr	35:18	since the days of the **p** Samuel;
1 Macc	14:41	until a trustworthy **p** should
Jer	1: 5	appointed you a **p** to the
Ezek	33:33	they shall know that a **p** has
Hos	9: 7	Israel cries, "The **p** is a fool,
Mal	4: 5	I will send you the **p** Elijah
Mt	11: 9	did you go out to see? A **p**?
Lk	4:24	no **p** is accepted in the **p**'s
Jn	1:21	Are you the **p**?"

PROSPER

Gen	39:23	the LORD made it **p**.
Ps	1: 3	all that they do, they **p**.
Isa	53:10	the will of the LORD shall **p**.

PROSTITUTE

Deut	23:17	Israel shall be a temple **p**;
Josh	6:25	But Rahab the **p**, with her
Prov	23:27	For a **p** is a deep pit;
1 Cor	6:16	whoever is united to a **p**
Heb	11:31	By faith Rahab the **p** did not

PROUD

2 Chr	32:25	for his heart was **p**.
Ps	94: 2	the **p** what they deserve!
Prov	16:19	divide the spoil with the **p**.
Sir	10:9	How can dust and ashes be **p**?
Ezek	28:17	Your heart was **p** because of
Hos	13: 6	and their heart was **p**;
Ob	1: 3	Your **p** heart has deceived you,
Rom	11:20	So do not become **p**, but
Jas	4: 6	God opposes the **p**, but gives

PROVIDE

Gen	22:14	The LORD will **p**";
1 Cor	10:13	he will also **p** the way out
1 Tim	5: 8	And whoever does not **p** for

PUNISH

Ex	32:34	I will **p** them for their sin."
2 Sam	7:14	I will **p** him with a rod
Isa	13:11	I will **p** the world for its evil
Jer	2:19	Your wickedness will **p** you,

PURE

Ex	25:11	shall overlay it with **p** gold,
2 Sam	22:27	the **p** you show yourself **p**,
Tob	8:15	O God, with every **p** blessing;
Job	4:17	human beings be **p** before
Prov	15:26	but gracious words are **p**.
Wis	7:25	a **p** emanation of the glory
Hab	1:13	Your eyes are too **p** to behold
Mt	5: 8	Blessed are the **p** in heart,
Phil	4: 8	whatever is just, whatever is **p**,
1 Tim	1: 5	that comes from a **p** heart,
Titus	1:15	To the **p** all things are **p**,
Jas	1:27	Religion that is **p** and
Rev	21:18	while the city is **p** gold,

PURPOSE

Ps	138: 8	The LORD will fulfill his **p** for
Prov	19:21	but it is the **p** of the LORD
Rom	8:28	are called according to his **p**.
Jas	1:18	fulfillment of his own **p** he

PURSUE

Ps	34:14	seek peace, and **p** it.
Isa	51: 1	me, you that **p** righteousness,
Rom	14:19	Let us then **p** what makes for
1 Cor	14: 1	**P** love and strive
1 Tim	6:11	**p** righteousness, godliness,
Heb	12:14	**P** peace with everyone,
1 Pet	3:11	let them seek peace and **p** it.

Q

QUESTION

Job	38: 3	I will **q** you,
Sir	19:15	**Q** a friend, for often it is
Mt	22:35	a lawyer, asked him a **q** to test
Mk	11:29	I will ask you one **q**; answer

QUICK

Prov	20: 3	but every fool is **q** to quarrel.
Eccl	7: 9	Do not be **q** to anger,
Jas	1:19	let everyone be **q** to listen,

QUIET

Eccl	9:17	The **q** words of the wise
1 Tim	2: 2	may lead a **q** and peaceable

R

RACE

Eccl	9:11	the **r** is not to the swift
2 Tim	4: 7	I have finished the **r**,
Heb	12: 1	run with perseverance the **r**

1 Pet	2: 9	But you are a chosen **r**,

RAIN

Gen	7: 4	seven days I will send **r**
Ex	16: 4	I am going to **r** bread from
Deut	11:14	he will give the **r** for your land
1 Kings	18: 1	I will send **r** on the earth."
Job	38:28	Has the **r** a father,
Isa	45: 8	skies **r** down righteousness;
Mt	7:25	The **r** fell, the floods came,
Jas	5:17	fervently that it might not **r**,

RAISE (D)

Deut	18:15	your God will **r** up for you a
Judg	2:18	Whenever the LORD **r** up

RANSOM

Ps	49: 8	For the **r** of life is costly,
Hos	13:14	Shall I **r** them from the power
Mk	10:45	to give his life a **r** for many."
1 Tim	2: 6	who gave himself a **r** for all

READ

Deut	17:19	and he shall **r** in it all the days
Josh	8:34	And afterward he **r** all the
Neh	8: 8	So they **r** from the book,
Isa	34:16	Seek and **r** from the book
Jer	36: 6	shall **r** the words of the LORD
Dan	5:16	if you are able to **r** the writing
Mk	12:10	Have you not **r** this scripture:
Lk	4:16	He stood up to **r**,

REAP

Lev	19: 9	When you **r** the harvest of
Ps	126: 5	those who sow in tears **r** with
Hos	8: 7	they shall **r** the whirlwind.
Lk	12:24	they neither sow nor **r**,
Jn	4:38	I sent you to **r** that
2 Cor	9: 6	who sows sparingly will also **r**
Gal	6: 7	for you **r** whatever you sow.
Rev	14:15	Use your sickle and **r**,

REBEL

Num	14: 9	do not **r** against the LORD;
Josh	22:18	If you **r** against the LORD today,

REBUKE

Ps	6: 1	O LORD, do not **r** me in your
Prov	17:10	A **r** strikes deeper
Eccl	7: 5	better to hear the **r** of the wise
Zech	3: 2	The LORD **r** you, O Satan!
Mk	8:32	took him aside and began to **r**
Lk	17: 3	you must **r** the offender.
Titus	1:13	For this reason **r** them sharply,
Jude	1: 9	The Lord **r** you!"

RECEIVE

Deut	9: 9	I went up the mountain to **r**
Ps	24: 5	They will **r** blessing from the
Mt	10:41	a prophet will **r** a prophet's
Mk	10:15	not **r** the kingdom of God
Lk	7:22	the blind **r** their sight,
Jn	16:24	Ask and you will **r**,
Acts	1: 8	But you will **r** power
Rom	11:31	they too may now **r** mercy.
1 Cor	4: 5	will **r** commendation from
Jas	1:12	and will **r** the crown of life
Rev	4:11	to **r** glory and honor and

RECONCILE

Acts	7:26	and tried to **r** them,
Col	1:20	God was pleased to **r** to

REDEEM (ER)

Ex	6: 6	**r** you with an outstretched
Ruth	4: 6	I cannot **r** it for myself
Ps	26:11	**r** me, and be gracious
Sir	51:12	*Give thanks to the **r** of Israel.*
Hos	13:14	Shall I **r** them from Death?
Lk	24:21	he was the one to **r** Israel.
Titus	2:14	might **r** us from all iniquity

REFINE (S)

Jer	9: 7	I will now **r** and test them,
Zech	13: 9	**r** them as one **r** silver
Mal	3: 3	and **r** them like gold and silver

REFUGE

Num	35:11	to be cities of **r** for you,
Josh	20: 2	Appoint the cities of **r**,
Ruth	2:12	wings you have come for **r**!"
2 Sam	22: 3	in whom I take **r**, my shield
Ps	2:12	Happy are all who take **r** in
Prov	14:32	but the righteous find a **r**
Isa	25: 4	you have been a **r** to the poor,
Jer	16:19	my **r** in the day of trouble
Nah	1: 7	he protects those who take **r**

REIGN

Ex	15:18	The LORD will **r** forever and
Deut	17:20	his descendants may **r** long
1 Sam	8:11	the king who will **r** over you:
Ps	146:10	The LORD will **r** forever,
Prov	8:15	By me kings **r**,
Isa	24:23	LORD of hosts will **r** on Mount
Jer	23: 5	he shall **r** as king and deal
Lam	5:19	But you, O LORD, **r** forever;
Mic	4: 7	LORD will **r** over them in
Lk	1:33	He will **r** over the house of
1 Cor	15:25	For he must **r** until he has
2 Tim	2:12	we will also **r** with him;
Rev	11:15	he will **r** forever and ever."

REJECT (ED)

Ex	20: 5	of those who **r** me,
Isa	30:12	Because you **r** this word,
Hos	4: 6	you have **r** knowledge,

REJOICE

Lev	23:40	shall **r** before the LORD your
1 Chr	16:10	those who seek the LORD **r**.
2 Chr	6:41	let your faithful **r** in your
Neh	12:43	God had made them **r** with
Ps	5:11	who take refuge in you **r**;
Prov	23:25	let her who bore you **r**
Sir	8:7	Do not **r** over any one's death;
Isa	35: 1	the desert shall **r** and blossom;
Hab	3:18	yet I will **r** in the LORD;
Zep	3:17	will **r** over you with gladness,
Zech	9: 9	**R** greatly, O daughter Zion!
Lk	6:23	**R** in that day and leap
Rom	12:15	**R** with those who **r**,
Phil	3: 1	**r** in the Lord.
1 Thess	5:16	**R** always,
1 Pet	4:13	**r** insofar as you are sharing
Rev	18:20	**R** over her, O heaven,

RELY

2 Kings	18:20	On whom do you now **r**,

2 Chr	14:11	for we **r** on you,
Prov	3: 5	do not **r** on your own insight.
Rom	2:17	a Jew and **r** on the law
2 Cor	1: 9	we would **r** not on ourselves
Gal	3:10	For all who **r** on the works

REMEMBER

Gen	9:15	I will **r** my covenant
Ex	20: 8	**R** the sabbath day,
Deut	5:15	**R** that you were a slave
Josh	1:13	**R** the word that Moses
1 Chr	16:12	**R** the wonderful works
Neh	13:31	**R** me, O my God,
Job	10: 9	**R** that you fashioned me like
Ps	77:11	I will **r** your wonders of old.
Eccl	12: 1	**R** your creator in the days
Isa	64: 9	and do not **r** iniquity forever.
Jer	31:34	and **r** their sin no more.
Lam	5: 1	**R**, O Lord, what has befallen
Ezek	36:31	Then you shall **r** your evil
Hos	7: 2	I **r** all their wickedness.
Hab	3: 2	in wrath may you **r** mercy.
Mk	8:18	And do you not **r**?
Lk	23:42	Jesus, **r** me when you come
Phil	1: 3	my God every time I **r** you,
2 Tim	2: 8	**R** Jesus Christ,
Heb	8:12	and I will **r** their sins no
Jude	1:17	**r** the predictions of the apostles
Rev	3: 3	**R** then what you received

REMNANT

Gen	45: 7	for you a **r** on earth,
2 Kings	19:31	from Jerusalem a **r** shall go
Ezra	9: 8	who has left us a **r**,
Isa	10:21	A **r** will return,
Jer	23: 3	I myself will gather the **r** of my
Zeph	3:13	the **r** of Israel;
Zech	8:12	I will cause the **r** of this people
Rom	9:27	only a **r** of them will be saved

REPENT

1 Kings	8:47	**r**, and plead with you
Job	42: 6	I despise myself, and **r**
Mt	4:17	**R**, for the kingdom of heaven
Mk	6:12	proclaimed that all should **r**.
Lk	13: 3	unless you **r**, you will all
Acts	2:38	**R**, and be baptized every one
Rev	2:21	time to **r**, but she refuses to **r**

RESCUE (D) (S)

2 Chr	32:17	other lands did not **r** their
1 Macc	2:48	They **r** the law out of the
Ps	31: 2	Incline your ear to me; **r** me
Sir	29:12	it will **r** you from every
Isa	1:17	seek justice, **r** the oppressed,
Ezek	34:10	I will **r** my sheep from their
Mt	6:13	but **r** us from the evil one
Rom	7:24	Who will **r** me from this body
2 Cor	1:10	continue to **r** us;
2 Pet	2: 7	if he **r** Lot, a righteous man

REST

Gen	8: 4	the ark came to **r** on the
Ex	31:15	a sabbath of solemn **r**,
Lev	25: 4	sabbath of complete **r** for the
Num	10:36	And whenever it came to **r**,
Deut	12:10	gives you **r** from your enemies
Josh	11:23	And the land had **r** from war.
2 Sam	7:11	I will give you **r** from all
1 Kings	5: 4	God has given me **r** on every

1 Chr	28: 2	build a house of **r** for the ark
Job	3:17	there the weary are at **r**.
Ps	95:11	They shall not enter my **r**."
Prov	6:10	folding of the hands to **r**,
Isa	11: 2	the LORD shall **r** on him,
Jer	6:16	and find **r** for your souls.
Mt	11:28	and I will give you **r**.
Mk	6:31	by yourselves and **r** a while."
1 Cor	2: 5	so that your faith might **r** not
Gal	3:12	But the law does not **r** on
Heb	3:11	They will not enter my **r**.'
Rev	14:13	they will **r** from their labors,

RESTORE

Deut	30: 3	God will **r** your fortunes
2 Chr	24: 4	Joash decided to **r** the house
Neh	4: 2	Will they **r** things?
1 Macc	4:57	they **r** the gates and
Ps	80: 3	**R** us, O God;
Isa	49: 6	**r** the survivors of Israel;
Lam	5:21	**R** us to yourself, O LORD
Dan	9:25	**r** and rebuild Jerusalem
Zech	9:12	I declare that I will **r** to you
Mt	17:11	and will **r** all things;
Acts	1: 6	will **r** the kingdom to Israel?"
1 Pet	5:10	will himself **r**, support,

RESURRECTION

2 Macc	7:14	you there will be no **r** to life!"
Mt	22:28	In the **r**, then, whose wife
Mk	12:18	who say there is no **r**,
Lk	14:14	the **r** of the righteous."
Jn	11:24	the **r** on the last day."
Acts	2:31	David spoke of the **r** of the
Rom	1: 4	holiness by **r** from the dead,
1 Cor	15:13	If there is no **r** of the dead,
Phil	3:11	I may attain the **r** from the
2 Tim	2:18	the **r** has already taken place.
Heb	6: 2	on of hands, **r** of the dead,
1 Pet	1: 3	through the **r** of Jesus Christ
Rev	20: 5	This is the first **r**.

RETURN

Gen	18:10	I will surely **r** to you in due
Num	10:36	he would say, "**R**, O LORD
Deut	30: 2	and **r** to the LORD your God
2 Sam	12:23	but he will not **r** to me."
2 Chr	30: 9	For as you **r** to the LORD,
Neh	1: 9	but if you **r** to me
Job	16:22	from which I shall not **r**.
Ps	104:29	they die and **r** to their dust.
Isa	10:21	A remnant will **r**,
Jer	4: 1	If you **r**, O Israel,
Lam	3:40	our ways, and **r** to the LORD.
Hos	6: 1	Come, let us **r** to the LORD;
Joel	2:12	says the LORD, **r** to me
Am	4: 6	yet you did not **r** to me,
Zech	10: 9	shall rear their children and **r**.
Mal	3: 7	**R** to me, and I will
Rom	9: 9	I will **r** and Sarah

REVEAL

Esth	2:10	Esther did not **r** her people
Sir	1:30	The Lord will **r** your secrets
Dan	2:11	and no one can **r** it to the king
Mt	11:27	whom the Son chooses to **r**

REVELATION (S)

2 Sam	7:27	have made this **r** to your
2 Cor	12: 1	to visions and **r** of the Lord.

REVERE

Josh	24:14	Now therefore **r** the LORD,
Tob	4:5	"**R** the Lord all your days
Ps	119:48	I **r** your commandments,
Mal	4:2	But for you who **r** my name

REWARD

Gen	15:1	your **r** shall be very great."
1 Sam	24:19	So may the LORD **r** you with
Ps	19:11	keeping them there is great **r**.
Prov	25:22	and the LORD will **r** you.
Sir	11:22	of the Lord is the **r** of the
Isa	49:4	and my **r** with my God."
Mt	5:12	for your **r** is great in heaven,
Lk	6:35	Your **r** will be great,
1 Cor	3:14	the builder will receive a **r**.
Col	3:24	the inheritance as your **r**;
Heb	11:26	looking ahead to the **r**.
2 Jn	1:8	but may receive a full **r**.
Rev	22:12	my **r** is with me,

RICH

Gen	26:13	the man became **r**;
2 Sam	12:1	the one **r** and the other poor.
Job	34:19	regards the **r** more than the
Ps	49:16	afraid when some become **r**,
Prov	13:7	Some pretend to be **r**, yet have
Eccl	5:12	the **r** will not let them sleep
Isa	53:9	and his tomb with the **r**,
Ezek	34:14	they shall feed on **r** pasture
Mt	19:23	will be hard for a **r** person
Lk	6:24	woe to you who are **r**,
2 Cor	8:9	that though he was **r**,
Eph	2:4	But God, who is **r** in mercy,
1 Tim	6:9	those who want to be **r** fall
Jas	2:5	to be **r** in faith
Rev	3:17	I am **r**, I have prospered,

RIGHT

Gen	13:9	I will go to the **r**;
Ex	15:6	Your **r** hand, O LORD,
Deut	6:18	Do what is **r** and good
Josh	1:7	turn from it to the **r** hand
1 Sam	12:23	in the good and the **r** way.
1 Kings	15:5	David did what was **r**
Neh	9:13	and gave them **r** ordinances
Job	42:7	spoken of me what is **r**,
Ps	4:5	Offer **r** sacrifices,
Prov	4:27	Do not swerve to the **r**
Isa	30:10	prophesy to us what is **r**;
Ezek	18:5	does what is lawful and **r**
Hos	14:9	the ways of the Lord are **r**,
Am	3:10	how to do **r**, says the Lord,
Jon	4:11	who do not know their **r** hand
Zech	3:1	Satan standing at his **r** hand
Mt	5:29	If your **r** eye causes you to sin
Mk	14:62	at the **r** hand of the Power,
Jn	7:24	but judge with **r** judgment."
Acts	7:55	Jesus standing at the **r** hand of
Rom	9:21	Has the potter no **r** over the
1 Cor	9:4	Do we not have the **r** to our
2 Cor	8:21	is **r** not only in the Lord's sight
Eph	6:1	the Lord, for this is **r**.
Col	3:1	seated at the **r** hand of God.
2 Thess	3:13	weary in doing what is **r**.
Heb	1:13	Sit at my **r** hand
1 Pet	3:14	for doing what is **r**,
1 Jn	3:7	who does what is **r** is righteous,
Rev	1:16	In his **r** hand he held seven

RIGHTEOUS

Gen	6:9	Noah was a **r** man,
1 Sam	24:17	You are more **r** than I;
Neh	9:8	for you are **r**.
Tob	3:2	"You are **r**, O Lord,
1 Macc	2:24	He gave vent to **r** anger
Job	4:17	Can mortals be **r** before God?
Ps	5:12	For you bless the **r**, O LORD;
Prov	4:18	But the path of the **r** is like
Eccl	3:17	God will judge the **r** and the
Wis	5:15	**r** live forever, and their reward
Isa	26:7	The way of the **r** is level;
Jer	33:15	I will cause a **r** Branch
Ezek	18:5	man is **r** and does what is
Hab	2:4	but the **r** live by their faith.
Zeph	3:5	The LORD within it is **r**;
Mal	3:18	between the **r** and the wicked,
Mt	5:45	rain on the **r** and on the
Mk	2:17	to call not the **r** but sinners."
Acts	3:14	rejected the Holy and **R** One
Rom	1:17	The one who is **r** will live by
2 Tim	4:8	the Lord, the **r** judge,
Heb	10:38	my **r** one will live by faith
Jas	5:16	The prayer of the **r** is powerful
1 Pet	3:18	the **r** for the unr,
2 Pet	2:7	if he rescued Lot, a **r** man
1 Jn	3:7	does what is right is **r**,
Rev	19:8	the fine linen is the **r** deeds

RISE (N)

Num	24:17	a scepter shall **r** out of Israel;
Ps	3:7	**R** up, O LORD! Deliver me
Isa	26:19	their corpses shall **r**.
Dan	12:13	you shall **r** for your reward
Am	8:14	they shall fall, and never **r**
Mal	4:2	of righteousness shall **r**,
Mt	27:63	After three days I will **r** again.'
Mk	13:8	For nation will **r** against
Lk	18:33	the third day he will **r** again."
Jn	20:9	that he must **r** from the dead.
Acts	17:3	and to **r** from the dead,
Eph	5:14	Sleeper, awake! **R** from the
1 Thess	4:16	the dead in Christ will **r** first.

RIVER (S)

Gen	2:10	A **r** flows out of Eden
Deut	1:7	as far as the great **r**,
Ps	46:4	a **r** whose streams make glad
Isa	48:18	would have been like a **r**,
Ezek	47:12	on both sides of the **r**,
Rev	22:1	the angel showed me the **r**

ROBE

Gen	37:3	him a long **r** with sleeves.
Ex	28:4	a breastpiece, an ephod, a **r**,
1 Sam	15:27	the hem of his **r**, and it tore.
2 Sam	13:18	wearing a long **r** with sleeves;
Isa	6:1	and the hem of his **r** filled the
Bar	5:2	on the **r** of the righteous
Lk	15:22	Quickly, bring out a **r**
Jn	19:5	of thorns and the purple **r**,
Rev	6:11	They were each given a white **r**

ROCK

Gen	49:24	the Shepherd, the **R** of Israel,
Ex	33:22	in a cleft of the **r**,
Num	20:8	command the **r** before their
Deut	32:4	The **R**, his work is perfect,
1 Sam	2:2	there is no **R** like our God.
2 Sam	22:2	The LORD is my **r**, my fortress,

Ps	18:2	The LORD is my **r**, my fortress,
Wis	11:4	was given them out of flinty **r**
Sir	51:12	Give thanks to the **r** of Isaac,
Isa	44:8	There is no other **r**; I know not
Mt	16:18	you are Peter, and on this **r**
Mk	15:46	hewn out of the **r**.
Rom	9:33	**r** that will make them fall
1 Cor	10:4	they drank from the spiritual **r**
1 Pet	2:8	and a **r** that makes them fall."

ROD

2 Sam	7:14	will punish him with a **r**
Ps	23:4	your **r** and your staff
Prov	13:24	Those who spare the **r** hate
Isa	11:4	the earth with the **r** of his
Heb	9:4	and Aaron's **r** that budded,
Rev	19:15	will rule them with a **r** of iron;

ROOT (ED)

1 Macc	1:10	them came forth a sinful **r**,
Prov	12:12	but the **r** of the righteous
Sir	47:22	to David a **r** from his own
Isa	53:2	like a **r** out of dry ground;
Mt	13:21	such a person has no **r**,
Rom	15:12	The **r** of Jesse shall come,
1 Tim	6:10	money is a **r** of all kinds of
Rev	5:5	the **R** of David,

RULE

Gen	3:16	and he shall **r** over you."
Deut	15:6	you will **r** over many nations,
Judg	8:22	**R** over us,
Ps	110:2	**R** in the midst of your foes.
Prov	17:2	who deals wisely will **r** over a
Isa	3:4	and babes shall **r** over them.
Zech	6:13	shall sit and **r** on his throne.
Rom	15:12	who rises to **r** the Gentiles;
1 Cor	7:17	my **r** in all the churches.
Eph	1:21	far above all **r** and authority
Col	3:15	let the peace of Christ **r**
Rev	12:5	who is to **r** all the nations

S

SABBATH

Ex	20:8	Remember the **s** day,
Num	15:32	gathering sticks on the **s** day.
Deut	5:12	Observe the **s** day and keep it
2 Chr	36:21	lay desolate it kept **s**,
Neh	13:17	profaning the **s** day?
Isa	56:2	keeps the **s**, not profaning it,
Jer	17:21	bear a burden on the **s** day
Mt	12:1	the grainfields on the **s**;
Mk	2:28	lord even of the **s**."
Lk	6:9	to do harm on the **s**,

SACRIFICE

Ex	5:17	Let us go and **s** to the LORD.'
Lev	3:1	If the offering is a **s** of well-
1 Sam	15:22	to obey is better than **s**,
Ps	50:14	God a **s** of thanksgiving,
Prov	15:8	The **s** of the wicked
Dan	9:27	he shall make **s** and offering
Hos	6:6	desire steadfast love and not **s**,
Zeph	1:7	the LORD has prepared a **s**,
Mt	9:13	I desire mercy, not **s**.'

Rom	3:25	God put forward as a **s** of
1 Cor	10:20	I imply that what pagans **s**,
Eph	5: 2	fragrant offering and **s** to God.
Phil	4:18	a **s** acceptable and pleasing to
Heb	9:26	remove sin by the **s** of himself.
1 Jn	2: 2	he is the atoning **s** for our sins,

SADDUCEES

Mt	16: 1	The Pharisees and **S** came;
Mk	12:18	Some **S**, who say there is no
Acts	23: 7	the Pharisees and the **S**,

SAINTS

Ps	31:23	all you his **s**.
Acts	9:13	done to your **s** in Jerusalem;
Rom	8:27	the Spirit intercedes for the **s**
1 Cor	6: 2	the **s** will judge the world?
Eph	1:18	inheritance among the **s**,
Col	1:12	inheritance of the **s** in the
1 Thess	3:13	Lord Jesus with all his **s**.
Philem	1: 7	the **s** have been refreshed
Jude	1: 3	for all entrusted to the **s**.
Rev	5: 8	are the prayers of the **s**.

SAKE

Gen	12:16	And for her **s** he dealt well
Josh	23: 3	all these nations for your **s**,
1 Sam	12:22	for his great name's **s**,
1 Kings	11:12	the **s** of your father David
Ps	25:11	For your name's **s**, O LORD,
Isa	43:25	transgressions for my own **s**,
Jer	14:21	spurn us, for your name's **s**;
Bar	2:14	and for your own **s** deliver us,
Ezek	20:14	But I acted for the **s** of my
Dan	9:17	and for your own **s**, Lord,
Mt	10:39	who lose their life for my **s**
Mk	13:20	but for the **s** of the elect,
Rom	8:36	For your **s** we are being killed
1 Cor	9:23	do it all for the **s** of the gospel,
2 Cor	4:11	given up to death for Jesus' **s**,
1 Pet	2:13	For the Lord's **s** accept the
3 Jn	1: 7	their journey for the **s** of Christ,

SALVATION

Gen	49:18	I wait for your **s**, O LORD.
Ex	15: 2	he has become my **s**;
Deut	32:15	at the Rock of his **s**.
2 Sam	22: 3	horn of my **s**, my stronghold
1 Chr	16:23	Tell of his **s** from day to day.
2 Chr	6:41	be clothed with **s**,
Job	13:16	This will be my **s**,
Ps	13: 5	heart shall rejoice in your **s**.
Wis	6:24	wise is the **s** of the world
Isa	12: 2	Surely God is my **s**;
Jer	3:23	God is the **s** of Israel.
Lam	3:26	quietly for the **s** of the LORD.
Bar	4:29	everlasting joy with your **s**.
Mic	7: 7	for the God of my **s**;
Hab	3:18	in the God of my **s**.
Lk	2:30	my eyes have seen your **s**,
Jn	4:22	for **s** is from the Jews.
Acts	4:12	There is **s** in no one else,
Rom	11:11	But through their stumbling **s**
2 Cor	6: 2	day of **s** I have helped you."
Eph	6:17	Take the helmet of **s**,
Phil	2:12	work out your own **s** with fear
1 Thess	5: 8	a helmet the hope of **s**.
2 Thess	2:13	the first fruits for **s**
2 Tim	2:10	the **s** that is in Christ Jesus
Titus	2:11	bringing **s** to all,

Heb	2: 3	if we neglect so great a **s**?
1 Pet	1: 9	the **s** of your souls.
2 Pet	3:15	patience of our Lord as **s**.
Jude	1: 3	to you about the **s** we share,
Rev	7:10	**S** belongs to our God

SAMARITAN

Lk	10:33	But a **S** while traveling came
Jn	4: 7	A **S** woman came to draw

SANCTIFY (SANCTIFIED)

Lev	11:44	**s** yourselves therefore, and be
Jn	17:17	**S** them in the truth;
1 Thess	5:23	the God of peace himself **s**
Heb	13:12	in order to **s** the people
1 Pet	3:15	in your hearts **s** Christ as Lord.

SANCTUARY

Ex	15:17	the **s**, O LORD,
Num	3:28	to the duties of the **s**.
1 Kings	6:19	The inner **s** he prepared
1 Chr	22:19	Go and build the **s** of the LORD
1 Macc	4:36	cleanse the **s** and dedicate it."
Ps	60: 6	God has promised in his **s**:
Isa	8:14	He will become a **s**,
Lam	1:10	invade her **s**,
Ezek	5:11	because you have defiled my **s**
Dan	8:11	overthrew the place of his **s**.
Heb	8: 5	They offer worship in a **s**

SATAN

1 Chr	21: 1	**S** stood up against Israel,
Job	1: 6	and **S** also came among them.
Zech	3: 2	the LORD said to **S**,
Mt	4:10	Away with you, **S**!
Mk	4:15	**S** immediately comes and
Lk	22: 3	Then **S** entered into Judas
Jn	13:27	**S** entered into him.
Acts	5: 3	why has **S** filled your heart
Rom	16:20	of peace will shortly crush **S**
1 Cor	7: 5	so that **S** may not tempt you
2 Cor	11:14	Even **S** disguises himself as an
2 Thess	2: 9	**S**, who uses all power,
1 Tim	5:15	turned away to follow **S**.
Rev	2: 9	but are a synagogue of **S**.

SAVE (D)

2 Sam	22: 3	my savior; you **s** me from
1 Chr	16:35	**S** us, O God
Ps	6: 4	O LORD, **s** my life;
Prov	6: 3	my child, and **s** yourself,
Isa	35: 4	He will come and **s** you."
Jer	15:20	I am with you to **s** you
Lam	4:17	a nation that could not **s**.
Ezek	7:19	Their silver and gold cannot **s**
Hos	1: 7	of Judah, and I will **s** them by
Zeph	1:18	nor their old will be able to **s**
Zech	8: 7	I will **s** my people from the
Mt	16:25	For those who want to **s** their
Lk	19:10	to seek out and to **s** the lost."
Jn	12:47	but to **s** the world.
Acts	2:40	**S** yourselves from this corrupt
Rom	11:14	and thus **s** some of them.
1 Cor	9:22	I might by all means **s** some.
1 Tim	1:15	Jesus came into the world to **s**
Heb	7:25	to **s** those who approach God
Jas	2:14	Can faith **s** you?
Jude	1:23	**s** others by snatching them

SAVIOR

2 Sam	22: 3	my **s**; you save me from
2 Kings	13: 5	the LORD gave Israel a **s**,
Jdt	9:11	**s** of those without hope.
1 Macc	4:30	"Blessed are you, O **S** of
Ps	106:21	They forgot God, their **S**,
Wis	16: 7	but by you, the **S** of all.
Isa	43: 3	Holy One of Israel, your **S**.
Jer	14: 8	its **s** in time of trouble,
Hos	13: 4	there is no **s**.
Lk	1:47	rejoices in God my **S**,
Jn	4:42	this is truly the **S** of the
Acts	13:23	to Israel a **S**, Jesus,
Eph	5:23	he is the **S**.
Phil	3:20	we are expecting a **S**,
1 Tim	2: 3	the sight of God our **S**,
2 Tim	1:10	our **S** Christ Jesus,
Titus	1: 4	Christ Jesus our **S**.
2 Pet	1: 1	God and **S** Jesus Christ:
1 Jn	4:14	sent his Son as the **S** of the
Jude	1:25	to the only God our **S**,

SCRIPTURE

Mk	12:10	Have you not read this **s**:
Lk	4:21	Today this **s** has been fulfilled
Jn	7:42	the **s** said that the Messiah
Acts	1:16	Friends, the **s** had to be
1 Tim	4:13	the public reading of **s**,
2 Tim	3:16	All **s** is inspired by God
2 Pet	1:20	no prophecy of **s**

SEA

Gen	32:12	as the sand of the **s**,
Ex	14:16	out your hand over the **s**
Num	34: 6	you shall have the Great **S**
Deut	30:13	Neither is it beyond the **s**,
1 Kings	7:23	Then he made the molten **s**;
2 Kings	25:13	and the bronze **s**
Neh	9:11	you divided the **s** before them,
Job	11: 9	and broader than the **s**.
Ps	74:13	You divided the **s** by your
Eccl	1: 7	All streams run to the **s**,
Isa	48:18	like the waves of the **s**;
Bar	3:30	Who has gone over the **s**,
Dan	7: 3	beasts came up out of the **s**,
Jon	1: 4	a great wind upon the **s**,
Mic	7:19	into the depths of the **s**.
Hab	2:14	as the waters cover the **s**.
Zech	9:10	dominion shall be from **s** to **s**.
Mt	18: 6	in the depth of the **s**.
Mk	11:23	up and thrown into the **s**,'
1 Cor	10: 1	all passed through the **s**,
Heb	11:29	passed through the Red **S**
Jas	1: 6	like a wave of the **s**,
Jude	1:13	wild waves of the **s**,
Rev	4: 6	like a **s** of glass,

SEAL

Esth	8: 8	and **s** it with the king's ring;
Song	8: 6	Set me as a **s** upon your heart,
Isa	8:16	**s** the teaching among my
Dan	8:26	As for you, **s** up the vision,
Jn	6:27	the Father has set his **s**."
1 Cor	9: 2	are the **s** of my apostleship
2 Cor	1:22	by putting his **s** on us
Eph	4:30	you were marked with a **s**
Rev	6: 3	When he opened the second **s**,

SEARCH

Deut	4:29	if you **s** after him with all your

Ezra 5:17 have a **s** made in the royal
Ps 139:23 **S** me, O God,
Prov 2: 4 and **s** for it
Jer 17:10 LORD test the mind and **s** the
Ezek 34:11 I myself will **s** for my sheep,
Mt 2: 8 Go and **s** diligently for the
Lk 15: 8 and **s** carefully until she

SEAT (S)
Ex 25:17 make a mercy **s** of pure gold;
Lev 16: 2 the mercy **s** that is upon the
2 Kings 25:28 gave him a **s** above the other **s**
Ps 1: 1 or sit in the **s** of scoffers;
Prov 31:23 taking his **s** among the elders
Mt 23: 2 Pharisees sit on Moses' **s**;
Rom 14:10 before the judgment **s** of God.
2 Cor 5:10 the judgment **s** of Christ,
Heb 9: 5 overshadowing the mercy **s**.

SEE
Gen 8: 8 to **s** if the waters had subsided
Ex 12:13 when I **s** the blood, I will pass
Num 14:23 shall **s** the land
Deut 34: 4 I have let you **s** it with your
Tob 11: 8 regain his sight and **s** the
Job 19:26 in my flesh I shall **s** God,
Ps 34: 8 O taste and **s** that the LORD is
Isa 40: 5 and all people shall **s** it
Ezek 8:12 The LORD does not **s** us,
Dan 3:25 But I **s** four men unbound,
Joel 2:28 young men shall **s** visions.
Mic 7: 9 I shall **s** his vindication.
Mt 7: 5 will **s** clearly to take the speck
Mk 14:62 you will **s** the Son of Man
Lk 3: 6 flesh shall **s** the salvation of
Jn 9:25 I was blind, now I **s**."
Acts 2:17 your young men shall **s**
1 Cor 13:12 For now we **s** in a mirror,
2 Cor 13: 5 Examine yourselves to **s**
Heb 12:14 no one will **s** the Lord.
1 Jn 3: 2 for we will **s** him as he is.
Rev 1: 7 every eye will **s** him,

SEED (S)
Gen 1:11 yielding **s**, and fruit trees
Eccl 11: 6 In the morning sow your **s**,
Isa 6:13 The holy **s** is its stump.
Mt 13:31 heaven is like a mustard **s**
Mk 4:31 It is like a mustard **s**,
Lk 8:11 The **s** is the word of God
2 Cor 9:10 He who supplies **s** to the
1 Pet 1:23 but of imperishable **s**,
1 Jn 3: 9 because God's **s** abides in

SEEK
Deut 4:29 you will **s** the LORD your God,
1 Chr 28: 9 If you **s** him, he will be found
2 Chr 7:14 pray, **s** my face,
Ezra 9:12 and never **s** their peace
Ps 4: 2 and **s** after lies?
Prov 17:11 Evil people **s** only rebellion,
Sir 24:34 but for all who **s** wisdom.
Isa 55: 6 **S** the Lord while he may be
Jer 29:13 if you **s** me with all your heart
Hos 10:12 it is time to **s** the LORD,
Am 5: 6 **S** the LORD and live,
Zeph 2: 3 **S** the LORD, all you humble
Lk 19:10 Son of Man came to **s** out and
Jn 5:30 because I **s** to do not my own
Acts 15:17 other peoples may **s** the Lord

Rom 10:20 those who did not **s** me;
1 Cor 7:18 Let him not **s** to remove
Heb 11: 6 he rewards those who **s** him.
1 Pet 3:11 let them **s** peace and pursue it.

SELF-CONTROL (LED)
Prov 25:28 is one who lacks **s**.
Acts 24:25 he discussed justice, **s**,
1 Cor 7: 5 because of your lack of **s**.
Titus 1: 8 upright, devout, and **s**.
2 Pet 1: 6 and knowledge with **s**, and **s**

SELFISH (NESS)
Ps 119:36 and not to **s** gain.
2 Cor 12:20 anger, **s**, slander,
Phil 1:17 Christ out of **s** ambition,
Jas 3:16 there is envy and **s** ambition,

SEND
Gen 7: 4 in seven days I will **s** rain on
Ex 33: 2 I will **s** an angel before you,
Deut 28:20 The Lord will **s** upon you
1 Sam 5:11 **S** away the ark of the God of
Ps 57: 3 He will **s** from heaven and
Eccl 11: 1 **S** out your bread upon the
Isa 6: 8 Whom shall I **s**, and who will
Mal 4: 5 Lo, I will **s** you the prophet
Mt 24:31 And he will **s** out his angels
Lk 20:13 I will **s** my beloved son;
Jn 3:17 God did not **s** the Son into the
Acts 3:20 that he may **s** the Messiah
1 Cor 1:17 For Christ did not **s** me

SERPENT
Gen 3: 1 Now the **s** was more crafty
Num 21: 9 So Moses made a **s** of bronze,
2 Kings 18: 4 broke in pieces the bronze **s**
Isa 27: 1 Leviathan the fleeing **s**,
2 Cor 11: 3 the **s** deceived Eve by its
Rev 12: 9 that ancient **s**, who is called

SERVANT
Ex 14:31 the LORD and in his **s** Moses.
Num 12: 7 Not so with my **s** Moses;
1 Sam 3:10 Speak, for your **s** is listening."
1 Kings 8:56 he spoke through his **s** Moses.
Job 1: 8 you considered my **s** Job?
Ps 19:13 Keep back your **s** also
Prov 11:29 the fool will be **s** to the wise.
Isa 42: 1 Here is my **s**,
Jer 30:10 have no fear, my **s** Jacob,
Ezek 34:24 my **s** David shall be prince
Zech 3: 8 going to bring my **s** the Branch.
Mt 8:13 And the **s** was healed in that
Lk 1:54 He has helped his **s** Israel,
Jn 12:26 where I am, there will my **s** be
Acts 3:13 has glorified his **s** Jesus,
Rom 1: 1 Paul, a **s** of Jesus Christ,
Gal 2:17 is Christ then a **s** of sin?
Col 1:23 I, Paul, became a **s** of this
1 Tim 4: 6 you will be a good **s** of Christ
2 Tim 2:24 the Lord's **s** must not be
Heb 3: 5 in all God's house as a **s**,
Rev 19:10 I am a fellow **s** with you

SERVE (D)
Gen 25:23 the elder shall **s** the younger."
Ex 28: 1 to **s** me as priests
Deut 10:12 to **s** the LORD your God
Josh 24:14 and **s** him in sincerity

1 Sam 12:20 but **s** the LORD with all your
2 Kings 17:35 bow yourselves to them or **s**
Neh 9:35 they did not **s** you
Job 36:11 If they listen, and **s** him,
Ps 2:11 **S** the LORD with fear,
Isa 60:12 that will not **s** you shall perish;
Jer 25: 6 other gods to **s** and worship
Dan 3:17 If our God whom we **s** is able
Mt 6:24 No one can **s** two masters;
Mk 10:45 to be **s** but to **s**,
Lk 16:13 No slave can **s** two masters;
Rom 12:11 be ardent in spirit, **s** the Lord.
1 Thess 1: 9 to **s** a living and true God
1 Tim 6: 2 they must **s** them all the more,
1 Pet 4:10 **s** one another with whatever

SEVEN (SEVENTH)
Gen 7: 2 Take with you **s** pairs of all
Ex 12:15 **S** days you shall eat
Num 23: 1 Build me **s** altars here,
Deut 7: 1 **s** nations mightier and more
Josh 6: 4 **s** priests bearing **s** trumpets
Judg 16:13 If you weave the **s** locks of my
1 Sam 2: 5 The barren has borne **s**,
1 Kings 19:18 Yet I will leave **s** thousand in
2 Kings 5:10 Go, wash in the Jordan **s**
Tob 3: 8 she had been married to **s**
1 Macc 6:53 because it was the **s** year;
Ps 119:164 **S** times a day I praise you
Prov 9: 1 she has hewn her **s** pillars.
Sir 40: 8 but to sinners **s** times more,
Isa 4: 1 **S** women shall take hold
Dan 3:19 the furnace heated up **s** times
Zech 4: 2 are **s** lamps on it, with **s** lips
Mt 18:22 Not **s** times,
Mk 12:20 There were **s** brothers;
Lk 11:26 brings **s** other spirits more evil
Rom 11: 4 I have kept for myself **s**
Rev 1:12 I saw **s** golden lampstands,

SEVENTY
Gen 46:27 who came into Egypt were **s**.
Ex 24: 1 and **s** of the elders of Israel
Num 11:25 and put it on the **s** elders;
2 Chr 36:21 to fulfill **s** years.
Ps 90:10 the days of our life are **s** years,
Jer 25:12 after **s** years are completed,
Dan 9:24 **S** weeks are decreed for your

SHAME
Ps 4: 2 shall my honor suffer **s**?
Prov 18:13 it is folly and **s**.
Isa 30: 5 everyone comes to **s**
Jer 8: 9 The wise shall be put to **s**,
Ezek 39:26 They shall forget their **s**,
Dan 12: 2 to **s** and everlasting contempt.
Hos 4: 7 changed their glory into **s**.
Joel 2:26 never again be put to **s**.
Rom 9:33 will not be put to **s**."
1 Cor 1:27 foolish in the world to **s** the
Phil 3:19 their glory is in their **s**;
Heb 12: 2 disregarding its **s**,
1 Pet 2: 6 will not be put to **s**."
1 Jn 2:28 and not be put to **s** before him

SHARE
Num 18:20 nor shall you have any **s**
2 Sam 20: 1 no **s** in the son of Jesse
2 Chr 10:16 What **s** do we have in David
Neh 2:20 but you have no **s** or claim

Prov	31:31	Give her a **s** in the fruit
Lk	3:11	Whoever has two coats must **s**
Acts	8:21	You have no part or **s** in this,
Rom	1:11	that I may **s** with you
2 Cor	1: 7	as you **s** in our sufferings,
Eph	4:28	something to **s** with the needy.
Col	1:12	to **s** in the inheritance
1 Tim	6:18	and ready to **s**,
2 Tim	2: 6	ought to have the first **s** of the
Heb	12:10	that we may **s** his holiness.
Jude	1: 3	about the salvation we **s**,
Rev	22:19	will take away that person's **s**

SHEEP

Gen	4: 2	Abel was a keeper of **s**,
Num	27:17	be like **s** without a shepherd."
Deut	17: 1	an ox or a **s** that has a defect,
1 Sam	15:14	is this bleating of **s** in my ears,
1 Kings	22:17	like **s** that have no shepherd;
Ps	44:22	as **s** for the slaughter.
Isa	53: 6	All we like **s** have gone astray;
Jer	50: 6	My people have been lost **s**;
Ezek	34:15	the shepherd of my **s**,
Zech	13: 7	that the **s** may be scattered;
Mt	9:36	like **s** without a shepherd.
Lk	15: 4	having a hundred **s** and losing
Jn	10: 3	and the **s** hear his voice.
Acts	8:32	Like a **s** he was led
Rom	8:36	accounted as **s** to be
Heb	13:20	the great shepherd of the **s**,
1 Pet	2:25	you were going astray like **s**,

SHEPHERD

Gen	48:15	God who has been my **s** all
Num	27:17	like sheep without a **s**."
2 Sam	7: 7	I commanded to **s** my people
1 Kings	22:17	like sheep that have no **s**;
1 Chr	11: 2	shall be **s** of my people Israel,
Ps	23: 1	The LORD is my **s**,
Eccl	12:11	that are given by one **s**.
Isa	40:11	feed his flock like a **s**;
Jer	31:10	will keep him as a **s** a flock."
Ezek	34: 5	because there was no **s**; and
Zech	11: 9	I will not be your **s**.
Mt	25:32	as a **s** separates the sheep
Mk	6:34	like sheep without a **s**;
Jn	10:11	I am the good **s**.
Heb	13:20	Jesus, the great **s** of the sheep,
1 Pet	5: 4	And when the chief **s** appears,
Rev	7:17	the throne will be their **s**,

SHINE (S)

Num	6:25	LORD make his face to **s** upon
Ps	37: 6	your vindication **s** like the
Isa	60: 1	Arise, **s**; for your light has
Dan	12: 3	Those who are wise shall **s**
Mt	5:16	let your light **s** before others,
2 Cor	4: 6	Let light **s** out of darkness,"
Eph	5:14	and Christ will **s** on you."
Phil	2:15	you **s** like stars in the world
Rev	21:23	sun or moon to **s** on it,

SHOW

Gen	12: 1	the land that I will **s** you.
Ex	9:16	to **s** you my power,
Deut	4: 6	for this will **s** your wisdom
1 Sam	20:14	**s** me the faithful love
2 Sam	9: 1	to whom I may **s** kindness
Ps	18:26	with the pure you **s** yourself
Prov	12:16	Fools **s** their anger at once,

Isa	30:18	he will rise up to **s** mercy to
Jer	32:18	You **s** steadfast love
Joel	2:30	I will **s** portents
Mic	7:20	You will **s** faithfulness to Jacob
Zech	7: 9	true judgments, **s** kindness
Mt	22:19	**S** me the coin
Jn	14: 8	Lord, **s** us the Father,
Acts	2:19	I will **s** portents in the heaven
1 Cor	12:31	And I will **s** you a still more
2 Cor	11:30	the things that **s** my weakness.
Eph	2: 7	he might **s** the immeasurable
Titus	3: 2	and to **s** every courtesy to
Jas	2:18	**S** me your faith apart from
Rev	4: 1	and I will **s** you what must

SICK

Prov	13:12	deferred makes the heart **s**,
Ezek	34: 4	you have not healed the **s**,
Mt	8:16	and cured all who were **s**.
Acts	19:12	were brought to the **s**,
Jas	5:14	Are any among you **s**?

SIGHT

Gen	6:11	earth was corrupt in God's **s**,
Ex	3: 3	look at this great **s**,
Ps	51: 4	what is evil in your **s**,
Prov	3: 4	in the **s** of God and of people
Jer	18:10	it does evil in my **s**,
Mt	11: 5	the blind receive their **s**,
Acts	4:19	Whether it is right in God's **s**
2 Cor	5: 7	walk by faith, not by **s**.
1 Pet	3: 4	is very precious in God's **s**.

SIGN

Gen	9:12	This is the **s** of the covenant
Ex	12:13	The blood shall be a **s** for you
Num	16:38	shall be a **s** to the Israelites.
Judg	6:17	show me a **s** that it is you
1 Kings	13: 3	He gave a **s** the same day,
Isa	55:13	for an everlasting **s**
Ezek	24:24	Ezekiel shall be a **s** to you;
Mt	12:38	we wish to see a **s** from you."
Mk	8:12	this generation ask for a **s**?
Lk	2:12	This will be a **s** for you:
Jn	2:18	What **s** can you show us
Rom	4:11	received the **s** of circumcision
1 Cor	14:22	a **s** not for believers
2 Cor	12:12	The **s** of a true apostle

SILENT

Ps	39: 2	I was **s** and still;
Prov	17:28	keep **s** are considered wise;
Isa	53: 7	before its shearers is **s**,
Jer	4:19	I cannot keep **s**;
Zeph	1: 7	Be **s** before the Lord GOD!
Mk	14:61	was **s** and did not answer.
Acts	8:32	lamb **s** before its shearer,
1 Cor	14:34	should be **s** in the churches.
1 Tim	2:12	she is to keep **s**.

SILVER

Gen	37:28	for twenty pieces of **s**,
Ex	20:23	shall not make gods of **s**
Deut	17:17	and gold he must not
Josh	7:21	two hundred shekels of **s**,
2 Chr	1:15	The king made **s** and gold as
1 Macc	1:23	He took the **s** and the gold,
Ps	66:10	you have tried us as **s** is tried.
Prov	3:14	her income is better than **s**,
Isa	48:10	but not like **s**;

Ezek	22:18	all of them, **s**, bronze,
Dan	5: 4	gods of gold and **s**, bronze,
Hag	2: 8	The **s** is mine, and the gold
Zech	11:12	my wages thirty shekels of **s**.
Mal	3: 3	a refiner and purifier of **s**,
Mt	26:15	paid him thirty pieces of **s**.
Acts	3: 6	I have no **s** or gold,
1 Cor	3:12	the foundation with gold, **s**,
2 Tim	2:20	not only of gold and **s**
1 Pet	1:18	perishable things like **s** or

SIN (S) (SINNED)

Gen	4: 7	**s** is lurking at the door
Ex	32:32	you will only forgive their **s**
Num	32:23	sure your **s** will find you out.
1 Sam	15:23	rebellion is no less a **s**
1 Kings	8:46	If they **s** against you
2 Chr	7:14	and will forgive their **s**
Neh	13:26	King Solomon of Israel **s**
Tob	12:10	but those who commit **s**
Job	1:22	In all this Job did not **s**
Ps	32: 5	I acknowledged my **s** to you,
Prov	5:22	in the toils of their **s**.
Eccl	5: 6	your mouth lead you into **s**,
Wis	10:13	but delivered him from **s**
Sir	7:8	Do not commit a **s** twice;
Isa	3: 9	proclaim their **s** like Sodom,
Jer	16:18	their iniquity and their **s**,
Dan	9:20	praying and confessing my **s**
Mic	6: 7	for the **s** of my soul?"
Mt	5:29	your right eye causes you to **s**,
Mk	3:29	is guilty of an eternal **s**"
Jn	8: 7	without **s** be the first to throw
Acts	7:60	Lord, do not hold this **s**
Rom	5:12	just as **s** came into the world
1 Cor	15:56	The sting of death is **s**,
2 Cor	5:21	him to be **s** who knew no **s**,
Eph	4:26	Be angry but do not **s**;
1 Tim	5:20	for those who persist in **s**,
Heb	4:15	as we are, yet without **s**.
Jas	1:15	it gives birth to **s**,
1 Pet	2:22	He committed no **s**,
1 Jn	1: 8	If we say that we have no **s**,

SINAI

Ex	19:20	descended upon Mount **S**,
Num	1:19	in the wilderness of **S**.
Ps	68:17	the Lord came from **S**
Gal	4:25	Hagar is Mount **S** in Arabia

SLANDER

Ps	15: 3	do not **s** with their tongue,
Prov	10:18	whoever utters **s** is a fool.
Sir	28:15	**S** has driven virtuous women
Mt	15:19	theft, false witness, **s**.
2 Cor	12:20	selfishness, **s**, gossip,
Eph	4:31	**s**, together with all malice,
Col	3: 8	malice, **s**, and abusive
1 Pet	2: 1	insincerity, envy, and all **s**.
2 Pet	2:10	they are not afraid to **s**
Jude	1: 8	and **s** the glorious ones.

SLAUGHTER

Ex	29:11	and you shall **s** the bull
Deut	12:15	you may **s** and eat meat
Prov	7:22	like an ox to the **s**,
Isa	53: 7	that is led to the **s**,
Jer	11:19	like a gentle lamb led to the **s**.
Zech	11: 4	of the flock doomed to **s**.
Acts	8:32	he was led to the **s**,

SLAVE (S) (SLAVERY)
Gen	9:26	and let Canaan be his **s**.
Mk	10:44	first among you must be **s** of
Lk	7: 2	A centurion there had a **s**
Jn	8:34	who commits sin is a **s** to sin.
Rom	7:25	I am a **s** to the law of God
1 Cor	7:21	Were you a **s** when called?
Gal	3:28	there is no longer **s** or free
Phil	2: 7	taking the form of a **s**,
Col	3:11	**s** and free
1 Tim	6: 1	are under the yoke of **s**
Philem	1:16	longer as a **s** but more than a **s**
2 Pet	2:19	for people are **s** to whatever
Rev	13:16	both free and **s**

SLEEP (ING)
Gen	2:21	LORD God caused a deep **s**
Ex	22:27	what else shall that person **s**?
Deut	24:12	shall not **s** in the garment
1 Sam	26:12	a deep **s** from the LORD
Ps	4: 8	both lie down and in peace
Prov	6:10	A little **s**, a little slumber
Eccl	5:12	Sweet is the **s** of laborers
Isa	29:10	a spirit of deep **s**
Dan	12: 2	who **s** in the dust of
Mt	9:24	girl is not dead but **s**.
Acts	20: 9	Overcome by **s**,
1 Thess	5: 7	those who **s s** at night.

SLOW
Ex	4:10	I am **s** of speech and **s** of
Num	14:18	The LORD is **s** to anger
Judg	18: 9	Do not be **s** to go
Ps	86:15	**s** to anger and abounding in
Prov	14:29	Whoever is **s** to anger
Joel	2:13	**s** to anger, and abounding in
Nah	1: 3	The Lord is **s** to anger but
Lk	24:25	how **s** of heart to believe all
Jas	1:19	**s** to speak, **s** to anger
2 Pet	3: 9	The Lord is not **s** about his

SON (S)
Gen	5: 3	became the father of a **s**'"
Ex	4:23	I will kill your firstborn **s**.
Deut	18:10	who makes a **s** or daughter
2 Sam	7:14	and he shall be a **s** to me.
1 Kings	3:23	and your **s** is dead
2 Kings	6:29	So we cooked my **s** and ate
1 Chr	22:10	He shall be a **s** to me
1 Macc	1:48	to leave their **s** uncircumcised.
Ps	127: 3	**S** are indeed a heritage
Prov	3:12	the **s** in whom he delights.
Isa	7:14	and shall bear a **s**
Jer	31:20	Is Ephraim my dear **s**?
Hos	11: 1	Out of Egypt I called my **s**.
Am	7:14	nor a prophet's **s**
Mal	1: 6	A **s** honors his father
Mt	1: 1	the **s** of David, the **s** of
Mk	1:11	"You are my **S**
Lk	1:32	the **S** of the Most High
Jn	1:34	this is the **S** of God."
Acts	7:56	the **S** of Man
Rom	1: 4	declared to be **S** of God
1 Cor	15:28	then the **S** himself
Col	1:13	the kingdom of his beloved **S**,
1 Thess	1:10	wait for his **S** from heaven,
Heb	1: 2	spoken to us by a **S**,
Jas	2:21	he offered his **s** Isaac
2 Pet	1:17	"This is my **S**,
1 Jn	1: 3	with his **S** Jesus

Rev	1:13	like the **S** of Man

SONG (SING)
Ex	15: 1	sang this **s** to the LORD.
Deut	31:21	this **s** will confront them
Jdt	16:13	I will **s** to my God a new **s**:
Ps	33: 3	**S** to him a new **s**;
Isa	54: 1	burst into **s**
Rev	5: 9	**s** a new **s**:

SOUL (S)
Deut	6: 5	with all your **s**,
2 Kings	23:25	with all his **s**,
Ps	16: 9	and my **s** rejoices;
Prov	13:19	sweet to the **s**,
Lam	3:20	My **s** continually thinks
Mic	6: 7	for the sin of my **s**?"
Mt	10:28	cannot kill the **s**;
Lk	1:46	"My **s** magnifies the Lord,
1 Thess	5:23	spirit and **s** and body
Heb	4:12	divides **s** from spirit,
Jas	5:20	save the sinner's **s**
1 Pet	2:11	war against the **s**.
3 Jn	1: 2	it is well with your **s**.
Rev	6: 9	**s** of those who had been

SOUND
Gen	3: 8	heard the **s** of the Lord
Ex	32:18	it is the **s** of revelers
Deut	4:12	the **s** of words
Ps	66: 8	let the **s** of his praise
Ezek	1:24	like the **s** of mighty waters,
Joel	2: 1	**s** the alarm
Jn	3: 8	hear the **s** of it,
Acts	2: 2	came a **s** like the rush
1 Cor	14: 8	gives an indistinct **s**,
1 Tim	1:10	contrary to the **s**
2 Tim	1:13	standard of **s** teaching
Titus	1: 9	preach with **s** doctrine
Rev	1:15	like the **s** of many waters.

SOW
Ex	23:10	shall **s** your land
Job	4: 8	and **s** trouble
Ps	126: 5	those who **s** in tears
Eccl	11: 6	In the morning **s** your seed,
Hos	8: 7	they **s** the wind,
Mt	6:26	they neither **s** nor reap
1 Cor	15:36	What you **s** does not come
2 Pet	2:22	"The **s** is washed only to

SPEAK
Gen	18:27	upon myself to **s** to the Lord
Ex	4:12	teach you what you are to **s**."
Num	12: 8	I **s** face to face
Deut	18:20	presumes to **s** in my name
1 Sam	3: 9	'**S**, LORD, for your servant
2 Kings	18:26	"Please **s** to your servants
Job	13: 3	I would **s** to the Almighty
Ps	49: 3	mouth shall **s** wisdom;
Prov	23: 9	Do not **s** in the hearing
Eccl	3: 7	and a time to **s**;
Sir	4:5	Never **s** against the truth,
Isa	28:11	he will **s** to this people,
Jer	10: 5	they cannot **s**;
Ezek	3:18	**s** to warn the wicked
Dan	7:25	shall **s** words against
Mt	13:13	I **s** to them in parables
Mk	7:37	the mute to **s**."
Jn	12:49	what to say and what to **s**.

Acts	2: 4	began to **s** in other languages
1 Cor	12:30	Do all **s** in tongues?
Eph	4:25	let all of us **s** the truth
Jas	1:19	quick to listen, slow to **s**,

SPIRIT
Gen	6: 3	"My **s** shall not abide
Ex	31: 3	filled him with divine **s**,
Num	11:25	the **s** rested upon them,
Deut	34: 9	full of the **s** of wisdom,
Judg	6:34	the **s** of the LORD took
1 Sam	10: 6	the **s** of the LORD will possess
2 Sam	23: 2	The **s** of the LORD speaks
2 Kings	2: 9	a double share of your **s**."
2 Chr	18:21	be a lying **s**
Neh	9:20	gave your good **s**
Job	33: 4	The **s** of God has made me
Ps	31: 5	I commit my **s**;
Wis	1:6	For wisdom is a kindly **s**,
Isa	11: 2	The **s** of the LORD shall rest
Ezek	3:12	the **s** lifted me up,
Dan	4: 8	endowed with a **s**
Joel	2:28	I will pour out my **s**
Mt	1:18	child from the Holy **S**.
Mk	1: 8	baptize you with the Holy **S**."
Lk	1:15	filled with the Holy **S**
Jn	1:33	you see the **S** descend
Acts	1: 5	baptized with the Holy **S**
Rom	7: 6	new life of the **S**.
1 Cor	2:10	the **S**; for the **S** searches
2 Cor	1:22	giving us his **S**
Gal	3: 2	receive the **S**
Eph	1:13	seal of the promised Holy **S**;
Col	2: 5	I am with you in **s**,
1 Thess	5:19	Do not quench the **S**.
2 Thess	2:13	sanctification by the **S**
1 Tim	3:16	vindicated in **s**,
2 Tim	1: 7	**s** of cowardice,
Heb	2: 4	by gifts of the Holy **S**,
1 Pet	1: 2	sanctified by the **S**
2 Pet	1:21	moved by the Holy **S**
1 Jn	3:24	by the **S** that he has given
Jude	1:20	pray in the Holy **S**;
Rev	1:10	in the **s** on the Lord's day

STAFF
Gen	38:25	cord and the **s**."
Ex	4: 4	became a **s** in his hand—
Num	17: 6	the **s** of Aaron was among
Ps	23: 4	your rod and your **s**—
Mic	7:14	your people with your **s**,
Zech	11:10	I took my **s** Favor

STAND (ING)
Gen	18:22	Abraham remained **s**
Ex	3: 5	on which you are **s** is holy
Num	22:23	saw the angel of the LORD **s**
Josh	4:10	remained **s** in the middle
2 Chr	18:18	host of heaven **s**
Sir	5:10	**S** firm for what you know,
Am	7: 7	Lord was **s** beside a wall
Zech	1: 8	He was **s** among the myrtle
Acts	7:55	Jesus **s** at the right hand
1 Cor	10:12	you think you are **s**
1 Tim	3:13	deacons gain a good **s**
Jas	5: 9	Judge is **s** at the doors!
Rev	3:20	I am **s** at the door,

STAR (S)
Gen	1:16	rule the night—and the **s**.

Num	24:17	a **s** shall come out of Jacob.
Deut	1:10	numerous as the **s** of heaven.
Job	38: 7	morning **s** sang together
Ps	148: 3	praise him, all you shining **s**!
Eccl	12: 2	and the moon and the **s** are
Isa	14:13	above the **s** of God;
Dan	12: 3	like the **s** forever
Joel	2:10	**s** withdraw their shining.
Mt	2: 2	observed his **s** at its rising,
Mk	13:25	the **s** will be falling
Phil	2:15	you shine like **s** in the world.
Rev	1:16	right hand he held seven **s**,

STEADFAST

Ex	15:13	"In your **s** love you led
Num	14:18	and abounding in **s** love,
2 Sam	7:15	will not take my **s** love from
Neh	9:32	keeping covenant and **s** love
Ps	13: 5	trusted in your **s** love;
Isa	26: 3	Those of **s** mind
Joel	2:13	abounding in **s** love,
Heb	6:19	sure and **s** anchor of the soul,
1 Pet	5: 9	**s** in your faith,

STONE (D) (S)

Gen	28:18	took the **s** that he had put
Ex	28: 9	take two onyx **s**,
Deut	4:13	he wrote them on two **s**
Josh	7:25	Israel **s** him to death;
1 Sam	7:12	Samuel took a **s**
Ps	91:12	dash your foot against a **s**.
Isa	8:14	a **s** one strikes against;
Jer	3: 9	committing adultery with **s**
Ezek	11:19	heart of **s** from their flesh
Zech	3: 9	a single **s** with seven facets,
Mt	4: 6	dash your foot against a **s**.'"
Mk	12:10	'The **s** that the builders
Lk	4: 3	this **s** to become a loaf of
Jn	8: 7	first to throw a **s** at her."
Acts	4:11	'the **s** that was rejected
Rom	9:32	stumbled over the stumbling **s**,
2 Cor	3: 3	not on tablets of **s**
1 Pet	2: 4	a living **s**, though rejected
Rev	2:17	I will give a white **s**,

STRAIGHT

Ps	107: 7	led them by a **s** way,
Prov	3: 6	he will make **s** your paths.
Isa	40: 3	make **s** in the desert
Mt	3: 3	Lord, make his paths **s**.'"
Jn	1:23	'Make **s** the way of the Lord
Acts	9:11	street called **S**,
2 Pet	2:15	left the **s** road

STRANGER (S)

Gen	23: 4	"I am a **s** and an alien
Deut	10:19	love the **s**, for you were **s**
1 Macc	1:38	she became a dwelling of **s**;
Mt	25:35	I was a **s** and you welcomed
Jn	10: 5	They will not follow a **s**,
3 Jn	1: 5	even though they are **s** to you;

STRENGTH (EN) (ENS) (STRONG)

Ex	15: 2	LORD is my **s**
Deut	33:25	as your days, so is your **s**.
Judg	16:15	what makes your **s** so great."
1 Sam	2: 1	my **s** is exalted in my God
2 Sam	22:33	girded me with **s**
1 Chr	16:11	Seek the Lord and his **s**,
Neh	8:10	LORD is your **s**."

1 Macc	3:19	but **s** comes from Heaven.
Job	12:13	"With God are wisdom and **s**;
Ps	18: 1	LORD, my **s**.
Prov	24: 5	those who have **s**;
Isa	12: 2	God is my **s**
Mic	5: 4	feed his flock in the **s**
Hab	3:19	Lord, is my **s**;
Mk	12:30	with all your **s**.'
Lk	1:15	never drink wine or **s** drink;
Acts	15:32	encourage and **s** the believers.
1 Cor	1:25	stronger than human **s**.
Phil	4:13	things through him who **s** me.
2 Tim	4:17	gave me **s**,
Heb	11:34	won **s** out of weakness,
1 Pet	4:11	with the **s** that God supplies,

STRIKE

Gen	3:15	he will **s** your head,
Ex	3:20	**s** Egypt with all my wonders
Isa	11: 4	he shall **s** the earth
Zech	13: 7	**S** the shepherd,
Mal	4: 6	**s** the land with a curse
Mk	14:27	'I will **s** the shepherd,
Rev	11: 6	to **s** the earth

STUMBLE (STUMBLING)

Ps	37:24	though we **s**, we shall not fall
Prov	3:23	foot will not **s**.
Jer	13:16	before your feet **s**
Ezek	14: 3	iniquity as a **s** block
Hos	14: 9	transgressors **s** in them
Mal	2: 8	caused many to **s**
Mt	18: 9	eye causes you to **s**,
Jn	11: 9	during the day do not **s**,
Rom	9:33	stone that will make people **s**,
1 Pet	2: 8	"A stone that makes them **s**,

SUFFER (ING) (INGS)

Job	2:13	his **s** was very great.
Zech	10: 2	they **s** for lack of a shepherd
Lk	22:15	with you before I **s**;
	24:26	Messiah should **s** these things
	24:46	Messiah is to **s**
Acts	3:18	Messiah would **s**.
Rom	5: 3	our **s**, knowing that **s**
1 Cor	3:15	builder will **s** loss;
Heb	9:26	had to **s** again
1 Pet	3:17	better to **s** for doing good,
Rev	2:10	you are about to **s**.

SUN

Josh	10:13	the **s** stood still,
Judg	5:31	like the **s** as it rises
Ps	72: 5	while the **s** endures,
Eccl	1: 9	nothing new under the **s**.
Song	6:10	bright as the **s**,
Isa	60:19	**s** shall no longer be your light
Joel	2:31	**s** shall be turned to darkness
Mic	3: 6	**s** shall go down
Mal	4: 2	the **s** of righteousness shall
Mt	5:45	makes his **s** rise
Mk	13:24	**s** will be darkened,
Acts	2:20	**s** shall be turned to darkness
Eph	4:26	do not let the **s** go down
Rev	1:16	face was like the **s**

SWEAR (SWORE) (SWORN)

Gen	22:16	"By myself I have **s**,
Ex	6: 8	land that I **s** to give
Deut	10:20	by his name you shall **s**.

Josh	2:12	**s** to me by the Lord
Ps	24: 4	do not **s** deceitfully.
Isa	45:23	every tongue shall **s**."
Mt	5:34	Do not **s** at all,
Heb	6:13	one greater by whom to **s**,
Jas	5:12	do not **s**, either by heaven

SWEET (ER)

Ex	15:25	water became **s**.
Judg	14:18	"What is **s** than honey?
Job	20:12	wickedness is **s** in their
Ps	119:103	How **s** are your words
Prov	9:17	"Stolen water is **s**,
Eccl	5:12	**S** is the sleep of laborers
Isa	5:20	who put bitter for **s** and **s**
Ezek	3: 3	as **s** as honey.
Joel	3:18	shall drip **s** wine,
Rev	10:10	it was **s** as honey

SWORD (S)

Gen	3:24	a **s** flaming and turning
Ex	18: 4	delivered me from the **s**
Num	14: 3	fall by the **s**?
Deut	32:41	when I whet my flashing **s**,
Josh	5:13	before him with a drawn **s**
1 Sam	17:45	come to me with **s**
2 Sam	12:10	the **s** shall never depart
1 Chr	21:30	he was afraid of the **s**
Neh	4:18	builders had his **s**
Ps	22:20	Deliver my soul from the **s**,
Prov	5: 4	sharp as a two-edged **s**.
Sir	21:3	lawlessness is like a two-edged **s**
Isa	2: 4	shall not lift up **s**
Jer	15: 2	destined for the **s**, to the **s**;
Lam	1:20	the **s** bereaves;
Ezek	5: 2	strike with the **s**
Hos	2:18	abolish the bow, the **s**,
Mic	4: 3	beat their **s** into plowshares,
Mt	10:34	bring peace, but a **s**.
Lk	2:35	a **s** will pierce your own soul
Acts	12: 2	killed with the **s**.
Rom	13: 4	does not bear the **s**
Eph	6:17	and the **s** of the Spirit, which
Heb	4:12	sharper than any two-edged **s**,
Rev	1:16	sharp, two-edged **s**,

SYNAGOGUE (S)

Mt	4:23	teaching in their **s**
Lk	4:16	he went to the **s**
Jn	18:20	taught in **s**
Acts	13:14	they went into the **s**
Rev	2: 9	but are a **s** of Satan.

T

TABERNACLE

Ex	25: 9	of the **t** and of all its furniture
Lev	8:10	anointed the **t**
Num	1:50	appoint the Levites over the **t**
1 Chr	6:48	of the **t** of the house of God.

TABLET (S)

Ex	31:18	two **t** of the covenant,
Prov	3: 3	write them on the **t**
Isa	30: 8	before them on a **t**,
Lk	1:63	asked for a writing **t**

2 Cor   3: 3 not on **t** of stone

TAKE (N)

Gen	2:23	for out of Man this one was **t**."
Ex	6: 7	I will **t** you as my people.
Num	1: 2	**T** a census
Deut	1: 8	**t** possession of the land.
1 Sam	8:11	he will **t** your sons
1 Kings	11:34	I will not **t** the whole kingdom
1 Chr	17:13	**t** my steadfast love
Job	23:10	he knows the way that I **t**;
Ps	2:12	Happy are all who **t**
Sir	44:16	pleased the Lord and was **t**
Hos	1: 2	**t** for yourself a wife
Mt	1:20	afraid to **t** Mary
Mk	2: 9	'Stand up and **t** your mat
Lk	21: 7	this is about to **t** place?"
Acts	1:20	'Let another **t** his position
Eph	6:13	Therefore **t** up the whole
1 Tim	3: 5	how can he **t** care of God's
Heb	11: 5	Enoch was **t**
Rev	1: 1	what must soon **t** place;

TASTE (D)

Ex	16:31	the **t** of it was like wafers
Ps	34: 8	O **t** and see that the Lord is
Prov	24:13	sweet to your **t**.
Song	2: 3	sweet to my **t**.
Mt	16:28	will not **t** death
Col	2:21	Do not **t**, Do not touch"?
Heb	6: 4	have **t** the heavenly gift

TEACH

Ex	4:12d	**t** you what you are
Deut	6: 1	God charged me to **t**
1 Kings	8:36	when you **t** them the good
Job	6:24	**T** me, and I will be
Ps	25: 4	**t** me your paths.
Prov	9: 9	**t** the righteous
Jer	31:34	they **t** one another,
Mic	4: 2	that he may **t** us his ways
Mal	4: 4	the **t** of my servant Moses, the
Mt	10:24	disciple is not above the **t**;
Lk	11: 1	"Lord, **t** us to pray,
Jn	14:26	will **t** you everything,
Ac	5:28	orders not to **t** in this name,
Rom	2:21	that **t** others, will you not **t**
1 Cor	11:14	nature itself **t** you
Col	3:16	**t** and admonish one another
1 Tim	1: 3	instruct certain people not to **t**
2 Tim	2: 2	able to **t** others as well.
Titus	2: 1	**t** what is consistent
Heb	5:12	**t** you again the basic
Jas	3: 1	we who **t** will be judged
2 Pet	2: 1	false **t** among you,
1 Jn	2:27	do not need anyone to **t** you.
Rev	2:20	is **t** and beguiling my servants

TEMPLE

Judg	4:21	drove the peg into his **t**,
1 Sam	3: 3	lying down in the **t**
1 Kings	6: 7	was heard in the **t**
2 Chr	2:12	build a **t** for the Lord,
Ezra	3:10	foundation of the **t**
Tob	14:5	they will rebuild the **t** of God,
1 Macc	4:48	and the interior of the **t**,
Ps	11: 4	Lord is in his holy **t**;
Isa	6: 1	his robe filled the **t**
Jer	7: 4	"This is the **t** of the Lord,
Ezek	8:16	entrance of the **t**

Dan	5: 2	taken out of the **t**
Mic	1: 2	Lord from his holy **t**.
Hab	2:20	Lord is in his holy **t**;
Mt	4: 5	pinnacle of the **t**,
Mk	15:38	curtain of the **t** was torn
Lk	21: 5	speaking about the **t**,
Jn	2:14	the found people selling
Acts	2:46	time together in the **t**,
1 Cor	3:16	you are God's **t**
2 Cor	6:16	we are the **t**
Eph	2:21	grows into a holy **t**
2 Thess	2: 4	seat in the **t**
Rev	3:12	pillar in the **t**

TEMPT (ED) (TEMPTER)

Mt	4: 1	to be **t** by the devil.
Mk	1:13	**t** by Satan;
Lk	4: 2	forty days he was **t**
1 Cor	7: 5	Satan may not **t** you
Gal	6: 1	you yourselves are not **t**.
1 Thess	3: 5	somehow the **t** had **t** you
Jas	1:13	God cannot be **t** by evil

TEST (ED)

Gen	22: 1	God **t** Abraham.
Deut	6:16	Lord your God to the **t**,
1 Kings	10: 1	she came to **t** him
1 Macc	2:52	found faithful when **t**,
Ps	26: 2	**t** my heart and mind.
Sir	44:20	he was **t** he proved faithful.
Jer	9: 7	refine and **t** them,
Mal	3:10	put me to the **t**,
Lk	4:12	God to the **t**."
Acts	5: 9	the Spirit of the Lord to the **t**?
1 Cor	3:13	fire will **t** what sort of work
2 Cor	13: 5	**T** yourselves.
Gal	6: 4	All must **t** their own work.
1 Thess	5:21	**t** everything; hold fast
Heb	3: 9	ancestors put me to the **t**,
Jas	1:12	stood the **t**
1 Jn	4: 1	**t** the spirits
Rev	3:10	**t** the inhabitants of the earth

TESTIFY (TESTIFIED) (TESTIFIES)
(TESTIMONY)

Isa	59:12	sins **t** against us.
Jer	14: 7	our iniquities **t**
Lk	22:71	What further **t** do we need?
Jn	1: 7	witness to **t**
Acts	10:43	prophets **t** about him
1 Jn	5: 6	Spirit is the one that **t**,
Rev	1: 9	the **t** of Jesus.

THANK (S)

Lev	7:12	offer with the **t** offering
1 Chr	16: 8	give **t** to the Lord,
2 Chr	29:31	brought sacrifices and **t**
Ps	52: 9	I will **t** you forever,
Isa	38:18	Sheol cannot **t** you,
Lk	18:11	'God, I **t** you
Jn	11:41	"Father, I **t** you for having
Phil	1: 3	I **t** my God every time
1 Thess	3: 9	can we **t** God enough

THIEF (THIEVES)

Ex	22: 1	**t** shall pay
Mt	6:19	where **t** break in
Lk	12:39	hour the **t** was coming,
Jn	10:10	**t** comes only to steal
1 Thess	5: 2	come like a **t** in the night.

THIRST (Y)

Ex	17: 3	livestock with **t**?"
Deut	28:48	hunger and **t**,
Ps	107: 9	he satisfies the **t**,
Mt	5: 6	those who hunger and **t**
Rom	12:20	if they are **t**,
Rev	7:16	**t** no more;

THOUSAND (S)

Deut	7: 9	to a **t** generations,
Josh	23:10	puts to flight a **t**,
1 Sam	18: 7	"Saul has killed his **t**,
Ps	50:10	cattle on a **t** hills.
Song	5:10	distinguished among ten **t**.
Mt	14:21	were about five **t** men,
2 Pet	3: 8	one day is like a **t** years,
Jude	1:14	Lord is coming with ten **t**
Rev	20: 4	reigned with Christ a **t** years.

THREE (THIRD)

Gen	6:10	Noah had **t** sons,
Ex	23:14	**T** times in the year
Deut	19:15	two or **t** witnesses
1 Sam	31: 8	Saul and his **t** sons
2 Sam	23: 9	among the **t** warriors
Job	2:11	when Job's **t** friends
Prov	30:15	**T** things are never satisfied;
Ezek	5:12	One **t** of you shall die
Dan	3:24	"Was it not **t** men
Am	1: 3	For **t** transgressions
Jon	1:17	of the fish **t** days and **t** nights
Zech	11: 8	disposed of the **t** shepherds,
Mt	12:40	Jonah was **t** days and **t** nights
Mk	8:31	after **t** days rise again.
Jn	2:19	in **t** days I will raise it
1 Cor	13:13	these **t**; and the greatest
2 Cor	12: 8	**T** times I appealed
1 Jn	5: 7	There are **t** that testify:
Rev	4: 7	**t** living creature

THRONE (S)

2 Sam	7:13	**t** of his kingdom
1 Chr	17:12	I will establish his **t**
Ps	11: 4	Lord's **t** is in heaven.
Prov	20:28	**t** is upheld by righteousness.
Isa	6: 1	Lord sitting on a **t**
Jer	33:21	reign on his **t**,
Ezek	1:26	something like a **t**,
Dan	7: 9	Ancient One took his **t**,
Mt	5:34	it is the **t** of God,
Lk	1:32	give to him the **t**
Acts	7:49	'Heaven is my **t**,
Col	1:16	whether **t** or dominions
Heb	1: 8	"Your **t**, O God, is forever
Rev	2:13	where Satan's **t**

TIME (S)

Gen	4:26	At that **t** people
Ex	23:14	Three **t** in the year
Deut	32:35	the **t** when their foot shall slip
Esth	4:14	at such a **t** as this,
Ps	119:126	It is **t** for the Lord
Eccl	3: 1	a **t** for every matter
Sir	20:12	but pay for it seven **t** over.
Dan	7:25	for a **t**, two **t**,
Hos	10:12	it is **t** to seek the Lord,
Lk	21: 8	'The **t** is near!'

1 Pet	4:15	a murderer, a **t**, a criminal,
Rev	16:15	I am coming like a **t**!

Rom	5: 6	right **t** Christ died
1 Cor	4: 5	judgment before the **t**,
2 Cor	6: 2	now is the acceptable **t**;
Gal	4: 4	fullness of **t** had come,
Eph	5:16	making the most of the **t**,
1 Tim	4: 1	in later **t** some will
Heb	9:28	appear a second **t**,
1 Pet	4:17	**t** has come for judgment
Rev	1: 3	for the **t** is near.

TONGUE (S)

Ex	4:10	and slow of **t**."
Job	33: 2	**t** in my mouth
Ps	34:13	Keep your **t** from evil,
Prov	6:17	a lying **t**,
Song	4:11	milk are under your **t**;
Isa	45:23	every **t** shall swear."
Jer	23:31	who use their own **t**
Mk	7:33	spat and touched his **t**.
Lk	16:24	cool my **t**;
Rom	14:11	every **t** shall give praise
1 Cor	14: 2	those who speak in a **t**
Phil	2:11	every **t** should confess
Jas	3: 5	**t** is a small member,

TOUCH (ED)

Gen	3: 3	nor shall you **t** it,
Ex	19:12	to **t** the edge of it.
Num	4:15	must not **t** the holy things,
1 Sam	10:26	whose hearts God had **t**.
Ps	105:15	"Do not **t** my anointed ones;
Wis	3:1	no torment will ever **t** them.
Isa	52:11	**T** no unclean thing;
Ezek	9: 6	**t** no one who has
Dan	10:16	one in human form **t** my lips,
Mt	9:21	"If I only **t** his cloak,
Lk	18:15	that he might **t** them;
2 Cor	6:17	**t** nothing unclean;
Col	2:21	Do not taste, Do not **t**"?
Heb	11:28	would not **t** the firstborn

TRANSFIGURED

Mt	17: 2	he was **t** before them,

TRANSGRESSION (S)

Ex	23:21	pardon your **t**;
Ps	19:13	innocent of great **t**.
Isa	53: 8	stricken for the **t**
Dan	9:24	finish the **t**, to put an end to
Mic	1: 5	**t** of Jacob
Gal	6: 1	anyone is detected in a **t**,
2 Pet	2:16	rebuked for his own **t**;

TREASURE (S) (D)

Ex	19: 5	you shall be my **t** possession
Deut	33:19	hidden **t** of the sand,
Ps	119:11	I **t** your word
Sir	41:14	wisdom and unseen **t**—
Isa	33: 6	fear of the Lord is Zion's **t**.
Mt	6:21	where your **t** is,
Lk	12:33	unfailing **t** in heaven,
2 Cor	4: 7	we have this **t** in clay jars,
1 Tim	6:19	the **t** of a good foundation
2 Tim	1:14	Guard the good **t** entrusted to

TREE (S)

Gen	1:29	every **t** with seed
Deut	21:23	night upon the **t**;

1 Kings	14:23	every green **t**;
Ps	52: 8	like a green olive **t**
Prov	3:18	She is a **t** of life
Isa	65:22	like the days of a **t**
Jer	17: 8	like a **t** planted by water,
	46:22	like those who fell **t**.
Ezek	17:24	bring low the high **t**,
Dan	4:10	a **t** at the center of the earth.
Hos	9:10	fruit on the fig **t**,
Hab	3:17	Though the fig **t** does not
Zech	3:10	under your vine and fig **t**."
Mt	3:10	root of the **t**;
Mk	11:13	fig **t** in leaf,
Lk	19: 4	climbed a sycamore **t**
Acts	5:30	hanging him on a **t**.
Rom	11:24	into their own wild olive **t**
Jas	3:12	Can a fig **t**,
Jude	1:12	autumn **t** without fruit,
Rev	2: 7	eat from the **t** of life

TRIBE (S)

Gen	49:28	these are the twelve **t**
Num	1: 4	man from each **t**
Josh	13:14	**t** of Levi
Judg	21: 6	**t** is cut off
1 Kings	11:13	give one **t** to your son,
Ps	122: 4	To it the **t** go up, the **t**
Heb	7:13	belonged to another **t**,
Rev	5: 5	Lion of the **t** of Judah,

TROUBLE (D)

Josh	7:25	"Why did you bring **t** on us?
Job	5: 7	are born to **t**
Ps	9: 9	stronghold in times of **t**.
Eccl	12: 1	days of **t** come,
Sir	51:10	forsake me in the days of **t**,
Isa	33: 2	salvation in the time of **t**
Nah	1: 7	stronghold in a day of **t**;
Mt	6:34	Today's **t** is enough
Jn	14: 1	not let your hearts be **t**.

TRUE (TRUTH)

Gen	42:16	whether there is **t** in you;
Num	11:23	word will come **t**
Deut	18:22	does not take place or prove **t**,
1 Sam	9: 6	he says always comes **t**.
1 Kings	10: 6	"The report was **t**
2 Chr	15: 3	without the **t** God,
Ps	119:151	commandments are **t**.
Prov	22:21	what is right and **t**,
Jer	10:10	Lord is the **t** God;
Lk	16:11	entrust to you the **t**
Jn	1: 9	The **t** light,
Rom	3: 4	let God be proved **t**,
Eph	4:24	likeness of God in **t**
Phil	4: 8	whatever is **t**,
1 Thess	1: 9	living and **t** God,
1 Jn	2: 8	commandment that is **t**
2 Jn	1: 1	I love in the **t**.
3 Jn	1:12	testimony is **t**.
Rev	3: 7	of the holy one, the **t** one,

TRUMPET

Ex	19:16	blast of a **t**
Isa	27:13	on that day a great **t**
Ezek	33: 5	sound of the **t**
Joel	2:15	Blow the **t** in Zion;
Zech	9:14	God will sound the **t**
Mt	24:31	angels with a loud **t**
1 Cor	15:52	at the last **t**. For the **t**

1 Thess	4:16	sound of God's **t**,
Rev	1:10	voice like a **t**

TRUST (TRUSTWORTHY)

Ex	19: 9	so **t** you ever after."
Num	20:12	you did not **t** in me,
Deut	1:32	you have no **t**
Judg	11:20	Sihon did not **t**
1 Sam	3:20	Samuel was a **t** prophet
1 Chr	9:22	them in their office of **t**.
Job	4:18	servants he puts no **t**,
Ps	4: 5	put your **t** in the Lord.
Prov	3: 5	**T** in the Lord
Sir	2:6	**T** in him, and he will help
Isa	26: 4	**T** in the Lord forever,
Jer	2:37	those in whom you **t**,
Mic	7: 5	no **t** in a friend,
Titus	1: 9	word that is **t** in
Heb	2:13	"I will put my **t** in him."

TURN (ED)

Ex	23:27	enemies **t** their backs
Num	32:15	you **t** away from following
Deut	5:32	you shall not **t**
Josh	1: 7	do not **t** from it
2 Chr	7:14	**T** from their wicked ways,
Ps	6: 4	**T**, O Lord, save my life
Isa	6:10	**t** and be healed."
Jer	31:	**T** now, all of you
Ezek	33: 9	warn the wicked to **t**
Joel	2:14	he will not **t** and relent,
Jon	3: 9	may **t** from his fierce anger,
Mal	4: 6	will **t** the hearts of parents
Mt	5:39	**t** the other also;
Lk	1:17	to **t** the hearts
Jn	12:40	with their heart and **t**—
Acts	3:19	**t** to God
Rom	3:12	All have **t** aside,
Gal	4: 9	how can you **t** back
2 Tim	4: 4	will **t** away from listening
1 Pet	3:11	let them **t** away

TWELVE

Gen	35:22	sons of Jacob were **t**.
Ex	24: 4	set up **t** pillars,
Josh	4: 3	Take **t** stones
1 Kings	11:30	tore it into **t** pieces.
Mt	10: 1	summoned his **t** disciples
Lk	9:17	**t** baskets of broken pieces.
Jas	1: 1	To the **t** tribes
Rev	12: 1	crown of **t** stars.

TWO (TWO-EDGED)

Gen	1:16	God made the **t** great lights
Ex	31:18	gave him the **t** tablets
Deut	4:13	wrote them on **t** stone
1 Kings	3:16	**t** women who were prostitutes
Prov	30: 7	**T** things I ask of you
Eccl	4: 9	**T** are better than one,
Isa	6: 2	with **t** they covered their faces,
Ezek	1:11	each creature had **t** wings,
Dan	8: 3	It had **t** horns.
Zech	4:11	**t** olive trees
Mt	6:24	"No one can serve **t** masters;
Mk	6: 7	send them out by **t**,
Lk	9:30	they saw **t** men,
1 Cor	6:16	"The **t** shall be one flesh."
Gal	4:24	women are **t** covenants.
Eph	5:31	**t** will become one flesh."
Heb	4:12	sharper than any **t** sword,

Rev 11: 3 my **t** witnesses authority

U

UNBELIEF (UNBELIEVER) (UNBELIEVERS)
Mk 6: 6 he was amazed at their **u**.
Rom 11:20 broken off because of their **u**,
1 Cor 7:12 wife who is an **u**,
2 Cor 4: 4 blinded the minds of the **u**,
1 Tim 1:13 acted ignorantly in **u**,
Heb 3:19 enter because of **u**.

UNCLEAN
Lev 5: 2 any of you touch any **u** thing
1 Macc 1:47 sacrifice swine and other **u**
Ps 106:39 became **u** by their acts,
Eccl 9: 2 to the clean and the **u**,
Isa 6: 5 man of **u** lips,
Mk 3:11 Whenever the **u** spirits
Acts 10:14 anything that is profane or **u**."
Rom 14:14 nothing is **u** in itself;
2 Cor 6:17 touch nothing **u**;
Rev 21:27 nothing **u** will enter it,

UNDERSTAND (ING)
Gen 11: 7 not **u** one another's speech,"
Ex 36: 1 skill and **u** to know how
Tob 4:19 For none of the nations has **u**,
Job 42: 3 have uttered what I did not **u**,
Ps 73:16 I thought how to **u** this,
Prov 2: 5 then you will **u** the fear
Isa 1: 3 people do not **u**.
Jer 17: 9 who can **u** it?
Dan 9:25 Know therefore and **u**:
Hos 14: 9 Those who are wise **u**
Mt 13:15 **u** with their heart
Mk 4:13 "Do you not **u** this parable?
Lk 24:45 minds to **u** the scriptures,
Jn 13: 7 later you will **u**."
Acts 8:30 you **u** what you are reading?"
Rom 7:15 I do not **u** my own actions.
1 Cor 2:12 so that we may **u**
Eph 5:17 **u** what the will
Heb 11: 3 By faith we **u**
Jas 3:13 Who is wise and **u**
2 Pet 1:20 you must **u** this,
1 Jn 5:20 and has given us **u**

UNRIGHTEOUS (NESS)
Ps 92:15 there is no **u** in him.
Mt 5:45 righteous and on the **u**.
1 Pet 3:18 righteous for the **u**,
2 Pet 2: 9 keep the **u** under punishment
1 Jn 1: 9 cleanse us from all **u**.

UPRIGHT
Gen 37: 7 sheaf rose and stood **u**;
Deut 32: 4 just and **u** is he;
Job 1: 1 man was blameless and **u**,
Ps 7:10 saves the **u** in heart.
Prov 2: 7 wisdom for the **u**;
Titus 1: 8 prudent, **u**, devout,

USE (FUL)
Ex 20: 7 make wrongful **u**

Deut 5:11 wrongful **u** of the name
Rom 9:21 **u** and another for ordinary **u**
Gal 5:13 do not **u** your freedom
Eph 4:29 only what is **u** for building up,
2 Tim 2:20 some for special **u**,

V

VAIN (VANITY)
Lev 26:16 sow your seed in **v**,
Ps 2: 1 peoples plot in **v**?
Eccl 1: 2 **V** of vanities,
Isa 65:23 shall not labor in **v**,
Ezek 6:10 not threaten in **v**
Mt 15: 9 in **v** do they worship me,
Acts 4:25 peoples imagine **v** things?
1 Cor 15: 2 have come to believe in **v**.
2 Cor 6: 1 grace of God in **v**,
Gal 2: 2 had not run, in **v**.
Phil 2:16 did not run in **v** or labor in **v**.

VENGEANCE
Gen 4:15 suffer a sevenfold **v**."
Num 31: 3 execute the LORD's **v**
Ps 94: 1 God of **v**, you God of **v**,
Sir 28:1 vengeful will face the Lord's **v**,
Isa 34: 8 day of **v**,
Jer 50:15 this is the **v** of the LORD:
Nah 1: 2 LORD takes **v**

VICTORY
1 Sam 2: 1 rejoice in my **v**.
2 Sam 8: 6 Lord gave **v** to David
Ps 33:17 vain hope for **v**,
Prov 21:31 **v** belongs to the LORD.
Zeph 3:17 warrior who gives **v**;
1 Cor 15:54 swallowed up in **v**."
1 Jn 5: 4 **v** that conquers the world,

VINE (YARD)
Gen 9:20 first to plant a **v**.
Deut 32:32 Their **v** comes
1 Kings 21: 1 had a **v** in Jezreel,
Ps 80: 8 brought a **v** out of Egypt;
Isa 36:16 eat from your own **v**
Jer 2:21 planted you as a choice **v**,
Ezek 17: 6 became a **v** spreading
Hos 10: 1 Israel is a luxuriant **v**
Mk 14:25 fruit of the **v**
Jn 15: 1 "I am the true **v**,
1 Cor 9: 7 Who plants a **v**
Rev 14:18 clusters of the **v**

VIOLENT (VIOLENCE)
Gen 6:11 earth was filled with **v**.
Prov 3:31 Do not envy the **v**
Ezek 18:10 son who is **v**,
Mt 11:12 **v** take it by force.
1 Tim 3: 3 not **v** but gentle,
Titus 1: 7 **v** or greedy for gain;

VIRGIN
1 Kings 1: 2 "Let a young **v**
Jer 31:21 Return, O **v** Israel,
Lam 2:13 O **v** daughter Zion?
Mt 1:23 **v** shall conceive

Lk 1:34 since I am a **v**?"
1 Cor 7:28 if a **v** marries,
2 Cor 11: 2 chaste **v** to Christ.

VISION (S)
Gen 15: 1 Abram in a **v**,
Num 24: 4 sees the **v** of the Almighty,
1 Sam 3:15 tell the **v** to Eli.
Ps 89:19 spoke in a **v**
Isa 22: 1 valley of **v**.
Jer 23:16 speak **v** of their own minds,
Dan 7: 2 saw in my **v**
Lk 1:22 he had seen a **v**
Acts 9:10 said to him in a **v**,
Rev 9:17 saw the horses in my **v**:

VOICE
Gen 3:17 listened to the **v**
Deut 4:33 heard the **v** of a god
1 Sam 15:22 obeying the **v**
Job 40: 9 thunder with a **v**
Ps 19: 4 their **v** goes out
Prov 1:20 she raises her **v**.
Isa 40: 3 A **v** cries out:
Jer 31:15 A **v** is heard
Dan 9:14 disobeyed his **v**.
Mt 2:18 "A **v** was heard
Mk 1: 3 **v** of one crying out
Jn 1:23 "I am the **v**
Rom 10:18 "Their **v** has gone out
Heb 3: 7 if you hear his **v**,
2 Pet 1:17 that **v** was conveyed
1:18 this **v** come from heaven,
2:16 with a human **v** and restrained
Rev 3:20 you hear my **v**

VOW (S)
Gen 28:20 Jacob made a **v**,
Num 6: 2 women make a special **v**,
Deut 23:21 If you make a **v**
Judg 11:30 Jephthah made a **v**
1 Sam 1:11 She made this **v**:
Ps 22:25 my **v** I will pay
Eccl 5: 4 make a **v** to God,
Sir 18:23 Before making a **v**, prepare
Jon 1:16 LORD and made **v**.
Acts 18:18 he was under a **v**.

W

WAIT (S)
Ps 27:14 **W** for the LORD;
Prov 1:18 they lie in **w**—
Sir 6:19 and **w** for her good harvest.
Isa 30:18 Therefore the Lord **w**
Lam 3:26 should **w** quietly
Hab 2: 3 **w** for it;
Acts 1: 4 **w** there for the promise
Rom 8:23 while we **w** for adoption,
Gal 5: 5 we eagerly **w** for the hope
1 Thess 1:10 **w** for his Son from heaven
Titus 2:13 we **w** for the blessed hope

WALK (ED) (ING)
Gen 5:24 Enoch **w** with God;
Deut 10:12 **w** in all his ways,

Josh	22: 5	**w** in all his ways,				Acts	1:10	men in **w** robes
Ps	15: 2	**w** blamelessly,				Rev	1:14	hair were **w** as **w** wool,
Prov	4:12	When you **w**,						

WALK — WILL

Josh	22: 5	**w** in all his ways,
Ps	15: 2	**w** blamelessly,
Prov	4:12	When you **w**,
Isa	2: 3	we may **w** in his paths."
Jer	6:16	**w** in it, and find rest
Dan	4:37	**w** in pride.
Am	3: 3	Do two **w** together
Mic	4: 5	**w** in the name of the Lord
Zech	10:12	**w** in his name,
Mt	14:26	disciples saw him **w**
Mk	2: 9	take your mat and **w**?
Jn	8:12	**w** in darkness
Acts	3: 8	stood and began to **w**,
2 Cor	5: 7	we **w** by faith,
1 Jn	1: 7	we **w** in the light
2 Jn	1: 6	we **w** according to his
3 Jn	1: 3	you **w** in the truth.
Rev	9:20	cannot see or hear or **w**.

WANT (ING)

Ps	23: 1	I shall not **w**.
Dan	5:27	on the scales and found **w**;
Lk	18:41	"What do you **w** me
Rom	7:15	do not do what I **w**,
2 Cor	12:14	I do not **w** what is yours
Phil	3:10	I **w** to know Christ

WAR (WARRIOR)

Ex	17:16	Lord will have **w**
Josh	11:23	rest from **w**.
1 Chr	28: 3	are a **w** and have shed blood.'
1 Macc	2:66	has been a mighty **w**
Ps	68:30	delight in **w**.
Eccl	3: 8	time for **w**,
Isa	2: 4	they learn **w** any more.
Dan	7:21	horn made **w**
Rom	7:23	another law at **w**
2 Cor	10: 3	we do not wage **w**
1 Pet	2:11	wage **w** against the soul.
Rev	12: 7	**w** broke out

WASH (ED)

2 Kings	5:10	**w** in the Jordan
Ps	51: 7	**w** me, and I shall be whiter
Jer	4:14	**w** your heart clean
Lk	11:38	he did not first **w**
Jn	9: 7	**w** in the pool
1 Cor	6:11	you were **w**, you were
Rev	22:14	those who **w** their robes,

WATER (S)

Gen	1: 2	over the face of the **w**.
Ex	7:20	struck the **w**
Num	5:19	be immune to this **w**
2 Kings	2: 8	struck the **w**; the **w** was parted
Ps	1: 3	planted by streams of **w**,
Prov	5:15	Drink **w**
Eccl	11: 1	bread upon the **w**,
Sir	15:3	him the **w** of wisdom to drink.
Isa	12: 3	With joy you will draw **w**
Jer	2:13	fountain of living **w**,
Ezek	36:25	sprinkle clean **w**
Mt	14:29	walking on the **w**,
Lk	5: 4	"Put out into the deep **w**
Jn	2: 9	steward tasted the **w**
Eph	5:26	washing of **w** by the word
Heb	10:22	washed with pure **w**.
Jas	3:11	brackish **w**?
1 Jn	5: 6	who came by **w**
Rev	7:17	springs of the **w**

WAY (S)

Gen	3:24	guard the **w**
Ex	13:21	lead them along the **w**,
Deut	1:33	before you on the **w**
1 Sam	12:23	right **w**.
2 Sam	22:31	his **w** is perfect;
1 Kings	8:36	good **w** in which they should
2 Chr	6:27	teach them the good **w**
Job	23:10	he knows the **w**
Ps	1: 6	over the **w** of the righteous
Prov	3: 6	In all your **w** acknowledge
Sir	2:15	who love him keep his **w**.
Isa	30:21	"This is the **w**;
Jer	21: 8	before you the **w** of life
Mal	3: 1	prepare the **w** before me,
Mt	3: 3	'Prepare the **w**
Lk	7:27	prepare your **w**
Jn	14: 6	"I am the **w**,
Acts	1:11	come in the same **w**
1 Cor	9:24	Run in such a **w**
Eph	4:20	That is not the **w**
Col	3: 7	These are the **w**
Heb	9: 8	indicates that the **w**
2 Pet	2:21	never to have known the **w**
Rev	15: 3	Just and true are your **w**,

WEAK

Judg	16: 7	I shall become **w**,
Ps	72:13	He has pity on the **w**
Ezek	34: 4	strengthened the **w**,
Mt	26:41	flesh is **w**."
Acts	20:35	we must support the **w**,
Rom	14: 1	**w** in faith,
1 Cor	1:27	God chose what is **w**
2 Cor	12:10	whenever I am **w**,
Gal	4: 9	turn back again to the **w**
1 Thess	5:14	help the **w**,
Heb	7:18	because it was **w**

WEALTH

Deut	8:17	hand have gotten me this **w**."
2 Chr	1:11	**w**, honor,
Ps	49: 6	trust in their **w**
Prov	13: 7	yet have great **w**.
Eccl	5:10	nor the lover of **w**,
Song	8: 7	all the **w** of his house,
Sir	11:14	and **w**, come from the Lord.
Mt	13:22	lure of **w**
Lk	16:11	dishonest **w**,
Rev	5:12	receive power and **w**

WEEP (ING)

Ps	6: 8	heard the sound of my **w**.
Eccl	3: 4	a time to **w**,
Jer	3:21	plaintive **w** of Israel's children,
Lam	1:16	For these things I **w**;
Lk	6:21	"Blessed are you who **w**
Rom	12:15	**w** with those who **w**,

WHEAT

Ex	34:22	fruits of **w** harvest,
Mt	3:12	gather his **w**
Lk	22:31	sift all of you like **w**,
Jn	12:24	unless a grain of **w**

WHITE (R)

Ps	51: 7	I shall be **w** than snow.
Dan	7: 9	clothing was **w** as snow,
Zech	1: 8	**w** horses.
Mt	5:36	make one hair **w**

WICKED (NESS)

Gen	13:13	people of Sodom were **w**,
Ex	23: 1	hands with the **w**
Num	14:35	all this **w** congregation
2 Kings	17:11	They did **w** things,
2 Chr	7:14	turn from their **w** ways,
Job	15:20	**w** writhe in pain
Ps	1: 1	advice of the **w**,
Prov	4:14	enter the path of the **w**,
Eccl	7:15	there are **w** people
Wis	2:21	for their **w** blinded them,
Sir	15:20	commanded anyone to be **w**,
Isa	11: 4	he shall kill the **w**.
Ezek	3:18	If I say to the **w**,
Dan	12:10	**w** shall continue to act **w**
Lk	6:35	ungrateful and the **w**.
Acts	1:18	with the reward of his **w**;
1 Cor	5:13	"Drive out the **w**
2 Tim	2:19	turn away from **w**."
Heb	1: 9	righteousness and hated **w**;

WIDOW (S)

Ex	22:22	shall not abuse any **w**
Deut	10:18	orphan and the **w**,
Ruth	4: 5	**w** of the dead man,
Jdt	8:4	Judith remained as a **w** for
Ps	68: 5	protector of **w**
Isa	1:17	plead for the **w**.
Lam	1: 1	How like a **w**
Ezek	22: 7	and the **w** are wronged in you.
Mk	12:19	marry the **w**
Lk	2:37	**w** to the age of eighty-four.
1 Tim	5: 4	**w** has children
Rev	18: 7	no **w**, and I will never see grief

WIFE (WIVES)

Gen	2:24	clings to his **w**,
Ex	20:17	covet your neighbor's **w**,
Num	5:12	man's **w** goes astray
Ruth	4:13	she became his **w**.
2 Sam	12:10	taken the **w** of Uriah
Ezra	10:11	from the foreign **w**."
Tob	8:6	his **w** Eve as a helper and
Ps	128: 3	**w** will be like a fruitful
Prov	5:18	rejoice in the **w** of your youth,
Eccl	9: 9	Enjoy life with the **w**
Sir	26:1	is the husband of a good **w**;
Hos	1: 2	take for yourself a **w**
Mal	2:14	between you and the **w**
Mt	1:20	take Mary as your **w**,
Mk	6:18	have your brother's **w**."
Lk	17:32	Remember Lot's **w**.
1 Cor	7: 2	man should have his own **w**,
Eph	5:23	head of the **w**
Rev	21: 9	**w** of the Lamb."

WILL (ING)

Num	30: 5	Lord **w** forgive her,
1 Sam	2:25	it was the **w** of the Lord
2 Kings	24: 4	Lord was not **w** to pardon.
1 Chr	13: 2	it is the **w** of the Lord
Ezra	7:18	according to the **w**
Tob	12:18	not acting on my own **w**,
2 Macc	12:16	the town by the **w** of God.
Ps	40: 8	delight to do your **w**,
Wis	14:5	your **w** that works of your
Isa	30:19	He **w** surely be gracious

Jer	3:17	follow their own evil **w**.
Ezek	16:27	up to the **w** of your enemies,
Dan	11:28	shall work his **w**,
Mt	6:10	Your **w** be done,
Mk	3:35	Whoever does the **w**
Lk	22:42	not my **w** but yours be done."
Jn	1:51	you **w** see heaven
Acts	21:14	"The Lord's **w** be done."
Rom	2:18	know his **w**
1 Cor	1: 1	by the **w** of God,
2 Cor	1:10	he **w** rescue us again,
Gal	1: 4	according to the **w**
Eph	1: 5	good pleasure of his **w**,
Phil	2:13	enabling you both to **w**
Col	1: 9	knowledge of God's **w**
1 Thess	4: 3	this is the **w** of God,
2 Tim	3: 1	distressing times **w** come.
Heb	2: 4	distributed according to his **w**.
Jas	3: 4	wherever the **w** of the pilot
1 Pet	2:15	it is God's **w**
2 Pet	1:21	ever came by human **w**,
1 Jn	2:17	those who do the **w** of God
Rev	4:11	by your **w** they existed

WIND (WHIRLWIND)

Gen	1: 2	**w** from God swept
1 Kings	19:11	there was a great **w**,
2 Kings	2:11	Elijah ascended in a **w**
Ps	1: 4	chaff that the **w** drives away,
Prov	11:29	households will inherit **w**,
Eccl	1:14	vanity and chasing after **w**.
Ezek	5: 2	shall scatter to the **w**,
Hos	8: 7	they sow the **w**,
Jon	1: 4	LORD hurled a great **w**
Nah	1: 3	His way is in **w** and storm,
Mk	6:51	the **w** ceased.
Jn	3: 8	**w** blows where it chooses,
Acts	2: 2	rush of a violent **w**,
Eph	4:14	every **w** of doctrine,
Jas	1: 6	tossed by the **w**;

WINE

Gen	9:21	drank some of the **w**
Num	6: 3	separate themselves from **w**
Deut	33:28	land of grain and **w**,
Judg	13: 4	be careful not to drink **w**
1 Sam	1:15	have drunk neither **w**
Neh	13:15	people treading **w** presses
Ps	4: 7	grain and **w** abound.
Prov	3:10	vats will be bursting with **w**.
Eccl	2: 3	cheer my body with **w**
Song	1: 2	love is better than **w**,
Sir	31:29	**W** drunk to excess leads to
Isa	1:22	**w** is mixed with water.
Dan	1: 8	rations of food and **w**;
Joel	2:24	overflow with **w** and oil.
Am	5:11	shall not drink their **w**.
Mic	2:11	preach to you of **w**
	6:15	tread grapes, but not drink **w**.
Zeph	1:13	they shall not drink **w** from
Mt	9:17	new **w** put into old **w**skins;
Lk	1:15	must never drink **w**
Jn	2: 3	"They have no **w**."
Acts	2:13	"They are filled with new **w**."
Rom	14:21	eat meat or drink **w**
Eph	5:18	Do not get drunk with **w**,
1 Tim	3: 8	not indulging in much **w**,
Rev	14: 8	nations drink of the **w**

WINGS

Ex	19: 4	on eagles' **w**
Ruth	2:12	under whose **w**
1 Kings	8: 7	spread out their **w**
Ps	17: 8	in the shadow of your **w**,
Isa	6: 2	each had six **w**:
Ezek	1: 6	each of them had four **w**.
Zech	5: 9	was in their **w**; they had **w**
Mal	4: 2	with healing in its **w**.
Lk	13:34	brood under her **w**,
Rev	4: 8	each of them with six **w**,

WISDOM

Deut	4: 6	show your **w** and discernment
1 Kings	4:29	gave Solomon very great **w**,
2 Chr	1:10	Give me now **w**
Job	11: 6	of **w**! For **w** is many-sided
Ps	37:30	righteous utter **w**,
Prov	1: 7	fools despise **w**
Eccl	1:13	search out by **w**
Isa	11: 2	spirit of **w**
Jer	9:23	boast in their **w**,
Bar	3:12	forsaken the foundatin of **w**
Ezek	28:12	full of **w**
Dan	5:14	excellent **w** are found
Mic	6: 9	is sound **w** to fear your name
Mt	11:19	Yet **w** is vindicated
Lk	2:52	Jesus increased in **w**
Acts	6:10	could not withstand the **w**
Rom	11:33	riches and **w**
1 Cor	1:19	destroy the **w**
Eph	1:17	spirit of **w**
Col	1: 9	all spiritual **w**
Jas	1: 5	lacking in **w**,
Rev	7:12	Blessing and glory and **w**

WISE

Gen	41:39	discerning and **w** as you.
Ex	7:11	Pharaoh summoned the **w**
Deut	4: 6	nation is a **w**
1 Kings	2: 9	you are a **w** man;
Job	9: 4	He is **w** in heart,
Ps	94: 8	when will you be **w**?
Prov	3:35	**w** will inherit honor,
Eccl	2:14	**w** have eyes in their head
Sir	7:19	Do not dismiss a **w** and good
Isa	29:14	wisdom of their **w** shall
Jer	8: 9	**w** shall be put to shame
Dan	2:21	gives wisdom to the **w**
Mt	25: 4	**w** took flasks of oil
Rom	1:22	Claiming to be **w**,
1 Cor	1:19	destroy the wisdom of the **w**,
Eph	5:15	unwise people but as **w**,
Jas	3:13	Who is **w** and understanding

WITNESS (ES)

Gen	31:44	**w** between you
Num	35:30	testimony of a single **w**.
Deut	19:15	evidence of two or three **w**
Josh	22:27	**w** between us and you,
Judg	11:10	LORD will be **w** between us;
1 Sam	12: 5	LORD is **w** against you,
Job	16:19	my **w** is in heaven,
Prov	12:17	false **w** speaks deceitfully.
Rom	2:15	conscience also bears **w**;
Heb	10:28	testimony of two or three **w**."
1 Pet	5: 1	**w** of the sufferings of Christ
Rev	1: 5	Christ, the faithful **w**,

WOMAN (WOMEN)

Gen	2:22	he made into a **w**
Ex	3:22	each **w** shall ask her neighbor
Num	30: 3	When a **w** makes a vow
Deut	20: 7	become engaged to a **w**
Judg	4: 9	into the hand of a **w**."
Ruth	3:11	you are a worthy **w**.
1 Sam	1:15	I am a **w** deeply troubled;
2 Sam	11: 2	from the roof a **w** bathing;
1 Kings	17:24	the **w** said to Elijah,
2 Kings	4: 8	where a wealthy **w** lived,
Jdt	8:31	a God-fearing **w**, pray for us
Job	2:10	speak as any foolish **w**
Ps	113: 9	gives the barren **w** a home,
Prov	11:16	gracious **w** gets honor,
Sir	9: 3	Do not go near a loose **w**,
Isa	54: 1	children of the desolate **w**
Mt	5:28	looks at a **w** with lust
Mk	7:25	**w** whose little daughter
Lk	1:42	"Blessed are you among **w**,
Jn	4: 7	Samaritan **w** came to draw
Acts	16:14	certain **w** named Lydia,
Rom	7: 2	married **w** is bound
1 Cor	14:34	**w** should be silent
Gal	4: 4	Son, born of a **w**,
1 Tim	2:11	Let a **w** learn in silence
2 Tim	3: 6	captivate silly **w**,
Titus	2: 3	tell the older **w** to be reverent
Rev	12: 1	**w** clothed with the sun,

WONDERFUL

Gen	18:14	anything too **w** for the LORD?
Judg	13:18	It is too **w**."
2 Sam	1:26	your love to me was **w**,
1 Chr	16: 9	tell of all his **w** works.
Job	42: 3	things too **w** for me,
Ps	105: 2	tell of all his **w** works.
Sir	11:4	works of the Lord are **w**,
Isa	9: 6	he is named **W** Counselor,
Lk	13:17	rejoicing at all the **w** things

WONDERS

Ex	3:20	strike Egypt with all my **w**
Ps	77:14	God who works **w**;
Sir	18:6	to fathom the **w** of the Lord
Dan	4: 3	how mighty his **w**!
Jn	4:48	"Unless you see signs and **w**
2 Cor	12:12	and **w** and mighty works.
2 Thess	2: 9	all power, signs, lying **w**,
Heb	2: 4	testimony by signs and **w**

WORD (S)

Gen	15: 1	After these things the **w**
Ex	20: 1	Then God spoke all these **w**;
Num	30: 2	he shall not break his **w**,
Deut	8: 3	every **w** that comes from the
1 Sam	3: 1	**w** of the LORD was rare
1 Kings	8:56	not one **w** has failed
1 Chr	17: 3	**w** of the LORD came
2 Chr	36:22	fulfillment of the **w** of the
Tob	14:4	None of all their **w** will fail
Ps	33: 4	**w** of the LORD is upright
Prov	12:25	a good **w** cheers it up.
Eccl	5: 2	therefore let your **w** be few.
Sir	32:8	Be brief; say much in few **w**;
Isa	1:10	Hear the **w** of the LORD,
Jer	5:13	the **w** is not in them.
Dan	9: 2	according to the **w** of the LORD
Mk	4:14	sower sows the **w**.
Lk	1: 2	servants of the **w**,

Jn	1: 1	was the **W**, and the **W**
Acts	4: 4	heard the **w** believed;
Rom	9: 6	not as though the **w** of God
2 Cor	2:17	peddlers of God's **w**
Gal	6: 6	taught the **w**
Eph	6:17	which is the **w** of God.
Phil	2:16	holding fast to the **w**
Col	3:16	Let the **w** of Christ dwell
2 Thess	2:15	either by **w** of mouth
Heb	1: 3	all things by his powerful **w**.
Jas	1:21	meekness the implanted **w**
1 Pet	1:23	enduring **w** of God.
2 Pet	3: 5	by the **w** of God
1 Jn	1: 1	concerning the **w** of life—
Rev	3: 8	you have kept my **w**

WORK (S)

Gen	2: 2	God finished the **w**
Ex	20:10	you shall not do any **w**—
Deut	14:29	bless you in all the **w**
1 Chr	22:16	Now begin the **w**,
2 Chr	2: 7	artisan skilled to **w** in gold,
Ezra	4:24	the **w** on the house of God
Job	1:10	You have blessed the **w**
Ps	8: 6	dominion over the **w**
Eccl	11: 5	you do not know the **w**
Isa	2: 8	they bow down to the **w**
Jer	48:10	slack in doing the **w**
Lk	13:14	six days on which **w**
Jn	6:27	Do not **w** for the food
Acts	13:25	John was finishing his **w**,
Rom	4: 6	righteousness apart from **w**:
1 Cor	3:13	**w** of each builder
Gal	6: 4	All must test their own **w**;
Eph	3:20	power at **w** within us
Phil	1: 6	one who began a good **w**
1 Thess	4:11	to **w** with your hands,
2 Thess	2: 7	lawlessness is already at **w**,
1 Tim	6:18	to be rich in good **w**,
2 Tim	2:21	ready for every good **w**.
Heb	6:10	overlook your **w**

WORLD

1 Chr	16:30	**w** is firmly established;
Ps	9: 8	the **w** with righteousness;
Isa	13:11	punish the **w** for its evil,
Mt	5:14	are the light of the **w**.
Jn	1:10	He was in the **w**, and the **w**
Acts	17:31	the **w** judged in righteousness
Rom	3:19	whole **w** may be held
1 Cor	1:27	foolish in the **w**
2 Cor	5:19	reconciling the **w** to himself,
Gal	6:14	by which the **w** has been
1 Tim	1:15	Jesus came into the **w**
Heb	1: 6	firstborn into the **w**,
Jas	1:27	unstained by the **w**.
1 Pet	1:20	foundation of the **w**,
1 Jn	2: 2	sins of the whole **w**.
Rev	11:15	"The kingdom of the **w**

WORSHIP

Ex	4:23	that he may **w** me."
Deut	12: 4	You shall not **w** the LORD
2 Kings	17:37	You shall not **w** other gods;
1 Chr	16:29	**W** the LORD in holy splendor
Ps	95: 6	come, let us **w**
Sir	35:10	Be generous when you **w** the
Dan	3:28	serve and **w** any god
Jon	1: 9	"I **w** the LORD,
Zech	14:17	go up to Jerusalem to **w**

Mt	4: 9	fall down and **w** me."
Lk	4: 8	'**W** the Lord your God,
Jn	4:24	who **w** him must **w** in spirit
Rom	12: 1	God, which is your spiritual **w**.
1 Cor	10:14	friends, flee from the **w** of idols.
Rev	4:10	**w** the one who lives forever

WORTHY

2 Sam	22: 4	who is **w** to be praised,
Mt	10:37	is not **w** of me;
Lk	15:19	I am no longer **w** to be called
Jn	1:27	I am not **w** to untie the thong
Eph	4: 1	lead a life **w** of the calling
Phil	1:27	manner **w** of the gospel of
Col	1:10	may lead lives **w** of the Lord,
Heb	3: 3	Yet Jesus is **w** of more glory
3 Jn	1: 6	on in a manner **w** of God;
Rev	5:12	"**W** is the Lamb that was

WRATH

Num	16:46	For **w** has gone out
1 Chr	27:24	yet **w** came upon Israel for
2 Chr	36:16	until the **w** of the LORD
1 Macc	1:64	Very great **w** came upon Israel
Ps	2: 5	speak to them in his **w**,
Prov	15: 1	A soft answer turns away **w**,
Isa	13:13	the **w** of the LORD of hosts
Jer	6:11	I am full of the **w** of the LORD;
Lam	4:11	gave full vent to his **w**;
Ezek	20: 8	I would pour out my **w** upon
Zeph	1:15	will be a day of **w**,
Mt	3: 7	flee from the **w** to come?
Jn	3:36	must endure God's **w**.
Rom	2: 5	storing up **w** for yourself
Eph	2: 3	were by nature children of **w**,
1 Thess	5: 9	has destined us not for **w**
Rev	6:17	great day of their **w** has come,

WRITE (WRITING) (WRITTEN)
(WROTE)

Ex	24: 4	Moses **w** down all the words
	34:27	LORD said to Moses: **W** these
Num	17: 2	**W** each man's name on his
Deut	10: 2	I will **w** on the tablets
1 Kings	2:3	as it is **w** in the law of Moses,
Prov	3: 3	**w** them on the tablet of
Jer	31:33	I will **w** it on their hearts;
Dan	5:7	"Whoever can read this **w**
Lk	1: 3	to **w** an orderly account for
Heb	8:10	and **w** them on their hearts,
1 Jn	2: 7	**w** you no new commandment,
Rev	21:27	are **w** in the Lamb's book of life

Y

YEAR (S)

Gen	1:14	seasons and for days and **y**,
Ex	12:40	was four hundred thirty **y**.
Num	1: 1	in the second **y** after they had
Deut	2: 7	These forty **y** the LORD your
2 Sam	21: 1	for three **y**, **y** after **y**;
2 Chr	36:21	sabbath, to fulfill seventy **y**.
Ezra	5:11	house that was built many **y**
Neh	9:21	Forty **y** you sustained them

Job	36:26	of his **y** is unsearchable.
Ps	90: 4	For a thousand **y** in your sight
Prov	9:11	and **y** will be added
Eccl	6: 6	live a thousand **y** twice over,
Jer	25:12	Then after seventy **y** are
Dan	9: 2	in the first **y** of his reign,
Joel	2:25	will repay you for the **y**
Mt	2:16	who were two **y** old or under,
Lk	3:23	Jesus was about thirty **y** old
Jn	2:20	construction for forty-six **y**,
Gal	4:10	months, and seasons, and **y**.
Heb	3:17	whom was he angry forty **y**?
2 Pet	3: 8	thousand **y**, and a thousand **y**
Rev	20: 2	bound him for a thousand **y**,

YEAST

Mt	16: 6	of the **y** of the Pharisees and
1 Cor	5: 6	little **y** leavens the whole

YOKE

Deut	28:48	He will put an iron **y** on your
1 Kings	12: 4	"Your father made our **y**
Mt	11:30	For my **y** is easy,
Gal	5: 1	submit again to a **y** of slavery.

YOUNG

Deut	22: 6	take the mother with the **y**.
Ruth	2: 5	"To whom does this **y** woman
1 Sam	2:17	sin of the **y** men was very great
2 Chr	10:14	with the advice of the **y** men,
Ps	37:25	I have been **y**, and now am
Prov	7: 7	a **y** man without sense,
Eccl	11: 9	**y** man, while you are **y**
Lam	1:18	my **y** women and **y** men
Dan	1: 4	**y** men without physical defect
Joel	2:28	your **y** men shall see visions.
Mk	14:51	A certain **y** man was following
Lk	2:24	turtledoves or two **y** pigeons."
1 Jn	2:13	I am writing to you, **y** people,

YOUTH

Gen	8:21	human heart is evil from **y**;
1 Sam	17:33	been a warrior from his **y**."
Ps	71: 5	my trust, O Lord, from my **y**.
Prov	2:17	forsakes the partner of her **y**
Eccl	4:13	is a poor but wise **y**
Isa	65:20	years will be considered a **y**,
Ezek	16:60	in the days of your **y**,
Mal	2:14	and the wife of your **y**,

Z

ZEAL (OUS) (ZEALOT)

Num	25:11	manifesting such **z** among
	25:13	because he was **z** for his God,
2 Kings	10:16	see my **z** for the LORD."
1 Macc	2:27	"Let every one who is **z** for the
Ps	69: 9	It is **z** for your house
Isa	37:32	The **z** of the LORD of hosts
Lk	6:15	Simon, who was called the **Z**,
Jn	2:17	"**Z** for your house will
Rom	10: 2	testify that they have a **z** for
2 Cor	7:11	alarm, what longing, what **z**,
Phil	3: 6	**z**, a persecutor of the church

ZION

2 Sam	5: 7	took the stronghold of **Z**,

Zion

2 Kings	19:31	Mount **Z** a band of survivors.	Lam	2:13	O virgin daughter **Z**?	Rom	9:33	"See, I am laying in **Z**
Ps	2: 6	set my king on **Z**, my holy	Joel	3:21	for the LORD dwells in **Z**.	Heb	12:22	you have come to Mount **Z**
Song	3:11	O daughters of **Z**, at King	Am	1: 2	The LORD roars from **Z**,	1 Pet	2: 6	"See, I am laying in **Z** a
Sir	24:10	and so I was established in **Z**.	Mic	3:12	**Z** shall be plowed	Rev	14: 1	Lamb, standing on Mount **Z**!
Isa	2: 3	of **Z** shall go forth instruction,	Zech	1:17	the LORD will again comfort **Z**			
Jer	50: 5	shall ask the way to **Z**,	Mt	21: 5	"Tell the daughter of **Z**,			

Map 1:
**THE WORLD OF
THE PATRIARCHS**

JAVAN   Descendants of Japheth (Gen. 10.2–5)
PUT   Descendants of Ham (Gen. 10.6–20)
LUD   Descendants of Shem (Gen. 10.21–31)
(Egypt)   Later biblical name
→   Abraham's route

GOMER

LUD
(Lydia)

JAVAN
(Greeks)

TOGARMAH

HITTITES

ASHKENAZ
(Scythians)

MADAI
(Medes)

The Great Sea (Mediterranean Sea)

KITTIM
(Cyprus)

ARAM
(Syria)

AMORITES

ASSHUR
(Assyria)

River Tigris

River Euphrates

ELAM
(Persia)

ARPHAXAD

Ur

Abraham and Sarah's
original home
(Gen 11.28)

Babylon

Mari

Haran

Paddan-Aram

Jacob meets
Leah and Rachel
(Gen, ch 29).

Abraham and Lot
first settle
(Gen 11.31).

Damascus

Penuel

Jacob wrestles
with God
(Gen 32.22–32).

Shechem

Hebron

CANAAN

Abraham and
Sarah's burial site
(Gen 25.9–10)

JOKTAN
(Arabia)

Beersheba

Gaza

PHILISTINES

Joseph is sold into
slavery in Egypt
(Gen, ch 37).

Zoan

On

MIZRAIM
(Egypt)

River Nile

PUT

Red Sea

Caspian Sea

*Persian
Gulf*

200 miles

200 kilometers

© 2001 by Thomas Nelson, Inc.
and Saint Mary's Press

maps.com

1569

35°N

30°

Map 2: THE EXODUS FROM EGYPT

A **B** **C** **D**

1

Moses' death (Deut, ch 34)

Ammon

Moab

River Jabbok

River Arnon

MT. NEBO +

Dead Sea (Salt Sea)

Zoar

Punon

Edom

Desert wandering (Deut, ch 2)

Midian

God gives the Ten Commandments (Ex, ch 20).

2

Hebron

Arad

Beersheba

Wilderness of Zin

Kadesh Barnea

Arabah

Ezion Geber

Gulf of Aqaba

1570

Gaza

Way of the Philistines

Way of Shur

Wilderness of Paran

Route from Egypt to Arabia

Miracles of manna and quail (Ex, ch 16)

Marah?

Elim?

MT. SINAI + HOREB

C

The Great Sea (Mediterranean Sea)

Baal Zephon

Avaris

Qantir

Pithom

Succoth

Land of Goshen

Memphis

River Nile

River Nile

Red Sea

3

31°E

33°

35°

37°

37°

31°N

29°

Route of the Exodus

Alternate routes of Red Sea crossing

Unsuccessful invasion of Canaan (Num. 14:39–45)

Trade routes

? Exact location questionable

0   75 miles

0   75 kilometers

Map 3:
THE KINGDOM YEARS

Probable extent of Israelite control during the Kingdom of Solomon, c. 950 B.C.

The Kingdoms of Israel and Judah, c. 860 B.C.

- - - - Boundary between Israel and Judah

? Exact location questionable

0 —————————— 75 miles
0 —————————— 75 kilometers

A 34° **B** 35° **C** **D** 37°E

1
Riblah

Zobah

34°N

Byblos

✝ MT. LEBANON

Sidon
Phoenicia   • Damascus   **2**

Tyre   ✝ MT. HERMON
                                Dan   **ARAM**
The Great Sea   Kedesh   **(Syria)**
(Mediterranean Sea)
                          Hazor   33°

Acco   *Sea of Chinnereth*   Ashtaroth

> Elijah confronts Baal's prophets (1 Kings 18.20–40).

✝ MT. CARMEL   *River Yarmuk*   Golan?
Dor   Jokneam   • Ramoth Gilead
      Megiddo   **Jezreel**
      Taanach   ✝ MT. GILBOA   **3**
      Dothan   • Jabesh Gilead

> Samuel is raised in the temple (1 Sam, chs 1–3).

         Tirzah   Zaphon
      Samaria•   Succoth   > Elijah ascends to heaven. Elisha picks up his mantle (2 Kings 2.1–14).
      Shechem
Aphek   Shiloh   **ISRAEL**   > Elijah, Elisha, Amos, and Hosea prophesy in Israel.
Joppa•   **Northern Kingdom**   32°

> Samuel proclaims Saul king (1 Sam 10.17–27).

         Bethel   *Ammon*
      Gezer   • Mizpah   Heshbon
Philistia   Azekah • Jerusalem   > David's capital (2 Sam 5.6–16); Solomon builds the Temple (2 Chr, chs 3–6).

> David defeats Goliath (1 Sam, ch 17).

Ashkelon   • Bethlehem   • Medeba
      Adullam   Tekoa
Gaza Eglon? Debir Hebron•   Dibon
                     Dead   Aroer   **4**
Ziklag?   Arad   *Sea*   *River Arnon*
      Beersheba   *(Salt Sea)* *Moab*

> Isaiah, Micah, Zephaniah, Jeremiah, Nahum, Habakkuk, and Ezekiel prophesy in Judah.

            Kir Hareseth
      Zoar *Brook Zered*   31°

> David defeats Aram, Ammon, Moab, Edom, and the Philistines (2 Sam, ch 8).

JUDAH
Southern Kingdom • Bozrah

Kadesh Barnea

Edom

      • Teman   **5**

Brook of Egypt

                                          30°

Ezion Geber • Elath
A   **B** 1571 **C** © 2001 by Thomas Nelson, Inc. and Saint Mary's Press **D** maps.com **6**

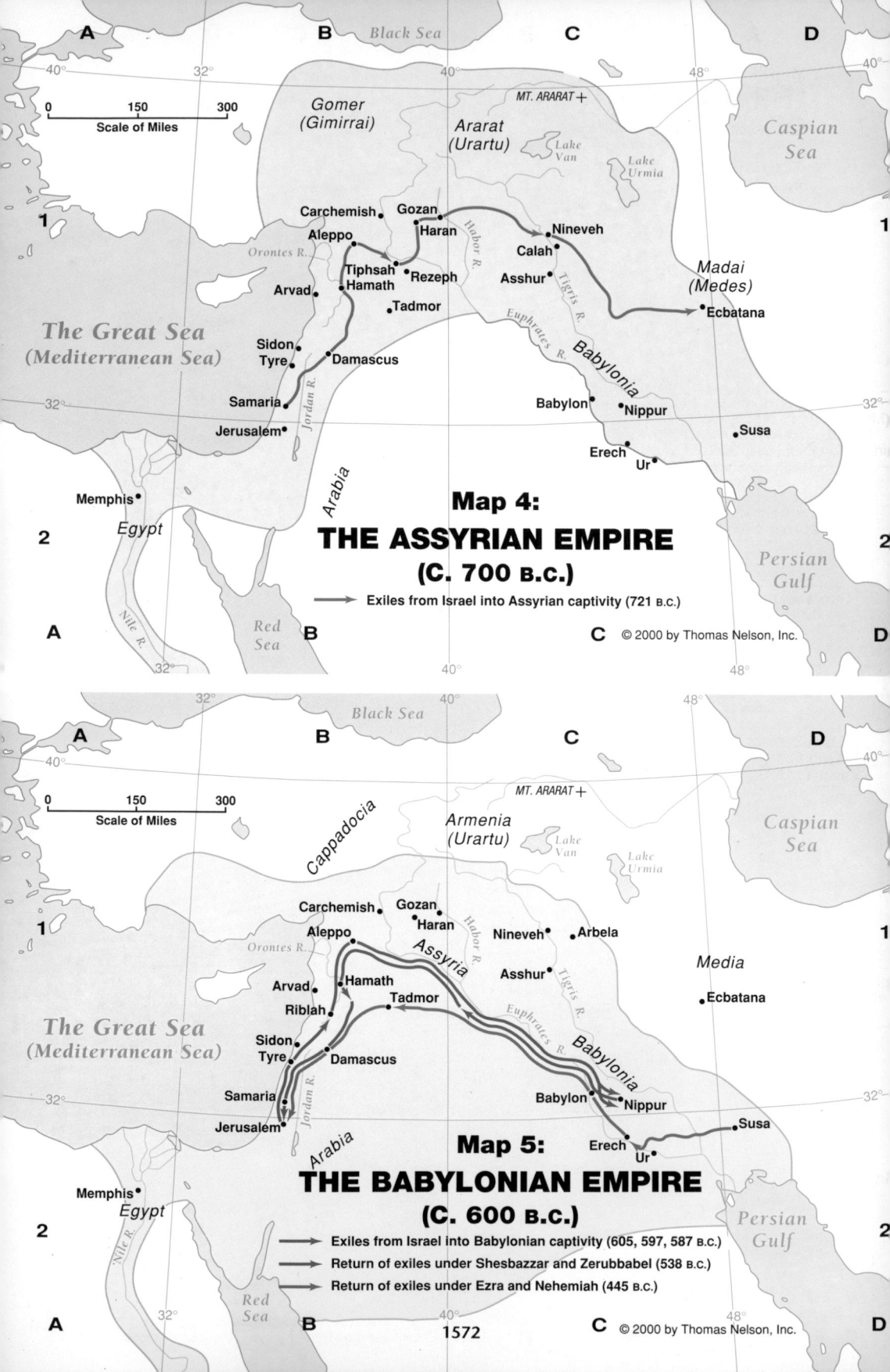

Map 4:
THE ASSYRIAN EMPIRE
(C. 700 B.C.)

→ Exiles from Israel into Assyrian captivity (721 B.C.)

© 2000 by Thomas Nelson, Inc.

Map 5:
THE BABYLONIAN EMPIRE
(C. 600 B.C.)

→ Exiles from Israel into Babylonian captivity (605, 597, 587 B.C.)
→ Return of exiles under Shesbazzar and Zerubbabel (538 B.C.)
→ Return of exiles under Ezra and Nehemiah (445 B.C.)

1572

© 2000 by Thomas Nelson, Inc.

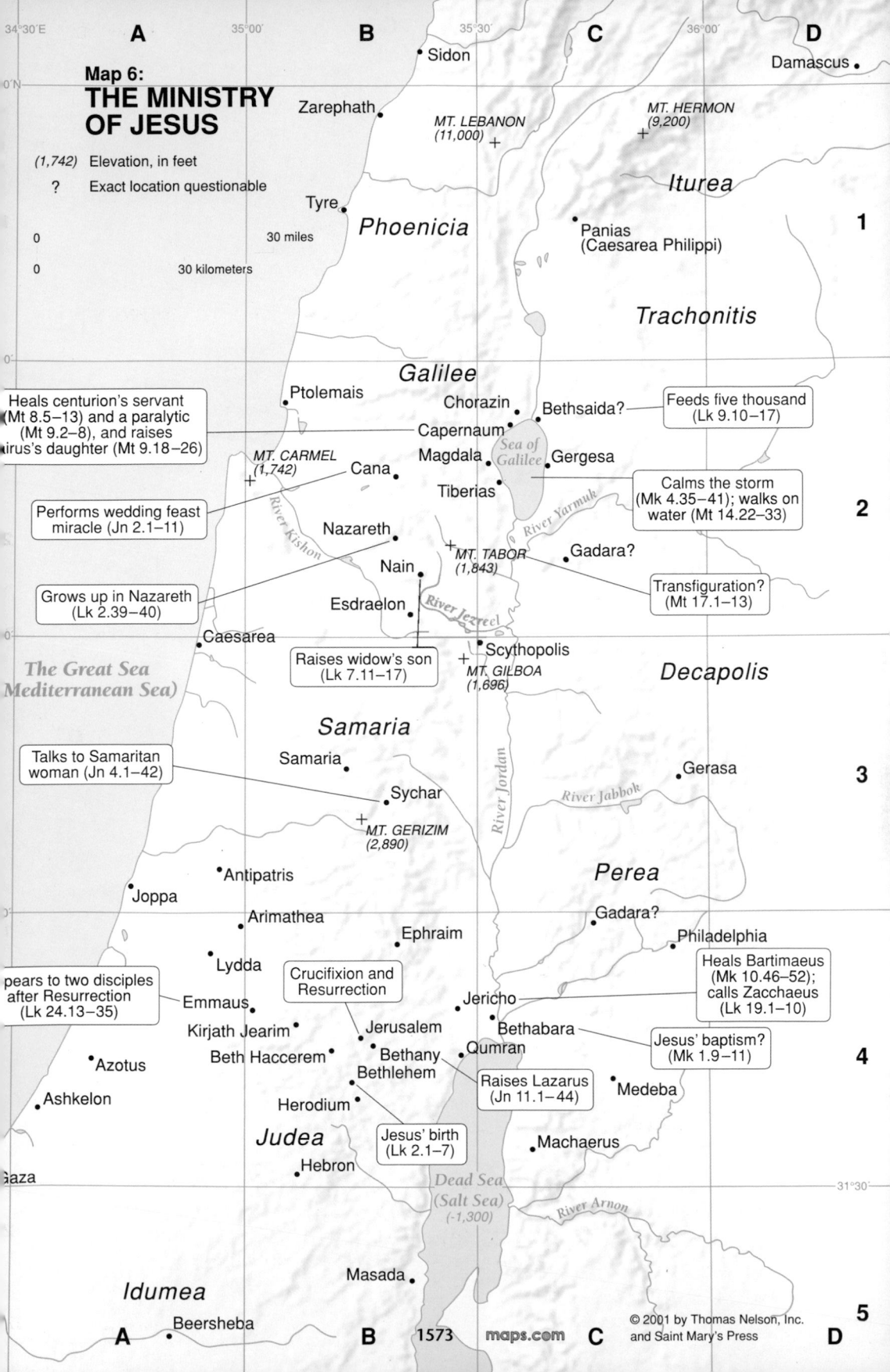

Map 6:
THE MINISTRY
OF JESUS

(1,742) Elevation, in feet

? Exact location questionable

0   30 miles

0   30 kilometers

Sidon

Damascus

Zarephath

MT. LEBANON
(11,000)

MT. HERMON
(9,200)

Iturea

Tyre

Phoenicia

Panias
(Caesarea Philippi)

Trachonitis

Galilee

Ptolemais

Chorazin

Bethsaida?

Feeds five thousand
(Lk 9.10–17)

Heals centurion's servant
(Mt 8.5–13) and a paralytic
(Mt 9.2–8), and raises
Jairus's daughter (Mt 9.18–26)

Capernaum

MT. CARMEL
(1,742)

Cana

Magdala

Sea of
Galilee

Gergesa

Tiberias

Calms the storm
(Mk 4.35–41); walks on
water (Mt 14.22–33)

Performs wedding feast
miracle (Jn 2.1–11)

River Kishon

Nazareth

Gadara?

MT. TABOR
(1,843)

River Yarmuk

Transfiguration?
(Mt 17.1–13)

Grows up in Nazareth
(Lk 2.39–40)

Nain

Esdraelon

River Jezreel

Caesarea

Raises widow's son
(Lk 7.11–17)

Scythopolis

MT. GILBOA
(1,696)

Decapolis

The Great Sea
(Mediterranean Sea)

Samaria

Samaria

Talks to Samaritan
woman (Jn 4.1–42)

Sychar

River Jordan

Gerasa

River Jabbok

MT. GERIZIM
(2,890)

Antipatris

Perea

Joppa

Arimathea

Ephraim

Gadara?

Philadelphia

Lydda

Heals Bartimaeus
(Mk 10.46–52);
calls Zacchaeus
(Lk 19.1–10)

Appears to two disciples
after Resurrection
(Lk 24.13–35)

Emmaus

Crucifixion and
Resurrection

Jericho

Kirjath Jearim

Jerusalem

Bethabara

Jesus' baptism?
(Mk 1.9–11)

Beth Haccerem

Bethany

Qumran

Azotus

Bethlehem

Raises Lazarus
(Jn 11.1–44)

Medeba

Ashkelon

Herodium

Herodium

Jesus' birth
(Lk 2.1–7)

Judea

Machaerus

Hebron

Dead Sea
(Salt Sea)
(-1,300)

River Arnon

Gaza

31°30'

Idumea

Masada

1573

© 2001 by Thomas Nelson, Inc.
and Saint Mary's Press

Beersheba

maps.com

Map 7:
PAUL'S FIRST AND SECOND JOURNEYS
(ACTS 13–14; 15.39—18.22)

→ First missionary journey, with Barnabas and Mark
(c. A.D. 46–48)

→ Second missionary journey, with Silas
(c. A.D. 49–52)

© 2001 by Thomas Nelson, Inc.

maps.com

Illyricum
Italy
Adriatic Sea
Black Sea
Sicily
Macedonia
Thrace
Amphipolis · Philippi
Thessalonica · Neapolis
Berea · Apollonia
Pontus
Bithynia
Troas
Galatia
Achaia
Phrygia
Antioch
Cappadocia
Corinth · Athens
Ephesus
Iconium
Lystra
Pisidia · Derbe
Tarsus
Attalia · *Pamphylia*
Antioch
Patmos
Lycia · *Cilicia*
Seleucia
Perga
Syria
Crete
Cyprus
Salamis
Paphos
The Great Sea
(Mediterranean Sea)
Caesarea
Jerusalem
Palestine

Map 8:
PAUL'S THIRD AND FOURTH JOURNEYS
(ACTS 18.23—21.16; 27—28.16)

→ Third missionary journey (c. A.D. 53–57)

→ Fourth missionary journey (c. A.D. 59–62)

© 2001 by Thomas Nelson, Inc.

maps.com

Illyricum
Italy
Rome · Three Inns
Appii Forum · Puteoli
Adriatic Sea
Black Sea
Rhegium
Sicily
Syracuse
Malta
Macedonia
Thrace
Amphipolis · Philippi
Thessalonica · Apollonia
Berea
Pontus
Bithynia
Troas
Assos
Galatia
Achaia
Mitylene · Colossae · Antioch
Chios
Phrygia
Cappadocia
Corinth · Athens
Ephesus
Pisidia · Iconium
Lystra · Derbe
Tarsus
Samos
Miletus
Pamphylia
Cos · Cnidus · *Lycia*
Cilicia
Antioch
Rhodes · Myra
Syria
Crete
Patara
Fair Havens
Cyprus
Sidon
The Great Sea
(Mediterranean Sea)
Tyre
Ptolemais
Caesarea
Antipatris · Jerusalem
Palestine

1574

Map 9:
THE HOLY LAND IN MODERN TIMES

Area occupied by Israel since June, 1967

0 — 75 miles
0 — 75 kilometers

The Great Sea
(Mediterranean Sea)

LEBANON

Tripoli
Beirut
Sidon
Tyre
Nahariyya
Akko
Haifa

LEBANON MOUNTAINS
BEKAA VALLEY
ANTI-LEBANON MOUNTAINS

Damascus
SYRIA

Dan
Qiryat Shemona
Quneitra
GOLAN HEIGHTS
Safad
Tiberias
Sea of Galilee
Nazareth
Afula
Beth Shean

1973 Line
1967 Cease-Fire Line

Dera
Ramtha

Hadera
Netanya
Tulkarm
Nablus
Herzliyya
Tel Aviv
Yafo
Petah Tiqwa
WEST BANK
River Jordan
Jarash
Amman
Rishon le Zion
Lod
Ramla
Ramalah
Ashdod
Jericho
Jerusalem
Madaba
Ashqelon
Bethlehem
Gaza
Qiryat Gat
Hebron
En Gedi
Dhiban
GAZA STRIP
Dead Sea (Salt Sea)
Beersheba
Karak
Al-Arish

ISRAEL

JORDAN

Negev
Arabah

EGYPT

Sinai

SAUDI ARABIA

Elat
Aqaba

1575

maps.com

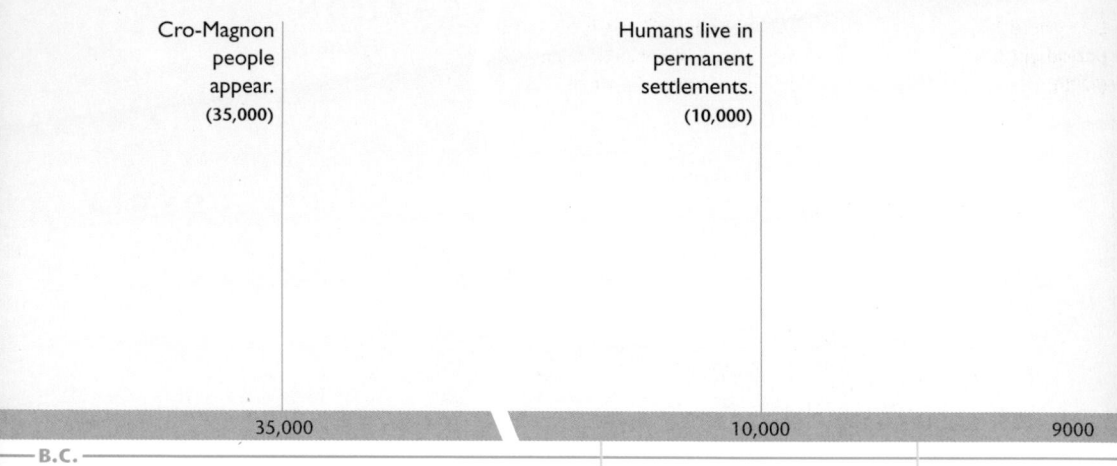

Timeline of Human History

Timeline of Biblical History

Cro-Magnon
people
appear.
(35,000)

Humans live in
permanent
settlements.
(10,000)

35,000   10,000   9000

PREHISTORY   2000   1900   1800   170

Jacob's
descendants
settle in Egypt.
(1750)

Abraham and Sarah
arrive in Canaan.
(1850)

BIBLICAL PREHISTORY

Important Biblical Figures
Adam and Eve
Cain and Abel
Noah

TIME OF THE PATRIARCHS
AND MATRIARCHS

Important Biblical Figures
Abraham and Sarah
Isaac and Rebekah
Jacob, Leah, and Rachel
Joseph and Asenath

Farming villages form;
goats, sheep, and oxen
are domesticated.
(7000)

| 8000 | 7000 | 6000 | 5000 |

B.C.

Timeline of Human History

Timeline of Biblical History

B.C.

Judges lead Israelite
tribes in Canaan.
(1200)

Moses leads Exodus from Egypt.
(1290)

Joshua invades
Canaan.
(1250)

TIME IN EGYPT AND THE EXODUS

Important Biblical Figures
Moses
Aaron
Miriam

TIME OF THE JUDGES

Important Biblical Figures
Deborah
Gideon
Samson
Samuel

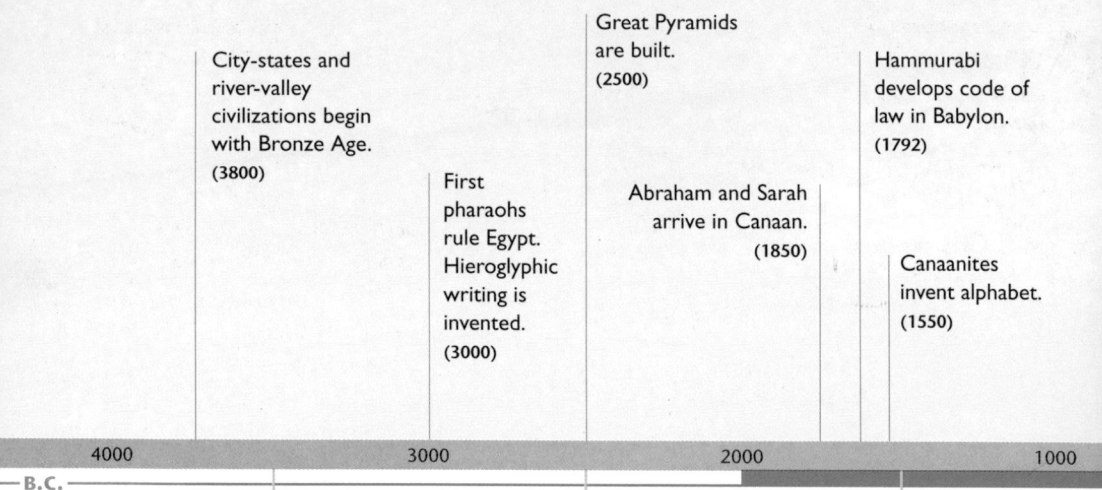

Timeline of Human History

4000	3000	2000	1000

City-states and river-valley civilizations begin with Bronze Age. (3800)

First pharaohs rule Egypt. Hieroglyphic writing is invented. (3000)

Great Pyramids are built. (2500)

Abraham and Sarah arrive in Canaan. (1850)

Hammurabi develops code of law in Babylon. (1792)

Canaanites invent alphabet. (1550)

B.C.

Timeline of Biblical History   PROPHETS   Prominent Kings of Israel   Prominent Kings of Judah

B.C.

1000	900	800	700	600	50

Kingdom divides into Israel and Judah. (922)

Solomon rules kingdom, builds Temple. (961)

David unites kingdom, takes Jerusalem as capital. (1000)

Saul is named first king of Israel. (1020)

Assyrians capture Samaria, ending the kingdom of Israel. (721)

Babylonians take Jerusalem. Exile of Judah begins. (587)

Cyrus of Persia frees Jews to return to Judah. (538)

People of Judah rebuild Temple. (515)

ELIJAH (865)

ELISHA (850)

AMOS (783)

HOSEA (755)

FIRST ISAIAH (740)

MICAH (720)

NAHUM (663)

ZEPHANIAH (630)

JEREMIAH (626)

HABAKKUK (609)

EZEKIEL (593)

ZECHARIAH (520)

HAGGAI (520)

SECOND ISAIAH (540)

TIME OF THE KINGS AND PROPHETS

UNITED KINGDOM	DIVIDED KINGDOM				PERSIAN DOMINATION

Saul   David   Solomon

Jeroboam I (922)   Ahab (869)   Ahaziah (850)   Jeroboam II (786)   Hoshea (732)

Rehoboam (922)   Ahaziah (842)   Jehoash (837)   Uzziah (783)   Hezekiah (715)   Josiah (640)   Jehoiachin (598)   Zedekiah (597)

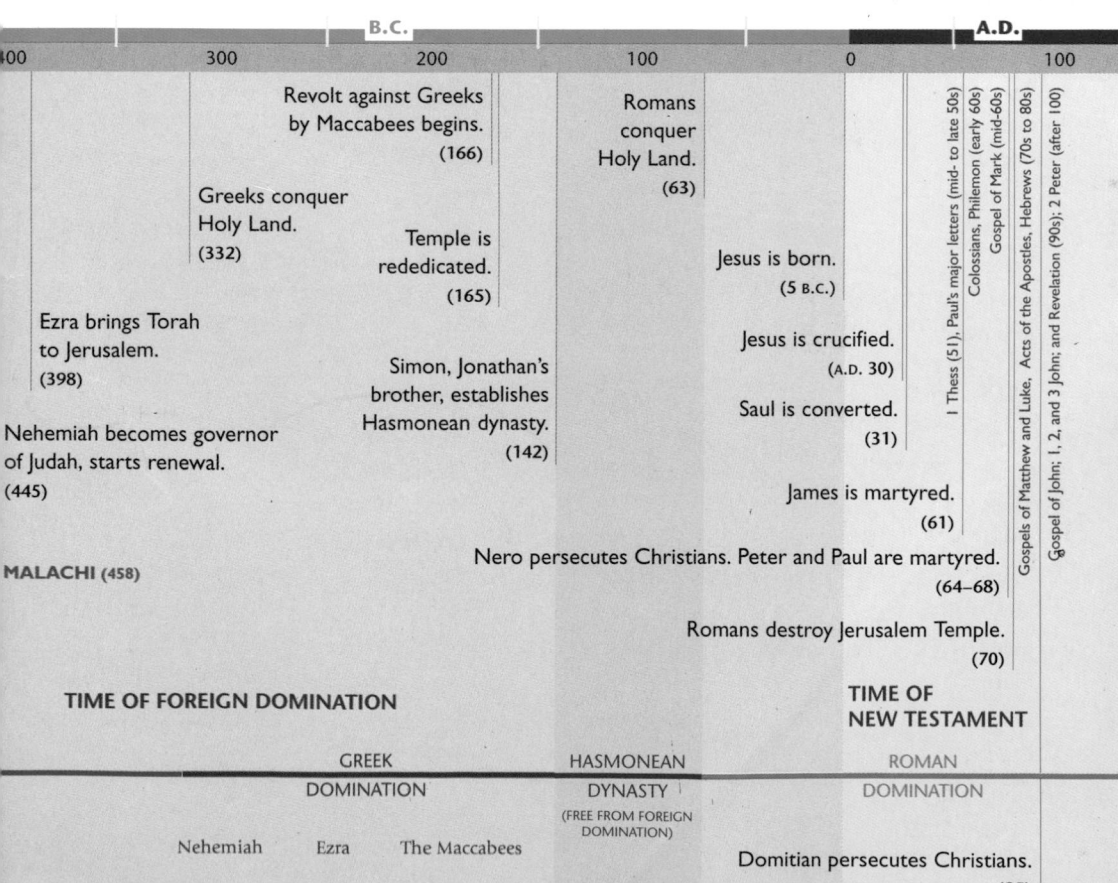

Timeline of Human History

Buddha is born in India.
(563)

Confucius is born in China.
(551)

Greece has golden age.
(400)

Crusades begin.
(1096)

Roman Empire is established.
(43 B.C.)

Jesus is crucified in Palestine.
(A.D. 30)

Roman Empire falls.
(476)

Muhammad founds Islam in Arabia.
(622)

Gutenberg invents printing press.
(1450)

Columbus sails to America.
(1492)

Personal computers become available.
(1972)

Luther starts Protestant Reformation.
(1517)

Declaration of Independence is signed.
(1776)

Dominion of Canada is created.
(1867)

World War II begins.
(1939)

| 0 | 1000 | 2000 |

A.D.

Timeline of Biblical History

New Testament Books

B.C. **A.D.**

| 400 | 300 | 200 | 100 | 0 | 100 |

Revolt against Greeks by Maccabees begins.
(166)

Greeks conquer Holy Land.
(332)

Temple is rededicated.
(165)

Romans conquer Holy Land.
(63)

Ezra brings Torah to Jerusalem.
(398)

Simon, Jonathan's brother, establishes Hasmonean dynasty.
(142)

Jesus is born.
(5 B.C.)

Jesus is crucified.
(A.D. 30)

Nehemiah becomes governor of Judah, starts renewal.
(445)

Saul is converted.
(31)

MALACHI (458)

James is martyred.
(61)

Nero persecutes Christians. Peter and Paul are martyred.
(64–68)

Romans destroy Jerusalem Temple.
(70)

1 Thess (51), Paul's major letters (mid- to late 50s)

Colossians, Philemon (early 60s)

Gospel of Mark (mid-60s)

Gospels of Matthew and Luke, Acts of the Apostles, Hebrews (70s to 80s)

Gospel of John; 1, 2, and 3 John; and Revelation (90s); 2 Peter (after 100)

TIME OF FOREIGN DOMINATION

TIME OF NEW TESTAMENT

| GREEK DOMINATION | HASMONEAN DYNASTY (FREE FROM FOREIGN DOMINATION) | ROMAN DOMINATION |

Nehemiah   Ezra   The Maccabees

Domitian persecutes Christians.
(95)

1579

Alphabetical List of Bible Books and Abbreviations

Book	Abbreviation	Page	Book	Abbreviation	Page
Acts	Acts	1265	1 Kings	1 Kings	322
Amos	Am	1040	2 Kings	2 Kings	352
Baruch	Bar	944	Lamentations	Lam	935
1 Chronicles	1 Chr	379	Leviticus	Lev	106
2 Chronicles	2 Chr	405	Luke	Lk	1178
Colossians	Col	1386	1 Maccabees	1 Macc	504
1 Corinthians	1 Cor	1328	2 Maccabees	2 Macc	532
2 Corinthians	2 Cor	1349	Malachi	Mal	1092
Daniel	Dan	1000	Mark	Mk	1148
Deuteronomy	Deut	172	Matthew	Mt	1100
Ecclesiastes	Eccl	712	Micah	Mic	1056
Ephesians	Eph	1371	Nahum	Nah	1064
Esther	Esth	491	Nehemiah	Neh	447
Exodus	Ex	60	Numbers	Num	135
Ezekiel	Ezek	953	Obadiah	Ob	1049
Ezra	Ezra	436	1 Peter	1 Pet	1441
Galatians	Gal	1363	2 Peter	2 Pet	1448
Genesis	Gen	4	Philemon	Philem	1417
Habakkuk	Hab	1068	Philippians	Phil	1380
Haggai	Hag	1078	Proverbs	Prov	682
Hebrews	Heb	1420	Psalms	Ps	590
Hosea	Hos	1022	Revelation	Rev	1466
Isaiah	Isa	810	Romans	Rom	1308
James	Jas	1434	Ruth	Ruth	259
Jeremiah	Jer	875	1 Samuel	1 Sam	265
Job	Job	558	2 Samuel	2 Sam	295
Joel	Joel	1034	Sirach	Sir	754
1 John	1 Jn	1452	Song of Solomon	Song	723
2 John	2 Jn	1459	1 Thessalonians	1 Thess	1392
3 John	3 Jn	1461	2 Thessalonians	2 Thess	1399
John	Jn	1226	1 Timothy	1 Tim	1403
Jonah	Jon	1052	2 Timothy	2 Tim	1410
Joshua	Josh	212	Titus	Titus	1414
Jude	Jude	1463	Tobit	Tob	461
Judges	Judg	235	Wisdom of Solomon	Wis	732
Judith	Jdt	476	Zechariah	Zech	1081
			Zephaniah	Zeph	1073

All scripture is inspired by God and is useful for teaching, for reproof, for correction, and for training in righteousness, so that everyone who belongs to God may be proficient, equipped for every good work.

(2 Tim 3.16–17)